Botanica

Botanica

The illustrated A–Z of over 10,000 garden plants and how to cultivate them

Chief Editors R. J. Turner Jr. and Ernie Wasson

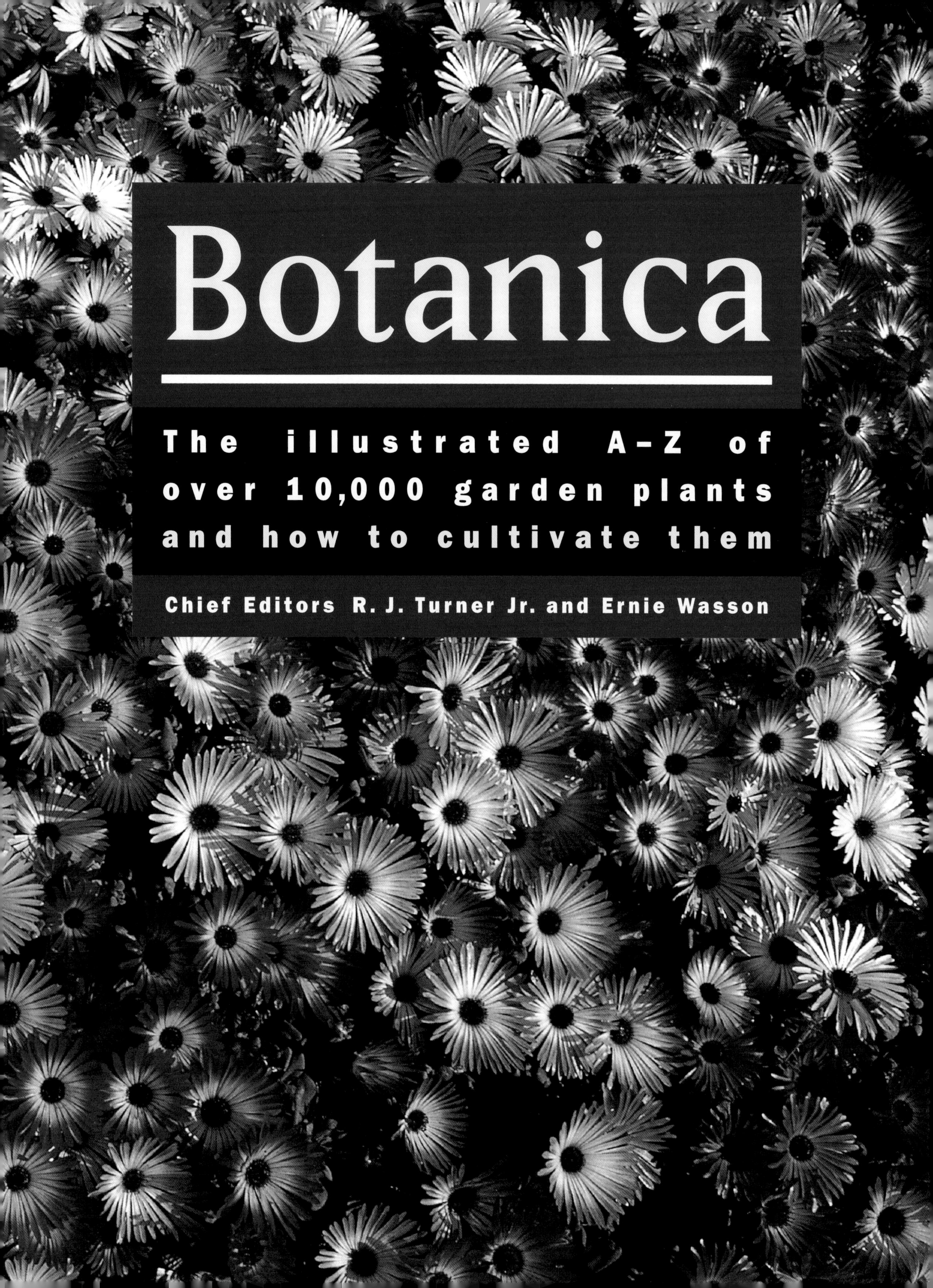

Publisher	Gordon Cheers
Chief editors	R. J. Turner Jr. and Ernie Wasson
Managing editors	Susan Page, Margaret Olds
Editorial consultants	Tony Rodd (Aust.) Geoff Bryant (NZ) Lynton Johnson (SA) Barbara Segall (UK)
Writers	Geoff Burnie Sue Forrester Denise Greig Sarah Guest Michelle Harmony Sue Hobley Gregory Jackson Dr Peter Lavarack Melanie Ledgett Dr Ross McDonald Stirling Macoboy Bill Molyneux Douglas Moodie Judy Moore Dalys Newman Tim North Professor Kristo Pienaar Graeme Purdy Julie Silk Stephen Ryan Gina Schien
Editors	Lisa Foulis Marlene Meynert Dee Rogers Janet Parker Kate Etherington Heather Jackson Siobhan O'Connor Marie-Louise Taylor Julie Stanton Loretta Barnard Louise Egerton Doreen Grézoux Gillian Gillett Denise Imwold Valerie Marlborough Gisela Mirwis Margaret McPhee Steve Samuelson Philippa Sandall Sarah Shrub Judith Simpson
Art directors	Stan Lamond, Bob Mitchell
Page layout	Joy Eckermann
Picture sizing	Jean Burnard
Publishing manager	Linda Watchorn
Publishing assistant	Sarah Sherlock
Maps	Stan Lamond, Graham Keane
Map zone consultant	Dr J. Gentilli
Picture research	Gordon Cheers
Photo library	Suzannah Porter
Chief photographer	James Young
Index	Lisa Foulis

First published in 1997
Second edition, revised, published 1998
Third edition, revised, published 1999

This edition published by Barnes & Noble, Inc.,
by arrangement with Random House Australia Pty Ltd
1999 Barnes & Noble Book:
ISBN 0760716420

Typesetting: Dee Rogers
Printed by Sing Cheong Printing Co. Ltd, Hong Kong
Film separation Pica Colour Separation, Singapore

Consultants

GEOFF BRYANT is a full-time garden writer and photographer in New Zealand who has worked for many years as a plant propagator, hybridizer and nurseryman. Geoff has a particular interest in evergreen azaleas and rhododendrons, and his first book, *The Azalea Grower's Handbook,* capitalized on this interest. Altogether he has written eight gardening books including the Montana Book Award finalist, *The Complete New Zealand Gardener,* and has edited, revised or contributed to many more. Geoff has a regular column in *Growing Today* (New Zealand) and a monthly diary entry for *Your Garden* (Australia). He also acts as a consultant for the New Zealand Consumers' Institute magazine, *Home and Garden.*

Photography is Geoff's other great love, and much of his work has been published worldwide. He lives in Christchurch, New Zealand.

TONY RODD is a graduate in botany and worked for many years at the Royal Botanic Gardens, Sydney, where among other tasks he catalogued the garden's collections, identified plants for the public, and explored for plants in the wild. He has co-authored a book on palms and one on rainforest gardens as well as contributing material to various other publications, including *Australian Encyclopedia* and *The Ultimate Book of Trees & Shrubs.* His special interest is the classification and nomenclature of ornamental plants, but he has long experience in their garden uses as well. He is also a photographer, managing his own library of botanical transparencies of which more than 2,000 have been published in books. Among his current activities are environmental consulting and the compilation of a database of early plant introductions to Australia.

Tony's leisure time is occupied by literature, bushwalking and fishing for trout in mountain streams.

BARBARA SEGALL is a horticulturist, award-winning freelance garden writer, editor and author based in the UK. She is a member of the Institute of Horticulture and a Fellow of the Linnean Society. She lectures on various subjects to gardening groups and specialist societies. Her horticultural expertise is supported by professional training in journalism and experience in international full-color magazine production, as well as editorial on various publications.

She writes regularly for a number of specialist publications such as *BBC Gardeners' World* magazine, the RHS Journal *The Garden, Country Life, The Kitchen Garden* and *Herbs,* of which magazine she is also editor. In addition, she contributes to gardening sections of consumer magazines and newspapers, including the Weekend Section of *The Times,* and has written for gardening partworks including *My Garden* and *Gardening Made Easy.* Barbara is also Editor of *The Horticulturist,* the quarterly journal of The Institute of Horticulture.

Barbara has written several books and is currently engaged in a book program that centers on her experience as a grower of herbs, flowers and potager-style gardens. She maintains a traditional, country-style garden at her Suffolk home.

R. G. TURNER JR. is a garden designer, educator, writer, photographer and tour leader. He has designed private and public gardens in Michigan, New Jersey and California. He taught at UC Berkley, Department of Landscape Architecture for six years; and gives occasional lectures throughout the Bay area on garden design and on the wildflowers of South Africa and Australia. He has served as Director of the San Francisco Landscape Garden Show and as Director of Education for the Strybing Arboretum Society. Most recently he was the Executive Director for the Ruth Bancroft Garden in Walnut Creek, California, the first private garden to be sponsored by the Garden Conservancy.

Some books he has contributed to include *The Nature Company Guide to Natural Gardening, The Ultimate Plant and Gardening Book* and *Sunset Western Landscaping Book.* He is currently the editor of *Pacific Horticulture,* one of the country's top garden magazines.

R. G. Turner Jr. has traveled extensively to study gardens, plants and wildlife in North America, Europe, Australia and South Africa. He lives in San Francisco.

ERNIE WASSON has gardened on both coasts of North America and is an alumnus of the Longwood Graduate Program in Ornamental Horticulture and Public Garden Management. Before entering graduate school Ernie was a horticultural instructor at College of the Redwoods and part-owner of a retail nursery, both in Humboldt County, California. After graduate school he spent five years in charge of Green Animals Topiary Garden, an historic garden in Rhode Island.

Since moving back west Ernie has worked at Berkeley Horticultural Nursery and done consultant work for *Books that Work,* on gardening software programs. He writes a monthly Internet column entitled "All Plants Considered" at <www.gardens.com>. Ernie traces his love of plants to his mother who always had something blooming in her Berkeley hills garden.

His professional interests include horticultural books, pruning, California native plants, fine foliage plants, ornamental grasses, salvias, South African restios and vegetables. He has always lived close to the ocean and his beloved fog.

Contents

Contents

How This Book Works

Botanica is an attractive and comprehensive guide to more than 10,000 plants, which are representative of all the major plant groups. The book contains three sections.

The first section gives full information on gardening and growing plants and a map which details the hardiness zones for the country. A full explanation of the hardiness zones is also given. Information on the major plant groups, such as annuals and perennials, bulbs, corms and tubers, and trees and shrubs is also included.

The second section is made up of the A to Z of the plants, and this makes up most of the book. More than 10,000 plants are listed. The plants are organized alphabetically by genus (the botanical name). The genus entries contain information on the group as a whole, including geographical origin, description, cultivation, propagation and pests and diseases.

These are followed by the species entries, which contain focussed information on particular species and on subspecies, varieties and cultivars. Each species entry finishes with a hardiness zone or range of zones. For more information on the hardiness zones, see page 16. Some genera, such as *Rhododendron, Rosa* and *Tulipa,* are broken down into the major groups within the genera. Synonyms and common names are also given. Each photograph is captioned with its botanical name; occasionally space constraints have meant that part of the caption is abbreviated.

The third section is made up of useful and interesting reference material. It includes information on plant names; a detailed glossary; a table of plant families and related genera arranged in both systematic and alphabetical order; and a comprehensive index of synonyms and common names.

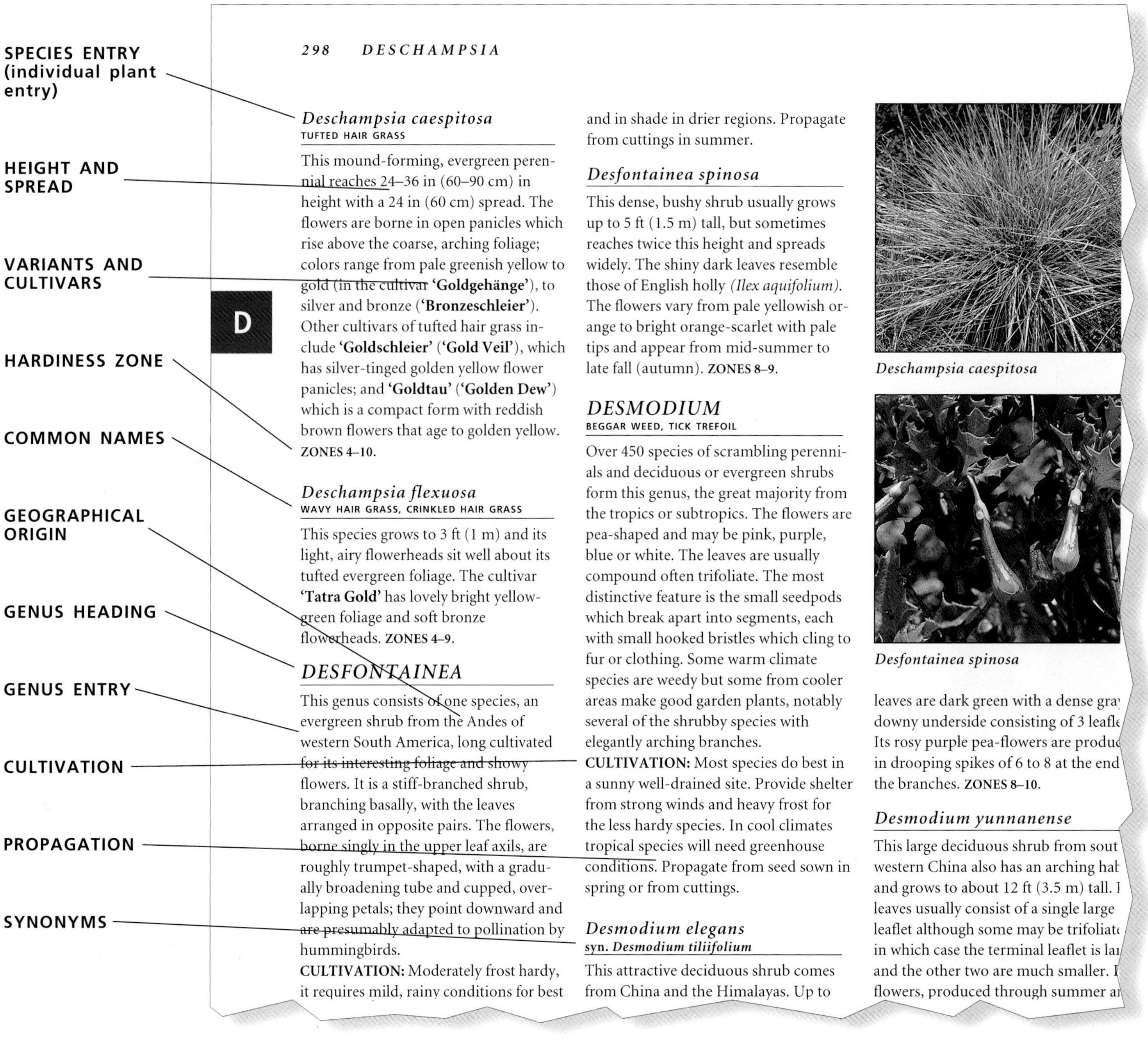

298 DESCHAMPSIA

Deschampsia caespitosa
TUFTED HAIR GRASS

This mound-forming, evergreen perennial reaches 24–36 in (60–90 cm) in height with a 24 in (60 cm) spread. The flowers are borne in open panicles which rise above the coarse, arching foliage; colors range from pale greenish yellow to gold (in the cultivar **'Goldgehänge'**), to silver and bronze (**'Bronzeschleier'**). Other cultivars of tufted hair grass include **'Goldschleier'** (**'Gold Veil'**), which has silver-tinged golden yellow flower panicles; and **'Goldtau'** (**'Golden Dew'**) which is a compact form with reddish brown flowers that age to golden yellow. **ZONES 4–10.**

Deschampsia flexuosa
WAVY HAIR GRASS, CRINKLED HAIR GRASS

This species grows to 3 ft (1 m) and its light, airy flowerheads sit well about its tufted evergreen foliage. The cultivar **'Tatra Gold'** has lovely bright yellow-green foliage and soft bronze flowerheads. **ZONES 4–9.**

DESFONTAINEA

This genus consists of one species, an evergreen shrub from the Andes of western South America, long cultivated for its interesting foliage and showy flowers. It is a stiff-branched shrub, branching basally, with the leaves arranged in opposite pairs. The flowers, borne singly in the upper leaf axils, are roughly trumpet-shaped, with a gradually broadening tube and cupped, overlapping petals; they point downward and are presumably adapted to pollination by hummingbirds.
CULTIVATION: Moderately frost hardy, it requires mild, rainy conditions for best and in shade in drier regions. Propagate from cuttings in summer.

Desfontainea spinosa

This dense, bushy shrub usually grows up to 5 ft (1.5 m) tall, but sometimes reaches twice this height and spreads widely. The shiny dark leaves resemble those of English holly *(Ilex aquifolium).* The flowers vary from pale yellowish orange to bright orange-scarlet with pale tips and appear from mid-summer to late fall (autumn). **ZONES 8–9.**

DESMODIUM
BEGGAR WEED, TICK TREFOIL

Over 450 species of scrambling perennials and deciduous or evergreen shrubs form this genus, the great majority from the tropics or subtropics. The flowers are pea-shaped and may be pink, purple, blue or white. The leaves are usually compound often trifoliate. The most distinctive feature is the small seedpods which break apart into segments, each with small hooked bristles which cling to fur or clothing. Some warm climate species are weedy but some from cooler areas make good garden plants, notably several of the shrubby species with elegantly arching branches.
CULTIVATION: Most species do best in a sunny well-drained site. Provide shelter from strong winds and heavy frost for the less hardy species. In cool climates tropical species will need greenhouse conditions. Propagate from seed sown in spring or from cuttings.

Desmodium elegans
syn. *Desmodium tiliifolium*

This attractive deciduous shrub comes from China and the Himalayas. Up to

leaves are dark green with a dense gra[y] downy underside consisting of 3 leafl[ets]. Its rosy purple pea-flowers are produ[ced] in drooping spikes of 6 to 8 at the end[s of] the branches. **ZONES 8–10.**

Desmodium yunnanense

This large deciduous shrub from sout[h-] western China also has an arching ha[bit] and grows to about 12 ft (3.5 m) tall. [Its] leaves usually consist of a single large leaflet although some may be trifoliat[e] in which case the terminal leaflet is la[rge] and the other two are much smaller. [Its] flowers, produced through summer a[nd]

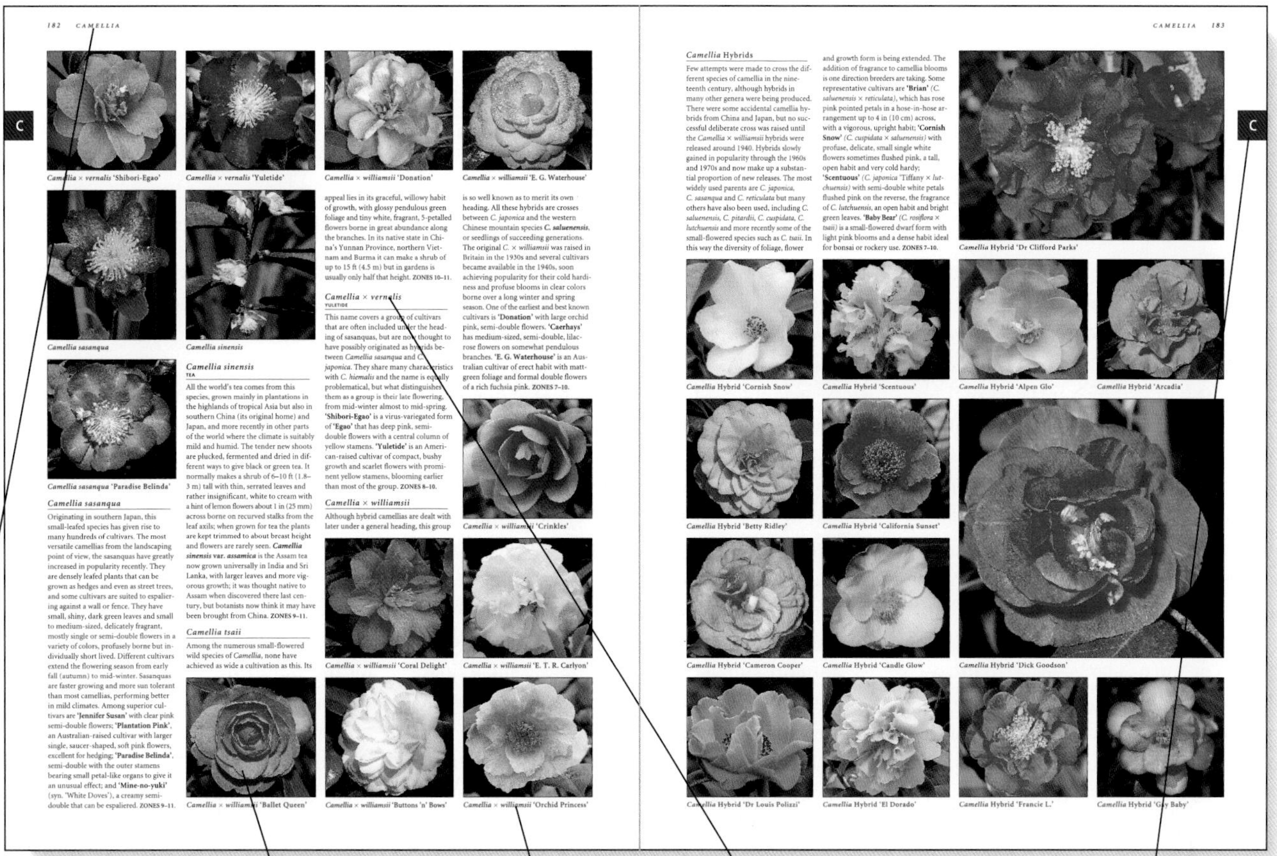

PAGE HEADINGS
To make it easy to find the plant you are looking for, page headings on each spread indicate the first genus described on the left-hand page, and the last genus on the right-hand page.

PHOTOGRAPHS
Photographs illustrate color, growth habit and other ornamental features of the plants.

CAPTIONS
Each photograph is captioned with the plant's botanical name.

GENUS AND SPECIES ENTRIES
In the A to Z section, plants are arranged in alphabetical order by genus. Entries include plant descriptions, geographical origin, cultivation, pests and diseases, height and spread and hardiness rating by zones.

MARGIN MARKERS
For ready reference, colored tabs in the margin show the letter of the alphabet.

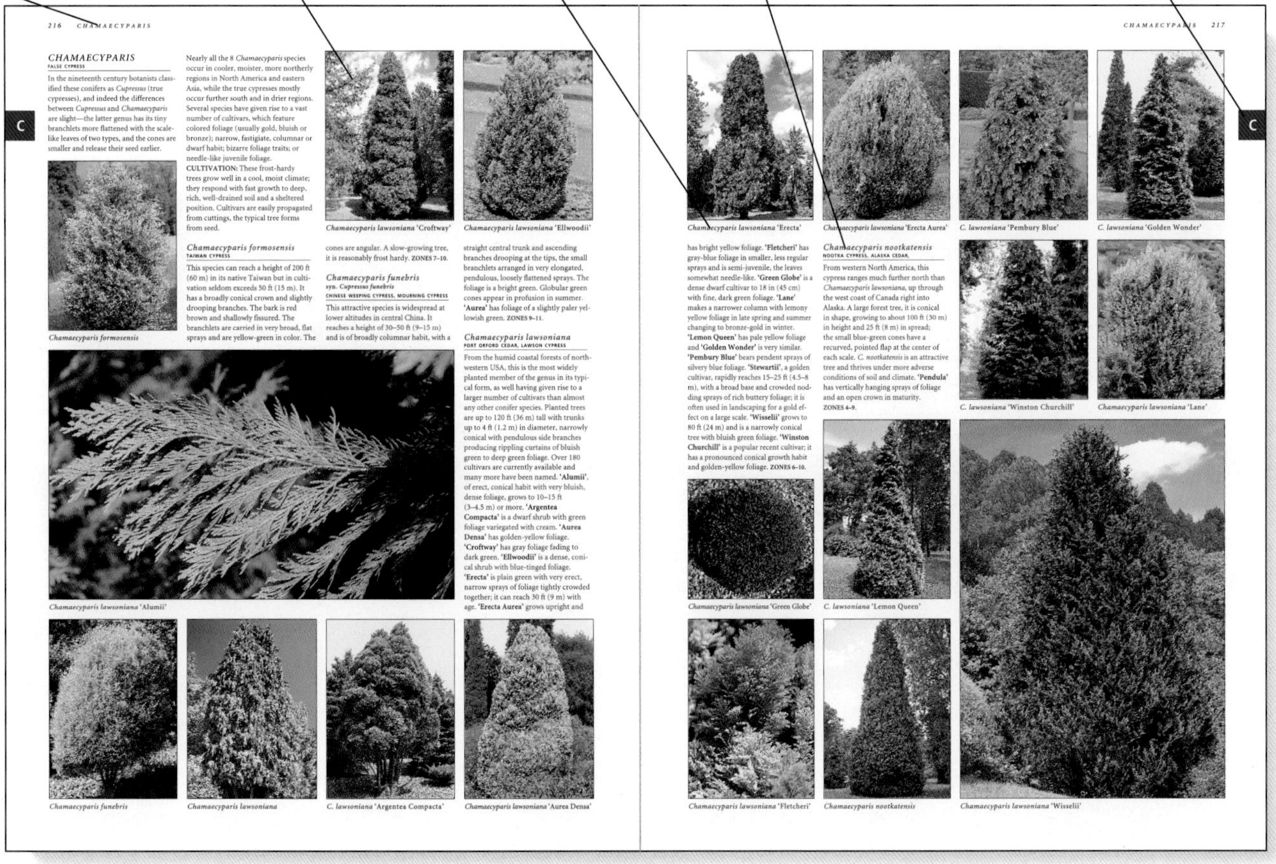

Introduction

Ernie Wasson

The Water Garden

Gardeners through the ages, notably the Persians, Romans and Spanish Moors, have used water as an integral part of their creations. English landscapers diverted rivers to form the lakes of their grand schemes, and all the while the gardeners of China and Japan delighted in the beauty of their near-natural water gardens.

The traditional ideas behind the pond as an oasis of tranquillity, serenity and capturing a small piece of nature are probably even more valid today. A water garden is a focal point that not only provides an opportunity to grow a completely different group of plants, but also introduces reflection and movement and is one of the best ways of encouraging birds and other wildlife into the garden. Most fortunate of all are those gardeners with natural ponds and streams, for with very little effort they can enhance what already exists.

The first consideration with a pond is to maintain its ecological balance. The presence of algae is normal and to be expected, but if there is an imbalance and nitrogen levels are high, algae can develop into an unsightly green scum. An ideal pool for fish is often said to be one where you lose sight of your hand at about 12 in (30 cm) depth. Most gardeners, however, prefer clearer water.

In a balanced pond community, surface leaves reduce the light in the water, limit algal growth and provide cover for fish to shelter beneath; plants rooted in the pond bottom use up nutrients that lead to excessive algae; and animals in the pond feed on algae. Achieving a balanced pond takes time and a little effort, but once the balance is there nature takes care of itself.

There are four main types of water garden plants:

- Permanently submerged plants that may or may not root in the pond soil and may occasionally produce surface leaves. These plants are primarily grown to oxygenate the water and include milfoil *(Myriophyllum)* and *Vallisneria.*
- Plants with floating leaves, which also may or may not be rooted in the bottom of the pond. These include waterlilies, most of the common ornamental aquatics, and the small floating plants like *Azolla* and duckweed *(Lemna).*
- Marginal plants that grow in permanently wet soil such as at the edges of large ponds or in very damp, low-lying areas. This group includes the reeds, rushes, gunneras and a few of the bog irises.
- Bog plants, which tolerate occasional periods with submerged roots but are really a transitional element between the pond margins and the rest of the garden. Plants like marsh marigold *(Caltha palustris),* Japanese irises, blue flag *(Iris versicolor),* bog primroses *(Primulas)* and rodgersias thrive in such conditions.

Bottom-rooting plants need soil in which to grow, and while it is possible to add a layer of soil at the bottom of the pond—the norm in a natural pond—many gardeners prefer to use movable cages or boxes to hold the soil and roots of their plants. This makes rearranging and cleaning easier and will help limit the size and spread of fast-growing, invasive aquatic plants.

The soil used should be low in organic matter. Twigs and leaves simply float to the surface and decomposing plant matter will foul the water. Natural pond or river silt is ideal, but failing that a fine clay soil will do. Expect some strong algal growth until the excess nutrients are exhausted.

True water plants largely take care of themselves. The real art in water gardening lies in blending the design with the garden. Many of the best water gardens owe their beauty to the skilful use of marginal and bog plants.

Those working on a large scale will have room for the giant rhubarb-like leaves of some of the *Gunnera* species or Indian rhubarb *(Darmera peltata)* and other large bog plants such as the various *Rodgersia, Aruncus* and *Filipendula* species, plus Canadian burnet *(Sanguisorba canadensis).* In smaller gardens primulas and the many *Astilbe* species and cultivars will be better.

The water garden should fit in with and be part of the overall garden scene, but even with limited space there is room to take advantage of water. A simple half-barrel with a pygmy waterlily *(Nymphaea)* will do.

Coastal Gardens

Gardening near the coast poses special problems of wind, salt spray and dry sandy soil. It is vital to realize that coastal conditions are unrelenting and are better accommodated than battled against. Inevitably, there are plants that simply

BELOW: ***Water gardens provide tranquillity, and allow the gardener to capture a piece of nature.***

will not survive coastal conditions, but a wide variety of interesting and unusual plants do thrive in a seaside garden.

Most coastal soils are sandy, prone to drought and liable to blow away. Soil must be stabilized and its structure improved. Fast-growing seaside ground covers, such as coastal grasses and perennials including sea hollies (eryngiums), sea lavendar (limoniums), trailing lantana *(Lantana montevidensis),* and shrubs including bearberry *(Arctostaphylos uva-ursii),* low-growing cotoneasters, bush lupines *(Lupinus arboreus)* and prostrate junipers such as shore juniper *(Juniperus conferta),* all help bind the sand together. The incorporation of organic matter such as compost, improves the structure and water-holding capacity of the soil.

Wind is a constant problem in coastal areas and shelter is essential. Fences, hedges and groups of large shrubs offer respite, but if there is enough room, layered semi-permeable shelter provides better protection and is often more attractive. Start with low-growing, soil-binding plants backed by soft billowy plants, such as grasses that move with the wind and absorb its strength. Next, plant tough coastal shrubs, and lastly, taller shrubs or small trees to act as your final buffer. Such a graduated planting all but eliminates the wind at ground level while allowing it to flow over the top of the shelter without creating excessive turbulence. Good shelter plants include Monterey cypress *(Cupressus macrocarpa),* escallonias, silk-tassel bush *(Garrya elliptica),* bayberry *(Myrica pensylvanica),* Holm oak *(Quercus ilex),* daisy bush *(Olearia),* shore pine *(Pinus contorta),* Scotch pine *(Pinus sylvestris),* pittosporums, saltspray rose *(Rosa rugosa)* and coast rosemary *(Westringia fruticosa).*

Gardens right on the seafront are plagued by salt spray. Any exposed plants are coated in a fine layer of salt water that quickly evaporates to leave salt-encrusted foliage. Coastal plants can cope with the salt deposits but the foliage of most inland plants becomes dry and burnt around the edges. Providing shelter will help in areas that are occasionally exposed to salty winds, but in very exposed sites there is no alternative but to choose salt-resistant plants.

In summer grow marginally hardy plants such as cordylines, cannas and abutilons in containers. Combine them with succulents including agaves, Mediterranean plants such as lavender and the dark foliaged aeoniums, as well as cotton lavender *(Santolina chamaecyparissus).*

Marguerite daisies *(Argyranthemum frutescens* cultivars) and pelargoniums are unrivalled for color and very much at home by the sea. In summer, regal pelargoniums add some height, growing to 18–24 in (45–60 cm) in a good season, and come in a huge range of flower colors. Ivy-leafed pelargoniums can be used as climbers, ground covers and even trained over frames as shelter plants. Gardeners in cold-winter climate regions must bring these plants indoors before the first killing frosts of fall (autumn) and keep them in a greenhouse over the winter.

ABOVE: ***Like other members of the protea family, leucospermums thrive in coastal conditions.***
RIGHT: ***Where not hardy, fuchsias make superb summer pot plants for the shaded garden.***

Succulents relish well-drained sandy soil and do particularly well where they receive the heat reflected off coastal cliffs. Aloes, agaves, aeoniums, echeverias, sempervivums and sedums grow in conditions that few other plants tolerate and are good choices for containers. Tender succulents must be protected or placed in sunny windows or greenhouses over the winter.

Many perennials are also suitable for coastal areas. Phlomises, catananches, helichrysums, mugwort *(Artemisia)* and yarrow *(Achillea)* will thrive, as will most thistle-like plants such as cynaras, eryngiums and globe thistle *(Echinops).*

Although there are climatic and geographic conditions to cope with, a coastal garden can still be full of interest and creativity. Large drifts of California poppy *(Eschscholtzia* species), waving grasses and flowering shrubs, including hedge fuchsia and escallonias and saltspray rose *(Rosa rugosa),* are just as effective as formal borders. For a more formal planting style, choose a Mediterranean theme. This usually involves the extensive use of lavender and other silver-gray foliaged plants combined with brightly colored shrubs and climbers. It also demands a strong architectural element using walls, steps and plenty of potted color.

However you approach it, coastal gardening comes down to learning to live with the environment rather than fighting against it.

Gardens in the Shade

All gardens have shaded areas that are sometimes difficult to deal with, yet they offer an opportunity to grow the many superb plants, including exquisite woodland perennials, that prefer shade.

Shade in the town and suburban garden tends to come from fences, walls, large trees and buildings. A garden shaded by a fence or wall will vary between total shade and full sun depending on how it is aligned to the sun. Afternoon shade suits summersweet *(Clethra alnifolia),* hydrangeas, rhododendrons, *Pieris,* Japanese anemones and woodland irises, while with morning shade and afternoon sun it is best to choose plants that prefer more sun, such as peonies, dahlias and deciduous azaleas.

Sun exposure within a garden changes throughout the year. During the long hot days of summer, many plants require overhead shade from the intense rays of the afternoon sun. Plants that can tolerate a wide range of sun exposure include evergreen azaleas, camellias, summer-dormant primroses, and most spring-flowering woodland bulbs. Keeping the soil mulched and humus rich will help shade- and moisture-loving plants endure periods of exposure and dryness.

The shade cast by evergreen trees is generally dense and the heavy foliage can also prevent light rain from reaching the ground. Careful thinning

ABOVE: *This closely planted herbaceous border efficiently suppresses weeds, those undesirable plants that compete for water.*
LEFT: *The blue columbine* (Aquilegia caerulea) *will grow and flower freely in light shade beneath trees.*

will let in more light and moisture without reducing the protection that the canopy affords. Evergreen trees often have leathery leaves that may take years to rot down, while conifer needles will form a thick mulch that can prevent moisture from penetrating. The soil under evergreen trees, particularly conifers, tends to become dry and acid. Mulch with a humus-rich compost. Rake off any fallen foliage and put it in the compost pile to speed its decomposition. When the partially decomposed compost is ready to return to the garden, lightly turn the soil and work in the organic matter as needed.

Deciduous trees are usually easier to work with, especially if they are well established and high-branched. In most cases enough light penetrates to ensure that the plants don't become scraggly; winter rains can reach the ground and deciduous foliage decomposes relatively quickly to eventually form a thick, black leaf mold. Such areas are tailor-made for a woodland garden and any gardener with such a site and established deciduous trees should be grateful indeed.

Your planting choice is largely governed by the degree of light. Rhododendrons, camellias and other large shrubs generally need reasonably bright conditions. They grow best around the outer edges of the woodland or under a very light canopy. Fuchsias will cope with some moist shade while the ferns and foliage shrubs already mentioned will tolerate full shade.

Primroses, meadow rue *(Thalictrum)*, dicentras and irises need bright shade; *Helleborus* and hostas will cope with slightly less light. Relatively few desirable perennials will grow well in deep shade. Columbines *(Aquilegia)*, ferns, *Lamium* cultivars and *Pachysandra terminalis* do an effective job of carpeting and filling in the darker sections of a shady garden.

Woodland bulbs seldom do well in the permanent shade of evergreens. They need spring sun and are most at home under deciduous trees that do not leaf up too early. The gradual increase in shade as the leaves develop creates perfect conditions for woodland bulbs such as bluebells *(Hyacinthoides)*, snowdrops *(Galanthus)*, wood anemones and grape hyacinths *(Muscari)*. Also use cyclamen, aconites, the hardy *Geranium phaeum*, lily-of-the-valley *(Convallaria majalis)*, Solomon's seal *(Polygonatum × hybridum)* and foxglove *(Digitalis)*.

Woodland flower gardens tend to be spring gardens and they can become somewhat colorless in summer. Make sure you have a good range of foliage types to ensure continued interest. Hostas are available in a huge range of leaf forms, and bold-foliaged perennials such as *Filipendula*, *Acanthus* and *Bergenia* will provide variety of shape and texture. Ferns are invaluable for adding variety of foliage in shaded areas. Tuberous begonias and shade-loving annuals, such as impatiens and mimulus, can be used to extend the flowering season in summer.

Water-efficient Gardens

Many gardeners are conscious of the need to conserve water resources and make every effort to recycle and store rain water, as well as some household water. Each year drought inspired water restrictions often affect gardeners well before other domestic water users. Ingenious and practical blueprints for keeping the garden looking good and conserving water have evolved. The various water authorities publish their own tips and suggestions for conserving: most are common sense and don't require elaborate equipment or extensive reorganization of the garden.

- Install collection barrels or cisterns to store winter rain water for gardening use.
- Group plants together according to their water needs.
- Choose perennials and shrubs that are drought-tolerant or are used to dry conditions. Plants with gray, leathery or hairy foliage are among the most drought-tolerant plants. Lavender, santolinas, cistus and Mexican orange blossom *(Choisya ternata)*, are some of the attractive plants that grow well in such situations.
- Make sure the top layer of the soil is not compacted or has a hard crust, as this will result in moisture loss from the soil. In fall (autumn) dig in organic matter which improves the soil structure and helps retain soil moisture. In spring or after winter rains, mulch beds to slow down evaporation of surface water.
- Water early in the morning and late at night to avoid rapid evaporation of water. Water onto the surface of containers and to the roots of plants. Attach a hose end shut-off valve so that you don't waste water as you move from bed to bed.
- If you plant annuals that need regular watering, group them in one area or in containers and place water trays under the containers.
- Don't waste water on the lawn, it will recover in fall (autumn).

- Keep competition from weeds to a minimum by weeding regularly or by planting strong-growing ground-cover plants that will outdo the weeds.
- Deeper, more infrequent waterings will encourage roots to grow deeper, making the plant less dependent on supplemental water and more drought tolerant.

Domestic irrigation systems that rely on simple timers are great water wasters. A system that detects if rain is falling before switching on is an improvement but is far from perfect because it still activates if rain has just fallen and regardless of the level of soil moisture. The only truly efficient automatic irrigation system is one that checks the soil moisture before switching on. Because hand watering is viewed as a chore it can be very efficient—we tend to water only those areas that really need it.

Sprinklers that spray over a wide arc waste water by wetting paths and areas of bare earth. Not only do the plants not receive all the applied water, much is lost to evaporation before it can be used. Soak hoses, drippers and micro-tube irrigation systems are more efficient because they apply moisture directly to the soil surface and may even target specific plants.

Increasing the organic content of the soil is the best way to achieve the ideal combination of good moisture retention and good drainage. Incorporating compost is moisture-efficient because it adds humus and adds to the moisture content of the compost itself. Mulches conserve moisture by reducing evaporation from the soil surface but must be applied after the soil has been made thoroughly moist.

Lawns need plenty of water to remain green in hot weather. It has been estimated that over half of the water used for garden irrigation goes to maintain lawns, yet many lawns are simply not used. Reducing your lawns to just those areas that are absolutely essential is one of the greatest water-saving measures you can take.

The type of grass is also important. The finest lawn grasses, like red fescue, usually demand the most water. Changing to a more drought-tolerant grass or one that can withstand drying off over summer will create a more efficient lawn without having to resort to coarse grasses.

Consider too the range of plants that are grown. *Brachyglottis* (syn. *Senecio*) species have moisture-conserving silver-gray felting on the underside of their leaves which helps them cope with drying winds. The leathery leafed *Pittosporum* species, such as *P. crassifolium* and *P. ralphii* are also drought resistant.

Cacti and succulents, silver-leafed plants, summer-dormant bulbs and plants with tap roots, including rock rose *(Cistus)* and santolinas, can survive extended periods without irrigation. Plants native to the Mediterranean climate regions of the world such as California, and parts of Chile, South Africa and Australia, tend to be naturally drought tolerant. Many however, will not survive through cold-climate winters or regions with abundant summer rainfall. Selecting plants from similiar climates and environments throughout the world helps reduce maintenance and ensure healthy, well-suited plants.

Group your plants according to their water use and they should all need watering at about the same time. Grouping plants from one geographic region is one of the best ways of achieving this, as such plants will have evolved to cope with similar conditions. Creating an oasis in an otherwise dry landscape enables the gardener to group together plants that need more water while creating a visually attractive and inviting cool, green sanctuary.

All these points can be summed up as simply taking the time to understand the effects of your cultivation techniques and your plant selection in terms of water usage. Get it right the first time and the work involved in garden maintenance is minimized while water efficiency is maximized.

Using Native Plants

Gardeners have always been excited by new plant introductions with the result that gardens are filled with a rich mixture of local and exotic plants.

Gardeners around the world have often been dismissive of their local flora, appreciating instead the dramatic appeal of exotics. It is often a case of one country's unappreciated native plants becoming the chosen exotics by gardeners in another country. In recent years, however, there has been increased interest in the use of native plants.

Apart from the conservation aspect of growing native plants, there are some considerable advantages in choosing natives over exotics: climate tolerance, pest resistance and the ability to be self-sustaining being the most important. The native flora varies considerably over the country, but by choosing plants endemic to your area, you can be almost certain of having hardy plants that will thrive in your garden. Native plants have evolved with native insects and plant diseases and can generally withstand their attacks.

North America has a great diversity of plants native to a wide variety of plant communities, landscapes, climates and soils. The humid coastal plains of the southern states are quite different from the arid intermountain ranges of the west. Likewise, the mild climate of the Pacific West Coast seems worlds apart from the harsh winters of New England or the upper Midwest.

The vibrant red berries of winterberry *(Ilex verticillata)* stand out in the snow-covered swamps of New England, while out west, the waxy yellows of flannel bush *(Fremontodendron)* and the rich blues of spring-blooming California lilac *(Ceanothus)* add color to the arid landscape. Down south the oak-shaped leaves of oakleaf hydrangea turn vibrant shades of red and purple in the fall (autumn), while in the spring woodlands of Washington, giant trilliums *(Trillium chloropetalum)* hold upright their distinctive three-petaled flowers. The beauty and diversity of the native landscape is year round and across every plain, mountain, seacoast and woodland of the continent.

Native plants offer benefits to residents other than gardeners. By planting a wide selection of nectar- and berry-producing natives you help the survival of birds, butterflies, moths, bees and many other beneficial insects, as well as bats. A stand of native plants in a garden can be a lifesaver for migratory birds, and if you are willing to provide supplementary feed, you may find that your garden takes on an exciting new dimension with regular visitors that may become permanent residents.

Fremontodendron californicum, ***the best known and hardiest of the flannel bushes.***

The Winter Garden

Winter is an unavoidable fact of life, but it is not all gloom as there are so many trees, shrubs, climbers and other plants that lighten the winter months with the color and texture of their bark, stems, foliage, hips, fruits and seed heads. Flowering plants include the fragrant winter daphne *(Daphne odora)*, silk-tassel bush *(Garrya eliptica)* with its long pendulent tassels, the long-lasting flowers and interesting foliage of the many different *Helleborus* species and the vibrant yellows, oranges and reds of the witch hazels *(Hamamelis)*. The bright yellows of winter hazel *(Corylopsis)* and winter jasmine *(Jasminium nudiflorum)* brighten the winter landscape as do the berries of holly *(Ilex)*, pyracanthas, cotoneasters and wintergreen *(Gaultheria procumbens)*.

Gardens in mild-winter climates can depend on fine foliage plants for winter interest. The colorful varieties of flax *(Phormium)*, the fine texture of evergreen grasses, the bold leaves of philodendrons and palms, along with the succulent rosettes of agaves and the long pointed leaves of yuccas, all provide interesting year-round foliage which is especially appreciated during the winter months.

All gardens contain many micro-climates that display varying characteristics. Some pockets may be less frosty, others will be exposed to almost continual breezes and some areas may hardly ever see rain.

Strong winds can be just as damaging as frosts, and continual cool sea breezes in particular can damage many otherwise well-adapted plants. Providing adequate wind shelter is vitally important, but take care that in so doing you are not reducing the air movement that helps prevent the formation of frost pockets.

There are always 'must-have' plants that are not hardy enough to survive winter outdoors and they will need the protection of a conservatory or greenhouse. Tender climbers, such as bougainvilleas and passifloras and many orchids, especially cymbidiums, thrive within a well-maintained greenhouse or sunroom.

In a conservatory or greenhouse you can enjoy the color and fragrance of early-flowering bulbs, such as daffodils *(Narcissus)* and hyacinths, plus the fragrance and fruit of citrus such as the dwarf Meyer lemon, which will grow in greenhouse temperatures down to around 25°F (-4°C).

It is important to keep the conservatory or greenhouse free of pest and disease as far as is possible. Hygiene and good air circulation will help. Blinds for shading and automatic roof vents will keep temperatures down in high summers, and will help prevent outbreaks of spider mite. In winter roll up shading and keep vents shut, but make sure there is still a good airflow while being careful to avoid damaging draughts.

The graceful arching foliage of palms offers a touch of tropical splendor under glass on chilly January nights. There are several that require only average light and warmth in winter. They can be grown in conservatories, sunrooms or as house plants depending on their size. Palms generally prefer shade when young and can be grown under a protective tree canopy or shading, and are usually good container plants.

Flowering plants, including gardenias, tibouchinas, bouvardias, hibiscus, *Iochroma cyaneum* or *Ruellia macrantha*, will transform the conservatory or sunroom into a subtropical paradise. They need shading and regular watering and feeding in the growing season. Check them closely for insects and deal with them as soon as they appear.

Cymbidiums thrive within a well-maintained greenhouse or sunroom. This is Cymbidium *Clarissa Carlton 'Shot Silk'.*

Courtyard and Patio Gardens

As cities become increasingly crowded, gardens inevitably become smaller. Many new houses that have little or no garden in the traditional sense often have courtyards and patios that can be made into attractive green and flowering areas. Larger gardens, too, often have enclosed areas that with attention to detail can be made just as interesting and practical as a large garden.

The first step is to break up and soften the rigid lines of the bare structure. Start by screening off any utility areas or unsightly objects such as garbage cans, drainpipes or air-conditioning units. This is most easily done with trellises and frames covered with climbers or upright shrubs grown as evergreen screens.

Often there will be existing features you can work around. A small tree or large shrub can be used as a background to a planter or a bench seat and the rest of the design developed from there. The entrance may be flanked by imposing pillars that can be reflected in the garden by the use of upright plants such as Italian cypress *(Cupressus sempervirens)* or columnar deciduous hornbeams or maples. Be careful where you plant trees that will develop large roots and may cause damage to foundations and waste pipes.

Paving is often already present and its color, texture and pattern may dictate how the garden is developed. Large areas of terracotta-colored paving suggest a hot environment that is often best planted with Mediterranean plants, such as lavender, cistus and oleanders. Gray paving is cooler and may be better suited to a shaded courtyard planted with rhododendrons, fuchsias and camellias.

Walls and fences, often a major feature of a patio or courtyard, are usually visible from any part of the garden so they should be made either as attractive or unobtrusive as possible. Cover fences with flowering climbers including honeysuckle, clematis or roses. Support them on the walls using a system of vine eyes and wires; then, if you have to do any maintenance of the walls, you can lift the plants away without damaging them. Walls can be patterned or textured to lessen their utilitarian appearance.

If they face south and are not over-shadowed by buildings, patios and courtyards are often summer heat traps. Shade trees may be too large or there may be no soil in which to grow them, and in any case it is not sensible to plant trees too close to the house. Although some trees can be grown in large containers, it may be better to consider alternatives. Pergolas may be erected as separate structures or attached to the house then covered in thin wooden laths to provide shade, or climbers can be grown over them. Artificial shading, such as awnings and umbrellas, is often best for very small patio gardens where evergreen overhead foliage can be cold and uninviting.

For quick color, fill pots or raised planters made from brick, concrete blocks or timber with vibrant annuals and perennials. Hanging baskets and window boxes attached to the house will add extra color.

You can also grow small quantities of fruit and vegetables in containers. Strawberries are very good container plants, as are dwarf fruit trees. Tomatoes, peppers and lettuces will provide the contents of a salad bowl and look good while they grow. Plant them up in growbags or the largest containers you can muster.

A small patio garden is often the perfect space for herbs. A bed edged with a low box hedge and planted with sage, rosemary, basil (in summer) and thyme provides interesting foliage colors and textures and superb fragrance while also being highly functional. Invasive herbs such as mint and lemon balm are more easily controlled when grown in containers. You could leave a few slabs of the patio floor unlaid and plant them up with lavender or thyme. The result is a fragrant or aromatic effect that incidentally softens the hard look of the patio.

Patio and courtyard gardens may be small, but the advantage is that they are easier to personalize and cheaper to experiment with. Be adventurous and the results should be every bit as satisfying as those from a larger garden.

ABOVE: *A garden that fits in with its environment requires less work than one that is fighting it.*
RIGHT: *Window boxes planted with annuals and perennials like these geraniums add extra color to the house and garden.*

Low-maintenance Gardens

Low maintenance is rather a subjective term: we all have our own ideas and limits with regard to the amount of work and time we are prepared to put into our gardens. Presumably, if you are reading this book you love plants and that inevitably leads to cultivating plants. Doubtless there are many aspects of gardening you enjoy, but there is no need to make more work for yourself: there are many labor-saving tricks and techniques that any gardener can use to good effect.

We have already looked at several of the main labor savers. In discussing water-efficiency we considered automated watering systems, mentioned mulching and reducing lawn areas; in considering patios and courtyards we looked at paving and raised planter beds; with native and coastal gardens the emphasis was on living with the climate and plants rather than trying to make them conform to your ideas; and nothing could eliminate hands and knees weeding more completely than a large water garden, although ponds usually require annual cleaning.

Weeding is probably the most loathed garden task. Routine mulching is the best way to cut down your weed problems while at the same time improving the health of your plants. The mulch forms a loose surface layer in which weeds, particularly those with strong tap roots, cannot get a firm hold. Pulling a dock or dandelion from a well-mulched garden is easily done by hand.

Remember, don't bury your shrubs and perennials in mulch. Keep the mulch clear of main trunks and keep it loose to prevent thatching. In heavily weed-infested areas it may be necessary to use a water-permeable membrane covered with bark to permanently discourage persistent perennial weeds. Layers of newspaper under the mulch will also act to prevent the development of weed seeds present in the soil.

The most attractive form of weed control is achieved by using clump- or mat-forming ground covering plants such as chamomile or creeping thyme. Ivy can also be used successfully as a ground cover to exclude light from, and weaken, competing weeds.

Back or knee injuries are among the hazards of gardening. Raised beds can lessen the problem while at the same time ensuring good drainage and making irrigation installation very straightforward. Certainly, there is considerable labor involved in making and filling the beds, but once they are made you may wonder how you ever managed without them. When you move plants in containers either use a handcart or move them as you would furniture, swivelling them on their bases. If the containers can be lifted make sure you pick them up correctly by keeping your back straight, bending the knees and lifting the pots up and in front of you.

A garden that fits its environment requires less maintenance. The desire to grow tender or difficult plants is something that all gardeners experience, but the frustration and work involved may not be worth it. Natural habitat gardeners have long realized this and have created many excellent examples of low-maintenance gardens that can serve as a guide and inspiration to us all.

Lawns are labor-intensive—all that mowing, top-dressing, moss and weed killing plus edge trimming. Low-maintenance planting can cut down the time spent on lawn care. Paving some of that lawn area may even be a good idea and it is certainly a more durable surface. Alternatively, lawns planted with meadow wildflower plugs or meadow sod can be managed like a meadow. Cut simple grass paths as needed, while the meadow should only be mown after flowers have bloomed and seeded.

Low-maintenance gardening is as much a matter of preventing future work as reducing frequent chores. Appropriate plants for specific garden situations and climates is essential. Always consider a plant's growth habit and the amount of space you are providing for the new garden plant. Trees that become too large or are poorly sited may have to be trimmed back every year; hedges that grow too wide or high require constant maintenance; and shrubs that become tall and lank overshadow smaller, more desirable plants that in turn also become rank growers.

As is so often the case with gardening, designing for low maintenance is just simple common sense. There is no such thing as a completely no-maintenance garden, but with a little forethought you can avoid making work for yourself and have more time to relax and enjoy the garden as your personal oasis.

Hardiness Zone Map

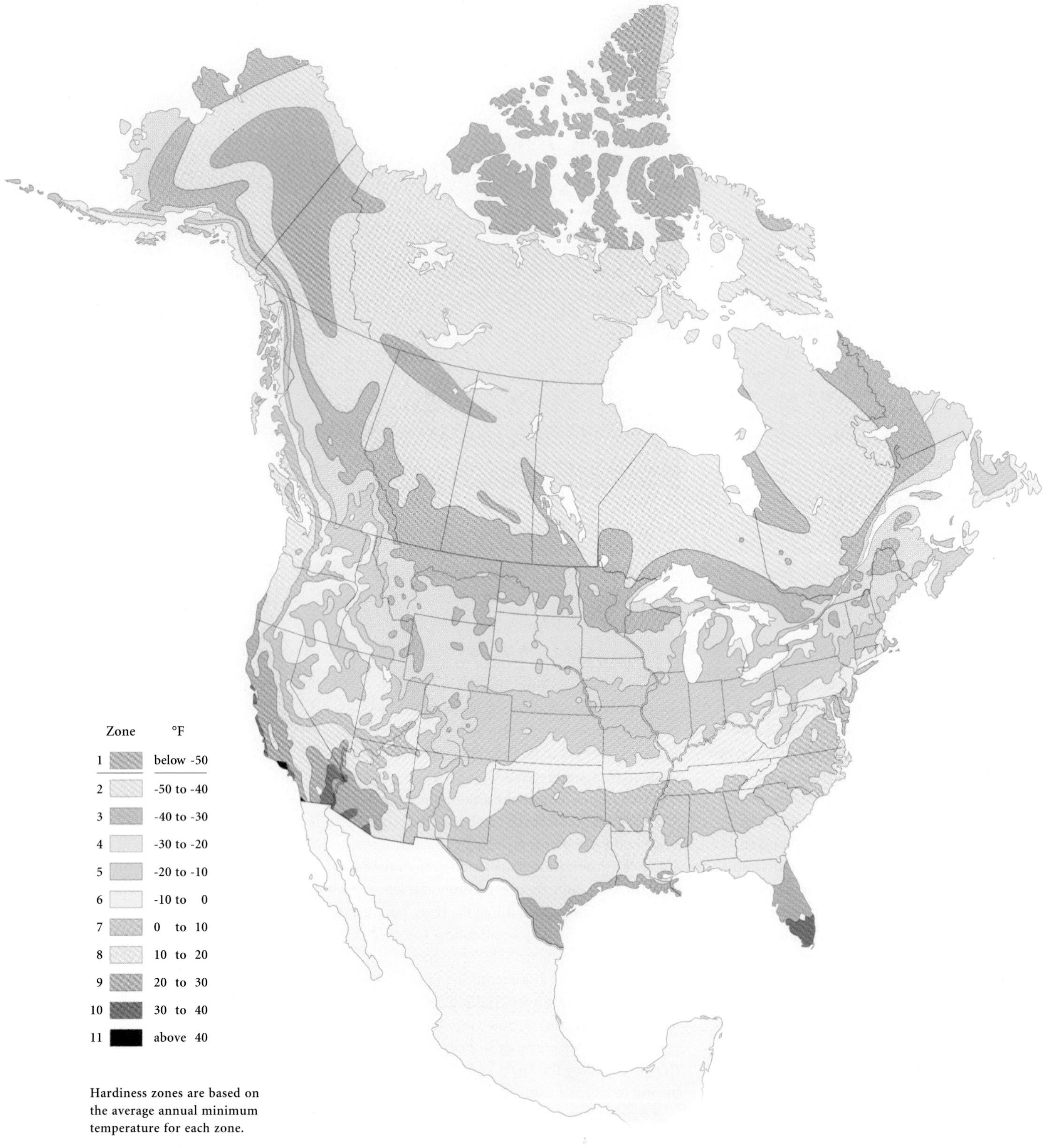

Hardiness zones are based on the average annual minimum temperature for each zone.

This map shows North America divided into zones of expected minimum winter temperatures, which may limit the survival of cultivated plants. This system of Plant Hardiness Zones was developed by the US Department of Agriculture. The coldest zone is Zone 1, corresponding to a subarctic climate such as central Canada or Siberia; the warmest zone is Zone 12, which covers much of the equatorial tropics (but not tropical highlands).

Each zone covers a range of 10 Fahrenheit degrees (5.5 Celsius degrees), as shown in the accompanying table (the Celsius rounded to the nearest degree). Zone 10 is the lowest zone in which frost and snow are not normally experienced.

For each plant listed in this book, both a minimum and maximum zone are indicated, for example ZONES 6–11 for *Magnolia grandiflora.* This means that the tree will survive the average winter frosts expected in at least the warmer parts of Zone 6, in which temperatures fall below 0°F (-16°C); but that it will also grow reasonably well in zones up to at least the cooler parts of Zone 11, where winter minimums are above 40°F (4°C). The indicating of a maximum zone goes beyond the original intent of the Plant Hardiness Zones, but we believe it serves a useful purpose here, in that most non-tropical plants have definite limits as to how warm a climate they will tolerate—in many cases they will survive in warmer zones but may fail to flower or fruit, or prove very short lived.

Major Plant Groups

Annuals and Perennials

Planting Combinations

By combining perennials with annuals in a more informal manner, the garden loses that 'all or nothing' effect which is so evident when a bed of annuals has 'finished' and is again planted out with tiny seedlings. By placing clumps of perennials beside drifts of annuals the eye is drawn from one accent to another, say from a group of low-growing annuals in front to the taller perennial flower spikes behind. Annuals are marvellous for providing a festive welcome to an entrance or a splash of color to a shrub border when the garden is to be used for a special event. For a continuous effect, group them with perennials, staggering the flowering times of the plants so that when a small pocket of annuals is nearly past its prime a perennial just behind is about to flower. This complementary display can take a few seasons to achieve, as many perennials need two years to bloom, but don't give up as experimenting in this way is one of the most rewarding aspects of gardening.

Apart from color combinations within a garden, try to tie in the house color to that of a garden display so they complement one another: a red or red-orange toned house looks good surrounded by bright oranges, yellows, rusty reds and creams, while a white or pastel painted house blends well with soft blue, mauve, pink and white flowers plus masses of silver foliage.

Just as important as linking the house to the garden, is the overall siting of the garden beds. Most annuals demand full sun to flower well so be sure to choose an aspect where the plants will receive as much light, particularly morning sun, as possible. Give them generously wide beds ensuring the colorful display will not be overwhelmed by shrub foliage or robbed of nutrients by the roots of nearby permanent plants.

Instant Color Effects

One of the most welcome developments in recent years has been the increase in the number of annuals and perennials available in 'instant color' pots. Once red geraniums were the only available way to provide a splash of color in early spring; now, right through the seasons a pot or tray of mature flowering annuals can be purchased to add instant color to a garden dead spot or patio. And don't overlook hanging baskets filled with annuals to highlight a garden color scheme. If potting up seedlings to make a basket full of your own instant color, take care to choose plants that will fall gracefully over the edge of the basket. If you are using large pots or tubs, both upright and sprawling plant types can produce a very decorative display.

Annuals, by their very nature, aim to set as many seeds as possible within a very short life span. Gardeners can extend the flowering period by cutting the blooms for indoor use or nipping off faded flowers before they set seed and so decide it's all over for another year. If you follow this procedure, remember it is good practice to provide regular nourishment to the plants in the form of a quick-acting fertilizer designed to promote flowers rather than foliage growth.

Soil Preparation and Planting

To ensure strong growth and maximum flowering, prepare your garden beds soundly. If the area to be planted has not been dug over before, it is a good idea to double dig. This means that the topsoil, say to a fork's depth, is weeded and put aside and the soil under this layer is dug over to the depth of a fork. Humus, such as well-rotted manure, or compost can be added to this layer to help break up heavy clay particles or to add moisture-retentive qualities to sandy soils. This double digging is particularly beneficial to perennials which may be left in the same position for some years. Replace the top layer of

RIGHT: *A display of annuals like these pansies and double daisies takes a lot from the soil, which you have to put back if you want to repeat it.*
BELOW: *With their large, brightly colored, showy pea flowers,* Lupinus *species and hybrids will enhance any garden.*

soil and prepare this surface in accordance with your planting needs. If planting perennials, a dressing of well-rotted manure or compost or a complete fertilizer can be added while roughly digging the soil over; if hardy annual seeds are to be sown directly into the soil in temperate areas, this top layer needs to be well dug over to remove any clods, then raked evenly to ensure a smooth, even surface.

In many areas the local climate determines when and if seeds can be planted directly into the ground. If a late frost is a possibility, a much greater success rate is ensured if seeds are sown in a greenhouse or on a warm, weather-proof verandah or similar sheltered spot. This guarantees that the seedlings are ready to be transplanted as soon as weather permits.

Annuals are grown from seed each season, but there are various ways to propagate perennials. Most can be grown from seed, however this usually takes longer for blooms to form. If established crowns or rhizomes are divided, new plants, true to form, are generally established more quickly and often produce flowers the following season.

For gardeners in all climatic zones annuals provide welcome displays of color, especially in early spring, while perennials put on a color parade once a year, often as a bonus to distinctive foliage. What's more, perennials pay handsome dividends, providing the gardener with a source of plant material with which to experiment with design and color combinations each season.

Bulbs, Corms and Tubers

Bulbs

True bulbs, of which the onion is an easily identified example, are made up of a series of scales joined at the base which enclose and protect a central bud. These scales collect and store food for the following year's growth and flowering, and for this reason it is necessary to allow the leaves of true bulbs to die down naturally as they continue to manufacture and store food for the following season, well after the flower has finished. This process also makes it possible for true bulbs such as hyacinths, narcissi and tulips to flower successfully in pots or jars as they use this stored energy to produce the current season's flowers. True bulbs reproduce by forming bulbils around the base of the plant and these can be easily removed when bulbs are lifted, even though they may take several years to flower.

Corms

A corm has a swollen base of solid storage tissue. Once flowering is over a new corm develops on top and the original one dies, often producing new corms or pips around the perimeter before it withers completely. Gladioli and freesias are good examples of a corm.

Tubers

Another form of food storage system is the tuber which can be formed from either stems or roots. 'Eyes' are produced from these swollen areas and form new plants. Dahlias are an example of this type of bulb as is the common potato which, if it has been sitting in the vegetable drawer too long, starts shooting new growth from the 'eyes'.

Creating Effects with Bulbs

Bulbs have evolved in response to long cold winters with a shortish warm season. They are able to store food for long, dry, dormant periods, then, in very quick time when the climate is right, shoot, flower then gather enough food for the following year. Some northern hemisphere bulbs like crocuses and fritillarias wait for the watering they receive as the snow melts to suddenly burst upon the scene. These and many other bulbs are very particular regarding their environment as many temperate climate gardeners have realized when they have omitted to chill their tulip bulbs in the refrigerator before planting. Other bulbs are far more accommodating and will often naturalize in the most unlikely places because the soil, combined with the surrounding ecosystem, is to their liking.

Even in small gardens, it can be easy to create a natural effect with bulbs. They are at their best under lightly foliaged deciduous trees as the roots of the trees ensure adequate drainage and there's less competition from grass. Choose these woodland companions giving consideration to their dormant period. Bulbs such as trilliums and scillas and many of the narcissus species, shoot and bloom early; then as they approach their dormant period the overhead canopy is beginning its active growth, creating interest and providing the shade the bulbs need at this time.

The informality of a woodland bulb display relies to a great extent on the naturalistic way in

ABOVE LEFT: *The sunny narcissus flowers are ideal for an informal garden display (seen here planted with a* Doronicum *cultivar) as well as for indoor decoration.*

ABOVE RIGHT: *A pleasing effect is achieved by planting bulbs in drifts of the same species, such as these* Cyclamen hederifolium.

LEFT: *The elegant shape and lovely range of colors of its flowers makes the tulip one of the most popular bulbs in the world.*

which the bulbs are planted. Planting in drifts, randomly scattering the bulbs and leaving them to grow where they land when thrown by the handful, is the best method of ensuring this. The size of the drift is governed by available space, of course, yet it is the very randomness of the display rather than its size that is the eye-catching element. Often gardeners in cold areas rely on bulb drifts to give a welcome color display in early spring and they are tempted to mix different species and colors. However, a more pleasing effect is achieved by having drifts of different color or species flowing on from one drift to the next rather than a multi-colored look. Bluebells look good in such a design with the blue species in the lighter, more open areas and the white flowering ones grouped closer to the dark green background of evergreen shrubs.

There are many hardy bulbs which we often associate with 'old' gardens. Long left to their own devices, they surprise us each year with their colorful appearance amid the shrubbery. Some of these, like *Amaryllis belladonna*, send up tall, single stems holding clusters of pale pink trumpets at the cusp of the summer–fall (autumn) season, while the snowdrop with its dainty green-tipped white bells lets us know when spring is almost here.

Planting bulbs among shrubs usually needs careful consideration because we can easily lose track of where they are while they are dormant, and gardeners everywhere have the tendency to fill any vacant space with something new which has taken their fancy. As always, competition from overhanging shrubs also has to be taken into account.

Many of the more delicate bulbs are overpowered by surrounding plants and are ideally suited to rock gardens where individual pockets can be given over to one particular species. Rockeries really need to be placed on an existing slope or where a change of level is being designed into the garden. If this is not an option, dwarf bulbs can be placed in spaces made in a brick or stone paved area where they can pop up in pockets from under a fine gravel scree. Provided drainage has been catered for, these pockets are ideal for dwarf tulips, crocuses, freesias, ixias, babianas, lachenalias and other delicate bulbs which would be lost in the general shrubbery.

Raised beds filled with good quality, free-draining soil, are a sure way of providing bulbs with the freedom from competition and drainage they need. These beds can be made using treated logs, railway sleepers or a couple of rows of old bricks. For a gardener wishing to perfect the hobby of growing prized, delicate bulbs rather than opting for a general garden display, these beds may well be the answer. Alternatively, these raised beds can be filled with free-draining sand and pots of bulbs plunged into them to ensure they don't dry out, then when the flowers appear each individual pot can be taken indoors or placed in a prominent position in the garden or on the patio where the blooms can be fully appreciated.

ABOVE: *The delicate mauve-pink flowers of* × Epicactus *'Bridesmaid' appear in spring. This semi-epiphytic cactus is ideal for pots and baskets.*
RIGHT: *Many* Parodia *species are ideal for beginners as they are very easy to grow. This one is* Parodia magnifica.

Growing Conditions

Generally bulbs prefer well-drained, slightly acidic soil. Most have evolved in areas with prolonged dry periods followed in the growing season by melting snow or good rains. Therefore, most are unable to withstand prolonged periods of waterlogged soil, but there are always exceptions to the rule and the arum lily thrives in moist sites as do the Japanese iris and the flag iris.

Similarly, there are few bulbs which can be grown in full shade and still flower well. Again, luckily for the gardener looking to highlight a shady spot with color throughout the year there is *Clivia miniata* which produces bright orange flowers each spring, or the more delicate lily-of-the-valley and snowdrop which can provide that wonderful flowering highlight of white blooms against green foliage that is so often employed by many a professional landscaper to such good effect.

Cacti and Succulents

Cacti

The cacti, a family from the Americas and distantly related to the carnation, show the succulent habit at perhaps its most wonderful. They have dispensed with leaves which would only transpire precious water during photosynthesis. To compensate for this the cacti stems are enormously swollen and spongy, often being almost spherical so they provide nearly as much light-catching area as leaves would. Many have developed ribbed forms, the ribs ensuring that at least part of the plant is in its own shade. A fat and tender plant full of stored water would be irresistible to thirsty desert animals so the typical cactus has given itself an armory of spines. Some have so many that they also serve to shade the body of the plant from the sun.

Other Succulents

Cactaceae is not the only family of succulent plants. There are succulent members of such well-known garden families as the lilies (agaves, aloes, gasterias) and even the daisies (kleinias, the succulent senecios) as well as families like Crassulaceae and Mesembryanthemaceae which are predominantly succulents. Most depart from the cacti in preferring to store their reserves of water in succulent leaves rather than stems, and these are often wonderfully shaped, colored and marked. Their habit varies from shrubby to just a few leaves on ground-hugging stems, and their flowers vary from the sheer brilliance of the mesembryanthemums and aloes to the delicate subtlety of some euphorbias.

This magnificent succulent, Euphorbia ingens, *comes from South Africa. In early summer it produces yellow-green flowers, often tinged red.*

Growing Cacti and Succulents

For all their diversity, cacti and succulents are surprisingly uniform in their cultivation needs, and their built-in tolerance of extreme drought makes them invaluable in arid climates. They ask only to be given sun, the more the better; perfectly drained but rich soil (desert soils are usually very fertile, as the prodigious crops they can yield under artificial irrigation show); and to be allowed to dry out completely while they are dormant in winter. Never mind that at this time they may shrivel alarmingly; they will recover almost fast enough to watch when you water them again in spring. Most can take a degree or two of frost as long as they are dry, but they are best considered tender and grown outdoors only in mild-winter climates. They differ so much in appearance from conventional plants that they need careful placement in the garden. Most people find it easiest to grow them on their own, but you don't have to grow them as single specimens; mass and group them, taking their different heights and colors into account just as you would in creating a border of more conventional perennials or shrubs. If you care to add a few desert-type (xerophytic) shrubs like *Senna artemisioides* as background and some carpeting annuals like portulacas, you'll find it easier to integrate the planting with the rest of the garden; but you need to exercise restraint—such lush growers as petunias would simply look silly.

Succulents grow happily in pots and, climate permitting, they can be the ideal choice for a pot placed where it is troublesome to water it frequently—on a roof or balcony for instance. In cold climates, especially those with wet winters, pot culture is the only way most people can grow succulents, either indoors or in a frost-proof greenhouse. Suit the size of the pot to the plant, and avoid plastic pots if you can—terracotta allows the soil to dry out faster. An open but still rich potting mix is best—you can try adding sand to a regular commercial mix, and mulching the plants with gravel to keep their collars dry. Give the plants as much sun and fresh air as you can, water and fertilize (artificial fertilizer is best) lavishly in spring and early summer while the plants are growing; and then tail off the watering until by the return of cold weather the plants are bone dry.

Almost all can be easily propagated from cuttings of side shoots, spring being the best time; the only thing to watch is that you don't over-water until the new roots are well developed. Indeed, over-watering is the main thing you can do wrong; it encourages the botrytis fungus to rot the roots and even the bases of the plants, and you can't always save them by making cuttings of unaffected parts of the plant after drenching everything in a strong fungicide. Mealy bug is the other main pest; it can eat out the growing point of a cactus but can also infest the roots of just about any succulent. As soon as you see it, spray the top and soak the roots in a powerful insecticide.

The only exception to this regime is the epiphytic forest cacti—the epiphyllums, the Christmas cacti, and their ilk. These are definitely frost tender, needing winter temperatures well above freezing, and are best grown in hanging baskets, as their usually flattened leaf-like stems tend to hang down. They like a fertile, well-drained soil and to be watered in warm weather, but again, don't water in winter.

All indoor grown cacti and succulents will benefit greatly from being taken outdoors for the summer, but bring them in the moment the weather forecast hints of cold and damp.

Climbers and Creepers

Climbers come mainly from temperate or tropical forests where competition has forced them to evolve various means of ensuring their lax stems reach the light that is essential for manufacturing food. These modifications allow some vines to twine around a host while others have thorns or hooks, tendrils, sucker discs or even aerial roots to reach out for an anchorage on supporting plants.

Arbors, Pergolas and Balcony Gardens

Arbors and pergolas are generally firm, solid structures built to last and can take strong growing twining plants such as wisteria and the ornamental grapes. Both of these are deciduous, providing shade in summer and allowing the sun to penetrate during the colder months. However, pergolas can be 'double planted' with less vigorous plants to give a combined show. For instance, a delicate, soft look can be achieved by highlighting the single yellow flowers of the rose 'Mermaid' against the small starry, white flowers of the dainty potato vine *(Solanum jasminoides)*. As well, these delicate vines can be used on a living frame such as an established flowering fruit tree and when the blossoms synchronize there are few more beautiful sights in the garden.

One of the joys of sitting under a pergola is being able to enjoy the flowers of the covering vine. Those with pendulous sprays such as *Akebia quinata* and *Thunbergia grandiflora*, as well as the superb wisterias, will certainly delight. However, some other vines will provide a carpet of fallen petals but the flowers remain hidden to all but those looking out from balconies or windows above the pergola. For this reason many vines are best grown on a vertical surface such as a trellis or lattice, or strands of wire stretched between two vertical posts, to form a screen or fence. This way the complete surface area of the plant provides a breathtaking display while taking up very little actual garden space. Consider aspect when growing climbers against a wall. In cold areas tender plants can be damaged if frozen tissue is thawed rapidly against a wall receiving early morning sun, while in warmer areas both the last rays of the sun and reflected heat from nearby paved areas can scorch new summer growth on plants.

Often the very reason for choosing to plant a vine against a wall is because it takes up very little space, yet this also could mean the root run is limited. Take care here with soil preparation and fertilizing to provide the best possible conditions for what is to be a feature plant. Often in these conditions, kept dry by eaves or next to a concrete slab, the climber is best planted a little away from the house then trained back against it. Cascading vines and shady canopies can be produced on balcony gardens to wonderful effect relying solely on pot culture. The risk of these pots overheating and drying out can be reduced by adding a creeping plant to cover the pot surface sides. In these sometimes exposed situations care should be taken never to allow the pots to dry out or their contents to become overheated—one cunning method to overcome this is to drop a plastic pot containing the plant into a more decorative one so the pot is insulated. Grouping three or five pots together to generate shade for one another is another way to ensure a successful high-rise or balcony garden.

Soil Preparation and Planting

As most climbers will be permanent, time spent preparing the soil well by digging it over will certainly be welcome. Like most plants, climbers need good drainage; this is especially important in those pockets against house walls. In these spots it is often worthwhile to dig deep and wide to unearth any leftover builder's rubble buried just beneath the surface. These positions can be a lot drier than the open garden so be generous with garden compost or animal manure to help the soil retain moisture.

Pruning

General pruning rules apply equally to climbers as to any other plant. In the very early stage of a climber's growth, finger or tip pruning encourages a single stem to branch out, giving more than one stem to be trained up a trellis—this can become the basis for an informal or stylized espaliered effect, say for a rose growing on stretched wire supports. As the climber matures, flowering can be encouraged by pruning; but, as in the case of shrubs, you have to be aware of the flowering characteristics of your chosen plant. Most will flower at the tips of branches, so, by pruning at nodes and allowing two or three extra branches to be formed, flowering can be increased. When planning pruning it must also be remembered that some vines flower on new or the present season's growth while others take till the next season to produce their blooms. Rambling type roses, for instance, flower on long new canes, and in general these can be cut well back after flowering. However, many of the climbing roses form a permanent mainframe of branches which adhere to horizontal trellising, then each year flowering side shoots appear and in turn these are pruned back to make way for further flowers. Even though they are prickly, roses trained in this way are easily managed and are long lived.

If a vine is tied onto a support be sure to check the ties regularly, particularly in the growing season, as they can injure the plant if they become too tight. Vines may take a little more of a gardener's time but results are most satisfying.

RIGHT: *Vines, such as this clematis with its pale yellow flowers and light green foliage, are ideal for softening a solid structure like a brick wall or fence.*
FAR RIGHT: *A vine grown against a wall provides a lovely display while taking up very little actual garden space.*
ABOVE RIGHT: *Ferns are greatly admired for their beautiful and diverse foliage. This lacy fern is* Asplenium lividum.

Ferns, Palms and Cycads

Ferns

Ferns are all perennials, mainly growing from creeping or clumpy rootstocks—although the tree ferns array their leaves atop palm-like trunks—and none has flowers. Their sex life is in fact rather complex and interesting. On the underside of their leaves (sometimes on special leaves which differ from the usual) they bear an array of what look like blisters. These are called sori, and they release spores, tiny clusters of cells which blow away on the wind. If they land in a favorable place, they germinate into curious little plants called prothalli, which usually look like little bits of leaf lying on the ground. These in turn bear male and female organs, the male releasing sperm which swim to the females to fertilize them. The fern plant then grows from the prothallus into its familiar form. The sperm need water to swim in, of course; and that is why ferns are almost all lovers of moist ground and shady places—in open areas the sun dries up the needed moisture too fast.

Ferns fall into two broad groups, the tropical and the temperate climate species, in each of which the variety of foliage forms and colors is quite staggering. You can have the usual once-divided fronds, twice or three times divided, crested, or even severely plain with no divisions at all. And they can be any shade of green or marked with color; in some species the sori are silver or gold and so abundant they color the leaf. The plants can be sedentary in habit or running about by their rhizomes, and they can be deciduous or evergreen. The tree ferns are mostly natives of warm-temperate to tropical climates and dislike frost, but they share the tribe's fondness for a shaded position, fertile soil and moisture.

Few ferns have big root systems, which makes them wonderful pot plants, although you need to choose your varieties with care if you want to grow them as house plants—most need more humidity than living rooms offer.

Ferns can be propagated from the spores, which are sown just like seeds in pots of moist soil, and most can be divided in the same way as any other perennial.

Palms

The palms are, by contrast to ferns, true trees, although usually they grow on a single unbranched trunk, with a crown of large leaves at the top. (Some form clumps of stems, but these are normally unbranched.) These leaves can be long and divided, like giant fern leaves, or they can be rounded and fan shaped, the two types being called 'feather' or 'fan' palms. They mostly grow in the company of other trees, so they like the shade, at least when they are young; but there are few among the taller palms that insist on it. Palms vary enormously in height; some of the clump-formers grow to only about 6 or 10 ft (1.8 or 3 m) tall and can be placed in the garden like shrubs; others can reach about 90 ft (27 m) and are sufficiently stately for the largest gardens. Alas, the most magnificent palms are strictly for frost-free climates, and the delights of a palm avenue are denied to the temperate climate gardener. He or she will have to be content with growing some of the more modest palms indoors; but they are among the most attractive of all house plants. They are mostly easy to grow; give them reasonable light, don't over-water them, and don't use a pot that is too large for the size of the palm.

There are few groups of trees as useful as palms in the countries where they grow; thatch is made from the leaves, the trunks provide timber, and dates and coconuts are significant commercial crops, both borne by palms. Some species can have their sap tapped to make palm wine or toddy; and there are those whose young shoots can be cut out and cooked like cabbage.

Cycads

Cycads are an ancient group of plants usually grouped like the conifers in the gymnosperms, but with palm-like fronds. They are only found in limited, warmer parts of the world. They bear large, nut-like seeds that are rich in starch. However, they are not for the vegetable plot—the raw seeds contain poisonous alkaloids which have to be destroyed by long and elaborate preparation for consumption. This varies with the species, but may involve pounding the seeds, steeping them in water for long periods or both. This is an art perfected by the indigenous peoples of Australia and Africa, where most cycads grow. Some species contain a great deal of starch (called sago) in their growing shoots, although as cycads grow so very slowly it is not economical to cultivate them commercially to harvest the sago. In fact, commercial sago (tapioca) comes from a totally unrelated plant.

It is their agonisingly slow growth that limits the popularity of cycads in gardens; sow a seed and it will be years before you are rewarded with a fully developed clump of glossy, palm-like leaves, let alone the curious flower cones, which can be far larger than any pine cone. The plants bear male and female cones, usually on the same plant, and the female cones can be a striking sight when the seeds ripen. Eventually, most will develop a short thick trunk, but don't hold your breath waiting—the magnificent specimens you see in botanic gardens are usually at least 50 years old. Cycads are not exactly abundant and are usually protected by law. If you do acquire one, give it a climate free of frost, or almost so, a place in light shade, and fertile soil. Grow it in a big pot by all means, and if you like you can bring it inside to a sunny room.

LEFT: Encephalartos friderici-guilielmi *is a striking cycad from South Africa. It is very hardy and adapts well to cultivation.*

BELOW: *Ferns and palms can be used to create an oasis in the suburban garden.*

Fruit and Nut Trees

Choosing a Fruit Tree

Fruit trees can be classed into two broad groups: the tropical fruits, members of several plant families, mainly evergreen, and often rather stately growers; and the temperate fruits, deciduous and almost all cousins of the rose. The citrus are a kind of link between the two; evergreen and with members that like hot climates and others that don't mind it coolish. Which to choose? Your own favorite, that goes without saying; but you need to take your climate into account. There is no joy in pining after mangoes if you suffer frost, or cherries if you can't provide them with the cold winters they need. Then, there is no point in growing just any sort of variety. Just about all types of fruit have been bred and improved by gardeners for centuries, and come in a bewildering number of varieties. Some of the tropical types (citrus too) can be grown from seed quite easily, but the resulting trees, while vigorous, almost always produce inferior fruit.

The named varieties are almost always grafted, and you may be offered the same one on several different understocks. Usually this is because by choice of a more or less vigorous stock you can tailor the final size of the tree, but sometimes one stock will be better than another in different soils. If in doubt, ask your supplier for advice, bearing in mind that bigger isn't necessarily better—you may prefer to have two smaller trees instead of one large one. That way you might have both a dessert and a cooking apple, or spread your crop by having an early-ripening variety and one that ripens later.

With some of the temperate fruits, notably apples, pears and sweet cherries, you need two trees in any case, as they are not 'self-fertile'—the flowers must receive the pollen of a different variety or there will be no fruit. Not that pollinating insects respect fences; the spouse tree could be in the garden of a co-operative neighbor. Or you might graft a branch of a compatible variety onto your main tree, being careful not to accidentally prune it off later.

Growing Fruit and Nut Trees

Almost all fruit trees need sun and fertile soil, and are best if they don't suffer undue drought while the fruit is ripening. They benefit too from some fertilizer in spring, but there is no need to grow them in mulched beds like vegetables; they can be grown in association with flowers and shrubs, in any way that suits your garden design. Careful and regular pruning will control the size of the tree and increase its fruitfulness, but you only have to come across some ancient apple tree, untouched by shears for years yet groaning with fruit, to realize that pruning is optional. Most warm-climate fruit trees need little pruning in any case. A specialized form of pruning is training the tree espalier, that is to grow the tree flat against a wall. The original idea was that in cooler climates, the warmth reflected from the masonry would encourage the fruit to ripen earlier. It is a lot of work as you will need to prune each year, but worth doing if you are short on space or want to grow a variety which is on the borderline of hardiness in your climate. Choose a tree grafted on a 'dwarfing' rootstock or it will be too vigorous.

All the above applies to nut trees too; after all they are just fruit trees from which we eat a different part of the fruit—the seeds rather than the fleshy covering. They aren't so popular, perhaps because we tend to regard nuts as an occasional luxury, but they are well worth growing, and the crop keeps without having to be preserved. As a group, they are less subject to pests and need less care generally.

Not all fruit grows on trees. There are for instance those that grow on vines, of which the grape is the supreme example; others are the kiwifruit (or Chinese gooseberry) and the granadilla, sometimes called the passionfruit, a great favorite in warm climates. All are great for covering fences and pergolas, and all are handsome plants. However selection of varieties is just as important as ever, especially with grapes; not only are varieties specially designed for wine, for eating fresh or for making raisins, they have very marked likes and dislikes about climate. All the fruiting vines need regular pruning to keep them under control, but no more than any other vigorous climber does.

Then there are the bush fruits, fruit shrubs rather than fruit trees. They can be the answer if you are short on space (although most like cool climates) and they are well worth growing, as their fruit tends to be soft and easily damaged on the way to market. Grow your own and you can have the very best. This is particularly true of strawberries, everyone's favorite—and everyone can grow them, for this is a creeping perennial, to be tucked in at the front of any convenient bed or container.

When is a fruit not a fruit? When it is a vegetable. The tomato is a fruit, but the plant is an annual to be grown in the vegetable patch rather than the orchard; and the fruit is a savoury one for main course dishes rather than dessert. The same is true of zucchini, bell peppers, squash, and even melons.

ABOVE: *Although pruning of fruit trees is optional, careful and regular pruning will control the size of the trees and increase their fruitfulness.*
RIGHT: *Like some other temperate fruits, apples are not 'self-fertile' so you need to grow two different varieties together to produce fruit.*

Indoor Plants

The Importance of Light

The first rule in growing any plant in the house is to give it adequate light. We almost always place our furniture in the best lit places in the room, but that often means that the corners where plants fit the decor best are the darkest in the room. The brightest place is in front of or just next to a window, but if you habitually keep your curtains drawn during the day for privacy, your room can be dim no matter how large your windows. There are plants that can take very low levels of light, but the range is limited, and pretty well confined to plants with plain green leaves. (Variegated leaves are almost always short on chlorophyll, and flowering takes a lot of energy which the plant can only derive from light.) You can overcome the forces of darkness by placing the plant under a lamp, but it will have to be fitted with a special bulb (a 'grow-light' or fluorescent bulb, available at most plant nurseries) that maximizes the frequencies of light that plants use—ordinary lights are of little use. Alternatively, have two plants and rotate them every week or two between the garden or greenhouse.

Humidity

The next requirement is adequate humidity, and here there can be real conflict between our ideas of comfort and those of our plants, many of which would be happiest in a Turkish bath rather than the average living room. If you have a well-lit bathroom or kitchen they can be good places for plants, but you can assist by growing several plants together—they will help humidify the air for each other—and by standing your pots on saucers filled with pebbles which you keep constantly moist (on the pebbles, not among them; you don't want the roots standing in water).

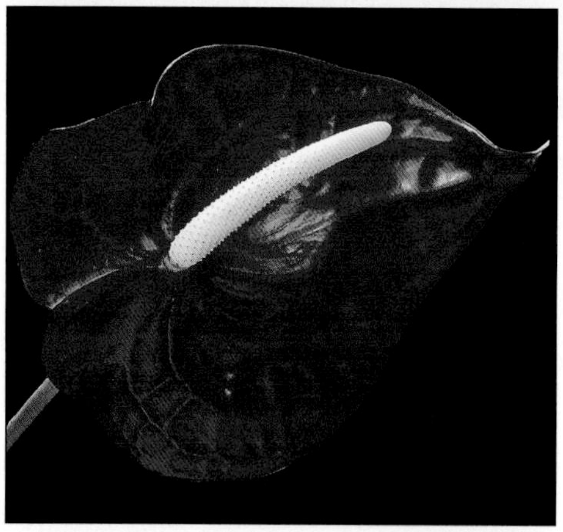

ABOVE: *Many indoor plants offer attractively colored foliage. This fine example is* Fittonia verschaffeltii.

LEFT: Anthurium andreanum *is grown for its brilliant red spathe. It blooms all year, making it popular as an indoor plant.*

Air-conditioning and central heating can dry out the air to desert-like levels. It is often said that house plants dislike air-conditioning, but this isn't strictly true. If they are standing on wet pebbles, they should be fine—and you'll be more comfortable too, and the piano will stay in better tune, for their presence. But you must keep your rooms at a reasonably even temperature. If you save energy by setting your system to come on and adjust the temperature by about 18°F (10°C) in the half-hour before you come home, your plants will resent it. Happily, about 64–70°F (18–21°C), the temperature that most people find comfortable, will suit most plants too, and if it falls by a couple of degrees during the night they'll appreciate it.

Watering

More house plants drown than die of thirst—water with care. Just about all should be allowed to dry out a little between waterings; but if you can't be so hard-hearted, pot them in terracotta pots, as their porosity makes it harder to over-water than impervious plastic. It looks better too. You can then use the best method of testing for dryness: tap the pot and if it rings, the plant needs water; if you hear a dull thud, it doesn't. This doesn't work with plastic! Alternatively, try one of the various self-watering pots, which allow the plants to draw just the water they need from a reservoir in the bottom. Or try concentrating on spathiphyllums, which are among the few house plants that like constant damp feet.

Temporary Plants

It is all very well to say that happiness comes from concentrating on the easy plants, but you would be less than human if you were not to fall sometimes for one of the difficult but spectacular flowering types like cyclamen, gloxinias or poinsettias. They aren't impossible—just difficult, needing warmer or cooler conditions than usual, high humidity and great care in watering—but they really aren't happy in the average room. Unless you have a greenhouse or sheltered, totally frost-free place in the garden to use as a convalescent home, resign yourself to these types being temporary delights. They'll still last longer than a bunch of cut flowers.

Fertilizing and Repotting

Sooner or later, if a plant flourishes the question of fertilizing or repotting will arise. The advent of slow-release fertilizers has made fertilizing easy. Just buy one formulated for indoor plants, and apply it in spring as growth begins (it's astonishing how even indoor plants remain aware of the seasons) according to the directions on the packet. As always, don't overdo the dosage. Fertilizer will usually allow you to at least put off the decision about repotting: but if you feel the plant's shoes really are getting too tight, do the job in spring, handle the plant gently, and don't go up to a pot more than a size bigger than the old one. If you like, you can tease off some of the old soil from the roots to allow more fresh soil, which should be the best premium grade potting mix you can buy. Naturally, you won't be tempted to put your plant in a container, no matter how beautiful, which has no drainage holes. If you can't resist, put some pebbles in the bottom, and use it purely as a decorative mask for the holey-bottomed one in which the plant is actually growing.

Pests

Alas, pests sometimes follow house plants indoors. The worst are mildew and root rot (almost always a result of over-watering), spider mite and mealy bug. All can be controlled by spraying with insecticides and fungicides, but who would be crazy enough to spray such poisons indoors, quite apart from the mess? If you can't take the plant outside to spray, you can use a systemic insecticide which is stirred into the soil. Fungi are more difficult, and if a plant really is severely infested, it might be wise to consider disposing of it, soil and all. (Wash the pot out with bleach and you can re-use it.)

A final word—dust. This settles invisibly on house plants and robs the leaves of light. Wipe it off regularly with a damp cloth, and, better yet, stand your plants out in the summer rain every so often. If you can bear to forego their company, a few weeks outside in the shadiest place in the garden each summer will do them a power of good; but bring them back in the instant you sense fall (autumn) in the air.

Lawns and Ground Covers

The universal favorite for flooring the main part of a garden is lawn. It is soft and quiet underfoot, it doesn't reflect glare, and its greenness is the most flattering backdrop imaginable for plants and flowers.

No one species will give a perfect, year-round sward—the finest lawns are the result of careful blending. Every area has its favorite lawn grass species, and these are the ones you should choose. We do suggest that if you choose the finest, slow-growing types you'll have less work to do in the long run, even if they are more trouble to establish than the faster growing meadow and pasture grasses.

Looking After a Lawn

Nonetheless the meadow grasses can become an acceptable lawn if they are regularly shorn, and that brings us to the least loved of all gardening tasks—mowing. No one enjoys it, and many shortcuts are devised by the lazy in the hope of having to take the mower out less frequently.

Most common is cutting the grass too short or leaving it to grow too long. Alas, none works. All weaken the grass and encourage the weeds: and so the time saved is spent (with interest) on weeding. A weedy lawn actually needs mowing more frequently than a clean one—the weeds grow faster than the grass so that unacceptable shagginess sets in sooner.

It's best to encourage a good, dense growing turf, by watering as needed, fertilizing at least once a year (in spring) and cutting short enough for neatness but not so short as to scalp the grass. With most fine grasses, about 1 in (25 mm) is short enough, and it is desirable not to let the grass get more than about twice as long as that so it won't be unduly shocked when it is cut. When you come to mow, you'll be grateful for having kept the lines of the lawn simple—getting the mower around wriggly edges and island flowerbeds is time consuming and frustrating. Whether you choose a rotary mower or a reel-cut type is up to you; the reel does give a more velvety finish (and is the only way to get that smart striped effect, caused by the way it 'lays' the grass like the pile of a carpet) but it is more trouble to maintain. Untidy edges will spoil the effect of the most immaculate mowing; allow time for trimming them, either with shears or a powered edging clipper. And don't be careless about safety. Turn the mower off whenever you leave it unattended, even for a minute; keep your hands and feet well away from the blades; and usher small children safely out of harm's way.

It can be tempting to allow the clippings to lie, to rot down and return the nourishment they contain; but this doesn't really work. They'll just make half-rooted 'thatch' and clog up the crowns of the grass plants. Off to the compost heap with them!

In nature, grass tends to grow in the spring and then brown off with summer's heat, to return green with the spring; but in gardens we want spring green all year. Except in the moistest of climates, this means watering. It is amazingly easy to do this wastefully—just sprinkle lightly until the lawn looks refreshed and repeat when it looks tired again. This will be pretty soon; light watering encourages the grass roots to linger near the surface. It is much better to water infrequently—even in the hottest, driest climates, this means no more than every ten days or so—but do it thoroughly so the water penetrates right into the soil and the roots go down deep after it.

The constant removal of foliage from the grass strips it of nutrients, and these ought to be made up to it by occasional fertilizing. This is easy; just buy a ready-made lawn fertilizer, sprinkle it on, and water heavily at once to wash it into the soil—if you don't it can burn the leaves. You can apply it at the manufacturer's suggested rate in one go, but it is more effective to divide the quantity in half and give two doses every couple of weeks.

If you started out with clean soil and keep the grass flourishing, weeds should cause little headache. If any get in, just dig them out (an old kitchen knife is a useful implement here) or spot treat them with glyphosate. The lawn will soon grow over the resulting bare patch, especially if you assist it with water and fertilizer.

Meadow Gardens

There is, however, one style of lawn to which all these rules don't apply, and that is the flowering meadow. Here, the grass is deliberately interplanted with 'weeds'—primroses, small bulbs, cornflowers, Flanders and Californian poppies, daisies and the like—the aim being to create an effect like the carpets of flowers you see in old tapestries. Very pretty and romantic it can be too. Here, you don't want the grass to flourish so much it smothers the flowers, so you start with rather poor soil, apply fertilizer with a sparing hand, water very judiciously, and mow only a few times a year.

Precisely when to mow depends on your chosen flowers: but as a guide, you'll probably mow in late winter to give the spring flowers a setting of short grass; again when they have shed their seeds and died down; and perhaps again in fall (autumn). Always keep the mower as high as it will go.

Ground Covers

It is a short step from the flowering meadow to leaving out the grass and carpeting the ground entirely with low-growing, easy-care plants, known, naturally enough, as ground covers.

You can use annuals as temporary ground cover—nasturtiums are excellent—but the best ground covers are spreading, evergreen perennials or dense, low-growing shrubs. Flowers are a feature of many, but far more important is the ability to make a carpet dense enough to smother weeds without growing too tall—ankle height is about right. Then a good ground cover needs to be presentable all year; to need little in the way of trimming or spraying; and to be easy to propagate to cut down on cost. It is possible to weave patterns with several species, but the stronger will tend to crowd out the weaker, and simplicity usually looks better anyway. Ground covers cannot be walked on.

Prepare your bed as thoroughly as for any other plant, plant at the appropriate season, and mulch at once; the last thing you want is weeds getting in between the young plants. If you like, you can plant some low-growing annuals between your permanent plants—and they will remind you to water and fertilize. Ground covers may be low, low maintenance when they are established, but when young they need care!

Ornamental Grasses

You can supplement the flowers in your meadow with grasses chosen for their ornamental foliage and flowers rather than their ability to stand

RIGHT: *With their airy grace, ornamental grasses look good beside a pond and as supplements to the flowers in a meadow.*

BELOW: *A healthy and well-manicured lawn can provide a flattering backdrop to flowers and foliage plants.*

cropping into lawn: but you will need to place them with care as many are quite tall. They can be placed anywhere in the garden that you want their airy grace, and it is currently fashionable to include them in plantings with more orthodox annuals and perennials. The important thing is to choose species that stay in sedate clumps; those that run about will turn themselves into weeds as soon as your back is turned. Most retain their form as they die off for the winter, and their golden and brown tints can be a lovely feature of the fall (autumn) and winter garden—but if they might be a fire hazard, by all means cut them down when they dry off.

Orchids

The orchid family is enormous (second only to the grasses as the largest in the plant kingdom), and wild orchids grow just about everywhere except in the Arctic and the Antarctic. The most admired and coveted may be those from the tropics and subtropics of the Old and New Worlds, but the more modest temperate climate orchids are delightful too, and not as well known as they should be.

Growing Orchids in the Garden

Most of these temperate orchids are terrestrial, that is they grow in the ground the way other plants do: but the glamorous warm-climate genera are mostly epiphytes, growing perched in trees (or on rock faces) where they derive nourishment from such debris as they manage to accumulate around their roots—fallen leaves, the occasional dead insect, that sort of thing—and storing water from rainy seasons in fleshy, almost succulent, stems called pseudobulbs. They can be grown very effectively thus in gardens where the climate is suitable; and it's not difficult to do. A not too shady tree, preferably with rather rough bark to which the roots can cling, is best. Attach the young plant in a suitable fork with twine, and pack sphagnum moss around its roots; water and fertilize as needed. The important thing is to match orchid to climate; but although we always think of epiphytic orchids as tropical plants, many grow in rather cool mountain regions and there is a surprisingly large range that can be grown outdoors wherever the temperature rarely falls to freezing and summer humidity is fairly high.

LEFT: Cattleya deckeri *is a member of the large genus of epiphytic cacti from Central and South America, perhaps the most admired of all orchids.*
BELOW: *The often fantastic shapes of column and labellum are designed to ensure that only the orchid's favorite insect is able to pollinate it.*

However, most of us will find it more convenient to grow our orchids in the conventional way in pots, which allows us to bring them into the living room when they flower, or to a sunroom for the winter. As long as it has ample drainage holes, the type of pot is immaterial; but terracotta not only looks better than plastic, it makes it easier to control the amount of water the roots receive. This is the most important aspect of growing orchids: most take rest periods, both in winter and for a short while after flowering, and dislike being over watered while they are not in active growth. This is critical in coolish climates or in an unheated greenhouse, for orchids can't cope with being both cold and wet—the roots go quite dormant in winter and will rot if they aren't kept dry. Don't pot them in soil or the roots will suffocate. Rather, choose a specially formulated orchid potting mix. Most of these are based on chopped up bark, the different types varying in how finely it is chopped. (Phalaenopsis and cattleyas, for instance, prefer a coarser mix than cymbidiums or paphiopedilums. If in doubt, choose the coarser mix.) The bark doesn't contain much nourishment for the plant, and you will need to fertilize. You can buy special orchid fertilizers, but a bit of well-rotted manure will be just fine.

Fertilize while the plants are growing, either making new leaves or flower buds; but not when the plants are resting. You can divide the plants like any other perennial when they outgrow their pots, after flowering is the best time. However there's no need, just put the plant (pot and all if its roots are clinging to the old one) into a bigger pot. Pests are few: the main ones are snails and caterpillars, which adore orchid flower buds; mealy bug; and spider mite.

Growing Orchids Indoors

If you can arrange the fairly high humidity they enjoy, there is no reason why you can't try orchids as house plants too, although it has to be admitted that out of flower few of them are especially decorative. Don't let direct sun strike them, but give them lots of bright light or they may grow furiously but never flower. Indoors or out, it's best to err on the side of too much light, even if the leaves then look a bit bleached. Lots of fresh air is desirable too—open the windows wide in warm weather.

If the orchid bug does bite, you will want to

consider a greenhouse. It is hard to do without one in cold climates, but even in mild areas it will considerably enlarge your scope. Whether it be timber or aluminum framed, plain or architecturally elaborate is up to you; but take as many ventilators as the makers offer. Not only do orchids like fresh air, you need to be able to keep the greenhouse temperatures from soaring on warm days, when the humidity should be kept up—spraying the plants with water every couple of days in summer is a good idea. Make sure too that the roof can be shaded from spring to fall (autumn). Heating can be by any means you find economical and convenient, the amount of heat needed depending on the plants.

Orchids are classified according to the minimum winter (night-time) temperatures they need, the convention being that 'cool growers' need about 46–50°F (8–10°C), 'intermediate growers' about 55–59°F (13–15°C), 'warm growers' as much as about 68°F (20°C), with daytime winter temperatures about 10°F (5°C) higher. (These classes are useful in determining the most suitable types to grow out of doors too, remembering that almost all orchids can take a couple of degrees less if they are kept dry in winter.)

Propagation

For all their variety, orchid flowers are built to a common pattern—three petal-like sepals and three petals, the lowest (the lip or labellum) being different in size, shape and often in color too. Above it, the stamens and stigma are fused into a single column, and the often fantastic shapes of column and labellum are designed to ensure that only the orchid's favorite insect gets a chance to pollinate it. Thus orchid hybrids are rare in the wild; but when gardeners perform the act, orchids interbreed with startling freedom, and hybrids uniting two, three, or even four genera (unheard of in other families) are common. These are usually given names combining those of their parents; for instance, cattleyas and their close relatives the laelias, brassavolas and sophronitis will cross among themselves, giving rise to brassocattleyas, brassolaeliocattleyas, sophrolaelias and so on. (When all four get into the act, a new name, *Potinara*, is used.) Actually pollinating is easy, but germinating the seeds is not; it needs laboratory conditions beyond the scope of most of us, who must rely on division. (Some tall growers such as vandas can be air-layered.)

Still, seed is the best way to propagate orchids in quantity, and this gives rise to a peculiarity in their nomenclature. If a breeder makes a particular cross, all the seedlings of that cross constitute a 'grex' and the grex is given a name, which by convention is not given the usual single quotes. The seedlings will be all of a kind, but some will likely be superior to their fellows; and if one of these is propagated vegetatively, it will be given a further (clone) name of its own, which does get quotes : and thus you get double-barrelled names such as *Brassolaeliocattleya* Sylvia Fry 'Supreme' or *Vuylstekeara* Cambria 'Plush'. (The system is sometimes used for rhododendrons and lilies too, as in *Rhododendron* Loderi 'King George'). These selected clones used to be frighteningly expensive, propagation by division being slow; but in recent years the technique of tissue culture has been applied to orchids with stunning success, enabling them to be quickly made available in large numbers. More than anything else, this has brought orchids from the gardens of the very rich to being flowers for all of us.

ABOVE: *This stunning woodland garden combines the lush green of trees with the brilliant colors of flowering shrubs, in this case rhododendrons.*
TOP LEFT: Rosa *'Claridge'. Roses are almost certainly the best loved of all flowers.*
TOP RIGHT: *Lavender is one of the many scented shrubs available to the gardener. These plants are ideally sited along a path, their fragrance welcoming anyone entering the house.*

Shrubs

Shrubs are generally classified as deciduous or evergreen, although in more temperate areas some fall between these two groups and are termed partly or semi-deciduous.

Evergreen shrubs provide the permanent structure of a garden so necessary in the overall landscape design, especially in winter when the deciduous types are dormant. In this regard they make excellent backgrounds for deciduous plants. Also, consider the advantage of permanent plant foliage against a plain house or fence wall or where a division of garden space is needed.

Deciduous shrubs can provide the contrast elements of garden design. Their ever-changing attributes give continued interest. In winter their bare branches can look magnificent against green backgrounds or a winter skyline, then plants such as the bright yellow forsythias and the flowering quinces in the pink shades tell us the cold is almost over. We can look forward to an unsurpassed parade of color through spring provided by a myriad of well-loved and proven shrubs. As summer progresses the shrub garden can form a dense, cool background highlighted by spectacular show stoppers like the crape myrtles, tibouchinas and oleanders.

Color through Foliage

Color is not the sole domain of flowers in the shrub garden. There are many plants clothed with a fantastic display of colored leaves. Many of these make striking accents in an otherwise green shrubbery, indeed in tropical and humid subtropical areas, plants such as acalyphas and crotons take the place of flowering plants and replace those that are traditionally used to provide fall (autumn) color in colder areas.

A selection of shrubs and small trees has been carefully combined to produce this attractive cottage garden.

Shrubs with silver or gray foliage can be used to create wonderful landscapes and are often combined with white flowering plants to great effect. Also there are the variegated forms, some of which need to be planted where they are sheltered from drying winds and hot afternoon sun otherwise they tend to burn. On the other hand, gold-leafed plants and those with gold markings need to be planted in full sun to retain their color. The shade-loving variegated forms of *Aucuba japonica* are the exceptions to this rule.

Remember also to include in your list of essential shrubs those plants with berries which highlight the foliage and make marvellous displays indoors. Holly is one cold country favorite. Then, in warmer climates, the golden dewdrop or star flower *(Durante erecta)* with its display of bright yellow berries can be a real eye stopper as can the showy ardisias with their long-lasting red or white berries providing added interest to a deeply shaded area.

Scented Shrubs

Plants not only give visual pleasure; a fragrant shrub can provide a subtle sense of joy as its scented foliage is brushed against or its flowers release their distinctive perfume. Daphne, boronias, lavenders, rosemary, gardenias and the lilacs are all beautifully scented and well worth including on your shopping list. They are examples of the many plants which can be placed near an outdoor living area where their perfume can be appreciated as you sit at leisure. Others, such as the night-scented *Cestrum nocturnum*, some may find overpowering on a summer's evening and are best positioned where you pass by, such as beside a front gate or entrance path.

Accent Points

The dramatic statements that an accent plant can provide are sometimes overlooked. These shrubs, used sparingly, act as a focal point, drawing the eye through the landscape to another section of the garden.

They are choice plants, chosen for a particular growth pattern such as a weeping standard, or for their arresting shapes like those of the *Acer palmatum* cultivars. Though usually more expensive, if well positioned they give a garden that individual look.

Soil

Most shrubs will tolerate a wide range of soil types, as long as it is well drained and reasonably fertile, however there are a number of garden favorites which need to have an acidic soil. Soil is measured on a pH scale ranging from very acid (1) to very alkaline (14) and although soil solutions don't reach these extremes, a plant is considered to be acid loving if it enjoys a pH level in the low 6 range. Three that immediately come to mind are camellias, azaleas and rhododendrons, but there are other shrubs which will thrive in similar conditions and help to give variety to a shrub border. Other shrubs to interplant with them include the heaths and ericas, magnolias, the American laurel *(Kalmia)* and the various species of *Pieris*. These plants thrive in soils that have had loads of compost, peat moss and organic mulches added to them.

Planting

A shrub border is best planned wide enough to accommodate at least two shrubs in depth, with the taller, easy care evergreens at the back and the plants which require more attention, in the form of pruning, or which are to be grown for cutting, planted towards the front. Often there is room to interplant these with ground-hugging shrubs to act as a mulch, keeping both weeding and watering requirements to a minimum. And it makes sound gardening sense to plant out a complete bed at the one time—not only do some plants resent being disturbed, but the ability for shrubs to establish a good root system within a well-established border is very limited.

Prepare a garden bed a few weeks prior to planting, digging it over well and adding well-rotted compost or other decayed organic matter. This humus helps to break up heavy soils making them more porous and so more easily drained and also provides light, sandy type soils with moisture-retentive materials.

Pruning

Pruning is often unnecessary for shrubs, but some do require annual attention to ensure continued high quality blooms. These shrubs can be divided into two categories—those that produce flowers on new or the current season's wood and those that form the flower buds in the previous season. Flowers that appear on last season's canes include forsythias, weigelas and kerrias. These and similar shrubs do best if the flowering canes are cut well back once the flowers are finished to give the developing new shoots ample room in which to develop.

When shrubs produce flowers on the current season's growth, the flowers usually appear towards the end of summer on spring growth. These are best pruned in late winter, or in colder areas once all possibility of frost is over. Shaping is the main requirement here, taking thin or dead wood back to the main trunk and shortening vigorous shoots. Plants in this category include the late summer flowering shrubs such as tibouchinas, fuchsias and abutilons as well as hibiscus and luculias. Bearing this in mind, it is possible to choose plants for a garden shrubbery that require very little attention and still be assured of a colorful display that is as easy care as a garden can possibly be.

Trees

A tree is a plant, either coniferous or broad leafed, with a single, woody stem reaching to a height of at least about 12 ft (3.5 m) when mature. Palms and tree ferns, although they do not have the same type of woody stem, are generally included for horticultural purposes because their growth habit and landscape uses are similar to that of trees.

Trees can form windbreaks in larger gardens, are invaluable as noise inhibitors, provide privacy from overlooking houses or apartment buildings and soften the skyline in the urban environment.

They are growing structures in gardens, chosen for a particular purpose, though many will provide bonus points to add to their initial attractiveness as they mature. Trees planted to provide shade may well provide a horizontal branch to support a swing, or branches to form a climbing frame for adventurous children. Birds will soon inhabit suitable trees for nesting or food gathering among blossom and fruits while keeping a sharp eye on the insect population in the garden below.

Choosing the Right Tree

Never buy a tree on impulse. It is a permanent part of the garden structure; after all, trees can take around 20 years to arrive at any semblance of maturity, so it is necessary to get the selection right first time. Take time before you go to the nursery, read as much as you can about a tree's growing habits such as its estimated mature height and spread, as well as its seasonal displays. What at first appears to be a bewildering choice will soon be whittled down to a couple of possible contenders for a particular spot in the garden.

Climate and soil requirements also need to be considered. It is preferable to grow a tree climatically suited to your area. If you're new to a neighborhood, walk through the parks and look over garden fences to see which trees are growing well.

Evergreen or Deciduous?

Trees are most often sought for their shade value. Consider then the choice of evergreen or deciduous. Perhaps an evergreen is what's needed in a screening situation or in the tropics where year-round sun protection over a patio is needed. A deciduous tree will provide summer shade and winter sun in cooler climates. There is an ever-changing display each season, ranging from the fine tracery of bare branches in winter to soft green new spring growth, a welcoming dense cover in summer then a wonderful fall (autumn) display, often with the added bonus of flowers and colorful fruit.

The colorful contribution trees make to the landscape often comes because of their foliage color. Consider the soft blue-gray foliage of some of the conifers and eucalypt species or *Pyrus salicifolia* which meld so well with the white and pastel blues and pinks favoured by cottage gardeners. Then there are trees with variegated foliage which provide a welcome accent in an otherwise green landscape, but it's the intensity of the yellow/orange/red tones that really capture a gardener's heart.

Cold country gardeners have any number of trees in all sizes and shapes from which to make a rich display of color before winter sets in. Temperate gardeners are not so fortunate. However, beautiful displays can be assured with *Nyssa sylvatica, Ginkgo biloba* or in larger gardens the majestic *Liquidambar styraciflua.*

Getting the Proportions Right

For the home gardener, perhaps the most important consideration in choosing a particular tree is its mature height and spread. Proportion is the catchword here for both aesthetic and practical reasons. A large, dense tree planted too close to a house may shade it too well, making rooms dark and cutting off any view from the windows. It may also rob the surrounding garden of light and root room. In such a situation it may be better to choose a smaller, more openly branched tree which both frames the view and allows ample light into a room: some examples include *Cassia fistula, Betula pendula, Pistacia chinensis* and *Zelkova serrata.*

Planting

It takes a few years for a tree to become self-sufficient even though it may be quite large when planted out. New roots need time to establish to forage for nutrients and to anchor the plant.

RIGHT: *Deciduous trees provide an ever-changing display each season. This is an avenue of* Ulmus procera *in fall (autumn).*
BELOW: *A show of fall (autumn) foliage color can indeed be spectacular, the intense yellow, orange and red tones taking one's breath away.*

ABOVE: *The Engelmann spruce* (Picea engelmannii) *is one of the most cold-tolerant evergreen trees. It also grows well in poor soil.*
LEFT: *Gardeners living in cold countries have any number of trees in all shapes and sizes from which to make a display of color before winter sets in.*

Consequently, all trees, but in particular those planted as specimen trees, need to be given great care in their early years. Before planting, check the tree will not be hindered above by overhead wires or that underground pipes will not be invaded by vigorous root systems.

Good drainage is essential as few plants will thrive with wet feet. Wide planting holes, ample surrounding soil cultivation and even raising the bed are some ways of overcoming a drainage problem. If the soil is very heavy, the addition of gypsum or coarse sand may be required as well. As soil in the container and the surrounding garden soil are often quite different in texture, it's important to combine these two to allow new roots to venture easily into their new surrounding. Do this by digging a shallow (just a little deeper than the container) yet wide hole, at least twice the diameter of the root ball, and fill the base with a friable mixture composed of about half the existing soil and a rich humus mix.

Carefully remove the plant from the container, taking special care not to damage the main trunk, and place the root ball in position, together with up to three stakes. At this point check that the roots are not tangled or wound round in circles. If they are they need to be gently teased out and straightened, otherwise they will continue in this circular fashion, eventually causing the plant to wither. Continue to fill the hole with the soil mix, firming it in and around the trunk by hand, but ensuring that the tree is planted only as deep as it was in the container. Once it is firmly in position water well to get rid of any remaining air pockets. The remaining soil mix can be used to form a raised circle around the plant. Then, to conserve moisture, a layer of organic mulch can be added. This mulch, weeds and low-growing ground covers should be kept well away from the trunk to discourage collar or other root-rot fungus.

If planting in a lawn, cut away a circle of turf at least about 3 ft (1 m) in diameter to ensure the tender roots of the newly planted tree will not have to compete with those of voracious lawn grasses. Keep the surface of this area well mulched to retain as much moisture as possible and to deter weeds competing for the available nutrients.

Trees need to be staked to ensure the leader (main trunk) is not damaged while still young and tender. Place the stakes in position at the time of planting, then attach the plant to these with tree ties or a length of old rag tied in a figure of eight to ensure the trunk remains steady when buffeted by strong winds. Don't use wire as it can cut into the trunk.

Deciduous trees are usually planted in the dormant state; evergreens in temperate areas are best planted out in fall (autumn) while the soil is still warm. In colder areas, evergreens with new tender growth will avoid frost damage if planted out in late spring.

Pruning

Trees rarely need pruning in maturity except after storm damage or for the removal of diseased branches, however young trees often benefit from being given a helping hand to balance their shape or to develop a higher branching system where they overhang a path. If noticed early enough unwanted new shoots can be rubbed off easily by hand, a technique which doesn't leave unsightly scars on the often beautiful trunks of these majestic garden plants.

Vegetables and Herbs

To be grown successfully, vegetables do need to be chosen with consideration to climate. Summer vegetables such as beans, tomatoes and the ground vine crops like cucumbers and squash are frost-tender and therefore need to be planted out when the prospect of frost is over. They like daytime temperatures of around 68°F (20°C) or higher to set fruit. On the other hand, many of the root crops (those with the edible parts underground), like carrots and potatoes, grow well in daytime temperatures of between 12–18°C (53–64°F) and are not as susceptible to frost. The cabbages, cauliflowers and brussels sprouts, all members of the same family, revel in cool temperatures and are quite frost-hardy.

All vegetables must have ample sunlight, and this factor more than any other can dictate the positioning of a vegetable garden. Other points to consider include competition from tree or shrub roots, prevailing winds and drainage, although this last factor can usually be rectified by raising the beds or by underground piping.

The size of the garden also needs careful thought. Depending on the space available and the time you are prepared to spend in the garden, any number of beds can be made, but it's a good idea to begin small. Beds are easily extended or new ones made. A bed of up to about 4 ft (1.2 m) wide is easily cultivated from both sides. Length can be determined by available space, but about 6 ft (1.8 m) gives ample room for the compact and quick growers. Others, like the vine crops, take up a lot more garden space and need the use of a bed the whole season to complete their cycle. The perennial plants such as rhubarb and asparagus, as well as many of the herbs which occupy the same space for many years, need a bed of their own or to be grouped at one end of a highly cultivated bed so that they are not interfered with when the rest of the garden is being prepared for the new season's crop.

Consider too the choice of vegetables you plan to grow. Yield per plant is a very important factor when space is limited. For instance beans take up relatively little space and their yield is tremendous over a season. Salad vegetables and the leaf crops too are worth considering before, say, a plot given over to potatoes which don't really spoil when left on the greengrocer's shelf.

One very practical way to overcome limited space is to build a trellis towards the back of a garden to hold climbing beans, peas, and even cucumbers. Sited correctly, this trellis will not shade the lower growing vegetables and it can act as a windbreak to a row of corn or some tomatoes.

Pots too can be used. They need not be restricted to growing herbs; they are also ideal for such long-cropping vegetables as bell peppers, tomatoes, eggplant or the 'bush' varieties of cucumbers or pumpkins. Placed on a sunny patio they can be easily observed and given immediate attention if this is required.

Planting Seeds

Some seeds, like the fast-growing radish or beans, melons and carrots, can be sown directly into their permanent garden positions. Finer seeds are better planted into seedbeds or frames where germination and early growth can be closely monitored. A seedbed needs to have soil of a fine consistency, perfect drainage and to be placed where it receives adequate sunlight and warmth and is well protected from any drying winds. The surface should be flat so that fine seeds are not washed away. Shallow grooves can be made with a length of dowel or similar, then the seeds carefully dropped into these miniature farrows and covered with a light soil layer. Water with a fine mist or spray, ensuring the surface is neither too wet nor allowed to dry out.

Gardeners in colder areas can sow seeds in frames in protected areas while it is still too early to plant outdoors. These plants are then transplanted into their permanent positions when all possibility of frost is over. When the weather warms up then it may be possible to sow another batch or two in a well-prepared, outdoor seedbed in the successive weeks. By making these regular small sowings the household won't be inundated by a glut of vegetables all maturing at the one time.

Planting Seedlings

Many gardeners prefer to buy their seedlings at the nursery. Transplanting should be done in the cool of the evening. Using a garden knife or small trowel, and holding the plants by their leaves, loosen them gently from the seedbed or punnet and place a bunch of them on a board—covering them with a cloth or damp kitchen paper towel will prevent them drying out. Use a piece of dowel to make a row of holes sufficiently deep so the tiny roots will not be bent or broken, then gently prize the seedlings apart and place single plants in the prepared holes, pushing the soil firmly around them with two fingers. Water each plant to ensure any air pockets are filled with soil. The seedlings do benefit from being given some protection in the form of a leafy branch, cut down milk carton or similar until they have time to become accustomed to their new surroundings.

Planting the same vegetables in the same position each year is not good garden practice as the plants of the same family are often prone to similar diseases and this only accentuates the problem. And, although chemicals can be used, one of the benefits of growing vegetables is that you can decide which, and indeed if any, chemicals to use. Plants of the same family also take up similar nutrients and it was for this reason that crop rotation was first introduced. Today these nutrients can be replaced by commercial fertilizers.

Fertilizing

Different crops require different types of fertilizers, the green plants grown for their leaves need a high nitrogen content, while plants grown for their fruit need a more balanced diet. When a garden is as intensively used as it is for vegetable growing it pays to supplement the use of chemical fertilizers with organic material to ensure its continued good health. Organic fertilizers such as compost can be dug into the soil at the changeover of the seasons. Straw or similar material used as a mulch during the growing season is usually sufficiently decomposed to be dug into the garden at the end of summer. You'll be amazed at the difference in soil texture and general health of the soil when this is done.

Vegetables need to be grown quickly to promote maximum quality in both leaf and fruiting types. To ensure this rapid, uninterrupted development it is necessary to keep soil adequately moist at all times. It follows then that sandy soil, which dries out more rapidly than heavy soil, needs to be watered more frequently. Many of the vine crops and tomatoes are prone to leaf diseases if leaves are subject to continued moisture, so in beds where these types of vegetables are to be grown, a trickle hose or a depression running the length of the bed and filled with water each morning could be used instead of sprinklers which spray moisture indiscriminately over foliage and ground alike.

Close planting and mulching are two ways to ensure moisture is conserved. Close planting may produce less vigorous plants or a marginally less prolific crop, but the home gardener can progressively use, and so thin out, rows as plants mature. Mulching saves the gardener time and energy in other ways as well. It helps the soil temperature control at both extremes and stops heavy rain washing away soil from around the fibrous roots which are often very near the surface of many of the annual vegetables. Mulching also limits weed growth. Many gardeners today rely solely on mulched or 'no dig' beds for successful vegetable growing.

Do try gardening with vegetables and herbs, as it really is the most satisfying of the stress-reducing hobbies and you'll glow with pleasure at the bountiful results of your leisure!

RIGHT: *Herb gardens are not only practical, they can also be an attractive feature in the overall garden design.*
BELOW: *A well-designed and accessible vegetable garden. Sunlight is the most important factor to consider when positioning a vegetable garden.*

A

Albelmoschus moschatus 'Pacific Orange Scarlet'

Abelia chinensis

Abelia floribunda

ABELIA

A genus of about 30 species of both deciduous and evergreen shrubs from eastern Asia and Mexico, the abelias are valued for their elegant growth and abundant small tubular or trumpet-shaped flowers over a prolonged summer season. They grow to about 6 ft (1.8 m) tall and have dark green foliage on arching canes.

CULTIVATION: Species vary from moderately frost hardy to somewhat tender. The frost-hardy species are trouble-free plants, capable of surviving harsh conditions. Abelias prefer sun or light shade, and need a well-drained soil with regular water in summer. They are easily propagated from cuttings and can withstand heavy pruning, for example, when used for low hedging.

Abelia chinensis

One of the hardier species, *Abelia chinensis* forms a spreading bushy shrub. It can be deciduous or semi-deciduous, and has reddish stems and small shiny leaves which turn bronze purple in fall (autumn). It blooms with a succession of small white flowers throughout summer and early fall, each conspicuous dull pink calyx persisting on the shrub long after the flower falls. **ZONES 8–10.**

Abelia floribunda

With the largest and most brightly hued flowers among the abelias, this species bears clusters of bright rose carmine, 2 in (5 cm) long flowers along arching branches in early summer. Only marginally frost hardy, in colder areas it is best grown in a warm sheltered spot such as against a wall or fence. **ZONES 9–11.**

Abelia × *grandiflora*

This hybrid between *Abelia chinensis* and *A. uniflora* grows to 6–8 ft (1.8–2.4 m) tall and wide. It has arching reddish brown canes and small, glossy dark green leaves. Small mauve and white flowers appear in early summer, usually with a second flush at summer's end. The dull pink calyces persist on the shrub after the flower falls, contrasting with the leaves which turn purplish bronze. The cultivar **'Francis Mason'** has yellow or yellow-edged leaves but it has a tendency to revert to plain green. **ZONES 7–10.**

Abelia schumannii

Less vigorous than *Abelia* × *grandiflora*, this deciduous shrub likes a sheltered situation. It has arching red canes and small pointed leaves; the upper part of each cane produces a succession of showy bell-shaped flowers from late spring to early fall (autumn). Flowers are rose pink with an orange blotch in the throat; the pale reddish calyx persists on the shrub after the flower falls. **ZONES 7–10.**

ABELMOSCHUS

This is a genus of around 15 species from the tropics of Africa and Asia. In older books all the species were included in the larger genus *Hibiscus.* They are annuals, biennials or short-lived perennials with tough bark (sometimes used for fiber) and maple-like leaves. Some species die back to a large tuber in the tropical dry season. The hibiscus-like flowers occur in shades of yellow, pink, orange or red. Several species make attractive ornamentals and the vegetable okra or gumbo *(Abelmoschus esculentus)* is grown for its edible young pods.

Abelia × *grandiflora*

CULTIVATION: They are mostly grown as summer annuals, requiring fertile, well-drained soil, a sheltered position in full sun, and plentiful water. Propagate from seed in spring. Rust disease can be a problem: spray with a fungicide.

Abelmoschus esculentus

syn. ***Hibiscus esculentus***

OKRA, GUMBO, LADY'S FINGERS

Long cultivated in parts of Africa and Asia (where it originated), this 6 ft (1.8 m) tall species was taken to the Americas with slaves from West Africa and has remained a traditional ingredient of many dishes in the USA's Deep South. It is an attractive plant with red-eyed yellow flowers. Both flower buds and the long starchy immature pods are eaten. Okra requires a long hot summer for successful growth. **ZONES 9–11.**

Abelmoschus manihot

AIBIKA

This is a perennial species 6–8 ft (1.8–2.4 m) tall. The stems are covered with small, bristly hairs and the 3- to 7-lobed leaves are up to 18 in (45 cm) across. The flowers are white to yellow with purple centers, borne singly or in small racemes, and followed by 3 in (8 cm) fruit. **ZONES 10–12.**

Abelmoschus moschatus

MUSK MALLOW

This tropical Asian species is very variable, with many wild and cultivated races. Some are used for fiber and the seeds (musk seeds) yield oils and fats (ambrette) used medicinally and in perfumery. The whole plant has a slight musky smell. The hairs on the leaves are often bristly and the large flowers are typically pale yellow with a purple eye. Ornamental cultivars have a range of flower colors. The cultivar **'Mischief'** is a compact plant that grows well in pots or can be naturalized in a sunny sheltered position; red, pink or white flowers are borne in summer and fall (autumn). **'Pacific Light Pink'** is an 18 in (45 cm) dwarf cultivar with 2-tone pink flowers up to 4 in (10 cm) wide. **'Pacific Orange Scarlet'** (syn. 'Oriental Red') is also very popular. **ZONES 8–12.**

Abelia × *grandiflora* 'Francis Mason'

ABIES

FIR

The true firs, sometimes known as silver firs to distinguish them from *Picea* (which have pendent, not upright, cones), comprise 40-odd species of evergreen conifers. Among the most stately of all conifers, firs come from cool- to cold-climate mountain areas of the northern hemisphere. The majority are from China and western North America, but a few species extend into the tropics on the high mountains of Central America and Southeast Asia. The short, stiff needles, which are distributed evenly along the twig, usually have 2 longitudinal blue bands on their undersides.

CULTIVATION: Their narrow shape and often slow growth allow many species to fit comfortably into the larger suburban garden, but they will not tolerate urban pollution and prefer a moist climate without extremes of heat. Soils must have adequate depth, drainage and moisture retention. Propagation is from seed. Grafting is used for selected clones, including named cultivars. The only pruning or shaping needed is the removal of twin leading shoots as soon as they appear.

Abies alba

EUROPEAN SILVER FIR

Originating in the mountains of central and southern Europe this conifer can grow to 180 ft (55 m). It has glossy dark

Abelia × *grandiflora* cultivar

Abies alba

green needles with whitish undersides, arranged in 2 rows on the lateral branches. The bark is a dark grayish color and the cones are up to 6 in (15 cm) long, changing from green to reddish brown as they ripen. It is capable of fast growth but may be damaged by unseasonal frost and is liable to attack by aphids. **ZONES 6–9.**

Abies amabilis
PACIFIC SILVER FIR, RED FIR

Native to the coastal mountains of northwestern USA, western Canada and southern Alaska, this species can grow to 260 ft (78 m) in the wild; in cultivation it seldom reaches 100 ft (30 m). Its glossy green leaves, deeply grooved above and banded bluish white beneath, give off a smell similar to orange peel when crushed. The cones, 4–6 in (10–15 cm) long, ripen from red to deep purple. **ZONES 5–9.**

Abies balsamea
BALSAM FIR

The 'balsam' in this fir's name is a clear, thin resin in its bark, once commercially important. The most widespread North American species, it extends from Canada (where it is a major source of paper pulp) south through the mountains of eastern USA as far as West Virginia. In cultivation, a short-lived slender tree, grown for its spicy fragrance, bluish green foliage and Christmas tree shape. Dwarf cultivars are most often seen in gardens with the most popular being **'Hudsonia'**, a compact miniature shrub up to 24 in (60 cm) high and **'Nana'**, a neat rounded shrub of similar size. **ZONES 3–8.**

Abies concolor var. *lowiana*

Abies amabilis

Abies borisii-regis
KING BORIS'S FIR

This rare species from Bulgaria and Greece was named after King Boris who ruled Bulgaria until 1943. Some botanists believe it to be an ancient hybrid between *Abies alba* and *A. cephalonica*, both of which it resembles. It has scented green leaves about 1 in (25 mm) long, resinous buds and barrel-shaped cones 4–6 in (10–15 cm) long. **ZONES 6–9.**

Abies bracteata
syn. *Abies venusta*
SANTA LUCIA FIR, BRISTLECONE FIR

Among the rarest *Abies* species in the wild, this fir comes from the higher parts of the Santa Lucia Mountains near the southern Californian coast. There it grows to 150 ft (45 m) tall. In cultivation it requires a mild climate, and may be short lived. It has a long-pointed crown, unusually long sharp needles, and egg-shaped cones covered in long appendages resembling the needles but narrower. **ZONES 7–10.**

Abies cephalonica
GREEK FIR, CEPHALONIAN FIR

This fir belongs to a group of Mediterranean firs with short, stiff, outward-pointing, prickly needles, and occurs naturally in the mountains of Greece and the Balkans. Widely grown, hardy and vigorous, it was introduced into Britain in the early 1800s, where native specimens have reached heights equal to those in the wild, about 120 ft (36 m). The brown cones are roughly cylindrical and about 4 in (10 cm) long. **ZONES 6–9.**

Abies concolor 'Glauca'

Abies bracteata

Abies concolor
COLORADO FIR, WHITE FIR

This species grows wild in the Rocky Mountains of western USA, where it reaches 150 ft (45 m), with a taller race, ***Abies concolor* var. *lowiana*** (Pacific fir), found closer to the coast in Oregon and northern California. The needles, which are bluish green on both sides and blunt tipped, exude a lemon scent when bruised. Cones range from deep dull purple to pale brown. A fine ornamental fir, it is also hardy and vigorous. Seedlings vary in the blueness of their foliage. Some of the best blue forms, propagated by grafting, are sold under the name **'Glauca'**; even more striking is the rare and slower-growing pale blue cultivar **'Candicans'**. **'Compacta'** also has quite blue foliage but is a dwarf cultivar, hardly exceeding 3 ft (1 m). **ZONES 5–9.**

Abies balsamea 'Nana'

Abies borisii-regis

Abies cephalonica

Abies balsamea 'Hudsonia'

A

Abies delavayi
DELAVAY'S FIR

This is one of a group of very similar species from the mountains of western China. It is a tall tree with very blunt-tipped needles $^1/_2$–1 in (12–25 mm) long, dark green above and whitish beneath, crowded densely on the twigs. The cones are fat, and purple when immature. The true *Abies delavayi* is hardly known in cultivation. **ZONES 7–9.**

Abies firma
MOMI FIR, JAPANESE FIR

With foliage of a deep shiny green, the momi fir reaches 150 ft (45 m) in the mountains of southern Japan. It is densely branched with stiff, leathery needles, up to $1^1/_2$ in (35 mm) long, in 2 rows forming a wide V on twigs of the lower branches. The brown, egg-shaped cones are up to 4 in (10 cm) long. **ZONES 6–9.**

Abies forrestii
syns. ***Abies delavayi*** **var.** ***forrestii, Abies delavayi*** **var.** ***smithii, Abies georgei***

This handsome fir from western China is similar to *Abies delavayi* (of which it is commonly but incorrectly treated as a variety) but it is much more widely grown in the West. It differs in having leaves, up to $1^1/_2$ in (35 mm) long, more inclined to be divided into 2 rows on the twig and curving up to display their white undersides. In cultivation it has proved vigorous and fast growing when young, but often goes into a decline and dies before reaching a mature size. **ZONES 7–9.**

Abies grandis
GIANT FIR, GRAND FIR, LOWLAND FIR

Among the world's tallest conifers, the giant fir reaches 300 ft (90 m) in forests on Vancouver Island, and its natural range extends south to Sonoma County in California. In cultivation it can grow 3 ft (1 m) a year in suitable climates, and is widely planted for its timber. It does best in deep, moist soils. The foliage resembles that of *Abies concolor* and when crushed smells like orange peel. The smallish cones ripen to dark brown. **ZONES 6–9.**

Abies holophylla
MANCHURIAN FIR

From Korea and northeastern China, this fir is rare in cultivation. It can grow to 60 ft (18 m) or more, with a spread of 20 ft (6 m) and a conical crown with bright green leaves. It resembles *Abies firma* but the leaf tips are pointed. Cones are green when young, turning light brown as they age. **ZONES 4–9.**

Abies homolepis
NIKKO FIR

Native to central Japan, this species grows well in Europe and North America and is more tolerant of urban pollution than most firs. It can exceed 100 ft (30 m) in height, and is broadly conical when young. The crowded needles, up to $1^1/_2$ in (35 mm) long, are dark green with broad blue-white bands on the undersides and blunt tips. The bark on young trees and immature cones is purplish gray. The shrub-sized cultivar **'Prostrata'** lacks erect leading shoots and is propagated from cuttings. **ZONES 5–9.**

Abies grandis

Abies holophylla

Abies forrestii

Abies homolepsis

Abies koreana
KOREAN FIR

In the wild known only from mountains in the far south of Korea, this fir has been grown in the West from the early 1900s. It is valued for its compact size, seldom exceeding 20–30 ft (6–9 m), and its early coning—it may produce its attractive small bluish cones when as little as 3 ft (1 m) high. The crowded needles are short and broad with notched tips and wide blue bands on the undersides. It is ideal for smaller gardens, or for a large rock garden. **ZONES 5–9.**

Abies koreana

Abies lasiocarpa
SUBALPINE FIR, ROCKY MOUNTAIN FIR

This species grows up to the tree line in the Rocky Mountains, from Arizona to southern Alaska. It may be a 100 ft (30 m) tall tree or a horizontal spreading shrub. The needles are crowded and overlapping, with bluish stripes on both surfaces. Cones are fat and dark purple. To the southeast of its range the typical species is replaced by ***Abies lasiocarpa*** **var. *arizonica*,** the corkbark fir, which has thick, corky, pale bark and blue-gray foliage. Selections of this variety valued as garden plants include **'Compacta'**, silver-blue and slow growing but difficult to obtain as it is propagated by grafting, and **'Aurea'**, which has yellowish foliage. **ZONES 4–9.**

Abies lasiocarpa

Abies firma

Abies magnifica
CALIFORNIAN RED FIR

This species occurs chiefly in cool, moist valleys on the higher slopes of the Sierra Nevada in California. In the wild it is a narrow conical or columnar tree to 200 ft (60 m) tall with reddish bark and deep blue-green foliage. Needles are narrow, blunt-tipped and curve upwards; cones are barrel-like and bluish purple ripening to pale brown. If cultivated in a moist climate it will grow to 65–100 ft (20–30 m), but is not as long lived as some other firs. **ZONES 5–9.**

Abies nordmanniana
CAUCASIAN FIR, NORDMANN FIR

This handsome fir can grow to 200 ft (60 m) and is native to the mountains of the Caucasus. Its densely crowded needles are dark glossy green, with rounded and slightly notched tips and whitish bands on the undersides. When crushed they smell like orange peel. The long fat cones ripen to reddish brown. Vigorous and adaptable, with a narrow shape and a long straight leading shoot, it is widely grown as an ornamental. **ZONES 4–9.**

Abies numidica
ALGERIAN FIR

In the wild this fir is known only from the Kabyle Ranges near Algiers, where it makes a broadly conical tree to 80 ft (24 m) tall. Its densely crowded needles, very flattened with broad blunt tips, are strongly banded with blue-white. Cones are long and narrow, ripening from deep green to dull brown. Very suitable for garden use, in cultivation it makes a cone of dense foliage. It needs adequate space to develop properly. **ZONES 6–9.**

Abies pinsapo
SPANISH FIR

A handsome column-shaped tree reaching 100 ft (30 m), often with multiple leaders and densely crowded branches, this fir adapts to a wide range of soils and climates. The very short, rigid needles are less flattened than in most firs, and have fine bluish white stripes on both surfaces. In spring small purple pollen cones appear on the lower branch tips. The seed cones, produced near the top of the tree,are brown when ripe. Seedlings are selected for bluish foliage, collectively referred to under the cultivar name **'Glauca'**. **ZONES 5–9.**

Abies procera
syn. *Abies nobilis*
NOBLE FIR

A very tall conifer from the high-rainfall coastal region of northwestern USA, this species reaches over 250 ft (75 m). Smooth-barked and broadly conical when young, it develops a mast-like trunk and a high, pointed crown with foliage in horizontal tiers. The narrow, bluntly pointed needles vary from bluish green to strong silvery blue. Cones are large, fat and purplish brown. It adapts well to cultivation in a cool, moist climate and good, deep soil. It is susceptible to aphid attacks in warmer climates. Blue-foliaged **'Glauca'** cultivars are usually grown. **ZONES 4–9.**

Abies spectabilis
HIMALAYAN FIR

This tall fir occurs in the Himalayas where it is found up to about 13,000 ft (4,000 m) in altitude; despite this it is not reliably frost hardy in the British Isles, being prone to damage by late frosts. It has long needles in 2 ranks forming a V between them. The needles are rather curved and tangled, with the white-banded undersides contrasting vividly with the dark green uppersides. The large, barrel-shaped violet-purple cones ripen to brown. In cultivation it forms a conical tree to 60–80 ft (18–24 m). **ZONES 7–9.**

Abies veitchii
VEITCH'S SILVER FIR

For most of the nineteenth and into the early twentieth century, Veitchs was the English nursery firm most renowned for introducing new plants from all parts of the world. John Gould Veitch found this beautiful fir in the mountains of central Japan in 1860. The smallest of the species from Japan, it grows to no more than 70 ft (21 m) and has a conical crown. The leaves are soft and blunt, curling to reveal blue-white undersides. The 2 in (5 cm) long cones are bluish purple when young, ageing to brown. A popular fir for gardens, it makes fast early growth but is not very long-lived. **ZONES 6–9.**

Abies numidica

Abies lasiocarpa var. *arizonica*

Abies spectabilis

Abies lasiocarpa 'Compacta'

Abies lasiocarpa 'Aurea'

Abies nordmanniana

Abies pinsapo 'Glauca'

Abies procera 'Glauca'

Abies pinsapo

A

Abutilon × hybridum 'Orange King'

Abutilon × hybridum

Abutilon × hybridum 'Souvenir de Bonn'

ABROMEITIELLA

The 2 species in this bromeliad genus, named after the German botanist J. Abromeit, are small ground-dwelling rosette plants from Bolivia and Argentina. A mature plant may consist of numerous small rosettes forming a mound up to 30 in (75 cm) in height; the leaves are triangular, fleshy and gray-green. The yellow-green, twisted flowers are grouped in threes on the inflorescence branches. They are followed by dull grayish green berries.
CULTIVATION: These frost-tender plants need moderately fertile, lime-free, well-drained soil and full sun. They are suitable as house plants if placed on a very sunny windowsill. Propagate from seed in spring or by rooting detached rosettes in spring and summer.

Abromeitiella brevifolia
syn. *Abromeitiella chlorantha*

This species from southern Bolivia produces cylindrical, intensely green flowers in summer. The densely arranged, triangular leaves are toothed at the base and have sharp tips. **ZONES 9–11.**

Abromeitiella lorentziana

This robust terrestrial bromeliad from northwestern Argentina is very similar to *Abromeitiella brevifolia* except that its leaves have more spines. In summer it bears tubular, yellow, green-tipped flowers. **ZONES 9–11.**

ABRONIA
SAND VERBENA

This is a genus of 35 species of trailing and spreading annuals and perennials from western North America. They have fleshy, oval leaves and in summer produce $^1/_2$–$1^1/_2$ in (12–35 mm) wide small, fragrant, tubular flowers in pink and yellow shades or white. The flowerheads are backed by small bracts. The stems, which are often sticky and tinted reddish or purple, spread to form mats up to 3 ft (1 m) wide.
CULTIVATION: Plant in light, gritty or sandy, well-drained soil in full sun. Some species are very tolerant of salt winds and are ideal plants for coastal gardens. Hardiness varies, though most are moderately frost hardy. Propagate the annuals from seed; the perennials from seed, layers or tip cuttings.

Abronia latifolia
YELLOW SAND VERBENA

Found in coastal areas from British Columbia to southern California, this perennial species has oval leaves $1^1/_2$ in (35 mm) long and sticky stems. The flowers are bright yellow. **ZONES 9–10.**

Abronia umbellata
PINK SAND VERBENA

Native to coastal areas from British Columbia to northern Mexico, this perennial has 1–2 in (25 mm–5 cm) long leaves on wiry, reddish stems. It spreads to around 24 in (60 cm) and has rose pink flowers with lighter bracts. It blooms all year round in mild climates. **'Rosea'** has pale pink flowers. **ZONES 8–10.**

Abronia villosa

An annual species very similar in appearance to *Abronia umbellata*, this species occurs in desert areas of Nevada, Arizona and California where it thrives in hot, dry conditions. The stems are tinted purple and the flowers are pale pink or white flushed with pink. **ZONES 8–11.**

ABUTILON
syn. *Corynabutilon*
CHINESE LANTERN, FLOWERING MAPLE

There are 100 or more species of mostly evergreen shrubs in this genus but only a few truly merit the name 'Chinese lantern'; that is only a few have flowers pendent on weak stalks and an inflated calyx above a bell of 5 overlapping petals. Such a flower type is adapted to pollination by hummingbirds. Most species, however, have a wide open flower like a small hibiscus, with petals most commonly yellow or orange. The genus is distributed widely through warmer countries but South America is home to the majority. One small group of species from the cooler parts of Chile is characterized by mauve flowers and deciduous foliage: these are sometimes placed in a separate genus, *Corynabutilon*.
CULTIVATION: They need well-drained soil and full sun or part-shade. In cooler climates they can be grown in containers in sheltered, sunny spots or in greenhouses. They need good watering, especially if in containers (in which they bloom best if root-bound). Propagate from cuttings in late summer. Flea-beetles, aphids and caterpillars can be problems in the garden.

Abutilon × hybridum
CHINESE LANTERN

Abutilon × hybridum is a collective name for cultivars derived from hybridizing some South American species. The lantern-like flowers, borne from spring to fall (autumn), come in yellow, white, orange, pink, mauve and scarlet. Named cultivars include **'Nabob'**; **'Golden Fleece'**, with rich golden yellow flowers; **'Kentish Belle'** with brilliant orange flowers; **'Orange King'**; **'Ruby Glow'**; **'Ashford Red'**; and **'Souvenir de Bonn'**, with variegated foliage and red-veined orange flowers. In warm climates they grow to 8 ft (2.4 m), some with a similar spread, and an open growth habit. Prune hard in early spring to keep growth in check; tip prune to promote bushiness and flowering. These cultivars can be grown indoors in a cool but sunny room. **ZONES 9–11.**

Abutilon megapotamicum
BRAZILIAN BELL-FLOWER

This species from southern Brazil and Uruguay comes in 2 growth forms: an almost prostrate shrub with branches that may self-layer, making it a good ground cover or rock-garden plant, and a vigorous shrub of up to 8 ft (2.4 m) tall with arching cane-like branches. Both have smallish, pendent, bell-shaped flowers with a deep red calyx larger than the pale yellow petals. In cooler climates it is usually grown as a pot plant but in zone 8 it can be grown outdoors against a warm wall. Cultivars include **'Marianne'**, **'Thomsonii'**, **'Super'**, **'Wisley Red'**, and **'Variegatum'**. The latter has leaves heavily blotched yellow and a prostrate growth habit. **ZONES 9–11.**

Abutilon megapotamicum

Abutilon × *suntense* 'Jermyns'

Abutilon megapotamicum 'Variegatum'

Abutilon × *suntense*

This cool-climate hybrid will tolerate lower temperatures than *Abutilon vitifolium;* its other parent is *A. ochsenii* from the colder south of Chile. It reaches 12 ft (3.5 m) tall and about 8 ft (2.4 m) wide, has dark green leaves and profuse purple or mauve flowers from spring to early summer. The cultivar **'Jermyns'** has deep mauve flowers fading with age. Moderately frost hardy, it requires shelter from strong winds. **ZONES 8–9.**

Abutilon vitifolium

syn. *Corynabutilon vitifolium*

A soft-wooded, short-lived, deciduous shrub from Chile, *Abutilon vitifolium* grows to 10–12 ft (3–3.5 m) and in summer bears profuse clusters of mauve-purple to white flowers up to 3 in (8 cm) wide. While needing a cool moist climate, it is one of the most cold hardy abutilons, but does best against a sheltered house wall or in a courtyard. Prune hard in early spring to prevent the shrub becoming straggly. Named cultivars include **'Veronica Tennant'** with fine, very pale lavender flowers; and **'Album'** with white flowers. **ZONES 8–9.**

Abutilon × *suntense*

ACACIA

WATTLE

This large genus contains over 1,200 species of trees and shrubs from warm climates. Some are deciduous but most are evergreen. Over 700 are indigenous to Australia. They range from low-growing shrubs to tall trees and many have been introduced to other countries for economic and ornamental purposes. Acacias are also common in tropical and subtropical Africa; most African species are characterized by vicious spines and referred to as 'thorn trees'. Acacias have either bipinnate leaves or their leaves are replaced by flattened leaf stalks, known as phyllodes, which perform the function of photosynthesis. The tiny flowers, ranging from deep golden yellow to cream or white, and crowded into globular heads or cylindrical spikes, are often fragrant and produce abundant, bee-attracting pollen. Fruit are either round or flattened pods.

CULTIVATION: The hard-coated seeds remain viable for up to 30 years. They should be treated by heating and soaking for germination in spring. Some need fire to germinate. In cultivation many species are fast-growing but short-lived (10–15 years). In their native regions they are often disfigured by insect or fungus attack. They do best in full sun and well-drained soil. Some will take part-shade.

Abutilon vitifolium

Acacia acinacea

GOLD-DUST WATTLE

This profusely branched shrub with very small, rounded phyllodes from the drier hill country of southeastern Australia grows to 6 ft (1.8 m) with a similar spread. It bears profuse bright yellow flower balls from mid-winter to spring. An ornamental, compact shrub wattle, it needs full sun for best flowering, is moderately frost hardy, and will also tolerate periods of dryness. **ZONES 8–11.**

Acacia amoena

BOOMERANG WATTLE

Growing to 10 ft (3 m) with a spread of 6 ft (1.8 m), this shrub native to the eastern Australian tablelands has broad, blunt, dark green phyllodes 2 in (5 cm) long. Bright golden flowerheads are borne in loose, narrow clusters in spring. It is moderately frost hardy and tolerant of dry conditions. **ZONES 8–11.**

Acacia acinacea

Acacia auriculiformis

EAR POD WATTLE

Native to far northern Australia and New Guinea, this tree grows to 30 ft (9 m) or more and has a broadly spreading crown. Its sickle-shaped phyllodes are 4–6 in (10–15 cm) long. Rods of dull golden flowers, 3 in (8 cm) long, borne in fall (autumn) are followed by twisted woody pods. Frost tender, it is widely planted in the tropics, preferring an open sunny position. Exceptionally fast-growing (though short-lived), it can drop most of its leaves in the dry season; fallen leaves and pods may thickly cover paths and lawns. **ZONES 10–12.**

Acacia amoena

Abutilion vitifolium 'Album'

Acacia baileyana
COOTAMUNDRA WATTLE, GOLDEN MIMOSA

A fast-growing, small, spreading tree to 20 ft (6 m), the Cootamundra wattle has a short trunk and arching branches, feathery, blue-gray leaves, and fragrant golden yellow flower clusters in late winter. Widely used in warm-temperate gardens as a feature or shade tree, a specimen in full bloom can be a spectacular sight. Like most acacias, it tends to be short lived and prone to borer attack when declining. The cultivar **'Purpurea'** has purplish foliage, especially on the growing tips. **ZONES 8–10.**

Acacia boormanii
syn. *Acacia hunteriana*
SNOWY RIVER WATTLE

This small, rounded, evergreen tree or shrub grows to a height and spread of 9–12 ft (2.7–3.5 m), and bears bright yellow balls of flowers in spring. It has narrow, dark green phyllodes and is best propagated from the suckers that appear around the main trunk. **ZONES 9–11.**

Acacia cultriformis

Acacia baileyana

Acacia cardiophylla
WYALONG WATTLE

Named for its fern-like leaves, each composed of tiny, heart-shaped leaflets in 12 to 18 pairs (*cardiophylla*: with heart-shaped leaves), this fast-growing wattle has smooth, gray, arching branches. It grows to a height of 9–12 ft (2.7–3.5 m) with a spread of 6 ft (1.8 m). In midwinter it bears small, bright yellow flowers. It is adaptable and can withstand moderate frosts. **ZONES 8–11.**

Acacia catechu
BLACK CATECHU, CUTCH

Native to southern Asia, this small, thickly barked tree has spreading branches armed with pairs of hooked spines, and bipinnate leaves. White to yellow flowers, crowded with 4 in (10 cm) spikes, are followed by flat pods. An astringent substance obtained from the bark and wood has been used medicinally and for tanning. **ZONES 10–12.**

Acacia cavenia
ESPINO CAVAN

This very thorny species from Chile and Argentina is closely related to *Acacia farnesiana* but is rather taller-growing,

Acacia elata

Acacia farnesiana

reaching a height of about 20 ft (6 m). At the base of each small, ferny leaf are paired thorns about 1 in (25 mm) long. Ball-like gold flowerheads about 1/2 in (12 mm) in diameter appear in spring. **ZONES 9–11.**

Acacia constricta
WHITETHORN ACACIA, MESCAT ACACIA

One of the few acacias occurring as a native in the USA, this species is found in arid regions from west Texas to Arizona but is more widespread in Mexico. It is a thorny shrub of up to about 10 ft (3 m) with small bipinnate leaves. Flowers are bright yellow, in small globular heads. **ZONES 8–11.**

Acacia cultriformis
KNIFE-LEAF WATTLE, KNIFE ACACIA

This 6–12 ft (1.8–3.5 m) tall shrub from the cooler tablelands of New South Wales, Australia, has blue-gray phyllodes, up to 1 in (25 mm) long and shaped like small paring-knife blades. These are stalkless, attached directly to the branches. The showy spring flowers are in profuse short sprays of round, fluffy yellow balls. It tolerates light frost and is happy in any sunny, well-drained position. **ZONES 8–11.**

Acacia dealbata
syn. *Acacia decurrens* var. *dealbata*
SILVER WATTLE, MIMOSA

In gardens this tree grows to 20–30 ft (6–9 m), though in the eucalypt forests of southeastern Australia, where it naturally grows, it is much taller. Fast-growing but rather short-lived, it has a single trunk with smooth gray bark. Each bipinnate leaf is made up of hundreds of tiny leaflets coated in white hairs, giving the foliage a silvery cast. In late winter or spring the domed crown is decked in sprays of small, globular, golden yellow

Acacia decurrens

Acacia greggii

Acacia cavenia

flowerheads. It is able to survive winter in southern England, but flowers better in climates with a longer, drier summer; in Europe it is known as mimosa. **ZONES 8–10.**

Acacia decurrens
GREEN WATTLE

This is an upright tree growing to 50 ft (15 m) tall. With its straight trunk, smooth brownish green bark, domed crown, and fine, feathery, rich green bipinnate leaves, it is one of the fastest-growing and most attractive of the tall wattles. In late winter it bears decorative, fragrant, golden yellow flowers. It prefers a warm-temperate climate and deep, moist soil. **ZONES 9–10.**

Acacia elata
CEDAR WATTLE

Native to warm-temperate east-coastal Australia, this is one of the taller acacias, making a tree to 80 ft (24 m), with a strong trunk and narrow conical crown. The fern-like leaves are larger than those of other bipinnate wattles. Long sprays of fragrant creamy yellow flowers appear in summer. Living for 25 years or more, it is one of the longer-lived wattles, but is less drought tolerant than many other acacias. **ZONES 9–11.**

Acacia farnesiana
MIMOSA BUSH, SWEET WATTLE

This spreading, many-branched shrub growing to 15 ft (4.5 m) tall is believed to come from tropical America but has now spread to drier tropical regions of all continents. Bipinnate leaves up to 2 in (5 cm) long with tiny leaflets are carried on spiny branches. Large golden, sweetly scented, globular flowerheads are borne in winter and spring. It is widely grown in southern France for the perfume industry. It can be used as a suitable hedge or screen plant. **ZONES 11–12.**

Acacia floribunda
WHITE SALLOW WATTLE

From higher-rainfall areas of eastern Australia, this bushy shrub or small tree flowers in late winter, producing abundant spikes of pale yellow flowers. Its somewhat drooping phyllodes are thin, smooth and green. Marginally frost hardy, it grows to a height of 20 ft (6 m) and a spread of 10 ft (3 m). **ZONES 9–11.**

Acacia greggii
CATCLAW ACACIA

A native of southwestern North America, this deciduous shrub reaches 6–8 ft (1.8–2.4 m) in height and spread and can be shaped into a small tree for patio gardens. Tiny, gray-green leaves appear in mid-spring, followed by fuzzy yellow catkins in late spring. The branches are covered with thorns, making the shrub useful as a barrier planting. It loves heat and is very drought tolerant once established. **ZONES 7–11.**

Acacia harpophylla
BRIGALOW

Native to eastern Australia's semi-arid interior and one of the longest-lived acacias, this handsome tree, grows to a height of 30–50 ft (9–15 m) or more. It has a low-branched trunk with an almost black, deeply furrowed bark, and a dense, spreading crown of blue-gray foliage. Flowers are in clustered yellow balls, usually appearing in late winter or early spring. The soft-coated seeds must be planted and watered straight away to achieve germination; alternatively,

Acacia iteaphylla

Acacia melanoxylon

Acacia longifolia

propagate by detaching lengths of root with sucker growths and treat like large cuttings. **ZONES 9–11.**

Acacia howittii
STICKY WATTLE

This is a dense evergreen shrub or tree to about 25 ft (8 m) tall, with weeping branches and small, slightly sticky phyllodes that give off an aromatic smell on warm days. Rare in the wild, it occurs in a small area near the southeastern tip of the Australian mainland. It flowers in spring, producing pale yellow balls on short stalks. Marginally frost hardy, it has become popular for large hedges, and is valued mainly for its attractive dense foliage. **ZONES 9–11.**

Acacia iteaphylla

Native to South Australia, this shrub has a weeping habit. It grows to 15 ft (4.5 m) tall and has very narrow gray-green phyllodes up to 4 in (10 cm) long. Pale yellow fragrant flowers borne in fall (autumn) and winter are followed by attractive, long-lasting seed pods. It is moderately frost hardy and tolerates quite dry conditions. A prostrate form is available. **ZONES 8–10.**

Acacia karroo
KARROO THORN

From South Africa, this species has become naturalized in parts of southern Europe where it was grown for ornament and hedging. If left unpruned it will grow fairly fast into a small or medium-sized tree to 25 ft (8 m), although it can be taller in the wild. It has a stiff, irregular growth habit, and the branches are armed with vicious long spines in V-shaped pairs. It bears small bipinnate leaves and a profusion of deep yellow sweetly scented ball-shaped flowerheads in summer. **ZONES 9–11.**

Acacia karroo

Acacia mangium

Acacia neriifolia

Acacia harpophylla

Acacia koa
KOA, HAWAIIAN MAHOGANY

Native to Hawaii, the koa's hard, dark red wood was once prized for the building of war canoes. In rich soil and a sheltered position, the tree can quickly reach 100 ft (30 m), with a broad, spreading crown; where buffeted by sea winds, it is apt to be shorter and crooked in growth habit. The evergreen phyllodes are long, narrow and dull green. The pallid flowers are of little account. In Hawaii it is highly regarded as a reafforestation tree, though it is not often planted elsewhere. **ZONES 11–12.**

Acacia longifolia
SYDNEY GOLDEN WATTLE

Occurring naturally along the eastern Australian coast, this shrub has a height and spread of up to 15 ft (4.5 m), with a short trunk and an irregularly shaped head. On exposed coastal dunes it may be represented by a semi-prostrate form, ***Acacia longifolia* var. *sophorae*.** It bears long fingers of fragrant, butter-yellow flowers from late winter to early spring and has narrow, oblong, dark green phyllodes. Excellent for a seaside hedge, windbreak, or street planting. **ZONES 9–11.**

Acacia mangium

From the tropical rainforests of far north Queensland, Australia, this acacia is a fine ornamental tree, notable for the size of its large, conspicuously veined phyllodes, up to 12 in (30 cm) long and 4 in (10 cm) wide. Planted in a sunny position, it makes a medium-sized tree with a straight trunk and dense pyramidal crown. Closer planting produces a tall, straight tree, reaching 80–100 ft (25–30 m). The cream flowers are not very showy. The pods are long and tangled together. **ZONES 11–12.**

Acacia mearnsii
LATE BLACK WATTLE

This acacia from the drier coastal woodlands of eastern and southern Australia grows to 30 ft (9 m) with a spreading crown. The blackish bark is finely ridged. The fern-like, bipinnate leaves are dark green above, paler and downy beneath. Racemes of pale yellow, ball-flowers borne in late spring and early summer are followed by brown, hairy pods. It is moderately frost tolerant. **ZONES 8–11.**

Acacia melanoxylon
BLACKWOOD

Unlike most acacias, this tree from the highland forests of mainland eastern Australia and Tasmania is long-lived and moderately frost hardy. The timber is highly valued for cabinetwork. Growing to 90 ft (27 m), it has dull, olive green phyllodes and profuse balls of pale yellow flowers appear in spring. Planted in the open, it has a spreading bushy crown and short thick trunk. Fertile, moist soil and humid climates suit it best, though it will survive on poorer soils. It is not drought resistant. **ZONES 8–11.**

Acacia neriifolia

This abundantly flowering wattle occurs naturally in the dry woodlands of eastern Australia. A tall shrub or small tree to about 25 ft (8 m) and with an erect, open growth habit, it has narrow, straight, grayish phyllodes and numerous sprays of bright golden yellow flowerheads in late spring and early summer. **ZONES 9–11.**

Acacia pycnantha

Acacia podalyriifolia

Acacia pendula

Acacia pendula
WEEPING MYALL, BOREE

Native to the plains country of inland eastern Australia, this small, densely crowned tree to 20 ft (6 m) has vertically drooping branchlets like a weeping willow and makes a good shade or ornamental tree in semi-arid areas. It has narrow, lance-shaped, silvery gray phyllodes and pale yellow flowers appear in spring. It can survive harsh climates with low rainfall, but prefers heavy clay soils. **ZONES 9–11.**

Acacia podalyriifolia
QUEENSLAND WATTLE, PEARL ACACIA, SILVER WATTLE

From the wooded hills of southeastern Queensland, Australia, this handsome small tree grows to about 20 ft (6 m) and spreads to about half that. It is fast growing but short lived. The silvery phyllodes are rounded and have a felty texture. Large sprays of fragrant golden flowers appear in winter and early spring. It prefers well-drained soil, full sun and a mild to warm climate. Staking is advisable for the first year or two. **ZONES 9–11.**

Acacia pravissima
OVENS WATTLE

This evergreen, bushy shrub native to the hills of southeastern Australia can grow to a height of 20 ft (6 m) and a spread of 15 ft (4.5 m) but is usually smaller. It has drooping branches and very distinctive small, triangular, olive green phyllodes. Small heads of golden yellow flowers appear in spring. The bronze buds and gold-tipped foliage are attractive throughout winter. There is a prostrate form. **ZONES 8–10.**

Acacia pycnantha
GOLDEN WATTLE

A medium shrub or small tree of up to about 20 ft (6 m) in height, this wattle is Australia's national floral emblem. In the wild it occurs mainly in Victoria and South Australia. It has a rounded crown with somewhat pendulous branches. Large, fragrant, golden, ball-shaped flowerheads appear in spring. Although not long lived it makes a fine garden specimen. It prefers sandy soils and it should be sheltered from heavy frost. Established trees tolerate quite dry conditions. **ZONES 9–11.**

Acacia redolens

Although a large, mounding shrub in its native Western Australia, the form of this species most common in gardens of the southwestern USA is a prostrate shrub useful as a ground cover. It reaches 24 in (60 cm) in height but spreads to 12–15 ft (3.5–4.5 m) wide and has gray-green leaves and yellow flowers like puffballs in spring. It is best in sun or dappled shade and can tolerate quite dry conditions and a range of soil types. **ZONES 9–11.**

Acacia roemeriana

Like *Acacia constricta* this species occurs as a native in the USA, in southern Texas, though its major occurrence is in Mexico. It is a shrub or small tree of about 15 ft (4.5 m) tall with ferny bipinnate leaves, the leaflets about $^1/_2$ in (12 mm) long, and pairs of hooked barbs at the base of each

Acacia pravissima

leaf. Globular yellow flowerheads only $^1/_4$ in (6 mm) in diameter are borne singly in the leaf axils in spring. **ZONES 8–11.**

Acacia sieberiana var. *woodii*

This fast-growing, flat-topped tree from the velds of southeastern Africa reaches a height of 30 ft (9 m) and spread of 50 ft (15 m). It has 4 in (10 cm) long bipinnate leaves with small leaflets covered in velvety golden hairs and yellowish brown, corky bark. In spring it bears a profusion of creamy white flowers. A hot-climate species, it is able to withstand very dry conditions and poor soil. It will also tolerate some frost. **ZONES 9–11.**

Acacia spectabilis
MUDGEE WATTLE

In gardens this species, which is from the inland slopes of eastern Australia, is normally a tall shrub of 8–10 ft (2.4–3 m) with an open growth habit, drooping branchlets and small bipinnate blue-green leaves. Masses of rich golden yellow, fragrant, ball-shaped flowerheads appear in winter and spring. It is valued for screening or specimen planting. Light annual pruning will help to maintain its shape. **ZONES 9–11.**

Acacia verticillata
PRICKLY MOSES

Indigenous to Tasmania and mainland southern Australia, this upright, bushy shrub grows to about 10 ft (3 m) tall. It has needle-sharp phyllodes arranged in distinct whorls and bears creamy yellow flowers in spring and summer. Moderately frost hardy, it can be grown in southern England, especially in seaside gardens. ***Acacia verticiallata* var. *latifolia*** is a name used for semi-prostrate forms that grow on exposed coastal cliffs and have broader, blunter phyllodes. **ZONES 8–10.**

Acacia spectabilis

Acacia xanthophloea

Native to southeastern Africa, this beautiful acacia has a straight main trunk and upright growth with sparse, thorny foliage. It can grow rapidly to 30–40 ft (10–13 m). Its most striking feature is its pale, ghostly yellow bark with its spongy texture. Golden yellow flowers, not very showy, are borne in spring. To thrive, it needs warm summers, and winters with no severe frosts, and can survive long periods of flooding. **ZONES 9–11.**

ACAENA

Around 100 species make up this genus of low-growing evergreen perennials. Related to the burnets *(Sanguisorba)*, they are native mainly to New Zealand and cooler parts of South America but with a few also in Australia and elsewhere in the Pacific region. Those grown in gardens all have thin, creeping stems or buried rhizomes that bear at intervals tufts of small pinnate leaves with toothed margins. Flowers are rather insignificant, green or purple-brown, in dense stalked heads or spikes, but are followed by small dry fruit with barbed hooks that cling to socks at the slightest touch. Acaenas are grown as rock garden plants or sometimes as ground covers, valued for their pretty, intricate foliage. Some more vigorous species are regarded as weeds, even in their native countries.

CULTIVATION: They are tough little plants, thriving in exposed places and poor soil, but do demand good drainage and summer moisture. Propagate from seed or by division.

Acaena argentea

This species from Peru and Chile has prostrate stems that spread to form a

Acacia xanthophloea

Acacia verticillata

24 in (60 cm) wide mat. The leaves, which are up to 6 in (15 cm) long, are pinnate with 9 to 15 leaflets, blue-gray above with silvery undersides. The flower and seed heads are purple. **ZONES 7–10.**

Acaena 'Blue Haze'

Thought probably to be a form of *Acaena magellanica*, which comes from the southern Andes of South America and subantarctic islands, this vigorous creeper can spread to an indefinite size, the stems rooting. The crowded leaves with roundish, toothed leaflets are an attractive pale blue-gray, and in summer it sends up 4 in (10 cm) high purplish flowerheads followed in fall (autumn) by red-spined fruit. A useful ground cover, it will spill over rocks or retaining walls. **ZONES 7–10.**

Acaena microphylla
NEW ZEALAND BURR

From the grasslands of New Zealand, this is one of the smallest-growing species. Forming a dense mat only about 1 in (25 mm) deep and usually no more than 1 ft (30 cm) or so across, the stems run beneath the soil and root. The tiny leaflets are only $^1/_8$ in (3 mm) across and are bronzy when young. Pink-spined fruiting heads add to the effect in fall (autumn). **ZONES 7–10.**

Acaena novae-zelandiae

This species from New Zealand, southeast Australia and New Guinea may be prostrate or mounding with wiry stems from 6–24 in (15–60 cm) long. The bright green leaves (sometimes tinted red) are up to 4 in (10 cm) long and composed of 9 to 15 leaflets. The flowerhead is cream and the immature fruiting heads have bright red spines on the burrs. It is a vigorous grower, sometimes becoming a nuisance. **ZONES 5–10.**

ACALYPHA

This genus of evergreen shrubs and subshrubs consists of over 400 species from most warmer countries of the world, but only a handful are grown as ornamentals. Some of these are valued for the decorative, narrow spikes of crowded, feathery flowers on the female plants (males are on different plants), while one species is grown only for its showy variegated foliage. The leaves are thin, usually with toothed margins.
CULTIVATION: They need a sunny to semi-shaded position, well-drained, light soil with plenty of water during summer, and protection from wind. Plants are frost tender. Prune lightly to shape in late winter, followed by additional feeding and watering. Propagate from cuttings in summer. Watch for mealybug, red spider mite and white fly.

Acalypha hispida
CHENILLE PLANT, RED-HOT CAT-TAIL

Thought to be from Malaysia, this upright, soft-stemmed shrub is grown for its striking, tiny, bright red flowers that in summer hang in pendulous, tassel-like spikes on the female plants. Leaves are large, oval and bright green to reddish bronze. It reaches a height and spread of 6 ft (1.8 m). Regular pruning will maintain a bushy shape. It does best in sheltered sites in full sun; in cool climates it needs a heated conservatory. **ZONES 11–12.**

Acalypha wilkesiana
FIJIAN FIRE PLANT, COPPER LEAF

Originating in Fiji and nearby islands, this shrub grows to a height and spread of 10 ft (3 m). With erect stems branching from the base, it is grown for its large, serrated, oval leaves which appear in a wide color range, some with contrasting margins. Inconspicuous tassel-like catkins of reddish bronze flowers appear in summer and fall (autumn). It prefers a warm, sheltered position and the foliage colors are best in full sun. Cultivars include **'Macrophylla'** with large leaves, each differently variegated with bronze, copper, red, cream and yellow blotches; **'Godseffiana'** with narrow, drooping green leaves edged with cream; **'Macafeeana'** with deep bronze leaves splashed with coppery red; and **'Marginata'** with bronze-red leaves edged with cream or pale pink. **ZONES 10–11.**

ACANTHOLIMON
PRICKLY THRIFT

This genus consists of around 120 species of curious prickly-leaved dwarf evergreen perennials and subshrubs from the eastern Mediterranean region and west and central Asia. Only a few have been successfully introduced to cultivation. These include some choice rock-garden plants. In the wild they inhabit dry mountain and desert areas, growing on screes, gravelly plains and the margins of salt lakes. Most species have crowded rosettes of stiff, harsh, needle-like leaves forming a mat or mound that may be very long lived, often with a thatch of old dead leaves built up beneath the living leaves. Some species have a whitish encrustation of mineral salts on the leaves. Related to armerias, acantholimons have similar pink or white flowers but they are grouped into short spikes rather than rounded heads; they may either nestle among the leaves or be held on stalks well above them.
CULTIVATION: These plants have specialized requirements. They dislike wetness persisting around their bases, especially when dormant in winter, so plant them in very coarse, gritty soil with the stems sitting on stones or rocks. A very hot, dry position suits them best. Propagate from tip cuttings.

Acaena argentea

Acantholimon glumaceum

From the Caucasus Mountains and adjacent parts of Turkey, this species makes a low mound of densely crowded rosettes only 2–3 in (5–8 cm) high and up to 12 in (30 cm) across. The showy deep pink flowers are produced in summer on numerous very short spikes, barely emerging above the rigid, prickly leaves. Where conditions suit it, it makes a fine rock garden subject. **ZONES 5–9.**

ACANTHOPHOENIX
BARBEL PALM

This genus consists of a single though variable palm species, confined to the Indian Ocean islands of Mauritius and Réunion. It has a solitary, ringed trunk swollen at the base and terminating in a 'crownshaft' of frond bases densely armed with long black needle-like spines. The pinnate fronds (leaves) have many narrow, drooping leaflets that are whitish on the undersides. Numerous small flowers are borne on large erect panicles among the leaves. The globular black fruit has a thin flesh enclosing a single seed.
CULTIVATION: This palm will grow outdoors only in the tropics and subtropics, preferring a sheltered position, fertile, sandy soil and full sun. In cooler climates it can be grown in a tub in a greenhouse or conservatory. Propagate from seed in spring.

Acanthophoenix rubra
syn. *Acanthophoenix crinita*

This elegant palm has a slender trunk and prickly, rich green leaves. The inconspicuous flowers are white, yellow, pink, red or purple and appear through summer. It grows to a height of 60 ft (18 m) with a 25 ft (8 m) spread. **ZONES 10–12.**

ACANTHOSTACHYS

This bromeliad genus from central South America consists of only one species, a plant of unusual growth form for this group. The plant spreads by short rhizomes which bear tufts of arching and drooping, very slender leaves like rats' tails, sprinkled with silvery scales. The inflorescence stalk resembles a leaf, and carries a small cone-like spike of yellow flowers among long-lived, bright orange or red bracts with spiny edges and tips. The flowers develop into sweet, edible fruit like small pineapples.
CULTIVATION: It needs an open, sunny position and fertile, well-drained, humus-rich soil. Keep it well watered in winter. It does well in hanging baskets. Propagate from seed or offsets.

Acaena 'Blue Haze'

Acaena novae-zelandiae

Acanthostachys strobilacea

This species grows to a height and spread of 3 ft (1 m) and bears tubular yellow flowers in dense inflorescences above leaf-like, reddish orange bracts. The leaves are spiny and bright green. **ZONES 10–12.**

Acalypha hispida

Acalypha wilkesiana 'Macrophylla'

Acalypha wilkesiana 'Macafeeana'

A

ACANTHUS

BEAR'S BREECHES

Around 30 species of perennials and shrubs from tropical Africa and Asia as well as Mediterranean Europe make up this genus. The genus name goes back to ancient Greek, and the large and colorful family Acanthaceae (mainly tropical) takes its name from the genus. The deeply lobed and toothed leaves of *Acanthus mollis* and *A. spinosus* have lent their shape to the carved motifs used to decorate the capitals of Corinthian columns. It is only the more temperate perennial species that have been much cultivated, valued for their erect spikes of bracted, curiously shaped flowers, as well as their handsome foliage. The flowers appear in spring and early summer, after which the leaves may die back but sprout again before winter.

CULTIVATION: Frost hardy, they do best in full sun or light shade. They prefer a rich, well-drained soil with adequate moisture in winter and spring. Spent flower stems and leaves can be removed if they offend. Snails and caterpillars can damage the new leaves. Propagate by division in fall (autumn), or from seed.

Acanthus mollis

Acanthus mollis 'Candelabrus'

Acanthus hungaricus

syn. *Acanthus balcanicus*

Despite its species name, this plant does not occur wild in present-day Hungary, though some of the Balkan countries to which it is a native were once part of the Austro-Hungarian Empire. It forms dense tufts of pinnately divided, soft, rather narrow leaves. The flower spikes may be up to 5 ft (1.5 m) tall, with vertical rows of white flowers almost hidden beneath dull pinkish bracts. It prefers a hot sunny position. **ZONES 7–10.**

Acanthus mollis

Occurring on both sides of the Mediterranean, this well-known species is somewhat variable, the form grown in gardens having broader, softer leaves and taller flowering stems than most wild plants. It is more of a woodland plant than other acanthuses, appreciating shelter and deep, moist soil. The large leaves are a deep, glossy green and rather soft, inclined to droop in hot dry weather.

Acanthus spinosus

Acanthus hungaricus

Flower spikes can be over 6 ft (1.8 m) tall, the purple-pink bracts contrasting sharply with the crinkled white flowers. Spreading by deeply buried rhizomes, it can be hard to eradicate once established. **'Candelabrus'** is one of several cultivars of *Acanthus mollis.* **ZONES 7–10.**

Acanthus spinosus

This eastern Mediterranean species has large leaves that are deeply divided, the segments having coarse, spine-tipped teeth. In summer it sends up flower spikes to about 4 ft (1.2 m) high, the individual flowers and bracts being very similar to those of *Acanthus mollis.* **ZONES 7–10.**

ACER

MAPLE

Maples are unrivaled for their fall (autumn) foliage coloring and variety of leaf shape and texture. They are also grown for shade and for timber. Many are compact enough for the average garden. The distinctive 2-winged fruit (samaras) are more noticeable than the flowers, which in most species are inconspicuous. Bark is a feature of some maples—although usually smooth and gray or greenish, in the group known as the 'snakebark maples' it has longitudinal gray or red-brown stripes and in others it is flaky or papery. Most species come from East Asia, particularly China (over 80 species), Japan (over 20) and the eastern Himalayas; 9 species are native to North America and a few to Europe, including ***Acer heldreichii* subsp. *trautvetteri*** (Greek maple). Most are deciduous but there are a few evergreen and semi-evergreen species from northern Turkey and the Caucasus.

CULTIVATION: Most maples prefer a cool, moist climate with ample rainfall in spring and summer. A planting position sheltered from strong winds suits them best. For best fall color, grow them in a neutral to acid soil. Propagation is generally from seed for the species, by grafting for cultivars. Cuttings are difficult to root, but layering of low branches can be successful. Seed germination can be aided by overwintering in damp litter, or by refrigeration. Some species produce few fertile seeds, so it may be necessary to sow a large quantity to obtain enough seedlings.

Acer heldreichii subsp. *trautvetteri*

Acer heldreichii subsp. *trautvetteri*

Acer buergerianum

Acer capillipes

Acer buergerianum

TRIDENT MAPLE

Although tall in its native forests of eastern China, in cultivation this species usually makes a bushy-topped small tree with a thick, strong trunk. The bark is pale brown and dappled and the smallish leaves usually have 3 short lobes close together at the upper end (hence the common name). Fall (autumn) coloring is often two-toned, with scarlet patches on a green or yellowish background. It tolerates exposed positions and poor soils and is a traditional subject for bonsai. **ZONES 6–10.**

Acer campestre

FIELD MAPLE, HEDGE MAPLE

A small to medium bushy-crowned tree, this European maple also occurs in western Asia and north Africa. In the UK it is also known as hedge maple, for its use in the traditional hedges that divide fields. It withstands heavy pruning and can be trimmed into dense, regular shapes. It has thick, furrowed corky bark; fall (autumn) brings golden yellow or slightly bronze tints to the foliage. It is easily grown from fresh seed. **ZONES 4–9.**

Acer capillipes

RED SNAKEBARK MAPLE

This fast-growing but short-lived (20 to 30 years) Japanese member of the snakebark group of maples makes a small spreading tree 15–20 ft (4.5–6 m) high, branching from just above the ground. Bark is striped pale gray and dull green and the broad, 3-pointed leaves turn yellow, orange and crimson in fall (autumn). It likes a sheltered, sunny position and is one of the few maples easily propagated from cuttings. **ZONES 5–9.**

Acer cappadocicum
COLISEUM MAPLE

This maple is found from southern Europe across temperate Asia to central China, with a number of geographic subspecies. Its smooth green leaves have regular, radiating triangular lobes, each lobe drawn out into a slender point. Fast growing, it can reach 100 ft (30 m) in the wild and is better suited to parks and streets rather than suburban gardens. Fall (autumn) color is a brilliant golden yellow. **'Rubrum'** has dark red new shoots, the young leaves expanding bright red before turning green. **ZONES 5–9.**

Acer carpinifolium
HORNBEAM MAPLE

This beautiful maple from the mountain forests of Japan has leaves finely toothed rather than lobed, with closely spaced veins and a corrugated surface. Both names refer to its resemblance to the hornbeams *(Carpinus)*. Spring leaves have a silky coating; in fall (autumn) they turn gold. A moderately slow-growing, upright, narrow-crowned tree, it can reach 20 ft (6 m) or more. Seeds have a low rate of germination, so it can be difficult to obtain. It is exceptionally cold hardy. **ZONES 3–9.**

Acer cissifolium

Acer cappadocicum 'Rubrum'

Acer circinatum

Acer circinatum
VINE MAPLE

Native to the west of North America, the vine maple belongs to the same group as *Acer palmatum*. Its roughly circular leaves have 7 to 9 short lobes, like small grape-vine-like leaves. A small, broadly spreading tree to 25 ft (8 m) high, branching at the base, its fall (autumn) tones are brilliant orange-scarlet to deeper red. It appreciates shelter from strong winds. Older specimens are often self-layering, a ready-made means of propagation. **ZONES 5–9.**

Acer cissifolium
VINE-LEAF MAPLE, IVY-LEAFED MAPLE

Rarely reaching 30 ft (9 m) and with a broadly spreading crown, the vine-leaf maple is native to Japan. Unlike most maples, it has compound leaves consisting of a number of separate leaflets. Fall (autumn) color is yellow and orange or red. Although easily grown, it can be hard to obtain: male plants are rare so fertile seed is unavailable, and nurseries must propagate by the slower method of layering. **ZONES 5–9.**

Acer crataegifolium
HAWTHORN MAPLE

This slender, deciduous tree from Japan has an open, spreading crown. The palmate leaves have shallow lobes. It bears pale yellow flowers in erect, terminal spikes and grows to 30 ft (9 m). **ZONES 6–9.**

Acer carpinifolium

Acer × *freemanii* 'Autumn Blaze'

Acer davidii

Acer davidii subsp. *grosseri*

Acer davidii
FATHER DAVID'S MAPLE

This Chinese maple of open habit and flat-topped outline is named for its discoverer, French missionary-naturalist Armand David. The scope of this name has now been widened to include a number of subspecies, previously treated as distinct species; David's original form is placed under ***Acer davidii* subsp. *davidii*.** A snakebark maple, it has bark striped silvery gray on an olive green background and leaves that are long pointed but mostly unlobed. The Dutch selection **'Serpentine'** has more strongly contrasting stripes on a deep purplish brown background. Fall (autumn) brings shades of yellow, orange and dull scarlet. In a cool, humid climate it grows rapidly to 20–25 ft (6–8 m). ***A. d.* subsp. *grosseri*** (syns *Acer grosseri, A. hersii*) differs in its shorter broader leaves with 2 short lateral lobes. This tree has an overall green coloring in summer, the bark striped paler gray-green; fall (autumn) tones are similar to subsp. *davidii*. Both subspecies are popular and are easily grown from fresh seed, but chance hybrids with other nearby snakebarks are likely. **'George Forrest'** is a broadly upright cultivar with mid- to dark green leaves. **ZONES 6–9.**

Acer × *freemanii*

This hybrid between *Acer rubrum* (the red maple) and *A. saccharinum* (the silver maple) was raised by O. M. Freeman at the US National Arboretum in 1933, but has since frequently been found to occur spontaneously. In foliage it is intermediate between these species, growing to 50 ft (15 m) or more quite rapidly with erect branches and a rounded crown. A half-dozen cultivars of *A.* × *freemanii* have been named including the colorful **'Autumn Blaze'.** They are suitable specimens for street planting. They are normally propagated by layering. **ZONES 5–9.**

Acer maximowiczianum

Acer japonicum 'Aconitifolium'

Acer japonicum 'Vitifolium'

Acer japonicum

Acer glabrum

ROCK MAPLE, ROCKY MOUNTAIN MAPLE

Within its vast range from Alaska down the Rocky Mountains to New Mexico are many variations and this maple has been divided into as many as 5 subspecies. It is nearly always low growing, usually with multiple stems from the base. It occurs as both an understory tree in forests and as lower scrubs on exposed hillsides. Not widely cultivated, its cold tolerance and small size may be useful in some situations. **ZONES 4–9.**

Acer griseum

PAPERBARK MAPLE

Prized for its bark—chestnut brown with paler corky dots which it sheds each year in wide curling strips—this narrow-crowned tree grows to 30 ft (9 m) with a fairly straight trunk. In fall (autumn) its small, dark green leaves turn deep scarlet. Under moist, sheltered conditions in good soil, growth can be rapid. No longer common in the wild in its native China, in cultivation it produces mostly infertile seed, so can be hard to obtain. **ZONES 5–9.**

Acer japonicum

FULL-MOON MAPLE

This maple's new growth is distinctive—very pale green with a coating of silky white hairs that disappear as the leaves mature into olive green tones. In fall (autumn) some leaves change early to orange or red, while others retain their summer colors into late fall. Slow growing and of narrow, shrubby habit, it is intolerant of drying winds and likes a moist, sheltered position. It has long been cultivated in Japan. Its many cultivars include **'Aconitifolium'**, with ferny leaves that turn crimson in fall, and **'Vitifolium'**, with leaves slightly more deeply lobed than the normal species and coloring more brilliant scarlet, orange or yellow. **ZONES 5–9.**

Acer griseum

Acer griseum

Acer macrophyllum

OREGON MAPLE, BIGLEAF MAPLE

This maple occurs wild from southern Alaska to southern California, usually as an understory tree, but it can make a fine 100 ft (30 m) forest tree with broadly domed crown and thick trunk. Leaves are up to 12 in (30 cm) wide, the yellowish flowers hang in dense sprays, and the 2- or 3-winged fruit are 3 in (8 cm) across; all larger than those of other maples. Fall (autumn) tones are gold and brown. It likes moderate shelter and deep, moist soil. **ZONES 6–9.**

Acer maximowiczianum

syn. *Acer nikoense*

NIKKO MAPLE

Native to Japan, this maple has compound leaves consisting of 3 leaflets, which are closely veined with whitish undersides. Slow growing and of neat appearance, it reaches 50 ft (15 m) in the wild but is commonly under 20 ft (6 m) in gardens. Like the related *Acer griseum*, it produces mainly infertile seed in cultivation and so can be difficult to obtain. The fall (autumn) foliage is in shades of yellow and deep red. **ZONES 6–9.**

Acer monspessulanum

MONTPELIER MAPLE, FRENCH MAPLE

Related to *Acer campestre* and occurring on stony hillsides around the Mediterranean, this bushy small tree of up to 30 ft (9 m) has dark green, rather thick leaves $1\frac{1}{2}$–2 in (35 mm–5 cm) long with 3 blunt lobes. It is tolerant of dry conditions and its compact crown makes it well suited for streets and suburban lawns. It turns reddish in fall (autumn). **ZONES 5–10.**

Acer negundo

BOX-ELDER MAPLE, BOX ELDER

The only North American maple to have compound leaves (consisting of 3 to 7 leaflets), this species can reach 50 ft (15 m) with a thick trunk and upright branching habit, but is more often seen as a smaller tree with cane-like, bright green branches. It is fast growing and tolerates poor conditions but its branches break easily in high winds. In some areas it is regarded as a weed because of its free-seeding habits. Its several subspecies cover the length and breadth of North America, extending south into Mexico and Guatemala. Favorite cultivars include **'Elegans'**; **'Variegatum'** and **'Aureo-marginatum'**, with leaflets edged white or gold respectively; **'Aureo-variegatum'** has leaflets with broader, deeper yellow margins, retaining this coloring into fall (autumn); the newer **'Flamingo'** is similar to 'Variegatum' but with leaves strongly flushed pink on new growth. The male clone **'Violaceum'** has purplish new shoots and twigs; the male flower tassels are also pale purple. None of these cultivars reach much more than half the size of the wild, green-leafed type. **ZONES 4–10.**

Acer oblongum

This very distinctive maple species has a wide distribution through the Himalayas and southern and central China, growing in warmer climates than most other maples. It is semi-deciduous, sometimes virtually evergreen, with pointed 2–5 in (5–12 cm) long leaves that are neither lobed nor toothed but smooth and leathery, with a thin bloom of wax on the underside. Some Chinese forms are more deciduous and cold hardy than the Himalayan ones. It is now being used as a street and park tree in mild climates such as California; usually no more than 20–25 ft (6–8 m) tall, it has a bushy, compact crown. **ZONES 8–11.**

Acer oliverianum

Native to central and eastern China and Taiwan, this maple makes a smallish tree of 12–25 ft (3.5–8 m) tall with a gracefully spreading crown. The leaves are 5-lobed, resembling those of *Acer palmatum* but slightly larger and more finely toothed, with more stiffly radiating lobes; in fall (autumn) they turn yellow, orange or deep bronze. **ZONES 6–9.**

Acer negundo 'Violaceum'

Acer negundo 'Variegatum'

Acer negundo

Acer negundo 'Flamingo'

Acer oliverianum

Acer palmatum

JAPANESE MAPLE

The Japanese maple is the most widely grown maple in gardens. It is valued for its compact size, delicate ferny foliage, and brilliant fall (autumn) coloring, from rich gold to deepest blood-red. In a garden it grows to 12–15 ft (3.5–4.5 m), branching low, with strong sinuous branches and a dense, rounded crown. Although more tolerant of warmer climates than most maples, it needs shade and shelter or leaves may shrivel. The more than 300 cultivars range from rock-garden miniatures to vigorous small trees, with a great variety of leaf shape, size and coloration. Nearly all need to be grafted to preserve their characteristics, so they are expensive. The most popular cultivar of tree size is **'Atropurpureum'**, dense and spreading, with dark purple spring foliage giving way to paler olive-purple in summer and deep scarlet tones in fall; it largely comes true from seed. **'Sangokaku'** ('Senkaki') has coral red branches and twigs, which are displayed bare in winter; in fall leaves have brilliant gold tones. **'Atrolineare'** has foliage color like 'Atropurpureum' but leaves divided almost to the base into narrow lobes. In the **Dissectum Group**, the primary leaf lobes are deeply cut into a filigree pattern; their fine, drooping twigs grow down rather than upward, so they are grafted onto a standard. The height of the standard determines the height of the dome-shaped shrub. **'Dissectum'** is a small cultivar with leaves turning yellow tinged with orange in fall. **'Dissectum Viridis'**, the original green cut-leaf maple, is slightly more able to withstand the sun than is **'Dissectum Atropurpureum'** ('Ornatum') which has purple leaves that are green in summer . Some other cultivars that are well-known include **'Bloodgood'**, **'Butterfly'**, **'Chitoseyama'**, **'Koreanum'**, **'Osakazuki'** and **'Shigitatsu Sawa'**. The finely cut leaves of **'Crimson Queen'** are red-purple, as are those of **'Garnet'** which persist through fall. **'Red Pygmy'** is a vase-shaped cultivar with red leaves in spring, turning to gold in fall. Some other popular forms include **'Linearilobum Rubrum'**, **'Trompenburg'** , **'Hessei'** and **'Lutescens'**. ZONES 5–10.

Acer p. 'Dissectum Atropurpureum'

Acer p. 'Dissectum Atropurpureum'

Acer palmatum 'Sangokaku'

Acer palmatum 'Butterfly'

Acer palmatum 'Dissectum Viridis'

Acer palmatum 'Linearilobum Rubrum'

Acer palmatum 'Trompenburg'

Acer pensylvanicum

Acer palmatum

Acer palmatum 'Dissectum'

Acer palmatum 'Atropurpureum'

Acer palmatum 'Bloodgood'

Acer palmatum cultivar

Acer palmatum 'Hessei'

Acer pectinatum subsp. *forrestii*
syn. *Acer forrestii*

This species from China has 3-lobed, ovate leaves that are dark green above and paler beneath; they turn orange-red in fall (autumn). It produces pendent racemes of brown-green flowers and grows to 30 ft (10 m) in height. ZONES 6–9.

Acer pensylvanicum
STRIPED MAPLE, MOOSEWOOD

Erect, vigorous and with a single main trunk, the striped maple is native to eastern North America. The bark striping on younger limbs is the most richly colored of any of the snakebark maples, suffused with red as well as olive and white. Fall (autumn) color is a bright golden yellow. The popular cultivar **'Erythrocladum'** has striking red branches in winter. ZONES 5–9.

Acer pentaphyllum

A rare and very distinctive maple species, this comes from a very limited area of central-western China. It has compound leaves, each consisting of 5 rather narrow leaflets arranged in digitate fashion around a central stalk, a unique leaf type among maples. It grows to about 30 ft (9 m) eventually, with spreading crown and pale gray bark. ZONES 6–9.

Acer platanoides
NORWAY MAPLE

This maple ranges from north of the Arctic Circle in Scandinavia (reduced almost to a shrub) across Europe from France to the Urals but not to the Mediterranean or the British Isles, though cultivated there for centuries. A large, round-headed tree, it thrives in a wide range of soils and situations, but not in warm climates. Yellow flowers appear before the leaves; fall (autumn) color is gold to reddish orange. Popular cultivars include **'Oregon Pride'**, **'Cleveland'**, **'Summershade'** and **'Drummondii'** which has variegated leaves. Cultivars with deep purplish foliage include **'Schwedleri'**, **'Faasen's Black'** and **'Crimson King'**. **'Columnare'**, with plain green leaves, has a narrow column shape. All except **'Oregon Pride'** are slow growing, and so suit smaller gardens. ZONES 4–9.

Acer pseudoplatanus
SYCAMORE MAPLE

This species, which occurs naturally from Portugal to the Caspian Sea and has been long established in England and North America, seeds so profusely as to be regarded a weed. Cultivated trees are usually 40–60 ft (12–18 m) tall and form a broad, dense crown of dark green. The thick, scaly bark is pale gray. Fall (autumn) color is not a feature. A useful park and street tree, it prefers a sheltered situation with deep moist soil, but tolerates more exposed sites. The cultivar **'Purpureum'** has leaf undersides of a deep plum, uppersides also slightly purplish. **'Erythrocarpum'** has red fruit in conspicuous clusters. The spring foliage of **'Brilliantissimum'** is pale creamy yellow flushed pink, changing in summer to whitish with green veining; it is slow growing and suits smaller gardens; **'Rubicundum'** has leaves flecked deep pink. **'Variegatum'** has cream markings. ZONES 4–10.

Acer rubrum
RED MAPLE, SCARLET MAPLE

This large maple from eastern North America displays brilliant fall (autumn) tones of deep red, contrasting with the blue-white undersides. In the wild it grows to 100 ft (30 m) in forests on deep alluvial soil. As a planted tree it makes rapid growth, with a straight trunk and narrow crown at first, but spreading broadly with age. Its timber is prized for furniture making. There are numerous popular cultivars including **'Bowhall'**, **'Red Sunset'**, **'Schlesingeri'**, the conical **'Scanlon'** and **'October Glory'**, which has glossy green foliage that turns a brilliant crimson in fall. ZONES 4–9.

Acer pentaphyllum

Acer platanoides

Acer rubrum

Acer platanoides 'Crimson King'

Acer pseudoplatanus

Acer platanoides 'Drummondii'

Acer pseudoplatanus 'Variegatum'

Acer platanoides 'Schwedleri'

Acer pseudoplatanus 'Erythrocarpum'

Acer rubrum 'Schlesingeri'

Acer rubrum 'October Glory'

Acer rufinerve

Acer shirasawanum 'Aureum'

Acer saccharum 'Globosum'

Acer saccharum

Acer tataricum subsp. *ginnala*

Acer saccharinum

Acer saccharum subsp. *nigrum*

Acer rufinerve

From the valleys of Japan, this is another of the snakebark maples, similar to *Acer capillipes*. A tree of upright habit, it reaches 20–30 ft (6–9 m), has downy, bluish new growths and the bark of young branches is attractively striped. Fall (autumn) foliage is a deep dull crimson with orange tones. The thickish, 3-lobed leaves are 3–6 in (8–15 cm) long, with the central lobe the largest. **ZONES 5–9.**

Acer saccharinum

syn. *Acer dasycarpum*

SILVER MAPLE

Ranging over eastern USA and Canada (except the arctic north), the silver maple grows large, branching low into several trunks with a broad crown of foliage. As an ornamental it is popular for its hardiness, rapid growth and rich golden fall (autumn) color. The cane-like branches are easily damaged by storms and heavy snow, but quickly grow back. American and European nurseries have developed many cultivars. **ZONES 4–9.**

Acer saccharum

SUGAR MAPLE

Commercially important for its sap (maple syrup) and durable timber, this maple ranges across eastern North America from Newfoundland and Manitoba in the north to Florida in the south, and west to Utah. In the south and west, regional subspecies occur, including *Acer saccharum* subspp. *floridanum, grandidentatum, leucoderme* and *nigrum:* all have been treated as distinct species by some botanists. Its leaf adorns the Canadian flag. Often slow growing in the first 10 years, in the garden it makes a low-branching, broad-crowned tree of 40–50 ft (12–15 m), though it will grow much taller in forests. Fall (autumn) color varies from tree to tree, with yellow, orange, scarlet and crimson all common. ***A. s.* subsp. *grandidentatum*** (bigtooth maple) is widely distributed in western North America. It has thicker leaves, and the bluish white undersides contrast with the deep green upper, and blunter, lobes. It makes a small, bushy-topped tree to 40 ft (12 m), and has pale bark. Attractive cultivars include **'Globosum'**, **'Green Mountain'**, **'Legacy'** and **'Monumentale'**. **ZONES 4–9.**

Acer shirasawanum

Native to the mountains of Japan, this smooth-barked maple is closely allied to *Acer palmatum* but its leaves have more lobes, usually 9 or 11. It has also been confused with *A. japonicum*, but its young leaves are not hairy. It normally grows to about 15–25 ft (5–8 m) and in fall (autumn) the leaves turn bright golden yellow. A well-known cultivar is **'Aureum'** (syn. *A. japonicum* 'Aureum') with lime-green new leaves turning to gold and scarlet in fall. **ZONES 5–9.**

Acer sikkimense

Acer sikkimense

syn. *Acer hookeri*

Native to the rainy eastern Himalayas, this species is frost tender, thriving in cooler countries only in the mildest coastal areas, or in humid highlands of the subtropics. It is fast growing, with long shoots and large oval leaves, and can reach 20 ft (6 m) in 10 years, but may prove short lived. Leaves are bronze-green in early spring and rich orange in fall (autumn) and often hang on into winter. It likes protection from strong winds, which damage the leaves. **ZONES 8–10.**

Acer tataricum

TATARIAN MAPLE, AMUR MAPLE

As now recognized, this is the maple species with the widest east–west distribution, occurring wild from Austria eastward across Europe and temperate Asia all the way to Japan and far eastern Siberia. Tataria was the name used in the eighteenth century for central Asia and eastern Russia, where it is a common tree. The species is divided into 4 geographic subspecies of which the most commonly cultivated is ***Acer tataricum* subsp. *ginnala*** (syn. *Acer ginnala*) from northeastern China, Japan, Korea and eastern Siberia: a large shrub or small tree of 15–30 ft (4.5–9 m), it often branches from the base into several long cane-like stems; leaves are long pointed and irregularly lobed, turning red in fall (autumn) and falling rapidly; red fruits are a summer feature. A quick grower, it is fully frost hardy; **'Flame'** is one of its cultivars. **ZONES 4–9.**

Acer tegmentosum

One of the snakebark maples, in this case a native of Korea, northeastern China and far eastern Siberia, *Acer tegmentosum* has green and white striped young branches and leaves up to 6 in (15 cm) wide with 3 or 5 rather shallow lobes. It makes a spreading tree 20–30 ft (6–9 m) tall and the foliage turns yellow in fall (autumn). **ZONES 5–9.**

Acer triflorum

Native to northeastern China and Korea, this maple makes a tree of rather upright habit with attractive brownish yellow bark that sheds in flakes. The leaves are compound, consisting of 3 leaflets, and turn dull orange to scarlet in fall (autumn). **ZONES 5–9.**

Acer triflorum

Acer truncatum

Achasma macrocheilos

Acer truncatum
SHANTUNG MAPLE

Occurring in eastern Siberia, Japan, Korea and northern China, the Shantung maple is a small tree with rough-barked trunk, a densely branched crown and rather tangled branches. In gardens it is often slow growing, remaining shrubby for many years. Fall (autumn) color is yellow. **ZONES 5–9.**

Acer velutinum
PERSIAN MAPLE

One of the largest species in the wild, *Acer velutinum* grows to 120 ft (36 m) tall in its native mountains of Iran's Caspian region and the Caucasus. In gardens it may reach 60 ft (18 m), with a broadly domed crown. It has 5-lobed leaves 6 in (15 cm) or more wide, hairy on the undersides. ***Acer velutinum* var. *vanvolxemii*** has even larger leaves, up to 12 in (30 cm) wide, hairless and with a bluish bloom on the undersides. **ZONES 7–9.**

ACHASMA

This genus of gingers from tropical Southeast Asia is hardly known in cultivation but often catching the eye of travelers through rich lowland rainforests. It is one of several genera that characteristically have very tall leafy shoots springing at intervals from a thick, usually buried rhizome, and quite separate flowering stems, from the same rhizome but often far shorter or sometimes virtually sitting on the ground. They often have brilliantly colored flowers, and yet it is suspected that they are pollinated by ground-dwelling fauna such as slugs and beetles, which one would not think very color conscious. Some botanists now regard *Achasma* as a synonym of *Etlingera*. **CULTIVATION:** *Achasma* species need very warm, humid and sheltered conditions beneath trees or in a courtyard,

Acer velutinum var. *vanvolxemii*

and a moist, humus-rich soil. Propagate by division of rhizomes.

Achasma macrocheilos
syn. ***Achasma megalocheilos***
YELLOW EARTH GINGER

Native to Malaysia, this species has leafy stems up to 20 ft (6 m) tall, but the small head of several flowers sits just above the litter of the forest floor. The large 'lip' of each flower is strikingly bicolored in scarlet and yellow. **ZONES 11–12.**

ACHILLEA
YARROW, MILFOIL, SNEEZEWORT

There are about 85 species of *Achillea*, most native to Europe and temperate Asia, with a handful in North America. Foliage is fern-like, aromatic and often hairy. Most species bear masses of large, flat heads of tiny daisy flowers from late spring to fall (autumn) in shades of white, yellow, orange, pink or red. Achilleas are suitable for massed border planting and rockeries, and flowerheads can be dried—retaining their color—for winter decoration. This genus is named after Achilles, who, in Greek mythology, used the plant to heal wounds.
CULTIVATION: These hardy perennials are easily grown and tolerant of poor soils, but they do best in sunny, well-drained sites in temperate climates. They multiply rapidly by deep rhizomes and are easily propagated by division in late winter or from cuttings in early summer. Flowering stems may be cut when spent or left to die down naturally in winter, when the clumps should be pruned to stimulate strong spring growth. Fertilize in spring.

Achillea ageratum
syn. ***Achillea decolorans***
SWEET NANCY

This spreading perennial from the western Mediterranean region and Portugal has yellowish white flowerheads 3 in (8 cm) wide appearing from mid-summer to fall (autumn) and sharply toothed, gray-white leaves. It grows to 24 in (60 cm) in height. **ZONES 6–10.**

Achillea 'Coronation Gold'

This vigorous hybrid cultivar originated as a cross between *Achillea clypeolata* and *A. filipendulina*. It has luxuriant grayish green foliage and flowering stems up to 3 ft (1 m) tall with large heads of deep golden yellow in summer and early fall (autumn). **ZONES 4–10.**

Achillea filipendulina

This species, native to the Caucasus, bears brilliant, deep yellow flowers over a long summer season. It grows to 4 ft (1.2 m) with flowerheads up to 6 in (15 cm) wide and is one of the most drought resistant of summer flowers. **'Gold Plate',** a strong-growing, erect cultivar reaching 4 ft (1.2 m), has aromatic, bright green foliage, and flat, rounded heads of golden yellow flowers, 4–6 in (10–15 cm) wide. **'Parker's Variety'** has yellow flowers. **ZONES 3–10.**

Achillea × *kellereri*

This unusual achillea is a hybrid between *Achillea clypeolata* and the rarely cultivated *A. ageratifolia*. It is a mat-forming plant, no more than 8 in (20 cm) tall even when flowering. It has massed rosettes of narrow gray-green leaves with comb-like toothing. In summer it produces on loosely branched stems daisy-like cream flowerheads $^3/_4$ in (18 mm) across, with a darker disc. **ZONES 5–10.**

Achillea × *lewisii* 'King Edward'

Growing to 6 in (15 cm) tall, this plant makes a mat of silver gray serrated leaves. Flowering stems rise above the foliage to a height of only 4 in (10 cm), topped with clusters of small, pale yellow flowerheads which fade as they age. It is well suited to rockeries. **ZONES 4–9.**

Achillea 'Coronation Gold'

Achillea × *kellereri*

Achillea filipendulina 'Gold Plate'

Achillea millefolium
MILFOIL, YARROW

Widely distributed in Europe and temperate Asia, this common species is hardy and vigorous to the point of weediness, and naturalizes freely. It grows to 24 in (60 cm) tall with soft, feathery, dark green foliage and white to pink flowers in summer. Cultivars include **'Cerise Queen'**, cherry red with pale colors; **'Fanal'** (syn. 'The Beacon'), bright red; **'Red Beauty',** silvery leaves and rose red flowers; the pink **'Rosea'**; and **'Apfelblüte'**, deep rose pink. Once established, plants can be difficult to eradicate. Most *Achillea* hybrids have this species as one parent. **'Paprika'** has orange-red flowerheads that fade with age. **ZONES 3–10.**

Achillea 'Lachsschönheit'

Achillea millefolium 'Fanal'

Achillea millefolium

Achillea millefolium 'Red Beauty'

Achillea millefolium 'Apfelblüte'

Achillea 'Taygetea'

Achillea tomentosa

Achillea 'Moonshine'

Achillea 'Schwellenberg'

Achillea 'Moonshine'

A cultivar of hybrid origin, this plant bears pretty flattened heads of pale sulfur yellow to bright yellow flowers throughout summer. It is a good species for cut flowers. It has delicate, feathery, silvery gray leaves and an upright habit, reaching a height of 24 in (60 cm). It should be divided regularly in spring to promote strong growth. **ZONES 3–10.**

Achillea ptarmica
SNEEZEWORT

This plant has upright stems springing from long-running rhizomes and in spring bears large heads of small white flowers amongst the dark green leaves which are unusual among achilleas, not being dissected, but merely toothed. It reaches a height of 30 in (75 cm), providing a quick-growing cover in a sunny situation. **'The Pearl'** is a double cultivar, widely grown. **ZONES 3–10.**

Achillea 'Lachsschönheit' ('Salmon Beauty')

This is one of the recently developed Galaxy hybrids. A cross between *Achillea millefolium* and *A.* 'Taygetea', this cultivar resembles the former in growth habit. In summer it produces masses of salmon pink heads which fade to paler pink, then almost to white. **ZONES 3–10.**

Achillea 'Schwellenberg'

A distinctive hybrid cultivar of spreading habit and grayish foliage, the leaf divisions are broad and overlapping. Tight heads of yellow flowers appear on short stalks through summer and into fall (autumn). **ZONES 3–10.**

Achillea 'Taygetea'

This popular achillea is known by the above for want of a better name. The true *Achillea taygetea* is a little known species from southern Greece (Taygetos Mountains), now treated as a synonym of *A. aegyptiaca*, whereas our *A.* 'Taygetea' is now thought to be a garden hybrid, its parents possibly *A. millefolium* and *A. clypeolata*. It is a vigorous grower with flowering stems about 24 in (60 cm) tall, the flowerheads pale creamy yellow in large flat plates. **ZONES 4–10.**

Achillea tomentosa
WOOLLY YARROW

Native to southwestern Europe, this is a low, spreading plant with woolly or silky-haired, finely divided gray-green leaves and flowerheads of bright yellow on 12 in (30 cm) stems. Tolerating dry conditions and hot sun, it is excellent in the rock garden or as an edging plant. **ZONES 4–10.**

ACHIMENES
HOT WATER PLANT

Traditionally grown as indoor plants in pots or hanging baskets, achimenes (pronounced with 4 syllables, emphasis on second) are tropical herbaceous plants that die back to small tubers in fall (autumn) and winter, or in the tropical dry season. The genus consists of about 25 species, all native to Central or South America. Their stems are soft and brittle, usually sprawling, and bear thin, hairy leaves arranged in opposite pairs. Brilliantly colored flowers appear from the upper leaf axils, each with a long narrow tube which flares abruptly into 5 flat, overlapping petals, forming an upward-turned disc in most species. Numerous hybrids were developed in Europe last century, some are still popular.
CULTIVATION: This follows an annual cycle, starting with the potting of dormant tubers in early spring at a temperature of 60°F (15°C), using a good quality indoor plant mix and placing plants in a strongly lit position. Increase watering gradually as summer approaches; at the same time add liquid fertilizer. After flowering finishes, cease watering so that plants return to dormancy by mid-fall. Propagate by tubers, which multiply during the growing season.

Achimenes erecta
syns *Achimenes coccinea, A. pulchella*

Native to Central America, this long-stemmed species grows to a height of 18 in (45 cm) with a 12 in (30 cm) spread and produces many solitary, long-tubed, red flowers $^1/_2$ in (12 mm) across. **ZONES 11–12.**

Achimenes grandiflora

Native to Honduras and southern Mexico, *Achimenes grandiflora* has sparsely hairy leaves that are dark green above and marked with red beneath. The flowers are spurred at the base and are maroon with purple spots. It reaches 24 in (60 cm) in height. **ZONES 11–12.**

Achimenes 'Little Beauty'

This bushy hybrid cultivar bears solitary, deep pink flowers with yellow eyes up to $1^1/_2$ (35 mm) across. It grows to 10 in (25 cm) with a 12 in (30 cm) spread. **ZONES 11–12.**

Achimenes longiflora 'Ambroise Verschaffelt'

This pretty cultivar bears a profusion of solitary, white flowers with purple stripes and dots and yellow throats. The leaves are coarsely toothed and are tinted red underneath. **ZONES 11–12.**

Achimenes 'Paul Arnold'

This is an erect, compact hybrid cultivar growing to a height and spread of 15 in (38 cm). It bears solitary, deep violet flowers with greenish yellow throats and dark green leaves that are red-purple beneath. **ZONES 11–12.**

Achimenes 'Purple King'

Solitary, ruffled, reddish purple flowers 2 in (5 cm) across appear on this vigorous hybrid cultivar. It grows to a height of 15 in (38 cm) and spread of 12 in (30 cm). **ZONES 11–12.**

ACINOS
CALAMINT

This genus of 10 species of annuals and woody, evergreen perennials gets its name from the Greek word *akinos*, the name of a small aromatic plant. Usually small, tufted, bushy or spreading plants growing to 8 in (20 cm), they come from central and southern Europe and western Asia. The 2-lipped, tubular flowers are borne on erect spikes in mid-summer.
CULTIVATION: Mostly quite frost hardy, they will grow in poor soil as long as it is well drained (they do not like wet conditions) and need full sun. Propagate from seed or cuttings in spring.

Acinos alpinus
syn. *Calamintha alpina*
ALPINE CALAMINT

Spikes of violet flowers 1 in (25 mm) wide and with white marks on the lower lips are borne on this spreading, short-lived perennial, a native of central and southern Europe. Growing from 4–8 in (10–20 cm) in height, it has rounded leaves with either pointed or blunt tips. **ZONES 6–9.**

Acinos arvensis
syn. *Clinopodium acinos*
MOTHER OF THYME, BASIL THYME

Widespread throughout Europe and western Asia, this annual or short-lived perennial is faintly aromatic and has erect to ascending, branching stems.

Aciphylla aurea

Aciphylla montana

It produces loose spikes of violet flowers marked with white on the lower lips. It spreads to 12 in (30 cm). **ZONES 5–10.**

ACIPHYLLA
SPEARGRASS, SPANIARD

This genus consists of 40 or so species of stiff-leafed perennials in the carrot family, mainly native to New Zealand with a few species in Australia. They are found mainly in alpine areas or windswept open grasslands at lower altitudes. Despite the common name speargrass, they are quite unrelated to grasses. They have deep tap roots that give rise to clusters of deeply divided basal leaves with long, narrow leaflets, often ochre in color with vicious spines at their tips. Strong, long-spined flower stems develop in summer and extend beyond the foliage clump. They carry masses of small white or yellow-green flowers. There are separate male and female flower stems.
CULTIVATION: The small to medium-sized species are not too difficult to cultivate but the larger species are liable to sudden collapse outside their natural environment. Plant in full sun with moist, well-drained soil deep enough to allow the tap root to develop. Do not remove the insulating thatch of dead leaves. Propagate from seed, or small suckers used as cuttings, or by division.

Aciphylla aurea
GOLDEN SPANIARD, TARAMEA

Found in drier conditions than most, this species from New Zealand's South Island forms a foliage clump around 3 ft (1 m) tall by 5 ft (1.5 m) wide. Its golden fan-shaped leaves have narrow 24 in (60 cm) long leaflets. The flower stems grow to around 4 ft (1.2 m) tall. **ZONES 7–9.**

Aciphylla hectori

Aciphylla hectori

A tiny species found in the southwest of the South Island of New Zealand, this plant consists of a tuft of stiff olive green foliage up to 4 in (10 cm) high and wide. The flower stem is up to 10 in (25 cm) tall; flowers are pale yellow to white. **ZONES 7–9.**

Aciphylla montana

Found in the southern half of the South Island, this species forms a clump of finely divided olive green leaves about 12 in (45 cm) high by 18 in (45 cm) wide. The flower stems, which are up to 18 in (45 cm) tall, are topped with a branched head of pale yellow flowers. Conspicuous sheath-like bracts surround the base of the flowerhead. **ZONES 7–9.**

ACMENA

This small genus of handsome evergreen trees has species in the rainforests of northern and eastern Australia, New Guinea and the Malay Archipelago. Like the related *Syzygium*, it was formerly included within the genus *Eugenia* (now restricted to mainly American species). The trees have smooth-edged leaves arranged in opposite pairs on the twigs, at the tips of which appear sprays of small white flowers followed by pink, purple or white berries with edible though spongy flesh which can be used for making jam. Charming street and garden trees, they are grown successfully in other warm-climate countries. Seeds are readily germinated but must be fresh.
CULTIVATION: They prefer a near frost-free climate and fertile, moist soil and will grow in sun or shade. Propagation is normally from seed, which is extracted from the fleshy fruit straight away. These trees prefer a humid, sheltered situation, at least when young.

Acmena smithii
LILLYPILLY

Native to eastern Australia from Queensland's Cape York Peninsula to southern Victoria, the lillypilly varies from a 70 ft (20 m) tree to a low shrub. Leaves are rather short and broad, narrowing to a fine point. Sprays of tiny white flowers with prominent stamens appear in early summer followed by white, pink or mauve fruits in late summer. A reliable garden plant, it is usually seen as a compact 20–30 ft (6–9 m) tree or grown as a tall screening shrub or hedge. It responds to clipping and extra water and fertilizer with flushes of coppery new growth. In more humid areas foliage is sometimes marred by sooty mold fungus. **ZONES 9–11.**

ACOELORRAPHE

A single species of elegant fan palm belongs to this genus, native to the far south of Florida and nearby shores of the Caribbean, including Central America. It is multi-trunked, the trunks quite slender and covered in fibrous remains of sheathing frond bases. The fronds are rather small, divided into many narrow segments drawn out into long thread-like points, and their stalks are spiny-edged. Flowers are in slender panicles projecting beyond the fronds and are followed by small orange-tan fruit that finally ripen black, making quite a fine display.
CULTIVATION: It is well suited to large-scale landscaping in tropical and subtropical areas and thrives in low-lying, swampy places, even tolerating slightly brackish groundwater; it will grow almost as well in well-drained soil, provided it gets ample water in summer. Propagate from seed, which should be freshly collected.

Acoelorraphe wrightii
syn. *Paurotis wrightii*
EVERGLADES PALM, SILVER SAW PALM

This palm grows to about 25 ft (8 m) tall, and with age can make a clump of even greater width. The fronds are a slightly grayish green, their blades 24–36 in (60–90 cm) long. Small cream flowers open in spring and the fruit ripen through fall (autumn). **ZONES 10–12.**

Acokanthera oblongifolia 'Variegata'

Acmena smithii

ACOKANTHERA
WINTERSWEET

This small genus of warm-climate evergreen shrubs and trees from southern Africa has poisonous milky sap. The flowers are narrowly tubular, clustered in the axils of leathery leaves which are arranged in opposite pairs on the twigs. The fruits are medium-sized drupes with a spongy, milky flesh that is poisonous.
CULTIVATION: Acokantheras prefer full sun and well-drained soil. Established plants need little watering and will tolerate salt-laden winds near the sea. Prune after flowering to prevent fruit from forming. Propagate from seed in spring, or cuttings in summer.

Acokanthera oblongifolia
syns *Acokanthera spectabilis, Carissa spectabilis*
WINTERSWEET, BUSHMAN'S POISON

This dense, spreading shrub to 12 ft (3.5 m) tall and somewhat less in width, has large, oblong, leathery, glossy, dark green leaves which become purplish in winter. Dense clusters of fragrant white flowers, dull pink on the outside, borne through spring and summer form into purplish black olive-sized fruit. It prefers a warm position. All parts of the plant are reputedly poisonous. The cultivar **'Variegata'** is smaller with gray-green and creamy white variegation; the young leaves have a pinkish tinge. Propagate by grafting. **ZONES 9–11.**

Acokanthera oblongifolia

Acoelorraphe wrightii

Acokanthera oppositifolia

From eastern tropical Africa and South Africa, the roots of this tree or shrub have been used to make poison for arrows. Growing to about 20 ft (6 m) it has deeply fissured bark and reddish branchlets. The shiny green leaves have a dull undersurface and more conspicuous veins than *Acokanthera oblongifolia*. The sweet-smelling flowers are white, tinged with pink and they are followed by a purple fruit. **ZONES 10–12.**

ACONITUM

ACONITE, MONKSHOOD, WOLFSBANE

Consisting of around 100 species of perennials scattered across temperate regions of the northern hemisphere, this genus is renowned for the virulent poisons contained in the sap of many. From ancient times until quite recently they were widely employed for deliberate poisoning, from execution of criminals to baiting wolves, or placing in an enemy's water supply. The poison has also been used medicinally in carefully controlled doses and continues to attract the interest of pharmaceutical researchers. The plants themselves are instantly recognizable by their flowers, mostly in shades of deep blue or purple or less commonly white, pink or yellow, with 5 petals of which the upper one bulges up into a prominent helmet-like shape. In growth habit and leaves the monkshoods show a strong resemblance to their relatives the delphiniums.

CULTIVATION: Monkshoods make attractive additions to herbaceous borders and woodland gardens. They prefer deep, moist soil and a sheltered position, partly shaded if summers are hot and dry. Propagate by division after the leaves die back in fall (autumn), or from seed.

Aconitum carmichaelii

Aconitum 'Bressingham Spire'

This cultivar, presumed to be of hybrid origin, bears erect spikes of purplish blue flowers in summer. Leaves are a glossy dark green and deeply divided. A compact plant with an upright habit, it reaches a height of 3 ft (1 m) with a spread of 18 in (45 cm). **ZONES 6–9.**

Aconitum × cammarum

This group of hybrid cultivars produces hooded white, violet or bicolored flowers in summer on upright branching stems. The deeply divided leaves are a glossy dark green. They have a compact habit and grow to a height of 4 ft (1.2 m) with a spread of 18 in (45 cm). **'Bicolor'** has flowers that are off-white with deep blue edges. **ZONES 3–9.**

Aconitum carmichaelii 'Arendsii'

Aconitum napellus

Aconitum 'Ivorine'

Acorus gramineus 'Variegatus'

Aconitum carmichaelii

syn. *Aconitum fischeri*

A native of northern and western China, this has become one of the most popular monkshoods by virtue of the rich violet-blue flowers, which are densely packed on the spikes in late summer. The leaves, thick, glossy and deeply veined, grow on rather woody stems. Several races and selections are cultivated, varying in stature from 3–6 ft (1–1.8 m). These include the **Wilsonii Group**, which contains, among others, the award-winning **'Kelmscott'**; **'Arendsii'** (syn. 'Arends') is another striking blue-flowered cultivar. **ZONES 4–9.**

Aconitum 'Ivorine'

This hybrid cultivar grows to about 3 ft (1 m) tall with dense foliage. The many spikes of pale ivory-yellow flowers rise a short distance above the foliage. **ZONES 4–9.**

Aconitum napellus

ACONITE, MONKSHOOD

Of wide distribution in Europe and temperate Asia, this is also the monkshood species most widely grown in gardens and is as handsome as any when well grown. The stems are erect, to 4 ft (1.2 m) or so high, with large leaves divided into very narrow segments and a tall, open spike of deep blue to purplish flowers. A vigorous grower, it likes damp woodland or stream bank conditions. **ZONES 5–9.**

Aconitum 'Spark's Variety'

A cultivar of garden origin, commonly regarded as a form of the Chinese *Aconitum henryi*, this monkshood makes a rather lanky plant with slender flowering stems up to 5 ft (1.5 m) tall, often scrambling and supported by other plants. In summer they terminate in widely branched panicles of deep purplish blue flowers, grouped in short clusters at the branch ends. **ZONES 6–9.**

Aconitum vulparia

syn. *Aconitum lycoctonum* subsp. *vulparia*

WOLFSBANE

Growing to over 3 ft (1 m) in height, this species has tall, erect stems and rounded, hairy leaves that are 6–8 in (15–20 cm) wide. Rather open spikes of pale yellow flowers, longer and narrower than those of most other species, are borne in summer. It is native to central and southern Europe. **ZONES 4–9.**

Acorus gramineus 'Ogon'

ACORUS

SWEET FLAG

This unusual genus consists of only 2 species of grass-like evergreen perennials from stream banks and marshes in the northern hemisphere. They are in fact highly atypical members of the arum family, lacking the large bract (spathe) that characteristically encloses the fleshy spike (spadix) of minute flowers. The flower spikes are inconspicuous and the plants are grown mainly for their foliage. The leaves are in flattened fans like those of irises, crowded along short rhizomes. Both leaves and rhizomes are sweet-scented, most noticeably as they dry, and have been used in folk medicine, perfumery and food flavorings.

CULTIVATION: Sweet flags are easily grown in any boggy spot or in shallow water at pond edges, needing no maintenance except cutting back to limit their spread. They are fully frost hardy. Propagate by division.

Acorus calamus

The most widespread of the genus, this species occurs through much of Europe, Asia and North America. The tough green leaves are up to 4 ft (1.2 m) long and 1 in (25 mm) wide with an off-centre midrib. From below the tops of apparent 'leaves' (actually flower stalks) emerge 3 in (8 cm) long pale green spikes in spring and summer. At one time the dried and candied rhizomes were a popular sweet. **'Variegatus'** has cream-striped leaves, the cream taking on a pinkish tint in spring. **ZONES 3–10.**

Acorus gramineus

Native to Japan, this is a miniature version of *Acorus calamus* with soft, curved leaves under 12 in (30 cm) long and about $^{1}/_{4}$ in (6 mm) wide; flower spikes are about 1 in (25 mm) long. **'Pusillus'**, popular in aquariums, is only about 4 in (10 cm) high; **'Variegatus'** has cream-striped leaves; **'Ogon'**, more recently introduced from Japan, has chartreuse and cream variegated leaves. **ZONES 3–11.**

ACRADENIA

This genus, related to *Boronia* and *Zieria*, consists of only 2 species of small to medium-sized evergreen trees: one from Tasmania, the other from mainland Australia on the subtropical east coast. The mainland species was until recently classified under the genus *Bosistoa*. The

leaves of both species are arranged in opposite pairs on the branches, and are divided into 3 leaflets which are pungent smelling when crushed. The small panicles of starry white flowers may be quite showy.
CULTIVATION: The Tasmanian species was introduced to the British Isles over 100 years ago and has proved to be an attractive garden subject in milder, moister regions there, though appreciating a sheltered position against a wall in areas where heavier frosts occur. Propagate from cuttings.

Acradenia frankliniae
WHITEY-WOOD

This small Tasmanian tree was named in honor of Lady Franklin, wife of an early British Governor. In gardens it seldom makes more than a shrub of 6–10 ft (1.8–3 m) in height, of dense growth and neat conical habit. The white flowers, few to a cluster in early summer, are only about $^{1}/_{4}$ in (6 mm) across but are quite pretty in mass. **ZONES 8–9.**

ACROCARPUS

This genus consists of only 2 species of large leguminous deciduous trees from tropical Asia, one of which is sometimes cultivated in warmer countries. Both have very large bipinnate leaves and massed spikes of densely packed scarlet flowers all along the branches and twigs. Seeds are borne in flattened pods.
CULTIVATION: Successful cultivation depends on an appropriate climate: although tropical, they do not like lowland areas with a very hot dry season, but prefer cooler hill country and deep moist soils. They also do well in warm-temperate coastal areas. Propagation is from seed, which may need soaking for good germination.

Acrocarpus fraxinifolius
PINK CEDAR

A rapid grower, this species can reach 12–15 ft (3.5–5 m) in two years or less; at this stage it is normally single stemmed with a palm-like appearance due to its huge bipinnate or tripinnate leaves. New leaves are attractively tinted bronze. In its native Southeast Asia it is said to reach 200 ft (60 m) in the wild with a massive trunk, but its size in cultivation is uncertain, although growth rates of 10 ft (3 m) per year have been recorded in the highlands of East Africa, where it has been planted for timber. It is deciduous in the dry or cold season, and towards the end of it produces a display of scarlet blossom (but may not bloom until a good size). **ZONES 10–11.**

Actaea rubra

ACTAEA
BANEBERRY

Only 8 species of frost-hardy perennials belong to this genus, which occurs in Europe, temperate Asia and North America, mostly in damp woodlands and on limestone outcrops. They are attractive plants with large compound leaves springing from a root-crown, the leaflets thin and broad with strong veining and sharp teeth. Flowers are in short, feathery spikes or heads, the individual flowers smallish with many white stamens among which the narrow petals are hardly detectable. The fruits are white, red or black berries, often on a stalk of contrasting color. All parts of the plants are very poisonous but particularly the berries, which may be attractive to small children.
CULTIVATION: Requiring a cool, moist climate, these plants grow best in sheltered woodland conditions or in a damp, cool spot in a rock garden. Propagate from seed or by division.

Actaea alba
WHITE BANEBERRY

From eastern USA, this summer-flowering perennial is most notable for its handsome berries, though its flowers and foliage are attractive too. It forms a clump of fresh green, divided leaves with a spread of 18 in (45 cm), from which rise the fluffy white flowers on stems up to 3 ft (1 m) high. By late summer they have developed into spires of small, gleaming white berries on red stalks. **ZONES 3–9.**

Actaea rubra
RED BANEBERRY, SNAKEBERRY

This North American species grows to 24–30 in (60–75 cm) tall and wide and has 6–18 in (15–45 cm) wide leaves. The mauve-tinted white flowers are about $^{1}/_{4}$ in (6 mm) in diameter and clustered in round heads on wiry stems. The berries are bright red. ***Actaea rubra* f. *neglecta*** is a taller growing form with white berries. **ZONES 3–9.**

ACTINIDIA

In recent years this east Asian genus of woody climbers has become familiar in the guise of the fruit of one species,

Actaea alba

Actinidia deliciosa

Acradenia frankliniae

Actinidia arguta 'Ananasnaya'

successfully promoted as 'kiwi fruit' by New Zealand orchardists who export them to many countries. An older generation first came across them as 'Chinese gooseberries', though the genus is quite unrelated to the gooseberry genus *Ribes* (or, for that matter, to kiwis). But *Actinidia* also contains a few fine ornamentals, treasured by discerning gardeners in regions of cool, moist climate. Mostly deciduous, they have tangled twining branches with widely spaced simple leaves; both branches and leaves often have bristly hairs. Male and female flowers usually occur on separate plants, with white, green or reddish petals, quite showy in some species. Fruit is a fleshy oval berry containing numerous tiny seeds.
CULTIVATION: If fruit is desired it will usually be necessary to plant at least one male vine close to one or more females. The vines need a strong trellis, a strong support or even a dead tree on which to climb. They grow best in moist, fertile soil in a sheltered but sunny position. Propagation is normally from cuttings.

Actinidia arguta

This deciduous species from China, Japan and southern Siberia is not only one of the largest and most vigorous actinidias but also the most cold hardy. It can grow to 50 ft (15 m) or more high over treetops and has very broad glossy leaves 3–5 in (8–12 cm) long, with fine bristle-tipped teeth. Flowers are greenish white, fragrant, borne in clusters of 3 in leaf axils in late spring or early summer and are followed on female plants by 1 in (25 mm) long yellow-green edible fruit. **'Ananasnaya'** is more cold hardy and has smaller fruit in larger clusters. **ZONES 4–9.**

Actinidia deliciosa
syn. ***Actinidia chinensis***
CHINESE GOOSEBERRY, KIWI FRUIT

Until recently this well-known fruiting vine, introduced in 1900 from China's Yangtze valley, was known as *Actinidia chinensis*. Recently a New Zealand researcher has drawn attention to significant differences between the cultivated plants and wild *A. chinensis*. In conditions that suit them the plants can astonish by their vigor and speed of growth, the long writhing canes reaching the thickness of a thumb in one season and forming a dense tangle that can break a trellis not built strongly enough. Leaves are oval, up to 8 in (20 cm) long, clothed in red bristles like the stems. Flowers, borne in late spring–early summer, are conspicuous with broad white petals, the males more showy with a boss of gold stamens as well. The fruits which follow in summer and fall (autumn) vary in shape and size and a number of selected clones have been named as cultivars. Chinese gooseberries tolerate only moderate frosts and require abundant water and nitrogenous fertilizer in summer. In winter the bare vines should be pruned back to a single branch along each trellis wire. **ZONES 8–10.**

Adansonia gregorii

Actinidia eriantha

Actinidia kolomikta

Actinidia eriantha

A recent introduction from China, this species is similar in habit and foliage to *Actinidia deliciosa* but grows only to about half the size. Its stems and leaves are clothed in furry whitish hairs and the summer flowers are an attractive reddish pink. The fruit has not yet been seen in cultivation. **ZONES 8–9.**

Actinidia kolomikta

KOLOMIKTA

Grown mainly for its spectacular foliage, this slender deciduous twiner forms a large mound-like mass but can be very successfully trained in elegant espalier fashion against a wall. The young leaves are reddish green, changing to bright green splotched with white or deep pink. The faintly fragrant small white flowers with pale yellow stamens are borne in late spring and summer, followed by small fruits. The plants color best in a cool temperate climate. **ZONES 5–9.**

ACTINOTUS

There are 11 species in the Australian genus *Actinotus*, of which the best known is *Actinotus helianthi*—a favorite wild-flower native to the open woodlands of the sandstone country around Sydney where it makes a great display in late spring and summer. In the structure of their flowerheads, members of this genus mimic those of the daisy (composite) family, but in fact they belong to the carrot (umbellifer) family. The leaves and flowerheads are both felted with dense hairs which help *Actinotus* species reduce moisture loss in a dry climate and grow in poor, scarcely water-retentive soils.

CULTIVATION: They demand light shade, a mild climate and very good drainage. Plants are is usually treated as a biennial. Propagate from seed or stem cuttings in spring or summer.

Actinotus helianthi

Adansonia digitata

Actinotus helianthi

FLANNEL FLOWER

This biennial or short-lived, evergreen shrub grows from 12 in–3 ft (30–90 cm) high with a spread of 24 in (60 cm). It has deeply divided gray-green foliage. Furry erect stems appear in spring and summer, topped by star-like flowerheads which consist of a cluster of pink-stamened, greenish florets surrounded by flannel-textured dull white bracts with grayish green tips. It prefers a well-drained soil in full sun and grows well in arid situations. **ZONES 9–10.**

ADA

The name of this South American orchid genus is among the shortest botanical names; like many others it was taken from classical mythology. Ada was the sister of the goddess Artemis of Caria (not the better known Artemis goddess of chastity)—what her relevance is to this genus is quite unclear, though the botanist Lindley who named it doubtless had his reasons. About 16 species make up the genus, most of them recently transferred from *Brassia*. All are epiphytes from tropical mist forests with fleshy pseudobulbs and leathery leaves. The arching flower spikes arise from pseudobulb bases and bear several to many flowers with narrow, pointed petals and sepals and broader, recurving labellums.

CULTIVATION: These are orchids for the cooler greenhouse, with the night temperature allowed to drop fairly low. Requiring similar treatment to miltonias and odontoglossum, they have no real rest period and should never be allowed to dry out.

Ada aurantiaca

This Colombian species is notable both for its lovely clear orange color and its habit of flowering in late winter and early spring. It is a compact plant with sprays of smallish flowers, and grows and looks best when allowed to make sizeable clumps. **ZONES 10–12.**

ADANSONIA

BAOBAB

These large trees, with trunks that become hugely swollen with age into a bottle or flask shape, amazed European explorers in Africa, Madagascar and northwestern Australia, the only regions where the 9 species are found growing wild (7 are endemic to Madagascar). They are usually deciduous in the tropical dry season. Leaves are divided into a number of leaflets radiating from the end of a common stalk. The cream flowers, which open only at night, are large and attractive and hang singly on pendulous stalks; they are adapted to pollination by nectar-feeding bats. The large oval fruits contain seeds embedded in a sour, edible pulp.

CULTIVATION: Propagate from seed or cuttings. Growth is slow until a good root system is established, but vigorous young trees with trunks beginning to swell make fine subjects for parks and streets. They are not too difficult to cultivate in the tropics or warmer subtropics and despite being from monsoonal climates with a long dry season, they adapt well to wetter regions.

Adansonia digitata

BAOBAB

The common name is thought to come from central Africa but this, the original baobab, ranges over most of Africa, from dry sub-Saharan scrubland to the veld of northern Transvaal. Old trees can reach monstrous proportions, often branching near the ground into several hugely swollen trunks each of which may be 80 ft (24 m) or more high. **ZONES 11–12.**

Adansonia gregorii

AUSTRALIAN BAOBAB, BOTTLE TREE, DEAD RAT TREE, BOAB

Confined in the wild to a small area of far northwestern Australia, this species is very closely related to the African baobab and young trees are hardly distinguishable. It does not generally grow quite as tall, but old trees reach an enormous girth. The unflattering name dead rat tree comes from the appearance of the gray seed pods. **ZONES 11–12.**

ADENANDRA

This genus of 18 species of small-leaved evergreen shrubs from the Cape region of South Africa is related to *Coleonema* and *Agathosma*. Like the latter, the aromatic leaves of some of its species have sometimes been used there as a herbal tea in rural areas. Two species are grown as ornamentals, seemingly better known to gardeners in some other countries than to South African gardeners. They are low, spreading shrubs producing very pretty 5-petalled white or pink flowers whose size seems out of proportion to that of the small, narrow leaves.

CULTIVATION: They are best suited to rock gardens, where they should have a

A

sunny position and gritty, well-drained soil, or they can be grown in pots or tubs. Water well in winter and spring but keep drier in summer. Propagate from seed or cuttings.

Adenandra uniflora
CHINA FLOWER

This twiggy shrub grows to 24 in (60 cm) high and 3 ft (1 m) wide, with small, aromatic, deep green leaves on fine reddish stems. Although not fragrant, the flowers are of great beauty—5-petalled, white and 1 in (25 mm) across, they have a porcelain-like appearance that gives the shrub its common name. **ZONES 8–10.**

ADENIUM

The name of this small genus of succulent shrubs is taken from their Arabic name *aden*, and these plants may also have given their name to the port city of Aden on the Arabian Peninsula, from where they first became known to the West. Shrubs and occasionally small trees, they are deciduous in dry seasons, and some develop very fleshy, swollen trunks. Vivid, funnel-shaped flowers are borne from mid-winter through to spring (or in the tropical dry season). Up to a dozen species of *Adenium* have been recognized in the past, but now they are regarded as constituting a single variable species which includes 6 subspecies, ranging widely through tropical and subtropical Africa, from South Africa's Cape Province to the Red Sea, as well as southern Arabia.

CULTIVATION: Popular in tropical gardens, they prefer a position in full sun or part-shade and thrive best in climates with a well-marked dry season. Kept dwarfed and rootbound in a pot, they will often flower more profusely. As they are very prone to rotting, they require a gritty, well-drained soil. Propagate from seed or cuttings.

Adenandra uniflora

Adenocarpus decorticans

Adenophora uehatae

Adenium obesum
syns *Adenium multiflorum, A. coetanum*

IMPALA LILY, DESERT ROSE

In the wild this species can make a small tree of 12 ft (3.5 m) or more with swollen trunk and thick, crooked limbs, but in cultivation it seldom exceeds about 5 ft (1.5 m), with a sparse branching habit. Whorls of lance-shaped to oval, glossy leaves are grouped at the branch tips, but when in flower in winter it is usually leafless. The very decorative, trumpet-shaped blooms are $1\frac{1}{2}$–2 in (38–50 mm) long and vary considerably in coloring; most popular is a very pale pink or white with deep pinkish red margins. Cultivar names have been given to a number of the color forms, most of which appear to be derived from ***Adenium obesum* subsp. *obesum***, which extends over the species' whole geographical range—some of the other subspecies are more succulent, and are sometimes grown by succulent collectors. **ZONES 11–12.**

ADENOCARPUS

Belonging to the Mediterranean-centered broom group of legumes, this genus consists of 20 or so species of deciduous and evergreen shrubs, some of which could pass for species of *Cytisus*, though the small leaves with 3 leaflets generally persist on adult shoots in contrast to the leafless twigs of many brooms. Flowers are yellow and fairly small, in narrow spikes terminating the branches. The genus ranges from the Canary Islands through north Africa and southern Europe as far as Turkey.

CULTIVATION: Some species are quite ornamental and can be grown in the shrub border; the more compact ones make interesting rock garden plants. They require a dry sunny position and soil needs to be very open and very well drained. Propagate from seed or cuttings.

Adenostoma sparsifolium

Adenium obesum

Adenocarpus decorticans

From Spain, this is one of the taller species, making an upright, open shrub to about 10 ft (3 m). It is deciduous, with very hairy young stems which develop a whitish bark as they thicken and age; the very narrow, crowded leaflets are $\frac{1}{2}$–$\frac{3}{4}$ in (12–18 mm) long and the golden yellow flowers are densely crowded on profuse short spikes in late spring and early summer. **ZONES 8–10.**

ADENOPHORA

A genus of around 40 species of herbaceous perennials closely related to *Campanula*, in fact distinguished from it only by an internal feature of flower structure. Most are native to eastern Asia but 2 species occur wild in Europe. One species is grown in Japan for its edible roots.

CULTIVATION: Cultivation requirements and mode of propagation are the same as for *Campanula*.

Adenophora bulleyana

Native to western China, this species has an erect growth habit with clustered stems bearing rather narrow, toothed leaves. The stems terminate in loose spikes of nodding small violet-blue bellflowers with reflexed petals, opening in late summer. The plant is usually 3–4 ft (1–1.2 m) tall. **ZONES 5–9.**

Adenophora liliifolia

Ranging in the wild from Europe to eastern Siberia and northern China, this species has only narrow stem leaves at the time of flowering. Stems are about 18 in (45 cm) tall and branched at the top, carrying pendulous, wide, pale blue bells about $\frac{3}{4}$ in (18 mm) long in summer. **ZONES 4–9.**

Adenophora uehatae

Native to eastern Asia, this is a charming dwarf species with large, pendulous pale mauve-blue bells borne on short leafy stems. It makes a fine rock garden subject. **ZONES 5–9.**

ADENOSTOMA

Only 2 species of evergreen shrubs belong to this genus of the rose family,

Adenium obesum

both occurring on dry hills of California and adjacent Baja California (northwestern Mexico). They have attractive peeling bark and tiny crowded leaves that are encrusted with sticky aromatic resin. Large foamy sprays of tiny white flowers project beyond the foliage.

CULTIVATION: These long-lived shrubs make unusual and attractive subjects for gardens in climates that experience only light frost but have hot dry summers. They do best in a sunny but sheltered position in light, well-drained soil. Propagate from seed or tip cuttings.

Adenostoma fasciculatum
GREASEWOOD, CHAMISE

Native to coastal hills of California and Baja California, this species makes a spreading shrub of up to 10 ft (3 m) high, though often much lower, its twisted branches clothed in reddish bark which shreds into narrow strips on the lower trunk. The resinous leaves are very small and crowded and the short but profuse sprays of white flowers appear in spring and summer. **ZONES 8–10.**

Adenostoma sparsifolium
RIBBONWOOD, REDSHANKS

From southern California and Baja California, this species is a shrub or sometimes a small tree of up to 20 ft (6 m) with thick, crooked, woody branches, the bark red and peeling in a very attractive manner. The resinous leaves are small and almost needle-like and the profuse sprays of white or slightly pinkish blossom are borne in late summer. **ZONES 9–10.**

A

ADIANTUM

MAIDENHAIR FERN

Among the best known ferns, even to many people who have never grown a fern, maidenhairs in their typical guise are recognizable by their billowy fronds of many delicate, membranous, almost circular fresh green leaflets, each connected by a very fine blackish stalk to a repeatedly branched main stalk which is also smooth and black. Spore-cases appear as tiny indentations with curled-over 'lips' around the edges of leaflets. The genus, consisting of over 200 species in all but the coldest parts of the world (the majority in the American tropics), is very varied and not all species conform to this frond pattern: some have larger, thicker, oblong or triangular leaflets without individual stalks. New growths may be pinkish or tinted bronze, though usually just a paler green. Maidenhairs include some of the most popular indoor ferns, and some of the more vigorous and decorative species have many named cultivars.

Adiantum peruvianum

CULTIVATION: The hardier species will thrive outdoors in shady areas, spreading by deep or shallow rhizomes to form a dainty ground cover, but they resent root disturbance so transplanting may be difficult. Tropical species, most with fronds in dense tufts, are usually grown indoors in pots or hanging baskets, appreciating strong light but not direct sun, and high humidity—the bathroom is a popular site; they don't like the dry atmosphere of heated rooms. Plant in a humus-rich indoor mix in a container that is not too large for the roots, which do not like too much wetness. Remove old fronds. Propagate from spores; division of rhizomes is possible but failures are common.

Adiantum aethiopicum

COMMON MAIDENHAIR

Occurring through much of Asia, Africa and Australasia, common maidenhair has some of the most delicate fronds of the genus with very rounded, pale green leaflets $^1/_4$ in (8 mm) or less in diameter. Its wiry rhizomes are deeply buried, and a plant can spread extensively. It often appears spontaneously in moist, shady spots in the garden, from wind-carried spores. It also flourishes in containers and hanging baskets, with frequent repotting. **ZONES 9–11.**

Adiantum capillus-veneris

VENUS-HAIR FERN, EUROPEAN MAIDENHAIR

Ranging through most warmer parts of the world and the only species native to Europe, this fern is similar to *Adiantum aethiopicum* but has shallowly lobed leaflets and a more clumping habit. *Capillus-veneris* literally means 'Venus' hair', referring to the fine, shiny frond stalks. Growing 12–24 in (30–60 cm) in height, it often occurs on limestone in the wild, and some growers recommend adding lime to the potting mix. **ZONES 8–11.**

Adiantum raddianum 'Tinctum'

Adiantum pedatum var. *aleuticum*

Adiantum raddianum 'Triumph'

Adiantum formosum

BLACK-STEM MAIDENHAIR, GIANT MAIDENHAIR

From New Zealand and Australia, this beautiful fern forms widespread colonies with long-reaching underground rhizomes. A tall species, reaching 2–4 ft (0.6–1.2 m) in height, it has verdant green fronds borne at widely spaced intervals. The fronds are 24–30 in (60–75 cm) long, paler green when immature, and are deeply and irregularly cut. It prefers a shady situation. **ZONES 9–11.**

Adiantum jordanii

CALIFORNIA MAIDENHAIR

A native of Oregon and the moist regions of California, this is one of the more cold-hardy maidenhairs. Its large fronds, up to 24 in (60 cm) arise from a shortly creeping rhizome and are divided into many semicircular leaflets. **ZONES 7–10.**

Adiantum pedatum

AMERICAN MAIDENHAIR

The most frost hardy species, this ranges in the wild across cooler parts of North America, also temperate East Asia and the Himalayas. The fronds, up to 2 ft (60 cm) high, are distinctive, with wedge-shaped leaflets arranged in neat rows along radiating 'spokes' from the main stalk. Its rhizomes can spread to form a large, dense patch in a shady spot. From cool mountain forests, it adapts poorly to cultivation in warmer areas. ***Adiantum pedatum* var. *aleuticum*,** now often treated as a distinct species, *A. aleuticum* from Alaska and western Canada has more erect fronds with fewer leaflets; it is even more cold hardy. ***A. p.* f. *billingsiae*,** a cultivated form, has broader, slightly ruffled segments of a bluish green hue. **ZONES 4–9.**

Adiantum raddianum

Adiantum pedatum forma *billingsiae*

Adiantum peruvianum

SILVER DOLLAR FERN

Valued for its silvery pink, slightly metallic looking new fronds, this fern comes from Ecuador, Peru and Bolivia. It has a stout rootstock and the fronds may ultimately reach up to 3 ft (1 m) in length. The diamond-shaped segments are fewer and larger than in most maidenhairs, up to 2 in (5 cm) long. Dormant during winter, it must only be watered sparingly during this time. It likes humidity and prefers a brightly lit situation with good air movement and neutral to alkaline soils. **ZONES 11–12.**

Adiantum raddianum

DELTA MAIDENHAIR

Larger and coarser than *Adiantium aethiopicum*, this tropical American species has vigorous, arching fronds making a dense, cascading tuft, the pale green, fan-shaped segments borne on fine, dark purple stems. Frost tender, it reaches a height and spread of 12–18 in (30–45 cm). Cut old fronds away in fall (autumn) to encourage new growth. The most popular species for indoor use, it has given rise to numerous cultivars such as **'Triumph'** and **'Tinctum'**. **ZONES 10–12.**

Adiantum venustum

EVERGREEN MAIDENHAIR

From the Himalayas and parts of China, where it grows among rocks at high altitudes, this species reaches a height of 1–3 ft (30 cm–90 cm). It is very decorative, with large coarsely divided fronds, the segments with bluish undersides. New growths are an attractive pink color. Very cold hardy, it makes an excellent ground cover in sheltered situations. **ZONES 8–10.**

ADLUMIA

CLIMBING FUMITORY, ALLEGHANY VINE, MOUNTAIN FRINGE

A single species from eastern USA and Canada belongs to this genus, which is related to *Fumaria.* A biennial, it is a weak, scrambling climber of unusual appearance, with very finely divided leaves of delicate, foamy texture. It climbs by using the leaf stalks as tendrils. Flowers are borne in weak drooping sprays: they are white to pale purple, narrowly heart-shaped, like a small bleeding-heart (*Dicentra*) flower.
CULTIVATION: It likes a sheltered, humid position in the shade of taller shrubs, and may be allowed to climb into their lower branches, otherwise it should be supported on thin stakes or wires, or on a fence. Soil should be moist but well drained. Propagate from seed in spring.

Adlumia fungosa

This slender climber normally grows to about the same height as a sweet-pea, around 6–10 ft (1.8–3 m), though it is capable of reaching greater heights. The flowers appear in summer and fall (autumn). **ZONES 3–9.**

ADONIS

This genus consists of 20 species of annuals and perennials from Europe and cooler parts of Asia, with brightly colored flowers similar to *Anemone*, to which it is closely related. The Greek god Adonis, beloved of Aphrodite, gave his name to the original annual species, whose red flowers were said to have sprung from drops of his blood when he was killed by a boar. The leaves are mostly finely divided, the uppermost ones on each stem forming a sort of 'nest' on which the single bowl-shaped flower rests. It is only the perennial species that are much cultivated, used in herbaceous borders and rock gardens.
CULTIVATION: *Adonis* require a cool climate with warm dry summers. They are best grown in a sheltered spot in full sun, and in moist, fertile soil with a high humus content. Propagate from fresh seed or by division of clumps.

Adonis aestivalis

PHEASANT'S EYE

An annual species from central Europe, this grows to about 18 in (45 cm) high; it has finely divided leaves and in summer bears smallish flowers with deep red petals blackish at the base (giving the flower a black 'eye'). Though seldom grown outside of wild gardens, it can make an effective border plant if sown densely. **ZONES 5–9.**

Adonis amurensis

A native of Manchuria, Japan and Korea, this very early blooming perennial has 20- to 30-petalled, bright yellow flowers. *Adonis amurensis* is particularly popular in Japan, where several cultivars have been raised. **'Benten'** has pale cream flowers with frilled edges; **'Fukujukai'** flowers extremely early; **'Pleniflora'** (syn. 'Plena') is a double-flowered cultivar;

Adromischus umbraticola

and the red-brown flowers of **'Ramosa'** are also double. **ZONES 3–9.**

Adonis annua

PHEASANT'S EYE

Quite different from most species, this is a summer-flowering annual with finely divided foliage and branching stems 12–15 in (30–38 cm) tall. The bright red, 5 to 8-petalled flowers are about 1 in (25 mm) wide with black centers. It occurs naturally in southern Europe and southwest Asia. **ZONES 6–9.**

Adonis vernalis

This European perennial species is rather like *Adonis amurensis* but has very narrow, almost needle-like, finely divided leaflets. Its 12- to 20-petalled, bright yellow flowers are large, up to 3 in (8 cm) across, and open in early spring. Both this species and *A. annua* have been used medicinally, but are now regarded as too toxic for general use. **ZONES 3–9.**

ADROMISCHUS

This genus comprises 30-odd species of dwarf succulents native to semi-desert areas in South Africa. They reach a height of about 4 in (10 cm) and a width of approximately 1–2 in (3–5 cm). The short-stemmed leaves are flat, oval to cylindrical and mottled in color. White-pink flowers are borne on long spikes, no more than $^1/_2$ in (12 mm), in summer.
CULTIVATION: They prefer well-drained soil in a partially shaded position and are frost tender. Propagate from stem or leaf cuttings, or from seed. All members of this genus are vulnerable to mealybug.

Adromischus cooperi

This succulent from southern Africa grows to a height of 4 in (10 cm) and has green spatulate leaves which reach 1–2 in (25 mm –50 mm) in length with purple markings on the upper part. In spring and fall (autumn) this plant produces purple and red trumpet-shaped flowers that grow to $^1/_2$ in (12 mm) long. Prune when required. **ZONES 10–11.**

Adromischus maculatus

During spring and fall (autumn) this small species, indigenous to Cape Province in South Africa, produces white trumpet-shaped flowers that grow up to 2 in (5 cm) long. The plant grows about 4 in (10 cm) high and has rounded or ovate green leaves which are mottled

Adonis vernalis

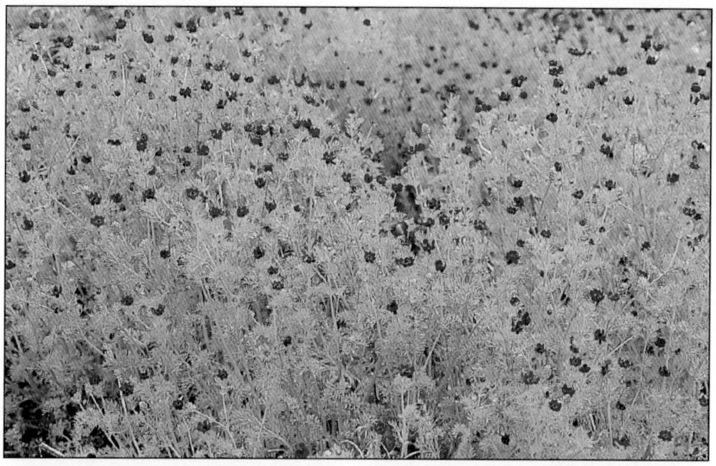

Adonis annua

Aechmea agavifolia

Aechmea 'Mary Brett'

dark red and grow up to 2 in (5 cm) in length. **ZONES 10–11.**

Adromischus umbraticola

syn. *Cotyledon trigyna*

Indigenous to the Transvaal area, *Andromischus umbraticola* has thick, oval-shaped green leaves with reddish orange margins. **ZONES 10–11.**

AECHMEA

Take your pick in pronouncing this name (of Greek origin)—regardless of whether you call it ike-maya, eek-mee-a, aitch-mee-a, ak-mee-a, or ek-mee-a, you will have company! One of the largest and most diverse bromeliad genera, as well as being one of the most popular among indoor plant growers, *Aechmea* consists of over 170 species from Central and South America. Most are epiphytes or rock-dwellers, conserving water in the vase-like structure formed by the rosette of stiff leaves, which may be barred, striped or otherwise patterned, and prickly margined in some such as ***Aechmea agavifolia.*** Flowers are small but often intensely colored, in dense spikes that vary greatly in size and structure but always with numerous overlapping bracts that usually contrast in color with the flowers— a typical example is ***Aechmea* 'Mary Brett'**. The berry-like fruits are often colorful as well.
CULTIVATION: How aechmeas are treated depends very much on the climate. In the humid tropics and subtropics they grow happily outdoors, most preferring filtered sun. Despite being epiphytes, they will grow on the ground as long as soil is open and high in humus, and the bed is raised slightly. Some tolerate surprisingly cool conditions and can be grown outdoors well into the temperate zones, so long as frost is absent. In more severe climates they are grown as indoor or conservatory plants, potted in a coarse medium just like many orchids. Propagate by division (separating 'pups' with a sharp knife), or from seed.

A

Aechmea fasciata

Aechmea chantinii 'Black'

Aechmea chantinii

Aechmea chantinii

Known as the Queen of the Aechmeas, this species from northwestern South America has vivid red and yellow flowers rising above long, drooping, salmon orange bracts. The rosettes consist of olive green leaves often with silvery gray dark green or almost black banding. The flowers appear in summer, followed by blue or white berries. It has an upright, urn-like habit and reaches a height and spread of 12–24 in (30–60 cm). **'Black'** is one of several cultivars of *Aechmea chantinii*. Ensure that growing conditions are not too moist in winter. This species is very cold sensitive. **ZONES 11–12.**

Aechmea fasciata
SILVER VASE

Reminiscent of a formal flower arrangement, this Brazilian species has a 'vase' of silvery gray leaves irregularly barred green, from which emerges in summer a short, broad cluster of mauve-blue flowers among crowded, spiky bracts of a most delicate clear pink. The rosettes, up to about 18 in (45 cm) high, do not clump up much. **ZONES 10–12.**

Aechmea 'Foster's Favorite'
LACQUERED WINE CUP

So named for its strap-like, arching, glossy wine red leaves, this bromeliad bears pendent spikes of dark blue, tubular flowers in winter, followed by chains of red pear-shaped berries. It has loosely formed rosettes and grows to a height and spread of 12–24 in (30–60 cm). This is a good plant for growing in pots on windowsills. **ZONES 11–12.**

Aechmea fulgens

From eastern Brazil, this popular species makes a rosette of rather thin leaves, bright green above but with a grayish waxy coating on the underside. The 18 in (45 cm) flowering stem terminates in a much-branched panicle without obvious bracts, the flowers with teardrop-shaped shiny red calyces and short violet petals. Most commonly grown is ***Aechmea fulgens* var. *discolor***, with leaves more purplish especially on the underside. **ZONES 11–12.**

Aechmea nidularioides

This species has strap-like leaves about 24 in (60 cm) long; the flowering stalk terminates in a rosette of red bracts at the center of which sit yellow flowers in an eye-catching display. **ZONES 10–12.**

Aechmea nudicaulis

One of the larger species, this attractive plant grows to a height and spread of 18–30 in (45–75 cm). The loose rosettes are made up of arching, yellow-green

Aechmea 'Shining Light'

leaves with spiny margins, often with gray scaly bands on the undersides. In spring and summer spikes of small yellow flowers are borne above large bright red bracts. Found growing on trees and rocks in its natural environments in central and northern South America, this species puts on the brightest display of all aechmeas but the floral spike is not as long lasting as the others. **ZONES 11–12.**

Aechmea pineliana

Attractive grown in bright light or full sun where the foliage takes on a deep rose color, this south Brazilian species grows to a height and spread of 12–15 in (30–38 cm). It has a dense upright habit with stiff, pointed gray-green leaves edged with red spines. The yellow flowers form a short, cylindrical head and are borne above the scarlet stems and bracts from winter through to spring. On maturity the flowers turn black. It is sun and cold tolerant and adapts well to outdoor conditions. **ZONES 10–12.**

Aechmea 'Royal Wine'

This is a popular hybrid cultivar which has adapted well to indoor culture. It has strap-like, bright green leaves with red bases and a slightly branched, pendent inflorescence with dark blue petals. The fruit is orange. **ZONES 11–12.**

Aechmea 'Shining Light'

This hybrid cultivar has a broad rosette of leaves that are glossy, pale green above and wine red on the undersides, It produces a large, about 24 in (60 cm) high, much-branched panicle, with bright red bracts and numerous small red flowers in summer. **ZONES 11–12.**

AEGOPODIUM

Consisting of 5 species of perennials in the carrot family, native to Europe and Asia, this genus is known in cool-temperate gardens only in the form of the common ground elder or goutweed—admittedly a moderately handsome plant, but detested by most for its rampant spread by underground rhizomes and the virtual impossibility of eradicating it. Resembling a lower-growing version of parsnip, it has compound leaves with large, toothed leaflets and rounded umbels of white flowers. Ground elder was for a long time used in herbal medicine, once thought effective against gout, and its young shoots can be used as a green vegetable.

CULTIVATION: Growing ground elder is far easier than stopping it, and it is difficult to see why anyone would wish to do so. However, it is undoubtedly an effective ground cover where space allows, smothering other weeds. It does best in moist soil and partial shade. Any piece of root will grow.

Aechmea pineliana

Aegopodium podagraria 'Variegata'

Aechmea nidularioides

Aechmea 'Royal Wine'

Aegopodium podagraria

GROUND ELDER, GOUTWEED

Spreading to an indefinite width, and up to 3 ft (1 m) high, ground elder sends up its pure white umbels of bloom in summer. **'Variegatum'** is sometimes grown as a ground cover: its leaflets are neatly edged white and it is slightly smaller and less aggressive than the normal green form. **ZONES 3–9.**

AEONIUM

Native to the Canary Islands, the Mediterranean and northern Africa, this genus contains 40 species of short-lived, perennial or shrubby evergreen succulents. The plants develop either as one large (or several smaller), compact, stemless rosette, or branch into several long, thick stems terminating in leaves; some are more closely branched, with many smaller rosettes. Attractive, star-shaped, pink, red, white or yellow flowers appear in dense pyramidal sprays, from small to very large, from the center of the leaf rosettes, usually in spring.

CULTIVATION: They prefer full sun or partial shade, light, well-drained soil and warmer temperatures. Some species tolerate light frosts. Prune off dead flower panicles after the blooms wither, although the flowering rosette will usually die and single-rosette species will die out completely. Propagate from seed or stem or leaf cuttings in spring and summer.

Aeonium arboreum

Native to the Atlantic coast of Morocco, this species grows to 24 in (60 cm) and develops a number of branches with rosettes of bright green leaves. In spring some branches produce dense conical clusters of golden yellow flowers, the whole branch dying back when they are spent. The cultivar **'Zwartkop'** has striking, reddish black leaves. **ZONES 9–11.**

Aeonium canariense

Notable for the large diameter of its rosettes, this low-growing, frost-tender perennial is native to the Canary Islands. The rosettes are only 6 in (15 cm) high but have a spread of up to 18 in (45 cm). The long, spoon-shaped leaves are plain green with red-tinted edges. After 2 or 3 years, the center extends to form a flower stem, terminating in a cluster of numerous yellow, starry flowers opening in spring; after blooming the whole plant expires. **ZONES 10–11.**

Aeonium haworthii

PINWHEEL

A native of the Canary Islands, this shrubby species has a dense, rounded, bushy habit and grows to a height of 24 in (60 cm). The short, erect, freely branching stems bear many rosettes of thick, spoon-shaped, bluish gray leaves with red margins, about 2 in (5 cm) long and almost as wide. Terminal clusters of pink-tinged, creamy yellow flowers are borne in spring and summer. This is a tough, long-lived species which is popular as a container plant for porches and patios. **ZONES 9–11.**

Aeonium tabuliforme

Endemic to Tenerife in the Canary Islands, this is one of the more striking species with a single leaf rosette up to 18 in (45 cm) in diameter, and as flat as a dinner plate. Sitting on a stalk no more than 8 in (20 cm) high, it consists of numerous, closely overlapping leaves. Growth is terminated by the inflorescence, about 18 in (45 cm) high, branching into sprays of yellow flowers in spring and summer, after which the plant dies. This remarkable species needs a semi-shaded position and perfect drainage. **ZONES 10–11.**

AERANGIS

A genus of about 50 species of epiphytic orchids, most of which are native to tropical Africa and Madagascar, but with a few found on other Indian Ocean islands as far east as Sri Lanka. The genus is closely related to *Angraecum* and features similar white or greenish white flowers with the rear of the labellum extended into a tubular nectar spur, very long in some species. They are sweetly scented in the evening and like angraecums are pollinated by long-tongued moths. In growth habit most are rather like a *Phalaenopsis*, with two to several broad, leathery leaves arising from a very short stem.

CULTIVATION: They prefer lower light levels than most other orchids, together with constant high humidity and warmth. They are best grown on bark or cork slabs or wooden rafts. They should be sprayed frequently with water while in active growth. Propagate by detaching offsets.

Aerangis ellisii

This is the largest-growing *Aerangis* species, with a stem of up to 24 in (60 cm) bearing leaves in two rows. The flowers, borne from summer to fall (autumn) on semi-pendulous racemes are pure white, about $1^1/_2$ in (35 mm) wide, with backward pointing petals and sepals and a slender spur about 6 in (15 cm) long, pointing downward. ***Aerangis ellisii* var. *grandiflora*** has larger flowers, with spurs up to 10 in (25 cm) long. **ZONES 11–12.**

Aeschynanthus javanicus

AERIDES

FOXTAIL ORCHID

There are about 50 species in this genus from tropical Asia. They are called foxtail orchids because of the way the sprays of flowers hang down from a rather upright plant which resembles a vanda in growth. The flowers mostly have a labellum with a large forward-pointing spur; they come in several colors, mostly in the delicate white to pink range, and usually have a pleasant, spicy odor. They can appear at any time from spring to fall (autumn).

CULTIVATION: They need intermediate to warm conditions and a coarse open compost. A hanging basket shows the pendent flowers to best advantage. They should be allowed to dry out a little in winter.

Aerides quinquevulnera

From the Philippines, this epiphytic orchid is intolerant of cold. Its short, erect stems bear 2 rows of strap-like leaves about 12 in (30 cm) long. The slender, erect flowering stem bears pendulous racemes of white flowers with red spots (though color can vary from white to pure purple), more or less continuously from spring to fall (autumn). They smell strongly of cinnamon. It reaches a height and spread of 18 in (45 cm).*Quinquevulnera* means 'with 5 wounds' (or marks, referring to the flower markings). **ZONES 11–12.**

AESCHYNANTHUS

Over 100 species of mostly epiphytic creepers and subshrubs in the African violet family make up this genus, ranging through rainforests of Southeast Asia and the Malay Archipelago. Some have become popular as indoor plants, suited to hanging baskets and flowering freely for months on end. The stems are tough and wiry, sometimes clinging by roots. Leaves are fleshy and pointed, arranged in opposite pairs, and the flowers, clustered at the ends of branches are trumpet-shaped but curved, often with the base enclosed in a conspicuous calyx.

CULTIVATION: Aeschynanthus grow happily outside in humid tropical and subtropical climates, preferring a position in part-shade and most at home in a hanging basket or established in the crotch of a large tree. In cooler regions they adapt well to indoor use, though requiring strong light. Pot in a coarse indoor plant mix and water freely in the growing period. Propagate from cuttings.

Aeschynanthus javanicus

LIPSTICK VINE

Native to Java and other islands of the Malay Archipelago, this species bears flowers shorter than in most others but of the most brilliant red or orange color, the cup-like calyx usually darker than the broadly lobed corolla and both covered in bristly hairs. Stems and flowers are both pendent, and a well-grown specimen in a basket can make a cascade of red and green. **ZONES 11–12.**

Aeschynanthus lobbianus

syn. ***Aeschynanthus radicans* var. *lobbianus***

LIPSTICK PLANT

An epiphyte native to Indonesian rainforests, this trailing species has rather broad leaves and pairs of bright red flowers about 3 in (8 cm) long, springing from the leaf-axils their bases enclosed by long, dull purple tubular calyces. **ZONES 11–12.**

Aeonium arboreum 'Zwartkop'

Aeonium tabuliforme

Aeonium arboreum

Aeschynanthus longicaulis

Native to Malaysia, this trailing species has clusters of short, orange-red flowers with green calyces appearing in summer and fall (autumn). The slender branching stems bear narrow waxy leaves mottled with light green. **ZONES 11–12.**

Aeschynanthus pulcher
LIPSTICK PLANT

A native of Java, this climbing or trailing species may reach a height of up to 10 ft (3 m) given a suitable support. The thick, oval leaves have purplish margins; terminal clusters of 2 in (5 cm) long bright red flowers with yellow throats are borne from summer to winter. **ZONES 11–12.**

Aeschynanthus speciosus

A summer-flowering plant, native to Borneo, this species bears large clusters of tubular, 4 in (10 cm) long orange flowers with yellow throats. With a somewhat trailing habit, it reaches a height and spread of 12–24 in (30–60 cm). Stems are slender and arching and the dark green, lance-shaped leaves are carried in pairs or whorls with a terminal rosette surrounding a cluster of flowers. **ZONES 11–12.**

AESCULUS
HORSE-CHESTNUT, BUCKEYE

These deciduous trees and shrubs have a finger-like arrangement in leaflets of their compound leaves, and eye-catching spikes of cream to reddish flowers at branch ends in spring or summer. The large, nut-like seeds, released from round capsules, resemble chestnuts but are bitter and inedible. At least half of the 20 or so species occur in North America, the remainder are scattered across temperate Asia and Europe. Renowned as majestic park and avenue trees in European cities, in the wild they are primarily trees of valley floors, where they grow in sheltered positions in deep soil with good moisture.
CULTIVATION: Although most are frost hardy, they perform best in those cool climates where seasons are sharply demarcated and summers are warm. They are propagated from seed or, in the case of selected clones and hybrids, by bud grafting.

Aesculus californica
CALIFORNIA BUCKEYE

Native to the hill slopes of California, where it can reach 40 ft (12 m), in gardens this is a large spreading shrub or small tree of 10–15 ft (3–5 m). Leaves are smaller than on most *Aesculus* species, the 5 to 7 narrow leaflets only 2–4 in (5–10 cm) long and grayish green. In summer it produces long, dense spikes of small, creamy white, often rose-flushed, fragrant flowers. More drought tolerant than other species, it is able to survive hot dry summers. **ZONES 8–10.**

Aesculus × *carnea*
RED HORSE-CHESTNUT

This hybrid tree, thought to have originated by chance in Germany in the early 1800s, grows to about 30 ft (9 m) and often comes true from seed. It gets the reddish pink of its flowers (produced in late spring) from one parent, *Aesculus pavia*; the other parent is *A. hippocastanum*. It adapts to warmer and drier climates than *A. hippocastanum*. The cultivar **'Briotii'** has larger spikes of brighter pink flowers. **ZONES 6–9.**

Aesculus flava
syn. *Aesculus octandra*
YELLOW BUCKEYE, SWEET BUCKEYE

This ornamental tree is native to fertile valleys in central-eastern USA, and grows to 90 ft (27 m) in the wild. Smallish creamy yellow or occasionally pinkish flowers appear in 6 in (15 cm) panicles from late spring to early summer, followed by fruits each with 2 to 4 seeds. The dark green leaves turn yellow before falling. The bark is dark brown, becoming furrowed with age. **ZONES 4–9.**

Aesculus glabra
OHIO BUCKEYE

This species is similar in range and appearance to *Aesculus flava*, though usually smaller and with rougher bark. In spring it produces greenish yellow flowers with protruding stamens, followed by prickly fruits. Its leaves have a disagreeable smell when crushed. Although a handsome tree with attractive foliage, the Ohio buckeye is found mainly in botanical gardens and other larger collections. **ZONES 4–9.**

Aesculus hippocastanum
HORSE CHESTNUT

This tree originated in the mountain valleys of the Greece–Albania border region and is now widely planted in parks, avenues and large gardens in Europe. It can reach 100 ft (30 m), though is usually half that and bears striking 'candles' of bloom in spring and early

Aeschynanthus speciosus

Aesculus flava

Aesculus californica

Aesculus californica

Aesculus glabra

Aesculus glabra

Aesculus × *carnea* 'Briotii'

Aesculus hippocastanum

Aesculus × *carnea*

Aesculus hippocastanum

summer; individual flowers have crumpled white petals with a yellow basal patch which ages to dull red. Fruit have a leathery case covered with short prickles and in fall (autumn) release large seeds, known as 'conkers' to British children. The dark green foliage turns yellow-brown in fall. **'Baumannii'** has longer-lasting double flowers. **ZONES 6–9.**

Aesculus indica
INDIAN HORSE CHESTNUT

From the northwest Himalayas, this tree tends to branch very low and produce a thick trunk and spreading crown when planted in the open. In early to mid-summer it produces 12–15 in (30–38 cm) spikes of white flowers with petals tinged yellow or red. The shiny leaves turn yellow in fall (autumn); the large fruit, brownish and slightly rough, lack prickles. It requires a sheltered but sunny position and reliable soil moisture. **ZONES 6–9.**

Aesculus × *neglecta*

Originating as a natural hybrid between the 2 American species *Aesculus flava* and *A. sylvatica*, this tree grows to 60 ft (18 m) or more and has pink new foliage and yellowish flowers. The cultivar **'Erythroblastos'** has carmine spring foliage and profuse peach to pink flowers borne in erect panicles during summer. **ZONES 5–9.**

Aesculus parviflora
BOTTLEBRUSH BUCKEYE

This many-stemmed shrub, native to the southeastern USA, grows 6–10 ft (1.8–3 m) tall, spreading into a broad clump by new growths from the roots. The 5 large, strongly veined leaflets are downy on the undersides. In late summer it produces spikes of spidery flowers

Aesculus indica

Aesculus parviflora

with small white petals and long, pinkish stamens. This species likes a hot humid summer, deep moist soil and a sheltered position. **ZONES 7–10.**

Aesculus pavia
RED BUCKEYE

From coastal plains and woodlands of eastern USA, this small tree to 20 ft (7 m) or frequently a shrub to 10 ft (3 m) with dense, rather cane-like branches, is valued for its deep crimson flowers borne in upright spikes in early summer, and the reddish fall (autumn) tones of its rather small leaves, each of 5 leaflets. Although it is easily grown, it is rarely available from nurseries. The cultivar **'Atrosanguinea'** has darker crimson flowers. **ZONES 7–10.**

Aesculus turbinata
JAPANESE HORSE CHESTNUT

Although closely resembling the common horse-chestnut *(Aesculus hippocastanum)* in shape, this tree is slower growing and differs in its larger leaves, slightly smaller panicles of cream flowers that open a few weeks later, in early summer, and its fruit lacking spines or prickles. Its handsome foliage turns a fine orange in fall (autumn). **ZONES 6–9.**

AETHIONEMA

Ranging through the Mediterranean region and into western Asia, the 30 or more species of this genus include evergreen perennials, subshrubs and low shrubs, all with small, narrow leaves and producing spikes or clusters of 4-petalled pink to white flowers in spring and summer. The genus belongs to the mustard family, falling into the same tribe as *Arabis* and *Alyssum*. A number of species are cultivated, prized mainly by rock garden enthusiasts for their compact habit and profuse display of bloom such as the

Aethionema 'Mavis Holmes'

Aesculus pavia

Aesculus turbinata

Aesculus turbinata

mauve-pink cultivar **'Mavis Holmes'**.
CULTIVATION: Aethionemas thrive best in a climate with cool, moist winter and a warm, dry summer. They should be grown in raised beds or rockeries in gritty, free-draining soil and exposed to full sun. Propagate from seed or cuttings.

Aethionema armenum

As its name suggests this species occurs in Armenia, also in nearby regions such as eastern Turkey. The most widely grown species, it is a spreading subshrub only about 6 in (15 cm) high with bluish green foliage. Short spikes of pale to deep pink flowers cover the plant in spring. **ZONES 7–9.**

Aethionema coridifolium
LEBANESE STONE CRESS

This perennial, native to the eastern Mediterranean region, bears prolific heads of rose pink flowers from spring to mid-summer. It has a branching, low habit with slender reddish brown stems and narrow, grayish blue leaves. It reaches a height and spread of about 10 in (25 cm). **ZONES 7–9.**

Aethionema grandiflorum
syn. *Aethionema pulchellum*
PERSIAN STONE CRESS

Grown for its sprays of dainty, phlox-like, pale pink to rose pink flowers in spring, this Middle Eastern species is a short-lived perennial. It has a loose habit, narrow, bluish green leaves and reaches a height of 12 in (30 cm). It makes a good rock garden specimen. **ZONES 7–9.**

Aethionema 'Warley Rose'

This low-growing, evergreen, short-lived subshrub is grown for its profusion of small, bright rose pink flowers in spring and summer. The handsome foliage is composed of narrow, elongated, bluish green leaves. It grows to a compact height and width of 6 in (15 cm). **ZONES 6–9.**

AFROCARPUS

Some 6 species make up this group of large, handsome conifers from the more humid mountain regions of southern and eastern Africa; they were previously included in the genus *Podocarpus* and for a short period in *Nageia*. As in those genera, male and female organs are borne on different trees. The female trees bear large naked seeds with a resinous, fleshy outer layer, on slender stalks quite different from the swollen, juicy stalks that characterize *Podocarpus*.
CULTIVATION: These trees appreciate a sheltered position when young, and are ideal for areas of high humidity and rainfall with deep fertile soil. Propagation is from seed or cuttings.

Agapanthus praecox subsp. *orientalis*

Agapanthus hybrid

Agapanthus 'Irving Cantor'

Agapanthus 'Loch Hope'

Afrocarpus falcatus
syns *Podocarpus falcatus, Nageia falcata*
OUTENIQUA YELLOWWOOD

In its native South African forests this erect tree reaches 100 ft (30 m) with a trunk diameter of 6 ft (1.8 m); planted in the open, it develops a dense, bushy crown. The brown bark exfoliates in fine plates. It has pointed, deep green leaves 1½–2 in (3.5–5 cm) long, and its round ¾ in (18 mm) diameter seeds ripen from dark green with a bloom of white wax, to pale yellow. This is a popular street and park tree in Australia, New Zealand and California. **ZONES 9–11.**

Afrocarpus gracilior
syn. *Podocarpus gracilior*
AFRICAN FERN PINE, MUSENGERA

In its native high mountain forests of tropical East Africa this tree grows to 65 ft (20 m) or more, with a straight trunk and smooth purplish bark. The foliage is dense and ferny with narrow, fine-pointed leaves 2 in (5 cm) or less long. The seeds are similar to those of *Afrocarpus falcatus* but ripen to purplish brown, with a waxy bloom. **ZONES 10–12.**

AGAPANTHUS
AFRICAN LILY, AGAPANTHUS, LILY-OF-THE-NILE

Native to southern Africa, these strong-growing perennials are popular for their fine foliage and showy flowers produced in abundance over summer. Arching, strap-shaped leaves spring from short rhizomes with dense, fleshy roots. Flowers are various shades of blue (white in some cultivars) in many flowered umbels, borne on a long erect stem, often 3 ft (1 m) or more tall. Agapanthus are ideal for background plants or for edging along a wall, fence or driveway, some hybrid examples are **'Irving Cantor'** and **'Storm Cloud'**. **Headbourne Hybrids** are especially vigorous and hardy. They grow to 3 ft (1 m) and come in a range of bright colors.
CULTIVATION: Agapanthus can thrive in conditions of neglect, on sites such as dry slopes and near the coast. They enjoy full sun but will tolerate some shade, and will grow in any soil as long as they get water in spring and summer. They naturalize readily, soon forming large clumps; they also make excellent tub and container specimens. Remove spent flower stems and dead leaves at the end of winter; frost hardy to marginally frost hardy. Propagate by division in late winter, or from seed in spring or fall (autumn).

Agapanthus campanulatus

Agapanthus africanus

This species from western Cape Province is moderately frost tolerant, but is not common in gardens. Often plants sold under this name turn out to be *Agapa–nthus praecox*. It produces blue flowers on 18 in (45 cm) stems from mid-summer to early fall (autumn); each flowerhead contains 20 to 50 individual blossoms, the color varying from pale to deep blue. The leaves are shorter than on *A. praecox*. **ZONES 8–10.**

Agapanthus 'Blue Baby'

Growing to 18–24 in (45–60 cm) high, this frost-hardy cultivar bears light blue flowers in small, rather open heads in summer. It is sometimes considered a form of *Agapanthus praecox*. **ZONES 9–11.**

Agapanthus campanulatus

Native to Natal in South Africa, this species makes a large clump of narrow, grayish leaves that die back in fall (autumn). In mid- to late summer, crowded umbels of pale blue flowers with broadly spreading petals are borne on 3 ft (1 m) stems. It is the most frost-hardy agapanthus. ***Agapanthus campanulatus* var. *patens***, smaller and more slender, is one of the daintiest of all the agapanthus. **ZONES 7–11.**

Agapanthus inapertus

From eastern South Africa, this is a distinctive species with very narrow, deep blue to purplish flowers that become pendent and hardly seem to open, nor do they face the sun as do other species. The bluish green leaves are held rather erect, and the flowering stems may be up to 5 ft (1.5 m) tall. It blooms in late summer and fall (autumn) and older plants can be deciduous. **'Albus'** has creamy white flowers. **ZONES 8–11.**

Afrocarpus gracilior

Agapanthus 'Loch Hope'

A late-flowering agapanthus, this cultivar grows to a height of 4 ft (1.2 m) and has abundant, large dark violet blue flowerheads. **ZONES 9–11.**

Agapanthus 'Peter Pan'

This dwarf, mid-blue variety will form a neat clump about 18 in (45 cm) high and wide after about 3 years. It is a good cut flower and excellent for planting in combination with daylilies. **ZONES 9–11.**

Agapanthus praecox

This is the most commonly grown species of agapanthus. Its glorious starbursts of lavender-blue flowers appear in summer, and its densely clumped evergreen foliage is handsome in the garden all year round. It is also available in white. ***Agapanthus praecox* subsp. *orientalis*** has large dense umbels of blue flowers. It prefers full sun, moist soil and is marginally frost hardy. **ZONES 9–11.**

AGAPETES
syn. *Pentapterygium*

These evergreen shrubs from the moist forests of southern Asia, mostly in the higher mountains, have leathery leaves and tubular flowers of a rather waxy texture. Most of the species grow as epiphytes in the forks of large trees, or frequently on cliffs or boulders. In some species the stems arise from a curious woody tuber which gets quite large with age.
CULTIVATION: They adapt to growing in the ground, but demand a well-drained soil of open texture and need

Afrocarpus falcatus

Afrocarpus falcatus

to be planted high, with the tuber or root bases exposed or covered only by coarse humus. They enjoy shelter and humidity, but adapt readily enough to garden conditions.

Agapetes incurvata
syn. ***Agapetes rugosa***

This species is native to the Himalayan slopes in Nepal and northern India. It is a shrub of about 3 ft (1 m) tall with long scrambling branches and strongly veined leaves 2–4 in (5–10 cm) long. From leaf axils near the branch tips it bears in summer groups of pendent tubular flowers about 3/4 in (18 mm) long, pale flesh pink with much darker transverse bars. **'Scarlet Elf'** has flowers of a stronger red shade. **ZONES 10–11.**

Agapetes 'Ludgvan Cross'

Agapetes 'Ludgvan Cross' is a hybrid between *A. incurvata* and *A. serpens.* It is rather similar to the latter except for its larger leaves and slightly larger, paler flowers. **ZONES 9–11.**

Agapetes serpens
syn. ***Pentapterygium serpens***

From the eastern Himalayas, this shrub with low-arching branches from a large woody tuber rarely exceeds 3 ft (1 m) in height but may be twice that in width. The bristly brown stems bear rows of small glossy leaves and single rows of tubular pale red flowers, each having 5 distinct angles and a pattern of V-shaped bars of darker red. **ZONES 9–10.**

AGARICUS
MUSHROOM

Mushrooms are among the few fungi actively cultivated. They are, of course, grown for their edible fruiting bodies, not their beauty. Mushrooms are all similar in general appearance but vary considerably in size: the white or pale pink to beige caps, with pink to brown undersides, range from 1/2 in (12 mm) to over 6 in (15 cm) diameter. As many fungi are highly toxic, take great care to accurately identify any collected in the wild before eating them—edible and inedible species are very similar in appearance.
CULTIVATION: Cultivating mushrooms is quite unlike growing any other garden crop. Generally grown in the dark, they require warm, moist conditions, a suitable growing medium, and care is needed with the compost mix to get the pH right. Once growing well, they are largely self sustaining, but it often takes considerable trial and error to get that first crop. Insects and rodents can be a problem, so it is important to keep the growing area clean.

Agaricus campestris
syn. ***Psalliota campestris***
MUSHROOM

This common fungus is happy to grow indoors or outdoors, under houses or in sheds, as long as it is darkish, humid and the temperature is constant, ideally between 50–55°F (10–13°C). The mushroom lives on different sorts of compost, and most home gardeners are best buying a mushroom kit from their nursery and following detailed instructions. Mushrooms are usually ready to harvest within 5 weeks—they can be harvested at the button, cap or flat stage of growth. Pick them by twisting out, not pulling. **ZONES 5–11.**

AGARISTA

The ever-wet mountain regions of Central and South America are home to a large and diverse array of shrubs and small trees in the erica family, though most are little known except to botanists. *Agarista* is one such, consisting of 20 or so species of evergreen shrubs from South America with an outlying species in the Indian Ocean island of Mauritius and another in southeastern USA. The genus is closely related to *Leucothöe*, in which its species were formerly included. They have similar leathery leaves and small urn-shaped flowers in drooping, often branched spikes, varying in color from greenish white to pink or red.
CULTIVATION: The South American species are frost-tender plants requiring a very sheltered, humid environment and soil rich in organic matter, but the single North American species has less specialised requirements and is moderately frost hardy. Propagate from cuttings.

Agarista populifolia
syn. ***Leucothöe populifolia***

Occurring wild in mountains of southeastern USA, this is a fairly hardy shrub of up to about 15 ft (4.5 m) high, though often much less in gardens, with long, arching, cane-like branches that are hollow in the center. The 3–5 in (8–12 cm) long leaves are bright green, strongly veined, finely toothed and drawn out into a long point at the apex. In late spring it bears small white flowers with a honey-like scent, crowded on numerous short spikes pendent from the leaf axils. It is an elegant shrub, but to see the flowers to best advantage, they need to be viewed from beneath. **ZONES 7–10.**

AGASTACHE

A genus of some 20 species of perennials found in China, Japan and North America. Most species are very upright with stiff, angular stems clothed in toothed-edged, lance-shaped leaves from 1/2–6 in (1.2 –15 cm) long depending on

Agastache rugosa

the species. Heights range from 18 in–6 ft (45 cm–1.8 m) tall. Upright spikes of tubular, 2-lipped flowers develop at the stem tips in summer. The flower color is usually white, pink, mauve or purple with the bracts that back the flowers being of the same or a slightly contrasting color.
CULTIVATION: Species are easily grown in moist, well-drained soil and prefer a sunny position. Hardiness varies, but most species will tolerate occasional frosts down to 20°F (–7°C). Propagate from seed or cuttings.

Agastache cana
MOSQUITO PLANT

This sage relative is popular with hummingbirds in its native New Mexico, producing bright rose-pink tubular flowers on 24–36 in (about 60–90 cm) stems through late summer and fall (autumn). It adapts well to cultivation in a cool, dry climate. The crushed foliage releases a distinct fragrance of bubblegum. It is a good plant for a mixed border. **ZONES 5–10.**

Agastache foeniculum
syn. ***Agastache anethiodora***
ANISE HYSSOP

This 18 in–4 ft (45 cm–1.2 m) tall, soft-stemmed North American species makes a clump of upright stems with 3 in (8 cm) leaves. Often treated as an annual, it is primarily grown for the ornamental value of its purple flower spikes. The anise-scented and flavored foliage is used to make a herbal tea or as a flavoring. **ZONES 8–10.**

Agastache mexicana
syns ***Brittonastrum mexicanum, Cedronella mexicana***

An erect, short-lived, aromatic perennial from Mexico, this species has ovate or lance-shaped leaves with serrated margins. It bears spikes of crimson flowers in mid- to late summer and grows to 3 ft (1 m) in height. **ZONES 9–11.**

Agastache rugosa

This species from China and Japan grows to 4 ft (1.2 m) tall with branching stems that make it more shrubby than most species. The leaves are around 3 in (8 cm) long and rather sticky. The flower spikes are up to 4 in (10 cm) long with small pink or mauve flowers that have white lobes. **ZONES 8–10.**

AGATHIS
KAURI

This remarkable genus of large conifers consists of 20 or so species scattered through the southwest Pacific region from New Zealand to the Malay Peninsula. Nearly all are tall with massive straight trunks and broad leathery leaves quite unlike the needles of more familiar conifers. The cones are curious too, nearly spherical with a criss-cross pattern of scales. *Agathis* is Greek for 'ball of twine'. Kauri (or kaori) is their Polynesian name. Timber and resin are economic products derived from them.
CULTIVATION: The trees are marginally frost hardy and prefer full sun, deep moist soil and high humidity. They can be pruned to limit size or to maintain shape. Propagation is from seed.

Agapetes serpens

Agapetes incurvata 'Scarlet Elf'

Agastache foeniculum

A

Agathis australis
NEW ZEALAND KAURI

The largest of New Zealand's native trees, this occurs in the North Island's lowland forests, reaching 150 ft (45 m) with 20 ft (6 m) trunk diameters and great spreading limbs. Slow growing in cultivation, even 50-year-old trees are still of modest size, with a dense, narrowly pyramidal crown. The short, blunt, stiff leaves are mid-green, turning coppery brown in colder weather. Kauris prefer moderate temperatures. **ZONES 9–10.**

Agathis robusta
QUEENSLAND KAURI

Native to coastal Queensland, Australia, and Papua New Guinea, this tall tree of up to 150 ft (45 m), has thick, deep green leaves about twice as large as those of the New Zealand kauri, and its growth is more vigorous. Young trees have straight trunks with short side branches. Its globular cones are the size of tennis balls. It prefers warm-temperate to tropical locations. **ZONES 9–12.**

Agathis australis

AGATHOSMA

A genus of over 130 species of aromatic erica-like shrubs, usually around 18–24 in (45–60 cm) tall and all native to southern Africa. The stems, which may be upright or spreading, are densely covered with tiny, narrow leaves, often rolled at the edges. Small flowers (always less than ½ in [12 mm] diameter) massed in umbels occur mainly at the branch tips, a good example is ***Agathosma dielsiana***, with a few in the upper leaf axils. Flower colors range from white through red to mauve and sometimes yellow.

CULTIVATION: Plant in full sun with a gritty, humus-enriched, well-drained, slightly acid soil. Where the winter climate is severe they may be grown in containers. Hardiness varies with the species, though most will tolerate occasional light to moderate frosts. Propagate from seed or tip cuttings.

Agathosma betulina
syn. ***Barosma betulina***
BUCHU

This species has rather large leaves for the genus, up to 1 in (25 mm) long, and is unusual in that its pink flowers are borne singly at the end of fine branchlets rather than in umbels. It is up to 3 ft (1 m) tall. The dried leaves were once widely used medicinally by the indigenous people of its native Cape Province and the Dutch settlers. **ZONES 9–10.**

Agathosma dielsiana

Agathosma ovata
FALSE BUCHU

This species has ½ in (12 mm) long leaves and clusters of tiny lilac flowers in the leaf axils near the branch tips. It grows to about 18 in (45 cm) tall. **ZONES 9–10.**

AGAVE

Occurring naturally in the Caribbean region including southern USA, Mexico and the West Indies, these perennial succulents are grown for their dramatic, sword-shaped, often sharply toothed leaves and tall flowering stems. The small species flower only after 5 to 10 years and the taller species may take up to 40 years to flower. All agaves flower only once and then the flowering shoot dies, leaving offsets (in most species) which continue the plant's growth. These plants are popular for use in Mediterranean styles of landscape design and for large rockeries and dry embankments.

CULTIVATION: Plant in a well-drained, gritty soil in full sun. Once established, water only in summer. Frost hardiness varies from species to species, but all are adapted to surviving very dry periods. Most species make excellent container plants. Propagate from offsets or from seed in spring or summer.

Agathosma ovata

Agathosma ovata

Agave americana
CENTURY PLANT, AMERICAN ALOE

From Mexico, this species consists of large, stemless rosettes of stiff, dull gray leaves with sharp tips and teeth. Each rosette grows to a height and spread of 6 ft (1.8 m) but an old clump may be 30 ft (9 m) or more across. The plant bears masses of yellow flowers on a branched flower stem rising to 20 ft (6 m) when about 10 years old. Popular cultivars include **'Marginata'** with yellow-edged leaves and **'Mediopicta'** with a broad yellow stripe down the center of the leaves. **ZONES 9–12.**

Agave attenuata

This spineless species has a thick stem to 5 ft (1.5 m) high, crowned by a compact rosette of broad, soft-textured pale green leaves. Its arched flower spike grows to 10 ft (3 m) and bears densely packed greenish yellow flowers which open in spring and summer. Lateral rosettes branch off the main stem making, in time, a large mound of rosettes. **'Nerva'** has bluish green leaves. **ZONES 9–12.**

Agathis australis

Agathis robusta

Agave americana

Agave americana 'Marginata'

Agave americana 'Mediopicta'

Agave bracteosa

From northeastern Mexico, this species has stemless rosettes with narrow, recurving yellow-green leaves, up to 30 in (75 cm) long, that taper into a fine, soft point. It normally suckers from the base before producing a narrow, unbranched spike of pale yellow flowers that open progressively from the base over a long period. **ZONES 10–12.**

Agave celsii

This eastern Mexican species has rosettes of succulent, greenish gray leaves, armed with closely set teeth and terminating in a 1 in (25 mm) brown spine. The 24 in

Agave attenuata 'Nerva'

Agave parryi var. *huachucensis*

Agave parryi

(60 cm) long leaves are spatula-shaped. The densely flowered yellow-green to purplish spike grows to 8 ft (2.4 m) high. The rosette produces basal suckers before flowering and dying. **ZONES 9–12.**

Agave ferox

Twenty or more 3–4 ft (1–1.2 m) long glossy dark green leaves form the rosettes of this large agave. The leaves are fiercely armed (*ferox* means 'fierce') with 1½ in (35 mm) long hooked marginal spines and 3 in (8 cm) long terminal spines. The 30 ft (9 m) high inflorescence is made up of panicles of 3 in (8 cm) long yellow flowers. **ZONES 9–12.**

Agave macroacantha

Macroacantha means 'large-spined' presumably referring to the fierce terminal spines on the 12 in (30 cm) long stiff gray-green to gray-white leaves of this Mexican species. They have marginal teeth at wide intervals and a gray to dark brown stout terminal spine. The inflorescence is about 6 ft (1.8 m) high with many reddish flowers. **ZONES 9–12.**

Agave neomexicana

As the name implies, this species is native to New Mexico. It makes a compact rosette of very broad bluish green leaves, about 16 in (40 cm) long with horny margins and several hooked teeth and a brownish black 2 in (5 cm) terminal spine. The branched inflorescence is up to 15 ft (4.5 m) high and the flowers are deep yellow with brownish red tinges. *Agave neomexicana* is sometimes treated as a synonym of *A. parryi.* **ZONES 8–11.**

Agave parryi

From arid mountains of Arizona, New Mexico and adjacent northern Mexico, this species varies in leaf shape, size and other features. The typical form has almost globular rosettes of many gray leaves up to 15 in (40 cm) long and 6 in (15 cm) wide, their margins with closely spaced and often curved prickles, or sometimes almost unarmed. The multi-branched inflorescence is up to 15 ft (4.5 m) tall, with dense clusters of yellow to dull orange flowers. ***Agave parryi* var. *huachucensis*** has larger leaves, sometimes over 24 in (60 cm) long, 8 in (20 cm) wide and broadest near the tip; it is known only from the Huachuca Mountains in southern Arizona. **ZONES 8–11.**

Agave macroacantha

Agave bracteosa

Agave attenuata

Agave neomexicana

Agave picta

This large agave from Mexico is similar to, and often confused with *Agave americana. Agave picta* is known mostly as a variegated form with cream marginal bands on the leaves. The thick, dark green, sword-shaped leaves are about 6 ft (1.8 m) long, their edges closely armed with strong, mostly hooked spines. The flowering stem is very similar to that of *A. americana* but even taller, up to 35 ft (10.5 m). **ZONE 10–12.**

Agave picta

Agave celsii

Agave potatorum

syn. *Agave scolymus*

The name of this species from central Mexico is Latin for 'of the drinkers', referring to its sap being used to make an alcoholic beverage (as is that of many other agaves). It forms a very symmetrical rosette of many broad, concave, dull blue-green leaves 24–36 in (60–90 cm) long and 8 in (20 cm) wide, their edges fiercely armed with large curved spines and terminating in a long spine. The narrowly branched inflorescence is up to 15 ft (4.5 m) high and the greenish yellow flowers open in summer. **ZONES 9–12.**

Ageratina ligustrina

Ageratina altissima

Ageratina occidentalis

Agave striata

This short-stemmed species from central Mexico has numerous stiff, very narrow 18 in (45 cm) long green leaves which are slightly incurved. They are smooth-edged with long, sharp terminal spines. The inflorescence is an 8 ft (2.5 m) erect spike with greenish yellow to somewhat purplish small flowers, not tightly packed. **'Nana'** is a dwarf variety with small, gray-tinted leaves. **ZONES 9–11.**

Agave stricta
HEDGEHOG AGAVE

Another Mexican species with very narrow, rigid leaves, the rosettes often growing into a clump when mature. The unbranched flowering spike reaches a height of 6–10 ft (1.8–3 m) and the reddish, once-only flowers appear in summer. The tapering leaves have finely toothed margins and are tipped with sharp, black spines, which may cause injury if the plant is badly positioned. One of the smaller species, it may flower when only 6–8 years old. **ZONES 10–12.**

Agave victoriae-reginae
ROYAL AGAVE

From Mexico, this slow-growing succulent is stalkless, up to 24 in (60 cm) in height and breadth, and its single rosette has dense, narrow, keeled leaves with white edges and surface lines. A flowering stem up to 12 ft (3.5 m) tall bearing pale greenish yellow flowers develops after 20 years. It is seldom attacked by pests and will tolerate light frosts but prefers a frost-free climate. Some people consider it the most beautiful of the agaves, but it must be renewed from seed after flowering. **ZONES 9–12.**

Agave vilmoriniana
OCTOPUS AGAVE

This species from northwestern Mexico makes a solitary rosette sitting on a short trunk. The green, fleshy channeled leaves are up to 6 ft (1.8 m) long with horny, wavy margins, free of marginal teeth but with a 1 in (25 mm) long terminal spine. The inflorescence is a 15 ft (4.5 m) high spike of crowded yellow flowers; after these drop, the spike sometimes produces vegetative buds, which can fall and take root. **ZONES 9–11.**

AGERATINA

This is just one of many genera, predominantly American, that has been split off the large and unwieldy *Eupatorium.* Although composites, that is, members of the daisy family, they have inflorescences consisting of many small fluffy heads without ray florets, and hence quite un-daisy-like in appearance. *Ageratina* consists of over 200 species from warmer parts of the Americas, a small number extending to somewhat cooler parts of eastern USA. Two Mexican species have become bad weeds in parts of Australia. The genus includes annuals, perennials and soft-wooded shrubs. Leaves are in opposite pairs on the cane-like stems and have a musky, slightly unpleasant smell. The small, soft flowerheads are in terminal panicles and are either white or pale pink.
CULTIVATION: They are easily grown in any sheltered spot in moist soil. The species from the USA are fairly frost hardy, others hardly at all. Propagate from seed, cuttings or by division.

Ageratina altissima
syn. *Eupatorium altissimum*

Native over a wide area of eastern and central USA, this perennial is one of the taller species, growing to about 8 ft (2.4 m) high. Its leaves are up to 5 in (12 cm) long, toothed in the upper part, and the numerous small white flowerheads appear in late summer. **ZONES 6–9.**

Ageratina ligustrina
syn. *Eupatorium ligustrinum*

A very distinctive shrubby species native to Central America, *Ageratina ligustrina* can reach as much as 15 ft (4.5 m) tall, with densely massed branches and glossy evergreen leaves reminiscent of privet leaves (hence *ligustrina,* 'privet-like'). The white flowerheads with pinkish enclosing bracts are borne in large panicles in fall (autumn). **ZONES 9–11.**

Ageratina occidentalis
syn. *Eupatorium occidentale*

Native to the northwestern states of the USA, this is a many-stemmed perennial about 30 in (75 cm) high, with small almost triangular leaves. The fluffy flowerheads, borne in late summer in numerous small panicles, vary in color from white to pink or purple. **ZONES 6–9.**

AGERATUM
FLOSS FLOWER

While undoubtedly best known for the annual bedding plants derived from *Ageratum houstonianum,* this genus includes some 43 species of annuals and perennials mostly native to warmer regions of the Americas. They are clump-forming or mounding plants up to 30 in (75 cm) tall with felted or hairy, roughly oval to heart-shaped leaves with shallowly toothed or serrated edges. The flowerheads are a mass of fine filaments, usually dusky blue, lavender or pink and crowded in terminal clusters.
CULTIVATION: Best grown in full sun in moist, well-drained soil. Regular deadheading is essential to prolong the flowering. Propagate by spring-sown seed, either raised indoors in containers or sown directly in the garden.

Ageratum houstonianum

Native to Central America and the West Indies, this annual ageratum is popular as a summer bedding plant. It is available in tall (12 in [30 cm]), medium (8 in [20 cm]) and dwarf (6 in [15 cm]) sizes and forms clumps of foliage with fluffy flowers in an unusual dusky blue that blends effectively with many other bedding plants. Pink and white forms are also available. **ZONES 9–12.**

AGLAONEMA

A genus of about 20 species of perennial subshrubs from the humid tropics of Southeast Asia. In growth form they are the old world counterparts of the tropical American *Dieffenbachia* and can be used for indoor decoration in a similar way. Some species are renowned for their tenacious hold on life and ability to grow in conditions of poor light and soil. The somewhat fleshy stems branch from the base and may root where they touch the ground. The broad, oblong leaves are often mottled or barred with cream. Tiny flowers are borne in a short fleshy spike within a furled spathe, an arrangement typical of the arum family. The spikes are more conspicuous in the fruiting stage, displaying oval berries that can be quite colorful.
CULTIVATION: In the tropics aglaonemas are easily grown in any

Agave striata

Agave victoriae-reginae

Agave stricta

Agave vilmoriniana

moist shady area beneath trees but in temperate regions they are grown indoors in containers. Propagation is normally by cuttings or offsets, which are easily rooted.

Aglaonema commutatum

Native to the Philippines and eastern Indonesia, this is the most widely grown aglaonema and has given rise to several cultivars, varying in their leaf markings. The fleshy stems, branching from the base, grow to about 18 in (45 cm) high, and bear slender-stalked leaves up to about 12 in (30 cm) long. The flowering stems have a narrow pale green spathe enclosing a small white spadix, and may appear through much of the year. In the original wild forms the leaves are dark green with subtle whitish feathering along the lateral veins, but cultivars have larger cream and yellow splashes. **ZONES 10–12.**

Aglaonema modestum
CHINESE EVERGREEN

From southern China and adjacent Southeast Asia, this species has long been cultivated in Chinese homes and was the first aglaonema known in the West. Though lacking the foliage variegation of some other species it has its own modest charm, with spreading stems to about 24 in (60 cm) long, declining as they grow and turning up at the tip, and very broad leaves drawn out into a long point at the tip and with wavy margins. It is a very hardy house plant, tolerating almost as much neglect as an aspidistra. A cut stem will grow for months in just water. **ZONES 9–12.**

AGONIS

This is a genus of about 10 species of warm-climate evergreen trees and shrubs indigenous to the southwest of Western Australia. They have narrow, thick-textured leaves, aromatic when crushed, and attractive small white flowers resembling those of tea-trees *(Leptospermum).* They are valued for their toughness and freedom from pests and diseases. Some species are used for cut flowers.
CULTIVATION: They do best in full sun and sandy soil that is well drained but preferably enriched with organic matter for moisture retention. They are frost tender, but tolerate droughts when established. Propagation is from seed or cuttings. Plants sometimes self-propagate from seed contained in their small woody fruit capsules.

Agonis flexuosa
WILLOW-MYRTLE, PEPPERMINT TREE

Growing to about 30 ft (9 m) tall and wide, this tree has a brown-barked trunk with a diameter up to 3 ft (1 m), quite disproportionate to its height. It has pendulous branches, rather like a small weeping willow. The narrow leaves are aromatic when crushed and in late spring the tree bears small white flowers along the branches. It is widely grown in parks and gardens in temperate areas of Australia, including seaside locations. The cultivar **'Variegata'**, with cream and pink-striped leaves, lacks vigor but is a very popular small tree. **ZONES 9–10.**

Agonis juniperina

Reaching a height of 15–25 ft (4.5–8 m), this tree is more slender and upright than others of its genus. Its deep green leaves are small and rather prickly, crowded into clusters along the twigs. The small white flowers appear through much of the year. This species has been grown for cut-flower production. **ZONES 9–10.**

Agonis parviceps

Not very common in the wild and even less so in gardens, *Agonis parviceps* grows to only about 10 ft (3 m) tall. Its leaves are even smaller than those of *A. juniperina*, and are prickly. From late winter to early summer it is a pretty sight with its masses of white flowers. Easy to grow and popular for cut flowers, it would be a good choice for a seaside garden. **ZONES 9–10.**

AGRIMONIA
AGRIMONY

About 15 species of perennials belong in this genus, occurring in temperate regions of the northern hemisphere. It is related to *Potentilla* but has its small yellow flowers in elongated spikes, opening progressively from the base, and its fruits are small spiny burrs. The pinnate leaves with thin, toothed leaflets are mainly basal. Agrimonias are plants of woodland verges and meadows and have little ornamental value, but they have a long history of medicinal use, the leaves and flowers making an infusion with astringent and diuretic properties due to their tannin content. They also yield a yellow dye.
CULTIVATION: They are very easily grown in any moist fertile soil, in full sun or light shade. Seed is difficult to germinate so propagation is usually by division of the rhizome.

Agrimonia eupatoria
COMMON AGRIMONY

Native to Europe, western Asia and North Africa, this species makes a sparse clump of foliage from a deeply buried rhizome; leaves consist of up to 13 leaflets, white-haired on the undersides, and the weak flowering stem is up to about 24 in (60 cm) tall. **ZONES 6–10.**

AGROPYRON
DOG GRASS, COUCH GRASS, WHEATGRASS

A genus of 40 species of perennial rhizomatous grasses spread over the temperate regions. Some are noxious weeds, particularly in parts of the USA. They form dense mats of creeping rhizomes, from which emerge upright leafy stems up to 3 ft (1 m) tall. In summer, spiky inflorescences develop at the top of the stems. The leaves of some of the species can be used in salads or juiced as a medicinal tonic.
CULTIVATION: These are very easily grown in any well drained soil in full sun. All are moderately to very frost hardy and are propagated from seed or by breaking up clumps or transplanting pieces of rhizome.

Agropyron repens
QUACKGRASS, COUCH GRASS, TWITCH

This 12–36 in (30–90 cm) tall grass has $\frac{1}{4}$–$\frac{1}{2}$ in (6–12 mm) wide, rough-textured leaves with a distinct mid-vein. There are small clasping auricles (ear-shaped structures) where the leaves join the stems. It has extremely vigorous, slender, branching rhizomes that can penetrate the hardest soils. It is widely regarded as a weed in farmland and gardens but does have some herbal uses. **ZONES 3–9.**

Agropyron smithii
WESTERN WHEATGRASS

This species has clasping auricles, but its leaves are a light blue-green color and are narrower than those of *Agropyron repens*. Its leaves also have several distinct ridges rather than a single prominent mid-vein. **ZONES 3–9.**

AGROSTEMMA

Two or possibly more species of slender annuals from the Mediterranean region belong to this genus, related to *Lychnis* and *Silene*. One of them is well known as a weed of crops in Europe, but is still a pretty plant with large rose-pink flowers and is sometimes used in meadow plantings and cottage gardens. Distinctive features of the genus are the long silky hairs on the leaves and the calyx consisting of 5 very long, leaf-like sepals radiating well beyond the petals.
CULTIVATION: They are very frost hardy, growing best in full sun in a well-drained soil. Young plants should be thinned to about 10 in (25 cm) spacing and may need light staking if growing in exposed areas. Propagate from seed sown in early spring or fall (autumn).

Agonis flexuosa

Agonis juniperina

Ageratum houstonianum

Agonis parviceps

Agrimonia eupatoria

A

A

Agrostemma githago
CORN COCKLE

This fast-growing showy annual reaches a height of 24–36 in (60–90 cm), making it ideal for planting at the back of an annual border. It has a slender, few-branched, willowy habit with long narrow leaves in opposite pairs. Broadly funnel-shaped pink flowers about 2 in (5 cm) in diameter appear on long hairy stalks from late spring to early fall (autumn). The tiny dark brown seeds are poisonous. **ZONES 8–10.**

AGROSTIS
BENT GRASS, BROWNTOP

This is a near-worldwide genus of some 120 species of annual and perennial grasses, both tuft-forming and stoloniferous. Those most widely cultivated have long, fine stolons which produce roots at every node, thus developing a dense sod of roots and mat of fine leaves. If left unmown, most species grow 12–24 in (30–60 cm) tall with feathery inflorescences of tiny seed heads from spring to fall (autumn). Various species of bent grass or browntop are widely used in cooler climates for lawns where a high-quality turf is required. They will grow even in light shade.
CULTIVATION: They need well-aerated and well-drained slightly acid to neutral soil (pH 5.6–7.0) with ample summer moisture and frequent feeding. They should be mown frequently and short. Propagate from seed. Watch out for fungal diseases such as brown patch and dollar spot.

Ailanthus giraldii

Agrostis aemula

This clump-forming annual species from temperate Australia and New Zealand is notable mainly for its broad, much-branched panicles of tiny delicate seed heads on hair-fine stalks, usually purple-fringed just before they mature in early summer. It grows to a height of around 18 in (45 cm). **ZONES 7–10.**

Agrostis capillaris
syn. *Agrostis tenuis*
BENTGRASS, BROWN TOP, COLONIAL BENT

Regarded highly for its tolerance of the cold, this attractive and durable perennial species from Europe is widely grown as a lawn grass in areas where summers are not too hot and dry. Although frost resistant, it is drought tender. Left unmown, it grows to 16 in (40 cm) in height. A recommended mowing height is about ¾ in (20 mm). A prodigious spreader, it has a creeping stem, with bright green, narrow leaves. Compared with other bent grasses, this more erect species needs less care. **ZONES 5–10.**

Agrostis aemula

Agrostemma githago

Ailanthus altissima

Agrostis stolonifera
CREEPING BENT GRASS

The premium lawn species, this is available in many different strains and requires constant care to maintain it at its best. Mow to a height of about ½ in (12 mm). **ZONES 3–10.**

AILANTHUS
TREE OF HEAVEN, SIRIS

This tree genus from eastern Asia and the Pacific region includes both winter-deciduous and dry-season-deciduous species, though only the former are generally known in cultivation. They are vigorous growers of medium size with long pinnate leaves and branches terminating in large flower clusters—male and female flowers are on separate trees and neither is very conspicuous, but those on female trees develop in summer into masses of winged, papery fruits that are very decorative. The winter-deciduous species are frost-hardy trees that adapt well to urban areas, even coming up from self-sown seed in the cracks of paving. They tolerate hard pruning, responding with vigorous new growths.
CULTIVATION: They do best in warm-temperate areas but will survive in most climates, preferring full sun or partial shade and deep, rich soil. Propagation is by means of seed in fall (autumn) and suckers or root cuttings from the female tree in winter.

Ailanthus altissima
syn. *Ailanthus glandulosa*
TREE OF HEAVEN

Native to China, in some cities this tree is valued for its ability to withstand urban pollution, in other areas it is scorned as a weed. Planted on a large lawn it shows little inclination to sucker, growing to 50 ft (15 m), its dome-shaped crown scattered with bunches of pale reddish brown fruits in summer. The deep green, pinnate leaves, up to 3 ft (1 m) long on young trees, smell unpleasant if bruised. **ZONES 6–10.**

Ailanthus giraldii

This is a tree very similar to *Ailanthus altissima*, but with slightly larger leaves and fruits. There is some debate as to whether it deserves to be treated as a distinct species or is just a form of *A. altissima*. **ZONES 6–10.**

AJANIA

This genus, consisting of 30 or so species from eastern and central Asia, is one of a number of genera now recognized in place of *Chrysanthemum* in its older, broader sense. *Ajania* is closest to *Dendranthema* and its species have similar bluntly lobed leaves usually with whitish-woolly hairs on the undersides. But their flowerheads are small and button-like, lacking ray florets and arranged in flattish panicles at tips of branches. The plants have extensively branching underground rhizomes, sending up numerous tough, wiry stems. Only one species, *Ajania pacifica*, has been widely cultivated for ornament in gardens and parks.
CULTIVATION: The plants are very hardy and easily grown in a wide range of situations, thriving in both poor and fertile soils, though preferring good drainage and full sun. If not cut back hard after flowering, including the rhizome, they may spread so rapidly that adjacent plants are smothered. Propagate from rhizome divisions.

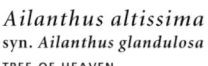

Ailanthus altissima

Ajania pacifica

Ajania pacifica

Ajania pacifica
syns *Chrysanthemum pacificum, Dendranthema pacificum*

An attractive plant, occurring wild in far eastern Asia, this species makes a spreading, loose mound of evergreen foliage up to about 18 in (45 cm) high. The leaves are deep green on the upper side and clothed in dense white hairs beneath; the white shows at the coarsely scalloped edges, making a striking contrast with the green. Sprays of brilliant gold flowerheads in fall (autumn) further enhance the effect. **ZONES 4–10.**

AJUGA
BUGLE

About 50 species of low-growing annuals and perennials make up this genus, which ranges through Europe, Asia, Africa and Australia, mainly in cooler regions. Although belonging to the mint family, their foliage is hardly aromatic. Rosettes of soft, spatulate leaves lengthen into spikes of blue, purple or pink (rarely yellow) 2-lipped flowers. In most perennial species the plants spread by runners or underground rhizomes, some forming extensive carpets. They make attractive ground covers, especially for shady places such as corners of courtyards.
CULTIVATION: These are frost-hardy, trouble-free plants requiring little but moist soil and shelter from strong sun, though the bronze and variegated forms develop best color in sun. The commonly grown species thrive in a range of climates, from severe cold to subtropical. Snails and slugs can damage foliage. Propagate by division.

Ajuga reptans 'Purpurea'

Ajuga reptans 'Atropurpurea'

Ajuga reptans 'Catlin's Giant'

Ajuga australis
AUSTRALIAN BUGLE

A variable species occurring over a wide area of southern and central Australia, from subalpine meadows to rocky desert gullies, this perennial forms compact clumps 3–15 in (8–40 cm) high; both the softly hairy leaves and the mauve or purple flowers vary greatly in size. As yet little cultivated, it grows vigorously but may be short lived. It flowers in spring through summer. **ZONES 8–10.**

Ajuga pyramidalis
PYRAMIDAL BUGLE

Widely distributed in Europe including parts of the UK, this attractive species makes a compact mat of rosettes, spreading by short underground rhizomes. The hairy dark green rosette leaves grade into the broad leafy bracts of the flowering stem to give it a narrowly pyramidal form, usually about 8 in (20 cm) tall. Flowers are mostly blue or mauve, and open from spring to mid-summer. **'Metallica Crispa'** is a curious miniature form, with rounded and somewhat contorted leaves showing a metallic purple sheen. **ZONES 5–9.**

Ajuga reptans
EUROPEAN BUGLE, COMMON BUGLE, BLUE BUGLE

The commonly grown ajuga, native to Europe, spreads by surface runners in the same way as a strawberry plant, making a mat of leafy rosettes only 2–3 in (5–8 cm) high and indefinite spread. In spring it sends up spikes of deep blue flowers, up to 8 in (20 cm) high in some cultivars. The most familiar versions are: **'Atropurpurea'** syn. **'Purpurea'** which has dark purple to bronze leaves; **'Burgundy Glow'**, with cream and

Ajuga reptans 'Jungle Beauty'

Ajuga reptans

Ajuga pyramidalis 'Metallica Crispa'

maroon variegated leaves; **'Multicolor'**, with white, pink and purple leaves; and **'Variegata'**, with light green and cream leaves. Rather different is **'Jungle Beauty'**, which is much larger, spreads more rapidly, and has dark green leaves tinged with purple. **'Catlin's Giant'** has much larger leaves and longer, to 8 in (20 cm), inflorescences. **'Pink Elf'** is a compact form with dark pink flowers. **ZONES 3–10.**

AKEBIA

There are 4 species in this genus, all deciduous or semi-evergreen twiners with slender, twining stems, occurring wild in China, Korea and Japan. Their compound leaves have rounded, sometimes lobed leaflets, the number varying with the species. In spring they produce racemes of slightly fragrant reddish purple to brown flowers of separate sexes (females larger). Large pulp-filled—edible but bland-tasting—blue to purple, sausage-shaped fruit follow. Two or more plants are needed for fruit production.
CULTIVATION: Plant in cool, moist, humus-enriched soil with the base of the plant in partial shade. They are moderately frost hardy and the extent of foliage loss in winter is largely dependent on how cold the weather is. Prune after flowering and cut down to the base every 3 or 4 years to remove tangled growth. Propagate from seed, layers or cuttings.

Akebia quinata
CHOCOLATE VINE

Deciduous (or semi-evergreen in warm areas), this decorative, twining climber

Akebia quinata

from Japan, China and Korea is grown for its attractive habit, leaves and flowers. The green leaves are divided into 5 leaflets and fragrant, purple-mauve, drooping flowers appear in late spring. Male and female plants are needed for the female plants to produce interesting sausage-shaped, edible fruits. It will grow to 10 m (about 30 ft) or more and will require a strong support.
ZONES 5–9.

Akebia trifoliata

This species is a native of China and Japan. Its leaves are composed of three $1\frac{1}{2}$–$2\frac{1}{2}$ in (35 mm–6 cm) long, shallowly lobed, light green leaflets. The brownish purple flowers are unscented and the fruit is up to 6 in (15 cm) long.
It is deciduous or semi-evergreen and can climb to 30 ft (9 m). **ZONES 5–9.**

ALBERTA

Three species make up this genus of subtropical evergreen trees, one from South Africa and two from Madagascar. They are noted for their handsome gardenia-like foliage and showy tubular flowers.
A curious feature is the way 2 of the 5 sepals enlarge after flowering to form colored wing-like flaps on the woody fruit. The name honours the famous medieval scholar Albertus Magnus.
CULTIVATION: Frost tender, this genus does best in a warm coastal climate with ample rainfall and protection from salty winds. All 3 species prefer a fertile, well-drained but moist soil and need plenty of water during summer. Propagate from fall (autumn) seed or root cuttings.

A

Alberta magna
NATAL FLAME BUSH

From South Africa, this species grows to a tree of 30 ft (9 m) in the wild but in gardens is generally only a shrub of 6–10 ft (1.8–3 m). The leathery leaves are shiny deep green, and from late fall (autumn) to summer it bears clusters of showy, upcurving scarlet flowers, followed by small fruits enclosed in pale red calyces. It is not frost hardy and requires a subtropical climate to perform well. **ZONES 10–11.**

ALBIZIA

For the most part *Albizia* species are quick growing tropical trees and shrubs with globular clusters of long-stamened flowers, rather like those of many *Mimosa* and *Acacia* species but larger. They have feathery leaves and densely clustered small flowers in which the stamens are far longer and more conspicuous than the petals. In nature they are often rather weedy small trees and frequently short lived, but can be shapely.
CULTIVATION: Springing up quickly from seed, *Albizia* species are easy to cultivate; their main requirements are summer warmth and moisture and a reasonably sheltered site.

Albizia julibrissin
SILK TREE

Ranging from Iran east to China, this deciduous tree is named for the long, silky stamens, creamy white to deep pink, the visible part of the flowerheads, borne in summer. Often less than 6 ft (1.8 m) tall, though flowering freely, in ideal conditions it becomes a flat-crowned tree of 20–25 ft (6–8 m) with luxuriant feathery foliage. It likes a warm-temperate climate and does very well in large containers but seldom lives beyond 30 years. Exceptionally richly colored specimens are usually given the name ***Albizia julibrissin* var. *rosea*.** **ZONES 8–10.**

Albizia lebbek
WHITE SIRIS, WOMAN'S TONGUE TREE, FRYWOOD TREE

This tree from tropical Africa, Asia and Australia reaches about 20–40 ft (6–12 m), developing quite early a broad, flat-topped crown. The bipinnate leaves, deciduous in the dry season, are composed of oblong leaflets up to 2 in (5 cm) long. In spring cream 'powderpuff' flowerheads appear, which darken to dull yellow then develop into long whitish papery pods that hang on the tree for months and make a rattling sound in the winter. **ZONES 11–12.**

ALBUCA

A genus of 30 or so species of bulbs, mainly native to South Africa with a few from elsewhere in Africa, or the Arabian Peninsula. They form clumps of sword-shaped bright green leaves from 4–36 in (10–90 cm) long depending on the species. In summer they produce stiffly upright flower spikes with conical heads of upward-facing, 6-petalled flowers. The flowers are usually white or pale yellow with a green stripe on the outer side of each petal.

Albizia julibrissin

Albizia julibrissin

Albizia julibrissin var. *rosea*

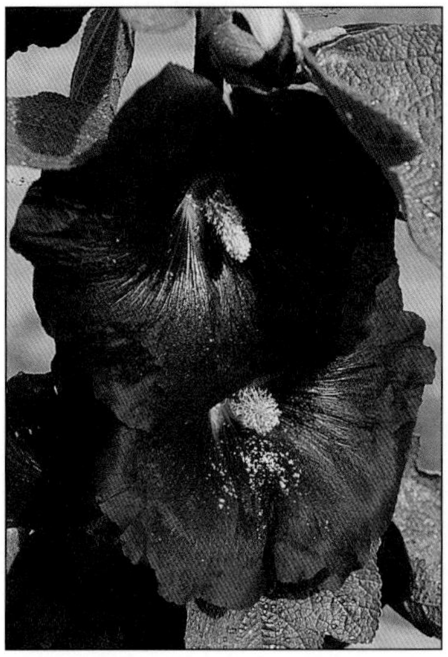
Alcea rosea

Alberta magna

Albuca canadensis

CULTIVATION: Plant in a bright, sunny position with light, well-drained soil. Although tolerant of light frosts, cold, wet conditions will lead to rotting. In such circumstances lift the bulbs after they die down at the end of summer. Plant again in early spring. Propagate from seed, dividing established clumps or by removing and growing on the small offset bulbils.

Albuca canadensis
SENTRY-IN-THE-BOX

This species is native to South Africa, even though its name suggests it is from Canada. *Albuca canadensis* grows up to about 3 ft (1 m) high with bright green leaves up to about 6 in (15 cm) long. The pendulous flowers, which appear in late spring, are 1 in (25 mm) long. The inner petals appear joined, as if forming a tube; the outer petals are yellow, with a green stripe on each petal. **ZONES 9–11.**

ALCEA
HOLLYHOCK

The botanical name *Alcea* is the old Roman one; Linnaeus adopted it although he also used the name *Althaea*, from the Greek *altheo*, to cure, in allusion to the plant's use in traditional medicine. Native to the eastern Mediterranean, hollyhocks were originally called holy hock or holy mallow; it is said that plants were taken to England from the Holy Land during the Crusades. There are about 60 species in the genus, all from western and central Asia. They bear flowers on spikes which may be 6 ft (1.8m) or more high, making them far too tall for the average flowerbed; even 'dwarf' cultivars grow to 3 ft (1m) tall.
CULTIVATION: Hollyhocks are quite frost hardy but need shelter from wind, benefiting from staking in exposed positions. They prefer sun, a rich, heavy well-drained soil and frequent watering in dry weather. Propagate from seed in late summer or spring. Rust disease can be a problem; spray with fungicide.

Albizia julibrissin

Alcea rosea
syn. ***Althaea rosea***
HOLLYHOCK

This biennial, believed originally to have come from Turkey or Palestine, is popular for its tall spikes of flowers which appear in summer and early fall (autumn), and come in a range of colors including pink, purple, cream and yellow; they can be either single, flat circles of color 4 in (10 cm) across, or so lavishly double that they are like spheres of ruffled petals. Foliage is roundish and rough and the plants may be as much as 10 ft (3 m) tall, erect and generally unbranched. The **Chater's Double Group** of cultivars have peony-shaped, double flowers that may be any color from purple-blue, purple, red, yellow and white to pink or apricot. There are many other cultivars and series including **Pinafore Mixed** and **Majorette Mixed** with lacy, semi-double flowers in pastel shades. **ZONES 4–10.**

Alcea rugosa

Similar to *Alcea rosea*, this species from the Black Sea region has longer hairs on its stems and leaves. The deeply lobed leaves are prominently veined on the underside and the flowers are a clear yellow or golden yellow. It has erect, unbranched stems. **ZONES 4–10.**

ALCHEMILLA

LADY'S MANTLE

There are around 300 species of herbaceous perennials in this Eurasian genus. There are also a few alpine species in Australia and New Zealand, but it is not clear if they are natives or naturalized introductions. They form clumps of palmate (hand-shaped) or rounded, lobed, gray-green leaves that often have a covering of fine hairs. Their spreading stems often root as they grow. Branched inflorescences of tiny yellow-green flowers develop in summer. Their sizes range from 6–30 in (15–75 cm) tall and wide. Many species have styptic and other medicinal properties.

CULTIVATION: They are very hardy and easily grown in any well-drained soil in afternoon shade. They may be grown in sun but the foliage will deteriorate in the summer heat. Propagate from seed or division in late winter to early spring.

Alchemilla alpina

ALPINE LADY'S MANTLE

This mat-forming perennial has an erect flowering stem and leaves that are grayish green above and silvery beneath. The flowers, which appear in summer, are very small and are greenish yellow. The species grows to 6 in (15 cm) in height with a spread of 18 in (45 cm). **ZONES 3–9.**

Alchemilla conjuncta

Native to the French and Swiss Alps, this 12 in (30 cm) tall species has 7 to 9 lobed, pale green leaves with toothed edges and a dense covering of silvery hairs on the undersides. The flowering stems are up to 15 in (38 cm) tall. **ZONES 5–9.**

Alchemilla ellenbeckii

This is a small, prostrate, sparsely haired perennial from east Africa with 5-lobed, kidney-shaped, pale green leaves and tiny, yellowish green flowers that are well hidden by the foliage. **ZONES 3–9.**

Alchemilla erythropoda

This clump-forming species grows to 12 in (30 cm) in height and bears greenish yellow flowers from late spring to late summer. The hairy, bluish green leaves are rounded and sharply toothed. **ZONES 3–9.**

Alchemilla lapeyrousii

A Pyrenean species with 7 to 9 lobed, roughly kidney-shaped leaves and flowering stems up to 12 in (30 cm) tall. **ZONES 5–9.**

Alchemilla mollis

LADY'S MANTLE

Sometimes sold as ***Alchemilla vulgaris***, this is the most widely cultivated species in the genus. It is a low-growing perennial ideal for ground cover, the front of borders or for rock gardens. It is clump forming, growing to a height and spread of 40 cm (about 16 in). It has decorative, wavy edged leaves which hold dew or raindrops to give a sparkling effect. In summer, it bears masses of small

Alectryon excelsus

Alchemilla mollis

Alchemilla rohdii

sprays of greenish yellow flowers, similar to *Gypsophila*. ***A. speciosa*** is very like *A. mollis* except that its leaves are more deeply lobed and the leaf stems have a covering of fine hairs. **ZONES 4–9.**

Alchemilla rohdii

One of the numerous European species that have at times been included under the name *Alchemilla vulgaris*, this makes a low spreading plant less than 8 in (20 cm) high with fresh green leaves, their short rounded lobes finely toothed. The greenish yellow flowers are not very showy. **ZONES 6–9.**

Alchemilla vetteri

This is a small species from the mountains of southwest Europe. Its flowering stems rarely exceed 8 in (20 cm) tall and the foliage clump is usually less than 12 in (30 cm) wide. The leaves have 7 to 9 lobes with toothed edges. **ZONES 4–9.**

ALECTRYON

Grown for their attractive dense foliage, these evergreen trees occur naturally through islands of the Pacific, Australia and the Malay region. Their name comes from the Greek for 'cock', referring to a crest on the fruit like a cockscomb. All species have pinnate leaves, divided into several somewhat leathery leaflets; flowers are small, in sprays at the branch tips, and are followed by berry-like capsules that split to reveal large seeds with succulent, showy appendages which attract birds.

CULTIVATION: Occurring in rainforest and coastal scrubs, they are tough trees surviving in exposed positions but will not tolerate severe frosts. Propagate from seed in fall (autumn).

Alectryon excelsus

TITOKI

Native to New Zealand, this spreading tree grows 20–30 ft (6–9 m) tall. Its squat trunk is covered with dark brown-black bark and branches are reddish brown and downy. Leaves are asymmetrically bipinnate and grow to 15 in (38 cm). Tiny red or cream-colored blossoms develop in multi-branched clusters, followed by brown seed pods which split to reveal a deep red interior and glossy black seed. **ZONES 9–11.**

ALEURITES

This small genus of evergreen or semi-evergreen trees ranges from Southeast Asia through Indonesia to Australia and

Alchemilla lapeyrousii

Alchemilla vetteri

Alchemilla speciosa

Alchemilla conjuncta

the Pacific Islands. Formerly included in the genus but now separated as *Vernicia* are some Chinese deciduous species including the tung-oil tree. Vigorous growers, *Aleurites* species have large, often lobed leaves and panicles of small cream, bell-shaped flowers. The fruits are fairly large, consisting of a ball-like outer husk, like a walnut, enclosing a hard stone which contains oily kernels. The oil can be extracted and was traditionally used in Asia for lamps or, after treatment to remove toxins, as a cooking oil. The fast-growing trees are suitable for use in streets and parks. The seeds of all species are poisonous.

CULTIVATION: They like a warm or hot climate. Young trees can be trained into a single trunk. Propagation is from seed, which germinates readily.

A

Allamanda cathartica

Aleurites moluccana

Allium aflatunense

Allamanda cathartica 'Hendersonii'

Allamanda schottii

Aleurites moluccana
CANDLENUT TREE

This evergreen tree grows rapidly to a height of 60 ft (18 m) or so, initially with a narrow, conical crown but with age spreading to a broader dome. It has a straight, thick trunk with smoothish brown bark and wide-spreading branches. The handsome, oval green leaves are lobed on young trees and are slightly aromatic when crushed. Panicles of creamy white flowers are borne in summer, followed by the large round fruits. **ZONES 10–12.**

ALISMA
WATER PLANTAINS

A genus of 9 species of herbaceous perennial aquatic and bog plants, most of them native to temperate regions of the northern hemisphere but 2 are found in Australia. They are known as water plantains because of a superficial resemblance to some members of the plantain genus *Plantago.* The plants consist of a basal rosette of leaves with usually broad, lance-shaped to heart-shaped blades. In summer a tall flowering panicle with whorled branches grows from the center of the rosette, bearing smallish 3-petalled white flowers. Small green fruits follow which disintegrate into many segments that can float away, each containing a seed. Some species are regarded as weeds by farmers and market gardeners, chiefly where crops are grown with irrigation. **CULTIVATION:** Alismas can grow submerged in shallow water in their younger stages but will not flower until the leaves are above water; they are mostly grown at pond edges or in boggy places. As landscape subjects they provide splashes of bold green foliage in the warmer months and require no maintenance. Propagate from seed or division.

Alisma plantago-aquatica
COMMON WATER PLANTAIN

The best known species, this has a wide distribution around temperate regions of the northern hemisphere and also occurs wild in South Africa and southern Australia. Its heart-shaped leaf blades are up to 8 in (20 cm) long and the much-branched flowering stems rise to a height of 24–36 in (60–90 cm). The white flowers are under ½ in (12 mm) in diameter and appear through summer. **ZONES 5–10.**

ALKANNA

This genus contains some 30 species of annuals or evergreen, clump-forming perennials ranging in the wild from southern Europe and northwest Africa to Iran, although only a few species are cultivated. Their leafy stems branch at the top into many one-sided spikes of funnel-shaped, usually blue or sometimes white or yellow flowers in early summer. The leaves are entire and hairy. **CULTIVATION:** *Alkanna* species are extremely tolerant of dry conditions, and thrive in dry, sunny locations in poor soil. They are very frost hardy and are propagated from seed or root cuttings.

Alkanna orientalis

This perennial species, which is native to southern Europe and southwest Asia, has an erect or ascending growth habit to 30 in (75 cm) in height. The white or yellow flowers are usually sweetly scented. **ZONES 6–9.**

Alkanna tinctoria
ALKANET, DYER'S BUGLOSS, SPANISH BUGLOSS

Purplish blue, funnel-shaped flowers are produced in profusion on this perennial species from the Mediterranean region and central Europe. It grows to a height of 12 in (30 cm) and has dull green, oblong, hairy, almost prickly, leaves. It has a deep tap root system and contains a red sap used to color food and beverages and to make a dye. Lift roots in fall (autumn) to dry for powders. **ZONES 5–9.**

ALLAMANDA

A dozen or so species of twining climbers and shrubs belong to this tropical American genus, a few of them widely planted in warm climates for their colorful trumpet flowers, mostly bright yellow. Glossy leaves are in whorls of 3 to 6 on the smooth stems, which bleed milky sap if cut. The climbing species are among the most popular ornamentals in the tropics, ideal for growing over fences or against walls. They produce a succession of flowers for much of the year. In cooler areas there may be some leaf fall. **CULTIVATION:** In warm climates grow outdoors in a sunny, sheltered position in rich soil, watering freely in summer. In cool climates they require a large container in a hothouse or conservatory. Prune heavily in spring to maintain shape and encourage flowering. Propagate from cuttings and watch for mites which disfigure the leaves.

Allamanda blanchetii
syn. ***Allamanda violacea***
PURPLE ALLAMANDA

Exceptional among the species of this genus in having flowers colored other than yellow, *Allamanda blanchetii* is of uncertain wild origin somewhere in South America. It is similar in foliage to the common *A. cathartica* but is a less vigorous twiner that can easily be trained to a 6 ft (1.8 m) shrub. The flowers, about 3 in (8 cm) across, are a somewhat dingy purplish mauve color but of heavy substance, borne freely through summer and fall (autumn). Some recently released hybrid cultivars have blended its coloring (in diluted form) with the vigor of *A. cathartica.* **ZONES 11–12.**

Allamanda cathartica
GOLDEN TRUMPET VINE

This vigorous climber, fast-growing to 15 ft (4.5 m), bears large, yellow, trumpet-shaped flowers to 6 in (15 cm) across in summer. It has whorls of lance-shaped leaves and makes a luxuriant cover for walls and strong fences in frost-free areas. The flowers of **'Hendersonii'** are yellow with white spotted throats. **ZONES 11–12.**

Allamanda schottii
syn. ***Allamanda neriifolia***
SHRUBBY ALLAMANDA

The only true shrub in the genus, this upright evergreen grows to a height and spread of 6 ft (1.8 m) and has glossy green leaves. Its trumpet-shaped golden-yellow flowers, occasionally streaked with orange, are borne in summer and into fall (autumn), sometimes followed by large, shiny seed pods. It prefers a sheltered sunny position. Prune in spring to control shape, and it often benefits from the stems being tied to supports. **ZONES 11–12.**

ALLIUM

This is a large genus consisting of more than 700 species of bulbous perennials and biennials that occur in temperate regions of the northern hemisphere and range in height from 4 in–5 ft (10 cm–1.5 m). Some species are edible, including onions, garlic and chives. The most ornamental species, which are brightly colored with beautiful flowers, mostly come from west and central Asia. Common to the genus is the oniony smell emitted when the leaves are bruised or cut. All species have flowers in an umbel terminating on a small, erect stalk and sheathed in bud by membranous bracts. Bulbs can be very fat or quite slender but generally produce new bulbils at the base, sometimes also in the flower stalks. **CULTIVATION:** They prefer a sunny, open position in fertile, well-drained, weed-free soil. Both edible and ornamental species have the same pest and disease enemies such as onion fly, stem eelworm, rust and onion white rot. Propagate from seed or bulbils.

Allium aflatunense

A large, summer-flowering species from central Asia, this grows to a height of 3–5 ft (1–1.5 m) or more. Over 50 tiny violet flowers, their petals with darker central stripes, are borne in 4 in

Allium cepa

Allium christophii

(10 cm) diameter umbels. The semi-erect, bluish leaves die away before the flowers appear. It has a muted garlic smell that is hardly detectable. **ZONES 7–9.**

Allium ampeloprasum
WILD LEEK, KURRAT

Ideal for rocky, coastal situations though equally adapted to many other environments, this allium has a tall, robust habit, its cylindrical stems reaching a height of up to 4 ft (1.2 m). Papery bracts enclose the globe-shaped umbels, dropping off as the hundreds of tiny dull pink flowers open. Leaves are grayish green, up to 18 in (45 cm) long with a waxy texture and rough margins. One of the larger, leafier Alliums, it has a bulb with garlic-like flavor—some strains are widely cultivated as vegetables in the Middle East. **ZONES 6–10.**

Allium beesianum

From China's Yunnan and Sichuan Provinces, this summer-blooming species bears few-flowered umbels of nodding, bell-shaped blue flowers above narrow grayish green leaves. Left undisturbed, it will form clumps to a height of 8–12 in (20–30 cm). **'Album'** is a white form. **ZONES 8–9.**

Allium caeruleum
syn. *Allium azureum*

This frost-hardy species from central Asia has very short, narrow leaves which wither by the time its 12–24 in (30–60 cm) flowering stalks have fully lengthened. These bear dense umbels of starry blue flowers in summer. **ZONES 6–9.**

Allium canadense
CANADA GARLIC, MEADOW LEEK

A summer-flowering species distributed widely through temperate North America, this allium bears white to pale

Allium cepa, **Proliferum Group**

pink, bell-shaped flowers on 12 in (30 cm) stems. The small, garlic-flavored bulbs were a favorite food of indigenous Americans, as well as being sought after by bears and other wild animals. The bulbils of this species are formed only on the flower stalks, the bulb remaining solitary. **ZONES 4–9.**

Allium carinatum
KEELED GARLIC

Native to southern Europe, this species is also naturalized in parts of the USA. It produces numerous bulbils, spreading rapidly. Leaves are linear and the 12–24 in (30–60 cm) tall flowering stems bear umbels enclosed in very long narrow bracts which drop away to reveal purplish pink flowers with protruding stamens. **ZONES 7–9.**

Allium cepa
ONION, SPRING ONION, SCALLION, SHALLOT

The onion was a popular vegetable among the Greeks and Romans but never eaten by the Egyptians who regarded it as sacred. The spring onion is an immature onion which has not yet made a bulb. This species has given rise to a vast number of cultivars, varying in size, shape, color and flavor. Bunching onions or shallots belong to the **Aggregatum Group**, which is distinguished by the cluster of small bulbs; these have a more delicate taste than spring onions and can be used instead of chives. The tree onion belongs to the **Proliferum Group** which bears small bulbs at the top of the flower stalk. Harvest onions in late summer when the leaves have begun to yellow. **ZONES 4–11.**

Allium cernuum
LADY'S LEEK, NODDING ONION

The distinctive feature of this North American species is the way the slender 12–24 in (30–60 cm) flowering stem

Allium cernuum

nods over at the top, as do the individual flower stalks, which bear white, pink or maroon bell-shaped flowers with protruding stamens. **ZONES 3–9.**

Allium christophii
syn. *Allium albopilosum*
STAR OF PERSIA

Growing to 24 in (60 cm), this species has broad leaves, green and shiny on top and white beneath, and the sturdy stem bears a rounded umbel of flowers up to 15 in (38 cm) wide in spring. Star-shaped individual violet flowers turn black as the seeds ripen and are useful for dried flower arrangements. Plant bulbs in fall (autumn), $2\frac{1}{2}$ in (6 cm) deep. This species grows best in full sun. **ZONES 7–9.**

Allium cyaneum

Cyaneus is Latin for blue, cyanide being named thus because it turns the lips blue. In summer, this northern Chinese species bears nodding, bell-shaped flowers that are a bluish purple color, their petals with dark blue or green center stripes. The leaves sheathe the base of the flowering stems which are up to about 18 in (45 cm) tall. **ZONES 7–9.**

Allium dichlamydeum
COAST ONION

This brightly colored species from California bears magenta-red, bell-shaped flowers on stout stems in summer. It

Allium fistulosum

Allium dichlamydeum

grows from 10–12 in (25–30 cm) in height and has very fine leaves the same height as the stems. **ZONES 8–9.**

Allium fistulosum
WELSH ONION, JAPANESE BUNCHING ONIONS

Growing to around 24 in (60 cm) tall, this species is distinctive for its hollow leaves and flowering stems and bears numerous green flowers in a dense umbel in summer. Of obscure origin and unknown in the wild, Welsh onion is grown as a green vegetable, used in salads and stir-fried dishes. **ZONES 6–9.**

Allium flavum
SMALL YELLOW ONION

A smaller, clump-forming species from Europe and western Asia, this plant is ideal for positioning at the front of a border. Leaves are grayish and cylindrical and in summer, small umbels of sweetly scented bell-shaped flowers appear on stems about 8 in (20 cm) high. They are lemony yellow, often tinged with red, green or brown. **ZONES 5–9.**

Allium giganteum
GIANT ALLIUM

Among the tallest of flowering alliums, this species has 4–6 ft (1.2–1.8 m) stems topped with dense, 4–6 in (10–15 cm) diameter umbels of violet to deep purple flowers in mid-summer. The leaves are gray-green, 18 in (45 cm) or more long. **ZONES 6–10.**

Allium giganteum

Allium giganteum

A

Allium insubricum
syn. *Allium narcissiflorum*

A native of northern Italy, this species grows up to 12 in (30 cm) with slender, gray-green leaves surrounding a stem bearing an umbel of up to 12 purple, bell-shaped flowers, appearing in summer. Plant bulbs and seeds in fall (autumn). This species will grow well in full sun. Propagate by division of bulbs. **ZONES 6–9.**

Allium karataviense

The most striking feature of this spring flowering species from central Asia is the 2–3 broad flat leaves that spread widely from the base, dull gray-green in color, flushed with purple. The short flowering stems terminate in dense umbels of star-shaped white to pale purple flowers, their petals with darker central veins. The name is a latinization of Kara Tau, the mountain range in Kazakhstan where the species was first found. **ZONES 3–9.**

Allium moly
GOLDEN GARLIC

Native to southern Europe, in some parts of which its appearance in a garden was regarded as a sign of prosperity, *Allium moly* grows to 15 in (45 cm). Broad, gray-green basal leaves surround stems which each bear an umbel of up to 40 flowers. The bright yellow, star-shaped flowers appear in summer. *Moly* was the classical name of a magical herb, fancifully applied to this species by Linnaeus. **ZONES 7–9.**

Allium moly

Allium 'Purple Sensation'

Allium neapolitanum
NAPLES ONION, DAFFODIL ONION

This easily grown flowering onion produces fragrant, usually white flowers in loose heads in early spring. Flowering stems are 12 in (30 cm) tall. The plant will spread from seed in favorable conditions. Plant 3 in (8 cm) deep in fall (autumn). It can also be potted up and grown indoors. **ZONES 7–9.**

Allium oreophilum

The name of this central Asian species means 'mountain loving'. A small clump-forming plant, its fine leaves are slightly longer than the 6 in (15 cm) flowering stems. Numerous bell-shaped pinkish purple flowers are borne in small, loose umbels in spring and summer. **'Zwanenburg'** has deep carmine flowers. **ZONES 7–9.**

Allium karataviense

Allium neapolitanum

Allium porrum

Allium porrum
syn. *Allium ampeloprasum* var. *porrum*
LEEK

Of uncertain origin but now widely distributed in cooler parts of the northern hemisphere, the leek has broad concave leaves, the sheathing bases of which form a tight cylinder, this being the edible part. The flowering stem can be 3 ft (1 m) or more tall, with a large, spherical head of tiny gray-green to dull reddish flowers. Leeks are easier to grow than onions and more suited to cold climates. Seeds are sown in spring or summer, and plants are harvested as needed once the base of the leek is at least 1 in (25 mm) thick. **'Giant Winter Wila'** is one of the blue-leafed cultivars that mature through winter; **'Mammoth Blanche'** is typical of the very fat leeks, the bases of which can be up to 2½ in (6 cm) in diameter. **ZONES 5–10.**

Allium 'Purple Sensation'

This cultivar is rather similar to *Allium giganteum*, from which it may possibly be derived, differing in the deep rosy purple color of its 3 in (8 cm) diameter spherical heads, which are carried on 3 ft (1 m) stems. **ZONES 6–9.**

Allium sativum

Allium porrum 'Giant Winter Wila'

Allium porrum 'Mammoth Blanche'

Allium sativum
GARLIC

The common garlic is quite like an onion above ground but the bulb is compound, its tight papery sheath enclosing several to many daughter bulbs or 'cloves', whose pungent flavor is valued around the world for cooking, to say nothing of its renown as a remedy for and preventative of infections. The species is unknown in the wild, but closely related plants are found in central Asia. Dainty deep pink to white flowers appear in summer in small umbels on a stalk about 18 in (45 cm) tall. Plant individual cloves 2 in (5 cm) deep in fall (autumn) in warmer areas or in spring where there is frost risk. Garlic takes up to 5 or 6 months to mature; harvest when the leaves have turned yellow. Garlic planted near roses helps to keep aphids away. **ZONES 7–10.**

Allium schoenoprasum
CHIVES

The narrow, cylindrical leaves of this perennial plant are used for flavoring and garnishing savory dishes. Growing to 10 in (25 cm) in small, neat clumps, it bears numerous balls of mauve flowers in late spring and summer which are edible. Plant in full sun or part-shade and keep well watered. Propagate from seed or division of small bulbs. Lift and divide the clumps every 2 or 3 years to invigorate the tufts. Chives makes an attractive edging for the herb garden and can be grown in window boxes, troughs and flower pots. Frequent cutting stimulates bushy growth and tenderer leaves. A vigorous cultivar, **'Forescate'** has rose-pink flowers. **ZONES 5–10.**

Allium subhirsutum

This sweetly scented Mediterranean species grows well in dry, stony and sandy sites. Its leaves are characterized by their distinctly hairy margins. Delicate star-shaped white flowers are borne in loose umbels in spring on slender stems, up to about 12 in (30 cm) tall. **ZONES 9–10.**

Allium triquetrum
THREE-CORNERED LEEK, THREE-CORNERED GARLIC

One of the most easily recognized alliums, on account of its sharply 3-angled thick flowering stems, *Allium triquetrum* is native to the western Mediterranean region. It can form dense clumps with flattish, soft green leaves rather like bluebell (*Hyacinthoides*) leaves, and the 10–18 in (25–45 cm) flowering stems bear small umbels of gracefully drooping $\frac{3}{4}$ in (18 mm) white, bell-shaped flowers in spring and early summer. It commonly naturalizes and may sometimes become a nuisance. **ZONES 7–10.**

Allium tuberosum
CHINESE CHIVES, GARLIC CHIVES

Cultivated for centuries in India and China, this edible species is now widely grown throughout Asia as well as other parts of the world for its leaves, used as a green vegetable. It grows up to 18 in (45 cm) in height and has flat, narrow leaves and angled flowering stems. Fragrant, star-shaped white flowers are borne from summer to fall (autumn). Although grown in the tropics, this species is fairly frost tolerant. Mature clumps are easily divided. **ZONES 7–11.**

Allium schoenoprasum

Allium schoenoprasum 'Forescate'

Allium subhirsutum

Allium ursinum
RAMSONS, WOOD GARLIC

From Europe and northern Asia, this species is found in dampish, shaded woods and may become invasive in gardens, spreading by slender rhizomes. It is easily recognised by its broad, deep green basal leaves, up to 3 in (7 cm) wide and which exude a powerful garlic smell when crushed. Flowering stems are 12–15 in (30–38 cm) in height and bear loose umbels of quite large, starry white flowers in spring and early summer. **ZONES 5–9.**

ALLOCASUARINA
SHE-OAK

The 60 species of this entirely Australian genus were until recently included in the genus *Casuarina*. Both genera are evergreen, with needle-like branchlets which serve the function of leaves, while the true leaves are rings of tiny triangular scales at joints of the branchlets, needing a hand lens to be seen readily. Small male and female flower spikes, adapted for pollination by wind, are usually carried on separate plants. Only the males are conspicuous, changing the branch tips to a rich brown when appearing in their countless thousands. With their attractive usually drooping foliage, she-oaks are grown as shade or windbreak trees, and for timber or firewood.

CULTIVATION: The taller species are very fast growing and may be quite long lived; some will survive very dry conditions. Propagate from seed in spring.

Allium ursinum

Allium tuberosum

Allium triquetrum

Allocasuarina littoralis

Allocasuarina littoralis

Allocasuarina decaisneana
syn. *Casuarina decaisneana*
DESERT OAK

One of the most beautiful of all the she-oaks, this species grows in the most extreme environment—the low-rainfall red dunes of central Australia—where its deep roots tap reservoirs of subsoil moisture concealed beneath the sands. It grows to 50 ft (15 m), with a thick straight trunk, deeply furrowed corky bark, dense crown of weeping gray-green branchlets and the largest seed 'cones' in the genus, making it a fine ornamental in hot, arid areas. **ZONES 9–11.**

Allocasuarina decaisneana

Allocasuarina littoralis
syn. *Casuarina littoralis*
BLACK SHE-OAK

Occurring along the east coast of Australia, this erect, evergreen tree grows to 30 ft (9 m) with an irregularly conical, pointed crown, though often smaller in exposed coastal situations. It has closely fissured gray-brown bark on a short trunk and very fine, dark green foliage. In winter male flower spikes may tint male trees brown. The cylindrical 'cones' on female trees are narrow and often densely clustered. Fast growing and ornamental when young, it becomes sparse and unattractive after 15 to 20 years. It thrives in poor soils and tolerates sea spray. **ZONES 9–11.**

Allocasuarina robusta

Allocasuarina tessellata

Allocasuarina verticillata

Allocasuarina luehmannii

Allocasuarina scleroclada

Allocasuarina torulosa

Allocasuarina luehmannii
BULL OAK

One of the larger *Allocasuarina* species, the bull oak occurs naturally in semi-arid areas of southeastern Australia and grows to 50 ft (15 m) with a stout, rough-barked trunk and thick ascending branches. The dense rather stiff branchlets are olive green and the seed 'cones' are smallish, usually wider than they are long. It adapts to poor soils and tolerates poor drainage and makes a useful shade tree for drier areas. **ZONES 9–11.**

Allocasuarina scleroclada

The weeping foliage of this shrub species is distinctive and makes an interesting feature in the garden. It grows to about 5 ft (1.5 m) and often twice this in width. Native to the western side of the Australian continent, it will tolerate arid conditions. ***Allocasuarina robusta*** is somewhat similar but with a more erect habit; to 10 ft (3 m). **ZONES 9–10.**

Allocasuarina tessellata

One of many smaller species from the southern part of Western Australia, this species makes a stiff erect shrub 10–15 ft (3–5 m) tall with rather coarse dull green branchlets. The persistent seed 'cones' are longer than in most species, up to 2 in (5 cm), with the close-packed bracts fitting neatly together to make a smooth surface. It grows on rocky hillsides in a semi-arid region. **ZONES 9–10.**

Allocasuarina torulosa
syn. ***Casuarina torulosa***
FOREST OAK, FOREST SHE-OAK

Fast growing to 40–50 ft (12–15 m) or more, this graceful tree has corky, deeply furrowed bark. The fine-textured, drooping branches and branchlets are green when young, turning a deep purple-bronze in winter. Occurring naturally in eastern Australia, it is useful for coastal planting on heavier soils, for ornament, or on farms for shade, shelter or fuel. Young trees can be lightly pruned to thicken growth. **ZONES 8–11.**

Allocasuarina verticillata
syns ***Casuarina stricta, C. verticillata***
DROOPING SHE-OAK

This spreading tree from southeastern Australia grows to 30 ft (9 m), forming a neat, mop-headed tree with densely weeping branchlets. Male flowers appear from winter to early spring, covering the tree in golden brown anthers. It tolerates most soils and aspects, and is fairly frost, wind and drought resistant. It is frequently found as a much smaller specimen on exposed sea-cliffs, especially on shales. **ZONES 8–10.**

ALLOXYLON

The few species in this genus of evergreen rainforest trees are native to the warm east coast of Australia and to Papua New Guinea. Until recently they were included in the genus *Oreocallis*, now restricted to South American species, and earlier still in *Embothrium* (listed later in this book). Not widely available in nurseries, they are worth seeking out for their magnificent heads of scarlet or crimson flowers.

CULTIVATION: While they can withstand very light frosts, they are really plants for tropical or subtropical gardens with regular summer rainfall. They do best on loamy or sandy, humus-rich soil and dislike root disturbance, so they should be planted while still small. Sudden and unexplainable death of sapling trees is a common problem, the more so in areas that experience dry spells. Trees should be trained to a single trunk for the first 6 ft (1.8 m) or so. Propagate in spring from fresh seed.

Alloxylon flammeum
syn. ***Oreocallis* 'Wickhamii'**
TREE WARATAH, SCARLET SILKY OAK

This species reaches a height of 30–50 ft (10–15 m), at first with a bushy, erect growth habit but with age developing a wide, irregular head of branches. The variably lobed leaves are dark green and leathery. Terminal clusters of nectar-rich, orange-red flowers which look like waratahs or spider chrysanthemums are borne in profusion in late spring or early summer. **ZONES 9–11.**

Alloxylon pinnatum
syn. ***Oreocallis pinnata***
DORRIGO WARATAH

Less well known than *Alloxylon flammeum* and more difficult to grow, this species makes a tree to 30–60 ft (9–18 m) in its natural rainforest, but in gardens it is usually an erect shrub of 12–20 ft (3.5–6 m). Shiny, dark green leaves are divided right to the midrib into narrow lobes, appearing to be pinnate. Striking heads of crimson-pink flowers are borne at the branch tips in mid-summer. **ZONES 9–11.**

ALNUS
ALDER

Upright trees related to the birches (*Betula*), alders come mainly from cool to cold climates of the northern hemisphere, though in the Americas they range south along the Andes into Argentina. Though less attractive than the birches, they are very fast growing and their roots contain micro-organisms that can fix nitrogen from the air, adding to soil fertility. Light-loving trees themselves, alders act as nurse trees for

Alloxylon flammeum

Alloxylon pinnatum

Alnus nepalensis

Alnus orientalis

slower-growing conifers but die after they are overtopped by them and shaded out. The female catkins are egg-shaped, hanging in groups at branch tips, becoming hard and woody in the seeding stage. The bark is brown or blackish and sometimes furrowed. Alders from cool-temperate regions are deciduous but produce little in the way of fall (autumn) color. A few species from subtropical mountain areas are evergreen or semi-evergreen.
CULTIVATION: Most alders require a cool-temperate climate, or at least one in which winters are distinctly cold. A common use is for windbreaks. They do best in soil that is permanently moist, and some species (notably *A. glutinosa*) thrive in valley bottom areas where soil is too waterlogged for good growth of most other trees; many alders will also grow in very infertile or polluted soils. When planted for ornament or shade the trees should be shaped early to a single trunk, and branches trimmed to above head height. Propagate from seed or hardwood cuttings.

Alnus acuminata
syn. ***Alnus jorullensis***
MEXICAN ALDER, EVERGREEN ALDER

This evergreen species ranges all the way from northern Mexico through the Andean mountain chain to northwest Argentina. Now a popular tree for mild coastal areas in Australia and New Zealand, it is valued for its fast growth and broad crown of attractively weeping, birch-like foliage. Of compact size, it does not usually exceed 30 ft (9 m); however, in a very favorable site it can

Alnus acuminata

grow rapidly to over 50 ft (15 m); it can be kept trimmed. **ZONES 9–11.**

Alnus cordata
ITALIAN ALDER

From the mountains of southern Europe, this large alder has dense foliage and grows to 30–40 ft (9–12 m), with short side branches and broad, rounded, shiny dark green leaves and smooth, gray bark. In late winter or early spring it produces yellowish male catkins 3–4 in (8–10 cm) long at branch tips, followed by 1 in (25 mm) long seed cones. Adapts well to most situations and soils but does best near water. **ZONES 7–9.**

Alnus firma
JAPANESE ALDER

This beautiful alder from the mountains of Japan has narrow, sharply toothed and prettily textured leaves on gracefully arching branches. It may remain a large shrub to 10 ft (3 m) for many years, though it can ultimately reach 30 ft (9 m). It has attractive bark, with older squares of gray flaking off to reveal reddish new bark. The leaves often remain green late into fall (autumn). This alder is not widely planted outside Japan. **ZONES 5–9.**

Alnus glutinosa
BLACK ALDER, COMMON ALDER

In cold, bleak climates and on poor, boggy soils the common alder of Europe is sometimes the only tree apart from certain willows that will thrive. It can reach heights of 60 ft (18 m) in the wild but planted trees are seldom more than half that. The dark brown bark becomes deeply furrowed and checkered and the high crown of the tree is often irregular and rather open. The leaves of the cultivar **'Imperialis'** are dissected into narrow, pointed lobes. **ZONES 4–9.**

Alnus rubra

Alnus nepalensis
NEPAL ALDER

Though from medium altitudes in the Himalayas and southern China, this alder is not very frost hardy, nor does it thrive in warm lowland climates. Of open, sparse branching habit with smooth, pale gray bark, it has broad oval leaves up to 8 in (20 cm) long, bright green above, pale and satiny below. The flowers appear in fall (autumn). The long, thin male catkins are borne at the branch tips. It needs shelter and humidity or its large leaves become torn and scorched. **ZONES 9–10.**

Alnus orientalis
SYRIAN ALDER

This handsome alder occurs wild along river banks in Syria, southern Turkey and Cyprus, where it can grow to 50 ft (15 m). Its glossy green leaves are irregularly toothed. The male catkins, appearing in early spring, are covered in a sticky exudation before they expand to release their yellow pollen. **ZONES 7–10.**

Alnus rhombifolia
WHITE ALDER

Of wide occurrence in the western regions of North America, this handsome alder may reach a height of 100 ft (30 m), though 30–50 ft (9–15 m) is more usual. It has a spreading, rounded crown with the smaller branches pendulous, and the 3–5 in (8–12 cm) long leaves are pointed and strongly toothed. It has long male catkins which appear before the leaves in early spring. White alder is rarely cultivated outside its native region. **ZONES 5–9.**

Alnus glutinosa

Alnus rubra
syn. ***Alnus oregona***
RED ALDER

Ranging from Alaska to central California, this tree grows to 40–50 ft (12–15 m), usually branching into several trunks with pendulous lower branches. Bark is thin and pale gray. The large leaves have coarse marginal teeth and are dark green above with paler gray-green undersides often covered with orange down. This alder produces profuse yellow male catkins at the branch tips in early spring. Reasonably frost hardy, it will soon outgrow a small garden. **ZONES 6–9.**

ALOCASIA
ELEPHANT'S EAR

There are some 70 species of large-leafed rhizomatous and tuberous perennials in this genus from tropical southern and Southeast Asia. They have heart-shaped to arrowhead-shaped leaves from 8 in–36 in (20–90 cm) long depending on the species. The leaves are often long-stemmed with distinctive red or purple markings. The long-stemmed arum-like flowers, often obscured by the foliage, are not very showy. Closely related to taro *(Colocasia)*, the roots of some species are edible, but most contain poisonous crystals which cause numbing and swelling of the tongue and throat.
CULTIVATION: Most species are totally intolerant of frost and do best when grown in a warm, humid climate with moist, humus-rich soil and ample feeding. They thrive in the close atmosphere of a warm greenhouse. Propagate from seed, stem cuttings with a leaf bud or by dividing or cutting up the rhizomes.

Alnus glutinosa 'Imperialis'

Alnus firma

A

A

Alocasia cuprea

This species from Borneo has striking foliage. The leaves are relatively small, usually less than 12 in (30 cm) long, but they have a silvery purple to copper metallic sheen with contrasting green veins and red reverse and are held on stems up to 24 in (60 cm) long. **ZONES 11–12.**

Alocasia macrorrhiza

GIANT ELEPHANT'S EAR, CUNJEVOI, GIANT TARO

This species has 3 ft (1 m) long stalks which carry broad, arrowhead-shaped, glossy green leaves up to 3 ft (1 m) long. It produces insignificant but fragrant flowers on a spadix enclosed in a leaf-like, yellow-green spathe. **ZONES 10–12.**

ALOE

Occurring wild in Africa , Madagascar and the Arabian Peninsula, this genus of succulent-leafed plants consists of over 300 species, including trees, shrubs and perennials. The 'aloes' of traditional medicine is a bitter drug obtained from some shrubby African species. All are evergreen, mostly with distinct rosettes of sword-shaped leaves terminating the stem or branches. Leaves vary greatly between species in size, color, degree of succulence, and presence and distribution of prickles on the margins or faces. The flowers are tubular to narrowly bell-shaped, in long-stemmed spikes on which they open progressively from the base. These are followed by oval fruits $\frac{1}{4}$–2 in (0.6–5 cm) long, usually ripening from green to brown. Aloes hybridize quite freely, some attractive examples include ***Aloe speciosa* × *A. ferox*** and ***A. splendens* × *A. speciosa*.**

CULTIVATION: Nearly all aloes prefer a warm dry climate and well-drained soil, but many will tolerate a few degrees of frost once established. The larger species of aloes can be grown in full sun, the smaller types in part-shade. Propagation is from offsets or stem cuttings. Infestation by mealybug can be a problem.

Aloe arborescens 'Compton'

Aloe arborescens

Aloe alooides

From eastern Transvaal, this aloe has a short, unbranched trunk up to 6 ft (1.8 m) high, usually half-hidden by dead leaves and topped by a dense rosette of narrow, deeply channeled leaves with small teeth on their red-tinged margins. In spring and summer it bears yellow-green tubular flowers on 3–4 ft (1–1.2 m) tall spikes. **ZONES 10–11.**

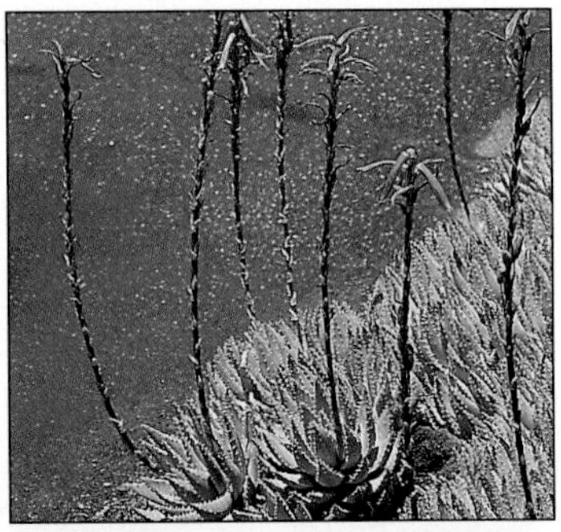

Aloe brevifolia

Aloe splendens × *Aloe speciosa*

Aloe alooides

Aloe buhrii

Aloe arborescens

CANDELABRA ALOE, KRANTZ ALOE

This shrubby species from south-eastern Africa can mound up to 6–10 ft (2–3 m) when in flower. The plants branch from the base into short, slender stems with both lateral and terminal rosettes, composed of rather narrow grayish blue leaves up to 24 in (60 cm) long, slightly downward curving and thorny edged. Branched spikes of scarlet red or yellow flowers appear from late winter to early spring. This species is both salt- and drought-resistant and marginally frost hardy. **'Pearson'** and **'Compton'** are just 2 of its cultivars. **ZONES 9–11.**

Aloe aristata

TORCH PLANT, LACE ALOE

Native to South Africa, this miniature aloe forms long-lived stemless clumps of rosettes only about 4 in (10 cm) high, and up to 12 in (30 cm) wide. Its finely tapering, deep green leaves have white surface spots, soft, serrated margins and are tipped by fine bristles. Loose spikes up to 24 in (60 cm) high of orange-red flowers develop in spring. Marginally frost hardy, it grows well in pots on window-ledges, or in rockeries. **ZONES 9–11.**

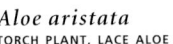

Aloe arborescens 'Pearson'

Aloe bainesii

Aloe aristata

Aloe bainesii

TREE ALOE

This is a large evergreen tree from South Africa which grows up to a lofty 70 ft (21 m) high with a 15 ft (4.5 m) spread. Long, narrow prickly leaves grow to 3 ft (1 m) in length. In spring and summer it bears medium-sized rose pink tubular flowers on a 24 in (60 cm) high flower spike. **ZONES 9–11.**

Aloe bakeri

Of somewhat sprawling habit, this rather rare species from Madagascar can form a dense mound if left undisturbed for many years. The narrow, twisting leaves are green-brown banded in a terracotta pink, often spotted on the upper side and with toothed margins. During the winter months the long, unbranched flower spikes carry racemes of tubular blooms in orange tones. **ZONES 10–12.**

Aloe brevifolia

A miniature aloe from South Africa's Cape Province, *Aloe brevifolia* forms tight clumps of fleshy rosettes only about 3 in (8 cm) in diameter, and its bluish green leaves are armed with many rather soft prickles. In early summer it produces unbranched flower spikes up to 18 in (45 cm) carrying dull scarlet bells tinged with green at the base. It has long been popular for growing in pots, window boxes and in rockeries. **ZONES 9–11.**

Aloe buhrii

An African evergreen plant with sword- or triangular-shaped leaves that grow to 16 in (40 cm). Foliage is tinged a bluish red color. Clusters of green-tipped, orange or red bell-shaped flowers, as well as brown seed capsules, appear in spring. **ZONES 10–11.**

Aloe marlothii

Aloe candelabrum

CANDELABRA ALOE

This species from Natal has an unbranched trunk 6–12 ft (1.8–3.5 m) high, usually covered with old, dry leaves and topped by a rosette of thick leaves up to 3 ft (1 m) long and 6 in (15 cm) wide, with sparse prickles on the undersides and finely toothed margins. As the species name suggests, the flowering stems are branched, with up to 12 upcurved spikes. The scarlet, orange or pinkish flowers open in winter. **ZONES 9–11.**

Aloe ciliaris

CLIMBING ALOE

This is unusual among aloes in being a scrambling climber that, with suitable support can reach 15 ft (4.5 m) in height. It branches freely from the base into many slender, elongated stems bearing well spaced short triangular leaves, edged with small white teeth, these longest where the sheath meets the stem. Short sprays of scarlet tubular flowers tipped with yellow open over a long period from spring to fall (autumn). It can be trained against a wall or trellis or left to cover large areas in an informal garden. **ZONES 9–11.**

Aloe claviflora

From Cape Province, South Africa, this species has blue-green foliage and reaches a spread of 3–7 ft (1–2 m). The 30 to 40 notched leaves are ovate to lanceolate and form a dense rosette. In spring and summer orange-red, tubular flowers open atop an 18 in (45 cm) tall flower spike. **ZONES 9–11.**

Aloe excelsa

Aloe cryptopoda

Aloe cryptopoda

Native to southern Africa, this species has green, pink-tinged lanceolate leaves 3 ft (1 m) long with marginal teeth forming a dense rosette. It bears red tubular flowers in spring and summer. **ZONES 9–11.**

Aloe dichotoma

Native to very arid areas of Namibia and adjacent Cape Province, this is one of the spectacular tree aloes of the rocky 'kopjes'. After many years' growth it can reach as much as 30 ft (9 m) with a dense, flat-topped crown of leaf rosettes topping a trunk that can measure 3 ft (1 m) or more in diameter. The blue-green leaves have finely toothed margins and in winter it produces 24 in (60 cm) branched spikes of crowded yellow flowers, the unopened buds green-tipped. **ZONES 9–11.**

Aloe excelsa

RHODESIAN TREE ALOE

Native to Zimbabwe, this species has fleshy, spiny lanceolate leaves growing to 30 in (75 cm) long in a single large rosette. The rosette grows atop a woody trunk that reaches 25 ft (8 m). It produces small, crimson tubular flowers in spring and summer from a central flower spike that grows 3 ft (1 m) tall. **ZONES 9–11.**

Aloe candelabrum

Aloe gariepensis

Aloe ferox

Aloe dichotoma

Aloe ferox

TAP ALOE, BITTER ALOE

From southern Africa, the single woody trunk of this frost-hardy species may grow to 15 ft (4.5 m) tall. The dense rosette of lance-shaped leaves, up to 3 ft (1 m) long, are bluish green with a spiny surface and reddish brown teeth on the margins. In spring, vivid orange-red blooms appear in a thick, round, brush-like terminal cluster on a single, slender stalk. **ZONES 9–11.**

Aloe gariepensis

Native to southern Africa, this succulent reaches 3 ft (1 m) tall. Its green, toothed leaves become reddish with age. A 4 ft (1.2 m) tall flower spike produces small, yellow tubular flowers in spring and summer. **ZONES 9–11.**

Aloe claviflora

Aloe harlana

This stemless rosette-forming aloe from Ethiopia can form a loose clump up to 2 ft (60 cm) across. The olive-green leaves are no more than 8 in (20 cm) long, and almost as broad at the base. In summer multi-branched flower spikes up to 3 ft (1 m) tall carry dark red, sometimes yellow blooms. **ZONES 9–11.**

Aloe humilis

Native to Cape Province in South Africa, this plant forms clusters of rosettes; each rosette is about 2½ in (6 cm) across. The green leaves have white toothed margins. In spring and summer small, coral red flowers open on 15 in (38 cm) tall flower spikes. **ZONES 9–11.**

Aloe marlothii

This aloe from Natal, Transvaal and Botswana forms a single very large rosette atop a trunk up to 8 ft (2.4 m) high, which is usually hidden by old dead leaves. The leaves are about 3 ft (1 m) long, dull gray-green and very thick, covered all over with short prickles. Orange-yellow flowers, held in tight cylindrical tapering spikes on a much-branched stalk, appear in winter. **ZONES 9–11.**

Aloe sessiliflora

Aloe pillansii

Aloe pluridens

Aloe petricola

From east Transvaal in South Africa, this succulent usually grows in large groups with bluish, lanceolate leaves reaching a length of 24 in (60 cm). Pale orange tubular flowers grow to $1\frac{1}{2}$ in (35 mm) in spring and summer. Scattered teeth appear along the margins of its 20 to 30 leaves. **ZONES 9–11.**

Aloe pillansii
TREE ALOE

This evergreen tree from western Cape Province in South Africa grows to a lofty height of 35 ft (about 10 m). Its stout trunk forms branches in the upper half. Gray-green leaves have curved teeth along their white margins and grow to 24 in (60 cm) long. **ZONES 9–11.**

Aloe plicatilis
FAN ALOE

With distinctive fan-like clusters of pale, blue-green succulent leaves, this shrub grows slowly to a height and spread of around 5 ft (1.5 m) with a stiff, multi-branched habit. Tubular scarlet flowers are borne in spring. Frost tender, it requires a sunny position with protection from hot afternoon sun and regular watering in winter and spring. **ZONES 9–11.**

Aloe pluridens

This is a shrubby species from Cape Province and Natal in South Africa that produces salmon-pink, tubular flowers in spring and summer from a 3 ft (1 m) tall flower spike. It grows to a height of 6–10 ft (1.8–3 m) with a single short trunk . Leaves are about 24 in (60 cm) long and rather narrow and channeled, the margins armed with numerous teeth. **ZONES 9–11.**

Aloe saponaria

Aloe rupestris

Aloe speciosa

Aloe speciosa × *Aloe ferox*

Aloe polyphylla

From the mountains of Lesotho comes this remarkable species, with clustered ball-like rosettes sitting directly on the ground, each consisting of numerous, crowded, incurved leaves arranged in 5 spiralling ranks. There is a tendency for its more distinctive features to be less evident in cultivation. In spring it produces branched flower spikes about 24 in (60 cm) high, the densely crowded flowers usually pale red to orange-pink. **ZONES 8–10.**

Aloe pratensis

This South African native has yellow-edged, bluish green ovate-lanceolate leaves. The leaf margins are rough with reddish, sharp teeth $\frac{1}{4}$ in (6 mm) long. In spring and summer this succulent produces a single inflorescence with a rounded head of green-tipped, tubular flowers. **ZONES 9–11.**

Aloe harlana

Aloe petricola

Aloe rupestris
syn. *Aloe pycnantha*

This tree-like succulent from Mozambique and Natal, South Africa, reaches a height of up to 25 ft (8 m). Small orange and yellow flowers open in spring and summer. Leaves are deep green, narrow, up to 30 in (75 cm) long, with small, red-brown teeth along the pink margins. **ZONES 10–11.**

Aloe saponaria
SOAP ALOE

Saponaria is Latin for 'soapy', and this well-known South African aloe was named thus because its leaf sap foams in water and can be used as a soap substitute. The plants form stemless rosettes of broad flat dark green leaves, usually closely flecked with white spots or streaks; the margins have close-set short teeth and the tips of the leaves soon die and curl, especially in dry conditions. The few-branched flowering stems are about 24 in (60 cm) high and bear very short head-like spikes of orange flowers in summer. This is one of the most easily grown aloes, surviving long periods without watering. **ZONES 9–11.**

Aloe plicatilis

Aloe polyphylla

Aloe pratensis

Aloe sessiliflora

This species is native to Transvaal and Natal. It has a large rosette with a central flower spike growing to 30 in (75 cm) tall. The leaves are green with red margins, the colour spreading with age; red flowers open in spring and summer. **ZONES 10–11.**

Aloe speciosa

This is a large aloe, reaching as high as 20 ft (6 m) with age in its native Cape Province, South Africa. Usually the trunk is unbranched and almost hidden by old dead leaves; it terminates in a dense rosette of fleshy dull green leaves 30 in (75 cm) long, with pale red margins and teeth. The short spikes of densely packed winter flowers are red in bud opening to greenish white. **ZONES 10–11.**

Aloe spectabilis
syn. *Aloe ferox* var. *xanthostachys*

A tree-like succulent from Natal in South Africa, this species varies in height from 6–12 ft (1.8–3.5 m), its spiny blue-green leaves have a reddish sheen. In spring and summer it bears red flowers. **ZONES 10–11.**

Aloe × spinosissima

This hybrid is one of the more manageably sized aloes, growing to about 3 ft (1 m) in flower and spreading into clumps of the same width. The name *Aloe × spinosissima* suggests something very spiny but the teeth that line the leaf margins are not very large or sharp. New rosettes grow from the base of the old ones. **ZONES 9–11.**

Aloe splendens

This medium-sized succulent from southwestern Arabia has dull green, triangular leaves that often have a purple sheen and grooves running towards the tip. Scarlet, tubular flowers appear in spring and summer. The Italian cultivar **'Spuria'** has reddish leaves 12–18 in (30–45 cm) long and pale red flowers. **ZONES 10–11.**

Aloe striata
CORAL ALOE

This species is distinctive for its usually stemless rosettes of broad, flattish, pink tinged, pale gray leaves with unarmed red margins and close-set, faint, green lines on the surface. The pendulous coral-red flowers are borne on multibranched upright stems in spring in loose, circular groups; they are unusually glossy and waxy, with a pouch-like swelling at the base of the tube. **ZONES 9–11.**

Aloe spectabilis (fruit)

Aloe striatula

From the mountains of South Africa, this shrubby, multi-stemmed aloe grows to about 6 ft (1.8 m) high. It has slender stems and bright green leaves about 10 in (25 cm) long with a distinct downward-curving habit and tiny teeth along the white margins. Short, dense spikes of yellow flowers grow from below the leaf rosettes on long, slender stalks during the summer months. **ZONES 9–11.**

Aloe umfoloziensis

This clump-forming aloe from Natal, South Africa has long, narrow, brown-green leaves have abundant white oblong marks and sharp serrations. Coral-red flowers open at the top of the flower spike which rises well above the plant, to a height of about 5 ft (1.5 m). **ZONES 10–11.**

Aloe variegata
TIGER ALOE, PARTRIDGE-BREASTED ALOE

Native to western South Africa and adjacent Namibia, this popular clump-forming species grows to around 12 in (30 cm) tall, its short erect stems concealed by very short overlapping pyramidal leaves that are boldly marked with white transverse bands and have finely serrated margins. In spring, clusters of rose-orange flowers appear at the ends of slender stalks. It has long been cultivated as an indoor and balcony plant in many parts of the world. **ZONES 9–11.**

Aloe vera
syn. *Aloe barbadensis*
MEDICINAL ALOE, MEDICINE PLANT, BURN PLANT

Renowned for its medicinal qualities, this short-stemmed species, its likely origin Arabia or northern Africa, grows to 24 in (60 cm) high and has rosettes of narrow, thick, lance-shaped, grayish green leaves with small whitish teeth on the margins. In summer, small orange-yellow flowers appear in spikes up to 3 ft (1 m) high. Its syrupy leaf juice is used in skin care products and for treatment of burns. **ZONES 8–11.**

ALONSOA
MASK FLOWER

This genus consists of some 12 species of perennials and subshrubs found in tropical western America from Mexico to Peru. They were named for Alonzo Zanoni, an eighteenth-century Colombian Secretary of State. The flowers are usually small, but often vividly colored, and open through most of the year.
CULTIVATION: Provide they receive some sun, mask flowers are very easily grown in any free-draining soil. Only very light frosts are tolerated, though plants can be propagated in autumn and overwintered under cover.

Aloe striata

Alonsoa warscewiczii

An evergreen perennial that in some climates (Zones 5–9) is short-lived and treated as an annual, this native of Peru can form a 24 in (60 cm) high subshrub in a frost-free climate. Named after botanist Joseph Warscewicz (1812–1866), it bears clusters of small, vivid orange-red flowers. Cultivars bear flowers in shades of pink and orange. **ZONES 9–11.**

ALOPECURUS
FOXTAIL GRASS

The 25 species of annual and perennial grasses from northern temperate regions that make up this genus include some species considered weeds, while others are ornamental with flowerheads suitable for use in dried-flower arrangements. They produce tufts of flat leaves and dense cylindrical flowering heads consisting of tightly packed small spikelets.
CULTIVATION: Frost-hardy plants, they need full sun or part-shade and moderately fertile, well-drained soil. Cut back in early summer before flowering. Propagate from seed or by division.

Alopecurus alpinus

This is a low-growing, loosely clumping perennial grass from subarctic Europe (extending to Scotland and northern England) with narrow leaves. In summer it produces stalked flowerheads that are purplish gray and softly hairy, oval in outline, and less than 1 in (25 mm) in length. **ZONES 3–8.**

Alopecurus lanatus
WOOLLY FOXTAIL GRASS

From mid-spring to mid-summer, this perennial species from the eastern Mediterranean produces very hairy, light green flowerheads only about $^3/_4$ in (18 mm) long but $^1/_2$ in (12 mm) wide. It is densely tufted and has felty, blue-green leaves with a silver-gray cast. It grows to around 12 in (30 cm) in height. **ZONES 6–10.**

Alopecurus pratensis 'Aureovariegatus'

This variegated cultivar of the common meadow foxtail of Europe, Asia and North Africa is a clump-forming perennial grass, spreading but non-invasive, the green leaves boldly striped and edged with gold. It bears pale green to purplish flowerheads to 4 in (10 cm) long in summer and reaches 4 ft (1.2 m). **ZONES 4–9.**

ALOYSIA

This genus consists of around 40 species of evergreen shrubs from North, Central and South America, grown for their aromatic foliage. The soft, cane-like branches have leaves arranged in opposite pairs or in whorls of three. Panicles of tiny flowers terminate the branches.
CULTIVATION: They prefer a well-drained, loamy or light-textured soil and plenty of summer watering. Tolerant of only mild frosts, they do best in sunny positions in warm, coastal environments. In cold areas they should be planted out new each year. Remove dead wood in early summer and prune well in late winter to maintain a bushy shape and encourage the flowers which are borne on current season's growth. Propagate by semi-hardwood cuttings in summer or soft-tip cuttings in spring.

Aloe vera

Aloe striatula

A

Aloysia triphylla
syn. *Lippia citriodora*
LEMON-SCENTED VERBENA

Grown for its heavily lemon-scented, crinkly pale to mid-green leaves, this shrub has an open, rather straggling habit and reaches a height and spread of 10 ft (3 m). Racemes of dainty, light lavender flowers appear in summer and fall (autumn). It needs regular pruning to improve its shape. Oil of verbena is produced from the leaves. **ZONES 8–11.**

ALPINIA
ORNAMENTAL GINGER

Of Asian and Pacific origin, these plants are widely cultivated in tropical and subtropical gardens, for their showy blooms, some as commercial cut flowers. They grow from fleshy rhizomes to form large clumps. The aboveground shoots are in fact pseudostems consisting of tightly furled leaf bases as in cannas and bananas. The large thin leaves form 2 rows. Although strictly speaking perennials, they do not die back and can be used in the garden like a shrub.

CULTIVATION: Alpinias are frost tender, but many will tolerate winter temperatures not far above freezing as long as summers are warm and humid. They appreciate part-shade, a warm, moist atmosphere and rich soil. Propagate by division.

Alpinia galanga

Alpinia galanga
GALANGAL, THAI GINGER

Although most alpinias are grown for ornament and are not regarded as edible, this Southeast Asian species is the source of an important spice, a vital ingredient of Thai cooking in particular. It is the thick, white-fleshed rhizome that is used, either freshly grated, dried or powdered ('laos powder'), to add a subtle piquancy to dishes such as curries. The plant makes a clump of leafy stems 6 ft (1.8 m) high. The flowers, white with pink markings, are not very showy. **ZONES 11–12.**

Alpinia purpurata
RED GINGER

From the Pacific Islands, this species produces showy spikes of small white flowers among vivid scarlet bracts throughout the year. The glossy leaves are narrow and lance-shaped. New plantlets sprout among the flower bracts and take root when the dying flower stems fall to the ground under the weight of the growing plantlets. The plants grow to 10 ft (3 m) tall. **ZONES 11–12.**

Alpinia purpurata

Alstonia pneumataphora

Alpinia zerumbet

Alstroemeria aurea

Alstroemeria aurea

Alpinia zerumbet
syns *Alpinia nutans, A. speciosa*
SHELL GINGER

This evergreen, clump-forming perennial grows to around 10 ft (3 m) with a spread of 5–10 ft (1.5–3 m). It has long, densely massed stems with broad, green leaves. The drooping sprays of flowers appear in spring and intermittently in other seasons, starting as waxy white or ivory buds, opening one at a time to reveal yellow lips with pink- or red-marked throats. **'Variegata'** has leaves irregularly striped yellow; it tends to be lower growing. **ZONES 10–12.**

ALSTONIA

A genus of 45 species of evergreen shrubs and trees found in Africa, Southeast Asia, Australasia and Central America. They have leathery, elliptical to lance-shaped leaves, often borne in whorls separated by intervals of bare stem. Inflorescences of small white, cream or green flowers are followed by long, bean pod-like fruits. All parts of these plants contain a milky sap rich in alkaloids which are poisonous.

CULTIVATION: These subtropical to tropical trees are largely frost-tender and should be grown in a mild, moist climate with humid, well-drained soil. They will grow in sun or part-shade. Propagate by cuttings or from seed, which should be sown immediately after ripening.

Alstonia scholaris
DEVIL TREE, PALI-MARI

Widely distributed through the Asian and African tropics, this species makes a 30–100 ft (9–30 m) tall, horizontally branching tree with a spread of up to 30 ft (9 m). It has glossy, deep green, lance-shaped leaves with heavy veining on the undersides. Its summer-borne creamy white flowers are tiny but profuse and are followed by deep blue fruit. Its bark is the source of a drug used to treat malaria. School students in southern India once used writing-tablets made from its pale lightweight timber; hence the species name. ***Alstonia pneumataphora*** which is similar to *Alstonia scholaris* is also grown in the tropics. **ZONES 10–12.**

Aloysia triphylla

ALSTROEMERIA
PERUVIAN LILY

Native to South America where they occur mostly in the Andes, these tuberous and rhizomatous plants with about 50 species are among the finest of all perennials for cutting, but they do drop their petals. Erect, wiry stems bear scattered, thin, twisted leaves concentrated on the upper half, and terminate in umbels of outward-facing flowers, usually with flaring petals that are variously spotted or streaked. They flower profusely from spring to summer.

CULTIVATION: All grow well in sun or light shade in a well-enriched, well-drained acidic soil. They soon form large clumps, bearing dozens of flowerheads. Propagate from seed or by division in early spring. They are frost hardy, but in cold winters protect the dormant tubers by covering with loose peat or dry bracken. Best left undisturbed when established, but one-year-old seedlings transplant well. Alstroemerias do well naturalized under trees or on sloping banks.

Alstroemeria aurea
syn. *Alstroemeria aurantiaca*

Native to Chile and the most common and easily grown species, this has heads of orange flowers, tipped with green and streaked with maroon. Leaves are twisted, narrow and lance-shaped. Several cultivars exist; **'Majestic'** and **'Bronze Beauty'** both have deep orange or bronzy orange flowers; they grow to 2–3 ft (0.6–1 m) with a similar spread. **ZONES 7–9.**

Alstroemeria, Dr Salter's Hybrids

This group of hybrid cultivars includes a wide range of colors. The flowerheads are more compact than in the Ligtu Hybrids, the flowers open more widely, and the 3 inner petals are more heavily marked. **'Walter Fleming'** has flowering stems up to 3 ft (1 m) tall and cream and gold flowers tinged with purple, the inner petals spotted red-purple. **ZONES 7–9.**

Alstroemeria, Dutch Hybrids

These are the alstroemerias that now dominate the cut-flower trade in many countries. They are bred mainly by one Dutch firm, and some of the newer cultivars are only made available to commercial cut-flower growers, who grow them under glass to avoid any rain damage to the blooms. The flowers, in compact umbels, are broad petalled and have heavily marked upper petals often in strongly contrasting colors. **'Friendship'**, **'Yellow Friendship'** and **'Mirella'** are examples of this type of hybrid. **ZONES 8–10.**

Alstroemeria haemantha
HERB LILY

This Chilean species has green leaves with a slightly hairy margin. The stiff flower stems up to 3 ft (1 m) tall carry up to 15 orange to dull red flowers during early summer, their upper petals splashed with yellow. The plants can spread by their fleshy rhizomes to form quite large patches. **ZONES 7–9.**

Alstroemeria ligtu
ST. MARTIN'S FLOWER

Also from Chile, this is one of the more cold-hardy species. Growing 24–36 in (60–90 cm) tall, it has very narrow leaves and large compound umbels of lilac, orange or red flowers which have purple or white streaks or spots. **ZONES 7–9.**

Alstroemeria, Dutch Hybrid, 'Mirella'

Alstroemeria psittacina

Alstroemeria, Dutch, 'Yellow Friendship'

Alstroemeria haemantha

Alstroemeria, Ligtu Hybrids

The well-known Ligtu Hybrids first appeared in Britain in the late 1920s, when *Alstroemeria ligtu* was crossed with *A. haemantha.* They come in a range of colors from cream to orange, red and yellow, but have been overshadowed in recent years as cut flowers by other hybrid strains derived from *A. aurea.* The plants die down soon after flowering. **ZONES 7–9.**

Alstroemeria psittacina
syn. *Alstroemeria pulchella*
NEW ZEALAND CHRISTMAS BELL

Though native to Brazil, *Alstroemeria psittacina* gets its common name from its popularity in New Zealand, where its narrow, crimson and green flowers are borne at Christmas. The well spaced stems, about 24 in (60 cm) high, spring from tuberous roots. Easily grown in warm-temperate climates, it can spread rapidly and prove difficult to eradicate. **ZONES 8–10.**

ALTERNANTHERA

Around 80 species from most warmer parts of the world make up this genus of annuals and perennials (and a few aquatics) allied to *Gomphrena.* They are mostly low sprawling or prostrate plants, with weak stems and simple leaves arranged in opposite pairs. Flowers are very small, concealed in dense clusters of chaff-like white or straw-colored bracts that appear at the leaf nodes. At least one species of *Alternanthera* is used in Asia as a green vegetable and for medicinal purposes. At least 2 species are grown for their colorful summer foliage.

CULTIVATION: Plant in humus-rich, well-drained soil in part-shade or full sun. Propagation is from cuttings or seed in spring.

Alstroemeria, Dr Salter's, 'Walter Fleming'

Alstroemeria Dutch Hybrid

Alyogyne huegelii

Alternanthera philoxeroides
ALLIGATOR WEED

This South American species is a noxious plant in some warm countries, second only to water-hyacinth (*Eichhornia*) among aquatic weeds that cause economic loss. **ZONES 10–12.**

ALYOGYNE

These hibiscus-like shrubs come from the drier regions of southern and western Australia and are fast-growing, erect, leggy plants about 6–10 ft (1.8–3 m) tall. The large, funnel-shaped flowers, borne singly near branch tips, are showy but delicate and short lived, usually in shades of lilac or mauve.

CULTIVATION: They will suit any frost-free warm climate and need full sun, shelter from strong winds and moderately fertile, well-drained soil. They can be improved by regular tip pruning after they have finished flowering. Propagate from seed or cuttings in summer.

Alstroemeria, Dutch, 'Yellow Friendship'

Alyogyne hakeifolia

Alyogyne hakeifolia
syn. *Hibiscus hakeifolius*
RED-CENTERED HIBISCUS

This Western Australian species grows to 10 ft (3 m) tall with upright habit and simple linear leaves. The funnel-shaped flowers are pale mauve (less commonly yellow or cream) with dark red centers, and appear in spring and summer. **ZONES 10–11.**

Alyogyne huegelii
syn. *Hibiscus huegelii*
LILAC HIBISCUS

Native to Western Australia, this spreading, semi-deciduous shrub grows to a height and spread of 8 ft (2.4 m) and blooms in late spring and summer, bearing lilac (sometimes pinkish) flowers up to 6 in (15 cm) across which open in succession from early spring to late summer. The deeply lobed leaves are slightly hairy with irregularly serrated margins. Prune often for compact growth. **ZONES 10–11.**

Alyssum spinosum

Alyssum murale

Amanita muscaria

Amaranthus tricolor 'Joseph's Coat'

Amaranthus caudatus

Amaranthus tricolor 'Flaming Fountain'

Amaranthus tricolor

ALYSSOIDES

The name of this genus of only 3 species of herbaceous perennials was intended to indicate a close relationship or resemblance to *Alyssum*. In appearance, though, they are more like wallflowers (*Erysimum*), being distinguished from these and most other crucifers by their fat, bladder-like fruits. They are natives of southern Europe and western Asia, growing in rocky places, and in the garden are likewise best suited to the rockery. Rare in cultivation, this genus is occasionally grown by enthusiasts. **CULTIVATION:** Propagation is normally from seed.

Alyssoides utriculata

This is a multi-branched, short-lived, shrubby species from southern Europe and Turkey with densely crowded leaves. It produces flowering stems of yellow blooms in spring and summer and also bears decorative seed pods. It does well on dry banks, in rock gardens and at the front of borders. **ZONES 6–9.**

ALYSSUM

MADWORT

The commonly grown bedding alyssum is now classified under *Lobularia*, but there are still some 170 species of annuals, perennials and subshrubs in this genus and many of them are superb rockery plants. They are mainly low spreaders with small elliptical leaves. In spring and early summer they are smothered in heads of tiny white, cream, yellow or pink flowers. Most are less than 8 in (20 cm) tall with a few of the shrubbier species reaching 24 in (60 cm). **CULTIVATION:** Plant in full sun with gritty, well-drained soil. Alyssums are ideal for growing in rock crevices and as dry-stone wall plants, though it is important that they are given an occasional soaking in spring and summer. Most species are fairly frost hardy and are propagated from seed or small cuttings.

Alyssum murale

YELLOW TUFT

One of the taller species, this native of southeastern Europe grows to around 18 in (45 cm) tall. Its leaves are gray-green and ½–1 in (12–25 mm) long. The flowers are yellow. **ZONES 7–9.**

Alyssum spinosum

Found naturally in southern France and southeastern Spain, this species is a twiggy subshrub that grows to 24 in (60 cm) tall. It has gray-green to silver foliage and the branches are spiny tipped. The flowers open white and become purple tinted as they age. ***Alyssum spinosum* var. *roseum*** has light to deep pink flowers. **ZONES 8–9.**

AMANITA

Mentioned here for their importance as poisonous plants and for their place in folklore and religious rituals, this genus includes some of the most notorious toadstools. Most deadly is the death cap, *Amanita phalloides*, which kills by inflicting irreversible liver damage on those unfortunate enough to eat it. Like most genera of fungi, *Amanita* occurs worldwide, the number of species difficult to estimate. They share with other toadstools the features of a 'veil' or torn ring of thin tissue encircling the stem below the cap, with a second one right at the base. These are danger signs of some of the most poisonous fungi, but it should be emphasized that *no* fungus should be eaten unless it is a kind with which you are closely familiar.
CULTIVATION: These fungi are never cultivated but grow naturally in grass and forest litter, usually beneath trees. Like all fungi they feed on other organic matter, either living or dead. Mushrooms, toadstools and other such larger fungi are merely the fruiting bodies sent up by the more extensive plant concealed below ground, in tree trunks or rotting logs, consisting of countless fine thread-like feeding cells.

Amanita muscaria

FLY AGARIC

This species, widely distributed in temperate regions of the northern hemisphere, may be familiar even to those who have never seen one growing, as the archetypal toadstool of children's books on elves and fairies—the elf or gnome is usually pictured sitting on top of one. It is in fact quite poisonous though not always fatally so. In some shamanistic religions of northern Asia it was consumed by the shaman to induce a trance-like state, and some botanists believe the *soma* of Sanskrit texts was this fungus. **ZONES 5–9.**

AMARANTHUS

The 60 or so species of annuals and short-lived perennials that make up this genus range through most warmer parts of the world and include weeds, leaf vegetables and grain crops as well as a few ornamentals, grown for their brilliant foliage, curious flowers and adaptability to hot, dry conditions. They are popular bedding plants, with large and attractively colored leaves and minute flowers borne in drooping tassel-like spikes.
CULTIVATION: A sunny, dry position with protection from strong winds is essential, and they enjoy a fertile, well-drained soil, mulched during hot weather. They are marginally frost hardy and in cool climates are usually brought on under glass before planting out in late spring. Prune when young to thicken growth. Prepare soil for planting with plenty of manure, and water seedlings regularly. Protect from snails when young and watch for caterpillars and aphids. Propagate from seed.

Amaranthus caudatus

LOVE-LIES-BLEEDING, TASSEL FLOWER

This species, growing to 4 ft (1.2 m) or more high, has oval, dull green leaves and dark red flowers in long, drooping cords, their ends often touching the ground. Flowers appear in summer through to fall (autumn). In many old gardens this plant was used to give height in the center of circular beds. **ZONES 8–11.**

Amaranthus tricolor

Native to tropical Africa and Asia, this quick-growing annual has given rise to many cultivated strains, some used as leaf vegetables (Chinese spinach), others as bedding plants with brilliantly colored leaves. They are bushy annuals, reaching about 3 ft (1 m) high and 18 in (45 cm) wide. Tiny red flowers appear in summer. **'Flaming Fountain'** has leaves that are deep green at the base, then bronze tinted higher up, and then entirely blood red at the top. **'Joseph's Coat',** has brilliant bronze, gold, orange and red variegated 8 in (20 cm) long leaves which retain their coloring into late fall (autumn). **ZONES 8–11.**

AMARYLLIS

'To sport with Amaryllis in the shade ... ' wrote Milton, referring to the supposed beautiful shepherdess of ancient times, and her name was adopted in the next century by Linnaeus for some of the most beautiful of all flowering bulbs. Linnaeus's concept of *Amaryllis* was in fact a mixed one, including the American plants we now know as *Hippeastrum* as well as the familiar South African belladonna lily. Earlier this century a battle raged among botanists and bulb enthusiasts over which of these plants the name should be restricted to, and the belladonna faction seems to have won. As now recognized the genus consists of a single species, occurring wild only in southwestern Cape Province. Its notable feature is the way its long-stemmed umbels of magnificent rose-pink flowers appear in late summer and early fall (autumn) from leafless bulbs, the bright green, rather succulent leaves emerging after the flowers wither. Occasionally grown are generic hybrids between *Amaryllis* and some related genera, the best known being × *Amarcrinum* (with *Crinum*) and × *Amarygia* (with *Brunsvigia*).

CULTIVATION: Plant large bulbs in late summer at soil level or just below, in well-drained soil. A fairly sunny position is best in cool areas, but they may need light shade in very warm areas. Cut down flower stalks once flowering is finished but ensure the plant is well watered through winter. Grown easily from seed, it often self-sows freely.

Amaryllis belladonna
syn. *Callicore rosea*
BELLADONNA LILY

This outstanding plant is a gardener's dream—moderately frost hardy, easy to grow and, as the name *belladonna* ('beautiful lady') implies, very beautiful. A sturdy, fast-lengthening stem up to 30 in (75 cm) high is topped with a glorious display of rosy pink, lily-like flowers about 4 in (10 cm) long. The strap-like basal leaves appear in a large clump after the long flowering period. Over a number of years the bulbs can multiply to form a clump up to 24 in (60 cm) or so in width. Many selections have been named as cultivars, among the best known being **'Hathor'**, large white, **'Capetown'**, dark crimson-pink, and **'Spectabilis'**, rose-pink and white, many-flowered. **ZONES 8–11.**

AMELANCHIER
SERVICEBERRY, SNOWY MESPILUS, JUNEBERRY

These shrubs and small trees, mostly native to cool climates of North

Amelanchier lamarckii

Amaryllis belladonna 'Hathor'

America, belong to the pome-fruit group of trees and shrubs in the rose family, which includes apples, pears and quinces as well as many 'berry' shrubs. Most *Amelanchier* species are deciduous, with simple oval leaves, clusters of white flowers, frequently with long narrow petals, and small rounded fruit ripening to purple or black and often sweet and edible. Some species make attractive, graceful trees, valued for the display of snowy white flowers in spring and for their fall (autumn) coloring.

CULTIVATION: They do best in moist, fertile soil in a grassy glade in the shelter of other trees but receiving ample sun. Propagation is normally from seed or by layering.

Amelanchier alnifolia
SASKATOON SERVICEBERRY, WESTERN SERVICEBERRY

Native to a wide area from central Alaska down the Rocky Mountains to Colorado, this species is commonly a shrub of 6 ft (1.8 m) or more, branching from the base. Clusters of white flowers, borne among its small, coarsely toothed leaves in late spring are followed by small, sweet, blue-black fruit. It is of limited value as an ornamental, but extremely cold hardy. **'Pembina'** is one of its cultivars. **ZONES 4–9.**

Amelanchier arborea
syn. *Amelanchier canadensis* of gardens
DOWNY SERVICEBERRY

Occurring naturally in the eastern USA, this easily grown tree reaches about 20 ft (6 m) in gardens, usually with a narrowish crown and drooping lower branches. The finely toothed, pointed leaves are covered with white down as they emerge

Amelanchier alnifolia

Amaryllis belladonna

Amelanchier arborea

in spring. Profuse flowers, in short upright sprays, are followed in early summer by small fleshy fruit. In fall (autumn) the foliage turns red, orange or yellow. **ZONES 4–9.**

Amelanchier × *grandiflora*
APPLE SERVICEBERRY

Amelanchier × *grandiflora* is a garden-origin hybrid between *A. arborea* and *A. laevis* and combines the most valued qualities of both parents: it has larger flowers in longer racemes than *A. arborea* and larger and better fruit than *A. laevis.* It is a low-branching shrub or small tree about 20 ft (6 m) tall, valued for its profuse flowers, fruit and leaf coloring. Quite a number of cultivars have been named. **ZONES 4–9.**

Amelanchier laevis
ALLEGHENY SERVICEBERRY

Valued as an ornamental, this species from eastern USA and Canada grows on sheltered slopes and in ravines. New leaves are bronze purple and almost hairless, and in spring fragrant white flowers appear among them. The sweet blackish fruit are traditionally used by American hill people for pies and preserves. Fall (autumn) foliage is usually red. **ZONES 4–9.**

Amelanchier lamarckii

The origin of this species has been the subject of speculation: in the past it has been much confused with *Amelanchier*

Amelanchier arborea

comedensis and *A. laevis.* It makes a spreading shrub or small tree to 30 ft (9 m). The leaves are broad and deep green, with a coating of silky hairs when young. White flowers appear in spring in drooping clusters; small edible fruit ripen to black. **ZONES 6–9.**

Amelanchier ovalis
syn. *Amelanchier vulgaris*
SNOWY MESPILUS

A large deciduous shrub growing to 10 ft (3 m). The only species of this genus from Europe, it often suckers from the roots and often occurs naturally on limestone. The new growth is covered with fine hairs but leaves soon become smooth and mid-green with the white spring flowers, clustered in groups of up to 8, followed by deep blue fruit. Although of less graceful habit than some other amelanchiers, this species has the largest flowers of any. **ZONES 6–9.**

A

Amelanchier utahensis
UTAH SERVICEBERRY, JUNEBERRY

Widely distributed in the Rocky Mountains at elevations up to 10,000 ft (3,000 m) this shrubby species is similar to *Amelanchier alnifolia* but the white flowers are smaller and in shorter sprays. The bluish purple berries are also smaller, but were valued highly as food both by Native Americans and European settlers. It grows to between 6 ft (1.8 m) and 15 ft (4.5 m) in height, branching from ground level. Its fragrant white flowers cover the bush in spring before the leaves appear. **ZONES 3–9.**

AMHERSTIA
PRIDE OF BURMA

The one species in this genus, considered among the most beautiful of all flowering trees, was named for Lady Sarah Amherst, a nineteenth-century botanist and collector whose husband became Viceroy of India. It is native to Burma.
CULTIVATION: A tropical tree, it succeeds only in equatorial regions with year-round rainfall, but even in these regions it is not common due to difficulties in propagation. Seed is almost impossible to obtain and cuttings are very difficult to strike, so layering of branches using pots raised on stands is usually the only way. *Amherstia* likes a very sheltered position, even part-shaded by larger trees.

Amelanchier utahensis

Amherstia nobilis

This spreading tree grows to 40 ft (13 m), with large bipinnate leaves up to 3 ft (1 m) long. Briefly deciduous in the dry season, the drooping leaflets have whitish undersides; new leaves are coppery pink. In the wet tropics, through much of the year, it bears sprays of orchid-like flowers 4 in (10 cm) across with crimson petals, the upper ones gold-tipped. **ZONE 12.**

AMMOBIUM
WINGED EVERLASTING

This genus from eastern Australia consists of 2 or 3 species of perennials, one of which (*Ammobium alatum*) has excellent flowers for cutting and drying; these should be harvested before the flowers fully open. The leaves are produced in basal rosettes and are lance-shaped and downy.
CULTIVATION: They are usually grown as annuals in cool-temperate zones, although if winter temperatures do not go below 20°F (–5°C) and soil is well drained they will survive quite well. Plant in full sun in light soil and propagate from seed.

Amorphophallus paeoniifolius

Amorphophallus bulbifer

Ammobium alatum

This upright plant grows to a height of 3 ft (1 m) and spread of 18 in (45 cm), and has silvery gray leaves that extend down the stems as narrow wings. The everlasting flowerheads are bright yellow with white, papery bracts, and are 1 in (25 mm) across. **ZONES 8–10.**

AMORPHOPHALLUS

The literal translation of the botanical name of this genus of bulbous plants is 'deformed penis'. The inflorescence structure consists of a large encircling bract (spathe) from the center of which emerges a fleshy spike of tiny flowers, the male and female flowers arranged in separate zones. The spike terminates in a bare portion called by botanists the 'sterile appendage'. In the case of *Amorphophallus* it is large and often knob-like, and is the source of the foul smell given off by many of this species' flowers. The whole arrangement may be of impressive size, and in the case of the renowned Sumatran species, ***A. titanum***, it may reach as much as 8 ft (2.4 m) tall and 5 ft (1.5 m) across. There is a famous specimen of this in the Tropical House at Kew Gardens, London, cultivated for over a century, which flowers every decade or so.

Most of the 100 or so species come from tropical Asia and Africa. They are leafless in the tropical dry season, dying back to a large underground tuber. At the start of the wet season they send up their flowers, shortly followed by a single, deeply lobed leaf that may be quite large and long stalked. These plants are grown mainly as curiosities in botanical gardens, except for a few grown for their edible roots, such as ***A. rivieri* 'Konjac'** and ***A. campanulatus. A. bulbifer*** is an easily grown species, though frost-tender, with an urn-like spathe of medium size.
CULTIVATION: Mostly tropical and frost tender, these plants prefer a sheltered, humid position and deep, fertile, humus-rich soil. Water well in the summer growing season. After the foliage dies back in fall (autumn) the tuber should be kept fairly dry. In colder climates the tubers can be lifted and stored over winter. Propagation is mainly by transplanted tubers, which usually multiply by small offsets.

Amorphophallus titanum

Amorphophallus paeoniifolius
ELEPHANT YAM, TELINGO POTATO

Of wide occurrence in tropical Asia and Australasia, this species has a solitary leaf up to 3 ft (1 m) long on a dark green, pale-spotted stalk. The purple and green, white-spotted spathe, up to 10 in (25 cm) across, has a protruding spadix with a very large, spongy, deep purple terminal knob. **ZONES 11–12.**

AMPELOPSIS

A genus of about 5 species of deciduous vines in the grape family, occurring wild in temperate Asia and North America. Climbing by tendrils, they have leaves that are compound with radiating leaflets, or simple and toothed. Insignificant flowers are followed by small, rather dry berries, mostly bluish or blackish. These climbers are valued for their fall (autumn) color as well as their decorative fruit.
CULTIVATION: Grow in a sunny or partially shaded position in a moisture-retentive, but well-drained soil. They are fully hardy, grow rapidly and need strong support with plenty of room to spread. Cut back hard to the main branches when berries have finished. Propagate from cuttings in summer or by layering in fall.

Ampelopsis brevipedunculata
syns *Ampelopsis heterophylla, Vitis heterophylla*
TURQUOISE-BERRY VINE, PORCELAIN VINE

This vigorous, deciduous climber will twine, with the aid of tendrils, 15 ft (4.5 m) or more. It has grape-like, lobed leaves, small greenish flowers in summer, and in fall (autumn) bunches of berries like miniature grapes that ripen from

Amherstia nobilis

Ampelopsis brevipedunculata 'Elegans'

Anacardium occidentale

Anagallis arvensis

Amsonia tabernaemontana

Amsonia tabernaemontana

pale green to turquoise, bright blue and violet. The leaves of ***Ampelopsis brevipedunculata* var. *maximowiczii*** are variable and larger than the species. The cultivar ***A. b.* 'Elegans'** has white and pink marbled leaves. **ZONES 4–9.**

AMPHITECNA

CALABASH

Grown for their ornamental fruit as well as their attractive white or greenish flowers, these small trees from Central and South America and the West Indies should not be confused with the true calabashes (*Crescentia*), the gourd-like fruit of which is hollowed out to make carrying receptacles. The gourds of *Amphitecna* are smaller and unsuited for such uses. The smallish evergreen leaves are simple.

CULTIVATION: These tropical plants demand steady, warm temperatures and regular water. They prefer a fairly light soil and most are at home in coastal conditions. Seed is the usual method of propagation.

Amphitecna latifolia

syn. ***Enallagma latifolia***

BLACK CALABASH, SAVANNA CALABASH

Occurring naturally in lowland tropical America from Costa Rica to Ecuador, this species grows to around 30 ft (9 m) high and has dark green leaves 3–8 in (8–20 cm) long. The white tubular flowers are carried singly or in groups of 2 or 3 and are followed by 3 in (8 cm) long, ball-like, purplish green fruit. **ZONES 11–12.**

AMSONIA

BLUE STAR

A genus of around 20 species of perennials and subshrubs native to southern Europe, western Asia, Japan and North America. They grow to around 3 ft (1 m) tall and have bright to deep green, narrow, lance-shaped leaves. Stems and leaves bleed milky sap when cut. The flowers, borne mainly in summer, are tubular with widely flared mouths. They are carried in phlox-like heads at the stem tips.

CULTIVATION: Amsonias are easily grown in any moist, well-drained soil that does not dry out in summer.
Plant in full sun or part-shade. They are moderately to very frost hardy and generally die back to the rootstock in winter. Propagattion is from seed, early summer cuttings or by division in late winter.

Amsonia orientalis

Almost extinct in its native northeastern Greece and northwestern Turkey, this somewhat shrubby species grows to 3 ft (1 m) tall. It has strong stems that become woody at the base. The leaves are about 2½ in (6 cm) long and the profuse flowers, which are purple-blue, are up to ½ in (12 mm) wide. **ZONES 5–10.**

Amsonia tabernaemontana

BLUE STAR, BLUE DOGBANE

Amsonia tabernaemontana is a delightful perennial from northeastern and central USA. Stiff stems, 24–36 in (60–90 cm) tall, are topped by pyramidal clusters of small, star-shaped flowers of pale blue from late spring to summer, flowering along with peonies and irises. The leaves are narrow to elliptical and about 2½ in (6 cm) long. This species needs minimal care if given a moist, fertile soil in full sun to light shade. It is good in the perennial border or in a damp wildflower meadow. The species name commemorates a famous sixteenth-century German herbalist, who latinised his name as Tabernaemontanus. **ZONES 3–9.**

AMYLOTHECA

AUSTRALIAN MISTLETOE

The Australian mistletoes (of which there are 10 or so different genera) are rather more showy in flower than the common European mistletoe, *Viscum album*, but grow in much the same way, attaching themselves to the branches of trees, especially eucalypts. Their sometimes green-tipped red or coral flowers appear in summer.

CULTIVATION: Mistletoe seeds arrive on tree branches by courtesy of birds who eat their juicy berries. They develop into bushy plants, almost like airborne shrubs, with pendulous branches. Although parasites, they do have leaves of their own and so can photosynthesize their own sugars. Their leaves often look very like those of the host tree. It is wise to remove them, as a heavy growth of mistletoe may seriously weaken or even kill a tree.

Amylotheca dictyophleba

This species is native to the rainforests of eastern Australia. It is shrub-like with thick stems up to 5 ft (1.5 m) long. The leaves are 3–4 in (8–12 cm) long and it bears green-tipped red flowers in summer and fall (autumn). **ZONES 10–11.**

ANACARDIUM

CASHEW

Although it includes 8 species of semi-deciduous small trees from tropical America, only one species of this genus has been much cultivated, namely *Anacardium occidentale*, the cashew. Both branches and foliage have a very awkward, untidy aspect so the cashew tree is rarely grown for its ornamental qualities. Stiff sprays of small pinkish flowers (fragrant at night) are followed by the curious fruits, consisting of 2 parts. The 'cashew apple', actually a swollen, fleshy stalk, is colored, edible and up to 4 in (10 cm) long and 2 in (5 cm) in diameter. Sitting in its hollowed apex is the true fruit, curved like the nut, with an outer fleshy husk containing an extremely acrid, resinous sap which can badly burn the skin; this must be removed before the edible kernel can be used, requiring gloves to protect the skin. Most of the world's cashew crop comes from India, where the long, hot dry season suits its cultivation. The young leaves are also used as a salad vegetable in some countries but they are only sweet and edible on selected trees.

CULTIVATION: Fast growing when young, cashews can be grown in the warmer subtropics as well as the tropics. Propagation is easy from fresh seed, planted directly into the ground.

Anacardium occidentale

Growing as tall as 25 ft (8 m) but usually about half that height with a spreading, irregular crown, the cashew produces flowers early in the wet season; fruit ripen later in the wet. **ZONES 11–12.**

ANAGALLIS

PIMPERNEL

These are low-growing, often mat-forming annuals and perennials with small, heart-shaped to elliptical, bright green leaves arranged in opposite pairs. In spring and summer small, 5-petalled flowers appear in profusion on short stems. The flowers usually arise from the leaf axils or occasionally in small racemes at the stem tips. They come in a variety of colors including pink, orange, red, blue and white.

CULTIVATION: Plant in full sun in any well-drained soil that does not dry out entirely in summer. The more attractive, less vigorous species are excellent rockery plants. Propagate annuals from seed; perennials from seed, by division or from small tip cuttings. Some of the weedy species self-sow only too readily.

Anagallis arvensis

SCARLET PIMPERNEL, COMMON PIMPERNEL

Widely regarded as a weed, this European native behaves as an annual, biennial or short-lived perennial depending on the climate. It is a sprawling plant with ½ in (12 mm) long, rounded, bright green leaves on stems up to 18 in (45 cm) long. Small, orange flowers appear in the leaf axils from spring to fall (autumn). Brilliant deep blue flowers are available in ***Anagallis arvensis* var. *caerulea*.** Both the orange and the blue forms are common in the wild. **ZONES 7–10.**

Ananas comosus

Anaphalis javanica

Anagallis monellii
syns *Anagallis linifolia, A. collina*

This charming little plant is grown for its brilliant blue or scarlet flowers of ½ in (12 mm) diameter, which appear during summer. This species grows to under 18 in (45 cm), with a spread of 6 in (15 cm) or more. ZONES 7–10.

Anagallis tenella
BOG PIMPERNEL

Found in western Europe, this prostrate perennial has stems up to 6 in (15 cm) long that root as they grow. It is seldom over 1 in (25 mm) high and has a spread of around 12 in (30 cm). The funnel-shaped flowers are soft pink, occasionally white, borne in summer. Growing in boggy spots in the wild, it is best suited to the edges of ponds and other damp, sheltered spots. **'Studland'** has scented, deeper pink flowers. ZONES 8–10.

ANANAS
PINEAPPLE

As well as its obvious importance as a commercial crop this genus of 8 species of South American bromeliads includes several ornamental plants that make an attractive addition to subtropical and tropical gardens. They have large rosettes of narrow, tapering, tough leaves with sharply toothed or spiny edges. The flowers, which develop into the familiar compound fruit shape, are usually reddish purple, each backed by a bract and borne in a crowded head at the top of a short, stout stem that emerges from the center of the leaf rosette.

CULTIVATION: All species are very frost tender and can be grown outdoors only in the tropics and subtropics; in cooler climates they can be grown as indoor or conservatory plants, but must have strong light. Plant in full sun in fertile, well-drained soil. They are usually propagated from the basal suckers that develop on mature rosettes. Alternatively you can remove the leafy top from the fruit and treat it as a cutting, either rooting it in soil or water.

Ananas bracteatus
RED PINEAPPLE, WILD PINEAPPLE

This 3 ft (1 m) tall species has basal leaves very like those of the common pineapple (*Ananas comosus*). The leaf edges and the floral and fruiting parts often develop pink tints. Summer-borne, 6 in (15 cm) inflorescences of lavender to red flowers are partially enclosed by red bracts. The small, orange-red fruit rarely reaches edible size but is an interesting feature. The cultivar **'Tricolor'** is the form in which this species is usually grown, with leaves edged and striped creamy white. ZONES 11–12.

Ananas comosus
PINEAPPLE

Cultivated by Central American Indians for centuries, the pineapple's wild origin is believed to be in Brazil. It was praised by early European visitors as the finest of all fruit and shipped back to the Old World. To offer the expensive exotic to a guest was a great compliment; hence the use of pineapple motifs in architecture to symbolize hospitality. The leaf rosettes are up to 30 in (75 cm) high and 4 ft (1.2 m) wide. The sword-shaped leaves are viciously edged with tiny thorns, but recently smooth-leafed cultivars have been developed. It has an inflorescence up to 12 in (30 cm) long with yellow to red bracts and grows up to 4 ft (1.2 m)

Anaphalis triplinervis 'Sommerschnee'

tall when in fruit. Fruit develop in the second year if conditions are suitable. **'Porteanus'** has leaves with a central yellow stripe, while **'Variegatus'** has leaves with cream marginal stripes and may develop red tints. ZONES 11–12.

ANAPHALIS
PEARLY EVERLASTING

A genus of around 100 species of gray-foliaged perennials. They occur over most of the northern temperate regions and at high altitudes in the tropics. The narrow, lance-shaped leaves are often clothed in cobwebby hairs attached directly to upright stems. Panicles on clusters of papery white flowerheads terminate the stems in summer or fall (autumn). The flowerheads may be small, resembling some achilleas, or large, with large papery bracts resembling helichrysums. Heights range from 6–30 in (15–75 cm) depending on the species. Like other everlastings they are useful for cut flowers, and the foliage and flowers are just as decorative when dried.

CULTIVATION: Plant in light, gritty, well-drained soil in full sun. They do not like being wet but when in active growth the soil should not be allowed to dry out completely. Prune back hard in winter. Propagate from seed or division.

Anaphalis javanica

From higher mountains of the Malay archipelago, this is a somewhat shrubby, evergreen species with a very dense coating of silver-gray hairs on the narrow leaves. It grows to about 18 in (45 cm) high and bears clusters of small, white flowerheads in summer. ZONES 9–10.

Anaphalis margaritacea
syn. *Anaphalis yedoensis*
PEARL EVERLASTING

Native to North America as well as Europe and Asia, this perennial is valued for its papery, small yellow flowers which can be dried for indoor decoration. It has lance-shaped, silvery gray leaves and the flowers are borne on erect stems in late summer. Bushy in habit, *Anaphalis margaritacea* grows to about 24–30 in (60–75 cm) high and about 24 in (60 cm) wide. Easily grown, it prefers a sunny situation (but will grow in part-shade) and well-drained chalky soil. ZONES 4–9.

Anaphalis nepalensis

A native of the eastern Himalayas, this low-growing species forms clumps of weak stems with narrow gray-green leaves that have woolly white hairs on the undersides and display 3 prominent veins. In late summer and early fall (autumn) it bears small terminal clusters of flowerheads with papery white bracts and yellow centers. It grows to no more than about 12 in (30 cm) high. ZONES 5–9.

Anaphalis triplinervis

This is a Himalayan species that grows to 30 in (75 cm) tall. It has daisy-like white bracts and leaves that are pale green above with felted undersides, broader towards the apex and usually with 3 prominent veins diverging from the base. **'Sommerschnee'** ('Summer Snow') grows only to a height of 12 in (30 cm) and has shorter, more heavily felted leaves. It may be, in fact, a hybrid with *Anaphalis nepalensis.* ZONES 5–9.

ANCHUSA
ALKANET, SUMMER FORGET-ME-NOT

This genus consists of about 50 species of annuals, biennials and perennials occurring in Europe, North and South Africa and western Asia. Although many have a rather weedy habit and undistinguished foliage, they bear flowers of a wonderful sapphire blue, which though individually not large are carried in clusters over a long spring and early summer season and do not fade easily. They are popular with bees. Anchusas are suitable for herbaceous borders, beds and containers, though the dwarf perennial species are more at home in the rock garden.

CULTIVATION: Frost hardy, they grow best in a sunny position in deep, rich, well-drained soil. In very hot areas planting in part-shade helps maintain the flower color. Feed sparingly and water generously. Taller species benefit from staking and the plants require plenty of

Anagallis monellii

Anagallis monellii

Andromeda polifolia

room as they make large root systems. Cut flower stalks back after blooming to promote new growth. Propagate perennials by division in winter, annuals and biennials from seed in fall (autumn) or spring. Transplant perennials when dormant in winter.

Anchusa azurea

syn. ***Anchusa italica***

ITALIAN ALKANET

Occurring wild around the Mediterranean and the Black Sea, this species is an upright perennial up to 3–4 ft (1–1.2 m) high and 24 in (60 cm) wide. It has coarse, hairy leaves and an erect habit with tiers of brilliant blue flowers borne in spring to summer. Its several cultivars differ in their precise shade of blue: rich blue **'Morning Glory'**, light blue **'Opal'** and the intense deep blue of **'Loddon Royalist'**. ZONES 3–9.

Anchusa capensis

CAPE FORGET-ME-NOT

From southern Africa, this species is biennial in cool climates, but in warm-temperate gardens it can be sown very early in spring to bear intense blue flowers in summer. It grows to 15 in (40 cm) tall and wide. Grown as an annual, **'Blue Angel'** reaches a height and spread of 8 in (20 cm) forming a compact pyramid of shallow, bowl-shaped sky-blue flowers in early summer. **'Blue Bird'** is taller, 24 in (60 cm), but equally striking. ZONES 8–10.

Anchusa cespitosa

Endemic to the island of Crete, this species is a dwarf perennial with rosettes of narrow leaves that build up into a mound. Clusters of brilliant blue flowers nestle among the leaves in spring. It requires a sunny spot in the rock garden with perfect drainage. ZONES 5–9.

Anchusa granatensis

This low-growing species from southwestern Europe is unusual in having flowers of a bright purplish red rather than the usual blue of other anchusas. The epithet *granatensis* means 'of Granada' referring in this case to the southern Spanish city. ZONES 6–9.

Anchusa leptophylla subsp. *incana*

This subspecies is somewhat similar to *Anchusa cespitosa* but it grows to 15 in (38 cm) with a rosette of narrow deep

Andropogon gerardii (immature)

green leaves, from which strong densely branched stems, holding masses of azure-blue flowers, arise in spring. ZONES 6–9.

Anchusa officinalis

BUGLOSS

Suited to the herbaceous border, the European *Anchusa officinalis* is a perennial but often treated as a biennial, up to 3 ft (1 m) tall with hairy mid-green leaves. The branched panicle bears myriads of tiny flowers, usually dark blue but violet, white or yellow blooms are not uncommon. This species has been used traditionally in herbal medicine, as a vegetable, and a dye is extracted from its roots. ZONES 6–10.

ANDROMEDA

BOG ROSEMARY

Only 2 species of low evergreen shrubs make up this genus from the colder parts of the northern hemisphere. They have tough short branches that root along the ground and small oblong leathery leaves. The small flowers, in short terminal sprays, are urn-shaped with a narrow aperture.

CULTIVATION: They are best grown in a shaded rockery, they prefer moist yet well-drained, acid conditions. They will tolerate any frosts and prefer a cold climate. Propagate from seed or small tip cuttings.

Andromeda polifolia

Growing to about 24 in (60 cm) high and wide, this species has narrow, deep green 1 in (25 mm) long leaves with pale undersides. The tiny white to pink flowers appear in sprays in spring. **'Compacta'** has a denser, more compact habit, with grayish leaves and pink flowers. ZONES 2–9.

Anchusa azurea 'Loddon Royalist'

ANDROPOGON

This genus includes some 100 species of annual and perennial grasses, most native to warmer regions of the Americas. Generally of vigorous, upright growth, they have short to elongated rhizomes. The dense tufts of leaves are often rather harsh textured, and often tinted bluish, purplish, or reddish, curling at the tips as they age. Seed heads are borne in summer and fall (autumn) on tall, feathery panicles, the individual spikelets usually with long bristles. The genus includes some weedy species but also some of the most handsome ornamental grasses.

CULTIVATION: Plant in moist, well-drained soil in full sun. Cold hardiness varies markedly with the species. Raise from seed or divide established clumps. The herbs lemongrass and citronella, sometimes included in this genus, are now classified as *Cymbopogon*.

Andropogon gerardii

BIG BLUESTEM, TURKEY FOOT

Native over a wide area of eastern and central North America, this clump-forming perennial grass is tolerant of harsh conditions. Easily identified by the blue color at the base of the stems, the narrow, erect foliage reaches 4–7 ft (1.2–2.1 m) in height and is tinged red when mature. The usually purplish seed heads turn a rich orange-wheat color in fall (autumn). It is useful where low water input is essential. ZONES 3–8.

Anchusa capensis

ANDROSACE

ROCK JASMINE

This genus consists of around 100 species of annuals and perennials from cooler regions of the northern hemisphere. It is mainly the low-growing perennials that are valued as garden plants, forming dense mats or cushions no more than 4 in (10 cm) high. Favorites for rock garden planting, they are rarely spectacular but are appealing. Most species have light green or silvery gray, loose rosettes of foliage crowded along prostrate stems, topped with umbels of small white or pink 5-petalled flowers in spring and summer.

CULTIVATION: Best in sunny, well-drained scree or rockery conditions with free-draining gravel-based soil and additional humus. Most are quite frost hardy but some may require alpine-house conditions in areas subject to heavy winter rains. Propagate from seed, cuttings or self-rooted layers.

Androsace carnea

This 2 in (5 cm) high, cushion-forming evergreen perennial from the mountains of southern Europe has fine, pointed leaves with hairy edges. Short-stemmed heads of pink flowers develop in spring. An excellent container or alpine-house plant. ***Androsace carnea* subsp. *laggeri*** has deep pink flowers on longer stems. ZONES 5–9.

Anchusa capensis 'Blue Angel'

Anchusa granatensis

A

Androsace lanuginosa

A spreading ground-cover or mat-forming perennial from the Himalayas with small deep green leaves that appear somewhat silvery due to a covering of fine silky hairs. Only about 2 in (5 cm) high, the plants can spread rapidly to 18 in (45 cm) or more wide. Heads of light pink flowers appear profusely in summer and fall (autumn). **ZONES 6–9.**

Androsace primuloides

A perennial species from the Himalayas with new rosettes of leaves forming on runners, like a strawberry plant. The foliage is densely covered in white hairs and

Androsace sarmentosa 'Brilliant'

Androsace lanuginosa

the flowers, clustered on 2 in (5 cm) stalks, are pink and a little less than $\frac{1}{2}$ in (12 mm) wide. **ZONES 6–9.**

Androsace sarmentosa

This is another Himalayan perennial species that spreads by runners. It forms patches of rosettes of small, oval leaves with a covering of fine silvery hairs. Large heads of yellow-centered, pink flowers on 4 in (10 cm) stalks are borne in spring. **'Brilliant'** has darker mauve-pink flowers. **ZONES 3–8.**

Androsace sempervivoides

A clump-forming perennial from Kashmir and Tibet, it is near prostrate and spreads slowly, though old clumps may mound up in the center. The small rosettes are connected by reddish stolons covered in fine hair. As new rosettes form they strike root and form new clumps. Mid-pink flowers are borne in primrose-like heads on 4 in (10 cm) stalks from early spring to early summer. **ZONES 5–9.**

ANEMIA

FLOWERING FERN

Although belonging to the true ferns, none of which actually flower, this genus gets its common name from the contrasting color and shape of the spore-bearing portions of the fronds and the green sterile portions. There are some

Androsace sarmentosa

Anemone coronaria St Brigid Group

90 species, mainly from tropical and subtropical parts of the Americas, with a few from Africa. Most species are soil dwelling but a few grow on rocks. They have creeping, hairy rhizomes and form small clumps of long-stalked fronds. The fronds are like those of many other ferns except for the more upright fertile portions which carry bunches of spore-bodies (sori) that resemble flower buds. **CULTIVATION:** These ferns are frost tender and should be grown in a sheltered shady position with moist, peaty soil. Propagate by division, or if very patient, from spores.

Anemia mexicana

FLOWERING FERN

No ferns have flowers, but this one bears its spores on special fronds which take the form of curly, tufted branches that do look a little like plumes of beige flowers arising from amidst the rich green of the other leaves. It is rather frost tender and likes the usual fern conditions of shade, fertile soil and regular watering. It grows about 18 in (45 cm) tall and in cooler areas dies down for the winter. **ZONES 10–11.**

ANEMONE

WINDFLOWER

This is a genus of over 100 species of perennials occurring widely in the northern hemisphere but with the majority in temperate Asia. Species include a diverse range of woodland plants as well as the more common florist's anemone (*Anemone coronaria*). All have tufts of basal leaves that are divided in palmate fashion into few to many leaflets. The starry or bowl-shaped flowers have 5 or more petals, their colors covering almost the whole range of flower colors. Anemones can be divided into the fall (autumn) flowering species with fibrous roots, such as *A. hupehensis* and *A.* × *hybrida*, and the tuberous and rhizomatous types, usually spring flowering, which include the ground-hugging *A. blanda* and *A. nemorosa*. There are other rhizomatous species which will tolerate less moisture and more open conditions. Given the right conditions and left undisturbed for many years many of these will form wonderful carpets of both leaf texture and color through their delicate flowers. The tuberous-rooted types, of which *A. coronaria* is best known, flower in spring and are best replaced every 1–2 years.

Anemone blanda 'Atrocaerulea'

CULTIVATION: Most woodland species are very frost hardy and do well in rich, moist yet well-drained soil in a lightly shaded position. Propagate from seed planted in summer or divide established clumps in early winter when plant is dormant. The tuberous-rooted types appreciate full sun and well drained soil, and welcome a dry dormancy period. They are more prone to frost damage and are often treated as annuals, both for this reason and the fact that tubers become weakened after blooming.

Anemone apennina

A 6 in (15 cm) tall, rhizomatous species from southern Europe, it has a clump of basal leaves, each divided into 3 segments which are themselves further divided. Blue flowers about 1 in (25 mm) wide on short stems open in spring. **'Petrovac'** is a vigorous cultivar with many-petalled, deep blue flowers. **'Purpurea'** has pinkish purple flowers, while ***Anemone apennina* var. *albiflora*** has all-white flowers. **ZONES 6–9.**

Anemone blanda

This delicate-looking tuberous species is frost hardy. Native to Greece and Turkey, it grows to 8 in (20 cm) with crowded tufts of ferny leaves. White, pink or blue star-shaped flowers, 1$\frac{1}{2}$ in (35 mm) wide, appear in spring. It self-seeds freely and, given moist, slightly shaded conditions, should spread into a beautiful display of flowers. Popular cultivars include the large-flowered **'White Splendour'**; **'Atrocaerulea'**, with deep blue flowers; **'Blue Star'**, with pale blue flowers; and **'Radar'** with white-centered magenta flowers. **ZONES 6–9.**

Anemone coronaria

WIND POPPY, FLORIST'S ANEMONE

This very frost hardy species, the most commonly planted anemone, is one that dies back to small woody tubers; these are sold in packets just like seeds, the plants being treated almost as annuals. They grow to about 10 in (25 cm) high, and the poppy-like flowers, up to 4 in (10 cm) wide can range in color from pink to scarlet, purple or blue. The 2 best known strains are the **De Caen** and **St Brigid Groups**, with single and double flowers respectively, and colors ranging from pink to purple to scarlet to blue. This species is excellent as a cut flower. **ZONES 8–10.**

Anemone hortensis

The finely dissected leaves of this low growing rhizomatous species from the Mediterranean regions makes a wonderful backdrop to the mauve-pink flowers held singly just above the foliage in spring. **ZONES 7–9.**

Anemone hupehensis

JAPANESE WIND FLOWER

A perennial with fibrous roots, this species from central and western China (long cultivated in Japan), can be almost evergreen in milder climates where, if conditions are to its liking it may spread and provide good ground cover, producing its single white to mauve flowers on tall, openly branched stems during the early fall (autumn). The cultivar **'Hadspen Abundance'** has deep pink petals edged with pale pink to almost white. **'September Charm'** has large pale pink flowers with 5 to 6 petals, while ***Anemone hupehensis* var. *japonica*** is the Japanese cultivated race, taller and with more petals than the wild Chinese plants. It includes **'Prinz Heinrich'** (Prince Henry) with 10 or more deep rose-pink petals, paler on the undersides. Most of the cultivars ascribed to this species are now placed under *Anemone* × *hybrida*. **ZONES 6–10.**

Anemone × *hybrida*

These popular hybrids are believed to have arisen as crosses between *Anemone hupehensis* and its close relative the Himalayan *A. vitifolia*, the latter distinguished by the dense woolly hair on its leaf undersides and usually white flowers. The hybrids generally have leaves that are hairier beneath than in *A. hupehensis*, and flowers in all shades from white to deepest rose, the petals numbering from 5 to over 30. They generally lack fertile pollen. The robust plants may reach heights of 5 ft (1.5 m) in flower. There are over 30 cultivars, among the most common being **'Honorine Jobert'** with pure white, 6–9-petalled flowers and very dark green leaves. Most nurseries do not list cultivar names but just sell the plants in flower, when they are easy to select both for color and flower type. **ZONES 6–10.**

Anemone × *lesseri*

This species, a cross between *Anemone multifida* and *A. sylvestris* but closely resembling the former, is an erect perennial with reddish pink, white, yellow or

Anemone h. 'Hadspen Abundance'

purple flowers and large, hairy, mid-green leaves. **ZONES 3–9.**

Anemone multifida

From Canada and northern USA this slender, fibrous-rooted species grows up to 24 in (60 cm) high. Its leaves are deeply divided with numerous segments coated in silky hairs, and with 2 or 3 smallish, white to cream, rarely red, flowers per stem. **ZONES 2–8.**

Anemone nemorosa
WOOD ANEMONE

As its common name implies, this European species is happiest in a moist, shaded position where its delicate creamy white early spring flowers delight the passer by. Usually under 4 in (10 cm) high, it has fine creeping rhizomes that will quickly cover a wanted area if conditions are suitable. Many named cultivars exist including **'Allenii'**, a rich lilac blue on the outside of the petals and pale lilac on the insides; **'Robinsoniana'**, with lavender-blue petals; and **'Vestal'**, a late-blooming white variety. **ZONES 5–9.**

Anemone pavonina
ANEMONE OF GREECE

Growing to 12 in (30 cm) high, this eastern Mediterranean species has deeply divided mid-green leaves and solitary single flowers up to 2½ in (6 cm) across in shades of pink, purple or red with a distinct white base. It is tuberous rooted with a graceful, slender habit and flowers in early spring. It requires a dry dormant period so is best lifted in fall (autumn), especially in humid areas or where frost could present a problem. It is generally represented by its **St. Bavo** strain with larger flowers in shades of pink or purple. **ZONES 8–9.**

Anemone ranunculoides

Slender creeping rhizomes ensure that this species will spread if conditions are to its liking. Around 6 in (15 cm) high, it has leaves divided into narrow, lobed leaflets. The deep yellow 5 to 6-petalled flowers about 1 in (25 mm) across are displayed in early spring. **ZONES 4–9.**

Anemone rivularis

Ranging from India to western China and flowering in late to mid summer, this fibrous-rooted species has leaves with broader, more rounded divisions

Anemone × *hybrida* cultivar

Anemone sylvestris

Anemone × *hybrida* 'Honorine Jobert'

Anemone rivularis

Anemone trullifolia

Anemone nemorosa

than most anemones. It grows to around 24 in (60 cm) tall, with white cup-shaped flowers tinted blue on the outside, and purple stamens. **ZONES 6–9.**

Anemone sylvestris
SNOWDROP ANEMONE

From Europe, this fibrous-rooted species is usually about 8 in (20 cm) tall, with deeply dissected glossy dark green leaves. The solitary, fragrant single white flowers have prominent yellow stamens and are borne over a long season in spring and early summer. Cultivars include **'Grandiflora'**, with large nodding flowers and **'Elisa Fellmann'**, with semi-double flowers. **ZONES 4–9.**

Anemone tomentosa
syn. ***Anemone vitifolia* 'Robustissima'**
GRAPELEAF ANEMONE

Native to central and northern China, this species is closely related to *Anemone hupehensis*, differing in the densely hairy undersides of its heavily veined leaves. Growing to 3 ft (1 m) or more, it has large

Anemone × *hybrida* cultivar

pale pink flowers, 5–6-petalled and up to 3 in (8 cm) in diameter, from late summer to early fall (autumn). **ZONES 4–9.**

Anemone trullifolia

Originating from the eastern Himalayas and western China, this fibrous-rooted anemone grows to around 12 in (30 cm) high with broadly lobed basal leaves. Delicate, long-stalked bluish, white or yellow flowers appear in summer. **ZONES 5–9.**

Anemonella thalictroides

Anemopsis californica

Anemopsis californica

ANEMONELLA

RUE ANEMONE

The name is a diminutive of *Anemone* and in fact the sole species of this North American genus is a more diminutive plant than most anemones, but in foliage and flowers it is more reminiscent of a *Thalictrum*. It is a tuberous-rooted perennial forming a small, dense clump of foliage, the compound leaves with few but rather large leaflets. The flowers are large for the size of the plant and few to each short flowering stem, with a variable number of overlapping petals in shades of white to pale mauve.
CULTIVATION: It makes a charming rock-garden plant but also adapts to moist, undisturbed spots in a woodland garden. It requires moist but very well-drained, humus-rich soil, and a semi-shaded position. Growth is slow and skilful management is needed to keep plants healthy for many years. Propagate by careful division of mature plants in fall (autumn) or from seed in spring.

Anemonella thalictroides

This beautiful plant occurs wild in eastern USA and southeastern Canada, in mountain woodlands. Usually 8 in (20 cm) or less in height, it has smooth blue-green leaves. In spring and early summer it bears delicate bowl-shaped flowers about $\frac{3}{4}$ in (18 mm) wide with 5 to 10 petals. **ZONES 4–9.**

ANEMONOPSIS

The single species in this genus from Japan is a rhizomatous, clump-forming perennial with alternate, glossy dark green leaves and loose racemes of pendent, pale purple to violet flowers. It looks best along terraces above paths, as the nodding flowers look very attractive when viewed from below.
CULTIVATION: It is fully frost hardy, and needs part-shade, deep, cool, moist, fertile, humus-rich, acidic soil, and protection from dry winds. Propagate from seed or by division.

Anemonopsis macrophylla

This species produces its cup-shaped flowers with 3 waxy sepals and rows of petals in mid- and late summer. It grows to a height of 30 in (75 cm) and spread of 18 in (45 cm). **ZONES 5–9.**

ANEMOPSIS

YERBA MANSA

Although its name means 'anemone-like', this genus of a single species from western USA and Mexico is quite unrelated to anemones, but related rather to the lizard's-tail genera *Saururus* and *Houttuynia*. The 'flowers' that look like those of some of the anemones with elongated receptacles are in fact inflorescences, with a group of petal-like white bracts at the base of a spike of tiny, fleshy greenish flowers. It is a creeping evergreen perennial that spreads both by thick underground rhizomes and surface runners that develop rosettes of leaves at intervals. The rhizome is used medicinally by Native Americans, who also use the small, hard fruits for beadwork.
CULTIVATION: It will grow equally well in boggy ground or in a well-drained raised bed or rockery, preferably in full sun. Although quite ornamental and unusual, it is a vigorous grower and can quickly become invasive, and is difficult to eradicate due to its tenacious rhizomes. A boggy stream or pond edge is perhaps its most appropriate placement. Propagate by division or from cuttings.

Angelica pachycarpa

Angelica archangelica

Anemopsis californica

Occurring wild in the southwestern states of the USA and adjacent Baja, California (Mexico), yerba mansa can rapidly spread over tens of feet (meters) when conditions suit it, mounding sometimes to about 18 in (45 cm) high. The spoon-shaped leaves become purple-tinged in the sun, and the curious white-bracted flower spikes develop over a long season in spring, summer and fall (autumn). **ZONES 8–11.**

ANETHUM

DILL

This well-known herb genus includes two species occurring wild in Europe and temperate Asia. The commonly cultivated dill (*Anethum graveolens*) is an annual, the other a biennial. Dill has a long, wiry root from which develops an upright, hollow stem with ferny foliage very similar to that of fennel (*Foeniculum vulgare*). Umbels of tiny bright yellow flowers develop at the stem tip and are followed by the pungent seeds. Dill is a culinary herb that is widely used in pickling and fish dishes. Both the foliage and the seeds are used. The foliage is best used before flowering. It also has medicinal uses, these days most notably as an indigestion remedy.
CULTIVATION: Only moderately frost hardy, dill is easily grown in any moist, well-drained, humus-rich soil in sun. The seed is best sown in spring where it is to grow, as seedlings are difficult to transplant. Dill often self-sows.

Anethum graveolens

DILL

Originally from southwestern Asia, this deliciously aromatic annual grows to about 3 ft (1 m) high with leaves divided into thread-like, fragile segments. Yellow flowers are borne in summer followed by the pungent dill seeds. Both leaves and seeds are used for flavoring. Since earliest times the seeds have been used to aid digestion. **ZONES 5–10.**

ANGELICA

This genus of 50 or so species is mainly indigenous to the cooler parts of the northern hemisphere. They are valued for the bold palm-like structure of their leaves, the bunches of pale green flowers on tall stems and the pleasant aroma.
CULTIVATION: They prefer moist, well-drained, rich soil in sun or shade. Plants die after flowering and setting seed and should then be removed. Angelica will self-sow or can be propagated from seed.

Angelica archangelica

A fast-growing, robust biennial, this species was for centuries valued for its medicinal uses—to relieve toothache, to dispel 'phrenzies of the head', and to protect against the plague. It is the young stems that are used, formerly cooked as a vegetable, nowadays most familiar as a candied green garnish for sweet dishes. It grows to 6 ft (1.8 m). Keep cutting back flowerheads to ensure leaf production. It has handsome, deeply divided, bright green leaves and umbels of small flowers in late summer. It does best in filtered sunlight with protection from strong winds. **ZONES 4–9.**

Angelica gigas

From China, Japan and Korea, this is a clump-forming biennial or short-lived perennial that grows to 3–6 ft (1–1.8 m). It produces umbels of rich red flowers on dark purple stems in late summer and early fall (autumn), and has toothed, mid-green leaves with lobed leaflets. **ZONES 5–9.**

Angelica pachycarpa

A species that has recently come into cultivation as an ornamental, this is semi-evergreen and remarkable for the succulence and glossiness of its compact foliage. The flowering branches barely rise above the foliage and rapidly develop clusters of small thick fruits. **ZONES 8–10.**

ANGOPHORA

APPLE GUM

Consisting of 13 species of evergreen trees from eastern Australia, often on sandstone-derived soils of low fertility, this genus is closely related to *Eucalyptus*. One way to distinguish the 2 genera is that *Angophora* has sharply ribbed fruit capsules and leaves in opposite pairs, while *Eucalyptus* has mostly smooth capsules and the adult leaves are arranged alternately. *Angophora* species vary considerably in size and habit, ranging from the almost shrubby dwarf apple to 100 ft (30 m) trees. The bark of most species is rough and scaly. Where space is available they make interesting subjects with their tortuous branches. Flowers are creamy white, usually profuse.

CULTIVATION: Easily grown in frost-free and near frost-free climates. Plant in light, well-drained soil, sheltered from strong winds. Propagate from seed.

Angophora costata

SYDNEY RED GUM, SMOOTH-BARKED APPLE

From Australia's east coast, this tree can reach 100 ft (30 m) with a sturdy trunk up to 4 ft (1.2 m) in diameter and a high, spreading crown of twisting branches. In spring it sheds its brownish pink bark to reveal salmon-pink bark. Narrow leaves are orange-red on the summer growth-flushes, changing to dark green as they mature. This tree is unpredictable in speed and form of growth. **ZONES 9–11.**

Angophora hispida

syn. ***Angophora cordifolia***

DWARF APPLE

This is a common large shrub or small tree of the dry sandstone ridges around Sydney, Australia, sometimes growing to 20 ft (6 m) tall but more often 8–10 ft (2–3 m). It has broad, stiff, grayish leaves, and the young flower buds, covered in russet bristles, open in early summer to big clusters of flowers. **ZONES 9–10.**

ANGRAECUM

COMET ORCHID

This very distinctive genus of orchids consists of 200 or so species from tropical Africa and Madagascar, but relatively few are grown in gardens. The flowers have long, backward-pointing spurs containing nectar and are pollinated by night-flying moths with exceedingly long tongues. Several hybrids are available. All are classed as warm growing and have scented flowers in white or combinations of white and pale green.

CULTIVATION: These plants like year-round warmth, humidity and moisture (which makes them difficult house plants) and a coarse potting mix. Give them plenty of light but not direct sunshine, and propagate from offsets. Outside the tropics they are normally grown in hothouses.

Angraecum eburneum

From Madagascar and the Mascarene Islands, this robust species eventually forms large clumps. The stiff strap-like leaves measuring up to 15 in (40 cm) in length are arranged in groups of 10 to 15 or so. Long racemes of evening-scented white and green flowers appear during the winter months. A number of subspecies and cultivars are available including ***Angraecum eburneum* subsp. *superbum***, distinguished by its larger, whiter flowers. **ZONES 11–12.**

Angraecum sesquipedale

The specific name of this Madagascan species means 'of one and a half feet', referring to the length of the nectar spur. Charles Darwin was impressed by this feature and predicted that there must exist a moth with a tongue of the same length to pollinate it, a prediction borne out soon afterwards. The white flowers are up to 8 in (20 cm) across, and have a spicy smell in the evening. **ZONES 11–12.**

ANGULOA

The eighteenth-century Spanish botanist Don Francisco de Angulo is commemorated in the name of this genus of 11 species of tropical orchids from South America. They include both epiphytic and ground-dwelling plants, with crowded short pseudobulbs, each carrying at the apex 3 large, thin, pleated leaves. The curious large flowers are borne singly on short erect stalks arising from among the pseudobulb bases. Mostly yellow or cream, they consist of thick fleshy petals that all curve in the one direction, the upper one strongly hooded. Within the cup that these form is a 'lip' that rocks back and forth at the slightest touch, a mechanism that brings large bees into contact with the sticky pollen masses, which they then carry to another plant of the same species.

CULTIVATION: Coming from mountain mist-forests, anguloas are easily grown in cool greenhouse conditions in a standard epiphytic orchid potting mixture. Propagate by division of established plants.

Anguloa clowesii

Native to Venezuela and Colombia, this beautiful and unusual orchid is a ground dweller with elongated pseudobulbs and pale green leaves about 24 in (60 cm) long and 6 in (15 cm) or more wide. The pale golden-yellow flowers, 3 in (8 cm) wide and upward-pointing, are borne singly on stalks about 8 in (20 cm) long with overlapping green bracts. They have a spicy perfume. **ZONES 11–12.**

× *ANGULOCASTE*

This name covers all hybrids derived from the crossing of any *Lycaste* species with any *Anguloa* species, both epiphytic orchids, and any later generations of seedlings. Some are deciduous, others evergreen. They have large pseudobulbs with strap-like leaves up to 18 in (45 cm) long. The flowers, carried singly and often yellow-green in color, are just slightly over 4 in (10 cm) wide and open in spring.

CULTIVATION: Plant in a very coarse, open soil mix and add extra drainage material such as crocks or styrofoam balls to the bottom of the pot. These hybrid orchids prefer cool to moderate conditions. Winter minimums around 50°F (10°C) are acceptable. Their culture is usually similar to that of the *Lycaste* parent. Deciduous plants prefer brighter light than the evergreens and will tolerate a greater temperature range. Feed frequently during the growing season. Propagate by dividing established clumps down to pairs of pseudobulbs.

× *Angulocaste* Hybrids

These orchid hybrids are derived from crosses between species of *Lycaste,* from Central America, and the less well known *Anguloa*, from South America. The plants are rather like large lycastes in habit, with fat pseudobulbs that usually lose their leaves in winter. The large flowers, which may be white, cream or yellow, appear from the bases of the naked pseudobulbs at the same time as the new shoots and last for several weeks. **ZONES 11–12.**

ANIGOZANTHOS

KANGAROO PAW

Native to southwestern Australia, these evergreen perennials are noted for their unique bird-attracting tubular flowers, the outsides coated with dense shaggy hairs and opening at the apex into 6 'claws', the whole resembling an animal's paw. Foliage is somewhat grass-like, and the various species can range in height from 1–6 ft (0.3–1.8 m). Flowers come in many colors including green, gold, deep red and orange-red; some species and hybrids are bi-colored. In recent years many hybrids have been produced, meeting the demands of the cut-flower industry and the florists' trade in potted flowers—an example is *Anigozanthos* **'Red Cross'**—though most will grow outdoors equally well.

CULTIVATION: They prefer warm, very well-drained sandy or gravelly soil and a hot, sunny, open position. Water well during dry seasons. Most will tolerate very light frosts and do well in coastal regions. Most tolerate drought, although flowering will be prolonged with summer water. Propagate by division in spring or from fresh seed. Plants are often affected by ink disease, a fungus which blackens the foliage. Watch for snails which can shred younger leaves overnight.

Angophora costata

Angophora costata

Anigozanthos 'Red Cross'

Angophora hispida

A

Anigozanthos Bush Gems Series

The best of the kangaroo paws for their resistance to ink disease, the Bush Gems hybrids are mostly of compact size, with flowers ranging from yellow, gold and green through to orange, red and burgundy. **'Bush Heritage'** is a small cultivar of 12–20 in (30–50 cm) in height with flowers of burnt terracotta and olive green. **'Bush Twilight'** grows 8–15 in (20–40 cm) tall, has prolific flowers in muted orange, yellow and green tones, appearing mainly in spring above the dull green, very narrow leaves. Other popular cultivars in the Series are **'Bush Glow'**, sunset-red, and **'Bush Gold'**, golden yellow. **ZONES 9–11.**

Anigozanthos 'Regal Claw'

Anigozanthos, BGS, 'Bush Heritage'

Anigozanthos flavidus

YELLOW KANGAROO PAW

Regarded as the hardiest of the kangaroo paws, this species has a vigorous clumping growth habit to 3 ft (1 m) across. With long, dull green leaves, flowering stems 3–5 ft (1–1.5 m) tall, and flowers in green, yellow or soft red tones, this species has proved adaptable to a range of soils and climates. Native to the far southwestern corner of Australia, where it is attractive to native birds, it is used extensively in hybridization programs. **ZONES 9–11.**

Anigozanthos humilis

This is a low, clumping perennial, growing no taller than 15 in (40 cm) but spreading anything up to 3 ft (1 m) if conditions are favorable. It can die back in summer and fall (autumn), so should be positioned so that it will not be overgrown while dormant. The flowering stems, often twice the height of the foliage, carry blooms in a wide range of colors from cream through dull orange to red. It prefers full sun. **ZONES 9-11.**

Anigozanthos manglesii

RED-AND-GREEN KANGAROO PAW

This striking plant has blue-green, strap-like leaves. Flowers are a deep green, contrasting vividly with a red base and stem, and appear mainly in spring. Flowering stems are 18–36 in (45–90 cm) in height and the plant has a spread at the base of about 18 in (45 cm). Unfortunately this spectacular species is one of the most difficult to cultivate, being very susceptible to ink disease as well as summer root rot. **ZONES 9–10.**

Anigozanthos flavidus

Anigozanthos humilis

Anigozanthos 'Pink Joey'

This is a hybrid cultivar with *Anigozanthos flavidus* as one of its parents. Low growing, no more than 20 in (50 cm) tall and with a spread of up to 3 ft (1 m), it blooms in smoky pink tones. **ZONES 9–11.**

Anigozanthos 'Regal Claw'

One of the many striking cultivars with parents listed as *Anigozanthos preissii* and *A. flavidus*, 'Regal Claw' is a dwarf plant with flowers of orange with a red felted overlay. **ZONES 9–11.**

ANISODONTEA

This genus of shrubby mallows from southern Africa have tough, wiry stems and small flowers like miniature hibiscus, carried on slender stalks from short lateral shoots near the tips of the branches. The leaves are small and irregularly lobed. In recent years they have been rediscovered and popularized as free-blooming indoor plants, or in warm-temperate climates as garden shrubs. However, if grown indoors they must receive some sun or very strong reflected light.

CULTIVATION: They need frequent watering in the warmer half of the year, little in the cooler. Light pruning after flowers finish produces a more compact plant and encourages subsequent flowering. Propagation is normally from summer cuttings, which strike readily. Grow them in a cold frame.

Anisodontea 'African Queen'

This recent cultivar is compact in habit with foliage much like *Anisodontea capensis*, but very profuse, slightly larger flowers of a soft, delicate pink. It is reported to have originated as a hybrid between *A.* × *hypomadarum* and *A. scabrosa*. **ZONES 9–11.**

Anisodontea capensis

syn. *Malvastrum capensis*

This species will quickly grow to a shrub about 6 ft (1.8 m) high with long straggling branches and rather sparse foliage. Flowers, $^{3}/_{4}$ in (18 mm) in diameter, appear in successive flushes from spring through summer or almost the whole year in warmer climates; flesh pink with darker veining on opening, they age to very pale pink. **ZONES 9–11.**

Anisodontea × *hypomadarum*

This evergreen bushy shrub has an erect habit, and can reach a height of 6 ft (1.8 m). Bowl-shaped, mid-pink flowers up to $1^{1}/_{2}$ in (35 mm) across with darker veins are borne from spring to fall (autumn). Although regarded as a probable hybrid, its true parentage is unknown. **ZONES 9–11.**

Anigozanthos, BGS,'Bush Twilight'

Anigozanthos,BGS, 'Bush Glow'

Anigozanthos, BGS, 'Bush Gold'

Anigozanthos manglesii

Anisodontea scabrosa

In its native habitat of South Africa's Cape Province, this soft-wooded shrubby species often reaches a height of 6 ft (1.8 m). The lobed leaves are attractive in themselves and the flowers, mostly borne singly but sometimes grouped in 4s or 5s, are of an open bell shape with petals in rose-purple tones, more intense towards the base. **ZONES 9–11.**

ANNONA

This genus of 100 or so species of evergreen trees from the American tropics and subtropics includes some of the most delectably sweet tropical fruits, notably the cherimoya, custard apple and sweetsop. The trees have broad, oblong, strongly veined leaves, and curiously shaped flowers, often with a pungent fruity aroma, which emerge from the old wood on short stalks. The fruits consist of many fused segments, with tough green or brownish skin which may be covered in soft prickles or other protrusions, and a pulpy white flesh containing many brown seeds.
CULTIVATION: *Annona* species are grown readily in most tropical and warmer subtropical areas. They prefer sheltered sunny positions and fertile well-drained soils. They may flower and fruit through much of the year. Propagation is easy from freshly extracted seed, or by grafting for selected varieties.

Annona muricata
SOURSOP

From northern South America, this grows to 15–20 ft (4.5–6 m), branching low with strongly ascending lateral growths. New growths have brownish silky hairs; older leaves are glossy bright green. The large green fruits are asymmetrically oval, covered in soft spines, and may be borne throughout the year. Despite the name, the fluffy white aromatic flesh is not very sour. **ZONES 10–12.**

Annona squamosa
CUSTARD APPLE, SUGAR APPLE

There are many varieties of custard apple, a popular fruit that originated in the tropical regions of Africa, Asia and the Americas. Its flowers are pale green and pleasantly scented. The large fruit has a custard-like texture and is delicious when eaten fresh. This is a semi-deciduous tree growing to 15 ft (5 m). Plant in a warm, sheltered position as the fruit yield may be damaged by low temperatures and the tree itself is frost tender. Propagate by grafting. **ZONES 10–12.**

ANOECTOCHILUS
JEWEL ORCHIDS

From tropical Asia and Australasia come the 25 or so species of small orchids that make up this genus. They are not often grown now, being regarded as too demanding in their requirements—most come from the deep shade and humidity of the rainforest floor—but were once a favorite subject for terrariums and wardian cases, where the atmosphere can be kept saturated with moisture. It is the

Anisodontea capensis

Anisodontea × *hypomadarum*

Anisodontea × *hypomadarum*

Anisodontea 'African Queen'

Anoectochilus regalis

Annona muricata

Annona squamosa

foliage that is the outstanding feature of most of them, the oval, rather fleshy leaves like purple-green velvet with crystalline surface cells and a reticulation of silver or gold veins. The short fleshy stems are creeping, with upturned tips, and the flowers, crowded near the tops of erect stalks, are rather small though the labellum may be prettily fringed and also has reflective surface cells.
CULTIVATION: When grown away from the wet tropics they need a well-warmed greenhouse and high humidity, or can be grown in a terrarium kept indoors or in a conservatory, out of direct sun, so long as winter temperatures are maintained fairly high. Plant in a pure organic mixture of leafmold and pulverised bark in a shallow pan with good drainage, keep moist at all times. Plants can seldom be maintained for many years. Propagate from sections of the creeping stem.

Anoectochilus regalis

This miniature orchid comes from the far south of India and Sri Lanka. It is grown primarily for its brilliantly variegated leaves, dark velvety green and netted in gold, each about 2 in (5 cm) long and arranged in a small rosette. The small white flowers are also interesting, with a fringed labellum, even though they are only about ½ in (12 mm) wide. **ZONE 12.**

ANOMATHECA

A genus of 6 species of cormous perennials native to southern and central Africa, closely allied to *Lapeirousia.* The plants have basal tufts of simple, grass-like, ribbed leaves up to 12 in (30 cm) long. In summer they produce a succession of flowering stems bearing starry, 6-petalled, ½–1 in (12–25 mm) wide flowers. The flowering stems are often branching and the flowers, which are occasionally fragrant, are mostly red, white or greenish, though often with darker markings in the throat.
CULTIVATION: Most species are very easily grown in well-drained soil in a sunny or part-shaded situation and will survive light frosts provided the soil does not freeze below their planting depth, which is around 2 in (5 cm). In cold areas they may be lifted and stored dry over winter. In milder climates plant in fall (autumn). Propagate from seed or by breaking up established clumps.

Anomatheca laxa
syn. *Lapeirousia laxa*
SCARLET FREESIA

This freesia-like native of South Africa grows to about 24 in (60 cm) with long, narrow basal leaves and produces one-sided spikes bearing up to 12 flowers. The tubular, star-shaped red to scarlet flowers, about 1½ in (35 mm) wide (although there is a form only half that size), appear in spring. If left undisturbed, it should self-seed readily. **ZONES 8–11.**

ANOPTERUS

This genus consists of only 2 species of small evergreen tree or shrub: one confined to Tasmania, the other to subtropical hill forests of mainland Australia's east coast. Both are very ornamental, with long, spatula-shaped leaves, deep red or bronze on new growth-flushes, and heavy-textured white flowers in short terminal sprays. It is only the Tasmanian species that has been brought into cultivation to any significant extent.
CULTIVATION: They require a very sheltered position, moist, humus-rich soil and a cool humid climate, but are not very frost hardy. Plants grown from cuttings of mature wood often flower when only 12 in (30 cm) or so high.

Anthemis tinctoria

Anthemis 'Moonlight'

Anthemis cretica

Antennaria dioica 'Australis'

Anopterus glandulosus

Anopterus glandulosus
TASMANIAN LAUREL

This shrub, normally about 6–8 ft (1.8–2.4 m) tall, is capable of growing to a tree of more than 20 ft (6 m) in moist Tasmanian forests. The glossy dark green leaves are very leathery, with blunt teeth, and the pure white cup-shaped flowers appear in spring in short sprays at branch tips. **ZONES 8–9.**

ANTENNARIA
CAT'S EARS, LADIES' TOBACCO

A genus of around 45 species of evergreen to near-evergreen perennials of the daisy family from temperate regions of the northern hemisphere, most species form dense mats of leaf rosettes that root as they spread; a few are mounding and up to 15 in (38 cm) tall. The narrow, crowded leaves are usually silver gray and hairy. The summer-borne flowerheads are of the 'everlasting' type with dry, papery bracts surrounding a disc of petal-less florets, the heads clustered on short stems that hold them clear of the foliage mat.

CULTIVATION: Most species are very frost hardy and are best grown in moist, well-drained soil in full sun or morning shade. They can be used in perennial borders or as rockery plants. Propagate from seed or division.

Antennaria dioica
CATSFOOT

A stoloniferous perennial occurring wild in the colder parts of the northern hemisphere. It forms a mat of rosettes of narrow spatula- to lance-shaped leaves, dark green above but white-woolly on the undersides. In summer strong 8 in (20 cm) tall flower stems develop bearing clusters of white, pink or yellow flowerheads. Catsfoot is unusual among composites (daisies) in having different sexes on different plants (dioecious), the female flowerheads larger than the male. An attractive ground cover or rock garden plant, it also has some medicinal uses. *Antennaria dioica* **'Rosea'** has deep pink flowerheads; and **'Australis'** silvery gray stems topped with clusters of white flowers. **ZONES 5–9.**

ANTHEMIS

In suitable conditions the 100 or so species of this genus of annuals and perennials from the Mediterranean region and western Asia are prolific in their flowering and this is what prompted the name, from the Greek *anthemon*. Belonging to the larger daisy family, the flowerheads have the typical daisy shape and are generally white, cream or yellow with distinctive contrasting disc florets; a typical example is ***Anthemis* 'Moonlight'**. Even when not in flower most species have somewhat aromatic, finely dissected foliage in shades of green or silver gray, which can be used to advantage in the mixed border or rockery. Formerly *Anthemis* was taken in a broader sense to include the herbal chamomile, which belongs to the genus *Chamaemelum*.

CULTIVATION: These plants flower best in full sun and like well-drained soil. The perennials can be short-lived and often become untidy, but cutting back after flowering in the fall (autumn) ensures a more shapely plant. They are easily replaced by cuttings taken in the warmer months or by division in fall or spring. Annual species can be grown from seed.

Anthemis cotula
STINKING CHAMOMILE, MAYWEED

This is an annual with strongly aromatic leaves that are sometimes considered to smell rather unpleasant. Growing to 24 in (60 cm) it bears in late summer loose masses of pure white flowerheads with gold centers on rather weak stems; it may need staking but grown hard, that is, in full sun in a well-drained position, stems should remain firm and less likely to sprawl. **ZONES 4–10.**

Anthemis cretica

A mound-forming perennial from southern Europe and Turkey, often with a gray down on its leaves, this species has white flowerheads with yellow discs held on solitary stems up to 12 in (30 cm) high during the spring and summer months. **ZONES 5–9.**

Anthemis punctata subsp. *cupaniana*

With its fine carpeting growth this perennial, native to Sicily, has finely cut silver gray foliage with white daisy flowers held on 6 in (15 cm) tall stems during the summer months. Either full sun or semi-shade will suit this species, and it can become invasive if conditions are to its liking. **ZONE 7.**

Anthericum liliago

Anthemis sancti-johannis

Bright golden-orange is the color of the 2 in (5 cm) wide flowerheads of this perennial species from Bulgaria. Introduced to gardens only shortly after World War I it has finely cut gray-green leaves, grows to 18 in (45 cm) high and is a good choice for borders or rockeries. The specific name is Latin for 'of St John', though the plant's connection with the saint is obscure. **ZONES 5–9.**

Anthemis tinctoria
DYER'S CHAMOMILE, GOLDEN MARGUERITE

Native to Europe and western Asia, this is a very hardy, easily grown perennial that is covered in late spring and summer with a dazzling display of daisy flowers above fern-like, crinkled green leaves. The plant mounds to as much as 3 ft (1 m) high if supported on a rockery or a bank. The epithet *tinctoria* signifies a dye plant, and indeed the flowers of this species were once used to make a yellow dye. The typical form with bright golden flowers is now less popular than some of the cultivars, notably **'E. C. Buxton'** with subtle soft yellow blooms blending beautifully with the fine foliage. **ZONES 4–10.**

ANTHERICUM
SPIDER PLANT

A genus of some 50 species of fleshy-rooted perennial lilies that form clumps of narrow, grass-like leaves. The flower stems are wiry and up to 3 ft (1 m) tall and by mid-summer are bearing their small, starry, 6-petalled, white flowers. They are natives of Europe, northern Africa and Asia Minor.

CULTIVATION: Plant in moist, well-drained soil in full sun or morning shade. Moderately frost hardy, they are propagated by sowing fresh seed or by division in late winter to early spring.

Anthericum liliago
ST. BERNARD'S LILY

This European species has 15 in (38 cm) long, gray-green leaves and in summer develops 3 ft (1 m) tall spikes of narrow-petalled, 1 in (25 mm) wide white flowers, each petal with a greenish midvein. **'Major'** has larger, pure white flowers. **ZONES 7–10.**

Anthericum liliago 'Major'

ANTHRISCUS

A genus of 12 species of annuals, biennials and perennials from Europe and temperate Asia, one of them used as a culinary herb. They are typical umbellifers, that is, members of the carrot family, with large, much-divided basal leaves and hollow, branched flowering stems terminating in large umbels of tiny white or greenish flowers. The small dry fruits are narrow, with a terminal 'beak'.
CULTIVATION: Apart from chervil *(Anthriscus cerefolium)* the species are easily cultivated in any garden soil, and in fact may prove invasive. They prefer full sun. The annual chervil is best grown in a sheltered though moderately sunny position, in light, well-tilled soil. Sow seed directly into the beds in spring or late summer, harvesting leaves as soon as large enough and before the flowering stem begins to extend. If some plants are allowed to reach flowering size they will usually self-seed.

Anthriscus cerefolium
CHERVIL

Resembling parsley, chervil grows to about 24 in (60 cm) and is grown as a cool-season annual. The light green, finely textured leaves and stems are harvested 2–3 in (5–8 cm) above the crown and are used in French cooking to give a delicate licorice flavor. The species is a native of Europe and western Asia. **ZONES 6–10.**

Anthriscus sylvestris
COW PARSLEY

One of the most familiar wild plants of European hedgerows and meadows, cow parsley is a vigorous perennial up to 4 ft (1.2 m) high, with large ferny leaves and widely branching flowering stems. In spring and early summer it bears numerous umbels of small white flowers. The species extends through most of Europe, also northwestern Africa and western Asia. **'Ravenswing'** has leaves that turn purple-black and tiny white flowers with pink bracts. **ZONES 4–9.**

ANTHURIUM
FLAMINGO FLOWER

This is a huge and diverse genus of evergreen, shrubby or climbing epiphytes in the arum family, all from tropical America. Familiar as florists' plants and cut flowers are 2 to 3 species with typically brilliant red flat spathes held above broad leathery leaves; selection and breeding has broadened the range of colors to include white, pink and orange. The actual flowers are the tiny bumps gathered around the central spadix.
CULTIVATION: Anthuriums are easy to grow in a tropical climate but elsewhere they are more likely to flourish in a greenhouse or indoors in containers. Indoors, they need bright light, high humidity and constant warmth and moisture to flower. Plant outdoors in a humid position, in well-drained, peaty soil in full or part-shade out of the wind. Keep soil moist but not soggy. Daytime temperatures should not fall below about 60°F (15°C). Propagate from rhizomes in early spring. Potted plants need dividing and repotting every few years.

Anthurium andraeanum

Grown for its large, brilliantly colored spathe with raised veining, this species grows to about 24 in (60 cm) high, with large heart-shaped leaves. The plants only produce one or two flowers at a time but they bloom all year. The spathes, so glossy they appear varnished, are typically bright red, but other colors have been bred including pink, and green marbled with red. **ZONES 11–12.**

Anthurium scherzerianum
FLAMINGO FLOWER

Growing to 24–30 in (60–75 cm) this species typically has red spathes, with curled spadices but cultivars vary from white to pink to very dark red, sometimes with paler spots. The elongated, rather dull green leaves are very thick and leathery. Although this is one of the more cold-hardy species, it must be protected from frost. **ZONES 10–12.**

ANTHYLLIS

This is a genus of around 25 species of leguminous annuals, perennials and small shrubs. The leaves are pinnate but the leaflets are often small and closely crowded, creating the appearance of coarsely serrated leaves. The individual flowers are small and pea-like but borne abundantly in dense, rounded heads from spring to summer. Flower colors include yellows, reds and pinks.
CULTIVATION: Easily grown in any well-drained soil in full sun. Cold hardiness varies with the species but most will tolerate moderate frosts. Propagate from seed or small cuttings.

Anthyllis montana

This perennial species from the mountains of southern Europe has ferny pinnate leaves and spreads to form a mat of foliage up to 10 in (25 cm) tall and 3 ft (1 m) wide. From late spring the plant is studded with profuse ½ in (12 mm) wide heads of pink and white flowers that from a distance resemble pink clover. **'Atrorubens'** has deeper pink to purplish flowers. **ZONES 7–9.**

Anthriscus cerefolium

Anthyllis vulneraria
KIDNEY VETCH, LADIES' FINGERS

This is a spreading, short-lived perennial ground cover native to Europe and North Africa. It forms crowded rosettes of silky-haired foliage and may sometimes mound up to about 18 in (45 cm) tall. The flowers, in ½ in (12 mm) wide heads, are cream and yellow, often with red or purple tints. The species is used medicinally as an astringent, laxative and cough remedy. It is also dried for use in flower arrangements. **ZONES 7–9.**

ANTIGONON
CORAL VINE

A Mexican and Central American genus of 3 species of tendril climber, only one of which is widely cultivated for its summer display of delicate coral-pink blossom. They are tender evergreens that behave as deciduous perennials in cold-winter areas if the roots are protected from freezing. The leaves are dark green and heart-shaped with wavy edges. The dense foliage canopy is decked with trailing sprays of clustered racemes of small flowers, appearing over a long season. Only the heart-shaped sepals, tightly pressed together, provide the color, which ranges from the deepest coral to quite pale pink or even white.
CULTIVATION: These climbers thrive in any well-drained soil in a warm spot but require ample summer moisture. The top dies back at temperatures just below freezing and the roots die if the soil freezes. Propagate from seed, cuttings or division of the rootstock.

Antigonon leptopus
CORAL VINE, CHAIN OF LOVE

This is a fast-growing, showy creeper that may grow to 25 ft (8 m) or more. It bears masses of deep pink, heart-shaped flowers from early summer to fall (autumn), and is ideal for trellises, pergolas and arbors where a light cover is desirable. **ZONES 9–11.**

ANTIRRHINUM
SNAPDRAGON

The resemblance of snapdragon flowers to the face of a beast was noted by the ancient Greeks, who called them *Antirrhinon*, nose-like. In French they are *gueule de loup*, wolf's mouth, and in German and Italian the name means lion's mouth. Closely related to the toadflaxes *(Linaria)*, the genus consists of about 40 species, most from the western Mediterranean region but with a few from western North America. They include annuals, perennials and evergreen subshrubs. The common snapdragon *(Antirrhinum majus)* is a perennial but it is normally treated as an annual in gardens.
CULTIVATION: They prefer fertile, well-drained soil in full sun. Propagate the garden snapdragon from seed in spring or early fall (autumn).

Anthurium andraeanum

Antigonon leptopus

Anthurium scherzerianum

Antirrhinum majus

Antirrhinum hispanicum

Antirrhinum majus Liberty Series

Aphelandra squarrosa

Antirrhinum braun-blanquetii

This perennial species from Spain and Portugal has erect, branched stems to 4 ft (1.2 m) in height, elliptical, acute leaves and bears 5 to 30 yellow flowers. **ZONES 7–10.**

Antirrhinum hispanicum

This short-lived perennial from Spain is a very pretty miniature species, 10 in (25 cm) tall with flowers about half the size of the garden snapdragon. Mauve-pink is its only color. **ZONES 7–10.**

Antirrhinum majus

GARDEN SNAPDRAGON

This bushy short-lived perennial is valued for its showy flowers, borne over a long period from spring to fall (autumn). The many named cultivars, usually grown as annuals, have a spread of 12–18 in (30–45 cm) and range from tall: 30 in (75 cm); to medium: 18 in (45 cm); to dwarf: 10 in (25 cm). Plant breeders have developed snapdragons with wide open or double flowers, but none have the charm of the traditional form, as exemplified by the strain called **Liberty**. Treat these garden snapdragons as annuals—they rarely flower well after the first year, and old plants are apt to succumb to the fungus, antirrhinum rust. Deadhead to prolong flowering and pinch out early buds to increase branching. The **Coronette Series** of F1 hybrids, bred as bedding plants, exemplifies some of the qualities plant geneticists are injecting into their breeding programs. These include tolerance of bad weather, extra large blooms on heavy spikes and uniformity from seedling stage. They can grow to 24 in (60 cm) or more tall and a number of individual colors are available, from bronze through shades of pink to deep red to yellows and white. Two popular cultivars of *Antirrhinum majus* are **'Flower Carpet'** and **'Madame Butterfly'**. **ZONES 6–10.**

APHELANDRA

This is a genus of around 170 species of subshrubs and shrubs, all native to tropical America. They have large, deeply veined, pointed leaves, usually deep green, sometimes with contrastingly colored veins, always arranged in opposite pairs on the stems. Dense terminal flower spikes have large, often brightly colored bracts from which protrude tubular orange, red or yellow flowers with a broad, 3-lobed lower lip. A handful of species have long been cultivated

Aphelandra squarrosa 'Dania'

as decorative indoor and conservatory plants, valued for foliage and flowers. **CULTIVATION:** These tropical plants are very cold sensitive and liable to drop foliage if exposed to temperatures below 60°F (15°C), or to cool draughts for prolonged periods. In the tropics they can be planted outdoors in moist, humus-enriched, well-drained soil in part-shade; otherwise they require a position indoors in strong light, though not direct sun. Cut back stems after flowering. Propagate from seed or cuttings.

Aphelandra squarrosa

ZEBRA PLANT

Widely grown as a house plant, this Brazilian species can grow to 6 ft (1.8 m) high under ideal conditions. It has green leaves up to 12 in (30 cm) long, white or cream veins and midribs. The flower spike is around 8 in (20 cm) long, bright yellow and often tinted red or maroon. There are a number of cultivars, varying in leaf size and pattern, and flower colors. **'Louisae'** is the cultivar most commonly grown, with bright creamy white main veins and midribs. **'Dania'** has yellow to orange-yellow flowers, which are rarely seen, and leaves with prominent white veins. **ZONES 11–12.**

APIUM

CELERY, CELERIAC

Over 20 species of biennials and perennials make up this genus in the carrot family, occurring through Europe, temperate Asia and cooler parts of the southern hemisphere. It is known in the guise of one species, celery, grown as an annual in the garden for its stalk, or petiole, which can be eaten raw or cooked. The wild *Apium* species have leaves in basal tufts, or spread along creeping stems; these are divided to varying degrees into somewhat fleshy segments. Tiny white flowers are borne in umbels. **CULTIVATION:** Celery needs plenty of moisture so it is important to provide soil with ample moisture-retentive humus. They are relatively shallow-rooted plants and it is essential that both water and fertilizer be provided on a regular basis to ensure stalks remain tender and succulent. Today many gardeners choose the self-blanching types which do not require trenching as was the case with earlier varieties. Sow seeds in a starter bed or tray and transplant seedlings to permanent beds ensuring that roots are disturbed as little as possible. Self-blanching types can be grown closer together to help keep light off stalks while the green or non-blanching types can be more widely spaced.

Apium graveolens

The wild celery of Europe is a strong-smelling biennial growing up to 3 ft (1 m). Occurring in marshy locations along the coasts, it has finely divided leaves; the late summer flowers are held in loose compound umbels. The species has been domesticated for over 2,000 years and selection and breeding has given rise to numerous cultivars which can be divided into 3 groups, traditionally designated as botanical varieties. ***Apium graveolens* var. *dulce*** is the common celery, characterized by its long, succulent, leaf stalks and limited leafy green tops. In a garden situation, it is cut before flowering, the timing of which to a great degree is governed by temperature, consequently it has quite a

Anthyllis montana 'Atrorubens'

Apium graveolens

Apium graveolens var. *dulce*

short growing season in many areas. ***A. g.* var. *rapaceum*** is celeriac and has a swollen, edible rootstock like a turnip and slender leaf stalks that are usually discarded. It requires similar growing conditions to celery but needs a long growing season to make a large root. Leaf celery or ***A. g.* var. *secalinum*** is the form from which the leafy tops are used in soups and stews. In China a similar type of celery is grown for its stalks and leaves. **ZONES 5–10.**

APONOGETON
WATER HAWTHORN

This genus of aquatic plants consists of 40-odd species, found wild in streams and lakes through tropical and subtropical regions of Africa, Asia and Australasia, but with the greatest concentration in Madagascar. The leaves are long-stalked, oval to narrowly oblong, with a close network of veining; they may be fully submerged, or most of the leaves may float on the surface. Long-stalked flowering heads emerge just above water, branched into short fleshy spikes of curious small white, pink or purplish flowers. The tuberous roots and flower buds are sometimes eaten in their native countries.

CULTIVATION: Aponogetons fall into 2 groups as far as cultivation is concerned. The larger group consists of choice subjects for the tropical aquarium, notably the magnificent Madagascar lace plant *(Aponogeton madagascariensis)* with its large lattice-like submerged leaves—not quite typical of this group, its requirements being very specialized—these require a fairly deep tank, the water kept to at least 60°F (16°C) in winter, higher in summer. The smaller group, typified by *A. distachyos,* are more cold hardy and vigorous, and are grown outdoors in temperate climates so long as the water has no more than a thin crust of ice from time to time in winter. They are easily grown, planted into the bottom mud or sand. Propagate by division of the tubers, or from seed.

Aponogeton distachyos
WATER HAWTHORN

From southern Africa, this plant makes an interesting ornamental for garden ponds, but is best not grown too close to waterlilies *(Nymphaea),* as its densely massed foliage tends to smother them. Hawthorn-scented white flower spikes, 2–4 in (5–10 cm) long and of a curious Y-shape, are produced from late spring to fall (autumn) and sometimes into winter, turning green as they age and bend into the water, where the fruit ripens. It will grow in temperate climates provided the water does not freeze. **ZONES 8–10.**

APOROCACTUS
RAT'S TAIL CACTUS

The name *Aporocactus* means the perplexing cactus, a comment on the difficulty of classifying these epiphytic cacti. Only 2 species belong to this genus from tropical Mexico; they have the usual round, spiny cactus branches, but so long, thin and weak that they cascade downwards. The pink or red flowers are large and showy, opening wide with a central small tuft of stamens; these are followed by small, reddish fruit.

CULTIVATION: Easy to grow, it is happiest in a hanging basket in fairly rich, freely draining potting soil and a place in the sun for about half the day, and no frost. Propagate from cuttings.

Aporocactus flagelliformis
RAT'S TAIL CACTUS

The unflattering common name comes from the long round branches of this epiphytic cactus. Shocking pink flowers are borne abundantly in spring and summer, crowded towards bases of stems. This species is one of the parents used in the colorful × *Epicactus* hybrids. **ZONES 10–12.**

Aporocactus martianus

Aporocactus martianus has a spread of about 3 ft (1 m) and height of 4 in (10 cm). In summer this cactus bears deep red flowers on grayish green tubular stems. **ZONES 10–12.**

APTENIA

The 2 species in this genus of mesembryanthemum relatives are native to South Africa. They are prostrate succulents with fleshy, heart-shaped to oval leaves, their surfaces having a slightly crystalline appearance. Solitary, small, pink to purplish-red, daisy-like flowers open after rain in desert areas or in summer elsewhere.

CULTIVATION: They are surprisingly hardy for South African succulents. If kept dry over winter they will tolerate temperatures down to 20°F (–7°C) or lower. Plant in gritty, very free-draining soil in full sun. They do well in dry rockeries, on retaining walls and in hanging baskets. Propagate from seed or cuttings.

Aptenia cordifolia 'Variegata'

Aptenia cordifolia

Aptenia cordifolia

This mat-forming succulent is quick growing, only about 2 in (5 cm) in height, but of indefinite spread. The creeping, weak stems bear green, heart-shaped leaves, up to 1 in (25 mm) long. Small, vivid, pink flowers (there is also a red-flowered form) appear mainly in summer, daisy-like in appearance with dense stamens. The leaves of **'Variegata'** have greenish white margins. **ZONES 9–11.**

AQUILEGIA
COLUMBINE

The common name comes from the Latin for dove, as the flowers were thought to resemble a cluster of doves. Native to Europe, North America and temperate regions of Asia, these graceful, clump-forming perennials are grown for their spurred, bell-shaped—single and double forms—flowers in a varied color range, and for their fern-like foliage. Some are also useful as cut flowers, and the dwarf and alpine species make good rock-garden plants. They flower mostly in late spring and early summer, and look best in bold clumps with a foreground planting of annuals.

CULTIVATION: Frost hardy, they prefer a well-drained light soil, enriched with manure, and a sunny site protected from strong winds and with some shade in hot areas. In cold climates columbines are perennials and need to be cut to the ground in late winter, but growing the larger-flowered cultivars as annuals usually gives best results. Propagate by division or from seed in fall (autumn) and spring; many of them self-seed readily.

Aquilegia alpina
ALPINE COLUMBINE

This upright species from the Alps of Europe grows to 18 in (45 cm) in height with a spread of 6 in (15 cm). It is similar to *Aquilegia caerulea* but has short spurs and usually all blue flowers. **ZONES 3–9.**

Aquilegia atrata
DARK COLUMBINE

Native to the alpine woodlands of Europe but tolerant of milder conditions, this species closely resembles the common columbine *(Aquilegia vulgaris)* but has dark violet-purple flowers with protruding yellow stamens, borne in late spring and early summer. Preferring part-shade in warmer areas, it grows to around 18 in (45 cm) tall. **ZONES 3–9.**

Aquilegia caerulea
BLUE COLUMBINE, ROCKY MOUNTAIN COLUMBINE

This short-lived, upright, alpine species from the Rocky Mountains grows to 24 in (60 cm) or more in height with a rather narrow growth habit. It is Colorado's state flower and arguably the

Aquilegia atrata

Aquilegia vulgaris, double form

Aponogeton distachyos

finest of the wild columbines. Large, powdery blue and white nodding flowers on branching stems appear in late spring and early summer. It sometimes produces a few blooms in fall (autumn). It does best in rich soil. **ZONES 3–9.**

Aquilegia canadensis
AMERICAN WILD COLUMBINE

This native of eastern North America produces masses of nodding, red and yellow flowers with medium-length spurs, on 18–24 in (45–60 cm) stems in late spring and early summer. It is tolerant of full sun, provided there is plenty of moisture. It will also tolerate heat if some shade is provided. Hummingbirds love the nectar-rich flowers. **ZONES 3–9.**

Aquilegia chrysantha
GOLDEN COLUMBINE

This is among the showiest of the North American columbines, with large, long-spurred, fragrant yellow flowers on stems often exceeding 3 ft (1 m) in height. Native to southwestern North America, it is more tolerant of sun and heat than most. White and double-flowered cultivars are available. **ZONES 3–10.**

Aquilegia 'Crimson Star'

These long-spurred aquilegias usually face their flowers upwards to the viewer, in contrast to the pendent flowers of the short-spurred granny's bonnets. The nectar spurs, which in other aquilegias normally match the color of the petals of which they are a prolongation, match the crimson of the sepals in this cultivar. **ZONES 3–10.**

Aquilegia 'Crimson Star'

Aquilegia elegantula

This species from the Rocky Mountains and northern Mexico is closely allied to *Aquilegia formosa* but is smaller, to 24 in (60 cm), and the pale orange or yellow flowers are slightly longer-spurred. **ZONES 5–9.**

Aquilegia flabellata

The soft, blue-green, ferny leaves and nodding, blue-purple flowers with short hooked spurs make this hardy alpine species from Japan and Korea a delightful addition to the rock garden. A summer-flowering species, it grows to about 18 in (45 cm) high. **ZONE 5.**

Aquilegia formosa
WESTERN COLUMBINE

This attractive species with long-spurred, nodding, pale scarlet flowers and protruding stamens comes from the Pacific Northwest of North America and is the parent of many popular garden cultivars. The flowering stems reach up to 3 ft (1 m) and are held above ferny leaflets. Its main flowering season is late spring and early summer. **ZONES 5–9.**

Aquilegia longissima

The species name means 'longest' and indeed this species from western Texas and adjacent Mexico has possibly the longest spurred flowers of any aquilegia, with spurs up to 6 in (15 cm) long. It resembles its close relative *Aquilegia chrysantha* but the pale yellow flowers are slightly narrower, and the spurs thinner and inclined to droop. **ZONES 5–10.**

Aquilegia chrysantha

Aquilegia caerulea

Aquilegia flabellata

Aquilegia canadensis

Aquilegia skinneri

Aquilegia formosa

Aquilegia McKana Hybrids

This, the best known strain of long-spurred columbines, is derived from North American species, chiefly *Aquilegia caerulea, A. chrysantha* and *A. formosa*. They bear flowers in a wide assortment of colors in late spring and early summer. Whatever the color of the sepals, the 5 petals that carry the spurs are usually white or yellow. Pinching off spent flowers will prolong the season. The plants grow to 3 ft (1 m) or more. **ZONES 3–10.**

Aquilegia saximontana

Native to Colorado, this is a dwarf alpine aquilegia usually less than 8 in (20 cm) high with small, short-spurred blue and yellow flowers. The specific name is a latinization of Rocky Mountains. **ZONES 4–9.**

Aquilegia skinneri

Suited to a moist, semi-shaded position, this species from New Mexico has finely divided, fern-like foliage and its pendulous green-yellow flowers have bright red, upward-pointing spurs up to 2 in (5 cm) long. Flowering over a long period during the summer months, it can grow to 3 ft (1 m) in height. **ZONES 6–9.**

Aquilegia viridiflora

This is an upright, short-lived perennial from Russia and western China that bears stems of nodding, perfumed flowers with green sepals and spurred, purplish brown petals. It grows to 12 in (30 cm) in height with a spread of 8 in (20 cm) and has mid-green leaves. **ZONES 4–9.**

Aquilegia elegantula

Aquilegia McKana Hybrid

Aquilegia vulgaris
GRANNY'S BONNETS, COLUMBINE

This is the true columbine of Europe, one of the parents of many hybrids. It grows to 3 ft (1 m) high with a spread of 18 in (45 cm) or more. On long stems from the center of a loose rosette of gray-green foliage, it bears funnel-shaped, short-spurred flowers, typically dull blue in wild plants but ranging through pink, crimson, white and purple in garden varieties. The cultivar **'Nora Barlow'** has double flowers of a curious form, with many narrow, greenish sepals and pink petals that lack spurs. **ZONES 3–10.**

Arabis caucasica

Arabis caucasica var. *brevifolia*

Arabis blepharophylla

Aquilegia vulgaris 'Nora Barlow'

ARABIS
ROCK CRESS

Over 120 species make up this northern hemisphere genus of annuals and perennials, the latter mostly evergreen. Although some can reach as much as 3 ft (1 m) in height, species grown in gardens are dwarf, often mat-forming perennials suited to the rock garden, dry walls and crevices. They spread by short rhizomes, producing crowded tufts of spatula-shaped leaves. Short sprays of delicate, 4-petalled flowers are held above the foliage in spring and summer.

CULTIVATION: They grow best in very well-drained soil in a sunny position. Propagation is from seed or from cuttings taken in summer, or by division.

Arabis blepharophylla
CALIFORNIA ROCK CRESS

This is a moderately frost-hardy species native to California, where it grows at low altitudes. Forming a compact clump 4–6 in (10–15 cm) high, it has tufts of toothed green leaves that extend into short, leafy spikes of pink to purple flowers during spring. It is best planted in a rockery or crevice where it will not be overrun. Most commonly available is the cultivar **'Frühlingszauber'** ('Spring Charm'), with rich, rose-purple flowers. **ZONES 7–10.**

Arabis caucasica
syn. *Arabis albida*
WALL ROCK CRESS

This tough, evergreen perennial is sometimes used to overplant spring-flowering bulbs. Easily grown, it forms dense clusters of thick foliage up to 6 in (15 cm) high with a spread of 18 in (45 cm). In spring it has white flowers on loose racemes above gray-green leaf rosettes. There are various forms of *Arabis caucasica* such as **'Pinkie'**, ***A. c.* var. *brevifolia*** and double-flowered forms such as **'Flore Pleno'** (syn. 'Plena'). **ZONES 4–10.**

Arabis procurrens
syn. *Arabis ferdinandi-coburgii*

This species from the mountains of southeastern Europe is similar in growth form to *Arabis caucasica*, though the leaves are smaller, hairless and press more closely against the soil. Profuse sprays of white flowers rise to 4 in (10 cm) above the foliage. It is available mainly in forms of the cultivar **'Variegata'**, with broad cream margins in the leaves. **ZONES 5–9.**

ARACHIS
PEANUT

Only one member of this genus of 20-odd species of annual and perennial legumes from South America is cultivated: the peanut *(Arachis hypogaea)*, an important crop plant though rarely grown in domestic gardens. Although treated as nuts, peanuts are more properly pulses that are eaten or processed after drying. All species have pinnate leaves with a variable number of leaflets. The pea-like flowers are usually yellow and rather small. As the flower fades, the stalk (or 'peg') of the developing pod lengthens and grows down and into the soil, ripening its seeds beneath the surface. Harvesting of the nuts is usually achieved by digging the whole plant, just as for potatoes.

CULTIVATION: Anyone can grow peanuts simply by purchasing *raw* peanuts from a health-food store and planting them just like beans, to which their cultivation requirements are very similar. The soil needs to be loose and open to allow the pegs to penetrate. They require a protected, sunny position and are quite frost tender.

Arachis hypogaea

The species name comes from the Greek for 'below the earth', referring to the unique botanical feature of this plant. It is an annual that requires a long, warm growing season for the fruit to mature fully. It grows to about 12 in (30 cm) tall and has leaves with 4 leaflets and the red-veined, yellow flowers. **ZONES 9–12.**

Aquilegia vulgaris hybrid

Aralia cachemirica

ARALIA

This genus of around 40 species of evergreen and deciduous shrubs and small trees and a few herbaceous perennials has a wide distribution in eastern and tropical Asia and the Americas. They have prickly stems, very handsome, large, compound leaves consisting of numerous leaflets, and large, terminal panicles of densely packed, small cream flowers. Younger plants of these woody species often make single, unbranched trunks with the leaves confined to the top, but as they age lateral branches develop and multiply to give a broad-headed small tree. Aralias can be eye-catching specimens when in full flower.

CULTIVATION: They need shelter from strong, drying winds and will tolerate full sun or part-shade beneath taller trees. While a moist, fertile soil suits them well, poorer soils are said to produce hardier, longer-lived specimens. Propagate from seed sown in fall (autumn) or suckers in spring.

Aralia cachemirica

Native to the Himalayas, this species is a shrub of no more than about 10 ft (3 m) with short stems lacking prickles, and large compound leaves with toothed leaflets up to 6 in (15 cm) long. *Aralia cachemirica* has white flowers which are borne on long arching sprays in summer. These are followed by tiny black fruit. **ZONES 7–9.**

Aralia californica
ELK CLOVER, SPIKENARD

Native to Oregon and moister parts of California, this aralia is a giant perennial, up to 8 ft (2.4 m) high, dying back to the ground in winter. *Aralia californica* has large coarse leaves which consist of broad, thin, toothed leaflets up to 12 in (30 cm) long, and its stems terminate in rather inconspicuous sprays of greenish flowers. The flowers are followed by small purplish fruit. A shade-loving plant, it has a large rhizome which was used medicinally in the past. **ZONES 8–10.**

Araucaria bidwillii

Araucaria bidwillii

Araucaria araucana

Aralia elata

Aralia chinensis

Araucaria angustifolia

Araucaria araucana

Aralia elata

Aralia chinensis
CHINESE ARALIA

As a young tree of up to about 10 ft (3 m), this species is usually single-stemmed with an irregular, umbrella-like crown of dark green leaves each about 4 ft (1.2 m) long, consisting of large, oval leaflets with closely toothed margins. It flowers in early fall (autumn), producing large panicles of creamy yellow umbels that droop over the foliage. With age it branches into smaller crowns, with smaller leaves and flower sprays, and may reach as much as 30 ft (9 m) in height. The leaves turn yellowish in fall. **ZONES 7–10.**

Aralia cordata
UDO

This species from Japan, Korea and China differs from most of the aralias described here in being a giant herbaceous perennial. In Japan the blanched shoots of udo are a popular vegetable, grown rather like celery or asparagus in mounded beds. The basal leaves are up to 6 ft (1.8 m) long with broad, rounded leaflets, and the arching flowering panicle is about 8 ft (2.4 m) long with umbels of modest cream flowers. **ZONES 4–9.**

Aralia elata
JAPANESE ANGELICA TREE

Native to Japan and mainland northeast Asia, this highly ornamental, frost-hardy species can grow to a spreading tree of up to 30 ft (9 m) but is most commonly seen as a shrub with few branches. Large sprays of tiny white flowers are carried into early fall (autumn), when the leaves have yellow and reddish tones. The leaflets of the cultivar **'Variegata'** have whitish markings. **ZONES 5–9.**

Aralia racemosa
AMERICAN SPIKENARD

This herbaceous perennial species, of wide distribution in North America, is valued more for its use in traditional medicine than as an ornamental. It is a woodland plant with compound leaves up to 30 in (75 cm) long, diminishing in size up the stems which are downy, 4–10 ft (1.2–3 m) in height and terminate in summer in narrow panicles of green to white flowers. The plant is many-stemmed from a branched rhizome. **ZONES 4–9.**

Aralia spinosa
DEVIL'S WALKING-STICK, HERCULES' CLUB

From the eastern USA, this species may remain a single-stemmed shrub for many years but with adequate light and nutrition it can make a tree of up to 30 ft (9 m). It has stout thorns on its trunk. The large, bipinnate leaves on younger trees are up to 3–4 ft (1–1.2 m) long, each consisting of many oval leaflets about 3 in (8 cm) long. A flowering panicle up to 4 ft (1.2 m) long bears numerous small, white flowers opening in late spring. **ZONES 6–9.**

ARAUCARIA

This remarkable, geologically ancient genus of evergreen conifers is confined in the wild to South America, Australia, Norfolk Island, New Guinea and New Caledonia. The last-mentioned island accounts for 13 of the 19 species of the genus. Most are large trees with massive, straight trunks that continue to the apex of the tree, sharply distinct from the crowded, shorter, lateral branches. The leathery leaves are incurved and densely overlapping in some species, flatter and spreading in others; male and female cones are on the same tree, the round, bristly seed cones developing right at the top of adult trees.

CULTIVATION: Most are too large for gardens but may be used as park and street trees. They will grow in a range of soil types but prefer a deep, moist, well-drained soil and full sun. Growth may be quite fast when conditions suit them. Propagate from seed in spring.

Araucaria angustifolia
PARANZA PINE

This species is native to the plateaus of southwest Brazil, where forests of it are managed for timber production. It makes a large tree with a very straight trunk and widely spreading branches, which in old trees produce an umbrella-shaped crown. The leaves are flat, prickly and rigid, up to 2½ in (6 cm) long. It adapts to climates from wet-tropical to moderately cool and will tolerate a few degrees of frost. **ZONES 9–12.**

Araucaria araucana
syn. ***Araucaria imbricata***
MONKEY PUZZLE

From South America, this tree enjoyed fad status in Britain in the 1840s. The remark that 'it would puzzle a monkey to climb it' gave rise to the common name monkey puzzle. It can grow to 80 ft (24 m) tall and 4 ft (1.2 m) in trunk diameter. Young trees have a dome-like shape with interwoven branches; with age, the crown retreats to high above the ground, so that old trees resemble long-stemmed parasols. The glossy, dark green leaves are rigid and fiercely prickly. Globular cones 4–6 in (10–15 cm) long are carried high on the crowns of mature trees. It needs a climate where the summers are cool and misty. **ZONES 8–9.**

Araucaria bidwillii
BUNYA PINE, BUNYA BUNYA

From the rainforests of southeast Queensland, Australia, this tree grows slowly to about 120 ft (36 m), developing a symmetrical, domed crown as it matures. The many long branches jutting out from the thick trunk have flat, dark green, prickly leaves about 2 in (5 cm) long. Mature trees bear huge, pineapple-like cones weighing up to 18 lb (8 kg) with large edible seeds. Ideal for large gardens in subtropical to warm-temperate climates with good rainfall, *Araucaria bidwillii* can adapt to somewhat cooler, drier conditions (but not seashores). **ZONES 8–11.**

Araucaria cunninghamii

Araucaria cunninghamii

Araucaria cunninghamii
HOOP PINE

Native to eastern Australian rainforests and found also in New Guinea, the hoop pine is moderately fast growing, reaching 100–120 ft (30–36 m) under good conditions. Not very frost hardy, it is fairly resistant to dry conditions in winter once established, though preferring good summer rainfall. The tiny, pointed scale leaves curve inwards on the branchlets, though on juvenile growths they are longer and very prickly. The new bark is copper-hued, but with age rougher, transverse ridges or 'hoops' develop. **ZONES 9–12.**

Araucaria heterophylla
syn. *Araucaria excelsa*
NORFOLK ISLAND PINE

Upright with a regular branching pattern, conical form and fast growing to 100 ft (30 m) or more, this Norfolk Island native is widely planted in subtropical coastal regions. The plants are wind tolerant, retaining their quite vertical and symmetrical habit even in the face of incessant onshore gales, and are able to thrive in deep sand; they need reliable water when young, but can tolerate dry spells once established. It is shade tolerant when young and can be long lasting in pots. **ZONES 10–11.**

ARAUJIA

Four species of evergreen, twining climbers with abundant milky sap belong to this genus, related to *Stephanotis.* They have terminal clusters of bell-shaped, sweet-scented flowers which attract moths in the evening; the moths have to wriggle into the throat of the bell to get at the nectar, and are imprisoned for a day or two until the flower withers. Pale green fruits, like a small pear in size and shape, split open to release the seeds, which are covered with downy hairs.

CULTIVATION: They spread rapidly by means of their fluffy seeds, which blow away on the slightest breeze. Marginally frost hardy, *Araujia* thrives in rich, well-drained soil in a sunny position. The seeds, thought to be poisonous to dogs and poultry, germinate readily and should be removed and disposed of carefully to prevent the plant from becoming invasive.

Araujia sericifera

Araucaria heterophylla

Araujia sericifera
syns *Araujia hortorum, A. sericofera*
CRUEL PLANT, KAPOK VINE

Native to Peru, this climbing vine grows to 20 ft (6 m) with broad, heart-shaped leaves, scented, white flowers in late summer and green, pointed seed pods that contain numerous silky seeds. In subtropical gardens it is regarded as a weed, but in cool-temperate climates it is often grown in conservatories. **ZONES 9–11.**

Arbutus canariensis

ARBUTUS
STRAWBERRY TREE, MADRONE

A dozen or more species of evergreen tree belong to this genus, the majority from Mexico and the remainder found in the Mediterranean region and North America. Most are smallish trees with thick trunks and somewhat sinuous limbs; the bark often peels attractively. The thick-textured leaves are usually finely toothed and the flowers are small, white or pinkish bells in compact clusters at the branch ends. A small proportion of flowers develop into fleshy but hard, reddish yellow globular fruit, often with wrinkled surfaces, which take almost a year to ripen. The 'strawberry' in the name refers to the fruit, which are edible but hardly palatable.

CULTIVATION: All *Arbutus* species prefer cool, humid climates, but tolerate dry conditions in summer; continental climates with extreme heat and cold do not suit them. They adapt equally to peaty, acid soils and limestone soil. Propagation is normally from seed, easily extracted from the fleshy fruit. Plant young: they dislike root disturbance.

Arbutus andrachne
GRECIAN STRAWBERRY TREE

From the eastern Mediterranean, this tree has smooth, reddish brown bark that peels to reveal the new cream or greenish bark. The glossy green leaves are smooth margined on adult trees, and the white flowers appear in early spring. The orange-red fruit, about $\frac{1}{2}$ in (12 mm) across, are quite smooth. It is rarely seen in cultivation. **ZONES 6–9.**

Arbutus × andrachnoides
HYBRID STRAWBERRY TREE

This hybrid of *Arbutus andrachne* and *A. unedo* is similar in size and ease of cultivation to the latter but usually has the smooth, peeling bark of the former. Clusters of white flowers appear in late fall (autumn). It is found wild in Greece, where the parent species grow together, and was introduced to England in the early 1800s. Selected clones are grafted onto stock of *A. unedo.* **ZONES 6–9.**

Arbutus canariensis
CANARY ISLAND STRAWBERRY TREE

From the Canary Islands, this species makes a neat, round-headed tree to 15 ft (4.5 m) high. In late summer and early fall (autumn) it produces pendulous clusters of small, light pink, lily-of-the-valley-like flowers that are followed by quite large bunches of soft green fruit about $\frac{1}{2}$ in (12 mm) in diameter, that ripen to red. The flaking, reddish brown bark is displayed throughout the year. **ZONES 8–10.**

Arbutus 'Marina'

Found as a chance seedling in a San Francisco garden, this presumed hybrid—showy, tough and relatively quick growing—is a large shrub that can be trained into a small tree of 20 ft (6 m) or more. The dark leaves serve as a backdrop for the soft pink flowers in large clusters in fall (autumn); these are followed by fruit like those of *Arbutus menziesii* but larger. **ZONES 9–10.**

Arbutus × andrachnoides

Arbutus × andrachnoides

A

A

Arctostaphylos densiflora 'Howard McMinn'

Arbutus unedo

Arbutus unedo 'Compacta'

Arbutus menziesii

Arbutus menziesii

MADRONE

Native from California to British Columbia, the madrone is the giant of the genus, reaching 100 ft (30 m) in height and 6 ft (1.8 m) in trunk diameter. In the wild it grows mostly in humid areas amongst tall conifers such as redwoods. It has beautiful, smooth, orange-brown bark and smooth-edged, glossy green leaves with whitish undersides, and produces large clusters of pure white flowers and profuse small, orange-red fruit. The American common name is a corruption of *madroño*, the Spanish name for *Arbutus unedo*. **ZONES 7–9.**

Arbutus unedo

ARBUTUS, STRAWBERRY TREE

Native to the western Mediterranean and Ireland, this bushy-crowned, small tree can attain 30 ft (9 m), though 10–15 ft (3–4.5 m) is more usual in gardens. The bark is dark gray-brown, rather fibrous and scaly, and the smaller branches and twigs have a reddish hue. In fall (autumn) the white or pinkish flower clusters, along with the 1 in (25 mm) orange fruit from the previous year, contrast with the dark foliage. It is fairly frost hardy and will tolerate neglect, but dislikes shade and damp ground. **'Compacta'** is a smaller cultivar. **ZONES 7–10.**

Arbutus xalapensis

syns *Arbutus glandulosa, A. texana*

A small tree to 40 ft (12 m) in the wild but usually less in gardens, from the highlands of Mexico, Guatemala and some southern border areas of the USA, this species is grown particularly for its distinctively beautiful, peeling bark which ages to a cinnamon or peach color, becoming more evident as the plant matures. The basal, leathery leaves are deep green above but pale brownish green beneath when young, and the pink or white summer flowers are held in loose panicles and are followed by dark red, rounded fruit. **ZONES 9–10.**

ARCHONTOPHOENIX

Majestic, subtropical palms from the rainforests of eastern Australia make up this genus of 6 species. All have tall, solitary trunks topped by a green crownshaft from which the long, gracefully arching fronds radiate. Old fronds fall cleanly from the trunk, leaving ringed scars. Large panicles of tiny but fragrant flowers burst from massive green buds that emerge at the base of the crownshaft, later becoming laden with cherry-sized red fruit.

CULTIVATION: These palms are not at all frost hardy but will grow in most fertile soil where organic matter and moisture are sufficient, even tolerating boggy conditions. They prefer part-shade when young, full sun as the crown gains height. They can also be grown as potted plants, but are not as satisfactory for this purpose as many other palms. Propagate from seed, which germinates readily in summer.

Archontophoenix alexandrae

ALEXANDRA PALM

Tall and elegant, this species from coastal north Queensland, Australia, has a straight trunk up to 50 ft (15 m) tall and arching fronds 10–12 ft (3–3.5 m) long. The silver-gray undersurface of the fronds catches the light, especially when the sun is low; the cream flowers appear mostly in fall (autumn). It thrives in wet, tropical climates but adapts well to warm-temperate climates. **ZONES 10–12.**

Archontophoenix cunninghamiana

BANGALOW PALM, PICCABEEN PALM

Similar in appearance and requirements to the Alexandra palm, this species differs in the green undersides of the fronds, the rusty scurf coating the crownshaft, and the longer, vertically pendulous panicles of pale lilac flowers. It is usually taller than the Alexandra palm at first flowering. From the subtropical Australian east coast, it prefers slightly cooler climates and can tolerate extremely light frosts. It is also more shade tolerant. **ZONES 9–11.**

ARCTOSTAPHYLOS

BEARBERRY, MANZANITA

Allied to *Arbutus*, this genus of around 50 species of evergreen shrubs or, rarely, small trees includes 2 species widely distributed through cool climates of the northern hemisphere; all others are native to western North America or Mexico. They are tough plants with very woody stems, smallish, leathery leaves and small clusters of white or pink, bell-shaped flowers. Some of the Californian species from the 'chaparral' evergreen scrub of the coastal ranges can survive the fires that periodically ravage it. They mostly have very ornamental bark, purple, red or orange and peeling in thin shreds or flakes.

CULTIVATION: They need full sun or part-shade and moist but well-drained, fertile, lime-free soil. The seed, enclosed in a small fleshy fruit, is difficult to germinate, which explains why manzanitas are propagated from tip cuttings hardened off in winter; treatment with smoke may assist germination.

Arctostaphylos alpina

ALPINE BEARBERRY, BLACK BEARBERRY

This is a dwarf shrub, native to subarctic regions of Europe, Asia and North America. It has a creeping habit, to about 6 in (15 cm) high and not spreading as extensively as the better known *Arctostaphylos uva-ursi*. The leaves, tapering to their bases and deeply veined above, are a fresh green in summer and color nicely before shrivelling in fall (autumn); they persist in plant through winter. The fruit ripen to black and are almost ½ in (12 mm) in diameter. **ZONES 2–8.**

Arctostaphylos densiflora

SONOMA MANZANITA

This is among the most adaptable and widely planted of native Californian shrubs. Ultimately growing to around 5 ft (1.5 m) tall and slightly wider, its flowers are produced in great quantity in late winter and are followed by dull red fruit in summer. **'Howard McMinn'** is a selected form of dense, mounding habit, a handsome shrub for full sun or dappled shade. **ZONES 8–10.**

Arctostaphylos 'Emerald Carpet'

A ground-covering form of manzanita thought to be a hybrid of two coastal Californian species, this plant grows to a height of 12 in (30 cm) although it may spread 6 ft (1.8 m) or more. The foliage is shining emerald green, and the pale pink flowers are relatively inconspicuous. It prefers a little shade in hotter regions and is an excellent bank cover. **'Winterglow'** is a low mounding shrub 24–36 in (60–90 cm) tall with striking reddish orange new growth maturing to dark green. **ZONES 8–10.**

Archontophoenix alexandrae

Archontophoenix cunninghamiana

Arctostaphylos hookeri

Arctostaphylos regismontana

Arctostaphylos 'Emerald Carpet'

Arctostaphylos 'Winterglow'

Arctostaphylos hookeri

Known in the wild only from a small stretch of the Californian coast, this low-growing, almost prostrate shrub has smooth, dark, reddish brown bark, a coating of downy hairs on the young branches and small, shiny, light green leaves. The clusters of waxy flowers are pinkish white; the fruit are small and pale red. It suits a situation where it can spill over rocks or a retaining wall. The cultivar **'Monterey Carpet'** makes an excellent compact bank cover 12 in (30 cm) tall and 6–8 ft (1.8–2.4 m) wide. ZONES 8–10.

Arctostaphylos manzanita

COMMON MANZANITA

Native to California, the common manzanita (Spanish for 'little apple') reaches 8 ft (2.4 m) in height and spread or sometimes much larger. A slow-growing, stiff, woody shrub, it has thick, oval leaves coated in a whitish scurf when young; the striking, reddish brown bark is sometimes hidden by peeling strips of duller, older bark. Tight clusters of small, urn-shaped, deep pink flowers in early spring are followed by $\frac{1}{2}$ in (12 mm) red-brown berries. It tolerates long dry periods in summer. **'Dr Hurd'** is an upright, tree-like selection to 15 ft (4.5 m) with striking cinnamon-colored branches. ZONES 8–10.

Arctostaphylos regismontana

From Californian coastal ranges, this species makes an upright shrub or small tree with beautiful smooth, purplish red bark that may peel off in flakes. The dense foliage is pale green with clasping leaves. ZONES 8–10.

Arctostaphylos uva-ursi

BEARBERRY, KINNIKINNICK

Found in the wild in the colder regions of the northern hemisphere, this species is best known as a completely prostrate form that can cascade over walls or embankments to form curtains of neat, dark green foliage that develops intense red tones in fall (autumn) and winter. In late spring it bears small clusters of dull pink, almost globular flowers, followed by green berries that ripen to red. *Arctostaphylos uva-ursi* is readily propagated from cuttings. Cultivars include **'Massachusetts'**, **'Radiant'**, **'Wood's Red'** which is a dwarf cultivar, and **'Vancouver Jade'** is an exceptionally vigorous and disease-resistant selection. **'Point Reyes'** is tolerant of coastal conditions. ZONES 4–9.

ARCTOTHECA

This is a South African genus composed of 5 species of rosette-forming perennials, some with prostrate short stems, others lacking any aboveground stem. The growth form is dandelion-like, with flower stems emerging from the center of the foliage rosette. The toothed or lobed leaves are densely coated in downy, white hairs, on the undersides only in some species and on both sides in others. The daisy-like flowerheads are borne singly on short stems. They are usually pale yellow or brownish yellow. In warmer temperate climates some species naturalize freely, in places becoming troublesome weeds.

CULTIVATION: *Arctotheca* species are very easily grown in any well-drained soil in full sun. They are marginally frost hardy and are propagated from seed or by removing small offset rosettes from established clumps.

Arctotheca calendula

CAPE DANDELION, CAPE WEED

A short-lived species that often pops up in lawns, Cape dandelion can be cultivated as a ground cover. In some parts of the world it is regarded as a troublesome weed, choking vegetable crops and tainting cows' milk. Its leaves are around 6 in (15 cm) long and the light yellow flowerheads, about 2 in (5 cm) in diameter, appear in continuous succession on short stems from the center of the rosette from spring to fall (autumn). Plants that are subjected to frequent mowing are far smaller than those that are left to develop naturally. ZONES 8–11.

Arctotheca populifolia

This species occurs naturally on beaches and coastal dunes, its prostrate stems becoming buried by loose sand. It has become naturalized along coasts of southern Australia. It has 3 in (8 cm) long leaves that are often elliptical in shape and unlobed with a dense felty coating of white hairs on both sides. The yellow flowerheads are small, $\frac{1}{2}$–1 in (12–25 mm) in diameter on very short stalks, and appear from summer to fall (autumn). ZONES 9–11.

ARCTOTIS

syns *Venidium*, × *Venidio-arctotis*

AFRICAN DAISY

This genus consists of about 50 species of annuals and evergreen perennials from South Africa. The stems and leaves are to varying degrees coated in matted downy hairs, giving them a gray-green or silvery gray color. The showy flowers are typical of the daisy family. They rely on the sun to open fully and come in a range of colors from creamy yellow often through orange to deep pinks and claret reds. Many hybrids are now available, their blooms with rings of darker color towards the center. Growth habit varies from compact and shrubby to quite prostrate, plants of the latter type making a faster-spreading and colorful ground cover. Some of the more distinctive *Arctotis* species include ***A. arctotoides***, with narrow, deeply lobed leaves, and ***A. cumbletonii*** with narrow disc florets.

CULTIVATION: Given plenty of space in full sun and well-drained, sandy soil, arctotises may be used as bedding plants or to cover a large area of dry bank. Flowering can be prolonged if blooms are deadheaded once the first flush of early summer flowers is finished. Propagate from seed or cuttings, which can be rooted at any time of year.

Arctostaphylos uva-ursi

Arctostaphylos manzanita

Arctotis cumbletonii

Arctotheca populifolia

Arctotis arctotoides

Arctotis acaulis

This perennial species flowers in fall (autumn) and is mostly treated as an annual in the garden. It is usually stemless with lobed leaves that are green above with a white downy coating beneath. The 4 in (10 cm) flowerheads, each held on a leafy stem, are in the yellow-orange to red range. **ZONES 9–11.**

Arctotis fastuosa

syn. ***Venidium fastuosum***

CAPE DAISY, MONARCH OF THE VELD

A perennial from the open veld in South Africa's western Cape Province, this is an adaptable plant and can be treated as an annual in colder regions. It will grow 24 in (60 cm) high, with silvery green, lobed leaves and glistening orange flowerheads with purple zones at the base of each of the many ray petals and a black central disc. It is a colorful choice for a sunny position in the garden. **ZONES 9–11.**

Arctotis hirsuta

This annual species of *Arctotis* has lobed, hairy, gray-green leaves. The flowers, in shades of orange and yellow to white, are borne in spring to mid-summer. *Arctotis hirsuta* is best propagated from seeds sown in early fall (autumn). **ZONES 9–11.**

Arctotis Hybrids

These plants were known until recently as × *Venidioarctotis* hybrids, one of the main parent species having being placed in the genus *Venidium* (now combined with *Arctotis*). They are grown as annual bedding plants in frost-prone areas but will overwinter in milder climates. Growing to a height and spread of around 18 in (45 cm), they have gray, lobed leaves that are quite downy beneath. In summer and fall (autumn) they produce a long succession of showy blooms, to 3 in (8 cm) across in a very wide range of colors, often 2-toned. **'Gold Bi-Color'**, **'Apricot'**, **'Flame'**, **'Dream Coat'** and **'Wine'** are among the more popular named hybrids. **ZONES 9–11.**

Arctotis Hybrid 'Flame'

Arctotis Hybrid 'Gold Bi-Color'

Arctotis Hybrid 'Dream Coat'

Arctotis venusta

syn. ***Arctotis stoechadifolia***

BLUE-EYED AFRICAN DAISY, FREE STATE DAISY

An annual growing to 24 in (60 cm), this species is readily identified by its strongly ribbed stems and mid-green leaves with a fine, hairy covering above, contrasting with the thick, white hairs on the undersides. The flowerheads range in color from white to salmon-pink or orange, usually with a yellowish inner ring and a distinctive blue-gray center. They bloom over a long period during summer and into fall (autumn). **ZONES 9–11.**

ARDISIA

MARLBERRY

This is a large genus consisting of over 250 species of evergreen trees and shrubs, widely distributed in tropical and subtropical regions of Asia and the Americas. The leathery leaves are mostly toothed in wavy margins. The smallish flowers are star-like, mostly white or pinkish, and the fruit are small, one-seeded berries (drupes), sometimes profuse and decorative.

CULTIVATION: When grown outdoors they are best suited to a moist, part-shaded position in well-drained, slightly acid soil that should have a high humus content. Some smaller-growing ardisias are well suited to pot culture for growing both indoors and in courtyards or patios, where they can be moved around to avoid sun and drying winds. Propagation is normally from cuttings, or by division in the case of rhizomatous species.

Ardisia crenata

syn. ***Ardisia crenulata***

CORAL BERRY

Growing up to 6 ft (1.8 m) but more often seen half that height or smaller, this shrub species has a wide distribution in Southeast Asia extending to eastern China and southern Japan. Its leathery leaves have attractively wavy margins and are densely massed above a short, single trunk. Small, white flowers emerge laterally in sprays during the summer months and are followed by densely clustered, bright red berries that persist over a long period during the fall (autumn) and winter months. **'Alba'** has white berries; **'Variegata'** has a narrow margin, red on new leaves but turning white as they mature. **ZONES 8–11.**

Ardisia crispa

There has long been uncertainty among botanists as to whether this should be regarded as a synonym of *Ardisia crenata* or as a distinct species, also from South-

Arctotis fastuosa

Arctotis Hybrid 'Apricot'

Arctotis hirsuta

Arctotis hirsuta

Arctotis Hybrid cultivar

Arctotis Hybrid 'Wine'

Arctotis venusta

Ardisia crenata

east Asia. Most plants cultivated under this name appear identical to plants grown as *A. crenata*. **ZONES 9–11.**

Ardisia japonica

Native to Japan and China, this is a low, evergreen shrub that spreads by underground rhizomes to create an attractive ground cover for shaded gardens in mild climates. The upright stems are only 8–12 in (20–30 cm) tall, although the plant spreads widely. Small, white flowers are produced at the tips of the stems in fall; these are followed by red fruit that remain colorful in winter. It is good for shaded areas with steady moisture and slightly acidic, loamy soil. **'Variegata'** has leaves marbled with cream and gray-green. **ZONES 8–10.**

ARECA

A palm genus of about 60 species, distributed through wetter regions of southern Asia and the Malay Archipelago, best known in the form of just one of its species the betel palm *(Areca catechu)*, from which betelnuts are obtained—chewed by many people in Asia and the Pacific as a mild narcotic. The species vary in growth habit and leaf type: from single-trunked to densely clumping, from tall and robust to almost stemless, and the fronds from long and regularly pinnate to small and almost undivided. The stem or trunk usually terminates in a 'crownshaft' of furled frond bases, with the flowering panicles emerging just below this. Flowers are not showy but the oval fruit can be brightly colored, usually red, orange or yellow.
CULTIVATION: These palms only grow well outdoors in the wet tropics, preferring sheltered conditions and moist soil. In cooler areas they are grown by palm enthusiasts in heated conservatories or greenhouses. Propagate from seed, which germinates readily if sown fresh.

Areca catechu
BETEL PALM, PINANG

A forest palm up to about 40 ft (12 m) tall with a single smooth, green trunk 4–6 in (10–15 cm) thick; its long feather-like fronds are rather erect but flop untidily with age. The yellow, orange or red fruit are egg-sized and may be borne at any time of year. The large white-fleshed seed is sliced and chewed together with lime and leaves of the betel pepper *(Piper betle)*. The wild origin of this species is not exactly known. **ZONES 11–12.**

ARENARIA
SANDWORT

This genus is composed of around 160 species of mainly mound-forming or ground cover perennials, some of which become shrubby with age. They are widespread in the northern hemisphere, with a few southern hemisphere species too. The plants commonly develop a dense mass of fine stems clothed with tiny, deep green or gray-green leaves and small, usually white, flowers in spring or summer. The flowers may be borne singly or in small clusters.

Areca catechu

CULTIVATION: They are easily grown in any moist, well-drained soil in full sun. They are ideal rockery or tub plants and are generally very frost hardy. Propagate from seed, self-rooted layers or small tip cuttings.

Arenaria balearica

Native to the islands of the western Mediterranean, this miniature species forms a mat of stems that root as they spread. The shiny, bright green leaves are less than ¼ in (6 mm) long and are almost circular. The plant is dotted profusely with ¼ in (6 mm) wide, green-centered, white flowers in spring and summer. **ZONES 7–9.**

Arenaria montana

This species from southwest Europe is larger than most arenarias in both leaves and flowers. It has gray-green leaves up to 1½ in (35 mm) long and mounds to about 6 in (15 cm) tall. Its flowering stems tend to be rather upright and extend slightly above the foliage clump. The abundant flowers are nearly 1 in (25 mm) in diameter, pure white with yellow-green centers. **ZONES 4–9.**

Arenaria tetraquetra

This is a densely foliaged, 1–2 in (2.5–5 cm) high, cushion plant from the mountains of southwest Europe. It has tiny overlapping leaves that give it a heather-like appearance. Small, white flowers are massed at the stem tips in spring. **ZONES 6–9.**

ARGEMONE
PRICKLY POPPY

This is a genus of 29 species of poppy-like plants native to the Americas, occurring mostly in drier subtropical regions. Most are annuals or perennials, but one is a shrub. They tend to be upright growers, many reaching 4 ft (1.2 m) or more tall, with strong stems and lobed leaves. In many species the stems, leaves and flowerbuds are a pale blue-gray and are covered in sharp prickles. The flowers, mainly yellow or orange, are from 2–6 in (5–15 cm) in diameter, usually 6-petalled and appearing throughout the warmer months. Several species, first grown as ornamentals, have become

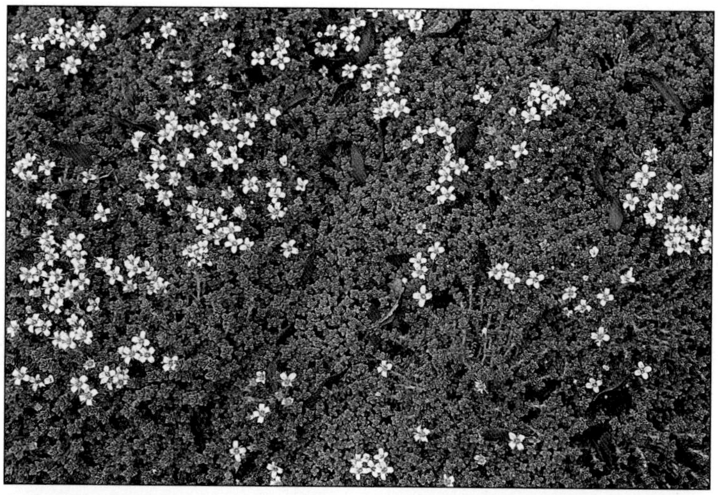

Arenaria tetraquetra

Arenaria balearica

Argemone mexicana

troublesome weeds of crops and waste places. They are all poisonous.
CULTIVATION: They are very easily grown in any well-drained soil in full sun. Hardiness varies with the species, though most will tolerate moderate frosts. Propagate from seed. Some species self-sow and become invasive.

Argemone mexicana

This annual species is native to Mexico and nearby areas of the Caribbean but has spread widely through warmer parts of the world as a weed of crops and waste ground. It has prickly, white-marked, grayish green leaves and fragrant, yellow, poppy-like flowers about 2 in (5 cm) wide appearing in summer. It has an erect habit, growing to 3 ft (1 m) high. **ZONES 8–11.**

Argemone platyceras

This annual (possibly at times a biennial) has white-marked, bluish green leaves with rather sparse prickles and bears in summer white to pale yellow, poppy-like flowers 4–5 in (10–12 cm) across. Its most distinctive feature is the seed capsule, so densely covered with spines that its surface is hardly visible. It has a spreading habit, growing to around 24 in (60 cm) high. **ZONES 8–11.**

ARGYRANTHEMUM
MARGUERITE

One of several horticulturally important genera now recognized in place of the once more broadly defined *Chrysanthemum*, this genus consists of 22 species of evergreen subshrubs from the Canary

Arenaria montana

Islands and Madeira. They tend to be upright, rarely over 3 ft (1 m) tall, and bushy with deeply lobed or divided, bright green to blue-green leaves. From spring to fall (autumn) in cool climates but mainly in winter–spring in warmer climates the bushes are covered in 1–3 in (2.5–8 cm) wide daisies in white and a wide range of pink and yellow shades. Marguerites are important as cut flowers and large numbers are sold as potted flowers by florists. In recent years there has been a renewed interest in breeding, resulting in many new cultivars.
CULTIVATION: Marguerites are very easy to cultivate in any light, well-drained soil in full sun. They grow particularly well near the sea and have naturalized in some coastal areas of the world. They should be cut back either in late winter or late summer to encourage fresh growth. Most species and cultivars tolerate light, irregular frosts only. Propagate from seed or cuttings.

A

Argyranthemum frutescens 'California Gold'

Argyranthemum frutescens

Argyranthemum frutescens 'Bridesmaid'

Argyranthemum f. 'Harvest Gold'

Argyranthemum frutescens 'Little Rex'

Argyranthemum frutescens 'Margaret'

Argyranthemum frutescens
syn. *Chrysanthemum frutescens*

Although the true species, a 3 ft (1 m) tall, white-flowered shrub from the Canary Islands, is now rarely cultivated, most of the commonly seen garden cultivars are classified under this name though many may in fact be hybrids with other species. There are numerous cultivars with a huge range of flower forms and sizes in a range of colors from white to deep pink and yellow. Some notable examples include **'Bridesmaid'**, **'California Gold'**, **'Harvest Gold'**, **'Jamaica Primrose'**, **'Little Rex'**, **'Margaret'**, **'Pink Lady'**, **'Rising Sun'**, **'Silver Leaf'**, **'Snow Man'**, **'Tauranga Star'** and **'Weymouth Pink'**. **ZONES 8–11.**

Argyranthemum maderense

Although its name implies it comes from Madeira, this species is in fact endemic to the island of Lanzarote in the Canaries. It makes a weak shrub of up to 3 ft (1 m) with broad green leaves, less deeply lobed than in most other species. The large flowerheads are pale golden yellow. **ZONES 9–11.**

ARGYREIA

Almost 100 species of rank-growing, tropical climbers make up this tropical Asian genus, closely allied to the morning glory genus *Ipomoea*. Their stems are twining, often becoming thick and woody with age, and the leaves are broad but unlobed. The flowers, carried in stalked clusters at the leaf axils, vary greatly in size, shape and color, while the fruit are red, purplish or yellow berries, not capsules as in *Ipomoea*, though they may have a leathery skin or even be quite woody. At least one species is popular for its decorative dried fruit, traded as 'wood

Argyranthemum frutescens 'Rising Sun'

Argyranthemum frutescens 'Snow Man'

rose' (or 'baby wood rose') on account of the overlapping, woody sepals that persist around the base of the fruit, giving them a shape reminiscent of double roses.

CULTIVATION: In a tropical climate cultivation is simple, the plants making very vigorous growth in a sunny position in moist soil. In cooler climates they can be grown in a sunny conservatory, but due to their rampant growth will need frequent cutting back. Propagate from seed or cuttings.

Argyreia nervosa
WOOLLY MORNING-GLORY

A native of eastern India and Bangladesh, this vigorous twiner will grow 30 ft (9 m) or more into the treetops, but can be trained over a post or stump and kept trimmed to a mound-like form. A dense white down covers both young stems and leaf undersides. The leaves are heart-shaped and up to 10 in (25 cm) wide, with lateral veins conspicuous on the undersides. Tight clusters of trumpet-shaped bright pink flowers about 2 in (5 cm) across appear among the foliage in spring and summer. **ZONES 11–12.**

ARGYROCYTISUS
MOUNT ATLAS BROOM

This genus of only one species was previously included with many other brooms in the genus *Cytisus*. A large evergreen shrub or small tree from the Atlas and Rif Mountains of Morocco, it is distinctive for its dense foliage with leaves of 3 leaflets that are exceptionally large for a broom and coated in silky hairs, giving them a beautiful silvery sheen. Spikes of yellow pea-flowers terminate the branches; they are followed by flattened, hairy pods.

CULTIVATION: It prefers a sunny position and rather dry atmosphere. It is more frost tender than most European brooms but nonetheless prefers a mild climate. It needs well-drained soil and is tolerant of a wide range of garden conditions. Propagate from seed or cuttings.

Argyrocytisus battandieri
syn. *Cytisus battandieri*

This shrub or small tree, 12 ft (3.5 m) high and wide, is mainly grown for the pineapple-shaped flowers, heavily scented with a pineapple perfume. **ZONES 8–10.**

ARGYRODERMA

From South Africa comes this genus of 10 species of very distinctive succulents. Although their foliage is somewhat variable, most often they have cleft pairs of very fleshy, gray-green leaves. The effect is something like a half-buried, small blue-green egg with a narrow wedge

Argyranthemum f. 'Tauranga Star'

Argyranthemum f. 'Weymouth Pink'

Argyranthemum maderense

Argyrocytisus battandieri

removed across the center. A white, purple-red or red, daisy-like flower develops in the cleft. As the plants age they develop into small clumps of the unusual paired leaves. At least one species has more elongated leaves. The name comes from the Greek words *derma*: meaning skin and *argyros* meaning silver, in reference to the foliage.
CULTIVATION: The key to success is a very light, gritty soil and mulching of gravel to prevent the foliage being splashed with water or remaining wet. Argyrodermas need full sun and are often better grown as house or greenhouse plants. They are hardy to only light frosts and are usually propagated from seed, though it is possible to divide large clumps.

Argyroderma delaetii
syn. *Argyroderma blandum*
LIVING STONES

This bizarre species has 2 succulent, frosted-green leaves, joined at the base, forming a rectangular mass $1\frac{1}{2}$ in (35 mm) high with a scooped-out center. In winter a single, deep crimson, daisy-like flower emerges from the middle of the plant, often completely covering the leaves. **ZONES 10–11.**

ARIOCARPUS
LIVING ROCK

This genus consists of about 6 species of bizarre, slow-growing cacti from arid hills of southern Texas and Mexico. They have no spines and their gray or green, overlapping tubercles are so well developed that they almost look like little agave leaves in some species, or like roughened pebbles in others. Some have tufts of downy hairs on the top of the plant or at the ends of the tubercles. The flowers, often quite showy, can be cream through yellow to pink or purplish.
CULTIVATION: Unless your garden is in a desert, they will need to be grown under glass, in strong light and in a very open cactus mixture kept virtually dry except in the summer growing season. Propagate from seed. In Europe it is illegal to offer *Ariocarpus* for sale.

Ariocarpus fissuratus

This striking species occurs on both sides of the border, in southwest Texas as well as northern Mexico. It has very short and broad, brownish green tubercles that are extraordinarily warty and fissured. The plant is almost globular, about 3–4 in (8–10 cm) in diameter, and bears a few large, pale to deep pink flowers right at the top in mid-summer. **ZONES 10–11.**

Ariocarpus retusus

Native to northern Mexico, this slow-growing species develops into a broad, brownish plant up to 10 in (25 cm) wide with triangular, grayish tubercles that terminate in strong, bony points. In nature the plant is usually half-buried in the soil. The smallish flowers, emerging at the plant's apex and opening only during the day, are white with pink midlines on the petals. **ZONES 10–11.**

Ariocarpus trigonus

From northern Mexico this compact cactus, up to 4 in (10 cm) high and 6 in (15 cm) across, has large, pointed, 3-angled, grayish-green tubercles and bears in summer showy, apricot-tinted cream flowers 2 in (5 cm) across in a ring around the top of the plant, which is virtually bare of wood. **ZONES 10–11.**

ARISAEMA
JACK IN THE PULPIT

This is a genus of the arum family, consisting of around 150 species of tuberous or rhizomatous perennials found in temperate to tropical parts of the northern hemisphere. Their foliage is variable and they often have only one or two leaves per shoot. The leaves are usually divided, sometimes very finely, and make a frilled base to the erect, flowering stem that emerges through the center of the foliage. The flowering stems vary considerably in height depending on the species, and carry a single flower spike in spring or early summer. The bloom is typical of the arum family, with a central spadix of minute, fleshy flowers surrounded by a greenish spathe. However, there is enormous variation in size, color and shape of the spathe. Heads of fleshy red fruit follow the flowers.
CULTIVATION: Most of the cultivated species tolerate moderate to severe frosts and prefer to grow in woodland conditions with cool, moist, humus-rich soil and dappled shade. Propagate from seed or offsets.

Arisaema elephas

This species from western China has a 12 in (30 cm) flower stem and a 3-parted leaf with leaflets up to 6 in (15 cm) long. The spathe is around 6 in (15 cm) long and deep purple with white striping at the base. The spadix develops a long, curved appendage that extends to the ground. ***Arisaema formosanum*** is another species of Chinese origin. **ZONES 5–10.**

Arisaema jacquemontii

With a flower stem from 4–30 in (10–75 cm) tall, this species produces one or two leaves divided into 3 to 9 leaflets up to 6 in (15 cm) long. The narrow, white-striped spathes are pointed and slightly hooded at the tip and up to 6 in (15 cm) long. It is found from Afghanistan to southeast Tibet. **ZONES 6–9.**

Arisaema serratum

Arisaema robustum

This is a Japanese species with flower stems up to 24 in (60 cm) tall. It has a single leaf with 3 leaflets up to 6 in (15 cm) long. The short spathe is green with white or purple stripes. **ZONES 7–10.**

Arisaema serratum

This northeast Asian species has a flower stem up to 3 ft (1 m) tall with 2 leaves each divided into 7 to 20 leaflets up to 6 in (15 cm) long. The spathe is 3–4 in (8–10 cm) long, pale green with purple spotting or purple all over, sometimes with white stripes. The spadix has a 2 in (5 cm) yellow appendage. **ZONES 5–9.**

Arisaema sikokianum

This Japanese native is probably the most widely cultivated species. Its flower stem is around 18 in (45 cm) tall and it has 2 trifoliate leaves with leaflets up to 6 in (15 cm) long. The spathe is 6–8 in (15–20 cm) long, deep purple on the outside with a stark white interior. The spadix is also pure white with an upright, club-shaped appendage. **ZONES 7–9.**

Arisaema triphyllum

This is one of the distinctive wildflowers of North America's northeastern woodlands, flowering in spring before the trees leaf. One or two medium green leaves, each divided into 3 leaflets, expand to a height of about 12 in (30 cm) after the flowers fade. The slender spadix is enclosed by a spathe of pale green to purple-brown. Bright scarlet berries ripen in fall (autumn), when the leaves have died down. **ZONES 4–9.**

Argyroderma delaetii

Ariocarpus retusus

Ariocarpus trigonus

Arisaema elephas

Arisaema formosanum

Arisaema robustum

Arisaema sikokianum

Arisaema triphyllum

ARISARUM

Only 3 species belong to this genus of small tuberous perennials in the arum family, native to the Mediterranean region and the Azores and Canary Islands. They are densely clumping plants with long leaf stalks springing directly from the ground, ending in smallish arrowhead-shaped or heart-shaped blades. Much shorter than the leaves, the flowering stems bear a small but curiously shaped spathe, with the tip hooded over so as to completely hide the short spadix. **CULTIVATION:** They are woodland plants that like a moist, sheltered situation, lightly shaded. They are best left undisturbed except for lifting and dividing clumps every few years, in fall (autumn) or winter. Propagate from seed or by division.

Arisarum proboscideum
MOUSE PLANT

Native to Spain and Italy, this is a charming miniature whose little spathes, with round purplish hoods prolonged into slender 6 in (15 cm) 'tails', never fail to arouse interest, though one may have to peer between the leaves to view them. Flowering in spring and dying back in fall (autumn), the plant is only about 6 in (15 cm) high but can spread to form a large patch. **ZONES 6–10.**

Armeria alliacea

ARISTEA

This genus contains around 50 species of mainly evergreen, rhizomatous, iris-like perennials from tropical and southern Africa and Madagascar. They form clumps of sword-shaped leaves from 8–36 in (20–90 cm) tall depending on the species. The ½–1 in (12–25 mm) wide, 6-petalled flowers are clustered along erect, cane-like stems and are usually in shades of blue or purple. The flowering season ranges from late winter to summer.
CULTIVATION: Aristeas thrive on stream banks, in moist, sandy, humus-rich soil in full sun or light shade. Most species are hardy to about 25°F (–4°C) but are damaged if subjected to frequent frosts. Older plants do not transplant well, so division may not always be successful. Propagate from seed—in fall (autumn) or spring—usually produced in abundance.

Aristea ecklonii

This vigorous, evergreen species from southeastern Africa is 18–24 in (45–60 cm) tall, forming tangled clumps of long, lanceolate green leaves, above which starry, deep blue flowers appear rather sparsely in summer. **ZONES 9–11.**

Aristea ensifolia

This elegant South African native grows to around 4 ft (1.2 m). The iris-like leaves surround stems on which 1 in (25 mm) purple-blue flowers are borne in summer. **ZONES 8–10.**

Aristea major
syn. *Aristea thyrsiflora*

This elegant, fall- (autumn) flowering native of South Africa's Cape Province grows up to 5 ft (1.5 m) tall. From clumps of iris-like leaves arise flowering stems terminating in dense spikes of 1 in (25 mm) wide, purple to blue flowers, which close at night. **ZONES 8–10.**

Arisarum proboscideum

Aristea ecklonii

Aristolochia clematitis

Aristolochia littoralis

ARISTOLOCHIA
DUTCHMAN'S PIPE, BIRTHWORT

This large genus of over 500 species comprises evergreen and deciduous, twining climbers and some herbaceous perennials, native to many different climatic regions. The climbers are most often cultivated, chosen for their heart-shaped leaves and unusually shaped tubular flowers, which have a swelling at the base and a hood above, usually with the tube between sharply bent. Insects are attracted into the mouth of the flowers by a strong scent, and pollen is scattered over their bodies. The fruit are also curiously shaped, dangling from slender stalks and splitting at maturity to spill fine seed as they rock in the breeze.
CULTIVATION: The plants require well-drained, humus-rich soil in a sunny position with some shade in summer, and support for their climbing habit. Many have some degree of frost tolerance and will grow vigorously in warm-temperate climates. In spring, prune the previous year's growth to 2 to 3 nodes. Propagate from seed in spring or from cuttings in summer. Watch out for spider mites.

Aristolochia californica

This deciduous, vigorous climber from California can clamber up to 15 ft (4.5 m) or more and has broad, heart-shaped leaves and distinctive, rather small, dull purple flowers with the upper lip divided into 2 lobes. **ZONES 7–10.**

Aristolochia clematitis
BIRTHWORT

Now seldom grown in gardens, this European species was used by medieval midwives, following the medieval Doctrine of Signatures—a belief that the Creator had marked plants in such a way that doctors could recognize diseases they were intended to cure. The womb-like shape of the birthwort flower indicated that the plant would help in problems of childbirth. **ZONES 5–9.**

Aristolochia grandiflora
PELICAN FLOWER

The curiously shaped flower buds of this Central American species resemble the neck of the pelican. The purple and green flowers, which at 6 in (15 cm) or more across are among the largest in the genus, appear in summer, emitting an odor that is attractive to pollinating flies, but not so appealing to humans. The vine grows very quickly from seed and can be treated as an annual in temperate climates. **ZONES 10–12.**

Aristolochia littoralis
syn. *Aristolochia elegans*
CALICO FLOWER

This creeper, fast-growing to 20 ft (6 m), is native to Brazil and needs high humidity and protection from frost. It has fleshy leaves and in summer bears strangely shaped, maroon flowers with white, thread-like markings. It is an interesting plant for verandah columns or a pergola and can be grown as an annual in cool climates. **ZONES 10–12.**

Aristolochia macrophylla
syns *Aristolochia durior, A. sipho*
DUTCHMAN'S PIPE

This vigorous, eastern North American, deciduous, twining vine reaches a height of 20–30 ft (6–9 m), crowding out other plants as it matures. The large, dark glossy green leaves tend to cover the pipe-shaped, purple-brown and yellow-green bicolor flowers borne in the leaf axils in late spring and early summer. Tolerant of a wide variety of soil types, it grows well in sun or shade. **ZONES 4–9.**

ARMERIA
THRIFT, SEA PINK

This genus of about 35 species of low-growing, tufted, early summer-flowering perennials is found in a wide variety of environments in the temperate zones of Eurasia, Africa and the Americas—from salt marshes and storm-swept headlands of the seashores to alpine meadows. The plants have crowded, narrow, mostly evergreen leaves, usually forming a dense mound, and small flowers crowded into globular heads, each atop a slender stalk.
CULTIVATION: They are suitable for rock gardens or borders and prefer exposed, sunny positions and rather dry soil with good drainage. They are generally frost hardy. Propagate from seed or cuttings in spring or fall (autumn).

Armeria alliacea

Occurring widely in the western half of Europe, this is one of the more robust species, with large tufts of long, soft, flat, deep green leaves and numerous bright reddish purple flowerheads on stems up to 18 in (45 cm) tall. **ZONES 5–9.**

Armeria 'Bee's Ruby'

From within the Bees Hybrid range of tall-stemmed armerias, 'Bee's Ruby' with its coloring of deep cerise pink bordering on ruby is ideal for cut flowers, either fresh or used in dried arrangements. The abundant flowering stems are about 12 in (30 cm) tall. **ZONES 5–9.**

Armeria juniperifolia
syn. *Armeria caespitosa*

A distinctive, dwarf species from the mountains of central Spain, this has very short, sharp-pointed fine leaves in dense rosettes crowded into small mounds no more than about 3 in (8 cm) tall. Tight heads of relatively large, pale to deep pink flowers are held on short stalks just above the foliage. The cultivar **'Bevan's Variety'** is even more compact in growth habit, with deeper pink flowers.
ZONES 5–9.

Armeria leucocephala

A dwarf, densely mound-forming subshrub from the Mediterranean islands of Corsica and Sardinia, this attractive species has tangled, fine, linear leaves up to 4 in (10 cm) long, often finely hairy, as are the fine flower stalks, up to 15 in (38 cm) tall. The small flowerheads vary in color; it is usually **'Corsica'** with brick-red summer flowers that is seen in gardens. **ZONES 7–9.**

Armeria maritima
COMMON THRIFT, SEA PINK

Native around much of the northern hemisphere and consisting of many wild races, thrift was in cultivation as early as 1578. Growing to 4 in (10 cm) high and spreading to 8 in (20 cm), it has a mound-like mass of narrow, dark green leaves, and dense flowerheads of small, white to pink flowers are produced in spring and summer. Most *Armeria* cultivars are derived from this species. **'Vindictive'** has vibrant rose-pink flowers. **'Alba'** has small white flowers. **ZONES 4–9.**

ARMORACIA
HORSERADISH

This is a genus of 3 species of vigorous, taproot-forming perennials found naturally from southeast Europe to Siberia, only one of which is cultivated. Horseradish is an extremely vigorous grower and even the most dedicated devotees of horseradish sauce should think twice before introducing it into their gardens. The tough, white roots are used to prepare the well-known condiment and also have some medicinal properties.
CULTIVATION: They are very easily grown in temperate climates, in any soil in sun or light shade. Propagate by dividing an established clump, however, this is seldom necessary as once you have it you have it for life.

Armoracia rusticana

This is the only commonly grown species and the one used for horseradish sauce. Native to southeast Europe, it has 12–18 in (30–45 cm) long, bright to deep green leaves with a puckered surface, sometimes lobed towards the base. Panicles of white flowers develop in summer but are usually removed to encourage root development. **'Variegata'**, as the name suggests, is a variegated form. Japanese horseradish, or wasabi, is a different plant, from the genus *Wasabia.* **ZONES 5–10.**

ARNEBIA

Related to the forget-me-not genus *Myosotis*, this genus consists of about 25 species of herbaceous perennials and annuals from the Mediterranean region, Africa and western Asia. Some are quite striking plants with basal rosettes of coarse, bristly leaves from which arise dense panicles of large, brilliant yellow or orange flowers, quite unlike their humble forget-me-not allies.
CULTIVATION: Coming from mountain areas where they grow on rocky screes and ledges in climates with dry summers, most species are difficult subjects in cultivation, requiring good drainage and a hot position as well as having a winter

Armoracia rusticana

chilling requirement. However, a few species are more adaptable, for example *Arnebia pulchra*, which can be grown in the perennial border. Propagate from seed or by division of the rootstock.

Arnebia pulchra

The only species at all likely to be grown in gardens, *Arnebia pulchra* is native to the Caucasus Mountains and nearby regions of Iran and Turkey. It is a perennial of up to about 15 in (38 cm) in height with densely tufted basal leaves and somewhat sprawling flowering stems that also bear leaves and are topped by dense heads of brilliant yellow flowers, each with 5 red-brown spots between the short rounded petals. **ZONES 6–9.**

ARNICA

This is an interesting genus of herbaceous perennials with yellow daisy flowers, the great majority of its 30-odd species native to cooler regions of North America but with 2 occurring in Eurasia. Many people are familiar with the name as that of an ointment and a tincture used for bruises and sprains, also in homeopathy—these are prepared from *Arnica montana*, a species occurring in northern parts of both eastern and western hemispheres. The plants are deep rooted, with tufts of narrow to broad, usually hairy, bright green leaves appearing in spring; the stems bear stem leaves in opposite pairs and in early summer terminate in showy yellow or orange flowerheads like small sunflowers.
CULTIVATION: Although quite ornamental, arnicas have never been popular as garden plants, probably due to their climatic requirements which make them prone to late summer rotting in lowland areas. They need full sun and moist, well-drained, humus-rich soil. Propagate from seed or by division.

Arnica montana
ARNICA

Although not the most ornamental of the arnicas, this well known medicinal species is nonetheless a pretty plant. It has a wide natural distribution in Europe and western Asia, common in wildflower meadows on treeless mountain slopes. The basal leaves are spoon-shaped with strongly marked veins, springing from a tenacious root system and forming extensive clumps. The golden-yellow flowerheads, 2–3 in (5–8 cm) across, are borne singly on strong hairy stalks 12–24 in (30–60 cm) tall. **ZONES 4–9.**

Armoracia rusticana 'Variegata'

Armeria leucocephala 'Corsica'

Aronia arbutifolia

Armeria maritima

Aronia melanocarpa

Aronia melanocarpa 'Nero'

ARONIA
CHOKEBERRY

A member of the pome-fruit group of the rose family, *Aronia* consists of only 3 deciduous shrub species from North America, but all these make fine garden shrubs of compact size with abundant displays of glossy red or black berries in late summer and fall (autumn). They have oval leaves with finely toothed margins, and bear small umbels of flowers like miniature apple blossoms in spring.
CULTIVATION: Frost hardy and not demanding as to soil, they will grow well in part-shade but respond to full sun with more profuse fruit and brighter fall foliage. Cut the oldest stems to the ground to encourage new growth. Propagate from seed or cuttings. The foliage is prone to disfigurement by the pear and cherry slug, the larva of a sawfly.

Aronia arbutifolia
RED CHOKEBERRY

Native to eastern North America, where it is a common understory plant, this species grows to 6 ft (1.8 m) with many vertical stems forming spreading clumps. White flowers in spring are followed by bright red berries in fall (autumn) and early winter, popular with birds. Narrow, oval leaves turn bright red in fall—this is best in **'Brilliant'** (sometimes listed as **'Brilliantissima'**). **ZONES 4–9.**

Aronia melanocarpa
BLACK CHOKEBERRY

Very similar in foliage and flowers to the red chokeberry *(Aronia arbutifolia)* and originating in the same region of the USA, the black chokeberry is a lower, more spreading shrub with more densely crowded stems. The leaves are less glossy and the berries, ripening a brilliantly glossy black, do not last long into fall (autumn) but drop soon after they ripen. **'Nero'** and **'Viking'** are well-known cultivars of *A. melanocarpa.* **ZONES 5–9.**

ARRHENATHERUM

This is a genus of 6 species of perennial grasses native to Europe and the Mediterranean, one of them widely distributed in cultivation and as a weed. The wild forms are rather nondescript grasses, somewhat resembling the oat grasses *(Avena)* or the fescues *(Festuca)*, with clumps of erect stems terminating in chaffy heads with protruding short bristles ('awns').
CULTIVATION: Cultivation is easy to say the least, with seed germinating freely and, in the case of the bulbous form, plants coming up wherever the bulbs are dispersed. As for most perennial grasses, the aboveground parts are killed off by winter frosts. They need full sun or part-shade and fertile, well-drained soil.

A

Artemisia absinthium

Artemisia absinthium 'Lambrook Silver'

Artemisia arborescens

Artemisia ludoviciana

Artemisia ludoviciana 'Valerie Finnis'

Artemisia ludoviciana 'Silver Queen'

Artemisia caucasica

Arrhenatherum elatius subsp. *bulbosum*
BULBOUS OAT GRASS

Both species and subspecies are native to Europe, the latter distinguished by the numerous small bulblike thickenings of the stem bases, allowing it to overwinter and be easily spread by disturbances such as cultivation of the soil. It normally makes a clump of rather ordinary, flattish grass leaves, in late spring and summer sending up seeding panicles to 3–4 ft (1–1.2 m) in height. Normally this grass is an undesirable weed, but the cultivar **'Variegatum'** is much less vigorous, only 12 in (30 cm) or so tall and rarely flowering; its leaves are conspicuously striped white. **ZONES 4–10.**

ARTEMISIA
WORMWOOD

This is a large genus of perennials and shrubs native to temperate regions of the northern hemisphere, many from arid and semi-arid environments. They are grown mainly for their decorative foliage which is often aromatic and sometimes repellent to insects; in many species it is coated with whitish hairs. An attractive addition to a flower border, the feathery foliage provides interest throughout the year. The small yellowish flowerheads are not showy. There are both evergreen and deciduous species.

CULTIVATION: Mostly quite frost hardy, they prefer an open, sunny situation with light, well-drained soil. Prune back lightly in spring to stimulate growth. Propagate from cuttings in summer or by division in spring. Transplant during winter.

Artemisia abrotanum
SOUTHERNWOOD, LAD'S LOVE, OLD MAN

The highly aromatic, frost-hardy shrub, growing to 3–5 ft (1–1.5 m), has naturalized through many parts of Europe although its exact origin has been lost in time. Although the finely incised, gray-green leaves are held erect, it is very brittle-stemmed so care should be taken in positioning it away from trafficked areas. Though grown mainly for its foliage, it does produce small, yellowish flowerheads in late summer. It may be deciduous or semi-evergreen depending on climate. **ZONES 4–10.**

Artemisia absinthium
COMMON WORMWOOD, ABSINTHE

Of wide natural occurrence in Europe and temperate Asia, common wormwood grows to 3 ft (1 m) though often rather lower, with much divided, dull gray foliage. It is a subshrub that spreads by rhizomes, the tangled, flopping stems also rooting as they spread. Inconspicuous, dull yellow flowerheads are borne in late summer. Trim after flowering to keep it neat. **'Lambrook Silver'** with its tidy habit is considered one of the better silver-leafed shrubs, providing a restful contrast to brightly colored flowers in a herbaceous border. **ZONES 4–10.**

Artemisia arborescens

This spreading, evergreen shrub from the Mediterranean region reaches a height of 4 ft (1.2 m) with a rounded habit and lacy, silver-gray foliage. Small, yellowish flowers are borne in summer and early fall (autumn). Only moderately frost hardy, it is a good plant for the back of a border. **ZONES 8–11.**

Artemisia caucasica
syns *Artemisia lanata, A. pedemontana*

Widely distributed through southern European mountains from Spain to the Ukraine and the Caucasus, this is a semi-deciduous or evergreen perennial less than 12 in (30 cm) high and of spreading habit, with soft, silvery grayish leaves divided into very narrow lobes. In summer it produces short spikes of dull yellow flowerheads. **ZONES 5–9.**

Artemisia dracunculus
TARRAGON

Native to central and eastern Europe and grown for its narrow, aromatic, green leaves which have a delicate, peppery aniseed flavor, tarragon grows up to 3 ft (1 m) in the warmer months, dying back to a perennial rootstock over winter. As it does not produce seed, propagate by division in early spring. The tarragon seed sometimes offered is the flavorless *Artemisia dracunculoides,* known as Russian tarragon. **ZONES 6–9.**

Artemisia frigida
FERN-LEAFED WORMWOOD, FRINGED SAGEBRUSH

This mat-forming perennial to 12 in (30 cm) high from southeastern Russia has silvery green, fine, long, fern-like leaves and nodding heads of yellow flowers in late summer. **ZONES 3–9.**

Artemisia pontica

Artemisia lactiflora
WHITE MUGWORT

This tall-growing, Chinese, herbaceous species has erect, many-branched panicles of tiny, milky white flowers in summer. The dark green foliage is cut into jagged segments. It contrasts well with stronger colors in a garden and grows to 4–5 ft (1.2–1.5 m) with a spread of 18 in (45 cm). It may need staking. **ZONES 5–9.**

Artemisia ludoviciana
syn. *Artemisia purshiana*
WESTERN MUGWORT, WHITE SAGE

Native to western North America and Mexico, this rhizomatous species is grown for its lance-shaped, sometimes coarsely toothed leaves, which are densely white-felted beneath and gray- to white-haired above. Bell-shaped, grayish flowerheads are produced in summer. A spreading, invasive species, it reaches a height of 4 ft (1.2 m) and is very frost hardy. **'Valerie Finnis',** with its jagged margined leaves, together with **'Silver Queen'** are 2 of several popular cultivars, while ***Artemisia ludoviciana* var. *albula*,** found naturally in California, has much smaller leaves. **ZONES 4–10.**

Artemisia pontica
ROMAN WORMWOOD

This vigorous plant from central Europe has upright growth and feathery silver-green foliage with creamy yellow flowers in summer. It is a rhizomatous herb growing to 30 in (75 cm) high and can be invasive, however, it usually dies back in winter. **ZONES 4–10.**

Artemisia 'Powis Castle'

This assumed hybrid between *Artemisia absinthium* and *A. arborescens* has finely dissected, silvery leaves, a gentle, 24–36 in (60–90 cm) mounding habit

Artemisia dracunculus

Artemisia 'Powis Castle'

Artemisia vulgaris 'Variegata'

and because it seldom flowers it remains more compact than other species; older plants benefit from a hard cutting back in early spring. It is useful in the garden for its distinctive foliage. In cold climates, grow indoors over winter for planting out in spring. **ZONES 6–10.**

Artemisia schmidtiana
SATINY WORMWOOD

This tufted, rhizomatous perennial herb grows up to 24 in (60 cm) with palmately lobed leaves and long, upright panicles of creamy white flowers in summer. **'Nana'** is a dwarf form, ideally suited to a well drained pocket in a rock garden. It grows to only 3 in (8 cm) high and forms a delicate mound of finely cut, fragrant silver leaves. **ZONES 3–9.**

Artemisia stelleriana
BEACH WORMWOOD, DUSTY MILLER

Excellent planted in light sandy soils, this evergreen perennial from sea coasts of northeast Asia has serrated, white-haired, silver leaves, and slender sprays of small yellow flowers are borne in summer. It has a compact habit and grows 12–24 in (30–60 cm) high and spreads up to 3 ft (1 m). It is very frost hardy. **ZONES 4–9.**

Artemisia vulgaris
MUGWORT

The leaves of this well-known species are green with hardly a hint of the much sought-after silver gray and are less divided than those of other species, so it is not as highly regarded by gardeners as other artemisias. **'Variegata'**, with its foliage marked with white specks, can make a useful addition to the garden in cooler areas. Mugwort was used to flavor beer before hops were so used, and in ancient times was believed to have magical properties. **ZONES 4–10.**

ARTHROPODIUM

The ungainly name *Arthropodium* is from the Greek and means having a jointed foot, referring to the way the footstalk of each flower has a joint in the middle. Of this genus of a dozen or so perennials from Australasia, only 2 or 3 are seen in gardens, the most ornamental being the New Zealand renga renga, *Arthropodium cirratum*.

CULTIVATION: They are essentially plants of warm-temperate climates; in cool areas they need a sheltered spot in fertile, well-drained soil. Propagate from seed or by division.

Arthropodium milleflorum

Arthropodium cirratum
RENGA RENGA LILY

This New Zealand species bears graceful sprays of starry white flowers on a 24 in (60 cm) stem above tufts of broad, handsome leaves in late spring. It looks a little like a hosta and is a good substitute in the hot-summer climates in which hostas languish. The Maoris made use of the fleshy roots in medicine. **ZONES 8–10.**

Arthropodium milleflorum

Native to Australia, this deciduous species with tuberous roots has long, narrow leaves and in late spring bears numerous, small pale lilac flowers on 24 in (60 cm) tall stems. The effect is rather like an ornamental grass and it would be a good choice for this role in warm-temperate flowerbeds. The species name means 'thousand-flowers', which is perhaps an exaggeration. **ZONES 8–11.**

ARTOCARPUS

Best known in the form of one of its many species, the breadfruit of Captain Bligh of the *Bounty* fame, *Artocarpus* is actually a very large tropical Asian genus of evergreen trees. It is closely related to *Ficus*, the fig genus, and in fact many of its species are hard to tell apart from figs when not in flower or fruit. The leaves, bark and twigs exude a milky sap when damaged, and the minute, greenish, female flowers are crowded onto short, fleshy spikes which after fertilization enlarge into aggregations of fleshy fruit, very large in the case of the species mentioned below.

CULTIVATION: Edible-fruited species are cultivated in the wet tropics, thriving best in deep, fertile, well-drained soil in sheltered positions. Propagation is from seed, or more commonly from root cuttings or aerial layers (marcotts), which perpetuate desirable clones.

Artocarpus altilis

Artocarpus altilis
syn. ***Artocarpus communis, A. incisa***
BREADFRUIT

Believed to be native to the Malay region and carried into the Pacific by colonizing Polynesians, this species has handsome foliage, with ascending branches bearing deeply incised fresh green leaves up to 30 in (75 cm) long. Fast growing when young, it reaches 25 ft (8 m) in 10 years; old trees are not much taller but develop a rounded, bushy crown. The flower spikes are inconspicuous, the female ones developing into yellowish green globular fruit with starchy flesh that is eaten after baking or boiling. **ZONE 12.**

Artocarpus heterophyllus
JACKFRUIT, JACA

This Southeast Asian species is easily confused with its close relative the chempedak *(Artocarpus integer)*; both have similar gigantic, compound fruit and leathery, unlobed leaves, but the chempedak's fruit are sweeter. The jackfruit grows to 30 ft (9 m) tall with a single main trunk and dense, rounded crown of dark green leaves. The fruit may be up to 24 in (60 cm) long and weigh up to 40 lb (18 kg). Their outer surface is creamy brown with small conical protuberances, and the sticky yellow or pink flesh contains many large brown seeds which are edible, as is the sweet though malodorous flesh. **ZONES 11–12.**

Artocarpus lingnanensis

Native to southern China, this species has no special value apart for its compact, glossy foliage. It could be used as a small shade tree. Short spikes of tiny cream flowers add interest in summer. **ZONE 10–12.**

ARUM

Although many plants are commonly called arums, only a few truly belong to this genus, consisting of some 25 species

Arthropodium cirratum

Artocarpus heterophyllus

from the Mediterranean region and western Asia. The white 'arum lily' of the flower shop is not among them—that is *Zantedeschia aethiopica*. All are curious and worth growing, but only 2 or 3 are widely available. They are tuberous perennials with broad, fleshy leaves, usually arrowhead-shaped and often variegated with a paler green along the veins. The true flowers are minute, carried in the finger-like spadix that terminates the thick flower stalk; the spadix in turn is encircled by the more conspicuous spathe, or bract.

CULTIVATION: The more leafy species, such as *Arum italicum*, are easily grown in part shade in moist but well-drained, humus-rich soil, and require no attention. Species from drier climates, such as *A. palaestinum*, require to be kept much drier during the dormant period. Propagate by division after the foliage dies back, or from seed in fall (autumn).

Arum creticum

This species has arrow-shaped, glossy, dark green leaves that emerge in fall (autumn) and reach 24 in (60 cm) in height. The flowering spikes consist of bright yellow to greenish white spathes and sweetly perfumed, pale yellow spadices. It is native to Crete. **ZONES 7–9.**

Arum italicum
ITALIAN ARUM

Growing to 12 in (30 cm), this species from Europe and North Africa has broad, arrow-shaped, marbled leaves in fall (autumn). Appearing in early spring, the flower spike has a light green, hooded spathe with a yellow spadix standing erect in the center. It is followed by orange berries that last until late summer. **ZONES 7–10.**

Arum italicum

Artocarpus lingnanensis

Arum maculatum

CUCKOO-PINT, LORDS AND LADIES, JACK IN THE PULPIT

This, the most northerly species, is a fairly common wildflower on wet ground in England and in much of Europe as well. It resembles *Arum italicum* but is smaller overall, the leaves often with dark flecks. The spathes are erect and hooded over at the top, pale green with purplish edges and sometimes spotted dark purple. **ZONES 7–9.**

Arum palaestinum

syns *Arum sanctum, Calla sancta*

This species, a native of Israel, is not really black but is as close to black as flowers get, and for that reason attracts gardeners who are not deterred by its musty smell. It is the inside of the spathe that is an extremely dark purple shade, the outside being greenish white. The plant is about 18 in (45 cm) tall. It prefers a mild-winter climate and flowers at the end of spring. **ZONES 9–10.**

Arum palaestinum

ARUNCUS

GOAT'S BEARD

There are 3 species in this genus of rhizomatous perennials, occurring widely over temperate and subarctic regions of the northern hemisphere. Their appearance is very much that of a giant astilbe, with ferny basal leaves up to 3 ft (1 m) long and summer plumes of tiny cream flowers in 8–18 in (20–45 cm) long, pyramidal panicles carried on wiry stems that hold them well above the foliage.
CULTIVATION: They are best grown in sun or part-shade in moist, humus-rich, well-drained soil around edges of ponds. Goat's beard is very frost hardy and is propagated from seed or by division.

Aruncus aethusifolius

This is a compact species, to 15 in (38 cm) in height and spread, with ovate, deeply incised leaves that turn yellow in fall (autumn). From Korea, it bears panicles of small, creamy white flowers in summer. **ZONES 4–9.**

Aruncus dioicus

syns *Aruncus sylvestris, Spiraea aruncus*

A graceful, woodland perennial, this clump-forming plant produces a mass of rich green, fern-like foliage and arching plumes of tiny, greenish or creamy white flowers in summer. It grows 6 ft (1.8 m) tall and 4 ft (1.2 m) wide. Cut flowering stems back hard in fall (autumn). **'Kneiffii'** reaches about 3 ft (1 m) and has cream-colored flowers. **ZONES 3–9.**

Aruncus dioicus

Aruncus dioicus 'Kneiffii'

ARUNDO

GIANT REED

Found through much of the Old World subtropics and warm-temperate regions, the 3 species in this genus are large, rhizomatous, perennial grasses. They have strong, upright, leafy stems reminiscent of bamboo but lacking the twiggy side branches of most bamboos. Thin, flat leaves, drooping at the tips, alternate in 2 rows up the stems which terminate in summer in large, feathery panicles of minute, chaffy flowers.
CULTIVATION: Unlike most reeds and rushes, they do not require waterlogged soil although they tolerate it well. Any well-drained soil that does not dry out entirely will do. They prefer full sun or light shade and may be propagated from seed or by division.

Arundo donax

GIANT REED

This giant grass from the Mediterranean region is one of the most striking of summer foliage plants. Growing to a height of 20 ft (6 m) and a similar spread, it is an excellent ornamental plant for large gardens. The drooping leaves are up to 24 in (60 cm) long by $2\frac{1}{2}$ in (6 cm) wide. In mild areas it can grow very vigorously and will need confining. In winter, when the foliage becomes untidy, it should be cut to the ground, creating luxuriant new spring and summer growth. **'Versicolor'** is a popular variegated cultivar, the leaves with longitudinal cream stripes. The reeds used in musical instruments such as organs and clarinets all come from carefully selected and cured stems of the giant reed, as did the pipes of Pan. **ZONES 9–11.**

Arundo donax

Asarum chinense

Asarum maximum

Asarum muramatui

Asarum sieboldii

Asarum arifolium

ASARINA

CREEPING GLOXINIA, TRAILING SNAPDRAGON

Some botanists have taken this genus name in a broad sense, including in it species that are treated here under *Lophospermum* and *Maurandya*, but in the narrow sense it consists of a single species only, a trailing perennial restricted in the wild to the Pyrenees region of Spain and France. It is an evergreen, with broadly heart-shaped leaves that are coarsely toothed and clothed in velvety hairs. Yellow snapdragon-like flowers appear in succession in the leaf axils.
CULTIVATION: The plants are moderately frost hardy and may be grown in sheltered pockets of rock gardens, or at the top of retaining walls. Some protection from hot sun may be necessary, and soil should be open textured and well drained. Propagate from seed or by carefully breaking off pieces of rootstock.

Asarina procumbens

The only species in the genus (as now conceived), this trailing perennial forms a dense mat of stems that become slightly woody at the base but younger growths are covered in velvety, slightly sticky hairs, as are the 2 in (5 cm) wide leaves. Short-stalked flowers appear singly from the leaf-axils in summer, pale yellow or sometimes pale pink with an orange blotch in the centre. **ZONES 7–10.**

ASARUM

WILD GINGER

This genus, belonging to the same family as *Aristolochia* (Dutchman's pipe), consists of over 70 species of rhizomatous perennials, both evergreen and deciduous, distributed widely through temperate areas of the northern hemisphere but most numerous in Japan and the USA. They are better known for their use in traditional medicine than as ornamental plants, though the foliage can make an attractive ground cover in shaded woodland gardens. The leaves are either kidney- or heart-shaped, and the small, bell-shaped flowers, which are usually hidden below the leaves, are mostly dull brownish or purplish and open at the mouth into 3 sharply reflexed sepals. Some examples include ***Asarum chinense***, ***A. maximum***, ***A. muramatui*** and ***A. sieboldii***. All 4 species have very attractive foliage.
CULTIVATION: These plants prefer a shady site in moist, well-drained soil and can be planted out any time between fall (autumn) and spring. They spread rapidly; divide the clumps every few years in spring. They can also be propagated from seed. They are prone to attack from slugs and snails.

Asarum arifolium

This is a variable, evergreen species from southeastern USA with large, elongated, heart-shaped leaves up to about 6 in (15 cm) long, marked with lighter green between the prominent veins. **ZONES 7–9.**

Asarum caudatum

Asarum europaeum

Asarum canadense

Asarum canadense
CANADIAN SNAKEROOT

This deciduous perennial native to the woodlands of eastern North America forms tufted mats with fleshy, creeping rhizomes and coarse-textured, heart-shaped leaves, 2–3 in (5–8 cm) wide rising on hairy stalks to 8 in (20 cm) high. Hidden beneath in spring are inconspicuous, brown, bell-shaped flowers. Decoctions of the rhizomes were used medicinally by Native Americans and white settlers. **ZONES 3–8.**

Asarum caudatum
BRITISH COLUMBIA WILD GINGER

Native to the coastal mountains of western North America, this ground-hugging, evergreen perennial grows in relatively deep shade on the forest floor. Spreading by rhizomes, it forms irregular, open patches and flowers from late spring into summer. Large, 6 in (15 cm) long, kidney-shaped leaves rise to 8 in (20 cm) above ground, hiding the brownish purple blooms. **ZONES 6–9.**

Asarum europaeum
ASARABACCA

Widely distributed in European woodlands, this species has conspicuous shaggy hairs on both the creeping rhizomes and the 4–6 in (10–15 cm) long leaf stalks. The deep-green, glossy leaves are kidney-shaped to almost circular, up to 3 in (8 cm) wide. The dull purplish flowers, hidden under the leaves, are insignificant, only about ½ in (12 mm) long. Asarabacca was formerly used medicinally and as an ingredient of snuff powders, but is moderately toxic. **ZONES 6–9.**

ASCLEPIAS
MILKWEED

Found naturally in the Americas, this genus consists of over 100 species of perennials, subshrubs and (rarely) shrubs and includes both evergreen and deciduous plants. Most have narrow, pointed elliptical to lance-shaped leaves and all have milky white sap. The flowers are borne in stalked clusters arising from the upper leaf axils. They are small, with 5 reflexed petals below a waxy corona, a feature characteristic of the milkwood family (see also *Hoya*). Elongated seed pods follow; the seeds have silky plumes and are dispersed on the breeze. Their sap is acrid and poisonous, and the butterfly larvae that feed on them are toxic to predators such as birds. A few species have become widespread weeds of warmer regions. Some African species with inflated, prickly pods are now placed in the genus *Physocarpus*.

CULTIVATION: They are easily grown in any well-drained soil in full sun. Hardiness varies considerably with the species. Some of the shorter-lived perennials may be treated as annuals, and are usually raised from seed. Some hardier North American species require a cool climate and will not survive in the dormant state where winters are too warm. Propagate from seed or semi-ripe cuttings.

Asclepias curassavica
BLOOD FLOWER

This frost-tender annual or short-lived perennial evergreen subshrub is a South American native that has become something of a weed in tropical areas. It grows to around 3 ft (1 m) tall and wide and has narrow, lance-shaped leaves up to 6 in (15 cm) long. From late spring to fall (autumn) it produces umbels of bright orange-red flowers followed by spindle-shaped, 3 in (8 cm) long seed pods. **ZONES 9–12.**

Asclepias speciosa

Asclepias speciosa

A 3 ft (1 m) tall perennial from eastern North America, this species has oval leaves up to 6 in (15 cm) long. The flowers are dull pinkish red and white and up to 1 in (25 mm) in diameter. The fruit have soft spines. **ZONES 2–9.**

Asclepias subulata
AJAMENTE, BUSH MILKWEED

An important food source for the monarch butterflies in its native arid regions of southwestern USA and western Mexico, this milkweed grows along desert washes, sending up numerous 3–5 ft (1–1.5 m) tall, pale green stems when there is moisture present. The stems are topped by clusters of curious yellowish flowers, which develop into characteristic milkweed pods filled with cottony seeds. It is very tolerant of dry conditions. **ZONES 9–11.**

Asclepias tuberosa
BUTTERFLY WEED

One of North America's brightest meadow wildflowers, this widely distributed, 24–36 in (60–90 cm), mounding perennial with a tuberous rootstock produces broad heads of small orange (sometimes yellow or red) flowers during summer. It is very popular with butterflies. Adaptable to both moist and very dry soils, it demands full sun and good drainage. **ZONES 3–9.**

× *ASCOCENDA*
MINIATURE VANDA

This is the name used for the hybrid genus of orchids that results when any *Ascocentrum* is crossed with any *Vanda*, and which must be used also for later generations of seedlings, including backcrosses. Most ascocendas resemble small-growing vandas (to about 60 cm [about 24 in] tall) and have very long lasting flowers about 4 cm (about 2 in) wide in clusters, in just about any color except green; the blues and purples are especially admired.

CULTIVATION: Mostly summer-flowering, they are warm-growing and cultivated in the same way as vandas. In the tropics they are commonly grown outdoors in more humid regions. Propagate by detaching lateral growths.

× *Ascocenda* Hybrids

These free-flowering orchids are popular with gardeners in the wet tropics as they take up less room in the greenhouse than full-size vandas, and they often feature among the bunches of 'Singapore orchids' imported from there and from Thailand and sold in flower shops. **ZONES 11–12.**

Asclepias curassavica

Asclepias curassavica

Asclepias curassavica

Ascocentrum Hybrid Kwa Geok Choo

Asperula arcadiensis

Asphodeline lutea

ASCOCENTRUM

This genus consists of five species of epiphytic orchids closely allied to *Vanda*, ranging in the wild from the Himalayan foothills to the Philippines. They have short, erect stems bearing 2 rows of closely overlapping short, strap-like leaves. The flowers are rather small, clustered on short stalks but in brilliant hues ranging from yellow to red, orange and purple. They flower in spring and summer. More widely grown are bigeneric hybrids with vandas (× *Ascocenda*), the ascocentrums contributing red and orange coloring.
CULTIVATION: These orchids require winter minimum temperatures above 60°F (15°C) with bright, indirect light. Plant them in very coarse, open, free-draining potting mix. Water and feed well during the growing and flowering season. Propagate from basal offsets.

Ascocentrum curvifolium

The best known member of this genus in cultivation, this lowland Himalayan species makes a bushy plant 15 in (38 cm) tall, with leathery leaves. It carries its

Asperula setosa

clusters of 1 in (25 mm) wide flowers in late spring or summer. Colored somewhere between red and orange, they are very long lasting. **ZONES 11–12.**

Ascocentrum Hybrids

There is a range of hybrids raised from some of the species of *Ascocentrum*, commonly grown in places such as Singapore for the cut flower trade. Typical examples of these hybrids are the ones pictured here, **Kwa Geok Choo** and **Thai Gold**. **ZONES 11–12.**

ASPARAGUS

This large genus not only includes the edible asparagus, *Asparagus officinalis*, but also up to 60 other perennial species. Many are commonly called ferns, but in fact they belong to the lily family in its broad sense, though botanists have recently recognized many smaller families in place of one large one, embracing very diverse elements. As interpreted here, the genus *Asparagus* includes only cool-temperate, herbaceous species, mainly from Europe and Asia. The shrubby and climbing species from Africa are removed to the genera *Protasparagus* and *Myrsiphyllum*.
CULTIVATION: For cultivation of the edible asparagus the selection of a suitable garden bed is critical as the crowns can grow undisturbed for up to 20 years or more. The chosen bed, in full sun, should be well dug over, manured and have good drainage. Seed can be sown; however, crowns if available will produce earlier cropping. Give asparagus 12 in (30 cm) between each plant and do not harvest the young shoots or spears until the third spring so as to allow the crowns

Ascocentrum Hybrid Thai Gold

to mature; always allow a few shoots to elongate to build up the plant's food reserves. If white spears are preferred cut well below the soil surface just as spears become visible.

Asparagus officinalis
ASPARAGUS

A frost-hardy perennial believed native to the Mediterranean region and western Asia, this vegetable seems to have been cultivated since before Christ, either for medicinal use or as a food crop. The emerging spear of asparagus will expand into a much-branched, ferny, erect stem with innumerable tiny, linear leaves if allowed to grow uncut. Female plants will produce many red-berried fruit which should be removed before self-seeding occurs. **'Mary Washington'** is a variety well liked for its long, thick spears, but the newer F1 hybrids will often provide higher yields. **ZONES 4–9.**

ASPERULA
WOODRUFF

There are around 100 species of annuals, perennials and small, twiggy subshrubs in this genus, distinguished from the closely related *Galium* by the generally longer tube of the small flowers. They occur mainly in temperate regions of Europe, Asia and Australasia. Most are densely foliaged mat- or tuft-forming perennials with tiny, narrow leaves arranged in whorls of 4 or more on the fine stems. In spring and summer the plants may be smothered in tiny flowers, usually white, pale pink or occasionally yellow. Most species spread by underground runners and a few of the woodland species grow to around 24 in (60 cm) high, with larger, bright green leaves. Like galiums, asperulas often develop fragrance as the cut foliage dries and some were once used as strewing herbs; at least one species yields a dye.
CULTIVATION: The small species generally do best in rockery conditions with gritty, well-drained soil in full sun. They can be raised from seed, from small rooted pieces removed from the clump, or by division.

Asparagus officinalis

Asperula arcadiensis

This perennial Greek species makes a woody based tuft of foliage up to 6 in (15 cm) high. The narrow leaves are gray and downy, ½ in (12 mm) or so long. The tiny flowers are pink to pale purple. **ZONES 5–9.**

Asperula setosa

Native to Turkey, this annual species grows to about 12 in (30 cm) high with very narrow, small leaves and lilac flowers arranged in dense clusters at the branch tips. **ZONES 5–9.**

Asperula suberosa
syn. *Asperula athoa* of gardens

This evergreen, perennial species from the Balkan Peninsula makes a dense mound up to 4 in (10 cm) tall and 12 in (30 cm) wide, with hairy, bluish green leaves. Masses of tubular, pale pink flowers smother the plant from late spring into early summer. **ZONES 5–9.**

ASPHODELINE
JACOB'S ROD

This is a genus of some 20 species of biennial and perennial lilies, native to the Mediterranean region and Asia Minor. The name indicates their close similarity to *Asphodelus*. They have thick, fleshy roots, from which sprout narrow, grassy to spear-shaped leaves that are usually bright green, sometimes with a bluish tint. Stiffly upright flower spikes up to 5 ft (1.5 m) tall develop in summer. They carry large numbers of star-shaped yellow, white or pale pink flowers on the upper half of the stem.
CULTIVATION: These plants are very frost hardy and easily grown in any well-drained soil in full sun. Propagate from seed or by division in winter or early spring. Try to avoid damaging the roots or they may rot.

Asphodeline lutea
ASPHODEL, KING'S SPEAR

A native of the Mediterranean region eastward from Italy, this fragrant, frost-hardy plant can grow to 5 ft (1.5 m),

Asparagus 'Mary Washington'

Asplenium australasicum

Asplenium bulbiferum

though usually rather less so. Tufts of narrow, glossy leaves appear below spear-like stems bearing spikes of yellow, star-shaped flowers, some $1\frac{1}{4}$ in (30 mm) wide. The plants should be kept moist before the flowering period in spring. **ZONES 6–10.**

ASPHODELUS

When Tennyson's lotus eaters 'rested weary limbs at last on beds of asphodel', it was the plant now known as *Asphodelus albus* on which they probably reclined—the name *asphodelos* goes back to the ancient Greeks. The genus consists of 12 species of fleshy-rooted annual and perennial lilies, native to the Mediterranean region and to western Asia as far as the Himalayas. They have basal tufts of narrow, grass-like leaves and 6-petalled, starry, white, green or pink flowers borne along stiff, upright stems, which may be branched. Spring and summer are the main flowering seasons.
CULTIVATION: Hardiness varies with the species, though most will tolerate moderate frosts. They require reasonably sunny, warm, dry summer conditions to flower well and prefer a light, sandy, humus-rich soil with good drainage. Propagate by division immediately after flowering or from seed.

Asphodelus acaulis

From the Atlas Mountains of northwest Africa, this near-evergreen species makes a grassy-foliaged clump about 10 in (25 cm) high and 15 in (38 cm) wide. It is distinctive for its very short, crowded spikes of $1\frac{1}{2}$ in (35 mm) diameter, pale pink flowers arising from the center of the foliage clump in early spring, often shorter than the leaves. This very attractive species needs dry summer conditions and good drainage. **ZONES 9–10.**

Asplenium daucifolium

Asphodelus aestivus

Widely distributed around the Mediterranean, this species grows to a height of about 3 ft (1 m), with broad, leathery basal leaves. The branched panicles, elongating in spring, bear white to very pale pink flowers as much as 3 in (8 cm) across, the petals with darker mid-lines. **ZONES 6–10.**

Asphodelus albus

Native to Europe and North Africa, *Asphodelus albus* is probably the most commonly cultivated species in the genus. It has thick, fleshy roots and sword-shaped leaves up to 24 in (60 cm) long. The 12–36 in (30–90 cm) tall flower stems bear pinkish brown striped, white flowers along most of their length in spring, those at the base opening first. The variable bracts—white or brown—are especially noticeable before the star-shaped flowers open. **ZONES 5–10.**

ASPIDISTRA

The very name aspidistra has become a byword for both ubiquity and indestructible toughness as an indoor plant, though it is only one species *(Aspidistra elatior)* that is being referred to in this context. In fact the genus consists of 8 species of leafy, evergreen, rhizomatous perennials occurring in the wild from the Himalayas to Japan. Long-stalked, deep green leaves with elliptical to lance-shaped blades spring directly from a thick, creeping rhizome. Aspidistras flower in spring and summer, producing small, inconspicuous, cream and red-brown to purple blooms virtually at ground level; they are pollinated by ground-dwelling fauna, including possibly snails and slugs.
CULTIVATION: Although widely grown as house plants, aspidistras will tolerate moderate frosts and in mild climates will thrive outdoors in a shady position in moist, humus-rich, well-drained soil. As indoor plants they are renowned for their tolerance of low light levels and poor air quality, but respond to more kindly treatment with more luxuriant growth. Water sparingly and avoid leaving the pot in standing water. Propagate by division in early spring.

Aspidistra elatior
ASPIDISTRA, CAST-IRON PLANT

The common aspidistra is now believed to be native to China, though it was first introduced to the west from Japan. Arising from short, rather woody, creeping rhizomes, the tough, dark green leaves are pointed at the tips and arch elegantly from 6 in (15 cm) leaf stalks to a height of about 24 in (60 cm). The cream to dark purple, bell-shaped flowers grow at soil level and are half-hidden by the leaves; it is something of an event to see them, as indoor plants seldom flower. There are several white- or cream-variegated cultivars, for example, **'Variegata'**, which, in order to prevent them reverting to green, should be grown in brighter light than the green-leafed species. **ZONES 8–11.**

ASPLENIUM
SPLEENWORT

This genus of some 700 species of mainly evergreen ferns is distributed widely through most of the world's land masses. Very diverse as to growth form, they include terrestrial and epiphytic species as well as many that grow on rocks. Some make dense tufts of fronds or rosettes, others creep across the surface with thick, scaly rhizomes. Most have feathery pinnate or bipinnate fronds but in some they are large and undivided: the 'bird's-nest ferns' are one such striking group. The fronds of many species develop small plantlets along the ribs. The spore-bodies are typically arranged in parallel or radiating lines on the undersides of the fronds.
CULTIVATION: Hardiness varies greatly with the species, as does the preferred growing environment. Most species prefer woodland conditions with cool, moist, humus-rich soil and dappled shade. A few species, however, need sunnier locations and are reasonably tolerant of dry conditions. Propagate by spores, by division of established clumps, removing rooted pieces of rhizomes, or by growing on the frond-borne plantlets.

Aspidistra elatior

Asphodelus albus

Asplenium australasicum
BIRD'S NEST FERN

Found in Australia and the South Pacific, this species has leathery, undivided fronds, somewhat V-shaped in cross-section and up to 5 ft (1.5 m) long by 8 in (20 cm) wide forming a dramatic large 'nest' or funnel. In the wild it grows on tree trunks or rocks. It is frost tender and requires warm, humid conditions to thrive. *Asplenium nidus* is a very similar species widespread in the tropics. **ZONES 10–12.**

Asplenium bulbiferum
HEN AND CHICKEN FERN, MOTHER FERN

This Australian and New Zealand native is one of the more widely cultivated species, easily grown in pots or hanging baskets. Typically fern-like in appearance, it has a tuft of arching, deep green, finely divided fronds up to 3 ft (1 m) long and 12 in (30 cm) wide. Small plantlets form on the fronds, mainly on the midrib. **ZONES 9–11.**

Asplenium daucifolium
MAURITIUS SPLEENWORT

Similar to *Asplenium bulbiferum*, this species from Madagascar and Mauritius has dark green, arching fronds up to 3 ft (1 m) long divided into very narrow segments, giving a delicate lacy effect. Numerous plantlets develop on the fronds and may be removed and grown on. It is at least as adaptable to indoor use as *A. bulbiferum*, though it is slightly less cold hardy. **ZONES 10–12.**

Asphodelus aestivus

Asphodelus albus

A

Asplenium nidus
BIRD'S NEST FERN

This pantropical, epiphytic fern colonizes trees, rock faces and boulders in humid, tropical rainforests. The glossy green, thin, tongue-like fronds have wavy margins and a prominent, almost black midrib. They arise from a densely hairy crown in a radial fashion, somewhat resembling a bird's nest. It requires warmth and ample humidity. *Asplenium australasicum* is a very similar species, adapted to slightly cooler conditions. **ZONES 11–12.**

Asplenium scolopendrium
HART'S TONGUE FERN

Found in North America, Europe and Asia, this is the species most commonly grown outdoors in cooler climates, occurring in a variety of forms. Typically it has broad, strap-shaped, undivided fronds up to 15 in (38 cm) long but cultivated forms may have divided fronds, ruffled edges, variegations or arrowhead-shaped fronds. A shortly creeping plant, it is very frost hardy. **ZONES 5–9.**

Asplenium trichomanes
MAIDENHAIR SPLEENWORT

This evergreen or semi-evergreen species has dark green pinnate fronds only 3–8 in (8–20 cm) long. It occurs mainly on limestone outcrops. **ZONES 3–9.**

ASTELIA

This genus of some 25 species of rhizomatous, evergreen perennials has a scattered distribution around the southern hemisphere including the Falkland Islands, Mauritius and Réunion, southeastern Australia and New Zealand, the latter being the richest in species. The bold, sword-shaped leaves are arranged in rosettes or tufts and the plants vary in stature from about 2 in (5 cm) to 8 ft (2.4 m) or even more. Most have a silvery coating of fine, silky hairs on the leaves, though this may be confined to the undersides. Habitats vary from alpine bogs to temperate rainforests, the larger-growing species generally in the latter, sometimes as epiphytes. Inconspicuous flowers are often hidden by the foliage but in many species are followed by showy clusters of brightly colored berries. There are separate male and female flowers, on the same plant in some species, on separate plants in others.
CULTIVATION: They are easily grown in moist, peaty, well-drained soil in full sun or part-shade; a few species will grow in boggy soil. Hardiness varies, though most species will tolerate light frosts. Propagate from seed or by division.

Astelia chathamica

From the remote Chatham Islands, this is the most striking of the 13 New Zealand species, with bright, almost metallic, silvery leaves. It forms a dense foliage clump up to 5 ft (1.5 m) high with a spread of up to 6 ft (1.8 m). The tiny flowers are followed by bright orange berries on female plants. These plants do best in full sun. **ZONES 9–10.**

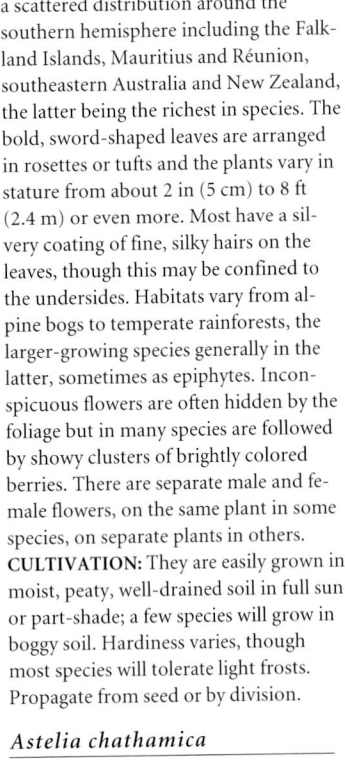

Asplenium nidus

Aster alpinus

Aster 'Coombe's Violet'

Aster amellus 'Violet Queen'

Astelia nervosa

Aster amellus 'King George'

Aster amellus 'Sonia'

Astelia nervosa
KAKAHA

Spreading 6 ft (1.8 m) or more and up to 36 in (90 cm) high, this vigorously clumping, New Zealand species is valued for its narrow arching leaves thinly coated with silvery hairs and growing 2–6 ft (0.6–1.8 m) long. In summer starry, light brown fragrant flowers form in clusters on the ends of long, slender stems. These are followed by small green fruit, which turn orange-red when ripe. **ZONES 9–10.**

ASTER
MICHAELMAS OR EASTER DAISY, ASTER

Native to temperate regions of the northern hemisphere (most numerous in North America), this large genus of perennials and deciduous or evergreen subshrubs contains over 250 species, ranging in height from miniatures suitable for rock gardens to 6 ft (1.8 m) giants. The leaves are simple and mostly smooth-edged, sometimes hairy, often quite small. Showy, daisy-like flowerheads are usually produced in late summer or fall (autumn) in a wide range of colors, including blue, violet, purple, pink, red and white, all with a central disc of yellow or purple. There are many aster cultivars once listed under the parent species, but this has become too complex and many now stand alone. A typical example is *Aster* **'Coombe's Violet'**. The 'China asters' grown as bedding annuals are now placed in the genus *Callistephus.*
CULTIVATION: Easily grown, they prefer sun (or part-shade in hot areas) in a well-drained soil, preferably enriched with compost. Keep moist at all times and shelter from strong winds and stake the taller species. Cut the long stems down to ground level and tidy the clumps when the flowers have faded. Propagate by division in spring or late fall, or from softwood cuttings in spring. Divide plants every 2 to 3 years, using the most vigorous outer part. Powdery mildew, rust, aphids and snails can be a problem.

Aster alpinus

From the higher mountains of Europe, this clump-forming plant, usually about 6–12 in (15–30 cm) high and spreading to 18 in (45 cm), bears large, violet-blue, daisy flowers with yellow centers from late spring until mid-summer; the foliage is dark green. It is a popular rock garden plant and is fully frost hardy. There are a number of named cultivars. **'Trimix'** grows to 8 in (20 cm) and has flowers that are a tricolor mix of pink, blue and white. **ZONES 3–9.**

Aster amellus
ITALIAN ASTER

The Italian aster, actually a native of the eastern half of Europe and also Turkey, is usually represented in gardens by its many cultivars. In its typical form it grows to 18–24 in (45–60 cm) with oblong basal leaves that can be somewhat hairy and erect stems which can become floppy if grown in too much shade. Although spreading by underground rhizomes, it is not considered invasive and is especially disease resistant. The large, fragrant flowerheads are pink and purple-blue, while popular cultivars are stronger in color and include **'King George'**, a deep violet, **'Violet Queen'**, somewhat paler, and the bright pink **'Sonia'**. **ZONES 4–9.**

Aster cordifolius
BLUE WOOD ASTER

Native to the eastern USA and Canada, this tall-growing species, to 5 ft (1.5 m), usually needs staking by the time its pale to dark blue flowers are at their best in late summer-early fall (autumn).

Aster ericoides

Aster divaricatus

However, it is one of the species that adapts to a woodland situation where its arching habit can be pleasantly informal. It is usually represented in gardens by its cultivar **'Silver Spray'**, a slightly more compact plant with feathery foliage and pale lilac-blue flowers. **ZONES 3–9.**

Aster divaricatus
WHITE WOOD ASTER

Also from eastern North America, this is a distinctive species with slender, wiry, dark mahogany stems to about 24 in (60 cm) tall that tend to twist and wander, broad-based leaves tapering to fine points, and delicate, open sprays of small, white flowerheads. Spreading by rhizomes to form loose clumps, it is essentially a plant for the woodland garden. Some forms are taller and more robust. **ZONES 3–9.**

Aster ericoides
HEATH ASTER

The specific name means 'with leaves like those of *Erica*', the heath genus, and indeed this species from eastern and central USA and northern Mexico has very small, narrow leaves, at least on the upper stems. With flowering stems rising up to 3 ft (1 m) high from tufted basal shoots towards mid-summer and into fall (autumn), it provides a wonderful display of massed, small, white flowerheads as does one of its more compact cultivars, **'White Heather'**. There are a number of cultivars of varied heights, mostly with pale pinkish or yellowish blooms. The cut flowers are popular with florists. **ZONES 4–10.**

Aster × frikartii

A garden hybrid between *Aster amellus* and the Himalayan *A. thomsonii*, the original cross with very large, violet-blue flowerheads is still popular despite the addition of a number of newer cultivars. It is a rather narrowly clumping plant

Aster ericoides 'White Heather'

about 30 in (75 cm) high. **'Mönch'** is a very free-flowering plant to 15 in (38 cm) with clear blue, long-lasting blooms; **'Wunder von Stäfa'** is taller, to 24 in (60 cm) with lavender blue blooms lasting throughout the summer months. **ZONES 5–9.**

Aster lateriflorus

This is a very decorative aster, native to eastern and central North America and grows to 4 ft (1.2 m) tall with spreading branches and small leaves turning copper purple in fall (autumn) as the crimson-centered, lilac flowerheads appear. **'Horizontalis'** is a lower, more broadly spreading form with almost white flowerheads with broad, brownish centers. **ZONES 2–9.**

Aster linariifolius
STIFF ASTER, SAVORYLEAF ASTER

Low, somewhat stiff mounds 12–24 in (30–60 cm) high and 12 in (30 cm) wide are covered in late summer and early fall (autumn) with 1 in (25 mm) daisies of soft lavender-pink. This species does not need staking, and makes a good low, flowering hedge. **ZONES 3–10.**

Aster linosyris
GOLDILOCKS ASTER

Very different from the usual concept of an aster, this species from Europe, North Africa and western Asia is a rather insignificant plant but good for areas where summers are hot and dry. Goldilocks aster grows to 24 in (60 cm) with very fine, dull gray-green foliage and erect sprays of small yellow flowerheads in late summer. The heads lack the usual ray florets—this trait has dominated in its hybrid with *Aster sedifolius (A. linosyris × A. sedifolius)*. **ZONES 4–10.**

Aster linosyris × Aster sedifolius

Aster novae-angliae 'Barr's Pink'

Aster novae-angliae
NEW ENGLAND ASTER

Originally native over a wide area of the eastern and central USA, this species is represented in cultivation by many cultivars, showing much variation in form and color of blooms. Vigorous clumps of mostly vertical, 3–5 ft (1–1.5 m) stems are likely to lean with the weight of large, loose clusters of daisies, making staking necessary. Cultivars include the late-blooming, clear pink **'Harrington's Pink'**; the rose-pink, mildew-resistant **'Barr's Pink'**; and the cerise **'September Ruby'**; while **'Andenken an Alma Pötschke'**, often shortened to **'Alma Pötschke'**, is a compact-growing, though 4 ft (1.2 m) tall plant with bright rose pink blooms, and **'Hella Lacy'**. These asters prefer a moist, rich soil in full sun. **ZONES 4–9.**

Aster novi-belgii
NEW YORK ASTER

Novi-belgii is Linnaeus' attempt to translate New Amsterdam (now New York) into Latin; the Belgii were the tribe encountered by Julius Caesar in the Low Countries. The New York aster in its wild form is native to the east coast, from Newfoundland to Georgia. It has given rise to innumerable garden forms in colors ranging from the palest mauve to violet and deep pink, and with varying degrees of 'doubling' of the flowerheads. They are among the most useful plants for the perennial border in cooler-temperate climates, responding to generous feeding and watering in spring and summer. Watch for mildew. Cultivars include **'Court Herald'**, **'Mulberry'** has large, semi-double, rich mulberry-red blooms. **'Ernest Ballard'**, named for a leading aster breeder, grows to 3 ft (1 m) with large, purple-red blooms. **'Audrey'** grows to a compact 12 in (30 cm) with double, lavender-blue fall (autumn) flowers. **ZONES 3–9.**

Aster novi-belgii 'Ernest Ballard'

Aster novi-belgii 'Court Herald'

Aster novi-belgii 'Audrey'

Aster novae-angliae 'Andenken an Alma Pötschke'

A

Aster sedifolius

Aster umbellatus

Astilbe chinensis var. *davidii*

Astilbe, Arendsii Hybrid, 'Europa'

Astilbe, Arendsii Hybrid, 'Brautschleier'

Astilbe, Arendsii Hybrid, 'Fanal'

Aster sedifolius

Native to central and southern Europe, this vigorous, spreading perennial, sometimes treated as an annual, grows to 3 ft (1 m) high. It has tiny leaves and masses of pink, violet-blue or purple flowerheads over a long flowering season that can extend from late spring through summer to fall (autumn). **ZONES 5–9.**

Aster umbellatus
FLAT-TOPPED ASTER

From eastern USA, this robust aster can grow up to 4 ft (1.2 m). By flowering time its rather broad basal leaves have withered, leaving only the smaller stem leaves. In summer it produces densely clustered white flowerheads ¾–1 in (18–25 mm) in diameter. **ZONES 3–9.**

ASTILBE
FALSE SPIRAEA

This genus of 14 species of pretty, early to late summer perennials comes mostly from eastern Asia, where they grow in the moist ground beside woodland streams though there are also 2 species occurring in the eastern USA. All astilbes have basal tufts of ferny, compound leaves, the leaflets usually sharply toothed. Pointed, plume-like panicles of tiny, white to pink or red flowers rise well above the foliage. Most usual in cultivation are the hybrids grouped under the name *Astilbe* × *arendsii*, though there are many recent hybrid cultivars of different parentage. The name 'spiraea' was mistakenly attached to this genus when they were introduced to England in the 1820s.

CULTIVATION: They need a lightly shaded place with rich, leafy soil that never dries out, though they do not like being actually flooded, especially in winter. Cooler climates suit them best; in hot summers they need constant watering to keep their roots cool. Good cut flowers, they also make pretty pot plants for bringing indoors for a while when the flowers are at their best. In a heated greenhouse they will flower early. Propagate by division in winter.

Astilbe, Arendsii Hybrids

This hybrid group, derived from four east Asian species, *Astilbe astilboides*, *A. japonica*, *A. davidii* and *A. thunbergii*, is named after German horticulturalist Georg Arends (1863–1952) to whom many of the finest cultivars are credited. Heights vary from 18–48 in (0.45 cm–1.2 m), with a spread of 18–30 in (45–75 cm). They produce feathery spikes in a wide color range from late spring to early summer. Cultivars are available in a range of colors from red through pink to white include **'Amethyst'**, with pale purple to pink flowers; **'Fanal'** with long-lasting scarlet flowers; **'Brautschleier'** ('Bridal Veil'), white; **'Rheinland'**, deep rose; and **'Europa'**, pale pink flowers. **ZONES 6–10.**

Astilbe 'Betsy Cuperus'

One of the larger hybrid cultivars, this plant grows to over 3 ft (1 m) and has deep green foliage and arching sprays of pale peachy pink flowers. **ZONES 6–10.**

Astilbe chinensis

A late-summer-flowering species native to China, Korea and eastern Siberia, this is an attractive, clump-forming plant reaching 24 in (60 cm) with toothed, hairy, dark green leaflets and dense, fluffy flower spikes of tiny, star-shaped, white, flushed with pink blooms. **'Pumila'**, a dwarf form growing to 12 in (30 cm) with pinkish mauve flowers, doesn't mind heavier clay soils and will spread quickly if conditions are to its liking. ***Astilbe chinensis* var. *davidii*** grows to 6 ft (1.8 m) with purple-pink flowers crowded on long, slender panicles; this variety has the added interest of bronze-toned new foliage, while ***A. c.* var. *taquetti*** has lavender-pink flowers on a plant about 3 ft (1 m) tall. **ZONES 6–10.**

Astilbe 'Perkeo'

This is one of a race of small garden hybrids, usually growing to no more than 10 in (25 cm) tall and wide with crinkled, deeply incised leaves. This cultivar has bronze new growths and narrow panicles of dark pink blooms. **ZONES 6–10.**

Astilbe 'Betsy Cuperus'

Astilbe rivularis

One of the larger-growing species of the genus, *Astilbe rivularis* from the Himalayas and western China is a clump-forming species growing to a height of 5 ft (1.5 m) with a spread of 3 ft (1 m) or more. It has very large compound leaves. Creamy white, feathery plumes are large and arching on well-defined branches. **ZONES 7–10.**

Astilbe simplicifolia

Rather than the feathery foliage associated with astilbes, this miniature Japanese species, growing to no more than 12 in (30 cm) tall, has deeply cut but simple leaves combined with narrow panicles of white flowers in the typical form, although several cultivars are available with pink flowers. **ZONES 7–10.**

Astilbe 'Straussenfeder'

Bred in Germany, 'Straussenfeder' grows to 3 ft (1 m) tall, with decorative leaves and distinctive flowering panicles with drooping branches, the blooms rose pink. The name is German for 'ostrich feather'. **ZONES 6–10.**

Astilbe thunbergii

This Japanese species is seldom found in gardens, but is an important parent of many hybrid astilbes. It grows to 24 in (60 cm) with a spread almost as wide, with olive green foliage. The small, white, ageing to pink, flowers are held on branching, pyramidal panicles in early summer. **ZONES 7–10.**

Astilbe 'Straussenfeder'

Astilbe chinensis 'Pumila'

Astrantia major

Astrantia major

A. major 'Sunningdale Variegated'

ASTRAGALUS
MILK VETCH

There are some 2,000 species of annuals, perennials and shrubs in this legume genus and they are found over much of the temperate zone of the northern hemisphere. The leaves are usually pinnate with up to 45 leaflets. A few have trifoliate leaves. Size varies considerably, from small cushion plants through to plants 5 ft (1.5 m) tall. The flowers are pea-like and are carried in spikes or racemes in the leaf axils near the top of the plant. A number of the west Asian species including ***Astragalus gummifer*** are the traditional source of gum tragacanth, a gelatinous gum used in cosmetics, pharmaceutical products and ice-creams, among other uses.
CULTIVATION: Plant in moist, well-drained soil in full sun. Most species will tolerate moderate to severe frosts. Propagate the annuals from seed, the perennials and shrubs from seed or small cuttings.

Astragalus angustifolius

A native of Greece and the Middle East, this species is an 18 in (45 cm) high, cushion-forming shrub with spiny stems. The leaves are pinnate with 5 to 12 pairs of leaflets. Racemes of 1 in (25 mm), cream to light purple flowers open in summer. **ZONES 7–9.**

ASTRANTIA
MASTERWORT

All 10 species of this genus, an unusual member of the carrot family, are herbaceous perennials that occur in mountain meadows and woodlands of Europe and western Asia. Gardeners delight in their delicate flowerheads surrounded by a collar of pointed bracts, carried on wiry stems above clumps of deeply toothed, lobed foliage of soft mid-green.
CULTIVATION: Keeping in mind their natural habitat, these plants are best suited to moist, fertile, woodland conditions, or near the edges of streams or ponds where the soil is always moist. As long as the roots are kept moist they will tolerate full sun, indeed the variegated species color much better in such a position. In a suitable position they will build up clumps. Propagate by division in early spring or from seed.

Astrantia major

Native to central and eastern Europe, this species has deeply lobed, palmate leaves forming a loose mound of foliage 18 in (45 cm) tall from which rise nearly bare stems to 24 in (60 cm) or more, each topped by intricately formed, soft pink or white, daisy-like flowerheads, surrounded by petal-like bracts in the same colors. The flowers are produced almost throughout summer. **'Rosea'** is slightly taller, with blooms of rich rose pink. **'Sunningdale Variegated'** is grown for the rich tapestry of its large yellow- and cream-marked leaves and for its delicate, pink-flushed white blooms. **ZONES 6–9.**

Astrantia maxima

Growing to almost 3 ft (1 m), this species likes a rich, fertile soil and will repay the nurturing gardener with splendid summer flowerheads of pale pink blooms above shell pink bracts. **ZONES 5–9.**

ASTROPHYTUM

This popular genus contains 6 species of slow-growing cacti, all native to Mexico. They differ in size and their form varies from star-shaped—hence the Greek genus name (star-plant)—to elongated or globular. The mostly unbranched plants are divided into 5 to 10 prominent, smooth ribs, some covered in thick hair, others patterned with minute white scales. The large flowers with shiny, lemon-yellow to golden-yellow petals, sometimes red at the base, appear from the top of the plant in summer or fall (autumn).
CULTIVATION: The plants are frost tender and prefer porous, alkaline soil and full sun. They should be kept fairly dry except during the mid-summer growing season. Propagate from seed in spring and summer. The tops of older plants can be grafted onto a hardier cactus, and the truncated base will then sprout new growths which can be rooted as cuttings.

Astrophytum asterias

Astrophytum asterias
SEA URCHIN CACTUS, SAND DOLLAR CACTUS

Resembling a sea urchin, this grayish green, globular, spineless cactus grows to no more than 3 in (8 cm) high and 4 in (10 cm) wide. It has smooth, vertical ribs with little white areoles and is covered with fine white scales. It bears yellow flowers with orange-red centers in summer. **ZONES 10–11.**

Astrophytum myriostigma
BISHOP'S CAP, BISHOP'S MITER

Also quite spineless, this odd-looking species grows up to 12 in (30 cm) high and 4 in (10 cm) wide. It has a grayish green body divided into 4 to 8 prominent ribs and typically is densely covered with tiny, white scales. Glossy yellow blooms appear in summer. It is quite variable and a number of varieties have been named. ***Astrophytum myriostigma* var. *quadricostata*** is distinctive for the fatness of each of its 4 ribs, separated only by shallow grooves. **ZONES 10–11.**

Astrophytum m. var. *quadricostata*

Astrophytum ornatum

One of the most commonly grown cacti in cultivation, this cylindrically shaped species has 5 to 8 rather sharp ribs lined with yellow spines. Small white scales on the ribs are arranged in interesting patterns, varying in density. It grows to 15 in (38 cm) high and 6 in (15 cm) wide. It bears yellow flowers in summer. **ZONES 10–11.**

ATHEROSPERMA
BLACK SASSAFRAS, SOUTHERN SASSAFRAS

This single species genus occurs in the cool-temperate rainforests of Tasmania and southeastern mainland Australia, commonly in association with the better known *Nothofagus* (southern beeches). Aromatic, oily substances produced in the wood, bark and foliage include the compound safrole, which is also found in the original North American sassafras *(Sassafras albidum).* It is these oils with their distinctive smell that earned it the name 'sassafras'. Sassafras oil, although

Astragalus angustifolius

Astrophytum myriostigma

Astrophytum ornatum

A

used in traditional folk medicine, is now regarded as dangerously poisonous.
CULTIVATION: Although rarely seen in cultivation, it is worth growing in a large collection for its symmetrical shape and scattered, small white flowers. It has been grown successfully in milder parts of the British Isles. A sheltered, humid location in deep, moist soil suits *Atherosperma moschatum* best. Propagate from seed or cuttings.

Atherosperma moschatum

This evergreen species, reaching almost 100 ft (30 m) in mountain gullies, appears conifer-like from a distance due to its fine grayish foliage and long-pointed crown. The musk-scented, narrow leaves in opposite pairs are dark green above and have a paler, furry coating beneath. Attractive white flowers are borne in spring. **ZONES 8–9.**

Atriplex cinerea

ATHROTAXIS

The island of Tasmania, Australia, with its cool-temperate rainforests, is unusually rich in conifers, including the extremely handsome *Athrotaxis.* The genus shows some resemblance in foliage and cones to the Japanese *Cryptomeria* and American *Sequoiadendron,* but its 3 species are much slower growing and more compact in habit though capable eventually of forming moderately large trees.
CULTIVATION: *Athrotaxis* species are not difficult to grow in a cool, moist climate. Do not expect them to reach tree size for at least 2 or 3 decades, but as dense, bushy saplings they are highly ornamental. Propagate from seed or cuttings.

Athrotaxis cupressoides
TASMANIAN PENCIL PINE

Occurring wild high in the mountains of western Tasmania, *Athrotaxis cupressoides* grows to 50 ft (15 m) but is usually much smaller with dense, symmetrical growth and paler green foliage than most conifers, even slightly yellowish. The branchlets, covered in appressed scale leaves, are much thicker and fleshier than in true cypresses. It can make a handsome garden tree, but may take 10 years or more to reach shrub size. **ZONES 7–9.**

Athrotaxis × *laxifolia*
TASMANIAN CEDAR

Although commonly treated as the third and least common of the wild species, this tree has long been suspected by botanists to be a natural hybrid between *Athrotaxis cupressoides* and *A. selaginoides,* since it is intermediate in most respects and occurs where both of them grow nearby. In cultivation it also combines vigor and hardiness, growing to 30 ft (9 m) or more with an attractive conical form. **ZONES 7–9.**

Athrotaxis selaginoides
KING BILLY PINE

The slow growth of the King Billy pine, a formerly important timber tree, is shown by the more than 30 annual growth rings per inch (25 mm) of diameter seen in some wood samples. Growing to 100 ft (30 m) with a trunk diameter of 8 ft (2.4 m), though half that height is more usual, its leaves are incurved and sharply pointed, bright green on top with contrasting white-banded undersides. Small, orange-brown cones appear in spring. The soft reddish brown bark is very thick. **ZONES 8–9.**

ATHYRIUM
LADY FERN

Consisting of around 180 species ranging through most of the world's lands, lady ferns can be found in temperate, tropical and even in alpine regions. Those from cooler climates are deciduous but many of the tropical and subtropical ones are evergreen. They have creeping rhizomes and upright, simple to tripinnate fronds with grooved stems.
CULTIVATION: These ferns, most of which are terrestrial although a few are epiphytic, thrive in a humid atmosphere and so should never be allowed to dry out. In the garden they need shade, moisture and fertile soil that is slightly acidic and rich in humus. Propagation is by spores or division. On some cultivars of the popular *Athyrium filix-femina* bulbils can form and then these can easily be pegged down to produce new plantlets.

Athyrium filix-femina
syn. *Asplenium filix-femina*

The lady fern was a great favorite in ferneries of the Victorian period, and a number of garden varieties with variegated or unusually shaped and feathered leaves and names like **'Fritzelliae', 'Pulcherrimum'** and **'Victoria'** were developed. The wild plant, native throughout temperate regions of the northern hemisphere, is as pretty as any, with much divided leaves in a delicate shade of green. It can vary in height from about 15 in (38 cm) to three times that, according to variety, and gradually spreads into large clumps. **'Minutissimum'** is a dwarf form needing a special position as it only grows 6 in (15 cm) high and wide and could easily be covered with more robust plants. **ZONES 5–10.**

Athyrium nipponicum 'Pictum'
JAPANESE PAINTED FERN

Prized for its soft, metallic-gray new fronds suffused with bluish or reddish hues, this Japanese native grows to 18 in (45 cm) in height. Locate in humus-rich loam with adequate moisture in a semi-sunny exposure; this will ensure the richest foliage color. **ZONES 4–9.**

ATRIPLEX
SALTBUSH

This is a genus of around 100 species of annuals, perennials, subshrubs and shrubs found throughout the temperate and subtropical zones, though most of the more ornamental or useful shrubby species come either from the western and central USA or from inland Australia. Most have an overall grayish white appearance due to a fine coating of scales or bladder-like surface cells. The leaves are variable and may be small and rounded or variously toothed and sometimes arrowhead-shaped. There are separate male and female flowers, both of which are usually small and insignificant; in some species the spongy fruit are a conspicuous feature. While scarcely spectacular these plants are mainly grown for their interesting foliage and form. They are also fire resistant and can withstand varied conditions, are often useful in erosion control, and some are nutritious fodder plants, valued for their ability to thrive in saline soils.
CULTIVATION: Some species of this genus are natural coastal plants and thrive where they are exposed to salt spray that would kill lesser plants. Many others are from arid environments, and these thrive best in a dry atmosphere. They are easily grown in any soil, in full sun. Frost hardiness varies with the species, though most will tolerate moderate frosts. Propagate from seed or cuttings.

Atriplex cinerea
GRAY SALTBUSH

The gray saltbush is an attractive subshrub from sea coasts of southern Australia which grows to 24–36 in (60–90 cm) in height and 6 ft (1.8 m) or more in spread, forming a loose mound. The narrowly tongue-shaped leaves are grayish and fleshy and the dull yellowish or reddish flowers are in short, dense, terminal spikes. **ZONES 9–10.**

Athrotaxis cupressoides

Athrotaxis × *laxifolia*

Athyrium filix-femina 'Minutissimum'

Athyrium nipponicum 'Pictum'

Atherosperma moschatum

Atriplex hortensis
ORACH, MOUNTAIN SPINACH

An annual of uncertain, probably central Asian origin, the edible leaves of this species are popular in various central European countries where they are used in salads or boiled. It grows to 8 ft (2.4 m) tall and produces heads of small yellow-green flowers from mid-summer. The lower leaves, somewhat like those of spinach *(Spinacia)*, are up to 4 in (10 cm) long, roughly triangular in shape with shallow lobes. ***Atriplex hortensis* var. *rubra*** (syn. *A. h.* var. *atrosanguinea*) is a purple-foliaged, red-stemmed variety. **ZONES 6–10.**

Atriplex lentiformis subsp. *breweri*
BREWER'S SALTBUSH, QUAIL BRUSH

This is a tough, gray-leafed shrub for the hot, dry regions of the southwestern USA where it is native. Growing to 6–8 ft (1.8–2.4 m) in height and width, this makes a very serviceable shrub for screen planting, for informal hedges or for wild gardens. The flowers and fruit are insignificant, although both are attractive to birds. It tolerates very hot, dry conditions and even highly alkaline soil. **ZONES 8–10.**

ATROPA

This genus of 4 species of perennials from Europe, western Asia and North Africa is closely related to the much larger genus *Solanum.* It is known mainly by one species, the famous deadly nightshade *(Atropa belladonna).* They are plants of rather shrubby habit, much branched, with thin, soft, smooth-edged leaves. Flowers are bell-shaped, borne singly near branch tips and are followed by black berries sitting on a large persistent calyx. All parts of the plants are poisonous and narcotic, containing a mixture of alkaloids but principally atropine, still used in medicine to dilate the pupils and relax muscles and blood vessels.
CULTIVATION: Nowadays grown mainly as curiosities and for educational value, they prefer sheltered, moist conditions and fertile soil. Propagate from seed.

Atropa belladonna
DEADLY NIGHTSHADE, BELLADONNA

Native to most of Europe except the north, also North Africa and southwest

Atriplex lentiformis subsp. *breweri*

Atropa belladonna

Asia, deadly nightshade grows to about 3 ft (1 m) high, with a spreading, bushy habit. In summer it produces nodding dark purplish flowers, followed in fall (autumn) by shiny black berries. The name *belladonna* ('beautiful lady') refers to its former use of enlarging the pupils to enhance a woman's beauty. **ZONES 5–9.**

AUBRIETA
ROCK CRESS

Although mountain flowers, aubrietas are not diminutive and temperamental as are many alpine plants. Rather they make carpets of color at the front of flowerbeds, or down retaining walls. Not very tall—6 in (15 cm) or so at most—they will happily sprawl to several times their height and in spring cover themselves with 4-petalled flowers, mainly in shades of purple. About a dozen species are native to stony hillsides and mountains from the Mediterranean area to as far east as Iran. The plants most often seen in gardens are hybrids mainly derived from *Aubrieta deltoidea.* The genus name honors the French botanical painter Claude Aubriet (1668–1743); it has sometimes been spelt *Aubrietia.*
CULTIVATION: They are easy to grow in cool-temperate climates (flowering is erratic in warm ones), asking only sunshine or a little shade and fertile, well-drained soil. They are short lived and it is wise to take a few cuttings in summer every 3 or 4 years; they are readily propagated also by division of the rhizomatous rootstock.

Aubrieta × *cultorum*

There are many garden hybrids that come under this heading, plants with unknown parentage and with a wide range

Atriplex hortensis var. *rubra*

Aubrieta × *cultorum* 'Cobalt Violet'

Aubrieta deltoidea

Aubrieta macedonica

of growth and flowering habit. The flower color varies from white through pinks and purples to almost violet, some double, and some with variegated foliage. Some examples include **'Cobalt Violet'**, **'Purple Gem'** and **'Doctor Mules'**, which has rich blue-violet flowers. **ZONES 4–9.**

Aubrieta deltoidea

Native to southeastern Europe and Turkey, this compact, mat-forming perennial has greenish gray leaves and masses of starry, mauve-pink flowers borne over a long period in spring. The species itself is now rare in gardens, most cultivated aubrietas being hybrids now known collectively as *Aubrieta* × *cultorum*, though they are often listed as *A. deltoidea.* **ZONES 4–9.**

Aubrieta gracilis

A delicate species forming thin mats, *Aubrieta gracilis* comes from Greece and Albania. The leaves are tiny and narrow and the slender 3–4 in (8–10 cm) flowering stems bear $\frac{1}{2}$–$\frac{3}{4}$ in (12–18 mm) wide purple flowers in summer. ***A. macedonica*** is a very similar species. **ZONES 5–9.**

AUCUBA
AUCUBA, SPOTTED LAUREL

This is an east Asian genus consisting of 3 species of shrubs, valued for their

Aubrieta gracilis

tolerance of heavy shade and large, often colorful, evergreen leaves. Clusters of large red berries appear in fall (autumn) but, with flowers of different sexes on different plants, it is only the females that fruit. The one species generally grown has given rise to many cultivars with variegated leaves in a range of patterns.
CULTIVATION: They are tough and resilient, tolerant of frost, neglect, pollution and heavy shading but responding to better treatment and stronger light with more luxuriant growth. The long-lasting but tender leaves should be protected from wind damage. Grow in full sun or part- or full shade, with filtered light for the variegated species, in any soil. Propagate from seed or cuttings.

Aucuba japonica 'Crotonifolia'

Aurinia saxatilis

Austrocedrus chilensis

Avena sativa

Aucuba japonica 'Variegata'

Austrocedrus chilensis

Aurinia saxatilis 'Citrina'

Aucuba japonica
JAPANESE AUCUBA

Usually a shrub of 4–6 ft (1.2–1.8 m), this species will continue to spread by basal sprouting and self-layering of its weak, soft-wooded stems and, as it thickens up, the mass of stems will support one another, allowing it to reach 10 ft (3 m). The thick, soft, glossy leaves are up to 10 in (25 cm) long and very variably toothed. Sprays of small, reddish flowers in spring may be followed by drooping clusters of ½ in (12 mm) long, red berries in early fall (autumn). **'Variegata'** (female) has leaves densely spotted with yellow, and **'Crotonifolia'** (male) has leaves heavily splashed with yellow. **ZONES 7–10.**

AURINIA

This is a genus of 7 species of biennials and evergreen perennials, formerly included in *Alyssum*, found from central and southern Europe to the Ukraine and Turkey. They are mainly small, spreading, mound-forming plants. The leaves are initially in basal rosettes, mostly fairly narrow. They bear elongated sprays of tiny yellow or white flowers in spring and early summer.

CULTIVATION: Plant in light, gritty, well-drained soil in full sun. They are ideal for rockeries, rock crevices or drystone walls. Most species are very frost hardy and are propagated from seed or small tip cuttings; they will self-sow in suitable locations.

Aurinia saxatilis
syn. ***Alyssum saxatile***
BASKET OF GOLD, YELLOW ALYSSUM

The only commonly grown species, it is a native of central and southeastern Europe. It has hairy, gray-green leaves, forms rather loose mounds to 10 in (25 cm) high and is smothered in bright yellow flowers in spring and early summer. It is very popular as a rockery or wall plant. There are a number of cultivars, including **'Argentea'** with very silvery leaves; **'Citrina'** with lemon-yellow flowers; **'Gold Dust'**, up to 12 in (30 cm) mounds with deep golden-yellow flowers; **'Sulphurea'** with glowing yellow flowers; and **'Tom Thumb'**, a 4 in (10 cm) high dwarf with small leaves. **ZONES 4–9.**

AUSTROCEDRUS
CHILEAN CEDAR

The only member of this temperate South American genus is a conifer of the *Thuja* type, with flattened sprays of branchlets that are themselves strongly flattened and with small, narrow cones consisting of weak, woody scales. In *Austrocedrus* the branchlets are quite fine and fern-like, attractively marked with bluish bands on the undersides. It is valued as a timber tree in its native Chile, where its fragrant, durable, easily worked, reddish wood is in demand for fine cabinet work.

CULTIVATION: It is a fairly frost-hardy conifer, able to survive in exposed positions but appreciating some shelter and deep, moist soil. Propagate from seed or cuttings.

Austrocedrus chilensis

Native to the Andean slopes of Chile and Argentina at altitudes of 3,000–6,000 ft (900–1,800 m), this moderately fast-growing species can reach 80 ft (24 m); young trees have a densely columnar habit but with age the crown lifts higher above a bare trunk and narrow cone of branches. The gray bark is finely scaled; some trees have more bluish foliage than others. **ZONES 7–9.**

AVENA
OATS

This grass genus of around 25 species from Europe and temperate Asia contains the important cereal oats *(Avena sativa)* as well as several of the more objectionable weeds of crops (wild oats). They are annuals of slender, erect habit, producing panicles of pendulous seed heads that open to reveal a grain surrounded by bristles and, in some species, long twisted 'awns' as well. Some of the weedy species make attractive dried decorations.

CULTIVATION: Only the cereal species in this genus is ever cultivated, grown as a spring and summer crop in a wide range of climatic conditions and tolerating quite poor soils. In smaller areas it may be grown for animal fodder. Sow seed in early spring.

Avena sativa
CEREAL OATS

Now believed to have evolved from wild oats *(Avena fatua)* by human selection in eastern Europe or western Asia, oats is an important grain crop, used mainly as livestock food but also for nutritious products such as rolled oats. With its drooping, pointed seed heads, arranged in elongated spikes, it is one of the most easily recognized cereals. **ZONES 5–10.**

AVERRHOA

These tropical fruit trees are close relatives of the humble *Oxalis* or wood sorrels, some species of which are detested weeds. Common to both are the flower structure of 5 overlapping pink or red petals and the 5-angled fruit, which in miniature in *Oxalis* split open to scatter tiny seeds rather than remaining fleshy as in *Averrhoa*. The genus consists of only 2 species, from Southeast Asia. These are small trees with densely twiggy crowns and short pinnate leaves, some of which yellow and drop in the dry season. The slightly fragrant flowers appear in short lateral clusters from the old wood and the slow-ripening fruit hang in clusters from the branches.

CULTIVATION: The trees are easily grown in full sun in tropical and warmer subtropical, humid climates, making fine small shade trees. Propagation is from seed or more commonly by grafts or air-layers (marcotts) which preserve desirable clonal characteristics.

Averrhoa bilimbi
BILIMBI, PICKLEFRUIT

Similar to the carambola but of lesser importance as a commercial fruit, the bilimbi is similar in growth habit but its pinnate leaves are longer, with up to 40 leaflets. The smaller fruit are only bluntly 5-angled and are generally not so sweet. **ZONES 11–12.**

Averrhoa carambola
CARAMBOLA, STAR FRUIT, FIVE-CORNER

In cultivation this species of rather upright form normally makes a small tree about 20 ft (6 m) high. The leaflets of the compound leaves have the curious habit of folding together after being touched or at night. It flowers and fruits through much of the year, but with major flushes

A

of flower in the middle of the wet and the middle of the dry season. The large, ornamental fruit ripen through pale yellow, when their flavor is pleasantly acid, to a deep golden orange color, when they become sweet and deliciously tangy, reminiscent of the taste of passionfruit. **ZONES 11–12.**

AVICENNIA

This mangrove genus of 6 species occurs on seashores and in estuaries throughout the tropics and elsewhere in the southern hemisphere, ranging as far south as New Zealand's North Island and the eastern shores of South Africa. They are small to medium-sized, spreading trees with smallish, glossy, thick-textured leaves in opposite pairs. The flowers are small in stalked clusters near branch tips and the dry fruit each contain a single large seed that actually germinates on the tree, producing a thick taproot. After falling the seeds may be carried away on receding tides, and if washed up elsewhere in the intertidal zone can rapidly take root. Another feature is the upward-growing aerial roots, stiff prongs that emerge from the mud to take in oxygen. **CULTIVATION:** Mangroves are rarely if ever cultivated.

Avicennia marina

GRAY MANGROVE

This species occurs in Asia, Africa and Australasia, with at least 3 regional subspecies. In temperate regions it forms pure stands in estuaries but in the tropics is mixed with unrelated mangroves. The leaves are whitish underneath and the small, yellow-orange flowers appear in late summer (late dry to early wet season in the tropics). The hard wood is so dense that it sinks in water. **ZONES 10–12.**

AZADIRACHTA

Only 2 species belong to this genus of trees from India and Southeast Asia. The genus is closely related to *Melia:* although similar in growth habit, *Azadirachta* is easily distinguished by its leaves being pinnate, not bipinnate as in *Melia*, with more regular ranks of leaflets which are curved in a sickle-like fashion. The leaves are deciduous in severe dry seasons but are evergreen in better-watered situations. Sprays of small white flowers at the branch tips are followed by profuse ovoid yellow fruits. Only one species, *Azadirachta indica*, is cultivated. Although planted as a shade tree and for streets and parks, it is more commonly grown in plantations for use as a natural, safe and efficacious insecticide. **CULTIVATION:** These plants have shallow roots, and need mulching or frequent watering in drier regions. They are susceptible to stem borers and termites. Propagate from seed, cuttings or suckers.

Azadirachta indica

NEEM TREE, NIM

In its natural habitat the neem tree grows in dry coastal forests on deep sandy soils. In the wild it can reach 50 ft (15 m), but planted specimens are usually under 30 ft (10m) tall with a spreading or rounded crown. Flowering occurs in the late dry season; the fruits appear shortly afterwards. In its native India, Burma and Sri Lanka *Azadirachta indica* has long been renowned for its medicinal and insecticidal uses, and its potential value is being increasingly recognized in other countries, so that it is now one of the more commonly planted trees in tropical regions. Its foliage is valued for both fodder and green manure. The neem tree is also a useful source of firewood and yields a high quality timber. **ZONES 11–12.**

AZALEA *see RHODODENDRON*

AZARA

The 15 or so species of this temperate South American genus of shrubs and small trees are characterized by neat, glossy, evergreen foliage and massed, small, yellow flowers and include trees from the Chilean subantarctic rainforests of the south as well as some from drier evergreen scrubs of the lower Andean slopes further north. A characteristic feature is the way each branch node has one small and one larger leaf. While they are quite attractive plants, azaras develop a certain 'legginess' with age. **CULTIVATION:** Azaras prefer cool but mild and humid climates and grow best in sheltered sites in moist soil. In colder areas they can be trained against walls to protect from severe frosts. Propagate from cuttings in summer.

Azara lanceolata

This species from southern Chile is graceful in growth habit and foliage, making a slender shrub or small tree to 20 ft (6 m) with weak, drooping branches. The narrow, toothed, glossy dark green leaves each accompanied by a smaller leaf make a distinctive pattern. In spring it produces short clusters of small, golden yellow flowers consisting mainly of stamens from the leaf axils. **ZONES 8–9.**

Azara microphylla

This fairly erect, small tree may reach 20 ft (6 m) in the garden, more in the wild in its native Chile and western Argentina. A vigorous grower with fine foliage, in late winter it produces numerous clusters of tiny, fragrant flowers half-hidden under the leaf sprays. The most adaptable member of the genus, but sometimes damaged by frost in southern England, **'Variegata'** has attractive cream variegations. **ZONES 7–9.**

Azara serrata

This small tree grows to 30 ft (9 m) in the wild, but in cultivation is usually a shrub of 10–15 ft (3–4.5 m), often with a twiggy habit and rather sparse foliage. The thick, glossy leaves have a broad, blunt apex and coarse teeth. Stalked clusters of fragrant, deep golden flowers appear in late spring or early summer. In cool climates it is easily grown in milder coastal areas. **ZONES 8–10.**

AZORELLA

A remarkable genus of cushion plants belonging to the carrot family, the majority of its 70 or so species are native to the South American Andes, often at high altitudes, but one species occurs on subantarctic islands right around the far southern hemisphere. The plants are evergreen perennials or long-lived subshrubs, the surface of the plant consisting of densely crowded tiny rosettes of fleshy leaves that may be toothed or lobed. Flowers are very small and fleshy, mostly yellowish, in profuse small umbels scattered over the surface of the cushion. They are aromatic, resinous plants and some have been used medicinally; one shrubby species is a source of firewood in the high Andes. **CULTIVATION:** They make appealing little rock garden plants, valued for the intricately patterned green foliage and neat habit. Requiring a very open, gritty, well-drained soil, they do best in full sun but can also be grown as alpines in a cool greenhouse. Propagate from seed, division, or cuttings.

Azorella trifurcata

One of the very few azorellas brought into cultivation, this species from Chile and Argentina makes a compact cushion up to about 4 in (10 cm) high, the tiny leaves deeply 3- or 5-lobed at their tips. In summer it produces rather insignificant umbels of tiny yellow flowers. **ZONES 6–9.**

Avicennia marina

Averrhoa carambola

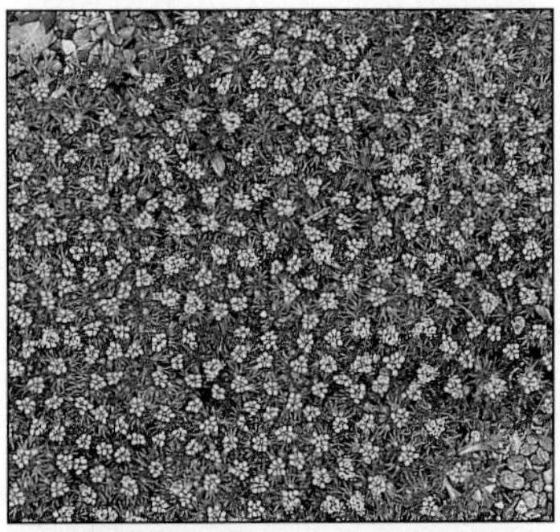

Azorella trifurcata

Azara microphylla

Azara lanceolata

Azara serrata

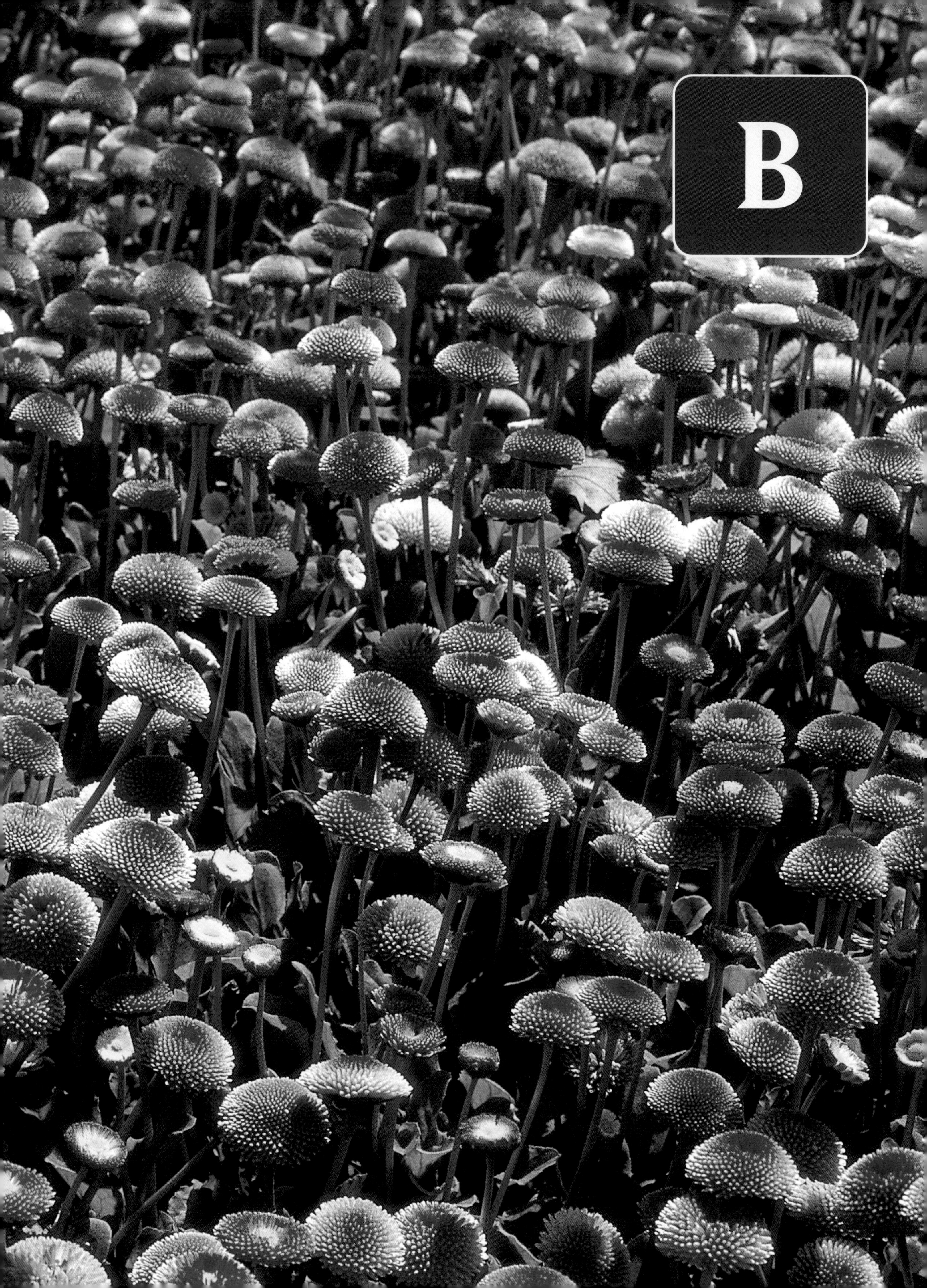

B

Babiana stricta

Babiana stricta 'Zwanenburg's Glory'

Baeckea virgata

BABIANA
BABOON FLOWER

Both the botanical and common names of this South African genus originate from the way baboons have often been observed digging up the corms of these spring flowers and eating them. They also formed part of the diet of the indigenous people. There are 50 or more species in the genus, but only a handful have found their way into general cultivation; however, quite a few more are grown by enthusiasts and are worth seeking out. These plants are rarely more than 12 in (30 cm) or so tall and look a little like miniature gladioli, with attractive flowers in shades of blue, yellow, pink and red borne on short spikes. Most of the corms supplied by bulb growers are hybrids derived mainly from *Babiana stricta.*

CULTIVATION: They are easy to grow in a warm-temperate climate and in cool areas they do very well in pots in a mildly warmed greenhouse. Plant the corms in fall (autumn) in light, rich, well-drained soil in a sunny position. Provide plenty of water during the growing season. Propagate from offsets or seed.

Babiana plicata

Baccharis pilularis 'Twin Peaks'

Babiana plicata
syn. *Babiana disticha*

This species is low growing, no more than about 8 in (2 cm) high, with hairy leaves that extend above the short flower spikes. The flowers, appearing in spring and scented of cloves, are pale blue, violet or white, often with yellow and purple markings. **ZONES 9–10.**

Babiana rubrocyanea
RED-EYED BABOON FLOWER

This species has purple-blue flowers with red centers. It grows to around 8 in (20 cm) tall with prominently veined leaves that bear fine hairs. It is similar to the more common *Babiana stricta* but it flowers several weeks earlier, often beginning in late winter. **ZONES 9–10.**

Babiana stricta

Together with its hybrids, this species is the most widely grown babiana. The vigorous, often rather untidy plants grow to about 10 in (25 cm) high with narrow, hairy, strongly ribbed leaves and branched spikes bearing cup-shaped flowers above the foliage in spring. The freesia-like flowers are blue to violet, but there are also white or cream forms; some are fragrant. The plants, which die back in summer, look best planted in large clumps. The hybrid cultivar **'Zwanenburg's Glory'** has purple-blue flowers with alternating pale bluish white petals, darker at the center. **ZONES 9–11.**

BACCHARIS

This genus of approximately 350 species of perennials and shrubs in the Compositae (daisy) family is native to the Americas. Most are evergreen, densely foliaged, wiry-stemmed plants, many from drier regions or locations with saline soil or exposed to salt spray. The leaves, arranged alternately on the branches, are mostly tough and leathery, very variable in shape but mostly toothed or lobed and often slightly resinous and sticky. The small, usually white or grayish flowerheads, which grow in panicles at the ends of branches, lack the ray-like flowers of typical daisies. Most species are rank-growing plants of no ornamental value but a few are useful in the garden.

CULTIVATION: Any sunny location with reasonable soil will do. Some salt-resistant species are ideal plants for coastal gardens. Some, too, will tolerate moderate to severe frosts but most are frost tender. Propagate from small tip cuttings or seed.

Baccharis pilularis
DWARF COYOTE BUSH

A native of California and Oregon, this evergreen shrub grows to a height of 24–36 in (60–90 cm). It has small, oval, bright green leaves on spreading branches and tiny white flowers. It is adaptable to most soils in any sunny position and is resistant to frost and to very dry conditions. **'Twin Peaks'** is a selected compact form under 30 in (75 cm) high and 10 ft (3 m) wide. It is valued as a hardy cover on dry slopes and for its fire-retardant qualities. **ZONES 7–10.**

BAECKEA

This is a genus of about 75 species of evergreen shrubs in the myrtle family, most native to Australia but a few occurring in New Caledonia and one extending to tropical Asia. They are found in many habitats from subalpine marshes to exposed coastal heaths. Mostly of heath-like habit, they vary in size from wiry prostrate plants to tall, erect shrubs, almost small trees. They are grown for their neat foliage and attractive flowers, which resemble tea-tree *(Leptospermum)* flowers but are mostly smaller; the dry fruits are small and thin-walled. Several species make good rock-garden plants.

CULTIVATION: They prefer full sun or part-shade, and moist but well-drained, moderately fertile soil. Plants benefit from a light pruning of the flowering shoots after the petals have fallen. Propagation is most readily achieved from cuttings.

Baeckea virgata
TWIGGY HEATH-MYRTLE, TALL BAECKEA

A bushy, erect shrub growing to a height and spread of 10 ft (3 m), or occasionally taller, this plant grows best on well-drained, sheltered sites. It is valued for its dainty white flowers, which are borne in abundance from late spring to late summer, and is useful for screening purposes. Some remarkable miniature cultivars with extraordinarily fine, dense foliage have appeared recently, an example being **'Howie's Sweet Midget'** which is normally under 18 in (45 cm) tall. **ZONES 8–11.**

BAILEYA

This is a genus of 4 annual or short-lived perennial species from southwestern USA and adjacent Mexico. They form clumps of wiry stems with narrow, deeply lobed or smooth-edged leaves densely covered in fine gray hairs. Coreopsis-like yellow flowerheads with up to 50 ray-like petals are borne singly at the stem tips and appear throughout the warmer months.

CULTIVATION: Easily grown in regions where summer humidity is low, baileyas will flourish in any light, well-drained soil in full sun. Since they tolerate moderately severe frosts, they may be planted in winter for early flowering and are ideal as a rather open ground cover for arid areas. Propagate from seed, which is best sown in place in early fall (autumn) or early spring.

Baileya multiradiata
DESERT MARIGOLD

Low mounds of silver-gray foliage mark this desert dweller, from southern USA. It is a perennial, though it sometimes behaves as an annual. Bright yellow 2 in (5 cm) wide blooms (also with yellow centers) rise above the foliage on slender stems to 18 in (45 cm) tall, over a long season. **ZONES 7–10.**

BALLOTA

This is a genus of about 35 species of perennials and deciduous or evergreen subshrubs in the mint family, mostly native to western Asia and the Mediterranean region but with one species extending to northern Europe, where it has been used in folk medicine. The aromatic foliage somewhat resembles that of horehound *(Marrubium).* The leaves are mostly rounded and bluntly toothed, arranged in opposite pairs on the stems which are squarish in cross-section and terminate in leafy spikes of small, 2-lipped flowers with prominent star-shaped calyces, clustered densely at the nodes. Most species have whitish hairy stems and leaves and these include some attractive garden plants of mound-like form used in rockeries and perennial borders.

CULTIVATION: Most ballotas are frost hardy and the hairy ornamental ones prefer a dry, sunny position and very well-drained soil. Evergreen species can be pruned to a more compact shape before spring growth starts. Propagate from seed or cuttings or by root division.

Ballota acetabulosa

This subshrub from Greece and Turkey grows to around 24 in (60 cm) high and wide. It has pale gray-green, downy, heart-shaped leaves around 2 in (5 cm) long. The spreading stems are also gray-green and downy. The purple-spotted white or mauve flowers, borne in summer, nestle in pale green 3 in (8 cm) wide calyces which produce the main decorative effect. **ZONES 8–10.**

Ballota nigra
BLACK HOREHOUND

Occurring widely through Europe, temperate Asia and North Africa, this species is a rank-growing perennial to about 3 ft (1 m) tall, the foliage rather like that of a nettle *(Urtica urens)* but more grayish

Ballota pseudodictamnus

Bambusa multiplex 'Alphonse Karr'

green. Clusters of small purple flowers with star-like brown calyces develop in the upper leaf axils in summer and fall (autumn). All parts of the plant have an unpleasant smell when crushed. Black horehound, which was used in herbal medicine, is very easily grown and spreads rapidly. **ZONES 5–10.**

Ballota pseudodictamnus

A native of Crete, Turkey and Libya, this species is very similar to *Ballota acetabulosa* except that it is smaller in all respects. It reaches a height of around 18 in (45 cm) and its pretty green calyces are only about ⅓ in (8 mm) wide. **ZONES 8–10.**

BAMBUSA

BAMBOO

This is a genus of around 120 species of clump-forming bamboos found in tropical and subtropical Asia. Many are very large, up to 80 ft (24 m) tall or even more, with strong, woody, hollow stems. In their native lands they are put to all sorts of uses, especially in construction, including scaffolding, and for piping and fencing. The upper parts of the stems are often arching, and branch at the nodes into wiry branchlets with masses of grass-like leaves. The flowers are rather insignificant, often half-hidden among the foliage on slender, arching panicles which are usually produced rather intermittently. *Bambusa* species have the advantage over some other bamboos of having short rather than long-running rhizomes and so are much less invasive. Some of the most popular ornamental bamboos in this genus are cultivars with striped variegation of the stems or leaves. **CULTIVATION:** They thrive in warm-temperate to tropical climates with humid conditions and deep, humus-rich soil. Plant young bambusas in part-shade. Propagate by division in spring.

Ballota acetabulosa

Bambusa multiplex

syn. *Bambusa glaucescens*

HEDGE BAMBOO

A native of southern China, this variable species has gracefully arching stems usually 10–30 ft (3–9 m) tall and 1–2 in (25–50 mm) in diameter topped with plumes of narrow, 6 in (15 cm) long leaves with silvery undersides. One of the more cold-tolerant *Bambusa* species, it is mostly represented in gardens by yellow-leafed and variegated cultivars. **'Alphonse Karr'** has yellow-striped stems, tinted pink when young. **'Riviereorum'** is a relatively dwarf cultivar with 5–10 ft (1.5–3 m) stems. **ZONES 9–12.**

BANKSIA

Named after the renowned English botanist Sir Joseph Banks, who discovered this genus at Botany Bay in 1770, *Banksia* consists of about 75 species of shrubs and small trees of wide occurrence in Australia—the majority, though, confined to the southwest. Habit and foliage vary, but all species have striking, dense, fuzzy spikes or heads of tightly packed small flowers, followed by woody fruits that protrude from among the dead flowers. The leaves are generally long and narrow, often with toothed edges, and contain much woody tissue, so they remain stiff and springy even when dead. Banksias vary in how well they adapt to garden conditions, but some are easily grown; the most decorative ones are now grown in plantations for the cut flower market. Some dwarf and prostrate ground cover forms of otherwise upright species are becoming popular as rock-garden plants. The flowers of all species are rich in nectar and attract birds. **CULTIVATION:** Most species prefer well-drained, sandy soil with low levels of major nutrients, especially phosphates. They do best in full sun, and some are moderately frost hardy. Regular, light tip pruning maintains shape and foliage density. Propagate from seed, which is best extracted from the 'cones' with the aid of fire or a hot oven.

Banksia burdettii

Banksia baxteri

BIRD'S NEST BANKSIA

This species from the far south of Western Australia is unusual in that the lemon-yellow flowers are in broad, almost hemispherical heads rather than cylindrical spikes. They appear in summer and fall (autumn) and are superlative as cut flowers, not least because the foliage is of striking form, the leaves cut to the mid-vein to form large triangular lobes. The young growths of this single-trunked shrub of 6–10 ft (1.8–3 m) are russet tinted. **ZONES 9–11.**

Banksia burdettii

BURDETT'S BANKSIA

Found naturally in sandy country north of Perth, Western Australia, Burdett's banksia grows 8–12 ft (2.4–3.5 m) tall with a dense spreading habit. The narrow olive-green leaves are blunt tipped and finely toothed. The 4 in (10 cm) erect blooms, borne at the tips of the branches in late summer and early fall (autumn), can look like giant acorns, opening progressively from the base and changing from pale gray in bud to pale orange. A useful species for cut flowers, it can make fast growth. **ZONES 9–11.**

Banksia coccinea

SCARLET BANKSIA

One of the most beautiful species and prized by the cut flower industry, the scarlet banksia from the far south of Western Australia has short, wide, erect cylinders of deep scarlet to orange flowers opening from downy gray buds, from winter through to early summer. The very broad, stiff leaves are gray on the undersides. It has a rather stiff, narrow habit, growing usually to 6–12 ft (1.8–3.5 m) in height. A difficult garden subject, it does not always flower readily and often succumbs to root-rot fungi in climates with wet summers. **ZONES 9–10.**

Banksia ericifolia

Banksia ericifolia 'Burgundy'

Banksia cunninghamii

syn. *Banksia spinulosa* var. *cunninghamii*

Coming from the same region of south-eastern Australia but in slightly moister and more elevated habitats, *Banksia cunninghamii* is very like *B. spinulosa* but is taller and more vigorous and has slightly broader, flatter leaves. Under good conditions it can reach a height of 20 ft (6 m). Another difference is that *B. cunninghamii* is unable to sprout from the roots when burnt or cut off, whereas *B. spinulosa* can repeatedly sprout from a woody rootstock. **ZONES 9–10.**

Banksia ericifolia

HEATH BANKSIA

From the Australian temperate east coast and adjacent ranges, this is the smallest-leafed banksia and also one of the most vigorous growers. It is a freely branching shrub with glossy deep green foliage and bears upright, bottlebrush-like spikes up to 10 in (25 cm) long in fall (autumn) and into winter. Their color varies from a washed-out orange to deep copper red, and the height of the plant from 6–12 ft (1.8–3.5 m). The heath banksia is one of the most easily cultivated banksias, surviving moderate frosts, salt spray on the coast, and adapting to richer soils. **'Port Wine'** has dull rose-pink spikes, and the striking **'Burgundy'** has flowers of a deeper red than most. **ZONES 8–11.**

Banksia baxteri

Banksia coccinea

B

Banksia 'Giant Candles'

A hybrid between *Banksia ericifolia* and *B. spinulosa*, 'Giant Candles' grows to about 12 ft (3.5 m). It is a dense shrub with abundant bronze-yellow flower spikes, which may be as long as 15 in (38 cm), in fall (autumn) and winter. Tough and vigorous like its parents, it is a bushier shrub than either. **ZONES 9–11.**

Banksia integrifolia
COAST BANKSIA

Of wide north-south distribution on the coast of eastern Australia, this salt-tolerant species forms at maturity a gnarled tree of up to 50 ft (15 m), with a trunk 18 in (45 cm) in diameter. Lime green flowers fading to dull yellow form cylindrical spikes about 4 in (10 cm) long from late summer to early winter. The distinctive silver-backed leaves, dull green above, are toothed only on young plants. In cultivation, *Banksia integrifolia* makes remarkably rapid growth, especially in deep sandy soil. **ZONES 9–11.**

Banksia integrifolia

Banksia cunninghamii

Banksia 'Giant Candles'

Banksia lemanniana

This is one of a small, unusual group of Western Australian banksias in which the flower spike points towards the ground. It makes a rather sparse shrub up to 15 ft (4.5 m) tall. The smallish, stiff leaves are jaggedly toothed, and the new growths are coated with rusty hairs. The 4 in (10 cm) long flower spikes are lemon yellow, appearing in late spring and early summer. **ZONES 10–11.**

Banksia marginata
SILVER BANKSIA

The most frost hardy of the banksias, this southeastern Australian species varies in growth form depending on its habitat. In lower regions with very poor soil it is commonly a dense, spreading shrub to about 6 ft (1.8 m), while in mountain forests it is an upright, small tree as much as 40 ft (12 m) high. The smallish dark green leaves are toothed at the apex and silvery white beneath. Small yellow-cream flower spikes appear from late summer to early winter. Compact forms make attractive shrubs, while taller forms are useful for screens and windbreaks. It is also a suitable coastal plant as it is resistant to salt damage. **ZONES 8–11.**

Banksia ornata

Banksia lemanniana

Banksia spinulosa

Banksia ornata
DESERT BANKSIA

Common in deep, sandy soil in western Victoria and adjacent South Australia, this species is normally a low-branching, bushy shrub of about 6 ft (1.8 m) in height. It has grayish green, closely toothed, narrowly wedge-shaped leaves. Stout silvery gray or pale yellow flower spikes appear in winter and spring, rich in nectar and attracting birds as well as honey-bees. This banksia is easily grown in well-drained sandy soil in an open sunny position. **ZONES 9–11.**

Banksia prionotes
ACORN BANKSIA

From the dry temperate west coast of Australia, this fairly fast-growing small tree is of rather open habit with long, narrow, toothed leaves. Spectacular orange-yellow flower spikes up to 6 in (15 cm) long opening from felty pure white buds are borne in fall (autumn) and winter. It can grow to 20 ft (6 m) or more, eventually forming a domed crown. Producing outstanding cut flowers, it thrives in sandy, alkaline soil in areas with dry summers but does poorly where summers are wet. **ZONES 10–11.**

Banksia prionotes

Banksia marginata

Banksia serrata

Banksia serrata
OLD MAN BANKSIA, SAW BANKSIA

This species is distinguished by its gnarled appearance with a short crooked trunk, thick, wrinkled, fire-resistant bark, and leathery, saw-toothed leaves. Large greenish cream flower spikes appear from summer through fall (autumn). Its bristly gray fruiting spikes, with protruding fruit-like small noses or chins, gave rise to the common name old man banksia. In the wild in its native southeastern Australia it grows on coastal dunes as well as sandstone ranges, reaching as much as 40 ft (12 m) in height; usually much smaller in cultivation, it is long lived and moderately frost hardy. **ZONES 9–11.**

Banksia spinulosa
HAIRPIN BANKSIA

This species is a common wildflower on the coastal hills of eastern Australia, and a favorite in Australian gardens. It does not grow as tall as other banksias, reaching about 4 ft (1.2 m), and develops a woody, underground rootstock which sprouts freely after fires. The flower spikes, which are usually dull yellow with hooked orange to bronze tips, nestle among the rather sparse, very narrow leaves. **'Birthday Candles'** is a dwarf cultivar with golden-bronze flower spikes. **ZONES 9–11.**

BAPTISIA
FALSE INDIGO

Baptisia is a genus of 20–30 species of pea-flowered perennials that grow naturally among the tall grasses of the prairies and woodlands of eastern and central USA. The common name arises from the former use of some species by dyers as a substitute for true indigo (*Indigofera*). Few of the species are grown much in gardens. Most are somewhat shrubby in habit, and the leaves are divided into 3 leaflets like a clover or a medic. The blue, purple, yellow or white pea-flowers are borne in terminal spikes over a fairly long summer season.

CULTIVATION: The plants prefer full sun and neutral, well-drained soil. They are not bothered by frost, nor do they resent very dry conditions in summer. As they have a deep root system they should not be transplanted or disturbed. Propagation is best done from seed in fall (autumn) or by division.

Baptisia alba

This bushy, upright species grows to around 5 ft (1.5 m). Its bluish green foliage provides a backdrop to the sprays of pea-like blooms, white sometimes streaked with purple, borne during early summer. **ZONES 7–10.**

Baptisia australis
FALSE INDIGO

This summer-flowering perennial is attractive in both flower and foliage. The leaves are blue-green and form a loose mound up to about 4 ft (1.2 m) high and 3 ft (1 m) across. The lupin-like flowers are borne on erect spikes from early to mid-summer and are an unusual shade of purplish blue. The seed pods can be dried for indoor decoration. **ZONES 3–10.**

BARBAREA

Found over much of the northern temperate zone, the dozen or so species of biennials and perennials in this genus are sometimes called land cress as they are somewhat similar in appearance and uses to watercress. They are most often found in damp soil along streamsides and in hollows. The smooth green leaves, initially in a basal rosette, are usually deeply lobed along the lower edges, leaving a large, rounded apical segment. Rosettes elongate into erect, leafy flowering stems branching into dense heads or spikes of small, bright yellow flowers.
CULTIVATION: Easily grown in damp soil in sun or part-shade, they may be invasive where conditions favor them. The foliage is gathered in winter and used in salads or boiled as a vegetable. Remove the flowerheads to encourage more luxuriant foliage. Propagate from seed.

Barbarea vulgaris
WINTER CRESS, YELLOW ROCKET

Occurring as a native in Europe and North Africa, this species has naturalized widely in other cool-temperate regions. It is a biennial or short-lived perennial making rosettes of glossy, deep green leaves with branching flower stems up to 3 ft (1 m) tall. The bright yellow flowers open from late spring. **ZONES 6–10.**

BARKLYA
GOLD BLOSSOM TREE

An Australian genus closely related to *Bauhinia* and consisting of one evergreen tree species only, *Barklya* is confined to a small area of coastal rainforest in Queensland, and is now rare in the wild. Producing a summer display of brilliant gold blossoms, it makes a handsome addition to warm-climate parks, gardens or streetscapes.
CULTIVATION: *Barklya* is subtropical and best grown in a frost-free climate; it requires full sun, fertile, well-drained soil and plentiful summer water. Growth can be slow; the tree may take many years to reach flowering size if conditions are less than ideal. Propagation is normally from seeds sown as soon as they ripen in fall (autumn).

Barklya syringifolia

This handsome tree has a dense, bushy, rounded crown and grows to around 50 ft (15 m) in its native habitat, although usually much smaller in gardens. It has glossy dark green, heart-shaped leaves, somewhat reminiscent of lilac leaves (hence the species name), and in early summer the crown is decked with stiff, erect spikes of crowded golden pea-flowers. They are followed by small seed pods. **ZONES 10–12.**

BARLERIA

This is a large genus of 250 or more species of evergreen shrubs and subshrubs from the tropics of Asia, the Americas and Africa. The plants have simple leaves arranged in opposite pairs on the stems. The flowers are generally tubular and 2-lipped, emerging from between overlapping bracts on short spikes on terminating branches or in the upper leaf axils. These are soft-stemmed, quick-growing plants, used in tropical and subtropical gardens for quick effect and as bedding plants, or they can be grown in the conservatory in cooler climates.
CULTIVATION: Barlerias are nearly all frost tender. In cooler climates they may be grown as indoor plants, but require strong light. Tip prune to encourage bushiness. The plants require full sun and fertile, moist but well-drained soil and look attractive when grouped together in a shrub border. They are easily propagated from cuttings in summer.

Barleria cristata
PHILIPPINE VIOLET

Despite its common name, this well-known tropical shrub is not native to the Philippines but to eastern India and Burma. It grows to around 3 ft (1 m) high and wide and is densely branched from ground level. For much of the year it produces small clusters of 2-lipped flowers from among bristly edged bracts in the upper leaf axils. Flowers vary from violet-blue to mauve, pink or white. It prefers a sheltered, humid position in part-shade. **ZONES 10–12.**

Barleria obtusa

This eastern South African shrub grows to 3 ft (1 m), with a spreading, bushy habit. Deep green, silky-haired leaves form a backdrop for the profuse white to pale mauve flowers, which appear in very short spikes in fall (autumn). **ZONES 9–11.**

BARRINGTONIA

This is a large genus of evergreen or dry-season deciduous trees with species scattered throughout the tropics, from Africa to northern Australia and the Pacific Islands. They occur mostly in lowland areas near water. Their branches have a distinctive habit of repeatedly forking in a candelabra-like fashion, terminating in

Baptisia australis

Barbarea vulgaris

Barleria cristata

Barringtonia asiatica

Baptisia alba

Barklya syringifolia

rosettes of paddle-shaped leaves. The striking flowers appear on usually pendulous spikes from the branch tips, with short petals and numerous long stamens. In many countries barringtonias are used as fish poisons: the bark, leaves or fruits are pounded or grated and then thrown in the water to stupefy the fish. Some of the species make fine ornamental trees for parks and streets in the tropics.
CULTIVATION: They require a completely frost-free climate and do best on sites with permanent subsoil moisture. Propagate from the large seeds which may take several months to germinate.

Barringtonia asiatica
syn. *Barringtonia speciosa*
FISH-KILLER TREE

Large brown seeds that are egg-shaped in outline but square in cross-section and with sharp angles are washed up on beaches all around the Pacific and Indian oceans. They are the fruit of this evergreen tree, which grows in coastal areas of tropical Asia, the Malay Archipelago and northern Australia. The buoyant seeds enable its dispersal across short ocean gaps. It normally grows to a height of about 20 ft (6 m) with multiple trunks and a vase-shaped crown. The leaves are dark green and glossy and the large flowers, appearing at the end of the dry season, are red and white. **ZONE 12.**

BASSIA

This is a widely distributed genus of some 26 species of annuals and perennials, most from warm-temperate northern hemisphere regions and most of them inconspicuous or weedy plants, but one sometimes cultivated for its delicate cypress-like foliage and bushy form. The genus belongs to the saltbush family and most of the species occur in somewhat saline habitats, for example around saltwater mudflats. Their growth form is usually shrubby, with small twiggy branches and narrow fleshy leaves. The flowers are very small, in leaf axils, and often pass unnoticed.
CULTIVATION: They are easily grown in any light, well-drained soil in full sun. Water well during spring and early summer, but allow to dry out slightly from mid-summer to encourage brighter foliage color. Propagate from seed sown under cover in late winter.

Bauhinia monandra

Bauhinia variegata

Bauhinia × blakeana

Barleria obtusa

Bauera sessiliflora

Bauera rubioides

Bassia scoparia f. *trichophylla*
syn. *Kochia scoparia* f. *trichophylla*
SUMMER CYPRESS, BURNING BUSH

A cultivated form of an annual species native to temperate Asia (naturalized in Europe and North America), this is the only *Bassia* normally grown in gardens. It grows from 2–5 ft (0.6–1.5 m) tall, making a rounded or somewhat columnar bush with very narrow bright green leaves. From late summer the fine foliage becomes orange- or red-tinted, sometimes even dull purple, depending on the climate. From a distance the plants resemble small conifers, hence the common name summer cypress. **ZONES 8–11.**

BAUERA

Occurring naturally in eastern Australia and much admired as wildflowers, the 4 species of this genus of evergreen shrubs are grown in gardens mainly for their star-shaped, deep pink to white flowers. The genus was named by Sir Joseph Banks in honor of the botanical artists Ferdinand and Franz Bauer. The branches are thin and wiry, often scrambling among other shrubs, and the small leaves appear as whorls of 6 at each node, though technically they are opposite pairs of compound leaves each with 3 leaflets; from their axils arise the flowers on very fine stalks.

CULTIVATION: Coming from mild, moist climates, the plants tolerate only light frosts and grow best in moist sandy or peaty soil in a sunny or part-shaded position. They appreciate soil kept cool by the shade of taller plants. Propagation is from cuttings in late summer. Light pruning after flowering produces a bushier plant and encourages abundant flowers.

Bauera rubioides
RIVER ROSE

Occurring in higher rainfall areas of southeastern Australia, including Tasmania, this attractive species grows in moist, shady places, mostly on the banks of small streams. It grows to a height of up to 3 ft (1 m) and usually greater spread; in some forms it is almost prostrate. The tiny, dark green leaves become reddish in winter, while the bowl-shaped, carmine-pink to white flowers appear from late winter to mid-summer. **ZONES 8–10.**

Bauera sessiliflora
GRAMPIANS BAUERA

This western Victorian species is the most colorful in flower, its long, scrambling branches strung with tight clusters of ½ in (12 mm) diameter bright rose-magenta flowers that appear in late spring and early summer. When supported by other shrubs it often scrambles to a height of 6 ft (1.8 m) or more, but can be kept trimmed if a neat bush is desired. Paler pink and white forms are also known. **ZONES 9–10.**

BAUHINIA

This is a variable genus of legumes, consisting of some 250 species of evergreen and dry-season-deciduous trees, shrubs and climbers, occurring in most tropical and subtropical regions of the world. Some botanists take a narrower view of the genus, splitting off about two-thirds of the species into other genera. All have characteristic 2-lobed leaves, but they are grown for their beautiful perfumed flowers whose likeness to orchids or butterflies has given rise to the common names of several species. The flattened brown seed pods that follow often persist on the branches for months.

CULTIVATION: Bauhinias do best in warm climates and need protection from frost and cold winds. Full sun and light, fertile, well-drained soil suit them best. Pruning is not usually necessary, but vigorous growth may be thinned out after flowering. Propagate from seed in spring.

Bauhinia × blakeana
HONG KONG ORCHID TREE

Bauhinia × blakeana is a presumed hybrid between *B. variegata* and the rather similar *B. purpurea.* It was first found in China in 1908, and was later adopted as Hong Kong's floral emblem. It resembles the more widely grown *B. variegata* but makes a taller, more densely foliaged and evergreen tree, with broader leaves. The slightly fragrant flowers, up to 6 in (15 cm) across on a healthy specimen, are a purplish red except for darker streaks on the inner petals, and are borne from late fall (autumn) through winter in shorter sprays than on *B. variegata.* It sets few seed pods. **ZONES 10–12.**

Bauhinia galpinii
syn. *Bauhinia punctata*
PRIDE-OF-DE-KAAP, RED BAUHINIA

One of the most colorful bauhinias, this evergreen scrambling shrub from south-eastern Africa has a sprawling, horizontal habit when grown out in the open, making a mound of dense foliage about 6 ft (1.8 m) high and up to 15 ft (4.5 m) wide. If grown beneath small trees, however, it may scramble through their branches to a height of 20 ft (6 m) or more, or it can be trained against a warm wall to good effect. The distinctive flowers, borne in showy clusters from late summer to fall (autumn), or spring in the tropics, are a rich apricot to brick red in color, their petals spoon-shaped with slender stalks. Fast growing, it will endure mild frosts and long periods without water. **ZONES 9–12.**

Bauhinia monandra

A rank-growing tropical species from the West Indies and northern South America, this species makes a multi-stemmed shrub or small tree to 20 ft (6 m) high. It has spreading branches and coarse foliage, with large pale green leaves. At the end of the dry season and well into the wet it produces a succession of flowers at the branch ends, with the large petals opening cream but ageing to flesh pink with a dramatic red splash on the upper petal. They are unusual in having only a single stamen. **ZONES 11–12.**

Bauhinia purpurea

This small, evergreen tree from southern Asia grows to around 20 ft (6 m) with an open upright habit and purple-toned, dark pink flowers. It is similar in appearance to *Bauhinia variegata,* but flowers in fall (autumn) rather than in spring, has fewer stamens, and its petals do not overlap. **ZONES 11–12.**

Bauhinia tomentosa
ST THOMAS TREE, YELLOW OR BELL BAUHINIA

This evergreen shrub grows to 15 ft (4.5 m) or more, with rather thin, pale green leaves. The pale yellow flowers, bell-shaped and somewhat drooping, have a dark brown blotch at the base of the upper petals and in the tropics are produced throughout the year, but mainly in spring and fall (autumn). **ZONES 10–12.**

Bauhinia variegata
ORCHID TREE, MOUNTAIN EBONY

This lovely small tree, native to India, bears abundant large, fragrant flowers in spring and intermittently in summer. These vary in hue from near white to rose pink, but always with a deeper shade on the broader upper petal. It grows 15–25 ft (4.5–8 m) tall, larger in the tropics, with a short trunk and spreading branches, and is marginally frost hardy.

In moist tropical climates it is semi-evergreen, but in cooler or drier locations it is almost deciduous, flowering on leafless branches. After flowering the branches of *Bauhinia variegata* usually become laden with masses of large, flat seed pods, which some gardeners find unsightly. **'Candida'** (syn. 'Alba'), commonly known as white mountain ebony, has fragrant white flowers with lemon-green markings. **ZONES 9–12.**

BEAUCARNEA

This genus consists of 20 or more species of evergreen trees and shrubs from semi-desert regions of Mexico and far southern USA, one of them widely sold as a decorative potted plant. Related to yuccas, they are grown for their remarkable thickened stems and long, thin, grass-like leaves. The numerous small white flowers are borne in large panicles arising from the centers of the leaf rosettes, though only on plants with trunks more than 3 ft (1 m) or so in height, which are generally at least 10 years old. The plant usually remains single stemmed until at least this height, but if the top is cut off it will sprout many new shoots. Some botanists treat *Beaucarnea* as a synonym of *Nolina*, others prefer to maintain them as different genera.
CULTIVATION: They can be grown outdoors in mild to warm climates, in full sun and well-drained, fertile soil. Water well while growing, but sparingly in winter or the stem may rot. As indoor potted plants they can reach ceiling height, flourishing in the warm, dry atmosphere of centrally heated rooms, though needing high light levels. Propagate from seed in spring or from suckers.

Beaucarnea recurvata
syns *Nolina recurvata, N. tuberculata*
PONYTAIL PALM

This slow-growing, evergreen tree is commonly sold in pots for the novel appearance of its swollen stem base; this tapers upward to a palm-like trunk bearing at its apex a dense crown of strap-like, downward-curving leaves up to 3 ft (1 m) long. Mature plants bear large feathery panicles of cream flowers in spring, followed by pinkish 3-winged fruit. Old specimens can achieve massive dimensions, the swollen base reaching up to 12 ft (3.5 m) wide, with multiple trunks 15–20 ft (4.5–6 m) tall. **ZONES 9–12.**

BEAUFORTIA

This is a genus of 18 species of evergreen shrubs from southwestern Australia, similar in many ways to the related genera *Callistemon, Melaleuca* and *Kunzea.* The flowers, in a range of colors from pink to orange, red or purple, are borne in small globular heads or bottlebrush-like spikes, often with slightly drooping filaments; they are followed by woody seed capsules. The leaves, aromatic when crushed, are small, linear to somewhat diamond-shaped and arranged usually in opposite pairs on the wiry branches.
CULTIVATION: These are easily grown shrubs that ask only for a sunny position with moist, well-drained soil and shelter from all but the lightest frosts. A light trim in spring will help to keep the growth dense and bushy. Unlike many Australian plants, beaufortias are not very tolerant of dry conditions. Propagate from seed or tip cuttings from non-flowering stems.

Beaufortia sparsa
SWAMP BOTTLEBRUSH

This heath-like shrub grows at the edges of swamps. It has small oval leaves and produces delightful feathery, vermilion to orange flowers in very short, bottlebrush-like heads in summer and fall (autumn). It grows to a height and spread of around 6 ft (1.8 m). **ZONES 9–11.**

BEAUMONTIA

This is a genus of 9 species of woody, evergreen, twining vines from the lower Himalayas and Indo-Malayan region. They have large, leathery, glossy leaves, arranged in opposite pairs on the stems, that bleed sticky sap when cut. The flowers are trumpet-shaped, quite large, mostly white and fragrantly scented, opening progressively from loose clusters that terminate leafy lateral branches.
CULTIVATION: In frost-free climates they may be planted outdoors in moist, humus-rich, well-drained soil in a sheltered position in full sun or light shade. The plants can be trained on a strong trellis or over a stump, or allowed to mound without support, trimming back longer growths. In cooler climates a large conservatory is required for plants to develop to flowering size. Prune immediately after flowering. Propagation is normally from cuttings.

Beaumontia grandiflora
HERALD'S TRUMPET

This beautiful, large, woody climber will climb to 20 ft (6 m) or more but needs strong support for its thick twining stems. It is valued for its large, fragrant, white trumpet flowers, 4–6 in (10–15 cm) long, which appear in late spring and summer, and its handsome, deep green leaves, prominently veined and up to 10 in (25 cm) long. **ZONES 9–12.**

BEGONIA
BEGONIA

Begonias are native to moist tropical and subtropical regions of all continents except Australia, and are most diverse in South America. There are over 1,500 known species, ranging from rhizomatous perennials a few inches (centimeters) high to 10 ft (3 m) shrubs. Many are grown as indoor plants, prized either for their beautifully colored and textured foliage or showy flowers, sometimes both present in the one species or cultivar. Mostly evergreen, they have broad, usually asymmetrical leaves of rather brittle and waxy texture. Female flowers, as distinct from male flowers which are on the same plant, have broad, colored flanges on the ovaries which develop into winged fruits.

Begonia enthusiasts divide the species and cultivars into a number of classes depending on growth habit and type of rootstock. The **cane-stemmed** begonias are erect growers, sometimes quite tall, with straight stems, fibrous roots, and usually pendent clusters of showy flowers; somewhat similar are some **shrubby** begonias, with a more closely branched habit (the bedding begonias belong here); another similar group but with lower, softer stems are known as the **winter-flowering** begonias, grown for their profuse and colorful flowers that peak in winter; the **rhizomatous** begonias are a large and varied class, with leaves arising directly from creeping, knotty rhizomes—they include the **Rex** begonias with colorfully variegated leaves and many others grown for foliage; and finally there are the **tuberous** begonias, now largely represented by hybrids of the **Tuberhybrida Group**; these plants die back to tubers in winter and bear large, showy, often double flowers in summer.
CULTIVATION: Many of the cane-stemmed, winter-flowering, shrubby and rhizomatous types can be grown outdoors in frost-free climates and make fine garden plants, though rhizomatous kinds in particular are prone to slug and snail attack. As indoor plants they do well in standard potting mix with peat moss or leafmold added to increase acidity. Grow in bright to moderate light, with good ventilation and above-average humidity, which can be maintained by standing pots on a tray of pebbles and water. Pinch back young plants of the shrubby type to keep them compact and to encourage flowers. Tuberous begonias require special treatment: tubers must be forced into growth in early spring at a temperature of 65°F (18°C) in peat moss or sphagnum, and kept in a cool, well-ventilated greenhouse for the summer flowering season. After flowering, plants die back and tubers are lifted in mid-fall (autumn) and stored dry. Propagate from tubers in the case of tuberous begonias. Other begonias may be propagated from stem or leaf cuttings (laying the cut leaf blades flat on damp sand and weighing them down with pebbles), or by division of rhizomes, or from seed. Begonias are susceptible to gray mold, powdery mildew and botrytis in the warmer part of the year if conditions are too damp.

Begonia auriculata

This rhizomatous begonia from tropical West Africa grows to a height of 12–15 in (30–38 cm) with short erect stems carrying smallish, very fleshy leaves in 2 distinct rows. The leaves are ear-shaped, shiny olive green with a central blotch of silver. This species bears small sprays of pink flowers in summer. **ZONES 10–12.**

Begonia boliviensis

From Bolivia, this is one of the major species from which the tuberous hybrid begonias have been bred. It is a summer-flowering, tuberous-rooted plant with stiffly erect, succulent, branching stems reaching to 3 ft (1 m); the stems soon become lax and may need to be staked. The large leaves are pointed and have toothed margins, and the orange-red blooms are held in freely drooping bunches. **ZONES 9–11.**

Begonia boliviensis

Beaucarnea recurvata

Beaufortia sparsa

Beaumontia grandiflora

Begonia × *cheimantha* 'Gloire de Lorraine'
CHRISTMAS BEGONIA, LORRAINE BEGONIA

One of the winter-flowering group, this hybrid cultivar has single, white to pale pink flowers, borne mainly in winter. The roundish leaves are bright green and the plant grows to a height of 12 in (30 cm). **ZONES 10–11.**

Begonia 'Cleopatra'

A rhizomatous begonia of uncertain origin, this is a popular, easy-to-grow plant with a dense mass of shortly creeping rhizomes that support crowded, sharply lobed, yellow-green and purplish brown leaves. Profuse, long-stalked sprays of pale pink flowers bloom in early spring. In warm climates it is a popular balcony plant, thriving in hot sun. **ZONES 10–12.**

Begonia coccinea
ANGEL-WING BEGONIA

The elegant, succulent stems, up to 4 ft (1.2 m) tall, of this cane-stemmed species from Brazil support leaves of deep green with red margins and dull red beneath. In spring and summer it bears masses of coral red flowers in long-lasting pendent clusters. Well suited to subtropical gardens or greenhouse cultivation, it prefers a humus-rich, well-mulched soil but will tolerate neglect. **ZONES 10–12.**

Begonia, Semperflorens-cultorum Group

Begonia 'Erythrophylla'
syn. *Begonia* 'Feastii'
BEEFSTEAK BEGONIA

This rhizomatous begonia is grown chiefly for its attractive foliage—the large, leathery leaves are some 4 in (10 cm) wide, bright green above and deep red-brown underneath, earning this species its unappetizing common name. The sprays of delicate pink flowers on 6 in (15 cm) stalks are a bonus. Apart from its popularity as an indoor plant, this easily grown cultivar makes an interesting garden plant for lightly shaded spots in frost-free climates. **ZONES 10–12.**

Begonia fuchsioides

Native to Venezuela, this shrubby begonia has small, crowded, oval leaves, flushed pink on new growths. Small coral-red to pale pink flowers are borne in numerous short sprays over a long season from fall (autumn) to spring. Suitable for outdoor use, it grows to 3 ft (1 m) tall with an erect, closely branched habit and gracefully drooping branchlets. It prefers good light. **ZONES 10–12.**

Begonia grandis subsp. *evansiana*
HARDY BEGONIA

Native to China, southern Japan and the highlands of Southeast Asia, this tuberous subspecies is the only begonia that can be expected to survive moderately cold winters outdoors. It is a low, bushy plant with red stems, growing to 24 in (60 cm) tall. The broad, somewhat fleshy leaves are a pale green above and flushed coppery red on the undersides. Fragrant pink flowers about 1 in (25 mm) across are produced in nodding clusters all summer. Preferring semi-shade, the plant dies back in winter. **ZONES 7–11.**

Begonia, S-c Group, 'Ernst Benary'

Begonia, Semperflorens-cultorum Group

Begonia 'Cleopatra'

Begonia × *hiemalis*

Begonia scharffii

Begonia × *hiemalis*
syn. *Begonia* × *elatior*
WINTER-FLOWERING BEGONIA

This name applies to a group of winter-flowering hybrid cultivars originating from crosses between *Begonia socotrana* and Tuberhybrida Group begonias, resulting in a range of easily grown plants with single or double blooms in subtle colors from white through yellow and orange to red and pink. They have fibrous rather than tuberous root systems and tend to die after flowering, though some newer cultivars have overcome this drawback. **ZONES 10–11.**

Begonia masoniana
IRON CROSS BEGONIA

Native to New Guinea, this rhizomatous species' common name is derived from the bold brown markings, reminiscent of the German Iron Cross, on the upper surfaces of the bright green, puckered, bristly haired leaves. With a mounding, knotty rhizome, this species grows to a height of 18–24 in (45–60 cm). The pinkish white flowers are insignificant and appear infrequently. **ZONES 11–12.**

Begonia metallica
METAL-LEAF BEGONIA

A tall-growing, shrub-like begonia from Mexico, this species has bronze-green, deeply veined leaves often splashed with white and red-veined on the undersides. It reaches a height of about 3 ft (1 m) and from summer to fall (autumn) bears pink flowers on stalks with bristly red hairs. **ZONES 10–12.**

Begonia 'Orange Rubra'

A long-established and popular cultivar of obscure origin, this cane-stemmed begonia is normally about 24 in (60 cm) tall, with rather weak stems. It has large, oval, light green leaves, sometimes with white spots that disappear with age. Pendent clusters of showy orange flowers are produced through the year. **ZONES 10–12.**

Begonia 'Pink Shasta'

Begonia 'Pink Shasta'

One of the 'angel-wing' type of cane-stemmed begonias, 'Pink Shasta' grows to 3–4 ft (1–1.2 m) high with branching stems and leaves slightly silver spotted. It produces pendulous panicles of light salmon-pink flowers through spring, summer and fall (autumn). It originated as a seedling of **'Shasta'**, which is derived from *Begonia coccinea.* **ZONES 10–12.**

Begonia Rex-cultorum Group
REX BEGONIA, BEEFSTEAK GERANIUM, PAINTED LEAF BEGONIA

This is a group of rhizomatous cultivars grown for their multicolored foliage. They are derived from the Himalayan *Begonia rex* and some related Asian species. They have short, knotty rhizomes and broad, very asymmetrical leaves usually with toothed or sharply lobed margins and often with a rather warty surface; the upper sides are variously colored and patterned with zones or spots of silver, pink, gray bronze, red or purple, while the undersides are mostly a dullish red. The flowers are relatively inconspicuous. **'Merry Christmas'** (syn. 'Ruhrtal') has leaves banded emerald green with a rose red center and silver highlights. **ZONES 10–12.**

Begonia scharffii
syn. *Begonia haageana*

This shrub-like begonia from Brazil grows to 24 in (60 cm) tall with a sprawling habit and has hairy stems and leaves. The large, olive-green leaves have pointed tips and are red-veined on the undersides. The flowers, pinkish white with pink-red hairs at the base like a beard, are produced throughout the year. **ZONES 10–12.**

Begonia Semperflorens-cultorum Group
BEDDING BEGONIA, WAX BEGONIA

Derived largely from the Brazilian ***Begonia semperflorens,*** the dwarf, shrubby begonias of this group are often grown as bedding annuals, for example, **'Ernst Benary'**, or for borders in shaded gardens, and are also popular as potted plants for window boxes or patio tubs. Freely branching plants with soft, succulent stems, they have rounded, glossy green (bronze or variegated in some cultivars) leaves about 2 in (5 cm) long. The flowers are profuse, opening progressively at the branch tips over a long summer and early fall (autumn) season (most of the year in warmer climates). The numerous cultivars include singles and doubles in colors of bright rose pink, light pink, white or red; they are generally released as a series, with mixed colors. They are grown from seed or stem cuttings and planted out in late spring in cooler climates; pinch out growing tips to encourage bushy growth. **Cocktail Series** are bushy miniatures with bronzy foliage and single flowers: **'Gin'** has metallic black-green leaves and deep pink flowers; **'Vodka'** produces deep red flowers against very dark green leaves; and the pale bronze leaves of **'Whiskey'** are offset by white flowers. **Thousand Wonders** is an older series consisting of compact, sun-hardy plants in mixed shades of pink and white. ZONES 9–11.

Begonia Tuberhybrida Group

These are the well-known tuberous begonias, sold in full bloom by florists and in an earlier era displayed in public conservatories designed especially for their needs. Their glorious large blooms come in almost every color of the rainbow except blues, as singles or doubles, with many variations of frills and ruffles. These hybrids are derived from a number of species native to the Andean region of South America. The tubers sprout in mid-spring, producing weak, brittle stems up to about 24 in (60 cm) long with rather sparse, mid-green

Begonia, Tuberhybrida Group

Begonia, Tuberhybrida, Picotee Type

leaves. The summer flowers can weigh down the stems, which may need staking. After flowering, plants enter their dormant stage and the tubers are normally lifted in mid-fall (mid-autumn) and stored dry. Several subgroups are recognised within the Tuberhybrida Group, based on growth form and flower type: most numerous are the **Camellia-flowered** and **Rose-flowered** cultivars, with very large, mostly double flowers up to 6 in (15 cm) across or even larger, in the full range of colors; examples are **'Fairy Lights'** and **'Mandy Henschke'**, their multiplicity of petals is developed only in the male flower, where the biggest flowers are obtained by removing buds, sacrificing the smaller single female flowers that grow on either side of the central male. **Picotee** group cultivars are mostly double blooms with petal edges washed in contrasting or deeper shades of the flower color. Cultivars of the **Multiflora** type are usually single-flowered and are grown mainly for their effect en masse. They are available in the same range of colors as the others and are grown in the same way, except that they need no bud removal. Plants can be floppy and will benefit from staking. The **Pendula Group** is a group of hybrids that carry their flowers in pendent sprays; known sometimes as 'basket begonias', they look best cascading from hanging baskets. The single or double flowers are usually smaller than the Camellia- and Rose-flowered types but come in the same range of colors and are grown in the same way. ZONES 9–11.

Begonia, Tuberhybrida Group

Begonia, Tuberhybrida Group, 'Fairy Lights'

Begonia, Tuberhybrida, 'Mandy Henscke'

Belamcanda chinensis

BELAMCANDA

This genus, native to southern and eastern Asia and belonging to the iris family, contains only 2 species. The plants are perennials but of weak growth and tending to be short lived, with flattened fans of thin-textured leaves arising from thin rhizomes. Slender flowering stems terminate in a few rather small flowers with 6 narrow petals; these are followed by seed pods which split widely to reveal rows of shiny black seeds, like small berries—these are popular for dried flower arrangements.

CULTIVATION: These are warm-temperate plants that require sunshine and rich, well-drained soil. Water well in summer. In a cold climate the dormant plants will need protection from heavy frosts. They are propagated by division or from seed, which should be sown every second or third year to ensure the plants' survival.

Belamcanda chinensis

LEOPARD LILY, BLACKBERRY LILY

This 24–36 in (60–90 cm) tall plant has something of the habit of an iris but the summer flowers are quite un-iris-like in appearance. Up to 2 in (5 cm) across, they come in a range of colors from cream to yellow, apricot or deep orange-red, usually with darker spotting, hence the common name leopard lily. The seed pods open to reveal tight clusters of seeds resembling the fruitlets of a blackberry, hence their other common name. ZONES 8–11.

BELLIS

DAISY

The little white flower that spangles lawns in spring is one of the best loved of European wildflowers. These, the true daisies, belong to the genus *Bellis* which consists of 15 species of small perennials that occur wild in Europe, North Africa and Turkey. *Bellis* is from the Latin *bellus* which means 'pretty' or 'charming', while the English 'daisy' is a corruption of 'day's eye', arising from the way the flower closes up at night, opening again to greet the sunrise. The plants form rosettes with small oval to spoon-shaped leaves; each rosette produces a succession of flowerheads on individual stalks in shades of white, pink, blue or crimson. Only one of the species is widely cultivated, mostly in the form of improved strains.

CULTIVATION: Daisies are favorite flowers for edging flowerbeds in spring and, while they are perennial in cool-temperate climates, it is usual to treat them as annuals or biennials, sowing seed in fall (autumn). They will thrive in any good garden soil in sun or part-shade; keep soil moist in winter and spring. Propagate from seed or by division.

Bellis perennis Pomponette Series

Bellis perennis

Bellis perennis 'Medicis White'

Bellis perennis

ENGLISH DAISY, COMMON DAISY

This daisy has become widely naturalized in temperate parts of most continents. The wild plants are small, forming carpets of crowded rosettes that spread through lawns by short runners. The 1 in (25 mm) wide flowerheads, appearing from late winter to early summer, are white with golden centers and pale purplish undersides. **'Medicis White'** is a white cultivar. The garden strains mostly have double flowerheads of red, crimson, pink or white, all with a gold center. **'Alba Plena'** is an old double white cultivar, very different from the **Pomponette Series** daisies now popular as bedding plants and cut flowers; these are a far cry from the wild flowers, making neat hemispherical flowerheads 1½ in (35 mm) wide with curled petals, on stems up to 10 in (25 cm) high, in mixed colors. **ZONES 3–10.**

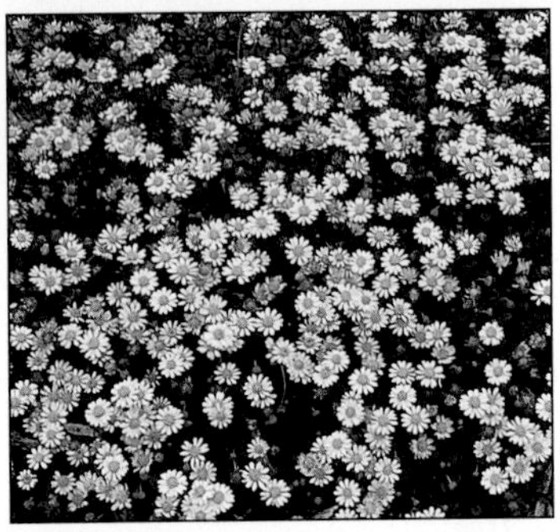

Bellium minutum

BELLIUM

This is a genus of 3 species of annual and perennial, trailing or mounding daisies native to southern Europe. The botanical name was intended to indicate their close similarity to *Bellis*, though in fine details of floral structure they are quite distinct. They are delightful miniature plants with very small, crowded, spatula-shaped leaves and tiny white flowerheads borne in profusion.

CULTIVATION: They prefer a sunnier, drier position than English daisies and thrive in well-drained rockeries. They should be mulched with fine gravel to prevent the foliage becoming mud-splashed during rain. All species will tolerate light to moderate frosts. Propagate from seed or by division.

Bellium minutum

A summer-flowering annual from the islands of the Mediterranean, this species has leaves that are slightly over ¼ in (6 mm) long. Its white flowerheads, which are carried on 2 in (5 cm) stems, are equally tiny, just over ½ in (12 mm) wide with purplish undersides. **ZONES 6–9.**

BERBERIDOPSIS

For most of the last 130 years this genus was believed to consist of a single species of woody, evergreen climber from southern Chile. The plant was much admired for its holly-like foliage, and sprays of deep scarlet flowers resembling those of some *Berberis* species but larger and fleshier. However, in 1984 a Dutch botanist drew attention to the similarities between this plant and a climber native to hill rainforests of eastern Australia,

Bellis perennis Pomponette Series

then classified in the genus *Streptothamnus*, and formally renamed it as a second species of *Berberidopsis*—thus the genus now has 2 species, one on either side of the Pacific. The ovate leaves are edged with spines and the flowers dangle from terminating stems.

CULTIVATION: These climbers are moderately frost hardy, though roots should be protected from frost by mulching. They thrive in mild, humid areas in peaty, well-drained soil but are quite adaptable. They are propagated mainly from cuttings.

Berberidopsis corallina

CORAL VINE

This Chilean native is a shrubby, scrambling climber with 3 in (8 cm) long, rather rigid, narrowly heart-shaped leaves with blunt-toothed edges. The waxy red, bell-shaped, long-stalked flowers resemble unopened fuchsia buds. It is not a brazenly showy, large-flowered climber but it is very elegant. Supported on trees it grows to at least 10 ft (3 m) high, or it can be trained into a shrub form with a dense canopy 6 ft (1.8 m) or more wide. **ZONES 8–9.**

BERBERIS

BARBERRY

This is a large genus consisting of well over 400 species of hardy shrubs, both evergreen and deciduous, mostly branching from below the ground into densely massed canes and with weak to quite fierce spines where the leaves join the stems. The leaves are generally rather leathery, of small to medium size and often with prickly marginal teeth. Clusters of small yellow, cream, orange or reddish flowers are followed by small fleshy fruits. Most species come from temperate East Asia, a few from Europe and several from Andean South America. North American species once placed in *Berberis* are now referred to *Mahonia*.

Berberidopsis corallina

CULTIVATION: Barberries are easy to grow and thrive in most soil types. Withstanding hard pruning, they are useful for hedges. Full sun suits them best. Propagate from seed or cuttings. In some countries there are restrictions on growing barberries because some species can harbor the overwintering phase of the wheat rust fungus.

Berberis calliantha

Native to the moist mountains of south-eastern Tibet, this dwarf, evergreen shrub grows to no more than 3 ft (1 m) high, often much less, with a spreading compact habit. The leaves are holly-like, about 1½ in (35 mm) long, glossy deep green above and waxy white beneath. The pale yellow flowers are large for a berberis, up to 1 in (25 mm) wide, borne on nodding stalks in spring; they are followed by deep purple berries with an attractive gray bloom. **ZONES 4–9.**

Berberis darwinii

DARWIN BARBERRY

The showiest of several evergreen species from Chile and Argentina, all with small leaves and neat clusters of deep yellow to orange flowers, *Berberis darwinii* has dark green, glossy leaves with holly-like toothing and dense short sprays of bright golden-yellow flowers in late winter and spring. These are followed by bluish berries. It grows 6 ft (1.8 m) or more high and wide with an irregular, open branching habit; branches are less spiny than most other species. **ZONES 7–10.**

Berberis × hybrido-gagnepainii

This hybrid between the 2 Chinese species *Berberis gagnepainii* and *B. verruculosa* includes many named cultivars. They are mostly low, dense, evergreen shrubs with rather long spines on the stems. The leaves are narrow and pointed with small spiny teeth on the margins. **'Parkjuweel'** ('Park Jewel')

Berberis darwinii

Berberis calliantha

Berberis × *s.* 'Corallina Compacta'

Berberis × *s.* 'Corallina Compacta'

Berberis × *stenophylla*

Berberis jamesiana

differs from most being semi-deciduous with small oblong leaves, mostly with smooth margins, that color vividly in fall (autumn). It grows to about 6 ft (1.8 m) high, with a broader spread. **ZONES 5–9.**

Berberis jamesiana

This deciduous shrub from western China grows to 6 ft (1.8 m) or more and has purplish new growths, stems armed with long spines, and thick, olive-green leaves that are strongly veined and bluish gray on the undersides. In early summer it bears masses of tiny golden-yellow flowers on spikes up to 4 in (10 cm) long, followed by globular white fruit ⅜ in (9 mm) in diameter that ripen to pale scarlet. A striking species, with fruit like redcurrants when ripe, the foliage also turns red in fall (autumn). **ZONES 6–9.**

Berberis × *mentorensis*
MENTOR BARBERRY

An extremely tough shrub resulting from the cross between the Chinese ***Berberis julianae*** and the Japanese *B. thunbergii*, this hybrid has an upright habit with densely crowded vertical stems bearing strong spines. The attractive foliage turns bright red in fall (autumn) in colder climates, but remains evergreen in mild-winter regions. The flowers and fruit are less showy than in other barberries. It is grown most frequently as an impenetrable hedge and thrives in regions with hot dry summers. **ZONES 5–9.**

Berberis × *ottawensis*

This hybrid between *Berberis thunbergii* and *B. vulgaris*, bred in Ottawa early this century, is best known in the form of the clone **'Superba'** (syn. 'Purpurea'), which is similar to and often confused with *B. thunbergii* 'Atropurpurea' but is taller, around 6 ft (1.8 m), and more vigorous, with the new growths bronze red rather than dark purplish. Its red berries appear in fall (autumn). It is a popular and very hardy, deciduous shrub with densely massed stems, useful for hedging or to provide contrast among green-leafed shrubs. It is also prized by flower arrangers. **ZONES 3–10.**

Berberis pruinosa

From western China, this distinctive evergreen shrub grows to 10 ft (3 m) with reddish new growths, the yellowish stems with spines up to 1½ in (35 mm) long. The dull green leaves, whitish beneath, are up to 3 in (8 cm) long and ¾ in (18 mm) wide, with fine spiny teeth toward the apex. Clusters of small, pale yellow flowers are borne in late spring followed by small blackish fruit covered in a thick white bloom. **ZONES 6–9.**

Berberis × *ottawensis* 'Superba'

Berberis × *ottawensis* 'Superba'

Berberis × *stenophylla*

This evergreen hybrid, a cross between *Berberis darwinii* and a related South American species ***B. empetrifolia***, has densely crowded, woody stems and arching branches. Growing to 8 ft (2.4 m) high and 10 ft (3 m) wide, it has narrow, deep green leaves, bluish beneath. A profusion of golden-yellow flowers appear in spring, followed by blue-purple berries. It makes a good specimen shrub or can be grown as a hedge. **'Corallina Compacta'** is a dwarf clone only 12 in (30 cm) or so in height, with yellowish leaves and coral fruit, and **'Crawley Gem'** is tall and very floriferous. **ZONES 6–9.**

Berberis thunbergii
THUNBERG BARBERRY, JAPANESE BARBERRY

This is one of the most widely planted barberries, usually in the guise of one of its cultivars. Native to Japan, it is a low-growing deciduous shrub (almost evergreen in warmer climates) only 5 ft (1.5 m) in height, with densely massed stems and small, neatly rounded leaves. Its spines are not particularly fierce. The small, not very decorative, bell-shaped flowers that appear in mid-spring are greenish yellow with dull red stripes. **'Atropurpurea'** has deep purplish brown foliage turning a metallic bronze black in late fall (autumn). **'Atropurpurea Nana'** (syns 'Crimson Pygmy', 'Little Favorite') is a neat, bun-shaped plant only 12–18 in (30–45 cm) high, with similar toning plus green tints. **'Keller's Surprise'** is compact and rather narrow, with green or bronze leaves splashed with pink. **'Rose Glow'** has rich purple leaves, which are also variously marked with pink, and have green margins. **'Red Pillar'** is an improved form of the earlier cultivar **'Erecta'** and has purple-red foliage and a very upright growth habit to around 4–5 ft (1.2–1.5 m) tall, **'Bagatelle'** is compact with purplish red foliage and **'Kobold'** is freely fruiting. **ZONES 4–10.**

Berberis thunbergii 'Atropurpurea Nana'

Berberis thunbergii 'Atropurpurea'

Berberis thunbergii 'Red Pillar'

Berberis thunbergii 'Rose Glow'

Berberis pruinosa

Berberis verruculosa
WARTY BARBERRY

This slow-growing, evergreen shrub from western China is normally about 5 ft (1.5 m) high with masses of strongly arching stems, their bark covered in small warty brown protuberances. The small, glossy leaves are crowded along the stems. Yellow flowers appear in late spring scattered singly among the leaves, followed by cylindrical purple-black berries with a blue bloom. **ZONES 5–9.**

Berberis vulgaris
COMMON BARBERRY

This is a common hedgerow plant in England. A deciduous shrub 6–10 ft (1.8–3 m) tall with crowded spiny canes and round-tipped leaves with bristly teeth, it makes a fine show of yellow blossom in late spring, but is at its most spectacular in fall (autumn) when laden with bright coral-red, cylindrical fruit. These have medicinal properties and are edible, but they have a strongly acidic taste. Easily grown, and extremely hardy and resistant to dry conditions, it is widely naturalized in North America and is the main species harboring wheat rust fungus there. **ZONES 3–9.**

Bergenia stracheyi

Berberis wilsoniae
WILSON BARBERRY

Deciduous, or almost evergreen in warmer climates, this Chinese species has small, narrow, toothless leaves with rounded tips and a densely bushy habit. It grows to 5 ft (1.5 m) but spreads into a broad mass of foliage, touching the ground. Rather inconspicuous yellow flowers from late spring to early summer are followed in fall (autumn) by abundant pink fruit which persist into winter, turning deeper red as the foliage takes on tints of yellow, orange and red. This highly ornamental species requires ample space. **ZONES 5–10.**

BERGENIA

Consisting of 6 or 7 species of rhizomatous, semi-evergreen perennials in the saxifrage family from eastern and central Asia, this genus is characterized by large, handsome, paddle-shaped leaves, arising from the ground on short stalks to form loose clumps. There are also many garden hybrids that have been developed over the last 100 years or so. Large clusters of flowers—mostly pale pink, but also white and dark pink—are borne on short, stout stems in winter and spring. An example is **'Eroica'**, with deep pink flowers. The foliage often develops attractive red tints in winter.

CULTIVATION: Bergenias make excellent ground cover and rockery plants, thriving in sun or shade and tolerant of exposed sites as well as moist ground beside streams or ponds, but leaves color most strongly when plants are grown under drier conditions. Water well in hot weather and remove spent flowerheads to prolong flowering. Propagate by division in spring after flowering, when the plants have become crowded.

Berberis verruculosa

Berberis wilsoniae

Bergenia purpurascens

Bergenia × *schmidtii*

Bergenia 'Eroica'

Bergenia cordifolia

Bergenia 'Beethoven'

This is one of a group of hybrid cultivars raised in England in the 1970s by Eric Smith who gave them names relating to classical music. It has deep green leaves and large heads of white flowers backed by reddish calyces, on dull red stems about 12 in (30 cm) tall. **ZONES 4–9.**

Bergenia ciliata

A native of the Himalayas, grown as much for its handsome rounded leaves, up to 12 in (30 cm) wide and fringed with fine reddish hairs, as for its delicate white to pinkish blooms; these appear in early spring, sometimes persisting to the beginning of summer, and deepen in color as they age. In cold climates the leaves may shrivel in winter. **ZONES 5–9.**

Bergenia cordifolia
HEARTLEAF SAXIFRAGE

Native to Siberia's Altai Mountains, this tough perennial has crinkly edged, more or less heart-shaped leaves up to 8 in (20 cm) wide, and produces panicles of drooping purple-pink flowers on 12–15 in (30–38 cm) stems in late winter and early spring. The plant is long flowering and the leaves remain green in winter. **'Purpurea'** has magenta-pink flowers and leaves tinged purple. **ZONES 3–9.**

Bergenia crassifolia

Bergenia crassifolia is one of the taller species, though the foliage is ground hugging with thick, blue-green leaves and bristly reddish margins. In early spring it produces nodding deep pink flowers in large dense clusters on stalks 12 in (30 cm) or more high. **'Aureo-Marginata'**, a cultivar with leaves streaked cream and dull purple, provides year-round color interest. **ZONES 3–9.**

Bergenia 'Morgenröte'

Bergenia 'Morgenröte' ('Morning Red')

This small-growing cultivar has plain green leaves under 6 in (15 cm) and dense small clusters of largish orchid pink flowers on deep red stalks in late spring, sometimes blooming again in summer. **ZONES 4–9.**

Bergenia purpurascens
syn. ***Bergenia beesiana***

The large fleshy, oval, purple-tinted leaves of this species develop a deeper color in winter, especially in a cold climate where frost occurs. Bright pink to reddish purple flowers are borne in late winter and spring on stems up to 18 in (45 cm) tall. **ZONES 5–9.**

Bergenia × *schmidtii*

Arguably the most vigorous and most widely planted bergenia, this old hybrid between *Bergenia ciliata* and *B. crassifolia* has large, rounded, fleshy, dull green leaves. Set among the foliage are rose-pink blooms on stalks up to 12 in (30 cm) long. The main flush of flowers occurs in late winter and early spring, frosts often damaging the blooms, though it often flowers sporadically at other times. The plant spreads to make a fine ground cover, and adapts well to warm-temperate humid climates. **ZONES 5–10.**

Bergenia 'Silberlicht' ('Silver Light')

This hybrid cultivar forms compact clumps of glossy green leaves up to 8 in (20 cm) long with scalloped margins. The large, pure white to palest pink flowers appear in late spring in compact clusters on a succession of flower stalks up to 18 in (45 cm) high. **ZONES 5–9.**

Bergenia stracheyi
syn. ***Bergenia milesii***

This species has relatively small leaves with hairs lining the edges and wedge-shaped at the base. Forming extensive clumps with age, it produces tight clusters of nodding, cup-shaped, deep pink to white flowers in early spring on stalks 10 in (25 cm) high. **ZONES 6–9.**

BERKHEYA

This is a genus of around 75 species of prickly leafed perennials and subshrubs from southern and tropical Africa. Although superficially resembling members of the thistle tribe (of the Compositae, or daisy family), they are closely allied to such genera as *Arctotis* and *Gazania*. Often beginning as a basal rosette of leaves with cottony white hairs on the undersides, they develop tall, leafy stems branching into globular flowerheads of yellow, white or purple florets surrounded by rows of spiny bracts. The leaves also are spiny toothed to varying degrees, depending on species.

CULTIVATION: Only a few species have been introduced to cultivation: these have proved easy to grow in sunny spots in mild, nearly frost-free climates with dry winters, providing bold foliage effects and a long succession of blooms in summer. Plant in any good garden soil, and propagate from seed or by root division. New introductions should be watched carefully for signs of weediness, at least in warm regions of the world.

Berkheya purpurea

This handsome, tall perennial comes from the cool mountain grasslands of the great escarpment of eastern South Africa. It has large basal leaves edged with spiny teeth and downy hairs on the undersides. In summer it sends up branched flowering stems to 3 ft (1 m) tall, terminating in prickly, pale purple flowerheads about 3 in (8 cm) across. **ZONES 7–10.**

BERLANDIERA

GREEN EYES

This is a genus of perennials from southern North America. Some species die back completely in winter, others maintain an evergreen basal rosette of foliage. The leaves are broadly lance-shaped with prominent veins and wavy to shallowly lobed edges. They are borne on rather woody stems that grow to around 3 ft (1 m) tall. The bright yellow daisy flowerheads each have a bright green 'eye' of disc florets which remain after the rays have dropped.

CULTIVATION: They are easily cultivated in any well-drained garden soil with added dolomite lime. They also prefer additional organic matter and occasional summer watering. Most species are hardy to moderate frosts. Propagate from seed or tip cuttings, or by division.

Berlandiera lyrata

CHOCOLATE DAISY

This species becomes fully dormant in winter and reshoots from its rootstock in spring, making a mound of foliage. Borne on 24–36 in (60–90 cm) tall stems, the yellow flowerheads open from mid-spring to late summer and have a mild chocolate scent. It is a popular plant with butterflies. **ZONES 8–10.**

BESCHORNERIA

This is a genus of 10 species of fleshy leafed, evergreen perennials related to agaves and all native to Mexico. They

Beschorneria chiapensis

form clumps with gray-green to blue-green sword-shaped leaves arranged in rosettes that usually sit on the ground but less commonly grow at the end of erect fleshy stems up to 3 ft (1 m) tall. The flowers, borne in clusters on large, fleshy, arching spikes or panicles, are tubular, fleshy, pale green and pinkish, and are often hidden by broad, overlapping, pinkish red bracts until the flowers are fully open.

CULTIVATION: Beschornerias are valued for the landscape effect they can provide in desert or Mediterranean-style gardens. They are vigorous, adaptable plants, able to thrive in a range of temperate to subtropical climates, though most require near frost-free locations—in cooler areas this may be achieved by growing them against warm walls or in courtyards. Most soils are suitable provided drainage is good and the position is sunny. Propagate by division or by removing basal offsets.

Beschorneria yuccoides

MEXICAN LILY

This spectacular lily-like plant can spread into a broad clump of evergreen foliage, reminiscent of some of the stemless yuccas, although the 24 in (60 cm) long, gray-green leaves are broader and softer, with the individual rosettes not very evident. In spring it sends up arching, very fleshy, pinkish flowering stems up to 6 ft (1.8 m) long with pendent, apple-green flowers and bright pink bracts. This is the most cold-hardy beschorneria. First discovered in the southernmost Mexican State of Chiapas, ***B. chiapensis*** is similar to *B. yuccoides* but has red bracts and flowers. **ZONES 9–12.**

BESSERA

One or possibly two species of bulb from southern Mexico make up this genus, allied to *Brodiaea* and *Triteleia* in the onion tribe. They have larger flowers and are more frost tender than most of their relatives. The bulb (more accurately a corm) itself is small, the basal leaves are long and very narrow, and the tall flowering scape terminates in an umbel of very long-stalked, pendent, 6-petalled, red to purplish flowers with green veining and protruding purple stamens.

CULTIVATION: Plant in light, very well-

Beta vulgaris subsp. *vulgaris* 'Pablo'

Beta vulgaris subsp. *maritima*

drained soil in full sun. While not very cold hardy, they may be lifted and stored dry over winter. Planted in early spring, they will flower in mid-summer. The plants produce many small cormlets, though seedlings are usually superior plants. Seedlings take 3 to 4 years to reach flowering age.

Bessera elegans

CORAL DROPS

This, the only commonly grown species of bessera, is quite a variable plant. The leaves are grassy and 24–30 in (60–75 cm) long. The flower stems are normally around 18 in (45 cm) tall but can reach 3 ft (1 m). The flowerheads carry anywhere from 2 to 30 blooms, each about 2 in (5 cm) wide. The flowers are usually bright red but they also occur in pink and purple shades, occasionally showing white or green markings. **ZONES 9–11.**

BETA

BEET

This genus of 6 species of broad-leafed annuals, biennials and perennials, native to Europe, west Asia and North Africa, is most familiar in the form of several important garden and commercial vegetables, all cultivated races of the one species, *Beta vulgaris*. The genus belongs to the saltbush family, as do spinach (*Spinacia*) and orache (*Atriplex*), and its species often grow in the wild in saline coastal habitats. They have a well-developed tap root and large basal leaves, from among which the flowering stems elongate, bearing numerous inconspicuous, greenish flowers followed by small, slightly prickly dry fruits, normally thought of as the 'seeds'.

CULTIVATION: All beets are relatively easy to grow, preferring a loose soil enriched with compost. Water well to

Beta vulgaris subsp. *vulgaris,* Swiss chard

Beta vulgaris subsp. *vulgaris,* ruby chard

encourage steady growth. Sow seeds in spring in cooler climates, all year round in warmer ones. Beetroot seeds are sown about 8 in (20 cm) apart; when the first leaves appear, weed out the weaker seedlings. Keep soil moist and harvest the beetroot by hand; in warm climates the beetroot can be harvested almost all year round, but in cold climates the roots are picked and stored over winter. Swiss chard (silver beet) is fast growing, so plant at a wider spacing in an open position in deep, fertile soil that has been previously cultivated. Water frequently—any check in growth or sudden change of conditions can lead to bolting (premature flowering). Propagate from seed.

Beta vulgaris

The original wild form of this well-known species, now classified as ***Beta vulgaris* subsp. *maritima***, is an erect or sprawling perennial of west European and Mediterranean seashores with succulent, salt-resistant foliage that can be gathered as a vegetable. Domestication has resulted in a number of cultivated races of food plants, most of which behave as biennials or annuals. ***B. v.* subsp. *vulgaris*** contains the most commonly grown vegetable (or crop) types. These include the familiar beetroot (and its cultivars such as **'Pablo'**), too well known to need description; sugar beet, similar but with pale roots that contain extremely high sugar levels; mangel-wurzel, used mainly for livestock fodder; the leaf vegetables, namely Swiss chard (including silver beet and ruby chard) with large, puckered leaves, popular as a spinach substitute in warm climates or grown partly for ornament if a red leaf-stalked form; and spinach chard with smaller, flatter leaves that can be harvested over a long period. **ZONES 5–10.**

Betula pendula

Betula pendula

Betula lenta

Betula albosinensis

BETULA

BIRCH

Deciduous trees extending to the far northern regions of the globe as well as lower-latitude mountains of the northern hemisphere, birches are among the most admired of all trees as landscape subjects despite having fairly inconspicuous flowers and fruits. Their appeal lies in their sparkling white to pinkish brown trunks, combined with vivid green spring foliage and delicate tracery of winter twigs. The short, broad, serrated leaves mostly turn gold in fall (autumn) before dropping. Their fast early growth, yet fairly modest final height, are added advantages for use in gardens or streets. In nature, birches often grow in dense stands rather than scattered among other trees.

CULTIVATION: To grow birches successfully, a climate cool enough for at least the occasional winter snowfall is needed. Birches are shallow-rooted and will need watering during dry periods. They grow best in full sun or dappled shade in deep, well-drained soil, but some adapt to poorer, shallower, even boggy soil. Propagation is normally from the small winged seeds, produced in vast numbers from the cylindrical female catkins.

Betula albosinensis

CHINESE RED BIRCH

The most beautiful feature of this western Chinese birch is its pale coppery orange-red bark; a thin bloom of white powder coats the new bark, which is revealed as large, loose plates of the shiny older bark layer peel-off. *Betula albosinensis* is a medium-sized tree of 30–40 ft (9–12 m), often branching low. Its jaggedly toothed leaves are up to 3 in (8 cm) long. A sheltered, sunny spot with moist soil suits it best. **ZONES 6–9.**

Betula alleghaniensis

syn. ***Betula lutea***

YELLOW BIRCH

Largest of the North American birches, the yellow birch can reach 100 ft (30 m) in its native mountains and valleys of eastern USA and southeastern Canada. The straight, high-branched trunk has smooth cream to golden-bronze bark that peels off in thin papery sheets. The leaves are more elongated than in most birches, strongly veined with sharply toothed margins; they turn a clear yellow in fall (autumn). The bark of the twigs is aromatic, containing an oil, very much like oil of wintergreen, that is distilled commercially. The timber is also valuable and the species is extensively cut for lumber. It makes a fine ornamental for large gardens or parks. **ZONES 4–9.**

Betula lenta

BLACK BIRCH, CHERRY BIRCH

This American species is closely related to the yellow birch and is rather similar in foliage, but only grows to 80 ft (24 m). The trunk is smooth and straight with shiny dark reddish brown to almost black bark, which does not peel but on older trees breaks up into scaly plates. It does not always thrive in cultivation but is worth growing with other birches for its contrasting bark color. **ZONES 5–9.**

Betula nana

DWARF BIRCH

This birch is abundant over large areas above the Arctic Circle. A low shrub only 2–4 ft (0.6–1.2 m) high, it forms extensive thickets on the tundra, in bogs or on low hills. Further south it is restricted to high, bleak regions. The leaves are much smaller than in other birches and rather thick textured. It can make an interesting garden shrub, especially for damp, boggy areas, but will not thrive in mild climates. **ZONES 1–7.**

Betula neoalaskana

syn. ***Betula papyrifera* var. *humilis***

YUKON WHITE BIRCH

This vigorous native of inland Alaska and western Canada is very similar in foliage to *Betula papyrifera* but is a smaller tree, mostly 20–40 ft (6–12 m) tall. Its papery bark is white to palest brown, and young stems are sticky and covered with small, warty excrescences. **ZONES 1–8.**

Betula alleghaniensis

Betula nigra

RIVER BIRCH

Widespread in warmer parts of eastern USA, this species' natural habitat is riverbanks. With maturity it becomes broader crowned, forking 10–20 ft (3–6 m) above ground into several arching limbs. Older trunks have dark, furrowed bark at the base, but in young trees the bark is smooth and whitish. The luxuriant leaves are triangular, with irregularly toothed edges. Though most at home beside water, the river birch thrives in well-drained soil and reaches 30 ft (9 m). **'Heritage'** has striking smooth bark—cream, salmon pink or pale brown, that peels off in large curling plates. **ZONES 4–9.**

Betula papyrifera

PAPER BIRCH, CANOE BIRCH

Famed for its tough papery bark, once used by Native Americans for their light but strong canoes, the paper birch is one of the most wide-ranging North American species and is extremely cold hardy. It reaches 60 ft (18 m) in cultivation, and has a sparse crown. The largish leaves are broadly heart-shaped or egg-shaped. The white or cream bark peels off in thin, curling layers, exposing new bark of a pale orange-brown. Its chief ornamental value is in the bark. From southern Alaska is a smaller-growing tree, ***Betula papyrifera* var. *kenaica***—up to 40 ft (12 m) with slightly smaller leaves and fissured bark at the base of older trees. **ZONES 2–9.**

Betula pendula

syns ***Betula alba, B. verrucosa***

SILVER BIRCH, WHITE BIRCH

The common birch of northern Europe, the silver birch is also one of the most

Betula nigra

Betula neoalaskana

Betula platyphylla

Betula papyrifera var. *kenaica*

Betula pendula 'Tristis'

Betula platyphylla

elegant species, with smooth gray-white bark and fine arching branchlets bearing small shimmering leaves. It is the most widely cultivated birch, ideal as a windbreak and generally trouble free in terms of pests and diseases. It reaches around 30–50 ft (9–15 m) in temperate climates; however, in Scandinavia it can reach 70–80 ft (21–24 m) and is an important timber tree there. Many cultivars have been named, including **'Purpurea'** with rich, dark purple leaves, **'Laciniata'** (commonly misidentified as 'Dalecarlica') with deeply incised leaves and weeping branches; **'Tristis'** with an erect trunk but weeping branchlets; and **'Youngii'** with growth like a weeping willow and no leading shoot, requiring it to be grafted on a standard. ZONES 2–9.

Betula platyphylla
JAPANESE WHITE BIRCH

Occurring widely through western and northern China, Japan, Korea, Mongolia and eastern Siberia, this species has several geographical varieties, of which the one common in the West is ***Betula platyphylla* var. *japonica*** (syn. *B. japonica*) from Japan and Siberia. In leaves and fruit this birch is similar to the silver birch, but it has dazzling pure white bark. A vigorous grower, it is a shapely tree of 40 ft (12 m) or more. **'Whitespire'** is a cultivar of very upright growth with clean white bark. ZONES 4–9.

Betula raddeana

Betula papyrifera

Betula populifolia
GRAY BIRCH

This is the North American equivalent of the European silver birch, growing in the most inhospitable climates and behaving as a pioneer tree on denuded lands such as eroded river floodplains. It is a 20–40 ft (6–12 m) tall tree with smooth, pale gray bark, a narrowly conical crown and slightly pendulous branch tips. The leaves are sometimes over 3 in (8 cm) long and are drawn out at the tips into fine points. ZONES 2–8.

Betula raddeana

Betula papyrifera

Betula pubescens
DOWNY BIRCH

Similar to the silver birch in geographic range, habitat and stature, this birch is less ornamental, usually with a more brownish cream bark (sometimes more whitish) and less pendulous branchlets. Its main distinction is the fine down on young twigs and it also tolerates more poorly drained soil. ***Betula pubescens* subsp. *carpatica*** is smaller with a more densely branched crown. ZONES 2–9.

Betula raddeana

Native to the Caucasus range between the Black and Caspian Seas and growing at moderately high altitudes, this birch is a large shrub or small tree of 10–20 ft (3–6 m) tall. Its silvery gray bark is often tinted pink and the young twigs have a velvety down. The pointed oval leaves are up to 2 in (5 cm) long and almost as wide, with serrated edges. It is a species little known in cultivation. ZONES 5–9.

Betula pubescens

Betula pubescens

Betula utilis
HIMALAYAN BIRCH

From the middle altitudes of the Himalayas, this tree up to 60 ft (18 m) has pale, smooth, peeling bark and a broadly domed crown. The leaves, dark green with paler undersides and irregularly toothed, are up to 3 in (8 cm) long. Most widely grown is ***Betula utilis* var. *jacquemontii*** with dazzling white or cream bark that peels in horizontal bands. Several clones of this variety with outstanding bark qualities have been named as cultivars. There are also forms with darker orange-brown bark. ***B. u.* var. *occidentalis*** normally has duller grayish white bark. **'Jermyns'** is a cultivar selected for the whiteness of its bark, uninterrupted by any darker markings or bands. ZONES 7–9.

Betula pendula 'Youngii'

Betula utilis

Betula utilis var. *jacquemontii*

BIDENS

TICKSEED, BEGGAR'S TICKS, BURR-MARIGOLD

This is a genus of around 200 species of annuals, perennials, subshrubs and shrubs that is closely related to *Cosmos* and occurs in most parts of the world except very cold regions. In most countries this genus is represented only by a weedy species. The majority are native to Mexico and adjacent regions of the Americas. The plants have erect leafy stems, usually much branched, with opposite pairs of leaves that are generally compound or deeply divided. Yellow daisy flowers (occasionally red to purple, for example, the purplish pink ***Bidens aequisquamea***), mostly with very few but broad ray florets, open in a long succession and are followed by burr-like seed heads containing narrow seeds, each tipped with 2-barbed bristles (*Bidens* means '2-toothed') that can stick to clothing and fur.

CULTIVATION: These plants are very easily grown in any well-drained soil. Plant in full sun or morning shade, and water well in summer. Although hardiness varies with the species, most will withstand moderate frosts. Propagate from seed or cuttings, or by division, depending on the growth form.

Bidens ferulifolia

Native to Mexico and Arizona, *Bidens ferulifolia* is a bushy, evergreen perennial 18–24 in (45–60 cm) tall, usually short lived. The leaves are small and fern-like, divided into narrow segments, and it bears golden-yellow, few-rayed flowerheads 1–1½ in (25–35 mm) wide in a long succession from late spring to fall (autumn). **'Arizona'** and **'Golden Goddess'** are both popular cultivars. **ZONES 8–10.**

Bidens aequisquamea

Bidens ferulifolia

Bidens triplinervia

Occurring in the wild from Mexico to Argentina, this species is a perennial growing to about 24 in (60 cm) tall. Its leaves are simple and oval with serrated edges, up to 3 in (8 cm) long, and its bright yellow flowerheads are around 1 in (25 mm) wide. **ZONES 9–11.**

BIFRENARIA

This is a genus of orchids consisting of around 20 epiphytic species from South America, grown for their striking, rather waxy flowers. They have crowded, egg-like pseudobulbs that tend towards being 4-sided, each terminating in a solitary, large, leathery leaf. Short, erect flower spikes arise from between the pseudobulbs, each carrying one or a few flowers of roughly triangular shape, with the lower sepals spreading horizontally and the upper ones hooded, while the short labellum and upper petals are folded inward. Colors range from white to pink, purplish or greenish.

CULTIVATION: They are normally grown in a moderately heated but well-ventilated greenhouse with a fair level of humidity. They do not need to undergo a dormant period and should not dry out completely. Pot in a standard orchid mix or grow on a raft, and keep them in strong light. To propagate, divide plants only after they have become rootbound, otherwise they will fail to flower.

Bifrenaria harrisoniae

This is the best known *Bifrenaria* and is typical of the genus, with large pseudobulbs in a compact clump and very broad leaves about 12 in (30 cm) long. The flowers are carried one to a stem but several to a pseudobulb in early summer. They look a little like cream-colored cymbidiums, but the purple labellum is delicately hairy; ***B. harrisoniae*** × ***furstenbergiana*** is yellow with a dark red labellum. **ZONES 10–11.**

Bifrenaria harrisoniae × *furstenbergiana*

BIGNONIA

CROSS-VINE, TRUMPET FLOWER

This genus was once taken in a much broader sense to include a wide range of trumpet-flowered climbers, mostly from the Americas; however all but one species have now have been reclassified. The genera they have been placed in include *Campsis, Clytostoma, Distictis, Macfadyena, Pandorea, Podranea* and *Pyrostegia.* The sole remaining species is an evergreen or semi-deciduous woody climber from southeastern USA.

CULTIVATION: Grow in any moist, well-drained soil in full sun. It is fairly cold hardy but inclined to lose much of its foliage in very cold conditions. If pruning is necessary, this should be done in spring. It may be grown from seed but is usually propagated from cuttings or by layering in winter.

Bignonia capreolata

syn. *Doxantha capreolata*

This creeper is commonly seen growing to 10–20 ft (3–6 m) on a trellis or wall, but is capable of climbing into 60 ft (18 m) tree tops. A distinctive feature of *Bignonia capreolata* is the cross shape revealed by a transverse cut through the stem, hence the common name of cross-vine. Its compound leaves consist of 4 leaflets, but the 2 furthest from the stem are modified into fine tendrils, by which the vine clings. The other 2 are about 3 in (8 cm) long and deep green. The narrowly bell-shaped flowers, which are 2 in (5 cm) long and may be densely clustered at the leaf axils, spread into 5 lobes at the mouth, where they are more yellowish than the orange-red tube. Borne in early summer, they are followed in fall (autumn) by pod-like fruit up to 6 in (15 cm) long. **ZONES 6–10.**

BILLARDIERA

This is an Australian genus of 9 species of slender twiners or subshrubs, valued in gardens for their mostly pendulous, bell-shaped flowers and elongated fleshy berries, which may also be quite ornamental as well as being edible when fully ripe. Some species with capsular fruits, formerly treated as the separate genus *Marianthus*, are now included in *Billardiera*. The genus name honors the French botanist de la Billardière, who discovered many new plants on an expedition to Australia in 1792–93. The plants have deep tap roots, from which they can rapidly regenerate after fire or drought have killed off the aboveground parts.

CULTIVATION: Most species occur in tall, moist forests or open woodlands, growing in very infertile soils. Grow in well-drained soil in a sheltered position, and protect from heavy frosts. Propagate from seed or cuttings.

Billardiera longiflora

PURPLE APPLE BERRY

This scrambling or twining climber grows to about 10 ft (3 m) high. The leaves are narrow and about 2 in (5 cm) long. Pendent, cream, bell-shaped flowers about 1 in (25 mm) long are followed by very ornamental large purple-blue berries with spongy flesh. **ZONES 8–9.**

Billardiera longiflora

BILLBERGIA

VASE PLANT

This genus of bromeliads consists of around 50 species of evergreen perennials from Central and South America. The majority of species are 'tank epiphytes', plants perched on trees with the bases of their broad, strap-like leaves tightly overlapping around a central hollow which fills with rainwater, providing a reservoir for the plant between rainfalls. The horny-textured leaves are often edged with small teeth and in many species have a coating of mealy, grayish white scales interrupted by greener bands. Showy, stalked flower clusters appear at any time of year from the centers of the leaf rosettes, with pink or red bracts often more conspicuous than the tubular flowers.

CULTIVATION: They are easy to grow and make ideal indoor plants, or can be planted outdoors in subtropical or tropical climates in sheltered, humid spots in the garden. A porous, fast-draining soil mix suits them, or they can be planted on a mound of stones. Some species soon form quite large clumps and can be propagated by division after flowering; the slower-growing ones are propagated by cutting off the basal 'pups', which are treated as cuttings. Scale insects and mealybugs can be a problem, and brown leaves may be the result of too much sun.

Billbergia amoena

The species name is Latin for 'delightful to the eye' and this Brazilian bromeliad is eye-catching when well grown. Its loosely clustered leaf rosettes consist of rather few, broad leaves up to 24 in (60 cm) long, making large 'tanks', and may be pale gray-green or various shades of purple with cream or green spotting. The flower spikes may rise as high as 3 ft (1 m) with very large dark pink bracts and a few chalky blue-green flowers about 2 in (5 cm) long. **ZONES 11–12.**

Billbergia leptopoda

Also from Brazil, this species makes a sparse clump of diverging leaf rosettes no more than about 12 in (30 cm) high. The broad gray-green leaves are heavily powdered with silver and spotted with cream, and their tips coil backwards like scrolls. The flowers are yellowish green, tipped dark blue, and are enclosed in salmon-pink bracts. **ZONES 11–12.**

Billbergia nutans
QUEEN'S TEARS, FRIENDSHIP PLANT

This popular species from southern Brazil and Argentina can be grown outdoors in sheltered rockeries or tubs, even in full sun and in places with occasional light frosts. Indoors it likes coarse potting mix and good light. Reaching a height of 24 in (60 cm) and spreading to make large dense clumps, its pale olive-green leaves are grass-like, tapering into long thread-like recurving tips, and pendent clusters of flowers appear in spring on long arching spikes. The curled-back petals are an unusual combination of pale green and navy blue, but it is the long pink bracts that catch the eye. **ZONES 10–12.**

Billbergia pyramidalis

Native to eastern Brazil, this is one of the more vigorous of the vase-forming species, making dense clumps about 18 in (45 cm) high and sometimes over 3 ft (1 m) across if allowed to spread unchecked in a sheltered part of the subtropical garden. Broad gray-green leaves with obscure transverse banding form wide rosettes. The showy flower spikes are erect and club-shaped, their stalks clothed with bright pink bracts, and the densely clustered flowers are pale bluish purple, appearing from late summer to mid-winter. The flowers of ***Billbergia pyramidalis* var. *concolor*** are rose red with purplish tips. **ZONES 10–12.**

Billbergia × windii

This interesting hybrid has green strap-like leaves to 24 in (60 cm) long, lightly banded on the underside with gray and forming a short 'vase' at the base. The nodding, flowering spike has large reddish pink bracts and bears several large, pendent flowers with green and red tubes and conspicuous blue petals. **ZONES 11–12.**

Billbergia amoena

Bixa orellana

BIXA
ANNATTO, LIPSTICK TREE

Only one species belongs to this tropical American genus. It is cultivated in warmer regions around the world for its ornamental value in gardens and for the fat-soluble orange dye its abundant seeds yield. The dye (annatto) is used to color foodstuffs and fabrics. South American Indians used it as body paint. The plant is very distinctive, with its large heart-shaped, bronze-tinged leaves, erect clusters of small, pink, rose-like flowers and large almond-shaped fruit capsules covered in dense red bristles. However, it is illegal in some parts of the world.
CULTIVATION: This plant does well in warm, frost-free climates, though in the warm-temperate latitudes it should be grown in a protected position, and may be trained into a small tree or kept as a bushy shrub. Propagation is best from cuttings, as seed-grown plants take longer to flower.

Bixa orellana

This colorful tree can sometimes reach a height of 30 ft (9 m) but is more commonly seen as a spreading shrub of about 10 ft (3 m) or slightly less. The pink and white flowers are borne throughout summer, overlapping with the clusters of bristly red fruit that persist on the branches long after they have released their seeds. **ZONES 10–12.**

BLANDFORDIA
CHRISTMAS BELLS

This is an eastern Australian genus of 4 species of grassy leafed perennials with deeply buried corm-like rhizomes. Prized for their beautiful, waxy red or red-and-yellow flowers that appear around Christmas in the southern hemisphere (early summer), they were traditionally included in the lily family but botanists in recent years have puzzled over their relationships to other genera. The plants are long lived, with tough, narrow basal leaves in sparse to dense tufts, from which arise one to several stiff flowering stems, bearing near the top semi-pendent flowers; these are bell-shaped and up to 3 in (8 cm) long, the 6 petals fused for most of their length.
CULTIVATION: Coming mainly from peaty coastal swamps in the wild, these are not easy plants to maintain in cultivation—they are prone to root-rot and are sensitive to nutrient imbalances. Plant in moist, peaty soil in full sun or light shade. Keep consistently moist. They tolerate light frosts and may be propagated by division or raised from seed. Seedlings develop slowly, taking 2 or more years to flower; divisions also may be slow to re-establish.

Billbergia nutans

Bixa orellana

Blandfordia grandiflora

Blechnum discolor

Blechnum fluviatile

Blandfordia grandiflora
syn. ***Blandfordia flammea***

This is the most colorful species and the one most prized for cut flowers. Its leaves are very narrow and rather rigid, and flowering stems are 24–36 in (60–90 cm) tall, carrying 3 to 10 flowers; these are up to 2½ in (6 cm) long, flared toward the mouth, and vary from deep pinkish red to red with yellow tips or sometimes pure yellow, always with a thin waxy bloom that enhances the flower's heavy substance. **ZONES 9–11.**

BLECHNUM
WATER FERN

This fern genus of 200 or more species is found around the world in both temperate and tropical climates, the majority in the southern hemisphere. Size and growth form vary but most species have very short rhizomes or vertical stems with rosettes of fishbone-type fronds. In a few species a short trunk develops. New fronds are usually pink, red or bronze. In many species the spore-bearing fronds are sharply distinct from the vegetative ones, more erect and with much narrower, thicker segments.
CULTIVATION: Blechnums are generally easy ferns to grow, especially outdoors in sheltered, moist areas, the edges of ponds and streams being the most favored spots. Most are ground dwellers that prefer humus-rich soil and part-shade, and form clumps that spread by runners. Most are frost tender and thrive in subtropical climates. Propagate from spores in late summer, or by division.

Blechnum discolor
CROWN FERN, PUI-PUI

So called because of the attractive crown of bright green radiating fronds, this New Zealand native has adapted well to gardens. Mature plants have trunks up to 12 in (30 cm) tall and a total height of 3 ft (1 m); they spread in time to produce large colonies of rosettes. The fronds are long and narrow with closely spaced segments, and the spore-bearing fronds are distinct with thicker, narrower segments. It likes a lot of water and will grow in sun, although it prefers a shady position. **ZONES 8–10.**

Blechnum fluviatile
RAY WATER FERN

Native to cooler parts of Australia and New Zealand, this fern extends itself by runners to form extensive colonies of rosettes. The fronds of each rosette are of firm texture andregular pattern, up to 18 in (45 cm) long, and radiate in a neat circle. The different spore-bearing fronds are numerous, in a tight group in the center of the rosette. Moderately frost hardy, it requires total shade. **ZONES 8–9.**

Blechnum penna-marina

Blechnum nudum

Blechnum gibbum
DWARF TREE FERN

Native to Fiji, this is one of the most widely cultivated blechnums, especially for indoor use. It is notable for its solitary trunk, which can reach a height of 24 in (60 cm), and is topped by a large rosette of many soft, fresh green, gracefully arching fronds 24–36 in (60–90 cm) long with numerous narrow segments that are only slightly narrower on the spore-bearing fronds. Easily grown as long as it can be protected from winter cold and harsh sun, it makes a long-lived plant for a large container, or can be grown outdoors in the tropics and subtropics. **ZONES 10–12.**

Blechnum nudum
FISHBONE WATER FERN

Occurring wild in southeastern mainland Australia and Tasmania, this species is a vigorous spreader with shuttlecock-like rosettes of fresh green fronds 24–36 in (60–90 cm) high, the new fronds delicately tinted pink. The frond midrib is blackish towards the base, and the rosettes often develop a short trunk. Spore-bearing fronds are much narrower and thicker, growing erect from the center of the rosette. It grows in damp places, often beside water, and will tolerate full sun. **ZONES 9–11.**

Blechnum penna-marina
ALPINE WATER FERN

A low-growing species native to New Zealand, southern Australia, South America and the subantarctic islands, this fern is often found in subalpine bogs where snow and frost are common. Growing in quick bursts in summer from creeping rhizomes, its narrow, dark

Blechnum spicant

Blechnum tabulare

green fronds, pink-tipped when young, are only about 8 in (20 cm) long and may form extensive mats. It prefers bright light and needs a temperate climate with cold periods. It makes an ideal ground cover. **ZONES 7–9.**

Blechnum spicant
DEER FERN, HARD FERN, LADDER FERN

One of the few blechnums from temperate regions of the northern hemisphere, this well-known species occurs in Europe, northern Asia and western North America. It makes a small rosette of neat, broadly radiating, leathery green fronds only about 6 in (15 cm) long, from the center of which arise a vertical group of very different spore-bearing fronds up to 30 in (75 cm) high. It is happiest planted in the shelter of rocks that have a constant supply of dripping water, but will grow in full sun if assured of permanent moisture. **ZONES 4–9.**

Blechnum tabulare
MOUNTAIN WATER FERN

This species takes its name from South Africa's famous Table Mountain but it is also common elsewhere on moist southern African mountains. It also occurs in Madagascar and on higher mountains of the West Indies, also on the Falkland Islands—a most unlikely distribution. It makes large, slow-growing rosettes of stiff, straight, diverging fronds of leathery texture up to 3 ft (1 m) long, often on short basal trunks. New fronds are brownish, and spore-bearing fronds have much narrower segments. Marginally frost hardy, it likes moist soil with plenty of compost and leafmold. **ZONES 9–10.**

BLETILLA

This orchid genus of about 10 East Asian species is usually represented in gardens by the species, *Bletilla striata*, which is one of the most easily grown of all orchids in temperate climates, as well as

Bloomeria crocea

being attractive in foliage and flower. **CULTIVATION:** The plants prefer a part-shaded situation and undisturbed, good garden soil, and are best suited to a woodland-style garden. Keep soil moist in spring and summer, and allow leaves to die back naturally in fall (autumn) to build up food reserves in the root. Propagate by careful division in early spring, but the plants are best left undisturbed to develop into clumps.

Bletilla ochracea

More recently introduced to cultivation than *Bletilla striata*, this attractive species comes from central China. It is a more erect plant, with sparser tufts of foliage and slender flowering stems 18–24 in (45–60 cm) high, rising well above the leaves. The late spring and early summer flowers are pale yellow and ochre. **ZONES 7–10.**

Bletilla striata
syn. *Bletilla hyacinthina*
HYACINTH ORCHID

This charming plant makes broad clumps of foliage, its broad, soft, pleated leaves sprouting abundantly from tubers in spring; these arching leaves are up to 18 in (45 cm) long. In early summer (mid- to late spring in warmer areas) it bears 12–15 in (30–38 cm) tall sprays of bright magenta-pink flowers of typical orchid shape but in miniature; the labellum is edged a darker purple-pink and is marked with white. **ZONES 7–10.**

BLOOMERIA

This genus of 3 species of bulbs, native to Mexico and southwestern USA and belonging to the allium (onion) tribe, is similar to *Triteleia*. Each small bulb

Bletilla striata

produces one or a few flat, narrow leaves and an erect flowering stem at the top of which is an umbel of long-stalked flowers, each with 6 narrow petals. **CULTIVATION:** Plants occur naturally among dry scrub or in semi-desert areas and prefer to be kept dry after flowering. Plant in a light, gritty, free-draining soil with a little humus added. They will tolerate occasional moderate frosts provided the ground is not too wet.

Bloomeria crocea

This species has very small bulbs, each of which produces a single long, narrow flat leaf and a flowering stem up to 12 in (30 cm) tall topped with an umbel of bright golden yellow flowers. The spring flowers are up to 1 in (25 mm) in diameter and open in spring. **ZONES 8–10.**

BOLAX

This is a genus of 2 or 3 cushion-forming perennials belonging to the carrot family, from the southern Andean regions of South America and the Falkland Islands. They have tiny, fleshy leaves and develop into clumps that resemble patches of moss until early summer, when they become studded with umbels of small greenish white flowers. They resemble the closely related genus *Azorella*. **CULTIVATION:** These are plants for cool, moist climates and are hardy to moderate frosts. They thrive in damp maritime or low alpine climates and do well in rockeries or alpine houses. Plant in gritty, humus-rich soil and water well in summer. Mulch with fine shingle chips. Propagate from seed or by removing and growing on rooted pieces.

Bolax gummifera

This species has 3-lobed, ¼ in (6 mm) long, leathery leaves and forms a cushion up to 3 in (8 cm) high at the center and 15 in (38 cm) wide. Its umbels carry up to 20 tiny flowers. **ZONES 7–8.**

Bolax gummifera

Bletilla ochracea

Borago officinalis

Borago officinalis

BOLTONIA

FALSE CHAMOMILE

This is a genus of 8 species of perennial daisies, all from eastern and central USA except for one species which comes from temperate East Asia. Very much like tall asters, they have in recent years become popular as background plants for perennial borders and as cut flowers. Over winter they die back to a clump of simple, narrow leaves. In late spring, tall flowering stems begin to develop and by late summer they carry hundreds of small daisies in shades of white, pink, lilac, violet or purple.

CULTIVATION: They are very easily grown in moist, well-drained soil in any sunny position. However, like many of the asters, they are prone to mildew from late summer, which cuts short the flower display. Frost hardy, they are propagated from seed or cuttings or by division.

Boltonia asteroides

This is the best known boltonia in gardens. It is widely distributed in northeastern USA. The flowering stems may be as much as 8 ft (2.4 m) tall, with the $\frac{3}{4}$ in (20 mm) flowerheads ranging in color from white through pale pink to mauve. **'Snowbank'** is a white-flowered selection with stems growing up to 6 ft (1.8 m) tall. ***Boltonia asteroides* var. *latisquama*** differs in its larger flowerheads, which are up to $1\frac{1}{4}$ in (3 cm) across in shades of mauve or purple. **ZONES 4–9.**

BOLUSANTHUS

AFRICAN TREE WISTERIA

This genus consists of one species: a small, leguminous, deciduous tree from the open woodlands and grasslands of subtropical southern Africa. Noted for its beautiful wisteria-like flowers, *Bolusanthus speciosus* is long lived. The name combines that of the nineteenth-century South African botanist Harry Bolus with the Greek *anthos*, meaning 'flower'.

CULTIVATION: This tree does best in full sun, light to medium, well-drained soil and an open position; it prefers a climate with hot, wet summers and dry winters and will tolerate very light frosts (but not while young). Propagate from seed in summer.

Bolusanthus speciosus

This small tree reaches a height of 20 ft (6 m) or more. It has a fairly erect habit, usually with a narrow crown and somewhat weeping branchlets. The pale to deep violet pea-flowers appear in spring in large pendent panicles on leafless branches, and are followed by the glossy, green pinnate leaves. Large bunches of dry pods remain on the tree throughout summer. Mature specimens have neatly fissured bark. **ZONES 9–11.**

BOMAREA

This genus of striking, tuberous-rooted climbers contains about 50 species, all of which are native to Central and South America. Closely related to *Alstroemeria*, they send up masses of wiry, twining stems with broad, thin, parallel-veined leaves in spring. The stems often reach a considerable height but they usually die back in winter. The bell-shaped flowers are usually in shades of green, yellow, orange or crimson, and are borne in hanging umbels.

CULTIVATION: Plants grow in any well-drained garden soil, but they need ample light and a support to climb on. The plants thrive in warm-temperate climates, but will grow in cooler climates if their roots are mulched in fall (autumn). If the soil is likely to freeze, the tubers can be lifted and stored. Water well when growing, and cut back hard after flowering to encourage new growth. Propagation is from seed or by division in early spring.

Bomarea caldasii

syn. *Bomarea kalbreyeri*

CLIMBING ALSTROEMERIA

This attractive evergreen climber grows to about 10 ft (3 m) and bears large clusters of pendulous bell flowers in summer. These usually have pinkish red outer petals and yellow to orange, spotted inner petals. It needs strong support and will form an attractive dense screen on a fence or trellis. The plant dies down in winter. **ZONES 8–10.**

Bomarea caldasii

Bomarea edulis

Of wide natural distribution in the highlands of Central America, the West Indies and northern South America, *Bomarea edulis* has edible roots, which are gathered for food in some regions. This climber grows to heights of 8 ft (2.4 m) or more, dying back in winter. The leaves are narrow, about 4 in (10 cm) long, and sometimes downy beneath. The dull pinkish orange flowers (actually yellowish with red flecks inside) are not so pendulous as those of *Bomarea caldasii*. The flowers are borne in large, open umbels in summer and fall (autumn). **ZONES 9–11.**

BOOPHONE

Related to *Amaryllis*, the 6 species of summer-dormant bulbs in this genus are native to southern and eastern Africa. They have a bizarre appearance with papery membranes sheathing the bulb. While still leafless in fall (autumn), a flowering stem is produced, topped by a large umbel of long-stalked, smallish flowers with narrow petals, which are usually in shades of pink, mauve or red. As the flowers wither, sword-like leaves appear in a broad fan from the top of the bulb.

CULTIVATION: Boophones are usually grown in pots, but they can be planted in gardens in more arid areas provided there is free-draining soil. Plant with the upper third of the bulb exposed and keep it dry in summer. They resent disturbance and it is usually best to partially replace the soil rather than attempt to repot the plants completely. The bulbs often take several years to bloom, though light feeding can speed them up. They are not frost tolerant. They are usually raised from seed, which should be sown uncovered on free-draining potting mix, as division is difficult.

Boophone haemanthoides

This cream and red-flowered species is rare in cultivation. Although not difficult to grow once established, it can be tricky when young, so keep plants shaded for their first year. **ZONES 10–11.**

BORAGO

This is a European genus of 3 species of annuals and short-lived perennials. The plants are generally erect with rather coarse growth and are covered with bristly hairs. They form clumps of lance-shaped basal leaves that rapidly develop in spring into branched, leafy flowering stems. By late spring the plants bear semi-pendulous, starry purple-blue or white flowers. The flowers are a rich source of nectar and are popular with beekeepers.

CULTIVATION: These plants are easily grown in any light, moist, well-drained soil in full sun. Usually they are propagated from seed, which often self-sows, so plants may become slightly invasive. Seed of the annual species can be sown in late winter for an early crop. Protect from snails.

Borago officinalis

BORAGE

This annual herb is grown for its cucumber-flavored leaves and pretty, purplish blue star-shaped flowers. The plant grows to around 30 in (75 cm) high with clusters of flowers in spring and summer. The fresh young leaves are used raw in salads and cool drinks or cooked with vegetables. The edible flowers have long been used to decorate salads. **ZONES 5–10.**

Bolusanthus speciosus

Borago pygmaea

This short-lived perennial starts out in spring as a ground-hugging plant, the broad basal leaves up to 8 in (20 cm) long. Weak flowering stems appear in succession into summer and fall (autumn) and the plant can develop into a loose mound up to 12 in (30 cm) high, with sparsely borne, light blue, bell-like flowers. Like borage, it self-seeds and is also propagated from stem cuttings taken in late summer. **ZONES 6–9.**

BORASSODENDRON

This genus consists of only 2 species of large tropical, fan-leafed palms from the Malay Peninsula and Borneo. The name reflects the close relationship between this genus and the more common Asian *Borassus*, large palms which yield sugar and palm wine. A feature of *Borassodendron* is the apparent disproportion between the slenderness of the tall, straight trunk and the massive size of the long-stalked fronds, the broad segments of which are tangled and drooping. Male and female flowers appear on different trees; the male on very long, pendulous, branched spikes that hang from among the frond bases, and the female in shorter, club-like spikes. The fruits are large nuts, packed in tight bunches.
CULTIVATION: These dramatic palms grow well only in the wet equatorial tropics, preferring very sheltered sites and deep, moist, alluvial soil or gravel. Propagate from seed, which must be freshly fallen, planting in a deep container or *in situ*.

Borassodendron machadonis

Named after an early twentieth-century amateur botanist, Machado, this species occurs sparsely in lowland rainforests of the Malay Peninsula. Its trunk is about 25 ft (8 m) tall with prominent rings, while the massive fronds are about 10 ft (3 m) long. Male flowers hang against the trunk in 5 ft (1.5 m) long branched spikes. The fruit have a diameter of 4 in (10 cm). **ZONE 12.**

Boronia heterophylla

Boronia 'Carousel'

BORONIA

Nearly all the 100-odd species of this genus of small- to medium-sized, compact evergreen shrubs are native to Australia, with 4 occuring in New Caledonia. They are noted for their aromatic foliage and for their attractive 4-petalled flowers, pink in the great majority though white, cream, brown or red in a few. The genus is named in honor of an eighteenth-century Italian botanist, Francesco Borone. Many of the species flower prolifically in the wild but do not adapt well to garden cultivation and are often short lived.
CULTIVATION: These shrubs do best in sheltered positions in sun or part-shade in moist, well-drained acid soil. Many species will tolerate very light frosts. Tip pruning after flowering will maintain shape. Seeds are very difficult to germinate, so propagation is best achieved using semi-hardened tip cuttings.

Boronia 'Carousel'

This hybrid boronia grows to around 5 ft (1.5 m) tall and has an upright, open growth habit. Blooming over a long season from early spring, its pink flowers are pleasantly scented and redden as they age. A light trimming after flowering will keep the plant compact and bushy. **ZONES 9–11.**

Boronia heterophylla
RED BORONIA, KALGAN BORONIA

This erect, compact shrub grows to 5 ft (1.5 m) tall and comes from the far south of Western Australia. Its dark green leaves are simple or less commonly

Boronia megastigma 'Harlequin'

Boronia 'Carousel'

Borassodendron machadonis

pinnate. Masses of rose-red, bell-shaped flowers, slightly aromatic, are borne in late winter and early spring, and the petals persist on the developing fruit. A popular commercial cut flower in Australia, it prefers a cooler climate than do some other boronias. Soil with added organic matter will ensure adequate moisture and a cool root run. **ZONES 9–10.**

Boronia ledifolia
SYDNEY BORONIA

This small, bushy evergreen shrub from the temperate east coast of Australia grows to a height and spread of 3 ft (1 m) and bears starry, bright pink flowers from mid- to late winter; the petals persist around the developing fruit through spring turning a deeper pinkish red. The flowers are faintly fragrant, but not so the trifoliate leaves, which emit an unpleasant odor when crushed. **ZONES 9–11.**

Boronia megastigma
BROWN BORONIA

It is the sweet, heady perfume of this species' flowers that is its main attraction, and their fragrance has been distilled for perfumery. Native to the far south of Western Australia, it bears hanging cup-shaped flowers, brownish purple to yellow-green outside and yellow-green inside, in late winter and spring. Growing to about 3 ft (1 m) and tolerating light frost, it is often difficult to grow and short lived. A number of varieties have been selected with different flower coloration, but they often lack the fragrance of the typical species. **'Lutea'** has yellow flowers and yellow-green leaves; **'Harlequin'** is a brownish pink-and-white candy-striped variety. **ZONES 9–10.**

Boronia mollis
SOFT BORONIA

This shrub grows to 6 ft (1.8 m) high with a spread of about the same. Its branches are covered with short fuzzy hairs, as are the bronze-green leaves which consist of 3 to 5 leaflets and give off a strong musky smell at the slightest brushing against, some people finding it quite unpleasant. Bright pink flowers, up to 1 in (25 mm) across, are borne in small groups in great abundance in spring. It prefers moist, semi-shaded habitats. **ZONES 10–11.**

Boronia molloyae

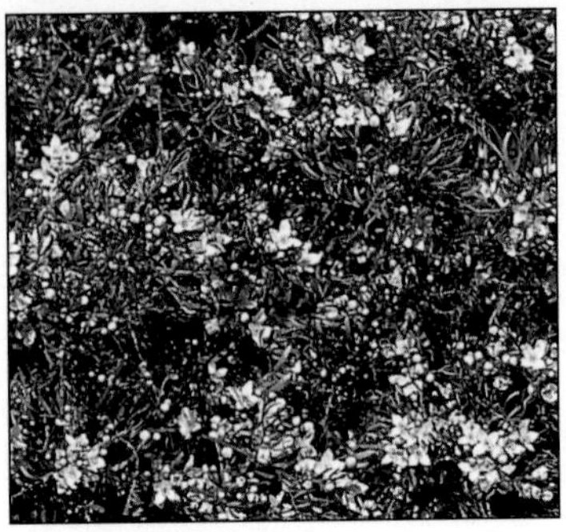

Boronia pinnata

Boronia molloyae
syn. *Boronia elatior*
TALL BORONIA

Named after Georgiana Molloy, one of the few female plant collectors in nineteenth-century Australia, this species from the moister forests of southwestern Australia grows to 5 ft (1.5 m) tall, with very aromatic, finely divided foliage. The bell-like scarlet blooms never fully open and hang singly from the axils of the leaflets. They make excellent cut flowers, as the petals do not fade or fall easily. **ZONES 9–11.**

Boronia pinnata
FEATHER-LEAFED BORONIA

One of the showiest boronias, this open, sometimes broadly spreading shrub from coastal New South Wales grows to a height of 5 ft (1.5 m). It has feathery, fern-like, strongly scented dark green leaves with very narrow, somewhat irregular leaflets. Fragrant light pink or white flowers are borne abundantly in loose sprays in spring. **'Spring White'** has clear white flowers. **ZONES 9–11.**

Boronia serrulata
AUSTRALIAN NATIVE ROSE

This upright small shrub, endemic to a small area around Sydney, grows to 3 ft (1 m) with a rather few-branched habit. It has unusual, almost diamond-shaped, finely toothed leaves that are arranged in the same vertical plane on the twig and which turn a distinctive bronze in the winter months. Clusters of fragrant bright pink flowers with overlapping petals, like a miniature rose blossom when in bud, appear in spring. Although one of the most beautiful boronias, it is not an easy subject in cultivation. **ZONES 10–11.**

BOUGAINVILLEA

Bougainvilleas are valued for their glorious, flamboyant display of blooms and their ability to cover a large area, of either ground or wall. The genus consists of 14 species ranging through tropical and subtropical South America, but only 3 or 4 have been grown as ornamentals. The numerous cultivars include many different kinds and colors. They are evergreen in the wet tropics, but may be deciduous in cooler climates or where there is a severe dry season. In more temperate climates the main flowering period is summer and fall (autumn), but in the tropics their finest display is in the dry season though they may flower on and off all year. The true flowers are tubular and rather insignificant, but the surrounding bracts are brilliantly colored, often changing color or shade as they age. The plants are essentially scrambling shrubs, producing long canes armed with strong woody thorns that act as an aid for climbing. The simple, broad leaves are soft and usually finely hairy. **CULTIVATION:** All species do best in warm to hot climates in full sun; they also do well in temperate frost-free areas. Only water when needed and do not over-fertilize, particularly with nitrogen, as this will produce luxuriant leaf growth but very little in the way of colorful bracts. Bougainvilleas need strong support for their vigorous growth, but can be controlled by pruning after flowering, when rampant plants can be ruthlessly cut back without harm. Flowers appear on the new wood. With regular heavy pruning, all bougainvilleas can be grown in large containers and kept to a height and width of about 3 ft (1 m) if desired. Propagate from cuttings in summer.

Bougainvillea × *buttiana*

This hybrid is a cross between *Bougainvillea glabra* and *B. peruviana* and includes many cultivars. They are large, woody, vigorous growers with dark green leaves and spines. The bracts vary in color from white to orange-pink and deep red. **'Mrs Butt'** with purplish red

Bougainvillea 'Temple Fire'

Bougainvillea × *buttiana* 'Mrs Butt'

Bougainvillea glabra 'Magnifica'

bracts was the original of this popular group, discovered by a Mrs Butt in a garden in Trinidad some time around 1900. **'Louis Wathen'** (syn. 'Orange King') has rounded orange bracts that change to a bright rose pink. **'Golden Glow'** (syn. 'Hawaiian Gold') has bracts that are a magnificent shade of orange-gold, turning more pinkish as they age. **ZONES 10-12.**

Bougainvillea glabra

A native of Brazil, this is one of the two common species that have been long established in gardens around the world. It includes many cultivars and is also one parent of the hybrid *Bougainvillea* × *buttiana*, which includes many more. It is a vigorous shrubby vine, growing to 30 ft (9 m), with masses of bright purple or white bracts. It has thin, curved spines and the leaves have tiny hairs. **'Alba'** (syns 'Snow White', 'Key West White') has white bracts with prominent green veins and smallish pale green leaves; it is not as vigorous as most other cultivars. **'Magnifica'** (syn. 'Magnifica Traillii') is the familiar bright magenta bougainvillea, blooming over a long summer season, with glossy, dark green leaves. **ZONES 10–12.**

Bougainvillea peruviana

This species from Peru, Colombia and Ecuador is little known in cultivation except in the form of its hybrid with *Bougainvillea glabra,* namely *B.* × *buttiana.* It has a less vigorous habit than the latter with greenish stems, more slender thorns and thin, hairless leaves. The bracts are small and pinkish magenta in color. **ZONES 10–12.**

Bougainvillea 'Scarlett O'Hara'

syns 'Hawaiian Scarlet', 'San Diego Red'

This popular free-flowering hybrid cultivar of uncertain origin is a large, vigorous grower, the new growths dark

Bougainvillea × *buttiana* 'Louis Wathen'

Bougainvillea glabra

Bougainvillea 'Scarlett O'Hara'

Bougainvillea glabra 'Alba'

red with many thorns. The leaves are large, dark green, rather rounded, and the almost circular crimson bracts are very large, orange-tinted before they mature and often appearing before the leaves. **ZONES 10–12.**

Bougainvillea spectabilis

A vigorous and fast-growing species from Brazil, this was the first of the bougainvilleas to be described in 1798, from dried specimens collected during a voyage commanded by Louis Antoine de Bougainville. Mainly evergreen, it can grow to 20 ft (6 m) and is armed with curved thorns. Its dark green leaves are hairier than those of other bougainvilleas, the undersides often quite velvety, and the showy bracts, which appear in summer in large panicles, are deep red and purple. There are a number of cultivars available and it is the parent of several hybrid cultivars with *Bougainvillea glabra* (known as *B.* × *spectoglabra*). **ZONES 10–12.**

Bougainvillea 'Temple Fire'

syn. 'Helen Johnson'

Of hybrid origin, this is one of the smallest bougainvilleas, growing to about 3 ft (1 m). It has small leaves and short thorns. The bracts are a reddish purple color with a hint of copper before they are fully expanded. This cultivar is well suited to growing in a tub. **ZONES 10–12.**

BOUTELOUA

GRAMA GRASS

Found throughout the Americas, except for the furthest northern and southern parts, the 40 or so species of annual and perennial grasses in this genus form clumps of stiff, narrow leaves, mostly basal and often finely hairy. The erect flowering stems bear a few reduced leaves but are most notable for their seed heads, which are usually branched into a number of dense, often drooping spikes. **CULTIVATION:** While some species are grown as ornamentals, most that are cultivated are used as pasture or coarse lawn grasses. They are tolerant of dry conditions once established but need water when young. Sow seeds in fall (autumn), in full sun in light, well-drained soil, to enable the young seedlings to take advantage of winter moisture. Although they are clumping grasses and rarely make a neat lawn, they thrive in tough environments such as very alkaline soils.

Bouteloua gracilis

BLUE GRAMA GRASS

This densely tufted perennial is one of the important native species of the shortgrass prairies that cover vast areas of the great plains of Canada, the USA and Mexico. A conspicuous grass with dense tufts of gray-green foliage, it withstands heat and extreme cold. Numerous delicate, wiry stems rise to about 18 in (45 cm) among the foliage, and terminate in groups of dangling finger-like purplish brown spikes. Well known as a pasture grass, it can grow with little or no irrigation and has been used extensively as a water-saving lawn grass for dry climates. **ZONES 3–10.**

BOUVARDIA

A genus of 30 or so species of softwooded evergreen shrubs and subshrubs from Mexico, Central America and far southern USA, these frost-tender plants,

Bouvardia ternifolia

Bouvardia longiflora

Brabejum stellatifolium

Bowkeria gerrardiana

Boykinia jamesii

popular with florists, are grown for their attractive, long-tubed, often fragrant flowers in a range of colors from white to red. The leaves are smallish, soft and smooth margined, arranged in opposite pairs on the stems or in whorls of 3 or more, while the flowers are held in loose to dense clusters at the end of the stems. **CULTIVATION:** These shrubs require a warm, sheltered position in part-shade, though in humid climates some can tolerate full sun. In cool climates they need a greenhouse or conservatory. The soil needs to be fertile and well drained. Water well and feed regularly during the growing period. Cut back stems by half after flowering to maintain shape, which can become straggly. Propagate from cuttings. They are susceptible to attack by sap-sucking insects such as white fly and mealybug.

Bouvardia jasminiflora

This perennial species produces fragrant, white tubular 4-petalled blooms. Growing to 24 in (60 cm), it is very free flowering and is tender to both frost and dry conditions. ZONES 10–11.

Bouvardia longiflora

syn. *Bouvardia humboldtii*
SCENTED BOUVARDIA

A favorite with florists, this tender, weak-stemmed evergreen shrub grows to a height and spread of 3 ft (1 m) or more. Very brittle, it is easily damaged by strong winds. The strongly perfumed, snow white flowers are up to 3 in (8 cm) long and 1 in (25 mm) wide, borne in fall (autumn) and winter. ZONES 10–11.

Bouvardia ternifolia

syn. *Bouvardia triphylla*

Although lacking scent, the striking red tubular flowers are an attractive feature of this species. Growing to 6 ft (1.8 m) but usually half that height, it needs a well-drained soil in part-shade sheltered from frost and prefers a moist soil. Many cultivars exist, ranging in color from palest pink to deep red. ZONES 9–11.

BOWKERIA

This is a South African genus of 5 species of shrubs and small trees. They have slightly hairy, bright green leaves with finely serrated edges, arranged in opposite pairs or whorls of 3 on the branches. Curious white to yellow pouch-shaped flowers, somewhat reminiscent of snapdragons (which belong to the same family), appear from late winter to spring and are followed by small, rounded seed capsules.
CULTIVATION: These plants are less tolerant of very dry conditions than many other South African trees and shrubs. They generally prefer cool, moist con-ditions with well-drained, humus-rich soil and a part-shaded position. They are not widely cultivated but appear to tolerate light frosts. Propagate from seed or cuttings.

Bowkeria citrina

YELLOW SHELLFLOWER BUSH

This 6–10 ft (1.8–3 m) tall shrub has 1½ in (35 mm) long narrow, drooping leaves in whorls of 3, lemon-scented when crushed. Its 2-lipped flowers, borne on slender stalks from late spring to early winter, gape narrowly at the mouth and are an attractive clear pale yellow. ZONES 10–11.

Bowkeria gerrardiana

This upright, open-branched shrub eventually reaches 10 ft (3 m) tall and produces, in short sprays, unusual flowers that resemble those of the shrubby calceolarias, having a glossy, almost artificial, waxy texture and being slightly sticky. The petals always seem about to burst open, but never do. Being small and partly hidden by the foliage they could be overlooked, but appearing as they do in winter, they attract attention. ZONES 9–11.

BOYKINIA

syn. *Telesonix*

A North American and Japanese genus of 9 species of woodland and alpine perennials, these plants spread by shortly creeping rhizomes. They resemble the closely related genera *Heuchera* and *Tiarella*, and have lobed and toothed, roughly heart- or kidney-shaped hairy leaves, varying in size depending on the species. Stalked panicles of small, 5-petalled, white, cream or reddish flowers open through spring or summer. While not spectacular, they are graceful plants that help to lighten shady corners. Botanists differ on the question of whether *Telesonix* should be united with *Boykinia*.
CULTIVATION: Plant in moist, humus-rich, well-drained soil in dappled shade. Hardiness varies, though all species will tolerate at least moderate frosts. Propagate by division in late winter.

Boykinia jamesii

syns *Boykinia heucheriformis*, *Telesonix jamesii*

A native of Colorado, this is one of the more cold-hardy species and also among the smallest. Its kidney-shaped leaves are usually less than 2 in (5 cm) wide and the plant forms a compact mound of fresh green foliage around 4 in (10 cm) high and up to 6 in (15 cm) in diameter. Its narrow 6 in (15 cm) stems bear purple-red flowers, larger than those of other boykinias, and it needs to be treated as an alpine. ZONES 5–8.

BRABEJUM

SOUTH AFRICAN WILD ALMOND

The South African 'wild almond' belongs to the macadamia tribe. Like the macadamia it has edible nuts, though the fruits are flattened and are not so hard shelled.
CULTIVATION: *Brabejum* has seldom been cultivated outside South Africa, but it is easily grown in a sunny position in a mild climate. It will endure long periods without water and makes a dense hedge or windbreak. Propagate from seed.

Brabejum stellatifolium

The first indigenous tree cultivated by South Africa's early colonists, this small, round-headed tree grows to about 15 ft (4.5 m), often branching from ground level into a number of short trunks. The leaves are arranged in whorls of up to 7 at regular intervals. In the axils of these appear short spikes, about 4 in (10 cm) long, of white sweetly scented flowers in summer. In fall (autumn) it bears fruit similar in shape to a cultivated almond. ZONES 9–11.

BRACHYCHITON

This genus consists of around 30 species of warm-climate, evergreen or dry-season deciduous trees and shrubs, all Australian except one or two found in New Guinea. Some brachychitons are noted for their spectacular flowers, which are bell-shaped, the apparent petals actually being colored calyces, and in most species appearing just before the new leaves of summer. The leaves are diverse in shape but are commonly lobed, though lobing tends to disappear on adult trees. The fruits consist of 5 stalked, boat-shaped carpels, rather woody when mature and splitting to release nut-like seeds that are edible but are surrounded by irritant hairs. Some species occur naturally in tropical and subtropical rainforests and others in semi-arid areas, where their leaves and bark may be used as fodder in dry seasons. Some of the arid-climate species have massive, swollen, water-storing trunks.
CULTIVATION: Noted for their drought-resistant qualities, brachychitons require light, well-drained soil, preferably acidic. They also prefer a sheltered position with protection from cold or salty winds and from frost when young. Several of the kurrajongs are widely planted in parks and streets. Propagate from fresh seed in spring or by grafting in the case of selected clones.

Brachychiton rupestris

Brachychiton populneus

Brachychiton discolor

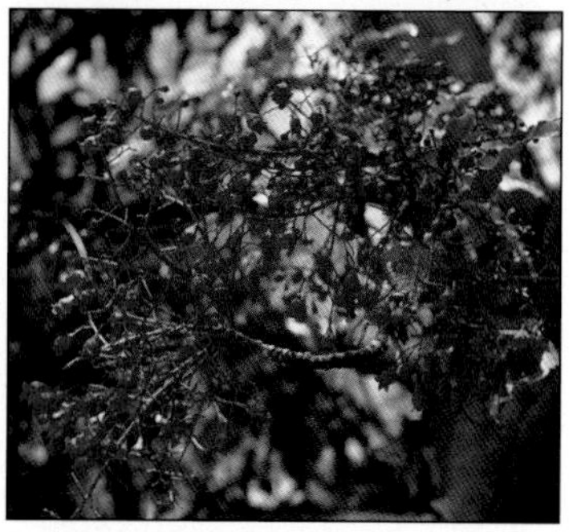

Brachychiton acerifolius

Brachychiton acerifolius
FLAME KURRAJONG, ILLAWARRA FLAME TREE

The flame kurrajong, at its best one of the world's most spectacular flowering trees, is indigenous to the warm, wet, coastal slopes of eastern Australia. It can reach 40–50 ft (12–15 m) in cultivation, taller in its native rainforests. Profuse foamy sprays of bright scarlet flowers are borne in late spring or early summer on the leafless crown, or on individual branches that shed their leaves just prior to flowering. Flowering is erratic from year to year and seems best following a dry, mild winter. **ZONES 9–12.**

Brachychiton discolor
LACEBARK KURRAJONG

A massive tree, to 80 ft (24 m) or more in its native rainforest, the lacebark kurrajong is smaller when seen in parks and gardens, though retaining its distinctive form. Its thick greenish trunk supports a dense canopy of large, maple-like leaves, dark green above and silvery beneath. Deep pink, velvety, bell-shaped flowers appear in early summer, while the tree is briefly leafless. **ZONES 10–12.**

Brachychiton populneus
syns *Brachychiton diversifolius, Sterculia diversifolia*

KURRAJONG

Widely distributed on rocky hillsides, this bushy headed evergreen tree is grown chiefly for shade, or on farms for its fodder value in times of scarcity. The deep olive-green leaves are variably lobed. During summer it produces, among the foliage, masses of greenish cream bell-shaped flowers, spotted inside with purple or yellow to attract bees. It will tolerate limestone soils. **ZONES 8–11.**

Brachychiton rupestris
QUEENSLAND BOTTLE TREE

Restricted in the wild to inland south-eastern Queensland where it grows in fertile soil in broad valleys or on low ridges, the Queensland bottle tree grows to 30–40 ft (9–12 m), developing a massive bulbous trunk with gray-green, slightly fissured bark. The moist, fibrous inner bark was used as food by Australian Aborigines. The deep green leaves make a dense crown and may drop in dry periods, though generally it is almost evergreen. In spring and early summer small yellowish flowers appear in clusters towards the branch tips. Grown in parks and streets for the unusual shape of its trunk, it can make surprisingly fast growth if well nourished. **ZONES 9–12.**

BRACHYCOME
syn. *Brachyscome*

Native to Australia, the low-growing annuals and evergreen perennials of this genus are attractive ground cover or rockery plants. Many of the perennials are mound-forming, spreading by underground runners and having finely divided, soft, fern-like foliage. They bear a profusion of daisy-like flowerheads in shades of blue, mauve, pink and yellow, with orange or brownish centers or yellow as in the hybrids **'Sunburst'** and **'Outback Sunburst'**, both with white ray florets. Australian botanists have disputed over the spelling of this genus, the debate hingeing on whether the nineteenth-century botanist who spelt it *Brachyscome* had the right to subsequently correct his bad Greek, as he did (it combines *brachys*, short, with *kome*, hair, referring to a seed feature, but the 's' is dropped when they are joined).
CULTIVATION: They require a sunny situation and a light, well-drained garden soil. Many are moderately frost hardy and some will tolerate coastal salt spray. Do not over-water as they prefer dry conditions. Pinch out early shoots to encourage branching and propagate from ripe seed or stem cuttings or by division in spring or fall (autumn).

Brachycome 'Amethyst'

A long-flowering perennial with purple-blue flowers, this recent hybrid grows to about 12 in (30 cm) tall and wide. **ZONES 9–11.**

Brachycome iberidifolia
SWAN RIVER DAISY

This daisy is a weak-stemmed annual, long grown as a bedding or border plant, that grows to a height and spread of around 12 in (30 cm), sometimes taller. It has deeply dissected leaves with very narrow segments. Small, fragrant, daisy-like flowerheads, normally mauve-blue but sometimes white, pink or purple, appear in great profusion in summer and early fall (autumn). **'Blue Star'** is a cultivar with massed small mauve to purple-blue flowers. **ZONES 9–11.**

Brachycome multifida

This perennial species is a charming ground cover in warm-temperate climates, though it is not long lived and should be renewed every few years. It grows about 4–6 in (10–15 cm) high and spreads to about 18 in (45 cm). The mauve-pink flowerheads bloom for weeks in late spring and summer. It likes sunshine and perfect drainage and is propagated by layers or from cuttings. **'Break O' Day'** is a selected form with finer leaves, profuse mauve-blue flowers and a very compact habit. **ZONES 9–11.**

Brachycome 'Sunburst'

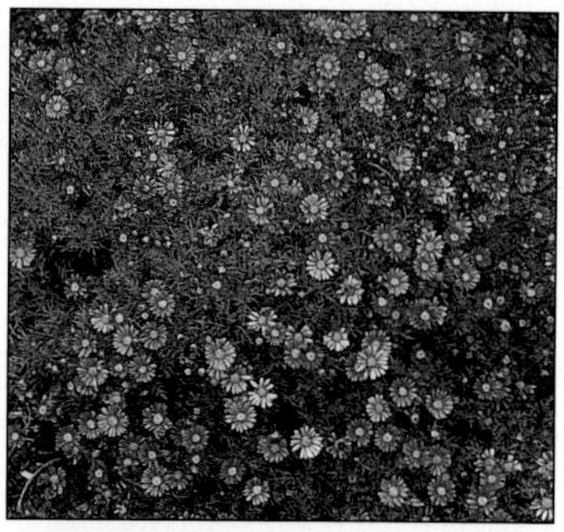

Brachycome 'Amethyst'

Brachycome multifida

Brachycome 'Outback Sunburst'

Brachycome multifida 'Break O' Day'

Brachycome iberidifolia 'Blue Star'

BRACHYGLOTTIS

This genus of low evergreen shrubs and small trees now includes many additional shrubby species transferred from *Senecio*, bringing the total number to around thirty. Most are New Zealand natives, but one or two occur in Tasmania. Apart from their flowers, many are valued for their attractive foliage, the stems and leaf undersides mostly having a dense coating of white wool. The flower- heads are in small to rather large panicles at the branch tips, and may be white or golden yellow with conspicuous petals (actually ray florets), or small and greenish white with no ray florets.
CULTIVATION: These are rewarding garden plants if climatic conditions are suitable—they do best in cool but mild and rainy climates, in a sunny position with well-drained soil. The shrubby species responds to heavy pruning. Propagation is from cuttings in late summer. Keep in shape by cutting it back.

Brachyglottis Dunedin Hybrids

Of mixed parentage involving 3 species, the Dunedin Hybrids resulted from a chance crossing early in the twentieth century at Dunedin in New Zealand. They are bushy, if somewhat open, shrubs to 5 ft (1.5 m) with dark green leaves having the characteristic felty white undersurface of the genus and the daisy-like yellow flowerheads. '**Sunshine**' has neat elliptical leaves and bright yellow flowerheads in large, loose terminal clusters. ZONES 7–9.

Bracteantha bracteata 'Diamond Head'

Bracteantha b. 'Dargan Hill Monarch'

Brachyglottis greyi
syn. *Senecio greyi*

This many-branched evergreen shrub grows into a large mound, anything up to 6 ft (1.8 m) high and greater than this in spread. Its small, bright yellow, daisy-like flowers appear in summer and fall (autumn) and are less interesting than its hair-covered leathery, green-gray leaves. This moderately frost-hardy species has long been grown in the UK. ZONES 7–9.

Brachyglottis laxifolia
syn. *Senecio laxifolius*
NELSON MOUNTAIN GROUNDSEL

This species is similar to *Brachyglottis greyi* except for a more open growth habit. It has heavily felted foliage and is relatively small growing, to 3 ft (1 m) high. The oval leaves are 2–3 in (5–8 cm) long, deep green above and silver gray below. The flowers, which are clustered in loose heads and open in mid-summer, are bright golden-yellow daisies up to 1 in (25 mm) in diameter. ZONES 7–9.

Brachyglottis monroi
syn. *Senecio monroi*

A neat, compact shrub, *Brachyglottis monroi* bears sprays of bright yellow flowerheads at the branch tips in summer. Moderately frost hardy, it grows to a height and spread of 3 ft (1 m). The small olive-green to brownish green leaves have crinkled margins. ZONES 7–9.

Brachyglottis greyi

Bracteantha bracteata

Brachyglottis repanda 'Purpurea'

Brachyglottis repanda
RANGIORA

The rangiora is a striking small tree of rapid growth, reaching about 20 ft (6 m), very different from most other *Brachyglottis* species. The saplings have straight, soft stems with opposite pairs of large, deep green, glossy leaves with wavy edges. In late winter to early spring each branch produces at its tip a large frothy panicle of thousands of small, greenish silver flowers. The large leaf size can be maintained by cutting branches back to the base after flowering, or the plant can be allowed to grow to a tree. **'Purpurea'** has the uppersides of the leaves deep purple. ZONES 9–11.

BRACTEANTHA
syn. *Helichrysum*
STRAWFLOWER, EVERLASTING DAISY

This Australian genus consists of 7 species of annuals and perennials, until recently classified under *Helichrysum*. They differ from true helichrysums in their large, decorative flowerheads carried singly or a few together at the end of the flowering branches, each consisting of golden-yellow to white bracts of straw-like texture surrounding a disc of tiny yellow or brownish florets. The leaves, mostly broad and thin, are often downy on their undersides, or can be very sticky in some species. Most of the cultivated forms and seedling strains are treated as forms of *Bracteantha bracteata*, but further botanical study is likely to result in new species being recognized.
CULTIVATION: Plant in moist, well-drained soil in full sun. The summer-flowering annuals may be planted from late winter for an early display. Provided they are not waterlogged, most species will tolerate light to moderate frosts. Propagate annuals from seed and perennials from seed or tip cuttings.

Brachyglottis laxifolia

Brachyglottis greyi

Brachyglottis repanda 'Purpurea'

Bracteantha bracteata
syn. *Helichrysum bracteatum*

This annual or short-lived perennial has an erect habit and grows to a height of around 3 ft (1 m). It has weak, hollow stems, thin green leaves and from summer to early fall (autumn) bears golden-yellow blooms up to 2 in (5 cm) in diameter at the branch tips. In the mid-nineteenth century annual strains with larger flowerheads in shades of pink, bronze red, cream, purple and yellow were developed; these plants were generally more vigorous; **Bright Bikinis Series** is a modern descendant of these. Some more spreading, shrubby perennial plants from eastern Australia, which may be recognized as distinct species, have been named as cultivars, including the popular **'Dargan Hill Monarch'**, with rich yellow blooms up to 3 in (8 cm) across, emerging over several months; **'Diamond Head'** is similar but lower and more compact. ZONES 8–11.

BRAHEA
syn. *Erythea*

This genus of 16 species of fan-leafed palms is related to *Washingtonia*, and comes from the same dry regions of western Mexico. They range from low-growing plants that develop no trunk, to quite tall, solitary-trunked palms with compact crowns. Tiny flowers are borne on panicles that may exceed the fronds in length and, as the date-like fruits develop, hang below the crown.
CULTIVATION: Most species can grow in inhospitable places, some even tolerating light frosts once established. Plants in containers should be watered frequently in summer. Propagation is from seed only, with rapid germination as palms go, but seedling growth is slow. Plants are prone to attack by scale insects and spider mites.

Brahea armata
syn. *Erythea armata*
HESPER PALM

The pale blue-gray color of the stiff fronds is the outstanding feature of this species. It grows slowly to a height of 20 ft (6 m), with a crown 10 ft (3 m) wide. In flower and fruit it is even more dramatic, with arching panicles 15 ft (4.5 m) long. It takes decades to reach flowering size, but even young plants are notable for their foliage. ***Brahea edulis***, differs from *B. armata* in having light green leaves and a stout trunk. It also grows taller: to about 30 ft (9 m). The flowers are similar but are more likely to be held within the crown of fronds, and the 1 in (25 mm) long dark brown fruit have a sweet, sticky edible flesh like dates. **ZONES 9–11.**

BRASSAVOLA

This genus contains up to 20 species of epiphytic or rock-dwelling orchids. They are found in Central and South America from sea level to as high as 6,000 ft (1,800 m). Flowering stems, carrying only one or up to 7 blooms, are produced from the top of a slender pseudobulb, from which also arises the single, fleshy leaf which can be almost circular in cross-section. White, ivory or green in color, the flowers may be as wide as 6 in (15 cm). The species formerly known as *Brassavola digbyana*, which has been crossed with cattleyas to produce the many beautiful × *Brassocattleya* hybrids, is now placed in the genus *Rhyncholaelia*.
CULTIVATION: Grow these frost-tender orchids in cool to intermediate orchid houses. They need moist, humid conditions and strong light all year. Grow in baskets with a very coarse orchid mix or on a bark slab. Water when growing, applying very dilute fertilizer with every third watering. As soon as new pseudobulbs are fully expanded, withhold water for up to a month. Propagate by division when plants fill their pots.

Brassavola nodosa
LADY OF THE NIGHT

The best known member of the genus, this orchid earns its common name from its sweet fragrance, which wafts about mostly at night. The plant makes a dense clump, with cylindrical leaves that look like green extensions of the pseudobulbs.

Brahea armata

Brassica juncea 'Red Giant'

The pendent sprays of white or white and pale green flowers with large white labellum can appear at any time from spring to fall (autumn). **ZONES 10–12.**

BRASSIA
SPIDER ORCHID

Around 25 species belong to this genus of easily grown epiphytic orchids from Central and South America and the West Indies. The plants form large clumps of cylindrical to conical pseudobulbs which arise at intervals from creeping rhizomes, each pseudobulb bearing 1 to 3 large, leathery leaves. They produce long, gracefully arching sprays of spidery flowers with long narrow petals and sepals.
CULTIVATION: Brassias are happy growing outdoors in a frost-free climate, but need the warmth and shelter of a greenhouse in cooler areas. They are among the easiest of orchids to grow as house plants. In winter brassias can be allowed to dry out a little. Propagate by division, but leave the plants undivided for years as they flower most freely when allowed to build up into sizeable clumps.

Brassia verrucosa

The most popular member of the genus in cultivation, this species makes a clump of elongated pseudobulbs with leaves up to 18 in (45 cm) long and 2 in (5 cm) wide, above which horizontally arching flower spikes about 24 in (60 cm) long arise in early summer. The flowers are greenish white or cream with petals and sepals up to 6 in (15 cm) long, darker spotted at their base and on the short triangular labellum. They are very fragrant, though the heavy, spicy perfume that develops as they age is not to everyone's liking. **ZONES 10–12.**

BRASSICA

This remarkable genus has produced a more diverse range of important vegetables than almost any other. It includes about 30 wild species of annuals, biennials and subshrubs, ranging through the Mediterranean region and temperate Asia. Thousands of years ago, botanists now believe, spontaneous hybrids between several of these appeared around human settlements and from one such hybrid arose all that major group of vegetables now classified under the name *Brassica oleracea*. Another large assortment are included under the name *Brassica rapa*. Then there are the mustards and rape, grown for the valuable oils in their seeds, hot-tasting in some. Yet other species are best known as common weeds of roadsides and crops: the wild mustards. The genus *Brassica* in its more primitive form is characterized by its usually lobed leaves, 4-petalled yellow to white flowers and small, spindle-shaped fruiting capsules containing rows of tiny seeds. Most parts of the plants have some hot-tasting mustard oils, which give the characteristic 'bite' to raw cabbage as well as the much more intense flavor to mustard.
CULTIVATION: Most brassicas love a lime-rich, moist, well-drained soil. Seedlings should be raised in seedbeds and then carefully planted out 6 to 8 weeks later in a sheltered, sunny spot in soil that has been used previously for a different crop. They are more prone to pests and diseases than other vegetables, and the use of insecticides is hard to avoid if undamaged vegetables are desired. Ensure soil is kept weed-free and not too wet. Club root is a common disease in these vegetables, and crop rotation should be practised.

Brassavola nodosa

Brassica napus

Brassica juncea
BROWN MUSTARD, INDIAN MUSTARD

This species, now thought to have originated as a hybrid between *Brassica rapa* and *B. nigra*, is cultivated for its pungent seeds used to flavor many dishes and for its seed oil, used in Asia for cooking. An annual that grows to 3 ft (1 m), it has bright yellow flowers that mature to $1\frac{1}{2}$ in (35 mm) long pods containing smooth brown seeds. The species has also given rise to a diverse range of leaf vegetables, little known in Europe but popular in east Asia, including the various Chinese mustard greens and the Japanese mizuna and cultivars such as ***B. juncea* 'Red Giant'**. **ZONES 6–11.**

Brassia verrucosa

Brassica napus
RAPE

This annual or biennial species in its more typical form includes the major oilseeds rape and canola, the latter being the product of recent breeding. In winter-rainfall temperate regions these crops are seen as a patchwork of brilliant yellow fields covering the countryside in spring. The **Napobrassica Group** consists of the root vegetable swede (Swedish turnips, rutabaga), mostly grown as an annual winter crop. Similar to turnips but larger and sweeter, swedes are frost hardy and prefer a fertile soil. **ZONES 5–9.**

B. oleracea, Gemmifera Group, 'Icarus'

B. oleracea, Capitata Group, 'Hawke'

Brassica oleracea, Acephala Group

B. oleracea, Capitata Group, 'Hardora'

Brassica oleracea, Capitata Group

Brassica nigra
BLACK MUSTARD

This annual, growing to 6 ft (1.8 m) or more, is a native of Europe. Four-petalled yellow flowers borne in long clusters in summer are followed by beaked pods each containing up to 12 brown to black seeds. The seeds are the major source of table mustard; the young leaves are edible. **ZONES 7–10.**

Brassica oleracea

Thought to have originated as an ancient hybrid between two or more of the wild Mediterranean species, this is the most important of the *Brassica* species and one of the most versatile of all cultivated food plants. In its various forms it yields edible roots (kohlrabi), leaves (cabbage), shoots (Brussels sprouts) and flower buds (cauliflower and broccoli), as well as a few ornamentals, for example the colored-leafed kales, and curiosities such as some forms of giant kale, the 'trunks' of which have been used as walking sticks! The vegetable brassicas associated with this species include thousands of named cultivars, which are most conveniently divided into the following cultivar groups. **ZONES 6–11.**

Acephala Group, the kales and ornamental kales—these are flat-leafed or curly-leafed cabbages that do not form a head, popular in northern Europe because of their tolerance to cold. Some forms can grow thick, knobby stems up to 6 ft (1.8 m) or more tall. Sow the flat-leafed kales from seed, as they do not tolerate transplanting. In Scotland, the broth made from their leaves is a traditional Highland dish. **'Tall Scotch'** is a typical cultivar, while **'Moss Curled'** is representative of the kales with tightly curled leaves looking a bit like parsley. Ornamental kales, used for bedding and also sold in pots by florists, have leaves usually lobed or dissected, and strikingly veined with purple, pink, yellow or white. **Osaka Series** is a modern strain of mixed colors, the leaves undivided but with frilled edges.

Botrytis Group, the ordinary white cauliflower, a popular vegetable with a history stretching back to the Renaissance. The densely massed, tiny, abortive flower buds and the stalk that bears them are white and tender, with a mild flavor. It is a vegetable that is not easy to grow to perfection, preferring a humus-rich soil for large, compact head production. The flower buds are easily bruised and damaged. Apart from white, cultivars with pale green, pink and purple heads are known. Typical white cultivars are **'Snowball'**, large headed and late maturing, and **'Mini'**, early maturing with heads of 4 in (10 cm) or so across. **'Early Purplehead'** is purple-green, but the purple disappears on cooking.

Capitata Group are the cabbages in all their diversity of form and coloring, possessing in common the tight, many-layered head of leaves. The innumerable cultivars, for example, **'Hardora'** and **'Hawke'**, vary in their seasonal tolerance, and this ensures that they can be grown worldwide in many different climatic zones. Their nutritional value is high. **'Golden Acre'** is a typical early-maturing, round-headed cultivar; **'Sugarloaf'** a spring type with conical head; and **'Greengold'** a large late-maturing F1 hybrid. Red cabbage, with its purplish leaves, is a slow-maturing cabbage that needs a long growing season, but its solid, chewy flesh makes it the best type for pickling and frying; **'Mammoth Red Rock'** is one of the best red cultivars. The Savoy cabbages (**Sabauda Subgroup**) have wrinkled, strongly veined leaves: they are extremely frost hardy and will thrive in very cold conditions. They tend to be larger and stronger flavored than ordinary cabbages. **'Drumhead'** is a favorite Savoy cultivar as is **'Karvoi'**.

Cymosa Group includes all the broccolis which, like cauliflower, are grown for their densely massed flower buds and fleshy stalks, but the buds are further advanced and are not pure white but green, purplish or yellow-green. 'Broccoli' is Italian, coming from *brocco*, 'sprout', and it was in Italy that nearly all the different types of this vegetable evolved. Calabrese is the common type with broad, fleshy, green or purplish heads maturing in summer. **'De Cicco'** is a pale green, early-maturing cultivar; **'Waltham 29'** is also popular. Romanesco broccolis are more cauliflower-like in both appearance and flavor, with tight, hemispherical heads consisting of many neat conical points, maturing later than Calabrese; usually pale yellow-green in color, they are very decorative. Sprouting broccoli is different again, with many narrow-headed buds on long, asparagus-like stalks, appearing among the leaves—they develop over winter and can be picked over a long season in spring and early summer; **'Italian Green Sprouting'** is the best known variety. All broccoli is best picked and eaten when young because once the yellow flowers begin to open it becomes coarse in both texture and flavor. It is ideally grown in raised beds. Do not allow the plant to flower, as it will stop growing. Grubs and waterlogging are 2 major problems.

Gemmifera Group equates with Brussels sprouts, cultivated as a biennial for the miniature cabbage-like heads which grow on the elongating stems, one below each of the large leaves. Timing is crucial when planting Brussels sprouts, since it needs to mature in the coldest part of the year in order to form compact hearts. In warm climates sow the plant in summer, in cold climates in mid-spring. In fall (autumn), remove any yellowing leaves and make sure the soil stays firm around the stem of the plant. There are many cultivars, suited to different soils, yielding smaller or larger sprouts. **'Long Island'**, **'Jade Beauty'**, **'Icarus'** and **'Troika'** are widely grown cultivars; **'Ruby Red'** has reddish sprouts.

B. oleracea, Gemmifera Group, 'Troika'

Gongylodes Group is the name that covers kohlrabi (a word of German origin). This root vegetable resembles beetroot in its growth form with a swollen, bulb-like stem base. With a slightly nutty flavor reminiscent of both turnip and cabbage, it can be eaten raw or cooked. Young leaves are edible. Weed lightly as root disturbance will slow growth. **'Purple Vienna'**, **'White Vienna'** and **'Earliest Erfurt'** are established cultivars.

Brassica rapa

After *Brassica oleracea*, this is the next most diverse of the brassica species in terms of the number of vegetables and crops it has given rise to. Its wild form, referred to as ***B. rapa* subsp. *sylvestris***, is a common weed of road verges and crops. In common with most of the cultivated races it has quite large flowers, about ½ in (12 mm) across and bright yellow. There are also some lesser-known cultivar groups in *B. rapa*, including additional leaf vegetables and oilseeds. **ZONES 7–11.**

Chinensis Group includes the Chinese vegetables known as pak-choi (bok-choi in Cantonese), annual plants with loose rosettes of bright green leaves with very broad white stalks, like silverbeet. The crisp stalks form the main bulk of the vegetable. The plants run to seed quickly, so should be sown in small groups every 10 days. Harvest the entire plant or take a few leaves as needed after 6 to 8 weeks. **'Joi Choi'** is a recent F1 hybrid with very white stalks.

Pekinensis Group equates to the Chinese pe-tsai, also known as wom-buk or Chinese cabbage. Somewhat resembling lettuce (especially cos lettuce) in growth form but with leaves very

B. oleracea, Cymosa Group

B. oleracea, Cymosa Group, Romanesco

strongly veined, this fast-growing vegetable was introduced to Europe only in the nineteenth century. It is easy to grow as long as it is kept moist. The leaves are commonly tied together around the developing heart, and the whole plant is harvested. **'Jade Pagoda'** and **'Hong Kong'** are modern, high-yielding F1 cultivars.

Rapifera Group, the turnips, is the best known cultivar group in the West. A moderately frost-hardy biennial, the turnip is grown as an annual for its fleshy roots. It was a staple food of the northern European working classes until the potato upstaged it. It is suited more to the cooler regions of the world. In order to produce a quick crop, grow turnips in fertile soil in rows and keep the young plants moist throughout the growing period. **'Scots Yellow'** is an old cultivar of carrot-like form; **'Purpletop White Globe'** is an early-maturing white turnip; while **'Shogrin'** is exceptional in being grown primarily for its edible leaves.

× *BRASSOCATTLEYA*

This hybrid orchid genus includes all crosses between the genera *Cattleya* and *Rhyncholaelia* and any later generations of seedlings. The orchids now classified under *Rhyncholaelia* were formerly placed in *Brassavola*, hence the name of the hybrid genus. Most of the earlier crosses had *Rhyncholaelia digbyana* as one parent; this species has a large, conspicuously fringed labellum, and the hybrids tend to have sumptuous flowers with the rich colorings of the cattleyas but with an extravagantly frilled and ruffled labellum. Often the flowers are fragrant, though usually only at certain times of the day.

CULTIVATION: Cultivate as for cattleyas; all require bright light and some will tolerate slightly cooler conditions than others.

× *Brassocattleya* Hybrids

Some of these, depending on their parentage, have a compact, free-flowering habit, with narrow leaves, and flowers with narrow petals and sepals and a large oval lip; others develop into much larger plants producing a single leaf on each pseudobulb with large, often frilled, flowers, for example, × ***B.* Donna Kimuna 'Susan'**. On orchid labels these hybrids are usually indicated by 'BC' before the grex and cultivar names. **ZONES 12–11.**

× *BRASSOLAELIOCATTLEYA*

This hybrid orchid genus is like × *Brassocattleya* above but with the addition of a third genus, *Laelia*, in the parentage. The plants usually look like cattleyas, while the genes of the laelias show in the broader petals and more richly colored labellum of the flowers, which are mostly in pink tones.

CULTIVATION: They are cultivated in the same way as cattleyas, protected from the elements and pests such as snails and are therefore usually grown under glass; they do not require direct sunlight, but lighting must be good. Provide a coarse potting mix, humid but airy atmosphere and rest them during the colder months for best results.

× *Brassolaeliocattleya* Hybrids

Often these and other multi-generic cattleya hybrids are sold simply as cattleyas, or on the labels their status is indicated by 'BLC' before the grex and cultivar names. **St Helier** has 4 large, mid- to dark purple flowers on each new stem. **ZONES 11–12.**

BRIMEURA

This southern European bulb genus includes just 2 species, which have at times been listed under *Scilla* and *Hyacinthus* but are now classified separately. They have narrow, fleshy, strap-like leaves and flower in spring. The flowers are pendulous and come in a range of purple, blue and pink shades and white. The overall appearance is very like that of a bluebell (*Hyacinthoides*).

CULTIVATION: Plant in fall (autumn) in moist, humus-rich soil in sun or part-shade. The bulbs are very hardy and can be left undisturbed for many years. Propagate from seed or by dividing well-established clumps.

Brimeura amethystina
syn. *Hyacinthus amethystinus*

This hyacinth-like species grows to about 10 in (25 cm). Slender, strap-like leaves surround upright 8 in (20 cm) tall flowering stems. These bear up to 8 delicate, about ½ in (12 mm) long, bell-shaped flowers ranging in color from white to blue. **ZONES 5–9.**

BRIZA

This is a genus of some 20 species of annual and perennial grasses, widely distributed in temperate regions. They form loose, small to large clumps of foliage and usually dry off soon after flowering.

Brassica rapa Pekinensis Group

Brassica rapa Chinensis Group

The flowers are carried in small panicles and soon mature into the seed heads, which are the main attraction: these are usually heart-shaped, pendulous on fine stalks and develop a pale golden-brown color as they mature. When moved by the wind they shiver and quake, and in some species make a rustling or rattling noise—this, combined with the shape, gave rise to one of its common names, rattlesnake grass.

CULTIVATION: They are fully frost hardy and easily grown in any well-drained soil in full sun. Propagate the annuals from seed, the perennials from seed or by division. Fungus diseases may cause problems.

Briza media
QUAKING GRASS

This is a tuft-forming perennial grass that grows to about 18 in (45 cm) high. It has mid-green leaves and in summer bears panicles of about 30 hanging, brownish purple seed heads. They make very good dried flower decorations and can be dyed different colors. **ZONES 6–11.**

Briza minor
LESSER QUAKING GRASS, SHIVERY GRASS

An annual grass from Europe, this species makes narrow tufts of around 12–18 in (30–45 cm) high with spreading, broad, rather short leaves. In summer and early fall (autumn) it produces its delicate seed heads in erect panicles up to 8 in (20 cm) wide. Each fine-stalked spikelet is only ⅛ in (3 mm) long, triangular in outline and pale green in color. In good soil it will grow larger and thicker, with large foamy masses of these tiny heads. **ZONES 5–11.**

BRODIAEA

The 15 species in this genus of perennials of the onion tribe, from western USA and parts of South America, have small corms rather than the bulbs found in *Allium*. The sparse, grass-like foliage usually dies off around flowering time. Umbels of starry pink, blue or purple flowers are carried on stems up to 30 in (75 cm) tall, mostly in late spring or summer. In older classifications *Brodiaea* included many of the plants now listed under *Dichelostemma* and *Triteleia*.

CULTIVATION: They are easily grown in any sunny area. Good drainage is vital. They require winter moisture but prefer to be kept dry over summer and usually survive well on natural rainfall. Most species are moderately frost hardy, provided the soil does not freeze for extended periods. Propagate from seed or by division after flowering.

× *Brassocattleya* Donna Kimuna 'Susan'

Briza minor

Brimeura amethystina

× *Brassolaeliocattleya* Hybrid St Helier

B

Brodiaea californica

This is the tallest brodiaea species. Its flower stems can reach 30 in (75 cm) tall and bear $1-1\frac{1}{2}$ in (25–35 mm) wide, pink to lavender-blue flowers in loose, open heads of 2 to 12 blooms. It prefers a warm, sunny position and will seed freely and naturalize where conditions suit it. **ZONES 8–10.**

Brodiaea minor
syn. *Brodiaea purdyi*

This species is considerably smaller than *Brodiaea californica.* Its 1 in (25 mm) wide, pink to purple-blue flowers are borne in a rounded head on a 3–5 in (8–12 cm) long stem. **ZONES 8–10.**

BROMELIA

This genus gives its name to the large family Bromeliaceae (the bromeliads). The 50 or so species of *Bromelia* are scattered widely through South America and parts of Central America and the West Indies. They are mostly ground-dwelling perennials resembling pineapple plants, with strong, hooked spines along the margins of their long, stiff leaves which generally turn a bronzy color in strong sun. The leaves form large rosettes, which in some species can multiply by sending out long rhizomes to make extensive clumps. A stout flower spike arises from the center of the rosette surrounded by leaf-like bracts that may be brilliantly colored; the flowers are tubular and densely packed and give way to large fleshy yellow fruits, which in some species are used medicinally.
CULTIVATION: *Bromelia* species are mostly grown outdoors in frost-free climates, thriving in full sun and well-drained soil. They are relatively free from diseases and pests. Propagate from offsets or seeds, keeping seedlings well ventilated to discourage damping off fungus.

Brodiaea californica

Brodiaea minor

Browallia americana

Bromelia balansae
HEART OF FLAME

This vigorous species reaches a height of 5 ft (1.5 m) and can spread extensively. Its flower spike is up to 3 ft (1 m) tall and is surrounded by glossy, brilliant scarlet, spiny-edged bracts, the longer, lower ones only colored at the base. The purple flowers, borne in late summer, are in a series of dense heads among shorter whitish bracts. The dull orange-yellow berries can form very large clusters, taking almost a year to ripen. This plant has been used in South America as an impenetrable living fence. **ZONES 10–12.**

BROMUS
BROME GRASS, PRAIRIE GRASS, RIPGUT

This genus, widespread in temperate regions of the world, includes some 100 species of annual, biennial and perennial grasses. Forming narrow to broad tufts, they have flat, narrow leaves and long-stalked panicles of seed heads that often terminate in dense bristles (awns). Though green when young, brome grasses are often drying off and brown by the time the seed heads ripen.
CULTIVATION: Most species are very frost hardy and easily cultivated in any moist, well-drained soil in full sun. Few are cultivated as ornamentals, and though some are browsed by livestock the rough awns can cause internal damage to the animals and may damage their pelts. Many species are considered to be minor weeds. They are usually propagated from seed.

Bromelia balansae

Browallia speciosa

Bromus interruptus

This brome grass has seed heads that are arranged along the main spikes in dense spikelets with gaps in between. **ZONES 5–10.**

BROUSSONETIA
PAPER MULBERRY

This genus consists of about 7 species of deciduous trees and shrubs from eastern Asia. They are closely allied to the true mulberries *(Morus),* but with thicker, pith-filled twigs and flowers of different sexes on different plants. Broussonetias are fast-growing, untidy trees with broad, thin-textured, toothed leaves. The small fruits are dry and unpalatable.
CULTIVATION: They are easily grown in a wide range of climates and soils, but prefer a sheltered, humid position. Propagate from cuttings in summer or from seed in fall (autumn).

Broussonetia papyrifera

Originating in China and Japan, this species has spread to other parts of the world including the South Pacific Islands. It yields a fine silky fiber from its inner bark, traditionally used in Japan to make paper; the renowned Polynesian 'tapa cloth' is also made from this fiber. Under suitable conditions it grows rapidly to a large tree of 40–50 ft (12–15 m) with a sparse, rounded crown and a dark trunk with an irregular surface. The leaves on saplings are up to 12 in (30 cm) long, often with 2 or 3 lobes; on adult trees, the leaves are smaller and seldom lobed. Male flowers are in long twisted catkins, with females in shorter, less conspicuous heads. **ZONES 7–12.**

Bromus interruptus

Broussonetia papyrifera

BROWALLIA
BUSH VIOLET

This is a genus of 6 species of bushy annuals and evergreen perennials, all native to tropical South America and the West Indies. They are densely foliaged with a compact habit, soft stems and simple, strongly veined, deep green leaves. The flowers, carried singly in the leaf axils, are like smaller versions of nicotianas (to which they are related) but with shorter tubes and generally in shades of blue, purple or white; they can be quite profuse on well-grown plants.
CULTIVATION: In cool climates browallias are grown as conservatory plants or treated as summer annuals. In frost-free climates they will grow well outdoors in moist, humus-rich, well-drained soil in a warm, part-shaded position sheltered from drying winds. Regular feeding with liquid fertilizer will keep the foliage lush and ensure steady flowering. Pinch back the stem tips to keep the plants bushy. Propagate the annuals from seed in spring, the perennials from seed or tip cuttings.

Browallia americana
syn. *Browallia elata*

This annual species makes a bushy plant of up to 24 in (60 cm) tall. In summer and early fall (autumn) it bears showy 2 in (5 cm) wide flowers, their color varying from a rare shade of intense blue through paler violet to white. It makes a good pot or basket plant and also grows well outdoors. **'Vanja'** has deep blue flowers with white eyes; **'White Bells'** has ice white flowers. **ZONES 9–11.**

Browallia speciosa

This shrubby perennial species grows to around 30 in (75 cm) tall and wide with leaves up to 4 in (10 cm) long. Its flowers are up to 2 in (5 cm) in diameter and purple-blue to deep purple. There are many cultivars, with flowers in all shades of blue and purple as well as white. **'Blue Troll'** is a 12 in (30 cm) dwarf with masses of blue flowers; **'White Troll'** is similar with white flowers. **'Marine Bells'** has deep indigo flowers; **'Sky Bells'** light blue flowers. **ZONES 9–11.**

BRUGMANSIA
syn. *Datura*
ANGEL'S TRUMPET

The large shrubs or small trees of this genus are grown for their very large, fragrant, pendent trumpet flowers. They are still often found under the name *Datura,* but the true daturas are short lived, herbaceous plants with smaller, more upright flowers and capsular fruits that are usually prickly (brugmansias

Brunfelsia australis

have fleshy, unarmed fruit that may be very long and narrow). Five or more species are currently attributed to *Brugmansia,* most originating in the Andes of northern South America, though even there they seem always to be associated with human habitation. They are evergreen or semi-evergreen and their leaves are large and soft, rather like tobacco leaves but smaller, and all parts of the plant are narcotic and poisonous.
CULTIVATION: Frost tender to marginally frost hardy, the plants prefer a warm to hot climate, a sunny sheltered site and a light, fertile, well-drained soil. Best grown as small trees, they can be shaped when young to obtain a single trunk or can be kept trimmed as dense, rounded shrubs. Water well during the growing season. Propagate from tip cuttings in spring or summer. Whitefly and spider mite can cause problems, as can snails.

Brugmansia aurea

This species grows to about 20 ft (6 m) with large, soft, downy leaves, serrated at the margins when young but becoming smooth-edged as they mature. The cream to pale golden yellow trumpet flowers, 10 in (25 cm) long with very wide mouths, hang beneath the foliage and appear to glow in the evenings when lit softly by garden lights. **ZONES 10–12.**

Brugmansia × *candida*

syn. *Datura candida*

This large shrub or small tree, 10–15 ft (3–4.5 m) high, of rather untidy habit, branches low from a short trunk and the long, oval, velvety leaves are confined to the branch tips. The pendulous white flowers, strongly scented at night, are up to 12 in (30 cm) long and have a widely flared mouth. They appear in summer and fall (autumn) but also at other times. Once the most commonly cultivated species, *Brugmansia* × *candida* is now believed to be a hybrid between *B. aurea* and *B. versicolor.* **'Plena'** has an extra frill of petals inside the main trumpet and **'Grand Marnier'** has flowers of soft apricot. **ZONES 10–12.**

Brugmansia 'Charles Grimaldi'

Named after a Californian landscape designer, this 6 ft (1.8 m) tall hybrid cultivar (**'Dr. Seuss'** × **'Frosty Pink'**) has very large, pendulous, fragrant, pale orange-yellow flowers, mainly from mid-fall (autumn) to spring. It has very large leaves and with age will form quite a thicket of stems. **ZONES 10–12.**

Brunfelsia pauciflora

Brugmansia 'Frosty Pink'

This hybrid has large, pale apricot-pink and white flowers and grows to around 6 ft (1.8 m) tall. It has large, pale green leaves and forms clumps of stems. **'Ecuador Pink'** is very similar, but has flowers of pastel pink. **ZONES 10–12.**

Brugmansia × *insignis*

This hybrid, growing to 12 ft (3.5 m), is a cross between *Brugmansia suaveolens* and *B. versicolor* and resembles the former most closely. The long tubular flowers are usually white, although very pale golden-yellow and pink clones are also available. **ZONES 9–12.**

Brugmansia sanguinea

syn. *Datura sanguinea*

RED ANGEL'S TRUMPET

This is the most distinctive of the brugmansias because of its usually orange-red flowers with yellow veins, narrower across the mouth than other species or hybrids. Reported to grow at altitudes up to 12,000 ft (3,600 m) in its native Andes and to become a tree as much as 40 ft (12 m) high, this is the most cold hardy of the brugmansias. It is normally seen in gardens as a many-stemmed shrub to about 8 ft (2.4 m) high. Flower color varies, some forms having paler orange or yellow flowers. **ZONES 9–11.**

Brugmansia suaveolens

syn. *Datura suaveolens*

This many-branched, spreading evergreen shrub or small tree, which reaches 15 ft (4.5 m), has downy, oval leaves up to 12 in (30 cm) long. The flowers are narrower than in *Brugmansia* × *candida,* and their tubes are heavily striped with green. They are profuse at various times of the year. Widely grown in tropical gardens, it is sometimes seen pruned to a round-headed shrub. In cool climates it does well in moderately heated greenhouses. **'Plena'** has semi-double blooms. **ZONES 10–12.**

Brugmansia versicolor

Very similar to *Brugmansia arborea,* which this species is often sold as in nurseries, *B. versicolor* has extremely long flowers, often 18 in (45 cm) or more, with the long-lobed cream petals spreading and recurving at the base. **ZONES 10–12.**

BRUNFELSIA

These evergreen shrubs or small trees from South and Central America bear delightfully fragrant flowers with a narrow tube flaring abruptly into 5 flat petals; these change color from their first day of opening through successive days, with flowers of different ages sprinkling the bush. Most species are slow growing and bushy, with simple, rather leathery leaves. The plants may all contain poisonous alkaloids, particularly in their berry-like fruits, which have been known to poison dogs.
CULTIVATION: These shrubs need a frost-free site, in full sun or with afternoon shade, and fertile, well-drained soil with adequate water in summer or during dry spells. They do well in pots and are widely grown in greenhouses in Europe. Prune after flowering to promote bushiness. Propagate from tip cuttings. Mealybug and white fly may present problems.

Brunfelsia americana

LADY OF THE NIGHT

This shrub or small tree grows to 15 ft (4.5 m) but is commonly less than half this height in gardens. It has mid- to dark green, smallish leaves. Night-scented white flowers, long tubed and faintly flushed purple near the center, turn cream and pale golden as they age; they are produced in summer. **ZONES 10–12.**

Brunfelsia australis

syns *Brunfelsia bonodora, B. latifolia*

YESTERDAY-TODAY-AND-TOMORROW

This attractive shrub grows to about 8 ft (2.4 m) tall and almost as wide, with a densely twiggy habit and slightly shiny leaves, purplish when young and in cool weather. At peak flowering, usually in mid-spring but sometimes in late winter or early summer, it bears masses of blossoms which open violet and fade to pale blue then white, all colors on the bush at the same time. It does well in coastal gardens as long as salt spray is not too heavy. **ZONES 9–12.**

Brunfelsia pauciflora

syns *Brunfelsia calycina, B. eximia*

BRAZIL RAINTREE

This small deciduous or semi-evergreen shrub is slower growing and less vigorous than *Brunfelsia australis,* with duller, dark green, leathery leaves, growing to about 5 ft (1.5 m) tall and wide but rather open branched. In bloom it is even more dramatic: large, abundant flowers open a rich purple and fade to mauve and white over successive days, all through spring and early summer. **'Floribunda'** has smaller leaves and extremely abundant pale purple flowers. **ZONES 10–12.**

Brugmansia 'Charles Grimaldi'

Brugmansia × *insignis*

Brugmansia × *candida* 'Plena'

Brugmansia aurea

Brugmansia 'Ecuador Pink'

Brugmansia 'Frosty Pink'

BRUNNERA

This is a genus of 3 species of perennials closely related to the forget-me-not *(Myosotis)* and *Anchusa*. They range in the wild from eastern Europe to western Siberia and form clumps of heart-shaped to rather narrow basal leaves on long stalks. Leafy, branched flowering stems bear panicles of tiny 5-petalled purple or blue flowers in spring and early summer. There are cultivated forms with white flowers and variegated foliage.
CULTIVATION: Essentially woodland plants, they prefer humus-rich, moist soil with a leafy mulch and a position in dappled shade. They are very cold hardy and in suitable conditions will self-sow and naturalize. Propagate from seed, by removing small rooted pieces or by taking cuttings of the soft spring shoots.

Brunnera macrophylla
SIBERIAN BUGLOSS

The small violet flowers of this species show their relationship to the forget-me-nots; they are held on slender stems 18–24 in (45–60 cm) tall above the bold mounds of heart-shaped leaves. When the flowers appear the new leaves grow to their full length of 4–6 in (10–15 cm). Clumps spread slowly underground but self-seed readily, making excellent ground cover under trees and large shrubs. **'Hadspen Cream'** has paler green leaves prettily edged with cream, and paler blue flowers. **ZONES 3–9.**

BRUNSVIGIA

Many gardeners have attempted to grow these large, interesting bulbs from South Africa, but not all have had the patience to wait while they put out leaves year after year with no sign of flowers. There are about 20 species in the genus, which is closely related to *Amaryllis*, but only one is widely available. The bulbs of some species can be huge; they send up tall flowering stems in late summer topped by umbels of flowers like smaller versions of the belladonna lily but on longer individual stalks. The strap-like leaves follow shortly after, staying green through winter and spring but dying back in summer.
CULTIVATION: They are marginally frost hardy and should be planted in rich, sandy soil in full sun. Water well in the growing season and feed with a soluble fertilizer of high potassium content (to promote flowering), but keep dry when dormant. Propagation is slow: seedlings usually take at least 4 years to flower, and offsets, which may also take years to flower, must be fairly large before undergoing division.

Brunsvigia josephinae
JOSEPHINE'S LILY

Empress Josephine was a patron of horticulture and in her great collection at Malmaison was this striking plant, which the great botanical artist Redouté named and painted. Its bulbs are huge, up to 12 in (30 cm) in diameter, sitting mostly above the soil. If mature and if conditions suit it, it may send up a thick flowering stem anywhere between 18 in (45 cm) and 3 ft (1 m) tall, bearing a large number of bright red, 3 in (8 cm) long, scented, funnel-shaped flowers on stalks up to 15 in (38 cm) long. The bulbs are expensive, and some growers have waited as long as 10 years for them to flower. **ZONES 9–11.**

Brunsvigia orientalis
syn. *Brunsvigia multiflora*
CANDELABRA FLOWER

Springing from a very large underground bulb, the sturdy stem of the candelabra flower grows up to 18 in (45 cm) and bears an umbel of flowers to 18 in (45 cm) wide. The narrow-petalled crimson flowers are about $2\frac{1}{2}$ in (6 cm) long and do not all open at once. The foliage often lies flat on the ground and is tender to frost. **ZONES 9–11.**

BRYA

This is a small genus of 4 species of pea-flowered trees from the West Indies, 3 of them endemic to Cuba. They have small, simple, stalkless leaves and small but abundant flowers, rather like those of some of the brooms, arising from the leaf axils. The genus name honors the seventeenth-century French engraver de Bry.
CULTIVATION: They appear to have potential as ornamentals for the tropics and warmer subtropics, growing well in sheltered coastal areas. Propagation is from seed.

Brya ebenus
JAMAICA EBONY, WEST INDIAN EBONY, COCUS WOOD

A tree of 20–30 ft (6–9 m) high when grown in the open, this species has a short trunk and an open crown of broadly spreading branches with stiffly diverging twigs. The round-tipped leaves are shiny, dark green and about 1 in (25 mm) long. Golden yellow flowers line the branches in fall (autumn) or late in the tropical dry season. Jamaica ebony yields a valuable timber with heartwood that becomes black with age. **ZONES 11–12.**

BUDDLEJA

The spelling *Buddleia* is often seen for this genus (named after seventeenth-century English botanist Adam Buddle), but *Buddleja* is now ruled the correct form. This genus consists of shrubs and small, mostly short-lived trees, both evergreen and deciduous. Most of the cultivated species originate in China, but the genus also occurs in Africa, Madagascar, southern Asia and South America and includes many tropical and subtropical species. The leaves are large, pointed and often crepe-textured, usually in opposite pairs. The spice-scented flowers are small and tubular, and occur in dense spikes at the branch tips or sometimes in smaller clusters along the branches. They range through pinks, mauves, reddish purples, oranges and yellows.
CULTIVATION: Buddlejas prefer full sun and good drainage, but thrive in any soil type. Fairly hard pruning in early spring controls their straggly appearance. Propagate from cuttings in summer.

Buddleja alternifolia

In full bloom in late spring and early summer, this tall deciduous shrub from northwestern China is transformed into a fountain of fragrant, mauve-pink blossom, the small individual flowers strung in clusters along its arching branches. It looks best trained to a single trunk so the branches can weep effectively from above, and should not be pruned back hard as it flowers on the previous summer's wood. **ZONES 6–9.**

Buddleja asiatica

This evergreen shrub from Southeast Asia and the lower Himalayas grows to around 10 ft (3 m) and has long, narrow grayish leaves in widely spaced pairs on the slender branches. Long, nodding spikes of fragrant white flowers appear in winter and spring; these last well as cut flowers. It is moderately frost hardy, but can be grown successfully in pots placed under cover in colder areas. **ZONES 8–10.**

Buddleja auriculata

An evergreen shrub from South Africa, this species has a rather scrambling habit with drooping branch tips and can reach a height of 12 ft (3.5 m). The leaves, glossy deep green and strongly veined above and white felted beneath, complement the numerous short drooping spikes of sweet-smelling cream, pale orange or lilac flowers in fall (autumn), winter or early spring. **ZONES 8–10.**

Buddleja colvilei

A small evergreen tree up to 20 ft (6 m) tall, this species from the Himalayas has the largest blooms of all the buddlejas and when in flower, during late spring and early summer, it makes a wonderful display. The bell-like blossoms, deep pink or crimson with white throats and up to 1 in (25 mm) across, are held in loose panicles near the ends of last season's drooping branches—a point to consider when pruning. **ZONES 7–9.**

Buddleja crispa

This deciduous, spreading shrub from the Himalayas and Afghanistan grows to

Brunnera macrophylla

Brunnera macrophylla

Brya ebenus

Brunsvigia orientalis

Buddleja alternifolia

Buddleja alternifolia

Buddleja davidii 'Cardinal'

about 12 ft (3.5 m), with rather short, broad leaves that are gray-felted beneath and coarsely toothed. It bears large, erect to drooping panicles consisting of tightly packed short spikes of fragrant lilac to pink flowers. It flowers on the current season's growth, so can be cut back hard in winter to stimulate flowering during the summer months. **ZONES 7–9.**

Buddleja davidii
BUTTERFLY BUSH

The common buddleja of gardens, *Buddleja davidii* is native to central and western China and was named after the French missionary–naturalist Father Armand David, who discovered it in 1869. It is a deciduous or semi-evergreen shrub of about 12 ft (3.5 m) with gray-green foliage. In late summer and early fall (autumn) its arching canes bear at their tips long, narrow cones of densely packed flowers, mauve with an orange eye in the original form. These are attractive to butterflies, which feed on the scented nectar. Prune in late winter to encourage strong canes with larger flower spikes. Cultivars with flowers in larger spikes and richer tones include **'Cardinal'**, rich purple-pink; **'Black Knight'**, dark purple; **'Empire Blue'**, purple-blue with an orange eye; **'Royal Red'**, magenta; and **'White Bouquet'**, cream with an orange eye. **'Dubonnet'** has large spikes of purple-pink flowers, and **'Pink Delight'** has long narrow spikes of bright pink ones. The flowers of **'White Profusion'** are white with golden-yellow centers. **ZONES 5–10.**

Buddleja fallowiana

Grown for its richly fragrant blossoms, this deciduous shrub from China grows to 15 ft (4.5 m) and is moderately frost hardy. The stems are white and felty, and the leaves are dull green and gray-felted beneath. In summer long panicles of very fragrant, pale lavender flowers with pale orange throats appear on the current season's growth. **'Alba'** has creamy white flowers with an orange eye. **'Lochinch'** has very fragrant violet-blue blooms featuring an orange eye. **ZONES 8–9.**

Buddleja globosa
ORANGE BALL TREE

Deep golden orange balls of tiny flowers, hanging like baubles from the branch tips in late spring and summer, make this deciduous or semi-evergreen species from temperate Chile and Argentina strikingly different from other buddlejas. The strongly veined leaves are soft and covered in white felty hairs, as are the twigs and flower stalks. It is a tall shrub of 10–15 ft (3–4.5 m), making fast growth under suitably sheltered conditions but inclined to be short lived. In cool but mild, moist climates it will do well close to the sea. **ZONES 7–10.**

Buddleja lindleyana

Occurring wild in southeastern China, this rather weak-stemmed evergreen or semi-evergreen shrub grows to about 12 ft (3.5 m). It has pointed, almost hairless leaves, and nodding, tapered spikes of violet flowers are borne in late summer. Individual flowers are ¾ in (20 mm) long and ⅓ in (8 mm) across at the mouth, but not many are open at the one time. **ZONES 7–9.**

Buddleja davidii 'Pink Delight'

Buddleja madagascariensis
syns *Buddleja nicodemia, Nicodemia madagascariensis*

From Madagascar, this evergreen species growing to 20 ft (6 m) with a vigorously scrambling growth habit makes a good wall shrub in cool but mild climates; in warmer climates, however, it is rampant and invasive. The branches are strikingly coated with dense white wool, and the leaves are dark green above and felty white on the underside. Long spikes of orange-yellow flowers in late winter and spring may be followed by tiny purple-blue or orange berries. **ZONES 9–12.**

Buddleja nivea

This deciduous shrub from western China grows 6–8 ft (1.8–2.4 m) tall, with white-downy branches and leaves up to 10 in (25 cm) long and 4 in (10 cm) wide; they are dull green and closely veined. In summer small white, or pink to pale purple flowers appear in narrow downy spikes about 6 in (15 cm) long, at the branch ends and arising from the upper leaf axils. **ZONES 7–9.**

Buddleja saligna
OLIVE BUDDLEJA, BASTARD OLIVE

In cultivation this species from southern Africa is a many-stemmed evergreen shrub around 10 ft (3 m) high; in the wild it grows 30 ft (9 m) or more. The narrow gray-green leaves, whitish underneath, are like olive leaves, though the name *saligna* signifies a likeness to willows. Borne in fall (autumn) in dense, broad panicles, the tiny, fragrant cream flowers have protruding stamens, an unusual feature among buddlejas. **ZONES 9–11.**

Buddleja salviifolia
SOUTH AFRICAN SAGEWOOD

Native to southern Africa, this dense, vigorous, semi-evergreen species bears abundant terminal clusters of sweet-smelling lilac flowers. It has 6 in (15 cm) long, finely serrated, deep gray-green leaves with a close network of deeply impressed veins. It grows to a height and spread of about 10 ft (3 m) with crowded stems from ground level. **ZONES 8–11.**

Buddleja × weyeriana

This name applies to hybrids between *Buddleja davidii* and *B. globosa*. In growth habit they resemble *B. davidii* though taller and with longer canes, but the flower spikes are broken up into globular bunches of cream or orange-yellow flowers reminiscent of the heads of *B. globosa*. **'Golden Glow'** has gold flowers, deep orange in the throat. **'Wattle Bird'** is a recent Australian hybrid with pale to rich yellow flowers in elongated spikes. **ZONES 7–10.**

Buddleja saligna

Buddleja × weyeriana 'Wattle Bird'

Buddleja globosa

Buddleja davidii 'Dubonnet'

Buddleja davidii 'Royal Red'

Buglossoides purpurocaerulea

Bupleurum fruticosum

Burchellia bubalina

Bulbine frutescens 'Hallmark'

Bulbinella floribunda

Bulbinella hookeri

BUGLOSSOIDES

This is a genus of around 15 species of annuals and perennials found over much of Europe and temperate Asia. The perennial species spread by rhizomes and may become slightly invasive. They have broad to narrow leaves on erect stems, mostly with bristly hairs. Small, starry, borage-like blue or purple flowers form in small heads at the top of the stems. **CULTIVATION:** These plants prefer a warm, dry position in part-shade. Plant in a sheltered, east-facing spot for the best results. They are very frost hardy and are usually propagated by division in late winter. Annuals are raised from seed.

Buglossoides purpurocaerulea
syn. *Lithospermum purpureocaeruleum*

This 30 in (75 cm) tall perennial species spreads to form a mat or clump of leafy stems 18–24 in (45–60 cm) tall with 3 in (8 cm) long, rather narrow leaves, and topped by small heads of ¾ in (20 mm) wide flowers that age to blue after opening purple-red. **ZONES 5–9.**

BULBINE

The majority of the 50 or so species in this genus of yellow-flowered lilies are native to southern or eastern Africa, with 5 native to Australia, where they occur widely in inland areas and include the only 2 annuals. The remainder are perennials and subshrubs, some of them having a succulent growth form while others have rather onion-like leaves arising from corms. The small star-shaped flowers with 6 petals are carried on stalked spikes that usually develop after rain in the wild. **CULTIVATION:** Plant in light, gritty, very well-drained soil in full sun. Water well in the growing season but allow to dry off after flowering. Most species tolerate only very light frosts. Propagate from seed or small tip or stem cuttings. Some of the succulent species may be grown from leaf-petiole cuttings.

Bulbine frutescens
syn. ***Bulbine caulescens***
STALKED BULBINE

This South African species is a fibrous-rooted subshrub whose stems branch above ground to form low-spreading clumps up to 12 in (30 cm) high and more in width. Its 6 in (15 cm) long succulent leaves are cylindrical and hollow, sometimes slightly bluish. The flowers, opening progressively up 18 in (45 cm) spikes in spring, summer and fall (autumn), may be various shades of orange and yellow, or white. **'Hallmark'** bears yellow flat-faced flowers in spring. **ZONES 9–11.**

BULBINELLA

This southern hemisphere genus has an unusual distribution, with 6 species endemic to New Zealand and the remaining 14 or so species native to southern Africa. They are fleshy-rooted perennial lilies similar to the related *Bulbine* but with mostly broader, thinner leaves and crowded spikes of golden yellow flowers terminating the long, hollow stems. They form clumps of somewhat untidy foliage. Some of the larger South African species, such as *Bulbinella floribunda*, make excellent cut flowers. The alpine species are much smaller but not so easily grown. **CULTIVATION:** In the wild, many species grow in very damp areas and in cultivation they demand moist, humus-rich soil that never dries out entirely in summer. A position in sun or semi-shade is best. Most species are at least slightly frost hardy and are propagated from seed or by dividing established clumps. The fleshy roots should be planted with the root-crown at soil level.

Bulbinella floribunda
CAT'S-TAIL

This native of South Africa produces 24–36 in (60–90 cm) tall flower stalks from late winter to mid-spring. Each stalk is topped with a broad, 10 cm (4 in) spike crammed with tiny orange-yellow flowers and terminating in tight green buds. Long, narrow basal leaves appear in winter, forming a large tangled clump. The plant dies back in summer and fall (autumn). It is excellent as a long-lasting cut flower. **ZONES 8–10.**

Bulbinella hookeri

Found in the subalpine grasslands of the main islands of New Zealand, this species has very narrow, grassy leaves and develops into a thick clump of foliage. The flower stems are around 24 in (60 cm) tall, half of which is the densely packed spike of ¼ in (6 mm) wide flowers. **ZONES 8–10.**

BUPLEURUM

Over 100 species belong to this genus, including annuals, perennials and shrubs ranging through Europe, Africa, Asia and some cooler parts of North America. They have undivided, untoothed leaves, mostly rather long and narrow but broader or even almost circular in some species. The small greenish or yellowish flowers are borne in rounded umbels, often with a circle or cup of pointed bracts, and the primary umbels are generally grouped into compound umbels. The common name 'thorow-wax' is sometimes used for the whole genus , but correctly applies only to *Bupleurum rotundifolium*, which has curious large, teardrop-shaped leaves through which the stems appear to grow. **CULTIVATION:** Some of the more shrubby evergreen species with leathery, salt-resistant foliage are useful plants for seaside gardens, while several herbaceous perennial species are sometimes grown as rockery plants. Plant in a sunny position in light, well-drained soil. Propagate shrub species from cuttings or by root division, herbaceous species from seed or by division.

Bupleurum fruticosum
SHRUBBY HARE'S-EAR

This southern European species is a 6–10 ft (1.8–3 m) tall, spreading evergreen shrub, though only 3 ft (1 m) or less in exposed positions. Its leaves are narrow and leathery with rounded tips, bluish green, especially on the undersides, and up to 3 in (8 cm) long with prominent midribs. From mid-summer it develops umbels of small, fleshy, yellow flowers at the branch tips. **ZONES 7–10.**

Bupleurum rotundifolium
THOROW-WAX

Occurring wild in Europe and northern Asia, this species is an annual or short-lived perennial of about 24 in (60 cm) in height. It has 1–2 in (2.5–5 cm) long leaves that are egg-shaped in outline with the slender stems appearing to penetrate them a little way in from the broader end; the leaves are often tinted pink when young. Small umbels of tiny yellow flowers with neat groups of pointed green bracts develop in summer. **ZONES 6–9.**

BURCHELLIA
SOUTH AFRICAN POMEGRANATE

This genus contains only one species. It is a slow-growing, evergreen shrub that deserves to be more widely cultivated for its neat, dark green leaves and showy, long-lasting late spring and summer flowers. These are tubular with 5 short pointed lobes and form a profusion of neat, tight clusters at the branch tips. Fleshy reddish fruit may follow. **CULTIVATION:** This shrub prefers a sheltered, sunny position and well-drained soil with added organic matter. Prune lightly after flowering to prevent fruit production. It is somewhat frost tender. Propagate from cuttings in summer.

Burchellia bubalina

A rounded to rather straggly, densely leafed shrub to 10 ft (3 m) high and almost as wide, *Burchellia bubalina* has faintly fragrant, vivid orange-red flowers about 1 in (25 mm) long. **ZONES 9–11.**

BURSARIA

Six species of evergreen shrubs and small trees make up this Australian genus. Most of them have thorny twigs and small leaves arranged in rosette-like small shoots along the branches. In summer they bear panicles of numerous sweet-smelling, small white flowers at the branch tips, attracting many insects, including butterflies. The flowers are followed by massed, small, flattened brown seed capsules. These plants are seldom cultivated, but can make useful screens or thorny hedges. **CULTIVATION:** They are not fussy about soil or position as long as there is adequate moisture. In cool climates give them a sunny position against a wall for winter warmth and a good display of flowers. Propagate from seed or cuttings.

Butia capitata

Butia eriospatha

Bursaria spinosa
AUSTRALIAN BOXTHORN

This is a shrub of erect but often crooked, irregular habit, occasionally becoming a small tree to 20 ft (6 m). It occurs widely in southeastern Australia as an understorey in open eucalypt forests. The masses of fruits are striking when immature and pinkish red. **ZONES 8–11.**

BUTIA

This small genus of marginally frost-hardy palms comes from central South America and is related to the coconut palm. They have short, thick trunks and thick-textured, elegantly arched fronds of the 'feather' kind (pinnate). They periodically produce among the fronds large panicles of fruity scented, small cream or purplish flowers, which are enclosed while in bud in a very long, woody bract; these are followed by abundant fruits with juicy but fibrous flesh around a very hard stone.
CULTIVATION: These tough palms are adaptable to a range of climates and soils. They are at their best when planted in full sun but tolerate part-shade well. They are deeper rooted than most palms, and once established need little watering as long as summer rainfall is not too low. Dead fronds can be cut off close to the trunk, but not before they turn brown as they continue to transfer nutrients to the new fronds. Propagate from seed in spring.

Butia capitata
syn. *Cocos capitata*
BUTIA PALM, JELLY PALM, PINDO PALM

This palm can be variable in shape, reaching a height of up to 20 ft (6 m). It has a rough gray trunk and long, gray-green fronds, which are arching and recurved. The fragrant yellow or purplish flowers are borne in very large panicles on a strong stalk, emerging among the frond bases, and may be followed by a

Butia yatay

large weight of juicy yellow or orange fruit up to 1 in (25 mm) wide; their sweet, edible pulp is used for jellies or fermented to make wine. Vigorous and easily grown, it is useful for landscaping. **ZONES 8–11.**

Butia eriospatha

This species is similar in most respects to *Butia capitata*, but has a very dense, pale brownish 'fleece' that coats the very large woody bract. A vigorous grower, it reaches first flowering just as the short, thick trunk begins to develop beneath the fronds. The fruit are smaller and less juicy than those of *B. capitata*. **ZONES 9–11.**

Butia yatay
YATAY PALM

At one time the commonly cultivated butia palm was called *Butia yatay*, but this was shown to be a wrong identification of what is in fact *B. capitata*. The true *B. yatay* is rare outside its native Argentina. Growing to 20 ft (6 m) or more, it has a gray trunk 18 in (45 cm) in diameter covered in persistent, overlapping bases of old fronds. Fronds and flowers are similar to those of *B. capitata*, but the edible yellow to orange-red fruit are only about ¾ in (20 mm) in diameter and proportionately longer. **ZONES 9–11.**

BUTOMUS
FLOWERING RUSH

A genus of just one species, this is an elegant, marginal water plant native to Europe and Asia. Belonging to a small family of its own though believed to be related to the lilies, it is a rush-like deciduous perennial and has narrow, twisted, 3-angled leaves with razor-sharp edges. Tall flowering stems are topped by umbels of faintly scented pink-and-white to rose pink flowers in summer.
CULTIVATION: Plant in a warm, sunny area along the shallow edges of a pool or in boggy soil. It is frost hardy in all but the coldest climates. Propagate from seed in spring or late summer, or by division in spring.

Butomus umbellatus

Growing to 4 ft (1.2 m) tall and 24 in (60 cm) wide, the flowering rush can be used to add height to plantings around large ponds or slow-moving streams. Its mid-green leaves are bronze when young, and the umbels of pink flowers are sometimes partially hidden by the foliage but often make a splash of color after showier spring flowers, such as irises, have finished. **ZONES 5–9.**

BUXUS
BOX

Traditional evergreens of cool-climate gardens, the boxes are grown for their small, neat, leathery leaves and dense, long-lived growth habit. The genus consists of around 30 species, only a few of which originate in Europe and temperate Asia; the majority are tropical and subtropical plants that come from Central America, the West Indies or southern Africa. The cultivated boxes, though regarded as shrubs, can (except for some dwarf cultivars) grow into small trees with strong, contorted trunks and branches. The profuse small flowers are greenish yellow and appear in small clusters in the leaf axils in spring; they attract bees.
CULTIVATION: These tough plants have simple requirements, thriving in most soils in sun or shade and adapting well to warmer climates. Boxes withstand regular close clipping, making them ideal for topiary, formal hedges and mazes. Pruning of hedges can be continued throughout the year. Propagate from cuttings.

Buxus balearica
BALEARIC BOXWOOD

From Spain, the Balearic Islands and northwestern Africa, this shrub or small tree of up to 30 ft (9 m) tall can be distinguished from the more popular Japanese or European box by its larger, thicker leaves; these are mostly 1–1½ in (25–35 mm) long and more or less oblong or wedge-shaped. An erect and vigorous grower, it has a narrow growth habit and gains height rather quickly; it can be used for hedging or topiary. It is less frost hardy than European box. **ZONES 8–10.**

Buxus microphylla
JAPANESE BOX

This east Asian box, long grown in Japan but unknown in the wild, first came to Western gardens as a dwarf cultivar with distorted leaves. Later, wild forms were discovered in Japan, Korea and China and named as varieties: ***Buxus microphylla*** **var.** ***japonica*** (syn. *B. japonica*), ***B. m.*** **var.** ***koreana*** and ***B. m.*** **var.** ***sinica*** respectively. The leaves of these are slightly glossier than the European box and usually more rounded at the tip, with the broadest part somewhat above the middle. A characteristic feature is the way the leaves turn pale yellow-brown in frosty winters. In North America *B. m.* var. *koreana* is popular for its compact, low-growing habit and cold hardiness. In milder climates *B. m.* var. *japonica*, with slightly larger, more rounded leaves, thrives, sometimes reaching 10 ft (3 m). **ZONES 6–10.**

Buxus microphylla var. *japonica*

Bursaria spinosa

Buxus sempervirens
EUROPEAN BOX, COMMON BOX

The common box can grow to 30 ft (9 m) with a trunk 12 in (30 cm) thick, but as a garden shrub it is commonly only 3–6 ft (1–1.8 m) high. It has a range of forms and cultivars, including the mound-forming **'Vardar Valley'**. The edging box, **'Suffruticosa'**, has a very dense, bushy habit and can be maintained as a dwarf hedge of 12 in (30 cm) or less. There are also many variegated clones, including **'Marginata'**, which has yellow-margined leaves, and **'Argenteovariegata'**, with white-edged leaves. **ZONES 5–10.**

Buxus wallichiana
HIMALAYAN BOX

Native to the western Himalayas, this box grows into a small tree up to 30 ft (9 m), though usually much smaller in gardens. It is distinguished by its leaves being longer than those of the other cultivated boxes, 1½–2½ in (3.5–6 cm) in length and proportionately rather narrow, tapering both to the base and the slightly squared-off tip. The young twigs are finely hairy. **ZONES 8–10.**

Buxus microphylla var. *koreana*

Buxus sempervirens 'Suffruticosa'

C

CABOMBA

This is a genus of 7 species of aquatic plants from warmer parts of the Americas, popular with aquarium fanciers and interesting for the contrast between their finely fern-like submerged leaves and the undivided floating leaves that develop where the plant reaches the surface. Rooting in the bottom sand or mud, they form long branching stems with crowded, finely dissected leaves; this foliage is valued for its oxygenating function in aquariums as well as being quite decorative. The floating leaves are oval to linear, joined at the middle to their slender stalks. In deeper water leaves of this type may never be produced. Another interesting feature is the gelatinous mucilage that coats the underwater stems. The flowers are smallish, 3-petalled and white, yellow or purplish, emerging just above the water.
CULTIVATION: Easily grown in the aquarium, cabombas' chief requirements are a humus-rich planting medium (not plain sand) and a high light level. They prefer still water less than 18 in (45 cm) deep. Propagate from cuttings.

Cabomba caroliniana
CAROLINA WATER SHIELD, FISH GRASS

Native to southeastern USA, this plant has branching underwater stems almost concealed by the ferny leaves, which are up to 3 in (8 cm) long and dissected into very fine segments. When the stems reach the surface these dissected leaves give way to $\frac{3}{4}$ in (20 mm) long, narrowly oval, floating leaves, giving an appearance of two different plants. Under suitable conditions in summer it produces at the surface solitary white or pinkish flowers up to $1\frac{1}{2}$ in (35 mm) wide, each petal with 2 yellow spots at the base. **ZONES 8–11.**

Caesalpinia gilliesii

Caesalpinia crista

CACCINIA

This little-known genus of the borage family consists of 6 species of biennials and perennials from western and central Asia. Several leafy stems, mostly with harsh bristly hairs, usually grow from the rootstock, though the narrow leaves themselves are mostly smooth and hairless. The star-shaped flowers, borne in short terminal sprays, are similar to those of borage *(Borago officinalis)* itself.
CULTIVATION: Caccinias are attractive, frost-hardy plants, suitable for sunny borders or hot positions in the rock garden. The soil must be open and well drained. They tolerate dry conditions but resent root disturbance. Propagate from seed.

Caccinia macranthera

Growing to around 24 in (60 cm), this species occurs wild in mountains from eastern Turkey to the western Himalayas. Its crowded oblong, gray-green leaves are up to 8 in (20 cm) long, and in spring and early summer it bears purplish blue flowers about $\frac{3}{4}$ in (20 mm) wide. Most often seen is ***Caccinia macranthera* var. *crassifolia*,** with thicker, shorter leaves. **ZONES 5–9.**

CAESALPINIA

Caesalpinia is a diverse genus of legumes found in warmer regions around the world and includes 70 or so species of trees, shrubs and scrambling climbers, the latter often very thorny. Most are evergreen, some lose leaves in the tropical dry season. Some shrub species from the Americas have been distinguished in the past as the genus *Poinciana* (not to be confused with the 'poinciana' tree, now *Delonix*). The leaves of all caesalpinias are bipinnate, some very large with numerous leaflets; the flowers are in spikes from the upper leaf axils and may be quite showy, mostly in shades of red, yellow or cream, with separate petals and often conspicuous stamens. The seeds are in typical leguminous pods.
CULTIVATION: Most species appreciate a sheltered sunny spot and deep, sandy soil. The majority are frost tender; none will tolerate more than a few degrees of frost. Propagation is from seed, which may need abrading and hot-water soaking to aid germination.

Caesalpinia ferrea

Caccinia macranthera

Caesalpinia crista

Widespread on the world's tropical coasts, this is a rampant, woody climber or scrambling shrub. Stems are somewhat thorny and the shiny, compound leaves, which can be up to 3 ft (1 m) long, are made up of up to 10 big leaflets, each 4 in (10 cm) long. In summer, the plant produces panicles of orange veined, yellow flowers at the tips of stems. These are both fragrant and showy. Frost tender, this species is best grown in the tropics at or near the coast. **ZONES 11–12.**

Caesalpinia decapetala
MYSORE THORN

Native to southern and eastern Asia, this is a prickly shrub with a distinct scrambling or climbing habit; it can reach 10 ft (3 m) or more in height, with large compound leaves that bear hooked prickles on their undersides. The flowers appear in summer and have creamy yellow petals and pink stamens. Restricted to China and Japan is ***Caesalpinia decapetala* var. *japonica*,** its leaves with larger and fewer leaflets; and more cold-hardy. **ZONES 9–12.**

Caesalpinia ferrea
LEOPARD TREE, BRAZILIAN IRONWOOD

A long-lived tree of up to 40 ft (12 m) high, native to eastern Brazil, this species is grown for its elegantly sinuous limbs, their smooth cream bark dappled with gray-green. The umbrella-shaped crown consists of ferny, unarmed, deep green leaves; in summer and fall (autumn) it is dotted with short, erect spikes of yellow flowers. Fast growing, the leopard tree is often untidily branched when young and should be trained to a single trunk at the base. **ZONES 10–12.**

Caesalpinia pulcherrima

Caladium bicolor

Caesalpinia gilliesii
syn. *Poinciana gilliesii*
DWARF POINCIANA, BIRD OF PARADISE BUSH

This shrub or small tree, native to subtropical Argentina and Uruguay, seldom exceeds 10 ft (3 m) in cultivation and flowers when less than 3 ft (1 m) high. The fern-like leaves are divided into tiny leaflets, and short spikes of pale yellow flowers with very long crimson stamens appear in summer. Evergreen in warm, wet climates, elsewhere it is semi-deciduous or deciduous. **ZONES 9–11.**

Caesalpinia pulcherrima
syn. *Poinciana pulcherrima*
PEACOCK FLOWER, BARBADOS PRIDE, RED BIRD OF PARADISE

Mostly seen as a shrub of about 8 ft (2.4 m), this tropical American species can grow to 15–20 ft (4.5–6 m). Short lived and fast growing, it has an open, moderately spreading habit with coarse, prickly leaves and branches with a whitish waxy bloom, which terminate from spring to fall (autumn) in tall, upright sprays of vivid, usually scarlet and gold blossom. There is also a yellow-flowered form and a darker red one. **ZONES 11–12.**

CAJANUS
PIGEON PEA, DHAL, RED GRAM, CAJUN, CATJANG

One or possibly two species of leguminous shrub from tropical Africa and Asia belong to this economically important genus. The Malay name for pea or bean is *kacang* (pronounced cut-jung), and this was Latinized to *Cajanus* by the botanist who named the genus last century. It is mainly the small bean-like seeds that are eaten, commonly dried and split as in the Indian 'dhal'; the immature pods are also eaten like French beans. Short-lived plants, they have compound leaves consisting of 3 narrow, hairy leaflets; yellow and red-brown pea-flowers are borne in loose clusters at the branch tips.
CULTIVATION: The pigeon pea is commonly treated as an annual. Seeds are sown in spring or at the start of the tropical wet season. It is not demanding as to soil and will grow in moderately acid, infertile soil and without irrigation unless rainfall is very low. Apart from its pods and seeds, which take 5 to 6 months to yield, the pigeon pea is useful as a green manure and soil stabilisation crop.

Cajanus cajan

Thought to have arisen in cultivation in India thousands of years ago, this makes a shrub up to about 10 ft (3 m) tall with a lanky but quite woody stem and long lateral branches. The leaflets of its compound leaves are 2–3 in (5–8 cm) long, and the flowers are a little over ½ in (12 mm) long. Weighing down the branch tips, the 2–4 in (5–10 cm) long pods are glossy green, turning dark brown at maturity; the 4 to 7 seeds are angled diagonally across the pod. **ZONES 10–12.**

CALADIUM

Now undergoing a slight revival in popularity, caladiums include some of the showiest but most tender tropical foliage plants, prized for the gorgeous colors and rich patterning of their large, thin leaves. Consisting of 7 species from tropical South America, the genus belongs to the arum family, resembling the taro genus (*Colocasia*) in growth habit with underground tubers and leaves of the 'elephant-ear' type. They are deciduous in the tropical dry season, the tubers going through a dormant stage. The flowering stems are typical of the arum type, not very showy, with a thin, greenish white spathe half-hidden under the leaves.
CULTIVATION: Caladiums are frost-tender plants, able to be grown outdoors only in moist tropical and subtropical climates. In cool climates they are best suited to heated conservatories and greenhouses, where the air can be kept humid during the growing season. They need bright light but not direct sun. Plant tubers in spring in peat moss or sphagnum, at a temperature of 70–80°F (21–27°C), transplanting when sprouted into a very humus-rich potting medium, fertilizing as the leaves expand and mist-spraying several times a day in summer. As the leaves die back in fall (autumn) allow the soil to dry and lift tubers over winter.

Caladium bicolor
syn. *Caladium* × *hortulanum*

ANGEL WINGS, ELEPHANT'S EARS, FANCY-LEAFED CALADIUM

Caladiums reached a height of popularity in the USA before World War II, when at least a thousand cultivars were listed. There has been debate as to whether the wild parents all belong to the South American *Caladium bicolor* in the broad sense, or whether they included several species (in which case many of the cultivars should correctly be treated as *C.* × *hortulanum*). Their leaves are typically arrowhead-shaped but some cultivars have narrower leaves, wedge-shaped at the base. Color varies from plain green with a red or pink center to intricate combinations of green, white, pink and red, usually with dark green veining. Plants reach 12–24 in (30–60 cm) high. In tropical climates they can remain in the ground year round, and may naturalize in damp areas. **ZONES 10–12.**

CALAMAGROSTIS

REED GRASS

This is a genus of over 250 species of perennial grasses, native to temperate regions of the northern hemisphere where they occur mainly in damp places. They mostly form dense, robust clumps with narrow arching leaves; the plume-like seed heads are carried on tall stems in summer and are quite decorative in some species. With the increased popularity of ornamental grasses, a number of *Calamagrostis* species and cultivars are to be found among the more widely grown grasses.
CULTIVATION: Almost any moist soil in full sun or part-shade suits these plants. If conditions are to their liking, some may become invasive so are best given ample space, for example, beside a pond. Regular division of clumps serves to keep growth in check. Seed heads and old leaves can be cut back to ground level in early winter. Propagate by division of clumps.

Calamagrostis × *acutiflora* 'Karl Foerster'

Calamagrostis × *acutiflora*

Calamintha nepeta

Calamagrostis × *acutiflora*

FEATHER REED GRASS

A hybrid between the Eurasian species *Calamagrostis arundinacea* and *C. epigejos*, this clump-forming grass has a strong, upright habit with thin, arching leaves up to about 3 ft (1 m) long. The somewhat silky, brown seed heads are borne on erect, much branched panicles 3–5 ft (1–1.5 m) tall, and persist into winter. **'Karl Foerster'** (syn. 'Stricta') is larger growing, to about 6 ft (1.8 m), with reddish pink seed heads that age more straw-colored. **ZONES 6–9.**

CALAMINTHA

CALAMINT

Seven species make up this genus of aromatic perennial herbs, occurring as natives mainly in Europe and temperate Asia but with 2 species confined to the USA. In growth habit they are quite like the true mints (*Mentha*), with creeping rhizomes and leaves in opposite pairs on square stems, but the white, pink or purplish flowers are mostly larger and are borne in looser terminal sprays. The leaves of several species are used in herbal medicine, as well as being infused to make herbal teas. The name *Calamintha* (beautiful mint) goes back to ancient Greek, referring originally to an aromatic herb of this general kind but now not identifiable.
CULTIVATION: Mostly fairly frost hardy, calaminthas are easily grown in moist but well-drained soil in a sheltered position; some species prefer woodland conditions in part-shade, others thrive best in full sun. Propagate by division of rhizomes or from seed sown in spring.

Calamintha nepeta 'White Cloud'

Calamintha grandiflora

LARGE-FLOWERED CALAMINT

With 1–1½ in (25–35 mm) long bright pink flowers, this species is used both as an ornament and as a herb. A woodland plant, it occurs wild in southern Europe, North Africa and Asia as far east as Iran. The tall stems spring from creeping rhizomes and bear pale green serrated leaves. The flowers are borne in summer in the uppermost leaf axils. **ZONES 7–10.**

Calamintha nepeta

LESSER CALAMINT

Native to much of Europe, also North Africa and western Asia, this is an unassuming plant 12–24 in (30–60 cm) tall that favors dry, well-drained conditions in full sun. Its small leaves are hardly toothed and the small summer flowers, held in long, erect, rather open sprays, are pale mauve or almost white. The epithet *nepeta* was presumably given to indicate its resemblance to the catmint genus *Nepeta*. ***C. n.* subsp. *glandulosa* 'White Cloud'** and **'Blue Cloud'** are popular cultivars. **ZONES 4–10.**

CALAMUS

RATTAN, ROTANG

The stems of this palm genus of 350-odd species are the source of the world's cane, or rattan, from which cane furniture is constructed. Most species are from the rainforests of tropical Asia and the Malay Archipelago, with a smaller number found in Africa, eastern Australia and the Pacific Islands. They are graceful feather-leafed palms, usually multi-stemmed from the base. The frond mid-rib may be extended into a whip-like, grappling appendage, or this may arise from the rim of the sheathing base of the frond. Similar whip-like panicles bear the tiny flowers, which are followed by small fruits with overlapping scales.
CULTIVATION: Many *Calamus* species adapt to cultivation in warm, wet climates and in their juvenile state can make attractive container plants, best grown in part-shade in moist, well-drained soil. Propagation is only possible from fresh seed.

Calamus australis

Calamus australis

This Australian species grows in dense rainforest in north Queensland. It is multi-stemmed with high-scrambling canes, and fronds about 6 ft (1.8 m) long. The long grappling appendages are armed with recurved hooks. The stalks and sheathing bases of the fronds also have spines. The juvenile, clumping phase is less ferocious and can be maintained for years in a pot. **ZONES 10–12.**

CALANDRINIA

ROCK PURSLANE

Closely related to *Portulaca*, this genus of 150 species of low-growing annuals and perennials is distributed around the Pacific, the majority being South American and favoring warmer, drier areas; Australia also has a good few species, some of them very succulent leafed and inhabiting very arid areas. The narrow fleshy leaves are usually densely clustered at the base. Short, weak flowering stems bear a succession of showy flowers, with 5 broadly overlapping petals, usually in colors of pink or purple though yellows and oranges are also known.
CULTIVATION: These vary in frost hardiness, some coming from high in the Andes and hence cold tolerant. Some species make attractive additions to the rock or scree garden, others are better as summer annuals or conservatory plants. They grow best in an open, free-draining soil with high humus content; perennial species should be kept fairly dry in winter. Propagate from seed in spring.

Calceolaria, Herbeohybrida Group

Calceolaria, Herbeohybrida Group

Calathea zebrina

Calathea burle-marxii

Calathea veitchiana

Calandrinia caespitosa

Native to cooler temperate areas of Chile and Argentina, right to the southernmost parts, this interesting perennial species makes a small, dense cushion of crowded, small, narrow leaves. In summer it is dotted with magenta-pink flowers about $\frac{1}{2}$ in (12 mm) across, borne singly on short stalks. **ZONES 7–9.**

CALANTHE

This orchid genus of around 150 species ranges widely through Asia, Africa and Australasia. It consists mostly of terrestrial plants with fleshy pseudobulbs bearing large, thin, pleated leaves which in some species die back in the tropical dry season. Tall spikes of yellow, white or pink flowers emerge from the bulb bases, which have elongated, downward-pointing labellum with 3 or 4 diverging lobes.

CULTIVATION: In the wild calanthes grow in thick forest floor litter. They are easily enough cultivated in an open but water-retentive medium; water freely as soon as new leaf growth appears and feed with liquid fertilizer. When the leaves begin to yellow, watering should be greatly reduced; flowering begins around this time. Some species will tolerate quite cold winters but not frost, while some more tropical species require a minimum temperature of around 50°F (10°C). Propagate by division.

Calanthe triplicata

Native over a large region in Southeast Asia, the west Pacific Islands and eastern Australia, this is an evergreen orchid with thin, dark green leaves up to 3 ft (1 m) long and 6 in (15 cm) wide arising from a small group of fleshy green

Calceolaria, Herbeohybrida Group

pseudobulbs. Summer flowering, its small pure white blooms are crowded at the top of a straight 3–5 ft (1–1.5 m) tall stem. **ZONES 10–12.**

CALATHEA

Consisting of 300 or so species of evergreen perennials of the arrowroot family, native to Central and South America and the West Indies, this genus is prized for its decorative foliage. At least one species is grown as a food crop, yielding small starchy tubers. The long-stalked, mostly upright leaves are usually large and often beautifully variegated in shades of green, white, pink, purple and maroon, and usually purplish on the undersides. The flowers are interesting but rarely showy, in short dense spikes with overlapping bracts that may be white or variously colored and often partly hidden beneath the foliage.

CULTIVATION: In the wet tropics and subtropics calatheas make attractive foliage plants for outdoor landscaping in shaded areas beneath trees or in courtyards. In colder parts of the world they are grown indoors. Many will thrive in low light levels. Plant in humus-rich, moist but well-drained soil. Water freely in warmer weather and fertilize regularly. Propagate by division of rhizomes. The sheathing leaf bases often harbor mealybugs, and the foliage is affected by aphids, spider mites and thrips.

Calathea burle-marxii

Named in honor of the renowned Brazilian landscape designer, Roberto Burle Marx, whose gardens featured dramatic swathes of plants such as calatheas, this east Brazilian species grows rapidly up to 5 ft (1.5 m) high, with short bamboo-like stems growing erect from the rhizomes. The leaves may be over 24 in (60 cm) long and half as wide, bright green with a yellowish central stripe on the upper surface, duller gray-green beneath. The $\frac{3}{4}$ in (20 mm) long pale violet flowers emerge from waxy white bracts grouped in a large spike. **ZONES 11–12.**

Calathea makoyana

PEACOCK PLANT, CATHEDRAL-WINDOWS

Also from eastern Brazil, this dwarf species grows to no more than 18 in (45 cm) but has the most gorgeously patterned leaves, well justifying its common name; they are broadly oval, with a feathery design of dark green markings on a pale creamy background grading to mid-green at the margins. The undersides have the same markings in purple. Makoy, after whom the species is named, was a renowned nineteenth-century Belgian grower of hothouse plants. **ZONES 11–12.**

Calathea veitchiana

One of the taller growing calatheas, to 3 ft (1 m) or more in height, this species from Peru has leaves blotched light green along the center, the blotches bordered by scalloped bands of dull green, these in turn are bordered greenish yellow, while on the underside the dark green areas become purple. The small white flowers are borne in a club-shaped spike with green bracts. This species is named after a horticulturalist, James Veitch, whose famous English nursery continued throughout the nineteenth century. **ZONES 11–12.**

Calathea zebrina

ZEBRA PLANT

This vigorous species from Brazil is usually 24–36 in (60–90 cm) tall, and can develop into a broad clump of crowded stems, its habit reminiscent of a dwarf canna except that the large, velvety, deep green leaves are marked by parallel stripes or bars of pale chartreuse; the undersides are purplish red. It will thrive in somewhat cooler climates than most calatheas, making a fine ground cover plant, though the leaves turn yellowish in winter; they can be trimmed away to reveal clusters of chocolate brown bracts which protect the spring flowers. **ZONES 10–12.**

CALCEOLARIA

LADIES' PURSE, SLIPPER FLOWER, POCKETBOOK FLOWER

Gardeners who know this genus only in the form of the gaudy 'slipper flowers' sold by florists may be surprised to learn that it contains upward of 300 species, ranging from tiny annuals to herbaceous perennials and even scrambling climbers and quite woody shrubs. All are native to the Americas, from Mexico southward to Tierra del Fuego, and all share the same curious flower structure, with a lower lip inflated like a rather bulbous slipper. Flower colors are mainly yellows and oranges, often with red or purple spots.

CULTIVATION: Calceolarias come from a wide range of natural habitats and vary greatly in cold hardiness. When grown outdoors they prefer a shady, cool site in moist, well-drained soil with added compost. Provide shelter from heavy winds as the flowers are easily damaged. Shrubby species may benefit from being pruned back by half in winter. Propagate from seed or softwood cuttings in summer or late spring. The Herbeohybrida Group, grown mainly in cool greenhouses, are fed and watered liberally in the summer growing season; they are subject to a number of diseases and pest infestations.

Calceolaria amplexicaulis

From the Peruvian Andes, this perennial has erect, branching stems to a height of

3 ft (1 m), and is covered in slightly sticky hairs. The soft, heart-shaped leaves wrap around the stems at the base. Bright yellow flowers $\frac{1}{2}$ in (12 mm) wide are borne in abundance, clustered on sticky stalks in late spring and summer. **ZONES 9–10.**

Calceolaria darwinii

This evergreen, rosette-forming perennial has pouch-shaped flowers appearing in summer in a strange blend of yellow, mahogany and white, and is a favorite of alpine plant lovers. It reaches 4 in (10 cm) in height. Its name honors Charles Darwin who, at the age of 23 during the *Beagle* voyage, travelled into the freezing mountains of this species' native Tierra del Fuego. **ZONES 7–9.**

Calceolaria, Herbeohybrida Group

These are the popular florists' calceolarias, a group of hybrids derived from 3 Chilean species. They are soft-stemmed, compact, bushy biennials often treated as annuals, producing in spring and summer blooms in a range of bright colors from yellow to deep red and so densely massed they almost hide the soft green foliage. Innumerable named varieties have appeared over the years, and they are now mostly sold as mixed-color seedling strains and series. Marginally frost hardy, they can be used for summer bedding but do not tolerate very hot, dry weather. The normal height is 12–18 in (30–45 cm) but dwarf strains can be as small as 6 in (15 cm). **'Sunset Mixed'** are bushy F1 hybrids 12 in (30 cm) tall with flowers in vibrant shades of red, orange and mixes of these two colors; they are useful in massed bedding. **'Sunshine'** is also an F1 hybrid of compact form around 10 in (25 cm) high, with bright golden-yellow blooms, bred for planting in massed displays or for use in borders. **ZONES 9–11.**

Calceolaria integrifolia

Native to Chile, this is a spreading shrub of rather loose and untidy habit though easily kept in shape by pruning, reaching a height of 6 ft (1.8 m). It has closely veined, slightly sticky leaves with an attractive, fine 'seersucker' texture, but is prone to insect damage. From late spring to early fall (autumn) a succession of bright yellow or bronzy yellow flowers appear in long-stalked clusters from the branch tips. It is the main parent of a group of hybrids, the Fruticohybrida Group. **ZONES 8–10.**

Calceolaria tomentosa

A native of Peru, this soft-stemmed perennial species grows to about 3 ft (1 m) with broad, soft, heart-shaped leaves with toothed margins. The golden-yellow flowers have an almost globular 'slipper' about $1\frac{1}{2}$ in (35 mm) wide. **ZONES 9–10.**

CALENDULA

MARIGOLD

It is thought that St Hildegard of Bingen (1098–1179) dedicated *Calendula officinalis* to the Virgin Mary and gave the flowers the name Mary's gold, or marigold. To gardeners of today 'marigold' generally signifies the unrelated *Tagetes* from Mexico (the so-called 'African' and 'French' marigolds). In the Middle Ages marigolds were considered a certain remedy for all sorts of ills ranging from smallpox to indigestion and 'evil humors of the head', and even today the marigold is a favorite of herbalists. The genus *Calendula* consists of 20-odd species of bushy annuals and evergreen perennials, occurring wild from the Canary Islands through the Mediterranean region to Iran in the east. They have simple, somewhat aromatic leaves and daisy-like, orange or yellow flowers. **CULTIVATION:** Calendulas are mostly fairly frost-hardy plants and are readily grown in well-drained soil of any quality in sun or part-shade. Flowering will be prolonged with regular deadheading. Propagate from seed, and watch for aphids and powdery mildew.

Calendula arvensis

FIELD MARIGOLD

This sprawling annual is a common wildflower in Mediterranean countries, where it grows among the long grass of fields and displays its golden flowers from spring to fall (autumn) and on into winter if the weather is mild. The name *Calendula* comes from the same root as calendar and refers to the almost all-year blooming. It is rarely cultivated but, transplanted to gardens, it can make a bright show. **ZONES 6–10.**

Calendula officinalis

POT MARIGOLD, ENGLISH MARIGOLD

Originally native to southern Europe and long valued for its medicinal qualities, this species is known in gardens only by its many cultivars and seedling strains, popular winter- and spring-flowering annuals that remain in bloom for a long time. There are tall and dwarf forms, all of bushy habit, the tall growing to a height and spread of 24 in (60 cm) and the dwarf to 12 in (30 cm). All forms have lance-shaped, strongly scented, pale green leaves and single or double flowerheads. Tall cultivars include **'Geisha Girl'** with double orange flowers; the **Pacific Beauty Series** with double flowers in a number of different colors including bicolors; **'Princess'** with crested orange, gold or yellow flowers; and the **Touch of Red Series** with double flowers in tones of deep orange-red. Dwarf cultivars include **'Fiesta Gitana'** with double flowers in colors ranging from cream to orange, and **'Honey Babe'** with apricot, yellow and orange flowers. **ZONES 6–10.**

Calceolaria integrifolia

C., Herbeohybrida, 'Sunset Mixed'

CALLA

WATER ARUM, BOG ARUM

This genus, a member of the arum family consists of a single species found in cool-temperate regions of the northern hemisphere. It is a semi-aquatic, deciduous or semi-evergreen perennial that grows in the boggy margins of lakes and swamps. It has thick rhizomes and long-stalked, smooth, heart-shaped leaves in a loose clump. The inflorescences are typical of the arum family, with a broad, rather flat white spathe and a short central spadix of very small fleshy cream flowers, which develop into closely packed small red fruits. The plants often called 'calla lilies' are in fact the African *Zantedeschia aethiopica*, not to be confused with the true genus *Calla*.

CULTIVATION: The water arum does best in boggy soil and will thrive when planted in up to 10 in (25 cm) depth of still or slow-moving water. It prefers full sun, but tolerates some shade in warmer areas. Propagate by division in early spring, or from seed in pots barely submerged in water. It will often self-seed if conditions are favorable.

Calla palustris

This plant grows to about 12 in (30 cm) high, and the dark green glossy leaves are up to 8 in (20 cm) long. The spathes, similar in shape to the upper stem-clasping leaves, are white flushed with green and appear through summer. Old spathes persist beneath the clustered head of bright red berries. **ZONES 2–9.**

CALLIANDRA

POWDERPUFF TREE

The great majority of the 200 or so species of this large genus of evergreen shrubs and small trees are native to the

Calendula arvensis

Calceolaria tomentosa

Calendula officinalis, Pacific Beauty Series

Calendula officinalis

Americas, mainly in the tropical regions, but a few are native to India, Africa or Madagascar. A small number are cultivated as ornamentals, valued for their showy flowerheads with numerous long stamens. The flowers are like those of the related acacias and mimosas but generally on a larger scale, usually in spherical or hemispherical heads. The leaves are always bipinnate but vary greatly in both number and in the size of the leaflets; in most species the leaves 'sleep' at night or in dull, stormy weather, the leaflets folding together.

CULTIVATION: Despite their often delicate appearance, many calliandras are tough, long-lived plants thriving in any well-drained, fertile soil in full sun. Cold hardiness varies between species, some tolerating a few degrees of frost as long as this is compensated for by hot summers. Water well in the summer growing season. Propagation is easiest from seed, but some produce few or no pods in cultivation and can be grown from cuttings.

Calliandra californica
BAJA FAIRY DUSTER

A native of Baja California (a state of northwestern Mexico), this is a shrub of about 4 ft (1.2 m) in height of rather upright habit and open branched, the branches with paired prickles at the leaf bases. The leaves are small, with narrow gray-green leaflets only $\frac{1}{4}$ in (6 mm) long. The flowerheads are small and deep red to purplish. **ZONES 10–12.**

Calliandra californica

Calliandra emarginata

A low-growing shrub, or occasionally taller to 10 ft (3 m) or so, this species is distinctive in having leaves with only 4 to 8 rather large leaflets; these are smooth and glossy and up to $2\frac{1}{2}$ in (6 cm) long. A native of Honduras, Guatemala and southern Mexico, the plant is dotted with globular flowerheads through much of the year. Color varies from almost white to deep reddish pink, the bases of the flowers are usually paler. **ZONES 10–12.**

Calliandra emarginata

Calliandra eriophylla
MOCK MESQUITE, FAIRY-DUSTER

Native to the far southwest of the USA and adjacent Mexico, this species makes a spreading low shrub, usually 24–36 in (60–90 cm) in height, with slightly hairy new growths and leaves only 1 in (25 mm) long with tiny gray-green leaflets. The flowerheads, appearing singly from the leaf axils, are about 1 in (25 mm) in diameter and consist of a few rosy pink to white flowers borne at various times of the year depending on climatic conditions. **ZONES 9–11.**

Calliandra eriophylla

Calliandra haematocephala
BLOOD-RED TASSEL-FLOWER, PINK OR RED POWDERPUFF

A native of tropical South America, this species produces large flowerheads around 3 in (8 cm) in diameter. The flowers appear almost year round but are most numerous in fall (autumn) and winter. It makes a large, broadly spreading shrub to a height of 12 ft (3.5 m) and an even greater spread with age. The leaves consist of rather few oblong leaflets about 2 in (5 cm) long, pink-flushed when first unfolding. It will grow and flower well in warm-temperate climates if sheltered from frost. **ZONES 10–12.**

Calliandra haematocephala

Calliandra tweedii

Calliandra surinamensis

Calliandra surinamensis
PINK TASSEL-FLOWER

This tropical species comes from the Guianas region of northern South America. It is an elegant shrub of erect, open habit up to about 10 ft (3 m) tall with arching branches and ferny foliage. The flowerheads are distinctive, forming narrow inverted cones that are scattered along the uppersides of the branches, white at the base but tipped rose pink. They appear through much of the year and attract butterflies. **ZONES 11–12.**

Calliandra tweedii
syn. *Inga pulcherrima*
RED TASSEL-FLOWER, TRINIDAD FLAME BUSH

Native to southern Brazil and Uruguay, this graceful shrub has a height and spread of 6–8 ft (1.8–2.4 m), with many tough stems arising from ground level. Its fern-like leaves consist of numerous tiny dark green leaflets, and striking scarlet pompon flowers appear among the foliage through spring, summer and early fall (autumn). It prefers full sun, a light, well-drained soil and copious summer water. Prune after flowering to promote bushiness. **ZONES 9–11.**

CALLICARPA
BEAUTY BERRY

Deciduous and evergreen shrubs and small trees occurring in tropical regions around the world as well as more temperate regions of east Asia and North America, the 140 or so *Callicarpa* species can be untidy in growth but appealing in flower and especially in fruit. The branches are long and cane-like and the leaves, in opposite pairs, are usually downy on their undersides. In the popular deciduous species, sprays of small pink to purple summer flowers are followed in fall (autumn) by dense clusters of small shiny berries, white or mauve to purple, which may persist into winter on the bare branches. Fruiting branches are often cut for indoor decoration.

CULTIVATION: Only 3 or 4 species are commonly grown in cool climates but others from subtropical and tropical regions make good garden subjects. *Callicarpa* species do best in full sun and fertile soil. Cut back older branches in late winter to encourage strong flowering canes. Propagate from tip cuttings.

Callicarpa americana

Callicarpa americana
AMERICAN BEAUTY BERRY

Not as commonly grown as it deserves, this deciduous species from southeastern and central USA makes a low, spreading shrub to 3–6 ft (1–1.8 m) in height. *Callicarpa americana* has broad, strongly veined leaves with downy undersides. The pink to violet-purple flowers are small but the brilliant mauve-magenta fruit are showy, in tight clusters like miniature bunches of grapes, and the fruit persist well into winter. **ZONES 7–10.**

C. bodinieri var. *giraldii* 'Profusion'

Callicarpa bodinieri
BODINIER BEAUTY BERRY

Very frost hardy and ornamental, this upright, deciduous bushy shrub from central China grows to about 6–10 ft (1.8–3 m) tall and wide. It has dark green leaves with paler, downy undersides, small, dense sprays of lilac flowers and bluish mauve to purple fruit. ***Callicarpa bodinieri* var. *giraldii*** differs in its less downy leaves and flower stalks and is the form most commonly grown; it fruits more abundantly in gardens than typical *C. bodinieri* does. ***C. b.* var. *giraldii* 'Profusion'** bears an abundance of rich lavender fruit. **ZONES 6–9.**

Callicarpa dichotoma
PURPLE BEAUTY BERRY

Native to China and Japan, this species grows only to about 4 ft (1.2 m). It is deciduous with rather glossy, strongly veined leaves and clusters of pink to purplish pink flowers in summer. The flowers are followed by small pale purple berries. **ZONES 8–10.**

Callicarpa japonica
JAPANESE BEAUTY BERRY

Another native of China and Japan, this species makes a shrub of up to 6 ft (1.8 m), the thin leaves drawn out into a long point and with finely toothed margins. Small clusters of pale pink flowers are followed in fall (autumn) by pink fruit. **'Leucocarpa'** has white fruit. **ZONES 6–9.**

Callicarpa macrophylla

This evergreen species from the Himalayas is a giant of the genus, both in stature, up to 20 ft (6 m) high and 30 ft (9 m) in spread, and in its large, pale green leaves which may be over 12 in (30 cm) long. In a warm climate it makes rapid growth, with outward-leaning stems that develop into trunks up to 6 in (15 cm) thick. The small, mauve flower clusters appear in fall (autumn) and are followed in winter and spring by whitish, pea-sized fruit in large clusters. **ZONES 10–12.**

Callistemon citrinus 'Burgundy'

Callistemon citrinus cultivar

Callistemon citrinus 'White Anzac'

CALLICOMA

BLACKWATTLE

This is a genus of one evergreen tree species from temperate eastern Australia, where it grows in moist forest along stream banks near the coast. It was the original 'wattle' of the first white settlers in Sydney, who used its flexible stems for the wattle-and-daub method of constructing dwellings. The similarity of the flowerheads of various species of *Acacia*, also common in the area, to the globular, creamy white flowerheads of *Callicoma* led to the use of the name 'wattle' for these as well, though *Acacia* and *Callicoma* are unrelated.

CULTIVATION: Blackwattle is easily grown in a mild climate, preferring a sheltered site with its roots shaded, a moist soil rich in humus and plenty of water in summer. It may be pruned when young into a dense shrub, or alternatively trained as a single-trunked tree. It is usually propagated from seed, collected in fall (autumn).

Callicoma serratifolia

The blackwattle grows to 30 ft (9 m) in the wild but is usually only half that height in gardens. It has slender, cane-like branches and the branchlets and leaf undersides are downy, somewhat rust-colored. The shiny dark green, sharply serrated leaves are borne in opposite pairs on the branchlets. Creamy white globular heads of blossom are clustered at the branch ends in spring and early summer. **ZONES 9–11.**

Callicarpa dichotoma

Callicoma serratifolia

Callicarpa macrophylla

Callisia fragrans

CALLISIA

Occurring as natives in tropical America, Mexico and far southern USA, the 20 or so species of this genus closely related to *Tradescantia* are evergreen perennials, mostly with trailing stems and rather succulent leaves. The flowers are mostly small and somewhat inconspicuous, 3-petalled and either white or pink.

CULTIVATION: Most callisias are very tough plants, almost as indestructible as tradescantias (wandering Jews), and can be used as ground covers in frost-free climates or grown in containers such as hanging baskets, either indoors or out. They do best planted in a lightly shaded position in moist soil. They may suffer from attack by scale insects and mealybug. Propagate from cuttings or by division.

Callisia fragrans

syn. *Spironema fragrans*

Native to southern Mexico, this species is remarkable for its robust growth and the extensive mats of foliage it can make in a relatively short time. Spreading by long surface runners, it produces numerous crowded rosettes of thick, strap-shaped green leaves up to 12 in (30 cm) long and tinged dull purple at the edges. In time it may mound up to 24 in (60 cm) high, and in winter and spring bears untidy stalked clusters of very small, fragrant white flowers. **'Melnickoff'** is a variegated form, with leaves striped yellowish. **ZONES 9–11.**

Callistemon citrinus 'Reeves Pink'

Callistemon citrinus 'Splendens'

Callisia navicularis

syn. *Tradescantia navicularis*

CHAIN PLANT

Grown for its interesting foliage, this species from eastern Mexico is sometimes found in succulent collections. The stems are quite prostrate, spilling over ledges, and the small oval leaves are very stiff and fleshy, arranged in two overlapping rows and each folded along its center line; in strong light they become tinged dull reddish and spotted beneath with purple-gray. From summer to fall (autumn) clusters of small, stalkless, pink to purple flowers appear from the leaf axils. **ZONES 10–12.**

CALLISTEMON

BOTTLEBRUSH

These evergreen Australian shrubs and small trees bear magnificent long-stamened, mostly red flowers in dense cylindrical spikes. The tips of the flower spikes continue to grow as leafy shoots, leaving long-lasting, woody seed capsules that eventually become half embedded in the thickening branch. Many species have a somewhat weeping habit and a few have striking papery bark, like that in the related genus *Melaleuca*. The flowers are nectar rich and attract birds, including small parrots (lorikeets) in their native regions. The 25 species hybridize freely and seed from mixed stands cannot be trusted to come true. In recent decades many hybrid cultivars have been named, most of uncertain parentage, with flowers in a variety of hues in the white, pink to red range.

CULTIVATION: The shrubby callistemons make a fine addition to the shrub border, where they attract birds. The larger species are popular as compact street and park trees for mild climates. In general, they are only marginally frost tolerant and prefer full sun and moist soil; some, however, will tolerate poor drainage. A light pruning after flowering will prevent seed capsules forming and help promote bushiness and flowering. Prune to establish a single trunk on tree-like species. Propagate species from seed (preferably wild collected), cultivars and selected clones from tip cuttings.

Callistemon citrinus

syn. *Callistemon lanceolatus*

SCARLET BOTTLEBRUSH, LEMON BOTTLEBRUSH

Widely distributed through coastal southeastern Australia, this stiff-leafed, bushy shrub was among the first bottlebrushes to be taken into cultivation. Its botanical epithet refers to a lemon scent in the crushed leaves, but this is barely detectable. A tough and vigorous plant, it usually grows quite rapidly to 10 ft (3 m) but may remain at much the same size for decades after, with a short basal trunk. The scarlet to crimson spikes are 4 in (10 cm) long and held erect, appearing in late spring and summer, often with a fall (autumn) flush as well. A variable species, it has a number of wild races as well as many cultivars, including **'Burgundy'**, with clustered, wine-colored brushes and leaves an attractive pinkish red when young; **'Mauve Mist'**, also with colored new leaves and abundant brushes that start mauve and age to a deeper magenta; **'Reeves Pink'**, a denser shrub with clear pink flowers; **'Splendens'** (syn. 'Endeavour'), an early cultivar making a compact bush bearing bright scarlet brushes over a long period; and **'White Anzac'** (syn. 'Albus'), with white flowers. **ZONES 8–11.**

C

Callistemon comboynensis
CLIFF BOTTLEBRUSH

Restricted in the wild to the cliffs of gorges and rocky stream banks in north-eastern New South Wales, this is a small shrub of up to about 5 ft (1.5 m), with glistening pink new shoots and stiff, often twisted mid-green leaves and rich crimson red flower spikes in summer and fall (autumn) or sporadically at other times. It has a somewhat straggly habit in the wild but this can be overcome by regular trimming. **ZONES 9–11.**

Callistemon formosus

Endemic to a small area of rocky forest country in southeast Queensland, this is a medium to tall shrub of up to 15 ft (4.5 m) in height. The new growths are red, maturing to stiff, flat, pointed, dull green leaves on pendulous branches. The small flower spikes are creamy yellow, rarely pinkish, and are borne in spring and summer. **ZONES 10–11.**

Callistemon comboynensis

Callistemon formosus

Callistemon linearis
NARROW-LEAFED BOTTLEBRUSH

This species occurs wild only in eastern New South Wales. Growing to a height of 6–8 ft (1.8–2.4 m) with a similar spread, it branches from the base with a rather open habit and thick linear leaves. The flower spikes are 4–6 in (10–15 cm) long, red with just a tinge of green, appearing from mid-spring to early summer. **'Pumila'** is a 24 in (60 cm) dwarf form. **ZONES 9–11.**

Callistemon phoeniceus

One of only two species from south-western Australia, where it is widely distributed along streams and swampy depressions, *Callistemon phoeniceus* has thick, usually curved, gray-green leaves and can grow to 10 ft (3 m) high. Its flower spikes are deep scarlet tipped with golden pollen and are 4–6 in (10–15 cm) long. It is one of the most intensely colored bottlebrushes. **ZONES 9–11.**

Callistemon pityoides
ALPINE BOTTLEBRUSH

One of the smallest growing species in the wild, this is often seen as a stunted shrub under 24 in (60 cm) high in its native southeastern Australia, but when cultivated under better conditions may reach as much as 10 ft (3 m). It is also one of the most frost-hardy bottlebrushes, growing at altitudes of up to 6000 ft (1800 m) in the Snowy Mountains. It has crowded, small, awl-shaped leaves only $\frac{1}{2}$–1 in (12–25 mm) long and bears narrow spikes of lemon-yellow flowers in summer. In the past it was known as *Callistemon sieberi.* **ZONES 7–10.**

Callistemon phoeniceus

Callistemon linearis

Callistemon subulatus

Callistemon salignus
WILLOW BOTTLEBRUSH, PINK TIPS, WHITE BOTTLEBRUSH

This attractive small tree has a wide natural distribution in coastal eastern Australia, growing along swampy stream banks. In the wild it may reach 60 ft (18 m) but in gardens and streets 15–30 ft (4.5–9 m) is more usual. It is one of the few species with papery, whitish bark. The narrow, pointed, dark green leaves are thinner than in most other species, and on new growth flushes are a striking pinkish bronze color. The profuse flower spikes that appear in spring and sparsely through summer are normally pale greenish yellow, though red-flowered plants are now also widely cultivated. **ZONES 9–11.**

Callistemon sieberi
syn. *Callistemon paludosus*
RIVER BOTTLEBRUSH

The natural habitat of this widespread southeastern Australian species is gravel banks and rock bars in the channels of strongly flowing streams, so it is adapted to surviving floods. It is a semi-erect shrub or small tree of variable habit, but usually around 6–10 ft (1.8–3 m) in height with silvery pink new growths. The leaves are smallish and gray-green while the cream flower spikes, commonly tinged flesh pink, appear over a long season from spring through summer and into fall (autumn). In the past the name *Callistemon sieberi* has been wrongly applied to the species now known as *C. pityoides.* **ZONES 8–11.**

Callistemon salignus

Callistemon viminalis

Callistemon viminalis 'Hannah Ray'

Callistemon subulatus

An attractive, spreading shrub from coastal valleys of New South Wales and eastern Victoria, this species produces its smallish, dark red brushes among fine, almost needle-like foliage through spring and summer. It usually only reaches a height of 5 ft (1.5 m) and, if desired, can be kept trimmed to a neat, rounded shape. **ZONES 9–11.**

Callistemon viminalis
WEEPING BOTTLEBRUSH

From coastal lowland streams of Queensland and northern New South Wales, this tree can reach up to 30 ft (9 m) in cultivation with a dense, domed crown and pendulous branchlets. The flowers, borne in profusion in spring with repeat flushes through to fall (autumn), have scarlet or crimson stamens. Often planted as a street tree or used for screening, this species is less frost hardy but more tolerant of poor drainage than some others. It has many regional forms and is the parent of many cultivars, some possibly of hybrid origin. **'Captain Cook'** forms a tree-like shrub to about 8 ft (2.4 m); the leaves are smaller than in the species and pinkish while young, becoming dark green. **'Hannah Ray'** grows to a height and spread of 10 ft (3 m) and has lance-shaped, gray-green leaves; the scarlet flowers grow up to 4 in (10 cm) long and appear in early summer and fall. **'Harkness'** grows as a tall shrub to 15 ft (4.5 m) on a short trunk with a dense crown and has abundant scarlet flower spikes up to 10 in (25 cm) long in spring and early summer. **ZONES 9–12.**

CALLISTEPHUS
CHINA ASTER

This genus contains just one annual species, native to China and once included in the genus *Aster.* It is a colorful garden flower, with summer blooms in a

wonderful array of shades from white to pink, blue, red and purple, popular both for bedding and as a cut flower. Long cultivation has given rise to many variants, and plant breeders add new strains just about every year. The 3–4 in (8–10 cm) flowerheads can be either yellow-centered single daisies or fully double. The doubles can have petals that are plume-like and shaggy, more formal and straight or very short, making the blooms like perfect pompons.
CULTIVATION: China aster is usually sown in spring to flower during summer, but the season of bloom is not long and it is usual to make successive sowings to prolong it. It is superlative for cutting and will grow in any climate, from the coolest temperate to subtropical. Give it sunshine and fertile, well-drained soil, and do not plant it in the same bed 2 years in a row—a rest of 2 or 3 years between plantings is desirable to guard against aster wilt, a soil-borne fungus.

Callitris rhomboidea

Callitris endlicheri

Callitris columellaris

Callitris columellaris

Callitris columellaris

Callistephus chinensis
syn. *Aster chinensis*

This erect, bushy, fast-growing annual has oval, toothed, mid-green leaves and long-stalked flowerheads. There are many seedling strains available, ranging from tall, up to 36 in (90 cm), to dwarf, about 8 in (20 cm). Stake tall cultivars and remove spent flowers regularly. The **Milady Series** are vigorous cultivars to 12 in (30 cm) in height with double flowerheads in pinks, reds, white, purplish blue and mixed colors. **ZONES 6–10.**

CALLITRICHE
WATER STARWORT, WATER CHICKWEED

This genus of annual and perennial aquatic plants consists of some 25 species found in temperate regions of all continents. Growing in still or slow-moving water, they have fine, elongated stems bearing opposite pairs of delicate, spoon-shaped leaves, the upper ones often floating on the surface in small rosettes. As pools dry out they often continue to grow on the exposed mud. The flowers are minute, borne singly in the leaf axils, and are soon followed by tiny nut-like fruits that are carried by the water.
CULTIVATION: These aquatics are used to oxygenate ponds and aquariums and to provide shelter for fish hatchlings and food organisms. Plants may rapidly outspread a given pool area and a close watch needs to be kept to ensure the entire surface of a pond is not covered. Place plants or weighted cuttings on the floor of the pond or aquarium or grow in gravel-topped pots set on the base of the pond.

Callistephus chinensis

Callitris verrucosa

Callitriche stagnalis

This annual or short-lived perennial may spread into a large mat in shallow water with weak stems and delicate pale green leaves, some floating by surface tension. The tiny greenish flowers and fruit are insignificant. **ZONES 8–11.**

CALLITRIS
CYPRESS PINE

The true cypresses *(Cupressus)* of warmer parts of the northern hemisphere have their counterpart in Australia in the genus *Callitris*, strikingly similar in foliage and cones and showing a similar range of growth forms. Close examination shows that *Callitris* has its tiny scale leaves arranged in whorls of 3, as opposed to pairs in *Cupressus*. The globular, woody cones likewise have 3 large seed-bearing scales alternating with 3 smaller ones. There is a total of 19 species in the genus, of which 2 are endemic to New Caledonia and the remainder to Australia. Only a few have been regularly cultivated, having similar requirements to *Cupressus*.
CULTIVATION: Cypress pines make attractive lawn specimens, most effective in small groups, and are useful also for screens and hedges. Full sun and a well-drained, light textured soil suit them best. They tolerate light frosts only, and respond to summer watering. Most species can be kept clipped to a compact shape if desired. Propagation is from seed or cuttings.

Callistephus chinensis Milady Series

Callitris columellaris
SAND CYPRESS PINE, BRIBIE ISLAND PINE

This species occurs wild mainly on old, wooded sand dunes of coastal southeast Queensland, where it makes a broad-headed tree of 70 ft (21 m) or more with dark, furrowed bark and very fine dark green foliage. In cultivation it is often strikingly different, making a dense column of slightly billowed form and retaining this shape even with age. **ZONES 9–11.**

Callitris endlicheri
BLACK CYPRESS PINE

The black cypress pine is a long-lived tree growing up to 60 ft (18 m) in its natural habitat in the dry stony ranges of eastern Australia but usually smaller in cultivation. It has a pointed, conical crown, deeply furrowed brown-gray bark, and the foliage can be dark green or slightly grayish. The cones are globular, about $^3/_4$ in (20 mm) diameter, with a minute prickle near the apex of each scale. **ZONES 8–11.**

Callitris glaucophylla
syns *Callitris glauca, C. huegelii*
WHITE CYPRESS PINE

This handsome tree occurs over the plains and low hills of inland eastern Australia and on scattered rocky ranges all the way to the far northwest of the continent. Growing to around 80 ft (24 m) tall with a straight trunk and short, spreading branches, the white cypress pine is an important timber tree in some regions. It has foliage which varies from deep green to a pale gray-green or somewhat bluish shade, and its abundant silver-gray cones release their seed as soon as they mature. **ZONES 9–11.**

Callitris rhomboidea
PORT JACKSON PINE, OYSTER BAY PINE

Occurring widely in the rocky hills and ranges of southeastern Australia, including Tasmania, this species makes a small, columnar tree of up to about 30 ft (9 m), with gracefully drooping shoots at the apex of the crown. The fine foliage is mid-green, changing in cold winters to a deep purplish brown. The woody, angular cones form clusters on the branches within the foliage and persist for years without releasing their seed. *Callitris rhomboidea* will tolerate light shade, and can be trimmed as a hedge. **ZONES 8–11.**

Callitris verrucosa
syn. *Callitris preissii* subsp. *verrucosa*
MALLEE OR SCRUB CYPRESS PINE

Occurring in a wide belt across the southern third or so of Australia, this species is similar in foliage to *Callitris glaucophylla* but makes a lower and broader tree, branching near the ground into several trunks. Its cones are very distinctive, around 1 in (25 mm) in diameter and covered in warty outgrowths. *C. verrucosa* grows naturally on loose sandy soils in areas of low rainfall. **ZONES 9–11.**

Calluna vulgaris 'Allegretto'

Calluna vulgaris 'Anchy Ann'

Calluna vulgaris 'Dark Beauty'

Calluna vulgaris 'Fred J. Chapple'

Calluna vulgaris 'Heidesinfonia'

Calluna vulgaris 'Kerstin'

Calluna vulgaris 'Multicolor'

CALLUNA

HEATHER, LING

The sole species of this genus, heather, is an evergreen shrub and is the dominant moorland plant of the colder parts of the UK and northern Europe; it is closely related to the heath genus *Erica*. White, pink, red or purple are the usual colors for the small bell-shaped flowers, borne in dense clusters. In winter the foliage turns brownish or dull purple. Mostly grown in gardens are the numerous cultivars, selected for dwarf or compact growth and for flower or foliage color. **CULTIVATION:** It is an extremely frost-hardy plant, thriving in very exposed situations and often performing poorly under kinder conditions. The soil should be acidic, gritty, and of low fertility. After flowering cut back to keep bushes compact. In areas with warm, humid summers it is prone to root- and stem-rot. Propagation is usually from tip cuttings or rooted branches can be detached.

Calluna vulgaris

Common heather makes a spreading shrub 12–36 in (30–90 cm) high. The flowers of wild plants are pale pink to a strong purplish pink, occasionally white. Flowering time is variable: some races and cultivars flower through summer, others from mid-summer to early fall (autumn). With over 400 cultivars available in the UK alone it is hard to decide which to mention, but the following are representative and will add interest and diversity to the garden. **'Allegretto'** is a low-growing compact form with cerise flowers. **'Allegro'** is medium sized with a neat habit and purple-red blooms. **'Anchy Ann'** has very long spikes of mauve flowers on 24 in (60 cm) bushes. **'Anthony Davis'** is a good variety for cutting with long sprays of single white flowers. **'Beoley Gold'** is 18 in (45 cm) tall with a spread of 24 in (60 cm) and has yellow-flushed foliage and single white flowers. **'County Wicklow'** is 10 in (25 cm) tall by 15 in (38 cm) and is a semi-prostrate shrub with double, pale pink flowers. **'Dark Beauty'** has rich, deep pinkish red flowers on small, compact plants. **'Darkness'** is 10 in (25 cm) tall with a spread of 15 in (38 cm) and has crimson-purple single blooms. **'Elsie Purnell'** is a somewhat larger bush growing to 15 in (38 cm) and spreading to 30 in (75 cm) with gray-green foliage and long spikes of silvery pink double blooms that are good for cutting and/or drying. **'Fred J. Chapple'** forms neat, dense mounds dusted with white flowers. **'Gold Haze'** has a height and spread of 18 in (45 cm), pale golden foliage and white single flowers. **'H. E. Beale'** is quite a tall specimen to 30 in (75 cm) with grayish green foliage and long racemes of silvery pink double flowers held late in the season. **'Heidesinfonia'** is one of the best of the mauve-pink forms; flowers are produced abundantly on long spikes that are good for cutting. **'J. H. Hamilton'** is a dwarf plant to 6 in (15 cm) with a spread of 10 in (25 cm) and needs careful siting to prevent it being overgrown by larger varieties; it has double pink flowers. **'Joy Vanstone'** has light-colored foliage turning orange in winter and produces single pink flowers. **'Kerstin'** has a spread of 18 in (45 cm) and foliage that turns deep lilac-gray in winter then cream to red as spring unfurls; flowers are mauve. **'Kinlochruel'** grows to 12 in (30 cm) tall with a spread of 15 in (38 cm) and has bright green foliage, turning bronze in the colder months, and double white flowers; it is very free flowering. **'Mair's Variety'** is an upright shrub which grows to 24 in (60 cm) in height with an almost identical spread and has pure white single flowers held on long stems, making it excellent for cutting. **'Mullion'** grows to 8 in (20 cm) with lilac-pink flowers held on short racemes. **'Multicolor'** is 4 in (10 cm) tall with a 10 in (25 cm) spread and is a compact variety with interesting yellow-green foliage tinged orange and red with racemes of mauve blooms. **'Orange Queen'** is a very compact plant grown for its foliage, golden yellow in summer changing to deep burnt-orange in winter; it has single pink flowers. **'Robert Chapman'** is 12 in (30 cm) tall by twice this in width and is an excellent accent plant with golden-yellow foliage in spring and summer turning to bronze shades during the colder months; it has lavender flowers. **'Silver Queen'** is 15 in (38 cm) tall and spreads to 24 in (60 cm) with downy, silver-gray leaves offset by pale mauve single flowers. **'Sir John Charrington'** is 15 in (38 cm) and has golden-yellow foliage during the summer turning to fall tones during winter with single mauve-pink blooms. **'Sister Anne'** is a compact bush that grows to only 4 in (10 cm) high but spreads to 10 in (25 cm) and is covered with mauve blooms offsetting the gray-green foliage, which becomes bronze during the colder months. **'Spring Cream'** is 15 in (38 cm) tall by 18 in (45 cm) wide with cream-tipped mid-green leaves in spring and white single flowers. **'Sunset'** is 10 in (25 cm) tall with golden-yellow spring foliage becoming deeper in summer and turning to vivid fall tones in winter; it has lilac-pink flowers. **'Tib'** has a more open habit with a spread of 15 in (38 cm) and deep pink double flowers during the height of summer. **'Velvet Dome'** is attractive in or out of bloom, forming tight buns of dense, deep green foliage. **'Walter Ingwersen'** has a loose, open habit and

Calluna vulgaris 'Walter Ingwersen'

Calluna vulgaris 'Orange Queen'

Calluna vulgaris 'Velvet Dome'

Calluna vulgaris 'Robert Chapman'

Calluna vulgaris 'Spring Cream'

Calocedrus decurrens

sprays of soft pink blossoms. **'White Lawn'** is 2 in (5 cm) tall with a spread of around 15 in (38 cm) and is a good trailing plant with fern green foliage and white single flowers. **'Wickwar Flame'** is 18 in (45 cm) tall with a 24 in (60 cm) spread and is a golden-leafed variety coloring to red in winter; its single flowers are lilac-pink. **ZONES 4–9.**

CALOCEDRUS

Calocedrus means 'beautiful cedar' and its 3 species, from western USA, Taiwan, western China and adjacent Burma, are indeed beautiful trees, though only the American one is well known in gardens. The branchlets are arranged in strongly flattened sprays, each branchlet with small scale leaves that alternate between large (lateral) and small (facial) pairs. The cones have only 4 seed-bearing scales, lying parallel in 2 opposite pairs, each scale with only 2 winged seeds. **CULTIVATION:** These trees do best in cool, moist mountain areas in full sun or part-shade and in deep, moderately fertile soil, but may still grow well under poorer conditions as small, bushy but attractive trees. If liberally watered when young they will cope better with dry conditions when larger. Propagate from seed in spring or cuttings in late summer.

Calocedrus decurrens

syn. ***Libocedrus decurrens***

INCENSE CEDAR

Valued for its shapely, conical habit and attractive foliage, this species is fully frost hardy and grows slowly to 40–70 ft (12–21 m). The foliage is a glossy dark green and the cylindrical cones open with 3 splayed segments. **'Intricata'** is a compact dwarf cultivar; its twisted branches turn brown in winter. **ZONES 5–9.**

CALOCHORTUS

MARIPOSA TULIP, MARIPOSA LILY, FAIRY LANTERN

Mariposa is Spanish for butterfly, an apt name for the richly colored and patterned flowers of this genus of over 50 species of bulbs, all native to the west coast of North America and Mexico. They produce goblet-shaped, often nodding flowers, with 3 large inner petals and 3 mostly smaller outer petals, on forked or branched, leafy stems in spring and summer. Flower colors range from white through yellow and pink to purple, commonly with red or chocolate brown

Calocedrus decurrens

markings on the inside of the inner petals. The leaves are usually narrow and grass-like—*Calochortus* is from the Greek, meaning 'beautiful grass'. **CULTIVATION:** They are not easy to grow and require care and attention. They are quite frost hardy and do best in a cool-temperate climate in a sunny situation. Bulbs should be planted in fall (autumn) in gritty, well-drained soil; a raised bed is ideal as good drainage is essential. Water through the growing season but allow to dry out for summer. Propagate by division or from seed.

Calochortus albus

WHITE GLOBE LILY

A native of central-southern California, this delightful spring-blooming species has globe-like, creamy white (rarely pinkish) flowers on slender nodding stalks, carried on a branched, leafy flowering stem up to 24 in (60 cm) high, though size varies greatly. The flowers are only about 1 in (25 mm) in diameter and can sometimes have a brownish blotch inside. **ZONES 5–9.**

Calochortus amoenus

PURPLE GLOBE LILY

Of wide distribution in the western USA, this species shares with *Calochortus albus* the feature of small globe-like 'fairy lantern' flowers, usually nodding, but in this case mauve-red to purple in color. The flowering stems are less branched and up to 18 in (45 cm) tall, and the plants bloom in spring. **ZONES 4–9.**

Calochortus clavatus

From southern California, this species carries upright flowers on strong stems that may be up to 3 ft (1 m) tall and sometimes much branched. The leaves are short in relation to the stem. In early summer large, deep yellow cup-shaped blooms with reddish brown markings in the throat are produced in clusters. **ZONES 5–9.**

Calochortus amoenus

Calochortus superbus

This is another Californian species. It has branched flowering stems, up to 24 in (60 cm) high, which bear upright poppy-like flowers in late spring. Their petals vary greatly in color from cream to pale violet or yellow, but are always spotted with purple towards the base and sporting a small chocolate spot in a broad orange basal blotch. **ZONES 5–9.**

Calochortus venustus

WHITE MARIPOSA LILY

Like *Calochortus superbus* this species, also Californian, has upright poppy-like flowers atop a branched stem, and their color likewise varies greatly, in this case from white to yellow or deep red. The petals also have basal markings, but the spots are larger and more reddish, on a smaller pale orange basal blotch. Blooming in late spring or summer, the slender plants grow 10–24 in (25–60 cm) tall, but are usually smaller. **ZONES 4–9.**

CALODENDRUM

CAPE CHESTNUT

This genus contains one beautiful evergreen tree species from South Africa, noted for its profusion of mauve-pink flowers covering the crown in late spring and early summer. It is widely cultivated as a street and park tree in the southern hemisphere and warmer parts of the USA. It needs protection from frost when young but once established will tolerate very light frosts. In cooler areas it may be deciduous or semi-deciduous. **CULTIVATION:** *Calodendrum* prefers full sun and a light, moist, fertile soil with good drainage, and adequate water in dry periods. Young trees can be pruned to shape. Propagate from fresh seed sown in fall (autumn); however, seedling trees may take up to 12 years to flower— grafted trees will flower sooner.

Calodendrum capense

This shapely tree grows to 50 ft (15 m) tall, developing a wide-domed crown. The glossy, oval leaves, dark green above and paler underneath, are dotted with translucent oil glands. The pale pink to lilac flowers with prominent stamens appear in large terminal panicles, and are followed by woody, pustular seed pods that split into a star-like shape to release their large, nut-like but intensely bitter seeds. **ZONES 9–11.**

Calochortus venustus

Calodendrum capense

Calochortus clavatus

Calochortus superbus

CALOMERIA

INCENSE PLANT

Only a single species belongs to this genus from the moist hill forests of southeastern Australia. It is closely related to the Australian everlasting daisies, which include genera formerly placed in the genus *Helichrysum*, some others of these being similarly aromatic. This unusual plant, marginally frost hardy, was introduced to cultivation in Europe in the nineteenth century and was at times quite popular as a biennial summer bedding plant under its obsolete synonym *Humea elegans*.

CULTIVATION: *Calomeria* is propagated only from fresh seed, although viable seed is usually difficult to obtain.

Calomeria amaranthoides

syn. *Humea elegans*

This is a vigorous but short-lived shrub with large tobacco-like leaves that give off an extraordinarily rank, musky smell at the slightest touch. After about 2 years growth a plant produces a giant feathery panicle at its apex with crowded, drooping, thread-like branches from which hang thousands of tiny, narrow, rusty red flowerheads; each head consists of only 2 to 4 tiny florets enclosed among dry chaffy bracts, representing one of the extremes of reduction in size of the typical Compositae (daisy) flowerhead. Growth can continue for several more years, with lateral branches producing panicles from their upturned ends. **ZONES 9–10.**

Calomeria amaranthoides

CALOPHYLLUM

Almost 200 species of evergreen trees, rarely shrubs, belong to this genus, related to the mangosteens (*Garcinia*) and occurring mainly in tropical Asia and the Pacific region with a few in tropical South America. Many are large rainforest trees, others grow on seashores and in mangrove swamps. Their most distinctive feature is their smooth-edged glossy leaves, arranged in opposite pairs and with close-set parallel veins at right angles to the midrib. The flowers are mostly white and fragrant, in short sprays borne near the branch tips, and are followed by smooth-skinned fruits containing a single oil-rich seed.

CULTIVATION: Only one species is widely grown in the tropics, valued as a shade tree and for sea-front planting. Like most tropical plants, they will not tolerate frost and require consistent warmth and moisture. Plant in humus-rich, well-drained soil in full sun. Propagate from seed or cuttings.

Calophyllum inophyllum

ALEXANDRIAN LAUREL, BEAUTY LEAF, OIL-NUT TREE

Occurring naturally from coastal southern India and Southeast Asia to northern Australia, this tree usually grows to about 40 ft (12 m) high with a broadly spreading, low-branched habit and dense dark green foliage. It commonly grows along beaches, providing an effective line of shelter. The blunt-tipped leaves are remarkably shiny and their lateral veins are so close they virtually touch one another. In summer it produces sprays of highly scented white flowers about 1 in (25 mm) in diameter, followed by 1½ in (35 mm) long yellow-brown fruit. **ZONES 11–12.**

Calophyllum inophyllum

Calostemma purpureum

CALOSTEMMA

GARLAND LILY

Only 2 species belong to this genus of bulbous plants in the amaryllis family. They occur in the arid interior of eastern Australia, in the alluvial soil of riverbanks and drainage channels. The deeply buried bulbs produce long, narrow, rather fleshy leaves, and the leafless flowering stems terminate in umbels of small bell-shaped flowers with stamens fused into a yellow corona. The flowers are yellow or reddish pink and are followed by papery-skinned fruits containing a single fleshy green seed, pea-sized or slightly larger, that will germinate without moisture. The genus name is from the Greek *kalos*, beautiful and *stemma*, crown or garland.

CULTIVATION: Calostemmas are easily grown in any sandy, well-drained soil in full sun, or in pots under glass in cooler climates. Plant bulbs in fall (autumn), water well through the spring–summer growing period and then allow to dry out. Propagate by dividing bulb clumps or from seeds, which often germinate on the plants.

Calostemma purpureum

From inland southeastern Australia, this species builds slowly into a tight clump of bulbs that in spring produce rather floppy dark green leaves about ½ in (12 mm) wide and up to 24 in (60 cm) long. The flowers appear from mid-summer to mid-fall (mid-autumn), in a tight umbel on a 12–18 in (30–45 cm) stem. They are normally reddish pink, rarely white, and up to 1 in (25 mm) long. There is a suspicion that the other species in the genus (*Calostemma luteum*) is no more than a color variant of *C. purpureum* with yellow or greenish yellow flowers. **ZONES 9–11.**

CALOTHAMNUS

NET BUSH, ONE-SIDED BOTTLEBRUSH

Some 40 species of evergreen shrubs make up this genus, which is endemic to Western Australia. They have narrow, almost needle-like, deep green leaves, 1–3 in (2.5 –8 cm) long. In flower they somewhat resemble the related bottlebrushes (*Callistemon*), except that the clusters of stamen filaments that make up each flower are fused for much of their length into a flat or concave portion, and flowers tend to be all on one side of the stem, usually the lower side, and open on older wood below the leafy branch tips. Most species of *Calothamnus* have red flowers that open in late winter and spring.

CULTIVATION: Plant in light, well-drained soil in full sun and protect from frost when young. All species tolerate poor soil and quite dry conditions. Although some may become rather woody, avoid pruning too heavily as the old wood is often reluctant to reshoot. They are propagated from seed or small, semi-ripe cuttings.

Calothamnus quadrifidus

COMMON NET BUSH

Widely distributed in the southwest corner of Australia, this is the most commonly grown species. It is a heavily wooded, erect or spreading shrub 6–8 ft (1.8–2.4 m) in height and nearly as wide, with dark green or gray needle leaves up to 3 in (8 cm) long. The flowers are bright red tipped with yellow pollen, their fused filaments divided to the base into 4 strap-like portions (hence *quadrifidus*, meaning 4-parted). **ZONES 8–11.**

Calothamnus quadrifidus

Calothamnus rupestris

CLIFF NET BUSH

Rare in the wild near Perth, Western Australia, this very handsome species makes a medium-sized shrub of up to 10 ft (3 m) tall and nearly as wide. The slender, sharp-pointed needle leaves are slightly curved and only about 1 in (25 mm) long. In spring *Calothamnus rupestris* bears broad clusters of showy flowers; velvety hairs on the large gray-green calyx contrast with the reddish pink bundles of stamens, their fused portions quite broad. **ZONES 9–11.**

Calothamnus rupestris

CALPURNIA

These small evergreen leguminous trees and shrubs are rather similar to the genus *Virgilia* so this genus was named after the second-rate Roman poet Calpurnius, who was an imitator of Virgil. The genus consists of 6 species, native to the wetter mountain areas of southern and eastern Africa, one found also in the mountains of southern India. They have pinnate leaves and pendulous clusters of yellow pea-flowers followed by flat, thin pods each holding a few seeds.

CULTIVATION: Preferring a sunny, sheltered position and reasonably fertile soil, these plants should be protected from frost when young and not allowed to dry out in summer, though they are more frost and drought tolerant at maturity. Propagate from seed sown in spring.

Calpurnia aurea

NATAL LABURNUM, EAST AFRICAN LABURNUM

Native to southeastern Africa and southern India, this small tree usually reaches a height of 15–20 ft (4.5–6 m) with a light, open crown of foliage. The leaves consist of two rows of 1–1½ in (25–35 mm) long oval, grayish green leaflets that may be downy on the undersides. Clear yellow flowers appear through summer in pendulous sprays up to 10 in (25 cm) long on the new growths, even on young plants. **ZONES 9–12.**

Calpurnia aurea

CALTHA

There are about 10 species of moisture-loving perennials in this genus of the ranunculus family, all occurring in cold marshlands and alpine bogs of the cool-temperate zones in both northern and southern hemispheres. With their cup-shaped, white or yellow flowers and kidney- or heart-shaped leaves, they bring bright color to the edges of garden ponds or to mixed borders in moist soil. They spread by thick rhizomes and often come into leaf and flower very early, appearing from beneath melting snow.

CULTIVATION: These very frost-hardy plants prefer full sun and rich, damp soil at the water's edge or in any damp spot. Propagate by division in fall (autumn) or early spring, or from seed in fall. Watch for rust fungus, which should be treated with a fungicide.

Caltha novae-zelandiae

This alpine species from New Zealand grows to about 8 in (20 cm) high and has curious leaves with stalks up to 4 in (10 cm) long but the heart-shaped blade is less than 1 in (25 mm) long and the two basal lobes fold back onto the leaf. From early to mid-spring it produces pretty, pale yellow flowers, borne singly on long stalks. **ZONES 6–9.**

Caltha palustris

MARSH MARIGOLD, KINGCUP

Occurring widely in temperate regions of the northern hemisphere, this semi-aquatic or bog plant is sometimes grown for its attractive flowers. It is deciduous or semi-evergreen with dark green, rounded leaves and glistening buttercup-like, golden-yellow flowers borne from early spring to mid-summer. It grows to a height and spread of 18 in (45 cm). The cultivars **'Monstrosa'** and **'Flore Pleno'** both have double flowers, while ***Caltha palustris* var. *alba*** has single white flowers with yellow stamens. **ZONES 3–8.**

Calycanthus floridus

Calycanthus occidentalis

Caltha palustris 'Monstrosa'

CALYCANTHUS

ALLSPICE

Only 2 or 3 species make up this genus of deciduous, cool-climate shrubs from North America. The leaves, bark and wood all have a spicy aroma when they are cut or bruised. They are grown for their curiously colored flowers, which appear singly among the leaves in late spring or summer and resemble small magnolia flowers with narrow petals that are deep red-brown or dull reddish purple; the flowers make interesting indoor decorations.

CULTIVATION: Undemanding shrubs, they flower best in a sunny but sheltered position in fertile, humus-rich, moist soil. Propagation is usually by layering branches, or from the seeds which are contained in soft, fig-like fruits.

Calycanthus floridus

CAROLINA ALLSPICE, SWEET SHRUB

A shrub from southeastern USA, this grows to about 6–9 ft (1.8–2.7 m) and has broad, glossy, pale green leaves with downy undersides. Its 2 in (5 cm) wide, early summer flowers consist of many petals that are dull brownish red, often with paler tips. **ZONES 6–10.**

Calycanthus occidentalis

SPICE BUSH, CALIFORNIAN ALLSPICE

This species, from the ranges of northern California, makes a shrub of rather irregular growth up to 12 ft (3.5 m) tall. The leaves are larger than those of *Calycanthus floridus* and their undersides are not downy. The flowers are also larger, sometimes 3 in (8 cm) across, but with similar coloring to those of *C. floridus*. **ZONES 7–10.**

CALYSTEGIA

BINDWEED

The English name bindweed is shared between this genus and the very similar *Convolvulus*, both consisting mainly of

Calycanthus occidentalis

Caltha palustris 'Flore Pleno'

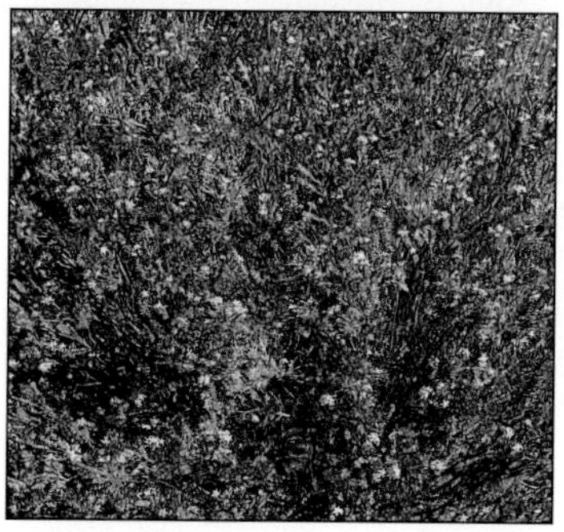

Calytrix tetragona

twining vines that wrap their cord-like stems around other plants. *Calystegia* includes about 25 species, found in most parts of the world, all perennial. The genus is easily distinguished by the large bracts covering the calyx, looking a little like extra sepals. The leaves are thin and vary from kidney- to heart- to arrow-head-shaped, while the flowers look just like those of *Convolvulus*, mostly white or pink. One species, *Calystegia soldanella* (sea bindweed), is prostrate and grows on beaches and coastal dunes.

CULTIVATION: These plants are only occasionally cultivated and are inclined to become weedy and hard to eradicate. They require no special treatment other than a sunny position. Propagation is from seed or by division of the roots.

Calystegia sepium

syn. ***Convolvulus sepium***

HEDGE BINDWEED, WILD MORNING GLORY

Occurring wild through temperate regions of both hemispheres, this is a vigorous climber that can reach a height of 10 ft (3 m) or more. The heart-shaped leaves are up to 4 in (10 cm) long and the white or pinkish flowers, borne in summer, are $1\frac{1}{2}$ in (35 mm) in diameter. It may be killed to the ground by cold winters but its hardy root system sprouts again in spring. **ZONES 5–10.**

Calystegia silvatica

GREAT BINDWEED

Native to southern Europe, this species is commonly naturalized elsewhere. It is similar to *Calystegia sepium* but the leaves are broader and the flowers larger, $2\frac{1}{2}$–3 in (6–8 cm) in diameter. More frequently grown as an ornamental, it is less cold hardy than hedge bindweed. **ZONES 7–10.**

Calystegia soldanella

SEA BINDWEED

This cosmopolitan species of sandy seashores is usually a small prostrate plant

Calystegia soldanella

Calytrix tetragona

but may climb on shrubs to 3 ft (1 m) or more. It has kidney- or heart-shaped leaves up to 2 in (5 cm) across. The mauve flowers are funnel-shaped and prettily striped with cream. **ZONES 6–10.**

CALYTRIX

FRINGE MYRTLE

Calytrix consists of about 70 species of wiry-branched evergreen shrubs in the myrtle family, found scattered across the Australian continent though most are confined to the southwest. The small leaves, often very narrow, contain aromatic oils that give the crushed foliage a slightly pungent smell. The flowers are very distinctive, with an extremely fine tube flaring into 5 pointed petals; alternating with these are 5 thread-like sepals that persist on the small, dry fruits, elongating into fine bristles. The flowers are often massed and very showy, colored white or in shades of pink, red, purple or yellow.

CULTIVATION: *Calytrix* species require very well-drained, light-textured soil of low nutrient content. Full sun and a rather dry atmosphere suit most species. Propagate from seed or cuttings.

Calytrix tetragona

This is the most wide-ranging *Calytrix* species, occurring in most parts of Australia except the central deserts and the monsoonal north. It is also very variable—from 2 to 6 ft (0.6–1.8 m) high—and has many stems from the base and narrow, heath-like leaves of variable length. The starry, white to pink flowers are densely massed in heads at all the branch tips. The bristly fruit, deep purple-brown, can also make a fine display. **ZONES 9–11.**

CAMASSIA

CAMAS, QUAMASH, BEARGRASS

The edible bulbs of these North American lilies were called *kamas* by the Native

C

Americans, written down variously as *camas, camash* or *quamash*, and this was Latinized to the generic name *Camassia.* The genus consists of 5 or more species, some divided into many subspecies and varieties, ranging in the wild from British Columbia to California and Utah, one extending to the upper Mississippi valley. They grow in moist meadows in very large numbers and the bulbs, like rather gummy potatoes when boiled, were an important food item of the indigenous people and indeed sustained the Lewis and Clark Expedition for part of their 1804–6 journey. The plants make tufts of rather coarse leaves from the midst of which rise the flower stems, studded along their length with clear blue, white or purple stars.

CULTIVATION: Camassias make attractive garden plants, very frost hardy and easily grown in most temperate climates. Bulbs should be planted in late fall (autumn) in well-drained, loamy, humus-rich soil. Position in part-shade, or full sun if the soil is very moist. Propagate by division or from seed; the latter may take up to 5 years to produce flowers.

Camassia cusickii

A native of eastern Oregon, this species tolerates drier conditions than most others and is easily grown over a wide moisture and temperature range. In late spring and early summer it produces star-like blue flowers about 2 in (5 cm) across in spikes 24–36 in (60–90 cm) tall. **ZONES 5–9.**

Camassia quamash

syn. *Camassia esculenta*

CAMASH, SWAMP SEGO

This is the most important edible species and also a fine ornamental. It occurs over a wide area of southwestern Canada and northwestern USA. The flowering stems are 12–36 in (30–90 cm) tall and are densely covered with 1–2 in (25–50 mm) wide star-shaped, pale to deep blue flowers in spring and early summer. It is a very variable species and a recent classification recognizes 8 subspecies, likely to differ in horticultural value as well as other features. ***Camassia quamash* var. *brevifolia*** has duller, more gray-green leaves and flowers that are a deeper shade of blue-violet. **ZONES 4–9.**

CAMELLIA

The camellia is one of the most popular of flowering shrubs with the profusion and beauty of garden varieties it has produced. A majority of the many thousands of cultivars now listed are descended from a single species, *Camellia japonica*, introduced to Europe in the early eighteenth century from China. Two other species, *C. sasanqua* and *C. reticulata,* have also produced many cultivars. But the genus *Camellia* has numerous additional species, most of which have never been cultivated. In the wild they are restricted to eastern Asia, ranging from Japan through southern and central China into Indochina, with a few outliers in the eastern Himalayas and the Malay Archipelago. Southern China accounts for the great majority of species, and discoveries by Chinese botanists in recent decades have tripled the number of known species, from under 100 in 1960 to almost 300 at the present time. All species are evergreen shrubs or small trees, the majority with small flowers of no great ornamental value, but there are nonetheless many beautiful species still awaiting introduction to gardens, some having foliage or bark rather than flowers as their chief attraction. The flower color of camellias is always in the white-pink-red range except for a small group of southern Chinese and Vietnamese species that have pale yellow to bronze-yellow flowers—their introduction to cultivation, starting in the 1970s, gave hope of introducing yellow into hybrid cultivars, but success has so far proved elusive. Hybridization between other species, however, has increased from a trickle in the 1930s (with the *C.* × *williamsii* hybrids) to an avalanche at the present time, and hybrid camellias (as opposed to straight japonicas, reticulatas or sasanquas) now account for a large proportion of new releases.

Apart from the ornamentals, there are camellias with economic importance of other kinds. Tea is the dried and cured young leaves of *C. sinensis*, now grown in many parts of the world in addition to its native southern China. Also from southern China is *C. oleifera,* grown there in plantations for the valuable oil pressed from its seeds, used in cooking and cosmetics; several other species are also grown for their oil.

CULTIVATION: Most camellias grow best in mild, humid climates and some species are very frost tender, but most of the cultivars are moderately frost hardy. They prefer well-drained, slightly acidic soil enriched with organic matter and generally grow best in part-shade, though some cultivars are quite sun tolerant. Good drainage is important to prevent phytophthora root rot, but they like to be kept moist. There are many varieties suited to pot culture and camellias make handsome tub specimens. Pruning is largely unnecessary, but plants can be trimmed after flowering or cut back harder if rejuvenation is required. Propagate from cuttings in late summer or winter, or by grafting.

Camellia cuspidata

Native to western and central China, this attractive species has become fairly widely grown in the West and is the parent of a number of fine hybrids. It extends further north in the wild than most other camellias, and is valued for its cold hardiness. A shrub of up to 10 ft (3 m), it has smallish dark green leaves with long fine points, copper colored on new growths. The white flowers, up to $1\frac{1}{2}$ in (35 mm) wide with broadly overlapping petals, are borne in profusion near the branch ends. **'Spring Festival'** has mid-pink flowers and narrow growth habit. **ZONES 7–10.**

Camellia granthamiana

This marginally frost-hardy species from Hong Kong and the adjacent Guangdong Province makes an open shrub of up to about 10 ft (3 m). It has distinctive, very glossy, leathery leaves with veins strongly impressed into the upper surface, and in late fall (autumn) bears large, flattish flowers with parchment-white petals with rolled-back edges and a central mass of gold stamens. It was discovered only in 1955 and named in honor of the Governor of Hong Kong at the time. **ZONES 9–11.**

Camellia hiemalis

The status of this camellia is problematic, and it has frequently been considered merely a cultivated form of *Camellia sasanqua* and indeed the cultivars associated with it are commonly listed as sasanquas. Long cultivated in Japan, it is known there as the 'cold camellia'. One school of botanical opinion now has it allied to *C. pitardii* and *C. hongkongensis* and native to eastern China, another that it is more likely a hybrid between *C. sasanqua* and *C. japonica* that arose in Japan. It is a large shrub with thick, deep green leaves and white to pink 7-petalled flowers up to $2\frac{1}{2}$ in (6 cm) across appearing mainly in winter. **'Shishigashira'** is the longest cultivated form, making a shrub with a dense, umbrella-shaped crown and smallish double reddish pink flowers; it is often grown in Japan as a neatly trimmed miniature. **'Showa-no-sakae'** has irregular double pale pink blooms with a musky fragrance; it has a vigorous spreading habit and can be used for ground cover or espaliered. **'Hiryu'**, an old favorite, is bushy and upright with bright to deep rosy red flowers. **'Somerset'** is a vigorous plant with lighter leaves than most and deep reddish pink, semi-double blooms. **ZONES 8–10.**

Camellia japonica

The wild plants of this, the best known camellia species, are small, scraggy trees 20–30 ft (6–9 m) tall in their natural habitats in Japan, Korea and China, usually with red, somewhat funnel-shaped, 5-petalled flowers only 2–3 in (5–8 cm) across. In Japan the typical form, ***Camellia japonica* subsp. *japonica***, is found in coastal scrubs of the south and is replaced in northwestern Honshu by the more cold-tolerant ***C. j.* subsp. *rusticana***, known as the 'snow camellia'. Selection of desirable garden forms of *Camellia japonica* began at least 300

Camassia cusickii

Camassia quamash var. *brevifolia*

Camellia hiemalis 'Somerset'

Camellia cuspidata 'Spring Festival'

years ago in both China and Japan, the Chinese favoring double flowers and the Japanese singles. After its introduction to Europe in about 1745 an increasing number of these cultivars were imported, mostly renamed with Latin names such as 'Alba Plena' and 'Anemoniflora' on their arrival in Europe, and in the early nineteenth century many new cultivars were raised in Europe also. It was dis covered that new flower types could be obtained both by seedling selection and by watching for branch sports (vegetative mutations). By the late nineteenth–early twentieth century thousands of cultivars had arisen, not only in Europe but in California, Australia and New Zealand not to mention Japan, where new cultivars were actively being produced. Camellias fell from fashion to some degree during the period between World War I and World War II, but the 1950s saw them come back strongly and the majority of known cultivars date from this time and later. Even though hybrid camellias make up an increasing proportion of new listings, cultivars of pure *C. japonica* origin remain as popular as ever. Camellia enthusiasts have devised classifications of the cultivars based on flower size and form: sizes run from **miniature** (under 2½ in [6 cm]) through **small**, **medium**, **medium-large** and **large** to **very large** (over 5 in [12 cm]); forms of flower are divided into **single**, **semi-double**, **anemone-form**, **informal double or peony-form**, **rose-form double** and **formal double**. By specifying their size class and form and describing the coloring, most cultivars can be pinned down at least to a small group. A subgroup of japonicas that deserve special mention are the **Higo camellias**, a collection of distinctively beautiful single cultivars that arose in the southern Japanese island of Kyushu in the nineteenth century, only reaching the West much later. *Camellia japonica* cultivars vary in flowering time from late fall (autumn) to early spring in mild climates, and from early to late spring in cooler climates. They will not survive outdoors where winter temperatures drop much below 15°F (–10°C). Among representative cultivars, some old favorites are **'Adolphe Audusson'** with large saucer-shaped semi-double dark red flowers sometimes with white markings and prominent yellow stamens; **'Chandleri'**, an anemone-form, bright red double of medium size; **'Magnoliiflora'** (syn. 'Hagoromo'), an elegant semi-double with blush pink blooms of medium size; **'Virginia Franco Rosea'**, a small formal double with many-rowed petals in soft pink with faint lines. Significant newer cultivars include **'Betty Sheffield Pink'**, a medium-large incomplete double anemone-form with wavy pink petals sometimes irregularly splashed white; **'Guilio Nuccio'**, a very large semi-double with very broad, irregular coral-red petals and prominent yellow stamens; **'Desire'**, a medium-large formal double with pale pink shading to darker pink or lilac on the outside; **'Erin Farmer'**, a large semi-double in orchid pink shading to almost white with golden stamens in the center. The best known miniature is **'Bokuhan'** (syn. 'Tinsie'), the tiny flowers having a ring of dark red petals surrounding a white bulb of petaloids; it is a very old Japanese cultivar. A fine Higo cultivar is **'Yamato Nishiki'** (syn. 'Brocade of Old Japan') with large single white flowers broadly streaked pink and red, and a very wide circle of gold stamens. Representing a group of cultivars with curious foliage is **'Kingyo-Tsubaki'** (syns 'Fishtail', 'Mermaid'), with leaves mostly 3-lobed; the flowers are medium-small, single and rose pink. **ZONES 5–10.**

Camellia japonica 'Guilio Nuccio'

Camellia japonica 'Erin Farmer'

Camellia japonica 'Bokuhan'

Camellia japonica 'Bienville'

Camellia japonica 'Bob Hope'

Camellia japonica 'Black Opal'

Camellia japonica 'Bob's Tinsie'

Camellia japonica 'Burnham Beeches'

Camellia japonica 'Chandleri'

Camellia japonica 'Berenice Perfection'

Camellia japonica 'Betty Sheffield Pink'

Camellia japonica 'Desire'

Camellia japonica 'Virginia Franco Rosea'

Camellia japonica 'C. M. Hovey'

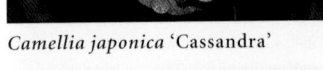

Camellia japonica 'Cassandra'

Camellia japonica 'Dahlohnega'

Camellia japonica 'Debutante'

C.j. 'Dona Herzilia de Freitas Magalhaes'

Camellia japonica 'Dr Burnside'

Camellia japonica 'Elegans Champagne'

Camellia japonica 'Elegans Splendor'

Camellia japonica 'De La Reine'

Camellia japonica 'Fire Dance'

Camellia japonica 'Elegans Supreme'

Camellia japonica 'Emperor of Russia'

C. j. 'Emperor of Russia Variegated'

Camellia japonica 'Erica McMinn'

Camellia japonica 'Forest Green'

Camellia japonica 'Grand Slam'

Camellia japonica 'Great Eastern'

Camellia japonica 'Gus Menard'

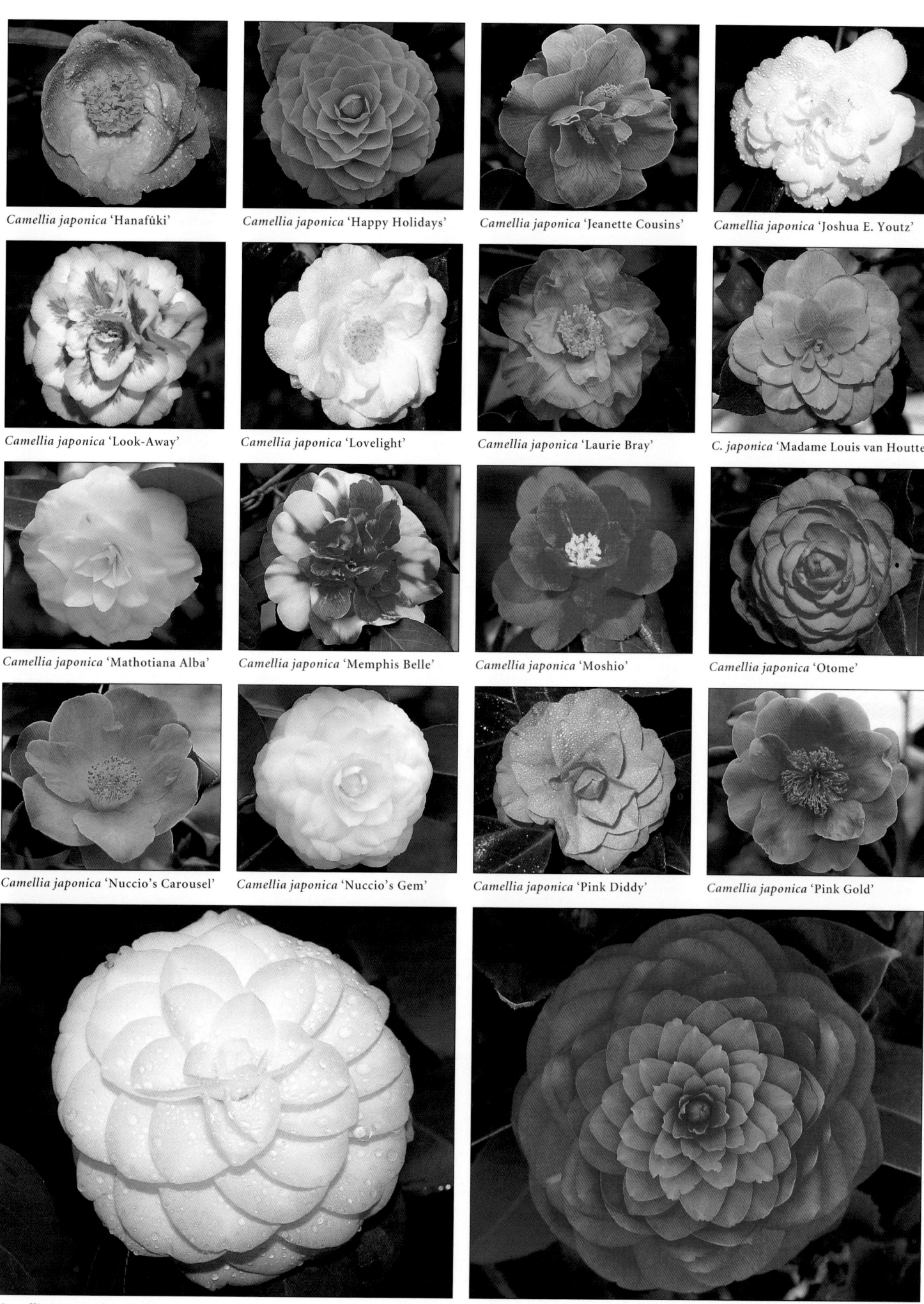

Camellia japonica 'Hanafûki'

Camellia japonica 'Happy Holidays'

Camellia japonica 'Jeanette Cousins'

Camellia japonica 'Joshua E. Youtz'

Camellia japonica 'Look-Away'

Camellia japonica 'Lovelight'

Camellia japonica 'Laurie Bray'

C. japonica 'Madame Louis van Houtte'

Camellia japonica 'Mathotiana Alba'

Camellia japonica 'Memphis Belle'

Camellia japonica 'Moshio'

Camellia japonica 'Otome'

Camellia japonica 'Nuccio's Carousel'

Camellia japonica 'Nuccio's Gem'

Camellia japonica 'Pink Diddy'

Camellia japonica 'Pink Gold'

Camellia japonica 'Mrs Bell'

Camellia japonica 'Lady Maude Walpole'

Camellia japonica 'Pope John XXIII'

Camellia japonica 'Pukekura'

C. japonica 'R. L. Wheeler Variegated'

Camellia japonica 'Red Red Rose'

Camellia japonica 'Roma Risorta'

Camellia japonica 'Rossii'

Camellia japonica 'Royal Velvet'

Camellia japonica 'Shikibu'

Camellia japonica 'Shishigashira'

Camellia japonica 'Silver Waves'

Camellia japonica 'Tama-no-ura'

Camellia japonica 'The Czar'

Camellia japonica 'White Nun'

Camellia japonica 'Wildfire'

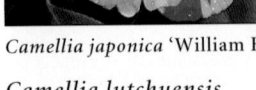

Camellia japonica 'William Honey'

Camellia japonica 'Yours Truly'

Camellia lutchuensis

The name of Japan's southernmost island group is now written as Ryukyu but in the past Liu-kiu or Lu-tchu were common Western spellings, hence this species' name. It occurs in the south of Japan's main islands as well as these subtropical islands, and has become popular in gardens for the delicious fragrance of its small white flowers, usually flushed pink on the outside. The plant is fairly fast growing, somewhat open and upright when young and spreading at maturity with small, dull green leaves which have a bronze tint as they unfurl. **ZONES 9–11.**

Camellia nitidissima

syn. *Camellia chrysantha*
YELLOW CAMELLIA

The first yellow-flowered camellia brought into cultivation, this species caused rather a sensation among camellia enthusiasts in the 1970s, who believed that its genes would allow a range of wonderful yellow hybrids to be created—sadly this expectation has not yet been fulfilled. It was realized from an early stage that the species in its typical form is not a good garden plant, being of weak, lanky form, shy flowering, and prone to sudden death from root rot. The spring flowers are only 2–2½ in (5–6 cm) across, and of a slightly washed-out golden yellow hue. The foliage, though, is very attractive, with large, strongly veined leaves that are very shiny (*nitidissima* means 'most shining'), and the repeated growth flushes are reddish purple. The species is native to southern China's Guangxi Province, close to the Vietnam border. **ZONES 10–11.**

Camellia oleifera

OIL-SEED CAMELLIA, TEA OIL CAMELLIA

This camellia is widely grown in southern China and parts of Indochina for its seed oil, used as a cooking oil and in cosmetics. Its wild origins are uncertain, but botanists believe that *Camellia oleifera* and *C. sasanqua* may have a common wild ancestor as they are without doubt very closely allied. As well as yielding oil, it makes a fine ornamental shrub or small tree and is one of the more cold-hardy camellias. The white flowers are up to 4 in (10 cm) across and fragrant, opening from early fall (autumn) to early winter. **ZONES 7–10.**

Camellia pitardii

An open-branched shrub or small tree to 20 ft (6 m), this species is native to southwestern and central China. Closely related to *Camellia reticulata* and blooming at the same time, it has smaller flowers and leaves than that species but is rather variable: the typical form has flowers 2 in (5 cm) or less in diameter with 5 or 6 rose pink to white petals; ***C. pitardii* var. *yunnanica***, the most widely cultivated form, has slightly larger flowers in the same color range—a very pretty plant, it is increasingly being used as a parent of hybrid cultivars. **'Gay Pixie'** is an Australian-raised cultivar with incomplete double flowers, the orchid-pink petals striped darker pink; **'Snippet'** has a dwarf habit and its flowers have notched margins on the delicate, pale pink colored petals. **ZONES 7–10.**

Camellia reticulata

This species includes some of the largest flowered camellia cultivars, and many of these were cultivated for centuries in southern China before one was brought to England in 1820 by Captain Rawes of the East India Company. It was not until much later that a much smaller flowered plant was discovered growing wild in Yunnan and determined by botanists to be the wild ancestor of these early Chinese cultivars. Many additional cultivars have since been documented, mostly in Yunnan and often as temple trees up to

Camellia pitardii 'Gay Pixie'

Camellia pitardii 'Snippet'

Camellia reticulata 'William Hertrich'

Camellia reticulata 'Cambria'

Camellia reticulata 'Blossom Time'

40 ft (12 m) tall and hundreds of years old—they are known as the **'Yunnan camellias'**. *Camellia reticulata* makes a more upright plant than *C. japonica,* with an open framework of sparser foliage and large, leathery leaves. They are late blooming for camellias, flowering from late winter to mid-spring. The wild form is sold as **'Wild Type'** and has rather irregularly cup-shaped single reddish pink flowers about 3 in (8 cm) wide. The original introduction from 1820, **'Captain Rawes'**, is still admired, with 6 in (15 cm) semi-double blooms of rich carmine-pink, the petals coarsely fluted. Newer cultivars are of more compact growth than this rather gaunt shrub, for example the American **'Lila Naff'**, a single but with multiple broad petals of a most delicate pink, and **'William Hertrich'**, a very large semi-double with deep red petals. Many cultivars that are usually treated as reticulatas are in fact hybrids, with influence from other species. ZONES 8–10.

Camellia reticulata 'Ellie's Girl'

Camellia reticulata

Camellia reticulata 'Lovely Lady'

Camellia reticulata 'Ellie's Girl'

Camellia reticulata 'Curtain Call'

Camellia reticulata 'K. O. Hester'

Camellia reticulata 'Mouchang'

Camellia reticulata 'Rhonda Kerri'

Camellia reticulata 'Ted Craig'

Camellia reticulata 'Zhangjia Cha'

Camellia × *vernalis* 'Shibori-Egao'

Camellia × *vernalis* 'Yuletide'

Camellia × *williamsii* 'Donation'

Camellia × *williamsii* 'E. G. Waterhouse'

Camellia sasanqua

Camellia sinensis

Camellia sasanqua 'Paradise Belinda'

Camellia sasanqua

Originating in southern Japan, this small-leafed species has given rise to many hundreds of cultivars. The most versatile camellias from the landscaping point of view, the sasanquas have greatly increased in popularity recently. They are densely leafed plants that can be grown as hedges and even as street trees, and some cultivars are suited to espaliering against a wall or fence. They have small, shiny, dark green leaves and small to medium-sized, delicately fragrant, mostly single or semi-double flowers in a variety of colors, profusely borne but individually short lived. Different cultivars extend the flowering season from early fall (autumn) to mid-winter. Sasanquas are faster growing and more sun tolerant than most camellias, performing better in mild climates. Among superior cultivars are **'Jennifer Susan'** with clear pink semi-double flowers; **'Plantation Pink'**, an Australian-raised cultivar with larger single, saucer-shaped, soft pink flowers, excellent for hedging; **'Paradise Belinda'**, semi-double with the outer stamens bearing small petal-like organs to give it an unusual effect; and **'Mine-no-yuki'** (syn. 'White Doves'), a creamy semi-double that can be espaliered. ZONES 9–11.

Camellia sinensis

TEA

All the world's tea comes from this species, grown mainly in plantations in the highlands of tropical Asia but also in southern China (its original home) and Japan, and more recently in other parts of the world where the climate is suitably mild and humid. The tender new shoots are plucked, fermented and dried in different ways to give black or green tea. It normally makes a shrub of 6–10 ft (1.8–3 m) tall with thin, serrated leaves and rather insignificant, white to cream with a hint of lemon flowers about 1 in (25 mm) across borne on recurved stalks from the leaf axils; when grown for tea the plants are kept trimmed to about breast height and flowers are rarely seen. ***Camellia sinensis* var. *assamica*** is the Assam tea now grown universally in India and Sri Lanka, with larger leaves and more vigorous growth; it was thought native to Assam when discovered there last century, but botanists now think it may have been brought from China. ZONES 9–11.

Camellia tsaii

Among the numerous small-flowered wild species of *Camellia*, none have achieved as wide a cultivation as this. Its appeal lies in its graceful, willowy habit of growth, with glossy pendulous green foliage and tiny white, fragrant, 5-petalled flowers borne in great abundance along the branches. In its native state in China's Yunnan Province, northern Vietnam and Burma it can make a shrub of up to 15 ft (4.5 m) but in gardens is usually only half that height. ZONES 10–11.

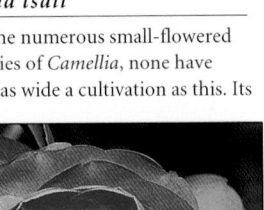

Camellia × *williamsii* 'Ballet Queen'

Camellia × *vernalis*

YULETIDE

This name covers a group of cultivars that are often included under the heading of sasanquas, but are now thought to have possibly originated as hybrids between *Camellia sasanqua* and *C. japonica*. They share many characteristics with *C. hiemalis* and the name is equally problematical, but what distinguishes them as a group is their late flowering, from mid-winter almost to mid-spring. **'Shibori-Egao'** is a virus-variegated form of **'Egao'** that has deep pink, semi-double flowers with a central column of yellow stamens. **'Yuletide'** is an American-raised cultivar of compact, bushy growth and scarlet flowers with prominent yellow stamens, blooming earlier than most of the group. ZONES 8–10.

Camellia × *williamsii*

Although hybrid camellias are dealt with later under a general heading, this group is so well known as to merit its own heading. All these hybrids are crosses between *C. japonica* and the western Chinese mountain species ***C. saluenensis***, or seedlings of succeeding generations. The original *C.* × *williamsii* was raised in Britain in the 1930s and several cultivars became available in the 1940s, soon achieving popularity for their cold hardiness and profuse blooms in clear colors borne over a long winter and spring season. One of the earliest and best known cultivars is **'Donation'** with large orchid pink, semi-double flowers. **'Caerhays'** has medium-sized, semi-double, lilac-rose flowers on somewhat pendulous branches. **'E. G. Waterhouse'** is an Australian cultivar of erect habit with matt-green foliage and formal double flowers of a rich fuchsia pink. ZONES 7–10.

Camellia × *williamsii* 'Coral Delight'

Camellia × *williamsii* 'Buttons 'n' Bows'

Camellia × *williamsii* 'Crinkles'

Camellia × *williamsii* 'E. T. R. Carlyon'

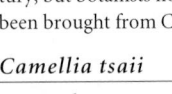

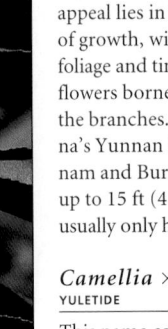

Camellia × *williamsii* 'Orchid Princess'

Camellia Hybrids

Few attempts were made to cross the different species of camellia in the nineteenth century, although hybrids in many other genera were being produced. There were some accidental camellia hybrids from China and Japan, but no successful deliberate cross was raised until the *Camellia × williamsii* hybrids were released around 1940. Hybrids slowly gained in popularity through the 1960s and 1970s and now make up a substantial proportion of new releases. The most widely used parents are *C. japonica*, *C. sasanqua* and *C. reticulata* but many others have also been used, including *C. saluenensis*, *C. pitardii*, *C. cuspidata*, *C. lutchuensis* and more recently some of the small-flowered species such as *C. tsaii*. In this way the diversity of foliage, flower and growth form is being extended. The addition of fragrance to camellia blooms is one direction breeders are taking. Some representative cultivars are **'Brian'** *(C. saluenensis × reticulata)*, which has rose pink pointed petals in a hose-in-hose arrangement up to 4 in (10 cm) across, with a vigorous, upright habit; **'Cornish Snow'** *(C. cuspidata × saluenensis)* with profuse, delicate, small single white flowers sometimes flushed pink, a tall, open habit and very cold hardy; **'Scentuous'** *(C. japonica* 'Tiffany *× lutchuensis)* with semi-double white petals flushed pink on the reverse, the fragrance of *C. lutchuensis*, an open habit and bright green leaves. **'Baby Bear'** *(C. rosiflora × tsaii)* is a small-flowered dwarf form with light pink blooms and a dense habit ideal for bonsai or rockery use. ZONES 7–10.

Camellia Hybrid 'Dr Clifford Parks'

Camellia Hybrid 'Cornish Snow'

Camellia Hybrid 'Scentuous'

Camellia Hybrid 'Alpen Glo'

Camellia Hybrid 'Arcadia'

Camellia Hybrid 'Betty Ridley'

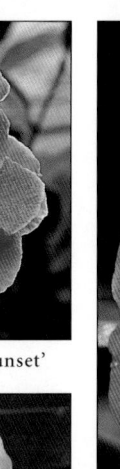

Camellia Hybrid 'California Sunset'

Camellia Hybrid 'Cameron Cooper'

Camellia Hybrid 'Candle Glow'

Camellia Hybrid 'Dick Goodson'

Camellia Hybrid 'Dr Louis Polizzi'

Camellia Hybrid 'El Dorado'

Camellia Hybrid 'Francie L.'

Camellia Hybrid 'Gay Baby'

C

Camellia Hybrid 'Howard Asper'

Camellia Hybrid 'Lasca Beauty'

Camellia Hybrid 'Lois Shinault'

Camellia Hybrid 'Warwick Berg'

Camellia Hybrid 'Nicky Crisp'

Camellia Hybrid 'Snow Drop'

Camellia Hybrid 'Tamzin Coull'

Camellia Hybrid 'Wirlinga Princess'

Camellia Hybrid 'Tom Knudsen'

Camellia Hybrid 'Valentine Day'

CAMPANULA

BELLFLOWER, BLUEBELL

Native to the temperate parts of the northern hemisphere, this large genus includes about 250 species of showy herbaceous plants, mostly perennials but a few annual or biennial. The leaves vary in shape and size, occasionally arising mainly from upright stems or sometimes only in basal clusters. The flowers are mostly bell-shaped but in some species are more tubular, urn-shaped or star-shaped, and come mainly in shades of blue and purple with some pinks and whites.

CULTIVATION: Campanulas are useful for rockeries, borders, wild gardens and hanging baskets. All do best in a moderately rich, moist, well-drained soil. They grow in sun or shade, but flower color remains brightest in shady situations. Protect from drying winds and stake the taller varieties, which make good cut flowers. Remove spent flower stems. Propagate from seed in spring (sow seed for alpines in fall (autumn), by division in spring or fall, or from basal cuttings in spring. They are very frost hardy to frost tender. Transplant during winter and watch for slugs.

Campanula alliariifolia

Native to the Caucasus region and adjacent parts of Turkey, this unusual bellflower has a basal tuft of large, heart-shaped, hairy leaves from which radiate several upcurving flowering stems about 24 in (60 cm) high, with pendulous white flowers about 1 in (25 mm) long hanging in rows from the lower side. The flower bases are enclosed in contrasting reddish brown calyces. **ZONES 5–9.**

Campanula betulifolia

The leaves of this dwarf perennial are often tinted purple while the nodding flowers held in broad clusters are white or faintly pink flushed. A native of Turkey and Armenia, this delicate species makes a dense clump no more than 4 in (10 cm) high and needs extremely well-drained soil. **ZONES 5–9.**

Campanula 'Birch Hybrid'

A hybrid between *Campanula portenschlagiana* and *C. poscharskyana*, this delightful miniature campanula grows up to 6 in (15 cm) high with blooms of a light blue color. **ZONES 4–9.**

Campanula 'Burghaltii'

This cross between *Campanula latifolia* and *C. punctata* has interesting flowers, up to 3 in (8 cm) long and amethyst purple in the bud stage opening to pale gray-mauve. Rhizomes do not creep to any great degree. It grows to a height of about 24 in (60 cm). **ZONES 4–9.**

Campanula carpatica

CARPATHIAN BELLFLOWER, TUSSOCK BELLFLOWER

The slowly spreading clumps of basal leaves of this species make it well suited for use as an edging or rock garden plant. From late spring through summer, 8–12 in (20–30 cm) stems rise above the foliage, carrying upward-facing, 1–2 in (2.5–5 cm) wide, bowl-shaped flowers in blue, lavender or white. The most common cultivars available are the compact-growing **'Blue Clips'** and **'White Clips'**, and the bright violet blue **'Wedgwood Blue'**. **ZONES 3–9.**

Campanula cochleariifolia

FAIRIES' THIMBLES

From the European Alps, this is a plant for the rock garden where good drainage is assured. Flowering during summer on wiry stems up to 6 in (15 cm), the dainty bell-shaped blooms are blue or mauve. The rhizomes creep and branch. **'Alba'** has white flowers. **ZONES 6–9.**

Campanula garganica

The trailing stems of this species can prove too invasive for the small rock garden, but it is an excellent plant for creeping between crevices in stone walls or paving. The open, star-like mauve-blue bells arise, over a long summer period, from mats of small light green leaves. **'W.H. Paine'** has more erect stems and starry blue flowers with a distinct white center. **ZONES 5–9.**

Campanula 'Birch Hybrid'

Campanula 'G.F. Wilson'

Of garden origin with rosettes of foliage arising from creeping rhizomes, this dwarf cultivar has yellow-tinged leaves and semi-pendulous or sometimes upturned, deep violet-blue bell-shaped flowers. **ZONES 4–9.**

Campanula glomerata

CLUSTERED BELLFLOWER

This variable species is found throughout Europe and temperate Asia. The violet-blue flowers are grouped in almost globular clusters on 10–15 in (25–38 cm) tall stems in early summer and again later if the spent flower stems are removed. **'Superba'** grows to 24 in (60 cm);

Campanula carpatica

Campanula 'Burghaltii'

Campanula glomerata 'Superba'

C. lactiflora 'Pritchard's Variety'

Campanula latifolia

Campanula portenschlagiana

Campanula glomerata* var. *dahurica is a deeper violet than the species. There are also double-flowered and white versions. ZONES 3–9.

Campanula isophylla
ITALIAN BELLFLOWER

This dwarf evergreen trailing perennial grows to 4 in (10 cm) high with a spread of 12 in (30 cm) or more. Native to the mountain slopes of northern Italy, it is only moderately frost hardy and is commonly grown indoors. It bears large star-shaped blue or white flowers in summer. The leaves are small and heart-shaped. **'Alba'** has white flowers. ZONES 8–10.

Campanula 'Joe Elliott'

A cross between two lime-loving species, *Campanula raineri* and *C. morettiana*, this dwarf cultivar has open, mid-blue flowers. ZONES 6–9.

Campanula lactiflora
MILKY BELLFLOWER

Native to the Caucasus region and eastern Turkey, this popular strong-growing perennial reaches a height of 5 ft (1.5 m) and spreads into a broad clump. The strong stems bear many narrowly oval leaves. In summer it produces very large and dense panicles of bell-shaped lilac-blue flowers (occasionally pink or white). If the flowering stem is cut back after flowering, side shoots may bear blooms in late fall (autumn). **'Loddon Anna'** has lilac-pink flowers; **'Pritchard's Variety'** has deep violet-blue flowers. ZONES 5–9.

Campanula latifolia
GREAT BELLFLOWER

Widely distributed in Europe and temperate Asia, this attractive species grows to 3 ft (1 m) tall with long-stalked basal leaves and strong leafy stems ascending from a compact rootstock. The upper leaves grade into bracts with lilac to white flowers arising from the axils; the flowers are up to 2 in (5 cm) across, bell-shaped and with elegantly recurved petals. ZONES 5–9.

Campanula medium
CANTERBURY BELL

A biennial species from southern Europe, this is a slow-growing, erect plant with narrow basal leaves. In spring and early summer it has stout spires up to 4 ft (1.2 m) tall of crowded, bell-shaped, white, pink or blue flowers with recurved rims and prominent large green calyces. Dwarf cultivars grow to about 24 in (60 cm), and double forms have a colored calyx like a second petal tube. Grow as border plants in part-shade. ZONES 6–10.

Campanula persicifolia
PEACH-LEAFED BELLFLOWER

Native to southern and eastern Europe and temperate Asia, this well-known species has large, nodding, bowl-shaped purplish blue or white flowers borne above narrow, lance-shaped, bright green leaves in summer. It is a rosette-forming perennial spreading by rhizomes and reaching a height of 3 ft (1 m). Pinch individual flowers off upright stems as soon as they fade. **'Alba'** has white flowers; **'Boule de Neige'** and **'Fleur de Neige'** have double white flowers. ZONES 3–9.

Campanula rapunculoides

Campanula portenschlagiana
syn. *Campanula muralis*
DALMATIAN BELLFLOWER

Native to a small area of the Dalmatian limestone mountains of Croatia, this is a dwarf, evergreen perennial growing to a maximum height of 6 in (15 cm) with an indefinite spread. It has crowded small violet-like leaves and a profusion of small, star-shaped, violet flowers in late spring and early summer. Best suited to rockeries and wall crevices, it likes a cool, partially shaded position with good drainage. ZONES 5–10.

Campanula poscharskyana
SERBIAN BELLFLOWER

This bellflower also occurs in Croatia but has a slightly wider distribution in this part of the Balkans. Also low growing, it is a more rampant spreader with larger, hairier leaves and bears sprays of starry mauve-blue flowers from late spring onwards. It can mound up to 12 in (30 cm) high with an indefinite spread and is ideal as a ground cover, on walls, banks and in the front of mixed borders. Part-shade will prolong flowering. ZONES 3–10.

Campanula rapunculoides
CREEPING BELLFLOWER, ROVER BELLFLOWER

Considered by some a weed on account of the difficulty of eradicating its long rhizomes, this common European native may conversely be useful for the wild woodland garden as it spreads and self-seeds easily. It sends up widely spaced stems to about 3 ft (1 m) tall with serrated nettle-like leaves and nodding violet-blue bell-shaped flowers during the summer months. ZONES 4–10.

Campanula persicifolia

Campanula persicifolia

Campanula rapunculus
RAMPION

This species from Europe, North Africa and temperate Asia is of little ornamental value but is of interest in that its parsnip-like tap roots, blanched shoots and young leave were once important food items. It is a biennial with a short tuft of basal leaves and a flowering stem to about 3 ft (1 m) tall carrying stalked white to light blue or lilac bells for several weeks in summer. ZONES 4–10.

Campanula rotundifolia
HAREBELL, SCOTTISH BLUEBELL

This variable species, widely distributed around the temperate northern hemisphere, has a hardy nature. Loose rosettes of rounded, long-stalked leaves arise from creeping rhizomes, followed by slender, wiry stems holding nodding lilac-blue to white bells during the summer months. ZONES 3–9.

Campanula rotundifolia

Campanula poscharskyana

Campanula medium

Campanula takesimana

A native of Korea, this striking perennial has unusually long bell-shaped flowers, satiny creamy white to lilac-pink outside but spotted with darker purple-brown inside. The large leaves form loose basal rosettes, and the roots tend to spread so the plant forms a large clump. The flowering stems are up to 3 ft (1 m) long but are usually weak and reclining. The cultivar **'Alba'** has white flowers. **ZONES 5–9.**

Campanula vidalii

syn. *Azorina vidalii*

AZORES BELLFLOWER

Campanula vidalii is so different from other campanulas that some botanists place it in a genus of its own *(Azorina)*. A shrubby evergreen perennial, it has crowded, narrow, fleshy leaves and bears nodding flesh pink or white bells of a remarkable waxy texture in early summer on 18 in (45 cm) tall stems. It is a garden plant for warm-temperate climates only—in cool climates it is best grown in a mildly warmed greenhouse. **ZONES 9–11.**

CAMPSIS

TRUMPET CREEPER, TRUMPET VINE

This genus, native to eastern USA and China, contains only 2 species of vigorous, woody stemmed, deciduous vines that climb by clinging roots. The species were formerly included in either *Bignonia* or *Tecoma*, both at one time catch-all genera in the bignonia family, and both now narrowed greatly in scope. *Campsis* species have pinnate leaves arranged in opposite pairs on the strong stems, and large, dull scarlet to orange trumpet-shaped flowers borne in summer and fall (autumn) in terminal panicles.
CULTIVATION: These plants require a sunny site, preferably with some shelter, with well-drained soil. They must be well watered in summer. They can be propagated from cuttings or seed, or by layering. Established plants may be cut back hard in late winter or early spring.

Campsis grandiflora

syns *Bignonia grandiflora, Campsis chinensis*

CHINESE TRUMPET CREEPER

This climber from China will reach up to 30 ft (9 m) with the aid of aerial rootlets clinging to a support. Deciduous and fast growing, it produces eye-catching clusters of scarlet to orange flowers up to 4 in (10 cm) long, the tube flattened and almost closed at the throat, in late summer and fall (autumn). **ZONES 7–11.**

Campsis radicans

***syns* Bignonia radicans, Tecoma radicans**

COMMON TRUMPET CREEPER

This native of southeastern USA can reach heights of 30–50 ft (9–15 m), though in the garden it can be kept much smaller. It differs from *Campsis grandiflora* in its narrower flowers which are open at the throat, usually dull orange or brick-red. Aerial rootlets are produced along the branches but are not strong enough to support the weight of the vine, especially in strong winds, so additional support is required. It flowers well against a warm wall. Considered a weed in the southeast, it is a popular garden specimen in other parts of North America. **'Crimson Trumpet'** has deep velvety red flowers and deep green leaves, while **'Flava'** (syn. 'Yellow Trumpet') has paler green leaves and golden-yellow flowers. **'Flamenco'** is a newer cultivar of particularly fine color. **ZONES 4–10.**

Campanula takesimana

Campanula takesimana 'Alba'

Campanula vidalii

Campsis × *tagliabuana*

Resulting from a cross between the two species, in some countries this hybrid is more commonly seen than either of its parents. It originated in Italy in the 1850s, in the nursery of the Tagliabue brothers near Milan. Often more shrubby in growth habit, it includes several attractive cultivars, most notably **'Madame Galen'** with spectacular salmon red flowers with deeper veining clustered in loose, open sprays throughout the summer months. **ZONES 6–11.**

CAMPTOTHECA

The single deciduous tree species in this Chinese genus comes from the low-altitude valleys of Yunnan and Sichuan and is not regarded as frost hardy in cool-temperate countries. A fast-growing tree in its first 10 years, its main attraction is its foliage, the leaves being large, glossy and strongly ribbed; on new growth flushes they are pale pinkish bronze. In summer *Camptotheca* bears stalked, spherical heads of tiny white flowers close to the branch tips, followed in fall (autumn) by enlarged heads of curious yellow-green, sharply angled fruit which finally turn brown before falling.
CULTIVATION: In a moist, warm-temperate climate and deep, moist soil it makes a handsome tree. It is too weak to tolerate strong winds, which break branches and disfigure the foliage. Propagation is from seed.

Campsis radicans

Campsis radicans 'Crimson Trumpet'

Campsis × *tagliabuana* 'Madame Galen'

Campsis radicans

Campsis radicans 'Flava'

Campsis radicans 'Flava'

Camptotheca acuminata

This tree grows to a height of about 40 ft (12 m) with a straight, gray-barked trunk and spreading lateral branches. Growth subsequently slows and some trees go into early decline. Its expected life span is still uncertain. It is reported to be widely cultivated in parts of China. **ZONES 10–11.**

CANANGA

This genus consists of 2 fast-growing evergreen tree species from tropical Southeast Asia, the Pacific islands and the north of Australia. They are prized for their 6-petalled, wonderfully fragrant flowers borne in pendent clusters. A perfumery oil is distilled from the flowers.
CULTIVATION: Like their relatives the custard apple and soursop (see *Annona*), they are easily cultivated in a sheltered, shaded position in tropical and warmer subtropical areas. They prefer a moist, humus-rich soil. Propagation is from seed or cuttings.

Cananga odorata
YLANG YLANG

This handsome tropical tree reaching 80 ft (24 m) in the wild has pendulous, rather brittle branches and large, glossy green leaves. The flowers, with their long, twisted, drooping, greenish yellow petals and extraordinarily heavy perfume, appear mostly in fall (autumn) in thick clusters at the leaf axils, and are followed by small greenish fruit. The ylang ylang (its Malay name) is widely cultivated in Hawaii for the perfume industry. **ZONES 11–12.**

CANARINA

Related to *Campanula*, this genus consists of only 3 species, one endemic to the Canary Islands, the other two occurring in tropical East Africa. They are deciduous weak climbers or scramblers, dying back to the tuberous rootstock in winter or the tropical dry season, with angular-toothed or shallowly lobed leaves. Large campanula-like bells in shades of red or orange appear singly in the upper leaf axils.
CULTIVATION: They prefer a sheltered, half-shaded position in moist, well-drained soil and must be kept fairly dry when dormant. In cool climates they grow well in an unheated conservatory. Propagate from seed or cuttings from stem bases.

Canarina canariensis
CANARY BELLFLOWER

Inside the 2 in (5 cm) pendent bells of *Canarina canariensis* can be seen a subtle and very beautiful pattern of dark scarlet veins on the orange background. The scrambling stems can grow to about 5 ft (1.5 m) long and produce their blooms in late winter and spring. **ZONES 9–11.**

CANAVALIA

About 50 species of bean-like creepers and climbers belong to this mainly tropical genus, found in all continents and many islands, though most abundant in the Americas. Most of them grow in dis-

Canarina canariensis

turbed habitats such as sandy river banks and seashores. They have compound leaves with 3 leaflets and erect spikes of white, pink or red pea-flowers followed by flattened, ribbed pods that may be quite large. The large flattish seeds are quite poisonous in most species, though several are cultivated for food.
CULTIVATION: Jackbeans and swordbeans can be grown just like ordinary climbing beans. They require a frost-free climate, though can be grown as annuals in cool climates that have long warm summers. Provide a support for plants to climb on. Propagate from seed sown in late spring.

Canavalia ensiformis
JACKBEAN

Native to tropical America, the jackbean is an erect, somewhat scrambling climber often no more than 6 ft (1.8 m) tall. It has large, thin leaflets and purplish pink flowers about 1 in (25 mm) long. The flat pods can be over 12 in (30 cm) in length and 1 in (25 mm) in width, with 2 slight ridges along one edge. The white beans can be eaten if collected when immature and then well boiled, but are poisonous when mature. **ZONES 10–12.**

Canavalia gladiata
SWORDBEAN

From tropical Africa and Asia, this species resembles *Canavalia ensiformis* but its pods are larger and up to 2 in (5 cm) wide, with a prominent ridge on each face. Flowers vary in color from white to red and seeds from white to deep red or brown. As a food it should be treated in much the same way as *C. ensiformis*. **ZONES 10–12.**

Canavalia rosea
syn. *Canavalia maritima*
BEACH BEAN

This species occurs on tropical and subtropical seashores around the world, growing on sandy beaches and ocean cliffs. Its stems are normally prostrate, radiating from a central rootstock and running for as much as 20 ft (6 m) to form large mats of fresh green foliage. The leaflets are rounded and leathery and the deep pink to lilac-pink flowers are borne on short erect spikes. The pods, up to 6 in (15 cm) long, contain poisonous seeds that have sometimes been eaten after roasting or boiling. This species is a useful ground cover and sand-binder for warm areas and will even survive occasional light frosts. **ZONES 9–12.**

Camptotheca acuminata

Camptotheca acuminata

Cananga odorata

Canavalia rosea

Canistrum lindenii

CANISTRUM

This bromeliad genus has 7 species, all native to eastern Brazil where they grow as epiphytes or rock dwellers. They are rosette plants rather like neoregelias, the rosette funnel-shaped and holding water in the base. In the center of the rosette appears a short flowerhead, consisting of a tight clump of small flowers enclosed by a neat ring of short but colorful bracts.
CULTIVATION: Usually grown as indoor plants in cooler climates, in the wet tropics and subtropics canistrums do well outdoors in a partially shaded position planted in low forks of trees or on rock piles, or in raised beds in a very open, humus-rich soil mixture. In dry summer weather, mist-spray frequently. Propagate from offsets or seed; protect seedlings from fungus and scale insects.

Canistrum lindenii
syns *Aechmea rosea, Canistrum roseum*

The stemless rosettes of this species consist of broad, spiny edged leaves up to 18 in (45 cm) long, green with silvery scales on the undersides. The crowded small flowers are white and the surrounding bracts are pale green to white (pink or reddish in **'Roseum'**); it blooms in summer. **ZONES 11–12.**

CANNA

This genus of robust rhizomatous perennials consists of about 25 species, all native to tropical and South America. Belonging to the same broad grouping as gingers and bananas, they resemble these in that their apparent aboveground stems are not true stems but collections of tightly furled leaf bases, rising from the thick knotty rhizomes. Slender flowering stems grow up through the centers of these false stems, emerging at the top with showy flowers of asymmetrical structure. Most of the wild species have rather narrow-petalled flowers in shades of yellow, red or purple. All garden cannas are hybrids with much broader petals, originating as

Canna × *generalis*

Canna × *generalis*

Canna × *generalis*

Canna × *generalis* 'Brandy Wine'

Canna indica

Canna × *generalis* 'Königin Charlotte'

Canna × *generalis* 'Lenape'

Canna × *generalis* 'Lucifer'

crosses between several species in the mid-nineteenth century. Early hybrids had fairly smooth petals in single colors but the addition of *Canna flaccida* genes resulted in larger, crumpled flowers with striking variegations ('orchid-flowered cannas'). The colors of cannas range from the common reds, oranges and yellows through to apricots, creams and pinks. The leaves can be green, bronze or purple, or sometimes white or yellow striped. Plants range in height from 18 in (45 cm) to 8 ft (2.4 m).
CULTIVATION: Cannas thrive outdoors in frost-free, warm climates but if grown outside in colder areas the roots need to be protected with thick mulch in winter, or else the rhizomes may be lifted in fall (autumn) and stored until spring—alternatively they can be grown in containers in a conservatory or greenhouse. They are sun-loving plants and thrive in hot dry weather as long as water can be kept up to the roots, and they respond well to heavy feeding. Cut back to the ground after flowers finish. Propagate in spring by division.

Canna × *generalis*

Canna × *generalis* is the name given to a large group of canna hybrids of unknown or complex parentage. Plants are extremely variable, ranging from dwarfs less than 3 ft (1 m) to large growers that reach 6 ft (1.8 m). Foliage is also variable and may be plain green, reddish, purple or variegated. Flowers come in all the warm shades, either in plain single colors such as the orange-red **'Brandywine'** or spotted or streaked as in the yellow and red **'King Numbert'**. **'Königin Charlotte'** has dazzling red flowers. **'Lenape'** is a dwarf hybrid cultivar with bright yellow flowers with a red throat and brownish red spots; it grows to a height of only 30 in (75 cm). **'Lucifer'** is a most attractive hybrid cultivar with yellow-edged red petals and purple-toned leaves. It is one of the newer dwarf types, growing to 3 ft (1 m) high. **ZONES 9–12.**

Canna indica

syn. *Canna edulis*

INDIAN SHOT

Despite the name, this species is native to northern South America although it is commonly naturalized in warm regions elsewhere. Growing to about 8 ft (2.4 m) tall, it has dark green leaves with purple tones and in summer bears dark red to yellow flowers with very narrow petals, followed shortly by fleshy spined capsules containing black seeds—their hardness and smooth spherical shape allowed them to be substituted for shotgun pellets, hence the common name. Some strains, once distinguished as *Canna edulis*, have been cultivated for the edible starch in their rhizomes, known as 'Queensland arrowroot'. **ZONES 9–12.**

CANNABIS

INDIAN HEMP, GANJA, KIF, MARIJUANA, DAGGA

The only species in this genus is a tall-growing annual from subtropical Asia that has been cultivated for many centuries for two purposes. First, the strong fibers in the stems are traditionally the best material for making rope and were also used by peasants to make coarse cloth. Second, the resin contained in all parts of the plant has a sedative, mildly intoxicating and hallucinogenic effect; dried leaves and flowers are smoked (marijuana), or resin is extracted to make hashish. The active drug is tetrahydrocannabinol (THC), most concentrated in the female flower buds; some fiber strains have almost zero content. Before its cultivation became illegal in most countries, Indian hemp was used by florists to provide greenery for cut flowers.
CULTIVATION: A summer-growing annual, *Cannabis* is adaptable to most soils and conditions and will grow virtually anywhere there is sufficient water, showing a strong response to fertilizer. However, the cultivation of this plant is largely prohibited, apart from a small amount grown for rope production.

Cantua buxifolia

Cannabis sativa

The foliage of this annual plant is rather pretty; the palmately divided leaves have a dark green upper surface and a paler green, downy undersurface. The small, green, unisexual flowers are borne on different plants. It can grow to a height of 10 ft (3 m) or more with a spread of 3 ft (1 m). **ZONES 6–12.**

CANTUA

SACRED FLOWER OF THE INCAS, MAGIC FLOWER

This small genus is made up of 6 species of semi-evergreen shrubs from the Andes of South America, characterized by pendulous, trumpet-shaped flowers on weak stalks. This characteristic is a feature of many unrelated flowers in the Americas that are pollinated by hummingbirds—with their amazing ability to hover they can obtain nectar from such flowers, which are inaccessible to other birds and insects. Only one species, *Cantua buxifolia,* is widely cultivated, valued for the elegance of its profuse flowers often in stark contrast with the bare, untidy stems and branches.
CULTIVATION: Cantuas require a mild climate without extremes of hot or cold, and a sunny open position; in colder areas they prefer a sheltered position against a warm wall. They do best in moist, well-drained, fertile soil. Shape can be improved by tying back stems and pruning back longer growths; however, keep in mind that flowers are borne on the previous season's twigs. Propagate from seed or cuttings, which strike fairly readily.

Cantua buxifolia

This species grows about 6–10 ft (1.8–3 m) high with erect stems and arching branches. The leaves are small, grayish green and rather fleshy. The flowers, borne in late spring, vary on different plants, most evident among plants raised from seed. In gardens a rose-purple shade is popular but pink, white and pink-and-white striped flowers are also

Cannabis sativa

seen. Sometimes the normal pink-flowering form also bears branches with yellow and white flowers and different foliage. **ZONES 8–9.**

CAPPARIS

This is a genus of around 250 species of shrubs, small trees and scrambling, prickly climbers, occurring in most warmer parts of the world. Only two species extend into Europe, one of them the caper bush (*Capparis spinosa*) of which the flower buds are used as a condiment. *Capparis* plants are distinctive for the paired, hooked spines at the base of each leaf, often only seen in the juvenile state, and the attractive, fragrant flowers with delicate white, cream or pink petals and brush of long showy stamens. The knobby fruits usually develop on a stalk that elongates above the persistent calyx. Except for the caper, few species are ever cultivated but they have some use as hedge or barrier plants in hot, dry areas and some are quite ornamental.
CULTIVATION: All species need a climate with long, hot summers, though their frost hardiness in winter varies considerably (zone 8 minimum). They need full sun with very free-draining soil and can be propagated from fresh seed or semi-ripe cuttings.

Capparis spinosa
CAPER BUSH

Capers are the unopened flower buds of this low, scrambling, evergreen shrub, which ranges in the wild from Mediterranean shores to southern Asia, Australia and the Pacific region, though divided into several subspecies. The leaves are roundish and leathery and the fluffy cream flowers are quite pretty. In cold climates it is most successfully grown as a container plant, overwintering under glass, but in frost-free zones it can be treated as a perennial. Harvest the flower buds before they show any color. Often pickled in wine vinegar, capers are used as garnish and in sauces and butters. **ZONES 8–12.**

CAPSICUM
PEPPER, CHILLI

This genus of about 10 species of annuals and shrubs from tropical America is renowned for the hot taste of its fruits, some varieties contributing the fiery hotness considered an essential element in so many of the world's cuisines. There is debate about how and when they reached Asia from the Americas, some claiming that their arrival predated Columbus, but there is no denying that most present-day eastern and southern Asian dishes would not be the same without them. The plants have soft but tough branches and smooth green leaves; inconspicuous white flowers are borne singly or in small groups in the leaf axils, followed by fleshy, hollow fruits that vary greatly in size, shape, color and flavor—generally, the smaller the fruit the hotter the taste. There has been much debate among botanists as to how to classify the innumerable cultivated races into species, though most now divide them among 3 or 4 species only. Some chillies are grown as ornamentals for their brightly colored fruits, though some similar ornamental solanums with poisonous fruits are easily confused with these.
CULTIVATION: The larger-fruited chillies and sweet peppers, as well as the shorter-lived of the small chillies, are grown in the vegetable garden as summer annuals, requiring a long, warm, humid season to ripen their fruit. Give plants a rich, friable soil as their roots are quite deep and ample water must be available to ensure growth is not checked. In warmer areas seed can be sown *in situ;* in colder areas sow under glass and transplant when frost danger is past. The shrubby chillies require only a sheltered spot against a wall in a warm climate, and are easily propagated from cuttings.

Capsicum annuum
PEPPER

This one species encompasses most of the variation in fruit characteristics found in the genus as a whole—from the large sweet bell peppers used in salads to some of the smallest and hottest of the chillies. Despite the specific name, the plants also vary from bushy annuals to quite long-lived shrubs up to 6 ft (1.8 m) tall. The species' main defining character is that the flowers are mostly solitary with recurved stalks. The many cultivars can be divided into a number of cultivar groups, depending on fruit size and shape. The well known **Grossum Group** includes the main salad peppers—pimento, bell and sweet peppers. The **Longum Group** includes the cayenne peppers and paprika and banana peppers, with elongated and usually curved, moderately hot to very hot fruits. The **Conoides Group** includes forms with erect, conical fruits, most small and hot, some grown as ornamentals with multicolored fruits—**'Red Missile'** is a typical example. Its fruit start out creamy white and ripen purple through red. The **Cerasiforme Group** (cherry peppers) have small, hot, globular to egg-shaped fruit; some of these are also used as ornamentals. The **Fasciculatum Group**, known as red cone peppers, have clustered, erect, elongated fruits. Within each group there is a range of cultivars of varying shades of red, yellow, green and purple, and in many shapes and sizes. **ZONES 8–12.**

Capsicum frutescens
TABASCO PEPPER, CHILLI PEPPER

This species consists of short-lived perennials and longer-lived shrubs, the latter sometimes growing to 8 ft (2.4 m) tall and becoming quite woody. They are distinguished from *Capsicum annuum* by having two to several flowers in most leaf axils, their stalks recurved only at the top and the leaves generally smaller. Grown as a perennial, *C. frutescens* has short stems, woody at the base, about 3 ft (1 m) high. Fruits vary considerably between the cultivars but all are small to very small and all very hot; they are used mainly for pickling or in hot sauces. The **Tabasco** strain comes from the town of that name in southern Mexico, while **Thai Hot** is a strain renowned in Southeast Asia for its fierce taste. **ZONES 9–12.**

CARAGANA
PEA SHRUB

About 80 species belong to this genus of pea-flowered deciduous shrubs and small trees from central and eastern Asia, of which several have been established in cultivation in Europe and North America. They are curious plants of a rather subdued attraction, with lemon yellow, orange or reddish flowers and small, pinnate leaves, in some species associated with weak spines. Slender, straw-colored pods appear in fall (autumn) after the flowers.
CULTIVATION: Although at their best in climates with cold winters and hot, dry summers, caraganas are adaptable in this respect with root systems not prone to rot diseases. Most are very frost hardy. They set plenty of seed in the pods, which ripen in mid-summer and provide an easy means of propagation.

Caragana arborescens
SIBERIAN PEA TREE

This is the tallest species, attaining a height of 12–20 ft (3.5–6 m). A native of central Asia, Siberia and Mongolia, it has been cultivated in western Europe for almost 250 years and is valued for its frost hardiness and tolerance of poor conditions. The leaves are soft and spineless, consisting of 8 to 12 fresh green leaflets. Loose clusters of slender-stalked, pale yellow flowers hang among the leaves from late spring to early summer. Several cultivars have been named, including **'Lorbergii'** with long narrow leaves and small flowers; **'Pendula'** with weeping branches, which is usually grafted onto a standard; and **'Walker'**, a dwarf spreading plant used as a ground cover. **ZONES 3–9.**

Caragana pygmaea
PYGMY PEA TREE

Found in temperate Asia from the Caucasus to eastern Siberia, this low-growing shrub of no more than 3 ft (1 m) high, is often semi-prostrate and with long, weak branches. The leaves are small, each with 4 narrow leaflets. One inch (25 mm) long yellow flowers hang on individual stalks from the leaf axils of the previous year's wood, in late spring and early summer. It is sometimes grafted onto a *Caragana arborescens* standard. **ZONES 3–9.**

CARDAMINE
BITTERCRESS

This genus of the mustard family includes 150 or more species of annuals and perennials from most parts of the world, usually with dissected or compound leaves forming basal tufts and on lower parts of the flowering stems. Small, 4-petalled, white, pink or purple flowers like small stocks open progressively up the stem and are followed by slender pods that split apart suddenly, flinging the minute seeds a short distance. They are found in shady, moist habitats, some forming large mats, but the genus also includes several common small weeds, for example ***Cardamine hirsuta*** which can be eaten like watercress.
CULTIVATION: Given moist soil and full or part shade, these soft-leafed plants can be planted in a woodland garden or in an informal border, where their foliage makes an attractive ground cover.

Cardamine californica
syn. ***Dentaria californica***
MILK MAIDS, TOOTHWORT

With leaves divided into 3 leaflets, this rhizomatous perennial, native to California, has light pink flowers crowded onto short stems during the spring. **ZONES 6–9.**

Capsicum annuum 'Red Missile'

Capparis spinosa

Capparis spinosa

Cardamine pratensis
CUCKOO FLOWER, LADY'S SMOCK

Native to Europe, temperate Asia and North America, this perennial is ideal for informal and woodland gardens. It has a graceful habit, forming a loose clump about 12 in (30 cm) high. The mid-green leaves are divided into rounded leaflets; pale pink to white flowers are borne in spring. **'Flore Pleno'** is a popular double-flowered pink form. **ZONES 3–9.**

Cardamine raphanifolia
syn. *Cardamine latifolia*

The botanical name of this species, native to southern Europe and western Asia, means 'radish-leafed' and its leaves do resemble those of a small radish plant. It is a perennial of up to about 24 in (60 cm) tall, the stems springing from a creeping rhizome. The flowers are pinkish purple, borne from late spring to mid-summer. Coming from stream banks and damp woodland, it will take sun as long as its roots are kept moist. **ZONES 7–9.**

CARDIOCRINUM

Knowing a little of how a plant's name is formed may enable us to picture the plant itself and *Cardiocrinum* is a good example, as it is made up from the Greek *kardia* meaning heart and *krinon*, a type of lily. The leaves are heart-shaped and the magnificent flowers are lily-like. This genus includes 3 species from cool-temperate regions of eastern Asia, all of which are monocarpic (the plant dies after flowering); however, many offsets are produced. **CULTIVATION:** The species occur naturally in moist forest areas, and this habitat can be duplicated in a woodland setting where deep soil and nutrient-rich humus is available, ideally on a gentle slope to ensure excess water drains away. Plant bulbs in fall (autumn) just below the surface, ensuring ample room between bulbs for best effect. Water and fertilize well once the shoots appear. The main bulb dies after flowering but propagation is possible from offsets (which flower in 3 or 4 years) and seed. Buying 3 sizes of bulbs will ensure some flowers each year. Snails and slugs can be a problem.

Cardiocrinum giganteum
syn. *Lilium giganteum*
GIANT LILY

Native to mountains of central and western China, this is a magnificent, summer-flowering plant reaching up to 12 ft (3.5 m). Unfortunately, the giant lily is not for the gardener who needs to see overnight results, as a small bulb planted today is unlikely to flower in less than 3 or 4 years. The tall, sturdy stem bears up to 20 trumpet-shaped flowers, each about 10 in (25 cm) long; they are cream, striped with maroon-red blotches in the throat and are heavily scented. **ZONES 6–9.**

Cardamine raphanifolia

Carex 'Everbright'

Carex 'Little Red'

Carex albula

Cardiocrinum giganteum

Cardiospermum halicacabum

CARDIOSPERMUM

This is a genus of 14 species of vigorous, fast-growing, evergreen climbers from tropical and South America one of them naturalized in all warm regions of the world. They climb by tendrils and need support. They have soft green foliage consisting of coarsely serrated leaflets and small white flowers, but it is the inflated, balloon-like seed pods that are their most distinctive feature—the pods split at maturity into 3 delicate segments, each with a hard black seed attached, that float to the earth with a spinning motion. They are grown as curiosities in cool-climate conservatories and one species is valued as a folk medicine in tropical Asia, but in some warm regions they can become troublesome weeds, smothering native trees and other vegetation. **CULTIVATION:** In warm climates these vines self-sow and regenerate from very small sections of root, however, in colder climates seed can be planted *in situ*. They need well-drained, fertile soil and a reasonably long, dry summer period to enable the seed cases to develop and dry to their attractive straw color.

Cardiospermum grandiflorum
HEART SEED, BALLOON VINE, LOVE-IN-A-PUFF

From South America, this tough-stemmed climber scrambles by tendrils up to the light to heights of 25 ft (8 m) or more, and can cover surrounding shrubs and trees in a very short time if not checked. However, contained on a lattice fence or similar the delicate foliage makes an attractive, light, quick cover and is interspersed with short sprays of creamy white, lightly fragrant, tiny blooms in summer, followed by the interesting golf-ball sized, green, 3-sided fruit capsules. These age to a straw color before releasing the rounded black seeds attached to a papery wing. **ZONES 10–12.**

Cardiospermum halicacabum
BALLOON VINE

Occurring widely through the world's tropics, this fast-growing vine climbs by tendrils and is usually grown in colder climates as an annual. It has hairy, pale green leaves with oblong, 3-lobed leaflets that are pointed and toothed. In summer there are clusters of inconspicuous white flowers. These are followed by papery, inflated, straw-colored fruit enclosing black seeds. The balloon vine is used in Indian traditional medicine. **ZONES 10–12.**

Carex comans

CAREX
SEDGE

This large genus of sedges contains over 1,500 species of deciduous or evergreen, usually clump-forming perennials. Most species have sharp-edged, grass-like leaves often with drooping tips, and tiny flowers arranged in catkin-like spikes. They occur worldwide but with the greatest concentration of species in cooler temperate parts of the northern hemisphere, including arctic and subarctic regions. The majority grow in bogs and swamps, and they form the characteristic vegetation of fens. With the growing interest in recent years in ornamental grasses and sedges, a number of species of *Carex* have been grown for their ornamental qualities; east Asian and New Zealand natives are prominent among them. There are also a number of attractive cultivars including **'Everbright'**, which forms a tussock of long, narrow leaves that are creamy white with green margins, and **'Little Red'**, resembling a tuft of dry grass; its long, very narrow leaves a reddish brown.
CULTIVATION: Their cultivation requirements vary, although most species need full sun or part-shade and watering only when surface roots seem dry. Propagate from seed or by division of clumps.

Carex albula
syn. *Carex* 'Frosted Curls'

This is one of the most striking sedges by reason of its pale buff-colored or almost silvery white, very fine and curly foliage. An evergreen, *Carex albula* grows wild in very dry tussock grassland on hills in the north of New Zealand's South Island, one of the country's lowest rainfall areas. It forms a soft, rounded tussock of up to 12 in (30 cm) high, and the inconspicuous summer-flowering stems are hidden beneath the leaves. This plant was introduced to gardens under the cultivar name 'Frosted Curls' before its correct botanical identity was established. **ZONES 7–9.**

Carex comans
NEW ZEALAND HAIR SEDGE

Native to New Zealand, *Carex comans* occurs there widely and in diverse habitats. It forms dense evergreen tufts about 12 in (30 cm) high of very fine foliage that varies in color from greenish yellow to reddish brown, deepening in winter. In summer it produces fine flowering stems shorter than the leaves but elongating and bending to the ground as they run to seed. **ZONES 6–10.**

Carex dipsacea

Another evergreen New Zealand species, *Carex dipsacea* is found in a wide range of natural habitats. It grows in large coarse tufts up to 30 in (75 cm) high, the foliage pale green to rather reddish and harsh to the touch. The summer-flowering stems are erect but shorter than the leaves and bear short brownish catkins. **ZONES 7–10.**

Carex elata

syn. *Carex stricta*

TUFTED SEDGE

Native to Europe and North Africa, this deciduous sedge is useful for growing in damp places and beside ponds. It is a fast-spreading plant with new shoots springing from rhizomes to form broad-based tufts of foliage about 18 in (45 cm) high, from which arise in summer erect flowering stems up to 3 ft (1 m) high with dark brown spikes. In gardens it is known by the cultivar **'Aurea'** (Bowles' golden sedge), with new foliage yellow-green changing to golden yellow in fall (autumn). **ZONES 3–9.**

Carex flagellifera

syn. *Carex lucida*

WEEPING BROWN NEW ZEALAND SEDGE

This New Zealand evergreen species forms tufts of fine, curled, bronze-brown foliage. It is remarkable for the way the leaf-like flowering stems elongate with the growing fruit, often to 3–4 ft (1–1.2 m), eventually becoming a tangled heap on the ground. The actual flowers and fruit are tiny and hardly noticeable. *C. flagellifera* is popular for planting in rockeries, pots and on banks, forming spreading clumps 12 in (30 cm) high. **ZONES 6–10.**

Carex elata 'Aurea'

Carex fraseri

Carex nudata

Carex fraseri

syn. *Cymophyllus fraseri*

Native to the Appalachian Mountains of eastern USA, this is distinctive among *Carex* species for its very broad deciduous leaves, about 1 in (25 mm) wide and mostly 10–18 in (25–45 cm) long, which emerge only after the flowering stems have elongated in spring and with only one leaf to each stem. Many botanists prefer to place it in a separate genus, *Cymophyllus*, on account of this unique characteristic. It is a woodland plant, liking moist soil and being tolerant of shade. **ZONES 5–9.**

Carex grayi

MACE SEDGE

A deciduous species of wide occurrence in eastern North America, *Carex grayi* makes an erect clump of coarse foliage 24 in (60 cm) or more high; the pale green leaves are harsh textured and about ⅓ in (8 mm) wide. Leafy flowering stems emerge in summer, with many heads of green flowers clustered at the ends; these quickly mature to long-pointed seed that give an interesting spiky effect to the heads, and they can be used for indoor decoration. **ZONES 3–9.**

Carex flagellifera

Carex morrowii 'Variegata'

Carex spissa

Carex testacea

Carex morrowii

JAPANESE SEDGE

Native to Japan, this evergreen sedge makes a soft clump of recurving, fine-pointed leaves 8–12 in (20–30 cm) high. Insignificant flowers appear in summer on short stems. Variegated cultivars are more popular. **'Variegata'** has white-striped, rich green leaves; **'Bressingham'** and **'Fisher'** are very similar. These are especially well suited to rock gardens, or among poolside rocks. **ZONES 7–10.**

Carex nudata

CALIFORNIA BLACK FLOWERING SEDGE

From the coastal hills of northern California, often along watercourses, this sedge has striking almost black flowers in early spring. Leaves are dull green, about 24 in (60 cm) long and ¼ in (6 mm) wide. In fall (autumn), the clump turns bright yellow with red tints, drying to brown in winter. It is fully frost hardy. **ZONES 7–9.**

Carex spissa

SAN DIEGO SEDGE

A native of boggy ground in southern California, this evergreen sedge produces a clump of upright blue-gray leaves 4 ft (1.2 m) or more tall. Golden tan flowers on tall stems appear in spring. It is moderately frost hardy. **ZONES 8–10.**

Carex testacea

This evergreen New Zealand species is fairly similar to *Carex flagellifera* with fine brownish foliage forming a clump about 24 in (60 cm) high, but its fine flowering stems elongate even more in the fruiting stage, sometimes to as much as 10 ft (3 m). **ZONES 7–10.**

Carex grayi

Carex tumulicola

Carex tumulicola

BERKELEY SEDGE

An evergreen from northern California, this sedge grows into a rounded tuft about 12 in (30 cm) tall and wide. In ideal conditions it can grow to twice those dimensions. Leaves are dark, glossy green and at least 12 in (30 cm) long, but very narrow. Insignificant flowers are held over the plant in spring. It is moderately frost hardy. **ZONES 8–10.**

CARICA

PAPAYA, PAWPAW

Large, succulent, edible fruits characterize this genus of 22 species from Central and South America. One species, *Carica papaya*, is grown throughout the tropics for its large, sweet fruit, and two or three others with slightly smaller fruit are cultivated to a more limited extent. Although ultimately tree sized, they remain soft wooded and are short lived. The very large leaves are mostly deeply lobed in a snowflake-like pattern. Male and female flowers are normally borne on separate trees, but hermaphrodite trees have been developed in cultivation. The small, cream, male flowers are in long-stalked panicles while the larger, fleshy females are stalkless and solitary. Female flowers are followed by pointed cylindrical fruits, which usually yellow as they ripen.

CULTIVATION: Papayas can only be grown outdoors in frost-free or near frost-free climates. The lowland tropical species are not really suitable for frost-free temperate regions but may be induced to ripen their fruits against a hot wall, or can be container grown in greenhouses. Plant in rich, moist, well-drained soil in sun or part-shade. Propagate from seed or cuttings or by grafting.

Carnegiea gigantea

Carissa macrocarpa

Carmichaelia odorata

Carmichaelia odorata

Carica papaya

Carica papaya

Carica papaya

This, the true papaya, is very much a tropical plant and will not tolerate freezing or even prolonged cold temperatures above freezing. It grows up to 20 ft (6 m) high with a single trunk and a palm-like head of foliage. The leaves are up to 24 in (60 cm) across and are carried on 24 in (60 cm) stems. Young plants fruit most heavily and it is wise to keep a succession of plants coming on as replacements. **ZONES 10–12.**

CARISSA

This genus is made up of 20 species of attractive evergreen, spiny shrubs that occur in eastern and southern Africa, Asia and Australia. They are grown as hedges and container plants in warm-climate areas, and are valued for their masses of sweet-scented flowers, mostly snow white, and for their neat appearance. All species bear edible fruits that are enjoyed by both humans and birds. The glossy green leaves are thick and tough; the leaves and stems exude a milky sap when they are cut or broken.
CULTIVATION: These shrubs prefer warm summers and moderate rainfall, and require full sun and well-drained soil. Plants in pots need moderate water in the growing season, less in winter. Propagate from seed when ripe in fall (autumn) or from cuttings in summer.

Carissa bispinosa
HEDGE THORN, NUM-NUM

Growing to 10 ft (3 m), this evergreen shrub from southern Africa is armed with repeatedly forked spines which, together with its being able to tolerate frequent clipping, makes it an ideal hedging shrub. Tiny white tubular flowers are held in clusters during summer and are followed by red fruit, ripening to purple as they mature. **ZONES 9–12.**

Carissa macrocarpa
syn. ***Carissa grandiflora***
NATAL PLUM

Occurring naturally on margins of evergreen forest on the east coast of southern Africa, this dense shrub grows quickly to a height of 10 ft (3 m) and a spread of 15 ft (4.5 m). The small, rounded leaves have long, sharp spines among them. The white flowers appear from spring to summer. The fruit that follow are red, fleshy and oval; they can be made into a delicious jelly. *Carissa macrocarpa* tolerates salt-laden winds. **'Horizontalis'** is a dense, trailing cultivar with bright red fruit. **'Emerald Carpet'** grows to about 60 cm (24 in). **ZONES 9–11.**

CARLINA
CARLINE THISTLE

Around 25 species belong to this genus of thistles, native to the Mediterranean region, Canary Islands and western Asia. The name has a romantic origin, based on the legend that Charlemagne (*Carolus* in Latin) had one of these thistles revealed to him by an angel as the plant that would avert a plague that was laying low his army. They include annuals and perennials with basal rosettes of leaves armed with sharp spines. The flowering stems bear one to several large flowerheads with densely massed florets surrounded by showy, pale papery bracts that are quite glossy. Like most thistle genera, it contains species regarded as troublesome weeds in some parts of the world, but some of them also make interesting ornamentals.
CULTIVATION: These thistles are easily grown in temperate climates in a dry, sunny spot in well-drained soil of low fertility; the smaller species are well suited to rock gardens. Propagate from seed sown in fall (autumn).

Carlina acaulis
STEMLESS CARLINE THISTLE

Native to southern and eastern Europe, where it grows on dry mountain slopes, this unusual species makes a rosette up to 24 in (60 cm) wide of grayish, spiny basal leaves. In late spring a single flowerhead appears in its center, about 4 in (10 cm) in diameter with silvery or pinkish bracts surrounding pale brownish disc florets. The flowerhead is normally stemless but may be supported on a short stem, and the plant may die after flowering and seeding. **ZONES 5–9.**

CARMICHAELIA

Apart from one species endemic to nearby Lord Howe Island, all 40 species of this genus of interesting deciduous pea-flowered shrubs and small trees are from New Zealand, where they occur in a wide range of habitats. Their small leaves, consisting of 3 leaflets, are scarce or absent on the adult plants of most species, the flattened green branchlets taking over their photosynthetic function. The flowers, mostly quite small, from white to pinkish or purplish, are freely produced in small clusters along the branchlets; they are often scented. Seeds are borne singly or a few together in small pods of unusual structure, the softer 'shell' shedding to expose the red or orange seed encircled by the persistent pod rim. Carmichaelias are not often cultivated outside their native areas, but many species have ornamental qualities.
CULTIVATION: Plant in sun or part-shade. They tolerate exposure and dry soil, but the taller species respond to shelter and better soil with denser foliage and more abundant flowers. Propagation is normally from seed, cuttings being difficult to strike.

Carmichaelia arborea

One of the largest growing species, *Carmichaelia arborea* can become a small tree of about 15 ft (4.5 m) with a woody, low-branching trunk and broad, bushy crown; more commonly it is seen as a broadly spreading shrub half that height. The massed branchlets are very narrow and dull olive green. The tiny purple and white flowers are borne in great profusion in summer. **ZONES 8–10.**

Carmichaelia odorata
SCENTED BROOM

This New Zealand species makes a shrub of 4–6 ft (1.2–1.8 m) tall with spreading branches and massed, drooping branchlets that are very narrow. In late spring and summer it bears an abundance of sweetly scented white flowers with purple veins on short, erect spikes. **ZONES 9–10.**

Carmichaelia williamsii

From northeast New Zealand, this species bears pink-veined, creamy yellow flowers from late spring to early summer with occasional flowers at other times. The slightly honey-scented flowers are followed by large seed pods. **ZONES 8–10.**

CARNEGIEA
GIANT SAGUARO

The sole species in this cactus genus is an upright plant of candelabra-like form that towers majestically over the low-growing shrubs common in its desert homelands of western Mexico, Arizona and southern California. Due to its slow growth this dramatic plant is seldom propagated and sold in ordinary nurseries, but mature plants are frequently poached from the wild, a cause of great concern to conservation authorities.
CULTIVATION: In a low-humidity, low-rainfall climate this cactus is suitable for garden or container cultivation, though it is not very easy to grow away from its native climate. Plant in humus-rich, gritty, very well-drained soil in full sun. Propagate from seed or offsets.

Carnegiea gigantea
syn. ***Cereus giganteus***
SAGUARO

This large, branching cactus can grow to 50 ft (15 m) high and has heavily fluted,

Carpinus japonica

Carpinus orientalis

Carpenteria californica

spine-encrusted stems. Growth is exremely slow: 50-year-old plants may be barely head high. The 4–6 in (10–15 cm) white flowers open at night in early summer and are followed by pulpy fruit that split when ripe. **ZONES 9–11.**

CARPENTERIA
TREE ANEMONE, BUSH ANEMONE

Only one species from California belongs to this genus, an evergreen shrub with pure white flowers like those of *Philadelphus* but with 5 to 7 petals rather than 4, and a more conspicuous cluster of golden stamens. The leaves are narrow and soft, deep green above but paler and felty beneath, arranged in opposite pairs on the soft-wooded branches. It is a beautiful shrub when in full flower in late spring and early summer. Named for the American Professor Carpenter, it should not be confused with the palm genus *Carpentaria.*
CULTIVATION: Although requiring a fairly cool climate, this species only flowers well in regions with warm dry summers and needs ample sunshine, well-drained, gritty soil that must not dry out too much and protection from strong winds. Propagation is usually from seed, as cuttings do not root easily.

Carpenteria californica

In the wild this very attractive shrub is known only from a small area of central California, on dry mountain slopes. It can grow to 20 ft (6 m) tall but in gardens is usually a sprawling shrub about 6–8 ft (1.8–2.4 m) tall that may need support and is best grown against a sunny wall. The flowers, solitary or in small groups, are normally 2–2½ in (5–6 cm) wide but may be up to 4 in (10 cm) wide with broadly overlapping petals. **ZONES 7–9.**

CARPINUS
HORNBEAM

The subtle beauty of hornbeams lies in their usually smoothly fluted trunks and limbs, their neatly veined, small, simple leaves that color attractively in fall (autumn), and their bunches of dry, winged fruit hanging from the twigs. *Carpinus* is a small genus of catkin-bearing, deciduous trees scattered across cool-climate areas of the northern hemisphere. In foliage and fruits there is not a huge variation between the species, though overall size and growth habit are distinct for each. Most, and in particular the European *Carpinus betulus*, yield a timber that is exceptionally strong, hard and close grained; it is much used in the mechanism of pianos. Long lived and often slow growing, hornbeams are useful small to medium-sized trees for parks, streets and lawns.
CULTIVATION: These grow best in well-drained, moderately fertile soil in a sunny or part-shaded position. Propagation is normally from seed except for certain named clones, which must be grafted.

Carpinus betulus
COMMON HORNBEAM, EUROPEAN HORNBEAM

Ranging from Asia Minor across Europe to eastern England, this species can grow to 80 ft (24 m) although 30 ft (9 m) is an average garden height. It has a broad, rounded crown and pale gray bark, fairly smooth and often fluted. The ovate leaves are ribbed and serrated, downy when young, and change from dark green in summer to yellow in fall (autumn). Inconspicuous flowers in early spring are followed by clusters of pale yellow winged fruit. *Carpinus betulus* likes cool, moist conditions. **'Columnaris'** is a compact grower to 30 ft (9 m) high and 20 ft (6 m) wide; **'Fastigiata'** (syn. 'Pyramidalis') develops into a taller, broadly conical tree. **ZONES 6–9.**

Carpinus caroliniana
AMERICAN HORNBEAM, BLUE BEECH

Often shrubby in habit and rarely reaching 40 ft (12 m), this tree is capable of rapid growth—in fact farmers and foresters consider it a weed. It is widely distributed in eastern North America but rarely cultivated. The bark is pale gray, the leaves large and pointed, turning deep orange or red in fall (autumn). The small catkins appear in mid-spring, lengthening in fruit to 6 in (15 cm). **ZONES 4–9.**

Carpinus caroliniana

Carpinus japonica
JAPANESE HORNBEAM

This species makes a medium-sized tree 30–40 ft (9–12 m) tall, forking rather low with broadly ascending branches. The smooth, dark gray bark often has lighter streaks and becomes scaly and furrowed with age. The leaves are larger than those of the common hornbeam, up to 4 in (10 cm) long and more closely veined, with edges more finely but sharply toothed and heart-shaped bases. The fruiting catkins are compact with broad, overlapping, jaggedly toothed bracts. **ZONES 5–9.**

Carpinus orientalis
ORIENTAL HORNBEAM

The 'oriental' in this name is used in its original sense, which meant anywhere east of the Adriatic. This species is native to the Balkans, Ukraine and Turkey. Often reaching 50 ft (15 m) in maturity, it is a densely branched tree with strongly veined leaves coloring well before dropping in fall (autumn). The fruit, in pendulous clusters 2½ in (6 cm) long, are accompanied by irregularly shaped oval bracts. **ZONES 6–9.**

CARPOBROTUS
PIGFACE, SOUR FIG, ICE PLANT

Valued for their abundance of vivid flowers, the 30 species in this genus of carpet-forming succulents of the mesembryanthemum family are predominantly native to South Africa, with a few in Australia, North America and the Pacific Islands, growing mainly on seashores. The completely prostrate, angled stems may be 6 ft (1.8 m) or more in length and become leathery with age. The deep green to gray-green fleshy leaves, arranged in pairs, vary from round to triangular in cross-section, sometimes with finely serrated margins. The large, solitary, daisy-like flowers are in varying shades of pink, red, purple or yellow. These are followed by soft, some-

Carpinus betulus

Carpinus betulus 'Columnaris'

Carpinus betulus 'Fastigiata'

Carpinus betulus

Carpinus caroliniana

times edible fruits, which gave rise to the genus name—*karpos* meaning fruit and *brota* meaning edible.

CULTIVATION: These marginally frost-hardy plants are easy to grow, requiring full sun and porous soil. They are very salt-tolerant, both as to soil salinity and coastal salt spray. They are suited to hanging baskets and make excellent sandbinders. Propagate from stem cuttings or seed in spring to early fall (autumn).

Carpobrotus acinaciformis
GIANT PIGFACE

This species is native to Natal and Cape Province, South Africa. It can mound to a height of 12 in (30 cm) and a spread of 3 ft (1 m) or often more. The leaves are gray-green, saber-shaped and up to 3 in (8 cm) long. From spring to fall (autumn) the plants bear purple flowers up to 6 in (15 cm) across, which open only in the sun. **ZONES 9–11.**

Carpobrotus aequilaterus

Thought to be native to Chile, this species has spread extensively along shorelines all around the Pacific and is highly regarded for its sand-binding qualities. Trailing stems, up to 6 ft (1.8 m) long bear thick, dull green leaves, and 2–3 in (5–8 cm) diameter light purple flowers, shading to white at the base of the petals, appear through summer. The reddish fruit are soft and edible when fully ripe and have 2 ear-like persistent sepals. **ZONES 9–11.**

Carpodetus serratus

Carpobrotus acinaciformis

Carpobrotus acinaciformis

Carthamus tinctorius

Carum carvi

Carum carvi

Carpobrotus edulis
HOTTENTOT FIG

Originating in South Africa, this prostrate succulent produces long, spreading, narrow stems with crowded, erect leaves with finely serrated reddish margins. In spring and summer it produces 3 in (8 cm) diameter pale yellow flowers that age to dull pinkish. Brownish, fig-like fruit follow. **ZONES 9–11.**

Carpobrotus glaucescens

Native to seashores of eastern Australia where it commonly grows on cliffs and salt marshes as well as sandy flats, this species is smaller than many others, making mats up to 3 ft (1 m) across and with narrow green leaves 2–3 in (5–8 cm) long. Purple flowers, $1\frac{1}{2}$–$2\frac{1}{2}$ in (3.5–6 cm) across, appear in summer, followed by reddish, cylindrical, edible fruit. **ZONES 9–11.**

Carpobrotus muirii
REAL SOUR FIG

Occurring wild only in South Africa's southern Cape Province, this fast-growing species forms a dense mat with leaves about 3 in (8 cm) long. In spring it bears pinkish purple flowers up to 4 in (10 cm) in diameter, followed by tasty fruit, the most edible of the genus. **ZONES 9–11.**

CARPODETUS

About 10 species make up this genus of small evergreen trees, distantly related to *Escallonia*, 9 in the mountains of Papua New Guinea and one in New Zealand; the latter is the only one of interest to gardeners. It makes an attractive bushy shrub when young, with interesting foliage and small but profuse white flowers.

CULTIVATION: The New Zealand species fits into various situations in mild-climate gardens, and makes vigorous growth if planted in deep, fertile soil in a reasonably sheltered position. Propagate from seed or cuttings.

Carpodetus serratus
PUTAPUTAWETA

This is a shapely small tree reaching heights of up to 30 ft (9 m) with grayish white bark and coarsely toothed, alternately arranged leaves that are often many lobed in the juvenile stages but rather leathery and elongated with a tapered base as the plant matures. White flowers are borne in panicles from late spring to early fall (autumn) and are followed by rounded, shiny black fruit. **ZONES 8–10.**

CARRIEREA

One of the best known names in nineteenth-century horticulture in Europe was that of Abel Carrière, French editor and publicist, whose name is preserved in many hybrids and cultivars of popular ornamentals. The genus that honors him, though, is still rare in cultivation, consisting of 3 species of deciduous trees from China and Southeast Asia. It is related to *Idesia*, having similar broad, long-pointed leaves with long stalks and toothed margins, but the flowers are larger and fragrant, borne in short upright sprays, and the fruits are large capsules containing winged seeds.

CULTIVATION: These are trees for mild temperate climates, tolerating only light frosts. In cultivation in the UK they have proved short lived. They appreciate a sheltered position and deep, moist soil of reasonable fertility. Propagate from seed, cuttings or root cuttings.

Carrierea calycina

Native to western and central China, this is a small deciduous tree of about 25 ft (8 m) with a broadly spreading crown. The leaves are almost heart-shaped, up to 6 in (15 cm) long, reddish when young ageing to glossy dark green. The curious yellowish flowers are about 1 in (25 mm) wide, consisting of a cup-shaped calyx surrounding a large downy ovary with long yellow styles and very short stamens, carried in an upright panicle in summer. **ZONES 8–10.**

CARTHAMUS

This genus of prickly composites of the thistle tribe consists of 14 species of annuals and perennials from the Mediterranean region and western Asia. Some are troublesome weeds but one species, safflower, is of commercial importance as an oil seed, and was also the source of red and yellow dyes used for rouge and food coloring. They are plants of upright growth with very sharp spines bordering the parchment-textured leaves; the thistle-like flowerheads are smallish, mostly with yellow florets surrounded by a ring of fiercely spiny bracts.

CULTIVATION: Not fussy as to soil but enjoying a full sun position, these plants need little care and their flowers make good, though not long lasting, cut flowers that can be easily dried. Propagate from seed in spring.

Carthamus tinctorius
SAFFLOWER, FALSE SAFFRON

A fast-growing annual 24–36 in (60–90 cm) tall, this thistle is valued for its orange-yellow flowers in summer and for the oil contained in its seeds. Its leaves are spiny and oblong, running down the stems. Safflower is frost hardy and grows best in fertile, well-drained soil. **ZONES 7–11.**

CARUM

About 30 species belong to this genus of annuals, biennials and perennials in the carrot family, one of them being the well known herb caraway (*Carum carvi*). The species are scattered through various temperate regions of the world, but caraway is the only one grown as a garden plant. They are typical umbellifers, with finely dissected basal leaves and hollow, branched stems bearing umbels of tiny white flowers, followed by aromatic, dry fruitlets. One of the essential herbs, caraway has been used as a condiment and medicinal herb since Ancient Egyptian times. It is still widely cultivated for its aromatic seeds, used mainly to flavor bread, cakes, sauces and pickles.

CULTIVATION: These frost-hardy plants grow well in deep, fertile, moist, well-drained soil in full sun. Propagate from seed in early fall (autumn) in mild winter areas, otherwise in spring.

Carum carvi
CARAWAY

A native of Europe and western Asia, this is an attractive biennial or perennial plant growing to about 3 ft (1 m) high with finely cut, lacy leaves. In its second year small white flowers are produced in umbels in early summer, followed in late summer by a crop of seeds. **ZONES 5–10.**

CARYA
HICKORY

These deciduous trees are valued for the toughness and strength of their wood as well as for their edible nuts. Some 20 species occur in eastern or central USA, one in Mexico and several in Asia. The medium to large trees have large, pinnate leaves that turn yellow, orange or rich gold in fall (autumn). The bark of most species is roughly textured. The male flowers appear in slender catkins at the base of the new year's growth, the female flowers in smaller clusters at its tip. The fruits are nuts enclosed in a leathery husk that divides neatly into 4 segments to open. *Carya* species are not commonly cultivated, with the exception of *Carya illinoinensis*.

CULTIVATION: Cold hardy and fast growing, hickory trees prefer sheltered, fertile sites with deep, moist soil in regions with cold winters and long, hot, humid summers. They should be grown from seed *in situ*, or planted out as very young seedlings.

Carya cordiformis
BITTERNUT HICKORY

Widespread through much of eastern USA, this fast-growing tree grows to 80 ft (24 m) with spreading limbs and a rounded crown. The gray or pale brownish bark is smooth except on quite old trees, when it becomes shallowly furrowed. In winter its twigs are distinguished by striking yellow dormant buds. The rounded nuts are smallish and thin shelled, their kernels too bitter to eat. The timber is used in smoking hams and bacon. **ZONES 4–9.**

Carya glabra
PIGNUT HICKORY

Occurring from Maine in the north to Alabama in the southern USA, this medium-sized tree has a tall, straight trunk and rather narrow crown. Its gray bark is deeply furrowed with scaly ridges. The leaves consist of 5 to 7 long, pointed leaflets that turn yellow or orange in fall (autumn). The nuts, enclosed in thin husks, are smallish and nearly spherical and contain a small but sweet kernel. In the wild, pignut hickory grows mainly on the wooded slopes of higher hills. It adapts readily to cultivation, making vigorous growth. **ZONES 4–9.**

Carya ovata

Carya ovata

Carya illinoinensis
PECAN

This species produces one the world's most popular edible nuts. From Indiana to Texas and Alabama, USA, it occurs along broad river valleys in deep, rich, alluvial soil, growing to 100 ft (30 m) tall with scaly gray bark. In cultivation it makes fast growth, becoming an open-crowned tree of about 30 ft (9 m) within 10 to 15 years. Although quite frost hardy, it needs long, hot summers to make growth and set fruit. The leaves are long, with many narrow, glossy gray-green leaflets. The elongated nuts occur in clusters. Many selections have been named and are propagated by grafting. **ZONES 6–11.**

Carya laciniosa
BIG SHELLBARK HICKORY

Found over much of eastern USA, this hickory is notable for its large, handsome leaves and its remarkable bark, hanging from the straight trunk in long, recurving plates. A vigorous grower, it reaches over 100 ft (30 m) in deep, rich soils and yields an important hickory timber. The leaves, up to 24 in (60 cm) long, are downy on their undersides and turn a magnificent clear yellow in fall (autumn). The nuts have a ridged shell and sweet, edible kernel. **ZONES 4–9.**

Carya ovata
SHAGBARK HICKORY, SHELLBARK HICKORY

This species has a similar striking bark to that of *Carya laciniosa.* In its native valley forests in central-eastern USA it grows as a tall, slender tree to 80 ft (24 m) with a long, straight trunk and high, narrow crown, but in the open it makes a much lower, broader column with foliage reaching almost to the ground. The leaves, of medium size with only 5 broad leaflets, turn a fine golden yellow in fall (autumn). The smallish nuts are edible. **ZONES 4–9.**

Carya tomentosa
MOCKERNUT HICKORY, WHITE HICKORY

This fine, large tree has a broad, rounded crown and very large winter buds with brown downy scales. Native to most of eastern USA, it favors drier hill slopes. The long leaves, dark green with downy undersides, have a distinct fragrance when handled. The dark gray bark is close textured, shallowly furrowed and very hard. A very thick husk encloses the smallish oval nuts; they contain sweet, edible kernels. **ZONES 4–9.**

Carya tomentosa

Caryopteris incana

Caryopteris × *clandonensis*

CARYOPTERIS
BLUEBEARD

This is a genus of 6 species of deciduous, erect subshrubs or woody perennials in the verbena family, all native to eastern Asia. They have slender, cane-like stems with thin, toothed leaves arranged in opposite pairs, and bear small blue or purple flowers in dense stalked clusters in the leaf axils. Only 2 species have been grown much in gardens and even these are now largely replaced by the hybrid between them, represented by a number of cultivars.

CULTIVATION: These plants are often included in shrub borders where their grayish foliage and white or blue flowers blend well with plants of more robust color. They need to be placed in a full sun position, in well-drained, humus-rich soil. Cut well back in early spring to ensure a good framework for the new season's growth and consequent late summer to fall (autumn) flowering. Seed can be used for propagation, but in the case of the many cultivars it is necessary to take soft-tip or semi-ripe cuttings.

Caryopteris × *clandonensis*
HYBRID BLUEBEARD, BLUE-MIST SHRUB

This subshrub, a cross between *Caryopteris incana* and *C. mongolica*, is prized for its masses of delicate, purple-blue flowers borne from late summer to fall (autumn). It grows to a height and spread of 3 ft (1 m), and the oval leaves are gray-green and irregularly serrated. **'Ferndown'** a popular choice among the many cultivars, with dark violet-blue flowers, while **'Heavenly Blue'** has blooms of deep blue. **'Kew Blue'** has darker green leaves and dark blue flowers. **ZONES 5–9.**

Carya cordiformis

Carya illinoinensis

Carya laciniosa

Caryopteris incana
syn. ***Caryopteris mastacanthus***
BLUEBEARD

This soft-stemmed shrub from China and Japan is often treated as a perennial in gardens. It reaches around 5 ft (1.5 m) in height with upright, leafy stems. The leaves are soft grayish, coarsely serrated and the clusters of bluish purple flowers display prominent stamen filaments, prompting the common name. **ZONES 7–10.**

CARYOTA
FISHTAIL PALM

Very unusual palms with bipinnate fronds make up this genus of 12 species from tropical Asia and Australasia. 'Fishtail' refers to the shape of the leaflets, which are usually wedge-shaped with the corners drawn out into points and veins radiating from the stalk end. They include both solitary-trunked palms, mostly large, and smaller multi-stemmed palms that sucker from the base. Flowering panicles first appear at the top of the trunk and continue opening successively lower down; after the last one sets fruit, the whole stem dies. Marble-sized fruits, usually ripening dark red, are formed on the female flowers. The fruits contain 1

Cassia javanica

Cassia fistula

Caryota urens

Caryota mitis

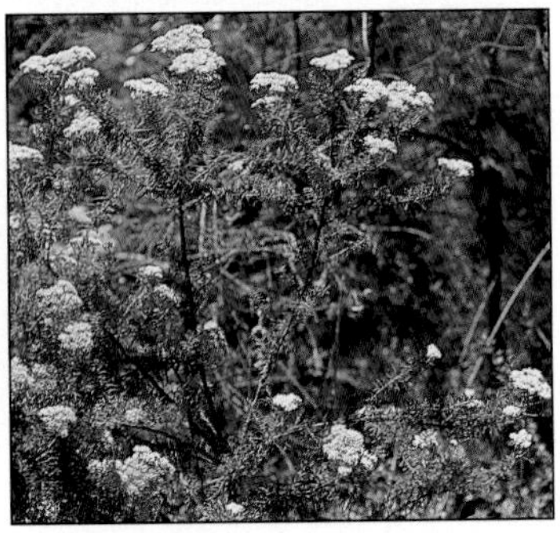
Cassinia aculeata

to 3 black seeds in a fibrous flesh that is quite irritating to the skin.

CULTIVATION: Fishtail palms originate in very moist tropical rainforests and require sheltered, humid environments, but most will tolerate a surprising degree of cold as well as poorly drained soils. They are easily propagated from seed.

Caryota mitis
CLUSTERED FISHTAIL PALM

This rainforest understory palm from Southeast Asia consists of a number of closely crowded stems up to about 30 ft (9 m) tall and 3–4 in (8–10 cm) in diameter, nearly always with a thicket of sucker growths at the base. The fronds are rather erect, up to about 8 ft (2.4 m) long, with widely separated leaflets. The flowers and fruit appear in succession throughout the year. It is the most widely grown species for ornament. **ZONES 10–12.**

Caryota no
GIANT FISHTAIL PALM

Native to Borneo, this is the largest of the fishtail palms, with a massive, solitary gray trunk to about 80 ft (24 m) tall and over 24 in (60 cm) in diameter. The vast fronds have stiffly spreading stalks but pendulous leaflets. The flowering and fruiting panicles may hang down almost 10 ft (3 m). It makes very fast growth in the wet, tropical lowlands and is therefore magnificent as an avenue palm. It can be grown successfully outside the tropics if protected from frost. **ZONES 10–12.**

Caryota urens
TODDY PALM, WINE PALM

This handsome, single-stemmed species is commonly grown for the drink toddy in its native India, Burma and Malaysia. Toddy is obtained by cutting off the young flower clusters and collecting the sugary, vitamin-rich sap that flows from the wound. The tree grows to about 40 ft (12 m) and is widely planted as an ornamental in tropical countries; though it is relatively not very long lived, its life span of about 30 years is long enough for most people. **ZONES 10–12.**

CASSIA

This genus, as now understood, consists of over 100 species of shrubs and trees from tropical and subtropical regions around the world. (Previously, *Cassia* was interpreted in a much broader sense, including a very large number of shrubs,

Caryota urens

small trees and herbaceous plants now separated as the genus *Senna*, listed later in this book.) Some are evergreen, some deciduous. Most have ferny, pinnate leaves and clusters of simple, bright golden-yellow flowers with prominent stamens, often borne for a long period; these are followed by bean-like seed pods which are often very large.

CULTIVATION: Cassias grow under a wide range of conditions, but most prefer well-drained soil and a sunny position. Propagation is from pre-soaked seed in spring or from cuttings in summer.

Cassia fistula
INDIAN LABURNUM, GOLDEN SHOWER TREE, PUDDING PIPE TREE, MONKEY-POD TREE

Native to tropical Asia, this widely cultivated species is a deciduous to semi-evergreen tree that can grow to around 60 ft (18 m) high though often only half that height or less in cultivation. It has pinnate leaves made up of 3 to 8 pairs of large leaflets. In summer it produces large, drooping clusters of fragrant, bright yellow flowers. It can be grown in a sheltered position in frost-free warmer temperate areas. **ZONES 10–12.**

Cassia grandis
PINK SHOWER TREE

This species from tropical America displays thick clusters of salmon pink flowers that open from pinkish mauve buds in spring. It has fern-like leaves composed of 10 to 15 green, oval leaflets and grows to a height of 50 ft (15 m). **ZONES 11–12.**

Cassia javanica
APPLE BLOSSOM TREE

This deciduous tree is native to Southeast Asia, where it may reach a height of 80 ft (24 m). Cultivated specimens are usually half that height, with a broad, flat-topped crown. *Cassia javanica* has long, pinnate leaves covered in fine down when young. The showy summer flowers are carried in large clusters and range from pale pink to red fading to cream or buff. **ZONES 11–12.**

Cassia leptophylla
GOLD MEDALLION TREE

This showy tree from Brazil is notable for its nearly evergreen pinnate leaves and bright golden-yellow flowers. A fast-growing species, it reaches 30 ft (9 m) in height and nearly as much in spread. Flowering in mid-summer with large clusters of bowl-shaped flowers, the fruit that follow are brown pods to 15 in (38 cm) long. It benefits from hard pruning after flowering. **ZONES 10–12.**

Cassia 'Rainbow Shower'

This hybrid cassia has been identified with Hawaii, where it blooms from March to August in a breathtaking display of cream, flesh pink and orange flowers, the color mixture varying from tree to tree. In growth habit it is somewhat intermediate between *Cassia fistula* and *C. javanica*. **ZONES 11–12.**

CASSINIA

This is a genus of around 20 species of evergreen shrubs from Australia and New Zealand closely related to *Helichrysum* and with similar straw-like bracts surrounding the flowerheads, but in *Cassinia* the heads are tiny and arranged in large, flat or elongated sprays, sometimes very tightly crowded. The twigs and leaves are very aromatic, usually coated with a sticky resin that gives off a strong musky smell most noticeable in hot weather. The leaves are variable in shape and size but in many species are small and heath-like. The color of the flowerheads, which are borne abundantly in summer and fall (autumn), varies from silvery white to deep yellow. These are vigorous shrubs, often short lived and of rather untidy habit.

CULTIVATION: Grow in full sun in fertile, well-drained, humus-rich soil. Heavy pruning after flowering may improve shape, and some species may have potential as commercial cut flowers. Propagate from seed or cuttings.

Cassinia aculeata

From eastern Australia, this shrub grows to around 5 ft (1.5 m) high with an erect, open habit and deep green, very narrow leaves. Massed heads of tiny, usually white flowers, sometimes pink, open during summer. In the wild this makes an open shrub but, with light pruning after flowering, a more compact bush can be achieved. **ZONES 8–11.**

CASSIOPE

Closely allied to the heathers, this genus of 12 species of dwarf evergreen shrubs is found in the arctic and alpine regions of the northern hemisphere, consequently it is only suited to gardens assured of moist, cool summers and moisture-retentive soil imitating the wild conditions. Cassiopes are low-growing plants, many stemmed from the base, with scale-like leaves and nodding, small, white or pink flowers. The name is taken from Greek mythology, Cassiope being the mother of Andromeda—her name was chosen for this genus because of its close relationship to the genus *Andromeda*. It should be pronounced with four syllables, like Penelope.

CULTIVATION: Cassiopes need to be grown in rather peaty soil to supply the

Cassiope 'Edinburgh'

Cassiope mertensiana 'Gracilis'

required acidity and moisture, and although they enjoy an open position they need to be protected from the sun and from reflected heat if growing in containers or among rocks. Propagation is from cuttings in summer, while the mat-forming types can be increased from self-rooted stems.

Cassiope 'Edinburgh'

This cultivar originated as a hybrid between *Cassiope fastigiata* and *C. lycopodioides*. It grows to about 12 in (30 cm) high with many stems from the base, in late spring bearing small white bells in rather tight clusters on short stalks. **ZONES 4–8.**

Cassiope fastigiata

From high elevations in the Himalayas, this is the most decorative *Cassiope* species. It makes a dense, erect shrublet around 10 in (25 cm) high and much the same in width, with stems hidden beneath the 4 rows of overlapping tiny leaves. The flowers appear singly from the leaf axils near the branch tips in spring; they are open white bells about $\frac{1}{3}$ in (8 mm) across, on downward-curved stalks. **ZONES 4–8.**

Cassiope lycopodioides

This species occurs both in Alaska and northeast Asia, extending into the high mountains of Japan. It is quite prostrate, forming a mat under 3 in (8 cm) in height but up to 3 ft (1 m) wide, and the stems, together with the tiny overlapping scale leaves, are only $\frac{1}{12}$ in (2 mm) thick. The $\frac{1}{4}$ in (6 mm) white bells are scattered along the branches on nodding, thread-like stalks in late spring and early summer, sometimes also in fall (autumn). **ZONES 2–8.**

Cassiope mertensiana
WHITE HEATHER

Native to mountains of western North America from Alaska to California, this is a semi-prostrate shrub 6–12 in (15–30 cm) high with stems hidden beneath 4-ranked, closely appressed scale leaves. In early spring it produces cup-shaped white flowers $\frac{1}{4}$ in (6 mm) across on short, recurved stalks. **'Gracilis'** makes more of a mound, and its profuse flowers have redder stalks. **ZONES 3–8.**

Cassiope 'Muirhead'

This cultivar originated from a cross between *Cassiope lycopodioides* and the east Himalayan *C. wardii*. It resembles the former in its very fine, flexible branches with flowers scattered along them, but its growth is more erect, to 8 in (20 cm) high, and the spring flowers are larger. **ZONES 3–8.**

CASTANEA
CHESTNUT, CHINQUAPIN

These cool-climate deciduous trees all bear edible nuts enclosed in a prickly, burr-like husk. The leaves are elliptical with regularly toothed margins and a regular feather-like arrangement of veins. In spring or early summer they produce showy clusters of stiff catkins of male flowers at the branch tips; the less conspicuous, small groups of female flowers among the foliage on the same tree develop into the nuts. Most of the 12 species are from North America; some are very small trees or large shrubs. Japan has 2 species and China at least 2, while *Castanea sativa* comes from the Mediterranean region. The larger species are important for the fine timber they produce. **CULTIVATION:** In a cool climate chestnuts are easily grown in full sun or part-shade in deep, fertile soil. Hot, dry summers suit them well as long as ample soil moisture is available in winter and spring. All species are readily propagated from fresh seed, and seedlings should be planted out early to avoid disturbing the tap root.

Castanea dentata

Castanea sativa

Castanea dentata
AMERICAN CHESTNUT

This tall chestnut, widely distributed in eastern North America, was decimated by the chestnut blight early this century, never to recover in anything like its previous numbers and sizes. It grew up to 120 ft (36 m) tall with a straight trunk 3–4 ft (1–1.2 m) thick and was one of the most important timber trees in eastern states of the USA. In foliage and fruit it closely resembles the sweet chestnut and the nuts are similarly edible. **ZONES 4–9.**

Castanea sativa
SWEET CHESTNUT, SPANISH CHESTNUT

This species comes from countries around the Mediterranean, Black and Caspian seas, but has been planted elsewhere in Europe for its edible nuts since time immemorial. Vigorous young trees have a pyramidal crown with erect leading shoots, but with age lower limbs become massive and broadly spreading and the bark deeply fissured. In fall (autumn), the leaves turn from yellowish green to gold and russet. When planting for nuts, buy grafted named varieties from a source certified free of disease. **ZONES 5–9.**

CASTANOSPERMUM
QUEENSLAND BLACK BEAN, MORETON BAY CHESTNUT

This genus consists of one species from the rainforests of northeastern Australia long valued for its beautiful chocolate brown timber. It is a slow-growing tree with a stout trunk and a dense, domed crown. The leaves are pinnate with glossy dark green, oblong leaflets, sometimes semi-deciduous in late winter. In early summer it produces showy large orange and yellow pea-flowers in stiff panicles within the foliage canopy. These are followed in fall (autumn) by huge hanging pods, deep green ripening to brown, each containing 2 to 5 brown seeds which are $1\frac{1}{2}$ in (35 mm) wide. **CULTIVATION:** This tree needs a frost-free climate, well-drained, fertile soil enriched with organic matter and regular watering. Pruning is rarely necessary. Propagate from seed in spring.

Castanospermum australe

This tree, widely planted in streets and for shade in parks and gardens on the east coast of Australia, commonly reaches a height of around 40 ft (12 m). The chestnut-like seeds are poisonous. **ZONES 10–12.**

Castanospermum australe

Castanea sativa

Castanospermum australe

Castanea sativa

Castanospora alphandii

Catalpa bignonioides

Catalpa bignonioides 'Aurea'

CASTANOSPORA

BROWN TAMARIND

Consisting of a single species of medium-sized evergreen tree, this is one of many genera of the soapberry family (Sapindaceae) found in rainforests of eastern Australia. Its chief attraction is its elegant foliage; the pinnate leaves curve downward and have 3 to 6 pairs of long, narrow, glossy leaflets, and new growth flushes are a very attractive paler green. Panicles of small, white, perfumed flowers appear at the branch tips in spring, followed by clusters of reddish brown, flattened seed capsules.
CULTIVATION: With its dense crown of foliage, this species makes a fine ornamental and shade tree but requires a sheltered position and deep, moist soil for good growth. It is propagated from seed.

Castanospora alphandii

From Queensland and northern New South Wales, this tree grows slowly to 30–40 ft (9–12 m) tall with a dense, dome-shaped crown of dark green foliage. The leaves consist of narrow, pointed leaflets about 8 in (20 cm) long. **ZONES 10–12.**

Casuarina cunninghamiana

Catalpa bignonioides

CASUARINA

SHE-OAK, AUSTRALIAN PINE

Members of this genus of evergreen trees earned the name Australian pine on account of their conifer-like appearance. It consists of 6 species of wide distribution in Australia, and about as many again in islands to the north. Many other species previously placed here are now classified under *Allocasuarina* or *Gymnostoma* (both listed elsewhere in this book). Despite bearing only inconspicuous (male and female) flowers, casuarinas are graceful trees, fast growing, tolerant of strong winds and adaptable, often to very dry conditions. Casuarina wood makes excellent firewood. They are grown as shade or amenity trees and are valued by some farmers for the shelter they provide for stock, while others maintain that they poison the ground; casuarinas do have nitrogen-fixing organisms in their roots and there is some evidence that compounds released from the fallen branchlets inhibit other plant growth.
CULTIVATION: Plant in full sun in fertile, moist, well-drained soil. Water well during the growing period, less so in winter. Propagate from seed in spring or cuttings in mid- to late summer. Pruning is rarely necessary.

Casuarina cristata

BELAH

Native to inland eastern Australia, this species makes a shapely tree of up to 80 ft (24 m) in height. It thrives in dry areas with heavy clay soils that may be inundated for short periods, making it a valuable shelter tree for livestock in low-lying areas. Fast growing, it can sucker to form copse-like colonies. **ZONES 9–11.**

Casuarina glauca

Casuarina cunninghamiana

RIVER OAK, RIVER SHE-OAK

The largest of the casuarinas, growing to 70–100 ft (21–30 m) tall, this species is much valued for its ability to stabilize riverbanks, its spreading roots helping to prevent erosion. Because of its rapid early growth with foliage persistent to ground level, it is useful for windbreaks. The tree requires adequate summer water; it will tolerate quite heavy frosts but growth will be slower and stunted in colder districts. **ZONES 8–12.**

Casuarina equisetifolia

BEACH SHE-OAK, HORSETAIL TREE

This tree of around 40–60 ft (12–18 m) tall, depending on soil and exposure, has a short trunk and long, weeping, silvery gray branchlets. It grows naturally on beaches and exposed coastal headlands, being very resistant to salt-laden winds and tolerant of poor, sandy soil. It is not at all frost hardy. Reputedly one of the best fuelwood trees in the world, beach she-oak is also used for boatbuilding, house construction and furniture-making. It has the widest natural distribution of any casuarina, occurring on tropical seashores around most parts of the Pacific and Indian oceans. **ZONES 10–12.**

Casuarina glauca

SWAMP OAK, SWAMP SHE-OAK

This upright tree with thick, grayish green to brown, weeping branchlets grows to 50–70 ft (15–21 m) and occurs along saline creeks, estuaries and seashores of eastern Australia. It can sucker freely from the roots, sometimes forming dense thickets in this way. Male flowers appear as reddish brown terminal spikes among the upper twigs, mostly in fall (autumn). **ZONES 9–12.**

CATALPA

CATALPA, INDIAN BEAN TREE

This genus consists of 11 species of fast-growing, deciduous trees from East Asia and North America. Catalpas have large, ovate leaves in opposite pairs, sprays of showy, bell-shaped flowers at the end of the branches, and extraordinarily long, thin fruits that open to release quantities of very light, winged seeds that float away on the breeze. At their best they are beautiful trees with a dense canopy of luxuriant foliage dotted with flower sprays and are capable of very fast growth, but may look scrappy if exposed to cold or dry winds or if the soil is too poor. Some species yield valuable timber.
CULTIVATION: Grow in moist, well-drained soil in a sunny but sheltered position. Propagate from seed in fall (autumn) or cuttings in late spring or summer, or by budding in late summer or grafting in winter.

Catalpa bignonioides

SOUTHERN CATALPA

This species comes from the warmer southeast of the USA, from Florida west to Mississippi, where it grows along riverbanks and around the edges of swamps. It makes a reasonably compact tree of 25–50 ft (8–15 m) with a rounded, irregularly shaped crown and is cultivated as an ornamental tree for streets, large gardens and parks. The heart-shaped leaves taper to a fine point and have downy undersides; they turn black before dropping in fall (autumn). Sprays of 2 in (5 cm), white flowers with frilled edges and orange blotches and purple spots on their lower lips appear in summer. **'Aurea'** has lime-yellow leaves. **ZONES 5–10.**

Catalpa bungei

BEIJING CATALPA

This very frost-hardy species from northeastern China makes a smallish tree with a dense bushy crown and has leaves with coarse teeth in the lower half, up to about 8 in (20 cm) long. The flowers are white and purple, of medium size and very few to a spray. Some trees grown in the West under this name have proved to be *Catalpa ovata* or small forms of *C. bignonioides*. **ZONES 4–9.**

Catalpa × *erubescens*

An interesting cross between *Catalpa ovata* and *C. bignonioides*, this hybrid has produced several attractive cultivars including **'Purpurea'** with its unfurling 3 in (8 cm) leaves and shoots of deepest purple, becoming the more usual light green as they mature. The flowers are white. **ZONES 5–9.**

Catalpa speciosa

NORTHERN CATALPA, WESTERN CATALPA

This handsome, fast-growing tree reaches over 100 ft (30 m) in its home region, the central Mississippi basin between Arkansas and Indiana, where it grows in forests in rich, moist soil in valley bottoms and on lower slopes. It is sometimes planted for its timber. The leaves are larger than those of *Catalpa bignonioides* but the flowers, borne in mid-summer, are similar though individually slightly larger. Northern catalpa is usually regarded as less decorative overall than the southern species. **ZONES 4–10.**

CATANANCHE

CUPID'S DART

Consisting of 5 species of annuals and perennials from the Mediterranean re-

gion, this genus of the daisy family is usually represented in gardens by only one of these, the common Cupid's dart *(Catananche caerulea)*. Their growth form is like a dandelion, with narrow basal leaves radiating from a root crown, and leafless flowering stems each terminating in a showy blue or yellow flowerhead. The heads are of a distinctive pattern with rather few ray florets that are broad and flat with 5 prominent teeth at the tip of each and a darker zone at the base; disc florets are absent. The genus name is from a Greek word meaning 'love potion', indicating its use in ancient times; the common name is a fanciful version of the same.
CULTIVATION: Grow in full sun in any soil as long as it is well drained. Propagate from seed or root cuttings or by division.

Catananche caerulea
COMMON CUPID'S DART

The common Cupid's dart is popular as a cottage garden plant or can be grown among grasses in a meadow garden. A fast-growing but usually short-lived perennial, it reaches 24 in (60 cm) in height with a spread of 12 in (30 cm). The narrow leaves are gray-green and thin, forming a dense basal clump. Lavender-blue flowerheads 1–2 in (2.5–5 cm) across are borne freely throughout summer on slender, weak, leafless stems. The flowers are suitable for drying. **'Major'** is a somewhat untidy cultivar with darker blue blooms, while in **'Bicolor'** they are white with a deep purple center or all white in **'Perry's White'**. **ZONES 7–10.**

CATHARANTHUS
MADAGASCAR PERIWINKLE

Although still referred to as *Vinca* by many gardeners, this genus is in fact quite distinct horticulturally and botanically. It consists of 8 species of annuals and evergreen perennials or subshrubs, all originally from Madagascar though one has spread throughout warmer regions of the world. It is this same widespread and often weedy species, *Catharanthus roseus,* that has given rise to many horticultural selections, grown as bedding and border plants or sold in pots by florists. They are plants with repeatedly branched, rather fleshy stems and plain, smooth-edged leaves. The flowers are clustered in the upper leaf axils and are somewhat oleander-like, with a short tube opening by a very narrow mouth into 5 flat, radiating petals, the whole effect being very neat and star-like.
CULTIVATION: In cooler areas *Catharanthus* can be can be grown in a sunny conservatory or as summer bedding plants. In warm climates they are moderately tolerant of deep shade, the fiercest sun, and a dry atmosphere. Grow in free-draining soil, which should be kept moist in the growing period. Tip prune to keep bushy, but not so heavily as to inhibit flowering. They can be propagated from seed or from cuttings in summer.

Catharanthus roseus
syns *Lochnera rosea, Vinca rosea*
PINK PERIWINKLE,

In its original form this shrubby perennial is a rather slender plant about 24 in (60 cm) high, with white to rose pink flowers shading to a darker red eye in the center. Garden forms are generally lower and more compact with larger flowers in a wider range of colors, blooming almost throughout the year in warm climates but mainly in spring and summer in cooler climates. Some mixed color series have flowers ranging from purple through pink to white, while others have mainly pale colors (or white) with prominent red eyes. All parts of the plant contain poisonous alkaloids from which drugs of value in the treatment of leukaemia have been refined. **ZONES 9–12.**

CATOPSIS

This is a bromeliad genus consisting of around 20 species of epiphytes of medium size from Central America and northern South America, most with the leaves arranged in rosettes that are tightly furled at the base to form a water reservoir. The leaves are broad and smooth, often with a coating of whitish powdery scales. The flowering stems are tall and leafy, branching into spikes of crowded flowers partially enclosed by small bracts.
CULTIVATION: Although frost tender, these plants are easily grown in a greenhouse or conservatory in filtered light in a typical coarse and fibrous bromeliad mixture. In the wet tropics and sub tropics they can be planted outdoors on low tree branches, piles of stones, or in raised beds with an open, humus-rich soil. Propagate by carefully detaching offsets or from seed.

Catopsis hahnii

Native to far southern Mexico and Central America, this species has rosettes

Catananche caerulea

Catalpa speciosa

about 24 in (60 cm) wide of crowded, finely pointed green leaves spotted with mealy white scales. In summer it sends up a panicle to about 24 in (60 cm) high with green leafy stem bracts, and branches with smaller yellow bracts enclosing the small white flowers.
ZONES 11–12.

CATTLEYA

The archetypal glamorous orchid flower is a cattleya, or one of its many hybrids with other orchid genera; ***Cattleya* Angel Heart 'Pink Cloud'** and ***C.* Little Susie 'Orchid Glen'** exemplify the beauty of these plants. The genus in its wild state consists of between 40 and 60 species (depending on which botanical classification you follow) of epiphytes from Central and South America, however from these have been bred countless hybrids, the flowers ranging from miniatures only 2 in (5 cm) or so across to giants of 6 in (15 cm) or more. Just about every color but blue is available. The flower characteristically has 3 fairly narrow sepals, in front of which are 2 broader upper petals often with frilled edges, and a showy central lip or labellum with frilled margin and variously marked and spotted, its edges folded over behind to form a tube. The plants have creeping rhizomes and narrow, erect pseudobulbs; in one group of species (the bifoliate cattleyas) there are 2 broad leaves arising from the top of each pseudobulb; in the other group (the unifoliates) there is only one leaf, usually narrower and more erect. The flower sprays, 1 or 2 to as many as 10 flowers, arise from the tops of the pseudobulbs. They appear, according to species or cultivar, in spring or fall (autumn). Many cattleya hybrids in the broad sense have other related genera in their parentage—see also × *Brassocattleya,* × *Brassolaeliocattleya,* × *Laeliocattleya,* × *Sophrolaeliocattleya.*
CULTIVATION: In cool climates cattleyas must be grown in a heated greenhouse or conservatory, the bifoliate species and hybrids requiring lower temperatures than the unifoliates. All prefer good light but not strong sunshine, a coarse potting mix and a winter rest. They are propagated by division just as growth begins, which may be either in spring or in early fall.

Cattleya bicolor

A charming species whose subdued coloring is at odds with the usual glamorous image of cattleyas, this native of Brazil is a bifoliate species with slender pseudobulbs less than 12 in (30 cm) long. *Cattleya bicolor* bears sprays of one or more flowers about 4 in (10 cm) in diameter; they have very fleshy petals and sepals and are a coppery green with a deep purple labellum, not with inrolled margins like most other species, leaving the large white staminal column as a prominent central feature.
ZONES 10–12.

Catharanthus roseus cultivar

Cattleya Angel Heart 'Pink Cloud'

Cattleya Little Susie 'Orchid Glen'

Cattleya, Bifoliate Hybrids
CLUSTER CATTLEYA

There are many of these hybrids available, with most of them having rather small flowers in clusters. They can be grown out of doors in a frost-free, humid summer climate and can be planted to good effect on low branches of trees, if the canopy is light and open. They can be spring or fall (autumn) flowering, and colors range from white through pink to magenta with some in the yellow to coral range, showing a genetic inheritance from the dainty orange-colored *Cattleya aurantiaca.* **Chocolate Drop**, which is an eye-catching hybrid grex between *C. aurantiaca* and *C. guttata,* is of such a deep, glossy maroon color it almost looks like chocolate. It has a small flower and grows to 18 in (45 cm) in height. It was raised in the 1960s. **Fascination**, which is a hybrid grex between ***Cattleya intermedia*** and ***C.* Irma**, was also raised in the 1960s. The plant is about 24 in (60 cm) high and the 2½ in (6 cm) wide flowers are pale mauve in color. **ZONES 10–12.**

Cattleya deckeri

Cattleya, Bifoliate Hybrid, Fascination

Cattleya bowringiana

This delightful bifoliate cattleya from Central America flowers in fall (autumn) and winter and is popular and easy to grow. The pseudobulbs are up to 24 in (60 cm) long and bear sprays of up to 15 flowers that are 3 in (8 cm) wide and deep pink in color. It looks best when allowed to make a large clump, when it will bloom profusely. It is the parent of several hybrids, some of which are optimistically described as 'blue'. **ZONES 10–12.**

Cattleya deckeri
syn. *Cattleya guatemalensis*

A bifoliate cattleya of fairly compact growth and with small flowers, *Cattleya deckeri* is widely distributed around the Caribbean from Mexico to the Guianas and on West Indian islands. Each pseudobulb bears a small number of 2 in (5 cm) wide flowers with rather narrow reddish purple petals and sepals and a deeper purple labellum. **ZONES 10–12.**

Cattleya dowiana
syns *Cattleya aurea, C. labiata* var. *dowiana*

A variable species, *Cattleya dowiana* ranges in the wild from Costa Rica to Colombia and is notable for the large size of its strongly frilled labellum. It is unifoliate with pseudobulbs less than 8 in (20 cm) long, thickest at the top, bearing a spray of several flowers in fall (autumn). Individual blooms are about 6 in (15 cm) wide with sepals and petals ranging from cream to golden yellow, sometimes red flushed, and a labellum 3–4 in (8–10 cm) wide of a rich velvety red with radiating yellow veins. It is a major parent of hybrid cattleyas. **ZONES 11–12.**

Cattleya Queen Sirikit 'Summer Stars'

Cattleya, Bifoliate Hybrid, Chocolate Drop

Cattleya labiata

Some present-day botanists use this name in a broad sense to cover a large group of unifoliate cattleyas from South and Central America, including *Cattleya mossiae,* ***C. warneri,*** *C. trianae,* ***C. gatskelliana*** and ***C. warscewiczii,*** all pink or white, as well as the yellow *C. dowiana*—but many other botanists still like to maintain at least some of these as distinct species. They are all intermediate growers with large flowers in spring or fall (autumn), and are collectively the most important parents of most cattleya hybrids. Pure-bred species of the group are not often available, but they are well worth growing. **ZONES 11–12.**

Cattleya mossiae
syn. *Cattleya labiata* var. *mossiae*

As noted in the previous entry, this species is sometimes treated as falling within the scope of *Cattleya labiata.* It is native to Venezuela and is that country's national flower. From a typical unifoliate pseudobulb it produces a spike of up to 7 flowers, each up to 6 in (15 cm) wide with broad, frilled, white to rose-purple petals and, usually, darker markings on the large labellum, which also has a yellow splash in the throat. **ZONES 11–12.**

Cattleya Queen Sirikit 'Summer Stars'

White cattleyas are favorite wedding flowers and this one is as lovely as any bride could desire. It is a purebred cattleya, with no *Laelia* or *Rhyncolaelia* blood, and grows in cooler temperatures than many hybrid cattleyas usually require. **ZONES 10–12.**

Cattleya skinneri
FLOWER OF SAN SEBASTIAN

This beautiful cattleya is the national flower of Costa Rica, though its range in the wild is more extensive: from southern Mexico to Venezuela. It is a bifoliate species, with thick pseudobulbs up to 15 in (30 cm) high and a spike of up to 12 flowers to 3 in (8 cm) wide. Color is normally rose pink to purple, sometimes with a white or cream labellum with orange in the throat; white forms are also grown. It flowers in winter and spring and can be grown into a large clump. **ZONES 10–12.**

Cattleya trianae

Native to the mountains of Colombia, this is one of the *Cattleya* species sometimes synonymized under *C. labiata,* which it resembles in growth form (a typical unifoliate species). A flowering stem can carry from 2 to 5 flowers up to 8 in (20 cm) across, varying in color from white to deep purple. The rather narrow labellum is even more variable in coloring, though usually with an orange-yellow central blotch. This is one of the most important parents of cattleya hybrids. **ZONES 11–12.**

Cattleya skinneri

Cattleya, Unifoliate Hybrids

These are the big, ruffled flowers of the flower shops, mainly in shades of pink or white. They can flower either in spring or fall (autumn); some grexes will bloom in both seasons if they are well looked after. The flowers, which can be as much as 6 in (15 cm) wide, are usually borne singly or in 2s or 3s. Many of these big cattleyas are more or less hybridized with laelias and rhyncolaelias, but famous names to look out for among the pure-bred cattleyas are **Bow Bells, Suzanne Hye** and **Bob Betts. ZONES 11–12.**

CAULOPHYLLUM

Two species of rhizomatous perennials, one from North America and one from East Asia, make up this genus of the berberis family. With compound leaves and lobed, strongly veined leaflets, they are not of great ornamental value but the American one is a traditional medicinal plant, used by Native Americans as well as white settlers. Each shoot bears a single leaf only, and the cluster of small green or dull reddish starry flowers appears to arise from the top of their central stalk (rachis). The berry-like seeds, two developing from each flower, are more ornamental than the flowers. The plants may spread underground with matted roots to form quite large patches, though their spread is very slow.
CULTIVATION: Suited to more heavily shaded areas of a woodland garden, these plants will tolerate dry soil but respond with faster growth to summer moisture and deep, humus-rich soil. Propagate by division or from ripe seed.

Caulophyllum thalictroides
BLUE COHOSH

The rich blue berries of this species, which are retained for a long period after the flowers are spent, are of interest to gardeners looking out for plants that will survive the deep shade of deciduous trees. Native to eastern USA and Canada, *Caulophyllum thalictroides* grows to around 30 in (75 cm) tall with mid-green 3-lobed leaflets, and has clusters of insignificant flowers in spring. **ZONES 4–9.**

CAVENDISHIA

The Andes of South America are the home of the 10 species that make up this genus, consisting of evergreen shrubs or small trees with bell-shaped or tubular flowers a bit like some *Erica* species but with broad, leathery leaves. Only one cavendishia has found its way into gardens in other parts of the world, and this has proved reasonably frost hardy and vigorous. Many are epiphytes, growing in cloud forests on mossy trees or sometimes on rocks.

CULTIVATION: All prefer filtered sun and peaty, humus-rich soil, a humid atmosphere and a climate without extremes of either heat or cold. Propagate from cuttings in summer or seed in spring or by layering in spring or fall (autumn).

Cavendishia acuminata
syn. *Cavendishia bracteata*

Native to Colombia and Ecuador, this is a shrub 3–6 ft (1–1.8 m) tall with somewhat scrambling, reddish brown branches, becoming pendulous at the tips. The new leaves are bronze-pink at the growing tips, hardening to glossy deep green. Clusters of tubular, waxy red to maroon flowers with paler yellowish tips burst from bud bracts from spring to late fall (autumn). **ZONES 9–10.**

CEANOTHUS
CALIFORNIA LILAC

Brilliant displays of blue or violet, or occasionally pink or white flowers are the chief attraction of most of the 50 or more species of this genus of evergreen and deciduous shrubs (some reaching small tree size), all of them North American but the vast majority confined to the coast ranges of California. Some species that grow on coastal cliffs develop dense, prostrate forms highly resistant to salt spray. The leaves are small to medium sized, blunt tipped and usually toothed. The flowers, individually tiny with thread-like stalks, are massed in dense clusters at the branch ends; they appear in spring in most species.

CULTIVATION: As garden plants these shrubs can be outstandingly ornamental

Ceanothus 'Blue Cushion'

but often short-lived, especially prone to sudden death in climates with warm, wet summers. They require full sun and prefer shelter, particularly from strong winds, in well-drained soil. Propagate from seed, often freely produced in small round capsules, or from cuttings.

Ceanothus arboreus
TREE CEANOTHUS, ISLAND CEANOTHUS

One of the largest-growing evergreen species, *Ceanothus arboreus* from islands off the south Californian coast makes an evergreen tree of up to 30 ft (9 m) but in gardens it is normally only half that, developing a thick, low-branching trunk. The leaves have downy undersides and are larger than in most species and the flowers, ranging from very pale blue to deep blue, are in loose clusters carried just above the leaves in spring and early summer. The plant makes fast early growth in suitable conditions. **'Mist'** is one of the palest forms with long spikes of delicate gray-blue blooms. **ZONES 8–10.**

Ceanothus 'Blue Cushion'

This hybrid grows only about 3 ft (1 m) tall, but its arching branches spread to

Ceanothus griseus

Ceanothus hearstiorum

Cavendishia acuminata

Ceanothus arboreus 'Mist'

8 ft (2.4 m) across. Unlike some other compact hybrids, it has an open appearance. Flowers, which are abundantly produced, are a soft pale lilac-blue. **ZONES 8–10.**

Ceanothus 'Blue Jeans'

A hybrid cultivar growing to 8 ft (2.4 m) tall and much the same spread, this evergreen is well suited to use as a hedge as it will tolerate clipping. The foliage is a leathery dark green, offsetting profuse blue flowers borne in late spring. **ZONES 8–10.**

Ceanothus 'Burkwoodii'
BURKWOOD CEANOTHUS

A hybrid between ***Ceanothus dentatus* 'Floribundus'** and ***C.* × *delilianus* 'Indigo'**, this cultivar is now more popular than either. It is moderately frost tolerant and forms a dense evergreen bush to around 6–8 ft (1.8– 2.4 m) with glossy green foliage and bright blue blooms in late summer and early fall (autumn). **ZONES 7–9.**

Ceanothus 'Concha'

Of chance origin in a garden, this highly floriferous evergreen hybrid grows up to 5–7 ft (1.5–2 m) tall and it has a spreading habit of at least 8 ft (2.4 m) wide. *Ceanothus* 'Concha' needs ample room to display its red-toned buds which open into large clusters of deep blue flowers. **ZONES 8–10.**

Ceanothus 'Delight'

Growing to 15 ft (4.5 m), this evergreen hybrid cultivar has glossy pale green leaves and flowers of deep blue held in long panicles. **ZONES 8–10.**

Ceanothus × *delilianus*

This old French hybrid makes a sturdy, vigorous, deciduous shrub with midgreen leaves that are broad and oval. It originated as a cross between the New Jersey tea (***Ceanothus americanus***) of eastern USA and the tropical ***C. coeruleus*** from Mexico and Guatemala, which has sky blue flowers in very large sprays. It includes a number of fine cultivars, the best known being **'Gloire de Versailles'**, an 12 ft (3.5 m) shrub with erect, loose panicles of pale blue, scented flowers from mid-summer to early fall (autumn). **ZONES 7–9.**

Ceanothus 'Frosty Blue'

A hybrid cultivar of broadly spreading habit, 'Frosty Blue' is an evergreen shrub of about 10 ft (3 m) in height and more in width, its deep blue flowers dusted with white. **ZONES 8–10.**

Ceanothus gloriosus
POINT REYES CREEPER

Known in the wild only from a short stretch of the central Californian coast, this species is a low, dense, evergreen shrub with leathery deep green leaves. Depending on exposure to wind and salt spray it develops local races anywhere between 12 in and 6 ft (30 cm–1.8 m) high, but usually broadly spreading or mat-forming. It bears profuse stalked clusters of dark blue to purple flowers in late spring and early summer. **'Emily Brown'** has smaller but more prominently toothed leaves and very dark blue flowers. **ZONES 7–9.**

Ceanothus griseus
CARMEL CEANOTHUS

A spreading, bushy shrub from the central Californian hills, this evergreen species grows to 8 ft (2.4 m) with rounded, dark green leaves, downy on the undersides. Starting in early spring, Carmel ceanothus produces abundant dense flower clusters of a pale violet-blue. ***Ceanothus griseus* var. *horizontalis*** is a name that covers various low-growing, densely spreading forms from coastal cliffs that make fine rock garden or ground cover plants for exposed sites; specific clones are grown under the names **'Yankee Point'** or **'Hurricane Point'**, referring to collection sites. **ZONES 8–10.**

Ceanothus hearstiorum
HEARST'S CEANOTHUS

Now recognized as a species in its own right, this low-growing ceanothus was named in honor of the Hearst family of newspaper fame, near whose coastal Californian home it was discovered. It is a semi-prostrate, evergreen shrub no more than 12 in (30 cm) high but spreading to 6 ft (1.8 m) or more; the leaves are small with deeply impressed veins and in late spring and early summer Hearst's ceanothus produces abundant small clusters of dark blue flowers. **ZONES 8–10.**

C

Ceanothus impressus 'Puget Blue'

Ceanothus thyrsiflorus

Ceanothus papillosus

Ceanothus thyrsiflorus var. *repens*

Ceanothus impressus
SANTA BARBARA CEANOTHUS

A free-flowering, small-leafed, evergreen species of dense, spreading habit, this is a first-class garden shrub under suitable conditions. The leaves are ½ in (12 mm) long or less, very thick and with the veins deeply impressed into the upper surface. In spring it produces a profuse display of small clusters of deep blue flowers. From 6–10 ft (1.8–3 m) in height, this coastal Californian species prefers tough, exposed conditions. **'Puget Blue'** features stunning blue flowers and is probably a hybrid with *C. papillosus*. **ZONES 8–10.**

Ceanothus papillosus

This vigorous evergreen shrub or small tree is endemic to the coast ranges of central California. It grows to around 12 ft (3.5 m) high and has bright green, leathery leaves to about 1½ in (35 mm) long that densely clothe its strong branches. In spring the plant is covered in heads of deep blue flowers. It is tough and adaptable, doing well in coastal conditions and withstanding regular trimming.

Ceanothus papillosus* var. *roweanus has narrower leaves and makes a lower, more spreading shrubless up to 6 ft (1.8 m) tall. **ZONES 8–10.**

Ceanothus 'Percy Picton'

Thought to be a cross between *Ceanothus impressus* and *C. papillosus*, this ceanothus makes a dense evergreen shrub to 10 ft (3 m), with small crowded leaves and early summer blooms of dark blue to lilac in very small but profuse clusters. **ZONES 8–10.**

Ceanothus prostratus
SQUAW CARPET, MAHALA MATS

This remarkable evergreen species differs from most of the others in being a subalpine plant, coming from high on the mountains of Washington, Oregon and California where it forms extensive mats that may be 10 ft (3 m) or more wide but only a few inches high, often rooting as they spread. The small, deep green leaves are thick and leathery and in spring the plants are covered in profuse small heads of pale lavender-blue flowers, sometimes darker blue or white, giving way to horned, bright red fruit. **ZONES 7–9.**

Ceanothus 'Ray Hartman'

Thought to be a cross between *Ceanothus arboreus* and *C. griseus*, this evergreen hybrid can reach 20 ft (6 m) in height at maturity and as much in spread. The leaves are largish, resembling those of *C. arboreus*. The early spring blooms of *C.* 'Ray Hartman' are grayish blue in stalked clusters terminating the branches. **ZONES 8–10.**

Ceanothus impressus

Ceanothus 'Percy Picton'

Ceanothus rigidus
MONTEREY CEANOTHUS

Found wild only on California's Monterey Peninsula, this is a much-branched evergreen shrub up to 6 ft (1.8 m) high. As the specific name suggests it has stiff branches, and the leaves are very small, wedge-shaped and prickly toothed. In spring and early summer the branches are clothed with abundant small umbels of a rich purplish blue. It is one of the most beautiful species but is not very frost hardy. **'Snowball'** is a form with white flowers. **ZONES 9–10**

Ceanothus thyrsiflorus
BLUE BLOSSOM CEANOTHUS

This is an evergreen shrub or small tree that grows to over 20 ft (6 m) in its native moist coastal forests of California, but the forms grown in gardens include some, for example ***Ceanothus thyrsiflorus* var. *repens,*** that are more compact shrubs of only 3–10 ft (1–3 m) with vigorous spreading branches. The shiny, oval, medium-sized leaves have 3 prominent longitudinal veins. In late spring and early summer the plant produces dense cylindrical clusters of lavender-blue to almost white flowers. **'Blue Mound'** is a low-growing hybrid of *C. thyrsiflorus* reaching 5 ft (1.5 m) in height and spreading to over 6 ft (1.8 m) wide, with medium blue flowers. **'Cascade'** on the other hand can grow to 25 ft (8 m) with broadly arching branches and pale blue flowers. **ZONES 7–9.**

Ceanothus × *veitchianus*

This hybrid, possibly of *Ceanothus griseus* and *C. rigidus*, carries the name of a famous English nursery family, a good indication that it arose in the nineteenth century when James Veitch & Son were most active. It is a popular evergreen shrub of up to 10 ft (3 m) in height. The small leaves are rounded and sharply toothed, with veins strongly impressed into the upper surface. The pale lilac-blue flowers are borne profusely in spring in cylindrical clusters. **ZONES 7–9.**

CECROPIA
CECROPIA

These fast-growing trees with large, umbrella-like leaves are a striking feature of the Amazonian rainforest. They are soft wooded, with large, open crowns that often project above the surrounding trees. The thick branches are often hollow, containing a series of chambers that are inhabited by fierce ants which attack intruders on the tree, including both humans and leafcutter ants that feed on the foliage. Some Amazonian Indians made trumpet-like instruments from the hollow stems. The genus is widespread in tropical America, including some species of smaller size and less striking form.

CULTIVATION: These trees are easily enough cultivated in warm climates in sheltered, sunny positions and deep, moist soil, but the rampant saplings are weak and easily damaged. Propagation is from seed.

Cecropia palmata
SNAKEWOOD TREE

This species from the West Indies and northeastern South America is particularly fast growing; the snakewood tree makes a tall, lanky tree of up to 50 ft (15 m) with few branches. The stems have a waxy blue coating and the leaves are about 24 in (60 cm) across, deeply segmented into 8 to 10 oblong lobes with rounded tips. The whole leaf is colored greenish white on the underside. **ZONES 11–12.**

Cecropia palmata

Cedrela mexicana

CEDRELA

CIGAR-BOX CEDAR

As formerly defined the tropical tree genus *Cedrela* included many species from Asia, Australasia and the Americas, but it is now treated as a purely American genus, the Old World species removed to the separate genus *Toona*. Both genera have long, pinnate leaves and panicles of inconspicuous greenish flowers, and the soft, aromatic, reddish timber of both is very valuable and has been exploited in the past to the point of scarcity. *Cedrela* timber is used to make traditional West Indian cigar boxes.

CULTIVATION: These trees are easily grown in any sheltered spot in a warm, humid climate, preferring deep, moist soil. They make fast growth in the first decade or two, slowing down thereafter and making fine shade trees. Propagation is normally from fresh seed.

Cedrela mexicana

An evergreen forest tree of 100 ft (30 m) or more in its native Central and South America, this species when grown in the open takes on a broader form with a stout, straight central trunk and widely spreading limbs. The crown is rather open and coarsely branched, the pinnate leaves being up to 24 in (60 cm) long with leaflets of a fresh green. **ZONES 10–12.**

CEDRONELLA

BALM OF GILEAD, CANARY BALM

The genus name is a diminutive of *Cedrus*, but there is no connection between these soft herbaceous perennials of the mint family and the large coniferous cedars except for the sweetly aromatic smell of their crushed leaves, which might be likened to that of the cedar's aromatic wood. The genus consists of a single species endemic to the Canary Islands. Its distinctive feature is the compound leaves consisting of 3 leaflets, unusual in the mint family which have mainly simple leaves. The leafy stems terminate in dense, short spikes of flowers with tubular 2-lipped blooms.

CULTIVATION: Grown outdoors in mild climates, these perennials need protection in a sunny position in the herb garden and moist, well-drained soil. In cool climates they can be grown in a sunny conservatory. Water freely in the growing season. Propagate from seed or cuttings.

Cedrus brevifolia

Cedronella canariensis

syn. *Cedronella triphylla*

The common name, of biblical origin, is even more fanciful than the genus name and is applied to several quite unrelated plants. Regardless of name, the plant is quite pretty, with cane-like stems to about 4 ft (1.2 m) tall, springing from a rather woody base, and fresh green leaves. The mauve-pink to white flowers, about ¾ in (18 mm) long, are borne in summer. The leaves are used in herbal teas and for potpourri. **ZONES 8–11.**

CEDRUS

CEDAR

This is a renowned genus of conifers belonging to the pine family; the 4 very similar species, from northwest Africa, Cyprus, Asia Minor and the Himalayas, are so similar that some botanists prefer to treat them as subspecies or varieties of a single species. All have needle-like leaves arranged in rosettes on the short but long-lasting lateral shoots, which arise from axils of the longer needles on stronger growths. The pollen cones, shaped like small bananas and up to 4 in (10 cm) long, release large clouds of pollen in early spring. The seed cones are broadly egg- or barrel-shaped, pale bluish or brownish; they eventually shatter to release seeds with broad papery wings. As cultivated trees the cedars are valued for the fine architectural effects of their branching, the texture and color of their foliage, and their vigorous growth.

CULTIVATION: In appropriate climatic conditions these conifers are long lived and trouble free, growing massive with age. They need full sun and well-drained, chalky soil. Propagation is normally from seed, though cuttings, layering and grafting are used for certain cultivars.

Cedrus atlantica

syn. *Cedrus libani* subsp. *atlantica*

ATLAS CEDAR

Native to the Atlas Mountains (*atlantica* is the adjectival form) of Morocco and Algeria, this tree in its younger stages has a neat, pyramidal shape with stiffly ascending branches, but with age it spreads into a broadly flat-topped tree with massive limbs up to 100 ft (30 m) or more high on good sites. The densely clustered needles are never more than 1 in (25 mm) long and vary from dark green to bluish, though it is mainly the bluish forms that are seen in gardens. This species prefers moderately cool climates. The collective cultivar name **'Glauca'** is used for selected seedling plants with bluish foliage. **'Glauca Pendula'** has long, completely pendulous branches and no leading shoot and is usually grafted onto a standard. **ZONES 6–9.**

Cedrus brevifolia

syn. *Cedrus libani* subsp. *brevifolia*

CYPRUS CEDAR

The rarest species in cultivation, this is known in the wild only from a small area of the mountains of Cyprus at an altitude of around 4,500 ft (1,350 m). Botanists have frequently treated it as no more than a variety of *Cedrus libani*, but it differs consistently in its shorter needles and smaller overall size. In the wild it grows to a maximum height of 60 ft (18 m) with a trunk of 4 ft (1.2 m) in diameter, although the oldest trees in cultivation are considerably smaller. **ZONES 6–9.**

Cedrus atlantica

Cedrus atlantica 'Glauca'

Cedrus atlantica 'Glauca Pendula'

Cedrus deodara
DEODAR, DEODAR CEDAR

The deodar (its Indian name) occurs in the western Himalayas, reaching over 200 ft (60 m) in the wild, but is now almost extinct over much of its former range. In cultivation it makes fast early growth. The long leading shoots nod over slightly, and smaller branches are quite pendulous. The foliage is a dark, slightly grayish green, with needles about $1\frac{1}{2}$ in (35 mm) long on strong shoots. The deodar is at its best in milder, humid climates in deep soil, making luxuriant growth and reaching 30 ft (9 m) in about 10 years. The most popular cultivar is **'Aurea'**, with golden branch tips. **ZONES 7–10.**

Cedrus libani
CEDAR OF LEBANON, LEBANON CEDAR

This magnificent tree has been all but wiped out in Lebanon, with only a few small groves surviving on Mount Lebanon; larger populations survive in Turkey. It was introduced to western Europe centuries ago, and trees in England are up to 120 ft (36 m) in height and 8 ft (2.4 m) in trunk diameter. As a young tree it has a narrow, erect habit but with age adopts a flat-topped shape with massive spreading limbs. The dark green needles are up to $1\frac{1}{2}$ in (35 mm) long. It prefers a moist, cool climate. **'Aurea-Prostrata'** is a dwarf form with golden foliage; **'Nana'** is a very dwarf, slow-growing cultivar of semi-prostrate habit suited to rock gardens; **'Pendula'** is a weeping form, usually grafted onto a standard. ***Cedrus libani* subsp. *stenocoma*** is the geographical race from mountains of southwestern Turkey; it has a more narrowly conical or columnar growth habit. **ZONES 6–9.**

Cedrus libani 'Pendula'

Cedrus libani 'Nana'

CEIBA
SILK COTTON TREE

This genus consists of 4 species of large, dry-season-deciduous trees with heavily buttressed spiny trunks, large palmate leaves and showy, 5-petalled flowers. The large football-shaped fruits split to release seeds embedded in kapok, a cottonwool-like fiber. They occur naturally in the tropics of Asia, the Americas and Africa and were once important as the main source of kapok, used for stuffing, insulation and flotation, still with some commercial uses though largely replaced by synthetics. The trees are widely used by local people as sources of fiber, fuel and timber.

CULTIVATION: These fast-growing trees can only be successfully cultivated in the wet tropics. They need regular rainfall, full sun, moist, well-drained soil and steady, warm temperatures. Propagate from seed or cuttings.

Cedrus libani subsp. *stenocoma*

Cedrus deodara

Ceiba pentandra
KAPOK

Reaching heights of over 200 ft (60 m) high, this African species is the tallest tree found in that continent. It also occurs wild in South America but in tropical Asia is considered introduced, having been planted for kapok production. Its trunk is spiny when young and the branches are held horizontally, giving the tree a distinctive pyramidal outline. Showy white, yellow or pale pink flowers, 6 in (15 cm) in diameter, are followed by 6 in (15 cm) long fruit. **ZONE 12.**

CELASTRUS
BITTERSWEET

Around 30 species of mostly deciduous shrubs and woody climbers from Africa, Asia, Australasia and North America belong to this genus, closely related to *Euonymus* but recognizable by their alternately placed leaves and distinctive capsular fruits that split open to reveal seeds enveloped in bright orange or red *arils*, oily edible appendages that attract birds. The most commonly grown species have the male and female flowers on separate plants, so one of each sex must be grown to produce the brilliantly colored fruits. Foliage color in fall (autumn) is quite good in some species. They are an excellent choice to cover an old tree stump or grow over a wall.

CULTIVATION: *Celastrus* species are easily grown in moist, well-drained soil in a sheltered position in full sun or part-shade. Plants will benefit from a spring trimming of the previous year's longer branches, and from occasional feeding. Propagate from seed or by layering in spring, or from cuttings in summer and fall.

Cedrus deodara 'Aurea'

Celastrus orbiculatus
syn. ***Celastrus articulatus***
ORIENTAL BITTERSWEET

Native to China, Japan and eastern Siberia, this is a vigorous climber that can cover small trees or old stumps to a height of 30 ft (9 m) or more. The thin leaves, sometimes almost circular in outline, are 3–6 in (8–15 cm) long and widely spaced on the twining longer shoots. The flowers, borne in summer, are green and inconspicuous, but in late fall (autumn) the profuse small fruit ripen and split to reveal brilliant red pea-sized seeds against the golden yellow interior of the capsule, the display retained through winter on leafless twigs. **ZONES 4–9.**

Celastrus scandens
AMERICAN BITTERSWEET, STAFF VINE

Native over much of eastern North America and climbing to heights of around 20 ft (6 m) or more, this twining shrub has oval leaves up to 4 in (10 cm)

Cedrus libani

Cedrus libani 'Aurea-Prostrata'

long. The insignificant greenish yellow flowers appear in summer and are followed by bunches of pea-sized fruit which split to reveal orange insides and bright red seeds. The fruit mature in fall (autumn) and can persist on the plants well into winter. **ZONES 3–9.**

CELMISIA

SNOW DAISY, MOUNTAIN DAISY, NEW ZEALAND DAISY

Sixty or so species of rhizomatous perennials and subshrubs with white daisy-like flowerheads make up this genus, the majority native to New Zealand but with a smaller number native to Tasmania and southeastern mainland Australia. Mostly occurring in higher mountain grasslands, meadows and rocky places, they are attractive evergreen plants with tufts of narrow silvery gray leaves and a profuse display of yellow-centered white flowers, mostly solitary on scaly stalks. The leaf undersides of most species are covered with a thick silvery white fur.
CULTIVATION: Most celmisias are true alpine plants that resent lowland conditions, but a few will grow successfully in rockeries, peat beds or scree gardens in temperate climates. They can be planted in full sun or part-shade and require moist, well-drained, gritty, acid soil. Protect from hot sun in drier areas and from excessive moisture in cool climates. Propagate from seed in fall (autumn) or by division in late spring.

Celmisia asteliifolia

SILVER SNOW DAISY

This species is native to Tasmania and southeastern mainland Australia, forming large swathes of silvery gray foliage over grassy mountain slopes above the treeline. A dense network of woody rhizomes connects tangled rosettes of narrow, curving leaves that are white-felty on the undersides and dark gray-green on the upper. In mid-summer appear profuse 2–3 in (5–8 cm) wide flowerheads with white ray florets that are purplish on the reverse, on stalks 8–12 in (20–30 cm) tall. **ZONES 6–9.**

Celmisia hookeri

From the South Island of New Zealand where it occurs in dry grasslands from the sea coast to lower mountain slopes, this is one of the larger-leafed species, with leaves up to 12 in (30 cm) long and 3 in (8 cm) wide, glossy deep green above and with thick white felt beneath. The flowerheads are up to 4 in (10 cm)

Celastrus scandens

Ceiba pentandra

across on short, thick stems, with a wide disc and a rather narrow rim of ray florets. **ZONES 7–9.**

Celmisia semicordata

syn. *Celmisia coriacea*

This is one of the largest-growing species, also from low to medium altitudes on the South Island of New Zealand. Forming with age large mounds of rosettes, the striking silvery leaves are stiff and straight, up to 18 in (45 cm) long and 1–3 in (2.5–8 cm) wide. The white flowerheads are up to 4 in (10 cm) across, on slender stems to 15 in (38 cm) long. Generally regarded as the easiest celmisia to grow, *Celmisia semicordata* is more tolerant than most of heat and dry conditions but likes ample summer moisture. **ZONES 7–9.**

Celmisia spectabilis

This alpine New Zealand species, found in high-altitude grasslands on the South Island, has been widely cultivated. Developing with age into a large patch, it has a few to many rosettes of very thick leaves that are dark green to somewhat silvery above and white-felty beneath. In early summer showy white and gold flowerheads about 2 in (5 cm) across appear, held above the leaves on stems 4–8 in (10–20 cm) high. **ZONES 6–9.**

CELOSIA

COCKSCOMB, CHINESE WOOLFLOWER

This genus of erect annuals, perennials and shrubs in the amaranthus family contains 50 or more species from warmer parts of Asia, Africa and the Americas, but only one *(Celosia argentea)* is widely cultivated as a bedding annual and for cut flowers. It has

Celmisia hookeri

Ceiba pentandra

Celosia argentea, Plumosa Group

evolved in cultivation into several different forms, hardly recognizable as belonging to the one species. It has simple, soft, strongly veined leaves; the variation is almost wholly in the structure of the heads of the small flowers, which have undergone proliferation and deformation in the two major cultivated races.
CULTIVATION: In cool climates celosias are treated as conservatory plants, or planted out for summer bedding after raising seedlings under glass in spring. They are better adapted to hot climates, withstanding the fiercest summer heat. They require full sun, rich, well-drained soil and constant moisture. Propagate from seed in spring.

Celosia argentea

syns *Celosia cristata, C. pyramidalis*

Probably native to tropical Asia, this erect, summer-flowering annual can reach 3 ft (1 m) or more in height. The leaves are mid-green; the silvery white flowers appear in summer in dense, erect, pointed spikes with a silvery sheen. The species is best known in the guise of two strikingly different cultivar groups, which in turn are hardly recognizable as belonging to the species. These are the **Plumosa Group**, with erect, plume-like heads of tiny deformed flowers in a range of hot colors, and the **Cristata Group** (cockscombs), with bizarre wavy crests of fused flower stalks also in many colors. Both have been developed in cultivation with a range of seedling strains, differing in height as well as size and the color of the flowerheads. The Plumosa Group in particular are favored for cut flowers and sale in pots for indoor decoration. Some dwarf strains are no more than 6 in (15 cm) tall, while the old-fashioned bedding strains are about 24 in (60 cm). Most strains are sold as mixed colors. **ZONES 10–12.**

Celtis occidentalis

Celtis jessoensis

Celosia spicata

Celosia spicata

Of uncertain origin, this annual species has appeared in recent years as a cut flower. Growing to 24 in (60 cm) or more, it has an erect, slender habit and much narrower leaves than *Celosia argentea*. The summer flowers are neatly crowded onto terminal spikes, opening progressively from the base with the buds purplish pink and the chaffy flowers ageing to pale silvery pink as the spikes elongate. The flowers last well when dried. **ZONES 10–12.**

CELTIS

NETTLE TREE, HACKBERRY

This large genus of 70 species includes many evergreens, occurring mainly in the tropics, but the cool-climate, deciduous species from North America, Europe and Asia are the ones mostly cultivated. They are medium to fairly large trees with smooth or slightly rough bark. The leaves are smallish, oval and pointed at the tip, with few or many marginal teeth. Insignificant flowers, of different sexes and lacking petals, appear with the new leaves, and the fruits are small, hard drupes carried singly in the leaf axils. Birds eat the fruits and disperse the seeds, and some species self-seed and can become a nuisance. *Celtis* species are planted mainly as shade trees in streets and parks, where they make shapely, long-lived and trouble-free specimens.

CULTIVATION: In cooler climates, these fully frost-hardy trees like dry soil and full sun; in warmer areas they prefer rich, moist, well-drained soil and part-shade. Propagate from seed in fall (autumn).

Celtis africana

A warm-climate, deciduous species from coastal forests and grassland areas of South Africa, this is a large, well-shaped tree with smooth, silvery white bark. It grows rapidly to a height and spread of 30–40 ft (9–12 m) in cultivation, much taller in the wild. Small, pale yellow flowers appear briefly in spring at the same time as the new foliage. Masses of orange or yellow berries ripen during summer. It tolerates dry conditions. **ZONES 9–11.**

Celtis australis

SOUTHERN NETTLE TREE, EUROPEAN HACKBERRY

This deciduous, small to medium-sized tree grows to 50 ft (15 m) in height and originates from southern Europe, North Africa and Asia Minor. It has broadly lance-shaped, serrated-edged leaves that are mid to dark green and rough to touch on the upper surface, paler green and downy on the underside. The small fruit, which turn purple-black in fall (autumn), are edible. **ZONES 8–10.**

Celtis jessoensis

syn. *Celtis bungeana* var. *jessoensis*

JESSO HACKBERRY

Indigenous to northeast Asia, this deciduous tree may reach 50 ft (15 m). It is densely clothed with toothed, lanceolate leaves carried on horizontal branches which give the tree a wide, squat appearance. **ZONES 6–10.**

Celtis laevigata

syn. *Celtis mississippiensis*

SUGARBERRY, SUGAR HACKBERRY

The handsome sugarberry is a valued deciduous street tree in its native midwestern and southeastern USA. In the wild it grows on riverbanks and moist ground. The thin leaves taper to a very fine point and usually lack marginal teeth. It grows fast when young, eventually making a shapely, round-headed tree of about 60 ft (18 m) or more in height with deep green foliage. In summer it has pea-sized orange-red fruit. **ZONES 5–10.**

Celtis occidentalis

AMERICAN HACKBERRY

This species comes from the east of the USA, the Mississippi Basin and eastern Canada. In its preferred habitat of forests in deep, rich, alluvial soils it can reach a very large size, but when planted in the open it makes a shapely, spreading tree of 40–60 ft (12–18 m). The bark, smooth on saplings, becomes rough as the tree matures. The pea-sized fruit ripen through red to dull purple. The foliage turns pale yellow in fall (autumn); it can become a pest along riverbanks and channels in some countries. **ZONES 3–10.**

Celtis sinensis

CHINESE HACKBERRY, CHINESE NETTLE TREE

Originating in China, Japan and Korea, this deciduous or semi-deciduous tree grows to 50–70 ft (15–21 m) with a rounded, broad crown. It is notable for its dark green, glossy leaves. Small, globe-shaped fruit start green and ripen to first dull orange then dull purple in mid-summer and fall (autumn). In warmer temperate climates this species has proved very tough and adaptable, tolerating infertile and poorly drained soil and urban pollution. In humid coastal areas it can rapidly become a weed. **ZONES 8–11.**

Celtis tenuifolia

GEORGIA HACKBERRY

Native to the southeast and Midwest of the USA, this small, rounded tree rarely reaches 30 ft (9 m). The leaves are about

Celtis africana

Celtis sinensis

Celtis tenuifolia

Cenia turbinata

2 in (5 cm) long, lanceolate and may be lightly toothed. They are somewhat rough to the touch. It is not a common tree in cultivation as it is a slow grower and not particularly showy in flower or fruit. **ZONES 6–9.**

CENIA

This genus of low-growing annuals and perennials in the daisy family is closely related to *Cotula*, in which they were formerly included. The plants have rather the aspect of *Anthemis* but the yellow flowerheads lack ray florets, appearing like large buttons, borne singly on slender stalks. The finely divided leaves are softly hairy and slightly aromatic.
CULTIVATION: Easily grown as rock-garden or edging plants, they produce a succession of cheerful blooms though the plants can become rather straggly as they age. Sow seed in fall (autumn), planting out in a sunny spot when seedlings are 1 in (25 mm) high.

Cenia turbinata

syn. *Cotula turbinata*
BACHELOR'S BUTTONS

Native to coastal areas of South Africa's Cape Province, this species is a short-lived perennial but in the garden is most often treated as an annual. The sprawling stems radiate from a central rootstock, concealed beneath the pale green, dissected, hairy foliage. In spring it produces a succession of bright yellow 'buttons' about $1\frac{1}{4}$ in (30 mm) in diameter on short, weak stalks. The plant grows 4–6 in (10–15 cm) high and spreads to about 24 in (60 cm).
ZONES 8–10.

CENTAUREA

CORNFLOWER, KNAPWEED

This genus, belonging to the thistle tribe of composites, is a huge one with around 450 species scattered all over the temperate, grassy regions of Eurasia and north Africa, with one or two strays in America. It includes annuals, biennials and perennials. Some spiny-leafed species are troublesome weeds in some parts of the world. Apart from the common annual cornflower, some of the perennial species are desirable garden plants; they come in various colors, from white through shades of blue, red, pink, purple and yellow. The flowerheads typically have an urn-shaped receptacle of fringed or spiny bracts, from the mouth of which radiate the quite large florets, each deeply divided into 5 colored petals; smaller florets occupy the center of the head, but do not form a distinct disc as in other members of the daisy or Compositae family.
CULTIVATION: Cornflowers do well in well-drained soil in a sunny position. Propagate from seed in spring or fall (autumn); perennials can also be divided in spring or fall.

Centaurea cineraria

Centaurea dealbata

Centaurea cineraria

syns *Centaurea candidissima* of gardens, *C. gymnocarpa*
DUSTY MILLER

A shrubby perennial from the Mediterranean region, *Centaurea cineraria* is grown mainly for its beautiful, much divided silvery white foliage. When not in flower the plant is easily mistaken for the unrelated *Senecio cineraria*, also known as dusty miller. Small thistle-like, lilac-pink flowerheads held on much-branched flower stems reveal delicate symmetry and color. The silveriness of the foliage can vary from plant to plant, the best being selected for propagation. **ZONES 7–10.**

Centaurea cyanus

BLUE-BOTTLE, BACHELOR'S BUTTON, CORNFLOWER

One of the best known wildflowers of Europe and northern Asia, this species is also a common weed of cereal crops. It is a weak-stemmed erect annual 24–36 in (60–90 cm) tall with very narrow leaves and small, rather untidy flowerheads that are typically a slightly purplish shade of blue. Garden varieties have been developed with larger flowers in shades of pale and deep pink, cerise, crimson, white, purple and blue, some of them dwarf and more compact. Best displayed in large clumps, it will flower for months if deadheads are removed regularly.
ZONES 5–10.

Centaurea dealbata

PERSIAN CORNFLOWER

Native to the Caucasus region and northern Iran, this very leafy perennial has deeply cut foliage that is grayish green underneath. Lilac-purple to lilac-pink flowerheads appear from late spring onwards. An erect plant, *Centaurea dealbeata* grows to 3 ft (1 m) high. **'Steenbergii'** has larger, deep pink flowers. **ZONES 4–9.**

Centaurea hypoleuca

Also from the Caucasus and Iran as well as eastern Turkey, this spreading perennial has fragrant pale to deep pink flowerheads, produced singly on stalks up to 24 in (60 cm) high in early summer often with a second flush in fall (autumn). It has long, lobed leaves, green on top and gray underneath, and forms a clump 18 in (45 cm) across. **'John Coutts'** bears deep rose pink flowers. **ZONES 5–9.**

Centaurea hypoleuca

Centaurea cyanus

Centaurea cineraria

Centaurea macrocephala
GLOBE CORNFLOWER

With foliage somewhat like a large dandelion, this perennial species originates in the subalpine fields of Armenia and nearby parts of Turkey. In summer stout leafy stems, up to 3 ft (1 m) tall, carry yellow flowerheads about 2 in (5 cm) across with a club-like base of shiny brown bracts. **ZONES 4–9.**

Centaurea montana
PERENNIAL CORNFLOWER, MOUNTAIN BLUET

From the mountains of Europe, this long-cultivated perennial species is up to 30 in (75 cm) high and has creeping rhizomes; it may form large clumps when conditions are to its liking. The leaves are usually smooth edged and green, and the 2 in (5 cm) wide violet flowerheads, borne in early summer, are distinctive for their widely spaced florets, giving them a delicate lacy effect. **ZONES 3–9.**

Centaurea moschata
syn. ***Amberboa moschata***
SWEET SULTAN

Some botanists now prefer to split off this and several other *Centaurea* species into a separate genus, *Amberboa*. A sweet-scented cottage garden plant introduced to cultivation over 350 years ago from the eastern Mediterranean, it is a fast-growing, upright annual to 24 in (60 cm) high with lance-shaped, grayish green leaves. Large, delicate, fluffy flowerheads to 3 in (8 cm) across are produced in a wide range of colors in summer and early fall (autumn). **ZONES 6–10.**

Centaurea simplicicaulis

From the Caucasus region and central Asia, this is a mat-forming perennial with a creeping rhizome and numerous miniature rosettes of dissected leaves that are gray-green above and felty white beneath. In early summer it sends up slender, unbranched flowering stems to 18 in (45 cm) high, each terminating in a $1\frac{1}{2}$ in (35 mm) wide flowerhead of delicate structure with rose pink florets. It is best suited to a dry sunny spot in the rock garden. **ZONES 3–9.**

CENTELLA

About 20 species of creeping annuals and perennials belong to this genus in the carrot family, most of them native to Africa but a few scattered through southern Asia and southern hemisphere countries. They have slender stems that root at the nodes, and leaves that are almost circular except for a notch where the leaf-stalk joins. Tiny, dull-colored flowers are borne on short stalks along the stems. Apart from *Centella asiatica*, none of the species is cultivated.
CULTIVATION: Easily grown in any small patch of moist soil in a frost-free climate, or can be grown in a pot. It can be invasive and growth needs to be kept in check. Propagate by division: any small piece of rooted stem will grow.

Centella asiatica
syn. ***Hydrocotyle asiatica***
INDIAN PENNYWORT, GOTU-KOLA

This humble perennial is one of the most widely used medicinal plants in southern Asia. Its original wild distribution is uncertain, but it is widespread in Australasia as well as Asia. It is mat-forming, often creeping through moist grass and only 1 in (25 mm) or so high, but when cultivated its leaf-stalks lengthen and it may exceed 6 in (15 cm). Tiny reddish flowers appear in spring. In parts of tropical Asia it is regarded as a general tonic and the green leaves are eaten daily with rice, but many other medicinal uses are recorded. **ZONES 9–12.**

Centaurea montana

Centella asiatica

Centaurea macrocephala

CENTRADENIA

About 5 species of weak-stemmed shrubs and subshrubs from Mexico and Central America make up this genus, which is allied to *Heterocentron*. Like other members of the melastoma family they have simple leaves arranged in opposite pairs and with long, curved veins strongly impressed into the upper surface. In *Centradenia* the leaves of each pair may be very different in size, and both leaves and stems may take on attractive reddish tones, especially on the undersides. The smallish flowers are pink or mauve, but often borne abundantly in panicles.
CULTIVATION: Centradenias are quick-growing plants suitable for indoor cultivation in pots or baskets, though requiring strong light, or for outdoors in warmer climates where they can be used to good effect on retaining walls or the edges of paths. Plants can be cut back when they become too straggly. Propagate from cuttings.

Centradenia floribunda

Native to Mexico and Guatemala, this little subshrub has narrow leaves up to 2 in (5 cm) long, dark green above and paler beneath with red veins. The pink flowers are less than $\frac{1}{2}$ in (12 mm) across but are borne in large panicles in winter and spring. **ZONES 10–12.**

Centradenia grandifolia

This Mexican species makes a weak shrub of up to 2–5 ft (0.6–1.5 m) tall, the reddish branches with 4 wing-like angles. The attractive leaves are up to 6 in (15 cm) long, very asymmetrical and with bright red undersides. Pink flowers only about $\frac{1}{4}$ in (6 mm) across are borne in short sprays in fall (autumn). **ZONES 10–12.**

CENTRANTHUS
VALERIAN

Around 10 species belong to this genus of annual and perennial herbs closely related to *Valeriana*, native to the Mediterranean region and western Asia, but only one, *Centranthus ruber*, is widely planted for ornament. They make tufts of soft leaves that may be simple and smooth edged or less commonly dissected, and the leafy, branched flowering stems bear many irregular heads of tiny tubular flowers.
CULTIVATION: Grow in full sun in moderately fertile, chalk or lime soil that is well drained. Deadhead regularly. These plants are not long lived and are best divided every 3 years to ensure a good display. Propagate from seed or by division.

Centranthus ruber

Centranthus ruber
RED VALERIAN, JUPITER'S BEARD, KISS-ME-QUICK

This perennial is often seen as a naturalized plant on dry banks and is ideal for dry rock gardens as well as borders. It forms loose clumps of somewhat fleshy leaves and grows to a height of 24–36 in (60–90 cm). From late spring to fall (autumn) it produces dense clusters of small, star-shaped, deep reddish pink to pale pink flowers that last for a long time. The cultivar **'Albus'** has white flowers. One of the easiest plants to grow, it requires sun and good drainage and will tolerate exposed positions and poor alkaline soil. **ZONES 5–10.**

CEPHALARIA

Closely related to *Scabiosa*, this genus of 65 species of annual and perennial herbs occurs wild in Europe, western Asia and temperate regions of Africa. They have basal tufts of pinnate or deeply dissected leaves, and usually smaller leaves on their branched flowering stems. The flowers, mostly yellow or white, are in heads like those of the daisy family but the florets have a different and distinctive structure in the scabious family.
CULTIVATION: These plants thrive in clay soil that can remain wet for some time, but are equally at home in well-drained, moist, fertile soil. They very rarely need staking even though they can become quite tall and lanky. Propagate from seed or by division.

Cephalaria gigantea
GIANT SCABIOUS, TARTARIAN CEPHALARIA

This handsome giant of a perennial is native to the Caucasus region including northern Turkey. It needs plenty of space to spread, as it can grow to 8 ft (2.4 m) high and 4 ft (1.2 m) across. It forms a robust clump of dark green, deeply divided leaves up to 18 in (45 cm) long, from which arise in summer many tough, thin stems topped with sulfur-yellow flowerheads about 2 in (5 cm) in diameter. **ZONES 3–9.**

CEPHALOCEREUS

Only 3 species of columnar cacti belong to this genus, both native to central Mexico. One of numerous groups of cacti once included in the catch-all genus *Cereus*, their present genus name means 'headed cereus', referring to a peculiar feature found in this and several other cacti genera, namely the cephalium, an

Cephalotaxus harringtonia 'Fastigiata'

Cephalotaxus harringtonia 'Fastigiata'

eruption of felt-covered tissue near the top of the stem from which flowers emerge year after year. In *Cephalocereus*, though, flowering generally occurs only on mature plants which may be decades old, and the average cactus grower may never see a cephalium develop. The main attraction of the genus is the snow white spines and bristles that cover the many-ribbed stems, especially near the apical growing point. The stems grow straight and erect and when they finally branch it is from the base, to form a small group of parallel stems.
CULTIVATION: These are subtropical cacti and will only tolerate the lightest of frosts, and then only if the climate is warm and dry. In cool climates they are grown indoors, requiring a window position with strong light or a sunny conservatory. They demand much the same well-drained soil mix as most cacti, though some growers recommend the addition of limestone chips, and are sensitive to over-watering. They are susceptible to mealybug and spider mite. Propagate from seed.

Cephalocereus senilis
OLD MAN CACTUS

In the wild on dry scrubby hills of the Mexican plateau, this cactus grows to over 40 ft (12 m) tall with multiple stems, but in cultivation specimens taller than 4 ft (1.2 m) are rarely seen. But even as a very young plant this cactus attracts attention by virtue of its long, tangled white bristles like an old man's whiskers that conceal the stem. It is sometimes

Cephalotaxus fortunei

sold as a novelty item complete with two glass eyes, spectacles, a pipe, etc. The trumpet-shaped white or somewhat yellowish flowers open only at night in summer. **ZONES 9–12.**

CEPHALOTAXUS
PLUM YEW

This is an interesting genus of conifers consisting of around 10 species of shrubs or small trees from eastern Asia, mostly with many stems sprouting from the base. The deep green, leathery leaves are rather like those of the true yews (*Taxus*), though usually longer. The fleshy 'fruits' develop in stalked globular heads and are more like olives than plums, ripening reddish brown. Male pollen sacs are also grouped in small, globular clusters on separate trees.
CULTIVATION: These conifers are tough, resilient plants, but do best in cool, fairly humid climates and in sheltered positions. The occasional free-seeding specimen can cause minor problems by the quantity of 'fruit' dropping to rot on the ground beneath. Propagate from seed, which may take 2 years to germinate, or from cuttings.

Cephalotaxus fortunei
CHINESE PLUM YEW

This species from northeastern China makes a spreading shrub or small tree to 20 ft (6 m) with brown bark peeling off in flakes. It was introduced to England in 1849 by Robert Fortune, the man who first brought the tea plant from China to India. The linear leaves, up to 4 in (10 cm) long, have fine sharp points. The oval fruit are about 1 in (25 mm) long. **ZONES 7–10.**

Cephalotaxus harringtonia
JAPANESE PLUM YEW

First known from Japan, this variable species also occurs in Korea and parts of China. The typical form is a spreading, bushy shrub 6–10 ft (1.8–3 m) tall with leaves up to 2½ in (6 cm) long. More commonly grown is ***Cephalotaxus harringtonia* var. *drupacea***, a dome-like shrub to about 10 ft (3 m) with short blunt leaves in 2 erect rows. The most remarkable and attractive form is **'Fastigiata'**: very erect, it sends up a dense mass of long, straight stems from the base, with radiating whorls of recurving leaves. It forms a tight column about 6 ft (1.8 m) or more high and 24–36 in (60–90 cm) across. **'Nana'** is a low-growing form, generally under 3 ft (1 m) high but spreading widely with almost prostrate branches, often self-layering. **'Prostrata'** forms a cushion of generally ascending branches to 24 in (60 cm) tall and spreads about 4 ft (1.2 m). **ZONES 6–10.**

CERARIA

About 5 species of succulent shrubs belong to this genus, allied to *Portulacaria* and likewise endemic to southern Africa, in this case restricted to the far west of Cape Province and nearby parts of Namibia. They are much-branched plants, sometimes with a very thickened basal trunk or 'caudex', the branches thick and fleshy or quite slender. The leaves are very small and succulent; the white or pink flowers are also very small.
CULTIVATION: These unusual plants require similar treatment to other South African succulents from the very low-rainfall areas of the Western Cape. They need a very open, gritty soil mix with perfect drainage and should be watered sparingly and then only in the spring growing season. Propagate from cuttings.

Ceraria pygmaea

Confined to South Africa's Little Namaqualand where so many other extreme succulent plants occur, this species makes a miniature shrub with branches springing from a short, thickened trunk with rough bark. The small succulent leaves are somewhat bluish or yellowish with a finely warty surface, and the tiny flowers are white to pale pink. **ZONES 9–11.**

CERASTIUM

Sixty or so species of low-growing annuals and perennials belong to this genus, occurring in most temperate regions of the world though mainly in the northern hemisphere, where some extend into arctic regions. The annuals include some common weeds of lawns (mouse-eared chickweeds), proliferating in winter and spring, but some of the perennials are useful garden plants grown as ground covers or rock-garden subjects, for example, ***Cerastium boissieri***. They have very weak stems from a network of thin rhizomes and small leaves tapering to narrow bases and usually clothed in whitish hairs. The flowers are white with 5 petals, each notched at the apex, held in stalked clusters above the leaves.
CULTIVATION: Easily cultivated, some cerastiums can be invasive if planted in confined spaces in a rock garden. All are frost hardy and like full sun and well-drained soil. Their foliage should, if possible, be kept dry both in winter and during humid summer weather as the fine hairs on the leaves tend to retain moisture and become mildewed. They are easily propagated by division of rhizomes.

Cephalotaxus harringtonia 'Prostrata'

Cephalocereus senilis

Cerastium boissieri

Cerastium tomentosum

Ceratonia siliqua

Ceratopetalum gummiferum

Cerastium alpinum

ALPINE MOUSE-EAR

This cold-loving perennial species is widely distributed across subarctic regions of the northern hemisphere, coming south in Europe in the mountains. Forming a mat or small hummock, *Cerastium alpinum* has hairy rounded leaves and in summer bears conspicuous white flowers with broad petals purple-lined in the throat, singly or in 2s or 3s on short, erect stalks. It does not adapt well to cultivation in warmer climates, requiring cool, humid summers. **ZONES 2–8.**

Cerastium tomentosum

SNOW-IN-SUMMER

A vigorous, fast-growing ground cover, this perennial is ideal for a well-drained, hot, dry bank or rockery. It has narrow silvery gray leaves, and masses of star-shaped white flowers are borne in loose heads in late spring and summer. It is

Ceratopetalum apetalum

Ceratopetalum apetalum

Ceratostigma griffithii

particularly attractive when used as an underplanting against darker backgrounds. The foliage is dense and an effective weed suppressant. It grows to 6 in (15 cm) high and spreads indefinitely, and is very cold hardy. In the wild this species is variable and some botanists have split off a number of species from it; taken in the broad sense, though, it has a wide distribution through the mountains of southern and eastern Europe and western Asia. **ZONES 3–10.**

CERATONIA

CAROB, ST JOHN'S BREAD

The single species in this genus comes from the eastern Mediterranean, where it forms a picturesque, round-headed tree of up to 40 ft (12 m). It is more commonly seen as a smaller tree or large shrub in cultivation and can be pruned hard to keep it in check. The bean-like pods, about 6 in (15 cm) long, commonly roasted and powdered as a chocolate substitute, can be picked in fall (autumn) when they are dark brown. They can also be eaten fresh and are used as stock fodder. **CULTIVATION:** While it requires hot, dry summers to perform well, the carob

Ceratopetalum apetalum

will survive in warm, sheltered positions in cooler climates. Marginally frost hardy, it does best in full sun although it will tolerate light shade and is also tolerant of dry conditions; a moderately fertile, well-drained soil suits it best. Propagate from seed in fall (autumn).

Ceratonia siliqua

A long-lived evergreen tree, this species is used as a shade tree for streets, parks and large gardens, and as a farm shelter and fodder tree. It has glossy pinnate leaves and clustered spikes of small greenish flowers in spring and fall (autumn), which may be ill-smelling at close quarters. As some plants bear only male or female flowers, interplanting of both sexes may be needed for production of the pods. **ZONES 9–11.**

CERATOPETALUM

Members of this small Australian genus come from the moist forests of the east coast; the 2 most important species are found in New South Wales, where they are valued for their timber and flowers. They are evergreen and bear flowers with small white petals but with sepals that enlarge and turn red as the small, nut-like fruits mature, appearing very flower-like and showy.
CULTIVATION: Ceratopetalums prefer a warm, almost frost-free climate and free-draining soil in a sunny or part-shaded position, with protection from salty winds and plenty of water in spring and summer. Propagation is from fresh seed or from cuttings.

Ceratopetalum apetalum

COACHWOOD

This tree with its tall, straight trunk and smooth, pale gray bark blotched with darker patches can reach a height of 80 ft (24 m) or more in deep-shaded rainforest gullies. The long, tapering leaves are dark green and heavily veined, and when crushed smell strongly of coumarin (like new-mown hay). Large clusters of small white flowers appear in late spring, the sepals enlarging and becoming red in early summer. A valuable timber tree, the coachwood is occasionally grown in parks and gardens. **ZONES 9–11.**

Ceratopetalum gummiferum

NEW SOUTH WALES CHRISTMAS BUSH

Occurring naturally in coastal gullies and on sheltered slopes in mostly sandstone soils, in the wild this species makes an upright tree to 30 ft (9 m) or more in height. In gardens it is often kept pruned as a shrub or small tree of about 12 ft (3.5 m), and is grown for its bright 'flowers' which start white and become pink or bright red in early summer. The shiny, soft green leaves are each divided into 3 serrated leaflets. As coloration is very variable from seedling stock, it is wise to buy plants when in flower or choose a clone such as **'Albery's Red'**. **ZONES 9–11.**

CERATOPHYLLUM

HORNWORT

Some 30 species of submerged aquatics make up this genus, sufficiently unique to merit a family of its own but related distantly to *Nymphaea* and *Cabomba.* They occur in most parts of the world, both tropical and temperate. The leaves are much divided, rather like those of *Cabomba,* but instead of being soft are remarkably rigid and brittle to the touch. The flowers are minute, in leaf axils, and the small fruits that follow have 2 or 3 horn-like spines. Hornworts have no true roots and usually grow suspended in still water, up to 30 ft (10 m) deep, which is commonly rich in lime; the leaves become encrusted with calcium carbonate, which forms a deposit on the beds of lakes or ponds as the leaves decay.
CULTIVATION: Hornworts are grown in aquariums or deep garden ponds and are regarded as useful oxygenating plants. They can be propagated from sections of a cut stem, anchored on the floor of a pond or aquarium in the warmer months.

Ceratophyllum demersum

RIGID HORNWORT

The most widespread species, rigid hornwort occurs in all continents. Its leaves, arranged in closely spaced whorls around the stem, are dark green and divided into thread-like segments. The tiny flowers, appearing in summer, are followed by hard fruit with 2 basal spines and a small terminal spine. **ZONES 8–12.**

CERATOSTIGMA

This genus of 8 species of herbaceous perennials and small shrubs is primarily of Himalayan and East Asian origin, with one species endemic to the Horn of Africa. Most of the species grown in gardens are small deciduous shrubs and from spring to fall (autumn) they produce loose heads of blue flowers that indicate the genus's relationship with *Plumbago.* The small leaves are deep green, turning to bronze or crimson in fall before dropping.
CULTIVATION: *Ceratostigma* species will grow in any moist, well-drained soil in sun or part-shade. Propagate from seed or semi-ripe cuttings, or by division. In cold climates they will reshoot from the roots even though the top growth may die back to ground level.

Ceratostigma griffithii

BURMESE PLUMBAGO

Native to the Himalayas, this is an evergreen shrub which makes a low mound

Ceratostigma plumbaginoides

Cerbera manghas

of foliage to about 36 in (90 cm) high and much greater spread, the densely massed, semi-prostrate stems all springing from the rootstock. The leaves are dull green and thick textured with purple-tinged margins. Bright purplish blue flowers are borne in clusters at the ends of the branches in summer. **ZONES 7–10.**

Ceratostigma plumbaginoides
syn. ***Plumbago larpentae***

CHINESE PLUMBAGO, PERENNIAL LEADWORT, DWARF PLUMBAGO

Native to western China, this bushy perennial grows to 18 in (45 cm) high with rather erect, crowded stems arising from much-branched rhizomes. It has oval, mid-green leaves that turn a rich orange and red in fall (autumn). The flowers are plumbago-like, with small clusters of single cornflower blue blooms appearing on reddish, branched stems in late summer and fall. **ZONES 6–9.**

Ceratostigma willmottianum
CHINESE PLUMBAGO

This 2–4 ft (0.6–1.2 m), deciduous shrub from western Sichuan, China, is prized for its small heads of lilac-blue flowers that open from late summer to fall (autumn). The leaves are deep green, roughly diamond-shaped and around 2 in (5 cm) long. **ZONES 6–10.**

CERBERA

Belonging to the oleander family, this genus consists of perhaps 4 species of evergreen shrubs and small trees, native to tropical Asia and Australasia, Madagascar and the Seychelles. They have a milky sap and are poisonous in all parts; one species from Madagascar was notorious for its use there as an 'ordeal' poison, administered to criminal suspects to test their guilt or innocence. Linnaeus took the genus name from that of Cerberus, the 3-headed dog guarding the entrance to Hades. The plants have broad, smooth

Ceratostigma willmottianum

leaves arranged in opposite pairs, fragrant white flowers and large egg-shaped fruits.
CULTIVATION: Apart from a warm, completely frost free climate, they need good light and a moist, humid atmosphere to prosper. Plant in well-drained, humus-rich soil. Propagate from seed or cuttings.

Cerbera manghas
syn. **Cerbera odollam**

Occurring over most of the range of the genus (except Madagascar), this species grows mainly at the edges of mangrove swamps. A tree or shrub to 20 ft (6 m) in height it has narrow, leathery leaves and highly fragrant white flowers, with either a pink or yellow center, held in large bunches. The large, single-seeded, egg-shaped fruit are 2–3 in (5–8 cm) long and ripen from green to red. **ZONES 11–12.**

CERCIDIPHYLLUM
KATSURA TREE

Consisting of a single species of deciduous tree native to Japan and China, this genus is placed in a family of its own, allied to the magnolia family. The dull red flowers are rather insignificant, with different sexes on different trees. On female trees clusters of small greenish pod-like fruit follow the flowers. The katsura tree is valued chiefly for its foliage, which is reddish when first expanding in spring, then dark green, changing in fall (autumn) to various mixtures of yellow, pink, orange and red. *Katsura* is its Japanese name.
CULTIVATION: This tree prefers rich, moist but well-drained soil in a sunny or part-shaded position. It is fully frost hardy but the spring foliage is easily damaged by late frost, very dry conditions or drying winds. Propagate from seed or cuttings.

Cercidiphyllum japonicum

In cultivation in the West *Cercidiphyllum japonicum* is known as a small, rather slender tree to about 40 ft (12 m) high, but in Japan and China it is the largest native deciduous tree—ancient specimens up to 130 ft (40 m) tall, with trunks over 15 ft (4.5 m) in diameter, are known. The trunk often forks at a narrow angle and the short branches spread horizontally in tiers. The heart-shaped leaves are mostly under 3 in (8 cm) wide, but larger in ***C. j.* var. *magnificum***; the Chinese ***C. j.* var. *sinense*** has slightly different leaves and flowers. **'Pendulum'** has a dome-shaped crown and pendulous branches. **ZONES 6–9.**

Cercidium floridum

CERCIDIUM

From the warmer and drier parts of the Americas, the legume genus *Cercidium* consists of small, wiry-branched trees that are commonly deciduous throughout dry periods, coming into leaf only after rain. The leaves are small and bipinnate, but for much of the time it is the wiry green branches that perform the function of photosynthesis. The fine-stalked flowers are yellow and cup-shaped, somewhat like *Cassia* flowers, and appear in profuse clusters all along the branches for a few weeks in spring. Some botanists suggest that all *Cercidium* species be transferred to *Parkinsonia*.
CULTIVATION: These trees can make fine ornamental and shade trees for very hot dry areas, though they do require a supply of deep subsoil moisture. Propagation is from seed, produced in small pods. They can become invasive, so excessive seedlings should be removed.

Cercidium floridum
PALO VERDE

The common name is Spanish for 'green stick' and describes the smooth bluish green bark and branches of this small tree. Native to the lower Colorado basin of southwestern USA and adjacent Mexico, *Cercidium floridum* matures into a broad-crowned small tree 25–30 ft (8–9 m) tall, with a short thick trunk and densely massed branches. In spring it is briefly transformed into a mass of golden yellow blossom. It is leafless for much of the time, unless regularly watered. **ZONES 8–11.**

Cercidiphyllum japonicum var. *sinense*

Cercidium floridum

CERCIS
JUDAS TREE, REDBUD

This genus is made up of small, deciduous trees or shrubs from North America, Asia and southern Europe. Their profuse clusters of pea-like flowers, bright rose pink to crimson, line the bare branches in spring; even the neat, pointed buds, slightly deeper in color, make an elegant display, hence the American name redbud. The handsome, heart-shaped to almost circular leaves follow, along with flat seed pods up to 4 in (10 cm) long.

Cercidiphyllum japonicum

Cercidiphyllum japonicum 'Pendulum'

Cercidiphyllum japonicum 'Pendulum'

CULTIVATION: All 7 or 8 species are worth cultivating, though not all are easily obtained. They resent disturbance to their roots, especially transplanting. A sunny position suits them best and they thrive in hot, dry summer weather, as long as the soil moisture is adequate in winter and spring. They are easily propagated from seed, though growth is usually slow and it may take many years for them to become larger than shrub size.

Cercis canadensis
EASTERN REDBUD

Native to eastern and central USA, this tree can reach 40 ft (12 m) in the wild and is strikingly beautiful in flower. In gardens it rarely exceeds 12 ft (3.5 m), branching close to the ground. The leaves are heart-shaped with a distinct point, and appear after the flowers. The buds are deep rose, and the paler rose flowers are profuse and showy; flowering may continue from spring into early summer. **'Forest Pansy'** has purple-colored leaves. In the southwestern part of its range the typical form is replaced by ***Cercis canadensis* var. *texensis*,** whose leaf undersides have a waxy bluish coating. **ZONES 5–9.**

Cercis chinensis
CHINESE REDBUD

This central Chinese species makes a large, densely branched shrub of up to about 15 ft (4.5 m) tall in cultivation, though in the wild it is reported to reach 50 ft (15 m). The glossy green heart-shaped leaves are up to 6 in (15 cm) long and have a short but distinct point. It produces bright pink, mauve or crimson flowers in spring or early summer. **ZONES 6–9.**

Cercis chinensis

Cereus granadensis

Cercis occidentalis
WESTERN REDBUD

Geographically this species takes over more or less where *Cercis canadensis* leaves off, occurring in the southwest of the USA where it grows on rocky slopes and in canyons. It is similar in growth habit and flowers to *C. canadensis* but usually remains shrubby. The leaves, more kidney-shaped and rounded at the apex, are bright green. **ZONES 5–9.**

Cercis reniformis

This interesting redbud is also from southern USA, its range in west Texas and New Mexico overlapping with both *Cercis canadensis* var. *texensis* and *C. occidentalis*. It is a small tree, said to reach as much as 40 ft (12 m) in the wild, but usually a large shrub in gardens, with kidney-shaped leaves that are finely hairy on the undersides. The pale pink spring flowers are in drooping sprays up to 4 in (10 cm) long, unlike the clusters of most other species. **ZONES 5–9.**

Cercis siliquastrum
JUDAS TREE, LOVE TREE

Native to regions close to the Mediterranean and Black Sea coasts, this tree seldom exceeds 25 ft (8 m) even after several decades. The leaves are slightly bluish green with rounded tips, and the late spring flowers, larger and deeper pinkish magenta than in other species, arise in clusters on previous years' growths. It is the most reliable ornamental species in regions where winters are mild. Forms with distinct flower coloration include the white **'Alba'** and the deeper reddish **'Rubra'**. **ZONES 7–9.**

Cercis siliquastrum

Cereus uruguayanus

Cercis canadensis

Cercis canadensis 'Forest Pansy'

CERCOCARPUS
MOUNTAIN MAHOGANY

These evergreen shrubs and small trees from western North America get their common name from their hard, strong, reddish wood and their occurrence high in the Rockies and Sierras. The small, thick-textured leaves with blunt teeth and crowded, parallel veins are carried on condensed, knotty side shoots that also produce tight clusters of tiny petal-less flowers in spring and summer. The nut-like fruits may persist into winter; each has a long, feathery plume, much more conspicuous than the small greenish flowers.

CULTIVATION: Successfully cultivated in Europe, *Cercocarpus* species remain rare there but are cultivated to a limited extent in their native regions. They are tough and tolerant of dry conditions. Grow in full sun in very well-drained soil. Propagate from seed or small tip cuttings. Shoots near the ground can be layered and sometimes self-layer.

Cercocarpus montanus
syns ***Cercocarpus alnifolius*, *C. betuloides***
HARD TACK, IRONWOOD

This species has a wide distribution in western USA and northern Mexico, and is divided into at least 7 geographic varieties, which some botanists prefer to treat as distinct species. Commonly shrub-like, it rarely reaches 20 ft (6 m) in height and has very hard, woody branches with smooth gray bark. The leaves are usually dark green above with paler downy undersides; depending on variety, they vary from about ½ in (12 mm) up to 2½ in (6 cm) in length, and their outline varies also. The small dull pinkish flowers open from late spring through summer, followed by the small dry fruit with decorative silvery plumes that can be over 3 in (8 cm) long. **ZONES 7–9.**

Cercocarpus montanus

Cercis occidentalis

CEREUS

In the early years of cactus classification *Cereus* was the name used for all cacti with columnar stems, *Echinocactus* for most of those with short fat stems, and *Opuntia* for the cacti with jointed stems. Today, botanists divide the cactus family into at least 130 genera and the once huge genus *Cereus* is now refined down to a group of about 40 species from South America and the West Indies. The name is still seen compounded in names of many other genera that would once have been included in it, for example, *Cephalocereus, Echinocereus, Heliocereus* and *Selenicereus*. The true cereuses are mainly erect, rarely trailing, multi-stemmed cacti with up to a dozen or so ribs running the length of each stem. The spine clusters are mostly rather sparse and the spines short and stiff. The flowers emerge from ribs at almost any point on the stem, or may be mainly toward the top; they are usually white or cream, of medium to large size, and open at night, closing late the next morning; a typical example, shown here, is ***C. granadensis***.

CULTIVATION: These cacti are mostly of tropical origin but are easily grown in most frost-free situations. The plants do best in full sun and well-drained, poor to moderately fertile, humus-rich soil. They include some of the most vigorous and disease-free cacti, popular as grafting stocks for other cacti difficult to grow on their own roots. Propagate from seed in spring or cuttings in summer.

Cereus uruguayanus
syn. ***Cereus peruvianus* of gardens**
PERUVIAN APPLE, PERUVIAN TORCH

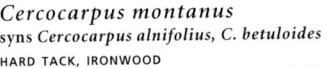

Native to southern Brazil and nearby parts of Argentina and Uruguay, this is the most commonly grown cereus and the one widely used as a cactus graft stock. It reaches about 15 ft (4.5 m) in height, branching from the base into stiff, gray-green stems which sometimes branch again higher up. The ribs usually number 8 and bear short, stiff, dark gray spines. The summer flowers are about 6 in (15 cm) long and as much across when fully open at night, white inside but red-brown outside; they are followed by yellow fruit about 1½ in (35 mm) long. Almost as widely grown is the bizarre cultivar **'Monstrosus'** with a proliferation of growing-points and few spines. **ZONES 9–12.**

CERINTHE

HONEYWORT

A genus of around 10 species of annuals, biennials and perennials, all native to Europe, *Cerinthe* belongs to the borage family but presents a rather different character from most of the harshly bristled plants that are normally found in the family. They have smooth, rounded leaves that tend to clasp the stem at their bases and short, uncurling spikes of tubular yellow flowers, usually with attractive markings in tones of dull pink, red or purple. They have a reputation for prolific honey production.

CULTIVATION: The annual species of *Cerinthe* are easily grown under similar conditions to many other flowering annuals, sowing seed in spring. The perennials have rootstocks that may rot off if too damp in fall (autumn) and winter, and are best suited to rock garden positions with good drainage. They will all grow in part-shade, or full sun if in a sheltered spot. Propagate perennials from seed or by division.

Cerinthe glabra

This perennial from southern and central Europe may sometimes be of only biennial duration. *Cerinthe glabra* is quite similar to *C. major* but has larger basal leaves and smaller flowers, only about ½ in (12 mm) long. **ZONES 5–9.**

Cerinthe major

This annual from southern Europe makes a bushy, rather succulent plant about 18 in (45 cm) high, branching into several or many stems from ground level. The leaves are strongly heart-shaped, bright green but often with whitish spots in the center. The flowers are pendent, about 1½ in (35 mm) long, golden yellow with a deep red or purplish band at the base. The leafy floral bracts of **'Purpurascens'** are tinged purple. **ZONES 7–10.**

CEROPEGIA

This genus of twining climbers and curious succulent shrubs and subshrubs belonging to the milkweed family consists of around 200 species widespread in warmer parts of the Old World but most diverse in Africa, Madagascar and the Canary Islands. It is related to stapelias and hoyas and like these attracts its own small band of dedicated collectors, some of whom have a good proportion of the species in cultivation. The flower structure is complex and bizarre, each flower having a trumpet-shaped tube, usually with a basal swelling, and expanded at the top into 5 lobes that commonly fold in and meet along their edges producing a variety of remarkable lantern-like and parasol-like structures. The smell is faintly putrid and the coloring mostly dull purples and yellows, the same as in some other plants adapted to pollination by carrion-feeding insects, which these flowers attract and force into carrying their pollen by an elaborate trapping mechanism. Many ceropegias have tuberous roots and some have small stem tubers, which can be detached and used for propagation.

CULTIVATION: Requirements vary according to origin and growth habit. Nearly all *Ceropegia* species are warmth-loving plants, requiring protection from frosts, and must be grown indoors in cool climates. A few are easily grown in any well-lit position, for example the well-known ***Ceropegia linearis***, but the more highly succulent species demand a perfectly drained, open soil mix with good humus content which should be kept fairly dry in winter. The more vigorously twining species need supporting wires. Propagate from seed, cuttings or stem tubers.

Ceropegia ampliata

This lightweight climber from South Africa bears heart-shaped leaves but these drop almost as soon as they mature. From the stringy, green stems which remain, curious white and green striped flowers emerge. They have an inflated base, a long tube and the green petals cover the opening in a cage-like structure. **ZONES 10–12.**

Ceropegia dichotoma

This erect succulent species is from the Canary Islands. The gray-green stems form clumps up to 3 ft (1 m) high and sometimes as much across and tend to branch dichotomously, as the name suggests. They carry very few, rather narrow leaves which are soon shed leaving leafless stems. The flowers, emerging in clusters at the nodes, are pale yellow and very slender, with lobes united at the tip. **ZONES 10–12.**

Ceropegia dichotoma

Ceropegia haygarthii

From South Africa's Cape Province, *Ceropegia haygarthii* is a semi-evergreen climbing succulent reaching a height of about 6 ft (1.8 m). It bears oval leaves and a profusion of small white to pinkish white flowers in summer. Each flower has a purple-spotted tube that widens towards the top and terminates in 5 abruptly narrowed segments whose fine tips are twisted together into a long, stalk-like structure with a hairy knob at the end. **ZONES 9–12.**

Ceropegia linearis subsp. *woodii*

syn. *Ceropegia woodii*

CHAIN OF HEARTS, HEARTS-ON-A-STRING, SWEETHEART VINE, ROSARY VINE

A favorite plant for hanging baskets, this native of southeastern Africa produces an abundance of slender, thread-like branches with small aerial tubers developing at some of the nodes. The small, heart-shaped leaves are bluish green mottled white. Pale purplish pink to purple, hairy, tubular flowers about ¾ in (20 mm) long appear in summer, poking out from among the leaves at the nodes. It is one of the most easily grown indoor and balcony plants, though demanding some sunlight each day. **ZONES 9–12.**

Ceropegia linearis subsp. *woodii*

Ceropegia haygarthii

Ceropegia ampliata

Cestrum 'Newellii'

Cestrum nocturnum

Cestrum parqui

Ceropegia sandersonii

syn. ***Ceropegia sandersoniae***

FOUNTAIN FLOWER, PARACHUTE PLANT, UMBRELLA FLOWER

A slender, twining climber, this species is popular for its white and green mottled flowers. These are funnels roofed with an umbrella giving the look of an unearthly parachute. Leaves are fleshy and heart-shaped and the whole plant may climb to 6 ft (1.8 m); it is frost tender. **ZONES 11–12.**

Ceropegia stapeliiformis

This highly succulent species is native to eastern South Africa. It has grayish brown stems about ½ in (12 mm) thick, the leaves reduced to small scales, and is commonly creeping or trailing, but with maturity can send up slender twining stems to 5 ft (1.5 m) in height. In spring and summer it produces tubular flowers 1½–2 in (3–5 cm) long, flaring at the top into a 5-pointed star and mostly off-white spotted dark purple. The creeping stems can take root, leaving older parts behind to wither and die. **ZONES 10–12.**

CESTRUM

This genus of the potato family is made up of almost 200 species of mostly evergreen shrubs native to Central and South America and the West Indies. The leaves are simple and smooth edged, often with a rank smell when bruised, and the smallish flowers are tubular or urn-shaped, gathered in clusters at the branch tips. The flowers vary in color from white to green, yellow, red and dull purplish, and some are night scented. Small round berries follow the flowers; these, as well as other parts of the plants, are poisonous.

CULTIVATION: Cestrums make rather straggly bushes but can be pruned hard to shape by removing older stems each year after flowering. In frost-free climates they are easily grown in full sun and moderately fertile, well-drained soil with plentiful water in summer and regular fertilizing. In cooler climates they can be grown in a conservatory or against a wall for frost protection. Some species are free seeding and invasive. Propagate from soft tip cuttings.

Cestrum elegans 'Smithii'

Cestrum fasciculatum

Cestrum aurantiacum

ORANGE CESTRUM

A native of Guatemala, this semi-scrambling shrub is deciduous in cool climates but almost evergreen in warm climates. It grows to a height and spread of 8 ft (2.4 m) though will stay a rounded shrub if cut back regularly. In summer and early fall (autumn) soft orange flowers appear in compact terminal sprays, followed by white berries. **ZONES 10–12.**

Cestrum elegans

syn. ***Cestrum purpureum***

PURPLE CESTRUM, RED CESTRUM

Native to Mexico, this vigorous evergreen grows to a height of 10 ft (3 m), forming a vase-shaped bush. The leaves are dark green, soft and velvety, but have an unpleasant odor when crushed. Dense sprays of faintly perfumed, nodding purplish red flowers are borne from late summer to winter; these are followed by drooping clusters of deep red fruit. **'Smithii'** has salmon-pink flowers. **ZONES 9–11.**

Ceropegia sandersonii

Cestrum fasciculatum

Also from Mexico, this species is similar to *Cestrum elegans* with scarlet flowers but they are borne in denser, more pendent clusters and are slightly more urn-shaped with conspicuous velvety hairs. It is a slender, fast-growing shrub to 10 ft (3 m) with arching branches and hairy, long-pointed leaves. The flowers are borne in summer and occasionally throughout the year. **ZONES 9–11.**

Cestrum 'Newellii'

This is a popular cultivar of hybrid origin, possibly between *Cestrum elegans* and *C. fasciculatum*—it takes an expert eye, in fact, to distinguish between these and *C.* 'Newellii'. It reaches about 6 ft (1.8 m) high and produces clusters of crimson, unscented flowers through much of the year, followed by matching berries. It is tougher than most cestrums and is regarded as a weed in some mild areas. **ZONES 9–11.**

Cestrum nocturnum

NIGHT-SCENTED JESSAMINE, LADY OF THE NIGHT

A rather untidy evergreen shrub to 12 ft (3.5 m) tall and almost as wide, this species has long, slender, arching branches springing densely from the base. Clusters of slender, pale green flowers appear in late summer and fall (autumn), strongly and sweetly perfumed at night but scentless during the day. The flowers are followed by berries that are green at first but a glossy china white when ripe in early winter. **ZONES 10–12.**

Cestrum parqui

GREEN CESTRUM, WILLOW-LEAFED JESSAMINE

Native to Chile, this species is a rather nondescript shrub of up to about 10 ft (3 m) tall that suckers from the roots and has foliage with a rank, unpleasant smell. In warm climates it blooms throughout the year with yellow green, night-scented flowers in dense clusters, followed by

Ceropegia stapeliiformis

Chamaebatiaria millefolium

small black fruit. In a mild, moist climate it self-seeds freely which, in combination with its tenacious root system, can make it a troublesome weed. **ZONES 9–11.**

CHAENOMELES

FLOWERING QUINCE

Related to the edible quince (*Cydonia*) with similar large, hard fruits, these many-stemmed deciduous shrubs are valued for their display of red, pink or white flowers on a tangle of bare branches in early spring or even late winter. Originating in China, Japan and Korea, they are very frost hardy and adapt to a wide range of garden conditions. The tough, springy branches are often thorny on vigorous shoots; the leaves are simple and finely toothed. The flowers appear in stalkless clusters on the previous year's wood, followed in summer by yellow green fruits with waxy, strongly perfumed skins that make fine jams and jellies. The wild forms have been superseded by a large selection of cultivars, of which only a few are generally available in any one place.
CULTIVATION: The flowering quinces perform best in a sunny spot in well-drained but not too rich soil and a dry atmosphere. To encourage vigorous, bushy growth, some of the older branches should be cut back hard each year. Propagate from cuttings.

Chaenomeles cathayensis

Believed native to central China, this is a rather sparsely branched shrub 10–15 ft (3–4.5 m) high, the branches armed with very long spines. The leaves are long, narrow and finely toothed, with a red-tinged felty coating on the undersides when young. The flowers are white flushed salmon pink and are borne in early spring. The fruit are large, sometimes up to 6 in (15 cm) long. **ZONES 5–10.**

Chaenomeles japonica

syn. ***Chaenomeles maulei***

JAPANESE FLOWERING QUINCE

This low-growing species, native to Japan, is usually no more than 3 ft (1 m) high, making a dense mass of horizontally spreading, thorny branches. The flowers, appearing long after the plant has come into leaf, are about $1\frac{1}{2}$ in (35 mm) across and usually orange-red

Chamaecereus silvestrii

but sometimes crimson; they are produced from spring to summer. The flowers are followed by small, round yellow fruit that have a pleasant fragrance. ***Chaenomeles japonica* var. *alpina*** is a dwarf form with semi-prostrate stems and small orange flowers; the fruit are also smaller. **ZONES 4–9.**

Chaenomeles speciosa

CHINESE FLOWERING QUINCE, JAPONICA

This species and its hybrids are the only flowering quinces usually grown. Shrubs of 5–10 ft (1.5–3 m) high, they spread by basal suckers to form dense thickets of stems. Their leaves are larger than in *Chaenomeles japonica*, up to 4 in (10 cm) long and $1\frac{1}{2}$ in (35 mm) wide, and the scarlet to deep red flowers, opening from late winter to mid-spring, are also larger. The many modern cultivars vary in availability, but several of the older ones are still widely grown, including **'Apple Blossom'**, white, flushed pink; **'Nivalis'**, white; **'Moerloosii'**, white flushed and blotched pink and carmine; and **'Rubra Grandiflora'**, crimson. **ZONES 6–10.**

Chaenomeles × superba

This is a hybrid between *Chaenomeles japonica* and *C. speciosa* with a height about midway between that of the two parents. It has given rise to a number of first-class cultivars like **'Knap Hill Scarlet'** with bright orange-scarlet flowers; **'Crimson and Gold'** with deep crimson petals and gold anthers; **'Nicoline'** which has a rather sprawling habit and scarlet flowers; **'Pink Lady'** with large, bright rose pink flowers; and **'Rowallane'** with blood crimson flowers. **ZONES 6–10.**

CHAMAEBATIARIA

FERNBUSH, DESERT SWEET

The mountains of western USA are home to several unusual genera of shrubs and small trees in the rose family, of which this is one of the most distinctive. It consists of only one species, a low shrub with several erect stems that are covered with sticky, aromatic hairs when young, giving off a balsamic smell. The leaves are finely dissected in a bipinnate pattern and covered in a sticky, whitish down. In summer the lateral branches terminate in short, crowded panicles of white flowers like small apple blossoms, opening among a mass of felty buds.
CULTIVATION: Fernbush adapts well enough to cultivation, preferring a dry, sunny spot and well-drained soil. It is best propagated from cuttings.

Chaenomeles cathayensis

Chamaebatiaria millefolium

A high-desert shrub scattered throughout the inner-mountain ranges of California and Oregon reaching east to Wyoming and Arizona. It reaches 2–6 ft (0.6–1.8 m) in height, depending on local conditions. The reddish bark is loose and shredded. **ZONES 5–9.**

CHAMAECEREUS

PEANUT CACTUS

If recognized as distinct this genus consists of only one species, native to northern Argentina, but many botanists now prefer to treat it as just another species of the large genus *Echinopsis*. It is a clustering cactus with slender, weak stems that flop over as they elongate and become prostrate or pendulous. The small, weak spine clusters are closely spaced and give the stems a whitish appearance. It has showy orange or red flowers that open wide in the sun.
CULTIVATION: This is an easily grown cactus, popular as an indoor and balcony plant and well suited to hanging baskets as well as pots. Grow in well-drained soil in a sunny spot and watch for infestations of mealybug, scale insects and spider mite. Propagate from offsets or seed.

Chamaecereus silvestrii

syns ***Echinopsis chamaecereus, Lobivia silvestrii***

This well-known cactus is composed of clusters of initially erect, finger-sized stems that are pale green with numerous soft, white bristles. Established plants can reach a height of 6 in (15 cm) and width of 12 in (30 cm), with many crowded stems. From an early age it flowers freely indoors if conditions suit it, producing vivid orange-red blooms about 2 in (5 cm) in diameter in spring and summer. **ZONES 10–12.**

Chaenomeles japonica

Chaenomeles speciosa 'Nivalis'

Chaenomeles speciosa 'Apple Blossom'

Chaenomeles × superba

CHAMAECYPARIS

FALSE CYPRESS

In the nineteenth century botanists classified these conifers as *Cupressus* (true cypresses), and indeed the differences between *Cupressus* and *Chamaecyparis* are slight—the latter genus has its tiny branchlets more flattened with the scale-like leaves of two types, and the cones are smaller and release their seed earlier.

Chamaecyparis formosensis

Nearly all the 8 *Chamaecyparis* species occur in cooler, moister, more northerly regions in North America and eastern Asia, while the true cypresses mostly occur further south and in drier regions. Several species have given rise to a vast number of cultivars, which feature colored foliage (usually gold, bluish or bronze); narrow, fastigiate, columnar or dwarf habit; bizarre foliage traits; or needle-like juvenile foliage.

CULTIVATION: These frost-hardy trees grow well in a cool, moist climate; they respond with fast growth to deep, rich, well-drained soil and a sheltered position. Cultivars are easily propagated from cuttings, the typical tree forms from seed.

Chamaecyparis lawsoniana 'Croftway'

Chamaecyparis lawsoniana 'Ellwoodii'

Chamaecyparis formosensis

TAIWAN CYPRESS

This species can reach a height of 200 ft (60 m) in its native Taiwan but in cultivation seldom exceeds 50 ft (15 m). It has a broadly conical crown and slightly drooping branches. The bark is red brown and shallowly fissured. The branchlets are carried in very broad, flat sprays and are yellow-green in color. The cones are angular. A slow-growing tree, it is reasonably frost hardy. **ZONES 7–10.**

Chamaecyparis funebris

syn. *Cupressus funebris*

CHINESE WEEPING CYPRESS, MOURNING CYPRESS

This attractive species is widespread at lower altitudes in central China. It reaches a height of 30–50 ft (9–15 m) and is of broadly columnar habit, with a straight central trunk and ascending branches drooping at the tips, the small branchlets arranged in very elongated, pendulous, loosely flattened sprays. The foliage is a bright green. Globular green cones appear in profusion in summer. **'Aurea'** has foliage of a slightly paler yellowish green. **ZONES 9–11.**

Chamaecyparis lawsoniana 'Alumii'

Chamaecyparis lawsoniana

PORT ORFORD CEDAR, LAWSON CYPRESS

From the humid coastal forests of northwestern USA, this is the most widely planted member of the genus in its typical form, as well having given rise to a larger number of cultivars than almost any other conifer species. Planted trees are up to 120 ft (36 m) tall with trunks up to 4 ft (1.2 m) in diameter, narrowly conical with pendulous side branches producing rippling curtains of bluish green to deep green foliage. Over 180 cultivars are currently available and many more have been named. **'Alumii'**, of erect, conical habit with very bluish, dense foliage, grows to 10–15 ft (3–4.5 m) or more. **'Argentea Compacta'** is a dwarf shrub with green foliage variegated with cream. **'Aurea Densa'** has golden-yellow foliage. **'Croftway'** has gray foliage fading to dark green. **'Ellwoodii'** is a dense, conical shrub with blue-tinged foliage. **'Erecta'** is plain green with very erect, narrow sprays of foliage tightly crowded together; it can reach 30 ft (9 m) with age. **'Erecta Aurea'** grows upright and

Chamaecyparis funebris

Chamaecyparis lawsoniana

C. lawsoniana 'Argentea Compacta'

Chamaecyparis lawsoniana 'Aurea Densa'

Chamaecyparis lawsoniana 'Erecta'

Chamaecyparis lawsoniana 'Erecta Aurea'

C. lawsoniana 'Pembury Blue'

C. lawsoniana 'Golden Wonder'

has bright yellow foliage. **'Fletcheri'** has gray-blue foliage in smaller, less regular sprays and is semi-juvenile, the leaves somewhat needle-like. **'Green Globe'** is a dense dwarf cultivar to 18 in (45 cm) with fine, dark green foliage. **'Lane'** makes a narrower column with lemony yellow foliage in late spring and summer changing to bronze-gold in winter. **'Lemon Queen'** has pale yellow foliage and **'Golden Wonder'** is very similar. **'Pembury Blue'** bears pendent sprays of silvery blue foliage. **'Stewartii'**, a golden cultivar, rapidly reaches 15–25 ft (4.5–8 m), with a broad base and crowded nodding sprays of rich buttery foliage; it is often used in landscaping for a gold effect on a large scale. **'Wisselii'** grows to 80 ft (24 m) and is a narrowly conical tree with bluish green foliage. **'Winston Churchill'** is a popular recent cultivar; it has a pronounced conical growth habit and golden-yellow foliage. **ZONES 6–10.**

Chamaecyparis nootkatensis

NOOTKA CYPRESS, ALASKA CEDAR,

From western North America, this cypress ranges much further north than *Chamaecyparis lawsoniana*, up through the west coast of Canada right into Alaska. A large forest tree, it is conical in shape, growing to about 100 ft (30 m) in height and 25 ft (8 m) in spread; the small blue-green cones have a recurved, pointed flap at the center of each scale. *C. nootkatensis* is an attractive tree and thrives under more adverse conditions of soil and climate. **'Pendula'** has vertically hanging sprays of foliage and an open crown in maturity. **ZONES 4–9.**

C. lawsoniana 'Winston Churchill'

Chamaecyparis lawsoniana 'Lane'

Chamaecyparis lawsoniana 'Green Globe'

C. lawsoniana 'Lemon Queen'

Chamaecyparis lawsoniana 'Fletcheri'

Chamaecyparis nootkatensis

Chamaecyparis lawsoniana 'Wisselii'

C

C

Chamaecyparis obtusa 'Spiralis'

Chamaecyparis obtusa 'Crippsii'

Chamaecyparis obtusa 'Kosteri'

Chamaecyparis obtusa 'Nana Gracilis'

Chamaecyparis obtusa 'Templehof'

Chamaecyparis obtusa (dwarf cultivar)

Chamaecyparis obtusa

HINOKI CYPRESS, HINOKI FALSE CYPRESS

The normal, tall form of this fine tree from Japan, with richly textured, deep green foliage, is seldom seen in gardens; the species is usually represented by its dwarf or colored cultivars. One of Japan's most valued timber trees, it reaches 120 ft (36 m) in the wild with a trunk to 4 ft (1.2 m) in diameter and thick, red-brown bark. In cultivation it grows 60 ft (18 m) high, broadly columnar with dense, spreading branches that touch the ground. **'Crippsii'** makes a broad, golden pyramid with a vigorous leading shoot and is usually about 10–15 ft (3–4.5 m) tall. **'Tetragona'** and **'Tetragona Aurea'** are of similar height but narrower and more irregularly branched, their scale leaves in 4 equal ranks and branchlets tightly crowded; the former is a deep, slightly bluish green, the latter green and gold. Of the dwarf cultivars, the smallest under 12 in (30 cm) in height, the best known are **'Flabelliformis'**, with pale green leaves to 6 in (15 cm); **'Kosteri'** with apple-green foliage; **'Minima'**, under 4 in (10 cm) after 20 years and with mid-green foliage; **'Nana'**, a spreading tree to 3 ft (1 m) in height with dull, dark green foliage; **'Nana Gracilis'** and its many variants, little bun-shaped plants normally 12–24 in (30–60 cm) high with crowded fans of tiny branchlets producing a richly textured effect; **'Nana Aurea'**, which has golden tips to the fans and more of a bronze tone in winter; **'Spiralis'**, an erect, stiff tree; **'Tempelhof'**, which grows to 8 ft (2.4 m) and has greenish yellow foliage that turns bronze in winter; and **'Verdon'** with yellow-green young growth. **ZONES 5–10.**

Chamaecyparis pisifera

SAWARA CYPRESS, SAWARA FALSE CYPRESS

Growing to 150 ft (45 m) in the wild, this vigorous Japanese species makes a broad, conical tree; the lower sides of the branchlets are strongly marked bluish white and the tiny scale leaves on juvenile growth are quite prickly. The cultivars fall into 4 groups: the **Squarrosa Group**, the **Plumosa Group** (the largest group), the **Filifera Group** and the **Nana Group**. **'Squarrosa'** itself is a broadly pyramidal, small tree to 65 ft (20 m) with pale bluish gray juvenile foliage that turns dull purple in winter. **'Squarrosa Intermedia'** is a dwarf cultivar. **'Boulevard'** is narrowly conical, to 10 ft (3 m), with foliage of a bright steel blue mixed with green. The Plumosa Group includes **'Plumosa'**, a conical or columnar tree to 20 ft (6 m) with mid-green foliage, the leaves shorter and less prickly than 'Squarrosa'; **'Plumosa Aurea'** with yellow-green foliage; and **'Plumosa Compressa'**, a dwarf cultivar to 18 in (45 cm) with yellowish green foliage. Of the Filifera Group, the best known are: **'Filifera'**, with slender shoots and dark green leaves, seldom grown now; **'Filifera Aurea'**, a broadly pyramidal shrub of up to 10 ft (3 m); its bright gold and green foliage has flattened fans of branchlets mixed with elongated 'rat's tail' branchlets that arch gracefully.

Chamaecyparis obtusa 'Flabelliformis'

Chamaecyparis obtusa 'Minima'

Chamaecyparis obtusa 'Tetragona Aurea'

Chamaecyparis pisifera 'Squarrosa'

Chamaecyparis thyoides 'Red Star'

'Nana' is a hemispherical shrub with very crowded, tiny sprays of deep blue-green foliage; it can take 10 years or more to reach 12 in (30 cm) in height. **ZONES 5–10.**

Chamaecyparis thyoides

ATLANTIC WHITE CEDAR, SOUTHERN WHITE CEDAR

From eastern North America, this very frost-hardy tree reaches about 60 ft (18 m) in the wild, less in cultivation. It is narrowly columnar when young. The dull gray-green branchlets are grouped into very small fans crowded irregularly on the branches and do not produce the rippled foliage effect of most other species. **'Andelyensis'** is a conical form with bluish green leaves. **'Ericoides'** makes a broad pyramid 6–8 ft (1.8–2.4 m) high; its soft, persistent, juvenile foliage is bronze-green in spring and summer, changing to deep plum tones in winter. **'Red Star'** is a compact tree to 6 ft (1.8 m) with soft, feathery, silvery green foliage turning rich purple in winter. **ZONES 4–9.**

CHAMAECYTISUS

A broom genus consisting of about 30 species of deciduous and evergreen shrubs from the Mediterranean region and the Canary Islands, *Chamaecytisus* is closely related to *Cytisus* and its species were formerly included in the latter genus. They range from dwarf to quite tall shrubs but all have leaves consisting of 3 leaflets and produce clusters of white, yellow, pink or purple pea-flowers. Some are attractive rock-garden subjects, while at least one taller

Chamaecyparis pisifera 'Boulevard'

species is grown as a fodder and green manure plant.

CULTIVATION: The smaller species should be grown in full sun in very well-drained soil, preferably in a raised position such as a rock garden. They seldom survive transplanting. The taller species are less fussy and will grow in most soils, fertile or infertile, and in a range of situations. Propagate from seed or cuttings.

Chamaecytisus palmensis

syn. *Chamaecytisus prolifer* var. *palmensis*

TAGASASTE, TREE LUCERNE

A native of the Canary Islands, this is one of the main species grown for livestock fodder and green manure. It makes a lanky evergreen shrub or even a small tree to about 15 ft (4.5 m) tall, with very leafy branches, often pendent at the tips. The leaves consist of 3 narrow, hairy leaflets to 1½ in (40 mm) long, and in winter and spring there appear numerous clusters of ½ in (12 mm) long narrow white pea-flowers, followed by profuse flat seedpods. Tagasaste often becomes naturalized in warm-temperate climates. **ZONES 8–10.**

Chamaecytisus purpureus

syn. *Cytisus purpureus*

PURPLE BROOM

Native to southeastern Europe this is a low-growing deciduous shrub reaching a height of about 18 in (45 cm), with broadly spreading habit. Showy lilac-purple flowers ¾ in (18 mm) in length are produced in late spring and early summer, in clusters of 1 to 3 at each leaf-axil. Flowering in the next season is promoted by cutting back as soon as flowering has finished. **ZONES 6–9.**

Chamaecyparis pisifera 'Plumosa Aurea'

Chamaecytisus × versicolor

syn. *Cytisus × versicolor*

This hybrid originated in a garden in England about 1850 and is probably a cross between *Chamaecytisus hirsutus* and *C. purpureus*. It is like the latter in habit but slightly taller, 24 in (60 cm) or more. The flowers are a pale buff-yellow shaded with lilac-pink and appear from late spring to early summer. **ZONES 6–9.**

CHAMAEDOREA

This genus consists of over 100 species of small to very small palms, most of them native to rainforests of Central America with a minority in northern South America. They include many very ornamental species with smooth, green, bamboo-like stems which can grow singly or in clusters; some species are virtually stemless. The fronds are mostly few to each crown and consist of thin segments arranged pinnately (in feather fashion), or in some species undivided apart from a shallow to deep notch at the apex. Flowering stems are mostly branched, appearing among or below the fronds, the tiny male and female flowers carried on different plants; females in particular often have stems that are bright red, orange or yellow, often contrasting with the color of the developing fruits, which are small berries.

CULTIVATION: They make first-class indoor plants, tolerating low humidity and dry soil better than many other palms and surviving for years in small containers. Plant in a humus-rich soil and keep in good light but out of strong sun. Water freely in summer, keep barely moist in winter. Outdoors, plant in humus-rich soil, in full sun or part-shade. Propagate from seed.

Chamaecytisus × versicolor

Chamaecyparis pisifera 'Nana'

Chamaecytisus purpureus

Chamaecyparis pisifera 'Filifera Aurea'

Chamaecyparis pisifera 'Plumosa'

Chamaedorea cataractarum
CASCADE PALM

This species from southern Mexico is found growing along banks of fast-flowing streams, sometimes half-submerged. Its stems are prostrate and branching, like thick green rhizomes, and each oblique shoot has only 4–5 dark green pinnate fronds up to 6 ft (1.8 m) long. The short green inflorescences are half-hidden beneath the leaves and bear small yellow flowers followed by reddish fruit about ¼ in (6 mm) in diameter on female plants. It is easily cultivated in a moist, sheltered spot, forming large clumps with age. **ZONES 10–12.**

Chamaedorea elegans
syns *Neanthe bella, Collinia elegans*
PARLOR PALM, MEXICAN DWARF PALM

One of the world's most popular palms for indoor use, this is a delicate little single-stemmed species from southern Mexico and Guatemala, usually under 3 ft (1 m) high though with age it can double this. Its has a compact crown of shiny deep green, very thin, pinnate fronds under 18 in (45 cm) in length, and bears insignificant yellow flowers in small panicles on stalks longer than the fronds; female plants bear ¼ in (6 mm) diameter black fruits on orange panicle branches. It is an ideal palm for a small pot indoors, tolerating low light levels and a degree of neglect. **ZONES 10–12.**

Chamaedorea erumpens
BAMBOO PALM

This species from Guatemala and Honduras has sickle-shaped pale green leaflets, up to a dozen or so on each side of the frond and often of varying width. Its bamboo-like, very slender stems are clustered from the base and up to 12 ft (3.5 m) in height; the short flowering panicles burst through the sheathing leaf bases, and the females bear black pea-sized fruit on orange panicle branches. This species makes an attractive landscape feature in tropical and subtropical courtyards, and also grows very well indoors. **ZONES 10–12.**

Chamaedorea microspadix
MEXICAN BAMBOO PALM

From the southeast of Mexico, this is an open clumping species somewhat like *Chamaedorea erumpens* but its inflorescences are longer and bear bright scarlet fruit about ½ in (12 mm) in diameter, often appearing freely even without the presence of a male plant. It is very easily cultivated in a semi-shaded or even quite sunny position outdoors or indoors, forming a clump to 6–8 ft (1.8–2.4 m) high with rather tangled stems. **ZONES 10–12.**

Chamelaucium drummondii

Chamaemelum nobile

Chamelaucium uncinatum

Chamelaucium uncinatum

Chamaedorea cataractarum

CHAMAEMELUM

Four species of weak annuals and perennials from the Mediterranean region and Europe make up this genus, closely allied to *Anthemis* and *Matricaria.* They have aromatic, finely divided leaves and smallish daisy flowerheads with white rays and a large, domed disc. Only one is much cultivated, used as a medicinal herb and for herbal teas, also grown as an ornamental and for ground cover.
CULTIVATION: They need a sunny position and moist, well-drained soil of light texture. Propagation is from seed sown in spring or fall (autumn), or from cuttings.

Chamaemelum nobile
syn. *Anthemis nobilis*
CHAMOMILE, ROMAN CHAMOMILE

There has for long been a debate among herbal enthusiasts as to which is the 'true' chamomile, this plant or *Matricaria recutita* (German chamomile), but the vote is generally in favor of the *Chamaemelum* as the plant with the stronger aroma and apparently greater herbal potency. It is a short-lived perennial growing to around 12 in (30 cm) high though inclined to flop over, with finely lobed leaves and white flowerheads a little over 1 in (25 mm) across, borne from late spring to early fall (autumn). Chamomile tea is made from the leaves and blossoms and has a mild sedative and soothing effect. Chamomile is also grown as a lawn substitute, the prostrate cultivar **'Treneague'** being most favored for this use; it creeps along the ground by runners which take root, and it rarely flowers. A chamomile lawn emits a wonderful odor when walked on. **ZONES 5–10.**

CHAMAEROPS
MEDITERRANEAN FAN PALM

Noteworthy as the only palm indigenous to Europe (except for a rare date palm on Crete), the single species of this genus occurs along all the warmer Mediterranean coasts, growing in seashore scrubs often on limestone and in northwest Africa on rocky slopes of the Atlas and Rif Mountains. Cultivated plants develop multiple trunks clothed in shaggy fiber and stubs of leaf stalks. The flowers are of different sexes on different plants, the male yellow in dense, short panicles, the female green in even shorter but sparser clusters, followed by shiny orange-brown fruit like short dates.
CULTIVATION: Easily cultivated in milder temperate climates, this palm will tolerate sun or shade and a wide range of soil types, but does best in warm, sunny positions. It takes many years to reach a respectable size and big specimens are prized for transplanting. Propagate from seed, which germinates readily, or by careful division of a clump.

Chamaerops humilis

Chamaerops humilis

Old plants of this palm have trunks up to about 12 ft (3.5 m) tall and 8–10 in (20–25 cm) in diameter, including the coating of fibers and old stalks. The fronds (leaves) are small for a fan palm, with stiff segments only 12–18 in (30–45 cm) long radiating from a stalk of about the same length, its edges fiercely armed. Fronds vary from plain olive green to a strong blue-gray shade in different races. The perfumed male flowers appear in late spring. **ZONES 8–11.**

CHAMELAUCIUM

This genus of 20 species of evergreen shrubs of the myrtle family is endemic to Western Australia. Their dainty flowers are among the best known of Australian commercial cut flowers and are grown in many countries. The narrow, almost needle-like leaves contain slightly aromatic oils; flowers are slender-stalked with 5 rounded, white or pink to purple petals around a central cup containing nectar. They are beautiful flowers, long-lasting when cut, but the shrubs have a reputation for being difficult to grow since they do not tolerate cold winters, wet summers or high humidity.
CULTIVATION: Try them in full sun and slightly alkaline, gravelly soil with perfect drainage and prune fairly hard after flowering, but do not be surprised if they are short-lived despite all your best efforts. Avoid any root disturbance. Propagate from cuttings in summer.

Chamelaucium drummondii

This is a rather rare species, differing from the better known *Chamelaucium uncinatum* in being a low-growing, compact bush rather than a tall, willowy one. It flowers abundantly in spring, and when better known may well prove popular for seaside gardens as it likes sandy soil. **ZONES 10–11.**

Chamelaucium uncinatum
GERALDTON WAXFLOWER

The common names refer to the town of Geraldton, north of Perth on the stretch of Western Australian coast where this species is most abundant. It is a commonly grown species and the chief parent of most recently bred cultivars. A brittle, spreading shrub of up 10 ft (3 m) tall and wide, it has fine needle-like foliage and large, airy sprays of waxy white, mauve or pink flowers borne profusely in late winter and through spring. New cultivars appear regularly but all seem prone to root-rot in wet soil. **ZONES 10–11.**

CHASMANTHE

This genus of 3 species of perennial cormous plants is indigenous to South Africa. In growth habit they resemble a gladiolus or watsonia, but the flowers are very narrow and distinctively curved, in attractive shades of yellow, orange or red. They bloom in fall (autumn), winter and spring.
CULTIVATION: They withstand only the lightest frosts and are cultivated mainly in warm-temperate or subtropical climates. Plant the corms in fall in moist, well-drained soil in sun or part-shade. Water well during the growing season. For best results leave plants undisturbed for several years. Propagate from offset cormlets or from seeds sown in fall.

Chasmanthe aethiopica

Despite its name suggesting Ethiopia, this species is native to South Africa's Cape Province. It has crowded fans of ribbed leaves up to 24 in (60 cm) long. From fall (autumn) to spring it produces slender one-sided spikes up to 2½ ft (75 cm) high of tubular red or orange flowers 2 in (5 cm) long. **ZONES 9–11.**

Chasmanthe floribunda
syn. *Antholyza floribunda*
AFRICAN CORNFLAG

Native in the southwestern Cape area of South Africa, this species has sword-shaped leaves up to 18 in (45 cm) long. The 3 in (8 cm) long orange-red flowers are arranged in 2 rows in zig-zag fashion on a spike about 24 in (60 cm) high, and borne in winter and spring. This species is free-seeding and is widely naturalized in southern Australia. **ZONES 9–11.**

CHASMANTHIUM

A genus of 6 species of perennial grasses from eastern USA and Mexico, forming large clumps or tussocks, the stems somewhat cane-like and the leaves rather short. The stems terminate in panicles of spikelets that are unusually broad and flat, and quite decorative.
CULTIVATION: These are very frost hardy grasses that prefer a sheltered, part-shaded position in moist, fertile soil. The old foliage of the previous year's growth should be cut off close to the ground each winter. Propagate from seed or by division of clumps.

Chasmanthium latifolium
syn. *Uniola latifolia*
SEA OATS, SPIKE GRASS

The only species generally cultivated, sea oats is grown for its unusual seedheads which can be used as dried decorations. It forms large tufts of leafy stems, the leaves mostly 8 in (20 cm) or less long, bright green but turning yellow in late fall (autumn). Flowering stems are up to 5 ft (1.5 m) tall, terminating in gracefully

Cheiridopsis pillansii

drooping panicles of flattish spikelets each up to 2 in (5 cm) long and 1 in (25 mm) wide. Apart from its decorative value, sea oats is a valuable fodder grass in its native USA and northern Mexico. **ZONES 4–10.**

CHEIRIDOPSIS

There are almost 100 species of compact succulents in this genus, one of many in the large mesembryanthemum group, nearly all them endemic to the drier western parts of South Africa and adjacent Namibia. Most species build up into small clumps of erect shoots, each shoot with a single pair of pale green or grayish leaves that are fused together for varying proportions of their length. New leaf-pairs grow from the center of the old, which shortly after shrivel and die, forming a short husk around the base of the shoot. White, yellow or pink daisy-like flowers also appear singly from the center of the leaf-pair.
CULTIVATION: The plants are marginally frost hardy and tolerant of arid conditions. They require a gritty, very well- drained soil and a position in full sun. In wet climates they will need to be kept under glass, especially in winter, to keep dry. Water sparingly in the growing season, and do not water after the old leaves begin to shrivel. Watch for mealybug infestation. Propagate from seed or by division.

Cheiridopsis pillansii
LOBSTER CLAWS

From western Cape Province (Little Namaqualand), this species makes a compact clump of shoots up to about 3 in (8 cm) high and 6 in (15 cm) wide. The blunt-tipped leaves are 1½ in (4 cm) long, fused for about half their length and very bluish when young but ageing to olive green. The pale yellow flowers are quite large and borne in summer. **ZONES 9–10.**

Cheiridopsis purpurea

Native to southern Africa, this species can mound up with age into a clump 12 in (30 cm) high and 18 in (45 cm) across. The 2½ in (7 cm) leaves are pale blue-green tinged with pink. Purplish pink flowers 2 in (5 cm) across appear in summer. **ZONES 9–10.**

CHELIDONIUM
GREATER CELANDINE, SWALLOWWORT

A single species of short-lived perennial belongs to this genus of the poppy

Cheiridopsis purpurea

Chelone lyonii

family, native to Europe and western Asia. It forms a clump of leafy stems, the slightly brittle leaves divided into several irregular leaflets with scalloped edges. Short sprays of small 4-petalled bright yellow flowers are produced over a long season, each flower soon succeeded by a slender pod that splits to release tiny black seeds. Broken leaves and stems bleed an orange latex which is irritating to the skin and has been used to cure warts; the plant has many other traditional medicinal uses but is quite poisonous.
CULTIVATION: The plant is very frost hardy and is easily grown in sun or light shade, adapting to all except very wet soils. Its duration may be only biennial, but it self-seeds readily and can become invasive. Propagate from seed or by division in fall (autumn) and cut back after flowering to keep under control.

Chelidonium majus

This quick-growing perennial can form an effective ground cover if planted closely. It is an erect to rather sprawling plant about 2–4 ft (0.6–1.2 m) high and wide, with attractive pale green foliage. From mid-spring to mid-fall (mid-autumn) it produces a continuous scatter of bright golden-yellow flowers about 1 in (25 mm) across; the slender seed capsules are 2 in (5 cm) long. **'Flore Pleno'** has double flowers. **ZONES 6–9.**

CHELONE
TURTLEHEAD

This genus of 6 species of rather coarse but showy perennials from North

Chasmanthe floribunda

Chasmanthe aethiopica

Chelidonium majus 'Flore Pleno'

America is related to *Penstemon*, which they resemble in growth habit and foliage. The name comes from the Greek *kelone* meaning a tortoise or turtle, and refers to the hooded, gaping flowers, borne in short terminal spikes. Leaves are toothed and shiny in most species.
CULTIVATION: They are best along streams or pond edges, but also adapt to a moist border planting with rich soil in full sun or part-shade. Propagate by dividing clumps in early spring, from cuttings in summer or from seed in spring or fall (autumn).

Chelone lyonii
PINK TURTLEHEAD

This species from mountains of south-eastern USA grows to a height of at least 3 ft (1 m), with erect, angled stems and dark green leaves up to 6 in (15 cm) long. The summer flowers are rosy purple and are produced in axillary and terminal spikes terminating the stems, and in upper leaf axils. **ZONES 6–9.**

Chelone obliqua

Chelone obliqua

Chilopsis linearis

Chilopsis linearis

Chelone obliqua
ROSE TURTLEHEAD

Also from southeastern USA, this is the showiest of the turtleheads and the best as a garden plant. Pairs of rich green leaves line 3 ft (1 m) tall vertical stems topped with short spikes of rosy-purple flowers in late summer and fall (autumn). **ZONES 6–9.**

CHIASTOPHYLLUM

This genus in the crassula family consists of a single species of somewhat succulent evergreen perennial native to the Caucasus Mountains. It has leafy stems arising from a rootstock, the rounded, blunt-toothed leaves arranged in opposite pairs. The stems terminate in branched, drooping spikes of small yellow, bell-shaped flowers.
CULTIVATION: Its natural habitat is cool, moist crevices among rocks, and this should be simulated in the garden, for example on the shady side of a stone wall or bank, or a cool position in the rock garden. Watch for snails and slugs. Propagate from seed in fall (autumn) or by division in summer.

Chiastophyllum oppositifolium
syn. *Cotyledon simplicifolia*

This plant grows to no more than 8 in (20 cm) high but can spread by rhizomes to make a mat of indefinite width. The leaves are rather like some of the herbaceous sedums, pale green and thinly succulent with scalloped margins, the rusty red lower ones about $1\frac{1}{2}$ in (38 mm) long. The golden-yellow flowers are $\frac{1}{4}$ in (6 mm) long, appearing in late spring and early summer. **ZONES 7–9.**

CHILOPSIS
DESERT WILLOW, DESERT CATALPA

Consisting of a single species that occurs wild in dry streambeds of inland southwestern USA and northern Mexico, *Chilopsis* belongs to the bignonia family and has the showy trumpet-shaped flowers typical of that family. Despite the common name it is quite unrelated to willows, though the leaves do resemble those of many willows, narrow and drawn out into a long point. The flowers are borne in short spikes at the branch ends, opening in succession. It is a lank, untidy shrub, worth growing only for its attractive flowers.
CULTIVATION: It does best in a hot, dry climate with cool, crisp nights. The soil should be open and well-drained but with deep subsoil moisture available. Propagation is from seed or cuttings.

Chilopsis linearis

The desert willow can make a tree of 30 ft (9 m) or more, but in gardens is usually a shrub of 10–15 ft (3–4.5 m) with an open habit of growth, the slender branches arching and twisted at odd angles. The sparse leaves are pale green, sometimes as much as 12 in (30 cm) long, and the 2 in (5 cm) flowers, borne through late spring and summer, can be white, pale pink or a deep cerise-pink, paler in the throat. **ZONES 7–10.**

CHIMONANTHUS
WINTERSWEET

This small genus of 6 species of deciduous shrubs from China belongs to a primitive flowering-plant family allied to the magnolia family; one species is popular in gardens for its deliciously scented flowers produced from early to midwinter. The leaves are simple and thin textured, clustered at the ends of the stiff branches. Smallish flowers are clustered just below the branch tips; they are multi-petalled and cup-shaped, with a translucent waxy texture, and are followed by leathery-skinned fruit of a strange shape, like little bags stuffed with balls, which turn out to be the large seeds.
CULTIVATION: This plant is quite frost hardy and will grow in most positions, but in cold climates should be positioned against a warm wall to protect the flowers. Pruning consists mainly of thinning out weaker stems and, if desired, shortening the larger stems, which should be done immediately after flowering. Propagate from seed or layer multiple stems by mounding with soil.

Chimonanthus praecox
syn. *Chimonanthus fragrans*

The wintersweet makes a thicket of stiff, angular stems 10–15 ft (3–4.5 m) high and wide, with harsh-textured, mid-green leaves. The flowers appear in abundance on bare winter branches or, in milder climates, among the last leaves of fall (autumn); the petals are pale yellow to off-white with a dull pink or red basal zone showing on the inside. The fruits are yellowish brown when ripe. **'Luteus'** has late blooming, buttercup-yellow flowers. **ZONES 6–10.**

CHIMONOBAMBUSA

A genus of bamboos from East and Southeast Asia, *Chimonobambusa* consists of possibly 20 species, many of which were previously included in the genus *Arundinaria*. The name is from the Greek and means 'winter bamboo', referring to the cold habitats of some species and their tendency to winter dormancy. They are bamboos of small to medium size with long-running rhizomes, which means the stems are widely spaced and the clumps may spread rapidly. The stems are slender but have very pronounced nodes, especially toward the base. The foliage is thin and graceful, though hardly distinguished from that of related bamboos. Flowering is rare in cultivation.
CULTIVATION: The species usually cultivated are fairly frost hardy as bamboos go, and are easily cultivated in any sheltered position in moist, well-drained soil. They will tolerate light shade. To keep spread of rhizomes in check it may be necessary to sink sheetmetal or concrete barriers in the soil to a depth of 24 in (60 cm); alternatively, plant in large shallow tubs or aboveground planting boxes. Propagate from rhizome divisions, which may be slow to establish unless quite large.

Chimonanthus praecox

Chimonobambusa quadrangularis
syn. *Arundinaria quadrangularis*
SQUARE-STEMMED BAMBOO, SHIKAKUDAKE

In gardens this bamboo from southeastern China and Taiwan usually grows to 6–12 ft (1.8–3.6 m) high, though in the wild it can reach at least twice this, and its spread is indefinite. Most distinctive are the stems, which are $\frac{1}{2}$–1 in (12–25 mm) thick, green and bluntly 4-sided in the lower part, with swollen nodes which may have small spine-like outgrowths; higher up there are 3 branches from each node. The leaves are bright green and up to 1 in (25 mm) wide. **ZONES 7–11.**

CHIONANTHUS
FRINGE TREE

Belonging to the olive family, the genus *Chionanthus* used to be regarded as consisting of only 2 species of deciduous tree, one from temperate North America and one from China, but botanists have now transferred to it a large number of tropical evergreens from the genus *Linociera*. The deciduous species, though, are of most interest to gardeners. In late spring the crowns of these small trees are sprinkled with clusters of delicate white flowers—each slender-stalked flower has 4 narrow, diverging white petals. A good specimen in full flower is outstandingly beautiful. The smooth-margined leaves are in opposite pairs; the summer fruits are like small olives.
CULTIVATION: These cool-climate trees are easily grown but may be slow to increase in size and can take 10 years to flower. A sunny but sheltered position with good soil and drainage suits them best. Propagate from seed in fall (autumn).

Chionanthus retusus
CHINESE FRINGE TREE

Native to China and Taiwan, this tree can reach 30 ft (9 m), developing a broad, umbrella-like crown with age. The shiny leaves vary in shape and size

Chiastophyllum oppositifolium

Chionodoxa luciliae 'Alba'

Chionodoxa luciliae

on the one tree. The flowers, with petals about 1 in (25 mm) long, are borne in profuse, upright clusters that stand above the foliage in late spring or early summer. This seems to be the more climatically adaptable of the 2 species, flowering equally well in both cool and warm, even subtropical regions. **ZONES 6–10.**

Chionanthus virginicus
AMERICAN FRINGE TREE

The individual flowers of this species are similar to those of *Chionanthus retusus*, but the leaves are larger and less shiny and the longer, drooping flower sprays appear among the foliage rather than standing above it. In its native forests of southeastern USA it grows in rich, moist soil close to streams, occasionally 30 ft (9 m) tall but often only a shrub. Away from its native regions it can be a shy bloomer, performing better in continental climates of central Europe than in the UK and not doing so well in climates warmer than that. **ZONES 5–9.**

CHIONOCHLOA

This southern hemisphere grass genus belongs to a group of very similar genera centered around *Danthonia*, and botanists are still trying to clarify their relationships. Around 20 species of large tussock-forming grasses belong to *Chionochloa*, all but 2 of them native to New Zealand: the exception is one species from higher mountains of southeastern Australia and one from Lord Howe Island. They are handsome grasses with dense clumps of fine, soft leaves. Their long-stalked plumes of small, rather silky seedheads sometimes reach over 6 ft (1.8 m) tall.

CULTIVATION: These are fine ornamental grasses for climates that are cool

Chionochloa rubra

but mild and fairly moist, though some will tolerate moderate frosts. Grow in a display of grasses, in a mixed border, rock garden, or in massed landscape planting. Plant in a sunny position in moist but well-drained soil. Propagate from seed or by division.

Chionochloa conspicua

This species, known in its native New Zealand as hunangamoho grass, will grow to a height of 4–6 ft (1.2–1.8 m) with a spread of about 3 ft (1 m). It makes a dense tuft of fine, arching leaves above which appear loose, open panicles of fine, drooping creamy-white seedheads in mid-summer. **ZONES 7–10.**

Chionochloa rubra

Another New Zealand native, this species makes a large clump with fine, reddish brown leaves and flowering stems rising to a height of around 5 ft (1.5 m) in summer. **ZONES 7–10.**

CHIONODOXA
GLORY-OF-THE-SNOW

The scientific name is a translation of the common one, or vice versa. Either way it is appropriate for these small bulbs, relatives of the hyacinth, which adorn the melting snows of Asia Minor with brilliant blue stars. There are only 6 species in the genus, restricted in the wild to mountains of southern Turkey, Crete and Cyprus, but their nomenclature is rather muddled; fortunately, they are all desirable garden plants. They should be planted in quantity to show off the wonderful clarity of the rich blue flowers with their white centers; lilac-pink flowers are also available. The flowers appear in late winter or early spring, depending on climate.

CULTIVATION: They need full sun or light shade, well-drained soil and cold winter temperatures; in warm-temperate or warmer climates they will languish and often fail to initiate flower-buds. Propagate from seed or offsets.

Chionochloa conspicua

Chionodoxa forbesii
syns *Chionodoxa luciliae* of gardens, *C. siehei*

From mountains of southwestern Turkey, this is the most widely grown species but has generally been misidentified as *Chionodoxa luciliae* in bulb catalogues. The plants are up to about 8 in (20 cm) high with broad, strap-shaped, fleshy leaves appearing with the flowers. The flowering stems can each carry up to 12 flowers about $\frac{3}{4}$ in (18 mm) across, very bright violet-blue except for the whitish center. **'Alba'** has pure white flowers. **ZONES 4–9.**

Chionodoxa luciliae
syn. *Chionodoxa gigantea*

Native to the same region of Turkey as *Chionodoxa forbesii*, this species resembles it in many respects but has only 2 to 3 flowers per stem and each flower has slightly broader, softer lilac petals and a smaller white central spot. **'Alba'** has all-white flowers. **ZONES 4–9.**

Chionodoxa sardensis

Sardes is a classical place-name from southwestern Turkey and *sardensis* is the Latin adjective referring to it. This species also comes from much the same region as *Chionodoxa forbesii*, and is a fairly similar plant but with narrower, more channeled leaves. The flowers are gentian-blue with a white eye, up to 12 per stem. It is rare in cultivation. **ZONES 4–9.**

× CHIONOSCILLA

This intergeneric hybrid between *Chionodoxa* and *Scilla* has arisen spontaneously both in gardens and in the wild, where the parent plants have been growing together. Though all from the same combination of parental species, the progeny show variation and a number of clones have been named. They have strap-shaped, deep green leaves that exceed the flower stem in height.

CULTIVATION: More free-flowering and climatically less demanding than *Chionodoxa*, these plants are easily grown in any well-drained soil in sun or part-shade. Plant bulbs 1–2 in (25 mm–5 cm) deep and propagate by breaking up established clumps in summer.

× *Chionoscilla allenii*

The presumed parent species are *Chionodoxa forbesii* and *Scilla bifolia* which both occur in mountains of southern Turkey. Its spring flowers are star-shaped, blue or lilac with paler centers, and $\frac{1}{2}$ in (12 mm) in diameter. They are carried in dense clusters on narrow 4–6 in (10–15 cm) tall stems. **ZONES 4–9.**

CHIRANTHODENDRON

The genus name is from the Greek, meaning 'hand flower tree', and its sole species was held in superstitious awe by the native peoples of southern Mexico and Guatemala, in which region it is native. It also aroused the wonderment of the Spanish conquerors, and various efforts were made to bring it into cultivation in Europe. It is a striking small tree

Chionanthus virginicus

Chionanthus retusus

Chionanthus retusus

related to cocoa, and the dull purple flowers might attract little attention if it were not for the long projecting stamens, fused at the base into a 'wrist' with the 5 huge anthers resembling fingers, each ending in a claw-like point.
CULTIVATION: Apart from being grown in European botanical gardens as a curiosity, *Chiranthodendron* has been cultivated mainly in Mexico and areas of southern USA that are almost frost free. It requires a sheltered position and deep, moist soil. Propagate from seed.

Chiranthodendron pentadactylon
syn. ***Cheirostemon platanoides***
HAND-FLOWER TREE, MEXICAN HAND PLANT

Although first found by Europeans in Mexico, the hand-flower tree is now believed to have been brought there from Guatemala where it is native. Fast growing when young, it can reach a height of 80 ft (24 m) in the wild but planted trees are mostly much smaller. It has gnarled branches and leaves 8 in (20 cm) wide, almost circular in outline but shallowly lobed, with rusty brown hairs on the undersides. Flowers are produced in the leaf axils from spring to fall (autumn), often partly hidden by the leaves. Each dull purplish red flower is about 3 in (8 cm) across, furry brown on the outside and with the long red and yellow 'hand' protruding 6 in (15 cm). In some tropical areas the hand-flower tree is evergreen but in cooler areas will usually lose its leaves in winter. It will tolerate the lightest frosts only. **ZONES 9–11.**

Chlidanthus fragrans

Chlorophytum comosum 'Mandaianum'

Choisya ternata

CHLIDANTHUS
SEA DAFFODIL, FAIRY LILY

Belonging to the amaryllis family, this bulb genus consists of only a single species, native to the Andes of Peru. The leaves are rather like daffodil leaves but the sweetly perfumed yellow flowers are trumpet-shaped with a long tube, the slightly recurving petals resembling those of a hemerocallis. The genus name is from the Greek, *chlide* meaning a costly ornament and *anthos* a flower. The common name 'sea daffodil' may be a result of confusion with the related *Pancratium.*
CULTIVATION: They are only marginally frost hardy and prefer a warm-temperate or even subtropical climate. They need a sheltered position in humus-rich, well-drained, sandy soil, or can be grown in pots in a conservatory in strong light. An annual dressing of potassium sulphate when in full leaf will promote the next year's flowering. Bulbs should be kept fairly dry after leaves die back in late summer. Propagate from seed or offset bulbs in spring.

Chlidanthus fragrans
PERFUMED FAIRY LILY

Appearing with the new leaves in early summer, the sea daffodil's flowering stems are 10–15 in (25–40 cm) tall, each topped by an umbel of up to 5 bright yellow, sweetly scented, trumpet-shaped blooms 3 in (8 cm) long. The sea daffodil makes a good cut flower. **ZONES 9–11.**

CHLOROPHYTUM

This is a large genus of lilies related to *Anthericum,* consisting of over 200 species scattered through parts of Africa, southern Asia, South America and Australia, though the vast majority are native to southern and tropical Africa. These are evergreen perennials with short rhizomes, the roots often swollen and fleshy. The strap-shaped, sword-shaped or lance-shaped leaves vary in size, thickness and coloration, while the small starry white or greenish flowers are hardly showy. Only one species is widely cultivated, regarded as one of the hardiest indoor plants.
CULTIVATION: Grown for their foliage, all chlorophytums are frost tender. Not fussy about soil or growing medium as long as drainage is adequate, they thrive in light to medium shade. Water freely during the growing season, sparingly at other times. Propagate from seed, by division, or by means of the plantlets that often form on flowering stems.

Choisya 'Aztec Pearl'

Choisya ternata 'Sundance'

Chlorophytum comosum
SPIDER PLANT, HEN-AND-CHICKENS

Native to moist coastal regions of South Africa, this species is widely grown for its attractive grass-like foliage and is one of the most popular plants for hanging baskets. In mild climates it can make a ground cover in the shade of trees, growing to a height of 12 in (30 cm). Rosettes of narrow leaves up to 18 in (45 cm) long multiply to form dense, untidy clumps. The long, weak, branched flowering stems carry small star-shaped white flowers through much of the year, and small plantlets develop on the stems after flowering, enabling the plant's rapid spread. The wild, green-leafed form is invasive in mild climates but several forms with cream- or yellow-striped leaves are more popular as garden or indoor plants: **'Mandaianum'** is a compact form, its narrower dark green leaves irregularly striped dull yellow-green; **'Picturatum'** has leaves with a broad yellow central stripe; **'Vittatum'** has leaves with a broad white central stripe, usually with finer stripes at the sides. **ZONES 9–11.**

CHOISYA

This genus of 8 species of evergreen shrubs belongs to the same family as citrus, from Mexico and the far south of the USA. One species is widely cultivated for ornament in warm-temperate climates. Their leaves are compound with 3 to 7 leaflets radiating from the stalk apex; from the leaf axils arise clusters of fragrant star-shaped white flowers, resembling orange-blossoms. The crushed or bruised leaves are also pleasantly aromatic.
CULTIVATION: They are excellent hedging plants as well as being attractive additions to shrub borders, growing best in full sun or part shade and a slightly acid, humus-rich, well-drained soil. Protect from strong winds, fertilize in spring and trim lightly after flowering to keep foliage dense and close to the ground. Propagate from tip cuttings in fall (autumn).

Choisya ternata 'Sundance'

Choisya 'Aztec Pearl'

This is a recently developed hybrid between *Choisya arizonica* and *C. ternata,* the first produced in this genus. It is an elegant shrub growing to 6 ft (1.8 m) or more, with aromatic leaves divided into 3 to 5 narrow, channelled leaflets. Flowers are similar to those of *C. ternata* but slightly larger, pink-flushed in the bud and opening white—it commonly produces 2 flushes of bloom, in early and late summer. **ZONES 8–11.**

Choisya ternata
MEXICAN ORANGE BLOSSOM

One of the most frost hardy evergreens to come from the highlands of Mexico, this popular species makes a compact, rounded bush to 6 ft (1.8 m) or more. Its attractive leaves consist of 3 glossy deep green leaflets (*ternata* means 'grouped in 3s'). Tight clusters of small white, fragrant flowers appear among the leaves in spring, and sometimes again in late summer. **'Sundance'** has golden-yellow foliage when young, maturing to yellow-green. **ZONES 7–11.**

CHONDROPETALUM

This genus of 12 species is endemic to South Africa's Cape Province. Perennials with a superficial resemblance to the sedges *(Carex)* or rushes *(Juncus),* they in fact belong to the southern hemisphere family Restionaceae, which has its main centers of diversity in South Africa and Australia; another South African genus is *Elegia.* They make tussocks of wiry leafless stems, each terminating in a short spike of tiny flowers nestled among chaffy brown bracts; male and female flowers are on different plants.
CULTIVATION: They make striking additions to collections of grasses and sedges but do not adapt readily to cultivation, the clumps resenting disturbance of any kind. They are also sensitive to fertilizers, especially those high in phosphorus. Grow in sandy soil that is moist but well-drained. Propagate from seed.

Chondropetalum tectorum
CAPE RUSH, DAKRIET

This robust species makes a broad, dense clump up to about 4 ft (1.2 m) tall and of greater width, with stiff gray-green stems and short dark brown flower spikes. **ZONES 8–10.**

CHORDOSPARTIUM

A genus consisting of only 2 species of small leguminous trees from New Zealand, now rare in the wild in

north-eastern South Island. The genus name is from *Spartium*, broom, modified by the Greek prefix *chord-*, string(-like), referring to the long thin branches. Like its close ally *Carmichaelia* and many other woody legumes from Australia and New Zealand, its resemblance to the Mediterranean brooms is superficial. Regardless of botanical position, *Chordospartium* species are viewed by discerning New Zealand gardeners as among their most beautiful native plants. The long, drooping, leafless branches burst out in late spring with a great profusion of small lavender-blue and mauve pea-flowers that continue opening almost until the end of summer. Tiny pods follow, each with a single seed.
CULTIVATION: Tolerating light frosts only, these lovely trees grow best in light soils with good drainage in places with moderately dry, sunny summer weather. They are often short-lived in cultivation. Propagate from seed or cuttings.

Chordospartium stevensonii
WEEPING BROOM

This is a deciduous, almost leafless shrub or small tree 10–15 ft (3–4.5 m) in height with arching branches. It has small pea-like flowers, pale lavender pink to purple in color and carried in dense drooping spikes from late spring to mid-summer. It is very rare in the wild. **ZONES 8–10.**

CHORISIA

This genus is made up of 5 species of deciduous South American trees with distinctively spiny, somewhat swollen trunks, the bark otherwise smooth and greenish. They belong to the kapok or silk-cotton family of tropical trees, with digitately compound leaves, hibiscus-like flowers, and large capsular fruit with silky fibres packed around the seeds. The showy flowers are borne on branches that may be leafless. In a recent botanical study *Chorisia* is treated as a synonym of *Ceiba*.
CULTIVATION: At least one species has gradually gained popularity in recent years, as a striking flowering tree for sunny, warm-temperate climates such as that of southern California. In more tropical climates they prefer those with a pronounced dry season. They do best in full sun and fertile, light, well-drained soil, with regular water in summer. Poorer or drier soils restrict the trees' size. Propagate from freshly collected seed or by grafting of selected clones.

Chorizema cordatum

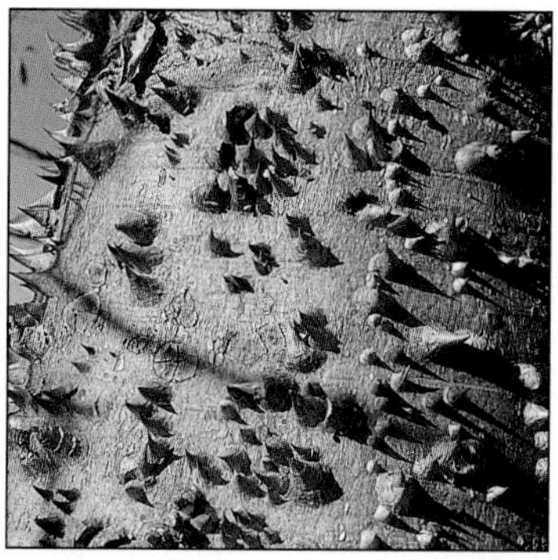
Chorisia insignis

Chorisia insignis
syn. ***Ceiba insignis***
SOUTH AMERICAN BOTTLE TREE, WHITE FLOSS SILK TREE

This species is worth growing for its thick green trunk alone. In young trees the trunk has scattered, conical spines but these tend to disappear with age. It grows fairly rapidly to a height of 30–40 ft (9–12 m), but growth then slows and the crown widens. The leaves are deep green with broad, overlapping leaflets. In fall (autumn) pale creamy yellow flowers, sometimes brown-blotched in the center, are borne in small groups at the branch ends. **ZONES 10–11.**

Chorisia speciosa
syn. ***Ceiba speciosa***
FLOSS-SILK TREE

Growing rapidly to 50 ft (15 m) or more with a spreading crown, this subtropical South American species is the one most commonly seen and is grown for its striking large flowers profusely scattered over the crown on bare or leafy branches from late summer to early winter. The saucer-sized flowers range from rose pink through salmon shades to burgundy, with gold or white throats. Flowers vary greatly from one seedling plant to another, also the density and persistence of spines on the trunk. **ZONES 9–11.**

CHORIZEMA
FLAME PEA

A genus of 18 species of evergreen pea-flowered subshrubs, all but one endemic to southwestern Australia the single exception occurring in coastal eastern Australia. The name comes from the Greek *choros*, 'dance', and *zema*, 'drink', because the French botanist-explorer Labillardière and his exhausted party danced for joy when they found water and this plant in the same location. The cultivated species are very floriferous, often with a combination of hot colors in each flower, hence the common name. Leaves are simple, the margins prickly toothed in some species.
CULTIVATION: These plants are marginally frost hardy and need full sun or very light shade and a well-drained, light soil. They should be kept well mulched in summer to prevent the roots from drying out. Propagate from seed sown in spring or cuttings in summer.

Chondropetalum tectorum

Chorisia speciosa

Chorisia speciosa

Chorizema cordatum
HEART-LEAFED FLAME PEA

This gaudy native of southwestern Australia bears sprays of yellow to orange-red pea-flowers with a pink to dark red central blotch, in spring. A thin-branched, scrambling shrub, it has heart-shaped, mid-green leaves with small prickly marginal teeth. It prefers shady conditions and grows to a height of 3–5 ft (1–1.5 m). Some botanists now treat *Chorizema cordatum* as a synonym of *C. ilicifolium*. **ZONES 9–11.**

CHRYSALIDOCARPUS

These feather palms from Madagascar and the nearby Comoros and Pemba Islands are very graceful plants that are most at home in tropical and subtropical areas. Although there are 22 species, only one, *Chrysalidocarpus lutescens*, is widely grown, though other species are equally attractive. The flowers and fruit are unremarkable—simple yellow flowers in branched sprays followed by small yellow fruit—but the foliage is very luxuriant. Recent intensive studies of Madagascan palms indicate that *Chrysalidocarpus* and several other genera may all have to be merged under the genus *Dypsis*.
CULTIVATION: All species are frost tender, but adapt well to warm-temperate climates as well as tropical. Plant in moist, well-drained soil in sun or light shade. Water freely in the summer growing season, keep soil slightly moist all year. Propagate from seed in spring; seeds can take up to 5 months to germinate.

Chrysalidocarpus lutescens

Chrysalidocarpus lutescens
syns ***Areca lutescens, Dypsis lutescens***
BUTTERFLY PALM, GOLDEN CANE PALM

This species is one of the most widely cultivated ornamental palms. It is a clump-forming feather palm with fairly short fronds that arch elegantly from cane-like stems 10–20 ft (3–6 m) high. The basal sheaths and frond stalks are yellow and the fronds themselves are yellowish in sun but when grown in shade are a beautiful light green. It responds well to container cultivation and can be grown as a house plant. **ZONES 10–12.**

C. monilifera subsp. *rotundata*

Chrysalidocarpus madagascariensis

Chrysalidocarpus madagascariensis

This Madagascan species may be either single-trunked or branch into several trunks from the base, the ringed trunks up to 30 ft (9 m) or more tall and 4–6 in (10–15 cm) in diameter. The large, plume-like fronds are arranged in 3 vertical rows at the top of the trunk, their broad, overlapping basal sheaths covered in gray scurf. The much-branched inflorescence bears tiny yellow flowers and the fruits, ½ in (12 mm) long, are also yellowish. **ZONES 10–12.**

CHRYSANTHEMOIDES

This southern African genus of evergreen shrubs contains only 2 species, of which one is widely cultivated and naturalized in other parts of the world. Somewhat short-lived and soft-wooded, they have leathery, toothed leaves. The yellow flowerheads are like small daisies and the fruitlets that follow are fleshy and juicy—these are attractive to birds, which effectively disperse the seed. **CULTIVATION:** Easily grown from seed or cuttings, they may be useful as summer bedding or tub plants in cool climates, but demand full sun. They have become pests in some areas, forming dense, impenetrable stands, and should be grown only in areas where they will not choke out native vegetation.

Chrysanthemoides monilifera

BUSH-TICK BERRY, BITOU BUSH, BONESEED

This fast-growing shrub has 2 subspecies, rather different in growth habit and ecology. ***Chrysanthemoides monilifera* subsp. *monilifera*** is an erect, bushy shrub of 4–6 ft (1.2–1.8 m) with dull green, thin-textured, coarsely toothed leaves and grows mainly away from the seashore. ***C. m.* subsp. *rotundata***, the coastal race, is usually 5–10 ft (1.5–3 m) tall and as much as 20 ft (6 m) across, forming a broad, dense mound of bright green foliage. The glossy leaves are rounded and barely toothed, with cobweb-like hairs on the undersides and young shoots. It can grow very quickly on dunes and seeds itself freely. Both subspecies can flower for most of the year. **ZONES 9–11.**

Chrysanthemoides monilifera

C. × *grandiflorum*, single form

CHRYSANTHEMUM

CHRYSANTHEMUM

Although the garden (or florists') chrysanthemums are so well known, the history of *Chrysanthemum* as a botanical name is very confusing. At one time this was used by botanists in a very broad sense to include not only the florists' chrysanthemums but several other related groups such as the Shasta daisies, marguerites, tansies and pyrethrums. After World War II the scientific evidence against this broad view began to mount, and a number of genera were split off *Chrysanthemum* to contain these rather distinct groups. For a while the florists' chrysanthemums themselves were given another genus name (*Dendranthema*) but a recent decision by an international committee on botanical nomenclature has brought their scientific name back into line with popular usage and they are now treated as the rightful claimants to the name *Chrysanthemum.*

The genus in this present, redefined sense consists of 37 species of perennials occurring wild mostly in eastern Asia, though two extend into northern Europe. They have lobed, somewhat aromatic leaves and panicles of daisy-like flowerheads in shades of red, purple, pink, yellow or white. Some of the species were taken into cultivation in China, possibly over 1,000 years ago, and by the seventeenth century hundreds of named cultivars were recorded. News of these gorgeous flowers reached the West and by the early nineteenth century a number of cultivars had been introduced to Europe. Breeding continued in both China and western countries to produce the extraordinary array of forms and colors available today. The largest and most striking cultivars are grown only for exhibition by chrysanthemum enthusiasts, but commercial growers raise other varieties by the millions for sale either as cut flowers or as flowering pot plants; their normal late summer–fall (autumn) flowering season is frequently extended by manipulation of day length and temperature in greenhouses.

Genera listed elsewhere in this book whose species were once classified under *Chrysanthemum* are: *Argyranthemum*, the marguerites, evergreen subshrubs from the Canary Islands and Madeira; *Leucanthemum*, white-flowered perennials from the Mediterranean and Europe, including the ox-eye and Shasta daisies; *Tanacetum*, perennials and subshrubs from temperate Eurasia and North Africa, with very aromatic foliage and yellow, red or white flowers—they include the insecticidal pyrethrum, tansy and feverfew; *Ajania*, perennials from eastern and northern Asia rather like the florist's chrysanthemums but with flowers in numerous yellow button-like heads. And finally, *'Chysanthemum'* in the sense recognised before the recent decision is the group of 5 annuals from Europe and North Africa including the crown daisy, corn marigold and painted daisy. The correct genus name for this group is still uncertain, so they are listed hereunder but with the genus in quotes, indicating they are no longer true *Chrysanthemum.* **CULTIVATION:** Chrysanthemums are generally frost-hardy, though some forms are a little more tender than others. They can be grown outdoors in most temperate climates but, for indoor use, exhibition purposes or choice cut flowers, are usually raised under glass. Plant outdoors in full sun in a well-drained, slightly acid soil improved with compost and well-rotted manure. For pot culture, use a rich, organic growing medium. Avoid excessive watering and in early summer feed with low-nitrogen, high-potassium fertilizer. Pinching out stem tips when they are 6–12 in (15–30 cm) high promotes flowering lateral stems with many flowers (known as 'sprays'), but for the largest exhibition blooms all lateral buds are removed at an early stage, leaving a single terminal bud—a 'disbudded chrysanthemum'. Stake tall plants with canes. Propagate bedding types from seed, named varieties from root divisions or basal cuttings of late fall (autumn) shoots. The annual species of *'Chrysanthemum'* are easily grown in any good garden soil in a sunny position, by sowing seed in spring in cool climates or in fall (autumn) in warmer climates.

Chrysanthemum × *grandiflorum*

syns ***Chrysanthemum morifolium*, *Dendranthema* × *grandiflorum***

FLORISTS' CHRYSANTHEMUM

Thought to be derived mainly from the Chinese species *Chysanthemum indicum*, this hybrid group includes most of the cultivated chrysanthemums, and all of those with large double blooms. A more recent development is the breeding of the 'Korean chrysanthemums', introducing genes from *C. zawadskii* for more compact plants with smaller single heads, good for bedding. The chrysanthemum plant can be up to 5 ft (1.5 m) tall though mostly smaller; it has rather woody stems rising from a mass of creeping rhizomes, bluntly lobed leaves up to 3 in (8 cm) long with grey felted undersides; flowerheads may be anywhere from 1 to 6 in (2.5–15 cm) across, borne on a broad panicle and ranging from white, pink or yellow through various bronze colors to deep red or purple. Most of the larger types are 'double' lacking disc florets.

Chrysanthemum enthusiasts and societies have classified the thousands of cultivars into 10 groups, based on the overall form of the blooms and the shape and orientation of the florets. The full range of colors is represented in each group. The groups are:

C. × *grandiflorum* 'Flame Symbol'

C. × *grandiflorum* 'Jane Sharpe'

C. × *grandiflorum* 'Elizabeth Shoesmith'

Anemone-centered: daisy-like but with a pincushion center and a single or double row of radiating flat florets; normally grown as sprays rather than single blooms.

Incurved: fully double globular blooms with firm-textured florets curving inward and packed closely together, used for cut flowers as well as exhibition, long-lasting when cut. Cream **'Gillete'** and yellow **'Max Riley'** are examples.

Intermediate: falling somewhat between incurved and reflexed, these have ball-like blooms, sometimes with recurving florets at the base. Pale bronze **'Crimson Tide'** and deep pink **'Elizabeth Shoesmith'** are examples.

Pompon: globular double blooms formed of numerous, tightly packed florets; normally grown as sprays rather than single blooms and make excellent cut flowers.

Quill-shaped: double blooms with narrow tubular florets that open out at the tips. **'Yellow Nightingale'** is an example.

Reflexed: rounded or dome-shaped, fully double blooms, the florets curved out and down, often with a curl or twist. Burnt-orange **'Flame Symbol'**, deep pink **'Matthew Scale'** and **'Yellow Symbol'** are examples.

Fully reflexed: perfectly rounded double blooms with florets that curve out and down, lowermost florets touching the stem.

Single: daisy-like blooms with up to 5 rows of radiating florets around a flattened yellow disc; excellent for massed planting.

Spider: double blooms with long narrow tubular florets that spread out in all directions, usually curled or twisted at the end. Golden-orange **'Dusky Queen'** and white **'Sterling Silver'** are examples.

Spoon-shaped: double blooms with radiating narrow, tubular florets with the tips expanded to form spoon shapes. **ZONES 4–10.**

C. × *grandiflorum* 'Yellow Nightingale'

Chrysanthemum weyrichii

syn. *Dendranthema weyrichii*

This is a mat-forming species from Japan that grows to 12 in (30 cm) tall by 18 in (45 cm) across. It has fleshy dark green leaves, the lower ones divided into about 5 lobes. The flowers, produced in fall (autumn), have yellow centers and pink or white ray florets. **ZONES 4–9.**

'Chrysanthemum' carinatum

syn. *Chrysanthemum tricolor*

PAINTED DAISY, SUMMER CHRYSANTHEMUM, TRICOLOR CHRYSANTHEMUM

This and the following 2 species are considered to belong to a separate genus from the florists' chrysanthemums but its name is yet to be determined, hence the quotes. It is a colorful garden flower from Morocco that grows to 24 in (60 cm), spreading to about 12 in (30 cm) wide with much-divided, rather fleshy leaves and banded, multicolored flowers in spring and early summer. **'Monarch Court Jesters'** comes in red with yellow centers or white with red centers, and the **Tricolor Series** has many color combinations. They are excellent as bedding plants and cut flowers. **ZONES 8–10.**

'Chrysanthemum' coronarium

CROWN DAISY

This is a fast-growing annual from the Mediterranean region that will grow to a height of about 3 ft (1 m). The light green leaves are deeply divided and feathery. Daisy-like flowerheads are single or double, very pale to deep yellow and up to 2 in (5 cm) across. The tender young shoots of selected strains are used in oriental cooking, known as *shungiku* or chop suey greens; they can also be used raw in salads but have a strong aromatic taste. **ZONES 7–11.**

'Chrysanthemum' segetum

CORN MARIGOLD

Originating from the eastern Mediterranean area and North Africa, this fast-growing annual is now widely naturalized in temperate regions. Up to about 24 in (60 cm) tall, it has gray-green leaves that are toothed or, on the lower stem, deeply cut. The daisy-like flowerheads, $1\frac{1}{2}$–$2\frac{1}{2}$ in (4–6 cm) across, appear in summer and early fall (autumn) in various shades of yellow. They make good cut flowers. **ZONES 7–10.**

CHRYSOCEPHALUM

All 8 species of this Australian genus of perennials were formerly included in *Helichrysum*, a genus of the daisy family that botanists are still in the process of redefining and narrowing in scope. *Chrysocephalum* species are mostly evergreens, with slender leafy stems arising from wiry rhizomes by which the plants may spread extensively, though some species have more compact rootstocks. The small 'everlasting' type flowerheads are mostly clustered at the stem apex, and have many rows of tiny yellow or white chaffy bracts surrounding a small group of orange disc-florets. Some species are vigorous growers and make useful ground covers, as well as providing spring and summer blooms.

CULTIVATION: These plants prefer a climate with warm, dry summers but are nonetheless fairly adaptable if grown in well-drained, open soil of moderate fertility and in a sunny spot. Propagate from seed, rhizome division, or cuttings from lower stems.

Chrysocephalum apiculatum

syn. *Helichrysum apiculatum*

YELLOW BUTTONS, COMMON EVERLASTING

Occurring over most of Australia, including Tasmania, this species is highly variable in growth-habit and foliage characters. Some forms are up to 24 in (60 cm) high, others much lower, some make compact clumps of basal rosettes, others spread extensively. The simple, flat leaves vary from gray-felted to green and only slightly hairy. Flowerheads are golden yellow, in small to large clusters, appearing mainly in spring or summer but can appear at any time of year. **ZONES 8–11.**

Chrysocephalum apiculatum

'Chrysanthemum' carinatum

C. × *grandiflorum* 'Dusky Queen'

C. × *grandiflorum* 'Sterling Silver'

Chrysanthemum' coronarium

C. × *grandiflorum* 'Matthew Scaelle'

C. × *grandiflorum* 'Yellow Symbol'

'Chrysanthemum' segetum

Chrysocephalum baxteri
syn. *Helichrysum baxteri*
FRINGED EVERLASTING, WHITE EVERLASTING

Native to southeast Australia, this compact perennial has narrow, dark green leaves, woolly white underneath, forming a mound to about 6 in (15 cm) high. The 4–8 in (10–20 cm) flowering stems each carry a single daisy-like flowerhead, with showy white or cream (sometimes buff or pinkish) papery bracts surrounding yellow disc-florets. This attractive rock-garden plant can flower at any time but peaks in spring. **ZONES 8–10.**

CHRYSOGONUM
GOLDEN KNEE, GOLDEN STAR

This genus has only a single species; an herbaceous perennial from eastern USA. Plants spread by long-running rhizomes, sending up short erect stems with heart-shaped leaves arranged in opposite pairs. The bright yellow flowerheads have only 5 broad ray-florets and are produced over a very long flowering season from spring to fall (autumn).
CULTIVATION: Easy to grow, it prefers light shade and a rather peaty, moist soil. Propagate from seed or by division.

Chukrasia tabularis

Cichorium intybus

Chrysolepis chrysophylla

Chrysogonum virginianum

This low growing, mat-forming perennial suitable for a rock garden spreads by underground runners, but is not normally invasive. It bears yellow daisy-like flowerheads from spring into fall (autumn). **ZONES 6–9.**

CHRYSOLEPIS
CHINQUAPIN, GOLDEN CHESTNUT

Although some botanists recognize a second species *(Chrysolepis sempervirens)* occurring on the Sierra Nevada, *C. chrysophylla* is normally considered the only species in this genus. From northern California and Oregon, it was formerly classified in the chestnut genus *Castanea*. The tree has a stout trunk and leathery leaves. The male flowers are in clusters of very short cream catkins at the branch tips; female flowers are clustered at the base of the current year's growth and develop in fruit into a tight group of spine-covered husks, each enclosing 2 to 3 edible nuts that are triangular in cross-section. This handsome tree is seldom cultivated.
CULTIVATION: Moderately frost hardy, it needs full sun or partial shade and fertile, moist, well-drained, neutral or acid soil and protection from strong winds. Propagate from fresh, ripe seed.

Chrysolepis chrysophylla

This species can reach 100 ft (30 m) in the wild, but usually forms a small, bushy tree of about 30 ft (9 m) in cultivation. The narrowly oval, leathery leaves are 2–3 in (5–8 cm) long, dark green above and golden brown beneath. Flowering in mid-summer, the tree takes another 15 months or so to ripen its small, pale brown nuts. **ZONES 7–9.**

CHUKRASIA

This genus, belonging to the mahogany family, consists of a single species of dry-season deciduous tree that occurs widely

Chrysocephalum baxteri

Chusquea culeou

Cichorium endivia

in Southeast Asia, from southern China to eastern India. It yields a valuable timber known variously as Chittagong wood, chikrassy, Indian redwood, or yonhin. The tree also produces a useful gum.
CULTIVATION: It requires a tropical or subtropical climate and does best in a sheltered situation in deep, moist, well-drained soil. Propagate from seed.

Chukrasia tabularis
INDIAN REDWOOD

This is a small to medium-sized tree that yields valuable timber. The leaves are spectacular, being tinted with pink, red and orange in spring. It is a useful shade tree in warm climates. **ZONES 11–12.**

CHUSQUEA

This genus of bamboos consists of 100 or so species from Central and South America, mainly occurring in 'cloud' or 'moss' forests in mountain regions with frequent mist and drizzle. Mostly of small to medium size, they are unique among bamboos in having solid stems, the centers filled with pith. The sheathing leaves persist on the stems, and the side-branches are 3 at each node, though each branches again not far from the node. The leaves are usually rather elongated and grass-like. Flowers are rarely seen in cultivation.
CULTIVATION: Outdoor cultivation requires cool but very humid conditions with high rainfall. They can also be grown in a cool greenhouse as long as summer temperatures are not too high. Propagate by division of clumps.

Chusquea culeou

A native of Chile, this is the most frost hardy species. Growing to a height of around 15 ft (4.5 m), it forms a dense clump with stems often arched over at the top, and drooping deep green foliage. The stems, half hidden beneath straw-colored sheaths, may have a bluish waxy coating. **ZONES 7–9.**

CICHORIUM

This genus of 8 species of annuals and perennials from Europe, western Asia and northern Africa is closely related to the lettuce genus *Lactuca*. Two species are grown in temperate-climate gardens mainly as salad plants, eaten in the same way as lettuce or sometimes blanched. The plants have slightly swollen taproots and basal tufts of large, crisp, tongue-shaped leaves, which exude pin-

Cichorium endivia 'Sally'

Cichorium intybus 'Palo Rosa Bella'

head drops of milky sap when broken. Their usually blue, dandelion-like flowerheads are borne on tall branched stems and open only for the morning.
CULTIVATION: Mostly very frost hardy, they need full sun. When growing as leaf vegetables plant in fertile, humus-rich, well-drained soil and keep moist, otherwise the plants will run to seed early. Sow the seeds 12–15 in (30–38 cm) apart in a shaded position in late summer. Use liquid fertilizer every now and then as the plants are growing. Watch for attack by slugs and for rust-fungus and mildew. They can also be propagated from root division.

Cichorium endivia
ENDIVE, SCAROLE

This close relative of chicory is an annual or biennial grown for its leaves, which are usually eaten green as a bitter salad; they resemble lettuce but are more sharply flavored. The plant typically is loose hearted, somewhat like a mignonette lettuce but all green. Most popular are varieties with more divided and crisped leaves, such as **'Sally'** and **'Green Curled'.** The wild origins of endive are uncertain, and it may be an old hybrid. **ZONES 4–10.**

Cichorium intybus
CHICORY, WITLOOF, RADICCHIO

In some countries chicory is best known as a coffee substitute or adulterant, the roots being roasted and ground for this purpose. But in France, Belgium and Italy this species has produced a whole range of leaf vegetables that have a firm place in the cuisines of those countries. They are grown like small lettuces and vary greatly in coloring and shape of the leaves (see for example **'Palo Rosa Bella'**), many having strong red or purple tones that add color to salads, others having curled or deeply cut leaves. In cooler regions blanched shoots or 'chicons' are produced by forcing the roots into growth in a dark cellar in winter, or by tying the leaves around the growing shoot. The true 'endive' of the French belongs to this species, not *Cichorium endivia.* It has the same geographical range as the genus as a whole, and is widely naturalized along roadsides in temperate regions of other continents, conspicuous by its pale blue flowers in summer and fall (autumn). **ZONES 4–10.**

CIMICIFUGA
BUGBANE

This genus of about 15 species of perennials in the ranunculus family, native to cooler regions of the northern hemisphere. The name literally means 'bug repellent', from the Latin *cimex*, the bedbug, and *fugare*, to repel, reflecting an early use of one species. The foliage is reminiscent of astilbes, having large compound leaves with toothed leaflets, but the branched flowering stems terminate in long, erect spikes of small white, cream or pinkish flowers, the many stamens being the conspicuous part of each flower. Some North American species are important in herbal medicine.

CULTIVATION: These plants are bold additions to the summer garden, at the back of borders or in open woodland situations. They prefer part-shade and a deep, rich soil and need regular watering but otherwise need little attention. Plant rhizome divisions in spring or fall (autumn), but do not disturb the root; they flower best when established, and seldom need staking.

Cimicifuga japonica
JAPANESE BUGBANE

From woodlands of Japan, this species is distinguished by its very long-stalked leaves with shallowly lobed leaflets up to 4 in (10 cm) wide. The flowering stems are slender and leafless, up to 4 ft (1.2 m) high, bearing rather undistinguished small white flowers from mid-summer to early fall (autumn). ***Cimicifuga japonica* var. *acerina*** (syn. *C. acerina*) has long drawn-out points on the leaf lobes. **ZONES 5–9.**

Cimicifuga racemosa
BLACK COHOSH, SQUAWROOT

From woodlands of eastern and central North America, this vigorous perennial has crowded, large, compound leaves arising from a knotted rhizome with densely massed fibrous roots. Flowering stems, leafy in the lower part, rise to a height of 5 ft (1.5 m) or more and bear spikes of cream flowers in summer and fall (autumn). The whole plant has an unpleasant smell when bruised. The rhizomes were used by Native Americans in childbirth and for menstruation problems and are now known to contain an oestrogen-like substance. **ZONES 3–9.**

Cimicifuga japonica var. *acerina*

Cimicifuga simplex
KAMCHATKA BUGBANE

From Japan and far eastern Siberia, this species is the latest to flower of the whole genus, the flowers coming in late fall (autumn). It is also smaller, reaching a height of about 4 ft (1.2 m). The flowers are white, carried on long arching wands, and the foliage is much divided. **'Elstead'** has purplish buds opening to pure white and is a very graceful plant. **ZONES 3–9.**

CINERARIA

This name has been the source of much confusion. The true *Cineraria,* as botanists understand it, is a genus of about 50 species from southern Africa and Madagascar, little known in gardens. The florists' 'cinerarias' are a colorful group of hybrids of Canary Island origin now referred to as *Pericallis* × *hybrida* though once placed in the genus *Senecio*; and the gray-leafed *Cineraria maritima* of gardens is correctly *Senecio cineraria*, a Mediterranean plant. The true (African) cinerarias are perennials and subshrubs with broad, rather fleshy leaves that are often heart-shaped or kidney-shaped and may be hairy or woolly. They produce numerous stalked flowerheads with yellow ray-florets, like small daisies.

CULTIVATION: Only a few South African species have ever been cultivated, making attractive low plants for rockeries or banks, or used as ground covers. They are not very frost hardy and like well-drained, humus-rich soil and plenty of sun. Propagate from seed, cuttings, or by root divisions.

Cineraria saxifraga

This South African subshrub is broadly spreading and usually about 8 in (20 cm) high, with prostrate branches that root into the soil. The pale green somewhat succulent leaves, to about 1½ in (38 mm) long, almost kidney-shaped and coarsely toothed. Numerous small, yellow, daisy-like flowerheads appear through spring, summer and fall (autumn), on weak slender stalks. **ZONES 9–11.**

Cimicifuga simplex

Cissus antarctica

Cineraria saxifraga

CINNAMOMUM

This genus of the laurel family consists of around 250 species of evergreen trees from tropical and subtropical Asia and Australasia with smooth, strongly veined leaves. Highly aromatic compounds are present in the leaves, twigs and bark of all species. The flowers are small and white or cream in delicate sprays and are followed by small fleshy berries containing a single seed. The genus includes *Cinnamomum zeylanicum*, the bark of which yields the spice cinnamon; ***C. cassia***, cultivated in China and Burma provides the spice cassia used in drinks and sweets. *C. camphora* is a source of commercial camphor and is traditionally used in China to make storage chests.

CULTIVATION: Most species require tropical or subtropical conditions, with fairly high rainfall; only *C. camphora* is adaptable to warm-temperate climates. They do best in full sun or dappled shade in deep, free-draining soil with plentiful water in summer. Propagate from seed sown in fall (autumn).

Cinnamomum camphora
CAMPHOR LAUREL, CAMPHOR TREE

Native to China, Taiwan and southern Japan, this fast-growing tree is known to reach 120 ft (36 m) in height with a rounded crown spreading to 50 ft (15 m) wide, but half this height is more usual in gardens. The short, solid trunk has scaly gray bark. The leaves, pinkish when young, turn pale green and finally deep green as they age. Widely grown for shade and as a street tree, it self-seeds freely and can become invasive in subtropical climates—in parts of east-coastal Australia it has become a serious pest. **ZONES 9–11.**

Cinnamomum zeylanicum
syn. *Cinnamomum verum*
CINNAMON

A 30 ft (9 m) high tree from southern India and Sri Lanka, this species has light brown, papery bark. Its large oblong leaves are bright red when young, maturing to deep green with conspicuous white veins. Loose panicles of inconspicuous yellow flowers are followed by purplish fruit in structures very like acorn cups. This species is the main source of cinnamon, obtained by peeling bark from smaller branches and letting it dry into 'quills'. **ZONES 11–12.**

CISSUS

Cissus consists of around 350 species occurring in all warmer parts of the

Cinnamomum camphora

world. They are varied in growth habit, though the majority are tendril climbers, including many that are among the largest woody lianes of rainforests. Some lower-growing species are adapted to very dry conditions, with very thick, swollen stems or large tubers. A number of the rainforest species are popular indoor plants, grown for their decorative foliage. The flowers are usually yellow or green and quite small, borne in modest panicles from the leaf nodes; they are followed by succulent fruits, showing a resemblance to small grapes but mostly hardly edible. Some species once included in *Cissus* are now placed in *Rhoicissus, Cyphostemma* or *Tetrastigma.*

CULTIVATION: All the climbing species need semi-shade in summer, when they need regular watering. Some means of support is necessary, though young plants can be allowed to spill from hanging baskets. Stems can be thinned out if necessary during spring. Propagation is from cuttings taken in summer.

Cissus antarctica
KANGAROO VINE

This native of moist eastern Australian forests gets no closer to Antarctica than southern New South Wales. In the wild it can grow into the tops of large rainforest trees, looping its massive stems below like Tarzan's 'jungle ropes', but grown as an indoor plant it will survive quite happily in a 6 in (15 cm) pot for years if fertilized occasionally. In the garden in mild climates it forms masses of foliage, rapidly climbing to 15 ft (4.5 m) or more on a fence or trellis, or left unsupported will scramble over rocky slopes and banks. Regular pruning will keep it more compact. Its distinctive features are the simple, toothed leaves and the rust-colored hairs on their undersides and on young stems. It bears thick-skinned, blackish fruit less than ½ in (12 mm) in diameter. **ZONES 9–11.**

C

Cissus rhombifolia

Cistus 'Snow Mound'

Cistus albidus

Cissus rhombifolia
GRAPE IVY

A native of tropical America, this commonly grown species might easily be mistaken for *Cissus antarctica* but a closer look will show that its leaves are compound, with 3 smallish, coarsely toothed leaflets that are roughly rhombic (diamond-shaped) in outline, hence the specific name. It is a moderately vigorous tendril climber that can be used in much the same ways as *Cissus antarctica*, though the foliage is denser and more compact, with less vigorous leading shoots. Even with support it does not often climb higher than about 12 ft (3.5 m). The cultivar **'Ellen Danica'** with larger, more deeply toothed leaflets is popular as an indoor plant, good for hanging baskets. **ZONES 10–12.**

CISTUS
ROCK ROSE

These evergreen shrubs from around the Mediterranean and the Canary Islands are valued for their attractive, saucer-shaped flowers, which have crinkled petals in shades of pink, purple or white and a central boss of golden stamens, like a single rose. Although short-lived, most bloom over a long season, some for almost the whole year, and they do very well in shrub borders, on banks or in pots; some examples include **'Peggy Sammons'**, **'Santa Cruz'**, **'Snow Mound'** and **'Warley Rose'**. Some species exude an aromatic resin which the ancient Greeks and Romans called *labdanum* and used for incense and perfumery, as well as medicinally.

CULTIVATION: These shrubs are easily cultivated provided they are given a warm, sunny position and very well-drained, even rather dry soil; they like being among large rocks or other rubble where their roots can seek out deep moisture. If necessary they can be tip pruned to promote bushiness, or main branches shortened by about a third after flowering. Most species are moderately frost hardy; all are resistant to very dry conditions. They will thrive in countries with cool- to warm-temperate climates, but not in subtropical regions with hot, humid summers. Propagation is normally from cuttings, although seed is readily germinated.

Cistus 'Peggy Sammons'

Cistus 'Warley Rose'

Cistus × *canescens* 'Albus'

Cistus × *aguilarii*

This plant is a spontaneous hybrid between *Cistus ladanifer* and *C. populifolius*. It is a bushy shrub with narrow, wavy-edged, slightly sticky, rich green leaves. The flowers are white and medium-small, produced in summer. **'Maculatus'** has flowers with a pattern of deep red spots at bases of petals. **ZONES 8–10.**

Cistus 'Santa Cruz'

Cistus albidus
WHITE-LEAFED ROCKROSE

This attractive species, with felty, gray-green foliage and large, lilac-pink flowers with a small yellow blotch at the base of each petal, is very sensitive to excess moisture. From the far southwest of Europe and northwest Africa, it grows to 4 ft (1.2 m) high and 8 ft (2.4 m) wide with foliage right down to the ground, concealing thick, twisted branches. The flowers appear mainly in spring. **ZONES 7–9.**

Cistus × *canescens*

This natural hybrid between *Cistus albidus* and *C. creticus* is usually found in the wild growing among both parents. It has gray-green leaves and usually pink flowers, about 2 in (5 cm) in diameter. **'Albus'** has white flowers. **ZONES 8–9.**

Cistus × *hybridus*
syn. *Cistus* × *corbariensis*
WHITE ROCK ROSE

A hybrid between *Cistus populifolius* and *C. salviifolius*, this mounding shrub is covered with pure white flowers from late spring into summer and occasionally beyond. The small, slightly furry leaves have an incense-like scent, most noticeable on a warm day. It may grow to 5 ft (1.5 m), although plants may be kept lower with light tip pruning. **ZONES 7–9.**

Cistus × *hybridus*

Cistus incanus

Cistus incanus
syn. *Cistus villosus*

Native to southern Europe, *Cistus incanus* makes a dense shrub of up to 5 ft (1.5 m) high, with an equal spread. The leaves are oval and crinkled, about 2 in (5 cm) long. Saucer-shaped rosy purple flowers about 2 in (5 cm) in diameter are produced in summer, the petals rumpled like tissue paper. **ZONES 8–10.**

Cistus ladanifer
CRIMSON-SPOT ROCKROSE

The most upright and slender species, *Cistus ladanifer* grows to around 5–6 ft (1.5–1.8 m) tall but quickly becomes sparse and leggy and does not take well to pruning. The whole plant, apart from the flower petals, is coated with a shiny resin that in the heat of the day becomes semi-liquid and very aromatic. Its leaves are narrow and dark green and the flowers, among the largest in the genus at 3–4 in (8–10 cm) across, have pure white petals each with a reddish chocolate basal blotch; they appear from mid-spring to early summer. The cultivar **'Albiflorus'** has pure white petals. **ZONES 8–10.**

Cistus laurifolius

The laurel-leafed cistus from south-western Europe and Morocco is not one of the largest in flower—the blooms are only about 2½ in (6 cm) wide—but it is a very beautiful, free-flowering plant. It has pure white flowers that are in gleaming contrast all through the summer against the leathery deep green leaves. Capable of growing to 6 ft (1.8 m) high, it has the best reputation for cold hardiness of any *Cistus*. **ZONES 7–9.**

Cistus ladanifer 'Albiflorus'

Cistus ladanifer 'Albiflorus'

Cistus × *laxus*

Cistus × *purpureus*

Cistus × *obtusifolius*

Cistus × *laxus*

This hybrid between *Cistus hirsutus* and *C. populifolius* is about mid-way in stature between that of the two parents. The flowers are white with a yellow center. **ZONES 8–9.**

Cistus × *lusitanicus*

This hybrid between *Cistus ladanifer* and *C. hirsutus* makes a densely foliaged shrub about 24 in (60 cm) high. It has narrow, dark green leaves and white flowers 2½ in (6 cm) across with a prominent crimson blotch at the base of each petal. **'Decumbens'** is a low, spreading form with flowers that have darker crimson blotches. **ZONES 8–9.**

Cistus × *obtusifolius*

This dwarf hybrid between *Cistus hirsutus* and *C. salviifolius* has a rounded growth habit. Flowers are white with a yellow basal stain and measure 1–1.5 in (2.5–3.5 cm) in diameter. **ZONES 8–10.**

Cistus × *pulverulentus*

A compact, spreading shrub, this hybrid between *Cistus albidus* and *C. crispus* bears small rose pink flowers in summer. The leaves are gray-green and about 1½ in (4 cm) long. It grows to a height of

Cistus × *lusitanicus*

Cistus × *pulverulentus* 'Sunset'

24 in (60 cm). **'Sunset'**, a superior cultivar has abundant rosy red flowers 2½ in (6 cm) in diameter. **ZONES 8–10.**

Cistus × *purpureus*
ORCHID ROCK ROSE

This hybrid between *Cistus ladanifer* and the eastern Mediterranean species *C. creticus* has deep pink flowers with prominent, dark reddish chocolate blotches on the petals. It is frost hardy and free flowering. Several clones have been named including **'Brilliancy'**, with clear pink petals, and **'Betty Taudevin'**, a deeper reddish pink. **ZONES 7–9.**

Cistus salviifolius
SAGELEAF ROCKROSE

This species has deeply veined leaves that are thinner than most other cistus, and smaller, slender-stalked flowers. It makes a rounded shrub of about 24–36 in (60–90 cm) high and reaching up to 6 ft (1.8 m) wide, with thin, densely massed twigs. The neat disc-like flowers, pure white except for a small, orange-yellow basal blotch on each petal, are scattered profusely over the plant from late winter to early summer. It can be cut back harder than other species. **'Prostratus'** is a dwarf form. **ZONES 8–10.**

Cistus × *skanbergii*

Cistus × *skanbergii*

A particularly beautiful cross between *Cistus monspeliensis* and *C. parviflorus*, this hybrid has been found in the wild in Sicily and Greece. It grows 3–5 ft (1–1.5 m) tall and up to 8 ft (2.4 m) wide. The flowers are a clear pink and are borne in large sprays. **ZONES 8–10.**

CITHAREXYLUM
FIDDLEWOOD

At least 70 species belong to this genus of tropical and subtropical trees and shrubs, native in Central and South America and the West Indies. Evergreen or semi-evergreen, they are grown for their handsome, glossy leaves and fragrant flowers as well as the fine quality wood which is used for cabinet work. *Citharexylum spinosum* received its common name from the use of its wood to make stringed instruments by the people of the Caribbean; it is not used in the manufacture of violins. All species have simple leaves arranged in opposite pairs, and spikes of very small flowers. **CULTIVATION:** Frost tender to marginally frost-hardy, they need full sun, a well-drained, humus-rich soil and plenty of summer water. Tip prune in early summer only if necessary to retain their shape. Propagate from ripe seed or from cuttings in spring.

Citharexylum spinosum
syns *Citharexylum quadrangulare, C. subserratum*
FIDDLEWOOD

This fast-growing, evergreen, often multi-stemmed tree with a rounded crown grows to about 40 ft (12 m) is native to the Caribbean. The glossy, oblong leaves are about 8 in (20 cm) long and turn from bright green in summer to copper and orange in winter and spring. Some leaves fall in spring, particularly in colder climates. Long racemes of tiny, yellow-white, fragrant flowers appear in late summer to winter. **ZONES 9–11.**

× *CITROFORTUNELLA*

This hybrid genus name includes any existing or potential hybrid between the genera *Citrus* and *Fortunella* (the cumquats), both of which are regarded as citrus fruits in a broad sense. The plants are intermediate in character between these, as might be expected, showing the

Cistus × *purpureus* 'Brilliancy'

Cistus salviifolius

Cistus laurifolius

Citharexylum spinosum

Citharexylum spinosum

influence of the *Fortunella* parent in a more shrubby habit, smaller leaves and less edible fruit than most *Citrus* plants. The calamondin is the only well-known hybrid of this type, but there is also a less well-known cross between a lime and a sweet cumquat.
CULTIVATION: All are sensitive to frost. Like all citrus they need ample water all year round and regular feeding. They are usually propagated by grafting onto a *Poncirus trifoliata* rootstock.

× *Citrofortunella microcarpa*
syn. *Citrus mitis*
CALAMONDIN, PANAMA ORANGE

A hybrid between a mandarin *(Citrus reticulata)* and a cumquat *(Fortunella margarita)*, this is the least edible of all citrus fruits. However, it makes an attractive ornamental shrub of up to about 8 ft (2.4 m) high with small bright orange fruits and is widely grown either as a tub specimen outdoors or, in cool climates, as a potted indoor plant. **ZONES 10–12.**

CITRULLUS

This Afro-Asian genus of the cucurbit family is remarkable for having produced from one of its 3 species some of the sweetest of all melons, namely the watermelons, though all its wild forms are very bitter and normally quite inedible. The plants are trailing annuals or perennials with very deeply lobed leaves and yellow flowers. The fruits have smooth but hard skins and the green, white or pink flesh has brown to black seeds embedded in it.
CULTIVATION: Only the watermelon is generally cultivated in this genus, grown in much the same way as pumpkins or cantaloupes. They require a friable, well-manured soil with good drainage and a long, warm growing season with plentiful irrigation—the longer and hotter the summer the better the crop will be. In cool climates they may be grown in a greenhouse but the space they need diminishes their value in terms of fruit production. Sow seed in spring. Watch for cucumber beetles.

Citrullus colocynthis
COLOCYNTH, BITTER APPLE

Native in warmer parts of North Africa and western Asia, the colocynth is now naturalized in other parts of the world, sometimes in very arid regions. It is a completely prostrate plant, the stems radiating from a tuberous, perennial rootstock. The deeply lobed leaves are small, under 4 in (10 cm) long, and the yellow and green striped fruit are only about 3 in (8 cm) in diameter. The intensely bitter fruits yield a drastic purgative which when taken to excess has sometimes proved fatal. It is believed to be the 'wild gourd' mentioned in the Bible. **ZONES 8–11.**

Citrullus lanatus
syn. *Citrullus vulgaris*
WATERMELON, CAMEL MELON

The original wild form of this species is believed to have come from southwestern Africa and is a prostrate annual vine with hairy stems, lobed leaves about 4 in (10 cm) long, and a spherical or oval melon 4–6 in (10–15 cm) long with moderately bitter flesh. It is a common weed in inland Australia. Apart from the watermelon, cultivated forms include some smaller melons with yellow or orange flesh, and the 'preserving melon' *(Citrullus lanatus* var. *citroides)* which is also small with white, hardly sweet flesh, used for pickling. **ZONES 8–11.**

Citrus limon

Citrus limon 'Eureka'

Citrus limon 'Meyer'

Citrus aurantifolia

Citrullus colocynthis

CITRUS

The number of original wild species in this genus of evergreen small trees, originally native in the Southeast Asian region, is very uncertain as many of the cultivated forms are probably of ancient hybrid origin following their domestication, which took place mainly in China and India. While largely cultivated for their fruit, citrus plants have the bonus of looking attractive in the garden, with glossy evergreen leaves and fragrant flowers. Most species are frost tender to some degree but a few tolerate very light frosts; the lemon is the most cold resistant, especially when grafted onto the related *Poncirus trifoliata* rootstock, and the lime is the least cold resistant, doing best in subtropical locations. All citrus can also be grown in pots, as long as the containers are large and the citrus are grown on dwarfing rootstocks.
CULTIVATION: Very well-drained, friable, slightly acid, loam soil is best. They need full sun, regular watering and protection from wind, especially during the summer months. Citrus also need regular feeding, including large amounts of nitrogen and potassium for good fruiting. Prune only to remove dead, diseased and crossing wood.
Subject to a range of virus diseases, they can be invaded by many pests including scale, leaf miner, bronze orange bug, spined citrus bug and fruit fly. They are rarely propagated by home gardeners as this is done by grafting, a specialist task.

Citrus aurantifolia
LIME

The lime is best suited to tropical and subtropical climates. The flesh and juice have a stronger acidity and flavor than the lemon. It is an erect tree growing up to 15–20 ft (4.5–6 m), more irregular and less ornamental than the lemon and with spiny branches. The Tahitian lime, the variety most commonly grown, bears fruit all year round. The Mexican lime has smaller fruit with high acidity and stronger flavor and is a thornier tree. **ZONES 10–12.**

Citrus aurantium
SOUR ORANGE, SEVILLE ORANGE

These marginally frost-hardy small trees are grown as ornamental shrubs or providers of fruit for marmalade and jelly. The heavy-fruiting '**Seville**' is the premium marmalade orange. **'Chinotto'** with small, dark green leaves and compact growth habit is excellent in containers or as border shrubs. The dwarf **'Bouquet de Fleurs'** is a more fragrant, ornamental shrub, smooth-stemmed and showy. Watch for melanose (dark brown spots on the wood and fruit) and citrus scab. **ZONES 9–11.**

Citrus limon
LEMON

The lemon tree does best in warm Mediterranean climates with mild winters. It grows to around 20 ft (6 m) and is prone to collar rot, so plant it with the graft union well above the soil and keep mulch away from the stem. **'Eureka'** is probably the most commonly grown cultivar, producing fruit and flowers all year round. It is an attractive, almost thornless tree, the best variety for temperate locations and coastal gardens. The smaller, hardier **'Meyer'** produces smaller fruit and is the better variety for growing in pots. **'Lisbon'** is popular with commercial growers and is reliable and heavy fruiting; it is good for hot areas but is thorny. **ZONES 9–11.**

Citrus medica
CITRON, CEDRAT

The fruit of this species is like a giant lemon, 6–12 in (15–30 cm) long, but of more irregular shape and with a rougher, highly fragrant skin. It has little juice and is used mainly for marmalade and candied peel. A tall shrub of rather ungainly habit, it has young foliage with a purplish tinge, also the flowers. This was the first citrus to reach the Mediterranean, some saying it came with Alexander's returning armies from India. It had many claimed medicinal virtues in earlier times and was also used in perfumery. The smaller-fruited **'Etrog'** has been grown in Israel for many centuries and has become part of Jewish religious custom. **ZONES 9–11.**

Citrus × *paradisi*
GRAPEFRUIT

Easily grown in mild areas, the grapefruit can make a dense, rounded tree to 20–30 ft (6–9 m) or more. Its large, golden-skinned fruits are well known and widely appreciated. Popular frost-hardy cultivars include **'Marsh'**, **'Morrison's Seedless'** and **'Golden Special'**. The seedless and **'Ruby'** cultivars are more tender, preferring a frost-free climate. All are usually grown from cuttings or grafts. **ZONES 10–12.**

Citrus reticulata
MANDARIN, TANGERINE

This, the most varied citrus species, has a wide range of climate tolerance among its varieties: some can survive an occasional light frost. Growing to 12–20 ft (3.5–6 m) or so high, it is a good fruit tree for the suburban garden. Similar to oranges, the fruit are smaller and looser skinned. It is slow growing and has heavily perfumed flowers. **ZONES 9–11.**

Citrus sinensis
ORANGE

Attractive trees to 25 ft (8 m) or more with a rounded head, glossy foliage and sweetly scented white flowers, oranges can be grown in most non-tropical climates. They will tolerate very light frosts. **'Valencia'** is perhaps the most frost hardy of all oranges, producing fruit in spring and summer that is most commonly juiced but can also be eaten fresh. **'Joppa'** is a good variety for tropical gardens. **'Ruby Blood'** has oblong fruit with reddish rind, flesh and juice; it is the best known and best tasting of the 'blood oranges'. The navel oranges are mutated forms with a 'navel' at the fruit apex and no seeds: **'Washington Navel'**, which fruits through winter, has very large and sweet, bright orange fruit and is best suited to slightly cooler areas. New varieties are available to commercial growers and gardeners could enquire at specialist nurseries about others that might suit their garden. **ZONES 9–11.**

Citrus × tangelo
TANGELO

An evergreen tree growing up to 20–30 ft (6–9 m) high and 10 ft (3 m) wide, this hybrid is derived from a cross between the tangerine *(Citrus reticulata)* and the grapefruit *(C. paradisi)*. Tangelo is renowned for its juicing properties and as a superb dessert fruit with a tart, yet sweet flavor. Plant in a warm site sheltered from frost. **ZONES 9–11.**

CLADANTHUS

Belonging to the compositae (daisy) family and allied to *Anthemis*, this is a genus of 4 species of attractive annuals with finely divided leaves and cheerful yellow flowerheads. All are native to the western Mediterranean region, but only one species has found its way into cultivation as a garden flower. The flowerheads resemble those of some *Coreopsis* species (though it is not closely related to that genus) and are borne singly at ends of long stalks terminating the leafy branches—*Cladanthus* means 'branch flower'. The leaves are aromatic when bruised.

Clarkia amoena (cultivar)

Cladrastis lutea

Clarkia unguiculata

CULTIVATION: Like most other annuals these are easily grown in a sunny spot in fertile, well-drained soil. Seed is sown in spring after all danger of frost has passed, for summer and fall (autumn) flowering.

Cladanthus arabicus

This is a moderately fast-growing annual that forms small hummocks about 24 in (60 cm) high. It has aromatic foliage and deep yellow, daisy-like flowers, each about 2 in (5 cm) in diameter, borne in summer and early fall (autumn) although the flowering season can be prolonged by regular dead heading. **ZONES 7–10.**

CLADRASTIS
YELLOWWOOD

This genus of 5 species of deciduous small leguminous trees occurs wild in eastern USA, Japan and China. The pinnate leaves have rather few leaflets and the pendulous sprays of small to medium-sized, fragrant white or pinkish pea-flowers that appear in summer are slightly reminiscent of *Wisteria* flowers. The flowers are followed by flattened pods, each containing a row of small, hard seeds. They are elegant trees, valued for their late flowering and, in the case of the American species, for their fall (autumn) foliage.
CULTIVATION: Fully frost hardy, they prefer full sun and fertile, well-drained soil. They also need protection from strong winds as the wood is brittle. Propagate from seed in fall or from cuttings in winter.

Cladrastis lutea
syn. ***Cladrastis kentukea***
AMERICAN YELLOWWOOD

The natural range of this species is from North Carolina to Alabama and Missouri, in rich soils on hill slopes or along ravines near streams. There it grows to 60 ft (18 m) with a trunk

Cladrastis lutea

Citrus × tangelo

Citrus sinensis

Citrus sinensis 'Valencia'

diameter to 3 ft (1 m), forking not far above the ground with steeply angled limbs. In cultivation it rarely exceeds 30 ft (9 m). The leaves consist of 5 to 9 broad, veined leaflets that are a fresh, rich green in summer turning yellow in fall (autumn). White flowers appear in early summer. Some trees flower only every second year. **ZONES 6–10.**

Cladrastis sinensis
CHINESE YELLOWWOOD

A medium-sized deciduous tree, this species grows to about 50 ft (15 m), rather more in the wild. The flowers are fragrant, white tinged with pink, appearing in large panicles in mid-summer. The leaves have 11 to 13 leaflets. The flowers are seldom produced on immature trees. **ZONES 6–10.**

CLARKIA
syn. *Godetia*

This genus, allied to the evening primroses (*Oenothera*) and consisting of about 36 species, was named in honor of Captain William Clark, of the famous Lewis and Clark expedition that crossed the American continent in 1806. They are bushy annuals, undistinguished in foliage but spectacular in their all too short flowering season when they are covered in showy funnel-shaped flowers in various shades of pink, white and carmine. The flowers can be 4 in (10 cm) across, and they look a little like azaleas—in Germany they are called *Sommerazalee*, the summer azalea. They are very good as cut flowers, borne on long stems and lasting a week in water.
CULTIVATION: They are easily grown in full sun in any temperate climate. They prefer moist but well-drained, slightly acid soil; soil that is too fertile will see good foliage but poor flower production. Propagate from seed in fall (autumn) or spring.

Clarkia amoena
syn. ***Clarkia grandiflora***
FAREWELL-TO-SPRING

A free-flowering annual, this Californian native is fast growing to a height of 24 in (60 cm) and spread of 12 in (30 cm). It has lance-shaped, mid-green leaves, thin upright stems, and in summer bears spikes of open, cup-like, single or double flowers in shades of pink; a number of cultivars have been produced from this species. Allow it to dry out between watering and watch for signs of botrytis. **ZONES 7–11.**

Clarkia unguiculata
syn. ***Clarkia elegans***
MOUNTAIN GARLAND

This species is usually taller than its fellow-Californian *Clarkia amoena* but with smaller flowers, only 1 in (25 mm) across, often frilled and doubled. The flowers, produced at the tops of slender, reddish stems 3 ft (1 m) or more in height, have a broader color range, including orange and purple. **ZONES 7–11.**

CLAUSENA
WAMPEE, WAMPI

A genus of tropical Asian trees related to *Citrus*, *Clausena* is usually known in the form of only one of its species, the Chinese wampee, cultivated for its edible fruit. It is a small, evergreen tree with pinnate leaves which release an aromatic oil when crushed. Small, white flowers like miniature orange blossom are borne in panicles terminating the smaller branches, followed by smallish, leathery-skinned, slightly downy fruit with a

Clematis 'Barbara Jackman'

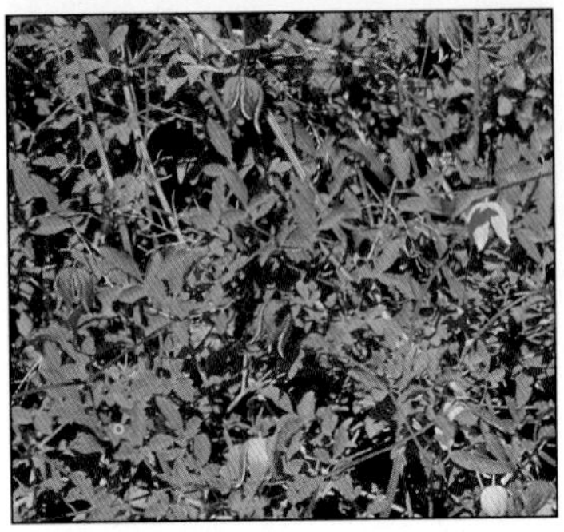

Clematis akebioides

sweet, slightly acid and aromatic white pulp in which are embedded green seeds. In southern China it is one of the most prized fruits, thought to aid digestion and to have other medicinal uses as well as having a delicious flavor.
CULTIVATION: A sheltered sunny position and deep, fertile soil will ensure good fruit production. It is propagated mainly from seed.

Clausena lansium

This small tree of about 15 ft (4.5 m) in height has a spreading, bushy crown and glossy foliage, the leaves consisting of 5 to 9 leaflets about 2 in (5 cm) long. The flowers appear in spring, followed in summer by yellow, oval fruits about 2 in (5 cm) long that can be eaten fresh or made into jam. **ZONES 10–12.**

CLAYTONIA

SPRING BEAUTY

About 15 species of small perennials with succulent leaves make up this genus which is allied to *Lewisia* and *Calandrinia* and occurs mainly in mountains of western North America. Botanists have varied in their classification of this and related genera, and some species at times included in *Claytonia* will be found under *Montia* and *Neopaxia*. Claytonias have swollen tap roots and sometimes spread by stolons; the fleshy leaves commonly form basal rosettes from which short, leafy flowering stems arise, bearing attractive white, pink, purple or yellow 5-petalled flowers.
CULTIVATION: Their requirements vary, as some species grow on mountain screes or cliffs, others in moist woodland or bogs. The mountain species should be grown in cool pockets in the rock garden with good drainage, preferably on a bed of stone chips, or can be grown in pots in a cool greenhouse; keep dry when dormant in winter. Propagate from seed or by division of offsets.

Claytonia megarhiza

As the botanical name suggests, this species from the Rocky Mountains of the USA has a very large tap root which grows deep into the alpine screes where it occurs. It makes a dense rosette of spoon-shaped leaves up to 6 in (15 cm) long, with many short spikes of white to pink flowers emerging in summer. Most commonly grown is ***Claytonia megarhiza* var. *nivalis***, with deeper purple-pink flowers. **ZONES 4–8.**

CLEISTOCACTUS

The 50 or so species of this cactus genus occur widely in South America, from Ecuador to Uruguay. They are slender-stemmed cacti, some columnar and reaching as much as 15 ft (4.5 m) tall, others with scrambling or almost prostrate stems. All species have ribbed stems, the ribs low and rounded and bearing numerous thin spines from closely spaced areoles. Flowers are often numerous, arising from the whole length of the stem or concentrated near the top, and are mostly rather narrowly tubular and slightly one-sided in the way they open—though in some species they hardly open at all (hence *Cleistocactus*, or 'closed cactus'). The outside of the flower tube is usually bristly or spiny. Most species grow rapidly and flower readily.
CULTIVATION: They are mostly robust plants which are easily grown in well-drained soil in a sunny spot. They are moderately frost and drought resistant but may be susceptible to mealybug and spider mite. Propagate from cuttings or seed.

Cleistocactus strausii

SILVER TORCH CACTUS

This erect columnar cactus is native to Bolivia and reaches up to 10 ft (3 m) in height. Quick and simple to grow, it has multiple, grayish green stems, covered with fine yellowish spines mixed with abundant long white bristle. Profuse deep red, cylindrical flowers develop straight from the stems in late summer, but only on older plants. This species likes full sun and extremely porous soil. Older plants may need staking or they tend to fall over. **ZONES 9–11.**

Cleistocactus strausii

CLEMATIS

VIRGIN'S BOWER, TRAVELLER'S JOY

The 200 or more species of mostly woody climbers in this genus are scattered throughout the world's temperate regions, but most of the popular, larger-flowered garden plants have come from Japan and China. They climb by twisting their leaf-stalk tendrils about a support and are ideal for training on verandah posts, arbors, bowers and trellises. Showy bell-shaped or flattish flowers with 4 to 8 petals (*sepals* really) are followed by masses of fluffy seed heads, often lasting well into winter.
CULTIVATION: The most important requirement for successful cultivation is a well-drained, humus-rich, permanently cool soil with good moisture retention. The plants like to climb up to the sun with their roots in the shade. Prune old twiggy growth in spring and propagate from cuttings or by layering in summer. In some areas where growing clematis is a problem, plants are often grafted. Clematis wilt can be a problem.

Clematis akebioides

This species from western China grows to a height of about 12 ft (3.5 m). The leaves are pinnate with up to seven bluish green and rather fleshy, toothed leaflets. Flowers are bell shaped, yellow and sometimes tinged green to purple inside; they are borne on long stems in late summer or early fall (autumn). **ZONES 5–9.**

Clematis alpina

This species, native to Europe and northern Asia, is very frost hardy and one of the earliest to flower. The lavender-blue to purple-blue flowers are carried on long stalks that arise singly from the leaf axils of the previous year's growth; they consist of 4 tapered petals forming spiky bells about 2 in (5 cm) wide. They are followed by prominent fluffy seed heads that persist until winter. There are several named cultivars, including **'Frances Rivis'**, with larger flowers. **ZONES 5–9.**

Clematis aristata

AUSTRALIAN CLEMATIS, GOAT'S BEARD

A native of Australian forests, this showy evergreen climber grows to 20 ft (6 m). It is often almost completely covered in masses of starry white flowers with narrow petals in spring and summer. Male and female flowers are on separate plants, the females bearing fluffy seed heads which are an additional decorative feature. **ZONES 8–10.**

Clematis armandii

EVERGREEN CLEMATIS

A vigorous evergreen climber from China, this clematis can grow to 25 ft (8 m) and spread twice as wide. Its lustrous deep green leaves have 3 leaflets with marked veining. The fragrant white flowers are saucer-shaped, around $2\frac{1}{2}$ in (6 cm) wide, and appear in spring. Although quite frost hardy, this species needs a protected site facing the sun. **'Apple Blossom'** is a popular cultivar and, as its name suggests, has pale pink flowers darker on the reverse but fading as they age. **ZONES 5–9.**

Clematis 'Ascotiensis'

This is one of the large-flowered hybrids that are the most spectacular of all clematis. It flowers late in the season, in summer, with mauve to blue flowers that change to mid-blue as they age. Each flower consists of 4 to 6 petals, which taper to points and are slightly wavy. It will climb to a height of about 12 ft (3.5 m). **ZONES 5–9.**

Clematis 'Barbara Jackman'

This large-flowered hybrid is a vigorous and quite bushy plant. Each flower has 8 petals which overlap and taper to the tips; each is about 4 in (10 cm) in diameter, purple-blue with a magenta bar but fading to a paler mauve-blue. The stamens are cream. **ZONES 5–9.**

Clematis 'Bees' Jubilee'

This large flowered hybrid has flat, rounded flowers 8 in (20 cm) wide, consisting of 8 overlapping, round-ended petals. The base color is mauve pink with a silver feathering towards each outer edge and overlaid with a central carmine bar. This clematis performs well if it is fertilized regularly. **ZONES 5–9.**

Clematis 'Bill Mackenzie'

This is a hybrid between *Clematis orientalis* and *C. tangutica*. It has yellow, lantern-shaped flowers that are borne over a long period. The seed heads are fluffy and grayish. It is a vigorous grower and very showy when in full bloom. **ZONES 5–9.**

Clematis 'Capitaine Thuilleaux'

This large-flowered hybrid has striped flowers, the central carmine bar occupying the greater part of each petal, with an outer edge of silver-gray. There are between 6 and 8 petals, forming a flower 6–8 in (15–20 cm) wide. It is a moderate grower, reaching a height of 5–6 ft (1.5–1.8 m). **ZONES 5–9.**

Clematis 'Capitaine Thuilleaux'

Clematis 'Duchess of Albany'

Clematis 'Duchess of Edinburgh'

Clematis × *durandii*

Clematis 'Comtesse de Bouchaud'

This is one of the oldest of the large-flowered hybrids and still the only one in this group with flowers of an overall pink color; they are 4–6 in (10–15 cm) wide and consist of 6 wide petals that are rounded and slightly reflexed with indented veins. The stamens are cream. This is an easily grown plant that reaches 6–8 ft (1.8–2.4 m) in height. **ZONES 5–9.**

Clematis 'Daniel Deronda'

This large-flowered hybrid has semi-double flowers, 6–8 in (15–20 cm) wide and consisting of 6 to 8 petals that taper to a point and a loose, irregular group of shorter petals in the center. The color is a deep purple-blue with a grayish midrib and brown-maroon shading. It flowers rather sparingly. **ZONES 5–9.**

Clematis 'Duchess of Albany'

This cultivar is the result of a cross between *Clematis texensis* and a large-flowered hybrid whose identity has been lost. The flowers are a clear pink with rose pink bars and cream stamens, with 4 to 6, quite fleshy petals. The leaves are divided into 3 or 5 heart-shaped leaflets, gray-green in color. It will climb to a height of 6–8 ft (1.8–2.4 m). **ZONES 5–9.**

Clematis 'Duchess of Edinburgh'

This large-flowered clematis grows to a height of 6–10 ft (1.8–3 m). It produces double white flowers with yellow anthers and green outer petals in spring and summer. It is very frost hardy but may sometimes be weak growing. **ZONES 5–9.**

Clematis × *durandii*

This hybrid between *Clematis integrifolia* and *C.* 'Jackmanii' has flowers that measure 4–6 in (10–15 cm) in diameter with 4 to 6 irregularly waved petals with 3 deeply grooved ribs. The flowers are an intense indigo blue, their stamens forming a yellowish tuft. This hybrid is easily grown but has a rather awkward habit and is best pruned right to the ground each year. It grows to 5–6 ft (1.5–1.8 m). **ZONES 5–9.**

Clematis 'Edith'

One of the large-flowered hybrids, this has 6-petalled flowers that are white with the faintest blush of pink, and a group of red stamens in the center. It is a seedling of **'Mrs Cholmondeley'**, growing to much the same size. **ZONES 5–9.**

Clematis 'Elsa Späth'

This is a very free-flowering hybrid that produces 8 in (20 cm) wide, lavender blue flowers with dark red anthers on white filaments in late spring, often with a second flush in mid-summer or later. The petals are broad and overlapping, tapering to the tips. The leaflets are heart-shaped. It will climb to a height of 6–8 ft (1.8–2.4 m). **ZONES 5–9.**

Clematis 'Ernest Markham'

This is one of the most vigorous of all the large-flowered hybrids and one of the most widely grown, although it is not all that free flowering. The flowers have 6 petals with fine points and impressed veins, bright magenta in color. It should be pruned quite lightly. It grows to a height of 15 ft (4.5 m). **ZONES 5–9.**

Clematis heracleifolia

Clematis 'Etoile Violette'

This is a hybrid from *Clematis viticella*, very vigorous and free flowering. The flowers are 3–4 in (8–10 cm) in diameter and consist of 6 petals, deep purple with cream stamens. It will grow to a height of 10–12 ft (3–3.5 m). **ZONES 5–9.**

Clematis florida

This native of Japan and China is a rather tender species that likes the protection of a warm wall; it is also suitable for growing in containers. It has a long flowering period in late spring and summer, the large, flat flowers appearing progressively on the ends of new growths. They have long stalks and a distinctive pair of leaf-like bracts. There are 4 to 6 petals, greenish white turning to cream and the stamens are purple. **'Sieboldii'** has stamens transformed into narrow, petal-like structures that form a central dome in each flower, turning a deep purple and persisting after the petals have fallen. **ZONES 8–9.**

Clematis 'General Sikorski'

This large-flowered hybrid was raised in Poland. The flowers are mid-blue with a reddish flush at the base of the petals. They measure about 6 in (15 cm) in diameter. **ZONES 5–9.**

Clematis 'Gillian Blades'

A large-flowered hybrid with flat petals that have frilled edges; color is pure white with golden stamens. **ZONES 5–9.**

Clematis 'Gipsy Queen'

This large-flowered hybrid blooms in early summer. The distinctive, rich red flowers have petals that are rounded at the ends but taper towards the base. This vigorous grower has a long flowering season, reaching a height of 10–12 ft (3–3.5 m). **ZONES 5–9.**

Clematis glycinoides

This is a small-flowered species from Australia not often encountered in gardens, though it is an attractive evergreen climber and makes a pretty show of white blossom in spring. The Australian Aborigines crushed the leaves and inhaled the aroma as a cure (or at least a palliative) for colds and headaches. **ZONES 9–11.**

Clematis 'Henryi'

This is one of the oldest of the large-flowered hybrids still in cultivation. The flowers are white with a touch of cream, and consist of 8 overlapping petals that are sharply pointed; they measure 6–8 in (15–20 cm) in diameter. The stamens are tipped with brown anthers. It will reach 6–10 ft (1.8–3 m) in height. **ZONES 5–9.**

Clematis heracleifolia
syn. *Clematis davidiana*

Hardly recognizable as a clematis, this semi-herbaceous perennial from China forms a woody base without dying down completely in winter and has velvet-textured, grayish green leaves. The small purplish-blue flowers are without stalks, arranged in whorls at the upper stem nodes; each consists of 4 petals formed into a tube and recurved at the tips. A number of improved forms are available, like **'Davidiana'** and **'Campanile'**. **ZONES 3–9.**

Clematis 'Gipsy Queen'

Clematis 'Gillian Blades'

Clematis 'Etoile Violette'

Clematis glycinoides

Clematis 'Horn of Plenty'

This hybrid clematis has purple flowers with a darker center. The flowers are single and each petal has a wavy edge. **ZONES 5–9.**

Clematis integrifolia

From southern Europe, this herbaceous clematis is hardly recognizable as belonging to this genus, at least until it flowers. It forms a gradually expanding clump with masses of stems arising from the base each spring, each one ending in a single, nodding flower of four 1 in (25 mm) long petals. It is normally purple-blue, deeper in the center. The stamens are creamy white and tightly packed. The flower stalks tend to flop and may need support. Improved forms like **'Hendersonii'**, **'Rosea'** and **'Tapestry'** are rather more reliable in this regard than the species. **ZONES 3–9.**

Clematis 'Jackmanii'

Produced in 1862 from a cross between *Clematis lanuginosa* and (probably) *C. viticella*, this was the first of the large-flowered hybrids and is still among the most popular. It will climb up to 10 ft (3 m), and produces spectacular purple flowers, 6 in (15 cm) across, in summer and fall (autumn). It is very frost hardy. **ZONES 5–9.**

Clematis lanuginosa 'Candida'

Clematis integrifolia

Clematis × *jouiniana* 'Praecox'

This is a hybrid between *Clematis vitalba* and probably *C. heracleifolia* 'Davidiana'. The flowers are 1–2 in (2.5–5 cm) in diameter with 4 to 6 narrow petals, off-white with mauve-blue tips and borne in axillary panicles of about 20 flowers on the upper part of the plant. The leaves are large, coarsely toothed, and turn yellow in fall (autumn). The plant forms a woody framework and it is best to prune back to this each year. A useful plant for covering an old tree stump or for trailing down a bank, it grows to 6–10 ft (1.8–2.4 m). **ZONES 4–9.**

Clematis 'Lady Betty Balfour'

This late-flowering clematis bears its velvety purple flowers entirely on the new growth in late summer and early fall (autumn). It can be pruned hard in early spring. This makes it one of the best cultivars for growing among the branches of climbing roses. It is easier to prune the roses if the clematis can simply be cut out of the way. **ZONES 5–9.**

Clematis lanuginosa

A native of China introduced to the West early in the nineteenth century, this species in its typical form is now rarely seen in gardens, but it is one of the most important parents of the large-flowered hybrids. A deciduous climber to about 6 ft (1.8 m) high, it bears white to pale lilac flowers up to 8 in (20 cm) wide from spring to fall (autumn). **'Candida'** has pure white flowers. **ZONES 6–9.**

Clematis 'Lasurstern'

Clematis 'Lady Betty Balfour'

Clematis mandshurica

Clematis 'Lasurstern'

This large-flowered cultivar produces lavender-blue flowers with 8 broadly overlapping petals in late spring and early summer. It grows up to 10 ft (3 m), and is very frost hardy. **'H. F. Young'** is a similar but more compact free-flowering form with smaller flowers. **ZONES 4–9.**

Clematis macropetala

DOWNY CLEMATIS

From northern China, Mongolia and Siberia, this low-growing climber has foliage of a pale to mid-green color, the leaves twice-divided into rather small leaflets. Borne profusely in spring and early summer, the rather spiky violet-blue flowers are 4 in (10 cm) across with 4 narrow petals and several rows of petal-like staminodes in a central cluster. **'Markham's Pink'** has deep rose-mauve flowers, softer pink on the undersides. **ZONES 5–9.**

Clematis mandshurica

syn. *Clematis recta* var. *mandshurica*

A native of China and Japan, this herbaceous perennial species has a sprawling habit or may climb to about 3–6 ft (1–1.8 m) in height. The small white flowers, about $1\frac{1}{4}$ in (3 cm) across, are borne in erect terminal umbels, while the smooth dark brown seeds have long yellowish tails. Plant in a protected, part-shaded position. **ZONES 7–9.**

Clematis 'Marie Boisselot'

This is one of the most popular whites in the large-flowered hybrid group. The flowers are large, 8 in (20 cm) in diameter with 6 very wide, overlapping petals. It will climb to a height of 8–12 ft (2.4–3.5 m). **ZONES 5–9.**

Clematis 'H. F. Young'

Clematis 'Marie Louise Jensen'

Clematis marmoraria

Clematis 'Marie Louise Jensen'

This large-flowered hybrid bears single, rich purple flowers with red anthers. Each flower has 6 wide, overlapping petals which taper to points. **ZONES 5–9.**

Clematis marmoraria

This New Zealand native, at about 6 in (15 cm) high, is the smallest species in the genus. *Clematis marmoraria* has a somewhat spreading habit and relatively large white flowers. **ZONES 8–9.**

Clematis microphylla

TRAVELLER'S JOY

Several small, white-flowered species of clematis, like this Australian one, share the common name traveller's joy, from the way they grow over trees and shrubs along roadsides to delight the traveller in spring with their massed white or cream flowers, and in fall (autumn) with their feathery white seeds. *Clematis microphylla* is distinctive for the small size of its leaflets, only about $\frac{3}{4}$ in (18 mm) long and $\frac{1}{8}$ in (3 mm) wide. **ZONES 8–11.**

Clematis 'Miss Bateman'

This is an early-flowering hybrid with 6 in (15 cm) flowers of 8 petals that are flat and overlapping. The central rib on each has a green stripe on the underside that shows through on the translucent white upper surface as a cream bar. The habit is quite compact, the plant bushing out at the sides and reaching to 6 ft (1.8 m) in height. **ZONES 5–9.**

Clematis montana

ANEMONE CLEMATIS

This vigorous species from the Himalayas will reach up to 30 ft (9 m) or more. It bears prolific, sweetly perfumed, white to pale pink flowers with yellow stamens in clusters in late spring. It is fast growing and very frost hardy, and ideal for

Clematis montana

Clematis montana 'Elizabeth'

covering a small shed or wall. The cultivars **'Elizabeth'**, **'Rubens'** and **'Tetrarose'** all produce pink flowers, the largest in 'Tetrarose', and purple-tinted leaves. Prune hard after flowering. **ZONES 6–9.**

Clematis 'Mrs Cholmondeley'

This large-flowered hybrid is very easy to grow. Opening in early summer, the flowers have 6 to 7 petals, widely spaced and tapering to the base, light to lavender blue and paler along the midribs; a network of veins stand out in a darker shade. It will reach 20 ft (6 m) in height. **ZONES 5–9.**

Clematis 'Mrs George Jackman'

Clematis 'Mrs George Jackman' is similar to 'Marie Boisselot' but is slightly creamy along the midribs and slightly less vigorous. It reaches 8 ft (2.4 m) in height. **ZONES 5–9.**

Clematis montana 'Tetrarose'

Clematis 'Mrs James Mason'

This hybrid has large flowers, 8 in (20 cm) across with 8 overlapping petals that are almost boat-shaped, with wavy edges. The flowers are violet-blue with a central dark red bar and a large boss of cream stamens. A vigorous and free-flowering plant, it grows to 6–10 ft (1.8–3 m). **ZONES 5–9.**

Clematis 'Nelly Moser'

Derived from *Clematis lanuginosa*, *C.* 'Nelly Moser' bears in early summer large flat flowers, pale pink with a deeper pinkish stripe in the center of each of its 8 petals. Grow in a part-shaded position that receives morning sun. Reaching up to 15 ft (4.5 m), it is very frost hardy. **ZONES 4–9.**

Clematis 'Niobe'

Each flower on this hybrid consists of 6 gently recurved petals, tapering to sharp points. The deep ruby red, almost black color, changes to bright ruby; the cream stamens form a contrast. It is a moderate grower, 8 ft (2.4 m), but with a long flowering season in summer. **ZONES 5–9.**

Clematis 'Mrs James Mason'

Clematis paniculata

syns *Clematis terniflora*, *C. dioscoreifolia*
PUAWHANANGA, SWEET AUTUMN CLEMATIS

This robust evergreen species, native to New Zealand, climbs up to 30 ft (9 m) with a main stem up to 4 in (10 cm) in diameter. The rather rigid, lustrous green leaves are divided into 3 leaflets. From late spring to early summer it bears fragrant white flowers up to 4 in (10 cm) across with yellow centers, frequently tipped with pinkish purple. The blooms are followed by downy seed heads in fall (autumn). **'Purity'** is a selected male form that bears very large white flowers in spring. It may spread to over 15 ft (4.5 m). **ZONES 5–9.**

Clematis 'Perle d'Azur'

This popular variety flowers profusely from mid-summer to fall (autumn). Each flower has 4 to 6 rounded petals, sometimes overlapping and corrugated along the midribs. The flowers measure 8 in (20 cm) across and are azure blue with a rosy flush at the base of the midrib. A very vigorous grower, it reaches 10–15 ft (3–4.5 m). **ZONES 5–9.**

Clematis 'Ramona'

syn. 'Sieboldii'

This large-flowered hybrid has overlapping petals of lavender blue forming a flower 6–8 in (15–20 cm) in diameter. A strong-growing plant, it reaches a height of 15 ft (4.5 m), blooming from mid-summer to fall (autumn). **ZONES 5–9.**

Clematis rehderiana

As a young plant, this species from western China starts slowly but if left unpruned will cover a small tree 15–20 ft (4.5–6 m) high. The leaves are quite large with 5 to 9 downy, slightly toothed leaflets. The pendent, bell-shaped flowers are borne in panicles up to 10 in (25 cm) long; they are predominantly yellow, fading to parchment. The 4 petals are tightly recurved at the tips. **ZONES 7–10.**

Clematis paniculata

Clematis rehderiana

Clematis paniculata

Clematis 'Ramona'

Clematis 'Nelly Moser'

Clematis 'Richard Pennell'

The early summer flowers on this variety are large, 8 in (20 cm) in diameter, and are a rosy purple, paler near the central ribs; there are 8 petals which are wide and overlapping, tapering to the tips. The red filaments with bright golden-yellow anthers are a special feature. A vigorous grower though not tall, it grows to 8 ft (2.4 m). **ZONES 5–9.**

Clematis spooneri
syn. *Clematis chrysocoma* var. *sericea*

This species comes from China and is rather similar to *Clematis montana*, climbing to a height of 20 ft (6 m). The flowers are carried on long stalks in axillary clusters of 1 to 5 flowers on the previous year's growth. Each flower has 4 round-ended, overlapping, white or very pale pink petals that are almost as wide as long. The young foliage is reddish bronze. **ZONES 6–9.**

Clematis 'Star of India'

This large-flowered hybrid has 4 to 6 petals that overlap and are widest near the apex; they are a red plum changing to violet purple. The 6 in (15 cm) flowers are borne profusely. It grows to a height of 12 ft (3.5 m). **ZONES 5–9.**

Clematis 'Star of India'

Clematis viticella 'Madame Julia Correvon'

Clematis spooneri

Clematis tangutica
LEMON PEEL CLEMATIS, GOLDEN CLEMATIS

This long-flowering species from China grows up to 20 ft (6 m). It bears curious, nodding, lantern-shaped flowers with clear yellow, 'thick-skinned' petals in summer and early fall (autumn). The flowers are followed by decorative, silky seed heads. Grow in a protected, part-shaded position; it is frost resistant but dislikes dry conditions. **ZONES 5–9.**

Clematis texensis
SCARLET CLEMATIS

As the name indicates, this species is native to Texas. It is the only species to have flowers of a true red color, this hue also being carried along the flower stalks. Borne in summer, the pendent flowers are pitcher-shaped, rather less than 1 in (25 mm) across at the base and narrowing to the mouth, with 4 rather thick petals. The foliage is smooth, glaucous and pinnate. The species is rare in cultivation but its influence shows in a number of hybrids, including **'Etoile Rose'** and **'Gravetye Beauty'**. **ZONES 5–9.**

Clematis 'The President'

This large flowered hybrid has deep purple flowers with a silvery reverse to each petal. Flowers measure 7 in (18 cm) across and are produced from midsummer to early fall (autumn). It is very free flowering. **ZONES 5–9.**

Clematis viticella
VIRGIN'S BOWER

This deciduous climber from southern Europe can reach 12 ft (3.5 m). Its dark green, pinnate leaves have ovate, sometimes lobed, leaflets; the nodding, bell-shaped violet or purple flowers appear in late summer and fall (autumn). The plant dies back in winter and should be pruned to within 24 in (60 cm) of the ground. **'Purpurea Plena Elegans'** has double flowers, with a mass of narrow, recurved petals, soft rosy purple and lavender gray on the reverse. *Clematis viticella* is the parent of many beautiful hybrids, including **'Abundance'**, light pink-purple; **'Alba Luxurians'**, white with a mauve tinge and dark stamens; **'Kermesina'**, deep crimson-purple; and **'Madame Julia Correvon'**, burgundy-red twisted petals. **ZONES 6–9.**

Clematis 'Wada's Primrose'

Cleome hassleriana

Clematis 'Vyvyan Pennell'

One of the best of the doubles in the large-flowered group, this hybrid will produce 2 flushes of bloom, the first in early summer being fully double lavender blue rosettes shaded with reddish brown, the second, from the current year's growth, being single and silver violet. This is a strong-growing plant, to 6–8 ft (1.8–2.4 m) in height and spread. **ZONES 5–9.**

Clematis 'Wada's Primrose'

The flowers of this hybrid have 8 slightly overlapping petals that taper to points. They are pale yellow to soft cream with a darker central stripe. A vigorous grower, it produces numerous, rather thin stems, to 6 ft (1.8 m) in height. **ZONES 5–9.**

CLEOME
SPIDER FLOWER, SPIDER PLANT

This genus of 150 species of bushy annuals and short-lived evergreen shrubs, from subtropical and tropical zones all over the world, is characterized by its spidery flowers with 4 petals that narrow into basal stalks and mostly long, spidery stamens and styles. The leaves are composed of from 5 to 7 palmate leaflets. One species is widely grown as a background bedding plant, useful for its rapid growth and delicate floral effect. **CULTIVATION:** Marginally frost hardy, they require full sun and fertile, well-drained soil, regular water and shelter from strong winds. Taller growth can be encouraged by removing side branches, and dead flowers should also be removed. Propagate from seed in spring or early summer. Check for aphids.

Clerodendrum buchananii

Cleome hassleriana

Cleome hassleriana
syn. *Cleome spinosa* of gardens

Native to subtropical South America, this fast-growing, bushy annual is valued for its unusual spidery flowers. An erect plant, it grows to 4 ft (1.2 m) tall with a spread of 18 in (45 cm). It has large palmate leaves and the hairy, slightly prickly stems are topped in summer with heads of airy, pink and white flowers with long, protruding stamens. Several strains are available as seed, ranging in color from pure white to purple. **ZONES 9–11.**

CLERODENDRUM

This genus of over 400 species ranges through the world's tropics and warmer climates. It contains trees, shrubs, climbers and herbaceous plants, both deciduous and evergreen, some with very showy flowers. The features that unite them are leaves in opposite pairs; tubular flowers, usually flared or bowl-shaped at the mouth and with 4 long stamens and a style protruding well beyond the tube; and fruit, a shiny berry sitting at the center of the calyx that usually becomes larger and thicker after flowering. **CULTIVATION:** They vary greatly in their cold hardiness, though only a few species from China and Japan are suited to cool climates. They all appreciate a sunny position, though sheltered from strong wind and the hottest summer sun, and deep, moist, fertile soil. Propagate from cuttings, which strike readily under heat; or many species sucker from the roots and a large root cutting can produce much quicker results.

Clerodendrum buchananii

This tropical species from Indonesia makes a tall, weak shrub of about 10 ft (3 m) with an open habit and large, heart-shaped leaves with downy undersides. The flowers appear through much of the year in terminal panicles, the stalks and flowers all scarlet. It is an unkempt shrub, fast growing but short lived. There may be confusion between this species and *Clerodendrum speciosissimum*. **ZONES 11–12.**

Clerodendrum bungei

syn. *Clerodendrum foetidum*

GLORY FLOWER

This suckering shrub from China and the Himalayas has many vertical stems topped in summer with wonderfully fragrant heads of rose pink flowers. The leaves are large and coarse, and have an unpleasant smell if crushed or bruised. The stems will reach 6 ft (1.8 m) unless cut to the ground each spring; new growths will then flower on 3 ft (1 m) stems. It will spread rapidly if not contained or controlled. **ZONES 7–10.**

Clerodendrum inerme

INDIAN PRIVET

This evergreen species is a sprawling shrub 3–6 ft (1–1.8 m) tall with smooth, evergreen leaves like those of some privets and inconspicuous small white flowers. It grows on seashores of tropical Asia and the Pacific region, tolerating salt spray and fierce sun. At Bombay's Hanging Gardens it is trained over wire frames into topiary shapes such as elephants. **ZONES 10–12.**

Clerodendrum paniculatum

PAGODA FLOWER

This fast-growing but short-lived species from tropical Asia is popular in the wet tropics for its huge panicles of small salmon pink flowers that terminate the erect shoots, appearing through much of the year. Growing to 6–8 ft (1.8–2.4 m), it branches from the roots into coarse, vigorous shoots with very large, deeply veined, glossy deep green leaves on long stalks. **ZONES 11–12.**

Clerodendrum bungei

Clerodendrum splendens

Clerodendrum trichotomum

Clerodendrum splendens

GLORY BOWER

From tropical West Africa, this evergreen, woody stemmed, twining plant grows to 10 ft (3 m) or more. It has rich green, oval or elliptic leaves and showy clusters of 1 in (25 mm) wide scarlet flowers from late winter to early summer. It will not withstand frost but grows happily in sheltered sunny positions in warm-temperate as well as tropical climates. **ZONES 10–12.**

Clerodendrum thomsoniae

BLEEDING HEART VINE, BLEEDING GLORY BOWER

A climbing, shrub from western tropical Africa, the popularity of this species derives from the clusters of deep crimson summer flowers emerging from pure white, bell-shaped calyces contrasted by large, oval, deep green leaves. The calyces persist in fruit, turning dull pinkish. Reaching 10 ft (3 m) in height, it requires high humidity. **ZONES 10–12.**

Clerodendrum trichotomum

HARLEQUIN GLORY BOWER

Native to Japan and China, this is one of the most frost hardy species. It makes an elegant deciduous tree to 15–20 ft (4.5–6 m) in height, of erect growth and sparse branching habit, drooping lower branches and thin, downy leaves. In late summer it produces at the branch tips

Clerodendrum paniculatum

Clerodendrum thomsoniae

Clerodendrum ugandense

Clethra barbinervis

gracefully drooping panicles of slightly upturned, sweet-scented white flowers, that age to pale mauve with large, dull pinkish calyces that are sharply ribbed. The small blue fruit, cupped in enlarged red calyces, are attractive. **ZONES 7–10.**

Clerodendrum ugandense

BLUE BUTTERFLY BUSH

While requiring a frost-free climate, this species from East Africa will take rather cooler conditions than most tropical clerodendrums. It is a rangy and open evergreen shrub to 10 ft (3 m) with a spread of 6 ft (1.8 m). Through summer and fall (autumn) its slightly arching branches bear terminal sprays of butterfly-shaped flowers in two shades of clear blue. It can be pruned back continually to keep the long branches in check. **ZONES 10–11.**

Clerodendrum zambeziacum

One of the lower-growing shrubby clerodendrums, this tropical African species puts up rather weak stems about 3–6 ft (1–1.8 m) tall from its spreading root system. The leaves are large, soft and heart-shaped. Throughout the warmer part of the year it produces a succession of pure white flowers with tubes about 4 in (10 cm) long and sometimes curled stamens. **ZONES 10–12.**

CLETHRA

A scattering of deciduous tree and shrub species across North America and eastern Asia, plus a larger number of evergreens in warmer climates, principally Southeast Asia, and one outlying species on the island of Madeira make up the total of 30 species in this genus. The frost-hardy deciduous species mostly behave as spreading shrubs in cultivation, producing a thicket of stems concealed by dense foliage. The leaves are thin textured with closely toothed margins. In summer and fall (autumn) small, white

Clerodendrum zambeziacum

Clethra arborea

flowers are borne in delicate loose sprays among the leaves, followed by numerous, tiny seed capsules.

CULTIVATION: Clethras prefer sheltered, moist spots half-shaded by taller trees and peaty, acid, moist but well-drained soil. They can be propagated from seed, cuttings or layers.

Clethra alnifolia

SWEET PEPPERBUSH, SUMMERSWEET CLETHRA

One of the very few temperate North American species, *Clethra alnifolia* occurs wild along the eastern seaboard of the USA, in moist woods. Making a broad, dense thicket up to 8–10 ft (2.4–3 m) high with thin green leaves, it bears profuse sprays of fragrant white flowers with rounded petals. **ZONES 4–9.**

Clethra arborea

LILY-OF-THE-VALLEY TREE

This species from Madeira requires milder conditions than others of the genus. An attractive densely leafed shrub or small tree 20–25 ft (6–8 m) tall, it has glossy leaves and long panicles of lily-of-the-valley-like flowers. Prune occasionally for shaping. **ZONES 9–10.**

Clethra barbinervis

JAPANESE CLETHRA

This species from mountain woodlands of Japan can make a 30 ft (9 m) tree in the wild with peeling orange-brown bark. In gardens it usually makes a shrub of less than 10 ft (3 m) with crowded stems that tend to lean outward and strongly veined leaves with a fuzz of very short hairs on the veins. The attractive flowers appear in short panicles at the branch tips. **ZONES 6–9.**

Clianthus puniceus

Clethra delavayi

Clianthus puniceus

Clethra delavayi

This large and beautiful shrub from Western China in its native habitat can reach a height of 30 ft (9 m) though in cultivation will seldom achieve more than half that. It produces long spikes of densely crowded, one-sided lily-of-the-valley flowers that can cover the whole plant. The dark green leaves are 4–6 in (10–15 cm) long and strongly veined. It may be cut back by severe frost. **ZONES 7–9.**

CLEYERA

A genus of evergreen shrubs and trees belonging to the camellia family, though within that family they are more closely related to *Ternstroemia*. It consists of one or perhaps two species from Japan, China and the eastern Himalayas, and 15 or more species from Mexico, Central America and the West Indies. So far only the Oriental species have been grown widely as ornamentals, valued for their glossy evergreen foliage rather than their very small white or cream flowers or their pea-sized blackish fruit. As with *Ternstroemia*, the older leaves often turn bronze or reddish before falling, adding to the plant's attraction.
CULTIVATION: The Asian species grow readily in any but the coldest temperate climates, a sheltered position being preferred with moist but well-drained soil of reasonable fertility. Propagation is normally from cuttings.

Cleyera japonica

syns *Cleyera ochnacea, Eurya ochnacea*

An evergreen, bushy shrub from Japan, Korea, China and Burma, this species grows to 10 ft (3 m) high. It produces small, fragrant, saucer-shaped white flowers only ½ in (12 mm) across from early to mid-summer; these are followed by small round black fruit. **'Tricolor'** has young leaves that are flushed with pink. It is very frost hardy. **ZONES 7–10.**

CLIANTHUS

Until recently this genus was regarded as including 2 species, one from Australia and one from New Zealand. The Australian species is the famous Sturt's desert pea, a prostrate hairy annual with spectacular red and black flowers; but

Clitoria ternatea

recent botanical study shows that its correct classification is with the large Darling-pea genus *Swainsona*, to which it has been removed, leaving only the rather different New Zealand species in *Clianthus*. This is an evergreen shrub or scrambling climber with pinnate leaves; it bears elongated pea-flowers in stalked clusters on short side branches.
CULTIVATION: Easily grown in mild climates, *Clianthus* is moderately frost tolerant. Often rather short-lived, it is inclined to become woody and occasional cutting back helps to rejuvenate it. It is prone to attack by leaf miners. Propagation is from seed or from semi-ripe cuttings.

Clianthus puniceus

KAKA BEAK, PARROT BEAK

The kaka is a New Zealand parrot and the long-pointed flowers of this shrub are reminiscent of its sharp beak. This species is now rare in the wild but is widely cultivated. In gardens it often grows into a shrub of about 5 ft (1.5 m) but is capable of climbing to 20 ft (6 m) if supported by other vegetation or a wall. The flowers, borne in spring and early summer, are normally red, but pink forms and white forms such as **'Alba'** are also available. **'Kaka King'** flowers heavily with lush foliage. **ZONES 8–10.**

CLINTONIA

Five species of woodland lilies from North America and eastern Asia make up this genus, all rhizomatous perennials with rich green smooth foliage rather like that of *Convallaria*, and erect spikes or umbels (solitary in one species) of small, starry 6-petalled flowers.
CULTIVATION: All species need a cool, peaty, lime-free soil and a shaded, humid position, and so are best suited to a woodland garden. Winter mulching will protect from frost. Propagate from seed or division of rhizomes.

Clintonia andrewsiana

Clintonia andrewsiana

A native of northern California and Oregon, this species has small bell-like flowers that are poised in a cluster at the top of the stems; they are colored a rich carmine red, the three inner petals with a central creamy vein. The flowers are followed by violet-blue berries. This plant increases slowly, reaching a height of about 24 in (60 cm). **ZONES 7–9.**

Clintonia borealis

CORN LILY, BLUEBEARD

From eastern and central North America, this species has loose clusters of yellowish white flowers with recurving petals and protruding stamens, followed by blue berries. It reaches a height of 6–12 in (15–30 cm) and blooms in late spring and early summer. **ZONES 3–9.**

Clintonia umbellulata

SPECKLED WOOD-LILY

From eastern USA, this is one of the prettiest species with dense umbels of fragrant white flowers, often speckled green or purplish, rising on stems up to 15 in (40 cm) tall above dense patches of luxuriant foliage. The flowers appear in late spring and early summer and are followed by black berries. **ZONES 4–9.**

CLITORIA

Eighteenth-century botanists such as Linnaeus (who named this genus) were less bothered than those of the present day at the thought of naming plants for their resemblance to intimate parts of the human anatomy, and *Clitoria* is one such case. There are some 70 species of evergreen leguminous climbers, perennials and shrubs in this genus, occurring in most tropical regions but predominantly in the Americas. They have pinnate leaves and the flowers are borne singly or in small clusters. Although their basic floral structure is of the pea-flower type, the flowers are presented upside down—

Clintonia umbellulata

Clintonia borealis

the 'keel' petal appears on the top rather than the underside and so insects are dusted with pollen on their backs instead of their bellies.
CULTIVATION: Clitorias prefer a tropical climate but can be grown in frost-free, warm-temperate areas. In cooler areas they can be treated as annuals or grown in a greenhouse. They need full sun, fertile, moist but well-drained, loamy soil. Provide good support for twining stems and thin out growth with annual spring pruning. Propagate from seed in spring.

Clitoria ternatea
BUTTERFLY PEA

This is a lovely evergreen twining up to 12 ft (3.5 m), with slender stems and fresh, green leaves divided into 3 or 5 oval leaflets. Flowers are quite large, about 2 in (5 cm) long, pale lilac with yellow centers; appearing in summer, they are followed by flat pods. There is also a double-flowered form. The specific name refers not to the commonly ternate arrangement of the leaflets, but to the Indonesian island of Ternate, where this species was first recorded. It occurs widely in tropical Asia. **ZONES 10–12.**

CLIVIA
KAFFIR LILY

This genus of southern African lilies was named after Lady Clive, Duchess of Northumberland, whose grandfather was the famous Clive of India. She was a patron of gardening and *Clivia nobilis* first flowered in the UK in her greenhouses. The genus consists of 4 species of evergreen perennials with thick, strap-like, deep green leaves springing from short rhizomes with thick roots. Flowers are borne in dense umbels terminating somewhat flattened stems and are funnel-shaped to trumpet-shaped, with 6 red to orange, sometimes green-tipped petals that are partially fused into a tube. They are sometimes followed by quite conspicuous, deep red, berry-like fruits.
CULTIVATION: They will grow well outdoors in a mild, frost-free climate, or in a conservatory or greenhouse in a colder climate. Plant in a shaded or part-shaded, position in friable, well-drained soil; they are surface-rooted and dislike soil disturbance. Keep fairly dry in winter and increase watering in spring and summer. Propagate by division after flowering. Seed can also be used but plants can be slow to flower.

Clivia caulescens

From South Africa where it often grows as a forest epiphyte, this is the rarest species in cultivation. The sheathing bases of the leaves form a basal 'neck' to each shoot, and the spreading, floppy leaves can sometimes reach as much as 6 ft (1.8 m) in length. Flowering stems are up to 18 in (45 cm) high, bearing an umbel of narrowly funnel-shaped, downward-curving flowers only 1½ in (38 mm) long, pale red with green tips and yellow protruding stamens. In its native habitat it flowers in fall (autumn) but is rare in cultivation. **ZONES 10–11.**

Clivia × cyrtanthiflora

Widely cultivated, this is a hybrid between *Clivia miniata* and *C. nobilis*. It produces dense umbels of pendulous, narrowly funnel-shaped, pale scarlet flowers about 2 in (5 cm) long with paler yellowish tips, borne from late winter to early summer. It grows to a height of 18–24 in (45–60 cm). **ZONES 10–11.**

Clivia gardenii

A native of South Africa, this species has reddish orange, sometimes yellow downward-curving flowers with green tips, 2–3 in (5–8 cm) long, on stems to 2½ ft (75 cm) tall. The leaves are rather narrow, about 24 in (60 cm) in length and deep green. It grows to 24 in (60 cm) in height and flowers in winter. **ZONES 10–11.**

Clivia miniata
BUSH LILY, FIRE LILY

This most commonly cultivated and showiest species is distributed widely in eastern South Africa. About 18 in (45 cm) in height, it has broad leaves, sometimes up to 3 in (8 cm) wide and bears clusters of broadly funnel-shaped flowers up to 3 in (8 cm) long, mostly orange to scarlet with a yellow throat, usually in spring but with the occasional bloom at other times. Many cultivars have been selected over the years, including yellow and cream forms. There is a group of especially prized forms commonly called 'hybrids' with tulip-shaped, deep, rich scarlet blooms. **ZONES 10–11.**

Clivia nobilis
DROOPING CLIVIA, NATAL CLIVIA

This attractive species, up to about 15 in (38 cm) tall, has a flowering stem usually shorter than the erect, dull green leaves. The pendulous flowers are in a fairly dense umbel, narrowly funnel-shaped, pale scarlet and prominently tipped with green; they are borne from late winter to early summer. **ZONES 10–11.**

CLUSIA

This is a very large genus of tropical American evergreen trees and shrubs, little known outside the Americas except as curiosities in botanical garden greenhouses but very diverse in their native rainforests. Many start life as epiphytes on other trees but soon put down a curtain of aerial roots to the ground, which may ultimately fuse together into a self-supporting trunk. The leaves of *Clusia* species may be quite large and are generally smooth and fleshy or leathery. The flowers, borne singly or in short sprays at the branch tips, are often large and showy, with male flowers more conspicuous than female ones though both appear on the same tree. They are cup or bowl shaped, often with 6 or more overlapping petals, and a dense, doughnut-shaped ring of stamens in the center; in females this is replaced by a broad, domed ovary with shiny stigmas fused to its surface.
CULTIVATION: Some species are vigorous trees tolerant of exposed coastal conditions, and these adapt well to street or park planting in tropical cities. All species prefer rich, moist but well-drained soil in a sheltered position. Propagation is from cuttings under heat, or by air-layering.

Clivia miniata

Clusia rosea
syn. *Clusia major*
COPEY, BALSAM APPLE

From the Caribbean region, this is one of the most widely planted species. It makes a tree of about 30 ft (9 m) tall with a broadly spreading crown of irregular shape and rather dense foliage, often forked into several trunks from ground level and sending down aerial roots, like some figs. The thick, olive-green leaves are paddle-shaped with broad, rounded tips. Pale pinkish flowers 2–3 in (5–8 cm) in diameter dot the crown in summer and early fall (autumn). **ZONES 11–12.**

CLYTOSTOMA

This South American genus consists of 9 species of evergreen, woody-stemmed climbers that were formerly included in the genus *Bignonia*. They have compound leaves with usually only 2 normal leaflets, and 2 others that are modified into tendrils, by which the plants climb. Showy, foxglove-like flowers are borne in pairs or clusters from the leaf axils.
CULTIVATION: These plants need well-drained soil and partial-shade in summer at least when young. They must be kept well-watered during hot weather and will need some support to climb on. Growth can become rather congested after a while and may need some thinning, which should be done immediately flowering has finished. Propagation is from semi-ripe cuttings taken in spring.

Clytostoma callistegioides
syn. *Bignonia lindleyana*
VIOLET TRUMPET VINE, ARGENTINE TRUMPET VINE

This creeper native to southern Brazil and Argentina has showy trumpet-shaped flowers which may be borne in great profusion. Fast growing and densely foliaged, it climbs to around 12 ft (3.5 m) and needs good support. In late spring and summer the pale lavender flowers with purple streaks are carried on short, drooping stems. It can be trained over fences and tall tree stumps in warm areas, to very good effect. **ZONES 9–12.**

Clusia rosea

Clytostoma callistegioides

Clivia miniata

CNEORUM

This, the only genus in the family Cneoraceae, consists of only 2 species of evergreen shrub, native to the western Mediterranean region and the Canary Islands. They have small gray-green, rather leathery leaves and small solitary yellow flowers with 3 or 4 narrow petals, followed by a small dry fruit. The leaves and fruit are used locally as a purgative but neither species is widely cultivated outside its native region.
CULTIVATION: They grow best in mild, rather dry climates, in a sunny position, for example in a rock garden. Coming from limestone terrain, they are very lime tolerant but will grow in a range of soils as long as drainage is very good. Propagate from seed or cuttings.

Cneorum tricoccon
SPURGE OLIVE

From the western Mediterranean, this species has pale gray-green leaves and 3-petalled bright yellow flowers only about 1/4 in (6 mm) across, followed by 3-sided, brownish red fruit that ripens to black. Multi-stemmed from ground level, it grows to 2–4 ft (60–120 cm) high and flowers in summer. **ZONES 9–10.**

COBAEA

Although there are about 20 species of *Cobaea*, only *C. scandens* is ever seen outside their homelands in tropical areas of the Americas. They are very fast-growing, somewhat untidy vines with compound leaves, the terminal leaflet modified into a tendril. Bell-shaped flowers, usually green, bluish or purplish, appear singly in the leaf-axils and have a prominent disc-like calyx. It is thought that the flowers are pollinated by bats as well as night insects.
CULTIVATION: Cobaeas are subtropical plants and they flower freely when grown outdoors as annuals in temperate climates. They prefer a sheltered, sunny position and fairly rich, moist but well-drained soil. Propagate from seed in spring or cuttings in summer.

Cobaea scandens
CUP AND SAUCER VINE

Native to Mexico, this vigorous perennial vine growing to a height of 12–15 ft (3.5–4.5 m) has dense foliage and abundant flowers to 2 in (5 cm) wide, each with a large calyx (the 'saucer'), that open yellow-green and turn from mauve to a translucent purple with age; they appear throughout the year in mild climates. In the evenings the young flowers emit a rather unpleasant odor that diminishes as they mature. **'Alba'** has white flowers that age to cream. **ZONES 9–11.**

COCCOLOBA

About 150 species of mainly evergreen shrubs, trees and vines make up this tropical American genus. They have leathery leaves of variable shape and produce spikes or panicles of very small separate male and female flowers. The flowers are succeeded by segmented purple fruit, edible in some species and of economic importance locally.
CULTIVATION: These tropical plants will not tolerate prolonged cool temperatures and do best in moist, well-drained soil in full sun. Some are highly adapted to seashore conditions. In cooler climates they are sometimes grown in greenhouses or conservatories. Propagate from seed or cuttings.

Coccoloba uvifera
SEA GRAPE, JAMAICAN KINO

From seashores of tropical America as far north as southern Florida, this striking small tree can grow to 30 ft (9 m) high, usually with a single trunk and broad crown. The glossy leaves are almost circular, about 8 in (20 cm) long, with prominent white or pinkish veins; new leaves are an attractive translucent bronze. In spring and summer it produces erect 8–12 in (20–30 cm) spikes of small white flowers, followed by green-spotted, edible purple fruit. It grows in the forefront of beach and dune shrubs. **ZONES 11–12.**

COCCOTHRINAX

This genus of slender fan palms consist of about 50 species distributed widely through the Caribbean region, most of them native to Cuba. Most are single-trunked, the upper trunk covered with fibrous remains of old leaf sheaths, sometimes forming interesting patterns. The fan-like fronds are smallish with blades divided to about midway into many pointed segments and are often coated with silvery scales on the underside. The inflorescences are mostly shorter than the fronds and moderately branched, with masses of fragrant white or cream flowers followed by small purple-black single-seeded fruits.
CULTIVATION: These make attractive ornamental palms for tropical gardens and parks, looking particularly effective when planted in groups. They tolerate poor soil and often boggy conditions, but need shelter in the early stages of growth. Propagation is from seed, which will usually germinate within 2 months.

Coccothrinax alta

A native of Puerto Rico, this species makes a medium-sized, rather slow-growing palm of up to 30 ft (9 m) with pale brown trunk about 4 in (10 cm) thick. It has graceful, drooping fan leaves that are glossy green on the upper surface, silvery underneath. The flowers are white and are followed by brownish to black shiny fruit. **ZONES 11–12.**

COCHLEARIA
SCURVYGRASS

From cooler temperate and subarctic regions of the northern hemisphere, this genus of cress relatives includes about 25 species of low annuals and perennials. The leaves are usually unlobed, kidney-shaped or heart-shaped, arranged in a basal rosette and in some species continuing up the flowering stems. Flowers are small and white with 4 petals, opening progressively on short to long spikes, and are followed by small, swollen, rounded pods. Some *Cochlearia* species have been used as a salad garnish and are a rich source of vitamin C, though they are not highly palatable. The common name goes back to a time when 'grass' meant any short green herbage.
CULTIVATION: Easily grown in the herb garden in moist light-textured soil in a cool, sheltered position, or in wall crevices, cochlearias are modestly attractive plants. Propagate from seed sown *in situ*, or by division of clumps.

Cochlearia officinalis
COMMON SCURVYGRASS

Native to northwestern and central Europe and commonly growing on coastal cliffs and shingle, this biennial or perennial species grows to 18 in (45 cm) high. The neat, fleshy basal leaves are kidney shaped and about 3/4 in (18 mm) long; the flowering stems branch into many spikes of small white flowers which open through spring and summer, followed by globular pods. At one time a preparation of this plant was used on long sea voyages to prevent scurvy, hence its common name. **ZONES 4–9.**

COCHLOSPERMUM

The 30-odd species of this genus of shrubs and small trees are scattered throughout the tropics, growing mainly in regions of strongly seasonal rainfall, and are mostly deciduous in the dry season. The leaves are lobed, rather like grape or maple leaves, and beautiful large cream to golden-yellow flowers are borne in clusters terminating the branches. The large seed pods are globular to sausage-shaped and split open in a most unusual pattern to reveal masses of seeds embedded in a kapok-like down. The roots of *Cochlospermum* are swollen and fleshy and are sometimes used as a food source, and other parts of the plants yield fibers and medicinal gums.
CULTIVATION: Although not difficult to cultivate under tropical conditions, these are shrubs of very open, ungainly habit, but respond to cutting back with denser growth. They need full sun and moderately fertile, well-drained soil. Propagate from seed or root-tuber cuttings.

Cochlospermum fraseri
YELLOW KAPOK

This, one of 3 species indigenous to far northern Australia, makes a crooked shrub or small tree up to 30 ft (9 m) high. The leaves are slightly hairy, up to 6 in (15 cm) wide, with 3 to 7 shallow lobes. The flowers are bright golden yellow, up to 3 in (8 cm) across, borne on leafless branches late in the dry season (spring). If kept watered in a garden the leaves may persist and be present with the flowers. **ZONES 11–12.**

COCOS
COCONUT

As now recognized, the only species in this genus of tropical feather palms is the

Coccothrinax alta

Cneorum tricoccon

Coccoloba uvifera

Cobaea scandens

Cochlospermum fraseri

coconut (*Cocos nucifera*), though many other palms were once included in it (see *Butia, Syagrus,* among others). It is the epitome of the tropical palm tree being a symbol of tropical seashores and a plant with many commercial and local uses. The genus is distinguished from its relatives, which share the hard blackish inner fruit shell with 3 pores or 'eyes', by the large size of the seed and the fact that its endosperm, or stored food material, is partly liquid (the 'coconut milk').
CULTIVATION: It is strictly a tropical plant and will not grow well where the temperature regularly falls below 60°F (15°C); it is occasionally grown in heated greenhouses in cooler climates but seldom achieves any size. It does best in full sun in deep, porous soil with ample moisture but will of course tolerate coastal conditions. It is raised from seed, which germinate in a few months if the whole unhusked nut is laid on its side on moist sand.

Cocos nucifera
COCONUT PALM

The coconut has now become distributed through most tropical lowland regions both through human agency and because its nut can survive for a month or so floating in the ocean. It is characterized by its slender, often curved trunk, up to as much as 100 ft (30 m) high, topped with a head of long, gracefully drooping fronds. It bears continuously large panicles of small creamy yellow flowers, a few of which develop into the familiar yellow-green fruit that dries and browns as it ripens. There are many selected strains, including **'Malay Dwarf'** with much shorter trunk and abundant golden-yellow nuts. **ZONE 12.**

CODIAEUM

This genus consists of about 15 species of evergreen shrubs and small trees native to southern Asia, the Malay region and Pacific Islands. One species, *Codiaeum variegatum*, has given rise to a large number of cultivars with highly colored and sometimes bizarrely shaped leaves. These are popular garden plants in tropical regions, and house or greenhouse plants in temperate climates. Where they can be grown outdoors, the larger-growing cultivars make good hedging plants. The small yellow flowers and tiny seed pods are quite insignificant—the plants are grown strictly for their magnificent foliage.
CULTIVATION: They will not withstand prolonged cold or dry conditions and prefer moist, humus-rich soil in sun or dappled shade. As indoor plants they are grown in a rich but freely draining potting mix, and watered and fed freely during the summer growing season. Propagate from tip cuttings or by air-layering.

Codiaeum variegatum
CROTON, GARDEN CROTON

This species occurs throughout the range of the genus, making a small tree with plain green leaves in the wild. Cultivated

Codonopsis clematidea

forms, though, show enormous variation of leaf color and pattern with shades of green, red, yellow, orange and purple, sometimes on the one plant. Some cultivars can grow to 8 ft (2.4 m) or more tall, with leaves up to 12 in (30 cm) long; they must be propagated vegetatively, usually by cuttings, to maintain their foliage color. **'America'** has green, red, orange and yellow leaves, the variegation following the veins and margins; **'Petra'** is similar to 'America' but has more clearly defined margins; **'Imperiale'** has yellow leaves with pink margins and green midribs; **'Interruptum'** has yellow, recurved leaves with green margins and red midribs; **'Mrs Iceton'** (syn. 'Appleleaf') has elliptic leaves, metallic purple at the edges, yellow to rose in the center. **ZONES 11–12.**

CODONOPSIS

Native to eastern Asia and higher mountains of the Malay region, this genus allied to *Campanula* consists of about 30 species of perennials with swollen roots, some with scrambling or climbing stems, and simple, broad to narrow leaves that smell slightly unpleasant when bruised. The flowers are pendent or nodding, basically bell-shaped but with many variations, and in many cases prettily veined.
CULTIVATION: They require a moist, cool-temperate climate and most species grow best in a light, well-drained soil in part or complete shade. For best effect, plant in a raised bed or on a bank where the insides of the nodding flowers can be seen. Propagate from seed or by division with care.

Codonopsis convolvulacea

This species from the Himalayas and Western China sends up twining stems to as much as 8 ft (2.4 m) high if a suitable support is available or it may hang down a bank or wall. The broadly bell-shaped flowers are up to 2 in (5 cm) across, range in color from violet to almost white and are carried singly on long stalks at ends of lateral branches. ***Codonopsis clematidea*** from central Asia is very similar but has nodding flowers with purple veining. **ZONES 5–9.**

COELOGYNE

This genus of epiphytic orchids, allied to *Cymbidium*, from tropical Asia and the Pacific Islands consists of over 100 species, though relatively few are in general cultivation. They have short, fat pseudobulbs, sometimes very smooth

Cocos nucifera with *Pandanus tectorius*

Codiaeum variegatum 'America'

Codiaeum variegatum 'Petra'

Coelogyne cristata

Codiaeum variegatum 'Interruptum'

and cylindrical, closely to widely spaced on a creeping rhizome. Each pseudobulb bears one or two leathery leaves. Flowering stems come from bases of pseudobulbs and are usually arching or pendulous, though sometimes with a single flower only. The flowers come in many shapes and sizes, mostly in shades of green, cream, brown and dull purple, sometimes pure white, often with orange markings on the labellum (lip).
CULTIVATION: Many of the coelogynes will grow into large, bulky plants, producing numerous sprays of blooms. Some do well in cool conditions and will happily grow outdoors in a sheltered spot protected from frost. They like a fairly coarse, soil-free compost and plenty of water while they are in active summer growth. However, they demand a winter rest if they are to flower freely. Propagation is by division after they have flowered.

Coelogyne cristata
ANGEL ORCHID

From the Himalayan hills, the angel orchid is the most popular member of the genus, and is one of the loveliest of all orchids. It makes a fine specimen plant with dozens of short sprays of scented white flowers touched with gold on the lip, among glossy deep green leaves. Cool growing, it likes summer shade and is one of the easiest orchids to grow as a house plant. It flowers at the end of winter and on into spring. **ZONES 10–11.**

Coelogyne dayana

This native of Borneo has pale buff-yellow flowers with chocolate-brown and white markings on the labellum, crowded on pendulous spikes that can sometimes hang down as much as 3 ft (1 m). It has longer pseudobulbs than most coelogynes, 6–10 in (15–25 cm) long, and the leaves are up to 30 in (75 cm) long. It flowers in late spring or early summer and requires fairly warm conditions. **ZONES 11–12.**

Colchicum agrippinum

Coelogyne mayeriana

Coelogyne pandurata

Coelogyne pandurata
BLACK ORCHID

The purple-black is only on the labellum; otherwise the scented, spidery flowers are pale green or yellowish green. They are borne on short arching sprays of a few blooms only in summer, among large leaves which spring from egg-shaped pseudobulbs. From Borneo and the Malay Peninsula, it prefers intermediate conditions. ***Coelogyne mayeriana*** is the same in most respects to *C. pandurata* except for its slightly broader labellum. **ZONES 10–11.**

COFFEA
COFFEE

This genus includes some 40 species of shrubs and small trees, native mainly to tropical Africa, with a few in Asia. Best known is *Coffea arabica*, the original source of coffee and still the most prized species. Most have tiered branches and deep green, smooth-edged leaves arranged in opposite pairs. Attractive white flowers are clustered in the leaf-axils, followed by small, fleshy, 2-seeded fruits that turn red as they ripen.
CULTIVATION: The preferred growing environment is humus-rich soil with

Colchicum autumnale

Coffea arabica

light shade and steady mild temperatures. Propagation is from seed or semi-ripe cuttings. As would be expected of tropical plants, most are frost-tender. They adapt well to being grown as house plants. Propagate from seed, which must be fresh but germinates very rapidly.

Coffea arabica
ARABIAN COFFEE

Originating in mountain rainforests of Ethiopia, this is the coffee of commerce and, while one or two are unlikely to supply your coffee needs, it is a very attractive evergreen shrub for frost-free gardens or for large containers. It can grow to around 15 ft (4.5 m) high. Small, fragrant white flowers are clustered along the branches behind the leaves and are followed by the dark red fruits; each contains 2 'beans' which, when extracted, dried and roasted are our familiar coffee beans. **ZONES 10–12.**

COIX

A genus of 5 species of rather unusual grasses from tropical Asia, including both annuals and perennials. They belong to the maize tribe of grasses and in foliage look rather like young maize plants. Their unique feature is the hollow, bead-like structure or 'receptacle' that encloses the base of each small group of spikelets. The genus name should be pronounced with 2 syllables, co-ix.
CULTIVATION: Easily cultivated in any sheltered, frost-free spot in moist, fertile soil and will usually self-seed in the same place. Propagate from seed.

Coix lacryma-jobi
JOB'S TEARS

This annual grass is native to Southeast Asia and grows to a height of around 3–6 ft (1–1.8 m), with knobbly, bamboo-like stems from the bases of which new 'tillers' arise, these sometimes

Colchicum autumnale 'Album'

self-layering. The glossy deep green leaves are up to 2 in (5 cm) wide with slightly wavy edges. The flowering and fruiting spikelets are insignificant, but the shiny, pea-sized receptacles that enclose their bases harden in fall (autumn) to a pale bluish gray and have often been used for beads and other decorative purposes. Some selected strains are cultivated for their edible grains. **ZONES 9–12.**

COLCHICUM
AUTUMN CROCUS

Although the flowers of these small 'bulbs' (actually corms) bear a strong resemblance to crocuses (*Crocus*), the likeness is only superficial as the two genera are not closely related. *Colchicum* consists of about 45 species, native to Europe, North Africa and west and central Asia, with the greatest concentration in Turkey and the Balkans; nearly all species have been cultivated by dwarf bulb and rock garden enthusiasts, but only a few are very widely grown. Despite the name 'autumn crocus', they bloom in either spring or fall (autumn), depending on species. All have flowers with a very long tube, the ovary at or below soil level and the petals spreading at the top into a usually narrow funnel. There are 6 stamens (*Crocus* always has 3). With few exceptions the leaves appear after the flowers and are mostly broad and fleshy. All parts of the plants are poisonous and even contact with the skin may cause irritation—the poisonous compound colchicine affects division of cell nuclei and is used in the treatment of certain forms of cancer; it is also used to create polyploids in plant breeding.
CULTIVATION: Frost hardy, they are easy to grow as long as winters are sufficiently cold. Some Mediterranean species like hot dry summer conditions and need a warm spot in the rock garden with good drainage. Plant corms in late

Colchicum byzantinum

summer in well-drained soil in full sun or part-shade. Corms can be flowered once without any soil, so they can be kept inside for display. Propagate from seed or by division in summer.

Colchicum agrippinum

Now believed to be an old hybrid, with *Colchicum variegatum* the only obvious parent, this is an easily grown plant of about 6 in (15 cm) height when in flower. Its most striking feature is the way the star-shaped flowers are finely checkered in light and deeper tones of lilac pink. They are about 3 in (8 cm) across and appear in fall (autumn). The tufts of broad leaves that follow are slightly taller. **ZONES 5–9.**

Colchicum autumnale
AUTUMN CROCUS, MEADOW SAFFRON

The best known species of the genus, *Colchicum autumnale* comes from Europe. The flowers rise to about 6 in (10 cm) above the ground and are about 3 in (8 cm) across. Appearing from late summer to mid-fall (mid-autumn), they vary a little in color but are usually a delicate shade of lilac pink. This is one of the most moisture tolerant species, and the one occurring furthest north. **'Album'** has white flowers, and there is also a double-flowered form. **ZONES 5–9.**

Colchicum byzantinum

The corms of this species are quite large, about 2–4 in (5–10 cm) long and almost as wide; each one can produce up to 20 or more flowers in early fall (autumn), the leaves following in winter. The flower tubes are about 5 in (12 cm) long, the 4 in (12 cm) wide flowers pale lilac to bright mauve with white centers. The leaves are ribbed and may be up to 12 in (30 cm) long and about 4 in (10 cm) wide. **ZONES 6–9.**

Colchicum 'Lilac Wonder'

One of a number of hybrid cultivars thought to be derived in part from *Colchicum speciosum*, 'Lilac Wonder' has large lilac flowers in fall (autumn). They are cup-shaped and about 4 in (10 cm) across, and stand about 8 in (20 cm) high. **ZONES 6–9.**

Colchicum speciosum

A native of the Caucasus region including northern Turkey and Iran, this is often regarded as the most beautiful species of colchicum, as well as one of

Colchicum 'Lilac Wonder'

Coleonema album

Coleonema pulchellum 'Sunset Gold'

the more easily grown. It bears goblet-shaped flowers the size of small tulips in a beautiful shade of rose pink, white in the throat, from late summer well into fall (autumn). **'Album'** has pure white flowers. **ZONES 6–9.**

Colchicum 'Waterlily'

Another probable derivative of *Colchicum speciosum* and flowering at the same season, 'Waterlily' is striking for its large double flowers often with up to 26 petals and lilac rose in color. The flowers often become top-heavy and flop over, and the untidy effect created by a clump may not please all gardeners, but they are eye-catching. **ZONES 6–9.**

COLEONEMA

These small, evergreen shrubs from South Africa are often wrongly referred to as diosmas, but *Diosma* is a different genus, rarely cultivated. There are 8 species, most of them restricted in the wild to western Cape Province. They have short, needle-like leaves on very fine, wiry twigs and tiny, starry flowers in winter and spring occasionally repeating through summer. The foliage is aromatic, smelling a little like ants.
CULTIVATION: They withstand regular trimming to shape, usually done immediately after flowering. Plant in light but moist, well-drained soil in full sun. If neglected, the foliage can become a rather sickly yellowish green—occasional applications of very dilute iron sulphate solution will keep it looking healthy. Propagate from cuttings.

Coleonema album
WHITE DIOSMA, WHITE BREATH OF HEAVEN

Often misnamed *Diosma ericoides*, this species has white flowers from mid-winter to mid-spring. It grows to about 5 ft (1.5 m) high and wide. The foliage is deep green, the individual leaves somewhat broader than those of the

Colletia paradoxa

Coleonema pulchellum 'Compactum'

more popular *Coleonema pulchellum*. **ZONES 9–10.**

Coleonema pulchellum
syn. *Coleonema pulchrum* of gardens
CONFETTI BUSH, PINK BREATH OF HEAVEN

This, the most widely grown species, is a 5 ft (1.5 m) high shrub with fine heathy foliage and profuse pink starry flowers in winter and spring. It was for long misidentified in gardens as *Coleonema pulchrum* but the true *C. pulchrum* is a different species, rare in cultivation. Several forms are cultivated with paler or deeper pink flowers. **'Compactum'** is a more compact form; **'Sunset Gold'** is a very popular cultivar with bright yellow foliage and light pink flowers. Also more compact, it usually grows as a low, flat-topped bush no more than 18 in (45 cm) high. **ZONES 9–10.**

COLLETIA
ANCHOR PLANT

This unusual genus consists of 17 species of stiff, woody, evergreen shrubs from temperate and subtropical South America with leaves and branchlets arranged in opposite pairs. The leaves are very small and in most species are present only on new growths; their photosynthetic function is taken over by the green branchlets, each tipped by a fierce spine. Small white bell-shaped

Colchicum speciosum

flowers appear in clusters at the branchlet junctions and have a sweet, honey-like smell. Colletias are curious plants that some people find attractive, others repellently fierce.
CULTIVATION: They can be grown in any average garden soil and prefer full sun. Few shrubs are so well suited to forming an intruder-proof barrier. Propagation is from cuttings or seed, produced in small, globular capsules. Plants can be pruned back to encourage denser growth.

Colletia paradoxa
syn. *Colletia cruciata*

Indigenous to Uruguay, Argentina and southern Brazil, this shrub grows to about 10 ft (3 m) tall with an erect, very irregular growth habit. Its leafless branchlets are deep gray-green with a slight waxy bloom and mostly flattened in the vertical plane, but sometimes it produces branches with shorter, narrower branchlets as well. The texture of the plant is remarkable—tapping it with a fingernail is like tapping a sheet of plywood. The flowers are white and appear in great abundance in fall (autumn). They are fairly long lasting. **ZONES 7–10.**

COLLINSIA

Around 20 species of annuals make up this genus from western North America. Belonging to the snapdragon family, they have whorls of colorful 2-lipped flowers which in structure are similar to those of *Linaria* but without the backward pointing spur; the enlarged lower lip and backward-folded upper lip give them the look of pea-flowers at first

Colchicum speciosum 'Album'

glance, and doubtless they attract similar pollinating insects.
CULTIVATION: Some Californian species are grown as garden flowers, adapting well to moist, semi-shaded positions. They may also be grown in pots in a conservatory, for floral display. Propagate from seed, sown in early spring or, in the case of the spring-flowering *Collinsia verna*, in fall (autumn).

Collinsia bicolor
syn. *Collinsia heterophylla*
CHINESE HOUSES

This Californian species is an annual that grows naturally in shady places, the weak stems up to about 24 in (60 cm) tall. The summer flowers are usually in shades of pink to pale purple with contrasting white upper lip. **ZONES 7–10.**

COLOCASIA

This genus of the arum family from tropical Asia consists of 6 species of evergreen tuberous perennials. The large leaves are arrowhead-shaped or heart-shaped, with prominent veins, supported on a tall stalk that joins the blade a little in from the edge. The flowering stems appear at any time of the year and are like small, pale yellow or cream calla lilies, with a delicate fragrance. At least 2 *Colocasia* species are grown for their edible tubers and others are occasionally grown as ornamentals.

Coleonema pulchellum

Colchicum 'Waterlily'

Columnea arguta

Colquhounia coccinea

Colocasia esculenta

CULTIVATION: Frost-tender plants, they like a sheltered but sunny position and fertile, humus-rich soil. Keep the soil around the base of the plant firm to support the slender stem. Water abundantly in the summer growing season and harvest tubers 8 months after planting. Young shoots can be cooked and eaten like asparagus, while the starchy tubers can be boiled or roasted like potatoes. Propagate by division.

Colocasia esculenta
syn. *Colocasia antiquorum*
TARO, DASHEEN, EDDOE, ELEPHANT'S EAR

Widely grown in many tropical and subtropical regions for the edible tubers, this species can stand 4–8 ft (1.2–2.4 m) tall, the long leaf-stalks supporting heart-shaped, mid- to dark green leaves up to 24 in (60 cm) long; the plants can spread by slender runners. ***Colocasia esculenta* var. *antiquorum*** (eddoe) has smaller but more numerous tubers. The ornamental cultivar **'Fontanesii'** has dark purple stalks and bronze-tinted leaves. There are innumerable edible cultivars of taro and one feature in which they vary is the presence and amount of irritant crystals in the tubers, which may need to be removed by repeated boiling. **ZONES 10–12.**

Colocasia gigantea

This species from the Malaysian region has pale green leaves up to about 5 ft (1.8 m) long and 3 ft (1 m) wide, their undersides with a whitish bloom. The whole plant can stand around 8 ft (2.4 m) high with a short basal trunk at the apex of which are produced a continuous succession of narrow cream spathes. It grows in slightly boggy clearings in rainforest and is easily cultivated in frost-free locations. **ZONES 10–12.**

COLQUHOUNIA

This genus consists of 3 species of evergreen or semi-evergreen shrubs or subshrubs in the mint family and comes from the Himalayas and Southeast Asia. The aromatic leaves are finely toothed and borne in opposite pairs on the square stems. The tubular, 2-lipped flowers are carried on terminal spikes. Pronunciation of the name might present problems to non-Scots—the surname of botanical collector Sir Robert Colquhoun, after whom the genus is named, was pronounced 'co-hoon', if present-day Scottish usage is a guide.
CULTIVATION: They need a sheltered position and well-drained soil in full sun. They may be cut down by frost in cold areas. Propagation is from cuttings in summer.

Colquhounia coccinea

This very handsome though rather sprawling shrub from the Himalayas, has large, felty, aromatic leaves and terminal clusters of pale pink to reddish orange flowers that are yellowish inside. It grows to 10 ft (3 m) high and wide. **ZONES 8–10.**

COLUMNEA

With over 150 species of shrubs, subshrubs and climbers from tropical America, this is one of the largest genera of the African violet and gloxinia family, as well as being one of the most important in terms of ornamental indoor plants. Coming from regions of high rainfall and humidity, many grow as epiphytes, with long trailing stems and rather fleshy leaves. The beautiful and unusual flowers, mostly in colors of red, orange and yellow, have a long tube and often a hooded or helmet-shaped upper lip; they are adapted to pollination by hummingbirds, which hover under the flower and brush pollen from anthers beneath the hood onto their heads while sipping nectar from the tube.
CULTIVATION: Some species demand constant high humidity, but many can grow outdoors in warm climates in a suitably sheltered spot in filtered light; in cooler climates they need the protection of a greenhouse or conservatory. Hanging baskets are ideal for most columneas, whether they are of the type with quite pendulous stems or more erect, scrambling plants. Grow in an open, fibrous compost, including, for example, sphagnum moss, peat and charcoal. Water freely in summer, reducing water as the weather cools. Propagate from cuttings.

Columnea arguta

A native of Panama, this is one of the most beautiful species which is at its best grown in a large hanging basket in a humid conservatory. The pendulous stems can grow up to 6 ft (1.8 m) long, forming a dense curtain of foliage; the small, crowded leaves are dark green on their convex uppersides with velvety purplish hairs, and the strongly hooded flowers, about 3 in (8 cm) long, make a display of brilliant color. **ZONES 11–12.**

Columnea gloriosa
GOLDFISH PLANT

Similar to its relative the lipstick plant (*Aeschynanthus*), this Central American native has semi-erect hairy stems and fleshy, convex leaves up to 1½ in (38 mm) long clothed in velvety hairs. Over a long period from spring to fall (autumn) it produces an abundance of brilliant scarlet and yellow flowers over 3 in (8 cm) long, from the leaf axils. **ZONES 11–12.**

COLUTEA

There are around 30 species of deciduous shrubs in this legume genus, mostly native to western and central Asia but with a few in China, the Mediterranean and North Africa. In the wild they grow mainly in dry mountain regions. Allied to *Clianthus* and *Sutherlandia*, the genus also has a bladder-like pod, quite large in some species, that produces a satisfying 'pop' when squeezed hard between the fingers. The leaves are pinnate, and pea-like flowers, in soft shades of yellow or coppery orange, are borne in short lateral sprays toward the ends of the season's growth.
CULTIVATION: Though not in the first rank of ornamental shrubs, coluteas have quite pleasant foliage and flowers, make vigorous growth even under poor conditions, and flower over a long season in the warmer half of the year. They do quite well in seashore plantings. *C. arborescens* is useful as a graft stock for the beautiful but difficult Australian annual *Swainsona* (*Clianthus*) *formosa.* Propagate from seed or cuttings.

Colutea arborescens
BLADDER SENNA

From southern Europe, this fast-growing, deciduous shrub has a rather open habit and can reach a height of 12 ft (3.5 m). The leaves are pale green and have many leaflets. The yellow pea-flowers are produced throughout summer and fall (autumn) and are followed by bladder-like seed pods. **ZONES 5–10.**

COLVILLEA
COLVILLE'S GLORY

This genus has only one species, endemic to Madagascar like its relative *Delonix regia*, but now widely planted in the tropics. It is a near-evergreen tree of medium size that makes a large spreading crown of fern-like, bipinnate leaves and often has a good height of clear trunk below the branches, making it an ideal shade tree and suitable for park and street planting in warm climates. The showy flowers are crowded on branched spikes held above the foliage and attract nectar-feeding birds, including parrots.
CULTIVATION: This tree does best in moist, well-drained soil in full sun. It needs a tropical or subtropical climate to grow well but will withstand very occasional light frosts. Propagation is from seed.

Colvillea racemosa

This tree can grow to 50 ft (15 m) though usually smaller in cultivation and has feathery bipinnate leaves up to 30 in (75 cm) long. In fall (autumn), long cylinders of bright orange flowers with yellow-tipped stamens open from pendulous silky buds. **ZONES 11–12.**

COMBRETUM

Members of this large genus occur across tropical and subtropical Africa, Asia and the Americas and include shrubs and small to medium-sized trees, as well as some climbers. While many are evergreen, some South African species are deciduous, the foliage coloring well in fall (autumn). The flowers appear in spikes, and in many species have inconspicuous petals but prominent, colorful stamens. The attractive, 4-winged fruit that follow persist on the branches until dispersed by the wind.
CULTIVATION: Combretums are adapted to summer-rainfall tropical and subtropical climates and will grow in most soils provided drainage is good. A position in full sun suits them best. They are easy to propagate from fresh seed or from cuttings.

Combretum bracteosum
HICCUP NUT

This evergreen scrambling climber is native to eastern South Africa and can climb into trees to a height of 15 ft (4.5 m) or even more. It has smooth, dull green leaves that are paler underneath, and in summer bears a profusion of orange-red flowers in rounded heads. The nut-like fruit that follow are said to either cause or cure hiccups. It can be grown as a wall climber or cascading down a bank. **ZONES 9–11.**

Combretum erythrophyllum
RIVER BUSHWILLOW

Of wide distribution in southeastern Africa, this species is a deciduous small, spreading tree to 30 ft (9 m) or more tall, often branching at ground level into several stout trunks with smooth yellow-brown bark. New growths are pale green, maturing mid-green, and the foliage turns yellowish then deep red in fall (autumn). Inconspicuous clusters of small greenish yellow flowers appear in winter and spring, followed in summer by masses of straw colored hop-like fruit

Convallaria majalis

that may be cut for dried decorations. It makes fast growth and the seeds germinate readily. **ZONES 9–11.**

COMMELINA

A widespread genus of about 230 species of perennial herbs from tropical and subtropical regions of the world, related to *Tradescantia.* They vary in growth habit, some sending up erect annual growths from tuberous roots, others with more evergreen and usually creeping stems which root at the nodes. Their distinctive features are the very asymmetrical boat-shaped bract that encloses each group of flower-buds, and the 3 petals of which often only 2 are conspicuous, each narrowed at the base into a fine 'claw', or stalk. Many species have petals of an intense, clear blue, though pinks and whites are also known.
CULTIVATION: A position in full sun is preferred and a well-drained soil is essential. Propagation is from cuttings or by division.

Commelina coelestis
MEXICAN DAYFLOWER

Native to Central and South America including Mexico, this species has vivid sky-blue flowers that close in the afternoon, each with 3 equal petals and about 1 in (25 mm) across. They open in late summer and fall (autumn). The weak, semi-erect stems with broad green leaves spring from a deep tuberous rootstock and may reach a height of 3 ft (1 m). It needs a warm position in full sun.
ZONES 9–11.

Commelina cyanea
SCURVY WEED

Native to eastern and northern Australia, this species occurs in many habitats and may become rather a nuisance in gardens. It has weak, prostrate stems which root at the nodes, at intervals forming masses of deep fleshy roots and rhizomes that will survive drought and frost. Leaves are narrow and strongly channelled, and flowers are intense sky blue to purple, borne sparsely from spring to fall (autumn). It is of little value as a garden plant, but early Australian settlers used it as a green vegetable to combat scurvy. **ZONES 8–11.**

CONSOLIDA
LARKSPUR

Botanists in the past often treated these annuals as species of *Delphinium,* but the consensus now is that the 40 or so

Convolvulus althaeoides

species constitute a distinct genus, occurring in the Mediterranean region and west and central Asia. The name *Consolida* was bestowed in the Middle Ages in recognition of the plants' use in the healing of wounds; they were believed to help the clotting (consolidating) of the blood. The larkspurs grown in gardens are mostly derived from the one species, *Consolida ajacis,* and include many strains, mostly grown as mixed colors. The flowers of the taller kinds will last a long time when cut. They have finely divided, feather-like leaves and poisonous seeds.
CULTIVATION: They are not difficult to grow, succeeding in any temperate or even mildly subtropical climate and liking full sun and rich, well-drained soil. Tall cultivars need to be staked. Propagate from seed and watch for snails and slugs and for powdery mildew.

Consolida ajacis
syns *Consolida ambigua, Delphinium consolida*

The name larkspur comes from the nectar spur at the back of the flowers, hidden in the open blooms but clearly visible on the unopened buds. This Mediterranean species originally had blue flowers. Present-day garden larkspurs are the result of hybridizing this species with *Consolida orientalis* to give the 'rocket larkspurs', or may be derived mainly from *C. regalis* in the case of the 'forking larkspurs'. Their blooms may be pink, white or purple and are usually double, borne mainly in summer. Some can reach a height of 4 ft (1.2 m).
ZONES 7–11.

CONVALLARIA
LILY-OF-THE-VALLEY

Some botanists have recognized several species of *Convallaria,* but most believe there is only one, occurring wild in forests from France to Siberia, also

Commelina cyanea

cooler parts of North America. The plant spreads over the forest floor by slender underground rhizomes which at intervals send up pointed oval leaves and slender flowering stems adorned with little white bells, shining like pearls against the dull green of the foliage. The red berries that follow have their uses in medicine, but they are poisonous—dangerously so, as they are sweet enough to tempt children to eat them.
CULTIVATION: The rhizomes, or 'pips' as they are commonly known from their growing tips, should be planted in fall (autumn) in a part-shaded position. Given the right conditions lily-of-the-valley spreads freely and in a confined space sometimes becomes overcrowded, when it will benefit from lifting and thinning. Grow in fertile, humus-rich, moist soil. They can be potted for display indoors, then replanted outdoors after flowering. Propagate from seed or by division.

Convallaria majalis

Renowned for its glorious perfume, this beautiful plant does best in cool climates. It is low growing, 8–12 in (20–30 cm) high but of indefinite spread, with dark green leaves. The dainty white bell-shaped flowers are $\frac{1}{4}$–$\frac{1}{2}$ in (6–12 mm) across and appear in spring. Pink-flowered variants are known, collectively referred to as ***Convallaria majalis* var. *rosea*,** and there are several cultivars with variegated or gold foliage. **ZONES 3–9.**

CONVOLVULUS

Found in many temperate regions of the world, this genus consists mainly of slender, twining creepers (the bind-

Combretum erythrophyllum

weeds) and small herbaceous plants. Only a few species are shrubby, and even these are soft stemmed and renewed by shooting from the base. They have simple, thin-textured, usually narrow leaves and the flowers are like morning glories, with a strongly flared tube that opens by unfurling 'pleats'. However, *Convolvulus* species differ from many true morning glories *(Ipomoea)* in having flowers that stay open all day, rather than shrivelling by mid-morning or early afternoon; they usually open in succession over a long season.
CULTIVATION: These easily grown plants adapt to most soils and exposed as well as sheltered positions, but always prefer full sun. They can be cut back hard after flowering if desired, to promote thicker growth. Propagation is from cuttings.

Convolvulus althaeoides

Native to the Mediterranean region, this is a perennial which can spread by underground rhizomes. It has trailing or twining stems and oval to heart-shaped leaves that may be strongly lobed and slightly overlaid with silver. The profuse bright pink flowers are 1–1$\frac{1}{2}$ in (25–38 mm) across, and they are borne in late spring and summer. In a mild climate the plants may become invasive. If not supported, they will mound untidily to about 6 in (15 cm) high.
ZONES 8–10.

Consolida ajacis

Combretum erythrophyllum

Convolvulus cneorum
BUSH MORNING GLORY

This attractive subshrub from Mediterranean Europe has crowded, weak, upcurving stems sprouting from the base to a height of 1–2 ft (30–60 cm). The leaves, in tufts along the stems, are soft and narrow with a coating of silky hairs which gives them a silvery sheen. The stems terminate in dense clusters of silky buds, each producing a long succession of flowers through spring and summer, flesh-pink in bud but opening pure dazzling white with a small yellow 'eye'. **ZONES 8–10.**

Convolvulus sabatius
syn. *Convolvulus mauritanicus*

MOROCCAN GLORY VINE, BINDWEED, GROUND MORNING GLORY

Widely distributed in northern Africa with a foothold in Europe in southern Italy, this densely trailing perennial bears profuse lilac-blue flowers from spring to fall (autumn). It has slender stems that may twine around twigs, and small oval green leaves. An excellent plant for draping over walls and hanging baskets, it grows to a height of 6–8 in (15–20 cm) and spreads extensively. **ZONES 8–11.**

Copernicia baileyana

Convolvulus sabatius

Convolvulus cneorum

Convolvulus tricolor
syn. *Convolvulus minor*

This bedding annual from the Mediterranean bears profuse deep purple- blue or white flowers with banded yellow and white throats. The small leaves are lance-shaped and mid-green. A slender, few-branched plant, it grows to a height of 8–12 in (20–30 cm) and blooms continuously from late spring to early fall (autumn) but individual flowers last only one day. **'Blue Ensign'** has very deep blue flowers with pale yellow centers. **ZONES 8–11.**

COPERNICIA

The majority of the 25 species of fan palms in this genus are endemic to Cuba, including some of bizarre appearance, but 3 species occur in eastern and central South America and 2 on Hispaniola. Their natural habitats include dry savanna at low elevations and areas subject to seasonal flooding. Their tall trunks may be covered with old frond sheaths or dead fronds, though these may be shed with age. The fronds are large and often very stiff, their outline varying from circular to wedge-shaped, with a long to very short, prickly stalk. In some species the lower frond surface has a thick coating of wax—the Brazilian *Copernicia prunifera* is the source of carnauba wax, used for car and furniture polishes. The inflorescences are much-branched and enclosed in bud in overlapping bracts that persist after flowering. The fronds are used for thatch and weaving, the trunks for fencing and the sheath fiber for making rope and brushes. **CULTIVATION:** Several of the Cuban species are prized as strikingly unusual garden subjects that can be grown outdoors in tropical and subtropical areas, though most are rather slow growing. Plant in a sheltered but sunny position in humus-rich, moist soil, preferably well

Coprosma acerosa f. *brunnea*

Convolvulus tricolor 'Blue Ensign'

Coprosma × kirkii 'Minogue'

spaced so their symmetry can be enjoyed. They grow well in low-lying ground and drainage lines. Propagate from seed.

Copernicia baileyana
YAREY

From Cuba, where it grows in savanna and woodlands, this stately palm develops with age a smooth, pale gray trunk of 30 ft (9 m) or more with a diameter of about 24 in (60 cm), but such specimens are rarely seen in cultivation. The fronds are notable for their large size and the way the numerous segments point upwards in a very regular comb-like fashion, the whole effect being very striking. It is popular in southern Florida and under ideal conditions can make reasonably fast growth. **ZONES 10–12.**

COPROSMA

Most of the 90 species of evergreen shrubs and small trees in this genus are native to New Zealand, though there are also a number in southeastern Australia and islands of the South Pacific. Several species are valued for their great tolerance of salt-laden winds and are commonly grown as coastal hedging and shelter planting. Leaves vary greatly in size and shape but are always borne in opposite pairs and are rather leathery and usually glossy; in some species the bruised foliage is unpleasant smelling. Flowers are inconspicuous, mostly greenish, reduced to bunches of stamens and long stigmas respectively in the male and female flowers which are always on separate plants. The small berry-like fruits, though, can be quite showy, in colors of red, white, blue or purple. **CULTIVATION:** They do best in full sun and in light, well-drained soil and are fast growing and easily maintained. Pruning will maintain foliage production. Propagate from seed in spring and semi-ripe cuttings in late summer.

Coprosma acerosa f. *brunnea*
syn. *Coprosma brunnea*

This species is native to New Zealand where it grows in dry gravelly stream beds. It is a wiry-stemmed prostrate shrub spreading to 10 ft (3 m) wide and no more than 6 in (15 cm) high. The tiny, narrow, olive green leaves are rather inconspicuous against the light brown stems. Minute cream flowers in spring are followed by beautiful translucent blue berries from late summer through fall (autumn). **ZONES 8–10.**

Coprosma 'Kiwi Silver'

Coprosma lucida

Coprosma × kirkii

This widely grown hybrid from New Zealand has narrow, oblong, glossy bright green or somewhat gray-green leaves arranged in numerous small rosettes. Squat and densely branched, this marginally frost-hardy shrub is useful as a dense ground cover and for erosion control, especially on coastal sites. It grows to 15 in (38 cm) high with a 3–6 ft (1–1.8 m) spread. **'Minogue'** is a green-leafed cultivar selected for its vigor. **'Variegata'** has leaves variegated gray-green and cream; several other cultivars have also been selected. **ZONES 8–11.**

Coprosma 'Kiwi Silver'

'Kiwi Silver' is a low, mound-forming plant to 12 in (30 cm) high and 3 ft (1 m) across. It bears elliptic, glossy mid-green leaves with pale yellow margins. **ZONES 9–11.**

Coprosma lucida
KARAMU

A very different New Zealand species, *Coprosma lucida* makes a large, open shrub or small tree to as much as 20 ft (6 m) tall, with broad glossy leaves up to 6 in (15 cm) long, broadest near the tips. Male flowers are yellow-green in dense clusters in the leaf axils, while female plants bear ½ in (12 mm) long orange-red fruits. **ZONES 8–10.**

Coprosma repens
syn. *Coprosma baueri* of gardens

TAUPATA, MIRROR BUSH, LOOKING-GLASS PLANT

Native to New Zealand seashores, this is the species most commonly planted to withstand coastal winds, growing where little else will survive. Usually shaped to a dense mound 3–6 ft (1–1.8 m) high, it will occasionally grow taller if left unpruned. It has brilliantly glossy, leathery, deep green leaves. Insignificant flowers are followed on female plants by small, orange-red fruit in late summer and fall (autumn). The leaves of **'Gold Splash'** are predominantly golden yellow; **'Marble Queen'** is a variegated form with paler green and cream leaves, often producing pure cream growths; **'Picturata'** has a central yellow blotch surrounded by dark glossy green; and **'Pink Splendor'** is a variegated form with pink-flushed leaves. ZONES 9–11.

CORDIA

This genus is made up of around 300 species of evergreen and deciduous shrubs and trees from most tropical and subtropical regions of the world. Some are used as timber trees, others hollowed out for canoes, and the leaves of a few species are used to make dyes. Most have large, smooth, oval leaves and small to moderately large, trumpet-shaped flowers that stand out against the dark foliage. The fruit is typical of the genus.
CULTIVATION: These plants require steady, warm temperatures and moist, well-drained soil. They are propagated from seed or semi-ripe cuttings.

Cordia dichotoma
BIRD LIME TREE

This handsome, evergreen tree from tropical Asia and Australasia grows to 30 ft (9 m) high with a broadly spreading habit and broad, shiny leaves to 8 in (20 cm) long. It produces both male and hermaphrodite orange flowers. These flowers are followed by 1 in (25 mm) long dull pinkish edible fruit with sticky flesh. ZONES 11–12.

Cordia sebestena
GEIGER TREE, SCARLET CORDIA

This evergreen shrub or small tree is native to the West Indies, Florida and Venezuela and is widely cultivated for ornament in the tropics. It grows to around 25 ft (8 m) high and has 8 in (20 cm) long, oval leaves. It produces tight clusters of bright orange-red flowers through much of the year, followed by 1 in (25 mm) oval, white, edible fruit. ZONES 10–12.

Cordia wallichii

Cordia wallichii

Cordia wallichii

A native of tropical Asia, this is a large shrub to small spreading tree, 12 to 20 ft (3.5 to 6 m) high. The leaves are broad and dark green. Flowers, borne in dense panicles in the upper leaf axils, measure rather less than 1 in (2.5 cm) across. It makes a bushy shrub that could be used as a screen or shelter plant in subtropical to tropical gardens. ZONES 10–12.

Cordia sebestena

Cordyline australis 'Albertii'

Cordyline australis

CORDYLINE
CABBAGE TREE, TI

Centered in the southwest Pacific region (one species in tropical America), most species of this genus of 15 or so species of somewhat palm-like evergreen shrubs and small trees are tropical or subtropical, but a few of the New Zealand species are moderately frost hardy. Cordylines resemble dracaenas in habit and foliage, but differ in the flowers which are small and starry, borne in large panicles, and in the red, black or whitish fruits. A peculiarity is their underground rhizome that grows downward, sometimes emerging through the drainage apertures of a pot; its main function appears to be food storage.
CULTIVATION: Cordylines do well in rich, well-drained soil. The narrower-leafed New Zealand species are the most sun hardy, and *Cordyline australis* tolerates salt spray near the ocean; the species with broader, thinner leaves prefer a sheltered position in part shade, though will tolerate full sun if humidity is high. Most can be kept in pots or tubs for many years as indoor or patio plants. Easily propagated from seed or stem cuttings.

Cordyline australis
syn. ***Dracaena australis***
NEW ZEALAND CABBAGE TREE, TI KOUKA

This striking New Zealand native is moderately frost hardy, occurring in some of that country's southernmost areas. The seedlings, with very narrow, elegantly arching leaves, are sold as indoor plants and last for years in this juvenile state; planted outdoors they begin to form a trunk and the brownish green leaves can be almost 3 ft (1 m) long and 2 in (5 cm) wide. The first large panicle of small white sweet-scented flowers, opening in summer, terminates the stem at a height of 6–8 ft (1.8–2.4 m); the stem then branches into several leaf rosettes, each in time flowering and branching again. It is the largest species, frequently reaching over 20 ft (6 m) tall with a stout trunk. **'Purpurea'** with bronze purplish leaves is popular. **'Albertii'**, a variegated cultivar with leaves striped cream, more pinkish on new growths, is less vigorous. ZONES 8–11.

Coprosma repens

Coprosma repens

Coprosma repens cultivar

Coprosma repens 'Gold Splash'

Coprosma repens 'Pink Splendor'

Cordyline banksii

Cordyline stricta

Coreopsis grandiflora

Cordyline banksii
TI NGAHERE

Also from New Zealand, this compact tree resembles *Cordyline australis* but has slightly broader, softer leaves, up to 3 in (8 cm) wide. It is usually a large shrub of about 10 ft (3 m) with a similar spread. The small, fragrant white flowers in long drooping panicles appear in late spring and summer. It does best in a protected position with regular water in the warm months. **ZONES 9–11.**

Cordyline fruticosa
syn. ***Cordyline terminalis***
TI NGAHERE

This well known species probably originated somewhere in the vicinity of Papua New Guinea but was long ago spread through the Pacific by Melanesians and Polynesians, who valued its starchy rhizomes as food. It grows to at least 10 ft (3 m) high, forming quite a strong, branched trunk, but is more often seen as a 3–6 ft (1–1.8 m) shrub in gardens or as a house plant. The thin, lance-shaped leaves are up to 30 in (75 cm) long and 6 in (15 cm) wide, clustered at the top of

Cordyline fruticosa cultivar

Coreopsis auriculata 'Nana'

the stem. The 12 in (30 cm) panicles of small, scented, white to dull mauve flowers, borne in summer, may be followed by crowded red berries. The many colored and variegated foliage forms are favorite landscaping plants in the tropics; they vary also in leaf size and shape. **'Imperialis'** has dark green leaves streaked pink and crimson. **ZONES 10–12.**

Cordyline indivisa
MOUNTAIN CABBAGE TREE, TOII, BLUE DRACAENA

Cordyline indivisa grows to 20 ft (6 m) in the wild, its stout trunk topped with clumps of heavily ribbed, light to mid-green leaves commonly 4–6 ft (1.2–1.8 m) long and 3–5 in (8–12 cm) wide. The small white flowers, massed on panicles 24–36 in (60–90 cm) long, appear in spring or early summer. It requires a cool, moist climate and does well in coastal fog belts. Light shade is best for young plants. **ZONES 9–10.**

Cordyline stricta
SLENDER PALM LILY

This shrub from subtropical eastern Australia makes a clump of weak cane-like stems to 6–8 ft (1.8–2.4 m) high with dark green, strap-like, floppy leaves no more than ¾ in (18 mm) wide. It reaches about the same height grown in a pot but makes a sparser plant. Long, drooping panicles of pale purplish flowers appear in late spring and early summer, followed by small black berries. It does best in moist, sheltered positions and is very shade tolerant. **ZONES 10–12.**

COREOPSIS

Around 80 species of annuals and perennials from cooler or drier regions

Cordyline indivisa

of the Americas make up this genus of the daisy family. The flowerheads, borne on slender stems mainly in summer, are mostly shades of gold or yellow, some bicolored. Leaves vary from simple and narrow, usually toothed, to deeply divided, and may be basal or scattered up the stems.

CULTIVATION: The annuals are grown as bedding plants, while the perennials are excellent for herbaceous borders. Perennials prefer full sun and a fertile, well-drained soil but also grow well in coastal regions and in poor, stony soil. Propagate by division of old clumps in winter or spring, or by spring cuttings. Annuals also prefer full sun and a fertile, well-drained soil; they will not tolerate a heavy clay soil. Taller varieties may need staking. Propagate from seed in spring or fall (autumn).

Coreopsis auriculata

This is a frost-hardy but short-lived perennial from southeastern USA that will grow to a height of 18 in (45 cm). The flowerheads are a rich yellow, produced through summer. The leaves are oval or lance-shaped. There are several improved forms, such as **'Perry's Variety'**, which has semi-double flowers. **'Nana'** is a compact form growing to 6 in (15 cm) tall. **ZONES 4–9.**

Coreopsis grandiflora
TICKSEED

Among the easiest of perennials, this bright golden-yellow daisy from southeastern and central USA provides color from late spring to mid-summer. Somewhat hairy leaves and stems form a loose mound to 12–24 in (30–60 cm) tall and

Coreopsis lanceolata

wide, the flower stems rising to nearly 24 in (60 cm) or usually flopping on their neighbors. Best suited to a meadow garden, it can be treated as an annual and self-seeds freely. Cultivars of more compact habit such as **'Badengold'**, **'Sunray'** or **'Early Sunrise'** are the best choices for the well-maintained border. **ZONES 6–10.**

Coreopsis lanceolata

Also from southeastern and central USA, this is a tufted perennial with long-stalked, lance-shaped basal leaves and bright golden-yellow flowerheads on leafy stems up to about 24 in (60 cm) high. It is extremely floriferous and when mass planted can make sheets of gold in spring and early summer. Short lived, it is very free-seeding, to the point that it has become an environmental weed in parts of Australia, on very poor soils. Double forms are sometimes grown. **'Baby Sun'** is a compact long blooming cultivar about 12 in (30 cm) high; suitable for bedding. **ZONES 3–11.**

Coreopsis maritima
syn. ***Leptosyne maritima***
WINTER MARGUERITE, SEA DAHLIA

Different from the other species here described, this perennial comes from coastal southern California. It grows to 30 in (75 cm) high and has a bushy habit with the stem rather succulent at the base and fern-like deeply divided leaves. Long flowering, it bears 4 in (10 cm) wide, yellow flowerheads on long bare stalks in late winter and spring. It can be treated as an annual and is sold in seed packets as 'leptosyne'. **ZONES 8–10.**

Coreopsis tinctoria
TICKSEED, PLAINS COREOPSIS, CALLIOPSIS

This fast-growing, showy annual produces clusters of bright yellow flowerheads with red centers throughout summer and fall (autumn). Of slender,

Coreopsis tinctoria

Coreopsis lanceolata 'Baby Sun'

Coreopsis verticillata 'Moonbeam'

weak habit, it grows to a height of 24–36 in (60–90 cm). The plants tend to incline over and may need staking. It provides good cut flowers. The species has a wide natural distribution in North America. **ZONES 4–10.**

Coreopsis verticillata

From southeastern USA, this perennial species produces crowded erect stems to 30 in (75 cm) tall from a tangled mass of thin rhizomes; the leaves, in whorls of 3, are divided into very narrow segments. The abundant bright yellow flowerheads are borne from late spring until fall (autumn). This species does best in light soil of low fertility. **'Moonbeam'** is slightly lower and more compact with lemon-yellow blooms. **ZONES 6–10.**

CORIANDRUM

Only 2 species make up this western Mediterranean genus of annuals in the carrot family, one of them renowned as a flavoring herb, now most widely employed in the cuisines of Southeast Asia and the Middle East. The plants have a fleshy tap root and much-divided leaves, the leaflets becoming much finer close beneath the umbels of numerous small white flowers.

CULTIVATION: The common coriander is the only species grown, usually in the herb garden. It requires a light but fertile, well-drained soil and full sun. Propagate from seed in early spring.

Coriandrum sativum

CORIANDER, KETUMBAR

This herb is grown mainly for its seed and aromatic leaves, although in Thai cuisine the whole of the coriander plant, including the roots, is used. It is a fast-growing annual reaching to 75 cm (about 30 in) high with parsley-like leaves and umbels of tiny white flowers in summer. The flowers are followed by small, round, aromatic seeds. Fresh leaves provide an exotic tang in Asian dishes. The dried seeds are used in curry powders, chutneys, confectionery, cakes and sauces. **ZONES 7–12.**

CORIARIA

A small genus of about 30 species of subshrubs, shrubs and small trees, *Coriaria* has a puzzling, patchy distribution around the world—New Zealand and South America account for most species, but others occur in Mexico, East Asia, the Mediterranean and Papua New Guinea. They have angled branchlets and

Coriaria japonica

usually a neat 2-rowed arrangement of the oval leaves. Flowers are inconspicuous, in short to long lateral spikes, but the tiny petals enlarge greatly after flowering, becoming thick, fleshy and colored enclosing the very small true fruits. The 'fruits' are poisonous and hallucinogenic, and have been used as an insecticide. Some species yield useful dyes.

CULTIVATION: They are easily grown in any normal garden soil, though appreciating some shelter. Most cultivated species will tolerate light to moderate frosts and even if damaged by frost will shoot again from the base if soil has not frozen. Propagate from seed, cuttings or by root division.

Coriaria japonica

From Japan, this species is a low subshrub with arching stems that makes a good ground cover. It has conspicuous red fruit and the leaves color well in fall (autumn). **ZONES 8–10.**

CORNUS

CORNEL, DOGWOOD

About 45 species of shrubs, trees and even 1 or 2 herbaceous perennials make up this genus, widely distributed in temperate regions of the northern hemisphere. They include deciduous and evergreen species, all with simple, smooth-edged leaves that characteristically have prominent, inward-curving veins. Flowers are small, mostly greenish, yellowish or dull purplish: few are decorative, but in one group of species they are arranged in dense heads surrounded by large white, pink or yellow bracts that can be showy. Another shrubby group has small panicles of flowers that are not at all showy, but the stems and twigs are often bright red or yellow, giving a decorative effect especially when leafless in winter. One such species is the common European dogwood, *Cornus sanguinea.* The fleshy fruits are also ornamental.

Coriandrum sativum

CULTIVATION: The various species all do best in sun or very light shade. Most appreciate a rich, fertile, well-drained soil, though some of the multi-stemmed shrub species will grow well in boggy ground. Many are quite frost hardy but *Cornus capitata* will tolerate only light frosts. The species with decorative red stems can be cut back annually almost to ground level to encourage new growths, which have the best color. Propagate from seed or rooted layers struck in a moist sand-peat mixture.

Cornus alba

RED-BARKED DOGWOOD, TATARIAN DOGWOOD

Shiny red branches and twigs, brightest in winter or late fall (autumn), are the feature of this northeast Asian deciduous shrub. It makes a dense thicket of slender stems 6–10 ft (1.8–3 m) high and often twice that in spread, with lower branches suckering or taking root on the ground. In late spring and summer it bears small clusters of creamy yellow flowers, followed by pea-sized white or blue-tinted fruit. It thrives in damp ground and is effective by lakes and streams. Cultivars include **'Elegantissima'**, with gray-green leaves partly white on their margins; **'Sibirica'**, with bright red leaves and stems; and **'Spaethii'**, with brilliantly gold-variegated leaves. **ZONES 4–9.**

Cornus alternifolia

GREEN OSIER, PAGODA DOGWOOD

From eastern USA and Canada, this species shares with the Asiatic *Cornus controversa* the distinction of having leaves arranged alternately, all other species of *Cornus* having them in opposite pairs. It is an attractive deciduous tree of up to 25 ft (8 m) with a layered or tiered

Cornus canadensis

Coriandrum sativum

arrangement of branchlets. In late spring it bears small clusters of cream flowers, followed by attractive bunches of blue-black berries on red stalks. The fall (autumn) foliage colors reddish. **'Argentea'** has leaves variegated with white, but is a weak grower. **ZONES 3–9.**

Cornus canadensis

syn. ***Chamaepericlymenum canadense***

CREEPING DOGWOOD, BUNCHBERRY, CRACKERBERRY

From eastern North America, this herbaceous species has its Eurasian counterpart in the subarctic *Cornus suecica.* Springing from a network of rhizomes, the stems form a thick mat, dying back each winter; each 4–8 in (10–20 cm) stem has a terminal rosette of deeply veined leaves, from the center of which appear the small cream flowerheads in summer, each with 4 conspicuous white bracts. The flowers are followed by bright red edible fruit in tight clusters. A woodland plant, it likes very sheltered, moist, cool conditions and can cover acres of ground. **ZONES 2–8.**

Cornus capitata

syns ***Benthamia fragifera, Dendrobenthamia capitata***

HIMALAYAN STRAWBERRY TREE, EVERGREEN DOGWOOD, BENTHAM'S CORNUS

From the Himalayas and China, this evergreen dogwood makes a rounded, low-branched tree of 30 ft (9 m) after many years, with dense grayish green foliage. In late spring and early summer its canopy is decked with massed flowerheads, each with 4 large bracts of a beautiful soft lemon-yellow. In fall (autumn) it has large, juicy (but tasteless), scarlet compound fruit. **ZONES 8–10.**

Cornus capitata

Cornus alba

Cornus controversa
TABLE DOGWOOD, GIANT DOGWOOD

Native to China, Korea and Japan, this handsome deciduous species makes a tree to about 40 ft (12 m) with age, with a straight trunk and horizontal tiers of foliage. The glossy, strongly veined leaves are arranged alternately on the reddish twigs, a feature shared by *Cornus alternifolia* only. In bloom it is one of the showiest of the species lacking large bracts, with white flowers in flat clusters about 4 in (10 cm) across borne in early summer. The fruit are shiny black, and fall (autumn) foliage is red to purplish. **'Variegata'** has leaves with creamy white margins. **ZONES 6–9.**

Cornus 'Eddie's White Wonder'

This hybrid between *Cornus florida* and *C. nuttalli* is a deciduous large shrub or small tree with an upright habit. Its small globular flowerheads produced in spring are each surrounded by 4 pure white bracts up to 3 in (8 cm) long. The leaves often color well in fall (autumn). **ZONES 6–9.**

Cornus kousa

Cornus florida
FLOWERING DOGWOOD

Popular for its beauty and reliability, this species reaches 20 ft (6 m) or more tall with a single, somewhat crooked trunk, and in mid-spring bears an abundance of flowerheads, each with 4 large white or rose pink bracts. In late summer the scattered red fruit make a fine showing, and in fall (autumn) the foliage is scarlet and deep purple with a whitish bloom on the leaf undersides. *Cornus florida* prefers a warm summer and may not flower well in cool-summer climates. **'Rubra'** has dark rose bracts that are paler at the base. **'Apple Blossom'** has pale pink flower bracts. **ZONES 5–9.**

Cornus kousa
JAPANESE FLOWERING DOGWOOD, KOUSA

Occurring wild in Japan, China and Korea, *Cornus kousa* can reach 20 ft (6 m) or more at maturity with dense, deep green foliage and tiered lower branches. In early summer when the leaves have fully expanded, the flowerheads with large, pure white bracts appear, each bract tapering to an acute point. The small compound fruit are dull red. As popular in gardens as the typical Japanese race is ***C. k.* var. *chinensis***, with slightly larger 'flowers' and more vigorous growth. **ZONES 6–9.**

Cornus kousa

Cornus kousa var. *chinensis*

Cornus florida

Cornus controversa

Cornus controversa 'Variegata'

Cornus mas
CORNELIAN CHERRY

When it flowers in late winter or early spring on the leafless branches, this tree species looks unlike most other dogwoods. The flowers are tiny and golden yellow, grouped in small clusters without decorative bracts, but so profuse on the small twigs as well as on thicker branches, that they make a fine display. Stiff and rather narrow at first, with maturity it becomes a spreading tree of 25 ft (8 m) or so. Edible fruit ripen bright red in late summer. Native to central and southeastern Europe, *Cornus mas* provides much-needed winter color for streets, parks and gardens. **'Variegata'** has white-margined leaves. **ZONES 6–9.**

Cornus 'Norman Hadden'

A hybrid between *Cornus kousa* and *C. capitata* that arose in the Somerset garden of Norman Hadden in the 1960s. It is a small, semi-evergreen tree of graceful, spreading habit, closer to *C. capitata* in both flower and fruit. Flowerheads open in mid-summer and the bracts later turn pinkish. An abundant crop of strawberry-like fruit are produced in fall (autumn). Some leaves may persist in winter and in mild areas even until the following spring; others turn red in fall. **ZONES 7–9.**

Cornus florida 'Rubra'

Cornus mas

Cornus nuttallii
PACIFIC DOGWOOD

In the wild, in the Pacific Northwest of North America, this is a slender tree to 50 ft (15 m), but in gardens is often only a tall shrub. The flowerheads are 4–5 in (10–12 cm) across with 4 to 7 pure white bracts, ageing pinkish, and the small cluster of flowers at their center is dull purple. Flowering occurs from mid-spring to early summer. The fall (autumn) foliage is yellow and red. This beautiful but short-lived tree is somewhat frost tender, but thrives in a cool, rainy climate in a part-shaded position. **ZONES 7–9.**

Cornus 'Norman Hadden'

Cornus 'Porlock'

This is a small spreading tree, similar to 'Norman Hadden'—it arose in the same garden, where the original plant still grows, and may have the same parentage. **ZONES 7–9.**

Cornus pumila
DWARF DOGWOOD

This unusual miniature species appeared in European gardens in the nineteenth century, but its origin is unknown. It has cane-like stems and inconspicuous flowers, and forms a dense mound of crowded suckers about 24 in (60 cm) high and twice as wide. The small pointed to oval leaves are slightly bronze tinted, turning bronze-yellow in fall (autumn). In winter the mass of fine reddish twigs is revealed. **ZONES 5–9.**

Cornus stolonifera
syn. ***Cornus sericea***
RED-OSIER DOGWOOD

This shrubby species is similar to *Cornus alba* but native to eastern North America and has a tendency to spread faster into large clumps. The winter stems are bright red, as are the fruit, while the flowers are white. Both species make excellent winter accent plants against white snow or dark evergreens. **'Flaviramea'** has yellow winter stems; **'Kelsey Gold'** has bright yellowish green leaves; **'Silver and Gold'** has variegated leaves with yellow winter stems. **ZONES 2–10.**

COROKIA

This small genus consists of 3 species of evergreen shrubs from New Zealand grown largely for their unusual angular, interlacing branch pattern. Attractive star-shaped, small yellow flowers are followed by colorful berries. Reasonably frost hardy, they suit mild coastal climates and can tolerate wind.
CULTIVATION: They should be planted in full sun or light shade and need moderately fertile, well-drained soil. A trim after flowering will maintain their shape and dense leaf growth. They are propagated from softwood cuttings in summer.

Cornus pumila

Cornus stolonifera

Coronilla emerus

Corokia buddlejoides

This densely foliaged shrub grows to about 10 ft (3 m) high and wide. It has long, narrow, bronze green leaves that are quite glossy when young. The flowers appear in spring and early summer and are followed by small red to black berries. A tough, adaptable bush that withstands regular trimming and is ideal for hedging, it also tolerates salt spray and is a very effective coastal plant. **ZONES 8–10.**

Corokia cotoneaster
WIRE-NETTING BUSH

With small, round, dark green leaves that resemble those of some small-leafed cotoneasters and a tangle of wiry, zigzagging branches that give rise to its common name, this species grows to 8 ft (2.4 m). It bears small, lightly fragrant flowers at most times of the year but most profusely in late spring and summer, followed in fall (autumn) by fleshy orange and red berries. **ZONES 8–10.**

Corokia × *virgata*

Originating in the wild as spontaneous crosses between *Corokia buddleioides* and *C. cotoneaster*, this hybrid is variable but its botanical characters are generally intermediate between the 2 parents. It bears its flowers in spring and early summer, followed by bright orange, egg-shaped berries. The glossy green leaves have a downy undersurface. It grows to a height and spread of 10 ft (3 m) and adapts to most soils and conditions, doing best in full sun. Cultivars include: **'Red Wonder'**, with bright red berries; **'Yellow Wonder'**, with golden berries; and **'Bronze Lady'**, so-called for its leaf color in maturity. **ZONES 8–10.**

Cornus stolonifera 'Kelsey Gold'

Coronilla varia

Coronilla valentina

Corokia buddlejoides

CORONILLA
CROWN VETCH

A legume genus of 20 or so species of annuals, perennials and low, wiry shrubs, native to Europe, western Asia and northern Africa. They have pinnate leaves with small, thin or somewhat fleshy leaflets, and stalked umbels of small pea-flowers a little like some clover or medic flowers. Certain perennial and shrub species are grown as ornamentals, valued for their profuse flowers blooming over a long season, though not especially showy. *Coronilla* is Latin for 'little crown', referring to the neat circular umbels of some species.
CULTIVATION: They need full sun, moderately fertile, well-drained soil and protection from cold winds. Cut leggy plants back to the base in spring. Propagate from seed, cuttings, or division of rootstock.

Coronilla emerus
SCORPION SENNA, FALSE SENNA

Of wide natural distribution in Europe, this low, somewhat sprawling deciduous shrub has bright yellow flowers borne in small groups from the leaf axils in spring. They are followed by slender seed pods that are articulated, like a scorpion's tail. The leaves are small with few, rounded, bright green leaflets. Normally less than 3 ft (1 m) high it will sometimes reach twice this height. **ZONES 6–9.**

Coronilla valentina
syn. ***Coronilla glauca***

This bushy, often short-lived evergreen shrub is a native of the Mediterranean region. If grown in a sunny spot in well-drained soil it will thrive and bear pretty heads of yellow, fragrant flowers in late winter and early spring and again in late summer. The leaves are dark green and have up to 13 leaflets. It grows to a height and spread a little over 5 ft (1.5 m). ***Coronilla valentina* subsp. *glauca*** has blue-green leaves with 5 to 7 leaflets. The epithet *valentina* means 'of Valencia' (Spain). **ZONES 9–10.**

Corokia × *virgata*

Coronilla varia
syn. ***Securigera varia***
CROWN VETCH

A sprawling perennial from Europe, crown vetch has run wild in some parts of the USA. It can spread quite rapidly by a deep network of thin rhizomes, the weak leafy stems rising to about 24 in (60 cm) tall. The soft pinnate leaves resemble those of the true vetches (*Vicia*) and the clover-like heads of pink to lilac-pink flowers appear throughout summer. Not suited to a formal garden, it can be rather invasive, but makes a good soil-binding plant for a sunny bank, stopping erosion while slower plants take hold. Some botanists now place it in the genus *Securigera*. **ZONES 6–10.**

Correa lawrenciana

Correa 'Mannii'

Correa reflexa 'Fat Fred'

Correa 'Dusky Bells'

Correa alba

CORREA

AUSTRALIAN FUCHSIA

This small Australian genus allied to *Boronia* consists of 11 species of evergreen shrubs, mostly of irregular habit, some semi-prostrate. They have smallish leaves arranged on the stems in opposite pairs, mostly felted with hairs on the underside and showing translucent oil dots when viewed against the light. The flowers, mostly borne singly in leaf axils, are bell-shaped or tubular with a thin felt of hairs on the outside and protruding stamens. Their habitats vary, some growing in cool, shaded spots near streams and under trees, others on exposed ocean headlands or dunes. The flowers attract nectar-feeding birds. The genus name honors the Portuguese botanist and diplomat José Francesco Correia da Serra, friend of Sir Joseph Banks.

CULTIVATION: Correas are not fussy, adapting to most mild, non-tropical climates. They do best in sun or part-shade in moderately fertile, free-draining but moist soil. Some species are inclined to be short lived, and plants should be replaced every 3–5 years. Tip prune to promote densely leafed bushes. Propagate from cuttings.

Correa alba

WHITE CORREA

A coastal shrub from southeastern Australia (including Tasmania), *Correa alba* grows on rocky sea-cliffs and sand dunes. It is a compact, spreading shrub to 5 ft (1.5 m) high with thick, rounded, gray-green leaves, downy underneath. The white flowers are borne mainly from late summer to early winter; they do not have a long tube as in most correas, but the 4 petals roll back into a star shape as the flower expands. This species is useful for mass planting in coastal gardens to bind the sand. **ZONES 9–10.**

Correa backhousiana

From coasts of Tasmania, this species resembles *Correa alba* in foliage and growth habit, making a densely spreading shrub about 4 ft (1.2 m) high. The thick, rounded leaves are about 1 in (25 mm) in length, with felty undersides. The solitary or clustered flowers are tubular, 1 in (25 mm) long, cream to pale green in color, and produced through winter. This species adapts to most soils and can tolerate salt spray as well as wet ground for short periods. **ZONES 8–10.**

Correa 'Dusky Bells'

Of uncertain origin but possibly a hybrid between *Correa pulchella* and *C. reflexa*, this spreading, dense shrub takes its name from the delightful dusky deep pink, narrowly bell-shaped flowers that appear from fall (autumn) to spring. It grows to 24 in (60 cm) with a spread of 3 ft (1 m). **ZONES 9–10.**

Correa lawrenciana

MOUNTAIN CORREA

The most variable *Correa* species as well as the tallest, *C. lawrenciana* is divided into 7 varieties based mainly on leaf width and flower color, ranging through wetter parts of southeastern Australia from the Queensland border southward, including Tasmania. Of erect habit, it occurs mainly in tall, mountain eucalypt forest or rainforest, and the tallest specimens are known to reach heights of 30 ft (9 m). Flowers are little more than 1 in (25 mm) long and rather narrow, from green to creamy yellow or dull reddish, pendent on fine stalks and with protruding stamens. It is an interesting but hardly showy shrub for sheltered situations. **ZONES 9–11.**

Correa 'Mannii'

This is a small to medium shrub, 3–4 ft (1–1.2 m) high with small, hairless leaves and tubular flowers about 2 in (5 cm) in length, red on the outside and pale pink inside, with reflexed tips. It is suspected to be of hybrid origin, the parents possibly *Correa pulchella* and *C. reflexa*. **ZONES 9–10.**

Correa pulchella

SALMON CORREA

Pulchella is Latin for 'pretty', which aptly describes this species from coastal South Australia. Occurring on better soils in sheltered places along stream banks, it is a semi-prostrate to erect, densely leafy shrub less than 3 ft (1 m) high. From fall (autumn) to spring it bears a profusion of attractive 1 in (25 mm) long bells in shades of pink, salmon or orange. **ZONES 9–10.**

Correa reflexa

COMMON CORREA, AUSTRALIAN FUCHSIA

This is the most widely distributed species of *Correa*, ranging from southern Queensland to Tasmania and South Australia, and from coastal dunes to semi-arid hills of the interior. Its habit can be prostrate or upright, from 12 in (30 cm) to more than 4 ft (1.2 m) in height. Leaves are in widely spaced pairs, rather harsh-textured and scattered with small rusty hair tufts, as are the outsides of the nodding or pendent flowers; these are tubular to bell-shaped, 1–1½ in (25–38 mm) long with the 4 petal tips gently reflexed. The color is variable, most commonly deep red with pale green tips, but pink and cream flowered forms are also found. **'Fat Fred'** is a cultivar with exceptionally wide, swollen, pink flowers with green tips; **'Salmon'** has slender salmon-pink flowers. **ZONES 9–10.**

Correa backhousiana

Correa schlechtendalii

From the dry, sandy inland of eastern South Australia, this upright shrub is 3–6 ft (1–1.8 m) tall with thin, almost hairless small leaves. Borne from fall (autumn) to late winter, the flowers are narrowly bell-shaped, well under 1 in (25 mm) long, pink or red with green tips and with prominently protruding stamens. This is a very adaptable shrub, pretty when in flower. **ZONES 9–10.**

CORTADERIA

This genus of giant tussock-forming evergreen perennial grasses contains around 20 species native to South America, 4 to New Zealand and one to Papua New Guinea. The leaves are long and finely tapering, of harsh texture and with sharp edges, and the tall flowering stems are reed-like and carry long terminal plumes of white to silvery or pinkish seedheads. Several of the larger South American species are known as 'pampas grass', a reference to the *pampas*—the grass plains extending across that continent's central southern region.The genus name comes from these grasses' Spanish-American name *cortadera*, the 'cutter', from their sharp leaves. They make striking ornamental plants, though the fashion for them has waned as gardeners discover the difficulty of maintaining them. In temperate southern hemisphere countries in higher-rainfall areas, they have become ecological weeds, invading native vegetation even without any human intervention. Worst as weeds are the well known *Cortaderia selloana*,

Correa pulchella

Cortaderia selloana

Corydalis flexuosa

which needs plants of both sexes to produce seed, and the very similar *C. jubata* which produces apomictic seed, that is seed which does not require fertilization.
CULTIVATION: Pampas grass is easily grown in any open sunny position, in almost any soil as long as moisture is adequate. It tolerates exposure to strong winds and even to salt spray. With age a clump will build up unsightly dead leaves and old flowering stems; if circumstances allow, these can be disposed of by setting fire to the clump in fall (autumn) or winter, otherwise it should be cut back 12 in (30 cm) or so high, preferably with a motorized slasher. Propagate by division of selected forms or cultivars, or from seed if obtainable.

Cortaderia selloana
syns *Cortaderia argentea, Gynerium argenteum*
PAMPAS GRASS

Native to Argentina and southern Brazil, this stately grass grows to a height of 10 ft (3 m) and similar spread, the pale green, rustling foliage forming a dense tangled clump about 6 ft (1.8 m) high. In summer and fall (autumn) the striking plume-like panicles appear above the leaves on pole-like stems, consisting of vast numbers of small silky spikelets varying in color from creamy white to purplish pink. In some regions this species has become very invasive. A number of clones have been named as cultivars. **'Aureolineata'** has bright green leaves with deep yellow edges. **ZONES 6–10.**

CORYDALIS

The 300 or so species that make up this genus, allied to the fumitories (*Fumaria*), occur widely as natives in temperate regions of the northern hemisphere, though with the greatest concentration in mountains of eastern Asia. They include some annuals but are mostly perennials, with basal tufts of ferny,

Cortaderia selloana 'Aureolineata'

deeply dissected leaves springing from fleshy rhizomes or tubers. The smallish tubular flowers have a short backward-pointing spur that may be curved; they are usually grouped in short spikes or clusters and come in a range of colors, mostly creams, yellows, pinks and purples but a few have clear blue flowers.
CULTIVATION: The sun-loving species do very well in rock gardens, while the shade lovers are best planted beneath shrubs in a border, or in a woodland garden. Soil should be well drained but moisture-retentive, rich in humus for the woodland species. Several species, such as *Corydalis lutea,* self-seed freely, coming up in cracks between paving or on walls. Propagate from seed or by division.

Corydalis cashmeriana

Native to the Himalayas, this tuberous perennial is one of the small group of species with brilliant blue flowers. It makes tufts of fresh green foliage and in summer the short flower spikes grow to 8–12 in (20–30 cm) high. Flowers are about ½ in (12 mm) long, with curved spurs. This species prefers a shaded, humid position in moist soil. **ZONES 5–9.**

Corydalis cava
syn. *Corydalis bulbosa*

From central Europe, this is an early spring-flowering, tuberous perennial 4–8 in (10–20 cm) high. The epithet *cava* means 'hollow' and refers to the tuber and stem base, which are hollow. The species is unusual in having no basal leaves but only 2 smallish, dissected leaves on each erect stem, which terminates in a crowded spike of pale purple to white flowers about 1 in (25 mm) long with short, curved spurs. It tends to die down in summer. **ZONES 6–9.**

Corydalis flexuosa

Another blue-flowered species, in this case from western China, which in size and profusion of its clear blue flowers outshines *Corydalis cashmeriana.* It forms a small clump of green foliage around 12 in (30 cm) tall, from which emerge in late spring and early summer short spikes of long-spurred tubular blue flowers, each flower about 1 in (25 mm) long. It requires a cool spot in part-shade and moist soil. **ZONES 5–9.**

Corylopsis glabrescens

Corydalis lutea
YELLOW CORYDALIS

The most easily cultivated species, this native of Europe's southern Alps region is widely naturalized in temperate climates around the world. A rhizomatous perennial, it makes broad clumps or mounds of fresh green foliage, to about 12 in (30 cm) high, and is dotted from spring to fall (autumn) with short sprays of soft yellow flowers. It will grow in many situations but often self-seeds in wall crevices or moist chinks in rockeries. In a woodland garden it makes an attractive ground cover. **ZONES 6–10.**

Corydalis solida
FUMEWORT

This species from northern Europe and Asia is similar to *Corydalis cava* differing, as its name suggests, in having a solid, not hollow, tuber and stem base. Each 6–10 in (15–25 cm) erect stem has only 2 or 3 dissected leaves, one at the base, and terminates in a dense spike of pink to purplish red flowers in spring. It dies back in summer. The cultivar **'George Baker'** has rich salmon-red flowers. **ZONES 6–9.**

Corydalis wilsonii

This species from China forms low mounds of blue-green foliage to 8 in (20 cm) high and wide. Loose spikes of bright yellow flowers are borne in spring. **ZONES 7–9.**

Corydalis lutea

CORYLOPSIS
WINTER HAZEL

These deciduous shrubs from China and Japan produce short, usually pendulous spikes of fragrant, 5-petalled, pale yellow or greenish flowers on the bare branches before the blunt-toothed leaves appear in late spring. The fruits, ripening in summer among the leaves, are small, woody capsules each containing 2 black seeds. The subtle appeal of these shrubs lies mostly in the repetitive pattern of flower spikes on the bare branches.
CULTIVATION: They are best suited to a woodland setting in a reasonably moist, cool climate, providing a foil for bolder shrubs such as rhododendrons. The soil should be fertile, moist but well-drained and acid. Propagation is normally from seed.

Corylopsis glabrescens
FRAGRANT WINTER HAZEL

Native to Japan where it grows in the mountains, this species makes a broadly spreading shrub of 15 ft (4.5 m) tall, sometimes more. The small flowers are lemon yellow with rather narrow petals and appear in mid-spring. **ZONES 6–9.**

Corylopsis pauciflora
BUTTERCUP WINTER HAZEL

As the specific name suggests, there are very few flowers to each spike on this native of Japan and Taiwan, but they open more widely and are a clearer yellow color than those of most other *Corylopsis* species, smelling of cowslips and borne from early to mid-spring. It has a spreading habit, reaching a height of 4–6 ft (1.2–1.8 m), with slender branches and bronze new growths. It does best in a very sheltered position. **ZONES 7–9.**

Corydalis wilsonii

Corylopsis pauciflora

C

Corylopsis sinensis

From western China, this is a variable species with several forms distinguished by name. It makes a spreading shrub 10–15 ft (3–4.5 m) high with pointed leaves. The flowers, borne in mid-spring on crowded spikes, have broad-tipped pale yellowish green petals with orange anthers. It is one of the most ornamental species. ***Corylopsis sinensis* f. *veitchiana*** is lower growing; the flowers have darker reddish anthers and there are fewer of them on the flower spikes. **ZONES 6–9.**

Corylopsis spicata

SPIKE WINTER HAZEL

This species from Japan was the first one known in the West. It is low growing, seldom exceeding 6 ft (1.8 m) and often less, and broadly spreading. The narrow, pale greenish yellow, spring flowers have red anthers, the short spikes bursting from particularly large, pale green bracts which persist on the spikes. The arrangement of flowers is more informal than that of some other species. **ZONES 6–9.**

CORYLUS

HAZEL, FILBERT

Ten or more species from temperate regions of the northern hemisphere make up this genus of deciduous trees and large shrubs, best known for their edible nuts. The commonly grown species have massed stems springing from ground level, but some others have a well developed trunk; the branches are tough and supple and the toothed leaves broad, somewhat heart-shaped and strongly veined. Male and female flowers grow on the same plant, the male in slender, pendulous catkins that shed their pollen before the leaves expand, the female in inconspicuous, small greenish clusters at the branch tips. The latter develop into the distinctive nuts, each enclosed in a fringed green husk and ripening in summer.
CULTIVATION: Plants are easily grown provided soil moisture is adequate and ample space is allowed. They need full sun or part-shade and fertile, well-drained, chalky soil. Propagation is often possible by detaching suckers, or by fresh nuts. For fruit set there is a cold requirement during winter of around 1,000 hours below 45°F (7°C), and cool, moist summers also assist nut production.

Corylopsis sinensis

Corylopsis spicata

Corylus avellana

COMMON HAZEL, COBNUT, EUROPEAN FILBERT

The common hazel occurs through most of Europe (including the UK) as well as in western Asia and northern Africa. It typically makes a broad mass of stems about 12–15 ft (3.5–4.5 m) high. In winter the bare twigs are draped with the developing male catkins, which start to show their yellow pollen at winter's end, making quite a display. The ripening nut is enclosed in a green, fringed tube that leaves the end of the nut showing. In fall (autumn) the leaves turn pale yellow. **'Contorta'** is a bizarre cultivar with branches that wander and wriggle in all directions; when leafless they are cut for sale by florists. **ZONES 4–9.**

Corylus maxima

FILBERT

The filbert, a native of southern Europe, is similar in most respects to the hazel but is more inclined to become tree-like and has sticky hairs on the young twigs. The most obvious difference, though, is the much longer tubular husk completely enclosing each nut, which is also more elongated. As an ornamental it is best known by the cultivar **'Purpurea'**, which has deep, dark purple, spring foliage, softening to a dull greenish purple in summer. **ZONES 4–9.**

Corylus avellana

Corymbia calophylla

CORYMBIA

The 113 species of trees from Australia and Papua New Guinea that make up this newly recognized genus are still treated as 'eucalypts' in the broad sense. Mainly tropical, they comprise mostly the 'bloodwood' group of eucalypts with soft, crumbly or corky bark and cream, pink or red flowers carried in showy clusters at tips of branches—the spectacular red-flowering gum of Western Australia, *Corymbia ficifolia*, is a typical example. But just to confuse the issue, some 'bloodwoods' (in the botanical sense) have smooth bark, for example the well-known lemon scented gum *(C. citriodora)*. Then there is another group of species known as the 'paper-fruited bloodwoods' which produce their smaller flowers and fruits usually in the space of one tropical wet season: these are little known in cultivation but one *(C. aparrerinja)* is the well-known 'ghost gum' of Central Australia.
CULTIVATION: The species vary in their requirements and ease of cultivation. Many come from tropical regions with a short wet season, and these rarely adapt well to more temperate climates. A number have proved more adaptable, though, and are popular in cultivation. They prefer full sun, and thrive in most soils, from heavy clay to light sand. All are drought tolerant once established. They are easily propagated from seed and should be planted in their permanent positions when not more than 24 in (60 cm) high.

Corylus avellana 'Contorta'

Corylus avellana 'Contorta'

Corylus maxima

Corymbia ficifolia

Corymbia citriodora

Corymbia aparrerinja

syn. ***Eucalyptus papuana***

GHOST GUM

Found near watercourses over much of northern inland Australia and around Port Moresby in Papua New Guinea, the ghost gum is a broad-crowned, single-trunked tree to 50 ft (15 m) high with an open, domed canopy of light green, lanceolate leaves. Its common name comes from the white, smooth, chalky bark. Small clusters of white flowers are produced in summer, followed by urn-shaped fruit. Well-drained soil and a warm, frost-free climate suit it best; it is tolerant of quite dry conditions. **ZONES 10–12.**

Corymbia calophylla

syn. ***Eucalyptus calophylla***

MARRI

From the south of Western Australia, this tree can grow to 200 ft (60 m) tall, though 40–80 ft (12–24 m) is more common. The thick, straight trunk has rough, grayish brown bark, often stained with red sap. Large cream or rarely pink flowers are borne in summer and fall (autumn), followed by 1 in (25 mm), goblet-shaped seed capsules. It hybridizes readily with *Corymbia ficifolia*, the hybrids usually being pink. **ZONES 9–11.**

Corymbia citriodora

syn. ***Eucalyptus citriodora***

LEMON-SCENTED GUM

This fast-growing adaptable tree from the open forests and dry slopes of tropical northeastern Australia is widely grown in more temperate areas. Tall and straight trunked, to 100 ft (30 m), it has smooth, sometimes dimpled bark in subtle shades of white, gray or pale pink that is shed during the summer months.

The foliage is held aloft on an open crown; when crushed, the long, narrow leaves have a lemony scent. The winter flowers are creamy white. **ZONES 9–12.**

Corymbia ficifolia
syn. *Eucalyptus ficifolia*
SCARLET-FLOWERING GUM, RED-FLOWERING GUM

The most spectacular of all the flowering eucalypts, *Corymbia ficifolia* bears large terminal clusters of scarlet to orange flowers in late spring or summer, followed by large, urn-shaped fruit. (Forms with crimson or pink flowers are suspected of being hybrids of *C. calophylla*.) It grows to about 30 ft (9 m) with rough bark and a spreading crown of lance-shaped foliage. It performs best in a winter-rainfall climate. **ZONES 9–10.**

Corymbia maculata
syn. *Eucalyptus maculata*
SPOTTED GUM

This 100 ft (30 m), straight-trunked, tree of broadly columnar or conical form occurs over much of the temperate east-coastal area of Australia. It has thick, mottled, gray-green bark that is shed in patches to create a patchwork of gray, green, pink and ochre. The pointed adult leaves are up to 8 in (20 cm) long. The large white flowers appear in winter, followed by small, urn-shaped seed capsules. Spotted gum yields a valuable, close-grained timber. **ZONES 9–11.**

Corymbia ptychocarpa
syn. *Eucalyptus ptychocarpa*
SPRING BLOODWOOD

Found in the extreme north of Western Australia and the Northern Territory,

Corypha umbraculifera

Corymbia ptychocarpa

Corymbia maculata

this species grows to 50 ft (15 m) and has some of the largest leaves among the eucalypts: they are dark green and up to 12 in (30 cm) long and 5 in (12 cm) wide. The fissured, gray-brown bark does not peel readily and remains attached even to the quite small twigs. The showy flowers are borne in pendent panicles and range from white or pink to apricot or red. Large, ribbed seed capsules follow. **ZONES 11–12.**

Corymbia torelliana
syn. *Eucalyptus torelliana*
CADAGA

This species is found on edges of rainforests in northern Queensland so it is fairly frost tender, but it performs well in warm-temperate climates. It has smooth, orange-brown bark that peels attractively in early summer to reveal pale green new bark. The broad, slightly hairy pale green leaves are heart-shaped at the base. It can grow to 100 ft (30 m). The small white flowers are produced in clusters at ends of branches. **ZONES 10–12.**

CORYPHA

From tropical Asia, this genus of 6–8 species includes some of the most massive of all palms, with huge, fan-shaped fronds. Their flowering is most remarkable: the growth of a mature palm, perhaps 30 to 40 years old, is terminated by a giant panicle of millions of small flowers, towering above the crown of fronds. The flowers are followed by an equally impressive crop of marble-sized fruit and after these ripen the whole palm dies, leaving the seeds to perpetuate the species. **CULTIVATION:** These are strictly tropical palms, growing normally in full sun in alluvial soil near rivers and swamps. They are usually seen in cultivation only in large parks and botanical gardens. Seed is easily germinated but even under the best conditions it will take 10 years at least before a trunk starts to elongate.

Cosmos atrosanguineus

Corymbia aparrerinja

Corypha umbraculifera
TALIPOT PALM

A seventeenth-century English traveller in southern India reported with astonishment that this palm had '… a single leaf so broad that it will cover some 15 to 20 men and keep them dry when it rains.' One of the most massive of all palms, it has a stout trunk up to 80 ft (24 m) tall supporting a crown of fronds with thick stalks about 12 ft (3.5 m) long from which radiate fan-like blades 15 ft (4.5 m) or more in length. The terminal panicle of flowers rises about 20 ft (6 m) above the leaves, with crowded masses of white flowers on drooping lateral branches. It is common in southern India and Sri Lanka where it has many traditional uses. **ZONE 12.**

COSMOS
MEXICAN ASTER

This genus of annuals and perennials, allied to *Dahlia*, contains 25 species native to warmer parts of the Americas but mostly to Mexico. Two of the species are well known garden flowers, grown around the world, and two or three others are occasionally grown. They have erect but weak, leafy stems and the leaves are variously lobed or deeply and finely dissected. Flowerheads, on slender stalks terminating branches, are daisy-like with showy, broad ray-florets surrounding a small disc; they range in color from white through pinks, yellows, oranges, reds and purples to deep maroon. **CULTIVATION:** They are only moderately frost hardy and in cold climates need protection in winter. Seedlings should be planted out only after all danger of frost has passed. They require a sunny situation with protection from strong winds and will grow in any well-drained soil as long as it is not over-rich. Mulch with compost and water well in hot, dry weather. Propagate annuals from seed in spring or fall (autumn), the

Cosmos bipinnatus

perennials from basal cuttings in spring. Deadhead regularly, and in humid weather check for insect pests and mildew.

Cosmos atrosanguineus
BLACK COSMOS, CHOCOLATE COSMOS

A tuberous-rooted, clump-forming perennial growing to 24 in (60 cm) in height and spread, the unusual black cosmos from Mexico has long-stalked, very dark maroon flowerheads that have a chocolate scent, most noticeable on warm days. It flowers from summer to fall (autumn). The leaves are rather few-lobed and tinged dull purplish. It normally dies back in fall and requires fairly dry soil if the rootstock is not to rot; alternatively the roots can be lifted and stored for the winter like dahlias. **ZONES 8–10.**

Cosmos bipinnatus
COMMON COSMOS, MEXICAN ASTER

This feathery-leafed annual from Mexico and far southern USA reaches 5–6 ft (1.5–1.8 m) in height with showy daisy-like flowerheads in summer and fall (autumn), in shades of pink, red, purple or white. Taller plants may need staking. Newer strains are usually more compact and can have double flowers and striped petals. **'Sea Shells'** has usually pink, sometimes crimson or white flowerheads with edges of ray-florets curled into a tube. **ZONES 8–11.**

Cosmos sulphureus

YELLOW COSMOS

This annual has a more sprawling habit and coarser foliage than *Cosmos bipinnatus* and blooms in many shades of yellow and orange in summer and early fall (autumn). It is fast growing, and height varies from 24 in (60 cm) to 5 ft (1.5 m) depending on the strain. In the wild it has a wide distribution from Mexico to northern South America. **ZONES 8–11.**

COSTUS

SPIRAL FLAG, SPIRAL GINGER

Belonging to the ginger family, this genus of clump-forming evergreen perennials consists of some 150 species scattered throughout the wet tropics, though concentrated mainly in tropical America and West Africa. They have ginger-like leaves arranged in an ascending spiral around the stem, and attractive terminal flowerheads with overlapping bracts, rather like a pine cone. The flowers which emerge between the bracts are orange, yellow, pink, red or white.
CULTIVATION: They are suitable for planting outdoors only in tropical or subtropical regions. In cooler climates they make showy indoor plants but require high humidity and a heated greenhouse or conservatory in winter. Grow in humus-rich soil in a well-lit position, but not direct sunlight. Propagate by division or from seed in spring. Plants grown indoors may be affected by red spider mite.

Costus speciosus cultivar

Costus speciosus

CREPE GINGER, SPIRAL GINGER

Of wide distribution in tropical Asia, this tall-growing species has short elliptic leaves running in a conspicuous spiral up the slender cane-like stems that are themselves gently twisted into a spiral, and up to 8 ft (2.4 m) tall. The large flowerheads consist of tightly overlapping green bracts tinged reddish, and white, sometimes pinkish flowers with yellow centers and petals like silky crêpe, emerging one or two at a time over much of the year. **ZONES 11–12.**

Costus spiralis

From northern South America and the West Indies, this handsome species is similar in growth habit to *Costus speciosus* but reaches only half its height. The cylindrical flowerhead is up to 10 in (25 cm) long, with pink to scarlet flowers emerging from between crimson bracts, which are the most conspicuous feature of the plant. **ZONES 11–12.**

Cotinus coggygria

Cotinus coggygria 'Velvet Cloak'

Cotinus obovatus

Cotoneaster apiculatus

Cotoneaster dammeri 'Coral Beauty'

Cotoneaster congestus

Cotoneaster conspicuus

COTINUS

SMOKE BUSH, SMOKE TREE

Only 3 species make up this genus of deciduous shrubs or small trees: one is from temperate Eurasia, one from eastern North America, and one confined to southwestern China. They have simple, oval, untoothed leaves. Their striking feature is the inflorescences, much-branched with delicate, thread-like dull purplish branchlets, only a few of which carry the small flowers; they produce a curiously ornamental effect like fine puffs of smoke scattered over the foliage. Both flowers and fruits are tiny and inconspicuous. The foliage is another attraction, coloring deeply in fall (autumn), and in some cultivars the spring foliage offers good color. In earlier times a commercial yellow dye was extracted from the wood of these trees.
CULTIVATION: Smoke bushes are easily grown, adapting to a range of temperate climates but most at home where summers are moderately warm and dry. Soil that is too moist or fertile discourages free flowering. Propagate from softwood cuttings in summer or seed in fall.

Cotinus coggygria

syn. *Rhus cotinus*

VENETIAN SUMAC, SMOKE TREE

Of wide distribution from southern Europe to central China, this bushy shrub is usually 10–15 ft (3–4 m) in height and spread, and has oval, long-stalked leaves. The inflorescences appear in early summer and are pale pinkish bronze, ageing to a duller purple-gray. Some of the flowers produce small, dry, flattened fruit in late summer. Fall (autumn) foliage has strong orange and bronze tones. **'Purpureus'** is widely grown—it has rich, purplish spring foliage becoming greener in summer and glowing orange and purple in fall; **'Royal Purple'** is very similar but spring and summer foliage is deeper purple; the leaves of **'Velvet Cloak'** are purple and turn dark reddish purple in fall. **ZONES 6–10.**

Cotinus obovatus

syns *Cotinus americanus, Rhus cotinoides*

AMERICAN SMOKE TREE

From southeastern USA, this species can make a small tree of up to 30 ft (9 m), though may remain a tall shrub. The leaves are larger than those of *Cotinus coggygria* and bronze pink when young, turning mid-green in summer and finally orange-scarlet to purple in fall (autumn). The inflorescences are also larger but sparser, and male and female flowers are on different trees. **ZONES 5–10.**

COTONEASTER

This temperate Eurasian genus of shrubs (rarely small trees) includes both deciduous and evergreen species and is one of the small-fruited genera of the pome-fruit group of the rose family, that includes *Pyracantha, Crataegus* and *Amelanchier*. The lower-growing species are popular for rockeries, embankments and foundation plantings. They are mostly very frost hardy, often of dense, spreading habit, and provide a good display of red berries. Some species make good hedges and espaliers.
CULTIVATION: The evergreen species especially provide fine displays of berries, even in warmer-temperate climates. All do best in full sun in moderately fertile, well-drained soil. They are prone to the bacterial disease fireblight. Propagate from seed or cuttings.

Cotoneaster apiculatus

CRANBERRY COTONEASTER

From western China and growing to about 3 ft (90 cm) high, this attractive shrub blooms in early summer, the petals mostly pinkish. The flowers and fruit are carried singly along the arching branches. It is deciduous, most of the leaves turning red before falling, though in warm climates it may not be fully so. **ZONES 6–9.**

Cotoneaster microphyllus

Cotoneaster microphyllus var. *cochleatus*

Cotoneaster lacteus

Cotoneaster horizontalis

Cotoneaster congestus
syn. ***Cotoneaster pyrenaicus***
PYRENEES COTONEASTER

This evergreen shrub, native to the Himalayas, forms compact mounds of small, bluish green leaves on arching branches with densely interlocking branchlets. It is rather variable in size but normally attains a height of 24 in (60 cm) and has pinkish red solitary flowers and bright red fruit $1/3$ in (8 mm) across. **ZONES 6–9.**

Cotoneaster conspicuus
WINTERGREEN COTONEASTER

A stiffly twiggy, evergreen shrub 4–6 ft (1.2–1.8 m) high (or in some forms almost prostrate) with small, thick leaves, this species comes from the mountains of western China. A tough shrub, its brilliant red fruit are scattered profusely all along the branches through late summer and fall (autumn). The small, solitary white flowers are borne in late spring. A lower-growing form is sometimes known as **'Decorus'**, though that name has also been applied to the taller form. **ZONES 6–10.**

Cotoneaster 'Cornubia'

This is a semi-evergreen, large rounded shrub or small tree 12–20 ft (3.5–6 m) tall with arching branches and leaves up to 5 in (12 cm) long. The dense clusters of bright red fruit are often so profuse that they weigh down the branches. It was raised at Exbury in England in 1930 and may be a hybrid between *Cotoneaster frigidus* and *C. salicifolius*. **ZONES 6–9.**

Cotoneaster dammeri
BEARBERRY COTONEASTER

Most distinctive of the fully prostrate cotoneasters, this central Chinese evergreen species has relatively large, round-tipped leaves with the veins deeply impressed into their dark green upper surfaces; the scattered starry white flowers appear through summer and are followed by solitary red fruit that last well into winter, when the leaves turn bronze. The varietal name *radicans* is often added, but there is confusion as to which form of the species it belongs; all cultivated forms have very similar qualities. **'Coral Beauty'** has profuse, bright orange fruit. **ZONES 5–10.**

Cotoneaster franchetii

This attractive evergreen from western China grows to about 10 ft (3 m) tall, with long, cane-like branches. The smallish, pointed leaves have curved veins strongly impressed into the glossy upper surface and woolly undersides. In early summer it bears small clusters of pink-tinged white flowers, followed by tight groups of salmon pink to pale orange berries which last into winter. A reliable shrub, it adapts to most garden conditions, in both warm and cool climates. **ZONES 6–10.**

Cotoneaster frigidus
HIMALAYAN TREE COTONEASTER

Deciduous or semi-evergreen, *Cotoneaster frigidus* can reach 20 ft (6 m) in gardens. Normally branching near the ground into multiple trunks, it can be trained into a single-trunked tree with an umbrella-like crown. The pointed leaves may turn yellow or reddish in fall (autumn). From late summer onwards profuse sprays of red fruit deck the branches and persist well into winter. They are preceded in early summer by the less conspicuous cream flowers. This beautiful tree, from cooler parts of the Himalayas, has proved easy and adaptable. **ZONES 6–9.**

Cotoneaster glaucophyllus
syn. ***Cotoneaster serotinus***
GRAY-LEAVED COTONEASTER

This large shrub species is variable in the wild in its native west and central China, but an evergreen (or semi-evergreen) form known as ***Cotoneaster glaucophyllus* f. *serotinus*** is best known in western gardens. Branching low, it forms an irregularly shaped, 10–12 ft (3–3.5 m) shrub. The leaves are broad and rounded, at first coated in woolly white hairs on the underside, but these soon wear off leaving only a thin bluish waxy bloom. Profuse but undistinguished white flowers appear in early summer, followed by an abundance of small, glossy red fruit that may persist through winter. Self-sown seedlings are often plentiful. **ZONES 6–11.**

Cotoneaster horizontalis
ROCK COTONEASTER

Popular in cooler areas where its fine foliage takes on bronze purple, orange and reddish fall (autumn) hues, this semi-prostrate shrub has horizontal, flattened sprays of branches building up in stiff tiers with age to 3 ft (1 m) high and up to 8 ft (2.4 m) wide. The small flesh pink summer flowers are followed by much showier, deep red fruit. Native to mountain areas of western China, it is deciduous in cool climates but only semi- deciduous in warmer climates. The named forms include **'Variegatus'** with leaves edged with white; ***Cotoneaster horizontalis*** var. ***perpusillus*** is a more compact, dwarf plant with tiny leaves. **ZONES 5–10.**

Cotoneaster 'Hybridus Pendulus'

This semi-deciduous hybrid is a shrub of high ornamental value, with weak, pendulous branches and rather narrow leaves, enlivened from late summer onward by loose bunches of bright red berries. Planted on its own roots, it mounds up eventually to about 3 ft (1 m) tall, and the branches can trail effectively over walls or rocks. Alternatively, grafted onto a standard of one of the taller species, it can make an attractive weeping specimen with curtains of foliage. **ZONES 6–9.**

Cotoneaster lacteus
syn. ***Cotoneaster parneyi***
ROCKSPRAY COTONEASTER

This evergreen Chinese shrub is similar to *Cotoneaster glaucophyllus* in many respects but has a more persistent coating of wool on its leaf undersides, and more conspicuous veining on the upper. The white flowers appear early in summer, followed by a fine display of orange-red fruit in large bunches, ripening at the end of summer and persisting through winter. It adapts well to warmer climates. **ZONES 7–11.**

Cotoneaster microphyllus

This compact, densely twiggy species from the Himalayas has small, thick, glossy evergreen leaves and plump crimson to purplish red fruit from late summer to winter. Its growth habit can vary from completely prostrate to upright or mound-like, sometimes 3–4 ft (1–1.2 m) in height; mature plants have a framework of tough, woody branches. Vigorous and very frost hardy, it needs a fairly exposed location in full sun. For a formal look, and to display its fruit more effectively, it can be clipped into dense mounds. ***Cotoneaster microphyllus*** var. ***cochleatus*** (syn. *Cotoneaster cochleatus*) is almost prostrate, with profuse fruit. ***C. m.*** var. ***thymifolius*** is a stiffly upright shrub to 24 in (60 cm) with a finely twiggy habit and narrow, wedge-shaped leaves. **ZONES 5–10**

Cotoneaster 'Hybridus Pendulus'

Cotoneaster franchetii

Cotoneaster glaucophyllus

Cotoneaster multiflorus
syn. *Cotoneaster reflexus*

Rather different from most cotoneasters, this is a deciduous shrub about 12 ft (3.5 m) in height with thin-textured, hairless leaves and arching branches with drooping tips. It produces a fine show of white blossom in late spring and small clusters of quite large, slightly pear-shaped, bright red fruit which ripen in mid-summer. It has a wide distribution, from the Caucasus across central Asia to western China, and is very cold hardy. **ZONES 5–9.**

Cotoneaster pannosus

This evergreen Chinese shrub to 12 ft (3.5 m) makes a tangle of tough, wiry branches with widely spaced, small, leathery, dull green leaves with white-woolly undersides. Clusters of small white flowers appear in late spring, followed by tight clusters of small pale red fruit that later deepen in color. A vigorous grower, it readily withstands trimming and is useful for hedges; it adapts to warm climates as well as cool, and has become naturalized in some places in the southern hemisphere. **ZONES 7–11.**

Cotoneaster salicifolius
WILLOWLEAF COTONEASTER

This attractive evergreen species from western China features narrow leaves with a network of veins deeply impressed into their convex, glossy upper surfaces. The profuse large bunches of bright red berries last long into winter, when the leaves may also take on bronze and yellow tones. It is variable in habit; some forms are low and spreading, others reach 10–15 ft (3–4.5 m) with long, arching growths. It takes well to trimming and makes a fine hedge plant. **'Herbstfeuer'** (**'Autumn Fire'**) is low and spreading and bears abundant orange-red fruit. **ZONES 6–10.**

Cotoneaster splendens

An attractive small-leafed but very vigorous deciduous shrub from northwestern China, this species was initially introduced to Sweden in the 1930s by the Swedish collector Harry Smith and was only popularized elsewhere in the West much more recently. It is a medium-sized shrub growing to 5–10 ft (1.5–3 m) with arching shoots, grayish green, glossy leaves that turn red in fall (autumn), solitary pinkish flowers in summer and reddish orange fruit up to almost ½ in (12 mm) long. **ZONES 5–9**

Cotoneaster salicifolius

Cotoneaster multiflorus

Cotoneaster pannosus

Cotyledon orbiculata

Cotoneaster splendens

Cotyledon orbiculata

Cotyledon campanulata

Cotoneaster × watereri

Believed to be a hybrid between *Cotoneaster frigidus* and *C. henryanus*, this is an evergreen or semi-evergreen shrub of up to about 20 ft (6 m), of broadly spreading habit with arching shoots. The leaves are dark green and up to 3 in (8 cm) long. Small white flowers are borne in summer followed by an abundance of small red fruit in large clusters. **'John Waterer'** is the original clone. **ZONES 6–10.**

COTULA

This is a genus of about 80 species of low-growing annuals and perennials in the daisy family, some of them marginal aquatic plants. They occur in many parts of the world but the majority are from temperate southern hemisphere regions of Africa, Australia and South America. The small, soft leaves are often deeply dissected, and the small flowerheads are button-like, lacking ray-florets though sometimes with the bracts forming a circle around the yellow or cream disc. Some species previously included in *Cotula* are now placed in the genus *Leptinella*.

CULTIVATION: They are grown as rock-garden plants or the semi-aquatic species can be grown in boggy areas at edges of ponds. They need full sun with some protection in very hot weather, and moist, humus-rich soil. Deadheading will extend the flowering season.

Cotula coronopifolia
WATER BUTTONS, BRASS BUTTONS

An annual or in warmer climates a short-lived perennial, water buttons is believed native to southern Africa but is now widely naturalized in other parts of the world. Growing naturally on mud-banks or in very shallow, often brackish water, it is easily grown in any moist soil or a shallow pond. It has creeping stems with erect shoots 6 in (15 cm) or more high and oblong bright green leaves usually toothed at the apex. The flowerheads are like neat golden buttons about ½ in (12 mm) across, appearing in succession from late winter to summer. **ZONES 8–11.**

COTYLEDON

This is a genus of the crassula family consisting of 9 species of evergreen succulent shrubs and subshrubs, from southern and East Africa and the Arabian Peninsula. In growth habit they range from highly succulent plants no more than 2 in (5 cm) high to larger shrubs that in rare cases can reach as much as 6 ft (1.8 m) high. They have fleshy leaves and tubular or bell-shaped, orange, yellow or red flowers.

CULTIVATION: Some species are marginally frost hardy, others quite frost tender. They prefer full sun or part-shade and humus-rich, very well-drained soil. Water only very lightly in winter. Propagate from seed, stem cuttings or leaf cuttings taken in spring or fall (autumn).

Cotyledon campanulata

This species from South Africa's Cape Province is virtually stemless, or at least its stems are not visible above ground. The clustered green leaves are cylindrical, 3–4 in long and about ½ in (12 mm) thick, with a pointed red tip. Flowering stems rise to as much as 18 in (45 cm) high, branching at the top into panicles of yellow flowers. **ZONES 9–10.**

Cotyledon orbiculata
PIG'S EAR

Native to southwestern Africa, this species is very variable and has been divided into a number of botanical varieties. Typically it is a shrub of around 18–24 in (45–60 cm), branching just above the ground with branches terminating in clusters of succulent leaves that vary from paddle-shaped to almost circular in outline, and from quite green and glossy to almost pure white from a thick waxy or powdery bloom; the leaf margins are often red-lined. In fall (autumn) long-stalked clusters of quite large, pendent orange flowers appear at the branch tips. **ZONES 9–11.**

COUROUPITA

Three species of trees from northern South America make up this genus. They have large, elliptical leaves, usually clustered at the branch tips. The flowers are large and complex in structure, usually 6-petalled, and sometimes smell like garlic. They are followed by spectacular large, spherical fruit.

CULTIVATION: These are plants for tropical or warm subtropical areas and will not tolerate frost or prolonged cold. They prefer to grow in deep, moist, humus-rich soil in full sun but in a sheltered position. Propagation is normally from seed.

Couroupita guianensis
CANNONBALL TREE

This species is an upright, evergreen tree capable of growing to 100 ft (30 m) high, though 30–40 ft (9–12 m) is a more usual size. Pendulous flowering branches emerge directly from the trunk, right down to the ground, and all year produce 3 in (8 cm) diameter, brilliant red and orange fragrant flowers with hundreds of stamens arranged in 2 groups, one in the flower's center and the other on a lower petal. Showy as the flowers are, the fruit are the main feature—they are brown spheres up to 10 in (25 cm) across filled with a smelly, soft red pulp, and one tree may bear hundreds of them. They look like small cannonballs and burst explosively on falling from the tree. **ZONES 11–12.**

COWANIA

This genus of 5 species of evergreen shrubs and small trees in the rose family is confined to the southwestern States of the USA and adjacent areas of Mexico. Species have very small leaves that are deeply lobed or dissected, usually woolly on the undersides, and both leaves and twigs are coated with sticky resin. The small white or pale yellow flowers are borne singly at ends of twigs and are followed by small dry fruits with persistent, plume-like styles that may be quite decorative. **CULTIVATION:** Grow in full sun, a well-drained soil and no more water than nature provides once the plant is established in the ground. Propagate from seed.

Cowania mexicana var. *stansburiana*
syn. *Cowania stansburiana*
CLIFF ROSE

A straggly shrub native to the deserts of the southwestern USA, this is a dependable addition to a desert garden. The rose-like, creamy white flowers in spring are followed quickly by feathery seed heads that soften the outline of the plant. The leaves are tiny, deeply toothed and evergreen. Ultimate height is around 6 ft (1.8 m) with a similar spread. **ZONES 5–9.**

CRAMBE

This genus, related to *Brassica*, consists of 20 species of annuals and perennials, ranging in the wild from central Europe to central Asia, also in parts of Africa. They have large, cabbage-like basal leaves that are shallowly to very deeply lobed, and large panicles of small, 4-petalled white flowers with a somewhat cabbage-like smell. They are attractive to bees. **CULTIVATION:** Mostly very frost hardy, they will grow in any well-drained soil and prefer an open, sunny position, although they will tolerate some shade. Propagation is by division in early spring or from seed sown in spring or fall (autumn).

Crambe cordifolia
COLEWORT

From the Caucasus region, this very spectacular perennial has lobed leaves up

Couroupita guianensis

to about 18 in (45 cm) long and almost as wide, forming a broad but untidy rosette. The stout, much-branched flowering stem bursts into a cloud of small, white, starry flowers, the whole measuring 4 ft (1.2 m) across with a total height of 6 ft (1.8 m). It is very deep rooted and will produce numerous offsets. **ZONES 6–9.**

Crambe maritima
SEA KALE

Occurring wild along cooler European coastlines, this robust small perennial forms a mound of broad bluish green or even purplish, cabbage-like leaves with curled and crisped margins. In late spring and summer it produces dense, erect panicles of honey-scented white flowers, as much as $2\frac{1}{2}$ ft (75 cm) tall. The young leafy shoots are used as a green vegetable, often blanched to lessen the bitterness. **ZONES 5–9.**

CRASPEDIA

A genus of around 30 species of perennials, all native to New Zealand or southeastern Australia including Tasmania. Most grow on higher mountains, at or above the tree-line in boggy meadows or on moist screes, but a few occur in grassy lowland areas. Belonging to the composite (daisy) family they have distinctive button-like to spherical flowerheads, consisting of a large number of tightly packed florets but lacking an outer circle of ray-florets. Color of heads varies from pale to deep yellow or even orange and they are borne singly at ends of erect stems, which arise from a basal tuft of broad, simple leaves. Some Australian species previously included in *Craspedia* are now placed in the genus *Pycnosorus*. **CULTIVATION:** Although little cultivated, many of the species are easily enough grown in cool areas and are potentially attractive subjects for herbaceous borders and rock gardens. Frost-hardiness varies but all can tolerate at least light frosts. Propagate from seed or by division.

Craspedia uniflora
BACHELOR'S BUTTONS, BILLY BUTTONS

The name *Craspedia uniflora* has been used in the past in a very wide sense to include plants from southeastern Australia as well as New Zealand. It is now narrowed to some New Zealand plants only, though still a very variable species and found in a range of habitats from seashore to alpine. It has a basal rosette

Couroupita guianensis

Crambe cordifolia

Crassula arborescens

of broad green leaves, their edges lined with tangled cottony hairs; in summer several flowering stems arise from the rosette to 12–18 in (30–45 cm) high, each topped by a single hemispherical, pale to deep yellow flowerhead up to about $1\frac{1}{4}$ in (30 mm) in diameter. **ZONES 7–9.**

CRASSULA

This diverse genus comprises about 300 species of annuals, perennials and evergreen shrubs, nearly all with succulent leaves. Some less highly succulent species are scattered widely around the world, but the great majority of species, including many of extreme succulent form, are confined to southern Africa. They range in habit from tiny prostrate or clump-forming plants to erect shrubs as much as 12 ft (3.5 m) high. A fairly constant feature is the arrangement of the leaves in opposite pairs, sometimes joining at the base around the stem. Flowers are grouped in terminal clusters or panicles and are only showy in a minority of species. The genus lends its name to the large family Crassulaceae, which includes other well known succulent genera such as *Sedum, Kalanchoe, Aeonium, Sempervivum* and *Echeveria*. **CULTIVATION:** Species range from marginally frost hardy to frost tender. Some of the more vigorous growers are tough, adaptable plants which will survive with almost no attention in pots, tubs or window boxes as long as soil is not waterlogged. At the other end of the scale are some of the more dwarf succulent South

Crambe maritima

African species, which are grown mainly by succulent collectors willing to meet their specialized requirements. Propagate from stem or leaf cuttings, or from seed.

Crassula arborescens
SILVER JADE PLANT, SILVER DOLLAR

Widely distributed in South Africa including the summer-rainfall eastern parts, *Crassula arborescens* can exceed 10 ft (3 m) in height and spread, though 24–36 in (60–90 cm) is more usual in cultivation. It is a much-branched shrub with thick brown stems and red-edged, almost circular leaves about $1\frac{1}{2}$ in (38 mm) wide with a powdery blue-gray coating peppered with small dark green dots. Panicles of small, starry pale pinkish flowers dot the plant in fall (autumn) and winter. It is a favorite tub plant for any sunny spot, thriving on minimal attention. A common 'jade plant' of gardens often known as *Crassula arborescens* is actually *C. ovata* (see overleaf). **ZONES 9–11.**

Crassula coccinea

Crassula 'Emerald'

Crassula 'Emerald Isle'

Crassula capitella

This subshrubby species from South Africa is variable and some of its subspecies were previously treated as distinct species. Its narrow, grooved leaves are usually red-spotted and form a basal rosette, from the center of which arises a slender flowering stem up to about 18 in (45 cm) tall bearing pale pinkish flowers through the spring and summer months. **'Campfire'** is a cultivar with deeper red foliage. **ZONES 9–11.**

Crassula coccinea

syn. *Rochea coccinea*

From mountains of South Africa's western Cape Province, this is a crassula grown mainly for its spectacular flowers. It is a succulent perennial up to 24 in (60 cm) high, branching from the base into several stems with crowded short green leaves sometimes tinged red. In late summer and fall (autumn) it bears an abundance of tubular, deep red flowers in dense, rounded panicles. It needs full sun and does best in a warm, dry spot in a rock garden with perfect drainage. Prune back stems to just above the base in late winter. **ZONES 9–10.**

Crassula capitella 'Campfire'

Crassula 'Emerald'

This dwarf cultivar appears to be derived from the fall- (autumn-) flowering *Crassula susannae*, from Cape Province. It is a real miniature, only 2–3 in (5–8 cm) high and the ends of its broad-tipped leaves are frosted with bluish gray. **'Emerald Isle'** is similar but the leaves are more tightly crowded. **ZONES 9–11.**

Crassula 'Green Pagoda'

This cultivar may merely be a form of the popular South African species *Crassula perforata*, or perhaps a hybrid. It has the leaves of each pair joined at the base, giving the impression of being threaded onto the stem and stacked into an upright column. The pretty pink flowers emerge from the crown. **ZONES 9–11.**

Crassula grisea

This species is endemic to Namaqualand in the far west of Cape Province, a region of very low rainfall that is home to an extraordinary array of extreme succulent plant forms. It grows to about 6 in (15 cm) high and has small, greenish yellow leaves only 1 in (25 mm) long. Small white flowers appear in spring and summer. It is a species found mainly in succulent collections. **ZONES 9–11.**

Crassula 'Morgan's Pink'

This cultivar reaches a height and width of 8 in (20 cm). It has gray-green, sickle-shaped leaves and features salmon pink flowers that bloom in spring and summer. **ZONES 9–11.**

Crassula multicava

FAIRY CRASSULA

One of the easiest of all crassulas to grow in mild climates, *Crassula multicava* is a

Crassula 'Green Pagoda'

spreading perennial 8–12 in (20–30 cm) high, its semi-prostrate stems taking root and spreading into a large patch. The thinly succulent gray-green leaves are densely dotted with dark green, and clusters of tiny star-shaped, pink and white flowers are borne on long, weak stalks in winter and spring, making a delicate gauze of color above the leaves when this species is grown as a ground cover. **ZONES 9–11.**

Crassula ovata

syns *Crassula argentea* of gardens, *C. portulacea*

JADE PLANT, JADE TREE, FRIENDSHIP TREE

This South African species should not be confused with *Portulacaria afra*, also known as 'jade plant' but easily distinguished by its much smaller leaves, not in opposite pairs. *Crassula ovata* has also been much confused with *C. arborescens*, the silver jade plant. It is a fast-growing, shrubby, succulent that can reach over 6 ft (1.8 m) in height, though 24–36 in (60–90 cm) is more usual. It has thick brownish stems and shiny, broadly wedge-shaped leaves that may be edged with red. In fall (autumn) and winter small, white to pale pink, starry flowers appear. It prefers full sun, and makes a good tub plant for growing on patios and balconies. **'Hobbit'** is a dwarf cultivar. **ZONES 9–11.**

Crassula grisea

Crassula ovata

Crassula perfoliata

PROPELLER PLANT

Native to southeastern South Africa, this interesting species is rather variable, some of its varieties having formerly been treated as distinct species. Stems are erect, branching from the base and up to about 3 ft (1 m) high. The long, fleshy leaves are in opposite pairs. In ***Crassula perfoliata* var. *perfoliata*** they are green and channelled, 4–6 in (10–15 cm) long, arranged in alternating planes and rather drooping. In ***C. p.* var. *minor*** (syn. *Crassula falcata*) they are pale gray-green and shaped like curved knife blades standing on edge; their bases overlap and all the leaves are squashed into one plane. Dense terminal panicles of quite showy deep red flowers are produced in summer. **ZONES 10–11.**

Crassula plegmatoides

Another species from Namaqualand in South Africa and extending into adjacent Namibia, this is a plant only about 6 in (15 cm) high with tiny blue-green, triangular leaves that are so tightly crowded they form a 4-angled column. In spring it bears sprays of very small white flowers. **ZONES 10–11.**

Crassula pruinosa

syn. *Crassula scabrella*

Native to southwestern Cape Province and reaching a height of 4 in (10 cm), this small species has green ½–1 in (12–25 mm) long leaves with a waxy whitish bloom. White bell-shaped flowers are borne in spring and summer. **ZONES 10–11.**

Crassula tetragona

From the southeast coast of South Africa this is a multi-stemmed shrub of about 24 in (60 cm) high. The leaves are distinctive, about 1 in (25 mm) long, almost circular in cross-section, curving upward and tapering to a fine point; they are

Crassula multicava

Crassula ovata 'Hobbit'

Crassula perfoliata var. *minor*

Crassula pruinosa

Crataegus arnoldiana

Crataegus 'Autumn Glory'

Crassula perfoliata

arranged in 4 neat vertical rows. Tiny cream flowers appear in short sprays in spring and summer. In mild climates this species naturalizes but is hardly invasive, building into a patch maybe 10–20 ft (3–6 m) across after many years as it self-propagates from fallen leaves. **ZONES 10–11.**

+ *CRATAEGOMESPILUS*

This is a hybrid between two genera, but in a sense is not a true hybrid. The symbol '+' in front of the name indicates that it is a *graft hybrid* rather than the more usual sexual hybrid denoted by a '×' sign. These result when the tissues of the stock and scion of a graft mix together and the new shoots that sprout from it show characteristics of both. Such a rare event came about in this case when a medlar (*Mespilus germanica*) was grafted onto a hawthorn (*Crataegus*). There are very few other examples of graft hybrids, the best known being + *Laburnocytisus*.

CULTIVATION: It is easily enough grown in a cool climate in a sheltered position with deep, moist soil. It is usually propagated by grafting onto a hawthorn rootstock.

+ *Crataegomespilus dardarii*
BRONVAUX MEDLAR

This first appeared in the garden of a M. Dardar of Bronvaux near Metz in France around 1895, as branches sprouting from a medlar grafted onto *Crataegus monogyna*. The first branch combined the leaf and fruit characters of the medlar with the thorns and flower umbels of the hawthorn; but the second branch from the same graft was more like the hawthorn in leaves, flowers and fruit, except that the young branches and flower stalks were coated with a gray wool like that of the medlar. Plants propagated from this second branch have been widely grown and have been given the cultivar name **'Jules d'Asnières'**. This makes an attractive small deciduous tree of 15–20 ft (4.5–6 m) with dense crown and somewhat pendulous branches. Leaves are downy on the undersides and variable in depth of lobing, and the white to pinkish white flowers, borne in late spring, are larger than those of hawthorn and have a woolly calyx. **ZONES 6–9.**

+ *C. dardarii* 'Jules d'Asnières'

CRATAEGUS
HAWTHORN, MAY

Native to cool-climate areas of Europe, Asia and eastern North America, *Crataegus* belongs to the pome-fruit group of the rose family and the resemblance of the fruits to miniature apples can easily be seen and tasted. Most of the 200 species have long, sharp thorns on the summer growths; the leaves are either toothed or lobed, and the white or rarely pink flowers are clustered in flat to rounded umbels in late spring or summer. They are followed in fall (autumn) by a display of fruits mostly in shades of red, often also with attractive foliage colors.

CULTIVATION: Hawthorns are robust, frost-hardy, deciduous trees, most of which are compact enough even for quite small gardens. They are sun-lovers and not very fussy about soil type or drainage. Some species sucker from the base, but suckers can be removed to produce a tree form. Some hawthorns are prone to fireblight, controlled only by prompt removal and burning of affected branches. Foliage may also be disfigured by the 'pear and cherry slug' (larva of a sawfly); spray severe attacks with an insecticide. Propagate from cold-stratified seed, or by grafting of named clones. In winter they are easily transplanted.

Crataegus arnoldiana
ARNOLD HAWTHORN

This small spreading tree from northeastern USA grows to about 20 ft (6 m) in cultivation and has gray scaly bark. The dark green, shiny leaves with paler undersides turn reddish in fall (autumn). Clusters of large white scented flowers with conspicuous deep pink stamens are strung along the branches in mid-spring, and are followed by small bunches of crimson fruit each about ¾ in (18 mm) in diameter. **ZONES 5–10.**

Crataegus 'Autumn Glory'

A cultivar of hybrid origin, 'Autumn Glory' is rather similar to the better known *Crataegus* × *lavallei* but has somewhat smaller, narrower leaves. Its large, brilliant crimson berries are borne in great profusion in fall (autumn). **ZONES 5–9.**

+ *Crataegomespilus dardarii* 'Jules d'Asnières'

Crataegus diffusa

Another species from northeastern USA, this makes a tree of up to 30 ft (10 m), the branches armed with long spines. Leaves are pale green and shallowly lobed. Umbels of smallish white flowers in late spring or early summer are followed by red fruit about 3/8 in (9 mm) in diameter. **ZONES 4–9.**

Crataegus flava

YELLOW HAW, SUMMER HAW

This species is believed native to eastern USA, but is not now found in the wild. It is a tree with smallish, smooth, toothed or shallowly lobed leaves, fairly large white flowers borne in early summer, and greenish yellow fruit about 5/8 in (15 mm) in diameter. It is not one of the more ornamental hawthorns. **ZONES 4–9.**

Crataegus flava

Crataegus laciniata

Crataegus laciniata

syn. *Crataegus orientalis*

ORIENTAL THORN

From Turkey and the Balkan and Caucasus regions, this species has been cultivated for ornament in western Europe for almost 2 centuries. It may reach 15–20 ft (4.5–6 m) but in gardens is frequently a spreading shrub, often virtually thornless. The broadly wedge-shaped leaves, green but frosted with whitish hairs, are deeply divided into narrow lobes. The large white flowers appear in early summer in small clusters, followed in fall (autumn) by 1 in (25 mm) red or yellowish fruit. **ZONES 6–9.**

Crataegus laevigata

syn. *Crataegus oxyacantha*

MIDLAND HAWTHORN, MAY, ENGLISH HAWTHORN

This small tree reaches 25 ft (8 m) or more in height and spread. Native to Europe and North Africa, it is easily confused with the English may (*Crataegus monogyna*), both these species having once been called *C. oxyacantha.* It has mid- to dark green, glossy leaves with shallow, rounded lobes and produces few thorns. Its abundant white flowers open in late spring. The cultivar **'Paul's Scarlet'** has bright crimson, double flowers opening in late spring; **'Punicea'** has deep pink single flowers with white centers; **'Punicea Flore Pleno'** is similar but with double flowers. **ZONES 4–9.**

Crataegus laevigata

Crataegus laevigata 'Punicea'

C. laevigata 'Punicea Flore Pleno'

Crataegus laevigata 'Paul's Scarlet'

Crataegus × *lavallei*

syn. *Crataegus* × *carrierei*

LAVALLE HAWTHORN, CARRIERE HAWTHORN

This hybrid originated in France in about 1880, the result of a cross between *Crataegus crus-galli* and *C. pubescens.* It forms a densely branched, almost thornless tree of 15–20 ft (4.5–6 m). The broad, irregularly toothed leaves are darker glossy green than most hawthorns and are semi-evergreen in warmer climates. The white flowers with red stamens open in loose clusters in early summer, and are followed by large yellow fruit, ripening to orange-red. Its fall (autumn) foliage tones intensify after the first hard frost. **ZONES 6–10.**

Crataegus mollis

RED HAW, DOWNY HAWTHORN

A widely spreading tree to 30 ft (10 m), this species from central USA has leaves 3–4 in (8–10 cm) long, broad and shallowly lobed and downy on both surfaces. In early summer it bears clusters of 1 in (25 mm) wide, white flowers, followed by deep red fruit up to 1 in (25 mm) in diameter. It has long been cultivated and is one of the best of the North American hawthorns. **ZONES 5–9.**

Crataegus monogyna

HAWTHORN, MAY

Native to Europe, this small tree is most commonly cultivated as a hedgerow, but when growing wild it can reach 30 ft (9 m). The leaves have 5 to 7 jagged lobes, and turn yellow-brown in fall (autumn). The fragrant single white flowers open in late spring, mid-May in England though according to the old calendar they opened around May Day (May 1). The small dark red fruit that follow hang onto the twigs into winter. *Crataegus laevigata* is very similar but *C. monogyna* is easily distinguished by its single style and fruit stone. ***C. monogyna* subsp. *azarella*** has leaves with very downy undersides. **ZONES 4–9.**

Crataegus persimilis 'Prunifolia'

syns *Crataegus* × *prunifolia*, *C. crus-galli* var. *prunifolia*

COCKSPUR HAWTHORN

Botanical opinion has changed back and forth as to the status of this North

Crataegus diffusa

Crataegus × *lavallei*

American hawthorn, which is clearly closely allied to *Crataegus crus-galli.* It is a very attractive small tree of up to about 20 ft (6 m) with a wide, rounded crown that may extend down to the ground, the branches armed with very sharp thorns up to 3 in (8 cm) long. The glossy green leaves are sharply toothed and the early summer flowers are $\frac{3}{4}$ in (18 mm) across. Glossy red fruit $\frac{1}{2}$ in (12 mm) in diameter are borne in abundant dense clusters in early fall (autumn). **ZONES 5–9.**

Crataegus phaenopyrum
syn. *Crataegus cordata*
WASHINGTON THORN

From southeastern USA, this elegant though very thorny tree reaches 20–30 ft (6–9 m), forming a round-headed, densely branched tree with long, sharp thorns. The leaves have 3 to 5 sharply toothed lobes, and are glossy green.

Crataegus phaenopyrum

Fragrant white flowers in mid-summer are followed in fall (autumn) by profuse clusters of small, shiny orange-red berries. **ZONES 4–10.**

× *Crataemespilus grandiflora*

Crataegus pubescens
syns *Crataegus mexicana, C. stipulacea*
MEXICAN HAWTHORN

This semi-evergreen species from the mountains of Mexico reaches 15–30 ft (4.5–9 m) and is often entirely thornless. The oblong, leathery leaves are coarsely toothed and dark satiny green with downy undersides. Clusters of white flowers with pink stamens are produced in mid-spring, followed in fall (autumn) by large edible fruit that ripen to butter yellow; they are sold in markets in some Mexican towns. **ZONES 7–10.**

Crataegus punctata
THICKET HAWTHORN

This species from eastern USA makes an attractive tree, growing to about 30 ft (9 m) with a stout trunk and crown of horizontally spreading branches. It has

Crataegus punctata

broad dark green leaves with toothed or slightly lobed margins and downy on the undersides. In early summer it produces clusters of white blossom up to 4 in (10 cm) wide. The fruit are large, slightly pear-shaped, dull crimson with paler dots. It is one of the most ornamental of the North American species. **'Aurea'** has yellow fruit. **ZONES 5–9.**

× *Crataemespilus grandiflora*

Crataegus pubescens

Crataegus monogyna

Crataegus viridis
GREEN HAWTHORN

Making a small tree of up to about 30 ft (9 m), this species from southeastern USA has fairly broad, glossy dark green leaves that are toothed or lobed in the upper half; in late spring–early summer it bears white flowers in small and rather sparse clusters, followed by smallish red fruit. **'Winter King'** is a superior cultivar with silvery bark, a vase-like form with relatively few thorns, good red fall (autumn) color and bright red fruit that last well into winter. **ZONES 4–9.**

× CRATAEMESPILUS

Not to be confused with + *Crataegomespilus*, which is a graft hybrid, this is a more normal, sexual hybrid between hawthorn and medlar. This hybrid genus name includes all known and potential crosses between the genera *Crataegus* and *Mespilus*, though so far only 2 have been recorded.

CULTIVATION: These hybrids are normally grown grafted onto a hawthorn.

Crataegus monogyna subsp. *azarella*

Crataegus viridis 'Winter King'

They like a sunny but sheltered position and a cool climate.

× *Crataemespilus grandiflora*

This hybrid between *Crataegus laevigata* and *Mespilus germanica* was found growing wild in France before 1800. Intermediate in character between these parent species, it is a small deciduous tree with downy leaves, sometimes few-lobed but only on vigorous shoots. Flowers are in pairs or 3s, about 1 in (25 mm) across, opening in late spring and early summer. The fruit is glossy brownish orange, about $\frac{3}{4}$ in (18 mm) in diameter, the mealy flesh more like hawthorn than medlar in flavor. The seeds appear to be sterile. Fall (autumn) tones are orange and yellow. **ZONES 4–9.**

CRATEVA

Six or more species of evergreen shrubs and small trees make up this genus, widely distributed through the tropics. They are closely related to the herbaceous genus *Cleome*, as is obvious from the flower structure. The flowers have large, stalked petals and very long, protruding stamens. Leaves are usually compound with leaflets radiating from a common stalk, also like *Cleome*. The foliage of some species can cause a form of contact dermatitis in humans.

CULTIVATION: These plants need warm, even temperatures year round and prefer rich, moist, well-drained soil with

Crateva religiosa

Crinodendron hookerianum

Crinum asiaticum

Crinodendron patagua

plenty of water in hot weather. Outside the tropics they can be grown and flowered in large containers in a heated conservatory or greenhouse. Propagate from seed or cuttings.

Crateva religiosa
SPIDER TREE, TEMPLE PLANT

Native to Southeast Asia, the Pacific region and northern Australia, this ornamental small tree grows to 20 ft (6 m) or more high. It has smooth gray bark with white spots and distinctive pale green young branches. Its handsome leaves are composed of 3 oval leaflets up to 6 in (15 cm) long. In winter it bears large flowers with creamy white petals aging to dull orange-yellow and long, dark red to violet stamen filaments. The flowers are followed by smooth green berries. **ZONES 11–12.**

CRINODENDRON
syn. ***Tricuspidaria***

This genus, allied to *Elaeocarpus*, consists of 4 species of shrubs and trees from South America, two of which are valued ornamentals where climatic conditions allow their cultivation. They are evergreens with leathery, toothed leaves and stalked, bell-shaped flowers pendent from the leaf axils.

CULTIVATION: Regions where they thrive best have cool but mild coastal climates with high rainfall or frequent mist, and include southwest England and Ireland, southern New Zealand, Tasmania, and the Pacific Northwest of the USA and Canada. In drier climates they are likely to be short lived, though a shaded, sheltered site with a humid microclimate and permanent soil moisture may increase their chance of survival. Propagation is normally from cuttings as the seeds, produced in a smallish capsular fruit, are rarely available.

Crinodendron hookerianum
syn. ***Tricuspidaria lanceolata***

This, the most admired species, is from the rainforests of southern coastal Chile on and about the island of Chiloe. In the wild it reaches heights of 30 ft (9 m) but in cultivation it is normally a bushy, upright shrub of 10 ft (3 m) or less with narrow, strongly veined, deep green leaves. Conspicuous crimson buds appear in fall (autumn) but the flowers do not reach their full size of up to 1½ in (35 mm) long until the next spring; they never open wide, retaining only a small aperture. **ZONES 8–9.**

Crinodendron patagua
syn. ***Tricuspidaria dependens***
LILY OF THE VALLEY TREE

Also from Chile, *Crinodendron patagua* comes from a region further north, in the hills around Valparaiso. It is a tree of similar size to *C. hookerianum*, but more vigorous and tolerant of drier conditions. The leaves are broader and flatter, dark green with downy undersides, and its 1 in (25 mm) white flowers are produced in late summer. **ZONES 8–9.**

CRINUM

This genus of beautiful large bulbous plants allied to *Amaryllis* consists of around 130 species, occurring wild in most warmer regions of the world. The bulbs are often quite large and may be deeply buried or sit virtually on the soil surface; in many species the bulb is elongated with a 'neck' of varying length on which the old dead leaf bases persist as papery sheaths. The lily-like flowers are borne in umbels at the apex of thick flowering stems and usually open progressively; usually white or pink, they have six broad petals, often upward-curving, and long stamen filaments. Globular, thin-skinned fruits contain large fleshy seeds that have no dormancy and will begin to germinate dry. Only a few species and 2 or 3 hybrids are widely grown in gardens, but some enthusiasts have amassed larger collections. It can be very difficult to locate sources of supply for many of the species.

CULTIVATION: Species vary in ease of cultivation, those from regions of highly seasonal rainfall being generally more difficult. Bulbs should be planted in rich, moist soil with the neck of the bulb above ground level. Some species do best in full sun, others appreciate a light shade. Propagation is best from seed as dividing the plants is difficult. The flowers usually take a few seasons to develop with either method. Most species are tender to frost and susceptible to caterpillars, slugs and snails.

Crinum asiaticum
ASIATIC POISON LILY, POISON BULB

This tropical Asian species can be a dramatic plant for a frost-free garden. It likes damp soil, and can be placed at the margins of a pond. Its long-necked bulbs sit on the surface and produce evergreen, fleshy, very broad leaves making a clump up to about 4 ft (1.2 m) high. The stout flowering stem can carry up to 50 sweetly scented white flowers with very narrow petals, opening through much of the year. There is a rare form with pale pink flowers, another with soft golden-yellow leaves, and one with its leaves boldly striped in green and cream. The poisonous bulbs were once used medicinally, as an emetic; they present little danger in the garden. **ZONES 10–12.**

Crinum bulbispermum
ORANGE RIVER LILY

This South African species is probably the most cold hardy of all crinums. It makes a clump of buried, rather short-necked bulbs which produce broad, channelled, recurving leaves with wavy edges which usually die back after the plant flowers in late spring or early summer. The flowering stem is up to 3 ft (1 m) tall and produces a succession of long-stalked, trumpet-shaped flowers that are white to pale pink but with a broad red stripe along the center of each petal. This species likes sun and grows well in wet ground. **ZONES 6–10.**

Crinum campanulatum
syns ***Crinum aquaticum, C. caffrum***
WATER CRINUM

This species from South Africa can be grown in shallow water during summer but the bulbs must be lifted and kept drier in winter if it is to bear flowers the following season. From buried bulbs it produces tufts of narrow, deeply channelled, recurving leaves. The funnel-shaped spring flowers are bright red to purple, paler at tips of petals, usually only about 2– 3 in long (5–8 cm) long; only a few are carried at the top of each reddish 12–18 in (30–45 cm) stem. **ZONES 9–11.**

Crinum flaccidum
MURRAY LILY, DARLING LILY

This Australian species is the most widely distributed of the few crinums native to that continent, occurring through much of the eastern and central inland, usually in deep alluvial soil along streams with intermittent flow. The bulb can be up to 3 ft (1 m) below the surface, connected by a long neck to the few narrow, channelled leaves that tend to flop on the ground and die back in summer or during long dry periods. The flowering stems reach a height of 18–24 in (45–60 cm), bearing in summer or fall (autumn) 6–12 delicate white or cream flowers that open widely in a star-like form, up to 6 in (15 cm) across. Cultivation of this species is not easy outside its native regions. **ZONES 9–11.**

Crinum macowanii
RIVER CRINUM

This South African species resembles *Crinum bulbispermum* but is a more robust plant and is dormant in winter, flowering while in leaf in spring and early summer. The flowering stem can reach as much as 4 ft (1.2 m) in height and produces a succession of large trumpet-shaped flowers with strongly recurved petal tips, their coloring much as in *C. bulbispermum.* The leaves form a wide rosette up to 3 ft (1 m) across. **ZONES 9–11.**

Crinum moorei
MOORE'S CRINUM, BUSH LILY

After *Crinum bulbispermum* this South African species is the next most cold hardy crinum and is popular on that account as well as for the delicate beauty of its large white to pale pink flowers, resembling those of some liliums. The very broad, weak leaves are usually beginning to die back as the flowers open in late summer and early fall (autumn), finally leaving a clump of large, very long-necked bulbs protruding above the ground. Flowering stems are up to 3 ft (1 m) tall and are topped by umbels of 4–5 in (10–12 cm) wide nodding flowers of very graceful appearance. It is easily grown in light to quite deep shade, preferring a friable, well-drained soil, but is highly prone to damage from snails and slugs. **'Cape Dawn'** is a delicate pink form. **ZONES 8–11.**

Crinum pedunculatum
BEACH LILY, SWAMP CRINUM

This eastern Australian species is similar to *Crinum asiaticum* but is a more robust plant. It makes large clumps of evergreen foliage, the long basal necks hardly distended at the base into proper bulbs; the dull green leaves are very thick and leathery, up to 4 ft (1.2 m) long. Through spring and summer it produces many stout flowering stems of up to 3 ft (1 m)

Crocosmia masonorum

Crocosmia × *crocosmiiflora*

high, each bearing a long succession of narrow-petalled white flowers with showy long stamens. The shiny greenish white fruit are up to 2 in (5 cm) wide. It thrives in almost any sunny situation, including exposed seashores and saline swamps. A mature clump can reach 6–8 ft (1.8–2.4 m) in width. **ZONES 10–12.**

Crinum × *powellii*
CAPE LILY

This well-known and easily grown hybrid between *Crinum bulbispermum* and *C. moorei* was bred in England in the nineteenth century. Strap-like foliage is produced from a long neck and dies back during late summer and fall (autumn). At about the same time the 3–4 ft (1–1.2 m) flowering stems are each crowned with up to 10 deep pink fragrant flowers, similar in shape and size to those of *C. moorei*. The flowers can become so heavy that the plant needs to be staked. **'Album'** has pure white flowers. **ZONES 6–10.**

CROCOSMIA
syns *Antholyza, Curtonus*
MONTBRETIA

These 7 species of South African cormous perennials have narrow, bayonet-shaped, pleated leaves. These fan out from the base of the plant, similar to a gladiolus. A branched spike of brightly colored flowers appears in summer.
CULTIVATION: Plant the corms in winter in rich soil with adequate drainage in a position that receives morning sun. Water well through summer. They will multiply freely and should not be divided unless overcrowded; this should be done in spring if necessary.

Crocosmia aurea

This species has a 3 ft (1 m) stem bearing a branching spike of yellow to orange,

Crocosmia × *crocosmiiflora* 'Lucifer'

3 in (8 cm), tubular flowers in early summer; these make good cut flowers. It likes a shaded position. **ZONES 8–11.**

Crocosmia × *crocosmiiflora*

Growing to 36 in (90 cm), the stem of this hybrid raised in France in the 1880s bears a branching spike of up to 40 orange-red, gladiolus-like flowers about 1 in (25 mm) wide. This species is frost hardy but needs full sun in cold climates. In cold-winter areas, lift the corms for the winter and replant them in spring. Recently, larger flowered hybrids in a wider range of colors (yellow to red) have been raised in England. They have names like **'Bressingham Blaze'** (bright orange-red) and **'Lucifer'** (bright red) and are a little hardier than the species itself. **ZONES 7–11.**

Crocosmia 'Walberton Red'

Crocosmia 'Emily Mackenzie'

Crocosmia 'Emily Mackenzie'

Raised in Northumberland in England in 1954, this vigorous and free flowering plant has large yellow to dark orange long lasting flowers with wallflower red splashes and a pale throat. The segments are well expanded. **ZONES 7–11.**

Crocosmia masonorum

This tall species grows up to 4 ft (1.2 m). The branched stem is topped with an arched display of tangerine flowers. The 6-petalled flowers are quite large, up to 3 in (8 cm) wide. It is useful as a cut flower. **ZONES 8–11.**

Crocosmia 'Walberton Red'

'Walberton Red' was the result of several years' crossing between *Crocosmia masoniorum, C. pottsii* 'Solfatare' and 'Her Majesty' by D. R. Tristram of Arundel in West Sussex. It has uplifted large flowers of a pure tomato-red color. The corms are also large and do not split into a mass of cormlets. **ZONES 8–11.**

CROCUS
CROCUS

There are about 80 species, as well as numerous garden forms and hybrids, in this genus of cormous perennials from Europe, North Africa and temperate Asia. Although belonging to the iris family, they differ in appearance from most other members of the family, with goblet-shaped flowers tapering at the base into a long tube that originates below the soil surface. Crocuses vary greatly in color, though lilac-blue, mauve, yellow and white are most usual. The species and hybrids can be divided into spring-flowering, the flowers appearing with or before the new leaves, and fall-(autumn-) flowering, blooming in full leaf. The foliage is grass-like, usually with a central silver-white stripe.
CULTIVATION: Very frost-hardy plants, they do best in a cool to cold area. In warm areas the corms may flower in the first season but may not flower again. They can be grown in pots in warmer areas, in a cool spot. Corms should be planted in early fall in moist, well-

Crinum moorei (white form)

Crinum pedunculatum

Crinum × *powellii* 'Album'

Crinum moorei 'Cape Dawn'

C

drained soil in full sun or part-shade. Keep well watered until the foliage begins to die. They do not spread very fast but clumps can be divided if they are overcrowded. Seed can be planted in fall, but plants grown from seed will usually not flower for 3 years.

Crocus angustifolius
syn. *Crocus susianus*
CLOTH OF GOLD

A native of Crimea and the Caucasus, this early spring-flowering species has deep golden-yellow flowers tinged with mahogany on the outside and an orange scarlet stigma. The leaves can be up to 10 in (25 cm) long but the flower stalks are much shorter. **ZONES 4–9.**

Crocus sieberi 'Firefly'

Crocus gargaricus

Crocus chrysanthus 'Gipsy Girl'

Crocus boryi
syns *Crocus cretensis, C. ionicus*

From western and southern Greece and Crete, this fall- (autumn-) flowering species has flowers that are creamy white, sometimes veined with purple and with a yellow throat. **ZONES 7–9.**

Crocus cartwrightianus

Native to Greece, this species flowers in late fall (autumn) or early winter, with the new leaves of the next season's growth, so it could be classed as very early rather than very late. The small flowers vary in color from mauve to white, with darker veining and suffused with purple toward the base. **ZONES 8–9.**

Crocus chrysanthus
syns *Crocus cannulatus* var. *chrysanthus, C. croceus*

This species from Turkey and the Balkan Peninsula has bright orange flowers feathered with bronze, and orange anthers; they appear in late winter or early spring. Leaves are up to 10 in (25 cm) long and appear at the same time as the flowers. There are a number of hybrid cultivars, including **'Cream Beauty'**, with creamy yellow flowers; **'Dorothy'**, with deep golden-yellow flowers; **'E. A. Bowles'**, with deep butter-yellow flowers with bronze feathering mainly at the base of the petals; **'Gipsy Girl'** produces yellow flowers, striped purplish brown on the outside; and **'Ladykiller'** has white flowers heavily suffused purple on the outside. **ZONES 4–9.**

Crocus sativus

Crocus chrysanthus 'Ladykiller'

Crocus chrysanthus 'Dorothy'

Crocus tommasinianus

Crocus etruscus

This spring-flowering species from Italy has quite large lilac to lavender flowers, variably striped with slightly deeper color and with a yellow throat. The leaves are 8 to 10 in (20 to 25 cm) long and have a white band. **ZONES 6–10.**

Crocus flavus
syn. *Crocus aureus*

A native of the Balkan region, this spring-flowering species bears a profusion of scented flowers, orange-yellow with an orange throat. It is easily grown from seed and adapts to somewhat warmer climates than most other yellow species. **ZONES 4–9.**

Crocus gargaricus

This is a rare species from western Turkey, where it grows in mountain meadows above the ancient city of Boursa. It bears golden-yellow flowers in spring, and rapidly builds into clumps by underground stolons. It tolerates slightly damper conditions than some of the other Asiatic crocuses. **ZONES 7–9.**

Crocus sativus
SAFFRON CROCUS

This small species is famous for the saffron, obtained from its reddish orange stigmas, which is used as a dye and to flavor food. *Crocus sativus* grows to 2 in (5 cm) high, and has lilac or purple flowers in fall (autumn). This species is known only in cultivation and does not set seed. Some botanists suggest that its wild ancestor is *C. cartwrightianus*. **ZONES 6–9.**

Crocus chrysanthus

Crocus tommasinianus 'Ruby Giant'

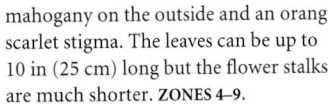

Crocus vernus 'Remembrance'

Crocus sieberi

This spring-flowering species from Greece and the Balkans has flowers that are pinkish lilac with yellow throats. **'Firefly'** bears a profusion of pale mauve flowers. **ZONES 7–9.**

Crocus tommasinianus

This dainty species from the northern Balkans grows about 4 in (10 cm) tall with lavender to purple, sometimes white-throated flowers with a very slender white tube, appearing in late winter. One of the more easily grown species, it does well in a rockery, or naturalized under deciduous trees. **'Ruby Giant'** has dark purple flowers. **ZONES 5–9.**

Crocus vernus
DUTCH CROCUS

There are many spring-flowering hybrid crocuses derived from *Crocus vernus* and known as Dutch crocuses. The species itself, a native of eastern and central Europe, grows to 4 in (10 cm) high and bears solitary white, pink or purple flowers from spring to early summer. The Dutch hybrids are vigorous plants with large flowers up to 6 in (15 cm) long, in a varied color range—white to yellow, purple or bluish; there are also some striped varieties. **'Remembrance'** has violet flowers with purple bases. **ZONES 4–9.**

CROSSANDRA

This genus of about 50 evergreen perennials, subshrubs and shrubs in the acanthus family ranges through subtropical and tropical regions of Africa and southwestern Asia. They have simple leaves arranged in opposite pairs and bear erect spikes of showy yellow to red flowers, opening progressively from the base of the spike, each flower with the petals opened out flat like a hand.

CULTIVATION: Some species are popular as potted plants for indoors or a heated greenhouse. They need to be watered freely when in full growth. Shoots that have flowered should be cut back by about half in late winter to promote branching. Propagation is from seed sown in spring or cuttings in late spring or summer.

Crossandra pungens

This tropical African species has rather narrow dull green leaves with a pattern of paler veins. The flowers are borne in spikes with broad, spiny-edged bracts and are orange in color. **ZONES 10–12.**

CROTALARIA

RATTLEBOX

This large genus of legumes consists of around 600 species, occurring in most warmer regions of the world but with the great majority confined to Africa and Madagascar. They include annuals as well as evergreen perennials, subshrubs and shrubs. The leaves are simple, or compound with 3 leaflets and the flowers are of the pea type, from medium-sized to quite large and mostly yellow or greenish yellow. The hard, inflated seed pods are a distinctive feature of the genus, with loose rattling seeds at maturity that give them their common name—when the seeds have dried out they rattle inside the pods.

CULTIVATION: They are nearly all frost-tender plants and need a sheltered location in full sun and moderately rich, well-drained soil. Pruning after flowering will keep them compact and encourage a second blooming. Propagate

Cryptanthus bivittatus 'Pink Starlight'

Crotalaria agatiflora

Crossandra pungens

from pre-soaked seed or from tip cuttings in spring or summer.

Crotalaria agatiflora

CANARY-BIRD BUSH, BIRD FLOWER

Native to upland areas of eastern Africa, this shrub of rather open habit is grown for its elegant, large greenish-yellow pea-flowers that appear from spring to fall (autumn) on ascending spikes. It has pale green leaves with 3 leaflets and grows to a height of 10–12 ft (3–3.5 m) and a spread of about 8 ft (2.4 m). The common names refer to the flowers' resemblance, before they open fully, to small birds perched on twigs. **ZONES 10–12.**

Crotalaria capensis

CAPE LABURNUM

This fast-growing, upright shrub from southern Africa can grow to about 10 ft (3 m) tall with a 6 ft (1.8 m) spread. It is much-branched with fine twigs and attractive trifoliate leaves. Smallish pale yellow pea-flowers are produced in spring and summer in profuse drooping spikes. It prefers moderate rainfall and does not tolerate dry conditions, but can withstand light frosts. **ZONES 9–11.**

Crotalaria semperflorens

A native of India, this species is a rank-growing shrub of up to 8 ft (2.4 m) with a spread of 6 ft (1.8 m), with an open branching habit. Its leaves are oval, 4–6 in (10–15 cm) long, bright green above but with whitish hairs on the undersides and accompanied by a pair of much smaller, stalkless leaflets at the base of the stalk. The bright yellow pea-flowers are $1\frac{1}{4}$ in (3 cm) wide, carried on long terminal spikes in winter and often

Crotalaria capensis

Crotalaria semperflorens

Crowea exalata

continuing sporadically through spring and summer. **ZONES 9–11.**

CROWEA

Four species of attractive small shrubs make up this temperate Australian genus, allied to *Boronia.* They are compact evergreens with narrow, mid-green leaves and masses of smallish, 5-petalled, usually pink flowers. These are borne most heavily in late spring, but plants are seldom without bloom.

CULTIVATION: They are easily grown in light but moist, well-drained soil in full sun or very light shade; a light trim after flowering helps to keep them neat. The dwarf cultivars make attractive rockery plants. Croweas are usually propagated from small cuttings.

Crowea exalata

This species from southeastern Australia is usually about 24 in (60 cm) high, with a bushy habit. Its leaves give off a slight aroma of aniseed when crushed. Its deep pink flowers are about $\frac{3}{4}$ in (18 mm) in diameter. **'Bindelong Compact'** is a recently introduced cultivar notable for its dwarf, bushy growth—to about 18 in (45 cm)—and lavish display of flowers, which give the appearance of being borne in clusters. **ZONES 8–10.**

Crowea saligna

RED WAX FLOWER

This species has the largest and most showy flowers; they are very bright pink, starry, and up to $1\frac{1}{2}$ in (40 mm) in diameter. Growing up to 3 ft (1 m) high, it flowers most profusely in fall (autumn) and demands perfect drainage. The hybrid ***Crowea exalata* × *C. saligna*** has similar bright pink flowers. **ZONES 9–10.**

Crowea exalata × *C. saligna*

Crowea exalata 'Bindelong Compact'

CRYPTANTHUS

EARTH STAR

One of the most distinctive and easily recognized genera of bromeliads, *Cryptanthus* consists of 20 or more species of rosette-forming perennials, all native to eastern Brazil where they reportedly grow on the ground, though in cultivation they are quite happy when treated as epiphytes. They have shortly creeping rhizomes that branch into small, flat rosettes of star-like form, usually with a small central funnel. The leaves have finely toothed, wavy edges and in many species and cultivars are striped or barred with white or red. Small white flowers emerge from the center of the rosettes.

CULTIVATION: They require similar growing conditions to most of the epiphytic bromeliads, but their compact size makes them especially suitable as indoor plants. Ensure a position in weak sun or partial shade, planting in a standard potting mix with some sphagnum moss or peat added. All need protection from frost and like a high level of humidity. They are susceptible to scale insect and mealybug. Propagate from seed or offsets.

Cryptanthus bivittatus

This species has not been found in the wild since its introduction to cultivation. The rosette is 12 in (30 cm) or more across, the dark green leaves each with longitudinal yellow stripes and very rippled edges. In ***Cryptanthus bivittatus* var. *atropurpureus*** the leaves are suffused with red and the stripes pale red, turning purple in full sun. **'Pink Starlight'** has pinkish white leaves with an olive-green central stripe. **ZONES 10–12.**

Cryptocoryne griffithii

Cryptomeria japonica 'Elegans'

Cryptomeria japonica var. *sinensis*

Cryptanthus bromelioides

This is one of the larger species and its rosette is less flattened than that of other species. Up to 15 in (38 cm) across and like a miniature agave in form, its leaves are thin-textured, hardly toothed, and gently wavy. More commonly grown is **'Tricolor'** with leaves striped cream-and-green with a red-pink blush when grown in high light. It requires very high humidity, and good light (though not direct sun) to bring out the pink coloring. It produces stolons from the base which make it easy to propagate. **ZONES 10–12.**

Cryptanthus zonatus

ZEBRA PLANT

This species is presumed to be native to Brazil but has not been found in the wild. It forms flattish rosettes of rather irregular shape and up to about 12 in (30 cm) in diameter. The attractive wavy-edged leaves are dark green to somewhat purplish and banded crosswise with silvery gray or pale brownish markings. In summer a cluster of tubular white flowers appears in the center of each rosette. **'Zebrinus'** has more highly colored leaves with a chocolate-brown background color. **ZONES 10–12.**

Cryptomeria japonica

Cryptomeria japonica 'Elegans'

CRYPTOCORYNE

The genus *Cryptocoryne* contains about 50 species of aquatic perennials in the arum family from tropical Asia. The interest comes not from the flowers themselves but from the colored, leaf-like spathe, which is sometimes twisted or folded and always unusually colored and which completely hides the spadix. The flowers produced in the spathe can be orange, red or purple. Although almost completely submerged, the stiff, leathery leaves are quite attractive.

CULTIVATION: Cryptocorynes are equatorial plants and need to be planted in full sun or part-shade in baskets containing humus-rich, sandy soil. They can also be planted in the mud at the water's edge. Propagate by division or by planting offsets.

Cryptocoryne griffithii

This curious plant bears its tiny flowers around a spadix completely hidden by the twisted, maroon-spotted spathe. It is a small plant—the leaves are some 2 in (5 cm) wide and the spathe about 1 in (25 mm) long. In the garden it grows best in damp soil at the edge of a pond or similar. **ZONES 11–12.**

CRYPTOMERIA

JAPANESE CEDAR, SUGI

Only one species is generally accepted in this conifer genus from China and Japan, though many variations have been named. Often fast-growing, the branches and branchlets of this evergreen, are clothed in short, leathery needle leaves that are densely overlapping and curve inward slightly. Male (pollen) and female (seed) cones are on the same tree, the former in profuse clusters and releasing clouds of pollen in spring, the latter in

Cryptomeria japonica var. *sinensis*

sparser groups behind the branch tips. Its handsome shape and uniformity of growth make it highly suitable for windbreaks, hedges and avenues. In Japan it is grown for its timber, but is also venerated in historic groves and avenues.

CULTIVATION: Very frost hardy, it prefers full sun or part-shade and deep, fertile, moist but well-drained soil. It likes plenty of water. Propagation is from seed, or from cuttings for the cultivars.

Cryptomeria japonica

This species can make rapid growth, to 20–25 ft (6–8 m) in 10 years; old trees in Japan are up to 150 ft (45 m) high, with massive trunks. The bark is thick and brown with straight, vertical furrows. Growth habit is conical with a long, pointed leader. The Japanese race has thicker branchlets and stiffer habit than the Chinese one, ***Cryptomeria japonica* var. *sinensis*.** There are at least 50 cultivars, most dwarf but a few approaching the wild types in size. The best known of the taller ones is **'Elegans'**, which makes a solid column of foliage of up to 30 ft (9 m) high and 8 ft (2.4 m) across; the needles remain long and soft, and in winter the whole tree turns a

Cryptomeria japonica 'Elegans Nana'

Cryptomeria japonica 'Globosa Nana'

striking dull bronze or plum color. **'Elegans Nana'** is similar but a dwarf form. **'Araucarioides'**, with a bizarre tangle of long rat's tail branches, reaches 10 ft (3 m) and makes an interesting foliage contrast in a mixed conifer planting. **'Globosa Nana'**, the most popular lower-growing cultivar, makes a dense ball with intricate branching that is soft to the touch; it is plain green, with paler green new growth in spring and summer. While listed as a dwarf, in good soil it may grow to 10 ft (3 m) across in only 15 years. **'Bandai-Sugi'** makes a globose plant that becomes irregular in shape after a time, to 6 ft (1.8 m); the foliage is thick and turns dull bronze in winter. **'Jindai-Sugi'** is a slow-growing bush, irregularly shaped with a flattish top; foliage is bright green and dense. The very tiny **'Vilmoriniana'** grows to about 12 in (30 cm) high and is suitable for rockeries. **ZONES 7–10.**

CTENANTHE

The ancient Greeks, it seems, could pronounce the 2 consonants that begin words such as this (*kteis*, comb; *anthos*, flower), but present-day English speakers normally pretend that the 'c' is not there. Around 15 species belong to this genus of tropical plants closely related to *Maranta* and *Calathea*, all but one of them native to Brazil (the exception is a native of Costa Rica). They are evergreen perennials or subshrubs with short rhizomes; the taller species produce forking, somewhat bamboo-like aerial stems with a single leaf at each node. The rather leathery, lance-shaped or almost oblong leaves are borne on slender stalks which broaden into sheathing bases. The flowers are borne in spikes with tightly overlapping bracts and are not showy.

Cryptomeria japonica 'Jindai-Sugi'

Cryptomeria japonica 'Globosa Nana'

CULTIVATION: Several species are widely grown as indoor foliage plants, or in frost-free climates they are easily grown outdoors in the shade of trees, requiring protection from drying winds. Indoors they require bright to moderate light but direct sunlight may cause the leaves to curl. They need ample water during the growing season and dislike low humidity. Propagation is usually from basal offshoots.

Ctenanthe lubbersiana
BAMBURANTA

Endemic to Brazil, this most commonly grown ctenanthe is a splendidly marked foliage plant, growing to 30 in (75 cm) with branching stems that spread laterally. The oblong green leaves are patterned in irregularly shaded bands of pale yellow-green, with pale green undersides. Small, white flowers on one-sided spikes are produced intermittently. **ZONES 10–12.**

Ctenanthe oppenheimiana

Also from Brazil, this widely grown species is normally about 18 in (45 cm) high but can grow taller under good conditions. Its 10–12 in (25–30 cm) long leaves are oblong and have a herringbone pattern of broad grayish bars on a dull green background, with dull red undersides. Most commonly grown is the cultivar **'Tricolor'** with irregular blotches of creamy yellow on its leaves; the red undersides give it a reddish glow from above. **ZONES 10–12.**

CUCUMIS
CUCUMBER, GOURD, MELON

Two genera of the cucurbit family are foremost in importance for the food plants they have produced, namely *Cucurbita* itself, and *Cucumis.* It is the latter genus that has given us most of the melons (except watermelon, which is *Citrullus*) and the cucumbers. It consists of 30 or more species and occurs wild in Africa, southern Asia and Australia. They are annual or perennial tendril climbers or prostrate scrambling vines with thin, lobed or angled leaves and white or yellow flowers, of different sexes but usually on the one plant.
CULTIVATION: Plant in humus-rich soil and water generously. A dry climate is preferable as humid conditions can affect the quality of the fruits and make the plants more prone to the fungus anthracnose. Hand pollinate if growing melons on a small scale. Propagation is from seed.

Cucumis melo
MELON

The wild forms of this species occur over the whole range of the genus, producing 2 in (5 cm) long melons that are barely edible. Long domestication has given rise to the sweet, delicious melons we know today. They have evolved into several major cultivar groups, according to the characteristics of their fruit. The **Cantalupensis Group** includes the cantaloupes, or rockmelons, compact plants with oval or round fruit with netted rinds and orange flesh. The **Inodorus Group** are the honeydew melons, small bushy plants producing melons with a hard rind making them suitable for long storage. The greenish white skin is usually smooth and the flesh is pale green or yellow. The **Reticulatus Group** are the netted melons, with net-like markings on the rind and orange flesh; they are widely grown in the USA. All melons need a long, hot growing season to produce sweet fruit, and in a cooler climate the vines should be encouraged to grow over concrete or rocks, or trained over black plastic in order for heat to circulate around the plant. **ZONES 8–11.**

Cucumis sativus
CUCUMBER, GHERKIN

A native of India, the cucumber is an annual trailing plant that grows to a height of 18 in (45 cm) with a 6 ft (1.8 m) spread. It has leaves with shallow, pointed lobes and yellow funnel-shaped flowers. The green-skinned fruit have a crisp white flesh with numerous seeds that are eaten with the flesh when immature. Cucumbers come in many different shapes and sizes, representing different cultivated races, though the flavor varies only slightly. Some smaller types have been developed for pickling and are known as gherkins. Some races have fruit with irregular rows of warty or prickly protuberances, others are completely smooth. In cool climates, cucumbers are normally grown in greenhouses, or the seedlings are raised under glass in winter or spring for summer planting. Train cucumber vines on a frame or trellis to keep the fruit away from the soil. They are quite vulnerable to downy mildew, though the long green kinds are more resistant than the short 'apple' cucumbers. All cucumbers are picked at an early stage of maturity, which encourages further fruit production as well as yielding tastier cucumbers. **ZONES 9–12.**

CUCURBITA
MARROW, PUMPKIN, SQUASH

All 27 species of this important genus are native to the Americas, mostly in the warmer, drier regions. Their history of domestication, established from archeological excavations, dates back to 7,000 BC in Central America and 1,000 BC in North America. Modern pumpkins and squashes come in a vast and bewildering array of shapes, sizes and colors and it is often difficult to assign a particular cultivar to a species. Some of the recognized species are believed to be of ancient hybrid origin. The cultivated species are annuals, generally with trailing stems radiating from a central root, and large, rough-textured leaves that are lobed in varying degree. The orange or yellow flowers are quite large and conspicuous, of different sexes but on the one plant; the fruits develop below the female flowers, which soon wither and drop off. Classification of cultivar groups is made difficult by the great variation in common names used in different countries: for example the 'pumpkin' of North America is usually one of the races of *Cucurbita pepo*, while in some other countries the most popular pumpkins are *C. maxima*. Some pumpkin varieties produce some of the largest of all fruits, some of those exhibited said to have exceeded 400 pounds (180 kg) in weight.
CULTIVATION: Most species of this genus are easy to raise and have the same need of a warm, rich soil. In warm climates sow from early spring to late summer; in cold climates sow indoors in early summer, watering all seedlings well before planting. They do best planted on raised mounds of soil mixed with well rotted compost and manure. Check for slugs and keep well irrigated as they are water hungry. Harvest in fall (autumn).

Cucurbita maxima
AUTUMN SQUASH, WINTER PUMPKIN, WINTER SQUASH

Originating in subtropical South America, this species has long-running stems and large, nearly circular leaves that are hardly lobed. The feature by which it is recognized is the fruit stalk, which is large, not ridged, and of a soft corky texture. It includes a large group of pumpkins with very hard blue-gray or orange skins, including the gigantic show pumpkins, some of the pumpkins used for livestock feed, and some of the winter squashes including a great variety of shapes, sizes and colors, often with ornamented skins. **ZONES 9–11.**

Cucurbita moschata
CROOKNECK SQUASH, PUMPKIN, WINTER SQUASH

Originating somewhere in Central America, this species was probably the earliest to be domesticated. The stems are long running or may climb by tendrils, and the leaves are shallowly 5-lobed. The fruits vary greatly but are often elongated or bottle-shaped and some are bent over at the top (crookneck squashes); they include also the butternut and other pumpkins. Most cultivars of this species ripen their fruit in fall (autumn) or winter. **ZONES 8–11.**

Cucurbita maxima

Cucurbita moschata

Ctenanthe oppenheimiana

Ctenanthe lubbersiana

Cucurbita pepo

GOURD, PUMPKIN, SUMMER SQUASH, VEGETABLE MARROW

Originating in Mexico and southern USA, and possibly an ancient hybrid, this species has given rise to a broader range of cultivars than any other. The plants can be either compact or have long trailing stems and the leaves are usually deeply lobed with overlapping lobes. The summer squashes vary from elongated to broad and flattened with scalloped rims, and may have ornamented skins, and there are also some crooknecked varieties. Vegetable marrows have long fruit with rather tender skins, usually green or yellow; a development from these, now of foremost importance among vegetables, are the zucchinis or courgettes, harvested when very immature and treated like a green vegetable. Vegetable spaghetti is a race of squashes with rather dry, shreddy flesh. Various kinds of pumpkin also belong to this species, some used mainly for stock food; they do not keep well and are normally eaten soon after picking. **'Atlantic Giant'** has large striped fruit. **'Rouge Vif d'Etampes'** has rich vermilion fruit. **ZONES 8–11.**

Cucurbita pepo

Cucurbita pepo

Cucurbita pepo (zucchini)

Cucurbita pepo (pumpkins)

Cucurbita pepo 'Atlantic Giant'

Cucurbita pepo 'Rouge Vif d'Etampes'

CUMINUM

Only 2 species of annuals in the carrot family belong to this species, native to the Mediterranean region and west and central Asia. They are slender plants with delicate, much-divided leaves and small umbels of tiny white or pink flowers. The small oval, dry fruits or 'seeds' are very aromatic. One species, *Cuminum cyminum* (cumin) is grown for its seeds, which are widely used as a flavoring herb, or sometimes classified as a spice. **CULTIVATION:** They are frost tender and grow best in warm climates. Grow in a light, well-drained soil in a sunny position. Propagate from seed sown in spring in a warm situation.

Cuminum cyminum

CUMIN

Cumin is grown commercially in India, China, Japan and the Middle East for its powerfully flavored seeds. It is a small annual which grows to 12 in (30 cm) high with leaves finely divided into thread-like segments and small white flowers in summer, followed by aromatic seeds. The dried seed is an important ingredient in curry powders. Both the Dutch and Germans flavor cheese with it, and it is used in many Mexican and Middle Eastern dishes. **ZONES 9–12.**

CUNNINGHAMIA

CHINESE CEDAR, CHINA FIR

This unusual conifer genus is native to China, Taiwan and Indochina. The stiff, springy, curved leaves taper to prickly points and have glossy upper surfaces. Dead leaves remain attached to the branches, making the interior of the trees untidy and prickly, but a well-grown specimen is among the more attractive conifers. Although quite handsome and not difficult to grow, *Cunninghamia* species are found mostly in botanical gardens and larger private collections. **CULTIVATION:** Fully frost hardy, they require adequate rainfall and deep, fertile soil. Propagation is normally from seed, though seed set may be poor, or from cuttings.

Cunninghamia lanceolata

Cunninghamia lanceolata

Cunninghamia lanceolata

COFFIN PINE, COFFIN FIR, CHINA FIR

In China, where it once had an extensive natural distribution, this tree provided a valued timber for coffins (it was thought the aromatic timber prevented bodies from decomposing), resulting in its over-exploitation. Trees of 150 ft (45 m) tall were recorded there, but in parks and gardens elsewhere it is mainly seen as a tree of 20–40 ft (6–12 m), sometimes multi-trunked and widest at the top, sometimes narrower with a single, straight trunk and scattered clumps of lateral branches. The growth rate is likewise unpredictable, and it may remain shrubby for many years. **ZONES 6–10.**

CUNONIA

One species in this small genus of evergreen trees and shrubs comes from South Africa, while most of the remaining 14 come from New Caledonia. They are evergreen, damp-loving trees with thick, leathery leaves and star-shaped, 5-petalled flowers. The genus is related to the Australian genus *Ceratopetalum*. **CULTIVATION:** Fairly frost tender, they do best in full sun in well-drained, fertile soil, but will grow in sandy or gravelly soil if given sufficient moisture. Prune to establish a single leader if a tree form is desired. Propagate from seed or cuttings.

Cunonia capensis

Cunonia capensis

Cunonia capensis

SPOON BUSH, RED ALDER

This species occurs wild in southern coastal districts of South Africa. It is quite fast growing and will become a rounded tree to 50 ft (15 m) with a single trunk where conditions suit it, or a bushy shrub in lesser conditions. It has attractive, shiny leaves that are divided into pairs of lance-shaped, serrated leaflets, dark green with a reddish tinge. From the tip of each branch projects a pair of large reddish stipules, closely

Cupaniopsis anacardioides

Cupaniopsis anacardioides

× *Cupressocyparis leylandii*

× *C. leylandii* 'Naylor's Blue'

Cuphea ignea

Cuphea micropetala

Cuphea micropetala

pressed together and shaped like a spoon, hence the common name. Tiny, creamy white flowers with long stamens appear in fall (autumn), densely crowded on long spikes. **ZONES 9–10.**

CUPANIOPSIS

These tropical and subtropical evergreen trees with pinnate leaves from Australia, Papua New Guinea, and islands of the southwest Pacific occur in rainforests and vine thickets, or in stunted coastal scrubs. Small flowers in shades of green or yellow are borne in panicles at the branch tips, followed by leathery, capsular fruits that split open to reveal 3 seeds, each cupped by a red or yellow fleshy appendage that is eaten by birds, thus dispersing the seeds.
CULTIVATION: They prefer an open, sunny position and well-drained, sandy soil. Some species are tough evergreens, coping with exposed situations including salt spray and urban pavements, often making surprisingly fast growth; their branches are very strong and resilient. Propagation is always from seed, which germinates readily if freshly collected.

Cupaniopsis anacardioides
TUCKEROO

A small to medium tree to about 50 ft (15 m) high with an irregularly spreading crown, the tuckeroo occurs right along the eastern and northern coastlines of Australia. The leaves consist of 5 to 9 oblong, leathery, shiny leaflets. The greenish yellow flowers appear in fall (autumn) and winter in panicles up to 12 in (30 cm) long, with yellow fruit ripening in summer. It makes an attractive small tree, planted in streets and plazas, and is popular in California as well as Australia. **ZONES 10–12.**

CUPHEA

From Central and South America, this genus consists of over 250 species of annuals, evergreen perennials, subshrubs and shrubs. They are mostly rather low growing with weak stems and smallish, simple leaves. The flowers have a long tubular calyx and small circular red, pink, yellow or white petals, the latter sometimes hardly visible. Most are frost tender but as they are fast growing they can be treated as annuals. The many species vary quite considerably in appearance, especially with regard to the flowers. They bloom almost throughout the year.
CULTIVATION: They prefer moist, well-drained soil in sun or very light shade. Propagation is usually from small tip cuttings, though they are also easily raised from seed, which often self-sows.

Cuphea hyssopifolia
FALSE HEATHER

A small shrub from Mexico and Guatemala, this species is popular worldwide as a pot plant for window ledges and balconies. It grows to about 2 ft (0.6 m) high, has a mound-like form and small dark green oblong leaves. The small flowers appear in the axils of the new shoots from late spring to winter; they have only a short tube and prominent pink to reddish purple petals. It is short lived but self-seeds very readily and may become a pest, especially in warm areas. **ZONES 10–12.**

Cuphea ignea
syn. *Cuphea platycentra*
CIGAR FLOWER, CIGARETTE PLANT

This species from Mexico and the West Indies gets its common names from the flowers, which are small, orange and tubular. Each has a white tip with a touch of black, suggesting the ash at the tip of a cigar or cigarette. The leaves are small, elliptical and bright green. A bushy subshrub, it grows up to about 24 in (60 cm) high and benefits from occasional trimming to keep it compact. **ZONES 10–12**

Cuphea micropetala

This Mexican species is like a larger version of *Cuphea ignea*. The leaves are up to 2½ in (6 cm) long, bright green and elliptical with a prominent midrib. The 1½–2 in (3.5–5 cm) tubular flowers occur in rows at the branch tips and are orange-red with golden yellow tones, tipped with greenish yellow. Tougher than most, this species will withstand occasional light frosts. Although in the wild *Cuphea micropetala* occurs on streamsides, it grows well in normal garden soils. **ZONES 9–11.**

Cuphea × *purpurea*

This hybrid between the shrubby *Cuphea llavea* and the annual *C. procumbens* includes several very attractive cultivars with brightly colored flowers. They are spreading subshrubs of up to about 18 in (45 cm) high with pointed elliptical leaves in 2 rows. The flowers have a narrow tube about 1 in (25 mm) long with purplish ribs, and 2 colored petals like little ears protruding from it; in the cultivar **'Firefly'** they are a brilliant blood red. It will flower freely from spring to fall (autumn) in a small pot. **ZONES 9–11.**

× *CUPRESSOCYPARIS*

The '×' in front of the name indicates that this is a bigeneric hybrid, that is, a hybrid between 2 different genera, in this case *Cupressus* and *Chamaecyparis*. Although the name applies to any hybrid between these genera (including later generations and backcrosses), it is best known in the form of the one which first appeared in England in 1888 as a chance hybrid between the frost-hardy *Chamaecyparis nootkatensis* and the less hardy *Cupressus macrocarpa*. Two additional hybrids have since been raised, their *Cupressus* parents being *C. glabra* and *C. lusitanica* respectively.
CULTIVATION: These conifers combine rapid growth with reasonable frost-hardiness, and adapt well to poorly drained soil but not to arid climates. They are widely planted for fast-growing hedges as they respond well to frequent trimming. However, if they are left untrimmed they rapidly grow to tree size. Propagate from cuttings, which strike readily under nursery conditions. Although seed is fertile, the resulting seedlings might vary.

× *Cupressocyparis leylandii*
LEYLAND CYPRESS

Representing the original cross between *Chamaecyparis nootkatensis* and *Cupressus macrocarpa*, this name encompasses a number of seedling clones, some of which have been named as cultivars. When used without specifying a cultivar name it usually refers to **'Haggerston Grey'** or **'Leighton Green'**, which both make very vigorous, upright trees with a long, open leading shoot and slightly irregular outline; foliage is deep green or slightly grayish. In good soil it will reach 30 ft (9 m) in 10 years and double that in 30 years, ultimately growing to 100 ft (30 m) or more. **'Naylor's Blue'** has more strongly bluish green foliage and is more columnar in habit. **ZONES 5–10.**

C

Cupressus bakeri subsp. *matthewsii*

Cupressus duclouxiana

Cupressus lusitanica

CUPRESSUS

CYPRESS

This important conifer genus has been cultivated since Classical times but its species are seldom planted where winters are severe due to their limited cold tolerance. The majority of the 20 or so species occur wild in western USA, Mexico and Guatemala, with a smaller number in the Himalayas and western China and a single species in the Mediterranean region. As well as the wild forms the cypresses include many cultivars. They are handsome ornamentals that come in many foliage hues; they range from tall to dwarf, from columnar to weeping or high-crowned and spreading. Their dense foliage and rapid growth makes them especially useful for screens and windbreaks.

CULTIVATION: Some species are very tolerant of dry conditions, others need a moister climate. Soil and sunlight requirements vary, although generally they prefer full sun, well-drained soil and protection from cold winds. They are easy to propagate from seed, always plentiful on adult trees, and cultivars are almost as easily raised from cuttings. However, some cypress species suffer from the disease cypress canker, which disfigures the trees and finally kills them.

Cupressus cashmeriana

Cupressus glabra

Cupressus lusitanica

Cupressus arizonica

ARIZONA CYPRESS, ROUGH-BARKED ARIZONA CYPRESS

Originating in Arizona, USA, and sometimes confused with *Cupressus glabra*, this pyramidal species will grow to 50 ft (15 m). Its mature foliage is gray-green and does not display the white spots of the smooth Arizona cypress. It has short-stalked, large, round cones, up to 1 in (25 mm) across, and a brown, stringy and furrowed bark. It is grown both as a specimen tree and as a hedge. **ZONES 7–10.**

Cupressus arizonica

Cupressus bakeri

MODOC CYPRESS

Rare in cultivation, this species is limited in the wild to the Siskiyou Mountains of northern California. It is a smallish tree of no more than 50 ft (15 m) with reddish brown bark and the gray-green foliage consists of very short, crowded branchlets. The cones are quite small. ***Cupressus bakeri* subsp. *matthewsii***, the Siskiyou cypress, is found in the northern end of the Siskiyou Mountains in Oregon. It grows to 100 ft (30 m) and has large, rather warty cones up to 1 in (25 mm) across. **ZONES 7–10.**

Cupressus cashmeriana

KASHMIR CYPRESS

Despite its name, this species is not native to Kashmir but to Bhutan, and was only rediscovered in the wild recently. It should by rights be called 'Bhutan cypress', except that *Cupressus torulosa* has a prior claim to this common name. This beautiful cypress has long, weeping sprays of blue-green, aromatic foliage, but is difficult to grow. In a suitable warm, moist climate it grows fast at first, attaining 20–30 ft (6–9 m) in 15 years, but is easily damaged by wind and may die in spells of hot or dry weather. In cooler mountain areas of the wet tropics are found some fine specimens, and it also does well in wetter hill areas of the Mediterranean, the western USA, eastern Australia and New Zealand. In the frost-prone areas of the UK it should be grown in a cool greenhouse. **ZONES 9–11.**

Cupressus duclouxiana

This very attractive cypress from the hills of western China is narrowly columnar, with dense, very fine-textured foliage. Although not widely grown, it appears to be a useful landscaping subject for warm climates, tolerant of dry or exposed conditions. It can reach 20 ft (6 m) in 10 years in good soil. **ZONES 9–10.**

Cupressus macrocarpa

Cupressus glabra

syn. *Cupressus arizonica* var. *glabra*

SMOOTH ARIZONA CYPRESS

This species is from the mountains of western Arizona, an area of low rainfall and quite low winter temperatures. With compact blue-gray foliage marked with white resin dots, waxy whitish twigs and reddish, flaking bark, it is very ornamental; it is popular in warm regions with hot dry summers. Under such conditions it makes vigorous growth, is long lived, and resistant to pests and diseases. Some cultivated forms are fairly narrowly conical, others have much broader, looser crowns. Mature specimens are usually 30–40 ft (9–12 m) in height. **'Limelight'** is a spectacular new cultivar that tolerates frost, heat and high humidity. It has glowing golden foliage and quickly makes a narrow conical tree. **ZONES 7–10.**

Cupressus lusitanica

CEDAR OF GOA, MEXICAN CYPRESS

This cypress is native to the mountains of western Mexico but was long ago introduced to Portugal (*Lusitania* in Latin), where it is now common in parts. In warm climates it is a vigorous grower, but also tolerates cold and dry conditions. It makes a bushy, broad-crowned tree with dense, grayish green foliage that has an attractive loose, foamy texture. ***Cupressus lusitanica* var. *benthamii*** has greener, more drooping foliage with branchlets in small, flat sprays. Both this and the typical form grow to 30 ft (9 m) or more in about 15 years. **ZONES 8–11.**

Cupressus macrocarpa

MONTEREY CYPRESS

Endemic to a very short stretch of the central Californian coast near Monterey, this grows into one of the largest of all cypresses, reaching 120 ft (36 m) tall

C. macrocarpa 'Greenstead Magnificent'

Cupressus macrocarpa 'Aurea'

Cussonia sphaerocephala

Cussonia spicata

with a trunk diameter of 8 ft (2.4 m). When planted in a grove it forms a tall, straight trunk, but in the open in good soil it branches low with massive, spreading limbs, producing a broad, dense crown of deep green with a rather spiky outline. Close up, the foliage is rather coarse, and it has a slightly sour smell when bruised. The cones are large and wrinkled. It grows best in cool but mild climates with winter rainfall and takes only 10 years or so to form a dense 30–40 ft (9–12 m) tree. It is one of the most popular farm hedging trees in New Zealand. Golden cultivars include **'Brunniana'**, somewhat columnar, the foliage ageing almost green; the vigorous **'Aurea'**, with long, golden spikes of foliage spreading almost horizontally; and **'Aurea Saligna'** with remarkable weeping, gold-tipped branchlets and elongated scale leaves. A lower-growing cultivar to 4 ft (1.2 m) is **'Greenstead Magnificent'**, which spreads to form a flat-topped, dense mat of pale gray-green foliage, drooping around the edges; as the plant ages the whole becomes raised above the ground on a short trunk. **'Goldcrest'** is a small conical form with golden foliage. **ZONES 7–10.**

Cupressus sempervirens

FUNEREAL CYPRESS, ITALIAN CYPRESS, MEDITERRANEAN CYPRESS

This species, a familiar tree in Italy, France and Spain, was introduced to these countries from the eastern Mediterranean. It has fine dark grayish green foliage with very tiny scale leaves in slightly flattened sprays, and large, slightly elongated, pale brown cones. In its growth habit the Mediterranean cypress exhibits a curious phenomenon: the form usually cultivated, known as **'Stricta'**, is narrowly columnar, but a proportion of its seedlings grow into trees with side branches at a wide angle to the trunk; this form is often known as **'Horizontalis'**. More tolerant of dry conditions and slower growing than most other cypresses, it makes quite vigorous growth under good conditions in a warm climate. The 'Stricta' form can reach 15–20 ft (4.5–6 m) in 10 years, often as a slim column at this stage, but old trees of 30–40 ft (9–12 m) are usually much broader. It takes well to topiary. **'Swane's Golden'**, an Australian cultivar with foliage flecked golden yellow with deeper gold tips, is slower growing than 'Stricta' but can still reach 20 ft (6 m) or more. It is rather frost tender. **'Gracilis'** is a narrowly columnar cultivar raised in New Zealand, slow growing and maturing at about 15 ft (4.5 m) with a width of about 3 ft (1 m). It has bright green foliage. **ZONES 8–10.**

Cupressus torulosa

BHUTAN CYPRESS, HIMALAYAN CYPRESS

This tall conifer reaches 150 ft (45 m) in its native Himalayas, though in cultivation 50–80 ft (15–24 m) is more usual. An elegant tree with a long-pointed crown broader at the base, it is valued for its fast growth and fragrant timber. Its small branchlets are slender and slightly curved, consisting of tiny deep green scale leaves that are blunt tipped. The small cones are purple when young but ripen shiny brown, and the brown fibrous bark peels into strips. It grows best in mild, very moist climates. **ZONES 8–10.**

CURCUMA

This genus of the ginger family consists of about 40 species of tuberous and rhizomatous perennials, ranging from tropical Asia to northern Australia in regions of very seasonal rainfall. They produce tufts of broad canna-like leaves which usually die back in the tropical dry season, and short erect spikes of small, often brightly colored flowers that emerge from between large bracts. Some are grown as ornamentals in tropical gardens or as curiosities in botanical garden greenhouses, but the genus is best known for the spices obtained from the rhizomes of several species, most notably turmeric from *Curcuma domestica.* **CULTIVATION:** In the tropics grow these plants in a well-tilled garden bed in moderately fertile soil. Plant rhizomes or tubers late in the dry season and water frequently when new leaves appear. Harvest turmeric rhizomes when the leaves die back.

Curcuma domestica

Curcuma domestica

syn. *Curcuma longa*

TURMERIC

Believed to have originated in India, turmeric is grown throughout tropical Asia for its bright orange rhizomes, which apart from their mildly spicy flavor are valued as a food coloring, providing a substitute for the very expensive saffron. It is also used for dyeing cloth. The broadly lance-shaped, bright green leaves can form large clumps up to about 3 ft (1 m) tall in hot areas. Short, dense spikes of pale yellow flowers are produced in summer. It prefers the warmth of the tropics but can be successfully grown in warm-temperate areas. The fresh or dried roots provide color and pungent fragrance to chutneys, pickles and curries; it is harvested when the foliage begins to dry off in fall (autumn). **ZONES 10–12.**

CUSSONIA

SOUTH AFRICAN CABBAGE TREE

The 20 species of small evergreen trees of this South African genus, related to *Schefflera,* have unbranched trunks in their younger stages. As these long-lived trees mature, they become multi-branched. They are topped by a thick mass of large, compound leaves; the leaflets radiate from a central point and are usually lobed or further divided into leaflets. Densely clustered spikes of small, greenish flowers stand well above the canopy; they are followed by the succulent fruits which are dull red to black. **CULTIVATION:** Though frost tender, they will grow in cooler areas in a sheltered, sunny location. They can be grown in containers provided they have adequate water in the growing season. Propagation is from fresh seed.

Cussonia paniculata

CABBAGE TREE

This upright tree from cool, mountainous areas of South Africa reaches a height of 12 ft (3.5 m); the trunk is thin and is topped by a narrow crown of foliage. The leaves, rich bluish green with a silvery bloom, are held on long stalks. The dense spikes of flowers appear like candelabras in summer above the foliage. **ZONES 9–11.**

Cussonia sphaerocephala

This rare species is similar in most respects to the better known *Cussonia spicata,* differing mainly in the larger, more rounded flowering panicle. The epithet sphaerocephala (sphere-headed) may refer to this feature or alternatively to the almost spherical crown of foliage that terminates each stem. **ZONES 9–11.**

Cussonia spicata

SPIKED CABBAGE TREE, KIEPERSOL

This is the only species to be widely cultivated and its juvenile form is well known as an indoor plant. Usually single trunked, it can grow to 20 ft (6 m) high and has 8 in (20 cm) diameter leaves that are divided into 5 to 9 leaflets and carried on long, thick stalks. The flowers are borne in spring and summer. Although often defoliated by heavy frosts, it can reshoot provided it is not repeatedly frozen. **ZONES 8–11.**

C. sempervirens 'Swane's Golden'

Cupressus torulosa

C. sempervirens 'Swane's Golden'

Cupressus sempervirens 'Gracilis'

CYANANTHUS

A genus of *Campanula* relatives from high mountain areas of western China and the Himalayas, *Cyananthus* consists of around 25 species of small carpeting or mound-forming perennials with small leaves and very pretty blue, purple, yellow or white bell-shaped to somewhat trumpet-shaped flowers held on short stems.

CULTIVATION: They are very pretty plants for the rock garden but their requirements are specialized and they are not always easy to grow successfully. Preferring a cool, damp climate, they should be planted in a gritty, humus-rich, slightly acid soil with very good drainage; a surface bed of gravel or rock chips may be an advantage. Some species may require the humidity and protection of an alpine house. Propagate from seed or stem cuttings in spring or summer.

Cyananthus lobatus

This species from the Himalayas makes a dwarf tuft or mound of foliage only 2–4 in (5–10 cm) high, the tiny, fleshy leaves cut into several lobes. Violet-blue flowers are borne singly on short stalks in late summer and are about $1\frac{1}{2}$ in (35 mm) long. **ZONES 5–9.**

Cyananthus microphyllus

A mat-forming species from the Himalayas of northern India and Nepal, this has tiny heart-shaped hairy leaves and bears small violet-blue funnel-shaped flowers in late summer and fall (autumn). It will grow to a height of no more than 6 in (15 cm). **ZONES 4–9.**

Cyananthus lobatus

Cyathea australis

CYANOTIS

Related to the wandering Jews (*Tradescantia*), this genus of about 30 species of creeping or clump-forming perennials is found mainly in the tropics of Africa and Asia. Some species have tuberous roots and die back in the tropical dry season but most are evergreen. Leaves are often quite hairy, with marginal fringes of white hairs a common feature. Small pink, bluish or purple flowers are borne in dense bracteate clusters. A few species have been cultivated as indoor plants and some are found in succulent collections. They can make attractive specimens for hanging baskets.

CULTIVATION: They are mostly frost tender and dislike excessive water, especially in winter. Grow in bright light in a coarse, gritty soil not too rich in nutrients. Propagate from cuttings.

Cyanotis kewensis

TEDDY BEAR PLANT

This evergreen perennial from southern India has trailing stems that carry 2 rows of overlapping oval fleshy leaves up to 2 in (5 cm) long, rather purplish with velvety brown hairs on the undersides. Stalkless clusters of 3-petalled violet-blue flowers appear among clusters of leaf-like bracts intermittently through the year. **ZONES 9–11.**

Cyanotis somaliensis

PUSSY EARS

From Somalia, this species has narrow 2 in (5 cm) long leaves, shiny green and edged with soft white hairs. Once established its creeping stems make vigorous growth. The pinkish blue summer flowers are very small and on some plants may never appear. **ZONES 9–11.**

Cyathea dregei

Cyathea brownii

Cyathea dealbata

CYATHEA

TREE FERN

Apart from *Asplenium* this is the largest genus of ferns, with over 600 species scattered through humid tropical and subtropical regions of the world. Some botanists have split off large groups of species into separate genera, notably *Alsophila* and *Sphaeropteris*, but most fern experts no longer agree with this. *Cyathea* species vary greatly in size, but most are single-stemmed with a trunk up to 50 ft (15 m) tall and an umbrella-like crown of very large fronds. The frond bases are usually covered in hairs or chaff-like scales which may be quite prickly. They often persist on the trunk but even after decaying, their scars make an interesting pattern on the trunk.

CULTIVATION: In warm-climate gardens few plants create such dramatic effects as these tree ferns, some of which are quite fast-growing under ideal conditions. They prefer a humid atmosphere, part-shade, and a moist, humus-rich soil. In warm weather they need plentiful watering and may need frequent mist-spraying during hot dry spells. When young many species make attractive indoor plants in a suitably humid environment. Propagate by spores in spring. Transplant established plants with care.

Cyathea australis

syn. *Alsophila australis*

ROUGH TREE FERN

A native of eastern Australia, this majestic fern grows to 20 ft (6 m) or more high, with a slender blackish trunk and fronds up to almost 10 ft (3 m) long; foliage is deep green in shady situations, more yellowish in full sun. The frond bases are covered in narrow dark brown scales and are quite prickly to the touch. It adapts better than most tree ferns to low humidity but still demands plentiful summer water to grow well. **ZONES 9–11.**

Cyathea brownii

syn. *Sphaeropteris excelsa*

This species from Norfolk Island is very similar to *Cyathea cooperi* but has a thicker trunk, more leathery fronds, and larger pale brown scales on the frond bases. In cultivation these differences are not always clear and intermediate hybrids may be found. **ZONES 10–12.**

Cyathea cooperi

syn. *Sphaeropteris cooperi*

STRAW TREE FERN, SCALY TREE FERN, AUSTRALIAN TREE FERN

Also from eastern Australia, this is one of the fastest-growing tree ferns outside the wet tropics, sometimes reaching 20 ft (6 m) in less than 15 years if moisture and nutrients are abundant. It has a crown of similar size to *Cyathea australis* but the frond bases are thicker and covered densely in chaff-like scales that are pale brown to straw-colored. The foliage is fairly tolerant of sun but is easily shrivelled by drying winds. **ZONES 10–12.**

Cyathea dealbata

syn. *Alsophila tricolor*

SILVER TREE FERN, PONGA

This attractive New Zealand species has distinctive silver-white undersides to its fronds. It is slow growing to about 15 ft (4.5 m) in cultivation. The slender erect trunk is topped by a crown of fronds up to 10 ft (3 m) long. One of New Zealand's national symbols, it is marginally frost hardy and needs shelter from wind. **ZONES 9–11.**

Cyathea dregei

syn. *Alsophila dregei*

A southern African native, this is a compact, slow-growing species with rather narrow fronds not much more than 3 ft (1 m) long, with a bright green upper surface and pale underside. The trunk is seldom higher than 10 ft (3 m). Its wild habitat is usually at the edge of streams and in the garden it prefers very moist, though well-aerated ground. **ZONES 9–11.**

Cyathea medullaris

syn. *Sphaeropteris medullaris*

BLACK TREE FERN

From New Zealand and other islands of the South Pacific, this species is one of the largest, most robust tree ferns known in cultivation. The trunk can reach 50 ft (15 m) or even more and 12 in (30 cm) diameter, with widely spaced frond scars.

The fronds can be up to 20 ft (6 m) long and more than 6 ft (1.8 m) wide, with black stalks up to 3 in (8 cm) thick covered in blackish chaff-like scales. It needs a sheltered position and responds with rapid growth to an abundant supply of water and nutrients. **ZONES 9–12.**

CYCAS
SAGO PALM

This geologically ancient genus of cycads has about 60 species from Australia, Southeast Asia, Madagascar and East Africa, as well as many of the islands in between, and out into the Pacific. They are palm-like plants with pinnate fronds spreading from the top of a thick trunk that is packed with starchy tissue; male and female organs are on different plants, the male in long, narrow cones terminating the stem, the female on the margins of furry, leaf-like organs that ring the trunk apex and may eventually hang in a 'skirt' below the trunk apex, as the hard, egg-like seeds mature. Trunk growth is normally very slow, so large specimens are prized and fetch high prices from collectors and landscape contractors.

CULTIVATION: With the exception of *Cycas revoluta,* most *Cycas* species do not thrive outdoors except in tropical and warmer subtropical areas. They like sunny positions but with some shade when young, and deep, well-drained soil. Propagation is from seed, detached offsets, or by cutting off a whole trunk and plunging the base in a trench filled with gravel and organic matter.

Cycas armstrongii

Cycas armstrongii

This species from the tropical 'Top End' of Australia's Northern Territory occurs in flat, sandy country in open eucalypt woodland. It is usually unbranched, with a straight, slender trunk 6–15 ft (1.8–4.5 m) tall, from the top of which emerges a circle of delicate, new, pale green fronds at the beginning of each wet season; during the long dry season they gradually shrivel and droop, hanging in a brown 'skirt'. Plants in moister positions may retain fronds for longer. Female trees mostly sport another 'skirt' of seed-bearing organs, each with 2 to 4 large, orange-brown seeds. **ZONES 11–12.**

Cycas circinalis
FERN PALM, QUEEN SAGO

Widely distributed in southern India, mainland Southeast Asia, the Malay Archipelago and islands of the South Pacific, this is a robust plant commonly suckering from the base with multiple trunks up to 15 ft (4.5 m) high and over 12 in (30 cm) thick, and dense crowns of bright green, glossy fronds 6–10 ft (1.8–3 m) long. The large seeds ripen to shiny reddish yellow and are able to float in water (this has aided their wide dispersal). **ZONES 10–12.**

Cycas revoluta

Cyclamen hederifolium

Cyclamen cilicium

Cyathea medullaris

Cycas revoluta
JAPANESE SAGO PALM

Endemic to the islands of southern Japan, this palm-like species is a popular ornamental plant in Japan. It grows slowly with short, single or multiple trunks to 10 ft (3 m) high with a compact crown of stiff pinnate leaves that have closely crowded, very narrow, spine-tipped leaflets. It is the most widely cultivated cycad in the world and is valued as a landscape subject, especially suited to courtyards and plazas. Slow growing, it is capable of living for 50 to 100 years or even more and is readily transplanted. **ZONES 9–12.**

CYCLAMEN
CYCLAMEN

This genus consists of about 20 species of tuberous perennials, native in the Mediterranean region and southwest Asia. They belong to the primula family, though the relationship to primulas is not at all obvious: the round tubers sit on or just below the soil surface and bear fleshy, heart-shaped leaves often with light or dark patterns on the upper surface. The very elegant flowers, borne singly on bare stalks, are downward-pointing but with the 5 twisted petals sharply reflexed and erect. They come in colors varying from crimson-red to pink or white and may be scented. Many of the smaller species are choice rock garden plants, while the larger florist's cyclamen (*Cyclamen persicum*) is grown in pots for indoor decoration.

CULTIVATION: Cyclamens vary from frost tender to very frost hardy. They should be planted in light, fibrous soil, rich in organic matter with good drainage and in sun or part-shade. Water regularly during growth but allow to dry out during summer. The tubers are best left undisturbed and should grow larger each year, flowering more abundantly each season. Propagate from seed in fall (autumn). Some cyclamens are susceptible to black rot.

Cycas armstrongii

Cyclamen cilicium

This species from southern Turkey has heart-shaped leaves that are slightly toothed. The flowers are borne on 4–5 in (10–12 cm) stems and are light pink with deeper rose pink at the base of the petals. The flowering period is from fall (autumn) through winter and into early spring. **ZONES 7–9.**

Cyclamen coum

This popular species from the Balkans, Turkey and Lebanon grows to 4 in (10 cm) with leaves that are round to heart-shaped, dark green and frequently marbled with light green or silver. The abundant winter or early spring flowers vary from pale mauve to deep pink, often stained crimson at the base. ***Cyclamen coum* subsp. *caucasicum*** has leaves marbled with silver; the dark pink flowers are stained crimson at the base. ***C. c.* subsp. *coum*** has elegant pink to crimson flowers. The Latin epithet *coum* refers to the Aegean island of Kos and should be pronounced co-um. **ZONES 6–10.**

Cyclamen persicum cultivar

Cyclamen persicum cultivar

Cyclamen persicum

Cyclamen pseudibericum 'Roseum'

Cyclamen hederifolium
syn. *Cyclamen neapolitanum*

This species flowers in fall (autumn) and can produce corms up to 6 in (15 cm) wide. Growing to 4 in (10 cm), it has dark green leaves heavily marbled paler green, with broad shallow toothing. The flowers are white to rose pink, darker at the base, and some strains are perfumed. It has a wide distribution in southern Europe and Turkey. **ZONES 5–10.**

Cyclamen libanoticum

This species from Lebanon has dark green leaves with a white zone on the upper surface and blotches of yellow green; the undersides are deep purple. The quite large and fragrant flowers are pure white to rose with darker markings round the mouth and are produced from late winter to early spring. **ZONES 9–10.**

Cyclamen mirabile

This species from western Turkey has small green leaves with pinkish gray markings on the upper surface, the undersides reddish. The pink flowers with red dots at the base of the petals appear in fall (autumn). **ZONES 7–9.**

Cyclamen persicum

Despite its botanical name this species is not found in Persia (now Iran), but occurs in woodlands from Greece to Lebanon and in North Africa. Selected strains of this species are the florists' cyclamens, commonly grown indoors. These plants can be quite large, up to 12 in (30 cm) tall and of similar spread. From among the crowded heart-shaped leaves, which are often marbled light and dark green with silver bands, rise large waxy flowers in shades of white, pink, red or purple, sometimes ruffled or edged with a contrasting tone. It flowers profusely over a long winter season; cool nights will ensure that flowering continues. **ZONES 9–10.**

Cyclamen pseudibericum

This species from Turkey has heart-shaped, patterned leaves with toothed, wavy margins. The small, deep pink flowers are produced in winter and spring. **'Roseum'** has paler purplish pink flowers with darker markings at the base of the petals. **ZONES 7–9.**

Cyclamen purpurascens

From central and eastern Europe, this species has rather large, glossy, dark green leaves that are purple beneath and may have faint silvery markings on the upper side. In summer it bears small purplish red or deep pink flowers on 4 in (10 cm) stalks; they are very sweetly scented. **ZONES 5–9.**

Cyclamen repandum

Cyclamen hederifolium

Cyclamen repandum
IVY-LEAFED CYCLAMEN

A native of southern Europe, this species has striking mid-green leaves that are heart-shaped and lobed, often marbled above and eventually become reddish purple below. The fragrant white, pink or red flowers with twisted petals appear on slender 6 in (10 cm) stalks in spring; the plant may continue flowering into summer in cool areas. **ZONES 6–9.**

CYDONIA
QUINCE

Quinces are familiar fruits, but the small deciduous trees from which they come are less well known tomost people, and at the same time quite unusual and ornamental. Native to temperate Asia, they belong to the pome-fruit group of the rose family. They are small, crooked, very woody trees with smooth bark and simple, oval leaves, downy at least on the underside and clustered on short spur-shoots (as in apples) except on the long summer growths. The flowers are solitary at the ends of the spur shoots, and have downy calyces and pink petals. The large fruits have waxy or almost greasy skins that are pleasantly aromatic.
CULTIVATION: Quinces only thrive in cooler-temperate climates, though the Chinese species tolerates warmer, more frost-free areas than the common quince does. They require moist, deep soil and a sunny position. Propagation is from seed, easily obtained from over-ripe fruit, or by grafting for named varieties.

Cydonia oblonga
COMMON QUINCE

A spreading, bushy tree of 12–15 ft (3.5–4.5 m), this species forks low into crooked limbs. The leaves are moderately large, deep green above but downy on the underside and on young twigs. The very attractive flowers, about 2 in (5 cm) in diameter and usually a clear pale pink, appear in late spring. The fruit, eaten cooked, ripen to pale or deep yellow and are up to 6 in (15 cm) long with hard flesh. The common quince is intolerant of summer humidity. **ZONES 6–9.**

CYLINDROPHYLLUM

This genus of the large mesembryanthum tribe, is made up of 6 species of low-growing succulents, all native to South Africa's Cape Province. Their leaves are cylindrical and may be quite elongated, up to about 4 in (10 cm) in length. The plants are long lived and build up into mats or small mounds of crowded leaf rosettes, each rosette consisting of a few leaves only. They produce quite large, solitary daisy-like flowers in summer in varying shades of

Cylindrophyllum dyeri

Cydonia oblonga

Cydonia oblonga

white or pink, opening in the afternoon. **CULTIVATION:** Frost-tender plants, they prefer a semi-shaded position and must have very well-drained soil. Water sparingly when new leaves are expanding and flowers are opening, hardly at all at other times. Insect pests include scale insects, mealybug and caterpillars. Propagate from seed or cuttings.

Cylindrophyllum dyeri

This plant forms a small mound to about 4 in (10 cm) high, its leaves are green with maroon tips, cylindrical and up to 3 in (8 cm) long. This species features medium-size, daisy-like pale pink flowers in summer. **ZONES 9–11.**

CYMBIDIUM

Although there are over 40 species of the orchid genus *Cymbidium*, ranging in the wild from south and East Asia to eastern Australia, few are found in orchid collections—it is their showy hybrids that are among the most widely grown of all orchids. They have long sprays of up to 30 graceful flowers in many combinations of green, yellow, white, pink, dull red or brown, with the labellum usually marked in red. Cymbidium plants have long, arching leaves arising in 2 rows from the edges of a short, slightly flattened pseudobulb, though some of the species have a scarcely developed bulb, their leaves forming grass-like tufts. The erect to pendulous flower spikes arise from the bases of the bulbs, which build up into large clumps as plants age. Flowers of the wild species are pretty in a subdued way with narrow, rather dull colored sepals and petals and most have a spicy fragrance. The result of 100 years of breeding, the larger modern hybrids have bowl-shaped flowers 4 in (10 cm) or more across on stems more than 3 ft (1 m) long, appearing mainly in spring. The best hybrids are kept for exhibition, but numerous others, generally unnamed, are sold by florists either as flowering plants or cut flowers. Over the last several decades miniature cymbidium hybrids have become very popular, bred from East Asian species with narrow, grassy leaves and erect spikes of smallish flowers.
CULTIVATION: Advances in propagation techniques have increased the availability of cymbidium plants at reasonable prices. In warm climates they are easily grown outdoors in sheltered spots, tolerating even very light frosts and some sun during the day (though sunlight can scorch pale-colored flowers). In cooler climates they need a mildly warmed greenhouse. Plant in pots with large drainage holes, in an orchid compost with more finely chopped bark or fiber than that used for epiphytes such as cattleyas. Apply weak liquid fertilizer frequently in the summer growing season. After flowering, divide large plants into groups of 2 to 3 leafy pseudobulbs, carefully cutting apart with a sharp sterilized knife, trimming off all dead roots, and discarding the old, leafless 'back-bulbs'; replant in a pot that is not too large. Propagation was traditionally from back-bulbs, but commercially this has given way to production of seedlings and mericlones on sterile media in laboratory flasks.

Cymbidium, Large-flowered Hybrids

These are the best known cymbidiums, and innumerable grexes (seedling families from the one cross) and cultivars (selected named seedlings) are available. The largest types can have flowers as much as 6 in (15 cm) wide, and their top-heavy, arching flower spikes benefit from staking. **Atlanta** has elegant cream and pink flowers about 4 in (10 cm) wide; **Claude Pepper** has clear crimson blooms, not like most red cymbidiums which tend more to mahogany, so is much sought after. **Valley Furnace 'Chocolate'** is an outstanding seedling clone of the grex Valley Furnace with large brown flowers. **ZONES 9–11.**

Cymbidium lowianum

From the mountains of southwestern China, Thailand and Burma, this was one of the earliest cymbidiums brought to the West and was also one parent of the first hybrid, made in England in 1889. It was named after the adventurer Hugh Low, associate of North Borneo's 'Rajah Brooke ' and a collector of tropical plants. It is a robust plant with well-developed pseudobulbs, and both leaves and flowering stems are up to 3 ft (1 m) long. Flowers normally have narrow, twisted green petals and sepals and a cream lip marked with red. **'Concolor'**, bronze-green with a greenish-cream lip, has been equally important in cymbidium breeding. **ZONES 9–11.**

Cymbidium lowianum

Cymbidium Swan Lake 'Margot'

C., L-fH, Valley Furnace 'Chocolate'

Cymbidium, L-fH, Claude Pepper

Cymbidium Leopard Lady 'Mary Smith'

Cymbidium Rothersay 'Black Label'

Cymbidium Sensation 'Marble Hill'

Cymbidium Valley Goddess 'Rajah'

Cymbidium Sleeping Nymph 'Perfection'

Cymbidium Clarissa × Volcano

C. Highland Lassie 'Mont Millius'

Cymbidium Ivy Fung 'Torch'

Cymbidium, Miniature Hybrids

These cymbidiums are usually only about 18 in (45 cm) tall, with many flowers about 2 in (5 cm) wide or less; some have the broad petals and rounded shape of the larger types, others are more spidery. All are charming, cool-growing plants that look best when allowed to grow into large, many-flowered clumps, for example, ***Cymbidium* Oriental Legend 'Temple Bells'** and ***C.* Lady Bug 'Drumm'**. Some of them have rather weak flower spikes which may need to be staked. **ZONES 9–11.**

CYMBOPOGON

At least 50 species of rather coarse grasses, native to warmer regions of Africa, Asia and Australia, belong to this genus. A feature of many species is the aromatic foliage, from essential oils in the tissues. They are densely clump forming, mostly with long, flattened leaves, and send up long-stalked seed heads with clustered spikelets that are woolly or silky-haired in some species. The genus includes several species of economic importance for their aromatic oils, and some that are potentially ornamental in warm-climate plantings.

CULTIVATION: Their main requirement is a climate with a long summer growing season, and a well-drained, light-textured but fertile soil. Some species including lemongrass may not overwinter successfully if winters are cool and wet, and should be replanted each year in late spring in such climates. Propagate from seed or by division of clumps.

C., MH, Oriental Legend 'Temple Bells'

Cymbidium, MH, Lady Bug 'Drumm'

Cymbidium, Miniature Hybrid

Cymbopogon citratus

LEMONGRASS

This valuable grass, believed to have originated in India, forms a dense clump of long, gray-green leaves reaching as much as 6 ft (1.8 m) high, though mostly smaller. It is rarely known to flower in cultivation, much less produce seed. The crushed or bruised leaves have a strong lemon fragrance but are very tough and inedible; it is the fleshy white bases of the shoots that are used in Southeast Asian cooking, collected and used fresh. The leaves can be used fresh or dried to make a herbal tea. **ZONES 10–12.**

CYNARA

A genus of 10 species of perennials, thistle relatives from the Mediterranean of statuesque proportions, grown both for their large silvery gray, deeply divided leaves and their thistle-like flowerheads. It includes the globe artichoke and the cardoon, both of which have edible parts, in one the immature flowerheads and in the other, the leaf stalks.

CULTIVATION: They should be grown in full sun and in a fertile well-drained soil. To be seen to best advantage they need plenty of space. Propagation is from seed by offsets that are formed around the crown.

Cynoglossum amabile

Cynoglossum amabile 'Firmamant'

Cynara cardunculus

CARDOON

Resembling its relative the globe artichoke, cardoon produces broad, fleshy, edible leaf stalks in a similar manner to celery. It also makes a fine ornamental, towering up to 8 ft (2.4 m) high with very coarse gray stems and leaves and multiple large mauve flowerheads. Most often grown from offsets, seed may be started indoors and planted out after all danger of frost has passed. Space plants 5 ft (1.5 m) apart in rows in well-drained, humus-rich soil. Leaf stalks can be blanched by enclosing them in cardboard tubes. Harvest stems by slicing under the crown through the roots. **ZONES 6–10.**

Cynara scolymus

GLOBE ARTICHOKE

The globe artichoke was once considered to be an aphrodisiac. It has delicate, gray-green leaves and is easy to grow in most soils and positions. Make sure it has enough space (one or two plants are enough in a small garden). A rich soil will mean better production. Plant suckers rather than seeds about 3 ft (1 m) apart in early spring. Remove yellowing leaves and stems in fall (autumn). Cut the plump flower buds from the plants in spring and summer before the flowers begin to open. Watch for leaf spot disease. **ZONES 6–10.**

Cynara scolymus

Cynodon dactylon

CYNODON

This genus consists of about 8 species of creeping perennial grasses, most native in southern and tropical Africa though one species, Bermuda grass, is now distributed through most warmer parts of the world. As well as surface runners they have deeply buried, knotty rhizomes; the leaves, on erect stems, are short and narrow, and the tiny seed heads are borne in an umbel-like inflorescence branched into 2 or more spikes.

CULTIVATION: Bermuda grass does not mind soils that are sandy or clayey and tolerates hot, dry weather so it does not require as much watering as other lawns. To propagate sow seeds; runners and turfs will also readily take. Not overly vulnerable to diseases, it will, however, suffer from exposure to cold weather and may turn brown in winter; it prefers sun.

Cynodon dactylon

BERMUDA GRASS, INDIAN DOUB, SOUTH AFRICAN COUCH

Considered a relatively minor weed in many parts of the world, this grass is at the same time highly regarded as a lawn grass in the right situation, in climates where winters are not too severe. A medium to fine-textured grass, it quickly spreads by underground and surface runners. **ZONES 9–12.**

CYNOGLOSSUM

A genus of 55 species of annuals, biennials and perennials from most temperate

Cynara cardunculus

Cynara cardunculus

regions of the world. All species are frost hardy and valued for their long flowering period. They are related to the common forget-me-not, which many resemble.
CULTIVATION: All species need a fertile but not over rich soil; if over-nourished the plants tend to flop over. Propagation is from seed sown in fall (autumn) or spring or, in the case of perennial species, by division.

Cynoglossum amabile
CHINESE FORGET-ME-NOT

This upright annual or biennial, growing to a height of about 20 in (50 cm) has dull green hairy lanceolate leaves and flowers in racemes, generally blue although white and pink forms can occur. Flowers are produced in spring and early summer. It self-seeds very readily. **'Firmament'** has pendulous sky-blue flowers. **ZONES 5–9.**

Cynoglossum nervosum
HIMALAYAN HOUND'S TONGUE

This species has narrow green leaves and intense blue forget-me-not flowers that are borne in profuse terminal clusters on slender branching stems in summer. It grows to a height of about 24 in (60 cm) and can spread to an equal distance. **ZONES 4–9.**

CYPELLA

This genus of the iris family is allied to *Tigridia* and consists of about 15 species, occurring wild in Central and South America. They have sparse basal leaves arising from small corms, and slender flowering stems usually branched into several flower clusters with tightly rolled bracts from which emerge a succession of colorful, delicate blooms with 3 long petals like a 3-pointed star. They come in yellows, oranges and blues, usually with darker brown or purplish markings.
CULTIVATION: These bulbs vary in frost hardiness, though none will survive in really cold climates. They should be planted in full sun in light, well-drained soil. Water well through the growing season and allow to dry out in winter. The bulbs should be lifted in areas with very wet winters. Propagate from offsets or from seed planted in winter or spring.

Cypella herbertii

This iris-like species is native to Uruguay and nearby parts of Argentina. The unusual flowers bloom only for a day, but new flowers appear through most of the summer months. The branched flowering stem is up to 24 in (60 cm) tall and bears $2\frac{1}{2}$ in (6 cm) wide triangular blooms. The larger outer petals are copper to tan; the much smaller inner petals are purple and gold. **ZONES 8–10.**

CYPERUS
UMBRELLA SEDGE, PAPYRUS

Cyperus is an enormous genus of over 600 species of sedges, including both annuals and evergreen perennials, found mainly in wet habitats in nearly all except the coldest parts of the world. They include some of the world's most troublesome weeds of crops and gardens, for example nutgrass, *Cyperus rotundus*. The broad clumps of thick, cylindrical or 3-angled, stems have grass-like leaves springing from the base and are topped by compact heads or large umbels of small chaff-like flower spikes.
CULTIVATION: Most ornamental species do well at water's edge or in boggy ground. Grow in rich compost and water well. Direct sunlight is tolerated. Repot when the plant fills the container. If the tips turn brown, the atmosphere may be too dry, while a lack of new stems may indicate too little light. Propagate from seed or by division.

Cyperus albostriatus

This dense perennial from southern Africa has thin stems with mid-green leaves and prominent veins. It grows to 24 in (60 cm) tall and bears its yellowish green flower spikes from mid-summer to early fall (autumn). **ZONES 10–12.**

Cyperus esculentus
CHUFA, NUT SEDGE

This species from western Asia and Africa is frost tender. The erect stems have a white stripe; the white flowers are borne in spikes and surrounded by long leaf-like bracts. The fibrous roots have small round tubers, about the size of a pea, hanging from them. These tubers are rich in oil and are edible, being sold commercially in southern Europe; in France they are known as 'Amandes de terre'. **ZONES 9–12.**

Cyperus involucratus
syns *Cyperus alternifolius, C. flabelliformis*
UMBRELLA SEDGE

Cyperus involucratus grows to about 3 ft (1 m) and sends up 3-cornered, hollow stalks crowned by a whorl of leaf-like bracts. The green flower spikes appear in summer. It is a densely tufted perennial from Madagascar, and is frost tender. **ZONES 10–12.**

Cyperus papyrus
PAPER REED, PAPYRUS

The papyrus of the ancient Egyptians is one of the stateliest of all water plants for mild climates. It is extremely rampant, growing 5–8 ft (1.5–2.4 m) tall with an indefinite spread. In summer its long, sturdy, leafless stems carry great starbursts of fine branchlets that carry the tiny brown flowers. It will grow in very shallow water and prefers a sunny position. **ZONES 10–12.**

Cyperus albostriatus

CYPHOMANDRA

This genus of about 30 species of evergreen shrubs, climbers and small trees from tropical America is closely related to *Solanum*. They have thin, usually hairy leaves, 5-petalled pink to purple flowers in branched sprays in the leaf axils, and berry-like fruits of varying size, some edible. *Cyphomandra betacea* (the tamarillo), is grown for its fruit.
CULTIVATION: The tamarillo is best suited to subtropical or frost-free warm-temperate climates. Train against a wire fence or stake to protect from wind as it is inclined to be top-heavy. It is a shallow-rooted plant which prefers moist but not wet soil. Prune lightly after fruiting and pinch out growing tips at 3 ft (1 m) high to encourage branching. Propagate from cuttings and plan to replace after 5 years or so as it is short lived.

Cyphomandra betacea
TAMARILLO, TREE TOMATO

This large shrub from South America grows to about 10 ft (3 m) tall, of tree-like form with a wide crown, large deep-green leaves and small sprays of pinkish flowers appearing from the branch forks over much of the year. It produces a succession of egg-shaped fruits about 2–3 in (5–8 cm) long with shiny dark red skin (yellow-orange in some varieties); tamarillos can be used for jam or the pulp can be eaten as a dessert. **ZONES 9–11.**

CYPHOSTEMMA

Closely related to *Cissus*, this genus consists of around 150 species of evergreen and deciduous climbers and shrubs, found in warmer parts of the world. Some of the many African species have swollen, succulent stems and are popular with succulent collectors. The leaves are usually compound, with several leaflets arranged in either a palmate or pinnate manner. Small flowers are borne on long-stalked, flattish panicles and are followed by grape-like fruits of varying size and degree of edibility.
CULTIVATION: These marginally frost-hardy to frost-tender plants need full sun and a very well-drained soil. They should be kept dry in winter. Propagate from seed in spring.

Cyphostemma juttae
syn. *Cissus juttae*

Native to southern Namibia, this long-lived, deciduous shrub grows eventually to about 6 ft (1.8 m) tall. It is a striking plant with a bloated, fleshy stem which branches near the top and is covered with brownish yellow peeling bark. The leaves are mostly divided into 3 pale bluish green leaflets that are quite fleshy and roughly saw-toothed, their downy undersides exuding droplets of resin. Small greenish yellow flowers appear in summer, followed by quite translucent red or yellow fruit which look very much like small bunches of grapes. **ZONES 9–11.**

Cyphomandra betacea

Cyperus papyrus

Cyphostemma juttae

Cyperus esculentus

Cyperus involucratus

Cypripedium calceolus var. *calceolus*

Cyrilla racemiflora

Cypripedium calceolus var. *pubescens*

Cypripedium japonicum var. *formosanum*

CYPRIPEDIUM

SLIPPER ORCHID

The 35 species of deciduous terrestrial orchids that make up this genus occur wild in cool-temperate Eurasia and North America and in mountains of southern Asia and Mexico. They take both their common and scientific names (meaning 'slipper of Venus') from the way the labellum (lip) of the flower is hollowed out to form a pouch, shaped like the toe of a slipper, albeit a very bulbous one. The broad, thin, pleated leaves emerge from rhizomes in spring and the curiously beautiful flowers are borne in summer on erect stems, either singly or several on the one stem. In the past many tropical orchids were also classified as cypripediums, but these have long since been split off into the genera *Paphiopedilum*, *Phragmipedium* and *Selenipedium*, though all are still known to orchid growers as the 'slippers'. In the past the true cypripediums were usually grown from wild-collected plants, resulting in many species now being threatened in the wild in their own countries. Since they mostly die sooner or later after transplanting to gardens, some are in danger of total extinction.

CULTIVATION: Difficulty of cultivation varies, some species being regarded as almost impossible. They require a cool-temperate climate and a rich, leafy, rather moist soil and a shaded position. Some growers construct artificial bogs with a saturated zone about 6 in (15 cm) below a well-drained surface zone. Some of the woodland species, for example *Cypripedium japonicum*, are best grown in a pot in a compost consisting of well-rotted leafmold, coarse, gritty sand and a light, loamy soil. They are generally intolerant of fertilizers and resent being disturbed. Propagation is by division of rhizomes in spring but, as with all terrestrial orchids, this must be done with care.

Cypripedium calceolus

YELLOW LADY'S SLIPPER

Native to Europe, Asia and North America, this species has bold, bright green leaves and flowers with deep yellow lips and purple or brown petals and sepals, borne singly or 2 to 3 together on 8–18 in (20–45 cm) stems from late spring to mid-summer. In the UK, renowned as the showiest native orchid, it has been collected almost to extinction. It is one of the most easily cultivated cypripediums. ***Cypripedium calceolus* var. *calceolus*** is the European race with usually solitary flowers, the lip bright yellow; ***C. c.* var. *parviflorum*** from eastern USA and Canada has slightly smaller flowers, sometimes 2 to a stem, the lip more golden yellow and spotted reddish on the inside; ***C. c.* var. *pubescens***, from North America as well as northeastern Asia, has larger flowers with more greenish petals and sepals, and its leaves are hairy and sometimes irritant. **ZONES 3–9.**

Cypripedium japonicum

This fine woodland species from Japan and China grows up to 18 in (45 cm) high, each stem with a pair of striking fan-shaped, strongly pleated leaves. The single large flower has pale greenish petals and sepals and a very wide, pale pink lip with corrugations running around its edge. ***Cypripedium japonicum* var. *formosanum*** from Taiwan has pale pink petals and sepals. **ZONES 8–9.**

Cypripedium reginae

SHOWY LADY'S SLIPPER

Native to eastern North America, this rather rare plant, often regarded as one of the most beautiful of all American wildflowers, is difficult to cultivate. Where it is happy it spreads into clumps; the fresh green leaves are adorned with a large white flower with a rose-pink labellum, borne singly on 18 in (45 cm) tall stems in early summer. **ZONES 3–9.**

CYRILLA

AMERICAN LEATHERWOOD, SWAMP CYRILLA

This genus consists of only one species of small tree or often only a shrub that includes both deciduous and evergreen races. This fact is partly explained by its very wide climatic range, from Virginia in eastern USA south through Florida and the West Indies, and into South America as far as Brazil. The plants usually grown in gardens are the northern, deciduous forms. They are tall shrubs with spatula-shaped leaves, producing many long, tapering racemes of tiny, white, fragrant flowers from just below the new leaves.

CULTIVATION: In the wild, cyrilla forms dense thickets along the margins of swamps, while in gardens it is an undemanding shrub worth growing for the elegance of its flowers. It does best in a sunny but sheltered spot in fertile, humus-rich, moist but well-drained soil. Propagation is normally from seed.

Cyrilla racemiflora

This shrub often only grows to about 5 ft (1.5 m) high, but under good conditions can reach 20 ft (6 m) or more with a central woody stem and open branching habit, the lateral branches wiry and tending to curve upward. The rather sparse leaves are glossy green and turn dull red one by one before falling in late fall (autumn). The white flower spikes start opening in early summer and may continue almost to fall. The flowers are followed by tiny, dry fruit. **ZONES 6–11.**

CYRTANTHUS

FIRE LILY

This genus of about 50 species is native to southern Africa and is related to Amaryllis. The scented, brightly colored flowers are usually tubular and curved, mostly grouped in an umbel at the top of a hollow stem and usually nodding. They bloom at various times, depending on the species. The fleshy, somewhat grass-like leaves usually die down over winter. They do well planted in pots and also make long-lasting, perfumed cut flowers. They hybridize freely, and nurseries may offer them by color rather than under specific names.

CULTIVATION: Most are somewhat frost tender and do best in areas where winters are mild. Although some species occur naturally in swamps, they are best planted in rich, well-drained soil in a sunny situation. The neck of the bulb should be at ground level and they should be watered well through the growing season. The bulbs are best left undisturbed but may need dividing if overcrowded. Propagate from bulb offsets or seed planted in spring.

Cyrtanthus brachyscyphus

Cyrtanthus brachyscyphus

syn. *C. parviflorus*

From Natal and Cape Province, this species has narrowly funnel-shaped bright red flowers in spring, occasionally in fall (autumn). It grows to a height of around 12 in (30 cm). **ZONES 9–11.**

Cyrtanthus elatus

syns *Cyrtanthus purpureus, Vallota speciosa*

SCARBOROUGH LILY

From western Cape Province, this species is different in appearance from most others in the genus, with clumps of crowded, fairly broad leaves and bright scarlet flowers opening out into broad funnels about 3 in (8 cm) wide in late summer. **ZONES 9–11.**

Cyrtanthus mackenii

IFAFA LILY

Popular and easy to grow, this species from eastern Cape Province has narrow leaves and flowering stems up to 16 in (40 cm) tall. The narrowly tubular flowers vary from white to yellow in color and are about 2 in (5 cm) long, appearing in spring and summer. **ZONES 9–11.**

Cyrtanthus ochroleucus

syn. *Cyrtanthus lutescens*

From Cape Province, this species has yellowish white flowers in early spring, on stems up to about 12 in (30 cm) tall. **ZONES 9–11.**

Cyrtanthus brachyscyphus

Cyrtanthus elatus

CYRTOMIUM

A genus of about 12 species of evergreen ferns from East and central Asia; some botanists include them in the genus *Phanerophlebia* which extends to Africa and the Americas. They are clump-forming, terrestrial ferns with pinnate fronds radiating from short erect rhizomes covered with scales. The broad segments may be toothed or cut, and on fertile fronds the rich brown spore-bodies are sprinkled densely over their undersides.
CULTIVATION: Most species are frost tender to moderately frost hardy and easy to grow. They grow well indoors in a well-lit position or in a conservatory or greenhouse. Propagate from spores, which germinate readily on moist bricks or mossy stones, or by division of clumps.

Cyrtomium falcatum
syn. ***Phanerophlebia falcata***
HOLLY FERN

A native of East Asia, this species is easily recognized by the holly-like form and texture of its tough, glossy frond segments, though their shape differs in some varieties. It forms a dense clump about 2–3 ft in (60–90 cm) high. The spores are easily carried by the wind, so it has naturalized in countries with mild climates, mainly on coastal cliffs. It tolerates light frosts though the upper fronds can burn. It will grow in quite deep shade, although one of the most sun-tolerant of the ferns. **ZONES 9–11.**

CYRTOSTACHYS

This genus has 8 species, occurring wild in the Malay Peninsula, Sumatra, Borneo and New Guinea, generally growing in coastal swamps. All are tall, slender, mostly clumping palms that will grow outdoors only in the tropics. The trunks are ringed with leaf scars and terminate in smooth 'crownshafts' of furled frond bases. The fronds are of the feather type (pinnate) with arching midribs. Branched inflorescences emerge below the fronds bearing numerous small flowers, followed by small single-seeded fruits. Only one species is widely cultivated, prized for its brilliantly colored crownshaft.
CULTIVATION: They require a tropical climate with year-round humidity to grow well, and rich, constantly moist soil. Outside the tropics they will only succeed in a heated greenhouse with winter temperature no lower than about 60°F (16°C). Propagate from freshly gathered seed.

Cyrtostachys renda
syn. ***Cyrtostachys lakka***
SEALING WAX PALM, LIPSTICK PALM, MAHARAJAH PALM

The contrast between the rich green of the leaves and the brilliant scarlet of the glossy leaf bases makes this clumping feather palm from swampy lowlands of Malaysia and western Indonesia one of the most ornamental of all palms. Needing constant hot weather for the color to develop properly, it grows to about 20 ft (6 m) tall and has the reputation of being rather difficult to transplant. **ZONE 12.**

CYTISUS
BROOM

The brooms, taking the word in its broad sense, are a diverse group of usually yellow-flowered, leguminous shrubs and subshrubs from Europe and the Mediterranean region which include a number of genera—the most important are *Cytisus* and *Genista*. *Cytisus* alone is a large and variable genus, in habit ranging from tall and erect to prostrate. Some of the 30 species have well-developed leaves, either simple and narrow or composed of 3 leaflets, while others are almost leafless with all photosynthesis performed by the green, angled branchlets. All have pea-flowers in small, profuse clusters along the current season's growths.
CULTIVATION: Generally easy garden subjects, they flower well under most conditions except deep shade, tolerating both dry and boggy soils, fertile or quite infertile. Some of the smaller species demand warm dry positions in a rock garden in pockets of well-drained soil. They are easily propagated from seed, cuttings or, in the case of some named cultivars, by grafting.

Cytisus ardoinoi

Native to the maritime Alps of France and Italy, this is a prostrate species with bright yellow flowers in spring and summer. It is a deciduous, hummock-forming shrub with arching stems. The leaves are divided into 3 leaflets and the flowers are produced in pairs in leaf axils. **ZONES 6–9.**

Cytisus × *beanii*

Believed to be a hybrid between *Cytisus ardoinoi* and *C. purgans*, this is a low-growing deciduous shrub with arching sprays of golden-yellow flowers, borne in spring on the previous season's growth. The leaves are divided into 3 leaflets and are small, linear and hairy. It grows to about 12 in (30 cm) high with a spread of up to 30 in (75 cm). **ZONES 5–9.**

Cytisus 'Burkwoodii'

Although similar to *Cytisus scoparius*, this reddish-flowered cultivar is believed to be a hybrid with *C. multiflorus*. It makes a vigorous, bushy shrub of around 5 ft (1.5 m) in height, starting to flower when quite small and developing arching branches as it ages. The upper petals (standards) are cerise, the inner (wings) crimson edged with yellow. It blooms in late spring and early summer. **ZONES 5–9.**

Cyrtomium falcatum

Cytisus fontanesii

A native of Spain, this broom is an erect deciduous shrub no more than about 3 ft (90 cm) high with crowded green twigs, rather like those of *Spartium junceum* with very sparsely scattered trifoliate leaves. The yellow flowers are borne at the branch tips in late spring. **ZONES 7–10**

Cytisus × *kewensis*

A hybrid between *Cytisus ardoinoi* and *C. multiflorus* raised at Kew Gardens. This is a deciduous, prostrate shrub 18–30 in (45–75 cm) in height with trailing stems that will cover an area about 6 ft (1.8 m) in diameter. Flowers are pale creamy yellow and slightly fragrant; they are produced in spring and are probably sterile. **ZONES 6–9.**

Cytisus multiflorus
syn. ***Cytisus albus***
WHITE SPANISH BROOM

From Spain, Portugal and northwest Africa, this is a deciduous shrub 6–12 ft (1.8–3.5 m) in height with small scented white flowers borne in the leaf axils in late spring and early summer. The upper leaves are simple and narrow, those nearer the base of the shoots have 3 leaflets. **ZONES 6–10.**

Cytisus × *praecox*
WARMINSTER BROOM, MOONLIGHT BROOM

This hybrid between the tall species *Cytisus multiflorus* and the lower-growing *C. purgans* includes several popular cultivars, all making free-flowering shrubs of 3–4 ft (1–1.2 m), with massed, slender branchlets arising from ground level and spreading gracefully. The original hybrid has cream and yellow flowers, with a heavy, perhaps overpowering, fragrance, borne in mid- to late spring. More recently developed cultivars include **'Allgold'**, with cascading sprays of soft, golden-yellow blossom, and **'Goldspear'**, a lower and broader shrub with deeper gold flowers. **ZONES 5–9.**

Cytisus fontanesii

Cytisus × *praecox* 'Allgold'

Cytisus scoparius
COMMON BROOM, SCOTCH BROOM

Widely distributed in central and western Europe including the UK, this is one of the taller and most vigorous species of *Cytisus*, reaching 6–8 ft (1.8–2.4 m) in height and making a great show of golden-yellow blossoms in late spring and early summer. The black seed pods may be abundant, ripening in midsummer and scattering their seed with a sharp, cracking sound in hot, dry weather. In cooler areas of some southern hemisphere countries it has become a troublesome weed. **'Pendulus'** is a rare cultivar with pendulous branches. **ZONES 5–9.**

Cytisus supranubius
TENERIFE BROOM

Endemic to the Canary Islands where it grows high on the Peak of Tenerife, this elegant broom makes an erect shrub of 6–10 ft (1.8–3 m) in height, with crowded, almost leafless blue-green branches. The profuse, fragrant flowers are white tinged with pink and appear in late spring. **ZONES 8–10.**

Cyrtostachys renda

Cytisus multiflorus

Cytisus scoparius 'Pendulus'

D

DABOECIA

ST DABEOC'S HEATH, IRISH HEATH

Only 2 species make up this genus of small-leafed, evergreen shrubs native to areas of western Europe and the Azores Islands. Low and spreading, they are commonly grouped with the heaths and heathers *(Erica* and *Calluna)* as suitable for heather gardens, rock gardens and retaining walls. Their conspicuous white to purple urn-shaped flowers, which contract to a small mouth, are borne on nodding stalks along bare stems that stand above the foliage. The petal tube falls after flowering, unlike that of many heaths and heathers.

CULTIVATION: Frost hardy to marginally frost hardy, they require permanently moist, acidic soil in a sunny position. Trim after flowering. Named varieties normally require propagation from cuttings, but they do produce fertile seed which may breed true to type.

Daboecia azorica

syn. ***Daboecia cantabrica*** **subsp.** ***azorica***

AZORES HEATH

Endemic to the Azores, this is the least widely grown and least frost-hardy species. It is most at home in the milder parts of cool-temperate zones. It has a prostrate or trailing habit to 8 in (20 cm) high and 16 in (40 cm) across and small dark green elliptic leaves with white down beneath. The deep red flowers are borne in racemes in early summer. **ZONES 8–9.**

Daboecia cantabrica

Dispersed along the Atlantic coasts of France and Ireland, this species grows up to 24 in (60 cm) high and has narrow, lance-shaped, dark green leaves with white hairs beneath. The rose-purple flowers, borne throughout summer and fall (autumn), are about ½ in (12 mm) long. **'Alba'** has pointed dark green leaves and white flowers; **'Atropurpurea'** has deep rosy purple flowers; **'Bicolor'** has white, purple and some striped flowers; **'Creeping White'** has white flowers and a low creeping habit. **ZONES 7–9.**

Daboecia × *scotica*

This hybrid of *Daboecia azorica* and *D. cantabrica* is a compact shrub up to 10 in (25 cm) high and 14 in (35 cm) across with elliptic to oval leaves that are dark green above and silvery beneath. It bears urn-shaped magenta flowers from late spring to mid-fall (autumn). **'Jack Drake'** is low and bushy to 8 in (20 cm) high and has rich ruby red flowers; **'William Buchanan'** grows to 14 in (35 cm) high and has deep, rosy red flowers. **ZONES 7–9.**

DACRYCARPUS

The genus name of these conifers, once included in *Podocarpus* and also related to *Dacrydium*, is a mixture of both and shows their affinity. The genus consists of about 9 species from the moist areas of Malaysia, the Philippines, New Caledonia, Fiji and New Zealand. Many are large forest trees which have at times been important timber trees. Most species are frost tender.

CULTIVATION: Although the species are rarely available, they could make attractive trees for damp to wet sites in frost-free environments. Propagate from seed or from cuttings.

Daboecia cantabrica

Daboecia cantabrica

Dacrycarpus dacrydioides

Dacrydium cupressinum

Daboecia cantabrica 'Alba'

Dacrycarpus dacrydioides

syn. ***Podocarpus dacrydioides***

KAHIKATEA, NEW ZEALAND WHITE PINE

Native to New Zealand, this species can reach 150 ft (45 m) or more in height with a trunk diameter of up to 5 ft (1.5 m) in the wild although it is unlikely to reach these dimensions in cultivation. Its habit is upright and conical and its foliage is fine and cypress-like when mature with an overall bronze color. The bark is gray and scaling off in flakes. Old specimens may have a buttressed trunk. **ZONES 8–10.**

DACRYDIUM

Of the original 15 species of *Dacrydium*, some are now reclassified as *Lagarostrobos* or *Halocarpus*. All come from the South Pacific, mostly from New Caledonia and New Guinea, but a few range as far as mainland Southeast Asia. These beautiful conifers all have graceful branchlets clothed in overlapping fine needle leaves. The small pollen cones are borne on male trees, and female trees produce solitary, large seeds each surrounded by fleshy scales.

CULTIVATION: *Dacrydium* species do not adapt well to cultivation; they require moderately cool climates without severe frosts or high summer temperatures, as well as adequate rainfall and humidity. Even then, growth is rather slow. Propagate from seed or cuttings.

Dacrydium cupressinum

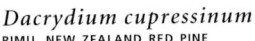

RIMU, NEW ZEALAND RED PINE

In the wild, the rimu is one of New Zealand's tallest natives, but in cultivation it rarely reaches 30 ft (9 m). In winter it turns a deep reddish brown. Adult trees have shorter, fleshier needles and are more closely branched than juvenile ones. Female trees bear small bluish seeds, each half-buried in a bright red fleshy cup. **ZONES 8–9.**

Dacrydium cupressinum

Daboecia cantabrica 'Creeping White'

Dactylorhiza maculata

DACTYLIS

COCKSFOOT, ORCHARD GRASS

This is a genus of 2 species of coarse perennial pasture grasses from Europe, North Africa and temperate Asia. The name comes from the Greek for 'finger', possibly a reference to the finger-thick aggregations of seed heads that are borne on tall stems. They make large, dense tussocks of foliage with flat, green leaf blades which often have a loosely tangled appearance. They are useful fodder when young but toughen with age and are difficult to mow. They are one of the more notorious hayfever grasses when flowering in spring.

CULTIVATION: Often sown in pastures to provide fodder, they prefer fertile, moist soils and respond vigorously to fertilizer application. The foliage is killed by winter frosts, though light frosts can leave the plants still green when other grasses are frost-killed. Propagate by division.

Dactylis glomerata

This grass is usually a pasture grass, not an ornamental. However, in its variegated forms it can be attractive and will make a ground cover in sun or semi-shade. **'Variegata'** has white-striped foliage and grows to about 10 in (25 cm) and **'Elegantissima'** has similar variegation but only grows to a dwarf hummock of 6 in (15 cm). **ZONES 6–10.**

DACTYLORHIZA

MARSH AND SPOTTED ORCHIDS

The genus *Dactylorhiza* occurs in Europe, western and northern Asia, and North America. The plants are terrestrial with 2 tubers which are divided like fingers, giving rise to the name. Many species have spotted leaves and most have pink flowers with darker spots. They grow in bogs, grasslands and pastures and there are at least 33 variable species which often tend to hybridize naturally, causing

problems in identification.
CULTIVATION: Members of this genus are fully frost hardy. They prefer part-shade and require some specialist potting mixtures usually including peat moss, leafmold, composted bark, sand and loam. The plants should be kept wet during the warm weather and somewhat drier during winter. Propagate by division in early spring.

Dactylorhiza elata
syn. *Orchis elata*
ROBUST MARSH ORCHID

This is a robust terrestrial species from southwestern Europe, Sicily and North Africa. There are 8 to 14 unspotted, lanceolate leaves. The inflorescence is from 12 in (30 cm) to over 3 ft (1 m) tall with numerous deep purple flowers about 1 in (25 mm) across, densely packed. *Dactylorhiza elata* flowers in spring and early summer. Repot in fall (autumn) after flowering and before the new leaves appear. **ZONES 4–9.**

Dactylorhiza foliosa
MADEIRAN ORCHID

This species is restricted to the island of Madeira where it grows in swampy grasslands. There are 2 fleshy tubers and several fleshy roots. The 4 or 5 lanceolate leaves are about $2\frac{1}{2}$ in (6 cm) long and $\frac{1}{2}$ in (12 mm) wide without spots. The inflorescence is 15–24 in (38–60 cm) tall with many densely packed, spotted, pink flowers each about $\frac{1}{2}$ in (12 mm) across. Flowering occurs in spring and early summer. **ZONES 8–10.**

Dactylorhiza maculata
HEATH SPOTTED ORCHID

This European orchid grows to 24 in (60 cm) high and has lance-shaped leaves which may be plain green or spotted. It bears a dense spike of white, pink, red or mauve flowers from mid-spring to late summer. **ZONES 4–9.**

Dahlia, Group 1, 'Yellow Hammer'

Dahlia, Group 3, cultivar

Dahlia, Group 5, 'Majuba'

Dahlia, Group 4, 'Gerrie Hoek'

Dactylorhiza majalis
BROAD-LEAVED MARSH ORCHID

Growing to 30 in (75 cm) high, this orchid has ovate to lance-shaped leaves which may be plain green or spotted deep red. Lilac to magenta flowers, spotted white and streaked purple are produced in dense spikes from late spring to mid-summer. **ZONES 4–9.**

DAHLIA

This comparatively small genus of about 30 species from Mexico and Central America has had as much impact on gardens as almost any other group of herbaceous perennials. Of this number only 2 or 3 species were used to create the thousands of named varieties of the past and present. Progeny of *Dahlia coccinea* and *D. pinnata* originally formed the nucleus of the modern hybrid dahlias. Others are derived from forms of *D. hortensis* such as the popular cultivar **'Ellen Huston'.** So many different flower forms have been developed that the hybrids are classified into about 10 different groups, determined by the size and type of their flowerheads. Some authorities suggest that there should be more, as group 10 consists of disparate classes as yet too small to give groupings of their own, known as the miscellaneous group. Most groups have small-, medium- and large-flowered subdivisions.
CULTIVATION: Dahlias are not particularly frost resistant so in cold climates the tubers are usually lifted each year and stored in a frost-free place to be split and replanted in spring. Most prefer a sunny, sheltered position in well-fertilized, well-drained soil. Feed monthly and water well when in flower. Increase flower size by pinching out the 2 buds alongside each center bud. All, apart from bedding forms, need staking. Propagate bedding forms from seed, others from seed, cuttings from tubers or by division.

Dahlia, Group 4, 'Cameo'

Dahlia, Group 5, 'Golden Ballade'

Dahlia, Group 5, 'Suffolk Punch'

Dahlia, Group 6, 'Rose Cupid'

The following are the 10 main classification groups of Dahlia hybrids.

Single-flowered (Group 1): As the name of this group suggests, these hybrids have a single ring of ray petals (sometimes 2) with an open center. Most singles are small plants usually growing no more than 18 in (45 cm) high, so they are ideal for bedding and are often sold as seed strains. **'Yellow Hammer'** is a popular bedding variety with bronze foliage and rich yellow flowers.

Anemone-flowered (Group 2): This group includes fewer cultivars than most of the others. They have one or more rows of outer ray florets; instead of the yellow center, these tiny flowers have mutated into outward-pointing tubular florets.

Collarette (Group 3): This group, once again becoming popular, has a single row of 8 outer large florets which are usually flat and rounded at the tips. Then comes a row of shorter tubular, wavy florets often in a contrasting color and finally the normally yellow center.

Waterlily or nymphaea-flowered (Group 4): These fully double-flowered dahlias have slightly cupped petals that have a more than passing resemblance to their namesakes, the waterlilies. The overall effect is of a flattish flower. **'Cameo'** has white flowers with a cream base; **'Gerrie Hoek'** has pink waterlily flowers on strong stems and is popular as a cut flower.

Decorative (Group 5): This group are fully double-flowered dahlias with no central disc showing. The petals are more numerous and slightly twisted making the flower look fuller than the waterlily types. This group, which can produce some truly giant forms, may be subdivided into formal decoratives and informal ones. Informal decoratives have petals that are twisted or pointed and of an irregular arrangement. **'Hamari Gold'** is a giant decorative with golden-bronze flowers. **'Evening Mail'** is also a giant decorative. **'Majuba'** is a very free-flowering compact, medium-sized decorative dahlia bearing deep red blooms on strong stems. Large informal decorative types include **'Almand's Climax'** which has lavender flowers with paler tips; **'Alva's Supreme'** with yellow flowers; **'Golden Ballade'** with deep golden flowers and **'Suffolk Punch'** with rich purple flowers.

Ball (Group 6): As the name suggests these dahlias are full doubles and almost ball-shaped. Miniature, small, medium and large forms are available. **'Rose Cupid'** is a medium-sized ball dahlia with salmon pink blooms; **'Wotton Cupid'** is a dark pink miniature.

Pompon (Group 7): These are similar to ball dahlias but even more globose and usually not much more than 2 in

Dahlia, Group 9, 'Brandaris'

Dahlia, Group 9, 'Salmon Keene'

Dahlia imperialis

(5 cm) across. They are sometimes called 'Drum Stick' dahlias. **'Buttercup'** is a yellow pompon form.

Cactus-flowered (Group 8): This group of fully double-flowered dahlias have long, narrow rolled petals giving the flowers a spidery look. This group can be divided further by size as well as into classes with straight petals, incurved petals or recurved petals. **'Hamari Bride'** is a medium-sized white form.

Semi-cactus (Group 9): As the name suggests this group is close to Group 8 but the petals are broader at the base and less rolled back at the edges. **'So Dainty'** is a miniature with golden bronze and apricot flowers; **'Brandaris'** is a medium form with soft orange and golden yellow flowers; **'Hayley Jane'** is a small form with purplish pink flowers and white bases; and **'Salmon Keene'** has large salmon pink to golden flowers.

Miscellaneous (Group 10): This category consists of small groups and unique forms of dahlias that do not fit into any of the above groups. If breeders

Dahlia, Group 10, 'Tally Ho'

increase the numbers in any of the forms in this category, they will probably be split off to form new groups. Under this heading can be found such forms as orchid types which are single with revolute petals: **'Giraffe'** with its banded yellow and bronze flowers is an example. The star dahlias are also single in appearance and produce very pointed, widely spaced petals. Peony-flowered dahlias, which are still kept as a separate group in some countries, usually have one or two rows of flat petals with a center which can be open or partly covered by small twisted petals; examples of this form include **'Bishop of Llandaff'** with its brilliant scarlet blooms above its beautiful deep burgundy leaves, **'Fascination'** with light pinkish purple flowers and dark bronze foliage, and **'Tally Ho'** with deep orange flowers and gray-green leaves, tinged with purple.

Dahlia imperialis
syn. *Dahlia excelsa*
TREE DAHLIA

Native to Central America, this tall woody perennial or subshrub has thick, bamboo-like stems to 15 ft (5 m) or more high. The large bipinnate leaves to 24 in (60 cm) long have up to 15 ovate leaflets with toothed margins. The large, single lavender-pink flowerheads with yellow centers are produced in fall (autumn). **ZONES 8–10.**

DAIS

This small genus consists of 2 species of evergreen or semi-deciduous trees and shrubs from southern and eastern Africa

Dahlia, Group 10, 'Bishop of Llandaff'

and Madagascar. One species is grown in warm climates for its showy pompon-shaped clusters of flowers. The branches have thin, very tough bark and the leaves are simple and oval. The silky-haired, tubular flowers have 5 spreading lobes and are borne in dense heads. **CULTIVATION:** Frost tender, they need full sun, moderate shelter, light, fertile, free-draining soil and adequate summer water. They maintain their shape well without pruning. Propagate from seed in spring or cuttings in summer.

Dais cotinifolia
POMPON BUSH, POMPON TREE

Native to Africa, this bushy, rounded shrub or small tree grows to about 12 ft (3.5 m). It has reddish bark and oval, blue-green leaves up to 3 in (7 cm) in length. In late spring it bears fragrant flower clusters of tubular pink blooms. It is evergreen in warm areas and deciduous in cool climates. **ZONES 9–11.**

DAMASONIUM
STAR FRUIT

A genus of 6 species of aquatic plants, these perennials have long-stalked, floating leaves on specimens growing in water or more erect, aerial ones on plants stranded out of water. Most species come from the northern hemisphere with one species extending to Australia. They are closely related to the water plantains, *Alisma*. White or pink cup-shaped flowers are produced in spring and summer, followed by star-shaped seed capsules, hence the common name. **CULTIVATION:** Marginally frost hardy, grow star fruits near or in water up to 6 in (15 cm) deep or in submerged containers. They prefer full sun. Propagate by division or from seed.

Damasonium alisma

This marginal aquatic species is native to Europe and grows to about 8 in (20 cm)

Dais cotinifolia

each way. It has oblong floating leaves up to 3 in (8 cm) long and produces numerous white flowers with a yellow spot at the base of each petal. **ZONES 5–10.**

DAMPIERA

This genus consists of about 70 species of herbaceous perennials or small erect shrubs endemic to Australia. Most of the species occur in southwestern Western Australia. Named after William Dampier, a seventeenth-century English navigator who explored Australia's west coast, dampieras have masses of brilliant blue or purple blooms. Many have a suckering habit making them excellent ground covers or rockery plants. **CULTIVATION:** Frost tender to marginally frost hardy, they require a very well-drained soil in full sun or part-shade. Propagate from cuttings or by division.

Dampiera diversifolia
KANGAROO LOBELIA

This prostrate perennial to 6 ft (2 m) across has narrow, mid-green leaves and a suckering habit. Masses of purple-blue flowers are produced in spring. It can be grown in containers and makes an excellent basket plant. **ZONES 9–10.**

Dampiera linearis
COMMON DAMPIERA

This species has a suckering habit with usually erect branches to 12 in (30 cm) high and a spread of up to 3 ft (1 m) in diameter. It is clothed with small mid-green leaves and produces rich purple-blue flowers in late spring and summer. Cut back after flowering to encourage vigorous new growth. **ZONES 9–10.**

DANÄE

This genus consists of only one species of evergreen clump-forming perennial from western Asia. It is grown for its

Dampiera linearis

Dampiera diversifolia

Daphne × *burkwoodii*

Danäe racemosa

elegant arching stems and its attractive foliage and fruit.
CULTIVATION: Frost hardy, it grows in a humus-rich, moist but well-drained soil in sun or shade. Old or damaged stems can be cut back to ground level if necessary in spring. Propagate from seed or by division.

Danäe racemosa
ALEXANDRIAN LAUREL

This native of Turkey and Iran makes an elegant evergreen plant to 3 ft (1 m) high and across. Its tiny greenish white flowers are produced in summer and followed by red berries that can persist well into winter. Whole branches can be cut and last well in a vase. **ZONES 7–10.**

DAPHNE
DAPHNE

Indigenous to Europe, North Africa and temperate Asia, this genus includes 50 or so deciduous and evergreen shrubs. They have simple, leathery leaves and small, highly fragrant flowers clustered at the shoot tips or leaf axils. Although the flower parts are not differentiated into true petals and sepals, for the sake of simplicity here they are called 'petals', of which there are always 4, characteristically pointed, recurving and rather fleshy. In the wild many daphnes occur on mountains in stony ground, often on limestone.
CULTIVATION: They prefer cool, well-aerated, gritty, humus-rich soil; intolerant of root disturbance, they are best planted out while small. The taller species are better adapted to sheltered woodlands, the smaller ones to rock gardens. Propagate from cuttings or layers. Fresh seed usually germinates readily but many species fail to fruit.

Daphne arbuscula

An attractive small evergreen shrub, this species grows up to 8 in (20 cm) tall and wider. It is a lovely rock garden subject,

Daphne caucasica

native to the mountains of Hungary. It produces its fragrant rich pink flowers in summer; its leaves are sometimes hairy and quite hard. A sunny aspect with a cool root run suits this plant. **ZONES 4–9.**

Daphne bholua

This species from the eastern Himalayas can be evergreen or deciduous depending on the form selected. It usually grows into an upright shrub up to 12 ft (3.5 m) tall and 5 ft (1.5 m) wide. It has clusters of highly scented soft pink flowers in late winter. Selected forms include **'Gurkha'**, which is deciduous, and **'Jacqueline Postill'**, which is evergreen. **ZONES 6–9.**

Daphne × *burkwoodii*

This popular hybrid (*Daphne cneorum* × *D. caucasica*) was raised early in the twentieth century by the Burkwood brothers, well-known English nurserymen. It is a low, rounded semi-evergreen shrub up to 3 ft (1 m) tall. Its pale pink flowers, darker in bud, appear in mid- to late spring, sometimes through summer. The most easily grown deciduous daphne, it flowers best in full sun. **'Somerset'** is slightly more vigorous and has deep pink flowers with pale pink lobes. **ZONES 5–9.**

Daphne caucasica
CAUCASIAN DAPHNE

A strong-growing upright deciduous species to 6 ft (1.8 m) tall, the flowers of this species are white, fragrant and produced in spring; these are followed by berries that can be either black or red. It sometimes produces late flushes of flowers into summer and is one of the parents of the much better known *Daphne* × *burkwoodii*. **ZONES 5–9.**

Daphne cneorum
GARLAND FLOWER, ROSE DAPHNE

This low-growing, to 16 in (40 cm), evergreen shrub from southern Europe has a

Daphne cneorum

loose, semi-prostrate habit, with trailing main shoots and dense lateral branches. It has small dark green leaves and bears fragrant rose pink flowers in mid-spring. It is a sun-loving plant but requires moist, well-drained soil. **ZONES 4–9.**

Daphne genkwa
LILAC DAPHNE

Indigenous to China but long cultivated in Japan, this small deciduous shrub tends to be short lived in cultivation. It is sparsely branched, producing long, wiry growths in summer which, next spring while still leafless, bear clusters of delicate, long-tubed, lilac flowers at every leaf axil. It prefers sheltered, sunny, frost-free conditions. **ZONES 5–9.**

Daphne laureola
SPURGE LAUREL

Although hardly one of the showiest species, *Daphne laureola* is an attractive evergreen shrub up to 5 ft (1.5 m) tall that will cope well with heavy shade. It is native to Europe including Britain. Its tiny green flowers are night scented and followed by black berries. The dwarf ***Daphne laureola* subsp. *philippi***, which rarely exceeds 15 in (38 cm), can sucker into substantial clumps making it a good ground cover. **ZONES 6–9.**

Daphne mezereum
MEZEREON, FEBRUARY DAPHNE

This slow-growing, short-lived, deciduous shrub grows to 5 ft (1.5 m) tall, and has long narrow leaves and purplish pink to purplish red, fragrant flowers clustering along bare twigs in early spring.

Daphne genkwa

Below the leaves, poisonous red fruit ripen in late summer. It needs moisture and shelter. **ZONES 5–9.**

Daphne × *napolitana*

A hybrid (possibly a natural one) between *Daphne sericea* and *D. cneorum*, this neat, compact evergreen shrub rarely exceeds 30 in (75 cm) each way. Its foliage is rich green and it produces terminal clusters of rose pink scented flowers in spring at times followed by further flushes through into fall (autumn). **ZONES 4–9.**

Daphne odora
WINTER DAPHNE

A Chinese evergreen shrub long cultivated in Japan, *Daphne odora* is too frost tender for many cooler regions of the northern hemisphere, but it thrives in temperate southern regions. It is a spreading, twiggy shrub to 4 ft (1.2 m), with dark green leaves. From late fall (autumn) to mid-spring its rose purple buds open to almost pure white, waxy flowers. **'Alba'** is wholly white; **'Aureo-marginata'** has yellow-edged leaves and flowers marked with reddish purple. **ZONES 8–10.**

Daphne petraea

From northern Italy, **'Grandiflora'** is a large-flowering selection. One of the alpine gems of the genus, it is very slow and not easy to propagate so is rarely available. An evergreen plant, it rarely exceeds 12 in (30 cm) tall and is usually much less. Its deep pink flowers are highly scented and are borne in dense terminal clusters in spring. **ZONES 6–9.**

Daphne odora

Daphne × *napolitana*

Daphne pontica

This evergreen shrub to 5 ft (1.5 m) comes from southeastern Europe, Turkey and the Caucasus. It is similar to *Daphne laureola* in many respects, preferring semi-shade and having greenish night-scented flowers in spring. Its berries are dark burgundy at first, turning black. **ZONES 5–9.**

Daphne retusa

This species may be a form of *Daphne tangutica*; authorities vary in their opinions. It makes a compact shrub to 30 in (75 cm) high with fragrant pale pink flowers in spring and glossy rich green foliage. **ZONES 6–9.**

Daphne sericea

Yet another compact evergreen shrub with deliciously scented pale pink-mauve flowers in spring, this species makes a lovely rock garden plant up to 20 in (50 cm) each way and its rich green foliage is slightly hairy. **ZONES 8–10.**

Daphne pontica

Daphne tangutica

Native to northwestern China, this very frost-hardy evergreen bears clusters of perfumed, white-stained, rose purple flowers in mid- to late spring. It has dark leaves, stout shoots and a bushy habit, growing to a height and spread of 3 ft (1m). **ZONES 4–9.**

DARLINGIA

This genus contains 2 evergreen tree species endemic to the tropical rainforests of northeastern Australia. They are grown for their handsome foliage and erect spikes of creamy white, grevillea-like flowers. The leaves are long and pointed, usually lobed on young trees; the waxy flowers, which are often scented, are borne in dense, erect spikes and are generally hairy. The fruits are follicles which contain thin, flat, winged seeds.
CULTIVATION: Frost tender, they are attractive specimen trees for large gardens or parks in subtropical and tropical regions. They need shelter, ample moisture and moderately rich well-drained soil. Propagate from fresh seed or cuttings.

Daphne retusa

Daphne sericea

Darlingtonia californica

Darlingia darlingiana

Darlingia darlingiana

Darlingia darlingiana
BROWN SILKY OAK

This handsome tree, growing to 80 ft (24 m) in the wild, has been exploited for its timber but it is not yet widely cultivated. Its shiny, dark green, variously lobed leaves with prominent veins can reach up to 15 in (38 cm) in length. Dense white flower spikes, about 10 in (25 cm) long, appear in spring. **ZONES 10–12.**

DARLINGTONIA
CALIFORNIA PITCHER PLANT, COBRA LILY

This genus has only one species, *Darlingtonia californica,* named after botanist William Darlington (1782–1863) of Philadelphia, USA, and it comes from the western Rocky Mountains foothills. The plant closely resembles *Sarracenia,* native to eastern North America, but whereas the sarracenia pitchers are like open trumpets, *Darlingtonia*'s pitchers bend over at the top. It ranges from 4 in (10 cm) to nearly 3 ft (1 m) tall, depending on soil richness, and, perhaps, on how many insects the plant catches. The flowers are a green and reddish brown blend, carried above the leaves, and lack the sarracenia's strange, umbrella-shaped stigma.
CULTIVATION: Grow in humus-rich, moist but well-drained, acidic soil in full sun. In cooler areas it does very well in greenhouses in bright light but shaded from hot sun. Keep well watered. Propagate from seed or by division in spring.

Darlingtonia californica

Greenish yellow sepals and purple petals give the flowers of this species an unusual, bicolored appearance. Each flower is about 3 in (8 cm) wide. **ZONES 7–10.**

DARMERA
syn. ***Peltiphyllum***
UMBRELLA PLANT, INDIAN RHUBARB

A genus of only one species, this is a herbaceous perennial with very large handsome leaves that follow the flowers in spring. The flowers, usually white or pink and in clusters on unbranched stems, are followed by attractive inedible fruit. It is native to northwestern California and southwestern Oregon.
CULTIVATION: As this plant comes from cool areas and damp to wet situations, it makes a good specimen in muddy banks and by streams. It is frost tolerant but not drought resistant. Propagation is by division or from seed.

Daphne tangutica

Darwinia homoranthoides

Darmera peltata
syn. ***Peltiphyllum peltatum***

This dramatic foliage plant can have leaves up to 24 in (60 cm) across on 6 ft (1.8 m) stalks. It bears attractive pink to white flowers in early spring. The dwarf form called **'Nana'** only grows to 12 in (30 cm). **ZONES 5–9.**

DARWINIA

This genus comprising about 60 species of evergreen shrubs is endemic to Australia. Most species occur in the far southwest, with fewer in the southeast, and grow among heath vegetation in sandy or peaty soil. Their small, narrow leaves have translucent dots containing aromatic oils. Although they belong to the myrtle family, they have atypical small, narrow, tubular flowers with long protruding styles, clustered on lateral branches. One group of southwestern species has flower clusters surrounded by large, colorful bracts, like a single bell-shaped flower. Some reach 10 ft (3 m) tall, but most are low and spreading.
CULTIVATION: Frost tender, they are well suited to growing in containers. Darwinias grow readily in light, well-drained soil and need moisture until established. A good mulch around the root area will keep the roots cool and moist during summer. Some tolerate coastal air. Propagate from cuttings in summer, or from seed or by layering in spring.

Darwinia citriodora
LEMON-SCENTED MYRTLE

A low, spreading evergreen shrub, this darwinia usually grows to about 4 ft (1.2 m) tall and up to 6 ft (2 m) across. The small oblong leaves are gray-green with reddish tones in fall (autumn) and winter and have a lemon smell when crushed. The small tubular flowers, produced mainly in spring are red and yellow and are surrounded by green and apricot bracts. Frost tender, it can be grown in coastal gardens with some protection. **ZONES 9–11.**

Darwinia homoranthoides

Growing to about 10 in (45 cm) high and up to 6 ft (2 m) across, this small spreading shrub has narrow, gray-green leaves and bears yellow and green tubular flowers with protruding styles in late spring and summer. It has self-layering branches and makes a good ground cover or rockery plant. **ZONES 9–11.**

Darwinia oxylepis
GILLIAM'S BELL

Despite its diminutive size, this shrub offers perhaps the best display of flowers in the genus. The flowerheads hang from the ends of pendulous branches, enclosed by brilliant scarlet, bell-like bracts. The small, pine-like leaves are crowded on the branchlets. Gilliam's bell grows to about 24 in (60 cm) high. **ZONES 10–11.**

DASYLIRION
SOTOL, BEAR GRASS

A genus of 18 species of yucca-like evergreens from southern USA and Mexico, some species can produce a short trunk of up to 12 ft (3.5 m) high. The long narrow leaves to 3 ft (1 m) in length are usually spiny. From among the leaves, established plants will send up flower spikes up to 12 ft (3.5 m) or more tall, bearing masses of small creamy white flowers. Male and female flowers are borne on separate plants.
CULTIVATION: These are plants of architectural quality for well-drained soils in hot sunny climates or large greenhouses elsewhere. Propagate from seed.

Dasylirion longissimum
MEXICAN GRASS PLANT

A fairly tall species with a trunk up to 12 ft (3.5 m) tall, has dull green leaves up to 6 ft (1.8 m) long, spread in all directions. The flower spike, reaching up to 15 ft (4.5 m) or more, is produced in summer on mature plants. **ZONES 10–12.**

Dasylirion wheeleri
DESERT SPOON, SOTOL

The gray-green, sword-like leaves of this species from southern USA develop thorny margins and grow to a length of 3 ft (1 m). Clusters of bell-shaped white flowers appear in spring on a spike up to 20 ft (6 m) high. **ZONES 9–11.**

DATURA
ANGEL'S TRUMPET

The tropical and subtropical genera *Brugmansia* and *Datura* are closely re-

Dasylirion longissimum

Darwinia oxylepis

lated; the taller, woody species with pendulous flowers are now included in *Brugmansia.* The genus contains 8 species of annuals or short-lived perennials, grown for their large, handsome and usually fragrant flowers. They bloom throughout summer and are white, sometimes blotched with purple, yellow or violet-purple. The foliage has an unpleasant odor, and all parts of the plants are narcotic and poisonous.
CULTIVATION: They need full sun and fertile, moist but well-drained soil. Propagate from seed.

Datura innoxia
syn. *Datura meteloides*

Though sometimes classed with *Brugmansia*, this bushy perennial from Central America is in fact a true *Datura.* It has pink or white flowers, the latter resembling those of *Datura stramonium,* but it is less poisonous, as its specific name suggests. If grown as an annual it makes a bush just under 3 ft (1 m) tall. **ZONES 9–11.**

Datura metel
HORN OF PLENTY, DOWNY THORN APPLE

An attractive annual to 5 ft (1.5 m) from southern China, this species resembles *Datura innoxia.* Although lovely to look at, it is quite poisonous and in some warm parts of the world it has potential as a weed. The flowers are up to 8 in (20 cm) long, can be double and may be in several shades, from dark purple to white or yellow. Cultivars include **'Alba'**, which is white; **'Aurea'**, which is yellow; **'Caerulea'**, which is blue and **'Flore-Pleno'**, which has double, off-white to purple flowers. **ZONES 9–11.**

Datura stramonium
JIMSON WEED, JAMESTOWN WEED, COMMON THORN APPLE

This American annual is a common weed in many countries. It grows to 6 ft (1.8 m) and its 3 in (8 cm) long trumpets, which are produced throughout summer and fall (autumn), can be white or purple. **ZONES 7–11.**

DAUCUS

This genus of about 25 species of annuals and biennials has a wide natural distribution and in the case of the carrot,

Dasylirion wheeleri

Daucus carota, an even wider man-made distribution. The wild species can be found in Europe, temperate Asia, Africa, Australia and New Zealand. Only one form is normally found in cultivation, the root vegetable carrot, which is not a wild species as such but a form of one developed over centuries by cultivation.
CULTIVATION: Carrots are raised from seeds best sown where they are to grow in rows about 10 in (25 cm) apart in deep, warm loam, making sure the earth is firmly compacted around the seeds. Keep the ground moist and thin the rows out when the seedlings are about 1 in (25 mm) high. The carrot gives a high yield even in a small garden and can be stored in bins or boxes between layers of sand. Once they are big enough to pick, avoid leaving them in the ground during wet weather as the root will split. The carrot is vulnerable to carrot-root fly, greenfly and aphids. A sunny well-drained aspect with a deep-dug fertile soil suits them best. Propagate from seed.

Daucus carota subsp. *sativus*
CARROT

This everyday root vegetable is thought to have originated in Afghanistan and was introduced to Europe 600 years ago. Many varieties are available including **'Nantes'** and **'Touchon'** which have a longish, cylindrical root with a distinct orange-yellow core and orange-red skin. **ZONES 3–11.**

DAVALLIA
HARE'S FOOT FERNS

This genus of ferns is very popular amongst gardens in warmer climates or with greenhouses. It consists of about 35

Datura innoxia

Datura stramonium

species many of which are epiphytic. They have creeping above-ground rhizomes, often covered in bronze, furry scales, hence the common name. They are native to many tropical and temperate parts of the world including tropical Asia, the Mediterranean region, North America, Australia and the Pacific Islands. Some temperate species are deciduous.
CULTIVATION: These soft fluffy ferns look best when grown in wire hanging baskets which they will eventually engulf with their creeping rhizomes. They require a moist environment, out of direct sunlight. Propagate by division of rhizomes.

Davallia canariensis
CANARY ISLAND HARE'S FOOT FERN, DEER'S FOOT FERN

This species is one of the more cold tolerant and comes from southwestern Europe and northwestern Africa. It will not, however, tolerate direct frost. It is deciduous or semi-evergreen with fronds up to 20 in (50 cm) long. Its rhizomes are covered with brown papery scales. **ZONES 9–11.**

Davidia involucrata

Davidia involucrata

Davallia fejeensis
RABBIT'S FOOT FERN

This epiphytic evergreen fern from Fiji has a woody rhizome covered with dark brown scales with long marginal hairs. The mid-green triangular fronds are up to 3 ft (1 m) or more in length and are very finely divided. **ZONES 10–12.**

Davallia mariesii
SQUIRREL'S FOOT FERN, BALL FERN

This deciduous species from east Asia has quite fine creeping rhizomes covered in brown scales. It is the most frost-hardy species. The fronds are up to 12 in (30 cm) long. **ZONES 8–11.**

Davallia pyxidata
HARE'S-FOOT FERN

A common fern in eastern Australia where it grows as an epiphyte on rocks or trees, it forms large clumps with spreading rhizomes covered with brown papery scales. The glossy dark green fronds, 3 or 4 times divided, are up to 3 ft (1 m) long. It is a popular plant for pots or baskets in Australia. **ZONES 9–11.**

Davidia involucrata var. *vilmoriniana*

Davallia trichomanoides
SQUIRREL'S-FOOT FERN

This species is native to Southeast Asia, where it grows as an epiphyte in rainforests. Furry, yellowish brown rhizomes produce lacy, glossy green, pinnate fronds around 15 in (38 cm) long. It demands a coarse, very well-drained, organic growing medium. Though deciduous for a short period, it quickly produces new fronds. **ZONES 10–12.**

DAVIDIA
DOVE TREE, HANDKERCHIEF TREE

Native to western China, this genus contains just one species, though some varieties occur. In China, it can reach over 60 ft (18 m), with a rounded crown, and in full flower it is one of the most striking of all deciduous trees outside the tropics. 'Like huge butterflies hovering' is how plant explorer E. H. Wilson described the long-stalked flowerheads, each nestled between 2 large, drooping white or cream bracts. The surface of the large, soft, toothed leaves is deeply creased by veins.

CULTIVATION: The tree is always raised from its large seeds, enclosed in a plum-like fruit about $1\frac{1}{2}$ in (35 mm) long. Cold treatment assists germination. It is frost hardy, but the bracts need protecting from wind. It needs rich, porous soil and full sun or part-shade. Propagate from the whole fruit, which may take up to 3 years to germinate.

Davidia involucrata

This conical tree has broad leaves up to 6 in (15 cm) long, and small, deep-set, brownish red flowers surrounded by 2 white bracts of unequal lengths. The greenish brown, pendent, ridged fruit are up to 2 in (5 cm) across. The more common cultivated form is ***Davidia involucrata* var. *vilmoriniana*,** which has paler and less downy leaf undersides. **ZONES 7–9.**

Davallia pyxidata

DECAISNEA

The well-known nineteenth-century French botanist Joseph Decaisne had many plant species named after him, but only in this one genus. It is one of 8 genera in the small family of Lardizabalaceae, which consists mostly of climbers and is regarded as one of the more primitive flowering plant families. *Decaisnea* consists of 2 species of erect, thick-branched, deciduous shrubs from western China and the Himalayas; their compound leaves have the leaflets pinnately arranged. The drooping panicles of 6-petalled, greenish yellow flowers are quite appealing but a greater attraction lies in the abundant sausage-like fruits, blue-gray in one species and yellow in the other.

CULTIVATION: Decaisneas are not too difficult to grow in cooler temperate climates, in a fertile, well-drained soil. They are quite frost hardy but may suffer damage from late frosts. Propagate from seed in fall (autumn).

Decaisnea fargesii

This upright sparsely branched shrub, which grows to about 20 ft (6 m), is of some architectural quality. Its large compound leaves are deciduous and up to 3 ft (1 m) long; they often have a faint blue-purple tinge to them particularly when young. Its cluster of small yellow flowers are followed by swollen sausage-like fruit that are a strange metallic blue-gray in color. **ZONES 5–9.**

DECUMARIA

A genus consisting of 2 species of self-clinging climbers with aerial roots, one from western China and the other from southeastern North America. This genus is closely related to *Hydrangea* and *Schizophragma* but it is generally less showy as all the flowers in the clusters are fertile and there are none of the larger sterile blooms that the other 2 genera have. They are, however, still quite decorative and have attractive leaves that can be evergreen or partially so.

CULTIVATION: Ideal for growing up walls or trees, they also serve well as a ground cover. Reasonably frost hardy they can be grown in any moist, well-drained soil. Propagate from seed, layers or cuttings.

Decaisnea fargesii

Decumaria barbara
WOOD VAMP, CLIMBING HYDRANGEA

Although one of its common names is misleading as it is not a hydrangea, it does look similar. This American member of the genus can reach up to 30 ft (9 m) on suitable supports. It is usually semi-deciduous and produces clusters of white scented flowers in summer. **ZONES 7–9.**

Decumaria sinensis

This is the Asian species which is not quite as cold tolerant as its American counterpart. It is usually evergreen and can reach up to 12 ft (3.5 m) or so. Its clusters of white flowers are produced in summer and have a musky scent. **ZONES 8–10.**

DEINANTHE

This genus consists of 2 perennials from Japan and central China. *Deinanthe* (pronounced with 4 syllables) is Greek for 'wondrous flower', which is perhaps an exaggeration. Though quite pretty, these plants are hardly outstanding for their floral beauty. They grow from a narrow rootstock, the few short stems bearing hydrangea-like leaves with finely toothed margins. Few-flowered panicles arise from the upper leaf axils on slender stalks; the individual flowers are white, blue or purple, with 5 large rounded petals, and point downward on short, curved stalks.

CULTIVATION: The plants require a cool, part-shaded, sheltered position in moist soil and are frost hardy except in very severe climates. Propagate from seed or by root division.

Deinanthe caerulea

This Chinese species is a clump-forming perennial to about 18 in (45 cm) high and across and has attractive, large compound leaves with serrated edges and prominent veins. The cup-shaped flowers are nodding, blue and white, and produced on stems that may hold quite a few in terminal panicles. **ZONES 6–9.**

DELONIX

Ten species make up this genus of tropical deciduous, semi-evergreen or evergreen trees from Africa, Madagascar, Arabia and India. The 5-petalled flowers

Delphinium cardinale

appear in terminal racemes, and the elegant leaves are bipinnate and fern-like. The fruits, typical of the legume group, are large, flattened, woody, bean-like pods. Frost tender, they do well as shade trees in warmer areas.

CULTIVATION: Plant in full sun in fertile, moist but well-drained soil and provide shelter from strong winds. Prune only when young to establish a single trunk. The vigorous roots can damage paths and foundations. Seedlings vary considerably in flower shape, color and size, and may take 10 or more years to flower. Propagate from seed or cuttings.

Delonix regia

POINCIANA, ROYAL POINCIANA, FLAMBOYANT TREE, FLEUR-DE-PARADIS, GUL MOHR, FLAME OF THE FOREST

This native of Madagascar grows only about 40 ft (12 m) tall, but its canopy may be wider than its height. The long, feathery leaves have lighter green undersides. Clusters of brilliant red or orange flowers, with one white petal marked with yellow and red, appear in late spring, followed by dark brown pods up to 12 in (30 cm) long. **ZONES 11–12.**

DELOSPERMA

Belonging to the large mesembryanthemum alliance, this is a genus of over 150 species of mainly shrubby succulents native to South and East Africa as well as Madagascar. Although these plants are usually quite drought tolerant and ideal for desert gardens, some are moderately frost tolerant as well. The leaves are borne in opposite pairs and can be triangular or circular in cross section. The flowers, which are usually produced in summer, are somewhat daisy-like and often brightly colored.

CULTIVATION: An aspect in full sun with good drainage and little frost will suit most species. Propagate from seed or cuttings.

Delosperma cooperi

A South African species to 24 in (60 cm) or more high, this is a good ground cover shrub for a sunny rock garden. Its bright magenta flowers are produced in mid- to late summer. **ZONES 9–11.**

D. grandiflorum 'Blue Butterfly'

Delosperma lineare

This species rarely exceeds 8 in (20 cm). Its branches are usually prostrate; the leaves are yellow-green and nearly cylindrical. Its white flowers are produced in summer. **ZONES 9–11.**

Delosperma nubigenum

This very prostrate trailing species makes a lovely ground cover or trailer. Its blooms are comparatively small but they are a bright yellow to orange-red. **ZONES 8–11.**

Delosperma vinaceum

This species' original habitat is unknown. It is a succulent creeper which produces small magenta flowers in summer .
Its green leaves reach 1 in (25 mm) in length. It propagates easily from cuttings. **ZONES 9–11.**

DELPHINIUM

This genus contains 250 or so species native to mainly northern hemisphere temperate zones, with a few found in scattered, high-altitude areas of Africa. They range from attractive self-seeding annuals or dwarf alpine plants up to statuesque perennials that can exceed 8 ft (2.4 m) in height. Nearly all start growth as a tuft of long-stalked basal leaves, their blades divided into 3 to 7 radiating lobes or segments. The tufts elongate into erect, sometimes branched flowering stems bearing stalked 5-petalled flowers each with a backward-pointing nectar spur. Garden delphiniums are mainly derived from *Delphinium elatum* and its hybrids. Recognized groups include the Belladonna, Elatum and Pacific hybrids. The annual larkspurs are now placed in the genus *Consolida*.

CULTIVATION: Very frost hardy, most like a cool to cold winter. They prefer full sun with shelter from strong winds, and well-drained, fertile soil with plenty of organic matter. Stake tall cultivars. Apply a liquid fertilizer at 2–3 weekly intervals.

Delonix regia

To maintain type, propagate from cuttings or by division though some species have been bred to come true from seed.

Delphinium cardinale

SCARLET LARKSPUR

This short-lived upright perennial to 6 ft (2 m) tall is native to California and Mexico. It has finely divided leaves and bears slender loose spikes of small, single red flowers with yellow centers in summer. Provide a rich, moist soil and a little shade. **ZONES 8–9.**

Delphinium formosum

This species from Turkey grows up to 6 ft (1.8 m). It is perennial and produces racemes of brilliant violet-blue flowers in summer. Its large, palmate leaves are quite handsome, with the segments deeply cut and toothed. **ZONES 5–9.**

Delphinium grandiflorum

syn. *Delphinium chinense*

BUTTERFLY DELPHINIUM, CHINESE DELPHINIUM

Native to China, Siberia, Japan and Mongolia, this tufted perennial grows to a height of 18 in (45 cm) and a spread of 12 in (30 cm), the leaf segments further divided into narrow lobes. Its large bright blue flowers with the long spurs finely warted blooms over a long period in summer. It is fully frost hardy. **'Azure Fairy'** is a pale blue-flowering form; **'Blue Butterfly'** has bright blue flowers. **ZONES 3–9.**

Delphinium macrocentron

This perennial from the mountains of East Africa can grow to 6 ft (1.8 m) tall and the leaf segments are divided into narrow lobes. The rather few flowers are nodding and can be dark blue to turquoise, white, or even green. The spur curves upwards and can be blue or white. **ZONES 8–10.**

Delosperma vinaceum

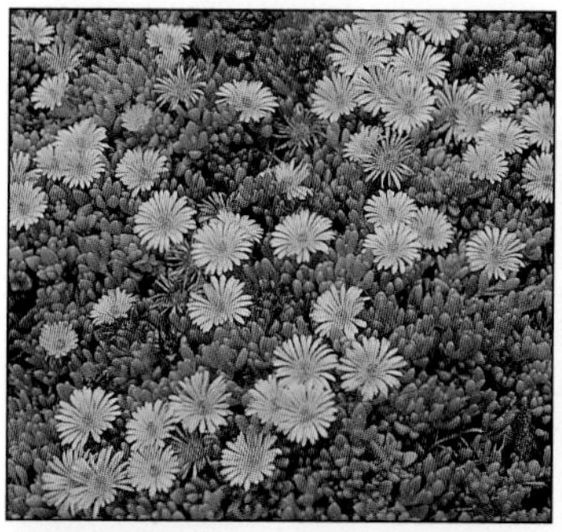

Delosperma nubigenum

Delosperma cooperi

Delonix regia

D

Delphinium semibarbatum
syn. *Delphinium zalil*

This short-lived, tuberous delphinium is indigenous to Iran and central Asia, where its flowers are used to dye silk. It is a rare plant of great beauty, producing spikes of sulfur yellow flowers with orange tips from spring to mid-summer. It grows to a height of 3 ft (1 m) with a 10 in (25 cm) spread. **ZONES 6–9.**

Delphinium, Belladonna Group

These frost-hardy perennials (*Delphinium elatum* × *D. grandiflorum*) have an upright, loosely branching form. Their widely-spaced blue or white flowers, 1 in (25 mm) or more wide, are single or sometimes semi-double and borne on loose spikes ranging in height up to 4 ft

Delphinium, Belladonna Group

(1.2 m). They bloom in early and late summer. Propagate by division or from basal cuttings in spring. **ZONES 3–9.**

Delphinium, Connecticut Yankees Group

These delphiniums are available in shades of blue, lilac, purple and white, and their graceful sprays of flowers are excellent for cutting. Even in mild-winter climates they should live 3 or 4 years. **ZONES 3–9.**

Delphinium, Elatum Group

This group whose main parent is *Delphinium elatum*, includes most of the tall delphiniums with flowers at least $2\frac{1}{2}$ in (6 cm) across, tightly packed on a tall flower stem that is usually unbranched. They bloom from summer to fall (autumn) and are excellent for picking. They can send up shorter later stems if cut back after the first ones are finished. Cultivars in this group include: **'Blue Bird'**, with clear blue flowers and white 'eyes'; **'Blue Dawn'**, with semi-double pale blue flowers and just a touch of pink; **'Blue Nile'**, with semi-double mid-blue flowers and a white center; **'Bruce'**, a tall variety with purple flowers and a brown center; **'Emily Hawkins'**, a medium grower with light violet flowers and a fawn center; **'Fanfare'**, a very tall

Delphinium elatum

Delphinium semibarbatum

grower with soft mauve semi-double flowers and a white eye; **'Fenella'**, a short variety with gentian blue flowers and black eyes; **'Gillian Dallas'**, a smallish variety with slate-gray to mauve white-eyed flowers; **'Loch Leven'**, with semi-double mid-blue flowers and white eyes; **'Lord Butler'**, a small variety with mid-blue flowers and white centers; **'Mighty Atom'**, a small variety bearing semi-double violet flowers and brown-streaked eyes; **'Sandpiper'**, a small-growing variety bearing semi-double white flowers with brown eyes; **'Spindrift'**, with semi-double rich blue flowers and creamy white centers, often with turquoise and green markings; and **'Sungleam'** a small-growing variety with semi-double cream flowers and pale yellow eyes. **ZONES 3–9.**

Delphinium, Pacific Hybrids

This group of short-lived perennials is usually grown as biennials. They were bred in California with the main parent being the perennial *Delphinium elatum*. They are stately plants to 5 ft (1.5 m) or more in height with star-like single, semi-double or double flowers of mostly blue, purple or white, clustered on erect rigid spikes. Some of the named cultivars are: **'Astolat'**, a perennial with lavender-mauve flowers with dark eyes; **'Black Knight'**, with deep rich purple flowers with black eyes; **'Galahad'** has pure white flowers. **'Guinevere'** bears pale purple flowers with a pinkish tinge and white

Delphinium, Pacific Hybrid, 'Galahad'

Delphinium, PH, 'Black Knight'

eyes; **'King Arthur'** has purple flowers with white eyes; and **'Summer Skies'** has pale sky-blue flowers. **ZONES 7–9.**

DENDROBIUM

This is one of the largest genera of orchids with about 1,200 species occurring from India to Japan, Australia, New Zealand and east to Fiji. The island of New Guinea, with at least 500 species, is particularly rich in *Dendrobium* species, as is the area from India across Thailand to southern China. Dendrobiums grow from hot steamy tropical lowlands to altitudes of 10,000 ft (3,000 m) and in semi-arid conditions in northern Australia. They grow epiphytically, on rocks and even in swampy ground, so it is difficult to generalize about cultivation. Clump formers make fat pseudobulbs; those with long, stem-like pseudobulbs often carry their flowers in sprays in the axils of the fallen leaves. These latter dendrobiums are divided into 'hard' (upright) and 'soft-caned' (floppy) types, but the distinctions are not very consistent. There are innumerable hybrids, both natural and cultivated. It is likely that the genus will be split up in the near future and many familiar names will be found under other genera. **CULTIVATION:** Generally they are divided into warm, intermediate and cool growing. For warm-growing species the temperature should not drop below about 60°F (15°C), for intermediate species temperatures down to about 35°F (2°C) are tolerated; and cool-growing species will tolerate still lower minimums but do not grow well in hot climates. A very well-drained mixture of bark and charcoal, often with a little added sphagnum moss, is preferred and most species should be given a dry resting period during winter if good flowering is required. Dendrobium resent disturbance. Most species should be repotted when the new shoots appear. Plants may be divided at this time; cuttings may also be taken. Watch for attack by spider mite, aphid and mealybug.

Dendrobium Hybrids

The genus has been very extensively used in hybridizing with several types now available for various climatic conditions and for different purposes such as hobby growing and the cut-flower industry, which is particularly well developed in Southeast Asia. Some of the hybrid types include 'soft cane' or 'nobile' types which are warm to intermediate growing; 'phalaenanthe' types which are mostly warm growers and widely used in the cut-flower industry; 'ceratobium' types which are warm growing and have interesting twisted floral segments. Recently a series of hybrids has been produced using Australian native species which are intermediate growing. **ZONES 10–12.**

Dendrobium antennatum
syn. *Dendrobium d'albertisii*
ANTELOPE ORCHID

A clump-forming epiphytic orchid, common in New Guinea and extending to northern Australia where it is rather rare. It has slender cylindrical pseudobulbs to 24 in (60 cm) long and about 12 thick-textured oblong leaves along the upper two-thirds of the pseudobulb. Up to 15 white or pale green perfumed flowers are borne on racemes, up to 14 in (35 cm) long, over a long period from fall (autumn) through to early summer. It is suitable for growing outdoors in tropical climates. **ZONES 11–12.**

Dendrobium bigibbum
COOKTOWN ORCHID

This beautiful epiphytic orchid occurs in Papua New Guinea and Australia, where it is common on Cape York Peninsula and is the floral emblem of Queensland. It forms small to medium clumps of erect, cane-like pseudobulbs to over 3 ft (1 m) in length. The dark green lance-shaped leaves are sometimes edged with purple. White, lilac, mauve or magenta flowers, up to 2 in (5 cm) across, are borne in racemes up to 16 in (40 cm) long in fall (autumn) and winter. **ZONES 11–12.**

Dendrobium chrysotoxum
syn. *Dendrobium suavissimum*
THE GOLDEN ARCH DENDROBIUM

This compact epiphytic species grows in the foothills of the Himalayas at moderate altitudes. The pseudobulbs are stout and about 8 in (20 cm) long with 2 to 4 leaves at the apex. The arching inflorescence arises from near the apex of the pseudobulb and is about 6–8 in (15–20 cm) long. The 12 to 20 flowers, each about 2 in (5 cm) in diameter, are golden yellow with a large dark orange spot on the tip. This species should be grown in full sun and requires only a short resting period in winter; it flowers in spring. **ZONES 10–11.**

Dendrobium formosum

Dendrobium lindleyi

Dendrobium cuthbertsonii

This miniature species comes from the high-altitude moss forests of Papua New Guinea. It is a clump-forming epiphytic orchid with short rounded or oval pseudobulbs. Plants have one to five dark green elliptic leaves that are sometimes warty on the upper surface and usually tinged purple on the underside. The solitary terminal flowers are usually red, but may be white, yellow, orange, pink or purple or sometimes bicolored. Cultivation is best on a slab of tree fern, kept evenly moist throughout the year in cool shady conditions. **ZONES 11–12.**

Dendrobium densiflorum

This spectacular epiphytic orchid is native to the Himalayas, Burma, Vietnam and Thailand. It forms dense clumps of erect, 4-angled pseudobulbs up to 20 in (50 cm) long with 3 to 5 narrowly elliptic leaves near the top. Pendent racemes to 10 in (25 cm) long bear many yellow flowers with fringed golden orange centers in spring. It prefers partly shaded intermediate conditions with plenty of water in summer and a dry rest in winter. **ZONES 10–11.**

Dendrobium kingianum

Dendrobium lawesii

Dendrobium formosum

From the Himalayas and Burma, this epiphytic orchid has erect cylindrical pseudobulbs up to 18 in (45 cm) long with leathery leaves about 5 in (12 cm) long. The large white flowers with an orange-yellow lip, up to 5 in (12 cm) across, are borne in small racemes from winter to late spring. It is one of the parents of many lovely hybrids including **'Fire Coral'** which has waxy white petals with a bright orange-red patch on the lower half of the lip. **ZONES 10–11.**

Dendrobium kingianum
PINK ROCK ORCHID

From eastern Australia, this very variable clump-forming species has numerous pseudobulbs of varying lengths and thin-textured leaves to 5 in (12 cm) long. The perfumed flowers range in color from deep rose to pale pink or, rarely, pure white. They appear in short racemes of 5 to 20 blooms in late winter and spring.

Dendrobium densiflorum

The plants should be given a dry rest during winter, intermediate to cool conditions, and strong light. **ZONES 9–11.**

Dendrobium lawesii

A native of New Guinea, this orchid has pendent pseudobulbs to 18 in (45 cm) long bearing thin-textured oval leaves to $2\frac{1}{2}$ in (6 cm) long. The white, red, orange, yellow or mauve flowers are produced on short racemes throughout the year but mainly in spring. **ZONES 11–12.**

Dendrobium lindleyi
syn. *Dendrobium aggregatum*

This is a small-growing species of wide distribution in mountains of Southeast Asia. The pseudobulbs are tightly crowded, small, spindle-shaped to 3 in (8 cm) long with a single, leathery leaf up to 6 in (15 cm) long. The inflorescences

Dendrobium rhodostictum

Dendrobium signatum

are 4–12 in (10–30 cm) long and pendulous with 5 to 15 flowers, each about 2 in (5 cm) across, fragrant and lasting more than a week. It requires strong light and is best grown on a slab of wood or cork. Flowers are borne in spring. ZONES 10–11.

Dendrobium nobile

This semi-deciduous species from parts of India and Southeast Asia, a parent of many fine hybrids, likes cool conditions and is a soft-cane type, about 15 in (38 cm) high. The fragrant flowers, which appear in spring, are pale pink with maroon and gold on the labellum; some forms have richer, darker color, some are white and gold. It likes strong light but some shade in summer, and an open compost. Water only when buds are well developed. ZONES 9–11.

Dendrobium rhodostictum

This orchid from Papua New Guinea and the Solomon Islands may be terrestrial or epiphytic. It has club-shaped pseudobulbs to 10 in (25 cm) long with 2 or 4 lance-shaped leaves near the top. Racemes, arising near the apex, carry slightly pendent white flowers with purple spots or markings on the edges of the lip. In cultivation it requires intermediate conditions. Flowering occurs mainly in winter and spring. ZONES 11–12.

Dendrobium signatum
syn. *Dendrobium hildebrandii*

This is a medium-sized orchid from mainland Southeast Asia with long, slender and pendulous pseudobulbs. The inflorescences are borne on the leafless stems with 2 or 3 flowers about 3 in (8 cm) across on each short stalk. The plants require intermediate to warm conditions with heavy watering during the growing season in spring and summer, but this should be greatly reduced in fall (autumn) and winter. Flowering occurs in spring. ZONES 10–11.

Dendrobium speciosum
KING ORCHID, ROCK ORCHID

Widely distributed along the eastern coast of Australia, this spectacular orchid grows on rocks and trees where it forms large spreading clumps. The pseudobulbs are usually large and thick, tapering to the apex and varying in length from 4 in (10 cm) to 3 ft (1 m). Two to five oval, thick dark green leaves are borne on the top of each pseudobulb. Racemes up to 24 in (60 cm) long are densely clustered with small fragrant flowers from pure white to cream or yellow, with the lip often marked with purple spots or stripes. They are produced freely from late winter through to late spring. ZONES 9–11.

Dendrobium taurinum

This large epiphyte occurs in the Philippines where it grows on low trees in mangrove forests. The pseudobulbs are crowded, cane-like and up to 3 ft (1 m) or more long and 1 in (25 mm) in diameter. The leaves are about 3 in (8 cm) long by 2 in (5 cm) wide. The inflorescences are up to 24 in (60 cm) long with numerous purple-pink, white and greenish colored flowers, each about $2\frac{1}{2}$ in (6 cm) long. This species should be kept warm and moist throughout the year. Flowers are produced in spring. ZONES 11–12

Dendrobium thyrsiflorum

From Thailand and moderate altitudes in the Himalayas, this species grows into large clumps on deciduous trees. The pseudobulbs are club-shaped up to 18 in (45 cm) long, with several leaves at the apex. The inflorescences are pendulous up to 10 in (25 cm) long with numerous creamy white fragrant flowers with bright golden yellow lips, about 2 in (5 cm) across, appearing in spring. It requires part-shaded intermediate conditions with plenty of water in summer and a dry rest in winter. ZONES 10–11.

Dendrobium, Yamamoto Hybrids

These soft-caned dendrobiums have undergone a great deal of development in recent years by Japanese breeders. The general name, Yamamoto hybrids, has been given to their creations, which are distinctive for their elegant shape and clear, brilliant colors. ZONES 10–11.

DENDROCHILUM
RICE ORCHIDS, GOLDEN CHAIN ORCHID

There are around 150 species in this orchid genus which occurs from Thailand to Papua New Guinea with the Philippines and Borneo being particularly rich. Most are epiphytes and most grow in the cloud forests of mountains. Dendrochilum generally have long pendulous inflorescences with many small fragrant star-shaped, usually

Deschampsia caespitosa

Desfontainea spinosa

yellow flowers. The inflorescences arise from the apex of the pseudobulbs which are crowded and squat with one or two long and moderately broad leaves. **CULTIVATION:** These frost-tender orchids require warm conditions to be grown outdoors. In temperate and cool climates they need to be grown under glass. Use a free-draining epiphytic orchid compost mix. They grow best in a small pot or basket. Care should be taken not to disturb the roots during repotting. Keep the plants moist throughout the year. In summer provide shade and liquid fertilize once every 2 to 3 weeks and not at all during winter. During the winter rest period ensure the plants get good light and water sparingly. Propagate by division.

Dendrochilum glumaceum
HAY-SCENTED ORCHID

This epiphytic orchid is native to the Philippines. It has short oval pseudo–bulbs and a solitary narrow elliptical leaf to 18 in (45 cm) long. The long pendent racemes of flowers, up to 20 in (50 cm) long, are produced in late summer and fall (autumn). The flowers are white to cream, with a pale green tip. **ZONES 11–12.**

Dendrochilum longifolium

Occurring naturally from Malaysia to Papua New Guinea, this epiphytic orchid has a short narrow pseudobulb to 3 in (8 cm) long, topped with a large, usually solitary elliptical leaf up to 15 in (40 cm) in length. The pendent raceme of flowers, up to 15 in (38 cm) long, is densely clustered with greenish yellow, chocolate-tipped flowers which occur mainly in late summer. **ZONES 11–12.**

DENDROMECON
TREE POPPY, BUSH POPPY

Native to southwestern USA and Mexico, this is a genus of two species of evergreen shrubs in the poppy family. They are

Deschampsia flexuosa 'Tatra Gold'

Desfontainea spinosa

much-branched, woody plants with simple, leathery leaves. The profuse golden flowers, borne singly and 4-petalled, are very like Californian poppies (*Eschscholtzia*) but larger. **CULTIVATION:** A frost-tender plant, the tree poppy requires a sunny, well-drained site and hot dry summers. In cool climates, grow in a cool greenhouse using a good potting mix. Ensure it receives direct sunlight and good air circulation. Propagate from seed or cuttings.

Dendromecon rigida

This lovely evergreen shrub can grow to 10 ft (3 m) or more tall. It has leathery gray-green leaves to 4 in (10 cm) long and masses of golden yellow poppy-like flowers throughout the warmer months. These are about 3 in (8 cm) across and are lightly fragrant. ***Dendromecon rigida* subsp. *harfordii*** (syn. *D. harfordii*) can grow to a small tree, with a rounded crown to 20 ft (6 m) high. **ZONES 8–10.**

DENMOZA

This cactus genus of 2 cacti species is native to Argentina. Both have erect, many ribbed spiny stems and red tubular flowers with protruding stamens, produced near the tops of the stems. The rounded fruits have tufted spines and later split to reveal black wrinkled seeds. **CULTIVATION:** These frost-tender cacti require full sun and excellent drainage when grown outdoors. In cool areas, grow in containers under glass in a standard cactus potting mix. They need full light and low humidity. Propagate from seed in spring or early summer.

Denmoza rhodacantha

A cactus to 12 in (30 cm) high with thick stems and up to 15 ribs, this species has up to 10 radial spines and usually one central spine. The red tubular flowers to 3 in (7 cm) long are produced in summer. **ZONES 10–11.**

DESCHAMPSIA
HAIR GRASS

This genus of mainly evergreen perennial grasses has a wide distribution in temperate zones. There are about 50 species although few are grown as garden plants. Those that are make attractive clumps with airy graceful flowerheads in summer that are often still attractive, albeit dead, into winter. They can be used fresh or dried for floral indoor arrangements. Much selection of superior garden forms has been carried out recently, so that new named varieties are becoming available. Plant in groups for a delicate, airy mass of blooms in the garden. **CULTIVATION:** These adaptable grasses usually do best in compost-enriched, moist soil in part-shade. Species can be raised from seed; propagate named clones by division in spring.

Deschampsia caespitosa
TUFTED HAIR GRASS

This mound-forming, evergreen perennial reaches 24–36 in (60–90 cm) in height with a 24 in (60 cm) spread. The flowers are borne in open panicles which rise above the coarse, arching foliage; colors range from pale greenish yellow to gold (in the cultivar **'Goldgehänge'**), to silver and bronze (**'Bronzeschleier'**). Other cultivars include **'Goldschleier'** (**'Gold Veil'**), which has silver-tinged golden yellow flower panicles; and **'Goldtau'** (**'Golden Dew'**) which is a compact form with reddish brown flowers that age to golden yellow. **ZONES 4–10.**

Deschampsia flexuosa
WAVY HAIR GRASS, CRINKLED HAIR GRASS

This species grows to 3 ft (1 m) and its light, airy flowerheads sit well about its tufted evergreen foliage. The cultivar

Dendromecon rigida

Dendrobium taurinum

'Tatra Gold' has lovely bright yellow-green foliage and soft bronze flowerheads. **ZONES 4–9.**

DESFONTAINEA

This genus has one species, an evergreen shrub from the Andes of western South America, long cultivated for its interesting foliage and showy flowers. It is stiff-branched, branching basally, with the leaves arranged in opposite pairs. The flowers, borne singly in the upper leaf axils, are roughly trumpet-shaped, with a gradually broadening tube and cupped, overlapping petals; they point downward and are presumably adapted to pollination by hummingbirds. **CULTIVATION:** Moderately frost hardy, it requires mild, rainy conditions for best results. Plant in moist, peaty, acidic soil and in shade in drier regions. Propagate from cuttings in summer.

Desfontainea spinosa

This dense, bushy shrub usually grows up to 5 ft (1.5 m) tall, but sometimes

Dendrochilum longifolium

Dendromecon rigida subsp. *harfordii*

Dendrobium, Yamamoto Hybrid

reaches twice this height and spreads widely. The shiny dark leaves resemble those of English holly *(Ilex aquifolium)*. The flowers vary from pale yellowish orange to bright orange-scarlet with pale tips and appear from mid-summer to late fall (autumn). **ZONES 8–9.**

DESMODIUM

BEGGAR WEED, TICK TREFOIL

Over 450 species of scrambling perennials and deciduous or evergreen shrubs form this genus, the great majority from the tropics or subtropics. The flowers are pea-shaped and may be pink, purple, blue or white. The leaves are usually compound often trifoliate. The most distinctive feature is the small seedpods which break apart into segments, each with small hooked bristles. Some warm climate species are weedy but some from cooler areas make good garden plants, notably several of the shrubby species with elegantly arching branches.
CULTIVATION: Most species do best in a sunny well-drained site. Provide shelter from strong winds and heavy frost for the less hardy species. In cool climates tropical species will need greenhouse conditions. Propagate from seed sown in spring or from cuttings.

Desmodium elegans

syn. *Desmodium tiliifolium*

This attractive deciduous shrub comes from China and the Himalayas. Up to

Deutzia crenata var. *nakaiana* 'Nikko'

Deutzia × *elegantissima*

5 ft (1.5 m) tall and of arching habit, its leaves are dark green with a dense gray downy underside consisting of 3 leaflets. Its rosy purple pea-flowers are produced in drooping spikes of 6 to 8 at the ends of the branches. **ZONES 8–10.**

Deutzia gracilis

Desmodium yunnanense

This large deciduous shrub from southwestern China also has an arching habit and grows to about 12 ft (3.5 m) tall. Its leaves usually consist of a single large leaflet although some may be trifoliate, in which case the terminal leaflet is large and the other two are much smaller. Its flowers, produced through summer and fall (autumn), are purple-pink and in dense panicles to 15 in (38 cm) long. **ZONES 8–10.**

DEUTZIA

These summer-flowering, deciduous shrubs from East Asia and the Himalayas are closely related to *Philadelphus* but they bear their smaller, white or pink flowers in more crowded sprays, with 5, rather than 4, pointed petals. Like *Philadelphus,* the plants have long, straight, cane-like stems. The leaves occur in opposite pairs and are mostly finely toothed. There are many frost-hardy species and fine hybrids available, especially those bred by the Lémoine nursery at Nancy, France, from 1890 to 1940.
CULTIVATION: Deutzias prefer a sheltered position, moist fertile soil and some sun during the day. Avoid pruning the previous year's short lateral shoots; thin out canes and shorten some of the thickest old stems after flowering. Propagate from seed or cuttings in late spring.

Deutzia crenata var. *nakaiana* 'Nikko'

syn. *Deutzia gracilis* 'Nikko'

One of the smallest deutzias, it makes a low spreading mound often rooting as it spreads. It is a good rock garden plant or ground cover in a shrub border, growing to about 24 in (60 cm) tall and as much as 4 ft (1.2 m) wide. The starry white flowers are produced in summer in spikes and the pale green foliage often turns burgundy before shedding. **ZONES 5–9.**

Deutzia gracilis

Deutzia × *elegantissima*

ELEGANT DEUTZIA

Including some of the finest and largest-flowered pinks among its clones, this hybrid of *Deutzia purpurascens* and *D. sieboldiana* reaches 4–6 ft (1.2–1.8 m) with purplish red twigs and flower stalks. The Lémoine nursery released the 2 original cultivars: **'Elegantissima'**, near-white inside and rose pink outside; and **'Fasciculata'**, with a slightly deeper rose flush. The Irish hybrid **'Rosealind'** has deeper flesh pink flowers. **ZONES 5–9.**

Deutzia gracilis

SLENDER DEUTZIA

A native of Japan, this popular species has a graceful, spreading habit and bears pure white flowers in slender, arching sprays during late spring and early summer. It grows to 3–6 ft (1–1.8 m) tall, and is one of the chief parent species of hybrid deutzias. **ZONES 4–10.**

Deutzia × *hybrida* 'Contraste'

This is a cross between *Deutzia longifolia* and *D. discolor* and 'Contraste' is but one named form. An arching shrub with rich green foliage, its flowers are star-shaped, rich pink to purplish pink with a wavy edge to the petals, and deeper pink bands on the petal backs. **ZONES 5–9.**

Deutzia × *kalmiiflora*

Only one clone of this early Lémoine hybrid between *Deutzia parviflora* and *D. purpurascens* is normally available, so a cultivar name is not used. It makes an erect shrub of about 6 ft (1.8 m) with small neat leaves and rather tight clusters of flowers whose pale pink outsides contrast with pale rose-colored insides. Flowering takes place from early to mid-summer. **ZONES 5–9.**

Deutzia longifolia

This Chinese species usually grows to 6 ft (2 m) tall by as much as 10 ft (3 m) wide. The flowers, about 1½ in (35 mm) across, are white. However, **'Veitchii'** has slightly larger blooms that are soft pink edged with white. **ZONES 5–9.**

Deutzia purpurascens

A graceful species from Yunnan discovered by the famous missionary-botanist Abbé Delavay, this slender arching shrub to 5 ft (1.5 m) tall has flowers that are white inside and purple on the outside. This species has been used extensively in hybridization. **ZONES 5–9.**

Deutzia × *rosea*

This was one of the earliest Lémoine crosses, involving the species *Deutzia gracilis* and *D. purpurascens*. It reaches a height and spread of 30 in (75 cm) and has the low, spreading habit of the former species with the pink coloration of the latter. The original clone has flowers of the palest pink, in shorter, broader sprays than in *D. gracilis*. **'Carminea'** has larger panicles of pink flowers with a stronger carmine pink on the back. **ZONES 5–9.**

Deutzia purpurascens

Dianella caerulea

Deutzia × *kalmiiflora*

Deutzia scabra

This is the longest established and most robust, cold-hardy species in Western gardens, with thick canes to about 10 ft (3 m) high, and long, dull green, rough-textured leaves. Large panicles of white, bell-shaped flowers terminate upper branches from mid-spring to early summer. **'Flore Pleno'** has double flowers, striped dull pink on the outside; **'Candidissima'** is a pure white double; **'Pride of Rochester'**, another double, has larger flowers faintly tinted mauve outside. **ZONES 5–10.**

Deutzia setchuenensis

This species from western China is a charming shrub to 6 ft (2 m) with clusters of small white star-shaped flowers in summer. It is comparatively slow growing but worth the wait. ***Deutzia setchuenensis* var. *corymbiflora***, with larger flowers in more substantial clusters, makes a beautiful specimen plant. **ZONES 5–9.**

DIANELLA

FLAX LILY

This genus of small-flowered lilies is named after Diana, the ancient Roman goddess of hunting. It consists of 25 to 30 species of evergreen, clump-forming perennials from Australia, New Zealand and the Pacific Islands; they grow in woodlands and are delightful plants for a shaded place in a warm-temperate garden. They are mostly under 3 ft (1 m) tall and are alike in their long leaves and sprays of small, deep or bright blue flowers in spring and early summer. The flowers are followed by long-lasting, bright blue berries.

CULTIVATION: They prefer sun or part-shade and a moderately fertile, humus-rich, well-drained, neutral to acidic soil. Propagate by division, or rooted offsets, or from seed in spring and fall (autumn). They naturalize well in mild climates.

Dianella tasmanica

Deutzia × *rosea* 'Carminea'

Deutzia × *rosea*

Dianella caerulea

BLUE FLAX-LILY

The evergreen foliage of this species from eastern Australia arisesin clumps from a creeping rhizome often with elongated, cane-like aerial stems. The grass-like leaves, up to 3 ft (1 m) long, have rough margins and the open panicles, up to 24 in (60 cm) tall, support small starry blue or, rarely, white flowers in spring and summer. These are followed in fall (autumn) by deep purple-blue berries which are sometimes more ornamental than the flowers. **ZONES 9–11.**

Dianella tasmanica

Native to southeastern Australia, including Tasmania, this species spreads from underground rhizomes and sends up arching, strap-like leaves that can be up to 4 ft (1.2 m) long and 1½ in (35 mm) wide. Nodding, star-shaped, bright blue or purple-blue flowers are borne in branching sprays up to 3 ft (1 m) tall in spring and early summer, followed by glossy, deep blue berries. **ZONES 8–10.**

DIANTHUS

CARNATION, PINK

This large genus consists of some 300 species. They mostly occur in Europe and Asia with a single species in Arctic North America and a few extending to southern Africa. Most are plants for the rock garden or edges of garden beds. Much hybridizing has created several different groups of pinks and carnations bred for specific purposes. Border Carnations are annual or perennial plants up to 24 in (60 cm) used as the name suggests as well as for cut flowers. Perpetual-flowering Carnations are mainly grown in the open but may be grown under cover to produce unblemished blooms;

Deutzia scabra

Deutzia scabra 'Pride of Rochester'

these are often disbudded leaving only the top bud to develop. American Spray Carnations are treated like perpetuals except that no disbudding is carried out. Malmaison Carnations, now undergoing a revival in popularity, are so-called because of their supposed resemblance to the Bourbon rose 'Souvenir de la Malmaison'; highly perfumed, they are grown in the same way as the perpetuals but need more care. Other groups of hybrids for the garden and cutting are the Modern Pinks and the Old-fashioned Pinks. Finally comes the Alpine or Rock Pinks bred from alpine species and used mostly in rock gardens. In all hybrid groups there are some cultivars that are self-colored (all the same color), and others that are flecked, picotee or laced, the latter two types having petals narrowly edged with a different color.

Dianthus caryophyllus cultivar

Dianthus barbatus

Dianthus chinensis 'Strawberry Parfait'

Dianthus erinaceus

CULTIVATION: Ranging from fully to marginally frost hardy, *Dianthus* species like a sunny position, protection from strong winds, and well-drained, slightly alkaline soil. Stake taller varieties. Prune stems after flowering. Propagate perennials by layering or from cuttings in summer; annuals and biennials from seed in fall (autumn) or early spring. Watch for aphids, thrips and caterpillars, rust and virus infections.

Dianthus alpinus

A native of the southeastern European Alps, this perennial to 8 in (20 cm) tall, makes a tight clump of fine dark green foliage with large flowers in summer ranging from deep pink to crimson, usually spotted and with toothed petals. This plant is normally short lived but readily raised from seed. It makes a charming rock garden subject. **ZONES 4–9.**

Dianthus armeria

DEPTFORD PINK

An annual or biennial species from Europe and western Asia, this species has basal rosettes of hairy dark green leaves up to 2 in (5 cm) long. In summer it produces terminal clusters of small flowers with narrow rose pink petals, that are dotted pale pink. It grows to about 16 in (40 cm) each way. **ZONES 6–9.**

Dianthus barbatus

SWEET WILLIAM

A slow-growing, frost-hardy perennial usually treated as a biennial, sweet William self-sows readily and grows to a height of 18 in (45 cm) and spread of 6 in (15 cm). The crowded, flattened heads of fragrant flowers range from white through pinks to carmine and crimson-purple and are often zoned in two tones. They flower in late spring and early summer and are ideal for massed planting. The dwarf cultivars, about 4 in (10 cm) tall, are usually treated as annuals. It has been crossed with Modern Pinks to produce a strain of hybrids, known as **'Sweet Wivelsfield'**. **ZONES 4–10.**

Dianthus carthusianorum

CARTHUSIAN PINK

This species from southern and central Europe makes a useful and attractive plant in the perennial border. A tufted perennial to about 8 in (20 cm) high, it has pale green, grass-like foliage. Its flowers, produced in summer, are borne in flattened terminal clusters and are up to 2 in (5 cm) across. The color is usually a deep pink to purple or occasionally white. **ZONES 3–9.**

Dianthus caryophyllus

WILD CARNATION, CLOVE PINK

The wild carnation is a loosely tufted woody-based perennial species from the

Dianthus 'First Love'

Mediterranean area with a history of cultivation dating back to classical times. It has pink-purple, pink or white flowers in summer, their perfume is sweet with a spicy overtone somewhat like cloves, and grows to about 30 in (75 cm) tall by 9 in (23 cm) wide or more. From this species have been raised over the years many varieties of Annual or Marguerite Carnations and the hardy Border Carnations, in addition to the modern Perpetual-flowering Carnations commonly grown for the cut-flower trade. **ZONES 8–10.**

Dianthus chinensis

CHINESE PINK, INDIAN PINK

This popular annual, originally from China, has a short, tufted growth habit, and gray-green, lance-shaped leaves. In late spring and summer it bears masses of single or double, sweetly scented flowers in shades of pink, red, lavender and white. It is slow growing to a height and spread of 6–12 in (15–30 cm), and is fully frost hardy. **'Strawberry Parfait'** has single pink flowers, lightly fringed with deep red centers. **ZONES 7–10.**

Dianthus deltoides

MAIDEN PINK

Ideal for a rock garden or ground cover, this dwarf mat-forming, evergreen perennial is easily grown from seed or cuttings. It has tiny, crowded leaves often with a purple tinge and bears small flowers with fringed petals in pink, cerise or white, mostly with a red eye, in spring and early summer. It grows to 6 in (15 cm) high with a spread of 12 in (30 cm), and is very frost hardy. Cut back after flowering. **ZONES 3–10.**

Dianthus erinaceus

This attractive cushion-forming species from Turkey forms a lovely rock garden plant that will trail over the top of rocks. It rarely grows more than 2 in (5 cm) tall but can exceed 24 in (60 cm) in spread and its gray-green foliage is surprisingly prickly. The small single pink flowers are produced on short stems not much above the mat in summer. **ZONES 7–9.**

Dianthus gratianopolitanus

Dianthus 'First Love'

There are many annual strains of Pinks, some descended from the Chinese Pink, *Dianthus chinensis*, others from sweet William (*D. barbatus*). 'First Love', a low grower at 6 in (15 cm), may be a cross between these groups. The fringed magenta and white flowers, often bicolored, are scented. **ZONES 6–10.**

Dianthus gallicus

JERSEY PINK

A native of the Atlantic coast of Europe from Portugal to northwestern France, this loose-tufted perennial grows to 18 in (45 cm) tall when in flower. The fragrant blooms are produced in summer at the tips of the stems, singly or in clusters of three. The pink petals are deeply toothed. **ZONES 8–10.**

Dianthus giganteus

As its name implies this is a comparatively tall species reaching up to 3 ft (1 m) tall. It comes from the Balkan Peninsula. In summer it produces dense heads of purple-pink flowers. **ZONES 5–9.**

Dianthus gratianopolitanus

syn. *Dianthus caesius*

CHEDDAR PINK

The English common name comes about because in the UK this species is only known from the limestone of Cheddar Gorge, but in fact it is widely distributed in continental Europe. It makes tidy mounds of blue-gray, linear leaves developing into broad mats 12 in (30 cm) or more wide. Delightfully fragrant, purplish pink blossoms with toothed ('pinked') petals are borne on 6–8 in (15–20 cm) wiry stems in spring; the flowers will often continue until frost. It

Dianthus, Ideal Series, 'Ideal Violet'

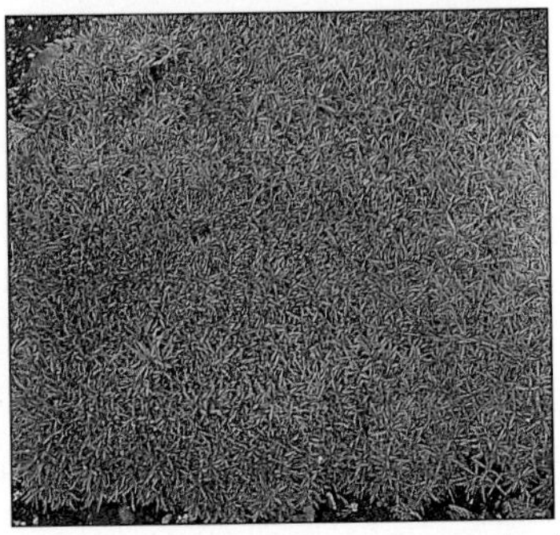

Dianthus gratianopolitanus 'Tiny Rubies'

Dianthus plumarius

Dianthus superbus 'Rainbow Loveliness'

Dianthus pavonius

Dianthus, Alpine Pink, 'Pike's Pink'

Dianthus superbus

requires a very well-drained, alkaline soil and full sun. **'Tiny Rubies'** is ideal as a neat compact ground cover. **'Tiny Tim'** has ½ in (12 mm), double, deep pink flowers on 4 in (10 cm) stems. ZONES 5–9.

Dianthus, Ideal Series

These short-lived perennial hybrids between *Dianthus barbatus* and *D. chinensis*, are usually grown as annuals or biennials, flowering in the first season. They grow to 14 in (35 cm) and have bright green leaves. They bear clusters of fringed, 5-petalled flowers in shades of deep violet, purple, deep pink and red in summer. **'Ideal Violet'** has deep purple-pink flowers with paler margins. ZONES 5–10.

Dianthus pavonius

syn. *Dianthus neglectus*

This is usually a tufted or mat-forming perennial to 6 in (15 cm) tall and up to 10 in (25 cm) across. It comes from the Alps of France and Italy. The flowers are usually solitary occasionally up to 3, pale pink with toothed petals. ZONES 4–9.

Dianthus plumarius

GARDEN OR COTTAGE PINK

A loosely tufted, evergreen perennial with pale pink or white flowers with strongly fringed petals, this species grows 12–18 in (30–45 cm) high and spreads to 10 in (25 cm) across. A native of Europe, this is one of the main parents of the Old-fashioned Pinks and Modern Pinks. There are many named cultivars, bearing sprays of single or fully double, sweetly scented flowers in red, pink, purple-red, mauve and white. Many have fringed petals and a contrasting eye. ZONES 3–10.

Dianthus superbus

Native to mountains in Europe and temperate Asia, this species is a loosely tufted perennial sometimes as much as 3 ft (1 m) high. Its leaves are mid-green and about 3 in (8 cm) long. The rich purple-pink fragrant flowers, produced singly or in pairs through summer, have petals deeply divided giving flowers a loosely fringed appearance. Seldom grown, it has been used in producing garden hybrids. It is better known as a parent of the Loveliness Strain which includes **'Rainbow Loveliness'**, with deeply fringed single flowers of mauve and pink shades carried on slender stems in spring. ZONES 4–10.

Dianthus, Alpine Pinks

Also known as Rock Pinks, the cultivars of this hybrid group are compact plants forming mounds or mats of crowded fine leaves. The flowers come in many colors and shapes and are usually held 6–12 in (15–30 cm) above the foliage. **'La Bourboule'** (syn. 'La Bourbille') bears a profusion of single clove-scented pink flowers with fringed petals; **'Pike's Pink'** has gray-green foliage and rounded double pink flowers with a darker zone at the base; **'Nancy Colman'** is very similar but without the darker zone. ZONES 4–9.

Dianthus, Annual or Marguerite Carnations

Although these are evergreen perennials, they are usually grown as annuals. They grow to 30 in (75 cm) high with a spread of 8 in (20 cm) and produce 2½ in (6 cm) wide flowers in sprays from spring to fall (autumn). **'Enfant de Nice'** has fancy or picotee flowers in attractive mixed colors. ZONES 5–9.

Dianthus, MP, 'Gran's Favourite'

Dianthus, Border Carnations

This large group of cultivars derives from the 'clove-scented Pink', *Dianthus caryophyllus*. Most carry a clove-like perfume. They grow to 24 in (60 cm) tall and spread to 12 in (30 cm). Frost hardy, they are best suited to cooler climates. The flowers produced in spring and early sum-mer are smooth edged or fringed, 3 in (8 cm) wide, and come in many colors. ZONES 6–9.

Dianthus, Modern Pinks

These are densely leafed, mound-forming perennials derived from crosses between cultivars of *Dianthus plumarius* and *D. caryophyllus*. The earlier hybrids were called *D.* × *allwoodii* but these hardly stand apart from the rest of the Modern Pinks now. Modern Pinks have gray-green foliage and many erect flowering stems, each carrying 4 to 6 fragrant, single to fully double flowers in shades of white, pink or crimson, often with dark centers and with plain or fringed petals. Most are 12–18 in (30–45 cm) tall with a spread of 18 in (45 cm) and flower from late spring until early fall (autumn); some are clove-scented. **'Allwoodii'** bears fringed, pale purple-pink flowers with deep red central zones; **'Becky Robinson'** bears laced pink, clove-scented double blooms with ruby centers and margins; **'Dick Portman'** bears double crimson flowers with pinkish cream centers and margins; **'Doris'** a scented pale pink double with deep pink center; **'Gran's Favourite'** is a sweetly scented, short-stemmed double, white with maroon centers and margins; **'Houndspool Ruby'** (syns 'Ruby', 'Ruby Doris') has rich pink double flowers with darker pink centers; **'Joy'** has semi-double carmine-pink flowers on strong upright stems; **'Laced Monarch'** bears deep pink to cerise double flowers with pale pink markings; **'Monica Wyatt'** has full double clove-scented pale pink flowers with dark centers; **'Valda Wyatt'** has clove-scented, rich pink double flowers with darker centers; and **'Warrior'** has double pink flowers with deep red centers and margins. ZONES 5–10.

Dianthus, Modern Pink, 'Allwoodii'

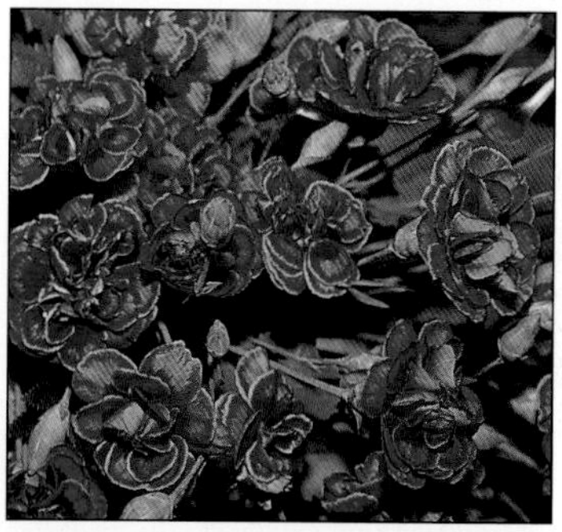

Dianthus, Modern Pink, 'Laced Monarch'

Dianthus, Modern Pink, 'Dick Portman'

Dianthus, Modern Pink, 'Doris'

Dianthus, Modern Pink, 'Joy'

Dianthus, Modern Pink, 'Warrior'

D

Dianthus, Old-fashioned Pinks

These are tuft-forming perennials that grow to 18 in (45 cm) high. In late spring and early summer they bear single to fully double, clove-scented flowers to 2½ in (6 cm) across in colors varying from white, through pale pink and magenta to red, often fringed and with contrasting centers. **'Mrs Sinkins'** is a famous Old-fashioned Pink with pure white shaggy flowers prone to split at the calyx; it is highly perfumed. **'Pink Mrs Sinkins'** is a pale pink form of 'Mrs Sinkins'. Other Old-fashioned Pinks include **'Clare'**, which produces bicolored clove-scented double pink fringed flowers with maroon centers, and **'Rose de Mai'**, which bears clove-scented single pink flowers with deep pink eyes. ZONES 5–9.

Dianthus, P-fC, 'Raggio di Sole'

Dianthus, Perpetual-flowering Carnations

These popular flowers are marginally frost hardy perennials that reach at least 3 ft (1 m) high with a spread of 12 in (30 cm). Their stems will need support. Fully double flowers, usually fringed, are produced all year. Disbud large-flowered varieties; spray types produce about 5 flowers per stem and do not need disbudding. Cultivars include **'Charlotte'** which bears cream flowers striped salmon pink; **'Malaga'** has salmon pink flowers; **'Olivia'** has salmon pink flowers with fringed petals; **'Raggio di Sole'** has bright orange flowers with red specks; **'Sofia'** bears white flowers with clear red stripes. ZONES 8–11.

DIASCIA

TWINSPUR

This is a genus of about 50 species of delicate but long-blooming perennials from South Africa that are popular in rockeries and borders and as potted specimens. They bear terminal racemes of flat, generally pink flowers with double nectar spurs on the back, and have erect or prostrate stems with toothed, mid-green leaves. A number of attractive cultivars are available including **'Kelly's Eye'**, and **'Rose Queen'** which is an excellent bedding plant.

CULTIVATION: Full sun is best, with afternoon shade in hot areas; most are frost hardy, but they dislike humidity. A fertile, moist but well-drained soil and regular summer watering are vital. Pinch out tips to increase bushiness and cut back old stems after flowering. Propagate from seed in fall (autumn), or cuttings in fall, to overwinter in a cool greenhouse.

Dianthus, O-fP, 'Pink Mrs Sinkins'

D. 'Pink Mrs Sinkins' and 'Mrs Sinkins'

Dianthus, Old-fashioned Pink, 'Clare'

Dianthus, O-fP, 'Rose de Mai'

Dianthus, P-fC, 'Charlotte'

Dianthus, P-fC, 'Olivia'

Diascia barberae

This low-growing, rather fragile perennial has small, heart-shaped, pale green leaves; it bears clusters of twin-spurred, salmon pink flowers from spring to early fall (autumn). It grows 6–12 in (15–30 cm) tall with a spread of 8 in (20 cm). **'Ruby Field'** has salmon pink, wide-lipped, flowers produced over a long period from summer to fall (autumn). ZONES 8–10.

Diascia 'Blackthorn Apricot'

This is probably another selection from *Diascia barberae.* It grows to 16 in

Dianthus, Perpetual-flowering Carnation, 'Malaga'

Diascia 'Rose Queen'

Dianthus, P-fC, 'Sofia'

Diascia barberae

Diascia barberae 'Ruby Field'

(25 cm) tall by at least 20 in (50 cm) wide and its apricot pink flowers, with downward-pointing spurs, are produced on loose spikes from summer well into fall (autumn). **ZONES 8–10.**

Diascia fetcaniensis
syn. *Diascia felthamii*

Indigenous to the Drakensburg Mountains, this fairly compact plant with ovate hairy leaves to 1 in (25 mm) long grows to a height of 12 in (30 cm) and spreads about 3–4 ft (1–1.2 m). It produces loose racemes of rose pink flowers with downward-curved spurs from summer well into fall (autumn). **ZONES 8–10.**

Diascia integerrima
syn. *Diascia integrifolia*

A creeping perennial to 18 in (45 cm) tall by 3–4 ft (1–1.2 m) wide, the leaves are linear to lance-shaped and up to 1 in (25 mm) long. The loose spikes of flowers are produced mainly in summer and are a vibrant rich purple-pink with downward-pointing spurs. **ZONES 8–10.**

Diascia rigescens

This vigorous twinspur has a sprawling form with dense 6–8 in (15–20 cm) spikes of pink flowers at the upturned ends of each stem; clumps may be 24 in (60 cm) across. It flowers nearly all summer if faded flower spikes are removed. **ZONES 8–10.**

Diascia 'Rupert Lambert'

This cultivar grows to about 10 in (25 cm) tall by 20 in (50 cm) wide and has narrow, shallowly toothed pointed leaves. The deep pink flowers with parallel spurs are produced during summer and fall (autumn). **ZONES 8–10.**

Diascia 'Rupert Lambert'

Dicentra formosa

Diascia fetcaniensis

Diascia stachyoides

Growing to 16 in (40 cm) tall, this perennial has slightly serrated leaves decreasing in size up the flower stems, which are sparsely clad in deep rose pink flowers in summer, their spurs pointing down and outwards. **ZONES 8–10.**

Diascia vigilis
syn. *Diascia elegans*

A vigorous plant with a strongly stoloniferous habit, it grows to 20 in (50 cm) tall. The foliage is light green and glossy. It produces loose racemes of clear pink flowers from summer into early winter with incurved spurs. This is one of the most frost hardy and floriferous species. **ZONES 8–10.**

DICENTRA
BLEEDING HEART

This genus consists of about 20 species of annuals and perennials much admired for their feathery leaves and the graceful carriage of their flowers, although they do not grow or flower well without a period of winter chill. The flowers, pendent and heart-shaped, come in red, pink, white, purple and yellow. They flower from mid-spring into early summer, though potted plants can be gently forced into early spring bloom if taken into a mildly warmed greenhouse at mid-winter. From Asia and North America, they are usually found in woodland and mountainous areas. **CULTIVATION:** Mostly quite frost hardy, dicentras love humus-rich, moist but well-drained soil and some light shade. Propagate from seed in fall (autumn) or by division in late winter.

Dicentra 'Bacchanal'

This bushy perennial has ferny bright green foliage and clusters of drooping heart-shaped, deep rich burgundy flowers. It grows to 18 in (45 cm) tall by at least 24 in (60 cm) wide. **ZONES 3–9.**

Dicentra formosa 'Alba'

Diascia 'Blackthorn Apricot'

Diascia stachyoides

Dicentra 'Bountiful'

The finely dissected blue-green foliage of this clump-forming perennial from America provides year-round interest. Narrow, heart-shaped, carmine to purple flowers hang on 12–15 in (30–38 cm) bare stems above the foliage through spring and summer. **ZONES 3–9.**

Dicentra cucullaria
DUTCHMAN'S BREECHES

This North American species is one of the daintiest in the genus. It grows only to about 8 in (20 cm) tall and makes slowly ever-increasing drifts. It grows from small pink to white oval tubers not much larger than a lemon pip. The foliage is fine and lacy, gray-green in color and disappears quickly after flowering. The flowers produced in early spring have two upward-pointing spurs that are pure white with yellow at the mouth. **ZONES 3–9.**

Dicentra formosa
WESTERN BLEEDING HEART

This spreading plant grows to about 18 in (45 cm) high with a spread of 12 in (30 cm). Dainty pink and red flowers appear on slender arching stems throughout spring and summer. **'Alba'** is a white-flowered form. **ZONES 3–9.**

Dicentra 'Langtrees'

A cultivar with silvery ferny foliage topped with white flowers tinged pink from mid-spring to mid-summer, this is a vigorous form, making luxuriant clumps 12 in (30 cm) tall by at least 18 in (45 cm) across. **ZONES 3–9.**

Diascia vigilis

Diascia rigescens

Dicentra 'Luxuriant'

This attractive spreading cultivar, to 12 in (30 cm) high and 18 in (45 cm) across, has rich green leaves to 12 in (30 cm) long. Drooping wine red flowers hover above the foliage from mid-spring into summer. **ZONES 3–9.**

Dicentra scandens
syn. *Dicentra thalictrifolia*

This perennial with a scrambling growth habit can climb as high as 12 ft (3.5 m) or more with the aid of tendrils; however, it is normally kept to a height of 3 ft (1 m) or so in gardens. It has light green foliage and throughout summer and fall (autumn) it produces clusters of yellow, green-tipped flowers. Though rare, there are forms with white flowers with pink or purple tips. **ZONES 4–9.**

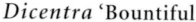

Dicksonia antarctica

Dicksonia fibrosa

Dichelostemma ida-maia

Dichondra micrantha

Dichorisandra thyrsiflora

Dicentra spectabilis

Dicentra spectabilis 'Alba'

Dicentra spectabilis
BLEEDING HEART

This popular garden perennial grows 24–36 in (60–90 cm) tall with a spread of 18–24 in (45–60 cm). Pink and white heart-shaped flowers on long arching stems appear in late spring and summer. After flowering, the foliage usually dies down to the ground. **'Alba'** is a pure white form with green-yellow markings and pale green leaves that will grow true from seed. **ZONES 2–9.**

DICHELOSTEMMA

This genus of about 7 species of summer-flowering bulbs and corms is related to *Brodiaea*, and some of its species were formerly classified under that genus. Native to the western USA, they bear dense, terminal clusters of tubular or star-shaped flowers on slender, erect, leafless stems that reach 3 ft (1 m). They have narrow, strap-like, basal leaves and are frost hardy if grown in a sunny, sheltered site. These dainty flowers look their best planted in groups.
CULTIVATION: Plant the corms in fall (autumn) in full sun in well-drained soil. Water regularly until the flowers die, then keep dry when dormant. Propagate from offsets in fall or sow seed in spring or fall (autumn).

Dichelostemma ida-maia
syn. *Brodiaea ida-maia*
CALIFORNIAN FIRECRACKER, FIRECRACKER FLOWER

The flowers of this species consist of a crimson tube with 6 yellow- and green-tipped petals. They are produced in clusters of up to 20 at the top of slender stems. The leaves of this marginally frost-hardy bulb are basal and semi-erect. **ZONES 8–10.**

Dichelostemma pulchellum
syns *D. capitatur, Brodiaea capitata, B. pulchella*
BLUE DICKS, WILD HYACINTH

The slender, leafless stem of this species grows to 24 in (60 cm) long. It carries dense clusters of pale lilac to mauve bell-shaped flowers, 1½ in (35 mm) long, with deep purple bracts. The narrow, basal leaves are semi-erect. **ZONES 8–10.**

DICHONDRA

This genus of some 10 species in the convolvulus family is not what one would call highly ornamental; the green and white flowers are tiny and not brightly colored. They can be useful ground covers and are often used as lawn substitutes in tropical and subtropical climates. Although they can be walked on they will not tolerate heavy foot traffic.
CULTIVATION: If using these plants as a lawn substitute make sure the ground is well cultivated and ample humus is incorporated. Be careful to destroy all weeds before planting dichondras as they will be difficult to eradicate later. Grow in a sunny position with plenty of water. Propagate from seed or by division.

Dichondra micrantha
KIDNEY WEED

A native of New Zealand and Australia, this perennial makes a good soft green lawn; it is good for a shady spot under a tree. It takes root at nodes on stems that spread widely; the leaves are kidney-shaped, and only about ½ in (12 mm) wide. In spring kidney weed produces small, green, insignificant flowers. *Dichondra micrantha* has been much confused with the very similar ***D. repens,*** which differs in the undersides of its leaves, which are green, not grayish. **ZONES 9–11.**

DICHORISANDRA

This genus of about 25 species from Central and South America, is related to the common wandering Jew *(Tradescantia).* The foliage of these soft-stemmed perennials may be glossy green or banded or striped with cream. The small cup-shaped flowers are purple or blue and are followed by fleshy orange fruits.
CULTIVATION: In warm-temperate climates they can be grown in well-drained, shady spots, however, they cannot survive frost and must be overwintered in a greenhouse in colder climates. They require adequate moisture at all times and high humidity in summer. Propagate by division in early spring or from cuttings in summer.

Dichorisandra reginae

This soft-stemmed clump-forming perennial to 12 in (30 cm) high has erect stems and dark green leaves to 7 in (18 cm) long that are purplish beneath and are often flecked with silver. Small dense spikes of purple-blue flowers are produced from summer to fall (autumn). **ZONES 11–12.**

Dichorisandra thyrsiflora
BLUE GINGER, BRAZILIAN GINGER

The common name for this species is a misnomer, and arises from its ginger-like stems, covered in tightly sheathing leaf bases. This perennial has glossy, dark green leaves 12 in (30 cm) long that are spirally arranged along the upright stems. It produces dense terminal clusters of deep purple-blue flowers in fall (autumn), and grows to a height of 8 ft (2.4 m) and spread of 3 ft (1 m). **ZONES 10–12.**

DICKSONIA
TREE FERN

Tree ferns are common in the wet tropics, among mountains where mist and drizzle are frequent. They are true ferns, distinguished from other ferns by their single bud terminating a vertical stem, at the core of which is a convoluted system of conducting and strengthening tissues, often clothed in matted aerial roots. The fronds are usually large and multi-pinnate, with downy bases. This genus contains 30 large, evergreen to semi-evergreen species, ranging from Malaysia to Australia. A New Zealand species, *Dicksonia squarrosa*, occurs up to latitudes equivalent to central Europe.
CULTIVATION: The plants, ranging from fully frost hardy to frost tender, require protection from wind and prefer peaty, damp soil and full or part-shade; they will not tolerate a dry atmosphere. Propagate from spores in summer.

Dicksonia antarctica
SOFT TREE FERN, TASMANIAN TREE FERN

Native to southeastern Australia, this tree fern can grow to 50 ft (15 m) with a trunk diameter of 3 ft (1 m) in the wild, with lacy dark green fronds up to 10 ft (3 m) long. In cultivation, it rarely exceeds 10 ft (3 m) in height. It is a marginally frost-hardy species requiring a moist, sheltered position. Its erect trunk is densely covered with fibrous roots and is an excellent host for epiphytic orchids and other ferns. **ZONES 8–10.**

Dicksonia squarrosa

Dicliptera suberecta

Dicksonia fibrosa
WHEKI-PONGA

This New Zealand tree fern grows slowly to a height of 20 ft (6 m) and produces dark green, arching fronds 5–8 ft (1.5–2.4 m) long. As it grows the stout stem becomes covered in thick, densely matted, fibrous, brownish red aerial roots. An easily grown species, it prefers cool, moist conditions. **ZONES 8–10.**

Dicksonia squarrosa
WHEKI, ROUGH TREE FERN

A marginally frost-hardy New Zealand fern, this species develops in colonies, discouraging other plants. The brownish red, downy trunk grows to over 15 ft (4.5 m) tall and 10 ft (3 m) in diameter. Its 3 to 4 deep green fronds, with a lighter colored underside, are over 3 ft (1 m) long. It needs humidity, part-shade, damp soil and shelter from frost and wind. **ZONES 8–10.**

DICLIPTERA

This genus of the acanthus family consists of some 150 species of annuals, perennials, subshrubs or scrambling climbers. The simple, smooth-edged leaves are arranged in opposite pairs. The tubular flowers are in terminal or sometimes axilary clusters. They range in the wild through most tropical and subtropical regions of the world.
CULTIVATION: In frosty areas lift and store in greenhouses for the winter or take cuttings which can then be held over indoors until after spring frosts. Propagate from cuttings.

Dicliptera suberecta
syns *Jacobinia suberecta, Justicia suberecta*

This is the only species commonly found in cultivation. It comes from Uruguay and makes a soft-wooded, sprawling subshrub up to about 24 in (60 cm) and sometimes wider. Its stems and leaves are covered with velvety gray felt which

Dictamnus albus

Dicliptera suberecta

makes a dramatic setting for the tubular orange-red flowers, which are produced through late summer and fall (autumn). It is a good pot plant and somewhat shade tolerant. **ZONES 8–11.**

DICTAMNUS
BURNING BUSH

The Book of Exodus tells how God spoke to Moses on Mount Sinai from a bush that burned yet was not consumed by the fire. Theologians point out that since this was a miracle the species is irrelevant. Gardeners insist that it must have been *Dictamnus albus*, the only species in its genus and indeed indigenous to the Mediterranean and temperate Asia. In still, warm conditions so much aromatic oil evaporates from the leaves that if you strike a match near it the vapor ignites and the bush is engulfed in flame, but so briefly that it is not damaged.
CULTIVATION: This perennial needs full sun and fertile, well-drained soil. It resents disturbance. Propagate from fresh seed in summer.

Dictamnus albus
syn. *Dictamnus fraxinella*
BURNING BUSH, DITTANY, GAS PLANT

This herbaceous, woody-stemmed perennial bears early summer spikes of fragrant, star-shaped, white, pink or lilac flowers with long stamens. It grows to 3 ft (1.2 m) tall with a spread of 36 in (90 cm) and has glossy light green leaves. It is quite frost hardy. ***Dictamnus albus* var. *purpureus*** (syn. *D. a.* var. *rubra*) bears purple-pink flowers with purple veins. **ZONES 3–9.**

Dierama pulcherrimum

DIEFFENBACHIA
DUMB CANE

A genus in the arum family of about 30 species from tropical America, these evergreen, tufted perennials are often grown as houseplants or under glass in frost-prone areas. Their large oval leaves are often heavily marked with creamy white or yellow stripes or patches. Their sap makes the mouth and tongue swell, rendering speech impossible.
CULTIVATION: Maintain humidity by mist spraying, and keep them away from windows in winter to minimize temperature extremes. Bright to moderate light suits them. Allow the surface soil to become dry in between thorough waterings as roots may rot if they are over-watered. Propagate from root cuttings or stem cuttings laid horizontally in compost.

Dieffenbachia seguine
syns *Dieffenbachia maculata, D. picta*

This robust plant of up to 10 ft (1.3 m) high has large, paddle-shaped, deep green leaves marked sparsely with white spots and blotches along the lateral veins and insignificant, greenish white flowers. It flourishes in poor light. **'Amoena'** has bold green leaves with creamy white bands and marbling between the veins; **'Rudolph Roehrs'** grows to 3 ft (1 m) with chartreuse leaves with green midribs and green edges; **'Tropic Marianne'** has yellowish green leaves, white midribs and green edges. **ZONES 10–12.**

Dierama pendulum 'Album'

Dierama pulcherrimum 'Album'

DIERAMA

This genus of about 40 species of evergreen perennials of the iris family is indigenous to tropical Africa and South Africa. Growing from corms, the plants produce tufts of upright, grass-like leaves up to 3 ft (1 m) long, and fine wiry flower stems which bend like fishing rods under the weight of the flower clusters. These charming plants thrive and also look good near a pool or water feature. Several fine hybrid cultivars have been raised.
CULTIVATION: These warm-temperate plants demand a sheltered, sunny spot in cool areas, and rich, moist, well-drained soil. They are marginally frost hardy and dislike being disturbed. Propagate by corm division in spring, or from seed in spring and fall (autumn).

Dierama pendulum
syn. *Dierama ensifolium*

This perennial from South Africa has flower stems up to 4 ft (1.2 m) high and grass-like leaves to 20 in (50 cm) or more long. The open bell-shaped flowers in shades of pink or magenta are produced on wiry pendulous stems in summer. **'Album'** produces white flowers. **ZONES 8–10.**

Dierama pulcherrimum
WANDFLOWER, ANGEL'S FISHING ROD

A South African species, this upright, summer-flowering corm has evergreen, strap-like foliage. The arching stems bear long tassels of tubular or bell-shaped deep pink, carmine or white flowers, larger than in *D. pendulum*. The flower stems can reach 5 ft (1.5 m). **'Album'** has white flowers. **ZONES 8–10.**

Dieffenbachia seguine 'Tropic Marianne'

Dieffenbachia seguine

DIERVILLA

BUSH HONEYSUCKLE

This genus of 3 species of deciduous shrubs from North America is a related to *Weigela* but has less showy flowers. Honeysuckle-like yellow flowers are borne in axillary or terminal clusters on new growth. Because they sucker they are useful to stabilize banks and as tall ground cover. Plants rarely exceed 3 ft (1 m). **CULTIVATION:** They are not fussy about soil types and are quite frost hardy. Grow in full sun or part-shade and well-drained soil. Cut back in late winter or early spring before new growth to encourage the best flowering. Propagate from cuttings or by division.

Diervilla sessilifolia

SOUTHERN BUSH HONEYSUCKLE

A native of southeastern USA, the bush honeysuckle grows to 5 ft (1.5 m) tall and at least 5 ft (1.5 m) wide. The foliage has reddish veins and produces its 2-lipped sulfur yellow flowers in pairs during summer. In exposed situations its foliage can take on attractive autumn tones. ***Diervilla* × *splendens*,** a hybrid of *D. sessilifolia* and *D. lonicera*, closely resembles the above but does not have the red leaf veins. **ZONES 4–9.**

Digitalis ferruginea

DIETES

FORTNIGHT LILY

Native to southern Africa and to Lord Howe Island off eastern Australia, this genus contains 6 species of evergreen rhizomatous perennials that are grown for their attractive, iris-like flowers. The flowers usually last only for a day but new buds open over a long period in spring and summer. They have leathery, erect, sword-like leaves which form large clumps. In the past the species were included in the genus *Moraea*, from which they differ in being rhizomatous. **CULTIVATION:** All species thrive in part-shade or full sun, and prefer humus-rich, well-drained soil that does not dry out too quickly. Marginally frost hardy, they are tough enough to serve as low hedges and, once established, self-seed readily. Propagate from seed in spring or fall (autumn) or by division in spring.

Dietes bicolor

syn. *Moraea bicolor*

Sometimes called the Spanish iris, though it is neither an iris nor Spanish (it comes from South Africa), *Dietes bicolor* has pale green sword-shaped basal leaves and pale yellow flowers that appear from spring to summer. Each of the 3 larger petals has a central brown mark. It grows to around 36 in (90 cm) in height. **ZONES 9–11.**

Digitalis grandiflora

Digitalis lanata

Digitalis grandiflora

Digitalis × *mertonensis*

Dietes bicolor

Dietes grandiflora

Dietes grandiflora

WILD IRIS

This species grows to a height and spread of 3 ft (1 m) and bears 4 in (10 cm) wide, white, iris-like flowers marked with mauve and orange-yellow. Its blooms last for several days in spring and summer. It has often been confused with the lower-growing *Dietes iridioides* and it is only in recent years that its identity has been clarified. **ZONES 9–11.**

Dietes iridioides

syns *Dietes vegeta, Moraea iridioides*

This species has branching, wiry stems that carry 2½–3 in (6–8 cm) wide, iris-like flowers that are white with central yellow marks. It grows to a height of 24 in (60 cm) and a spread of 12–24 in (30–60 cm), forming dense clumps of basal leaves in a spreading fan. Its preferred habitat is in semi-shade under tall, open trees. **ZONES 8–11.**

Dietes robinsoniana

syn. *Moraea robinsoniana*

The tallest growing species with broad mid-green upright leaves that can exceed 6 ft (1.8 m) long by 3 in (8 cm) wide. This species is endemic to Lord Howe Island off the east coast of Australia. It is one of the most frost-tender species and requires warm-temperate or subtropical conditions to be grown outdoors. It produces quite large pure white flowers with pale yellow central blotches on erect panicles to 5 ft (1.5 m) tall. Each flower is short lived, but they are produced over a long period. **ZONES 9–11.**

DIGITALIS

FOXGLOVE

Natives of Europe, northern Africa and western Asia, these 22 species of biennials and perennials, some of them evergreen, are grown for their tall spikes of tubular, 2-lipped flowers which come in many colors including magenta, purple, white, cream, yellow, pink and lavender. The leaves are simple, mid-green and entire or toothed. The medicinal properties of digitalis have been known since ancient times, and these plants are still used in the treatment of heart ailments. **CULTIVATION:** Marginally frost hardy to fully frost hardy, they grow in most

Dietes iridioides

sheltered conditions, doing best in cool climates in part-shade and humus-rich, well-drained soil. Cut flowering stems down to the ground after spring flowering to encourage secondary spikes. Propagate from seed in fall (autumn) or by division; they self-seed readily.

Digitalis ferruginea

RUSTY FOXGLOVE

A biennial or short-lived perennial, this robust plant can reach 4 ft (1.2 m) or so tall. The leaves are comparatively narrow and rich green. The trumpet-shaped flowers are golden brown with darker red-brown veins and are produced in summer. **ZONES 7–10.**

Digitalis grandiflora

syns *Digitalis ambigua, D. orientalis*

YELLOW FOXGLOVE

A charming pale lemon-flowered foxglove, this species grows to 3 ft (1 m) when in flower from early to mid-summer and has rich green, prominently veined leaves. It can be a biennial or a short-lived perennial. **'Dwarf Temple Bells'** (syn. 'Temple Bells') is a smaller form but with larger pale yellow flowers. **ZONES 4–9.**

Digitalis lanata

GRECIAN FOXGLOVE

A clump-forming biennial or short-lived perennial, this subtle species produces flowers in mid- to late summer on stems up to 36 in (90 cm) tall. The flowers are strange but appealing: they are pale cream to fawn, finely veined with brown inside and a lighter cream lower lip. **ZONES 4–9.**

Digitalis lutea

This foxglove is a 24 in (60 cm) tall, clump-forming, summer-flowering perennial from Europe. It is admired for its elegance and unusual color, which varies from almost white to canary yellow, and there are usually purple spots in the flowers' throats. It has hairless, glossy, dark green leaves and is sometimes cultivated for medicinal use. **ZONES 4–9.**

Digitalis × mertonensis

A hybrid of *Digitalis grandiflora* and *D. purpurea*, this frost-hardy perennial forms a clump about 36 in (90 cm) tall and 12 in (30 cm) wide. Summer flowering, it bears spikes of tubular, pink to salmon flowers above a rosette of soft, hairy, oval leaves. Divide after flowering. **ZONES 4–9.**

Digitalis purpurea

This is the common foxglove, a short-lived, frost-hardy perennial with an upright habit, a height of 3–5 ft (1–1.5 m) and a spread of 24 in (60 cm). The flowers come in purple, pink, rosy magenta, white or pale yellow, above a rosette of rough, oval, deep green leaves. All parts of the plant, especially the leaves, are poisonous. Many seedling strains are available, grown as bedding annuals, the **Excelsior Hybrids** in mixed colors being very popular. ***Digitalis purpurea* f. *albiflora*** has pure white flowers sometimes lightly spotted brown inside; it will usually come true from seed especially if it is isolated from other colored forms. **ZONES 5–10.**

DILLENIA

A genus of some 60 species of evergreen trees and shrubs, mostly from tropical Asia, Africa, Madagascar and Australia. The large leathery leaves have prominent veins, and the showy yellow or white, 5-petalled flowers are produced singly or in loose panicles. They are followed by fleshy fruits enclosed by enlarged, fleshy sepals. They make good shade trees and

Digitalis purpurea

Digitalis purpurea f. *albiflora*

Dillenia alata

are grown for their handsome foliage, showy flowers and decorative fruits. The fruits are used in tropical countries for curries, jellies and preserves.
CULTIVATION: These frost-tender plants are moderately fast growing, transplanting easily when young. They need sun, a tropical or subtropical climate, fertile, humus-rich, moist but well-drained acidic to neutral soil, ample water and some shelter when young. Propagate from seed.

Dillenia alata
RED BEECH

Indigenous to the wet tropical regions of northern Australia, this evergreen tree grows to 25 ft (8 m) or more with a crooked, low-branching trunk and red, flaking bark. It has thick, glossy leaves; flat-opening yellow flowers, 3 in (8 cm) across; and bright red seed pods. It is best suited to tropical regions and will withstand some salty winds. **ZONE 12.**

Dillenia indica
ELEPHANT APPLE

This spectacular tree found in India and Southeast Asia grows to 50 ft (15 m) tall, with a broad canopy of large, dark green leaves up to 30 in (75 cm) long, with prominent parallel veins. The 6 in (15 cm) wide creamy yellow flowers are fragrant. The developing fruit resemble green apples. Mature fruit, measuring up to 6 in (15 cm) across, are edible, and so are the mature fruit bracts. **ZONE 12.**

Dillenia suffruticosa

This species from the Malay Archipelago can grow up to 30 ft (9 m) or more tall. Its leaves are about 10 in (25 cm) long with conspicuous parallel veins. The yellow flowers can be 4 in (10 cm) wide. **ZONE 12.**

Dillenia indica

Dillenia suffruticosa

Dimorphotheca pluvialis

Dionaea muscipula

DIMORPHOTHECA
AFRICAN DAISY, CAPE MARIGOLD

These 7 species of annuals, perennials and evergreen subshrubs from South Africa have colorful, daisy-like flowers from late winter. Related to *Osteospermum*, they are useful for rock gardens and borders.
CULTIVATION: They need an open sunny situation and fertile, well-drained soil; they are salt tolerant. The flowers only open in sunshine. Prune lightly after flowering; deadheading prolongs flowering. Propagate annuals from seed in spring and perennials from cuttings in summer. Watch for fungal diseases in summer rainfall areas.

Dimorphotheca pluvialis
syn. *Dimorphotheca annua*
RAIN DAISY

This bedding annual produces small flowerheads in late winter and spring that are snow white above, purple beneath, with brownish purple centers. Low growing, it reaches 8–12 in (20–30 cm) in height with a similar spread. **ZONES 8–10.**

Dimorphotheca sinuata
syns *Dimorphotheca aurantiaca* of gardens, *D. calendulacea*

This erect annual grows to 12 in (30 cm) tall and wide. Its roughly serrated, spoon-shaped leaves are up to 3 in (8 cm) long. Daisy-like flowerheads with yellow centers and orange outer petals (occasionally with yellow bases) appear in winter and spring in milder areas or from spring through summer elsewhere. **ZONES 8–10.**

DIONAEA
VENUS FLYTRAP

This genus contains only one species, the best known of all carnivorous plants, though it is quite small. The rosettes of leaves rarely exceed 8 in (20 cm) across, while the flower stems reach about 12 in (30 cm) high; and the white, 5-petalled flowers are about ½ in (12 mm) wide. Each leaf has 2 flattened lobes with stiff spines along the margins. Minute glands secrete insect-attracting nectar; when the insect alights, it stimulates 3 hairs on each lobe, and the trap closes shut. The nectar digests the insect by liquefying it. When only the hard bits are left, the leaf opens and the remains are blown away.
CULTIVATION: Marginally frost hardy, grow in peat kept saturated by standing the pot in a saucer of rainwater in full sun. Pinching out emerging flower stems and removing dead traps will encourage new traps to grow. Feed plants tiny pieces of meat or cheese and watch the flytrap in action. Without some animal protein, it will not flower. Propagate from seed or leaf cuttings or by division in spring.

Dionaea muscipula

This rosette-forming perennial comes from southeastern USA, where it grows in mossy bogs. The rounded leaves are yellow-green or red and have winged stalks. Like so many carnivorous plants, it is very sensitive to pollution and is becoming rare in the wild. **ZONES 8–10.**

Dionysia involucrata

Diospyros virginiana

Diospyros kaki

DIONYSIA

A genus of 42 species in the primula family from the arid mountains of southwestern and central Asia, these tufted or cushion-forming alpine plants, much admired by alpine plant enthusiasts, usually grow in moist shaded crevices. The flowers are tubular and flared out nearly flat at the end. **CULTIVATION:** Only grown in climates with cool to cold winters and needing protection from excessive damp on the foliage, these plants are normally grown under cover in pots or in the hollows of tufa rocks. Make sure that the cushions are sitting up on a bed of coarse gravel to stop crown rot. Propagate from seed or by division.

Dionysia aretioides

This lovely plant makes tight cushions of gray-green rosettes that are covered with numerous bright yellow flowers in early spring. Considered to be one of the easier species in the genus to grow, it reaches a height of 2½ in (6 cm) and a width of 12 in (30 cm). **ZONES 5–9.**

Dionysia involucrata

Considered to be relatively easy to grow, this species forms a dense cushion of rich

Dioon edule

Diospyros virginiana

green foliage from which are borne in early summer masses of violet to violet-purple flowers with white eyes that darken with age. **ZONES 4–9.**

DIOON

Cycads are among the most ancient groups of plants, and dioons are grown for their primeval appearance. Endemic to Mexico and Honduras, most of the 10 species are now rare in the wild. The Greek genus name, meaning 'two eggs' (referring to the paired seeds), is pronounced di-o-on. Their evergreen, pinnate fronds, with spiny toothed leaflets arise from a rosette at ground level or topping a rough trunk as tall as 30 ft (9 m). Cycads have no flowers. Mature specimens produce a large seed cone on female plants, or a pollen cone on males. **CULTIVATION:** Mostly frost tender, they grow in well-drained soil, in sun or light shade. Pruning ruins their symmetry. Propagate from seed or offsets.

Dioon edule
MEXICAN FERN PALM

From Mexico, *Dioon edule* is the most widely grown species. It has handsome, gray-green leaves and spine-tipped leaflets. The thick trunk may grow 10–12 ft (3–3.5 m) tall. It produces edible seeds from a 12 in (30 cm) diameter cone. It can be grown almost indefinitely in a container but is difficult to transplant. **ZONES 10–12.**

DIOSCOREA
YAMS

Named after the Greek physician Dioscorides, this very large genus of about 600 species is found throughout the tropics as well as in some more temperate regions. Many produce poisonous tubers, but there are about 10 species that are regularly cultivated and are

Dioscorea elephantipes

edible after being cooked. Yams are slender climbing plants and the tubers can be formed both below and above ground. The alternate leaves are heart-shaped and the spikes of tiny flowers are either solitary or clustered. The fruits are capsules containing winged seeds. **CULTIVATION:** These frost-tender plants require good drainage and a fertile soil with a high organic content of well-rotted manure or compost dug in at planting time. Each plant should be staked. The period of growth is from 7 to 12 months varying with the species. If the tubers are not dug up they continue to grow for years. Propagate from seed, by division or by slicing small pieces, each with 2 or 3 dormant buds, from the upper part of an old tuber.

Dioscorea alata
GREATER YAM

Widely grown in the West Indies and in West Africa, this is by far the most important of the cultivated yams. It has pointed heart-shaped leaves and bulbils are frequently borne on the stem. These can be used in propagation. Each plant may produce up to 3 tubers which have a brown outer skin and white flesh; they are high in starch and contain about 70 percent water. Different cultivars produce tubers of different shapes. The tubers store well. **ZONES 10–12.**

Dioscorea bulbifera
AERIAL YAM

A slender twining plant with wiry stems to 3 ft (1 m) high, the bright green heart-shaped leaves of this species have prominent veins. Aerial bulbils are present in the leaf axils. A native of tropical Africa, Asia and northern Australia, this is a decorative, non-vigorous climbing plant for tropical gardens. The plants die back to a perennial root system each year after flowering and fruiting. **ZONES 10–12.**

Dioscorea elephantipes
syn. ***Testudinaria elephantipes***
ELEPHANT'S FOOT, HOTTENTOT BREAD

Although this species was once cooked and eaten by the indigenous people of southern Africa, it is now grown primarily by succulent plant enthusiasts. *Dioscorea elephantipes* is a twining plant with heart-shaped leaves, but its most striking feature is the enormous tuber, which sits on the ground; its thick corky bark is broken up into broad plates or ridges. It requires deep soil, good drainage and ideally, semi-arid conditions. It is also suitable for growing as a greenhouse plant. **ZONES 10–11.**

DIOSPYROS
PERSIMMON, EBONY

This genus consists of several hundred species of mostly evergreen trees from the tropics and subtropics, as well as several deciduous species in temperate Asia and America. *D. ebenum* from Sri Lanka provides the now rare timber ebony. Some species bear edible fruit, notably the black sapote *(D. digyna)* and the Japanese and American persimmons. All have strong branches, smooth-edged leaves, and flowers with rolled-back petals and a leaf-like calyx that enlarges as the pulpy fruit develops; the fruits of most species are edible. For good crops, grow plants of both sexes. **CULTIVATION:** Fully frost hardy to frost tender, these trees prefer well-drained, moist soil, with ample water in the growing season and, being brittle, need shelter from strong wind. Propagate from seed.

Diospyros digyna
BLACK SAPOTE

This evergreen grows to 60 ft (18 m) tall in the wild in Mexico and Central America; it has also naturalized in tropical Asia. The leaves reach 8 in (20 cm) long; the flowers are small, white and fragrant. The fruit, about 4 in (10 cm) across, ripen quickly from olive green to black and are high in vitamin C. **ZONES 11–12.**

Diospyros kaki
CHINESE PERSIMMON, KAKI

A native of China and cultivated in Japan for centuries, this deciduous tree grows to about 20 ft (6 m) with spreading branches. Its dark green oval leaves turn yellow to deep orange in fall (autumn). It has small cream flowers and orange or yellow fruit about 3 in (8 cm) across with delicious sweet flesh when ripe. There are many cultivars. **ZONES 8–10.**

Diospyros virginiana
AMERICAN PERSIMMON, POSSUM WOOD

This spreading tree can reach over 100 ft (30 m) in its native eastern USA, in alluvial river valley forests, but in cultivation it usually reaches 20–30 ft (6–9 m). It has cream flowers and sweet edible fruit, 1½ in (35 mm) across, ripening to orange or purple-red. The timber (white ebony) is valued for its durability. **ZONES 5–9.**

DIPELTA

Only 4 species from China make up this genus of deciduous shrubs, and only one is well established in Western gardens—but even that is uncommon. They are related to and resemble *Weigela* and *Kolkwitzia*, with richly marked, bell-shaped flowers in large clusters. The fruits are partly concealed by two rounded bracts enlarging at their base after the flowers are shed. **CULTIVATION:** They are frost hardy, and prefer a sunny position with moist, fertile, well-drained soil and shelter from strong winds. Propagate from seed or cuttings.

Dipelta floribunda

Dipelta floribunda

From the lower mountains of China, this shrub grows to about 10 ft (3 m), with woody stems and pale peeling bark. It bears broad, soft leaves and large, drooping clusters of pale pink, fragrant flowers, $1\frac{1}{2}$ in (35 mm) long; these are deeper pink on the outside of the tube and have orange-yellow markings in the throat. **ZONES 6–9.**

DIPHYLLEIA

There are only 3 species of these large-leaved herbaceous perennials, 2 from eastern USA and one from Japan and China. The botanical name is Latinized Greek for 'two-leafed', referring to the fact that each stem that emerges from the large, knotted rootstock bears only 2 leaves with no further leafy growth possible. The leaves are held more or less horizontally, giving an umbrella-like effect, and are jaggedly toothed or lobed; a single leaf may be as much as 18 in (45 cm) across. From the fork between the leaves emerges a cluster of starry white flowers on a long stalk, their size overshadowed by that of the leaves.
CULTIVATION: Diphylleias are frost-hardy plants that are fairly easily grown in woodland conditions in moist, humus-rich soil in full or partshade. Propagate by division of the rootstock.

Diphylleia cymosa
UMBRELLA LEAF

A species from the eastern USA, this plant grows to about 3 ft (1 m) tall with handsome leaves up to 24 in (60 cm) across, cut into 5 or 7 lobes. The white flowers are produced in late spring and early summer, and are followed by blue berries that are attached to red stems at the time the fruit ripens. **ZONES 5–9.**

DIPLARRENA

This Australian genus of the iris family contains 2 species of rhizomatous, evergreen perennials with iris-like flowers. The long, flat, sword-shaped leaves occur in basal tufts. The fragrant, short-lived flowers are produced in clusters in late spring and early summer.
CULTIVATION: Diplarrenas are marginally to moderately frost hardy and can be grown outdoors in cool climates, but where winters are severe they need a greenhouse. Grow in moist but well-drained, sandy, humus-rich soil in full sun or part-shade. Propagate from seed or by division in spring.

Diplarrena latifolia

Diplarrena latifolia

Endemic to the mountains of Tasmania, this tufted perennial bears white, iris-like flowers marked with purple and yellow on wiry stems in summer. The leaves are grayish green, shorter and broader than those of *Diplarrena moraea.* It reaches a height of about 12 in (30 cm) and a spread of 10 in (25 cm). **ZONES 7–9.**

Diplarrena moraea
BUTTERFLY FLAG

This species from Tasmania and south-eastern mainland Australia has white flowers with purple and yellow centers in clusters of 2 to 3, borne on wiry, erect stems in spring and summer. The leaves are thin and strap-like. It grows to 24 in (60 cm). **ZONES 8–10.**

DIPOGON

This genus consists of a single species, a leguminous perennial climber. It is native to South Africa but has naturalized to weed proportions in some areas of Australia. This densely foliaged plant can be used as a green manure.
CULTIVATION: It thrives in a well-drained, sunny position and prefers a warm climate. Propagate from seed.

Dipogon lignosus
syn. *Dolichos lignosus*

This twining plant with stems to 10 ft (3 m) high has compound leaves consisting of 3 oval leaflets. The attractive purple-pink pea-flowers are produced in clusters of 3 to 6 blooms during summer. **ZONES 9–11.**

DIPSACUS
TEASEL

Related to *Scabiosa*, this genus consists of 15 species of biennials and short-lived perennials from Europe, North Africa and temperate Asia. They have harsh bristly or prickly leaves arranged in opposite pairs on the strong stems, which branch into long-stalked, erect, barrel-shaped flowerheads. At the base of each flowerhead is a circle of long, springy, spine-like bracts. The small white, pink or purple flowers open progressively from the base of the head; an additional short springy bract accompanies each small flower. Apart from fuller's teasel, they are known as wildflowers or weeds. They are popular with landscape designers because of their statuesque habit.
CULTIVATION: Teasels are happy in well-drained garden soil of moderate fertility, in sun or light shade. They are frost hardy and will generally self-seed freely in the garden. Propagate from seed.

Dipogon lignosus

Dipsacus fullonum
syn. *Dipsacus sylvestris*
WILD TEASEL

Native to Europe and western Asia, this common wildflower is a prickly biennial up to 6 ft (1.8 m) tall, initially with a basal rosette of long, pointed leaves though these shrivel by the time the plant flowers; the stem leaves are shorter. The long-stalked flowerheads, borne mid- to late summer, are about 3 in (8 cm) long, with mauve-pink flowers emerging between small, curved, springy bracts which persist long after the flowers are gone. In more recent times *Dipsacus sativus* has been the species principally used for fulling—the dressing of cloth after it is woven. **ZONES 4–10.**

Dipsacus sativus
syn. *Dipsacus fullonum* subsp. *sativus*
FULLER'S TEASEL

This biennial species is known only as a cultivated plant, though botanists now believe it may be derived from the wild Mediterranean species *Dipsacus ferox.* It is similar in most respects to *D. fullonum* but the small bracts that cover the flowerheads are shorter and broader and slightly hooked at the apex—it is the dried heads of this teasel, gathered after flowering, that are used to 'card' woollen cloth, the springy hooks raising the nap as the cloth is dragged past. It is also grown as a curiosity and for dried flowers. **ZONES 5–10.**

Dipsacus fullonum

Dipsacus sativus

DISA

This is a terrestrial genus of about 125 species of orchids from southern and eastern Africa and Madagascar. The plants arise from tuberous roots and consist of a leafy stem and a single terminal inflorescence. The 6 species from western and southwestern Cape Province in South Africa have been successfully cultivated. The species from other habitats have proved extremely difficult to grow. These plants are noted for their often large, colorful flowers in shades of red, pink, yellow and white.
CULTIVATION: *Disa* once had a reputation for being difficult to grow, but the 6 commonly grown species and their hybrids are readily cultivated if care is taken. The growing mixture, coarse sand or a mixture of peat and perlite, should be well drained, but it should not be allowed to dry out. High humidity levels, along with good air circulation, are required. Regular watering with water with a pH of 4.5 to 6 is best and salts must not be allowed to build up. Broken shade is best and cool to warm conditions are required, with as little fluctuation in temperature as possible. Watch for thrips. Propagate by division.

Disa Diores

This grex name is used for hybrids between *Disa* Veitchii and *D. uniflora. D.* Veitchii is itself the cross between *D. racemosa* and *D. uniflora. D.* Diores dates back to 1898. There are up to 10 long-lasting flowers about 10 cm across, in shades of pink to red, occasionally with some yellow. It is popular for cut flowers and has been used in making more complex hybrids. **ZONES 10–11.**

Disa Diores

Diplarrena moraea

Disa Hybrids

The six cultivated species have been used to create over 80 hybrids which are now well established in many collections. The species used are *Disa cardinalis, D. caulescens, D. racemosa, D. tripetaloides, D. uniflora* and *D. venosa.* The colorful and long-lasting flowers are suitable for the cut-flower industry. **'Inca Princess'** bears racemes of pink and cream flowers with faint purple veining. **ZONES 10–11.**

Disa uniflora

syn. *Disa grandiflora*

PRIDE OF TABLE MOUNTAIN

This is a terrestrial species which occurs in the Cape Province of South Africa where it grows along stream banks and in seepages at low altitudes. The stem is robust and leafy to about 30 in (75 cm) tall. The inflorescence has 1 to 4 large, long-lasting flowers which are about 4 in (10 cm) across; the flowers are usually red but there are yellow and orange forms. This spectacular species has been central to the development of *Disa* hybrids. Flowering occurs in summer and fall (autumn). **ZONES 10–11.**

DISANTHUS

Just a single species of deciduous, ornamental shrub belongs to this Japanese genus in the witch-hazel family. Its leaves are almost circular with pronounced bluish undersides; the flowers, appearing in fall (autumn) as the leaves color, are small, with strap-like purplish red petals, borne in pairs along the old wood. Even in summer the strongly veined leaves are bronze tinted but by early fall they turn a deep metallic bronze purple and finally fade to red or orange before falling. **CULTIVATION:** Although fairly frost hardy, *Disanthus* requires sheltered conditions and deep, moist, friable soil. The seeds, produced in small capsules, can be used for propagation, but cuttings or ground layering are more effective.

Disa Hybrid 'Inca Princess'

Disanthus cercidifolius

Disanthus cercidifolius

This slow-growing, spreading shrub eventually reaches 10 ft (3 m) or more. It has stiff, wiry branches, usually with a number of stems diverging from the base. The flowers, ½ in (12 mm) across, are slightly fragrant. **ZONES 8–10.**

DISCARIA

This genus of thorny, evergreen shrubs is closely related to *Colletia,* though not quite so fiercely spiny. It consists of 15 species, one is native to New Zealand, two to cooler areas of southeastern Australia, and the remainder to the southern part of South America. With a distribution of this sort, it can be inferred that the plant group evolved on the ancient southern supercontinent of Gondwana, from which these landmasses later split away. Discarias are rather straggling shrubs with lateral branchlets modified into thorns, arranged in opposite pairs with successive pairs at right angles to one another. Some species have well-developed leaves, smooth and shiny, while in others the leaves are almost absent and the green branches are the only photosynthetic organs. Flowers are tiny white or greenish yellow bells, usually sweet-scented and clustered profusely along the branches; they may be followed by numerous knobbly seed capsules. **CULTIVATION:** Moderately frost hardy once established, these tough plants tolerate poor, even boggy soils and exposed positions. Propagate from seed or cuttings.

Discaria toumatou

WILD IRISHMAN

This tangled prickly shrub can reach 15 ft (4.5 m) although it is usually a small mound at higher altitudes in its native New Zealand habitat. It produces very few leaves and photosynthesizes using its stems. It can be interesting in a large rock garden and its tiny white flowers are fragrant. **ZONES 8–10.**

Discaria toumatou

Disporum flavens

Distictis buccinatoria

DISPORUM

FAIRY BELLS

Disporum is a genus of between 10 and 20 species of elegant and attractive woodland plants related to and similar to Solomon's seal (*Polygonatum*). Species are native to the USA, eastern Asia and the Himalayas. They have creeping rhizomes that can travel some distance but they are not invasive. The arching stems are often slightly branched and clothed with attractive alternating leaves. The flowers are bell-shaped and hang under the stems. They can be white to green-yellow.
CULTIVATION: As these are woodland plants give them a cool part-shaded position with ample organic material like leafmold. They are definitely not for tropical or arid zones. Propagate from seed or by division.

Disporum flavens

This Korean woodland perennial grows in neat clumps to 30 in (75 cm) high by 12 in (30 cm) across. It has attractive lance-shaped leaves and in early spring will produce up to 3 drooping soft yellow flowers per stem. These are followed in fall (autumn) by small black berries. **ZONES 5–9.**

Disporum smilacinum

Also from Korea as well as Japan, this species grows to about 16 in (40 cm) tall and will spread to at least 12 in (30 cm) wide. It is sparsely branched with oval and oblong-shaped leaves to 3 in (7 cm) long. It produces one or two drooping cup-shaped white flowers per stem in mid- to late spring. **ZONES 5–9.**

DISTICTIS

syn. *Phaedranthus*

The 9 species in this genus of vigorous showy climbers in the bignonia family from Mexico and the West Indies are only suitable for nearly frost-free climates.

Disporum smilacinum

Dodecatheon jeffreyi

Dodecatheon meadia

The tubular or trumpet-shaped flowers are produced in spring and throughout summer and can vary from white through mauves to deep reds, depending on species. They are usually self-clinging as long as the support has a rough surface. **CULTIVATION:** These useful plants for a sunny position, they like moist, but well-drained soil. Prune in early spring and water well during summer. Propagate from seed or cuttings, or by layering.

Distictis buccinatoria

syns *Bignonia cherere, Phaedranthus buccinatorius*

MEXICAN BLOOD FLOWER, CHERERE, BLOOD-RED TRUMPET VINE

A native of Mexico, this marginally frost-hardy, evergreen, woody climber reaches about 15 ft (4.5 m) and bears large clusters of trumpet flowers in bright shades of purple-red in early spring and summer. A vigorous vine, its tendrils cling to brick and stone surfaces. **ZONES 9–11.**

Distictis 'Mrs Rivers'

syn. *Distictis* 'Rivers'

A cultivar or hybrid with deep green foliage; its flowers, produced throughout late spring and summer, are deep mauve with a yellow throat. **ZONES 9–11.**

DODECATHEON

SHOOTING STAR

The shooting stars (about 14 species) are western North America's equivalent to Europe's cyclamens and, like them, they are perennials and cousins of the primrose. Most are rosette-forming and grow to about 15 in (38 cm) high, with pink or white flower clusters. They have swept-back petals and protruding stamens. **CULTIVATION:** Fully frost hardy, they prefer part-shade in moist, well-drained acidic soil. Most require a dry dormant summer period after flowering. They resent disturbance. Propagate from seed in fall (autumn) or by division in winter.

Dodonaea boroniifolia

Dolichandrone heterophylla

Dodecatheon hendersonii
syn. *Dodecatheon latifolium*
SAILOR'S CAPS, MOSQUITO BILLS

A rosette-forming perennial from California, this species grows to 16 in (40 cm) tall and 10 in (25 cm) wide when in flower in early summer. Its sturdy stems support up to 5 purple-pink flowers, each with a white or yellow ring at the base and a dark center. **ZONES 6–9.**

Dodecatheon jeffreyi
SIERRA SHOOTING STAR

Occurring from California to Alaska, this plant grows to about 18 in (45 cm) tall. Its flower spike is topped with many red-purple flowers with deep purple stamens. Its leaves are slightly sticky and about 12 in (30 cm) long. **ZONES 5–9.**

Dodecatheon meadia

From eastern North America, this is the best-known species, bearing white, rose pink or cyclamen pink, nodding flowers. It has primula-like, clumped rosettes of pale green leaves, and ranges from 6–18 in (15–45 cm) high with a spread of 18 in (45 cm). It was named for English scientist Richard Mead (1673–1754), a patron of American botanical studies. **ZONES 3–9.**

Dodecatheon pulchellum
syns *Dodecatheon amethystinum*, *D. pauciflorum*, *D. radicatum*

Native to the mountains of western North America, this clump-forming perennial has mid-green 8 in (20 cm) long leaves in rosettes and produces up to 30 deep cerise to lilac flowers per stem. White forms are known as well as a form named **'Red Wings'** which has magenta-pink flowers on strong stems in late spring and early summer. **ZONES 4–9.**

DODONAEA
HOPBUSH

This is an almost entirely Australian genus of about 60 species of evergreen

Dolichandrone heterophylla

trees and woody shrubs. Its common name refers to the abundant, winged, capsular, hop-like fruits once used for brewing beer by early European settlers. In many species, male and female flowers appear on separate plants. The flowers are small and insignificant, but the fruits are large on some species.
CULTIVATION: Hopbushes grow in full sun or part-shade and prefer moderately fertile, light, free-draining soil. They are frost tender, but some will withstand drought and coastal salty winds. Lightly prune in early spring. Propagate from seed in spring or cuttings in summer.

Dodonaea boroniifolia
FERN-LEAF HOPBUSH, HAIRY HOPBUSH

A bushy shrub to 5 ft (1.5 m), this species has dark green, fern-like leaves with sticky leaflets. The insignificant flowers are followed in summer by attractive 4-winged red fruit capsules. This species will tolerate extended dry periods. **ZONES 9–11.**

Dodonaea viscosa

This variable species grows throughout Australia and in New Zealand, as well as in the tropical regions of America, Africa and Asia. It has elliptic to linear, slightly sticky, light green leaves with wavy margins. The showy yellowish 3-winged capsules, produced in terminal clusters, turn brown, pink or purple at maturity. Dense and fast growing, prune to an upright shrub form around 10 ft (3 m) or more tall; it is useful for screening and hedging. **'Purpurea'**, a popular bronze-leafed cultivar from New Zealand, has purplish red fruit capsules. **ZONES 9–12.**

DOLICHANDRONE

This small genus in the bignonia family consists of 9 species of shrubs and small trees from tropical areas of Africa, Asia, Australia and some Pacific islands. Most species are quite heavily wooded with dull to dark brown, attractively patterned bark. The leaves are pinnate and trumpet-shaped flowers appear in clusters at the branch tips; they are usually white and night scented.
CULTIVATION: They prefer moist, humus-rich, well-drained soil in sun or dappled shade. Propagate from seed or cuttings.

Dolichandrone heterophylla
LEMONWOOD

From dry monsoonal woodland areas of northern Australia, this species is a 20 ft (6 m) tree with deeply furrowed, dark brown bark. It has either lance-shaped simple leaves or pinnate leaves composed of leaflets up to 4 in (10 cm) long. The white tubular flowers, about $1\frac{1}{2}$ in (35 mm) long, have spreading lobes with frilled margins. They are highly fragrant and are produced from mid-spring to mid-summer. **ZONES 11–12.**

DOMBEYA
WEDDING FLOWER

This genus of about 200 species of evergreen, deciduous or semi-deciduous shrubs and small trees has some species in Africa but many more in Madagascar; only a few species from the eastern summer-rainfall regions of southern Africa are widely cultivated. The leaves are mostly circular, heart-shaped or maple-like in outline, and have a scurf of downy hairs at least on the underside. The flowers are very pretty, cup-shaped with overlapping white, pink or red petals, in small to large clusters all over the crown. The petals persist while the small capsular fruits are ripening, turning a rusty brown.
CULTIVATION: Dombeyas thrive in most warm-temperate and subtropical climates with good summer moisture; some species are moderately frost hardy. Grow in moist but well-drained, fertile soil in sun or part-shade. Propagate from seed in spring or cuttings in summer.

Dombeya burgessiae
PINK DOMBEYA

From parts of Natal, Transvaal and Zimbabwe, this species is often only a shrub of 10–15 ft (3–4.5 m) with a dense mass of stems from ground level. The large leaves are hairy, with shallow, maple-like lobes. From mid-summer to mid-fall (autumn) loose clusters of bell-shaped flowers appear, varying from palest pink to deep pinkish red. **ZONES 9–12.**

Dombeya rotundifolia

Dombeya tiliacea

Dombeya × *cayeuxii*

Of uncertain origin, this shrub possibly has *Dombeya burgessiae* as one parent; it is of similar growth habit but the leaf lobes have longer points. Profuse, pale pink flowers are borne on large, hemispherical heads at all branch tips from summer to fall (autumn). **ZONES 10–12.**

Dombeya rotundifolia
SOUTH AFRICAN WILD PEAR

This deciduous or semi-deciduous small tree from southeastern Africa grows to about 20 ft (6 m) tall with a dense canopy, rough leaves, fissured bark, a thick crooked trunk and profuse white flowers in early spring. Trees cultivated in Australia with pale pink flowers have been identified as this species. **ZONES 9–12.**

Dombeya tiliacea
syn. *Dombeya natalensis*
NATAL WEDDING FLOWER

This evergreen with slim, blackish, multiple trunks comes from Natal in eastern South Africa. It is a bushy-crowned tree of 20–25 ft (6–8 m). From fall (autumn) to early spring it bears small pendulous clusters of pure white flowers. Some leaves may turn red in fall. **ZONES 9–11.**

Dombeya wallichii

This species from East Africa and Madagascar usually makes a large shrub or small branched tree to 25 ft (8 m). Its evergreen foliage is bright green with leaves up to 8 in (20 cm) long. The 1 in (25 mm) wide deep pink to red flowers are crowded into dense globular heads hanging on long stalks. **ZONES 10–12.**

Dombeya × *cayeuxii*

Dombeya burgessiae

Doodia aspera

Doodia media

Doronicum pardalianches

Doronicum columnae 'Miss Mason'

Doronicum orientale 'Magnificum'

DOODIA

This fern genus was named after English chemist and botanist Samuel Doody and contains 11 species of tufted, terrestrial ferns native to Australia, New Zealand and some Pacific islands. The slender, pinnate fronds are harsh to the touch and have heavily serrated leaflets, vivid red-pink when immature. They are attractive small ferns suitable for gardens or containers.
CULTIVATION: Species range from frost tender to marginally frost hardy and prefer a cool, not cold, climate. Plant in fertile, damp soil and avoid direct sunlight. They thrive in humidity, but tolerate dry conditions once established. Propagate from spores or by division in spring.

Doodia aspera
PRICKLY RASP FERN

Native to eastern Australia, Norfolk Island and New Zealand, this small fern proliferates in open forests. It has a short, creeping rhizome and grows to about 12 in (30 cm) tall. The upright fronds which widen at the base have serrated margins and a harsh, raspy texture. New growth is pink or red. It thrives in shade or sun if kept moist. **ZONES 9–11.**

Doodia media
COMMON RASP FERN

This low-tufted, clump-forming Australian and New Zealand fern has an underground creeping rhizome and grows 8–12 in (20–30 cm) tall, spreading up to 24 in (60 cm). The immature, rich reddish pink, pinnate fronds are covered in scales and hairs. They are at their most vivid in full sun, turning deep green with maturity. **ZONES 9–11.**

DORONICUM
LEOPARD'S BANE

The 35 species of herbaceous perennials that make up this genus extend from Europe through western Asia to Siberia. Species are grown for their attractive, bright yellow daisy-like flowers which are produced in spring and summer above fresh bright green foliage. Most species make attractive border plants of restrained habit and are also good as cut flowers.
CULTIVATION: Doronicums will cope with a range of habitats, but for best results give them a moisture-retentive but not wet soil, high in humus; part-shade or morning sun is preferred but never heavy dark shade. Propagate from seed or by division.

Doronicum columnae 'Miss Mason'

This is a large-flowered selection with blooms about 3 in (8 cm) across in mid- to late spring. Its bright yellow daisies are held well above its heart-shaped leaves on stems up to 24 in (60 cm) tall. **ZONES 5–9.**

Doronicum orientale 'Magnificum'

This clump-forming perennial grows to about 20 in (50 cm) tall and has bright green ovate leaves. The flowers, up to 2 in (5 cm) across, are produced in mid- to late spring. This cultivar apparently comes true from seed. **ZONES 4–9.**

Doronicum pardalianches
syn. *Doronicum cordatum*
LEOPARD'S BANE

Doronicum pardalianches is a spreading, clump-forming perennial to 3 ft (1 m) tall and wide. The oval basal leaves, to 5 in (12 cm) long, have heart-shaped bases. Bright yellow daisy-like flowers are borne on slender, branching stems from late spring to mid-summer. **ZONES 5–9.**

DOROTHEANTHUS
ICE PLANT, LIVINGSTONE DAISY

A genus of about 10 species of succulent annuals from South Africa, these mat-forming plants bear masses of daisy-like flowers in bright shades of red, pink, white or bicolored with dark centers in summer. Ideal for borders and massed displays.
CULTIVATION: Marginally frost hardy, grow in well-drained soil in a sunny position. Deadhead to improve appearance and prolong flowering. In frost-prone areas plant out after the likelihood of frost has passed. Propagate from seed.

Dorotheanthus bellidiformis
ICE PLANT, LIVINGSTONE DAISY, BOKBAAI VYGIE

This small succulent annual has daisy-like flowerheads in dazzling shades of yellow, white, red or pink in summer sun; flowers close in dull weather. It grows to 6 in (15 cm) tall and spreads to 12 in (30 cm) and has fleshy light green leaves to 3 in (7 cm) long with glistening surface cells. **ZONES 9–11.**

DORSTENIA

The 170 or more species in this genus which is related to *Ficus*, have a scattered natural distribution including the Arabian Peninsula, northeastern Africa, Madagascar, India and South and Central America. They include low-growing ground covers, shrubby perennials and upright succulents with a thickened stem or fleshy thick leaves to preserve moisture. Minute petal-less flowers are embedded in flat, saucer-like receptacles. Members of this genus are mainly grown as curiosities. Plants are almost always poisonous.
CULTIVATION: Wherever frosts are experienced or the climate is too wet, these frost-tender species are best grown in heated greenhouses. Propagate from seed, cuttings or by division.

Dorstenia contrajerva
CONTRA HIERBA, TORUS HERB

This ground cover from the Caribbean is often used under greenhouse benches as it tolerates reduced light. The deeply lobed leaves to 8 in (20 cm) long have been used as a febrifuge, a snake bite antidote and to flavor tobacco. **ZONES 10–12.**

Dorotheanthus bellidiformis

DORYANTHES

The 2 species of *Doryanthes* are large evergreen perennials indigenous to the east coast of Australia. Somewhat resembling agaves in growth habit, they have loose rosettes of sword-shaped leaves and bear large red flowers with spreading petals, at the end of very tall stalks. The nectar attracts birds. Although requiring up to 10 years to bloom, they are popular in warm-climate public gardens.
CULTIVATION: Frost tender, they do best in full sun or part-shade in warm, frost-free conditions in light, humus-rich, well-drained soil. Water well during the growing season. Propagate from seed or by division.

Doryanthes excelsa
GYMEA LILY

The larger and more common of the 2 species, *Doryanthes excelsa* is one of the largest lilies in the world. The large rounded head of deep red, torch-like flowers is borne terminally on a stem that can reach 20 ft (6 m) tall, arising from a rosette of sword-shaped leaves that can spread to about 8 ft (2.4 m) wide. It makes a spectacular feature plant for the large garden. **ZONES 9–11.**

Doryanthes palmeri

This species forms a dense rosette of lance-shaped, bright green leaves up to 10 ft (3 m) long. The flower stalk, up to 18 ft (5 m) tall, carries numerous scarlet, funnel-shaped flowers with white throats arranged along the upper part of the stalk and appear in spring. **ZONES 9–11.**

Doryanthes excelsa

Doryanthes palmeri

Dovyalis caffra

Dovyalis hebecarpa

DORYOPTERIS

This is a genus of about 25 species of tropical ferns, with few found regularly in cultivation. They are tufted ferns with the spores collected into sori which run right around the margins on the undersides of the lobed fronds. Usually fairly small growing, they are suitable for containers and rockeries.

CULTIVATION: These are frost-tender plants so must be grown in a greenhouse except in frost-free regions. Unlike many ferns, they prefer moderate water and fairly low humidity. Shade them from excessive direct sunlight. Propagate by spores or bulblets.

Doryopteris pedata
HAND FERN

Native to tropical regions in America, this attractive plant is the most commonly grown species. It is easily identified by its dark green, triangular fronds which are deeply palmately lobed. Mature fronds have small bulblets at the base of the leaf. With an average growth rate, it reaches a height and width of some 12 in (30 cm). **ZONES 10–12.**

DOVYALIS

This genus of about 22 species of trees and shrubs is largely restricted to Africa, with a few species in Madagascar and Sri Lanka. Most are spiny, particularly on coppice shoots and young growth. The leaves are simple and alternately arranged. The small flowers are greenish or yellowish in clusters along the branches. Male and female trees are separate. The globular fruits are edible, mostly pale yellow when ripe. *Dovyalis* species are occasionally grown for their fruits, used in pickles and preserves. Heavily pruned, they make a formidable spiny hedge.

CULTIVATION: Frost tender, the plants are suitable for subtropical climates. Plant in fertile, humus-rich, well-drained soil in full sun. If they are grown for fruit

Dovyalis caffra

it is usual to bud females onto seedling stocks, with one or two male trees present for pollination. Propagate from seed or by layering.

Dovyalis caffra
KEI APPLE

From southern Africa, this evergreen shrub or small tree grows to about 20 ft (6 m) in height and width. Of upright habit, it has thorny stems and small, shiny, oval leaves, usually at the base of the spines. The tiny, yellowish flowers are followed by rounded yellow fruit that are edible but acidic. **ZONES 9–11.**

Dovyalis hebecarpa
CEYLON GOOSEBERRY

This bushy, small tree grows vigorously, reaching about 20 ft (6 m) in height. The velvety leaves have an undulating surface, and red stalks and veins. The green flowers appear in summer and fall (autumn) in leaf axils followed by velvety fruit about 1 in (25 mm) in diameter, which ripen from yellowish green to dull purple. The fruit are not highly palatable, but this species has been crossed with *Dovyalis abyssinica* to give a better-tasting hybrid. **ZONES 10–12.**

DRABA

Draba is a mainly Arctic and alpine genus of perennial or occasionally annual tufted or cushion plants. There are about 300 species and they range through the northern temperate regions as well as some of the mountains of South America. Some of the very tight cushion-forming species are much prized by alpine plant enthusiasts.

CULTIVATION: Most are frost hardy but they do require ample light, good drainage and protection from winter wet. They are handsome plants in rock gardens, troughs or individually in shallow terracotta pots. Propagate from seed, cuttings or by careful division.

Draba aizoides

Draba aizoides
YELLOW WHITLOW GRASS

A variable species native to the UK and the mountains of central and southern Europe, this tufted plant usually grows 4 in (10 cm) tall by 10 in (25 cm) wide. Its bright yellow flowers are borne in late spring. This is one of the most easily grown species. **ZONES 5–9.**

Draba longisiliqua

This tufted perennial grows 4 in (10 cm) tall by up to 10 in (25 cm) across and comes from the Caucasus region. It forms tight rosettes of tiny hairy gray leaves and it produces bright yellow flowers on long stalks in late spring. **ZONES 5–9.**

Draba rigida var. *bryoides*
syn. *Draba bryoides*

From Turkey and Armenia this species makes tufts about 3 in (8 cm) each way. Its bright yellow flowers are produced on stems up to 4 in (10 cm) long. It forms tight rosettes of minute dark green leaves with inrolled margins. **ZONES 6–9.**

Draba sachalinensis

From the far northeast of Asia, this is a tufted perennial with velvety mid-green obovate to spoon-shaped leaves. Its small white flowers are borne in dense racemes up to 8 in (20 cm) tall. **ZONES 5–9.**

DRACAENA
syn. *Pleomele*

This genus of some 40 species of evergreen trees and shrubs, many originating from equatorial Africa and Asia, is grown for foliage, often as greenhouse or indoor plants. Those grown indoors are sometimes confused with species of *Cordyline* and are often termed 'false palms' because of their cane-like stems and crowns of sword-like leaves.

CULTIVATION: Outdoors, dracaenas need warm-temperate to subtropical

Dracaena draco

Dracaena draco

conditions, full sun or part-shade and well-drained soil. Cut back to almost soil level in spring. Propagate from seed or by air-layering in spring or from stem cuttings in summer. Watch out for mealybugs.

Dracaena draco
DRAGON'S-BLOOD TREE, DRAGON TREE

This slow-growing tree from the Canary Islands is long lived. It may reach 30 ft (9 m) high with a trunk to 3 ft (1 m) in diameter and a crown of rosettes of stiff, lance-shaped, blue-green leaves to 24 in (60 cm) long and nearly 2 in (5 cm) wide. It bears insignificant flowers followed by orange berries in summer. **ZONES 10–11.**

Dracaena fragrans 'Massangeana'

This variegated form of a species native to tropical Africa, is a shrubby sparsely branched plant that can reach 50 ft (15 m) or more in the wild but seldom reaches half this height in cultivation. Its clusters of small cream flowers are very fragrant and are followed by orange-red berries. This form is marked by a central stripe of yellow on each leaf. **ZONES 10–12.**

Dracaena hookeriana

An erect shrub to 6 ft (1.8 m), this species from South Africa is only occasionally branched, its foliage clustered towards the tops of the stems. The leaves are up to 30 in (75 cm) long, spreading to recurved with a white translucent margin. Its tiny flowers are white followed by orange-red berries. **ZONES 9–11.**

Dracaena marginata

A slow-growing tree or shrub from Madagascar, this species reaches 15–20 ft (4.5–6 m) in warm climates. Its narrow, sword-like leaves have red margins. The cultivar **'Tricolor'** with a cream stripe and red edge is commonly grown as a house plant. This species tolerates some shade and quite low winter temperatures but not frost. **ZONES 10–12.**

Dracaena marginata

Draba sachalinensis

Dracaena sanderiana
BELGIAN EVERGREEN, RIBBON PLANT

A slender erect shrub branched at the base with upright branches, this species usually has silver variegated leaves up to 10 in (25 cm) long; they are often reflexed, wavy edged and the variegation consists of stripes usually along the leaf edges. This attractive plant, ideal for pot culture, is native to Cameroon. **ZONES 10–12.**

DRACOCEPHALUM
DRAGON'S HEAD

Related to mints, this genus consists of 50 or more species mainly from temperate Asia but with a few native to Europe and North Africa and one to North America. *Nepeta* is its closest ally, but in general appearance *Dracocephalum* shows parallels with salvias. The common name is merely a translation of the botanical name (of Greek origin) and refers to a fancied resemblance of the flower to a miniature dragon's head. The plants include annuals and perennials and, like most other members of the mint family, have stems that are squarish in cross-section and leaves that are aromatic when crushed and are arranged in strictly opposite pairs. The stems terminate in whorls of 2-lipped flowers, mostly blues and purples, the upper lip hooded and the lower 3-lobed.
CULTIVATION: Frost-hardy and easily cultivated in a temperate climate in reasonably fertile soil with ample moisture in spring and summer. A sunny but sheltered position suits them best. Propagate by division of established clumps.

Dracocephalum forrestii

This clump-forming perennial from western China grows 18 in (45 cm) tall by 12 in (30 cm) wide. Its stems are erect and densely leafy. It produces deep purple-blue flowers with a white hairy exterior from late summer until mid-fall (autumn). **ZONES 4–9.**

Drimys winteri

Drimys winteri

Dracocephalum moldavica
syn. *Dracocephalum moldavicum*

A branched erect aromatic annual to 24 in (60 cm) tall by 12 in (30 cm) wide, this species has violet-blue to purple flowers although a white form also exists. It is useful and attractive as a summer-flowering filler in garden beds. Originally from eastern Europe, central Asia and Siberia, it has naturalized in parts of North America. **ZONES 3–9.**

Dracocephalum ruyschianum
SIBERIAN DRAGON'S HEAD

This perennial species from Europe and northern Asia grows to 24 in (60 cm) tall. It has lance-shaped leaves with inrolled margins and upright felted stems. The flowers are a rich blue-purple and produced in short spikes from mid- to late summer. **ZONES 3–9.**

DRACULA

This genus of epiphytic orchids was so named because its rather strange flowers supposedly resemble a dragon. There are about 60 species occurring from southern Mexico to Peru in moist forests at mainly moderate altitudes. They are particularly well represented in Colombia. The plants are mostly small with short stems and long, strap-like leaves. The flowers are most distinctively shaped, with the 3 sepals joined in their basal part to form a broad cup, with the ends drawn out into long fine points.
CULTIVATION: These grow best in a hanging basket as the flowers in many species are pendent and poke through the bottom of the basket. The mixture should be well drained. Watering should be consistent throughout the year and shaded conditions with good air movement are best. Propagate by division.

Dracunculus vulgaris

Dracocephalum forrestii

Drosanthemum speciosum

Drosanthemum candens

Drosanthemum bellum

Dracula bella
syn. *Masdevallia bella*

The leaves of this medium-sized epiphytic or terrestrial orchid are about 6–8 in (15–20 cm) long and 1 in (25 mm) wide and arise from a short stem. The inflorescence comes from the leaf base and is pendulous, about 6 in (15 cm) long with a single, large, fragrant, showy flower about 8 in (20 cm) long including the drawn out tips of the sepals. It flowers from summer to winter. Cool humid conditions are required for its cultivation. **ZONE 11.**

DRACUNCULUS

A genus of 3 species, these tuberous-rooted perennials are from the Mediterranean region, the Canary Islands and Madeira. They are closely related to the genus *Arum*, but the leaves are palmately divided and the spadix is much longer.
CULTIVATION: Grow in a well-drained soil in full sun or part-shade. Water well through the growing season, but allow to dry out after flowering in summer. Although *Dracunculus* species are moderately frost hardy, protect plants in cold areas with a dressing of mulch in winter. Propagate from seed or offsets.

Dracunculus vulgaris
syn. *Arum dracunculus*
STINK LILY, DRAGON LILY

This species is not a plant you would want to grow beside your front door; it emits a potent, foul odor which attracts flies for pollinating. A native of the Mediterranean region, it grows to about 3 ft (1 m). The large leaves are red-veined and deeply divided. In late spring, a thick stem bears one or more large spathes, up to 15 in (38 cm) tall, green on the outside and red to purple or black on the inside, with a purple to black spadix. **ZONES 9–11.**

Drosanthemum barwickii

DRIMYS
WINTER'S BARK

This genus of 30 species of evergreen shrubs or small trees from South and Central America belongs to the small family Winteraceae, which is related to the magnolias and believed to be one of the most primitive flowering plant families. *Drimys* species produce terminal clusters of small, star-shaped flowers and have aromatic leaves. Plants from Australia and New Guinea formerly placed under *Drimys* are now placed in the genus *Tasmannia*.
CULTIVATION: These cool-climate plants require sheltered situations in the garden and fertile, moist but well-drained soil. Propagate from cuttings in summer; established plants can be layered.

Drimys winteri
WINTER'S BARK

This is the only species well known in cultivation. It is native to Chile and Argentina and can reach over 50 ft (15 m); some shrub forms remain under 6 ft (1.8 m). The handsome oblong leathery leaves to 8 in (20 cm) long are dark green above with a bluish undersurface. It bears large clusters of fragrant multi-petalled, cream flowers from spring to early summer. **ZONES 8–9.**

DROSANTHEMUM

This genus of the mesembryanthemum alliance contains approximately 95 species of perennial, mostly creeping succulents native to South Africa. *Drosanthemum* species have a spreading habit and vary in height, some reaching 3 ft (1 m). The fleshy leaves are densely covered in minute protuberances and

daisy-like flowers range from pink and yellow to deep purple.
CULTIVATION: Frost tender, they requires bright sunlight for flowers to open fully. Pots can be kept indoors in winter in a warm, sunny position. Plant in well-drained, compost-enriched soil. Water sparingly in summer and keep fairly dry in winter. Propagate from seed or cuttings in spring or summer and replace plants about every 3 years.

Drosanthemum barwickii

This species has violet-pink, daisy-shaped flowers, appearing from spring through to fall (autumn). The plant grows to 15 in (38 cm) with a spread of 3 ft (1 m). Its small green leaves are narrow and elongated. **ZONES 9–11.**

Drosanthemum bellum

This plant produces yellow to pink, daisy-like flowers up to 2 in (5 cm) across in spring, summer and fall (autumn). Its green, lance-shaped leaves vary in length; the entire plant reaches a spread of 3 ft (1 m) and a height of 12 in (30 cm). **ZONES 9–11.**

Drosanthemum bicolor
BICOLORED ICE-PLANT

This fast-growing, short-lived plant has a stiffly branched, thick, rounded habit to 12 in (30 cm) high and small greenish yellow leaves; it bears golden-centered, purplish red-tipped flowers in spring. **ZONES 9–11.**

Drosanthemum candens
syn. ***Drosanthemum floribundum***
ROSEA ICE PLANT

This low-growing, mat-forming plant reaches 4–6 in (10–15 cm) in height and has an indefinite spread. Its creeping branches take root as they grow and are covered with pairs of pale, gray-green, cylindrical leaves. A profusion of pinkish purple, daisy-like flowers are borne in summer. Excellent for hanging baskets, pots or as ground cover, it thrives in exposed coastal situations. **ZONES 9–11.**

Drosanthemum speciosum

In summer this species features orange-red, daisy-like flowers up to 2 in (5 cm) across. Its has tiny pale green, cylindrical leaves with blunt tips. The plant measures 24 in (50 cm) in height and 3 ft (1 m) across. **ZONES 9–11.**

Drosera binata

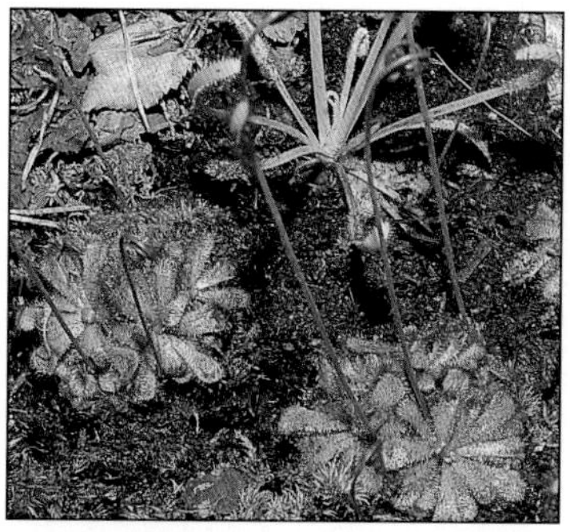

Drosera aliciae

DROSERA
SUNDEW, DAILY DEW

This genus of carnivorous perennials consists of around 100 species; more than half of these are indigenous to Australia, and the rest are widely distributed throughout the world. They usually grow in highly acidic, damp to wet soils. Sticky glandular hairs on the leaf surfaces attract and catch insects, closing over the prey and slowly absorbing its nutrients. The fork-leafed sundews are among the easiest to cultivate and include the very attractive **'Marston Dragon'** with narrow green leaves glistening with red glandular hairs.
CULTIVATION: Due to their wide distribution, great differences in hardiness exist. Some species require heated greenhouse conditions if taken from their tropical home; others are very cold tolerant. Grow in damp to wet conditions in a nutrient-deficient mix of peat moss and sand. Most like plenty of light. Propagate from seed, by division or root cuttings.

Drosera aliciae

This is a South African species with a rosetting habit to 2 in (5 cm) across and dark green leaves with bright red glandular hairs. Flowers are pink and produced on fine stems up to 18 in (45 cm) tall. **ZONES 9–11.**

Drosera anglica
ENGLISH SUNDEW, GREAT SUNDEW

Although its name suggests it is native to England, it also ranges through Europe, Asia and North America. Its linear pale green leaves are covered in bright red glands. The flowers are white and produced in summer on stems up to 10 in (25 cm) tall. **ZONES 4–10.**

Drosera binata
FORKED SUNDEW

A native of southeastern Australia, this erect growing sundew has once- or

Dryandra nobilis

Drosera capensis

Dryas octopetala var. *argentea*

twice-forked leaves to 24 in (60 cm) long. They are pale green to reddish and are covered in glandular hairs. Numerous white or pink flowers are borne on erect stems to 30 in (75 cm) tall from spring to mid-fall (autumn). **ZONES 9–11.**

Drosera capensis
CAPE SUNDEW

This species grows to 6 in (15 cm) tall, with small rosettes of narrow linear leaves covered in sensitive, red, glandular hairs which secrete fluid. In summer many small, purple flowers are produced on leafless stems. Water only with rainwater as it is very sensitive to the impurities found in tapwater. **ZONES 9–11.**

DRYANDRA

This genus, closely related to *Banksia*, consists of about 60 species of evergreen, bushy shrubs and small trees native to Western Australia. They range in size from prostrate shrubs to small trees, but the majority grow as small shrubs. The highly decorative leaves vary greatly in shape, but are generally stiff, lobed or toothed and are often prickly. The yellow, gold, orange or bronze flowers are grouped together in large rounded heads with a collar of persistent bracts, sometimes in contrasting colors. The flowers are long-lasting when cut and make excellent floral decorations, in both fresh and dried arrangements.
CULTIVATION: Frost tender, dryandras are most reliable in a warm Mediterranean-type climate with a dry summer season. They prefer full sun or part-shade and do best in well-drained, light, sandy soil without a large amount of nitrates or phosphates. Water moderately. Propagate from seed in spring.

Dryandra nobilis
GOLDEN DRYANDRA

This bushy rounded shrub to 10 ft (3 m) high and across has dark green leaves to

Dryas octopetala

Dryas octopetala 'Minor'

12 in (30 cm) long, divided to the midrib with prickly triangular lobes and whitish undersides. The golden yellow flowerheads to 3 in (8 cm) across are produced along the branches in winter and spring. **ZONES 9–11.**

DRYAS
MOUNTAIN AVENS

A small genus of 3 species from alpine and Arctic regions of the northern hemisphere, *Dryas* species make dense mats of evergreen foliage somewhat like tiny oak leaves; these often turn dark bronze in winter. Although the foliage and stems hug the ground, the showy flowers and seed heads sit up well above them.
CULTIVATION: Completely cold tolerant they may be less than satisfactory in warm climates. They make attractive rock garden or ground cover plants and are also useful between paving slabs. Grow in full sun or part-shade in a well-drained, humus-rich soil. Propagate from seed or cuttings.

Dryas octopetala
MOUNTAIN AVENS

This lovely European alpine plant can make evergreen mats up to 4 in (10 cm) tall in flower with a spread exceeding 3 ft (1 m). It has dark green scalloped leaves to $1\frac{1}{2}$ in (4 cm) long. The pure white flowers, $1\frac{1}{2}$ in (4 cm) across and with a boss of golden stamens in the center, are produced in late spring and early summer and followed by equally ornamental fluffy silver seed heads. ***Dryas octopetala* var. *argentea*** (syn. *lanata*) has felted leaves on both sides; **'Minor'** has smaller flowers and leaves. **ZONES 2–9.**

Dryas × suendermannii

This cross between *Dryas octopetala* and *D. drummondii* bears slightly nodding creamy white flowers, yellow in bud. It grows to about 4 in (10 cm) tall and is of garden origin. **ZONES 2–9.**

Dryopteris erythrosora

Dryopteris filix-mas

Dryopteris affinis

Dryopteris filix-mas **'Grandiceps Wills'**

Dryopteris filix-mas **'Depauperata'**

DRYOPTERIS

SHIELD FERN, WOOD FERN

This genus of about 200 species of deciduous or semi-evergreen terrestrial ferns is found mainly the northern hemisphere woodlands by streams and lakes. Most cultivated species have elongated fronds that are pinnately divided. Many make excellent garden ferns and handsome pot plants.

CULTIVATION: They require part-shade and moist, humus-rich soil. Remove fading fronds regularly. Protect from wind damage and do not overwater established plants. Propagate from spores in summer or by division in fall (autumn) or in winter.

Dryopteris affinis

syns *Dryopteris borreri, D. pseudomas*

GOLDEN SHIELD FERN, GOLDEN MALE FERN

This cold-hardy species makes a neat erect cluster of fronds up to 4 ft (1.2 m) tall. The new fronds are golden in color due to golden scales on the midrib, hence the common names. It is native to Europe and Asia and has given rise to many aberrant forms with curled, twisted, fasciated and plumed fronds; **'Cristata'** (syn. 'Cristata The King') is one such form with crested tips and pinnae. **ZONES 4–9.**

Dryopteris erythrosora

AUTUMN FERN, JAPANESE SHIELD FERN

Native to eastern Asia, this fern produces new fronds that range from copper to very bright red. As the fronds age they become glossy green. Bright red spor-masses dot the undersides of the pinnules. A mature fern reaches 18 in (45 cm), spreading to 12 in (30 cm). **ZONES 5–9.**

Dryopteris filix-mas

MALE FERN

Common to Europe, Asia and North America, this deciduous or semi-evergreen fern has lanceolate, pinnate, elegantly arching fronds that arise from crowns of large, upright rhizomes. It grows up to 4 ft (1.2 m) high and 3 ft (1 m) wide. **'Grandiceps Wills'**, the crested male fern, has a lovely form with a crested top almost as wide as the frond as well as finely crested leaflets. **'Depauperata'** grows to 15 in (38 cm) high and has rich green fronds that blend together at the top. **ZONES 2–9.**

Dryopteris goldieana

GOLDIE'S SHIELD FERN, GOLDIE'S WOOD FERN

This North American species has evergreen (sometimes deciduous) fronds up to 4 ft (1.2 m) tall. The rhizome is stout and slightly creeping and the bipinnate pale green fronds have dark brown glossy scales with pale margins. **ZONES 3–9.**

Dryopteris marginalis

MARGINAL SHIELD FERN, LEATHER WOOD FERN

This fern from North America has stiffly upright, slightly arching, olive green bipinnate fronds arising from a tight, central crown to a height of 12–24 in (30–60 cm). The spore-masses are borne along the margins of the leaflets. **ZONES 4–8.**

DUCHESNEA

INDIAN STRAWBERRY, MOCK STRAWBERRY

There are 6 species of these perennial plants, closely related to and very similar in appearance to the true strawberries. The leaves are divided into 3 to 5 leaflets and the plant spreads vegetatively with long fine stolons that produce more rosettes. Native to eastern and southern Asia, they differ from strawberries in having yellow flowers instead of white flowers and the red fruits are dry and unpalatable.

CULTIVATION: These frost-hardy plants can be quite aggressive so they should be placed with care; they are probably best as ground covers in less cultivated parts of the garden. They prefer part-shade and are not really fussy about the soil. Propagate by division.

Duchesnea indica

syn. *Fragaria indica, Potentilla indica*

A semi-evergreen trailing perennial, this species grows to a height of 4 in (10 cm) and multiplies rapidly by runners to an indefinite spread. It is useful as a ground cover and for bed edges, hanging baskets and pots. It has dark green leaves and bright, 1 in (25 mm) wide, yellow flowers from spring to early summer. Ornamental, strawberry-like small red fruits appear in late summer. **ZONES 5–11.**

Duchesnea indica

DUDLEYA

LIVEFOREVER, BLUFF LETTUCE

Native to southwestern USA and western Mexico, this genus is closely allied to *Echeveria* and consists of 40 species of rosetted glabrous succulents. They are generally low growing with oval to strap-like leaves and characteristic white, waxy frosting which repels water. Panicles of flowers in shades of red, white or yellow are produced from the leaf axils.

CULTIVATION: Frost-tender, these plants need to grow in well-drained, humus-rich soil in full sun. In containers, use cactus potting mix and ensure plants receive plenty of light. Propagate from seed. Watch for mealybugs on indoor plants.

Dudleya brittonii

CHALK DUDLEYA

This Mexican species forms rosettes of powdery white, broad, oblong leaves, to 10 in (25 cm) long and bears masses of star-shaped yellow flowers in spring and summer on a branched stem growing up to 3 ft (1 m) high. **ZONES 10–11.**

Dudleya caespitosa

This species is native to central California. It has a spread of up to 8 in (20 cm) and its fleshy, oblong leaves have pointed tips. Leaves vary in length from 2–6 in (5–15 cm). White, yellow or red star-shaped flowers are borne in panicles to 24 in (60 cm) tall in late spring and early summer. **ZONES 9–11.**

Dudleya pulverulenta

CHALK LETTUCE

Native to Mexico, this plant forms a solitary rosette with a 24 in (60 cm) spread. It reaches 3 ft (1 m) high, has silver-gray oblong pointed leaves and produces red to yellow, star-shaped flowers in panicles up to 30 in (75 cm) high in spring or early summer. **ZONES 10–12.**

Dudleya caespitosa

Dudleya brittonii

Durio zibethinus

Duranta erecta

Dudleya virens

ALABASTER PLANT, ISLAND LIVEFOREVER

Native to coastal California, this succulent forms rosettes of oblong pointed leaves 3–10 in (8–25 cm) long. White flowers on stems up to 24 in (60 cm) in height appear in spring and summer. **ZONES 8–11.**

DURANTA

This is a genus of about 30 species of evergreen trees and shrubs from the American tropics and subtropics, although only one of its many species is commonly grown. The more vigorous growths have spines; the whorled or opposite leaves are smallish, often toothed; and the 5-petalled flowers, narrowing to a short tube, appear in delicate sprays from the upper leaf axils. The firm, fleshy, orange berries are alleged to be poisonous.

CULTIVATION: *Duranta* species are vigorous, equally at home in the tropics and frost-free temperate regions. Grow in a fertile, well-drained soil in full sun. They can be trained to become small trees or can be kept cut back as shrubs; they make useful hedges. Propagate from seed or cuttings. They may be bothered by whiteflies.

Duranta erecta

syns *Duranta plumieri, D. repens*

GOLDEN DEWDROP, SKY FLOWER

This species, with dense, slightly pendulous branches, can reach to 15–25 ft (4.5–8 m) if trained to a single-trunked tree. The flowers are a pale mauve-blue with darker streaks on the two lower petals and a cream 'eye', borne from late spring to fall (autumn). The fruits, ½ in (12 mm) long, overlap with the flowers in late summer and fall and often persist into winter. The cultivar **'Variegata'** has cream-edged leaves with purple tinges. The white-flowered **'Alba'** has almost entire leaves. **ZONES 10–12.**

Dymondia margaretae

DURIO

There are 20 or more species in this genus of tall evergreen trees, native to tropical Southeast Asia. They have elliptical, dull green, scaly leaves and produce their usually creamy white, heavily scented flowers on the old wood and often bloom twice a year. Some flowers develop into large, prickly fruits that have a strong-smelling, edible pulp.

CULTIVATION: As tropical plants, they are not happy in areas where the temperature falls much below 65°F (18°C). They prefer moist, humus-rich soil with full sun or dappled shade. Plants may be propagated from seed but the best fruiting cultivars are grafted or budded.

Durio zibethinus

DURIAN

The durian, notorious for its putrid smell, is widely cultivated as a fruit tree in Asia. The tree grows to 120 ft (36 m) in the wild. The leaves are 8 in (20 cm) long, dark green above and paler on the undersides. The greenish white or pink flowers, in clusters of 3 to 30, grow directly on the trunk and branches. The large, spiny, green to yellow fruits are up to 15 in (38 cm) long. **ZONE 12.**

DUVERNOIA

Only 3 or 4 species make up this genus of evergreen shrubs indigenous to tropical and southern Africa, and belonging to the acanthus family. Their large leaves have wavy margins, slightly ovate and smooth. The 2-lipped flowers are borne in short, dense spikes, closely packed in the axils of the upper leaves. They are minutely hairy, as are the club-shaped fruit capsules.

CULTIVATION: They prefer a frost-free environment, humus-rich soil, part-shade or full sun, with plenty of water, especially in summer. They are wind resistant. Propagate from cuttings in summer.

Dyckia brevifolia

Duvernoia adhatodoides

Duvernoia adhatodoides

PISTOL BUSH

A sturdy, evergreen shrub to 10 ft (3 m) tall and 3 ft (1 m) wide. The ovate leaves are about 10 in (25 cm) long. During summer and fall (autumn) it bears an abundance of slightly aromatic, white to mauve flowers with purple stripes, particularly on the throat, in densely packed racemes. The ripe seed pods burst open with a loud crack. **ZONES 9–11.**

DYCKIA

A genus of about 100 species of rosette-forming terrestrial bromeliads, native chiefly to Brazil, Paraguay and Argentina. The leaves are stiff, linear and spiny-margined and are often strongly tinged reddish or brownish, or may be coated in silvery scales. Bell-shaped flowers can be shades of yellow or orange through to red, borne on spikes or panicles. They form large clumps and are suitable as bedding or rock garden plants in frost-free climates. They are good for containers and can be grown indoors in a very bright room.

CULTIVATION: They require warm frost-free conditions in full sun and well-drained soil. During the growing season water moderately and keep completely dry in winter. Use an open bromeliad or cactus potting mix if growing in containers. Whether in a container or garden do not plant too deeply. Propagate from seed or by division.

Dyckia brevifolia

syn. *Dyckia sulphurea*

PINEAPPLE DYCKIA

This native of south-eastern Brazil forms stiff open rosettes of narrowly triangular leaves to 8 in (20 cm) long. Spikes of rich yellow flowers are produced on stems to 18 in (45 cm) high in spring. **ZONES 9–11.**

Dyckia encholirioides

This native of coastal areas of southern Brazil forms large rosettes of narrow tapering leaves to 3 ft (1 m) long. The bronzy purplish leaves are toothed, smooth above and scaly beneath. It produces upright panicles of numerous red or yellow flowers in spring. **ZONES 9–11.**

Dyckia rariflora

syn. *Dyckia remotiflora*

This attractive species forms a mat of small rosettes; the narrow, recurved leaves are 4–6 in (10–15 cm) long. A 24 in (60 cm) unbranched spike bears a few orange-red flowers about ½ in (2 cm) long. **ZONES 9–11.**

DYMONDIA

A South African genus of one species, this mat-forming plant is ideal for rock gardens, borders, edging and ground cover.

CULTIVATION: In frost-prone climates grow in hanging baskets and containers. In warmer areas plant in the rock garden or in paving crevices in well-drained, moderately fertile soil in full sun. Propagate from seed or by division.

Dymondia margaretae

This prostrate ground-covering perennial will spread to 20 in (50 cm) in diameter. The linear dark green leaves to 2 in (5 cm) or less long have 2 or 3 teeth and silvery undersides. Very small bright yellow daisy-like flowerheads on very short stalks are produced in spring. **ZONES 8–11.**

Dudleya pulverulenta

E

Echeveria derenbergii

Eccremocarpus scaber

Echeveria 'Baron Bold'

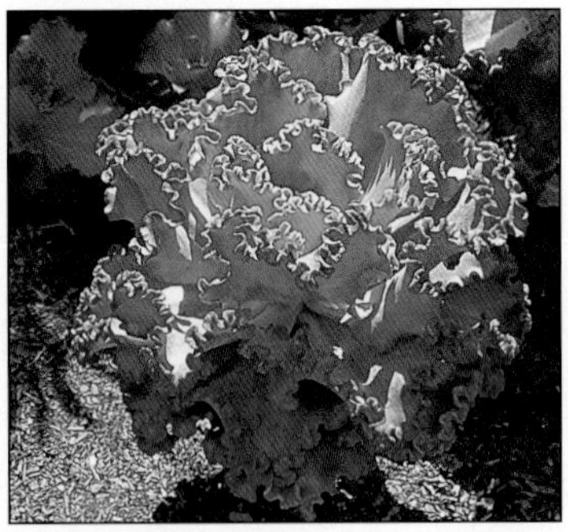

Echeveria 'Delight'

ECBALLIUM

EXPLODING CUCUMBER, SQUIRTING CUCUMBER

This is a genus of only one species native to the Mediterranean region. A trailing to slightly bushy perennial that has wet, messy, exploding seed pods, it is more a gardener's practical joke than a major garden ornament. The trailing habit could lend itself to ground cover or for running up low fencing. Its leaves are palmately lobed and bristly, and both male and female flowers appear on the one plant; they are yellow and about 1 in (25 mm) across. *Ecballium* looks somewhat like its more useful relatives the cucumbers and pumpkins.

CULTIVATION: Little more than a sunny well-drained site is required to grow *Ecballium*. Although frost will kill it back to the roots in fall (autumn), if it is well covered it will often return the following year. In warm, frost-free climates it may become invasive. Propagate from seed in spring.

Ecballium elaterium

This plant produces funnel-shaped flowers with deep yellow centers throughout summer. It grows to a height of 18 in (45 cm) with a 3 ft (1 m) spread. The hairy seed pods are blue-green. **ZONES 9–11.**

ECCREMOCARPUS

GLORY FLOWER

There are about 5 species in this genus of climbing perennials, but only 2 are commonly seen away from their homelands of Chile and Peru. They have bipinnate leaves, each with a terminal tendril. The small, tubular flowers are constricted at the base and mouth. These rather dainty climbers can twine attractively around a pillar or trellis, enhancing it with handsome leaves and small, cheerful flowers.

CULTIVATION: Marginally frost hardy, glory flowers are short-lived vines usually grown as annuals in cold areas; they also grow well in temperate climates. They grow best in full sun in light, well-drained soil. Keep moist during the growing season and support with small sticks until attached to the main trellis. Propagate from seed in early spring.

Eccremocarpus longiflorus

This evergreen vine will climb to a height of 10 ft (3 m). It has a woody, twining stem and heart-shaped leaflets. The yellow flowers, which appear for a long time from summer, are 1 in (25 mm) long and occur in pendent clusters. As it is only marginally frost hardy it can be treated as an annual in cold areas. **ZONES 9–11.**

Eccremocarpus scaber

CHILEAN GLORY FLOWER

This evergreen, tendril climber is grown for its attractive flowers, which bloom over a long season from spring into fall (autumn). It has dainty, heart-shaped leaflets and racemes of small, orange-red, tubular flowers, followed by fruit pods containing winged seeds. It grows sparsely to a height of 6–8 ft (1.8–2.4 m). In cold climates it can be grown as an annual. **ZONES 8–10.**

ECHEVERIA

Native to the Americas (mostly to Mexico), *Echeveria* takes its name from Spaniard Atanasio Echeverria Codoy, an eighteenth-century botanical artist. This large genus contains over 150 species of ornamental, perennial succulents valued for their habit, foliage and flowers. The leaves form symmetrical rosettes either sitting on the soil or as terminating erect stems; plants may form multi-stemmed bushes up to 3 ft (1 m) tall. They have fleshy, usually, smooth-edged leaves that are particularly vivid during the colder months; some plants, for example the hybrids **'Baron Bold'** and **'Delight',** have attractive crimped-edged leaves. Bell-shaped to cylindrical flowers bloom at different times of the year.

CULTIVATION: Marginally frost hardy to frost tender, *Echeveria* requires full sun or semi-shade, very porous soil and plenty of water from spring to late summer reducing to little or none in winter. Propagate from seed, offsets or cuttings, or by division in spring and summer.

Echeveria agavoides

syns *Echeveria obscura, E. yuccoides*

This hardy succulent is native to Mexico and grows to a height of 6 in (15 cm) and spread of about 4 in (10 cm). The leaves, arranged in rosettes, are triangular with stiff, reddish tips and reach 4 in (10 cm) in length. Dark pink, bell-shaped flowers are produced from spring to fall (autumn). It tolerates both frost and very dry conditions. **'Prolifera'** has dark pink, $\frac{1}{2}$ in (12 mm) long flowers, while **'Victor Reiter'** has larger red flowers and foliage tipped brown-red. **ZONES 8–11.**

Echeveria agavoides

Echeveria agavoides 'Prolifera'

Echeveria derenbergii

From Oaxaca State in Mexico, this succulent offshoots freely and the central rosette is always surrounded by little ones—the hen and chicks effect of the common name given to several species of *Echeveria*. In spring it bears reddish yellow blooms of the vivid intensity unique to desert flowers. **ZONES 9–11.**

Echeveria elegans

PEARL ECHEVERIA, HEN AND CHICKS

This marginally frost-hardy succulent develops into a dense mound of small rosettes up to 2 in (5 cm) tall and 18 in (45 cm) in diameter. Its leaves are frosted blue-green with red margins. The bell-shaped, pinkish red flowers have yellow petal tips. **'Kesselringii'** has gray-blue leaves in a loose rosette. **ZONES 8–11.**

Echeveria harmsii

syn. *Oliveranthus elegans*

A small, branched, shrubby succulent native to Mexico, this species reaches a spread of 12 in (30 cm). The leaves are green and lance-shaped and up to $1\frac{1}{2}$ in (35 mm) long. Medium-sized scarlet flowers bloom in late summer. **ZONES 8–11.**

Echeveria × *imbricata*

HEN AND CHICKS

Echeveria glauca and *Echeveria gibbiflora* var. *metallica* are the parents of this attractive and widely grown hybrid.

Echeveria elegans

Echeveria agavoides 'Victor Reiter'

Echeveria × imbricata

Echeveria pulvinata

It has gray-green, obovate leaves and produces red trumpet-shaped flowers in spring and summer. **ZONES 8–11.**

Echeveria pulvinata

PLUSH PLANT, CHENILLE PLANT

This shrubby succulent produces loose, silvery gray-green rosettes up to 4 in (10 cm) in diameter atop short, brown downy stems. The leaves are dense, silky soft, inversely egg-shaped and covered with white down. Red or yellowish red flowers appear from winter to late spring on 12 in (30 cm) tall stems. It is rather frost tender. **ZONES 9–11.**

Echeveria secunda

BLUE ECHEVERIA, HEN AND CHICKS

This small species has pointed, roundish leaves arranged in neat, slightly flattened rosettes with a spread of 4 in (10 cm); the leaf margins often become reddish as the plant matures. Small, red and yellow, bell-shaped flowers are borne in spring; it is an ideal indoor specimen. ***Echeveria secunda* var. *glauca*** is distinguished by its finer leaves. **ZONES 8–11.**

Echeveria setosa

MEXICAN FIRECRACKER

Native to Mexico, this rosetted succulent to 2 in (5 cm) high has a spread of 12 in (30 cm) across. The spoon-shaped leaves to 3 in (8 cm) long are densely covered with white bristles. Red-yellow, trumpet-shaped flowers bloom in spring and summer. **ZONES 9–11.**

ECHINACEA

CONEFLOWER

The 9 coneflower species, all native to the USA, share their common name with their close cousins the rudbeckias; some botanists still prefer to include them in that genus. They are clump-forming plants with thick edible roots. The daisy-like flowerheads are usually mauve-pink or purple, with darker and paler garden

Echeveria secunda

forms available. The dried root and rhizome of *Echinacea angustifolia* and *E. purpurea* are used in herbal medicine and allegedly increase the body's resistance to infection.
CULTIVATION: Very frost hardy, these plants like full sun and fertile soil, and resent disturbance—divide them only to increase stock, otherwise leave them alone and mulch each spring. Deadhead regularly to prolong flowering. Propagate by division or from root cuttings from winter to early spring.

Echinacea pallida

PINK CONEFLOWER

This species is an upright perennial to 4 ft (1.2 m) differing from *Echinacea purpurea* in that its petals are longer and tend to hang down. The petal (ray floret) color is usually a pink-mauve, although purple and white forms are known. **ZONES 5–9.**

Echinacea purpurea

syn. ***Rudbeckia purpurea***

PURPLE CONEFLOWER

This showy, summer-flowering perennial has dark green, lance-shaped leaves and large, daisy-like, rosy purple flowers with high, orange-brown central cones. The flowerheads, about 4 in (10 cm) wide, are borne singly on strong stems and are useful for cutting. Of upright habit, it grows to 4 ft (1.2 m) tall and spreads about 18 in (45 cm). **'Robert Bloom'** has dark pink flowers with orange-brown centers, while **'White Swan'** has large, pure white flowers with orange-brown centers. **ZONES 3–10.**

Echinacea pallida

ECHINOCACTUS

This is a genus of 12 species of very spiny cacti native to Mexico and southwest USA. Generally slow growing, they can eventually reach a height of 6 ft (1.8 m) and a width of 3 ft (1 m) and feature prominently spined ribs. Yellow, pink or red flowers are produced at the crown of mature plants in summer.
CULTIVATION: Frost tender but tolerant of very dry conditions, they grow best in well-drained soil and a position in full sun, which will help to maintain the lustre of the spines and longevity of the flowers. Young plants are prone to mealybug and spider mite. Propagate from cuttings or seed.

Echinocactus grusonii

GOLDEN BARREL CACTUS

Originating in Mexico, this popular cactus reaches up to 3 ft (1 m) in height and spread. It has a single, globe-shaped, pale green body that elongates in maturity, becoming barrel-shaped. This stem is heavily ribbed with numerous areoles sprouting yellow radial spines. In summer, larger specimens produce a circle of vivid yellow flowers from a crown at the top of the plant. **ZONES 9–12.**

Echinocactus platyacanthus

Echinocactus platyacanthus

syn. ***Echinocactus ingens***

This Mexican species has a downy apex, a green stem with long sharp spines and up to 50 ribs. It reaches a height of 5 ft (1.5 m). Yellow, mid-sized, funnel-shaped flowers blossom from spring to fall (autumn). **ZONES 9–12.**

ECHINOCEREUS

This large and popular genus of about 45 species of small cacti from Mexico and south to southwestern USA has a varying habit. The stems are many-ribbed and spiny with new stems bursting forth from inside existing ones. In spring and summer large, brightly colored, trumpet-shaped enduring blooms appear, followed by small, spiny, globular fruits. The genus name comes from the Greek *echinos* meaning hedgehog.
CULTIVATION: Species range from marginally frost hardy to frost tender and need extremely porous soil with full sun. Propagate from seed or cuttings in spring and summer.

Echinocactus grusonii

Echinacea purpurea

Echinocereus reichenbachii
LACY CACTUS

This frost-tender cactus is globe-shaped when immature, becoming elongated and cylindrical with age. Typically single stemmed, it reaches a height of up to 8 in (20 cm) and a width of 4 in (10 cm). Close-set areoles sprout abundant yellow or white spines, giving it a lacy appearance. In spring large, vivid, rose-pink to purple flowers appear. **ZONES 10–11.**

Echinocereus subinermis

This attractive, frost-tender species from New Mexico grows to about 12 in (30 cm) in height, usually as a single, fluted, gray-green plant. It bears lovely cream or yellow flowers in spring. **ZONES 10–11.**

Echinocereus triglochidiatus

This evergreen succulent grows in Arizona, Texas and Colorado, USA. The 4 in (10 cm) long green stems form large mats that spread along the ground. Funnel-shaped scarlet flowers are produced in summer and reach 2 in (5 cm) in diameter. The red fruit of this species can be made into jam when fully ripened. ***Echinocereus triglochidiatus* var. *harvensis*** grows to 6 in (15 cm) with a 5 ft (1.5 m) spread. **ZONES 8–11.**

Echinocereus viridiflorus

This clump-forming, globe-shaped cactus is the shortest species in the genus, its 3 in (8 cm) high stems spreading in colonies to about 6 in (15 cm). The stems are covered in red-brown or white radial spines with up to 16 ribs. Vivid green flowers bloom in spring. **ZONES 8–11.**

ECHINOPS
GLOBE THISTLE

This is a genus, related to thistles, of some 120 species of erect perennials, biennials and annuals, the perennials being the ones usually met with in gardens. They are native to southern Europe, central Asia as well as some of the mountainous areas of tropical Africa. The cultivated species are considered bold attractive additions to mixed or herbaceous borders and many are used in dried flower arrangements. The foliage is usually gray-green and thistle-like though usually not as spiny. The ball-shaped flowerheads can be blue, blue-gray or white, the rich blues being the most favored, and up to 2 in (5 cm) in diameter. Most cultivated species grow to 4 ft (1.2 m) or more.
CULTIVATION: These plants are usually fully frost hardy and heat tolerant, requiring nothing more than a sunny aspect with a well-drained soil of any quality. Like most herbaceous perennials, cut them to the ground in fall (autumn) or early winter. Propagate by division or from seed.

Echinops bannaticus

Native to southeastern Europe, this perennial grows to 4 ft (1.2 m) tall and bears spherical, blue-toned flowers during mid- to late summer. It has downy stems and gray-green leaves up to 10 in (25 cm) long. **'Taplow Blue'** is taller and produces vivid blue flowers. **ZONES 3–10.**

Echinopsis arachnacantha

Echinopsis 'Attila'

Echinopsis bruchii

Echinocereus reichenbachii

Echinocereus triglochidiatus

Echinocereus subinermis

Echinocereus subinermis

Echinops ritro

This perennial is a useful plant for the herbaceous border, and its globe-like, spiky flowers can be cut and dried for winter decoration. It has large, deeply cut, prickly leaves with downy undersides, silvery white stems and round, thistle-like, purplish blue flowerheads in summer. Of upright habit, it grows 30 in (75 cm) tall and wide. **ZONES 3–10.**

ECHINOPSIS
syn. *Trichocereus, Lobivia*
SEA URCHIN CACTUS

This popular genus contains up to 120 species of cacti native to South America. Ranging from single, globe-shaped stems to readily colonizing, columnar and even tree-like plants, these cacti are mostly densely covered with spines and have pronounced ribs. Many species are valued for their funnel-shaped, brilliantly colored flowers, up to 8 in (20 cm) long. Some bloom at night and are very short lived. There are numerous hybrids.
CULTIVATION: In the garden these frost-tender cacti require full sun, a rich, well-drained soil and should be watered sparingly. Under glass they need bright light, a fairly dry atmosphere and warmth if they are to reach their full potential and bear flowers. Use a free-draining cactus potting mix and keep dry during winter. Propagate in spring and summer from seed and offsets.

Echinops ritro

Echinopsis arachnacantha
syn. *Lobivia arachnacantha*

This short, spherical, frost-tender cactus is up to $1\frac{1}{2}$ in (35 mm) tall and 2 in (5 cm) in diameter. Numerous undulating, creamy white ribs cover the deep green stem. Downy, golden-yellow flowers 2 in (5 cm) in diameter bloom in abundance from the crown. **ZONES 9–11.**

Echinopsis 'Attila'

This erect-stemmed, dark green hybrid has big, showy cerise-pink flowers in spring, sometimes with a second flush in fall (autumn). Ribs are prominent and the plant can grow 10 in (25 cm) or more tall. **ZONES 9–11.**

Echinopsis aurea
syn. *Lobivia aurea*

From Argentina, this simple or clump-forming cactus with rounded to elongated stems to 10 in (25 cm) high has up to 16 straight ribs densely covered with white radial spines and a longer central spine to 1 in (3 cm) long. In summer it produces lemon-yellow flowers with darker yellow throats. **ZONES 9–11.**

Echinopsis bruchii
syn. *Lobivia bruchii*
GOLDEN BARREL OF THE ANDES

This is one of the larger species, the many-ribbed stems growing to as much as 12 in (30 cm) thick. It has yellow spines and flowers that are colored brilliantly red. **ZONES 9–11.**

Echinopsis camarguensis
syn. *Trichocereus camarguensis*

From Bolivia, this clump-forming cactus has upright cylindrical stems to 18 in (45 cm) high. It has 14 ribs densely covered in yellowish spines, and white flowers to 8 in (20 cm) across. **ZONES 9–11.**

Echinopsis candicans
syn. *Trichocereus candicans*

White, perfumed, funnel-shaped flowers open at night in summer on this cactus. Clump forming, it will reach a height of 3 ft (1 m) with an indefinite spread. Plant in full sun in well-drained soil. **ZONES 9–11.**

Echinopsis chiloensis
syn. *Trichocereus chiloensis*

Native to Chile, this large shrub or small tree has branching upright stems to 12 ft (3.5 m) high. It has up to 16 ribs with areoles bearing 12 strong radial spines and one longer central spine. The diurnal funnel-shaped flowers are white, tinged maroon. **ZONES 9–11.**

Echinopsis cinnabarina
syn. *Lobivia cinnabarina*

From Bolivia, this flattened spherical or spherical cactus has dark green stems to 6 in (15 cm) high and in diameter and up to 20 irregular, warty ribs. The white areoles produce somewhat curved spines. From the crown of the plant short, tubular, scarlet flowers are produced in spring and summer; they are diurnal. **ZONES 9–11.**

Echinopsis 'Green Gold'

While the most ardent cactophiles prefer to grow purebred species, most cacti will hybridize in cultivation and the resulting hybrids are often very pretty, easily grown plants. *Echinopsis* 'Green Gold' is a neat, clump-forming cactus about 8 in

Echinopsis terscheckii

Echinopsis 'Stars and Stripes'

Echinopsis camarguensis

(20 cm) high with abundant lime-yellow flowers in summer. It is marginally frost hardy. **ZONES 9–11.**

Echinopsis huascha
syns *Lobivia huascha, Trichocereus huascha*

This attractive plant to 3 ft (1 m) high and across has stout stems, symmetrical ribs and brilliant red or yellow flowers in summer. They are scentless and diurnal. **ZONES 9–11.**

Echinopsis kuehnrichii
syn. *Lobivia densispina*

The wonderful flower of this species is twice the size of its parent plant—a columnar, spiny cactus that is only $2\frac{1}{2}$ in (6 cm) or so across. *Echinopsis kuehnrichii* has spring flowers in shades of orange, pale yellow, red or crimson, always set off by creamy stamens. **ZONES 9–11.**

Echinopsis lageniformis
syn. *Trichocereus bridgesii*

Originating in the Andes of South America, this cactus has an erect,

Echinopsis oxygona

Echinopsis subdenudata

Echinopsis pasacana

Echinopsis kuehnrichii

Echinopsis lageniformis f. *monstrosus*

cylindrical stem up to 12 ft (3.5 m) in height. The greenish blue body freely branches from its base and has up to 8 ribs, sparsely lined with areoles bearing up to 6 spines. In summer white, trumpet-shaped flowers open widely at night and emit a very strong fragrance. Spreading only to 3 ft (1 m), this cactus makes an excellent conservatory specimen. ***Echinopsis lageniformis* f. *monstrosus*** is a large, pale green cactus to 15 ft (4.5 m) with very long, yellowish spines in clusters of two to six. **ZONES 9–11.**

Echinopsis oxygona
syn. *Echinopsis multiplex*
EASTER LILY CACTUS, BARREL CACTUS

Originating in Brazil, this spherical, multi-branched cactus grows to about 6 in (15 cm) in maturity and with age forms dense clumps up to 3 ft (1 m) in diameter. The stems are covered with brown, black-tipped spines; these sprout fragrant, pinkish white flowers from the tips in summer. **ZONES 10–12.**

Echinopsis pasacana
syn. *Trichocereus pasacana*

This is one of the larger species, indigenous to Bolivia and Argentina and growing to 30 ft (9 m). It has yellow spines and its 4 in (10 cm) long flowers bloom at night; these are followed by edible green fruit. **ZONES 9–11.**

Echinopsis 'Stars and Stripes'

The semi-prostrate 4 in (10 cm) long stems of this hybrid branch from the base. Stems are prominently ribbed and have bristly, silver-gray spines. Coral-pink, star-like flowers are borne in summer. **ZONES 9–11.**

Echinopsis subdenudata

Featuring a flower around 8 in (20 cm) long, this medium-sized cactus has a dark green stem and grows to 3 in (8 cm) in height and 6 in (15 cm) in spread. **ZONES 9–11.**

Echinopsis terscheckii
syn. *Trichocereus terscheckii*

Native to northern Argentina, this species, the giant of the genus, grows up to 40 ft (12 m) high with a trunk up to 18 in (45 cm) thick. Clusters of 8 to 15 spines sprout from light brown areoles. The dark red to green bell-shaped flowers have white throats. **ZONES 9–11.**

ECHIUM

Indigenous to the Mediterranean, Canary Islands, western Europe and Madeira, the 40 or so species of annuals, perennials and shrubs in this genus are grown for their spectacular bright blue, purple or pink flowers in late spring and summer. The hairy leaves form rosettes at the bases of the flowering stems. They look best in mixed borders; ingestion of the plants can cause stomach upsets.

CULTIVATION: Very frost hardy to frost tender, they require a dry climate, full sun and a light to medium, well-drained soil. They become unwieldy in soil that is too rich or damp. Prune gently after flowering to keep them compact. Coastal planting is ideal. Propagate from seed or cuttings in spring or summer. In mild climates they self-seed readily.

Echium candicans

Echium thyrsiflorum

Echium candicans
syn. ***Echium fastuosum***
PRIDE OF MADEIRA, TOWER OF JEWELS

This soft-wooded shrub from Madeira has fuzzy gray-green leaves that are broadly sword-shaped and clustered in large rosettes at the branch ends. In spring and summer, 24 in (60 cm) spires of sapphire-blue to violet-blue flowers with crimson stamens are produced, each flower only about ½ in (12 mm) wide but borne by the hundreds together. Sprawling in habit, it grows to about 6 ft (1.8 m) tall but spreads wider. ***Echium thyrsiflorum*** is quite similar to *E. candicans* but has taller, straighter spikes of pale lavender flowers; it is a less showy species and the spikes look untidy as they mature. **ZONES 9–10.**

Echium pininana

Indigenous to La Palma in the Canary Islands, this biennial species bears striking tapered spires of funnel-shaped lavender-blue flowers, soaring to 10 ft (3 m) or more in height. The leaves appear in the first year, the flowers the next, and after flowering the plant dies. **ZONES 9–10.**

Echium plantagineum

Echium plantagineum
syn. ***Echium lycopsis***

This annual or biennial to 24 in (60 cm) and native to warm, dry areas of Europe produces a basal rosette of bristly leaves up to 6 in (15 cm) long. The flower stems produced in late spring and summer form a panicle of rich blue-purple, occasionally red flowers. This is an attractive bedding plant but it tends to self-seed in dry climates; in southern Australia it has become a notorious weed known as Paterson's curse. **ZONES 9–10.**

Echium vulgare
VIPER'S BUGLOSS

This spectacular European biennial to 3 ft (1 m) tall has erect leafy stems. The funnel-shaped flowers, borne in spikes or panicles, are usually a rich violet, although white and pink forms exist. A dwarf form is available with white, blue, pink or purple flowers. **ZONES 7–10.**

Echium wildpretii
syn. ***Echium bourgaeanum***
TOWER OF JEWELS

A striking biennial from the Canary Islands, this evergreen plant makes a

Echium pininana

rosette of narrow, silvery leaves and, in its second season, bears a single, bold spike of small, funnel-shaped, rich coral flowers. It has an erect habit, growing to 6 ft (1.8 m) or more high and about 24 in (60 cm) wide. **ZONES 9–10.**

EDGEWORTHIA
PAPER BUSH

This genus comprises 3 deciduous shrub species related to *Daphne* and native to China and the Himalayas. Only the Chinese species is widely cultivated, famous for its traditional use in Japan as a source of high-quality paper; it is also an ornamental shrub of some distinction. Tight heads of small tubular flowers cluster on the ends of the bare branches in spring; the outside of each flower is concealed by a layer of silky white hairs, the yellow, orange or red color only appearing on the inner faces at the tip. **CULTIVATION:** They are moderately hardy but easily damaged by late frosts. They prefer a sheltered, sunny spot in well-drained soil. Pruning is not normally necessary. Propagation is usually from cuttings.

Edgeworthia chrysantha
syn. ***Edgeworthia papyrifera***

From central China, this low-branching, single-stemmed shrub may grow to about 6 ft (1.8 m) high and wide, but is usually seen at 3–5 ft (1–1.5 m). The red-brown twigs are extraordinarily tough and flexible and the soft, pale green leaves are inclined to wilt and shed in hot weather. The tips of the flowers, borne in mid-spring, are normally golden yellow, contrasting prettily with the pure white silky tubes. Red-flowered forms are also grown, including **'Red Robin'** and **'Red Dragon'**. **ZONES 7–9.**

Edgeworthia chrysantha

EDMONDIA

This genus contains 3 species of perennials or subshrubs from South Africa. The daisy-like flowerheads are entirely composed of disc florets, but the surrounding bracts are papery and petal-like, making them excellent, long-lasting cut flowers that are dried as everlastings. Plants are good rockery subjects. **CULTIVATION:** Marginally frost hardy, they grow best in well-drained soil in a sunny position. In cold climates they can be overwintered in a greenhouse. Propagate from seed in spring or from cuttings in summer or fall (autumn).

Edmondia pinifolia
syn. ***Helichrysum humile***

This evergreen subshrub with a height and spread of 12 in (30 cm) has small narrow leaves, deep green above and white-felted beneath. The papery oval flowerheads are surrounded by crimson bracts and are borne singly at the ends of branchlets in spring. **ZONES 8–9.**

EDRAIANTHUS

This genus consists of about 24 species of very low-growing perennials from southern Europe and the Caucasus; they are ideally suited to rock or scree gardens and for growing in dry stone walls or troughs. *Edraianthus* species all produce neat clumps of grassy or cushiony strap-shaped leaves and starry or bell-like flowers in blue, violet or white. Some species are densely covered with silver hairs, which gives them an attractive sheen. Species are related to and sometimes included in *Wahlenbergia.* **CULTIVATION:** In cooler climates, full sun is best but the plants will tolerate midday shade in hotter areas. Good soil drainage is essential; the plants thrive in gritty, alkaline soil containing rotted organic matter. Water liberally from late spring to summer, decreasing to almost

Echium vulgare

Edgeworthia chrysantha

Elaeagnus pungens

Elaeagnus pungens 'Variegata'

nothing in winter. Propagate from seed or cuttings of side shoots taken in spring.

Edraianthus pumilio

Rarely taller than 2 in (5 cm), this beautiful silver-leafed perennial from the coastal mountains of Croatia spreads to form a soft cushion about 12 in (30 cm) across. The leaves are narrow and densely hairy, and the campanula-like flowers are usually violet but may also be blue. It is frost hardy as long as it is kept dry in winter. **ZONES 6–9.**

EICHHORNIA

WATER HYACINTH

This is a genus of 7 species of aquatic perennials native to tropical America. They form rosettes of stalked, broadly oval or heart-shaped leaves and terminal spikes of showy, funnel-shaped flowers. They grow floating in water, with no need to anchor their roots; a raft of connected plants can rapidly cover a large area of water, choking rivers and blocking sunlight to other marine life. Grow only where they can be controlled and never in open watercourses.
CULTIVATION: Reasonably frost hardy, they thrive in warm, slowly moving water in full sun. Propagate by division.

Eichhornia crassipes

This species from South America spreads to around 18 in (45 cm). The pale violet flowers are marked with bright blue and gold, and occur in upright terminal spikes. The rounded, glossy green leaves are arranged in rosettes. Its cultivation is prohibited in most warmer countries. **ZONES 9–12.**

EKEBERGIA

This small genus of 15 species from tropical and southern Africa and Madagascar includes trees and small to large shrubs with smooth, compound leaves composed of 1 to 7 pairs of leaflets

Elaeagnus umbellata

and a terminal leaflet; the midrib is sometimes winged. The flowers are borne in branching heads in the leaf axils, male and female flowers on different trees. The 4- to 5-lobed calyces are saucer-shaped and there are 4 to 5 petals. These are followed by succulent fruits which contain one or more woody seeds.
CULTIVATION: Fast growing, wind resistant and able to tolerate some frost, they make useful specimens for parks and open spaces. Propagate from seed.

Ekebergia capensis

CAPE ASH

This attractive tree, the most widely cultivated species, is a useful shade tree growing to 30–70 ft (9–21 m) with a spreading crown. Generally evergreen, it may be semi-deciduous in cooler regions depending on rainfall, but new foliage quickly develops. The small white spring flowers are sweetly scented but insignificant; they are followed by fruit that ripen glossy red. **ZONES 9–11.**

ELAEAGNUS

This genus of about 45 species of deciduous and evergreen shrubs, small trees and scrambling climbers comes from Europe, Asia and North America, with one species extending to Australia. All have alternate, entire leaves which, together with the young stems, flower buds and fruits, glisten with tiny silvery or rusty brown scales. Small flowers, clustered in the leaf axils, are tubular at the base with 4 spreading petals. The fruits, pale fleshy drupes, are edible in some species.
CULTIVATION: Frost hardy and generally vigorous and trouble free, they thrive in most soils and positions. The evergreen species will tolerate shade. Most species can be cut back heavily if a bushy shape is desired. Propagate from seed for deciduous species (which fruit freely) and cuttings for the evergreens.

Ekebergia capensis

Elaeagnus angustifolia

OLEASTER, RUSSIAN OLIVE

This deciduous species extends from southern Europe to China. A large shrub or small tree, it grows to 30 ft (9 m) high, the new branches and the undersides of the narrow leaves coated in silvery scales. In late spring and early summer clusters of small, perfumed, pale yellow flowers appear, followed in late summer by edible yellowish fruit, also coated in silvery scales. It makes a striking ornamental but needs warm, dry summers to bring out its silvery foliage. **ZONES 7–9.**

Elaeagnus × *ebbingei* 'Gilt Edge'

This shrub grows to 10 ft (3 m) and is usually evergreen. It will sometimes shed foliage in very cold climates. Its dark metallic sea-green leaves have a narrow golden margin. The undersurface is silvery and scaly. The flowers, produced in fall (autumn), are very small but sweetly scented. It makes a good bushy screening plant or clipped hedge. **ZONES 6–9.**

Elaeagnus pungens

SILVERBERRY, THORNY ELAEAGNUS

The most common species of the genus, this frost-hardy, evergreen bush or scrambling climber has long, prickly, horizontal branches and glossy, oval leaves which are dark green above and silvery beneath. It is excellent for hedges, growing to a height and width of 10–15 ft (3–4.5 m). In fall (autumn) it bears fragrant, tiny, bell-shaped, cream flowers. Among a number of cultivars with variegated foliage are **'Variegata'**, with narrow, irregular, cream-margined leaves, and **'Maculata'**, whose leaves have a central splash of gold. **ZONES 7–10.**

Elaeagnus umbellata

AUTUMN ELAEAGNUS, AUTUMN-OLIVE

From the Himalayas, China and Japan, this deciduous or semi-deciduous species is a large, spreading shrub 12–15 ft (3.5–4.5 m) high with broad, green leaves that have wavy margins and silvery, reflective undersides. In late spring and early summer it bears numerous clusters of scented cream flowers in the upper leaf axils, followed in fall (autumn) by crowded, small, berry-like fruit that are initially silvery green but ripen eventually to pale red, blending attractively with the pale yellow fall foliage. **ZONES 7–10.**

ELAEIS

OIL PALM

This is a tropical genus of 2 species of palms with narrow, straight trunks topped with long, drooping fronds. The individual leaflets also droop, which creates a soft, graceful effect. Small yellow flowers in large inflorescences are followed by the oil-bearing fruits.
CULTIVATION: A warm, humid, tropical climate is necessary to grow these plants outdoors, though they may be container grown indoors in temperate zones. Plant in rich, moist soil in full sun. They are tender to both frost and dry conditions. Propagate from seed.

Elaeis guineensis

AFRICAN OIL PALM

The fruit and seeds from this species yield palm oil. Originally from West Africa but planted by the millions in tropical countries to satisfy commercial demand, it is sometimes seen as a threat by conservationists because it is replacing rainforests. It grows to 70 ft (21 m) high with fronds up to 15 ft (4.5 m) long. The all-important fruit occur in large, tightly packed bunches and change from red to black when ripe. **ZONES 11–12.**

Elaeis guineensis

Eichhornia crassipes

ELAEOCARPUS

This genus of over 200 species of evergreen trees and tall shrubs ranges widely through tropical Asia and Australasia, including Pacific Islands as far south as New Zealand. Most species are slender and graceful with sprays of cup-shaped flowers with fringed petals, followed by colorful berries with thin flesh around a large stone. They make good specimen plants for warm-temperate gardens.
CULTIVATION: Mostly frost tender, they prefer full sun or part-shade and fertile, well-drained but moist soil. Prune only to establish a single trunk. Plants in containers require a plentiful supply of water during the growing season. Propagate from seed sown in spring and soaked in warm water for 24 hours, or from cuttings in summer.

Elaeocarpus reticulatus
syn. *Elaeocarpus cyaneus*
BLUEBERRY ASH

The most commonly grown, this frost-tender Australian species is a slender tree to 30 ft (9 m) tall with shiny, leathery leaves. Racemes of white flowers are borne from spring to summer, followed by globular, deep blue fruit. It grows well in a container and can be pruned to form a 10 ft (3 m) shrub. **'Prima Donna'** has pink flowers. **ZONES 9–11.**

Elegia persistens

Elegia grandispicata

Elegia cuspidata

ELAPHOGLOSSUM

This is a large genus of 400 species of epiphytic ferns mostly found in tropical America. They have a creeping rhizome and simple, stalked fronds; in some species the fronds are repeatedly forked into narrower lobes. They are rarely encountered in cultivation. Frost tender, they make interesting container plants for a greenhouse and indoors.
CULTIVATION: Use an epiphyte potting mixture that is open and coarse and high in organic material. Keep the mixture evenly moist but well drained. Provide good, indirect light, high humidity and avoid extremes in temperature. Propagate by division.

Elaphoglossum peltatum
syn. *Peltapteris peltata*

The rhizomes of this species from tropical America often form colonies. It has repeatedly forked sterile fronds to 6 in (15 cm) long and smaller almost translucent fertile fronds. **ZONES 11–12.**

ELATOSTEMA
syn. *Pellionia*

There are at least 50 species in this genus native to Asia and Australasia. They are low, spreading or trailing evergreen perennials with brittle, fleshy stems and ornamental leaves. Plants take root wherever the stems touch the ground. Useful as ground cover in shady tropical and subtropical gardens, they also make attractive indoor or greenhouse plants in cooler climates.
CULTIVATION: In tropical and subtropical areas plant in rich, fertile soil in bright shade; plants will take some sun but not during the hottest hours of the day. Keep moist and feed once or twice during the warmer months with a liquid organic fertilizer. To propagate simply remove rooted sections from the parent plant and transplant.

Elegia capensis

Elegia stipularis

Elatostema repens
syn. *Pellionia repens*
TRAILING WATERMELON BEGONIA

This attractive ground-hugging species, spreading to about 24 in (60 cm), has wavy edged, lanceolate leaves with blotchy dark green margins and pale gray-green centers. An unusual ground-cover or hanging basket specimen, the latter displays its pink-flushed, fleshy stems to better effect. **ZONES 10–12.**

ELEGIA
CAPE REED

This genus consists of 32 species restricted to the Fynbos (a type of heath-like vegetation) region of southern Africa. Fynbos is typified by poor soils, wet periods and hot, dry, fire-prone seasons. In their native home, many species have been used as thatching and for making brooms. They are also becoming very popular in the florist trade as foliage; the strong, fine stems of ***Elegia grandispicata*** makes excellent accent foliage as does ***E. persistens*** with its terminal ochre-colored bracts. Some species can exceed 10 ft (3 m), although most are smaller. Most are soft rush-like plants that look good by ponds or among rocks. Some species may have weed potential in Mediterranean climates.
CULTIVATION: Most are sun-loving plants requiring nothing more than some moisture and good drainage in a frost-free climate. Cut back any old stems that are dying off. Propagate from seed or by division of young plants.

Elegia capensis
BESEMRIET, BERGBAMBOES

This is possibly the most attractive and one of the easiest species to grow. It has fluffy, branching, green stems that perform the function of leaves (the leaves are attractive bronze bracts that run up the stems at the nodes). These stems are usually about 5 ft (1.5 m) tall, although they can reach nearly 10 ft (3 m) under ideal conditions. Tiny brown flowers are produced at the ends of the stems. **ZONES 9–10.**

Elegia cuspidata
BLOMBIESIES

This species rarely exceeds 3 ft (1 m) tall. The sturdy upright stems support dense bronze flowerheads surrounded by papery brown bracts. **ZONES 9–10.**

Elaphoglossum peltatum

Elegia stipularis

Growing to 3 ft (1 m), this species produces attractive golden-brown sheaths surrounding the flowerheads at the tops of the stems. Due to its size it is ideal as a feature in a sunny rock garden or by a pond in a smaller garden. **ZONES 9–10.**

ELEOCHARIS
SPIKE-RUSH

This genus contains about 150 species of rhizomatous sedges occurring in most parts of the world. They have erect, green cylindrical stems, each topped by a short spike of tiny flowers among flat, overlapping bracts. One species is cultivated in China and southern Asia for its edible tubers, which are eaten fresh or cooked. ***Eleocharis acicularis*** is fully hardy and grown as an ornamental.
CULTIVATION: Species of *Eleocharis* need a rich soil and a hot summer. Traditionally the tubers are planted about 3 ft (1 m) apart and the soil flooded to a depth of about 4 in (10 cm). In fall (autumn) the field is drained and the tubers dug up. In warm areas plants can be raised in shallow water or ponds. Propagate from tubers .

Eleocharis dulcis
CHINESE WATER CHESTNUT

This is the species most commonly grown in Asia for its dark brown edible tubers, which have a nut-like texture and a sweet taste. Each tuber produces a tuft of long tubular leaves and numerous slender horizontal rhizomes. It grows to a height of 3 ft (1 m). **ZONES 9–12.**

ELEUTHEROCOCCUS
syn. *Acanthopanax*

This is a genus of about 30 species of deciduous shrubs and small trees mostly from China, but a few extending to nearby Southeast Asia as well as Japan, Korea and eastern Siberia. They have prickly or bristly stems and palmate leaves with up to 7 leaflets. The small white, greenish or purplish flowers, arranged in terminal umbels, are followed by showy, black, berry-like fruits. A few species have been grown as ornamentals in cool-temperate climates, valued mainly for their foliage.
CULTIVATION: Very frost hardy, they need friable, humus-rich, well-drained soil and full sun. Propagate from seed in spring or fall (autumn) or from cuttings in early summer.

Eleutherococcus senticosus
SIBERIAN GINSENG

The root of this species, a shrub 4–6 ft (1.2–1.8 m) high from northern China and eastern Siberia, shares many properties of the renowned medicinal herb ginseng (*Panax ginseng*). More readily cultivated than ginseng, it was adopted with enthusiasm by the Russians, used as a daily tonic and supplied to athletes training for the Olympic Games. **ZONES 4–9.**

ELODEA

WATERWEED, PONDWEED, DITCHMOSS

These submerged freshwater perennials are native to North America and subtropical South America. Some 12 species have been described and most have a reputation for becoming weedy and difficult to control. They are, however, useful in small ponds or even indoor aquariums as fish shelter and oxygenating plants. The stems are long, clothed in crowded, small oblong leaves, often slightly spiralling as they rise toward the surface.

CULTIVATION: Grow in ponds or aquariums in a clay base or in a pot of soil set on the bottom in a sunny or part-shaded position. Propagate by division or from cuttings in summer.

Elodea canadensis

CANADIAN PONDWEED

As both the species and common name would suggest, this plant is native to Canada as well as the USA. It has branching stems up to 12 ft (4 m) long and small, curling, translucent leaves. Canadian pondweed is too vigorous for an aquarium and can become quite invasive in large bodies of water. **ZONES 3–9.**

ELYMUS

LYME GRASS, WILD RYE

This genus of creeping or clump-forming perennial grasses consists of about 150 species, occurring in temperate regions throughout the world. They produce flowering stems with rows of long bristles on the spikelets.

CULTIVATION: These frost-hardy grasses need full sun and fertile, well-drained soil. In late fall (autumn) they may be cut down to ground level. In places where the warmer months are dry, a deep soaking once a week will keep them fresh looking and prevent the early onset of dormancy. Propagate from seed in fall or spring or by division in summer.

Elymus hispidus

syn. ***Elymus glaucus*** **of gardens**

HAIRY COUCH

This native of Eurasia has erect, hairy stems and greenish blue, long, linear leaves. The summer flowers occur in densely packed, cylindrical heads. It grows to a height of 30 in (75 cm) with a 15 in (38 cm) spread. **ZONES 5–9.**

Elymus magellanicus

This species reaches 6 in (15 cm) in height. From Chile and Argentina, it has attractive bluish leaves and its virtually prostrate flower spikes are produced throughout summer. **ZONES 7–10.**

EMBOTHRIUM

Consisting of 8 species of evergreen trees and shrubs from the Andes in South America, this genus includes one species grown for its striking scarlet flowers, often borne in great profusion. It is one of the few tree members of the spectacular protea family that can be grown in cool climates. The trees are relatively fast growing and in 10 years will provide a good floral display. The handsome, lance-shaped or oblong leaves are leathery in texture.

CULTIVATION: Provide deep, moist but well-drained soil and a sunny or part-shaded position. Grow in a sheltered position if frosts are heavy. Propagate from seed in spring, cuttings or detached suckers in summer.

Embothrium coccineum

FLAME FLOWER

Coccineum is Latin for 'scarlet', which aptly describes this tree's flowers, borne freely in late spring and early summer. Cultivated specimens seldom exceed more than 30 ft (10 m). It is an upright tree bearing deep green lance-shaped leaves to 6 in (15 cm) long, and abundant scarlet flowers are produced in loose clusters. It grows wild in southern Chile and adjacent Argentina. **'Norquinco Valley'** has longer, narrowly lance-shaped leaves; it was named after the locality on the Andean slopes of Argentina from where it was collected. **ZONES 8–9.**

EMMENOPTERYS

The great plant explorer Ernest Wilson, who collected hundreds of garden plants in China in the early twentieth century, described one of the 2 known species of this genus as 'one of the most strikingly beautiful trees of Chinese forests'. The genus, allied to *Luculia*, occurs in central and southwestern China and also in northern Burma and Thailand. It consists of deciduous trees of small to medium size with oppositely arranged pairs of broad, smooth-edged leaves. The flowers are funnel-shaped with 5 spreading petals, borne terminally on the branches in large clusters; some flowers in each cluster have one of their 5 sepals greatly enlarged (as in the genus *Mussaenda*).

CULTIVATION: Frost hardy, grow in a deep, moist soil in full sun and shelter from cold, drying winds. Propagate from cuttings in summer.

Emmenopterys henryi

This medium to large tree of spreading habit grows to about 40 ft (12 m) in cultivation. It is a lovely tree with attractive bronze-red new growth that matures to dark green with a paler undersurface. The flowerheads consist of quite large white blooms surrounded by even larger white sepals. They are produced in summer, but only on mature trees. **ZONES 6–9.**

Encephalartos altensteinii

ENCELIA

This genus of shrubby or herbaceous daisies native to southwestern North America, Chile, Peru and the Galapagos Islands is generally found in dry to desert habitats. There are 15 species few of which are in general cultivation. The flowers are either yellow or purple. One species *(Encelia farinosa)* was used by early Spanish settlers. The stems are highly resinous and make a form of incense.

CULTIVATION: Frost tender, these plants prefer full sun and a well-drained to dryish sandy soil. The shrubby species may need pruning after flowering to keep them tidy. Propagate from seed.

Encelia farinosa

BRITTLEBRUSH, INCIENSO

From southwestern deserts of the USA and Mexico, this mounding shrub covers itself with bright yellow daisies from late winter through spring. It remains low and compact—little more than 2 in (5 cm)—on natural rainfall but with irrigation it may become a lanky 6 ft (1.8 m) shrub. The silvery leaves usually drop in hot summers, when it is best to cut the stems to the ground to encourage new growth for next season's flowers. **ZONES 8–10.**

ENCEPHALARTOS

The 60 or more species of slow-growing cycads in this genus come mostly from southern Africa with a minority scattered through tropical Africa. They are commonly found on rocky outcrops, among coastal dunes or on mountainsides. They appear as large tufts of spiky fronds for many years before eventually developing a stout trunk, up to 10–12 ft (3–3.5 m) high. The stiff, palm-like leaves are pinnate, with leaflets that are spine tipped and often toothed. As with all cycads, there are both male and female plants; the latter produce spectacular cones either singly or in groups of up to 5 from the center of the crown.

CULTIVATION: These plants tolerate an occasional frost, but will do best in subtropical areas with full sun and plenty of moisture; they can withstand strong winds. Propagate from seed, which germinates easily, although seedlings take many years to develop.

Encephalartos altensteinii

PRICKLY CYCAD, BREAD TREE

This cycad from moist coastal areas of South Africa is extremely slow growing. The rigid, palm-like fronds are about 6 ft (1.8 m) long, with numerous stiff, spiny-toothed leaflets. A female specimen may produce cones resembling giant, elongated pineapples 18 in (45 cm) long. **ZONES 10–11.**

Embothrium coccineum

E. coccineum 'Norquinco Valley'

Embothrium coccineum

E

Encephalartos transvenosus

Encephalartos friderici-guilielmi

Encephalartos friderici-guilielmi

Encephalartos arenarius

This rare species from South Africa's eastern Cape Province has an erect stem to 3 ft (1 m) tall. The arching fronds, to 5 ft (1.5 m) in length, have lobed, blue-green leaflets. Mature specimens of *Encephalartos arenarius* bear solitary green cones with red glossy seeds. **ZONES 10–11.**

Encephalartos friderici-guilielmi
WHITE-HAIRED CYCAD

This species from eastern Cape Province can produce more cones per stem than any other species—up to 12 male cones, or 5 to 6 female cones, in both cases densely covered in felty pale brown hairs. The solitary or clustered trunks are up to 12 ft (3.5 m) tall and 24 in (60 cm) thick, each with a crown of rather stiff, upright fronds with closely crowded narrow leaflets; the younger fronds are a pale green or blue-green color. It adapts well to cultivation and is very hardy, thriving in poor sandy soil and needing very little water. **ZONES 9–11.**

Encephalartos horridus
FEROCIOUS BLUE CYCAD

Native to eastern Cape Province, this unusual species forms at maturity dense clumps of short stems, up to 24 in (60 cm) high, and has very prickly fronds of a striking ice-blue or blue-green shade; the leaflets are very rigid, with often one to several large spine-tipped lobes. It prefers very hot conditions. **ZONES 9–11.**

Encephalartos longifolius

This cycad eventually reaches 10 ft (3 m) high. Arching, deep green fronds up to 6 ft (1.8 m) long are composed of overlapping lance-shaped leaflets. Brownish cones are borne on mature specimens in summer. From eastern Cape Province, this is a moisture-loving species that prefers acid soil conditions and full sun. **ZONES 9–11.**

Encephalartos natalensis
NATAL CYCAD, THOUSAND HILLS CYCAD

This cycad grows to 12 ft (3.5 m) tall with an erect stem—over many decades

Encephalartos arenarius

Encephalartos horridus

some do reach 20 ft (6 m). In summer, the downy female cones turn dark yellow. The fronds are dark green and up to 10 ft (3 m) in length, the leaflets either entire or with a few small, spiny prickles. It comes from subtropical valleys behind Durban, South Africa, and likes rich, deep soil and plenty of water; it does best in a sheltered position, in sun or part-shade. **ZONES 10–12.**

Encephalartos transvenosus
MODJADJI CYCAD

Reaching 25 ft (8 m) high, this species from northern Transvaal has arching fronds to 8 ft (2.4 m) long divided into broadly lance-shaped, sparsely toothed leaflets. Mature specimens produce colorful golden cones that are felty when young. The tallest species, it occurs in a number of remarkable stands in northern Transvaal, consisting of pure forests of this cycad numbering many thousands of mature plants, now strictly protected. In cultivation it prefers a sheltered position with plentiful moisture. **ZONES 10–12.**

Encephalartos trispinosus

This species has an erect stem to 3 ft (1 m) and erect, ascending then arching fronds to 4 ft (1.2 m) long with recurved tips. They are composed of gray-green leaflets that usually have 3 spiny lobes at the tip. Bright yellow, solitary cones with orange-red seeds are usually produced in summer. Growing in hot, dry situations in eastern Cape Province, it is a hardy, sun-loving plant that responds to plentiful watering. **ZONES 9–11.**

Encephalartos trispinosus

Encephalartos woodii

From Natal, this tall cycad has a stem to 20 ft (6 m) high and dark green fronds to 8 ft (2.4 m) long. They are composed of numerous leaflets that are distinctly toothed when young, becoming entire with age. Bright orange cones are borne in clusters of up to six. The rarest of all cycads, it was only ever known as a single male plant in the wild, from which offsets were removed as long ago as 1899 and grown in several botanical gardens. It is easily grown in a sheltered situation in deep, moist soil. **ZONES 10–12.**

ENKIANTHUS

About 10 species of deciduous shrubs from East Asia make up this genus, valued for their small, bell-shaped flowers, densely clustered and prettily marked in most species, and their fine fall (autumn) foliage colors. Growth is rather open and the smallish leaves are clustered at the end of each season's growth, producing a layered effect. The stalked, pendulous flowers are produced in numerous short sprays from just below the leaves.

CULTIVATION: Very frost hardy, they like similar conditions to many rhododendrons and azaleas: moist woodland with humus-rich but not too fertile, acid soil. They will not thrive in heavy shade. Pruning into a rounded shape should be avoided, or the flowers will not be so well displayed. Propagate from seed or cuttings in summer.

Encephalartos longifolius

Encephalartos woodii

Enkianthus campanulatus

Enkianthus campanulatus var. *palibinii*

Enkianthus campanulatus
REDVEIN ENKIANTHUS

From Japan and southern China, this is the most popular species, reaching 8–12 ft (2.4–3.5 m) high, of narrow, open habit and rather slow growing. The flowers, cream but heavily striped and tipped dull crimson, are produced in abundance in spring. In fall (autumn) the leaves turn to shades of gold, scarlet and dull purple. ***Enkianthus campanulatus* var. *palibinii*** has more strongly reddish flowers. ZONES 6–9.

Enkianthus cernuus

Both the typical species and ***Enkianthus cernuus* var. *rubens*** are native to Japan. The only difference between them is the color of the broadly bell-shaped flowers. The species has white flowers, while *E. c.* var. *rubens* has rich red ones. The shrub can reach 10 ft (3 m) tall and nearly as wide although it rarely attains these dimensions in cultivation. Its fall (autumn) color is brilliant red. ZONES 6–9.

Enkianthus deflexus
BENT ENKIANTHUS

This shrub or small tree from the Himalayas and western China grows to 12 ft (3.5 m) or more high. The oval, bright green leaves with a felted undersurface turn orange and red in fall (autumn). The bell-shaped, pink-tinged cream flowers have broad petals. ZONES 6–9.

Enkianthus perulatus
WHITE ENKIANTHUS

From Japan, this is rather distinctive among *Enkianthus* species in its lower, bushier habit and more sparsely scattered urn-shaped flowers that are pure white or greenish white, without markings and contracted at the mouth. They are borne on nodding stalks in early spring. This species likes a very cool, sheltered position and has brilliant red fall (autumn) foliage color. ZONES 6–9.

Enkianthus cernuus var. *rubens*

Enkianthus quinqueflorus

This species is unique in the genus due to its being almost fully evergreen. Its leaves are quite large and up to 4 in (10 cm) long and are a lovely coppery-pink while young. Its largish pink bell flowers are thick and waxy in texture and the shrub will grow to 10 ft (3 m) or so. This is probably the rarest species and is only found in small areas of southeastern China and Hong Kong. It is the least frost-hardy species. ZONES 8–10.

ENSETE

At one time the 7 species of this remarkable genus of gigantic tropical herbs were included in the banana genus *Musa*, of which they are undoubtedly the closest relatives. They are native to tropical Africa and Asia and have a non-branching underground stem, resulting in only a single, trunk-like false stem being produced by the plant. The flowering stem grows through the middle of the crown of large spreading leaves, producing a pendulous spike of flowers half-hidden among large bracts. After the small banana-like fruits mature the whole plant dies. They make dramatic if short-lived ornamentals.
CULTIVATION: Frost-tender, they should be grown in full sun or part-shade in a rich, moist but well-drained soil and given shelter from winds. Propagate from seed in spring; germination can be erratic without a warm seed-bed.

Ensete ventricosum
ABYSSINIAN BANANA, WILD BANANA

Native to tropical Africa, this large leafy perennial to 30 ft (9 m) tall has huge leaves up to 12 ft (3.5 m) long with a bright red midrib. In late spring, flowers surrounded by deep red bracts droop in spikes to 10 ft (3 m) long. The fruit are not edible. ZONES 10–12.

EOMECON
SNOW-POPPY, POPPY OF THE DAWN

The single species in this genus from the woodlands of eastern China is a vigorous rhizomatous perennial with heart-shaped leaves and poppy-like flowers. It has an indefinite spread and grows well as a ground cover on shady banks.
CULTIVATION: This frost-hardy plant needs part-shade and moist but well-drained, humus-rich soil; it can tolerate full sun if kept damp. Propagate from seed or by division in spring. It may be prone to attack by snails and slugs.

Eomecon chionantha

This rhizomatous plant bears its 1–2 in (2.5–5 cm) wide, pure white flowers from late spring to summer. It has dull green, 4 in (10 cm) wide, toothed, almost circular leaves and grows to a height of 12 in (30 cm). ZONES 7–10.

EPACRIS

This genus of heath-like shrubs contains 38 species from Australia and New Zealand. They are wiry-stemmed evergreens with small, crowded, sometimes prickly leaves and tubular or star-shaped flowers. Those with tubular flowers are reminiscent of the showy southern African ericas. Cultivated species may grow to around 5 ft (1.5 m) high but are usually clipped back to keep them tidy.
CULTIVATION: They thrive in moist, slightly acidic, well-drained soil in sun or part-shade. They will tolerate occasional light frosts, but prefer a warm-temperate climate. Propagate from seed in spring or from cuttings in summer.

Epacris impressa

Native to southeastern mainland Australia and Tasmania, this species has wiry stems that arch up from the base of the plant and small, pointed, deep green leaves. From late winter, 1 in (25 mm) tubular flowers in 4–8 in (10–20 cm) terminal spikes develop. They range from white through light pink to reddish purple. ZONES 9–10.

Epacris longiflora

This species from eastern Australia blooms in spring and summer and has $1\frac{1}{2}$ in (35 mm) red tubular flowers with white tips. The pendulous blooms hang from the undersides of the stems and may occur in such profusion that the branches bend under their weight. The $\frac{1}{2}$ in (12 mm), roughly diamond-shaped leaves have sharp tips. ZONES 9–11.

EPHEDRA
JOINT-FIR, MORMON-TEA

Ephedra is a genus of around 40 species of gymnosperms from southern Europe, North Africa, temperate Asia and the Americas. They show no close relationship with other major plant groups and are presumed to be an evolutionary dead end. These near-leafless shrubs form a mass of slim, dull green, jointed stems—such as those of ***Ephedra californica***—and are tolerant of dry conditions. Tiny scale-like leaves are present for a brief period after rain. They do not produce true flowers but have separate male and female, yellow, flower-like cones

Epacris impressa

Ensete ventricosum

Epacris longiflora

Enkianthus perulatus

(strobili) that are usually followed by berry-like fruits. This genus is best known for its association with ephedrine, used as an allergy and asthma treatment, a stimulant and a metabolic accelerator. Some herbal extracts of ephedrine are known as Ma Huang or Mormon tea.

CULTIVATION: Very frost hardy to marginally frost hardy, they demand a light, stony or sandy soil with good drainage and full sun. No pests or diseases are known. Propagate from seed.

Ephedra americana var. *andina*

syn. *Ephedra chilensis*

This variety is native to the Andes mountain range, from Ecuador to Patagonia, and is usually a sprawling shrub to 8 ft (2.4 m), although it is sometimes a small tree to 12 ft (3.5 m) high. The young shoots are green and finely ridged. The leaves when present are small, no more than ¼ in (6 mm). Its berries are vivid red to orange and up to ½ in (12 mm) long. **ZONES 6–9.**

Ephedra equisetina

Ephedra major subsp. *procera*

Ephedra distachya

Found from southern Europe to Siberia, this shrub often has a sprawling growth habit and is usually less than 3 ft (1 m) high. The stems are bluish green and sprout from rhizome-like roots. The tiny cones develop into very small, globose, red fruit. **ZONES 4–9.**

Ephedra equisetina

This species makes an upright shrub to 6 ft (1.8 m) with bright green branches. It is native from Turkestan to Mongolia and northern China. It has quite large berries for this genus, red with the seed only slightly exserted. **ZONES 4–9.**

Ephedra gerardiana

This species, native to China and the Himalayas, can be a tiny creeping shrub as low as 2 in (5 cm) in height, although it can be found up to 24 in (60 cm) high with a spread of up to 10 ft (3 m). The fruit are red and to ¼ in (6 mm) long. **ZONES 7–10.**

Ephedra major subsp. *procera*

This is an erect, wiry shrub to 6 ft (1.8 m) in height ranging from the Mediterranean to the Himalayas. Its smooth branches support small red or sometimes yellow berries up to ½ in (12 mm) long. Its tiny leaves are scale-like and opposite. **ZONES 6–10.**

× *EPICACTUS*

This name, applied to many hundreds of cactus hybrids with flattened stems and large, brightly colored flowers, is used more as a matter of horticultural convenience than in the precise sense of a hybrid between 2 specified genera. What they have in common is that an *Epiphyllum* is one of the parents: other parent genera include *Echinopsis*, *Heliocereus* and *Nopalxochia*, though several generations of crossing are generally involved, making the original parentage almost impossible to pin down. The plants are semi-epiphytic, mostly only 12–24 in (30–60 cm) high, with a trailing habit. The large flowers, borne in spring and early summer, are basically funnel-shaped and come in a wide range of colors, from white to yellow, pink, orange, red or rosy purple. A few are night blooming and fragrant, but most are day bloomers.

Ephedra gerardiana

× *Epicactus* 'Bridesmaid'

Ephedra californica

Ephedra distachya

Ephedra americana var. *andina*

Ephedra americana var. *andina*

CULTIVATION: Frost tender, they are nearly always grown in pots or baskets and require indoor or greenhouse conditions except in tropical or subtropical climates. They need a coarse, open mixture and strong light for flower production. Feed and water plants freely as soon as buds appear, reducing the amount of water in winter but never allowing plants to dry out completely. Propagate from cuttings.

× *Epicactus* 'Ackermannii'

syns *Epiphyllum ackermanii*, *Nopalxochia ackermannii*

This freely branching cactus grows up to 12 in (30 cm) tall with a spread of around 24 in (60 cm). Its succulent, arching stems are up to 18 in (45 cm) long with notched margins. Bright red, trumpet-shaped flowers arise from these notches from spring to summer. **ZONES 10–12.**

× *Epicactus* 'Ackermannii'

× *Epicactus* 'Bridesmaid'

This pendulous cultivar has flattened stems over 24 in (60 cm) in length. Its leaves have wavy edges. In early to mid-spring, flower buds appear along the leaves, opening into large, lightly fragrant mauve-pink flowers. **ZONES 10–12.**

× *Epicactus* 'Deutsche Kaiserin'

syns *Epiphyllum* 'Deutsche Kaiserin', *Nopalxochia phyllanthoides* 'Deutsche Kaiserin'

This semi-erect epiphytic cactus grows up to 24 in (60 cm) and spreads to around 3 ft (1 m). The fleshy, vivid green, pendulous stems have wavy margins. Numerous pink, bell-shaped flowers with white centers bloom in spring. **ZONES 10–12.**

EPIDENDRUM

This is one of the largest of the orchid genera with about 1,000 species recognized, though in recent years several genera including *Encyclia* have been split from it. The genus is variable, with some species having cane-like stems and others having stout pseudobulbs. They range through the Americas from Florida to Argentina at a variety of altitudes and in habitats ranging from rainforests to rocky, arid hills.

CULTIVATION: Epidendrums thrive outdoors in a warm, frost-free climate in sun or light shade; in colder climates they need the protection of a sunny room or greenhouse. Water and fertilize plants from spring to fall (autumn). Propagate by division or by removing rooted offsets.

Epidendrum ibaguense
syn. *Epidendrum radicans*
CRUCIFIX ORCHID

This common species from Mexico to Colombia has long, slender, cylindrical stems to over 3 ft (1 m) long with short leathery leaves along most of their length. The orange, red or mauve flowers, which can appear at any time of year, are only about 1 in (25 mm) wide, but each flower stem will have up to 20 open at any one time. In cooler climates, it should be grown in a greenhouse and given strong light. The common name is inspired by the shape of the labellum, which looks like a tiny golden cross standing in the center of each flower. **ZONES 9–12.**

Epidendrum 'Joseph Lii'

Like many of the hybrid epidendrums, 'Joseph Lii' has bigger individual blooms than the parent species, in this case a brilliant fiery orange. This hybrid grows to around 3 ft (1 m) tall. **ZONES 10–12.**

Epidendrum pseudepidendrum

Admired for their striking and unusual colors, the flowers of this species arch gracefully from narrow, 3 ft (1 m) high pseudobulbs. The bright green, 2 in (5 cm) wide flowers are in clusters of up to 6, have a bright orange lip, and are produced from summer to fall (autumn). It is from low altitude regions in Costa Rica and Panama. **ZONES 10–12.**

EPILOBIUM
syns *Chamaenerion*
WILLOW HERB

This is a large genus of about 200 species of annuals, biennials, perennials and subshrubs in the evening primrose family, widely distributed throughout the temperate and cold zones of both hemispheres. Most species are invasive, but some are valued in cultivation for their pretty deep pink or white flowers

Epimedium alpinum

Epimedium davidii

Epimedium acuminatum

produced over a long period from summer to fall (autumn).
CULTIVATION: Plant in sun or shade in moist, well-drained soil. They are mostly quite frost hardy. Remove spent flowers to prevent seeding. Propagate from seed in spring or fall, or from cuttings.

Epilobium angustifolium
syn. *Chamaenerion angustifolium*
FIREWEED, ROSE BAY WILLOW HERB

This is a tall, vigorous perennial to 5 ft (1.5 m) found throughout the northern and mountainous parts of Eurasia and North America, most widespread in areas that have been recently burned or logged. Drifts of rose-pink flowering spikes are produced in late summer. It will spread indefinitely unless confined by pruning or containing the root system and self-seeds freely. **ZONES 2–9.**

Epilobium latifolium
RIVER BEAUTY

This perennial species from northern Eurasia and North America grows to 18 in (45 cm) from spreading rhizomes. The lance-shaped leaves are dull blue-green and the pink or white funnel-shaped flowers occur from mid-summer to early fall (autumn). **ZONES 5–9.**

Epilobium nummularifolium

This creeping perennial, native to New Zealand, grows on sandy riverbanks and in boggy ground. The leaves are tiny, shining and coppery colored and the tiny white flowers are borne on about 2 in (5 cm) stems in spring and summer. Of a creeping, mat-forming habit, it grows 1–1½ in (25–35 mm) high with a spread of 3 ft (1 m) or more. **ZONES 7–9.**

EPIMEDIUM
BARRENWORT

This genus of about 40 species comes mainly from temperate Asia with a few species extending to the Mediterranean.

Epimedium diphyllum

Epidendrum 'Joseph Lii'

Epidendrum ibaguense

Epidendrum pseudepidendrum

Among the most useful low-growing perennials for shady situations, the barrenworts produce elegant foliage, sometimes evergreen, the compound leaves composed of heart-shaped leaflets. Delightful sprays of delicate, often spurred flowers appear in late spring or early summer just above the foliage. Slowly spreading to form a broad mound or mat, they serve well as ground covers in open woodland or in the foreground of borders and rockeries.
CULTIVATION: Frost hardy, most species are tolerant of dry conditions, especially in the shade. All prefer woodland conditions and well-drained soil. Old leaves are best cut back in early spring to better display the new foliage and flowers. Propagate from ripe seed or by division in fall (autumn).

Epimedium acuminatum

The flowers of this clump-forming plant to 12 in (30 cm) high from western and central China can be pale purple or pink and up to 1½ in (35 mm) across. Its attractive leaflets are on stems up to 18 in (45 cm) long and are a reddish tone while young. **ZONES 7–9.**

Epimedium alpinum

An evergreen, low-growing perennial from southern Europe, this plant makes a good ground cover under azaleas and rhododendrons. The finely toothed, glossy leaves are bronze-red when young, turning to mid-green with age. In spring it bears racemes of pendent yellow and crimson flowers. It grows to a height of 10 in (25 cm) and spread of 12 in (30 cm). It prefers cooler climates. **ZONES 5–9.**

Epilobium angustifolium

Epimedium × *cantabrigiense*

This rhizomatous hybrid between *Epimedium alpinum* and *E. pubigerum* bears profuse brownish pink and yellow flowers in spring. Growing to a height and spread of 24 in (60 cm), its leaves are divided into 7 to 17 hairy leaflets. **ZONES 7–9.**

Epimedium davidii

This species from China is a tufted plant with stems to 12 in (30 cm) high. The foliage is coppery when young, becoming a soft green later. It has yellow flowers with long curved spurs from mid-spring to early summer. **ZONES 6–9.**

Epimedium diphyllum

From Japan, this dainty semi-evergreen plant to 12 in (30 cm) tall and wide has leaves divided into 2 leaflets. The small, bell-shaped, pure white, spurless flowers are borne in spring. Purple flowering forms are also known. **ZONES 5–9.**

Epimedium grandiflorum

Epimedium × versicolor

Epimedium perralderianum

Epimedium grandiflorum
syn. *Epimedium macranthum*
BISHOP'S HAT, LONGSPUR EPIMEDIUM

This species from northern China, Korea and Japan is deciduous, except in mild climates. It has toothed leaflets often edged with red. Spidery pink or purple flowers with white spurs are held above the foliage on 12 in (30 cm) slender stems in spring. It is best displayed as a clump rather than as a ground cover. **'Rose Queen'** bears clusters of cup-shaped rose-pink flowers with long, white-tipped spurs. **'White Queen'** has large pure white flowers. **ZONES 4–9.**

Epimedium × perralchicum

This hybrid between *Epimedium pinnatum* subsp. *colchicum* and *E. perralderianum* was found in Wisley Gardens, England, where both parents were growing together. It grows to 18 in (45 cm) tall and has evergreen, spiny-edged leaflets up to 3 in (8 cm) long. Bright yellow flowers with short brown spurs are borne in spring. **'Fröhnleiten'** has 1 in (25 mm) wide flowers and elongated leaflets. **ZONES 6–9.**

Epimedium × rubrum

Epimedium × versicolor 'Sulphureum'

Epimedium perralderianum

Native to Algeria, this species forms a carpet of large, glossy green leaves about 12 in (30 cm) high. Small, bright yellow flowers are borne on thin, wiry stems in early spring. As with all epimediums, it is best to cut off the old foliage by late winter so the flowers can be seen at their best. **ZONES 7–9.**

Epimedium pinnatum

Native to northeastern Turkey, this carpeting perennial grows to about 12 in (30 cm) high and wide. The leaflets are 3 in (8 cm) long and are somewhat leathery, evergreen and with spiny edges. The bright yellow flowers with purplish brown spurs are produced in late spring and early summer. ***Epimedium pinnatum* subsp. *colchicum***, the Persian epimedium, has showy panicles of larger, yellow flowers with short brown spurs. **ZONES 6–9.**

Epimedium × rubrum
RED BARRENWORT

This hybrid can be variable, but generally has spiny leaves that are strikingly veined in red. Low mounds are topped by 12 in (30 cm) stems with crimson and white, 1 in (25 mm) wide flowers in spring. It can be used as a ground cover. **ZONES 4–9.**

Epimedium × versicolor

This hybrid of *Epimedium grandiflorum* and *E. pinnatum* is the best known of the epimediums. It is a carpeting perennial to 12 in (30 cm) high and wide. The green, heart-shaped leaves are tinted reddish when young. Clusters of pendent pink and yellow flowers with red spurs are produced in spring. **'Sulphureum'** has sulfur-yellow flowers and reddish bronze-tinted young foliage. As summer advances it turns green, then russet again in fall (autumn). **ZONES 5–9.**

Epimedium × warleyense

This is a spreading perennial to 18 in (45 cm) high and 30 in (75 cm) wide. It works well in a woodland garden and produces beautiful flowers that combine coppery red with yellow centers. The leaves are spiny and semi-evergreen. It is one of the best hybrid epimediums. **ZONES 4–9.**

Epimedium × youngianum

This hybrid between *Epimedium diphyllum* and *E. grandiflorum* is possibly of wild origin. It forms attractive, neat clumps 18 in (45 cm) high and 30 in (75 cm) wide. The leaves can have up to 9 leaflets and are tinted red in spring and fall (autumn). The flowers come in colors varying from white through to pink-mauve and may have spurs or may not. **'Niveum'** is a lovely, white-flowered form with bronze-tinged foliage in spring. **'Roseum'** (syn. 'Lilacinum') has soft pink-mauve flowers. **ZONES 5–9.**

EPIPACTIS
HELLEBORINES

This orchid genus of 24 species extends from Europe south to Ethiopia, through northern parts of Asia to Japan and to northern America. The plants are terrestrial, usually in wet habitats and have fleshy rhizomes and leafy stems often to 3 ft (1 m) tall. The terminal inflorescence bears a few to several colorful flowers which may be up to 2 in (5 cm) across.
CULTIVATION: Species of *Epipactis* can be grown in a bed or rock garden of leafmold and peat in sun or shade. Frost hardy, they should be kept moist throughout the year. Propagate by division in spring.

Epipactis gigantea
CHATTERBOX, STEAM ORCHID

This species grows to about 3 ft (1 m) tall and occurs in the western states of the USA and northern Mexico. It has 4 to 12 leaves clasping the stem and a terminal inflorescence with up to 15 flowers, each about $1\frac{1}{2}$ in (35 mm) across. It commonly grows on the banks of streams and in soaks. **'Serpentine Night'** is an especially attractive cultivar of *Epipactis gigantea*. It flowers in spring and summer. **ZONES 6–10.**

EPIPHYLLUM
ORCHID CACTUS

This genus from tropical and subtropical regions of the Americas consists of 20 species of epiphytic cacti. They have a shrubby, prostrate or pendent growth habit and are virtually spineless when mature. The much-branched, flattened stems have undulating margins and may be mistaken for leaves. In spring or summer large funnel-shaped flowers arise from the edges of the stems. They may be nocturnal or diurnal.
CULTIVATION: Frost tender, species of *Epiphyllum* require a dry, cool spell during winter, a light, sandy soil and strong light for optimum flowering. These cacti are ideal hanging basket plants, their trailing stems seeming to grow better if the roots are restricted. Propagate from seed in spring and cuttings in summer.

Epiphyllum oxypetalum
BELLE DE NUIT

Ranging from Mexico to Brazil, this popular species has an upright growth habit to 6 ft (1.8 m) in height. Its multiple stems are up to 4 in (10 cm) wide, tapering to their bases and arching in maturity. The nocturnal, 6 in (15 cm) wide, white flowers have long, slightly curved tubes. They are intensely fragrant. **ZONES 10–12.**

Epimedium × youngianum

Epimedium × youngianum 'Niveum'

Epimedium pinnatum

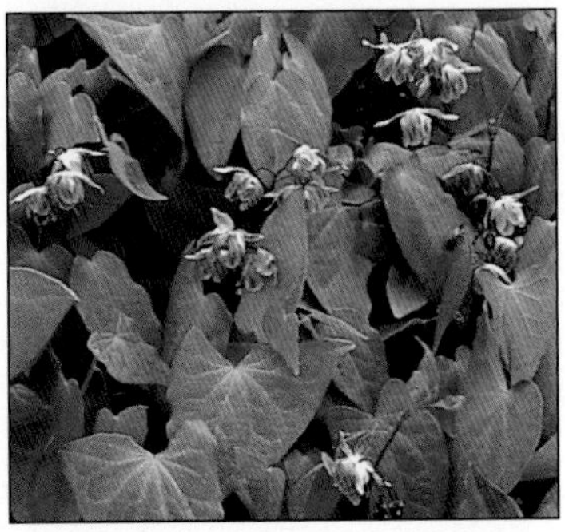

Epimedium × youngianum 'Roseum'

EPIPREMNUM

This is a genus of 8 species of evergreen climbing plants from tropical areas of Southeast Asia and the western Pacific. Cultivated for their attractive foliage, they climb by using adhesive aerial roots and can reach great heights in forests. In the home or greenhouse they are easily pruned at any time to control growth. The foliage goes through both juvenile and adult forms and adult leaves of some species can be up to 24 in (60 cm) long. They are usually somewhat heart-shaped. They rarely flower until they produce adult foliage so don't often bloom in non-tropical areas.
CULTIVATION: Frost tender, most species are easy to grow indoors in bright, indirect light. Grow in a good, moisture-retentive potting mix. Water regularly during spring and summer, less in winter. Provide the support of a moss pole, and to encourage branching pinch out shoot tips. Propagate from cuttings or by layering.

Epipremnum pictum 'Argyraeum'
syn. *Scindapsus pictus* 'Argyraeus'
SILVER VINE

This is a slow-growing, woody stemmed, root climber to 10 ft (3 m) or more. It is cultivated for its satiny dark green juvenile leaves which are heart-shaped with irregular silver spots. **ZONES 10–12.**

Epipremnum pinnatum
syn. *Raphidophora pinnata*

Up to 60 ft (18 m) tall in its native forests from Southeast Asia to tropical Australia, this species can be kept to a manageable size in cultivation. The juvenile leaves are usually entire, although they are sometimes perforated or lobed. The perforated, adult leaves are up to 3 ft (1 m) long by 18 in (45 cm) wide and often have translucent spots along the midrib. **'Aureum'** (syns *Epipremnum aureum, Pothos aureus, Rhaphidophora aurea, Scindapsus aureus*), devil's ivy or pothos, has apple-green, heart-shaped leaves marbled with creamy white or gold. **ZONES 10–12.**

EPISCIA

From the jungles of tropical America and the West Indies, the 6 species of this genus are related to the African violet and make ideal plants for hanging baskets. Long runners bear tufts of ornamental leaves, which are hairy and produced in whorls or rosettes; they cascade down the sides of the pot or basket, and given the right conditions produce long-lasting, colorful flowers. The flowers, either solitary or in small racemes, have 5 lobes and appear from spring to fall (autumn).
CULTIVATION: Plant in African violet mix or porous, peaty, indoor plant mix in bright indirect light. Poor light may result in few flowers. They require constant warmth and humidity, so are well suited to a sunny bathroom or conservatory. Keep moist at all times, but take care not to over-water as it leads to rotting. Pinch back stems after flowering to encourage branching, and repot every year in spring. Propagate in summer by laying runners in compost, from cuttings or by division.

Episcia cupreata
FLAME VIOLET

This evergreen creeper, native to northern South America, grows to a height of about 6 in (15 cm). The attractive, felted, bronze leaves have silver veins. It intermittently produces tubular, scarlet flowers with yellow centers. **'Mosaica'** has dark, almost black leaves with an embossed appearance. **ZONES 10–12.**

Episcia dianthiflora
LACE FLOWER VINE

A native of Central America and Mexico, this evergreen, low-creeping perennial has rooting stems that provide an easy means of propagation. Its small leaves, to 2 in (5 cm) long, are dark green often with red veins. Its pure white flowers have purple spotting at the base and inside the spur. The edges of the petals are deeply and attractively fringed. **ZONES 10–12.**

Episcia 'Pink Brocade'

The runners of this evergreen, creeping perennial bear deep copper-green leaves variegated in silver and pink. Small pink flowers appear in summer but not freely. It reaches a height of 4 in (10 cm) with an indefinite spread. **ZONES 10–12.**

EPITHELANTHA

The striking miniature cacti in this genus from northern Mexico and southwestern USA are sometimes regarded as a single species consisting of 3 varieties, or alternatively 3 separate species. Closely related to *Mammillaria*, they are characterized by a dense covering of short white spines, around the tops of the numerous, spirally arranged tubercles. The spines are all in the same plane and may overlap with spines of adjacent tubercles, forming a smooth white coating. In spring and summer a few small white, pink or pale orange flowers emerge from the apex of the plant. Epithelanthas sometimes remain solitary for many years, but some plants can produce basal offsets and build up into mounds of many small globes.
CULTIVATION: Grow in very gritty, open soil mix with perfect drainage, full sun and a dry atmosphere. Frost tender, they do best under glass in cooler areas. Propagate from seed or offsets or by grafting.

Epithelantha micromeris
BUTTON CACTUS

This is a small, slow-growing, spherical cactus to 2 in (5 cm) high with tiny, overlapping, white spines completely covering the gray-green stem. Pale pink flowers are produced from the felty crown in summer. **ZONES 10–12.**

EQUISETUM
HORSETAIL, SCOUR RUSH

Some 25 species of rush-like perennials belong to this ancient group of plants, distantly related to the ferns. They occur mainly in the northern hemisphere although a few cross the Equator to Africa and South America. The cylindrical stems are usually erect and may be unbranched or have whorled branches at the nodes. They rarely exceed 10 ft (3 m) tall and grow from vigorous creeping rhizomes. Although quite ornamental, their use in gardens is limited because they can become invasive and are difficult to eradicate. Horsetails have been used since Roman times to scour pots and medically as a general tonic and an astringent.
CULTIVATION: Most species are very frost hardy. Grow plants in containers and make sure the rhizomes don't escape out the drainage holes. Give them a sunny aspect and plenty of water. Propagation is usually by division.

Equisetum hyemale
ROUGH HORSETAIL

This species, native to both Eurasia and North America, is the one once used to scour pots and pans. Its stems can reach 5 ft (1.5 m) tall and are usually unbranched. **ZONES 5–10.**

Equisetum scirpoides
DWARF SCOURING RUSH

This is a fairly small species to 6 in (15 cm) or so tall from Eurasia, Greenland and North America. Its stems are very fine and not usually branched, with 3, or rarely, 4 ridges. This is not a very ornamental species. **ZONES 2–9.**

Equisetum trachyodon

Similar to *Equisetum hyemale* but not as tall, this horsetail is also unbranched. It makes an attractive potted specimen and needs shade during the hottest hours. **ZONES 5–9.**

ERANTHEMUM

This genus of around 30 species of tropical Asian shrubs and subshrubs in the acanthus family are grown for their attractive pink or blue flowers or in some cases for their decorative foliage. They have simple, smooth-edged leaves

Episcia dianthiflora

Epipremnum pinnatum 'Aureum'

Epiphyllum oxypetalum

Equisetum trachyodon

Episcia cupreata 'Mosaica'

arranged in opposite pairs on the branches, and clustered flowers with tubular bases and 5 flat spreading petals. The fruits are small club-shaped capsules that split explosively into two halves.

CULTIVATION: Frost tender, eranthemums are easily grown in tropical and subtropical climates, preferring a sheltered, part-shaded position in good soil and plentiful watering during the growing season. If a more compact shape is desired they can be cut back fairly hard after flowering. Indoors, provide bright, indirect light and water freely in spring and summer, less in winter. Propagate from cuttings in spring.

Eranthemum pulchellum
syn. *Eranthemum nervosum*
BLUE SAGE

This is a colorful evergreen shrub to 4 ft (1.2 m) from tropical India that has naturalized in many other frost-free countries. Its erect stems are well clothed with rich green leaves to 8 in (20 cm) long with conspicuous veins. The flowers, usually produced in winter or early spring, are a violet blue and arranged in dense spikes. The individual blooms have a slender tube with widely flared lobes. **ZONES 10–12.**

Eranthis hyemalis

Eranthemum pulchellum

ERANTHIS
WINTER ACONITE

From Europe and temperate Asia, these 7 species of clump-forming perennials have been grown for centuries and are valued for their ability to naturalize under deciduous trees and their habit of flowering in late winter and early spring. The short-stemmed, yellow, buttercup-like flowers are surrounded by a ruff of green leaves. They mix pleasantly with other early-flowering, bulbous plants.

CULTIVATION: Very frost hardy, grow in full sun or part-shade. Slightly damp conditions during the summer dormancy and an alkaline, well-drained soil are conducive to good growth and plentiful flowers. Propagate from seed in late spring or by division in fall (autumn).

Eranthis cilicica

Native to the Middle East, this species grows on open hillsides in sparse pine forests. The flowers are bright yellow and held close to the ground on 2 in (5 cm) long stalks. They are surrounded by a ruff of finely dissected, glossy leaves. **ZONES 4–9.**

Eranthis hyemalis

Native to Europe, this ground-hugging perennial with knobbly tubers grows to a height of 3 in (8 cm). The yellow, cup-shaped flowers to 1 in (25 mm) across are borne above a ruff of lobed leaves. **ZONES 5–9.**

Eremophila 'Roger's Pink'

Eranthis × *tubergenii* 'Guinea Gold'

This tuberous perennial to 4 in (10 cm) high bears golden flowers above a ruff of bronze-green leaves cut into narrow lobes. **ZONES 5–9.**

ERCILLA

From temperate regions of the Americas, this genus is allied to the inkweeds (*Phytolacca*) and contains only 2 species of evergreen perennial climbers that cling by aerial roots. Plants produce dense spikes of small flowers without petals and have alternate, leathery leaves. Without a strong support to cling to, ercillas will form a ground cover.

CULTIVATION: Marginally frost-hardy, they need full sun or part-shade and fertile, moist but well-drained soil. They should be protected from strong winds and pruned if necessary after flowering. Propagate from cuttings or by layering.

Ercilla volubilis
syns *Bridgesia spicata, Ercilla spicata*

This vigorous species from the Andes of Peru and Chile grows to a height of 30 ft (10 m). With age, it bears numerous spikes of green to purple flowers in spring, followed by small, deep purple berries. It has heart-shaped, shiny deep green leaves with pale veins. **ZONES 8–10.**

EREMOPHILA
EMU BUSH

This is a large, diverse genus of about 200 species of evergreen shrubs and small trees from arid and semi-arid interior regions of mainland Australia. The flowers are conspicuous: arising from the leaf axils on thin stalks, they are tubular at the base and are commonly 2-lipped, the lips and throat mostly spotted. The fruits are like small berries but ripen hard and dry, often flattened and sitting in an enlarged calyx. A number of garden forms are available including **'Roger's Pink'**.

Eremophila maculata

Eremophila glabra 'Murchison River'

CULTIVATION: Marginally frost hardy to frost tender, some species only grow in desert conditions while others adapt well to moister climates. They do best in full sun and well-drained, slightly alkaline soil. They resent summer humidity. Once plants are established, water sparingly or not at all. Prune lightly after flowering to maintain bushiness. Propagate from seed or cuttings in fall (autumn).

Eremophila glabra
COMMON EMU BUSH

This shrub grows to a height of 4 ft (1.2 m) and has an erect, downy, grayish white stem. The linear, lance-shaped leaves to 2 in (5 cm) long may be smooth to densely hairy. The green, yellow or red, tubular, 5-petalled flowers are borne singly in the leaf axils mainly in spring and summer. **'Murchison River'** has beautiful silver-green foliage and scarlet flowers. **ZONES 9–11.**

Eremophila maculata
SPOTTED EMU BUSH

The most commonly grown species, spotted emu bush makes a rounded shrub 3–6 ft (1–1.8 m) high and wide with green to gray-green leaves. Yellow, red, pink or white tubular flowers with recurved petals and spotted throats appear most of the year, especially in winter and spring. **'Aurea'** is a smaller-growing, golden-yellow flowering form with light green leaves. **ZONES 9–11.**

Eremophila polyclada
FLOWERING LIGNUM

This unusual species makes a tangled mound of green branches 3–6 ft (1–1.8 m) high and at least as much in spread, with very narrow, dark shiny green leaves to 2½ in (6 cm) long. It grows in clay soils on flood plains over a large area of eastern and central Australia. The large white tubular flowers with pinkish brown spots on the lower lip appear for most of the year but mainly in spring and fall (autumn). It is a fine ornamental shrub for arid areas. **ZONES 9–11.**

EREMURUS
FOXTAIL LILY, DESERT CANDLE

This is a genus of 50 or so species, all native to the cold, high plains of central and western Asia. Among the most dramatic of early summer perennials, they are mainly clump forming with a rosette of strap-shaped leaves. Their flower spikes, each of which can contain hundreds of flowers in pale shades of white, yellow or pink, rise to well over head height. The foliage is luxuriant but low so the flower stems rise almost naked, which makes them all the more imposing.

CULTIVATION: In the wild these cool- to cold-climate plants are protected from the winter cold by a thick blanket of snow; in milder climates they must be given a winter mulch to ensure the soil does not freeze. The other requirements are sun, a well-drained soil and shelter

Eremophila polyclada

Eremurus × *isabellinus,* Shelford Hybrid

Eremurus aitchisonii

from strong winds. Propagate from fresh seed in fall (autumn) or by careful division after flowering.

Eremurus aitchisonii

syn. *Eremurus elwesii*

From Afghanistan, this is a clump-forming perennial to 6 ft (1.8 m) tall with glossy, narrow, lance-shaped leaves to 24 in (60 cm) long and spikes of pale pink flowers in late spring to early summer. **ZONES 6–9.**

Eremurus himalaicus

This clump-forming, upright perennial from the western Himalayas has strap-shaped basal leaves. Its star-shaped, pure white flowers with long stamens are borne in erect, terminal spikes up to 3 ft (1 m) tall in late spring and early summer. It requires staking. **ZONES 3–9.**

Eremurus × *isabellinus,* Shelford Hybrids

These frost-hardy perennials are grown for their lofty spikes of close-packed flowers, magnificent for floral displays. They produce rosettes of strap-like leaves and in mid-summer each crown yields spikes of bloom with strong stems and hundreds of shallow cup-shaped flowers in a wide range of colors including white, pink, salmon, yellow, apricot and coppery tones. **'Shelford Desert Candle'** is a particularly lovely pure white form. They grow to about 4 ft (1.2 m) in height with a spread of 24 in (60 cm). **ZONES 5–9.**

E. × *isabellinus* 'Shelford Desert Candle'

Eremurus olgae

Fragrant, star-shaped, white flowers tinged with the palest pink appear on this plant on erect spikes in summer. The leaves are green and strap-like. It will reach a height of 5 ft (1.5 m). **ZONES 6–9.**

Eremurus robustus

The tallest of the foxtail lilies, this upright perennial from central Asia flowers profusely in early summer. The individual flowers are smallish stars in palest peach-pink and are produced by the hundreds in spires that can reach nearly 10 ft (3 m) in height. They need to be staked. **ZONES 6–9.**

Eremurus spectabilis

This is a tufted perennial with strap-like, rough-margined, gray-green leaves. In mid-summer it sends up rigid spikes of sulfur-yellow flowers to 4–6 ft (1.2–1.8 m). The individual blooms are star-shaped and ½ in (12 mm) across. This species ranges from Turkey to Pakistan. **ZONES 6–9.**

Eremurus stenophyllus

This species from southwestern or central Asia has tufted basal leaves that are gray-green in color. The flowers are bright yellow and produced on spikes up to 3 ft (1 m) tall. **ZONES 5–9.**

ERICA

HEATH

This large genus is made up of more than 800 species of small-leafed, free-flowering, evergreen shrubs. The vast majority are native to South Africa, but a relatively small number of species occur in Europe and elsewhere in Africa. In Europe, several *Erica* species plus the closely related *Calluna* (heather) dominate moorland vegetation. The Cape heaths from South Africa, often with long, tubular flowers, are fine garden plants in mild-winter climates where summer humidity is low. The European species bear smaller, bell-shaped flowers in a more limited white to deep pink color range but are frost hardy and are very popular garden plants.

CULTIVATION: Most heaths like full sun, well-drained, neutral to acid soil and dislike lime and animal manure. Prune after flowering to keep plants bushy and compact. Propagate from seed or from cuttings in late summer.

Erica australis

Erica arborea

TREE HEATH, BRUYÈRE

The largest of the heaths, this frost-hardy species also has the widest distribution, from the Canary Islands and Portugal right across to Iran and south through the high mountains of Arabia, Ethiopia and equatorial Africa, where it forms mist-shrouded forests of trees 20 ft (6 m) high with stout trunks. It has contorted woody stems, finely fibrous bark and dark green needle-like leaves. It bears masses of small white flowers in spring. **'Alpina'** is less than 6 ft (1.8 m) high, has bright green foliage and white flowers in dense cylindrical racemes. **ZONES 8–10.**

Eremurus robustus

Erica australis

SPANISH HEATH, SOUTHERN HEATH

This marginally frost-hardy, erect shrub to 6 ft (1.8 m) tall and about 3 ft (1 m) wide is native to the western Iberian Peninsula and Morocco. It produces tiny tubular to bell-shaped flowers of a bright magenta-pink in spring and summer. A number of selections have been named, in colors from white to deep pink. The foliage is very fine and dark green. **ZONES 9–10.**

Eremurus spectabilis

Eremurus robustus

Erica arborea 'Alpina'

Erica bauera
BRIDAL HEATH

More cold hardy than some other South African species, the bridal heath also has the most beautiful flowers of all. The waxy tubes are china white to soft rose pink, 1½ in (35 mm) long and narrowed toward the mouth, opening progressively along the erect branches from spring to fall (autumn). It makes a small, slender shrub only about 3 ft (1 m) high and appreciates a sheltered position. **'Alba'** has pure white flowers. **ZONES 9–10.**

Erica bauera 'Alba'

Erica canaliculata
CHANNELLED HEATH, PURPLE HEATH

This is the tallest and most floriferous of the South African ericas grown in frost-free gardens, usually reaching about 6 ft (1.8 m) but much taller in the wild. It has an open growth habit and dark green narrow leaves in whorls of three. The massed bell-shaped, small flowers vary from pale pink to rose purple, with darker anthers protruding from the mouth. They are produced in late winter and early spring. **ZONES 8–10.**

Erica carnea
syn. *Erica herbacea*
WINTER HEATH, SNOW HEATH

From the mountains of central and southern Europe, this frost-hardy species and its numerous cultivars are among the few heaths that will thrive in chalk soils. It forms a low, spreading subshrub usually less than 12 in (30 cm) high with densely crowded branches. Through most of winter and into early spring it produces a fine display of small, urn-shaped, purple-pink flowers with protruding darker stamens. This is an ideal ground cover between taller shrubs or beneath deciduous trees, or in rock gardens. Well-known cultivars include **'December Red'** with purplish pink flowers and **'March Seedling'**, which flowers until late spring. Others are **'Myretoun Ruby'**, with very dark green leaves against bright rose-pink flowers; **'Ruby Glow'** with deep rose-red flowers; **'Springwood Pink'** with a vigorous trailing habit and rose-pink flowers; and **'Springwood White'** with a spreading habit, vigorous growth and white flowers. **ZONES 5–9.**

Erica carnea cultivar

Erica carnea 'Springwood White'

Erica carnea 'March Seedling'

Erica × *darleyensis*

Erica cinerea 'Crimson King'

Erica cinerea 'Kerry Cherry'

Erica casta

This marginally frost-hardy species from the mountains of South Africa's Cape Province has recently come into cultivation. It is already popular for its lavish late spring flowers, which vary in color from white to deep purple-pink. It grows to about 18 in (45 cm) tall and makes a very pretty pot plant. **ZONES 9–10.**

Erica casta

Erica cerinthoides
SCARLET HEATH, FIRE HEATH

This South African species is one of the showiest of all ericas, with bright orange-scarlet flowers about 1½ in (35 mm) long, clustered at the ends of long, straight or slightly arching branches through winter and spring. There are also forms with white, pink and crimson flowers. It is no more than 3 ft (1 m) high and wide. **ZONES 9–10.**

Erica cerinthoides

Erica ciliaris
DORSET HEATH

This is a fully frost-hardy, small, spreading shrub to 30 in (75 cm) tall from southwestern Europe, southwestern England and Ireland. The flowers that are produced from mid-summer to mid-fall (mid-autumn) are urn-shaped and usually deep pink. Many selections have been made of this species that include white to pink flowers as well as gold foliage. **ZONES 7–9.**

Erica × *darleyensis* 'Darley Dale'

Erica × *darleyensis* 'Epe'

Erica × *darleyensis* 'Dunwood Splendour'

Erica × *darleyensis* 'White Perfection'

Erica doliiformis

Erica erigena 'Mrs Parris White'

Erica erigena 'W. T. Rackliff'

Erica cinerea
BELL HEATHER, TWISTED HEATH

Native throughout western Europe including the British Isles, the bell heather is one of the prettiest of the frost-hardy heaths. Its small, crowded, rose-pink bells are produced over a long season from early summer to early fall (autumn). Low and spreading, the stiff ends of the twisted branches ascend to 12–18 in (30–45 cm) high. Bell heather dislikes hot summer weather, which scorches its foliage and may kill the plant. There are many named cultivars, varying chiefly in flower color from white to rich rose purple; some also have golden or coppery foliage. **'Kerry Cherry'** has deep pink flowers, **'Crimson King'** is crimson; **'Golden Drop'** has summer foliage gold with coppery tints, turning red in winter. ZONES 5–9.

Erica erigena 'Hibernica'

Erica formosa

Erica erigena 'Alba Compacta'

Erica × darleyensis
DARLEY DALE HEATH

Erica × darleyensis is a hybrid of the two frost-hardy species *Erica erigena* and *E. carnea* and has proved to be a valuable garden plant. It forms a dense, bushy shrub to 24 in (60 cm) high with dark green foliage, and from late fall (autumn) through spring is covered in crowded, short spikes of cylindrical, pale rose flowers with protruding, darker stamens. It tolerates chalk soils. The original clone is now known as **'Darley Dale'** but others, with flowers ranging from white to deep pink, are listed: **'Dunwood Splendour'** spreads widely and produces a spectacular display of mauve-pink flowers; **'Epe'** is relatively low growing with white flowers tinged pink; **'George Rendall'** is a compact grower with purplish pink flowers throughout winter; **'Jack H. Brummage'** has golden to red-tinted winter foliage and purplish pink flowers; and **'White Perfection'** has bright green foliage and pure white flowers. ZONES 6–9.

Erica grandiflora

Erica erigena 'Ewan Jones'

Erica erigena 'Hibernica Alba'

Erica doliiformis
syn. *Erica blanda*

This native of South Africa is a small upright shrub to 12 in (30 cm) high with crowded, hairy tipped leaves and umbels of tubular rose-pink flowers. ZONES 9–10.

Erica erigena
syns *Erica hibernica, E. mediterranea*
IRISH HEATH, MEDITERRANEAN HEATH

This western European species has deep green foliage and massed, urn-shaped, bright pink flowers in winter and spring. It grows to 6 ft (1.8 m) high and 3 ft (1 m) wide. Cultivars include **'Alba Compacta'**, a compact, white-flowered form; **'Ewan Jones'**, a vigorous grower with mauve-pink flowers set against dark green leaves; **'Hibernica'** with shell-pink flowers; **'Hibernica Alba'**, a spectacular white-flowered form growing about 3 ft (1 m) tall. **'Irish Dusk'** with rose-pink flowers and gray-green leaves; **'Mrs Parris Lavender'** an upright form to 18 in (45 cm) tall with mauve flowers; **'Mrs Parris White'**, an albino form of the

Erica erigena 'Mrs Parris Lavender'

Erica erigena 'Superba'

previous cultivar; **'Silver Bells'** with white, scented flowers; **'Superba'** with pale pink, perfumed flowers; and **'W. T. Rackliff'**, a compact grower with white flowers. ZONES 7–9.

Erica formosa

This is an erect, much-branched shrub to 3 ft (1 m) from South Africa with fine leaves arranged in whorls of three. The pendent flowers, also arranged in 3s and produced from winter into early summer, are small, fluted, pure white and slightly sticky to the touch. ZONES 9–10.

Erica grandiflora
LARGE ORANGE HEATH

Occurring naturally on mountain slopes of western Cape Province in South Africa, this sturdy, upright shrub grows to 3 ft (1 m) tall and wide. The attractive orange, tubular flowers, borne in midsummer, are up to 1½ in (35 mm) long and are slightly sticky. The leaves are stiff and needle-like. It is marginally frost hardy. ZONES 9–10.

Erica perspicua

Erica regia

Erica peziza

Erica mammosa

Erica mammosa 'Jubilee'

Erica linnaeoides

Erica linnaeoides

This South African species grows to no more than 3 ft (1 m) tall and is noteworthy for its delicate color. Like all its tribe, it flowers in early spring and makes a fine pot plant. Give it a light trim when the flowers are finished to keep it compact. **ZONES 9–10.**

Erica lusitanica
PORTUGUESE HEATH, SPANISH HEATH

From Portugal, Spain and France, this erect shrub, seldom more than 6 ft (1.8 m) high, has extremely fine, delicate, mid-green foliage. Through winter it bears densely massed, small, tubular flowers, dull pink in bud but opening white flushed pale pink, the pink soon disappearing. This species is lime tolerant but not very frost hardy. It has become naturalized in the USA, Australia and New Zealand. **ZONES 8–10.**

Erica mackaiana
syns *Erica crawfordii, E. mackaii, E. mackayana*
MACKAY'S HEATH

This neat little shrub from Spain and Ireland grows to about 18 in (45 cm) tall and 30 in (75 cm) wide. Its branches are hairy while young and its dark green leaves are arranged in whorls of four. The flowers are usually pink and produced in terminal clusters from summer to early fall (autumn), although many different colors have been selected and named. **'Galicia'** grows less than 8 in (20 cm) tall and has mauve-pink flowers that open from orange buds; **'Maura'** is a small form to 6 in (15 cm) tall with gray-green foliage and semi-double purple flowers; **'Shining Light'** grows to 10 in (25 cm) tall by 24 in (60 cm) wide and has pure white flowers. **ZONES 6–9.**

Erica mammosa
RED SIGNAL HEATH

This South African species has bright green foliage and massed terminal clusters of red to deep pink tubular flowers, 1 in (25 mm) long, in spring. It grows to about 3 ft (1 m) high and 18 in (45 cm) wide. **'Coccinea'** is a particularly heavy-flowering cultivar, while **'Jubilee'** has pink flowers. **ZONES 9–10.**

Erica melanthera

This species from South Africa has small, bell-shaped flowers reminiscent of the European ericas. It is a bushy shrub 3 ft (1 m) high and wide, with bright green foliage that from late fall (autumn) disappears beneath the pinkish purple flowers. This species is widely grown as a cut flower. **ZONES 9–10.**

Erica mackaiana 'Shining Light'

Erica perspicua
PRINCE OF WALES HEATH

This is a much-branched, upright shrub from South Africa to 6 ft (1.8 m). The soft leaves are produced in whorls of three or four. Its tubular flowers stick straight out from the branches and can be white, pale pink tipped white, pink, deep mauve or red and white. It usually flowers from fall (autumn) into winter and likes a moist soil. **ZONES 9–10.**

Erica peziza
KAPOKKIE HEATH

This shrub is native to the western Cape area of South Africa and makes a bushy shrub to 24 in (60 cm) high and wide. Its leaves are mid-green and its cup-shaped, spring flowers are pure white and covered with downy hairs. **ZONES 9–10.**

Erica quadrangularis

This compact bushy shrub grows to 24 in (60 cm) tall and 18 in (45 cm) wide. The cup-shaped flowers range in color from white through pink to red and are produced from late winter into summer. Its mid-green leaves are arranged in whorls of four. Native to the western Cape region of South Africa, this species is frost tender. **ZONE 10.**

Erica regia
ELIM HEATH

This shrub from southern parts of South Africa's Cape Province is widely cultivated. It grows to about 6 ft (1.8 m) high and 3 ft (1 m) wide, is wind resistant and tolerates some frost. The flowers, which

Erica lusitanica

Erica mackaiana 'Galicia'

Erica mackaiana 'Maura'

Eucalyptus caesia subsp. *magna*

leaves that tend to hang vertically so the foliage provides only partial shade; the leaves contain aromatic oil in small translucent cavities, eucalyptus oil being an important product of certain species. The nectar-rich flowers are abundant, mostly white, but yellow, pink or red in a minority of species, with the massed stamens the most conspicuous part. Petals and sepals are fused into a cap-like structure (operculum) that is shed as the stamens unfold; the fruits are woody capsules, mostly quite small. The bark of many eucalypts is smooth and shed annually, and the new and old bark can make a colorful contrast while this is happening. Other groups of eucalypts have persistent bark of varying texture, examples being the stringybark and ironbark groups. In cooler countries eucalypts are often seen only as cut foliage, sold by florists; this foliage is the juvenile type characteristic of many species, with rounded, stalkless, waxy-bluish leaves, and mostly gives way to adult leaves that are narrow, stalked, and greener. A distinctive growth form seen in many of the smaller-growing eucalypts is what Australians call a 'mallee', in which a large woody tuber gives rise to a number of slender trunks; it is characteristic of many species, but seedling plants may not display this feature in cultivation.

A recent development in the botanical study of eucalypts is the splitting off of 112 species into the newly named genus *Corymbia*, consisting mainly of the 'bloodwoods'. Only a small number of cultivated species are affected by this reclassification—in this book they are found under *Corymbia,* with the old *Eucalyptus* botanical name indicated as a synonym.

CULTIVATION: There are species to suit most climates except those where winter temperatures fall below about 10°F (−12°C), but the great majority of species will tolerate only the lightest frosts. Drought hardiness also varies greatly, some species requiring fairly moist conditions. With rare exceptions eucalypts are grown from seed, which germinates freely. They should be planted out into the ground when no more than 18 in (45 cm) high, ensuring that roots have not coiled in the container at any stage. They seldom survive transplanting, and are not long-lived as container plants. They prefer full sun at all stages of growth.

Eucalyptus brevifolia
SNAPPY GUM

From the gravel plains, ridges and woodlands of northwestern Australia, the snappy gum grows to 40 ft (12 m) and has blue-green adult foliage. The attractive bark is white with darker patches that are shed in flakes. **ZONES 11–12.**

Eucalyptus caesia

This graceful, weeping tree that grows to 25 ft (8 m) bears pendent clusters of pink blossoms. The red-brown bark peels away to reveal a green trunk. ***Eucalyptus caesia* subsp. *magna*** reaches about 15 ft (4.5 m) with silver-gray foliage and larger red flowers. **ZONES 9–11.**

Eucalyptus calycogona
SQUARE-FRUITED MALLEE

This shrubby small tree found on poor soils over much of southern Australia grows to around 25 ft (8 m) tall. The smooth gray bark often sheds in strips or flakes. The narrow adult leaves are up to 4 in (10 cm) long. Small flowers open in spring and summer. **ZONES 9–11.**

Eucalyptus camaldulensis
RIVER RED GUM

The river red gum can grow up to 150 ft (45 m) tall with a generous spread and trunk to 12 ft (3.5 m) in diameter. It is valued for its impressive appearance. Occurring along watercourses over much of inland Australia, it is an invaluable shade and shelter tree able to cope with extended dry periods or waterlogging. It is widely cultivated in warm-climate areas of Africa and Asia. **ZONES 9–12.**

Eucalyptus cinerea
ARGYLE APPLE

From tablelands of southeastern Australia, this eucalypt is familiar to flower arrangers for its silver-blue circular leaves. On some trees these juvenile-type leaves are replaced by sickle-shaped adult leaves, also silver-blue. Rather insignificant cream flowers appear in early summer. It has a somewhat twisted growth habit, reaching 50 ft (15 m) in height. Suited to most well-drained soils, it can be kept pruned. **ZONES 8–11.**

Eucalyptus cladocalyx
SUGAR GUM

Often branching quite low, this fast-growing eucalypt from South Australia reaches 50–100 ft (15–30 m) and usually forms a wide, dense crown. The reddish brown outer bark is shed in patches to reveal the smooth, chalky white new bark. The leaves are dark green and glossy, and the new growths are bronze-pink. The small white flowers are borne in large clusters to make a pleasing display in summer. Sugar gum trees should not be lopped as their coppice branches are brittle at the base. **ZONES 8–10.**

Eucalyptus coccifera
TASMANIAN SNOW GUM

This gum comes from the mountains of Tasmania and due to its high altitude range is one of the most cold-resistant of all eucalypt species. It can grow to 30 ft (9 m) but in the wild at its highest altitudes can often be no more than a tiny gnarled shrub. It has smooth bark, white-gray with yellow and pink toning. Its leaves are stiff and up to 4 in (10 cm) long, and its summer blossoms are white. **ZONES 8–9.**

Eucalyptus cladocalyx

Eucalyptus camaldulensis

E

Eucalyptus curtisii
PLUNKETT MALLEE

This tough little mallee species from southeast Queensland grows to 20 ft (6 m) high, forming a thicket of smooth stems mottled grayish green and white. The narrow leaves are dark green and the yellow buds open in spring in a profusion of pretty white blossoms held in terminal clusters. It makes an excellent low screen. **ZONES 9–12.**

E

Eucalyptus dalrympleana
MOUNTAIN GUM

This species comes from the mountains of southeastern Australia. It can grow 70 ft (21 m) or more tall and has creamy white bark blotched with yellow, pink and olive green (even red in cold climates). Its white flowers are produced in summer and it has narrow, gray-green adult foliage and broader blue-green juvenile leaves. **ZONES 8–9.**

Eucalyptus curtisii

Eucalyptus desmondensis
DESMOND MALLEE

Endemic to the Ravensthorpe Range in the south of Western Australia, this is a slender, willowy, large shrub or small tree that grows to around 15 ft (4.5 m) high. It has powdery white bark and twigs, and 4 in (10 cm) long, narrow adult leaves. The pale yellow flowers appear in large clusters in late summer and are quite showy. **ZONES 9–11.**

Eucalyptus diversicolor
KARRI

An important timber tree from the southwest of Western Australia, the karri can grow to a height of almost 300 ft (90 m) with a massive trunk. It requires fertile, well-drained soil with assured moisture. The smooth, brown-tinted cream or blue-gray bark is shed in irregular patches, and the crown is relatively open atop the straight trunk. **ZONES 9–10.**

Eucalyptus elata
RIVER PEPPERMINT

Sometimes growing to over 100 ft (30 m), this is a fast-growing shade tree for large gardens or farms in temperate regions where the soil is moist but well drained. The lower trunk is covered with rough blackish bark, while the upper trunk and branches are smooth and almost greenish white, blending well with the pendulous, dark gray-green leaves. The creamy white late spring flowers are an attractive feature. **ZONES 9–11.**

Eucalyptus desmondensis

Eucalyptus erythrocorys

Eucalyptus eremophila

Eucalyptus eremophila
TALL SAND MALLEE

Like other mallees, this species from semi-arid areas of Western Australia forms a thick clump about 10 ft (3 m) wide, and its numerous stems, to 30 ft (9 m) tall, are clothed in smooth gray bark. The narrow adult leaves are blue-green. The horn-shaped, yellow or reddish buds open to reveal bright yellow flowers, $1\frac{1}{2}$ in (35 mm) across, which hang from the branches in fluffy clusters through winter and spring. It dislikes humid summers. **ZONES 9–11.**

Eucalyptus erythrocorys
ILLYARRIE, RED-CAP GUM

This Western Australian eucalypt is of the mallee type, a spreading shrub or small tree with thin stems rising from a swollen woody base below ground level. The name *erythrocorys* refers to the red flower cap, which provides an interesting contrast to the yellow flowers in early summer. Growing usually to about 25 ft (8 m), it is suited to warm climates without summer humidity, requiring good drainage. Prune to prevent top-heaviness. **ZONES 9–11.**

Eucalyptus globulus

Eucalyptus globulus
TASMANIAN BLUE GUM

The first eucalypt to be introduced to Europe and North America, this large tree can grow to over 200 ft (60 m), with a trunk to 6 ft (1.8 m) in diameter. The bluish bark is shed in long strips. Juvenile leaves are silvery blue and rectangular, while the adult form is deep green and sickle shaped, to 18 in (45 cm) long. A distinctive feature is the solitary, stalkless flowers in the leaf axils, with broad, wrinkled, bluish bud caps. Occurring naturally in coastal areas of Tasmania and far southern Victoria, it prefers moist conditions. It is used for timber, paper pulp and as a source of eucalyptus oil. **'Compacta'** reaches only 30 ft (10 m) and retains its silvery blue juvenile foliage for some years. **ZONES 8–10.**

Eucalyptus gracilis
YORRELL

Widespread in semi-arid, sandy regions across southern Australia, this tree is commonly 15–25 ft (4.5–8 m) tall. It has rough, flaky bark on the base of the trunk, and smooth, gray to reddish brown bark above. The glossy adult leaves are very narrow and around 3 in (8 cm) long. Tiny cream flowers are followed by equally small seed capsules. It is tolerant of dry conditions and salt winds. **ZONES 9–11.**

Eucalyptus gracilis

Eucalyptus grandis
FLOODED GUM

One of the noblest of the large eucalypts, flooded gum comes from high-rainfall regions of the Australian east coast and can achieve a height of 200 ft (60 m) and a trunk up to 10 ft (3 m) in diameter in suitably deep, rich, moist soil. The base of its shaft-like trunk is blackish and rough, with smooth, whitish or blue-gray bark above. The thin leaves are dark green and shiny on top, paler beneath.

Clusters of white blossoms are borne in winter. It is much cultivated for its timber in South Africa. **ZONES 10–11.**

Eucalyptus gunnii
syn. ***Eucalyptus divaricata***
ALPINE CIDER GUM

From the highlands of Tasmania, this 80 ft (24 m) tall tree is sometimes multi-trunked. It has light reddish brown bark that peels irregularly revealing white new bark. Young trees have the 'silver dollar' style foliage: opposite pairs of rounded, gray-green leaves. Mature trees have narrower stalked leaves. Small cream flowers in spring and summer are followed by tiny, goblet-shaped seed capsules. It is perhaps the most frost-hardy eucalypt and the most commonly grown in the British Isles. **ZONES 7–9.**

Eucalyptus haemastoma
BROAD-LEAFED SCRIBBLY GUM

This species often has multiple twisted trunks in its limited native region around Sydney, Australia, and the white bark is marked by ornate 'scribbles' caused by burrowing larvae of a tiny moth. It grows to about 30 ft (9 m) with an uneven crown of thick, sickle-shaped leaves about 6 in (15 cm) long, and bears nectar-rich white blossoms from late spring to early fall (autumn). It is best suited to well-drained, sandy soil. **ZONES 9–11.**

Eucalyptus leucoxylon
YELLOW GUM, SOUTH AUSTRALIAN BLUE GUM, WHITE IRONBARK

A tree from high rainfall regions of South Australia, this shapely eucalypt grows to 100 ft (30 m) with an open canopy. Its distinctive bark is fissured at the base but above this is smooth and dappled with yellowish white and blue-gray spots. The leaves are grayish or bluish green and taper to a point. The large, 1½ in (35 mm) wide flowers, which may be cream or dark pink, are borne in small clusters from fall

Eucalyptus grandis

Eucalyptus mannifera subsp. *maculosa*

(autumn) through to spring. Crimson-flowered plants have often been sold under the name ***Eucalyptus leucoxylon* 'Rosea'**. **ZONES 9–11.**

Eucalyptus macrocarpa
MOTTLECAH

This species from southwestern Australia has the largest flowers and fruit of the genus. Of sparse, mallee-type growth with multiple arching stems, it reaches 12 ft (3.5 m) tall and wide. Both the juvenile and adult leaves are broad and silvery, held close to the branch. The large, bright red or sometimes pink blossoms are about 3 in (8 cm) across, nestling among the leaves, and are followed by broadly conical, very woody fruit of similar diameter. It must have well-drained, slightly acid soil and low summer humidity; it has a reputation for being difficult. **ZONES 9–11.**

Eucalyptus mannifera
BRITTLE GUM

Erect, with an open, spreading crown and contorted limbs, this frost-hardy tree from cooler southeastern areas of Australia grows quickly to about 40 ft (12 m). Its powdery whitish bark takes on orange-red tones in summer before being shed in strips. The sickle-shaped, blue-green leaves are narrow and thin. Small creamy white flowers appear in clusters, usually from late spring to summer. ***Eucalyptus mannifera* subsp.**

Eucalyptus nicholii

Eucalyptus mannifera

maculosa is the form most commonly grown and perhaps has the most attractively colored bark. **ZONES 8–10.**

Eucalyptus microcorys
TALLOW-WOOD

This tree from New South Wales and Queensland coastal areas displays creamy white flowers from late winter to mid-summer. It has a densely spreading crown and will grow to 120 ft (36 m). The brown bark is fibrous and soft. The valuable, tough timber contains a natural wax, giving it a greasy feel, hence the common name. **ZONES 10–12.**

Eucalyptus microtheca
COOLIBAH

The coolibah comes from semi-arid northern regions of Australia, where it is usually found near waterholes and on river floodplains. A medium-sized tree to about 50 ft (15 m) high, it branches fairly low with a twisted trunk. The narrow, blue-green leaves are very thin and the tiny white flowers are insignificant. The seed capsules are among the smallest of all eucalypts. The bark varies from fibrous to hard and furrowed, often smooth on upper branches. This tree is extremely tolerant of dry conditions and of heat. Botanists now recognize a number of species of coolibah, and have revived the name ***Eucalyptus coolibah*** for a widely distributed tree of Queens-

Eucalyptus leucoxylon

land and northern New South Wales. **ZONES 9–12.**

Eucalyptus nicholii
NARROW-LEAFED BLACK PEPPERMINT, WILLOW LEAF PEPPERMINT

With its fine, sickle-shaped, blue-green leaves held aloft on a high crown, this fibrous-barked species from the highlands of northeastern New South Wales makes an excellent shade or street tree. It bears white flowers that can only be appreciated when the tree is small. *Eucalyptus nicholii* withstands mild frosts and strong winds. It usually reaches 40–50 ft (12–15 m) in height. **ZONES 8–11.**

Eucalyptus pauciflora subsp. *niphophila*

Eucalyptus nitens

Eucalyptus nitens
SHINING GUM

This cool-climate species grows in high-rainfall mountain areas of New South Wales and Victoria. It grows to over 200 ft (60 m) and is little known in cultivation. It has shining, green adult foliage, while the juvenile leaves are grayish. **ZONES 8–9.**

Eucalyptus nova-anglica
NEW ENGLAND PEPPERMINT, BLACK PEPPERMINT

This medium-sized tree to 60 ft (18 m) high has persistent, finely fibrous bark. In the wild it often grows with snow gums and is frost hardy. Its adult leaves are bright shiny green and quite narrow, and clusters of small white flowers are produced in summer. **ZONES 8–10.**

Eucalyptus pauciflora
syn. *Eucalyptus coriacea*
SNOW GUM

This 30–60 ft (9–18 m) tree is found in southeastern Australia, commonly grow-

Eucalyptus nova-anglica

ing in frost-prone highland valleys. It tends to have a rather twisted trunk, with reddish brown or gray bark peeling in irregular strips to reveal white and beige under-bark. Small cream flowers are borne in spring and summer. Alpine snow gum, ***Eucalyptus pauciflora* subsp. *niphophila*** (syn. *E. niphophila*), occurs at altitudes over 5,000 ft (1,500 m) where snow lies through most of winter; it is smaller and lower branching. **ZONES 7–9.**

Eucalyptus perriniana
SPINNING GUM, ROUND-LEAFED SNOW GUM

This small, rather straggly tree grows to around 30 ft (9 m) high, often with multiple trunks. It has silver-gray, rounded, juvenile leaves, the bases of each pair fused to form a disc encircling the twig, and 6 in (15 cm) long, pointed adult leaves. Small white flowers in clusters of 3 appear in summer. This species can be grown as a shrub, cut back hard each year, and is popular for cut foliage. **ZONES 8–9.**

Eucalyptus polyanthemos
RED BOX, SILVER DOLLAR GUM

A single-trunked tree growing to about 80 ft (24 m), the red box has distinctive bark: gray and scaly on the lower trunk but subtly mottled above with gray, pink and cream. The leaves are gray-green to quite bluish and on some trees are almost circular, though tapered at the base into a slender stalk. They are used for cut foliage. The creamy white flowers, borne in fine pendulous sprays, are nectar bearing and will encourage birds. It often grows naturally in very shallow, stony sites where it produces a short, crooked trunk but, given better soil conditions, the trunk is usually upright. **ZONES 9–11.**

Eucalyptus regnans
MOUNTAIN ASH

This magnificent species which reigns over the mountain forests of far southeastern Australia and Tasmania is the tallest hardwood tree in the world, specimens of over 320 ft (96 m) tall being known. It has a long, straight trunk and relatively small, open crown, the bark being almost white and shed annually in long ribbons. The white flowers are small and rarely noticed. Despite the great beauty of mountain ash forests and the value of its timber, it is seldom cultivated. **ZONE 9.**

Eucalyptus perriniana

Eucalyptus torquata

Eucalyptus rubida
CANDLEBARK

Found in cooler regions of southeastern Australia, this is an open-crowned tree that is usually 40–80 ft (12–24 m) tall. It has narrow leaves to 6 in (15 cm) long and grayish brown old bark which may turn deep pink or red in winter before revealing the cream new bark. Small cream flowers open from late summer. **ZONES 8–9.**

Eucalyptus saligna
SYDNEY BLUE GUM

This magnificent tree grows to well over 100 ft (30 m) and has ornamental, smooth, bluish white bark. Its pointed leaves are deep green and prominently veined, paler green beneath. Dense white blossoms appear in summer and fall (autumn), attracting an abundance of bees. This marginally frost-hardy tree prefers deep, fertile soil. It is grown for timber and honey. **ZONES 10–11.**

Eucalyptus salmonophloia
SALMON GUM

From inland Western Australia, this handsome eucalypt is mostly 30–40 ft (9–12 m) tall with a long, sinuous, smooth trunk topped by a dense, umbrella-shaped crown. The new bark is an attractive salmon pink, turning gray as it ages before

Eucalyptus rubida

Eucalyptus pauciflora

Eucalyptus woodwardii

Eucalyptus salmonophloia

being shed. The mature leaves are shiny, green and tapering, and the small, white flowers appear in spring and summer. It can be grown in areas of very low rainfall and can withstand some frost. **ZONES 9–11.**

Eucalyptus sideroxylon
RED IRONBARK, MUGGA, PINK IRONBARK

This species from temperate eastern Australia is closely allied to *Eucalyptus leucoxylon* but its bark is black, deeply furrowed and never shed. The leaves can be bluish to dull green and diamond-shaped to slightly sickle-shaped. The showy, pale pink to near-crimson flowers, about 1 in (25 mm) across, open from fall (autumn) to spring, followed by small, goblet-shaped seed capsules. Forms with deeper pink flowers are selected for cultivation, but flower color of seedlings cannot be predicted. **ZONES 9–11.**

Eucalyptus sideroxylon

Eucalyptus tereticornis
FOREST RED GUM

Found throughout east-coastal Australia and in southern New Guinea as well, this tree grows up to 150 ft (45 m) tall. It is open headed and single trunked, though it often branches quite low. Its outer bark is shed in irregular patches, showing a grayish white under-bark. The green adult leaves are narrow and up to 8 in (20 cm) long. Small cream flowers open from pointed buds from mid-winter. **ZONES 9–12.**

Eucalyptus tereticornis

Eucalyptus tetraptera
SQUARE-FRUITED MALLEE

In nature this species is a straggly, untidy shrub rarely more than 6 ft (1.8 m) tall, growing in poor sandy soil along the southern coast of Western Australia. Its large leaves are thick and leathery and its big 4-winged flowers are bright red with pink stamens. These are produced in fall (autumn) and early winter. This species is not frost tolerant but in hot, dry climates it could be worth growing. Light pruning will moderate its straggly habit. **ZONES 10–11.**

Eucalyptus tetraptera

Eucalyptus torquata
CORAL GUM

This small tree from Western Australia grows to about 20 ft (6 m) high with a fairly narrow, upright habit, though it may droop under the weight of its flowers and seed capsules. Its blue-green, sickle-shaped leaves are 4 in (10 cm) long, and the rough brown bark flakes rather than peels. Orange-red, lantern-shaped buds, 1 in (25 mm) long, develop during spring, opening to a mass of creamy orange and yellow or pink and yellow stamens. The flowers are followed by large seed capsules. It can withstand dry conditions but does better with regular moisture. **ZONES 9–11.**

Eucalyptus viminalis

Eucalyptus viminalis
MANNA GUM, RIBBON GUM, WHITE GUM

This species has a wide distribution in the cooler hill country of southeastern Australia. It has smooth, whitish bark except for some roughish bark at the base of the trunk. The upper limbs shed bark in long ribbons, hence the common name ribbon gum. It is a favored food tree of the koala and can grow to 180 ft (55 m) tall. Small white flowers are produced in summer. It makes a fine shade tree but the fallen bark can be messy. **ZONES 9–10.**

Eucalyptus woodwardii
LEMON-FLOWERED GUM

The outstanding feature of this eucalypt is its showy, bright yellow flowers, up to 2 in (5 cm) across, which are borne on reddish twigs through winter and spring. The long, leathery leaves are dull green, often covered with a silvery bloom. It grows to about 50 ft (15 m), with an attractive weeping habit and a smooth, grayish trunk. From arid areas of Western Australia, the lemon-flowered gum is successful in dry areas and prefers low summer rainfall. **ZONES 9–11.**

Eucalyptus regnans

E

EUCHARIS

AMAZON LILY, EUCHARIST LILY

Natives of South America, these bulbous perennials look somewhat like tropical daffodils with large, icy-white flowers marked with pale green. They are sweetly scented like jonquils and, in the right conditions, will flower several times a year; the main flowering season is in summer. The flowers are usually borne in bunches of four. The genus name has no religious connotations: *eucharis* simply means 'elegant'.

CULTIVATION: Frost tender, *Eucharis* are flowers of the rainforest floor and do best in hot, moist conditions, growing well even in deep shade. Provide plants with a humus-rich, well-drained soil. The foliage is attractive and the bulbs look effective massed in a tropical garden. In temperate areas they require a well-warmed greenhouse. Propagate from seed when ripe or from offsets in spring.

Eucharis amazonica

Native to Colombia and bordering areas of Peru, this is a clump-forming bulb with broad, paddle-shaped, dark green basal leaves. Fragrant white flowers in umbels of 3 to 6 are produced in late summer. It reaches 24 in (60 cm) in height. **ZONES 11–12.**

Eucharis × *grandiflora*

A natural hybrid from Colombia, this plant is grown commercially for the cut flower trade. The scented blooms, carried on strong, straight, flowering stems, have pale creamy white petals and appear in early summer. The dark green, well-displayed, glossy foliage is also decorative. It reaches 18 in (45 cm) in height. **ZONES 11–12.**

EUCOMIS

PINEAPPLE LILY

The 15 species of pineapple lily, all deciduous and native to southern Africa, bear spikes of small, star-shaped flowers with crowning tufts of leaves resembling a pineapple. They grow from enlarged bulbs, and the basal rosette of glossy foliage is both quite handsome in itself and rather bulky—these are not bulbs to slip in among other plants but rather substantial border plants in their own right. The Xhosa people used the bulbs, boiled into a poultice, as a cure for rheumatism.

CULTIVATION: Marginally frost hardy, they do best in warm-temperate climates in full sun in moist but well-drained soil; they dislike water during the dormant winter months. Where there is a danger of frost reaching the bulbs they are best grown as pot plants and wintered safely indoors. Propagate from seed or by division of clumps in spring.

Eucomis autumnalis

syn. *Eucomis undulata*

Greenish white, pendent flowers appear on this plant in dense terminal spikes in summer and fall (autumn). The bright green leaves have undulating margins. It grows to 12 in (30 cm) in height. **ZONES 7–10.**

Eucomis bicolor

Eucharis amazonica

Eucomis comosa

Eucommia ulmoides

Eucomis bicolor

This summer-flowering bulb bears spikes of green or greenish white flowers with purple-margined petals; these are topped by a cluster of leaf-like bracts. It grows to 18–24 in (45–60 cm) tall and 24 in (60 cm) wide. **ZONES 8–10.**

Eucomis comosa

syn. *Eucomis punctata*

This species grows to about 30 in (75 cm) in height. Dark green, crinkly, strap-like leaves surround the tall, purple-spotted scapes. The hundreds of flowers, white to green and sometimes spotted with purple, are borne in late summer and fall (autumn). Water well through the growing season. It makes an excellent, long-lasting cut flower. **ZONES 8–10.**

Eucomis pole-evansii

This species grows to a height of 6 ft (1.8 m) with a spread of 3 ft (1 m). In late summer it bears soft green, bell-shaped flowers with creamy centers crowded onto long spikes with a quite large cluster of bracts at the top. The long green leaves form basal rosettes. **ZONES 9–10.**

EUCOMMIA

This deciduous tree genus from China consisting of a single species is placed in a family of its own, rather distantly related to the elm and witch-hazel families. While widely grown in northern and eastern China, it is not known in the wild, but fossil leaves of the genus have been found. A remarkable feature of this plant is the presence of latex in the leaves and bark, and earlier this century it was considered a potentially commercial rubber-yielding species. In China it is grown almost entirely for its medicinal properties; the dried bark is used in herbal medicine.

Eucryphia cordifolia

Eucommia ulmoides

CULTIVATION: Very frost hardy, it should be planted in light to medium, well-drained soil in a sheltered, sunny position. Propagate from cuttings or from seed.

Eucommia ulmoides

GUTTA-PERCHA TREE

This is usually a slender tree to 50 ft (15 m) high of open habit with furrowed, gray bark; the crown becomes broader and more rounded with age. The shiny green leaves are narrow and pointed. Male and female flowers, both inconspicuous, are carried on different trees and the winged fruit, rather like the 'keys' on an ash, are seldom seen on planted trees. This is a vigorous tree, though not an especially ornamental one. **ZONES 5–10.**

EUCRYPHIA

This small genus of about 6 species is made up of evergreen or semi-deciduous trees from the southern hemisphere. All species have pure white flowers of singular beauty, rather like small single roses with 4 petals and a 'boss' of red-tipped stamens. There are 2 species indigenous to Chile and 4 indigenous to Australia. Eucryphias have been grown in the British Isles for more than a century, especially in mild, moist, Atlantic coastal districts where the climate suits them well. Several garden hybrids are more vigorous and floriferous than the species.

CULTIVATION: Frost hardy, they require a humid microclimate and constant soil moisture combined with good drainage. Good flowering demands that the tree crown be in the sun but the roots shaded. Propagate from seed or cuttings in summer.

Eucryphia cordifolia
ULMO

Growing to a medium to large tree in the wettest coastal rainforests of southern Chile, this tree was called ulmo (meaning elm) by the Spanish settlers. The simple, oblong, wavy edged, shiny dark green leaves are gray beneath. White flowers 2 in (5 cm) across are borne singly in late summer. In cultivation this evergreen species has proved more tender than the others and, while its foliage is interesting with reddish new growths, it is not very free flowering. In very mild, wet climates it grows tall and slender, up to 20–25 ft (6–8 m) in under 10 years. **ZONE 9.**

Eucryphia glutinosa
HARDY EUCRYPHIA

Also endemic to Chile but from slightly drier mountain regions than *Eucryphia cordifolia*, this is the only deciduous species, though in mild climates it may be semi-evergreen. It is the most frost-hardy and most ornamental species, forming a small, shrub-like tree with erect branches, slow growing to 20 ft (6 m) or more. Young shoots are coated in a sticky resin, hence the name *glutinosa*, and the leaves are compound with 3 to 5 glossy green leaflets that may turn orange and red before dropping in fall (autumn). The flowers are borne in profusion along the branches in late summer. **ZONES 8–9.**

Eucryphia × *intermedia*

This hybrid between the Chilean *Eucryphia glutinosa* and the Tasmanian *E. lucida* first appeared as a chance seedling at Rostrevor in Ireland; several clones are available but **'Rostrevor'** is the most widely planted. It makes an upright tree of slender habit, reaching 30 ft (9 m) in time, and under good conditions makes a profuse show of flowers in late summer. **ZONES 8–9.**

Eucryphia lucida
TASMANIAN LEATHERWOOD

From Tasmanian rainforests, this slender evergreen tree can reach 100 ft (30 m) in the wild and has been felled for its close-grained, pinkish timber, but it is best known for the aromatic honey that the introduced honeybee makes from its abundant, fragrant, early summer flowers. It has sticky buds and the small, shiny leaves are simple, not compound. In cultivation it is rather slow growing, seldom exceeding 20 ft (6 m). **'Pink Cloud'** is a pink-flowered cultivar recently introduced, while **'Leatherwood Cream'** has leaves irregularly margined with cream. **ZONES 8–9.**

Eucryphia moorei
PINKWOOD

From the far southeast of mainland Australia, this species grows in sheltered gullies in the coastal ranges. It reaches 25 ft (8 m) in height and has pinnate leaves, each leaf consisting of about 5 to 7 neat, oblong leaflets with white undersides. The shoots and leaves are less sticky and shiny than on other eucryphias. The flowers are about $1\frac{1}{2}$ in (35 mm) wide, borne among the ferny foliage from mid-summer to early fall (autumn). Pinkwood is very ornamental and sometimes grows vigorously in cultivation. **ZONES 9–10.**

Eucryphia × *nymansensis*

This name covers all hybrids between the 2 Chilean species *Eucryphia glutinosa* and *E. cordifolia* and arose first at Nymans, Sussex, in 1914. A small, compact tree of narrow habit, in time it may exceed 30 ft (9 m). The leaves vary in shape and size and can be simple or composed of 3 leaflets. It flowers in late summer, and in a sunny spot the tree may be covered in white blossoms. Several clones have been raised but the most popular in Britain is still one of the original seedling clones now known as **'Nymansay'** (from its initial tag 'Nymans A'). **ZONES 8–9.**

EUGENIA

This is a very large genus of up to 1,000 species, even after the splitting off of numerous Old World species into other genera like *Syzygium*. They are evergreen or deciduous shrubs or trees mostly from the Americas with a few extending to Africa, Asia and the Pacific Islands. The flowers, arising singly or in small groups from the leaf axils, are white usually with small petals and many stamens. The fruits are berries which in some cases are edible. The foliage is usually rich deep green, often bronze or red tinged when young.
CULTIVATION: With such a large genus from so many places their needs will vary. However, most are frost tender or only marginally frost hardy. Some species can be employed as screening plants or for formal hedges. Most will tolerate full sun to part-shade and prefer moist, humus-rich but free-draining soil. They are usually slow growing and in cool areas can be grown as container plants. Propagate from seed or summer cuttings.

Eugenia brasiliensis
BRAZIL CHERRY, GRUMICHAMA

This small evergreen tree is native to southern Brazil. It has leathery deep green elliptical leaves about 4 in (10 cm) long, the new growths bronze-tinted. In summer it bears masses of small, pure white flowers, followed by sweet black cherry-sized fruit that ripen in only one month and are very tasty. **ZONES 10–12.**

Eugenia uniflora
SURINAM CHERRY, PITANGA, FLORIDA CHERRY

Indigenous to South America, this tree is popular in subtropical and tropical zones for its bright red new foliage which replace the dark green leaves of the previous season. It grows very slowly to 20 ft (6 m) high but may be kept trimmed to 8 ft (2.4 m). Small, fragrant white flowers with a mass of central stamens open in summer. They are followed by sweet, ribbed, red fruit the size of small tomatoes. The darker the fruit, the better the taste. **ZONES 10–12.**

Eulychnia acida

Eucryphia × *nymansensis*

Eucryphia lucida 'Leatherwood Cream'

Eucryphia × *intermedia* 'Rostrevor'

Eucryphia moorei

EULYCHNIA

From Chile and Peru, this is a genus of about 8 species of shrubby or tree-like cacti with conspicuously ribbed stems and strong bristly spines. Short, bell-shaped flowers are produced from felty white areoles near the tops of the stems.
CULTIVATION: In frost-prone areas grow in a temperate greenhouse or conservatory in a gritty cactus compost in full light. Water freely in the growing season and keep almost dry from mid-fall (mid-autumn) to late winter. Outdoors grow in a light, well-drained soil in full sun. Propagate from seed in early spring or cuttings in late spring.

Eulychnia acida

From Chile, this shrubby cactus may develop a tree-like habit to 12 ft (3.5 m) or more. It has thick ribs and radiating spines with a central spine up to 8 in (20 cm) long. The white, bell-shaped summer flowers have a pink mid-stripe. **ZONES 9–11.**

EUMORPHIA

There are 4 species of *Eumorphia*, all of which come from South Africa. They are shrubby members of the daisy family but with their tiny, crowded leaves, which may be smooth or silky hairy, they may be mistaken for heaths when not in flower.
CULTIVATION: Grow in full sun in very well-drained, sandy loam to which has been added a proportion of rotted organic matter. Plants will easily tolerate light frosts but where temperatures drop below 26°F (–3°C) protect from wind and keep dry. Where winters are cold and wet they can only be grown under glass. Propagate from cuttings.

Eumorphia prostrata
SILVER CLOUD

Fast growing to 18 in (45 cm) and spreading to 3 ft (1 m) or more, *Eumorphia prostrata* has attractive silvery green foliage and yellow-eyed, white, daisy-like flowers. This species is useful as a ground cover, especially when planted en masse. Flowering occurs from mid-summer to late fall (autumn). The species is native to mountain regions of Natal, Lesotho and eastern Cape Province. **ZONES 8–10.**

Euonymus alatus

Euonymus japonicus

Euonymus alatus

Euonymus 'Red Chief'

Euonymus bungeanus

EUONYMUS

SPINDLE TREE

This genus of about 175 species consists of both deciduous and evergreen trees, shrubs and creepers from the northern hemisphere, centered mainly in East Asia including the Himalayas. All have simple leaves in opposite pairs, usually with toothed margins. The flowers are inconspicuous, greenish or yellowish, in small groups along the lower parts of the current year's growth. While deciduous plants, such as **'Red Chief'**, have rich fall (autumn) foliage, it is the capsular fruits that provide the main interest, splitting open in fall to reveal bright yellow, red or orange seeds against a contrasting capsule. Birds, attracted by their nutritious, oily outer layer, distribute the seeds. **CULTIVATION:** Mostly frost hardy, they grow best in a sheltered position with ample sun and fertile, well-drained soil. Propagate from seed or cuttings.

Euonymus alatus

WINGED SPINDLE, WINGED EUONYMUS

From Japan, China and Korea, this decorative, spreading, much-branched, deciduous shrub grows to about 15–20 ft (4.5–6 m) tall, the small branches distinctive for the broad 'wings' of corky tissue attached to either side of the green twig (the specific name *alatus* means 'winged'). In late spring it bears small, green flowers in inconspicuous sprays and by fall (autumn) the small, purplish, 4-lobed capsules start splitting to reveal orange-red seeds. At the same time the leaves turn the most vivid deep red, sometimes showing paler scarlet tones as they are about to fall. ***Euonymus alatus* var. *apterus*** has equally good fall color but has a more lax habit and rarely produces the corky wings of bark; **'Compactus'** grows to around 6 ft (1.8 m) tall. **ZONES 5–9.**

Euonymus bungeanus

WINTERBERRY EUONYMUS

This species, native to China, is a large deciduous shrub or small semi-evergreen tree to 20 ft (6 m) and 15 ft (4.5 m) wide. Its tiny, insignificant flowers are followed by 4-lobed fruit which are yellow tinged pink. When these split they expose seeds with bright orange arils. The fruit are formed in summer and persist into fall (autumn). The leaves turn yellow and pink before shedding. ***Euonymus bungeanus* var. *semipersistens*** is a semi-evergreen form, or at least hangs on to its leaves until well into winter; it is also later fruiting. **ZONES 4–9.**

Euonymus europaeus

EUROPEAN SPINDLE TREE

This deciduous shrub or small tree is usually single stemmed at the base and occasionally reaches 20 ft (6 m). It is native to Europe, including the UK, and can be found growing in woodlands and often on limestone or chalk soils. The wood of this and the few other European species was once used to make spindles, used in spinning wool. It has inconspicuous flowers followed in fall (autumn) by pink or red fruit that split open to reveal the large orange seeds. At the same time the leaves turn to shades of yellow and scarlet. **'Aldenhamensis'** is a form selected for the larger size and brilliant pink coloring of its fruits; **'Red Cascade'** is often pendulous with the weight of its large red, orange-seeded berries. **ZONES 6–9.**

Euonymus fortunei

syn. *Euonymus radicans*

WINTERCREEPER EUONYMUS

This prostrate to shrubby creeper spreads or climbs by aerial roots like ivy and can climb on a brick or stone wall as high as 20 ft (6 m). As a ground cover it has an indefinite spread, but it is mostly more compact forms that are grown in gardens. From early to mid-summer it bears greenish white flowers on the branching, non-clinging adult stems. **'Emerald Gaiety'** is a small, compact cultivar with dark green leaves margined with white and often pink tinged in winter; it grows to 3 ft (1 m) tall and 5 ft (1.5 m) wide. **'Emerald 'n' Gold'** is a very bushy, small form with broad gold edges to its rich green leaves often tinged pink in winter; it grows to about 12 in (30 cm) tall and 3 ft (1 m) wide. **'Silver Queen'** has broad white margins to its leaves which are pink tinged in winter; it is a bushy shrub up to 6 ft (1.8 m) tall and wider than its height. **'Variegatus'** (syn. 'Gracilis') is a climbing or trailing form with larger leaves with white margins, often pink tinted. **ZONES 5–9.**

Euonymus europaeus

Euonymus japonicus

JAPANESE SPINDLE TREE

Generally known in gardens by its variegated cultivars, this spreading, evergreen shrub from Japan has shiny, dark green leaves in its typical state, reaching heights of 10–12 ft (3–3.5 m). Pale greenish flowers appear in early summer, and the fall (autumn) foliage may be enlivened by scattered pinkish capsules opening to reveal orange seeds. The variegated cultivars are all lower and denser: **'Albomarginatus'** has irregular, white-margined leaves. **'Aureomarginatus'** has oval, yellow-margined leaves and small, star-shaped, green flowers in summer; it makes a suitable choice for a hedge. **'Microphyllus Variegatus'** is a small, dense shrub to 3 ft (1 m) tall with small, crowded leaves with white margins. **'Ovatus Aureus'** has broad, irregular margins of bright yellow. All forms of the species are adapted to somewhat exposed seashore conditions. **ZONES 8–10.**

Euonymus lucidus

syn. *Euonymus pendulus*

This Himalayan species is a broad, spreading, evergreen shrub or small tree that can reach 30 ft (10 m) tall and 25 ft (8 m) wide. Its leaves are glossy green, to 4 in (10 cm) long, with regular serrations. Its new foliage is bronze-red. The berries are yellow with seeds attached to orange arils. **ZONES 9–11.**

Euonymus oxyphyllus

This bushy, deciduous shrub to 8 ft (2.5 m) tall or more comes from Korea and Japan. It is slow growing but ornamental with rich red-purple fall (autumn) foliage and lovely red berries dangling on long stems. These split to expose brilliant orange-covered seeds. **ZONES 5–9.**

Euonymus fortunei 'Emerald 'n' Gold'

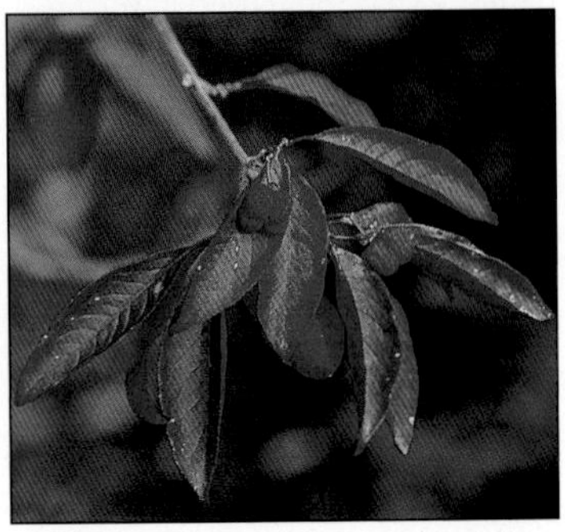

Euonymus europaeus 'Red Cascade'

Euonymus japonicus 'Ovatus Aureus'

Euonymus oxyphyllus

Euonymus planipes
syn. ***Euonymus sachalinensis***

This large and handsome deciduous shrub or small tree grows to 10 ft (3 m) or more high and wide. It comes from northeastern China, Japan and Korea and is similar to, but more spectacular than, the European spindle tree *(Euonymus europaeus)*. It has brilliant red fall (autumn) color and quite large 4- to 5-lobed deep pink to scarlet fruit splitting to expose the orange-covered seeds. **ZONES 4–9.**

EUPATORIUM

This genus contains about 40 species of perennials and subshrubs, mainly from the Americas but a few from Asia and Europe. Only a few are cultivated for their large terminal panicles of small flowerheads, which come in white or shades of purple, mauve or pink. **CULTIVATION:** Mostly quite frost hardy, they need full sun or part-shade and moist but well-drained soil. The shrubs should be pruned lightly in spring or after flowering. Propagate from seed in spring, from cuttings in summer or by division in early spring or fall (autumn).

Eupatorium cannabinum
HEMP AGRIMONY

This is a very robust, herbaceous perennial to 5 ft (1.5 m) tall or more and 4 ft (1.2 m) wide. It is native to many areas of Europe and is not generally considered to be as good a garden plant as the similar *Eupatorium purpureum* from North America. It produces large, flat-topped heads of tiny, fluffy, very pale dusty pink or whitish flowers in late summer to fall (autumn). **ZONES 5–9.**

Eupatorium coelestinum
syn. ***Conoclinium coelestinum***
MIST FLOWER, HARDY AGERATUM

Native to eastern USA, this is a robust herbaceous perennial with large heads of

Eupatorium fistulosum

clear blue fluffy flowers in late summer. It is suited to naturalizing in damp places near water. **ZONES 5–9.**

Eupatorium fistulosum
JOE PYE WEED

Native to the southeastern states of the USA, this variable perennial grows 3–10 ft (1–3 m) tall and about as wide. It enjoys constantly moist, humus-rich soil and will tolerate periods of wetness. It produces heads of rosy-mauve flowers from mid-summer to early fall (autumn). It can be invasive in rich, moist soil but is easily controlled by division every second year. **'Filigrankuppel'** is an improved flowering form. **ZONES 7–10.**

Eupatorium maculatum

This perennial has stems marked with purple blotches and serrated, lance-shaped leaves in whorls of three or four. In late summer and fall (autumn) rose-purple flowers are produced in rather flattened terminal clusters. **ZONES 5–10.**

Eupatorium megalophyllum
syn. ***Bartlettina megalophylla***
MIST FLOWER

A native of Mexico, this species grows to a height of 5 ft (1.5 m) and spreads—branching at the ground—to 6 ft (1.8 m). In spring it bears dramatic, wide heads of lilac flowers. The very large leaves, up to 10 in (25 cm) long and 8 in (20 cm) wide, are dark green and velvety on the uppersurface and paler on the underside. Immature stems are covered in fine purple hairs. This species will not survive even the mildest of frosts. ***Eupatorium sordidum*** is a similar species but with smaller leaves and flowerheads. **ZONES 10–11.**

Eupatorium purpureum
JOE PYE WEED

This robust perennial grows to a height of 5–8 ft (1.5–2.4 m) with a spread of about 4 ft (1.2 m) or more. It provides a bold accent for the fall (autumn) garden, with 12 in (30 cm) long leaves and large heads of tiny, purplish flowers. Native to eastern and central North America, it is usually found where there is plenty of water and needs lots of moisture for full growth. **ZONES 4–9.**

Euphorbia 'Excalibur'

EUPHORBIA
MILKWEED, SPURGE

The genus is a very large one with close to 2,000 species, among them annuals, herbaceous perennials, shrubs and numerous succulent species that at first sight look remarkably like cacti. This variety of forms has suggested to many botanists that the genus should be divided; but the flowers of all species are almost identical in structure. They are very much reduced, consisting of only a stigma and a stamen, always green, and usually carried in small clusters. Many species have showy bracts, these are the most widely cultivated; examples include ***Euphorbia cognata*** and ***E.* 'Excalibur'**. Mainly tropical and subtropical, the genus also includes many temperate species. All euphorbias have milky sap which is corrosive to sensitive areas of the skin; some can cause temporary blindness if sap contacts the eyes. **CULTIVATION:** Plant species of *Euphorbia* in sun or part-shade in moist, well-drained soil. Cold tolerance varies greatly depending on the species; the more highly succulent species are generally frost tender. Propagate from cuttings in spring or summer, allowing succulent species to dry and callus before placing in barely damp sand, by division in early spring or fall (autumn) or from seed in fall or spring.

Euphorbia abyssinica

This upright, succulent tree grows to a height of 30 ft (9 m). The leafless trunk and branches are made up of multi-angled, somewhat flattened, jointed, spiny segments. It makes an interesting architectural addition to the warm-climate garden, where its form contrasts well with more conventional plants. **ZONES 10–12.**

Euphorbia ammak

This tree-like succulent from southern Arabia has a branched green stem up to 8 in (20 cm) thick with short spines. It reaches a height of 15 ft (4.5 m) or more and produces small flowers and brown, oval fruit in spring and summer. **'Variegata'** has the stem variegated with cream. **ZONES 10–12.**

Eupatorium maculatum

Eupatorium megalophyllum

Eupatorium purpureum

Euphorbia cognata

Euphorbia amygdaloides
WOOD SPURGE

Native to much of Europe and also Asia Minor, this erect perennial to 3 ft (1 m) high has dark green leaves to 3 in (8 cm) long and flowerheads with yellowish green bracts from mid-spring to early summer. It is generally represented in cultivation by its frost-hardy, selected, colorful varieties and forms. ***Euphorbia amygdaloides* var. *robbiae*** (syn. *E. robbiae*), Mrs Robb's bonnet, forms spreading rosettes of dark green leaves to 24 in (60 cm) high and wide and bears rounded heads of lime-green floral bracts; **'Rubra'** has light green leaves heavily suffused with burgundy and acid green floral bracts. ZONES 7–9.

Euphorbia caerulescens

Standing up to 5 ft (1.5 m) tall, this cactus-like succulent from the dry parts of Cape Province, South Africa, forms an expanding clump of segmented, vertical stems. Each is ribbed, very spiny and gray-green in color. In spring tiny bright yellow flowers cover the tops of the stems. It is tolerant of light frosts but can be grown in colder climates in a warm dry greenhouse. ZONES 9–11.

Euphorbia characias subsp. *wulfenii*

Euphorbia ammak 'Variegata'

Euphorbia caerulescens

Euphorbia cooperi

Euphorbia canariensis

This erect, tree-like succulent from the Canary Islands normally grows to about 8 ft (2.4 m) tall and forms large clumps or colonies of sharply angled and spiny, bright green stems. Cup-shaped, reddish green floral bracts are produced in summer. This makes a fascinating specimen plant for the frost-free desert garden. ZONES 10–11.

Euphorbia caput-medusae
MEDUSA'S HEAD

This South African succulent has a thick basal stem up to 6 in (15 cm) tall, from which radiate numerous thinner but still succulent branches up to about 18 in (45 cm) long, like the tentacles of an octopus. Short-lived, narrow leaves grow only at the branch extremities, where green flowers with white, lacy margins appear in summer. ZONES 8–11.

Euphorbia characias

This is a sun-loving, frost-hardy subshrub usually up to 3 ft (1 m) or so. It is native to the Mediterranean region from Portugal and Morocco west to Turkey. It likes a sunny, well-drained site and where happy will self-seed. It has deep brown nectaries giving a brown spot in the center of each yellow-green bract. ***Euphorbia characias* subsp. *wulfenii*** (syn. *Euphorbia wulfenii)* has blue-green leaves densely clothing the erect stems, which in spring are topped by dome-like chartreuse flowerheads. ZONES 8–10.

Euphorbia colliculina

Euphorbia enopla

Euphorbia esculenta

Euphorbia flanaganii

Euphorbia colliculina

This is one of the deciduous species of *Euphorbia*, from the Cape region of South Africa. Its branches vary in length from 2–6 in (5–15 cm). The main root and stem form the caudex of the plant. The flowers appear in spring. ZONES 7–9.

Euphorbia cooperi

This tree-like succulent has branches that grow at right angles to the stem then curve upwards like a candelabrum. The branches are usually 4- or 5-angled and have paired spines along the ridges. Yellowish flowers are clustered along ridges between the spines. ZONES 9–11.

Euphorbia amygdaloides 'Rubra'

Euphorbia caput-medusae

Euphorbia dulcis

This perennial species from Europe grows to 12 in (30 cm) high and wide with a slowly creeping root system. The bronze-green foliage forms a dense mound, and in summer the stems terminate in flowerheads with broad yellow-green bracts. In the cultivar **'Chameleon'** the leaves are burgundy colored in spring, and in fall (autumn) both leaves and floral bracts turn a rich purple before dying down. ZONES 6–9.

Euphorbia enopla

This cactus-like species, native to the Karoo Desert in South Africa, grows to 3 ft (1 m) high with broadly ribbed, much-branched blue-green stems with rows of long reddish spines. Tiny flowers bloom in spring. ZONES 9–11.

Euphorbia esculenta
syn. *Euphorbia inermis* var. *laniglans*

Native to the Karoo region of South Africa, this species is used as cattle fodder. The trunk grows up from a basal swelling that thickens out to 4–8 in (10–20 cm) across. Tuberculate branches reach a maximum length of 8 in (20 cm), and tiny flowers are produced in spring and summer. ZONES 8–10.

Euphorbia flanaganii

This is a small succulent to about 6 in (15 cm) high with many slender branches arising from a central stem. The bright yellow floral bracts appear in summer. It is marginally frost hardy and comes from Cape Province in South Africa. ZONES 8–10.

Euphorbia fulgens
SCARLET PLUME

A native of Mexico, this deciduous shrub grows to a height of about 5 ft (1.5 m) with arching branches. In winter and spring it bears sprays of flowers with showy bright red bracts in the upper leaf axils. It has mid- to deep green, narrow leaves. This species is frost tender and is suited to warmer areas only. **ZONES 10–12.**

Euphorbia glauca
MAORI SPURGE, WAINATUA, SHORE SPURGE

This shrubby perennial species is native to New Zealand and is that country's only member of the genus; its Maori name means 'milk of the demons'. It is an erect plant to about 24 in (60 cm) tall with blue-green foliage. Its flowerheads are only fractionally paler in color than the leaves, but it has tiny red nectaries. **ZONES 9–11.**

Euphorbia grandicornis
COW'S HORN EUPHORBIA

This bright green South African succulent has flattened triangular stems edged with strong white spines up to 2 in (5 cm) long. Mature plants are around 4 ft (1.2 m) high with stems up to 6 in (15 cm) in diameter. Occasionally small, oval leaves will develop after warm, moist weather. It has yellowish green flower bracts followed by 1 in (25 mm) diameter red fruit. This frost-tender species requires bone-dry conditions in winter. **ZONES 9–11.**

Euphorbia grandidens

Native to South Africa, this giant, cactus-like species can grow to a towering 30–50 ft (9–15 m) in height and is covered with short brown thorns. The long, flexuous branches are mostly 3-angled with coarse teeth on the angles, and are arranged in whorls. **ZONES 8–11.**

Euphorbia horrida

Euphorbia griffithii **'Fireglow'**

Euphorbia grandicornis

Euphorbia glauca

Euphorbia griffithii

This perennial from the eastern Himalayas, which grows to a height of 3 ft (1 m), produces small, yellow flowers surrounded by brilliant orange bracts in summer. The lanceolate, green leaves have prominent pinkish midribs and turn red and yellow in fall (autumn). **'Fireglow'** produces orange-red floral bracts in early summer. **ZONES 6–9.**

Euphorbia horrida

This cactus-like species up to 10 in (25 cm) high from South Africa may form a clump up to 15 in (38 cm) across. Its striped stems are covered in sharp spines, and very small green and yellow flowers are borne in summer. **ZONES 8–11.**

Euphorbia inermis
syn. ***Euphorbia viperina***

The tuberous root of this succulent shrub from the Karoo region of South Africa, merges with the main stem to form a swelling at the base of the plant. Green branches grow to 12 in (30 cm) long and flowers appear in spring and summer. **ZONES 8–11.**

Euphorbia griffithii

Euphorbia ingens

Euphorbia inermis

Euphorbia ingens
TREE EUPHORBIA, NABOOM

This is a succulent tree from eastern South Africa that can reach up to 40 ft (12 m) high. It has a very short trunk and a massive crown made up of many much-branched, 4-sided stems. The straight, dark brown spines are borne together in pairs. Yellow-green flowers, often tinged with red, develop in groups of 3 close to the spines in early summer. **ZONES 9–11.**

Euphorbia knuthii

This species, a dwarf succulent native to Mozambique and South Africa, features gray-green stripes on its light-green, 3-angled, sinuate stems. It is thickened at its base and bears short brown thorns. **ZONES 10–11.**

Euphorbia lambii

This shrub from the Canary Islands grows to 5 ft (1.5 m) in height. Its stems are thick and light brown in color and have conspicuous scars left by shedding leaves. The leaves are clustered at the ends of its stiff branches. Its flowerheads feature large yellow-green bracts. It is hardly frost tolerant. **ZONES 9–11.**

Euphorbia ledienii

Brown thorns grow in pairs on this South African succulent species. It reaches 6 ft (1.8 m) in height and has gray-green branches up to $2\frac{1}{2}$ in (6 cm) thick. The flowers are produced in spring. **ZONES 9–11.**

Euphorbia lambii

Euphorbia grandidens

Euphorbia longifolia

From Bhutan, *Euphorbia longifolia* is a perennial plant to 3 ft (1 m). In early summer it produces attractive yellow flowers that are surrounded by yellow bracts. The lanceolate green leaves have prominent white midribs. **ZONES 7–9.**

Euphorbia marginata
SNOW ON THE MOUNTAIN, GHOSTWEED

Native to central areas of North America, this bushy annual makes an excellent foil for brighter flowers. It has pointed oval, bright green leaves, sharply margined with white, and broad, petal-like white bracts surrounding small flowers in summer. *Euphorbia marginata* is fairly fast growing to about 24 in (60 cm) tall with a spread of about 12 in (30 cm). It will endure cold conditions. **ZONES 4–10.**

Euphorbia mauritanica

Euphorbia marginata

Euphorbia mellifera

Euphorbia × *martinii*

This is a naturally occurring hybrid from southern France. The parents are *Euphorbia characias* and *E. amygdaloides* and the hybrid can more closely resemble one or other parent. Its stems are usually red and its foliage is somewhat like *E. characias*, though less blue in color. It does best in a sunny, sheltered garden. **ZONES 7–10.**

Euphorbia mauritanica

MILK TREE, PENCIL TREE, FINGER TREE

Native to southwestern Africa, this is a thornless, leafless succulent that reaches a height of 5 ft (1.5 m) in cultivation and branches freely from the base. Its milky, poisonous sap should be kept away from cuts and from the eyes. **ZONES 9–12.**

Euphorbia mellifera

HONEY SPURGE

This handsome evergreen shrub usually grows little more than 6 ft (1.8 m) tall and as wide in cultivation. It has soft green leaves up to 8 in (20 cm) long with a conspicuous, whitish midrib. The honey-scented spring flowers consist of rounded heads of bronze-green bracts

Euphorbia × *martinii*

Euphorbia longifolia

surrounding the tiny green flowers. Although not very frost hardy, in favorable positions in a sunny, sheltered garden it will make an impressive feature plant. It is native to Madeira and is quite rare in the wild. **ZONES 8–10.**

Euphorbia meloformis

From South Africa, this is one of the more extreme succulent forms found among euphorbias. It is more or less globular with 8 or more broad ribs and is up to about 4 in (10 cm) in diameter. Green or purplish flowers are produced at the top of the plant in summer. **ZONES 9–11.**

Euphorbia milii

syn. *Euphorbia splendens*

CROWN OF THORNS

This slow-growing, ferociously thorny, semi-succulent shrub with bright green leaves is a native of Madagascar. Deciduous in cooler areas, it tolerates dry conditions and grows to a height of about 3 ft (1 m). It is excellent in frost-free rock gardens or sunny courtyards and is often used as a low hedge in coastal areas. Throughout the year, and especially in spring, it bears tiny yellowish flowers among bright red bracts, borne in showy flat sprays. ***Euphorbia milii* var. *splendens*** is a semi-prostrate form with oblong leaves. **ZONES 10–12.**

Euphorbia myrsinites

This trailing species is only 6–8 in (15–20 cm) tall but spreads to over 24 in (60 cm) wide. Blue-green, oval leaves spiral around the stems, each stem ending in a rounded flowerhead of soft chartreuse in spring. It is excellent in a rock garden or at the top of a low wall. It ranges in the wild from southern Europe

Euphorbia ledienii

to central Asia. It self-seeds readily and will tolerate frost, poor soil, heat and dry conditions. **ZONES 5–10.**

Euphorbia obesa

GINGHAM GOLF BALL, BASEBALL PLANT

Almost perfectly spherical at first, becoming slightly elongated with age, this unusual frost-tender succulent is native to South Africa. It grows up to 8 in (20 cm) tall and 6 in (15 cm) in diameter, and is quite spineless. The pale green stem has 8 almost flat ribs and red-brown horizontal and vertical lines making a checkered pattern similar to gingham. Small, yellow-green, cup-shaped flowers appear at the apex in summer. **ZONES 10–11.**

Euphorbia palustris

This bushy, evergreen perennial occurs through most of Europe and western Asia. It grows to about 3 ft (1 m) tall and has mid-green, lance-shaped foliage and flattish heads of deep yellow flowers and bracts in late spring. Frost hardy, this is one of the few euphorbias that will grow well in damp soil. Prune out flowered stems to ground level. **ZONES 5–9.**

Euphorbia pentagona

syns *Euphorbia heptagona, E. tetragona*

This tall, thorny succulent, native to the Karoo region of South Africa, grows 10 ft (3 m) tall. It has stiff green stems, $1\frac{1}{2}$ in (35 mm) thick, with branches that form in irregular whorls and are edged with downturning thorns. **ZONES 9–11.**

Euphorbia polychroma

syn. *Euphorbia epithymoides*

CUSHION SPURGE

Native to central and southern Europe, this frost-hardy, clump-forming perennial is grown for its heads of bright chrome-yellow flowers produced from spring to summer. It has softly hairy, deep green leaves and a rounded, bushy habit, reaching a height and spread of about 18 in (45 cm). **'Major'** has yellowish green flowers in loose clusters. **ZONES 6–9.**

Euphorbia polygona

This is a thick-stemmed, medium-sized, thorny succulent from South Africa. It is multi-ribbed in form, with up to 30 ribs, sometimes making a spiral pattern. The plant branches basally and has a dark gray-green stem that thickens up to 4 in (10 cm) in diameter. **ZONES 9–11.**

Euphorbia pulcherrima

POINSETTIA, MEXICAN FLAME TREE

Potted poinsettias are a familiar Christmas decoration all over the northern hemisphere, but this native of Mexico is only a garden plant in frost-free climates.

Euphorbia palustris

Euphorbia milii

Euphorbia myrsinites

Euphorbia pentagona

Euphorbia milii cultivar

Euphorbia polygona

Euphorbia sikkimensis

Euphorbia schillingii

Euphorbia seguieriana subsp. *niciciana*

It makes a rather open shrub up to 12 ft (3.5 m) tall, usually dropping its leaves as flowering commences. The broad bracts, which give each flower cluster the appearance of a single, huge flower, last many weeks. There are many named cultivars, which extend the color range from the original blood red to pink and cream. It thrives best in subtropical regions and likes fertile soil and sunshine. The leaves are large but not especially attractive. Cultivars of the normal tall-growing poinsettia include **'Henrietta Ecke'** with additional smaller red bracts. Most cultivars now sold for indoor use are semi-dwarf: **'Annette Hegg'** is red, while **'Rosea'** (pink) and **'Lemon Drop'** (pale yellow) are similar except for color. **ZONES 10–12.**

Euphorbia punicea

This evergreen species is native to Jamaica, Cuba and the Bahamas. It has gray-green branches ascending from the stem and growing up to 18 in (45 cm). The plant's total height at maturity is 3 ft (1 m). Red flowerheads bloom in spring and summer. The foliage is green and lance-shaped, with the broadest part of the leaf above the middle. **ZONES 10–12.**

Euphorbia resinifera
syn. *Euphorbia sansalvador*

This species is the source of the drug euphorbium, which has been in use since ancient times. It is a spiny shrub that can reach 6 ft (1.8 m) in height in its native Morocco, and grows in clusters of gray-green, 4-angled stems 18 in (45 cm) long. Short brown thorns grow from the stem in pairs; the flowers are produced in spring and summer. **ZONES 8–11.**

Euphorbia rigida
syn. *Euphorbia biglandulosa*

This evergreen perennial grows to 24 in (60 cm) with rigid but semi-trailing stems clothed in grayish, somewhat succulent foliage. The stems are topped with heads of lime-yellow bracted flowers in spring. This native of the Mediterranean and parts of the Middle East is a frost-hardy plant ideal for a sunny rock garden. **ZONES 7–10.**

Euphorbia schillingii
SCHILLING'S SPURGE

This is a frost-hardy, clump-forming, perennial species to 3 ft (1 m) tall. It is a comparative newcomer to horticulture, discovered in Nepal by Tony Schilling in 1975. It has unbranched, well-clothed stems with foliage of a soft green with a white midrib. The flat flowerheads are produced from mid-summer to mid-fall (autumn). In some climates—usually with dry fall weather—its foliage will color well before dying. **ZONES 5–9.**

Euphorbia schimperi

From southern Arabia, this shrubby succulent grows to 6 ft (1.8 m) high. Its tiny leaves are oblong. Not often found in cultivation, material sold with this name is more likely to be ***Euphorbia nubica***. **ZONES 10–12.**

Euphorbia triangularis

Euphorbia seguieriana subsp. *niciciana*
syn. *Euphorbia reflexa*

This perennial plant has several slender stems arising from a central woody crown. Its foliage is fine and blue-green and in late summer it bears terminal heads of small yellow-green bracts, sometimes ageing reddish. This frost-hardy plant is a good rock garden subject or for the edge of a border where it can trail out over gravel or paving. It is native to southeastern Europe and southwestern Asia. **ZONES 5–9.**

Euphorbia sikkimensis

This herbaceous perennial from the eastern Himalayas has a somewhat suckering, spreading root system that produces upright stems to 3 ft (1 m) tall. In late winter its foliage is rich burgundy, fading to green as the season progresses although it keeps a lovely pinkish midrib. By mid-summer it produces flat heads of lime-yellow bracts. **ZONES 6–9.**

Euphorbia tirucalli
CAUSTIC BUSH, PENCIL EUPHORBIA

This generally shrubby succulent is from eastern and southern Africa as well as the Arabian peninsula. Once used as a source of latex, it grows to a height and spread of about 15 ft (4.5 m), its twiggy stems bearing tiny, deciduous leaves. The flowers are minute and insignificant. **ZONES 10–12.**

Euphorbia triangularis

This giant, thorny succulent is native to Natal in South Africa and grows from 30–60 ft (9–18 m) high. The stems are 6-angled, becoming rounder towards the top. The branches form in tiers and whorls, with ½ in (12 mm) thorns in pairs ¾ in (20 mm) apart on the ribs. **ZONES 9–11.**

Euphorbia trigona
AFRICAN MILK TREE

This 3–6 ft (1–1.8 m) tall, cactus-like succulent from Namibia is a popular indoor plant—it looks dramatic with its bolt upright, 3-angled stems and oval leaves standing horizontally at intervals from the angles. By the end of summer most of the leaves drop. The insignificant green flowers are not often seen on indoor plants. It is frost tender and needs good light indoors, light shade in the garden. **ZONES 10–12.**

Euphorbia tuberculata

This succulent comes from the semi-arid northwest of South Africa's Cape Province. It has cream flowers with scarlet tips and grows to 30 in (75 cm). **ZONES 9–11.**

Euphorbia tirucalli

Euphorbia punicea

Euphorbia polychroma 'Major'

Euphorbia pulcherrima

E

Euphorbia valida

This succulent from South Africa is similar to *Euphorbia meloformis* but grows to a height of 12 in (30 cm) and diameter of 8 in (20 cm). It branches basally, with blue-green bands often appearing on the body. Small flowers appear in spring and summer. **ZONES 9–11.**

Euphorbia viguieri

This spiny succulent from Madagascar grows to 5 ft (1.5 m) in height. Its stems are 6-angled and ridged and bear triangular leaf scars and rows of irregular spines along the ridges. The leaves, clustered towards the tips of the branches, are red in color with green midribs. Its floral bracts are yellow-green. **ZONES 10–12.**

EURYA

One of the larger genera in the camellia family, *Eurya* consists of about 70 species of evergreen trees and shrubs from eastern Asia and the western Pacific region. They favor high-rainfall habitats, growing in densely forested hill country, low scrub on misty mountaintops, or sometimes on windswept sea coasts. Most have rather leathery leaves, commonly with small, blunt teeth and tending to turn a dull reddish or bronze color before falling or, sometimes, in winter. Male and female flowers are borne on separate plants. The flowers are very small with overlapping, whitish petals and carried on short, recurving stalks in the leaf axils. The fruits are small, black berries.

CULTIVATION: Growing requirements and cold hardiness vary between species, though generally they do well in moist, well-drained, leafy, humus-rich, acid soil in full sun or part-shade. Propagate from ripe seed or cuttings in summer.

Euryops pectinatus

Euryops virgineus

Euryops linearis

Eurya japonica

This shrub can be up to 30 ft (10 m) tall and wide in the wild although it is not likely to exceed 10 ft (3 m) in cultivation. It has leathery, deep green leaves. The tiny white flowers produced in spring are followed by small, black fruit that are not very showy and which have a slightly offensive smell. It is native to Japan and Korea and is moderately frost hardy. **ZONES 8–10.**

EURYALE

FOX NUTS, GORGON PLANT

This genus consists of a single species, a remarkable spiny water lily related to the huge-leafed *Victoria*. Native to China, Japan and northern India, it has long been cultivated for its edible seeds ('fox nuts') and rhizomes. Its stems, leaf undersides and club-like flower buds and fruits are all armed with fierce-looking long prickles, though these are somewhat flexible and are not needle sharp. The large, floating leaves have a bubbly upper surface. The flowers themselves are comparatively small, with deep purple petals.

CULTIVATION: It requires about 24 in (60 cm) or more depth of water maintained at a temperature of 60°F (15°C) or higher during summer, with heavy feeding in the form of well-rotted manure held beneath sand. In cool climates it is occasionally grown in a large pool in conservatories. Propagate from seed in late spring.

Euryops chrysanthemoides

Eurya japonica

Euphorbia valida

Euryale ferox

This handsome, large aquatic plant is suitable for warm to tropical climates or a heated pond in a tropical greenhouse. An interesting perennial, it has flowers with petals that can be red, purple or lilac and are shorter than the 4 sepals, which are green. The flowers appear in summer, followed by prickly berries. **ZONES 10–12.**

EURYOPS

Part of the large daisy family, this genus consists of around 100 species of annuals, perennials and evergreen shrubs, most of which come from southern Africa. They are grown for their colorful yellow to orange flowerheads which are held above fern-like foliage; a typical example, shown here, is ***Euryops linearis***.

CULTIVATION: Frost hardiness varies between species. Generally, a well-drained soil and a position in full sun are the main requirements of these attractive plants, otherwise the shrubs tend to grow leggy and the flowers are not as plentiful. They respond to light pruning after the flowers have faded but do not respond well to root disturbance. Propagate from seed in spring or cuttings in summer.

Euryops acraeus

syn. ***Euryops evansii* of gardens**

Native to South Africa, this showy species is a very dense, dome-shaped shrub to 3 ft (1 m) high and wide. Its foliage is dense, the leaves narrow and intensely silvery white. The bright yellow daisy flowers are produced through spring and summer. It is marginally frost hardy and somewhat short-lived. **ZONES 8–10.**

Euryops chrysanthemoides

syn. ***Gamolepis chrysanthemoides***

PARIS DAISY

Growing to around 3 ft (1 m) high, this shrub has soft, irregularly serrated leaves and in winter is covered with yellow daisy-like flowerheads; these continue sporadically through most of the year. It does well in warm, dry climates; in cool areas it makes an attractive pot plant. **ZONES 9–11.**

Euscaphis japonica

Euphorbia viguieri

Euryops pectinatus

GRAY-LEAFED EURYOPS

This widely cultivated, frost-tender shrub from the southwestern Cape region of South Africa, grows well in most temperate conditions. From winter to spring it bears bright yellow daisies up to 2 in (5 cm) across, for which the finely cut, gray-green leaves are an attractive foil. It is a single-stemmed, bushy shrub growing up to 4 ft (1.2 m), and can be lightly pruned to maintain a rounded shape. It likes to be kept moist during dry weather. **ZONES 9–11.**

Euryops virgineus

RIVER RESIN BUSH

A species easily distinguished by its small, bright green leaves and upright habit, this 4 ft (1.2 m) high shrub has stiff branches densely clothed in fine foliage. Flowering throughout the year, it blooms most heavily in late winter and spring, when it produces masses of small daisies at the branch tips. It is very much at home in seaside gardens. **ZONES 9–10.**

EUSCAPHIS

This genus contains just a single species. It is a small, deciduous tree with short, weak branches and attractive foliage, flowers and fruit. While none of these features is outstanding on its own, they combine to make an appealing, undemanding tree.

CULTIVATION: Any well-drained soil in sun or dappled shade will do. Propagation is from seed, which may require two periods of stratification, or from cuttings taken in early summer.

Euscaphis japonica

Endemic to China and Japan, this species grows to 30 ft (9 m) high. It has 10 in (25 cm) long pinnate leaves made up of 7 to 11 leaflets, each 2–4 in (5–10 cm) long. In spring it produces small yellow flowers in long panicles that develop into attractive hollow red fruit. When the leaves fall, the white-striped, purple bark is an interesting and unusual feature. **ZONES 6–10.**

EUSTOMA

syn. ***Lisianthius***

Belonging to the gentian family, this genus consists of 3 species of annuals, biennials and perennials, ranging in the wild from southern USA to northern South America. One species, *Eustoma grandiflorum,* has very showy, tulip-like flowers that have become popular as cut flowers in recent years, and has been the subject of considerable breeding work. Japanese plant breeders extended the pastel color range to white, pale blue and pink as well as the original violet, and also developed double-flowered strains. Any unopened buds on the spray develop beautifully in water, so these give pleasure for an extended period.

CULTIVATION: Usually regarded as frost tender, the plants are easy to cultivate in any warm-temperate climate. Give them sun, perfect drainage and fertile soil; they rarely perform well after their first year. Propagate from seed in spring or from cuttings in late spring or summer.

Eustoma grandiflorum

syn. ***Lisianthus russellianus***

PRAIRIE GENTIAN, TEXAS BLUEBELL, LISIANTHUS

Native to America's Midwest from Nebraska to Texas, this biennial's flowers last up to 3 weeks in water after cutting. It can also be grown as a container plant. It has gray-green leaves and 2 in (5 cm)

Euscaphis japonica

wide, flared, tulip-like flowers in colors of rich purple, pink, blue or white. Of an upright habit, the plant is slow growing to a height of 24 in (60 cm) and spread of 12 in (30 cm). **ZONES 9–11.**

Eustoma grandiflorum cultivar

EXACUM

Like *Eustoma,* this genus belongs to the gentian family; it consists of about 25 species of annuals, biennials or perennials, widely distributed through tropical Africa and Asia. They have mostly yellow, white, blue or purple flowers that are often broadly cup-shaped or flat, unlike the tubular flowers of gentians. Only one species, *Exacum affine,* has become widely cultivated, a miniature from the hot dry island of Socotra that sits just off the horn of Africa at the mouth of the Red Sea; it is grown as an indoor plant, popular for its neat shrub-like growth habit and long succession of flowers.

CULTIVATION: These plants can only be grown outdoors in warm, frost-free climates, where they do best in a sunny position in rich, moist but well-drained soil. Indoors they like diffused sun and a night temperature not below 50°F (10°C). Propagate from seed in early spring.

Exacum affine

Exacum affine

PERSIAN VIOLET, GERMAN VIOLET

This showy miniature has shiny, oval leaves and bears a profusion of small, 5-petalled, saucer-shaped, usually purple-blue flowers with yellow stamens throughout summer. A biennial usually treated as an annual, *Exacum affine* grows to a height and spread of 8–12 in (20–30 cm). **'Blue Midget'** grows to only half as big and has lavender-blue flowers, while **'White Midget'** has white flowers. **ZONES 10–12.**

EXBUCKLANDIA

This genus consists of only 2 species in the witch hazel family. They are evergreen trees with broad, sometimes 3-lobed leaves, leathery and pink tinged while young. They are native to the eastern Himalayas, southern China and Southeast Asia.

CULTIVATION: These trees require a mild climate to grow well as they are not very cold tolerant. They like a moist soil with high humus content and a sheltered position. Propagate from seed or cuttings.

Exbucklandia populnea

Exbucklandia populnea

syn. ***Bucklandia populnea***

This tree can grow up to 100 ft (30 m) tall although it is unlikely to reach these proportions in cultivation. The heart-shaped leaves have conspicuous stipules to 1 in (25 mm) long, the blade up to 6 in (15 cm) long and red beneath when young with red veins and stalks. The flowers are small and of little value. *Exbucklandia populnea* ranges from the eastern Himalayas to Java. **ZONES 10–12.**

EXOCHORDA

PEARL BUSH

There are 4 species of deciduous shrubs in this genus from central Asia and northern China. They have weak, pithy branches and thin-textured, paddle-shaped leaves. In spring the branch ends are clustered with 5-petalled, white flowers of delicate, informal beauty. The fruits are capsules with wing-like segments, splitting apart when ripe to release flattened seeds.

CULTIVATION: Species of *Exochorda* are quite frost hardy but they prefer climates with sharply defined seasons and dry summers for the best display of flowers. A sheltered position in full sun and well-drained soil are desirable. Prune older stems back to their bases after flowering to encourage vigorous new growth and abundant flowers. Propagate from seed in fall (autumn) or from cuttings.

Exochorda racemosa

Exochorda × *macrantha*

Exochorda × *macrantha* 'The Bride'

Exochorda × *macrantha*

This hybrid was raised in France around 1900 by crossing *Exochorda racemosa* with the central Asian *E. korolkowii.* Sometimes reaching 10 ft (3 m) tall, in mid- to late spring it produces elongated clusters of pure white flowers, each about $1\frac{1}{2}$ in (35 mm) across, from every branch tip. **'The Bride'** is one of the loveliest varieties of pearl bush. It makes a weeping shrub up to 6 ft (1.8 m) or so tall and about as much in width. 'The Bride' produces masses of large white flowers on arching stems in spring. **ZONES 6–9.**

Exochorda racemosa

From northern China this species, long established in western gardens, makes a lovely display when well grown. It grows to about 10 ft (3 m) high with arching branches and has narrow, pale green leaves to 3 in (8 cm) long. The flowers are borne in late spring, with loose, slender sprays appearing from the branch tips, each flower being $1\frac{1}{2}$ in (35 mm) wide with narrow petals. **ZONES 6–9.**

F

FABIANA

From temperate South America, this genus contains about 25 species of heath-like shrubs. Only one species is generally cultivated: *Fabiana imbricata*, grown for its attractive deep green foliage and pure white flowers. The genus, which is named after Spanish archbishop and patron of botany Francisco Fabian y Fuero (1719–1801), is grown for its small, overlapping, needle-like leaves and single, bell-shaped or tubular flowers.
CULTIVATION: They are frost hardy, but are liable to damage during severe winters. In cold areas plant in a sheltered position. They require full sun and fertile, well-drained soil. Propagate from cuttings in summer.

Fabiana imbricata

This is an erect or spreading shrub to 8 ft (2.4 m) high with branches densely covered with small, mid-green, overlapping leaves. The slender tubular white or pale pink flowers are borne in profusion in summer. Prune after flowering. ***Fabiana imbricata* f. *violacea*** has horizontal branches and mauve-blue flowers. ZONES 8–11.

FAGOPYRUM

BUCKWHEAT

This small genus of annuals and perennials are grown for their richly flavored, highly nutritious seeds which are processed into grits or flour. It is unsatisfactory for bread, but is used to make pancakes and ordinary cakes particularly in Europe and eastern Asia; it is also used to make buckwheat pasta. In the USA and Canada the flour is used in griddle cakes and in Japan it is made into thin green-brown noodles called soba. The leaves are alternate, and the small white flowers appear in racemes or corymbs.
CULTIVATION: Buckwheat are frost-hardy plants that will grow in poor soil. They mature within 2 months, which makes it possible to harvest 2 crops per season. Propagate from seed in spring and summer.

Fagus grandifolia

Fagus grandifolia

Fagopyrum esculentum

syn. *Polygonum fagopyrum*

BUCKWHEAT

A native of northern Asia, this annual species grows to 3 ft (1 m) tall. It has reddish stems and short dense racemes of white fragrant flowers followed by triangular fruit that are enclosed in a tough, dark-brown rind. ZONES 3–9.

FAGRAEA

This genus contains about 35 species of evergreen trees and shrubs, the latter generally epiphytic. Species are found naturally throughout the Pacific region, East and Southeast Asia. The opposite leaves are large and leathery and the terminal clusters of tubular, fragrant flowers are followed by fleshy, multi-seeded, often brightly colored, berry-like fruits. While *Fagraea* species are relatively uncommon in cultivation, they make fine ornamentals and shade trees; they are also suitable to control soil erosion.
CULTIVATION: Plants are best suited to tropical regions, but can be successfully cultivated under glass in frost-prone areas. They prefer a shady, somewhat protected situation and freely draining, sandy soil. Propagate from seed or cuttings in spring.

Fagus orientalis

Fagus sylvatica

Fabiana imbricata

Fagraea fragrans

From India and Southeast Asia, this many-stemmed shrub or single-trunked tree to 70 ft (21 m) tall has a wide-spreading crown of leathery, elliptic leaves to 6 in (15 cm) long. In summer it bears clusters of fragrant long-tubed flowers that open white and fade to cream. ZONES 11–12.

FAGUS

BEECH

Although these long-lived, deciduous trees, to 130 ft (40 m), are scattered across Europe, the UK, Asia and North America, most of the 10 species are confined to China and Japan. They occur in a rather narrow climatic zone, being absent from far northern forests as well as the lowland Mediterranean-type forests. Most species have a rounded crown of delicate foliage that turns golden brown in fall (autumn) and smooth, gray bark. They bear brown-scaled, pointed winter buds and prominently veined, ovate to elliptic leaves. In spring new leaves are briefly accompanied by small, individual clusters of male and female flowers. In early fall, small shaggy fruit capsules split open to release angular, oil-rich seeds (beech nuts) that are a major food source for wildlife. Their valuable timber is close-grained and readily worked; it is used for flooring and furniture, and for making kitchen utensils.
CULTIVATION: Frost hardy, beeches require well-drained, reasonably fertile soil and some shelter from strong wind; they will do best in areas with long, warm summers. Purple-leafed forms prefer full sun and yellow-leafed forms a little shade. Propagate from seed as soon as it falls; cultivars must be grafted. They may be attacked by aphids and are prone to powdery mildew.

Fagraea fragrans

Fagopyrum esculentum

Fagus grandifolia

syn. *Fagus americana*

AMERICAN BEECH

From eastern USA, Canada and the highlands of Mexico, this species grows with a long straight trunk to about 80 ft (24 m) in its native forests, but in the open it develops low branches and a broad crown and reaches only 30 ft (9 m). Root suckers are often present beneath mature trees. The foliage and nuts resemble those of Europe's *Fagus sylvatica*. It is not commonly cultivated outside North America. ZONES 4–9.

Fagus orientalis

ORIENTAL BEECH

This species once formed extensive forests in Greece, Turkey, northern Iran and the Caucasus, replacing *Fagus sylvatica* at low altitudes. It resembles that species except that it has noticeably longer leaves that turn brownish yellow in fall (autumn) and larger nuts. In a suitably warm climate it can grow vigorously to 70 ft (21 m) in height and 50 ft (15 m) in spread. ZONES 5–10.

Fagus sylvatica

COMMON BEECH, EUROPEAN BEECH

Although regarded as one of the most 'English' natives, this species ranges across Europe and western Asia, with an average height of about 80 ft (24 m). In spring it bears drooping balls of yellowish male flowers and greenish clusters of female flowers. Many cultivars have been selected for their habit, intricately cut leaves and colorful foliage, including **'Aspleniifolia'**, a fern-leafed beech with narrow, deeply cut leaves; **'Dawyck'** with a narrow columnar habit to 50 ft (15 m) and dark purple foliage; **'Pendula'** with branches that droop from a mushroom-shaped crown; ***Fagus sylvatica* f. *purpurea*** (syn. 'Atropunicea'), the copper beech, a round-headed form with purple-green leaves that turn copper and which does best in full sun; **'Riversii'**, the purple beech, with very dark purple leaves; **'Rohanii'** with brownish purple deeply cut leaves; **'Rotundifolia'** with strong upright growth and small

Fagus sylvatica 'Tricolor'

Fagus sylvatica 'Aspleniifolia'

Fagus sylvatica 'Pendula'

Fagus sylvatica 'Rotundifolia'

rounded leaves; **'Tricolor'** (syn. 'Roseomarginata'), a smaller tree with purplish leaves edged and striped pink and cream; and **'Zlatia'** which bears yellow young foliage that later becomes mid- to dark green. ZONES 5–9.

FALLOPIA

syns *Bilderdykia, Reynoutria*

This genus consists of 7 species of herbaceous annuals and woody-based perennials with twining or trailing stems, from northern temperate regions. Whitish flowers borne in spike-like panicles in late summer or fall (autumn) are followed by nut-like fruits. These vigorous but often invasive growers, ideal for covering a shed or old deciduous tree, need to be kept under control.
CULTIVATION: Very frost hardy, they will grow in any moderately rich, well-drained soil in full sun or part-shade. Plants like plenty of moisture. Propagate from seed or by division in spring. Trailing species are propagated from cuttings.

Fallopia aubertii

syns *Bilderdykia aubertii, Polygonum aubertii*

SILVER LACE VINE, MILE-A-MINUTE PLANT

This deciduous, vigorous, twining climber from China can reach 40 ft (12 m). The leaves are broad and heart-shaped, and panicles of small, white to green

Fagus sylvatica f. *purpurea*

flowers, maturing to pink, are borne in summer. Small white fruit follow in fall (autumn). Keep under control with hard pruning. Unlike other species in the genus, it can tolerate an alkaline soil. ZONES 4–10.

Fallopia baldschuanica

syns *Bilderdykia baldschuanica, Polygonum baldschuanicum*

RUSSIAN VINE, BOKHARA FLEECE FLOWER

This woody twining deciduous climber from central Asia reaches 40 ft (12 m) or more. The dark green leaves are heart-shaped, up to 4 in (10 cm) long, and drooping panicles of minute, pink-

Fagus sylvatica 'Zlatia'

tinged white flowers are borne in late summer and fall (autumn). The flowers are followed by pinkish white fruit. ZONES 4–10.

Fallopia japonica

syns *Polygonum cuspidatum, Reynoutria japonica*

JAPANESE KNOTWEED

Reaching 10 ft (3 m) tall with a creeping rhizome, often forming extensive colonies, this species has elliptic to broadly ovate leaves to 6 in (15 cm) long. White flowers are borne in the upper leaf axils in late summer to fall (autumn). ZONES 4–10.

FALLUGIA

APACHE PLUME

This genus contains just one species, a small deciduous shrub from arid regions of southwestern North America. It is grown for its attractive foliage and flowers and as a source of oilseed.
CULTIVATION: It is moderately frost hardy, but not in areas with wet winters. Grow in full sun in a sharply drained soil with shelter from cold winds and severe frosts. Propagate from seed or cuttings.

Fallugia paradoxa

This shrub reaches 8 ft (2.4 m) high with slender branches and shedding white bark. The finely cut dark green leaves are downy underneath. Single white flowers, borne on slender stalks in summer, are followed by leathery nutlets, each with a purplish, feathery plume. ZONES 7–10.

Fagus sylvatica 'Rohanii'

FARFUGIUM

From temperate Asia and closely allied to *Ligularia*, the 2 species of evergreen perennials in this genus are grown for their large, leathery foliage and daisy-like, yellow flowerheads. They are suitable for growing in containers.
CULTIVATION: These frost-hardy plants do best in part-shade in fertile, moist but well-drained soil. Propagate from seed in spring or by division of variegated cultivars in spring.

Farfugium japonicum

syns *Farfugium tussilagineum, Ligularia tussilaginea*

Native to Japan, this clump-forming perennial to 24 in (60 cm) high has glossy, kidney-shaped leaves on long stalks, above which arise downy branched stems bearing clusters of flowers from fall (autumn) to winter. **'Aureomaculatum'**, the leopard plant, has variegated leaves with circular yellow blotches. ZONES 7–10.

Fallopia aubertii

Farfugium japonicum 'Aureomaculatum'

Fallugia paradoxa

Farfugium japonicum

Fascicularia bicolor

Fatsia japonica

Fatsia japonica

Fargesia nitida

FARGESIA

This genus consists of about 4 species of evergreen, clump-forming bamboos from China and the northern Himalayas. They have narrowly oblong leaves, and grass-like flowers that are rarely produced in cultivation and then generally only on long-established specimens. **CULTIVATION:** Grow these marginally to fully frost-hardy plants in fertile, moist soil in full sun or part-shade (depending on the species) and shelter from strong cold winds. Propagate from cuttings or by division in spring.

Fargesia murieliae

syns *Arundinaria murieliae, Fargesia spathacea* of gardens

UMBRELLA BAMBOO

Native to China, this fully frost-hardy species grows to 12 ft (3.5 m) or more high and has bright green leaves to 4 in (10 cm) long. The canes, which are yellowish green when young, branch in the first year and turn yellow with age. This is an attractive specimen or accent foliage plant. **ZONES 6–10.**

Fargesia nitida

syns *Arundinaria nitida, Sinarundinaria nitida*

FOUNTAIN BAMBOO

Originating in China, this slow-growing bamboo can eventually reach about 12 ft (3.5 m) in height. It has small tapering mid-green leaves, purple canes, and after the first year a number of branches that grow out from the nodes. The insignificant flowers appear only rarely. *Fargesia nitida* is particularly effective as a screen or hedge and is fully frost hardy. **ZONES 5–10.**

FASCICULARIA

This genus is made up of 5 species of evergreen, rosette-forming, perennial plants of the bromeliad family. They all originate from Chile and are valued for their spreading leaves which form large rosettes and for their exotic, long-lasting blue flowers, which are followed by scaly fruits. **CULTIVATION:** These frost-tender plants are best grown in a greenhouse in cool climates. In warmer areas grow outside in poor, very well-drained soil in full sun. Water moderately during the growing season and sparingly in winter. Propagate from seed or by division in spring or summer.

Fascicularia bicolor

syn. *Fascicularia andina*

So named because of its green and red inner leaves, this vigorous bromeliad is one of the most attractive of Chile's native plants when in full flower. It has compact clusters of narrow, gray-green leaves with serrated edges which form a large rosette. Its inner leaves turn a vivid fiery red in fall (autumn). The flowers are borne in dense corymbs in summer. **ZONES 8–11.**

× *Fatshedera lizei*

× FATSHEDERA

TREE IVY

The one species of this hybrid genus, combining *Fatsia* and *Hedera*, is an evergreen erect or scrambling shrub grown mainly for its foliage and often used as a conservatory or house plant in cool climates. It grows to 6 ft (1.8 m) or more high with palmately 5- or 7-lobed lustrous dark green leaves. Rounded heads of small greenish white flowers are borne in terminal panicles in fall (autumn). **CULTIVATION:** Grow this frost-hardy plant in fertile, well-drained soil in full sun or part-shade. It will withstand coastal exposure and can be grown in seaside gardens. Propagate from cuttings in summer.

× *Fatshedera lizei*

This is a spreading open shrub with glossy lobed leaves to 10 in (25 cm) across. It is used extensively as ground cover, or it can be trained against a wall or tree trunk. **'Variegata'** has leaves with a narrow, creamy white edge. To encourage bushy growth, regularly pinch back when young. **ZONES 7–11.**

FATSIA

The 2 or 3 species of evergreen shrubs or small trees that make up this genus come from Japan, Korea and Taiwan. They are closely related to ivy (*Hedera*), a relationship evident in the flowers and fruit as well as in leaf texture. *Fatsia*, however, have thick, erect stems, small branches and deeply lobed leaves larger than those of ivy. Rounded heads of creamy white flowers occur in large panicles and are followed by small black berries. Their affinity with *Hedera* is demonstrated by the hybrid × *Fatshedera lizei*. **CULTIVATION:** They tolerate cold better than most other evergreens with leaves of this size, yet adapt to warm climates if shaded and moist. In mild areas grow in well-drained, humus-rich soil in sun or light shade. In very cold regions they are usually grown as indoor plants. Propagate from seed in fall (autumn) or spring, or from cuttings in summer.

Fatsia japonica

syns *Aralia japonica, A. sieboldii*

JAPANESE ARALIA, JAPANESE FATSIA

This handsome shrub or small tree reaches a height of 5–12 ft (1.5–3.5 m). The lustrous, palmately lobed leaves are 12 in (30 cm) or more across. The flowers appear in fall (autumn). Though tough, this frost-hardy species needs to be protected from fierce summer sun, making it suitable for a position beneath trees or in a courtyard. **'Variegata'** has leaves with creamy white margins. **ZONES 8–11.**

FAUCARIA

TIGER JAWS

There are about 30 species of these clump-forming, stemless, perennial succulents from South Africa. They have unusual fleshy, boat-shaped leaves with formidable-looking teeth along their margins (hence the common name) and daisy-like yellow, pink or white flowers that open in the afternoon from summer to fall (autumn). These dwarf plants are ideal for a raised rockery or desert garden. **CULTIVATION:** Faucarias do best in warm climates although they will tolerate light, infrequent frosts; they need a position in full sun in poor, well-drained soil. They need to be kept dry in winter but well watered in spring and occasionally in summer. Propagate from seed or stem cuttings in spring or summer.

Faucaria britteniae

syn. *Faucaria grandis*

The leaves of this species are fleshy, diamond-shaped and gray-green with gray dots. They reach 2 in (5 cm) long and have reddish margins and several fine recurved teeth. The large yellow flowers, tinged purplish pink beneath, are borne in late summer to mid-fall (mid-autumn). **ZONES 9–11.**

Faucaria tigrina

This easy to cultivate, attractive succulent grows to 4 in (10 cm) in height and spreads to 8 in (20 cm). The triangular, fleshy leaves are covered with white dots, occasionally tinted red, and bear up to 10 pointed teeth on their margins. Large, deep yellow flowers bloom in fall (autumn). **ZONES 9–11.**

Faucaria britteniae

Faucaria tigrina

Fenestraria aurantiaca

FEIJOA
PINEAPPLE GUAVA

Named after Brazilian botanist de Silva Feijo, this genus of 2 species from subtropical Brazil and Argentina consists of evergreen shrubs that reach about 15 ft (4.5 m) tall with a similar spread; they are grown for their showy, edible flowers and guava-like fruits. The fruits appear only after a hot summer and may be damaged by fall (autumn) frosts. The oval, glossy green leaves have a silvery underside. Some botanists prefer to classify this genus as *Acca*.
CULTIVATION: Feijoas prefer a warm, frost-free climate, but can grow in areas with very mild frosts in a sheltered, sunny spot. In colder climates they are best grown in a greenhouse. Plant in well-drained, humus-rich soil and ample water while the fruits mature. They are easily propagated from seed but cultivars produce better fruits. Fruit fly is a problem in some areas.

Feijoa sellowana
syn. *Acca sellowiana*
PINEAPPLE GUAVA, FEIJOA

This species, with pruning, can be formed into a single-trunked small tree or it can be clipped as a hedge. The flowers, carried on the new season's growth, have red petals that are white underneath and almost overshadowed by prominent, dark red stamens. The elongated fruit have a tangy flavor and are eaten raw or made into jam. **ZONES 9–11.**

FELICIA
BLUE DAISY

This genus, which ranges from southern Africa to Arabia, consists of 80 species of annuals, perennials and evergreen subshrubs. Named after Herr Felix, mayor of Regensburg on the Danube (about 1845), they are sprawling plants with aromatic foliage; in mild climates they flower on and off almost all year. The daisy-like, usually blue flowerheads with yellow disc florets are borne in masses.
CULTIVATION: They are fully frost hardy to frost tender and require full sun and well-drained, humus-rich, gravelly soil; they do not tolerate wet conditions. In all but the mildest areas the frost-tender perennial species need protection in winter with open-ended cloches. Deadheading prolongs the flowering season. Prune straggly shoots regularly. Propagate from cuttings taken in late summer or fall (autumn) or from seed in spring.

Feijoa sellowana

Felicia aethiopica

This bushy evergreen to 24 in (60 cm) high has small, smooth, obovate leaves to 1 in (25 mm) long. It bears solitary blue flowerheads to 1½ in (35 mm) across on glandular stalks in summer. **ZONES 9–11.**

Felicia amelloides
BLUE MARGUERITE

This bushy, evergreen subshrub has a spreading habit, growing to 24 in (60 cm) in height and twice as wide. It has roundish, bright green leaves and sky blue flowerheads with bright yellow centers borne on long stalks from late spring to fall (autumn). Frost tender, it is fast growing in temperate climates and is suitable for seaside gardens. It is often grown as an annual in cool areas. **'Santa Anita'** has extra large blue flowers and **'Alba'** is a white form. ***Felicia pappei*** is like a miniature version of *F. amelloides* in growth, foliage and flower except that the flowerheads are an even richer, purer blue. It reaches 20 in (50 cm) in height. **ZONES 9–11.**

Felicia bergeriana
KINGFISHER DAISY

This mat-forming annual has hairy, lance-shaped, gray-green leaves and bears a mass of cobalt blue yellow-centered flowerheads above the foliage. The flowers open only in sunshine, so plant in a sunny situation. It is fast growing to a height and spread of 6 in (15 cm). **'Variegata'** has variegated leaves and blue flowers. **ZONES 9–11.**

Felicia echinata

Felicia echinata is a rounded bushy subshrub to 24 in (60 cm) high, with small, recurved sometimes toothed leaves which taper to sharp points. Lilac to white flowerheads are borne in groups of up to 6 in summer. **ZONES 9–11.**

Felicia aethiopica

Felicia filifolia

This many-branched subshrub to 3 ft (1 m) high has alternate needle-like leaves. Axillary mauve to white flowerheads are borne in profusion along the length of the stems in spring. **ZONES 9–11.**

Felicia fruticosa
syns *Aster fruticosus, Diplopappus fruticosus*

A bushy perennial 2–4 ft (0.6–1.2 m) high, *Felicia fruticosa* has tiny heath-like, linear leaves and pink, white or purple flowerheads in spring and early summer. The flowering period is long and extremely abundant. After flowering cut back to encourage compact growth and a good crop of flowers the following year. **ZONES 9–11.**

Felicia heterophylla

This dome-shaped, mat-forming annual from South Africa grows to 20 in (50 cm) high and wide. It has lance-shaped, gray-green leaves and solitary blue flowerheads in summer. **ZONES 9–11.**

Felicia petiolata

This mat-forming prostrate perennial with a spread of up to 3 ft (1 m) has small, sparsely lobed leaves and bears solitary white to violet flowerheads in summer. **ZONES 9–11.**

FENESTRARIA

This Namibian genus is made up of one or two species of tiny clump-forming, perennial succulents with basal rosettes of fleshy pebble-like leaves that have a translucent patch at the tips. They have bright yellow or white daisy-like flowers. In warm areas they make fascinating rock- or desert-garden plants.
CULTIVATION: These frost-tender plants can be grown outdoors in mild areas in a porous, very well-drained soil in full sun. Water sparingly during the growing season and not at all in winter. In frosty climates grow as house plants or in a greenhouse. Propagate from seed in fall (autumn) or spring or by division in spring or summer.

Felicia heterophylla

Felicia amelloides

Fenestraria aurantiaca
WINDOW PLANT

This small succulent forms cushions up to 2 in (5 cm) tall and 8 in (20 cm) across composed of upright, circular to almost triangular, smooth, gray-green leaves approximately 1½ in (35 mm) long. Large, vivid yellow flowers appear from late summer to fall (autumn). **ZONES 10–11.**

FEROCACTUS
syn. *Hamatocactus*
BARREL CACTUS

The name of this genus from North and Central America translates as 'fierce cactus', an apt title for plants protected by 4 in (10 cm) long sturdy spines that can be yellow, red, brown or white. There are about 30 species of these spherical cacti, which become columnar with age. They are slow growing and can take 15 years to flower. The flowers are usually yellow, red, orange or brown. The plants vary in size and shape according to age and

Felicia petiolata

Felicia fruticosa

Felicia echinata

F

species, ranging in height from 12 in (30 cm) to 6 ft (1.8 m). When young they make excellent container plants.
CULTIVATION: They require full sun, porous, well-drained soil and free air circulation. They must be protected from frost and from excessive rain. Propagate from seed in spring.

Ferocactus gracilis

This solitary cactus, with a stem at first globular and later cylindrical to 10 ft (3 m) tall, comes from northwestern Mexico. It has up to 32 prominent ribs and 8 to 12 slender white radial spines and 4 to 12 longer, curved and twisted red central spines. Yellow, red-tinged, bell-shaped flowers are borne in summer, followed by yellow, squarish fruit. **ZONES 10–11.**

Ferocactus haematacanthus

Not to be confused with the following better known species, this cactus native to eastern Mexico, reaches 4 ft (1.2 m) high and 10 in (25 cm) wide. It is armed with short, reddish brown spines and has up to 27 ribs, patterned in slightly wavy lines. Medium-sized, purple-pink, daisy-shaped flowers appear in summer, and are followed by purplish oval seed pods in summer. **ZONES 10–11.**

Ferocactus wislizenii

Ferocactus gracilis

Ferocactus hamatacanthus
syn. *Hamatocactus hamatacanthus*
TURK'S HEAD

This fiercely spined, globe-shaped Mexican and southwestern USA species reaches 24 in (60 cm) in height and diameter. It has up to 17 prominent ribs and numerous tubercles sprouting hooked, brownish red, yellow-tipped spines. In summer to fall (autumn) it bears a single yellow flower with a red interior, and then a pulpy, round seed pod. It may develop black areoles as a result of fungus. **ZONES 10–11.**

Ferocactus schwarzii

Native to Mexico, this pale-green cactus grows up to 24 in (60 cm) high and 18 in (45 cm) wide. Large, yellow, daisy-like flowers bloom in spring and globular red fruit follow in summer. This plant has between 13 and 19 ribs, bearing 2 in (5 cm) long spines which, after their initial yellow color, turn brown. **ZONES 10–11.**

Ferocactus stainesii
syn. *Ferocactus pilosus*

In the wild this species forms massive clumps, although in cultivation it is usually smaller—to 10 ft (3 m). When mature it bears many orange flowers. **ZONES 10–11.**

Ferocactus wislizenii
FISH HOOK CACTUS

Named for its strongly hooked spines which are up to 6 in (15 cm) long, this slow-growing, spherical cactus is native to southwest USA and Mexico. It grows up to 5 ft (1.5 m) tall and bears large, funnel-shaped orange or yellow flowers in spring and yellow fruit in summer. The spines of this species are said to be used as fish hooks in their native habitat. ***Ferocactus wislizenii* var. *herrerae*** has 13 ribs and the spines are not flattened. **ZONES 10–11.**

Ferocactus haematacanthus

Ferocactus stainesii

Ferula communis

FERRARIA

Ten species of small perennials with curious flowers make up this genus, all endemic to South Africa except for one species in tropical Africa. The flowers are remarkable for the intricately frilled and crisped margins of their 6 petals (3 long and 3 short), which are also strongly marked and mottled in shades ranging from gray to purple or chocolate. Each flower lasts only one day and they only open in fine weather.
CULTIVATION: Ferrarias are marginally frost hardy to frost tender and need to be overwintered indoors in cool climates. They are easily grown in a sunny position in any well-drained soil of reasonable fertility. Plants die down during summer, at which time watering should be withheld. Propagate from seed or from corms, which can be lifted and divided in fall (autumn).

Ferraria crispa
STARFISH LILY, SPIDER FLOWER

This odd-looking South African plant, to about 15 in (38 cm) high, is able when conditions are unfavorable to extend its dormancy for at least a year. The deep brown and pale yellow flowers, which are unpleasantly scented, are short lived but bud formation continues over a prolonged but unpredictable period. **ZONES 9–11.**

Ferocactus schwarzii

Festuca amethystina 'Superba'

FERULA
GIANT FENNEL

This genus consists of about 170 species of aromatic herbaceous perennials from central Asia to the Mediterranean, with finely cut pinnate leaves and large rounded umbels of greenish white or yellow flowers borne on tall branching stems. These plants are grown for their strong architectural form and are ideal for the back of a border. They should not be confused with culinary fennel *(Foeniculum).*
CULTIVATION: Grow these frost-hardy plants in full sun in fertile, well-drained soil. Plants often die after seeding. Propagate from seed in late summer. They are prone to attack from aphids and slugs.

Ferula communis
GIANT FENNEL

Found in most parts of the Mediterranean region, this tall robust perennial to 15 ft (4.5 m) high has narrowly lobed leaves and leaf stalks that sheath the stems. The 5-petalled yellow flowers appear in early summer. Plants may take several years to flower. **ZONES 8–10.**

FESTUCA
FESCUE

Native to temperate zones worldwide, this genus consists of about 300 to 400 species of tuft-forming perennial grasses with evergreen linear leaves, often very narrow and sometimes rolled under. The panicles of flowerheads composed of generally small and flattened spikelets are produced from spring to summer. Several fescues are grown as fine lawns, others are grown for their ornamental gray-blue foliage which is attractive all year round.
CULTIVATION: Grow in any well-drained soil. They do best in full sun but will tolerate semi-shade and withstand dry conditions and the severest frosts. Propagate from seed in spring or fall (autumn) or by division in spring. Disease and pests rarely affect them.

Festuca amethystina
LARGE BLUE FESCUE, TUFTED FESCUE

A native of the Alps and southern Europe, this fescue is named for its violet-tinged spikelets of flowers which appear in late spring and early summer. It grows to 18 in (45 cm) high and forms tufts of slender, blue-green, rough-edged leaves. ***Festuca amethystina* 'Superba'** has blue leaves and amethyst colored flowers. **ZONES 3–10.**

Festuca elatior
TALL FESCUE

This species from Europe and northern Asia has a tendency to clump, making it suitable for turf on playing fields and for controlling erosion. It grows to a height of 4 ft (1.2 m). Its leaves are tough and it will grow in compacted soil. As it does not send out runners, sow thickly for a close turf. **ZONES 5–10.**

Festuca eskia
syns ***Festuca scoparia, F. varia* var. *scoparia***
BEARGRASS, BEARSKIN GRASS

This species from the Pyrenees reaches only 6 in (15 cm) high, but spreads to 10 in (25 cm) to form an attractive cushion of spiky, dark green, needle-like leaves. Slender, pendent flowerheads appear in summer. **ZONES 5–10.**

Festuca glauca
syn. ***Festuca ovina* var. *glauca***
BLUE FESCUE, GRAY FESCUE

This clump-forming European grass reaches a height and spread of 12 in (30 cm). The very narrow leaves range in color from silvery white to blue-gray, and insignificant flowers bloom in summer. It is suitable as an edging or ground cover. Cultivars include **'Blaufuchs'** ('Blue Fox') with vivid blue leaves; **'Blausilber'** ('Blue Silver') with intensely silver-blue leaves; **'Elijah Blue'** with paler silver-blue leaves; **'Seeigel'** ('Sea Urchin') which forms a tight, compact tuft of soft, silver-blue leaves; and **'Golden Toupee'** which has rounded tufts of bright green and yellow leaves. **ZONES 3–10.**

Festuca glauca 'Seeigal'

Festuca glauca

Festuca glauca 'Elijah Blue'

Festuca glauca 'Golden Toupee'

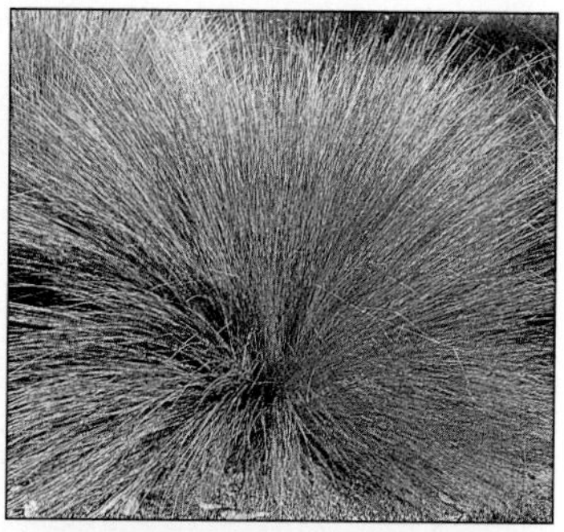

Festuca ovina var. *novae-zelandiae*

Festuca mairei

Festuca mairei
ATLAS FESCUE

This clump-forming grass, which is native to Morocco, has gray-green, rough-textured leaves to 24 in (60 cm) long. *Festuca mairei* has open panicles of spikelets on flowering stems to 4 ft (1.2 m) high. **ZONES 7–11.**

Festuca ovina
SHEEP'S FESCUE

Native to cooler temperate regions of the world, this clump-forming grass to 12 in (30 cm) high may form dense tussocks. It has stiff, very narrow green to gray-green leaves. In mid- to late summer it bears narrow open panicles with purple-tinged spikelets of 4 to 5 flowers. It is cultivated mainly as a forage and meadow grass. The New Zealand native ***Festuca ovina* var. *novae-zelandiae*** (syn. *F. novae-zelandiae*) has very narrow leaves to 18 in (45 cm) long and spikelets of 5 to 7 flowers. **ZONES 5–10.**

Festuca eskia

Festuca rubra var. *pruinosa*

Festuca vivipara

Festuca rubra
CREEPING RED FESCUE

A meadow grass native to Europe, this species is easily identified by the red or purplish sheath circling the base of the stem. Wiry slender green leaves rise to 6 in (15 cm), overtopped by narrow panicles of purple-tinged flowers. Rhizomatous and tolerant of dry conditions, it is suitable as a lawn grass and requires low maintenance. **'Commutata'** is a tuft-forming cultivar that makes an appealing ground cover. It is also extensively grown as a lawn grass. ***Festuca rubra* var. *pruinosa*** has glaucous foliage with a whitish or bluish sheen. **ZONES 3–9.**

Festuca vivipara

Native to northern Europe, this small, clump-forming plant forms dense tussocks of stiff, very narrow leaves. The spikelets produce small plantlets instead of flowers. **ZONES 5–10.**

FICUS
FIG

This large, varied genus consists of about 800 species of evergreen and deciduous trees, shrubs and climbers from tropical and subtropical areas throughout the world. It includes the common fig, *Ficus carica*, which bears edible fruit, but most species are grown for their ornamental foliage and for shade. The tiny flowers are completely enclosed in the developing fruits which are borne in the leaf axils and are produced all year. Ripe fruits are eaten by bats and birds and the seeds of many species are often dropped into the branches of other trees where they germinate, sending down roots to the ground. These eventually form secondary trunks that kill the host tree.
CULTIVATION: Some grow to great heights in gardens and most have vigorous, invasive root systems. Marginally frost hardy to frost tender, many make excellent pot and house plants when young. Figs prefer full sun to part-shade and humus-rich, moist but well-drained soil and shelter from cold winds. Water potted specimens sparingly. Propagate from seed or cuttings, or by aerial layering.

Ficus cordata subsp. *salicifolia*

Ficus benjamina 'Exotica'

Ficus benghalensis

Ficus benjamina

Ficus aspera 'Parcellii'
MOSAIC FIG

The wild form of this species comes from islands of the southwest Pacific. This evergreen shrub or small tree has large, roughly oval, dark green leaves mottled with white and with rather hairy undersides. Reaching 10 ft (3 m) in height, it is grown as a house plant in cool climates. This cultivar has pronounced foliage markings and pink to purple instead of orange-red fruit. **ZONES 11–12.**

Ficus aurea
GOLDEN FIG, STRANGLER FIG

This tree from the West Indies and Florida reaches 60 ft (18 m) high, sometimes originating as a strangler. It has thick elliptic leaves to 4 in (10 cm) long and it bears tiny yellow figs. **ZONES 11–12.**

Ficus benghalensis
BANYAN, INDIAN BANYAN

From southern Asia, the banyan is outstanding for its aerial roots, which descend from the branches to the ground and eventually form secondary trunks. An old tree, though reaching only about 70 ft (21 m) in height, can spread widely enough to shelter an entire village. The banyan has pale gray bark, large glossy mid-green leaves, bronze when young, and round red figs borne in pairs. **ZONES 11–12.**

Ficus benjamina
WEEPING FIG, WEEPING CHINESE BANYAN

A tropical Asian evergreen tree, the weeping fig can reach 50 ft (15 m) in

Ficus aurea

height and a much greater spread, sometimes supported by aerial roots. It has shiny, pointed, oval leaves, insignificant fruit and an invasive root system. This species and its cultivars are used extensively as potted house plants; they need adequate water in summer, less in cooler months. **'Exotica'** has twisted leaf tips; **'Variegata'** has rich green leaves splashed with white. **ZONES 10–12.**

Ficus carica
COMMON FIG

The edible fig with its distinctive 3-lobed leaves is indigenous to Turkey and western Asia and has been cultivated for millennia. A small deciduous tree, it reaches 30 ft (9 m) and needs a sunny position in a warm climate with dry summers, as rain can split the ripening fruit. There are many named cultivars. **'Black Mission'** is the well-known black fig grown in California; the fruit is of excellent quality and in warm regions it bears 2 crops per year. **'Brown Turkey'** is a productive, vigorous tree with large purplish brown fruit with pink flesh and a rich flavor. **'Genoa'** bears greenish yellow fruit with a rich flavor and amber flesh. **ZONES 8–11.**

Ficus cordata subsp. *salicifolia*
WILLOW-LEAFED FIG

This shrub or small tree has leathery oval leaves to 6 in (15 cm) in length with a rounded or heart-shaped base. The small fruit are shining red with white specks when ripe and are borne singly or in pairs in the leaf axils. They are an important food source for birds, monkeys and baboons in tropical Africa. **ZONES 10–12.**

Ficus aspera 'Parcellii'

Ficus dammaropsis
DINNERPLATE FIG

From the mountains of New Guinea, this small tree grows to 30 ft (9 m). Unlike many *Ficus* species it is single-trunked, forming neither buttresses nor aerial roots. The large rough leaves, up to 24 in (60 cm) long, with deeply corrugated surface, are deep green above and paler beneath, sometimes with red veins. The large figs ripen to a deep purple and are clothed in overlapping scales. **ZONES 10–12.**

Ficus deltoidea
MISTLETOE FIG

This slow-growing evergreen shrub reaches 20 ft (6 m). It has bright green, broadly spoon-shaped leaves with a reddish brown undersurface. Profuse greenish white small fruit that mature to orange and red are produced in pairs. **ZONES 11–12.**

Ficus elastica
INDIA RUBBER TREE, RUBBER PLANT

From tropical Asia, this tree can reach 100 ft (30 m) tall and forms massive

Ficus carica

Ficus dammaropsis

Ficus religiosa

Ficus elastica 'Decora'

aerial roots and high buttresses with age. *Ficus elastica* has an agressive root system and a site must be chosen with care. Outside the tropics it is usually seen as a potted plant. Its rosy new leaves make an attractive contrast to the deep green mature leaves. Cultivars include **'Decora'** with bronze new leaves, and **'Doescheri'** with variegated gray-green and creamy white leaves with light pink midribs. **ZONES 10–12.**

Ficus lyrata

syn. ***Ficus pandurata***

BANJO FIG, FIDDLELEAF FIG

This spreading, evergreen tree from tropical Africa can reach a height of 100 ft (30 m). It features broad, violin-shaped leaves: they are bright glossy green, heavily veined, and up to 15 in (38 cm) long. Figs are long and green. *Ficus lyrata* is often seen as a house plant. **ZONES 10–12.**

Ficus pumila 'Quercifolia'

Ficus macrophylla

MORETON BAY FIG, AUSTRALIAN BANYAN

This large, spreading evergreen tree occurs in coastal rainforests of eastern Australia. It grows to about 130 ft (39 m) tall with a spread nearly as great and a buttressed trunk. It bears large, leathery, dark green leaves with rust-toned undersides, and abundant figs that turn reddish brown when ripe. **ZONES 10–12.**

Ficus microcarpa

syn. ***Ficus retusa***

CHINESE BANYAN, INDIAN LAUREL FIG

When mature, this large evergreen tree reaches 100 ft (30 m) and can form dense curtains of aerial roots. The small, pointed oval leaves are held on ascending branches, the tips of which have a weeping habit. A native of Australia, ***Ficus microcarpa* var. *hillii*** is used for multiple plaited plantings or as a single standard either in a container or in a garden. The Indian laurel fig, ***F. m.* var. *nitida***, has dense, upright branches. **ZONES 9–12.**

Ficus opposita

SANDPAPER FIG

Widely found in tropical northern Australia, this tall shrub or small tree to 30 ft (9 m) has mid-green leaves. Their raspy surfaces were used by Aborigines for smoothing wooden implements. The small, edible fruit are pear-shaped. This tree may become completely deciduous during the dry season. **ZONES 11–12.**

Ficus petiolaris

From Mexico, this small to large freely suckering tree bears heart-shaped, pale green leaves to 4 in (10 cm) long, often

Ficus petiolaris

Ficus opposita

with a pattern of red veins above. The leaves are carried on stalks up to 4 in (10 cm) long. Almost rounded, downy figs are produced in pairs, maturing with pink or white spots. **ZONES 10–11.**

Ficus pumila

syn. ***Ficus repens***

CLIMBING FIG, CREEPING FIG

From Japan, Vietnam and China, this vigorous evergreen climber clings by aerial roots along the stems. It has attractive small, bright green, heart-shaped juvenile leaves that turn bronze. Remove any mature woody branches that stand out strongly from the support to retain juvenile leaves. **'Minima'** has much

Ficus rubiginosa 'Variegata'

Ficus lyrata

smaller, daintier foliage and is less rampant; **'Quercifolia'** has lobed leaves; **'Variegata'** is more vigorous with leaves mottled white to cream. **ZONES 8–11.**

Ficus religiosa

BO TREE, PEEPUL, SACRED FIG

Indigenous to India and Southeast Asia, this species resembles the banyan although not as tall. It has an open crown and poplar-like leaves with long thread-like tips and bears small purple figs. It is believed that Buddha was meditating beneath a bo tree when he received enlightenment. Many trees have been propagated from the tree at Anaradhapura, Sri Lanka, recorded as having been planted in 288 BC. **ZONES 11–12.**

Ficus rubiginosa

RUSTY LEAF FIG, PORT JACKSON FIG

This salt-resistant evergreen, native to Australia, grows 30–50 ft (9–15 m) tall and almost as wide. The main trunk is buttressed and sometimes aerial roots are produced. The foliage is shiny deep green on top, downy and rust-colored underneath. Pairs of globular yellow fruit mature in fall (autumn). **'Variegata'** has prominent golden markings on the leaves. **ZONES 10–11.**

Ficus macrophylla

Ficus sur
syn. ***Ficus capensis***
BROOM CLUSTER FIG, CAPE FIG

This semi-deciduous to evergreen tree of wide distribution in Africa grows to 70 ft (21 m) tall with a wide, spreading crown, and bears large leaves that are reddish brown when young. The edible fruit, about ½ in (12 mm) in diameter, are borne in large panicles from the trunk and limbs. This makes a fine shade tree for a large garden or park. **ZONES 10–12.**

Ficus sycomorus
SYCAMORE FIG, MULBERRY FIG

Widespread through Africa, this tree has a huge spreading crown and a very thick trunk with narrow buttresses. The large leaves are slightly rough with entire margins. Unlike most fig species, the fruit are borne in clusters on fruiting branchlets on the trunk and main branches. The figs are fairly large, up to 2 in (5 cm) across, and are yellowish red when ripe. **ZONES 10–12.**

Ficus virens
GRAY FIG, JAVA WILLOW, SPOTTED FIG, STRANGLER VINE

Ranging from India to the Solomon Islands and northern Australia, this briefly deciduous strangler often starts life as an epiphyte. Cultivated plants, however, are usually more conventional single-trunked trees growing to about 50 ft (15 m) tall with a broad crown and heavy limbs. It has pointed-tipped, poplar-like leaves up to 6 in (15 cm) long and produces pairs of small, red-spotted white figs at the branch tips. **ZONES 10–12.**

Ficus virens

FILIPENDULA

This is a genus of 10 species of herbaceous perennials from northern temperate regions. All except *Filipendula vulgaris* occur naturally in moist waterside habitats. They have alternate pinnate leaves and erect stems bearing large panicle-like clusters of tiny, 5-petalled flowers with fluffy stamens. They do well at the back of large perennial borders and in waterside positions.
CULTIVATION: Grow these fully frost-hardy plants in full sun or part-shade in any moisture-retentive but well-drained soil. *F. rubra* and *F. ulmaria* will thrive in swampy, boggy sites. Propagate from seed or by division in spring or fall (autumn). Check for powdery mildew.

Filipendula kamtschatica
syn. ***Filipendula camtschatica***

Occurring naturally from far eastern Siberia to China and northern Japan, this popular garden plant to 10 ft (3m) tall has palmately lobed leaves. Large fluffy heads of white or pink-tinted, scented flowers are produced from mid-summer to early fall (autumn). **ZONES 3–9.**

Filipendula purpurea
JAPANESE MEADOWSWEET

From Japan, this upright clump-forming perennial reaches 4 ft (1.2 m) high with deeply divided toothed leaves. In

Filipendula purpurea 'Elegans'

Ficus sur

Filipendula ulmaria 'Aurea'

Filipendula ulmaria 'Variegata'

Firmiana simplex

summer it bears large terminal heads composed of masses of tiny crimson-purple flowers. This is a beautiful plant for growing near a water feature. **'Elegans'** has light, greenish yellow foliage, and ***Filipendula purpurea* f. *albiflora*** has white flowers. **ZONES 6–9.**

Filipendula rubra
QUEEN OF THE PRAIRIES

This North American species, up to 8 ft (2.4 m) high, is grown for its attractive, deeply cut, fern-like foliage and showy, crowded heads of tiny peach-blossom pink flowers. The flowers are long lasting and the foliage remains lovely long after flowering. These plants do well in waterside positions and in damp meadows. **'Venusta'** has deeper pink flowers in very large clusters. **ZONES 3–9.**

Filipendula ulmaria
syn. ***Spiraea ulmaria***
MEADOWSWEET, QUEEN-OF-THE-MEADOW

Native to Europe and western Asia, this clump-forming perennial grows to 6 ft (1.8 m) high. It has pinnate leaves to 12 in (30 cm) long with sharply toothed ovate leaflets. The creamy white flowers are borne in dense heads to 10 in (25 cm) across in summer. **'Aurea'** has golden-green leaves that are yellow when young; the leaves of **'Variegata'** are striped and mostly blotched yellow. **ZONES 2–9.**

Filipendula vulgaris
syn. ***Filipendula hexapetala***
DROPWORT

From Europe and Asia, this species reaches about 24–36 in (60–90 cm) high and has fleshy swollen roots. It is grown for its attractive, deeply cut, fern-like foliage, and showy, crowded heads of tiny white flowers; some garden varieties are pink. This species will tolerate fairly dry conditions and must have good drainage. **ZONES 3–9.**

Filipendula vulgaris

FIRMIANA

This genus was named after the eighteenth-century patron of the Padua botanic gardens, Karl Josef von Firmian. It comprises 9 species of trees and shrubs, mostly deciduous, grown for their attractive foliage and to provide shade. The leaves are entire or palmately lobed and small, showy, bell-shaped flowers are followed by papery, leaf-like fruits. The beautiful Chinese parasol tree, *Firmiana simplex*, is widely grown and is a great favorite in China; it was commonly planted in the gardens of scholars and poets, who made it their emblem.
CULTIVATION: Warm, frost-free conditions are best. Plant in moist but well-drained, fertile soil in full sun or part-shade. In frost-prone areas grow in containers and overwinter in a greenhouse and water well in summer. Prune only if necessary. Propagate from ripe seed in spring.

Firmiana simplex
syns ***Firmiana platanifolia, Sterculia platanifolia***
CHINESE PARASOL TREE, WU TREE

From Vietnam to Japan, this deciduous tree grows to about 50 ft (15 m), with smooth green bark, large, maple-like leaves and sprays of small, greenish yellow spring flowers. The pinkish gold fruit are also of interest. **ZONES 9–11.**

FITTONIA
NERVE PLANT, PAINTED NET LEAF

This genus consists of 2 species of evergreen, creeping perennials from tropical rainforests in South America. They are grown mainly for their opposite, short-stemmed leaves, with their brightly colored veins, most often as conservatory

and house plants. Occasionally white to reddish white, insignificant flowers are borne on short spikes. In warm, frost-free climates they make excellent ground covers or trailing plants.
CULTIVATION: Grow in part-shade and provide a humus-rich, well-drained soil and plenty of water. Where temperatures drop below 50°F (15°C) grow indoors in a good potting mix and keep evenly moist. They make excellent hanging basket subjects. Cut back straggly stems in spring. Propagate from cuttings or by layering stems in summer.

Fittonia verschaffeltii

This species reaches about 6 in (15 cm) high with an indefinite spread and has dark green oval leaves with conspicuous red veins. The insignificant flowers are irregular and best removed if they form. ***Fittonia verschaffeltii* var. *argyroneura*** (syn. *F. argyroneura*), the silver net leaf, has rooting stems and mid- to dark green leaves with conspicuous white veins. **ZONES 11–12.**

FITZROYA

Named after Captain Robert Fitzroy, commander of HMS *Beagle* and companion of Charles Darwin, this genus consists of a single species, an important conifer of the cool-temperate forests of southern Chile and Argentina. It yields a valuable reddish, straight-grained timber prized for its strength and durability. Wild specimens, some thought to be as old as 3,000 years, often reach a great size, but even very old cultivated trees rarely exceed 50 ft (15 m) in height.
CULTIVATION: Moderately frost hardy, it does best in fertile, moist but well-drained soil in full sun with protection from cold winds. Propagate from seed in spring or cuttings in late summer or fall (autumn).

Foeniculum vulgare 'Purpurascens'

Foeniculum vulgare

Fittonia verschaffeltii var. *argyroneura*

Fitzroya cupressoides
syn. *Fitzroya patagonica*
PATAGONIAN CYPRESS

Usually seen as a strongly upright, single-trunked tree, this evergreen has fibrous reddish bark and rather pendulous branches of small juniper-like oblong leaves arranged in whorls of three. Small globular cones are borne in abundance, maturing rapidly and shedding their seed from early fall (autumn). **ZONES 8–10.**

FLINDERSIA

Named after the explorer Matthew Flinders, this genus comprises 17 species of evergreen trees of which all but 2 are indigenous to the Australian mainland. Several are valued for their timber. The attractive foliage is similar to that of the northern hemisphere ash trees (*Fraxinus*), hence the common names crow's ash for *Flindersia australis* and silver ash for ***F. schottiana***. The flowers are small and white, and the woody fruits that follow are often covered with small sharp prickles.
CULTIVATION: While most species are from the tropical and subtropical rainforests and are best suited to high rainfall areas, one popular species, ***F. maculosa***, the leopard tree, can tolerate drier inland areas. Frost tender, they require full sun, moist but well-drained soil and regular water. Propagate from seed in spring.

Flindersia australis
CROW'S ASH, AUSTRALIAN TEAK

This evergreen tree from eastern Australia's subtropical rainforests grows to 120 ft (36 m) in the wild, less in cultivation, forming a sturdy trunk with scaly brown bark and a dense multi-branched crown. The large pinnate leaves consist of shiny green leaflets. Small white flower clusters appear in spring. The large fruit have 5 prickly, boat-shaped segments. **ZONES 10–11.**

Foeniculum vulgare var. *azoricum*

Fittonia verschaffeltii

Flindersia australis

Flindersia maculosa

Flindersia maculosa
LEOPARD TREE

Native to inland eastern Australia, this slow-growing tree reaches 50 ft (15 m) high with a symmetrical crown of delicate foliage and bark mottled with cream, gray and white. The juvenile plant is bushy but develops a straight, slender trunk. *Flindersia maculosa* bears profuse panicles of small, creamy white flowers in summer. **ZONES 10–11.**

FOENICULUM
FENNEL

This genus of one species of aromatic biennial or perennial is grown for its yellow flower umbels and finely cut, aniseed-flavored leaves, which are used in cooking; it also has edible stems and seeds. Darker-leafed cultivars provide attractive contrast in the herb garden or flower border.
CULTIVATION: Grow this frost-hardy plant in full sun in fertile, moist but well-drained soil and remove spent flowers to prevent self-seeding. Propagation is from seed in spring or fall (autumn).

Foeniculum vulgare

This tall, graceful perennial grows to 6 ft (1.8 m) tall with thick, hollow stems, masses of feathery foliage and flat clusters of yellow flowers on tall, erect stems during summer. The flowers are followed by brown seeds. Both the leaves and seeds have a strong aniseed taste and are used for flavoring fish and other savory dishes. ***Foeniculum vulgare* var.**

Fitzroya cupressoides

azoricum (syn. *F. v.* var. *dulce*), Florence fennel, has a crisp white 'bulb' with the texture of celery. ***F. v.* subsp. *piperitum*** has fleshy leaves with segments less than ½ in (12 mm) long. Its lateral clusters of flowers are longer than those produced terminally. **'Purpurascens'** has finely divided bronze-purple foliage when young. **ZONES 5–10.**

FOKIENIA

This coniferous genus contains one species only, discovered in 1908 in Fokien Province (now Fujian), China. It is a densely foliaged tree resembling a *Chamaecyparis*. The foliage consists of flattened sprays of tightly appressed scales. The cones are also similar to those of *Chamaecyparis* except that they are larger.
CULTIVATION: Plant in moist, well-drained soil in sun or dappled shade. Propagation is from seed or small cuttings.

Forsythia × *intermedia* 'Spectabilis'

Forsythia × *intermedia* 'Lynwood'

Forsythia × *intermedia*

Forsythia suspensa

Forsythia × *intermedia* 'Beatrix Farrand'

Fokienia hodginsii

Usually reaching 10–20 ft (3–6 m), this pyramidal tree can grow to 100 ft (30 m) in the wild. It has light olive-green foliage and a solid trunk, reddish brown bark that peels off in small strips, and near-spherical cones up to 1 in (25 mm) in diameter. **ZONES 8–10.**

FONTANESIA

From China, this genus of a single species of deciduous shrub is closely related to privet, *Ligustrum*, and similarly can be used for hedging. The small greenish white 4-petalled flowers with protruding stamens are borne in panicles and are followed by a flat-winged nutlet.
CULTIVATION: Frost hardy, this plant does best in moderately rich, well-drained soil in full sun or part-shade. Propagate from seed in spring or cuttings in late summer or fall (autumn).

Fontanesia phillyraeoides

This dense, spreading shrub to 5 ft (1.5 m) has dull green oval to lance-shaped leaves to 4 in (10 cm) long with finely toothed margins. The greenish white flowers appear in early summer. Growing to 10 ft (3 m) or more high, ***Fontanesia phillyraeoides* subsp. *fortunei*** has glossy, smooth margined, lance-shaped leaves. **ZONES 6–9.**

FORESTIERA

From North and Central America, and like *Fontanesia* a privet ally, this genus of deciduous and occasionally evergreen shrubs and trees comprises about 20 species. They have small, opposite leaves that may be entire or minutely toothed, and small yellowish flowers borne on the branches of the previous year's growth; small black drupes follow.
CULTIVATION: Mostly marginally frost hardy, they grow well in moist but well-drained soil in full sun. Propagate from ripe seed or cuttings in summer.

Forestiera neomexicana
DESERT OLIVE, NEW MEXICAN PRIVET

This deciduous shrub to 10 ft (3 m) high has dull green oval to lance-shaped leaves to 2 in (5 cm) long. Axillary clusters of tiny yellowish white flowers are produced in spring. Its attractive black fruit are frosted blue. Frost tender, it will withstand dry conditions. **ZONES 9–10.**

FORSYTHIA

Since their introduction to Western gardens from China and Japan in the nineteenth century, the 7 species of forsythia have been popular shrubs valued for their brilliant yellow or gold blossoms in mid-spring. They make excellent cut flowers. Deciduous or sometimes semi-evergreen and of medium stature, they have soft-wooded stems branching from near the ground. The rather narrow, bluntly toothed leaves appear after the 4-petalled flowers, which are paired or clustered at the twig nodes.
CULTIVATION: Fully frost hardy, they are not fussy about soil type but fertilizer and compost encourage growth. They prefer a sunny position, but climate is crucial: they seldom flower in warm climates, requiring winter temperatures well below freezing point. Prune only to remove older branches. Propagate from cuttings in early summer.

Forsythia × *intermedia*
BORDER FORSYTHIA

An arching or spreading deciduous shrub with dark green, lance-shaped leaves, this species grows 8–10 ft (2.4–3 m) tall and slightly wider. A hybrid between *Forsythia suspensa* and *F. viridissima*, it was first recorded in Germany in about 1885. Some fine cultivars include **'Lynwood'** and **'Spectabilis'**. In 1939 Karl Sax at the Arnold Arboretum in Massachusetts created the first artificial tetraploid, **'Arnold Giant'**, and subsequently bred **'Beatrix Farrand'** and **'Karl Sax'**, all carrying large, brilliant gold flowers. **ZONES 5–9.**

Forsythia suspensa
WEEPING FORSYTHIA

Indigenous to China, this deciduous species was cultivated for centuries in Japan before being taken to Europe. It makes a shrub of 8–10 ft (2.4–3 m), or taller if supported, with dense, slender, arching branches. From early to mid-spring the branches carry profuse golden flowers with narrow petals. **ZONES 4–9.**

Forsythia viridissima
GREENSTEM FORSYTHIA

This deciduous or semi-evergreen species from China is neither as tall nor as graceful as *Forsythia suspensa*; it grows

Fokienia hodginsii

Forestiera neomexicana

Fokienia hodginsii

Fontanesia phillyraeoides subsp. *fortunei*

Fothergilla major

Fothergilla gardenii

to 6–10 ft (1.8–3 m) with thicker and more stiffly ascending branches. The yellow flowers, held close to the branches, appear from mid- to late spring. The hybrid cultivars are generally preferred and include **'Bronxensis'**, a small-growing variety that rarely exceeds 12 in (30 cm) in height with primrose-yellow flowers. **ZONES 5–9.**

FORTUNELLA

KUMQUAT, CUMQUAT

The renowned Scottish plant collector Robert Fortune (1812–80) introduced the kumquat to the conservatories of the UK, where it has flourished ever since. The genus comprises 5 evergreen shrubs or small trees, most of which have a small spine at the junction of leaf and branch. Originally they were included in the *Citrus* genus, to which they are closely related. They make compact, small shrubs bearing fragrant white flowers in spring and small, edible orange fruits from summer to fall (autumn). They make perfect container plants for small gardens or sunny patios. **CULTIVATION:** Frost tender, kumquats require an open position in full sun and fertile, moist but well-drained soil. Apply fertilizer in spring and water during the growing season, especially when the fruits are forming. In frost-prone areas grow in containers and overwinter in a greenhouse. Propagate species from seed or cuttings and varieties by budding onto rootstock in fall or spring.

Fortunella japonica

ROUND KUMQUAT, MARUMI CUMQUAT

Reaching 8–12 ft (2.4–3.5 m), although smaller when grown in a container, this species from China bears decorative small golden-orange fruit. They remain on the plant for a considerable time, but are best picked as they ripen to maintain the tree's vigorous growth. **ZONES 9–11.**

Fothergilla gardenii

FOTHERGILLA

From southeastern USA, this genus consists of 2 species of deciduous shrubs grown for their spring flowers and fall (autumn) foliage color. The fragrant, petal-less flowers are in upright, conical, brush-like spikes with conspicuous creamy white stamens. They appear before the foliage, which is roughly diamond-shaped, heavily ribbed and hazel-like. The leaves start out bright green, mature to deep green and develop intense yellow, orange and red fall tones. **CULTIVATION:** Frost hardy, they do best in humus-rich, moist but well-drained, acidic soil in sun or light shade and can be trimmed to shape after flowering if necessary. Propagate from seed or cuttings or by layering.

Fothergilla gardenii

WITCH ALDER, DWARF FOTHERGILLA

A small bushy shrub 24–36 in (60–90 cm) high from coastal plain areas of eastern USA, this species thrives in a cool climate with moist, well-drained soil. It produces fragrant white flowers 1½ in (35 mm) long in early spring, and the 2–3 in (5–8 cm) long leaves that follow develop brilliant fall (autumn) colors. **ZONES 5–10.**

Fothergilla major

syn. *Fothergilla monticola*

MOUNTAIN WITCH HAZEL, ALABAMA FOTHERGILLA

This shrub thrives in cool, shady mountain areas. The best known of the genus, it grows to 6–10 ft (1.8–3 m) tall and nearly as wide. Fragrant, white, puffball flowers appear in spring and again in fall (autumn). The dark green leaves, slightly blue beneath, turn vibrant yellows, oranges and reds in fall. **ZONES 5–9.**

FOUQUIERIA

This genus from southwestern USA and Mexico consists of some 10 species of woody, resinous, often succulent shrubs with upright, narrow, spiny stems. Some species reach 50 ft (15 m) high and produce small, bright green, oval leaves. The mass of thorny stems makes a formidable hedge. Terminal clusters of showy tubular flowers, usually borne after spring rains, are red, pale purple, cream or yellow, depending on the species. **CULTIVATION:** Frost tender, these desert or near-desert plants need a very dry winter, soil with good drainage and a position in full sun. Propagate from seed or cuttings taken from the short side branches in spring.

Fouquieria splendens

OCOTILLO, SLIMWOOD, CANDLEWOOD, COACH WHIP, FLAMING SWORD

This species briefly bursts into leaf and flower in spring and occasionally blooms later as well if rainfall allows. It has gray-green, grooved, thorny stems that can reach 30 ft (9 m) high. The 1 in (25 mm) long red flowers, in clusters, have prominent pollen-tipped stamens. **ZONES 9–11.**

FRAGARIA

STRAWBERRY

The dozen or so species in this genus are native to temperate areas of the northern hemisphere with one species from South America. They are low-growing, creeping or tufted perennials grown as ornamental ground covers and for their fleshy red fruits. The palmate leaves are composed of 3 toothed leaflets, and the white or pink, 5-petalled flowers appear in cymes. The strawberry itself is a false fruit consisting of tiny pips on a large fleshy receptacle. Modern, more robust strawberry plants can produce fruit for 6 months, or all year round in a warm climate. There are many named varieties, and flavor also varies. **CULTIVATION:** Grow these frost-hardy plants in beds or containers lined with straw, in free-draining, acidic soil. The plants need full sun or light shade and protection from wind; in cold climates grow them in slits in sheets of plastic. Propagate from seed in spring or fall (autumn) or by runners and replant with fresh stock every few years. Protect them from snails, strawberry aphids and birds. Botrytis can be a problem in high rainfall areas.

Fragaria × *ananassa*

GARDEN STRAWBERRY

The name ananassa means 'pineapple-flavored', a curious description for the modern, large-fruited garden strawberry that arose from crossing American species. It has ovate leaflets that are glaucous above and white beneath. A wide range of strawberry cultivars have been developed to suit differing climatic conditions. **ZONES 4–10.**

Fragaria chiloensis

SAND STRAWBERRY

This species grows wild in coastal North and South America and is one of the parents of modern strawberries. It spreads by runners in dense tufts, the lower leaves forming rosettes. It reaches a height of 12 in (30 cm) and spreads to 18 in (45 cm). The 2 in (5 cm) long, obovate, trifoliate leaves are a lustrous deep green, and hairy underneath. **ZONES 4–10.**

Fragaria moschata

HAUTBOY, HAUTBOIS

This European strawberry makes few runners. It grows to about 12 in (30 cm) high and has leathery wrinkled leaves with silky undersides. As the botanic name suggests, the fruit are musk-scented. They are pinkish red with a persistent calyx. The seeds are grouped more densely towards the tips of the fruit. **ZONES 4–10.**

Fragaria 'Pink Panda'

This spreading, ground cover perennial to 6 in (15 cm) high with an indefinite spread is grown for its pretty bright pink flowers to 1 in (2.5 cm) across, which appear from late spring to fall (autumn). It rarely bears fruit. **ZONES 4–10.**

Fortunella japonica

Fragaria chiloensis

Fragaria × *ananassa*

Fragaria chiloensis

Fragaria 'Pink Panda'

Fragaria vesca
WOODLAND STRAWBERRY

Prior to the cultivation of strawberries, which began in the sixteenth century, this was the species gathered from European woodlands. It is a spreading perennial with white flowers and grows to 12 in (30 cm) high; its red fruit are larger than those of the alpine strawberry. **'Temptation'** and **'Sweetheart'** are just two of the many popular garden forms of this species. **'Semperflorens'** (syn. *Fragraria alpina*) has few runners and bears small tangy red or yellow fruit in early summer through to fall (autumn). **ZONES 4–10.**

FRAILEA

Around 10 to 15 species of small cacti belong to this genus, found through the Andean regions of South America from Colombia to Argentina and into southern Brazil and Uruguay. The stems can be globular to shortly cylindrical, seldom more than 4 in (10 cm) tall. The spines range from short to long, are variously colored, and sometimes arranged in comb-like rows. The spine clusters radiate from the tips of protuberances along the tops of vertical ribs. The funnel-shaped flowers are pale to deep yellow, and are fairly large for the size of the plants. They emerge from close to the crown in summer. The flowers open only during the afternoon if there is sufficient sunshine. These cacti flower at an early age and seed can set in the small bristly fruits even without the flowers opening.
CULTIVATION: These frost-tender plants require a very well-drained, gritty soil mixture with high humus content and do best in part-shade. In frost-prone areas grow in containers indoors in a fairly dry atmosphere with good ventilation and bright light. Propagate from seed.

Frailea pygmaea
syn. *Frailea pulcherrima*

This small, spherical cactus, which is native to Uruguay and Argentina, has a light gray-green body and short white spines. Each head grows to a height of $1\frac{1}{2}$ in (35 mm) with a similar spread, with yellow flowers blooming in spring and round fruit following in summer. **ZONES 9–10.**

Francoa sonchifolia

Franklinia alatamaha

Franklinia alatamaha

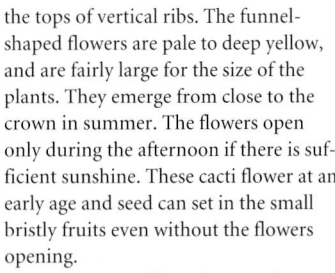

FRANCOA
MAIDEN'S WREATH, BRIDAL WREATH

The 5 species of evergreen perennials that make up this genus from Chile are grown for their flowers, which are used in floral arrangements. The plants form a basal rosette of wavy, lobed leaves, each with a large terminal lobe. The 5-petalled bell-shaped flowers in white, pink or red with darker markings at the base are borne in terminal, spike-like racemes in summer and early fall (autumn).
CULTIVATION: Mostly frost hardy, but in very cold climates plants make good potted specimens for a cool greenhouse. Outdoors grow in humus-rich, moist but well-drained soil in a sheltered sunny or part-shaded position. Water sparingly in winter. Propagate from seed or by division in spring.

Francoa ramosa
syn. *Francoa glabrata*

This clump-forming perennial to 3 ft (1 m) tall and 12 in (30 cm) wide has broadly lance-shaped basal leaves. Branched flowering stems of white flowers marked with deep pink are produced in summer. **ZONES 7–10.**

Francoa sonchifolia

This species to 3 ft (1 m) tall has oblong to oval, crinkled dark green basal leaves. The pale pink flowers, spotted deep pink within, appear on erect, sparsely branched stems from summer to early fall (autumn). **ZONES 7–10.**

FRANKENIA
SEA HEATH

The 80 or so species in this genus are widely distributed in the world's subtropical and temperate zones including Europe and the Mediterranean region, Asia Minor and Australia, which is home to nearly 50 species. They are all low, sometimes prostrate, evergreen shrubs or perennials densely clothed with tiny gray or gray-green leaves. The flowers are produced in spring, summer or sporadically throughout the year, depending on species. Although small and simple, they are generously produced and may be pink, purple or white. *Frankenia* inhabit dry, salty areas including coastal dunes and salt marshes and the shores of inland salt lakes.
CULTIVATION: Full sun and reasonable soil are essential but other than that, the plants are not particularly fussy; they are able to live in a wide range of soil types including heavy clays. They make attractive additions to the dry rock garden and can be massed for ground cover in a hot, sunny spot. They can also be grown in containers. Once established, they do not need a lot of watering. European species are moderately frost hardy. Propagate from seed or by division.

Frankenia laevis

This is a low, wiry shrub usually less than 8 in (20 cm) tall with hairy, reddish green, heath-like leaves and $\frac{1}{4}$ in (6 mm) pink flowers. These appear in early summer. The plant occurs naturally in coastal areas from the southern UK to the Mediterranean and western Asia. **ZONES 9–10.**

Frankenia thymifolia

From southwestern Europe and North Africa, this is a ground-hugging shrublet with small, stiff, hairy leaves and rose-pink flowers. **ZONES 9–10.**

FRANKLINIA
FRANKLIN TREE

Named for Benjamin Franklin and consisting of a single species, this genus became extinct in the wild shortly after its discovery in about 1765 in Georgia, USA, due to the rapid spread of white settlement and clearing of the forests. It is a small deciduous tree with large white flowers with crinkled, overlapping petals and a central bunch of golden stamens similar to those of the closely related *Camellia*. The fruit, large woody capsules, have 5 compartments and split to release 2 flattened seeds.
CULTIVATION: Frost hardy, it prefers humus-rich, moist but well-drained soil and a sheltered, warm position in full sun. Growth is slow. Climates with long, hot, humid summers produce the best flowering. Propagate from fresh ripe seed.

Franklinia alatamaha

The name is taken from the Altamaha River in Georgia, where this species was first discovered. It makes a small, spreading tree of about 15–20 ft (4.5–6 m), often several trunked. The glossy, bright green leaves turn scarlet in fall (autumn), while the 3 in (8 cm) wide fragrant flowers open in late summer and early fall. **ZONES 7–10.**

FRAXINUS
ASH

This genus consists of 65 species of mainly deciduous, fast-growing trees, ranging throughout the northern hemisphere except for the coldest regions and lowland tropics. It differs from other woody members of the olive family (Oleaceae) in having pinnate leaves consisting of several leaflets, small insignificant flowers that in most species lack petals, and single-seeded, winged fruits botanically called samaras. One group of species known as the 'flowering ashes', typified by *Fraxinus ornus*, produces showier flowers with small petals in large terminal panicles at the tips of the branches. Several larger species are valued for their tough, pale timber.
CULTIVATION: Ashes are mostly quite frost hardy and can survive exposed or arid conditions, but thrive in shelter and in fertile, moist but well-drained soil. They are widely planted as street and park trees and are seldom affected by pests and diseases. Propagate from seed in fall (autumn); for cultivars, graft onto seedling stock of the same species.

Fraxinus americana
WHITE ASH

The most valued ash in North America, this species occurs naturally through eastern USA and in southeastern

Fraxinus americana var. *juglandifolia*

Fraxinus americana 'Autumn Purple'

Canada. In the wild it reaches about 80 ft (24 m) with a long straight bole and furrowed gray-brown bark and a somewhat domed canopy. The pinnate leaves have 7 to 9 large, dark green leaflets with silvery undersides. The inconspicuous flowers appear before the leaves. Fall (autumn) color is most commonly a fine yellow. A number of forms are available including ***Fraxinus americana* var. *juglandifolia*,** which has a slender, columnar habit, and **'Autumn Purple'** with leaves that turn reddish purple in fall. **ZONES 4–10.**

Fraxinus angustifolia
syn. *Fraxinus oxycarpa*
NARROW-LEAFED ASH

This species is related to *Fraxinus excelsior*, with similar foliage, flowers and fruit but darker bark and leaves in whorls of 3 to 4, not in pairs. It can grow in semi-arid climates and has a broadly columnar to rounded crown. ***F. a.*** subsp. ***oxycarpa*** (the desert ash), has leaves with up to 7 leaflets, hairy under the midribs. **'Raywood'**, apparently a clone of subspecies *oxycarpa*, is called the claret ash for its wine-purple fall (autumn) foliage. **ZONES 6–10.**

Fraxinus excelsior 'Jaspidea'

Fraxinus americana 'Autumn Purple'

Fraxinus japonica

Fraxinus excelsior
EUROPEAN ASH, COMMON ASH

One of Europe's largest deciduous trees, this species can reach 140 ft (42 m); in the open it is usually 50–60 ft (15–18 m), with a broad crown. It bears dark green leaves with 9 to 11 narrow, toothed leaflets that turn yellow in fall (autumn). Velvety, blackish flower buds are noticeable in winter. **'Aurea'** and the more vigorous **'Jaspidea'** have pale yellowish green summer foliage that deepens in fall; the twigs turn yellow in winter.

Fraxinus excelsior 'Pendula'

Fraxinus excelsior

Fraxinus latifolia

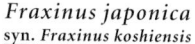

'Pendula', the weeping ash, has branches often weeping to the ground. **ZONES 4–10.**

Fraxinus griffithii

An evergreen or semi-evergreen tree from Southeast Asia growing to 40–60 ft (12–18 m), this ash has gray bark. The leaves are pale green above and silvery beneath. Its young, brown, square shoots are downy. White flowers appear in spring in long panicles at the branch tips. It prefers dry, warm regions and deep soil. **ZONES 8–11.**

Fraxinus japonica
syn. *Fraxinus koshiensis*

From Japan, this deciduous tree has pinnate leaves composed of up to 9 ovate to lance-shaped toothed leaflets with a downy midrib beneath. The flowers appear in panicles on the new shoots. **ZONES 7–10.**

Fraxinus excelsior 'Aurea'

Fraxinus latifolia
OREGON ASH

This species comes from the West Coast forests of North America. Valued for its timber, it can grow to 80 ft (24 m) tall with a 3 ft (1 m) trunk diameter, but cultivated trees seldom exceed half that size. Its closest relative is *Fraxinus pennsylvanica*, which it resembles except that the leaflets do not narrow into stalks at the base. **ZONES 5–10.**

Fraxinus mandshurica
MANCHURIAN ASH

This bushy-headed deciduous tree to 100 ft (30 m) has pinnate leaves about 15 in (38 cm) long composed of up to 11 lance-shaped, toothed leaflets that are downy on both sides and have sunken veins. The flowers appear before the leaves in spring. **ZONES 6–10.**

Fraxinus mandshurica

Fraxinus angustifolia 'Raywood'

Fraxinus angustifolia subsp. *oxycarpa*

Fraxinus pennsylvanica

Fraxinus tomentosa

Fraxinus uhdei

Fraxinus ornus

Fraxinus quadrangulata

Fraxinus velutina

Fraxinus ornus
FLOWERING ASH, MANNA ASH

From southern Europe and Asia Minor, the widely cultivated flowering ash makes a round-topped tree of 30–50 ft (9–15 m) with a short, fluted trunk and smooth gray bark. The leaves have 5 to 9 oval leaflets, dull green with downy undersides. In late spring it bears foamy panicles of white blossoms all over the crown, and then small, narrow fruit. **ZONES 6–10.**

Fraxinus pennsylvanica
RED ASH, GREEN ASH

Similar to *Fraxinus americana*, this tree is also a fast-growing native of North America but is not as large; it reaches 70 ft (21 m) in height with a similar spread. Its green leaves are divided into 5 to 9 leaflets and are sometimes hairy, resembling stalks. This species prefers a moist soil. **'Summit'** has an upright, cylindrical habit with leaves turning yellow in fall (autumn); ***F. pennsylvanica* var. *subintegerrima*** has long, narrow, sword-shaped leaves. **ZONES 4–10.**

Fraxinus quadrangulata
BLUE ASH

From southeastern and central USA, this ash has exceptionally durable wood. Usually 50–70 ft (15–21 m) tall with a slender but open, rounded crown, it has thin gray bark breaking up into large flattened scales. A distinctive feature is the 4-angled twigs often drawn out into wings. The leaves consist of 7 to 9 largish leaflets. Purplish stamened flowers appear in spring before the leaves. **ZONES 4–10.**

Fraxinus tomentosa
PUMPKIN ASH

This deciduous tree to about 120 ft (36 m) high has swelling at the base of the trunk with knobbly growths. The pinnate leaves to 18 in (45 cm) long have up to 9 lance-shaped, deep olive-green leaflets with a pale, downy undersurface. White flowers are borne in crowded panicles in spring, followed by oblong, winged fruit. This is a good shade tree that will tolerate poorly drained, swampy situations. **ZONES 6–10.**

Fraxinus uhdei
EVERGREEN ASH, SHAMEL ASH

From Mexico and Central America, this evergreen grows to 80 ft (24 m) or more and thrives rapidly in warm moist climates. It bears dark green leaves with up to 7 very large leaflets. The dense flowerheads are followed by winged fruit. Cultivars include **'Majestic Beauty'**, a vigorous, larger tree with a rounded crown and deep green leaves; and **'Tomlinson'**, a more compact, upright tree that can grow to 12 ft (3.5 m). **ZONES 8–11.**

Fraxinus velutina
VELVET ASH, ARIZONA ASH, DESERT ASH

From the southwestern USA and Mexico, this species is a useful shade tree in hot, dry regions. Its common name, velvet ash, derives from the thick downy coating on the twigs and leaf undersides. Reaching 30 ft (10 m) or more with a bushy crown, it has silvery gray bark, smallish leaves consisting of 3 to 5 thick, grayish green leaflets, inconspicuous flowers and wedge-shaped fruit with notched tips. **'Modesto'** has smaller, downy leaflets. **ZONES 7–10.**

FREESIA

There are around 6 species of these South African cormous perennials extensively grown for their bright, goblet-shaped, deliciously scented spring flowers. The wild species can have blooms of yellow, pink or purple, but the many hybrids have extended the range to most colors as well as pure white. The narrow, sword-shaped leaves fan out at the base of the plants. They make excellent cut flowers and in the garden look best in a massed display. **CULTIVATION:** Freesias are marginally frost hardy and grow satisfactorily in containers in a greenhouse. In warm climates, plant corms outdoors in fall (autumn); plant in mid-spring in colder climates. Grow in full sun in fertile, moist but well-drained soil. Water well through the growing season but allow to dry out once flowering finishes. Leave the clumps undisturbed for 3 years, and then divide them in fall. In cold climates the corms need to be lifted for the winter. Propagate from seed in spring or offsets in fall.

Freesia Hybrids

Over 300 hybrids have been raised and come in a wide range of brilliant colors, although the scent of some has been diminished. The showy flowers are borne on wiry, arching stems, easily flattened by rain or wind, so some form of shelter or staking is advisable. **ZONES 9–10.**

Freesia lactea
syns *Freesia alba* of gardens, *F. refracta* var. *alba*

This widely grown, highly scented species flowers in early spring. The creamy white flowers are 2 in (5 cm) long and are borne in a loose spike. Slender, bayonet-shaped leaves surround wiry stems up to 12 in (30 cm) long. **ZONES 9–10.**

FREMONTODENDRON
syn. *Fremontia*
FLANNEL BUSH

This unusual small genus consists of 2 species of evergreen or semi-evergreen shrubs or small trees from the far south-

Freesia lactea

Freesia Hybrids

Fritillaria acmopetala

Fritillaria camschatcensis

Fritillaria glauca 'Goldilocks'

Fritillaria imperialis 'Lutea'

western USA and Mexico. The young stems have a felty coating of hairs, as do the lobed leaves on their pale undersides. The large bowl-shaped flowers consist of 5 petal-like, large golden sepals. They are named after Major-General John Charles Fremont (1813–90), an American explorer and distinguished amateur botanist. **CULTIVATION:** Frost hardy, these plants are not difficult to grow in a sheltered, sunny position with neutral to alkaline, well-drained soil, but they tend to be short lived. Plant out in spring when the danger of frost has passed. They do not perform well in climates with hot, wet summers. Propagate from seed in spring or cuttings in summer.

Fremontodendron 'California Glory'

Fremontodendron californicum has been crossed with the larger-flowered but less hardy *F. mexicanum* to produce the hybrid 'California Glory', which is hardier than both parents and has bowl-shaped lemon flowers tinged with red. **ZONES 8–10.**

Fremontodendron californicum

This is the best known and hardiest species, ranging along California's Sierra Nevada foothills and coast ranges. It can reach 30 ft (9 m), but is usually a sparse, crooked shrub 20 ft (6 m) tall with dark brown bark. It produces a succession of 2 in (5 cm) wide golden flowers from mid- to late spring. ***Fremontodendron californicum* subsp. *decumbens*** has a dwarf habit and orange-yellow flowers. **ZONES 8–10.**

Fremontodendron mexicanum

This upright, long-flowering shrub to 20 ft (6 m) tall has thick-textured leaves to 3 in (8 cm) long. Deep gold, almost orange flowers are produced from late spring to mid-fall (mid-autumn). **ZONES 9–11.**

Fremontodendron 'San Gabriel'

This spreading, rounded evergreen shrub has rounded 3- or 5-lobed dark green leaves. In summer it produces saucer-shaped bright yellow flowers with long, slender-pointed lobes. **ZONES 8–10.**

FRITILLARIA

FRITILLARY

There are about 100 species in this genus of bulbs, relatives of the lily and the tulip, native to temperate regions of the northern hemisphere. Christian tradition has it that the fritillaries refused to bow their heads at the crucifixion but, in shame, have bowed them ever since. They are not easy to grow, but their nodding, bell- or goblet-shaped flowers borne mainly in spring are worth the trouble.

Fremontodendron 'San Gabriel'

CULTIVATION: Mostly quite frost hardy, they do best in areas with cold winters. Plant bulbs in early fall (autumn) in part-shade in rich, organic, well-drained soil. Water well through the growing season but allow to dry out after flowering. In areas with high summer rainfall, lift bulbs gently and keep them out of the ground for as short a time as possible. Propagate from offsets in summer, but do not disturb clumps for a few years. Seed can be sown in fall but will take 4 to 5 years to bloom.

Fritillaria acmopetala

This species, to 15 in (38 cm) high, comes from southwestern Turkey, Cyprus, Syria and Lebanon where plants are found in cedar forests and on limestone escarpments. The bells have 3 green outer segments and 3 inner segments that are green stippled with brownish purple. The inside of the bell is a glowing shiny yellow-green. The foliage is a dull gray-green. **ZONES 7–9.**

Fritillaria affinis

syn. *Fritillaria lanceolata*

CHECKER LILY, RICE-GRAIN FRITILLARY

From northwestern USA, this is one of the easier species to grow if kept dry during summer when bulbs are dormant. Stems reach 24 in (60 cm) tall, carrying whorls of broadly lance-shaped, blue-green leaves topped by goblet-shaped flowers of a curious purple-brown mottled with yellow spots. **ZONES 6–9.**

Fritillaria camschatcensis

BLACK SARANA

This fritillary to about 18 in (45 cm) high is found, in the wild, in both north-western USA and northeastern Asia and grows in moist subalpine meadows, in open woods and on lightly grassed slopes close to the sea. The drooping, half-closed bells of flower vary in color between maroon-brown, purple-green and black and are borne during the summer months. **ZONES 4–9.**

Fritillaria glauca

SERPENTINE FRITILLARY

This low-growing American mountain species is often only 3–4 in (8–10 cm) high. The flowerheads are large for a plant of its stature and are variously described as greenish yellow with purple-brown markings or purple-brown with greenish yellow markings. **'Goldilocks'** is a selected garden form in which yellow hues predominate. **ZONES 7–9.**

Fritillaria imperialis

CROWN IMPERIAL

Native to Turkey, Iran, Afghanistan and Kashmir, this is the tallest of the species and the easiest to grow. The leafy stems up to 5 ft (1.5 m) high bear whorls of lance-shaped pale green leaves. Pendent clusters of up to 8 yellow, orange or red bell-shaped flowers appear in late spring and early summer. The flowers have an unpleasant odor. The popular garden form **'Lutea'** bears bright yellow flowers. **ZONES 4–9.**

F. californicum subsp. *decumbens*

Fremontodendron 'California Glory'

Fremontodendron californicum

F

Fritillaria meleagris
SNAKE'S HEAD FRITILLARY, CHECKERED LILY

In spring this common European species produces slender stems reaching 12 in (30 cm), each bearing one nodding, goblet-shaped bloom that is maroon, green or white, 1 in (25 mm) long, and blotched or checkered. A few slender leaves grow along the stem. It thrives under deciduous trees or in a rock garden, if it has plenty of moisture while growing. **ZONES 4–9.**

Fritillaria messanensis
syn. *Fritillaria oranensis*

Originating in Greece, this rare but easy to grow species reaches 12 in (30 cm). In early spring it bears brown and pale green, bell-shaped flowers. **ZONES 9–10.**

Fritillaria michailovskyi

This small, 8 in (20 cm) high mountain plant from northeastern Turkey carries yellow-tipped bells of maroon brown in summer. The plant needs a loose gritty soil. **ZONES 7–9.**

Fritillaria meleagris

Fritillaria pallidiflora

A native of northwestern China and Siberia, this robust fritillary to 15 in (38 cm) high is easily grown in gardens in a rich peaty soil and part-shade. The gray-green leaves are broad and glaucous and the broadly bell-shaped flowers are pale or bright yellow. **ZONES 3–9.**

Fritillaria persica

This species from southern Turkey can grow in warmer areas than most other species. It reaches about 3 ft (1 m) and has narrowly lance-shaped leaves along the stem. In spring it bears a spike of up to 25 nodding, narrow, bell-shaped flowers that range from dark purple to brown to blackish purple. **ZONES 5–9.**

Fritillaria pontica

This species, which ranges from Bulgaria to the mountains of Turkey, grows to 18 in (45 cm) high and has lance-shaped to oval, gray-green leaves. The usually green flowers are sometimes purple-stained at the throat. Like *Fritillaria messanensis* and *F. strausii*, it is quite rare in the wild. **ZONES 6–9.**

Fritillaria uva-vulpis

Fuchsia arborescens

Fritillaria strausii

Fritillaria pyrenaica

From the subalpine meadows of northwestern Spain, this elegant plant to 18 in (45 cm) high bears narrow, alternate leaves. The squarish bells are brown-purple, slightly checkered with yellow on the outside. The interesting coloring is reversed on the inside of the bell. Good drainage is essential. **ZONES 5–9.**

Fritillaria strausii

The checkerboard pattern that marks the flowers of so many *Fritillaria* species is especially distinctive in the rare *F. strausii*, which has chocolate and cream checks on purple petals. It grows about 10 in (25 cm) tall and comes from Turkey. The name honors botanist Heinrich Strauss (1850–1922). **ZONES 6–9.**

Fritillaria uva-vulpis
syn. *Fritillaria assyriaca* of gardens

The name of this diminutive species means 'fox's grapes'. In its native Turkey, Iraq and Iran it grows in abundance in cornfields, bearing gray-purple and gold flowers in spring. It reaches a height of 8 in (20 cm) with a 2 in (5 cm) spread. **ZONES 7–9.**

Fritillaria pontica

Fritillaria messanensis

Fritillaria verticillata

Fritillaria verticillata

Native to the mountains of central Asia, this fritillary to 24 in (60 cm) high has slender mid-green leaves in whorls along the stem. In spring it bears a loose spike of up to 15 broadly bell-shaped white flowers, faintly checkered or veined green. **ZONES 5–9.**

FUCHSIA

This genus consists of about 100 species and thousands of hybrids and cultivars developed for their pendulous flowers, which come in a fascinating variety of forms (though usually with a long or short perianth tube, spreading sepals and 4 broad petals) and a wonderful range of colors in shades of red, white, pink and purple. They are deciduous or evergreen trees, shrubs or perennials treated almost as herbaceous plants. The genus is confined to South and Central America except for 4 species in New Zealand and one in Tahiti. Most of the larger-flowered American species inhabit areas of very high rainfall, sometimes growing as epiphytes or on boulders in moss forests; they are pollinated by hummingbirds. Habit varies from upright shrubs to spreading bushes. Trailing lax varieties are ideal for hanging baskets or are trained as weeping standards. Strong upright types may be trained as compact bushes, standards or espaliers.

CULTIVATION: Moderately frost hardy to frost tender, these plants require moist but well-drained, fertile soil in sun or partial shade and shelter from hot winds and afternoon sun. In most cases, pinching back at an early age and then pruning after flowering will improve shape and flower yield. Propagate from seed or cuttings, and check for white fly, spider mite, rust and gray mold.

Fuchsia arborescens
syn. *Fuchsia arborea*
LILAC FUCHSIA, TREE FUCHSIA

This large erect evergreen shrub from Mexico and Central America grows to about 18 ft (5.5 m) with narrow, elliptic deep green leaves offset by small rose-purple tubular flowers in erect clusters from late spring to early autumn. Marginally frost hardy, it tolerates a warmer climate than most other species but needs a humid, protected position. **ZONES 9–11.**

Fuchsia boliviana

Native to the forested foothills of the Peruvian Andes, this frost-tender shrub or

Fuchsia campos-portoi

Fuchsia denticulata

Fuchsia magellanica 'Versicolor'

Fuchsia procumbens

Fuchsia paniculata

small tree grows to 12 ft (3.5 m) high. It has soft, gray-green leaves, sometimes with reddish veins, and pendent clusters of long-tubed scarlet flowers. ***Fuchsia boliviana* var. *alba*** has flowers with white tubes and sepals with scarlet markings at the base. ZONES 10–11.

Fuchsia magellanica

Fuchsia magellanica 'Thompsonii'

Fuchsia campos-portoi

Occurring naturally at altitudes above 7,000 ft (2,100 m) in Brazil, this shrub has small flowers with red tubes and sepals and purple petals. ZONES 9–11.

Fuchsia denticulata

From Peru and Bolivia, this species grows to 8 ft (2.4 m) high and has large leaves up to 6 in (15 cm) long. The long-tubed flowers have bright red petals and sepals that fade to cream and green at the tips. ZONES 9–11.

Fuchsia excorticata
NEW ZEALAND TREE FUCHSIA, KOTUKUTUKU

From New Zealand, this is the giant of the genus, a slow-growing tree reaching 40 ft (12 m) in the wild with a trunk diameter of over 24 in (60 cm) and peeling bark. When cultivated it usually only makes a shrub of 10–15 ft (3–4.5 m) tall. In cool climates it is deciduous. The small, greenish purple or dull red flowers often sprout directly from the branches. ZONES 8–10.

Fuchsia boliviana

Fuchsia boliviana var. *alba*

Fuchsia fulgens

A native of Mexico, this upright shrub to 5 ft (1.5 m) high has spreading branches and ovate to heart-shaped leaves to 10 in (25 cm) or more long. Terminal drooping clusters of slender scarlet flowers with green-tipped sepals are produced in summer. It is frost tender. ZONES 9–11.

Fuchsia magellanica
LADIES' EARDROPS, HARDY FUCHSIA

From Chile and Argentina, this vigorous erect shrub grows up to 10 ft (3 m) tall. It has lance-shaped to ovate leaves usually held in whorls of three. The pendulous red tubular flowers with red sepals and purple petals are produced over a long period in summer and autumn; black fruit follow. Prune it back to maintain its shape. **'Alba'** can grow to a considerable size and bears white flowers. **'Thompsonii'** has scarlet tubes and sepals and pale purplish petals, although the flowers are smaller than type, they are more profuse. **'Versicolor'** (syn. 'Tricolor') has gray-green leaves flushed red when immature and irregularly white-splotched margins when mature; the flowers are small and deep red. ZONES 7–10.

Fuchsia paniculata

Native to southern Mexico and Panama, this unusual species has foliage resembling that of *Fuchsia magellanica* but its pink flowers are very small and are

Fuchsia fulgens

massed in large panicles. It bears rounded, deep purplish red berries that are often more conspicuous than the flowers. ZONES 9–11.

Fuchsia procumbens
TRAILING FUCHSIA

Native to New Zealand, this prostrate, spreading, evergreen subshrub grows to 6 in (15 cm) tall at the very most with an indefinite spread. It bears erect, orange-tipped, purple and green flowers among small, heart-shaped leaves. Large, bright red berries follow. Frost hardy, it is excellent as a vigorous ground cover or in rock gardens and hanging baskets. ZONES 9–10.

Fuchsia 'Blue Satin'

Fuchsia 'Cara Mia'

Fuchsia 'Bicentennial'

Fuchsia splendens

This upright shrub has pale green foliage and small single flowers with broad orange tubes and short green sepals and petals. It is marginally frost hardy. ZONES 9–11.

Fuchsia thymifolia

Native to Mexico, this upright shrub to 3 ft (1 m) tall has small, opposite leaves. The small flowers have white tubes, pinkish white sepals and pinkish white petals that gradually darken with age. ZONES 8–11.

Fuchsia triphylla

HONEYSUCKLE FUCHSIA

From the West Indies, this evergreen shrub grows to a height of 30 in (75 cm) and has pairs or whorls of lance-shaped

Fuchsia 'Baby Blue Eyes'

leaves with a purple undersurface. The orange-scarlet flowers have a slender tapered tube and small petals. They are borne in dense terminal clusters. The leaf color is most intense if the plant is grown in light shade. The honeysuckle fuchsia grows best in a frost-free climate. ZONES 10–11.

FUCHSIA Hybrids

syn. *Fuchsia* × *hybrida*

This useful gardener's name covers the thousands of modern large-flowered hybrid cultivars derived mainly from *Fuchsia magellanica* and *F. fulgens*. Those derived from *F. triphylla* have slender, long-tubed, single flowers and the leaves usually have a purplish undersurface. All cultivars may be grown in pots, hanging baskets or planted in the garden. Those of upright habit may be trained as standards, while trailing cultivars look very attractive in hanging baskets and window boxes.

Fuchsia 'Beacon Rosa'

Frost hardiness varies slighty between cultivars, as the hardiness zones indicate.

Fuchsia 'Annabel'

This upright shrub to 24 in (60 cm) high bears abundant double, pink-striped white flowers. ZONES 9–11.

Fuchsia 'Baby Blue Eyes'

This free-flowering, upright, compact shrub bears single flowers with red tubes and sepals and purple-pink petals. It makes an excellent pot plant. ZONES 8–11.

Fuchsia 'Beacon Rosa'

This upright, compact shrub with dark green foliage with wavy edges bears single flowers with rose-red tubes and sepals and pink petals with red veins. ZONES 8–11.

Fuchsia 'Bicentennial'

Of lax habit, this shrub grows to 18 in (45 cm) high and 24 in (60 cm) wide.

Fuchsia 'Candy Bells'

The double flowers have white tubes, orange sepals and magenta corollas. ZONES 9–11.

Fuchsia 'Blue Satin'

This free-flowering trailing shrub has dark green foliage and bears double flowers with white tubes and sepals and satiny, blue petals that shade to white at the base. It is an ideal hanging basket specimen. ZONES 9–11.

Fuchsia 'Brutus'

This vigorous, upright, bushy shrub has mid-green leaves with darker-colored veining. The single flowers have short crimson tubes and recurving sepals and deep purple petals that shade to carmine at the base. It flowers profusely and makes an excellent standard or garden specimen. ZONES 8–11.

Fuchsia 'Candy Bells'

This branching shrub has small, shiny mid-green leaves with toothed margins. The small single flowers have pink waxy tubes and sepals and pink petals. ZONES 8–11.

Fuchsia 'Cara Mia'

Free-flowering, this vigorous, trailing shrub has semi-double, medium-sized flowers composed of pale pink tubes, reflexed sepals and deep crimson petals. They are produced generously along the branches, making this a superb pot plant or basket specimen. ZONES 9–11.

Fuchsia 'Celia Smedley'

An upright shrub, this species bears dainty single or semi-double flowers with greenish white tubes, pale pink

Fuchsia 'Chillerton Beauty'

sepals and red petals. It grows to a height and spread of 30 in (75 cm). **ZONES 9–11.**

Fuchsia 'Chillerton Beauty'

This vigorous, upright, bushy shrub grows to about 3 ft (1 m) high with small shiny green leaves. The small single flowers, which are freely produced, have pale pink tubes and sepals and purple petals with pink veins. It is suitable as a hedge or compact garden shrub. **ZONES 8–11.**

Fuchsia 'Cloverdale Pearl'

This is an upright, self-branching shrub bearing medium-sized, single flowers which have white tubes, pink reflexed sepals shading to white with green tips and white petals with pink veins. It flowers freely and is easy to shape. **ZONES 9–11.**

Fuchsia 'Dark Eyes'

This bushy, upright shrub which grows to 24 in (60 cm) high bears medium-sized double flowers with deep red tubes and sepals and deep violet-blue petals. **ZONES 9–11.**

Fuchsia 'Display'

A strong, upright, branching shrub which grows to 30 in (75 cm) high, 'Display' bears medium-sized, single saucer-shaped flowers in shades of pink. **ZONES 9–11.**

Fuchsia 'Dollar Princess'
syn. *Fuchsia* 'Princess Dollar'

This upright shrub to 18 in (45 cm) high produces small to medium double flowers with cerise-red tubes and sepals and purple petals that turn deep pink at the base. **ZONES 8–11.**

Fuchsia 'Flash'

Fuchsia 'Fanfare'

This is a vigorous tall grower with drooping stems and large deep green leaves. The single flowers have long, slender, deep pink tubes to 3 in (8 cm), short, deep pink sepals and short scarlet petals. The flowers appear in late fall (autumn) and sometimes in winter. **ZONES 10–11.**

Fuchsia 'Flash'

An upright bushy shrub with small, finely serrated, light green leaves, 'Flash' has single, small but profuse flowers. The tubes and short sepals are light magenta and the petals red. **ZONES 8–11.**

Fuchsia 'Garden News'

Fuchsia 'Garden News'

A free-flowering upright shrub to 24 in (60 cm) high, this hybrid bears double pink flowers with pale pink tubes and sepals. **ZONES 8–11.**

Fuchsia 'Gartenmeister Bonstedt'

A vigorous hybrid of *Fuchsia triphylla,* this is a spreading shrub with red-tinted bronze leaves. The flowers are long-tubed and bright red overall. **ZONES 10–11.**

Fuchsia 'Gartenmeister Bonstedt'

Fuchsia 'Cloverdale Pearl'

Fuchsia 'Dark Eyes'

Fuchsia 'Fanfare'

Fuchsia 'Display'

Fuchsia 'Dark Eyes'

Fuchsia 'Genii'

This upright shrub to 3 ft (1 m) high and wide has light greenish yellow leaves and small single flowers with deep pink tubes and sepals and purple petals. **ZONES 8–11.**

Fuchsia 'Golden Marinka'

This small trailing shrub to 12 in (30 cm) high has a spread of 18 in (45 cm) across. It has variegated golden-yellow leaves with red veins and bears abundant single red flowers with darker red petals. It is an excellent hanging basket subject. **ZONES 9–11.**

Fuchsia 'Hidcote Beauty'

This upright shrub grows to a height and spread of up to 24 in (60 cm). The single flowers have creamy white tubes and sepals and pinky salmon petals. It is marginally frost hardy. **ZONES 9–11.**

Fuchsia 'Jack of Hearts'

This free-flowering trailing shrub has mid-green serrated leaves. The large, double flowers have thick pink tubes, pink sepals with green tips and numerous white petals flushed with pink. It makes a good basket specimen. **ZONES 9–11.**

Fuchsia 'Jack Shahan'

This vigorous trailing shrub grows to 18 in (45 cm) high and 24 in (60 cm) wide. It bears large, single, pale pink to deep pink flowers. **ZONES 9–11.**

Fuchsia 'Joanne'

This is a bushy trailing shrub with mid-green leaves to $2\frac{1}{2}$ in (6 cm) long. The single flowers have short, thin pink tubes, pink sepals with green tips and reddish purple petals. It makes a good basket plant or can be clipped as a compact garden specimen. **ZONES 9–11.**

Fuchsia 'John Grooms'

This vigorous, free-flowering, upright shrub has toothed, emerald-green leaves. The double flowers have short greenish white tubes, pink reflexed sepals and purple petals. **ZONES 9–11.**

Fuchsia 'Joy Patmore'

This upright shrub to 18 in (45 cm) high bears single flowers with waxy white tubes and sepals and deep carmine petals. **ZONES 9–11.**

Fuchsia 'La Campanella'

This trailing shrub to 12 in (30 cm) high and 18 in (45 cm) wide bears small, semi-double flowers with white tubes and sepals and purple petals. *Fuchsia* 'La Campanella' is free-flowering and makes an excellent hanging basket subject. **ZONES 9–11.**

Fuchsia 'Lady Thumb'

This upright shrub to 12 in (30 cm) high bears abundant small, semi-double flowers which have deep pink tubes and sepals and white to pale pink petals. It makes an attractive container plant. **ZONES 8–11.**

Fuchsia 'Lena'

This trailing shrub to 24 in (60 cm) high with a spread of up to 30 in (75 cm) bears single to semi-double flowers with white tubes and sepals and magenta petals that are a lighter shade at the base. Its abundant flowers make it a good garden specimen. **ZONES 8–11.**

Fuchsia 'Leonora'

This is a vigorous upright shrub to 30 in (75 cm) tall. The single soft pink flowers

Fuchsia 'John Grooms'

Fuchsia 'Joy Patmore'

Fuchsia 'Leonora'

Fuchsia 'La Campanella'

Fuchsia 'Hidcote Beauty'

Fuchsia 'Jack of Hearts'

Fuchsia 'Lord Byron'

have green-tipped sepals. It makes a delightful standard. ZONES 9–11.

Fuchsia 'Lisa'

This low-growing, compact shrub bears abundant flowers with rose-pink tubes and sepals and lavender-blue petals. ZONES 9–11.

Fuchsia 'Lord Byron'

This free-flowering upright bushy shrub has mid-green serrated leaves. The single flowers to 3 in (8 cm) long have short, thin cerise tubes, scarlet sepals and very

Fuchsia 'Mrs Popple'

Fuchsia 'Mrs Marshall'

dark purple petals with red veining that shade to a paler purple at the base. The petals are expanded to an open saucer shape. ZONES 8–11.

Fuchsia 'Madeleine Sweeney'

This upright shrub has toothed emerald-green leaves and large double flowers. They have bright cerise tubes and sepals and purple petals. ZONES 8–11.

Fuchsia 'Marcus Graham'

This shrub has widely flared double flowers with pale pink sepals and reddish pink petals. The flowers are very large and showy. ZONES 9–11.

Fuchsia 'Marin Glow'

This shapely upright bush bears masses of medium-sized single flowers with waxy white tubes and sepals and rich purple petals that gradually fade to magenta. It makes an excellent garden specimen and will train as a standard. ZONES 9–11.

Fuchsia 'Marinka'

A trailing shrub to 12 in (30 cm) high with a spread of up to 24 in (60 cm), this hybrid bears abundant, single, red flowers with petals of a deeper red. It makes an excellent pot plant or an attractive hanging basket specimen. ZONES 8–11.

Fuchsia 'Orange Drops'

Fuchsia 'Madeleine Sweeney'

Fuchsia 'Marcus Graham'

Fuchsia 'Marinka'

Fuchsia 'Mrs Marshall'

This upright, bushy, free-flowering shrub bears masses of single flowers with creamy white tubes and sepals and rose-cerise petals. It makes an excellent garden specimen and can be easily trained as a standard. ZONES 9–11.

Fuchsia 'Mrs Popple'

A vigorous bushy shrub which grows to a height and spread of about 3 ft (1 m), this hybrid has single flowers with scarlet tubes and sepals and purple petals with a deep pink center. This fuchsia is more frost hardy than most. ZONES 8–11.

Fuchsia 'Natasha Sinton'

This very free-flowering trailing shrub bears toothed mid-green leaves. The medium-sized double flowers have pale pink tubes, sepals and petals. ZONES 9–11.

Fuchsia 'Nellie Nuttall'

This is an early flowering upright shrub that reaches a height and spread of about 18 in (45 cm). The single flowers face outwards and have red tubes and sepals and white petals with red veins. ZONES 9–11.

Fuchsia 'Natasha Sinton'

Fuchsia 'Orange Drops'

This bushy upright or semi-trailing shrub is probably one of the best orange-flowering fuchsias. The single flowers have light orange tubes and sepals and darker rich orange petals. The flowers tend to hang in clusters. ZONES 9–11.

Fuchsia 'Pacquesa'

An upright, free-flowering shrub to 24 in (60 cm) tall, this hybrid bears large, single flowers with deep red tubes and red reflexed sepals and red-veined white petals. It is suitable for growing as a bush or standard. ZONES 9–11.

Fuchsia 'Tango Queen'

Fuchsia cultivar

Fuchsia 'Sealand Prince'

Fuchsia 'Swingtime'

Fuchsia 'Strawberry Sundae'

Fuchsia 'Phyllis'

Fuchsia 'Phyllis'

This upright shrub to 5 ft (1.5 m) tall bears abundant semi-double rose-red flowers. It is suitable for a hedge or garden shrub. **ZONES 8–11.**

Fuchsia 'Riccartonii'
syn. *Fuchsia magellanica* 'Riccartonii'

A tall upright shrub to 10 ft (3 m) high, this plant has bronze-tinted green leaves and masses of small single flowers with red tubes and sepals and dark purple petals. It is frost hardy in sheltered areas and it may be grown as a hedge. **ZONES 7–10.**

Fuchsia 'Rose of Castile'

A tall upright shrub, this cultivar bears single flowers with white tubes, green-tipped white sepals and purple petals with pink markings. It is good for training as a standard. **ZONES 8–11.**

Fuchsia 'Royal Velvet'

A vigorous upright shrub to 30 in (75 cm) high, this plant has large double flowers with waxy red tubes and red reflexed sepals and deep purple petals. This is an excellent variety for training as a standard. **ZONES 9–11.**

Fuchsia 'Sealand Prince'

This upright bushy shrub bears medium-sized, single bell-shaped flowers. The tubes and long upturned sepals are light red and the violet-purple petals gradually fade to reddish purple. It is best grown in an open garden. **ZONES 8–11.**

Fuchsia 'Sierra Blue'

This free-flowering bushy trailing shrub bears large double flowers. The tubes and slightly upturned sepals are white and the silver-blue petals with pinkish veining gradually fade to a soft lilac. **ZONES 9–11.**

Fuchsia 'Superstar'

Fuchsia 'Strawberry Sundae'

A free-flowering trailing shrub with large double flowers, this plant has broad pinkish green sepals and the petals are pinkish lilac. It makes a good basket subject. **ZONES 9–11.**

Fuchsia 'Superstar'

This upright, freely branching shrub has deep green leaves and bears medium-sized single, pale purple flowers which have strongly reflexed sepals. **ZONES 8–11.**

Fuchsia 'Swingtime'

This vigorous shrub has medium to large double flowers with red tubes and sepals and creamy white, red-veined petals. With its spreading habit, it is considered one of the best choices for a hanging basket or window box. It grows to 24 in (60 cm) in height. **ZONES 9–11.**

Fuchsia 'Tango Queen'

This trailing shrub has toothed mid-green leaves and bears medium-sized, semi-double flowers with pale pink tubes and sepals and purple petals with white veining. **ZONES 9–11.**

Fuchsia 'Royal Velvet'

Fuchsia 'Thalia'

Fuchsia cultivar

Fuchsia 'Thalia'

An upright bushy shrub to 3 ft (1 m) tall, this hybrid has velvety dark green leaves with purplish undersides and bears masses of small, orange-red flowers with very long tubes. **ZONES 10–11.**

Fuchsia 'Tom Thumb'

This small upright bushy shrub to 12 in (30 cm) high bears profuse small, single flowers with pinkish red tubes and sepals and pinkish purple petals veined red. This free-flowering plant makes an excellent miniature standard. **ZONES 8–11.**

Fuchsia 'Vivienne Thompson'

This upright, self-branching shrub produces semi-double flowers over a long period. The tubes and strongly reflexed sepals are pink and the petals are white with rose-pink veins at the base. It is suitable for growing as a bush or standard and is reasonably heat tolerant if shaded. **ZONES 9–11.**

Fuchsia 'Vivienne Thompson'

Fuchsia 'White Pixie'

Fuchsia 'Waltzing Matilda'

This trailing shrub has dark green leaves with finely toothed edges. The medium-sized double blooms are pale pink with faint deep pink veins. The wavy sepals are green tipped. **ZONES 9–11.**

Fuchsia 'Westminster Chimes'

A trailing, cascading shrub with small almond-shaped leaves, this hybrid bears smallish but profuse semi-double flowers. The tubes are deep pink, and spreading deep pink sepals fade to pale pink. The violet-blue petals gradually fade to magenta with a lighter pink at the base. **ZONES 9–11.**

Fuchsia 'White Ann'

syn. *Fuchsia* 'Heidi Weiss'

An upright shrub to 24 in (60 cm) high, this plant has small dark green leaves and bears double flowers with crimson tubes and sepals and white petals veined red. **ZONES 8–11.**

Fuchsia 'White Pixie'

This upright, bushy free-flowering shrub has yellowish green leaves with red veins. The smallish single flowers have red short tubes, red upturned sepals and white petals with reddish pink veins. It will grow up to 3 ft (1 m) high and would be suitable as a medium hedge or garden shrub. **ZONES 8–11.**

Fuchsia 'White Spider'

Fuchsia 'Waltzing Matilda'

Fuchsia 'White Spider'

This vigorous, upright, branching shrub bears abundant single pale pink flowers with pink tubes and some pink veining. It is good for training as a standard. **ZONES 9–11.**

FURCRAEA

This genus closely allied to *Agave* consists of about 12 species of perennial succulents with terminal or basal rosettes of sword-shaped, long fleshy leaves. Large panicles of broad, short-tubed flowers are produced in summer. Bulbils are often borne between the flowers. These plants occur naturally in semi-arid regions of the West Indies, Central and South America. They are suitable for large rock gardens or desert gardens.
CULTIVATION: Grow in a very well-drained soil in full sun. Keep dry in winter. In frosty areas grow in containers in a greenhouse in a dry atmosphere with good ventilation and bright light. Propagate from seed in spring or by division.

Furcraea foetida

syn. *Furcraea gigantea*

GREEN ALOE

This giant species is the largest of the genus. It has a rosette of broad, sword-shaped, green leaves that may bear a few spines at the base. In summer fragrant, bell-shaped, green flowers with white centers are produced on a giant panicle up to 30 ft (9 m) high. **ZONES 10–12.**

Furcraea selloa var. *marginata*

The leaves of this species grow to 3 ft (1 m) or more in length. They have a sharp tip and pale yellow margins with widely spaced, hooked spines. The panicles, to 20 ft (6 m) high, bear faintly scented, greenish white, bell-shaped flowers in summer. **ZONES 10–12.**

Furcraea selloa var. *marginata*

Fuchsia 'Tom Thumb'

F

G

GAILLARDIA

BLANKET FLOWER

This genus of around 30 species of annuals, perennials and biennials are all native to the USA, with the exception of 2 South American species. The perennials are better suited to cool-temperate climates. All plants bloom for a very long season from summer until the first frosts. The daisy-like flowers are either single, like small sunflowers, or double and as much as 6 in (15 cm) wide. The common name arose because the colors of the flowers resemble the bright yellows, oranges and reds of the blankets traditionally worn by Native Americans. Gaillardias are a colorful addition to the flower border and meadow garden, they are also very good for cutting.
CULTIVATION: Among the hardiest of garden flowers, they tolerate extreme heat, cold, dryness, strong winds and poor soils. Plant in full sun in well-drained soil and stake if necessary. In cool climates the stems of perennials should be cut back in late summer in order to recover before frosts. Propagate from seed in spring or early summer. Perennials may be divided in spring.

Gaillardia × *grandiflora* cultivar

Gaillardia amblyodon

This annual species from Texas grows to a height of 3 ft (1 m) with a similar spread. It has grayish green oblong leaves and bears maroon, daisy-like flowers in fall (autumn). **ZONES 8–11.**

Gaillardia aristata

This showy perennial from the prairies of central USA grows to 24 in (60 cm) tall and 18 in (45 cm) wide and has aromatic grayish, downy leaves, sometimes shallowly lobed or deeply divided. The decorative large, single, red-centered yellow flowers are borne freely from early summer until fall (autumn). Fully frost hardy, it may be short lived, especially in damp conditions. **ZONES 6–10.**

Gaillardia × *grandiflora*

These hybrids of *Gaillardia aristata* and *G. pulchella* are the most commonly grown of the blanket flowers. The plants form mounds up to 3 ft (1 m) high and wide and have narrow, slightly lobed hairy leaves. The flowerheads, 3–4 in (8–10 cm) in diameter, come in hot colors: red, yellow, orange and burgundy. They are propagated by division or from cuttings to provide named cultivars. **'Burgunder'** ('Burgundy') has deep maroon-colored flowers; **'Dazzler'** has bright orange-yellow flowers with maroon centers; **'Kobold'** ('Goblin') has compact growth to 12 in (30 cm) high and rich red flowers with yellow tips. **ZONES 5–10.**

Gaillardia pulchella

A frost-hardy annual or, rarely, short-lived perennial, this fast-growing upright species to 18–24 in (45–60 cm) high and spread of 12 in (30 cm) has hairy, lance-shaped, gray-green leaves. The flowers' ray-florets are red with yellow tips or self-colored red or yellow with a cone-shaped purplish disc-floret. This is a very long-blooming summer flower, especially when deadheaded regularly. **ZONES 8–10.**

Gaillardia × *grandiflora* cultivar

Gaillardia × *grandiflora* 'Kobold'

GALANTHUS

SNOWDROP

This genus of about 19 species of small bulbs is native to Europe and western Asia. Small, white, nodding, sometimes perfumed flowers appear above leaves like those of daffodils but much shorter. The 3 inner petals, much shorter than the outer 3 and usually with green markings, are the feature by which this genus is recognized. Snowdrops are beautiful for naturalizing in grass or lightly shaded woodland. They also do well in a rockery and are excellent cut flowers. They flower in late winter and herald the coming of spring.
CULTIVATION: Very frost hardy, they do best in cooler climates. Grow in rich, moist but well-drained soil in part-shade. In very cold areas they may be planted in full sun. Water adequately during the growing period for good establishment and increase. Propagate from fresh ripe seed or divide clumps immediately the flowers fade and while still in leaf.

Galanthus elwesii

GIANT SNOWDROP

This species from Turkey and the Balkans multiplies well in temperate climates and has distinctive gray-blue leaves folded one inside the other at the base. It bears nodding white flowers with the inner petals marked by 2 green spots (these spots sometimes join to form a single V-shaped mark). They flower in late winter and spring and grow to 10 in (25 cm) tall. **ZONES 6–9.**

Galanthus ikariae

syn. *Galanthus latifolius* of gardens

A native of Turkey and the Caucasus, this species to 6 in (15 cm) high has rich green, strap-like leaves and delicate, nodding, bell-shaped flowers. The outer petals are pure white, and the inner petals are green at the tip. **ZONES 6–9.**

Galanthus nivalis

COMMON SNOWDROP

This most commonly grown species reaches 6 in (15 cm) tall. The erect leaves are bluish green. Each stem bears a nodding, bell-shaped, 1 in (25 mm) wide scented flower in late winter. The outer petals are white, and the inner petals have a green marking at the tip. There are many cultivars, including the double-flowered **'Flore Pleno'**. **ZONES 4–9.**

Galanthus plicatus

CRIMEAN SNOWDROP

This species from Turkey and eastern Europe is up to 8 in (20 cm) high with broadly strap-shaped, erect dull green leaves. The white flowers borne in late winter and early spring have a green patch at the tip of each inner petal. The flowers of ***Galanthus plicatus* subsp. *byzantinus*** differ in having green marks at both the base and tip of each inner petal. **ZONES 6–9.**

GALAX

BEETLEWEED, WANDFLOWER

This genus consists of a single species, a shade-loving perennial from the moist, humid woodlands of southeast USA. It has tough, glossy, almost circular leaves with toothed edges. Although evergreen, the leaves take on a bronzy sheen during the cooler months. In late spring or early summer leafless flower stems rise well above the foliage and open into spikes of small, pure white flowers.
CULTIVATION: Grow in shade or part-sun in moist but well-drained, humus-rich soil. It will not tolerate lime (alkaline) soil. Keep the organic content of the soil high by mulching each spring with leafmold or rotted manure. Propagate from seed sown in fall (autumn) or by dividing established plants in early spring.

Galax urceolata

syn. *Galax aphylla*

A 12–18 in (30–45 cm) high perennial that spreads by creeping rhizomes, this species makes a beautiful ground cover beneath deciduous or lightly foliaged evergreen trees. Its low growth makes it an ideal edging plant in shady areas and it looks particularly lovely by ponds. **ZONES 4–9.**

GALEGA

GOAT'S RUE

This legume genus consists of 6 species of herbaceous perennials originating from southern Europe and western Asia. They are clump forming with erect stems, pinnate, soft green leaves and erect racemes of small pea-flowers. They are excellent cottage garden plants and are good for borders.
CULTIVATION: Frost hardy, they prefer an open, sunny or part-shaded position in any well-drained, moisture-retentive soil. Plants will require staking. Cut back faded flower stems to the ground. Propagate from seed in spring or by division in late fall (autumn) and spring.

Gaillardia × *grandiflora* 'Kobold'

Galanthus nivalis 'Flore Pleno'

Galega officinalis

This species reaches a height of 3–5 ft (1–1.5 m) and has light green leaves with lance-shaped leaflets. It bears spikes of small, pea-like, mauve, pink or white flowers over summer. These are followed by erect, long, narrow pods. It has an upright habit with erect stems. **ZONES 5–10.**

Galega orientalis

This rampantly spreading perennial, growing to about 4 ft (1.2 m) high and 24 in (60 cm) wide, has soft pinnate leaves with larger leaflets than those of *Galega officinalis.* The erect spikes of violet-blue pea-flowers are carried for many weeks in late spring. **ZONES 6–10.**

GALIUM

BEDSTRAW

This genus contains about 400 species of annuals and perennials of cosmopolitan distribution, of which some have become naturalized beyond their native regions and are weeds. They have weak sprawling stems and whorls of narrow green leaves. Many species spread by slender, much-branched rhizomes. The small star-shaped flowers are white, pink or yellow. **CULTIVATION:** Grow these frost-hardy plants in part-shade in well-drained but moist soil. Propagate from fresh ripe seed or by division in early spring or fall (autumn).

Galium aparine

GOOSE GRASS, CLEAVERS

Native to Europe and temperate Asia, this trailing or scrambling annual to 5 ft (1.5 m) high has narrow, lance-shaped leaves about 1 in (25 mm) long with fringed margins in whorls of up to eight. Stems and leaves are armed with stiff hooks, causing them to cling to clothing or even to bare skin, hence the common name 'cleavers'. Tiny white flowers are borne in groups of 3 in spring and summer. It is invasive and is considered a weed in some areas. **ZONES 7–10.**

Galium odoratum

syn. *Asperula odorata*

SWEET WOODRUFF

This delicate European perennial produces a beautiful pattern of whorled leaves, making a dense mass of foliage about 12 in (30 cm) high and greater spread. The tiny white flowers appear in few-flowered clusters in late spring. The fragrant foliage was traditionally added to white wine to produce May wine in Europe. **ZONES 5–10.**

Gardenia augusta

Galium verum

Galium verum

LADY'S BEDSTRAW

This sprawling perennial from temperate Eurasia and North America grows to about 12 in (30 cm) high forming a dense mass of fine foliage up to 4 ft (1.2 m) across. It has linear leaves arranged in whorls and tiny bright yellow flowers borne in dense terminal heads in summer and early fall (autumn). **ZONES 3–10.**

GALTONIA

This genus of 4 species of frost-hardy bulbs, native to South Africa, is named after Francis Galton (1822–1911), an explorer, scientist and student of all things African. Summer flowering, they are closely related to *Ornithogalum* though their more bell-shaped flowers set them apart. They have semi-erect strap-like leaves in rosettes and elegant tall spikes of pendent, funnel-shaped flowers. **CULTIVATION:** Plant in a sheltered site in full sun and fertile, well-drained soil; winter damp will rot them. They tend to die down in winter and may be lifted for replanting in spring. Propagate from fresh ripe seed in spring or by offsets in fall (autumn) or spring. Snails may be a problem.

Galtonia candicans

BERG LILY, SUMMER HYACINTH

This species is up to 4 ft (1.2 m) high with fleshy gray-green leaves and erect stems bearing loose spikes of up to 30 pendent bell-shaped white flowers, sometimes shaded or marked with green. They are produced for about 6 weeks from the middle of summer. **ZONES 6–10.**

Galtonia viridiflora

This species has lance-shaped, gray-green leaves and reaches a height of 3 ft (1 m). It bears arching stems of nodding, trumpet-shaped, pale green flowers in late summer. **ZONES 8–10.**

Gardenia augusta 'Magnifica'

Galium odoratum

Galtonia candicans

GARCINIA

This is a genus of some 200 species of slow-growing evergreen trees or shrubs mostly from tropical Asia with a few from Africa. They are grown for their thick foliage and edible fruits. The mangosteen, ***Garcinia mangostana***, is considered by many to be one of the world's most delicious fruits. Some are cultivated for the yellow latex in their stems, which has been used in dyeing and is said to have medicinal properties. **CULTIVATION:** Plant in part-shade in moist, well-drained soil and water regularly. Male and female flowers are on separate trees, but male trees are rare and most fruits are formed without fertilization. They thus contain no seeds. Propagation from cuttings or by layering is difficult and the trees bear fruit only in equatorial climates, so they are rarely seen away from their origins.

Garcinia xanthochymus

GAMBOGE

A straight-trunked tree from northern India and the western Himalayas, this species reaches 40 ft (12 m) with a dense, rounded, low canopy. The glossy green, narrow leaves are up to 18 in (45 cm) long. It bears small white flowers and dark yellow fruit, the sap of which yields the yellow pigment gamboge, now superseded by the more durable chrome and cadmium yellows. **ZONES 11–12.**

GARDENIA

Evergreen shrubs or small trees with glossy deep green leaves and fragrant white or cream flowers, gardenias provide some of the most fragrant of all flowers and are popular in warm-climate gardens worldwide. The genus includes some 200-odd species, most of them from tropical Asia or southern Africa. **CULTIVATION:** They need well-drained, neutral to acid soil and prefer light shade. Generous water in the warmer

Galtonia candicans

Garcinia xanthochymus

Garcinia xanthochymus

months and a regular dressing of compost and fertilizer ensures good flowering and keeps foliage a deep glossy green. Frost tender and lovers of humidity, they are best grown in heated greenhouses in cooler climates. Gardenias are easily propagated from cuttings in summer.

Gardenia augusta

syns *Gardenia florida, G. grandiflora, G. jasminoides*

COMMON GARDENIA, CAPE JASMINE

This is the best known species of the genus, an evergreen, glossy-leafed shrub from southern China, though long supposed native to the Cape of Good Hope, hence the name Cape jasmine. It is commonly seen in gardens and flower shops in one of its double-flowered cultivars, all with white, strongly perfumed flowers changing to pale yellow as they age. The best known is **'Florida'**, a 3 ft (1 m) tall shrub with flowers about 3 in (8 cm) wide; **'Magnifica'** is larger in all its parts though less generous with its flowers; **'Radicans'** is almost prostrate, with small flowers and leaves. Flowers appear over a long season from late spring. **ZONES 10–11.**

Gaultheria fragrantissima

Gardenia thunbergia

Garrya elliptica

Gardenia thunbergia
STARRY GARDENIA

From the humid forests of southern Africa, this erect shrub grows to 10 ft (3 m) or more high and almost as wide with stiff, erect branches. The large fragrant white flowers are held singly towards the branch tips in early summer. Being surface rooted, *Gardenia thunbergia* appreciates regular fertilizing, ample water and a yearly mulch of compost. **ZONES 9–11.**

Gardenia volkensii
syn. *Gardenia spatulifolia*
TRANSVAAL GARDENIA

Of wide distribution in the grasslands of southeastern Africa, this many-branched evergreen shrub or small tree up to 20 ft (6 m) tall has leaves in whorls of 3 at the branch ends. The single white flowers have petals with overlapping edges appearing from late winter to early summer. **ZONES 9–11.**

Gardenia thunbergia (fruit)

GARRYA

The only genus in its family, *Garrya* comprises some 13 species of evergreen shrubs and small trees from western USA, Mexico and the West Indies. They are cultivated for their handsome leaves and pendent catkins, which are longer and more attractive on male plants. The most important species in gardens is the silk-tassel bush, *Garrya elliptica.*
CULTIVATION: They require a mild-temperate climate with shelter from freezing winds. Grow in rich, well-drained soil in full sun or part-shade. Slow growing, they need little pruning and dislike being transplanted. Propagate from cuttings in summer.

Garrya elliptica
SILK-TASSEL BUSH

This dense, bushy shrub from California and Oregon grows to 8–25 ft (2.4–8 m) high and wide. It can be trained in espalier form. The leaves are broadly oval, dark green, leathery and wavy edged. Curtains of tassel-like, cream and dull pink catkins are borne from mid-winter to early spring on male plants (which are the only ones normally cultivated). The cultivar **'James Roof'** has silvery catkins with golden anthers. **ZONES 8–9.**

GASTERIA

Indigenous to South Africa, this genus of perennial succulents is closely allied to *Aloe.* Gasterias are grown for their interesting tongue-like leaves, usually marked with whitish dots or warty protuberances and showy spikes of narrowly bell-shaped flowers. The leaves mostly form a rosette or fan, making them useful for the rock garden or containers.

Gaultheria mucronata 'Bell's Seedling'

CULTIVATION: These frost-tender plants need to be grown indoors in climates with severe winter frost. Outdoors, grow in well-drained soil in full sun or part-shade. Propagate from leaf cuttings in spring and summer or by division.

Gasteria carinata var. *verrucosa*
syn. *Gasteria verrucosa*
WARTY ALOE, OX TONGUE

This South African fan-shaped succulent grows up to 4 in (10 cm) high and 12 in (30 cm) wide. Its long, thick, tapering leaves are deep green and densely sprinkled with white, wart-like tubercles. The leaves are in 2 opposing ranks and have incurved edges. In spring racemes of tubular orange and green flowers appear from the center. **ZONES 9–11.**

GAULTHERIA
syns × *Gaulnettya, Pernettya*

Named after Dr Gaultier, an eighteenth-century physician, this genus of 170 or so species of evergreen shrubs are widely distributed in moist temperate regions of the world, also in higher mountain areas of the tropics. They have attractive glossy leaves which may be aromatic when crushed. The flowers are pink or white and are usually bell- or urn-shaped. The fruits, though capsules, are berry-like and aromatic.
CULTIVATION: Marginally to very frost hardy, they prefer well-drained, humus-rich, acid soil, and a sheltered position in part-shade. Propagate from seed in fall (autumn) or cuttings in summer or by division of suckers in fall or spring.

Gaultheria cuneata

From China, this small compact shrub to 12 in (30 cm) high has stiff stems and dark green, oval leaves. In late spring and early summer it bears white urn-shaped flowers followed by white globose fruit in fall (autumn). **ZONES 7–9.**

Gaultheria procumbens

Gaultheria fragrantissima

From the mountains of southern Asia, this large, dense shrub or small tree reaches 10 ft (3 m). The leathery, elliptical leaves, 4 in (10 cm) long, smell strongly of oil of wintergreen when crushed. In maturity the green adult leaves develop a brown underside. In spring fragrant, bell-shaped flowers, white or pale pink, appear on last season's growth. The rounded fruit ripen mid- or pale blue. **ZONES 8–10.**

Gaultheria mucronata
syn. *Pernettya mucronata*
PRICKLY HEATH

This thicket-forming, suckering shrub from Chile and Argentina grows to 5 ft (1.5 m) high and wide and has deep green, glossy leaves ½ in (12 mm) long with sharp tips. It bears clusters of small, white, pendulous flowers and small, fleshy, pinkish purple fruit. There are separate male and female plants. Cultivars include **'Bell's Seedling'** with deep dusky pink berries; **'Mother of Pearl'** with pale pink berries; **'Mulberry Wine'** with purple berries; and **'White Pearl'** with white berries. **'Wintertime'** has pure white berries. **ZONES 7–9.**

Gaultheria procumbens
WINTERGREEN, CHECKERBERRY

From the woodlands of eastern North America, this prostrate shrub grows only 6 in (15 cm) tall but spreads widely by trailing stems. It bears 1 in (25 mm) elliptical, glossy green leaves and single, drooping white flowers in summer. The flowers are followed by small scarlet berries that hold their color well into winter. This species was the original source of oil of wintergreen, used in liniments. **ZONES 4–9.**

Gaultheria pumila

From the southernmost tip of South America and the Falkland Islands, this

Gaultheria shallon

Gaultheria pumila var. *leucocarpa*

Gazania 'Double Orange'

Gazania 'Gwen's Pink'

prostrate shrub has small oval leaves crowded along the stems in 2 almost opposite rows. Small white, bell-shaped flowers, borne singly in the leaf axils, are followed by white to reddish fruit. ***Gaultheria pumila* var. *leucocarpa*** from southern Chile has white fruit. **ZONES 6–9.**

Gaultheria rupestris

A native of New Zealand, this erect, branching shrub grows to a height and spread of 6 ft (1.8 m), and bears clusters of tubular white flowers amid oblong, leathery leaves. Succulent berries follow the blooms. **ZONES 7–9.**

Gaultheria shallon

SHALLON

From northwestern North America, this suckering shrub grows to 4–10 ft (1.2–3 m) high and wide. In spring it produces terminal panicles of small, pinkish white, lily-of-the-valley flowers. These are followed by $\frac{1}{2}$ in (12 mm) fleshy, purple fruit. **ZONES 5–9.**

Gaultheria × *wisleyensis*

syn. × *Gaulnettya wisleyensis*

These vigorous hybrids, bred in England from *Gaultheria shallon* and *G. mucronata,* though variable are usually dense and less than 6 ft (1.8 m) high. They have small leathery leaves, white flowers and large bunches of dark red berries that persist until late winter. Several named cultivars are available. **ZONES 7–9.**

GAURA

Related to the evening primrose *(Oenothera),* this genus of about 20 species of annuals, biennials, perennials and subshrubs from North America are apt to be weedy, despite their showy flowers and the genus name that translates as 'gorgeous'. They have simple, narrow leaves and either racemes or

Gazania 'Flore Pleno'

panicles of flat, star-shaped, pink or white flowers.

CULTIVATION: They prefer full sun and light, well-drained soil. Cut ruthlessly to the ground when flowering has finished. Propagate from seed in fall (autumn) or spring, or from cuttings in summer.

Gaura lindheimeri

Native to the USA–Mexico border region, this clump-forming, long-flowering perennial is useful for backgrounds and mixed flower borders. It has loosely branched stems covered with tiny hairs, and from spring to fall (autumn) produces long sprays of beautiful flowers which open white from pink buds. It grows to 4 ft (1.2 m) in height with a spread of 3 ft (1 m). **ZONES 5–10.**

GAZANIA

From tropical and southern Africa, this genus consists of about 16 species of low-growing annuals and perennials grown for their bright colorful flowers. The genus name honors the medieval scholar Theodore of Gaza (1398–1478). The leaves are entire or deeply lobed, long and narrow, often dark green on top and white- or silver gray-felted beneath or in some species silvery haired on both sides. The flowerheads borne singly on short stalks range from cream to yellow, gold, pink, red, buff, brown and intermediate

Gazania rigens var. *leucolaena*

Gazania hybrid cultivar

shades, usually with contrasting bands or spots at the petal bases. They appear from early spring until summer. Most modern varieties are hybrids from several South African species; they are marginally frost hardy and useful for coastal areas for bedding, rock gardens, pots and tubs and for binding soil on slopes. Cultivars include **'Double Orange'** bearing large orange flowers with double centers on short stems just above the leaves; **'Flore Pleno'** with bright yellow double flowers; and **'Gwen's Pink'** with salmon pink single flowers with yellow centers and dark brown rings. Plants in the **Chansonette Series** are strong but low growers, reaching just 8 in (20 cm) in height. There are many color varieties, mostly with contrasting dark centers.

CULTIVATION: Grow in full sun in sandy, fairly dry, well-drained soil. Mulch with compost and water during dry periods. Propagate by division or from cuttings in fall (autumn), or from seed in late winter to early spring.

Gazania, Daybreak Series

These carpeting perennials grow to a height and spread of 8 in (20 cm). In cooler districts they are often grown as annuals and bear large orange, yellow, pink and bronze daisy-like flowers. Unlike most gazanias, the flowers of this series remain open even in cloudy weather. **ZONES 9–11.**

Gazania krebsiana

From South Africa, this stemless perennial has slender lance-shaped leaves with a smooth upper surface and white downy underside. The flowers range from yellow to orange-red with a contrasting darker color around their centers. **ZONES 9–11.**

Gazania rigens

This perennial species grows to a height of 12 in (30 cm) with a similar spread. It

Gaultheria × *wisleyensis*

Gazania krebsiana

is a mat-forming plant with crowded rosettes of mostly unlobed leaves that are green above and whitish beneath, and orange flowerheads with a black eye spot at petal bases. The leaves of ***Gazania rigens* var. *leucolaena*** are silvery green on both sides and the flowers are yellow; ***G. r.* var. *uniflora*** has flowers that are smaller and short stalked. **ZONES 9–11.**

Gazania, Sunshine Hybrids

These mat-forming perennials may be grown as annuals. The height and spread is around 8 in (20 cm) and solitary flowers, borne in summer, range in color with the disc-florets usually ringed in a darker color. **ZONES 9–11.**

GEISSORHIZA

Consisting of 60 to 70 species of small bulbs (or more accurately corms), almost all from the winter rainfall parts of the southwest of South Africa, *Geissorhiza* is a spring-blooming genus that is dormant from late spring to mid-fall (mid-autumn). Plants grow from small, hard corms producing one or a few small, grassy leaves. The flowers are produced on simple or branched stems and although each bloom is only 1 in (25 mm) across they can be exquisite.

CULTIVATION: Sow seeds or plant corms in small pots in mid-fall. Seed germinates well if sown onto a mix of fine gravel and sand. Corms need only be pushed just below the surface. Keep cool and lightly moist until growth begins, when watering can be increased slightly. Do not overfeed, especially with fertilizers high in nitrogen. They are best grown in a cool greenhouse in climates where severe frost is experienced, and can be started in earliest spring for

Gaura lindheimeri

Gazania, Sunshine Hybrids

bloom in early summer. After bloom gradually reduce water and, when plants begin to yellow, let them go dry. Potted plants can be stored dry in their containers over summer.

Geissorhiza aspera

One of the more cold-hardy species, *Geissorhiza aspera* rewards growers with sprays of dainty, starry flowers that are a satiny blue-violet color. The flowers appear in late winter or early spring in mild climates, a little later in cooler areas. **ZONES 9–10.**

GELSEMIUM

This genus contains 3 species of evergreen, twining climbers, 2 of them native to the southern states of the USA of which one extends to Central America, and the third native to Southeast Asia. Moderate growers, they produce lavish displays of sweet-scented, bell-like flowers in spring. They do well as ground covers and growing over verandahs and pergolas. In cool climates they can be grown as pot plants in a greenhouse or conservatory. All parts of the plants are poisonous and extracts from the Asian species were used for murder and suicide, but in the garden they present little threat.

CULTIVATION: Gelsemiums need fertile, well-drained soil, full sun and shelter from drying winds. The stems may need support and can be pruned if necessary after flowering. Propagate from seed in spring or from cuttings in summer.

Gelsemium sempervirens

Genista falcata

Genista horrida

Gelsemium sempervirens
CAROLINA JASMINE

Carolina jasmine has glossy green leaves and fragrant, small yellow trumpet flowers, which appear for many months in spring and again in fall (autumn). This species grows quickly but tidily to 10 ft (3 m) and can be trained on fences, walls or a pergola near the house, where the perfume can be enjoyed. **ZONES 8–11.**

GENISTA
syns *Chamaespartium, Teline*
BROOM

From Europe and the Mediterranean to western Asia, this legume genus consists of about 90 species of deciduous and evergreen shrubs, grown for their profuse, fragrant, pea-like flowers. Many of the species have very reduced leaves, sometimes bearing their flowers on leafless green branches. In ancient times their flowers were used to make dyes.

CULTIVATION: Many are only marginally frost hardy; they prefer a temperate climate and some are good seaside plants. Full sun and a not-too-rich, well-drained soil suit them best. The frost-tender species can be grown in a well-ventilated greenhouse. They resent being transplanted. Prune to encourage a compact, bushy shape. Propagate from seed in spring or cuttings in summer.

Genista aetnensis
MOUNT ETNA BROOM, SICILIAN BROOM

This rounded, somewhat weeping deciduous shrub or small tree is native to Sicily and North Africa. Growing to 30 ft (9 m) high and wide, it is almost leafless but in summer bears an explosion of small, golden-yellow flowers. It is marginally frost hardy. **ZONES 8–10.**

Genista hispanica

Genista lydia

Genista lydia

Genista pilosa 'Vancouver Gold'

Genista × spachiana

Genista × spachiana 'Nana'

Genista × spachiana

Genista falcata

From western Spain and Portugal, this erect deciduous shrub, to around 24 in (60 cm) high, has axillary spines to 2 in (5 cm) long and small, narrow elliptic leaves. The young branches and undersides of the leaves are covered in silk-like hairs. In spring it produces small pea-like yellow flowers in clusters or dense panicles. **ZONES 9–10.**

Genista hispanica
SPANISH GORSE

From southwestern Europe, this dwarf deciduous shrub is ideal for rockeries and dry, sunny banks. It has few leaves and many spines. It grows 30 in (75 cm) tall and 5 ft (1.5 m) wide, forming a neat dome covered in spring and early summer with dense clusters of tiny, golden-yellow flowers. **ZONES 6–10.**

Genista horrida

A native of the Pyrenees, this spiny domed shrub can grow to 24 in (60 cm) high and bears opposite, trifoliate leaves with minute linear leaflets. Downy, yellow pea-like flowers are borne in terminal heads. The oblong fruit are also downy. **ZONES 7–9.**

Genista lydia

This mound-forming, deciduous shrub from the Balkans reaches 24–36 in (60–90 cm) tall and wide; it has arching branches and bluish green leaves. Bright yellow pea-like flowers are borne in abundance in early summer. Fully frost hardy, this is an excellent plant for rockeries, banks and for trailing over walls. **ZONES 7–9.**

Genista pilosa

This deciduous, prostrate to erect European species grows to 16 in (40 cm) high and twice as wide. Fully frost hardy, it bears small, narrow, lance-shaped, dark green leaves with a silky undersurface and profuse small yellow pea-flowers in early summer. **'Vancouver Gold'** has a domed habit to 18 in (45 cm) high and golden-yellow flowers. **ZONES 5–9.**

Genista sagittalis
syn. *Chamaespartium sagittale*

This prostrate shrub from Europe reaches 6–12 in (15–30 cm) high with a spread of up to 3 ft (1 m). It has very distinctive, broadly winged stems, sparsely scattered dark green oval leaves and dense terminal clusters of deep yellow pea-flowers in early summer. **ZONES 4–9.**

Genista × spachiana
syns *Cytisus fragrans, C. racemosus, Genista fragrans*

This dense, evergreen broom is a hybrid between *Genista canariensis* and

Genista sagittalis

Gentiana acaulis

Gentiana andrewsii

Gentiana farreri

Gentiana 'Inverleith'

G. stenopetala. Although frost tender, it tolerates dry, windy conditions and infertile soils, growing quickly to about 6 ft (1.8 m). The dark green leaves are shiny above and pale and silky beneath. A profusion of fragrant yellow pea-flowers appear in long spikes in winter and spring; **'Nana'** is similar but has a smaller growth habit. Both are widely sold as a flowering pot plant. **ZONES 9–11.**

Genista stenopetala
syns *Cytisus stenopetalus*, *Teline stenopetala*

From the Canary Islands, this species has silky leaves and spikes of sweetly scented bright yellow flowers in spring. It grows to about 10 ft (3 m) tall. **ZONES 9–11.**

Genista tenera

This is a graceful, arching shrub from the Canary Islands and Madiera to 10 ft (3 m) high with narrow, gray-green leaves and dense clusters of fragrant bright yellow pea-flowers in summer. **'Golden Showers'** has profuse, bright golden-yellow flowers. **ZONES 9–11.**

Genista tinctoria
DYER'S BROOM, WOADWAXEN

Used as a medicinal herb and as a source of yellow dye, this tough, deciduous, green-stemmed 3 ft (1 m) shrub ranges from Europe to Siberia. It has 1 in (25 mm) long leaves with fine hairs beneath. Golden yellow, pea-flowers appear in summer after other brooms have finished flowering. **'Flore Pleno'** (syn. 'Plena') is a dwarf cultivar, 12 in (30 cm) high, with double flowers. **'Royal Gold'** has golden-yellow flowers arranged in conical panicles to 3 in (8 cm) long. **ZONES 3–9.**

Genista 'Yellow Imp'

'Yellow Imp' is one of a group of beautiful hybrid brooms. It is a sprawling shrub 5–6 ft (1.5–1.8 m) tall that flowers in late spring. The flowers can be pure yellow, or variously flushed and tinted with maroon or cream. **ZONES 8–10.**

GENTIANA
GENTIAN

Occurring worldwide, mostly in alpine meadows and occasionally in woodlands, this is a genus of around 400 species of annuals, biennials and perennials, some of them evergreen. Intense deep blues and sky blues are the usual flower colors, but whites, creams, yellows and even red are also found. The mostly trumpet-shaped flowers are borne from spring to fall (autumn). They are useful in rock gardens and sloping hillside gardens.
CULTIVATION: They prefer cooler regions and well-drained, but moisture-retentive soil rich in humus. Some species grow naturally in limestone soil. Plant in either sun or semi-shade. Propagate by division in spring or from fresh seed in fall. Divide fall-flowering species every 3 years in early spring, planting out in fresh soil.

Gentiana acaulis
syns *Gentiana excisa*, *G. kochiana*
STEMLESS GENTIAN, TRUMPET GENTIAN

The stemless gentian is an evergreen, rhizomatous perennial from southern Europe. It makes a striking carpet of small, crowded leaves and disproportionately large vivid blue trumpet flowers with green-spotted throats in spring and early summer. The foliage is only about 1 in (25 mm) high. It needs a deep root run and benefits from a light application of lime. **ZONES 3–9.**

Genista 'Yellow Imp'

Gentiana andrewsii
BOTTLE GENTIAN, CLOSED GENTIAN

This perennial plant is native to the moist meadows and woodlands of eastern North America. The dark green foliage is borne on stems 12–24 in (30–60 cm) tall, and it has a narrow, erect habit. The bottle gentian is distinguished from other species by bearing, in mid-summer, dark violet-blue tubular flowers that never open fully. **ZONES 5–9.**

Gentiana asclepiadea
WILLOW GENTIAN

The arching stems of this perennial bear slender, willow-like leaves. In early fall (autumn) many rich violet-blue flowers appear in the leaf axils on the upper stems. It forms a loose clump 3 ft (1 m) high and 24 in (60 cm) wide. **ZONES 6–9.**

Gentiana bellidifolia

The 'daisy-leafed' gentian is typical of the New Zealand species in having white flowers in clusters. It is variable, reaching 6 in (15 cm) at the most. The flowers appear in summer, and the leaves are usually brown tinted. **ZONES 7–9.**

Gentiana dinarica

From Italy and the Balkans, this small, tufted perennial grows to about 6 in (15 cm) high with a basal rosette of broadly elliptic leaves to 1½ in (35 mm) long. In summer it bears solitary, deep blue, narrowly bell-shaped flowers on stems to 3 in (8 cm) long. **ZONES 6–9.**

Genista tinctoria (with seed pods)

Gentiana asclepiadea

Gentiana farreri

This 4 in (10 cm) tall semi-evergreen perennial from the borders of China and Tibet is one of the most beautiful of the Asiatic gentians. It has trailing stems with rosettes of small lance-shaped leaves. The turquoise blue, trumpet-shaped flowers with a white stripe appear in fall (autumn). **ZONES 5–9.**

Gentiana 'Inverleith'

This robust hybrid of *Gentiana farreri* and *G. veitchiorum* has trailing stems with basal rosettes of linear, lance-shaped leaves. The pale blue trumpet-shaped flowers have deep blue stripes and appear in fall (autumn). **ZONES 5–9.**

Gentiana lutea
GREAT YELLOW GENTIAN

This robust, erect, clump-forming perennial from the mountains of Europe produces tubular yellow flowers in clusters in the upper axils of tall stems in summer. It grows to 3–6 ft (1–1.8 m) high and 24 in (60 cm) wide and has oval, stem-clasping leaves to 12 in (30 cm) long. This is the main commercial source of gentian root, used medicinally and to flavor vermouth. **ZONES 5–9.**

Gentiana bellidifolia

Gentiana dinarica

G

Gentiana paradoxa

Geranium 'Brookside'

Geranium cinereum subsp. *subcaulescens*

Geranium cinereum 'Ballerina'

Gentiana paradoxa

This beautiful perennial species has prostrate stems with linear, lance-shaped, finely pointed leaves up to 2 in (5 cm) long. The trumpet-shaped, bright blue flowers have deep purple and white stripes at the throat. ZONES 6–9.

Gentiana septemfida
CRESTED GENTIAN

Native to mountains of western and central Asia, this sun-loving perennial grows about 8 in (20 cm) tall and has paired oval leaves. The rich blue flowers with white throats are borne in terminal clusters of up to 8 in summer. ZONES 3–9.

Gentiana septemfida

Geranium goldmanii

Geranium cinereum subsp. *subcaulescens*

Gentiana sino-ornata

This evergreen perennial from western China flowers in fall (autumn), bearing deep blue trumpet flowers that are paler at the base and banded purplish blue. It has a prostrate, spreading habit, reaching 2 in (5 cm) tall and 12 in (30 cm) wide. **'Alba'** has white flowers. ZONES 6–9.

Gentiana verna
SPRING GENTIAN

This spring-flowering perennial to 2 in (5 cm) high has a scattered distribution in mountainous regions in Europe from Ireland to Russia. Often short-lived, it forms compact clumps of basal rosettes of broadly ovate leaves. Short, erect stems bear solitary brilliant blue flowers with a white throat and spreading petals in early spring. **'Angulosa'** has larger, more robust flowers. ZONES 5–9.

GERANIUM
CRANESBILL

Over 300 species of annual, biennial and perennial geraniums, some evergreen, grow all over the world mainly in cool-temperate regions. The leaves are on long stalks, broadly circular in outline but usually palmately lobed. They make small, showy clumps with pink to blue or purple and white, 5-petalled flowers. The true geraniums or cranesbills, so-called for the shape of their small, dry fruitlets, are often confused with species of the genus *Pelargonium*, also commonly known as 'geraniums'. Symmetrical flowers are their chief point of distinction from pelargoniums, which produce irregularly shaped or marked flowers. With their attractive flowers they are useful for rock gardens, ground covers and borders. Compact species and hybrids such as **'Brookside'** and ***Geranium goldmanii*** are also good for containers.
CULTIVATION: Mostly quite frost hardy, they prefer a sunny situation and damp, well-drained soil. Transplant during winter. Propagate from cuttings in summer or seed in spring, or by division in fall (autumn).

Gentiana sino-ornata 'Alba'

Geranium 'Ann Folkard'

This free-flowering, spreading perennial to 24 in (60 cm) high and up to 3 ft (1 m) wide has deeply lobed, light yellowish green leaves. Dark magenta saucer-shaped flowers with black centers and veining are borne from mid-summer to mid-fall (mid-autumn). ZONES 6–9.

Geranium × *cantabrigiense*

This hybrid between *Geranium dalmaticum* and *G. macrorrhizum* to 12 in (30 cm) high spreads by runners to 24 in (60 cm) wide. It has aromatic, light green basal leaves and bright purplish pink flowers in summer. **'Biokovo'** has pink-tinged, white flowers. ZONES 5–9.

Geranium cinereum

From southern Europe, this small, tufted perennial to 6 in (15 cm) tall forms a basal rosette of soft, deeply divided leaves. The cup-shaped flowers, white or pale pink often with purple veins, are produced in late spring or early summer. **'Ballerina'** bears purplish pink flowers with distinct purple veins; ***Geranium cinereum* subsp. *subcaulescens*** has darker green leaves and vivid magenta flowers with a striking black center. ZONES 5–9.

Geranium × *cantabrigiense*

Gentiana verna 'Angulosa'

Geranium clarkei

From the western Himalayas, this perennial is up to 18 in (45 cm) high with spreading stems and deeply divided leaves. Its saucer-shaped flowers, borne in summer, are white or violet with pink veins. **'Kashmir Purple'** bears lilac-blue flowers with red veins. ZONES 7–9.

Geranium dalmaticum

This mat-forming perennial from the coastal Balkans grows to 6 in (15 cm) high. It spreads slowly and has glossy, deeply divided leaves. Long-stemmed clusters of soft pink flowers are held above the foliage from spring to mid-summer. It is a good rock garden plant. **'Album'** has white flowers. ZONES 5–10.

Geranium endressii

From the Pyrenees, this rhizomatous perennial forms clumps to 18 in (45 cm) high and 24 in (60 cm) across. The leaves are deeply lobed and toothed and pale pink flowers, becoming darker with age, are produced from early summer to early fall (autumn). ZONES 5–9.

Geranium clarkei 'Kashmir Purple'

Geranium × *cantabrigiense*

Geranium erianthum

Geranium himalayense

Geranium himalayense 'Plenum'

Geranium erianthum

This is a clump-forming perennial from northeastern Asia and northwestern North America. It has erect stems to 24 in (60 cm) tall and light green, deeply lobed and toothed leaves, which have a rich fall (autumn) coloring. Clusters of saucer-shaped, violet flowers are borne in early summer. **ZONES 3–9.**

Geranium farreri

From northwestern China, this dwarf, tufted perennial has erect red stems to 5 in (12 cm) high and kidney-shaped leaves with up to 7 deeply cut lobes. Pale pink or lilac flowers with black anthers are borne in mid-summer. **ZONES 4–9.**

Geranium fremontii

This clump-forming perennial to 18 in (45 cm) high is native to North America. It has light green, broadly toothed basal leaves with a sticky underside and bears flat purplish pink flowers from early summer to early fall (autumn). **ZONES 4–9.**

Geranium himalayense
syn. *Geranium grandiflorum*

This clump-forming perennial has cushions of neatly cut leaves and grows to an 18 in (45 cm) high and 24 in (60 cm) wide. In summer large cup-shaped violet-blue flowers with white centers

Geranium fremontii

Geranium himalayense 'Gravetye'

appear on long stalks. **'Gravetye'** (syn. *Geranium grandiflorum* var. *alpinum*) has lilac-blue flowers with reddish centers and leaves that turn russet before dying down in fall (autumn). **'Plenum'** (syn. 'Birch Double') has double, purplish pink flowers with darker veins. **ZONES 4–9.**

Geranium ibericum

Although 'ibericum' is normally taken to mean 'Spanish' in Latin, it can also refer to the Caucasus region, where in fact this species comes from. This clump-forming perennial grows to a height and spread of 18 in (45 cm). It has heart-shaped, hairy leaves and produces large sprays of saucer-shaped violet flowers with faint darker veins in early summer. **ZONES 6–9.**

Geranium incanum

This South African evergreen perennial grows up to 15 in (38 cm) high and 3 ft (1 m) wide. Its grayish green leaves are deeply cut and feathery and have a spicy aroma. The cup-shaped blooms are deep pink with deeper colored veins. It is marginally frost hardy. **ZONES 8–10.**

Geranium 'Johnson's Blue'

This rhizomatous perennial may be merely a form of *Geranium himalayense.* It has deeply divided leaves and bears cup-shaped lavender-blue flowers with pale centers throughout summer. It has a spreading habit, reaching 18 in (45 cm) tall and 30 in (75 cm) wide. **ZONES 5–9.**

Geranium lucidum

Geranium lucidum
SHINY CRANESBILL

This widespread annual from Europe, North Africa and Asia has reddish, smooth stems and grows to around 18 in (45 cm) high. The somewhat succulent, glossy leaves up to 2 in (5 cm) across are shallowly lobed. The shiny cranesbill produces small deep pink flowers in spring and summer. **ZONES 7–10.**

Geranium macrorrhizum

This clump-forming perennial often forms large colonies in its shady mountain habitats of southern Europe. The sticky, deeply lobed leaves are aromatic, often turning red or bronze in fall (autumn). The flowers appear on 12 in (30 cm) stems above the foliage in spring and early summer. Flower color varies from pink or purplish to pure white. It makes an excellent ground cover for a dry, shady site. **'Album'** has white petals with reddish calyces; **'Ingwersen's Variety'** has pale pink flowers and smoother glossy leaves. **'Spessart'** is an attractive German cultivar. **ZONES 4–9.**

Geranium maculatum

Native to eastern American woodlands, this species is best used in woodland gardens as it is less showy and more open in habit than others. It is an erect, clump-forming perennial to 30 in (75 cm) tall with deeply lobed, glossy leaves and bears saucer-shaped, lilac-pink flowers with white centers in late spring to mid-summer. **ZONES 6–9.**

Geranium maderense

Native to Madeira, this short-lived, evergreen bushy perennial to 5 ft (1.5 m) tall has huge leaves for a geranium, often 12 in (30 cm) or more across, divided in a striking snowflake pattern and turning reddish in fall (autumn). Shallowly cup-shaped pinkish magenta flowers with darker centers are borne in tall panicles from late winter to late summer. Old leaves should not be removed too soon, as the plant props itself on them to resist wind-loosening. **ZONES 9–10.**

Geranium 'Johnson's Blue'

Geranium maderense

Geranium ibericum

Geranium incanum

G. macrorrhizum 'Ingwersen's Variety'

Geranium maculatum

G

Geranium × *magnificum*

This vigorous garden hybrid of *Geranium ibericum* and *G. platypetalum* forms clumps to 24 in (60 cm) high. It has hairy deeply cut leaves that color in fall (autumn). Abundant, violet-blue, reddish veined, saucer-shaped flowers appear in mid-summer. Propagate by division or from cuttings. **ZONES 5–9.**

Geranium malviflorum

syn. *Geranium atlanticum* of gardens

From southern Spain and northern Africa, this tuberous perennial to 12 in (30 cm) tall has deeply cut dark green leaves and violet-blue, red-veined, saucer-shaped flowers in spring. It flowers best in a poor soil, although better soil promotes a fine display of foliage. **ZONES 9–10.**

Geranium psilostemon

Geranium × *oxonianum*

This vigorous upright hybrid of *Geranium endressi* and *G. versicolor* forms clumps to 30 in (75 cm) high; it has light green wrinkled leaves with conspicuous veining. Trumpet-shaped flushed pink flowers with darker veins are produced over a long period from late spring to mid-fall (mid-autumn). **'Claridge Druce'** has mauve-pink darker veined flowers in summer; **'Wargrave Pink'** has bright pink flowers. **ZONES 5–9.**

Geranium palmatum

syn. *Geranium anemonifolium*

This bushy perennial from Madeira is related to *Geranium maderense* and has similar leaves, over 12 in (30 cm) wide. Masses of purplish pink, saucer-shaped flowers are carried on tall, central panicles to 4 ft (1.2 m) high throughout summer. **ZONES 9–10.**

Geranium phaeum

MOURNING WIDOW, DUSKY CRANESBILL

From Europe and western Russia, this clump-forming perennial to 30 in (75 cm) high and 18 in (45 cm) wide has soft green, densely lobed leaves. Its flowers are a deep, brownish purple with a paler center ring, borne in late spring or early summer. **'Lily Lovell'** has large white flowers; ***Geranium phaeum* var. *lividum*** has pale pink or lilac flowers; **'Variegatum'** has leaves with yellow margins and pink splotches. **ZONES 5–10.**

Geranium malviflorum

Geranium × *oxonianum*

G. × *oxonianum* 'Claridge Druce'

G. × *oxonianum* 'Wargrave Pink'

Geranium platypetalum

This hairy perennial from Turkey and the Caucasus forms clumps up to 18 in (45 cm) high and wide bearing deeply divided, wrinkled leaves. Flat, saucer-shaped violet-blue flowers with darker veins appear in summer. **ZONES 5–9.**

Geranium pratense

MEADOW CRANESBILL

From Europe, Siberia and China, this clump-forming perennial species reaches 3 ft (1 m) in height. It has hairy stems and the leaves are deeply lobed almost to the base. They become bronze in fall (autumn). Saucer-shaped, violet-blue flowers are carried on erect branching stems in summer. **'Plenum Violaceum'** (syn. 'Flore Pleno') has double, deep violet-blue flowers. **ZONES 5–9.**

Geranium psilostemon

syn. *Geranium armenum*

ARMENIAN CRANESBILL

This robust clump-forming perennial grows 2–4 ft (0.6–1.2 m) high and 24 in (60 cm) wide; it has lobed, deeply toothed leaves, often reddish in fall (autumn). Striking, large cup-shaped magenta flowers with a black eye appear in summer. **ZONES 6–9.**

Geranium renardii

This clump-forming perennial develops into a neat mound to 12 in (30 cm) high and wide. It has lobed, circular, finely wrinkled leaves with a velvety underside. The saucer-shaped white flowers with bold purple veins are borne in early summer. **ZONES 6–9**

Geranium × *riversleaianum* 'Russell Prichard'

This cultivar is a garden hybrid between *Geranium endressii* and *G. traversii.* It is a low-growing, mound-forming perennial

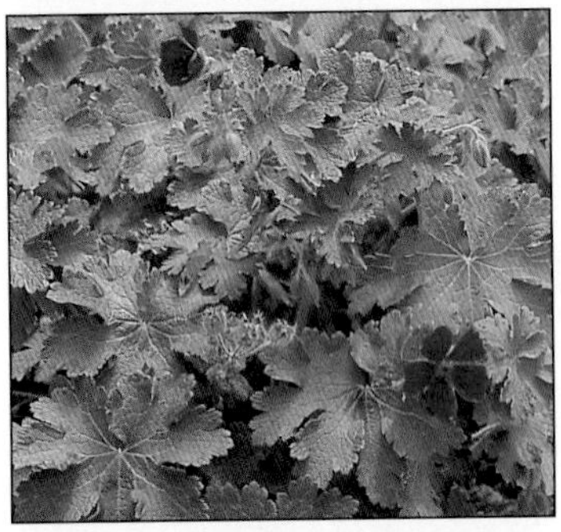

Geranium × *magnificum*

Geranium platypetalum

Geranium phaeum

Geranium phaeum

Geranium renardii

Geranium phaeum 'Lily Lovell'

Geranium phaeum var. *lividum*

Geranium phaeum 'Variegatum'

G. × *riversleaianum* 'Russell Prichard'

to 12 in (30 cm) high and has silvery, gray-green toothed leaves and rose magenta, funnel-shaped flowers from early summer to fall (autumn). **ZONES 7–9.**

Geranium robertianum
HERB ROBERT, RED ROBIN

Late in the season, this scrambling annual or biennial, found widespread in regions of the northern hemisphere, takes on an overall red color. The 'Robert' in the name is in fact a corruption of *ruberta,* from the Latin adjective *ruber* meaning 'red'. Herb Robert derived its traditional uses from the medieval Doctrine of Signatures which stated that a plant's medicinal qualities were revealed in its external features—in this case for diseases of the blood. The plant has deeply cut ferny leaves with a rather strong, not altogether pleasant, scent. Small star-shaped pink or rose flowers are produced from summer to fall (autumn). It is self-seeding, often to the point of being a nuisance. **ZONES 6–10.**

Geranium sanguineum
BLOODY CRANESBILL

In flower color this European species is often less 'bloody' than many other geraniums, but then coiners of English plant names had a weakness for translating the Latin name wherever possible. It is a low-growing perennial of around 8 in

Geranium sylvaticum

Geranium wallichianum 'Syabru'

Geranium sanguineum 'Vision'

Geranium sylvaticum 'Album'

Gerbera jamesonii cultivar

(20 cm) tall spreading by rhizomes. The dark green leaves are deeply cut into toothed lobes. Abundant cup-shaped bright magenta flowers with notched petals are produced during summer. ***Geranium sanguineum* var. *striatum*** is a pink version; **'Vision'** is a compact form with deep pink flowers. **ZONES 5–9.**

Geranium sylvaticum
WOOD CRANESBILL

Another well-known European species, this upright, clump-forming perennial to 30 in (75 cm) tall has deeply divided basal leaves from which arise branching stems carrying bluish purple, cup-shaped flowers with white centers from late spring to summer. **'Album'** has white flowers; **'Mayflower'** has rich violet-blue flowers with white centers. **ZONES 4–9.**

Geranium traversii

From coastal cliffs on the Chatham Islands off southern New Zealand, this perennial of up to 6 in (15 cm) high forms mounds of silvery, gray-green, lobed leaves. The pink or sometimes white saucer-shaped flowers are carried on slender stems above the foliage in summer to fall (autumn). It is ***Geranium traversii* var. *elegans*** rather than the type that is found in cultivation; **'Seaspray'** has small, pale pink flowers on short stems. **ZONES 8–9.**

Geranium sanguineum var. *striatum*

Geranium sylvaticum 'Mayflower'

Geranium traversii 'Seaspray'

Gerbera jamesonii cultivar

Gerbera 'Brigadoon Red'

Gerbera jamesonii cultivar

Geranium wallichianum

From the Himalayas, this tufted perennial to 12 in (30 cm) high has trailing branches to 4 ft (1.2 m) long. The lobed and toothed leaves have prominent veins. The violet-blue saucer-shaped flowers with white centers and darker veins are produced from mid-summer to mid-fall (mid-autumn). **'Buxton's Variety'** (syn. 'Buxton's Blue') has flowers which are a deeper blue with a large white center. **'Syabru'** has magenta flowers with darker veins and a small white center. **ZONES 7–9.**

GERBERA

This genus of around 40 perennial species is from Africa, Madagascar and Asia. The showy flowerheads, in almost every color except blue and purple, are carried on bare stems 18 in (45 cm) long. Linnaeus named the genus to honor a German colleague, Traugott Gerber. They are ideal rockery plants in frost-free climates. Only one species, *Gerbera jamesonii,* is commonly cultivated, along with its numerous hybrids.

CULTIVATION: They need full sun to part-shade in hot areas and fertile, composted, well-drained soil. Water well during summer. Gerberas make good greenhouse plants, where they require good light and regular feeding during the growing season. Propagate from seed in fall (autumn) or early spring, from cuttings in summer or by division from late winter to early spring.

Gerbera jamesonii
BARBERTON DAISY, TRANSVAAL DAISY

Native to South Africa, this is one of the most decorative of all daisies and is an excellent cut flower. From a basal rosette of deeply lobed, lance-shaped leaves, white, pink, yellow, orange or red flowerheads, up to 3 in (8 cm) wide, are borne singly on long stems in spring and summer. Modern florists' gerberas derive from crosses between *Gerbera jamesonii* and the tropical African *G. viridifolia.* Some have flowerheads as much as 12 in (30 cm) across, in a wide range of colors, as well as double, for example **'Brigadoon Red',** and quilled forms. **ZONES 8–11.**

Gillenia trifoliata

Geum chiloense 'Lady Stratheden'

GEUM

AVENS

This genus of 50 or so herbaceous perennials is from the temperate and colder zones of both northern and southern hemispheres. Species form basal rosettes of hairy, lobed leaves and bear masses of red, orange and yellow flowers with prominent stamens from late spring until early fall (autumn), and almost all year in frost-free areas. They suit mixed herbaceous borders and rock gardens, but may require a lot of room.
CULTIVATION: Frost hardy, they prefer a sunny, open position and moist, well-drained soil. Propagate from seed in fall or by division in fall or spring.

Geum chiloense

syns *Geum coccineum* of gardens, *G. quellyon*

SCARLET AVENS

This Chilean native reaches a height of 24 in (60 cm) with a spread of 12 in (30 cm). It forms a basal rosette of deep green, pinnate leaves to 12 in (30 cm) long. The vivid scarlet, cup-shaped flowers appear in terminal panicles in summer. **'Lady Stratheden'** (syn. 'Goldball') has semi-double, golden-yellow flowers. **'Mrs Bradshaw'** bears rounded semi-double scarlet flowers. **ZONES 5–9.**

Geum coccineum

syn. *Geum borisii* of gardens

This perennial from southeastern Europe is up to 18 in (45 cm) high with soft, hairy, irregularly lobed basal leaves. From late spring to late summer it bears open, 5-petalled red flowers with yellow central filaments on erect, branching stems. **'Werner Arends'** is a low-growing cultivar to 12 in (30 cm) with bright orange flowers. There has been confusion in the past between cultivars of this species and of *Geum chiloense.* **ZONES 5–9.**

Gilia capitata

Geum triflorum

Geum montanum

ALPINE AVENS

From mountainous regions of southern and central Europe, this clump-forming perennial forms mats of up to 6 in (10 cm) high and 12 in (30 cm) wide. The basal leaves are pinnately divided, each with a large, rounded, terminal lobe. Solitary golden-yellow flowers are carried on short stems from spring to early summer. **ZONES 6–9.**

Geum reptans

CREEPING AVENS

This rhizomatous perennial from central and eastern Europe makes a good ground cover, reaching 6 in (15 cm) in height and spreading 8 in (20 cm). It has pinnate leaves with deeply toothed, rounded leaflets arranged in rosettes. The mostly solitary bright yellow flowers are borne on short stems in early summer. **ZONES 6–9.**

Geum rivale

WATER AVENS

This clump-forming perennial from Europe is up to 15 in (40 cm) high forming a basal rosette of hairy, deeply divided dark green leaves. Nodding, bell-shaped pink and orange flowers are carried on reddish stalks from late spring to mid-summer. **'Leonard's Variety'** (syn. 'Leonardii') has coppery pink flowers in summer. **ZONES 3–9**

Geum triflorum

PRAIRIE SMOKE, PURPLE AVENS

Geum triflorum, native to northern USA and Canada, is a plant of 12–18 in (30–45 cm) with crowded leaves that have regularly incised margins. In summer it bears sprays of nodding, pinkish white flowers with long protruding styles. The floweres are followed by feathery, smoky gray seed heads that make a striking display in fall (autumn). **ZONES 3–9.**

Gibbaeum gibbosum

GEVUINA

This genus consists of only one species of evergreen tree allied to *Lomatia,* native to Chile. It is fast growing when young, with new growth densely covered with rust-colored felty hairs. It is cultivated for its ornamental qualities and its relative cold hardiness. In its native country the seeds are gathered as edible nuts and have a flavor like hazelnuts.
CULTIVATION: It requires a mild climate with cool, humid summers. Grow in a sheltered spot with deep, rich, well-drained soil that never dries out. Propagate from freshly gathered seed.

Gevuina avellana

CHILEAN HAZEL, CHILE NUT

A medium-sized evergreen tree or large shrub to 30 ft (10 m) high and similar width, the leathery leaves of this species are pinnate or sometimes bipinnate with up to 30 glossy, toothed oval leaflets. In summer, erect spikes of spidery, white, cream or greenish flowers arise from the leaf axils. These are followed by slightly elongated small fruit that are blue-black when ripe. **ZONES 9–10.**

GIBBAEUM

Another of the many South African genera of succulents of the mesembryanthemum tribe, *Gibbaeum* consists of about 20 species, all from the western Cape region. Although rather variable in shape and size, they share the feature of paired leaves of unequal length and fused together for at least part of their length; the longer leaf often resembles a long nose, with the shorter like a chin beneath it. The flowers are smallish, white, pink, red or purplish, a single one to each leaf pair. These are frost-tender succulents from extreme desert conditions, with only a few inches of rain annually in winter.
CULTIVATION: They do best in a small pot with a deep surface layer of coarse gravel, and kept in strong light and watered very sparingly. Propagate from seed or by division of offsets in spring or summer.

Gibbaeum gibbosum

syns *Gibbaeum marlothi, G. muirii, Mesembryanthemum gibbosum*

This clump-forming succulent grows to $2\frac{1}{2}$ in (6 cm) high and $2\frac{1}{2}$–6 in (6–15 cm) across. The half-cylindrical leaves grow in pairs, and pink or purple, daisy-like flowers appear in spring and summer. **ZONES 9–10.**

Gibbaeum velutinum

This is a carpeting succulent to 3 in (8 cm) high and 12 in (30 cm) wide. It has unequal pairs of gray-green leaves and bears pink, lilac or white flowers, 2 in (5 cm) across, in spring. **ZONES 9–10.**

GILIA

From temperate western regions of both North and South America, this is a genus of about 30 species of annuals, biennials and perennials in the phlox family. The basal leaves are feathery and finely divided, and erect panicles of small, funnel- to trumpet-shaped flowers, often densely clustered, appear in spring and summer.
CULTIVATION: Moderately to very frost hardy, gilias prefer a climate with cool wet winters and hot summers, and well-drained soils in full sun. Water lightly and regularly. They are particularly sensitive to drought and heat and wilt rapidly. Light stakes may be needed for support on windy sites. Propagate from seed in spring directly where they are to grow when the soil has warmed up.

Gilia capitata

QUEEN ANNE'S THIMBLES, BLUE THIMBLE FLOWER

Native to the west-coastal ranges of Canada, the USA and Mexico, this erect, branching annual to 24 in (60 cm) high has mid-green, fern-like leaves and tiny, soft lavender blue flowers that appear in a pincushion-like mass in summer and early fall (autumn). It is a good cut flower and useful border plant. **ZONES 7–9**

Gilia tricolor

BIRD'S EYES

This Californian native is an upright bushy annual of up to 18 in (45 cm) tall with mid-green, finely divided leaves. The small blue $\frac{1}{2}$ in (12 mm) flowers have purple spots around orange centers and are borne either singly or in clusters from late spring to early summer. **ZONES 7–10.**

GILLENIA

This genus of the rose family consists of 2 species of rhizomatous perennials from temperate North America. They are clump forming with stalkless leaves consisting of 3 leaflets and starry, 5-petalled flowers. After flowering the sepals enlarge and turn red. They are easy to grow in a shady position and make good cut flowers.
CULTIVATION: Very frost hardy, they prefer humus-rich, moist but well-drained soil, preferably in part-shade. Propagate from seed in spring or by division in spring or fall (autumn).

Gillenia trifoliata

INDIAN PHYSIC, BOWMAN'S ROOT

This species is up to 4 ft (1.2 m) tall and has reddish stems and bronze green leaves composed of 3 oval toothed leaflets, each 3 in (8 cm) long. Open panicles of white or pale pink starry flowers are produced throughout summer. **ZONES 3–9.**

Ginkgo biloba

Ginkgo biloba

GINKGO

GINKGO, MAIDENHAIR TREE

The Ginkgoales, seed-bearing plants more primitive than the conifers and even more ancient, first appeared in the Permian Period (about 300 million years ago) and flourished all through the Jurassic and Cretaceous periods. About 100 million years ago they began to die out, leaving the maidenhair tree as the sole survivor—and then only in China. It is now unknown in a wild state, and probably would no longer exist if ancient trees had not been preserved in temple grounds and young ones planted there. The 'maidenhair' in the common name refers to the leaf shape and vein pattern, resembling some of the maidenhair fern (*Adiantum*) species. Male trees bear small spikes of pollen sacs, females solitary naked seeds ('fruits') with an oily flesh around the large kernel.

CULTIVATION: A tree of temperate climates, it resists pollution and seems to have outlived any pests it may have once had. It does, however, need shelter from strong winds and does best in deep, fertile soil. City authorities prefer to grow male trees, as females drop smelly fruit; in China female trees are preferred as the seeds are edible and nutritious. Fruit do not appear before the tree is at least 20 years old, however. Propagate from seed or fall (autumn) cuttings.

Ginkgo biloba

The ginkgo grows at least 80 ft (24 m) tall, upright when young and eventually spreading to 30 ft (9 m) or more. Deciduous, the 4 in (10 cm) long, matt green, fan-shaped leaves turn golden yellow in fall (autumn). A fleshy, plum-like orange-brown fruit with an edible kernel appears in late summer and fall if

Ginkgo biloba 'Fastigiata'

male and female trees are grown together. **'Fastigiata'** is a slender, erect cultivar that reaches 30 ft (9 m). **'Princeton Sentry'** has a narrow, upright habit and is male. **ZONES 3–10.**

GLADIOLUS

syns *Acidanthera, Homoglossum*

This is a genus of about 180 species of cormous perennials with sword-shaped leaves in fan-like tufts native to Africa, Europe and the Middle East, though the species with the most conspicuous and colorful flowers nearly all come from South Africa. The cultivated gladioli are mainly large-flowered hybrids, grown for their showy, funnel-shaped flowers both for garden display and as cut flowers. Plants in this genus vary greatly from the very small and sometimes fragrant species to the spectacular, colorful spike of the florists' gladiolus. The 3 main hybrid groups are the **Grandiflorus** (or Large-flowered) **Group**, the **Primulinus Group** and the **Nanus** (or Butterfly) **Group**.

CULTIVATION: Plant corms about 4 in (10 cm) deep in well-drained, sandy soil in a sunny position. In cool areas plant in early spring; in warm areas plant from fall (autumn). Water well in summer and cut off spent flower stems. Tall stems may need staking. When picking for indoors, cut when the lower flowers open. Lift corms over winter in cold climates; lift large-flowered corms in all areas, especially those with high winter rainfall; store when perfectly dry. Propagate from seed or cormlets in spring.

Gladiolus alatus

KALKOENTJIE

This small, short-lived species from South Africa grows to about 12 in (30 cm). It shows much variation in the wild and has been divided by botanists into 5 varieties, differing in flower size and color markings. Typically the fragrant flowers, up to 10 on a spike, are red to orange and yellow at the base and are borne from late winter to spring, or later in cool climates. Good drainage is essential. A pretty plant for the rock garden, its leaves die back in summer. **ZONES 8–10.**

Gladiolus carneus

Gladiolus callianthus

syn. *Acidanthera bicolor* var. *murieliae*

PEACOCK FLOWER, ABYSSINIAN SWORD LILY

This beautiful species from the mountains of East Africa has flowering stems up to 3 ft (1 m) tall. The sweetly scented white flowers, borne few to a stem, often have a dull crimson blotch in the throat; they are 2–3 in (5–8 cm) wide with elegantly pointed, spreading petals and a tube about 6 in (15 cm) long. It flowers in fall (autumn) and the leaves die back in winter. **ZONES 9–11.**

Gladiolus cardinalis

WATERFALL GLADIOLUS

Flowering in summer, *Gladiolus cardinalis* has arching stems bearing spikes of up to 6 funnel-shaped, bright red flowers with white markings on the 3 lower petals. It grows to 4 ft (1.2 m) with a spread of 6 in (15 cm). In its native Cape Province this colorful species grows thickly on rock ledges beside waterfalls and cascades. It is one of the most important parent species of modern hybrid gladioli. **ZONES 9–10.**

Gladiolus carneus

syn. *Gladiolus blandus*

PAINTED LADY

This is a lovely, spring-flowering species from western Cape Province with arching spikes of white, pink or mauve, funnel-shaped flowers blotched with purple or yellow. It reaches a height of 12–24 in (30–60 cm) and has narrow leaves which die back in summer. **ZONES 8–10.**

Gladiolus × *colvillei*

BABY GLADIOLUS

The dainty *Gladiolus* × *colvillei* was the earliest known gladiolus hybrid, originating in England in 1823 as a cross between *G. cardinalis* and the cream *G. tristis.* It bears up to 10 elegant, 3 in (8 cm) dark pink, yellow or white blooms on an 18 in (45 cm) spike, usually in late spring. **'The Bride'** has white flowers. There is now a range of similar hybrids, all about 15 in (38 cm) tall, with similarly blotched flowers in shades of white and pink. **'Peach Blossom'** has pale pink flowers suffused with mauve or purple. **ZONES 8–10.**

Gladiolus communis

From spring to summer this vigorous species from southern Europe produces spikes of pink flowers streaked or blotched with white or red. It grows to a height of 3 ft (1 m) and has very narrow, tough leaves. ***Gladiolus communis* subsp. *byzantinus*** (syn. *G. byzantinus*) bears up to 15 pink to magenta blooms from late spring to early summer. All forms of the species are hardier than any of the South African gladioli. **ZONES 6–10.**

Gladiolus communis subsp. *byzantinus*

Gladiolus, Grandiflorus, 'Red Majesty'

Gladiolus cardinalis

G

Gladiolus dalenii
syns *Gladiolus natalensis, G. primulinus, G. psittacinus, G. quartinianus*

Of wide distribution in tropical Africa and the summer-rainfall regions of South Africa, this is a vigorous, summer-flowering specie. It produces up to 25 yellow and orange or red flowers with the hooded upper petals often spotted red. It reaches 5 ft (1.5 m) in height and the leaves die back in winter. **ZONES 9–11.**

Gladiolus, Grandiflorus Group

These very large-flowering hybrids produce long, densely packed spikes of broadly funnel-shaped flowers in summer. The sometimes ruffled flowers are arranged in alternating fashion mostly on one side of a 3–5 ft (1–1.5 m) stem. They are regarded as too demanding for normal garden use, in terms of pest and disease control, as well as requiring support to keep upright. They are therefore grown mainly for exhibition or as commercial cut flowers. **'Green Woodpecker'** bears medium-sized, ruffled greenish flowers with red markings at the throat; it is very good for exhibition. **'Red Majesty'** has lightly ruffled red flowers. **ZONES 9–11.**

Gladiolus illyricus

This attractive species ranges from southern England to the Caucasus. It has narrow, gray-green leaves and bears 2 in (5 cm) wide magenta to purple flowers with white-streaked lower lobes on loose spikes up to 3 ft (1 m) tall in early summer. **ZONES 6–9.**

Gladiolus tristis

Gladiolus × colvillei 'The Bride'

Gladiolus imbricatus

This spring- to summer-flowering species from central and southern Europe has pale crimson to red-purple flowers, and lobes that have a white central mark outlined in purple. **ZONES 6–9.**

Gladiolus liliaceus

This rarely cultivated species from western Cape Province grows to about 24 in (60 cm) tall with only 3 very long narrow leaves to each shoot. The strongly scented flowers, very few to a stem, are dull yellow with brown, pink, red or purple specks, changing to a blue color after sunset and back to yellow as the sun rises. **ZONES 9–10.**

Gladiolus, Nanus Group

Also known as Miniature Hybrids and Butterfly Group, in a broad sense these also include *Gladiolus × colvillei*, listed separately. The loosely arranged flower spikes to 12–15 in (30–38 cm) long bear up to 7 flowers, smaller and neater than those of the Grandiflorus Group, and often blotched or ruffled. **ZONES 9–11.**

Gladiolus, Primulinus Group

This hybrid group has rather small flowers, often blotched, arranged irregularly on a stem up to 24 in (60 cm) long, each bearing up to about 20 blooms. The flowers are never ruffled and have strongly hooded upper petals. They bloom from early to late summer. **ZONES 9–11.**

Gladiolus tristis

In late winter or early spring each 24 in (60 cm), slender stem of this species carries up to 6 white, cream or pale yellow 3 in (8 cm) wide flowers; their strong fragrance is released only at night.

Gladiolus × colvillei 'Peach Blossom'

Gladiolus cardinalis

Glechoma hederacea

Glechoma hederacea 'Variegata'

Glaucidium palmatum var. *leucanthum*

Glaucium flavum

It prefers rich soil, but is adaptable and in favorable conditions it self-sows freely. Many spring-flowering hybrids derive from this popular species. **ZONES 7–10.**

GLAUCIDIUM

This genus of a single species is indigenous to northern Japan. A rhizomatous perennial, its large pink to lilac flowers are somewhat poppy-like but in fact the genus is a relative of *Paeonia*.
CULTIVATION: Plant in rich, peaty soil with plenty of moisture. It prefers part- to deep shade and shelter from drying winds. Propagate from seed in spring or by careful division in early spring.

Glaucidium palmatum

This clump-forming perennial has a height and spread of 15 in (40 cm). It has light green, palmately lobed leaves with crinkly surfaces and irregularly toothed edges. The large, cup-shaped, 4-petalled lilac or mauve flowers are borne in late spring and early summer. ***Glaucidium palmatum* var. *leucanthum*** (syn. 'Album') has white flowers. **ZONES 6–9.**

GLAUCIUM
HORNED POPPY, SEA POPPY

This is one of the most distinctive genera of poppy relatives, consisting of 25 species of annuals, biennials and perennials from temperate Asia and the Mediterranean region (with one extending to Atlantic coasts). Their characteristic feature is the up to 12 in (30 cm) long, narrow seed capsule that rapidly elongates after the petals fall from the flowers. Showy flowers terminate the leafy branches and may be yellow, red or white, usually with a darker blotch at the base of each petal.
CULTIVATION: Fairly frost hardy, they prefer a sunny position and sandy, well-drained soil. Propagate from seed in spring or fall (autumn).

Glaucium corniculatum
syn. *Glaucium phoenicium*
RED HORNED POPPY

From Europe and southwestern Asia, this hairy biennial or perennial has a basal rosette of pinnately lobed, silver gray leaves. It grows up to 18 in (45 cm) high and wide and bears orange to red flowers, usually with a black spot at the base of each petal, from summer to early fall (autumn). The flowers often hardly emerge above the foliage. This species has been confused with ***Glaucium grandiflorum*** from western Asia which has larger, better-displayed flowers. **ZONES 7–10.**

Glaucium flavum
YELLOW HORNED POPPY

This native of western and southern Europe and northern Africa occurs naturally in coastal areas and is widely naturalized elsewhere. It is a slightly hairy short-lived perennial with a basal rosette of pinnately lobed, glaucous gray-green leaves. The golden-yellow or orange flowers, to 3 in (8 cm) across, are produced in summer. **ZONES 7–10.**

GLECHOMA

This genus consists of 12 species of creeping, perennial plants found through much of Europe. The stems root at the nodes, often forming extensive mats of coarsely toothed, rounded or broadly oval, soft hairy leaves. Ascending shoots bear pairs of small, tubular, 2-lipped flowers in the leaf axils in summer. They make good carpeting ground covers, but can be very invasive and should be kept away from heavily planted beds. They are quite suitable for containers and hanging baskets.
CULTIVATION: They prefer full sun or part-shade and moderately fertile, moist but well-drained soil. Propagate from cuttings in late spring or by division in spring or fall (autumn).

Glechoma hederacea
GROUND IVY, RUNAWAY ROBIN

This prostrate species has stems that take root at the nodes, often forming mats to 6 ft (1.8 m) or more across and producing an unpleasant smell when bruised. The opposite, almost kidney-shaped leaves have scalloped margins. Small violet flowers are borne in the upper leaf axils in late spring and early summer. **'Variegata'** is commonly grown and has pretty, soft pale green leaves with white marbling. **ZONES 6–10.**

GLEDITSIA
LOCUST

Occurring in temperate and subtropical regions of both North and South America as well as parts of Africa and Asia, this genus consists of about 14 species of deciduous, broadly spreading, usually thorny trees. They are grown for their attractive foliage, ease of cultivation and usefulness as shade trees. They have pinnate or bipinnate leaves, inconspicuous flowers and large, often twisted, hanging seed pods that are filled with a sweetish, edible pulp. The locust referred to in the Bible is the related *Ceratonia siliqua*, but in North America 'locust' has been used for both *Gleditsia* and *Robinia*, the latter not closely related.
CULTIVATION: Gleditsias grow best in full sun in rich, moisture-retentive soil and will tolerate poor drainage. They are fast growing and mostly quite frost hardy, although young plants may need protection from frost. Prune young trees to promote a single, straight trunk; thorns on the lower trunk can be removed. Propagate selected forms by budding in spring or summer and species from seed in fall (autumn).

Gleditsia aquatica
WATER LOCUST

As the common name suggests, this species from southeastern USA likes wet ground; it grows in swamps in Texas and is widely planted in Florida and North Carolina. It reaches a height of 60 ft (18 m) and is not as thorny as the similar *Gleditsia triacanthos*. **ZONES 6–11.**

Gleditsia caspica
CASPIAN LOCUST

From Iran, Azerbaijan and Georgia, this is a short, broadly spreading tree up to 40 ft (12 m) high with large spines on the trunk. It has glossy, pinnate leaves that turn yellow in fall (autumn). The tiny green flowers are borne on axillary spikes

Gleditsia caspica

Gleditsia triacanthos 'Stevens'

Gleditsia triacanthos 'Shademaster'

up to 4 in (10 cm) long in summer, followed by curved, twisted seed pods. **ZONES 6–10.**

Gleditsia triacanthos
HONEY LOCUST

Native to eastern and central USA and reaching 100 ft (30 m) high, this species has an open, vase-shaped canopy and a thorny trunk. Fern-like, shiny, dark green bipinnate leaves with small leaflets turn deep yellow in fall (autumn). Twisted black pods, up to 18 in (45 cm) long and $1\frac{1}{2}$ in (35 mm) wide, hang in large numbers from the branches in fall and winter. ***Gleditsia triacanthos* f. *inermis*** is thornless as are most present-day cultivars. **'Imperial'** has rounded leaves and few seed pods; **'Ruby Lace'** has reddish young growth turning dull bronze in fall; **'Shademaster'** is fast growing and broadly conical with bright green leaves; **'Skyline'** has dark green leaves that turn golden yellow in fall; **'Stevens'** is wide spreading with bright green leaves turning yellow in fall; and **'Sunburst'** has bright yellow young leaves that turn pale green in summer. **ZONES 3–10.**

GLOBBA

There are around 70 species of these aromatic, clump-forming perennials belonging to the ginger family, scattered

Gleditsia caspica

Gleditsia triacanthos 'Skyline'

Gleditsia triacanthos 'Shademaster'

through wetter parts of southern Asia and the Malay Archipelago. The genus name is taken from a Malay vernacular name. Like other members of the ginger family they grow from a branching rhizome, but the leafy shoots are mostly small and slender with leaves narrowed abruptly at their bases into long, thin stalks. The flowering branch emerging at the top of each shoot is characteristically bent downward, bearing overlapping bracts that are large and colorful in some species. The flowers, arising on slender spikes from between these bracts, are of a complex structure with small, spreading sepals at the base and petals fused into a very thin tube that is bent like a fish-hook, with short petal lobes and stamens at its apex. In many species small bulbils replace some of the lower flower spikes.
CULTIVATION: Grow in part-shade and humus-rich, well-drained soil. Plants should remain dry during winter. Frost tender, grow globbas in a warm greenhouse or conservatory in cooler climates; they require sustained warmth, filtered light, a potting mix with high humus content and a rest period in winter when the leaves die back. Propagate by division or by planting the bulbils.

Globba winitii

A native of Thailand, this species has large, lance-shaped leaves to 8 in (80 cm)

Gleditsia triacanthos f. *inermis*

Gleditsia triacanthos 'Sunburst'

long that are heart-shaped at the base. It bears pendent racemes of tubular yellow flowers with large deep pink or purplish reflexed bracts from fall (autumn) to early winter. **ZONES 10–12.**

GLOBULARIA
GLOBE DAISY

The 20 or so species of this genus of mainly evergreen, tufted or sometimes mat-forming perennials or subshrubs are grown for their neat rounded habit and compact heads of many tiny tubular flowers in shades of blue. Many are suitable for a rock garden or container, such as the tight, cushion-forming **'Hort's Variety'**. The bushy subshrubs such as ***Globularia* × *indubia*** and ***G. sarcophylla*** are attractive planted among other small shrubs or against low walls.

Gloriosa superba 'Rothschildiana'

Gloriosa superba 'Rothschildiana'

Globularia punctata

Globularia 'Hort's Variety'

Globularia × *indubia*

Globularia sarcophylla

Globularia cordifolia

Globularia gracilis

CULTIVATION: Most cultivated species are only moderately frost hardy. Grow in full sun in well-drained soil. Water sparingly and keep dry in winter. Propagate from seed in fall (autumn) or by division in spring and early summer.

Globularia cordifolia

This evergreen miniature subshrub, found in central and southern Europe, has creeping woody stems with unusual tiny, spoon-shaped leaves, and produces solitary, stemless, fluffy blue to pale mauve flowerheads from late spring to early summer. It forms a dense mat or hummock, growing to a height of only 1–5 in (2.5–12 cm) and gradually spreading to 8 in (20 cm) or more. **ZONES 6–9.**

Globularia gracilis

This tufted, upright perennial has dark green, spoon-shaped leaves on long stalks. The lavender-blue flowerheads are borne in summer. **ZONES 7–9.**

Globularia punctata

syns *Globularia aphyllanthes, G. wilkommii*

Native to Europe, this is a tufted perennial to 12 in (30 cm) high with a basal rosette of long-stalked, somewhat spoon-shaped leaves. Indigo flowerheads are produced in summer. **ZONES 5–9.**

GLORIOSA

GLORY LILY, CLIMBING LILY

This genus contains one variable species of tuberous climbing lily from Africa and western Asia. Although its flowers resemble some of the *Lilium* species with strongly reflexed petals, the genus is actually more closely related to *Colchicum* and the plants contain the same highly poisonous compound colchicine. They climb over low shrubs and through long grass by means of the coiled, tendril-like tips of the leaves. They are widely grown for their decorative, brightly colored flowers which make long-lasting and most attractive cut flowers. The plants die back in fall (autumn) or in the tropical dry season to dormant tubers.

CULTIVATION: Glory lily is a tropical plant and will thrive outdoors only in a frost-free, warm climate; in colder areas it can be grown indoors in pots. Plant the tubers in late spring in full sun and rich, well-drained soil, fertilizing as the stems begin to elongate. Protect from wind and provide support. Propagate from seed or dormant tubers.

Gloriosa superba

TIGER'S CLAWS

This tropical species can climb to a height of 6–8 ft (1.4–2.4 m) under suitable conditions. The brilliant red and gold flowers resemble tiger lilies in shape with reflexed, wavy edged petals and conspicuous stamens. **'Rothschildiana'** has larger, pinkish red flowers with petals yellow-edged; **'Simplex'** has similar but smaller flowers in deep orange and yellow. **ZONES 10–12.**

GLOTTIPHYLLUM

This is a genus of about 60 species of dwarf succulents in the mesembryanthemum tribe, native to the drier areas of South Africa's Cape Province. The name is derived from the Greek *glotta,* tongue and *phyllon,* leaf, referring to the leaf shape of these almost stemless, clump-forming plants. The more commonly grown species have bright green leaves in 2 rows, and produce yellow daisy-like flowers in summer. They are easily grown in rockery pockets or in a desert garden in mild climates, though their tender foliage is often scarred and chewed, detracting from their neat appearance.

CULTIVATION: In warm climates grow in a gritty, very well-drained soil in full sun. In colder areas they can be grown in a greenhouse and require a standard cactus potting mix, low humidity and a rest period when dormant in fall (autumn) to late winter. They are vulnerable to attack from snails, mealybugs and caterpillars. Propagate from seed or root cuttings.

Glottiphyllum cruciatum

This species has light green, semi-cylindrical leaves 3–4 in (8–10 cm) long. Large yellow daisy-like flowers are produced in spring. **ZONES 9–11.**

Glottiphyllum latum

This species is characterized by its sickle-shaped 3 in (8 cm) long leaves. It produces yellow daisy-like flowers in late spring. **ZONES 9–11.**

Glottiphyllum linguiforme

This species grows to $2\frac{1}{2}$ in (6 cm) high with a spread of 12 in (30 cm). It has 2 rows of incurved, strap-shaped, bright

Glottiphyllum cruciatum

Glottiphyllum latum

green leaves with rounded tips and bears daisy-like bright yellow flowers to 3 in (7 cm) across, from fall (autumn) to late winter. This is the most commonly listed *Glottiphyllum*, but most of the rather vigorous plants in cultivation are now regarded as hybrids. **ZONES 9–11.**

GLYCERIA

MANNA GRASS

Around 16 species belong to this genus of aquatic and meadow grasses, distributed throughout the world with the majority in the northern hemisphere. They are vigorous growers with creeping rootstocks and flat, juicy leaf blades. The greenish flowers and seed heads are borne on narrow panicles, generally not rising above the leaves. The genus name comes from the Greek word for 'sweet', referring to the sweet-tasting seed grains of some of the European species; the name 'manna grass' also refers to this quality. Apart from their use as fodder, glycerias can be grown as aquatics in large ponds or lakes and their long-running rhizomes can stabilize muddy banks; occasionally their dense growth may be nuisance in irrigation canals.
CULTIVATION: Grow in permanently boggy soil in full sun. Plants can also be grown at the edge of ponds in 6 in (15 cm) of water. To restrict spread, grow in containers. Propagate from seed or runners.

Glyceria maxima

syns *Glyceria aquatica, Poa aquatica*

REED SWEET GRASS, REED MEADOW GRASS

This species from temperate Eurasia, which spreads by rhizomes, has stems to 3 ft (1 m) or more tall with flat, arching leaves 24 in (60 cm) long and ¾ in (18 mm) wide. Branched panicles of green to purplish spikelets are produced in late summer. **'Variegata'** is a popular ornamental grass with cream- or white-striped foliage, sometimes flushed pink when young. **ZONES 5–9.**

GLYCINE

This is a genus of 18 species of slender, twining or trailing perennial legumes, the majority native to Australia but extending to eastern Asia and the Pacific islands. They have alternate compound leaves composed of 3 leaflets and pea-like flowers followed by narrow, oblong seed pods. The only cultivated species is *Glycine max*, the soya bean from Asia.
CULTIVATION: Frost tender, the soya bean thrives in climates with hot humid summers in fertile, well-drained soil. Water well during very dry periods. Propagate from seed.

Glycine max

SOYA BEAN, SOYBEAN

The soya bean is an ancient Chinese crop and has been used for at least 5,000 years as a food and medicine. The origins of the plant are obscure, but it is believed to have derived from *Glycine soja* (syn. *G. ussuriensis*), a wild plant of eastern Asia. It is a branching, twining perennial with a varying height of up to 6 ft (1.8 m). The alternate, trifoliate leaves are softly pubescent. Small white or lilac pea-flowers borne in summer are immediately followed by hairy pods containing 2 to 4 seeds. Numerous cultivars of this important agricultural crop have been developed. **ZONES 9–11.**

GLYCYRRHIZA

LICORICE

This genus consists of around 20 species of perennial legumes from the Mediterranean region, Asia, Australia and the Americas. Species have pinnate leaves with oval leaflets and axillary spikes of small pea-like flowers. *Glycyrrhiza glabra* is cultivated for its soft, fibrous roots which are a source of licorice used for flavoring, confectionery and medicine. The wild licorice of North America is ***G. lepidota***.
CULTIVATION: Moderately frost hardy, they prefer full sun and deep, humus-rich, well-drained soil that should be kept evenly moist. The roots are harvested in fall (autumn). Propagate from seed sown in spring or fall or by division in early spring.

Glycyrrhiza glabra

LICORICE

This perennial, native to the Mediterranean region and western Asia, has short, tough stems springing from a rather woody rootstock and feathery mid-green leaves. It bears pea-like, bluish purple and white flowers on short upright spikes in late summer. Licorice grows to a height and spread of 3 ft (1 m). **ZONES 8–10.**

GLYPTOSTROBUS

This genus consists of a single species of deciduous conifer, allied to *Taxodium*. Its named is derived from the Greek for 'carved cone'. Believed native to southern China and North Vietnam, it may now be extinct in the wild, but has been widely planted to stabilize riverbanks and rice paddy walls in eastern Asia. In foliage it resembles most closely the now much better known *Metasequoia* but its cones are smaller and less woody and borne in profuse clusters on mature trees. It will thrive in waterlogged ground.
CULTIVATION: This marginally frost-hardy species does best in warm, wet areas where humid summer temperatures can be expected for at least 3 months. Grow in any moist or wet soil in full sun or part-shade. Propagate from seed or by grafting.

Glyptostrobus pensilis

Glyptostrobus pensilis

CHINESE SWAMP CYPRESS

This medium-sized, upright conifer with a distinctive conical outline can grow up to 80 ft (24 m) tall. It has attractive new spring growth and rich, red-brown fall (autumn) colors. It is a single-stemmed tree but can become multi-stemmed if damaged by frost. **ZONES 8–11.**

GOMPHRENA

This genus of about 90 species of prostrate or erect annuals or perennials is related to *Alternanthera* and *Celosia* and is found mainly in Central and South America but also extends to Australia. They have opposite, usually hairy leaves and papery flowers forming terminal oval or globular heads. If picked before fully open the flowers are good for drying.
CULTIVATION: Marginally frost hardy to frost tender, they require a sunny position, reasonably fertile, well-drained soil and plenty of water during active growth. The plants benefit from mulching in hot weather. Propagate from seed in early spring.

Gomphrena globosa

GLOBE AMARANTH, BACHELOR'S BUTTONS

A good bedding plant, this bushy annual from Southeast Asia reaches a height of up to 24 in (60 cm). It has oval, hairy leaves and produces flowerheads in shades of pink, purple, yellow, orange or white in summer and early fall (autumn). These papery, pompon-like flowerheads are attractive when dried: cut flowering stems just before blooms are fully open and hang upside down in a cool, well-ventilated place until dry. **ZONES 9–12.**

GOODENIA

This genus of about 170 species of perennials or shrubs is mostly found in Australia with 3 species extending to Papua New Guinea and Indonesia. The growth habit is extremely variable but most are dwarf evergreen perennials or subshrubs, some with a basal rosette of leaves and well-displayed, mostly bright yellow flowers, their 5 petals spreading like the fingers of a hand. Some bear flowers in various shades of pink, mauve or blue. Only a few species are cultivated and most of these make good rock garden, ground cover or container subjects.
CULTIVATION: Frost tender to moderately frost hardy, most goodenias require good drainage and a sunny or part-shaded position. Prune back after flowering to encourage compact growth. Propagate from seed or cuttings.

Goodenia hederacea

FOREST GOODENIA, IVY GOODENIA

This prostrate perennial from eastern Australia normally forms a delicate rosette of somewhat spoon-shaped leaves, from which spread wiry, prostrate stems that sometimes take root; they bear leaves of decreasing size, from the axils of which arise slender stalks and yellow flowers in spring and summer. ***Goodenia hederacea* subsp. *alpina*** is a higher-mountain race that is prostrate, its rooting stems forming mats to about 3 ft (1 m) across; leaves are neater and thicker. **ZONES 8–11.**

Goodenia macmillanii

PINNATE GOODENIA

This small shrub with a suckering habit may reach up to 3 ft (1 m) high. It has pinnate basal leaves to 3 in (8 cm) and small lobed leaves on the stems. The fragrant flowers, borne in spring and summer, are pink with purple streaks and about 1 in (25 mm) across. **ZONES 9–11.**

Goodenia macmillanii

Glycyrrhiza glabra

Glycine max

Glottiphyllum linguiforme

Goodenia ovata

From moister areas of eastern Australia, this compact, evergreen shrub grows to a height of 3–4 ft (1–1.2 m). In spring and summer it bears clusters of fan-shaped, bright yellow flowers. The ovate leaves, 4 in (10 cm) long, are bright green with finely-toothed margins and are slightly sticky. A good ground cover, it is a useful plant for a shaded rock garden or slope. Prostrate and semi-prostrate forms from exposed coastal cliffs have been introduced, some no more than 6 in (15 cm) high but spreading extensively. **ZONES 9–11.**

GOODYERA

About 40 species make up this genus of orchids named after British botanist John Goodyer. Most are ground-dwelling but a few may be found growing on trees or rocks. They are found in all warmer parts of the world except Africa. Plants spread by creeping rhizomes and produce rosettes of fleshy, sometimes furry leaves that may be patterned in a contrasting color. Flowers are borne on tall spikes that carry dozens of small to medium-sized, hooded blooms.

CULTIVATION: Hardiness varies with the species but all will tolerate at least some frost. Grow in shallow pots or pans of moist, leafy compost or in similarly humus-rich soil in the garden in dappled shade. Plants need moisture year-round but watering should be much more generous in the warmer months than in winter. Feed 2 or 3 times from mid-spring to late summer with a dilute solution of liquid organic fertilizer. Mulch around the plants in spring with leafmold to maintain a high content of organic matter in the soil. Propagate by division in spring.

Goodyera pubescens

RATTLESNAKE PLANTAIN

From northern Europe, this species grows to about 18 in (45 cm) and features netted, bluish leaves and stems of white flowers in summer. **ZONES 6–9.**

GORDONIA

This genus of about 70 species of evergreen trees and shrubs allied to *Camellia*, is native to Southeast Asia, except for one North American species. Their handsome, white-petalled, camellia-like flowers and glossy, dark green leaves make them popular ornamental plants for warm climates.

CULTIVATION: They do best in sun or dappled shade in friable, slightly acidic soil—they enjoy conditions similar to those preferred by camellias. Mulch, feed and water regularly. Tip pruning during the first few years of growth will improve their slightly open habit. Propagate from seed in fall (autumn) or spring, or from cuttings in late summer.

Goodenia ovata

Gordonia axillaris

Graptopetalum bellum

Graptopetalum paraguayense

Gossypium sturtianum

Gordonia axillaris

Though it can become a tree about 25 ft (8 m) tall and wide, this beautiful evergreen from China with dappled orange-brown bark grows slowly, usually as a tall shrub. The dark green, glossy leaves to 6 in (15 cm) long turn scarlet before they fall, a few at a time, throughout the year. The white flowers are about 4 in (10 cm) wide with broad, crumpled petals and golden stamens. **ZONES 9–11.**

Gordonia lasianthus

LOBLOLLY BAY

From southeastern USA, this species grows to 80 ft (24 m) tall, with a dense, narrow crown and finely toothed, glossy leaves. Scented white, saucer-shaped flowers, about 2½ in (6 cm) in diameter, are borne on short stalks in summer. **ZONES 6–9.**

GOSSYPIUM

This genus contains 40 species of annuals, subshrubs or shrubs found in warm-temperate and tropical regions worldwide. Best known are the 4 to 5 species grown as commercial crop plants (cotton). The flowers resemble those of *Hibiscus* (to which it is closely related) and may be cream, yellow or rose colored, sometimes with a dark spot at the base. They are followed by globular pods which split open to release their oily seeds, embedded in cotton fibers. Apart from the cotton-yielding species, several others are grown as ornamental plants, mostly the Australian species with pink or mauve flowers. These are best suited to fairly hot, semi-arid climates.

CULTIVATION: Frost tender, they need moist but well-drained soil, long, hot summers and a sheltered position in full sun. Propagate from seed or cuttings.

Gossypium arboreum

TREE COTTON

One of the cotton-yielding species, this is a large shrub, reaching 12 ft (3.5 m) in height with an upright branching habit. It has deeply lobed leaves and in summer bears yellow or dull red, hibiscus-like flowers with purple spots at the base. Although regarded as an Asian native, some botanists now believe it is a cultivated derivative of the African *Gossypium herbaceum*. **ZONES 9–11.**

Gossypium arboreum

Gossypium barbadense

SEA ISLAND COTTON

This erect annual or perennial to 5 ft (1.5 m) high is native to South America but was long ago introduced to the southern States of the USA, becoming established first on Sea Island in Georgia. It is still one of the major cotton-yielding species. It has reddish stems and lobed leaves to 5 in (12 cm) long. The white to yellow hibiscus-like flowers turn pink with age, and are borne mainly in winter. **ZONES 9–12.**

Gossypium herbaceum

COTTON, LEVANT COTTON

This native of southern Africa is the traditional cotton plant of western Asia and northern Africa. It is an annual or perennial plant growing to a height of 6 ft (1.8 m). It has hairy, lobed leaves and yellow flowers with purple basal spots. **ZONES 9–11.**

Gossypium sturtianum

STURT'S DESERT ROSE

This species, the floral emblem of the Northern Territory, Australia, is an evergreen shrub that grows over 6 ft (1.8 m) high and wide. It has oval, gray-green leaves and beautiful large mauve flowers with overlapping petals that are darker at the base. It is a useful ornamental plant for hot, arid regions, surviving with minimal irrigation, but adapts well enough also to higher-rainfall areas and tolerates light frosts. **ZONES 9–11.**

GRAPTOPETALUM

This genus of about 12 species of perennial succulents related to *Echeveria*, is native to Mexico and Arizona, USA. They are mainly rosette-forming on short stems with bluish gray leaves and bear star-shaped or tubular flowers in spring or summer. Frost tender, many of these species are grown as house plants or in temperate greenhouses. In frost-free areas they are ideal for rock and desert gardens.

CULTIVATION: Grow in very well-drained soil in full sun or very light shade. Propagate from seed or cuttings in spring or summer.

Graptopetalum bellum

syn. *Tacitus bellus*

Recently discovered in Mexico, this little succulent has rapidly become popular on account of the rather startling disproportion between the size of its bright pink flowers and its miniature rosette of leaves. The stemless rosettes are composed of dull gray, triangular leaves hardly more than 1 in (25 mm) long from between which emerge short sprays of starry flowers, each about 1 in

(25 mm) across, from spring to summer. It makes an ideal windowsill specimen in a small pot or shallow pan. **ZONES 9–11.**

Graptopetalum paraguayense
syn. *Sedum weinbergii*
GHOST PLANT, MOTHER-OF-PEARL PLANT

In spite of its specific name implying it is native to Paraguay, the mother-of-pearl plant is now known to be native to Mexico. Dense rosettes of thick, blunt-tipped leaves are borne on fleshy stems at first erect then bending down with age. The leaves are gray with a reddish cast and a silvery blue bloom. Showy sprays of white, star-shaped flowers bloom in spring, rising well above the rosette; they are very long lasting. **ZONES 9–11.**

GRAPTOPHYLLUM

Generally seen as house plants, this genus of evergreen shrubs in the acanthus family comprises 10 species from tropical Australia and the Pacific islands. They are admired chiefly for their decorative foliage, which is often marked with various colors. The tubular, 2-lipped flowers are borne mainly in late spring and summer.
CULTIVATION: Frost tender, they need a tropical climate to succeed as garden plants, doing best in dappled shade and fertile, well-drained soil. They respond well to gentle pruning to control their tendency to legginess. As house plants they need regular watering except in winter, when they should be kept on the dry side. Propagate from cuttings at any time in the tropics, in spring or summer elsewhere.

Graptophyllum pictum
CARICATURE PLANT

This species has an erect, open habit and reaches a height of 5 ft (1.5 m) with a spread of about 30 in (75 cm). Its leaf coloration varies but typically it has mid-green, oval leaves with creamy central blotches. The tubular purplish red flowers are borne on terminal spikes in spring and summer. **'Tricolor'** has cream and green leaves, heavily flushed pink especially when young; **'Purpureum Variegatum'** is similar but replaces the pink with purple-red. **ZONES 11–12.**

GREENOVIA

Similar to *Sempervivum*, this genus of 4 species of succulent perennials comes from the Canary Islands. They form neat rosettes of gray-blue or dark green leaves from which the flowering stems emerge in spring. Up to 40 small yellow flowers are produced on each head of bloom. The plants can be quite small, anything from 1 in (25 mm) to 2 in (5 cm) across.
CULTIVATION: They will tolerate light frosts so long as they are kept dry. In areas of continuous winter frosts they are best grown under glass but kept cool and shaded during the hottest part of the day. In frost-free climates they can be grown in full shade. Grow in very well-drained, gritty soil that contains plenty of leafmold. Water regularly from mid-fall (mid-autumn) until early spring, then sparingly or not all over summer. Propagate from seed or cuttings.

Greenovia aizoon

This species forms a clump of tiny, dark green rosettes, the dead leaves persisting on the much-branched stems. It is easy to grow and is a good choice for stone steps, dry walls or pots. The flowering stem is about 6 in (15 cm) high, terminating in a flat head of small yellow flowers. **ZONES 9–11.**

GREVILLEA

Some 250 species of evergreen shrubs and trees in the protea family make up this genus. Variable in habit, foliage and flowers, most grevilleas are native to Australia with a few from New Caledonia and Papua New Guinea. The small flowers are mostly densely crowded into heads or spikes, their most conspicuous feature being the long styles which are at first bent over like a hairpin and then straighten out. Many are adaptable and easy to grow, with a long flowering period, and are popular with nectar-seeking birds. The leaves are commonly deeply divided and may be very decorative in their own right, the foliage of some species being grown for cutting. In the last several decades hundreds of hybrid grevillea cultivars have been bred, nearly all in Australia, and many are extremely floriferous. Some of the most beautiful species are low growing or prostrate; these may be planted in a rock garden, as ground cover or in pots.
CULTIVATION: Moderately frost hardy to frost tender, grevilleas do best in well-drained, slightly dry, neutral to acid soil in full sun. Strong roots develop early and it is important not to disturb these when planting out. Pruning of the shrubby species and cultivars is recommended immediately after flowering to promote healthy new growth and a compact habit. They are generally pest free although scale insects and leaf spot may pose a problem. Propagate from seed in spring, from cuttings in late summer, or by grafting for some of the species most prone to root-rot.

Grevillea annulifera
PRICKLY PLUME GREVILLEA

A very rare species from Western Australia, this dense shrub to 10 ft (3 m) or more high has pinnate leaves divided into narrow pointed segments. Strongly scented plumes of cream flowers, ageing to red, are carried high above the foliage throughout spring. This plant is marginally frost hardy and is difficult to establish in summer-rainfall climates unless grafted onto a hardier eastern species. **ZONES 9–10.**

Grevillea beadleana

Grevillea banksii
BANKS'S GREVILLEA

Named after Sir Joseph Banks, this subtropical Australian east coast species is a variable shrub or small open-branched tree growing 8–30 ft (2.4–9 m) tall, though some forms from coastal headlands are almost prostrate. The gray-green leaves are deeply divided; the branches terminate in large, cylindrical, cream, red or rich pink flowerheads, which appear profusely in spring and summer. It adapts well to coastal climates in mid-temperate zones. **ZONES 9–11.**

Grevillea baueri
BAUER'S GREVILLEA

This small shrub to 3 ft (1 m) high has closely packed, light green oblong leaves to 1 in (25 mm) long, often bronze on new growths. Deep pink and cream flowers are carried in tight globular heads on short branches in winter and spring. It is moderately frost hardy and may be lightly trimmed to form a neat small hedge. **ZONES 8–10.**

Grevillea baueri

Grevillea beadleana

A rare species from the highlands of northeastern New South Wales, this makes a bushy shrub to 5 ft (1.5 m) high with a similar spread. The deeply lobed, dark gray-green leaves to 2 in (5 cm) long have soft points and are densely hairy beneath. Profuse dark red toothbrush-shaped flowerheads to 2 in (5 cm) long are produced over a long period from spring to fall (autumn). It is moderately frost hardy and reasonably long lived. **ZONES 8–10.**

Grevillea biternata

This fast-growing native of Western Australia is a vigorous, prostrate shrub during its first few years, with densely massed branches and small leaves deeply divided into narrow lobes. The flowering branches, though, are up to 8 ft (2.4 m) high, bearing in winter and spring masses of fragrant, small white flowers that attract large numbers of insects. Occurring naturally in moist hollows, it is resistant to root-rot and can tolerate some frost. **ZONES 9–10.**

Grevillea annulifera

Grevillea banksii

G

Grevillea 'Coconut Ice'

Grevillea 'Bonnie Prince Charlie'

Grevillea 'Boongala Spinebill'

Grevillea 'Bonnie Prince Charlie'

This free-flowering cultivar is a small compact shrub to 3 ft (1 m) high with a similar spread. The dark green oblong leaves to 2 in (5 cm) long have whitish undersides. Pendent, spidery clusters of red and yellow flowers are produced from late winter to mid-summer. It is marginally frost hardy and is well suited to growing in a container. **ZONES 9–10.**

Grevillea 'Boongala Spinebill'

This attractive cultivar bears long, dense heads of deep red toothbrush-like flowers for most of the year. A spreading, marginally frost-hardy shrub, it has serrated green leaves, reddish on new growth. It grows to 6 ft (1.8 m) tall and 12 ft (3.5 m) wide with foliage to ground level. **ZONES 9–10.**

Grevillea 'Canberra Gem'

syn. ***Grevillea juniperina*** **'Pink Pearl'**

This dense, bushy shrub grows to 8 ft (2.4 m) with a similar spread, its erect stems crowded in a hedge-like form. It has narrow, pointed, dark green leaves and is irregularly scattered with small clusters of bright pink and red flowers from winter to late summer. A hybrid between *Grevillea juniperina* and *G. rosmarinifolia*, it is moderately frost hardy and responds well to hard pruning. It can be grown as a hedge, though not very long-lived. **ZONES 7–10.**

Grevillea 'Clearview David'

This free-flowering hybrid cultivar is an erect bushy shrub to about 10 ft (3 m) high and across. It has crowded, needle-like, deep green leaves with silky undersides. Abundant deep red, pendent,

Grevillea 'Canberra Gem'

spider-type flowerheads are borne along the branches in winter and spring. Marginally frost hardy, it responds well to regular pruning and is suitable as a hedging plant. **ZONES 8–10.**

Grevillea 'Coconut Ice'

A spreading bushy shrub, this attractive hybrid cultivar is very similar to the better known **'Robyn Gordon'**, but its large flowerheads are cream and pale pink. It blooms almost throughout the year. **ZONES 9–11.**

Grevillea dimorpha

FLAME GREVILLEA

A native of sandstone hills of western Victoria, this shrub grows to 10 ft (3 m). It has stiff, long, narrow, undivided, deep green leaves with silky whitish undersides and bears masses of bright red spider-type flowerheads at the branch tips in spring and summer. It is moderately frost hardy and prefers part-shade. **ZONES 8–10.**

Grevillea fasciculata

This southern Western Australian shrub grows to less than 3 ft (1 m) high, spreading up to 8 ft (2.4 m) wide. It has small, deep green, roughly elliptical leaves with faint pale brown felting underneath. In late winter and spring it bears bright red, spider-type flowerheads with yellow tips. It is marginally frost hardy and is useful for covering dry banks. **ZONES 9–10.**

Grevillea × *gaudichaudii*

This naturally occurring hybrid between ***Grevillea acanthifolia*** and ***G. laurifolia*** is well established in cultivation as a prostrate ground-cover plant and will spread up to 10 ft (3 m) or more across. The irregularly lobed dark green leaves of up to 4 in (10 cm) long have a reddish tint during the cool months. Deep pinkish red toothbrush-type flowerheads are borne freely from spring through to fall (autumn). **ZONES 8–10.**

Grevillea 'Clearview David'

Grevillea glabrata

Fast growing, this species reaches 10 ft (3 m) tall and has a spread of up to 12 ft (3.5 m) across, with slightly weeping branches. It bears lobed, prickly, gray-green leaves and, for most of the year, dainty white perfumed flowers. It is marginally frost hardy and can be kept compact by regular pruning. **ZONES 9–11.**

Grevillea hilliana

WHITE YIEL-YIEL

In rainforests of Australia's east coast, this tree grows up to 70 ft (21 m) or more high but commonly makes a smaller, more compact tree in cultivation. It has deeply lobed, glossy green juvenile leaves with silky undersides that give way to unlobed, wavy adult leaves to 8 in (20 cm) long. Tightly packed, cylindrical rods to 8 in (20 cm) long are made up of hundreds of small, curled, greenish white flowers. They appear in late spring or early summer. Established plants will tolerate light frosts. **ZONES 9–11.**

Grevillea 'Honey Gem'

This hybrid cultivar grows to 12 ft (3.5 m) or more tall and 6 ft (1.8 m) or more wide. It carries large orange toothbrush-like flower-spikes for most of the year with the main flush in early spring. The finely divided, dark green leaves up to 12 in (30 cm) long have silvery undersides. Frost tender, it is best suited to warm-temperate and tropical climates. **ZONES 10–12.**

Grevillea hilliana

Grevillea glabrata

Grevillea lanigera 'Mt Tamboritha'

Grevillea johnsonii

Grevillea johnsonii
JOHNSON'S GREVILLEA

From drier valleys of eastern New South Wales, this is a dense shrub of up to 15 ft (4.5 m) high with dark green leaves to 10 in (25 cm) long divided into very narrow lobes. Erect clusters of pinky cream and orange-red flowers are produced throughout spring. Moderately frost hardy, it makes an outstanding specimen or screening plant. The name honors Dr Lawrence Johnson, former Director of the Sydney Botanic Gardens and foremost expert on eucalypts. **ZONES 8–10.**

Grevillea juniperina
PRICKLY SPIDER FLOWER

This semi-prostrate to upright rounded shrub to 6 ft (1.8 m) or more high from temperate eastern Australia has bright green, crowded, needle-like leaves. Profuse scarlet to orange or pale yellow, spider-like flowerheads appear from late winter to early summer. This is one of the most variable grevilleas and many forms and cultivars are grown. Most are moderately frost hardy and long lived. ***Grevillea juniperina* f. *sulphurea*** (sometimes sold as **'Aurea'**) has an erect habit to 4 ft (1.2 m) high and pale yellow flowers. **'Molonglo'** is a semi-prostrate cultivar to 30 in (75 cm) high with a spread of 6 ft (1.8 m) or more across; it produces abundant apricot flowers and is a popular ground cover for large areas. **'Pink Lady'** is a low-spreading shrub to 24 in (60 cm) high and 10 ft (3 m) across; it has pale pink flowers that are not always borne freely. **ZONES 8–10.**

G. longistyla × *johnsonii*

Grevillea juniperina

Grevillea lanigera
WOOLLY GREVILLEA

This species from mountains of southeastern Australia has narrow, grayish, furry leaves and red and cream flower clusters from late winter to spring. It varies in size—some forms are prostrate and others grow to about 3 ft (1 m) tall and wide. This is one of the most frost-hardy species, but it does resent summer humidity. **'Mt Tamboritha'** is a popular, small, prostrate form with soft gray-green foliage and reddish pink and cream flowers. **ZONES 7–9.**

Grevillea lavandulacea
LAVENDER GREVILLEA

This is an attractive but extremely variable species from western Victoria and adjacent parts of South Australia, ranging from an almost prostrate plant to a bushy suckering shrub up to 3 ft (1 m) high. It bears small clusters of crimson to pink and, occasionally, white flowers in winter and spring. The narrow gray-green leaves are usually hairy. It is marginally frost hardy and resistant to dry conditions. Several forms and cultivars are available including **'Penola'** with soft, gray foliage and profuse red and cream flowers and **'Tanunda'** with downy, silver gray leaves and large clusters of pinkish mauve flowers. **ZONES 8–10.**

Grevillea lavandulacea 'Penola'

Grevillea longistyla × *johnsonii*

This unnamed hybrid between 2 closely related eastern Australian species grows vigorously to 15 ft (4.5 m) or more tall. It has finely divided leaves and masses of showy pinkish red flowers, with long red styles, from late winter to late spring. This grevillea prefers a fairly warm climate. **ZONES 9–11.**

Grevillea lavandulacea

Grevillea 'Honey Gem'

Grevillea 'Robyn Gordon'

Grevillea 'Mason's Hybrid'

Grevillea 'Mason's Hybrid'
syn. *Grevillea* 'Ned Kelly'

This spreading shrub is a hybrid cultivar very similar to the better known **'Robyn Gordon'**, having the same parentage. It has dark green divided leaves and grows to a height of 3 ft (1 m) or more. Orange-red flower spikes appear intermittently throughout the year. **ZONES 9–11.**

Grevillea oleoides

Native to a restricted area of coastal New South Wales, this is an erect, often suckering shrub up to 6 ft (1.8 m) high with entire, linear leaves to around 6 in (15 cm) long with a silky undersurface. The brilliant crimson flowers are borne in loose, spider-like heads from winter to early summer. **ZONES 9–10.**

Grevillea 'Poorinda Constance'

This hybrid cultivar is a bushy shrub up to 10 ft (3 m) high with a spread of up to 15 ft (4.5 m) across. The small, dark green, oblong leaves are silky haired beneath. Bright orange-red flowers are borne in terminal clusters from winter to early summer. It is marginally frost hardy. **ZONES 9–10.**

Grevillea 'Poorinda Queen'

One of the earliest named hybrid cultivars , this large, spreading shrub has glossy green elliptic leaves to 1½ in (35 mm) long with silky undersides. Clusters of pendent apricot flowers with a pinkish tinge are produced throughout spring with a repeat flowering in fall (autumn). It grows to 8 ft (2.4 m) high with a 10 ft (3 m) spread and is moderately frost hardy. **ZONES 8–10.**

Grevillea 'Poorinda Royal Mantle'

This prostrate shrub is similar to *Grevillea* × *gaudichaudii* and will eventually form a dense mat up to 15 ft (4.5 m) across. Throughout the year, but especially in spring and summer, it bears red, toothbrush-like flowerheads. Its dull green leaves to 6 in (15 cm) long are sometimes lobed. It is sometimes grafted onto a *Grevillea robusta* stock to form a weeping standard. This grevillea is suited to warm-temperate climates where it will make an exceptional ground cover for large areas. **ZONES 9–10.**

Grevillea 'Poorinda Royal Mantle'

Grevillea pteridifolia
GOLDEN GREVILLEA

Occurring widely across Australia's monsoonal north, this is a variable shrub usually making a small tree with an erect, open habit to 15 ft (4.5 m) and more tall. It has fern-like, finely divided silvery foliage and long, golden flowerheads from fall (autumn) to spring. All forms are frost tender and are suited only to warm temperate and tropical climates. There are some prostrate forms from coastal headlands that make attractive rockery plants. **ZONES 10–12.**

Grevillea robusta
SILKY OAK

From subtropical rainforests of the Australian east coast, this tree grows to 100 ft (30 m) and has long been valued for its beautiful timber, used for furniture making. The fern-like leaves with silvery undersides are partly shed just before the branches are almost hidden by the masses of long, golden-yellow blooms which appear in late spring. Moderately frost hardy once established, it will tolerate fairly dry conditions—in fact it will hardly succeed without a warm, dry summer. **ZONES 8–11.**

Grevillea 'Robyn Gordon'

This free-flowering offspring of *Grevillea banksii* and *G. bipinnatifida* is widely regarded as the best hybrid grevillea. It makes a rather dense bush a little more than 3 ft (1 m) tall and 6 ft (1.8 m) wide. The olive green leaves, russet when young and sometimes turning gray, are much divided and, though stiff and prickly, look fern-like. The cylindrical, soft red flowerheads appear almost all year, peaking in spring and fall (autumn). It is marginally frost hardy. Its foliage is reported to provoke allergic reactions in some people. **ZONES 9–11.**

Grevillea rosmarinifolia
ROSEMARY GREVILLEA, SPIDER FLOWER

This dense, spreading shrub to 6 ft (1.8 m) tall from cooler parts of south-

Grevillea oleoides

Grevillea robusta

Greyia radlkoferi

eastern Australia has bright green, needle-like leaves mostly under 7 in (25 mm) long. The pendent, red spider-like flowerheads are produced mainly from early winter to late spring. Moderately frost hardy, it takes well to being clipped to shape as a hedge. **'Jenkinsii'** is a decorative cultivar that is a little less prickly than its parent. **ZONES 8–10.**

Grevillea thelemanniana
SPIDER NET GREVILLEA

This southwestern Australian species may be prostrate and spreading or upright to about 3 ft (1 m) high. There are both green and gray foliage forms. The green form is slightly more upright and generally compact, while the prostrate form has long prostrate stems. The waxy, salmon-red spider-type flowerheads appear in spring and summer and sometimes again in late fall (autumn). It is marginally frost hardy. **ZONES 9–11.**

Grevillea victoriae
ROYAL GREVILLEA

This variable species from the mountains of southeastern Australia makes an upright, spreading shrub to 6 ft (1.8 m) high and 10 ft (3 m) across. It has ovate gray-green leaves to 6 in (15 cm) long with silvery undersides. Pendent clusters of rusty red, spider-type flowerheads appear in spring and again in late summer and fall (autumn). Occurring at elevations of up to 6,000 ft (1,800 m), it is one of the most frost-hardy grevilleas. **ZONES 7–9.**

GREWIA

Although there are over 150 species of this genus of deciduous and evergreen trees, shrubs and climbers from tropical and subtropical regions of Africa, southern Asia and Australia, only one species, *Grewia occidentalis* from southern Africa, is commonly found in gardens. The genus is named after Nehemiah Grew, who was famous for his botanical drawings. They have simple, toothed leaves and starry, 5-petalled flowers borne singly or in small groups in the leaf axils.
CULTIVATION: They are mostly frost tender to marginally frost hardy and require a sheltered, sunny position with well-drained, humus-rich soil. Prune

Greyia sutherlandii

frequently to maintain a compact habit. Propagate from cuttings or seed.

Grewia flava
RAISIN BUSH, BRAND BUSH

This deciduous shrub from summer-rainfall regions of southern Africa grows to 6 ft (1.8 m) high with young branches and leaves covered with grayish hairs. The pale green leaves have finely toothed margins and a velvety underside. The starry yellow flowers have a central mass of prominent gold stamens. These are followed by reddish brown, 2-lobed berries. **ZONES 9–11.**

Grewia occidentalis
FOUR CORNERS, LAVENDER STARFLOWER

Of wide occurrence in southern Africa, this adaptable evergreen shrub with deep green, oval, toothed, leathery leaves can grow to 10 ft (3 m) high and even greater spread. It bears star-shaped, mauve-pink flowers about $1\frac{1}{2}$ in (35 mm) across during spring and summer; they have pink sepals the same size and color as the petals, making them appear 10-petalled. They are followed by brownish, 4-lobed berries. **ZONES 9–11.**

GREYIA

This South African genus encompasses 3 species of evergreen or semi-deciduous shrubs or small trees grown for their attractive, bottlebrush-like clusters of bell-shaped flowers with protruding stamens, and their colorful fall (autumn) foliage. The genus is named in honor of Sir George Grey, governor of the Cape in the nineteenth century. Only one species, *Greyia sutherlandii,* is generally cultivated, although ***G. radlkoferi*** is also occasionally cultivated.
CULTIVATION: Marginally frost hardy, they are best suited to warm, dry climates and need full sun and fertile, well-drained soil. Lightly prune after flowering to keep them compact. Water generously during the growing season, less while the shrub is dormant in winter. Propagate from seed in spring or from cuttings in summer.

Greyia sutherlandii
NATAL BOTTLEBRUSH

This dome-shaped, rather gaunt, woody evergreen shrub from the drier hills of South Africa grows to 10 ft (3 m) or more high. Its almost circular shallowly toothed leaves turn red in fall (autumn), but it is mainly grown for its brilliant orange-red flowers. Appearing in late winter and early spring, the dense spikes of many small flowers with protruding stamens are borne at the ends of the bare branches. **ZONES 9–11.**

GRINDELIA
GUM PLANT, ROSINWEED, TARWEED

This genus of the daisy family consists of around 60 species of annuals, perennials and subshrubs from dry areas of North, South and Central America. The plants are usually covered in a sticky white resin

Grevillea thelemanniana

Grevillea victoriae

Grewia occidentalis

Grevillea rosmarinifolia

and have yellow, daisy-like flowers. The simple, sometimes stalkless leaves are also resinous.
CULTIVATION: Marginally frost hardy, they grow well in poor to moderately fertile, well-drained soil in full sun. Propagate from seed in spring or cuttings in summer.

Grindelia stricta
PACIFIC GRINDELIA

This frost-hardy, clump-forming perennial is a native of western North America. It grows to 3 ft (1 m) high, has oblong leaves to 10 in (25 cm) long and solitary 2 in (5 cm) yellow, daisy-like flowers from summer to early fall (autumn). **ZONES 8–10.**

GRISELINIA

This genus is made up of 6 species of evergreen shrubs and trees from New Zealand, Chile and Brazil, of which only the 2 New Zealand species are commonly cultivated. They are grown for their foliage and bushy habit, the pale greenish flowers being tiny and inconspicuous. The flowers are followed by black berries on female plants only.
CULTIVATION: They are only moderately frost hardy and require a temperate climate, well-drained soil and sunshine. They are resistant to salt and are suitable for coastal areas. With a little trimming the shrubs make good hedges. Propagate from summer cuttings or seed.

Griselinia littoralis
KAPUKA

Growing 20–40 ft (6–12 m) tall, this spreading tree or shrub from New Zealand has dense, bright green foliage and yellow-green flowers. It withstands salt-laden winds and dry conditions and, although frost hardy, appreciates the protection of a wall in colder areas. If used as a hedge, the plants are best trimmed in summer. The leaves of **'Dixon's Cream'** are splashed creamy white, while **'Variegata'** has blotched white variegations. **ZONES 8–10.**

Griselinia lucida 'Variegata'

Griselinia lucida

Griselinia lucida
PUKA

This fast-growing species from New Zealand is somewhat more erect and open branching than *Griselinia littoralis.* It grows to 20 ft (6 m) high, with larger, more glossy and darker green leaves. The leaves of the frost-tender **'Variegata'** are marked creamy yellow. **ZONES 8–10.**

GUNNERA

This is a genus of around 45 species of rhizomatous perennials from temperate regions of Africa, Australasia and South America. Occurring in moist habitats, they range in size from small, mat-forming plants to very large, clump-forming plants with some of the largest leaves of any broad-leafed plants. They are grown mainly for their striking foliage, although some species have attractive flower spikes and fruits.
CULTIVATION: Most species enjoy moist but well-aerated soil at the edge of a pond or stream. Plant in rich soil in full sun, although they may need shelter from very hot sun (which can scorch the leaves) and wind (which can reduce the leaves to tatters). Propagate from seed in fall (autumn) or spring, or by division in early spring. Protect from slugs and snails.

Gunnera manicata

Griselinia littoralis

Gunnera magellanica

From southern South America, this rhizomatous, clump-forming perennial grows to only 6 in (15 cm) high with a spread of up to 12 in (30 cm) or more. It has stalked, kidney-shaped, scalloped leaves and bears tiny green flowers in short, rounded spikes in summer. **ZONES 7–9.**

Gunnera manicata
syn. ***Gunnera brasiliensis***
GIANT ORNAMENTAL RHUBARB

Native to the high mountain swamps of Brazil and Colombia, this huge plant thrives in boggy soil and is usually grown on the margins of a pond. The massive leaves quickly unfurl in spring to a width of as much as 8 ft (2.4 m) on prickly stalks about 6 ft (1.8 m) high. Long spikes of greenish red flowers are borne in summer. Give the dormant crown a protective mulch of straw in winter. **ZONES 7–9.**

Gunnera perpensa
RIVER PUMPKIN

This rare species from South Africa grows naturally in marshy areas and

Gunnera manicata

Grindelia stricta

along streams. It has pumpkin-like leaves up to 12 in (30 cm) wide and nodding spikes of tiny reddish brown flowers up to 3 ft (1 m) tall. **ZONES 8–9.**

Gunnera prorepens

This creeping, ground-covering species from New Zealand spreads to 18 in (45 cm). The leaves, only about 1½ in (35 mm) wide, have scalloped edges and a purplish tinge. Insignificant flowers are followed by tiny, bright red fruit that are quite decorative. **ZONES 8–9.**

Gunnera tinctoria
syn. *Gunnera chilensis*

Next in size to *Gunnera manicata*, this is a slow-growing species from Chile with large, heart-shaped, sharply toothed, deep green leaves up to 5 ft (1.5 m) wide and borne on prickly stalks to 5 ft (1.5 m) in length. Numerous tiny, rusty flowers are borne on erect cylindrical panicles up to 24 in (60 cm) high; they are followed in summer by rounded green fruit suffused with red. **ZONES 6–7.**

GUZMANIA

The 120 species in this genus of evergreen, mostly epiphytic bromeliads have lance-shaped leaves that form funnel-shaped rosettes, and flowerheads of tubular white or yellow flowers usually surrounded by colorful bracts on yellow, orange or bright red stems. Guzmanias are mostly rainforest plants from the American tropics and are frost tender.
CULTIVATION: They require a position in part-shade in a well-drained compost. Water moderately during the growing season, less at other times, but always keep the leaf vases filled with water. If potting, leave enough room for just one year's growth and then repot. They make good indoor or greenhouse plants where they need plenty of indirect light. Fertilize only when in full growth, during the warmer months. Propagate from seed or offsets in spring or summer.

Guzmania lingulata

Ranging in the wild from Honduras to Bolivia, this is the most commonly grown species. It has basal rosettes of strap-like, apple-green leaves and grows to 12–18 in (30–45 cm) tall. Striking colored bracts surround clusters of tubular, white to yellow flowers in summer. ***Guzmania lingulata* var. *minor*** grows to 12 in (30 cm) high and across and has creamy yellow flowers and orange-red bracts; it is easily grown in a greenhouse. **'Indiana'** has erect golden-yellow bracts tipped with orange-red. **ZONES 10–12.**

Guzmania monostachia
syns *Guzmania tricolor, Renealma monostachia, Tillandsia monostachya*

Equally wide-ranging in the Americas, this densely rosetted epiphyte to 15 in (40 cm) high has strap-shaped, pale green leaves. The cylindrical flowering spike is tricolored, green at first, then the lower half takes on red or black lines, the upper part vivid red with snowy white tubular flowers. **ZONES 10–12.**

Guzmania sanguinea
syns *Caraguata sanguinea, Tillandsia sanguinea*

This basal rosette-forming epiphyte grows to 8 in (20 cm) high and up to 5 in (8 cm) wide. The broadly lance-shaped leaves, tinted with red in the early stages, gradually become spotted with violet-red, changing later to deep red. A compact cluster of tubular yellow flowers surrounded by red bracts is borne within the leaf rosettes of *Guzmania sanguinea* in summer. **ZONES 11–12.**

Guzmania 'Squarrosa'

This cultivar is a clump-forming epiphyte with rosettes of colorful bronzy leaves that grow up to 3 ft (1 m) in length. The center of the foliage flares a brilliant red for a short period during bloom time. The bright red inflorescence is borne on a short erect stem, and the flowers are white. **ZONES 11–12.**

GYMNOCALYCIUM
CHIN CACTI

This genus consists of about 50 species of low, round cacti with shallow, sometimes spirally arranged ribs and usually developing a protrusion or 'chin' below each areole. The spines are slightly curved and rather sparse, and the funnel-shaped flowers are large for the size of the plants. These small cacti are native to subtropical South America and make excellent house plants, although they can be grown outdoors in frost-free or near frost-free areas.
CULTIVATION: In the garden chin cacti need full sun and poor, well-drained soil. Indoors use a cactus potting mix and provide plenty of light and water during spring and summer. Keep dry in winter. Propagate from seed in spring or from offsets in summer.

Gymnocalycium andreae

From Argentina, this small clustering cactus reaches 2 in (5 cm) high and 4 in (10 cm) wide. The shiny, green-blue stems are globe-shaped with 8 ribs. Seven yellowish radial spines and 3 upwardly curving central spines sprout from whitish areoles. Vivid yellow trumpet-shaped flowers appear from the flat crown in spring and summer. It is frost tender and requires full sun. **ZONES 9–11.**

Gymnocalycium baldianum

This small cactus has a gray to blue-green stem and areoles with 5 to 7 creamy white radial spines. Abundant, 2 in (5 cm) long flowers in various shades of red appear throughout summer. It grows to a height and spread of 3 in (8 cm). **ZONES 9–11.**

Gymnocalycium denudatum

This rounded, clump-forming cactus to 3 in (8 cm) tall and 6 in (15 cm) wide has a dark green glossy stem and sharp but rather sparse, reflexed spines. White to pale pink tubular flowers, up to 3 in (8 cm) across, appear in spring, followed by oblong green fruit. **ZONES 9–11.**

Gymnocalycium horstii

This species is native to Brazil and has a glossy green, rounded body growing 3 in (8 cm) high and 4 in (10 cm) wide. It features light yellow spines and large pink flowers that are seen to best advantage in strong sunlight. Oval green fruit appear in summer. **ZONES 9–11.**

Gymnocalycium horstii

Gymnocalycium andreae

Guzmania lingulata 'Indiana'

Guzmania 'Squarrosa'

Gymnocalycium baldianum

Gunnera tinctoria

Guzmania lingulata

Gymnocalycium mihanovichii

Gymnocladus dioica

Gymnostoma australianum

Gymnocalycium mihanovichii
PLAID CACTUS

This Paraguayan species has flattened, grayish green, globular stems 2 in (5 cm) in diameter. These have 8 ribs and horizontal grooves above and below the areoles which bear short brownish yellow spines. Pink or greenish yellow flowers appear in early summer. A number of cultivars with stems of different colors or variegated have become popular. Some lack chlorophyll and so must be grafted onto a normal green cactus to survive; the best known is the brilliant red **'Red Head'** (syn. 'Hibotan'). **'Variegatum'** has stems irregularly blotched red and bronzy green. **ZONES 9–11.**

Gymnocladus dioica

Gymnocalycium quehlianum

From Argentina, this cactus grows to 2 in (5 cm) high and 3 in (8 cm) across. It has a gray-green stem with up to 15 ribs. Pale brown spines develop in whorls, but there are no central spines. It bears white funnel-shaped flowers with pinkish throats in early summer. **ZONES 9–11.**

Gymnocalycium saglionis

Native to northwestern Argentina, this rounded cactus grows to 4 in (10 cm) high and up to 12 in (30 cm) wide. It has a mid-green stem with 30 or more ribs with prominent tubercles. Reddish brown spines develop in whorls and there are about 3 central spines. It bears small, very pale pink to almost white flowers in early summer. **ZONES 9–11.**

Gymnocalycium tillianum

This short, squat Argentinian cactus grows 4 in (10 cm) tall and 6 in (15 cm) wide. It has long, black-brown spines and small pink flowers in spring. Spherical fruit follow in summer. **ZONES 9–11.**

GYMNOCARPIUM

Consisting of 5 species, this genus of deciduous, ground-covering ferns that spread by creeping rhizomes can be found on all northern continents. All are attractive and useful ferns, 12–15 in (30–38 cm) tall with triangular fronds that may be bluish, green or yellow-green in color. Rhizomes are tough and tenacious and the plants should only be

G. mihanovichii 'Variegatum'

grown where they can be contained or where they will not become a nuisance. **CULTIVATION:** Best and most luxuriant in full shade but tolerant of a few hours of daily sun, these ferns need moist, fertile soil that contains plenty of rotted organic matter. They are an appropriate ground cover under groups of trees or large shrubs so long as their water needs are not neglected. Hardiness varies with species but all will take at least some frost. Propagate by sowing spores or by division.

Gymnocarpium dryopteris
OAK FERN

From Europe, Asia and North America, this is a lovely fern with yellowish fronds about 15 in (38 cm) long. The creeping rhizome by which it spreads is wiry, black and shiny and the triangular fronds unroll from a tight sphere. **'Plumosum'**, with its larger, denser fronds, is generally thought to be even more attractive. **ZONES 3–9.**

GYMNOCLADUS

Distinctive for their enormous, handsome bipinnate leaves, the 4 deciduous trees of this genus, allied to *Gleditsia*, come from North America and East Asia. Small, greenish white flowers appear only in prolonged warm weather. The seeds and pods of different species have been used for soap and as a coffee substitute. Only female trees bear fruits. **CULTIVATION:** Cool-climate plants, they require full sun and deep, well-drained, fertile soil. Propagate from seed in fall (autumn).

Gymnocladus dioica
KENTUCKY COFFEE TREE

From moist woodland areas of the eastern USA, this slow-growing tree reaches 70 ft (21 m) tall and 50 ft (15 m) wide. The large compound leaves, up to 3 ft (1 m) long, are pinkish bronze when young. The small, star-shaped white flowers are fragrant and are borne in early summer followed, on the female plants, by pendent reddish brown pods to 10 in (25 cm) long. The seeds were once roasted and ground for a coffee-like beverage. **ZONES 4–10.**

Gymnocalycium saglionis

GYMNOSTOMA

This genus of about 20 species of attractive cypress-like trees occurs in islands of the southwest Pacific and Malay Archipelago; a single species occurs in northern Australia. They are not conifers but are close relatives of *Casuarina*, in which genus they were formerly included. They differ from *Casuarina* and *Allocasuarina* by having only 4 tiny scale leaves at each joint of the slender needles, and by the long 'beaks' radiating from the cone-like structures containing the seeds. One or two species are planted for ornament and shade in wetter parts of the Asian tropics, and the Australian species is becoming well known in cultivation. **CULTIVATION:** They prefer sheltered, humid situations and deep, moist, humus-rich soil. Propagation is from seed or cuttings.

Gymnostoma australianum

This is Australia's only member of the genus, known in the wild solely on one high granite mountain near the mouth of the Daintree River in northeastern Queensland. It can become a small, bushy crowned tree of about 20 ft (6 m), but is usually grown as a neat, conical, 10 ft (3 m) shrub with dense, deep green foliage. **ZONES 10–12.**

GYNANDRIRIS

This genus of 9 species of iris-like cormous plants is native mainly to South Africa, but also occurs in the Mediterranean region and southwest Asia. They have one or two narrow, channelled basal leaves and produce a succession of short-lived flowers. Each flower consists of 3 long, spreading outer petals and 3 smaller, erect inner petals. **CULTIVATION:** Moderately frost hardy, they require well-drained soil in full sun. They are from winter rainfall areas and need dry summer conditions. Propagate from seed or cormlets.

Gynandriris sisyrinchium
syn. *Iris sisyrinchium*

This species from the Mediterranean and western Asia grows to 8 in (20 cm) high and bears violet-blue, iris-like flowers

Gymnocalycium tillianum

Gypsophila paniculata 'Bristol Fairy'

Gymnostoma australianum

with white, yellow or orange patches on the 3 outer petals; they are produced in spring. They open mid-afternoon and fade by midday of the following day. **ZONES 8–10.**

GYNURA

Related to *Senecio*, this genus is native to tropical Africa, Asia and Australia. It consists of about 50 species of evergreen perennials, shrubs and scrambling climbers grown for their attractive foliage and colorful small cylindrical flowerheads.

CULTIVATION: Frost tender, they are suitable for growing outdoors only in tropical and subtropical areas where they need fertile, well-drained soil and some shade. Scrambling species will need some support for the stems. Tip prune regularly to encourage compact growth. Indoors use a good potting mix and keep moist during the growing season. Avoid wetting the foliage. Propagate from cuttings in late spring or summer.

Gynura aurantiaca

PURPLE VELVET PLANT, ROYAL VELVET PLANT

Native to Java, this evergreen perennial or subshrub to 24 in (60 cm) high has weak, scrambling stems covered with purple hairs. The ovate, toothed leaves to 8 in (20 cm) long also have a downy covering of purple hairs. Clusters of narrow orange-yellow flowerheads are produced mainly in winter. **'Purple Passion'** has more elongated or pendent stems and smaller, more jaggedly-toothed leaves that have reddish purple hairs on the underside. It is popular as an indoor plant, often incorrectly identified as *Gynura sarmentosa*. **ZONES 10–12.**

GYPSOPHILA

Native to Europe, Asia and North Africa, there are over 100 species of these annuals and perennials, some of which are semi-evergreen. They are grown for their masses of small, dainty, white or pink flowers, often used by florists as a foil for bolder flowers or foliage. The narrow leaves are borne in opposite pairs.

CULTIVATION: Plant in full sun with shelter from strong winds. Fully frost hardy, they will tolerate most soils but do best in deep, well-drained soil lightened with compost or peat and grow well in limy soil. Cut back after flowering to encourage a second flush. Transplant when dormant during winter. Propagate from cuttings in summer or from seed in spring or fall (autumn).

Gypsophila cerastioides

A native of the Himalayas, this low-growing, mat-forming perennial to 3 in (8 cm) high twice as wide has small, grayish green, spoon-shaped basal leaves. Abundant small white flowers with purple veins are produced from late spring to early summer. **ZONES 5–10.**

Gypsophila elegans

This bushy, erect annual grows to 24 in (60 cm) tall and half as wide. Making delicate, pretty clumps in the garden, it bears masses of tiny purplish white flowers in branching heads from summer to early fall (autumn). The lance-shaped leaves are grayish green. **ZONES 6–10.**

Gypsophila paniculata

BABY'S BREATH

This short-lived perennial, mostly treated as an annual, has small, dark green leaves and sprays of tiny white spring flowers. It reaches a height and spread of 3 ft (1 m) or more. **'Bristol Fairy'** has double white flowers. **'Compact Plena'** has double white or soft pink flowers. **ZONES 4–10.**

Gypsophila repens

This prostrate perennial has stems forming low mounds up to 8 in (20 cm) high and 18 in (45 cm) wide. It has narrow, bluish green leaves and bears panicles of star-shaped white, lilac or pale purple flowers in summer. It is an ideal plant for trailing over rocks. **'Dorothy Teacher'** has abundant pale pink flowers ageing to deep pink. **'Rosea'** has deep pink flowers. **ZONES 4–9.**

Gypsophila 'Rosenschleier' ('Veil of Roses')

This perennial produces masses of tiny, ½ in (12 mm), rose-like double flowers in summer. They open white, becoming pink as they age. The leaves are grayish green. It grows to about 18 in (45 cm) high and spreads to 3 ft (1m). **ZONES 5–9.**

Gypsophila repens 'Rosea'

Gypsophila paniculata

Gypsophila paniculata 'Compacta Plena'

Gypsophila repens

H

HAAGEOCEREUS

This genus, native to Chile and Peru, consists of up to 10 species of cacti with ribbed, thickly spined stems that branch from the base; the spines vary in color from creamy yellow to reddish brown. They generally reach up to 6 ft (1.8 m) in height and 1½–4 in (3.5–10 cm) in thickness. Large, funnel-shaped flowers bloom in spring, varying in color from white to red. Usually these cacti will not start to produce flowers for many years. The flowers are followed by round red fruit in summer.

CULTIVATION: These are frost-tender cacti that do best in full sun and very well-drained soil. Propagate from cuttings or seed. They are susceptible to mealybug and spider mite.

Haageocereus pseudoversicolor

This columnar cactus from Peru is thickly covered with yellow-brown

Haageocereus pseudoversicolor

spines. It reaches a height of 4 ft (1.2 m) with stems that grow up to 4 in (10 cm) thick. White, tubular flowers appear in spring. Large, green-red berries follow in summer. **ZONES 10–11.**

Haageocereus versicolor

In cultivation, this Peruvian cactus has clumps of upright, tubular stems to 5 ft (1.5 m) tall and 3 in (8 cm) in diameter. The compact, downy stems have about 20 light ribs and are thickly covered with areoles bearing up to 30 golden yellow-red, whorled spines. At night during summer, long, white, trumpet-like flowers appear. **ZONES 10–11.**

HABERLEA

Of the more than 2,000 species of the large African violet and gloxinia family (Gesneriaceae) only a small proportion extend beyond the tropics, and of these a mere half-dozen are native to Europe. The European species are shared among 3 genera, *Ramonda, Jankaea* and *Haberlea*, all perennials and restricted to small regions in the Pyrenees or the Balkans. *Haberlea* consists of 2 species only, occurring in Bulgaria and northern Greece. They are rosette plants that grow on rock ledges and in crevices, resembling some of the smaller *Streptocarpus* species in leaf and flower.

CULTIVATION: They require a climate with warm dry summers and cool wet winters but dislike excessive wetness around the roots at any time. Plant in freely draining crevices in a rock garden or a stone wall, or grow in pots with coarse gravel in an alpine house. Choose an aspect where the roots remain shaded but foliage gets some sun. Propagate from seed, by division of rhizomes, or from leaf cuttings.

Haberlea rhodopensis

Haemanthus coccineus

Habranthus brachyandrus

Habranthus robustus

Haberlea rhodopensis

This pretty plant grows only to about 4–6 in (10–15 cm) in height, with spatulate, scalloped leaves arising from a short rhizome. In spring and early summer it produces stalked umbels of lilac flowers about 1 in (25 mm) across, the 3 lower petals much longer than the 2 upper. There is also a pure white-flowered form, **'Virginalis'**. **ZONES 6–9.**

HABRANTHUS

PAMPAS LILY

There are around 10 species of *Habranthus*, mainly from South and Central America but with one species from Texas. They are neat floriferous plants closely related to *Hippeastrum* and *Zephyranthes*. They have strap-shaped linear leaves and produce their crocus-like blooms successively from mid-summer to late fall (autumn), usually after rain. In late winter the plants die back but are rarely completely dormant and resent dry storage.

CULTIVATION: *Habranthus* species are not generally fully frost hardy and prefer full sun and any well-drained, moderately fertile soil. Once planted, do not disturb other than to divide the bulbils. They also grow well in pots. Propagate from seed or by division of the bulbils.

Habranthus brachyandrus

Free flowering, these plants produce their elegant, funnel-shaped flowers, 2 to 4 to a stem, throughout the summer months. The flowers are 2½–4 in (6–10 cm) in length and the petals are a soft pink touched with beetroot at the base. Each stem rises to a height of about 12 in (30 cm). The leaves are linear, usually in groups of three, but rarely on display during the flowering season. **ZONES 10–12.**

Habranthus robustus

syns *Habranthus tubispathus, Zephyranthes robusta*

This beautiful plant comes from Brazil and Argentina and bears a trumpet-shaped flower about 3 in (8 cm) long on each 12 in (30 cm) stem. The flowers, which appear in summer, are rose pink, often fading to white. The glossy, green basal foliage is narrow and strap-like. It is a good pot plant for a bright, sheltered position. **ZONES 10–12.**

HACQUETIA

syn. *Dondia*

There is one species only in this genus: a tiny perennial from the woodlands of eastern Europe. At most it grows to 4 in (10 cm) tall, spreading very slowly into a small mat. The flowers appear in spring before the leaves and the plant is usually grown in rock gardens or in small pots in collections of alpine plants. It requires a cold winter for success.

CULTIVATION: Grow in porous, gritty soil that contains leafmold or other rotted organic matter in part- or dappled shade. Keep moist always but give more water from the time the flower buds appear until the leaves begin to yellow in fall (autumn). Propagate from seed sown as soon as it is ripe or by division of clumps in late winter, before flower buds appear. Divide infrequently as it resents root disturbance.

Hacquetia epipactis

syn. *Dondia epipactis*

The pinhead-sized, bright yellow flowers of this species are surrounded by glossy green bracts, giving the effect of a most unusual bright green flower. Appearing straight from the ground in earliest spring, they are followed by 3-lobed leaves. This is a most unusual and desirable plant for cooler areas. **ZONES 6–9.**

HAEMANTHUS

BLOOD LILY

The blood lilies are remarkable deciduous or evergreen bulbous plants from South Africa, the genus containing about 20 species. They flower—from summer to fall (autumn)—on naked stems that rise straight from mostly leafless bulbs. Though the flowers themselves are neither very large nor showy, they are cupped in bracts that give the whole inflorescence considerable distinction. Most of them are red, hence the origin of both the Latin and common names. Many of the species once placed in *Haemanthus* are now reclassified under *Scadoxus*.

CULTIVATION: Plant these bulbs in fall or spring in part-shade in light but compost-rich, well-drained soil. In wet summer climates or in well-watered gardens, it is best to grow the plants in pots and bring them under cover when the leaves wither. In frost-prone climates grow in pots and remove to a greenhouse in winter. They only need sufficient warmth to keep from freezing. Water and feed during the growing season, but keep deciduous species completely dry when dormant and evergreens dry but not parched. The plants are best left undisturbed for a few years, after which they can be propagated from offsets or from seed; either way the resulting plant will take a few years to flower.

Haemanthus albiflos

Native to South Africa's Cape Province, the bizarre, shaving brush-like flowers of this species are greenish white and are produced in summer. The large, paired leaves are evergreen and leathery with fine hairs along their edge; unfortunately they are often damaged by slugs and snails. The plants grow to a height of 12 in (30 cm). **ZONES 9–10.**

Haemanthus coccineus

BLOOD LILY

The blood lily grows to 15 in (38 cm) tall. From summer to fall (autumn) its sturdy, purple-spotted stems bear clusters of slender, bright red flowers enclosed by waxy, scarlet to pink bracts. The flowers are followed by 2 broadly oval, dark green leaves that are hairy on the underside and which lie on the soil. **ZONES 9–10.**

Haemanthus deformis
syn. ***Haemanthus baurii***

This lovely bulb comes from Natal in South Africa and was introduced to cultivation in 1869. It has broad, dark green leaves to 4 in (10 cm) in length and numerous white flowers on a 3 in (8 cm) stem. It flowers in spring. **ZONES 10–11.**

Haemanthus montanus

A deciduous species from highland parts of eastern South Africa, this bulb produces pleasantly fragrant white flowers in spring. Leaves are grayish green and held erect. **ZONES 9–11.**

HAKEA

This genus consists of 130 species of evergreen shrubs and small trees from Australia. They are closely allied to the grevilleas and, like them, are well-regarded garden plants in their home country, though the most easily grown species are not necessarily the most spectacular. They are popular in California also, though are rather frowned on in South Africa where several species have become weeds. There is great variety in the foliage, from needle-like to broad, though the leaves are always stiff and leathery. The flowers are borne in small clusters, and the bracts are woody follicles, sometimes quite large. The bushier species are suitable for informal hedges, those with prickly leaves being impenetrable.

CULTIVATION: Fast growing but not always long lived, they prefer mild-winter climates, sunshine and well-drained soil and dislike phosphorus-rich fertilizers. Some tend to do poorly in summer-rainfall climates, especially the Western Australian species. Propagation is usually from seed; outstanding forms can be perpetuated from summer cuttings. Watch for root-rot in moist soil.

Hakea bucculenta
RED POKERS

This medium shrub from Western Australia grows to 20 ft (6 m) tall and half as wide. It has long, somewhat

Haemanthus montanus

Hakea nitida

prickly leaves and magnificent spikes of nectar-rich orange-red blooms in winter. A useful plant for semi-arid, warm areas, it withstands moderate frosts, and it is relatively long lived. Prune lightly to keep it compact. **ZONES 9–11.**

Hakea eriantha
TREE HAKEA

This slender, fast-growing shrub or small tree reaches to 15–25 ft (4.5–8 m) and has clusters of small white flowers in spring. The narrow leaves, about 4 in (10 cm) long, are often tinged pink when young. **ZONES 9–10.**

Hakea laurina
PINCUSHION BUSH, SEA URCHIN

This shrub or small tree from Western Australia grows to 20 ft (6 m) tall and 10 ft (3 m) wide. The long, narrow leaves are gray-green and leathery. During winter and spring its fragrant, ball-shaped, crimson flowerheads appear, with long creamy styles protruding like pins from a pincushion. Useful for hedges and screens, this hakea must have perfect drainage, and if grown too fast it may become top heavy and liable to being toppled by strong winds. **ZONES 9–11.**

Hakea microcarpa
NEEDLE BUSH

The most cold-hardy hakea, this open, rounded shrub from mountains of southeastern Australia grows to 6 ft (1.8 m) in height and spread. The green leaves are variable, but are usually needle-shaped with sharp points. The small, creamy white flowers appear from

Haemanthus deformis

Hakea laurina

Hakea microcarpa

late winter to summer; they have a honey-like fragrance. **ZONES 8–10.**

Hakea nitida

One of the lesser known hakeas, *Hakea nitida* is indigenous to Western Australia. The white flowers, which appear in late winter to spring, tend to hide among the dull green leaves, but the plant is of shapely, upright habit and makes a fine informal hedge about 8 ft (2.4 m) high. **ZONES 10–11.**

Hakea purpurea

This small dense shrub from southern Queensland grows to about 5 ft (1.5 m) high. The leaves are needle-shaped, up to 4 in (10 cm) long, and clusters of vivid red flowers appear during winter and spring. It prefers a dry climate and, once established, is hardy both to dry conditions and moderate frosts. **ZONES 9–11.**

Hakea salicifolia
syn. ***Hakea saligna***
WILLOW HAKEA

With narrow deep green leaves, which are bronze-red when young, this eastern Australian shrub grows to 20 ft (6 m). Its delicate creamy white flowers appear in clusters in spring and fall (autumn), and are followed by small, woody fruit. It grows naturally in moist gullies as well as in shallow, dry soil, and so has adapted well to a wide range of warm-climate garden conditions. It tolerates strong winds and makes a good hedge plant as it benefits from pruning. **ZONES 8–9.**

Hakea purpurea

Hakea bucculenta

Hakea sericea

This evergreen, rounded shrub from eastern Australia grows to a height of 10–15 ft (3–4.5 m) and a spread of 6–12 ft (1.8–3.5 m). It bears clusters of small, fragrant, white or palest pink flowers in fall (autumn) and winter. Its needle-like leaflets are very sharply pointed and the plant makes a good burglar-proof hedge. **ZONES 9–10.**

Hakea suaveolens
syn. ***Hakea drupacea***
SWEET HAKEA

With its sharply pointed, bright green leaves, this Western Australian hakea makes an excellent hedge. Though it will reach as much as 20 ft (6 m) high and wide, it can be pruned to stay under 10 ft (3 m). The fluffy white, sweetly scented flowers, hidden within the foliage, are borne in fall (autumn). **ZONES 9–10.**

Hakea victoria

Halesia carolina

Halimium lasianthum

Halesia carolina

Hakonechloa macra 'Aureola'

Hakea victoria
ROYAL HAKEA

This upright, 10 ft (3 m) tall shrub has spectacular foliage. The leathery leaves have a similar shape to scallop shells and display striking variegations in shades of yellow or orange on a gray-green background, those on the long-flowering branches being the brightest. The flowers are pale pink and inconspicuous. It is difficult to propagate and grow, needing a dry climate with little frost, sandy (or at least very well-drained) soil and abundant sunshine. **ZONES 9–11.**

HAKONECHLOA

This tufted perennial grass genus occurs in Japan and has only one species. It grows to a height of 12–18 in (30–45 cm) and has bright green leaves that turn orange-bronze in fall (autumn) in cooler climates. There are a number of very attractive variegated forms that tend to be more compact and look best in light shade.

CULTIVATION: This frost-hardy grass prefers full sun or part-shade and fertile, humus-rich, moist but well-drained soil. Propagate the species from seed, the cultivars by division.

Hakonechloa macra 'Aureola'
GOLDEN VARIEGATED HAKONECHLOA

This slowly spreading, perennial grass from the mountains of Japan provides a striking accent to the garden. The narrow, 8 in (20 cm) long, bright yellow leaves are lined with fine green stripes with a pink-red tint in fall (autumn). It can be used as a specimen or planted in drifts. Reaching heights of 24 in (60 cm), it is very good in a pot. **ZONES 5–11.**

HALESIA
SILVERBELL, SNOWDROP TREE

The 5 species of this genus of deciduous trees and shrubs are found in eastern USA and in China in rich, moist woodlands and beside streams. They are grown mainly for their attractive bell-shaped flowers, opening in clusters as the leaves unfold, and the unusual winged fruit capsules that follow.

Halesia monticola

CULTIVATION: Cool-climate plants, they prefer a sheltered position in part- to full sun and grow best in well-drained, moist, neutral to acid soil. Propagation is from seed in fall (autumn) or from softwood cuttings in summer. Halesias have little trouble with pests and diseases.

Halesia carolina
syn. *Halesia tetraptera*
CAROLINA SILVERBELL

This ornamental, spreading tree grows 25–40 ft (8–12 m) high and somewhat wider. It flowers profusely, even when young, producing masses of drooping, bell-shaped white or pink-flushed flowers in mid- to late spring. The flowers are followed by 4-winged green fruit that ripen to pale brown. The mid-green leaves are downy when they first appear and turn yellow in fall (autumn). **ZONES 3–9.**

Halesia monticola
MOUNTAIN SILVERBELL

Taller and more cone-shaped than the other species, this tree is fast growing to 40–60 ft (12–18 m) high. The pendent, bell-shaped white flowers are borne in profusion in late spring before the leaves, and the characteristic 4-winged fruit ripen in fall (autumn). The rare ***Halesia monticola* var. *vestita* 'Rosea'** has pale pink flowers and a white down on the new growth. **ZONES 4–9.**

× *HALIMIOCISTUS*

This is a small group of intergeneric hybrids between *Halimium* and *Cistus* that have arisen both in the wild and in cultivation. They are all smallish evergreen shrubs that in appearance are intermediate between their 2 parents.

CULTIVATION: They prefer mild winters, full sun and well-drained soil and will thrive in warm, dry climates. Propagation is from tip cuttings in summer.

× *Halimiocistus sahucii*

This naturally occurring hybrid between *Halimium umbellatum* and *Cistus salviifolius* is found in southern France. It is a low-spreading shrub growing 18–24 in (45–60 cm) high and 3 ft (1 m) or more wide. The lanceolate leaves, 1 in (25 mm) long, are coated in fine hairs. Many pure white $1\frac{1}{4}$ in (30 mm) flowers are borne in summer. **ZONES 8–10.**

× *Halimiocistus wintonensis*

This unusual and beautiful plant originated in Hillier's nursery in England, probably as a cross between *Halimium ocymoides* and *Cistus salviifolius.* It grows to 24 in (60 cm) and has grayish, lanceolate leaves. The flowers are 2 in (5 cm) across with white petals each with a crimson-maroon blotch at the base, streaked with yellow; they appear in late spring to early summer. It is moderately frost hardy. **ZONES 8–9.**

HALIMIUM
SUN ROSE

This useful genus is very similar to the popular *Cistus* and *Helianthemum* and some species have even been included in these other genera. It comes from the Mediterranean region and has about 14 species. They are herbaceous perennials or dwarf shrubs with small, narrow leaves and 5-petalled, white or yellow flowers with a reddish, purple or brown blotch at the base of the petals.

CULTIVATION: They prefer full sun and a moderately fertile, well-drained soil and are frost hardy. Water sparingly and prune regularly to maintain shape and encourage flowering. Propagation is from cuttings.

Halimium lasianthum
syn. *Halimium formosum*

This low-spreading evergreen is a native of Spain and Portugal. It has gray-green foliage and in spring and summer bears rich yellow flowers, each petal marked with a central crimson blotch. Although frost hardy, it needs shelter in colder areas. Like *Cistus*, it is admirably suited to coastal gardens. It grows to a height of 3 ft (1 m) and can spread to 5 ft (1.5 m). **ZONES 8–9.**

Halimium ocymoides
syns *Cistus algarvensis, Helianthemum ocymoides*
PURPLE SPOT SUNROSE

This lovely low shrub from Spain and Portugal can grow to 3 ft (1 m) and has a spread of 5 ft (1.5 m). It has downy gray leaves and single, bright yellow, rose-like flowers with a purple eye. In a sunny location it will flower for most of the year. **'Susan'** is more compact with broader leaves and has numerous, single or semi-double bright yellow flowers with a deep purple-red throat. **ZONES 8–9.**

HALIMODENDRON
SALT TREE

Belonging to the pea family, this genus of only one species, is found in Siberia, southwest Russia and central and southwest Asia, and is grown for its flowers and attractive foliage.

CULTIVATION: The salt tree requires well-drained soil in an open sunny position. As its name suggests, it is tolerant of salty soil and only needs to be watered during very dry conditions. Propagation is from seed, cuttings, by layering or grafting onto *Laburnum* stock.

Halimodendron halodendron

Halleria lucida

Halimodendron halodendron
syn. *Halimodendron argenteum*

This shrub grows to 6 ft (1.8 m) and has deciduous pinnate leaves with 2 to 3 pairs of oblanceolate silky leaflets and a terminal spine. It produces many purple-pink pea-flowers in summer. ***Halimodendron halodendron* var. *purpureum*** has bright rosy purple flowers. ZONES 2–8.

HALLERIA

This is a genus of about 4 species of evergreen shrubs or small trees from Africa and Madagascar. They have ovate or elliptic, entire or serrated leaves and trumpet- or funnel-shaped flowers that appear either singly or in terminal cymes.

CULTIVATION: Species of *Halleria* generally require a warm climate, full sun and light, fertile soil. Propagation is from seed or cuttings.

Halleria lucida
TREE FUCHSIA

Halleria lucida is a much-branched shrub or small tree to 30 ft (10 m), native to southern and eastern Africa, and the only commonly cultivated species. In its native habitat it grows in or near forests on the slopes of mountains. It has ovate, 1–4 in (2.5–10 cm) leaves and in summer has red or orange tubular flowers in axillary clusters followed by edible, dark purple berries. The flowers arise mostly on old stems. African honeysuckle tolerates a wide climatic range from tropical to cool-temperate. ZONES 8–11.

HAMAMELIS
WITCH HAZEL

This genus contains 5 species of deciduous shrubs or small trees from East Asia and North America. They are prized for their fragrant flowers, borne on bare stems through winter, and for their foliage, which turns yellow with red and orange tints in fall (autumn). The fruits are small capsules containing 2 black seeds.

CULTIVATION: *Hamamelis* are good shrubs for cool-climate gardens, preferring an open, sunny position (although they will tolerate semi-shade) in fertile, moist but well-drained, loamy, acid soil. Propagate selected forms by grafting in winter, from heeled cuttings in summer or by budding in late summer. Species can be raised from seed, but germination may take a full year. Check for coral spot and honey fungus.

Hamamelis × *intermedia*

The name covers a group of cultivars derived from *Hamamelis japonica* and *H. mollis*, deciduous shrubs with oval leaves 3–6 in (8–15 cm) long that color well in fall (autumn). Fragrant flowers appear on bare twigs in winter, their color varying from light yellow to deep orange depending on the cultivar. **'Arnold Promise'** has bright yellow flowers; **'Diane'** has fragrant, spidery, deep red flowers in late winter and large leaves that turn red and yellow in fall; **'Jelena'** is bright orange; and **'Ruby Glow'** (syn. *H. japonica* 'Rubra Superba') has coppery red flowers and rich foliage colors in fall. ZONES 4–9.

Hamamelis japonica
JAPANESE WITCH HAZEL

This open, upright shrub grows to a height of 10–15 ft (3–4.5 m) and about as wide. Its perfumed yellow flowers with twisted petals are carried in clusters on the bare branches from mid- to late winter. Flowering branches are often cut for indoor decoration. The oval, mid-green leaves appear in spring and turn yellow before dropping in fall (autumn). ZONES 4–9.

Hamamelis mollis
CHINESE WITCH HAZEL

This upright, open shrub has extremely fragrant, golden-yellow flowers, borne on bare branches from mid-winter to early spring. It grows to a height and spread of 10–15 ft (3–4.5 m) and the large, thick leaves are mid-green above and downy beneath; they turn deep golden yellow in fall (autumn). **'Coombe Wood'** has slightly larger flowers; **'Pallida'** has dense clusters of large, sweetly scented sulfur-yellow flowers and yellow leaves in fall. ZONES 4–9.

Hamamelis vernalis
OZARK WITCH HAZEL, VERNAL WITCH HAZEL

This upright, suckering shrub is a smaller species, growing to a height and spread of about 6 ft (1.8 m). It flowers in spring with a profusion of sweet-smelling cream or dull yellow flowers with dark red centers. The leaves that follow are green above and grayish below, and turn yellow in fall (autumn). **'Sandra'** has purplish new leaves that turn orange, scarlet and red in fall and brilliant yellow flowers. ZONES 4–9.

Hamamelis japonica

Hamamelis × *intermedia* 'Ruby Glow'

Hamamelis mollis

Hamamelis × *intermedia* 'Ruby Glow'

Hamamelis × *intermedia* 'Jelena'

Hamamelis vernalis

Hamamelis virginiana
VIRGINIAN WITCH HAZEL, COMMON WITCH HAZEL

This witch hazel has an open, upright habit and grows to a height and spread of 12–20 ft (3.5–6 m) but can be readily adapted to tree-like form by training to a single trunk in early years. Small, fragrant, curled and twisted yellow flowers appear in fall (autumn) as the leaves fall. The dark green, broadly oval leaves turn a bright buttercup yellow in fall. **ZONES 7–9.**

HAMELIA
RAT POISON PLANT

This is a genus of about 40 evergreen shrubs and small trees from tropical America, of which only a few of the shrubby species are encountered in tropical and subtropical gardens. The attraction is the clusters of flowers, borne over a long summer season. The inelegant common name comes from the poisonous nature of the fruit.
CULTIVATION: They prefer rich soil, light shade and plenty of moisture, and are propagated from cuttings in summer.

Hamelia patens
FIREBUSH, SCARLET BUSH

This dense, soft-wooded shrub grows to about 10 ft (3 m). The leaves are pale green with downy undersides, and the bright scarlet tubular flowers are held in clusters towards the ends of the branches. The flowers are followed by yellow-green berries that ripen to purple-black. **ZONES 10–11.**

HAPLOPAPPUS

There are 160 species of annuals, perennials and shrubs in this genus in the daisy family, all of which are found in mild, sunny, relatively dry habitats in the Americas. In gardens they are used in similar situations or are grown in rockeries or pots.
CULTIVATION: Grow in well-drained, sandy or gravelly soil that contains some rotted organic matter but not a lot of rich manure or fertilizer. Water deeply but not frequently. Full sun is essential, and in cooler areas a position against a sunny wall helps preserve them from frosts. Plants are generally only marginally frost hardy but there are one or two exceptions which are frost hardy. Propagate from fresh seed or cuttings rooted in a warm, humid atmosphere.

Haplopappus glutinosus
syn. *Haplopappus coronopifolius*

This is a tufted perennial from Argentina and Chile that reaches a height of 8 in (20 cm). It produces yellow flowers over a long season in winter. **ZONES 9–11.**

HARDENBERGIA
CORAL PEA, FALSE SARSAPARILLA

The 4 species of this Australian genus of legume are twining climbers of modest size, usually with leaves divided into 3 leaflets that have closely reticulated veining. They are much admired in their native country for their clusters of small purple or pink pea-flowers, and they are occasionally seen in other countries where a mild winter allows their cultivation.
CULTIVATION: Hardenbergias prefer moist, well-drained, lime-free soil. They will grow in full sun or part-shade. Propagation is from seed sown in spring at 68°F (20°C); the seed should be presoaked for 24 hours to allow for germination. Watch for scale insects.

Hardenbergia violacea

Hardenbergia violacea

Hardenbergia comptoniana

Hamelia patens

Hardenbergia comptoniana
LILAC VINE

This most decorative species is the right size for a front fence or for training over shrubs. The small flowers can be soft purple or lilac pink; there is a white variety also. Happiest in a mild-winter climate, it flowers in spring. **ZONES 9–11.**

Hardenbergia violacea
syn. *Hardenbergia monophylla*
PURPLE CORAL PEA

Used as a ground cover for scrambling over banks or as a climber when given support, this beautiful twining plant will withstand dry conditions and some frost, and will grow in most soil with good drainage. Lovely sprays of purple pea-flowers are borne in winter and spring; there is also a pink form. **ZONES 9–11.**

HARPEPHYLLUM
SOUTH AFRICAN WILD PLUM

There is only one species in the genus—a handsome evergreen tree widely grown in subtropical climates both as a shade tree and for its edible fruit; both male and female trees are needed if the female trees are to bear fruit. It is a fine street tree, but is less desirable in a small garden as its dense shade makes it difficult to grow other plants beneath it. It is not a plum but is a relative of the cashew nut and mango.
CULTIVATION: *Harpephyllum caffrum* will tolerate a range of soils in full sun in frost-free areas. In colder climates, it grows best in a greenhouse. Propagate from seed or by grafting.

Harpephyllum caffrum

Hamelia patens

Hamamelis virginiana

Harpephyllum caffrum

This dense, broadly domed tree grows to 40 ft (12 m) tall and about as wide, with an erect, short trunk. Its deep green, compound leaves resemble those of an ash *(Fraxinus)*, and inconspicuous whitish green blossoms appear near the branch tips. On fertilized female plants the blossoms are followed by small, oval fruit the size of a small plum that ripen to orange-red; these are tart tasting but make excellent jam. **ZONES 10–11.**

HATIORA
syn. *Rhipsalidopsis*

Native to Brazil, this genus consists of 10 species of epiphytic or terrestrial, freely branching cacti. Ideally situated in hanging baskets, these plants have pendulous, jointed stems and yellow, pink or red funnel-shaped flowers. These are followed by pale white or yellow berries.
CULTIVATION: Plant these frost-tender cacti in porous soil in full sun or part-shade. Propagate from cuttings or seed. Prune when required.

Hatiora gaertneri
syns *Rhipsalidopsis gaertneri*, *Schlumbergera gaertneri*

This segmented, epiphytic cactus has flat, deep green stems, erect at first but soon arching outwards and downwards under their own weight. The plant is not spiny and bears spectacular, brilliant orange-scarlet flowers in winter and spring. **ZONES 10–11.**

Hatiora rosea
syn. *Rhipsalidopsis rosea*
EASTER CACTUS

This species is similar to *Hatiora gaertneri* except that the segmented branches may be flat or angled and are usually edged in red. Starry mauve-pink flowers are produced towards the ends of branches in early spring. It is native to southern Brazil. **ZONES 10–11.**

Hatiora salicornioides
syn. *Hariota salicornioides*
BOTTLE PLANT, DRUNKARD'S DREAM

This small, perennial, epiphytic cactus has a narrow, shrubby habit and reaches 15 in (38 cm) in height and spread. The slender stems are densely branching and divided into segments shaped like tiny bottles. In spring tiny, deep yellow flowers appear at the swollen stem tips. Maintain moisture during the hotter months and water only occasionally during winter. **ZONES 10–12.**

HAWORTHIA

This genus consists of 150 perennial succulents from South Africa, resembling miniature aloes. They are predominantly clump forming, developing in basal or short-stemmed rosettes. The small leaves vary in shape and may be marked with white dots or darker green translucent streaks. Racemes of insignificant white, or occasionally yellow, 6-petalled flowers appear in summer. **CULTIVATION:** These frost-tender succulents require semi-shade to maintain healthy leaves, and porous, well-drained soil. Keep slightly moist during the hotter months and totally dry in winter. Propagate by division or from offsets during spring to fall (autumn).

Haworthia attenuata
ZEBRA PLANT

This evergreen, clump-forming succulent owes its common name to the white bands that appear across its dark green, oblong-triangular leaves. White, tubular flowers are borne in spring. **ZONES 9–11.**

Haworthia bolusii

Growing to about $2\frac{1}{2}$ in (6 cm) high and 4 in (10 cm) in diameter, this attractive succulent develops in a compact, stemless

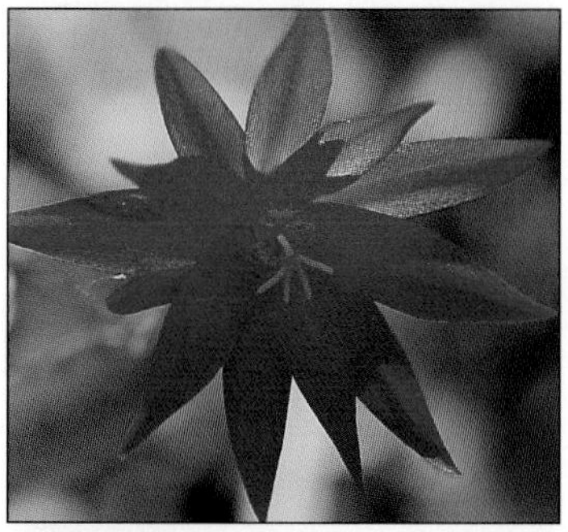

Hatiora gaertneri

Haworthia bolusii

Haworthia fasciata

rosette. The crowded gray-green leaves are long-pointed and their margins fringed with long silvery hairs. Slender racemes of white flowers appear from spring to fall (autumn). **ZONES 9–11.**

Haworthia coarctata
syn. *Aloe coarctata*

This small evergreen succulent grows in a tight rosette shape to 8 in (20 cm) tall. Its medium-sized, white-dotted, pointed leaves form in a dense spiral. Small white tubular flowers appear in spring and last until fall (autumn). **ZONES 9–11.**

Haworthia fasciata
ZEBRA HAWORTHIA

This almost stemless succulent is grown for its interesting leaves, which stand upright in neat rosettes, showing off the rows of white dots on their undersides and giving a gray and white effect. The tiny white flowers appear in early summer on 15 in (38 cm) tall bare stems. **ZONES 9–11.**

HEBE
VERONICA

The large genus *Veronica* used to be interpreted more broadly to include all

Hatiora rosea

Hebe 'Alicia Amherst'

H

Hebe armstrongii

Hebe albicans

these shrubby species (native to New Zealand and nearby islands, with a couple in Chile also) and some older gardeners still know them as veronicas. With over 100 species of evergreen shrubs, the hebes include many first-rate garden plants. They have neat, attractive leaves and often showy flower-spikes, which arise in the axils of the leaves, as in ***Hebe* 'Wiri Joy'**, **'Autumn Beauty'** and **'Pamela Joy'**. There are 2 main groups: the broad-leafed hebes, fast-growing shrubs with pleasing foliage and abundant spikes of small flowers ranging from white through pink to violet and blue over a long summer to fall (autumn) season; and the whipcord hebes with small leaves that give them the appearance of dwarf conifers, and white or pale mauve flowers. **CULTIVATION:** Most hebes are best suited to temperate to warm climates. In warm climates they grow equally well in sun or shade; in cooler climates sun is preferred. They like moist but well-drained soil and the broad-leafed types benefit from a post-flowering trim. Many of the whipcord hebes are mountain plants and tricky to grow at low altitudes. Propagate from cuttings in summer.

Hebe albicans

This distinctive, frost-hardy species has $\frac{1}{2}$ in (12 mm) blue-gray leaves that are coated with a fine grayish, grape-like bloom. The leaves are tightly packed on the stems. This very neat plant grows to about 18 in (45 cm) high and wide, and rarely needs trimming. The flowers, which appear in early summer, are white with purple anthers and are carried in short spikes. **'Boulder Lake'** is a low, spreading cultivar. **ZONES 8–10.**

Hebe 'Alicia Amherst'
syn. *Hebe veitchii*

This robust, frost-hardy shrub, with a height and spread of 4 ft (1.2 m) has mid- to dark green leaves about 4 in (10 cm) long. From late summer to fall (autumn) racemes of violet-purple flowers appear. **ZONES 9–10.**

Hebe × andersonii

This is a bushy, frost-tender shrub that grows to a height and spread of about 6 ft (1.8 m). It bears dense spikes of small lilac flowers in summer. The leaves are dark green. **'Variegata'** (syn. 'Argenteovariegata') has cream variegated leaves. **ZONES 9–10.**

Hebe armstrongii
syn. *Hebe lycopodioides*

From summer to early winter this frost-hardy, rounded, bushy shrub bears dense clusters of tiny, 4-petalled, white flowers. One of the whipcord group, its narrow oval leaves are bronze when young and the twigs are a distinctive greenish gold. It has a height and spread of less than 3 ft (1 m). **ZONES 8–10.**

Hebe cupressoides 'Boughton Dome'

Hebe haastii

Hebe 'Hagley Park'

Hebe glaucophylla

Hebe cupressoides

Hebe × *franciscana* 'Blue Gem'

Hebe elliptica

Hebe diosmifolia

Hebe 'Autumn Glory'

syn. *Hebe* 'Autumn Gem'

This lovely small, frost-hardy shrub grows 2–4 ft (0.6–1.2 m) high and has thick glossy obovate leaves and reddish bronze stems. The flowers, which are presented on short, dense, axillary racemes, are a very pretty shade of violet blue and appear in late summer and fall (autumn). **'Autumn Beauty'** has longer spikes of paler blue blooms and more elongated leaves. **ZONES 9–10.**

Hebe cupressoides

This unusual, densely branched whipcord hebe comes from the South Island of New Zealand and may grow 3–6 ft (1–1.8 m) in height with a spread of up to 10 ft (3 m). It has tiny, ¾ in (18 mm), glaucous, cypress-like leaves and in summer bears small, pale lilac flowers that fade to white. It is resistant to both frost and dry conditions. **'Boughton Dome'** is a dwarf form with a more rounded appearance and a less glaucous tinge to the leaves. **ZONES 8–10.**

Hebe diosmifolia

This densely foliaged twiggy shrub grows 2–4 ft (0.6–1.2 m) high and 3–5 ft (1–1.5 m) wide. The dark green leaves are about ½ in (12 mm) long. The branches tend to lie flat, creating a tiered effect. The pale mauve flowers, occurring from spring to fall (autumn), are carried in short spikes near the branch tips. This usually compact species requires little trimming, but is short lived and best replaced after about 10 years. **ZONES 8–10.**

Hebe 'Autumn Glory'

Hebe elliptica

syn. *Hebe decussata*

This attractive shrub occurs mainly in New Zealand but is also found in Chile and the Falkland Islands. It has elliptic leaves ¾–1½ in (18–35 mm) long and usually forms a profusely branched bush to 6 ft (1.8 m) but can also be a small tree to 20 ft (6 m). The flowers are fragrant, large and white or sometimes bluish. **ZONES 8–10.**

Hebe × *franciscana* 'Blue Gem'

syn. *Hebe latifolia*

From summer to early winter, this spreading evergreen bears dense spikes of small, violet-pink flowers and has oblong, densely arranged, mid-green leaves. Frost hardy, *Hebe* × *franciscana* 'Blue Gem' grows to a height of about 24 in (60 cm) with a spread of about 3 ft (1 m). **ZONES 8–10.**

Hebe glaucophylla

This is a bushy, frost-hardy shrub from the South Island of New Zealand. It grows to only 3 ft (1 m) and has narrow, bluish leaves and small white flowers. **ZONES 8–10.**

Hebe 'Autumn Beauty'

Hebe 'Great Orme'

This is a neat, low, frost-hardy shrub that can grow to 3 ft (1 m). The leaves are lanceolate and the lovely pink flowers, which fade to white, are produced on long racemes. **ZONES 8–10.**

Hebe haastii

This low, woody shrub is from the mountains of the South Island of New Zealand and grows 12–24 in (30–60 cm) in height. It has broad, overlapping ¼–½ in (6–12 mm) leaves and white flowers in dense clusters at the ends of the branches in late summer. **ZONES 6–9.**

Hebe 'Hagley Park'

syn. *Hebe* 'Lady Hagley'

This cultivar makes a small, low-growing shrublet with elliptic to ovate leaves that have a prominent midrib and seam outlined in black. The dainty flowers are pastel pink and appear in open, airy clusters. **ZONES 8–10.**

Hebe 'Hartii'

This is a prostrate, spreading shrub to 4 in (10 cm) in height with a spread of up to 3 ft (1 m). It has ½ in (12 mm)

Hebe 'Hartii'

Hebe leiophylla

Hebe macrocarpa var. *brevifolia*

Hebe ochracea 'James Stirling'

lanceolate, glossy green leaves, tinged purple. It bears many pale, mauve flowers in summer. **ZONES 8–10.**

Hebe hulkeana

This upright, open, frost-hardy shrub bears masses of small, pale lilac flowers in spring and early summer. Its attractive, oval, serrated, glossy dark green leaves have red margins. It grows to a height and spread of about 3 ft (1 m). **ZONES 8–10.**

Hebe 'La Séduisante'

syn. *Hebe speciosa* 'Ruddigore', *H. s.* 'Violacea'

This is a low, frost-hardy shrub 3–6 ft (1–1.8 m) in height with thick, narrow, glossy green, 3–4 in (8–10 cm) leaves and 4 in (10 cm) spikes of violet-purple flowers in summer and intermittently through to late fall (autumn). **ZONES 8–10.**

Hebe leiophylla

This plant is from the South Island of New Zealand, although there are some doubts about the validity of its specific name. *Hebe leiophylla* is a low shrub 3–6 ft (1–1.8 m) tall with narrow leaves and densely flowered 4 in (10 cm) racemes of white flowers in late summer. **ZONES 6–9.**

Hebe macrantha

This hebe is from the mountains of the South Island of New Zealand and grows 12–24 in (30–60 cm) in height with a spread of 3 ft (1 m). It has thick, elliptical, 1 in (25 mm) leaves and large white flowers from late spring to early fall (autumn). **ZONES 6–9.**

Hebe macrocarpa

From the far north of New Zealand's North Island, this hebe is a large, rather coarse shrub of up to 8 ft (2.4 m) in height with leathery, oblong dark green leaves $2^{1}/_{2}$–5 in (6–12 cm) long. From midwinter to early summer it produces 4 in (10 cm) dense spikes of white flowers. It is very tolerant of coastal conditions. **'Latisepala'** has deep purple-blue flowers, the darkest in color of any hebe. ***Hebe macrocarpa* var. *brevifolia*** has reddish purple flowers and shorter leaves. **ZONES 9–11.**

Hebe menziesii

syn. *Hebe divaricata*

This medium shrub is from the South Island of New Zealand where it grows to 10 ft (3 m) in height. Like *Hebe buxifolia* it is likely to be just another form of *H. odora.* It has wide-spreading, narrow leaves and lateral inflorescences with small white or pale lilac flowers. **ZONES 6–10.**

Hebe 'La Séduisante'

Hebe 'Midsummer Beauty'

This is one of the most rewarding of all hebes and deserves a place in most temperate gardens. Frost hardy, it grows to 4 ft (1.2 m) with a similar spread and has green leaves with a red underside. Its lavender-blue flowers are displayed on long racemes throughout summer. **ZONES 8–10.**

Hebe ochracea

A frost-hardy whipcord species with olive green to golden brown stems, *Hebe ochracea* is most commonly represented by **'James Stirling'**, a particularly bright golden cultivar. The shrub grows to about 18 in (45 cm) high and 3 ft (1 m) wide. The inflorescences of about 10 white flowers are rarely seen in cultivation. Do not prune this species unless absolutely necessary as it may lead to dieback. **ZONES 6–10.**

Hebe odora

syn. *Hebe anomala*

Growing to about 5 ft (1.5 m), this frost-hardy, evergreen species from New Zealand has tightly packed, neat green leaves arranged in a symmetrical pattern and spikes of white flowers during summer. Nurseries sometimes label this species as *Hebe buxifolia.* **ZONES 7–10.**

Hebe 'Pamela Joy'

This rounded shrub presents its vibrant violet-purple flowers in compact spikes at the ends of the branches. The leaves are elliptic and mid-green. **ZONES 8–10.**

Hebe pimeleoides

This charming, frost-hardy, small, much-branched hebe comes from drier mountain parts of the South Island of New Zealand east of the divide. It grows 18 in (45 cm) high with a spread of 3 ft (1 m). It has small gray-green leaves on purple branches, and in summer bears deep blue flowers in spikes to 1 in (25 mm) long. **ZONES 7–10.**

Hebe pimeleoides

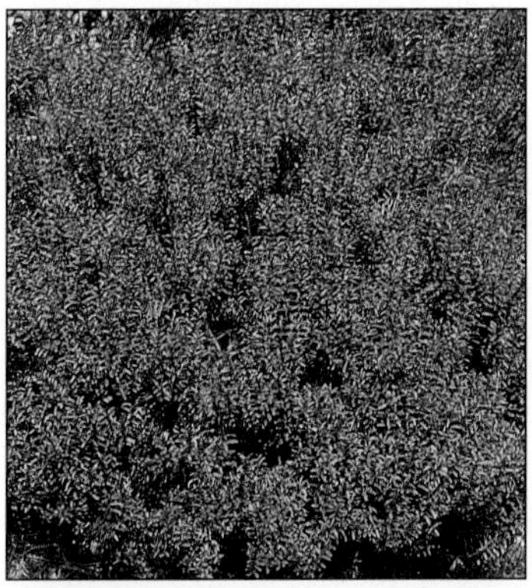
Hebe odora

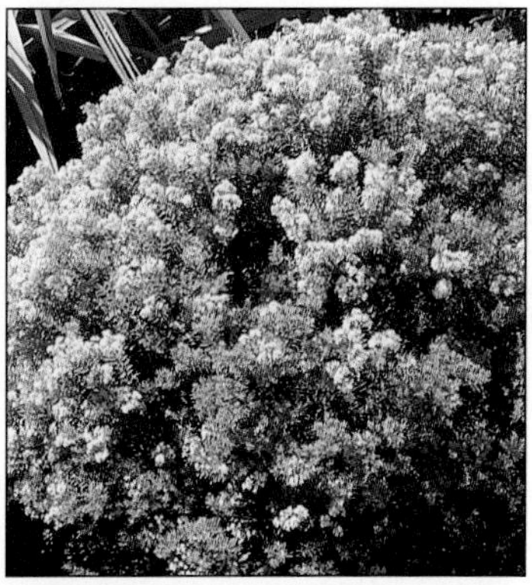
Hebe odora

Hebe 'Pamela Joy'

Hebe pinguifolia

This variable and adaptable small shrub from the drier mountain districts of the South Island of New Zealand can grow to 3 ft (1 m) high and wide. The pale blue-green leaves are margined with red and the white flowers are borne in small dense terminal spikes. It can tolerate a wide range of growing conditions and is frost hardy. **'Pagei'** is a low, spreading form with small, blue-gray leaves and many small white flowers in spring. It is an ideal rock garden plant. **ZONES 6–10.**

Hebe propinqua

This dwarf shrub from the mountains of the South Island of New Zealand forms a flat-topped cushion 3 ft (1 m) high and wide, although in cultivation it may not exceed 12 in (30 cm). It resembles *Hebe cupressoides* except that its tiny, triangular leaves are a bright yellow-green color. The flowers are white. **ZONES 6–9.**

Hebe speciosa

Hebe rakaiensis

syn. *Hebe subalpina*

This is a low shrub to 3 ft (1 m) in cultivation, although in its native habitat on the South Island of New Zealand it may grow to 6 ft (1.8 m). It has small, glossy, bright-green elliptic leaves and white flowers in short racemes during summer and can be used as a ground cover or as a low hedge. It is frost hardy. **ZONES 7–9.**

Hebe ramosissima

This prostrate hebe grows naturally on Mount Tapuaenuku on the South Island of New Zealand. It forms dense mats to 12 in (30 cm) in diameter. The leaves are obovate and the terminal flower spikes have small white flowers. **ZONES 7–9.**

Hebe salicifolia

KOROMIKO, KOKOMUKA

This frost-hardy, spreading evergreen shrub, up to about 10 ft (3 m) tall and wide, is from New Zealand's South Island and Chile and is tolerant of pollution and salt winds. Of dense habit, it makes an effective screen. The narrow, waxy leaves may be up to 6 in (15 cm) long. The fragrant white flowers, tinged with lilac, are produced in showy spikes up to 8 in (20 cm) long. **ZONES 7–9.**

Hebe speciosa

SHOWY HEBE

This evergreen, compact shrub grows 2–5 ft (0.6–1.5 m) high, spreading to 4 ft (1.2 m) wide in a broad, bun shape. It has oval, glossy foliage and bears a profusion of reddish purple flowers in terminal clusters from early summer to late fall (autumn). This species is more prone to wilt than other hebes. Many attractive cultivars exist, including **'Variegata'** with creamy white leaf margins. Hardiness depends on which cultivar is planted but all will tolerate some frost. **ZONE 9.**

Hebe stricta

This is a variable species from New Zealand that can grow to more than 10 ft (3 m) in the wild. The leaves are lanceolate to 6 in (15 cm) long and the flowers are white or pale bluish in racemes. There are a number of forms in cultivation. **ZONES 9–11.**

Hebe venustula

This is a tough whipcord hebe that develops into a 3–4 ft (1–1.2 m) ball of twigs and foliage. The leaves are a light yellowish green on whippy, upright stems. The white to pale mauve flowers appear in early summer carried in loose clusters at the branch tips. It is a very free-flowering shrub. Prune lightly to shape each year after flowering. **ZONES 9–10.**

Hebe propinqua

Hebe pinguifolia

Hebe salicifolia cultivar

Hebe 'Wiri Joy'

Hebe venustula

Hebe 'Wiri Mist'

Hebe salicifolia

Hebe 'Wiri Joy'

This showy, large-flowered hybrid grows into a rounded shrub densely clothed with glossy oblong leaves. Purple-pink flowers appear in summer. **ZONES 8–10.**

Hebe 'Wiri Mist'

This low shrub grows to 18 in (45 cm) and can spread to 3 ft (1 m). It has thick, green leaves margined with yellow and is covered with white flowers towards the end of spring. **ZONES 8–10.**

HEDERA

IVY

There are about 10 species of ivy from Europe, temperate Asia, North Africa, the Canary Islands and the Azores, but the most familiar and the only one to thrive indoors is *Hedera helix*, which is available in many named varieties. Evergreen, woody-stemmed climbers, ivies can be used for ground cover, clothing walls and fences, covering tree stumps and arches, growing up pillars and posts and edging of borders, and for trailing from containers and as indoor specimens. Ivy topiary has been revived; as the ivy grows over the shape the side shoots are clipped regularly to produce a dense cover.

CULTIVATION: In sun or shade ivies are adaptable to a wide variety of conditions, soils and climates. Regular pruning is recommended so that the attractive, lobed juvenile leaves are retained and no flowers are produced. If the mature growth, which produces tiny green flowers in fall (autumn) followed by black berries, is struck as cuttings, the resultant plants remain as shrubs. Propagate from cuttings or rooted stems. Pests afflicting ivy include spider mites, scale, thrips and aphids.

Hedera canariensis
CANARY ISLAND IVY, ALGERIAN IVY

This species from Tunisia and Algeria has bright green, leathery, 3-lobed leaves about 4 in (10 cm) long. Small red hairs cover the undersides of young leaves and the stems. The foliage is easily frost-damaged but soon recovers. **'Gloire de Marengo'**, a good cover for sheltered walls, has silver-green leaves with cream-white markings. **'Ravensholst'**, useful for a wall or as a ground cover, has dark green leaves. **'Variegata'**, particularly showy and a good cover for large areas of walls or fences, has leaves that are dark green in the middle shading to silver-gray and bordered with cream or white. **ZONES 8–11.**

Hedera colchica
PERSIAN IVY

This frost-hardy, vigorous creeper comes from the Caucasus region and has large heart-shaped, dark green leaves that are mostly lobed. It prefers a moist, well-drained position, and strikes readily from cuttings. **'Dentata'** is densely foliaged with leaves that are paler than the species. **'Dentata Variegata'** has cream variegation on the leaves. **'Sulphur Heart'** is like the species but has attractive yellow variegation on the leaves. **ZONES 6–11.**

Hedera helix
COMMON IVY, ENGLISH IVY

This very frost-hardy species from Europe will produce a dense, dark green cover. It is often used as a ground cover

Hedera hibernica 'Sarniensis'

Hedychium coccineum

in shade where grass has difficulty thriving, and is also excellent for climbing up walls and hiding paling fences, although may eventually damage woodwork or masonry that is not sufficiently strong. There are innumerable named varieties with a range of leaf shapes, some variegated. Many cultivars of ivy with variegated leaves are suitable for growing indoors. **'Atropurpurea'** has purple stems and leaves that change from green to reddish purple in winter. **'Baltica'** is a form from Latvia that differs from normal ivy in its smaller, more deeply cut leaves and paler veins. **'Buttercup'** has beautiful golden new growth that shades to green with age. **'Erecta'** is a form from Japan that has stout stems and broadly triangular pointed leaves arranged regularly up the stem. **'Glacier'** has gray-green leaves with silver-gray variegations. **'Goldheart'** is perhaps the best of the green and gold cultivars. **'Ivalace'** is a very attractive branching vine with 5-lobed leaves with a lacy edge. **'Manda's Crested'** has leaves with long undulate lobes that grow on erect red petioles; the overall effect rather resembles seaweed. **'Pedata'** has elongated lobes and prominent veins. **'Pittsburgh'** (syn. 'Hahn's Self-branching') has closely set, small, deep green leaves. **'Silver Queen'** (syn. 'Tricolor') has shallowly lobed, triangular leaves that are gray-green with cream markings that are tinged pink in winter. **ZONES 5–11.**

Hedera colchica 'Sulphur Heart'

Hedera helix 'Goldheart'

Hedera helix 'Silver Queen'

Hedera hibernica
syn. *Hedera helix* subsp. *hibernica*

This is a rampant climber with shallowly lobed, triangular leaves. **'Sarniensis'** is mid-green with lighter colored veins. **ZONES 5–11.**

HEDYCHIUM
GINGER LILY

Ginger lilies, like frangipanis and hibiscus, are associated with the tropics because of their lush foliage, glamorous flowers and heady scent. Yet, of the 40 species of *Hedychium* native to southern Asia, many grow quite high on the mountains, indicating their tolerance for cooler weather. Some recently introduced species are hardy enough to be grown even in temperate gardens. They are perennials that grow from rhizomes to form clumps up to 6 ft (1.8 m) high and 4 ft (1.2 m) wide, and for most of the year in warm climates (summer elsewhere) bear spikes or heads of fragrant flowers that last well and are good for cutting.
CULTIVATION: They prefer humus-rich, moist but well-drained soil in a part-shaded position. They flower in summer and spent stems should be cut out each season to ensure vigorous growth—or cut blooms for indoors. Propagate from fresh seed or by division.

Hedychium coccineum
RED GINGER LILY

This species from the Himalayas forms a low clump with spreading stems and

Hedera helix 'Atropurpurea'

narrow leaves. Its spectacular erect flower spikes, which carry only a few flowers, can reach 10 in (25 cm) high. The blooms vary from pale coral to a bright red, always with the exaggerated stamen in pink. The cultivar **'Tara'** has brilliant orange flowers and is more frost hardy than the species. **ZONES 9–11.**

Hedychium coronarium
WHITE GINGER LILY, GARLAND FLOWER

In summer this Indian species bears dense spikes of butterfly-like, satiny white flowers with pastel yellow blotches and a sweet scent. The leaves are lance-shaped with downy undersides. It has an upright habit and grows to about 5 ft (1.5 m) in height with a spread of up to 3 ft (1 m). It is frost tender and in cool climates needs the protection of a well-warmed greenhouse. **ZONES 10–12.**

Hedychium densiflorum

Surprisingly cold tolerant for a ginger, the Himalayan *Hedychium densiflorum* develops into a dense clump of tall, leafy stems topped with orange or yellow-orange flowers in late summer and fall (autumn). **'Stephen'** has longer, looser flower spikes of a stronger orange shade. **ZONES 8–11.**

Hedychium gardnerianum

Hedyscepe canterburyana

Hedychium gardnerianum

KAHILI GINGER

This species from the Himalayas grows to 8 ft (2.4 m) tall with long, bright green leaves clasping the tall stems. This is the most widely cultivated species; it prefers a warm climate although it will grow outside in temperate areas that have light, infrequent frosts. The fragrant red and pale yellow flowers, held in dense spikes, appear towards the end of summer. This species is considered a weed in some regions such as in the north of New Zealand. **ZONES 9–11.**

Hedychium greenei

This spectacular ginger lily comes from Bhutan where it may reach a height of 6 ft (1.8 m). Its leaves are 10 in (25 cm) in length and about 2 in (5 cm) wide while its flowers, produced in dense spikes, are bright red. Bulbils sometimes form in the leaf axils. **ZONES 10–11.**

HEDYOTIS

A large genus of mostly low-growing annuals and perennials, together with a few soft-stemmed shrubs and even one or two climbers. Around 150 species are known, scattered mainly through warmer parts of the world. Some botanists include in *Hedyotis* a group of North American species that others prefer to treat as the separate genus *Houstonia*. The herbaceous species occasionally grown in gardens are small plants with weak, often creeping stems that bear small, narrow leaves arranged in opposite pairs. Slender-stalked small flowers are borne in the leaf-axils, often only one to each leaf but sometimes in tight clusters or loose short sprays; each flower has a short tube and 4 spreading petals, which most commonly are white.
CULTIVATION: *Hedyotis* species are mostly quick-growing but short-lived plants that require little apart from warmth, good soil and abundant summer moisture to thrive and flower. Their climatic requirements vary according to origin. Propagate from seed or division.

Hedyotis michauxii

syns *Houstonia caerulea, Hedyotis caerulea*

CREEPING BLUETS

A native of southeastern USA, this is a mat-forming plant with densely branched stems that root into the soil, and tiny rounded leaves. The small, almost stalkless flowers dot the mat of foliage profusely in late spring and early summer: each has 4 sky-blue petals forming a cross, with a creamy yellow center. **ZONES 6–10.**

HEDYSARUM

Over 100 species belong in this genus of pea-flowers from temperate regions of the northern hemisphere, most of them annuals, biennials and perennials but a few of them soft-wooded deciduous shrubs. The name is latinized Greek and goes back to ancient times, the *hedy-* part of it meaning 'sweet' in reference to the sweet-smelling flowers of some species. With their pinnate leaves and narrow, crowded spikes of flowers, they are reminiscent of the vetches *(Vicia)* though lacking the tendrils characteristic of that genus. Only a few species are known in gardens, valued for their bold display of red, pink or purple flowers. Apart from their ornamental value, some species are grown as fodder plants, and the thick tap roots of some North American and subarctic species have been used as a food by native peoples.
CULTIVATION: Frost hardy, all species require a sunny position and freely draining sandy or gravelly alkaline soil. Water regularly in spring and summer. Propagate from seed or by careful division in spring.

Hedysarum coronarium

FRENCH HONEYSUCKLE, SWEETVETCH

Growing about 3 ft (1 m) tall and easily as wide, the perennial French honeysuckle is popular for its summer display of fragrant, dark red flowers. These are attractive to bees and nectar-feeding birds and are shown off well against the gray-green, compound leaves. **ZONES 5–10.**

HEDYSCEPE

BIG MOUNTAIN PALM, UMBRELLA PALM

Hedyscepe is a genus of one species of palm from Lord Howe Island, off the east coast of Australia. The name comes from the Greek for 'pleasant shade'. It occurs mainly at altitudes from 1,400–2000 ft (420–600 m).
CULTIVATION: *Hedyscepe* makes a handsome pot or tub plant or a useful, if slow-growing, palm for warm-temperate zones. It prefers full sun or part-shade and fertile, humus-rich, moist but well-drained soil. Protect it from wind. Propagate from seed in spring.

Hedyscepe canterburyana

This solitary feather palm grows to about 30 ft (9 m) and features a thick crown of strongly recurving dark green fronds and a silver crownshaft. The small creamy yellow flowers are followed by egg-sized dark red fruit, borne in short panicles below the crownshaft. **ZONES 10–11.**

HELENIUM

SNEEZEWEED, HELEN'S FLOWER

This genus, native to the Americas, consists of about 40 species of annual, biennial or perennial herbs. The mid-green leaves, which are alternate on erect stems, are oval to lance-shaped. The daisy-like flowerheads appear in summer and have yellow, red-brown or orange ray florets and yellow, yellow-green, red or brown disc florets. The flowers make a good border and are ideal for cutting.
CULTIVATION: Frost hardy, heleniums are easy to grow in any temperate climate as long as they get sun. The soil should be moist and well drained. Remove spent flowers regularly to prolong the flowering period. Propagate by division of old clumps in winter or from seed in spring or fall (autumn).

Helenium amarum

syn. *Helenium tenuifolium*

BITTERWEED, BITTER SNEEZEWEED

This strongly smelling annual comes from the southeast of the USA. Growing to 30 in (75 cm), this plant produces golden-yellow ray florets. It is said that some Native American tribes used to sniff the dried and powdered flowers of this species like snuff if they were suffering from blocked sinuses. **ZONES 4–11.**

Helenium autumnale

COMMON SNEEZEWEED

This perennial from North America grows about 5 ft (1.5 m) tall. The flowers occur from late summer to mid-fall (mid-autumn). This species has given

Helenium autumnale

Heliamphora heterodoxa

Helenium 'Moerheim Beauty'

rise to a number of named garden forms whose flowers range from yellow to maroon, with many being a blend of yellow and russet tones. **ZONES 3–9.**

Helenium bigelovii
BIGELOW SNEEZEWEED

This unbranched perennial from California and Oregon grows to about 4 ft (1.2 m). It has lanceolate leaves up to 10 in (25 cm) long and 2½ in (6 cm) solitary yellow-rayed flowerheads with a yellow or reddish center in summer and fall (autumn). There are a number of cultivated forms. **ZONES 7–9.**

Helenium 'Moerheim Beauty'

This upright perennial has sprays of daisy-like, rich orange-red flowerheads with prominent, chocolate-brown central discs. They are borne in summer and early fall (autumn) above mid-green foliage. Easily grown, it gives color to borders and is useful for cut flowers. Slow growing to 3 ft (1 m) high and 24 in (60 cm) wide, it enjoys hot summers. **ZONES 5–9.**

HELIAMPHORA
SUN PITCHERS

This genus contains 6 species of rhizomatous, carnivorous plants, allied to sarracenias, and is found on very wet mountains in Venezuela and Guyana. They have funnel-shaped, green to reddish leaves with, in most cases, a small overhanging cap. Each leaf has a nectar-secreting gland designed to attract small insects to their last meal. The flower stems may be up to 24 in (60 cm)

Heliamphora nutans

tall, each with several delicate white flowers changing to pink with age.
CULTIVATION: These plants grow naturally in wet, peaty soil and prefer warm, humid conditions, though preferably less than 86°F (30°C); they tolerate a minimum temperature of 40°F (5°C). They are best grown in a pot with a mixture of peat, sand and sphagnum moss placed in a saucer of water. Propagate by division of rhizomes in spring or from seed.

Heliamphora heterodoxa

This sun pitcher is from the swampy mountains of Venezuela and grows to about 15 in (38 cm) in height. It has funnels up to 2 in (5 cm) in diameter and white to pink flowers in early winter. There are a number of forms. **ZONES 11–12.**

Heliamphora nutans

This is an intriguing sun pitcher with green, basal, pitcher-shaped leaves with red margins and a constriction in the middle. It grows 4–8 in (10–20 cm) high and has large, nodding white to pink flowers on 6–12 in (15–30 cm) stalks. **ZONES 11–12.**

Helianthemum 'Fire King'

HELIANTHEMUM
ROCK ROSE, SUN ROSE

Helianthemum means flower of sunshine, an appropriate name for flowers that only open in bright sunlight. Allied to *Cistus,* the genus contains over 100 species found on rocky and scrubby ground in temperate zones around the world. Sun roses are sturdy, short-lived, evergreen or semi-evergreen shrubs or subshrubs. Their bushy foliage ranges in color from silver through mid-green. There are many garden forms, mostly of low, spreading habit. Wild plants have flowers resembling 1 in (25 mm) wide wild roses, but garden forms can be anything from white through yellow and salmon-pink to red and orange, and some varieties have double flowers.
CULTIVATION: Plant in full sun in freely draining, coarse soil with a little peat or compost added during dry periods. They should be cut back lightly as flowers fade to encourage a second flush of bloom in fall (autumn). Propagate from seed or cuttings.

Helianthemum apenninum
WHITE ROCK ROSE

Helianthemum apenninum is an evergreen low shrub originating in southern and western Europe and Turkey where it grows on dry hillsides. It grows to 18 in (45 cm) with a similar spread. The leaves are variable, gray-green and downy. The 1 in (25 mm) white flowers with yellow centers appear in summer. The white rock rose likes an open sunny position and tolerates both dry conditions and frost. **ZONES 6–10.**

Helianthemum 'Coppernob'

'Coppernob' is a delightful, creeping subshrub with gray-green leaves and deep copper flowers with a bronze-crimson center. The flowers are rather fleeting, but a succession appears all through mid-spring and summer. **ZONES 6–10.**

Helianthemum 'Fire Dragon'
syn. ***Helianthemum* 'Mrs Clay'**

Helianthemum 'Fire Dragon' is one of the best rock roses, with its scarlet flowers on display from late spring into summer. The leaves are a pleasant gray-green shade. It may grow to 12–18 in (30–45 cm) with a spread of 24 in (60 cm). **ZONES 6–10.**

Helianthemum 'Fire King'

This cultivar is similar to *Helianthemum* 'Fire Dragon' but its flowers are a brighter orange. This plant forms low, spreading mounds of gray-green leaves. **ZONES 6–10.**

Helianthemum 'Jubilee'

This is a very pretty low shrub that grows to only 12 in (30 cm) high and 18 in (45 cm) wide. It has small dark green leaves and double, primrose-yellow flowers from spring to late summer. **ZONES 6–10.**

Helianthemum nummularium

A variable species from Europe and Turkey, *Helianthemum nummularium* has a neat, prostrate habit and grayish foliage. Its small but profuse flowers vary in color from yellow or cream to pink and orange. Most of the cultivars traditionally listed under this name are in fact of hybrid origin and are given separate entries here. **ZONES 5–10.**

Helianthemum 'Coppernob'

Helianthemum nummularium

Helianthemum 'Rhodanthe Carneum'
syn. *Helianthemum* 'Wisley Pink'

This subshrub grows to 12 in (30 cm) high and wide and has narrow gray leaves. In spring and summer it has delicate pastel pink flowers shading to orange at the center. **ZONES 5–10.**

Helianthemum 'Wisley Primrose'

This vigorous small subshrub has narrow, entire, gray-green leaves and primrose-yellow flowers in spring and summer. **ZONES 5–10.**

HELIANTHUS

This genus of the daisy family includes one of the world's most important oilseed plants, also used for livestock fodder, as well as the Jerusalem artichoke with edible tubers, and many ornamentals. Consisting of around 70 species of annuals and perennials, all native to the Americas, they have large daisy-like, usually golden-yellow flowerheads, which are on prolonged display from summer to fall (autumn). The plants have hairy, often sticky leaves and tall, rough stems.

CULTIVATION: Frost hardy, they prefer full sun and protection from wind. The soil should be well drained. Fertilize in spring to promote large blooms and water generously in dry conditions. Perennials should be cut down to the base when they finish flowering. Propagate from seed or by division in fall or early spring.

Helianthus maximilianii

Helianthus annuus
COMMON SUNFLOWER

This fast-growing, upright annual can reach a height of 10 ft (3 m) or more. Large daisy-like, 12 in (30 cm) wide yellow flowerheads with brown centers are borne in summer. They are tall, leggy plants with broad, mid-green leaves. This species produces one of the world's most important oilseeds. It can be a little large for small gardens, but newer varieties have been developed that grow to a more manageable size, about 6 ft (1.8 m), including **'Autumn Beauty'** with medium-sized flowers usually brownish red, deep red, light yellow or golden yellow; and **'Teddy Bear'**, a compact grower with double, dark yellow flowers. **ZONES 4–11.**

H. × *multiflorus* 'Triomphe de Gand'

Helianthus × *multiflorus*

Helianthus annuus

Helianthemum 'Rhodanthe Carneum'

Helianthus decapetalus
THIN-LEAF SUNFLOWER

This strong-growing perennial from central and southeastern USA grows up to 5 ft (1.5 m) high. The leaves, smooth above and hairy underneath, are lance-shaped. The flowerheads, yellow with yellow-brown centers and up to 3 in (8 cm) in diameter, appear in summer and fall (autumn). **'Maximus'** is a popular cultivar. **ZONES 5–9.**

Helianthus maximilianii

Growing to at least 10 ft (3 m) tall, this perennial has rough stems densely covered with spearhead-shaped leaves about 8 in (20 cm) long. Golden-yellow flowers 4–6 in (10–15 cm) across appear in summer and fall (autumn). **ZONES 4–9.**

Helianthus × *multiflorus*

Helianthus × *multiflorus* is a clump-forming perennial to 6 ft (1.8 m) in height and 3 ft (1 m) in spread. The domed flowers can be up to 6 in (15 cm) across and appear in late summer to mid-fall (mid-autumn). Popular cultivars include **'Capenoch Star'**, **'Loddon Gold'**, **'Soleil d'Or'** and **'Triomphe de Gand'**. **ZONES 5–9.**

H. × *multiflorus* 'Loddon Gold'

Helianthus tuberosus

Helichrysum argyrophyllum

Helianthus salicifolius
syn. *Helianthus orgyalis*

This upright perennial, valued for background planting, grows to 6 ft (1.8 m) high and bears brilliant yellow, 3 in (8 cm) wide, single daisy-like flowers on branching stems in late summer or fall (autumn). The rich, dark green, shiny leaves are willow-like and looks good planted with late-flowering blue asters or salvias. **ZONES 4–9.**

Helianthus tuberosus
JERUSALEM ARTICHOKE

The 'artichoke' in the common name of this sunflower relative comes from a fancied resemblance in flavor of its edible tubers to those of the true artichoke *(Cynara scolymus)*; the 'Jerusalem' has resulted from a mis-hearing of the Italian for sunflower, *girasole*. Native to the USA and Canada, it is sometimes regarded as a weed; it spreads rapidly, making a forest of slender stems terminating in small yellow flowerheads. A popular vegetable in some parts of Europe, it is not always realized that the tubers contain the carbohydrate inulin, not used by the human digestive system, therefore having little food value. Native Americans fermented the tubers in pits, converting inulin to digestible sugars. **ZONES 4–10.**

HELICHRYSUM
EVERLASTING, PAPER DAISY, STRAWFLOWER

As understood until recently, this is a genus of around 500 species of annuals, perennials and shrubs, their highest concentration being in southern Africa followed by Australia, with smaller numbers in the Mediterranean, west and central Asia, and New Zealand. Belonging to the daisy family, they all have flowerheads with no ray florets or 'petals' but instead papery, mostly whitish bracts that are long-lasting when dried, hence the common names. But study by botanists has shown this to be an unnatural group, and they have been busy carving off both large and small groups of species and renaming them as distinct genera. This study is ongoing, and many species still in *Helichrysum* will eventually be reclassified, particularly among the South African species. The 'true' helichrysums include the Mediterranean and Asian species and an uncertain number from southern Africa; some well-known Australasian species have been reclassified under genera such as *Bracteantha, Ozothamnus* and *Chrysocephalum.*

Helichrysum bellidioides

CULTIVATION: Most species will tolerate only light frosts and are best suited to mild climates with low summer humidity, but a few are more frost hardy. They are mostly rock garden plants, requiring gritty, well-drained soil that is not too fertile and a warm, sunny position. A few, such as *Helichrysum petiolare* and *H. splendidum* are more adaptable as border shrubs or ground covers. Propagate from seed, cuttings, or rhizome divisions.

Helichrysum argyrophyllum

This shrubby perennial from eastern South Africa grows to 4 in (10 cm) and is used as a ground cover. It has silvery leaves and clusters of yellow flowers from summer to early winter. The 'petals' are in fact brightly colored bracts surrounding the central florets. **ZONES 9–11.**

Helichrysum bellidioides

This prostrate perennial comes from New Zealand and subantarctic islands to the south of that country where it grows to a height of only 6 in (15 cm), with a spread of up to 24 in (60 cm). It has tiny—¼ in (6 mm) long—spoon-shaped leaves that are light green above and clothed in cobweb-like white hairs beneath, and stems that develop roots where they touch the ground. It produces many ¾–1¼ in (18–30 mm) white strawflowers on tall stems in spring and summer. **ZONES 7–9.**

Helichrysum italicum
syn. *Helichrysum angustifolium*
CURRY PLANT

This clump-forming perennial herb from the Mediterranean grows 4–24 in (10–60 cm) tall with a spread of up to 3 ft (1 m). It has grayish, linear, downy leaves that have an intense curry aroma—the new, more tender leaves can be used to flavor salads and cooked meat dishes. The very small, darkish yellow flowerheads are crowded into long-stemmed flattish sprays terminating the branches throughout spring and summer. **ZONES 8–10.**

Helichrysum milfordiae
syn. *Helichrysum marginatum* of gardens
SILVER STRAWFLOWER

This cushiony, creeping perennial comes from subalpine areas of South Africa and Lesotho where it generally grows to only 2 in (5 cm) with a spread of 12 in (30 cm). It has densely packed, tiny, gray-green leaves. It is one of the finest species for a rock garden; the flowerheads, with a neat golden disc and broad funnel of lustrous, fine-pointed white bracts with crimson undersides, open only in sunny weather. **ZONES 7–10.**

Helichrysum splendidum

Helichrysum petiolare
syn. *Helichrysum petiolatum* of gardens
LICORICE PLANT

This South African evergreen is an excellent foliage plant; its gray, heart-shaped leaves and its stems are covered with cobweb-like white hairs. It is a sprawling subshrub forming dense mounds 24 in (60 cm) or more high and 6 ft (1.8 m) or more wide, with new stems springing from a network of rhizomes. It is well adapted to sun or shade and to dry conditions. The flowers, only occasionally produced, are not showy. **'Limelight'** has pale chartreuse foliage, and **'Variegatum'** has a creamy variegation. Both of these cultivars do better in shade and are superb summer container plants in cold climates. **ZONES 9–10.**

Helichrysum retortum

This prostrate perennial from the Cape region of South Africa can grow to 8 in (20 cm) with a spread of 18 in (45 cm). It has contorted stems with bright, silvery-gray oval leaves and pretty, white papery flowers in spring. It is marginally frost hardy. **ZONES 9–11.**

Helichrysum splendidum
syns *Helichrysum alveolatum*, *H. trilineatum*

This dense evergreen shrub occurs in the mountains of Africa from Ethiopia to the Cape. It grows to 5 ft (1.5 m) high and wide. It has crowded narrow leaves clothed in cobweb-like white hairs. Profuse small heads of golden-yellow flowers are borne from summer through fall (autumn). Frost hardy, it should be kept compact with regular pruning. **ZONES 7–10.**

HELICONIA
LOBSTER CLAW, FALSE BIRD-OF-PARADISE

From tropical America, Southeast Asia and some Pacific Islands, these beautiful, exotic plants have large leaves and spikes of colorful bracts enclosing relatively insignificant flowers. There are around 100 evergreen perennial species and hybrids in this genus, which is related to bananas and strelitzias. Planted *en masse,* heliconias create an eye-catching show of color all year round. The bracts may be red, yellow or orange, or scarlet tipped with yellow and green, or lipstick red and luminous yellow. The leaves are spoon-shaped and grow to 6 ft (1.8 m) long. Heliconias make excellent cut flowers.

CULTIVATION: Grow only in warm, tropical gardens with a winter minimum of 64°F (18°C). Plant in humus-rich, well-drained soil in filtered sun and with summer humidity. Water well during the growing season. To encourage new growth remove all dead leaves and flowers. Propagate by division of rootstock in spring, ensuring there are two shoots on each division. Check for spider mites, snails and mealybugs.

Heliconia bihai
syns *Heliconia humilis, H. jacquinii*
FIREBIRD, MACAW FLOWER

The large, paddle-shaped, green leaves of this species surround a flower stem of pointed, scarlet bracts tipped with green and inconspicuous white flowers. This is the most familiar species and is popular for flower arrangements. **ZONES 11–12.**

H

Heliconia bihai

Helichrysum retortum

Helichrysum petiolare 'Limelight'

Helichrysum petiolare

Heliconia caribaea
BALISIER, WILD PLANTAIN

As its specific name suggests, this plant is from the Caribbean Islands. It can grow to 8 ft (2.4 m) with a spread of 6 ft (1.8 m) and has glossy dark green banana-like leaves. The inflorescence is 3–5 ft (1–1.5 m) long and has white, inconspicuous flowers within red or yellow spathes. **ZONES 11–12.**

Heliconia collinsiana
COLLINS' HELICONIA, HANGING HELICONIA

Growing to around 12 ft (3.5 m) tall, this heliconia grows into a dense clump of thin stems from which the pendulous flowers hang in long strings. Bracts are 8–10 in (20–25 cm) long, bright red and sheath the golden yellow true flowers. The whole plant is dusted with a staining, powdery bloom. **ZONES 11–12.**

Heliconia latispatha

This big, vigorous plant of wide occurrence in tropical America needs plenty of room to spread. It has showy bracts that may be yellow, red or a combination of both. Bracts appear atop tall, erect stems, each pointing in a different direction. In the wild, they are pollinated by hummingbirds. **ZONES 11–12.**

Heliconia psittacorum
PARROT FLOWER

Ranging from eastern Brazil to the West Indies, this smaller species is good for mass planting. It has long-stalked, lance-like, rich green leaves. Narrow, pinkish, orange or pale red bracts surrounding yellow or red flowers with green tips are produced in summer. It is usually 3–5 ft (1–1.5 m) tall. **ZONES 11–12.**

Heliconia caribaea

Heliconia collinsiana

Heliconia psittacorum

Heliconia rostrata
FISHTAIL HELICONIA

Possibly the most striking of the heliconias, this species from Peru and Argentina has a large, pendulous cascade of alternating bracts of scarlet tipped with yellow and green. It grows 3–20 ft (1–6 m) in height. **ZONES 11–12.**

Heliconia stricta

This heliconia from South America grows in clumps to 6 ft (1.8 m) with a spread of 5 ft (1.5 m). It has 6 ft (1.8 m) long banana-like leaves. Each inflorescence has red or orange bracts edged with green. **ZONES 11–12.**

Heliconia wagneriana
RAINBOW HELICONIA, EASTER HELICONIA

From steamy Central America, this magnificent heliconia with its cream, red and green bracts cannot fail to impress. They grow at least 12 ft (3.5 m) tall, but the spring flowering season is relatively short for heliconias. **ZONES 11–12.**

Heliconia rostrata

Heliconia wagneriana

Heliconia stricta

Helictotrichon sempervirens

Heliconia latispatha

HELICTOTRICHON
OATGRASS

This is a genus of about 50 species of tussocky grasses from temperate Europe, North America and western Asia, some growing over 3 ft (1 m) tall. The long, narrow leaves may be flat or creased. The flowers, which appear in summer, may be either upright or arching. **CULTIVATION:** Grow all species in very well-drained, sandy or gravelly soil in full sun. In very cold climates plants should be sheared to the ground in late fall (autumn) and covered with a thick layer of straw or bracken. In warmer areas, shear to the ground in late winter to make room for new growth. Propagate by division of established clumps or by sowing seed in spring saved from the previous summer's flowers.

Helictotrichon sempervirens
syns *Avena candida, A. sempervirens*
BLUE OAT GRASS

This evergreen, perennial grass from central and southwest Europe is the most commonly grown and should be given prominence in a garden planting. It has arching blue-gray leaves that grow to about 3 ft (1 m). The oat-like summer flowers are produced in drooping panicles on stems that can reach a height of 4 ft (1.2 m). This frost-hardy grass looks good when contrasted with purple and pink low-growing plants. **ZONES 4–9.**

HELIOPSIS

ORANGE SUNFLOWER, OX EYE

The name *Heliopsis* means resembling a sunflower, and these perennials from the North American prairies do look like sunflowers, though on a rather reduced and more manageable scale. There are about 12 species, with stiff, branching stems and toothed, mid- to dark green leaves. The solitary, usually yellow flowers are up to 3 in (8 cm) wide and make good cut flowers.

CULTIVATION: These plants are easily grown, and for a while even tolerate poor conditions; however, they thrive in fertile, moist but well-drained soil and a sunny position. They are all very frost hardy. Deadhead regularly to prolong the flower display and cut back to ground level after flowering finishes. Propagate from seed or cuttings in spring, or by division in spring or fall (autumn).

Heliopsis helianthoides

This species grows to 5 ft (1.5 m) tall and 3 ft (1 m) in spread. It has coarse, hairy leaves and golden-yellow flowers in summer. The cultivar **'Patula'** has semi-double orange flowers. **'Light of Loddon'** has rough, hairy leaves and strong stems that carry dahlia-like, bright yellow, double flowers in late summer; it grows to a height of 3 ft (1 m) and a spread of 24 in (60 cm). **ZONES 4–9.**

HELIOTROPIUM

HELIOTROPE

This genus consists of over 250 species of annuals, perennials, shrubs and subshrubs from most warmer parts of the world. The leaves are simple and usually alternate. The clusters of flowers can be purple, blue, white or yellow and are deliciously scented. They appear in summer and are attractive to butterflies. The smaller varieties make excellent pot plants.

CULTIVATION: Heliotropes grow wild in both subtropical and cooler temperate climates and hence vary in frost hardiness. They prefer moist, well-drained, moderately fertile soil. Cut plants back by about half in early spring to promote bushiness. Propagate from seed in spring or cuttings in early fall (autumn).

Heliopsis h. 'Light of Loddon'

Helleborus argutifolius

Heliotropium arborescens

syn. ***Heliotropium peruvianum***

CHERRY PIE, COMMON HELIOTROPE

This attractive, soft-wooded evergreen shrub bears clusters of fragrant, purple to lavender flowers, with a delicate scent similar to stewed cherries, from late spring to fall (autumn). From the Peruvian Andes, it grows fast to 30 in (75 cm) tall and 3 ft (1 m) wide. It has dark green, wrinkled leaves, golden to lime-green in the cultivar **'Aurea'** and dark purplish green in **'Lord Robert'**. In cold climates it is grown as a conservatory or summer bedding plant. **ZONES 9–11.**

Heliotropium europaeum

This erect or lax, branched annual occurs in Europe and central Asia. Growing to 18 in (45 cm), it has softly hairy, oval, green leaves and small white or pale lilac flowers in forked spikes. The flowers appear in spring and fall (autumn). A common weed in Europe and Australia, it is toxic to livestock. **ZONES 4–11.**

HELLEBORUS

HELLEBORE

Native to areas of Europe and western Asia, these 15 perennial or evergreen species are useful winter- and spring-flowering plants for cooler climates. They bear beautiful, open flowers in white or shades of green, red and purple and are effective planted in drifts or massed in the shade of deciduous trees. All hellebores are poisonous.

CULTIVATION: Grow in part-shade and moist, well-drained, humus-rich soil; do not let them completely dry out in summer. Cut off old leaves from deciduous species just as the buds start to appear. Remove flowerheads after seeds drop. A top-dressing of compost or manure after flowering is beneficial. Propagate from seed or by division in fall (autumn) or early spring. Check for aphids.

Heliotropium arborescens

Helleborus argutifolius

Helleborus foetidus

Helleborus lividus

Helleborus argutifolius

syns ***Helleborus corsicus, H. lividus* subsp. *corsicus***

CORSICAN HELLEBORE

This is one of the earliest flowering hellebores, with blooms appearing in late winter and early spring. It is a robust evergreen that produces large clusters of cup-shaped, nodding, 2 in (5 cm) wide green flowers on an upright spike above divided, spiny, margined, deep green foliage. It has a clump-forming habit, growing to a height of 24 in (60 cm) and a spread of 24–36 in (60–90 cm). This is the most sun- and drought-tolerant species of the genus. **ZONES 6–9.**

Helleborus foetidus

STINKING HELLEBORE

This clump-forming perennial has attractive, dark green, divided leaves that remain all year. In winter or early spring the clusters of pale green, bell-shaped flowers, delicately edged with red, are borne on short stems. Established plants will often self-seed readily. **ZONES 6–10.**

Helleborus lividus

This species from the islands of the western Mediterranean has deep green or bluish green leaves and bowl-shaped,

Helleborus orientalis **hybrid**

creamy green flowers from winter to spring. It is slow to establish after being transplanted. **ZONES 7–9.**

Helleborus niger

CHRISTMAS ROSE

Popular for its white, mid-winter flowers, often appearing in the snow, this is one of the more temperamental species. It is often worth covering the plant with a cloche before the flowers open, to protect them from the winter weather. The mid-green, deeply lobed leaves are evergreen; mounds are 12 in (30 cm) high with a spread of 12–18 in (30–45 cm). They need steady moisture. **ZONES 3–9.**

Helleborus orientalis
LENTEN ROSE

The most widely grown of the genus, this evergreen, clump-forming species from Greece, Turkey and the Caucasus grows to 24 in (60 cm) high and wide. The large nodding flowers come in a great variety of colors from white, green, pink and rose to purple, sometimes with dark spots. Very frost hardy, it flowers in winter or early spring. The dense foliage fades and can be trimmed back before flowering. **ZONES 6–10.**

Helleborus purpurascens

Flowering from about mid-winter, even in cool climates, this frost-hardy, deciduous perennial from eastern Europe blooms before the new season's leaves appear. Plants grow anywhere up to 12 in (30 cm) tall but often less and the clumps spread at least 12 in (30 cm) across. The compound leaves are big and lobed and the flowers are an odd gray-green-pink combination. **ZONES 6–9.**

Hemerocallis forrestii

Helleborus 'Queen of the Night'

Possibly a hybrid between *Helleborus orientalis* and *H. purpurascens,* this plant produces simple, open-faced flowers that are a brownish purple color. **ZONES 6–10.**

HELONIAS

This genus, which is allied to *Veratrum* and *Narthecium,* consists of one species of lily, from swamps and marshes of eastern USA. The name comes from the Greek word *helos,* for 'marsh'. This evergreen perennial has a short swollen rhizome from which sprouts a tuft of broad sword-shaped, rather weak and floppy leaves; offsets may be produced, building up into a larger clump. A single, stout flowering stem arises from the center of each shoot, bearing at the top a short almost globular spike of crowded small purplish pink 6-petalled flowers. Fruits are small capsules that split open to release many seeds.
CULTIVATION: Grown mainly by collectors and bog-garden enthusiasts, *Helonia* species are not difficult to grow in moist, peaty soil in a sheltered spot, and are quite frost hardy. Propagate from seed or by division.

Helonias bullata
SWAMP PINK

This species occurs over a limited area of eastern USA, from southern New York State to North Carolina. The shiny, rather fleshy leaves can be up to 3 ft (1 m) long and 2 in (5 cm) wide. The thick flowering stems are also up to 18 in (45 cm) high; these terminate in a pin-cushion-like head 1–3 in (2.5–8 cm) long of densely packed small flowers, borne in late spring. **ZONES 6–9.**

HELONIOPSIS

Closely related to *Helonias* (the suffix *opsis* indicates resemblance) and of similar growth form, this genus consists of 4 species occurring wild in Japan, Korea, Taiwan and far eastern Siberia. In both foliage and flowers they are more decorative and graceful than *Helonias.* The drooping, leathery leaves taper more to both base and apex, and may be suffused with pink or marbled darker green. The starry flowers are larger than those of *Helonias,* in a looser spike and attractively drooping: they are white, pink, greenish yellow or purplish.
CULTIVATION: Grow *Heloniopsis* species in moist, peaty soil in a sheltered spot; they are shade-loving and intolerant of hot dry conditions. Propagate from seed or by division.

Heloniopsis orientalis

A variable species in growth habit and foliage as well as flower size and color, this has broad, long-pointed leaves that are gray-green, often suffused with red, and sometimes lightly barred with yellow-green. The rather few flowers per stem are nodding and funnel-shaped, with narrow petals, broadest near their ends; they vary from white to dull pink or greenish yellow. It grows 12–24 in (30–60 cm) in height. **ZONES 6–9.**

HEMEROCALLIS
DAYLILY

Native to temperate east Asia, these perennials, some of which are semi-evergreen or evergreen, are grown for their showy, often fragrant flowers which come in a vibrant range of colors. Individual blooms last only for a day, but are borne in great numbers on strong stems above tall, grassy foliage and continue flowering from early summer to fall (autumn). The flower size varies from 3 in (8 cm) miniatures to giants of 6 in (15 cm) or more, single or double; and plant height ranges from about 24 in (60 cm) to 3 ft (1 m). Grow in the herbaceous border, among shrubs or naturalize in grassy woodland areas.
CULTIVATION: Position carefully when planting as the flowers turn their heads towards the sun and the equator. Most daylilies are fully hardy; they prefer sun but will grow well and give brighter colors in part-shade. Plant in a reasonably good soil that does not dry out. Propagate by division in fall or spring and divide clumps every 3 or 4 years. Cultivars raised from seed do not come true to type. Check for slugs and snails in early spring. Plants may also suffer from aphid or spider mite attack.

Hemerocallis aurantiaca

This species forms a clump of long, linear foliage about 24 in (60 cm) high, with orange flowers about 12 in (30 cm) above the clump height. Grow it in borders, among shrubs or in large containers. **ZONES 6–10.**

Hemerocallis forrestii

Collected from the Yunnan Province of China by the plant hunter George Forrest in 1906, this species grows to 18 in (45 cm) with evergreen leaves to 12 in (30 cm). The flower stem rises from the outer foliage and bears 5 to 10 yellow, funnel-shaped flowers. It is less frost hardy than most other species. **ZONES 5–10.**

Hemerocallis fulva
TAWNY DAYLILY

This clump-forming species grows to 3 ft (1 m) high and 30 in (75 cm) wide. Rich orange-red, trumpet-shaped, 3–6 in (8–15 cm) wide flowers are borne from mid- to late summer. This plant has been in cultivation for centuries and in China and Japan the flower buds are sold as a food item. **'Flore Pleno'** (syn. 'Kwanzo') has 6 in (15 cm) double orange flowers with sepals curved back and a red eye. **'Kwanzo Variegata'** bears similar flowers to 'Flore Pleno' and has leaves with a white margin. **ZONES 4–11.**

Hemerocallis Hybrids

Almost all the cultivated species of *Hemerocallis* have played their part in producing the vast range of modern daylily hybrids. Most have been bred for size and texture of blooms, together with rich or delicate coloring, often with an 'eye' of contrasting color in the center; but some others are grown more for the massed effect of smaller or more spidery flowers which can be of great elegance. A recent development is a range of miniatures, in many colors and with either broad or narrow petals: one of the most popular is **'Stella d'Oro'** with clear golden-yellow flowers of almost circular outline. **ZONES 5–11.**

Helleborus 'Queen of the Night'

Helleborus purpurascens

Helleborus orientalis

Hemerocallis fulva 'Flore Pleno'

Hemerocallis Hybrid 'Stella d'Oro'

Hemerocallis Hybrid 'Apricot Queen'

Hemerocallis Hybrid 'Chemistry'

Hemerocallis Hybrid 'Christmas Day'

Hemerocallis Hybrid 'Coquetry'

Hemerocallis Hybrid 'High Priestess'

Hemerocallis Hybrid 'Holy Mackerel'

Hemerocallis Hybrid 'Memories'

Hemerocallis Hybrid 'Russian Rhapsody'

Hemerocallis Hybrid 'Rose Tapestry'

Hemerocallis Hybrid 'Constant Eye'

Hemerocallis Hybrid 'Custom Design'

Hemerocallis Hybrid 'Esau'

Hemerocallis Hybrid 'Florisant Snow'

Hemerocallis Hybrid 'Golden Wonder'

Hemerocallis Hybrid 'Mama Joe'

Hemerocallis Hybrid 'Scarlet Pansy'

Hemerocallis Hybrid 'Velvet Shadow'

Hemerocallis Hybrid 'Wynnson'

Hemerocallis Hybrid 'So Excited'

Hemerocallis Hybrid 'Silver Threads'

Hemerocallis lilioasphodelus

syn. *Hemerocallis flava*

PALE DAYLILY, LEMON DAYLILY

This is one of the first daylilies used for breeding and is found across China. It forms large spreading clumps with leaves up to 30 in (75 cm) long. The lemon-yellow flowers are sweetly scented and borne in a cluster of 3 to 9 blooms. It has a range of uses in Chinese herbal medicine: some parts may be eaten, while others may be hallucinogenic. **ZONES 4–9.**

HEMIANDRA

SNAKEBUSH

The 8 species in this genus are restricted to southwestern Western Australia. They are all prostrate to smallish shrubs allied to *Westringia*. The red, lilac, pink or white flowers are 2-lipped, the lower lip enlarged and spotted. The stiff, narrow leaves often have prickly tips.

CULTIVATION: They need very well-drained, preferably sandy soil and prefer a sunny spot, although they will tolerate some shade. They prefer drier, temperate zones and need only be watered sparingly. Prune regularly to keep them tidy and to prolong flowering. Propagate from fresh seed or cuttings. They are prone to fungal diseases in humid conditions. Some success has been had by grafting them onto *Westringia* stock.

Hemiandra pungens

SNAKEBUSH

This is the most commonly grown *Hemiandra* and, while not necessarily the most spectacular, it is still very ornamental. It is a variable species across its natural range where it grows in sandy soil. A number of prostrate forms are grown. They can form mats up to 12 ft (3.5 m) across and bear white or pink flowers with a darker throat. The more upright forms may grow to 5 ft (1.5 m). All forms have stiff, pointed, narrow linear to lanceolate leaves. Prostrate forms are best grown over a mulch of gravel or cascading down a wall to minimize the likelihood of fungal attack. **ZONES 9–11.**

Hemerocallis lilioasphodelus

HEMIGRAPHIS

There are more than 60 species of these annuals and evergreen perennials in this genus of the acanthus family, native to tropical Asia. They are strictly for subtropical and tropical gardens, where their attractive foliage forms and colors make them valuable as ground covers. Although not a major feature, their flowers are held in terminal heads.

CULTIVATION: Species of *Hemigraphis* are frost tender and enjoy good light, though not direct sun, and moist, well-drained soil. Water well in summer. Propagate from cuttings.

Hemigraphis alternata

syn. *Hemigraphis colorata*

RED IVY, RED FLAME IVY

This creeping or trailing perennial has heart-shaped or oblong, deeply puckered, metallic, purplish gray leaves with wine red undersides and stems. The white summer flowers hardly show at all. In warm climates red ivy can be grown as a colorful ground cover; in cooler areas it must be grown indoors or in a greenhouse. **ZONES 11–12.**

HEMIONITIS

STRAWBERRY FERN

There are 7 species of these small, terrestrial evergreen ferns. They are found in tropical Asia and America. Their leaves are palmately or pinnately divided or arrowhead shaped.

CULTIVATION: All species are easily grown in greenhouses or outdoors in frost-free areas. They grow best in warm, humid climates and like moist soil that should be allowed to almost dry out between waterings. They can take full shade. They make excellent terrarium specimens. Propagate from spores or from the plantlets that form on the fronds of some species.

Hemionitis arifolia

This unusual, delicate fern is found in tropical Asia. It has 2 types of frond: sterile, heart-shaped ones with stalks 2–4 in (5–10 cm) long, and fertile, arrowhead-shaped ones on stalks about 12 in (30 cm) long. **ZONES 10–12.**

Hemiandra pungens

HEMIPTELEA

The single species in this genus, *Hemiptelea davidii,* is a spiny deciduous tree in the elm family. It comes from northern China, Mongolia and Korea.
Its leaves are medium to dark green, elliptic in shape and have toothed edges. Although the flowers and fruit are both insignificant, this is a dense, attractive shade tree that is almost always smaller than 50 ft (15 m) in height.
CULTIVATION: Grow in average garden soil that drains freely in an open, sunny position. It is fully frost hardy and grows easily from seed sown in spring.

Hemiptelea davidii

The more vigorous branches of this small tree are armed with long, sharp thorns like those of a hawthorn. The oval leaves are only 1–2 in (2.5–5 cm) long, and their upper surfaces bear small stiff hairs which fall off leaving small darker green pits. The nut-like fruit are 2-edged with slight wings, only about $\frac{1}{4}$ in (6 mm) wide. **ZONES 3–9.**

HEPATICA

LIVERLEAF

Hepatica is closely related to *Anemone*, as the flower shape suggests. There are 10 species from North America, Europe and temperate Asia. They are all small, hairy, spring-flowering perennial herbs. The supposed resemblance of their leaves to a liver gave them their common and botanical names: *hepar* is Latin for liver. They have medicinal uses in liver and respiratory complaints, as well as for indigestion. There are a number of garden varieties with white, blue or purple flowers, sometimes double.
CULTIVATION: They occur naturally in woodlands so prefer part-shade and rich, moist but well-drained soil. Propagate from seed or by division, especially for the double varieties.

Hepatica nobilis

syns *Anemone hepatica, Hepatica triloba*

An inhabitant of mountain woods across much of Europe, this small perennial has solitary blue, pink or white $\frac{1}{2}$–$1\frac{1}{4}$ in (12–30 mm) flowers on long stalks. It has evergreen leaves with 3 broad, rounded lobes, usually purplish beneath. Although the plant is poisonous, it has been used as a herbal remedy for coughs and chest complaints. **ZONES 5–9.**

HERACLEUM

HOGWEED

The botanical name *Heracleum* derives from Heracleon, the ancient Greek name for this plant, named after the hero Hercules. There are 60 to 70 species of these herbaceous biennials and perennials occurring throughout Eurasia and North America. They have large compound leaves and produce white or pinkish, greenish or yellowish umbelliferous flowers. *Heracleum mantegazzianum,* which is dramatic in appearance, is considered a dangerous weed—contact with it can cause severe dermatitis and photosensitizing of the skin.
CULTIVATION: They prefer full sun and fertile, well-drained soil. Some hogweeds are useful additions to the less formal garden and look impressive at the back of a herbaceous border. They are propagated readily from seed and are fully frost hardy.

Heracleum spondylium

COW PARSNIP, KECK

Found throughout Europe, Asia and North America, cow parsnip is an upright perennial that grows to a height of 10 ft (3 m) or more with a spread of 3 ft (1 m). It has large pinnate leaves 6–12 in (15–30 cm) in length, and in summer produces large pink or white umbels up to 8 in (20 cm) wide. It is a variable species with many forms. Contact with the sap or the leaves can cause dermatitis. **ZONES 6–9.**

HERBERTIA

There are 6 species of cormous perennials in this genus of the iris family, from southern USA, Mexico and temperate South America. They grow in summer rainfall zones and produce attractive iris-like flowers in shades of blue, pale blue and purple. The flowers consist of 3 larger outer petals and 3 small petals inner ones. Each bloom only lasts for a day, but the tightly bracted clusters produce a long succession of new flowers. The leaves are linear and pleated along their entire length. The plants are dormant in winter and flower in spring and summer.
CULTIVATION: Hardy to moderate frosts, the plants are easily grown in full sun in humus-rich, well-drained soil. They have become minor weeds in some warm countries. Propagate from seed in fall (autumn).

Herbertia drummondii

syns *Alophia drummondii, Herbertia caerulea*

BLUE TIGER FLOWER

This cormous species comes from the grasslands and prairies of southern Texas and Mexico. The leaves grow from 6–12 in (15–30 cm) and resemble those of the iris, being sword-shaped and pleated. The stems reach to 12 in (30 cm) and bear short-lived flowers about 2 in (5 cm) across in spring and summer. The outer petals are violet blue and the smaller inner petals are often spotted white. **ZONES 9–11.**

HERITIERA

There are over 30 species of tropical trees from Africa, tropical Asia, Australia and the Pacific Islands in this genus. They are noted for their hard, durable timber, impressively buttressed trunks and curious leaves, the undersides of which are silvery and reflective.
CULTIVATION: In tropical climates grow in fertile, well-drained soil in full sun. Frost tender, they can be grown in part-shade but will grow much taller there as they reach for the light. In cool climates they must be grown in a heated greenhouse. Water well during the summer, much less in winter. Propagate from fresh seed.

Heritiera littoralis

LOOKING GLASS MANGROVE

Widespread along tropical coasts of the Old World, this spreading tree grows in mangroves and coastal swamps. A large specimen can measure 70 ft (21 m) with a spread of 40 ft (12 m). The flowers are insignificant but the tree's buttressed roots are an impressive feature. **ZONES 11–12.**

Hemiptelea davidii

Hepatica nobilis

Heritiera littoralis

HERMANNIA

This genus of evergreen perennials, shrubs and subshrubs with tough fibrous stems consists of over 100 species distributed widely through tropical and subtropical regions of the world, the majority from Africa. The leaves are characteristically hairy with small hair tufts scattered over the surface—in some species so densely that the leaf is gray and felty—and vary greatly in shape and size. The flowers are small but quite colorful, mostly yellow, orange or red. They are bell-like in form with 5 twisted petals, and are borne singly or in small clusters in the leaf axils. The flowers are followed by small capsular fruits.
CULTIVATION: Although little known as yet in gardens, some species make quite decorative plants for outdoor use in warmer climates and have also been grown as conservatory plants in cooler climates. They require a warm, sunny position and sandy, well-drained soil, and should be freely watered in the summer growing season. Propagate from seed or cuttings.

Hermannia incana
syn. *Hermannia candicans*

Native to South Africa's Cape Province, this erect shrub grows to over 3 ft (1 m) in height, with a rather lanky habit of growth. The small leaves, around 1 in (25 mm) in length, are green above and clothed with felted white hairs beneath. In spring and summer it produces terminal sprays of ½ in (12 mm) long pendent flowers with yellow petals. **ZONES 9–11.**

HERMODACTYLIS
SNAKE'S HEAD IRIS, WIDOW IRIS

The single species of herbaceous, tuberous-rooted perennial in this genus comes from countries surrounding the Mediterranean Sea. *Hermodactylus tuberosus* is grown for its pleasantly scented, iris-like flowers. The blooms, which appear atop tall stems, are produced in late winter in mild climates, spring in cooler areas. Leaves are long and narrow and the irregularly cylindrical tubers creep so that plants appear to move over time.
CULTIVATION: Grow this frost-hardy plant in full sun in very well-drained, preferably alkaline soil. Keep moist from about mid-fall (mid-autumn) to early spring but try to keep as dry as possible over summer as this simulates its natural conditions. Plant tubers in early fall, about 3 in (8 cm) deep. Propagate from seed sown in spring or by division in spring or early summer when the leaves have died off. It is not well suited to areas that are rainy and humid in summer.

Hermodactylus tuberosus
syn. *Iris tuberosa*

This relative of the iris gets its common names from the appearance and unusual colors (greenish yellow and blackish brown) of its flowers. Its stems and blue-green leaves grow to 20 in (50 cm) tall. **ZONES 7–10.**

HERNANDIA

This small genus of broad-leafed, evergreen trees scattered through the wet tropics is rarely cultivated but some species have the potential to make fine ornamental and shade trees. They have rather large, often heart-shaped leaves, panicles of numerous small flowers and hard, nut-like fruit, each enclosed in a hollowed reddish or yellowish structure formed from fused bracts; the structure may be a conspicuous and decorative feature.
CULTIVATION: Cultivation of these trees is not difficult in humid tropical or subtropical regions. A sheltered position and deep, moist but well-drained soil are preferred. Propagation is from fresh seed.

Heterocentron elegans

Hermodactylus tuberosus

Hesperis matronalis, purple form

Hesperis matronalis, white form

Hernandia bivalvis
GREASE NUT

This small tree, rare in the wild in a small area of southeast Queensland is fast becoming a popular ornamental, reaching 30 ft (9 m) or more with a compact, bushy crown. In late spring it bears many panicles of cream flowers slightly above the foliage, followed in late summer and fall (autumn) by a fine show of orange to red bladder-like fruit about 2 in (5 cm) long, each consisting of 2 'valves' enclosing a large nut with very oily flesh. **ZONES 10–11.**

HESPERALOE

The name of this small genus is made up of the word *Aloe* and the Greek prefix *hesper-*, meaning 'of the west' (or the sunset), and refers to its geographical distribution in southwestern USA and northern Mexico. In fact the genus, consisting of 3 species of perennials, is most closely related to *Yucca* and its resemblance to the African *Aloe* is superficial. The plants have deeply buried rootstocks with narrow, tough, grass-like leaves whose margins have a fibrous texture with some fibers detaching as curled grey or white hairs. The flowers, borne in spikes from 4–8 ft (1.2–2.4 m), are tubular and more or less pendulous in shades of dull pink, red and green, and may be followed by capsular fruit.
CULTIVATION: These are long-lived evergreen plants that require a dry climate and very open, well-drained soil; their most appropriate use is in a desert garden or, in wetter regions, in a large succulent house. Normally raised from seed, they usually take several years to reach flowering size.

Hesperaloe funifera
syns *Agave funifera*, *Yucca funifera*

A small succulent from northern Mexico, this species features long, narrow, green leaves. It blooms from spring to fall (autumn), bearing greenish, bell-shaped flowers roughly ½ in (12 mm) across. **ZONES 7–11.**

Hesperaloe parviflora
syns *Aloe yuccaefolia*, *Yucca parviflora*

Native to Mexico and southwest Texas, this succulent has long, narrow, green leaves. In spring it bears pinkish red, bell-shaped flowers 1½ in (35 mm) wide. **ZONES 7–11.**

HESPERIS

From the Mediterranean and temperate Asia, this genus consists of 60 species of biennials and herbaceous perennials allied to stocks *(Matthiola)*. They have narrow, usually undivided leaves that may be toothed or toothless, and showy pink, purple or white flowers in long racemes. The flowers of some species are fragrant.
CULTIVATION: The species are readily grown in temperate areas and will naturalize, but cultivars sometimes prove more difficult. Frost hardy, they prefer full sun and moist but well-drained, neutral to alkaline, not too fertile soil. Propagate from seed or cuttings and check regularly for mildew and also for attack from slugs and snails.

Hesperis matronalis
DAME'S ROCKET, SWEET ROCKET

Ranging from Europe to central Asia, *Hesperis matronalis* is grown for its flowers which become very fragrant on humid evenings. It has smooth, narrowly oval leaves and branching flowerheads with white to lilac flowers borne in summer. Upright in habit, this species grows 12–36 in (30–90 cm) in height with a spread of about 24 in (60 cm). Plants lose their vigor after a time and are best renewed every 2 to 3 years. **ZONES 3–9.**

HESPEROCALLIS
DESERT LILY

This genus consists of a single species of bulbous lily from arid areas of southwestern USA. The plant has a deeply buried bulb from which arises a basal tuft of long, slender leaves that tend to flop on the ground; they have whitish undulating margins. The thick, erect flower spikes bear upward-facing fragrant white flowers with a green central stripe on each petal.
CULTIVATION: They prefer full sun and gritty, dry soil. Successful cultivation requires fairly warm, dry conditions and in colder, wetter climates these plants can probably only be grown well in a cactus house or in a very hot, dry position against a wall. Propagate from seed or bulb offsets.

Hesperocallis undulata
DESERT LILY

This lily is usually no more than 12 in (30 cm) high when in flower in late spring or summer. The flowers are funnel-shaped and about 3 in (8 cm) in diameter. **ZONES 9–11.**

HETEROCENTRON
syn. *Schizocentron*

About 27 species of shrubby or creeping plants make up this genus which is allied to *Tibouchina*. Originating in Mexico and Central and South America, *Heterocentron* are grown for their showy, 4-petalled, white, pink, mauve or purple flowers which appear from summer to winter.
CULTIVATION: These plants grow well in sun or part-shade in well-drained soil. They are frost tender, and need a minimum temperature of 40°F (5°C). Propagate from cuttings in late winter or early spring.

Heterocentron elegans
syn. *Schizocentron elegans*
SPANISH SHAWL

Native to Central America, *Heterocentron elegans* is a prostrate, evergreen perennial. It is a popular ground cover in areas of warm climate. The foliage is dense, trailing and mid-green, and masses of bright carmine-purple flowers cover the plant in summer. This plant grows to a height of 2 in (5 cm) with an indefinite spread. **ZONES 10–11.**

Heterocentron elegans

Heteromeles arbutifolia

Heterocentron macrostachyum
syn. *Heterocentron roseum*
PEARL FLOWER

This small evergreen shrub from Mexico has handsome red-edged leaves that are small, hairy and oval. It bears clusters of cerise flowers blooming in fall (autumn). It grows to a height of 3 ft (1 m) and spreads easily to 24 in (60 cm). **ZONES 10–11.**

HETEROMELES
CALIFORNIA HOLLY, CHRISTMAS BERRY, TOYON

This genus consists of one species, an evergreen tall shrub or small tree that was formerly included in *Photinia*. Indigenous to the drier regions of California, it is often planted as an informal screen, and can be clipped to form a tall hedge. It grows to 30 ft (9 m). When young it can be pruned to maintain a single trunk if a tree form is desired. A member of the rose family, its name comes from the Greek words for 'different' and 'apple tree'.
CULTIVATION: *Heteromeles arbutifolia* needs full sun or part-shade and moderately fertile, well-drained soil. It is frost hardy, although in colder regions it needs protection. Propagate from cuttings in summer or seed in fall (autumn).

Heteromeles arbutifolia
syn. *Photinia arbutifolia*

This shrub or tree has thick, leathery, glossy dark green leaves with quite sharply toothed margins. The flattened heads of flowers appear in summer. They are followed by bright red berries that persist, as they are not eaten by birds until winter in its native habitat. **ZONES 9–11.**

HETEROTHECA

From the southern parts of the USA and Mexico comes this genus of around 20 species of annuals and perennials in the daisy family. The leaves, which may be silvery or green, smooth edged or toothed, form a basal clump from which (usually) branched flower stems arise. Species vary in height from about 8 in (20 cm) to 5 ft (1.5 m).
CULTIVATION: They are best grown in dry, sandy or gravelly soil in full sun. Where winters are always frosty, plants may rot if that season is also rainy and will need some shelter. In areas with milder winters, rain has no ill-effect so long as soil drains fast. Propagate annuals from seed sown in spring; perennial species by division in spring.

Heterotheca villosa
syn. *Chrysopsis villosa*
HAIRY GOLDEN ASTER

A variable perennial from Texas and New Mexico, this species is sometimes erect, sometimes sprawling, and has hairy, gray-green leaves and 1 in (25 mm) wide golden-yellow flowerheads in summer and fall (autumn). In hot, dry locations, this species may only reach a height of 8 in (20 cm) but in better soil with regular water it may grow over 30 in (75 cm) tall. It is frost hardy. **'San Bruno Mountain'** is a form selected for attractive foliage and profusion of flowers. **ZONES 5–9.**

Heterotheca v. 'San Bruno Mountain'

HEUCHERA
ALUM ROOT, CORAL BELLS

There are about 55 species of these evergreen and semi-evergreen perennials, native to North America and Mexico. They form neat clumps of scalloped leaves, often tinted bronze or purple, from which arise stems bearing masses of dainty, nodding, white, crimson or pink bell flowers often over a long flowering season. They make useful ground covers and woodland plants, or they may be used as rock garden or edging plants.
CULTIVATION: Mostly very frost hardy, they grow well in either full sun or semi-shade and like well-drained, coarse, moisture-retentive soil. Propagate species from seed in fall (autumn) or by division in spring or fall; cultivars by division in fall or early spring. Remove spent flower stems and divide established clumps every 3 or 4 years.

Heuchera × *brizoides*

This group are all complex hybrids involving *Heuchera sanguinea* and several other species. Highly attractive plants, they produce mounds of rounded, lobed leaves that are prettily marbled. Above these rise tall, slender, arching stems bearing dainty bell-like flowers in white, as in **'June Bride'**, or shades of pink or red. Foliage mounds are about 12 in (30 cm) tall with flower stems rising at least another 12 in (30 cm). **ZONES 3–10.**

Heuchera maxima

Heuchera × *brizoides* 'June Bride'

Heuchera maxima
ISLAND ALUMROOT

Found only on the islands off the southern Californian coast, this species has big, coarse, deeply lobed and cut leaves and bears its small, pinkish white flowers on thick, sturdy stems. It grows well in dry, dappled shade and is marginally frost hardy. **ZONES 9–10.**

Heuchera micrantha var. *diversifolia* 'Palace Purple'

This cultivar is grown for its striking, purple, palmate leaves and panicles of tiny white flowers in summer. It is clump forming, with a height and spread of about 18 in (45 cm). The leaves last well as indoor decoration. **ZONES 5–10.**

Heuchera m. var. *d.* 'Palace Purple'

Heuchera × *brizoides*

× *Heucherella tiarelloides*

Heuchera pilosissima

Heuchera 'Pewter Veil'

Heuchera 'Pewter Veil'

This beautiful hybrid has silvery green leaves with a contrasting network of deep green veins. Pinkish red flowers appear on stout, red stems. **ZONES 5–10.**

Heuchera pilosissima
SHAGGY ALUMROOT

Compact and free flowering, this Californian species has maple-like lobed and toothed leaves that are rather hairy to the touch. In late spring, pink or white flowers are generously borne on the tall stems typical of the genus. **ZONES 6–10.**

Heuchera sanguinea
CORAL BELLS

This, the most commonly grown species, occurs naturally from Arizona to New Mexico. It grows to 18 in (45 cm) and has sprays of scarlet or coral red flowers above toothed, deeply lobed leaves. British and American gardeners have developed strains with a wider color range—from pale pink to deep red—and slightly larger flowers. Bressingham hybrids are typical. **ZONES 6–10.**

Heuchera sanguinea

Heuchera 'Taff's Joy'

This clump-forming hybrid bears panicles of delicate pink flowers in early summer, and features leaves with cream and pink variegations. **ZONES 3–10.**

Heuchera villosa

From the mountains of eastern USA, this species has glossy, bronze-green leaves with pointed, triangular lobes. The flowers are usually white but may be pink. **ZONES 5–10.**

× HEUCHERELLA

This hybrid genus is the result of a cross between *Heuchera* and *Tiarella*, both members of the saxifrage family. Plants are evergreen, clumping or ground-covering perennials with tall, airy stems of dainty pink or white flowers. These are produced over a long season beginning in late spring. The leaves are rounded, lobed and have distinct veins. When young they are bronze-red, turning green during summer then reddish in fall (autumn).
CULTIVATION: Heucherellas are easy to grow and enjoy leafy, rich, moist but well-drained soil. Where summers are mild, full sun is best, but in hotter areas dappled or part-shade suits them and they will do reasonably well in full shade that is not too dark. Propagation by division is easy and this should be done in fall or winter in mild areas, spring in cooler places.

× *Heucherella tiarelloides*

Growing about 12 in (30 cm) tall with flower stems rising a further 12–15 in (30–38 cm), this fully hardy perennial

Heuchera villosa

spreads by creeping stolons. The leaves are lobed and toothed and form a dense, rounded mound. Small pink flowers appear on red stems. In the cultivar **'Bridget Bloom'** the flowers are a soft, pastel pink and very freely produced. **ZONES 5–9.**

HEVEA

Nine species make up this tropical American genus, which includes the rubber tree, *Hevea brasiliensis*, the major source of natural rubber. All species, as with others of the euphorbia family, have a milky sap. The flowers are small, fragrant and pale yellow, and the leaves are compound with 3 large leaflets.
CULTIVATION: Tropical heat and humidity are essential to the commercial cultivation of these trees, although they can be grown as curiosities in large heated greenhouses where they should be pruned in late winter to restrict size and maintain a neat shape. They need moist, free-draining soil and part-shade in the heat of summer. Propagate from seed, which must be very fresh.

Hevea brasiliensis
PARA RUBBER TREE

This tree, native to the Amazon and Orinoco rivers in South America, reaches 120 ft (36 m) but elsewhere it seldom exceeds 60 ft (18 m). The thick, leathery leaves are divided into 3 leaflets and the greenish white perfumed flowers appear before or with the new growth, which is a distinctive bronze-purple. It is rarely grown other than in commercial plantations or in botanical gardens. **ZONES 11–12.**

Hevea brasiliensis

HIBBERTIA
GOLDEN GUINEA FLOWER

There are more than 120 species of these evergreen shrubs and climbers with their pretty yellow flowers, and almost all are indigenous to Australia. They are known as guinea flowers because the buttercup-like blooms are as yellow as a golden guinea. They are related to dillenias and the flowers look very similar though they are smaller.
CULTIVATION: Any moderately fertile, well-drained soil is suitable. Hibbertias will grow in full sun or semi-shade and are a good choice for sandy, coastal gardens as they tolerate salt spray. Marginally frost hardy, they are ideal for warm climates. Lightly prune to shape in spring and propagate from cuttings in late summer. Gray mold can be a problem in winter.

Hibbertia cuneiformis
syns ***Hibbertia obcuneata, H. tetrandra***
CUTLEAF GUINEA FLOWER

This small to medium shrub comes from the southwest of Western Australia where it grows up to 10 ft (3 m) with a spread of up to 6 ft (1.8 m). It has bright green, 1 in (25 mm), oblong, wedge-shaped leaves with a few apical teeth, and produces 1–2 in (2.5–5 cm) golden yellow flowers on axillary shoots, mainly in spring. **ZONES 10–11.**

Hibbertia procumbens

This prostrate shrub has characteristically yellow flowers, $1\frac{1}{2}$ in (35 mm) across, borne profusely in summer. It grows as a tangled mat of weak branches with narrow leaves, seldom more than 6 in (15 cm) in height and is a good choice for rockeries. **ZONES 10–11.**

Hibbertia scandens
GUINEA GOLD VINE

This soft twining climber or trailing plant can grow up to 20 ft (6 m) high or can be trained along the ground as an effective ground cover. It has broad, dark green leaves and large, showy, buttercup yellow flowers from spring through the warmer months. It looks very effective trained over a pergola or arch. **ZONES 9–11.**

Hibbertia cuneiformis

Hibiscus heterophyllus

Hibiscus cisplatinus

HIBISCUS

While the genus name conjures up the innumerable cultivars of *Hibiscus rosa-sinensis*, the genus of around 220 species is quite diverse, including hot-climate evergreen shrubs and small trees and also a few deciduous, temperate-zone shrubs and some annuals and perennials. The leaves are mostly toothed or lobed and the flowers, borne singly or in terminal spikes, are of characteristic shape with a funnel of 5 overlapping petals and a central column of fused stamens.

CULTIVATION: Easy to grow, the shrubby species thrive in sun and slightly acid, well-drained soil. Water regularly and feed during the flowering period. Trim after flowering to maintain shape. Propagate from seed or cuttings or by division, depending on the species. Check for aphids, mealybugs and whitefly. The *H. rosa-sinensis* cultivars make greenhouse subjects in frosty climates, and compact-growing cultivars are gaining popularity as house plants.

Hibiscus arnottianus

This shrub of variable size, up to 20 ft (6 m), has long, arching branches covered with mid-green leaves and lightly scented, white single flowers with 5 petals surrounding a central red column. It is a warm-climate shrub suited to full sun; it can stand neglect, but responds well to regular watering and feeding. **'Wilder's White'** is a free-flowering cultivar now regarded as belonging to this species rather than to *Hibiscus rosa-sinensis*. **ZONES 9–11.**

Hibiscus calyphyllus

This tropical African species is a shrub of 3–6 ft (1–1.8 m) with 3–4 in (8–10 cm)

Hibiscus mutabilis

blooms distinguished by a purple-brown eye contrasting with the yellow of the petals. **ZONES 10–11.**

Hibiscus cisplatinus

This is a shrub growing at least 10 ft (3 m) tall with thorny branches and curious, rectangular-petalled flowers. These are large and pink with each petal being longitudinally veined in a darker pink. The leaves are dark green, up to 6 in (15 cm) long and somewhat variable in shape. The plant is native to Argentina and Brazil and is tolerant of the occasional light frost only. **ZONES 10–11.**

Hibiscus coccineus

This tall perennial species from the marshes of Georgia and Florida in the USA has distinctively shaped petals, each petal narrowing at the base to a slender basal stalk. The elegant flower, up to 8 in (20 cm) wide, also has the long column of stamens typical of many hibiscus, which dusts the head and back of birds with pollen. **ZONES 7–11.**

Hibiscus heterophyllus
AUSTRALIAN ROSELLA, SCRUB KURRAJONG

This tall, evergreen shrub to 20 ft (6 m) high has narrow, heavily veined leaves with serrated margins or deeply 3-lobed on stronger shoots. The flowers, usually white or pale pink but sometimes yellow with a darker center, appear in summer and fall (autumn). The flower buds and young shoots are edible, cooked or raw; however, the small prickles on the stems and leaves can cause skin irritation. **ZONES 9–11.**

Hibiscus insularis

Hibbertia scandens

Hibiscus insularis
PHILLIP ISLAND HIBISCUS

Endemic to tiny Phillip Island, which lies off Norfolk Island in the southwest Pacific, this species is now close to extinction in the wild. It is a spreading shrub up to 12 ft (3.5 m) tall, branching low into a tangle of very woody stems supporting a twiggy canopy of fine foliage. The leaves are coarsely toothed and the 2 in (5 cm) diameter flowers appear all through fall (autumn) and winter and sporadically at other times; they open lemon yellow with a maroon center and age to dull pink. **ZONES 10–11.**

Hibiscus moscheutos
COMMON ROSE MALLOW, SWAMP ROSE MALLOW

Native to North America, this herbaceous perennial grows to 8 ft (2.4 m) high and 3–5 ft (1–1.5 m) wide. Single, hollyhock-like flowers 4–8 in (10–20 cm) wide are carried on robust, unbranched stems in late summer and fall (autumn). Colors vary from white to pink, some with deeper throat markings. The leaves are large, toothed and softly hairy beneath. A range of lower-growing cultivars with dramatic large flowers has been bred from this species, including **'Southern Belle'** with rose-pink blooms up to 10 in (25 cm) across. **ZONES 5–9.**

Hibiscus mutabilis
CONFEDERATE ROSE, COTTON ROSE

A multi-branched shrub or small deciduous tree with a low-branching habit, the cotton rose comes from China and grows to about 12 ft (3.5 m) tall and almost as wide. The large flowers open white and age from pale pink to deep pink; they appear in fall (autumn) and are held among the felty, multi-lobed leaves. **'Plenus'**, with its double flowers, is the most commonly grown cultivar. **ZONES 8–10.**

Hibiscus moscheutos 'Southern Belle'

Hibiscus arnottianus

Hibiscus coccineus

Hibiscus calyphyllus

H

Hibiscus rosa-sinensis
CHINESE HIBISCUS, RED HIBISCUS, SHOEFLOWER

The name shoeflower is Jamaican, from the unromantic use of crushed flowers to polish black shoes. The species itself is of ancient hybrid origin from the Indian Ocean region and is a glossy leafed evergreen shrub, sometimes as much as 15 ft (4.5 m) high and wide, with blood-red flowers borne just about all year. It is less often seen than its numerous garden cultivars, some pure-bred and others, like the enormous blooming Hawaiian hybrids, carrying the genes of other species. These plants grow 3–10 ft (1–3 m) high, and the flowers can be 5-petalled singles, semi-double or fully double, the colors ranging from white through pinks to red; the Hawaiian hybrids offer yellow, coral and orange, often with 2 or 3 shades in each flower. The flowers range upwards in size from about 5 in (12 cm): some of the Hawaiian hybrids are as large as dinner plates. Each flower only lasts a day, opening in the morning and withering by evening, but they appear in long succession as long as the weather is warm. All the *Hibiscus rosa-sinensis* cultivars like a frost-free climate. They include **'Surfrider'** with single flowers that are deep orange with a red center; **'Fiesta'** with dark apricot flowers with red and white centers; **'Covakanic'** with flowers in beautiful varying tones of orange and apricot; as well as **'Apple Blossom'**, **'Cooperi'**, **'Madonna'** and **'Sabrina'**. ZONES 10–12.

Hibiscus rosa-sinensis Hawaiian Hybrid

Hibiscus rosa-sinensis Hawaiian Hybrid

Hibiscus schizopetalus

From tropical Africa, this evergreen shrub grows to 12 ft (3.5 m) with rounded, toothed, deep green leaves and long-stemmed, pendulous, scarlet flowers; their petals are recurved and much cut, and the staminal column hangs as though on a silken thread. Pruning is not necessary as its natural, somewhat slender, drooping habit is part of this plant's charm. This species is closely allied to *Hibiscus rosa-sinensis* and has interbred with it. ZONES 10–11.

Hibiscus syriacus
BLUE HIBISCUS, ROSE OF SHARON

This upright, deciduous shrub (evergreen in warmer climates) from temperate Asia is the most frost hardy of the genus. It flowers freely in summer in varying shades of white, pink, soft red, mauve and violet blue. The single, semi-double and double flowers are bell-shaped and are borne in the axils of the leaves. It has small, hairless leaves and grows to 12 ft (3.5 m) tall with a spread of 3–6 ft (1–1.8 m). Prune to shape in the

Hibiscus rosa-sinensis 'Covakanic'

Hibiscus syriacus 'Woodbridge'

Hibiscus syriacus cultivar

Hibiscus rosa-sinensis 'Surfrider'

Hibiscus syriacus 'Diana'

Hibiscus schizopetalus

Hibiscus syriacus 'Blue Bird'

first 2 years of growth, trimming lightly thereafter to maintain compact form. Popular cultivars include **'Ardens'** with large, mauve flowers with crimson centers; **'Blue Bird'** with single, violet blue flowers with red centers; **'Diana'** with broad, pure white flowers; and **'Woodbridge'** with 2-toned pink blooms at least 4 in (10 cm) across. **ZONES 5–10.**

Hibiscus tiliaceus

COTTONWOOD TREE, MANGROVE HIBISCUS, SEA HIBISCUS

This evergreen tree from tropical seashores of the Indian and Pacific Oceans grows to a height and spread of about 30 ft (9 m). It has large, heart-shaped, soft mid-green leaves with whitish undersides and bears scattered clear yellow flowers with large crimson centers turning orange as they fade. There are cultivars with purple and variegated leaves. It flowers for most of the year, prolifically in summer. **ZONES 10–11.**

Hibiscus trionum

BLADDER KETMIA, FLOWER-OF-AN-HOUR

This weed of cultivation and waste places is cosmopolitan, being found throughout warm parts of the world. It may be an annual or biennial herb or subshrub to 3 ft (1 m) high and 24 in (60 cm) wide. The hairy leaves are usually divided into deep lobes, with these further lobed or toothed. Each morning in summer and fall (autumn) it produces a sprinkling of smallish pale yellow flowers with a deep crimson, almost black center. It self seeds readily. **ZONES 9–11.**

HIERACIUM

HAWKWEED

Hawkweeds are found throughout most of the world excluding Australasia. Few genera of temperate herbaceous plants have caused botanists as many headaches as this genus of dandelion relatives, on account of its rapidly evolving forms especially in the post-glacial landscapes of Europe and northern Asia. Thousands of names have been given to small variations, treated by some botanists as species but by others as mere 'microspecies'. At present about 250 groups of these microspecies can be distinguished. They are mostly perennials, the majority small and often weedy, but including a few of some worth as ornamentals. The plants have a strong tap root and a rosette of basal leaves; from this arise one or more flowering stems each with a single flowerhead like that of a dandelion, or branching into several smaller flowerheads; the colors are mostly yellow, orange or red.

CULTIVATION: The species with more attractive foliage make good rock garden plants, thriving in well-drained, poor soil in a sunny position. Propagate from seed or by root division.

Hibiscus tiliaceus, variegated

Hibiscus tiliaceus

Hibiscus trionum

Hippeastrum 'Apple Blossom'

Hippeastrum 'Carnival'

Hippeastrum 'Cocktail'

Hippeastrum 'Kalahari'

Hieracium lanatum

This perennial from limestone mountains of France and northern Italy has striking, broadly spoon-shaped leaves 4–6 in (10–15 cm) long with a short dense coating of whitish hairs that give the leaf a pale gray hue. The flowering stems branch into loose panicles up to 18 in (45 cm) tall of golden-yellow flowerheads about 1 in (25 mm) across, opening in late spring and early summer. **ZONES 5–9.**

HIPPEASTRUM

AMARYLLIS, BARBADOS LILY

These spectacular trumpet-shaped tropical lilies, indigenous to South America, are cultivated virtually everywhere as pot plants. There are more than 80 species but it is the intensely developed hybrids that are most often grown. These have been bred mainly by the Dutch and are known as Dutch Hybrids; they include **'Apple Blossom'** and **'Cocktail'**. Other striking cultivars include **'Carnival'**, **'Desert Dawn'**, the beautiful red **'Kalahari'** and **'Red Lion'**. Nurseries sometimes use their old genus name, *Amaryllis*. The flowers can be up to 12 in (30 cm) across and are borne, before the leaves develop, in clusters of 3 or 4 atop a large hollow stem. Colors include white, pink, red and pink, and red streaked with white. Hippeastrums normally flower at the end of spring, but in the northern hemisphere potted plants can be coaxed into flowering out of season to make colorful Christmas decorations. They generally grow to 24 in (60 cm) high and 12 in (30 cm) wide.

CULTIVATION: Hippeastrums grow outdoors in a frost-free, warm climate. Bulbs should be planted in fall (autumn) in well-drained soil rich in organic matter, with just the tip of the bulb exposed, in full sun or part-shade. Water and feed well through the growing season and allow the bulb to dry after the foliage dies down. Protect from snails.

Hippeastrum 'Desert Dawn'

Hoheria populnea

Hoheria sexstylosa

Hippeastrum 'Belinda'

'Belinda' has broad, deep crimson petals that shade to scarlet towards the base of each petal. **ZONES 10–11.**

Hippeastrum 'Christmas Gift'

This early-flowerer grows 18 in (45 cm) high and bears its white, 6 in (15 cm) flowers in early winter. **ZONES 10–11.**

Hippeastrum 'Orange Sovereign'

Reaching a height of 18 in (45 cm) and with a 12 in (30 cm) spread, this bulbous perennial bears its large orange-red flowers in winter. **ZONES 10–11.**

Hippeastrum 'Picotee'

'Picotee' has white flowers with red margins; the flowers are 6 in (15 cm) wide and appear in winter. **ZONES 10–11.**

HIPPOPHAE

These 3 species of thorny, deciduous shrubs and trees are valued for their toughness and their showy fall (autumn) berries. Both male and female plants must be grown together to obtain the fruit. Inconspicuous flowers appear in spring. Indigenous to cold-climate regions of Asia and northern Europe, they are found along the coast or river banks and in sandy woodlands. They are wind and salt resistant and make excellent hedges for coastal areas.
CULTIVATION: Species of *Hippophaë* grow best in full sun and tolerate dry or very sandy soil. Propagation is from seed in fall or from cuttings in summer.

Hoheria populnea

Hoheria lyallii

Hippophaë rhamnoides
SEA BUCKTHORN

Growing to a height and spread of about 20 ft (6 m) with a bushy, arching habit, this shrub or small tree has very narrow, gray-green leaves with paler undersides. Insignificant, yellowish flowers appear in clusters in spring, before the leaf growth. The bright orange berries are borne in dense clusters on the shoots of female plants and usually persist through winter. **ZONES 2–9.**

HOHERIA

This genus consists of 5 species of evergreen and deciduous small trees native to the forests of New Zealand. Of slender, upright habit, they are grown for their showy clusters of faintly perfumed white flowers which appear in summer and fall (autumn). Plants can be anywhere between 20–50 ft (6–15 m) high and flowering is usually followed by the appearance of fruit capsules.
CULTIVATION: Happiest in warm-temperate climates, they grow in sun or semi-shade in fertile, well-drained soil in areas with high summer rainfall. Straggly plants can be pruned by about one-third in winter and all plants benefit from a light annual pruning of the outer branches to maintain a tidy shape and abundant foliage. They are propagated from seed in fall or from cuttings in summer.

Hoheria lyallii
syn. ***Plagianthus lyallii***
LACEBARK

This deciduous tree from New Zealand can grow to 20 ft (6 m) tall. It has thick, fibrous bark, which gives it its common name. The toothed, oblong leaves are gray-green with a felty white underside; they are up to 4 in (10 cm) long. Fragrant white flowers appear in late summer and are followed by leathery, capsular fruit. The lacebark prefers a sunny position and soil rich in humus; it tolerates alkaline soil. **ZONES 7–10.**

Hoheria populnea
HOUHERE, NEW ZEALAND LACEBARK

A fast-growing evergreen, this tree forms a slender dome about 20 ft (6 m) high. The attractive, glossy, toothed leaves resemble those of a poplar. Glistening white, 5-petalled flowers with golden stamens are borne in profuse clusters on the younger shoots in late summer and early fall (autumn), followed by winged fruit capsules. Mature trees have distinctive, often flaky, pale brown and white bark. **ZONES 9–11.**

Hoheria sexstylosa
RIBBONWOOD

Narrowly conical in habit, this evergreen tree grows to 20 ft (6 m) tall; it has an erect trunk and main branches with drooping branchlets. The leaves are bright green and oval, with sharply toothed margins. Small clusters of sweetly fragrant star-shaped white flowers are borne abundantly in late summer and fall (autumn), followed by small, brown, winged fruit capsules. When young the plant is bushy and has more deeply toothed leaves. **ZONES 7–10.**

HOLBOELLIA

Except for the shrubby *Decaisnea,* the small lardizabala family consists of climbers, and *Holboellia,* with 5 species from China and the Himalayas, is a fairly typical genus quite similar in appearance to its allies *Stauntonia* and *Akebia.* The plants are evergreen, twining vigorously into the tops of small trees if allowed, and have compound leaves with 3 or more leathery leaflets. The flowers are whitish or purplish, the female flowers borne in small clusters near the base of new growth, the males in short drooping sprays at the ends of the previous year's growth. Narrow fleshy sepals, darker on the inside, form the bell-shaped flowers, which lack petals. They are sweetly fragrant on some plants. The purple fruits are plum-sized and contain black seeds; they are said to be edible, but are rarely produced freely in cultivation.
CULTIVATION: Although uncommon in gardens, these frost-hardy climbers are not difficult to grow in full sun or part-shade in well-drained, fertile, humus-rich soil—the main problem with established plants may be controlling their rampant growth. Propagate from seed or cuttings or by layering.

Holcus mollis 'Albovariegatus'

Holboellia latifolia

A native of the Himalayas, this climber makes luxuriant growth over the crowns of small trees if permitted, but can be kept to a smaller size on a trellis, post or stump. The leaves consist of 3 to 7 leathery, oblong leaflets up to $3\frac{1}{2}$ in (9 cm) long. Small pendent sprays of fleshy bell-shaped flowers appear in spring, the males white, the larger female flowers greenish white flushed purple. The purple fruit are cylindrical, about 2 in (5 cm) long and 1 in (25 mm) in diameter. **ZONES 8–10.**

HOLCUS
VELVET GRASS

This is a genus of 8 species of hairy annual or perennial grasses from Europe, temperate Asia and Africa. They have soft, mid-green or bluish green leaves and flat or folded leaf blades. Panicles of 2-flowered spikelets appear in summer.
CULTIVATION: Although some species have uses in landscaping, they are not commonly grown. Some have become weeds, especially in pasture situations, so they should not be planted near farmland or natural areas. They grow best in moist, rich soil in full sun and are fully hardy. Propagate by division.

Holcus mollis 'Albovariegatus'

Holcus species have a reputation for becoming invasive but this variegated form is far better behaved. It grows to about 15 in (38 cm) high and, unusually for an ornamental grass, it can be mowed into a lawn. Left to grow, the leaves are long, narrow and attractive as each blade is edged with wide white bands. The feathery flowerheads, which are not always produced by the variegated form, are typical of the grass family but not particularly showy. **ZONES 5–9.**

HOLMSKIOLDIA

This genus of 10 species of evergreen, sprawling shrubs or scrambling climbers is indigenous to warm-climate coastal regions from southeastern Africa and Madagascar to India. They are fast growing and generally suit tropical or subtropical gardens, but their range can be extended slightly by planting near a

Holmskioldia sanguinea

sheltering wall. The flowers are usually trumpet-shaped with a coral-red calyx. **CULTIVATION:** Full sun and well-drained, fertile soil suit them best, and ideally some type of support that allows their attractive and unusual flowers to be viewed from below. They are propagated from cuttings or from seed in summer. In cooler climates, they grow in greenhouse conditions.

Holmskioldia sanguinea

CHINESE HAT PLANT, PARASOL FLOWER

Its unique flowers are the main interest of this scrambling shrub: each is a narrow, orange-scarlet tube backed by a broad, circular calyx, appearing in dense terminal clusters through summer and fall (autumn). The mid-green leaves are pointed, oval and slightly serrated. Its long, trailing canes make it ideal for espaliering. Contain rampant growth by pruning after flowering and remove old canes. There are also yellow- and bronze-flowered forms. **ZONES 10–11.**

HOLODISCUS

The 8 or so members of this genus in the rose family all come from the western side of North America and extend through Central America as far south as Colombia. They are deciduous shrubs popular for their billowing habits and masses of small, usually creamy white flowers which are produced in great, hanging clusters. The often hairy leaves are rounded or spearhead-shaped and sometimes lobed and toothed. **CULTIVATION:** Grow in sun, part- or dappled shade in deep, fertile soil that contains plenty of rotted organic matter. In nature they are woodland plants, and in gardens they enjoy the company of other shrubs or trees. They make excellent screening or background shrubs but are graceful enough to be a feature shrub on their own. Prune right after bloom by removing about a quarter of the oldest stems at ground level. Shorten remaining branches. Propagate from ripe seed, from cuttings of semi-mature wood or by pegging down branches so that they form roots.

Holodiscus discolor

syn. *Spiraea discolor*

OCEAN SPRAY, MOUNTAIN SPRAY, CREAM BUSH

Ranging in the wild from British Columbia in Canada to southern California and New Mexico, this attractive shrub varies in size from 5–20 ft (1.5–6 m) in height and usually wider. The leaves, up to 3 in (8 cm) long, are shallowly lobed, deep green above and paler to whitish beneath. The tiny white flowers are massed in pendulous sprays up to 12 in (30 cm) long on all the branch tips, producing a wonderful foamy effect in summer. It occurs from sea-level to over 7,000 ft (2,100 m) in altitude in the Rocky Mountains. **ZONES 4–10.**

HOMALOCLADIUM

RIBBON BUSH, TAPEWORM PLANT

One species of evergreen shrub, alternatively included in the genus *Muehlenbeckia,* makes up this genus from the islands of the western Pacific Ocean. It is sometimes grown in tropical and subtropical gardens for foliage contrast. Although it does have leaves, these usually fall quickly after forming. What is left is a rounded, somewhat tangled mass of flat, segmented bright green stems which sometimes scramble into nearby shrubs. Insignificant greenish flowers appear along the edges of the stems in spring. **CULTIVATION:** In frost-free and warmer areas, grow this frost-tender plant in moisture-retentive, leafy, rich soil in sun or part-shade. Keep evenly moist but apply most water during the warmer half of the year, decreasing as winter approaches. Where winters are frosty, it can be grown in a heated greenhouse. If plants become untidy they can be trimmed to shape in mid- to late spring. Propagate from cuttings taken in summer; in warm climates these root easily, but in cooler areas bottom heat may be necessary.

Homalocladium platycladum

syn. *Muehlenbeckia platyclada*

There is some doubt as to the original home of this unusual shrub, as it has long been cultivated by villagers in New Guinea and the Solomon Islands but does not appear to grow wild there. In gardens, it grows 3–5 ft (1–1.5 m) tall with a similar spread. **ZONES 10–12.**

HOMERIA

CAPE TULIP

There are around 31 species of cormous perennials in this South African genus. They are winter-growing, spring-flowering, summer-deciduous plants that produce bright, star-like flowers in shades of orange, yellow and salmon pink. The leaves are grass-like and the corms carry a distinctive brown papery sheath. Most species, notably *Homeria collina* and *H. miniata,* are reported to be poisonous to livestock. **CULTIVATION:** Given the right climate and conditions (good drainage and plenty of sunlight) *Homeria* species grow well and can be invasive. Four species have become weeds in Australia so they should not be planted near natural areas outside their native habitat. Being from winter rainfall areas, they prefer dry summers. Propagate from seed or offsets.

Homeria collina

Homeria collina

syn. *Homeria breyniana*

Among the easiest of the South African bulbs for mild climates, this species presents a glorious display of salmon pink or yellow flowers in spring. Each bulb produces only one narrow leaf, which quickly withers after the flowers fade. The stems are 18 in (45 cm) tall, the flowers 2 in (5 cm) across. **ZONES 9–10.**

HOMORANTHUS

The 7 species of spreading or ground-covering shrubs in this genus of the myrtle family are all native to Australia, mostly along the east coast. All are evergreen with tiny, heath-like leaves and clusters of small, mostly yellowish blooms which have long, protruding styles. The stems are generally horizontal so the shrubs have a low, layered look. **CULTIVATION:** Grow in very well-drained soil of poor to average fertility. In humid areas an open, sunny position is best but in warm, dry climates a little afternoon shade is welcome. Although plants are tolerant of long dry periods, they always look better with consistent, even moisture. Low phosphorus, slow-release fertilizer may be lightly applied. Lightly trim if necessary but do not cut back hard as the plants may not regrow successfully.

Homoranthus flavescens

Ranging in height from 8–15 in (20–38 cm) but spreading as much as 5 ft (1.5 m), this makes an attractive ground cover especially for well-drained banks or other dryish, sunny areas. From spring to summer orange-yellow flowers dust the flat top of the plant, which remains dense and attractive without pruning. It tolerates light frosts. **ZONES 9–11.**

HOODIA

These 20 or so species of succulent, leafless perennials allied to *Stapelia* are natives of southern Africa. They are unusual plants composed of a series of angular, serrated-edged, gray-green stems covered with small tubercles that are often spine- or bristle-tipped. The stems range from 4–15 in (10–38 cm) long and 1–4 in (2.5–10 cm) in diameter. Large, multi-petalled, flat flowers develop between the angles of the stems near the tips. The flowers occur in a wide range of colors, often with contrasting markings. In the wild they appear after rain; in cultivation usually in late spring. **CULTIVATION:** Typical desert plants, these succulents prefer gritty, well-drained soil and a position in full sun. They prefer occasional deep watering to

Homalocladium platycladum

Homalocladium platycladum

Homoranthus flavescens

frequent sprinkling. Propagation is generally from seed, though large clumps may be carefully divided. Most species will tolerate light but not repeated freezing.

Hoodia bainii

This evergreen succulent is native to South Africa and has a cylindrical stem with spiralling tubercles. Yellow bell-shaped flowers up to $2\frac{1}{2}$ in (6 cm) across appear in spring. **ZONES 10–11.**

HORDEUM
BARLEY

Hordeum is a genus of 20 species or so of annual or perennial grasses from temperate regions worldwide. They have flat or rolled, light to mid-green or blue-green leaves. The flowers are suitable for use in dried flower arrangements, but the plants are free-seeding and often weedy.
CULTIVATION: These grasses are frost-hardy. Any temperate climate suits, but they prefer well-drained, fertile soil and full sun. Some species can become invasive.

Hordeum jubatum
SQUIRREL TAIL GRASS

Hordeum jubatum is quite densely tufted and has light green leaves growing to 6 in (15 cm). The stems bear dense, nodding panicles of long-bristled, soft spikes in mid-summer. Place these ornamental grasses where the light can shine through them, emphasizing their delicacy.
ZONES 5–10.

Hordeum junceum
FOXTAIL BARLEY, SQUIRREL GRASS

Growing 12–18 in (30–45 cm) tall (depending on the fertility of the soil), this is one of the best grasses for growing near flowers as it maintains a neat clump form. It has feathery flower clusters from summer to fall (autumn). The flower clusters retain their silkiness when dried.
ZONES 5–10.

Hordeum vulgare
BARLEY

An annual grass to 4 ft (1.2 m) tall grown as a grain or fodder crop, barley has been an important grain throughout recorded history, growing in areas too cold for wheat, corn and rice. It is sometimes grown as an ornamental or a curiosity in gardens but there are better, more attractive grasses for this purpose. Being a warm season annual it can be grown in most areas. **ZONES 3–11.**

HORMINUM

Horminum pyrenaicum is the only species in this genus found high on the rocky slopes and grasslands of Europe's Pyrenees and Alps. It is a perennial which produces rosettes of glossy deep green, quilted, toothed, ovate leaves from which rise stems bearing tubular or bell-shaped, lipped flowers.
CULTIVATION: Grow in peaty, well-drained but not overly rich soil in full sun. This is an alpine plant best suited to areas with mild summers where nights are cool. Keep evenly moist and feed once at the start of the growing season with a ration of slow-release fertilizer. Propagate from seed sown in fall (autumn) and exposed to low winter temperatures, or by dividing established clumps in spring.

Horminum pyrenaicum
DRAGON'S MOUTH, PYRENEAN DEADNETTLE

This perennial from the mountains of France and Spain produces rosettes of erect stems to 18 in (45 cm). It flowers in early summer, producing spikes of rich blue-violet flowers with a white striped throat. **ZONES 7–9.**

Hornstedtia scyphifera

Hordeum jubatum

Hosta 'Birchwood Parky's Gold'

Hordeum vulgare

HORNSTEDTIA

This genus is composed of 60 species of rarely seen rhizomatous perennials that are mostly native to tropical Asia, with one species found in far northern Australia. They are members of the ginger family and have upright, fleshy pseudostems up to 20 ft (6 m) tall. The leaves are large and simple, typical of the family. The flowers arise directly from the rhizome, separate from the leafy pseudostems.
CULTIVATION: Grow these frost-tender plants in rich, moisture-retentive yet well-drained soil in part- or dappled shade. Plants need plenty of water year round and require a steamy tropical climate for success. Propagate from fresh seed or by division of established clumps in early spring.

Hornstedtia scyphifera

Occurring wild in Malaysia, this species has pseudostems up to about 15 ft (4.5 m) tall. The flower clusters arise directly from a thick rhizome, surrounded by a goblet-shaped sheath of brown bracts spotted with small white scales—*scyphifera* is Latin for 'cup-bearing', referring to this sheath—and the glossy red flowers that emerge from the top are small and tubular. The plant grows in rainforest understory and is seldom cultivated. **ZONES 11–12.**

HOSTA
PLANTAIN LILY

Natives of Japan and China, the 40 species in this genus of easily grown, frost-hardy perennials are valued for their decorative foliage. They all produce wide, handsome leaves, some being marbled or marked with white and others a bluish green. All-yellow foliage forms are also available. They do well in large pots or planters, are excellent for ground cover, and add an exotic touch planted on the margins of lily ponds or in bog gardens. Tall stems to about 18 in (45 cm) of nodding white, pink or shades of purple and blue, bell- or trumpet-shaped flowers appear in warmer weather. Both the leaves and the flowers are popular for floral arrangements.
CULTIVATION: They grow well in shade and rich, moist, neutral, well-drained soil. Feed regularly during the growing season. Propagate by division in early spring, and guard against snails and slugs.

Hosta 'Birchwood Parky's Gold'
syn. *Hosta* 'Golden Nakaiana'

The big leaves of this hybrid open yellowish green but turn golden with age and as summer progresses. It is a strong-growing plant up to 18 in (45 cm) tall that slowly spreads to form large colonies. Mauve flowers are produced in late spring or summer. **ZONES 6–10.**

Hosta crispula

Hosta fortunei 'Albopicta'

Hosta fortunei 'Aureomarginata'

Hosta 'Gold Edger'

Hosta fortunei 'Albomarginata'

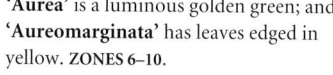

Hosta fortunei 'Aurea'

Hosta fortunei

Hosta crispula

This handsome species has elongated, lanceolate, distinctly pleated leaves. They are gray-green with creamy white margins. Pale lavender flowers are produced in early summer but it is the foliage that is the chief attraction. ZONES 6–10.

Hosta 'Eric Smith'

This hybrid has big, rounded leaves with a blue-green bloom and is best grown where summers are mild with cool nights. ZONES 6–10.

Hosta fortunei

This strong-growing perennial has given rise to many hybrids. It has ovate or broad lanceolate, pleated and pointed leaves that are a dull mid-green. In summer tall flower stems are produced from which hang lavender flowers. Plants grow at least 18 in (45 cm) tall but spread nearly twice as wide. **'Albomarginata'** has gray-green leaves with creamy yellow to white margins; **'Albopicta'** has leaves marbled or irregularly marked in 2 shades of green; **'Aurea'** is a luminous golden green; and **'Aureomarginata'** has leaves edged in yellow. ZONES 6–10.

Hosta 'Golden Sculpture'

Hosta 'Gold Edger'

Hosta 'Gold Edger' forms a 12 in (30 cm) tall mound of broad, yellowish green leaves and produces tall spikes of almost white flowers in summer. ZONES 6–10.

Hosta 'Golden Sculpture'

This big-leafed plant with quilted foliage is a combination of yellow and green overlaid with a powdery bloom. It is a vigorous grower. ZONES 6–10.

Hosta 'Golden Tiara'

'Golden Tiara' forms a dense mound of dull green leaves edged in golden green. As a bonus, it produces unusual striped purple flowers in summer. A compact plant, it rarely exceeds 12 in (30 cm) in height. ZONES 6–10.

Hosta 'Eric Smith'

Hosta 'Golden Tiara'

Hosta 'Halcyon'

Striking gray-blue leaves make 'Halcyon' an arresting sight, especially when contrasted against green or yellow foliage. Its summer flowers are a dusty mauve color. ZONES 6–10.

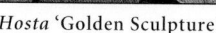

Hosta 'Halcyon'

Hosta 'June'

Hosta 'Pearl Lake'

Hosta 'Honeybells'

Hosta plantaginea

Hosta tokudama

Hosta tokudama 'Aureonebulosa'

Hosta lancifolia

Hosta 'Honeybells'

'Honeybells' has oval to heart-shaped leaves, about 10 in (25 cm) long, with strong veins. The short lived white flowers, opening from mauvish buds, are borne in late summer. Some are pleasantly scented in the evening. **ZONES 6–10.**

Hosta 'Hydon Sunset'

The leaves of this hybrid open lime green but age to yellow, creating a dense clump of various shades of yellow-green. The flowers are a deep lavender purple. **ZONES 6–10.**

Hosta 'June'

'June' has similar gray-blue leaves to its parent *Hosta* 'Halcyon', overlaid with splashes of yellow and green. **ZONES 6–10.**

Hosta 'Krossa Regal'

This hybrid has beautiful powdery gray-green leaves that are upward folded, wavy edged and distinctly pleated. **ZONES 6–10.**

Hosta lancifolia

NARROW LEAFED PLANTAIN LILY

This smaller-leafed species forms a clump to 18 in (45 cm) high and 30 in (75 cm) wide. It has narrow, lance-shaped, glossy mid-green leaves. It bears racemes of trumpet-shaped, pale lilac flowers in late summer and early fall (autumn). **ZONES 6–10.**

Hosta 'Pearl Lake'

The 4 in (10 cm) long leaves of this hybrid are plain gray-green with a slight powdery bloom. The lavender-blue flowers are are quite showy. **ZONES 6–10.**

Hosta plantaginea

AUGUST LILY, FRAGRANT PLANTAIN LILY

Popular for its pure white, fragrant flowers on 30 in (75 cm) stems, this species has mid-green leaves forming a mound 3 ft (1 m) across. It flowers in late summer. **ZONES 3–10.**

Hosta sieboldiana

This robust, clump-forming plant grows to 3 ft (1 m) high and 5 ft (1.5 m) wide. It has puckered, heart-shaped, bluish gray leaves and bears racemes of mauve buds opening to trumpet-shaped white flowers in early summer. **'Frances Williams'** has heart-shaped, puckered blue-green leaves with yellowish green margins. ***Hosta sieboldiana* var. *elegans*** also has heart-shaped, puckered leaves. **ZONES 6–10.**

Hosta 'Hydon Sunset'

Hosta tokudama

This very slow-growing perennial, native to Japan, has racemes of trumpet-shaped, pale mauve flowers that are borne above cup-shaped blue leaves in mid-summer. Clump forming, it reaches a height of 18 in (45 cm) and a spread of 30 in (75 cm). There are several cultivars available: **'Aureonebulosa'** has leaves splashed with green and yellow; **'Flavocircinalis'** has heart-shaped leaves with creamy margins. **ZONES 6–10.**

Hosta sieboldiana

Hosta 'Krossa Regal'

Hosta plantaginea

Hosta undulata

Hosta undulata
WAVY LEAFED PLANTAIN LILY

Hosta undulata has creamy white, wavy or twisted leaves that are splashed and streaked green along their edges. Mauve flowers on tall stems in summer complete this attractive and desirable specimen. **ZONES 6–10.**

Hosta ventricosa
BLUE PLANTAIN LILY

From China and Korea, this plant forms a tall clump of shiny, dark green leaves that are strongly veined and broadly heart-shaped. Tall stems of purple flowers appear in summer. **ZONES 6–10.**

HOTTONIA
FEATHERFOIL, WATER VIOLET

This genus comprises 2 species of aquatic perennials related to primulas and native to eastern USA, Europe and northern Asia. They develop a mat of small rosettes that may be submerged in shallow water or grow in mud at the water's edge. Leaves are divided into narrow lobes, the submerged leaves more finely than the emergent ones. Each plant produces numerous erect flowering stems.
CULTIVATION: Hottonias grow in still or gently moving water and are useful for oxygenation. Fish will also spawn around them. Some sun is needed to prevent the stems becoming stringy. Propagate by breaking off rooted pieces. They are frost hardy in any pond or stream that does not freeze solid. Like all water plants, they should not be introduced to waterways outside their native habitat.

Hottonia palustris
WATER VIOLET

This pretty plant is native through much of Europe as well as northern Asia. The many flowering stems are usually about 24 in (60 cm) high, with widely spaced whorls of starry flowers: these are up to 1 in (25 mm) across, white to lilac with yellow centres. The American featherfoil, ***Hottonia inflata***, is a smaller plant no more than about 8 in (20 cm) tall, with white flowers less than $^3/_8$ in (9 mm) across. **ZONES 6–9.**

HOUTTUYNIA

There is only one species in this genus, a wide-spreading, creeping herbaceous perennial from moist or wet, part- or fully shaded parts of eastern Asia. It is a good ground cover in moist, woodland gardens or beside ponds and can also grow in shallow water or boggy ground. The wild form has dark green, heart-shaped, red-margined, plain green leaves, and in summer bears spikes of tiny yellowish flowers with 4 pure white bracts at the base of each spike.
CULTIVATION: Grow this frost-hardy plant in moist, leafy rich soil. In cooler climates the plant will tolerate sun so long as the ground is moist, but in hotter places some shade is desirable. Where winters are always cold, reduce water in winter or cover the roots with a thick layer of straw. Propagate from ripe seed or from cuttings in late spring and early summer, or by division in spring.

Houttuynia cordata

Houttuynia cordata

Ranging from the Himalayas to Japan, this water-loving deciduous perennial makes a good ground cover but may become invasive. It is a vigorous plant, growing to 12 in (30 cm) in height with an indefinite spread. It grows from underground runners which send up bright red branched stems bearing aromatic green leaves. However, the most popular form, **'Chameleon'** (syns 'Tricolor', 'Variegata') is strikingly variegated in red, cream, pink and green. **ZONES 5–11.**

HOVENIA

This genus consists of 2 species of deciduous trees from Asia, only one of which is widely grown. They have small fragrant yellow flowers and small, spherical, capsular fruits held in branched stalks which become thick and fleshy. The leaves are toothed and oval to heart-shaped.
CULTIVATION: Graceful trees for temperate-climate gardens, they prefer full sun and well-drained, reasonably fertile soil. Protect from dry winds. Propagate from fresh seed in fall (autumn) or from cuttings in summer. Where wood is not fully ripened, check for coral spot.

Hovenia dulcis
JAPANESE RAISIN TREE

Indigenous to China and Japan, this tree grows to 50 ft (15 m). Its large, heart-shaped leaves produce brilliant fall (autumn) hues. The summer flowers are inconspicuous and lightly fragrant and are borne in clusters on thick stalks. As the small capsular fruit ripen, the stalks become fleshy and are also edible; they have a sweet taste like raisins. **ZONES 8–10.**

HOWEA
syn. *Kentia*

This genus of palms has only 2 species, both native to Lord Howe Island off eastern Australia and both widely cultivated. They have graceful, feather-like fronds on long, smooth stalks and a smooth, ringed, single trunk. The flowers are small and fleshy, borne in long, arching spikes that emerge among the frond bases and are followed by small red fruit. Lord Howe Islanders successfully export the seeds.
CULTIVATION: These palms are frost tender and need moist, humid conditions and some shade if they are to be kept outdoors. They are more commonly grown indoors, tolerating less light and needing less heat than most other palms. They can be kept in the same pot or tub for years, as long as the potting mix is well drained and contains some humus. Provide part-shade while they mature. They are propagated from seed in spring; constant warmth is required for germination.

Howea belmoreana
CURLY PALM, SENTRY PALM

Less commonly grown than *Howea forsteriana,* this species also tolerates a substantial amount of neglect. Outdoors, it may grow to 25 ft (8 m) high. It is a slender plant with a ringed trunk and strongly recurving, feather-shaped, dull green fronds. Long, flowering spikes bear the glossy, brown to red fruit. **ZONES 10–11.**

Hovenia dulcis

Houttuynia cordata 'Chameleon'

H

Howea forsteriana
KENTIA PALM, THATCH PALM

Growing wild in natural groves, this palm is best known as an indoor plant. Outdoors in warm climates it is slow growing to about 30 ft (9 m) with a slender trunk, and can withstand coastal conditions. Most effective when planted in groups, it needs to be protected from the sun when young. Provide adequate water during dry periods. **ZONES 10–11.**

HOYA
WAX FLOWER

Twiners or root climbers (sometimes both) with waxy foliage native to Southeast Asia, New Guinea and tropical Australia, hoyas all bear clusters of scented, star-shaped flowers in summer. They are waxy and resemble cake ornaments, one star sitting atop a larger one. If plants are supported on a frame and are also slightly potbound they are more likely to flower, but may not do so for several years. There are about 200 species. **CULTIVATION:** Plant in any potting soil that drains well in bright to very bright light, with moderate temperatures and humidity. Allow the soil surface to become quite dry between waterings. As the new flowers come from the same spurs as the old ones, it is best not to prune or pick. Propagate from semi-ripe cuttings in summer. Be careful where you place the plant as sticky nectar drips from the flowers. Check for mealybugs under glass.

Hoya carnosa
WAX PLANT

Native to eastern India, southern China and Burma, this twining plant can be grown against a small framework. It has dark green, glossy, oval leaves from summer to fall (autumn) and bears scented, star-shaped flowers, white to pink in color and with dark pink centers. **'Compacta'** has twisted, upward-folded leaves that give the plant a curious rope-like appearance. **ZONES 10–11.**

Hoya lanceolata subsp. *bella*
syn. ***Hoya bella***
BEAUTIFUL HONEY PLANT, MINIATURE WAX PLANT

This compact, shrubby Himalayan species has arching stems and bright green, narrow, lance-shaped leaves. It looks best when grown in a hanging pot or basket where the summer flowers can be admired. Star-shaped white flowers, with red or purplish pink centers, hang in flattened clusters. **ZONES 10–11.**

Hoya lanceolata subsp. *bella*

Hoya santos × *cumingiana*

This lovely hybrid has flowerheads that look like a cluster of sugared shooting stars. Each bloom has a small, reddish star attached to backward-pointing creamy beige petals. **ZONES 10–11.**

Hoya santos × *cumingiana*

Hoya serpens

The flowers of some hoyas are covered with minute hairs to give a soft downy effect. Such is the case with *Hoya serpens*, a rather rare species from the Indian state of Sikkim with flowers about ½ in (12 mm) wide. **ZONES 10–11.**

HUERNIA
DRAGON FLOWER

These small, grayish evergreen succulents, related to stapelias, are native to South and East Africa; the genus consists of some 60 to 70 species. Reaching no more than 6 in (15 cm) high, they are known for their slightly carrion-smelling, bell-shaped flowers which are spotted and up to 1½ in (35 mm) across. **CULTIVATION:** All species enjoy part-shade and moderately fertile, sandy, very well-drained soil. Propagate from seed or cuttings. They are susceptible to caterpillars and mealybug.

Howea forsteriana

Hoya serpens

Hoya carnosa 'Compacta'

Hoya carnosa

Huernia zebrina
OWL EYES

Native to South Africa, this small evergreen grows to a height of 3 in (8 cm). The flowers are greenish yellow closely barred with maroon and 1½ in (35 mm) wide. **ZONES 10–11.**

HUMULUS
HOP

Two species of herbaceous perennial twiners from northern temperate regions comprise this genus. These members of the hemp family produce annual vines from an overwintering rootstock and have palmate or heart-shaped leaves and rough stems that are prostrate if not supported. Male and female flowers occur on separate plants. The heads and fruits of *Humulus lupulus* are used throughout the world to give the bitter flavor to beer. **CULTIVATION:** Hop plants require a cool-temperate climate with plenty of moisture in spring and a warm summer. They grow best in deep, well-drained, loamy soil. Plant in early spring once frosts are finished. Propagate from seed or by division in spring. They are useful for screening. Hops may suffer from a number of fungal diseases as well as occasionally being troubled by aphids and spider mites in drier weather.

Humulus lupulus
COMMON HOP

This species is native to Europe, Asia and North America, although the North American form is sometimes classified as *Humulus americanus.* It has rough stems that allow the plant to climb, always twining in a clockwise direction, to around 30 ft (9 m). Its mid-green, heart-

Humulus lupulus 'Aureus'

shaped or lobed leaves are up to 6 in (15 cm) wide. The small, green-yellow male and female flowers are carried on separate plants; the males are held in panicles, while the females are in a cone-shaped cluster and covered with scales. Borne in late summer, it is the female flowerheads that develop into hops, and it is for this essential part of the brewing industry that it has been cultivated for centuries. **'Aureus'** has yellow-green foliage, making it a highly desirable screen for sheds and fences. **ZONES 5–9.**

Hunnemannia fumariifolia

Hyacinthoides hispanica

HUNNEMANNIA
MEXICAN TULIP POPPY, GOLDEN CUP

This genus consists of one species of poppy found in dry, elevated parts of Mexico. It has an upright habit and is fast growing to a height of 24 in (60 cm) with a spread of 8 in (20 cm). It has decorative, oblong, finely dissected, bluish green leaves and bears rich, glowing yellow, single or semi-double, 3 in (8 cm) wide, poppy-like flowers in summer and early fall (autumn). **CULTIVATION:** Grow in full sun in free-draining, sandy or gravelly soil. Plants do not enjoy cold, wet winters although they can withstand considerable frost in their native range where winter days are sunny. In the UK and similar cool, rainy climates they are often grown as annuals, the seed sown under glass in late winter or early spring. Deadhead plants regularly to prolong flowering and provide support in exposed areas. Water liberally during hot weather.

Hunnemannia fumariifolia

One of the best yellow-flowered perennials, this relative of the California poppy

Hyacinthoides non-scripta

Humulus lupulus 'Aureus'

Humulus lupulus

Huernia zebrina

(Eschscholzia californica) is grown as an annual in frost-prone areas. **ZONES 8–10.**

HYACINTHOIDES
syn. **Endymion**
BLUEBELL

The frost-hardy European bluebells, vigorous, bulbous perennials with attractive, scented flowers, are popular with gardeners in temperate regions worldwide. They have strap- to lance-shaped, basal leaves. The flowers are usually blue or white but sometimes pink. The 3 or 4 species are equally happy in a rock garden, naturalized under deciduous trees or in flower borders. **CULTIVATION:** They thrive in moist, part-shaded conditions. Bulbs should be planted in fall (autumn) in rich, moist soil. Water well until the flowers start to die. They should multiply freely but are best left undisturbed for a few years, and then divided in late summer.

Hyacinthoides hispanica 'Azalea'

Hyacinthoides hispanica
syns ***Endymion hispanicus, Scilla campanulata, S. hispanica***
SPANISH BLUEBELL

The most popular and most easily grown species, *Hyacinthoides hispanica* grows to about 12 in (30 cm) and flowers in spring. The 1 in (25 mm) wide, nodding, bell-shaped flowers are lilac to blue. The bright green foliage is strap-like. It multiplies freely. **'Azalea'** is a compact, free-flowering form with many shorter spikes of pink-lilac flowers. **ZONES 5–10.**

Hyacinthoides non-scripta
syns ***Endymion non-scriptus, Scilla non-scripta***
ENGLISH BLUEBELL

This plant flowers from early spring to summer. The fragrant, semi-pendulous, bell-shaped flowers in lavender blue, pink or white are about ½ in (12 mm) long and hang off one side of the fine, nodding stems that grow to about 12 in (30 cm) tall. The slender, strap-like foliage is glossy green. **ZONES 5–10.**

Hyacinthus orientalis 'King of the Blues'

Hyacinthus orientalis 'Columbus'

Hyacinthus orientalis 'Lady Derby'

Hyacinthus orientalis

HYACINTHUS

HYACINTH

There are 3 species in this genus of bulbs from Asia Minor and central Asia, all spring flowering. Bulbs are squat and have a tunic of fleshy scales. The glossy green leaves, which appear just as the flower spike is emerging, are narrow and strap-like while the blooms themselves are crowded onto a short spike. The individual flowers are either tubular or strongly reflexed and are sweetly and pervasively perfumed.

CULTIVATION: Plant bulbs about 4 in (10 cm) deep in fall (autumn) or at the start of winter in mild climates. Water in but do not keep watering unless winters are very dry. They do best in full sun except in marginal climates (those with mild winters) where some shade helps keep the bulbs cool. After bloom, bulbs can be left where they are but the following year's flowers are usually fewer and not so crowded on the spike. For a reliable display, it is best to dig and discard the bulbs after bloom, replacing with fresh stock the following fall.

Hyacinthus orientalis

Popular with gardeners all over the world, the many named varieties of hyacinth are cultivars of *Hyacinthus orientalis* which originally comes from the Middle East and Mediterranean region. The wild form has far fewer flowers and rather more leaves than the cultivated varieties. A spike of flowers is massed atop a 12 in (30 cm) stem. The spring flowers vary enormously in color. **'King of the Blues'** is a favorite, but many others are available in white, pale yellow, pink, red or purple. **'City of Haarlem'** produces a strong spike of creamy yellow flowers late in the season. **'Columbus'** has creamy white blossoms that are long and tubular without reflexed petals. **'Lady Derby'** has flowers in the softest pastel pink. **ZONES 5–9.**

HYDRANGEA

These deciduous or evergreen shrubs, climbers and sometimes small trees occur over a wide area of temperate Asia and North and South America. Most species have large oval leaves with serrated edges; some develop good fall (autumn) foliage color. The flower clusters contain tiny fertile flowers and showy sterile ones with 4 petal-like sepals. Although most species produce panicles of flowers with few sterile flowers, many cultivated forms have heads composed almost entirely of sterile flowers and are called by gardeners mob-caps, mopheads or hortensias (for *Hydrangea macrophylla* cultivars only). Intermediate forms with a ring of sterile flowers surrounding fertile flowers are called lacecaps. Flower color may vary with the acidity or alkalinity of the soil: blue in acid soil, pink or red in alkaline; white cultivars do not change. In some but not all cultivars the old flowers gradually fade to shades of green and pink, this color being independent of soil type.

CULTIVATION: Except in cool, moist climates, they need shade or part-shade or both leaves and flowers will scorch; and though soil should be constantly moist and rich in humus, it should be well drained. Pruning is best done immediately after bloom, cutting out all stems that have just flowered and leaving the others alone. Propagate from cuttings or seed. Check regularly for powdery mildew, leaf spot, honey fungus and aphids, scale insects and spider mites.

Hydrangea arborescens 'Annabelle'

Hydrangea arborescens

SNOWHILL HYDRANGEA, SMOOTH HYDRANGEA

This frost-hardy, shade-loving shrub from eastern USA grows 6–8 ft (1.8–2.4 m) tall, usually with a greater spread. It forms a lax mound from many suckering stems which are clothed in big, simple, serrated leaves up to 6 in (15 cm) long. Hemispherical heads of many small white flowers are produced in late spring and summer; these turn green as they age. **'Grandiflora'** is commonly sold but **'Annabelle'** is an improved variety with bigger blooms that are produced about 2 weeks later. **ZONES 6–9.**

Hydrangea aspera

This species occurs naturally over much of southern and eastern Asia, showing much variation in the wild. In cultivation it grows to around 10 ft (3 m) high and wide. Its serrated-edged leaves vary from narrow to oval, and are 3–10 in (8–25 cm) long. The large flowerheads that occur in summer are lacecap style with pale, sterile flowers

Hydrangea arborescens 'Grandiflora'

Hydrangea aspera

Hydrangea heteromalla 'Bretschneideri'

and tiny, purplish blue, fertile flowers. The flower color varies little with soil type. The **Villosa Group** bear broad heads of blue or purple flowers in the center of the shrubs and larger white flowers towards the periphery. Deciduous and upright, they grow to a height and spread of 10 ft (3 m) and are very frost hardy. **ZONES 7–10.**

Hydrangea heteromalla

Growing to a height of around 10 ft (3 m), this deciduous shrub from western China and Tibet produces many stems from ground level to form a loose, rounded shrub. The leaves are broadly lanceolate or narrowly ovate, pointy and toothed along their edges. The flowers are of the lacecap variety with a cluster of tiny fertile flowers surrounded by bigger, more showy infertile, white or pink flowers. Blooming occurs in summer. The cultivar **'Bretschneideri'** is shrubbier than the species and has narrower leaves, peeling, reddish brown bark and flatter flower sprays. **ZONES 6–9.**

Hydrangea luteovenosa

This unusual hydrangea from southern Japan is regarded by some botanists as no more than an odd form of *Hydrangea scandens.* It is a shrub of semi-prostrate or scrambling habit with very slender, weak stems; the leaves are little more than 1 in (25 mm) long, and are veined or blotched with yellow, hence the specific name. The flowering panicles of *H. luteovenosa* are very modest, less than 3 in (8 cm) wide and with very few white sterile flowers. This plant is not often found in cultivation. **ZONES 7–9.**

Hydrangea luteovenosa

Hydrangea macrophylla

BIGLEAF HYDRANGEA, GARDEN HYDRANGEA

This species in its typical wild form comes from Japan and is rather rare in cultivation. The name also covers a large race of garden varieties derived from it, though in fact many of these may have originated as hybrids between *Hydrangea macrophlla* and *H. aspera.* The major group known as 'hortensias' (once *H. hortensia)* have flowerheads of the 'mophead ' type, with densely massed sterile florets. A smaller group are the 'lacecaps' with a circle of sterile florets around a flat head of tiny fertile florets; examples of the lacecaps are **'Blue Sky'** and **'Blue Wave'**. There are a large number of named cultivars, ranging in growth from less than 3 ft (1 m) tall and wide to twice that size; 5 ft (1.5 m) is the average. As a rule, the deeper the color the smaller the growth. **'Geoffrey Chadbund'** is a lacecap form with rich, bright red flowers; **'Libelle'** (also a lacecap) has extra large, pure white infertile flowers that give the head a crowded, full look; **'Altona'** is a hortensia form with flowers that vary from deep pink to purplish blue; **'Générale Vicomtesse de Vibraye'** (also a hortensia) bears large flowerheads in pink or pale blue. **'Lilacina'** (lacecap) has pink flowers that may be tinged purple; **'Shower'** (lacecap) produces elegant heads of clear, hot pink blooms; **'Sir Joseph Banks'** (hortensia) is pink flowered; **'Sunset'** (lacecap) is a big, vigorous shrub which often grows to over 5 ft (1.5 m) across and produces many heads of rich pinkish scarlet blooms; **'Taube'** is similar to 'Sunset' but does not grow quite as large and has softer pink blooms; and **'Veitchii'** (lacecap) bears flowers that open white but as they age they turn soft pink. **ZONES 6–10.**

H. m. 'Générale Vicomtesse de Vibraye'

Hydrangea macrophylla

Hydrangea macrophylla 'Blue Sky'

Hydrangea macrophylla 'Blue Wave'

Hydrangea macrophylla 'Altona'

Hydrangea macrophylla 'Libelle'

Hydrangea macrophylla 'Geoffrey Chadbund'

Hydrangea macrophylla 'Sir Joseph Banks'

Hydrangea macrophylla 'Veitchii'

Hydrangea macrophylla 'Taube'

Hydrangea macrophylla 'Lilacina'

Hydrangea macrophylla 'Shower'

Hydrangea paniculata
PANICLE HYDRANGEA

This large deciduous shrub from China and Japan grows to 15 ft (4.5 m) or more, with a broad, dome-shaped crown the same in width. It has large, oval, dark green leaves and in mid-summer bears small cream, fertile flowers and larger flat, creamy white, sterile flowers that turn rose purple as they age. Prune back hard in late winter or spring if larger flowerheads are preferred. **'Grandiflora'** (the peegee hydrangea) is the form most commonly grown. **'Tardiva'** does not flower until fall (autumn). **ZONES 5–9.**

Hydrangea petiolaris
syn. *Hydrangea anomala* subsp. *petiolaris*
CLIMBING HYDRANGEA

This deciduous, self-clinging climber from Japan and northeast Asia grows up to 50 ft (15 m) or more and bears beautiful flattened heads of small white flowers in summer. It has oval, finely toothed leaves and is very frost hardy. Provide some protection from hot afternoon sun, and water regularly in summer. Prune after flowering, trimming close to the support. **ZONES 5–9.**

Hydrangea 'Preziosa'

This shrub is sometimes regarded as a cultivar of *Hydrangea macrophylla.* It has reddish foliage and big heads of usually pink flowers. **ZONES 6–10.**

Hydrangea quercifolia
OAK-LEAF HYDRANGEA

Native to the USA, mostly to the southeast of the Mississippi River Valley, this deciduous shrub grows to a height of 6–8 ft (1.8–2.4 m), spreading by stolons

Hydrangea paniculata 'Grandiflora'

Hydrangea macrophylla 'Sunset'

Hydrangea paniculata

to 12 ft (3.5 m) or more. The deeply lobed, dark green leaves change to orange-scarlet in fall (autumn). The flowers, borne from mid-summer to mid-fall, are a mixture of small, fertile and sterile flowers. The white, sterile flowers eventually fade to pink and violet. This species does best in dappled shade. **ZONES 5–9.**

Hydrangea serrata

This species, a lacecap style hydrangea, is very closely allied to *Hydrangea macrophylla* and sometimes included there as a subspecies. It grows into a rounded shrub up to 5 ft (1.5 m) tall with a similar spread. The leaves are more narrowly ovate than in *H. macrophylla* and are prominently toothed. **'Bluebird'** is typical of the species with wide, flattish flowerheads over most of summer. **ZONES 6–10.**

HYDROCLEYS

This is a genus of 9 species from South America, only one of which is often cultivated. They are tender rhizomatous annuals and perennials that prefer shallow water. The name water poppy comes from the 3-petalled, deep yellow, 2–3 in (5–8 cm) diameter flowers that resemble the blooms of the California poppy (*Eschscholzia californica*). Each flower lasts only a day but they appear in succession throughout summer. The shiny mid-green leaves are 1–3 in (2.5–8 cm) in diameter and resemble the foliage of water lilies, although smaller.
CULTIVATION: Water poppies thrive in warm-climate pools or in tubs that can be sheltered in winter. They are not frost tolerant, need full sun and water less than 18 in (45 cm) deep. Plant in loamy silt with a topping of sand or gravel. Propagate by breaking up the rhizomes in spring. Do not plant near waterways outside their native habitat.

Hydrangea quercifolia

Hydrangea serrata 'Bluebird'

Hydrocleys nymphoides
WATER POPPY

This fast-spreading, aquatic perennial is grown in both cool and warm climates and is at home in either the muddy margins of ponds or fully submerged in water. Where winters are frosty, the plant becomes dormant in early fall (autumn) and may be lifted and stored moist, above freezing, until late the following spring. In subtropical and tropical gardens it remains evergreen. **ZONES 10–11.**

HYDROCOTYLE
PENNYWORT

This large and varied genus contains well over 100 species of mostly creeping perennials in the carrot family that are found in habitats ranging from sand dunes to bogs and from sea level to alpine areas. They have rounded often almost circular leaves though in a few species they are deeply lobed or divided in a palmate manner, but none has flowers of any significance. Some make useful soil or sand binders, others make low ground cover in shady or moist areas.
CULTIVATION: Hydrocotyles are easy to grow in appropriate positions. There are both sun and shade lovers and species for moist or dry areas. Propagate from seed or by division. Hardiness varies with species, but most will tolerate some frost.

Hydrangea 'Preziosa'

Hydrangea paniculata 'Tardiva'

Hydrocotyle bonariensis

A running, ground-covering perennial from South America, this species has become naturalized in dunes and coastal sandy soils in many parts of the world. The leaves are tough, leathery and almost circular, with scalloped edges. The insignificant flowers are produced in compound umbels. It is marginally frost hardy. **ZONES 9–11.**

HYDROPHYLLUM
WATERLEAF

Eight species of perennials comprise this genus, which is indigenous to the USA and Canada. They are understory plants found in permanently damp places in woodlands, and in gardens can be used as ground cover beneath trees or in other moist, shady places. Plants spread by creeping rhizomes and have medium to large, lobed leaves. The flowers may be mauve, violet or white depending on the species.
CULTIVATION: Grow in leafy or humus-rich soil kept constantly moist but not sodden. Full or part-shade suits these plants so long as their soft leaves are not exposed to sun during the hottest hours. They are easily raised from seed in spring or propagated by dividing established plants in fall (autumn).

Hydrophyllum virginianum
VIRGINIAN WATERLEAF, SHAWNEE SALAD

Native to northeastern USA and Canada, this plant grows to no more than 24 in (60 cm) tall, with fleshy compound leaves divided into 5 to 7 oblong leaflets. The erect flowering stem terminates in a loose umbel of violet-purple flowers with protruding stamens. The tender new shoots were used as za salad or pot herb by early white settlers. **ZONES 3–9.**

Hydrocleys nymphoides

Hydrocotyle bonariensis

Hydrangea petiolaris

HYLOCEREUS

QUEEN OF THE NIGHT

This genus comprises 20 species of climbing epiphytic cacti, indigenous to Mexico and parts of Central America. Some of these are commonly used as grafting stock. The broadly winged or flattened stems grow to 4 in (10 cm) across. The large flowers, which open at night in spring and summer, are white and funnel-shaped.

CULTIVATION: Grow these cacti in sun (or in a heated greenhouse in cooler climates) in very well-drained, acid soil. Frost tender, they are most vulnerable to caterpillars, mealybug and scale insects. Propagate from seed or cuttings.

Hylocereus polyrhizus

This species is native to Colombia and Panama in South America. Its 1½ in (35 mm) thick, reddish green stems bear long, light brown spines. This cactus produces large cream flowers opening from red buds. **ZONES 11–12.**

Hymenocallis caribaea

Hylocereus undatus

NIGHT-BLOOMING CEREUS, HONOLULU QUEEN

Of unknown origin, this tropical cactus develops long, multiple stems up to 15 ft (4.5 m) in length. These vivid green stems have 2 to 3 angles and tough, undulating margins with widely spaced, single-spined areoles. In late spring or summer 12 in (30 cm), creamy white, fragrant flowers appear. These are followed by red, edible, egg-shaped fruit. The species is easy to cultivate and will readily climb trees if allowed to grow freely. **ZONES 10–12.**

HYMENANTHERA

The 10 evergreen shrubs in this genus are found in eastern Australia, Norfolk Island and New Zealand; they belong to the violet family but it would take a botanist to see the resemblance to violets. All are dioecious, that is, there are separate male and female plants. The leaves vary considerably in size and shape. The flowers are small and insignificant, and they are followed by white, purple or white-flecked purple berries. Recent botanical opinion is that *Hymenanthera* cannot be distinguished from *Melicytus,* and all its species should be transferred to the latter genus.

CULTIVATION: Most species tolerate occasional light frost. They prefer a cool but frost-free climate and thrive in coastal gardens. Any position in sun or part-shade with moist, well-drained soil will do. Light trimming in late winter will maintain neatness. Propagate from cuttings or seed.

Hymenocallis × *festalis*

Hylocereus undatus

Hymenanthera dentata

syn. *Melicytus dentatus*

TREE VIOLET

In its alpine habitat, this variable shrub may only grow 24 in (60 cm) tall, but in lowland parts of its range it can easily reach 12 ft (3.5 m). It is spiny and well clothed with narrow leaves which are shallowly toothed. In spring small, yellow, very strongly fragrant flowers appear along the branches; these are followed by spherical purple fruit about ¼ in (6 mm) long. It is native to southeastern Australia. **ZONES 8–11.**

HYMENOCALLIS

syn. *Ismene*

SPIDER LILY, FILMY LILY, SACRED LILY OF THE INCAS

The unusual, beautiful white flowers of the spider lilies resemble daffodils except for the delicate, spider-like petals surrounding the inner corona. Native to Central and South America, there are about 40 species of *Hymenocallis.* Some are evergreen and all are deliciously scented.

CULTIVATION: Most species are tropical plants and prefer a warm, frost-free climate; in colder areas they need the shelter of a greenhouse. They can also be grown as indoor pot plants. Bulbs should be planted in winter, about 6 in (15 cm) deep in well-drained soil. A part-shaded position is best. Water very well during growth and never allow to dry out completely. Offsets form quickly and should be divided in winter.

Hymenocallis caribaea

This evergreen species from the West Indies has strap-like leaves to 24 in (60 cm) long. The large flowers, about 6 in (15 cm) across, with long, narrow petals that look like white spiders perched atop glossy green foliage, appear from summer to fall (autumn). **ZONES 10–12.**

Hymenocallis × *festalis*

This marginally frost-hardy plant grows to about 18 in (45 cm). The glossy green leaves are slender and strap-like. Each stem bears up to 5 white flowers 4 in (10 cm) wide. The inner trumpet-shaped cup of petals is surrounded by 6 slender, recurving petals. **ZONES 9–11.**

Hymenanthera dentata

Hylocereus polyrhizus

Hymenocallis littoralis

Pure white, trumpet-shaped flowers surrounded by 6 thread-like petals are borne on 30 in (75 cm) stems on this tropical species. The almost strap-like foliage is bright green. It is frost tender. **ZONES 10–12.**

Hymenocallis narcissiflora

syn. *Ismene calathina*

BASKET FLOWER, PERUVIAN DAFFODIL

Hymenocallis narcissiflora is the most widely grown species, often planted as a summer bulb like *Gladiolus.* It is native to the Peruvian Andes, and is at home in gardens of the southern hemisphere. Its broad, white flowers are very showy, with wide petals reflexed behind the green-tinged cup. The flowers appear in early summer; a pale yellow form exists. **ZONES 9–11.**

HYMENOLEPIS

syn. *Athanasia*

Fewer than 10 species of somewhat weedy looking shrubs comprise this genus from South Africa's Cape Province. Only one species, *Hymenolepis parviflora,* is ever seen in gardens. All species have alternate leaves but the shape varies considerably from species to species. The flowers are tiny and yellow and are produced in heads at the tops of the branches.

CULTIVATION: They are easy to grow in average garden soil that drains freely. Full sun is usually the best aspect except in hot, inland areas where dappled or part-shade during the middle of the day is helpful. The plants should be kept well watered from about mid-fall (mid-autumn) until spring but need much less water in summer. Propagate from seed sown in fall or from cuttings taken in mid-spring.

Hymenolepis parviflora
syn. *Athanasia parviflora*
COULTER BUSH

This spreading, slightly woody shrub comes from the southwestern Cape region of South Africa. It grows 5–8 ft (1.5–2.4 m) high and bears small, golden-yellow flowers on large, flattened heads in early summer. The leaves are needle-like and branched. It will tolerate light frosts. Prune regularly to remove old stems and maintain shape. **ZONES 9–11.**

HYMENOSPORUM
AUSTRALIAN FRANGIPANI, SWEETSHADE

This genus consists of a single species of evergreen tree originating in the subtropical rainforests of east coast Australia and New Guinea. It has showy tubular flowers and oval to oblong, glossy leaves. The name comes from the Greek *hymen*, a membrane, and *sporos*, a seed, referring to the winged seeds.
CULTIVATION: A relatively fast-growing tree, it adapts to most soil types but prefers moist, humus-rich soil where it is less likely to be checked by long dry spells. It flowers best in a sheltered position in full sun, but will tolerate some shade. Propagation is easily done from seed or from cuttings.

Hymenosporum flavum

Growing to 30 ft (9 m), taller in its natural rainforest environment, this tree develops a straight, smooth trunk and open, columnar shape, with widely spaced horizontal branches and dark green glossy leaves clustered towards the ends. In spring it bears profuse clusters of very fragrant cream flowers that age over several days to deep golden yellow. They are followed by flattish seed pods with small, winged seeds. **ZONES 9–11.**

HYOPHORBE
syn. *Mascarena*

This genus of 5 species of unusual palms is now endangered in its natural homeland—the tropical Mascarene Islands of the western Indian Ocean. All are feather-leafed palms with ringed trunks which, in some species, are very swollen. They have smooth crownshafts from which emerge relatively few, stout,

Hymenosporum flavum

Hypericum androsaemum

strongly recurved fronds. The branched, broom-like inflorescences, each containing hundreds of tiny flowers, encircle the top of the trunk where it meets the crownshaft.
CULTIVATION: These frost-tender palms prefer lowland tropical or subtropical climates. In their native ranges, they grow in fertile volcanic soil but in gardens will do well in any reasonably fertile, well-drained soil. Usually grown in full sun, they do tolerate part-shade. Propagate from seed sown in spring.

Hyophorbe lagenicaulis
BOTTLE PALM

This slow-growing species is probably the most popular due to its prominently swollen, bottle-shaped trunk. Even mature specimens usually have fewer than 10 fronds which gives the palm an attractive and elegant silhouette. It is almost extinct in the wild but its popularity in tropical gardens ensures its survival. **ZONES 11–12.**

HYPERICUM
ST JOHN'S WORT

This is a large and varied genus of 400 species of annuals, perennials, shrubs and a few small trees, some evergreen but mostly deciduous, grown for their showy flowers in shades of yellow with a central mass of prominent golden stamens. They are found throughout the world in a broad range of habitats. Species range in size from diminutive perennials for the rockery to over 10 ft (3 m) tall.
CULTIVATION: Mostly cool-climate plants, they prefer full sun but will tolerate some shade. They do best in fertile, well-drained soil, with plentiful water in late spring and summer. Remove seed capsules after flowering and prune in winter to maintain a rounded shape. Cultivars are propagated from cuttings in summer, and species from seed in fall (autumn) or from cuttings in summer. Some species are susceptible to rust.

Hymenolepis parviflora

Hypericum beanii 'Gold Cup'

Hypericum cerastoides

Hypericum androsaemum
TUTSAN

Native to both sides of the Mediterranean Sea and extending into western Asia, this bushy, deciduous shrub usually grows less than 3 ft (1 m) tall with a slightly wider spread. It is dense and leafy, the broad leaves being produced on the many stems that arise from the base. The stems are reddish and odd leaves are margined or flushed purplish red. In summer, clusters of 1 in (25 mm) wide, golden-yellow flowers appear all over the plant. These are followed by globular red fruit that ripen to black. This species is considered a troublesome weed in Australia and New Zealand. The common name is a corruption of *toutsain,* referring to the medicinal uses of the plant. **ZONES 6–10.**

Hypericum beanii

A vigorous, evergreen shrub from western China, this variable species may grow to 6 ft (1.8 m) tall with dense, arching branches. The mid-green leaves are usually elliptical and paler beneath. Large, star-shaped, golden yellow flowers with showy stamens appear in summer. This species is often used for bank

Hyophorbe lagenicaulis

retention. **'Gold Cup'** (syn. *Hypericum* × *cyathiflorum* 'Gold Cup') grows to 5 ft (1.5 m) tall and produces 2 in (5 cm) wide, cup-shaped, golden-yellow flowers in summer. **ZONES 7–10.**

Hypericum calycinum
AARON'S BEARD, CREEPING ST JOHN'S WORT

One of the best of all ground covers for temperate climates, this species from Turkey is a low-growing evergreen shrub only about 15 in (38 cm) tall but spreading rapidly by creeping, runner-like stems to cover quite a large area. The mid-summer flowers are about the size of a rose and have long stamens. Any sort of soil suits and, though the plant will grow happily in the dry shade beneath deciduous trees, it flowers more profusely if given sunshine. **ZONES 6–10.**

Hypericum cerastoides
syn. *Hypericum rhodoppeum*

This densely mounding perennial has oval, gray-green leaves and terminal clusters of bright yellow, cup-shaped flowers in late spring and early summer. It has an upright, slightly spreading habit and grows to 12 in (30 cm) tall with an 18 in (45 cm) spread. Frost hardy, it is useful in rock gardens. **ZONES 6–9.**

Hypericum kouytchense

Hypericum monogynum

Hypericum 'Hidcote'

Hypericum × *moserianum* 'Tricolor'

Hypericum frondosum
GOLDEN ST JOHN'S WORT

A rounded deciduous shrub from the southeastern States of the USA, golden St John's wort grows up to 4 ft (1.2 m) tall with a similar spread. The many stems are upright and densely clothed with curving, oblong leaves that are a blue-green color with a powdery bloom. In summer clusters of showy, bright yellow flowers are produced. The cultivar **'Sunburst'** is an improvement on the species and worth seeking out. **ZONES 5–10.**

Hypericum 'Hidcote'

This dense bushy shrub reaches 4 ft (1.2 m) in height and has a spread of 5 ft (1.5 m). It bears large, cup-shaped, 2½ in (6 cm) golden-yellow flowers from mid-summer to early fall (autumn) and has lance-shaped, dark green leaves. **ZONES 7–10.**

Hypericum kouytchense

This broad semi-evergreen shrub grows to 5 ft (1.5 m) tall, spreading to 6 ft (1.8 m). The golden-yellow flattish flowers with showy long styles and stamens are carried in profusion on the drooping branchlets in summer. **ZONES 6–10.**

Hypericum lancasteri

At least 3 ft (1 m) tall and wide, this deciduous shrub comes from the mountains of southwestern China and was introduced to the West by renowned plantsman Roy Lancaster. It has erect stems, slightly blue-green leaves and terminal clusters of starry yellow flowers with prominent stamens. **ZONES 7–10.**

Hypericum monogynum
syn. *Hypericum chinense*

This long-flowering, semi-evergreen shrub is from China, Japan and Taiwan. It grows to 5 ft (1.5 m) tall and 18 in (45 cm) wide. There is also a low-growing form. The thick, rounded, leathery leaves are mid-green on their upper surface, paler beneath. Lemon or golden-yellow, star-shaped summer flowers, 2½ in (6 cm) across, crowd towards the outer parts of the plant; they are followed by capsular fruit. **ZONES 9–10.**

Hypericum × *moserianum*
GOLD FLOWER

This species bears star-shaped, bright yellow flowers. **'Tricolor'**, with its green, cream and pink leaves, is one of the most desirable of variegated-leafed shrubs; it grows 24–36 in (60–90 cm) tall and rather wider, bearing modest bowl-shaped flowers from summer to fall (autumn). **ZONES 7–10.**

Hypericum olympicum

This low, spreading deciduous shrub to 12 in (30 cm) tall is native to Greece and Turkey and has many erect, outward arching or near horizontal branches. The leaves are about 1 in (25 mm) long, oblong and gray-green. The flowers are quite large and showy and very generously produced in summer. **ZONES 6–10.**

Hypericum patulum

This evergreen, upright shrub from China bears large, golden-yellow, erect flowers from mid-summer to mid-fall (mid-autumn). It has dark green oval leaves and grows to a height and spread of between 3 ft (1 m) and 5 ft (1.5 m). *Hypericum patulum* is frost hardy. **ZONES 7–10.**

Hypericum reptans

From both sides of the Himalayas comes this spreading, mat-forming, deciduous ground cover. The leaves are small, triangular or oval and gray-green in color. The propeller-shaped, 5-petalled flowers appear in summer, individually rather than in clusters, and in great profusion. Plants spread to at least 3 ft (1 m) across. **ZONES 7–9.**

Hypericum revolutum
CURRY BUSH

Growing to about 8 ft (2.4 m) high, this dense, bushy shrub from south-eastern Africa has drooping branches. The green pointed leaves smell like curry after rain or when crushed. The large, bright yellow flowers with their masses of long golden stamens are loosely grouped at the branch tips. This shrub is easy to grow but does best in rich, well-drained soil in full sun. **ZONES 9–11.**

Hypericum frondosum

Hypericum lancasteri

Hypericum olympicum

Hypericum patulum

Hypericum 'Rowallane'

Hypericum 'Rowallane'

This semi-evergreen, arching shrub bears large, bowl-shaped, deep golden-yellow flowers from mid-summer to fall (autumn). The oval leaves are a rich green. It reaches a height and spread of 5 ft (1.5 m). **ZONES 8–10.**

HYPOESTES

This is a genus in the acanthus family consisting of 40 species of evergreen perennials, shrubs and subshrubs from South Africa, Madagascar and tropical Asia, some of which have become popular house and garden plants. Some species, such as the polka-dot plant (*Hypoestes phyllostachya*), have attractively spotted leaves and this is their chief attraction. Others are grown for their pleasant fall (autumn) flowers, which are densely clustered along the upper stems.
CULTIVATION: Grow in sun or part-shade in well-drained soil of average fertility. Give increasing water as the weather warms, decreasing in fall (autumn) and winter. These plants are not fussy or hard to grow, and in warm climates with regular rainfall can largely look after themselves. In cold climates they are grown as house or greenhouse plants. Propagate from stem cuttings in spring or summer, or seed sown in spring.

Hypoestes aristata
syn. ***Hypoestes antennifera***
RIBBON BUSH

This soft-wooded shrub is native to Natal in South Africa, and grows to a height of around 3 ft (1 m) with a spread of 24 in (60 cm). In late fall (autumn) and into winter, it bears profuse terminal spikes of attractive small tubular pink to purple flowers, set among 3 in (8 cm) mid-green, oval leaves. It prefers light shade and a moist, well-drained soil. Prune as required. **ZONES 10–11.**

Hypoestes phyllostachya
syn. ***Hypoestes sanguinolenta***
POLKA-DOT PLANT, FRECKLEFACE

A native of Madagascar, this popular indoor plant is grown for its colorful carmine pink spotted leaves. The small pink flowers are insignificant. Though it can grow to 3 ft (1 m), it is best kept pruned to 12–18 in (30–45 cm). Average temperatures and filtered to bright light produce the most colorful leaves. Allow the soil to dry between waterings. The cultivar **'Splash'** has larger areas of carmine pink on the leaves, often merging into the dots. **ZONES 10–12.**

HYPOXIS
STAR GRASS

There are around 150 species in this genus of perennials, found in Africa, Australia, tropical Asia and North America. Their corms produce tufts of grassy foliage 3–12 in (8–30 cm) long depending on the species. The leaves are sometimes ribbed and are often covered with fine hairs. The flowers, which are carried singly or loosely clustered on wiry stems, are starry, usually bright yellow and $\frac{1}{2}$–$1\frac{1}{2}$ in (12–35 mm) in diameter. They usually appear in mid-summer.
CULTIVATION: Most species tolerate only light frosts, but those that become fully dormant in winter are happy anywhere the soil does not freeze or become very wet. A light, gritty soil with excellent drainage is important, as is a position that receives at least half-day sun. Propagate from seed or by breaking up established clumps.

Hypoestes phyllostachya

Hypoxis hemerocallidea
syn. *Hypoxis rooperi*

From grasslands of South Africa, this is one of the showiest members of the genus. It has a large corm from which emerge spreading and deeply channeled leaves up to 18 in (45 cm) long and 3 in (8 cm) wide, of a rich shade of green. The bright yellow flowers are crowded onto curving stems up to 18 in (45 cm) high and are each up to $1\frac{1}{2}$ in (35 mm) in diameter. It flowers profusely throughout summer. **ZONES 8–10.**

HYSSOPUS
HYSSOP

This genus of aromatic culinary and medicinal herbs belongs to the mint family and includes about 5 species of herbaceous perennials and shrubs. All are found in poor soils around the northern Mediterranean coasts and also in Asia Minor. The leaves vary with species from linear to ovate and may be green or blue-green in color. The flowers are small, tubular with protruding stamens, and usually a shade of blue although they may also be white or pink.
CULTIVATION: All species do best in full sun and although they will grow in dry sandy soil, in gardens they look much better when grown in friable, fertile loam though good drainage is essential. Ensure adequate water particularly in fall (autumn) and winter. Propagate from cuttings taken in early summer or from seed sown in fall. Prune by shearing plants all over.

Hyssopus officinalis
HYSSOP

This bushy perennial herb grows to 24 in (60 cm) and has narrow, pointed, dark green leaves. Spikes of small violet-blue flowers, which are attractive to bees and butterflies, are borne in late summer. White and pink flowering forms are also available. Fully frost hardy, hyssop is evergreen in mild climates; in cool areas it dies down for the winter. The slightly bitter leaves are used in small quantities with fatty meats and fish. The essential oil made from the leaves has antiseptic properties and is used in the manufacture of perfumes. **ZONES 3–11.**

Hyssopus officinalis

Hypericum reptans

I

IBERIS

This genus consists of around 50 species of annuals, perennials and evergreen subshrubs are mainly from southern Europe, northern Africa and western Asia. Highly regarded as decorative plants they are excellent for rock gardens, bedding and borders. Showy flowers are borne in either flattish heads in colors of white, red and purple, or in erect racemes of pure white flowers.
CULTIVATION: Fully to marginally frost hardy, they require a warm, sunny position and a well-drained, light soil, preferably with added lime or dolomite. Propagate from seed in spring or fall (autumn)—they may self-sow, but are unlikely to become invasive—or cuttings in summer.

Iberis amara
CANDYTUFT, HYACINTH-FLOWERED CANDYTUFT

Native to the UK and Europe, this is a fast-growing and erect bushy annual. Frost hardy, *Iberis amara* has lance-shaped mid-green leaves and reaches a height of 12 in (30 cm), with a spread of 6 in (15 cm). It produces large racemes of small, fragrant, pure white flowers in early spring and summer. Various strains are available. The **Hyacinth-flowered Series** has large fragrant flowers in varying shades of pink; these are sometimes used as cut flowers. **ZONES 7–11.**

Iberis amara cultivar

Iberis gibraltarica

Iberis pruitii

Iberis gibraltarica
GIBRALTAR CANDYTUFT

This species, a sprawling, bushy perennial from Gibraltar and southern Spain grows to 12 in (30 cm) in height. It has narrow, dark green leaves and produces clusters of pink- or red-tinged white flowers in summer. Although normally frost hardy, it is susceptible to damage when frost is combined with wet winter conditions. **ZONES 7–11.**

Iberis pruitii
syn. *Iberis jordanii*

A short-lived perennial or occasionally an annual, this species is native to the Mediterranean. It grows to about 6 in (15 cm) tall with a spread of 8 in (20 cm). *Iberis pruitti* has slightly fleshy, dark green rosette-forming leaves and produces tight clusters of lilac to white flowers in summer. It is frost hardy, but is susceptible in wet winter conditions. **ZONES 7–11.**

Iberis sempervirens
CANDYTUFT, EVERGREEN CANDYTUFT

A low, spreading, evergreen subshrub, this species from southern Europe is ideal for rock gardens. It has narrow, dark green leaves and dense, rounded heads of unscented white flowers in spring and early summer. It is frost hardy, and grows 6–12 in (15–30 cm) high with a spread of 18–24 in (45–60 cm). The cultivar '**Snowflake**' is most attractive, with glossy, dark green leaves and semi-spherical heads of white flowers. Lightly trim after flowering. **ZONES 4–11.**

Iberis sempervirens

Idesia polycarpa

Idiospermum australiense

Iberis umbellata
GLOBE CANDYTUFT

Native to the Mediterranean region, this upright bushy annual has lance-shaped, mid-green leaves. Flattish heads of small, mauve, lilac, pink, purple, carmine or white flowers are produced in late spring and summer. *Iberis umbellata* grows to a height of 6–12 in (15–30 cm) and a spread of 8 in (20 cm). It is frost hardy and is a useful cut flower. The **Fairy Series** has flowers in shades of pink, red, purple or white which appear in spring. Bushes in this series grow to a height and spread of 8 in (20 cm). Lightly trim after flowering. **ZONES 7–11.**

IDESIA
WONDER TREE, LIGIRI

This genus consists of a single species of deciduous tree. Indigenous to central and western China, Korea, Japan and neighboring islands, it is grown for its striking foliage and fruit, and makes a handsome shade tree. To obtain the fruit, both male and female plants are needed.
CULTIVATION: It will grow in either sun or part-shade. Moderately fertile, moist but well-drained neutral to acid soil and a cool to warm-temperate climate suit it best. It can be pruned when young to establish a single main trunk, which will promote a shapely crown. Propagate from seed in fall (autumn) or cuttings in summer.

Idesia polycarpa

This fast-growing, shapely tree grows to a height of 40 ft (12 m), with a broadly conical crown spreading to 20 ft (6 m). It has large heart-shaped, red-stalked dark green leaves; fragrant, greenish flowers are borne in spring and summer. *Idesia polycarpa* is frost hardy, particularly after long, hot summers which promote well-ripened wood. The female plants produce large hanging clusters of pea-sized berries that turn deep red in fall (autumn) and are not eaten by birds. **ZONES 6–10.**

Idesia polycarpa

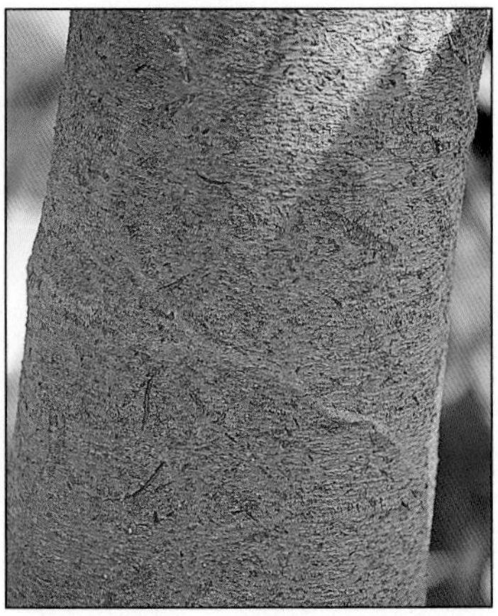
Idiospermum australiense

IDIOSPERMUM

In 1912 a German botanist named a new plant from the rainforests of northeastern Queensland as *Calycanthus australiensis*, this being the first record of the genus *Calycanthus*, and of the family Calycanthaceae, from Australia. But the plant was not found again until 60 years later, when a few cattle were poisoned by eating the seeds from what turned out to be a quite large evergreen tree, with a flower structure quite similar to the deciduous shrubby *Calycanthus* from North America, but with a quite unique fruit containing a single very large, globose seed, deeply cleft into 3 to 4 wedge-shaped cotyledons. On the basis of these differences an Australian botanist reclassified the species into the new genus *Idiospermum*. Its single species appears to be a primitive member of what is already regarded as one of the oldest and most primitive flowering plant families.
CULTIVATION: It is quite easy to cultivate in any moist, frost-free climate, preferring a deep, reasonably fertile soil that remains moist. It makes quite fast early growth. Propagate from fresh seed.

Idiospermum australiense

The sole species of the genus, this tree grows up to 50 ft (15 m) tall with a girth of up to 18 in (45 cm); the bark is dark gray and slightly rough. The glossy elliptical leaves are up to 10 in (25 cm) long and 4 in (10 cm) wide. The $^3/_4$ in (20 mm) diameter flowers, borne singly on the branches below the leaves, are like miniature magnolia flowers with purplish burgundy petals. The globular brown fruit are up to 3 in (8 cm) in diameter. **ZONES 10–12.**

ILEX
HOLLY

The 400 or so evergreen and deciduous trees and shrubs that make up this large genus come predominantly from the temperate regions of the northern hemisphere. They are grown for their foliage and clusters of small glossy berries. Hollies make excellent hedges, border plants, tub plants or screens for privacy according to their height. Male and fe-

Ilex aquifolium 'Aurea Marginata'

male plants must be grown together to obtain the berries. Produced in summer, fall (autumn) or winter, the berries are either red, yellow or black, and clusters of small, insignificant, greenish white flowers precede them.

CULTIVATION: Hollies grow well in deep, friable, well-drained soils with high organic content. They are fully to marginally frost hardy. An open, sunny position is best in cool climates. Water in hot, dry summers. Hollies do not like transplanting. Prune carefully in spring to check vigorous growth. Propagate from seed or cuttings. Check for signs of holly aphid and holly leaf miner.

Ilex × *altaclerensis*
HIGHCLERE HOLLY

This group of evergreen hybrid hollies, reaching a height of about 50 ft (15 m), has larger, variable leaves and larger flowers and berries than the English holly *(Ilex aquifolium)*. Its many cultivars include **'Belgica Aurea'** (syn. 'Silver Sentinel'), an upright female with few-spined leaves which have a gray-green center and irregular yellow margin; **'Camelliifolia'**, a female with purple-tinged shoots, leaf stems and petal bases,

Ilex × *altaclerensis* 'Hendersonii'

Ilex × *altaclerensis* cultivar

Ilex aquifolium 'Silver Milkmaid'

Ilex aquifolium

larger berries and long leaves with only a few spines; **'Golden King'**, a frost-hardy female with smooth-edged, deep green leaves with yellow margins which makes an excellent hedge (requires pollination with a male cultivar such as **'Silver Queen'**, a cultivar of *I. aquifolium*, to bear its red berries); **'Hendersonii'**, a compact female with long-lasting red berries and dull green foliage; **'Hodginsii'**, a robust male clone with dark purple twigs and glossy, very deep green foliage; **'Lawsoniana'** a sport of 'Hendersonii' which has good crops of red berries and sparsely spined leaves with irregular light green and gold centers; and **'Wilsonii'**, a moderately frost-hardy female growing to 20 ft (6 m) with a spread of 12 ft (3.5 m), broad, spiny, dark green leaves and masses of large scarlet fruits which

Ilex × *altaclerensis* 'Lawsoniana'

Ilex × *altaclerensis* 'Wilsonii'

Ilex aquifolium 'Pyramidalis Fructu Luteo'

Ilex aquifolium 'Ferox Argentea'

Ilex × *aquipernyi* 'Meschick'

make it good for hedging. Able to resist pollution and harsh coastal conditions, this is a useful plant for industrial and maritime areas. ZONES 6–10.

Ilex aquifolium
ENGLISH HOLLY

Native to Europe, north Africa and western Asia, this evergreen species—a popular Christmas decoration in the northern hemisphere with its glossy, spiny-edged dark green leaves and bright red winter berries—reaches 40 ft (12 m) with a spread of about 15 ft (4.5 m) or more and has an erect, branching habit. The most commonly grown cultivars include **'Amber'**, which has lovely yellow fruit and almost thornless leaves; **'Angustifolia'**, which has green or purple twigs and lanceolate dark green foliage with a neat pyramidal shape; **'Aurea Marginata'**, a small, bushy, silver holly with yellow margins on its spiny foliage and red berries on the female form; **'Ferox'**, the hedgehog holly, a male with more compact growth to a height of 20 ft (6 m) and leaves with spines over their entire surface; **'Ferox Argentea'**, a male with purple twigs and small, cream-edged dark green leaves; **'Golden Milkboy'**, with variegated golden leaves; **'Golden Queen'**, a dense male clone with spiny, dark green leaves with pale green and gray shadings and a substantial yellow margin; **'Handsworth New Silver'**, a

Ilex aquifolium 'Pyramidalis'

Ilex aquifolium 'Amber'

Ilex aquifolium 'Golden Queen'

free-fruiting clone whose leaves have a creamy white margin while its twigs are purple; **'J. C. van Tol'**, which grows to 15 ft (4.5 m) tall with dark green, almost spineless leaves and crimson berries; **'Madame Briot'**, a female clone with large, strongly spined, glossy green leaves which are broadly edged in gold and scarlet berries; **'Pyramidalis'**, a good fruit-bearing female clone that bears well and has a conical habit whilst young, but broadens with age; **'Pyramidalis Fructu Luteo'**, much the same as the previous clone, but with yellow fruit; **'Silver Milkmaid'**, with scarlet fruit and green-edged golden leaves, that are prone to revert to green and must be cut out if they do so; and **'Silver Queen'**, a male, non-berrying shrub with leaves that are pink when young, maturing to a very dark green in the middle with creamy white margins and gray-green in between. ZONES 6–10.

Ilex × *aquipernyi*

This hybrid between *Ilex aquifolium* and *I. pernyi* is a conical evergreen small tree. It grows to 20 ft (6 m), with a spread of 12 ft (3.5 m). It has glossy, dark green spiny leaves and bears red fruit. **'Meschick'** colors a pinkish bronze. ZONES 6–10.

Ilex cornuta

Ilex decidua

Ilex glabra 'Compacta'

Ilex cornuta
CHINESE HOLLY

Self-fertile and better suited than other species to mild-winter climates, this fully frost-hardy, dense, rounded shrub from China grows to 12 ft (3.5 m) with a spread of 15 ft (4.5 m). The thick glossy leaves are almost rectangular, with spiny points; the berries, while not as profuse as on the English holly, are larger and borne throughout summer. Water when newly planted. **ZONES 6–10.**

Ilex crenata
JAPANESE HOLLY

From Japan, this frost-hardy, compact evergreen shrub has stiff branches, small scalloped leaves, dull white flowers and glossy black berries. It is often used for clipped hedges and topiary. Although it can grow to 15 ft (4.5 m) in height with a spread of 10 ft (3 m), it is usually smaller in cultivation. Cultivars include '**Convexa**', which has almost spineless, glossy black-green leaves and purplish stems; '**Golden Gem**', a compact but rarely flowering shrub, with soft yellow foliage; '**Green Lustre**', a compact male shrub with very dark green leaves which does not produce fruit; '**Helleri**', a female clone of spreading habit that can

Ilex crenata 'Helleri'

Ilex cornuta

reach 5 ft (1.5 m) in height and spread, with sparsely spined leaves and black fruit; and '**Schwoebel's Compact**', a low-spreading dwarf form to 3 ft (1 m) tall. Variegated or pale-leafed forms do best in full sun; green-leafed forms do well in partial shade. **ZONES 6–10.**

Ilex decidua
POSSUM HAW

From southeastern USA, this frost-hardy shrub or small tree usually grows to 10 ft (3 m), but can become tree-like and reach 30 ft (9 m) in height. It is deciduous with a short trunk, slender pyramidal head, toothed leaves, slender stems and bright orange or red berries that last well into winter. **ZONES 6–10.**

Ilex glabra
INKBERRY

An evergreen from eastern North America, this erect shrub reaches 10 ft (3 m) tall and has narrow, deep green leaves; glossy black fruit follows the inconspicuous white flowers. Cultivars include '**Compacta**' and '**Nordic**', both ideal for hedging; and '**Ivory Queen**', a white-berried form. It can be propagated from seed, but germination is slow; cuttings, taken in late summer, are faster and more reliable. The species is surface rooted and easily damaged by digging around its feet. **ZONES 3–9.**

Ilex × *meserveae*
MESERVE HYBRID HOLLY

This group of hybrids was derived from *Ilex aquifolium* and *I. rugosa*. It is noted for the bluish green foliage, purple stems, red berries and frost hardiness of its members. Most have a dense, pyramidal shape and make attractive, strong-growing hedges. The cultivars '**Blue Girl**', '**Blue Boy**' and '**Blue Angel**' are the most commonly available. Others include '**Blue Prince**', a male plant of spreading habit which grows to 10 ft (3 m) in height and spread, and has glossy bright green leaves; and '**Blue Princess**', with extra glossy foliage and very abundant red berries on a shrub up to 10 ft (3 m) tall. **ZONES 5–9.**

Ilex mitis
CAPE HOLLY

One of the few African hollies, this evergreen species ranges widely through the wetter forest regions of southern and eastern Africa. It can grow to over 30 ft (9 m) in height, with a thick trunk and spreading dense crown. Leaves are quite smooth-edged, about 3 in (8 mm) long and tapering to a fine point; young leaves and twigs are red. Small white flowers in spring and early summer are followed by red berries. **ZONES 8–11.**

Ilex opaca
AMERICAN HOLLY

The best known American species, this evergreen tree grows to a height and

Ilex crenata

Ilex crenata 'Golden Gem'

Ilex crenata 'Convexa'

Ilex × *meserveae* 'Blue Angel'

Ilex pernyi

Ilex opaca

spread of about 30 ft (9 m); it has an erect habit and produces red berries in winter. The leaves are dull green above and yellowish underneath, with spiny or smooth edges. It prefers a sunny position and acid soil, and does not do well near the sea. **ZONES 5–10.**

Ilex paraguariensis
MATÉ, PARAGUAY TEA, YERBA MATÉ

This frost-tender, slow-growing, evergreen tree reaches 20 ft (6 m) tall and has a spread of 30 ft (10 m). Its indented leaves are deep green; the offset flowers are greenish white. The flowers are borne in the leaf axils and are followed by clusters of deep red berries. In its native South America, the dried leaves are used to make maté, a drink rich in caffeine. **ZONES 9–11.**

Ilex pernyi
PERNY'S HOLLY

From central and western China, this densely branched evergreen tree was named after the French missionary Paul Perny. It grows to a height of 30 ft (9 m), with distinctive, diamond-shaped, triangular-spined leaves and oval red berries. The flowers are yellowish. This species is very frost hardy, but does not tolerate dry conditions; water well in summer. **ZONES 5–10.**

Ilex serrata
JAPANESE WINTERBERRY, FINETOOTH HOLLY

Originating in Japan, this deciduous shrub reaches a height of 15 ft (4.5 m), with spreading branches, egg-shaped leaves, pale pink flowers and an abundance of tiny red berries. **'Sparkleberry'** is a vigorous hybrid between *Ilex serrata* and *I. verticillata*. A female clone, it has deep green leaves and glossy brilliant red berries. It grows to a height of 15 ft (4.5 m). **ZONES 5–10.**

Ilex × *meserveae* 'Blue Prince'

Ilex verticillata
WINTERBERRY, BLACK ALDER, CORAL BERRY

From eastern USA, this deciduous shrub grows 6–10 ft (1.8–3 m) high and has a spread of 4–10 ft (1.2–3 m). The toothed leaves are purple-tinged in spring and turn yellow in fall (autumn). The bright red berries stay on the bare branches for a long period, persisting until spring. This shrub tolerates wet conditions. Cultivars include **'Cacapon'**, a female which produces abundant berries when grown with a male; **'Nana'** (syn. 'Red Sprite'), a dwarf female which reaches 4 ft (1.2 m) tall and has a spread of 5 ft (1.5 m); and **'Winter Red'**, an extra vigorous female with a height and spread of 10 ft (3 m) and good crops of bright red berries when grown with a male plant. **ZONES 3–9.**

Ilex serrata

Ilex vomitoria
CAROLINA TEA, YAUPON HOLLY

An evergreen tree from southeastern USA and Mexico, this holly grows to a height of 20 ft (6 m) and has red berries and shallowly round-toothed glossy dark green leaves. A quick-growing species, it makes a good hedge or screen. Its leaves contain an emetic substance and were infused by Native Americans to prepare a purgative drink. The cultivar **'Fructoluteo'**, as the name would suggest, is a yellow-fruited clone. **ZONES 6–10**

ILLICIUM

This interesting genus originates from the temperate to subtropical regions of East Asia and the Americas. It contains about 40 frost-hardy evergreen shrubs and small trees, grown for their handsome foliage and fragrant flowers. The flowers are not unlike magnolias, to which the genus is related closely enough to have been included, at one time, in the family Magnoliaceae. They are followed by distinctive woody fruit shaped like 8-pointed stars, each lobe containing a seed. The largest species, *Illicium verum*, is the source of star anise, a spice much used in Chinese cooking. The name *Illicium* itself comes from a Latin word meaning 'alluring', especially in the sense of having an alluring fragrance.

CULTIVATION: Moderately to marginally frost hardy, the *Illicium* species grow best in part-shade or shade. They prefer moist, sandy, lime-free soil with added leafmold. Propagate them from cuttings in summer or by layering in fall (autumn).

Ilex verticillata 'Cacapon'

Ilex verticillata

Illicium anisatum
syn. ***Illicium religiosum***
FALSE ANISE, JAPANESE ANISE TREE

Notable for its aromatic bark, which was used for incense in Japan and China, this moderately frost-hardy species grows slowly to a height and spread of 20 ft (6 m) and has a conical form. The daphne-like leaves are aromatic and glossy dark green, and the fragrant greenish yellow, many-petalled flowers are borne in mid-spring; the fruit are poisonous if eaten in quantity and should not be used in cooking. *Illicium anisatum* prefers a sheltered position. **ZONES 8–11.**

Illicium floridanum
PURPLE ANISE, FLORIDA ANISE TREE

This marginally frost-hardy, bushy evergreen shrub from southern USA reaches a height and spread of 10 ft (3 m). The highly aromatic leaves (not always pleasantly so) are deep green, leathery and lance-shaped. It has spectacular, star-shaped, red or purplish red flowers with numerous narrow twisted petals, borne in late spring and early summer. **ZONES 9–11.**

Illicium verum
CHINESE ANISE

This native of China and Vietnam is a handsome evergreen shrub or tree which grows to 60 ft (18 m) tall and has a spread of 22–40 ft (7–12 m). Moderately frost hardy, it has leathery, deep green, elliptic leaves and bears fragrant, many-petalled white flowers in spring and summer. The flowers are commonly red- or pink-tinged inside. They are followed by distinctive star-shaped fruit which, in addition to being used as a spice, are often substituted for the more expensive aniseed oil. **ZONES 8–11.**

Illicium anisatum

IMPATIENS

This large genus of around 850 species of succulent-stemmed annuals, evergreen perennials and subshrubs is widely distributed, especially in the subtropics and tropics of Asia and Africa. They are useful for colorful summer bedding displays and for indoor and patio plants. The flowers come in an ever-increasing range of colors. Many hybrid strains are perennial in mild climates, but in colder climates are usually grown as annuals. Their botanical name, *Impatiens*, refers to the impatience with which they grow and multiply.

CULTIVATION: Frost hardy to frost tender, they will grow in sun or part-shade; many species do well under overhanging trees. They prefer a moist but freely drained soil, and need protection from strong winds. Tip prune the fast-growing shoots to encourage shrubby growth and more abundant flowers. Propagate from seed or stem cuttings in spring or summer.

Impatiens balfourii

A native of the Himalayas, this frost-tender annual species reaches 24–36 in (60–90 cm) in height and has a spread of 12 in (30 cm). In all but very cold climates, *Impatiens balfourii* will self-seed, thus becoming a prominent summer and fall (autumn) feature. Its flowers are a combination of white and rich mauve. The leaves are alternate, recurved and ovate to elliptic. Seedlings should be thinned each year to allow space for those left to mature properly. **ZONES 10–12.**

Impatiens, New Guinea Hybrid

Illicium floridanum

Impatiens pseudoviola

Impatiens pseudoviola 'Woodcote'

Impatiens balsamina
GARDEN BALSAM

This species from India, China and Malaysia is an erect, bushy annual that grows fairly quickly to a height of 12–18 in (30–45 cm) with a spread of 8–10 in (20–25 cm). It has lance-shaped bright green leaves and produces small, camellia-like single or double spurred flowers throughout summer and early fall (autumn). Colors include blood red, purple-red, pink and white; some flowers are spotted. *Impatiens balsamina* is marginally frost hardy and is a good species for bedding displays in sunny situations. **ZONES 9–12.**

Impatiens capensis
JEWEL WEED, LADY'S EARRINGS, ORANGE BALSAM

This frost-hardy annual from eastern North America is now naturalized in Europe, including the UK. It has ovate to elliptic, coarsely-toothed leaves. It grows to 5 ft (1.5 m) tall and produces its orange-yellow, brown-spotted flowers throughout summer and fall (autumn). *Impatiens capensis* will self-seed, perhaps somewhat too well, and can become invasive. **ZONES 4–10.**

Impatiens, New Guinea Hybrid 'Tango'

Impatiens, New Guinea Hybrid 'Concerto'

Impatiens glandulifera
syn. ***Impatiens roylei***
POLICEMAN'S HELMET, HIMALAYAN BALSAM

A native of the Himalayas, this plant has naturalized in both the UK and northern North America. A frost-hardy annual with a strong self-seeding tendency, it grows to about 6 ft (1.8 m) tall. It has thick fleshy stems, particularly at the bottom, and produces masses of flowers during summer. Its flowers are rose-purple to lilac or even white with a yellow-spotted interior. **ZONES 6–10.**

Impatiens mirabilis

Mirabilis means wonderful or amazing, and this plant is quite unlike other *Impatiens* species. An obscure but striking plant from Malaysia, it has curiously formed golden-yellow flowers that look almost like orchids and appear in summer and oval leaves arranged in terminal clusters. It grows to a height of 6 ft (1.8 m) and has a similar spread. **ZONES 10–12.**

Impatiens, New Guinea Hybrids

Hybrids from a New Guinean species, members of this group of fast-growing perennials are also grown as annuals in cool climates. They are frost tender and grow to a height and spread of 12–18 in (30–45 cm). The leaves are oval, pointed and bronze green, or may be variegated with cream, white or yellow. The flat, spurred flowers are pink, orange, red or cerise, sometimes with white markings. Cultivars include 'Cheers', with its coral flowers and yellow leaves; **'Concerto'**, with crimson-centered deep pink flowers; **'Tango'**, with deep orange flowers and bronze leaves; and **'Red Magic'**, which has scarlet flowers and bronze-red leaves. They do well in brightly lit positions indoors in cooler climates or on enclosed verandahs or patios in warmer areas. **ZONES 10–12.**

Impatiens niamniamensis

An unusual frost-tender succulent shrub from tropical East Africa, this species grows to 3 ft (1 m) tall. Each flower has a curled spur and the color changes along their length; the flower color also varies from plant to plant. The combinations of color include red to purple, red and pink, or red and yellow as in the cultivar *Impatiens niamniamensis* **'Congo Cockatoo'. ZONES 10–12.**

Impatiens noli-tangere
TOUCH-ME-NOT

An annual from Europe and Asia, this species grows up to 4 ft (1.2 m) in height and has a spread of 3 ft (1 m). Its flowers are produced in groups of 3 or 4, and are yellow with a red-spotted interior. The leaves are alternate and have coarsely toothed margins. **ZONES 8–12.**

Impatiens pseudoviola

This semi-trailing East African species is a perennial. It produces white flowers suffused with rose pink, with violet-rose central stripes on the wing petals. **'Woodcote'** is a shrubby, pale pink-lilac form. **ZONES 10–12.**

Impatiens repens
GOLDEN DRAGON

This evergreen, creeping perennial is native to Sri Lanka. It bears golden, hooded flowers with a large hairy spur in summer; these stand out against the small, kidney-shaped leaves with red stems. *Impatiens repens* is frost tender, and grows to a height of 2 in (5 cm). This species is especially suited to hanging baskets. **ZONES 10–12.**

Impatiens sodenii
syn. *Impatiens oliveri*
POOR MAN'S RHODODENDRON

Native to tropical East Africa, this vigorous and profusely flowering, soft-wooded, evergreen bushy perennial grows at least 4–8 ft (1.2–2.4 m) tall with a spread of 24 in (60 cm). Frost tender, it has whorls of 4 to 10 waxy, oval, pale green leaves with toothed margins. Flat, white or pale lilac, single flowers appear in fall (autumn) to winter. **ZONES 10–12.**

Imperata cylindrica 'Rubra'

Impatiens usambarensis

This tropical African species gets its name from the Usambara Mountains on the borders of Kenya and Tanzania, where it was first discovered. It is related to the better known *Impatiens walleriana* and has been used in the breeding of the many colorful 'busy lizzie' hybrids in this group. ***I. u* × *walleriana*,** seen here, displays just one of the many possible color outcomes in such crosses. **ZONES 10–12.**

Impatiens walleriana
syn. *Impatiens sultanii*
BUSY LIZZIE

From tropical East Africa, this succulent, evergreen perennial has soft, fleshy stems with reddish stripes and oval, fresh green leaves. Flattish spurred flowers ranging through crimson, ruby red, pink, orange, lavender and white, some variegated, are produced from late spring to late fall (autumn). There are many cultivars. It is marginally frost hardy, fast growing and bushy, and grows to a height and spread of 12–24 in (30–60 cm); water well. **ZONES 9–12.**

Imperata cylindrica 'Rubra'

Impatiens zombensis

Another tropical African species, *Impatiens zombensis* comes from the highland region around Zomba in Malawi. It is a shrubby species that reaches about 3 ft (1 m) tall and bears purplish flowers with white-spotted throats. **ZONES 10–12.**

IMPERATA

This grass genus consists of a single species, a moderately frost-hardy perennial with creeping underground rhizomes. The wild forms are usually of little horticultural merit, however, the colored-leaf types are uniquely attractive plants. *Imperata* ranges widely through eastern and southern Asia and southward to Australia.

CULTIVATION: They prefer full sun or dappled shade and humus-rich, moist but well-drained soil. Propagation is usually by division for colored-leaf forms or from seed for wild types.

Imperata cylindrica

This plant has slender leaf tufts to 30 in (75 cm) in height and in late summer produces 2 in (5 cm) long panicles of silver-white feathery spikelets. **'Rubra'** (syn. 'Red Baron'), the Japanese blood grass, has erect, mid-green leaves; in mid- to late summer their ends turn the color of blood, hence the common name. By fall (autumn) the whole plant has turned this vibrant color. This is an excellent plant for providing color contrast. **ZONES 8–12.**

INCARVILLEA

This genus of the bignonia family (Bignoniaceae) consists of 14 species native to central and East Asia, including the Himalayas, and are suitable for rock gardens and borders. The taller species are more at home in herbaceous borders. Some species are annuals, although those in cultivation are usually perennial. From mountain habitats, some of the shorter growing species from higher altitudes have, strangely enough, the largest and most exotic flowers. Most species flower in shades of magenta and deep rose pink although one or two species come in shades of yellow or white.

CULTIVATION: Most species of *Incarvillea* are frost hardy, but do not tolerate overly wet or waterlogged soil in winter. They usually require an aspect that has rich, moisture-retentive, well-drained soil, in a position that receives ample sun except in the very hottest part of the day. These plants prefer cold to temperate climates. Propagation is usually by seed in fall (autumn) or spring; division in spring or fall is possible, but difficult, as mature plants resent disturbance.

Impatiens repens

Impatiens zombensis

Impatiens walleriana

Impatiens usambarensis × *walleriana*

Incarvillea delavayi

Inula helenium

Incarvillea arguta

This hardy species from the Himalayas and western and southwestern China grows to about 3 ft (1 m) tall with a spread of 12 in (30 cm). It is more suitable for a border than a rock garden, although it will grow in a crevice in a wall. It will flower in the first year from seed and although perennial is sometimes treated as an annual. Its 1½ in (35 mm) long trumpet-shaped flowers are usually deep pink or sometimes white, and are produced through summer. **ZONES 8–10.**

Incarvillea delavayi

PRIDE OF CHINA, HARDY GLOXINIA

This fleshy-rooted, clump-forming perennial is useful for rock gardens and borders. It has handsome, fern-like foliage and erect stems bearing large, trumpet-shaped, rosy purple flowers in summer. It grows to a height of 24 in (60 cm) with a spread of 12 in (30 cm), but dies down early in fall (autumn). It is very frost hardy, but should be protected with a compost mulch during cold winters. **ZONES 6–10.**

INDIGOFERA

Members of this large leguminous genus of more than 700 species come in just about every form imaginable: annuals, perennials, shrubs and small trees. Most come from tropical and subtropical regions, with species found in both hemispheres. The cultivated species are generally subshrubs or small, deciduous, woody plants with smallish pinnate leaves and panicles of pea-like flowers, usually produced in summer.

CULTIVATION: Frost-tender to moderately frost hardy, they tend to prefer light yet moist, well-drained soil in sun or part-shade. Propagate from seed in fall (autumn) or cuttings or basal suckers in summer.

Indigofera australis

AUSTRALIAN INDIGO

Native to Australia, this elegant, smooth, spreading shrub grows to a height and spread of 6 ft (1.8 m); it has blue-gray leaves divided into leaflets and is moderately frost hardy. It bears small, mauve-pink flowers in long heads in winter to summer, followed by brown pods. **ZONES 9–11.**

Indigofera decora

syn. *Indigofera incarnata*

This bushy deciduous shrub from China and Japan grows to 24 in (60 cm) high with a spread of 3 ft (1 m); wider in mild climates. This species is moderately frost hardy and stems may die back to ground level, but the plant usually shoots again from the rootstock. The glossy dark green pinnate leaves, up to 10 in (25 cm) long, are composed of 7 to 13 oval leaflets. Long wisteria-like spikes of mauve-pink pea-shaped flowers appear throughout the warmer months. The cultivar **'Alba'** is a white-flowering form of this species. **ZONES 7–11.**

Indigofera heterantha

syn. *Indigofera gerardiana*

This elegant, deciduous, slightly arching shrub grows up to 10 ft (3 m) in height and spread. Its fine pinnate foliage is gray-green and sets off well the dainty,

Incarvillea arguta

semi-erect spikes of purple-pink pea-shaped flowers. This plant is native to the northwestern Himalayas and blooms from early summer to early fall (autumn). It is moderately frost hardy and likes a sunny position. **ZONES 7–10.**

Indigofera tinctoria

A deciduous, shrubby perennial, this plant has been grown and traded since ancient times for the intense blue dye extracted from its leaves. In frost-free climates, it can grow 6–8 ft (1.8–2.4 m) tall with a similar spread. The compound leaves, smooth above but hairy beneath, are made up of about a dozen leaflets. Its flowers, typical of the pea family in shape, are a pretty red and blue combination. **ZONES 10–12.**

INDOCALAMUS

Consisting of 20 or so species, *Indocalamus* is a genus of small running bamboos (and these can be invasive if not contained) from central and eastern China, Japan and Malaysia. Its most notable feature is that it has very big leaves relative to the size of the plant and the weight of these can cause some species to arch downwards.

CULTIVATION: These plants do best in sheltered positions protected from wind, in dappled or part-shade. They need constant moisture around their roots, but will not tolerate boggy or wet ground. Growth is most rapid and luxuriant in fertile, humus-rich soil. Propagation is by division of existing clumps in late winter or early spring, before new stems emerge from the ground.

Indocalamus tessellatus

This species can grow to 8 ft (2.4 m) but is usually somewhat shorter than this in cultivation. It spreads quickly to form open stands and because its leaves are so big and heavy—more than 24 in (60 cm) long—the stems are always bent over. Of interest to bamboo enthusiasts, this species is perhaps a little unkempt for most gardens. **ZONES 8–9**

Indigofera australis

INULA

Native to Asia, Africa and Europe, this genus of about 90 species in the daisy family are mostly herbaceous perennials, although some are subshrubs, biennials or annuals. The different species vary in size from quite tiny plants suited to the rock garden up to towering perennials that can exceed 10 ft (3 m) tall. Often in the case of the larger species, the leaves can also be impressive if somewhat rank. Inulas are well known for their fine-petalled, invariably yellow daisies, some species of which are quite large and showy. Several species have been in cultivation since ancient times and the name *Inula* was in use in Roman times.

CULTIVATION: Inulas are frost hardy plants. They will grow in any well-drained or moist but not wet soil that is reasonably deep and fertile. They prefer a sunny to part-shaded aspect. Propagation is usually from seed or by division in spring or fall (autumn).

Inula helenium

ELECAMPANE, SCABWORT

Believed to have originated in central Asia, this plant has become widely naturalized. It is one of the largest *Inula* species at 8 ft (2.4 m) tall with a spread of 3 ft (1 m). As it is rhizomatous, it is also one of the most invasive. It produces its large, yellow daisy-like flowers in summer and should be planted with due deference to its invasive potential. *Inula helenium* was used in medicine as a tonic, astringent, demulcent and diuretic and, because of this, is often planted in herb gardens. **ZONES 5–10.**

Indigofera decora

Indigofera decora 'Alba'

Iochroma fuchsioides

Iochroma grandiflorum

Iochroma cyaneum

Inula oculis-christi

EYE OF CHRIST

This showy, daisy-like perennial is a spreading, fleshy-rooted plant growing to 18 in (45 cm) in height with a spread of 24 in (60 cm). It has lance-shaped, hairy, mid-green leaves and blooms freely in summer, producing wide, yellow flowerheads. **ZONES 6–10.**

IOCHROMA

Members of the nightshade family, these brittle-wooded evergreen shrubs from tropical and subtropical areas of Central and South America are best suited to warm, humid climates. Usually erect, with softwooded, arching branches, they carry clusters of long tubular flowers in shades of blue, purple, red or white throughout summer and fall (autumn). Grown for their showy flowers, these plants are suitable for the garden, the greenhouse or as potted plants.
CULTIVATION: These frost-tender plants need full sun to part-shade and fertile, well-drained soil. In the garden, a sheltered position is best for protection from wind. Young plants can be pruned lightly to make them bushy, and flowered stems should be cut back heavily in early spring. Propagate from cuttings or seed. Potted plants should be watered well in summer. They may be prone to attack from white fly and spider mites.

Iochroma cyaneum

syns ***Iochroma tubulosum, I. lanceolatum***

VIOLET TUBEFLOWER

This fast-growing, semi-erect shrub grows to 10 ft (3 m) high with a spread of 5 ft (1.5 m). *Iochroma cyaneum* brings a deep purple accent to the warm-climate garden; it can be grown in a greenhouse in cooler areas. It has gray-green felty leaves; deep purple-blue flowers are borne in large pendent clusters through summer and fall (autumn). Prune to shape in early spring. **ZONES 9–11.**

Iochroma fuchsioides

This species from the South American Andes is similar in its habit to *Iochroma cyaneum.* However, its tubular flowers are scarlet to bright red with a yellow throat. *Iochroma fuchsioides* is marginally less frost tolerant than other species. **ZONES 10–12.**

Iochroma grandiflorum

Indigenous to Ecuador, this shrub or small tree grows 10–20 ft (3–6 m) high and 6–12 ft (1.8–3.5 m) wide. Its soft, deep green, pointed oval leaves are up to 8 in (20 cm) long and are slightly downy when young. The flowers, borne in late summer and fall (autumn), are long, pendent, bright purple tubes with widely flared mouths. They are followed by pulpy, purplish green, berry-like fruit. **ZONES 9–12.**

IPHEION

SPRING STARFLOWER

These small spring bulbs from Argentina present such a simple picture of starry pale blue flowers set among grassy leaves that it is hard to credit that for 160 years science has been unable to decide where they fit into the scheme of things and what their correct name should be. Since they were first described in 1830, they have been shunted from one genus to the next, been demoted to a subspecies or alternatively given a genus of their own, and been assigned no fewer than 8 generic names. Gardeners have barely had time to get used to each new name before botanists present them with a newer one.
CULTIVATION: Frost hardy, they are easily grown in any temperate climate. They prefer a sheltered position in dappled shade and well-drained soil, but can be grown in full sun in cooler areas. Propagate from offsets in late summer or early fall (autumn).

Ipheion uniflorum

syns ***Brodiaea uniflora, Tristagma uniflorum, Triteleia uniflora***

SPRING STARFLOWER

One of the longest blooming of the spring bulbs, each bulb of this plant produces a succession of dainty flowers on 4 in (10 cm) stems for several weeks from late winter to spring. The most common color is pastel blue, but forms are also available in white and deep, purple-tinted blue. The flowers are delicately and pleasingly scented; the grass-like leaves have a garlic odor when bruised. **ZONES 6–10.**

IPOMOEA

syns ***Calonyction, Mina, Pharbitis, Quamoclit***

MORNING GLORY

This large genus of some 300 mostly climbing, evergreen shrubs, perennials and annuals is widespread throughout the tropics and warm-temperate regions of the world. It includes sweet potato and some of the loveliest of the tropical flowering vines. Most species have a twining habit and masses of funnel-shaped, flowers which in many species wither by midday. The flowers are usually short lived, lasting only one day (or night), but blooming prolifically and in succession. They are useful for covering sheds, fences, trellises and banks, and may also be grown in containers.
CULTIVATION: Marginally frost hardy to frost tender, they are best suited to warm coastal districts or tropical areas. They prefer moderately fertile, well-drained soil and a sunny position. Care should be taken when choosing species, as some can become extremely invasive in warm districts. Propagate in spring from seed which has been gently filed and pre-soaked to aid germination, or from cuttings in summer (for perennial species).

Ipomoea alba

syns ***Calonyction aculeatum, Ipomoea bona-nox***

MOON FLOWER

From tropical America, this fast-growing, soft-stemmed, evergreen perennial vine grows up to 20 ft (6 m) or more. It is cultivated for its large, fragrant, pure white flowers, which are borne in summer and open at night. It is frost tender, but is easily grown as an annual in cool climates where summers are warm. **ZONES 10–12.**

Ipomoea batatas

SWEET POTATO, KUMARA

From Central America and the Pacific islands, this perennial climber comes in both white-fleshed and orange-fleshed forms. It has entire, toothed or 3-lobed leaves and flowers with a lavender to pale purple tube that is darker on the inside. Plant cuttings in soil that has been fertilized and dug thoroughly; water well while the tubers grow. **ZONES 9–12.**

Ipomoea alba

Ipomoea batatas

Ipheion uniflorum

I

Ipomoea cairica
syn. *Ipomoea palmata*

This herbaceous perennial climber is from tropical and subtropical Africa and parts of Asia. It grows from a tuberous rootstock and reaches about 15 ft (4.5 m) in height. It can be used as a climber or trailing plant. The funnel-shaped flowers are red, purple or white, with purple inside the tube. **ZONES 9–12.**

Ipomoea hederacea

This annual, twining, frost-tender climber has slender, hairy stems and rounded, 3-lobed, mid- to deep green leaves. It bears from 2 to 5 funnel-shaped, blue flowers with white tubes in summer and grows to 20 ft (6 m) or more. **ZONES 10–12.**

Ipomoea horsfalliae
CARDINAL CREEPER

Native to the West Indies and other tropical regions, this beautiful evergreen flowering vine grows up to 10 ft (3 m) and requires warm, frost-free conditions. From summer through to winter, *Ipomoea horsfalliae* bears stalked clusters of long, tubular, deep rose-pink or rose-purple flowers, which give it its common name. **ZONES 11–12.**

Ipomoea indica
syns *Ipomoea acuminata, I. learii*
COMMON MORNING GLORY, BLUE DAWN FLOWER

The blooms of this frost-tender perennial climber open a rich blue color in the morning, fade to purple during the heat of the day, then crumple and die in the evening. There are also white and pink forms. The vine is very rampant and can become a pest in frost-free climates; in parts of Australia, people can be fined for harboring *Ipomoea indica* in their gardens, yet in the UK it is cherished and cosseted as an annual or greenhouse plant. **ZONES 10–12.**

Ipomoea horsfalliae

Ipomoea indica

Ipomoea × multifida

Ipomoea nil

Ipomoea cairica

Ipomoea lobata
syns *Ipomoea versicolor, Mina lobata, Quamoclit lobata*

Native to Mexico and Central America, this vigorous, short-lived twining climber is a perennial usually grown as an annual. It is deciduous or semi-evergreen with 3-lobed bright green leaves, and bears racemes of small, tubular, dark red flowers fading to orange then creamy yellow. The flowers appear from late summer until late fall (autumn). This marginally frost-hardy plant climbs to a height of 15 ft (4.5 m) and quickly provides a dense leafy cover over a suitable supporting structure. **ZONES 8–12.**

Ipomoea × multifida
syn. *Ipomoea × sloteri*
CARDINAL CLIMBER

This is a hybrid of *Ipomoea coccinea* and *I. quamoclit* of garden origin. A frost-tender annual climber with slender twining stems, it reaches 10 ft (3 m) in height. The foliage is mid-green and divided into several lobes. Its tubular flowers, produced during summer, are crimson-red with white throats. **ZONES 9–12.**

Ipomoea nil
syns *Ipomoea imperialis, Pharbitis nil*

This soft-stemmed, short-lived, twining perennial is best treated as an annual. Marginally frost hardy, it grows to 12 ft (3.5 m) in height. Its stems are covered with hairs, and the leaves are heart-shaped. Large, trumpet-shaped flowers appear from summer through to early fall (autumn) in a variety of shades. **'Scarlett O'Hara'** is a cultivar with dark crimson blooms. **ZONES 9–12.**

Ipomoea pes-caprae
syn. *Ipomoea biloba*
BEACH MORNING GLORY, RAILROAD VINE

A prostrate or climbing perennial, *Ipomoea pes-caprae* has 2 in (5 cm) wide flowers that can be pink to light purple with a dark throat. This species is found in tropical beaches around the world, its stems rooting at the nodes. The plant's distinctive leaf shape, with 2 rounded lobes, is referred to in the name *pes-caprae*, which means goat's foot. **ZONES 10–12.**

Ipomoea pes-caprae

Ipomoea purga
syns *Ipomoea jalapa, Convolvulus jalapa*
JALAP

This marginally frost-hardy, evergreen climber reaches a height of 10 ft (3 m). It has purple-red, twining stems and pointed ovate to heart-shaped leaves. The purple-pink, funnel-shaped flowers are produced in fall (autumn) The turnip-like tuber and its resin is sometimes used medicinally in laxative and carminative preparations, and can be used to treat intestinal parasites. Its use is restricted in some countries. **ZONES 9–12.**

Ipomoea quamoclit
syn. *Quamoclit pennata*
CYPRESS VINE

Looking quite unlike other morning glories, this annual climbing vine can grow to 12 ft (3.5 m) in height when planted in a warm, sheltered site. From tropical South America, its bright green leaves are finely dissected into linear lobes. The narrow, orange and scarlet tubular flowers are produced from summer to early fall (autumn). **ZONES 8–12.**

Ipomoea tricolor
syns *Ipomoea rubrocaerulea, I. violacea, Pharbitis tricolor*

This Mexican perennial is more often grown as an annual. It can reach a height of 10 ft (3 m) with a spread of 5 ft (1.5 m), and has cord-like, twining stems and heart-shaped, light green leaves. From summer to early fall (autumn), *Ipomoea tricolor* bears large blue to mauve, funnel-shaped flowers which open in the morning and gradually fade during the day. Widening to a trumpet as they open, they can reach 6 in (15 cm) across. The cultivar **'Heavenly Blue'** is particularly admired for its color, as is the very similar **'Clarke's Himmelblau'**. **ZONES 8–12.**

IPOMOPSIS

This genus of perennials and biennials in the phlox family consists of 24 species from the USA—from the Pacific Coast to Florida and South Carolina—with one outlying species from southern Argentina. The leaves are usually in a basal rosette, with smaller leaves on the flower spikes. Few species are grown in cultivation, but they can be useful as summer bedding plants in cold climates and are also grown as pot plants in greenhouses and conservatories.

CULTIVATION: These mostly frost-hardy plants prefer a sunny aspect or full light with fertile, well-drained soil. They should be grown in cool, airy conditions. Propagation is from seed in early spring or early summer, or by division of the perennial species.

Ipomopsis aggregata
syn. *Gilia aggregata*
SCARLET GILIA, SKYROCKET

Native to the mountains of western North America, this showy, slow-growing biennial adapts easily to gardens where the summer humidity is low. It grows to 3 ft (1 m) tall with a spread of 12 in (30 cm). Finely divided leaves delicately clothe its slender stems. Terminal clusters of fragrant, trumpet-shaped flowers appear in summer and are usually bright scarlet, sometimes with yellow mottling, but can be silvery pink, yellow or white. ZONES 4–11.

Ipomoea tricolor 'Heavenly Blue'

Ipomoea tricolor 'Clarke's Himmelblau'

Ipomoea tricolor 'Heavenly Blue'

IRESINE

Belonging to the amaranthus family, these tropical perennials from the Americas and Australia—some 80 species in all—are sometimes treated as annuals. They vary in habit from upright to ground-hugging. The flowers are insignificant and not the reason for which these plants are grown. It is for their often brilliantly colored leaves that they merit attention.
CULTIVATION: These frost-tender plants only make permanent garden plants in tropical to warm temperate climates where there is no incidence of frost. In cooler areas they can be grown in greenhouses and planted out once all chance of frost has passed. They prefer good loamy, well-drained soil and must be kept moist during the growth period. They also need bright light, with some sun, to retain the brilliant color in their leaves. Tips should be pinched out in the growing season to encourage bushy plants. Propagate from cuttings in spring.

Iresine herbstii
syn. *Iresine reticulata*
BEEFSTEAK PLANT, BLOODLEAF

Native to Brazil, this species makes an attractive tropical bedding or pot plant. Although perennial, it is often treated as an annual that is overwintered as struck cuttings in a greenhouse in cold areas. It grows to 24 in (60 cm) tall with a spread of 18 in (45 cm), but usually much less if grown as an annual. It has red stems and rounded purple-red leaves up to 4 in (10 cm) long, with notches at the tips and yellowish red veins. Garden forms have a range of colors: from bright green leaves with bright yellow veins through to cultivars such as **'Brilliantissima'** with its rich purple-green leaves with beetroot-pink veins. ZONES 10–12.

Iresine herbstii 'Brilliantissima'

Iresine herbstii

IRIS

This wide-ranging genus of more than 200 species, native to the temperate regions of the northern hemisphere, is named for the Greek goddess of the rainbow and is valued for its beautiful and distinctive flowers. Each flower has 6 petals: 3 outer petals, called 'falls', which droop away from the center and alternate with the inner petals, called 'standards'. There are many hybrids. Irises are divided into 2 main groups, **rhizomatous** and **bulbous**.

Rhizomatous irises have sword-shaped leaves, are sometimes evergreen, and are subdivided into 3 groups: **bearded** (or flag) irises, with a tuft of hairs (the 'beard') on the 3 lower petals; **beardless** irises, without the tuft; **crested** or **Evansia** irises, with a raised crest in lieu of a beard.

The bearded types include the rare and beautiful **Oncocyclus** and **Regelia** irises, native to the eastern Mediterranean and Central Asia and so needing cold winters and hot, dry summers to flourish. Hybrids between these 2 groups are called **Regeliocyclus** irises, while hybrids between either of them and other bearded irises are called **Arilbred** irises. But the main group of bearded irises consists of numerous species with thick, creeping rhizomes, mainly from temperate Eurasia, and countless hybrids bred from these: both species and hybrids can be subdivided into the 3 classes **Tall Bearded**, **Intermediate Bearded** and **Dwarf Bearded** irises, depending mainly on height of plant but some other characteristics as well. Tall bearded irises are the most popular class of irises, with by far the largest number of hybrid cultivars.

The beardless irises are mostly plants with long narrow leaves and include several identifiable groups of species and hybrids, most notably the East Asian **Laevigatae** or **Water** irises including the large-flowered **'Kaempferi'** irises derived from *I. ensata*, the **Louisiana** irises from southeastern USA and their hybrids, the **Pacific Coast** irises from the west side of North America, also with many hybrids, and the Eurasian **Spuria** and **Siberian** irises, consisting of numerous species and a scattering of hybrids.

The bulbous irises are divided into 3 groups, the **Juno, Reticulata** and **Xiphium** irises, the first 2 consisting of beautiful but mostly difficult bulbs from west and central Asia. The Xiphium irises, though, are centered on the Mediterranean and are more easily grown; they have given rise to a group of bulbous hybrids including the so-called **English, Spanish and Dutch** irises; it is the latter that are commonly seen in florist shops.
CULTIVATION: Growing conditions vary greatly, however, as a rule rhizomatous irises, with the exception of the crested or Evansia irises, are very frost hardy and prefer a sunny position; some of the beardless types like very moist soil. Bulbous irises are very frost hardy, and prefer a sunny position with ample moisture during growth, but very little during their summer dormancy; plant in fall (autumn). Bulbous irises are prone to virus infection and so need to be kept free of aphids, which will spread the infection. Propagate irises by division in late summer after flowering or from seed in fall; named cultivars by division only.

Iris aphylla
syns *Iris benacensis, I. bohemica, I. melzeri*

Native to central and eastern Europe, this bearded iris reaches only 6–12 in (15–30 cm) in height. It has broad deciduous leaves and branched flowering stems which produce up to 5 typical bearded iris flowers each in late spring and occasionally again in fall (autumn). The flowers range in color from pale purple to a deep blue-violet, but are usually a rich dark purple. This is one of the species that have been used in the breeding of semi-dwarf and dwarf hybrids. Although it prefers good summer drainage, it is the most tolerant of winter wet of all the bearded irises. This species contains many regional varieties, some of which were once considered separate species. ZONES 5–9.

Iris bakeriana

This bulbous Reticulata iris has narrow, almost cylindrical leaves that are very short at flowering time, but which grow longer later on. A solitary, pale blue flower with a dark blue blotch and a spotted, deep blue center is borne in late winter. A cold-climate species, it grows to 4 in (10 cm) in height and prefers an open, sunny, well-drained position. ZONES 5–9.

Iris bracteata

Iris cristata

Iris danfordiae

Iris bracteata
SISKIYOU IRIS

So called because its leaves on the flowering stems are short and bract-like, this native of Oregon inhabits dry conifer forests. Its flowers are usually predominantly cream or yellow, but some plants with reddish toned flowers exist. The falls are flared with reddish veins, and its standards are erect. The flowers are held on stems 12 in (30 cm) tall. Although frost hardy, this species is not easy to grow; it resents being lifted and divided, so is best raised from seed. **ZONES 7–9.**

Iris bucharica
syn. ***Iris orchiodes***
BOKHARA IRIS

This bulbous Juno iris from central Asia grows to 18 in (45 cm) tall and its growth form is quite uncharacteristic. It has broad, strongly channeled leaves progressing up the stem in 2 rows, their bases overlapping. The 2½ in (6 cm) scented flowers—2 to 6 blooms borne in

Iris cristata 'Alba'

spring—vary in color. Standards and falls can be white to golden yellow, or standards can be white and falls yellow. It requires a rich soil and is slow to multiply. Although easier to grow than other Juno irises, take care not to damage the thick lateral roots when transplanting or dividing clumps. **ZONES 5–9.**

Iris cristata
CRESTED IRIS

A woodland crested or Evansia iris native to southeastern USA, this creeper grows 4–9 in (10–22.5 cm) in height. In spring, it bears faintly fragrant, pale blue to lavender or purple flowers held just above the foliage; each fall has a white patch with an orange crest. It prefers a moist soil in part-shade, making it suitable as a ground cover in shaded gardens; it spreads slowly by rhizomes. **'Alba'** is a vigorous cultivar with white flowers. **ZONES 6–9.**

Iris danfordiae
DANFORD IRIS

This bulbous Reticulata iris, native to central Turkey, has narrow, quadrangular leaves which are very short during flowering, but later grow longer. It bears a usually solitary yellow flower with green spots on each fall in late winter. It produces masses of small bulblets and should be deeply planted. It reaches a height of 2–4 in (5–10 cm). **ZONES 5–9.**

Iris douglasiana
DOUGLAS IRIS

One of the chief parents of the Pacific Coast irises, this evergreen, rhizomatous beardless species comes from the coastal mountain ranges of California. It reaches

Iris douglasiana

10–30 in (25–75 cm) in height and its branched stems produce 1 to 3 flowers in early spring. The flowers are variable in color, from rich blue-purple to almost white, while the leathery, dark green leaves are stained with maroon at the base. It readily hybridizes with other species from its region. **ZONES 8–10.**

Iris ensata
syn. ***Iris kaempferi***
JAPANESE FLAG, HIGO IRIS

Native to Japan and cultivated there for centuries, this beardless iris grows to 3 ft (1 m) tall. It has purple flowers with yellow blotches on each fall, which appear from late spring to early summer; the leaves have a prominent midrib. The many named varieties bear huge flowers, up to 10 in (25 cm) wide, in shades of white, lavender, blue and purple, often blending 2 shades and some with double flowers. These plants prefer part-shade in hot areas, rich, acid soil and plenty of moisture, and can even grow in shallow water provided they are not submerged in winter; the foliage dies down for the winter. **'Exception'** has particularly large falls and deep purple flowers; **'Mystic Buddha'** has purple-blue flowers with red edging. **ZONES 4–10.**

Iris foetidissima
STINKING IRIS, GLADWYN OR GLADDON IRIS, ROAST BEEF PLANT

This widespread European rhizomatous, beardless species is found growing in open woods, scrub and hedges. Its rich green foliage is evergreen and reaches a height of 30 in (75 cm) or more. The whole plant is fully hardy. The small flowers, which appear in late spring, are usually pale lemon to fawn or purple gray in color and veined with brown. In winter, the plant's large green pods open to expose masses of orange seeds that are highly ornamental. Due to its ability to grow in dry shade, it is a very useful

Iris ensata

plant in cultivation. It also tolerates damp conditions. **ZONES 7–9**

Iris forrestii

A dainty, slender rhizomatous, beardless Siberian iris, this species grows to 15 in (38 cm) tall. Native to China and northern Burma, it is fairly easy to grow and requires little more than a sunny site with moist to damp soil; it will even grow well on the margins of ponds. Its fragrant flowers, usually 2 per stem, are a soft yellow; the falls are marked with black lines and dark brown spots along the veins. The standards are erect or somewhat closed in, and occasionally flushed with brown. **ZONES 6–9.**

Iris × *fulvala*

This is a hybrid between *Iris fulva* and *I. brevicaulis* (syn. *I. lamancei*), which belong to a small group of North American beardless irises including the Louisiana irises. It has purple-red flowers and, like its parent *I. fulva*, appreciates a moist to wet aspect. It will grow to 30 in (75 cm) tall. **ZONES 7–10.**

Iris germanica
COMMON FLAG, GERMAN IRIS

The putative ancestor of the modern bearded irises, this rhizomatous, bearded species is easy to grow in just about any temperate climate, its creeping rhizomes multiplying rapidly into large clumps. The sparsely branched stem produces up to 6 yellow-bearded, blue-purple to blue-violet flowers in spring. ***Iris germanica* var. *biliottii*** (syn. *Iris biliottii*) occurs naturally in the Black Sea region of Turkey. It grows to about 3 ft (1 m) tall and, like *I. germanica*, has scented flowers. This variety has reddish purple falls with standards of a more blue-purple shade;

Iris ensata 'Exception'

Iris ensata cultivar

Iris innominata

Iris × fulvala

the beard is white with yellow tips. Another form of *I. germanica* is **'Florentina'**, which has scented white flowers with a bluish flush and a yellow beard. Its bracts are brown and papery during flowering. This latter species is cultivated in Italy, particularly around Florence, for its perfume (orris root), which is released when the roots are dried. An early-flowering variety, 'Florentina' prefers a position with full sun. **ZONES 4–10.**

Iris graminea
syn. *Iris colchica*

This species of rhizomatous, beardless Spuria iris is widespread from Spain to western Russia, usually growing in part-shade. In cultivation, it also likes a moist but not soggy soil. In spring, its fine lance-shaped foliage partially obscures up to 10 fragrant, 3 in (8 cm) wide flowers. These vary considerably in color from violet-blue to purple, but usually have wine-purple standards and veined, violet-blue falls. Although the small flowers overtopped by foliage make it a less showy species, it still makes a pretty and dainty subject for a moist rock garden or border's edge. It should be noted

Iris lactea

Iris japonica

that *Iris graminea* does not like to be disturbed. **ZONES 5–9.**

Iris histrio

This beautiful bulbous Reticulata iris is found in Turkey, Syria and Lebanon, and is possibly the largest flowered of its group. It is not an easy plant to cultivate as it is easily damaged by late frosts and its bulbs tend to break down into tiny non-flowering ones. The flowers, which are produced from late winter to very early spring, are in shades of blue fading to white in the center, with large blue blotches and a yellow ridge. The leaves are quadrangular in cross-section. **ZONES 4–9.**

Iris histrioides

Closely allied to *Iris histrio*, this Turkish species is distinguished by its broader-petalled flowers and leaves which are taller than the flowers though usually absent when the first flowers appear in late winter. In gardens it is usually represented by a large deep violet-blue form known as **'Major'**; there is some confusion over this name as it was originally described as a pale blue form. It requires a well-drained, sunny aspect. **ZONES 5–9.**

Iris innominata
DEL NORTE COUNTY IRIS

Native to the northwest coast of the USA, this rhizomatous, beardless iris is one of the parent species of the Pacific Coast Hybrids. It reaches 6–10 in (15–25 cm) in height. Its evergreen, narrow, deep green leaves are up to 12 in (30 cm) long and are purple at their bases. The unbranched stems bear 1 or 2 flowers in early summer. They range in color from

Iris germanica var. *biliottii*

bright yellow to cream, and from pale lavender-blue to purple. The falls may be veined with brown or maroon. **ZONES 8–10.**

Iris japonica
syn. *Iris fimbriata*
CRESTED IRIS

From Japan and the lowlands of China, this is the best known of the crested or Evansia species. It grows to 18–32 in (45–80 cm) in height, forming large clumps of almost evergreen, glossy mid-green leaves. In late winter and spring, it bears sprays of 2½ in (6 cm) wide, ruffled, pale blue or white flowers; each fall has a violet patch around an orange crest. It prefers an acidic soil, a lightly shaded position, and a mild climate. It must be kept shaded from afternoon sun. A variety with white-striped leaves, it is rather shy flowering. **ZONES 8–11.**

Iris kamaonensis

A clump-forming iris from the Himalayas, this belongs to a small group of bearded species allied to the Oncocyclus and Regelia irises. Its leaves grow up to 18 in (45 cm) long when they mature. Its scented, blue-purple striped flowers nestle amongst the leaves; they are 2 in (5 cm) across and have dark blotches and white to yellow-tipped beards, with paler standards. *Iris kamaonensis* prefers a slightly shaded aspect, with moist but well-drained gritty soil. **ZONES 6–9.**

Iris lactea

This widespread beardless species allied to *Iris ensata* is found from central Russia to Korea and the Himalayas. It has stiff, upright, gray-green leaves up to about 2 in (5 cm) wide which can overtop the 12 in (30 cm) tall flower spikes. These are produced in early summer and have 1 or 2 fragrant pale lavender-blue or rarely white flowers. This strong plant will cope with both frost and heat, but is one of the less spectacular irises. **ZONES 4–9.**

Iris germanica

Iris germanica 'Florentina'

Iris laevigata

RABBIT-EAR IRIS

This rhizomatous, beardless species native to Japan is similar to *Iris ensata*, but has slightly smaller blooms and its leaves do not have a prominent midrib. Its sparsely branched stems bear 2 to 4 purple flowers with yellow blotches from mid-spring to early summer. It thrives in sun or part-shade in moist conditions, and will also grow in shallow water all year. Both *I. laevigata* and *I. ensata* feature in traditional Japanese paintings. **ZONES 4–9.**

Iris latifolia

syn. *Iris xiphioides*

ENGLISH IRIS

Most of the bulbous English irises (so-called because of their great popularity in eighteenth-century England) are derived from this bulbous Xiphium species native to Spain. It grows to 30 in (75 cm), with lance-shaped, mid-green leaves. In late spring, it bears purple-blue or white 4 in (10 cm) flowers. The very wide falls are 'winged' and often have a golden blotch running down their center. **ZONES 7–10.**

Iris orientalis

Iris lutescens

syn. *Iris chamaeiris*

Iris lutescens is a variable rhizomatous, dwarf bearded iris from southwestern Europe similar to *I. pumila*. It is fast growing and can have foliage that is less than ½ in (12 mm) to more than 1 in (2.5 cm) wide and up to 12 in (30 cm) long. The flowers, borne in early spring, can be yellow, violet blue, white or bicolored; the beard is yellow. This is an easy-to-grow and showy species, but it does need winter cold to flower well. **'Caerulea'** is a bluish version of *I. lutescens*. **ZONES 5–9.**

Iris maackii

This little known and comparatively newly described species from China is related to *Iris laevigata*. The flowers are more than 2 in (5 cm) wide and completely yellow. It should prove to be a hardy and dainty iris, growing up to about 12 in (30 cm) tall. **ZONES 4–9.**

Iris milesii

This Evansia species comes from the Himalayas and varies little in form. It thrives well in a sunny bed and will seed readily. It is similar to but not as showy as *Iris tectorum*, the Japanese roof iris. *I. milesii* has creeping fat rhizomes that are slightly green, and these support fans of rich green foliage up to 24 in (60 cm) long. The flowers are soft lavender-blue in color, with darker markings on the falls and yellow markings within. **ZONES 7–10.**

Iris lutescens 'Caerulea'

Iris pseudacorus

Iris pseudacorus 'Variegata'

Iris missouriensis

syn. *Iris tolmeiana*

MISSOURI FLAG, ROCKY MOUNTAIN IRIS

A widespread rhizomatous, beardless iris extending through western and central North America from Mexico to British Columbia, this is a very frost-hardy and easy-to-grow plant, although quite variable in appearance. It reaches 30 in (75 cm) in height. It likes moist soil up until it flowers in early spring and drier conditions during summer. This species can make substantial clumps with slender leaves. Its flowers vary in color from very pale blue through to deep blue or lavender, with some white forms. The falls, veined with deep purple, usually have a yellow blaze. **ZONES 3–9.**

Iris pallida

Iris missouriensis

Iris maackii

Iris pallida 'Variegata'

Iris munzii

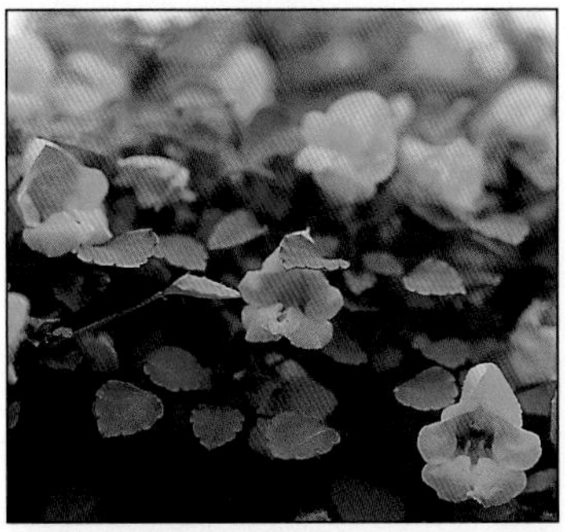

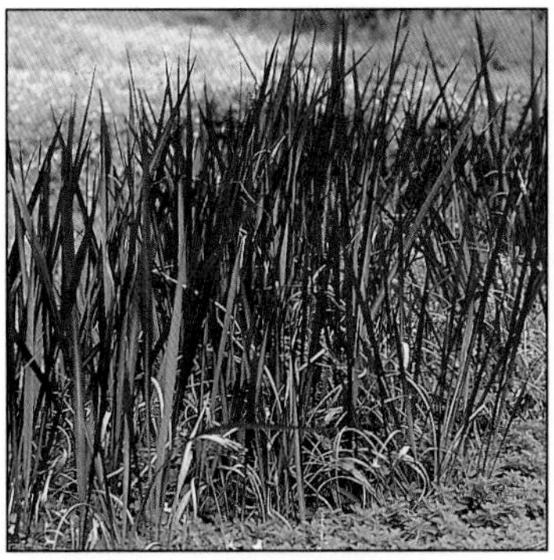

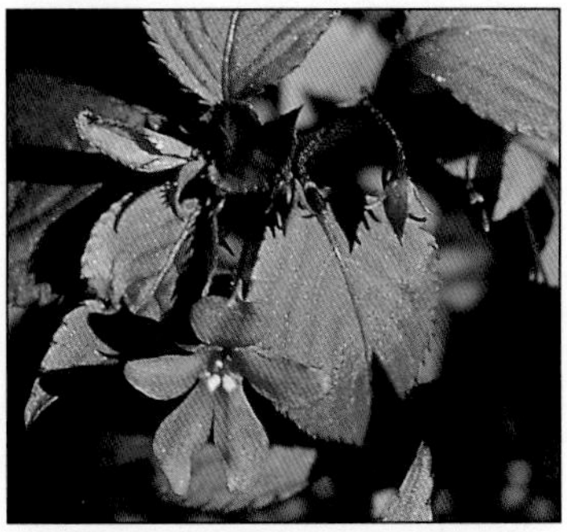

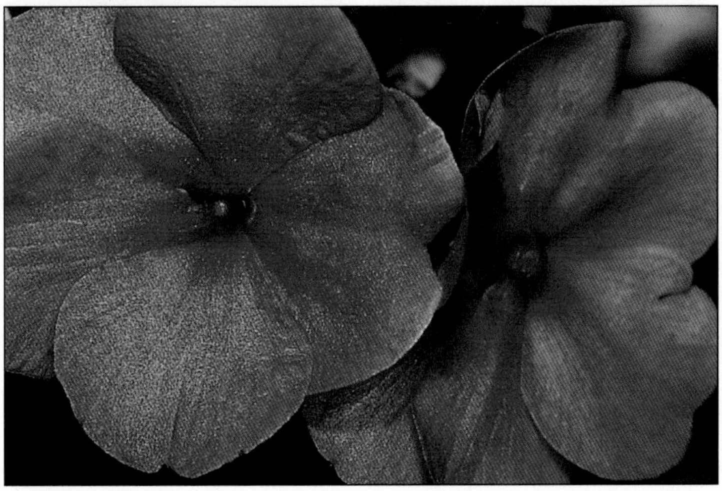

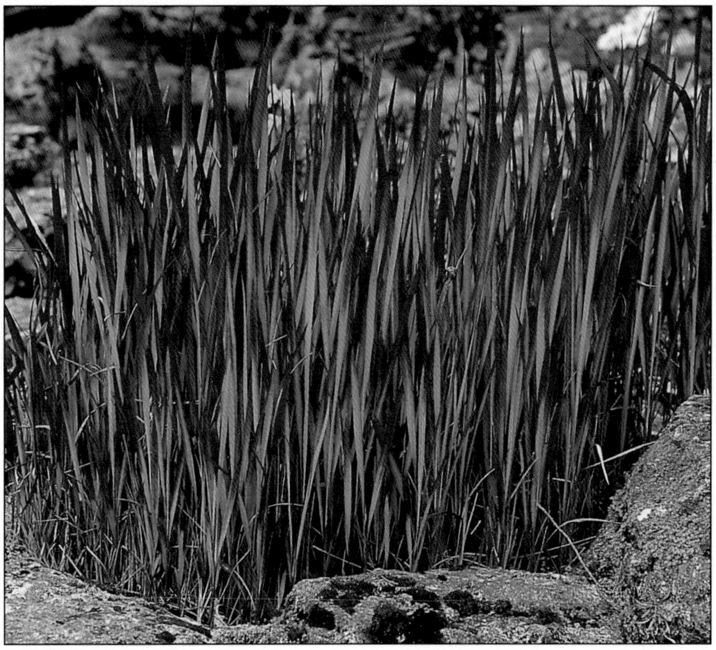

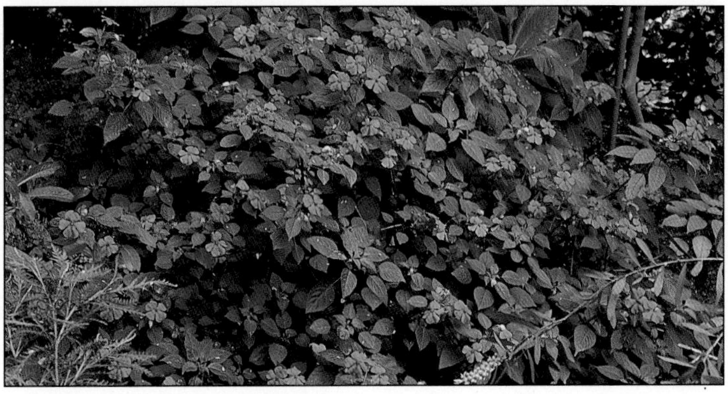

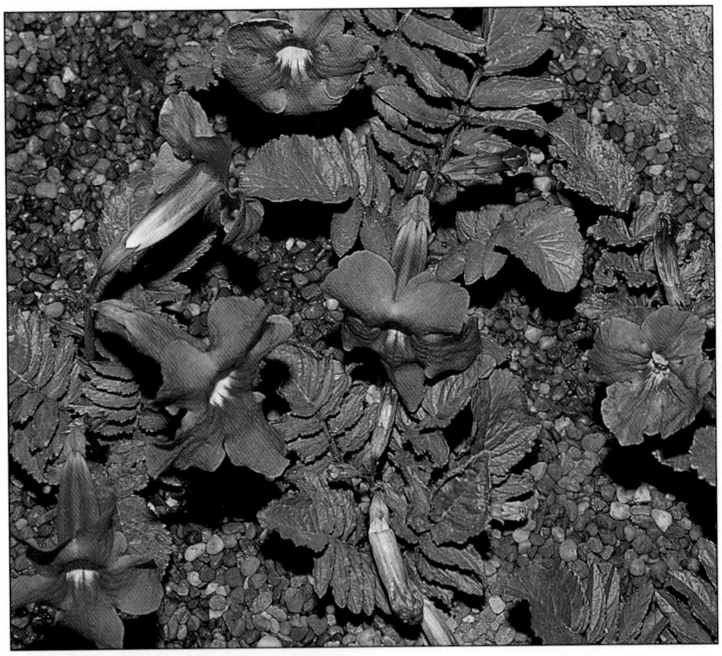

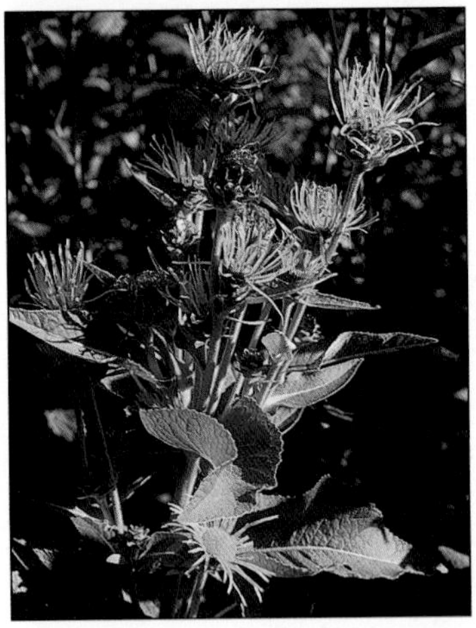

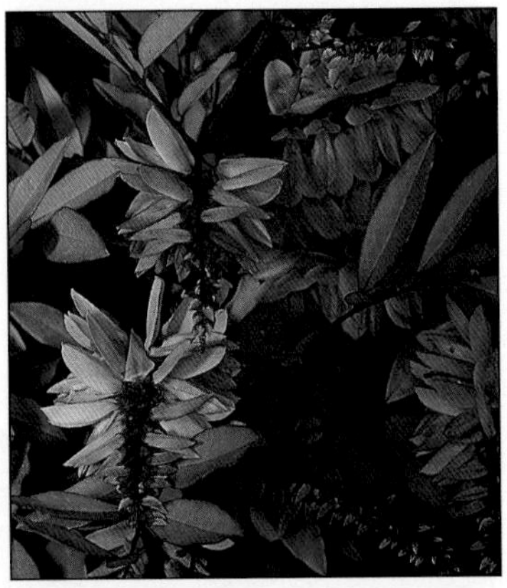

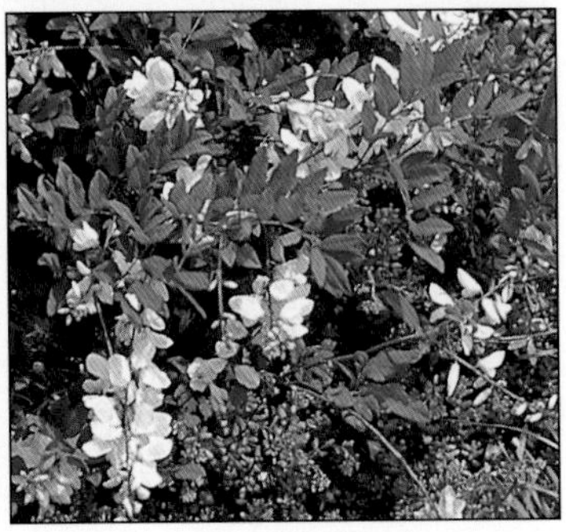

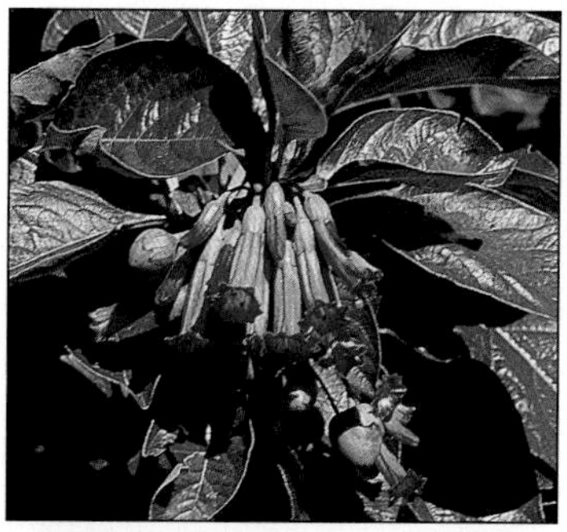

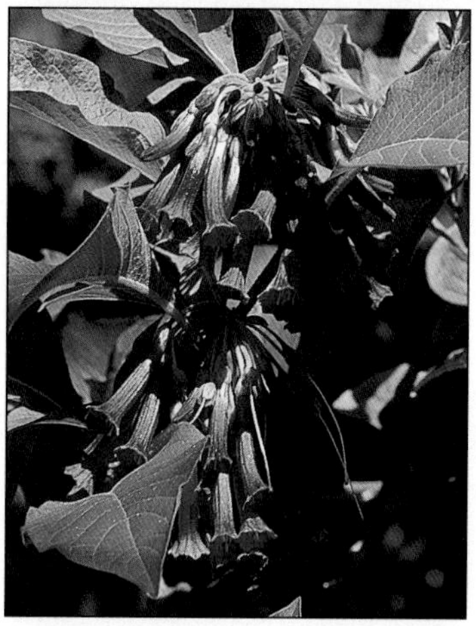

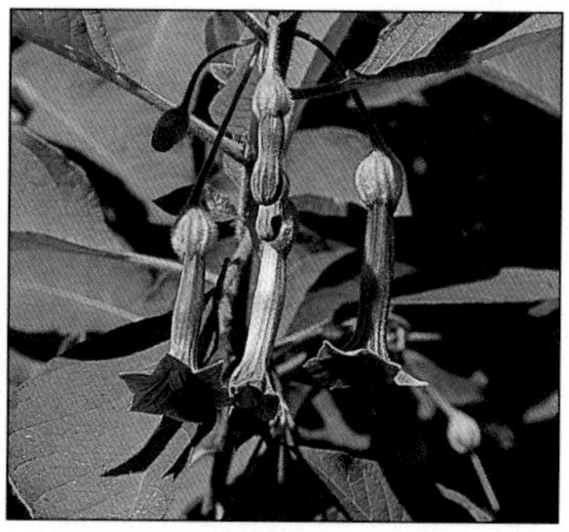

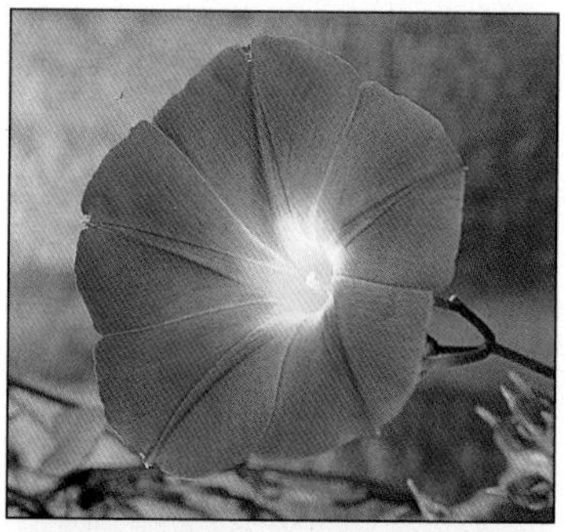

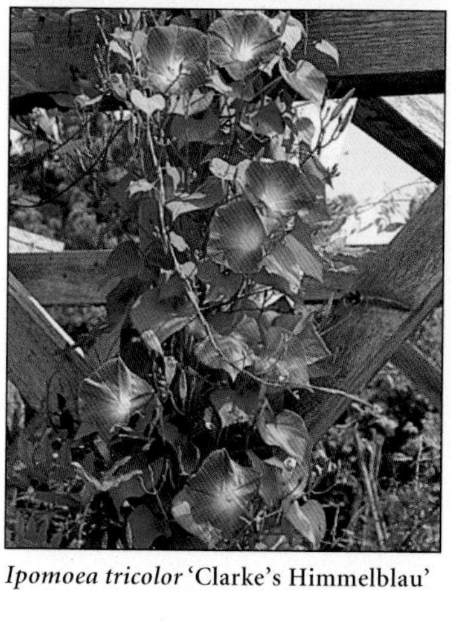

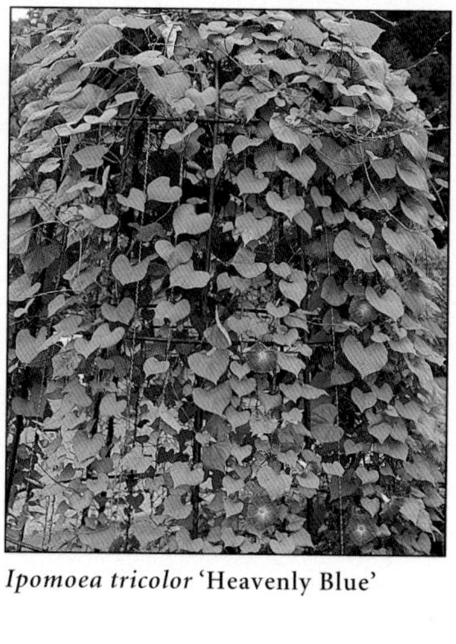

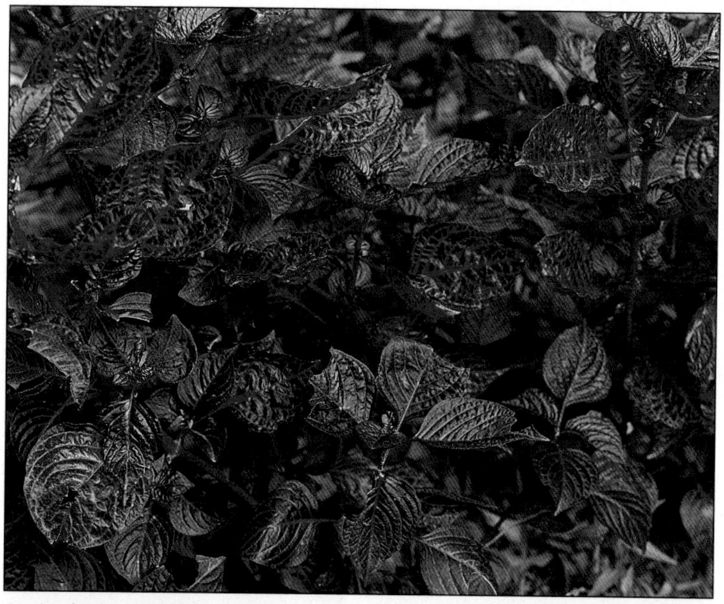

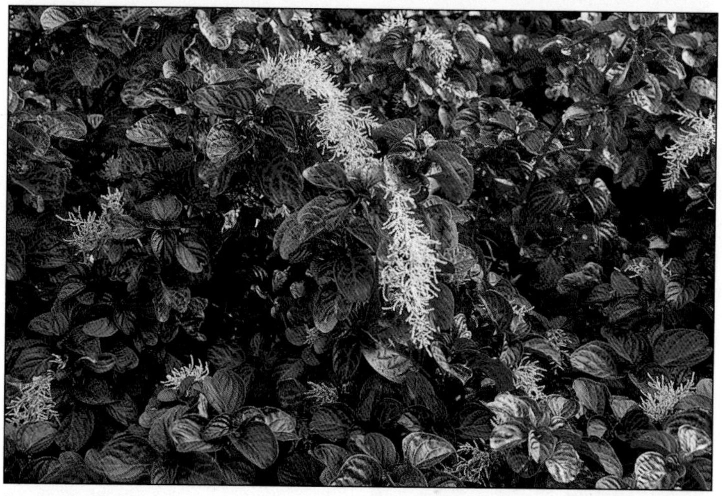

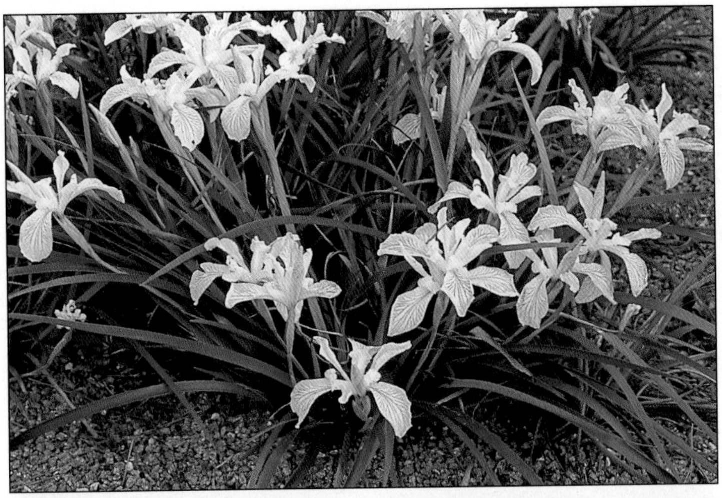

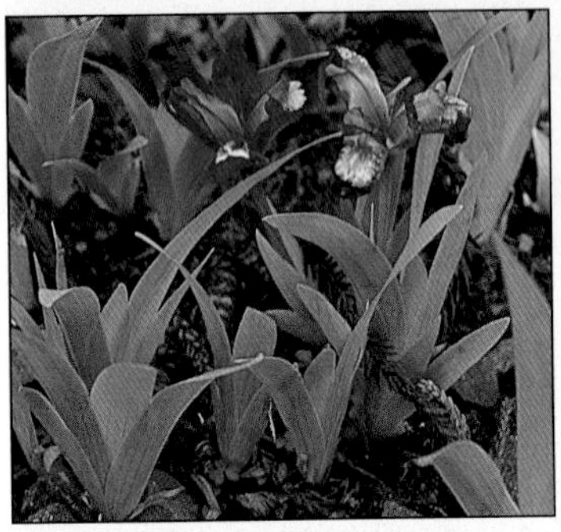

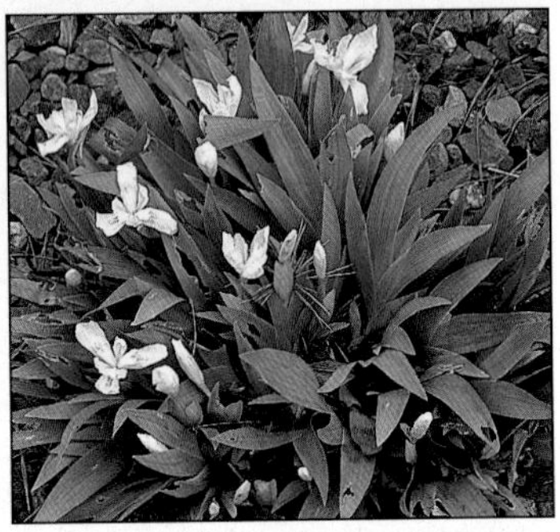

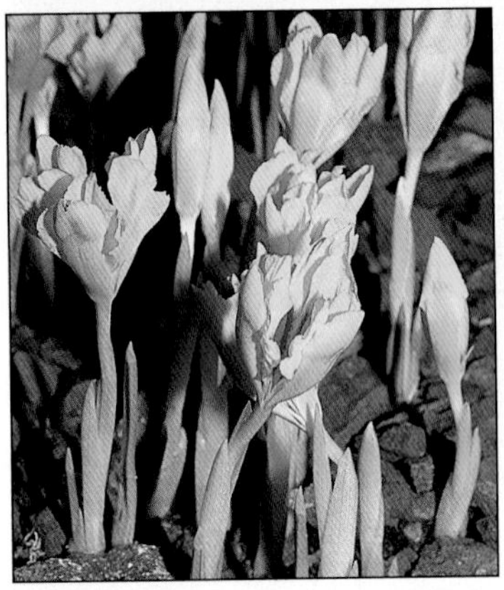

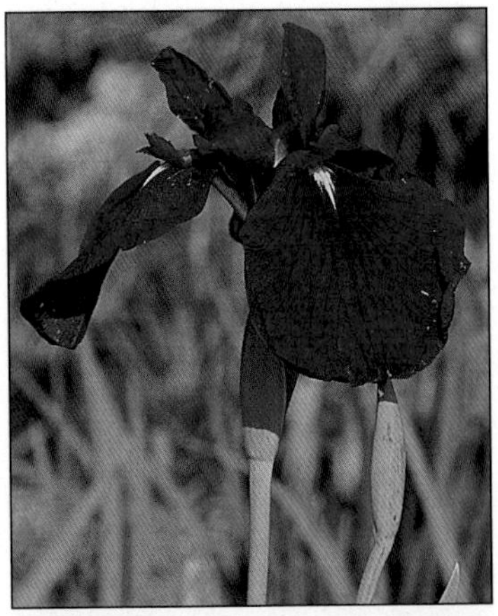

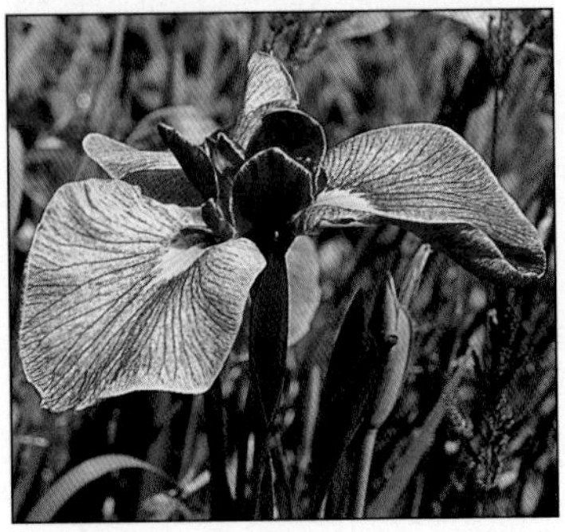

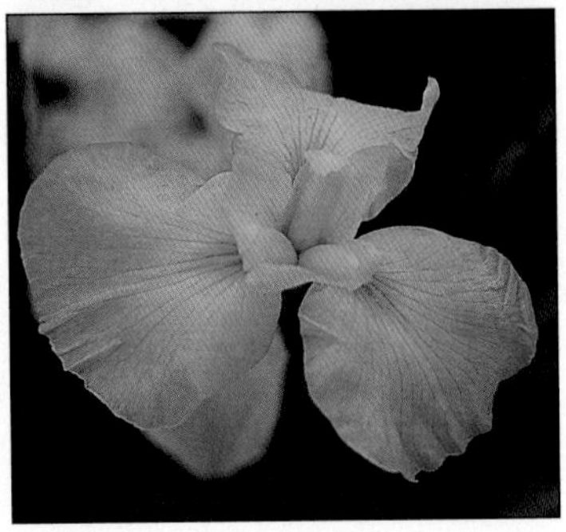

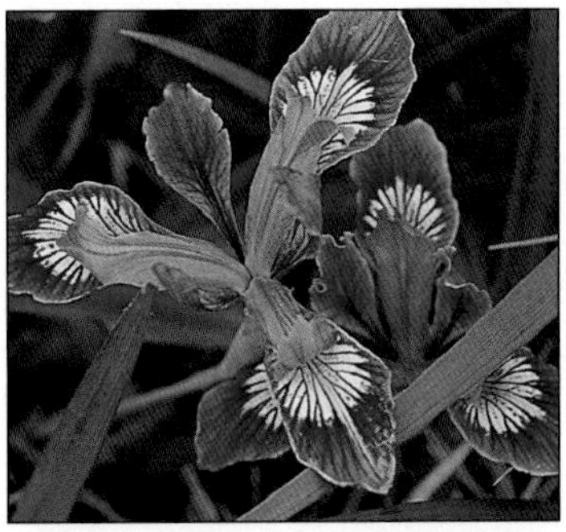

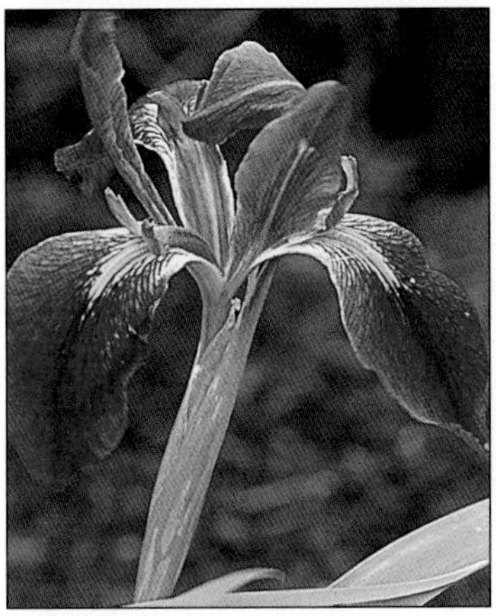

Iris pallida

Iris missouriensis

Iris maackii

Iris pallida 'Variegata'

Iris munzii

Iris munzii
MUNZ'S IRIS

One of the largest flowering of the Pacific Coast irises, this species grows up to 30 in (75 cm) tall. Flowers up to 3 in (8 cm) wide are borne in summer. The flowers vary in color from pale blue through lavender to dark red-purple, with the veins often darker. This species is not very frost hardy. **ZONES 8–10.**

Iris orientalis
syn. ***Iris ochroleuca***
SWAMP IRIS

This 4 ft (1.2 m) tall, almost evergreen, rhizomatous beardless iris from western Asia has mid-green leaves and white and yellow flowers in early summer. ***Iris orientalis* var. *monnieri*** is an all-yellow form. Although these plants will grow in damp ground, they are perfectly happy in any rich, well-watered garden soil in a sunny position. **ZONES 6–9.**

Iris pallida
DALMATIAN IRIS

This bearded iris from the Dalmatian region of Croatia has fragrant, pale blue flowers with yellow beards, which are borne on 4 ft (1.2 m) high stems in late spring. It is often grown as a source of orris (also obtained from *I. germanica* 'Florentina'), a volatile substance that develops in the dried and aged rhizomes and is used in perfumes, dental preparations and breath fresheners. **'Variegata'** (syn. 'Aurea Variegata') has handsome leaves striped in gray-green and cream. **ZONES 5–10.**

Iris pseudacorus
WATER FLAG, YELLOW FLAG

A robust beardless iris from Europe, the water flag has handsome, mid-green leaves and profuse bright yellow flowers on 3 ft (1 m) stems which are borne in early spring. The flowers usually have brown or violet veining, with a darker yellow patch on the falls. It prefers to grow in shallow water and rich soil; plant in fall (autumn) in a box of rich earth and place in a sunny position in the garden pond. The cultivar **'Variegata'** has yellow- and green-striped foliage during the spring months, often turning green in summer; it is less vigorous than the species. **ZONES 5–9.**

Iris reticulata 'Joyce'

Iris reticulata 'Edward'

Iris reticulata 'Gordon'

Iris reticulata 'Purple Gem'

Iris setosa subsp. *canadensis*

Iris pumila 'Purpurea'

Iris pumila

This dainty little bearded iris is distributed throughout central and eastern Europe and Turkey, varying considerably over its range. It has thick fleshy rhizomes and, in flower, rarely exceeds 6 in (15 cm) in height. The color also varies greatly and may be white, yellow, violet, purple or blue, with yellow or blue beards on the falls. It prefers a sunny position and well-drained, slightly alkaline soil. **'Purpurea'** is a deep purple form. **ZONES 4–9.**

Iris reticulata
NETTED IRIS, RETICULATED IRIS

Another highly variable species from the Caucasus region, this bulbous Reticulata iris grows to 4 in (10 cm) high when in flower. Several named varieties are available, differing mainly in the shade of blue of the showy flowers. The foliage is short during the late winter to early spring-flowering time, becoming longer after bloom. The leaves are quadrangular in cross-section and although often scarcely visible at flowering, some forms will have leaves taller than the flowers. It prefers sun and perfectly drained soil; it is very frost hardy and does best in cold winter climates. Its flowers are scented. It makes a delightful pot plant. Some of its hybrids and forms (often crossed with *Iris histrioides*) include **'Cantab'**, with very pale Cambridge-blue flowers; **'Edward'**, which has a rich, dark blue flower with orange marks; **'Gordon'**, with its light blue flowers with an orange blotch on a white background; **'Joyce'**, which has lavender-blue standards and sky-blue falls marked with gray-brown and yellow; and **'Purple Gem'**, with flowers with violet standards and extremely dark purple falls blotched with lighter purple and white. **ZONES 3–10.**

Iris 'Roy Davidson'

Iris 'Roy Davidson'

This beardless iris is a hybrid of *Iris pseudacorus* and as such is a suitable plant for a boggy site, although it is equally happy in moist garden conditions. It grows to slightly more than 3 ft (1 m) tall and has yellow flowers very like its parent, except that they last longer and are about 4 in (10 cm) across. **ZONES 5–9.**

Iris setosa subsp. *canadensis*

This subspecies of a more widely spread species is found from Newfoundland to Ontario and south to Maine in North America. It grows to 24 in (60 cm) tall, although it is often shorter. A beardless iris, it flowers from late spring to early summer. Its flowers are usually solitary and are lavender-blue in color. This is a tough, easy-to-grow plant ideal for rock gardens. **ZONES 3–9**

Iris sibirica
SIBERIAN FLAG

Despite the name, this well-known species has a natural distribution across temperate Eurasia from France to Lake Baikal. It is one of the most popular beardless irises, usually found in gardens in one of its cultivars rather than its wild form. The plants make strongly vertical clumps of slender bright green leaves 2–4 ft (0.6–1.2 m) high. In late spring or early summer, flowering stems rise above the foliage with narrow-petalled, blue, purple or white flowers, often veined in a deeper color. It prefers full sun to very light shade (particularly in hot areas), a moderately moist, rich soil that may be slightly acid and water during the hottest periods. It will grow in a wet soil and does best in cold winter climates. Some of the available cultivars include **'Cleave Dodge'**, with mid-blue flowers; **'Perry's Blue'**, which has rich lilac-blue flowers with yellow markings and netted brown towards the base of the falls; **'Ruby'**, which has purplish blue flowers; **'White Swirl'**, which has pure white flowers with yellow at the base and flared, rounded petals; and **'Vi Luihn'**, with flowers in a rich violet shade. **ZONES 4–9.**

Iris tectorum
JAPANESE ROOF IRIS, WALL FLAG

So-called because in Japan this species was said to have been grown on thatched roofs in times of hardship when all available ground was needed for food crops. Originally native to China, it is a hardy crested or Evansia iris with thick rhizomes and broad, bright green leaves in fans to 12 in (30 cm) long. The flowers, produced in spring and early summer, are about 4 in (10 cm) across and are lilac-blue with darker veins and blotches, and a white crest on each fall. It prefers part-shade in a sheltered position with protection from afternoon sun. It also has a white form called **'Alba'**. **ZONES 5–10.**

Iris tenax
syn. *Iris gormanii*
OREGON IRIS

This is a deciduous beardless Pacific Coast iris from Oregon and Washington which grows to about 15 in (30 cm) tall. Its dark green foliage is stained pink at the base. It flowers from mid-spring into summer; the blooms are about 3½ in (9 cm) across and can be blue, lavender, yellow or white, and often have yellow and white markings on the falls. This species is relatively easy to grow and prefers sun or part-shade. **ZONES 8–10.**

Iris tingitana
TANGIERS IRIS

From northwest Africa, this robust, bulbous Xiphium iris has 6 in (15 cm) wide, pale blue flowers and silvery gray, lance-shaped leaves. The leaves appear in fall (autumn) and are susceptible to frost, so a sheltered position is best. It grows to 30 in (75 cm) tall and bears 4 in (10 cm) light blue flowers on each stem from late winter to early spring. It is cultivated in the same manner as the Dutch hybrids but is temperamental in cultivation and now seldom grown in gardens. **ZONES 7–10.**

Iris tectorum

Iris tenax

Iris typhifolia

This recently named species from China is related to *I. sibirica*. It is moderately frost hardy and grows to about 12 in (30 cm) tall. The flowers, produced in late spring, are usually dark violet. **ZONES 7–9.**

Iris typhifolia

Iris unguicularis
syn. *Iris stylosa*
WINTER IRIS, ALGERIAN IRIS

This evergreen, beardless species from northern Africa is notable for its habit of bearing its flowers deep down among the clumps of grassy, dark green leaves, on stems no more than 8 in (20 cm) long. Flowers are typically pale blue, but white and darker blue varieties are also available; the falls have yellow centers. It blooms from fall (autumn) to spring and flowers are primrose-scented. Although moderately frost hardy, it does best in a warm, sheltered, sunny position, in slightly alkaline soil. Flowers will be more conspicuous if the tough foliage is cut back in early winter. **ZONES 7–10**

Iris versicolor
BLUE FLAG, WILD IRIS, POISON FLAG

This robust beardless iris is an eastern North American species found from Labrador through to Virginia. It was commonly used as a medicinal plant

Iris sibirica 'Ruby'

Iris sibirica

Iris sibirica 'Perry's Blue'

Iris sibirica 'Vi Luihn'

Iris sibirica 'Cleave Dodge'

Iris, Arilbred Hybrid, 'Vera'

Iris, Tall Bearded, 'Cannington Skies'

among native Americans—the Creek people found it so vital they cultivated it near their villages. *Iris versicolor* grows to about 30 in (75 cm) tall and its flowers, produced in spring, can be violet-purple or lavender-blue with an area on each fall that is purple with white veins. This species is very frost hardy and thrives in wet to moist soils or will grow in shallow water. It prefers part-shade. ZONES 3–9.

Iris xiphium
SPANISH IRIS

This bulbous Xiphium iris from the western Mediterranean region is the main parent species of the Spanish and Dutch hybrids. It reaches a height of 30 in (75 cm) or slightly more, and has narrow, lance-shaped mid-green leaves which are scattered up the flower stem. Flowers, borne in early spring, may be blue to mauve, or occasionally white or yellow; the falls have a yellow or orange blotch and are not winged like those of the English irises, which are derived chiefly from the related *Iris latifolia*. ZONES 6–10.

Iris, Arilbred Hybrids

This is a somewhat varied group of hybrids resulting from crosses between the 'arillate' group of bearded irises (principally the Oncocyclus, Regelia and Regeliocyclus irises) and any other bearded irises not of this group. **'Vera'** has chocolate-brown flowers tinged with purple; the beards are purple. ZONES 5–9.

Iris, Bearded Hybrids

Often classed under *Iris germanica* or *I. pallida,* which are only 2 of their ancestral species, the bearded irises are among the most widely grown of late-spring flowers, with fat creeping rhizomes, handsome sword-shaped, grayish foliage and stems bearing several large flowers. They are available in an enormous range of colors—everything but true red—with many varieties featuring blended colors, contrasting standards and falls, or a broad band of color around basically white flowers (this pattern is called 'plicata'). Some of the newer varieties, described as 'remontant', flower a second time in late summer or fall (autumn), though rather erratically. All prefer a temperate climate, sun and mildly alkaline, well-drained soil, and flower most freely if not over-watered in summer. Bearded irises are subdivided into 3 groups:

Dwarf Bearded, which grow 6–15 in (15–40 cm) tall and flower earlier than the others.

Intermediate Bearded, about 24 in (60 cm) tall, which flower a fortnight or so later than the dwarf varieties. **'Sunny Dawn'** is typical, with yellow flowers with red beards.

Tall Bearded irises are the last to bloom and grow to 3 ft (1 m) tall or

Iris, I. Bearded, 'Sunny Dawn'

Iris, Tall Bearded, 'Blue Shimmer'

Iris, Tall Bearded, 'Supreme Sultan'

Iris, Tall Bearded, 'Dancer's Veil'

Iris, Tall Bearded, 'Light Beam'

Iris, Tall Bearded, 'Sun and Sand'

Iris, Tall Bearded, 'Orange Celebrity'

slightly higher. Representative Tall Bearded cultivars include **'Almaden'** with standards and falls in a rich burgundy; **'Beyond'** with a creamy apricot background color and red-brown plicata edging; **'Blue Shimmer'** has white flowers with lilac-blue stitching; **'Dancer's Veil'**, to 3 ft (1 m) tall, has white flowers with plicata edges in blue-violet; **'Jelly Roll'** has pink flowers with a red beard; **'Light Beam'** has yellow standards and white falls edged with yellow; and **'Orange Celebrity'** is renowned for its ideal form and brilliant yet delicate colors, including apricot and pink shades with a flaming orange beard. **'Stepping Out'** produces 8 to 11 white flowers with purple plicata edges on each stem; it reaches 3 ft (1 m) in height and bears flowers in mid-spring. **'Blue-eyed Brunette'** has coppery brown standards and falls, with a blue spot on each fall. **'Cannington Skies'** has mid-blue standards and falls. **'Early Light'** has lemon-flushed cream standards, with slightly darker falls, and yellow beards.

Iris, Louisiana, 'Art World'

'Supreme Sultan' has butterscotch-yellow standards and crimson-brown falls. ZONES 5–10.

Iris, Dutch Hybrids

These bulbous irises of the Xiphium group derive their purity of color from the northern African *Iris tingitana;* their other main parent, *I. xiphium,* tends towards purple. They are very easy to grow and do well in temperate climates. They prefer sun and well-drained, slightly alkaline soil, but will also grow in acidic soil. Ranging from pale blue to almost violet, the hybrids include **'Blue Magic'**, with flowers in the middle of the color range; the purplish blue **'Professor Blaauw'**, one of the most widely grown flower shop irises in the world and named for A. H. Blaauw (1882–1942), whose pioneering studies led to the modern techniques of inducing irises to bloom in all seasons; and the pale, almost turquoise, **'Wedgwood'**. ZONES 7–10.

Iris, Louisiana, 'Vermilion Treasure'

Iris, Louisiana Hybrids

This extremely colorful group of rhizomatous, beardless hybrid irises include *Iris fulva* and *I. brevicaulis* among their ancestral species. They are evergreen with fine strap-like foliage and can build into substantial clumps; divide after 2 to 3 years. The Louisiana hybrids are not fully frost hardy in very cold climates, but are becoming increasingly popular in Australia and southern parts of the USA. Although basically swamp or water irises, they will happily grow in the garden if kept very well watered. They do best in a sunny position with average to damp, humus-rich garden soil. This

Iris, Dutch, 'Blue Magic'

Iris, Louisiana, 'Insider'

Iris, Louisiana, 'Exclusive Label'

Iris, Tall Bearded, 'White City'

Iris, Dutch, 'Professor Blaauw'

Iris, Louisiana, 'Bluebonnet Sue'

Iris, Louisiana, 'Guessing Game'

Iris, Louisiana, 'Sierra Amarillo'

group rarely exceeds 3 ft (1 m) in height and is usually much shorter. Some of the available hybrids include '**Art World**', with mauve-pink duo-toned flowers; '**Bluebonnet Sue**', with rich violet-blue blooms; '**Designer's Dream**', which has a light yellow flower with ruffled petals; '**Dural Dreamtime**', with its fine white flower with green veins; '**Exclusive Label**', with a rich burgundy flower with a fine yellow edge; '**Guessing Game**', with a pale mauve flower with darker violet veins and irregular markings; '**Icarus**', which has a bright yellow flower; '**Insider**', a new Australian hybrid which has yellow-edged reddish brown standards and falls of reddish brown with yellow spray patterning; and '**Vermilion Treasure**', with a red-violet flower with lighter spray patterning. **ZONES 7–10.**

Iris, Spuria Hybrids

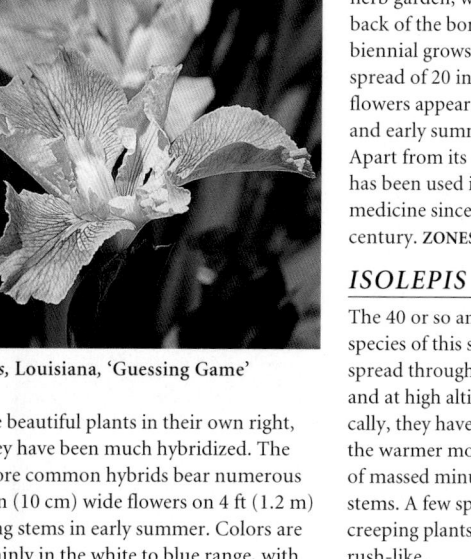

While *Iris spuria* (from northern Africa and southern France), *I. sibirica* (from eastern Europe) and their allied species are beautiful plants in their own right, they have been much hybridized. The more common hybrids bear numerous 4 in (10 cm) wide flowers on 4 ft (1.2 m) long stems in early summer. Colors are mainly in the white to blue range, with some yellow and white forms. All prefer sun, rich soil and lavish watering while they are growing and flowering. **ZONES 4–9.**

ISATIS

This genus of about 30 species of annuals, biennials and perennials is widespread over southern Europe and western Asia, and often found in stony ground and waste places. The plants form a rosette of oblong to lance-shaped leaves which become stem-clasping and decrease in size along the stem. The masses of small 4-petalled flowers are borne in loose panicles. They are usually yellow and are attractive to bees.
CULTIVATION: Fully frost hardy, they grow in a sunny position in a moderately fertile, well-drained soil. Propagate from seed in fall (autumn) and spring.

Isatis tinctoria
WOAD, COMMON DYER'S WEED

Isatis tinctoria is one of the oldest dye plants of Europe and Asia, where it was especially valued for its precious blue dye. This is the dye with which Celtic warriors traditionally painted their faces and bodies, a practice still occurring at the time the Romans invaded Britain in the first century AD. Queen Elizabeth I found the pungent smell of the fermenting dye so offensive she banned its production within 5 miles of her palaces. This plant makes a novel addition to the herb garden, where it is best suited to the back of the border. This vigorous upright biennial grows to 4 ft (1.2 m) high with a spread of 20 in (50 cm). Bright yellow flowers appear in profusion in spring and early summer. It will self-sow freely. Apart from its use as a dye, *I. tinctoria* has been used in traditional Chinese medicine since at least the sixteenth century. **ZONES 7–10.**

Isatis tinctoria

ISOLEPIS

The 40 or so annual and perennial species of this sedge genus are widespread throughout the temperate regions and at high altitudes in the tropics. Typically, they have grass-like foliage and in the warmer months they produce heads of massed minute flowers on slender stems. A few species of *Isolepis* are tiny, creeping plants while some others are rush-like.
CULTIVATION: *Isolepis* species are often to be found in moist conditions, including bogs and alpine fellfields. In cultivation, they thrive in full sun in most garden soils and can often be grown around pond margins. They are undemanding plants that need minimal care. Propagate by division in spring or from seed, which often self-sows, sometimes invasively. Most species will tolerate occasional light frosts.

Isolepis cernua

This small rush-like plant grows to about 12 in (30 cm) tall and comes from western and southern Europe as well as northern Africa. Its stiff foliage is dark green and its tiny greenish flowers, which appear in summer, are followed by smooth brownish seeds. **ZONES 8–11.**

Isolepis nodosa
syn. *Scirpus nodosus*
KNOBBY CLUB-RUSH

Occurring around most temperate coastal regions of the southern hemisphere, this is one of the more robust *Isolepis* species, forming a dense clump of erect, dark green leafless stems to about 3 ft (1 m) tall. The flowers are borne in tight spherical clusters of brown spikelets about ½ in (12 mm) diameter just below the stem apex. It is highly tolerant of both salt spray and waterlogged or saline soil and is easily cultivated, making fast growth. **ZONES 9–11.**

ISOPLEXIS

This is a small genus of 3 species of soft-wooded evergreen subshrubs, native to Madeira and the Canary Islands, and are related to the foxgloves (*Digitalis*). They are under pressure in their native habitat, as is much of the world's island flora. They are showy plants suitable for shrub borders in virtually frost-free climates.

Isolepis nodosa

Iris, Louisiana, 'Impressioned'

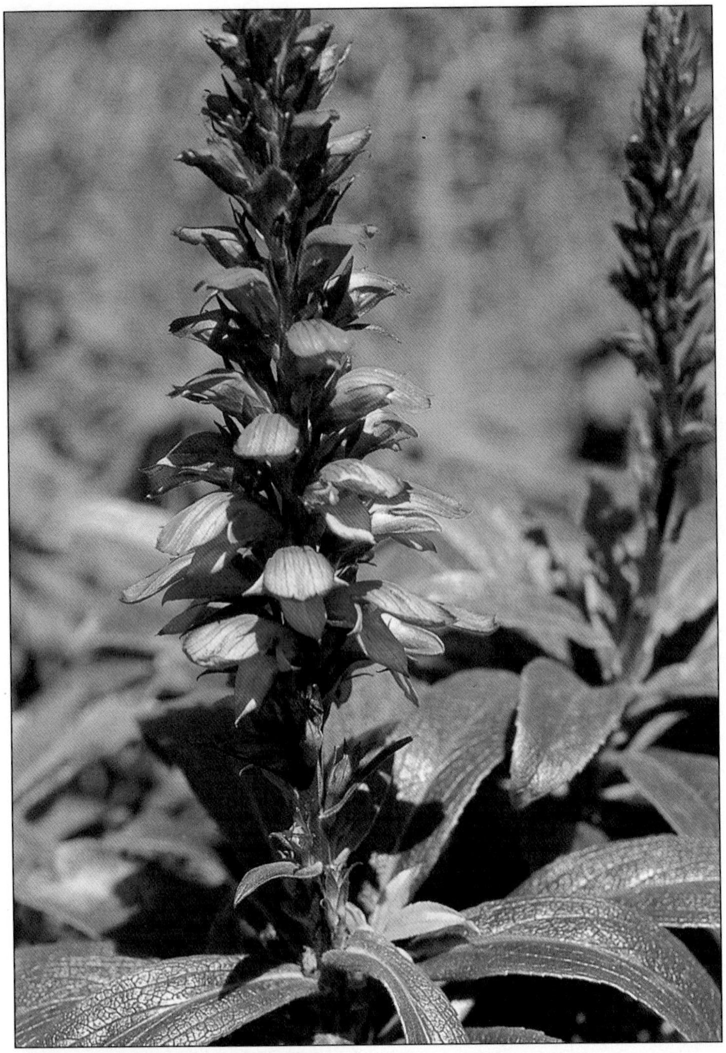

Isoplexis canariensis

Isopogon anemonifolius

Isopogon dawsonii

CULTIVATION: Although marginally frost hardy to frost tender, these are reasonably undemanding plants. They prefer a well-drained soil and must be adequately watered in summer. Plant in sun or part-shade and regularly remove any spent flower spikes. Propagation is usually from seed in spring, although cuttings taken in summer will also give good results.

Isoplexis canariensis

This is the showiest species in the genus and comes from Tenerife in the Canary Islands. Frost-tender, it is an erect shrub which grows to 5 ft (1.5 m) tall and with a similar spread as it matures. The leaves are long and narrow, and almost leathery and slightly felty in texture. Its spikes of flared tubular flowers are produced mainly in summer and come in shades of orange-yellow through rusty orange to yellow-brown. **ZONES 9–11.**

ISOPOGON

DRUMSTICKS

With around 30 species of evergreen shrubs from Australia, this genus is admired for its attractive light green foliage which, though frequently dissected and ferny in appearance, is hard and prickly—like that of many Australian shrubs—and their globular heads of fragrant white, cream or pink flowers

Isopogon anemonifolius

Isopogon formosus

Itea virginica

borne in spring or summer. Plants of quiet charm, they are somewhat overshadowed by their more spectacular relatives the grevilleas and banksias, and even in their native land are not widely grown. The flowers are followed by woody, knob-like fruiting heads resembling small pine cones or drumsticks—hence the common name. These may persist on the bare, straight stems after both flowers and leaves have died.
CULTIVATION: Marginally frost hardy, they need a sunny spot and well-drained soil, and a dry-summer climate. Water freely during dry periods. Propagate from ripe seed in winter or from cuttings in late summer and fall (autumn).

Isopogon anemonifolius

DRUMSTICKS

From eastern Australia, this upright bushy species grows to a height and spread of 6 ft (1.8 m), although low-growing, prostrate forms are also seen. In spring it bears prominent, cone-shaped, creamy yellow flowerheads, followed by cones. Marginally to moderately frost hardy, it needs generous watering in dry periods. **ZONES 9–11.**

Isopogon dawsonii

Native to the Blue Mountains of New South Wales, this attractive species is found on sandstone slopes and cliffs. It is an, open tall shrub which reaches 10 ft (3 m) in height and has divided leaves with flattened segments. Its pale yellow, pink-tinged flowers are followed by silver-gray fruiting cones. **ZONES 9–11.**

Isopogon formosus

ROSE CONE FLOWER

Native to southern parts of Western Australia, this is quite a variable species. It usually makes a bushy shrub up to 5 ft (1.5 m) in height and spread. Its dark green, much-divided foliage is stiff and prickly. The heads of dainty rose-pink flowers are about 2 in (5 cm) across and usually borne in spring. **ZONES 9–11.**

ITEA

Of the 10 species of evergreen and deciduous shrubs and trees in this genus, most are from tropical and temperate Asia but 1 species is native to North America. They are grown for their showy, fragrant fall (autumn) flowers. They are frost hardy, although in some colder areas they need the protection of a wall. These are useful plants for specimens or for growing in a shrubbery. The botanical name *Itea* comes from the Greek, meaning 'willow', to which some species bear a slight resemblance.
CULTIVATION: They will thrive in anything but very dry soil and prefer a part-shaded position, but will tolerate full sun. Propagate from cuttings in summer and plant out in fall or spring.

Itea ilicifolia

HOLLY SWEETSPIRE

This handsome, bushy, evergreen shrub from western China grows to a height and spread of 10 ft (3 m). The leaves, borne on arching branches, resemble those of holly, only narrower. In late summer to early fall (autumn), it bears long racemes of small, greenish or cream flowers. It does best in moist, deep, rich soil, preferring partial shade. **ZONES 7–10.**

Itea virginica

SWEETSPIRE, VIRGINIA WILLOW

The best known member of the genus, this deciduous North American shrub of upright, slender form grows 3–5 ft (1–1.5 m) tall and in summer bears fragrant, creamy white flowers in semi-erect panicles. Its finely toothed, deciduous, bright green leaves do not fall until early winter, when they sometimes turn red. It is suitable for mass planting, particularly in wet, low places and is more frost hardy than *Itea ilicifolia*. **ZONES 5–9.**

IXIA

AFRICAN CORN LILY

This genus of 40 to 50 deciduous cormous perennials is confined to the winter rainfall region of South Africa. These relatives of the iris family produce masses of delightful, star-shaped flowers on wiry stems in spring and early summer—these flowers close in the evening and on cloudy days; the leaves are

Ixia maculata, garden form

Ixia viridiflora

usually long and slender. The tallest species grows to 24 in (60 cm).
CULTIVATION: Marginally frost hardy, they are easy to grow in temperate to warm areas. In frost-prone areas, they should be grown in a cool greenhouse. The bulbs should be planted in early fall (autumn) in well-drained soil. Bonemeal mixed into the soil before planting will help produce good blooms. A sunny position is ideal, except in warm areas where they will need protection from hot sun. Water well through winter and spring, but allow to dry out after flowering. These plants are suitable for growing in containers. Propagate from offsets in fall (autumn). If sown from seed in fall, they should flower in the third year.

Ixia maculata
YELLOW IXIA

The most commonly grown species, this has wiry stems growing to 18 in (45 cm) tall with a spread of $1\frac{1}{2}$–2 in (3.5–5 cm). The 2 in (5 cm) flowers are clustered along the top, and have brown or black centers and orange to yellow petals, sometimes with pinkish red undersides. Garden forms come in white, yellow, pink, orange or red. **ZONES 9–10.**

Ixia paniculata
syns *Morphixia paniculata, Tritonia longiflora*
BUFF IXIA

The slender stems of this species grow to 24 in (60 cm) with a spread of 10 in (25 cm). The stems are topped with spikes of creamy white, sometimes pink-suffused, or pale yellow blooms with a purplish black blotch at their bases. These are often tinged pink or red on the outside. The 2 in (5 cm) flowers, star-shaped and tubular at the base, appear in late spring to early summer. **ZONES 9–10.**

Ixia 'Uranus'

This is one of many selected cultivars; some are of hybrid origin and some are selections of species. It has rich, dark yellow flowers with red-black centers. **ZONES 9–10.**

Ixia viridiflora
GREEN IXIA

This species is popular for its jewel-like, star-shaped, 2 in (5 cm) flowers—turquoise with a purple-black center—which are borne on a spike atop the 24 in (60 cm) stem. It has very narrow, erect leaves, which mostly appear at the base of the stem. **ZONES 9–10.**

IXORA
JUNGLE FLAME

From tropical regions of Africa, Asia and islands of the Pacific, this is a large genus of about 400 species of evergreen shrubs and small trees, some with spectacular heads of scarlet, orange, yellow, pink or white flowers. They have glossy, deep green leaves. In Asia, the roots of ixoras are used to make a medicine said to alleviate stomach ailments and cure dysentery. These shrubs are used for massed bedding, hedges and screens, and can be grown in containers.
CULTIVATION: Ixoras need a warm, frost-free climate to grow outdoors as they are frost tender; in the tropics, they appreciate a part-shaded position, and in cooler climates they are grown in greenhouses. Humus-rich, moist but freely drained, friable soils and high humidity suit them best, and they need regular water during the warmer months. Light pruning after flowering in fall (autumn) or late winter will maintain shape; spent flowerheads should also be removed. Propagate from cuttings in summer or from seed in spring.

Ixora chinensis

This evergreen shrub grows to a height and spread of 4 ft (1.2 m), its densely packed, erect branches clothed with narrowly pointed, deep green leaves. The large terminal clusters of tubular flowers are borne from spring to fall (autumn) and vary from bright orange-red, yellow and white to pink. **'Lutea'** has yellow flowers; **'Prince of Orange'** has larger orange-scarlet flowerheads that almost cover the bush in summer. **ZONES 10–12.**

Ixora coccinea
JUNGLE GERANIUM

From tropical Southeast Asia, this neat, rounded evergreen shrub reaches a height of 3 ft (1 m) with a spread of 5 ft (1.5 m). Small, scarlet, tubular flowers borne through summer in dense, ball-like clusters among the 4 in (10 cm) long, dark green leaves may be followed by cherry-sized black fruit. **ZONES 11–12.**

Ixora javanica
syn. *Ixora amoena*
RED IXORA, JAVANESE IXORA

Native to Java and the Malay Peninsula, this small evergreen tree grows up to 15 ft (4.5 m) in the wild but rarely reaches more than 5 ft (1.5 m) in cultivation. Its heads of small, tubular flowers are usually red, although orange and pink forms are known. **ZONES 11–12.**

Ixora 'Sunkist'

The cultivar 'Sunkist' originated in Singapore and grows to 24 in (60 cm) tall. It has narrow, shiny green leaves and massed heads of apricot-pink flowers which later turn brick red. It prefers sun or part-shade in the tropical garden; it is not tolerant of frost. Prune away half its growth after the flowers have finished or in late winter. Propagate from cuttings in spring. **ZONES 11–12.**

Ixora chinensis

Ixora coccinea

Ixora chinensis 'Prince of Orange'

Ixora 'Sunkist'

J K

JABOROSA

There are about 20 species of these tomato cousins, all relatively low-growing perennials from the drier parts of South America. The leaves are roughly oval in shape and may be cut, toothed or lobed depending on the species. Flowers may be white, cream or yellow. Only one species has found its way into gardens, where it is mainly used as a ground cover on sunny, well-drained sites.

CULTIVATION: Good drainage is essential and the plants thrive in sandy soil that contains a proportion of rotted organic matter. Once established, they need little in the way of water, usually managing on natural rainfall. If water is given, apply mostly during the warmer half of the year. In average garden soils, no fertilizer is needed. Propagate from seed sown in spring or by division of existing plants in late winter or early spring.

Jaborosa integrifolia

This moderately frost-hardy, stemless perennial is found in southern Brazil, Uruguay and Argentina where it grows naturally on the pampas or in damp fields. It reaches a height of 6 in (15 cm) and has a spreading habit. The plant spreads by underground rhizomes, which produce rosettes of fleshy, dark green leaves on short stems. The leaves are up to 8 in (20 cm) long. Its tubular, star-shaped greenish white flowers are borne from late spring to early summer, and are fragrant at night. This species can become invasive, so site carefully. **ZONES 8–10.**

Jasminum humile

JACARANDA

This genus consists of about 50 species of medium to large deciduous and evergreen trees from Brazil and other parts of tropical and subtropical South America. All species have fern-like, bipinnate leaves and bell-shaped flowers which may be white, purple or mauve-blue. The best known species, the mauve-blue *Jacaranda mimosifolia*, is one of the most widely planted and admired of all warm-climate flowering trees. It yields a richly figured timber, although as the tree is so valued as an ornamental it is rarely cut; the timber, Brazil rosewood, is usually that of ***J. filicifolia***, a larger but less decorative species with white flowers.

CULTIVATION: Marginally frost hardy, they grow in fertile, well-drained soil and full sun. Young plants need protection from frost. Potted specimens should be watered freely when in full growth, less so at other times. Propagate from seed in spring or from cuttings in summer.

Jacaranda mimosifolia

syns ***Jacaranda acutifolia, J. ovalifolia***

JACARANDA

From the high plains of Brazil, Paraguay and Argentina, this fast-growing, deciduous tree can reach 50 ft (15 m) in height with a spread of up to 40 ft (12 m), and has a broad, rounded crown. The vivid green, fern-like foliage is bipinnate, with 12 or more leaflets. Depending on climate, the leaves may be shed in winter or early spring before the flowers—mauve-blue to lilac terminal clusters of trumpet-shaped blossoms—appear; flat, leathery seed pods follow. Pruning is not desirable; if branches are removed, they are replaced by vertical shoots which spoil the shape of the tree. The trees are shallow rooted, which can pose problems for underplanting. **ZONES 9–11.**

Jacaranda mimosifolia

Jacksonia scoparia

Jasminum azoricum

Jasminum fruticans

JACKSONIA

Belonging to the pea family, this genus of some 50 species of erect to prostrate evergreen shrubs is native to temperate, arid and tropical areas of Australia. The leaves have been replaced by cladodes and many species are spiny, although some are unarmed. The flattened green stems perform the functions normally carried out by leaves in other plant species. The plants bear pea-like flowers in shades of red, orange or yellow.

CULTIVATION: A well-drained, rather infertile soil and a Mediterranean-type climate generally suit these mostly frost-tender shrubs best. If well hardened during hot, dry summers, they tolerate very light frosts. Propagate from seed that has been stratified or treated with hot water. Cuttings are also an option.

Jacksonia scoparia

Native to New South Wales and Queensland, this species grows 10 ft (3 m) tall with a spread of 7 ft (2 m). It has an elegant habit with numerous angular, arching branches and leaves on young plants only. Its small, pea-shaped flowers are bright yellow and are produced in quantity during summer, making quite a show. **ZONES 9–11.**

JASIONE

SHEEP'S BIT

Found in temperate Europe and the Mediterranean region, the 20 species of annuals, biennials and perennials in this genus of meadow plants form small, grassy tufts of foliage. In summer, tiny, 5-petalled spherical flowerheads appear and are normally blue in color. They are borne on erect, wiry stems that are up to 18 in (45 cm) tall, although 4–8 in (10–20 cm) is more common. The taller species tend to have broader leaves with larger flowers. They are grown for their attractive flowers, and are often planted in rock gardens.

CULTIVATION: *Jasione* thrives in most well-drained garden soils in sun or part-shade. A dash of dolomite lime is beneficial, but do not overfeed as they do not like rich soil. The biennial and perennial species are frost hardy unless they become waterlogged in winter. Propagate annual and biennial species from seed in fall (autumn); the perennial species from seed in fall or by division in spring.

Jasione laevis

syn. ***Jasione perennis***

SHEPHERD'S SCABIOUS

This perennial species from the Mediterranean grows 2–12 in (5–30 cm) tall with a spread of 4–8 in (10–20 cm). It has narrow, oblong gray-green leaves which are either very hairy or glabrous. Masses of spiky, jacaranda-blue, spherical flowers appear in early summer in a short-lived but profuse display. This species is particularly suitable for rock gardens. **ZONES 5–10.**

Jasione montana

An annual or biennial species from the mountains of Europe, *Jasione montana* grows to 18 in (45 cm) in height. Its tiny flowers, produced in summer in dense rounded heads surrounded by bracts, are usually blue and are sometimes tinged with red or white. This is not one of the most ornamental species of *Jasione* and is not often seen in cultivation. **ZONES 6–10.**

JASMINUM

JASMINE

The name jasmine is synonymous with sweet fragrance, although among this large genus of some 200 deciduous, semi-evergreen and evergreen shrubs and vines, mostly from Asia and Africa, there are many that offer nothing to the nose. The leaves are usually compound, the flowers white, yellow or more rarely reddish pink. Most of the species cultivated for their fragrance are climbing plants.

CULTIVATION: Some species are frost hardy, although most thrive best in subtropical to tropical areas. Plant in full sun in fertile, moist but well-drained soil. Prune as required after flowering. Propagate from cuttings in summer.

Jasminum azoricum

syn. ***Jasminum fluminense* of gardens**

LEMON SCENTED JASMINE

This lovely, marginally frost-hardy evergreen climber is from the Azores. Its leaves are a rich green and composed of 3 leaflets. The flowers, borne in summer, are deep pink when in bud, opening to white; they are highly fragrant. A lovely, controllable climber, it is ideal for growing up a post or fence in a warm, sunny aspect with protection from frost. It can also be grown as a shrub if kept pruned. **ZONES 9–11.**

Jasminum fruticans

This large, spreading evergreen or semi-deciduous shrub is native to the Mediterranean and Asia Minor. It reaches 10 ft (3 m) in height and spread, although it can grow taller if trained as a wall shrub. Its foliage is bright mid-green and usually composed of 3 leaflets. The bright yellow flowers are scentless, produced in clusters of 5 or so, and are in evidence throughout spring, summer and fall (autumn); in mild climates, flowers may even appear in winter. **ZONES 8–11.**

Jasminum humile

ITALIAN YELLOW JASMINE

This large evergreen, bushy shrub can exceed 12 ft (3.5 m) in height and spread. A moderately frost-hardy species, it has bright green leaves. Its bright yellow, occasionally scented flowers are produced from early spring to late fall

Jatropha integerrima

(autumn) and can be $\frac{1}{2}$ in (12 mm) or more across. Although commonly called Italian yellow jasmine, it actually comes from the Middle East, Burma and China—another case of a deceptive common name. The cultivar **'Revolutum'** has larger leaves and fragrant flowers up to 1 in (25 mm) across. **ZONES 8–11.**

Jasminum mesnyi
syn. ***Jasminum primulinum***
YELLOW JASMINE, PRIMROSE JASMINE

This marginally frost-hardy evergreen shrub from western China grows to 6–10 ft (1.8–3 m) in height and spread. Its long, arching canes eventually form a wide, fountain shape. The deep green leaves are made up of 3 leaflets, and bright yellow, scented blooms appear during late winter and early spring. Remove old canes to thin, crowded plants. **ZONES 8–10.**

Jasminum nitidum
ANGEL WING JASMINE

The star-shaped, white flowers of this frost-tender species are large, about 2 in (5 cm) across, and, like many jasmines, sweetly scented. Borne in small sprays, they appear from late spring and throughout summer. A strong-growing climber for subtropical climates, it has glossy, oval leaves and reaches a height of 10–20 ft (3–6 m). **ZONES 10–11.**

Jasminum nudiflorum
WINTER JASMINE

This rambling, deciduous, arching shrub from China has oval, dark green foliage and grows 6–10 ft (1.8–3 m) tall with a similar spread. It is best suited to a cool or cold climate, where it will bear masses of bright yellow flowers on slender, leafless, green shoots in winter and early spring. Frost hardy, it prefers a well-drained soil and full sun. **ZONES 6–9.**

Jasminum officinale
COMMON JASMINE, POET'S JASMINE, JESSAMINE

Introduced to Europe from China in the sixteenth century, this deciduous or semi-evergreen shrubby climber can be maintained as a neat 3–5 ft (1–1.5 m) shrub or allowed to ramble. The dark green leaves have 7 to 9 leaflets; clusters of deep pink buds followed by very fragrant, starry white flowers occur through summer and fall (autumn). This frost-hardy species likes full sun, well-drained, fertile soil and ample water in warmer months. It is an excellent container plant for a sunny terrace.

Jatropha multifida

The essential oil of this species is used in perfume and as a food flavoring, such as in maraschino cherries. Pink-flowered and variegated-foliage forms are also available. **ZONES 6–10.**

Jasminum parkeri
DWARF JASMINE

Native to the high mountains of northwestern India, this is a dwarf, mounded, evergreen shrub that reaches 12 in (30 cm) in height with a spread of 18 in (45 cm) or more. Its leaves, which appear only sparsely on the green branches, are small with 3 to 5 leaflets. Small, yellow, scentless flowers are borne in summer and this species is a good subject for a sunny rock garden. **ZONES 7–10.**

Jasminum polyanthum
PINK JASMINE

This vigorous, scrambling, evergreen climber from China is fast growing but only maginally frost hardy, and best suited to mild climates. In cool areas, it makes a pretty pot plant. Fragrant white flowers with pink buds are produced in spring and summer. It grows to a height of 20 ft (6 m) and can become invasive. Prune after flowering to keep under control. **ZONES 8–11.**

Jasminum rex

This vigorous, evergreen tropical climber from Thailand has dark green foliage consisting of one leaflet. Its unscented white flowers, mostly borne in summer, can be more than 2 in (5 cm) across. The attractive floral display makes up for its lack of perfume. **ZONES 9–12.**

Jasminum sambac
ARABIAN JASMINE

This rather weak evergreen climber grows to only 10 ft (3 m). Frost-tender, it has large, glossy green leaves, and in spring and summer bears sweetly perfumed white flowers. In China the flowers are used for perfuming tea, while in India they are made into garlands. **'Grand Duke of Tuscany'** is a double-flowered form, rather less vigorous. Often confused with *Jasminum sambac* is ***J. multiflorum***, with denser flower clusters and downy stems. **ZONES 10–11.**

Jasminum mesnyi

Jasminum × *stephanense*

This evergreen hybrid between *Jasminum beesianum* and *J. officinale* is of garden origin, although it is said to also appear in the wild where both parents grow. Moderately frost hardy, it is a fast-growing climber and reaches 20 ft (6 m) in height. Clusters of lightly scented, pale pink flowers are produced in summer; the downy leaves are gray-green and composed of 5 leaflets. **ZONES 7–11.**

JATROPHA

This genus of evergreen and deciduous shrubs, small trees and herbs originates in warm-temperate and tropical regions of Asia and the Americas. The plants have a distinctive milky sap and are grown primarily for the unusual, large, deeply divided leaves which can have 5 lobes. The flowers may be yellow, purple or scarlet, and male and female flowers are generally borne on separate plants; they are not especially ornamental. Due to their strong sculptural form, some *Jatropha* species are often cultivated as part of a collection of succulents—although they are not related.
CULTIVATION: They do best in full sun, but will tolerate light shade, and need fertile, humus-rich, well-drained soil. Propagation is from seed or cuttings in spring.

Jatropha integerrima
syns ***Jatropha pandurata, J. pandurifolia***
PEREGRINA, SPICY JATROPHA

Indigenous to the West Indies and Peru, this narrow-domed, evergreen tree grows to 20 ft (6 m) tall with a spread of 6 ft (1.8 m), but can be kept trimmed to shrub size. Its glossy green leaves are mostly unlobed; bright red, funnel-shaped flowers are grouped in clusters towards the ends of the branches. **ZONES 10–12.**

Jasminum polyanthum

Jasminum nitidum

Jatropha multifida
CORAL PLANT, GUATEMALA RHUBARB

This shrub from Central America grows to 6 ft (1.8 m) tall. Its large leaves, up to 12 in (30 cm) wide, are deeply incised, with as many as 12 narrow lobes. Clusters of red flowers are borne on long, thin stalks high above the foliage. It likes a sheltered position; it tends to shed leaves as a response to either dryness or cold. All parts of the plant are highly poisonous. **ZONES 10–12.**

JEFFERSONIA
TWIN LEAF

This genus of just 2 species of herbaceous perennials is named after Thomas Jefferson, the third president of the USA. The species are dainty woodland plants—one from North America, the other from northeast Asia. Although they are part of the Berberis family, this fact is not at all obvious to most gardeners. The rounded, mid-green leaves consist of 2 even lobes, hence the common name.
CULTIVATION: As much as possible, try to simulate their natural woodland homes. They are fully hardy plants and

Jasminum multiflorum

Jasminum polyanthum

Jasminum × *stephanense*

Jubaea chilensis

Jovibarba hirta

Jeffersonia diphylla

prefer a cool, part-shaded position and humus-rich soil; top-dress with leafmold regularly. Propagation is usually from fresh seed in fall (autumn) or by careful division in late winter or early spring.

Jeffersonia diphylla
RHEUMATISM ROOT, TWIN LEAF

This North American species grows in rich woodland from Ontario to Tennessee. Slow-growing, its attractive kidney-shaped, deeply incised leaves are about 6 in (15 cm) across and gray tinted. The dainty, white, cup-shaped flowers are 1 in (25 mm) wide and produced in late spring or early summer; they have prominent yellow stamens. The plant increases in height after flowering and can reach 18 in (45 cm) with a similar spread by the time it sets seed. Do not disturb its roots. **ZONES 5–9.**

JOVELLANA

A small genus of some 6 species of perennials or subshrubs, it is related to *Calceolaria*, but lacks its pouched shape. One species is native to New Zealand, while the rest are found in South America. The flowers are unusual, looking like a series of open mouths

Juglans ailantifolia

Jovibarba hirta

with spotted throats. Only *Jovellana violacea* is regularly found in cultivation. **CULTIVATION:** Jovellanas like a cool, moist soil in a sunny, sheltered position with protection from heavy frosts. Propagation is usually from cuttings with the shrubby species or by division in early spring; plants can also be propagated from seed.

Jovellana violacea
syn. *Calceolaria violacea*

This attractive, suckering subshrub from Chile has brittle, upright stems clothed in small toothed or lobed mid-green leaves. It can grow up to 3 ft (1 m) or more tall; with age, it can sucker out to a spread greater than this. Profuse, small mauve flowers with purple spots and yellow blotches in their throats appear in summer. Remove old canes in spring to rejuvenate the plant. **ZONES 9–11.**

JOVIBARBA

This small genus of 5 species of evergreen, succulent perennials has a rosette-forming habit much like the closely related *Sempervivum* genus. Some species have attractive colored leaves, which are the reason why these plants are grown; all have pale yellow flowers, but these are insignificant. The rosettes die after flowering, but the gaps are soon filled with new growth.
CULTIVATION: Unlike many succulents, these plants are fully frost hardy and only require a well-drained, sunny aspect in temperate to cold climates to succeed. Some shade is necessary in warmer areas. They are ideal in rock gardens, troughs or in dry stone walls packed with a little soil. Propagate from offsets in summer. Simply remove a rosette with a piece of stem; once planted, it will quickly take root.

Juglans major

Jovibarba hirta
syn. *Jovibarba globifera*

The rosettes of this mat-forming species are usually about 2 in (5 cm) across. If the plants become dry, their leaves will curl up; otherwise, they radiate outwards. The thick, fleshy leaves are mid-green and often tipped red or reddish brown; star-shaped flowers are borne in summer. ***Jovibarba hirta* subsp. *arenaria*** has smaller rosettes—usually only about 1 in (25 mm) across, with occasional red tips on the leaves. These plants dislike winter-wet conditions. **ZONES 7–10.**

JUBAEA
CHILEAN WINE PALM, COQUITO PALM

Consisting of one species of palm, this genus is named after King Juba of the old African kingdom of Numidia, although the plant itself comes from coastal Chile. It is now very rare in its natural habitat as it has been consistently cut for its sugary sap, which is distilled as palm wine or boiled down to make palm honey.
CULTIVATION: Slow growing when young, this palm's growth is much quicker once a trunk has formed. More frost tolerant than most palms, and widely grown in temperate climates, it needs full sun and deep, fertile, well-drained soil. As both male and female flowers are held on the same plant, fertile seed is easily obtained in fall (autumn); it must be sown while fresh, but can take 6 to 15 months to germinate.

Jubaea chilensis
syn. *Jubaea spectabilis*

With maturity, this handsome palm reaches 80 ft (24 m), with a distinctive thick, cylindrical gray trunk topped with a dense mass of long, straight, feathery, deep green fronds. The yellowish flowers are borne in spring and are followed in fall (autumn) by woody, yellow fruit that look like small coconuts. **ZONES 8–11.**

JUGLANS
WALNUT

This genus, consisting of 15 species of deciduous trees, is distributed from the Mediterranean region and the Middle East to East Asia and North and South America. They are grown for their handsome form and elegant, aromatic foliage. All species bear edible nuts—usually produced within 12 years—and several yield fine timber used in furniture making. Greenish yellow male catkins and inconspicuous female flowers appear on the same tree in spring before the large pinnate leaves. They are followed by the hard-shelled nuts. The fallen leaves are said to be toxic to other plants (so do not put them on the compost heap). The name *Juglans* is derived from the Latin *Jovis glans*, meaning 'Jupiter's acorn'. These are excellent ornamental trees for parks and large gardens.
CULTIVATION: Cool-climate trees, they prefer a sunny position. Although quite frost hardy, young plants and the new spring growth are susceptible to frost damage. Deep rich alluvial soil of a light, loamy texture suits them best, and they need regular water. Propagate from freshly collected seed in fall (autumn).

Juglans ailantifolia
syn. *Juglans sieboldiana*
JAPANESE WALNUT

Occurring naturally beside streams in Japan, this species grows to 50 ft (15 m) and has gray-brown bark and large, hairy, toothed, dark green leaves. Catkins are greenish and the fruit is a shallow, pitted brown nut, enclosed in a sticky green husk. The husk is poisonous and is traditionally used in Japan to catch fish. The nuts are edible and the wood is used for carving. **ZONES 4–9.**

Juglans cinerea
BUTTERNUT, WHITE WALNUT

From the rich woodlands and river valleys of eastern North America, this species reaches 60 ft (18 m) and has gray, furrowed bark. The dark green pinnate leaves are up to 18 in (45 cm) long and hairy on both sides. Male and female catkins, borne in late spring to early summer, are followed by clusters of 2 to 5 strongly ridged, edible, sweet-tasting, oily nuts, each enclosed in a sticky green husk. Native Americans used this tree as a digestive remedy and it was also widely used as a laxative in the nineteenth century. **ZONES 4–9.**

Juglans hindsii
syn. *Juglans californica* var. *hindsii*
NORTHERN CALIFORNIAN BLACK WALNUT

This tree from California will grow to about 50 ft (15 m) tall; if given space, it can spread nearly as far. Its leaves, composed of 15 to 19 leaflets, measure about 12 in (30 cm) long. The fruit are spherical and 1 in (25 mm) or more wide. Both the new growth and the fruit are covered with fine hairs. **ZONES 8–10.**

Juglans major
syn. *Juglans microcarpa* var. *major*
ARIZONA WALNUT

Native to western Texas, New Mexico, Arizona and Mexico, this narrow-crowned tree can reach 50 ft (15 m) in height. Its thick-shelled nuts are brown to black in color, grooved and enclosed in a rusty brown fruit up to 1½ in (35 mm) wide. **ZONES 9–11.**

Juglans nigra
BLACK WALNUT, AMERICAN WALNUT

From central and eastern USA, this large, handsome, fast-growing tree reaches

Juglans regia

Juglans nigra

100 ft (30 m) with a spread of 80 ft (24 m). It has a single, erect trunk and a broad, rounded crown. Greenish brown catkins appear in spring with the early leaves, followed by dark brown edible nuts enclosed in a green husk. The leaves are made up of glossy, dark green leaflets. This species is valued for both its nuts and its dark wood. **ZONES 4–10.**

Juglans regia

COMMON WALNUT, PERSIAN WALNUT, ENGLISH WALNUT

From southeastern Europe and temperate Asia, this slow-growing tree reaches 50 ft (15 m) tall with a spread of 30 ft (9 m). It has a sturdy trunk, a broad, leafy canopy and smooth, pale gray bark. The leaves are purplish bronze when young, maturing to a mid-green. Yellow-green flowers are borne in catkins in late spring to early summer, followed by the edible nut, enclosed in a green husk that withers and is cast off. The timber is valued for furniture making. Cultivars include **'Wilson's Wonder'**, which fruits younger than the norm at about 7 years old. **ZONES 4–10.**

JUNCUS

RUSH

This genus contains about 225 species of grass-like plants from damp to wet habitats around the world, although they are rare in tropical countries. Most have little or no horticultural potential and some can become invasive weeds away from their natural habitats. If controlled, they can be used around the edges of ponds and lakes.

Juglans regia

CULTIVATION: Most species grow well, perhaps too well, in any moist to wet position in heavy clay soil. Propagation, particularly of named cultivars, is by division.

Juncus effusus

COMMON RUSH, SOFT RUSH

This everergreen plant's range extends from Europe to North America. It grows to about 3 ft (1 m) tall and has little to offer the gardener. However, several cultivars are of some interest, including variegated plants such as **'Aureus Striatus'** and **'Zebrinus'**. The bizarre **'Spiralis'** has stems that are curled and twisted like a corkscrew; it rarely attains much height due to the curled leaves; any rhizomes that produce straight stems must be promptly removed to prevent the plant reverting to type. **ZONES 4–10.**

JUNIPERUS

JUNIPER

Slow growing and long lived, the 50 or so species of evergreen shrubs and trees in this conifer genus are occur throughout the northern hemisphere. Juvenile foliage is needle-like, but at maturity many species develop shorter scale-like leaves, closely pressed to the stem and exuding a pungent smell when crushed. Both types of foliage are found on adult trees of some species. Male and female cones usually occur on separate plants. The bluish black or reddish seed cones have fleshy, fused scales; known as berries, those of some junipers are used to flavor gin. The fragrant, pinkish, cedar-like timber is soft but durable.

Juniperus chinensis

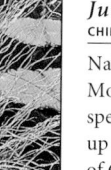

Juncus effusus 'Spiralis'

Various species of juniper are used medicinally with a range of applications from antiseptic to diuretic.

CULTIVATION: Easily cultivated in a cool climate, they prefer a sunny position and any well-drained soil. Prune to maintain shape or restrict size, but do not make visible pruning cuts as old, leafless wood rarely sprouts. Propagate from cuttings in winter, layers if low-growing, or from seed; cultivars can be propagated by grafting.

Juniperus chinensis

CHINESE JUNIPER

Native to the Himalayas, China, Mongolia and Japan, this frost-hardy species usually matures to a conical tree up to 50 ft (15 m) in height with a spread of 6–10 ft (1.8–3 m). Sometimes, however, it forms a low-spreading shrub. Both adult and juvenile foliage may be found on adult trees. The berries are fleshy and glaucous white. **'Aurea'** grows to at least 35 ft (11 m) tall, with a conical habit and soft, golden foliage; **'Blaauw'** is somewhat spreading when young, but becomes an upright 5 ft (1.5 m) shrub; **'Kaizuka'** is a small tree to 20 ft (6 m), with twisted spear-like branches; **'Obelisk'** is an attractive plant of upright form that can reach 10 ft (3 m) in height and has bluish green juvenile foliage; **'Pyramidalis'** grows to 15 ft (4.5 m) tall, with dense, blue-green leaves and a columnar habit; and **'Variegata'** grows to 20 ft (6 m) tall, glaucous with white markings. **ZONES 4–9.**

Juncus species

Juncus species

Juniperus chinensis 'Blaauw'

Juniperus chinensis 'Aurea'

Juniperus chinensis 'Kaizuka'

Juniperus communis
COMMON JUNIPER

Ranging widely through northern Europe, North America and western Asia, this is either an upright tree growing to 20 ft (6 m) or a sprawling shrub with a height and spread of 10–15 ft (3–4.5 m). It has brownish red bark and grayish green leaves. Fleshy, greenish berries take 2 to 3 years to ripen to black and are used for flavoring gin. Hardiness varies considerably depending on the subspecies or cultivar. Among popular cultivars are '**Compressa**', a dwarf, erect form suitable for the rock garden, growing to 30 in (75 cm) tall and 6 in (15 cm) wide with silvery blue needles; '**Depressa Aurea**', a dwarf form growing to 24 in (60 cm) tall and 6 ft (1.8 m) wide with bronze-gold foliage; '**Hibernica**', growing 10–15 ft (3–4.5 m) tall and 2–4 ft (0.6–1.2 m) wide, forming a dense column of dull, blue-green foliage when young but becoming broader and conical with age; and **'Hornibrookii'**, an excellent prostrate shrub with gray-green foliage that rarely exceeds 10 in (25 cm) in height, but will spread to more than 4 ft (1.2 m) wide. ZONES 2–9.

Juniperus conferta
JAPANESE SHORE JUNIPER

This prostrate, spreading shrub from Japan grows to a height of 6–12 in (15–30 cm) with a spread of 6–8 ft (1.8–2.4 m). The soft foliage is a mixture of fresh, clear green and pale blue, aromatic, needle-like leaves. The berries are pale green. It tolerates seaside conditions and grows rapidly, making it a first-rate ground cover. ZONES 5–10.

Juniperus davurica 'Expansa Aureovariegata'

A wide-spreading ground cover, this plant can exceed 24 in (60 cm) in height and spread to more than 5 ft (1.5 m) wide. Its blue-gray foliage is irregularly mottled with sprays of pure butter-yellow foliage. ZONES 3–9.

Juniperus deppeana var. *pachyphlaea*
ALLIGATOR JUNIPER, CHEQUERBOARD JUNIPER

Rarely growing higher than 20 ft (6 m) with a spread of 5 ft (1.5 m), this conical small tree has a sharply pointed crown, silvery blue-gray foliage and reddish brown bark, divided into small square scales, hence the common names. Native to low alpine areas of southwest USA and Mexico, it prefers a cool, dry climate. ZONES 8–10.

Juniperus 'Grey Owl'
syn. *Juniperus virginiana* 'Grey Owl'

This is a low-spreading, fan-shaped shrub with soft silvery gray foliage. It grows to more than 3 ft (1 m) tall with a spread of 6 ft (1.8 m). This species looks at its best when planted so that it fans out over a large rock. ZONES 6–10.

Juniperus horizontalis 'Bar Harbor'

Juniperus horizontalis 'Blue Chip'

Juniperus horizontalis 'Douglasii'

Juniperus horizontalis 'Glauca'

Juniperus horizontalis

This cold-climate prostrate shrub from northern North America is fast spreading and tough. Its branches form a mat of blue-green or gray leaves up to 18 in (45 cm) thick. Cultivars include '**Bar Harbor**', with grayish green foliage, turning mauve in winter; **'Blue Chip'**, with blue-green foliage; '**Douglasii**', with glaucous gray-blue leaves, turning plum purple in winter; **'Glauca'**, a prostrate form that exceeds 6 ft (1.8 m) in spread with a height of only 2 in (5 cm) or so, with blue-gray foliage often tinged purple in winter; **'Plumosa'**, which has an ascending habit unlike other forms of this species and spreads to about 10 ft (3 m) across by 24 in (60 cm) tall in a star-shaped pattern, with blue-gray foliage turning rich purple in winter; and **'Wiltonii'**, blue, with trailing branches. ZONES 4–10.

Juniperus horizontalis 'Wiltonii'

Juniperus × media

This group of cultivars, mainly derived from *Juniperus chinensis* and valued in cool to cold climates for their foliage, are all spreading shrubs, 1 or 2 being semi-prostrate. Their mainly scale-like, gray-green leaves have an unpleasant smell when crushed; the berries are white or blue-black. '**Blaauw**' grows to a height and spread of 6 ft (1.8 m) with blue-green foliage; **'Gold Coast'**, possibly the finest golden form of this group, makes a neat, spreading ground-cover shrub to 3 ft (1 m) in height and spread; **'Dandelight'** grows to 24 in (60 cm) tall with a 6 ft (1.8 m) spread and has golden-yellow new growth ageing to yellow-green; **'Old Gold'**, a sport of 'Pfitzeriana Aurea', makes a neat plant ideal for large rock gardens or as a tall ground cover reaching 30 in (75 cm) tall with a spread of 5 ft (1.5 m) and attractive golden foliage; '**Pfitzeriana**', by far the best known cultivar, grows to 10 ft (3 m) tall with a spread of 10–15 ft (3–4.5 m) and is broadly pyramidal with wide-spreading branches with weeping tips and gray-green leaves; **'Pfitzeriana Aurea'**, only for those with plenty of space, is a hardy juniper with spray-like branches that reach up to 3 ft (1 m) in height with a spread of more than 10 ft (3 m); '**Plumosa Aurea**' reaches a height

Juniperus conferta

J. davurica 'Expansa Aureovariegata'

Juniperus deppeana var. *pachyphlaea*

Juniperus communis

Juniperus communis 'Depressa Aurea'

Juniperus communis cultivar

Juniperus communis cultivar

Juniperus × media 'Gold Coast'

Juniperus × media 'Dandelight'

Juniperus × media 'Old Gold'

Juniperus × media 'Pfitzeriana'

Juniperus × media 'Plumosa Aurea'

J. × media 'Plumosa Aurea-Variegata'

Juniperus × media 'Pfitzeriana Aurea'

of 3 ft (1 m) and spread of 6 ft (1.8 m) with arched, weeping tips to the branches and green-gold foliage turning bronze in winter; and **'Plumosa Aurea-Variegata'** will grow to 12 in (30 cm) tall with a spread of more than 3 ft (1 m) and has gray foliage with sprays of creamy yellow foliage splashed throughout. **ZONES 4–10.**

Juniperus monosperma

REDBERRY JUNIPER, ONE-SEED JUNIPER

From southwestern USA and northeastern Mexico, this tree reaches a height of 25–50 ft (8–15 m). Both adult and juvenile foliage appear on the adult tree, the prickly juvenile foliage eventually being replaced by scale-like leaves. The fruit ripens to gray-blue and contains only one seed. **ZONES 6–10.**

Juniperus monosperma

Juniperus rigida

Juniperus sabina

Juniperus occidentalis

WESTERN JUNIPER

Native to North America, this juniper can grow up to 40 ft (12 m) in height and has a spreading crown and branches that are horizontal to pendulous. The scale-like leaves are blue-green. **ZONES 5–10.**

Juniperus procumbens

This prostrate, shrubby juniper builds up to 30 in (75 cm) high and 10–15 ft (3–4.5 m) wide. It has tufts of prickly, needle-like, bluish green foliage and brown or black berries. Its long, thick branches are held parallel to and slightly above the ground. '**Nana**', mat-forming and less vigorous, reaches 12 in (30 cm) high and 5 ft (1.5 m) wide. **ZONES 7–11.**

Juniperus sabina 'Tamariscifolia'

Juniperus procumbens

Juniperus procumbens 'Nana'

Juniperus recurva

COFFIN JUNIPER, HIMALAYAN JUNIPER

Native to Burma, southwest China and the Himalayas, this shrub or tree grows to 50 ft (15 m) tall and 15 ft (4.5 m) wide. It has spreading, pendulous branches and needle-like, aromatic, gray- or blue-green incurved leaves. The reddish brown bark peels in vertical strips; its glossy berries are dark purple. Its aromatic wood was used in China to make coffins, hence the common name. ***Juniperus recurva* var. *coxii*** has smaller leaves. **ZONES 7–11.**

Juniperus rigida

NEEDLE JUNIPER

From Japan and Korea, this cool-climate tree grows to 20 ft (6 m) in height, although it often forms a shrub when grown in gardens. It has pendulous branches and needle-like leaves with a band of white on the upper surface. The fruit ripens through brown to blue-black. **ZONES 4–9.**

Juniperus recurva var. *coxii*

Juniperus sabina

SAVIN JUNIPER

This spreading shrub from cold-climate Europe and Asia reaches 12 ft (3.5 m) high and 10–15 ft (3–4.5 m) wide. It has flaking, reddish brown bark and deep green, mainly scale-like leaves; the berries are blue-black. It does well in limestone soil. '**Tamariscifolia**' makes a broad mound to 3 ft (1 m) with a spread of 5–10 ft (1.5–3 m). **ZONES 3–9.**

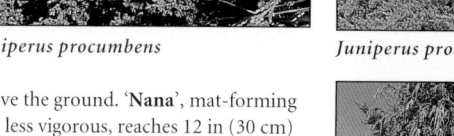

Juniperus thurifera

Juniperus squamata 'Blue Carpet'

Juniperus squamata 'Blue Star'

Juniperus scopulorum
syn. ***Juniperus virginiana scopulorum***
ROCKY MOUNTAINS JUNIPER

Slow growing to 30–40 ft (9–12 m) with a spread of 12 ft (3.5 m), this cold-climate tree has a rounded crown and scale-like, aromatic, gray-green to dark green leaves. The bark is reddish brown and peels on the branches; the berries are blue and fleshy. **'Blue Heaven'** is a silvery blue, conical form to 20 ft (6 m); **'Repens'**, a prostrate form, is less than 8 in (20 cm) high with a spread of 5 ft (1.5 m) and has blue-green foliage; **'Skyrocket'** has a narrow, columnar habit, reaching 15 ft (4.5 m) in height, with silvery blue foliage. ZONES 3–9.

Juniperus squamata
HOLLYWOOD JUNIPER

This species ranges in height from 1–20 ft (0.3–6 m) with a spread of 3–15 ft (1–4.5 m) depending on the variety. Needle-like green or blue-green leaves clothe densely crowded branchlets and the bark is flaky and reddish brown; the berries are fleshy and black. **'Blue Carpet'** is another blue-needled juniper which makes a mat of foliage about 10 in (25 cm) deep with a spread of up to 3 ft

Juniperus virginiana

Juniperus virginiana 'Sulphur Spray'

(1 m). **'Blue Star'**, a dense, rounded shrub with blue foliage, grows to 18 in (45 cm) tall and 24 in (60 cm) wide. **'Holger'** is a lovely shrub with a spreading, star-shaped habit that grows up to 24 in (60 cm) tall and 6 ft (1.8 m) wide. Its steely blue needles are attractively ornamented in spring by its golden tips. **'Meyeri'** has steely blue foliage with a rich silver sheen and reaches a height and spread of 15 ft (4.5 m). ZONES 4–10.

Juniperus thurifera
SPANISH JUNIPER

Native to Spain, southeastern France and the Atlas Mountains in northwestern Africa, this large shrub or tree reaches up to 60 ft (18 m) in height. It has a conical crown while young, broadening with age. Its branches are horizontal with upswept tips; the juvenile leaves are spreading, becoming small stem-clasping scales in the adult form. ZONES 8–10.

Juniperus virginiana
EASTERN RED CEDAR, PENCIL CEDAR

From North America, this is the tallest of the junipers commonly grown in gardens, reaching 50–60 ft (15–18 m) in height. It has a conical or broadly columnar habit and both scale- and needle-like, gray-green leaves. The berries are fleshy, small, glaucous and brownish violet. The wood is used in making lead pencils, hence the common name. **'Glauca'**, a columnar form with blue-green foliage, grows to 25 ft (8 m) tall with a spread of 8 ft (2.4 m); **'Hetzii'** has layers of gray-green foliage and reaches 10–12 ft (3–3.5 m) high and wide; **'Sulphur Spray'** (syn. *Juniperus chinensis* 'Sulphur Spray') is a popular sport of 'Hetzii' with soft yellow-green new growth ageing to gray-green. ZONES 2–9.

Juniperus virginiana 'Glauca'

JUSTICIA
syns ***Adhatoda, Beloperone, Drejerella, Jacobinia, Libonia***

This genus of about 420 species of shrubs and evergreen perennials is found in subtropical and tropical areas of the world, especially the Americas. They are widely grown in gardens in most warm areas, and in greenhouses in cooler climates. The leaves are simple and in opposite pairs, and the tubular flowers, in shades of cream, yellow, pink, orange or red, are mostly held in upright terminal spikes or clusters.
CULTIVATION: Frost tender, they prefer well-drained soils in full sun or bright filtered light. They require shelter from the wind as many species have somewhat brittle stems. Plants can be kept neat and bushy by pinching out the growing tips. They are easily propagated from cuttings of non-flowering shoots taken in spring.

Justicia adhatoda
syn. ***Adhatoda vasica***

This erect evergreen shrub from Sri Lanka and India can reach 10 ft (3 m) in height. Its leaves are mid-green and up to 8 in (20 cm) long. The flowers, borne in summer, are white with a curved upper lip and are veined red or purplish pink. This plant is used in Indian traditional medicine. ZONES 10–12.

Justicia brandegeana
syns ***Beloperone guttata, Drejerella guttata***
SHRIMP PLANT

The curved spikes of salmon to rose-pink or pale yellow bracts surrounding the white flowers of this attractive, evergreen shrub resemble shrimps—hence its common name. Reaching a height of 3 ft (1 m) and a spread of 24 in (60 cm) or more, it flowers mainly in summer.

Justicia carnea

It can survive temperatures as low as 25°F (–4°C) by behaving like a perennial when the tops are frozen back. A weak, sprawling plant, it needs regular pruning. ZONES 9–11.

Justicia californica
syn. ***Beloperone californica***
CHUPAROSA, BELOPERONE

Justicia californica is a desert shrub from southwestern North America. It is mostly leafless, the simple paired leaves appearing only for a short time after heavy rain. The stems are dense and green, creating a mounding shrub to 5 ft (1.5 m) or more in height and spread. In spring, masses of narrow red flowers attract hummingbirds. ZONES 9–10.

Justicia carnea
syns ***Jacobinia carnea, J. pohliana***
BRAZILIAN PLUME

This handsome, evergreen shrub bears dense, erect spikes of white, pink or rose-purple flowers in summer to fall (autumn). It grows to a height of 5 ft (1.5 m) with a spread of 30 in (75 cm), and has pointed, veined, deep green leaves. It is frost tender; potted specimens need to be watered freely in full growth, less so at other times. Prune back hard in early spring to encourage branching. Caterpillars and snails can be a problem. ZONES 10–12.

Justicia rizzinii
syns ***Libonia floribunda, Jacobinia pauciflora***

This attractive Brazilian shrub will grow to about 24 in (60 cm) in height and spread. It has comparatively small leaves—less than 1 in (25 mm) long—and in summer and fall (autumn) it produces scarlet tubular flowers with a yellow tip. **'Firefly'**, though apparently differing little from the species, is reputed to be particularly heavy flowering. ZONES 9–11.

Justicia spicigera
syn. ***Justicia ghiesbreghtiana***
MOHINTLI

Found from Mexico to Central America, *Justicia spicigera* is an erect, bushy shrub growing to 6 ft (1.8 m) tall. The mid-green leaves are oval and deeply veined. Loose, few-flowered terminal clusters of orange to red tubular flowers, about 1½ in (35 mm) long, are produced in succession all through the warmer months. ZONES 10–12.

Justicia brandegeana

KADSURA

This genus of Asian evergreen climbers consists of 22 species, valued for their attractive foliage and small, scented flowers, as well as their red berries—although both male and female plants are needed to produce these. They make useful subjects to cover fences, grow up posts or clamber through small trees.
CULTIVATION: Although these plants are reasonably frost tolerant a sheltered site in sun or part-shade is best. They prefer a well-prepared, humus-rich, neutral to acid soil. Prune if needed in late winter and propagate from plants of known sex by cuttings taken in late summer.

Kadsura japonica

Valued for its bright red berries which appear in fall (autumn), this evergreen, twining climber grows to 10 ft (3 m) tall. Its attractive, rich green, oval leaves and lightly perfumed, small cream flowers are borne in summer. Fully frost hardy, this plant does best in semi-shade in a well-drained soil. **ZONES 7–11.**

KAEMPFERIA

This is a large genus of about 50 species of rhizomatous perennials in the ginger family and the plants will grow up to 18 in (45 cm) tall. Found naturally in the tropical forests of Asia and Africa, they are grown in cultivation for their aromatic leaves and flowers. The roots of some *Kaempferia* species are used as spices and the Swazis have used the rhizomes as a treatment for malaria.
CULTIVATION: These plants are frost tender and like a shaded, moist aspect during summer growth and a dry resting period in winter. They are usually grown in a greenhouse in cool to cold climates. Propagate by division in late spring. Fresh seed sown in warm conditions as soon as collected is also an option.

Kaempferia rotunda
ORIENTAL CROCUS, RESURRECTION LILY

This species reaches 12 in (30 cm) high and wide. A delightful cluster of stemless flowers appears in spring before the large, patterned foliage which usually has a purple underside; the delicate purple and white flowers are scented. This plant is very sensitive to frost, so grow in a greenhouse in cool areas. It does best in subtropical conditions. **ZONES 9–12.**

KALANCHOE

This genus, native to subtropical and tropical Africa and Madagascar, with a scattering of species in Asia, consists of 150 species of perennial succulents, climbers or shrubs. These vary from small, leafy succulents to tree-like shrubs. They are mainly valued for their decorative foliage. Plants grow from 6 in (15 cm) to 12 ft (3.5 m) high and bear white, yellow or orange to brown, red or purple, tubular or bell-shaped flowers in early spring, followed by small seed-bearing capsules.
CULTIVATION: These succulents need full sun or part-shade and well-drained soil, and only light watering in the colder months; they range from marginally frost hardy to frost tender. Propagate from stem or leaf cuttings in late spring to summer, seed at the end of spring, or pot up plantlets that may form along leaf margins.

Kalanchoe beharensis
syn. *Kalanchoe vantieghemi*
VELVET ELEPHANT EAR

Native to Madagascar, this slow-growing shrub features olive-green, slightly triangular leaves with a soft, velvety texture. Treelike, it may grow to an eventual height and spread of 12 ft (3.5 m) or more. Once mature, it produces panicles of small greenish yellow flowers in late winter. **ZONES 10–12.**

Kalanchoe blossfeldiana
FLAMING KATY

This small, shrubby African species reaches 12 in (30 cm) high and wide. Its multiple, upstretched branches are covered with round to rectangular, deep green leaves with red margins and notched tips. Thick racemes of small, deep red, cylindrical flowers appear from winter to early summer; cultivated strains may be pink, yellow and also orange. Frost tender, it requires part-shade, and is a popular pot plant. **ZONES 10–12.**

Kalanchoe fedtschenkoi
SOUTH AMERICAN AIR PLANT

Despite the common name, this compact succulent is native to Madagascar. It reaches 12–18 in (30–45 cm) in height and spread, with upturned branches which put out profuse aerial roots from their lower parts. Fleshy, blue-green leaves are rounded to rhombic and have scalloped margins; a form with cream edges is very popular. Terminal panicles of reddish orange, bell-shaped flowers appear in late winter. It requires a warm dry position in full sun. **ZONES 9–12.**

Kalanchoe grandiflora
syn. *Kalanchoe nyikae*

Originating from East Africa, this succulent grows to 3 ft (1 m) tall on an erect stem in its native habitat. The foliage is blue-green with oval-shaped leaves. The small yellow tubular flowers are produced from late spring to summer. **ZONES 11–12.**

Kalanchoe blossfeldiana cultivar

Kalanchoe pumila

This small succulent shrub is native to central Madagascar and grows to a height of 4–8 in (10–20 cm). It has a creeping habit and its green, ovate leaves are offset by small, urn-shaped flowers which bloom in late winter and are reddish violet in color. It prefers part-shade. **ZONES 11–12.**

Kalanchoe 'Tessa'

A cultivar of uncertain origins, 'Tessa' has a trailing habit and grows to about 12 in (30 cm) tall by 24 in (60 cm) long. Its leaves are oval, mid-green and often have red edges. Its flowers, which open from late winter, are orange, tubular and borne in pendent panicles. **ZONES 11–12.**

Kalanchoe thyrsiflora

This species is native to South Africa and grows to 24 in (60 cm) tall. Rounded whitish leaves, often with faintly red margins, are up to 6 in (15 cm) long; the young growth is bright red. *Kalanchoe thyrsiflora* dies after producing clusters of yellow, tubular flowers in spring. **ZONES 11–12.**

Kalanchoe tomentosa

Kalanchoe tomentosa
PANDA PLANT, PUSSY EARS

This erect, shrubby Madagascan species grows gradually to 18 in (45 cm) tall with a spread of 8 in (20 cm). Its spoon-shaped, light gray-green leaves, covered with white felt, often have rusty brown spots along the margins. Yellowish green flowers tinged with purple on the lobes appear in early spring, although flowering is rare in cultivation. **ZONES 11–12.**

Kalanchoe 'Wendy'

This late winter-flowering hybrid bears panicles of purple-red, $1\frac{1}{2}$ in (35 mm) long, bell-shaped flowers, reflexed and yellow at the petal tips. Up to 6 in (15 cm) tall with a 24 in (60 cm) spread, its growth may be pendent or semi-erect. The leaves are mid-green with shallow, irregular teeth. **ZONES 11–12.**

KALIMERIS

A small genus of perennials from China, Korea and Japan, its 10 species are members of the large daisy family. Leaves vary from species to species, and

Kadsura japonica

Kalanchoe thyrsiflora

Kalanchoe blossfeldiana

Kalanchoe grandiflora

K

may be long and narrow or rounded, toothed or lobed. Flowers, which appear from summer to fall (autumn), are always yellow-centered, but the petals or ray florets may be white, mauve or purple. All the species grow to about 3–5 ft (1–1.5 m) in height.
CULTIVATION: Easily grown in any average, well-drained garden soil, they do best in full sun and with shelter from strong winds. Tip pruning when young encourages a compact, bushy shape and more flowers. After bloom, the plants can be tidied up with a light shearing. After about 3 years, they will become woody and old, but are easily replaced from cuttings taken in spring. All are fully frost hardy to at least –5°F (–20°C).

Kalimeris incisa

From northeast Asia, this 5 ft (1.5 m) tall species forms a clump of 4 in (10 cm) long, oblong leaves with finely-toothed edges. During summer the clump enlarges and produces billowing sprays of small purple or white daisies. **ZONES 4–9.**

Kalmia latifolia 'Ostbo Red'

Kalmia latifolia

Kalmia latifolia

Kalmia latifolia 'Ostbo Red'

KALMIA

From North America, this genus contains some very beautiful spring-flowering evergreen shrubs, although the 6 species in the genus are poisonous. English writer and critic John Ruskin waxed eloquent about *Kalmia latifolia*, describing its flowers as little bowls 'of beaten silver, the petals struck by the stamens instead of with a hammer'. However, they are not silver but a very delicate pale pink. The 2 common species are quite different in their general appearance, but both bloom in late spring and early summer and bear heads of pink flowers that open from buds that look as if they were made by a cake decorator. The flowers of *K. angustifolia* are far smaller than those of *K. latifolia.*
CULTIVATION: They prefer to grow in a cool, moist climate in lime-free, humus-rich, well-drained soil and a position in part-shade. They are among the hardiest of broad-leafed evergreens. Propagate from seed in fall (autumn) or cuttings in summer, or by layering.

Kalmia angustifolia
SHEEP LAUREL, HOBBLE BUSH, LAMBKILL

This open, twiggy shrub growing to 3 ft (1 m) tall and 4 ft (1.2 m) wide can be kept in a neat, compact shape suitable for shrubberies, rockeries or containers if trimmed after flowering. The leaves are 1–2 in (2.5–5 cm) long, and bright green

Kalmiopsis leachiana

to bluish green. The flowerheads, usually bright reddish pink, appear in late spring and early summer. In its native USA, it acquired its common names because sheep were often caught in the low, sprawling branches. Propagate by layering. ***Kalmia angustifolia* f. *rubra*** has deeper, almost red flowers. **ZONES 2–9.**

Kalmia latifolia
MOUNTAIN LAUREL, CALICO BUSH

While its leathery, evergreen leaves are quite attractive (and are the reason for the common name 'laurel'), this shrub is grown mainly for its flowers which appear in late spring to early summer—clusters of distinctive, bright pink buds that open to heads of small, pale pink flowers with stamens arranged like umbrella ribs. Mountain laurel can grow to 12 ft (3.5 m), but is more commonly 5 ft (1.5 m) in height and spread. **'Ostbo Red'** is a cultivar with deeper pink flowers which open from red buds; **'Carousel'** has purple-striped white flowers; and **'Elf'** is a pink-flowered dwarf form. **ZONES 3–9.**

Kalmia microphylla
syn. ***Kalmia polifolia* var. *microphylla***
WESTERN LAUREL, ALPINE LAUREL

This plant extends from Alaska to California and is a small, evergreen shrub rarely more than 24 in (60 cm) tall. It grows in very damp to boggy conditions in its natural habitat. Clusters of tiny, deep pink flowers are produced in late spring and early summer. Not as showy as some of its larger relatives, it is still an attractive addition to a moist rock garden. **ZONES 2–9.**

KALMIOPSIS

Descriptions of the single *Kalmiopsis* species, a native of Oregon, USA, usually refer to it as resembling a miniature rhododendron. Its 1in (25 mm) long elliptical leaves are deep green and densely clothe its wiry stems to form a 12 in (30 cm) mound of foliage. In spring, racemes of wide, flat, 5-petalled flowers open, they are around ½ in (12 mm) in diameter and have prominent stamens.
CULTIVATION: A plant for the rockery and alpine connoisseur, it is not difficult to cultivate in peaty, lime-free soil. Good winter drainage and shelter from hot summer sun are important requirements. Use a 50/50 mixture of rhododendron potting mix and fine grit, and cultivate it in a pot if drainage is likely to be a problem. It is very frost hardy. Propagate from seed or cuttings.

Kalmia angustifolia

Kalopanax septemlobus

Kalopanax septemlobus

Kalmiopsis leachiana

This aristocratic dwarf shrub is found naturally on rocky ledges in Oregon, where it is a protected species. It rarely exceeds 12 in (30 cm) in height. Its tiny, bright green leaves are a good foil for the open, cup-shaped, rich pink rhododendron-like flowers produced in spring. A slightly temperamental plant for the collector of dwarf shrubs, it is suitable for cold-winter, cool-summer climates. **ZONES 7–9.**

KALOPANAX
TREE ARALIA

This genus now contains only a single species, the deciduous tree aralia, indigenous to the cool deciduous forests of China, Korea, Japan and eastern Siberia. It is grown for its attractive foliage and fruit.
CULTIVATION: When grown in moist but well-drained, fertile soil, it develops into a good shade tree. It enjoys full sun, but will also grow well in part-shade. Propagate from fresh seed collected in fall (autumn) or from cuttings in summer.

Kalopanax septemlobus
syn. *Kalopanax pictus*

This tree develops a single stout trunk and a low-branching habit with a dense, rounded crown, and may grow 40–50 ft (12–15 m) high in gardens. When mature it will generally retain prickles on its trunk, branches and new growth. The maple-like leaves are usually large, dark green and coarsely lobed, and may be as much as 15 in (38 cm) across on young saplings. The white summer flowers are held in large sprays radiating from the ends of branches. The small blue-black fruit, borne in fall (autumn), are slightly split at the apex. **ZONES 5–9.**

KECKIELLA

This is a small group of 7 species of shrubs formerly in the genus *Penstemon*. Keckiellas are grown for their brightly colored, tubular flowers which attract birds. Found mostly in the California chaparral community, they also are native to Arizona and Baja, Mexico.
CULTIVATION: All keckiellas need well-drained soils and part-shade to full sun. Only occasional watering is required in summer. Shrubby keckiellas tend to become scraggly and require pruning to promote compact growth. Propagation is from seed or cuttings.

Keckiella antirrhinoides var. *antirrhinoides*
syn. *Penstemon antirrhinoides*

BUSH SNAPDRAGON, SNAPDRAGON KECKIELLA, YELLOW PENSTEMON

This species is a large, well-branched, spreading to erect shrub reaching 5–8 ft (1.5–2.4 m) tall and wider. Leafy clusters of bright, yellow, snapdragon-like flowers appear from scarlet buds in spring. The bush snapdragon prefers hot locations; it sheds many leaves during the hot dry months. **ZONES 9–11.**

Keckiella corymbosa
syn. *Penstemon corymbosa*

RED-FLOWERED ROCK PENSTEMON

Summertime clusters of tubular, wide-mouthed, scarlet flowers grace this sprawling, much-branched shrub, which grows up to 18 in (45 cm) tall and wider. Native to rocky slopes in northwest and central western California, it tolerates abundant winter rains when planted in well-drained soils; it is an excellent rock garden plant. **ZONES 8–11.**

Kennedia rubicunda

Kerria japonica 'Pleniflora'

Kedrostis nana var. *zeyheri*

KEDROSTIS

This genus from tropical Africa and southern India consists of 23 species of climbing or creeping, succulent perennials. The 3 ft (1 m) stems, are often very swollen at the plant base; small green leaves radiate out like fingers. Small green, white or yellow, beak-shaped flowers appear in spring. Most species have the male and female flowers on the same plant. Reddish orange berries appear in summer.
CULTIVATION: These frost-tender plants enjoy part-shade and well-drained soil. Water well in summer. Propagate from seed in spring; some species from cuttings. Cut back climbing stems when necessary. They are susceptible to scale.

Kedrostis nana var. *zeyheri*

Native to the South Africa's Cape Province, this deciduous climber has heart-shaped, medium-sized pale green leaves. Its tiny, greenish yellow flowers blossom in spring and are followed by red, ovoid fruit in summer. **ZONES 10–12.**

KENNEDIA

This Australian genus consists of 16 species of evergreen, woody stemmed, climbing or trailing plants, named after John Kennedy, a London nurseryman. They are cultivated for their showy, pea-like flowers, which attract birds.

Kennedia nigricans

Kerria japonica 'Pleniflora'

Keckiella corymbosa

K. antirrhinoides var. *antirrhinoides*

CULTIVATION: Marginally frost hardy to frost tender, they thrive in a light, well-drained soil and a sunny situation, but will tolerate light shade. Plant growth can be very vigorous and a strong climbing support is necessary. In spring or after flowering, invasive growth can be cut back reasonably hard without harming the plant, but keep well watered until new growth is established. Propagate from pre-soaked seed in spring or cuttings in summer.

Kennedia nigricans

BLACK CORAL PEA

This robust but frost-tender climber can quickly cover an area of up to 20 ft (6 m) in diameter. It has dark green leaves divided into 3 leaflets and unusual black and yellow pea-flowers which appear in spring and summer. It is ideal for covering a large area on a fence or shed in a fairly open position. **ZONES 10–12.**

Kennedia rubicunda

RUNNING POSTMAN, DUSKY CORAL PEA

This vigorous, marginally frost-hardy species grows up to 15 ft (4 m) in height and should be kept well away from nearby shrubs and trees, as it will quickly climb over anything in reach. Suitable as a ground or bank cover, it bears dark coral-red pea-flowers in small sprays in spring and early summer. **ZONES 9–12.**

KERRIA

JAPANESE ROSE

This genus from China and Japan contains only a single species, a deciduous shrub with many upright 6 ft (1.8 m), deep green stems emerging directly from the ground. The leaves are 1 in (25 mm) long, bright green and roughly diamond-shaped with finely serrated edges. The true species has simple, bright golden-yellow flowers up to 2 in (5 cm) across.
CULTIVATION: This is a very tough, fully frost-hardy, adaptable plant that does well in any moist, well-drained soil in dappled shade. Trim lightly after flowering to thin out some of the older canes. Propagate from basal suckers or cuttings in summer or by division in fall (autumn).

Kerria japonica

The bright golden blossoms of this shrub, which appear in spring on lateral shoots along its branches, make delightful cut flowers; the small leaves that follow only sparsely clothe the arching branches. Although *Kerria japonica* is single-flowered, the double form '**Pleniflora**' is more common in gardens and was introduced to European gardens nearly 50 years before the wild species was discovered. **ZONES 5–10.**

K

Kigelia africana

Kingia australis

Knautia macedonica

KIGELIA

This African genus consists of a single species of tropical and subtropical trees, extending into northern South Africa. The pinnate leaves are made up of oval leaflets and the large, bell-shaped flowers are borne in long pendent racemes and are mostly orange or red. The large, woody, sausage-shaped fruit have a smooth skin enclosing a woody, fibrous pulp.
CULTIVATION: These frost-tender trees require a warm climate, full sun, well-drained soil and plenty of water, and do best in areas of high humidity. Propagate from seed or cuttings in spring.

Kigelia africana
syn. *Kigelia pinnata*
SAUSAGE TREE

This evergreen tree grows to about 40 ft (12 m) and has a wide crown of spreading branches. The leaves are about 12 in (30 cm) long. The flowers, borne in panicles up to 6 ft (1.8 m) long in early

Kigelia africana

Knightia excelsa

summer, open at night and are crinkled and rich dark red inside, but duller outside. They have an unpleasant smell which attracts bats for pollination. The light brown fruit, up to 18 in (45 cm) long and weighing up to 8 lb (4 kg), are not edible. It grows vigorously in fertile, well-drained soil with adequate water. **ZONES 10–12.**

KINGIA
SKIRTED GRASS-TREE

This single species genus is from higher rainfall areas in southwestern Australia. It is very slow growing: the tallest plants are thought to be up to 1,000 years old.
CULTIVATION: Rarely cultivated, it thrives in sandy loam with good drainage and is happiest in full sun or light shade. Young plants can be grown in pots, but larger plants resent transplanting. Propagation is from seed, which may take up to 6 months to germinate.

Kingia australis

This plant eventually reaches 20 ft (6 m) in height, with a cylindrical, distinctively textured trunk topped by a dome-shaped tuft of smooth, needle-like leaves up to 24 in (60 cm) long. The dead leaves persist for some time, hanging down like a skirt around the trunk. Creamy white flowers are clustered in ball-shaped heads on upright stems which appear in a ring among the upper leaves. **ZONES 9–11.**

KIRENGESHOMA

This aristocrat from the cool forests of Japan and Korea is represented by only one species, although the Korean form is sometimes accorded species status. An upright perennial, it has arching, usually black stems with large, lobed, soft green

Kirengeshoma palmata

leaves and flowers in summer.
CULTIVATION: This fully frost-hardy perennial suits cool to cold areas in part-shade. It also requires a moist, humus-rich, lime-free soil and complements plants such as hostas and rodgersias. Propagation is from seed or by careful division in fall (autumn) or spring.

Kirengeshoma palmata
YELLOW WAXBELLS

This unusual perennial thrives in cool, moist conditions. In late summer to fall (autumn), it bears sprays of pale yellow, narrow, shuttlecock-shaped flowers on arching stems 3 ft (1 m) high, forming a clump about the same distance across. **ZONES 5–10.**

KLEINIA

This is a genus of around 40 species of succulent daisies. They are widespread in tropical and southern Africa and are also found in Madagascar, northwestern Africa, the Canary Islands, western Asia, India and Sri Lanka. They vary greatly in size, but are usually shrubby with simple, often rather flattened leaves. The small, cream, thistle-like flowerheads soon develop into a mass of fluffy seeds.
CULTIVATION: Other than being generally frost tender, most species are easily grown in any very well-drained soil in full sun. Propagate from seed or cuttings, or by layering.

Kleinia stapeliiformis
syn. *Senecio stapeliiformis*

This medium-sized perennial is native to South Africa and reaches a height of 8 in (20 cm). Red, daisy-like flowers grow to 2½ in (6 cm) across in spring. **ZONES 9–11.**

KNAUTIA

Consisting of 60 species of annuals and perennials, this genus is found extensively throughout temperate Eurasia, from the Mediterranean to Siberia. Their flowers are very like the related *Scabiosa*, but few are ornamental enough to be grown in gardens except for the 2 described here. These have a rosette of basal leaves through which the flower stems grow; these are branched and support some leaves.
CULTIVATION: Occurring in meadows, hedgerows and open woodland, these frost-hardy plants prefer sun or part-shade. Although often found growing in limy soil in their natural habitat, they will grow happily in any well-drained loam, but require staking. Propagate from seed in fall (autumn) or by basal cuttings in spring.

Knautia arvensis
syn. *Scabiosa arvensis*
FIELD SCABIOUS, BLUE BUTTONS

Native to Europe, the Mediterranean and the Caucasus and naturalized in parts of North America, this is a good subject for wild or meadow gardening; it self-seeds lightly in the garden. Erect branched stems up to 5 ft (1.5 m) tall come from basal rosettes of lyre-shaped foliage. These support pale purple-blue, pincushion-like flowerheads produced in summer and fall (autumn). **ZONES 6–10.**

Knautia macedonica

A showy species from the central Balkans to Romania, this makes an attractive subject for herbaceous borders. Its habit is similar to *Knautia arvensis*, but it grows to only 30 in (75 cm) tall, although it has larger and more attractive flowers which are usually deep purple-red, and occasionally pale pink or white. **ZONES 6–10.**

KNIGHTIA

This is a genus of just 3 species, 2 native to New Caledonia and the other *(Knightia excelsa)* from New Zealand. They are large evergreen shrubs or trees with leathery leaves that may be smooth edged or coarsely toothed. Their flowers, which are usually red to red-brown, are individually simple—very narrow petals curl back to expose 4 stamens and a style—but they are massed in bottlebrush-like racemes from late spring to early summer.
CULTIVATION: The New Caledonian species are rare in cultivation, but the New Zealand species is relatively widely available. It tolerates light frost, becoming hardier with age, and prefers a well-drained soil low in phosphates. Drought tolerant when established, it prefers ample summer moisture. Propagate from seed sown in spring or from semi-ripe cuttings.

Knightia excelsa
REWA REWA, NEW ZEALAND HONEYSUCKLE

This 30–80 ft (9–25) m) tree has coarsely toothed leathery leaves up to 8 in (20 cm) long and the new growth is red-brown. The scented flowers have recurved, deep red, petal-like segments and are massed in dense clusters. **ZONES 9–11.**

KNIPHOFIA
RED-HOT POKER, TORCH LILY, TRITOMA

There are 68 species in this genus of stately perennials, some of which are evergreen. They are native to southern and eastern Africa. Upright, tufted plants with long leaves, in summer they carry showy, brightly colored, tubular flowers in dense spikes on tall bare stems; some cultivars flower in winter and early spring. Originally the flowers were mostly flame colored, but cultivars bear flowers of pink, orange or yellow. Ranging from head-high to miniature types growing to 24 in (60 cm) or less, they are attractive to nectar-feeding birds.
CULTIVATION: Frost hardy to somewhat frost tender, they require an open position in full sun, well-drained soil and plenty of water in summer. In areas with winter temperatures below 5°F (–15°C)

Kniphofia 'John Benary'

Kniphofia 'Gold Crest'

they can be carefully lifted and stored indoors to be planted again in spring, although heavy mulching is preferable. They will tolerate wind and coastal conditions. From spring onwards, fertilize monthly. Remove dead flower stems and leaves in late fall (autumn). Propagate species from seed or by division in spring; cultivars by division in spring.

Kniphofia 'Atlanta'

One of many fine hybrids and selected forms, 'Atlanta' grows to 4 ft (1.2 m) tall. It has gray-green leaves and orange-red flowers fading to lemon yellow. **ZONES 7–10.**

Kniphofia caulescens

This majestic, frost-hardy evergreen grows on mountainsides up to altitudes of 10,000 ft (3,000 m). The 12 in (30 cm) rust-colored stems are topped with cream to coral pink flowers that fade to yellow; these appear from late summer to mid-fall (mid-autumn). The narrow leaves are blue green. It reaches 4 ft (1.2 m) in height. **ZONES 7–10.**

Kniphofia 'Cobra'

'Cobra' is a compact form with relatively short-stemmed, pale orange flowers that age to cream. **ZONES 7–10.**

Kniphofia 'Maid of Orleans'

Kniphofia 'Lemon Green'

Kniphofia ensifolia
WINTER POKER

This moderately frost-hardy evergreen perennial forms a dense clump, growing to 5 ft (1.5 m) tall with a spread of 24 in (60 cm). It has slender, sword-shaped, mid-green leaves and bears torches of prolific, lemon-yellow flowers in late fall (autumn) and winter. **ZONES 8–10.**

Kniphofia 'Erecta'

'Erecta' is an unusual deciduous form with orange-red flowers that point upwards when open. It grows to 3 ft (1 m) and flowers from late summer to mid-fall (mid-autumn). **ZONES 7–10.**

Kniphofia 'Express'

This hybrid has wide-based, triangular flower spikes of greenish yellow blooms, each tipped with red. **ZONES 8–10.**

Kniphofia 'Gold Crest'

This cultivar forms a clump of bright green, grassy foliage with fine-stemmed, somewhat loose flowerheads that open orange and age to bright yellow. **ZONES 8–10.**

Kniphofia 'Atlanta'

Kniphofia 'Little Maid'

Kniphofia 'John Benary'

'John Benary' grows to 5 ft (1.5 m) tall and has loose spikes of deep scarlet flowers. **ZONES 7–10.**

Kniphofia 'Lemon Green'

Yellow green in bud, the flowers of this form open soft yellow and become brighter with age. **ZONES 8–10.**

Kniphofia 'Little Maid'

'Little Maid' is a dwarf form that reaches a height of 24 in (60 cm). It has buff-tinted soft-yellow flowers opening from pale green buds. **ZONES 7–10.**

Kniphofia 'Erecta'

Kniphofia ensifolia

Kniphofia × *praecox* cultivar

Kniphofia 'Maid of Orleans'

This summer-flowering upright cultivar has dense racemes of yellow buds that open into creamy yellow flowers. It is frost hardy and grows to a height of 4 ft (1.2 m). Basal, strap-shaped leaves spread to 18 in (45 cm). **ZONES 7–10.**

Kniphofia × *praecox*
RED-HOT POKER

This South African perennial is the most common species in the wild and reaches up to 5 ft (1.5 m) tall when in bloom. Its slender leaves, up to 24 in (60 cm) long, are heavily keeled and serrated. Vivid red or yellow flowers appear in early summer. It is able to survive long dry periods and enjoys full sun. **ZONES 7–10.**

Kniphofia caulescens

Kniphofia 'Cobra'

Kniphofia 'Royal Standard'

This upright perennial reaches 4 ft (1.2 m) in height with a spread of 24 in (60 cm). Moderately frost hardy, it has grass-like leaves and bears terminal spikes of scarlet buds, which open to lemon-yellow flowers in late summer. In cold areas, use a winter mulch to protect the crowns. **ZONES 7–10.**

Kniphofia 'Samuel's Sensation'

Up to 5 ft (1.5 m) tall, 'Samuel's Sensation' has bright orange-red flowers tinged with yellow as they age. **ZONES 7–10.**

Kniphofia 'Royal Standard'

Kniphofia tuckii

Kniphofia 'Star of Baden-Baden'

Forming large clumps with age, this cultivar has 5 ft (1.5 m) flower stems with flowerheads that are mainly bright orange to-red except for the oldest flowers, which fade to yellow. **ZONES 7–10.**

Kniphofia triangularis

syns *Kniphofia galpinii* of gardens, *K. macowanii*, *K. nelsonii*

This poker from South Africa grows to about 3 ft (1 m) tall and is usually deciduous. Its flowers are a rich orange, yellowing slightly with age. This species has probably contributed the coral shade to the gene pool of hybrids. **ZONES 7–10.**

Kniphofia tuckii

This species closely resembles *Kniphofia ensifolia*, the winter poker, with its heads of greenish white flowers from reddish buds. However, it is not as tall, reaching only 4 ft (1.2 m) in height. **ZONES 7–10.**

Kniphofia 'Underway'

'Underway' has slightly blue-green foliage with small flowerheads that open rusty orange and fade to buff yellow. **ZONES 8–10.**

Kniphofia uvaria

This tall perennial, the source of many hybrids, grows to 4 ft (1.2 m) high and 18 in (45 cm) wide. It has thick, strongly channeled leaves. In late summer and fall (autumn), it bears dense racemes of tubular scarlet flowers becoming orange-yellow with age. It is fully frost hardy. ***Kniphofia uvaria* var. *maxima*** is slightly larger, reaching 6 ft (1.8 m) in height. It also has larger, rich orange-red flowers which fade slightly with age. **ZONES 5–10.**

Kniphofia 'Underway'

Kniphofia 'Star of Baden-Baden'

Kniphofia 'Winter Cheer'

Kniphofia 'Winter Cheer'

syn. *Kniphofia* 'Zululandiae'

This evergreen, upright perennial reaches 5 ft (1.5 m) in height with a spread of 3 ft (1 m). It is fairly frost hardy and bears large torches of orange-yellow flowers in winter that gradually turn yellow. It has narrow, grass-like leaves. **ZONES 7–10.**

Kniphofia 'Yellow Hammer'

This pale yellow *Kniphofia* hybrid, one of the best of the shorter-growing plants, raises its 3 ft (1 m) flower stems in summer. The flowers are excellent for cutting. **ZONES 7–10.**

Kniphofia triangularis

Kniphofia uvaria var. *maxima*

Kniphofia 'Yellow Hammer'

Koelreuteria bipinnata

KOELREUTERIA

Grown for their foliage, flowers and decorative fruit, this small genus of 3 species of deciduous trees is from dry valley woodlands in East Asia. They are useful small trees with pyramid-shaped panicles of long, bowl-shaped flowers followed by inflated fruit capsules. **CULTIVATION:** Moderately frost hardy, they thrive in full sun in fertile, well-aerated soil with free drainage. They can withstand hot, dry summers, but seaside conditions do not suit them. Propagate from root cuttings in late winter or from seed in fall (autumn). Prune in the early years to establish a single trunk.

Koelreuteria bipinnata

PRIDE OF CHINA, CHINESE FLAME TREE

From central and western China, this shapely tree grows 30–50 ft (9–15 m) tall with a single trunk and broadly conical crown. The bipinnate leaves are a clear yellow-green, turning deep golden in fall (autumn). Bright yellow flowers, blotched scarlet at the base, are borne during summer. The fruit are like miniature Chinese lanterns, green at first then turning bright pink in fall and paper-brown in winter. **ZONES 8–11.**

Koelreuteria elegans

FLAMEGOLD TREE

From Taiwan, this species is suited to most tropical and subtropical climates. It grows to 40 ft (12 m), forming a spreading, flat-topped tree with large, mid-green, ferny, compound leaves. In late summer to fall (autumn), long panicles of rich yellow flowers open towards the branch ends, followed by bladder-like pods that split into 3 rose-hued segments and turn brown in winter. **ZONES 9–12.**

K

Koelreuteria paniculata

GOLDEN RAIN TREE, VARNISH TREE

From China and Korea, this slow-growing, wide-spreading tree can reach 30–50 ft (9–15 m), but is often smaller in gardens. It has a convex crown and a single or divided main trunk. The bark is furrowed and the branches droop at the ends. The mid-green leaflets turn deep golden yellow to orange in fall (autumn). Large clusters of clear yellow flowers are borne in summer and are followed by papery, bladder-like, pinkish brown pods. It does well in alkaline soil. **'September'** (syn. 'September Gold') is similar to the species, except that it flowers late in the season. **ZONES 4–10.**

Koelreuteria paniculata

Koelreuteria paniculata 'September'

Koelreuteria paniculata 'September'

KOHLERIA

This attractive genus of the African violet family consists of about 50 species of rhizome-forming perennials or subshrubs from tropical regions of the Americas. Their tubular flowers are usually felty, pendulous, single or in clusters, in an outrageous array of gaudy colors. The entire plant, including the flowers, is covered in bristles.

CULTIVATION: These plants are tropical and frost tender; in all but tropical climates they are treated as plants for heated greenhouses or as indoor plants. In the tropics, give them a moist shaded site in which to grow. Water sparingly in winter. Propagation is by division of clumping species in spring or soft cuttings from shrubby types.

Kohleria digitaliflora

This Colombian perennial species has an erect to spreading habit and grows to at least 24 in (60 cm) tall. Its flowers are nodding, rich purple, furry trumpets borne from summer to fall (autumn). They are pinched in towards the ends, then flare out to expose the internal color, which is green-white with masses of dark purple freckles. **ZONES 10–11.**

Kohleria eriantha

A robust, shrubby perennial to 4 ft (1.2 m) or more tall, this species has a rhizomatous root system. Its foliage is lance shaped and up to 5 in (12 cm) long. It produces brilliant orange to orange-red pendulous trumpets, either singly or in clusters of 3 to 4, in summer. **ZONES 10–11.**

Kohleria eriantha

KOLKWITZIA

BEAUTY BUSH

This genus consists of a single species of deciduous shrub from China, much admired in temperate and cool-climate gardens for its lavish spring display. However, as its foliage is undistinguished for the rest of the summer, it should be placed where other plants can attract the eye.

CULTIVATION: Fully frost hardy, *Kilkwitzia* grows in any well-drained soil and does well in sun or light shade. It can become very untidy if old wood is not removed from time to time; winter pruning will simply cut away the flowering wood. Propagation is from cuttings in summer.

Kunzea ericoides

Kunzea parvifolia

Kolkwitzia amabilis

Kolkwitzia amabilis 'Pink Cloud'

Kolkwitzia amabilis

This bushy shrub develops into a mass of upright, cane-like stems to 12 ft (3.5 m) high, with small side branches. The leaves are in opposite pairs, oval, 1½ in (35 mm) long and deep green. The pale pink, trumpet-shaped flowers, which open in spring as the new leaves are developing, form profuse clusters at the ends of the side branches. They are followed by small fruit covered with bristles. **'Pink Cloud'** has clear pink flowers and is slightly larger than the type. **ZONES 4–9.**

KUNZEA

This Australasian genus of the myrtle family is made up of 30 species of small evergreen shrubs with small heath-like leaves that are pungently aromatic when crushed. Their individual flowers consist mainly of fluffy bunches of stamens, but in their spring season these cover the bushes and are usually pale—white, pink or lilac—though *Kunzea baxteri* has bright crimson flowers.

CULTIVATION: The need for these plants to be grown *en masse* to make an impact has led to their not being cultivated as widely as they might be, even in Australia. They also tend to be short lived and straggly, which can be overcome by a post-flowering trim. Moderately frost hardy to frost tender, these plants do best in mild climates, moist but well-drained soils and light shade. Old bushes are easily replaced from late-summer cuttings; they can also be propagated from seed in spring.

Kunzea baxteri

SCARLET KUNZEA

Growing to 8 ft (2.4 m) or more tall, this open, wiry-stemmed shrub from Western Australia is notable for the fluffy, crimson flowerheads it bears in spring and early summer. The stiff, narrow leaves are dull green, and the small fruit are red. It tolerates light frosts and sandy, coastal conditions. Tip-prune or clip lightly as the flowerheads are fading. **ZONES 9–11.**

Kunzea ericoides

syn. ***Leptospermum ericoides***

KANUKA

Found over much of New Zealand and southeastern Australia, *Kunzea ericoides* is a wiry-stemmed large shrub or small tree that has tiny, narrow, bronze-green leaves. A rapid-growing colonizer of cleared land, it is often treated as a near weed, but is a valuable pioneer and nurse plant in forest regeneration. Its tiny cream flowers are an important food source for nectar-feeding geckoes and are also favored by apiarists for the rich honey that bees produce from the nectar. **ZONES 8–11.**

Kunzea parvifolia

VIOLET KUNZEA

This spreading shrub from cooler hill areas of southeastern Australia grows to about 5 ft (1.5 m) tall with a spread of 10 ft (3 m). Often fairly open, it can be kept compact by regular clipping, making it useful as a hedge. The tiny, heath-like leaves are hairy when young, and in late spring and early summer the shrub bears masses of showy, violet balls of blossoms towards the ends of the branches. **ZONES 8–10.**

L

LABLAB

HYACINTH BEAN, LABLAB BEAN, BONAVIST BEAN

This genus of beans consists of only one species, a fast-growing but short-lived climbing perennial that probably originated in tropical Africa, though now widely cultivated in warmer parts of the world. A vigorous twiner, it has typical bean leaves consisting of 3 broad leaflets, and large pea-like flowers in long, erect spikes. The pods are flattened, with a line of bumps along the edge. Both pods and seeds are edible. The roots are thick and fleshy and are sometimes eaten.
CULTIVATION: Apart from being frost tender, hyacinth bean is easily grown in any moist but well-drained soil and in a sunny position. In cool climates it can be grown as an annual, though needing a long warm summer for best development. Propagate from seed or cuttings.

Lablab purpureus

syns *Dolichos lablab, Lablab niger*

This very attractive bean can be used as a quick cover to hide unattractive fences, walls and sheds. Its stems twine for up to 20 ft (6 m), with a dense canopy of purple-tinged foliage, the leaflets up to 4 in (10 cm) wide and strongly veined. Through summer it bears clustered 6 in (15 cm) spikes of fragrant white and mauve flowers, followed by 6 in (15 cm) maroon seed pods. **ZONES 9–12.**

Lablab purpureus

+ LABURNOCYTISUS

This genus name is based on a single plant, a curious small tree that is one of the few familiar examples of a graft hybrid, something that happens very rarely indeed; normally stock and scion remain distinct and their genetic material does not blend. It arose in a Paris nursery in 1826, when it was fashionable to create standard brooms by grafting *Cytisus purpureus* onto the stems of the closely related *Laburnum anagyroides.* In one plant the two fused to create this hybrid, which has been perpetuated more as a curiosity. The hybrid is unstable, odd branches reverting to one parent or the other, so the trees usually show the golden laburnum flowers and the purple ones of the broom, as well as the parti-colored blossoms of the hybrid.
CULTIVATION: This tree is propagated by grafting onto laburnum stock, and can be grown fairly easily in fertile soil in a sunny position in temperate climates.

+ *Laburnocytisus adamii*

This graft hybrid resembles one parent, the popular laburnum, in overall habit, being a shrub or small tree to 20 ft (6 m) high. Three leaflets about 2 in (5 cm) long make up each compound leaf. The drooping flowerheads are somewhat smaller than those of laburnum and the flowers are purple, salmon pink or bronze. **ZONES 5–9.**

+ *Laburnocytisus adamii*

Laburnum anagyroides

Laburnum × watereri 'Vossii'

Lachenalia aloides 'Quadricolor'

LABURNUM

GOLDEN CHAIN TREE

Two species of deciduous small trees from Europe and western Asia make up this genus of legumes, allied to *Cytisus* and other brooms. They have compound leaves with 3 leaflets that are larger and thinner than other members of the broom tribe, and the bright yellow pea-flowers borne in profuse pendulous sprays are also relatively large; they are followed by brown seed pods. All parts of the tree are very poisonous; handle with gloves.
CULTIVATION: Cool-climate plants, they prefer full sun, some humidity and tolerate any moderately fertile soil with free drainage—they do not like being waterlogged. Prune competing leaders in the early years to establish a tree-like form. Owners of large gardens may create 'laburnum arches' of 2 rows of trees tied down over a trellis, so that the flower sprays hang below like wisterias. Watch for leaf miner insects; protect young trees from snails. Propagate species from seed in fall (autumn), cultivars by budding in summer.

Laburnum alpinum

SCOTCH LABURNUM

Native to southern and central Europe, this broadly spreading small tree can reach a height of about 25 ft (8 m). Delicate, pendulous racemes 10–15 in (25–38 cm) long of golden-yellow flowers are borne in spring and early summer. They are followed by hairless brown pods containing brown seeds. The deep green leaves are smooth and glossy on the undersides. The bark is smooth and dark gray, shallowly fissured with age. **ZONES 3–9.**

Laburnum × watereri 'Vossii'

Lachenalia bulbifera

Laburnum anagyroides

COMMON LABURNUM, GOLDEN CHAIN TREE, GOLDEN RAIN

From the mountain regions of central and southern Europe, this small, spreading tree grows to a height and spread of 25 ft (8 m). The gray-green leaves are downy on the undersides. The densely clustered flowers are borne on 6–10 in (15–25 cm) long pendulous racemes in late spring and early summer, and are followed by hairy brown pods containing black seeds. The cultivar **'Aureum'** has pale yellowish green foliage. **ZONES 3–9.**

Laburnum × watereri

VOSS LABURNUM, WATERER LABURNUM

Now the most commonly grown laburnum, this hybrid between *Laburnum anagyroides* and *L. alpinum* makes a tree of similar size to the parent species. It has dark green leaflets and in late spring and early summer it produces dense racemes up to 18 in (45 cm) in length of fragrant rich yellow flowers. **'Vossii'**, the cultivar most commonly seen in nurseries, produces rich, buttercup-yellow flowers on racemes up to 24 in (60 cm) in length. **ZONES 3–9.**

LACHENALIA

CAPE COWSLIP, SOLDIER BOYS, VIOOLTJIE

Massed in clumps or planted in window boxes, these South African bulbs make a striking display. Short spikes of nodding to pendulous, tubular flowers in bright colors stand erect above narrow, sometimes marbled, strap-like foliage. The genus includes some 90 species, many of which are from the southeast Cape region.
CULTIVATION: Plant bulbs in fall (autumn) in well-drained, humus-rich soil. They like a sunny position and lots of water until the foliage begins to die off. Keep dry when dormant; they may need lifting in areas with high summer rainfall. They are frost tender, so plant in pots or window boxes or in greenhouses in cool areas. They spread quite freely and can be propagated by division in fall.

Lachenalia aloides

syn. *Lachenalia tricolor*

This species grows to around 12 in (30 cm). From winter to spring, flower spikes appear above the green or mottled red-brown foliage bearing nodding, tubular flowers that are usually greenish to golden yellow flaring out to red tips with sometimes red to orange petal bases. There are various forms of this species as well as a number of hybrids.

'Quadricolor' is one of the most unusual, with maroon, orange, yellow, green and crimson rainbow-like flowers. ZONES 9–11.

Lachenalia bulbifera
syn. *Lachenalia pendula*
RED LACHENALIA

This species grows to about 10 in (25 cm) in height, with a spike of flowers appearing from winter to spring. The flowers are pink to red to yellow, and the flared tips are green to purple. ZONES 9–11.

Lachenalia orchioides var. *glaucina*
syn. *Lachenalia glaucina*

Each 12 in (30 cm) flower spike on this species bears up to 25 bell-shaped blooms. The 1 in (25 mm) flowers are usually pale blue to violet and are scented; the leaves are often spotted with purple. ZONES 9–11.

LACTUCA
LETTUCE

This widespread genus of around 100 species is best represented in temperate Eurasia. It includes a number of common weeds but is best known in the form of *Lactuca sativa*—the common lettuce—which appears to have been in cultivation for at least 5,000 years and is

Lactuca sativa 'Lollo Rossa'

Lactuca sativa ' New Red Fire'

Lactuca sativa Oak Leaf type

thought to be derived from the weedy 'prickly lettuce', ***L. serriola,*** whose seeds also yield an edible oil. Species may be annual, biennial or perennial and range in size from 4 in (10 cm) to over 6 ft (1.8 m) high. If allowed to flower, it quickly becomes apparent that lettuces are in the daisy family; they have large sprays of small blooms, often mauve or yellow. The non-edible species contain very bitter compounds that have sedative properties and some have been used medicinally.

CULTIVATION: They are easily grown in any moist but well-drained soil in full sun or part-shade. In cool climates sow seed from early spring to late summer, in warm climates from fall (autumn) to mid-spring, though some heat-tolerant varieties can be grown in summer. For tender, succulent leaves it is important that there be no check in growth, so ensure soil remains moist. Shade young plants in hot weather and feed at intervals with weak liquid manure. Propagate from seed.

Lactuca sativa 'Red Sails'

Lactuca sativa 'Rouge d'Hiver'

Lactuca sativa 'Simpson Flute'

Lactuca sativa 'Target'

Lactuca sativa 'Black Seeded Simpson'

Lactuca sativa
COMMON LETTUCE

This leafy annual, grown for its succulent crisp leaves, comes in a large number of shapes and flavors. Popular types include the common iceberg or crisphead with globular heads like pale green cabbages; cos or Romaine lettuce with tall upright growth and crisp well-flavored leaves; butterhead, a small variety with waxy light green outer leaves and a firm heart; and the popular loose-leaf varieties with leaves that can be picked a few at a time as they mature. All come in an array of cultivars. **'Black Seeded Simpson'**, a loose-leaf variety with good vitamin C content, is popular in the USA. **'Bubbles'** is a compact semi-cos with blistered leaves, sweet and nutty. **'Frisby'** has tight heads of bright green, crinkly leaves. **'Green Salad Bowl'**, a loose-leaf variety with bright green frilly leaves, is good for cutting all summer. **'Lakeland'** is an excellent, crisp-leafed iceberg variety that is similar to **'Great Lakes'**. **'Lolli Bionda'** is a loose-leaf, non-hearting variety with decorative frilly leaves that can be used as an ornamental edging plant. **'Lollo Rossa'** is another loose-leaf variety; its rich reddish purple curly leaves may be cut at any time of year. **'New Red Fire'** is an iceberg with a green heart and reddish bronze outer leaves. The **Oak Leaf** types are loose-leafed, the leaves divided into narrow, finger-like lobes: **'Red Oak Leaf'** has reddish brown leaves. **'Red Salad Bowl'** has reddish brown leaves with a hint of bitterness. The Batavian loose-leaf **'Red Sails'**, with its crinkled dark reddish bronze leaves, has the advantage of being longstanding and slow to bolt. **'Rouge d'Hiver'** is smooth-leafed and among the hardier red lettuces for winter cutting. **'Saladini'** is sold as a seed mixture of many different types of loose-leaf lettuces and lettuce-like greens. **'Simpson Flute'** has bright green frilly leaves. **'Target'** is a tight-hearted, almost cabbage-like lettuce. Celtuce, ***Lactuca sativa* var. *augustana*** (syn. *L. s.* var. *asparagina*), has an edible stem, similar to celery stalk and edible bright green, curled leaves. It is sold in the UK as seed only. ZONES 7–12.

Lactuca sativa 'Bubbles'

Lactuca sativa 'Frisby'

Lactuca sativa 'Green Salad Bowl'

Lactuca sativa 'Lakeland'

LAELIA

These orchids, found in Central and South America and the West Indies, are closely allied to the cattleyas and rather resemble them, both in growth and in the shape and colors of their flowers. Their reputation does not compare well with their more glamorous relatives but they are still an attractive group of epiphytes in their own right and many of the 50 species and their hybrids are well worth growing. They interbreed easily with the cattleyas, bringing to the hybrids their richly colored labellum and also a neater flower shape—some of the larger cattleya species have distinctly floppy petals. Laelias bloom from fall (autumn) to spring, depending on the variety. Most bear their flowers in short sprays, although one group (formerly treated as *Schomburgkia*) has sprays of

× *Laeliocattleya* Hybrid

Laelia anceps

Laelia gouldiana

blooms up to 3 ft (1 m) long. They are spectacular for a large greenhouse.
CULTIVATION: Laelias like subtropical to warm-temperate, frost-free climates. Grow in strong light in a very open orchid compost in a small pot or, for some creeping species, establish the plant on a slab. In cooler climates grow indoors or in a cool to intermediate greenhouse. A dry resting period during dormancy is essential for many species. Propagate by division when the first roots appear on the new shoots.

Laelia anceps

This medium-sized species grows epiphytically or on rocks at moderate altitudes in Mexico where it is often exposed to full sunlight. The pseudobulbs are well separated, about 2½ in (6 cm) long and 1 in (25 mm) in diameter with a single stiff, leathery leaf 8 in (20 cm) long. The 3 in (8 cm) wide lilac-pink flowers with purple labellums are carried several together on 3 ft (1 m) long flower stems in winter. There are several named clones available, chosen for their larger or more shapely flowers. **ZONES 10–12.**

Laelia cinnabarina

From Brazil, this compact species grows on trees or rocks at moderate altitudes. The cylindrical pseudobulbs, 4–8 in (10–20 cm) long, grow close together; the single, purple-tinged leaf is 6 in (15 cm) long. The long-lasting inflorescence bears 1 to 2 flowers about 2½ in (6 cm) in diameter in summer. After flowering, until new shoots appear, water the plants only when the pseudobulbs have shrivelled. **ZONES 11–12.**

Laelia 'Coronet'

This representative of a group of miniature hybrids raised from *Laelia cinnabarina* has dainty sprays of 2 in (5 cm) wide flowers in shades of deep yellow or orange. The plants grow about 10 in (25 cm) tall, and look best in generous, many-flowered clumps in spring or summer. Some of these miniatures have cattleya genes and thus are officially classed as laeliocattleyas. **ZONES 11–12.**

Laelia gouldiana

The 4 in (10 cm) pinkish mauve flowers of *Laelia gouldiana* appear in early winter and look marvellous when brought indoors for a splash of seasonal color. The species, which comes from Mexico, grows to a height of 3 ft (1 m). Some authorities regard *L. gouldiana* as a natural hybrid between *L. anceps* and ***L. autumnalis***. **ZONES 11–12.**

× *Laeliocattleya* Hybrid 'Chic Bonnet'

× *Laeliocattleya* Hybrid 'Orange Crush'

Laelia purpurata

This orchid well deserves the honor of having been selected as the national flower of Brazil, a country with many beautiful wildflowers. Its 6 in (15 cm) wide flowers with their white or pale mauve petals and vivid purple labellums are quite magnificent. They appear in small clusters in early spring. This species has been much used in crossing with cattleyas. **ZONES 11–12.**

× LAELIOCATTLEYA

The laelias have been much crossed with the cattleyas, giving rise to this hybrid genus of evergreen orchids with over 2,000 names registered. The name applies to any cross between any member of each genus, plus all backcrosses and later generation seedlings. They vary from cool to intermediate growing, and can have dainty, almost miniature flowers or enormous ruffled ones in the full range of cattleya colors. The pseudobulbs bear only one leaf; it is lance-shaped and leathery.
CULTIVATION: These frost-tender plants should be grown in a very open orchid compost in bright, filtered light. Water well in summer, then sparingly in winter. Propagate by division and watch for aphids, spider mites and mealybugs.

× *Laeliocattleya* Hybrids

These colorful hybrids cover a wide range of plant size and flower color. Many have a large labellum (lip) that is often frilled and contrasts in color with the rest of the flower. They bloom primarily in spring and summer with occasional flowers throughout the year; the blooms are long lasting and make good cut flowers. Among the wealth of hybrids are **'Chic Bonnet'**, a bright pink flower with a magenta to crimson lip; and **'Orange Crush'**, an overall orange flower with relatively narrow petals.
ZONES 11–12.

LAGAROSTROBOS

This genus, allied to *Podocarpus* and *Dacrydium*, consists of 2 species of evergreen conifers, one endemic to the cool, moist forests of southwestern Tasmania and the other to New Zealand. They are long-lived trees with fine cypress-like foliage. Female (seed) and male (pollen) cones are carried on separate trees and are both very small and inconspicuous. The fine-grained, fragrant, pale yellow wood is highly prized; it is used for turning and is considered an excellent timber for boat-building.
CULTIVATION: These trees require a mild climate with high, year-round rainfall, high humidity and cool summers, and do best in deep, rich, well-drained, moist soil. Tolerant of shade, they need protection from drying winds. Propagate from seed (if available) or cuttings.

Lagarostrobos franklinii
syn. *Dacrydium franklinii*
HUON PINE

This Tasmanian species lives for hundreds, sometimes thousands of years in cool-temperate rainforests but is now scarce in the wild due to past

Lagarostrobos franklinii

Lagarostrobos franklinii

Lagunaria patersonia

exploitation. Extremely slow growing, it reaches a height of 50–80 ft (15–24 m) with a somewhat conical growth habit. Its slim, pendent, gray branchlets are covered in fine, scale-like, dark green leaves; the bark is smooth and silvery to gray-brown. On female trees, the small, erect seed cones appear near the ends of the branches by fall (autumn). It makes a good container specimen.
ZONES 8–10.

LAGENARIA

WHITE-FLOWERED GOURD

This genus of 6 species of annual or perennial climbers from South America have soft hairy leaves, which are malodorous when bruised, and large white flowers. The various species have differently shaped gourds commonly named for their appearance or use, and edible when young.
CULTIVATION: Lagenarias require light, well-drained soil, regular water and part-shade. They tolerate little or no frost and are propagated from seed.

Lagenaria siceraria

TRUMPET GOURD

This frost-hardy annual vine grows to 10 ft (3 m) and has hairy, dark green leaves and white trumpet-shaped flowers in summer. The gourd is edible when young; the hard shell can be fashioned into a receptacle. The gourds vary in shape and it is sometimes possible to buy seed that produces a mixture of shapes.
ZONES 10–12.

LAGERSTROEMIA

CRAPE (OR CREPE) MYRTLE

From southern and eastern Asia and ranging as far as northern Australia, this is a genus of around 50 species of evergreen and deciduous small to large trees, a few grown in warm and hot climates for their showy flowers. Their most distinctive feature is the crinkly margin and slender basal stalk of each of the 5 petals that make up a flower; the flowers in turn are massed into large, dense panicles at the branch tips. The 'crape' (alternatively crepe) in the name arose from the flowers' texture being reminiscent of the once popular fabric crape, while 'myrtle' alludes to their being close relatives to the large myrtle family. They make fine garden plants and are easily grown. Some species have attractive smooth bark, colored green, brown or reddish. The timber of some species is highly prized for shipbuilding.

Lagurus ovatus

CULTIVATION: They thrive in full sun in well-drained, humus-rich soil. Shelter from strong summer winds, which destroy the delicate flowers. Propagate from cuttings in summer or from seed in spring. Watch for powdery mildew.

Lagerstroemia indica

CRAPE (OR CREPE) MYRTLE, PRIDE OF INDIA

This deciduous tree, now believed to have originated in China, grows to about 25 ft (8 m) tall with an open, spreading, rounded head and smooth beige-colored bark streaked red-brown. In mid- to late summer it bears large clusters of frilly pink to deep red flowers. In cooler areas, the small oval leaves turn gold in fall (autumn). Flowerheads appear at the tips of the current season's growth; they are largest on strong growths, encouraged by pruning the main branches in winter; if not pruned, the tree develops an attractive, open shape, with massed smaller heads. The typical form of this species is now almost forgotten in cultivation, replaced by an array of cultivars (including some of dwarf habit), not all of which live up to the claims of their promoters. **'Petite Snow'**, of dwarf habit, has white flowers; **'Ruby Lace'** has frilly, deep red blooms. Some cultivars, such as **'Eavesii'** with its broad, open habit and pale mauve flowers and **'Heliotrope Beauty'** with pale lilac-pink flowers, are believed to be of hybrid origin: *Lagerstroemia indica* × *L. speciosa* hybrids re-crossed with *L. indica*. Some modern American cultivars are hybrids between *L. indica* and ***L. fauriei***, such as **'Natchez'** with creamy flowers; **'Seminole'** with mid-pink flowers; and **'Tuscarora'** with crimson flowers. **ZONES 6–11.**

Lagerstroemia speciosa

syn. ***Lagerstroemia flos-reginae***

QUEEN'S FLOWER, QUEEN CRAPE MYRTLE

This deciduous species from the humid jungles of India, Sri Lanka and Burma can reach a height of 80 ft (24 m) in the wild, with a single trunk and a spreading broad head. It has long, leathery leaves that turn copper red in fall (autumn) before dropping. Showy panicles of large, rose-pink to lilac and lavender-purple flowers are borne from summer to fall. The bark is shed in irregular patches, giving the smooth gray trunk an yellowish, mottled appearance. **ZONES 11–12.**

Lagerstroemia indica

LAGUNARIA

NORFOLK ISLAND HIBISCUS, COW ITCH TREE, WHITE OAK

This genus, closely allied to *Hibiscus*, consists of a single species that occurs wild on Australia's east coast near the Tropic of Capricorn as well as on the far offshore Norfolk and Lord Howe Islands. A densely foliaged tree of neat proportions, it is well suited to seaside situations as its gray-green foliage seems to be immune to salt spray; it is often planted as a street and park tree in such areas. The seed pods contain spicules, or tiny needles, which can cause extreme skin irritation.
CULTIVATION: This tree needs full sun, well-drained soil and adequate water; it can tolerate the occasional very light frost once established. Pruning is not usually necessary. Propagate from seed, but take care when handling the irritant seed pods.

Lagunaria patersonia

syn. *Hibiscus patersonius*

Usually seen as a neat, pyramid-shaped tree 15–30 ft (4.5–9 m) high, this warm-climate evergreen has somewhat oval, leathery leaves with a coating of grayish hairs, denser on the undersides. Profuse pale pink to almost purplish flowers that appear in the leaf axils during summer look like small hibiscuses, about 2 in (5 cm) across, with 5 reflexed petals surrounding a central column of stamens. The seed pods contain bright orange seeds among irritant bristles.
ZONES 10–11.

Lagerstroemia indica 'Tuscarora'

Lagerstroemia indica

LAGURUS

HARE'S TAIL GRASS

Often found growing on coastal dunes, the single species of Mediterranean annual that makes up this grass genus is popular for dried arrangements and has naturalized in many other parts of the world. It is a wiry grass with very thin leaves up to 10 in (25 cm) long. The foliage is briefly green in late winter and spring but soon dries to a pale golden brown. The main feature is the mass of soft, downy seed heads carried on wiry stems just above foliage height; these last indefinitely when dried. Their shape and texture are reminiscent of a rabbit's or hare's tail, hence the common name.
CULTIVATION: Frost hardy, it is easily grown in any light, even sandy, well-drained soil in full sun. Propagate from seed in late summer or fall (autumn).

Lagurus ovatus

This ornamental, sparsely tufted grass grows to 18 in (45 cm) tall, spreading into a broad clump only if given ample space and nutrition. The panicles of downy spikelets begin pale green, sometimes with lilac tinges, and mature to a creamy white; they appear from mid-spring to summer. **ZONES 9–10.**

L

Lagerstroemia speciosa

Lagerstroemia indica 'Seminole'

Lagerstroemia indica 'Heliotrope Beauty'

LAMARCKIA

GOLDEN TOP, SILVER GRASS, TOOTHBRUSH GRASS

There is only a single species in this grass genus, native in the Mediterranean region. It is a small summer-growing annual with a tuft of broad, tender green leaves and short brush-like spikes of densely crowded, fine, soft flower spikelets. Although commonly naturalized in many warm-temperate regions of the world, usually in sandy soils, it also makes a pretty ornamental for use in borders or as a filler in areas with difficult, dry soil. The seed heads can be used for dried decorations.

CULTIVATION: It requires a light, sandy, well-drained soil and full sun. It is an undemanding plant that progresses quickly to flowering and seeding provided it has moisture when young. Propagate from seed from mid-spring onward.

Lamarckia aurea

Growing to no more than 12 in (30 cm) tall and often flowering when only a few inches high, golden top makes a sparse tuft of diverging, slightly twisted leaves. A succession of flowering spikes are at first pale silvery green changing to pale yellowish, sometimes with a purple hue when mature; they appear from mid-spring to early summer, or winter to spring in warmer climates. **ZONES 7–11.**

Lamarckia aurea

Lamium album

LAMIUM

syns *Galeobdolon, Lamiastrum*

DEADNETTLE

This genus of over 50 species of annuals and rhizomatous perennials, native to Europe, Asia and North Africa, belongs to the mint family, not the nettle family as the common name would seem to indicate. They include some common weeds and hedgerow plants as well as a handful cultivated for ornament. Some have astringent properties and have been used in folk medicine, or have been grown as pot herbs in parts of Europe. Some are an important source of nectar for bees. They have leaves with toothed margins, arranged in opposite pairs and sometimes splashed with paler gray-green or white, and short spikes or axillary whorls of white, yellow, pink or purple 2-lipped flowers, the upper lip curved over in a helmet-like shape.

CULTIVATION: Lamiums are frost hardy and grow well in most soils. Flower color determines planting season and light requirement: white- and purple-flowered species are planted in spring and prefer full sun; the yellow-flowered ones are planted in fall (autumn) and prefer shade. They often have invasive habits and need plenty of room. Propagate from seed or by division in early spring.

Lamium album

WHITE DEADNETTLE, ARCHANGEL

Ranging right across Europe and northern Asia, this species has foliage that superficially resembles that of the common nettle (*Urtica urens*). An erect perennial of 12–24 in (30–60 cm) high, it produces whorls of pure white flowers from late spring to early fall (autumn). It became known as archangel because it flowers around the 8th of May, the feast day of the Archangel Michael in the old calendar. It is known to sometimes flower in mid-winter. **ZONES 4–10.**

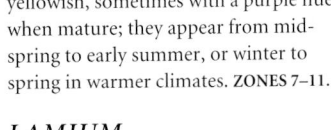

Lamium galeobdolon 'Hermann's Pride'

Lamium galeobdolon 'Hermann's Pride'

Lamium maculatum 'Beacon's Silver'

Lamium galeobdolon

syns *Galeobdolon luteum, G. argentatum, Lamiastrum galeobdolon*

YELLOW ARCHANGEL

This perennial species from Europe and western Asia spreads both by rhizomes and surface runners to form extensive, loose mats of foliage usually about 12 in (30 cm) deep, spreading over moist, shady areas beneath trees. Its leaves are variably splashed with silvery gray and in summer it bears leafy spikes of bright yellow flowers each about $\frac{3}{4}$ in (18 mm) long. **'Florentinum'** has leaves splashed with silver that becomes purple-tinged in winter. **'Hermann's Pride'** is densely mat forming and has narrow leaves streaked and spotted with silver. **ZONES 6–10.**

Lamium garganicum

The specific name refers to the Garganian Promontory which extends into the Adriatic from Italy, whence this species extends eastward to Turkey and Iraq. It is a mound-forming perennial up to 18 in (45 cm) tall with toothed, heart-shaped leaves and produces pink, red, purple or, rarely, white flowers in early summer. **ZONES 6–10.**

Lamium maculatum

SPOTTED DEADNETTLE

Its wild forms often regarded almost as weeds, this semi-evergreen perennial is native to Europe and western Asia and naturalized in North America. A variable species, it may have erect stems to 24 in (60 cm) tall, or have a lower, more spreading habit. The strongly toothed leaves have a central blotch or stripe of pale silvery green, and leafy whorled spikes of very pale pink to deep rose flowers appear in spring and summer. The cultivars are more desirable garden plants, mostly with a compact mat-forming habit and not more than 6 in (15 cm) high. **'Pink Pewter'** has silvery leaves which highlight the beautiful pink flowers; **'Beacon's Silver'** has purplish flowers with silvery green leaves edged dark green; **'Roseum'** has silver-striped foliage and pinkish lilac flowers; and **'White Nancy'** has silvery green leaves and white flowers. **ZONES 4–10.**

Lamium garganicum

Lamium maculatum 'Roseum'

Lamium maculatum 'White Nancy'

LAMPRANTHUS

ICE PLANT, PIGFACE, VYGIE

This South African genus of wiry stemmed succulents with bright, daisy-like flowers is one of many that once went under the name of *Mesembryanthemum*. These are perhaps the most dazzling in flower of the succulents known as ice plants—the flowers are brilliantly colored in orange, yellow, pink or red. The 180 or more species and numerous garden forms vary in habit, from creeping ground covers to bushy little shrubs. All have pairs of narrow succulent leaves, triangular to almost circular in cross-section. *Lampranthus* thrive in seaside gardens and flower most profusely where conditions are harshest; however, they may be rather short lived, or at least become straggly after a few years.

CULTIVATION: They prefer a warm, frost-free climate. They thrive in dry conditions and, once established in a warm-climate garden in full sun in well-drained soil, can exist on rainfall without any extra watering. In cooler climates they can be placed outdoors once frosts are past, in pots or tubs in the sunniest available spots, and overwintered in a conservatory. Propagate from seed or stem cuttings in spring or fall (autumn).

Lampranthus aurantiacus
ORANGE ICE PLANT

Reaching about 18 in (45 cm) in height and 30 in (75 cm) in width, this species has small, gray-green, cylindrical leaves that narrow towards the tip. In summer it bears an abundance of vivid dark orange flowers with a spot of purple at their centers. **ZONES 9–11.**

Lampranthus aureus
ORANGE VYGIE

This upright subshrub reaches about 15 in (38 cm) in height. The bluish green leaves are up to 2 in (5 cm) long and are covered in fine translucent spots. In summer, vivid yellow or orange flowers up to 2½ in (6 cm) in diameter appear in profusion. **ZONES 9–11.**

Lampranthus blandus
PINK VYGIE

One of the larger-growing species, this makes a spreading, mound-like shrub 12–18 in (30–45 cm) tall and about 3 ft (1 m) wide with pale gray-green foliage, the whole plant covered in a sheet of pale pink blossom in spring. The flowers have multiple rows of very narrow petals giving a semi-double effect. It is a favorite plant for large coastal rock gardens in warm climates, but will also thrive in dry inland areas. **ZONES 9–11.**

Lampranthus coccineus
RED VYGIE

This spectacular plant resembles *Lampranthus aurantiacus* except that the leaves are a little shorter. In late spring it is a dazzling sight—literally so, as the

Lantana montevidensis

Lantana camara 'Radiation'

Lampranthus hybrid

brilliant red flowers are iridescent and flash purple, pink or orange as the sun strikes them. It is marginally frost hardy. **ZONES 9–11.**

Lampranthus spectabilis
ICE PLANT, TRAILING ICE PLANT

Growing 10 in (25 cm) high with an indefinite spread, this species has large daisy-like flowers with glossy pinkish lilac petals, appearing profusely in spring and summer. It also has edible fruit. **ZONES 9–11.**

Lampranthus veredenbergensis

This succulent has a compact habit, growing to about 6 in (15 cm) across. Its small green leaves are in pairs and tiny pink flowers appear in spring. **ZONES 9–11.**

LANTANA

This genus of the verbena family consists of around 150 species of evergreen shrubs and cany stemmed perennials, native to warmer parts of the Americas except for a few in southern Africa. Several species are notorious weeds of tropical and subtropical regions, most notably *Lantana camara*. The plants have rough, slightly prickly stems with oval leaves in opposite pairs, their surfaces harsh and closely veined. Very small, trumpet-shaped flowers in compact button-like heads open progressively from the center of each head, their color changing in the older flowers towards the perimeter. Tiny fruits like blackberry drupelets may follow. Several species and their cultivars are useful greenhouse or conservatory plants in cool climates, where they may also be treated as summer bedding plants, or in warm-climate gardens they are grown as outdoor shrubs or ground covers.
CULTIVATION: These plants prefer fertile, well-drained soil and full sun. Plants in containers should be top-dressed

Lantana camara 'Chelsea Gem'

Lampranthus aurantiacus

Lampranthus spectabilis

Lampranthus veredenbergensis

annually in spring and watered well when in full growth, less at other times. Tip prune young growth to promote a bushy habit and propagate from cuttings in summer or from seed in spring. They are generally little affected by pests, but check regularly for white fly and spider mite.

Lantana camara
COMMON LANTANA, SHRUB VERBENA

This is the Dr Jekyll and Mr Hyde of the plant world, reviled in warmer, wetter parts of the world for its rampant invasion of forests and pastures and poisoning of cattle, but valued as an ornamental especially in cooler or drier regions. Much of this split personality is accounted for by its great variability, causing botanists to doubt whether it is in fact a single species. At least 25 weedy strains have been identified in Australia, only a few of which were introduced as ornamentals; many of the ornamental cultivars show no signs of becoming weedy. The weedy forms produce long scrambling canes and can mound up to 20 ft (6 m) even without trees to climb over, but garden forms are mostly rounded or spreading shrubs 2–6 ft (0.6–1.8 m) high. The tiny flowers typically open cream, yellow or yellow-red and age to pink, red, orange or white, the heads appearing in a long succession from spring to fall (autumn). There are many cultivars ranging in color from the golden orange and red of **'Radiation'** and the yellow of **'Drap d'Or'** to the white blooms of **'Snowflake'**. **'Chelsea Gem'** is one of the oldest, an excellent compact shrub with profuse orange and red flowerheads—it makes an attractive standard. **ZONES 9–12.**

Lantana montevidensis
syn. ***Lantana sellowiana***
TRAILING LANTANA

The slender, weak stems of this trailing species mound up into a dense mass making it a wonderful plant for a ground cover or low hedge. It grows 18–36 in (45–90 cm) tall and 6 ft (1.8 m) wide or often more, with small, neat, closely veined dark green leaves. Throughout the year, but particularly in summer, it bears bright mauve-pink flowerheads, each with a yellow eye. A white-flowered cultivar has recently appeared and can make an attractive combination planted with the pink. **ZONES 9–11.**

LAPAGERIA
CHILEAN BELLFLOWER, COPIHUE

The scientific name of this remarkable genus of a single species of climbing lily honors the Empress Josephine of France (*née* Tascher de la Pagerie, 1763–1814) and her ardent devotion to botany. It was she who first grew this flower in Europe, taken to France from its native Chile by one of the empress' botanists. It is a vine with a reputation for being difficult; once established, however, it usually grows and flowers easily.
CULTIVATION: It needs a rich, leafy, very well-drained soil, some shade and a climate free from temperature extremes. In cool-temperate climates it is best grown under glass, although the greenhouse only needs sufficient heat to exclude severe frost in winter. Propagate from seed or cuttings.

Lapageria rosea

Larix decidua

Larix gmelinii

Lapageria rosea

The national flower of Chile, to whose woodlands it is native, this is a strong-growing, twining climber with evergreen, glossy leaves. Borne from summer to late fall (autumn) in 2s and 3s, the bell- or trumpet-shaped pale pink to red flowers are 3 in (8 cm) long with petals of such heavy texture they appear molded from wax. It can reach 25 ft (8 m) high but will flower well if kept trained to a height of about 8 ft (2.4 m) on a post . **'Superba'** has a slender, twining stem, glossy bright green leaves and bell-shaped, deep rose-red flowers. **ZONES 9–10.**

LARIX

LARCH

From cool mountainous regions of the northern hemisphere, these deciduous, fast-growing conifers have a handsome, graceful form and fresh green spring foliage as well as strong, durable timber; the bark also is used for tanning and dyeing. Mainly conical in shape, they lose

Lapageria rosea 'Superba'

Larix decidua

their leaves in fall (autumn), bursting into leaf in early spring. With the new foliage appear both drooping yellow male (pollen) cones and upright red female cones, which mature over the following summer to short, erect seed cones with thin scales; these persist on the tree after shedding their seeds. Up to 15 species of *Larix* have been recognised, but recent studies have merged some of these, reducing this number to as few as 9 species. **CULTIVATION:** Cold- to cool-climate plants, they do best in well-drained, light or gravelly soil; most resent waterlogged soil. Propagation is from seed. Check regularly for larch canker or blister and infestation by larch chermes (a type of aphid).

Larix decidua

EUROPEAN LARCH

From the mountains of central and southern Europe, this tree reaches a height of 100 ft (30 m); it has a conical crown when young, spreading with maturity. The branches are widely spaced and the branchlets have a graceful, weeping habit. The soft, bright green, needle-like leaves turn yellow in fall (autumn) before dropping. The mature seed cones are egg-shaped, brown and upright. The gray bark becomes red-brown, fissured and scaly with age. **ZONES 2–9.**

Larix gmelinii

DAHURIAN LARCH

This northeastern Asian species reaches 100 ft (30 m) in the wild. It has finely hairy branchlets, needle-like leaves and

Larix potaninii

the dark reddish brown bark is broken into long scales. The cones ripen through summer from reddish to purple and finally brown. ***Larix gmelinii* var. *japonica*** from far eastern Siberia and the Kurile Islands is an equally tall tree, suited to very cold winters. Its branchlets are covered in brown hairs and the cones are nearly 1 in (25 mm) long. **ZONES 2–9.**

Larix kaempferi

syn. *Larix leptolepis*

JAPANESE LARCH

This fast-growing Japanese species is widely used for ornamental landscaping and is grown in forestry plantations in the UK. Broadly conical, it grows to a height of 100 ft (30 m) and a spread of 20 ft (6 m). Its soft needle-like leaves are gray- to blue-green and the mature cones are brown and almost globular, their broad scales spreading at the tips to give a rosebud appearance. The scaly bark is reddish brown, or orange-red on older branches. **ZONES 4–9.**

Larix laricina

TAMARACK, AMERICAN LARCH, EASTERN LARCH

This, the most widespread and abundant larch in North America, ranges from Alaska through Canada to northeastern USA. It reaches 60–80 ft (18–24 m) high and has blue-green, needle-like foliage that turns yellow in fall (autumn). The mature cones are smaller than those of the other larches and have fewer, thinner scales. The bark is scaly and pinkish to reddish brown. **ZONES 2–8.**

Larix potaninii

CHINESE LARCH

From cool climates of western China (where it is an important timber tree), this compact larch reaches a height of 60–70 ft (18–21 m). Similar in appearance to the European larch, it has needle-like foliage on rather stout shoots, giving off a strong, distinctive smell when crushed. The seed cones are large for a larch, about 2 in (5 cm) long, with shiny brown scales that bear long flap-like appendages or 'bracts'. The bark is dark pinkish gray with scaly cracks. **ZONES 5–9.**

Lathraea clandestina

LATHRAEA

The name of this genus comes from the Greek *lathraios*, meaning hidden, because most of the plant is underground. In fact the 7 species of this Eurasian genus are parasites, lacking chlorophyll of their own and attaching to the roots of trees and shrubs. The fleshy, ivory to mauve leaves are borne in 4 rows on subterranean rhizomes; the interesting fleshy flowers are borne on stems arising from the rhizome and, together with the capsular fruits that succeed them, are the only parts of the plant normally visible. **CULTIVATION:** These frost-hardy plants can sometimes be induced to grow in a woodland setting if the right host genera are present. Scatter seed among the tree roots in shade, in moist but well-drained soil with a mulch of leaves in fall (autumn).

Lathraea clandestina

PURPLE TOOTHWORT

This parasitic plant from southwestern Europe bears dense clusters of showy purplish flowers with hooded apices just 2 in (5 cm) above the soil. The scale-like leaves are kidney-shaped and white. The host trees for this species are poplars, willows and alders. **ZONES 6–10.**

Larix kaempferi

Larix kaempferi

Lathyrus latifolius

Lathyrus nervosus

Lathyrus odoratus 'Esther Ranson'

LATHYRUS

Closely allied to the garden peas *(Pisum)* and vetches *(Vicia)*, this genus consists of 150 or so species of annuals and perennials, many of them tendril climbers and some of them edible, native mainly in temperate northern hemisphere regions but with a significant number of species also in Andean South America. The leaves are pinnate with the uppermost pair of leaflets usually modified into tendrils. The pea-shaped flowers come in a wide range of colors, from red, mauve and white to blue and even pale yellow. Flat seed pods follow the flowers. *Lathyrus odoratus*, the sweet pea, has a proud place in the history of science, for it was one of the chief plants used by Gregor Mendel (1822–84) in his hybridizing experiments which laid the foundations for the science of genetics.

CULTIVATION: Plant these frost-hardy plants in fertile, well-drained soil in full sun. Stake or train on wires and deadhead regularly. Propagate annuals from seed in early summer or early fall (autumn), and perennials from seed in fall or by division in spring. They may be affected by mildew and botrytis.

Lathyrus latifolius
PERENNIAL PEA, EVERLASTING PEA

This perennial tendril climber from Chile grows to about 6 ft (1.8 m) high,

Lathyrus odoratus 'Apricot Sprite'

Lathyrus odoratus 'Elegance'

with many stems and densely massed foliage. It has dense heads of pink, rose or white, scentless pea-flowers in spring and summer. The dull green leaves have narrow leaflets. Feed and water regularly when the buds are forming. **ZONES 5–10.**

Lathyrus nervosus
syn. *Lathyrus magellanicus* of gardens

This perennial climber from temperate South America can grow to a height of 10 ft (3 m) and has conspicuously veined, leathery leaves. The racemes of fragrant, purplish blue flowers are borne in summer. **ZONES 8–10.**

Lathyrus odoratus
SWEET PEA

Native to Italy but much improved upon by gardeners, this vigorous, climbing

Lathyrus odoratus 'Felicity Kendall'

Lathyrus odoratus 'Kiri Te Kanawa'

Lathyrus odoratus 'Bandaid'

annual is grown for its abundant, sweetly scented flowers. The $1\frac{1}{2}$ in (35 mm) wide flowers in colors of white, cream, pink, blue, mauve, lavender, maroon and scarlet bloom several to the stem from late winter to early summer and make excellent cut flowers. The plant grows to 6 ft (1.8 m) or more in height, although there are dwarf, non-climbing cultivars available. The climbers will need a good support, such as wire netting or lattice, and are ideal for covering sunny walls or fences. Over many years of development sweet peas have become less scented. Also, mixed color seedling strains, for example, **'Carnival'**, tended to predominate. With the resurgence of interest in cottage gardens, breeders, mainly in the UK and New Zealand, developed a range of very fragrant cultivars in single colors. These include **'Apricot Sprite'**, deep apricot fading with age; **'Bandaid'** with pale pink flowers; **'Elegance'** with pure white flowers; **'Esther Ranson'** with mauve flowers; **'Felicity Kendall'** with deep purplish pink flowers; **'Hampton Court'**, with purple to mauve flowers; **'Katherine'** with bright red-pink flowers; **'Kiri Te Kanawa'** with pinkish purple flowers; and **'Lucy'** with apricot-pink flowers. The **Knee-hi Group**, although a little taller than the name suggests—around 24–30 in (60–75 cm) high—is a bushy strain that flowers heavily in colors from white through red to blue. Cultivars in the **Supersnoop Group** have no tendrils and may be grown as bushes rather than as climbers. **ZONES 4–10.**

Lathyrus odoratus

Lathyrus odoratus 'Hampton Court'

Lathyrus odoratus 'Lucy'

LAURUS

This genus consists of 2 species of evergreen shrubs and trees from the Mediterranean region, Canary Islands and the Azores. The common laurel *(Laurus*

Lathyrus odoratus 'Carnival'

Lathyrus odoratus 'Katherine'

L. odoratus Supersnoop Group cultivar

nobilis) has been grown as an ornamental since ancient times and has always had great symbolic significance. Among other uses, its dark green leaves have been used in funeral and remembrance wreaths, though the glossy leaves of the unrelated cherry laurel *(Prunus laurocerasus)* are now generally substituted. The highly aromatic leaves are also dried and used as a culinary herb (an essential ingredient in bouquet garni). Both species are useful evergreen screen plants and tub specimens, and are often used for topiary.
CULTIVATION: Cool- to warm-climate plants, they are moderately frost hardy and do best in sheltered positions in sun or part-shade in fertile, well-drained soil. They are tolerant of coastal conditions. Propagation is from seed in fall (autumn) or from cuttings in summer.

Laurus azorica
syn. *Laurus canariensis*
AZORES BAY, CANARY ISLAND BAY

Similar to *Laurus nobilis,* this species is a large tree up to 70 ft (21 m) high. Its flowers are a mass of yellow filaments $\frac{1}{2}$ in (12 mm) long and carried in clusters of 5 to 9 blooms; they are followed by small black berries. The leaves, which are evergreen, are elliptical and up to 6 in (15 cm) long. **ZONES 8–11.**

Laurus azorica

Laurus nobilis
SWEET BAY, BAY TREE, BAY LAUREL, LAUREL

A broadly conical tree, this species grows up to 40 ft (12 m) high and 30 ft (9 m) wide, but is generally smaller in cultivation. Its glossy, dark green leaves are smooth and leathery and in Classical times were used to make the victor's 'crown of laurels'. It produces small, star-shaped, fragrant yellow flowers in late spring to early summer, followed by small, round, green berries that ripen to dark purplish black in fall (autumn). This tree is suited to clipping and shaping. **'Aurea'** is a yellow-leafed form and **'Saratoga'** is best suited to training as a single-trunked tree. **ZONES 7–10.**

Laurus nobilis 'Saratoga'

LAVANDULA
LAVENDER

These fragrant, evergreen, aromatic shrubs of the mint or labiate family occur naturally from the Mediterranean region through the Middle East to India. There are around 25 species, several of which are cultivated in southern Europe and elsewhere for the perfume industry; they are also valued for their attractive lacy, fragrant, usually grayish foliage. Most species grow 24–36 in (60–90 cm) high and a similar width. The small mauve-purple or bluish purple flowers emerge from between bracts in erect, short spikes held on stalks above the foliage, mostly in spring. There are oil glands at the bases of the flowers that produce the pungent oil of lavender, obtained commercially by distillation from *Lavandula angustifolia* and *L. stoechas.*
CULTIVATION: These plants prefer full sun and fertile, well-drained soil; they will thrive in both acid and alkaline soils. The woodier species such as *L. dentata* are excellent as low hedges, and a light trim after blooming keeps them neat. Hardiness varies with the species, although most are moderately frost hardy if the growth is well ripened by warm fall (autumn) weather. Propagate from seed or cuttings in summer.

Lavandula dentata

Lavandula × intermedia 'Provence'

Lavandula angustifolia
syns *Lavandula officinalis, L. spica, L. vera*
LAVENDER

This dense, bushy subshrub is not native to England despite its English common name, but comes from the Mediterranean region of southern Europe. It grows to about 3 ft (1 m) tall though usually lower, with narrow, furry gray leaves. It is grown mainly for the long-stemmed heads of purple, scented flowers that appear in summer and through the warm months; these are easily dried for lavender sachets, potpourri and the like. *Lavandula angustifolia* makes an attractive low hedge and can be trimmed after flowering. There are a number of selected cultivars, of which **'Munstead'** and the dwarf **'Hidcote'** are outstanding. **'Alba'** grows to 2 ft (60 cm) with a 3 ft (1 m) spread; it has yellowish gray bark on its woody stems, pale gray-green foliage and white flowers in whorls. **'Jean Davis'** grows to 15–18 in (38–45 cm) and has attractive blue-green foliage and tall pinkish white flowers. **ZONES 6–10.**

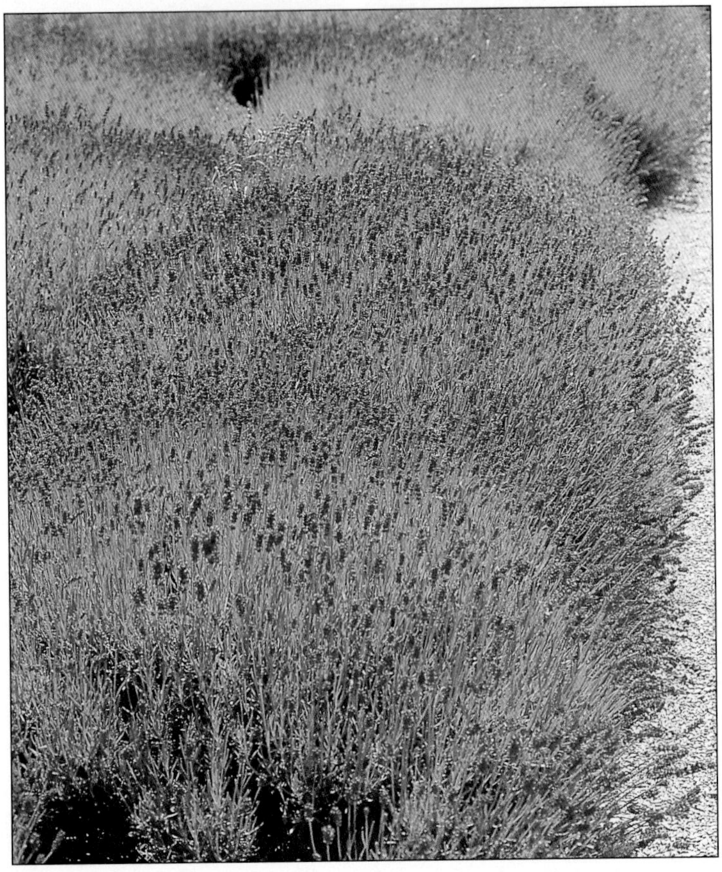

Lavandula angustifolia 'Munstead'

Laurus nobilis

Lavandula angustifolia 'Alba'

Lavandula dentata
FRENCH LAVENDER

Densely packed, soft spikes of mauve-blue flowers remain on this shrub from fall (autumn) through to late spring in warm climates. A native of the western Mediterranean and Atlantic islands, its gray-green aromatic leaves are fern-like with blunt teeth or lobes. It grows to a height and spread of 3–4 ft (1–1.2 m). This marginally frost-hardy species is resistant to dry conditions and adaptable to most soils, and is often used as an edging plant to soften the harsh lines of paving. **ZONES 8–10.**

Lavandula × intermedia
ENGLISH LAVENDER, LAVANDIN

These naturally occurring and cultivated hybrids between *Lavandula angustifolia* and *L. latifolia* show considerable variation in plant size and flower form. Few exceed 3 ft (1 m) tall but they are otherwise something of a catch-all group. **'Provence'** has green foliage and small-bracted spikes of mauve-pink flowers. **ZONES 6–10.**

Lavandula latifolia
SPIKE LAVENDER

This subshrubby species is very like *Lavandula angustifolia,* differing in its slightly wider leaves but narrower floral bracts. A rounded clump rarely reaching 3 ft (1 m) high and wide, its gray stems

Lavandula pinnata

Lavandula stoechas 'Marshwood'

Lavandula stoechas subsp. *lusitanica*

and foliage are downy and fragrant. The heavily scented, light purple flowers appear in spikes in summer. Its compact form makes it an ideal specimen for containers and dwarf hedges. ZONES 7–10.

Lavandula 'Sidonie'

This is a hybrid lavender that originated in Australia, the seed parent reportedly ***Lavandula pinnata***. It makes a soft, mound-like shrub of loose form with grayish leaves that are deeply divided into narrow lobes. A long succession of flower spikes, held above the foliage on long, rather weak stalks, bear strongly scented, rich blue flowers from late winter to early fall (autumn). It is a vigorous grower but is rather frost-tender. ZONES 9–11.

Lavandula stoechas subsp. *pedunculata*

Lavandula stoechas
SPANISH LAVENDER, FRENCH LAVENDER

Native to the western Mediterranean, this marginally frost-hardy species is the most striking in flower of all lavenders, at least in some of its varied forms. A small neat shrub 20–30 in (50–75 cm) high, it has pine-scented, narrow silvery green leaves with inward-curling edges. In late spring and summer it is covered with spikes of deep purple flowers. Several bracts at the apex of each spike are elongated into pinkish purple 'rabbit ears' of varying size. **'Merle'** is a compact bush with long-eared, magenta-purple flowerheads. **'Marshwood'** is a particularly heavy flowering, long-blooming cultivar. ***Lavandula stoechas* subsp. *lusitanica*** has very narrow leaves and dark purple flowers with paler 'rabbit ear' bracts. ***L. s.* subsp. *pedunculata***, (syn. *L. pedunculata*) from Spain, North Africa and the Balkans, grows 18–24 in (45–60 cm) tall. It has flower stalks that grow to 2–3 in (5–8 cm). It has greenish foliage and the flower spikes are plump and pale green after the flowers have dropped. ***L. s.* subsp. *luisieri***, which is a native of Portugal, is an upright bush with green rather than silver-gray foliage and large purple flower spikes. ZONES 7–10.

Lavandula latifolia

Lavandula stoechas subsp. *luisieri*

Lavandula viridis

Lavandula viridis
GREEN LAVENDER

This upright, bushy shrub from Spain, Portugal and Madeira is a most unusual lavender, having green leaves and the palest green flowers. These emerge from short-stemmed dense spikes from mid- to late summer. It grows to a height of 30 in (75 cm). **'Pippa White'** has flowerheads with large bracts. ZONES 8–10.

Lavandula viridis 'Pippa White'

LAVATERA

Closely related to the mallows and hollyhocks, this genus of 25 species of annuals, biennials, perennials and soft-wooded shrubs has a scattered, patchy distribution around temperate regions of the world, mostly in Mediterranean or similar climates; some of them favor seashores. A few species are cultivated for their colorful mallow flowers, generally produced over a long season. These plants are upright in habit with simple to palmately lobed leaves, often downy to the touch. The shrubs and perennials in this genus are not very long-lived.

CULTIVATION: Moderately to very frost-hardy, these plants prefer a sunny site with any well-drained soil. Prune after a flush of blooms to encourage branching and more flowers. Propagate annuals, biennials and perennials in spring or early fall (autumn) from seed sown *in situ* (cuttings do not strike well), and shrubs from cuttings in early spring or summer.

Lavandula stoechas 'Merle'

Lavandula stoechas

Lavatera arborea
TREE MALLOW

This is an annual, biennial or short-lived perennial from western Europe and the Mediterranean growing to a height of 10 ft (3 m) and a spread of 5 ft (1.5 m). Adaptable to moist, well-drained soil in full sun, it has large velvety leaves and reddish purple, hibiscus-like flowers. **ZONES 8–10.**

Lavatera assurgentiflora
MALVA ROSE, ISLAND MALLOW

A frost-tender, deciduous shrub native to the offshore islands of southern California and growing to as much as 20 ft (6 m) tall, this plant will have excessive growth of foliage at the expense of flowering if grown in too rich a mix. Used in coastal gardens and as a windbreak, it is tolerant of dry conditions. It has gray twisted trunks and rich red-purple flowers. **ZONES 9–11.**

Lavatera maritima

Lavatera trimestris

Lavatera 'Barnsley'

This semi-evergreen soft shrub grows to 6 ft (1.8 m) and bears sprays of pale pink flowers with deep pink centers throughout summer. It is very frost hardy. **ZONES 6–10.**

Lavatera 'Bredon Springs'

This vigorous cultivar, which reaches 6 ft (1.8 m) in height and spread, is a semi-evergreen soft shrub with gray-green leaves and rich pink flowers in summer. **ZONES 6–10.**

Lavatera 'Kew Rose'

This moderately frost-hardy shrub bears its bright pink flowers in profuse tall sprays throughout summer. It grows to a height and spread of 6 ft (1.8 m) and has gray-green leaves. **ZONES 6–10.**

Lavatera trimestris 'Mont Blanc'

Lavatera 'Kew Rose'

Lavatera 'Barnsley'

Lavatera maritima
syn. ***Lavatera bicolor***

This vigorous species from the western Mediterranean region is noted for its gray-green foliage and a nearly continuous production of hollyhock-like, soft lavender flowers with purple centers. A broad shrub, it will quickly reach 6 ft (1.8 m) or more in height with a somewhat greater spread. The peak of flowering is in spring, and it may be relatively short lived. **ZONES 8–11.**

Lavatera 'Rosea'
syn. ***Lavatera olbia* 'Rosea'**

This frost-hardy cultivar reaches 6 ft (1.8 m) in height and spread. It is a semi-evergreen shrub with deep pink flowers borne over a long period in summer. **ZONES 6–10.**

Lavatera thuringiaca

This perennial from central and south-eastern Europe produces a glorious display of rose-pink, hollyhock-like flowers all summer on sturdy bushes up to 5 ft (1.5 m) in height. Softly mid-green leaves are an attractive foil for the flowers. Use at the back of a border or as a colorful hedge. Several cultivars with distinct flower colors are available. **ZONES 6–10.**

Lavatera trimestris
ANNUAL MALLOW

This shrubby annual, native to the Mediterranean, is grown mainly for its silken, trumpet-shaped, brilliant white or pink flowers. The flowers are 3 in (8 cm) wide and appear from summer to early fall (autumn). They are short lived but are borne in profusion, benefiting from regular deadheading. The annual mallow has an erect, branching habit and is moderately fast growing to a height of 24 in (60 cm) and a spread of 18 in (45 cm). **'Mont Blanc'** (syn. *Lavatera* 'Mont Blanc') has pure white flowers; **'Silver Cup'** has lovely dark pink flowers. **ZONES 8–11.**

Lavatera thuringiaca

Lavatera 'Barnsley'

LAWSONIA
HENNA

This genus, allied to *Lagerstroemia*, consists of a single species: a variable, somewhat open evergreen shrub or small tree. Widely distributed in hot, semi-arid regions of northern Africa and south-western Asia, it is cultivated for orange dye called henna which is obtained from its crushed leaves. Hindu women in India traditionally use henna to stain the palms of their hands and the soles of their feet for religious purposes.
CULTIVATION: It requires a tropical or subtropical climate, full sun and well-drained soil. Light pruning in late spring encourages dense, more compact foliage. Propagation is from seed or cuttings in fall (autumn).

Lawsonia inermis

The henna plant grows 12–25 ft (3.5–8 m) tall and has a loosely branching habit. Its gray twigs are covered with fine silvery gray-green foliage and the small, fragrant flowers, white, pink or red, are borne in terminal panicles. The fruit are tiny capsules. **ZONES 10–12.**

LAYIA

This genus of the daisy family consists of 15 species of annuals, native to western USA. They develop into small, mounding bushes with narrow, toothed or lobed leaves. From spring they bear a mass of small yellow daisy-like flowers.
CULTIVATION: They are best grown in full sun in rich, moist but well-drained soil and develop quickly. Sow seed in late winter or early spring and then thin out the seedlings to 18 in (45 cm) spacing. They need feeding monthly and the roots should be kept moist.

Layia platyglossa
TIDY TIPS

This Californian species, the only one widely cultivated, has fine, grass-like foliage and in summer and fall (autumn) is smothered in 2 in (5 cm) golden flowerheads with white-tipped petals. The blooms are so profuse they can be regularly cut for indoor display, while leaving the summer garden a blaze of color. They also look spectacular in window boxes and other containers. **ZONES 8–11.**

LEDEBOURIA

There are 16 species of bulbs in this genus, closely allied to *Scilla* and native to South Africa. Each bulb produces 1 to 7 narrow leaves up to 15 in (38 cm) long and sometimes slightly fleshy. Often the foliage is the most attractive part of the plant; leaves of some species have prominent veins, others attractive pink and gray markings. The flowers, which appear after rain in the wild or in late summer, are tiny but massed in racemes of up to 150 blooms. They are usually gray or green in color with pink or purple markings.
CULTIVATION: Mainly arid-zone plants, they require gritty, well-drained soil and a position in full sun. Most will withstand light frosts provided the soil is dry and the bulbs properly ripened. Propagate from seed or by division of established clumps.

Ledebouria cooperi
syn. *Scilla adlamii*

This species grows to 4 in (10 cm) tall at the most and has pale gray-green leaves striped with brownish purple. *Ledebouria cooperi* has short spikes of bell-shaped green and purple flowers only ¼ in (6 mm) or less long . They appear in summer. **ZONES 9–11.**

Ledebouria socialis
syn. *Scilla violacea*

This little evergreen bulb grows 2–4 in (5–10 cm) high, multiplying into compact clumps in time. It has pale gray-green leaves heavily spotted with grayish purple, and produces short spikes of bell-shaped purple-green flowers no more than ¼ in (6 mm) long in late spring and summer. **ZONES 9–11.**

LEDUM

Resembling small examples of their close relatives the rhododendrons, the 4 species in this genus are bushy evergreen shrubs. They range widely around the cooler northern temperate regions and into subarctic territories. They vary in height from 1–6 ft (0.3–1.8 m) depending on the harshness of the environment in which they are grown. In spring and summer the bushes are covered in small, 5-petalled white flowers with protruding stamens.
CULTIVATION: Treat *Ledum* in the same way as a cool-climate rhododendron: plant in cool, humus-rich, moist but well-drained soil in shade or morning sun. They are among the frost hardiest of broad-leafed evergreen plants. Propagate from seed or cuttings or by layering.

Ledum palustre

Ledum groenlandicum
LABRADOR TEA

One of the few shrubs to survive the rigorous climate of Greenland, this species is also found in northern North America. It grows 3 ft (1 m) high and 4 ft (1.2 m) wide. The wiry branches are covered in red-brown hair, as are the undersides of the 1–2½ in (2.5–6 cm) long leaves. Clusters of flowers open at the branch tips from late spring. The leaves and stems are used in folk medicine as inhalants or insect repellents. **ZONES 2–8.**

Ledum palustre
MARSH TEA

This evergreen shrub comes from northern parts of North America, Europe and Asia and grows 3 ft (1 m) high and wide. It grows well in peat bogs, so prefers moist soil in full shade. The white, cream or rose flowers appear from spring until early summer and are followed by small, capsular fruit. The plant has narcotic qualities and its leathery leaves were used in Germany to increase the intoxicant properties of beer. ***Ledum palustre* var. *diversipilosum*** bears dense corymbs of white flowers. **ZONES 2–8.**

LEIOPHYLLUM

This genus consists of one species, a charming evergreen shrub from eastern USA. A rhododendron relative resembling a small evergreen azalea, it is low growing or prostrate and is suitable for rockeries or a peat terrace. The leaves are simple and usually less than ½ in (12 mm) long. It bears massed heads of tiny, pale pink and white flowers which form at the branch tips and open from late spring.
CULTIVATION: Although small, *Leiophyllum* has an extensive system of fine, hair-like roots and requires cool, moist, humus-rich soil conditions with minimal root disturbance. Plant in shade or morning sun. It is fully frost hardy. Propagate from seed or cuttings.

Ledum palustre var. *diversipilosum*

Ledum groenlandicum

Leiophyllum buxifolium var. *prostratum*

Leiophyllum buxifolium
BOX SAND MYRTLE

The specific name means 'with leaf like that of box' *(Buxus)*, and when not in flower this shrub of up to 18 in (45 cm) high is as neat and compact as a dwarf box. However, it has the advantage of a delightful spring flower display. ***Leiophyllum buxifolium* var. *prostratum***, the Allegheny sand myrtle, is similar but has rounded, downy leaves. **ZONES 5–10.**

LEMNA
DUCKWEED, DUCKMEAT, FROG'S BUTTONS

These 13 species of tiny aquatic plants, found naturally in most parts of the world, float on or below the water surface. The whole plant consists of no more than a leaf-like, egg-shaped 'frond'; new fronds bud from the base and soon break free, giving rise to large colonies which form a green film on still water. Flowering fronds produce 1 to 2 minute flowers in marginal pouches, but are rarely seen. Each frond has only one root, which has a tubular sheath at the tip. Duckweeds provide food for fish, ducks and other birds. Some of the most common duckweeds belong not to *Lemna* but the closely related *Spirodela*, distinguished by its fronds usually having multiple roots.
CULTIVATION: They enjoy plenty of light and can be invasive, forming a thick green carpet rapidly across a pond. They are good aquarium specimens tolerating both tropical and cold-water conditions. Their growth can be thinned by frequent skimming. Propagate by throwing small colonies onto still water that is rich in nitrates and somewhat alkaline.

Ledebouria cooperi

Lemna minor
COMMON DUCKWEED

This species often forms large colonies on the surface of still water. Rarely cultivated, it is useful for covering the surface of a pond in a sunny position, helping cool the water. It has shiny, paper-thin fronds that can sometimes be tinged red. **ZONES 4–11.**

LENS
LENTIL

Six species of annual legumes from the Mediterranean, western Asia and Africa make up this genus, including *Lens culinaris,* which is among the most ancient of cultivated food plants—it has been grown in the eastern Mediterranean region since the Bronze Age. Among the most nutritious of pulses, it is now cultivated in many parts of the world for its edible seeds, which are dried and used like dried beans. Lentils are a staple food throughout the Middle East, where herdsmen and traders considered them an ideal food to carry on long journeys.

Lepidozamia peroffskyana

Leontopodium alpinum

Leptinella potentillina

Esau's 'mess of pottage' was probably lentil porridge. Members of this genus resemble vetches *(Vicia)* and have flattened fruit and pods containing 2 flat, orbicular seeds. *Lens* is the plant's classical name and the words 'lens' and 'lenticular' both originate from the shape of lentil seeds.
CULTIVATION: Lentils are marginally frost hardy and, being a cool-season crop, are best planted very early in spring in cold areas. In warmer areas they may be planted in winter. A light, sandy, well-drained soil in full sun is preferred. Propagate from seed. Seed saved for planting the following year will keep well if stored in its own pod.

Lens culinaris
syn. ***Lens esculenta***

This annual grows to about 18 in (45 cm) high and has compound leaves comprising 6 pairs of oblong leaflets, the upper ones modified into tendrils. The pale blue pea-flowers are followed by slightly inflated pods containing 2 seeds. After harvesting the seeds are dried in the pod before being threshed, shelled and split. **ZONES 8–11.**

Leonotis leonurus

Leontopodium ochroleucum var. *campestre*

LEONOTIS

This genus of the mint family consists of around 30 species of annuals, perennials, subshrubs and shrubs, native to tropical and southern Africa except for one species that extends to tropical Asia and America. One species is widely grown as an ornamental, with showy 2-lipped flowers that are densely hairy on the outside (said to resemble lion's fur). The leaves are arranged in opposite pairs on square stems.
CULTIVATION: Plant in full sun in rich, well-drained soil. Do not over-water. The plants can be cut back quite heavily in early spring. Propagate from seed in spring or from softwood cuttings in early summer.

Leonotis leonurus
LION'S EAR, WILD DAGGA, LION'S TAIL

This semi-evergreen, shrubby perennial from South Africa is popular in all countries with warmer temperate or subtropical climates. A striking plant growing to 6 ft (1.8 m), its tall straight stems bear whorls of tawny orange, furry, tubular flowers in late summer and fall (autumn). The leaves are lance-shaped and aromatic. This plant is fairly resistant to dry conditions and does well in coastal situations. **'Harrismith White'** is a white-flowered cultivar. **ZONES 9–11.**

LEONTOPODIUM
EDELWEISS

Occurring wild in the mountains of Europe and temperate Asia, this genus consists of about 35 species of short-lived, downy perennials in the daisy family. Their distinctive feature is the flowerheads, with a central disc of rather inconspicuous cream florets surrounded

Leonotis leonurus

by a ring of overlapping, pointed bracts of unequal length and coated with sparse to dense white wool. The simple, lance-shaped leaves are also covered with white hairs, which protect the plant from cold and from intense ultraviolet sunlight. They are suitable for rock gardens in cool to cold climates.
CULTIVATION: Plant in full sun or part-shade (in hot climates) in gritty, well-drained soil. They are very frost hardy but need shelter from winter rain. Propagate from fresh seed or by division in spring.

Leontopodium alpinum

Much loved by the Swiss, the European edelweiss is often regarded as a symbol of the Alps. It reaches a height and spread of around 8 in (20 cm). Each silvery white flowerhead is 2–3 in (5–8 cm) across, the bracts so thickly felted they look like strips of flannel. It blooms in spring or early summer. **ZONES 5–9.**

Leontopodium ochroleucum var. *campestre*
syn. ***Leontopodium palibinianum***

This species from Asia is a loosely tufted perennial growing 6–15 in (15–38 cm) tall. It has attractive yellowish, nearly white bracts that almost enclose the inconspicuous disc florets. **ZONES 4–9.**

LEPIDOZAMIA

Four species have been named in this cycad genus, but 2 of them exist only as fossils, while the remaining pair can be found growing in the moist forests of Australia's east coast. Among the tallest known cycads, they are palm-like in appearance with a usually unbranched, straight trunk and dark green, glossy pinnate fronds that are produced in annual whorls, with 3 to 5 years' whorls present at any one time. Like all cycads they produce male (pollen) and female (seed) cones on separate plants, and both are exceptionally large in this genus, sitting singly and erect in the center of the circle of fronds: the female cones are coated in brown felt, with pointed flaps projecting, while the narrower males are green, releasing vast quantities of pollen through a spiral split when mature.
CULTIVATION: Attractive garden and container plants in warm climates, they tolerate an occasional very light frost. Grow in moderately fertile, moist but well-drained soil. They transplant easily and are best grown in the shelter of taller trees, as the leaves tend to become faded and yellowish in full sun. Propagate from seed in spring or summer.

Lepidozamia peroffskyana
syn. ***Macrozamia denisonii***
PINEAPPLE ZAMIA

Named for a Russian patron of botany, the pineapple zamia from subtropical eastern Australia will in time grow to more than 25 ft (8 m), but in gardens it is more commonly seen with no trunk or a very short one. The glossy fronds are about 5 ft (1.5 m) long with curved, smooth-edged leaflets about ½ in (12 mm) wide. The huge female cones are up to 30 in (75 cm) long. The second species, ***Lepidozamia hopei*** from tropical Queensland rainforests, differs mainly in its broader leaflets and is known to reach a height of over 60 ft (18 m). **ZONES 10–12.**

LEPTINELLA

This Australasian and South American genus of the daisy family consists of 30 species of creeping or tufted perennials, formerly included in the genus *Cotula*. They are usually aromatic with deeply toothed or dissected small leaves giving the foliage a fern-like appearance. The small flowerheads lack ray florets and resemble small, rounded buttons. They are mainly summer flowering and are a common feature of the New Zealand alpine flora.
CULTIVATION: They grow well in full sun in humus-rich soil with added shingle or grit to ensure good drainage. Some species will grow in paving crevices and can withstand light foot traffic. Most are frost hardy. Propagate from seed or by division.

Leptinella potentillina
syn. ***Cotula potentillina***

This New Zealand species forms a wide-spreading mat of 4 in (10 cm) long, pinnately dissected leaves. The foliage mounds up to as much as 8 in (20 cm) in the center of the mat. It bears ½ in (12 mm) wide white flowerheads in summer. **ZONES 8–10.**

Leptinella squalida
syn. ***Cotula squalida***
COTULA WEED

Although a rather inconspicuous small, mat-forming plant, this New Zealand species has found a niche in cultivation as a grass substitute for bowling greens. Left unmown, its 4 in (10 cm) ferny leaves mound to 6 in (15 cm) in height. The flowerheads are yellow-green and less than ¼ in (6 mm) wide. **ZONES 5–10.**

LEPTOSPERMUM
TEA TREE

This genus of evergreen shrubs or small trees in the myrtle family is unrelated to tea *(Camellia sinensis);* the name 'tea tree' arose when Captain Cook and his crew used the aromatic leaves to make a 'tea' on their landfalls in both Australia and New Zealand, believing it would protect them from scurvy. The genus consists of 80-odd species, the great

Leptospermum laevigatum

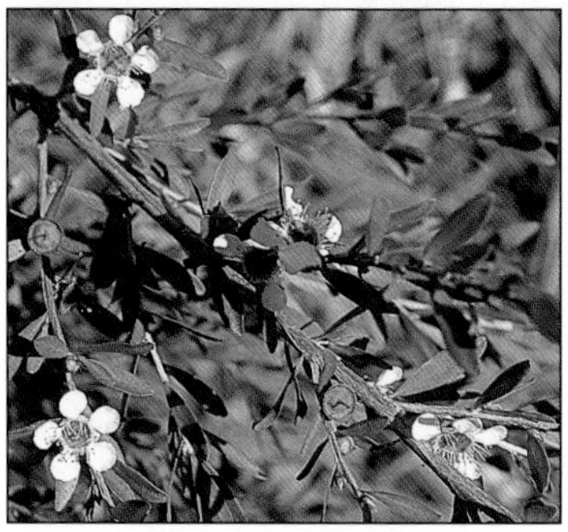
Leptospermum petersonii

majority Australian but with 1 or 2 in New Zealand and a handful scattered through mountains of the Malay Archipelago and Peninsula. They are mainly upright growers with small, sometimes prickly leaves and bear 5-petalled, white or pale pink flowers along the branches in spring or summer, followed by small capsules that release fine, elongated seeds—*Leptospermum* means 'slender seed'. Tea trees are widely planted in their native countries, also in California, for their rapid growth, pretty flowers and graceful habit. A few of the most frost-hardy species can be grown outdoors in the UK. Many cultivars have been named, mostly derived from the red-flowered New Zealand forms of *L. scoparium*, some with double flowers in shades from white to red.

CULTIVATION: They prefer a mild-winter climate, full sun and well-drained soil; some tolerate poor soils, dry conditions, or ocean spray. In cool climates they can be grown as conservatory plants or placed outdoors in tubs in summer. Prune lightly, if at all. Propagate from seed or cuttings in summer.

Leptospermum brevipes

This frost-hardy, evergreen shrub from the rocky hills of southeastern Australia is adaptable to most soils and tolerant of dry conditions. It grows to 12 ft (3.5 m) in height with a spreading, bushy habit. The white flowers, $\frac{1}{2}$ in (12 mm) across, are borne from spring to early summer. **ZONES 8–11.**

Leptospermum laevigatum
COAST TEA TREE, AUSTRALIAN TEA TREE

Growing naturally among sand dunes along much of the east coast of Australia, this tall, bushy shrub or small tree bears attractive white flowers in profusion in spring and early summer. The small leaves are rounded at the tips and grayish green. It grows to about 20 ft (6 m) tall

Leptospermum macrocarpum

with a similar spread, and has a shaggy-barked trunk that becomes gnarled and twisted with age, especially when buffeted by salt-laden winds. It is one of the best shrubs for coastal shelter; however, in South Africa it has become a much-hated weed. **ZONES 9–11.**

Leptospermum macrocarpum
syn. *Leptospermum lanigerum* var. *macrocarpum*

This shrub is known only from a small area of the sandstone Blue Mountains near Sydney, Australia. Mostly 2–6 ft (0.6–1.8 m) high and becoming very woody, it adapts to a range of soils and climates. The broad leaves are purplish green while the flowers are remarkable for the size of their greenish yellow central receptacle, up to $\frac{3}{4}$ in (18 mm) across and glistening with nectar; it is out of proportion to the circular petals which are usually flesh pink. The woody capsules are correspondingly large. It withstands pruning and can even make a bonsai specimen. **ZONES 8–11.**

Leptospermum petersonii
syn. *Leptospermum citratum*
LEMON-SCENTED TEA TREE

From the subtropical east coast of Australia, this frost-tender shrub or small tree grows to a height of 25 ft (7.5 m) with an open branching habit and rather pendulous branchlets, giving it a willow-like appearance. The narrow leaves have a characteristic lemon scent when crushed; new foliage is bronze red. A vigorous grower, it bears pendent sprays of small white flowers in spring and early summer. **'White Swan'** grows to 20 ft (6 m) tall; it responds well to pruning and is covered with a mass of white flowers. **ZONES 9–11.**

Leptospermum scoparium 'Red Damask'

Leptospermum scoparium
MANUKA, NEW ZEALAND TEA TREE

This species occurs throughout New Zealand and in the far southeast of Australia (mainly Tasmania). It is an adaptable plant, growing to 10 ft (3 m) tall, with mainly erect growth, small, broadly needle-like leaves and sweetly scented, white or pale pink flowers. The numerous cultivars have been selected or bred mainly in New Zealand, though in California the famous rose and camellia breeder Walter Lammerts created a number in the 1950s. Cultivars include **'Abundance'** with salmon-pink double flowers in winter; **'Gaiety Girl'** with dark-centered deep pink flowers; **'Keatleyi'** with pale pink flowers; **'Kiwi'**, a dwarf form with crimson flowers; **'Pink Cascade'** with horizontal branches and pink flowers; **'Pink Pixie'** with pink blooms; **'Ray Williams'** with dark-centered white flowers striped with pink; **'Red Damask'** with double crimson blooms; **'Ruby Glow'** with dark foliage and double, dark red blooms over winter and spring; and **'Helene Strybing'**, especially popular in the USA. **ZONES 8–10.**

Leptospermum spectabile

Recently discovered and named, this species, like its relative *Leptospermum macrocarpum*, is known only from a small area of Australia's Blue Mountains, growing on sandy stream banks. Its outstanding feature is the blood-red petals of its medium-sized flowers. It makes a shrub 3–8 ft (1–2.4 m) tall with erect branches and long-pointed leaves. The flowers are about 1 in (25 mm) across and their pale pink sepals contrast prettily with the red petals, making them attractive as cut flowers. It is adaptable to most soils and will grow in full sun or part-shade. Its flower color is already being exploited in hybrid cultivars. **ZONES 8–11.**

Leptospermum scoparium 'Pink Cascade'

Leptospermum scoparium 'Ruby Glow'

Leptospermum squarrosum
syn. *Leptospermum persiciflorum*
PEACH-FLOWERED TEA TREE

A native of New South Wales, this pretty 6–10 ft (1.8–3 m) tall shrub grows in poorly drained, peaty soil in the wild but in cultivation prefers good drainage. Its foliage is almost identical to that of *Leptospermum scoparium* but the pale to deep pink flowers are more abundant on the older, thicker branches. At higher altitudes it is represented by forms with smaller white flowers. **ZONES 9–11.**

Leptospermum scoparium 'Ray Williams'

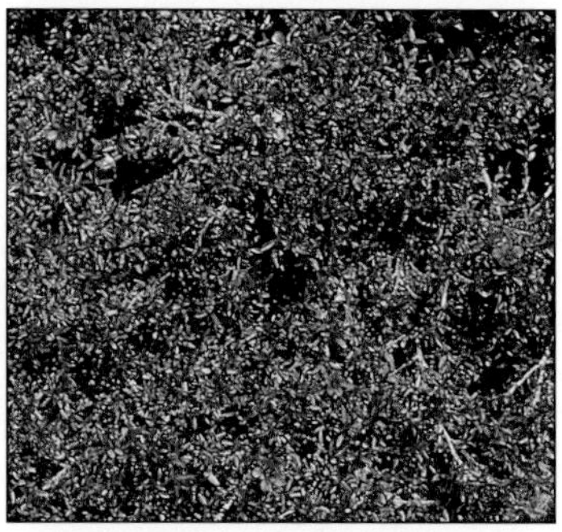
Leptospermum scoparium 'Kiwi'

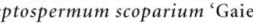

Leptospermum scoparium 'Gaiety Girl'

LESCHENAULTIA

syn. *Lechenaultia*

This genus of 26 species of small evergreen shrubs, subshrubs and perennials, is from Australia; most species, including the most attractive ones, come from southwestern Australia where they grow in very poor sandy soil. Weak-stemmed plants, often with a suckering habit, they have small flat or needle-shaped leaves. The flowers have 5 radiating petals each with a smooth central portion and broad crinkled margins, and broadly notched at the tips; some are brilliantly colored, in shades of blue, yellow, orange or red. **CULTIVATION:** Not the easiest plants to grow but they are worth trying in areas with mild winters, low summer humidity and well-drained, sandy soil. Plant in full sun or part-shade and provide moderate water. Potted specimens should be moderately watered during growth, less at other times. Propagate from seed in spring or from cuttings in summer.

Leschenaultia biloba

BLUE LESCHENAULTIA, FLOOR OF THE SKY

With flowers among the most brilliant blues of any plant, this native of Western Australia's Perth region is an erect or straggling shrub growing to a height and spread of 24 in (60 cm). It has small, soft, grayish green leaves and from late winter to late spring bears terminal groups of flowers that vary from pale to deep blue, sometimes with a central splash of white or sometimes all white. It needs a dry, sunny position and usually proves short lived in cultivation, but is easily grown from cuttings, so that young plants can be held in reserve; cut back over-long stems after blooming. **ZONES 10–11.**

Lespedeza thunbergii

Lespedeza thunbergii

Leucadendron eucalyptifolium

Leschenaultia formosa

RED LESCHENAULTIA

Common on poor soils in the far south of Western Australia, this suckering subshrub makes a low mound seldom more than 12 in (30 cm) high and sometimes with a much wider spread. The gray-green leaves are tiny and crowded and the showy scarlet, orange or yellow flowers appear from late winter to early summer, sometimes so profuse as to almost hide the foliage. It needs warm, dry summer conditions and a very free-draining gritty soil. **ZONES 9–11.**

LESPEDEZA

This legume genus was named in honor of the Spanish governor of Florida in 1790, whose name was in fact de Céspedes but the botanist Michaux got it wrong—however the mistaken version became so familiar that botanists eventually voted to retain it. It includes about 40 species of annuals, perennials and deciduous shrubs and subshrubs from across the northern hemisphere, extending to Southeast Asia and Australia. The leaves are made up of 3 leaflets, while the small pea-flowers are held in long sprays.

Leucadendron argenteum

Leucadendron argenteum

Leschenaultia biloba

The pods are small and one-seeded, falling without opening. Some species are grown for fodder or green manure. **CULTIVATION:** These plants do best in a sunny position in well-drained soil, and prefer warmer climates where cold winters will not cut them back. Mulch well, especially at the limit of frost hardiness, and prune to rejuvenate in spring. Propagate from seed or cuttings, or by division.

Lespedeza thunbergii

BUSH CLOVER SHRUB BUSH CLOVER

This erect, open subshrub grows 3–6 ft (1–1.8 m) tall and has bright green leaves. The pendulous sprays of rose-purple flowers appear in late summer and are followed by flattish seed pods. **'Alba'** bears white flowers. **ZONES 6–10.**

LEUCADENDRON

Closely allied to the proteas, this South African genus consists of 84 species of shrubs and small trees, the great majority of them confined in the wild to western Cape Province. They are popular garden plants where soil and climate allow, and are grown commercially for cut flowers. The leaves are simple and leathery, varying greatly in shape and size and sometimes clothed in silvery hairs. The flowers are small, in dense globular or conical heads terminating the branches, but the heads are usually surrounded by a flower-like collar of bracts that also vary greatly in size and color. Male and female flowerheads are borne on separate plants. A number of hybrid cultivars have appeared in recent years, some bred for the cut flower industry. **CULTIVATION:** Frost tender to marginally frost-hardy, they do best in full sun and perfectly drained, sandy or gritty soil with added humus, preferably with low levels of phosphorus and nitrogen. Potted specimens should be well watered in periods of growth, less at other times. They are propagated from seed or cuttings.

Leucadendron laureolum

Leschenaultia formosa

Leucadendron argenteum

SILVER TREE

One of South Africa's rarest and most beautiful trees, the silver tree survives in the wild only on some slopes of Table Mountain. It grows 20–30 ft (6–9 m) tall, unbranched when young but later forming a narrow crown of erect branches, all covered in large, pointed gray leaves clothed in long silky hairs that give a silver cast to the whole tree. The bracts around the rather insignificant flowerheads, borne in winter and early spring, are hardly different from the normal leaves. Silver tree can only be raised from seed and makes fast growth, but is often very short lived in cultivation; it does not tolerate any root disturbance. **ZONES 9–11.**

Leucadendron comosum

YELLOWBUSH

Endemic to the mountains of southwestern Cape Province, this shrub grows to about 5 ft (1.5 m) high and much the same in width. The small, incurved leaves almost needle-shaped on male plants, but significantly wider on the females, and the light green or yellow bracts around the red flowerheads follow the same pattern. It grows very easily from seed. **ZONES 9–10.**

Leucadendron eucalyptifolium

This vigorous species is common in the wild in the coastal ranges of Cape Province, growing in deep, sandy soils. It makes an erect shrub up to 15 ft (4.5 m) tall with a single trunk at the base and a dense, bushy crown. Despite the name, the narrow leaves are no more eucalyptus-like than those of many other members of the protea family. A profusion of small flowerheads with long, narrow, bright yellow bracts surrounding the yellow-cream knob of flowers is produced in winter and spring. This easily grown species is becoming important in the cut flower trade. **ZONES 9–10.**

Leucadendron laureolum

Confined to the Cape Town region, this is one of the most widely grown species in many parts of the world and has given rise to a number of cultivars. Growing to 6 ft (1.8 m) high, this bushy shrub has leathery oblong leaves and flowerheads with bracts cupped at the base, the color typically grading from soft yellow in the center to pale green outside; some forms have deeper gold bracts. It is a moisture-loving plant. **ZONES 9–11.**

Leucadendron 'Safari Sunset'

A hybrid between *Leucadendron salignum* and *L. laureolum*, 'Safari Sunset' was developed in New Zealand, where it is much grown for use as a cut flower. A vigorous erect shrub, it grows rapidly to about 5 ft (1.5 m) with a densely branched, bushy habit. The deep green, oblong leaves are flushed with red, and the stems and bracts are a deep wine red in fall (autumn) to winter, at the height of the flowering season; these turn pale to golden yellow as the season progresses. Full sun is needed for maximum color. **ZONES 9–11.**

Leucadendron salignum

Rather similar to *Leucadendron laureolum* and just as widely grown, this species has a much wider natural distribution in Cape Province and differs in its often red-tinged foliage, reddish buds, and bracts with reddish tips, though plain yellow-and-green forms are also known, as well as forms with rich red bracts. The bracts spread widely, especially on male plants; female flowers have a strong yeasty smell. It usually grows only to about 3 ft (1 m) and has many erect, branching stems This species does poorly in humid-summer climates. **ZONES 9–11.**

Leucadendron 'Silvan Red'

'Silvan Red' is a vigorous hybrid of the same parentage as 'Safari Sunset' and is similar in style and coloring, but with more slender branches and narrower floral bracts. **ZONES 9–11.**

Leucanthemum paludosum

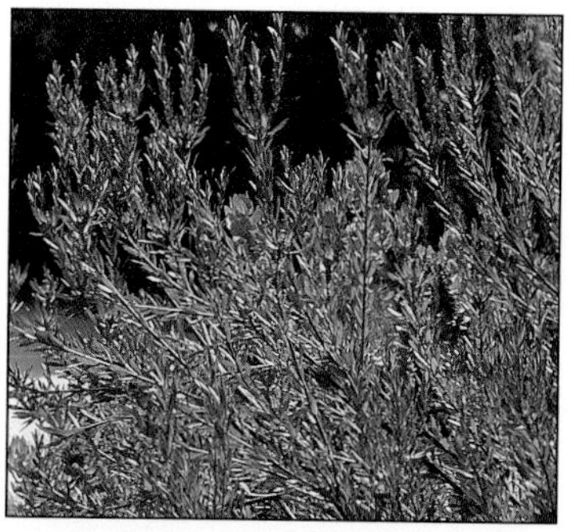

Leucadendron 'Silvan Red'

Leucadendron salignum

Leucadendron stelligerum

This rare and endangered species is known only from the vicinity of Cape Agulhas at the southernmost tip of Africa. It is a 4–5 ft (1.2–1.5 m) tall shrub has thin wiry branches and narrow 1 in (25 mm) long leaves. The red-tipped creamy bracts form starry cups around the small flowerheads, which develop in winter and have an unpleasant smell. **ZONES 9–11.**

Leucadendron strobilinum

Known only from the Cape Peninsula near Cape Town, this very attractive species is endangered in the wild. It is a shrub growing to more than 6 ft (1.8 m) with broad, incurved leaves. The conspicuous spring flowerheads likewise have very broad, creamy yellow bracts that overlap and form a smooth cup around the fat, globular flowerhead. **'Waterlily'** is a selected female form with large bracts that pass through several color changes: initially bright green, they become cream at the center, then light yellow, and finally red-edged; the flowerhead itself is reddish brown. **ZONES 9–11.**

Leucadendron 'Safari Sunset'

Leucadendron strobilinum 'Waterlily'

Leucadendron tinctum

Leucadendron tinctum
TOLBOS

Common in the hills and mountains of southwest Cape Province, this species grows to 4 ft (1.2 m) tall and much the same width, and both male and female flowerheads are beautiful. The female cones are dark red, the males yellow, and both are enclosed by broad, red-suffused yellow bracts. It is a popular garden specimen in South Africa on account of its beauty as well as its tolerance of wind and some frost. **ZONES 9–11.**

Leucadendron stelligerum

LEUCANTHEMUM

There are about 25 species of annuals or perennials in this genus from Europe and temperate Asia, all previously included in *Chrysanthemum* by many botanists, though some botanists always treated them as a distinct genus. They are clump-forming plants with variably toothed or lobed leaves that are neither grayish hairy nor aromatic, unlike those of other chrysanthemum relatives. Long-stalked daisy-like flowerheads arise from leafy stems, with white or yellow ray florets and yellow disc florets. While mostly vigorous, adaptable plants, some do not do well in warmer climates.
CULTIVATION: These plants are largely undemanding, growing well in a perennial border or garden bed in full sun or morning shade in moderately fertile, moist but well-drained soil. Propagate from seed or cuttings, or by division.

Leucanthemum paludosum
syn. *Chrysanthemum paludosum*

This southern European annual grows to 6 in (15 cm) in height. It has pale yellow or white-tinged yellow flowers. **'Show Star'** has bright yellow flowers and wavy edged leaves. **ZONES 7–11.**

Leucanthemum × *superbum*

L. × *superbum* 'Wirral Pride'

Leucanthemum × *superbum* 'Tinkerbell'

Leucogenes grandiceps

Leucanthemum × *superbum*

syns ***Chrysanthemum maximum*** **of gardens,** ***C.*** **×** ***superbum***

SHASTA DAISY

Growing to a height and spread of 2–3 ft (60–90 cm), this robust perennial has large, daisy-like white flowerheads with pale golden centers; these may be 3 in (8 cm) across and are carried high above the dark, shiny, toothed leaves in summer and early fall (autumn). The Shasta daisies were once thought to be ***Leucanthemum maximum***, a native of the Pyrenees but are now believed to be hybrids between that species and the Portuguese ***L. lacustre***; they were first noticed naturalized on the slopes of Mount Shasta in Washington State, USA and attracted the attention of the famous plant breeder Luther Burbank. There are now many cultivars, always white-flowered, but including doubles as well as singles, some with fringed petals. **'Aglaia'** grows to 12 in (30 cm) tall and is noted for its semi-double flowers that last throughout summer; **'Esther Read'** grows to 3 ft (1 m) tall with a profusion of semi-double flowers; **'Wirral Pride'** reaches 30 in (75 cm) in height with double white flowerheads; and **'Wirral Supreme'** is noted for its anemone-centered double flowers. **'Tinkerbell'** and **'Snow Lady'** are low-growing forms with single flowers. **ZONES 5–10.**

Leucanthemum vulgare

syn. ***Chrysanthemum leucanthemum***

OX-EYE DAISY, MOON DAISY

This native of Europe and temperate Asia is like a small version of the Shasta daisy, though the pretty white flowerheads, borne in early summer, are no more than 2 in (5 cm) in diameter. A clump-forming perennial up to 30 in (75 cm) tall, it is freely self-seeding and has become abundantly naturalized in parts of North America, Australia and New Zealand. **ZONES 3–10.**

LEUCHTENBERGIA

AGAVE CACTUS, PRISM CACTUS

This genus contains a single, quite remarkable species of cactus, native to northern Mexico. Other cactus genera (*Mammillaria* for example) have ribs broken up into knobby tubercles, but in Leuchtenbergia this structure is carried to an extreme, with tubercles so elongated and knife-edged that they look like the leaves of a miniature agave, except that each ends in a tuft of twisted, somewhat papery spines. Large lemon-yellow flowers are produced from the tips of younger tubercles in summer, usually only one at a time.

CULTIVATION: Like most cacti, *Leuchtenbergia* requires gritty, very well-drained soil and a position in full sun.

Leucanthemum vulgare

It grows quite quickly in summer if kept moist, but should be kept dry and near dormant in winter. Under glass in a cool climate the minimum winter temperature should be around 50°F (10°C), but lower temperatures are tolerated in a desert climate. Propagate from seed.

Leuchtenbergia principis

Young plants of this cactus are about 8 in (20 cm) in diameter with only the tubercles visible, but with age the older tubercles wither and fall, revealing a shaggy 'trunk' that may be up to 24 in (60 cm) high in very old specimens. The glossy yellow flowers are sweet-smelling and 2 in (5 cm) or more in diameter. **ZONES 10–11.**

LEUCOCORYNE

This genus of the onion tribe consists of 12 species of bulbous perennials found exclusively in Chile in areas where the rains come in fall (autumn), winter and spring and the summers are both hot and dry. They have scented blue, white or lilac flowers borne in umbels in late winter and spring. The linear basal leaves smell like garlic.

CULTIVATION: These frost-tender plants are best established in full sun and in very well-drained loam. During their summer dormancy the plants should be kept fairly dry. Regrowth begins with the fall rains. Propagate from ripe seed or offsets.

Leucocoryne ixioides

GLORY-OF-THE-SUN

This species is a bit of a gamble for the gardener: one year you may get a magnificent display of blooms, and the next spring it may refuse to flower at all. The flowers are borne in clusters on wiry stems up to 18 in (45 cm) tall. The 2 in (5 cm), sweetly scented, milky blue or purple flowers are reflexed and star-shaped, white in the center and graduating to blue at the tips with prominent yellow anthers. The foliage is long and slender. **ZONES 9–11.**

LEUCOGENES

NEW ZEALAND EDELWEISS

This very small genus consists of 3 or 4 species of evergreen, woody based perennials, first cousins of the helichrysums or everlasting daisies. Although not closely related to the European edelweiss, they resemble it both in their mountain habitat and small, furry, white flowers. The resemblance is close enough that the name *Leucogenes* is the Greek translation of the German word edelweiss, meaning 'the noble white flower'. They are excellent rock-garden plants.

CULTIVATION: The mountains of New Zealand being less frigid than the Alps, *Leucogenes* species are a little less dependent on cold winters to flourish than their European counterparts. Winter-wet feet are their enemy, so they need very good drainage. Plant in full or filtered sun in gritty, peaty soil. Propagate from fresh, ripe seed or from cuttings in late spring or early summer.

Leucogenes grandiceps

Leucogenes grandiceps has felty, white bracts enclosing golden-yellow flowerheads and downy silver leaves. It is dense and low growing, reaching a height and spread of 6 in (15 cm). **ZONES 7–9.**

Leucogenes leontopodium

NORTH ISLAND EDELWEISS

This species reaches 6 in (15 cm) in height and has silvery white to yellow leaves. Its small, star-shaped, downy, yellow flowers are surrounded by thick, felted white bracts. **ZONES 7–9.**

LEUCOJUM

SNOWFLAKE

This genus consists of 10 species of bulbous perennials, resembling the snowdrop, which bear delightful flowers that bloom in spring and fall (autumn). They are native to North Africa and the

Leucogenes leontopodium

southern Mediterranean. The pendent, bell-shaped flowers consist of 6 petals, borne singly or in 2s and 3s at the top of a thin stem growing up to 24 in (60 cm). The mid-green to deep green leaves are narrow and strap-like. The bulbs multiply freely, and large clumps of nodding blooms make a glorious display.
CULTIVATION: Some of the species prefer part-shade in moist soil, while others thrive in sunny positions with well-drained soil; they are moderately to fully frost hardy. The bulbs should be planted in late summer or early fall and only lifted for dividing when they produce few flowers and many leaves. Propagate from offsets in spring or early fall or from seed sown in fall.

Leucojum aestivum
SUMMER SNOWFLAKE, GIANT SNOWFLAKE

This dainty, spring-flowering bulb is native to Europe and western Asia. The fragrant flowers are white with a green spot near the tip of each petal and are borne in clusters atop 18 in (45 cm) stems. The blue-green leaves are long and slender. Frost hardy, the small bulbs are best planted under a deciduous tree. ***Leucojum aestivum* var. *pulchellum*** is found in the wild near or in water in the southern parts of Europe and western Asia. Growing to a height of 24 in (60 cm), it naturalizes freely in similar situations and climates and grows in sun or shade. The flowers, 3 to 6 per stalk, carry 6 white, green-spotted petals of equal length and appear in late spring and early summer. The strap-shaped leaves, which are poisonous to stock, form voluminous clumps. **ZONES 4–10.**

Leucojum autumnale
AUTUMN SNOWFLAKE

This species has delicate white flowers flushed with pink that appear singly or in 2s and 3s at the top of a thin, 10 in (25 cm) high stem. Its erect, very fine basal leaves, which usually follow the flowers, add to the plant's dainty air. As both common and scientific names imply, the flowers appear in late summer or early fall (autumn). The bulbs should be planted 2 in (5 cm) deep in well-drained soil in a sunny position. **ZONES 5–10.**

Leucojum vernum
SPRING SNOWFLAKE

A native of central Europe that blooms in late winter and early spring, this species grows to a height of 18 in (45 cm). The plant naturalizes freely in damp conditions, in sun or shade, and survives dry summers in style. The leaves are strap-like and the bell-shaped flowers, 2 to a stalk, carry white petals of equal length that are marked with either a green or yellow spot. **ZONES 5–10.**

LEUCOPHYLLUM

There are 12 species of lslow-growing, low, spreading, evergreen shrubs in this genus from the Chihuahuan Desert of western Texas and northern Mexico. They have soft gray foliage and complement hedges or clumps of green shrubs.
CULTIVATION: They prefer a warm, sunny position, sheltered and frost free, in sandy, well-drained soil. Propagate from seed or cuttings.

Leucophyllum candidum
VIOLET SILVERLEAF

This desert shrub grows from 24–36 in (60–90 cm) tall with a spread of 3 ft (1 m). It likes part-shade. **'Silver Cloud'** has spiky, silvery leaves and small, violet, bell-shaped flowers. **ZONES 9–11.**

Leucophyllum frutescens
TEXAS RANGER, TEXAS SAGE, SILVERLEAF, CENIZO

This species is the most frost hardy and the most commonly seen in gardens. Its dense, upright form—usually 6–8 ft (1.8–2.4 m) tall and almost the same in width—is covered with reddish lavender flowers following a good rain. Very tough and tolerant of heat and dry conditions, nurseries are now offering selections with flowers of pink, white or purple on plants that may be low and compact or tall and slender. **ZONES 8–11.**

Leucophyllum laevigatum
CHIHUAHUAN RAIN SAGE

This desert species enjoys quite dry conditions from shade to sun. It has perfumed pale blue to lavender flowers. **ZONES 9–11.**

LEUCOPHYTA
CUSHION BUSH

This genus of the daisy family consists of a single species of evergreen subshrub, native to the southern seashores of Australia and formerly included in the genus *Calocephalus*. It is an intricately branched plant of mound-like form with small scale-like leaves; all parts of the plant are clothed in silvery hairs that reflect light strongly, even the small knob-like flowerheads though these give glimpses of cream florets. It is among the plants most highly resistant to ocean spray, growing on the most exposed headlands and dunes, but also adapts well to garden conditions in mild climates, though shelter results in looser growth.
CULTIVATION: It prefers light, open soils of moderate fertility and must have sun. Once established the plants seldom need watering; they are not very long lived, being inclined to rot off at the base after a few years. Propagate from cuttings in summer.

Leucophyta brownii
syn. *Calocephalus brownii*

This spreading shrub has a dense, rounded habit, growing at the most to 3 ft (1 m) high but sometimes of greater width, making a silvery mound with its intricate, silvery gray branches. It flowers in summer with creamy white, rounded knobs that appear silver when in bud. The race from Western Australia has longer, slightly recurving leaves and is even more silvery. **ZONES 9–11.**

LEUCOSPERMUM
PINCUSHION

This genus might be confused with *Leucadendron*, another genus of protea allies from South Africa, but a quick look will show that their flowerheads are quite different in structure. It consists of about 50 species of woody evergreen shrubs, all but a very few restricted in the wild to western Cape Province with only about 4 from the summer-rainfall eastern regions, one of them extending just into Zimbabwe. Unlike proteas and leucadendrons they do not have showy bracts surrounding their terminal flowerheads, the flowers themselves being the showy part. Borne in tight clusters, they have long projecting styles giving the whole inflorescence the appearance of a pincushion. Long lasting and often brilliantly colored, they are favorite cut flowers in any place where a mild winter and a rather dry but not too hot summer provide the conditions needed for their successful cultivation. The leaves are usually stiff and leathery and often toothed around the tip. They are much grown in Australia and New Zealand, in the highlands of Hawaii from where they are exported to the flower shops of the USA, and in Israel for the European market. Florists usually sell them as 'proteas' rather than accustom their buyers to the long Greek name, which means 'white seed' from the shining seed vessels.
CULTIVATION: They are mostly compact, attractive bushes full of flowers, the only pruning needed to keep them so being the cutting of the flowers. They need well-drained, slightly acidic soil and sunshine in a warm-temperate climate with low summer humidity. Propagate from seed or cuttings, the latter being the best way to perpetuate the attractive hybrids now being produced.

Leucojum aestivum

Leucophyta brownii

Leucophyllum frutescens

Leucojum aestivum var. *pulchellum*

Leucojum autumnale

L

Leucospermum cordifolium
syn. *Leucospermum nutans*
NODDING PINCUSHION

Growing 3–6 ft (1–1.8 m) tall with a spread of about 3 ft (1 m), this species has a well-branched habit with sturdy, flowering branches bearing gray-green, very broad leaves and terminal flowerheads. These distinctive, dome-shaped blooms in yellow, orange and red tones are held over a long period through summer. **'Flame Spike'** has deep orange-red flowerheads. **'Red Sunset'**, a hybrid with ***Leucospermum lineare***, bears red and gold flowers in spring. **ZONES 9–11.**

Leucospermum mundii

Leucospermum oleifolium

Leucospermum reflexum

Leucospermum erubescens

A somewhat rare species in the wild, *Leucospermum erubescens* is restricted to the Langeberg Mountains east of Cape Town, where it grows on dry rocky hills. It is an erect, rather stiff shrub up to 6 ft (1.8 m) high with narrow, blunt leaves toothed at the apex. From late winter to early summer it produces clusters of flowerheads at the branch tips, opening honey yellow but ageing dull pink. This is only one of many beautiful *Leucospermum* species that await more general cultivation. **ZONES 9–10.**

Leucospermum grandiflorum

Leucospermum tottum 'Scarlet Ribbon'

Leucospermum reflexum var. *luteum*

Leucospermum formosum

Closely allied to and very similar to the green-leafed ***Leucospermum catherinae***, this native of the southwest Cape has hairy gray-green leaves and in spring produces hemispherical flowerheads with pale orange-yellow styles. **ZONES 9–10.**

Leucospermum glabrum

This shrub measures 10 ft (3 m) and has bright green leaves. The flowers have bright scarlet styles and deep red ribbons. **ZONES 9–10.**

Leucospermum grandiflorum

Found in the hills and mountains of southeastern Cape Province, this 5 ft (1.5 m) tall species is notable for its unusual flowerheads. They open from mid-winter to early summer and have relatively few styles. The styles, which are yellow, point almost directly upwards and are tipped with red pollen receptacles. **ZONES 9–11.**

Leucospermum mundii

This species, another from the Langeberg Mountains, has light green leaves with up to 17 notch-like teeth at their tips. The small brush-like flowerheads occur in clusters at the stem tips and open pale yellow then age to golden brown. They appear from mid-winter to late spring. **ZONES 9–10.**

Leucospermum tottum

Leucospermum oleifolium

This shrub grows 3–5 ft (1–1.5 m) tall and has clusters of flowers that are pale yellow changing to orange then deep crimson. **ZONES 9–10.**

Leucospermum glabrum

Leucospermum erubescens

Leucospermum formosum

Leucospermum reflexum
ROCKET PINCUSHION

This species makes an erect shrub up to 10 ft (3 m) tall with a spread of 6 ft (1.8 m). The small, silvery leaves are clasped to the stems in a compact manner while the terminal crimson, yellow-tipped, spiky, reflexed flowers are borne profusely through spring and summer. ***Leucospermum reflexum* var. *luteum*** grows to over 12 ft (3.5 m) tall and has light, gray-green foliage and clear light yellow flowers. **ZONES 9–10.**

Leucospermum tottum
syn. *Leucospermum gueinzii*
FIREWHEEL PINCUSHION

This dense shrub grows to 5 ft (1.5 m) high and wide. Its long, narrow, gray-green, oblong leaves are covered with fine, short hairs. The dome-shaped flowerheads, 3–4 in (8–10 cm) wide and opening in spring and summer, are pinkish red with numerous cream styles radiating from the central boss. **'Scarlet Ribbon'** is a cross between *Leucospermum tottum* and *L. glabrum* with bright pink flowers and yellow styles. **'Golden Star'**, a cross between *L. tottum* and *L. cordifolium*, has light yellow flowers on long slender stems. **ZONES 9–11.**

Leucospermum cordifolium

Leucospermum cordifolium 'Flame Spike'

LEUCOTHOE

This genus, containing about 50 species of deciduous and evergreen shrubs allied to *Pieris*, is widely distributed in cool- to warm-climate regions from southern USA to the mountains of South America, with a few in East Asia. They have simple, alternate leaves and produce white or pink flowers in short axillary or terminal spikes. The fruits are small capsules containing many seeds.
CULTIVATION: These shrubs prefer moist, acidic, well-drained soil and a sheltered position in sun or part-shade. Propagation is from seed, cuttings or from the suckering root sections of the plant, or by division.

Leucothoë davisiae
SIERRA LAUREL

An evergreen shrub from the USA, this species will grow 3 ft (1 m) tall with a spread of 5 ft (1.5 m). In summer, it has 6 in (15 cm) long clusters of white, bell-shaped flowers and needs regular water during the growing season. **ZONES 5–10.**

Leucothoë fontanesiana
syn. *Leucothoë catesbaei*
PEARL FLOWER, DROOPING LEUCOTHOE

Indigenous to the southeastern states of the USA, this evergreen shrub grows 3–5 ft (1–1.5 m) tall. The arching stems bear leathery, long-pointed dark green leaves and pendulous spikes of small bell-shaped white or pinkish flowers through spring. **'Rainbow'** (or 'Golden Rainbow'), is a very popular cultivar, with cream and pink-mottled green leaves. **ZONES 6–10.**

LEVISTICUM
LOVAGE

This genus consists of one species, a bright green perennial herb up to 6 ft (1.8 m) high with celery-like leaves divided into wedge-shaped segments. Umbels of small greenish yellow flowers are borne in summer, followed by ribbed aromatic seeds in early fall (autumn). When crushed the leaves release a strong balsamic odor. This is a traditional cottage garden plant and its tall stature makes it a good background specimen in the herb garden.
CULTIVATION: Grow this fully frost-hardy plant in deep, humus-rich soil with good drainage in full sun or part-shade. Keep soil evenly moist, especially when grown in full sun. Protect from strong winds. Propagate by root division or from seed in spring.

Lewisia columbiana

Levisticum officinale

Levisticum officinale

This robust species from the eastern Mediterranean has dark green leaves and a thick, erect, hollow stem. The roots and shoots are used in salads. **ZONES 4–10.**

Lewisia cotyledon

Lewisia cotyledon hybrid

Lewisia cotyledon var. *howellii*

Lewisia cotyledon 'Pinkie'

Lewisia 'Ben Chase'

Leucothoë davisiae

Leucothoë fontanesiana

LEWISIA
BITTER ROOT

This genus, which honors the explorer Meriwether Lewis (1774–1838), contains about 20 species of small perennials with deep tap roots, leathery leaves and starry flowers, all native to the Rocky Mountains of the USA. The roots are endowed with wonderful powers of survival: Lewis returned to civilization in 1806 and it is said that a botanist in London, studying his dried plant specimens nearly 5 years later, found that one was trying to grow. He planted it and it duly revived, and the following summer bore its beautiful pink flowers. Hybrid lewisias such as **'Ben Chase'**, flower over a long period in summer in a range of colors—pink, white, apricot, red or flame.
CULTIVATION: Give them a cool climate, full sun or part-shade in warm climates and excellent drainage, so there will be no chance of winter-wet rotting the roots. Propagate herbaceous species from seed in spring or fall (autumn), and evergreen species from seed in spring or offsets in summer.

Lewisia columbiana

Named after the Columbia River region whence it originates, this evergreen species forms a clump of narrow, fleshy basal leaves. The foliage clump is around 6 in (15 cm) high with an 8 in (20 cm) spread and in summer it produces heads of pink-veined white to pale pink flowers on 12 in (30 cm) stems. **ZONES 5–9.**

Leucothoë fontanesiana

Lewisia cotyledon

This evergreen, which hybridizes readily, has rosettes of fleshy, toothed leaves and bears clusters of white to yellow, apricot and pink to purple flowers on upright stems. It grows to a height of 12 in (30 cm). ***Lewisia cotyledon* var. *howellii*** spreads to 6 in (15 cm). **'Pinkie'**, with pink flowers grows 1 in (25 mm) tall and 2 in (5 cm) wide. **ZONES 6–10.**

Lewisia rediviva

The specific epithet means 'brought back to life', referring to the capacity of this rosette-forming species to revive after desiccation. It bears clusters of grass-like, deciduous leaves and large, multi-petalled pink flowers and reaches to 2 in (5 cm) in height. There is also a white form. **ZONES 4–10.**

Liatris spicata 'Floristan Violett'

Liatris spicata 'Kobold'

Libertia peregrinans

Lewisia tweedyi

Growing to 8 in (20 cm) tall and 12 in (30 cm) wide, this evergreen species has succulent stems, small fleshy leaves and pale to peach-pink open-faced flowers from spring to summer. **ZONES 5–9.**

LEYCESTERIA

This genus of 6 deciduous or semi-evergreen shrubs from the western Himalayas and western China form clumps of arching, suckering, cane-like stems and grow from 4–8 ft (1.2–2.4 m) tall, depending on the species. The leaves are from 2–8 in (5–20 cm) long, oval with pointed tips and finely serrated edges. They are usually borne in pairs. The small, tubular or trumpet-shaped flowers, carried in whorls on pendulous or arching racemes, may be partly obscured by colored bracts and are followed by clusters of soft berries. The flowers open over a long period and the berries ripen quickly, so racemes may bear flowers and fruit at the same time.

Liatris spicata

Leycesteria formosa

Lewisia tweedyi

CULTIVATION: They are easily grown in any well-drained soil in sun or part-shade. In cool but mild, wet climates some species can become weeds of disturbed forests. Most are frost hardy. Propagate from seed or by removing rooted suckers.

Leycesteria formosa

HIMALAYAN HONEYSUCKLE

This deciduous shrub from the Himalayas measures 8 ft (2.4 m) tall and 6 ft (1.8 m) wide. It has a woody stem, leafy chains of purple and white flowers and interesting fruit of purple-black berries in purple leafy sheaths. In a favorable climate it can become an invasive weed. **ZONES 7–10.**

LEYMUS

EUROPEAN DUNE GRASS, WILD RYE

This genus of 40 species of rhizomatous perennial grasses is found over much of the northern hemisphere temperate region, with one species from Argentina. They form clumps of erect foliage, the narrow leaves often with inrolled edges. The largest species has leaves around 30 in (75 cm) long with flower spikes over 6 ft (1.8 m) tall. The dried seed

Liatris punctata

heads remain on the plants for some time and can be an attractive winter feature. The name of the genus is an anagram of the related genus *Elymus*.
CULTIVATION: These grasses are easily grown in any well-drained soil in full sun or part-shade. The foliage may be cut back in winter to keep the clumps under control and to encourage fresh shoots in spring. Frost hardiness varies but most will tolerate heavy frosts. Propagate from seed or by division.

Leymus arenarius

syn. *Elymus arenarius*

LYME GRASS

This species from Europe and northern Asia grows to 5 ft (1.5 m) tall with spreading clumps of blue-gray leaves. It can be sheared for a lawn and as it is a natural coastal species is an excellent choice for stabilizing dunes or as a foundation plant when establishing a garden in sandy soil. The spikelets appear in spike-like racemes in summer. **ZONES 6–10.**

LIATRIS

BLAZING STAR

These 40 species of perennials come from the central and eastern regions of North America. In summer they shoot up tall, cylindrical spikes of fluffy flowers from a knobby rootstock that remains visible during the rest of the year. They belong to the daisy or composite family but their spike-like inflorescences, with crowded small flowerheads opening from the top downward, are so unlike those of other daisies that it is hard to recognize their affinity.
CULTIVATION: These plants will grow in most soils and conditions including damp places such as stream banks and ditches, although they do best in climates with low humidity. They thrive with minimum care and attention, making excellent border plants. Propagation is from seed or by division of old clumps in winter.

Liatris punctata

SNAKEROOT

Ranging from eastern Canada to New Mexico, this species reaches nearly 3 ft (1 m) in height and has purple, occasionally white, flowers in fall (autumn). Flowering is prolonged by cutting and the stems make an attractive indoor display. They perform best in fertile, well-drained soil. **ZONES 3–10.**

Liatris spicata

syn. *Liatris callilepis* of gardens

GAY FEATHER, SPIKE GAY FEATHER

This low-growing species is a desirable cut flower and a good butterfly- and bee-attracting plant. The flowers are lilac purple, although they can occur in pink and white. They are produced in crowded, fluffy spikes—like a feather duster—in late summer, opening from the top downwards, the opposite of most flowering spikes. It grows to a height of 24 in (60 cm), with thickened, corm-like rootstocks and basal tufts of grassy, mid-green foliage. **'Floristan'** is a seedling strain growing to 5 ft (1.5 m) tall; it is available in 2 colors: deep violet (**'Floristan Violett'**) and white (**'Floristan Weiss'**). **'Kobold'** is a dwarf cultivar reaching 15 in (38 cm) and producing bright purple flowers. **ZONES 3–10.**

LIBERTIA

These 20 species of perennials in the iris family have tufts of grass-like leaves springing from rhizomes which may be very short or long creeping. They are found on both sides of the Pacific Ocean in New Zealand, Australia, New Guinea and the Andes of South and Central America. They grow easily in a temperate climate, producing erect, wiry stems bearing clusters of small white iris-like flowers in spring and summer.
CULTIVATION: Moderately frost hardy, they require a sheltered, sunny or part-shaded position and well-drained, peaty soil with plenty of moisture in spring and summer. Propagate by division in spring or from seed in spring or fall (autumn). Some species naturalize freely.

Libertia grandiflora

NEW ZEALAND IRIS

This easily grown rhizomatous perennial is native to New Zealand and is valued for its foliage, decorative seed pods and flowers. It has grass-like, brown-tipped, dark green leaves over 24 in (60 cm) long. In early summer it produces tall, wiry, lightly branched flower stems with dainty white flowers, followed in fall (autumn) by golden-brown seed capsules. Loosely clump forming, it grows to a height of 3 ft (1 m) and has a spread of 24 in (60 cm). **ZONES 8–11.**

Libertia ixioides

Growing 8–15 in (20–38 cm) tall and wide, this New Zealand species has dark green leaves and stems from 12–24 in (30–60 cm) high with clusters of white flowers. **ZONES 8–10.**

Libertia peregrinans

This New Zealand species is remarkable for its long, branching rhizomes which send up sparse tufts of narrow, strongly veined leaves at intervals, these turning a striking orange-brown shade in fall (autumn) and winter. It reaches 30 in (75 cm) in height and grows in moist, slightly acidic, well-drained soil in full or part-shade. It has a yellowish bronze-green shorter flowering stem with white flowers with orange-brown anthers. **ZONES 8–10.**

LIBOCEDRUS

These evergreen trees and shrubs belonging to the cypress family are from high-rainfall areas of New Zealand, New Caledonia and temperate South America. There are 6 species with short, needle-like juvenile leaves and scale-like adult ones. Male and female cones appear on small branchlets arranged in flattened sprays on the same tree. Their pleasantly aromatic timber has been used in building construction and for making pencils.
CULTIVATION: Fully frost-hardy, cool-climate plants, they prefer a sheltered position in full sun and fertile, moist soil. Propagate from seed or cuttings. Watch for dry rot.

Libocedrus plumosa

KAWAKA

This narrowly upright conifer from New Zealand grows very slowly to a height of 40 ft (12 m) with a spread of about 8 ft (2.4 m). It has tiny, bright yellow-green scale leaves on flattened, fern-like branchlets. The bark is stringy and the timber is deep red and beautifully grained. An excellent lawn specimen, it also does well in containers. **ZONES 8–10.**

LICUALA

There are around 100 species in this genus of fan palms from the wet tropics of Southeast Asia and Australasia, varying greatly in stature. Their fronds are very distinctive, from circular to fan-shaped in outline with regularly radiating ribs and toothed around the perimeter; in most species they are divided by splits into pie-wedge segments, often of unequal widths and with few to many ribs each. Slender flowering panicles arise from the frond axils, bearing numerous tiny yellowish flowers followed by small red or orange berries.
CULTIVATION: Frost tender, they prefer part-shade and sandy, well-drained soil. Where temperatures fall below 60°F (15°C) most species need the shelter of a warm greenhouse, though the Australian ***Licuala ramsayi*** will survive night-time temperatures only slightly above freezing-point. Propagate from seed or suckers.

Licuala spinosa

This is a Southeast Asian evergreen species reaching 20 ft (6 m) with a 10 ft (3 m) spread. It has clumps of slender stems and frond segments like the spokes of a wheel, 3 ft (1 m) across, and fruit of bright orange berries carried on an arching inflorescence up to 8 ft (2.4 m) long. **ZONES 10–12.**

LIGULARIA

There are at least 150 species of perennials in this genus which is closely related to *Senecio* and is found mainly in temperate eastern Asia, though a smaller number occur in northern Asia and Europe. Many species are large-leafed, clump-forming plants that produce tall spires of daisy-like flowerheads, mostly in shades of yellow or orange. The cultivated ligularias are stately plants and vigorous growers, adapted to moist, sheltered sites such as stream banks and woodland glades and flowering mainly in summer and early fall (autumn). The spring foliage can be almost as ornamental as the summer blooms.
CULTIVATION: Quite frost hardy, they prefer moist, well-drained soil and will grow in either sun or part-shade. Propagate by division in spring or from seed in spring or fall. They are prone to attack by slugs and snails.

Ligularia dentata

syns *Ligularia clivorum, Senecio clivorum*

This compact species from China and Japan is grown for its striking foliage and showy flowerheads. It grows to a height of 4 ft (1.2 m) and a spread of 3 ft (1 m). It has kidney-shaped, long-stalked, leathery, brownish green leaves and bears clusters of large, 3 in (8 cm) wide, orange-yellow flowerheads on long branching stems in summer. It will grow happily at the edge of ponds. Cultivars worth growing are **'Othello'** and **'Desdemona'**, which has green leaves heavily overlaid with bronze and maroon. **'Gregynog Gold'** has round green leaves and orange flowers. **ZONES 4–9.**

Ligularia przewalskii

This northern Chinese species has round, deeply cut, dark green leaves. It raises spires (rather than domes) of small, yellow flowers on dark purple stems from mid- to late summer, and reaches a height of 6 ft (1.8 m). **ZONES 4–9.**

Ligularia stenocephala

This species from Japan, China and Taiwan grows to 5 ft (1.5 m). It has dark purple stems and bears slender racemes of yellow flowers in summer. The leaves are triangular and toothed. **ZONES 5–10.**

LIGUSTRUM

PRIVET

For many temperate-climate gardeners the words 'hedge' and 'privet' are synonymous, but this genus of some 50 or so species of shrubs and trees from temperate Asia, Europe and North Africa offers more than simply the ability to grow in almost any soil or position and to take regular clipping without protest; some species are in fact rather decorative. They range from shrubs to small trees, some evergreen, others deciduous; all grow very rapidly and bear abundant sprays of small white flowers in summer, almost always scented, though sometimes unpleasantly. The flowers are followed by black berries, which can look very striking against the gold-splashed leaves of the variegated cultivars. Birds feast on these and can easily overpopulate the whole district with privet seedlings. In parts of the USA, Australia and New Zealand several privet species have become detested weeds of native woodland.
CULTIVATION: Grow in sun or part-shade in moist, well-drained soil. The roots are very greedy, usually making growing anything else within their reach a frustrating exercise. Privets grow all too easily from seed in fall (autumn) or spring or by division, but selected varieties need to be propagated from cuttings. They may be damaged by aphids, scale insects and leaf miner.

Licuala spinosa

Ligularia dentata

Libocedrus plumosa

Libocedrus plumosa

Ligustrum delavayanum

A compact, evergreen shrub from China, this species grows to 6 ft (1.8 m) tall with a 10 ft (3 m) spread. It has a slender stem with dark green leaves and white flowers tinged with purple on terminal panicles. The summer flowers are followed by blue-black fruit. **ZONES 7–11.**

Ligustrum ibota

This is a bushy, deciduous shrub from Japan reaching 6 ft (1.8 m) in height. The glossy green leaves and young stems have a covering of fine hairs. It bears white flowers in summer. **ZONES 5–10.**

Ligularia stenocephala

Ligularia dentata 'Desdemona'

Ligustrum ibota

Ligustrum delavayanum

Ligustrum japonicum
JAPANESE PRIVET

This bushy, evergreen shrub with a dense habit reaches 10 ft (3 m) tall with a spread of 8 ft (2.4 m). From Asia, it has oval, glossy, dark green leaves and bears large conical panicles of flowers from mid-summer to early fall (autumn), followed by blue-black berries. It can be used as a hedge plant. **'Rotundifolium'** is dense and slow growing, with thick, rounded leaves. ZONES 7–11.

Ligustrum lucidum
GLOSSY PRIVET, WAXLEAF PRIVET

This upright evergreen shrub from China, Japan and Korea reaches a height of 30 ft (9 m) and a spread of 25 ft (8 m). It has large, pointed, glossy dark green leaves and bears large panicles of small creamy white flowers in late summer and early fall (autumn). It has been declared a weed in some areas of warm, wet climate. The leaves of **'Tricolor'** are variegated with yellow, pink when young. **'Excelsum Superbum'** is a vigorous cultivar with flecked deep yellow leaves and small, cream-edged, tubular white flowers. Although the blue-black fruit are poisonous, they are used medicinally in China, claimed to prevent bone marrow loss in chemotherapy patients, as well as a potential treatment for AIDS, respiratory infections, Parkinson's disease and hepatitis. ZONES 7–11.

Ligustrum lucidum 'Tricolor'

Ligustrum obtusifolium

This deciduous Japanese shrub reaches 10 ft (3 m) in height. It has graceful mid-green foliage and white flowers in summer. ***Ligustrum obtusifolium* var. *regelianum*** is frost hardy and has a horizontal branching pattern, growing 5–6 ft (1.5–1.8 m) tall. Its leaves may turn purplish in spring and fall (autumn), and the white flowers produce black berries that last into winter. ZONES 3–10.

Ligustrum ovalifolium
CALIFORNIA PRIVET

Although native to Japan, this shrub is so entrenched in parts of the USA that it is known as California privet. This species and *Ligustrum japonicum* are now weeds in New Zealand. Growing to about 12 ft (3.5 m) tall, it is usually seen in its variegated form **'Aureum'**. Partly deciduous, it can form a thick mass of upright branches and is often used as hedging. The leaves need full sun to become variegated yellow; if green-leafed shoots appear, they should be cut out or they will eventually take over. ZONES 5–10.

Ligustrum quihoui

A native of China, this elegant, evergreen shrub is one of the best species of the genus, producing panicles of white flowers up to 18 in (45 cm) long in fall (autumn). It has dark green, oval leaves and grows to a height of 8 ft (2.4 m) with a spread of 6 ft (1.8 m). ZONES 6–10.

Ligustrum sinense
CHINESE PRIVET

This semi-evergreen or deciduous, bushy shrub from China bears large clusters of fragrant white flowers in mid-summer, set among small dark green leaves. Small, black-purple berries follow. Frost hardy, *Ligustrum sinense* grows to a height of 12 ft (3.5 m). In eastern Australia it has invaded native vegetation to an alarming degree. ZONES 7–11.

Ligustrum japonicum 'Rotundifolium'

Ligustrum lucidum 'Tricolor'

Ligustrum quihoui

Ligustrum 'Vicaryi'
GOLDEN VICARY PRIVET

Popular for its solid yellow leaves, this cultivar has a natural vase-like shape and grows to nearly 10 ft (3 m) in height and spread. It must be grown in full sun to ensure a good yellow color, otherwise any conditions will suit it. It bears panicles of white flowers in summer, followed by blue-black fruit. ZONES 5–10.

Ligustrum vulgare
EUROPEAN PRIVET, COMMON PRIVET

This bushy shrub from Europe, North Africa and temperate Asia is deciduous or semi-evergreen and reaches a height and spread of 10 ft (3 m). It has dark green, pointed, oval leaves and bears panicles of small, strongly perfumed white flowers from early to mid-summer, followed by black berries. There are several cultivars with variegated leaves. If using as a hedge, prune back hard for the first few years of growth then trim regularly. ZONES 4–10.

LILIUM
LILY, LILIUM

Many plants are referred to as 'lilies', usually signifying that they belong to the lily family or one of its allied families, but in the narrowest sense this word means a member of the bulbous genus *Lilium*; this consists of around 100 species, native in temperate Eurasia (extending to high mountains of the Philippines) and North America, with the largest number found in China and the Himalayas. All species grow from buried bulbs consisting of overlapping fleshy scales which do not encircle one another as in the classical onion-type bulb. The stems are elongated with spirally arranged or whorled leaves that vary from narrow and grass-like to very short and broad. One to many 6-petalled flowers are borne in terminal sprays, the blooms erect, nodding or pendent and often with strongly recurved petals—the so-called 'Turk's cap' type.

Lilies of various species have been in cultivation for centuries and have acquired many religious and mystical associations. *Lilium candidum*, for example, was the flower of the Virgin Mary and so became a symbol of purity. In the Middle Ages the lily was the symbol of peace. Botanically, lilies are varied both in their growth habit, their method of reproduction and the shape, size and color of their flowers. The great majority flower in summer. Lilies have been extensively hybridized, especially in recent years. A formal classification of hybrids was published in 1968 but more recent hybridizing and the introduction of tetraploid varieties has already blurred the distinctions between the various groups.

CULTIVATION: Lilium bulbs, unlike those of many other genera, have no outer protective coat so should be out of the ground for the shortest possible time. The most important requirement of lilies is good drainage. A few have a preference for an alkaline soil, others will not tolerate it. Almost all like sun but a cool root area, which means they should be planted quite deeply; a general guide is to plant so that there is a minimum of 4 in (10 cm) of soil over the bulb. Most can be left undisturbed for many years and allowed to multiply naturally. Liliums can be propagated by means of offsets from the main bulb, from bulb scales or seed or, in some species, from bulbils which form in the leaf axils up the stem.

Ligustrum obtusifolium

Ligustrum vulgare

Lilium auratum
GOLDEN-RAYED LILY OF JAPAN

This magnificent lily caused a sensation when it was first exhibited in England in 1862. The downward- and outward-facing, bowl-shaped flowers are very large, 8–10 in (20–25 cm) in diameter and have a wonderful spicy fragrance. The gold band on the white petals can be variable and sometimes there may also be a red band. They can reach 10 ft (3 m) in height but are normally less. This is one species that will not tolerate lime. ***Lilium auratum* var. *platyphyllum*** is very vigorous, with a deep yellow band in the center of each petal. **ZONES 6–10.**

Lilium × *aurelianense*

This is the original cross between *Lilium henryi* and ***L. sargentiae*** but, like most of the original interspecific crosses, it has now been almost totally superseded by later hybrids (see Trumpet and Aurelian Hybrids below). **ZONES 5–10.**

Lilium bulbiferum

This species from southern Europe has upward-facing 4–6 in (10–15 cm) wide flowers, bright orange to fire red in color, with the inner portions of the petals spotted with dark maroon. It will grow to a height of 4 ft (1.2 m), bears 15 to 20 flowers on each stem and produces bulbils in the leaf axils on the upper part of the stem. The leaves are short and dark green. ***Lilium bulbiferum* var. *croceum*** from southern Germany, southern France and Italy has orange flowers. **ZONES 7–10.**

Lilium canadense
MEADOW LILY

This eastern North American species was the first American lily to be introduced into England, in 1800. The lemon-yellow bell-shaped flowers, speckled with deep crimson spots on the inside and widely spreading, gracefully drooping petals, are 3–4 in (8–10 cm) in diameter. It prefers light shade and a moist soil. ***Lilium canadense* var. *editorum*** has red flowers and rather broader leaves. **ZONES 5–10.**

Lilium candidum
MADONNA LILY

This beautifully scented species from southern Europe is probably the oldest species in cultivation. It grows to 6 ft (1.8 m) high and bears up to 20 trumpet-shaped blooms in summer. The pure white flowers can be 6 in (15 cm) long and are slightly reflexed, held close to the stem. The bulb produces basal leaves and a few leaves are scattered along the length of the stem; the basal leaves normally persist over winter. This is one lily that should not be planted deeply, in fact the nose of the bulb should be almost at ground level. It prefers an alkaline soil. **ZONES 6–10.**

Lilium chalcedonicum

Native to Greece, this species has been in cultivation for a long time. The stems, well clothed with leaves, reach 4 ft (1.2 m) tall and carry up to 10 brilliant red, Turk's cap flowers in late summer; the flowers have a lacquer sheen. It prefers a position in full sun. **ZONES 5–10.**

Lilium × *dalhansonii*

This is a cross between *Lilium hansonii* and *L. martagon* var. *cattaniae*. In

Lilium candidum

mid-summer it produces up to 50 maroon to yellow-orange, spotted and bordered flowers. It grows to a height of 5 ft (1.5 m). **ZONES 5–10.**

Lilium davidii

This species from western China flowers in late summer with up to 40 Turk's cap flowers on a stem. These are orange red, heavily spotted with raised black spots and 3 in (8 cm) in diameter. The stems are thin but strong, up to 4 ft (1.2 m) tall. A characteristic of this species is that the longest leaves are at the base of the stem, decreasing in length as they rise up the stem. It is stem rooting and likes full sun. **ZONES 5–10.**

Lilium formosanum

Native to Taiwan, this species grows up to 6 ft (1.8 m) and flowers in late summer. The trumpet-shaped flowers have recurving, highly fragrant petals, pure white on the inside, pink or purple brown on the outside. Up to 8 in (20 cm) long, the glossy, narrow leaves can cover the whole stem. It is easily grown from seed. In Australia it has become abundantly naturalized. **ZONES 5–11.**

Lilium hansonii

This species is indigenous to the Isle of Dagelet off the coast of Korea. It has a 4 ft (1.2 m) tall stem carrying up to 12 pendulous orange flowers, spotted with brown; the petals are thicker than in most *Lilium* species. The leaves are produced in whorls. It is stem rooting and enjoys some shade. **ZONES 5–10.**

Lilium henryi

From central China, this species grows to 10 ft (3 m) in cultivation, but much less in the wild. It can have as many as 40 reflexed flowers, bright orange with carmine spots, in late summer. It is stem rooting so the bulbs, which are larger than those of most species, should be planted deeply. The flowers may be bleached by hot sun but otherwise this species is adaptable to a wide range of climates and is exceptionally vigorous. **ZONES 5–10.**

Lilium humboldtii

The Turk's cap flowers on this species from central and northern California can be variable in color, but are normally pale orange with maroon dots, 4 in (10 cm) in diameter and arranged pyramidically. The stems are up to 4 ft (1.2 m) tall and the leaves may be in

Lilium martagon

Lilium bulbiferum

whorls or scattered along the stems. It prefers some shade. **ZONES 5–10.**

Lilium lancifolium
syn. ***Lilium tigrinum***
TIGER LILY

This species from Japan, Korea and eastern China is one of the most widely grown and also one of the oldest in cultivation. It grows to a height of 4 ft (1.2 m) and produces numerous bright orange pendulous flowers, spotted with purple on the lower parts of the petals, in mid- to late summer. The stems are black and large quantities of dark purple bulbils are produced in the leaf axils. This is a vigorous lily and will thrive even in poor soils. The bulbs and flower buds of tiger lily are food items in Japan and China. **ZONES 4–10.**

Lilium longiflorum
EASTER LILY, ST JOSEPH LILY, BERMUDA LILY

In summer this beautiful, pure white lily, which grows to 4 ft (1.2 m) tall, produces up to 8 slender, funnel-shaped and fragrant flowers, each 6–8 in (15–20 cm) in length. The shiny leaves are up to 8 in (20 cm) long and 1 in (25 mm) wide. It is native to the islands to the south of Japan and is one of the best species for warmer climates. **ZONES 6–11.**

Lilium mackliniae

This comparatively small species from northeastern India has nodding pink Turk's cap flowers, 2 in (5 cm) in diameter. The stems are 12–18 in (30–45 cm) tall and carry only 2 to 3 flowers on each stem in mid-summer. **ZONES 5–10.**

Lilium formosanum

Lilium × *dalhansonii*

Lilium lancifolium

Lilium martagon
COMMON TURK'S CAP LILY

This species is widely distributed over Europe, northern Asia Minor and as far east as Mongolia. It will grow to 6 ft (1.8 m) and can produce as many as 50 blooms. The flowers are pendulous and generally creamy white to pale purple with darker spots, although many forms exist, some with deep burgundy or mahogany red flowers. It is fully frost hardy and will grow in sun or shade. ***Lilium martagon* var. *album*** bears pure white flowers. **ZONES 4–10.**

Lilium monadelphum
syn. ***Lilium szovitsianum***

This is an early-flowering species, native to the Caucasus. The stems are 4 ft (1.2 m) tall and carry up to 40 flowers. The flowers are fragrant, lemon yellow with dark spots on the outer edges of the petals; the stamens are fused into a tube. The leaves are scattered along the stem. It likes some shade and resents transplanting. **ZONES 5–10.**

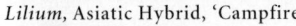

Lilium, Asiatic Hybrid, 'Campfire'

Lilium pitkinense

Lilium pardalinum

Lilium ocellatum
syn. ***Lilium humboldtii* var. *ocellatum***

Previously listed as a variety of *Lilium humboldtii*, this species has flowers of a rich tangerine color, heavily spotted with maroon, each spot often ringed with crimson. Sometimes the spots tend to run into each other around the tips, which then become fairly solidly red. It is more strongly stem rooting than *L. humboldtii* and therefore more amenable in cultivation. **ZONES 5–10.**

Lilium pardalinum
LEOPARD LILY

This native of California can grow to 8 ft (2.4 m). The flowers, between 6 and 10 on each plant, are salmon pink and may be yellow towards the tips spotted with crimson-brown. Appearing in summer, they are pendulous and variably recurving, sometimes fragrant. The leaves are produced in whorls, sometimes almost in a spiral. This species is fully frost hardy and prefers some shade in summer. **ZONES 5–10.**

Lilium philippinense

This species is native to the northern part of the Philippines, growing on the higher mountains. *Lilium philippinense* grows to about 3 ft (1 m) and bears up to 6 fragrant, funnel-shaped flowers in late summer, white on the inside, flushed with green and red on the outside. The leaves are scattered along the stem, 6 in (15 cm) long and narrow. This species needs some protection in cold climates. **ZONES 9–11.**

Lilium pitkinense

Closely resembling *Lilium pardalinum*, this species is native to Sonoma County in California and has fiery orange-red flowers with purple-black spots and a yellow zone. The stems are 3 ft (1 m) tall and the flowers are produced in mid-summer. **ZONES 5–10.**

Lilium pumilum

This species is indigenous to North Korea, Siberia and China. *Lilium pumilum* has nodding, recurving red flowers with a few black spots on each, about 1 in (25 mm) in diameter. Up to 20 flowers are produced on each 18 in (45 cm) stem in mid-summer. The stems are strong and wiry with grass-like foliage clustered in the middle. It likes full sun. **ZONES 5–10.**

Lilium, Asiatic Hybrid, 'Cinnamon'

Lilium pyrenaicum

From Spain and southwest France, this species has long been in cultivation. Up to 15 pendulous, pale yellow flowers with dark, almost black spots, are produced on 4 ft (1.2 m) stems in early summer. The flowers are about $1\frac{1}{2}$ in (35 mm) in diameter and sharply recurving. It likes some shade in very hot areas but otherwise is easily grown. **ZONES 3–10.**

Lilium regale
REGAL LILY, CHRISTMAS LILY

This species from western China is one of the best of the trumpet-flowered species. Growing to 6 ft (1.8 m) in height, it bears up to 30 blooms. The heavily scented flowers are white on the inside with a yellow base, flushed with carmine on the outside; each is about 6 in (15 cm) long and they are normally crowded together. The leaves are dark green and lanceolate. This species is stem rooting and produces a number of stem bulblets. **ZONES 5–10.**

Lilium speciosum

Growing 6 ft (1.8 m) tall, this species from Japan, eastern China and Taiwan produces up to 12 fragrant, pendent flowers with petals strongly recurved though not quite in the Turk's cap style. There are many forms, and flower color can vary from white to crimson, sometimes with contrasting spots. The leaves are 6–8 in (15–20 cm) long and 2 in (5 cm) wide. It flowers from late summer to early fall (autumn) and is marginally frost hardy. ***Lilium speciosum* var. *rubrum*** has deep crimson flowers and is the form most commonly grown. All forms are stem rooting. **ZONES 8–10.**

Lilium superbum
AMERICAN TURK'S CAP LILY

This late summer-flowering species from eastern USA has 10 ft (3 m) tall stems. The flowerheads form a pyramid with up to 40 blooms on a plant. They are orange, turning to crimson at the tips, the lower part of the petals dotted with maroon. The flowers are pendulous and recurving with 4 in (10 cm) long petals. The leaves are produced in whorls. **ZONES 3–10.**

Lilium regale

Lilium × *testaceum*
NANKEEN LILY

This was a chance cross between *Lilium candidum* and *L. chalcedonicum* that appeared in a German garden over 100 years ago, making it probably the first *Lilium* hybrid. It is almost midway between its 2 totally dissimilar parents, about 4–5 ft (1.2–1.5 m) tall with apricot-yellow, recurving flowers. It is still an outstanding garden plant. **ZONES 6–10.**

Lilium, American Hybrids

These are derived from various American species and include the popular Bellingham Hybrids—all have Turk's cap flowers. **'Shuksan'** is a very fine variety with tangerine-gold flowers, 4–6 in (10–15 cm) across, spotted with a darker hue and with crimson tips to the petals. **ZONES 5–10.**

Lilium, Asiatic Hybrids

These have been bred from various central and west Asian species and form by far the largest hybrid group. They include most of the varieties grown commercially as cut flowers or potted plants as well as the widely grown Mid-Century hybrids. Most, however, lack fragrance. The group has been divided into 3 subgroups:

Upward-facing: This group is of upright habit to 30 in (75 cm) and normally flowers in early summer. Examples include **'Campfire'** with deep, almost russet-red flowers 6 in (15 cm) in

Lilium ocellatum

Lilium speciosum

Lilium, Asiatic Hybrid, 'Golden Pixie'

diameter that glow under artificial light; **'Cinnamon'** with creamy white flowers spotted with brown; **'Connecticut King'**, a popular variety with bright yellow flowers, and 8 in (20 cm) in diameter; **'Enchantment'**, one of the best known of all lily hybrids, bears up to 20 nasturtium-red flowers spotted with deep maroon, 6–8 in (15–20 cm) in diameter; **'Golden Pixie'** with deep golden-yellow flowers; **'Red Carpet'**, a strong-growing variety derived from *Lilium pumilum*, with deep red flowers; **'Roma'**, with creamy white flowers, lightly spotted and with lemon nectary channels and a ring of spots in the center of the flower; and **'Sterling Star'** is compact with white flowers up to 6 in (15 cm) across, spotted brown—it was one of the first white-flowered hybrids in this group.

Outward-facing: This group is also early flowering and with an upright habit. Examples include **'Connecticut Lemon Glow'**, a popular cut-flower variety with bright yellow unspotted flowers and quite short stems, usually only 18 in (45 cm) tall.

Downward-facing: Normally a little later to flower than the others, this group includes **'Citronella'**, a strain rather than a single variety with flowers ranging from pale lemon to yellow, spotted with purple-black and slightly recurving petals—there will normally be a large number of flowers on one stem; and **'Rosemary North'**, one of a range of Asiatics bred by Dr North at the Scottish Crop Research Institute producing dull buff-orange flowers. All the North hybrids have more or less pendulous flowers with recurving petals and are usually scented, which is unusual among the Asiatics. ZONES 5–10.

Lilium, Candidum Hybrids

This is a small group derived from *Lilium candidum* or other European species other than *L. martagon*.

Lilium, Asiatic Hybrid, 'Roma'

The apricot-flowered ***L.* × *testaceum*** is one such hybrid. ZONES 6–10.

Lilium, Longiflorum Hybrids

Derived from *Lilium longiflorum* and *L. formosanum*, these hybrids all have trumpet-shaped flowers. This is a small group and none are widely grown. ZONES 5–10.

Lilium, Martagon Hybrids

These have been bred from *Lilium martagon* and *L. hansonii*. Examples are the Backhouse and Paisley groups of hybrids. All have reflexed ('Turk's cap') flowers. **'Marhan'** is a cross between *L. martagon* var. *album* and *L. hansonii*; it is a very strong plant with hanging or slightly outward-facing flowers, the petals strongly recurving and the mauve-pink buds opening to a tawny gold with chocolate spots, the tips overlaid with maroon that fades in strong sunlight. ZONES 5–10.

Lilium, Oriental Hybrids

Not to be confused with the so-called Asiatic hybrids, these are hybrids bred from East Asian species such as *Lilium auratum*, *L. speciosum* and ***L. japonicum*** and include hybrids between these and *L. henryi*. Collectively they comprise the most spectacular of all lily hybrids. They are late flowering and may carry several flowerheads on one stem, which is inclined to make them top heavy and in

Lilium, Asiatic Hybrid, 'Sterling Star'

Lilium, Asiatic Hybrid, 'Red Carpet'

Lilium, Asiatic Hybrid, 'Connecticut King'

L

need of support. All are intolerant of lime. There are 4 sub-groups:

Trumpet-shaped flowers: None of these are widely grown at present.

Bowl-shaped flowers: 'Carmen' with petals that are deep pink in the center and paler on the margins; **'Esperanto'** with mid-pink flowers with a yellow midrib and orange spots; **'Evelina'** and **'Ghia'** which are very similar to **'Esperanto'**; **'Louvre'** with creamy pink flowers and dark pink spots; and **'Stargazer'**, one of the most commonly grown in the whole group and the first to have upward-facing flowers—these are a rich crimson with darker spots and paler on the margins of the petals.

Flat-faced flowers: Examples include **'Acapulco'** with vivid hot-pink flowers with darker spots and frilled petals; **'Capitol'** with pure white flowers; **'Imperial Silver'** with large, shining white 6–8 in (15–20 cm) flowers with little or no other coloring apparent, although some may have small crimson dots; **'Jillian Wallace'**, whose 8 in (20 cm) flowers are watermelon pink with deep crimson spots and white margins; **'Laura Lee'** with deep pink flowers with white edges and dark pink spots; **'Maharajah'**, a short and stocky variety with flowers in 3 shades of rose pink, with no spots and very wide leaves; **'Mona Lisa'**, deep pink with white margins; and **'Yasuko'**, in which the purple spots of *L. auratum* and *L. speciosum* are minimized and the softer shades of ***L. rubellum*** predominate—the flowers are wide, up to 10 in (25 cm) in diameter and have a fine fragrance.

Recurved flowers: An example is **'Shooting Star'**, a variety with strong sturdy stems whose petals are sharply reflexed, cerise in color and 4 in (10 cm) across. ZONES 6–10.

Lilium, Oriental Hybrid, 'Stargazer'

Lilium, Oriental Hybrid, 'Mona Lisa'

Lilium, Oriental Hybrid, 'Yasuko'

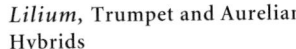

Lilium, Oriental Hybrid, 'Maharajah'

Lilium, Oriental Hybrid, 'Laura Lee'

Lilium, Oriental Hybrid, 'Carmen'

Lilium, Oriental Hybrid, 'Esperanto'

Lilium, Oriental Hybrid, 'Evelina'

Lilium, Oriental Hybrid, 'Ghia'

Lilium, Trumpet and Aurelian Hybrids

These are derived from various species with trumpet-shaped flowers such as *Lilium regale*, ***L. sulphureum*** and *L. henryi*. Most are strongly perfumed. They are divided into 4 sub-groups: **Trumpet-shaped flowers:** An example is **'Black Dragon'**, with up to 20 fragrant white flowers with maroon on the reverse of the petals that open from deep wine-red buds 6–8 in (15–20 cm) in diameter. **Bowl-shaped, outward-facing flowers: 'Hearts Desire'** has wide-flared flowers that range in color from white through yellow to gold and tangerine. **Pendent flowers: 'Thunderbolt'** has delicate pale orange flowers, up to 8 in (20 cm) across. **Star-shaped flowers: 'Sunburst'** has large, gold or orange, pink and silver flowers up to 8 in (20 cm) across with widely flared, slightly reflexed petals. ZONES 5–10.

Lilium, Oriental Hybrid, 'Louvre'

LIMNANTHES

MEADOW FOAM, POACHED EGG FLOWER

These western North American meadow plants are annuals more often cultivated in other countries. The genus consists of 7 species of plants with 5-petalled, cup-shaped flowers and bright green leaves and can be relied on to provide color from spring to fall (autumn).

CULTIVATION: They prefer damp soil and full sun as long as the roots are cool. Sow seed directly in fall or early spring and lightly cover. Staggered sowing ensures a constant display best suited to the rockery or along the pavement edge.

Lilium, Oriental Hybrid, 'Acapulco'

Lilium, Oriental Hybrid, 'Capitol'

L., Oriental Hybrid, 'Imperial Silver'

Limnanthes douglasii
MEADOW FOAM

Delightful and delicate, this 6 in (15 cm) tall plant has pale green fern-like foliage and masses of 1 in (25 mm) slightly perfumed, white-edged, golden-centered flowers. There is also a pure gold form. It is named after the early nineteenth-century collector David Douglas, who made many important finds in western North America. **ZONES 8–10.**

LIMONIUM
STATICE, SEA LAVENDER

Statice is an obsolete botanical name of this genus of around 150 species, scattered around the world's temperate regions mostly in saline coastal and desert environments, with major concentrations in the Mediterranean, central Asia and the Canary Islands. They include evergreen and deciduous subshrubs, perennials, biennials and annuals, some of the latter grown as border plants and popular for their many-colored heads of small papery flowers which can be cut and dried for decoration. The flowers should be cut just as they open and hung upside down to dry in a cool, airy place. The tapering, almost stalkless leaves appear in basal rosettes.

CULTIVATION: Statices are easily grown in full sun and well-drained, sandy soil. Their tolerance to sea spray and low rainfall make them a good choice for seaside and low-maintenance vacation house gardens. Plants will benefit from light fertilizing in spring, while the flowerheads are developing. Propagate by division in spring, from seed in early spring or fall (autumn) or from root cuttings in late winter. Transplant during winter or early spring.

Limonium brassicifolium

Limonium minutum

Limonium perezii

Limonium brassicifolium

A perennial from the Canary Islands to 8–18 in (20–45 cm) tall, this species has thick, woody stems and purple to white, tubular flowers. **ZONES 9–11.**

Limonium gmelinii

This robust perennial from eastern Europe and Siberia grows to 24 in (60 cm) tall in any deep, well-drained soil in full sun. It has leaves in spikelets and lilac tubular flowers. **ZONES 4–10.**

Limonium latifolium
syn. *Limonium platyphyllum*

From eastern Europe, this tall-stemmed perennial bears clusters of lavender-blue or white flowers over summer. Clump forming and large leafed, it grows 24 in (60 cm) tall and spreads 18 in (45 cm). The dried flower stems have a delicate appearance. **ZONES 5–10.**

Limonium gmelinii

Limnanthes douglasii

Limonium perezii

Limonium sinuatum

Limonium minutum

This spreading perennial from southern Europe reaches 4 in (10 cm) tall and is suited to rockeries. It has tiny rosettes of leaves and lilac flowers. **ZONES 8–10.**

Limonium perezii

Limonium perezii comes from the Canary Islands and is a species of more or less shrubby habit with glossy leaves. The leafless flower stems bear many small flowers, whose insignificant white petals make less impact in the garden than the long-lasting, deep mauve-blue calyces. It grows about 24 in (60 cm) tall and flowers in summer. **ZONES 9–11.**

Limonium sinuatum
syn. *Statice sinuata*

This Mediterranean species is a bushy, upright perennial almost always grown as an annual. It produces dense rosettes of oblong, deeply waved leaves and bears masses of tiny papery flowers on winged stems. It flowers in summer and early fall (autumn) and is fairly slow growing, reaching a height of 18 in (45 cm) with a spread of 12 in (30 cm). One of the most popular cut flowers, seedling strains are available in a rainbow of colors. The **Petite Bouquet Series** are dwarf plants to 12 in (30 cm) in height and with golden- or lemon-yellow, white, cream, salmon-pink, purple or blue spikelets. **ZONES 9–10.**

Limonium latifolium

L. sinuatum, **Petite Bouquet Series**

LINARIA
EGGS AND BACON, TOADFLAX

Native mainly in the Mediterranean region and western Europe, these 100 species of adaptable annuals, biennials and perennials are related to snapdragons and have naturalized in many places. They grow to 18 in (45 cm) with masses of tiny snapdragon-like blooms in many colors. The erect stems have stalkless, usually gray-green leaves. They

Lindera obtusiloba

Linaria purpurea

Linaria vulgaris

Linaria purpurea 'Canon J. Went'

are ideally suited to rock gardens, borders and cottage gardens. **CULTIVATION:** They require rich, well-drained, preferably sandy soil, moderate water and full sun. Seed sown directly in fall (autumn) or very early spring will germinate in 2 weeks. Seedlings need to be thinned to a 6 in (15 cm) spacing and weeded to ensure no over-shadowing of these fine plants. Cutting back after the first flush will produce more flowers.

Linaria alpina

This trailing perennial from Europe grows to about 3 in (8 cm) in height with a 6 in (15 cm) spread. It has violet, yellow, white or pink flowers and narrow blue-gray leaves. **ZONES 4–10.**

Linaria maroccana
BABY SNAPDRAGON, TOAD FLAX

Native to Morocco and naturalized in northeastern USA, this fast-growing, bushy annual is a useful bedding plant, giving a long and colorful display of small flowers in colors of gold, pink, mauve, apricot, cream, purple and yellow in spring. It has lance-shaped, pale green leaves and grows to a height of 4–6 in (10–15 cm) and spread of 4 in (10 cm). **Fairy Bouquet** is a mixed-color strain. **ZONES 6–10.**

Linaria purpurea
PURPLE TOADFLAX

This perennial from Europe is naturalized in some areas and grows to 3 ft (1 m). It bears violet-tinged purple flowers in summer. **'Canon J. Went'** is a tall example of the species with tiny pale pink flowers. **ZONES 6–10.**

Linaria vulgaris

A 3 ft (1 m) tall perennial that occurs wild in the Mediterranean and much of Europe, this species has reddish brown stems, numerous pale blue-green leaves and yellow flowers appearing in summer and fall (autumn). It can be grown from seed and will self-seed. It has traditional uses as a medicinal herb. **ZONES 4–10.**

LINDELOFIA

Lindelofia includes 12 species of hairy perennials native from central Asia to the Himalayas. Relatives of borage, they grow in open, rather dry areas of average to poor soil. Their basal leaves are spearhead-shaped and about 4 in (10 cm) long, while those on the branching stems are smaller and more rounded. Tubular, 2-lipped flowers in shades of bright blue or purple appear from spring to fall (autumn). **CULTIVATION:** Grow in full sun in free-draining, sandy or gravelly soil. It should

Linaria alpina

not be completely dry and a proportion of rotted organic matter worked into the soil will help retain necessary moisture. Lay straw thickly around plants in winter in cold areas. Propagate by dividing established clumps in late winter.

Lindelofia longiflora
syns *Cynoglossum longiflorum, Lindelofia anchusiflora* of gardens, *L. spectabilis*

Saved from obscurity by deep, gentian-blue flowers, this 24 in (60 cm) tall perennial forms a clump of mid-green basal leaves. In late spring and summer branching stems bear funnel-shaped, 5-lobed flowers. Grow it in mixed flower borders or in rockeries that simulate its natural environment. **ZONES 7–10.**

LINDERA

This genus of the laurel family consists of 80 species of evergreen and deciduous trees and shrubs, indigenous to eastern Asia and North America. Only a handful of cool-climate, deciduous species are grown in gardens, and these are valued for their fall (autumn) foliage. The leaves are variable, often lobed; when crushed, the foliage releases a pungent and distinctly spicy odor. Male and female flowers, both yellow, are borne on the bare branches of separate plants in early spring. The fruits are globular and berry-like.
CULTIVATION: *Lindera* species grow naturally in part-shade in acidic, humus-rich soil. Though tolerant of extreme cold, they do best if protected from late spring frosts. Plants can be propagated from seed, which should be cleaned of pulp and sown fresh. Cuttings taken in late summer are also used.

Lindera benzoin
SPICE BUSH, BENJAMIN BUSH

This deciduous shrub occurs in damp woodland areas along much of the east coast of North America. Rounded in shape, it can grow up to 10 ft (3 m) tall. Small clusters of yellow-green flowers appear in spring, followed by berries that ripen glossy bright red in late summer. The leaves, unlike those of other species, are thin and unlobed and up to 6 in (15 cm) long; they turn orange and gold in fall (autumn). **ZONES 2–10.**

Lindernia americana

Lindera obtusiloba

Native to Korea, China and Japan, this shrub or small tree may grow as high as 20 ft (6 m). The leaves, usually 3-lobed, turn pale gold in fall (autumn). The small, yellow-green flowers appear in spring, followed by shiny, black, globose fruit that are about ½ in (12 mm) in diameter. **ZONES 6–10.**

LINDERNIA

A genus of annuals and perennials from most warmer parts of the world, *Lindernia* consists of about 50 species. Related to the snapdragons and toad-flaxes, they have colorful flowers on erect racemes or arising singly from leaf axils, and fruits that are narrow capsules.
CULTIVATION: They grow well in moist soil, some liking almost boggy situations, in full sun. Propagate from fresh seed.

Lindernia americana

This species from North America has bright green, rounded, fleshy leaves. Long-tubed, violet-like flowers are borne in the leaf axils and open from spring. **ZONES 9–11.**

LINDHEIMERA
STAR DAISY

This genus consists of a single species of annual from the limestone soils of Texas, USA. It grows to just over 24 in (60 cm) tall, and has yellow flowers suitable for cutting and bright green, bract-like leaves that obscure the seed heads.
CULTIVATION: Grow this plant in moderately fertile, well-drained soil in full sun. Propagate from seed sown direct.

Lindheimera texana

This frost-hardy annual is grown for its dainty, daisy-like yellow flowers, borne in late summer and early fall (autumn). It is moderately fast growing, with hairy stems and pointed to oval, serrated, hairy fresh green leaves. Of an erect, branching habit, it grows from 12–24 in (30–60 cm) in height with a spread of 12 in (30 cm). **ZONES 6–10.**

Lindheimera texana

Linum capitatum

LINNAEA

TWIN-FLOWER

The famed eighteenth-century botanist Linnaeus named all plant genera then known, many of the names honoring his scientific contemporaries; he named this one for himself, its humble stature signifying his modesty. The sole species of the genus is a creeping evergreen shrub found in cooler northern temperate and arctic regions. It has wiry stems that spread across the ground to make a mat, and sparse pairs of circular to oval leaves. Flowering stems develop from the leaf axils, each bearing 2 pink, pendent, bell-shaped flowers marked with deep pink on the inside.

CULTIVATION: As expected of a plant from the far north, *Linnaea* is very frost hardy; indeed, it soon suffers in warm summer conditions. Plant it in a cool, moist area with loose, peaty soil and part-shade. Propagate from seed or cuttings, or by rooted runners.

Linnaea borealis

This is a tiny, mat-forming perennial that spreads to over 12 in (30 cm). It has small leaves around ½ in (12 mm) long and in summer produces pairs of small, fragrant pale pink and white flowers about ½ in (12 mm) long perched on thread-like stems 2–3 in (5–8 cm) tall. **ZONES 2–8.**

LINUM

FLAX

This genus contains 200 species of annuals, biennials, perennials, subshrubs and shrubs, some of which are evergreen, distributed widely in temperate regions. It includes the commercial flax, *Linum usitatissimum*, grown for fiber and oilseed. Several ornamental species are grown for their profusely blooming, 5-petalled flowers, which can be yellow, white, blue, red or pink. They are useful plants in a rock garden or border.

CULTIVATION: They are mostly quite frost hardy; some species need shelter in cool climates. Grow in a sunny spot in humus-rich, well-drained, peaty soil. After perennial species flower, prune them back hard. Propagate the annuals, biennials and perennials from seed in fall (autumn) and perennials by division in spring or fall. Most self-sow readily. Transplant from late fall until early spring.

Linum campanulatum

Linum arboreum

From the northern hemisphere, this sticky stemmed shrub grows to 12 in (30 cm) and has whorls of 1 in (25 mm), spatula-shaped leaves and compact heads of yellow flowers. **ZONES 8–10.**

Linum campanulatum

This small southern European perennial is reminiscent of some of the oxalises or of California poppy *(Eschscholzia californica)*. It has small, slightly glaucous leaves and during summer produces small, 3- to 5-flowered heads of yellow to orange flowers. **ZONES 7–10.**

Linum capitatum

This European rhizomatous perennial grows to about 18 in (45 cm) high. When in flower, it forms a basal clump of foliage from which emerge leafy flower stems bearing heads of 5 or more flowers. **ZONES 7–10.**

Linum flavum

GOLDEN FLAX, YELLOW FLAX

A 12–24 in (30–60 cm) tall, somewhat woody perennial with a strongly erect habit, this southern European species has dark green, pointed or blunt-ended leaves about 1 in (25 mm) long. The golden-yellow, trumpet-shaped flowers, many to each stem, appear in summer. **'Compactum'** is a dwarf variety growing just 6–8 in (15–20 cm) tall. **ZONES 5–10.**

Linum 'Gemmell's Hybrid'

This semi-evergreen perennial grows to 6 in (15 cm) and has gray-tinted, ovate leaves and yellow flowers that are borne profusely throughout summer. **ZONES 6–10.**

Linum grandiflorum

FLOWERING FLAX

Native to Algeria, this annual has small, rounded, flattish, pink to red flowers and lance-shaped, gray-green leaves. It flowers best in cool summers; the short flowering period can be extended by sowing seed at monthly intervals. It has a slim, erect habit and is fairly fast growing to a height of 18 in (45 cm) and spread of 6 in (15 cm). **'Rubrum'** has deeper crimson-red flowers. **ZONES 6–10.**

Linum narbonense

A perennial native of the Mediterranean region, this most handsome of all the blue flaxes has violet, funnel-shaped flowers borne on slender stems. The flowers last for many weeks in summer. It has soft, green leaves and forms clumps 18 in (45 cm) high and wide. **ZONES 5–10.**

Linum perenne

syn. *Linum sibiricum*

Of wide occurrence in Europe and temperate Asia, this is a vigorous, upright perennial that forms a shapely, bushy plant 24 in (60 cm) high with a spread of 12 in (30 cm). It has slender stems with grass-like leaves and clusters of open, funnel-shaped, light blue flowers are borne throughout summer. **'Alba'** is a pure white form. **ZONES 7–10.**

Linum usitatissimum

FLAX

This important fiber plant species is now thought to have originated in cultivation, its wild ancestor possibly the Mediterranean **Linum bienne**. It is a 3 ft (1 m) tall annual with lavender-blue flowers having darker veins and is grown from seed. This is the flax of commerce; the fiber from the stems is used in linen manufacture and the seeds are the source of linseed oil. It requires a rich, moist soil in full sun. **ZONES 4–11.**

LIQUIDAMBAR

This is a genus of 4 species of deciduous trees from Turkey, East Asia, North America and Mexico belonging to the witch-hazel family, grown for their shapely form, handsome foliage and superb fall (autumn) colors. The leaves are deeply lobed, resembling a typical maple leaf. Some species produce a resinous gum known as liquid storax that is used to scent soap, as an expectorant in cough remedies and in the treatment of some skin diseases.

Liquidambar formosana

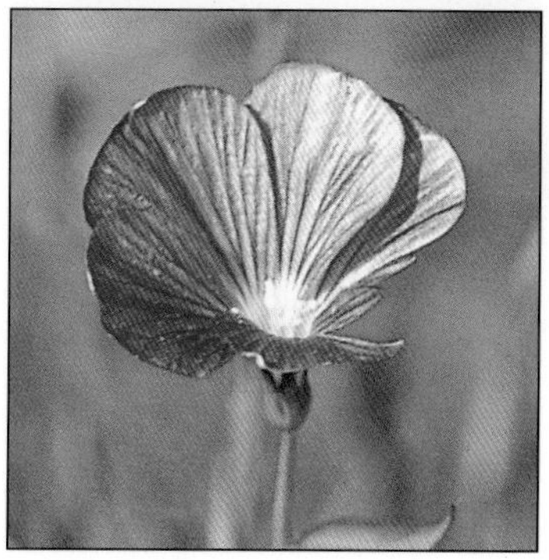

Linum narbonense

CULTIVATION: They are temperate-climate plants, requiring sun or part-shade and fertile, deep, loamy soil with adequate water during spring and summer. They will not thrive in shallow, sandy soil. The trees are best allowed to develop their lower branches to ground level. Propagate by budding in spring or from seed in fall.

Liquidambar formosana

From central and southeastern China and Taiwan, this broadly conical species grows to 40 ft (12 m) with a spread of 30 ft (10 m). Its single trunk is erect, and the horizontal branches bear large, 3-lobed, toothed leaves that are bronze when young, dark green when mature, then turn red, gold and purple in fall (autumn). The bark is grayish white. Small, yellow-green flowers appear in spring, followed by spiky, globular fruit clusters. The wood is used for making tea chests. **ZONES 7–10.**

Liquidambar orientalis

ORIENTAL SWEET GUM

This broadly conical tree from southwestern Turkey reaches 20 ft (6 m) tall with a spread of 12 ft (3.5 m). Slow growing, it bears bluntly lobed, smooth, matt green leaves that turn orange with purplish tones in fall (autumn). Small yellow-green flowers appear along with the new leaf growth, followed by clusters of small, brown, rounded fruit. Thick, orange-brown liquid storax is obtained from the bark of this species. **ZONES 8–11.**

Liquidambar orientalis

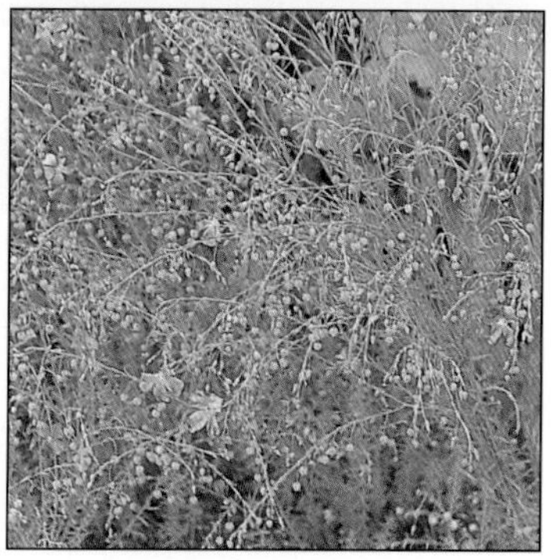

Linum usitatissimum

Liquidambar styraciflua
SWEET GUM

This widely grown deciduous tree is native to eastern USA and Mexico and reaches a height of 80 ft (24 m) and spread of 40 ft (12 m). The young branches and twigs often have distinctive ridges of corky bark and the wood of this species, known commercially as satin walnut, is used for furniture-making. It bears glossy dark green leaves that color orange to red and purple in fall (autumn). Globular heads of small yellow-green flowers appear in spring, followed by spiky, ball-like fruit clusters. Some *Liquidamber styraciflua* cultivars valued for their rich fall coloring include **'Moraine'**; **'Burgundy'**: deep purple-red; **'Festival'**: pink through yellow; **'Palo Alto'**: orange-red; **'Rotundiloba'**, an odd form with the leaves having very rounded lobes, as the name suggests; **'Variegata'**: streaked yellow; and **'Worplesdon'**: purple through orange-yellow. ZONES 5–11.

LIRIODENDRON
TULIP TREE

Some botanists dispute there being 2 species in this genus; they prefer to recognize only one, *Liriodendron tulipifera,* regarding *L. chinense* as a variety of this. The majority, however, accept the two. Their 4-lobed leaves distinguish them at once from all other trees: they look as though someone has cut their ends off with scissors. The flowers are distinctive too, in pale green with orange at the bases of their petals and numerous stamens. They do not, in fact, look very much like tulips, but are more like their cousins the magnolias. They are both handsome trees, with straight boles and symmetrical crowns, though they are too large, and fast growing to be suitable for any but the largest of gardens.
CULTIVATION: They prefer a temperate climate, sun or part-shade and deep, fertile, well-drained, slightly acidic soil and are propagated from seed or by grafting. They are difficult to transplant.

Liquidambar styraciflua 'Worplesdon'

Liriodendron chinense
CHINESE TULIP TREE

From China, this deciduous tree is the smallest and denser of the 2 species, reaching a height of 80 ft (24 m) and a spread of 40 ft (12 m). Fast growing with a broadly columnar habit, it bears dark green, lobed leaves that turn yellow in fall (autumn). The leaf undersides are gray-blue and covered with minute hairs. The flowers are borne singly on the ends of shoots in mid-summer, followed by conical, pale brown clusters of fruit that fall apart when ripe. ZONES 8–10.

Liriodendron tulipifera

From eastern USA, this is an outstanding tree for cool climates, reaching 100 ft (30 m) or more with a spread of about 50 ft (15 m). A vigorous grower with a broadly conical habit, it bears deep green, lobed leaves that turn rich golden yellow in fall (autumn). Its summer-blooming flowers are followed by conical brown fruit. The pale timber, called 'yellow poplar', is not very hard or durable but is fairly light and strong and much used in furniture-making. **'Aureomarginatum'** has green leaves heavily edged with yellow; **'Fastigiatum'** is about half the size, with an erect, columnar form. ZONES 4–10.

Liquidambar styraciflua 'Rotundiloba'

Liquidambar styraciflua 'Variegata'

Liquidambar styraciflua

Liquidambar styraciflua 'Variegata'

Liriodendron chinense

Liriodendron tulipifera

Liriodendron tulipifera

L. tulipifera 'Aureomarginatum'

LIRIOPE

This genus contains 5 species of clump-forming, rhizomatous, evergreen perennials native to Vietnam, China, Taiwan and Japan. Some cultivars are so dark in leaf they are practically black, a most unusual color for the designer to play with. They do not creep, and for ground cover have to be planted 6 in (15 cm) apart. *Liriope* flowers range from white through to pale purple.
CULTIVATION: Grow in full sun or part-shade in well-drained soil. In early spring cut back shabby leaves, just before the new ones appear. Propagate from seed in fall (autumn) or by division in early spring.

Liriope muscari 'Variegata'

Liriope muscari
syns *Liriope platyphylla, L. graminifolia*

This clumping, evergreen perennial is a useful casual ground cover or path edging. It has grass-like, shining, dark green leaves and bears erect spikes of rounded, bell-shaped, violet flowers in late summer. It grows to a height of 12–24 in (30–60 cm) with a spread of 18 in (45 cm), with flower spikes held just above the foliage. **'Lilac Beauty'** comes from China and Japan and is a larger example of the species; the leaves are 1 in (25 mm) wide and 12–18 in (30–45 cm) long with stiff lilac flowers rising above the foliage. **'Majestic'** has large violet-blue flowers. **'Variegata'** is the most common of the variegated forms—the leaf margins are lined with cream and it has lovely lilac flowers. ZONES 6–10.

Liriope spicata
syn. *Ophiopogon spicatus*

There is some confusion between the closely related genera *Liriope* and

Liriope muscari

Liriope muscari 'Lilac Beauty'

Ophiopogon, and it is possible to buy this evergreen species under either name. It has 10 in (25 cm) tall tufts of grassy, dark green leaves and can grow in either bright shade or in gloomy positions. Spikes of bell-shaped, pale lilac flowers appear in late summer. **'Silver Dragon'** is an evergreen, creeping perennial with grass-like, variegated leaves 18 in (45 cm) long and a mat of lilac flowers in summer. **ZONES 4–10.**

LITCHI

LYCHEE

This genus consists of just one evergreen tree from southern China and Southeast Asia, which is grown throughout the subtropics for its foliage and delicious fruit. The lychee is grown commercially by air layering or grafting of superior named varieties.
CULTIVATION: It requires full sun and shelter from wind and cold, although it can withstand an occasional light frost, and it prefers deep, moist soil and regular water. Propagate from seed in summer or by budding in spring. Trees raised from seed start to bear fruit after about 5 years.

Litchi chinensis

A graceful, slim-trunked tree, the lychee reaches a height of 30 ft (9 m) and a spread of 10–15 ft (3–4.5 m). Bright green compound leaves, gold or pink when young, form a low-spreading crown. Clusters of small, petal-less, greenish yellow flowers are borne in abundance in spring, followed by the bright red, edible fruit which enclose a brown seed. The fruit contain a sweet whitish pulp reminiscent in texture and flavor to that of grapes. **ZONES 10–11.**

LITHOCARPUS

This large genus comprises 300 species of evergreen trees and shrubs from Asia, plus a single species, *Lithocarpus densiflorus*, from California and Oregon. In appearance they fall somewhere between the oak and the chestnut. Their flower clusters are similar to that of the chestnut and their fruits, like those of the oak, are acorns.
CULTIVATION: Grown for their foliage, these cool-climate plants require sun or part-shade and well-drained, neutral to acidic soil. Young trees should be sheltered from strong winds. Propagation is from seed in fall (autumn); the trees are difficult to transplant.

Lithocarpus densiflorus

Lithodora diffusa

Lithocarpus densiflorus

TANBARK OAK, TAN OAK

This species from western USA reaches a height of 80 ft (24 m) or more. The leaves are covered with thick, pale orange felt when young, becoming smooth and glossy green with maturity. The tiny, pale yellow male flowers, densely packed in narrow catkins, are borne in spring and often again in fall (autumn). The female flowers and acorns, which mature in their second year, come in stout, stiff spikes below the male catkins. Tannins used in the leather industry are obtained from the thick, scaly bark. **ZONES 7–10.**

Lithocarpus edulis

This small tree or shrub, native to Japan, grows to 30 ft (9 m) in cultivation and has leaves that are a glossy yellow-green above and gray-green below. The flowers are grouped together in 2s or 3s on a glabrous spike. **ZONES 7–10.**

LITHODORA

This genus of 7 species of dwarf evergreen subshrubs and shrubs from Europe, Turkey and North Africa is well suited to rockeries. Most are known for their 5-lobed, funnel-shaped intense blue flowers, borne over a long season in small sprays at the growth tips. The deep green leaves are hairy.
CULTIVATION: Most species prefer well-drained, alkaline soil; water lightly even in summer. They do well in full sun if grown in not too hot an area. Shearing after flowering will promote a compact habit and encourage dense flowering the following year. Propagate from cuttings of last year's growth and strike in a mix of peat and sand.

Lithocarpus densiflorus

Lithodora diffusa 'Grace Ward'

Lithodora diffusa 'Heavenly Blue'

Lithodora 'Star'

Lithodora diffusa

syn. *Lithospermum diffusum*

This spindly subshrub cannot tolerate lime at all and is suited to cool-temperate gardens. It grows to 4–12 in (10–30 cm) tall with masses of vivid blue flowers, somewhat star-shaped, and makes a stunning ground cover or rockery specimen. **'Grace Ward'**, an evergreen, semi-prostrate shrub, grows to 6–12 in (15–30 cm) tall with a spread of 12 in (30 cm). It has trailing stems, hairy dull green leaves and masses of funnel-shaped deep blue flowers. **'Heavenly Blue'** is similar, although perhaps slightly more compact. **ZONES 7–10.**

Lithodora oleifolia

This spreading, evergreen shrub grows 6–18 in (15–20 cm) tall and 3 ft (1 m) wide. It has oval silky leaves, curving stems and small, funnel-shaped, light blue flowers. **ZONES 7–10.**

Lithodora 'Star'

syn. *Lithospermum* 'Star'

This shrub grows to 12 in (30 cm) in height and has star-shaped, lilac flowers with a purple stripe down the center of each lobe. **ZONES 7–10.**

LITHOPS

LIVING STONES, STONEFACE

Confined in the wild to the driest western part of South Africa's Cape Province and the adjacent part of Namibia, this fascinating genus of the mesembryanthemum alliance contains about 40 extreme succulents, which develop singly or in colonies. They are composed of pairs of extremely fleshy, upright leaves fused together to form a cylindrical or hemispherical mass with a deep crevice running across the top. New leaf-pairs and white or yellow daisy-like flowers grow up through the fissure. The plants look like smooth river stones, explaining the genus and common names, and often have translucent upper surfaces.
CULTIVATION: These frost-tender succulents are easy to grow but require very dry conditions, so need to be kept under shelter in all but arid climates. Plant in coarse, gritty soil and allow full sun. Water only in spring and propagate in summer from seed or by dividing bodies and treating them like cuttings.

Litchi chinensis

Lithops divergens

This species from Cape Province has the shoots more deeply divided than most into 2 distinct, semi-cylindrical leaves. Yellow daisy-like flowers are produced in fall (autumn). **ZONES 9–11.**

Livistona rotundifolia

Lithops divergens

Lobelia cultivar

Lithops karasmontana subsp. *bella*
syn. *Lithops bella*

This cluster-forming perennial has egg-shaped bodies up to $1\frac{1}{2}$ in (35 mm) tall and 1 in (25 mm) in diameter. These are composed of yellowish brown, compressed leaves with dark brown lines on the markedly curving crown. In summer to fall (autumn), snow-white flowers appear from the crown's crevice. **ZONES 9–11.**

Lithops turbiniformis

Lithops turbiniformis forms in small clumps of paired leaves. Egg-shaped and orange-brown in color, they are up to 1 in (25 mm) in height. The flattened surface is scored with a shallow, transverse crevice and brown linear markings. Vivid yellow flowers up to 2 in (5 cm) in diameter bloom from white buds. **ZONES 9–11.**

Livistona australis

Livistona chinensis

LITTONIA

This genus, allied to *Gloriosa*, consists of 8 species of tuberous perennial climbers from southern Africa, tropical West Africa and the Arabian peninsula that cling by means of tendrils that extend from the leaf tips; they require a trellis or wires around which to twine. Their pendent, bell-shaped flowers are borne in summer.
CULTIVATION: Grow in full sun in moist, peaty, well-drained loam with some sand and leaf litter compost. They require regular watering and misting to increase humidity once established. Littonias thrive in pots on terraces and can be grown in the open if the winters are mild. Propagate from seed or by dividing tubers.

Littonia modesta
CLIMBING LILY, CLIMBING BELL

This southern African species reaches 6 ft (1.8 m), climbing up stakes or other plants by means of leaf tendrils that wind around the supports. In summer it produces masses of $1\frac{1}{2}$ in (35 mm) yellow-orange, bell-shaped, nodding flowers at the leaf axils. The leaves are a bright glossy green. **ZONES 9–11.**

LIVISTONA

This is a genus of about 30 species of medium to tall fan palms, about half of them endemic to Australia, the remainder scattered through the Malay Archipelago and southern Asia with a single species recently identified in desert oases of southern Arabia and Djibouti. Most feature large, almost circular, pleated fronds up to 5 ft (1.5 m) across forming a dense crown from which dead fronds may remain hanging for some time. The frond stalks are usually long and are edged with sharp prickles. These palms are widely used for outdoor landscaping; their clusters of blue, black or rarely reddish fruits and tapering frond segments are shown to great effect.
CULTIVATION: Some species will tolerate frosts down to about 25°F (–4°C), although they do best in subtropical, frost-free areas. Slow growing, they prefer deep, sandy soil and, while they tolerate full sun, they produce more vigorous, deeper green foliage in dappled shade. They make excellent indoor or outdoor container plants. Propagate from seed in summer.

Livistona australis
AUSTRALIAN FAN PALM, CABBAGE-TREE PALM

Widely distributed along the east coast of Australia south of the Tropic of Capricorn, this is one of the tallest species, growing to 80 ft (24 m) in the wild. The slender brown trunk shows the scars left by the shed fronds. The large, rounded leaves are held at the apex of the trunk, allowing understory plants such as ferns to grow under mature specimens. Long sprays of small yellow flowers are borne in spring. The common names refer to the highly nutritious apical bud, which was eaten by Aborigines and early European settlers. **ZONES 9–12.**

Livistona chinensis
syn. *Livistona oliviformis*
CHINESE FAN PALM, CHINESE FOUNTAIN PALM

This palm from islands to the south of China and Japan will reach a height of 20–40 ft (6–12 m); it is quite fast growing in the tropics, slow in temperate climates. Its single trunk is rough textured, and the large fronds held on relatively short stalks have very long, attractively drooping segments giving a curtain-like effect. The fruit are somewhat elongated, about $\frac{3}{4}$ in (18 mm) long and ripen to china blue. A useful container specimen, it is one of the most frost-hardy palms and has been grown outdoors in sheltered gardens in southern England. **ZONES 8–11.**

Livistona rotundifolia

This attractive fan palm from the Philippines and Indonesia grows to 80 ft (24 m). It has spherical scarlet fruit that eventually ripen black and will grow in moist soil in the tropics. The seed remains viable for a longer period than most palms, and it can be grown from seed in a deep container. **ZONES 11–12.**

Lithops turbiniformis

Livistona saribus
syn. *Livistona cochinchinensis*

This fan palm from tropical Asia and the Malay Archipelago grows to 80 ft (24 m) tall. It has quite large blue fruit like those of *Livistona chinensis* and small clusters of yellow flowers. It is distinctive for the frond stalks of younger trees being wickedly armed with very large, curved prickles. **ZONES 11–12.**

LOBELIA

This genus of 370 species of annuals, perennials and shrubs is widely distributed in temperate regions, particularly the Americas and Africa. Growth habits vary from low bedding plants to tall herbaceous perennials or shrubs. They are all grown for their ornamental flowers and neat foliage and make excellent edging, flower box, hanging basket and rock-garden specimens. Some are suitable in wild gardens or by the waterside.
CULTIVATION: These frost-hardy to somewhat frost-tender plants are best grown in well-drained, moist, light loam enriched with animal manure or compost. Most grow in sun or part-shade but resent wet conditions in winter. Prune after the first flush of flowers to encourage repeat flowering, and fertilize weekly with a liquid manure during the season. Propagate annuals from seed in spring, perennial species from seed or by division in spring or fall (autumn) and perennial cultivars by division only. Transplant from late fall until early spring.

Lobelia alata
ANGLED LOBELIA

Native to temperate southern parts of Australia, Africa and South America, this slender, creeping species grows to 15 in (38 cm) tall with a spread of 3 ft (1 m), making a tangle of soft, angled stems with very narrow leaves. It bears tiny blue or lilac flowers in summer. It grows well in moist soil in full sun or shade. In the wild it commonly grows in damp spots on rocky seashores, tolerating salt spray. **ZONES 9–11.**

Lobelia cardinalis
CARDINAL FLOWER

This clump-forming perennial from eastern North America is useful for growing in wet places and beside streams and ponds. From late summer to mid-fall (mid-autumn) it produces spikes of brilliant, scarlet-red flowers on branching stems above green or deep

Littonia modesta

Lobelia laxiflora

Lobelia cardinalis

bronze-purple foliage. It grows to a height of 3 ft (1 m) and a spread of 12 in (30 cm). **ZONES 3–10.**

Lobelia erinus
EDGING LOBELIA

This slow-growing, compact annual is native to South Africa and grows to a height of 4–8 in (10–20 cm) and spread of 4–6 in (10–15 cm). It has a tufted, often semi-trailing habit, with dense oval to lance-shaped leaves tapering at the base. It bears small, 2-lipped pinkish purple flowers continuously from spring to early fall (autumn). **'Cambridge Blue'** is a popular hybrid along with **'Color Cascade'**, with a mass of blue to violet to pink and white flowers. **'Crystal Palace'** is a very small variety with dense foliage and is smothered in deep violet-blue flowers. **ZONES 7–11.**

Lobelia × *gerardii*

A hybrid between the North American species *Lobelia cardinalis* and *L. siphilitica*, this robust perennial can grow as tall as 5 ft (1.5 m). It has pink, violet or purple flowers and makes a beautiful garden specimen. **'Vedrariensis'** is its best-known cultivar, producing racemes of violet-blue flowers in late summer; its leaves are dark green and lance-shaped. These hybrids prefer to grow in moist but well-drained soil in full sun. **ZONES 7–10.**

Lobelia erinus 'Crystal Palace'

Lobelia membranacea 'Blue Carpet'

Lobelia siphilitica

Lobelia gibberoa

This spectacular giant lobelia from the mountains of Africa can reach 30 ft (9 m) in height. It is rarely seen away from its homelands as it is not very amenable to cultivation. **ZONES 9–10.**

Lobelia × *gerardii* 'Vedrariensis'

Lobelia × *gerardii*

Lobelia keniensis

Kilimanjaro, Kenya, Ruwenzori, Elgon—these and other volcanic massifs reaching heights of more than 10,000 ft (3,000 m) in tropical eastern Africa are the habitats of the giant lobelias, each massif having its own distinct group of species. As the name suggests, *Lobelia keniensis* comes from Mt Kenya, where it occurs in large numbers in the heath zone not far below the permanent snow. **ZONES 9–10.**

Lobelia laxiflora
TORCH LOBELIA

This clump-forming evergreen subshrub from Mexico and Guatemala grows to more than 3 ft (1 m) high and 24 in (60 cm) wide and has arching leafy canes with axillary clusters of slender-stalked tubular red and yellow flowers. It is marginally frost hardy and blooms for much of the year in warm climates; in cooler areas it is grown as a conservatory plant. An annual trim will keep it from becoming leggy. **ZONES 9–11.**

Lobelia membranacea

This mat-forming perennial is a native of tropical Queensland, Australia, where it grows in rainforest clearings. It has fine creeping stems that root as they spread and tiny dark green leaves. Pale blue flowers are borne singly on short stalks just above the foliage in spring and summer. **'Blue Carpet'** is a trade name for a form which is hardly distinguishable from the species in general, though the flowers are profuse and a fine blue. It requires moist, humus-rich soil and regular watering. **ZONES 10–12.**

Lobelia 'Queen Victoria'

Spikes of blood-red flowers on branching stems appear from late summer to mid-fall (mid-autumn) on this clump-forming perennial. The foliage is a deep purple-red and it grows to 3 ft (1 m) high and 12 in (30 cm) wide. **ZONES 3–10.**

Lobelia siphilitica
BLUE CARDINAL FLOWER, BIG BLUE LOBELIA

This frost-hardy perennial from eastern USA bears racemes of 2-lipped violet-blue flowers in late summer and fall (autumn). It reaches a height of 2–3 ft (60–90 cm) and does well in moist, heavy soil. Along with other North American lobelias this was formerly employed as a powerful drug, allegedly effective in treatment of syphilis among other diseases, but they are all quite toxic. **ZONES 5–9.**

Lobelia erinus 'Cambridge Blue'

Lobelia erinus

Lobelia gibberoa

Lobelia keniensis

L

Lobelia × *speciosa*

This is one of a group of hybrid lobelias derived from the American species *Lobelia cardinalis, L. splendens* and *L. siphilitica*, noted for their tall spikes of flowers that range in color from pink to mauve, red or purple. **ZONES 4–10.**

Lobelia splendens

syn. ***Lobelia fulgens***

SCARLET LOBELIA

Native to southern USA and Mexico, *Lobelia splendens* bears tubular, 2-lipped, scarlet flowers in one-sided racemes in late summer. It has lance-shaped, mid-green leaves that are sometimes flushed red, and grows 3 ft (1 m) tall. **ZONES 8–10.**

Lodoicea maldivica (fruit)

Lodoicea maldivica

Lobelia tupa

This vigorous, upright perennial from Chile is a rather coarse plant with large, light gray-green leaves and grows to about 6 ft (1.8 m) in height. In late summer and fall (autumn) the stems terminate in striking many-flowered erect racemes of tubular, 2-lipped flowers in shades from scarlet to deep, dull scarlet. **ZONES 8–10.**

LOBULARIA

This genus consists of 5 species of frost-hardy, dwarf plants from the Mediterranean and the Canary Islands; they are useful for rockeries, window boxes and borders. Although there are both annual and perennial forms, the annuals are most commonly grown. They bear tiny 4-petalled, fragrant flowers in compact, terminal racemes in summer and early fall (autumn).

CULTIVATION: Grow in full sun in fertile, well-drained soil. Continuous flowering can be encouraged by regular deadheading. Propagate from seed in spring or, if used outdoors, from late spring to fall.

Lobularia maritima

syn. ***Alyssum maritimum***

SWEET ALYSSUM, SWEET ALICE

This fast-growing, spreading annual is a widely popular edging, rock-garden or window box plant. It produces masses of tiny, honey-scented, 4-petalled white

Lobularia maritima 'Violet Queen'

Lobularia maritima

Lobelia × *speciosa*

Lobelia splendens

flowers over a long season, from spring to early fall (autumn). Lilac, pink and violet shades are also available. It has a low, rounded, compact habit with lance-shaped, grayish green leaves, and grows to a height of 3–12 in (8–30 cm) and a spread of 8–12 in (20–30 cm). **'Violet Queen'** is the darkest of the garden varieties of sweet Alice. **ZONES 7–10.**

LODOICEA

SEYCHELLES NUT, COCO-DE-MER, DOUBLE COCONUT

This remarkable palm genus consists of a single species, the famous 'double coconut', found only on the small islands of Praslin and Curieuse in the Indian Ocean Seychelles group. Despite the common name, it is not closely related to the feather-leafed coconut palm but is a close ally of the African doum palms *(Hyphaene)* and like them has massive fan-like fronds that radiate from the top of a tall trunk, unbranched in the case of *Lodoicea*. It is famous for having the largest single-seeded fruit of any plant, with a curious 2-lobed shape resembling large buttocks; these roll down the steep slopes of their native islands and may be carried away by the ocean—they were familiar as flotsam centuries before the palms were discovered, and were the source of several strange myths. Germination of the seeds is a remarkable process, with a cotyledon the thickness of a man's arm and up to 12 ft (3.5 m) long emerging over a period of months and finally producing roots and shoots from its tip.

CULTIVATION: It is suitable for outdoor growth only in the humid tropics in full

Lobularia maritima

Lobelia tupa

sun in deep, moist, fertile loam. Propagate from seed, for which special provision needs to made on account of its mode of germination and which requires warmth and high humidity.

Lodoicea maldivica

This palm, healthy specimens of which can be seen in a number of tropical botanical gardens, grows to 100 ft (30 m) tall and has large 18 in (45 cm) fruit that resemble a wooden heart and weigh up to 40 lb (18 kg). The main source of seed is still the wild stands of palms in the Seychelles, the islands government selling them to tourists at quite high prices. **ZONE 12.**

LOLIUM

RYE GRASS

There are about 8 species of annual or perennial grasses in this Eurasian genus. They have no ornamental value but are frequently cultivated as pasture grasses and are often found in lawns, although their presence may be unwelcome; they bear characteristic spikes with 2 appressed rows of green spikelets, which shed abundant pollen in late spring or early summer, a prime cause of hay fever in some parts of the world. The small grains that follow are carried by wind or water and germinate freely.

CULTIVATION: These are adaptable grasses and will grow in most well-drained soils in full sun; they benefit from regular watering. Propagation is from seed.

Lolium perenne
PERENNIAL RYE GRASS

This short-lived, clumping perennial species, originating in Europe and naturalized in most other temperate regions of the world, grows up to 18 in (45 cm) tall and 12 in (30 cm) wide. It has smooth, whippy stems that tend to lie down under the lawn mower, springing back up later. The flat blades are glossy and dark green. The tiny flowers, which appear in late spring and summer, are borne in narrow spikes 6 in (15 cm) long. It is a very coarse grass needing frequent mowing, and best for rough areas rather than for fine lawn. **ZONES 5–10.**

LOMANDRA
MAT RUSH

This genus of grass-like rhizomatous perennials and subshrubs consists of 50 species, all native to Australia though 2 extend to New Guinea and one to New Caledonia. Its relationships have long been a matter of debate and it has variously been grouped with the rushes, the lilies and the Australian grass-trees (*Xanthorrhoea*) but it is now placed in a family of its own together with several other small Australian genera of similar form. The tough, leathery leaves are either flat, channelled or cylindrical. Male and female flowers, mostly cream to yellow and often inconspicuous, are borne on separate plants.
CULTIVATION: Mostly rather frost-tender these plants prefer full sun (or part-shade where heat is extreme) and well-drained, fairly poor soil. They are tolerant of dry conditions. Propagate from seed or by division.

Lomandra longifolia
SPINY HEADED MAT RUSH, HONEY REED

A ubiquitous native of coastal eastern Australia and growing to over 3 ft (1 m) high and 4 ft (1.2 m) wide, this species makes dense tussocks of narrow strap-like leaves, varying from deep green to somewhat bluish green. The yellow or cream blossoms have a strong honey smell and are carried on dense, flattened panicles with many spiny (though not fiercely so) bracts. Only recently brought into general cultivation, it has been taken up enthusiastically by public authorities in Australia for mass planting on highway embankments and median strips, and for large-scale landscaping in parks, requiring no maintenance once established. **ZONES 9–11.**

Lonicera etrusca

Lomandra longifolia

LOMATIA

From both sides of the South Pacific in eastern Australia and Chile, these 12 species of evergreen shrubs and trees are members of the protea family. They have leathery leaves which vary from toothed to deeply and finely dissected, and grevillea-like flowers which have distinctive spidery, twisted petals and styles which uncurl from the buds. The fruits are pod-like, somewhat woody follicles.
CULTIVATION: Mostly plants for cool but mild, humid climates, they require sun or part-shade and sandy, acidic, well-drained soil, preferably rich in organic matter. Some are moderately frost hardy but will need shelter from cold winds. Propagate from cuttings or seed in summer.

Lomatia ferruginea
RUST BUSH

Native to southern Chile and Argentina, this tall shrub or small tree grows to 30 ft (9 m) tall often with erect branches from the base. The new growths are covered with a brown, felt-like down; the fern-like, divided leaves consist of many olive-green leaflets. The flowers, which appear in late winter and spring, are produced in dense, branched spikes from the leaf axils; each flower has a red base, grading to yellow-green at the petal tips.
ZONES 8–10.

Lomatia silaifolia
CRINKLE BUSH

From coastal areas of southeastern Australia, this several-stemmed shrub grows from a woody root-mass to about 5 ft (1.5 m) tall and has 8 in (20 cm), deeply dissected leaves that are silky when young. It produces showy long terminal panicles of white flowers in summer. **ZONES 9–11.**

Lonicera × americana

Lomatia ferruginea

Lonicera deflexicalyx

Lomatia tinctoria
GUITAR PLANT

This low shrub from Tasmania has a dense, suckering habit with often rather tangled stems and smallish gray-green leaves that are variably dissected into narrow segments. In summer creamy white flowers are borne on erect sprays above the foliage. It grows to about 3 ft (1 m) tall; this shrub is quite easily cultivated and tolerates moderate shade to full sun. **ZONES 8–10.**

LONICERA
HONEYSUCKLE, WOODBINE

This diverse genus, of wide occurrence in the northern hemisphere, consists of around 180 species of shrubs and woody twining climbers, both evergreen and deciduous. They have leaves in opposite pairs and mostly smooth-edged, and flowers that are 2-lipped with a short to long tube, usually sweetly scented and yielding nectar to visiting bees or birds. Many honeysuckle species and their hybrids are valued garden plants, hardy, long lived and disease free though often becoming straggly unless pruned annually. The shrub species are excellent for borders, while the climbers can be used to cover trellises, walls or fences.
CULTIVATION: They are plants of temperate climates, easily grown in sun or light shade and not fussy about soil. They benefit from regular pruning to keep them from becoming hopeless tangles. Propagate from seed in fall (autumn) or spring or from cuttings in summer or late fall. Watch for aphids.

Lonicera × americana

Despite its name this deciduous, twining honeysuckle is a hybrid between 2 European species, *Lonicera caprifolium* and *L. etrusca*. It can grow up to 25 ft (8 m) high, though usually trimmed to lesser height. It has oval leaves and clusters of strongly perfumed, yellow flowers flushed red-purple. **ZONES 6–10.**

Lomatia silaifolia

Lolium perenne

Lonicera caprifolium
ITALIAN HONEYSUCKLE

Native to southern Europe and growing up to 20 ft (6 m), this species has light green, oval, pointed leaves that are joined at the base. Highly scented, yellow flowers tinted with pink on the outside appear in spring, followed by orange fruit that are very attractive to birds.
ZONES 5–9.

Lonicera deflexicalyx

Native to China and Tibet, this species is a 5 ft (1.5 m) tall deciduous shrub with purple-red stems, 3 in (8 cm) long, pointed oval leaves and paired, small yellow flowers. The flowers are produced in the leaf axils in spring and summer and are followed by small pink berries.
ZONES 5–10.

Lonicera etrusca
ETRUSCAN HONEYSUCKLE

This is a deciduous or semi-evergreen vine from the Mediterranean growing to just over 12 ft (3.5 m). It has slender woody stems, dull green leaves and tubular, scented, cream tinged with purple flowers in spring and summer; small red berries follow. This species requires protection where late frosts are likely. **'Superba'** bears clusters of creamy flowers that eventually turn orange.
ZONES 7–10.

L

Lonicera × heckrottii

Lonicera korolkowii

Lonicera japonica

Lonicera henryi

Lonicera hispida var. *bracteata*

Lonicera fragrantissima

Lonicera fragrantissima

WINTER HONEYSUCKLE

From China, this bushy, deciduous or semi-evergreen shrub reaches a height of 6–8 ft (1.8–2.4 m) with a spread of 10 ft (3 m). The most fragrant of the shrubby species, winter honeysuckle bears short creamy white flowers in pairs, in some forms stained with rose carmine, in winter and early spring. The berries are dark red. The new dark green oval leaves appear shortly after the flowers and except in the coldest climates, many of these will hang on the plant through winter. **ZONES 4–10.**

Lonicera × heckrottii

EVERBLOOMING HONEYSUCKLE, GOLDFLAME HONEYSUCKLE

Believed to have originated from a cross between *Lonicera × americana* and *L. sempervirens* this deciduous, woody vine is valued for its magnificent flower colors and exceptionally long bloom period: late spring through summer with an occasional recurrent bloom in fall (autumn). In bud the flowers are brilliant carmine, revealing a lustrous yellow throat as the corolla opens. Once opened the outside changes to a true pink. The fruit are red. The foliage emerges reddish purple and matures to a lustrous blue-green. It reaches 10–20 ft (3–6 m) in height. **ZONES 5–9.**

Lonicera henryi

A 30 ft (10 m) evergreen vine from China, this species has vigorous woody stems, glossy green leaves and red or yellow tubular flowers in spring and summer, followed by purple-black berries. **ZONES 4–10.**

Lonicera hildebrandiana

GIANT HONEYSUCKLE, BURMESE HONEYSUCKLE

This evergreen or semi-evergreen climber from southern China and Southeast Asia, reaches up to at least 30 ft (9 m), with vigorously twining branches and large glossy leaves. It has the longest flowers in the genus, about 4 in (10 cm) long with a curved tube and recurving lips, cream at first but soon aging to orange; borne through summer, they are only faintly scented and are followed by green fruit. It needs strong support and is marginally frost hardy. **ZONES 9–11.**

Lonicera hispida var. *bracteata*

This deciduous shrub grows to 5 ft (1.5 m) high with an equal or slightly wider spread. A native of Turkestan, it has 3 in (8 cm) long leaves and funnel-shaped, pale yellow flowers a little over 1 in (25 mm) long, followed by bright red berries. **ZONES 6–10.**

Lonicera involucrata

TWINBERRY

From western North America and Mexico, this deciduous shrub has fascinating flowers, with 2 tubular, red-suffused yellow blooms, each around ½ in (12 mm) long, almost joined at the base and backed by broad green bracts that redden with age. They are followed by round black berries still surrounded by the bright red bracts. **ZONES 4–10.**

Lonicera japonica

JAPANESE HONEYSUCKLE

This vigorous climber from eastern Asia, growing to 30 ft (9 m), has glossy, dark green leaves. Pairs of fragrant white flowers, ageing yellow or sometimes purple tinged, appear in late summer to fall (autumn); black berries follow. This species can become an invasive weed, although it is very useful as a ground cover or to quickly hide fences and posts. **'Aurea-reticulata'** has attractive, gold-veined leaves but bears only a few flowers; **'Halliana'** with bright green oval leaves and perfumed, small white flowers that age to yellow, has been used in Chinese medicine since the Tang dynasty in 659 AD. **ZONES 4–10.**

Lonicera korolkowii

From Turkestan, this deciduous shrub grows to 10 ft (3 m) high and wide. It has bluish green heart-shaped leaves, tubular reddish pink flowers and red berries in fall (autumn). It is grown from cuttings. **ZONES 5–10.**

Lonicera ledebourii

syn. *Lonicera involucrata* var. *ledebourii*

This is a large deciduous shrub from California, its upright branches wreathed in early summer with scentless but brightly colored yellow and orange flowers that grow in pairs in the axils of the leaves. Black berries are backed with red bracts. It can grow to well over head height; prune after blooming to control its size. **ZONES 6–10.**

Lonicera nitida

Lonicera hildebrandiana

Lonicera maackii

Growing to 15 ft (4.5 m) high, this deciduous shrub from China, Korea and Japan has white fragrant flowers that yellow with age and dark red fruit. It can be grown from seed. **ZONES 2–9.**

Lonicera myrtillus

This Himalayan shrub grows to 3 ft (1 m) tall and has 1 in (25 mm) long oval leaves. The fragrant cream flowers are just over ¼ in (6 mm) long. These are followed by orange-red fruit that can be as much of a feature as the flowers. **ZONES 6–10.**

Lonicera nitida

BOX HONEYSUCKLE

An evergreen shrub endemic to Yunnan and Sichuan, China, this is possibly the smallest-leafed honeysuckle, forming a dense bush composed of masses of fine twigs bearing tightly packed, ½ in (12 mm) long, leathery, dark green glossy leaves. Gold and variegated foliage forms, such as **'Aurea'**, are available. The small, creamy white, spring-borne flowers are not showy and the purple fruit are rarely seen in cultivation, so it is best regarded as a foliage plant. It withstands heavy trimming and is often used for hedging. **'Baggesen's Gold'** has tiny, bright yellow leaves, insignificant yellowish green flowers and mauve fruit. **ZONES 6–10.**

Lonicera oblongifolia

SWAMP FLY

This shrubby species from northeastern North America grows to 5 ft (1.5 m) in height and has yellowish white flowers and red fruit. **ZONES 3–10.**

Lonicera periclymenum

WOODBINE

This deliciously scented climber has long been a favorite for its delightful scent. It is a vigorous, twining, evergreen climber

Lonicera oblongifolia

Lonicera maackii

Lonicera tatarica

Lonicera sempervirens 'Superba'

Lonicera myrtillus

Lonicera quinquelocularis

Lonicera × *tellmanniana*

native to the UK and much of Europe, opening its small white and cream, sometimes pink and cream, flowers at mid-summer. It reaches 20 ft (6 m) in height. **'Graham Thomas'** has oval to oblong leaves and fragrant white flowers; it has been used in folk medicine for many centuries but the red berries are harmful if eaten untreated. **'Serotina'**, known as late Dutch honeysuckle, has fragrant, tubular, dark purple flowers with pink centers. **ZONES 4–10.**

Lonicera pileata

PRIVET HONEYSUCKLE

An evergreen shrub from China, this species grows to 24 in (60 cm) high and 8 ft (2.4 m) wide. It has glossy deep green leaves and tiny, tubular, yellow flowers; the fruit are lovely violet berries. **ZONES 5–10.**

Lonicera × *purpusii*

This deciduous or semi-evergreen hybrid bears small clusters of fragrant, creamy white, short-tubed flowers with yellow anthers in winter and early spring. The berries are bright red. It is a dense, bushy shrub with a height and spread of up to 6 ft (1.8 m). The oval leaves are dark to mid-green. It is frost hardy. **ZONES 6–10.**

Lonicera quinquelocularis

This deciduous shrub from the Himalayas and China grows to 12 ft (3.5 m) in height. The oval leaves are dull green above and gray beneath and the creamy white flowers turn yellow with age. The oval fruit are translucent white in color. **ZONES 5–9.**

Lonicera sempervirens

TRUMPET HONEYSUCKLE, CORAL HONEYSUCKLE

From eastern and southern USA, this twining, woody vine has pairs of glaucous, blue-green leaves, united to form a disc at least toward the ends of the thin stems, where clusters of long-tubed orange to red flowers are produced. The throat of the tube opens to reveal a bright yellow to yellow-orange interior. Bright red fruit follow. Climbing to 12 ft (3.5 m) or more, it is evergreen in milder climates but deciduous in colder regions. **'Superba'** produces brilliant crimson blooms, while **'Sulphurea'** produces a pure yellow flower. **ZONES 4–10.**

Lonicera standishii

This 6 ft (1.8 m) deciduous or semi-evergreen Chinese shrub has peeling bark, bristly dark green leaves, perfumed creamy white flowers and red berries. **ZONES 6–10.**

Lonicera tatarica

TATARIAN HONEYSUCKLE

This deciduous, bushy, medium-sized shrub ranges from the Caucasus region to central Asia. It grows to a height of 12 ft (3.5 m) and spreads to 10 ft (3 m). In late spring and early summer the dark green foliage is covered with trumpet-shaped flowers in shades from white to deep pink; these are followed by red berries. **'Arnold Red'** has darker green leaves and red flowers. **ZONES 2–9.**

Lonicera × *tellmanniana*

Although virtually scentless, this deciduous hybrid is one of the most colorful of the climbing honeysuckles, with its yellowish orange flowers. It has circular leaves and is quite vigorous, reaching a height of 15 ft (4.5 m). **ZONES 5–9.**

Lonicera webbiana

Lonicera tragophylla

Lonicera tragophylla is one of the parents of *L.* × *tellmanniana*, and is a fine plant in its own right, the flowers making up for their lack of scent by their size and brilliant orange-yellow to red color; red fruit follow. A strong-growing, deciduous vine, it comes from central China and flowers in summer. **ZONES 6–10.**

Lonicera webbiana

Found from southeastern Europe to the Himalayas, this is a deciduous shrub up to 10 ft (3 m) tall. In spring its 4 in (10 cm) long leaves partially obscure the small, greenish white flowers. Red berries follow the blooms. **ZONES 6–10.**

Lonicera xylosteum

FLY HONEYSUCKLE

Found naturally from Europe through the Caucasus to China and Siberia, this is a dense, deciduous upright shrub growing to 10 ft (3 m) high and wide. It has gray-green leaves and in late spring and early summer bears smallish 2-lipped creamy white flowers that are scentless and pollinated by flies rather than the bumble-bees that visit most of the other honeysuckles; they are followed in fall (autumn) by red berries that can make an attractive display. **ZONES 6–10.**

Lonicera periclymenum

Lonicera × *purpusii*

LOPHOCEREUS

From the southern areas of the USA down to Mexico, this genus consists of 10 species of cacti, all with narrow columnar stems from 10–20 ft (3–6 m) tall in their natural habitat. Some botanists now classify them under *Pachycereus*. They bear pink, medium-sized, funnel-shaped flowers that bloom at night during spring and are followed by red berries in summer.

CULTIVATION: Plant in full sun and well-drained soil. Marginally frost hardy, they can be propagated from seed or cuttings. Mealybugs can be a problem.

Lophocereus schottii

syn. *Pachycereus schottii*

WHISKER CACTUS, SENITA

This cactus grows up to 15 ft (4.5 m) tall and its sallow to bright green stem tends to branch out from below after several years. The body has 5 to 7 ribs and varying areoles. The higher, flowering areoles sprout bristly gray spines radiating around one central spine. The smaller, non-flowering areoles bear up to 10 dense, tapering, grayish black spines. Small, tubular, night-opening flowers appear in spring and summer, followed by globular fruit. **ZONES 9–10.**

Lophocereus schottii

Lonicera tragophylla

Lonicera nitida 'Baggesen's Gold'

LOPHOMYRTUS

This genus of 2 species of evergreen shrubs or small trees from New Zealand, has been included in the genus *Myrtus* by many botanists. They are grown for their decorative foliage, which can be colorful and attractively aromatic, and for their small white flowers and dark red berries. **CULTIVATION:** Moderately frost hardy, they prefer full sun, well-drained, fertile soil and ample water in the warmer months. Tip pruning in spring will keep them compact. Propagate in summer from seed or cuttings for the species, and from cuttings for the cultivars.

Lophomyrtus bullata
syn. ***Myrtus bullata***
RAMARAMA

This species grows to 25 ft (8 m) high and is characterized by its 1–2 in (2.5–5 cm) long, puckered (bullate), oval leaves. The foliage varies in color depending on where the plant is grown: in shade it is deep green, in the sun it develops purple and red tones. Small cream flowers open in summer, followed by reddish purple berries. **'Variegatum'** has cream-edged leaves. **ZONES 9–10.**

Lophomyrtus obcordata

Lophomyrtus bullata 'Variegatum'

Lophomyrtus × *ralphii* 'Variegata'

Lophomyrtus × *ralphii* 'Lilliput'

Lophomyrtus obcordata

This erect, bushy shrub grows to about 6 ft (1.8 m) high, its many twiggy branches holding small, notched leaves. Young foliage turns bronze purple during the winter months; small, white, summer flowers are followed by red berries that ripen black. **ZONES 8–10.**

Lophomyrtus × *ralphii*

The many naturally occurring hybrids between the 2 species of this genus must all take the name *Lophomyrtus* × *ralphii*. Selected clones grown in New Zealand include the widely seen **'Purpurea'**, to about 6 ft (1.8 m) high, with puckered or crinkly leaves of a deep purple bronze throughout the year; **'Lilliput'**, a dwarf, compact shrub with tiny red and green leaves; **'Pixie'**, with leaves that are pinkish red; and **'Variegata'** with rounded, deep green leaves with cream variegations. These forms are propagated from cuttings, best taken in early fall (autumn) as the new season's growth hardens. **ZONES 8–10.**

LOPHOPHORA
PEYOTE, MESCAL

This is a genus of 2 species of slow-growing, perennial cacti from Mexico and southern USA. Spineless and with up to 10 plump ribs separated by a slight groove, they resemble small bluish dumplings. Short white hairs are produced from flowering areoles. Short-lived, bell-shaped flowers appear at the stem tips from spring to fall (autumn). The genus is famous for its content of the powerful hallucinogenic drug mescalin, long used by Native Americans in the USA and Mexico in religious ceremonies; analysis of its chemical structure led to the synthesis of LSD. In many countries these cacti are now prohibited plants.
CULTIVATION: Plant in full sun in very well-drained soil, as the plants are prone to rotting; allow to dry out in winter. Propagate from seed in spring or summer.

Lophophora williamsii
MESCAL BUTTON, DUMPLING CACTUS

Native to a limited area either side of the Texas-Mexico border, this slow-growing, flat-crowned cactus may be solitary or branch into tight colonies, up to 2 in (5 cm) tall. The dumpling-like, bluish green, ribbed stem is lightly covered with areoles sprouting short white hairs. Beautiful light pink flowers sprout from

Lophophora williamsii

the crown center. This species has quite potent narcotic properties. **ZONES 9–10.**

LOPHOSPERMUM

This genus, in the past variously included in *Maurandya* or *Asarina*, contains 8 species of deciduous and evergreen climbers and shrubs from North and Central America, with pretty white to purple foxglove-like flowers. Often having scandent stems, they may die back in winter in cold climates.
CULTIVATION: They are moderately frost-hardy to frost-tender. Grow in full sun in reasonably fertile, moist but well-drained soil. Water regularly in summer. Propagate from seed in spring or from cuttings in late summer.

Lophospermum erubescens
syns ***Asarina erubescens, Maurandya erubescens***
CLIMBING GLOXINIA

This dainty evergreen climber has velvety, heart-shaped leaves and bears pink, tubular flowers resembling gloxinias in late spring and early summer. It has twining stems up to 10 ft (3 m) tall, and adapts well to hanging baskets and window boxes. **ZONES 11–12.**

LOPHOSTEMON

The 6 species of evergreen trees in this genus are related to *Metrosideros* and *Tristania* and occur mainly in tropical Australia and subtropical eastern Australia, also in southern New Guinea. Only the most southerly species, *Lophostemon confertus,* is widely grown, and it is also the tallest and most handsome. They have simple, leathery leaves grouped in pseudowhorls (like rhododendron leaves) on the branchlets, and white to cream flowers with 5 delicately fringed petals. The flowers are followed by woody seed capsules, very like those of *Eucalyptus*. In warm climates *L. confertus* is widely planted as a street or shade tree, and also for timber.
CULTIVATION: Frost-tender, they require a humid climate with ample summer rainfall. Plant in full sun or part-shade in fertile, well-drained, neutral to acid soil. Propagate from seed in spring or from cuttings in summer.

Lophostemon confertus
syn. ***Tristania conferta***
BRUSH BOX, BRISBANE BOX

Tall and massive in its natural habitat, the brush box, in a more open position, is usually a dome-headed tree with

Lophostemon confertus

Lophostemon confertus

dense, mid-green foliage. The bark is smooth and pinkish tan, peeling in summer to reveal greenish cream new bark. The white flowers, although profuse, are hidden among the leaves. It grows to a height of over 100 ft (30 m) and is native to coastal Queensland and New South Wales. **'Variegata'** has cream central markings on the leaves, while **'Perth Gold'** has yellow coloration towards the leaf margins. **ZONES 10–12.**

LOROPETALUM
FRINGE FLOWER

Possibly 2 or 3 species (or a single variable species) make this genus from the Himalayas, China and Japan. The name derives from the Greek *loron*, a thong or a strap, referring to the masses of flowers with twisted, strap-like, creamy white petals that hang on the shrub in spring.
CULTIVATION: The plant has a distinctly horizontal branching habit, which means it can be easily trained as an espalier or pruned after flowering to emphasize the habit. It does best in a warm-temperate climate in sun or dappled shade and prefers well-drained, slightly acidic soil. Propagate from cuttings in summer.

Loropetalum chinense

This is an evergreen shrub reaching 6 ft (1.8 m) in height with horizontally inclined branches often forming a very wide profile. The small, neat, oval leaves are mid- to deep green and form a pleasant background to the fragrant, pendent flowers. While undemanding, it does respond to regular water and fertilizer. **'Burgundy'** has deep green oval leaves and tufted clusters of deep pink flowers. **ZONES 9–11.**

LOTUS

This legume genus of 150 species from temperate regions worldwide includes summer-flowering annuals, short-lived perennials and deciduous, semi-evergreen and evergreen subshrubs. They are grown for their foliage and pea-like flowers which come in a range of colors. They should not be confused with the aquatic plants *(Nelumbo* and *Nymphaea)* commonly known as lotus.
CULTIVATION: Fully frost hardy to frost tender, they prefer moderately fertile, well-drained soil in full sun. Propagate from cuttings in early summer or from seed in fall (autumn) or spring.

Lotus berthelotii
CORAL GEM, PARROT'S BEAK, PELICAN'S BEAK

Native to the Cape Verde and Canary Islands, this semi-evergreen, trailing subshrub is suitable for hanging baskets, ground cover or spilling over rockeries, banks or the tops of walls. It has hairy, silvery branches of fine needle leaves, and clusters of 1 in (25 mm), pea-like orange to scarlet flowers cover the plant in spring and early summer. It grows to 8 in (20 cm) tall with an indefinite spread. Frost tender, it suits warm coastal gardens. Tip prune young shoots to encourage dense foliage. **ZONES 10–11.**

Lotus maculatus

This trailing perennial from the Canary Islands grows to 8 in (20 cm) high and has silver needle-like leaves and claw-like tawny yellow flowers. It also has trailing, cascading fruit. **'Gold Flame'** has golden-yellow to orange flowers. **ZONES 10–11.**

LUCULIA

This is a genus of 5 species of deciduous and evergreen shrubs and small trees from the foothills of the Himalayas. They are very much admired by gardeners for their attractive large pointed leaves and clusters of scented pink or white flowers, but they have a reputation for being difficult to grow.
CULTIVATION: They need a humid warm-temperate climate free of both severe frost and dry conditions, acidic soil and perfect drainage, or there will be trouble with root-rot. If the plants grow straggly—as they often do—they can be

Luma apiculata

Lotus maculatus 'Gold Flame'

pruned gently after flowering. In cooler climates they succeed in mildly warmed greenhouses, altering their natural flowering season from earliest spring to summer. Propagation is from seed or summer cuttings.

Luculia grandifolia
syn. *Luculia tsetensis*

This deciduous, upright, vigorous shrub from Bhutan can grow to 20 ft (6 m) tall, though 4–8 ft (1.2–2.4 m) is its usual garden height. It bears terminal clusters of fragrant tubular white flowers in summer and has green, oval leaves with red veins and stalks. **ZONES 9–11.**

Luculia gratissima

Said to reach 20 ft (6 m) in height in its native eastern Himalayas, this semi-evergreen or evergreen shrub is normally no more than 8 ft (2.4 m) tall in gardens. It is grown in mild climates for its large, viburnum-like heads of fragrant pink flowers, up to 8 in (20 cm) across, which appear from mid-fall (mid-autumn) to early winter. The leaves are bronze green, soft and up to 10 in (25 cm) long. **ZONES 10–11.**

Luculia intermedia

This beautiful evergreen shrub from China and the Himalayas reaches 12 ft (3.5 m) in height. It has perfumed pale pink flowers. **ZONES 9–11.**

LUFFA
LOOFA

Belonging to the melon and gourd family, *Luffa* contains a single species of useful fruiting vine that has been used in China as medicine since the tenth century AD. The fruit has also been used as a vegetable, and its dried skeleton of conducting tissues is used as sponge and as a shock absorber in helmets; its most popular use is as an exfoliant. The seeds may be pressed for oil.

Luma apiculata

Lotus berthelotii

Loropetalum chinense 'Burgundy'

Luculia intermedia

CULTIVATION: This frost-tender plant prefers rich, sandy soil and full sun. Growth is encouraged by pruning. Propagate from seed sown in spring.

Luffa cylindrica
syn. *Luffa aegyptiaca*

This is an annual, 10 ft (3 m) tall vine from Egypt. It has yellow tubular flowers and the fruit are club-shaped gourds, edible when young. **ZONES 9–11.**

LUMA

This genus consists of 4 species of evergreen shrubs and trees from Argentina and Chile, closely related to *Myrtus* in which genus they were formerly included. They have small, leathery, pointed, oval, deep green leaves and a dense, bushy growth habit. The small, creamy white, starry flowers appear from mid-summer. The attractive bark of most species is a year-round feature; it is a reddish brown and flakes off to reveal white to pink new bark.
CULTIVATION: Although generally shrubby, old specimens can eventually grow to tree size; with trimming they can be kept to shrubs. Some species are suitable for hedging. They prefer moist, well-drained soil in sun or light shade. Propagate from seed or cuttings in late summer.

Loropetalum chinense

Loropetalum chinense 'Burgundy'

Luculia gratissima

Luma apiculata
syns *Myrtus luma, Eugenia apiculata,*

An upright, bushy shrub or small tree, this species grows to around 50 ft (15 m) tall in the wild but can be kept to 10 ft (3 m) high with regular trimming and may be used for hedging. The small leaves are aromatic and the flaking bark is cinnamon brown with white wood underneath. The flowers have conspicuous stamens and smother the bush from mid-summer to mid-fall (mid-autumn). The fruit are dark purple berries. **ZONES 9–11.**

LUNARIA
HONESTY

The origin of the common name for this genus, allied to stocks *(Matthiola)*, of 3 species of annuals, biennials and perennials is uncertain, although it could be from the way the silver lining of the seed pods is concealed in the brown husk like a silver coin, the reward of virtue that does not flaunt itself. Sprays of honesty have been popular as dried flower arrangements since the eighteenth century.
CULTIVATION: Plant in full sun or part-shade in fertile, moist but well-drained soil. Propagate perennials from seed or by division in fall (autumn) or spring, biennials from seed. They self-seed quite readily.

Lunaria annua

Lunaria rediviva

Lupinus hartwegii

Lupinus, Russell Hybrid

Lupinus, Russell Hybrid, 'Noble Maiden'

Lunaria annua
syn. *Lunaria biennis*

A fast-growing biennial native to southern Europe and the Mediterranean coast, this plant is grown for its attractive flowers and curious fruit. It has pointed, oval, serrated, bright green leaves and bears heads of scented, 4-petalled, rosy magenta, white or violet-purple flowers in spring and early summer. These are followed by circular seed pods with a silvery, translucent membrane. Erect in habit, it grows to a height of 30 in (75 cm) and a spread of 12 in (30 cm). **ZONES 8–10.**

Lunaria rediviva
PERENNIAL HONESTY

This perennial grows to 3 ft (1 m) high with a spread of 12 in (30 cm). It has hairy stems, heart-shaped leaves and pale violet flowers; the fruit are silver pods. **ZONES 8–10.**

LUPINUS
LUPIN, LUPINE

This legume genus of 200 species of annuals, perennials and semi-evergreen and evergreen shrubs and subshrubs, is mainly native to North America, southern Europe and North Africa. They are popular for their ease of culture, rapid growth and long, erect spikes of showy pea-flowers in a range of colors including blue, purple, pink, white, yellow, orange and red. Apart from being ornamentals, they are used for animal fodder, as a 'green manure' crop (because of their nitrogen-fixing capacity), and a few species are grown for grain, used as food by both humans and livestock. The compound leaves are distinct among legumes in being palmate, with 5 or more leaflets radiating from a common stalk, rather than the usual pinnate arrangement.
CULTIVATION: Most lupins prefer climates with cool wet winters and long dry summers. They should be planted in full sun and in well-drained, moderately fertile, slightly acidic, sandy soil. They like plenty of water in the growing season and should be mulched in dry areas. Spent flowers should be cut away to prolong plant life and to prevent self-seeding. The foliage adds nitrogen to the soil when dug in. Propagate species from seed in fall (autumn) and Russell lupin cultivars from cuttings or by division in early spring. Watch for slugs and snails.

Lupinus albifrons var. *collinus*

This evergreen subshrub from the USA reaches just 4 in (10 cm) in height. It has 7 to 10 silvery, silky leaves and bears its red-purple or blue flowers in racemes in summer. **ZONES 8–10.**

Lupinus arboreus
TREE LUPIN, YELLOW BUSH LUPINE

From coastal California, this evergreen or semi-evergreen shrub grows to 8 ft (2.4 m) tall and 3 ft (1 m) or more wide. It has hairy gray-green leaves and fragrant, usually pale yellow flowers in many short spikes. The pods are up to 3 in (8 cm) long. **ZONES 8–10.**

Lupinus argenteus
SILVERY LUPIN

Native to western USA and Canada and growing only 6–12 in (15–30 cm) tall, this perennial has silvery leaves, white, rose, blue or violet flowers and hairy 1 in (25 mm) long fruit. **ZONES 4–10.**

Lupinus hartwegii
HAIRY LUPIN

Native to Mexico, this fast-growing annual has a compact, erect growth habit and reaches 30 in (75 cm) in height with a spread of 15 in (38 cm). It has hairy dark green leaves, and slender spikes of flowers in shades of blue, white or pink are borne abundantly in late winter, spring and early summer. **ZONES 7–11.**

Lupinus nanus

This easy-to-grow Californian annual reaches 18 in (45 cm) in height. It has numerous short flower spikes that are bright blue or purple with white spots or splashes. **ZONES 7–11.**

Lupinus odoratus
MOJAVE LUPINE

Widely distributed in western USA, this lupin grows to 3 ft (1 m) in height, and has golden fragrant flowers. **ZONES 5–9.**

Lupinus perennis
SUNDIAL LUPIN, WILD LUPIN

This perennial species from eastern and central USA reaches 24 in (60 cm) in height and has blue and white or pink and white flowers in racemes up to 12 in (30 cm) long. **ZONES 4–10.**

Lupinus, Russell Hybrids

George Russell was a gardener fond of growing lupins, and over the years selected the best seedlings from open-pollinated plants of *Lupinus polyphyllus*. Around 1937 a colorful selection of his perennial lupins was released and rapidly became popular, known as 'Russell lupins'. It is thought that they are hybrids, the other major parent being the annual *L. hartwegii*. This fine strain of strong-growing lupins bears long spikes of large, strongly colored flowers in cream, pink, orange, blue or violet, some varieties bicolored, in late spring and summer. They produce a magnificent clump of deeply divided, mid-green leaves, growing to a height of 3 ft (1 m). **'Noble Maiden'**, one of the Band of Nobles series, has cream flowers; **'Polar Princess'** has white flowers; and the blooms of **'Troop the Colour'** are bright red. There are also dwarf strains, such as the 24 in (60 cm) high **'Lulu'**. **ZONES 3–9.**

Lupinus, Russell H., 'Troop the Colour'

Lupinus sparsiflorus
COULTER'S LUPINE

Reaching 8–15 in (20–38 cm) in height, the annual *Lupinus sparsiflorus*, a native of western USA and northwestern Mexico, has light blue to lilac flowers. **ZONES 9–11.**

Lupinus succulentus
ARROYO LUPINE

With silky hairy leaves and deep blue to purple flowers with yellow centers, this handsome species from southern California and nearby parts of Mexico grows to around 24 in (60 cm) tall. **ZONES 8–11.**

Lupinus texensis
TEXAS BLUE BONNET

A bushy annual reaching a height of 12 in (30 cm), this species has bright green leaves divided into 5 small leaflets that are hairy on the undersides, and bears dark blue and white flowers in late spring. Easily grown, it thrives in poor soil and is quick to flower from seed. This is the state flower of Texas, beyond which it does not occur wild. **ZONES 8–10.**

LUZULA
WOODRUSH

This genus of some 80 species of rushes is found in temperate regions of both the northern and southern hemispheres. They differ from most of the familiar rushes of the related genus *Juncus* in having grass-like, flat or channelled leaves with long silky hairs fringing the edges. Most are perennials and evergreen, forming tufts or clumps, some are stoloniferous and may be slightly invasive. The wiry, flowering stems extend above the foliage and bear clusters of tiny pale gray to golden-brown flowers,

Lupinus, Russell Hybrid, 'Polar Princess'

Lupinus texensis

Lychnis viscaria 'Splendens Plena'

Lychnis chalcedonica

sometimes tinted pink. Several cultivars with variegated foliage are grown. **CULTIVATION:** Most species prefer a moist position but are not fussy about soil type or aspect provided they are not in deep shade. Most are frost hardy. Propagate from seed or by division.

Luzula nivea

SNOWY WOODRUSH

This slow-spreading evergreen perennial from central and southern Europe reaches 24 in (60 cm) in height and can spread to 24 in (60 cm) or more. The narrow grassy leaves are edged with white hairs and the flowers are borne in dense clusters of shining white. **ZONES 6–9.**

LYCASTE

This orchid genus consists of about 45 species of epiphytes that grow on trees and rocks in mountains of tropical America from Mexico to Peru. The pseudobulbs are crowded into a compact clump, each with 2 to 4 large plicate leaves that are deciduous in many species. The showy flowers are borne singly, or occasionally 2 together, on many short stems arising from the bases of the pseudobulbs. Flower shape is more or

Luzula nivea

less triangular dominated by the 3 sepals, the petals and labellum mostly smaller and of contrasting color. There is a wide range of flower colors with oranges and greenish yellows the most common, but pinks, reds, greens and white also occur. There has been some hybridizing, for example, **'Diana'** and **'Erin Harmony'**, and a few hybrids have been registered. **CULTIVATION:** These orchids like cool to intermediate growing conditions with a minimum winter temperature of around 50°F (10°C). They prefer a rather fine-textured orchid compost, and a well-lit position with good air movement. Water frequently during the growing period though allowing plants to almost dry out between waterings. Allow a dry resting period during winter. Propagate by division.

Lycaste cruenta

The pseudobulbs of this prolific flowerer from Central America are up to 4 in (10 cm) long and 2 in (5 cm) wide with several leaves 15 in (38 cm) long and 6 in (15 cm) wide. The greenish yellow flowers with bright orange petals and labellum are borne singly in spring on stems up to 6 in (15 cm) high; they are about 3 in (8 cm) wide and develop a sweetly aromatic scent like cinnamon toward the evening. A plant with several pseudobulbs can have 20 or more flowers and, as the leaves are shed before flowering, it is a spectacular sight on such a small plant. **ZONES 10–12.**

Lycaste skinneri

syn. *Lycaste virginalis*

This is the largest-flowered and arguably most beautiful of the lycastes. It grows at moderate altitudes in Central America and has been collected to the point of extinction in Mexico. The pseudobulbs are up to 4 in (10 cm) long with several broad, pleated, deciduous leaves up to 30 in (75 cm) long. The pale rose-pink flowers, borne singly on stems up to 12 in (30 cm) tall, can be as much as 6 in (15 cm) across. The flowering season is mostly in late fall (autumn) and winter. A white form of this species is the national flower of Guatemala. ***Lycaste skinneri* × *dowiana*** has flowers with pink sepals, white petals and pale pink labellum. **ZONES 11–12.**

LYCHNIS

CAMPION, CATCHFLY

Native to temperate regions of the northern hemisphere, these 15 to 20 species of biennials and perennials include some that have been cultivated for many centuries, grown for their summer flowers that range in color from white through pinks and oranges to deep red. All have flat 5-petalled flowers but in many species the petals are notched or deeply forked or sometimes divided into narrow teeth. The genus is related to *Silene,* and the boundary between the 2 genera has shifted with varying botanical opinion. **CULTIVATION:** They are frost hardy and easily grown in cool climates, preferably in sunny sites, and in any well-drained soil. The higher mountain species do best in soil that is protected from being excessively warmed by the sun. Remove spent stems after flowering and deadhead frequently to prolong the flowering period. Propagate by division or from seed in fall (autumn) or early spring. Some species self-seed readily.

Lychnis alpina

ALPINE CAMPION, ALPINE CATCHFLY

Ranging right around the northern hemisphere on higher mountains and in subarctic regions, this 6 in (15 cm) tall perennial bears rosy purple flowers with frilled petals in summer. The dark green leaves appear in rosettes. **ZONES 2–8.**

Lychnis chalcedonica

MALTESE CROSS

This perennial species from far eastern Europe has been a favorite with gardeners since the seventeenth century. Its color is such a dazzling orange-red that its garden companions should be chosen with care. It flowers for a rather short season in early summer, grows about 4 ft (1.2 m) tall, and takes its common name from the shape of the flower. White and pink varieties and one with double flowers exist, but these are fairly rare. **ZONES 4–10.**

Lycaste skinneri × *dowiana*

Lycaste 'Diana'

Lycaste 'Erin Harmony'

Lychnis coronaria
ROSE CAMPION, DUSTY MILLER, MULLEIN PINK

A clump-forming perennial sometimes grown as a biennial, this striking plant grows to a height of 30 in (75 cm) and a spread of 18 in (45 cm). It forms a dense clump of silvery white downy leaves, and many-branched gray stems carry large, deep rose-pink to scarlet flowers throughout summer. **'Alba'** is a white-flowered cultivar. In ancient times the flowers were used for garlands and crowns. It is drought tolerant, requires little or no cultivation or watering, and often self-seeds. **ZONES 4–10.**

Lychnis flos-jovis
FLOWER OF JOVE, FLOWER OF JUPITER

This perennial species from the Alps grows to a height of 18 in (45 cm). It has tufts of ground-hugging leaves, from the midst of which the flower stems arise to carry the flowers in clusters in summer. The leaves are gray and downy and the flowers are bright pink. **ZONES 5–9.**

Lychnis coronaria 'Alba'

Lychnis coronaria

Lychnis × *haageana*

This garden hybrid between *Lychnis fulgens* and *L. sieboldii* is a short-lived, clump-forming perennial growing to a height of about 18 in (45 cm). In summer it bears clusters of large white, salmon red or scarlet flowers. It is weak growing and needs to be regularly propagated from seed. **'Vesuvius'** is very striking, with deep bronze-green foliage and large, vivid orange flowers. **ZONES 6–10.**

Lychnis viscaria
GERMAN CATCHFLY

This perennial is widely distributed through Europe and western Asia. Growing to 18 in (45 cm) tall and with a similar spread, it is a densely clumping plant with bronze stems and narrow dark green leaves with sticky hairs. It produces spike-like panicles of mauve to magenta flowers in early summer. **'Splendens Plena'** (syn. 'Flore Pleno') has larger, bright magenta double flowers. **ZONES 4–9.**

LYCIUM
BOXTHORN

Around 100 species of erect or sometimes scrambling shrubs belong to this genus, widely scattered throughout sub-tropical and temperate regions of the world. They belong to the potato family and are most closely allied to *Atropa*, the deadly nightshade. Including both evergreen and deciduous species, they have simple, elliptical leaves clustered on small rosette-like spur shoots along the branches, which are often armed with strong, sharp thorns. The small flowers, carried singly or in small clusters, are bell -shaped and are followed by ovoid berries.
CULTIVATION: These plants will grow in full sun in poor but well-drained soil. Cold-hardiness varies with the species. They often grow in coastal areas and tolerate salt spray and saline soil. Dead wood should be removed after winter. Propagate from seed in fall (autumn) or cuttings in winter.

Lycium barbarum
syns *Lycium chinense, L. hailimifolium*
CHINESE BOXTHORN, MATRIMONY VINE

This is a variable species, one widely cultivated form of which was commonly distinguished under the name *Lycium chinense*. It is native to China but reached Europe in the eighteenth century; in England it was believed at first to be the tea plant but the mistake was soon realized and it became known, ironically perhaps, as the 'Duke of Argyle's tea tree'. It is a deciduous shrub of up to 12 ft (3.5 m) in height with arching, rarely spiny branches, bright green or grayish leaves, pink or purple flowers only $\frac{1}{4}$ in (6 mm) long, and orange-red berries about $\frac{3}{4}$ in (18 mm) long. **ZONES 6–10.**

LYCOPERSICON
TOMATO

There are 7 species in this Central and South American genus of annuals and short-lived evergreen perennials, closely allied to the much larger genus *Solanum* which includes the potato and the eggplant. The plant known as the tomato was cultivated at the time of the Spanish conquest by the Incas in Ecuador and Peru and the Aztecs in Mexico. For centuries the tomato was regarded with suspicion by Europeans and it was not until the early nineteenth century that it finally gained worldwide acceptance as a food plant. The genus name *Lycopersicon* is from the Greek meaning 'wolf peach' and applied originally to an unrelated Egyptian plant; Linnaeus somewhat arbitrarily named the tomato *Solanum lycopersicum* and the name stuck.
CULTIVATION: Tomatoes require a long, warm growing season, and in cool climates the seedlings need to be started under glass in spring so fruit development can take place in the brief summer. Plant in fertile, well-drained soil that is warmed by at least 6 hours of direct sunlight. Position stakes before planting and set plants about 24 in (60 cm) apart when all danger of frost is over; in cool climates use cloches to protect young seedlings. Keep soil moist but not too wet and feed regularly while fruit are developing. A variety of pests and diseases attack tomatoes, and disease resistance is one of the main aims of breeders.

Lycopersicon esculentum

Lycium barbarum

Lycopersicon esculentum
syn. *Lycopersicon lycopersicum*

This soft-stemmed, spreading plant up to 6 ft (1.8 m) high has strong-smelling, deeply lobed leaves and yellow flowers followed by soft succulent fruit. The fruit are generally red or yellow and vary considerably in size and shape among the numerous cultivars. At harvest time, vine-ripened fruit are definitely the best. Among the most widely grown traditional red cultivars are **'Beefsteak'**, tall, with large rounded fruit, **'Grosse Lisse'**, very sweet with large, soft fruit, and **'Rouge de Marmande'** with large, ribbed fruit. **'Yellow Pear'** yields big crops of 2 in (5 cm), golden-yellow, pear-shaped fruit. **'Red Pear'** is similar except that the fruit are red. The elongated Roma tomatoes, popular in Italy, include **'Super Roma'** and **'Plumito'**. A novel group in gardens of the West are the eastern European black tomatoes, an example being **'Black Russian'**. Cherry tomatoes, sometimes designated by the name ***Lycopersicon esculentum* var. *cerasiforme***, bear long decorative strings of cherry-size red, orange or yellow fruit. Another small-fruited species ***L. pimpinellifolium*** is sometimes cultivated and has been used by plant breeders in recent years to introduce new genes to cherry tomatoes. **ZONES 8–12.**

LYCOPODIUM
CLUBMOSS

Widespread throughout most moister regions of the world, the 100 or more species in this genus are an ancient group of plants whose larger ancestors, along with those of the horsetails *(Equisetum)*, dominated the world's vegetation around 250 million years ago. Considered more primitive than the ferns but more advanced than the mosses, they range from tiny thread-stemmed plants that grow in boggy ground below heath, to large epiphytes that form curtains of ferny foliage on the limbs of tropical rainforest trees. All share similar cord-like stems clothed with overlapping, bright green or golden-green scale-like leaves. Club mosses do not flower but instead bear tiny spore capsules between the scales of delicate small cones (strobili).

CULTIVATION: Only the epiphytic species are cultivated to any extent, mainly by fern enthusiasts. Outdoors in the tropics they prefer part-shade and a permanently moist niche in the fork of a tree. Elsewhere they require a greenhouse or conservatory maintained at high humidity, and can make dramatic specimens in hanging baskets. Hang in positions with some air movement; they are sensitive to excess water around the roots. Propagate from cuttings or by layering fertile stem tips.

Lycopodium phlegmaria
LAYERED TASSEL FERN

This elegant species is widely distributed in rainforests of tropical Asia and the South Pacific. It features small, shiny, lacquered leaves that line the long, pendent stems in 4 rows. In this and many related species the ends of the stems branch into groups of fine, elongated strobili-like green tassels, earning this group the name tassel ferns. They form large clumps of hanging stems that make them suited to basket culture. **ZONES 11–12.**

LYCORIS
SPIDER LILY, SURPRISE LILY

With spider-like flowers, these 10 to 12 species of East Asian amaryllids are rather like the better known nerines but are mostly more robust plants. The name comes from Roman history—Lycoris, famed for her beauty, was a mistress of Marc Antony. The strap-like foliage of these bulbs dies back during summer, reappearing after they bloom in summer or early fall (autumn). Each smooth stem carries an umbel of trumpet-shaped flowers with narrow, strongly recurved petals that usually have wavy margins, and long, showy stamens and styles contributing to the spidery appearance.
CULTIVATION: Plant the bulbs in a sunny position in rich, well-drained soil. The plants like plenty of water during their winter growing season but need warm, dry conditions when dormant. They are only moderately frost hardy and need protection from cold winds. Clumps are best left undisturbed for a few years; they can then be divided when dormant in summer. They may also be propagated from seed.

Lygodium japonicum

Lycoris aurea
GOLDEN SPIDER LILY

A native of China and Japan, this lily grows to 24 in (60 cm) tall and bears a cluster of 4 to 5 golden-yellow flowers in summer. The 3 in (8 cm) wide flowers have narrow, sharply recurved petals and long, straight stamens. **ZONES 7–10.**

Lycoris radiata

Lycoris radiata
RED SPIDER LILY

Also from China and Japan and the most commonly grown species, this has 12–18 in (30–45 cm) stems bearing in late summer or early fall (autumn) clusters of 4 or 5 rose-red, 2–3 in (5–8 cm) wide flowers with strongly curled petals and very long, slightly upward-curving stamens. **ZONES 7–10.**

Lycoris squamigera
RESURRECTION LILY, MAGIC LILY

This Japanese native grows up to 30 in (75 cm) in height. Appearing in late summer or early fall (autumn), the inflorescence is made up of 6 to 8 scented, funnel-shaped flowers, pink with yellow throats and with much shorter stamens than *Lycoris aurea* or *L. radiata*. The flowers can be up to 4 in (10 cm) across. **ZONES 7–10.**

LYGODIUM
CLIMBING FERN

About 35 to 40 species of unusual climbing ferns make up this genus, scattered widely through warmer and moister regions of the world. Including both deciduous and semi-evergreen species, they have much-branched rhizomes beneath the soil. Young plants at first produce short pinnate fronds, but they soon send up fronds with the unusual property of being able to grow indefinitely from the tips, their mid-stalks twining around twigs, shrubs and saplings and sometimes forming large masses of foliage. The leaflets vary from almost circular to narrow and lobed, and on fertile portions of the frond are usually edged with narrow comb-like teeth bearing small spore-bodies. In some tropical regions the tough 'stems' are used for cordage, nets, mats or baskets.
CULTIVATION: They require moist humus-rich, peaty soil and will grow in sun or part-shade. Frost hardiness varies with the species. They may need support as they grow, or can be allowed to drape from hanging baskets. Propagate by division in spring or from spores in summer.

Lygodium japonicum
JAPANESE CLIMBING FERN

This deciduous species is widespread in Asia from Japan southward, extending to northern Australia. It can climb to more than 12 ft (3.5 m) and the apparent fronds (actually pinnae of the climbing frond) are bright green and divided into many long leaflets that are toothed and basally lobed. The spore-bearing leaflets are sharply distinct. **ZONES 10–12.**

LYONIA
HUCKLEBERRY, FETTERBUSH

This genus, allied to *Pieris* and *Gaultheria*, is composed of 35 species of deciduous and evergreen shrubs and small trees, with a distribution covering East and Southeast Asia, eastern North

Lycopodium phlegmaria

Lycopodium phlegmaria

Lyonothamnus floribundus subsp. *aspleniifolius*

L. floribundus subsp. *aspleniifolius*

America, and parts of the Caribbean. The leaves are usually pointed, often with small scales or spots on the undersides, and the white or cream flowers are cylindrical or bell-shaped, usually pendent on racemes that develop from the leaf axils in spring.

CULTIVATION: In common with most ericaceous plants, they prefer moist, well-drained soil with ample humus and no lime. A position in part-shade is best. Frost hardiness varies considerably among the species. Propagate from seed or cuttings or by layering.

Lyonia mariana
STAGGER BUSH

This deciduous, frost-hardy shrub from eastern USA grows to 6 ft (1.8 m) tall and spreads to 4 ft (1.2 m). It bears clusters of ½ in (12 mm) long white or pink-tinged, bell-shaped flowers from late spring into summer, and has rich red leaves in fall (autumn). It is able to grow in quite boggy ground. **ZONES 5–9.**

LYONOTHAMNUS
CATALINA IRONWOOD

An early resident of Los Angeles, W. S. Lyon, discovered in 1884 the single species of evergreen tree that makes up this genus, on Santa Catalina Island off the coast of southern California. The *-thamnus* part of the name comes from the Greek for shrub, so the name means 'Lyon shrub'. Belonging to the rose family, it is a tree-like relative of the potentillas, with very distinctive pinnate leaves with usually toothed leaflets and large terminal panicles of small white flowers.

CULTIVATION: Grow in fertile, well-drained soil and protect from cold, drying winds. It does well in coastal conditions where frost is not a problem. This is a tree for a sunny or part-shaded position in a warm climate. Propagate from seed in fall (autumn) or cuttings in summer. Propagation may prove difficult; try seed if available or take cuttings in summer.

Lyonothamnus floribundus

This slender, narrow-crowned tree grows to about 50 ft (15 m) tall and has attractive reddish brown bark, shed in slender strips. The supposedly typical form has simple leaves with virtually untoothed edges, but this may merely be a very adult phase of growth; the form usually grown is that known as ***Lyonothamnus floribundus* subsp. *aspleniifolius*** with ferny compound leaves in which the long, narrow leaflets are divided into many regular, pointed lobes. The early summer flowers are a soft creamy white, held in large clusters towards the ends of the branches, and are followed by brown seed capsules. **ZONES 9–11.**

LYSICHITON
syn. *Lysichitum*
SKUNK CABBAGE

This unusual genus of the arum family is composed of 2 species of rhizomatous perennials, one from northeastern Asia, the other from western North America. They flower in spring as or before the new foliage develops. The stout-stemmed, pointed, heart-shaped leaves are quite large, sometimes as much as 4 ft (1.2 m) long when fully expanded. The spathes, white or yellow depending on the species, are around 15 in (38 cm) long and partially enclose the flower spike (spadix). The flowers have a musky smell that is nowhere near as bad as the common name suggests.

CULTIVATION: Skunk cabbages are frost-hardy plants suited only to cool climates. They normally grow in damp or boggy ground and are best positioned at the edges of ponds or streams. Propagate from seed or by division.

Lysichiton americanus
YELLOW SKUNK CABBAGE

This species ranges in the wild from coastal Alaska to northern California and east to Montana. It has large butter-yellow spathes that appear in mid-spring before the leaves, though still present when the leaves have expanded, making a dramatic contrast. It grows to a height of around 3 ft (1 m). **ZONES 5–9.**

Lysichiton camtschatcensis
WHITE SKUNK CABBAGE

As the name suggests, this species occurs on the Kamchatka Peninsula of far eastern Siberia, but its range includes other nearby parts of Siberia and northern Japan. The name skunk cabbage is not at all apt for this species, as its pure white spathes are odorless or even slightly sweet-scented. They appear before the leaves in early spring and stand about 24 in (60 cm) high. The conspicuously veined leaves are up to 3 ft (1 m) long. **ZONES 5–9.**

Lysimachia nummularia 'Aurea'

LYSIMACHIA
LOOSESTRIFE

Ranging through temperate and subtropical regions of the northern hemisphere, this genus of mainly evergreen perennials and shrubs of the primula family consists of around 150 species, of which about 130 are found in China. There are also a few species in Africa, Australia and South America. They vary greatly in growth habit from low, creeping plants to stately clumps with tall, spike-like racemes of crowded flowers. The 5-petalled flowers are mostly yellow or white, less commonly pink or purple. The botanical name is Latinized Greek for 'ending strife' and the English common name is a version of the same, though why these plants deserve such a name is now unclear.

CULTIVATION: They prefer slightly acidic soil with a good mix of organic matter and medium to moist conditions in sun or part-shade. Some species are marsh plants that grow best at the edge of a pond or stream. Propagate from seed or cuttings, or by division.

Lysimachia ciliata

This North American species is an upright perennial around 3 ft (1 m) high. Its leaves, which are up to 6 in (15 cm) long, are borne in closely spaced whorls of up to 4 along the stems. Throughout summer, small yellow flowers are carried singly or in pairs in the upper leaf axils. ***Lysimachia ciliata* var. *purpurea*** has reddish purple foliage that contrasts well with the yellow flowers. **ZONES 4–10.**

Lysimachia clethroides
JAPANESE LOOSESTRIFE

This somewhat hairy perennial from China, Korea and Japan grows to 3 ft (1 m) high making a broad, leafy clump of erect stems. In summer it produces tapering terminal spikes, gracefully nodding in bud but becoming erect with maturity, of crowded starry white flowers. **ZONES 4–10.**

Lysimachia ephemerum

A native of southwestern Europe, this handsome summer-flowering perennial

Lysimachia clethroides

Lysimachia vulgaris

has stems up to 3 ft (1 m) tall, rather narrow gray-green leaves and erect, tapering spikes of ½ in (12 mm) wide, starry white flowers at the stem tips. **ZONES 6–10.**

Lysimachia nummularia
CREEPING JENNY, MONEYWORT

Native to much of Europe and also Turkey and the Caucasus, this vigorous creeping perennial has become widely naturalized in North America. Various medicinal properties were attributed to it by herbalists. The prostrate stems take root wherever they touch damp ground, forming a dense, rapidly spreading mat usually no more than 3 in (8 cm) deep. The paired leaves are almost circular, hence *nummularia* from the Latin for coin-like, also the English 'moneywort'. The deep yellow bowl-shaped flowers are up to 1 in (25 mm) wide, borne singly on short stalks from the leaf axils over a long summer period. **'Aurea'**, golden creeping Jenny, is a popular cultivar with pale yellow-green leaves and stems; when grown in shade it turns an interesting lime green. Both green and gold forms are useful ground-cover plants for moist or even boggy soil and can tolerate occasional light foot traffic. **ZONES 4–10.**

Lysimachia punctata
GOLDEN LOOSESTRIFE, GARDEN LOOSESTRIFE

A vigorous clump-forming perennial, this species is native to central and southern Europe and Turkey. It grows erect to a height of 3 ft (1 m) with broad mid-green leaves in whorls of 4, grading into floral bracts on the upper stems which carry in summer a massed display of brilliant yellow starry flowers, each about 1 in (25 mm) across. Golden loosestrife looks best planted in large groups. It is suitable for bedding, large rock gardens, or pool and streamside plantings. **ZONES 5–10.**

Lysimachia vulgaris
YELLOW LOOSESTRIFE

This perennial is a common wildflower in Europe and western Asia, growing in wet meadows and along streams. It has creeping rhizomes with erect stems that can be 4 ft (1.2 m) or more in height, with broad green leaves in whorls of three or four. The starry golden-yellow flowers, about ¾ in (18 mm) wide, are borne in loose terminal spikes in summer. **ZONES 5–10.**

LYTHRUM
LOOSESTRIFE

This genus of annuals, perennials and subshrubs shares the common name 'loosestrife' with *Lysimachia*, though the 2 genera are quite unrelated; however, the long, erect flower spikes of some *Lythrum* species and their boggy habitats are like those of some lysimachias. There are around 35 species, scattered through all continents except South America. They vary from small creeping plants with stems rooting in the mud of ditches, to plants 6 ft (1.8 m) or more tall with showy spikes of pink to purple flowers. **CULTIVATION:** These plants will grow in most soil conditions as long as mois-

Lysimachia punctata

ture is adequate, and in bogs and other wetlands some species can be quite invasive. Propagation is very easy from seed or by division.

Lythrum salicaria
PURPLE LOOSESTRIFE

A native of Europe, North Africa and western Asia, this perennial always grows in wet ground, often spreading into the shallow water at the edges of ponds. Erect stems arise from a knotty rhizome to a height varying from 3–6 ft (1–1.8 m) depending on soil moisture and fertility. It produces showy long spikes of pink to magenta flowers from mid-summer to fall (autumn). In eastern North America it has become widely naturalized and in some areas is detested as a weed, displacing native wildflowers. Purple loosestrife was used in folk medicine for centuries; its tannins have coagulent properties, hence staunching the flow of blood; treatment of cholera was one of its uses. There are a number of garden forms, with flowers in the deep rose-red to deep pink range, some double-flowered. **'Feuerkerze'** ('Firecandle') is a cultivar with more reddish flowers. **ZONES 3–10.**

Lythrum virgatum

This species extends in the wild from central Europe through central Asia as far as northern China. It is a handsome, vigorous perennial growing to as much as 6 ft (1.8 m) tall, with pretty pinkish red flowers arranged rather loosely in erect spikes. Like the similar *Lythrum salicaria*, it has become a weed in North America. Cultivars include **'Morden Gleam'** with rich crimson-red flowers, **'Morden Pink'** with pretty pink flowers, and **'The Rocket'** has purple-tinged foliage and deep mauve-pink flowers. **ZONES 4–10.**

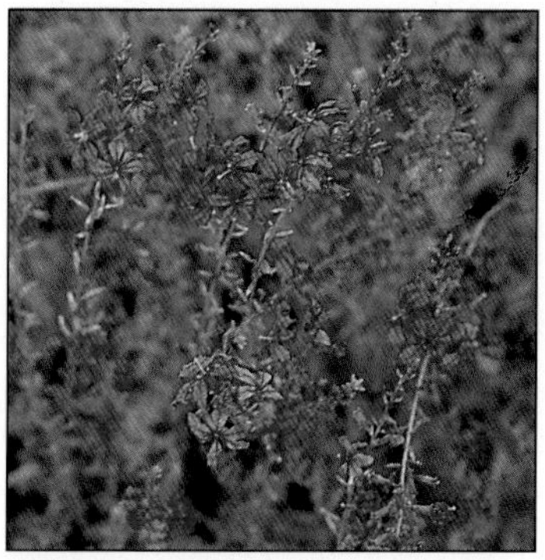

Lythrum virgatum

Lythrum salicaria

M

MAACKIA

Eight species of deciduous shrubs and trees make up this genus from China and East Asia. The pinnate leaves have 7 to 13 narrow leaflets with fine hairs on the undersides. The pea-like flowers are carried in dense, branching racemes in summer. They are usually white, cream or yellow in color. Flattened, winged seed pods, about 2 in (5 cm) long, follow the flowers.
CULTIVATION: Plant in well-drained, humus-rich soil in sun or part-shade. Trim lightly after flowering to maintain compact growth. Most species are very frost hardy. Propagate from seed in fall (autumn).

Maackia amurensis
AMUR MAACKIA

This elegant tree from northeast China has an attractive, open, spreading habit. It grows to 50 ft (15 m) tall and about 30 ft (9 m) wide. Upright spikes of white to creamy yellow flowers are produced in summer; these are followed by the seed pods. **ZONES 4–10.**

MACADAMIA

Consisting of 11 species, this relatively small genus from Australia, Sulawesi in Indonesia and New Caledonia is made up of small to medium evergreen rainforest trees. Their leathery, narrow leaves, usually in whorls of 3 or 4 on the twigs, have smooth or toothed edges. They bear small flowers, crowded on cylindrical spikes, and nuts that take up to 9 months to mature.
CULTIVATION: These frost-tender trees require sun, plenty of water and fertile, moist but well-drained soil. They flower and fruit year-round in the tropics and in summer in temperate climates, with the nuts ripening in late summer, usually 5 years after planting. The best crops come from selected cultivars commonly grafted onto seedlings. Propagate from ripe seed in fall (autumn).

Macadamia integrifolia
SMOOTH SHELL MACADAMIA NUT, QUEENSLAND NUT

This spreading tree has whorls of leathery, glossy leaves and produces panicles of small, creamy white flowers 4 in (10 cm) long. It reaches 70 ft (21 m) in height and has edible round, brown nuts. **ZONES 9–11.**

Macadamia tetraphylla
ROUGH SHELL MACADAMIA NUT, BOPPLE NUT

Growing to about 40 ft (12 m) in height with a bushy habit when given room, this handsome tree has pink or white flowers on long, pendulous spikes. Its toothed, dark green leaves may be prickly. The young branchlets are pinkish red before darkening with age. **ZONES 10–11.**

MACFADYENA
syn. *Doxantha*

This small genus consists of 3 or 4 species of climbing plants ranging from Mexico to Uruguay, their countries of origin giving a hint of their frost-tender nature. In subtropical climates, some can become vicious engulfing weeds. The leaves have 2 opposite leaflets with terminal claw-like tendrils, which they use to cling onto any support within reach. The showy trumpet-shaped flowers bloom abundantly in spring and summer.
CULTIVATION: The plants prefer frost-free areas with full sun and a moist, well-drained site, protection from cold winds and ample water during the summer months. Prune to control after flowering. Propagate from seed or cuttings or by layering.

Macfadyena unguis-cati

Mackaya bella

Macadamia tetraphylla

Macleaya cordata

Macfadyena unguis-cati
syns *Bignonia tweediana*, *Doxantha unguis-cati*
CAT'S CLAW CREEPER, YELLOW TRUMPET VINE

This beautiful, evergreen vine is grown for its large, bright yellow flowers in the shape of a flattened trumpet. They reach up to 4 in (10 cm) across and are borne in profusion in late spring. These are followed by bean-like seed pods. Tiny, 3-pronged tendrils, like little claws, cling to supporting surfaces and the vine climbs to a height of up to 30 ft (9 m). It is an excellent climber for covering a high fence or garden shed. **ZONES 9–12.**

MACKAYA

A member of the acanthus family, this genus consists of a single species of evergreen shrub. Native along stream banks in forests of southern Africa, it has lustrous, deep green leaves. The short racemes of pale lilac, trumpet-shaped flowers with 5 large flared lobes with deep purple veining add to its attractive appearance.
CULTIVATION: To flower profusely, this frost-tender plant needs a semi-shaded position in a warm-climate garden or a sheltered microclimate and moist, well-drained, fertile soil. Propagate from cuttings in spring or summer, or seed in spring.

Mackaya bella
FOREST BELL BUSH

This shrub is erect when young but develops a more spreading habit with maturity and eventually reaches 8 ft (2.4 m) in height. From spring to fall (autumn), spikes of 5-petalled, funnel-shaped, pink flowers with dark veins are borne; it will flower into winter in warm climates. The leaves are glossy, deep green and oval shaped. **ZONES 10–11.**

MACLEANIA

This is a genus of 40 evergreen shrubs with somewhat pendulous branches. They are natives of Central and South America and vary in height, depending on the species. The simple, short-stemmed, elliptical leaves are 1–4 in (2.5–10 cm) long, leathery and often tinted red when young. The pendent, 1 in (25 mm) long tubular flowers are carried in small groups or racemes of up to 10 blooms.
CULTIVATION: While not frost tolerant, this genus does not need a hot climate; a winter minimum of 40°F (5°C) will do. Plant in moist, well-drained, humus-rich soil in sun or part-shade. Propagate from seed or cuttings.

Macleania insignis

This open-growing shrub can reach 12 ft (3.5 m) in height, but is more commonly 6 ft (1.8 m) and 5 ft (1.5 m) wide. It originates from southern Mexico, Honduras and Guatemala. Its flowers are borne mainly during summer and consist of orange to scarlet tubes with a hairy interior to $1\frac{1}{2}$ in (35 mm) long. The lax, open habit of this shrub means it can also be trained up a wall as a semi-climber or espalier. **ZONES 10–12.**

MACLEAYA
PLUME POPPY

This genus honors the services to botany of Alexander Macleay (1767–1848), for many years Colonial Secretary of New South Wales, Australia. The plants are sometimes offered under the name *Bocconia*, a closely allied genus whose members are all American. The genus consists of 2 or so species of rhizomatous perennials from China and Japan that in fact do not really resemble poppies; the deception arises because the tubular flowers shed their petals as they open. The heart-shaped leaves are gray-green to olive green.
CULTIVATION: These fully frost-hardy plants prefer full sun and moderately fertile, moist but well-drained soil. Protect from cold winds. Propagate from seed or cuttings or by division.

Macleaya cordata
syn. *Bocconia cordata*

This tall perennial, growing to 5–8 ft (1.5–2.4 m) in height, has large, rounded, deeply veined, heart-shaped, gray-green leaves. Large, feathery, terminal flower spikes of cream tinted with pink are borne in summer. It is one of the most attractive foliage plants for the herbaceous border. It exudes a yellow sap when cut. This plant spreads from rhizomes and may become invasive. **ZONES 3–10.**

Macleaya microcarpa

This species is very similar in general appearance to *Macleaya cordata* except that it is a little shorter, at 6–7 ft (1.8–2.1 m) tall. It is also more invasive, spreading quickly by running roots, and its flowers are beige with a pink flush. **'Coral Plume'** has flowers that are a richer pink than the species. **ZONES 5–10.**

MACLURA
syn. *Cudrania*

This genus of 15 species of deciduous and evergreen thorny trees, shrubs and scrambling climbers is scattered widely throughout warmer parts of the world. The usually green flowers appear in racemes or clusters. Both male and female trees bear flowers and both are needed for fruits to grow; on female trees, the flowers are followed by compound fruits.
CULTIVATION: Fully frost hardy, they do best in full sun and in areas with hot summers. They will grow well in a wide range of soils. They have spreading roots and are resistant to very dry conditions. Propagate from seed in fall (autumn), or from cuttings in summer or late winter.

Maclura pomifera
OSAGE ORANGE

This deciduous tree from southern USA can reach 50 ft (15 m) in height with a

Maclura pomifera

Macropiper excelsum

spread of 40 ft (12 m). It has dark brown, fissured bark, and its thorny branches form an open, irregular crown with oval, dark green leaves. Tiny yellow flowers, borne in summer, are followed by large, wrinkled, pale green fruit. The hard, flexible timber is used for archery bows. Young plants may be susceptible to frost damage. **ZONES 7–10.**

MACROPIPER

This genus consists of 9 species of evergreen shrubs or small trees from the South Pacific, where they grow in low-altitude, humid forests. The large, soft leaves are held alternately along the branches and have unbroken margins; tiny yellow flowers are crowded into fleshy, cylindrical spikes that stand out from the foliage. These are followed by small, round, soft fruits.
CULTIVATION: Marginally frost hardy, they prefer well-drained, moderately fertile soil and a part-shaded position. During the growing season they require evenly moist soil; they also benefit from mulching. Propagate from seed or from cuttings in the cooler months.

Macropiper excelsum
KAWA KAWA, PEPPER TREE

A shrub or small tree reaching 20 ft (6 m) in height, this native of Australia, New Zealand and nearby Pacific islands has dark green, heart-shaped leaves, tiny yellow flowers and orange fruit that cluster on spikes. **ZONES 10–12.**

MACROZAMIA

This genus consists of about 24 species of cycads from Australia. Their stems vary from cylindrical to almost globose, above or below ground level, and are topped with palm-like fronds of evergreen foliage reaching up to 8 ft (2.4 m) long. The trunks are clothed in persistent dead frond bases. They produce large light green, pineapple-shaped, male and female cones, the individual cone scales tipped with a sharp spine; the mature female cones contain bright orange, red or yellow seeds. The starchy kernels were eaten by the Australian Aborigines after lengthy preparation that removed toxic substances. They cannot be eaten fresh.
CULTIVATION: Marginally frost hardy, they prefer temperate to subtropical areas and open, well-drained soil in part-shade. Propagate from fresh seed, which may take up to 18 months to germinate. Growth is very slow in cooler areas.

Macrozamia communis
BURRAWANG

Extensive stands of this species occur in coastal New South Wales. The trunk, though usually underground, may reach 6 ft (1.8 m) high. The crown carries up to 100 bright green, palm-like fronds about 6 ft (1.8 m) long. It produces multiple male and female cones 18 in (45 cm) long; the female cones contain oblong orange or red seeds. It tolerates light frosts and transplanting. **ZONES 9–11.**

Macrozamia miquelii
ZAMIA

This cycad occurs only in southeastern Queensland forests. Its trunk reaches 24 in (60 cm) high; the dark green, 5 ft (1.5 m) long fronds have many crowded leaflets, 10–15 in (25–38 cm) long, with white or reddish bases. The barrel-shaped female cones, 15 in (38 cm) long, contain oblong red or orange seeds. Male cones are the same length, but banana-shaped. **ZONES 10–12.**

Macrozamia spiralis

This small cycad from New South Wales grows to 3 ft (1 m) with a 6 ft (1.8 m) spread. It has a very short, mainly underground stem and produces rosettes of deep green fronds, each with a spirally twisted midrib and narrow, leathery leaflets. **ZONES 9–11.**

MAGNOLIA

This large, varied genus of 100 or more species of deciduous and evergreen trees and shrubs from East Asia and the Americas was named after French botanist Pierre Magnol. Magnolia leaves are usually oval and smooth edged. The flowers are generally large, fragrant and solitary, come in white, yellow, pink or purple, and vary in shape from almost flat and saucer-like to a narrow goblet shape. The fruits are cone-like or roughly cylindrical.

Macrozamia communis

CULTIVATION: Magnolias require deep, fertile, well-drained soil. Some species require alkaline soil while others prefer a mildly acid, humus-rich soil. The roots are fragile so the plants do not transplant readily. They thrive in sun or part-shade but need protection from strong or salty winds. The flower buds are frost sensitive. Propagate from cuttings in summer or seed in fall (autumn), or by grafting in winter.

Magnolia acuminata
CUCUMBER TREE

This most stately of American deciduous magnolias reaches 90 ft (27 m) in the wild and develops a wide pyramid shape. The 10 in (25 cm) long, mid- to dark green leaves have downy undersides. The cup-shaped, slightly fragrant, greenish yellow flowers with erect petals appear singly in early summer; the green cucumber-shaped fruit ripen to red. **ZONES 4–9.**

Magnolia campbellii

This deciduous Himalayan species grows 80 ft (24 m) tall with a 40 ft (12 m) wide crown. Slightly fragrant flowers appear on leafless branches from late winter to mid-spring. Plants raised from seed take 20 or more years to flower. **'Alba'** has pure white flowers; **'Charles Raffill'** is white and rose purple; **'Lanarth'** is a deeper rose purple; and ***Magnolia campbellii* subsp. *mollicomata*** flowers at an earlier age. **ZONES 7–10.**

Magnolia cylindrica

From eastern China, this large deciduous shrub or small tree grows up to 20 ft (6 m) high and wide. The typical form has 6 in (15 cm) long leaves that are dark green above, lighter below; its cup-shaped flowers are produced just before or with the new spring leaves. The flower color is creamy white often flushed pink at the base of the petals. **ZONES 6–9.**

Magnolia campbellii

Macrozamia miquelii

Magnolia delavayi

This evergreen species from China is spectacular in both flower and leaf. The foliage is impressive and is produced in large rosettes, each leaf is more than 12 in (30 cm) long, hard and leathery. Its open cup-shaped flowers are pale buff-yellow and slightly fragrant. They are produced in late summer, and individual flowers are short-lived. *Magnolia delavayi* is not frost hardy and in frost-prone areas will need protection. **ZONES 9–11.**

Magnolia denudata
syns *Magnolia conspicua*, *M. heptapeta*
YULAN MAGNOLIA

This small deciduous tree from central China grows 30 ft (9 m) in height and the same in width. Masses of scented, pure white flowers are borne from mid- to late spring before the mid-green leaves and rectangular cones containing orange seeds appear. The Chinese have cultivated the Yulan magnolia for centuries as a symbol of purity and candor. *Magnolia denudata* is closely related to *M. sprengeri* 'Diva', a taller plant bearing rose-pink flowers. **ZONES 6–10.**

Magnolia acuminata

Magnolia campbellii 'Lanarth'

Magnolia denudata

Magnolia grandiflora

Magnolia liliiflora

Magnolia globosa

Magnolia globosa

This deciduous large shrub or small tree can exceed 20 ft (6 m) in height and grows even wider than it is tall. Its leaves are attractive and up to 8 in (20 cm) long, often with brown felt on the underside. It is a summer-flowering species with pendent white cup- to egg-shaped blooms enclosing its burgundy stamens. This species is not often grown as it is usually considered to be less ornamental and frost hardy than relatives such as *Magnolia sieboldii*. ZONES 9–11.

Magnolia grandiflora

SOUTHERN MAGNOLIA, BULL BAY

One of the few cultivated evergreen magnolias, this southern USA species forms a dense 60–80 ft (18–24 m) dome of deep green leathery leaves, rust-colored underneath. Cup-shaped white or cream blooms 10 in (25 cm) across appear during late summer, followed by reddish brown cones. It usually prefers warm, moist conditions, but many cultivars (including the Freeman hybrids with *Magnolia virginiana*) are hardier; others, such as **'Exmouth'**, have a more conical habit and fragrant flowers from an early age. **'Edith Bogue'** is renowned for its cold tolerance. **'Little Gem'** is a narrow semi-dwarf selection with smaller flowers produced on young plants; it will reach up to 12 ft (3.5 m) tall or so in 15 years.

Magnolia sieboldii

Magnolia liliiflora 'Nigra'

'Russett' was selected because of its compact upright habit and the beige suede-like undersides of the leaves; it also has comparatively large flowers to 12 in (30 cm) across. **'St Mary'** is a slow growing compact form with profuse blooms and shiny green leaves, rust colored underneath. ZONES 6–11.

Magnolia hypoleuca

syn. *Magnolia obovata*

This large, magnolia, beautiful and rare, comes from Japan and will grow up to 100 ft (30 m) tall in the wild although rarely more than 30 ft (10 m) in cultivation. It is deciduous and its mid-green spatula-shaped leaves can exceed 15 in (38 cm) long. Its large cup-shaped flowers are produced in late spring and early summer. They are sweetly scented, 8 in (20 cm) across and creamy white with burgundy stamens. ZONES 6–10.

Magnolia kobus

KOBUS MAGNOLIA

Deciduous and conical, this Japanese species can reach 30 ft (10 m) or so tall, although it is not often seen this big in cultivation. Its aromatic leaves are 8 in (20 cm) long and mid-green in color. The flowers are produced in early spring before the foliage and have long, narrow petals sometimes stained pink at the base. It is similar to *Magnolia stellata*, but is a much larger plant. Once extensively used as a grafting stock, its suckering roots have reduced its popularity for this purpose. ZONES 5–9.

Magnolia liliiflora

syn. *Magnolia quinquepeta*

LILY MAGNOLIA

A deciduous, bushy shrub, this Chinese species reaches 10 ft (3 m) tall and 15 ft (4.5 m) wide. The mid- to dark green leaves, downy on the undersides, taper to a point. Fragrant, narrow, purplish pink flowers, whitish inside, are borne among the leaves from mid-spring until mid-summer. **'Nigra'** has large, dark wine purple flowers that are pale purple inside. ***Magnolia lilliflora* × *stellata* 'Rosea'** was produced in the USA in the 1950s. ZONES 6–10.

Magnolia × *loebneri*

LOEBNER MAGNOLIA

A deciduous hybrid between *Magnolia kobus* and a pink form of *M. stellata*, this species grows 30 ft (9 m) tall and 25 ft (8 m) wide. The blunt leaves range from dark to paler green. Variable white to pink star-like flowers open from early to mid-spring. **'Leonard Messel'** is a compact form bearing many-petalled lilac pink flowers in early to late winter and early spring, before and after the leaves emerge. **'Merrill'** has large white flowers faintly flushed pink. ZONES 5–9.

Magnolia macrophylla

BIGLEAF MAGNOLIA

This deciduous American 50 ft (15 m) tree has a broad, columnar shape. Its rather thin, oval leaves can grow to 3 ft (1 m) long. Large, fragrant, cup-shaped, creamy white to yellowish flowers, with pink or purple shading at the petal bases, appear with the leaves in mid-summer. ZONES 6–10.

Magnolia officinalis

A deciduous tree to 60 ft (18 m) tall from western and central China, this species is similar to *Magnolia hypoleuca*. However, as its flowers are smaller and irregularly shaped with less substantial petals, it is considered to be inferior. The flowers are beige or light brown and are produced in mid-summer. The scent is almost overpowering. ZONES 8–10.

Magnolia salicifolia

WILLOW-LEAFED MAGNOLIA, ANISE MAGNOLIA

This is a very dainty, usually conical, deciduous small tree from Japan. It grows up to 40 ft (12 m) tall although usually less in cultivation. As its name suggests, it has quite narrow small leaves, at least for this genus; they are up to 6 in (15 cm) long and 2 in (5 cm) wide. It produces its dainty narrow-petalled white flowers in early spring. ZONES 6–10.

Magnolia × *soulangeana*

Magnolia × *soulangeana* 'Lennei'

Magnolia sargentiana var. *robusta*

Magnolia sargentiana is a superb shrub to medium tree from western China. It grows up to 30 ft (10 m) tall and wide. As spring approaches, mature specimens produce large rose-pink waterlily-like flowers. *M. s.* var. *robusta* is a compact, bushy grower bearing large blooms that can be 12 in (30 cm) across. ZONES 9–11.

Magnolia sieboldii

OYAMA MAGNOLIA

This smallish tree or large shrub is one representative of a group of deciduous, summer-flowering species from China. Their pendent flowers distinguish them from the upright ones of the better known spring-flowering species. The white blooms are beautifully fragrant. ZONES 7–10.

Magnolia × *soulangeana*

SAUCER MAGNOLIA

This deciduous hybrid between *Magnolia denudata* and *M. liliiflora* first appeared in Europe in the 1820s and is now represented by many cultivars. It is an erect tree which grows to 25 ft (8 m) tall and 15 ft (4.5 m) wide, usually single trunked. The dark green leaves are tapered at the base and rounded at the tip, with a short point. Blooms in goblet, cup or saucer shapes and in white, pink or deep purple-pink appear from late winter to mid-spring, before and after the leaves emerge. **'Alexandrina'** flowers are pure white inside, flushed rose purple outside; and **'Brozzonii'** has very large white flowers, purple at the base.

Magnolia × *soulangeana*

Magnolia × *soulangeana* 'Lennei Alba'

Mahonia fortunei

Mahonia aquifolium

Goblet-shaped cultivars include **'Lennei',** purplish pink outside, white to pale purple inside; **'Lennei Alba'** with pure white flowers; and **'Rustica Rubra'**, rose red outside and pink and white inside. **ZONES 5–10.**

Magnolia sprengeri

From central China, this deciduous, spreading tree reaches a height of 70 ft (21 m) with a spread of 30 ft (9 m). Closely related to *Magnolia denudata*, it bears large, bowl-shaped, fragrant, rose-pink flowers from early to mid-spring, before the oval, dark green leaves appear. Popular cultivars include **'Wakehurst'** and **'Diva'**. **ZONES 8–10.**

Magnolia stellata
STAR MAGNOLIA

This many-branched, compact, deciduous shrub from Japan grows 10–15 ft (3–4.5 m) tall and wide, with aromatic bark when young, and narrow dark green leaves. Fragrant, star-like, pure white flowers open from silky buds in late winter and early spring, before the leaves. It flowers when quite young, and has several cultivars in shades of pink, including **'Rosea'**. **'Waterlily'**, the most prolific flowerer, has more petals and slightly larger white flowers. **ZONES 5–9.**

Magnolia 'Susan'

This upright, deciduous shrub has fragrant red-purple flowers with slightly curled petals, paler on the inside. It grows to 12 ft (3.5 m) in height. **ZONES 6–10.**

Mahonia bealei

Magnolia × *veitchii*
VEITCH MAGNOLIA

This hybrid was produced in 1907 by Peter Veitch when he crossed *Magnolia campbellii* with *M. denudata*. It makes a sizeable plant, very slowly reaching 100 ft (30 m). Several selections have been made from this cross including **'Isca'**, which has white flowers with pink stains at the petal bases, and **'Peter Veitch'**, which is soft pink shaded to white towards the petal tips. **ZONES 7–10.**

Magnolia virginiana
SWEET BAY

From eastern America, this evergreen to semi-evergreen tree reaches a height of 20 ft (6 m) in gardens. In cooler climates it may become deciduous. Fragrant, creamy white, goblet-shaped flowers are produced in summer and are followed by red fruit 2 in (5 cm) long with scarlet seeds. The leaves of this species are smaller than those of most other magnolias. **ZONES 5–10.**

Magnolia 'Wada's Memory'

Probably a hybrid between *Magnolia kobus* and *M. salicifolia*, this deciduous cultivar was selected in Seattle from seed sent by well-known plantsman Koichiro Wada of Yokohama. The petals of the fragrant white blooms are narrow but larger than either potential parent. It is an attractive small tree up to 30 ft (9 m) tall and 20 ft (6 m) wide. **ZONES 6–10.**

Magnolia wilsonii
WILSON'S MAGNOLIA

From China, this spreading, deciduous shrub or small tree grows to 20 ft (6 m) high and wide. In late spring and early summer fragrant cup-shaped white flowers with red or magenta stamens hang from arching branches among narrow mid- to dark green leaves that are velvety beneath. Pink fruit follow, ripening to release shiny red seeds. It tolerates alkaline soil. **ZONES 7–10.**

MAHONIA

The 70 species of evergreen, low-growing to tall-flowering shrubs that make up this genus come from East Asia, and North and Central America. They have beautiful foliage, often fragrant yellow flowers, blue-black, dark red or purplish fruits that usually have a bloom of whitish or blue-gray wax on some taller species and cultivars, and interesting bark. The berries resemble miniature grapes and make an excellent jelly. They make useful hedges, windbreaks and ground covers. Some botanists still include these plants in the genus *Berberis*. **CULTIVATION:** Cool-climate shrubs, they require a sunny aspect and well-drained, fertile soil with adequate water. In warmer climates they do better in shade or part-shade. They seldom need pruning, but old canes can be cut out at ground level. Propagate species from cuttings, basal suckers or seed; selected forms from cuttings or basal suckers.

Mahonia aquifolium
OREGON GRAPE, HOLLY GRAPE

From western North America, this dense, bushy species grows 6 ft (1.8 m) high and wide. Its 8 in (20 cm) long deep green pinnate leaves each consist of 5 to 9 holly-like leaflets; in the cooler months, these develop purple tones. Clustered heads of small, bright yellow flowers appear in spring, before the fruit. **'Compacta'** is a more compact form growing to about half the size of the species. **ZONES 5–10.**

Mahonia bealei
LEATHERLEAF MAHONIA

This species is sometimes listed as a form of *Mahonia japonica* and differs mainly in its shorter, stiffer flower spikes and the fact that its leaflets often overlap and have a broader base. The leaf color is also deeper. *Mahonia bealei* is native to western China. **ZONES 6–10.**

Mahonia fortunei
CHINESE MAHONIA

This erect shrub grows to 6 ft (1.8 m) or so. The mat green leaves consist of 7 or more leaflets. Although toothed, they are not as sharply spiny as some other species. Its usually yellow flowers appear in late fall (autumn). This is one of the most restrained species, making it ideal where space is limited. **ZONES 7–10.**

Mahonia fremontii
DESERT MAHONIA

From southwestern USA and Mexico, this open, branching shrub grows to 12 ft (3.5 m) tall. It has glaucous, yellow-green leaves with spiny leaflets and bears racemes of buttercup-yellow flowers in late winter and early spring, before the fruit. If pruned, it makes an attractive hedge for dry-climate gardens. **ZONES 8–11.**

Magnolia sprengeri 'Diva'

M

Magnolia wilsonii

Magnolia virginiana

Magnolia stellata

Mahonia 'Golden Abundance'

'Golden Abundance' is a hybrid seedling of several *Mahonia* species, including *M. amplectans*, *M. aquifolium* and *M. piperiana*. It is a vigorous, dense, upright shrub which grows to more than 6 ft (1.8 m) tall and wide. It has glossy, leathery green leaves and large clusters of showy yellow flowers which develop into purple fruit. It is well adapted to drier, warmer climates. **ZONES 6–9.**

Mahonia haematocarpa

syn. *Berberis haematocarpa*

A more sun-loving species than many of those native to southwestern parts of the USA, this shrub is quite closely related to *Mahonia fremontii*. However, it has longer, narrower leaves that are richer green in color and it also has plum-colored berries. **ZONES 8–11.**

Mahonia lomariifolia

Mahonia japonica

An upright, spreading shrub growing to a height of 6 ft (1.8 m) and a spread of 10 ft (3 m), this species has deep green leaves with numerous spiny leaflets. It bears long, slender, drooping sprays of fragrant yellow flowers from fall (autumn) to spring, followed by the fruit. It prefers a partly shaded position. **ZONES 6–10.**

Mahonia lomariifolia

From central and western China, this is one of the tallest and most elegant mahonias, growing 10–15 ft (3–4.5 m) tall and 6–10 ft (1.8–3 m) wide. Its long, dark green leaves, borne mostly at the ends of the bamboo-like shoots, have narrow, holly-like spiny leaflets. Dense, upright racemes of fragrant, bright yellow flowers appear during late fall (autumn) and winter, before the purplish fruit. **ZONES 7–10.**

Mahonia × *media*

This hybrid between *Mahonia japonica* and *M. lomariifolia* is one of several named cultivars of this cross that has been repeated several times in England to produce plants with the good foliage of the latter and the hardiness of the former. **'Charity'** has flowers in densely clustered racemes; **'Buckland'** bears its flowers in arching racemes. **ZONES 6–10.**

Mahonia nervosa

LONGLEAF MAHONIA

From northwest America comes this suckering dwarf shrub up to 2 ft (0.6 m) or more tall and 3 ft (1 m) wide. It has rich dark green foliage often turning dark burgundy with winter cold. Its yellow flowers are produced in dense racemes up to 8 in (20 cm) long in spring, followed by blue-black berries. **ZONES 6–9.**

Mahonia × *media*

Mahonia japonica

Mahonia nevinii

Mahonia nevinii

NEVIN MAHONIA

This is a small erect shrub to 8 ft (2.4 m) tall from California, with leaves consisting of up to 7 narrow lanceolate leaflets of a pleasant gray-blue color with a lovely white underside. Its flowers, produced in quite small clusters, are typically yellow and are followed by dark red berries. **ZONES 8–11.**

Mahonia pinnata

CALIFORNIAN HOLLY GRAPE

This species, related to *Mahonia aquifolium*, is a strong suckering shrub with prickly leaflets usually a dull green in summer but turning maroon and red in winter. Its flowers, produced in late winter, are yellow and appear in dense clusters followed by blue-black berries. The plant often sold as this species is actually a hybrid with *M. aquifolium* called *M.* × *wagneri* **'Pinnacle'**. **ZONES 7–10.**

Mahonia repens

CREEPING MAHONIA

From western USA, this shrub grows to only 18 in (45 cm) or less in height. Its creeping habit makes it a useful ground cover, especially on uneven, rocky ground. The glaucous green leaves, with spiny leaflets, often turn a reddish shade in colder winters. Bunches of small, fragrant, yellow flowers are borne in spring, followed by the globular fruit. **ZONES 6–9.**

MAIANTHEMUM

TWO-LEAFED SOLOMON'S SEAL, MAY LILY, FALSE LILY-OF-THE-VALLEY

This genus of 3 rhizomatous perennials comes from temperate zones of the northern hemisphere. Fully dormant over winter, the foliage develops in spring; it consists of a small number of heart-shaped leaves on each wiry stem. The stems produce spikes of small white starry flowers at their tips. Small red berries follow the flowers and can be the showiest feature.

CULTIVATION: These fully frost-hardy woodland plants thrive in cool, moist soil rich with leaf mold and prefer shade. In very loose, open soil the rhizomes can spread quickly and become invasive. Propagate from seed or by division.

Mahonia repens

Maianthemum bifolium

FALSE LILY-OF-THE-VALLEY

This is the most commonly grown species and is a dainty herbaceous ground cover for shade with a creeping rootstock very like that of the true lily-of-the-valley. It comes up in spring and produces 2 attractive bright green heart-shaped leaves per stem. Between these is a spike of tiny white flowers followed by red berries. It rarely exceeds 6 in (15 cm) in height, but can make quite extensive colonies. **ZONES 3–9.**

Maianthemum canadense

This vigorous ground cover has slender stems bearing spikes of small white flowers in late spring and early summer; these are followed by red berries. The large, wavy edged, upright, oval leaves are glossy green. It reaches only 4 in (10 cm) in height. **ZONES 3–9.**

Maianthemum dilatatum

This low-growing perennial to 15 in (35 cm) high bears 2 heart-shaped leaves to 8 in (20 cm) long and short terminal spikes of white flowers followed by red berries. **ZONES 3–9.**

MALCOLMIA

MALCOLM STOCK

This genus consists of 35 species of bushy or prostrate annuals and perennials from the Mediterranean region. The flowers, usually quite small although often sweetly fragrant, are 4-petalled and white or shades of red or purple; they appear from spring to fall (autumn).

CULTIVATION: These fully frost-hardy plants prefer full sun and fertile, well-drained soil that is not too rich as this will encourage leaf growth at the expense of flowers. Propagate from seed in spring, summer or early fall; they self-seed freely.

Malcolmia maritima

VIRGINIA STOCK, VIRGINIAN STOCK

An attractive, low-growing annual, this plant is valued for its ability to flower quickly from seed—as soon as 4 to 6 weeks after seed is sown. It has oval, gray-green leaves and bears 1 in (25 mm) wide fragrant flowers in pink, red, mauve and white. It has an erect habit and is fast growing to a height of 8 in (20 cm) and spread of 2–3 in (5–8 cm). For a long flowering season, sow seed at frequent intervals. It is very useful for edging, for paths, crevices and window boxes, and for combining with spring-flowering bulbs. **ZONES 8–11.**

MALEPHORA

This is a southern African genus of 15 species of spreading or shrubby perennials with gnarled stems and more or less succulent, fleshy leaves that are triangular to cylindrical in cross-section and have a blue-gray, powdery surface bloom. The leaves are small, usually under 2 in (5 cm) long, and may develop red tints in cold or dry conditions. From late summer to early winter bright yellow, orange or red daisy-like flowers develop in the leaf axils and at the stem tips.

Malosma laurina

Malosma laurina

CULTIVATION: Grow in light, gritty, well-drained soil in full sun and keep dry over winter. They will tolerate occasional light frosts, but prolonged cold or wet weather causes rotting. Propagate from seed or by breaking off the fleshy leaves and treating them as cuttings in spring or summer.

Malephora crocea

Native to Western Cape in South Africa, this succulent has mid-sized green leaves and produces yellow, daisy-like flowers in spring. It grows to a height of 8 in (20 cm). **ZONES 9–11.**

Malephora lutea

This spreading plant from South Africa has yellow-green foliage growing up to 2 in (5 cm) long. Orange and yellow daisy-shaped flowers, 1 in (25 mm) across, appear in spring. **ZONES 9–11.**

MALOSMA

This genus consists of only one species of evergreen shrub or small tree native to California. *Malosma* is grown in warm-temperate areas for its attractive foliage and flowers and decorative clusters of berry-like fruits.
CULTIVATION: In frost-free climates grow in a moderately fertile, well-drained soil in full sun. Water freely during growth. In frost-prone areas, grow in a cool or warm greenhouse. Propagate from seed or root cuttings.

Malosma laurina
LAUREL SUMAC

Malosma laurina is a shrub or small tree growing to 6–18 ft (1.8–5.5 m) tall. It has alternate, ovate leaves with a slight reddish tinge and white margins. In spring or early summer, it bears compact, pyramidal clusters of small flowers with spreading petals. These are followed by clusters of small white berries. **ZONES 9–11.**

MALPIGHIA

Several of the 45 species of this genus of hot-climate evergreen trees and shrubs are grown for their delicate flowers and attractive foliage. Originating in the West Indies and Central and South America, they have distinctive flowers—pink, rose or red, with 5 slender-stalked petals—which are followed by edible berries in shades of orange, red or purple. The leaves are leathery and are usually toothed.
CULTIVATION: These frost-tender plants need regular feeding and watering, and do best in an open, sunny position in well-drained, moderately rich, moist soil. If desired, prune to maintain a dense habit. Propagate from seed or cuttings.

Malpighia coccigera
BARBADOS HOLLY, SINGAPORE HOLLY

This beautiful little shrub from the West Indies grows slowly to a height and spread of 30 in (75 cm). It has small, shiny, holly-like leaves and in summer neat, pale pink flowers with fringed petals and golden stamens are crowded along the branches. These are followed by the red berries. It makes an excellent miniature clipped hedge in the tropics. **ZONES 10–12.**

Malpighia glabra
BARBADOS CHERRY, ACEROLA, WEST INDIAN CHERRY

A shrub from tropical America, this species grows 5–10 ft (1.5–3 m) tall with smooth-edged leaves. In summer it produces clusters of small, pale pink flowers. It bears red, cherry-sized fruit; though tart in flavor, these are rich in vitamin C and much used in the plant's native lands in cooking and for making jams and preserves. **ZONES 9–12.**

MALUS
APPLE, CRABAPPLE

This genus of 35 species of deciduous flowering and fruiting trees from the northern temperate zones contains the diverse crabapple as well as the many varieties of the long-cultivated edible apple, probably derived from crosses between several species and usually named *Malus* × *domestica* or *M. pumila*. The leaves are simple and toothed, sometimes lobed, and the flower clusters vary from white to deep rose pink or deep reddish purple. They are valued for their shapely form, moderate size and delicate spring blossom.
CULTIVATION: Very frost hardy, they prefer a cool, moist climate and full sun (but tolerate part-shade) and need fertile, well-drained, loamy soil with protection from strong winds. They grow in poorer soils if fertilized annually. Cut out dead wood in winter and prune for a balanced shape. Propagate by budding in summer or grafting in winter. Watch for aphids and fireblight.

Malus × *arnoldiana*
ARNOLD CRABAPPLE

Malus × *arnoldiana* is a low-spreading tree growing to 20 ft (6 m) tall but is substantially broader. A hybrid between *Malus baccata* and *M. floribunda*, it is not a particularly profuse grower but it does make quite ashow with its pink buds opening to off-white flowers. The fruit are also attractive, are about ½ in (12 mm) or more in diameter and are yellow-green flushed red. **ZONES 4–9.**

Malus × *atrosanguinea*
CARMINE CRABAPPLE

This hybrid, a cross between *Malus halliana* and *M. sieboldii*, looks something like *M. floribunda* in habit with its spreading, slightly pendulous shoots. Its flowers, however, are much more deeply colored. The leaves are glossy green, the flowers almost crimson until they open rose pink; they are followed by red-blushed yellow fruit in fall (autumn). This plant can reach 20 ft (6 m) in height and spread. **ZONES 4–9.**

Malus baccata var. *mandschurica*
MANCHURIAN CRABAPPLE

This form of Siberian crabapple is only different from the typical species in that its leaves are more sparsely toothed and are downy beneath. Otherwise it has the same masses of white blossoms followed by small red or yellow fruit usually about ½ in (12 mm) in diameter. It can reach 50 ft (15 m) in height and spread although pruning can control this. **ZONES 2–9.**

Malus baccata var. *mandschurica*

Malus baccata var. *mandschurica*

Malpighia coccigera

Malpighia glabra

Malus × *domestica* 'Jonamac'

Malus × *domestica* 'Golden Delicious'

Malus × *domestica* 'Granny Smith'

Malus × *domestica* 'McIntosh Rogers'

Malus × *domestica* 'Delicious'

Malus × *domestica* 'Jonathan'

Malus × *domestica* 'Discovery'

Malus coronaria

AMERICAN SWEET CRAB

This small, vigorous species grows 30 ft (9 m) tall. It has fragrant white flowers and green, unpalatable, acid crabapples. The shoots bear slightly lobed, broad, short, bright green leaves. **ZONES 4–9.**

Malus × *domestica*

COMMON APPLE

This large hybrid group includes upright and spreading trees, usually with dark, gray-brown scaly bark and gray to reddish brown twigs. They can grow 30 ft (9 m) tall and 15 ft (4.5 m) wide. Their leaves are usually downy underneath and the white flowers are usually suffused with pink. The juicy, sweet fruit are green or yellow to red. These common orchard trees are distinguished from the wild crab *(Malus sylvestris)* by their downy shoots, blunter leaves and juicy fruit that sweeten on ripening. Apples are not completely self-fertile and for fruit production a different cultivar growing nearby is needed. Advice on compatible pollinating cultivars should be obtained before buying apple plants. There are hundreds of cultivars; some of the best known are **'Crofton'**, **'Cox's Orange Pippin'**, **'Discovery'**, **'Delicious'**, **'Golden Delicious'**, **'Golden Harvest'**, **'Granny Smith'**, **'Gravenstein'**, **'James Grieve'**, **'Jonathan'** and **'McIntosh Rogers'**. Many relatively new varieties are grown for their greater disease resistance. **'Gala'** is a somewhat small dessert fruit with excellent flavor and good storage qualities; **'Jonagold'** has large, yellow, red-striped fruit with good flavor and crisp texture; and **'Liberty'**, a highly productive and especially disease-resistant tree bears striped dark red fruit with pale yellow crisp flesh.

The above are generally accepted varieties grown commercially to supply year-round fruit. But there are many fine old apples worthwhile for home gardens and small orchards with special markets. **'Adam's Pearman'** is a quality dessert apple with golden-yellow skin flushed bright red; **'Ashmead's Kernel'** is an upright spreading tree with light greenish yellow fruit and sweet white flesh; **'Blenheim Orange'** has yellow fruit with one-half flushed dull orange red; **'Bramley's Seedling'** has large, late-ripening fruit best suited to cooking; and **'Ellison's Orange'** bears light greenish yellow fruit with soft juicy flesh and a rich flavor.

Some apple varieties have been bred as single-stemmed columnar forms, enabling the trees to be grown close together in a row without occupying a lot of ground. Named varieties include **'Starkspur Compact Mac'** and **'Starkspur Supreme Red Delicious'.** Some tall forms such as **'Jonamac'** can be trained over a path to make an arch. **ZONES 3–9.**

Malus florentina

syn. × *Malosorbus florentina*

This species from northern Italy may be a natural hybrid between *Malus sylvestris* and *Sorbus torminalis*. It is a small round-headed tree with white flowers followed by small bright red berries. Its serrated gray-green foliage is similar to that of a hawthorn *(Crataegus)*. **ZONES 6–9.**

Malus florentina

Malus × *domestica* 'Ashmead's Kernel'

Malus × *domestica* 'Ellison's Orange'

M. × *d.* 'Starkspur Supreme Red Delicious'

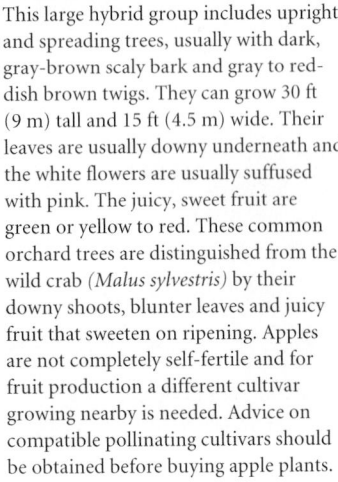

Malus × *domestica* 'Blenheim Orange'

Malus × *domestica* 'Bramley's Seedling'

M. × *d.* 'Starkspur Compact Mac'

Malus, ornamental crabapple, 'Red Jade'

Malus pumila 'Dartmouth'

Malus floribunda

JAPANESE CRAB

This parent of many hybrids grows 25 ft (8 m) tall with a broad 30 ft (9 m) crown and arching branches. It bears profuse, pale pink flowers, red in bud, and tiny, pea-shaped, yellowish blushed red fruit. It is thought to have been introduced to Japan from China. **ZONES 4–9.**

Malus hupehensis

syn. ***Malus theifera***

HUPEH CRAB, TEA CRABAPPLE

From the Himalayas and China, where a tisane ('red tea') is made from the leaves, this vigorous, spreading crabapple grows 30 ft (9 m) tall and wide. The leaves are dark green, tinged purple when young. It bears large, fragrant white flowers, pink in bud, and small yellow and orange fruit that ripen to red. **ZONES 4–10.**

Malus ioensis

IOWA CRAB

Growing 20 ft (6 m) tall and 25 ft (8 m) wide, this leafy tree has a shrubby habit and good fall (autumn) color. Its heavy crop of large, fragrant, pale pink flowers is borne in late spring—it is one of the last crabapples to flower, and one of the finest. **'Plena'** has double flowers followed by green fruit; **'Prariefire'** has glossy bark, red-purple single flowers and deep purple-red fruit. **ZONES 2–9.**

Malus × *magdeburgensis*

This hybrid crabapple has as its parents *Malus pumila* and *M. spectabilis*, most closely resembling the latter. It makes a bushy spreading tree to 20 ft (6 m) in height and spread with deep green foliage. Its deep pink semi-double flowers are sometimes followed by ½ in (12 mm) yellow fruit. **ZONES 4–9.**

Malus × *micromalus*

MIDGET CRABAPPLE

This cross between *Malus baccata* and *M. spectabilis* makes an attractive, small, erect tree with small deep pink flowers produced in enough quantity to make it showy en masse. Its berries are red or yellow and slightly pointed. **ZONES 4–9.**

Malus, ornamental crabapples

This group includes **'Beverly'**, an upright spreading tree to 20 ft (6 m) high with white single flowers and excellent, small bright red fruit; **'Butterball'**, up to 25 ft (8 m) tall with pink-tinged white flowers and bright orange-yellow fruit; **'Candied Apple'**, a small, spreading tree with pink flowers and red fruit; **'Dolgo'**, to 40 ft (12 m) with white flowers and purple-red fruit; **'Golden Hornet'**, to 25 ft (8 m), with pink-flushed flowers and edible golden fruit; **'John Downie'**, conical when mature, with red-flushed orange fruit; **'Katherine'** with semi-double pink flowers and rich red fruit blushed yellow; **'Naragansett'**, a good disease-resistant tree to 13 ft (4 m) high with showy red buds, white single flowers and pendulous clusters of cherry-red fruit; **'Pink Perfection'** with pale pink and white double flowers; **'Prince Georges'** with sterile, scented fully double pale pink flowers; **'Profusion'** with rich, dark wine red flowers and cherry-like, red-purple fruit; **'Radiant'**, to 25 ft (8 m) high with deep red buds, deep pink single flowers and bright red fruit; and **'Red Jade'**, a weeping tree to 12 ft (3.5 m) with white- to pink-flushed flowers and glossy red fruit. **ZONES 3–9.**

Malus hupehensis

Malus floribunda

Malus × *purpurea* 'Aldenhamensis'

Malus pumila

This tree grows 12–15 ft (3.5–4.5 m) high and half as wide. It bears lance-shaped leaves with serrated margins, and pink and white flowers. The small, attractive fruit are ideal for stewing and have been used for generations for jellies and jams. **'Dartmouth'**, an open, spreading tree to 25 ft (8 m) with white flowers from pink buds and large crimson fruit. **ZONES 3–9.**

Malus × *purpurea*

These hybrid trees have very dark, sometimes glossy, bark and bronze or purple-red foliage. The flowers are large, red to purple-red, followed by small fruit of a similar color. Cultivars include **'Aldenhamensis'**, a spreading tree to 25 ft (8 m) with semi-double, wine-red flowers and purple-red fruit; and **'Eleyi'**, with purple leaves, deep crimson flowers and purple-red fruit. **ZONES 4–9.**

Malus × *magdeburgensis*

M., ornamental crab., 'Golden Hornet'

M., ornamental crabapple, 'Butterball'

M., ornamental crab., 'Pink Perfection'

Malus, ornamental crabapple, 'Prince Georges'

M

Malus × *robusta*

These hybrids between *Malus baccata* and *M. prunifolia* are known as Siberian crabapples, although this makes little sense as they don't originate there. Two cultivars are regularly met with: **'Yellow Siberian'** and **'Red Siberian'**, named obviously after the color of their fruit. Both grow into vigorous small trees of spreading habit to 30 ft (9 m) high and wide and their flowers are pink-tinged white. **ZONES 3–10.**

Malus sargentii
SARGENT'S CRABAPPLE

A spreading shrub, this species reaches a height of 8–10 ft (2.4–3 m) and spread of 12–20 ft (3.5–6 m). It bears oval, dark green leaves with serrated margins, masses of white flowers and tiny, deep red fruit that last well into winter. Some branches may carry thorns. **ZONES 4–9.**

Malus sieboldii 'Gorgeous'

A cultivar whose breeder had no modesty, this green-leafed form has white blossoms from pink buds followed by good crops of green-red to deep red crabapples. This variety is considered a good one to harvest for jellies and preserves. **ZONES 5–10.**

Malus sylvestris
WILD CRABAPPLE, COMMON CRABAPPLE

From Europe, this parent of orchard crabapples can grow 30 ft (9 m) tall and 10 ft (3 m) wide, and has a rounded crown and dark bark. It bears white flowers flushed with pink and its yellow, flushed orange-red fruit, although rather sour and bitter, make delicious conserves. The leaves have a partly red stalk and some branches may bear thorns. **ZONES 3–9.**

Malus toringoides

From China, this very attractive small tree grows 25 ft (8 m) tall and has wide-spreading branches. The distinctive leaves are small and narrow and often 2- or 3-lobed. Creamy white flowers are followed by round or pear-shaped red and yellow fruit. **ZONES 5–10.**

Malus transitoria

This elegant species resembles *Malus toringoides* and is also Chinese. It differs in its smaller, narrower habit and more narrowly lobed, smaller leaves. Its flowers are white and are followed by small round yellow fruit and rich fall (autumn) foliage. **ZONES 5–10.**

Malus tschonoskii

This Japanese species makes a quick-growing, upright conical tree to 40 ft (12 m) tall and about 20 ft (6 m) wide. Its flowers are white with a pink flush and are followed by yellowish green fruit with a red tinge. Its foliage is mid-green and large, up to 5 in (12 cm) long. In fall (autumn), it is the tree's crowning glory; it turns brilliant orange, red and burgundy, making it a spectacular sight. **ZONES 6–10.**

Malus × *zumi* var. *calocarpa*

A hybrid between *Malus baccata* var. *mandshurica* and *M. sieboldii*, this form resembles the latter parent and is often included as a variety of it. A small, spreading tree, it has mid-green foliage, small fragrant white flowers from pink buds and very small, persistent, glossy red fruit that can be still evident at the end of winter, birds allowing. **ZONES 5–10.**

Malus toringoides

Malus sieboldii 'Gorgeous'

Malus sargentii

Malva sylvestris

Malva moschata 'Alba'

MALVA
MALLOW

This genus is made up of 30 species of annuals, biennials and perennials that originate in Europe, North Africa and Asia, but have in some cases naturalized elsewhere. The flowers are similar to but smaller than the popular *Lavatera* to which the malvas are related; they are single, 5-petalled flowers in shades of white, pink, blue or purple. Although they may not be quite as showy as those of *Lavatera,* they do make attractive subjects for the border or wild garden.
CULTIVATION: These plants flourish in sunny, well-drained aspects and tend to be more robust and longer lived in not too rich soil. They are fully frost hardy. Cut plants back after the first flowers have faded. Propagate from cuttings or seed in spring; the perennials often self-seed. Watch for rust disease in spring.

Malva alcea
HOLLYHOCK MALLOW

This short-lived perennial species from southern Europe grows to about 4 ft (1.2 m) tall and 24 in (60 cm) wide. Its foliage is large—up to 12 in (30 cm) wide toward the base of the plant—and heart-shaped with scalloped edges. The leaves get smaller and more serrated the farther up the stem they are. The purple-pink flowers are produced throughout summer and well into fall (autumn). **ZONES 4–10.**

Malva moschata
MUSK MALLOW

Useful for naturalizing in a wild garden or odd corner, this perennial has narrow, lobed, divided leaves with a sticky, hairy texture which emit a musky, cheesy odor when crushed. A native of Europe, *Malva moschata* bears profuse spikes of saucer-shaped pink flowers in summer. **'Alba'**, a white cultivar, is also very popular. It has a bushy, branching habit and can grow to a height of 3 ft (1 m). **ZONES 3–10.**

Malva sylvestris
TALL MALLOW, HIGH MALLOW, CHEESES

This erect perennial species grows to 3 ft (1 m) tall, often behaving as a biennial. Its leaves are broad and heart-shaped to rounded, slightly lobed and mid- to dark green. The flowers are produced from late spring to mid-fall (mid-autumn) and in the wild form are mauve-pink with dark purple veins. Cultivars have been selected with flower colors from pure white through blues to deep purple. **ZONES 5–10.**

MALVASTRUM

This genus is made up of 30 species of mostly shrubs and spreading to erect evergreen perennials from drier tropical and subtropical regions of the world. They produce colorful small flowers like miniature *Hibiscus.* The leaves vary with the species, but are usually lobed and more or less rounded.
CULTIVATION: They are most successful in sandy or gravelly, well-drained soil in full sun. Plants are not particularly heavy feeders, neither do they demand a lot of water although consistent moisture during the warmer months does produce a fuller, more luxuriant plant. Hardiness varies with species, some being intolerant of all but the lightest frosts. Prune to shape in early spring and propagate from seed sown in spring or from soft tip cuttings taken in early summer.

Malvastrum lateritium

From Argentina and Uruguay comes this low-growing, spreading perennial with lobed leaves that are about 4 in (10 cm) long. The flowers, 2 in (5 cm) wide, dot the plant in spring and summer. They are a reddish yellow color with darker, outlined centers. Plants grow to 10 in (25 cm) in height and spread to 6 ft (1.8 m) across and are moderately frost hardy. **ZONES 8–10.**

MALVAVISCUS

This genus of 3 species of soft-wooded, frost-tender evergreen shrubs and small trees from tropical North and South America is named from the Latin *malva* (mallow) and *viscidus* (sticky). They have heart-shaped, light to mid-green leaves and long-stemmed, hibiscus-like flowers in red, pink or white.
CULTIVATION: These frost-tender plants prefer a warm, humid climate but thrive in subtropical frost-free areas. They need well-drained, loamy soil and ample summer moisture. If container-grown, they must be well watered. Prune flowering wood in winter to maintain shape. Propagate from seed or cuttings in late summer, which strike easily.

M

Malvaviscus arboreus
SLEEPY MALLOW, WAX MALLOW

This vigorous rounded shrub has serrated, bright green, softly hairy leaves and grows to a height of 10 ft (3 m) with a similar spread. From summer to fall (autumn), small bright red flowers with protruding stamens appear. **ZONES 9–12.**

Malvaviscus penduliflorus
syn. ***Malvaviscus aboreus* var. *penduliflorus***
CARDINAL'S HAT, SLEEPING HIBISCUS

This rounded, warm-climate shrub from Mexico grows 10 ft (3 m) tall and wide. It bears large, mid-green leaves and long, pendulous, bright red flowers 2–3 in (5–8 cm) long. It grows in sun or part-shade. In early spring, prune back half the last season's growth to ensure good flowering in the later summer months. **ZONES 10–12.**

MAMMILLARIA
PINCUSHION CACTI

This genus of cacti contains around 150 dwarf species mostly native to Mexico. The short, globular or clump-forming, erect columns up to 12 in (30 cm) tall have stems with raised, horny tubercles and downy areoles sprouting silky bristles or tough, curving spines. In spring and summer, funnel- or daisy-shaped flowers appear in a circle around the crown, followed by light green or reddish fruits. **CULTIVATION:** These marginally frost-hardy cacti require full sun for maximum flowering. Easy to grow, they prefer light, sandy soil and occasional water, particularly in the growing season. Most species will only tolerate frost in a dried-out state. Propagate from seed in spring and summer, or from offsets in summer. Mealybug and spider mite can be a problem.

Mammillaria bocasana
POWDER PUFF, SNOWBALL CACTUS

The white, hooked spines of this spherical cactus were used as fish hooks in its native Mexico. It grows 8–12 in (20–30 cm) high and 8 in (20 cm) across, with offsets measuring 2 in (5 cm) across each head. Off-white, daisy-like flowers appear in spring and fall (autumn) and oblong red berries follow in summer. **ZONES 9–11.**

Mammillaria bombycina
SILK PINCUSHION

Native to Mexico, this single, spherical cactus has short, pillar-like stems that grow up to 8 in (20 cm) tall and have spirally arranged tubercles with numerous whorls of white spines and yellowish brown central spines. If allowed full sun, purple-pink flowers bloom around the fleecy crown from winter into spring. **ZONES 9–11.**

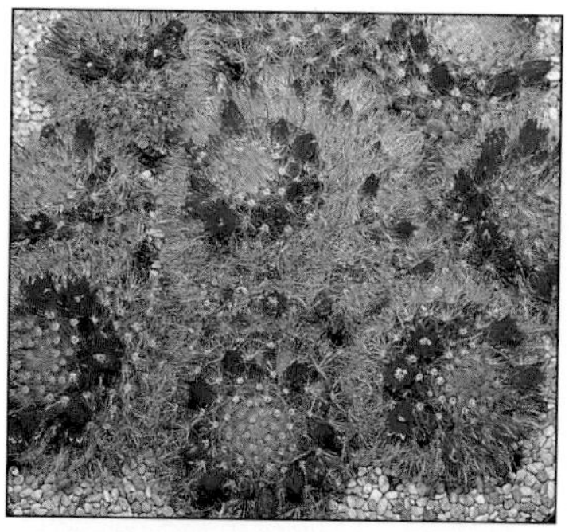
Mammillaria bocasana

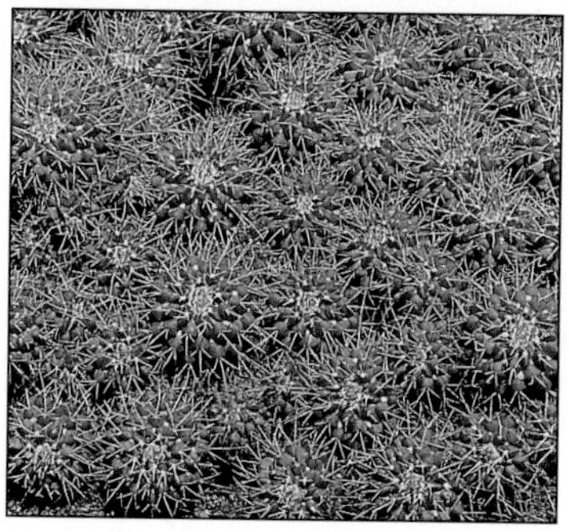
Mammillaria compressa

Malvaviscus arboreus

Mammillaria candida
SNOWBALL CUSHION CACTUS

A pale, bluish green spherical cactus from Mexico, this species grows 6 in (15 cm) tall and 8 in (20 cm) wide and is covered with short spines. Pink, daisy-like flowers develop in spring and are followed by red berries in summer. **ZONES 9–11.**

Mammillaria carmenae

This central Mexican species produces numerous spherical stems covered in fine white to buff spines, up to 100 per cluster. Its white to pale pink flowers are produced in spring and summer and are followed by light green fruit. **ZONES 9–11.**

Mammillaria compressa

This species offsets freely into small pincushion clumps covered in long white spines. The body is colored a light bluish green to gray-green and the head of each offset can grow to 8 in (20 cm) high and 2–3 in (5–8 cm) wide. This plant develops dark purple, daisy-shaped blossoms in spring and large red berries in summer. **ZONES 9–11.**

Malvaviscus arboreus

Mammillaria candida

Mammillaria carmenae

Mammillaria guelzowiana

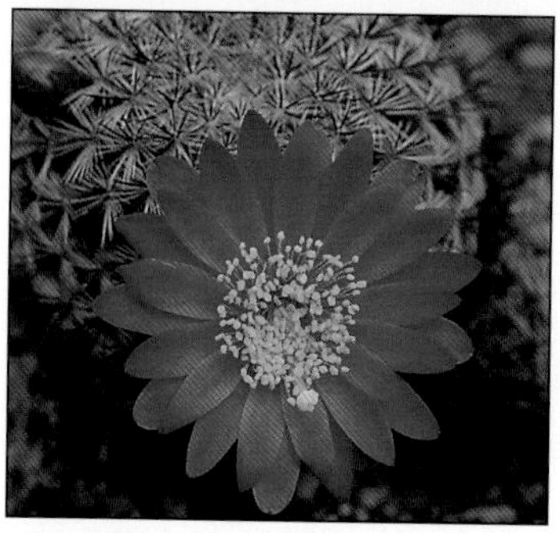
Mammillaria deherdtiana

Mammillaria geminispina

Mammillaria deherdtiana

The spines of this small, spherical, clumping cactus from Mexico are light yellow, turning white with reddish tips as it matures. Each head grows 1 in (25 mm) high and 2 in (5 cm) across. Pink, funnel-shaped flowers 2 in (5 cm) long appear in spring, followed by tiny light green fruit in summer. **ZONES 9–11.**

Mammillaria elongata
LADY FINGERS, LACE CACTUS

This cylindrical, yellow-spined cactus from Mexico has numerous finger-like stems growing out from the base in varying thicknesses. Small light yellow flowers develop in spring and fall (autumn). They are followed by very elongated little red fruit. **ZONES 9–11.**

Mammillaria geminispina

This light green Mexican cactus offsets into spiny, spherical clumps. It bears small, creamy, daisy-shaped flowers in spring and red berries in summer. **ZONES 9–11.**

Mammillaria guelzowiana

This species bears 2 in (5 cm) fluorescent pink flowers with golden stamens, and grows 4 in (10 cm) tall and 3 in (8 cm) wide. It is not easy to cultivate, and needs very strong light. **ZONES 9–11.**

Mammillaria haageana

Mammillaria haageana
syn. ***Mammillaria elegans***

This marginally frost-hardy Mexican species is singular and globular, later clustering in short columns up to 8 in (20 cm) tall and 4 in (10 cm) wide. Four black-pointed central spines and many shorter white bristles cover the blue-green stems. In spring it bears tiny, vivid red flowers in coronets around the top of the plant. **ZONES 9–11.**

M

Mammillaria hahniana

Mammillaria microhelia

Mammillaria plumosa

Mammillaria hahniana
OLD LADY CACTUS

The light green body of this species is covered in white felty hair and fine white spines. The globular offsets grow up to 4 in (10 cm) in height and spread. It bears attractive purple flowers in spring and fall (autumn) and small red berries in summer. **ZONES 9–11.**

Mammillaria lloydii

This is a dark green spherical cactus from Mexico with attractive reddish brown spines. The white, daisy-shaped flowers appear in spring, and are followed by small pink berries. **ZONES 9–11.**

Mammillaria microhelia

The creamy spines of this solitary or clustering cactus are so profuse that they dominate the small, pale yellow flowers. The thick stems are cylindrical and grayish green. As this cactus matures, it slowly produces offsets in a clump that can reach 15 in (38 cm) across. **ZONES 9–11.**

Mammillaria pectinifera
syn. ***Solisia pectinata***

The lovely flowers of this species, pale pink with a pale brown mid-stripe,

Mammillaria lloydii

Mammillaria rhodantha 'Rubra'

crowd around the stem in a lavish coronet. At 1 in (25 mm) across, they are nearly as wide as the stem itself. **ZONES 9–11.**

Mammillaria plumosa
FEATHER CACTUS

This curious cactus, native to Mexico, readily forms a thick, felty, mound-like cluster 6 in (15 cm) high and 15 in (38 cm) wide. The stems are blanketed with feather-like radial spines, which sprout from downy areoles. In winter, creamy green, pink or yellow flowers appear, but rarely under cultivation. It prefers fertile, alkaline soil. **ZONES 9–11.**

Mammillaria prolifera
LITTLE CANDLES

Native to southwestern USA, northeastern Mexico and the West Indies, this spherical, self-fertilizing cactus offsets strongly to form cushions 2½ in (6 cm) tall and 2 in (5 cm) wide. Creamy white daisy-like flowers appear in spring while small red berries stay on the plant all year round. **ZONES 9–11.**

Mammillaria rhodantha 'Rubra'

Each head of this spherical, offsetting cactus, native to Mexico, reaches a height of 12 in (30 cm) and grows 4 in (10 cm) across. It has a profusion of attractive, dark red spines with pink funnel-shaped flowers blooming in summer followed by oval red fruit. **ZONES 9–11.**

Mammillaria scrippsiana var. *rooksbiana*

This Mexican cactus, which reaches a height of 2½ in (6 cm), has a spherical, blue-green body and long spines with downy axils. It usually grows in clumps and produces deep pink, funnel-shaped flowers in spring. **ZONES 9–11.**

Mammillaria pectinifera

Mammillaria sempervivi

This is a dark blue-green, spherical cactus with short, reddish spines. Reaching 3 in (8 cm) wide, it has small pink flowers in spring and tiny red fruit appearing in summer. **ZONES 9–11.**

Mammillaria silvatica

This species forms clumps of cylindrical stems 6–8 in (15–20 cm) high. The tops of the stems are ringed by minute pink flowers that develop into reddish pink fruit. **ZONES 9–11.**

Mammillaria zeilmanniana
ROSE PINCUSHION

From Mexico, this marginally frost-hardy cactus has globular stems up to 6 in (15 cm) high and spreads out, in colonies, to 12 in (30 cm). Silky brown and white radial spines and reddish brown central spines cover the green stems. Rings of dark purple flowers appear around the crown in spring. **ZONES 9–11.**

MANDEVILLA
syn. ***Dipladenia***

Native to Central and South America, many of these fast-growing, woody stemmed climbers come from the Organ Mountains forests near Rio de Janeiro, home of many exotic plants admired worldwide. They bear profuse pink or

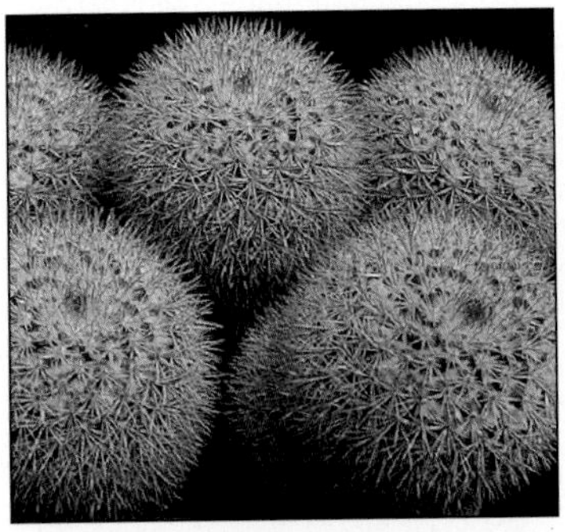

Mammillaria scrippsiana var. *rooksbiana*

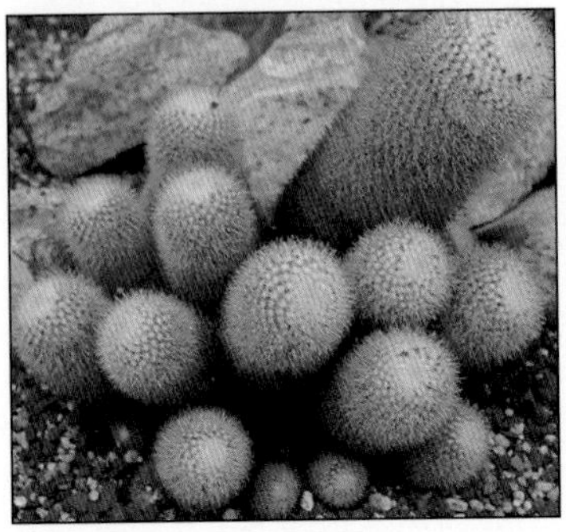

Mammillaria silvatica

white trumpet-shaped flowers, fragrant in some species. They were named after British diplomat and gardener Henry Mandeville (1773–1861).

CULTIVATION: Although tropical, mandevillas grow at high altitudes so they prefer temperate, frost-free climates with part-shade in summer and deep, rich, well-drained soil. Provide ample water on hot days. In cool areas, they grow very well in greenhouses. Propagate from seed in spring or cuttings in spring or summer.

Mandevilla × *amoena* 'Alice du Pont'
syns ***Mandevilla* × *amabilis* 'Alice du Pont', *Dipladenia* 'Alice du Pont'**

Growing up to 20–30 ft (6–9 m) tall (much less in containers), this twining climber produces handsome, oval, glossy leaves and clusters of large, deep pink, scentless flowers over a long period in summer. It is frost tender and needs a warm, protected position with midday shade. **ZONES 10–11.**

Mandevilla laxa
syn. ***Mandevilla suaveolens***
CHILEAN JASMINE

From Argentina, this marginally frost-hardy vine reaches 20 ft (6 m) or more

Mandevilla × *amoena* 'Alice du Pont'

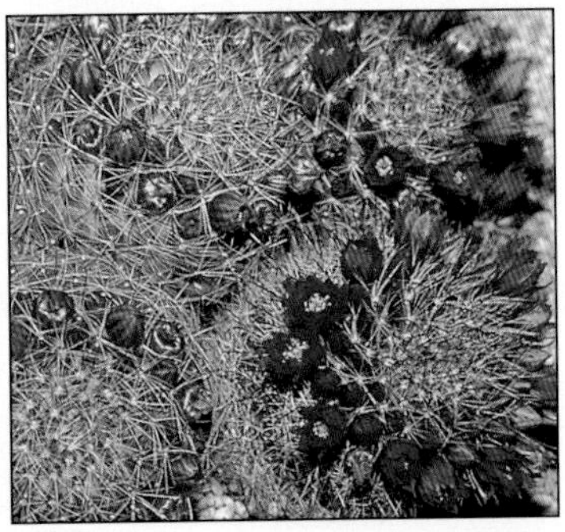

Mammillaria zeilmanniana

Mammillaria sempervivi

and is deciduous in cool areas. In summer it produces heavily perfumed white flowers in profusion—these make good cut flowers. The plant can be pruned heavily in early spring to shape it and to encourage new growth. **ZONES 9–11.**

Mandevilla sanderi
syn. *Dipladenia sanderi*
BRAZILIAN JASMINE

This vine climbs by twining around its support up to 15 ft (4.5 m) in warm, virtually frost-free climates. Its foliage is rich glossy green and up to $2\frac{1}{2}$ in (6 cm) long. In the wild form, the flowers are usually rose pink and 3 in (8 cm) wide. Several named cultivars have recently been released, including **'My Fair Lady'**, which is pink in bud opening white with pink shadings; **'Red Riding Hood'** with rich bright pink flowers from late spring to winter; and **'Scarlet Pimpernel'** which can flower throughout the year in warm climates and is the darkest form so far discovered with rich scarlet flowers with a yellow throat. **ZONES 10–11.**

Mandevilla splendens
syn. *Dipladenia splendens*

One of the showiest species of its genus, this evergreen twining climber, native to Brazil, reaches 10 ft (3 m) in height. Its lustrous green leaves are wide and elliptical to rectangular, and 8 in (20 cm) long. From late spring to early summer, it bears pink flowers with yellow centers. It prefers temperatures above 50°F (10°C). **ZONES 10–12.**

MANDRAGORA
MANDRAKE

This genus consists of 6 species of low-growing perennials from the Mediterranean and the Himalayas which bear pale blue flowers in spring followed by yellow fruits a little like cherry tomatoes. The Ancient Greeks used the roots as an anesthetic, and their curious forked shape gave rise to many legends. The plants were thought to resemble the human body—some male, others female—and people believed that if they were not gathered very carefully they would scream and anyone hearing them would go mad.

CULTIVATION: They are happiest in a warm-temperate climate, but grow in a cool-temperate one if mulched in winter. Plant in full sun or part-shade in deep, humus-rich, well-drained soil. They resent being transplanted. Propagate from seed in fall (autumn) or cuttings in winter. Check for slugs and snails.

Mandragora officinarum

This is the most common species that is cultivated. It grows 10 in (25 cm) tall and a little wider. The flowers appear in early spring, followed almost at once by the berries, green at first and ripening to yellow. **ZONES 8–10.**

MANETTIA

This is a genus of some 80 species of evergreen, mainly climbing plants valued for their vibrantly colored flowers. They are native to tropical America and, in climates where they grow well, are usually well-behaved, thin-stemmed moderate climbers ideal for posts or fences. The flowers are produced throughout the year in suitable climates and are tubular, usually in shades of orange and red.

CULTIVATION: A well-drained site in semi-shade is appropriate in frost-free climates, otherwise they can be grown in a heated greenhouse. They will clamber up through trellis or wire netting. Propagate from cuttings in summer or from seed in fall (autumn).

Manettia cordifolia
FIRECRACKER VINE

This species found from Bolivia to Argentina and Peru, is quite similar to the better known *Manettia luteorubra*. It grows to about 6 ft (1.8 m) and the flowers are brilliant red to orange and sometimes tipped yellow. **ZONES 10–11.**

Manettia luteorubra
syns *Manettia bicolor, M. inflata*
BRAZILIAN FIRECRACKER

This twining climber reaches 6 ft (1.8 m) in height and produces small decorative flowers, bright red and tipped with gold, in spring and summer. It looks attractive trained up a pillar, over a trellis or trailing from a hanging basket. Originally from South America, this plant does best in a warm climate. If grown as an indoor plant, it should be given plenty of bright light. **ZONES 10–11.**

MANGIFERA

This is a genus of evergreen trees from India and Southeast Asia. Their dense, glossy leaves are drooping and tinged strongly with red when young; this feature of tropical trees is thought to protect them from sun and heavy rain. The fruits, which are drupes, consist of a big central stone usually containing 3 embryos: the first 2 result from pollination, the third arises entirely from the mother tree. If the first 2 are removed as the seed germinates, the third grows and replicates the parent fruit. Nonetheless, it is customary to graft selected varieties.

CULTIVATION: These trees tolerate subtropical conditions, but prefer tropical, monsoonal climates. Rain at flowering time can rot the blossoms and ruin the crop. Plant in full sun in deep, rich soil; they need protection from strong winds. Prune when young to encourage a single trunk. In addition to grafting, they can be propagated from ripe seed from summer to fall (autumn). Check for fruit fly and fungal diseases.

Mangifera caesia

This attractive tree can be planted as an ornamental in tropical parts of the world. It grows to about 120 ft (36 m) and its trunk at maturity can be attractively buttressed with fissured gray-brown bark. The fruit are elipsoid and 8 in (20 cm) long and 4 in (10 cm) wide, rough and yellow-brown. **ZONES 11–12.**

Mangifera indica
MANGO

The mango can grow 80 ft (24 m) tall and wide, though grafted trees are normally smaller. The tiny, greenish spring flowers are borne in large sprays. The fruit resemble enormous peaches, though the skin is smooth, ripening to orange or red. Seedling trees tend to have furry seeds, making juice extraction awkward, and their flavor is often marred by a bitter aftertaste. Selected cultivars have superior fruit, sweet to the last, with smooth pits; **'Alphonso'** is universally regarded as the finest. **ZONES 11–12.**

MANGLIETIA

This genus, closely related to *Magnolia*, includes some 25 species of spreading, evergreen shrubs and trees. They occur naturally from Southeast Asia through to the eastern Himalayas and southern China. The leaves are an elongated oval shape, usually glossy above with blue-green undersides. The flowers, which open in spring, differ only in minor details from those of the magnolia. They are held erect, are about 3–4 in (8–10 cm) in diameter and may be white or various shades of pink or mauve.

CULTIVATION: Most species tolerate light frosts only and are best grown in warm-temperate, frost-free climates with regular rainfall. The ideal soil is moist, humus-rich and well drained, with a neutral to slightly acid pH. Propagate from seed or cuttings.

Mangifera indica

Mangifera caesia

Mandragora officinarum

Manettia luteorubra

Mandevilla sanderi 'My Fair Lady'

Mandevilla × *amoena* 'Alice du Pont'

Manglietia insignis

Native to areas of the Himalayas, western China and northern Vietnam, this attractive evergreen tree starts out as an upright conical plant but eventually becomes somewhat spreading and can grow to 40 ft (12 m) tall with a spread of 15 ft (4.5 m). Its leathery leaves are felted while young and glossy rich green when mature, and are up to 8 in (20 cm) long. Its cup-shaped flowers can be white-tinged, pinkish or reddish and are produced throughout spring. **ZONES 9–11.**

MANIHOT

There are about 100 species of trees and shrubs in this genus, all attractive foliage plants found in tropical and warm-temperate America. Several species have significant economic importance as a food crop. The alternate leaves are 3- to 9-lobed, while the large flowers appear in racemes or panicles.
CULTIVATION: These plants require a warm wet growing season followed by a dry period. Good drainage is required. Propagate from cuttings of mature stem about 6 in (15 cm) long.

Manihot esculenta
syn. ***Manihot utilissima***
CASSAVA, TAPIOCA

A variable species, cassava is a shrubby perennial 3–10 ft (1–3 m) high with palmately lobed leaves of up to 9 lance-shaped leaflets. The roots, which radiate from the base of the plant, may grow up to 4 ft (1.2 m) long and contain about 30 per cent starch. Cassava meal, obtained from the tuberous roots, is used in soups and puddings, to preserve meat and sauces and as a glue. A form of sugar, various alcoholic drinks and acetone are other end products. Cyanide is also obtained from the roots. **ZONES 10–12.**

Manglietia insignis

Maranta leuconeura 'Erythroneura'

Manihot esculenta

MARANTA

This is a genus of 32 species of evergreen rhizomatous perennials from the tropical forests of Central and South America. Apart from the beautifully marked and textured leaves, they are known for their habit of 'going to sleep' at night. The leaves spread by day and stand erect at night. One species, ***Maranta arundinacea***, is an important crop plant; it is better known to cooks as arrowroot.
CULTIVATION: Except in tropical climates, to which these plants are native, they are usually grown in greenhouses or as indoor plants. They like humidity and bright light without direct sunlight. In tropical areas, they make a good ground cover under large trees. Propagation is usually done by dividing established clumps or from basal cuttings struck on bottom heat.

Maranta leuconeura
PRAYER PLANT, TEN COMMANDMENTS

This variable species contains most of the best foliage forms of this genus. It usually grows to about 12 in (30 cm) in height and spread, and produces its inconspicuous white flowers with foliate spots in slender spikes during summer. The dark green leaves are usually about 6 in (15 cm) long. They have silver to pink veins and the reverse side can be purple or gray-green. In the cultivar **'Erythroneura',** the herringbone plant, the leaves are velvety and very dark black-green with a brilliant green irregular zone along the midrib. It also has bright pink veins and a deep red reverse. **'Kerchoviana',** known as rabbit tracks, has oval, light green leaves with green to brown blotches on either side of the central vein; the insignificant white to mauve flowers appear intermittently. **ZONES 11–12.**

Maranta leuconeura 'Kerchoviana'

Margyricarpus pinnatus

Markhamia zanzibarica

MARGYRICARPUS

The only species in the genus is a ground cover or small shrub growing to about 12 in (30 cm) high and 5 ft (1.5 m) wide. It is a native of Chile. The bright green leaves are needle-like and somewhat flattened. They are about ½ in (12 mm) long and occur in clumps at intervals along wiry brown stems. In spring, ¼ in (6 mm) filamentous green flowers are produced. These could easily pass unnoticed, but are followed by ½ in (12 mm) white berries with touches of purple. The berries are unattractive to birds and last well into winter.
CULTIVATION: *Margyricarpus pinnatus* is easily grown in any well-drained soil in sun or light shade. It is hardy to around 20°F (–7°C) and dislikes wet soil in winter. It is ideal for planting at the tops of dry banks. Propagate from cuttings, layers or seed.

Margyricarpus pinnatus
syn. ***Margyricarpus setosus***
PEARL FRUIT

For most of the year, this species makes a good but uninspiring ground cover with a spread of 3 ft (1 m) or more. The leaves are small and mid-green, and the tiny green flowers almost invisible. When fall (autumn) arrives, the plant is covered in almost pea-sized pearly white berries. **ZONES 9–10.**

MARKHAMIA

This small genus of about 13 species is mainly from tropical Africa and Asia; they are grown as small to medium trees with handsome flowers in similar climates. They are not often grown in the greenhouses of colder climates as they are not prolific flowerers when container-grown.
CULTIVATION: A well-drained but moist soil in full sun is all that is needed to grow these attractive specimen plants. In a cold climate under glass, they are better planted into a border than in tubs and unless you have a huge greenhouse, some restrictive pruning will be necessary. Propagate from seed in spring or from cuttings.

Markhamia lutea

Markhamia lutea

Markhamia lutea
syn. ***Markhamia platycalyx***

This species is native to areas of central Africa and usually grows into a small spreading tree to 30 ft (9 m). Its leaves are divided into 7 to 13 mid-green leaflets. The flowers are up to 1 in (25 mm) across, cup-shaped and yellow with red veining in the throat. **ZONES 11–12.**

Markhamia zanzibarica
BELL BEAN TREE

Native to southern Africa, this small tree has a short trunk and usually grows to 20–25 ft (6–8 m) high. The compound leaves to 15 in (38 cm) long are divided into 3 to 5 faintly glossy leaflets. The bell-shaped flowers with spreading lobes are up to 2 in (5 cm) across and are pale yellow speckled with red dots on the outside, with deep maroon at the throat. The spirally twisted capsules with grayish speckles are up to 24 in (60 cm) long. **ZONES 10–12.**

MARRUBIUM
HOREHOUND

This genus of around 40 species of aromatic perennial herbs is found in temperate regions of Europe and Asia, often by the roadside and in wastelands. *Marrubium* is a member of the mint family and characteristically has square branching stems and opposite pairs of toothed, ovate leaves with soft hairs and conspicuous veining. The whorls of small flowers are borne in the leaf axils. The botanical name is believed to have evolved from *marob*, a Hebrew word meaning a bitter juice, as this was one of the bitter herbs eaten by Jews to commemorate the feast of Passover.
CULTIVATION: These fully frost-hardy plants prefer full sun in poor,

well-drained soil. Although trouble free, avoid planting them in an over-rich soil and protect from drying winds. Propagate by root division in mid-spring or from seed in late spring.

Marrubium kotschyi
syn. ***Marrubium astracanicum***

This native of Iraq and Kurdistan grows up to 15 in (38 cm) in height. It has elliptic-toothed leaves and whorls of reddish purple flowers are produced in summer. **ZONES 7–10.**

Marrubium supinum

A native of mountainous regions in central and southern Spain, this species grows to 18 in (45 cm) in height and has kidney-shaped, toothed leaves and pink or lilac flowers in summer. **ZONES 7–10.**

Marrubium vulgare
WHITE HOREHOUND

Native to most of Europe and northern Asia, this quite invasive species is now naturalized in many other countries and grows wild in the USA. It grows up to 18 in (45 cm) or more, has downy, heart-shaped leaves and clusters of small white flowers which appear from the second year from mid-summer to early fall (autumn). Once a popular herbal remedy, it is still occasionally used, primarily as an expectorant. **ZONES 3–10.**

MARSILEA
NARDOO, WATER CLOVER

This is a genus of about 65 species of aquatic, amphibious and terrestrial plants that look like clovers but are actually ferns. When the rhizomes are submerged the leaves float on the water surface. They come from warm-temperate areas of Europe, northern Asia, tropical West Africa, eastern USA and Australia. They are attractive plants but in temperate to tropical climates are quite invasive and difficult, if not

Marrubium kotschyi

Marrubium supinum

Marrubium vulgare

impossible, to eradicate so they should be used with discretion.
CULTIVATION: Most species are frost tender or only marginally frost hardy. They are fully aquatic or marginal plants for the muddy edges of a pool. They need fertile soil, slightly acid water and full sun. Their rhizomes spread through the mud, and division of these is the best way to propagate.

Marsilea drummondii
COMMON NARDOO

This Australian species is an important wild food for the Aborigines, who grind the hard spore cases (sporocarps) to make a type of flour. The leaflets are in 4s and are fan-shaped. The leaf stems are usually about 12 in (30 cm) long, although they can be substantially longer if in deeper water. **ZONES 9–11.**

MARTYNIA
UNICORN PLANT, DEVIL'S CLAW

This genus includes just one species, an annual climber from Central America and the West Indies with large deltoid (poplar-shaped) leaves up to 12 in (30 cm) wide. *Martynia annua* is grown for its seed pods which, if picked while young and tender, may be pickled like gherkins. The pods are about 1 in (25 mm) in diameter and 4–6 in (10–15 cm) long. About half of the length is a curved

Marsilea drummondii

Masdevallia coccinea

beak—the 'unicorn' and 'claw' of the common names. The pods develop from orchid-like flowers. As the flowers are attractive, this plant is grown as an ornamental as well as for cropping.
CULTIVATION: Plant in a warm, sunny location with moist, well-drained soil that has been enriched with compost or other organic matter. Propagate from seed sown in spring as soon as any danger of frost has passed.

Martynia annua
ELEPHANT'S TUSK, PROBISCUS FLOWER

Throughout summer, this frost-tender climber produces attractive creamy white flowers with purple lobes and yellow to red spotting. It can grow to 3–6 ft (1–1.8 m) or more on a suitable support and likes a sunny aspect. It has naturalized in many tropical countries. **ZONES 10–12.**

MASDEVALLIA

These cool-growing evergreen epiphytic or terrestrial orchids from the mountains of South America bear dainty, 2½ in (6 cm) wide flowers from winter to spring. The petals and labellum are tiny, so the sepals resemble a triangular flower, held on a slender stem 15 in (38 cm) above the lowly foliage. The iridescent sepals glitter with different colors as they catch the light, even in the white varieties, but they are especially striking in the red and orange types. Several hybrids occur in yellow and hot pink.
CULTIVATION: Masdevallias grow in the wild mainly in cloud forests of high tropical mountains and do not adapt well to climates with seasonal contrasts. Away from their natural habitat, they need a temperature-controlled greenhouse and the correct amount of fresh air. They should not be given a winter rest, so it is important that winter temperatures do not fall near freezing. Propagate by division after flowering.

Masdevallia coccinea 'Splendens'

Masdevallia coccinea

This beautiful species is found at high altitudes in the Andes in Colombia and Peru. The plants grow into large clumps with stems about 2½ in (6 cm) long. The leaves are 6–8 in (15–20 cm) long and 1½ in (35 mm) wide. The large showy flowers are variable in color from white, yellow, purple and red, and are borne in spring and summer. **'Splendens'** is a cultivar with bright magenta flowers. **ZONE 11.**

Masdevallia Hybrids

Masdevallias are popular with orchid growers and there are many cultivars available. Some are selected forms of the species, but many are hybrids. Cultivars include **'Ayabacora'**, which has dusky red sepals with long filamentous tips; **'Circe San Barbara'**, with golden-yellow centered orange-red sepals that taper to threads; and **'Southern Son'**, which has bright orange flowers with only the upper sepal filamentous. **ZONE 11.**

MATRICARIA

This extensively revised genus of aromatic annual herbs consists of 5 species, native to the temperate regions of the northern hemisphere. They have finely dissected leaves with numerous linear segments and produce terminal, white daisy-like flowerheads from spring to late summer.

Masdevallia Hybrid

Masdevallia Hybrid 'Ayabacora'

Masdevallia Hybrid 'Circe San Barbara'

Masdevallia Hybrid 'Southern Son'

Matthiola incana

Matricaria recutita

Maurandya barclayana

They can be grown in a rockery, herb garden or as a border edging. Some species produce good cut flowers and *Matricaria recutita* is valued for its herbal use.
CULTIVATION: These fully frost-hardy plants prefer well-drained, light sandy soil in full sun. Propagate from seed in summer.

Matricaria recutita
syn. *Matricaria chamomilla*
GERMAN CHAMOMILE

This is an aromatic annual with stems to 24 in (60 cm) and finely divided, light green leaves. It has white daisy-like flowers with golden centers. The flowers appear in summer and fall (autumn), during which period the fully opened flowers can be harvested and dried. This species is used in a similar fashion to *Chamaeleum nobile,* chamomile. Use

Matucana weberbaueri f. *flammea*

discarded tea flowers on the compost pile to activate decomposition. **ZONES 6–10.**

MATTEUCCIA

This genus of deciduous ferns consists of about 4 species native to temperate North America, Europe and eastern Asia. All are attractive garden plants producing tall sterile fronds in a neat shuttlecock shape in spring, followed later in the season by the smaller overwintering fertile fronds.
CULTIVATION: These impressive frost-hardy ferns prefer a moist but not wet soil that is neutral or slightly acidic. Add ample leaf mold and shelter from excessive direct sunlight, which will burn the fronds. Propagation is usually done by dividing established clumps in late winter. Although they can be raised from spores, this is a slow process.

Matteuccia struthiopteris
syn. *Matteuccia pensylvanica*
OSTRICH FERN

Native to temperate northern hemisphere, this rhizomatous fern produces clusters of tall, plume-shaped, sterile fronds 2–5 ft (0.6–1.5 m) high. Each cluster eventually forms a dense, raised crown. Persistent, fertile fronds arise from the crown and provide engaging winter scenery. Clumps can spread rapidly and become invasive. **ZONES 2–8.**

Matteuccia struthiopteris

MATTHIOLA
STOCK, GILLYFLOWER

This is a genus of some 55 species of annuals, biennials and subshrubby perennials, few of which are grown in gardens with the exceptions of the night-scented stock *Matthiola longipetala* subsp. *bicornis* and the cultivars of *M. incana,* the much-loved stock that has many forms in both double and single flowers. The species are native to Europe, central and southwestern Asia and North Africa. The leaves are usually gray-green and the perfumed flowers can be produced from spring to fall (autumn). They are attractive both for bedding out and as cut flowers but be warned, stocks are prone to quite a few pests and diseases, including downy mildew, club-root, gray mold and cabbage root fly.
CULTIVATION: *Matthiola* prefer a sunny aspect in moist but well-drained, neutral or alkaline soil. Shelter from strong winds and stake some of the larger forms and the top-heavy large doubles. Propagate from seed sown in situ for night-scented stock—this should be staggered to increase flowering season—or in spring sow seed of *M. incana* types into seed trays and prick out into beds later.

Matthiola incana

This upright biennial or short-lived perennial is best grown as an annual. It has a bushy habit and grows up to 24 in (60 cm) in height with a spread of 12 in (30 cm). Fully frost hardy, it has lance-shaped, gray-green leaves and fragrant, 3–6 in (8–15 cm) long spikes of mauve flowers borne in spring. Many varieties and strains are available, the best selected for a high percentage of double flowers. **'Mammoth Column'** grows taller, reaching 30 in (75 cm) in height, and produces a single, 12–15 in (30–38 cm) tall spike of scented flowers in spring in mixed or separate colors. **ZONES 6–10.**

Matthiola longipetala subsp. *bicornis*
syn. *Matthiola bicornis*
NIGHT-SCENTED STOCK

This erect, usually branched annual to 15 in (38 cm) tall produces its flowers in shades of pink, mauve or purple throughout summer and into fall (autumn) if sown regularly throughout spring. Although the blooms are not very showy the scent, only detectable at night, is strong and sweet. **ZONES 6–10.**

MATUCANA

There are 20 species in this cactus genus from Peru. They are globular in form, reaching a maximum height of 24 in (60 cm) and width of 6 in (15 cm). Most species bear a dense profusion of spines and produce large, funnel-shaped spring flowers varying in color combinations from yellow and orange to red and violet. Round greenish fruits follow in summer.
CULTIVATION: Marginally frost hardy, these cacti prefer full sun. Plant in well-drained soil. Propagate from seed. They are susceptible to root mealybug and spider mite.

Matucana weberbaueri f. *flammea*

This small cactus grows to a height of 3 in (8 cm) and features reddish brown spines. Yellow and orange, funnel-shaped, 2 in (5 cm) flowers bloom in spring. **ZONES 9–11.**

MAURANDYA

This genus consists of 2 species, both climbing plants of light and graceful habit from Mexico and Central America. They will twine up through shrubs or small trees as well as over fences. They are not very frost hardy but are worth growing in frost-free to tropical climates; in such situations they can flower practically all year round. In cold areas they can be treated as annuals. The foliage is a soft green and the flowers are tubular.
CULTIVATION: They prefer moist but not wet soil in a warm aspect with full sun. Propagate from seed or cuttings in spring.

Maurandya barclayana
syn. *Asarina barclayana*
CLIMBING SNAPDRAGON

This pretty free-flowering climber can reach up to 15 ft (4.5 m) on a suitable support. Its soft green leaves are shallowly lobed and its $1\frac{1}{2}$ in (35 mm) long tubular flowers can be white, pink or deep purple, usually with a paler throat. **ZONES 9–12.**

MAXILLARIA

Among the largest orchid genera, *Maxillaria* is estimated to contain anywhere between 250 and 700 species, distributed through the Americas from Mexico and Florida to northern Argentina. Nearly all epiphytic or rock-dwelling and evergreen, they mostly have short pseudobulbs bearing a single strap-like, leathery leaf, though some have leaves springing directly from a creeping rhizome or from short erect stems. Flowers are carried singly on short stalks arising from the pseudobulb base (or from leaf axils in species lacking pseudobulbs); in some species there are several flowers per pseudobulb. Three large, fleshy, spreading sepals dominate

Mazus pumilio

Maytenus boaria

each flower, the 2 petals and labellum usually smaller and directed forward; they occur in a range of colors, mostly reds, purples, oranges and yellows, often with markings on the labellum.
CULTIVATION: The species vary in climatic requirements, some needing sustained warmth and humidity and others tolerating warm-temperate though frost-free conditions. Pot in standard orchid compost and keep moist all year, watering more freely in the summer and feeding with dilute liquid fertilizer. They mostly prefer strong light but not direct sun, and dislike disturbance of the roots. Propagate by dividing clumps.

Maxillaria picta

From southeastern Brazil, this is one of the cooler-growing species that will live happily outdoors in a warm-temperate climate. It forms dense clumps of small pseudobulbs with leaves about 8 in (20 cm) long, and in late fall (autumn) and winter it produces a profusion of fragrant small yellow flowers on short stalks from the pseudobulb bases. In cultivation it has sometimes been confused with the similar *Maxillaria porphyrostele*. **ZONES 10–12.**

Maxillaria sanderiana

With possibly the showiest flowers of the genus, this species comes from lower mountain areas of Peru and Ecuador. The plants form large, dense clumps with each flattened pseudobulb bearing a leaf about 15 in (40 cm) long. The solitary, scented flowers are up to 5 in (12 cm) across; they are pure white except for the bases of both petals and sepals which are heavily blotched with red. **ZONES 11–12.**

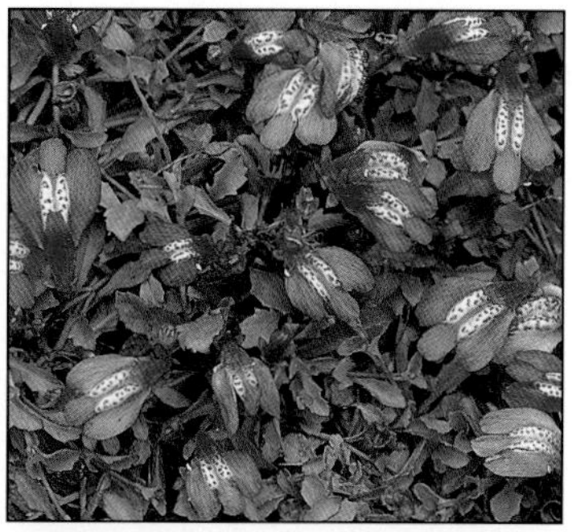

Mazus reptans

Maytenus boaria

MAYTENUS

This genus contains more than 225 species of evergreen trees and shrubs, mainly from South America and the Caribbean. They have variably shaped, alternate leaves and tiny, star-shaped or tubular flowers. Some shrubby species bear decorative red or yellow seedpods in fall (autumn).
CULTIVATION: Long, hot summers are needed for these very frost-hardy to frost-tender plants to produce flowers and fruits. They also need full sun and fertile, moist, well-drained soil. Propagate from seed in fall or from cuttings in summer.

Maytenus boaria
MAITEN, MAYTEN TREE

Growing to 30–50 ft (9–15 m) tall and almost as wide, this Chilean tree's graceful, weeping habit makes it look like an evergreen weeping willow. Its narrow, glossy green, finely serrated leaves hang from slender shoots. In spring, inconspicuous star-shaped flowers, white tinged with green, cluster in small groups; these are followed by red and yellow seed pods. This species tolerates frost. **ZONES 8–10.**

MAZUS

Consisting of around 30 species, this genus comes from usually damp habitats in lowland or mountain regions of the Himalayas, China, Japan, Southeast Asia, Australia and New Zealand. They can be annuals but those grown in gardens are perennial ground-hugging plants that root at the nodes as they grow, making them ideal in between paving slabs and as low ground cover for rock gardens.
CULTIVATION: Most are reasonably frost tolerant and like fertile, moist but well-drained soil in full sun. Propagate by division in late winter or early spring.

Mazus pumilio

This almost completely prostrate species comes from Australasia. Its 2 in (5 cm) long leaves are spatulate and its summer flowers are usually blue with a yellow throat although a white-flowered form, **'Albus'**, exists. Like *Mazus radicans*, this is a useful rock-garden plant and filler of cracks between paving slabs. **ZONES 7–11.**

Mazus radicans
SWAMP MUSK

This prostrate, carpet-forming New Zealand perennial has short, upright branches. The limbs are covered with egg-shaped to linear foliage that often has a downy underside. In summer, bluish purple to pink or white 5-lobed cylindrical flowers with a yellow center appear. These are followed by egg-shaped seed pods containing many seeds. **ZONES 6–10.**

Mazus reptans

This prostrate, carpet-forming, Himalayan perennial has stems that root as they trail and are lined with 1 in (25 mm) long bright green leaves. Small flowers appear in spring on short, upright stems; they are lavender with white and yellow spots. Only 2 in (5 cm) tall but spreading to 12 in (30 cm) or more, this species will often invade nearby lawns but looks attractive there and will tolerate light foot traffic. **ZONES 3–11.**

MECONOPSIS

This genus consists of about 45 species of annuals, biennials and short-lived perennials that are mostly native to the Himalayas. They bear large, exotic flowers with papery petals and a bold, central boss of stamens on tall stems. The flower stalks lengthen after flowering as the fruits develop. The hairy leaves are either simple or pinnate.
CULTIVATION: Mostly frost hardy, they need a moist but not over-wet, lime-free, humus-rich soiland a cool site in part- or full shade with shelter from strong winds. Propagate from seed in late summer.

Meconopsis betonicifolia
syn. *Meconopsis baileyi*
BLUE POPPY, TIBETAN POPPY, HIMALAYAN POPPY

This clump-forming woodland species bears sky blue, saucer-shaped, 2–3 in (5–8 cm) wide satiny flowers with yellow stamens in late spring and early summer. Oblong, mid-green leaves occur in basal rosettes. It grows 3–5 ft (1–1.5 m) tall and 18 in (45 cm) wide. It does not bloom in the first season, and dies down completely over winter. **ZONES 7–9.**

Meconopsis cambrica
WELSH POPPY

Native to western Europe and the UK, this species is more easily grown than *Meconopsis betonicifolia*. The slightly hairy, deeply divided, mid-green leaves form basal rosettes. Lemon yellow or rich orange blooms are freely borne from mid-spring to fall (autumn). It has a spreading habit, reaching 12–18 in (30–45 cm) tall and 12 in (30 cm) wide. Though short lived, it self-seeds readily, given the right conditions. **ZONES 6–10.**

Meconopsis grandis
HIMALAYAN BLUE POPPY

This stunning rich blue poppy is more solidly perennial than the better known *Meconopsis betonicifolia*. It has rosettes of irregularly toothed, deciduous green leaves with red-brown or rust colored hairs. The brilliant, early summer flowers can be up to 6 in (15 cm) across on stems up to 4 ft (1.2 m) tall. **ZONES 5–9.**

Meconopsis grandis

Meconopsis cambrica

Meconopsis betonicifolia

M

Meconopsis horridula

This monocarpic (flowers once then dies) species from western Nepal to China can also behave as a short-lived perennial. The foliage, stems and even buds are covered in spines, hence the species name. These appendages can be yellow to purple in color. The cup-shaped blooms are produced from early to midsummer, several to the stem. They are usually deep blue, 3 in (8 cm) across and on stems up to 3 ft (1 m) tall. **ZONES 6–9.**

Meconopsis integrifolia
YELLOW CHINESE POPPY

Native to Tibet and Burma, this species is usually monocarpic. It grows to about 3 ft (1 m) tall and usually has bright yellow poppies in late spring and early summer, although white forms have been grown. The lance-shaped leaves and the stems are covered in yellow hairs; these are almost all shed at maturity. **ZONES 7–10.**

Meconopsis pseudointegrifolia

As the name suggests, this species is similar to *Meconopsis integrifolia.* However, it differs in bearing heads of downward-facing blooms at the top of strong stems.

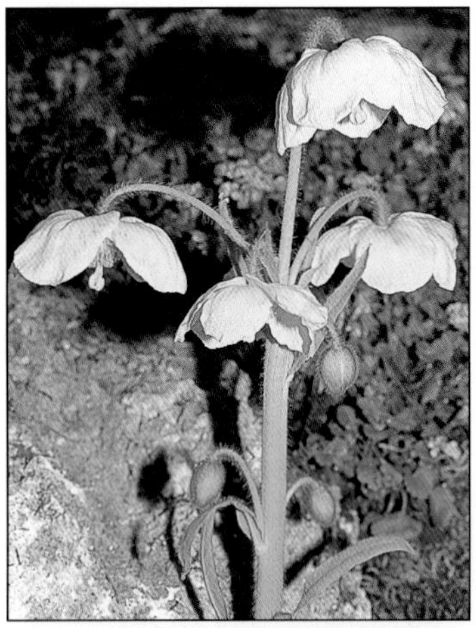

Meconopsis pseudointegrifolia

The flowers are soft yellow with conspicuous golden stamens and are borne in late spring and early summer. The plant is covered in fine golden-brown hairs. **ZONES 7–9.**

Meconopsis quintuplinervia
HAREBELL POPPY

A clumping perennial from Tibet and western China, this species will slowly build up into a reasonable patch in ideal cool, moist conditions. Its rosetting leaves are lance-shaped, mid- to dark green and are covered in golden bristles. Its cup-shaped summer flowers are usually produced singly and normally a soft lavender blue. **ZONES 8–10.**

Meconopsis × *sheldonii*

These hybrids between *Meconopsis betonicifolia* and *M. grandis* are rosette-forming, hairy perennials with 12 in (30 cm) leaves. They can grow up to 5 ft (1.5 m) tall in good conditions. The blue flowers are borne from late spring to early summer. **'Slieve Donard'** is a vigorous brilliant blue form with long pointed petals, growing to 3 ft (1 m) tall. **ZONES 6–9.**

MEDICAGO
MEDIC, MEDICK

This genus of 50 to 60 species of annuals, perennials and small shrubs originates in Europe, Africa and Asia. They are quite variable in size and form, although trifoliate leaves with fine hairs are common throughout. The foliage color may be bright green to silver gray. The pea-like flowers, which are most commonly yellow, are carried in racemes of a few and up to 50 blooms. Summer is the main blooming season. *Medicago sativa* is an important commercial crop.
CULTIVATION: Most are easily grown in full sun in any well-drained soil. They need occasional watering in summer. Their roots are able to fix nitrogen from the atmosphere, which reduces their nutrient requirements. Hardiness varies with the species. Propagate from seed, or from division or cuttings, in the case of the perennials.

Meconopsis × *sheldonii* 'Slieve Donard'

Medicago sativa

Megaskepasma erythrochlamys

Megaskepasma erythrochlamys

Melaleuca argentea

Melaleuca argentea

Medicago sativa
ALFALFA, LUCERNE

Native to Europe, this perennial clover-like plant of the pea family has a long tap root and short clusters of purplish flowers. From time immemorial it has been used as forage for cattle, but is now also eaten in the form of sprouting seeds. Delicious in salads and on sandwiches, the sprouted seeds produce very fine shoots with a delicate, pea-like flavor. **ZONES 6–10.**

MEDINILLA

This genus of about 150 species of evergreen shrubs and climbers, some of which are epiphytic, native to Southeast Asia, the Pacific islands and tropical Africa. Size varies but the most commonly grown species are around 5–10 ft (1.5–3 m) tall. The leathery, oval leaves are heavily veined and deep green. Pendulous panicles of flowers form at branch tips. The flowers, usually pink, are tiny, but when combined with the large colorful bracts they produce a showy display.
CULTIVATION: Most species only grow outdoors in the tropics. They can be cultivated as greenhouse and house plants, but will not tolerate winter minimums below 64°F (18°C). Plant in rich, moist, well-drained, humus-rich soil in part-shade. Water and feed well in the growing season. Propagate from seed or cuttings.

Medinilla magnifica

This erect shrub to 6 ft (1.8 m) tall is usually found as an epiphyte in its native Philippinesd. Its stems may be ribbed or even winged, and its rich glossy green leaves grow to about 12 in (30 cm) long and have obvious paler veins. *Medinilla magnifica* has small pink flowers which are produced throughout spring and summer in long pendulous panicles to 18 in (45 cm); these are made even more obvious because of the large pink bracts attached to the flower clusters. **ZONES 11–12.**

MEGASKEPASMA
BRAZILIAN RED CLOAK, MEGAS

Originally from Venezuela, the single species in this genus is a hot-climate, spreading shrub grown for its display of red flowers. It can reach 10 ft (3 m) in height and has simple, entire leaves.
CULTIVATION: Plant this shrub in sun or part-shade and light, moist, well-drained soil rich in organic matter. It benefits from regular watering and fertilizing. Protect from snails. Propagate from seed or cuttings.

Megaskepasma erythrochlamys

The mid-green, oval leaves of this evergreen shrub are up to 12 in (30 cm) long, with prominent veining. It forms spreading clumps, and the erect stems bear spikes of deep red flowers in summer; these are up to 12 in (30 cm) long and are held above the foliage. **ZONES 10–12.**

MELALEUCA
PAPERBARK

The evergreen trees and shrubs that form this large genus are indigenous to Australia, except for a handful of species found in Papua New Guinea, Indonesia and coastal Southeast Asia. Some species have beautiful papery bark which peels off in large sheets. They bear profuse, brush-like flowers with showy stamens, and their nectar provides food for birds and small animals. The leathery leaves are small and are either cylindrical or flat.
CULTIVATION: Adaptable plants, they can tolerate wet and even boggy conditions (but prefer well-drained soil), pollution, salt winds and saline soil. Although they are warm-climate plants, most species withstand very ligh frosts if given full sun. Propagate from seed or cuttings taken just as the current season's growth begins. Shrubby species benefit from light pruning straight after the main flowering period. Melaleucas are remarkably free from pests and disease.

Melaleuca alternifolia
TEA-TREE

From coastal swamps of subtropical eastern Australia, this tall shrub or small bushy tree to 25 ft (8 m) high has narrow linear leaves to $1\frac{1}{2}$ in (35 mm) long. Rich in essential oils, the leaves are used commercially for oil extraction. Profuse white flowers are borne from late spring to mid-summer. Marginally frost hardy, it succeeds best in a warm climate. As it tolerates heavy pruning, it makes a good hedge or screening plant. **ZONES 9–11.**

Melaleuca argentea
SILVER-LEAFED PAPERBARK

This pendulous, spreading tree reaches a height of 80 ft (24 m) and a spread of 25 ft (8 m). It has an attractive papery bark and narrow, silvery green leaves up to 4 in (10 cm) long. Spikes of cream flowers are borne in winter and spring. **ZONES 11–12.**

Melaleuca armillaris
BRACELET HONEY MYRTLE, DROOPING MELALEUCA

This small to medium-sized 30 ft (9 m) tree has a spreading canopy of deep green needle-like leaves. The buds are usually pink or red, opening to white flowers in cylindrical spikes up to 2 in (5 cm) long in spring and summer. The gray, furrowed bark peels off in strips. This fast-growing species adapts to a wide range of soil types. **ZONES 9–11.**

Melaleuca linariifolia

Melaleuca linariifolia

Melaleuca nesophila

Melaleuca erubescens

Melaleuca bracteata
BLACK TEA-TREE, RIVER TEA-TREE

This 30 ft (9 m) tree has dark gray, fissured bark and gray to deep green leaves scattered along the branches. Creamy white flowers are held at the branch tips in summer. It adapts well to various soil and climatic conditions. Three cultivars suitable for warm-climate gardens are **'Revolution Gold'**, with red stems and golden foliage that scorches in very hot weather; **'Revolution Green'**, 12 ft (3.5 m) tall with bright green foliage; and **'Golden Gem'**, 6 ft (1.8 m) tall. **ZONES 9–11.**

Melaleuca capitata

This rounded bushy shrub grows to about 6 ft (1.8 m) high and wide. It has dark green linear leaves to 1 in (25 mm) with a pointed tip. Terminal cream flowers are borne in dense rounded heads in late spring and summer. **ZONES 9–11.**

Melaleuca erubescens
syn. *Melaleuca diosmatifolia*

This dense, upright shrub reaches 10 ft (3 m) in height and has small, tightly

Melaleuca incana

Melaleuca thymifolia

Melaleuca armillaris

Melaleuca bracteata

arranged, narrow, rounded leaves ½ in (12 mm) long. The yellowish green flowers are 2 in (5 cm) long and appear in summer. **ZONES 9–11.**

Melaleuca hypericifolia
DOTTED MELALEUCA

This rounded, many-branched shrub grows up to 15 ft (4.5 m) tall. It has oblong to elliptic, mid- to pale green leaves. The flowers, which are composed of a 1 in (25 mm) long brush of pale red stamens, are borne in summer in bottlebrush-like spikes 3 in (8 cm) long. **ZONES 9–11.**

Melaleuca incana
GRAY-LEAFED HONEY MYRTLE

This 10 ft (3 m) shrub usually has a low-branched main trunk and forms a spreading bush 6 ft (1.8 m) across. Slender, arching branches carry narrow, hairy leaves; these are reddish green at first, becoming gray-green with a red edge and turning grayish purple in winter. Creamy yellow flower spikes appear in spring. It tolerates most soils. **ZONES 9–11.**

Melaleuca leucadendra
WEEPING PAPERBARK, CAJEPUT TREE

This tree species ranges from northern Australia to eastern Indonesia. It has thick, pale, spongy bark, a tall, open crown and weeping branches. It grows at least 70 ft (21 m) tall and 40 ft (12 m) wide, with narrow, dull green leaves to 6 in (15 cm) long. Fuzzy, creamy white fragrant flower spikes appear in summer and fall (autumn). It thrives in waterlogged soil. Cajeput oil, distilled from the foliage, is used in medicine. **ZONES 10–12.**

Melaleuca linariifolia
FLAX-LEAFED PAPERBARK, SNOW-IN-SUMMER

A fast-growing 30 ft (9 m) tree with a spreading crown and white, papery bark, this species derives one of its common names from its flax-like leaves. Short white

Melaleuca capitata

Melaleuca hypericifolia

flower spikes bloom at the branch tips from late spring into summer. It grows naturally around swamps, but adapts to most garden soil types. An essential oil is extracted from its leaves. **'Snowstorm'** is a dwarf, heavy-flowering form that grows to around 6 ft (1.8 m) tall. **ZONES 9–11.**

Melaleuca nesophila
syn. *Melaleuca nesophylla*
WESTERN TEA MYRTLE, PINK MELALEUCA

This bushy shrub, native to Western Australia, bears summer flowers that are brushes of mauve, gold-tipped stamens, fading to white, giving the plant a multicolored effect. Its leaves are oval, narrow, smooth and gray-green. It grows 10 ft (3 m) tall and 6 ft (1.8 m) wide. **ZONES 9–11.**

Melaleuca quinquenervia
BROAD-LEAFED PAPERBARK, PUNK TREE

The best known of the broad-leafed melaleucas, this is a popular street and park tree in warm climates. In the Florida Everglades it has become thoroughly naturalized, to the concern of environmentalists. It is native to east-coastal Australia and New Caledonia, usually growing in swamps, but adapts to quite dry soil in cultivation. The cream bark is very thick and papery, the leaves stiff and flat, and the white flowers appear in spring and sporadically at other times. It grows to 60 ft (18 m) or more tall. **ZONES 10–12.**

Melaleuca thymifolia
THYME HONEY MYRTLE

An upright or spreading shrub, this species grows to 3 ft (1 m). Its small, erect, blue-green leaves give off a spicy aroma when crushed. Pale to bright purple flowers with incurving stamens appear from late spring to fall (autumn). It tolerates most soils, but thrives in a wet position in full sun. **ZONES 9–11.**

Melaleuca quinquenervia

Melia azedarach

Melianthus major

Melaleuca viridiflora
BROAD-LEAFED PAPERBARK

Closely allied to *Melaleuca quinquenervia*, and *M. leucadendron*, this species occurs across the tropical north of Australia in poorly drained soil. It makes a tree of up to about 30 ft (9 m) of open, crooked habit and with thick papery bark. The leaves are large, up to 4 in (10 cm) long and 2 in (5 cm) wide. The bottlebrush-type flower spikes are usually greenish cream, but pink and red forms also occur. It provides food for bats and nectar-eating birds. **ZONES 10–12.**

MELAMPODIUM

This is a genus of daisies native to all warmer parts of the Americas. There are about 37 species of annuals, perennials or subshrubs up to 3 ft (1 m) tall. The ray florets are usually white or lemon yellow and the center is usually yellow. **CULTIVATION:** Although not often cultivated, this genus of plants is quite tolerant of dry conditions and will still flower well over quite a period even in poor soils. They are ideal on sunny banks and in rock gardens as long as their deep tap roots have enough loose soil to grow in. They resent disturbance. Propagate from seed.

Melaleuca quinquenervia

Melia azedarach

Melampodium leucanthum
BLACKFOOT DAISY

This subshrub, found from Mexico to Colorado, USA, grows to around 24 in (60 cm) high and wide. It has narrow, 2 in (5 cm) long leaves that may be smooth edged or with up to 6 lobes. Cream, 1½ in (35 mm) wide flowers open continuously from spring to fall (autumn). **ZONES 4–10.**

MELASTOMA

This genus consists of 70 species of evergreen shrubs and small trees, all native to tropical regions. They have large, soft leaves with prominent veins. White, pink or purple terminal flowers bloom for most of the year in tropical climates, and in summer in subtropical areas. These are followed by fleshy berries. **CULTIVATION:** Frost tender, they require full light or part-shade in fertile, well-drained soil. If necessary, they can be pruned in late winter. Propagate from cuttings taken in spring or summer.

Melastoma affine
syns *Melastoma denticulatum*, *M. polyanthum*

This tropical, bushy shrub from Southeast Asia and Australia grows 5–8 ft (1.5–2.4 m) tall. The rough-textured leaves are bright green, with 3 to 5 prominent veins. Its mauve or, more rarely, white flowers up to 3 in (8 cm) wide are borne in terminal clusters; they are short lived but bloom for most of the year, peaking in summer. They are followed by edible purple berries. This species has often been confused with *Melastoma malabathricum*. **ZONES 10–12.**

Melastoma affine

Melastoma malabathricum
INDIAN RHODODENDRON, PINK LASIANDRA

This low-branched, tropical Asian shrub with large, soft leaves bears profuse clusters of distinctive, almost flat, 3–4 in (8–10 cm) mauve flowers—often mistaken for those of a *Tibouchina*—in summer and fall (autumn). The reddish berries have long been used medicinally in India and Southeast Asia. **ZONES 10–12.**

MELIA
BEAD TREE, CHINABERRY, PERSIAN LILAC, ROSARY TREE, WHITE CEDAR

This genus of only one very variable species of deciduous tree ranges across Asia from Iraq to Japan and south to Australia. *Melia azedarach* has many common names; 2 of them, bead tree and rosary tree, arise from the way the seeds have a hole through the middle, convenient for bead-making. The trees were formerly grown in southern Italy for making rosaries. *Melia* is Greek for 'ash' *(Fraxinus)*, although the only connection is that the pinnate or doubly pinnate leaves are vaguely similar. **CULTIVATION:** It grows in warm climates and readily tolerates dry conditions and poor soil. It is a favorite street tree in arid climates. Propagate from seed in fall (autumn).

Melia azedarach
syn. *Melia azedarach* var. *australasica*

This is a fast-growing, spreading tree which grows to 30 ft (9 m) tall. The young leaves appear in late spring or early summer, with large sprays of small, delicately scented lilac flowers; these are followed by bunches of pale orange or cream berries, each containing a single woody seed, which persist after the leaves fall. They are poisonous to humans but much eaten by birds. **'Umbraculiformis'** has a curious yet attractive habit, like a blown-out umbrella. **ZONES 8–12.**

MELIANTHUS

This small genus contains 6 species, all native to South Africa. Although they are shrubs, because of their often leggy growth, particularly the stunning *Melianthus major*, they are usually cut down to start again. Although grown for their foliage, the spikes of brownish red bracted flowers are attractive, as well as drawing nectar-feeding birds; the flowers are followed by papery seed pods. **CULTIVATION:** Grow in full sun or part-shade in moist but well-drained, fertile soil. They are only marginally frost hardy but a thick winter mulch will give added protection; they also need shelter from cold winds. Propagate from seed or cuttings in summer.

Melianthus major
HONEY FLOWER, TOUCH-ME-NOT, HONEY BUSH

This sprawling, bush grows to a height and spread of 6–10 ft (1.8–3 m). It is prized for its luxuriant foliage and for the brownish red, tubular flowers on terminal spikes that appear in spring and summer. The leaves have blue-gray, serrated leaflets. If pruned hard in early spring it will remain compact, but it will then flower less freely. The leaves have a strong, unpleasant smell when bruised, hence the common name touch-me-not. This species is slightly invasive in favored climates. **ZONES 9–11.**

Melianthus minor

This species is both smaller and less ornamental than *Melianthus major*. It reaches 6 ft (1.8 m) in height, has gray-green foliage and 15 in (38 cm) long brownish red flower spikes. **ZONES 9–11.**

MELICA
MELICK

This genus of some 75 species of perennial grasses is native to most of the temperate regions except Australia. Most species are 2–5 ft (0.6–1.5 m) tall and form clumps of arching leaves with strong stems. The summer flowerheads, are erect spikes, usually with lax or drooping spikelets that often develop attractive pink or purple tints. Several species with variegated leaves and unusual flowers are cultivated. **CULTIVATION:** Species of *Melica* will grow in any reasonably fertile, well-drained soil in full sun or very light shade. They are generally quite frost hardy. Propagate from seed in summer or by dividing large clumps.

Melica altissima
SIBERIAN MELICK

This is an elegant ornamental grass with tufted foliage to 8 in (20 cm) long. The leaves are mid-green and rough. The flower stems have spikelets hanging on one side of the stem. In the wild form these are green, while the cultivars have different colored spikelets: **'Alba'** has pale leaves and greenish white spikelets; and **'Atropurpurea'** has purple spikelets. **ZONES 5–10.**

Melica uniflora

Growing to 24 in (60 cm) tall but often less, this species makes an open clump or tuft of rich green, hairy leaves. The flowers are small and reddish brown in color and are produced in loose panicles. *Melica uniflora* occurs naturally from Europe to western Asia. **'Variegata'** has leaves striped white and darker colored flowers. **ZONES 7–10.**

MELICOPE

This genus of about 150 species of evergreen shrubs and small trees comes from tropical Asia and Australia. The leaves

are opposite or alternate, can be trifoliate or simple, and all have glands dotted over them. Most have brightly colored seeds that hang from the ripe pods.
CULTIVATION: These frost-tender plants prefer well-drained but moist, acidic soil and tolerate heavy pruning well. Propagate from seed or summer cuttings.

Melicope elleryana
PINK-FLOWERED CORKWOOD

This fast-growing tree to 80 ft (24 m) tall is native to the rainforests of eastern Australia, New Guinea and the Solomon Islands. The trifoliate leaves to 3 in (8 cm) long have dark green, shiny oval leaflets. It is often cultivated as an ornamental tree in subtropical regions for its showy clusters of pink flowers that are produced in summer to early fall (autumn). **ZONES 10–12.**

MELINIS

This genus is made up of 15 species of annual or short-lived perennial grasses native to open grasslands and disturbed places of tropical Africa and Southeast Asia. They usually form tufts of very narrow thread-like leaves and produce panicles of white or silvery pink spikelets from summer to fall (autumn). *Melinis repens* is the only species in cultivation and looks particularly attractive in a woodland setting. It also makes a handsome pot specimen.
CULTIVATION: These marginally frost-hardy plants will grow in any reasonably fertile, well-drained soil in full sun or very light shade. Propagate from seed or by division.

Melinis repens
syn. ***Rhynchelytrum repens***
NATAL GRASS, NATAL RED TOP

This native of tropical Africa is a tuft-forming annual or short-lived perennial grass to 4 ft (1.2 m) tall with bright green flat leaves to 12 in (30 cm) long. The flowering stems, produced from mid-summer to early fall (autumn), bear attractive silvery pink spikelets, fading to white. **ZONES 8–12.**

MELISSA
BALM

This genus of 3 species of perennial herbs has representatives from Europe to central Asia. The name *Melissa* is derived from a Greek word meaning bee, owing to the abundance of nectar in the flowers which attracts bees. Borne in opposite pairs on square stems, the crinkled ovate or heart-shaped leaves emit a lemony odor when bruised. Axillary spikes of white or yellowish flowers appear in summer. These quick-growing, decorative foliage plants look good along paths, in herb gardens, among ferns and when grown in pots.
CULTIVATION: Very frost hardy, they prefer full sun or light shade if summers are hot. Slightly moist, well-drained soil is best. Propagate from seed sown in spring. Variegated forms are propagated by root division or from young spring cuttings.

Melissa officinalis
LEMON BALM, BEE BALM

A native of southern Europe, this perennial to 24 in (60 cm) high is grown for its fresh, lemon-scented and lemon-flavored leaves. Small white flowers appear in late summer and attract pollinating bees into the garden. Lemon balm spreads rapidly, dies down in winter but shoots again in spring. The leaves are valued as a calming herbal tea. They also give a light, lemon flavor to fruit salads, jellies, iced tea and summer drinks, and can be used as asubstitute for lemon peel in cooking. **ZONES 4–10.**

MELOCACTUS
TURK'S CAP CACTUS

The 30 cactus species in this genus are generally globose, unbranched and only rarely exceed 3 ft (1 m) tall. They are natives of tropical America. Usually deep green, ribbed and formidably armed with curved spines, they bear small, white, pink, red or purple tubular flowers that are followed by $\frac{1}{2}$–1 in (12–25 mm) berry-like fruits. All species have a conspicuous disc of dense, felty hairs known as a cephalium at the top of their stems; this is often a fleshy pink color.
CULTIVATION: Grow these plants in full sun in gritty, well-drained soil that is moist during the growing season and dry in winter. Few species will tolerate any but the very lightest frosts, and they need warm summer temperatures to grow well. Propagate from seed in spring.

Melocactus matanzanus

This globular cactus grows 4 in (10 cm) high and slightly wider. As it matures, it produces a cephalium from which grow pink, mid-sized flowers and narrow red fruit. Both flowers and fruit last from spring through to fall (autumn). **ZONES 10–12.**

Melocactus salvadorensis

Ranging from Brazil to El Salvador, this 4 in (10 cm) high cactus grows out to about 6 in (15 cm). Long-lasting red flowers and elongated pink fruit appear from spring to fall (autumn). **ZONES 10–12.**

MENISPERMUM
YELLOW PARILLA, MOONSEED

This is a genus of 2 climbers, one from eastern North America and the other from East Asia. They tend to be straggly plants that climb to around 20 ft (6 m) high. The leaves are roughly heart-shaped, sometimes with shallow lobes, and up to 8 in (20 cm) long; they have a dark green upper surface with lighter underside that is downy when young. Tiny yellow-green flowers are borne on racemes that develop in the leaf axils in spring. The inconspicuous flowers are followed by grape-like bunches of $\frac{1}{2}$ in (12 mm) fruits that are toxic and possibly fatal to children.
CULTIVATION: Primarily plants of deciduous woodlands, these climbers are easily cultivated in any humus-rich, well-drained soil in sun or part-shade. They are very frost hardy. Propagate from seed or cuttings or by layering.

Menispermum canadense
CANADIAN MOONSEED

This rampant suckering climber usually has persistent stems, although in very cold climates it can be cut to the ground by winter cold. It will grow up to 20 ft (6 m) tall and has inconspicuous yellow-green flowers. When both male and female forms are present, the females will produce glossy black fruit with crescent-shaped seeds. **ZONES 5–9.**

MENTHA
MINT

This genus contains 25 species of aromatic, perennial herbs, some evergreen and some semi-evergreen, from Europe, Asia and Africa. Most are cultivated for their fragrance, some for their flavor or ornamental appeal. Several species make attractive ground covers. They vary in size from tiny creeping forms to bushy plants, and vary in flavor from refreshing to very strong.
CULTIVATION: Most are very frost hardy, like sunshine and rich soil and need lots of moisture (poor drainage matters not at all). They are invasive, spreading rapidly by runners; to keep them under control, try growing them in large pots, watering regularly and repotting annually. Propagate from seed or by root division in spring or fall (autumn).

Mentha aquatica
WATER MINT, WILD MINT, MARSH MINT

During the Middle Ages, this species was known as menastrum and was a popular strewing herb. It is an aromatic, pubescent plant up to 3 ft (1 m) tall with short-stalked, lance-shaped to oval leaves with serrated edges. Heads of small lilac flowers are borne at the tops of the stems or in whorls in the leaf axils from late summer to late fall (autumn). **ZONES 6–10.**

Mentha arvensis
CORN MINT, FIELD MINT

This erect hairy perennial reaches up to 24 in (60 cm) in height. It occurs throughout most of Europe on disturbed, often damp ground. The lance-shaped leaves are shallowly toothed. The lilac flowers appear in dense axillary whorls from mid-summer until fall (autumn). This species has the property of being able to prevent milk from curdling and was once cultivated solely for this purpose. **ZONES 4–10.**

Melicope elleryana

Melicope elleryana

Melissa officinalis

Mentha arvensis

Mentha × piperita
PEPPERMINT

This spreading perennial, grown for its aromatic foliage and culinary uses, grows to 24 in (60 cm) high and wide. Using underground stems, it forms a carpet of oval, toothed, mid-green and reddish green leaves. Purple flowers appear in spring. ***Mentha × piperita* f. *citrata***, Eau de Cologne mint, is too strong and bitter for culinary use but is grown for its distinctive perfume. **ZONES 3–10.**

Mentha pulegium
PENNYROYAL, EUROPEAN PENNYROYAL MINT

A native of Asia and Europe with small, elliptical, gray-green, hairy leaves, this species has spreading stems that form a foliage clump around 4 in (10 cm) high and 18 in (45 cm) wide. In summer and early fall (autumn), the plant produces upright spikes with whorls of white to pale lilac to soft purple-pink flowers. Plant in shade if the soil is inclined to dry out. Prostrate dwarf forms grow well in hanging baskets. It is renowned for its curative value in treating colds, nausea, headaches, nervous disorders and various skin conditions. **ZONES 7–10.**

Mentha requienii
syn. ***Mentha corsica***
CORSICAN MINT

This semi-evergreen, creeping species grows only ½ in (12 mm) high and has small, round, pale green leaves with a peppermint aroma and light purple, tiny flowers that appear in summer. Unlike most of the genus, it needs a shaded site. It tolerates light foot traffic and looks good planted between paving stones. It self-seeds freely, but is not difficult to control. **ZONES 8–10.**

Mentha spicata
SPEARMINT

Reaching 24 in (60 cm) in height, this fast-growing mint with dark, crinkly leaves thrives in a sunny or part-shaded position. This is the mint used in mint sauce, mint jelly and to flavor and garnish new potatoes, green peas, fruit drinks and desserts. It is best grown in a container as it is highly invasive. **ZONES 3–10.**

Mentha × piperita

Mentha pulegium

Mentha suaveolens
syn. ***Mentha rotundifolia*** **of gardens**
APPLE MINT

This vigorous suckering perennial grows to 3 ft (1 m) tall with felted gray-green apple-scented leaves. Although its foliage looks and smells good and can be used in the kitchen, it is a plant best kept in a container with no contact with the ground as it suckers strongly and is difficult to control. **ZONES 6–10.**

Mentha × villosa f. *alopecuroides*
BOWLES' MINT, WINTER MINT

This mint is a hybrid between *Mentha spicata* and *M. suaveolens*; it is sometimes sold in nurseries as *M. cordifolia*. It is a vigorous, erect plant to 3 ft (1 m) high with ovate or rounded mid-green leaves with a distinct spearmint scent. Pink flowers are produced in dense spikes during fall (autumn). This is an excellent culinary mint and may be used in any dishes where spearmint is called for. In warm-temperate climates it will keep growing through winter. **ZONES 5–10.**

MENTZELIA
BLAZING STAR, STARFLOWER

This genus of some 60 species of biennials, perennials and shrubs is found over much of southwestern USA, Mexico and the West Indies. Species range from 2–4 ft (0.6–1.2 m) tall. The foliage is simple or coarsely toothed and is often whitish green when young or at the base of the plant. The leaves and stems are covered with fine hairs. The summer-borne flowers, which in some species open at night, are 5-petalled, sometimes

Mentha × piperita f. *citrata*

Mentha pulegium

Mentha suaveolens

fragrant, usually bright yellow and range from 1–4 in (2.5–10 cm) in diameter depending on the species.
CULTIVATION: Plant in full sun in light, well-drained soil and water occasionally in summer. Species from southwestern USA tolerate sandy or saline clay soils. Hardiness varies with the species. Propagate the biennials from seed and the perennial and shrubby species from seed or cuttings.

Mentzelia laevicaulis
BLAZING STAR

This frost-hardy biennial from southwestern USA grows to 4 ft (1.2 m) tall. It has white stems and toothed foliage, and produces pale yellow flowers to 4 in (10 cm) across during summer; these open in the morning. **ZONES 8–11.**

Mentzelia lindleyi
syn. ***Bartonia aurea***
BLAZING STAR

This annual species from California grows to about 30 in (75 cm) tall. It has mid- to gray-green foliage up to 6 in (15 cm) long and produces night-scented bright yellow flowers to 3 in (8 cm) across through summer. The petals have an orange flush at their base. **ZONES 8–11.**

MENYANTHES

There is only one species in this genus, with a very wide distribution through Europe, northern Asia, northwestern India and North America. It is an aquatic or marginal water plant with creeping rhizomes to 4 ft (1.2 m) long. This plant has long been used in herbal medicine to relieve gout and fever. The Inuit ground it into a flour and the leaves have been used in Scandinavia to make beer.
CULTIVATION: This plant is fully frost hardy and is happy grown in wet mud in, or on the edge of, water. Propagate from seed sown in wet soil or cuttings of pre-rooted rhizomes in spring.

Mentha spicata

Mentha × villosa f. *alopecuroides*

Menyanthes trifoliata

Menyanthes trifoliata
BOG BEAN

This plant has attractive foliage divided into 3 leaflets of rich green supported by dark-colored stems. The tiny fringed flowers are produced in erect spikes and are white, but pink in bud. This species grows to about 12 in (30 cm) tall and spreads out over a considerable area of water. **ZONES 3–10.**

MENZIESIA
MINNIE BUSH, FOOL'S HUCKLEBERRY, MOCK AZALEA

This is a genus of 7 deciduous shrubs from the cool-temperate regions of North America and East Asia. They range in size from 12 in (30 cm) to 8 ft (2.4 m) tall and usually have an erect growth habit. The leaves, which are often clustered at the branch tips, are oval and seldom more than 2 in (5 cm) long. They have a covering of fine hairs or down, especially when young. The flowers, which form at the branch tips, are clusters of pendulous, ¼–½ in (6–12 mm) tubular bells. They come in shades of cream, pink, red or purple.
CULTIVATION: In common with other plants from the erica family, *Menziesia* species prefer moist, humus-rich, well-drained, acid soil. Plant in sun in cool areas, afternoon shade elsewhere. They are hardy to at least –10°F (–23°C). Propagate from seed or cuttings taken in late spring.

Menziesia ciliicalyx

This is a Japanese species of great charm and quiet elegance to 3 ft (1 m) tall. Its branches are arranged in layers, supporting clusters of small leaves towards their tips. In late spring and early summer, it produces clusters of drooping purple-pink flowers. The foliage turns yellow before shedding. **ZONES 6–10.**

MERREMIA

This genus of some 70 species is closely related to *Ipomoea* (morning glory) and is only separated from this latter genus due to the difference in pollen grains. They are generally climbing plants and can be herbaceous or woody. The leaves can be entire, lobed or compound with up to 7 leaflets. The funnel-shaped flowers can be white, yellow or purple. They are pantropical in distribution.
CULTIVATION: Most are vigorous, sun-loving vines for basically frost-free climates, although some of the herbaceous species will survive if covered in winter. They prefer fertile, moist but well-drained soil and need protection from cold winds. Propagate from seed sown in spring.

Merremia tuberosa
syn. *Ipomoea tuberosa*
WOOD ROSE, YELLOW MORNING GLORY, SPANISH MORNING GLORY

This woody vine from Mexico and tropical South America grows to 70 ft (21 m) in height if suitable supports and climate exist. Its 6 in (15 cm) leaves are deeply 7-lobed and it produces its yellow flowers in summer. These are followed by a ball-shaped brown, woody seed capsule surrounded by woody sepals; dried, these are used for floral work. **ZONES 9–12.**

MERTENSIA

This genus from northern temperate areas consists of about 50 species of herbaceous perennials. The foliage is usually lanceolate and hairy. They produce terminal panicles of tubular flowers, usually blue, in spring.
CULTIVATION: Some species are small alpines ideal for cool rock gardens; others are taller, making them suitable for most borders and woodland gardens. All species prefer full sun and moisture-retentive soil but in most cases, especially the alpines, sharp drainage is important. All are fully frost hardy. Propagate from seed, although some species can be carefully divided. Check for slugs and snails.

Mertensia ciliata
CHIMING BELLS

This species from western USA grows to about 24 in (60 cm) tall. Its leaves are lanceolate and bluish green. The flower stems support nodding, blue, trumpet-shaped flowers, $\frac{1}{3}$ in (8 mm) long during summer. **ZONES 4–10.**

Mertensia pulmonarioides
syn. *Mertensia virginica*
VIRGINIA BLUEBELLS

Native to the cooler parts of North America, this perennial is one of the loveliest of all blue spring flowers. It has smooth, oblong, soft blue-green foliage, and bears clusters of rich blue, tubular 1 in (25 mm) long flowers, 20 or more on each stem. It is effective planted with daffodils and polyanthus, and is seen at its best naturalized in woodlands or alongside streams. It grows to a height and spread of around 18 in (45 cm). **ZONES 3–9.**

MERYTA
PUKA

This genus of around 30 species of evergreen, large-leafed shrubs and trees from the Pacific Islands is found as far south as the north of New Zealand. These spectacular foliage plants have simple oval leaves, up to 18 in (45 cm) long, that are very glossy and leathery. The leaves are clustered at the branch tips, which produce a round-headed tree. Variegated foliage forms are occasionally available. The panicles of tiny greenish white spring and early summer flowers and the fleshy $\frac{1}{2}$ in (12 mm) blackish fruits that follow are conspicuous but not really a feature.
CULTIVATION: Plant in moist, humus-rich, well-drained soil in light to moderate shade. When grown in full sun, the foliage is smaller and tends to look bleached. As most species will not tolerate frosts, they thrive as greenhouse or house plants in tubs. Propagate from seed or cuttings (these are large and difficult to handle).

Meryta sinclairii
PUKA PUKANUI

This is a very handsome, small, round-headed tree to 25 ft (8 m) only suitable for frost-free climates if grown outdoors. It is found wild only on the Three Kings Islands and the Hen and Chicken Islands, both small island groups to the north of, and part of, New Zealand. The big bright, glossy green, paddle-shaped leaves can exceed 24 in (60 cm) in length and 8 in (20 cm) in width. **ZONES 10–12.**

MESEMBRYANTHEMUM
ICE PLANT

Once treated as a much larger genus that included most of the small succulents with daisy-like flowers commonly referred to as ice plants, *Mesembryanthemum* is now regarded as containing only a few species of creeping or prostrate succulent annuals or biennials from South Africa.

Meryta sinclairii

These are characterized by leaves covered with glistening, swollen surface cells, giving the plants a crystalline appearance. The small flowers are white, pink or red, very rarely, yellow. They have naturalized in southern California and Australia, where they were cultivated as ornamentals.
CULTIVATION: Mesembryanthemums will only tolerate the lightest frost. They require very light soil and full sun at all times. Propagate from seed in spring.

Mesembryanthemum crystallinum

This is the best known species of the *Mesembryanthemum* genus. It is an annual, carpet-forming succulent that grows 4 in (10 cm) high. It has dense, flat leaves with undulating edges. The small, shiny papillae (glands) covering the leaves, the flower stems and cups glisten in the sun. Groups of 3 to 5 white, narrow-petalled flowers 1 in (25 mm) wide appear in summer. **ZONES 9–11.**

MESPILUS
MEDLAR

Allied to the pears, the medlar, the single species in this genus from Europe and southwest Asia, has been cultivated for hundreds of years. A deciduous, sometimes thorny tree, it is grown primarily for its brown fruit, edible only after they are 'bletted' (almost rotten), which remain on the tree until well into fall (autumn). Its large hairy leaves form a dense canopy.

Merremia tuberosa

CULTIVATION: Slow growing, the medlar resents being transplanted, but is easy to cultivate; it needs a temperate climate, well-drained soil and shelter from strong wind. It must not be allowed to dry out. Lightly prune for shape in early winter. Propagate from seed or by grafting.

Mespilus germanica

In early summer, this species bears large, single, unperfumed white flowers, and its gnarled branches make it look ancient even when young. Its dark green leaves turn russet in fall (autumn), particularly if the tree is grown in full sun. It spreads to 25 ft (8 m). **ZONES 4–9.**

Mespilus germanica

Mespilus germanica

Metrosideros excelsus

Metrosideros excelsus 'Variegata'

Metrosideros excelsus

Metrosideros kermadecensis 'Variegatus'

METASEQUOIA

DAWN REDWOOD

Until shortly after World War II, *Metasequoia glyptostroboides*, the single species of the genus, was known only as a fossil conifer. Then a stand of living trees was discovered in western China; from these it has been propagated and widely planted in temperate-climate areas. It is notable for its gold and russet foliage in fall (autumn)—it is one of the few deciduous conifers. It grows very rapidly and, as the timber is durable and of fine quality, it is a very promising tree for cool-climate forestry.
CULTIVATION: It prefers full sun, deep fertile soil, good summer rainfall and shelter from strong winds. It is fully frost hardy. Propagate from seed or cuttings from side shoots in fall.

Metrosideros carmineus

Metasequoia glyptostroboides

Its gracefully conical outline and delicate foliage, light green in spring and summer, have made the dawn redwood a popular tree. It grows unusually fast in favorable conditions, and old trees may reach 200 ft (60 m) in height. As the tree matures, the rough-textured bark turns from reddish to dark brown to gray. It can be clipped to make a tall hedge. **ZONES 5–10.**

METROSIDEROS

The 50 or so species in this South Pacific genus are not all trees; some are shrubs or clinging vines. They are especially important in New Zealand where several species yield rata—the hard, dark red timber prized by the Maoris for sculpture—and where they range from the very edge of the sea to the high mountains. They have hard, leathery, evergreen leaves, often gray tinged, and red (sometimes bright yellow) summer flowers whose chief beauty, like those of the related *Eucalyptus* of Australia, comes from their long colored stamens.
CULTIVATION: Moderately frost hardy to frost tender, they do best in subtropical or warm-temperate climates, in full sun or light shade and fertile, well-drained soil. The shrubby species do very well as container plants. Propagate from seed in spring or cuttings in summer.

Metrosideros carmineus

AKAKURA

This New Zealand species is a self-clinging evergreen climber that, like ivy, starts as a juvenile non-flowering form while climbing. Later, as the branches grow out from it to support it, it starts to flower. If propagated from adult wood, it will make a small bush ideal for a rock garden. This species does best in moist semi-shade and is frost tender. **ZONES 9–11.**

Metrosideros excelsus

syn. ***Metrosideros tomentosus***

POHUTUKAWA, NEW ZEALAND CHRISTMAS TREE,

Reaching 40 ft (12 m) in height, this tree begins as a shrub with dense masses of spreading branches, then develops a stout main trunk and umbrella-shaped canopy. The oblong leaves are dull deep green above and gray and felty underneath. The crimson stamens stand out from the flowers, borne from late spring to mid-summer in warm zones. The pohutukawa will survive in the most exposed seashore situations, as long as the soil is not saline. **'Variegata'**, with creamy yellow-edged leaves, is a popular cultivars. **ZONES 10–11.**

Metrosideros kermadecensis

KERMADEC POHUTUKAWA

Though very similar to *Metrosideros excelsus*, the leaves of this species are slightly smaller and more oval, and the flowering season is usually longer. Much the same height as *M. excelsus*, it is more often seen in its variegated-leaf forms. **'Variegatus'** forms a neat shrub for many years, eventually reaching about 20 ft (6 m); the gray-green leaves are edged with an irregular creamy yellow margin. **'Sunninghill'** has the creamy yellow marking towards the middle of the leaf. **ZONES 10–11.**

Metrosideros robustus

Metrosideros robustus

NORTHERN RATA

This slow-growing species from New Zealand's North Island and northern South Island is a heavily wooded tree 70 ft (21 m) high. In the wild, it is usually

Metasequoia glyptostroboides

Metasequoia glyptostroboides

Michelia champaca

Michelia figo

covered with epiphytes and often begins its own life as an epiphyte, eventually sending roots to ground level. Masses of brilliant orange-red flowers open in summer. **ZONES 9–11.**

Metrosideros umbellatus

SOUTHERN RATA

Similar to the northern rata, although not as large, this species occurs almost throughout New Zealand and extends into higher alpine regions. It produces masses of intensely scarlet blooms from late spring to fall (autumn) and its flowering is a feature of the bushlands of the Southern Alps. It grows very slowly. **ZONES 8–10.**

MEUM

BALDMONEY, SPIGNEL

There is only one species in this genus of the carrot family. It is a clump-forming herbaceous perennial to 24 in (60 cm) tall with attractive foliage and umbels of small white flowers in summer. This plant occurs naturally in western and central Europe.

CULTIVATION: An attractive addition to the perennial border or wild garden, it is simple to grow in any well-drained but moist soil in full sun and does best in temperate to cold climates. It is very frost hardy. Propagate from fresh seed. It will often self-seed if happy.

Meum athamanticum

The pretty soft mid-green basal foliage is the major asset of this plant. In early summer it will start to produce its tiny white or purple-tinged white flowers in small umbels. It spreads to 12 in (30 cm). The foliage is aromatic. **ZONES 4–9.**

MICHAUXIA

These are strong-growing perennials from the eastern Mediterranean and western Asia. There are only 7 species, but all are impressive plants with interesting, sometimes reflexed flowers. The genus belongs to the campanula family, and its species often attain heights of 5 ft (1.5 m) or more. The hairy leaves are produced in basal rosettes and are always lobed or toothed. The flowers appear on tall, branching, leafy stems.

CULTIVATION: Full sun and shelter from strong wind is essential for success with these fully frost hardy plants. Soil must drain freely, but need only be moderately fertile. Raised from seed, plants take at least 2 years to bloom, sometimes 3, after which they promptly die. Where winters are cold, mulch around plants with straw in late fall (autumn). Propagate from seed sown in spring where it is to grow.

Metrosideros umbellatus

Michelia doltsopa

Michauxia tchihatchewii

From Turkey, this perennial grows to 6 ft (1.8 m) tall, sometimes more. It has 8 in (20 cm) toothed leaves that form a rosette at ground level. In summer, each of these rosettes produces a thick branching stem on which develop numerous long-petalled white flowers. As these age, the petals reflex (bend backwards). This is an impressive plant for the back of a border and looks especially good in groups. **ZONES 7–10.**

MICHELIA

Closely related to the magnolias, the 45 or so species of *Michelia* are found in tropical and subtropical Asia, with a few species in the cooler foothills of the Himalayas. They range from shrubs to substantial trees, mainly evergreen, and many bear intensely fragrant flowers. Some species are widely cultivated in India for their fragrant oil, which is extracted from the blooms for use in perfume and cosmetics.

CULTIVATION: They like frost-free climates and a position in full sun or part-shade in humus-rich, well-drained, neutral to acid soil; they resent being transplanted. Propagate from seed in fall (autumn) or spring, or from cuttings in summer.

Michelia champaca

CHAMPAK, CHAMPACA

From the lower Himalayas, this upright, conical tree reaches 100 ft (30 m) in its native habitat, but cultivated trees usually reach only a third of this height. Its long, slender, mid-green leaves droop from the somewhat horizontal branches. Cup-shaped creamy orange petals on a bed of recurved sepals are borne upright on the branch tips during late summer. The flowers are particularly fragrant. **ZONES 10–11.**

Michelia doltsopa

This 30 ft (9 m) tree from the eastern Himalayas is slender while young, developing a broader crown with age. The large, scented white flowers, resembling those of *Magnolia denudata*, appear in the axils of the grayish green leaves in late winter and early spring. **'Silver Cloud'** was selected due to its incredibly abundant flower production; otherwise it is identical to the species. **ZONES 9–11.**

Michelia figo

syns ***Magnolia fuscata, Michelia fuscata***

PORT-WINE MAGNOLIA, BANANA SHRUB

A slow-growing, compact shrub from western China, the port-wine magnolia usually grows as a dense 10 ft (3 m) shrub. It bears small, shiny, deep green leaves and tiny spring-blooming heavily scented cream flowers streaked with purple. Pruning produces abundant new flowering growth. **ZONES 9–11.**

Meum athamanticum

Metrosideros umbellatus

Michelia yunnanensis

In spring, this small, open-crowned 15 ft (4.5 m) tree produces along its branches furry brown buds which open to large, round, perfumed clusters of cream flowers with prominent yellow stamens. It is well suited to cool climates if protected from strong winds. Slow growing, it is a good tree for small gardens and for containers if consistently watered during its growing season. **ZONES 9–11.**

MICROBIOTA

There is just one species in this genus, a dwarf evergreen conifer that is excellent as a ground cover, as a specimen on its own, or grouped with other low-growing conifers or heathers. It also makes a good foil for other more colorful plants, such as bulbs.

CULTIVATION: Very frost hardy, it does best in free-draining soil with an open aspect, although it tolerates extremes of temperature and high altitudes. Prune only if absolutely necessary and then only into the new wood. Propagate from seed or from tip cuttings.

Microbiota decussata
RUSSIAN ARBORVITAE

This conifer from Siberia grows to only 18 in (45 cm) high with a spread of up to 10 ft (3 m). Its branches nod at the tips and bear flat sprays of scale-like, yellowish green leaves (bronze in winter). Its small, round cones are pale brown and contain one fertile seed each. **ZONES 3–9.**

MICROSORUM

This genus consists of perhaps 40 species of ferns, mainly creeping or climbing rhizomatous plants, often epiphytic, mainly from tropical Africa, Asia, Australasia and Polynesia. The fronds are simple and entire in some species, deeply lobed in others, leathery and lance-shaped. ***Microsorum diversifolium***, has variously shaped fronds.

CULTIVATION: Like most fern species, moist, well-drained, cool, shaded aspects suit them best. Most are frost tender and in cold climates can be greenhouse grown. They can be grown up a trunk or in hanging baskets which they will engulf. Propagate by dividing rooted rhizomes.

Microsorum howeanum
syn. ***Phymatosorus pustulatus*** **subsp.** ***howensis***

Native to Lord Howe Island off the east coast of Australia, this species has leathery, long-stemmed fronds. The fronds are pinnately lobed with broad, pointed lobes. Some botanists now prefer to call it by its synonym. **ZONES 10–11.**

Microsorum howeanum

Millettia grandis

Microbiota decussata

Michelia yunnanensis

Microsorum scolopendrium
syn. ***Phymatosorus scolopendria***
WART FERN

Probably the most widespread species, being found in tropical Africa through Asia to Australasia and the islands of Polynesia, this species has broad, tongue-shaped fronds that are light green and deeply cut. The fronds arise from a spreading rhizome. **ZONES 9–12.**

MILIUM

Some 6 species of annual or perennial grasses native to Europe, Asia and eastern North America comprise this genus. The only species usually grown is ***Milium effusum,*** which has been planted in woods as a food plant for game birds. It is grown as an ornamental for its flowers and foliage, especially the variegated forms.

CULTIVATION: They are easily grown in semi-shade, are frost tolerant and prefer moisture-retentive soil. Propagate by division or from seed in spring. The golden form described below comes true from seed as long as it isn't growing near the wild green form.

Milium effusum 'Aureum'
BOWLES' GOLDEN GRASS, MILLET GRASS, GOLDEN WOOD MILLET

This evergreen, tuft-forming perennial grass is grown for its yellow foliage and flowers. It is good in perennial borders, water gardens or as a ground cover, and effective when planted under white-variegated shrubs. Its flat leaves are golden yellow in spring, fading to yellowish green in summer. Panicles of greenish yellow spikelets are produced in summer; they can be cut and used for dried arrangements. It grows to a height of 2–3 ft (0.6–1 m) and a spread of 12 in (30 cm). It self-seeds readily. **ZONES 6–10.**

MILLA

The 6 species of bulbs that make up this genus are natives of southern USA, Mexico and Central America. They have narrow, arching, blue-green, grassy leaves up to 24 in (60 cm) long. Well-established clumps can be more than 3 ft (1 m) across. In spring, each bulb produces a wiry stem bearing bell- or funnel-shaped flowers, each up to $1\frac{1}{2}$ in (35 mm) long. Some species formerly included in *Milla* are now listed under *Brodiaea, Leucocoryne* and *Ipheion.*

CULTIVATION: Easily grown in any free-draining soil in sun or morning shade, these bulbs are hardy in any place where the soil does not freeze to the planting depth of the bulb. Propagate from seed or by dividing established clumps.

Milium effusum 'Aureum'

Milla biflora
MEXICAN STAR

This is a bulb of limited horticultural merit from Mexico, southern USA and Central America. It has a cluster of semi-erect narrow mid-green basal leaves through which the flower spike appears in summer to fall (autumn). Its blooms consist of 6 spreading petals, usually white or flushed lavender or pink and produced in umbels of up to 8 flowers; the center of the petal is usually striped green. **ZONES 9–11.**

MILLETTIA

This legume genus consists of more than 90 species of vines, shrubs and trees occurring throughout the tropics together with several species from humid coastal South Africa and eastern Australia. All species, both evergreen and deciduous, thrive in warm, humid areas where their large compound leaves and trusses of pea-shaped flowers demand admiration.

CULTIVATION: Mostly frost tender, they prefer moist, well-drained soil and full sun; the trees in the genus are ideal as shade trees. Prune only to keep them shapely. Propagate from ripe seed.

Millettia grandis
syn. ***Millettia caffra***
SOUTH AFRICAN IRONWOOD, UMZIMBEET

The most popular tree species of *Millettia* for warm, humid areas, the ironwood's dense, evergreen crown consists of long glossy leaves each with up to 15 pairs of leaflets. Growing to 30 ft (9 m), it begins to branch at head heightand in late spring carries large rose-purple flower spikes above the foliage. Flat furry pods develop after the flowers have faded. **ZONES 10–12.**

Millettia megasperma
AUSTRALIAN WISTERIA

This fast-growing vigorous climber to 30 ft (9 m) or more is native to moist forests of subtropical eastern Australia. It has glossy pinnate leaves consisting of 7 to 13 oblong leaflets and large drooping panicles of purple, pea-shaped flowers in winter and spring, followed by furry, woody pods, up to 6 in (15 cm) long which contain large brown seeds. It needs solid support and room to spread. **ZONES 10–12.**

MILTONIOPSIS

This genus was created for the pansy orchids still commonly called miltonias. There are about 5 species, from South America, but the hybrids are more commonly grown. With their flat, almost circular flowers and vivid markings, they resemble pansies, but are much larger—up to 6 in (15 cm) across—and come in stronger colors than pansies usually do: bright yellow, white, red and pink, often with gold, purple or brown flashes. Many are sweetly scented. Low-growing, clumping plants, they have round

Miltoniopsis Hybrid Bel Royal

M. Hybrid Charlotte's Delight

Miltoniopsis Hybrid × *Miltassia* Anne Warne 'Alii'

M. Hybrid Hudson Bay 'Judith'

Miltoniopsis Hybrid Sao Paulo

pseudobulbs and pale green, strap-like leaves. The flowers are borne in small clusters, mostly in mid-summer, but they can appear at any time from spring to fall (autumn). Many plants flower twice a year.

CULTIVATION: The plants like open compost and light shade. They can grow outdoors in tropical and subtropical climates; elsewhere they need a greenhouse. Unlike most orchids, they do not take a winter rest. Propagate by division after flowering.

Miltoniopsis Hybrid Rozel

Miltoniopsis Hybrids

Numerous complex intergeneric hybrids have been made using *Miltonia, Miltoniopsis, Odontoglossum, Oncidium, Cochlioda* and *Brassia*. Most members of the tribe Oncidiinae are interfertile. These hybrids go by names such as *Miltonidium, Odontonia, Miltonioda* and *Miltassia*. Among the multitude of forms and color resulting have been the so-called pansy orchids, which are derived from *Miltoniopsis phalaenopsis* and other species. Most of these are cool-growing species requiring shady, moist conditions. Hybrids include: **Anjou 'Red Mask',** deep red with a golden-yellow center and dark markings; **Bel Royal,** crimson with a white picotee edge; **Charlotte's Delight,** white with a large lower lip and crimson markings; **Grouville,** deep purplish pink with a fine white edge, darker markings and a golden center; **Hudson Bay 'Judith',** deep pink with a white-edged red center; **Sao Paulo,** relatively narrow, soft-pink petals with a large deep-pink lip and a dark center; and **Rozel,** small red petals with a large red-veined and pink-edged lip. Typical of the *Miltonia* × *Brassia* hybrids, × ***Miltassia* Anne Warne 'Alii'** has strap-like leaves and differs from the *Miltoniopsis* hybrids in having relatively narrow petals and a prominent lower lip. The magenta flower has a darker throat and yellow markings. **ZONES 10–11.**

Miltoniopsis Hybrid Grouville

Miltoniopsis Hybrid Anjou 'Red Mask'

Miltoniopsis phalaenopsis
syn. *Miltonia phalaenopsis*

This species occurs in Colombia at altitudes of 4,000–5,000 ft (1,200–1,500 m). The pseudobulbs are ovoid, about $1\frac{1}{2}$ in (35 mm) long, compressed, with a single narrow, strap-like leaf 4–8 in (10–20 cm) long. The inflorescence is shorter than the leaves, with 3 to 5 flowers about $2\frac{1}{2}$ in (6 cm) wide. **ZONES 11–12.**

MIMETES

This is a small genus of South African evergreen shrubs in the Protea family, about 11 in all. They are usually sparsely branched, and are well clothed with lance-shaped to ovate leaves. Those leaves towards the branch tips, between which the small flowers emerge, are often brightly colored. Most species grow on exposed heathland in phosphorus-poor soil. Like the related leucodendrons, these plants can be useful for floristry.

Mimetes cucullatus

CULTIVATION: In Mediterranean climates with only light frosts, *Mimetes* will do well if given full sun, good drainage and a nutrient-deficient soil. The flowerheads can rot in prolonged wet conditions. Propagate from ripe seed. Seedlings should be potted individually without delay as they resent disturbance.

Mimetes cucullatus
ROOISTOMPIE

This handsome shrub from the southwestern and southern Cape area of South Africa reaches 5 ft (1.5 m) in height. Striking bright red and yellow and white inflorescences are produced from midwinter to early summer. Plant in marshy, slightly acidic soil in full sun. **ZONES 9–10.**

Mimetes fimbrifolius

Mimulus cardinalis

Mimetes fimbrifolius

This species resembles the better known *Mimetes cucullatus,* but is larger and more vigorous, although less colorful. It can grow to around 8 ft (2.4 m) tall with a slightly wider spread. **ZONES 9–10.**

MIMOSA

Allied to *Acacia*, this large and diverse genus consists of about 480 species of annuals, evergreen perennials, shrubs and small trees. All but a few are from the Americas, in habitats varying from rainforest to dry savannah. The usually thorny stems bear bipinnate leaves, while the minute, 4- or 5-petalled flowers have long stamens and appear in rounded heads. Florist's mimosa is actually the Australian acacia.
CULTIVATION: These frost-tender plants prefer full sun and moderately fertile, well-drained soil. Water well during the growing period, sparingly in winter. Propagate from seed, although summer cuttings are also practical.

Mimosa pudica
HUMBLE PLANT, SENSITIVE PLANT, TOUCH-ME-NOT

Native to Brazil, this short-lived evergreen subshrub is usually treated as an annual. It is grown for its curiosity value—the fern-like leaves close up and

Mimulus aurantiacus

droop when touched, usually re-opening within minutes. It has prickly stems and small, fluffy, ball-shaped pink flowers in summer. It grows to a height and spread of around 3 ft (1 m). In some areas, this plant is becoming a noxious weed. **ZONES 10–12.**

MIMULUS
syn. *Diplacus*
MONKEY FLOWER, MUSK

The 180 or so species of annuals, perennials and shrubs are characterized by tubular flowers with flared mouths, often curiously spotted and mottled, which have been likened to grinning monkey faces. The flowers come in a large range of colors, including brown, orange, yellow, red, pink and crimson. Mainly native to the cool Pacific coastal areas of Chile and the USA, most species are suited to bog gardens or other moist situations, although some are excellent rock-garden plants.
CULTIVATION: Grow these plants in full sun or part-shade in wet or moist soil. Propagate perennials by division in spring and annuals from seed in fall (autumn) or early spring.

Mimulus 'Andean Nymph'

Possibly a hybrid between *Mimulus luteus* and *M. guttatus*, this is a spreading herbaceous perennial which grows to 8 in (20 cm) tall by at least 12 in (30 cm) wide. It produces its soft pink trumpets, stained and patched white, for a prolonged period in summer. **ZONES 6–10.**

Mimulus guttatus

Mimulus aurantiacus
syns *Diplacus aurantiacus, D. glutinosus, Mimulus glutinosus*
MONKEY MUSK

This marginally frost-hardy, evergreen shrub is native to North America. It bears crimson or yellow-orange flowers in spring and summer. The sticky, glossy, lance-shaped, rich green leaves have margins that roll slightly inwards. It grows 3 ft (1 m) tall and wide. **ZONES 8–10.**

Mimulus bifidus

This sticky-leafed shrub to 30 in (75 cm) has elliptic-oblong serrated leaves to $2^1/_2$ in (6 cm) long. Pale yellow flowers are borne in spring and summer. It is native to California. **ZONES 9–11.**

Mimulus cardinalis
CARDINAL MONKEY FLOWER, SCARLET MONKEY FLOWER

From southwestern USA and Mexico, this herbaceous perennial grows at least 3 ft (1 m) tall and 12 in (30 cm) wide. It has sharply toothed, hairy, mid-green leaves and produces racemes of yellow-throated scarlet flowers from summer through to fall (autumn). Found on banks of streams and ponds, it needs a sheltered position as it tends to sprawl if battered by rain and wind. **ZONES 7–11.**

Mimulus guttatus
syn. *Mimulus langsdorfii*
COMMON MONKEY FLOWER

A vigorous, very frost-hardy, semi-herbaceous perennial native to the Americas from Alaska to Mexico, this species grows well in damp to wet sites and has naturalized in areas well away from its natural habitat. It grows to about 12 in (30 cm) or so tall and spreads to at least 4 ft (1.2 m) and produces its bright yellow flowers, spotted or blotched brown-red, throughout the summer months. **ZONES 6–10.**

Mimulus × *hybridus* cultivar

Mimulus × *hybridus* Hybrids

These popular hybrids between *Mimulus guttatus* and *M. luteus* blend parental characters in various ways. The funnel-shaped, open-mouthed flowers can be up to 2 in (5 cm) wide and come in red, yellow, cream and white, or mixed variations of these colors, plus red mottling, spotting or freckling. Although reasonably hardy and perennial, they rapidly deteriorate in hot sunlight and become straggly after a few months, and so are treated as annuals. **'Ruiter's Hybrid'** bears orange trumpet-shaped flowers with wavy petal margins. **ZONES 6–10.**

Mimulus lewisii
GREATER PURPLE MONKEY FLOWER, MOUNTAIN MONKEY FLOWER

An upright perennial found from Alaska to California, this species bears pink-purple to rose-pink trumpet flowers with a white throat throughout summer. Its leaves are soft and hairy, mid-green and sticky to 3 in (8 cm) long. The plant grows to 24 in (60 cm) tall by at least 18 in (45 cm) wide. **ZONES 5–10.**

Mimulus longiflorus
SALMON BUSH MONKEY FLOWER

This shrubby species grows to about 3 ft (1 m) in height and spread, and has sticky 3 in (8 cm) long mid-green leaves. Its flowers, produced in spring and summer, can be from cream through yellow to orange and dark red. It is native to California and northwest Mexico. **ZONES 9–11.**

Mimulus luteus
YELLOW MUSK, GOLDEN MONKEY FLOWER

A spreading perennial often grown as an annual, this plant bears a profusion of

Mimulus longiflorus

Mimulus × *hybridus* 'Ruiter's Hybrid'

Mimulus moschatus

Mimulus luteus

yellow flowers above mid-green foliage throughout summer. It grows to a height and spread of 12 in (30 cm). It is very frost hardy, and needs part-shade and moist soil. **ZONES 7–10.**

Mimulus moschatus

MONKEY MUSK

This small, creeping, water-loving perennial grows to a height and spread of 6–12 in (15–30 cm). It bears pale yellow flowers, lightly dotted with brown, in summer to fall (autumn). It is very frost hardy. This plant was once grown for its musk scent but, mysteriously, it has been odorless for many years. **ZONES 7–10.**

Mimulus 'Whitecroft Scarlet'

syn. *Mimulus cupreus* 'Whitecroft Scarlet'

This brilliant deep scarlet flowered selection grows to about 4 in (10 cm) tall by 6 in (15 cm) wide. It blooms over a long period from late spring through summer. Take cuttings regularly as it is somewhat short lived. **ZONES 6–10.**

MINUARTIA

SANDWORT

This genus consists of about 100 species closely related to *Cerastium*. They are mostly perennials; although some annual species occur, they are of little horticultural interest. The genus has a wide distribution through much of the temperate and arctic regions of the northern hemisphere. The tight mat-forming species can make attractive subjects for rock gardens.
CULTIVATION: These very frost-hardy plants are easy to grow in temperate to cold climates in a sunny, moist aspect where the roots can get in under rocks to stay cool. Propagate by division, though cuttings and seed are both possible.

Minuartia recurva

Native to the mountains of south and central Europe, *Minuartia recurva* makes an attractive dense tuft of fine hairy foliage topped by white flowers on ½ in (12 mm) long stems. These stems usually support 2 to 8 flowers, although they can be solitary. It flowers in summer. **ZONES 5–9.**

Mirabilis jalapa

MIRABILIS

UMBRELLA WORT

This Central and South American genus consists of about 50 species of annuals or herbaceous perennials that make showy garden plants in virtually frost-free climates. Some can become invasive and difficult to eradicate as they can be quite deep rooted. The flowers are often brightly colored and in one case at least are variegated in bold colors like magenta and orange. Most have a pleasant fragrance.
CULTIVATION: In frost-free and dry tropical climates, they are quite easy plants to grow. All that is required is a sunny, well-drained aspect. In colder climates, the tubers of perennial species can be lifted and stored over winter like dahlias. Propagate from seed or by division of the tubers.

Mirabilis jalapa

MARVEL OF PERU, FOUR-O'CLOCK FLOWER

This bushy tuberous perennial, native to tropical America, is grown for its fragrant, trumpet-shaped, crimson, pink, white or yellow flowers that open in late afternoon and remain open all night, closing again at dawn. It is good as a pot or bedding plant or as a dwarf hedge. It is summer flowering and grows to around 3 ft (1 m) high with a spread of 24–30 in (60–75 cm). **ZONES 8–11.**

Mirabilis multiflora

This perennial species from southern USA makes a much-branched plant to 3 ft (1 m) tall. The leaves are ovate and gray-green. The flowers, borne in summer, consist of magenta bracts and a pink to purple trumpet-shaped flower about 2 in (5 cm) long. ***Mirabilis multiflora* var. *pubescens*** varies only in that its foliage is slightly sticky and covered in fine short hairs whereas the species has smooth leaves. **ZONES 8–11.**

Minuartia recurva

MISCANTHUS

This is a genus of ornamental grasses occurring naturally from Africa to eastern Asia. They are highly desirable and well-behaved herbaceous plants, ideal in a perennial border or by the edge of water. Most are tall-growing grasses that can reach up to 12 ft (3.5 m) or more. There are 17 to 20 species, usually neatly clump forming with upright reed-like stems and narrow arching leaves. The flowerheads are produced in late summer and fall (autumn) and make attractive fluffy plumes at the tops of the stems. They make good cut flowers.
CULTIVATION: Moderately frost hardy, they prefer full sun and fertile, moist but well-drained soil. Cut them down to ground level in late winter when the dead stems start to collapse. Propagate by dividing larger clumps in late winter.

Miscanthus sacchariflorus

SILVER BANNER GRASS, AMUR SILVER GRASS

This robust, clump-forming deciduous grass can exceed 8 ft (2.4 m) in height and 4 ft (1.2 m) in width. Its foliage is bright green with a white midrib. In late summer, it produces fluffy panicles of silvery pale green spikelets. Although native to Asia, it has naturalized in North America. **ZONES 8–10.**

Mirabilis multiflora var. *pubescens*

M

Miscanthus sinensis

EULALIA

Probably one of the most beautiful and least invasive of ornamental grasses, this Asian species has undergone more selection of cultivars than probably any other grass. The wild form makes neat, upright to slightly arching clumps up to 12 ft (3.5 m) tall although usually less. Its leaves have a white midrib and die to a soft straw color in winter. The flowerheads are usually soft gray tinted purple-brown. **'Gracillimus'** has very fine leaves that color well in fall (autumn), have a white mid-rib and arch elegantly; it rarely exceeds 4 ft (1.2 m) in height. **'Kleine Fontaine'** has arching leaves and flowers in early to mid-summer. **'Morning Light'**, similar to 'Gracillimus', has a fine silver variegated leaf edge. **'Silberfeder'** (syn. 'Silver Feather') grows to 8 ft (2.4 m) and produces a generous crop of light, open, silvery pink flowers on slender, erect stems in fall. **'Variegatus'** has creamy white leaves with pale green bands. **'Yaku Jima'** is a dwarf form to about 30 in (75 cm) or so with narrow arching leaves. **'Zebrinus'** is a tall variety with bands of gold irregularly positioned across the leaf blade, giving it the common name of zebra grass. **ZONES 4–10.**

Miscanthus sinensis 'Variegatus'

MITCHELLA

PARTRIDGE BERRY

Two species of evergreen perennials make up this genus: one a native of North America, the other found in Japan and South Korea. They trail across the ground and have glossy, deep green, oval leaves up to 1 in (25 mm) long. In spring, they produce pairs of 4-lobed, funnel-shaped flowers about ½ in (12 mm) long. The American species has white flowers; the Asian pink. The flowers are followed by ½ in (12 mm) 2-lobed white or red berries, rather like 2 berries fused together.

CULTIVATION: Plant in moist, well-drained soil in sun or part-shade. They are fully frost hardy. Propagate from seed, layers or cuttings.

Miscanthus sinensis 'Zebrinus'

Miscanthus sinensis 'Kleine Fontaine'

Miscanthus sinensis 'Gracillimus'

Mitchella repens

TWO-EYED BERRY, RUNNING BOX, PARTRIDGEBERRY

This North American species grows into a prostrate mat of dark green foliage with white veins to ¾ in (18 mm) long. Its small white flowers are often tinged pink; they are produced in early summer and are followed by bright red berries. It prefers acid soil and plenty of moisture. **ZONES 3–9.**

Miscanthus sinensis 'Morning Light'

MITELLA

BISHOP'S CAP, MITREWORT

This genus of some 20 species of rhizomatous perennials originates in North America and northeast Asia. Allied to *Heuchera* and *Tiarella*, and very similar in appearance, they form clumps of roughly heart-shaped leaves with shallow lobes and a covering of fine hairs. The leaf size varies from ½–4 in (1.2–10 cm) across, depending on the species. The tiny green, white or pink flowers are carried in spikes on upright, wiry stems that extend well above the foliage clump. Up to 60 flowers per spike appear in spring.

CULTIVATION: These woodland plants prefer moist, well-drained, humus-rich soil in sun or part-shade. They will not tolerate prolonged dry conditions, but will withstand temperatures down to −10°F (−23°C). Propagate from seed or by dividing established clumps in late winter to early spring.

Mitella breweri

A dainty if somewhat inconspicuous clumping plant from North America, this species has pleasant light green foliage that is slightly hairy and about 4 in (10 cm) long. Through these densely furnished leaves erupt its fine erect flower stems supporting tiny green flowers, hardly showy but en masse an attractive sight. If grown in a moist, semi-shaded aspect it will self-seed and make a good ground cover. It grows to 6 in (15 cm) tall in bloom. **ZONES 6–10.**

Mitraria coccinea

MITRARIA

This genus includes just one species, an evergreen scrambling or climbing subshrub from the south of Chile and Argentina. Its wiry stems are clothed in pointed elliptical leaves with toothed edges. The leaves, around 1 in (25 mm) long, have fine hairs along their midribs and petioles. From late spring to fall (autumn), it produces 4- or 5-lobed, narrow-mouthed, orange-red tubular flowers that are up to 1½ in (35 mm) long. The flowers are followed by ½ in (12 mm), fleshy, berry-like fruits.

CULTIVATION: This climber is very easy to grow, if a little untidy. Plant it in cool, moist, humus-rich, peaty soil. Provided the roots are cool, its foliage will tolerate full sun and the plant flowers better for it; otherwise grow in part-shade. Propagate from seed, layers or cuttings.

Mitraria coccinea

This is a useful and attractive subshrub with rich glossy green leaves and a long flowering season. It can be allowed to trail over the ground, spill over banks, cascade from a hanging basket or climb up a fence through trellis or wire. It stems can grow to 6 ft (1.8 m) or more in length. **ZONES 9–11.**

MOLINERIA

This small tropical genus of about 7 species of lily-like perennials is distrib-

uted from India to Australia. They have spreading underground stolons, somewhat palm-like leaves and short clusters of yellow flowers borne at or near ground level. Only one species, *Molineria capitulata,* is generally cultivated, valued for its highly ornamental foliage. Frost tender, it makes an attractive indoor specimen.
CULTIVATION: Suited to tropical, subtropical and warm-temperate regions, *Molineria* can be grown in a rich, moist soil in shade or sun. Propagate by division or from fresh seed.

Molineria capitulata
syn. *Curculigo recurvata, C. capitulata*
WEEVIL LILY

This widespreading, clump-forming perennial to 3 ft (1 m) tall grows in sheltered gullies in rainforests from Southeast Asia to northern Queensland, Australia. It has distinctive pleated, bright green leaves to 3 ft (1 m) long. Its bright yellow, widely opening flowers are borne in a short dense spike from between leaf bases near ground level. The flowers appear in summer to late fall (autumn) and are followed by rounded succulent fruit. **ZONES 10–12.**

MOLINIA

Only consisting of 2 or 3 species, this small grass genus has little ornamental value in its wild forms; in fact, wild plants can act as a host to ergot fungus which is a disease a variety of grasses and food crops. They are native to Eurasia and rarely exceed 4 ft (1.2 m), although the cultivated forms are often smaller. The attractive flowers in some forms are a purple shade.

Moltkia doerfleri

CULTIVATION: These grasses are fully frost hardy and grow happily in moist, neutral to acidic soil in a sunny aspect. They are especially effective near water or between large rocks in a rock garden. Propagate from seed or by division of cultivars and colored-leafed forms in spring.

Molinia caerulea
MOOR GRASS, PURPLE MOOR GRASS

A native of acid heathlands in Europe and southwestern and northern Asia, this tuft-forming perennial grass forms large tussocks 18 in (45 cm) high when in flower. It has broad, flat, mid-green leaves and in summer bears panicles of purplish spikelets. It has swollen stem bases which at times have been used as pipe cleaners and toothpicks. It is one of the most attractive garden grasses, especially in its finest variegated forms. **'Variegata'** is a compact type with cream-striped leaves and purplish flowers that grows to 24 in (60 cm) tall. **ZONES 5–10.**

MOLTKIA

This genus of 6 species comes from northern Italy to northern Greece and southwestern Asia. All are perennials or small shrubs found on rocky, sunny hillsides. They have lance-shaped, hairy, mid- to dark green leaves. The flowers are usually tubular and pendulous in shades of blue, purple and occasionally yellow. These attractive plants can be useful in rock gardens as ground covers or in the front of perennial borders.

Molineria capitulata

Molinia caerulea 'Variegata'

Monarda citriodora

CULTIVATION: They all like full sun and alkaline, well-drained soil, especially in winter. Some species can be invasive and are best in wilder parts of the garden. Propagate from seed or cuttings or by layering the woody species.

Moltkia doerfleri
syn. *Lithospermum doerfleri*

This is a suckering herbaceous species to 18 in (45 cm) in height and spread with unbranched, erect stems topped with drooping clusters of deep purple flowers from late spring to mid-summer. From Albania, it can be invasive in gardens and swamp smaller plants. **ZONES 6–10.**

Moltkia × *intermedia*

This hybrid between *Moltkia petraea* and *M. suffruticosa* most resembles the latter and arose as a garden hybrid. It makes an attractive bun-shaped subshrub to 12 in (30 cm) in height and spread, and produces drooping, funnel-shaped, rich blue flowers to $\frac{1}{2}$ in (12 mm) long that can be pink tinged in bud. **ZONES 6–10.**

MOLUCCELLA

The origin of this genus name is a puzzle, since none of its 4 species get any closer to the Moluccas than northwestern India, from where they extend to the eastern Mediterranean. They are annuals or short-lived perennials, although it is only the annual species that are usually grown. They are tall, upright, branched plants to 3 ft (1 m) or more with toothed leaves and small white fragrant flowers. It is, however, for the large green calyces that *Moluccella* species are grown; these are attractive in the garden or as cut flowers, fresh or dried.
CULTIVATION: Marginally frost hardy, these plants prefer full sun and moderately fertile, moist but well-drained soil. Propagate from seed.

Moluccella laevis
BELLS OF IRELAND, SHELL FLOWER

This summer-flowering annual, native to Turkey, Syria and the Caucasus, is grown for its flower spikes, surrounded by shell-like, apple green calyces, which are very popular for fresh or dried floral work; the tiny white flowers are insignificant. Its rounded leaves are pale green. This plant is fairly fast growing to a height of 3 ft (1 m) and spread of 12 in (30 cm), and has an erect, branching habit. **ZONES 7–10.**

MONARDA
BERGAMOT, HORSEMINT

This is a genus of 15 species of perennials or annuals from North America with green, sometimes purple-tinged, veined, aromatic leaves. They are much loved by bees and are used for flavoring teas and in potpourris, as well as for their ornamental value, flower color and scent. Plants can be single stemmed or sparsely branching, and bear 2-lipped, tubular flowers from mid-summer to early fall (autumn).
CULTIVATION: They are very frost-hardy plants best planted in full sun although some shade is acceptable. They must be well drained; in fact the annual species do best on sandy soil. The perennials are happy in moist soil and in some climates like a good feed of manure or compost. Annuals are sown directly into their permanent spot, and perennials are usually grown by division of established clumps.

Monarda citriodora
LEMON MINT

This annual species from central and southern USA and northern Mexico grows to 24 in (60 cm) tall. Its curved tubular flowers are scented and usually white, pink or purplish, and have a hairy mouth. **ZONES 5–11.**

M

Monarda didyma

Monarda didyma 'Aquarius'

Monarda 'Mahogany'

Monstera deliciosa

Monopsis lutea

Montanoa bipinnatifida

Monarda didyma
BEE BALM, OSWEGO TEA

This herb was used by the American Indians and early colonists as a tea. With its spidery white, pink or red flowers borne in late summer, it is one of the showiest of the culinary herbs. The young leaves may be used in salads or as a soothing tea; they can also be used as a stuffing for roast meat. The species grows 3 ft (1 m) or more tall. **'Aquarius'** has deep, purple-lilac flowers with purplish green bracts. **'Cambridge Scarlet'** is a vigorous perennial to 3 ft (1 m) with dark green, slightly toothed leaves that when crushed or brushed against emit an exotic, citrus-like scent. **'Croftway Pink'** grows to 30 in (75 cm) tall and has rose-pink flowers from mid-summer to early fall (autumn). **ZONES 4–10.**

Monarda fistulosa
WILD BERGAMOT

This perennial species from eastern North America has hybridized naturally and in gardens with *Monarda didyma* to produce a range of hybrids. The wild species grows to about 4 ft (1.2 m) tall and less than half that in width. The flowers produced in late summer and early fall (autumn) are usually light purple or pale pink with purple-stained bracts. **ZONES 4–10.**

Monarda 'Mahogany'

This is one of the above-mentioned hybrids between *Monarda didyma* and *M. fistulosa* and is a tall variety to 3 ft (1 m) with handsome wine-red or lilac flowers from mid-summer well into fall (autumn). **ZONES 4–10.**

Monarda punctata
SPOTTED BEE BALM

This very diverse species can be perennial, biennial or annual depending on the form selected. It usually grows to 3 ft (1 m) tall and the flower color can be yellow or pink, usually spotted with purple. **ZONES 6–10.**

MONARDELLA

This is a small genus of annuals and perennials from western North America, some 20 species in all. They are grown for their highly aromatic foliage, which in some species is used for herbal teas. The 2-lipped, tubular flowers are formed in terminal clusters and are most usually red, pink or purple in color.
CULTIVATION: Most like a sunny, sharply drained site and can be attractive in a rock garden or pot in the alpine house if smaller species are selected. The taller ones can be used at the front of a dry sunny border. They have reasonable frost resistance, but do resent dampness in winter. Propagate from seed or summer cuttings of perennial species or by division.

Monardella macrantha

From California, this suckering, trailing subshrubby perennial to 6 in (15 cm) tall and at least 8 in (20 cm) wide has slightly hairy mid-green leaves. By mid-summer it produces its whorls of orange-red ½ in (12 mm) long flowers set off by the purplish bracts. **ZONES 9–11.**

Monardella villosa
COYOTE MINT

This species is a trailing, woody stemmed, suckering perennial from California. The flowers are usually pale pink to rose purple. It can vary in height from 4 in (10 cm) up to 24 in (60 cm). **ZONES 8–11.**

MONOPSIS

This is a genus of 18 species of annuals from tropical and southern Africa that are quite similar to the annual lobelias. They can be used in much the same way in borders of flower beds. The tubular flowers flare at the tips into spreading lobes and are usually in shades of blue or yellow. The tube is split all the way to the base on the top side.
CULTIVATION: They do best in climates with cool summers and prefer full sun or part-shade and well-drained soil of moderate richness. Propagate from seed either planted *in situ* or raised under glass and planted out after frosts are over.

Monopsis lutea

This spreading, trailing plant has thin wiry stems to 12 in (30 cm) or more long, sometimes taking root from the lower nodes. It has alternate, linear to lance-shaped leaves with toothed margins. In spring and summer, bright yellow flowers are produced towards the ends of the stems. This is a pretty cascading plant for a rock garden or wall. **ZONES 10–11.**

MONSTERA

This is a genus of 25 species of often very large-growing evergreen tropical climbers, usually with long aerial roots and often epiphytic or becoming so as they clamber up forest trees. The foliage has both juvenile and adult forms: juvenile leaves are usually much smaller and entire, often growing flat to the trunk of the host plant; adult leaves are much larger and often perforated. The flower spikes are enclosed in a spathe to 18 in (45 cm) long that is sometimes shed and is usually white or greenish cream. The fruits, which often mature to white, are edible in some species. They are native to tropical America and the West Indies.
CULTIVATION: Species of *Monstera* are usually grown as indoor plants in all but tropical countries, where they can climb trees to 70 ft (21 m) or more. They can be controlled by pruning. They prefer part-shade and humus-rich, moist but well-drained soil. Propagate from ripe seed or cuttings or by layering.

Monstera deliciosa
FRUIT SALAD PLANT, SWISS CHEESE PLANT, SPLIT-LEAF PHILODENDRON

A close relative of *Philodendron* and native to the West Indies and tropical America, the huge, broad, glossy, perforated and deeply cut leaves of *Monstera deliciosa* grow from thick stems with aerial roots. Mature plants bear thick, cream spathes followed by sweet-smelling cones of edible fruit that take about a year to ripen and usually only outdoors. It is easy to grow, and adjusts to all but the coldest indoor conditions. **ZONES 10–12.**

MONTANOA

This striking genus of around 25 species of large evergreen daisies from tropical America includes some shrubs that can reach a height of 20 ft (6 m) and which may be treated as herbaceous plants. The leaves of most species are deeply indented, giving a pleasant appearance for a shrub border. The daisy-like flowers can be white or cream to rose or purple.
CULTIVATION: As these plants are frost tender, a position in full sun will produce a good floral display provided the soil is well drained and has ample humus and water added. After flowering, the plants should be cut back hard. Propagate from seed or root cuttings.

Montanoa arborescens
DAISY TREE

This is a multi-trunked shrub to over 12 ft (3.5 m) tall with oval, slightly toothed leaves. Clusters of small white, daisy-like flowers bloom in winter. **ZONES 10–12.**

Montanoa bipinnatifida
MEXICAN DAISY TREE

This 15 ft (4.5 m) species with large, soft green, deeply indented leaves comes

Monardella macrantha

Monardella villosa

M

Morina longifolia

Moraea spathulata

from Central America. In late fall (autumn) and winter, large clusters of white, daisy-like, single flowers appear on long, branching canes. The canes tend to be brittle, so plant in a sheltered position. **ZONES 10–12.**

Montanoa grandiflora
DAISY TREE

This species from Central America is an upright shrub with thick, cane-like stems to 12 ft (3.5 m) or more. Rising above the large, deeply cut leaves are fall (autumn) and winter blooming, large, daisy-like, fragrant white flowers with yellow centers. **ZONES 10–12.**

MORAEA
FORTNIGHT LILY

These beautiful, iris-like cormous perennials are native mainly to southern Africa. The genus contains about 120 species, although not many are in cultivation. The flowers are often short lived, usually lasting only a couple of days; they vary greatly in size, flowering time and color.
CULTIVATION: The bulbs should be planted in full sun, although in warm areas they may need some protection from hot afternoon sun. They like a fairly rich soil and good drainage is essential. They need plenty of water during growth, but must be kept dry when dormant. Propagate from offsets when dormant or from seed.

Moraea neopavonia
PEACOCK IRIS

This attractive species grows to about 18 in (45 cm) tall. The 2 in (5 cm) flowers, borne in spring, have 3 large outer petals and 3 tuft-like inner petals. The outer petals may be white or orange, and each has a bright blue 'peacock eye' outlined in black. The foliage is long and narrow. It is frost tender. **ZONES 9–11.**

Moraea spathulata
syn. *Moraea spathacea*
LARGE YELLOW TULIP

This marginally frost-hardy species grows to 4 ft (1.2 m). It has long, tough, strap-like leaves, which usually lie on the ground. The 3 in (8 cm) wide, bright yellow, iris-like flowers appear in spring. **ZONES 8–11.**

MORINA

This is a small genus of 4 species of prickly, rosette-form perennials that until they flower look for all the world like some species of thistle. The tall flower spikes produce whorls of long tubular curved flowers supported by collars of prickly bracts. These cold-hardy perennials come from mountainous regions of eastern Europe and the Himalayas and make statuesque foliage and flowering plants for the flower border.
CULTIVATION: They prefer full sun and very well-drained soil enriched with compost. Propagate from ripe seed or from root cuttings.

Morina longifolia
WHORL FLOWER

Probably the best known species in the genus, this plant grows to 4 ft (1.2 m) or more tall. Its foliage is mainly basal and spiny. The flowers start pure white and turn deep cerise; after pollination both colors will be seen together. The flowers are supported by bronze-tinged spiny bracts and the bronze calyxes stay ornamental even after flowering. **ZONES 6–10.**

MORINGA

Originating in the hotter, drier parts of western Asia and northeastern Africa, this genus consists of 14 species of small deciduous trees that are admired for their soft, corky bark, attractive foliage and fragrant flowers. The fruits are pod-like capsules. They are ideal for sunny, protected gardens.
CULTIVATION: Species tolerate most soil types and grow well in full sun. Water regularly and protect from wind and frost; in cooler climates, they can be grown in warmed greenhouses. Propagate from seed or cuttings.

Moringa oleifera
DRUMSTICK TREE, HORSERADISH TREE

This small tree, to 25 ft (8 m) tall and 10 ft (3 m) wide, bears large, much-divided leaves, sprays of white and gold, honey-scented spring flowers and fluted, bright green 18 in (45 cm) fruit. The seeds and asparagus-flavored pods are much used in Indian curries and the roots were once used as a substitute for horseradish. **ZONES 11–12.**

Morus alba 'Pendula'

MORUS
MULBERRY

There are about 10 species of deciduous shrubs and trees in this northern hemisphere genus, most of them from eastern Asia. They bear broad, roughly heart-shaped leaves with closely toothed margins and inconspicuous greenish male and female flowers separately, each on a short catkin. On female catkins, tiny fruits closely packed together appear as a single fruit, the mulberry. The leaves on seedlings may be deeply lobed. Some species have been cultivated for centuries, for their edible fruits and for silk production; the silkworm larvae feed on the leaves.
CULTIVATION: They thrive under a wide range of conditions, but do best in fertile, well-drained soil and a sunny, sheltered position. Propagate from cuttings in winter, which can be quite large branches.

Morus alba
syn. *Morus bombycis*
WHITE MULBERRY, FRUITLESS MULBERRY, SILKWORM MULBERRY

This vigorous, low-branching tree has sustained the silk industry of China and Japan. It grows up to 40 ft (12 m) tall, and has a broadly spreading crown and rather pendulous smaller branches. The leaves, almost hairless, are a fresh green to yellow color, strongly veined, with sharp marginal teeth. The rather rubbery fruit are cylindrical, sometimes lanceolate, and color varies from white through pink or red to purple-black. **'Fruitless'** is a very fast-growing, sterile clone to 60 ft (18 m) and is a good silkworm feeder. **'Pendula'** is a mushroom-shaped weeping form usually grafted onto standards to give initial height. **'Stribling'** (syn. 'Striblingii') is also sterile, due to the early shedding of its male flowers. **ZONES 5–10.**

Morus nigra
BLACK MULBERRY

Grown primarily for its fruit, this is the common mulberry of Britain and northern Europe, believed to have come from China or central Asia. It is similar to *Morus alba* but has a thicker trunk, a more compact crown and darker leaves with velvety down underneath and blunt marginal teeth. The fruit are dark red or almost black, sweet when ripe. **ZONES 6–10.**

Morus rubra
RED MULBERRY

The ruby-red fruit of this North American mulberry are relatively tasteless; it is mostly cultivated for its shape. As *Morus rubra* reaches its mature height of 70 ft (21 m) it twists, giving it a characteristic, grotesque appearance. The trunk bears a spreading crown with serrated, heart-shaped leaves with a rough upper surface. **ZONES 3–10.**

MUCUNA

There are some 100 species in this legume genus of herbaceous and woody stemmed, evergreen, twining climbers and shrubs, occurring throughout the tropics and subtropics of both hemispheres. Mucunas belong to the bean tribe and have rather showy pea-flowers in pendent sprays, and thin-walled pods

Morus nigra

Morus rubra

Morus alba

Morus alba

that may be clothed in irritant hairs. Only one species is outstanding as an ornamental.
CULTIVATION: Mucunas grow rampantly in the tropics, but languish in cooler climates except in large heated greenhouses. They like their roots kept cool and shaded, and prefer well-drained soil rich in humus. Propagate from seed in spring or by layering in late summer.

Mucuna bennettii
NEW GUINEA CREEPER

The leaves of this strong, fast-growing climber divide into 3 oval leaflets, and in summer it bears large, pendent clusters of pea-like, brilliant orange-scarlet flowers. It will grow only in climates like those of its native Papua New Guinea, is cold sensitive and needs abundant water during growth. It requires a well-supported, large area for climbing. Crowded stems may be thinned out in spring. **ZONES 11–12.**

MUEHLENBECKIA

This genus of 20-odd species is restricted to the southern hemisphere, especially South America, Papua New Guinea, Australia and New Zealand. Some are tiny alpine mat-forming plants, whereas others are vigorous vines with masses of dark stems and small bronze-tinged leaves. In mild, moist climates, rampant species can become weedy and difficult to eradicate. However, a well-trimmed climbing *Muehlenbeckia* on a wire fence can make a remarkably good screen. They can also be grown over frames of any shape to make fanciful topiaries. They are usually dioecious, that is, there are separate male and female flowers, and the fruits on female plants are normally white with a visible dark brown seed.
CULTIVATION: These frost-hardy plants prefer full sun (with some midday shade) and moderately fertile, moist but well-drained soil. Prune to keep in bounds and shape. Propagate from seed or summer cuttings or pre-rooted layers.

Muehlenbeckia astonii

Muehlenbeckia axillaris

Mucuna bennettii

Muhlenbergia pubescens

Muhlenbergia rigens

Muehlenbeckia astonii

Now very rare in the wild, this New Zealand species grows naturally in exposed, windswept locations. It is a very compact, often near-leafless plant—a dense mound of tangled, zigzagging twigs. The flowers and fruit are inconspicuous. Cultivated specimens tend to become open-growing and lank, up to about 8 ft (2.5 m) tall, destroying the rugged character of the plant that is its main appeal. **ZONES 8–9.**

Muehlenbeckia axillaris
CREEPING WIRE VINE

Native to southeastern Australia and New Zealand, this small, deciduous, prostrate or sprawling shrub can form mats more than 3 ft (1 m) wide. Its stems are black or golden brown with sparse, tiny dark green leaves with a gray reverse. The tiny summer flowers are yellowish and are followed by black glossy fruit. **ZONES 8–10.**

Muehlenbeckia complexa
MAIDENHAIR VINE, WIRE VINE, MATTRESS VINE

This vigorous New Zealand species is probably the best for trimming and topiary. Semi-deciduous, it grows to 15 ft (4.5 m) or more up suitable supports, and produces spherical, waxy, swollen white berries with black seeds. It can become quite weedy in suitable climates if not restrained. **ZONES 8–10.**

MUHLENBERGIA
MUHLY GRASS

This genus consists of around 150 species of tufted or rhizomatous annual or perennial grasses from Mexico, southern North America and Asia. They are low or moderately tall with slender stems bearing flat or rolled, thread-like leaves. Flowerheads at the end of the stems form clusters of spikelets in late summer.

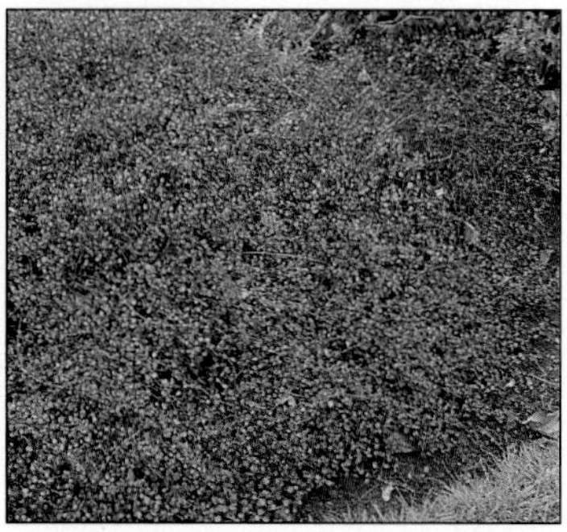
Muehlenbeckia complexa

Muhlenbergia racemosa

CULTIVATION: These marginally frost-hardy grasses prefer full sun or part-shade and moderately fertile, moist but well-drained soil. In frost-prone areas, overwinter in large pots in a greenhouse and place outside in summer. Propagate from seed.

Muhlenbergia dumosa
BAMBOO MUHLY

This tall perennial grass with robust stems 3–10 ft (1–3 m) tall has the appearance of a miniature bamboo. The rolled leaves are mostly less than 2 in (5 cm) long and numerous flowerheads produced in late summer are thickly set with nodding spikelets. Its native habitat ranges from southern Arizona to Mexico. **ZONES 9–11.**

Muhlenbergia pubescens
SOFT BLUE MEXICAN MUHLY

This 3 ft (1 m) tall clump-forming perennial grass has flat, arching, somewhat blue-green leaves. Massed gray-brown spikelets appear in summer. **ZONES 9–11.**

Muhlenbergia racemosa

This perennial grass to 3 ft (1 m) tall has creeping rhizomes, erect stems and flat leaves to 6 in (15 cm) long. The thick compact flowerheads to 6 in (15 cm) long, often purplish, are produced in late summer. **ZONES 9–11.**

Muhlenbergia rigens
DEERGRASS

This grass to 5 ft (1.5 m) tall forms small clumps of slender stems that are initially erect, but as they lengthen soon become slightly pendulous to create an attractive weeping effect. The slender spikelets to 24 in (60 cm) long are composed of masses of tiny pale gray spikelets. **ZONES 9–11.**

MUNDULEA

This legume genus consists of 15 species of more or less evergreen shrubs and small trees, all from Madagascar except one in tropical Africa and western Asia, and one in South Africa. Their pinnate leaves consist of many small leaflets, and distinctive purple-blue pea-shaped flowers are borne in clusters at the ends of the branches.
CULTIVATION: They occur naturally in the dappled shade of taller trees in warm temperatures. Cultivated plants do well if planted in similar conditions, including a well-drained, humus-rich soil. Prune lightly to maintain shape. Propagate from seed soaked in hot water or from cuttings of short side shoots taken with a heel.

Mundulea sericea
SOUTH AFRICAN CORKBUSH

This slow-growing shrub reaches 10 ft (3 m) in height. Its young branches are tough and flexible. It bears masses of pea-shaped, purple-blue flowers with 3 in (8 cm) long tapering seed pods covered with velvet-like hairs. It is the only species of this genus found in South Africa. **ZONES 9–11.**

MURRAYA

Allied to *Citrus*, this small genus of evergreen trees and shrubs comes from India and Southeast Asia. They have aromatic foliage and attractive creamy white flowers, which resemble those of their relative the orange and are often strongly scented. The fruits are small, oval berries. They were named after John Andrew Murray, a pupil of Linnaeus.
CULTIVATION: Species of *Murraya* flourish in warm, frost-free climates in full sun or part-shade and humus-rich, moist but well-drained soil. When grown in borderline temperate situations, they need shelter. Early pruning ensures a shrub thickly branched from the ground up; clipping after the late flowering season will keep their shape. Gardeners in cooler areas should substitute the similar (though not so tall growing) *Choisya ternata*, from Mexico. Propagate from seed or cuttings.

Murraya koenigii
CURRY LEAF TREE, KARAPINCHA

The leaves of this species are used in curries and other spicy dishes. From the Indian subcontinent, this aromatic shrub grows to about 10 ft (3 m). Loose sprays of small, fragrant, creamy white flowers stand out against the fresh green foliage in summer and are followed by small black fruit. **ZONES 10–12.**

Murraya paniculata
syn. *Murraya exotica*
ORANGE JESSAMINE, MOCK ORANGE

Widely distributed in tropical Asia, this compact, rounded bush up to 10 ft (3 m) tall is densely covered with shiny, dark green leaflets. The small, creamy white, perfumed flowers are held in dense clusters at the branch tips in spring and at intervals thereafter. Red berries may appear after each flowering. **ZONES 10–12.**

MUSA
BANANA, PLANTAIN

Bananas, originally native to southeast Asia are now cultivated throughout the tropics; and since they can ripen in transit, they are a familiar fruit in temperate countries also. Nearly all the edible varieties, including red and green fruit, entirely lack seeds. The genus includes several other important species: ***Musa textilis*** yields strong fiber known as Manila hemp; others are grown for their enormous leaves or colored flowers. The flowers are borne in large terminal spikes, erect or pendulous depending on species, the buds enclosed in large purplish bracts. Female flowers are borne at the base of the spikes, male ones further up. Classification of the genus is difficult due to 3,000 years of cultivation and hybridization and because hybrids can be so easily propagated clonally by dividing the rootstock. Though they often grow to tree size, they are really giant herbaceous perennials; each 'trunk' is composed of leaf bases and, when the flowering shoot has risen and borne fruit, it dies.
CULTIVATION: Some of the smaller species can be cultivated as house plants or in greenhouses in temperate climates. Banana crops require fertile, moist soil and full sun. Protect from winds, which will cause new growth to shred. Propagate from ripe seed or by division of clumps.

Musa acuminata
BANANA

One of the most widespread wild species in tropical Asia, *Musa acuminata* is believed to be the main parent of most edible bananas (some classified under *M.* × *paradisiaca*). It normally forms a clump of several false stems up to about 20 ft (6 m) tall, with long arching leaves and a pendulous flower spike with dull reddish bracts. The fruit are long and curved, seedless in cultivated forms. **'Dwarf Cavendish'** grows only 6–10 ft (1.8–3 m) high with short, broad leaves. **ZONES 10–12.**

Murraya koenigii

Murraya paniculata

Musa velutina

Musa velutina

Musa × *paradisiaca*

Musa × *paradisiaca*

Musa ornata
FLOWERING BANANA

From Bangladesh and Burma, this species bears erect spikes of yellow flowers emerging from pink bracts. It grows 10 ft (3 m) tall, two-thirds of this consisting of mid-green leaves, red-tinged along their midrib. It has crowded, slender, false stems that are waxy and pale green mottled with black. **ZONES 11–12.**

Musa × *paradisiaca*

This hybrid name covers the banana cultivars containing genes of *Musa acuminata* and *M. balbisiana*. Plants are up to 25 ft (8 m) tall, often flowering and bearing fruit 18 months or less after the shoot appears from the rootstock. **'Lady Finger'**, 15 ft (4.5 m) tall, is better suited to domestic gardens, being less vulnerable to bunchy top virus; it also tolerates cooler, more temperate weather. **ZONES 10–12.**

Musa uranoscopus
syn. *Musa coccinea*

The pseudostem or trunk of this Indochinese species has a lovely glossy red-green color while young. The leaves are 30 in (75 cm) long by 12 in (30 cm) wide, bright green above and waxy beneath. The flower spike is erect with large magenta to scarlet bracts 6 in (15 cm) by 3 in (8 cm) each with 2 attendant small flowers. The fruit are 4 in (10 cm) long, pink to green ripening to yellow-brown. **ZONES 10–12.**

Musa velutina

Banana flowers are admired more for their curiosity value than their beauty. This dwarf species grows no higher than 6 ft (1.8 m) with yellow flowers highlighted by red bracts and small, velvety, red bananas. The fruit unpeel themselves when ripe, hence one common name of self-peeling banana. **ZONES 9–12.**

MUSCARI
GRAPE HYACINTH

The 30 or so species of this genus are natives of the Mediterranean region and western Asia. The slender, strap-like leaves appear soon after planting, as the summer dormancy period is very short. Spikes 4 in (10 cm) long bear grape-like clusters of bright blue, pale blue, pale yellow or white flowers in early spring.
CULTIVATION: Frost hardy, they prefer cool areas. They look best planted in clumps and need rich, well-drained soil. Plant the bulbs in fall (autumn) in a sunny or part-shaded position, but protect from hot sun in warm areas. The rapidly multiplying clumps should spread freely and are best left undisturbed for a few years. Divide the bulbs if they become overcrowded. They can also be grown from seed.

Muscari botryoides

Muscari azureum 'Album'

Muscari botryoides 'Album'

Muscari armeniacum

Growing to about 8 in (20 cm) high and 2 in (5 cm) wide, *Muscari armeniacum* is one of the best loved of spring bulbs. The flowers may be blue or white and there are several named cultivars, of which **'Heavenly Blue'**, with its delicate, musky fragrance, is the best known; it is sometimes assigned to *Muscari botryoides*. **'Blue Spike'** bears clusters of rounded, bell-shaped double blooms; the flowers, borne on 8 in (20 cm) stems, are blue rimmed with white. **ZONES 4–10.**

Muscari aucheri
syn. *Muscari tubergenianum*

Common in cultivation, *Muscari aucheri* is easily grown, free-flowering and has foliage that is neater during the post-flowering phase than that of most *Muscari* species. The pale turquoise-blue buds are eye-catching and as the flowers open, the pale top knot makes an interesting contrast to the darker open bells. It reaches a height of 8 in (20 cm). **ZONES 6–10.**

Muscari armeniacum 'Heavenly Blue'

Muscari armeniacum

Muscari azureum

From the damp mountain meadows of northwest Turkey, this plant thrives in similar situations. It can, however, be slow to multiply and may fail in prolonged dry conditions. As the name suggests, the florets are sky blue with those at the base of the stem being darker than those at the top. A small plant well suited for naturalizing, it is fairly neat at flowering time but a voluminous leafy mess thereafter. **'Album'** bears white flowers and grows to 8 in (20 cm). **ZONES 8–10.**

Muscari botryoides

This species from central and southeastern Europe is one of several species that could be defined as a classical grape hyacinth. It grows to about 8 in (20 cm) tall with semi-erect channeled mid-green leaves and spherical bright blue flowers with a white constricted mouth. **'Album'** bears racemes of scented white flowers. **ZONES 3–10.**

Muscari comosum
syn. *Leopoldia comosa*
TASSEL GRAPE HYACINTH, FRINGE HYACINTH

The tassel grape hyacinth is a strangely attractive species from North America and southern and central Europe. It grows to about 24 in (60 cm) tall and has a flower stem supporting both fertile and sterile blooms. The sterile flowers are at the top of the stems and consist of fine blue tassels. The lower fertile flowers are urn-shaped and creamy brown with restricted mouths. The cultivar **'Plumosum'** (syn. 'Monstrosum') has strap-shaped leaves and curious flowers whose petals are so elongated that the

Muscari comosum

Muscari neglectum

inflorescence looks like a plume of lavender feathers. **ZONES 3–10.**

Muscari macrocarpum
syns *Muscari moschatum* var. *flavum*, *M. muscarimi* var. *flavum*

This is a strangely colored species from Greece and western Turkey. The buds are purplish brown opening to soft yellow-green fragrant flowers on stems up to 6 in (15 cm) tall. The leaves are gray-green. This species requires a hot, dry dormancy in summer to flower well the next spring. **ZONES 7–10.**

Muscari neglectum
syn. *Muscari racemosum*
COMMON GRAPE HYACINTH

This is a variable species native to Europe, North Africa and southwestern Asia. The tiny urn-shaped flowers are deep blue to blue-black with a white mouth. The leaves can be erect or spreading, and are bright green sometimes stained red at soil level. **ZONES 4–10.**

MUSSAENDA

This is a genus of about 100 species of evergreen shrubs, subshrubs and climbers from tropical Africa, Asia and the Pacific Islands, widely cultivated throughout the tropics and subtropics for their year-long display. Their chief feature is not so much the petals of the small red or yellow flowers but the way a single sepal is greatly enlarged into a kind of bract, which can be white, red or pink. The shrubs themselves are attractive, with bright green leaves, but tend to become straggly and need regular trimming to keep them compact and 3–5 ft (1–1.5 m) tall.

CULTIVATION: Frost tender, they prefer a sunny or part-shaded position and fertile, well-drained soil. Propagate from seed or cuttings in spring. Spider mite and white fly may be troublesome.

Mussaenda erythrophylla

Mussaenda 'Aurorae'
syn. *Mussaenda phillippica* 'Aurorae'

This is a shrubby hybrid with evergreen rounded leaves to 6 in (15 cm) long. The small trumpet-shaped flowers are bright golden yellow surrounded by large white bracts to 3 in (8 cm) long. These flower clusters are produced mainly in summer but can be seen all year round in warm climates. **ZONES 11–12.**

Mussaenda erythrophylla
ASHANTI BLOOD, RED FLAG BUSH

Occurring naturally in tropical west and central Africa, this twining woody shrub usually climbs to 6 ft (1.8 m) on slender strong stems. It bears large, rounded, bright green leaves covered with silky hairs and, in late summer, clustered creamy yellow flowers with a red-felted middle accompanied by blood red bracts up to 3 in (8 cm) long. **ZONES 11–12.**

Mussaenda frondosa
DHOBI TREE

Native to India, this shrub grows to a height and spread of 6 ft (1.8 m). In

Mussaenda philippica

Mussaenda philippica

Myoporum laetum

Myoporum parvifolium

Myoporum floribundum

Myoporum floribundum

summer, it bears clusters of orange-yellow tubular flowers beside large, white bracts, set among pale green, oval leaves; berries follow the bloom. The erect, branching stem has a shrubby crown. ZONES 11–12.

Mussaenda philippica
LADY FLOWERS

The name is a botanical convenience, applied to a group of presumed hybrids. These have much tighter flower clusters than usual, so the 'bracts' resemble large, many-petalled flowers and are usually pink. Most are named after prominent ladies, hence the common name *dona flores* (lady flowers). Cultivars include the bright pink **'Dona Imelda'**; **'Dona Luz'**, which is pink with red edges; and the pale pink and crimson **'Queen Sirikit'**. They may have been derived from *Mussaenda erythrophylla* and *M. frondosa*. ZONES 11–12.

MUTISIA
CLIMBING GAZANIA

These unusual climbers and shrubs are natives of South America. The most commonly cultivated of the roughly 60 species can best be described as climbing daisies. The foliage varies greatly between the species: some have pinnate foliage, others elliptical, heart-shaped or linear. Those with lobed leaves sometimes bear spines at the points of the lobes. Undersides of leaves often have closely appressed hairs or scales; species that climb often have tendrils at the leaf tips. The flowers also vary: the smaller ones resemble daisies, the larger blooms are more like dahlias. They appear throughout the growing season and occur in many colors.
CULTIVATION: Frost tolerance varies, though few species will tolerate regular frosts of any more than a few degrees. Plant in moist, well-drained soil in sun or part-shade and water during the growing season. In most cases, propagation is difficult unless fresh seed is available; otherwise propagate from cuttings or by layering.

Mutisia decurrens

This species from Chile and Argentina is a suckering climber with sparsely branched stems up to 10 ft (3 m) on a suitable support. Its narrow leaves are sometimes toothed and end in tendrils by which it climbs. Its large, bright orange daisies can be 6 in (15 cm) wide and are produced mainly in summer. ZONES 8–11.

MYOPORUM

About 30 species of evergreen trees and shrubs from a wide area throughout the southern hemisphere make up this genus. Myoporums can reach 30 ft (9 m) tall and produce small, mostly white flowers. These plants are named from the Greek *myo* (to close) and the Latin *porum* (a pore), because of the high number of glands or transparent spots on their leaves. They make quick-growing screens and hedges, and are especially useful where salt-laden winds are a problem.
CULTIVATION: These frost-tender plants prefer full sun and well-drained soil of any quality. For a dense windbreak, the plants need clipping, although this may interfere with the attractive display of the fruits which follow the flowers. Propagate from seed or from cuttings taken from young firm growth.

Myoporum floribundum
WEEPING BOOBIALLA

This small to medium-sized, short-lived shrub reaches a height and spread of 10 ft (3 m) and has slender, weeping branches lightly clothed in long narrow leaves. During spring and early summer, it is covered with tiny, white, strongly scented blossoms. ZONES 9–11.

Myoporum insulare
BOOBIALLA

This 3–20 ft (1–6 m) species has spreading, upright branches holding fleshy, dark green leaves with toothed margins. The small, white, purple-spotted flowers are clustered towards the branch tips. They are followed by succulent, purple-streaked white fruit. This species is highly adaptable, even withstanding wet periods in heavy soils. ZONES 9–11.

Myoporum laetum
NGAIO

Varying from 15–30 ft (4.5–9 m) tall, this wind-resistant small tree is native to New Zealand. It has mid-green leaves, 3–4 in (8–10 cm) long and lightly toothed towards their tips, and sticky shoots at the branch ends. It bears small white flowers, liberally purple dotted, and maroon fruit. It responds well to trimming, although in exposed conditions this tree is often shaped by prevailing winds. ZONES 9–11.

Myoporum parvifolium
CREEPING BOOBIALLA

This spreading to prostrate shrub, native to southern and western Australia, grows 6 in (15 cm) tall and 30 in (75 cm) wide. Clusters of white, tubular, honey-scented flowers appear in summer, followed by purple, globular berries. The semi-succulent leaves are narrow, blunt and thick. ZONES 9–11.

MYOSOTIDIUM
CHATHAM ISLAND FORGET-ME-NOT

Though the Chatham Islands lie east of New Zealand, this forget-me-not gives a glimpse of what Antarctic flora might have been like before the continent settled at the South Pole. The scientific name of the only species of the genus, *Myosotidium hortensia,* emphasizes the plant's close relationship to the true forget-me-not, *Myosotis*.
CULTIVATION: The instructions that accompanied the plant's introduction to England in 1858 were to give it a cool, rather damp position and mulch it twice a year with rotting fish, a practice that has happily proved unnecessary. Salt tolerant and marginally frost hardy, it requires semi-shade and a humus-rich, moist soil. Propagate by division in spring or from seed in summer or fall (autumn). Once growing well, it should not be disturbed and will naturalize freely.

Myosotidium hortensia

Myosotidium hortensia

This evergreen, clump-forming perennial is the giant of the forget-me-not family, growing to a height and spread of 24 in (60 cm). It has a basal mound of large, glossy, rich green, pleated leaves, and in spring and summer bears large clusters of bright purple-blue flowers, slightly paler at the edges, on tall flower stems. A white-flowered cultivar is also grown. ZONES 9–11.

MYOSOTIS
FORGET-ME-NOT

This genus of annuals and perennials includes 34 New Zealand natives among its 50 or so species, but the most commonly cultivated are from the temperate regions of Europe, Asia and the Americas. Their dainty blue (sometimes pink or white) flowers bloom in spring, and most species are useful in rock gardens and borders, or as ground cover under trees and shrubs. The plants fade after flowering. *Myosotis*, from the Greek for 'mouse ear', refers to the pointed leaves. The flowers have long been associated with love and remembrance.
CULTIVATION: Mostly quite frost hardy, they prefer a semi-shaded setting or a sunny spot protected by larger plants, and fertile, well-drained soil. They are rarely affected by pests or diseases and like fertilizing before the flowering period. Propagate from seed in fall (autumn). Once established, they self-seed freely.

Myosotidium hortensia

M

Myosotis alpestris
ALPINE FORGET-ME-NOT

This short-lived perennial from Europe (usually grown as an annual or biennial) forms clumps to a height and spread of 4–6 in (10–15 cm). In late spring and early summer, it bears clusters of dainty, bright blue, pink or white flowers with creamy yellow eyes. **ZONES 4–10.**

Myosotis colensoi
NEW ZEALAND FORGET-ME-NOT

The best known New Zealand forget-me-not, this species is much more adaptable to garden conditions than most of the other species. It has rounded, slightly hairy, grayish green to silver leaves and small white flowers in late spring and summer. It forms a dense clump 2 in (5 cm) tall and 12 in (30 cm) wide. **ZONES 8–10.**

Myosotis scorpioides
syn. ***Myosotis palustris***
WATER FORGET-ME-NOT

A deciduous to semi-evergreen perennial, this species from North America and Eurasia grows as a marginal water plant for muddy situations or in very shallow water. It grows to a height and spread of 12 in (30 cm), and bears small blue flowers with a yellow, pink or white eye throughout summer. **ZONES 5–10.**

Myosotis sylvatica 'Blue Ball'

Myosotis sylvatica

Myrica californica

Myosotis sylvatica
GARDEN FORGET-ME-NOT

This European biennial or short-lived perennial is usually grown as an annual for its bright lavender-blue, yellow-eyed flowers in spring and early summer. It forms mounds of fuzzy foliage 18 in (45 cm) tall and 12 in (30 cm) wide, with taller stems uncurling as the flower buds open. There are many named selections; some more compact, some pink or white. **'Blue Ball'** has tiny, deep blue flowers and is good for edging. **ZONES 5–10.**

MYRICA

Myrica is a genus of about 50 species of evergreen or deciduous shrubs and trees of worldwide distribution ranging in height from 5 ft (1.5 m) to 100 ft (30 m). Their fruits are clusters of bluish black berries enclosed in a white waxy crust. Tiny flowers appear in late spring; both sexes are borne on the one plant, the males in elongated catkins and the females in globular clusters.
CULTIVATION: Moderately frost hardy to frost tender, they thrive in part-shade, but will not grow in alkaline or chalky conditions, and must never be allowed to dry out. Propagate from seed or cuttings, or by layering in summer.

Myrica californica
PACIFIC WAX MYRTLE

An evergreen shrub or small tree, this native of the West Coast of the USA has dark green leaves and a decidedly upright habit, except where sheared by coastal winds. *Myrica californica* grows 25 ft (8 m) or more in height, less in spread. **ZONES 7–10.**

Myrica cerifera
WAX MYRTLE

This evergreen shrub flourishes in south-eastern North America, where it enjoys swampy conditions, peaty soil and the shade of taller trees. Reaching 30 ft (9 m)

Myrica cerifera

Myrica californica

Myosotis alpestris

tall, *Myrica cerifera* bears narrow, glossy dark green leaves with unusual downy undersides. Its golden brown catkins are followed by the fruit, the wax on which is used in the manufacture of candles. **ZONES 6–10.**

Myrica gale
SWEET GALE, BOG MYRTLE

Indigenous to northern Asia and northern regions of North America, this erect, deciduous shrub grows to 5 ft (1.5 m) tall and wide. It has oval leaves, dark green on top and paler underneath. Its tiny fruit, crowded in dense spikes, are greenish yellow. Bushy and compact, it makes a useful screen in damp, peaty areas. **ZONES 1–8.**

Myrica pensylvanica
BAYBERRY

Like the wax myrtle, the bayberry is a coastal native that occurs among the sand dunes of North America's eastern coast. It is a deciduous shrub 10 ft (3 m) tall and wide. The wax on its berries is the source of the fragrance in bayberry candles. It spreads slowly by suckers. **ZONES 2–8.**

MYRIOPHYLLUM
MILFOIL

This genus consists of 45 species, mainly aquatic annuals and perennials with representatives worldwide. They are usually submerged plants rooted in the bottom silt of ponds or slow-moving streams. As their wiry stems elongate they reach the surface, where they float and produce emergent leaves. The submerged leaves are very finely cut, feathery and whorled around the stems, while the emergent leaves are often simple and narrow. Spikes of minute flowers develop in summer, usually at the tips of the emergent stems.
CULTIVATION: Little effort is required in cultivation provided a species appropriate to the climate is chosen. As long as the stems have soil to root in, they should thrive. They prefer sun, but will tolerate part-shade. Hardiness varies with the species. Propagate by breaking off rooted pieces of stem.

Myriophyllum aquaticum
syns ***Myriophyllum brasiliense, M. proserpinacoides***
PARROT FEATHER, DIAMOND MILFOIL

This perennial species found wild in Australia, New Zealand and South America produces stems up to 6 ft (1.8 m)

Myriophyllum aquaticum

Myristica fragrans

long often with their tips well up out of the water. The finely dissected foliage appears yellow-green if submerged, blue-green out of the water. Tiny, bright yellow-green flowers appear among the submerged leaves in summer. **ZONES 10–12.**

Myriophyllum verticillatum
MYRIAD LEAF

This aquatic perennial hails from Europe, Asia and North America. It has usually unbranched stems to 3 ft (1 m) long. Its submerged leaves are larger than its emergent ones. Its bright yellow flowers are produced on spikes to 6 in (15 cm) long just above the water level. **ZONES 3–10.**

MYRISTICA

Native to tropical Asia, northern Australia and Pacific islands, *Myristica* consists of about 80 species of tropical evergreen trees that grow to 100 ft (30 m). Only the flowers of the female trees produce the large, succulent fruits, but do so several times a year. The leaves are usually waxy white underneath.
CULTIVATION: They must be protected from frost and dry conditions, and planted in rich, moist, well-drained soil if they are to flourish outside their homelands. They need a hot, humid position away from sun, strong winds and pollution. Propagate from seed or cuttings or by grafting in spring and fall (autumn).

Myristica fragrans
NUTMEG

The fruit of this tree from Indonesia is nutmeg, now cultivated commercially mainly in Indonesia and Grenada. A slender, evergreen tree reaching 50 ft (15 m), it has distinctive whorls of spreading branches, smooth gray bark, aromatic leaves and small, pale yellow flowers. Ripe nutmegs are fleshy, pear-shaped, brilliant scarlet berries. Their jackets are harvested to make mace, a milder spice. ZONE 12.

MYROXYLON

Indigenous to tropical America, the 2 or 3 *Myroxylon* species are spreading, evergreen trees grown for their attractive foliage and white flowers. The pinnate leaves are glossy green, and the fruits consist of 2-winged pods that appear in profusion in late summer.
CULTIVATION: They need moist, fertile soil and plenty of warmth and humidity. Water well when in full growth. Propagate from scarified seed or from cuttings.

Myroxylon balsamum
TOLU BALSAM

This native of Venezuela bears masses of white, butterfly-like fragrant flowers if grown in a hot, steamy environment. The glossy leaves have up to 13 oblong, alternate leaflets. It also needs heat to produce its seed pods, which are about 3 in (8 cm) long. ***Myroxylon balsamum* var. *pereirae*** (syn. *M. pereirae*) differs in its small leaflets and attenuate fruit. ZONES 11–12.

MYRRHIS
SWEET CICELY, MYRRH

This is a genus of only one species, an attractive long-lived perennial in the carrot family, native to southern Europe. It has aromatic, fern-like leaves and fragrant creamy white flowers in flattened heads in early summer, followed by ribbed, shiny brown seeds that have a very brief viability. The leaves and seeds have a sweet aniseed flavor and are cooked with fruit as a sugar substitute. They are also good in raw vegetable juices.
CULTIVATION: Fully frost hardy, they should be grown in part-shade in moist but well-drained, fertile soil. Propagate from fresh seed in fall (autumn) or spring or by division in fall or early spring.

Myrrhis odorata

This graceful perennial to 6 ft (1.8 m) high is excellent as a background plant in the herb garden or mixed flower border. It will tolerate shade and can be sited beneath garden trees. It self-seeds readily and the strongest seedlings may be transplanted. ZONES 5–10.

Myroxylon balsamum

MYRSINE

This is a small genus of 5 species, all evergreen shrubs or small trees with inconspicuous flowers—male on one plant, female on another. If both sexes are present attractive berries will form, but it is for the pleasant foliage that these plants are usually grown. The leaves alternate up the stems and can be linear or lance-shaped or even rounded. The genus has a disjunct distribution in Africa, the Azores, the Himalayas and China. Sometimes the genus *Rapanea* is merged with *Myrsine*, resulting in a genus of over 150 species.
CULTIVATION: Species vary from fully frost hardy to frost tender. They will grow in sun or part-shade, and are not fussy about soil types, although do not thrive in shallow, dry soil. They can be raised from seed, but plants of known sex are probably better struck from summer cuttings.

Myrsine africana
CAPE MYRTLE, AFRICAN BOXWOOD

Although its botanical and common name suggests an African origin, this species is also native to the Himalayas and China. It is a slow-growing, upright, leafy shrub to 4–8 ft (1.2–2.4 m) tall by 30 in (75 cm) wide. The aromatic foliage is $\frac{3}{4}$ in (18 mm) long and glossy dark green, and the berries are $\frac{1}{4}$ in (6 mm) across and pale blue in color. ZONES 9–11.

MYRSIPHYLLUM

One of the genera resulting from the breaking up of the genus *Asparagus*, it includes a few twining rhizomatous species. They have wiry, sometimes sticky stems and much-reduced scale-like leaves. The fleshy green structures, up to $1\frac{1}{2}$ in (35 mm) long, appear to be leaves but are actually cladodes. Small insignificant flowers are followed by red berries.
CULTIVATION: Only marginally frost hardy, they may be grown as house plants in areas with cold winters. The cut 'foliage' is used in floral decorations. Plant in moist, humus-rich soil in part-shade. Propagate from seed or by carefully dividing the rootstock in spring.

Myrsiphyllum asparagoides
syn. ***Asparagus medeoloides, Medeola asparagusoides***
FLORISTS' SMILAX

This scrambling, twining plant from South Africa grows to around 5 ft (1.5 m) tall. It has profuse bright green, oval to pointed, heart-shaped cladodes. **'Myrtifolius'** is a compact dwarf form sometimes known as baby smilax. ZONES 10–11.

Myroxylon balsamum

Myrrhis odorata

Myrsine africana

Myrtus communis

Myrtus communis

MYRTILLOCACTUS

The 4 species of cacti in this genus from Mexico and Guatemala are quite bushy and, under ideal conditions, can become tree-like. Their spiny, branching stems have few ribs and are usually bright green or blue-green. The flowers, in clusters of up to 9, develop from black, downy tufts known as areoles. Usually less than 1 in (25 mm) long, the funnel-shaped flowers are $\frac{1}{2}$ in (12 mm) in diameter. These are followed by fleshy fruits.
CULTIVATION: While tolerant of occasional light frosts, *Myrtillocactus* species grow best in a warm dry climate with free-draining, gritty soil and in full sun or morning shade. Water during the growing season and keep dry in winter. Propagate from seed or basal and stem offsets.

Myrtillocactus cochal

This small branching tree-like cactus from northwestern Mexico grows to about 3 ft (1 m) tall by 18 in (45 cm) wide. Its thick bright green stems have shallow grooves and gray or black spines, 3 to 5 per cluster often with a longer central one. The flowers are white or soft yellow with green or purple shading and are 1 in (25 mm) across. They are produced in early summer and can be night or day flowering. ZONES 9–11.

Myrtillocactus geometrizans

This bluish green, tree-like cactus from central Mexico grows about 15 ft (4.5 m) high and 10 ft (3 m) wide. It is strongly branching. Greenish white flowers appear in spring and summer, as do purple fruit. ZONES 9–11.

MYRTUS
MYRTLE

The Ancient Greeks and Romans knew these shrubs as *Myrtus*, from which 'myrtle' derives, via Old French. Contemporary botanists classify the southern

Myrtus communis 'Microphylla'

hemisphere myrtles into several other genera, including *Lophomyrtus, Luma* and *Ugni*, leaving *Myrtus* with only 2 Mediterranean species. Myrtles are usually dense, evergreen shrubs with small, deep green, pointed leaves and starry white flowers in spring, sometimes followed by blackish purple berries.
CULTIVATION: True myrtles prefer moist, well-drained soil and grow in sun or light shade. Trimming keeps them compact. They can be used for hedging or as container plants, clipped into a ball or pyramid. In cooler areas, container plants need protection during winter. Some foliage cultivars are available, but there is little variation in the flowers. Propagate from cuttings or from seed.

Myrtus communis
TRUE MYRTLE

This erect shrub, to around 10 ft (3 m), has highly perfumed white flowers in spring, followed by edible berries ripening to blue-black with a delicate whitish, waxy bloom. The leaves, when crushed, are also very fragrant. Several cultivars exist including **'Compacta'**, a dwarf form with smallish leaves; **'Flore Pleno'** with double white flowers; **'Microphylla'** with tiny leaves and flowers; **'Variegata'** with leaves edged white; and **'Tarentina'** with creamy white flowers and needle-like leaves. ZONES 8–11.

NO

NANDINA

SACRED BAMBOO, HEAVENLY BAMBOO

This is a single species genus from China and Japan. Despite its rather bamboo-like habit and the elegance of its leaves it is actually related to the barberries. It grows as a clump of thin, upright stems, and bears sprays of white flowers in summer and red berries in fall (autumn) and winter. Plants are either male or female, and both are needed for the berries to develop; hermaphrodite cultivars are available. The scientific name is a corruption of the Japanese name *nanten*, and the common name comes from the Oriental tradition of planting it in temple gardens; it is also popular in secular gardens.

CULTIVATION: This moderately frost-hardy species likes some shade, fertile soil and a warm-temperate or subtropical climate. In spring, prune straggly stems to the base on established plants. Propagate from seed or cuttings in summer.

Nandina domestica

This shrub has strongly upright, cane-like stems and grows to 6 ft (1.8 m) high. The evergreen foliage is usually bipinnate and composed of many 1 in (25 mm), elliptical leaflets. These are red when young, becoming green and then developing intense yellow, orange and red tones when the cold weather arrives. The small white flowers appear in terminal panicles in summer. **'Nana'** (syns 'Compacta', 'Pygmaea') is a widely grown dwarf form, making a rounded shrub about 18 in (45 cm) in height and width, often taking on deep scarlet and red tones in fall (autumn) and winter; **'Firepower'** is similar in form, with bright pink or red winter foliage; **'Harbor Dwarf'** is a cultivar no more than 24 in (60 cm) high that spreads extensively by rhizomes to make a useful ground cover; **'Richmond'** is an erect hermaphrodite raised in New Zealand that produces abundant dense clusters of fruit without the need of a pollinating plant; **'Umpqua Chief'** is a vigorous plant 5–6 ft (1.5–1.8 m) tall with good winter color. **ZONES 5–10.**

Narcissus, Div. 3, 'Amore'

Narcissus, Div. 1, 'Las Vegas'

Nandina domestica 'Richmond'

Nandina domestica

NARCISSUS

DAFFODIL, NARCISSUS

Members of this well-known genus of bulbs from Europe, Asia and North Africa are easy to grow, multiply freely and bloom year after year. The wild species number about 50 and are mostly native to the western Mediterranean region. Many thousands of cultivars have been named, and horticultural authorities have grouped these into 12 divisions or classes, the most important of which are: the Trumpet narcissi (Division 1) which have trumpets as long as the outer petals or perianth; the Large-cupped narcissi (Division 2), with trumpets from one-third to two-thirds as long; the Small-cupped narcissi (Division 3), with trumpets less than one-third the length of the petals; and the Double-flowered narcissi (Division 4) with double flowers, either one or several per stem. Divisions 5 to 9 cover hybrids and cultivars of important species such as *Narcissus triandrus*, *N. cyclamineus*, *N. jonquilla*, *N. tazetta* and *N. poeticus* respectively; Division 10 covers the wild species; Division 11 the split-corona hybrids; and Division 12 consists of daffodils not included in any other division, such as *N. bulbocodium* hybrids. Flower colors range from white to yellow, although individual varieties may have white, yellow, red, orange or pink trumpets.

CULTIVATION: Frost hardiness of these bulbs varies, but all will tolerate at least light frosts and they grow best in cool areas. Plant in fall (autumn), 4–6 in (10–15 cm) deep in rich, well-drained soil. They enjoy full sun in cool areas, and some shade in warmer areas. Water well during growth and allow to dry out once the leaves die down. Remove spent flowers. Clumps will multiply freely and should be left undisturbed for a few years; thereafter lift and divide in fall.

Narcissus, Div. 2, 'Fortune'

Narcissus, Div. 2, 'Ambergate'

Narcissus, Div. 2, cultivar

Narcissus, Trumpet daffodils (Division 1)

These are the best known of all the daffodils with their solitary large flowers and long trumpets. They are derived mainly from the wild daffodil *Narcissus pseudonarcissus*. There are innumerable named cultivars, which may be all yellow, white with yellow trumpets, all white, or white with pale pink trumpets. They are the first of the big daffodils to flower. The all-gold **'King Alfred'**, raised in 1890, is the classic cultivar, but its name has been very loosely applied, and some authorities consider the original variety may be extinct. **'Arctic Gold'** and **'Kingscourt'** have deep golden-yellow flowers; **'Spellbinder'** has sulfur-yellow flowers. **'Las Vegas'** and **'Ptolemy'** have white growth and yellow trumpets. **'Empress of Ireland'** has a white perianth and trumpet. **'Dutch Master'** has many golden flowers in mid-spring, each up to 4 in (10 cm) wide; it grows 18–20 in (45–60 cm) tall. **'Little Gem'** is a dwarf only 6 in (15 cm) tall or less that produces its 2 in (5 cm) wide golden flowers in early spring. **'Rijnveld's Early Sensation'** is an award-winning, early-blooming daffodil growing about 12 in (30 cm) tall. **ZONES 4–10.**

Narcissus, Large-cupped daffodils (Division 2)

Flowering a week or two later than the trumpets, this is a large division with many named varieties. They originate mainly from the cross *Narcissus poeticus* × *pseudonarcissus* (or *N.* × *incomparabilis*). The popular pink-cupped cultivars with their white perianths mostly belong here, but there are many others in various combinations of white or yellow perianths with cups in white, yellow, orange or red. **'Exotic Pink'** and **'Passionale'** are pink-cupped daffodils, while **'Ambergate'** and **'Fortune'** have brilliant orange coronas. Both the perianth and the corona of **'Ice Follies'** are white. **ZONES 4–10.**

Narcissus, Small-cupped daffodils (Division 3)

Of similar origin to Division 2, these resemble the Trumpet and Large-cupped daffodils except for their smaller cups. Like them, they come in many named cultivars. They flower at the same time as the Large-cupped types. **'Merlin'** has flowers with pure white perianths and pale yellow cups; **'Amore'** has a white perianth and a primrose cup that fades to orange at the rim; **'St Keverne'** has a white perianth and cup. **ZONES 4–10.**

Narcissus, Double-flowered daffodils (Division 4)

These daffodils can have either a solitary large flower or several smaller ones, with the perianth segments or the corona, or both, doubled. Some of the oldest narcissus cultivars are the double-flowered daffodils. They are less popular than many other types because they tend to be late flowering and their buds will not open properly if they have undergone dry conditions while developing. **'Acropolis'** has pure white segments interspersed with orange-red segments; **'Tahiti'** has a yellow perianth with an orange corona; and **'Unique'** has a white perianth and wavy, yellow corona segments. **ZONES 4–10.**

Narcissus, Triandrus daffodils (Division 5)

The type species *Narcissus triandrus* is native to Spain; it is rarely cultivated but this division includes garden forms of the species. All have pendent, nodding flowers, a straight-edged cup and slightly reflexed petals. There are usually several blooms per stem. The forms vary in height from 6–18 in (15–45 cm). **'Hawera'** has yellow flowers. **'Thalia'** has pale yellow petals and a white cup with 3 or more blooms per stem. **ZONES 4–9.**

Narcissus, Cyclamineus daffodils (Division 6)

These hybrids bear the characteristics of *Narcissus cyclamineus* and grow to 15 in (38 cm) high. Their trumpet-shaped cups are longer than those of *N. triandrus*, and their petals are narrow and strongly reflexed. They flower in early to mid-spring. Popular hybrids are **'February Gold'**, an early bloomer that naturalizes well and has single, lasting flowers with yellow petals and slightly darker yellow trumpets; **'Dove Wings'**

Narcissus, Div. 8, 'Geranium'

Narcissus, Div. 8, 'Geranium'

Narcissus, Div. 8, 'Erlicheer'

Narcissus, Div. 4, 'Acropolis'

with small flowers comprising white petals and a long, primrose-yellow trumpet; and **'Tête-à-Tête'**, a profuse and early flowerer with lasting blooms consisting of golden-yellow petals and an orange, frilled corona. **'Charity May'** has long-lasting, vivid, pure yellow flowers. **ZONES 6–9.**

Narcissus, Jonquilla daffodils (Division 7)

Possessing the characteristics of the wild jonquil of southern Europe and northern Africa, *Narcissus jonquilla*, these narcissi are scented, with the cups shorter than the flat petals. There are often 2 or more blooms on a stem, which grows to 15 in (38 cm). **'Suzy'** flowers in mid-spring and has 2 or more fragrant blooms on its sturdy stem, the flowers having golden petals and a deep orange cup. **'Stratosphere'** has 3 blooms with a cup of a deeper golden yellow than its petals. **'Trevithian'** flowers early in spring and produces up to 3 large, rounded, primrose-yellow blooms. The flowers of **'Sweetness'** are rich gold with pointed petals. **ZONES 4–9.**

Narcissus, Tazetta daffodils (Division 8)

These sweetly scented narcissi flower from fall (autumn) to spring and have many-flowered stems; they grow up to 15 in (38 cm). The cup is small and straight-sided, with broad, often frilled petals. This class can be further subdivided into those similar to *Narcissus tazetta* and those resulting from a cross between *N. tazetta* and *N. poeticus* and referred to as *poetaz narcissi.* **'Avalanche'** bears 15 white flowers with soft yellow cups on a single stem. **'Erlicheer'**, a double, cluster-flowered daffodil, has flowers as perfect (and nearly as sweetly scented) as gardenias. **'Geranium'** has a rich orange cup in a soft white perianth. **'Minnow'** has lemon-yellow cups and lighter yellow petals. **'Silver Chimes'** has creamy white flowers. **'Soleil d'Or'** is another beautiful cultivar. **ZONES 8–10.**

Narcissus, Div. 8, 'Avalanche'

Narcissus, Div. 8, 'Silver Chimes'

Narcissus, Div. 4, 'Tahiti'

Narcissus, Div. 4, 'Unique'

Narcissus, Poeticus daffodils (Division 9)

This is a late spring- to early summer-flowering division showing the features of *Narcissus poeticus* of southern Europe. The plants grow to 18 in (45 cm) and produce one, sometimes two, blooms per stem. The petals are white and the small cup often has a frilled red or orange rim. **'Actaea'** produces fragrant flowers in late spring with a flat, yellow cup rimmed with orange. **'Cantabile'** is completely white. **ZONES 4–9.**

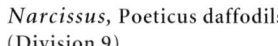

Narcissus, Div. 8, 'Soleil d'Or'

Narcissus, Div. 7, 'Suzy'

Narcissus, Div. 9, 'Cantabile'

Narcissus, Wild species and variants (Division 10)

Horticultural societies have decreed that all the wild *Narcissus* species be lumped under this division, at the tail end of the daffodils along with the next 2 divisions. In this book, though, the wild species are listed separately. ***Narcissus* × *odorus*** is an old hybrid with large, 2 in (5 cm) wide fragrant, bright yellow flowers; **'Rugulosus'** is a more robust form with up to 4 flowers per stem. **ZONES 6–9.**

Narcissus, Split-corona daffodils (Division 11)

Characterized by having coronas or cups that are split along at least a third of their length, these narcissi are also referred to as Collar, Papillon, Orchid or Split-cupped daffodils. The edges of the split coronas bend back towards the petals, and are sometimes frilled. They all flower in spring. **'Baccarat'** is yellow; **'Ahoy'**, **'Cassata'** and **'Pink Pageant'** have soft yellow cups and broad white petals; and **'Orangery'** and **'Pick Up'** have orange cups and white petals. ZONES 4–10.

Narcissus bulbocodium

HOOP-PETTICOAT DAFFODIL

This species, widespread in the western Mediterranean, grows to 6 in (15 cm) and has many forms. Bright yellow flowers, with a long trumpet and sharply reflexed, usually insignificant petals, appear in spring. ZONES 6–9.

Narcissus papyraceus

PAPER WHITE, JOSS FLOWER

Often regarded as a mere cultivar of the Tazetta daffodil group (Division 8), this species is now known to occur wild in the western Mediterranean. Growing to 15 in (38 cm), the white, fragrant flowers have pointed petals, the corona is frilled and the stamens are orange-yellow. It flowers in late winter to spring and is an attractive indoor display grown in a bowl of gravel; in China it is grown in pots to celebrate the new year. ZONES 8–10.

Narcissus pseudonarcissus

WILD DAFFODILS, LENT LILY

This is a very variable species, native to western Europe including the British Isles. It bears nodding yellow trumpet flowers with cream perianths in spring and has erect, strap-shaped leaves. This species naturalizes easily. ZONES 4–9.

Narcissus bulbocodium

Narcissus papyraceus

Narcissus, Div. 1, 'Chivalry'

Narcissus, Div. 2, 'Bantam'

Narcissus, Div. 1, 'Golden Lion'

Narcissus, Div. 1, 'Irish Luck'

Narcissus, Div. 1, 'Golden Riot'

Narcissus, Div. 2, 'Flower Record'

Narcissus, Div. 2, 'Charter'

Narcissus, Div. 2, 'Craigie Warren'

Narcissus, Div. 2, 'Easter Bonnet'

Narcissus, Div. 2, 'Elysian Fields'

Narcissus, Div. 2, 'Galway'

Narcissus, Div. 2, 'Holiday Fashion'

Narcissus, Div. 3, 'Blarney'

Narcissus, Div. 2, 'Pipe Major'

Narcissus, Div. 2, 'Stromboli'

Narcissus, Div. 4, 'Gay Time'

Narcissus, Div. 3, 'Whitbourne'

Narcissus, Div. 3, 'Rob Roy'

Narcissus, Div. 3, 'Eminent'

Narcissus, Div. 4, 'Obdam'

Narcissus, Div. 4, 'Pink Pageant'

Narcissus, Div. 11, 'Palmares'

Narcissus, Div. 8, 'St Agnes'

Narcissus, Div. 10, 'Magnificum'

Narcissus, Div. 11, 'Tiri Tomba'

Nauclea orientalis

Nassella trichotoma

Nectaroscordum siculum

N. siculum subsp. *bulgaricum*

NASSELLA

A genus of perennial grasses closely related to *Stipa*, *Nassella* consists of 15 species from South America, mostly from the Andes. They are tussock formers with fine, thread-like leaves and weak, rather inconspicuous flowering panicles; the seed heads are sparse and each seed has a long, fine bristle (awn). Although at least one species has been grown as an ornamental grass in the northern hemisphere, *Nassella* species should be treated as potential weeds.
CULTIVATION: They have similar requirements to other tussock-forming grasses, preferring full sun and a rather dry, well-drained soil of medium fertility. Foliage is killed by winter frosts and should be cut back close to the ground before spring growth begins. Propagate from seed.

Nassella trichotoma
SERRATED TUSSOCK

Native to Argentina and some adjacent countries, this grass forms a tussock to about 24 in (60 cm) high of very fine, green foliage that is slightly rough to the feel. In late spring and summer, it produces numerous weak panicles of very delicate seed heads that hardly rise above the foliage. As they mature, the panicles break off and may be blown considerable distances by the wind, dispersing the seed. Serrated tussock is a feared weed of pastures in parts of the USA, Australia and New Zealand, unpalatable to livestock and crowding out more useful grasses. **ZONES 7–10.**

NASTURTIUM
WATERCRESS

There are 6 species of watercress. The one most commonly cultivated is *Nasturtium officinale*, an aquatic plant with longish stalks and dark green rounded leaf segments. White roots form on the leaf nodes. Originally a marsh plant from Europe and northern Asia, watercress is now a river weed in North America and temperate southern hemisphere regions. It is mainly used as a salad herb or cooked as a vegetable in Asian dishes. Rich in vitamins and minerals, watercress is a popular sharp-tasting garnish for salads. It is also used for stimulating the digestion and to ease severe headaches.
CULTIVATION: Watercress must have clean running water or be watered copiously to grow well; an old laundry tub is ideal as the old water can be regularly drained and the tub refilled with fresh water when needed. These plants flourish in damp, shaded corners of the garden as well as in ponds. Plant from cuttings about 4 in (10 cm) apart in early fall (autumn), making sure the soil has been thoroughly and deeply manured. Water thoroughly and constantly, and prune the shoots to keep growth thick. Propagate from seed or cuttings.

Nasturtium officinale
syn. *Rorippa nasturtium-aquaticum*
COMMON WATERCRESS

This species has creeping stems up to 30 in (75 cm) in length that become erect with age. The small white flowers appear in racemes, but should be cut back when they appear in order to promote vegetative growth. **ZONES 6–10.**

NAUCLEA

This genus, named from the Greek *naus* (ship) and *kleio* (to close) because the seeds resemble the hull of a ship, contains about 10 species. These evergreen shrubs and trees found from tropical Africa to Asia, Australia and Polynesia have smooth, leathery leaves. They are cultivated in warmer areas for their fragrant flowers and edible red fruits.
CULTIVATION: Naucleas require filtered light and moist soil enriched with organic matter, and are good for binding riverbanks. Propagate from ripe seed or cuttings taken towards the end of summer.

Nauclea orientalis
LEICHHARDT TREE

Growing to around 50 ft (15 m) tall, this widely distributed tree has a conical shape and spreading branches. Its bark is deeply furrowed and the heart-shaped, deep green leaves are up to 10 in (25 cm) long. If there is a shortage of water, the tree may drop its leaves. Attractive yellow flowers are borne in clusters during late spring and summer. **ZONES 11–12.**

NAUTILOCALYX

Occurring over much of tropical America, this genus is composed of 38 species of evergreen perennials and subshrubs that form spreading clumps up to 18 in (45 cm) high and 3 ft (1 m) wide. Their usually succulent stems are clothed with opposite pairs of fleshy, oval leaves, $\frac{1}{2}$–2 in (1.2–5 cm) long. The leaves are often bronze when young and develop red tints in sunlight, and those of some species have puckered surfaces or an indumentum on the undersides. The flowers, which appear throughout the growing season, are 1–2 in (2.5–5 cm) long, tubular and borne in small clusters that develop in the leaf axils. Most often they are white to cream with purple markings.
CULTIVATION: Intolerant of frost but otherwise easily grown in humus-rich, moist, well-drained soil in part-shade, they are also excellent greenhouse plants. Propagate from seed, layers or cuttings.

Nautilocalyx lynchii

This species from Colombia is favored as an indoor plant in cooler areas, but will grow outdoors in more humid regions. It grows to a height of 24 in (60 cm) with glossy dark green or reddish purple fleshy, puckered leaves and insignificant, yet interesting, tubular cream and red flowers marked with purple flecks on the inner surface. **ZONES 10–12.**

NECTAROSCORDUM

Native to a large area of southern Europe, western Asia and Iran, this genus is represented by 3 species of bulbs akin to the *Allium* (onion) genus; all parts of the plant emit a strong onion scent when bruised. In fact, the genus name means 'nectar-bearing onion'. The gray-green, strap-like leaves which emerge from solitary bulbs in spring die back at or shortly after blooming. The flowers appear in late spring and are held atop single stems. They not only look well in the herbaceous border, but also in cut flower arrangements.
CULTIVATION: These plants are ideal for naturalizing, but care should be taken in siting as, in full sun, they tend to become invasive. They are happy in a friable, well-drained soil, either in full sun or part-shade, and can be propagated from seed sown in spring or from bulbils.

Nectaroscordum siculum
syn. *Allium siculum*

In the wild these plants are found growing sparsely in damp, shaded places, but under garden conditions they thrive and may become invasive. The flowering umbels, which unfold from a tissue-like covering, are held on naked upright stems 30 in (75 cm) tall. They consist of drooping, bell-shaped flowers of variable coloring and markings; the range is between beige, flesh pink and red, with green to brown-green markings. ***Nectaroscordum siculum* subsp. *bulgaricum*** bears elegant, pendent, bell-shaped flowers, pale pink tinged with purple and green. **ZONES 6–10.**

NELUMBO
LOTUS

This is a genus of 2 species of deciduous, perennial water plants found in North America, Asia and northern Australia. Lotuses resemble waterlilies but differ in that they raise both their leaves and flowers well clear of the muddy water of the ponds and ditches in which they grow, blossoming unsullied. The leaves are waxy and almost circular, while the solitary, fragrant flowers are borne on long stalks. Flowers left on the stem develop into decorative seed pods; when

Nelumbo lutea

Nematanthus gregarius

dried they can be used in flower arrangements. Lotus seeds found in Japan and shown by carbon dating to be 2,000 years old have germinated and borne flowers.
CULTIVATION: Frost hardiness varies, some tropical forms of *Nelumbo nucifera* being quite frost tender. They prefer an open, sunny position in 24 in (60 cm) of water. Plant in large pots in heavy loam and submerge. Propagate from seed or by division in spring.

Nelumbo lutea
WATER CHINQUAPIN, AMERICAN LOTUS

This American species, suitable for larger waterscapes, has leaves almost 24 in (60 cm) across emerging 6 ft (1.8 m) or more above the water surface. Pale yellow, 10 in (25 cm) wide summer flowers, held on solitary stalks, are followed by attractive seed heads. **ZONES 6–11.**

Nelumbo nucifera
SACRED LOTUS, INDIAN LOTUS

The sacred lotus has leaves that emerge 6 ft (1.8 m) or more above the water. The plant spreads to 4 ft (1.2 m) wide. Large, fragrant, pink or white, 10 in (25 cm) wide flowers are borne above large, shield-shaped, pale green leaves. This vigorous plant from Asia and northern Australia grows well in large ponds; Buddha is often depicted in the center of such a lotus. **ZONES 8–12.**

NEMATANTHUS

Members of this genus, which is in the popular Gesneria family, come from the tropical zones of South America. The 30 species of evergreen subshrubs are at home in humid zone gardens or they can be used as indoor or greenhouse plants in cooler areas, where their trailing stems, thickly clothed in small leaves, are highlighted by tubular flowers in yellow, orange, pink or purple.
CULTIVATION: These tropical forest plants require indirect light and ample

Nelumbo nucifera

humidity in their active growth period to prosper. They are fibrous, shallow-rooted plants, so are best grown in wide shallow pots in a moisture-retentive yet porous potting mix. Do not repot too often as these plants tend to bloom better if slightly potbound. They can be grown outdoors in part-shade, but are frost tender. Mealybug, spider mite, whitefly and scale insects may cause problems. Propagate from stem cuttings.

Nematanthus gregarius
syns *Hypocyrta radicans, Nematanthus radicans*
CLOG PLANT

A relatively easy-to-grow, trailing plant mostly grown in containers, this species from Brazil has closely set, glossy, dark green leaves. The dark yellow or orange flowers look puffy and bloom throughout the year, especially if it is slightly potbound. It prefers an African violet potting soil mix, and bright light with some cool morning sun. Keep the soil moist and the atmosphere humid by placing the container on a tray of pebbles and water, or mist frequently. **ZONES 10–12.**

NEMESIA

This genus of 50-odd species of annuals, perennials and subshrubs comes from South Africa. Their flowering period is short, although if they are cut back hard when flowering slows down they will flower again. The flowers are showy, being trumpet-shaped and 2-lipped, and are borne singly in the upper leaf axils or in terminal racemes. The leaves are opposite and simple.
CULTIVATION: These plants need a protected, sunny position and fertile, well-drained soil. They cannot tolerate very hot, humid climates. Pinch out growing shoots on young plants to ensure a bushy habit. Propagate from seed in early fall (autumn) or early spring in cool areas.

Nemesia strumosa 'Prince of Orange'

Nemesia strumosa 'Red and White'

Nemesia caerulea
syn. *Nemesia fruticans*

This perennial can grow up to 24 in (60 cm) in height if conditions are to its liking. Becoming slightly woody at the base, it tends to sprawl, branching into erect stems holding small mid-green leaves and terminal heads of soft pink, lavender or blue flowers. **'Elliott's Variety'** is very free-flowering, with bright mauve-blue flowers with a white eye. **ZONES 8–10.**

Nemesia strumosa

Nemesia strumosa is a colorful, fast-growing, bushy annual, popular as a bedding plant. It has lance-shaped, pale green, prominently toothed leaves, and grows to a height of 8–12 in (20–30 cm) and a spread of 10 in (25 cm). Large flowers in yellow, white, red or orange are borne in spring on short terminal racemes. **'Blue Gem'** is a compact cultivar to 8 in (20 cm), with small, clear blue flowers. **'Prince of Orange'** also grows to about 8 in (20 cm), but has orange flowers with purple veins. **'Red and White'** has flowers strikingly bicolored, the upper lip bright red and the lower lip white. **ZONES 9–11.**

Nemesia caerulea 'Elliot's Variety'

Nemesia caerulea

Nemesia strumosa

NEMOPHILA

This is a group of 11 species of annuals grown for their bright, open, 5-petalled flowers. Originating from western USA, these annuals make good borders and are attractive in window boxes. They produce colorful spring–summer blooms in a range of mainly blues.

CULTIVATION: These quick-growing annuals grow best in full sun or part-shade in friable, moisture-retentive soil. As the foliage is rather soft, provide protection from wind and position plants away from high-traffic pathways. Regular watering will help prolong blooming. Check for aphids. Propagate from seed which can be sown *in situ* during the fall (autumn) months.

Nemophila maculata
FIVE SPOT

Commonly referred to as five spot because each veined, white petal has a prominent deep purple blotch at its tip, this plant grows to 12 in (30 cm) tall. It is used extensively in massed displays as plants hold their profusion of blooms above the ferny foliage over a long period during summer. **ZONES 7–11.**

Nemophila menziesii
syn. ***Nemophila insignis***
BABY BLUE-EYES

A charming little Californian wildflower, this spreading annual is a useful ground cover under shrubs such as roses, as well as in rock gardens and around edges; it is particularly effective overplanted in a bed with spring bulbs. It bears small, bowl-shaped, sapphire-blue flowers with a well-defined concentric ring of white in the center. It has dainty, serrated foliage, and grows to a height and width of 6–10 in (15–25 cm). These plants dislike heat and transplanting. **ZONES 7–11.**

NEODYPSIS

These feather-leafed palms from Madagascar are closely related to the genus *Dypsis;* in fact, recent botanical studies show that they may be reclassified as *Dypsis.* Only one species is commonly cultivated, valued for its elegant fronds, strikingly arranged in 3 vertical ranks, the large, sheathing frond bases making a triangle in cross-section. The trunk itself is short and stout, and ringed with scars from the fallen fronds. Short panicles of small, cream flowers protrude from among the frond bases, with small, oval fruits following, although these are rare in cultivation.

CULTIVATION: These palms require a tropical or subtropical climate free of frost, but have proved surprisingly hardy under dry or exposed conditions if the roots are well watered. Plant in full sun in rich soil and water freely in summer. Propagation is only possible from seed.

Neodypsis decaryi
THREE-CORNERED PALM

This palm seldom reaches more than 6 ft (1.8 m) high, but it is topped by a vase-shaped crown of large fronds up to about 12 ft (3.5 m) long with elegantly recurved tips and very narrow leaflets arranged in 2 regular rows. The lowest leaflets are extended into long, thread-like appendages that hang down to the ground. The broad frond bases are clothed in thick, blue-gray felt with rusty tinges, and the fronds are also a pale grayish green. **ZONE 11.**

Neodypsis decaryi

Neomarica northiana

Nemophila menziesii

NEOMARICA

Related to irises, the 15 species in this genus are herbaceous perennials from tropical America and western Africa. The strappy leaves rise from a basal rhizome in fan formation to a height of around 3 ft (1 m); flowering stems bear masses of short-lived blooms. The flowers have 3 distinct, somewhat flattened outer petals in intense colors, with the central segments having interesting markings.

CULTIVATION: They are easily grown plants, but frost tender. Grow in part-shade or full sun in well-drained, humus-rich soil. Water well in summer and ensure the soil does not dry out during the winter months. Propagate by division of the rhizomes, or from seed in spring. Transplant from late fall (autumn) until early spring.

Neomarica caerulea

Native to Brazil, this species yields an amazing number of flowers, but it is essentially a garden plant as the flowers are not suitable for cutting. It has tall, straight, sword-like leaves, and produces a succession of triangular sky blue flowers with white, yellow and brown central markings. The flowers are short lived, but are borne over a long period in summer. The plant grows to a spread of 3–5 ft (1–1.5 m). **ZONES 10–11.**

Neomarica northiana
WALKING IRIS, APOSTLE PLANT

With long, heavily ribbed leaves up to 24 in (60 cm), this plant from Brazil provides textural interest to the warm-climate garden. Plants flower for a long period during the spring–summer months, with each stem carrying scented multi-colored blooms in white, mottled crimson with a violet-blue banding. **ZONES 10–11.**

NEOPAXIA
syns *Claytonia, Montia*

This genus contains a single species, a low, spreading perennial found in moist to wet soil and in shallow water mostly in highland or alpine areas of Australia and New Zealand. It is not easy to grow, although gardeners successful with other alpine species should have little difficulty. It has long, narrow, somewhat succulent leaves and simple, 5-petalled white or soft pink flowers that are produced in summer.

CULTIVATION: Most successful in highland areas or cooler climates, this fully frost-hardy plant grows best in peaty soil kept permanently moist from mid-spring to mid-fall (mid-autumn), drier during winter. Propagate from seed or by division in fall.

Nemophila maculata

Neopaxia australasica

In Australia there are 2 forms of this species, one from alpine areas and the other from lower elevations. The alpine form is mat forming and more compact. It has grayish leaves, and is covered in summer with simple white flowers. The lower altitude form has longer, narrower, dark green leaves and similar white flowers that are not as generously produced. It sometimes grows in shallow water. **ZONES 6–10.**

NEOPORTERIA

Around 25 species belong to this genus of cacti, all from western South America. They are all small, globular to shortly columnar plants, with many ribs that may be divided into tubercles.
Numerous spines radiate from closely spread areoles. The flowers are medium sized and colorful, in shades of pink, red, orange, yellow or lemon, usually clustered at the top of the plant.

CULTIVATION: Most species tolerate very light frosts when grown outdoors in a dry climate. When grown indoors, they should be in strong light and planted in a normal, gritty cactus compost, and kept cool and dry in winter. Propagate from seed in spring or summer.

Neoporteria chilensis
syn. *Neochilenia chilensis*

This greenish, spherical cactus from Chile grows in time to about 6 in (15 cm) tall and 4 in (10 cm) wide, with closely spaced green ribs and numerous white spines up to ¾ in (18 mm) long. It produces mid-sized, pale red, funnel-shaped flowers in spring and summer, and red elongated fruit less than 1 in (25 mm) long. **ZONES 9–11.**

NEOREGELIA

The members of this stemless bromeliad genus containing about 70 species vary greatly in size, texture and color. Native to South America, the genus was named after Edward von Regel, Superintendent of the Imperial Botanic Gardens in St Petersburg, Russia. Many species turn a brilliant rose, violet or red color in the center of the rosette when flowering approaches. The flowers may be blue or white and the spined foliage ranges from green to maroon, striped, spotted or marbled. The leaves form a wide funnel-shaped or tube-like rosette which ranges from 6 in (15 cm) to 5 ft (1.5 m) across.

CULTIVATION: Neoregelias prefer well-drained soil and dislike strong light, but they require some direct light to maintain their color. This genus thrives in a humid atmosphere and is best grown in pots or hanging baskets where it will enjoy good air circulation. Do not allow the center cup to dry out and ensure it stays warm in winter. Propagate from offsets in spring or summer.

Neoregelia carolinae
HEART OF FLAME, BLUSHING BROMELIAD

This is the most widely cultivated species of the genus and forms a spreading rosette 15–24 in (38–60 cm) across, composed of light olive-green, strap-shaped, saw-toothed leaves. Immediately before flowering, which can be at any time of the year, the youngest inner leaves turn deep red. The cluster of inconspicuous, blue-purple flowers is surrounded by crimson-red bracts. **'Fendleri'** has leaves neatly edged with bands of cream, although otherwise bright green. ***Neoregelia carolinae* × *concentrica***, an unnamed cross between 2 of the most colorful species, displays the variegation found in some forms of *N. carolinae*, combined with the purple leaf tips of *N. concentrica*. **'Tricolor'**, seen more often than the species itself, has cream-striped foliage; the inner leaves turn a rich crimson before producing purple flowers and the entire plant turns pink. **'Tricolor Perfecta'** is a variety susceptible to cold. **ZONES 10–12.**

Neoregelia chlorosticta
syn. *Neoregelia sarmentosa* var. *chlorosticta*

This species from Brazil is distinguished by its green-lilac-brown leaf blotching. The flowers are white, opening on short stalks 1 in (25 mm) long. **ZONES 10–12.**

Neoregelia concentrica

This Brazilian species has a flat, outstretched funnel-shaped rosette 30–36 in (75–90 cm) across. It has broad, leathery leaves with a center becoming deep purple as the flower buds form. The flowers are blue. **'Aztec'** is possibly of hybrid origin, but shows a strong influence of this species; its leaves are heavily blotched with deep purple. **ZONES 10–12.**

Neoregelia concentrica 'Aztec'

Neoregelia chlorosticta

Nepenthes maxima

Neoregelia marmorata

Spreading 18–24 in (45–60 cm) across, the rosettes of this species are mottled in reddish brown and the pale green leaves are tipped with red. The white flowers bloom from spring to summer. **ZONES 10–12.**

NEPENTHES
PITCHER PLANT

These are perhaps the easiest of all the carnivorous plants to grow; they come from a genus of nearly 70 species, mainly from Indonesia and tropical Asia. They include some tall climbers, capable of ascending nearly 70 ft (21 m) into any handy tree, but their preference for swampy land means they often have to make do without support. Some species grow at lower altitudes, others in tropical highlands. They bear inconspicuous purple or brownish flowers in spikes among the upper leaves; the leaves often terminate in pendulous, colored 'pitchers' with lids strikingly tinted in shades of russet, green or even red and pink. Insects are attracted to them and drown in the liquid held in the pitcher before being absorbed into the plant as food. **CULTIVATION:** They require a very humid atmosphere, part-shade and moist, fertile soil. The species from tropical lowlands require higher temperatures (minimum winter temperature of 65°F/18°C) than those from the tropical highlands (minimum winter temperature of 50°F/10°C). Propagate from seed in spring or from stem cuttings in spring or summer, although air layering may prove more successful.

Neoregelia carolinae 'Tricolor Perfecta'

Nepenthes rafflesiana

Nepenthes × *coccinea*

Nepenthes × *coccinea*

A garden crossing of 2 tall climbers, *Nepenthes* × *coccinea* produces pitchers measuring up to 6 in (15 cm) in length. These are yellow-green in color, mottled with purple-red streaks and blotches. **ZONES 11–12.**

Nepenthes maxima

As its name implies, the pitchers on this species are extremely large, often measuring up to 8 in (20 cm) in length. Because this species comes from the high-altitude areas of Indonesia and New Guinea, its temperature requirements are lower than the lowland species. **ZONES 11–12.**

Nepenthes rafflesiana

This is a tall, climbing species that can clamber up to 30 ft (9 m) by means of long tendrils, but it can withstand quite severe pruning in cultivation. The large leaves can camouflage the elegant green pitchers with their heavily spotted and ribbed mouths, often measuring up to 6 in (15 cm) in length. **ZONES 11–12.**

Neoregelia carolinae 'Fendleri'

Neoregelia carolinae × *concentrica*

NEPETA

This large genus of more than 200 species of perennial, rarely annual, plants is used extensively in herbaceous borders and for edgings or as ground-cover plants. Some species have highly aromatic silver-gray foliage and are naturally compact, while others tend to be taller growing plants and may benefit from staking. Originating from a wide area of Eurasia, North Africa and the mountains of tropical Africa, many species have been extensively hybridized to produce exceptional garden plants. **CULTIVATION:** Provide a well-drained soil in a sunny position. Some of the vigorous herbaceous species make good

N

Nepeta × *faassenii*

Nepeta × *faassenii* 'Dropmore Blue'

Nepeta cataria

single species ground covers as they have a tendency to overpower less robust plants. However, they can be kept in check by light trimming during the growing season and can be cut back each year to prevent the plants from becoming too straggly. Propagation is by division, from cuttings taken during the late spring–summer months or from seed.

Nepeta cataria

CATNIP, CATMINT

A native of Europe, catnip is a frost-hardy perennial with branching, upright stems growing up to 3 ft (1 m). It has aromatic, gray-green leaves and whorls of white flowers from late spring through to fall (autumn). Cats are attracted to this plant and will lie in it or play in it and sometimes dig it up. A tea made from the leaves is said to be relaxing. ZONES 3–10.

Nepeta clarkei

This species from Pakistan and Kashmir forms large clumps up to 30 in (75 cm) high. The leaves are green and the upright flowering stems hold masses of lilac-blue blooms, each with a white patch on the lower lip. This is an very cold-hardy species. ZONES 3–9.

Nepeta × *faassenii*

CATMINT

This is a bushy, clump-forming perennial, useful for separating strong colors in the shrub or flower border, and very effective when used with stone, either in walls, paving or rock gardens or as an

Nepeta × *faassenii* 'Walker's Blue'

Nepeta clarkei

edging plant. It forms spreading mounds of grayish green leaves that are aromatic when crushed, and the numerous flower stems carry hundreds of small, violet-blue flowers throughout summer. It grows to a height and spread of 18 in (45 cm). Many cultivars are available, including **'Dropmore Blue'** with upright, tall flower spikes of lavender blue; and **'Six Hills Giant'**, a robust plant growing to around 18 in (45 cm) with gray foliage complemented by tall spikes of lavender-blue flowers that will bloom continuously throughout the summer if spent flowers are kept clipped. **'Walker's Blue'** has finer foliage and flowers than the other 2 hybrids. ZONES 3–10.

Nepeta nervosa

This showy species forms a bushy habit to 24 in (60 cm) tall. It has long, narrow, deeply veined leaves and dense spikes of purplish blue flowers, although they can occasionally be yellow in the wilds of its native Kashmir. ZONES 5–9.

Nepeta racemosa

syn. *Nepeta mussinii*

Native to the Caucasus region and northern Iran, this ornamental species has generally been known as *Nepeta mussinii* in gardens, though many of the plants sold under that name are in fact the hybrid *N.* × *faassenii*. It is a vigorous perennial up to about 12 in (30 cm) high with gray-green, densely hairy leaves and lavender-blue summer flowers in long racemes. **'Blue Wonder'** is a very free-flowering form of spreading habit with violet-blue flowers; **'Snowflake'** has pure white flowers. ZONES 3–10.

Nepeta nervosa

Nepeta tuberosa

One of the few nepetas with tuberous roots, this native of Portugal, Spain and Sicily is more at home in warmer climates than many other species within this genus. With upright stems growing to 3 ft (1 m), it has violet-purple flowers. ZONES 8–10

NEPHELIUM

Related to the lychee *(Litchi chinensis)*, this Southeast Asian genus consists of about 35 species of evergreen trees, with densely foliaged spreading crowns. Some species are grown in subtropical and tropical regions for their sweet-tasting edible fruits.

CULTIVATION: Being frost-tender plants, they will not tolerate low temperatures at any stage of growth and require a tropical climate with an even rainfall throughout the year. Full sun and a fertile, well-drained soil enriched with plenty of compost and well-rotted manure is important. Continue using manure annually. These trees can be propagated from seed, although propagation by grafting is generally preferred for named varieties.

Nepeta × *faassenii* 'Six Hills Giant'

Nepeta racemosa 'Blue Wonder'

Nepeta racemosa 'Snowflake'

Nepeta tuberosa

Nephelium lappaceum
RAMBUTAN

This tree grows to a height of 15 ft (4.5 m), bearing clusters of white flowers in spring, followed by orange-red fruit in summer. Similar to lychees, they are among the sweetest and most delicious of all tropical fruit, with a translucent flesh of more delicate flavor, encased in soft, prickly skin. **ZONE 12.**

NEPHROLEPIS
SWORD FERN

Commonly found in the tropics and subtropics on edges of rainforests or in open forests, this genus of 30 species of frost-tender, evergreen or semi-evergreen ferns has fishbone-shaped fronds. These may be erect, spreading or pendent and with short, upright rhizomes.
CULTIVATION: For ferns, they are extremely tolerant of dry conditions and are fast growing, provided they are given enough room to spread out and have well-composted, moist soil. Since they are sensitive to cold, these ferns are ideal for indoors, but be sure to provide lots of water in warm conditions. Propagate from spores or tissue culture, or by division.

Nepeta racemosa

Nephrolepis cordifolia
FISHBONE FERN, SOUTHERN SWORD FERN

Naturally found among rocks at the edges of rainforests, this fast-growing fern can survive in fairly dry and dark positions as well as in full sun. It is one of the toughest species in cultivation and a very easily grown plant—so much so that it can become a pest. Fronds grow to 3 ft (1 m). **'Plumosa'** is a slow-growing cultivar with lobed pinnae. **ZONES 10–12.**

Nephrolepis exaltata
BOSTON FERN, SWORD FERN

This evergreen fern is less often grown than its many cultivars, which have more luxuriant foliage that is sometimes lacy or tinted yellow. The species has erect, lance-shaped, pale green fronds on wiry stems and grows to a height and spread of 3 ft (1 m) or more. They can be attractive in hanging baskets. **ZONES 10–12.**

NEPTUNIA

Named after the Roman god of the sea, many species of this perennial herb, which is a member of the pea family, are found on the margins of slow-moving water in the tropics; others prefer dry land. They are prostrate, spreading plants with deep tap roots which anchor them, allowing the branches to float—sometimes they become weeds in tropical irrigation channels. However, contained in an aquarium or tank in the heated greenhouse they are of interest as some species are sensitive to touch, closing up their foliage on contact as do other members of this family.
CULTIVATION: Members of this genus are easily grown in tropical areas, but be careful they do not become weeds. In cooler areas, however, provided warmth and humidity are assured, plants can be grown in pots and partly submerged in an aquarium. Propagate from seed or by detaching floating rooted branches.

Neptunia oleracea

This species is best suited to planting near the water's edge in a slow-moving watercourse or pond so that the stems, often reaching 5 ft (1.5 m), can float. These stems develop spongy tissue in water and often detach from the mother plant. The foliage is finely divided, and the rounded flowerheads are green. **ZONES 9–12.**

NERINE
SPIDER LILY, GUERNSEY LILY

About 30 species of *Nerine* are grown for their heads of pretty, narrow-petalled, trumpet-shaped flowers in pink, red or white. From southern Africa, they bloom in fall (autumn), usually before their leaves appear. Some are evergreen; others die down in summer. They can reach up to 24 in (60 cm) in height and 12 in (30 cm) in width. Species vary in the wild and readily interbreed in gardens, so not all can be easily identified. They are good plants for pots, and can be brought inside when in flower.
CULTIVATION: Plant the bulbs in well-drained, sandy soil in a sunny position. Water them well during growth, but allow them to dry out over the summer dormancy period. They are not suitable for areas with high summer rainfall or very severe frosts. They can be propagated from seed or offsets inn fall, but the plants do not like being disturbed and may take a couple of years to flower.

N

Nephrolepis cordifolia

Nephelium lappaceum

Nerine bowdenii

PINK SPIDER LILY, LARGE PINK NERINE

This species has a sturdy stem up to 24 in (60 cm) that bears as many as 12 pink blooms. The flowers have split, reflexed petals with a crimson rib running along their center and frilled edges. There is also a white form. **ZONES 8–11.**

Nerine filifolia

GRASS-LEAFED NERINE

This plant grows to 10 in (25 cm) and bears a 4 in (10 cm) cluster of rosy pink blooms. The flowers have slender, reflexed petals and the foliage is grass-like and almost evergreen. **ZONES 9–10.**

Nerium oleander 'Album'

Nerine flexuosa

syn. *Nerine pulchella*

On this species, a sturdy stem up to 24 in (60 cm) bears a cluster of up to 15 pink flowers with narrow, reflexed petals that have a deeper pink mid-vein. The foliage is narrow and strap-like and appears before the flowers. **'Alba'** is a white form. **ZONES 8–10.**

Nerine fothergillii

syn. *Nerine curvifolia*

This perennial species has scarlet, spider-like flowers with 6 expanding petals in terminal clusters. It grows to a height of 18 in (45 cm) and a spread of 12 in (30 cm). **ZONES 8–10.**

Nerine sarniensis

RED NERINE, GUERNSEY LILY

This delightful species grows up to 24 in (60 cm). The sturdy stem bears up to 20 bright red, 3 in (8 cm) flowers with sharply reflexed petals and prominent stamens. The strap-shaped leaves usually appear after flowering. **ZONES 9–11.**

Nerium oleander 'Punctatum'

Nerine undulata

syn. *Nerine crispa*

This evergreen bulb is native to the eastern Cape Province of South Africa, where most rain falls in summer. Plants vary in height from 10–18 in (25–45 cm). The flowers appear in fall (autumn), a cluster of wavy petalled, soft pink blooms atop each sturdy, leafless stem. This species is not particularly hardy, but will accept lows of 32°F (0°C). **ZONES 10–11.**

NERIUM

ROSE LAUREL, OLEANDER

This small genus consists of one or two species of evergreen shrubs native to northern Africa and southwestern Asia. They bear brightly colored, funnel-shaped flowers with 5 broad petals; these are followed by bean-like seed pods containing plumed seeds. The leaves are narrow, leathery and lance-shaped. *Nerium oleander* and its cultivars are those plants most commonly seen in gardens. All neriums are very poisonous; all parts of the plant are so very bitter that even goats will not eat them.

CULTIVATION: Plant these shrubs in full sun and in well-drained soil. If they get overgrown and leggy, they can be rejuvenated by severe pruning in spring. In frosty climates, they can be grown in containers and overwintered under glass. Propagate from seed in spring or from summer cuttings.

Nerine flexuosa 'Alba'

Nerium oleander

Depending on the cultivar selected, these plants can grow from 6–12 ft (1.8–3.5 m) tall. As the species is often used for hedging, it is wise to keep the varying growth habits of the cultivars in mind if a uniform appearance is wanted. The blooms can be single or double, and some cultivars have variegated foliage. Some popular cultivars include: **'Album'**, with single, white flowers and a cream center; **'Little Red'**, with single red flowers; **'Luteum Plenum'**, with creamy yellow double flowers; **'Mrs Fred Roeding'**, with salmon-pink double blooms and a relatively small growth habit; **'Petite Pink'**, with single pale pink flowers and growing only 3–6 ft (1–1.8 m) tall; **'Punctatum'**, a vigorous plant with single, pale pink blooms; **'Splendens Variegatum'**, with pink double flowers and variegated gold-green foliage borne at the expense of the profuse flowering habit of its parent 'Splendens'; **'Algiers'**, with its flowers of the darkest red; and **'Madonna Grandiflora'**, which has white double flowers. **'Casablanca'** (syn. 'Monica') has single, very pale pink, almost white flowers. **ZONES 9–11.**

NERTERA

These neat perennial plants, with their prostrate or creeping habit, are native to a number of cool, moist regions of the world, including southern Australia and New Zealand, and the Andes of Central and South America. There are 15 species, all of which form small mats

Nerine sarniensis

Nerine filifolia

Nerine bowdenii

N

Nerium oleander 'Algiers'

Nerium oleander 'Madonna Grandiflora'

Nertera granadensis

Neviusia alabamensis

or hummocks of moss-like foliage. It is their bead-like fruits that attract the gardener's interest. Some species make excellent alpine-house plants or they can be used in rock gardens where frosts are only light and infrequent.
CULTIVATION: Nerteras thrive in a cool, sheltered, part-shaded site with gritty, moist but well-drained sandy soil such as that which can be provided in a sink garden. Water well in summer but keep dryish in winter. Propagate by division or from seed or tip cuttings in spring.

Nertera granadensis
syn. *Nertera depressa*
BEAD PLANT, CORAL MOSS

This carpeting species is grown for the masses of spherical, orange or red, bead-like berries it bears in fall (autumn). It has a prostrate habit, growing to ½ in (12 mm) in height with a spread of 4 in (10 cm), and forms compact cushions of tiny bright green leaves with extremely small, greenish white flowers in early summer. A variety with purple-tinged foliage is also available. **ZONES 8–11.**

NEVIUSIA
SNOW-WREATH

This genus of only 2 species, is found on the cliffs above the Black Warrior River in Alabama, USA. A member of the rose family, it is a very frost-hardy plant, admired for its beautiful spring flowers.
CULTIVATION: This plant prefers reasonably fertile, well-drained soil but appreciates extra water in dry periods. After flowering, remove old wood by cutting back to the lowest outward-facing bud. Propagate by division or from cuttings or seed.

Neviusia alabamensis
ALABAMA SNOW-WREATH

This deciduous shrub grows to around 5 ft (1.5 m) and has a stoloniferous root system. This means that it has a spreading, multi-stemmed habit, and needs ample room to develop. The spring-borne flowers, with distinctive spreading stamens, are pure white in their natural habitat, but usually creamy white in cultivation unless grown under glass. **ZONES 5–10.**

NICOTIANA
FLOWERING TOBACCO

The 67 species of annuals, biennials, perennials and shrubs in this genus are from America and Australia and include the commercial tobacco plant. Earlier introduced species are grown for the fragrance of their warm-weather flowers, usually opening at night; flowers of newer strains remain open all day but have limited perfume. They are good for cutting, although the plants are sticky to handle.
CULTIVATION: Marginally frost hardy to frost tender, they need full sun or light shade and fertile, moist but well-drained soil. Propagate from seed in early spring. Check for snails and caterpillars.

Nicotiana alata
syn. *Nicotiana affinis*

A short-lived perennial often grown as an annual, this marginally frost-hardy plant bears clusters of attractive, tubular flowers in white, red or various shades of pink. The flowers open towards evening and fill the garden with scent on warm, still nights. Rosette forming, it has oval leaves and grows to a height of about 3 ft (1 m) with a spread of 12 in (30 cm). It flowers through summer and early fall (autumn). **ZONES 7–11.**

Nicotiana bigelovii
syn. *Nicotiana quadrivalvis*

This annual species from California grows to 6 ft (1.8 m) and is rather ill-smelling. It bears racemes of white flowers tinged with green. **ZONES 6–11.**

Nicotiana glauca
TREE TOBACCO, MUSTARD TREE

Considered a soft-wooded shrub, this species often grows to a tree-like 6 ft (1.8 m) or more in height and bears large glaucous leaves and heads of green-tinted, creamy yellow tubular flowers in fall (autumn). Native to Bolivia and Argentina, it has become naturalized in much of the USA. **ZONES 8–11.**

Nicotiana langsdorfii

This annual species grows to 5 ft (1.5 m) tall and has erect and branching stems that produce masses of fine, tubular lime-green flowers during the summer months. Do not be in a hurry to deadhead the last of the blooms as they may self-seed if conditions are favorable, even though the seeds themselves are extremely small. **ZONES 9–11.**

Nicotiana langsdorfii

Nicotiana glauca

Nicotiana alata

N

Nicotiana sylvestris

Nicotiana × sanderae 'Falling Star'

Nicotiana tabacum

Nicotiana rustica
WILD TOBACCO

This South American native, with an erect, branching stem and large green leaves, grows to 3 ft (1 m) in height. The pinkish white, tubular flowers appear in terminal clusters. ZONES 8–11.

Nicotiana × sanderae

This hybrid is a slow-growing, bushy annual reaching a height of 15 in (38 cm) and spread of 8 in (20 cm). In summer and early fall (autumn) it bears long, trumpet-shaped flowers in shades of white, pink, red, cerise, bright crimson and purple. The flowers stay open during the day and are fragrant in the evening. Many cultivars have been developed from this garden hybrid, including **'Lime Green'**, which has abundant, vivid lime-green blooms held over a long summer season. The flowers of **'Falling Star'** range from white to pale pink to deep pink. ZONES 8–11.

Nicotiana sylvestris

One of the few summer-flowering annuals which thrive in shade, *Nicotiana sylvestris* is one of the taller-growing species with flowers remaining open even in deep shade or on overcast days. This robust, though tender, species grows to 5 ft (1.5 m) or more with tall, stately flowering stems that arise from a mass of large, bright green lush foliage. Terminal groups of long, tubular white flowers are particularly fragrant on warm summer evenings so plant it where the scent can be appreciated. ZONES 8–11.

Nicotiana tabacum
TOBACCO

In close-up the flowers of this, the commercial tobacco plant, are rather pretty and offer a pleasant, if faint, perfume. Rather small, about 1 in (25 mm) wide, they are borne atop a head-high plant with coarse leaves. The plant is scarcely decorative enough for a flower garden, but the leaves provide the reason for its cultivation. Although different cultivars have been developed for processing into cigarettes, pipe tobacco or cigars, the way the leaves are processed determines their ultimate use. ZONES 8–11.

NIDULARIUM

From the Latin *nidulus* meaning little nest, this genus of bromeliads is characterized by an inflorescence which, in most species, nestles in the rosette. There are 46 species, native to eastern Brazil. The flowers vary in color from red to white.

CULTIVATION: These frost-tender plants grow best in moist, rich soil. They prefer warm temperatures in semi-shady to shady positions. Position in an area of bright light for good foliage and color. Water regularly, keeping the rosettes full from spring to the end of summer. Propagate from offsets or seeds.

Nidularium fulgens
BIRD'S NEST BROMELIAD, BLUSHING BROMELIAD

Sometimes called the 'friendship plant' and resembling the genus *Neoregelia*, *Nidularium fulgens* has dense rosettes of strap-shaped, saw-toothed, glossy, yellow-green foliage with dark green spots. A rosette of scarlet bracts surrounds the white and violet flowers, which appear mainly in summer. ZONES 10–12.

Nidularium innocentii
syns *Karatas innocentii*, *Regelia innocentii*

The rosette of this stemless species of bromeliad has a spread up to 24 in (60 cm) across. Its leaves are dark green to reddish brown on the upper side and brown-violet on the underside. White flowers appear on red-brown primary bracts. ZONES 10–12.

Nidularium purpureum

The rosette of this species grows out to a spread of 24 in (60 cm). Its leaves grow to 18 in (45 cm) long, with small-spined margins. They are a dull green to purple on the upperside and purple-brown on the underside. Depending on the variety, the flowers are red or white in color and grow to 2 in (5 cm) long. ZONES 10–12.

NIEREMBERGIA
CUPFLOWER

Comprising 23 species within the Solanaceae family, these annual and perennial herbs and subshrubs make ideal plants for borders or rock garden pockets where the somewhat invasive types such as *Nierembergia repens* can be contained. They are slender plants with generally fine foliage found growing naturally in moist, sunny places in the more temperate regions of South America. They come in a variety of colors, the most popular garden types bearing white or purple-blue, open, cup-shaped flowers.

CULTIVATION: Provide friable, well-composted soil in a full sun position for best results; water well and feed to prolong flowering. The annual varieties will flower from seed during their first year. In colder areas, the perennial types are often grown as annuals, but in more temperate regions they can be overwintered outdoors. Propagate the annuals from seed, the perennials by division in spring and the subshrubs from cuttings towards late summer.

Nierembergia caerulea 'Purple Robe'
syn. *Nierembergia hippomanica*

This small, bushy perennial, best grown as an annual, is ideal for edgings, massed beddings, rockeries and window boxes. In summer and early fall (autumn), it bears a profusion of open, dark bluish purple flowers with yellow throats. It has much-branched, thin, stiffly erect stems and narrow, lance-shaped, deep-green, slightly hairy leaves. It grows to a height and spread of 6–8 in (15–20 cm). Cut back after flowering. ***Nierembergia caerulea* var. *violacea*** is similar, but has longer leaves. ZONES 8–10.

Nierembergia repens
syn. *Nierembergia rivularis*
WHITECUP

This perennial species spreads by underground stems to form clumps of about 2 in (5 cm) high by 18 in (45 cm) wide. This species is best grown in a contained area or rock garden as it may become invasive. It has small, spatula-shaped bright green foliage covered, in summer, with a mass of single, open flowers, white with a golden center. ZONES 8–10.

Nierembergia repens

Nidularium innocentii

NIGELLA

The nigellas are a genus of about 15 species of annuals from the Mediterranean countries and western Asia. They have a long history of use in folk medicine. The flowers are attractive and are suitable for cutting. They have ornamental seed pods which hold their shape and are popular for flower arrangements.
CULTIVATION: Nigella seedlings hate being transplanted, but if seeds are sown where the plants are to grow and some of the flowers are allowed to go to seed, new plants will come up of their own accord for years. Plant in full sun in fertile, well-drained soil and deadhead to prolong flowering if the seed pods are not needed. Propagate from seed in fall (autumn) or spring.

Nigella damascena
LOVE-IN-A-MIST, DEVIL-IN-A-BUSH

This fully frost-hardy annual is grown for its attractive flowers. It bears spurred, many-petalled, pale to lilac-blue or white flowers in spring and early summer, almost hidden in the bright green, feathery foliage; these are followed by rounded, green seed pods that mature to brown. Upright and fast growing, it reaches 24 in (60 cm) in height with a spread of 8 in (20 cm). **'Miss Jekyll'** is a double blue form. **ZONES 6–10.**

Nigella sativa
BLACK CUMIN, NUTMEG FLOWER, ROMAN CORIANDER

This species was cultivated by the Romans for its jet black seeds, which have a flavor described as being like strawberries and pepper. They are still used as a spice in Middle Eastern cooking under the name of 'black cumin'. It grows to a height of 24 in (60 cm) and the flowers are small and whitish. **ZONES 7–10.**

NOLANA

Found in Chile, Peru and the Galapagos Islands, this genus consists of 18 species of annuals, perennials and subshrubs. Most are clump forming to semi-trailing and rarely exceed 8 in (20 cm) in height, although they may spread to 18 in (45 cm) or more. The bright green foliage can be slightly succulent, is elliptical and 1–2½ in (2.5–6 cm) long. Long-tubed, bell-shaped flowers, carried singly or in small clusters, develop in the leaf axils near the stem tips. They are up to 1½ in (35 mm) in diameter and appear throughout the growing season. They are generally white to purple with yellow throats.
CULTIVATION: Plant in humus-rich, well-drained soil in sun or part-shade. The semi-trailing types grow well in hanging baskets. Pinch the stem tips back occasionally to keep them bushy. They are only hardy to the lightest frosts. Propagate from seed, layers or tip cuttings.

Nolana paradoxa

This annual has a dwarf, creeping habit, and is ideal as a colorful ground cover in an open sunny position or for pots and hanging baskets. Low growing, up to 10 in (25 cm) high and 15 in (38 cm) wide, it produces masses of trumpet-shaped, purple-blue flowers, each with a pronounced white throat, over the summer. Many hybrids have evolved: **'Blue Bird'** has flowers in a rich, deep blue shade, again with the white throat. **ZONES 8–11.**

NOLINA

Related to the yuccas, these evergreen perennials, shrubs or small trees have adapted to their dry habitat in southern USA and Mexico. Some species produce thick corky bark on swollen bases with tapering trunks sprouting long, narrow leaves, often quite pendulous. Most only flower in maturity but the inflorescences are distinctive long panicles. Some well-known species formerly included in *Nolina* are now placed in the genus *Beaucarnea.*
CULTIVATION: These plants need to be provided with well-drained soil and, although they will respond to being watered during summer, they should be kept dry during winter. They can be successfully grown outdoors in frost-free regions but require a greenhouse where winters are more severe. Propagation is from seed or offsets taken from the parent plant in spring.

Nolina longifolia
syn. *Dasylirion longifolium*
MEXICAN GRASS TREE

In maturity, this species can reach a height of 6 ft (1.8 m). Thin, dark green leaves, gracefully recurved, hang in thick rosettes from the many short branches. Its 6 ft (1.8 m) long panicle is made up of numerous, small white individual flowers. **ZONES 10–11.**

Nolina parryi
PARRY'S NOLINA

Growing up to 10 ft (3 m) tall and with a mass of rigid leaves in terminal rosettes, this species makes a striking accent plant. The leaves, with finely notched margins, tend to persist around the trunk; in a garden situation these can be cut away with no ill effects. **ZONES 10–11.**

NOMOCHARIS

Aptly named from the Greek for pasture and loveliness, one can immediately visualize these lilies growing in fields and woodlands across the mountainous regions of northern India, Tibet and western China. The 7 species of bulbous herbaceous perennials have saucer- or bell-shaped blooms in white, pink or pale yellow, often spotted with purple.
CULTIVATION: Preferring acidic, woodland conditions in part-shade, these plants thrive where good drainage is assured and where an even, cool, slightly humid atmosphere can be maintained. *Nomocharis* can be propagated by division or from seed, although plants grown from seed may take up to 4 years to flower. Advanced plants can be expensive to buy.

Nolana paradoxa

Nomocharis aperta

Growing to 30 in (75 cm) high, the stems of this species have whorls of bright green leaves scattered along their length while towards the tips flowers appear in the terminal leaf axils. The flattened blooms, up to 4 in (10 cm) across, are pale pink to red with spots and blotches of deeper red and maroon splashed across the petals. **ZONES 7–10.**

Nomocharis pardanthina
syn. *Nomocharis mairei*

The slender stem of this frost-hardy species grows to about 3 ft (1 m) and bears whorls of leaves and up to 12 blooms in summer. The nodding, 4 in (10 cm) wide flowers are white to rose and spotted with crimson. **ZONES 7–10.**

NOPALXOCHIA

This genus of 4 species of epiphytic, perennial cacti is native to Central America; it is very closely related to the genus *Epiphyllum.* The species have flat, ribbon-like, spineless stems with heavily undulating margins. Pinkish red flowers appear from the edges of the stems, then after 3 or 4 days both flowers and stems perish. The flowers are followed by red fruits with seeds encased in a jelly-like pulp.
CULTIVATION: These frost-tender plants are readily cultivated, provided temperatures do not drop below 41°F

Nomocharis aperta

Nomocharis pardanthina

Nigella damascena

(5°C); they require porous, fertile soil in semi-shade. Propagate from stem cuttings in spring and summer.

Nopalxochia phyllanthoides
POND LILY CACTUS

This cactus grows up to 24 in (60 cm) tall and 3 ft (1 m) wide. The cylindrical base bears vivid green, pendulous stems with wavy margins. Numerous rose-pink, tubular-stemmed flowers bloom in spring. This species is easily confused with the cultivar **'Deutsche Kaiserin'**, now placed in × *Epicactus*. **ZONES 10–12.**

NOTHOFAGUS
SOUTHERN BEECH

Wide ranging in the southern hemisphere from South America to southeastern Australia, *Nothofagus* is a genus of more than 25 species of evergreen and deciduous trees. Fast growing, they have dark green leaves often with toothed margins. The foliage of several of the deciduous species displays rich bronze hues before dropping. The small fruits each contain 3 triangular seeds known as beechnuts.

CULTIVATION: Southern beeches can be cultivated in a variety of climates provided they have protection from strong winds. They prefer acidic soil deep enough to support their large root system and should be planted out when small and never transplanted. Position in full sun and water well when young. Propagate from cuttings in summer or seed in fall (autumn).

N

Nothofagus fusca

Nothofagus antarctica
ANTARCTIC BEECH

This is a deciduous tree or large, multi-stemmed shrub from the cool, rainy forests of the far southern regions of Chile and Argentina. In the wild, old specimens up to 100 ft (30 m) tall are known, but in gardens they are unlikely to exceed 30 ft (9 m). It is variable in habit—anything from widely conical to contorted and irregular—and is generally rather slow growing. The flowers are insignificant but the wavy edged, toothed leaves turn buttery yellow in fall (autumn) before dropping. It is moderately frost hardy. **ZONES 7–9.**

Nothofagus cunninghamii
TASMANIAN BEECH, MYRTLE BEECH

This magnificent tree attains a height of more than 150 ft (45 m) when grown in the cool, mountainous regions of its native southern Australia. An evergreen, it is one of the faster growing species in the genus, and is valued for its reddish timber. Its small, triangular-toothed leaves are held in fan-shaped sprays and the young foliage is a deep bronze shade in spring. Small catkin flowers are borne in early summer. **ZONES 8–9.**

Nothofagus fusca
NEW ZEALAND RED BEECH

This attractive, erect evergreen has a dome-shaped crown and averages 20–40 ft (6–12 m) in height when cultivated and up to 120 ft (36 m) in the wild. The egg-shaped, roughly serrated foliage is up to 2 in (5 cm) long; immature leaves turn reddish bronze in cooler weather. Small, green flowers are followed by seed cups, each containing 3 angular seeds. **ZONES 7–10.**

Nopalxochia phyllanthoides

Nothofagus fusca

Nothofagus menziesii

Nothofagus moorei

Nothofagus menziesii
NEW ZEALAND SILVER BEECH

Famed for its beautiful silver bark, this evergreen species from New Zealand bears a mass of small, dense leaves with coarsely serrated margins. Reaching a height of 70 ft (21 m), it needs plenty of sun and protection from wind. The flowers appear as small catkins in summer. **ZONES 7–10.**

Nothofagus moorei
AUSTRALIAN BEECH, ANTARCTIC BEECH

This Australian evergreen tree prefers a part-shaded, frost-free position where its roots can stay moist during dry spells. It grows to a mature height of over 70 ft (21 m) with a broad head, and bears finely serrated, pointed ovate leaves up to 4 in (10 cm) long. Its massive trunk is covered with brown, scaly bark. The tiny, insignificant flowers appear in early summer. **ZONES 9–11.**

Nothofagus obliqua
ROBLE

Deriving its name from its characteristic, oblique leaf base, the roble is a deciduous species from Chile and Argentina.

Nothofagus cunninghamii

Nothofagus obliqua

Nothofagus procera

Growing to more than 150 ft (45 m), it has a broad spread of 20 ft (6 m) and is suitable for cold regions. Its deeply toothed leaves and attractive drooping habit make it one of the most popular *Nothofagus* species in cultivation. Its leaves turn a deep reddish orange before dropping. The roble is now grown as a plantation crop for its fine timber and exceedingly rapid growth. **ZONES 8–10.**

Nothofagus procera
RAULI

Common on the wetter Andean slopes of Chile, this is one of the best timber species of the genus and also the fastest growing. The rauli thrives in moist climates and is moderately frost hardy. It is also the longest leafed of the temperate species, with strongly veined leaves 3–6 in (8–15 cm) long which turn a pleasant russet shade in fall (autumn). It is also susceptible to pollution. **ZONES 7–10.**

Nothofagus solandri
BLACK BEECH

A 60 ft (18 m) high evergreen tree native to New Zealand, the black beech has small leaves, around ½ in (12 mm) long, but they are densely packed in fan-like sprays. The young growth is soft and downy. Small, reddish brown flowers, heavy with pollen, open in spring. Although individually the flowers are not very significant, when in full bloom the tree develops a reddish cast.

Nothofagus solandri* var. *cliffortioides has twisted and more sharply pointed leaves. **ZONES 7–10.**

NOTOSPARTIUM

The 3 species of broom-like shrubs that comprise this genus are medium sized, reaching a maximum of 10 ft (3 m). They grow naturally in New Zealand, but have become popular in mild-winter climates elsewhere because of the profusion of charming, pea-shaped flowers that appear in mid-summer. The shrubs are leafless at maturity and attain their shape from graceful arching branches, which can spread to 6 ft (1.8 m).
CULTIVATION: They thrive in any well-drained soil, but must have full sun to flower. They may require staking. Propagate from seed in fall (autumn) or from cuttings taken in late summer.

Notospartium carmichaeliae
NEW ZEALAND PINK BROOM

This deciduous shrub bears leaves only when the plant is young, and spends the rest of its life as a flat-stemmed, erect, slender bush. When in full spring flower, the shrub is smothered in lilac-pink blossoms which appear all along the branches. If protected from wind, flowering will continue for many weeks during warm weather. **ZONES 8–10.**

NUPHAR
SPATTERDOCK, POND LILY, YELLOW POND LILY

Made up of 25 species of perennial aquatic herbs with creeping rhizomes, these pond lilies from the temperate northern hemisphere have large, floating and submerged leaves. The flowers, usually in yellow or green tones, are held on stalks above the water surface.
CULTIVATION: Requirements are very similar to the hardy species of *Nymphaea* with the additional benefit that they will flower in shade and some are suited to being planted in slow-moving water. They prefer to be planted in pots of rich soil and carefully submerged to around 24 in (60 cm) deep, depending on the species. Propagation is by division and best carried out in spring.

Nuphar lutea
YELLOW POND LILY

This species is native to eastern USA, the West Indies, northern Africa and large

Nothofagus solandri

tracts of Eurasia. It thrives in deep water and has large orbicular leaves that emerge when the water is shallow or float when planted in deeper ponds. Summer-flowering, deep yellow-orange blooms held just above the surface emit a distinct odor. This is a vigorous species. **ZONES 4–11.**

Nuphar polysepala

In this species from the USA, the large, round, floating leaves, with their distinct V-shaped lobe, offset the greenish blooms which are tinged with purple-brown. **ZONES 4–9.**

NUXIA

There are about 15 species in this genus of evergreen trees and shrubs spread throughout Africa, Madagascar and the Mascarene Islands. The leaves are simple and generally arranged in 3s around a node, very occasionally alternate or sometimes opposite. Smooth or hairy, the sticky leaves can be toothed or lobed, either wavy or with entire margins. Small, sweet-smelling flowers are borne terminally. The fruits are capsules with small and numerous seeds.
CULTIVATION: As these plants do not grow easily from seed, cuttings are the best method of propagation. Plant in large holes in fertile, humus-rich soil. Fast growers, they like plenty of sun and a frost-free winter.

Nuxia floribunda
FOREST ELDER

This decorative tree grows to about 25 ft (8 m) tall with a spread of 12 ft (3.5 m) and a rounded crown when mature. The glossy leaves are simple, oblong and 6 in (15 cm) long. From fall (autumn) to spring, the tree bears large clusters of

Nothofagus solandri

Nuxia floribunda

fragrant, creamy white flowers, up to 12 in (30 cm) long, that give it a hazy, almost lacy, beauty. **ZONES 9–11.**

NUYTSIA
WESTERN AUSTRALIAN CHRISTMAS TREE

This genus, consisting of a single species from Western Australia, was named after the Dutch navigator Pieter Nuyts. It is a terrestrial shrub or small tree that parasitizes the roots of grasses.
CULTIVATION: It seems that in cultivation this plant is not particular as to its host type—it germinates easily as long as a tuft of grass is added to the potting mix of young seedlings. Plant out when quite young in full sun, in combination with the initial host plant and in the vicinity of another likely companion. Propagate from seed or by root division.

Nuytsia floribunda

An evergreen species growing to 30 ft (9 m), *Nuytsia floribunda* has widely spreading branches and slender leaves about 3 in (8 cm) long. A magnificent

Nuytsia floribunda

display of honey-scented, orange-yellow flowers are borne in elongated clusters towards the end of the branches during the summer months. As the plants grow naturally in a moist position, cultivated specimens will need to be well watered, especially while young. **ZONES 9–11.**

NYMPHAEA
WATERLILY

This worldwide genus of 50 species of deciduous and evergreen perennial aquatic plants with fleshy roots is named after the Greek goddess Nymphe. They are grown for their rounded, floating leaves which are cleft at the base and for their attractive large flowers which come in shades of white and cream, brilliant yellows and oranges, pinks and deep reds, blues and purple. They may be night blooming, depending on species,

Nuphar polysepala

Notospartium carmichaeliae

N

Nymphaea, Hardy Hybrid, 'Lucida'

Nymphaea, HH, 'Atropurpurea'

Nymphaea gigantea

Nymphaea capensis

and sometimes fragrant. The berry-like fruits mature underwater. There are both frost-hardy and tropical varieties.
CULTIVATION: Frost-hardy waterlilies grow in most climates and flower freely throughout summer, both flowers and foliage floating on the water surface; remove faded foliage. Divide the tuber-like rhizomes and replant in spring or summer every 3 or 4 years. Tropical waterlilies are all frost tender, requiring a very warm, sunny situation. They flower from mid-summer into fall (autumn), and have large, scented flowers held above the water surface. In cooler areas, the tubers of tropical waterlilies should be lifted and stored in moist sand over winter. All species need still water and annual fertilizing as they are gross feeders. Propagate from seed or by separating plantlets in spring or early fall. Check for insects, particularly aphids; goldfish kept in the pool will eat most pests.

Nymphaea alba
EUROPEAN WHITE LILY

This is a deciduous, frost-hardy species from Europe, North Africa and Asia with dark green leaves and fragrant, semi-double, 4–8 in (10–20 cm) wide white flowers with golden centers. It spreads to 10 ft (3 m). **ZONES 6–10.**

Nymphaea caerulea
syn. *Nymphaea nouchali* var. *caerulea*
BLUE LOTUS, EGYPTIAN LOTUS

This waterlily species is widely distributed in Africa and has often been misidentified as *Nymphaea capensis.* It has floating leaves up to 15 in (38 cm) in diameter with toothed edges. Pale blue flowers, held well above the water have narrow, pointed petals paler towards the center and yellow stamens. It is a day-blooming waterlily. **ZONES 9–12.**

Nymphaea candida

This dainty, dwarf species from northern Europe and Asia is ideal for a miniature pond. Closely related to *Nymphaea alba,* it bears small, pure white flowers 3–5 in (8–12 cm) across and its leaf lobes touch or overlap at the base. Plant with around 6–10 in (15–25 cm) of water over the crown of the plant. **ZONES 4–9.**

Nymphaea capensis
CAPE BLUE WATERLILY

This bright blue, fragrant day-opening waterlily from southern and eastern Africa has floating leaves up to 15 in (38 cm) in diameter with acute, overlapping petals. When young, its foliage is spotted with purple below. Some plants grown as *Nymphaea capensis* may in fact be *N. caerulea.* **ZONES 9–11.**

Nymphaea, Hardy Hybrid, 'Attraction'

Nymphaea gigantea
AUSTRALIAN WATERLILY

This tuberous-rooted plant from the tropical areas of Australia and New Guinea has large leaves, often up to 24 in (60 cm) in diameter. Day-blooming, 12 in (30 cm) flowers range from sky to deeper purple-blue. **ZONES 10–12.**

Nymphaea, Hardy Hybrids

These cold-hardy and colorful hybrids have been bred from several European and North American species, principally *Nymphaea alba, N. odorata* and *N. mexicana.* The day-blooming flowers are 3–6 in (8–15 cm) across, mostly in shades of white, yellow, pink or red, set on or just above the surface of the water. **'Atropurpurea'** has reddish purple foliage complementing its dark red, wide-open flowers with golden stamens. **'Attraction'** will grow in quite deep water; its crimson-red flowers with contrasting white sepals deepen to a rich garnet red as they age. **'Aurora'** is smaller, spreading to 30 in (75 cm), and has olive-green leaves blotched with purple; its semi-double flowers are star-shaped, 2 in (5 cm) wide and they turn from cream to yellow, to orange, to blood red as they age. **'Escarboucle'**, with masses of blooms and a long flowering season, has wine-crimson flowers with contrasting golden stamens. **'Formosa'** is a profuse bloomer, producing many large flowers in a soft rosy pink shade on opening, becoming deeper in coloring as the flower ages. **'Gladstoniana'** is generally a very hardy and vigorous plant, its deep red foliage contrasting with very large, pure white flowers that have thick and incurving petals. **'Gonnère'**, once known as **'Snowball'**, is a multi-petalled or double hybrid in pure white with a moderately contained leaf spread. **'James Brydon'** flowers in part-shade, its scented blooms opening pink and ageing to rosy red. **'Lucida'** has large green leaves and attractive deep red flowers with paler outer petals, 5–6 in (12–15 cm) across; **'Mme Wilfon Gonnère'** produces 6 in (15 cm) wide flowers in 2 shades of pink; reddish leaves age to bright green. **'Rose Arey'** has dark pink, sweetly fragrant flowers; leaves are reddish purple ageing to reddish green. The compact-growing **'Paul Hariot'**, suited to small and medium ponds, has foliage streaked maroon and flowers that open pale peach and darken to rich coppery red with maturity. The compact **Laydeckeri hybrids** are very free flowering yet produce comparatively little foliage. Colors range from soft rose pink to deep pink and rosy crimson, and they have a spread of around 24 in (60 cm). **'Fulgens'** has star-shaped, semi-double, crimson to magenta flowers. The **Marliacea hybrids** are among the most elegant of all the hardy waterlilies, raised by M. Latour-Marliac in the 1880s. They have dark green leaves and star-shaped, semi-double, soft pink flowers with golden centers, which appear in summer. The large flowers stand slightly above the water. **'Albida'** is a strong-growing plant bearing free-blooming white flowers. **'Chromatella'** is a very free-flowering and reliable hybrid, even flowering in part-shade; it has creamy yellow blooms and foliage marked with bronze. **ZONES 5–10.**

Nymphaea, Hardy Hybrid, 'Albida'

Nymphaea lotus
EGYPTIAN WATERLILY, LOTUS

This very robust plant from Egypt and tropical and southeastern Africa has large leaves forming a backdrop to the emergent, slightly fragrant white blooms up to 10 in (25 cm) across. These open at night, closing around noon the following day. **ZONES 10–12.**

Nymphaea nouchali
SHAPLA

This tropical species has a wide distribution from southern Asia to northern Australia. Its flower is the national emblem of Bangladesh and it is used there and in India in perfumery and cosmetics. It is a rather small waterlily with floating leaves normally only 3–6 in (8–15 cm) across, and 3 in (8 cm) wide flowers held at or just above the water surface; they open during the day and have 10 or fewer pointed petals that may be blue, pink or white, with a distinct gap between the petals and the bunch of yellow stamens. **ZONES 11–12.**

Nymphaea, Hardy Hybrid, 'Formosa'

Nymphaea, TD-bH, 'Margaret Randig'

Nymphaea, TD-bH, 'St Louis Gold'

N., TN-bH, 'Emily Grant Hutchings'

Nymphaea, TN-bH, 'H. T. Haarstick'

Nymphaea, TD-bH, 'Pink Platter'

Nymphaea, TD-bH, 'Director Moore'

Nymphaea, TD-bH, 'Blue Beauty'

Nymphaea, TD-bH, 'St Louis'

Nymphaea nouchali

Nymphaea odorata

POND LILY, WHITE WATERLILY

This native of North and tropical America has white fragrant, many-petalled flowers 3–5 in (8–12 cm) across, appearing by day in summer. The leaves are thick, glossy and mid-green. It spreads to 4 ft (1.2 m). **ZONES 3–11.**

Nymphaea tetragona 'Helvola'

This true miniature waterlily bears soft yellow, star-shaped, semi-double flowers only 2–3 in (5–8 cm) across. The leaves are handsome, too, being dark olive green splashed with maroon. The species is widely distributed around the temperate northern hemisphere. Plant with around 10 in (25 cm) of water over the crown of the plant. It is the smallest of the miniature waterlilies. **ZONES 7–10.**

Nymphaea, Tropical Day-blooming Hybrids

Tropical hybrids can bear day- or night-time flowers. **'Blue Beauty'** is a deciduous or evergreen, day-blooming waterlily with large, brown-speckled, dark green leaves with purplish undersides; the flowers are rounded, semi-double, 12 in (30 cm) across, and deep purple-blue with yellow centers and it spreads to 8 ft (2.4 m). Another day-blooming hybrid, **'Director Moore'**, with deep blue petals surrounding purple stamens and a yellow center, lasts well indoors when cut. The day-blooming **'Margaret Randig'** has mottled-purple foliage with fragrant large, open, sky-blue petals with yellow centers and blue-tipped stamens. Bright green leaves mottled with rich brown offset the open, soft pink daytime blooms of **'Pink Platter'**; those of **'St Louis'** are scented and pale yellow. **'St Louis Gold'**, with abundant daytime blooms of deep gold, is a good variety for smaller pools or tubs. **ZONES 10–12.**

Nymphaea, Tropical Night-blooming Hybrids

Of the night-bloomers, **'H. T. Haarstick'** and **'Wood's White Knight'** are notable. Both have tall stems, the former carrying deep red flowers over deep coppery red leaves with very serrated edges, the latter bearing creamy white flowers over mid-green leaves, also with serrated margins. **'Emily Grant Hutchings'** has enormous deep pink flowers that can reach 12 in (30 cm) across. **ZONES 10–12.**

Nymphaea, TD-bH, 'Isabelle Pring'

Nymphaea, TD-bH, 'Bob Trickett'

Nymphaea, TD-bH, 'William B. Shaw'

N., Hardy Hybrid, 'Caroliniana Perfecta'

N., Hardy Hybrid, 'Colonel Welch'

Nymphaea, Hardy Hybrid, 'Colossea'

Nymphaea, Hardy Hybrid, 'Rosea'

NYMPHOIDES

FAIRY WATERLILY, WATER SNOWFLAKE

Resembling miniature waterlilies, the 20 species of rhizomatous, aquatic perennials in this genus are distributed throughout the world. Their rootstocks embed in the pond bottom while the long-stalked, oval, round or kidney-shaped, wavy-edged leaves float on the surface. The foliage ranges in diameter from 1–6 in (2.5–15 cm), and is usually slightly glossy and olive green, occasionally purple mottled. The ½–1 in (12–25 mm) diameter flowers, with 5 often fimbriated (fringed) petals, may be white or yellow; they appear in summer and are held just above the foliage.
CULTIVATION: Plant in soil with a water depth of 4–18 in (10–45 cm) in full or half-day sun. The runners can spread to 6 ft (1.8 m), so allow room for development. Propagate by dividing the rootstock in late winter or early spring.

Nymphoides indica

WATER SNOWFLAKE, FALSE INDIAN WATERLILY

These plants are found throughout the tropics with separate subspecies found in different continents. This hardy perennial has rounded surface leaves ranging from 2–8 in (5–20 cm) across with a heart-shaped base. The flowers are white with a deep yellow center and the petals have characteristic fringed margins. **ZONES 10–12.**

Nymphoides peltata

WATER FRINGE, YELLOW FLOATING HEART

This is a very hardy species from a vast area of Eurasia and Japan. The small, heart-shaped submerged leaves grow near the very long rhizomes, while surface leaves are bright green with blackish markings on their upper sides and reddish tinges below. The flowers are bright golden yellow. **ZONES 6–10.**

Nyssa sylvatica

Nymphoides indica

NYSSA

TUPELO

Occurring naturally in southern Asia and North America, this genus is named after Nyssa, the water nymph, because the trees insist on adequate year-round water to survive. Fast growing and wind tolerant, they must be left undisturbed after planting and may reach a maximum height of 120 ft (36 m) with a broad-based, conical shape. Small clusters of greenish white flowers appear during summer, to be followed by vivid, dark purple berries up to 1 in (25 mm) long which provide an effective contrast to the stunning foliage. Few trees attract as much attention as these when they are clad in their spectacular red, crimson, yellow and orange fall (autumn) foliage.
CULTIVATION: They need fertile, moist but well-drained, neutral to acidic soil, sun or part-shade and a cool climate. Prune only to remove dead or crowded branches. Propagate from cuttings in summer or from seed in fall.

Nyssa aquatica

WATER TUPELO

This species can commonly be found in swamps or shallow water where it develops a sturdy, buttressed trunk. Its leaves are diamond-shaped, green and 10 in (25 cm) long. The honey made by bees from the nectar of tupelo flowers has a distinctive and delicious taste. An important timber tree, it is pyramid-shaped and reaches 120 ft (36 m) in optimum conditions. **ZONES 5–10.**

Nyssa sinensis

CHINESE TUPELO

This is a smaller growing species than the popular black tupelo—in maturity it will reach between 30–50 ft (9–15 m) with a more spreading habit and narrowly oval pointed leaves. Spring foliage is tinged red and in fall (autumn) the leaves turn brilliant red and yellow. **ZONES 7–10.**

Nyssa sylvatica

Nymphoides peltata

Ochna serrulata

Nyssa sylvatica

BLACK TUPELO, SOUR GUM, PEPPERIDGE

This elegant tree is one of the most decorative and useful of all deciduous plants, as it flourishes in swampy conditions. The glossy, 4 in (10 cm) long leaves, which are slightly wider towards the tip, are dark or yellowish green then turn brilliant red, often with shades of orange and yellow as well, before dropping. It grows to 70 ft (21 m) with a broad columnar conical habit and has an unusual trunk covered with brownish gray bark, which breaks up into large pieces on mature specimens. **ZONES 3–10.**

OCHNA

The 90 or so species of this genus of evergreen and deciduous trees and shrubs occur wild in tropical and subtropical regions of Africa and Asia. The leaves are mostly finely toothed and may be shed briefly in late winter or spring, the new growth flush being translucent bronze. Flowers are mostly yellow, like small hypericums but in tight clusters. Fruits consist of an enlarged red calyx and receptacle with several green to black drupelets, each containing one seed.
CULTIVATION: Grow in full sun in any fertile, moist but well-drained soil. Prune during spring, and propagate from seed in spring or from cuttings in summer.

Ochna pulchra

This rather lovely small deciduous tree comes from the subtropical savannah lands of northern South Africa and Zimbabwe. Stout-trunked, it grows into an elegant, spreading tree, up to 20 ft (6 m) tall. In winter and spring, clusters of golden-yellow flowers appear along with the reddish bronze new foliage, followed in summer by decorative red and black fruit. The bark of mature trees is attractive, creamy white with peeling flakes of brownish older bark. **ZONES 10–11.**

Ochna serrulata

CARNIVAL BUSH, MICKEY MOUSE PLANT

A native of southern Africa, this shrub can grow up to 8 ft (2.4 m) with a rather open habit and has narrow, glossy mid-green leaves. The spring flowers are butter yellow and are followed in summer by red and black fruit; these are eaten by birds which distribute the seed widely causing the plant to become a pest in warm climates. **ZONES 9–11.**

Ocimum tenuiflorum

Ocimum basilicum

OCIMUM

BASIL

This genus of approximately 35 species of rather frost-tender annuals, perennials and shrubs is native to tropical Asia and Africa. They are now widely cultivated in many other countries for their highly aromatic leaves, which are used for medicinal purposes or to flavor salads, soups, sauces, stews and curries. They have mostly oval leaves in opposite pairs and small tubular flowers borne in whorls towards the ends of the stems in late summer.
CULTIVATION: Grow in a protected, warm, sunny position in a moist but well-drained soil. Regularly pinch back plants to encourage bushy growth and to prevent them going to seed quickly. Propagate from seed in mid-spring. Protect from late frosts and check for chewing insects and snails.

Ocimum basilicum

BASIL, SWEET BASIL

This native of tropical Asia, together with its cultivars, is the most commonly grown and most widely used basil. A favorite with cooks, it is one of the most widely used herbs in Mediterranean cooking. Fresh leaves are best; freeze them for the winter as they lose their flavor when dried. It is a tender annual plant growing to about 18 in (45 cm) with light green, oval leaves that have a delicious warm, spicy fragrance. Small white flowers are carried in whorls towards the ends of the stems in late summer. There are a number of varieties of basil including a compact small leaf type; a crinkled, lettuce leaf variety and the beautiful **'Dark Opal',** which has rich purple stems and leaves. There are perennial varieties also, but their flavor is inferior. **'Minimum'** is a dwarf form with tiny leaves, used in the Greek Orthodox Church for sprinkling holy water. As a summer annual, basil can be grown in cooler climates. **ZONES 10–12.**

Ocimum tenuiflorum
syn. *Ocimum sanctum*
HOLY BASIL

This popular aromatic herb from India is an important sacred plant in the Hindu religion. It is a short-lived perennial that dies back to a few woody stems near ground level. It grows to about 3 ft (1 m) tall with many upright stems clothed in oval, toothed leaves. Small, not very showy flowers appear on a spike from the tips of the branches. It is not particularly frost hardy and in cooler areas is usually raised as a summer annual. **ZONES 10–12.**

× *ODONTIODA*

A hybrid genus created through the crossing of 2 closely related orchid genera, *Odontoglossum* and *Cochlioda.* The resulting plants are evergreen epiphytes with egg-shaped pseudobulbs that each produce 2 narrow, strap-like leaves up to 10 in (25 cm) long. Usually in spring, but in warm climates at any time, long stems emerge from the pseudobulbs and from these are produced 10 to 20 starry, often spotted or patterned flowers in shades of pink, red and yellow. **CULTIVATION:** In frost-free or nearly frost-free climates, these orchids can be grown outdoors year round. Where heavier frosts occur, grow in a cool greenhouse kept above freezing point. Everywhere, raise in pots of fine orchid compost and keep relatively dry over winter, giving increasing water as summer approaches. The plants do best with dappled shade in summer, slightly more sun in winter. They are not well suited to lowland tropical regions as they like relatively cool nights in summer.

× *Odontioda* Heatonensis

This was one of the first crosses that created the hybrid genus × *Odontioda.* It produces long sprays of red spotted, pink blooms and is easy to grow. It is tolerant of the lightest frosts only. **ZONES 10–11.**

× *ODONTOCIDIUM*

This is a hybrid genus of orchids created by crossing 2 closely related genera of epiphytic orchids from South America, *Odontoglossum* and *Oncidium.* All of the resulting plants produce egg-shaped pseudobulbs from which emerge 2 narrow, strap-like leaves. Several times a year in warm climates, but usually in spring in cooler areas, the plants produce long sprays of at least a dozen starry flowers, each with a prominent lip. Flowers are in red and yellow shades and usually spotted or patterned. **CULTIVATION:** These cool-growing orchids can be grown outdoors in highland tropical, subtropical or warm temperate areas. Where winters are frosty, they are grown in a cool greenhouse kept above freezing point. Fine grade orchid compost suits them and they should be given the most water in summer, least in winter, gradually increasing and decreasing as the months grow warmer and cooler. Bright dappled shade is best in summer, but the plants will tolerate more sun in winter.

× *Odontocidium* Susan Kaufmann

This hybrid has flowers in the typical colors of the genus. Each bloom is on the small side, but many are produced. **ZONES 10–11.**

ODONTOGLOSSUM

The most widely grown plants of this genus of 200 species from Central and South America are epiphytes, although terrestrial species are known. They are admired for their usually ruffled flowers borne in long sprays, and the wonderful variety of colors and markings displayed thereon. They produce egg-shaped pseudobulbs, from the bases of which the flower stems appear; flowering is from early spring to fall (autumn), depending on variety. The genus is closely related to *Oncidium,* and some botanists consider that they cannot be separated. Some well-known *Odontoglossum* species are now separated off into the genera *Lemboglossum* and *Rossioglossum.* **CULTIVATION:** Few odontoglossums are difficult to grow: most are cool growing, and need only the usual orchid cultivation of coarse compost, plenty of water in summer and light shade. They do not need as definite a winter rest as cattleyas, but do not over-water then. They can be divided after flowering.

Odontoglossum crispum

This high-altitude epiphyte from Colombia is a variable species with many named forms, very popular in cultivation and with hybridists. The pseudobulbs are compressed, about 3 in (8 cm) long with 2 strap-like leaves to 15 in (38 cm) long and 1½ in (35 mm) wide. The inflorescence is arching or pendulous, with 8 to 25 showy flowers each about 2½–4 in (6–10 cm) across. Flowering is in fall (autumn) to winter. **ZONES 10–11.**

× *Odontioda* Heatonensis

Odontoglossum Hybrids

Thousands of colorful hybrids have been developed suitable for greenhouse culture using *Odontoglossum.* Many other genera have also been utilized in the production of hybrids including those with *Cochlioda* (× *Odontioda*), *Oncidium* (× *Odontocidium*) and *Miltonia* (× *Odontonia*). Virtually all these are cool-growing species with similar requirements to the genus. **'La Houge Bie'** is notable for its very broad, overlapping petals giving the bloom a full, rounded look. Extravagant **'Samares'** is another fine example. Its pure white petals are wavy and frilly-edged and each is decorated with a blood-red spot. **ZONES 10–12.**

OENANTHE
WATER DROPWORT

Native to very damp areas of the northern hemisphere and tropical Africa, this genus of the carrot family consists of about 30 species of perennials, found mainly in damp habitats such as marshland and water meadows. Tiny white flowers appear in umbels, while the leaves are divided into many small leaflets. Care must be taken with these plants, as some species are quite toxic. **CULTIVATION:** These plants can be naturalized in informal situations, requiring moist, fertile soil and doing well in either shade or sun. Propagate from seed or stem tip cuttings or by division or layering.

Oenanthe crocata
HEMLOCK, WATER DROPWORT

This European species is extremely poisonous and dangerous to livestock, so care should be taken when planting. It grows to a height of 5 ft (1.5 m) with a robust branching habit and has a very strong smell. Terminal heads of white flowers are borne in winter. **ZONES 5–10.**

Oenanthe javanica
syn. *Oenanthe japonica*

With its celery-like leaves consisting of small toothed leaflets, this species from eastern and southern Asia is grown as a leaf vegetable, usually eaten with rice. Growing to a height of 15 in (38 cm), it bears its flowers in late summer. **ZONES 10–12.**

OENOTHERA
EVENING PRIMROSE

Native to temperate regions of both North and South America but widely naturalized elsewhere, this genus consists of more than 120 species of annuals, biennials and perennials. Their short-lived flowers, borne during summer, have 4 delicate petals, yellow or less commonly pink, red or white, and a long basal tube. Most species are pollinated by nocturnal insects and only release their fragrance at night. Some do not even open their petals during the day. Evening

Oenanthe crocata

Odontoglossum Hybrid 'La Houge Bie'

Odontoglossum Hybrid 'Samares'

× *Odontocidium* Susan Kaufmann

primrose oil is extracted from the plants' tiny seeds; it contains certain fatty acids believed to be beneficial to health if consumed regularly in modest quantities.
CULTIVATION: They are mostly frost hardy and grow best in a well-drained, sandy soil in an open, sunny situation. They will tolerate dry conditions. Propagate from seed or by division in spring or fall (autumn), or from softwood cuttings in late spring.

Oenothera biennis
COMMON EVENING PRIMROSE

A showy plant, this upright, hairy biennial has large, scented yellow flowers in tall spikes, opening in the evening and shrivelling before noon. It is erect and fast growing to a height of 5 ft (1.5 m). **ZONES 4–10.**

Oenothera caespitosa
TUFTED EVENING PRIMROSE

A clump-forming, stemless perennial, this species has mid-green leaves that are sometimes toothed. The flowers appear in summer at sunset, and are fragrant and white, turning pink with age. This plant is frost hardy and is suitable for use in a rock garden. It grows to height of 4 in (10 cm) and has a spread of 8 in (20 cm). **ZONES 4–9.**

Oenothera macrocarpa

Oenothera odorata

Oenothera speciosa 'Rosea'

Oenothera drummondii
BEACH EVENING PRIMROSE

A native of coastal Texas to northwestern Mexico, this species is usually treated as an annual in cultivation, but grows as a biennial or perennial in the wild. It has soft, hairy, oblong to lance-shaped leaves and very decorative bright yellow flowers that open in the evening. A broadly spreading plant, it reaches a height of 12–24 in (30–60 cm). It grows on beaches and other sandy places and has become naturalized in other countries. **ZONES 6–10.**

Oenothera elata subsp. *hookeri*
HOOKER'S EVENING PRIMROSE

This species from western North America grows to a height of 6 ft (1.8 m). An erect perennial or biennial, it bears its lemon-gold turning to red-orange flowers in summer; the flowers open just as the sun sets. **ZONES 7–9.**

Oenothera erythrosepala

This handsome North American perennial has erect stems, with large, rough leaves. The flowers have conspicuous reddish sepals and large, pale yellow petals which redden as they shrivel in the afternoon. This plant is very adaptable to most conditions and resists both dry conditions and frost. It grows to a height and spread of 3–4 ft (1–1.2 m). **ZONES 3–10.**

Oenothera speciosa 'Rosea'

Oenothera biennis

Oenothera elata subsp. *hookeri*

Oenothera speciosa 'Siskiyou'

Oenothera stricta

Oenothera fruticosa
SUNDROPS

This biennial or perennial species from eastern North America sometimes grows to a height of 3 ft (1 m), but is usually smaller. It has a reddish, erect, branching stem and narrow leaves. Deep yellow 1–2 in (2.5–5 cm) wide flowers open by day. ***Oenothera fruticosa* subsp. *glauca*** has broader, less hairy leaves with red tints when young. **'Fyrverker'** (syn. 'Fireworks') has yellow flowers that open from red buds. **ZONES 4–10.**

Oenothera macrocarpa
syn. *Oenothera missouriensis*

OZARK SUNDROPS, MISSOURI PRIMROSE, FLUTTERMILLS

This perennial is usually almost stemless with large rosettes of narrow tapering leaves. The flowers are large, reaching 4 in (10 cm) in diameter, lemon yellow in color and open in the evening in summer. This plant reaches a height of no more than 6 in (15 cm), but spreads to 24 in (60 cm) or more across, the flowers appearing singly from between the leaves. **ZONES 5–9.**

Oenothera odorata

This perennial, native to South America, was introduced into England by Sir Joseph Banks in 1790. It has erect red-tinted stems with a rosette of narrow leaves at the base. The fragrant yellow flowers appear in summer, turning red with age and opening at dusk. It reaches a height of 24–36 in (60–90 cm) and a spread of 12 in (30 cm). **ZONES 7–10.**

Oenothera speciosa 'Rosea'

Oenothera rosea
PINK EVENING PRIMROSE, ROSE OF MEXICO

With profuse but pink to reddish flowers less than 1 in (25 mm) across and opening during the day, *Oenothera rosea* has a dainty appearance that belies its toughness and ease of culture. The species comes from northern Mexico and south-central USA. **ZONES 6–10.**

Oenothera speciosa
WHITE EVENING PRIMROSE, SHOWY EVENING PRIMROSE

This short-lived, rhizomatous perennial native to southern USA and Mexico bears spikes of profuse, fragrant, saucer-shaped, pink-tinted white flowers. Fresh flowerheads open daily during summer. The small leaves often turn red in hot or cold weather. Clump forming, it grows to 18–24 in (45–60 cm) in height with a spread of 18 in (45 cm) or more. **'Rosea'** (syns 'Childsii', *Oenothera berlandieri*) is lower growing, with flowers edged and heavily veined rose pink, yellow in the center. **'Siskiyou'** is similar but with larger flowers. These pink forms have often been confused with *O. rosea*, which has much smaller flowers. **ZONES 5–10.**

Oenothera stricta

This South American species is very similar to *Oenothera odorata*, but has flowers of a more golden yellow shade. It is commonly naturalized in southern Australia. **ZONES 8–10.**

OLDENBURGIA

There are only 4 species in this South African genus of slow-growing, evergreen shrubs and perennials in the daisy family. They are grown more for their

interesting foliage and irregular, picturesque habit than for their fluffy flowerheads which are reminiscent of thistles. Rather coarse plants, they are useful in dry parts of the garden or in areas that call for strong, stark plants.
CULTIVATION: Grow in full sun and for best results plant in reasonably fertile, moisture-retentive yet well-drained soil. Plants will tolerate poorer soils provided drainage is good. Propagate from seed sown as soon as it is ripe.

Oldenburgia grandis
syn. *Oldenburgia arbuscula*

This evergreen shrub has erect, sparsely branched woody stems, and large leaves that are stiff, oblong, oval and glossy green with prominent mid-veins. Its flowerheads are up to 4 in (10 cm) across with purple and white ray florets. It reaches a height and spread of 6 ft (1.8 m). **ZONES 9–11.**

OLEA
OLIVE

There are about 20 species in this genus, all long-lived, evergreen trees from Africa, Asia and Australasia. They have leathery, narrow to broad leaves and tiny, off-white flowers which are followed by the fruits, known botanically as drupes. The important species is the common olive *(Olea europaea)* which, in its many cultivars, is the source of olive oil. Since ancient times it has been cultivated around the Mediterranean for its nourishing oil-rich fruit. The fruits are too bitter to be eaten fresh; they must be treated with lye (sodium hydroxide) before being pickled or preserved in their own oil. The wood of the olive tree is prized for carving and turning.
CULTIVATION: Generally these plants require a mild climate, but the winters need to be sufficiently cool to induce flowering, while the summers must be long and hot to ensure development and growth of the fruits. Although olives can survive on poor soils, better cropping will result if the trees are given well-drained, fertile loam where ample moisture is available when the fruits are forming. Propagate from seed in fall (autumn), from heel cuttings in winter or from suckers.

Olea europaea
COMMON OLIVE

Olea europaea is a tree of wide distribution in Africa, Arabia and Himalayan Asia. The cultivated olive, ***O. e.* subsp. *europaea*,** is believed to have derived from smaller-fruited plants thousands of years ago. A slow grower to about 30 ft (9 m), it is very long lived, to compensate for its not coming into full bearing until it is at least 10 years old. Its picturesque habit, rough, gray bark and gray-green leaves, touched with silver on their undersides, make it a beautiful sight.
O. e.* subsp. *africana has pea-sized black fruit and glossy dark green leaves, brown on the undersides. It makes a handsome small shade tree with a thick, gnarled trunk, but seeds itself so profusely as to

Olea europaea subsp. *europaea*

Olea europaea subsp. *europaea*

become a problem weed in subtropical climates. **ZONES 8–11.**

OLEARIA
DAISY BUSH

Indigenous to Australia and New Zealand, this genus consists of 130 or more species of evergreen shrubs and small trees. The plants are characterized by daisy-like flowerheads which can be white, cream, blue, lavender, purple or pink and which appear from spring to fall (autumn).
CULTIVATION: *Olearia* species need full sun and fertile, well-drained soil; many species are tolerant of salt, wind and atmospheric pollution. Many species with dense foliage make excellent shrubs for hedging, particularly if pruned hard after flowering to encourage growth. Propagate from seed or cuttings in summer.

Olearia arborescens
TREE DAISY

In summer, this many-branched, spreading, tree-like shrub bears white, daisy-like flowerheads in panicles at the ends of the branches. It has oval, serrated leaves and grows to 15 ft (4.5 m) tall and 10 ft (3 m) wide. It is native to New Zealand. **ZONES 8–10.**

Olea europaea subsp. *africana*

Olearia argophylla

Oldenburgia grandis

Olearia argophylla
MUSK TREE

Deriving its name from the strong musk-like scent of its stems, this species can make a low-branched tree of more than 50 ft (15 m) tall in its native southern Australian forests, with a trunk up to 3 ft (1 m) in diameter. The large leaves have silvery undersides. The small flowerheads are creamy white and are held in long terminal clusters. It grows well in a part-shaded position. **ZONES 8–9.**

Olearia avicenniifolia
AKEAKE

This New Zealand species prefers well-drained soil and constant moisture during dry spells. It grows to a height of 12 ft (3.5 m) and has arching branches spreading from an erect stem. The leaves are an intense green with a white downy underside and the fragrant, white flowerheads are borne in profusion. Remove spent flowers to prolong flowering during summer. **ZONES 8–10.**

Olearia phlogopappa

Olearia ilicifolia

Olearia cheesemanii

Olearia macrodonta

Olearia cheesemanii
STREAMSIDE TREE DAISY

This evergreen spreading shrub or small tree from lowland stream banks in New Zealand is multi-branched with rounded, glossy green leaves with a downy undersurface. It has a profusion of white flowerheads that completely cover the plant in mid-spring. This species prefers a moist soil, needs some protection and is affected by dry conditions but resists frost. It reaches a height of 10 ft (3 m) and a spread of 6 ft (1.8 m). **ZONES 8–11.**

Olearia ilicifolia
MOUNTAIN HOLLY, HAKEKE

This species earns both its botanical and common names from the resemblance of its leaves to those of the holly, *Ilex aquifolium*. It is a 10 ft (3 m) daisy bush with a rounded crown made up of stiff, dull, grayish green leaves with undulating margins. This is one of the few species in this genus whose white flowers are fragrant. From New Zealand, it prefers light soils and a protected position. **ZONES 8–10.**

Olearia macrodonta

This New Zealand shrub has 2–4 in (5–10 cm) long, somewhat glossy, holly-like leaves. They are deep green above with grayish white hairs below. The flowerheads are white and yellow in the middle and the bush blooms heavily from early summer. It grows to about 6 ft (1.8 m) in cultivation; if necessary, trim to shape after flowering. **ZONES 8–10.**

Olearia × *mollis* 'Zennorensis'

A hybrid between the New Zealand species *Olearia ilicifolia* and *O. laeunesa*, this shrub reaches a height of 6 ft (1.8 m) and bears many clusters of white flowers in spring. It has narrow, dark olive-green leaves with whitish, downy undersides. **ZONES 8–10.**

Olearia nummulariifolia

Olearia nummulariifolia comes from subalpine mountain areas of New Zealand and is distinguished by its tiny leaves, dark green above and densely white or yellowish hairs on the undersides. During summer, it bears fragrant cream to pale yellow solitary flowerheads. It reaches a height of 10 ft (3 m) with a dense, many-branched form. ***Olearia nummulariifolia* var. *cymbifolia*** is a form with slightly larger leaves, but with their edges curled under and almost touching beneath. **ZONES 8–9.**

Olearia paniculata

Olearia paniculata
AKIRAHO

Native to New Zealand, *Olearia paniculata* can grow to 20 ft (6 m), but is more usually seen as a shrub half that height. The bark is coarsely grooved and the pale yellow-green, wavy-edged leaves are grayish white on the undersides and up to 2½ in (6 cm) long. The clustered, creamy white flowerheads appear in fall (autumn) and, while lacking conspicuous ray florets, they are pleasantly scented. This species is tolerant of exposed coastal positions and can be planted as a windbreak or clipped hedge. **ZONES 9–11.**

Olearia phlogopappa
syn. ***Olearia gunniana***
DUSTY DAISY BUSH

This 6–10 ft (1.8–3 m) high, erect shrub from southeastern Australia bears numerous white flowerheads up to 1 in (25 mm) across in late spring; in some selected forms they are mauve-blue or purplish. The oblong leaves are grayish green, under 2 in (5 cm) long with serrated margins. Its height makes it an effective screen or windbreak for seaside gardens or parks. Prune hard or it can become very straggly. **ZONES 8–10.**

Olearia pimeleoides

This evergreen shrub is native to eastern and southern Australia, and has erect stems and densely crowded branches. The leaves are very small, gray-green and rounded. The solitary flowerheads are pure white with few ray florets, and appear in profusion in spring. It reaches a height of 5 ft (1.5 m) and a spread of 6 ft (1.8 m). **ZONES 8–10.**

Olearia × *scilloniensis*

This dense, upright to rounded hybrid originated in Tresco in the Scilly Isles as a cross between the southeastern Australian species *Olearia lirata* and *O. phlogopappa*. Small white flowers are borne in spring. It grows to a height and spread of 6 ft (1.8 m). **ZONES 8–10.**

Olearia semidentata

This rounded shrub to 12 ft (3.5 m) tall comes from the Chatham Islands off eastern New Zealand. It has solitary flowerheads with purple centers and lilac ray florets, and small, white-felted, lance-shaped, gray-green leaves. **ZONES 8–9.**

Olearia 'Talbot de Malahide'

This hybrid of *Olearia avicenniifolia*, sometimes sold as *O. albida*, makes a

Olearia × *scilloniensis*

Olearia pimeleoides

Olearia × *scilloniensis*

Omphalodes cappadocica

dense, bushy shrub of up to 10 ft (3 m) with a spread of 15 ft (4.5 m). It is clothed in dark green, leathery, oval leaves with silvery undersides. Its fragrant, creamy white flowerheads appear in late summer in large, showy clusters. It is one of the best of the genus for coastal plantings in cooler climates. **ZONES 8–9.**

Olearia tomentosa

This rather short-lived species is usually under 3 ft (1 m) tall with fuzzy, olive-green leaves. In spring and summer, it bears graceful erect panicles of white to pale blue-mauve flowerheads, the ray florets darker on the reverse. *Olearia tomentosa* comes from New South Wales, Australia. **ZONES 9–11.**

Olearia traversii

Endemic to the Chatham Islands off eastern New Zealand, this species has a pale, furrowed bark. Its $2\frac{1}{2}$ in (6 cm) oval leaves are deep glossy green above with fine, grayish white hairs below. It can grow to 20 ft (6 m), but is often seen as a 6 ft (1.8 m) high, trimmed hedge, for which it is ideal especially in coastal areas. Despite producing numerous cream flowerheads in summer, it is primarily a foliage plant. **ZONES 8–10.**

OLNEYA

DESERT IRONWOOD

The single species of small, prickly evergreen tree in this legume genus comes from the deserts of southwestern North America. It has pinnate leaves with small leaflets, and short sprays of pinkish pea-flowers form in the axils.
CULTIVATION: Grow in any moderately fertile, very well-drained soil in full sun. Although tolerant of the odd light frosts, it will not live through extended freezes. In the wild, this tree grows in desert washes where its roots can reach underground water. A good choice for arid-area gardens. Propagate from seed.

Olneya tesota

A tough evergreen, the ironwood gets its name from its very heavy heartwood. Reaching 25–30 ft (8–9 m) tall with a rounded canopy, it is at its best in early summer when covered with pinkish lavender blossoms $\frac{1}{2}$ in (12 mm) long.

Omphalodes cappadocica

Old leaves drop shortly after flowering, but are quickly replaced with a new crop. **ZONES 9–10.**

OMALANTHUS

These evergreen shrubs and small trees, from Australia and the Asian tropics, are grown for their heart-shaped leaves which turn bright red, one by one, as they age. Their tiny yellowish flowers are borne in tassel-like, terminal clusters without petals. In the warm-temperate areas of the east coast of Australia, they tend to appear as spontaneous seedlings in gardens near bushland and are ideal pioneer plants for a rainforest-type garden.
CULTIVATION: They are not long lived, but after about 5 years will usually have self-seeded. They prefer a shaded site with moist, well-drained soil. Prune to shape if necessary, and propagate from seed or cuttings if self-seeded plants are not available.

Omalanthus populifolius

BLEEDING HEART TREE, QUEENSLAND POPLAR

This large shrub or small tree grows rapidly to around 12 ft (3.5 m) with erect stems, but becomes spreading and rounded with age. The heart-shaped leaves are up to 5 in (12 cm) wide. Small purple capsules follow the flowers, which are borne in spring to summer. This species is a rewarding indoor plant. **ZONES 10–12.**

OMPHALODES

NAVELWORT

From Europe, Asia and Mexico, this genus consists of 28 species of forget-me-not–like annuals and perennials that are either evergreen or semi-evergreen. These plants make excellent ground covers, and they are most suited to rock gardens.
CULTIVATION: These plants prefer shade or part-shade with moist but well-drained soil (except for *Omphalodes linifolia*, which prefers a sunny position). They are mostly frost hardy. Propagate from seed in spring or by division in fall (autumn).

Olearia traversii

Omphalodes cappadocica

This spreading perennial from Turkey has creeping underground stems. It produces numerous sprays of flat, bright purple-blue flowers in spring that arise from clumps of densely hairy, oval to heart-shaped leaves that are found at the base of the plant. This plant reaches a height of 6–8 in (15–20 cm) and a spread of 10 in (25 cm) and is fully frost hardy. **'Cherry Ingram'** is a vigorous grower to 10 in (25 cm) in height with purplish blue flowers. **'Starry Eyes'** has relatively big flowers, with each blue petal edged in white giving a starry effect. **ZONES 6–9.**

Omphalodes linifolia

VENUS' NAVELWORT

A fairly fast-growing annual from south-western Europe, this species has leaves that are lance-shaped, upright and gray-green in color. The flowers are produced in profusion during summer, and are very small, slightly scented and white, sometimes tinged with blue. This plant reaches a height of 6–12 in (15–30 cm) and a spread of 10 in (25 cm). **ZONES 7–9.**

Omphalodes verna

BLUE-EYED MARY, CREEPING FORGET-ME-NOT

This semi-evergreen thrives in shady conditions. During spring, it produces long, loose sprays of flat, bright blue flowers with white eyes. This plant has heart-shaped, mid-green leaves that form clumps. It reaches a height and spread of 8 in (20 cm). **ZONES 6–9.**

ONCIDIUM

This is a huge and varied genus of orchids (more than 450 species) from Central and South America, allied to *Odontoglossum* and *Miltonia* (although different in appearance) and able to be crossed with them to give odontocidiums and such multi-generic hybrids as *Wilsonara*. The species usually grown are epiphytes, and vary in their temperature requirements according to species (or parentage); they can be cool, intermediate or warm growing.
CULTIVATION: They all like light shade and only a short winter rest, an open, coarse potting mix and high humidity; most species intensely dislike being over-watered. In the wild, many have a

Omphalodes cappadocica 'Cherry Ingram'

Omphalodes cappadocica 'Starry Eyes'

Olearia tomentosa

tendency to climb up their host tree, and are best potted with a slab of tree fern trunk to which it can cling. In humid subtropical regions, some species are easily established outdoors on trunks and branches of corky barked trees such as jacarandas. They can be propagated by division in spring.

Oncidium varicosum

This species from Brazil is typical of a large group that bears small flowers in large, branched sprays which dance in the slightest breeze. The most prominent feature of each flower is the brilliant yellow labellum, the other parts being small and brownish. The flowering season runs from spring to fall (autumn). The flowers are popular with florists, as the airy sprays last for weeks in water. **ZONES 10–11.**

Onopordum acanthium

Oncidium varicosum

ONCOBA

Tropical and southern Africa is the natural home of this genus of slow-growing, spiny, evergreen trees. In the wild, some species may reach 70 ft (21 m) tall, but in a garden 20 ft (6 m) is more common. Although not widely cultivated outside their native region, the trees are attractive and may be found in subtropical botanic gardens. The flowers can be white, yellow or light red and are followed by globular, gourd-like fruits.
CULTIVATION: These trees need shelter from strong winds and a warm, sunny position to flower. They prefer moist, well-drained soil with a generous application of mulch. Propagate from seed or cuttings in summer and fall (autumn).

Oncoba spinosa
SNUFF-BOX TREE

This species from southeastern Africa has large camellia-like, fragrant white flowers with showy, yellow stamens and glossy serrated leaves. These, together with the roots of the tree, are used for medicinal purposes in Africa. Its golden-yellow fruit are $2\frac{1}{2}$ in (6 cm) in diameter and contain an edible, though rather unpalatable, pulp. The hard shells will last indefinitely and are used for rattles and snuff containers. The trunk and branches are armed with 2 in (5 cm) long spines. **ZONES 10–12.**

ONIXOTIS
WATERFLOWER, DIPIDAX

This is a genus of 2 species of winter-growing, early spring-blooming bulbs from South Africa, each shoot with 1 or 2 erect, rush-like leaves about 18 in (45 cm) tall. The flower stems are sheathed by the leaf bases and each stem bears many starry flowers over a long season starting in late winter or early spring.
CULTIVATION: Plant bulbs in fall (autumn) in pots or garden beds. In nature, these bulbs are found in seasonally wet places, often standing in water and must be kept well watered from the time growth begins until flowering finishes. If growing in pots, stand the pot in a saucer of water. Full sun is essential and although the plants will tolerate the odd light frost, in cold areas they should be grown in a cool greenhouse. Keep the bulbs as dry as possible over summer; potted bulbs can be stored dry in their pots.

Onixotis triquetra

Oncoba spinosa

Onixotis triquetra

This is the most commonly seen species and a thick clump makes a very attractive potted display. It is also a good choice for the wet soil beside ponds so long as the bulbs are dried out after bloom. Flowers are starry, white, usually with maroon centers, although there is a pure white form. **ZONES 9–11.**

ONOCLEA
SENSITIVE FERN

The single species in this genus is a deciduous fern from eastern North America and temperate East Asia. It very rapidly colonizes in wet conditions. The long-stalked fronds are crowded onto creeping rhizomes and in spring are all sterile, with broad thin segments; later in the season, more finely divided spore-bearing or fertile fronds are produced.
CULTIVATION: This fully frost-hardy fern thrives in both sunny and shady conditions in moist, fertile, acidic soil. Fronds should be removed as they begin to die off, which they will do at the first sign of frost. Propagate from ripe spores or by division in fall (autumn) or winter.

Onoclea sensibilis

This deciduous, water-loving fern is quick spreading. The sterile bipinnate fronds are large and wide, while the fertile fronds look like a small group of green balls growing on the leaf stalk. It is suitable for cool climates. **ZONES 4–10.**

ONOPORDUM
syn. *Onopordon*

Found naturally in Europe, North Africa and western Asia, this is a genus of about 40 species of large biennial thistles. They have a basal rosette of large, gray-green, lightly felted leaves, deeply toothed, with a spine at the tip of each tooth. The flowerheads are of typical thistle form: globose with a dense tuft of purple florets at the top and covered in spiny bracts. They are borne at the top of branched stems up to 10 ft (3 m) tall, and mature in mid-summer. On drying, they release downy seeds. In the first year the plants form an attractive foliage clump with a few flowerheads. In the second year they grow rapidly to full height, flower heavily then die.
CULTIVATION: Onopordums are easily cultivated in any well-drained soil in full sun with shelter from strong winds. Offsets and seedlings often naturally replace spent plants. They are frost hardy and are propagated from seed.

Oncoba spinosa

Onopordum acanthium
SCOTCH THISTLE, COTTON THISTLE

Despite its common name, it is doubtful that this European and west Asian species is a true native of Scotland or indeed of the British Isles, but it is the thistle usually regarded as the one shown on the Scottish royal emblem. It has a thick, downy stem with many wing-like ridges on its numerous branches. Its leaves are large and also downy, with wavy, sharply prickly edges. The flowers appear in late summer and fall (autumn) and are light purple in color. It reaches a height of up to 10 ft (3 m) and a spread of 6 ft (1.8 m) or more. **ZONES 6–10.**

ONOSMA

This genus comprises 150 species of semi-evergreen biennials, perennials and subshrubs, allied to the comfreys *(Symphytum)*, cultivated particularly for their gracefully pendent, tubular flowers. The densely tufted leaves are tongue-like with rather stiff, prickly hairs. Native to the Mediterranean region, they are most useful in rock gardens and along banks.
CULTIVATION: They are moderately frost hardy. Full sun is essential, although in warmer climates some shade must be provided for them to flourish. They prefer well-drained soil and dislike wet summers. They can be propagated from cuttings in summer or from seed in fall (autumn).

Onosma alborosea

This semi-evergreen perennial is covered with fine hairs that may be an irritant to some people. The drooping tubular flowers open as white and then turn pink and appear for a long period during summer. Clump forming, it reaches a height of 6–12 in (15–30 cm) and spread of 8 in (20 cm). **ZONES 7–9.**

Onosma tauricum
GOLDEN DROP

Nodding spikes of pale yellow flowers are borne on this 12 in (30 cm) tall perennial. The erect stems are sparsely branched and the lower surfaces of the leaves have minute tufts of short, spreading hairs. **ZONES 6–9.**

ONYCHIUM

CLAW FERN

This genus of about 6 small, lacy-leafed ferns is from tropical and subtropical regions of Asia and Africa. They spread by creeping rhizomes and produce triangular fronds that are very finely divided. These pretty ferns make a good ground cover in bright, moist shade.

CULTIVATION: In frost-free or near frost-free areas, grow in moist, leafy-rich soil in dappled shade. Where winters are cold, raise in pots in a greenhouse kept above freezing point. In all areas, give more water as the weather warms, decreasing as winter approaches. Plants can be kept near dry in winter, but may lose some leaves, especially in cooler areas.

Onychium japonicum

CARROT FERN

Native to Japan, this is a vigorous, low-growing fern that spreads widely, sometimes rampantly, by thin rhizomes that run across or just beneath the soil surface. Fronds are smooth, triangular and about 6 in (15 cm) long. In frost-free gardens, it is best contained within a wide, shallow pot. **ZONES 9–11.**

OPHIOPOGON

MONDO GRASS, SNAKEBEARD, LILYTURF

This genus contains 50 or so species of evergreen perennials from eastern Asia. They are valued for their attractive, long-lived clumps of grass-like foliage springing from underground rhizomes. They are not grasses but lilies, allied to lily-of-the-valley *(Convallaria)*. The summer flowers are small and can be white or blue through to purple. The berry-like fruits each contain one seed. They are trouble-free plants that will last indefinitely, providing an attractive ground cover that effectively suppresses leaves.

CULTIVATION: These plants are mostly fairly frost hardy and will tolerate sun or part-shade in moist, well-drained soil. Propagate by division of clumps in spring, or from seed in fall (autumn). To establish a quick ground cover, plant divisions at 8 in (20 cm) intervals.

Ophiopogon jaburan

WHITE LILYTURF

This Japanese species has rather loose, spreading tufts of deep green leaves up to ½ in (12 mm) wide. It is popular with landscape gardeners for ground cover in shaded areas, and grows well under deciduous trees. It is sometimes grown as a pot plant indoors in shade and can grow to a height of up to 24 in (60 cm). Loose, drooping sprays of bell-shaped, white flowers are borne in early summer, followed by shiny deep blue berries. **'Vittatus'** (syn. 'Variegatus') is more commonly grown than the plain green form and has leaves variably striped cream or butter yellow. **ZONES 7–11.**

Ophiopogon japonicus

syn. *Liriope japonica*

MONDO GRASS

This fine-leafed species is native to Japan and Korea. The dark green recurving foliage arises from deep rhizomes, spreading to form dense, soft mats up to about 8 in (20 cm) deep. Pale purple flowers are hidden among the leaves in mid-summer, followed by bright blue, pea-sized fruit. **'Kyoto Dwarf'** is only 2–4 in (5–10 cm) high, with very short leaves. **ZONES 8–11.**

Ophiopogon planiscapus 'Nigrescens'

syn. *Ophiopogon planiscapus* 'Ebony Night'

BLACK MONDO GRASS

This cultivar is grown particularly for its distinctive purple-black rather stiff leaves about ¼ in (6 mm) wide which form slow-growing, sparse clumps. Its lilac flowers appear in clusters along the flowering stem in summer. These are followed by black fruit. It reaches a height of 10 in (25 cm) and a spread of 12 in (30 cm). *Ophiopogon planiscapus* is native to Japan. **ZONES 6–10.**

OPHRYS

This genus of 30 species of tuberous orchids is found naturally in Europe, North Africa and western Asia. They have broad, oval leaves forming basal rosettes from which arise erect flower spikes up to about 24 in (60 cm) tall depending on the species. The flowers are rarely much over 1 in (25 mm) wide but have a lower lip (labellum) often as large as the rest of the flower. The base color is most often green, yellow or pink with the lip a contrasting, usually darker, color. All flowers in this genus mimic insects to effect pollination.

CULTIVATION: They are very difficult to cultivate; some success may be had in a leafy, moist, gritty, well-drained soil in part-shade. Propagation is equally difficult and seed sown in sterile flasks or tissue culture is the best option. Most species are quite frost hardy.

Ophrys apifera

BEE ORCHID

Widely distributed from the UK to the Mediterranean and North Africa, this orchid grows in grasslands and forest margins. They are 8–18 in (20–45 cm) tall with 5 to 9 broadly lance-shaped leaves and an inflorescence of 2 to 10 flowers 1 in (25 mm) across. It flowers in spring and summer. **ZONES 7–9.**

OPHTHALMOPHYLLUM

Sometimes included in *Conophytum*, the 20 or so species of *Ophthalmophyllum* are miniature, ground-dwelling, succulents from dry parts of southwestern Africa. In appearance, they closely resemble *Lithops*, with fused leaf-pairs looking just like pebbles, except for the translucent 'windows' at the apex which allow light into the plants' photosynthetic tissues.

CULTIVATION: Grow them in gritty, very well-drained soil in full sun. In cool climates, do not water in winter; resume watering when new leaves emerge, but always sparingly. Propagate from seed or by division of clumps.

Onosma tauricum

Ophthalmophyllum longum

syn. *Conophytum longum*

This tiny, clump-forming succulent is from South Africa's Little Namaqualand Desert. Each leaf pair, less than 1½ in (35 mm) high and 1 in (25 mm) wide, is brownish green with translucent dark green tips. It produces white, daisy-like flowers in spring. **ZONES 10–11.**

OPLISMENUS

BASKET GRASS

The 6 species in this grass genus are native to shady areas in the tropics and subtropics in both hemispheres. The genus name is derived from the Greek *hoplismos* meaning armed, referring to the plants' bristle-tipped spikelets. They are quick-growing trailing plants, with wiry stems rooting at the nodes and shorter, broader leaves than most grasses. They make useful specimens for hanging baskets and window boxes.

CULTIVATION: These frost-tender grasses flourish in well-drained, moderately moist soil. They respond well to liquid fertilizer and a humid atmosphere and will thrive in a sheltered position in sun or part-shade. Tip prune to promote bushiness. Propagate from seed or cuttings, or by division.

Oplismenus hirtellus

Oplismenus hirtellus is an evergreen perennial grass of wide distribution in the tropics with very fine wiry stems. The leaves are lance-shaped with wavy margins. This plant produces flower spikelets that are inconspicuous and appear in spring and summer. Preferring part-shade, it reaches a height of 8 in (20 cm) with an indefinite spread. **'Variegatus'** is the form usually cultivated, with white-striped leaves often tinged pink. **ZONES 10–12.**

OPUNTIA

PRICKLY PEAR, CHOLLA

This is the largest and most widespread genus of cacti, numbering more than 200 species and occurring in the wild from southern Canada almost to the southern tip of South America, as well as the West Indies and Galapagos Islands. They range from tiny prostrate plants with tuberous roots to trees over 30 ft (9 m) tall. The branches are constricted at regular intervals to form 'joints' that may be broad and flattened or cylindrical and sometimes covered in tubercles. All

Ophiopogon japonicus 'Kyoto Dwarf'

Ophiopogon japonicus

Ophiopogon planiscapus 'Nigrescens'

have small, fleshy leaves at the growing tips that usually fall off soon after they appear. Most species have sharp spines (sometimes barbed), as well as small bristles that are extremely hard to remove from the skin, so position these plants away from areas where children or animals play. The flowers are generally yellow or red, sometimes quite showy, followed by edible fruits (prickly pears), which range from green to yellow to red. Several species have become serious pests with some being declared noxious weeds in some warmer countries. The spread of *Opuntia stricta* in Australia and South Africa was eventually checked by biological control, using the cochineal insect and the cactoblastus moth.

CULTIVATION: These plants thrive in hot, dry conditions in moderately fertile, gritty, humus-rich, well-drained soil and full sun, but many species adapt to less optimal conditions indoors and can tolerate much neglect. Propagate from seed or detached joints in spring or summer. The cultivation of all or some of the species is prohibited in certain countries.

Opuntia bigelovii
TEDDY BEAR CHOLLA

In Mexico and southwestern USA, 'cholla' (pronounced hol-ya) is the name given to the opuntias with cylindrical joints, usually very spiny. This 3–5 ft (1–1.5 m) tall shrub has its elongated joints densely covered in vicious yellow spines—'teddy bear' is used in an ironic sense, as it appears woolly only from a distance. Native to southern California, Arizona and Baja California, it bears pale green to yellow flowers striped with lavender. **ZONES 9–11.**

Opuntia ficus-indica
INDIAN FIG CACTUS

This species, native to Mexico, has been cultivated in Mediterranean countries and India for centuries for its delicious fruit. It grows to 10–18 ft (3–5.5 m) tall and wide, each branch made up of several flat, oval segments that may be almost the size of a tennis racquet head, and bears rather attractive yellow flowers in early summer. These develop into the oval, red or orange fruit 2–3 in (5–8 cm)

Opuntia imbricata

in diameter, their skin studded with bristles which must be carefully stripped (wearing gloves) before the white sweet pulp can be enjoyed. Spineless cultivars exist, but connoisseurs insist they are not as sweet as the prickly ones. **ZONES 9–11.**

Opuntia macrocentra

Opuntia macrocentra

Opuntia marnieriana

Opuntia imbricata
CHAIN-LINK CACTUS, TREE CHOLLA

From Mexico and southwestern USA, this cactus can eventually grow to 10 ft (3 m), with a tree-like form. It has long, cylindrical branch segments with very prominent tubercles and brownish white spines about 1 in (25 mm) long. Its flowers are yellowish, pink or red and are followed by rounded, spineless, yellow fruit. **ZONES 8–11.**

Opuntia macrocentra
syn. ***Opuntia violacea* var. *macrocentra***
PURPLE PRICKLY PEAR

Native to southern USA and Mexico, this low-growing cactus has purple-tinged segments that are almost circular in outline and about 6 in (15 cm) wide, with blackish spines up to 2½ in (6 cm) long. It grows 2–6 ft (0.6–1.8 m) in height. Coming from very hot, dry areas, it needs full sun. Medium-sized yellow flowers appear in summer, followed by purple berries in late summer and fall (autumn). **ZONES 9–11.**

Opuntia marnieriana

This species, native to Mexico, was named after the noted plant collector Juan Marnier-Lapostelle, whose family created the liqueur Grand Marnier. It is a

Opuntia bigelovii

low shrub with bluish green flattened segments. Orange-red, funnel-shaped flowers, which grow about 3 in (8 cm) long, are borne in summer. Large purple berries follow in late summer and fall (autumn). **ZONES 9–11.**

Opuntia microdasys
BUNNY EARS, DWARF PRICKLY PEAR

The crowded branches of this small cactus from Mexico, to only about 24 in (60 cm) tall, consist of flattened, oval, pale to mid-green pads densely dotted with small tufts of tiny golden spines. Each pad or segment is 3–5 in (8–12 cm) wide; in spring and summer they produce bright yellow flowers about 2 in (5 cm) across. These may be followed by reddish fruit more than 1 in (25 mm) in diameter, but these are rarely seen in cultivation. ***Opuntia microdasys* var. *albispina*** has clusters of white spines on

Opuntia microdasys var. *albispina*

Opuntia microdasys

darker green pads. Its flowers are also a paler yellow. Both are widely grown as pot plants, but the tiny spines stick into the skin at the slightest touch. **ZONES 8–11.**

Opuntia stricta
syn. *Opuntia inermis*

This species, which forms large colonies, was one of the plants that over-ran pastoral land in subtropical eastern Australia. Native to the Caribbean, it forms pale green, thin, oblong segments 4–8 in (10–20 cm) long. Yellow funnel-shaped flowers appear in summer, followed by purplish fruit. The plants have a rather sprawling habit, branching from the base and usually only 3 ft (1 m) or less tall. The pads take root wherever they fall. **ZONES 9–12.**

Opuntia tunicata

A native of Mexico and southwestern USA, this is one of the 'cholla' species resembling *Opuntia bigelovii*, growing to 24 in (60 cm) high, the cylindrical joints densely clothed in long spines which have papery yellowish sheaths. In summer, it produces cup-shaped flowers about $2\frac{1}{2}$ in (6 cm) long and green, globular fruit that last until fall (autumn). **ZONES 9–11.**

Opuntia verschaffeltii

This dwarf opuntia from Bolivia and Argentina makes an irregular, spreading subshrub only about 6 in (15 cm) high, the branches consisting of globular joints under $1\frac{1}{2}$ in (35 mm) long, although in cultivation these often elongate. They bear fleshy, narrow leaves that may persist, and sparse long spines. From spring to summer, it produces cup-shaped, red or orange flowers whose size is out of proportion to the small joints; these are followed by round, spineless red fruit. **ZONES 9–11.**

Opuntia vulgaris

Orbea variegata

Opuntia vestita
COTTON POLE CACTUS, OLD MAN OPUNTIA

This unusual species from Bolivia is usually found only in specialist cacti collections. Growing to only about 18 in (45 cm) high, it has unjointed cylindrical stems about 1 in (25 mm) thick, covered in long white hairs and with long fleshy leaves that may persist. Dark red flowers about $1\frac{1}{2}$ in (35 mm) wide are borne in summer. **ZONES 9–11.**

Opuntia vulgaris
SMOOTH PRICKLY PEAR, BARBADOS FIG

This tree-like species was once widely planted to feed the cochineal insect which produces a red dye. A native of Brazil, Uruguay and Argentina, it is an erect shrub or small tree to 20 ft (6 m) tall with elongated but thin, flattened, glossy green joints with sparse yellowish brown spines. The 3 in (8 cm) flowers are golden yellow, sometimes tinged with red, and appear from summer to fall (autumn). **ZONES 9–11.**

ORBEA

This genus of about 20 species of curious creeping succulents is closely related to *Stapelia* and its species have often been placed in that genus. They occur wild in drier parts of southern and eastern Africa. They are low plants, usually forming a cluster of leafless, semi-erect stems armed with ridges of soft fleshy spines. A milky sap exudes from cut or broken stems. In summer and early fall (autumn), they produce flat, star-shaped flowers that are spotted or patterned and smell faintly of rotting meat in order to attract the flies which pollinate them.
CULTIVATION: Grow in full sun in sandy or gritty, very well-drained soil. Where summers are very hot and dry, the plants appreciate light shade in the afternoon. They do not require much water at any time of the year and outdoors will usually get by on rain. They are not frost hardy and in cold climates must be grown indoors, watering sparingly especially in winter. Propagate by cuttings, dried off for a few days before inserting in sand.

Opuntia vulgaris

Opuntia tunicata

Opuntia vestita

Orbignya cohune

Orbea variegata
syn. *Stapelia variegata*
TOAD CACTUS, STAR FLOWER, STARFISH FLOWER

Grown for its curious flowers, this South African succulent has much-branched, finger-shaped, creeping stems to 3 in (8 cm) tall with upturned ends; they are often marked with purple and have pointed tubercles in 4 rows. From summer to fall (autumn), striking starfish-shaped, individual flowers appear, with a kaleidoscopic pattern of reddish brown, yellow and purple. **ZONES 9–11.**

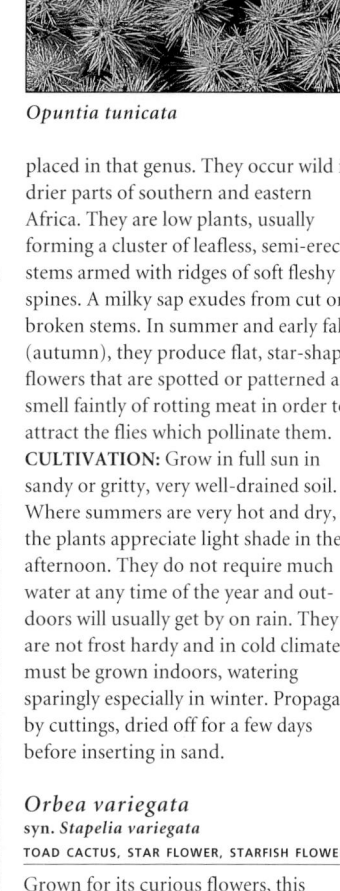

ORBIGNYA
BABASSU PALM

This genus, native to tropical America, occurs naturally in humid tropical forests as well as in more open habitats in high rainfall areas, though often with a distinct dry season. Some species are of commercial importance, the kernel oil being used in the manufacture of soap and margarine. These imposing, slow-growing palms with erect to arching pinnate fronds of great size require many years to produce an emergent trunk.
CULTIVATION: These plants need tropical conditions with high humidity, moist, well-drained soil and respond well to liquid fertilizer. Propagate from seed.

Orbignya cohune
COHUNE PALM

Native to Central America, this palm reaches a height of 50 ft (15 m) with a stout trunk. The plume-like fronds are up to 30 ft (9 m) long and the leaflets are dark green. The 5 ft (1.5 m) long inflorescence bears thousands of cream-colored flowers. The 3 in (8 cm) long fruit contain cohune oil, which is used commercially. **ZONES 11–12.**

O

Orchis militaris

Oreocereus celsianus

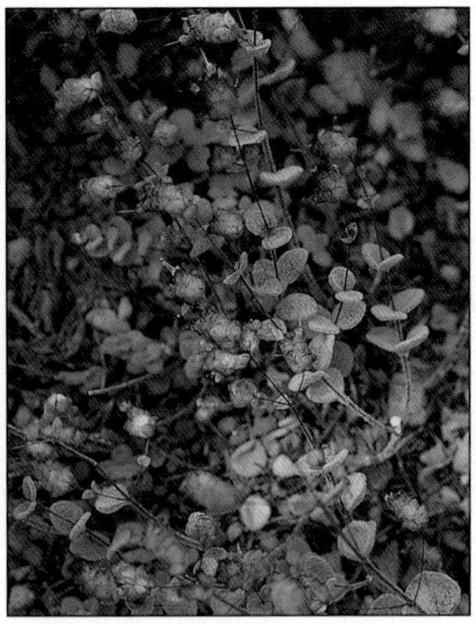

Origanum dictamnus

Origanum 'Barbara Tingey'

Origanum calcaratum

ORCHIS

MARSH ORCHID, MAY ORCHID

The medieval herbalists saw a resemblance between the paired tubers of these common European plants and the testicles of animals, hence the name *Orchis* (Greek for testicle); the genus gave its name to the huge plant family Orchidaceae and thence to the English word orchid, meaning any member of this family. *Orchis* consists of 35 species of deciduous, terrestrial orchids that have strong green leaves and bear tall spikes of small magenta or white flowers in early summer. Many of the more attractive members of the genus have been transferred to the genus *Dactylorhiza*.
CULTIVATION: *Orchis* plants prefer part-shaded positions and soil that is deep, rich and slightly limy. They dislike being disturbed so transplanting is best done when the tubers are fully grown, in fall (autumn). Propagation is by division.

Orchis mascula

EARLY PURPLE ORCHID

This species, which stands up to 18 in (45 cm) tall, is distributed widely through Europe in grasslands, pastures and open woodlands. It has glossy, tongue-shaped leaves about 3–6 in (8–15 cm) long with many dark purplish blotches. The flowering stem bears up to 20 flowers, each about 1 in (25 mm) long with an odor resembling cat's urine. This relatively common species flowers in spring and early summer. **ZONES 5–9.**

Orchis militaris

MILITARY ORCHID, SOLDIER ORCHID

This species, which grows to about 18 in (45 cm) tall, is widespread over most of Europe and eastward to the Caucasus and Russia, in grasslands and open woodlands. The 2 tubers give rise to unspotted leaves about 4–6 in (10–15 cm) long and an inflorescence of many purplish pink and white flowers, each about 1 in (25 mm) long. Flowering occurs in spring and summer. **ZONES 5–9.**

OREOCEREUS

syn. *Borzicactus*

The 6 species of small to medium-sized cacti in this genus all come from the Andes, hence the name *Oreocereus* (from the Greek *oros*, mountain, prefixed to the cactus genus *Cereus*). They branch mainly from the base and have few to many ribs, sometimes divided into tubercles, and bearing sparse to dense spines and sometimes long white hairs or dense wool. Flowers are narrow and trumpet-shaped, appearing from one side of the stem near the top, and are mostly red or pink.
CULTIVATION: These cacti require full sun and moderately fertile, humus-rich, very well-drained soil; water well in spring and summer, sparingly at other times. The taller species should not be encouraged to grow too quickly or they become unstable and unable to stand upright. Propagate in spring or summer from seed. They are frost tender.

Oreocereus celsianus

syns *Borzicactus celsianus, Pilocereus celsianus*

OLD MAN OF THE ANDES

Native to the Andes of Bolivia and northern Argentina, this slow-growing cactus reaches heights of up to 5 ft (1.5 m). The erect stems have 10 to 18 ribs and rust-colored spines, with long white hairs that completely cover the upper stems, hence the common name. Older specimens produce reddish pink summer flowers that close up at night. **ZONES 9–11.**

ORIGANUM

syn. *Majorana*

MARJORAM, OREGANO

Native to the Mediterranean region and temperate Asia, these perennials and subshrubs in the mint family have aromatic leaves and stalked spikes or heads of small tubular flowers with crowded, overlapping bracts. Some species are grown as culinary herbs, while others are grown for their decorative pink flowerheads. With arching or prostrate stems arising from vigorously spreading rhizomes, they make useful plants for trailing over rocks, banks and walls.
CULTIVATION: These plants like full sun and a moderately fertile, well-drained soil. Trim excess growth regularly and propagate from seed in spring or by root division in fall (autumn) or spring.

Origanum amanum

From the eastern Mediterranean, this dwarf evergreen subshrub has a rounded, compact habit. The long-tubed, pink or white flowers are funnel-shaped, appearing in spring and summer above the small heart-shaped, pale green leaves. An attractive rock-garden subject, it reaches a height and spread of 6–8 in (15–20 cm) and prefers dry atmospheric conditions. **ZONES 8–10.**

Origanum 'Barbara Tingey'

This cultivar of possible hybrid origin is another miniature subshrub with rounded, felty, blue-tinged leaves that are reddish purple beneath. In summer, pink flowers appear nestled in bracts which are green at first, but age to a purplish pink color. It grows 4–6 in (10–15 cm) tall, but spreads to at least 10–12 in (25–30 cm) across. **ZONES 7–9.**

Origanum calcaratum

This dense, shrubby perennial has heart-shaped to almost circular leaves densely clothed in white, woolly hairs. These help protect the plant from water loss during the hot, dry summers experienced on the islands of the Aegean Sea, where it occurs naturally. Small pink flowers are produced in summer, but this plant is more usually grown for its foliage. **ZONES 9–11.**

Origanum dictamnus

CRETAN DITTANY

This semi-prostrate shrub has arching branches clothed in aromatic, hairy, gray-white leaves. The heads of purple-pink flowers that appear in summer and fall (autumn) have inflated purplish bracts. This native of Crete is frost hardy and suitable for window boxes, hanging baskets and containers. It reaches a height of 6–12 in (15–30 cm) and a spread of 15 in (38 cm). **ZONES 7–9.**

Origanum × hybridum

This hybrid is a result of crossing *Origanum dictamnus* with *O. sipyleum*. **'Santa Cruz'** is a cultivar with dusky purple flowers held on stems well above the foliage. **ZONES 9–11.**

Origanum 'Kent Beauty'

This prostrate subshrub with low, arching stems is grown for its charming, almost globular heads of tubular pale pink flowers which peep from between darker pink and pale green bracts. The leaves are hairless and very pale green, almost circular in outline. Reaching a height of 6–8 in (15–20 cm), its habit makes it suitable to grow on a wall or spill over a ledge. **ZONES 8–10.**

Origanum laevigatum

This vigorous and ornamental species has spreading woody rhizomes and densely massed evergreen leaves, from which arise numerous flowering stems 18–24 in (45–60 cm) high. Tiny flowers with purple bracts create a cloud of lavender at the top of the stems all summer long, and provide nectar for bees and butterflies. An excellent filler

Origanum × hybridum 'Santa Cruz'

Origanum laevigatum

Ornithogalum montanum

Ornithogalum arabicum

for the perennial border as well as the herb garden, it also makes a delightful addition to dried flower arrangements. **'Hopleys'** and **'Herrenhausen'** are recent cultivars with richer flower color. ZONES 7–11.

Origanum libanoticum

From Lebanon, this 24 in (60 cm) tall species produces nodding spikes of quite large pink flowers with dull pink bracts in summer. ZONES 8–10.

Origanum majorana

syns *Majorana hortensis*, *Origanum hortensis*

SWEET MARJORAM

A highly aromatic plant up to 24 in (60 cm) high, marjoram originates in the Mediterranean, but has long been grown elsewhere in Europe for its sweet and spicy, small gray-green leaves. The tiny white flowers are borne in short spikes with very tightly packed bracts. The leaves are used fresh or dried for savory foods and are said to aid digestion. Marjoram has a special affinity with tomatoes and goes well with many meats. ZONES 7–10.

Origanum onites

syn. *Majorana onites*

FRENCH MARJORAM, POT MARJORAM

Origanum onites is a small, rounded, aromatic shrub that grows to around 18 in (45 cm) tall with wiry, hairy stems and bright green heart-shaped leaves. White or pale pink flowers are borne in clusters at the ends of the branches in late summer. A native of Sicily, this popular herb is used in Mediterranean cooking. Taller than the type, **'Aureum'** has golden-green foliage and pink flowers. ZONES 8–11.

Origanum pulchellum

Similar to *Origanum dictamnus*, this southwest Asian species has rose-colored flowers. The leaves are smaller than those of *O. dictamnus* and not as hairy. ZONES 7–9.

Origanum rotundifolium

A deciduous species from Turkey and the Caucasus, this subshrub with small, rounded green leaves reaches a height and spread of about 12 in (30 cm), spreading by rhizomes. It bears nodding spikes of white or pale pink flowers with inflated pale green bracts in late summer and early fall (autumn). ZONES 8–9.

Origanum vulgare

COMMON OREGANO, WILD MARJORAM

The common oregano has a sharper, more pungent flavor than marjoram. It has a sprawling habit and grows to 24 in (60 cm) high with dark green, oval leaves and small, white or pink flowers in summer. The leaves are used, fresh or dried, in many Mediterranean-inspired dishes. In Italy, oregano is used in pizza toppings and pasta dishes. **'Aureum'** has a less sprawling habit and bright greenish gold leaves. **'Thumble's Variety'** is a low, mound-forming selection with yellow-green leaves. ZONES 5–9.

ORNITHOGALUM

STAR-OF-BETHLEHEM

This large genus contains 80 or so species of spring- to summer-flowering bulbs native to Africa, Europe and western Asia. Star- to cup-shaped, mostly white and sometimes scented flowers are borne on short to tall stems. The leaves, which occasionally have a silver stripe down the center, are all basal. The sap may irritate the skin.

CULTIVATION: Marginally to moderately frost hardy, they are easy to grow. Plant bulbs in fall (autumn) or spring in well-drained soil. They like full sun but will need part-shade in warm areas. Keep the plants moist until the leaves begin to die off, and dry when dormant. Frost-tender species should be lifted in winter. They multiply quite freely and clumps should be divided every 1 to 2 years to prevent overcrowding. Propagate also from seed sown in fall or spring.

Origanum vulgare 'Thumble's Variety'

Ornithogalum arabicum

Flowering in early summer, this Mediterranean species is one of the most striking in flower. It carries as many as 15 scented white flowers up to 2 in (5 cm) across with large black ovaries in their centers. The basal leaves are strap-like and about 1 in (25 mm) wide. Reaching a height of 18 in (45 cm) or more, these plants prefer a sheltered position. They are often grown as pot plants so their climatic needs can be more easily met. ZONES 9–11.

Ornithogalum montanum

This species grows on open grassy slopes of southern Europe and south-western Asia. In cultivation, this spring-flowering plant thrives and displays an abundance of long-lasting, white, star-like flowers. The reverse of each petal is handsomely marked with a green stripe. Good drainage is essential if the plant is to survive winter conditions. It grows to a height of 8 in (20 cm); it is often short lived. ZONES 6–9.

Ornithogalum nutans

Occurring wild in waste ground in southern Europe and western Asia, this plant flowers in late spring and early summer. It will naturalize in similar conditions, preferring a semi-shaded situation and a poorish, well-drained soil. The nodding flowers with recurved green and white petals have a distinctive silvery sheen. The leaves are a deep green, channelled and arranged in an informal basal rosette. This species grows 12–24 in (30–60 cm) tall. ZONES 6–10.

Ornithogalum saundersiae

GIANT CHINCHERINCHEE

This species from South Africa is one of the tallest in the genus, growing to as much as 5 ft (1.5 m) tall. The long bare stem is topped by a flattish cluster of waxy, star-shaped, creamy white blooms about 1 in (25 mm) across with black to green centers. The basal leaves are glossy and strap-shaped up to 2 in (5 cm) wide. ZONES 9–11.

Origanum libanoticum

Origanum vulgare

Origanum rotundifolium

Origanum vulgare 'Aureum'

O

Ornithogalum thyrsoides
CHINCHERINCHEE

This South African species acquired the odd common name 'chincherinchee', which according to one dictionary is 'said to be imitative of the flower-stalks rubbing together in the wind'. The most ornamental member of the genus, it has dense clusters of up to 20 star- to cup-shaped white flowers borne on spikes about 18 in (45 cm) tall. The basal leaves are strap-shaped. As cut flowers they last for weeks, even out of water; the flowers absorb dye and bunches of them are sold in a range of colors. **ZONES 9–11.**

Ornithogalum umbellatum
COMMON STAR-OF-BETHLEHEM

The leaves of this frost-hardy, clump-forming perennial are mid-green with a central white stripe. The loose clusters of white flowers with green striping appear at the top of the 12 in (30 cm), erect stems in early summer and open only in sunshine. This species can become invasive. **ZONES 5–10.**

ORONTIUM
GOLDEN CLUB

The single species in this genus is an unusual member of the arum family from eastern USA. An aquatic perennial, it has thick rhizomes and broad spatulate leaves on long-stalked spadices of minute flowers surrounded by a membranous spathe that shrivels at an early stage.
CULTIVATION: This very frost-hardy plant will overwinter in any pond or slow-moving stream with water over 6 in (15 cm) deep that does not freeze solid. The roots need to be in soil, either in silt at the pond bottom or in tubs. The foliage is best in sun or morning shade. Propagate by breaking up the rhizome in late winter as dormancy finishes.

Orontium aquaticum

This species has simple, leathery leaves up to 10 in (25 cm) long that may be submerged, floating or held erect above the water surface. The leaves have metallic blue-green upper surfaces, purple undersides and stalks up to 15 in (38 cm) long. Flower spikes appear in summer and are short lived; the papery spathe is insignificant and quickly withers, but the bright yellow spadix, around 6 in (15 cm) long, is held above the surface on a long stem. **ZONES 7–9.**

ORPHIUM
STICKY FLOWER

The only species in this genus of the gentian family from southwestern South Africa is a small evergreen shrub, very soft stemmed and inclined to be short lived. It has pale green, smooth-edged and somewhat twisted leaves and bears very pretty flowers with 5 glossy, slightly sticky petals clustered at the branch tips.
CULTIVATION: Sticky flower is grown in subtropical gardens for its compact habit and long, summer display of flowers. Marginally frost hardy, plant in a sunny, frost-free site in well-drained but reasonably moist soil. Pinch out tips in spring to promote bushy growth. Propagate from cuttings in late summer.

Orthophytum navioides

Orthophytum gurkenii

Ornithogalum umbellatum

Orphium frutescens

Orphium frutescens

Growing to no more than 24 in (60 cm), this erect, soft-wooded shrub bears its 1 in (25 mm) pink-purple flowers towards the tips of the branches from late spring through summer. **ZONES 9–11.**

ORTHOPHYTUM

This bromeliad genus is endemic to eastern Brazil and consists of about 17 species, all terrestrial and forming rosettes of stiff, prickly edged leaves, spreading by stolons and sometimes forming extensive mats. The flowering stems may rise well above the leaf rosettes with interesting broad bracts, or the flowers may be in stemless clusters in the center of the rosette.
CULTIVATION: These plants are frost tender and should be grown in fertile, well-drained soil in full sun. Water moderately in the growing season and keep dry in winter. Propagate from seed in early spring. They are susceptible to aphids while flowering.

Orthophytum gurkenii

This curious bromeliad has purple-bronze leaves strikingly barred with rows of silvery scales. The erect flowering stem bears bracts like the leaves but broader, and the upper bracts have brilliant green bases the same color as the small tubular flowers. **ZONES 9–12.**

Orthophytum navioides

Found in the wild in rocky crevices, this species has long narrow leaves edged with very short, delicate spines. The white flowers are borne in a dense hemispherical cluster in the center of the rosette, the inner leaves turning deep reddish purple at flowering time. It is easy to grow but needs strong light. **ZONES 9–12.**

ORTHROSANTHUS

Found in the mountains of Central and South America and the sandy plains of southern Australia, the 7 species of this genus of the iris family are grass-like perennials with short, woody rhizomes and flattened fans of sword-shaped leaves up to 18 in (45 cm) long. Blue or

Orthrosanthus multiflorus

Orthrosanthus multiflorus

O

yellow 6-petalled flowers up to 2 in (5 cm) in diameter open in spring and summer. In some species, the flowers have dark veining. They are carried in clusters of 2 to 8 blooms on wiry stems. **CULTIVATION:** Plant in moist, well-drained soil in sun or part-shade. Light frosts are tolerated, but *Orthrosanthus* species are best grown in a mild, frost-free climate. They are often short lived. Propagate from seed or by division of the rhizomes in late winter.

Orthrosanthus multiflorus

This native of southwestern Australia makes an erect tufted plant with narrow, grass-like leaves and spikes of starry blue to purple flowers which appear in spring. It reaches a height of 24 in (60 cm) and a spread of 12 in (30 cm). **ZONES 9–10.**

ORYZA

RICE

Rice *(Oryza sativa)* is one of about 20 species of aquatic or swamp-dwelling, annual or perennial grasses in this genus, occurring wild in warmer parts of Africa, Asia and Australia. They have loose panicles of compressed flowering spikelets that ripen to edible grains. The only species to have been domesticated, rice is thought to have been cultivated in China for about 5,000 years. Today, almost all of East Asia is wholly dependent upon rice as a staple food.
CULTIVATION: Rice needs a long hot growing season and abundant water. The seeds are sown in nursery beds or trays; when about 6 in (15 cm) high, they are transplanted in spring to a well-fertilized level plot or 'paddy' which must be submerged under water about 2–4 in (5–10 cm) deep for a large part of the summer growing season. When the rice is ready to harvest, the water is drained from the field. For ornamental purposes, rice can be grown in pots that are submerged in shallow water in a sunny position near a water feature or pond. Mountain rice is grown in 'dry' conditions, but needs high rainfall.

Oryza sativa

This is an annual grass to about 3 ft (1 m) high with long flattened leaves and spikelets of flowers which produce yellow or brown seeds. **'Nigrescens'** is an ornamental form grown for its purplish colored leaves. **ZONES 9–12.**

OSBECKIA

This genus of 40 to 60 species of evergreen perennials, subshrubs and shrubs occurs wild in warmer parts of Asia, Africa and Australia. It belongs to the same family as the tibouchinas, which it resembles, although the leaves and flowers are smaller on most species. Like the tibouchinas, these plants are grown for their brightly colored flowers which can be pink, purple or red, appearing for long periods in spring and summer.
CULTIVATION: These plants are easily grown in tropical and subtropical climates in a sunny position. Soil should be light and friable, and well drained.

Oryza sativa

They dislike dry conditions and frost equally. Prune lightly in late winter to maintain density. Propagate from soft-tip cuttings taken during spring and placed in a sand and peat mixture in humid greenhouse conditions.

Osbeckia stellata

A native of Southeast Asia, this shrub has erect, freely branching stems and long, narrow leaves. The flowers are lilac-pink and appear in profusion in spring and summer. It requires a protected, shaded position in the garden, and reaches a height of 6 ft (1.8 m). **ZONES 9–12.**

OSCULARIA

This is a genus of only 2 species belonging to the large mesembryanthemum tribe of succulents; they are included by some authorities in the genus *Lampranthus.* Both species are low-growing, bushy succulents from South Africa that form dense carpets of bloom in spring and early summer. Both the flowers and the foliage are decorative and the small blooms are also fragrant.
CULTIVATION: Grow in full sun or part-shade in soil that drains freely. They are easily propagated from cuttings taken in spring or from ripe seed.

Oscularia caulescens

syn. ***Lampranthus deltoides***

An evergreen succulent native to the Cape region of South Africa, this is a spreading plant with small, grayish leaves. Tiny yellow, daisy-like flowers appear profusely in spring. **ZONES 9–11.**

OSMANTHUS

syn. ***Siphonosmanthus***

Except for one from the Caucasus region, all 30 or so species of evergreen shrubs and trees in this genus are native to the Himalayas, China and Japan. Several are prized for the fragrance of their flowers, which some consider the sweetest and most attractive of all flowers. The white or cream flowers of most species are rather inconspicuous, but their fragrance is reminiscent of jasmine or gardenia. The Chinese use the flowers to enhance the scent of tea. Many Chinese species have longer tubular flowers that are more decorative. Belonging to the olive family, they are slow growing, with some

Osmanthus delavayi

Osbeckia stellata

Osmanthus × fortunei

Osmanthus fragrans

eventually reaching 50 ft (15 m). The thick, rigid leaves may be edged with stout, even hooked, spiny teeth.
CULTIVATION: Plants should be clipped after flowering to maintain their compact shape. Plant in rich, well-drained soil in a sheltered position in either sun or part-shade. Propagate from seed or cuttings or by layering.

Osmanthus × burkwoodii

syn. ***× Osmarea burkwoodii***

This is a hybrid between *Osmanthus delavayi* from China and the rare ***O. decorus*** from the Caucasus. Grown for its profusion of small, very fragrant flowers which appear in the latter half of spring, it reaches a height of 6 ft (1.8 m). It has a dense, rounded habit with glossy, dark green foliage. **ZONES 6–9.**

Osmanthus delavayi

syn. ***Siphonosmanthus delavayi***

DELAVAY OSMANTHUS

This species grows to a height and spread of around 6 ft (1.8 m). It has serrated, oval, dark green leaves, 1 in (25 mm) long, held on arching branches. The white flowers are tubular, about $\frac{1}{2}$ in (12 mm) long, and are borne profusely in the leaf axils and at ends of branches during summer. **ZONES 7–9.**

Osmanthus × fortunei

An old cross between *Osmanthus fragrans* and *O. heterophyllus*, this upright shrub has similar small, fragrant flowers to the former and the more strongly and irregularly toothed leaves of the latter. It grows to a height and spread of 10 ft (3 m) and its small clusters of white flowers appear sporadically through much of the year in a mild climate. **ZONES 7–11.**

Osmanthus fragrans

SWEET OSMANTHUS, SWEET OLIVE

Usually seen as a shrub with a height of around 10 ft (3 m), this species can be trained as a small tree and can also be grown in containers. Its broad, deep green leaves act as a foil to the clusters of very small creamy white or yellow flowers, which are held towards the ends of the branches. It flowers intermittently from spring to fall (autumn). ***Osmanthus fragrans* f. *aurantiacus*** has dull orange flowers. **ZONES 7–11.**

Osmanthus heterophyllus

Osmunda regalis

Osmanthus serrulatus

Osteomeles schweriniae

Osteospermum 'Whirligig'

Osteospermum ecklonis 'Starshine'

Osmanthus heterophyllus
syn. ***Osmanthus ilicifolius***
HOLLY OSMANTHUS, HOLLY TEA OLIVE

Native to Japan and Taiwan, this shrub produces leaves of rather variable shape, some toothed like holly leaves and others only toothed at the tip. It grows to a height and spread of some 15 ft (4.5 m), and is sometimes grown as a hedge. It bears sparse rather inconspicuous white flowers in early summer. **'Gulftide'** has very spiny leaves; **'Purpureus'** has very dark purple leaves; and **'Variegatus'** has leaves irregularly edged in white. **ZONES 7–10.**

Osmanthus serrulatus

From western China, this evergreen shrub has erect branches and narrowly oval leaves with closely spaced small prickly teeth, at least in the young stages. The flowers are small, white and fragrant; it reaches a height of around 10 ft (3 m). **ZONES 8–10.**

OSMUNDA

This is a genus of about 12 species of large, deciduous ferns that occur naturally near water in the Americas, Europe and Asia. The fronds are erect and rather narrow in outline, forming dense tufts or rosettes and turning yellow or golden brown in fall (autumn). Spore-bearing fronds (or portions of fronds in some species) are very distinct, the green leaflets replaced by reddish brown spore cases. Osmunda fiber is used as a potting medium for orchids among other uses, and consists of the densely matted roots of *Osmunda regalis*.
CULTIVATION: These fully frost-hardy ferns require a position in shade (with the exception of *Osmunda regalis*, which tolerates sun and very wet conditions) in moist, fertile, humus-rich soil. Propagate by division in fall or winter or from spores as soon as they ripen.

Osmunda cinnamomea
CINNAMON FERN

This species occurs in both Asia and the Americas, including moist tropical mountains as well as cool-temperate regions. It produces stiffly erect clusters of fronds up to 4 ft (1.2 m) tall that arch gracefully from a stout, crown-forming rhizome. The sterile fronds are bluish green from spring to summer, while the smaller fertile fronds are the color of cinnamon, expanding in the center of each crown in summer. Though slow to establish and gain stature, this is a long-lived fern. **ZONES 3–10.**

Osmunda claytonia
INTERRUPTED FERN

This fern, native to North America as well as temperate East Asia, resembles the cinnamon fern, but has much broader leaflets which are pale green in color. The unusual name derives from the fertile fronds bearing normal, sterile segments among the crown segments on the same frond. As the frond matures in mid-summer the fertile segments fall off, giving an 'interrupted' appearance to the frond. Growing up to 5 ft (1.5 m) in height, the young fiddleheads emerge covered with pinkish hairs. **ZONES 3–9.**

Osmunda regalis
ROYAL FERN

Native to Asia, the Americas and Europe, this is the largest species of the genus. It grows to a height of 6 ft (1.8 m) with long bipinnate fronds. It is commonly found in large groups in swamps and other boggy areas, and so is suitable for wet gardens. The inner fronds in the crown are divided into a sterile, leafy lower portion and a crown spore-bearing upper portion. **ZONES 3–9.**

OSTEOMELES

This genus, allied to *Sorbus*, consists of 3 species of evergreen, deciduous or semi-deciduous shrubs with an unusual distribution: China and Japan and the Pacific islands from the Philippines to Hawaii and New Zealand. Capable of reaching 10 ft (3 m) tall but more commonly around 3 ft (1 m), the twiggy bushes have small pinnate leaves composed of many rounded leaflets. The white, slightly fragrant flowers are carried in clusters at the branch tips. They appear from mid-spring to early summer and are followed by small brown or black fruits.
CULTIVATION: Easily cultivated in any fertile, well-drained soil in full sun or part-shade, they are only moderately frost hardy. Propagate from seed or cuttings in summer.

Osteomeles schweriniae

This deciduous or semi-evergreen arching shrub from southwestern China bears clusters of small white flowers in early summer, followed by red fruit that turn blue-black. The arching branches bear leaves with 2 rows of dark green leaflets only about $\frac{1}{4}$ in (6 mm) long. This shrub prefers full sun and will reach a height of 5 ft (1.5 m) with a spread of 10 ft (3 m). **ZONES 8–10.**

OSTEOSPERMUM

This genus of 70 or so species of evergreen shrubs, semi-woody perennials and annuals is mostly indigenous to South Africa. Allied to *Dimorphotheca*, they have irregularly toothed leaves and produce a profusion of large, daisy-like flowerheads in the white, pink, violet and purple range. Most of the commonly grown osteospermums are cultivars of uncertain origin, suspected to be hybrids. Tough plants, they are useful for rock gardens, dry embankments or the front rows of shrub borders, particularly as temporary filler plants.
CULTIVATION: Osteospermums are marginally to moderately frost hardy and do best in open, well-drained soil of medium fertility. An open, sunny position is essential. Light pruning after flowering helps maintain shape and extend the plants' lifespan. Propagate from cuttings of non-flowering shoots or from seed in summer.

Osteospermum 'Buttermilk'

This erect shrub has flowerheads which are pale yellow with darker centers and appear from mid-summer through to fall (autumn). It has gray-green foliage and an upright bushy habit, reaching a height of 24 in (60 cm). **ZONES 8–10.**

Osteospermum 'Cannington Roy'

A woody based perennial of almost prostrate habit, this cultivar produces masses of showy daisy flowers from late spring to fall (autumn). Each bloom is about 3 in (8 cm) across, the petals opening white with purple tips but ageing to mauve. **ZONES 8–10.**

Osteospermum ecklonis
syn. ***Dimorphotheca ecklonis***
BLUE-AND-WHITE DAISYBUSH, SAILOR BOY DAISY

Native to eastern Cape Province, this shrub is variable in growth habit, with some erect forms of up to 5 ft (1.5 m) tall and other forms that are lower and more spreading, or even semi-prostrate. From late spring to fall (autumn), it bears profuse 3 in (8 cm) wide daisies, sparkling white with deep reddish violet centers and streaked bluish mauve on the undersides of petals. **'Starshine'** is a more compact plant with white flowers and more bluish centers. **ZONES 8–10.**

Osteospermum fruticosum
syn. ***Dimorphotheca fruticosa***
FREEWAY DAISY, TRAILING AFRICAN DAISY

Of wider distribution across southern South Africa, this is a perennial with prostrate or trailing stems that spread to

Ostrya virginiana

cover large areas when planted along freeways in coastal California. Masses of palest lilac daisies are borne on stalks up to 12 in (30 cm) above the ground; the heaviest bloom is in winter, with some blossoms year-round. Named selections are available with pure white, burgundy or purple flowers. **ZONES 9–11.**

Osteospermum jucundum

syns *Dimorphotheca barberae* of gardens, *Osteospermum barberae*

TRAILING MAUVE DAISY, PINK VELD DAISY

This semi-prostrate perennial species from the mountains and grasslands of South Africa's inland makes a low clump often no more than 8 in (20 cm) high and up to 3 ft (1 m) across. It produces abundant purplish pink daisies with darker central discs throughout fall (autumn), winter and spring. The flowers close on cloudy days. **ZONES 8–10.**

Osteospermum 'Pink Whirls'

This new pink-flowering cultivar has a slight constriction in each petal on some flowerheads, although others may have more normal petals. It reaches a height of about 18 in (45 cm) and spread of 3 ft (1 m). **ZONES 8–10.**

Osteospermum 'Whirligig'

syn. *Osteospermum* 'Starry Eyes'

This somewhat bizarre cultivar is close to *Osteospermum ecklonis* and may belong in this species. Its petals, white above and gray-blue beneath, each have their edges pinched together in the outer part, but remaining flat right at the tip; the effect is curious but quite decorative. It reaches a height of about 24 in (60 cm) with a loosely spreading habit. **ZONES 8–10.**

OSTROWSKIA

GIANT BELLFLOWER

This is a genus of just one species, a tall, tap-rooted perennial from central Asia closely related to and very similar to *Campanula.* Its leaves are whorls of 4 or 5, widely spaced on the thick unbranched stem, terminating in a spray of very large 5- to 9-petalled flowers.

CULTIVATION: Plant in full sun in light, well-drained soil with well-rotted manure. The plants should be allowed to dry off after flowering and should remain dry through the winter while

Ostrya carpinifolia

dormant. The plants are sensitive to disturbance and are most easily propagated from seed.

Ostrowskia magnifica

The rootstock of this species produces a few very strong, unbranched stems 4–6 ft (1.2–1.8 m) tall that bear simple, blue-green leaves up to 6 in (15 cm) long. There are rarely more than 4 to 6 of the bell-shaped flowers at the top of each stem, but they are up to 6 in (15 cm) in diameter, varying in color from pale to deep blue. **ZONES 7–9.**

OSTRYA

HOP-HORNBEAM

There are 10 species of deciduous trees in this genus scattered through temperate regions of the northern hemisphere. Allied to the true hornbeams *(Carpinus)*, they have similar toothed leaves that are prominently veined and tapered to a point. In spring, the yellow male catkins look attractive against the bright green new leaves; these are followed in summer by the shorter fruiting catkins, each small nutlet enclosed in a bladder-like bract like those of hops *(Humulus)*, hence the common name. Hop-hornbeams may be rather slow growing in the early stages but are attractive small- to medium-sized trees, usually with a good fall (autumn) coloring.

CULTIVATION: To flourish, these frost-hardy trees need a sheltered position in full sun or part-shade and fertile, well-drained soil. Prune only to remove dead branches. Propagate from seed in spring.

Ostrya carpinifolia

HOP-HORNBEAM

Native to southern Europe and Turkey, the hop-hornbeam forms a compact tree of up to 60 ft (18 m) with a conical crown. Its toothed, dark green leaves turn a clear yellow before falling and look very attractive against the smooth gray bark of its trunk. The pendent fruiting catkins are cream to straw-colored, about 2 in (5 cm) long. **ZONES 2–9.**

Otacanthus caeruleus

Ostrya virginiana

AMERICAN HOP-HORNBEAM, IRONWOOD

Comparatively rare outside its native eastern North America, this tree is very similar to *Ostrya carpinifolia* except for its dark brown bark. The deeply saw-toothed, dark green leaves are up to 5 in (12 cm) long and turn a rich yellow. The wood is prized for carpentry. **ZONES 3–9.**

OTACANTHUS

The 4 species of this genus of soft-wooded evergreen shrubs are all native to Brazil. When first known, they were placed in the acanthus family and named *Otacanthus* (Greek *otus*, ear, and *acanthus)* on account of their somewhat ear-like flower shape with 2 almost semi-circular lips flaring from the end of a narrow tube. Later it was realized that they really belong in the same family (Scrophulariaceae) as the foxgloves and snapdragons, and in fact a close look reveals that the mouth of the flower tube is closed together in much the same way as a snapdragon.

CULTIVATION: Frost-tender plants, they are easily grown outdoors in a warm climate in any moist, reasonably fertile and well-drained soil in a sheltered sunny position. In cool climates, grow in a sunny conservatory or place outdoors from late spring onwards. Propagate from cuttings.

Osteospermum 'Pink Whirls'

Otacanthus caeruleus

This 3 ft (1 m) tall shrub is grown for its almost year-round display of violet-blue, flowers. It produces many weak erect branches terminating in a short, bracted spike of flowers with slender, curved tubes about 1 in (25 mm) long which flare abruptly into 2 flat lips about $\frac{3}{4}$ in (18 mm) wide. **ZONES 10–12.**

OTANTHUS

COTTONWEED

This genus consists of a single species of low-growing rhizomatous perennial from seashores of western Europe and the Mediterranean region. *Otanthus* is allied to *Achillea,* but has leaves that are neither toothed nor divided and flowerheads that lack ray florets. The stems, leaves and undersides of the flowerheads are all coated in matted white hairs like cotton wool.

CULTIVATION: Although not commonly cultivated, cottonweed is an interesting plant for rock gardens and dry banks in exposed places, especially near the sea. It prefers sandy, dry soil and full sun, and will not tolerate long wet periods. Propagate from seed or cuttings or by division.

Osteospermum jucundum

Osteospermum fruticosum cultivar

Otanthus maritimus
COTTONWEED

This tufted, creeping perennial reaches up to 18 in (45 cm) high with erect stems and small spatula-shaped leaves. Flat-topped clusters of dull orange-yellow flowers are borne in late summer and early fall (autumn). **ZONES 8–10.**

OTHONNA

The 150 species of perennials, subshrubs and small shrubs in this genus are native to Africa. Many have succulent leaves, stems or rootstocks, and may be found in large succulent collections. Shape, size and structure of the leaves varies greatly, but all species produce daisy-like flowerheads rather like those of *Senecio*. The flower color is nearly always yellow.
CULTIVATION: Plant the highly succulent species in gritty, very free-draining soil in full sun and keep dry after flowering and during winter. Some more vigorous species can be grown outdoors as ground cover and rock-garden plants and will tolerate occasional light frosts. Propagate from seed or cuttings. Succulent species also grow from leaf cuttings, budding from the stalk end of the detached leaves.

Othonna capensis
syn. *Othonna crassifolia*

From South Africa's Cape Province, this trailing succulent grows to little more than 6 in (15 cm) in height, but will spread over a large area or hang from a basket. Its cylindrical, pale green leaves are about 1 in (25 mm) long, and the small yellow flowerheads bloom profusely in summer on short slender stalks. **ZONES 9–11.**

Othonna cheirifolia

Othonna cheirifolia

A native of Algeria and Tunisia, this bushy evergreen shrub has spoon-shaped, somewhat fleshy, gray-green leaves about 3 in (8 cm) long. The bright yellow flowerheads are borne singly on erect stalks in early summer. Of low, spreading habit, it reaches a height of 8–12 in (20–30 cm). **ZONES 8–10.**

OXALIS
WOOD-SORREL

This is a large genus of 500 or so species of bulbous, rhizomatous and fibrous-rooted perennials and a few small, weak shrubs. Though found around the world, the greatest number of *Oxalis* species are native to South Africa and South America. Some have become garden and greenhouse weeds which, though pretty in flower, have given a bad name to the genus; most species listed here are more restrained in growth and make choice additions to the garden. The leaves are always compound, divided into 3 or more heart-shaped or more deeply 2-lobed leaflets in a palmate arrangement (like clover). The funnel-shaped flowers are usually pink, white or yellow, and are carried in an umbel-like cluster on slender stalks.

Oxalis adenophylla

Oxalis massoniana

Oxalis oregana

CULTIVATION: Most species grow from bulbs or corms, which multiply readily. A position in sun or part-shade suits most, along with a mulched, well-drained soil and moderate water. Propagate by division of the bulbs or from seed in fall (autumn).

Oxalis acetosella
WOOD SORREL

Native to temperate North America and Eurasia, this delicate perennial has a creeping, prostrate habit and bears nodding white flowers with purple veining in spring and early summer. It is a woodland plant growing in cool, moist soil often in quite deep shade. A modestly pretty plant, it is seldom more than 4 in (10 cm) high. Pink-flowered forms are sometimes cultivated. **ZONES 3–10.**

Oxalis adenophylla

This bulbous species from the southern Andes of South America makes a small mound to 3 in (8 cm) high. The leaves consist of up to 12 two-lobed leaflets. Suitable for a rockery, it bears open, purple-pink flowers with darker centers from late spring to early summer. **ZONES 5–9.**

Oxalis articulata

This Paraguayan species has numerous fleshy, caterpillar-like rhizomes which readily disperse when soil is disturbed. In some mild, moist climates it has become a minor nuisance. The 3-lobed, hairy edged leaves are long stalked and the rose-pink flowers are borne above the foliage in dense, showy sprays in summer and fall (autumn). **ZONES 8–11.**

Oxalis citrina

A native of cooler areas of South Africa and the Americas this charming little plant has the brightest golden-yellow flowers of any oxalis and is prized by collectors of rare bulbs. It flowers in spring or early summer. **ZONES 8–10.**

Oxalis citrina

Oxalis hirta

Oxalis enneaphylla
SCURVY GRASS

Native to the far south of South America and the Falkland Islands, this clump-forming perennial produces tufts of fleshy, hairy, blue-gray leaves with up to 20 folded leaflets and grows only to about 3 in (8 cm) high. It bears fragrant, large, white to deep pink-red flowers from late spring into early summer; it spreads slowly by deep scale-covered rhizomes. **ZONES 6–9.**

Oxalis hirta

Most oxalises have leaves like clovers, but this perennial from South Africa's western Cape Province is different. Growing from bulbs, it produces elongated, closely crowded stems, to about 8 in (20 cm) long, making a bushy, crinkly leafed plant that covers itself for weeks in fall (autumn) and winter with deep pink flowers with yellow throats about ¾ in (18 mm) wide. **ZONES 9–11.**

Oxalis 'Ione Hecker'

Believed to have originated as a hybrid between the South American species *Oxalis enneaphylla* and ***O. laciniata***, this summer-flowering plant bears funnel-shaped, lilac-blue flowers marked with darker veins. It makes a tiny mound of gray foliage only 2 in (5 cm) high and about 2–3 in (5–8 cm) across. **ZONES 6–9.**

Oxalis massoniana

Its orange-toned flowers make *Oxalis massoniana* something of a novelty. From southern Africa, it was named after Francis Masson, a Scot who made notable collections in South Africa in the late eighteenth century. **ZONES 9–10.**

Oxalis oregana
REDWOOD SORREL

This species from western USA and Canada spreads by creeping rhizomes and forms large, dense mats in moist, shady woodlands and forests. It grows 10 in (25 cm) high and has 1 in (25 mm) or more long, broadly heart-shaped dark green leaflets. Rosy pink to white flowers are borne on solitary stems from spring to fall (autumn). **ZONES 7–10.**

Oxalis pes-caprae
BERMUDA BUTTERCUP, SOURSOB

In frost-free climates, this South African species will take over the garden; in fact it has become a bad agricultural weed in some winter-rainfall areas with light-textured soils. It is a bulbous, stemless perennial that grows to 18 in (45 cm) tall with tufts of crowded, erect or spreading, succulent bright green leaves on long stalks. Its bright yellow flowers appear in great profusion in spring or early summer on tall stems. **ZONES 7–10.**

Oxalis purpurea
syn. *Oxalis variabilis*

One of the showiest species in the genus, this South African native has large flowers in pink, rose, lilac or white; all have soft yellow centers. Clover-like leaves arise from bulbs to form a mound only 4 in (10 cm) high; the deep green leaflets have purple undersides and the flowers appear from late fall (autumn) until early spring. It spreads slowly, but is not invasive. **ZONES 8–10.**

Oxalis tetraphylla
syn. *Oxalis deppei*
LUCKY CLOVER, GOOD LUCK PLANT

This Mexican species is a tuft-forming, bulbous perennial. Its crowded leaves are usually divided into 4 roughly triangular leaflets up to 2½ in (6 cm) long with a basal blotch of dull purple. It produces loose sprays of funnel-shaped, deep reddish pink flowers with a yellow throat in spring and summer. This plant needs a protected position. It reaches a height of 6 in (15 cm) and a spread about the same. 'Iron Cross' has a dark purplish mark at the base of each leaflet. **ZONES 8–10.**

Oxalis pes-caprae

Oxalis tuberosa
OCA

Believed to have originated in the northern Andes, this species is second only to the potato in importance as a root vegetable in the cooler parts of South America. Its knobbly translucent tubers are up to about 2 in (5 cm) in diameter and may be round or elongated with color varying from white to yellow or pink, sometimes with darker streaks. Only the white-tubered form will flower. Above ground, it forms a tangle of weak stems with plain green 3-pointed leaves; the small flowers are yellow. It is hardy to most frosts. **ZONES 7–10.**

OXYDENDRUM
SORREL TREE, SOURWOOD

The single deciduous tree species in this genus is a native of eastern USA and is grown for its fall (autumn) foliage and flowers. The leaves are alternate and finely toothed; the fragrant, small urn-shaped flowers are held in drooping terminal panicles. The genus takes its name from Greek words meaning 'sour tree', a reference to the sour-tasting foliage.
CULTIVATION: For the best fall colors, it should be planted in an open position in sun or part-shade in moist soil. An occasional dressing of iron and/or ammonia after flowering may be required. Propagate from cuttings in summer or seed in fall.

Oxydendrum arboreum

Making a small, 20–40 ft (6–12 m) tree, this cool-climate species tolerates frost better than it does dry conditions. The trunk is slender and the crown pyramid-shaped. Streamers of small white lily-of-the-valley-like flowers appear in late summer sometimes prior to, sometimes coinciding with, the display of deep scarlet foliage. **ZONES 3–9.**

OXYTROPIS
POINT VETCH, LOCOWEED, CRAZY WEED

Consisting of 300 species of perennials in the pea family, *Oxytropis* is closely related to the even larger genus *Astragalus* and has a similar wide distribution around the temperate northern hemisphere. Leaves are usually in a basal rosette and are pinnate, with mostly narrow leaflets that are often silky haired. Smallish pea-like flowers are crowded onto short spikes, often held on long stems. They occur mostly in cold, rather dry climates in well-drained gravels and sandy soils. The common names refer to the toxicity of some species, which can cause an apparent madness in cattle and horses if eaten.
CULTIVATION: Very good drainage is essential for success with these plants. Grow on sloping ground or in raised beds of gritty soil. Full sun and a cold winter are both necessary; where winters are also rainy and damp, plants should be grown under glass as many species do not enjoy cold, wet conditions. Propagate from seed sown in spring and transplant into individual pots as soon as they are big enough to handle.

Oxalis purpurea

Oxalis tuberosa

Oxalis tetraphylla 'Iron Cross'

Oxytropis campestris
YELLOW MILK-VETCH

Occurring right around colder parts of the northern hemisphere, this species has loose rosettes of furry leaves each about 6 in (15 cm) long. In summer it sends up flowering stems to a height of about 12 in (30 cm) carrying more than a dozen pale yellow and sometimes pale violet flowers. **ZONES 3–8.**

OZOTHAMNUS

This genus consists of about 50 species of evergreen shrubs from Australia and New Zealand, all of them until recently classified in the genus *Helichrysum.* Their foliage is aromatic, even quite resinous and sticky in some species; individual leaves are mostly small and whitish on the undersides or reduced to tiny scale-leaves in some species. Flowerheads are tiny, with white or yellowish papery bracts, but often massed into large flat or domed sprays.
CULTIVATION: Some of the smaller-growing species make attractive rock-garden plants. They prefer freely draining soil and shelter from cold, drying winds. Most species will tolerate light frosts and some are moderately frost hardy. Prune leggy specimens before spring growth and propagate from cuttings in summer.

Ozothamnus ledifolius

Oxydendrum arboreum

Ozothamnus hookeri
syn. *Helichrysum hookeri*

From Tasmania and cooler parts of mainly southeastern Australia, this shrub has a compact habit, growing to 3 ft (1 m) tall with a spread of 24 in (60 cm). Clusters of white flowerheads with greenish yellow bracts are borne in summer. The foliage is cypress-like, with tiny dark green scale-leaves. **ZONES 8–9.**

Ozothamnus ledifolius
syn. *Helichrysum ledifolium*
KEROSENE BUSH

From the mountains of Tasmania, this species bears small white flowerheads from reddish buds in early summer. The small blunt-tipped leaves, dark green above and yellow beneath, are crowded onto the yellowish twigs. It has a neat, rounded habit, with a height and spread of 3 ft (1 m). Plant in a sheltered situation to take full advantage of its sweetly aromatic foliage. Its common name comes from its highly resinous and hence inflammable foliage, used for kindling in Tasmania. **ZONES 8–9.**

O

P

PACHIRA

From tropical America, this genus consists of 24 species of evergreen and deciduous trees that can reach 90 ft (27 m). They are grown for their large, compound leaves and unusual flowers, which are followed by big, woody pods. The flowers, which have a large number of protruding stamens, appear throughout the year, each bloom lasting only a short time. These trees make excellent bonsai or container specimens.
CULTIVATION: Frost tender, they need moist soil, full sun and preferably a tropical environment. Propagate from seed or cuttings in late summer.

Pachira aquatica

SHAVING BRUSH TREE, GUIANA CHESTNUT, PROVISION TREE

This evergreen tree can vary in height from 15 ft (4.5 m) to 60 ft (18 m). *Pachira aquatica* is grown for its fruit, which can be roasted and eaten the way sweet chestnuts are. This species has compound leaves consisting of up to 9 leaflets to 12 in (30 cm) long, and greenish or cream flowers with red-tipped stamens resembling long brushes. Its large brown fruit are 12 in (30 cm) long and 6 in (15 cm) round. This tree is suitable for boggy areas. **ZONES 10–12.**

Pachira aquatica

PACHYCEREUS

This genus from semi-desert regions of the USA and Mexico consists of about 9 species of cacti. They are either single stemmed or form clusters of tall stems. The stems are studded with felted areoles along their ribs. In some species, the entire stem is felted, especially heavily near the tip. Each areole bears small radial spines with larger central spines up to 4 in (10 cm) long in the larger species. They produce cream to red, funnel- or bell-shaped, or tubular flowers with slightly protruding, massed anthers from felty buds at the apex of the stems.
CULTIVATION: Plant in full sun in light, gritty, very free-draining soil. Hardiness varies with the species, but few tolerate anything more than occasional light frosts. Wet winter conditions can cause rotting. Propagate from seed as rooted basal offsets are rare. Some species produce cristate growths that are grafted onto normal stems.

Pachycereus marginatus

syn. *Stenocereus marginatus, Lemaireocereus marginatus*

ORGAN-PIPE CACTUS

From Mexico, this dramatic large cactus, with many vertical stems branching from a short basal trunk and reaching up to 25 ft (7.5 m) tall, is often planted closely in rows to form a living fence. The dull yellowish green stems, up to 6 in (15 cm) thick, have 5 to 7 broad, angled ribs. Short spines are restricted to the upper parts of each stem, soon falling and leaving just the small furry aeroles that are so closely spaced they form a continuous band along the margin of each rib. Small pinkish cream flowers are scattered over the whole length of the ribs in summer, appearing from the same band of aeroles year after year. **ZONES 10–12.**

Pachyphytum fittkaui

Pachyphytum oviferum

Pachycereus marginatus

Pachypodium namaquanum

PACHYPHYTUM

This succulent genus, native to Mexico, consists of 12 species. They are generally medium-sized plants with a height and spread of up to 24 in (60 cm). Their leaves are fleshy and sometimes form stemless rosettes that appear, depending on the species, as green, blue or purple. Diurnal, pendent flowers are produced in spring, summer or fall (autumn), and are followed by tiny seeded capsules. Some species are slow growers.
CULTIVATION: These frost-tender plants need full sun, with some shade during the hottest part of the day. Grow in moderately fertile, very well-drained soil. Propagate from seed or cuttings.

Pachyphytum fittkaui

An evergreen succulent with a pendulous habit, this species reaches 18 in (45 cm) in height; its stem then bends and trails to a length of 3 ft (1 m). It has green, narrow to oval leaves growing to about 3 in (8 cm) long, and bears small, deep pink flowers in spring and summer. **ZONES 9–11.**

Pachyphytum oviferum

SUGAR ALMOND PLANT, MOONSTONES

This beautiful perennial succulent colonizes in stemless rosettes of bloated, spoon-shaped, blue-green leaves with a whitish red, powdery coating. Deep red-orange or pale green flowers appear in short-stemmed, pendent clusters from the end of winter to early spring. It grows to a height of 4 in (10 cm) with a 12 in (30 cm) spread. **ZONES 9–11.**

PACHYPODIUM

Native to Madagascar and South Africa, these 17 species of upright, perennial succulent shrubs grow to 20 ft (6 m) tall. They tend to grow as single, fleshy, spine-covered columns, sometimes with 2 or 3 main branches; the whole structure often leans towards the sun. The stem is usually armed with vicious thorns. The leaves sprout from the top and frangipani-like flowers in white or red nestle among them in summer. They do not flower until the plants are mature and at least 3 ft (1 m) tall, which can take 10 years or even longer in a greenhouse.

Pachypodium lamerei

CULTIVATION: Essentially tropical plants, they are frost tender and require full sun and porous soil. They can be grown in pots indoors or in a greenhouse in cooler climates. Water only when they are in leaf. Propagate from seed in spring and summer.

Pachypodium baronii var. *windsori*

This attractive dwarf species has an almost spherical main stem and short, spiny branches. The distinctive flowers are a beautiful shade of scarlet and have a white eye. **ZONES 9–11.**

Pachypodium lamerei

This, the best-known species, has a spiny or cactus-like trunk and develops multiple stems that readily divide after each flowering. It grows to 20 ft (6 m). Long, slender leaves sprout from the crown and fall at the end of summer. Fragrant flowers—white with a yellow center—appear from the stem tips on mature specimens in summer. **ZONES 9–11.**

Pachypodium namaquanum

CLUB FOOT, ELEPHANT'S TRUNK

Originating in southwest Africa, this tree-like succulent grows 3–6 ft (1–1.8 m) tall. It features a profusion of long, brown spines growing in spiralled ribs along the stem. Long, narrow green leaves form in clusters at the crown of the plant. Reddish brown, funnel-shaped flowers are produced in spring. **ZONES 9–11.**

PACHYRHIZUS

This genus of 6 species of tuberous-rooted, herbaceous, twining legumes is native to tropical America. They have trifoliate leaves and 6–8 in (15–20 cm) long racemes of white to deep purple, pea-like flowers appear in summer, followed by flat seed pods up to 12 in (30 cm) long. The roots of some species are important vegetable crops, not only in their homelands, but also in many tropical areas. After cropping the dried plants are used as fodder.
CULTIVATION: The plants need a rich, moist, well-drained soil, a position in full sun or part-shade and protection from frost. They grow rapidly and need strong support if grown as climbers. They are usually treated as annuals in warm summer areas. The tubers take 4 to 7 months to mature. Propagate from seed.

Pachyrhizus tuberosus

JICAMA, YAM BEAN, POTATO BEAN

Native to the Amazon Basin, this species is grown in Central America and the southern USA for its edible tubers. A twining vine, it can grow to 20 ft (6 m) and requires staking in the garden. Its flowers, ½–1 in (12–25 mm) wide, are a whitish purple in color and have a green blotch on the base of the standard. **ZONES 10–12.**

PACHYSANDRA

Widely used as ground covers in shady areas, the 4 evergreen or semi-evergreen subshrubs in this genus from China, Japan and southeastern USA are tough and thrive in dry shade where few others will grow. They form mats or mounding clumps of fleshy, rhizome-like stems clothed at the tips with whorls of 2–4 in (5–10 cm) long, oblong, deep green, toothed leaves. Small spikes of tiny, scented, cream flowers develop in spring. **CULTIVATION:** Frost hardy, all species will grow in most soils in sun or part-shade. The more sun they receive, the more moisture they require. They are usually propagated by removing self-rooted layers or from cuttings.

Pachysandra procumbens
ALLEGHENY SPURGE

This semi-evergreen species, native to eastern USA, is a clumping ground cover that is slower growing than the more common *Pachysandra terminalis* and also less invasive. It produces upright inflorescences of cream and pink flowers in early spring before the new growth develops. In fall (autumn), the foliage develops a silvery marbling. **ZONES 6–10.**

Pachysandra terminalis

This creeping evergreen perennial, a native of Japan, has leathery, ovate leaves with saw-tooth tips, clustered at the ends of short stems. Tiny white flowers, sometimes pink or purple tinted, appear in terminal clusters in early summer. It is frost resistant and makes a good ground cover, growing to 4 in (10 cm) high with a spread of 8 in (20 cm). **'Variegata'** has cream, gray-green and green variegated foliage. **ZONES 5–10.**

PACHYSTACHYS
GOLDEN CANDLES

This genus of 12 species of evergreen perennials and small shrubs is native to tropical Central and South America, and the West Indies. In tropical and subtropical areas, they can reach 6 ft (1.8 m) in height and are grown for the splashes of bright yellow and red they add to gardens. Elsewhere they are popular as indoor or greenhouse plants. They are erect growers with large, bright green leaves and yellow floral bracts that almost hide the true flowers, which are small, white and tubular. The flowers themselves last only a few days, but the bracts are colorful over several weeks. **CULTIVATION:** They require frost-free conditions in at least a warm-temperate climate, preferably subtropical, full sun and fertile, moist but well-drained soil.

Pachysandra procumbens

Pachystachys lutea

If used as indoor plants, they prefer warm, well-lit, humid conditions. Cold winter drafts will cause foliage loss. Propagate from seed or cuttings.

Pachystachys lutea

This small, shrubby plant forms a clump of upright stems with a 'candle' of bright golden yellow bracts at the tip of each stem. The creamy white flowers within do not reveal themselves until the bracts are fully developed. The leaves are a deep matt green, lance-shaped, up to 6 in (15 cm) long and have prominent veins. Widely grown as a house plant, it makes a cheerful display all summer and can be treated as a bright summer annual in warm climates. **ZONES 10–12.**

PACHYSTEGIA

The status of this New Zealand genus is somewhat confused. Some botanists include it with *Olearia*; some suggest there are up to 5 species while others regard it as just one highly variable species. It is closely allied to the New Zealand bush daisies and is found in the coastal region of the northeast of the South Island. The large, thick, leathery leaves have glossy, wax-coated upper surfaces and felted undersides—superb protection against salt spray and coastal storms.The showy, white, daisy-like flowers, produced in summer, are followed by rounded, fluffy, brown seed heads.
CULTIVATION: Moderately frost hardy, they grow in any well-drained soil in sun or light shade, and are ideal for exposed coastal gardens. Propagate from seed or cuttings.

Pachystegia insignis
syn. ***Olearia insignis***
MARLBOROUGH ROCK DAISY

This evergreen shrub ranges in height from 1–5 ft (0.3–1.5 m) and can spread to 3 ft (1 m). White flowerheads with golden yellow central florets open in

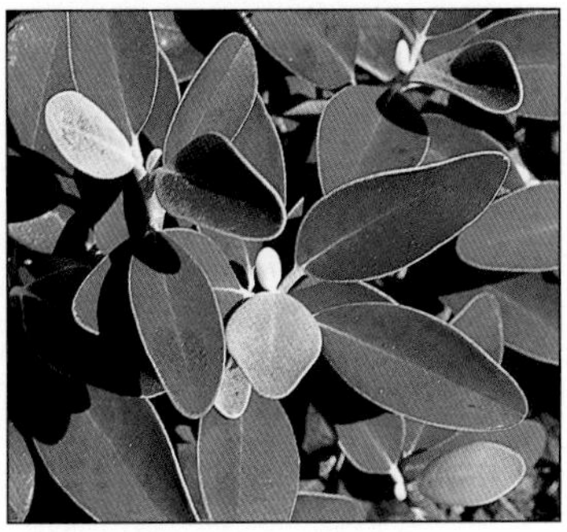
Pachystegia insignis

Pachystachys lutea

Pachysandra terminalis

Pachysandra terminalis 'Variegata'

summer. Its leaves, 3–8 in (8–20 cm) long, are deep glossy green above with white or beige felting below. **ZONES 8–11.**

× *PACHYVERIA*

This hybrid genus consists of 8 species of rosette-forming succulents obtained by crossing species of 2 Mexican genera, *Echeveria* and *Pachyphytum*. The 2–4 in (5–10 cm) long, fleshy, spatula-shaped leaves usually end in a fine point. They may be gray to bright green, often with a powdery bloom, and commonly develop reddish purple tints in the sun. From late spring, the $\frac{1}{2}$–1 in (12–25 mm) long tubular flowers are carried in groups of 1 to 3 on upright, wiry stems and are orange, red-tinted yellow or purple.
CULTIVATION: Plant in light, gritty, well-drained soil in full sun. They tolerate occasional light frosts but rot in cold, wet conditions. Propagate by replanting rooted rosettes or from leaf cuttings.

× *Pachyveria glauca*

This hybrid grows 12 in (30 cm) tall and has red-tipped, blue-gray, oblong-shaped leaves reaching a length of $2\frac{1}{2}$ in (6 cm). The parents are *Pachyphytum compactum* and *Echeveria glauca*. Star-shaped, pendent, yellow flowers are produced in spring. **ZONES 9–11.**

PAEONIA
PEONY

There are 33 species in this genus of beautiful perennials and shrubs, all native to temperate Eurasia apart from 2 that occur on the west coast of North America. The genus name goes back to classical Greek and arose from the supposed medicinal properties of some species. Peonies are all deciduous and have long-lived, rather woody rootstocks with swollen roots, and large compound leaves with the leaflets usually toothed or lobed. Each newly elongated stem in spring terminates in one to several large, rose-like flowers, their centers with a mass of short stamens almost concealing the 2 to 5 large ovaries that develop into short pods containing large seeds. The flowers are mostly in shades of pink or red, but there are also white and yellow-flowered species. The great majority of the species are herbaceous, dying back to the ground in fall (autumn), but there is a small group of Chinese species known as the 'tree peonies' that have above-ground woody stems, although no more than about 8 ft (2.4 m) in height, so strictly they are mere shrubs; cultivars of this group produce the largest and most magnificent of all peony flowers, some approaching a diameter of 12 in (30 cm), mostly double and often beautifully frilled or ruffled.
CULTIVATION: Most peonies will only succeed in climates with a cold winter, allowing dormancy and initiation of flower buds; but new foliage and flower buds can be damaged by late frosts. They appreciate a sheltered position in full or slightly filtered sunlight, but with soil

Paeonia bakeri

Paeonia delavayi

Paeonia lactiflora Hybrid

Paeonia lactiflora 'Beacon Flame'

Paeonia lactiflora 'Bowl of Beauty'

Paeonia lactiflora 'Cora Stubbs'

Paeonia lactiflora 'Kelway's Glorious'

Paeonia lactiflora 'President Roosevelt'

Paeonia lactiflora Hybrid

kept cool and moist. Mulch and feed with well-rotted manure when leaf growth starts, but avoid disturbing roots. Pruning of the tree peonies should be minimal, consisting of trimming out weaker side shoots. Propagate from seed in fall, or by division in the case of named cultivars. Tree peony cultivars are best propagated from basal suckers, but few are produced and plants on their own roots are hence very expensive; a faster and cheaper method is to graft them onto herbaceous rootstocks, but the resulting plants are often short lived.

Paeonia bakeri

This species grows to 24 in (60 cm) tall with leaves composed of two sets of three, 3–4 in (8–10 cm) long leaflets. The leaves are dark green above, blue-green below. The flowers, over 4 in (10 cm) in diameter, open from late spring and have rounded purple-red petals and bright golden anthers. ZONES 5–9.

Paeonia cambessedesii

MAJORCAN PEONY

Native to Majorca, this herbaceous species is 18 in (45 cm) tall with rather sticky leaves and stems. The dark green leaves are up to 10 in (25 cm) long, red-tinged above with purple undersides. The leaflets are smooth edged and 4 in (10 cm) long. Deep pink 4 in (10 cm) wide flowers open from late spring. ZONES 8–10.

Paeonia delavayi

The tree peonies have similar flowers to the herbaceous perennials, but differ in their growth habit: they are large, deciduous shrubs and do not die back to a rootstock in winter. Among the most common and easiest of the tree peonies to cultivate, this 6 ft (1.8 m) Chinese species bears bright to very deep black-red flowers in early spring. The flowers open as the light green foliage develops. ZONES 6–9.

Paeonia lactiflora Hybrids

The herbaceous Chinese peonies, derived mainly from *Paeonia lactiflora*, have handsome foliage—maroon tinted when it first appears in spring—and usually scented flowers in a huge range of colors and forms. **'Beacon Flame'** has deep red semi-double flowers. **'Bowl of Beauty'** grows to 3 ft (1 m) tall and between late spring and mid-summer bears dense clusters of slender, creamy white petaloids nesting in the center of broad, pink outer petals. **'Coral Charm'** has deep apricot buds fading to soft orange-pink as they mature. **'Cora Stubbs'** has broad outer petals and smaller central ones in contrasting tones. **'Duchesse de Nemours'** is a fairly tall grower with fragrant, white to soft yellow flowers with frilled incurving petals. **'Félix Crousse'** is a deep pink double with a red center. **'Festiva Maxima'** has large fully double flowers with frilled petals; the scented flowers are white with red flecks. **'Inspecteur Lavergne'** is a late-flowering, fully double red. **'Kelway's Glorious'** has highly scented creamy white double flowers. **'Miss America'** has large, highly scented white flowers with gold stamens. **'Monsieur Jules Elie'** has very deep cerise-pink single flowers. **'President Roosevelt'** is a luxuriant 'rose' or 'bomb' double peony. **'Sarah Bernhardt'** has scented, double, rose-pink flowers with silvery margins. **'Whitleyi Major'** has single, ivory-white flowers with yellow stamens. ZONES 6–9.

Paeonia lutea

YELLOW TREE PEONY

This shrub from western China was introduced to the West in the late nineteenth century. It grows to a height and spread of 5 ft (1.5 m) and from late spring to early summer bears single, clear yellow flowers about 6 in (15 cm) across. The leaves are dark green with saw-toothed margins. ***Paeonia lutea* var. *ludlowii*** grows to 8 ft (2.4 m) tall and produces bright yellow flowers in late spring. ZONES 6–9.

Paeonia mascula

Found from the northwest Balkans to the Himalayas, this herbaceous perennial is a very variable species. It usually has very stout stems 10–24 in (25–60 cm) tall. The leaves vary considerably, some

Paeonia lutea var. *ludlowii*

Paeonia lactiflora 'Moonstone'

Paeonia lactiflora 'Scarlett O'Hara'

Paeonia lutea

Paeonia lactiflora 'Yangfeichuyu'

Paeonia mlokosewitschii

Paeonia officinalis 'Rosea'

Paeonia officinalis

Paeonia officinalis 'Rubra Plena'

forms having broad leaflets, others narrow and some with serrated edges. The flowers are deep pink, red or white, more than 4 in (10 cm) wide and open early. **ZONES 8–10.**

Paeonia mlokosewitschii
CAUCASIAN PEONY

From late spring to mid-summer, this European peony bears big, open, pale to bright yellow flowers atop soft green leaves that have hairy undersides and are sometimes tinged purple at the edges. An erect, herbaceous perennial, it grows to 30 in (75 cm) high and wide, enjoys semi-shade and is resistant to frost. The seed pods split open to reveal black seeds on a red background. **ZONES 6–9.**

Paeonia mollis

Of unknown origin and considered to be a garden variety rather than a true species, this 18 in (45 cm) tall herbaceous peony has biternate (made up of two, 3-leaflet sections) leaves with lobed leaflets up to 4 in (10 cm) long. Its 3 in (8 cm) wide, deep pink or white flowers open from early summer. **ZONES 6–9.**

Paeonia officinalis

Of European origin, this herbaceous perennial reaches a height and spread of 24 in (60 cm) and from spring to mid-summer bears single, purple or red, rose-like flowers. Although poisonous, it has been used medicinally. Of similar size, **'Rubra Plena'** bears flowers that consist of clusters of many small, mid-magenta petals. The more compact **'China Rose'** bears darker green foliage and salmon-pink flowers with yellow-orange anthers. **'Rosea'** has deep pink flowers. **ZONES 8–10.**

Paeonia peregrina

Native to southern Europe, this 18 in (45 cm) herbaceous species has sticky stems and leaves made up of 15 to 17 leaflets. The leaves have a blue-green tinge. Cup-shaped, 4 in (10 cm) wide, deep red flowers with golden anthers open from late spring. **'Sunshine'** (syn. 'Otto Froebel') is an early-flowering cultivar with vivid deep orange-red flowers. **ZONES 8–10.**

Paeonia suffruticosa
TREE PEONY, MOUTAN

Native to China, this handsome deciduous shrub has been so enthusiastically transplanted into gardens it is probably extinct in the wild. It reaches a height and width of 3–6 ft (1–1.8 m) and produces very large single or double cup-shaped flowers in spring. Depending on the variety, these are white, pink, red or yellow, and are set among attractive, large, mid-green leaves. ***Paeonia suffruticosa* subsp. *rockii*** has semi-double white flowers with a maroon blotch at the base of each petal. **ZONES 4–9.**

PALIURUS

This genus is made up of 8 species of deciduous or evergreen spiny shrubs or trees from the Mediterranean region. The trees can reach 20 ft (6 m) or more in height. Because of their thorns, the shrubs have long been used as hedging plants. The leaves are oval and glossy green. The yellowish green star-shaped flowers appear in summer; they are followed by small, winged fruits.
CULTIVATION: They require a position in full sun and well-drained, fertile soil. Propagate from cuttings taken in late summer or from seed in fall (autumn).

Paeonia mollis

Paliurus spina-christi
CHRIST'S THORN

This is one of the plants thought to have been used for Christ's crown of thorns. It can be grown as a small tree, but is usually seen as a deciduous tall shrub or hedge plant. Its branches, covered with pairs of long thorns, form an excellent barrier. Erect when young, these spiny branches arch over as side branches appear. Tiny yellow blooms are followed by decorative fruit. The foliage turns a rich yellow before dropping in the cooler months. **ZONES 8–11.**

PANAX
GINSENG

This genus consists of 5 or so species of perennial herbs, 2 of which are cultivated for their economic significance. Chinese or Asian ginseng *(Panax ginseng)* has been used for centuries by the Chinese and Koreans as a medicinal herb. North American ginseng *(P. quinquefolius)* has similar properties to the Asian species; both have a sweetish aromatic flavor. It is the roots that are valuable: graded according to age, color and their distinctive man-like shape; the older the root and the more human its shape, the more highly it is valued.
CULTIVATION: These plants require a humus-rich, well-drained soil. As woodlands are their native habitat, it is important to provide adequate shade, especially during the summer months. Also ensure good air circulation around the plants. Ginseng may be propagated from fresh seed or root stocks.

Paliurus spina-christi

Paeonia suffruticosa cultivar

Panax ginseng
syn. *Panax pseudoginseng*
CHINESE GINSENG, ASIAN GINSENG

Native to northeastern China and Korea, this fully frost-hardy perennial grows to about 8 in (20 cm) tall. The dark green leaves are divided into 5 toothed leaflets. The small greenish white flowers have 5 petals and appear in late summer; these are followed by bright red berries in fall (autumn). **ZONES 6–9.**

PANCRATIUM
SEA LILY

The 'trumpet' that characterizes the daffodils is also seen on near relatives such as *Pancratium*, a genus of about 16 species of bulbous perennials from the Canary Islands, West Africa, tropical Asia and the Mediterranean shores. The trumpet is a development of the bases of the stamens; in *Pancratium* the trumpet remains attached, so that the stamens seem to be growing from the serrated edge of the trumpet. The flowers are almost always white (never deeper than cream) and come in bunches atop a bare stem that rises straight from the bulb in the midst of the leaves.
CULTIVATION: These plants of the seaside thrive in full sun in sandy, perfectly drained soil. They should be kept dry in summer. Propagate from seed or offsets.

Pancratium maritimum

This species bears umbels of sweetly scented flowers in late summer. It flowers most freely when the long-necked bulbs have multiplied into tight clumps. It grows to a height and spread of 12 in (30 cm). **ZONES 8–11.**

Pancratium maritimum

Paeonia suffruticosa subsp. *rockii*

Pandanus tectorius

Panicum virgatum

PANDANUS

SCREW PINE

This genus from East Africa, Malaysia, Australia and the Pacific contains about 600 species, a few of which make decorative trees for seaside gardens and swampy areas in frost-free climates. Palm-like evergreens, some grow 50 ft (15 m) or more tall. They may appear shorter, as they often lean at an angle. The sword-shaped, spiny-edged green leaves, are long and narrow andarranged spirally at the ends of the branches. The white flowers are very small; the fruits are aggregations of reddish or yellow berries, up to 12 in (30 cm) in diameter, and resemble a pineapple.
CULTIVATION: *Pandanus* require a tropical or subtropical climate, full sun or part-shade, and moist, well-drained soil. They can be treated as house plants when young if they are given ample water. Keep the plants tidy by removing dead and damaged leaves. Propagate from seed, soaked for 24 hours before planting, or by detaching rooted suckers.

Pandanus odoratissimus

Found through the tropical Asian and Pacific region, this species is up to 20 ft (6 m) tall and has long slender leaves edged with sharp spines. It has strong aerial roots that form a stout buttress base. Male trees have showy white flower bracts, while female trees bear pineapple-like fruit. The foliage is used for weaving and thatching. Male flowers and foliage also have culinary uses. **ZONES 11–12.**

Pandanus tectorius

HALA SCREW PINE, PANDANG

This species, found on seashores around the western Pacific, is often wider than its height of 25 ft (8 m), and the weight

Pandorea jasminoides

Papaver alpinum

of its branches is supported by stout, buttress-like aerial roots. Male flowers are sweetly scented. The leaves have long spines on their edges and on the undersides of the midrib; they are also used for thatching and weaving. **ZONES 11–12.**

PANDOREA

Named after Pandora of Greek mythology, this genus, native to Australia, the Malay Archipelago and New Caledonia, contains around 6 species of twining climbers. They are grown for their spectacular, long-lasting displays of tubular bell- or trumpet-shaped flowers and make good pergola or trellis subjects. They also have a dense covering of deep green, leathery, pinnate leaves and are attractive even when not in flower.
CULTIVATION: Frost tender, they are ideal for warm-temperate or tropical areas and require well-drained, humus-rich soil. They do best with abundant moisture and a sunny, protected position. Propagate from fresh seed in spring or from cuttings throughout the year.

Pandorea jasminoides

syns ***Bignonia jasminoides, Tecoma jasminoides***

BOWER PLANT, BOWER VINE

This attractive climber from Australia, up to 15 ft (4.5 m) tall, has deep green, glossy leaflets. Showy, pale pink trumpet flowers with deep carmine throats are borne from late spring to fall (autumn) in warm climates. **'Lady Di'** has white flowers with yellow throats. **ZONES 9–11.**

Pandorea pandorana

syns ***Bignonia pandorana, Tecoma australis***

WONGA WONGA VINE

From Australia, this robust, woody climber up to 20 ft (6 m) tall bears

Pandorea pandorana

masses of showy, tubular flowers in spring and summer; they are usually creamy white with reddish throats. Several cultivars are available, one with pure white flowers and another with gold and brown flowers. It is good for covering arches and pergolas or for disguising wire mesh fences. **ZONES 9–11.**

PANICUM

PANIC GRASS, CRAB GRASS

This is a genus of around 470 species of annual and perennial grasses found throughout the tropics and in warm-temperate parts of the northern hemisphere. Some are cropped, others are ornamental and more than a few are weeds. They range in size from 2–10 ft (0.6–3 m) tall and form clumps of fine stems with long, very narrow leaves often covered with fine hairs when young. Erect to nodding panicles of loose flower spikes open in summer. The flower panicles, which are up to 18 in (45 cm) long, are often bronze or red tinted.
CULTIVATION: They are easily grown in any moist, well-drained soil in full sun. Most of the perennial species will tolerate heavy frost. Propagate the species from seed and the cultivated forms by division.

Panicum virgatum

SWITCH GRASS

Found from Central America to southern Canada, this 6 ft (1.8 m) tall perennial forms clumps of blue-green to purple-green stems with sticky, bright green leaves up to 24 in (60 cm) long. Stiff, 18 in (45 cm) long flower panicles open from late summer. The leaves yellow in fall (autumn), the flowers develop red to bronze tones. **'Heavy Metal'** has erect blue-green leaves that yellow in fall. **'Rubrum'** has red-green leaves that turn bright red in fall and fine sprays of deep brown flower spikelets. **ZONES 5–10.**

Papaver atlanticum

PAPAVER

POPPY

The 50 or so annual, biennial or perennial species of the genus *Papaver* are mainly from the temperate parts of Eurasia and Africa, with a couple from eastern USA. With their characteristic cupped petals and nodding buds turning skywards upon opening, they are popular bedding flowers. Several of their close relatives take their name in common usage, such as the tree poppy *(Romneya)*, the Californian poppy *(Eschscholzia)* or the blue poppy *(Meconopsis)*.
CULTIVATION: Poppies are fully frost hardy and prefer little or no shade and deep, moist, well-drained soil. Sow seed in spring or fall (autumn); many species self-seed readily.

Papaver alpinum

A short-lived perennial, this tuft-forming semi-evergreen alpine poppy (a miniature Iceland poppy) grows to 8 in (20 cm) high with a spread of 4 in (10 cm) and has fine, grayish leaves. It bears white or yellow flowers in summer. This species prefers a little lime in the soil. Use on banks or in rock gardens. **ZONES 5–10.**

Papaver atlanticum

This perennial from Morocco has a woody rhizome and 6 in (15 cm) long, toothed-edged, downy leaves. The flowers are borne on 18 in (45 cm) stems and are pale orange to red, around 4 in (10 cm) wide, and open in summer. **'Flore Semi-Pleno'** has semi-double flowers on slightly shorter stems than the species. **ZONES 6–10.**

Papaver bracteatum

Occurring naturally from the Caucasus to the Himalayas, this summer-flowering species is very similar to *Papaver orientale*. It is a perennial with 3 ft (1 m) tall flower stems and 18 in (45 cm) long pinnate leaves. The foliage and stems are covered with white hairs. The flowers, usually red with purple centers, are 4 in (10 cm) wide. **ZONES 5–10.**

Papaver commutatum

A close relative of the blood-red *Papaver rhoeas*, this annual species can be massed in a garden to create an effect resembling an Impressionist painting. The flowers, bright red on hairy stems, appear in summer but only last for about 3 weeks. **ZONES 8–10.**

Papaver atlanticum **'Flore Semi-Pleno'**

Papaver commutatum

Papaver bracteatum

Papaver nudicaule
ICELAND POPPY

This tuft-forming perennial from North America and Asia Minor is almost always grown as an annual. It is good for rock gardens and for cutting. Large scented flowers, borne in winter and spring, are white, yellow, orange or pink, and have a crinkled texture; the leaves are pale green, the stems long and hairy. It grows 12–24 in (30–60 cm) tall with a 6–8 in (15–20 cm) spread. **ZONES 2–10.**

Papaver orientale
ORIENTAL POPPY

This herbaceous perennial is native to southwest Asia. In summer it bears spectacular flowers as big as peonies in shades of pink through to red with 4 in (10 cm) diameter dark centers. The cultivated varieties, sometimes double, come in a wide range of colors and many feature a dark basal blotch on each petal. It has hairy, lance-like, bluish green leaves and can become straggly. According to variety, it grows from 18 in (45 cm) to more than 3 ft (1 m) tall. **'Cedric Morris'** is a big-flowered form with individual blooms up to 6 in (15 cm) across; the shell-pink flowers have frilly petals, each with an almost black blotch at the base. **'Mrs Perry'** has large, coral pink flowers. **ZONES 3–9.**

Papaver rhoeas
CORN POPPY, FIELD POPPY, FLANDERS POPPY

The cupped flowers on this fast-growing annual from Asia Minor are small, delicate, scarlet and single. The cultivated varieties (**Shirley Series**) come in reds, pinks, whites and bicolors; they have a pale heart instead of the black cross that marks the center of the wild poppy. The leaves are light green and lobed. This

Papaver rhoeas Shirley Series

Papaver orientale

species grows to 24 in (60 cm) high with a 12 in (30 cm) spread. Double-flowered strains are also available. **'Mother of Pearl'** has gray, pink or blue-purple flowers. **ZONES 5–9.**

Papaver somniferum
OPIUM POPPY

The grayish green leaves on this fast-growing annual from the Middle East are lobed and elliptical with serrated edges. It blooms in summer, displaying big flowers in white, pink, red or purple, usually as doubles. Opium poppies are cultivated for the milky sap produced in their seed capsules; this is the source of the narcotic drug opium and its derivatives. The flowers of **'Hungarian Blue'** are more intense in color than those of the wild plants. **ZONES 7–10.**

Papaver rhoeas 'Mother of Pearl'

Papaver rhoeas Shirley Series

PAPHIOPEDILUM
SLIPPER ORCHID, LADY'S SLIPPER

This orchid genus extends from India through Southeast Asia, including southern China, to the Philippines and New Guinea. The plants grow mostly at moderate altitudes in dense shade on the rainforest floor or in leaf mold on rock faces and occasionally as epiphytes. They are usually compact, consisting of fleshy roots, a short stem and a few large, often mottled leaves with a terminal inflorescence of one or a few large flowers with a characteristic pouched lip. There are about 60 species, although some authorities recognize many variations as species.
CULTIVATION: Cultivation depends on the origin of the plants, but most are best grown in intermediate temperatures and part-shade. They should be kept evenly moist throughout the year with well-drained potting mixture. Difficult to grow from seed, many species are threatened by over-collecting from the wild. They are propagated by division; mericlonal propagation does not suit them, and so selected clones and hybrids remain expensive.

Paphiopedilum callosum

This attractive species grows to about 18 in (45 cm) tall and occurs at low altitudes in Thailand, peninsular Malaysia, Laos and Cambodia. There are 3 to 5 leaves about 4–8 in (10–20 cm) by 1–2 in (2.5–5 cm), lightly mottled on the upper surface. The inflorescence has a single showy flower, 3–4 in (8–10 cm) across and long lasting. In cultivation, this species requires warm conditions; it flowers in early summer. **ZONES 11–12.**

Paphiopedilum insigne

This species occurs in Nepal and northern India at about 6,660 ft (2,000 m) in limestone soils. It is a vigorous grower, about 12–18 in (30–45 cm) tall and often forms large clumps. The few strap-like leaves are up to 15 in (38 cm) long and 1 in (25 mm) wide. The inflorescence is 12 in (30 cm) long with 1 or 2 glossy flowers 4–6 in (10–15 cm) long, which appear in fall (autumn) and winter. This species is the basis of many modern hybrids. Named forms combine shades of green, russet, cream and white in various patterns and markings. **ZONES 10–12.**

Paphiopedilum insigne

Paphiopedilum callosum

Papaver somniferum

Papaver somniferum 'Hungarian Blue'

Papaver nudicaule

Paphiopedilum lawrenceanum

This plant grows to about 15 in (38 cm) tall and occurs at low altitudes in Borneo, in deep leaf litter in rainforests or on mossy limestone rocks. There are 5 to 6 mottled, dark green leaves up to 8 in (20 cm) long and 2 in (5 cm) wide. The inflorescence is up to 12 in (30 cm) long with a single flower up to 4 in (10 cm) across. It flowers in spring and early summer. **ZONES 11–12.**

Paphiopedilum malipoense

This is one of a group of species from southwest China having been discovered only recently, growing in cracks on rocks at moderate altitudes. It has 7 or 8 mottled leaves about 4–8 in (10–20 cm) by 1–2 in (2.5–5 cm) wide. The inflorescence is about 10–12 in (25–30 cm) tall with a single flower about 3 in (8 cm) across with a prominent pouched lip about 2 in (5 cm) long. **ZONES 10–12.**

Paphiopedilum rothschildianum

This large clump-forming species occurs only on Mt Kinabalu in Borneo, where it grows at low altitudes terrestrially or on rock ledges. It is regarded as one of the most threatened orchid species in the world as it is known from only 2 sites and is much sought after. There are several leaves, strap-like and up to 24 in (60 cm) long and 2 in (5 cm) wide. The inflorescence is up to 18 in (45 cm) long with 2 to 4 flowers about 12 in (30 cm) in diameter. Cultivation is as for the genus, but higher levels of light are recommended. Flowering occurs in spring. **ZONES 11–12.**

Paphiopedilum superbiens

Paphiopedilum rothschildianum

Paphiopedilum lawrenceanum

P. Hybrid King Arthur 'Burgoyne'

Paphiopedilum superbiens

syn. *Paphiopedilum curtisii*

This species occurs on the island of Sumatra at an altitude of 3,000–4,330 ft (900–1,300 m), growing terrestrially in coniferous forests. There are 4 to 5 leaves, mottled light and dark green, about 6–10 in (15–25 cm) long and $1\frac{1}{2}$–$2\frac{1}{2}$ in (3.5–6 cm) wide. The inflorescence is up to 12 in (30 cm) tall with a single flower $2\frac{1}{2}$–3 in (6–8 cm) across. It flowers in summer. **ZONES 11–12.**

Paphiopedilum malipoense

P. Hybrid 'Broadwoodwidger' × 'Momag'

P. Hybrid Copperspice 'Vulcano'

Paphiopedilum Hybrid Grande Jersey

Paphiopedilum Hybrids

Thousands of hybrids have been produced, many in an attempt to achieve a more rounded flower shape. Other goals include increased vigor and flower size, and interesting color combinations. Many will bloom several times a year. Another trend in hybridizing has been to produce novelties, generally ignoring size and rounded shape. More hybrids have been registered in *Paphiopedilum* than in any other orchid genus. Unfortunately many attempts have not resulted in improvements over the original species, although there are some outstanding exceptions. Most of the hybrids come from about 25 species. **King Arthur 'Burgoyne'**, a typical hybrid, shows a strong influence of *P. insigne*; it has flowers of a rich coppery red except for the white tip of the broad dorsal sepal. **Grande Jersey** is a hybrid grex of a quite different kind, bred from the small group of species with very elongated, twisted petals; some of these have more than one flower per stem, a feature also apparent in this hybrid. **ZONES 10–12.**

Paphiopedilum Hybrid Ernest Reed

P. Hybrid Chouvetti 'Van Dyke'

PARADISEA
ST BRUNO'S LILY, PARADISE LILY

This genus consists of 2 species of rhizomatous perennials from the mountains of southern Europe. They form small clumps of grassy to strap-like bright green leaves and from late spring produce erect stems topped with heads of 6-petalled, funnel- to bell-shaped white flowers up to 1½ in (35 mm) long. The flower stems are from 1–5 ft (0.3–1.5 m) tall depending on the species and carry 4 to 25 blooms.
CULTIVATION: Both species will tolerate moderate frosts and prefer to be grown in moist, humus-rich soil in full sun, though they do not always respond well to cultivation. They must not dry out in summer. Propagate from seed or by dividing well-established clumps.

Paradisea liliastrum

In early summer, this species bears racemes of 4 to 10, 1–2 in (2.5–5 cm) long, scented, white, funnel-shaped flowers blooming on wiry, 12–24 in (30–60 cm) stems. The strappy, grayish green leaves are arranged in a basal rosette. It is a beautiful plant but not always amenable to cultivation. **ZONES 7–9.**

PARAHEBE
VERONICA

This genus of 30 species is native mainly to New Zealand with a few species in New Guinea and Australia (most of the Australian species hitherto included in this genus have now been placed in the genus *Derwentia,* including *Parahebe perfoliata*). They are dense, subshrubby evergreens with a low, spreading habit, making them excellent for border edgings or rockeries. Their leaves are usually small and round with toothed edges, and along with the wiry stems make a dense mounding mat of growth.

Parahebe × bidwillii

In spring and summer they bear small white, pink, mauve or blue flowers in sprays held above the foliage.
CULTIVATION: Hardy to moderate frosts, they prefer full sun and good drainage. Most grow best in humus-rich soil, although some prefer gravelly conditions. Many self-layer freely where the stems touch the ground, or they may be propagated from seed or cuttings.

Parahebe × bidwillii

A hybrid between 2 New Zealand species *(Parahebe decora* and *P. lyallii),* this mat-forming plant to 6 in (15 cm) high has wiry stems clothed with leaves less than ½ in (12 mm) long. In summer, it bears showy 8 in (20 cm) racemes of tiny, lilac-veined white flowers. **ZONES 8–10.**

Parahebe catarractae

Perhaps the most decorative, this species has a rapid, spreading habit at first and then grows upwards. In spring it bears racemes of small, white, funnel-shaped flowers tinged with purple among oval, serrated leaves. It grows to a height and spread of 12 in (30 cm). **ZONES 8–10.**

Parahebe linifolia

This New Zealand species is a wiry-stemmed, 8 in (20 cm) tall subshrub.

P. Hybrid 'Iolanthe' × 'Daiboth'

Paphiopedilum Hybrid Pinocchio

Paphiopedilum Hybrid 'Burnea'

Paphiopedilum Hybrid 'Western Port'

Parahebe linifolia

It may be rounded or spreading, and has ½ in (12 mm) long, shallowly toothed leaves. In summer it bears racemes of small white to pink flowers. **ZONES 8–10.**

Parahebe lyallii

This semi-evergreen, marginally frost-hardy, prostrate shrub fromNew Zealand, grows to a height of 6 in (15 cm) with a spread of up to 10 in (25 cm). In early summer it bears terminal spikes of small white or pink flowers set among oval, serrated, leathery green leaves. **ZONES 8–10.**

PARASERIANTHES

This genus consists of 4 species of evergreen trees that were formerly included in the genus *Albizia.* They occur wild in Australia and the islands to its north. All have feathery bipinnate leaves with small crowded leaflets and mimosa-like flowers that are crowded into dense spikes. The taller tropical species are grown for fuel and timber, while the smaller *Paraserianthes lophantha* is used in gardens for instant effect and to provide shelter for slower-growing plants.
CULTIVATION: *P. lophantha,* the only species seen in gardens, is not particular as to soil and will thrive in full sun or part-shade. Marginally frost-hardy, it may be grown as a greenhouse plant in cold climates. Propagate from seed in fall (autumn). The hard seeds, held within long flat pods, germinate more quickly if gently nicked or filed before planting.

Paraserianthes lophantha
syn. *Albizia lophantha*

CAPE LEEUWIN WATTLE, CRESTED WATTLE, TREE-IN-A-HURRY

This tree grows very quickly to 25 ft (8 m). The yellowish green brush-like

Paraserianthes lophantha

flower spikes appear in late winter and spring. The feathery grayish green leaves have the unusual habit of folding up at night. Crested wattle may grow to 12 ft (3.5 m) during its first summer and often flowers in its first year. **ZONES 9–11.**

PARIS
syn. *Daiswa*

This genus consists of 20 species of herbaceous, rhizomatous perennials and is closely related to the trilliums. It is found from Europe to eastern Asia. They form clumps and their leaves are carried in whorls at the top of stems up to 3 ft (1 m) long. Unlike trilliums, the 1–4 in (2.5–10 cm) long, oval to lance-shaped leaves are not always in 3s, but in groups of 4 to 12 depending on the species. The flowers, borne singly at the stem tips in spring and summer, have 4 to 6 petals and sepals that are usually green or yellow-green.
CULTIVATION: Plant in cool, moist, woodland conditions in dappled shade. Most species are vigorous and are not difficult to cultivate. They are very frost hardy. Propagate from seed or by dividing established clumps. Divide only every 3 to 4 years or the plants may be weakened.

Paris japonica

Paris lanceolata

Paris polyphylla var. *yunnanensis*

Paris polyphylla

Paris japonica
syn. *Kinugasa japonica*

This Japanese species has stems up to 30 in (75 cm) tall and whorls of 8–12 in (20–30 cm) long elliptical leaves. The flowers are borne singly on 1–3 in (2.5–8 cm) pedicels at the stem tips and have white sepals up to 2 in (5 cm) long. The petals are much reduced or absent. The flowers are followed by small, fleshy red fruit. **ZONES 8–10.**

Paris lanceolata

This species has long, narrow leaves that form a very distinct collar around a central stem. At its tip, the stem carries a flower with golden anthers and petals reduced to filaments. **ZONES 7–10.**

Paris polyphylla
syn. *Daiswa polyphylla*

This Chinese species grows to 3 ft (1 m) tall with 6 in (15 cm) leaves. The flowers have very narrow, almost filamentous petals up to 4 in (10 cm) long. Although scarcely a feature, they are yellow-green while the center of the flower is purple with brown stigmas. The flowers are followed by red fruit. ***Paris polyphylla* var. *yunnanensis* f. *alba*** is a white form with slightly broader petals. **ZONES 7–10.**

Paris quadrifolia

This very frost-hardy species from Eurasia, which grows to 15 in (38 cm) in height, bears its star-shaped, green and white flowers in late spring. The mid-green leaves are from 2–6 in (5–15 cm) long. **ZONES 8–10.**

PARKINSONIA

Related to *Cassia*, this genus consists of only 2 species of thorny, deciduous trees and shrubs from subtropical and tropical America and Africa respectively, but

Paris quadrifolia

some botanists now interpret *Parkinsonia* more broadly, transferring to it the 10 species hitherto included in *Cercidium*. If grown in full sun they can reach 30 ft (9 m). The leaves are pinnate but the small leaflets are very short-lived, so for most of the year only the slender bare stems and leaf-stalks are present. These set off to good effect the delicate golden flowers produced in spring. The fruits are brownish pods.

CULTIVATION: Frost tender but very drought and heat tolerant, they prefer full sun and fertile, well-drained soil. Keep them reasonably dry in winter. Scarified seeds germinate rapidly when sown in spring.

Parkinsonia aculeata
JERUSALEM THORN, HORSE BEAN, MEXICAN PALO VERDE

Occurring widely as a native through warmer drier parts of the Americas, the Jerusalem thorn has naturalized in other continents in regions of similar climate, being regarded as a troublesome weed. However, it is quite ornamental and valued for its tolerance of extreme conditions. This graceful shrub or small tree of 12–25 ft (3.5–7.5 m) has an umbrella-shaped crown and drooping branchlets bearing small thorns. The pinnate leaves consist of a flattened green central stalk (rachis) which persists after the tiny round leaflets have fallen. In spring and summer it bears short sprays of 1 in (25 mm) wide fragrant golden flowers. *Parkinsonia aculeata* is also a useful hedge plant. **ZONES 9–12.**

PARNASSIA
BOG STAR, PARNASSUS GRASS

This is a genus of around 15 species of perennials found over much of the northern temperate zone. They have long-stemmed, kidney-shaped to near round, 1–4 in (2.5–10 cm) long leaves in basal rosettes. The wiry flowers stem, which grow up to 24 in (60 cm) tall, bear a single, 5-petalled, 1–1½ in (25–35 mm) wide flower backed by a single bract. The flowers open in summer.

CULTIVATION: Plant in moist, well-drained soil in sun or part-shade and do not allow to become dry in summer. Some species are very difficult to cultivate and will only grow well in naturally damp, grassy meadows or damp, peaty soil. All species are very hardy. Propagate from seed in fall (autumn) or by very careful division of established clumps.

Parnassia grandifolia

This species from central and south-eastern USA grows to 24 in (60 cm) tall. It has rounded 1½–4 in (3.5–10 cm) long leaves on 1½–6 in (3.5–15 cm) stems. Its flowers are white with very narrow petals. **ZONES 6–10.**

Parnassia palustris
GRASS OF PARNASSUS

This species grows to 8 in (20 cm) in height with a 4 in (10 cm) spread. It has 1½ in (35 mm) long, light to mid-green leaves. White, saucer-shaped flowers with dark green or purplish green veining appear from late spring to early summer. **ZONES 4–9.**

PAROCHETUS
SHAMROCK PEA, CLOVER PEA, BLUE PEA

This genus contains a single species, a prostrate perennial with clover-like trifoliate leaves composed of leaflets slightly more than ½ in (12 mm) long. It occurs naturally in the mountains of tropical Africa and Asia and for most of the year looks exactly like a small patch of clover. However, from late summer to winter, depending on the climate, it is studded with ½–1 in (12–25 mm) wide bright blue pea-like flowers borne singly or in pairs.

CULTIVATION: It is an excellent plant for rockeries or an alpine house or as an unusual subject for a hanging basket. It prefers to grow in moist, humus-rich soil in sun or part-shade. Although it tolerates only light frosts, in the right conditions it can spread quickly. Propagate from seed or by division.

Parochetus communis

From southwest China, Southeast Asia and the Himalayas to Sri Lanka, this

Parkinsonia aculeata

Parkinsonia aculeata

Parnassia grandifolia

deciduous species grows to a height of 4 in (10 cm) with a 12 in (30 cm) spread. The flowers are produced in succession throughout late summer and fall (autumn). **ZONES 9–11.**

PARODIA

syns *Eriocactus, Notocactus, Wigginsia*

BALL CACTUS

Mostly native to the mountains of equatorial South America, the 50 or so species in this cactus genus vary from those that are singular and globe-shaped, to those that colonize in dense clusters of short cylindrical stems. These stems are ribbed with transverse rows of prominent tubercles with fleecy areoles sprouting brilliantly colored, curving spines. From a relatively young age, red, yellow and orange trumpet-shaped flowers bloom from the crown. **CULTIVATION:** These frost-tender plants prefer full sun with protection from the midday heat. Easy to grow, they mostly require well-drained soil and plentiful water during the summer months, with a dry spell during winter. Propagate from seed in spring or from cuttings in summer.

Parodia chrysacanthion

A small, globe-shaped cactus from northern Argentina, *Parodia chrysacanthion* grows to a height of 1½ in (35 mm) and spread of 4 in (10 cm). Its deep yellow, funnel-shaped flowers are a feature in the warmer months and cream-colored fruit, ½ in (12 mm) long, are produced in fall (autumn). **ZONES 9–11.**

Parodia concinna

syns *Notocactus apricus, N. concinnus*

Native to Brazil and Uruguay, this spherical cactus grows to 2½ in (6 cm) high and 4 in (10 cm) wide. Large, yellow, funnel-shaped flowers and green globular fruit dominate in the summer months. **ZONES 9–11.**

Parodia formosa

Parodia formosa, native to South America, is less flamboyant in bloom than other species of the genus—its orange flowers are small in comparison with its 12 in (30 cm) diameter body. However, the plant is noteworthy for its spiral ribs and short, white spines. **ZONES 9–11.**

Parochetus communis

Parodia graessneri

syn. *Notocactus graessneri*

Closely resembling *Parodia haselbergii* and also from southern Brazil, this species has a spherical, deep green stem with yellowish spines up to 1 in (25 mm) long. Its 1 in (25 mm) wide yellow-green flowers are borne in spring. It grows to a height and spread of 6 in (15 cm). **ZONES 9–11.**

Parodia grossei

syns *Notocactus grossei, N. schumanniana*

This cactus from Paraguay is one of the larger of the genus, with a dark green, rounded body growing up to 3 ft (1 m) high. Funnel-shaped, 1½ in (35 mm) yellow flowers develop in summer at the crown of the plant and are followed by round green fruit. **ZONES 9–11.**

Parodia haselbergii

syn. *Notocactus haselbergii*

This species from southern Brazil usually has a single stem up to 6 in (15 cm) in diameter with 30 to 60 or more ribs. Its spines, up to 60 per tubercle, are around ½ in (12 mm) long and white or yellow tinted. In winter and spring the stem produces around 15, ½ in (12 mm) long orange-red flowers. **ZONES 9–11.**

Parodia chrysacanthion

Parodia grossei

Parodia herteri

syn. *Notocactus herteri*

Reaching a height of 18 in (45 cm), this pale green cactus is native to Uruguay. It grows to a width of 6 in (15 cm) and bears reddish brown spines that develop in clusters along raised ribs. The summer flowers are funnel-shaped and red with a yellowish throat, while the fruit are green and spherical, growing to 1½ in (35 mm) in diameter. **ZONES 9–11.**

Parodia leninghausii

syns *Eriocactus leninghausii, Notocactus leninghausii*

GOLDEN BALL

This green cactus is initially spherical, but becomes column-shaped with maturity. Bearing pale yellow spines, it grows up to 3 ft (1 m) tall and 4 in (10 cm) wide. Deep yellow flowers, 2 in (5 cm) across, and green spherical fruit develop in summer. **ZONES 9–11.**

Parodia magnifica

syn. *Notocactus magnificus*

Native to Brazil, this rounded cactus usually forms in clusters and has a blue-green body. It grows 3 ft (1 m) high and 6 in (15 cm) wide. Yellow, 2 in (5 cm) wide, funnel-shaped flowers appear in summer, along with rounded green fruit. **ZONES 9–11.**

Parodia mammulosa

syn. *Notocactus mammulosus*

This is a small globular cactus with a maximum height of 4 in (10 cm) and width of 2½ in (6 cm). In summer, its dark green body bears a cluster of yellow, funnel-shaped flowers at its crown. **ZONES 9–11.**

Parodia haselbergii

Parodia leninghausii

Parodia herteri

Parodia magnifica

Parodia graessneri

Parodia microsperma
syn. *Parodia sanguiniflora*

From northern Argentina, this green cactus is initially globular but later becomes cylindrical in shape with a maximum width of 2 in (5 cm). It is crowned by a cluster of blood-red flowers in summer. **ZONES 9–11.**

Parodia scopa
syn. *Notocactus scopa*

With a body densely covered in white radial spines, this cactus is native to southern Brazil and Uruguay. It grows up to 10 in (25 cm) tall and 4 in (10 cm) wide, with yellow, funnel-shaped flowers appearing in summer. **ZONES 9–11.**

PARONYCHIA
WHITLOW WORT

This widespread genus consists of around 50 species of usually mat- or clump-forming, dianthus- or thyme-like annuals or perennials. Most occur naturally in the Mediterranean region and have wiry stems and tiny linear to rounded leaves, often in pairs. The minute flower inflorescences, in themselves quite inconspicuous, smother the plants in early summer and are highlighted by the surrounding silvery bracts.
CULTIVATION: These are very much plants for well-drained, sunny positions and are at home in rockeries or alpine houses. Most are quite frost hardy, but suffer if kept wet and cold in winter. Propagate from seed or by layering (they are often self-layering) or by division.

Paronychia argentea

This species from southern Europe, North Africa and southwest Asia forms a mat of wiry stems with rounded leaves. In summer, it is smothered in small, dull yellow inflorescences partially covered by silvery bracts. **ZONES 7–11.**

Paronychia capitata

This Mediterranean species is very similar to *Paronychia argentea*. However, its leaves are linear to lance-shaped rather than rounded and its bracts are an even brighter silver. **ZONES 5–10.**

Parodia microsperma

Parodia scopa

Parrotia persica

Parthenocissus henryana

PARROTIA
PERSIAN WITCH-HAZEL

This genus from Iran and the Caucasus was named after F. W. Parrot, a German botanist. It consists of a single tree species cultivated for its rich hues in fall (autumn) and unusual flowers. The petal-less flowers consist of upright, wiry, dark red stamens enclosed in brown bracts. They appear in early spring before the leaves, which are about 4 in (10 cm) long and have undulating edges. The branches on older trees dip down towards the ground.
CULTIVATION: A lime-tolerant tree, it is said to achieve its best colors when grown in slightly acid soil. It grows well in full sun, fertile soil and temperate climates. Propagate from softwood cuttings in summer or from seed in fall—germination can take up to 18 months.

Parrotia persica

This spreading, short-trunked, deciduous tree with flaking bark can reach 40 ft (12 m) in the wild; in a garden it is unlikely to grow above 25 ft (8 m). The roughly diamond-shaped leaves turn magnificent shades of yellow, orange and crimson in fall (autumn). **ZONES 5–9.**

Parrotia persica

Paronychia capitata

Parthenocissus tricuspidata

PARTHENOCISSUS

These 10 species of charming climbing plants from North America and Asia have deciduous, attractively cut leaves, some with magnificent fall (autumn) coloring. The genus name is from the Greek *parthenos*, meaning 'virgin', and *kissos*, meaning 'creeper'. They climb by tendrils with tiny disc-shaped suckers and are perfect for growing on building facades and walls.
CULTIVATION: Very frost hardy, they grow best in humus-rich, well-drained soil in filtered sunlight with protection from hot winds. Propagate from cuttings in late winter or early spring.

Parthenocissus henryana

Native to China, this species climbs to around 25 ft (8 m) high and wide. Its leaves consist of 3 to 5 leaflets, 2–4 in (5–10 cm) long with dark green, silver-veined upper surfaces and purple undersides. The leaves redden in fall (autumn), but are seldom very vibrant. The spring foliage, which is the main attraction, often does better in part-shade. **ZONES 7–10.**

Parthenocissus quinquefolia
syns *Ampelopsis quinquefolia*, *Vitis quinquefolia*
VIRGINIA CREEPER, WOODBINE

This high climber from eastern North America grows to 50 ft (15 m) or more. It has handsome compound leaves with 5 leaflets and makes an attractive green wall cover in summer, turning brilliant red in fall (autumn). **ZONES 3–9.**

Parthenocissus tricuspidata
BOSTON IVY, JAPANESE IVY

Ideal for covering large walls, this ivy reaches up to 60 ft (18 m) or more. The 3-lobed leaves, 8 in (20 cm) across, turn spectacular shades of red and purple in fall (autumn); the tiny flowers are greenish yellow. The smaller leaves of **'Veitchii'** (syn. *Ampelopsis veitchii*) are purple when immature. **ZONES 4–9.**

PASSIFLORA
syn. *Tacsonia*
PASSION FLOWER, GRANADILLA

This genus contains over 400 species of mostly evergreen or semi-evergreen, tendril-climbing vines, primarily native to tropical South America. They are grown for their ornamental blossoms and their pulpy fruit, notably the passionfruit. Flowers range from pale pink to purple-red and fruits from pale yellow through to purple-black, depending on the species. Two examples of beautiful hybrids are **'Coral Seas'**, which is a deep red, and **'Lilac Lady'** (syn. 'Lavender Lady'), with its delicate light lilac petals fading to white at their tips. **CULTIVATION:** Very frost hardy to frost tender, these climbers are best suited to warm areas. Plant in rich, well-drained soil in full sun and provide support. Water regularly in summer. Prune congested or overgrown plants in spring. Propagate from seed in spring, or from cuttings or by layering in summer. They are susceptible to nematodes.

Passiflora caerulea 'Constance Elliott'

Passiflora 'Lilac Lady'

Passiflora 'Coral Seas'

Passiflora × *alato-caerulea*

This is a frost-tender hybrid between *Passiflora alata* and *P. caerulea* with 3-lobed, smooth-edged leaves. The 4 in (10 cm) wide flowers are pinkish purple and white outside with white interiors and violet filaments. **ZONES 9–11.**

Passiflora × *allardii*

This hybrid between *Passiflora caerulea* **'Constance Elliott'** and *P. quadrangularis* was raised at Cambridge University in 1907. It has 3-lobed leaves and strikingly colored flowers just over 4 in (10 cm) wide. The flowers are white suffused pink with contrasting deep blue filaments. It blooms from late summer and is marginally frost hardy. **ZONES 9–11.**

Passiflora × *exoniensis*

Passiflora antioquiensis
syn. *Tacsonia van-volxemii*
RED BANANA PASSION FLOWER

This strong grower from Colombia has 3-lobed oval to lance-shaped leaves up to 6 in (15 cm) long. The leaves are downy when young and felted on their undersides. Pendulous, bright red flowers up to 6 in (15 cm) wide open in summer. Long, elliptical, edible yellow fruit follow. It is frost tender. **ZONES 9–11.**

Passiflora aurantia

Native to Queensland, Australia, this species has 3-lobed leaves up to 3 in (8 cm) long. Its flowers are 4 in (10 cm) wide with pale pink ageing to orange-red sepals, orange to brick red petals and deep red filaments. It blooms in summer and is frost tender. **ZONES 10–12.**

Passiflora × *allardii*

Passiflora caerulea

Passiflora caerulea
BLUE PASSION FLOWER, BLUE CROWN PASSION FLOWER

In summer, this marginally frost hardy, fast-growing, 30 ft (9 m) evergreen or semi-evergreen climber produces beautiful flowers with pale pink petals, with filaments banded with blue or purple. These are followed by edible, egg-shaped, yellow fruit. **'Constance Elliott'** has all-white flowers. **ZONES 8–11.**

Passiflora × *caeruleoracemosa* 'Eynsford Gem'
syn. *Passiflora* 'Eynsford Gem'

This frost-tender hybrid between *Passiflora caerulea* and *P. racemosa* has 5-lobed blue-green leaves and mauve-pink flowers with white filaments. **ZONES 9–11.**

Passiflora coccinea

Passiflora coccinea
RED GRANADILLA, RED PASSION FLOWER

This robust, evergreen, woody stemmed climber reaches 12 ft (3.5 m) in height. It is grown for the brilliant, large, scarlet flowers with red, pink and white crowns it bears in summer and fall (autumn), set among large, dark green, crinkly leaves. It is frost tender and also needs protection from hot winds. **ZONES 10–12.**

P. × *caeruleoracemosa* 'Eynsford Gem'

Passiflora edulis
PASSIONFRUIT

This frost-tender species is valued for its glossy, bright green leaves, purple-white flowers and flavorsome fruit. It grows to 15 ft (4.5 m) and has white flowers that are green beneath. Train on a pergola or trellis and prune to prevent tangling as this encourages insect infestation. Pick fruit when the skin has turned purple and is still smooth, but do not eat until the skin is wrinkled. This species is self-fertile. **ZONES 10–12.**

Passiflora × *exoniensis*

This is a hybrid between *Passiflora antioquiensis* and *P. mollissima*. It has wide, 3-lobed, rather hairy leaves and pendulous flowers up to 6 in (15 cm) wide. The flowers are red on the outside with a pink interior and violet-tinted petals. It is frost tender. **ZONES 10–12.**

Paulownia tomentosa

Paulownia tomentosa

Passiflora laurifolia
YELLOW GRANADILLA, JAMAICA HONEYSUCKLE

This species, found through much of northern South America and the West Indies, has oval 4 in (10 cm) long leaves and flowers to 3 in (8 cm) wide. The sepals have red upper surfaces, green below. The petals are a similar color but filaments have red, blue or white banding. The summer flowers are followed by 3 in (8 cm) long ovoid yellow fruit. **ZONES 11–12.**

Passiflora manicata

Found in Colombia and Peru, this frost-tender species has 3-lobed, 3 in (8 cm) long leaves with felted undersides. Its flowers are bright red, bell-shaped and relatively small; the interiors are blue and white. The flowers are followed by 2 in (5 cm) long green fruit. **ZONES 9–11.**

Passiflora mollissima
syn. *Tacsonia mollissima*
BANANA PASSION FLOWER

This attractive, fast-growing vine does well in cool climates and features pink flowers and long, golden-yellow fruit. Train against a support to show the fruit and flowers to advantage. Generous in its crop, it often fruits in the first year; the fruit are not as sweet as the ordinary passionfruit. This frost-tender vine can spread like a weed. **ZONES 8–11.**

Passiflora quadrangularis
GIANT GRANADILLA

This vigorous, scrambling vine grows to 50 ft (15 m) or more in height. It has bright green oval leaves and bears large, deep red flowers with a conspicuous ring of purplish filaments from mid-summer to fall (autumn). The oblong to oval fruit, to 12 in (30 cm) long, have a thick yellowish rind and a sweet pulp. This frost-tender plant needs both high temperatures and high humidity to set fruit. **ZONES 10–12.**

Passiflora racemosa
RED PASSION FLOWER

This is a frost-tender Brazilian species with 3-lobed, 4 in (10 cm) long leaves. The bright red or white flowers are held in 12 in (30 cm) long pendulous racemes. The outer filaments are white with purple bands; the inner filaments are short and red. **ZONES 10–12.**

Passiflora vitifolia

Native to Central and South America, this spring- and summer-flowering species has 6 in (15 cm), 3-lobed grape-like leaves with shiny upper surfaces and finely hairy undersides. The flowers are up to 4 in (10 cm) wide, bright red or deep orange with red or yellow filaments. The fruit that follow are edible and have a mild strawberry flavor. It is frost tender. **ZONES 10–12.**

Paulownia fortunei

Pastinaca sativa

PASTINACA

Only one species is cultivated in this genus of 14 species of biennials or perennials found throughout Eurasia. It is the parsnip, grown for its fleshy white root with a distinctive flavor. It has simple or pinnate leaves and yellow flowers.
CULTIVATION: Grow in full sun in well-drained, deep, friable, stone-free soil that has been well dug. Improve poor soil with plenty of compost, but do not use fresh manure as it may cause misshapen roots. Propagate from seed in spring. Watch for slugs, canker, celery fly or greenfly.

Pastinaca sativa
syn. *Peucedanum sativum*
PARSNIP

A hardy root vegetable related to the carrot, the parsnip is nutritious, sweet and can be grown year round in warm climates and from mid-spring in cold climates. A strong-smelling biennial that reaches 3 ft (1 m) in height, it has pinnate leaves 4–12 in (10–30 cm) long and flowers in summer. Harvest when the leaves start to yellow. **ZONES 7–10.**

PAULOWNIA

Originating in eastern Asia, this genus of 17 species of deciduous trees is named for Anna Paulowna, daughter of Paul I, Tsar of Russia. Some fast-growing species reach 8 ft (2.4 m) in their first year, eventually growing to 50 ft (15 m). Their big, heart-shaped leaves and dense clusters of elegant flowers make them distinctive shade trees. Conspicuous, attractive buds appear in fall (autumn), opening in spring to foxglove-like flower spikes; these are followed by the leaves and capsules containing winged seeds. Some species are grown for timber in China and Japan.
CULTIVATION: These very frost-hardy trees do best in well-drained, fertile soil, with ample moisture in summer and shelter from strong winds. Propagate from seed or root cuttings taken in late summer or winter.

Paulownia fortunei
POWTON

This spreading tree to 40 ft (12 m) tall has broad, oval, mid-green leaves, 6–8 in (15–20 cm) long and half as wide with the midribs and major veins clearly visible on the hairy undersides. The leaves turn dull yellow before dropping in fall (autumn). Fragrant, 3 in (8 cm) long, bell-shaped flowers, cream to pale mauve with a creamy, purple-spotted throat, are borne in clusters in spring. **ZONES 6–10.**

Paulownia tomentosa
syn. *Paulownia imperialis*
PRINCESS TREE, EMPRESS TREE

This tree can reach a height and width of 40 ft (12 m) and is valued for its large,

Passiflora laurifolia

Passiflora manicata

Passiflora mollissima

Passiflora quadrangularis

paired, heart-shaped leaves, up to 12 in (30 cm) wide, and erect, fragrant, pale violet flowers. Grown in both cool- and warm-temperate climates, it can suffer frost damage to the flower buds. If pruned almost to the ground each winter, the tree will develop branches about 10 ft (3 m) long with enormous leaves, but will not flower. **ZONES 5–10.**

PAVONIA

This is a genus of around 150 species of perennials, subshrubs and shrubs widespread in the tropics and subtropics, particularly in the Americas. They usually have strongly upright, cane-like stems clothed with simple oval, occasionally lobed, leaves from 1–10 in (2.5–25 cm) long depending on the species. The flowers usually occur singly in the leaf axils and have a very distinctive structure: the petals enclose a central column of stamens and fold back to form a starry flower that leaves the staminal column exposed. It is rather like a hibiscus with daisy-like ray petals.
CULTIVATION: Provided they are given moist, well-drained soil and a warm, frost-free climate, most species are not difficult to cultivate. They grow in sun or part-shade. Propagate from seed in spring or cuttings in summer.

Pavonia × gledhillii
syn. *Pavonia intermedia* of gardens

This hybrid between 2 Brazilian species (*Pavonia makoyana* × *P. multiflora*) is probably the most widely cultivated and has produced several cultivars. It forms a shrub to 6 ft (1.8 m) tall and has serrated-edged, elliptical to lance-shaped leaves up to 6 in (15 cm) long. The flowers, borne singly, are bright pink, starry and up to 1½ in (35 mm) wide. The staminal column bears conspicuous blue-gray pollen. **'Kermesina'** is a dwarf cultivar with very bright magenta to carmine flowers. **'Rosea'** has deep pink flowers. **ZONES 10–12.**

Pavonia lasiopetala

This 3–4 ft (1–1.2 m) tall South American shrub bears bright pink, 1–2 in (2.5–5 cm) wide flowers throughout the warmer months. It is one of the hardier species and grows well in sun or shade. **ZONES 10–12.**

PAXISTIMA
syn. *Pachystima*
MOUNTAIN LOVER

This is a genus of 2 species of dwarf evergreen shrubs from North America. They have narrow, 4-sided stems with a corky bark covered in small protuberances. The simple oval to linear leaves are leathery and have finely serrated edges. The tiny 4-petalled flowers occur singly in the leaf axils in spring and summer, and are followed by tiny, 2-valved seed capsules.
CULTIVATION: Easily grown in any well-drained soil in sun or part-shade, they prefer summer moisture. They are very frost hardy, and may be used as low hedges if trimmed heavily. Propagate from seed, cuttings or self-rooted layers.

Paxistima canbyi
syns *Canbya paxistima, Pachystima canbyi*

This low, shrubby native from the mountains of Virginia is a useful ground cover for east coastal gardens. Adaptable throughout the Midwest and northeastern USA, it is grown for its narrow, evergreen leaves and mounding habit; its flowers and fruit are insignificant. It reaches around 12 in (30 cm) high and 3–5 ft (1–1.5 m) wide. **ZONES 3–8.**

Paxistima myrtifolia
OREGON BOXWOOD

This spreading, multi-branched species is found over much of western North America from California to British Columbia. It grows to around 3 ft (1 m) tall and has finely serrated, glossy green, rounded leaves up to 1½ in (35 mm) long. The flowers are minute, red tinted and open in spring. **ZONES 6–10.**

PEDILANTHUS
RICK RACK PLANT

This succulent genus, closely allied to *Euphorbia,* is native to the Caribbean, southern USA and northern South America. It consists of about 14 species, all bushy in appearance, growing to a maximum height of 8 ft (2.4 m) with a spread of 5 ft (1.5 m). Species differ mainly in their green-white flowers, borne in summer and fall (autumn), and enclosed by bracts shaped like a bird's head. The foliage is green or variegated.
CULTIVATION: Ensure a sheltered spot as these frost-hardy plants are sensitive to cold. They prefer well-drained soil and part-shade. Propagate from cuttings.

Pedilanthus bracteatus
syn. *Euphorbia bracteata*

This evergreen succulent shrub, originally from Mexico, grows to a height of 10 ft (3 m). Its long green leaves are ovate to inversely lance-shaped, reaching a length of 6 in (15 cm). The small green flowers are produced in summer. **ZONES 9–11.**

Pedilanthus tithymaloides
ZIGZAG PLANT, DEVIL'S BACKBONE, JACOB'S LADDER

Popular as a greenhouse plant in the UK in the nineteenth century, this slow-growing succulent from the West Indies can reach a height of 6 ft (1.8 m) in cultivation. The fleshy, erect stems change direction at each node, hence the common name zigzag plant. The mid-green leaves sprout from the stems in 2 rows, resembling ribs on a backbone. Variegated cultivars are popular. Showy red bracts encase small, scarlet flowers, but such flowers are rarely produced indoors. The stems, when cut, secrete a poisonous milky sap. **ZONES 9–11.**

PELARGONIUM

The widely grown hybrid pelargoniums are popularly known as 'geraniums', but should not be confused with members of the genus *Geranium* of the same plant family. The genus *Pelargonium* consists of perhaps 280 species, the vast majority endemic to South Africa and adjacent Namibia, but a sprinkling of species are found elsewhere in the world including other parts of Africa, southwest Asia, Arabia, Australia, New Zealand and some Atlantic Ocean islands. Although pelargoniums are mostly soft-wooded shrubs and subshrubs, some are herbaceous perennials or even annuals; there is also a large but little known group of species that have succulent stems, leaves or roots and are grown by succulent collectors. The leaves of pelargoniums are often as broad as they are long and are variously toothed, scalloped, lobed or dissected, depending on species; they are usually aromatic, containing a wide range of essential oils, and may secrete resin droplets which give the leaves a sticky feel. Flowers of the wild species have the 2 upper petals differently colored or marked from the 3 lower ones, a feature that distinguishes pelargoniums from true geraniums. Their seeds are plumed like thistledown, another distinguishing feature.

Only a few groups of hybrid pelargoniums are widely grown in gardens and as indoor plants, originating in the early nineteenth century from a small number of South African shrub species. The common garden and pot 'geraniums' are the **Zonal pelargoniums**, once known botanically as *Pelargonium × hortorum*. They have almost circular leaves with scalloped margins, often with horseshoe-shaped zones of brown, red or purple, and flower almost continuously. This group has the largest number of cultivars, and recent breeding has developed some very attractive subgroups. Somewhat similar are the **Ivy-leafed pelargoniums**, with their semi-scrambling habit and leaves that are fleshier with more pointed lobes; these are also the subject of intensive breeding, and are tending to merge with zonals in some of their characteristics. Another major group is the **Regal pelargoniums**, sometimes known as the **Martha Washington geraniums** or *Pelargonium × domesticum*; these have woody stems and sharply toothed and creased leaves, and the large flowers come in a range of gaudy colors and patterns. There are some smaller groups of hybrids bred for their flowers, most significant being the **Unique** and **Angel pelargoniums**. And then there is a large and varied group, grown primarily for their foliage, known as the **Scented-leafed pelargoniums**: these are mostly shrubby and usually have deeply lobed or dissected leaves that give off a quite remarkable range of odours when bruised or crushed, depending on the variety. They include both species and hybrids, and some also have quite pretty flowers. Some of these are grown commercially for 'geranium oil', used in perfumery.
CULTIVATION: These frost-tender plants are often treated like annuals for summer bedding in colder climates. In warmer climates with long hours of daylight they flower almost all the time, although they do not do well in extreme heat and humidity. Plant in pots or beds. The site should be sunny with light, well-drained, neutral soil. If grown in pots, fertilize regularly and cull dead heads. Avoid over-watering; Zonals in particular rot at the base if soil remains wet, although stems re-root higher up (but weaker plants result). Propagate from softwood cuttings from spring to fall (autumn).

Pedilanthus tithymaloides

Pavonia lasiopetala

P

Pelargonium alternans

This semi-succulent species has a definite period of dry season dormancy. Its stems are short and woody, bearing small, finely divided leaves at their tips. Its flowers are carried in clusters of up to 4 blooms and are white or pink. Do not water or feed this plant too much or it will become sprawling with lax, rangy growth. **ZONES 9–11.**

Pelargonium, Angel Hybrids

This small group of hybrids was initially developed in the 1930s in London, with *Pelargonium crispum* one of the parent species. These small plants, seldom more than 10 in (25 cm) high, have toothed, crinkled leaves; the flowers are large in proportion and often very prettily marked, rather like Regal pelargoniums. **'Captain Starlight'** and **'Roller's Echo'** are typical cultivars. **ZONES 9–11.**

Pelargonium australe

This species is widely distributed across the southern half of Australia, often on

Pelargonium alternans

Pelargonium crispum

Pelargonium, Angel Hybrid, 'Captain Starlight'

Pelargonium cucullatum

sea cliffs and sand dunes. It is an herbaceous perennial forming a mound of pale green foliage about 12 in (30 cm) high; the long-stalked leaves are rather hairy and shallowly lobed. Small pink flowers in tight heads are borne from spring to early fall (autumn). **ZONES 9–11.**

Pelargonium betulinum
BIRCH LEAF PELARGONIUM

This shrubby species from South Africa grows to around 24 in (60 cm) tall, but can become sprawling in moist conditions. It has small, almost hairless, oval leaves with toothed edges. The leaves are slightly blue-green and become red tinted at the edges in very sunny or cool conditions. The pink or purple, sometimes white flowers are 1 in (25 mm) wide and are borne in clusters of 3 to 4 blooms. **ZONES 9–11.**

Pelargonium crispum
LEMON GERANIUM, FINGER-BOWL GERANIUM

A distinctive species from South Africa's southwest Cape Province, *Pelargonium*

Pelargonium crispum 'Variegatum'

Pelargonium, Angel Hybrid, 'Roller's Echo'

crispum is an erect, few-branched shrub to 3 ft (1 m) high, its straight stems regularly lined with small lobed leaves with crinkled margins, lemon-scented when bruised. The scattered pink flowers appear large in proportion, up to 1 in (25 mm) across with darker markings. **'Variegatum'** (syn. 'Prince Rupert Variegated') is a widely grown form with cream-edged leaves. **'Prince Rupert'** is a vigorous, larger-leafed form. **ZONES 9–11.**

Pelargonium cucullatum
WILDEMALVA

This South African species is one of the original parents of the Regal pelargonium hybrids; like many other significant species it is restricted in the wild to the southwest Cape Province. It makes a very attractive shrub of sprawling habit to around 3 ft (1 m) in height; the downy gray-green leaves are sharply toothed and lobed and somewhat cupped. In spring and summer, it bears clusters of bright reddish mauve flowers with darker veins, up to 2 in (5 cm) in diameter. **ZONES 9–11.**

Pelargonium echinatum
syn. *Pelargonium reniforme*
SWEETHEART GERANIUM, CACTUS GERANIUM

This unusual species, from arid regions of South Africa's northern Cape Province, has tuberous roots and a swollen stem from which several grayish, prickly branches emerge. The plant reaches no more than 18 in (45 cm) tall. At the end of the growing season, its somewhat kidney-shaped, shallowly lobed leaves drop off, leaving bare branches. White, pink, mauve or purple flowers bloom from late winter to early summer, the

Pelargonium betulinum

Pelargonium australe

upper petals often carrying a heart-shaped red blotch. Water it less for the 3 months after the leaves yellow. **ZONES 9–11.**

Pelargonium grandicalcaratum

Only rarely seen in cultivation, this species comes from near-desert regions of South Africa's Cape Province and Namibia. An 18 in (45 cm) tall deciduous shrub, it has peppery scented leaves that are rather fleshy, 3-lobed and seldom over ½ in (12 mm) long. The flowers have a ½ in (12 mm) long tube-like base that, along with the calyx and stem, is red tinted. The small, mauve flowers with purple markings never open fully; the upper petals are inward-curled, but the lower petals remain folded over one another. **ZONES 9–11.**

Pelargonium graveolens
ROSE GERANIUM

The deeply lobed, furry leaves of this species give off an aroma of roses when crushed. It is a shrubby plant, growing 12–24 in (30–60 cm) tall and wide. The smallish flowers are rose pink with a purple spot on the upper petals. The common 'rose geranium' of gardens is not the same as the original South African *Pelargonium graveolens* and is probably of hybrid origin. **ZONES 9–11.**

Pelargonium, Ivy-leafed Hybrids

These are derived mainly from the South African *Pelargonium peltatum*, which has a scrambling or trailing habit with fleshy, pointed-lobed, hairless leaves and small pink flowers. The many cultivars retain the leaf characteristics, but have larger flowers in conspicuous long-stalked

Pelargonium, I-lH, 'Blooming Gem'

Pelargonium, I-lH, 'Laced Red Cascade'

Pelargonium, Ivy-leafed Hybrid, 'Harlequin Mahogany'

Pelargonium, I-lH, 'Lilac Cascade'

Pelargonium, I-lH, 'Chic'

heads, often double and in a wide range of colors. Easily grown, they tolerate wetter conditions than the zonals, and are especially suited to hanging baskets, window boxes and the tops of retaining walls. Recent developments include variegated leaves and compact or miniature plants. Hybridizing of Ivy-leafed and Zonal pelargoniums has resulted in plants with leaves like the former and flowers more like the latter. The popular **'Amethyst'** has massed clusters of semi-double purple-pink flowers. **'Blooming Gem'** has bright pink flowers.

The **Cascade Series** of miniature ivy-leafed pelargoniums have small leaves and masses of small flowers; they include **'Laced Red Cascade'** with red flowers flecked with white, and **'Lilac Cascade'** with lavender-pink flowers. **'Chic'** has deep pink double flowers. **'Crocetta'** has red-edged semi-double white flowers. **'Galilee'**, one of the best known ivy-leafed cultivars, is compact and has leaves that may be variegated with cream or cream and pink; its densely massed double flowers are flesh pink. **'Harlequin Mahogany'** has flowers with white

Pelargonium, I-lH, 'Crocetta'

Pelargonium, I-lH, 'Galilee'

variegations caused by a virus transmitted through the seed; this has enabled the breeding of a full range of colors from pink and white to red and white. **'Mutzel'** has bright red flowers and pale green variegated leaves. **ZONES 9–11.**

Pelargonium, I-lH, 'Mutzel'

Pelargonium graveolens

Pelargonium odoratissimum

Pelargonium magenteum

syn. *Pelargonium rhodanthum*

This woody stemmed shrub, to about 3 ft (1 m) tall, has hairy, rounded to kidney-shaped, gray-green leaves slightly over $\frac{1}{2}$ in (12 mm) wide. The flowers, in clusters of 3 to 9 blooms, are up to 2 in (5 cm) wide, bright pink with a darker center. This plant has been used medicinally for intestinal complaints. **ZONES 10–11.**

Pelargonium 'Mrs Taylor'

This hybrid or cultivar of *Pelargonium ignescens* has pungent-smelling, deeply divided, lobed leaves and vivid scarlet flowers. **ZONES 10–11.**

Pelargonium × *nervosum*

This scented-leafed hybrid has small, deep green, lobed, slightly curled, toothed-edged leaves with a strong lime scent. It grows to about 15 in (40 cm) tall with an erect yet compact growth habit. The darkly veined, deep pink single flowers are borne in clusters of 3 to 7 blooms. **ZONES 9–11.**

Pelargonium grandicalcaratum

Pelargonium magenteum

Pelargonium 'Mrs Taylor'

Pelargonium odoratissimum

APPLE GERANIUM

A strong, sweet smell of apples comes off the small, roughly heart-shaped, lobed, gray-green leaves of this very bushy, many-branched geranium. It reaches a height and spread of 12 in (30 cm). The flowers are small and white, sometimes with red veins in the upper petals. In warm-temperate climates, flowers may be borne almost continuously, although it dislikes hot, humid conditions. **ZONES 10–11.**

Pelargonium peltatum

Pelargonium quercifolium

Pelargonium, RH, 'Lord Bute'

Pelargonium, RH, 'Lyewood Bonanza'

Pelargonium, Regal Hybrid, 'Rosmaroy'

P., RH, 'Monkwood Bonanza'

Pelargonium, RH, 'Morwenna'

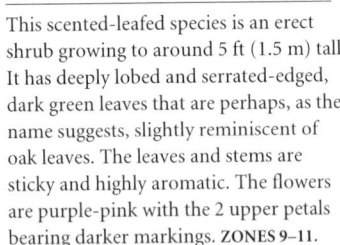

Pelargonium, Regal Hybrid, 'Parisienne'

Pelargonium, RH, 'Rembrandt'

Pelargonium, RH, 'Spot-on-Bonanza'

Pelargonium, RH, 'Vicky Clare'

Pelargonium peltatum
IVY-LEAFED GERANIUM

From coastal areas of South Africa's Cape Province, this species has trailing or scrambling stems up to 3 ft (1 m) long. Its bright green leaves have 5 sharp lobes, the shape reminiscent of ivy leaves, and are up to 3 in (8 cm) across. The flowers of the original wild form are pale pink and have quite narrow petals, appearing mainly in spring and summer. This species is the chief ancestor of the Ivy-leafed hybrids. ZONES 9–11.

Pelargonium quercifolium
OAK-LEAFED GERANIUM, ALMOND GERANIUM

This scented-leafed species is an erect shrub growing to around 5 ft (1.5 m) tall. It has deeply lobed and serrated-edged, dark green leaves that are perhaps, as the name suggests, slightly reminiscent of oak leaves. The leaves and stems are sticky and highly aromatic. The flowers are purple-pink with the 2 upper petals bearing darker markings. ZONES 9–11.

Pelargonium, Regal Hybrids
MARTHA WASHINGTON GERANIUMS, REGAL GERANIUMS, REGAL PELARGONIUMS

The spectacular large blooms of these hybrids make them suitable for exhibiting in flower shows and conservatories, as well as for sale as flowering pot plants. Originally derived from the South African mauve-flowered *Pelargonium cucullatum*, further breeding brought in red, purple and white coloring from *P. fulgidum*, *P. angulosum* and *P. grandiflorum* respectively. Sprawling shrubs about 24 in (60 cm) high, they have strong woody stems and stiff, pleated, sharply toothed leaves. In late spring and summer, they bear clusters of large flowers, wide open and often blotched or bicolored. Frost tender, in cool areas they need a greenhouse. Cut back hard after blooming to keep the bushes compact. **'Grand Slam'** is heavy flowering and compact, deep pinkish red suffused salmon pink with darker markings and a small white center. **'Kimono'** is bright pink with darker markings and a white center. **'Lord Bute'** is black-red with lighter edges. **'Lyewood Bonanza'** is white with apricot-pink markings on the upper petals. **'Monkwood Bonanza'** is pale pastel pink with darker markings. **'Morwenna'** (syn. 'Morweena') has deep maroon flowers shading to near black. **'Parisienne'** has mauve flowers with purple and blackish red markings on the upper petals. **'Rembrandt'** has some of the largest and most richly colored flowers—3 in (8 cm) wide and deep purple edged with lavender, the edges frilled. **'Rosmaroy'** is bright pink with reddish markings. **'Spot-on-Bonanza'** is white or pale pink with flecks or sectors of apricot pink. **'Vicky Clare'** has multi-colored blooms, deep purple-red on the upper petals, pink veining on the lower and the whole edged in white. **'White Glory'** is pure white. **'Starlight Magic'** has velvety purple-pink petals on the top half of the flower, and a paler shade on the bottom half. ZONES 9–11.

Pelargonium, RH, 'White Glory'

Pelargonium, RH, 'Kimono'

Pelargonium, RH, 'Starlight Magic'

Pelargonium 'Splendide'

P., Scented-leafed Hybrid, 'Fragrans'

Pelargonium rodneyanum

Native to southeastern Australia, this attractive species grows on hot, dry outcrops of hard rock. It has tuberous roots and forms dense mounds, usually no more than 8 in (20 cm) high, of long-stalked, heart-shaped green leaves with finely toothed margins. Through spring and summer, it bears clusters of small but vivid magenta flowers. It is best suited to rock gardens and must have very well-drained soil, preferably among sun-warmed rocks. **ZONES 8–10.**

Pelargonium, Scented-leafed Hybrids

This varied group of hybrids derives from quite a few wild South African species. Many of them are primary hybrids whose origins go back to the early nineteenth century, although there are also a good number of more recent cultivars. Most are vigorous shrubs with dense branches and shallowly to deeply lobed or dissected leaves that in some are quite hairy. The range of essential oils in the leaves is very large, their scents ranging through peppermint, eucalyptus, lemon, cloves, aniseed, apple, rose and even coconut. Often a hot day will bring out the aroma, but it is released most strongly when the foliage is bruised or crushed. Some have quite showy flowers, in others they are small but still pretty. **'Fragrans'** (apple geranium) is a bushy, many-branched shrub reaching 12 in (30 cm) high and wide. A strong spicy smell like green apples comes off the small, roughly heart-shaped, lobed, gray-green leaves. Its flowers are small and white, sometimes with red veining on the upper petals. **'Mabel Grey'**, a vigorous cultivar, has lemon-scented leaves that are rough, serrated-edged and deeply lobed, and pale purple flowers with red markings. Considered to be the most strongly scented pelargonium, it grows to 15 in (38 cm) high. **ZONES 8–11.**

Pelargonium 'Pretty Lady'

Pelargonium 'Splendide'

Believed to be a hybrid between the South African species *Pelargonium tricolor* and *P. ovale*, this subshrubby 6–12 in (15–30 cm) tall plant, often sold as *P. tricolor* **'Arborea'**, has knotted woody stems with toothed, long-stalked, oval, hairy gray-green leaves. It produces branched flowering stems ending in 2- to 3-flowered clusters of striking bicolored flowers with red upper petals dark purple at the base, and pure white lower petals, about 1½ in (35 mm) wide. **'Pretty Lady'** is a similar cultivar. **ZONES 9–11.**

Pelargonium tomentosum

PEPPERMINT GERANIUM

A strong, refreshing smell of peppermint comes from the large pale green, velvety leaves of this sprawling, soft-stemmed pelargonium from South Africa's southwest Cape Province. It produces tiny, insignificant, purple-veined white flowers in clusters. It reaches 24 in (60 cm) in height, spreading widely or hanging over a ledge, and is shade tolerant but will also grow in full sun if sheltered from wind. If required, its spread can be limited by pinching out the growing tips; older plants are often better replaced. **ZONES 10–11.**

Pelargonium tricolor

This species is a sprawling, wiry-stemmed shrub about 12 in (30 cm) tall. It has narrow, hairy, gray-green leaves with a few deeply cut teeth, and are seldom more than 1½ in (35 mm) long. The distinctive flowers are pansy-like, 1½ in (35 mm) wide; the upper petals are red with a black base and the lower petals are white. **ZONES 9–11.**

Pelargonium, Unique Hybrids

This is a small group of hybrids that goes back to the early nineteenth century, with one of the parent species believed to be *Pelargonium fulgidum*. They have been the subject of renewed interest in recent years and a number of new cultivars have appeared. They are erect, shrubby plants of around 18 in (45 cm) in height with sharply toothed leaves that have a strong musky smell, and heads of fairly large flowers with marked upper petals, a little like some Regal pelargoniums. **'Paton's Unique'** is typical, with fruity, verbena-scented leaves and rose-pink single flowers borne over a long season. **'Scarlet Pet'** has quite showy, 1 in (25 mm) wide red flowers, borne in bunches of 12 or so for most of the year. It grows to 15 in (38 cm) tall, sprawling rather wider, and makes a good knee-high ground cover in dry-summer climates. **ZONES 9–11.**

Pelargonium tomentosum

Pelargonium xerophyton

This stiff, erect shrub seldom exceeds 18 in (45 cm) high but has very thick, rather woody stems with spine-like persistent stipules. Native to the semi-desert regions of South Africa's northwest Cape Province and Namibia, it is usually found in the shelter of rocks and small trees. Its leaves, less than ½ in (12 mm) wide, are blue-green and almost circular in outline, with small teeth. The flowers are about 1 ½ in (35 mm) wide, white with red spots and with narrow upper petals. It is mainly grown by succulent collectors. **ZONES 9–11.**

Pelargonium zonale

This South African species is rarely seen in gardens, being best known for its genetic contribution to the Zonal pelargonium hybrids. **ZONES 9–11.**

Pelargonium, Zonal Hybrids

ZONAL PELARGONIUM, BEDDING GERANIUM

This large group of hybrids, which have been known collectively as *Pelargonium × hortorum*, are derived principally from *Pelargonium inquinans*, which occurs wild in southeastern South Africa, but their parentage includes several other species as well, including *P. zonale* and *P. frutetorum*. They are compact plants, usually less than 24 in (60 cm) tall, with succulent green to pale bronze stems and almost circular to kidney-shaped, undulating leaves that have distinctive darker markings or 'zones'. The flowers, massed on long-stemmed heads, may be single or double, are usually brightly colored and appear over a long season. Although shrubs, Zonal pelargoniums may be treated as bedding annuals. Besides the vast number of typical Zonal cultivars, there are a number of distinct subgroups that are recognized by enthusiasts. **Variegated** or **Fancy-leafed** zonals have foliage banded and dappled with red, purple, orange and yellow, sometimes with all these colors showing; **Miniature** and **Dwarf** varieties are very compact plants, the leaves sometimes

Pelargonium, Unique Hybrid, 'Scarlet Pet'

Pelargonium xerophyton

Pelargonium zonale

quite small and often purple tinged; flowers vary, but include some with narrow petals, some of these are referred to as **Frutetorums**, reflecting the dominance of this parent species. **Stellars** (or 'Staphs') are an increasingly popular group with narrow, pointed, sometimes forked petals giving the flowers a very distinctive appearance; they come in both singles and doubles, in many colors. **Formosums** have very narrow petals and deeply lobed leaves. **Rosebuds** are a distinctive type of double with, as the name suggests, double flowers like a miniature rose bloom in bud. **Cactus-flowered** zonals have flowers with quilled petals like the cactus-flowered dahlias. Another recent development has been the appearance of Zonal pelargoniums sold as seed, usually as mixed-color series. The following is just a selection of the thousands of zonal cultivars available. **'Caroline Schmidt'** (syn. 'Wilhelm Langguth') is a compact plant with white-edged, pale-centered, bright green leaves and bright red double flowers. **'Dolly Varden'** is a fancy-leafed cultivar with striking cream, bronze and green foliage and single red flowers. **'Flower of Spring'** is an upright grower with cream-edged leaves and vermilion single flowers. **'Francis Parrett'** is a miniature with deep green leaves and tight clusters of double fuchsia-pink flowers. **'Frank Headley'** is a miniature with cream-edged leaves and soft pink single flowers. **'Irene'**, which gives its name to a group of hybrids, has red semi-double flowers and clearly zonal, downy green leaves. **'Mr Henry Cox'** (syn. 'Mrs Henry Cox') is a fancy-leafed type with dark-zoned leaves edged in gold and shadowed with red; the flowers are dark-centered bright pink singles. **'Mrs Parker'** has white-edged gray-green leaves with darker markings and deep pink double flowers in tight heads. **'Orange Ricard'** is a compact plant with tight heads of orange-red flowers. **'Apple Blossom Rosebud'** is one of the most popular rosebud zonals, the flowers are white, and pink-flushed white and the foliage bright green with little zonation; **'Gemini'** is a stellar cultivar with white-centered, pink flowers. **'The Boar'** is a miniature of the Frutetorum group with small salmon-pink flowers and toothed-edged, rounded leaves. ZONES 10–11.

P., Zonal Hybrid, 'Caroline Schmidt'

Pelargonium, Zonal Hybrid cultivar

P., Zonal Hybrid, 'Flower of Spring'

P., Zonal Hybrid, 'Frank Headley'

Pelargonium, Zonal Hybrid, 'Mrs Parker'

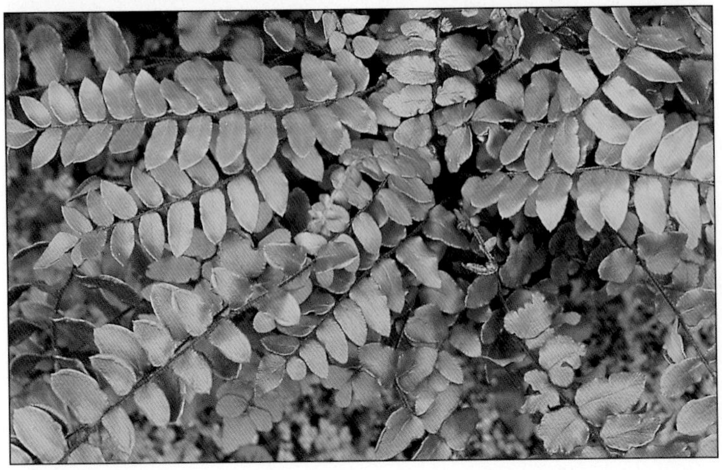
Pellaea falcata

Pellaea rotundifolia

PELECYPHORA

HATCHET CACTUS, LIVING ROCK

There are 2 species of this very distinctive cactus genus from Mexico. They are small and many shed their spines as the plants mature. Like mammillarias, pelecyphoras have prominent tubercules, but these are flattened; in one species in the verticle plane, and in the other in the horizontal plane. The pink or white flowers almost look like miniature water lilies; they emerge from the top of the plants in summer.

CULTIVATION: They grow among rocks and stones of the desert where they are well camouflaged and are rare in cultivation. They prefer full sun and a standard cactus compost. Propagate from seed, although this is difficult.

Pelecyphora aselliformis

Found in eastern and central Mexico, this species may be single stemmed or clustering with stems up to 2 in (5 cm) in diameter. The crowded tubercles are flattened vertically and bear neat, comb-like rows of short white spines. Its purple-pink flowers open in summer. ZONES 9–11.

Pelecyphora aselliformis

PELLAEA

BRAKE FERN, CLIFF BRAKE

This genus of ferns is widespread in tropical to warm-temperate areas and includes some 80 species. They are rhizomatous, creeping and usually evergreen, and have generally pinnate fronds in a wide variety of forms. The rhizomes are usually brown and scaly and spread across the surface of the ground or through crevices in rocks. The fronds, which are rarely over 18 in (45 cm) tall, are often leathery and are held erect.

CULTIVATION: Although hardiness varies with the species, these ferns are generally quite sun tolerant provided they do not dry out. They will grow in fairly poor soil and often thrive in exposed positions and hard clay that would defeat most ferns. Propagate by breaking off rooted pieces of rhizome.

Pellaea falcata

SICKLE FERN, AUSTRALIAN CLIFF BRAKE

Found from India to Australia, this species has 12–15 in (30–38 cm) fronds with 1–2 in (2.5–5 cm) leaflets. They have dark green upper surfaces, brownish undersides and are carried on 2–6 in (5–15 cm) stems. ZONES 10–12.

Pellaea rotundifolia

BUTTON FERN, ROUND-LEAFED FERN, TARAWERA

Native to Australia and New Zealand, this species is a very popular garden plant. It is a small, dark green, ground-dwelling fern found in damp, open forests or drier woodlands. It has pinnate fronds with deep green, glossy round leaflets and long-creeping rhizomes. Suitable for a garden or fernery with filtered sunlight and protection from drafts, it also does well in rock gardens. ZONES 9–11.

Pellaea viridis

syn. ***Pellaea adiantoides***

GREEN CLIFF BRAKE

This African species has some of the largest fronds in the genus; they are bright green, very broad and more than 24 in (60 cm) long, held on 12 in (30 cm) stems. ZONES 10–12.

PELTARIA

This is a genus of 7 species of sticky stemmed, aromatic perennials from the Middle East and central Asia. They form a clump of basal leaves from which develops a strong upright flower stem with a large head of tiny white flowers. The flowers open in spring and summer.

Pennisetum alopecuroides

Pennisetum alopecuroides 'Moudry'

CULTIVATION: Members of the cabbage family, they thrive in slightly alkaline, well-drained soil and prefer full sun. They are very frost hardy and can sometimes be divided, although seed is a more reliable method of propagation.

Peltaria turkmena

This central Asian species has flower stems up to 30 in (75 cm) tall and entire to shallowly toothed leaves. **ZONES 6–10.**

PELTOPHORUM

At home in the tropical regions of the world, these 15 species of evergreen, leguminous trees are grown primarily for the dense shade they cast. In the wild some species can reach 100 ft (30 m), but in cultivation they are more usually 60 ft (18 m) tall. The fern-like leaves are deep glossy green, with individual leaflets measuring up to 1 in (25 mm) long. Impressive spikes of perfumed yellow flowers, borne in summer, develop into long, brown pods.
CULTIVATION: These trees prefer fertile, moist but well-drained soil and a sheltered, part-shaded position, although they can tolerate full sun if well watered. Propagate from pre-soaked or scarified seed or cuttings taken during the wet season.

Peltophorum africanum

Native to the tropics and subtropics of Africa, this species reaches 40 ft (12 m) in height. In summer, pale yellow flowers are borne in terminal clusters.
ZONES 10–11.

Peltophorum pterocarpum
syns *Peltophorum ferrugineum, P. inerme*
RUSTY-SHIELD TREE, YELLOW FLAME TREE, YELLOW POINCIANA

Growing to 60 ft (18 m) tall with a crown up to 25 ft (8 m) wide, this species is a good shade tree for tropical gardens. Clusters of heavily perfumed flowers with unusual crinkled petals open in early summer from vivid rust-red buds. The abundance of rust-red, flattened seed pods that follow persist on the tree until the next flowering. **ZONES 11–12.**

Peltaria turkmena

Peltophorum pterocarpum

PENNISETUM

This genus consists of about 80 species of tuft-forming, rhizomatous or stoloniferous, annual or perennial grasses found in tropical, subtropical or warm-temperate regions around the world. The leaf blades are usually flat. They are mostly grown for their dense flower clusters of brush-like spikelets, which appear in summer and fall (autumn) and are used in floral arrangements both fresh and dried.
CULTIVATION: Most species are very frost hardy and prefer full sun and fertile, well-drained soil. Dead foliage may be cut back when the plants are dormant. Propagate from seed in early spring or by division in late spring or early summer.

Pennisetum alopecuroides
syn. *Pennisetum compressum*
SWAMP FOXTAIL, FOUNTAIN GRASS

This perennial grass from Asia and parts of Australia has mid- to dark green leaves, which grow to 24 in (60 cm) long and form a dense clump. In summer to fall (autumn), yellow-green to dark purple bristle-like spikelets appear. **'Hameln'** is a shorter form, to 18 in (45 cm) high, flowering in early summer; its spikelets are white, tinted green. **'Moudry'** is a low grower with wide, deep green leaves and purple to black flowerheads. **ZONES 7–10.**

Pennisetum clandestinum
KIKUYU GRASS

This species from the East African highlands is so unlike other pennisetums that only a botanist specializing in grasses could detect any resemblance. It has both deep-running and surface rhizomes that form a dense, hard-wearing turf of a rich, slightly yellowish green. Its flowers are almost completely hidden (hence *clandestinum*) among the sheathing leaf bases, only evidenced by the very fine but remarkably long white stigmas or stamens that appear briefly in summer. Most plants are functionally either male or female, and a kikuyu turf rarely seeds, but bisexual strains have been developed. This grass is popular in Australia for its vigor and drought tolerance, but can be very invasive in gardens; unmown, it will build into hummocks about 24 in (60 cm) high.
ZONES 9–12.

Pennisetum alopecuroides 'Moudry'

Pennisetum setaceum 'Burgundy Giant'

Pennisetum setaceum

Pennisetum setaceum 'Rubrum'

Pennisetum orientale

Found in central and southwest Asia, *Pennisetum orientale* is a deciduous perennial that forms a clump of 4–8 in (10–20 cm) leaves. From these develop 3 ft (1 m) tall plumed flower stems. The flower plumes are an attractive silvery pink shade. Cultivated plants are often far smaller than the wild species.
ZONES 7–10.

Pennisetum setaceum
syn. *Pennisetum ruppellii*
AFRICAN FOUNTAIN GRASS, FOUNTAIN GRASS

Pennisetum setaceum is a deciduous perennial grass from tropical Africa that grows into tufts 3 ft (1 m) high with a spread of 18 in (45 cm). It has rough stems and long, narrow leaf blades. In summer, it produces arching, coppery spikes with bearded bristles forming brush-like flower clusters that last into winter. It is not suitable as a lawn grass, but makes an attractive tall ground cover or a feature plant in a border. In warm climates it will self-seed freely and can become a nuisance. **'Burgundy Giant'** grows to 4 ft (1.2 m) tall and has purple-red foliage. **'Rubrum'** is a tall-growing cultivar with bronze leaves and purple-red flower plumes.
ZONES 9–12.

Pennisetum villosum
FEATHER TOP

Sometimes grown as an annual in cool climates, this species from the mountains of tropical Africa is a deciduous perennial. It forms a loose clump of 6 in (15 cm) leaves with 24 in (60 cm) white to brownish flower plumes.
ZONES 8–11.

PENSTEMON

This large genus consists of 250 species of deciduous, evergreen or semi-evergreen subshrubs and perennials, mostly native to Central and North America. The leaves appear in opposite pairs in whorls, while the flowers have 2 lobes on the upper lip and 3 on the lower. Hybrids are grown worldwide for their showy flower spikes in blues, reds, white and bicolors. Tall varieties suit sheltered borders; dwarf strains are bright in bedding schemes. **'Bev Jensen'** is a red hybrid and **'Holly's White'** is a favorite in the USA.

Penstemon 'Andenken an Friedrich Hahn'

Penstemon cardwellii

Penstemon 'Cherry Ripe'

Penstemon 'Connie's Pink'

CULTIVATION: These marginally to very frost-hardy plants do best in fertile, well-drained soil and full sun. Cut plants back hard after flowering. They can be propagated from seed in spring or fall (autumn), by division in spring, or from cuttings of non-flowering shoots in late summer (the only method for cultivars).

Penstemon ambiguus
PRAIRIE PENSTEMON, BUSH PENSTEMON

Native to central and southwestern USA and Mexico, this 24 in (60 cm) tall subshrub has very narrow ½–2 in (1.2–5 cm) long leaves and lax heads of rose-pink flowers that age to white. It blooms from early summer until fall (autumn). **ZONES 3–10.**

Penstemon 'Andenken an Friedrich Hahn'
syn. *Penstemon* 'Garnet'

This very frost-hardy perennial, which grows to 30 in (75 cm) with a 24 in (60 cm) spread, bears its dark pink flowers from mid-summer to fall (autumn). **ZONES 7–10.**

Penstemon 'Apple Blossom'

'Apple Blossom' is a narrow-leafed cultivar that grows to just 24 in (60 cm) high. Its flowers are pale pink with white throats. **ZONES 8–10.**

Penstemon barbatus
syn. *Chelone barbata*
CORAL PENSTEMON, BEARD-LIP PENSTEMON

The scarlet flowers on this semi-evergreen, very frost-hardy perennial are tubular with 2 lips. They bloom on racemes from mid-summer to early fall (autumn) above narrow, lance-shaped, green leaves. The plant grows to 3 ft (1 m) high, with a spread of 12 in (30 cm). **ZONES 3–10.**

Penstemon 'Beech Park'
syn. *Penstemon* 'Barbara Barker'

Named after David Shackleton's garden near Dublin, this is a frost-hardy perennial hybrid with white-throated pink flowers. Although its breeder did not rate it highly, it is a reliable, heavy-flowering cultivar, the blooms appearing from mid-summer to fall (autumn). **ZONES 7–10.**

Penstemon 'Blue of Zurich'
syn.* Penstemon *'Zuriblau'

This 18 in (45 cm) tall cultivar has particularly bright blue flowers. **ZONES 8–10.**

Penstemon campanulatus

This frost-hardy, semi-evergreen perennial from Mexico and Guatemala is 12–24 in (30–60 cm) tall with narrow, serrated, 3 in (8 cm) long leaves. Its flowers are funnel- to bell-shaped,

Penstemon digitalis

Penstemon digitalis 'Husker's Red'

reddish purple to violet and are carried on a lax inflorescence. They open from early summer. **ZONES 9–11.**

Penstemon cardwellii

From northwestern USA, this very frost-hardy evergreen subshrub forms broad 4–8 in (10–20 cm) high clumps with ½–2 in (1.2–5 cm) long, elliptical, serrated-edged leaves. Its flowers are 1–1½ in (25–35 mm) long, bright purple and open in summer. **ZONES 8–10.**

Penstemon centranthifolius
SCARLET BUGLER

Ranging from 1–4 ft (0.3–1.2 m) tall, this perennial species from California and Baja California has 1½–4 in (3.5–10 cm) long lance-shaped leaves and 1–1½ in (25–35 mm) long scarlet flowers. It blooms from early summer. **ZONES 9–11.**

Penstemon 'Cherry Ripe'

This is a 4 ft (1.2 m) tall hybrid with narrow, warm red blooms on wiry stems. **ZONES 7–10.**

Penstemon 'Chester Scarlet'

This 24 in (60 cm) tall perennial bears its tubular, bright red flowers from mid-summer to fall (autumn). It is marginally frost hardy. **ZONES 8–10.**

Penstemon 'Connie's Pink'

This 4 ft (1.2 m) tall hybrid has fine wiry stems with a coating of hairs. Its flowers are rose pink and rather narrow. **ZONES 7–10.**

Penstemon davidsonii

This evergreen subshrub from the West Coast of the USA is very similar to *Penstemon menziesii* except that its leaves are not serrated. It is a very frost-hardy, clump- or mat-forming species with ½–1½ in (12–35 mm) long purple flowers. **ZONES 6–10.**

Penstemon digitalis

Native to eastern North America, this very frost-hardy perennial species is usually seen with white or pale lavender flowers, neither particularly exciting. **'Husker's Red'**, however, is notable for

Penstemon 'Blue of Zurich'

Penstemon campanulatus

Penstemon 'Bev Jensen'

Penstemon barbatus

Penstemon 'Evelyn'

Penstemon glaber

its deep reddish purple foliage. A robust plant, it reaches a height of 30 in (75 cm) and spread of 24 in (60 cm), and is attractive to hummingbirds. **ZONES 3–9.**

Penstemon 'Evelyn'

This is a 30 in (75 cm) tall perennial hybrid with very narrow leaves and masses of slightly curved pale pink flowers. It was raised by the famous Slieve Donard nursery of Northern Ireland and is very frost hardy. **ZONES 7–10.**

Penstemon 'Firebird'

syn. 'Schoenholzen'

This cultivar grows to around 30 in (75 cm) and has vivid orange-red flowers. **ZONES 7–10.**

Penstemon glaber

A woody based species from Wyoming, this perennial grows to about 24 in (60 cm) tall. Its leaves are 1½–4 in (3.5–10 cm) long and lance-shaped. The inflorescence is up to 10 in (25 cm) long and is composed of 1–1½ in (25–35 mm) flowers that are purple-red at the base and white near the tips. It blooms from late summer. **ZONES 3–10.**

Penstemon × *gloxinioides*

BORDER PENSTEMON

This name applies to a group of hybrids raised in the middle of the nineteenth century from the species *Penstemon cobaea* and *P. hartwegii.* They have some of the largest and showiest flowers of any penstemons, mainly in rich reds and pinks and usually with a white throat. However, they are often short lived and not so cold hardy as other penstemons, and so have declined in popularity. **ZONES 7–9.**

Penstemon 'Firebird'

Penstemon heterophyllus

FOOTHILL PENSTEMON, BLUE BEDDER PENSTEMON

From California, this very frost-hardy, summer-flowering subshrub grows to about 18 in (45 cm) tall. Its leaves are 1–2 in (2.5–5 cm) long, lance-shaped and slightly blue-green. The 1–1½ in (25–35 mm) long flowers vary from deep violet-pink to near blue. ***Penstemon heterophyllus* subsp. *purdyi*** (syn. *P. h.* 'Blue Bedder') is a semi-evergreen shrub with blue tube-shaped flowers and pale green leaves. **ZONES 8–10.**

Penstemon 'Hidcote Pink'

Up to 4 ft (1.2 m) tall, this narrow-leafed perennial has gray-green foliage and rose-pink flowers with deep pink streaks. It is very frost hardy. **ZONES 7–10.**

Penstemon hirsutus

A penstemon from the northeastern and central states of the USA, this species reaches about 24 in (60 cm) in height and has hairy stems and rather narrow, dark green leaves. The flowers, crowded at the ends of the stems in summer, are pale purple outside with a coating of fine fuzzy hairs, and white in the throat. ***Penstemon hirsutus* var. *pygmaeus*** is a loosely mat-forming plant no more than 4 in (10 cm) high with short, spreading flowering stems and purple-flushed foliage; it is popular as a rock-garden plant. **ZONES 3–9.**

Penstemon isophyllus

From Mexico, this 30 in (75 cm) tall evergreen subshrub has very distinctive narrow flowers. They are up to 2 in (5 cm) long and are pale pink or cream at the base, deepening to rich red at the lobes. The leaves are 1½ in (35 mm) long, lance-shaped and rather thick. It is marginally frost hardy. **ZONES 9–11.**

Penstemon 'Pennington Gem'

Penstemon menziesii

This little mat-forming, semi-evergreen subshrub from western North America has ½ in (12 mm) long leaves with finely serrated edges. In summer, it is studded with 1–1½ in (25–35 mm) long, violet-purple flowers; it is very frost hardy and is a marvellous rockery plant. **ZONES 7–10.**

Penstemon 'Midnight'

This cultivar has large leaves and grows to 3 ft (1 m) tall. Its flowers are deep purple-blue. **ZONES 8–10.**

Penstemon newberryi

MOUNTAIN PRIDE

Native to California and Nevada, USA, this rather woody evergreen subshrub forms mats of foliage 6–12 in (15–30 cm) high. It leaves are elliptical, 1–1½ in (25–35 mm) long with finely serrated edges. Its rose-red flowers are around 1 in (25 mm) long and open in late spring and summer. It is moderately frost hardy. **ZONES 8–10.**

Penstemon × *gloxinioides*

Penstemon parryi

PARRY'S PENSTEMON

This 12–24 in (30–60 cm) tall species from southern Arizona forms clumps of erect stems clothed with spatula-shaped 2–3 in (5–8 cm) long blue-green leaves. Its flowers are less than 1 in (25 mm) long, cerise to magenta and funnel-shaped with large lobes, opening in spring. **ZONES 8–10.**

Penstemon 'Pennington Gem'

This 30 in (75 cm) tall, frost-hardy perennial has deep pink, white-throated flowers with a few purple-red stripes. **ZONES 7–10.**

Penstemon hirsutus var. *pygmaeus*

Penstemon 'Hidcote Pink'

Penstemon heterophyllus

Penstemon pinifolius

This sprightly evergreen subshrub is best suited to a well-drained rock garden. A moderately frost-hardy native of southwest USA and Mexico, it thrives in heat and needs little water beyond the normal rainfall. The flowers are typically 2 lipped and bright orange-red, and are produced for much of the summer. The leaves are needle-like. **ZONES 8–11.**

Penstemon 'Rubicundus'

Not to be confused with the species *Penstemon rubicundus*, this hybrid grows to 4 ft (1.2 m) tall and has broad, bright red flowers with pure white mouths. The flower are among the largest on any hybrid, but the plant is rather frost tender. **ZONES 5–10.**

Penstemon rupicola
ROCK PENSTEMON

This very low-growing, mat-forming evergreen subshrub is from the west coast of the USA. Its ½–1 in (12–25 mm) long leaves have finely toothed edges. The flowers are up to 1½ in (35 mm) long, deep pink and open from late spring. It is very frost hardy. **ZONES 7–10.**

Penstemon scouleri
syn. *Penstemon fruticosus* subsp. *scouleri*

From the western half of North America, this evergreen subshrub forms dense clumps of stems up to 18 in (45 cm) tall. Its narrow, lance-shaped leaves are slightly glossy and have serrated edges. The lavender-blue to purple flowers are 1½–6 in (3.5–15 cm) long. They open in summer. **ZONES 5–10.**

Penstemon serrulatus
CASCADE PENSTEMON

Found from Oregon to southern Alaska, this 12–30 in (30–75 cm) tall, very frost-hardy subshrub has broad, lance-shaped, 1–4 in (2.5–10 cm) long leaves with serrated edges. The flowers, in dense clusters, are less than 1 in (25 mm) long, tubular- to bell-shaped, deep blue to purple and open from late summer. **ZONES 5–10.**

Penstemon 'Sour Grapes'

This large-leafed perennial has pinkish purple flowers tinged with green in bunched clusters from mid-summer to fall (autumn). It grows to 24 in (60 cm) in height with an 18 in (45 cm) spread, and is frost hardy. **ZONES 7–10.**

Penstemon pinifolius

Penstemon 'White Bedder'

Pentas lanceolata

Penstemon serrulatus

Penstemon spectabilis

This Californian species has erect stems to 4 ft (1.2 m) tall and leaves up to 4 in (10 cm) long with coarsely serrated edges. The foliage is sometimes tinted blue-green. The flowers, which are wide throated, are around 1½ in (35 mm) long. Lavender-purple with blue lobes and white interiors, they open from early summer. **ZONES 7–10.**

Penstemon 'Stapleford Gem'

A very frost-hardy strong grower to 4 ft (1.2 m) tall, this perennial has flowers in a glowing shade of purple-pink. The color varies somewhat with the climate and soil pH. **ZONES 7–10.**

Penstemon 'Thorn'

This hybrid grows to 3 ft (1 m) in height and has narrow pink and white flowers. **ZONES 7–10.**

Penstemon 'White Bedder'
syns *Penstemon* 'Burford White', *P.* 'Royal White', *P.* 'Snow Storm'

This frost-hardy, 30 in (75 cm) tall perennial has white flowers with a pale yellow-cream tinge and an occasional hint of pale pink. The buds are often pink tinted. **ZONES 7–10.**

PENTAPHRAGMA

This genus of about 25 species from the rainforests of Southeast Asia is related to the bellflowers (*Campanula*) but the relationship would only be evident to a botanist. They evergreen perennials have fleshy, creeping stems, broad, simple leaves that are often one-sided at the base, and dense clusters of rather insignificant circular flowers in the leaf axils.

Pentaphragma horsfieldii

Penstemon 'Thorn'

Penstemon 'Stapleford Gem'

Foliage of some species is gathered by local people for use as a green vegetable. **CULTIVATION:** These plants are seldom cultivated except in botanical gardens, and outside the wet tropics would need a heated greenhouse.

Pentaphragma horsfieldii

Native to Java, Sumatra and the Malay Peninsula, this low-growing plant has creeping stems and broad, heavily veined green leaves. The tightly clustered small flowers are fleshy, disc-shaped and cream in color, changing to green as they age. **ZONES 11–12.**

PENTAS

This genus of around 40 species of biennials, perennials and subshrubs is found in tropical parts of Arabia and Africa. They have bright green, lance-shaped, 3–8 in (8–20 cm) long leaves, sometimes coated with a fine down or tiny hairs. The small, starry, long-tubed flowers are massed in flat-topped heads and appear throughout the warmer months. They are usually bright pink, but also occur in red and purple shades and white. **CULTIVATION:** Although very frost tender and only suitable for outdoor cultivation in very mild climates, pentas are easily grown as house plants; the new dwarf strains can be treated as bedding or pot annuals. Plant in moist, well-drained soil in full sun or part-shade and pinch back regularly to maintain a compact habit and to encourage bloom. Deadhead as required and trim lightly in early spring. Water well when in full growth. Propagate from seed in spring or from softwood cuttings in summer. Watch for aphids and red spider mites.

Pentas lanceolata
syn. *Pentas carnea*
EGYPTIAN STAR, STAR CLUSTER

This erect, straggling shrub grows to a height of 2–3 ft (0.6–1 m) with a slightly wider spread. It is grown for the spring–summer appearance of its clusters of tubular, red, pink, lilac or white flowers, set among bright green, hairy leaves. **ZONES 10–12.**

PEPEROMIA

RADIATOR PLANT

This genus from tropical and subtropical regions worldwide contains 1,000 species of evergreen or succulent perennials. Ideal in terrariums or dish gardens, they have diverse and beautifully marked and shaped, fleshy, usually long-stalked leaves. Long-stemmed spikes of minute, greenish white to cream flowers are produced in late summer, although flowering can be erratic.

CULTIVATION: Frost tender, these make good house plants. Peperomias like bright light (but not direct sun), especially near a window, with high humidity in summer. Keep moist in warm weather, and be sure to water them from below as the leaves mark easily; in winter, allow the plants to dry out between waterings. Use a half-strength, soluble fertilizer once a month in spring and summer. Peperomias are easily propagated from leaf or stem cuttings in spring or summer, and should be repotted annually. Watch for mealybugs, spider mites and white fly.

Peperomia argyreia

WATERMELON PEPEROMIA

Found from northern South America to Brazil, this is a compact, nearly stemless perennial with rosettes of glossy, rounded, 3–4 in (8–10 cm) long, gray-striped leaves on long red stems. The flower spikes are small, but extend beyond the foliage. **ZONES 11–12.**

Peperomia argyreia

Pericallis × *hybrida*

Peperomia caperata

EMERALD RIPPLE

This perennial species has oval, deeply corrugated and veined, heart-shaped, dark green leaves that are pale green underneath and about $1\frac{1}{2}$ in (35 mm) across, carried on the pinkish stems. Tight clusters of white flower spikes appear irregularly. **'Silver Ripples'** has silver-gray markings on the ridges of the corrugations. **ZONES 11–12.**

Peperomia obtusifolia

BABY RUBBER PLANT

This is a bushy perennial with fleshy leaves and occasional spikes of minute flowers. The plain green species is a handsome plant growing 12 in (30 cm) tall. More common are the variegated cultivars, with leaves marbled in gray-green and cream or gold. Good light but not direct sun is needed. Cut back if the plants grow straggly. **ZONES 11–12.**

Peperomia scandens

This species is a trailing perennial with stems 24 in (60 cm) or more tall. The leaves are 3 in (8 cm) long and nearly as wide, on $1\frac{1}{2}$ in (35 mm) stems. It produces spikes of green flowers. This species is usually grown as a house plant and trained up a wire frame or length of tree-fern trunk. **ZONES 11–12.**

Peperomia 'Sweetheart'

Typical of the hybrid peperomias that appear from time to time, this one is named for its heart-shaped leaves. ***Peperomia marmorata***, the silver-heart peperomia, resembles it except that the leaves have silver markings. Both are a shade larger than *P. caperata.* **ZONES 11–12.**

Peperomia caperata

Pericallis × *hybrida*

Pericallis × *hybrida*

Pericallis × *hybrida* (dwarf form)

PERESKIA

Unusual in that they are cacti with leaves, the 16 species of this genus are distributed in the Americas from southern Mexico to Brazil. Most are spiny stemmed shrubs or small trees, but a few scramble or climb. The leaves are generally elliptical, tapering to a point, and often rather fleshy. They are $1\frac{1}{2}$–10 in (3.5–25 cm) long. In spring and summer the flowers, in a wide variety of colors, open from downy buds. They may be carried singly or in clusters, ranging from $\frac{1}{2}$–$2\frac{1}{2}$ in (1.2–6 cm) in diameter, followed by berry-like fruits.

CULTIVATION: Plant in light, well-drained soil in sun or morning shade and keep dry during winter. Most species are intolerant of all but the lightest frosts. Propagate from seed or cuttings.

Pereksia grandifolia

This Brazilian shrub or small tree reaches 15 ft (4.5 m) or more tall. It has narrow, 8 in (20 cm) long leaves and $\frac{1}{2}$–$1\frac{1}{2}$ in (12–35 mm) long thorns. In the warmer months, it bears large sprays of pink to purple pink flowers. **ZONES 9–11.**

Peperomia caperata 'Silver Ripples'

PERICALLIS

CINERARIA

This is a genus of some 15 species of perennials and subshrubs closely allied to *Senecio,* where they were once included. They are distributed throughout the mid-latitude islands of the Atlantic, especially the Canaries. Best known in cultivation for the florist's cineraria (*Pericallis* × *hybrida*), the wild species are nowhere near as fancy. The leaves, which may be in basal rosettes in the perennials, are usually oval to lance-shaped, 2–6 in (5–15 cm) long, with finely toothed edges and covered in small hairs. The flowers are usually pink, mauve or purple, $\frac{1}{2}$–2 in (1.2–5 cm) wide and carried in open heads.

CULTIVATION: Although easily cultivated in any moist, well-drained soil in part- to full shade, few species will tolerate anything other than very light frosts. The florist's strains are often used as winter-flowering house plants. Propagate from seed or cuttings or by division, depending on the growth form.

Pericallis × *hybrida*

syns ***Senecio cruentus, S.*** × ***hybrida***

This hybrid reaches 12 in (30 cm) tall and wide. It is a multi-purpose bloomer for grouping or for formal bedding in part-shaded spots, for window boxes or for containers on balconies or in protected courtyards. The color of the daisy-like flowers ranges from pink, red, purple and crimson through to white, as well as the traditional blue. They are very tolerant of heat, salt air and poor soil, but suffer in high humidity or excessive rain. **ZONES 9–11.**

Perovskia abrotanoides

Perovskia 'Hybrida'

Pericallis lanata

Pericallis lanata
syn. *Senecio heritieri*

This 3 ft (1 m) tall subshrub from Tenerife in the Canary Islands has flexible stems that may be upright or spreading. It leaves, which are hairy and up to 6 in (15 cm) long, are usually oval and finely toothed, but sometimes have 5 to 7 deep lobes. The flowers may be borne singly or in loose heads and are mauve to purple, up to 1½ in (35 mm) wide and sweetly scented. **ZONES 9–11.**

PERILLA

This genus consists of 6 species of annuals distributed from India to Japan, including one that is cultivated as a salad herb and foliage bedding plant. They have glossy, heavily veined, toothed, deep green, oval leaves up to 6 in (15 cm) long. There are now many cultivars, mainly with purple foliage, and various

Perovskia atriplicifolia

Persea americana

leaf shapes. The foliage is aromatic and is used as a garnish or flavoring. Spike-like inflorescences up to 4 in (10 cm) long develop at the stem tips and bear tiny white flowers; these are usually removed from cultivated plants to prevent seeding and to prolong plant life.
CULTIVATION: Plant in moist, well-drained soil in sun or part-shade. Young plants tolerate light frost and may be planted in late winter to ensure a long season. Propagate from seed.

Perilla frutescens
CHISO, SHISO

Found from the Himalayas to eastern Asia, this species, usually treated as a summer annual, grows to 3–5 ft (1–1.5 m) tall. Its coleus-like leaves are just over 4 in (10 cm) long, deeply serrated and sometimes spotted purple. The flower spike is about 4 in (10 cm) long and the tiny summer flowers are white or red tinted. The foliage is used as a herb in Japanese dishes and has medicinal properties. **ZONES 8–11.**

PERIPLOCA
SILK VINE

This is a genus of around 11 species of sticky-stemmed and leafed, sometimes twining or scrambling evergreen or deciduous shrubs. They are found from the Mediterranean region to East Asia and tropical Africa; several species have medicinal herbal uses. The leaves are

Periploca sepium

usually deep green, oval to lance-shaped and 1–3 in (2.5–8 cm) long. The starry flowers are yellow-green on the outside with maroon to deep purple interiors. They are followed by bean pod-like fruits known as follicles.
CULTIVATION: Although often tropical in origin, several species are reasonably frost hardy. They prefer moist, well-drained soil in full sun or part-shade and can become rampant. Propagate from seed in spring or from cuttings in summer.

Periploca sepium

Native to China and Taiwan, this deciduous species scrambles to about 15 ft (4.5 m) tall. It has short-stemmed, 2–3 in (5–8 cm) leaves and its flowerheads carry only a few ½ in (12 mm) wide purple flowers from late spring. The roots and bark are used for treating rheumatoid arthritis and injuries. **ZONES 6–10.**

PEROVSKIA

Found in western Asia and the Himalayan region, the 7 species of deciduous subshrubs in this genus have gray-white stems and aromatic leaves that are covered with gray felt when young. As they mature, the deeply lobed, 2–3 in (5–8 cm) long leaves lose the felting and become gray-green. The stems form large clumps, grow 3–5 ft (1–1.5 m) tall and are topped in late summer with 12–18 in (30–45 cm) panicles of tiny purple-blue flowers.
CULTIVATION: They are very easily grown in any well-drained, rather dry soil in a sunny position. It is often best to contain their growth by planting them beside a path, wall or border edge. If allowed free rein smaller, less vigorous plants may be smothered. They are very frost hardy and may be propagated from seed or cuttings of non-flowering stems.

Perovskia abrotanoides

Native to Afghanistan and the western Himalayas, this 3 ft (1 m) tall species has 3 in (8 cm) long, deeply cut, oval, gray-green leaves. The small tubular flowers, in whorls of 4 to 6 blooms on 15 in (38 cm) panicles, are violet to pink. It blooms in late summer. **ZONES 5–9.**

Perovskia atriplicifolia
RUSSIAN SAGE

This tall, tough species produces soft, gray-green foliage that beautifully complements the haze of pale lavender-blue flowers that appear on panicles in late summer and fall (autumn). The plants are upright to 5 ft (1.5 m), with a spread of 3 ft (1 m) or more. They are long lived. **ZONES 6–9.**

Perovskia 'Blue Spire'

This upright hybrid grows to 4 ft (1.2 m) in height and has deeply cut, almost pinnate foliage. The large panicles of lavender-blue flowers are produced in late summer and early fall (autumn). **ZONES 6–9.**

Perovskia 'Hybrida'

This hybrid between *Perovskia abrotanoides* and *P. atriplicifolia* grows to around 4 ft (1.2 m) tall and has deeply cut, gray-green, 2 in (5 cm) long leaves. Its flowers, a deep lavender blue, are held in 15 in (38 cm) panicles. **ZONES 5–9.**

PERSEA

This genus is made up of about 150 species of evergreen trees and shrubs mostly from tropical parts of Central and South America with a few from Asia and one, *Persea indica*, indigenous to the Azores and Canary Islands. The best known member of the genus is the avocado. They are large trees with deep green, elliptical leaves and inconspicuous unisexual flowers followed by the familiar large, rough-surfaced, pear-shaped fruits, which have a very high fat content.
CULTIVATION: Frost tender and fast growing, they can be untidy trees as they drop leaves constantly. Although self-fertile, at least 2 trees are required for good crops. *Persea* demand rich soil, perfect drainage, ample moisture when fruiting and full sun and are best sheltered from strong winds. Cutting-grown or grafted plants are superior to seedlings.

Persea americana
syn. *Persea gratissima*
AVOCADO

This species can reach a height of 60 ft (18 m). Its glossy, dark green leathery leaves are shed all year. The small greenish flowers, held in the axils, are followed by pear-shaped, nutritious, green or black fruit. The stem is usually erect. The avocado is tender to both frost and dry conditions, and can be nurtured in mild climates well south and north of the tropics. There are many named cultivars, each with different growth patterns and requirements. **ZONES 10–11.**

Persea indica

This tree can reach 70 ft (21 m) tall with great age and has 3–8 in (8–20 cm) long, leathery, deep green leaves. The 6 in (15 cm) panicles of small yellow-green flowers are followed by very large, 10 in (25 cm) long, pear-shaped fruit that are blue-black when ripe. **ZONES 10–11.**

PERSICARIA
syns *Aconogonon, Bistorta, Tovara*
KNOTWEED

This is a genus of 50 to 80 species of evergreen, semi-evergreen or deciduous

Persicaria affinis

Persicaria affinis 'Donald Lowndes'

annuals, perennials or subshrubs, nearly all species of which were formerly included in *Polygonum*. They are found in most parts of the world and have strong wiry stems with rounded, lance- or heart-shaped leaves 1½–10 in (3.5–25 cm) long depending on the species. The foliage often has purple-gray markings and may develop red and gold tints in fall (autumn). The flowers, usually pink or cream, are small and are borne in sometimes showy panicles or spikes in the leaf axils and at stem tips.

CULTIVATION: Most species are vigorous and very frost hardy and easily cultivated in any well-drained soil in sun or part-shade; indeed, some are too vigorous and may become invasive. The stronger growers are best planted where they can be contained. Propagate from seed in spring or by division in spring or fall.

Persicaria affinis
syn. *Polygonum affine*

This evergreen perennial has small, shiny green, lance-shaped leaves that become bronze in winter. It forms a mat 12 in (30 cm) or more high with a similar spread. In late summer and fall (autumn), it bears dense spikes of small, red, funnel-shaped flowers. **'Darjeeling Red'** (syn. *Polygonum affine* 'Darjeeling Red') has elongated leaves that turn bright red in fall. **'Donald Lowndes'** (syn. *P. a.* 'Donald Lowndes') is a compact cultivar with salmon-pink flowers that age to deep pink. **'Superba'** (syn. *P. a.* 'Superbum') is a strong-growing cultivar with lustrous brown fall foliage color and pink to red flowers. **ZONES 3–9.**

Persicaria affinis 'Superba'

Persicaria amplexicaulis
syns *Bistorta amplexicaulis, Polygonum amplexicaule*
BISTORT, MOUNTAIN FLEECE

Persicaria amplexicaulis is a clump-forming, leafy, semi-evergreen perennial from the Himalayas. It has oval to heart-shaped mid-green leaves and grows to a height and spread of 4 ft (1.2 m). Its profuse spikes of small, rich red flowers are borne from summer to fall (autumn). *P. amplexicaulis* **'Firetail'** (syn. *Polygonum amplexicaule* 'Firetail') is a low grower with vivid crimson flowers. **'Inverleith'** (syn. *P. a.* 'Inverleith') is a dwarf cultivar with short spikes of deep crimson flowers. **ZONES 5–9.**

Persicaria campanulata 'Rosenrot'

Persicaria capitata

Persicaria bistorta
syn. *Polygonum bistorta*
BISTORT, SNAKEWEED

A vigorous perennial with heavy rootstock, *Persicaria bistorta* is found from Europe to western Asia. This species grows to around 24 in (60 cm) tall. Its leaves are oblong with wavy margins and grow 4–8 in (10–20 cm) long. The flowers open in summer and are white or pink. **'Superba'** (syn. *Polygonum bistorta* 'Superbum') is a tall form which has densely packed spikes of pink flowers. **ZONES 4–9.**

Persicaria campanulata
syn. *Polygonum campanulatum*
LESSER KNOTWEED

This Himalayan species is a spreading perennial that forms a clump of unbranched wiry stems. Its leaves are 1½–4 in (3.5–10 cm) long and are lance-shaped, bright green on top with pale gray to pink undersides. The flowering stems are erect, 2–4 ft (0.6–1.2 m) tall with pink or white flowers from late summer. **'Rosenrot'** (syn. *Polygonum campanulatum* 'Rosenrot') is an upright grower with deep pink flowers. **ZONES 8–10.**

Persicaria amplexicaulis 'Firetail'

Persicaria capitata
syn. *Polygonum capitatum*

This is a spreading Himalayan evergreen or deciduous perennial that forms a mat which is normally about 6 in (15 cm) deep, and of indefinite spread. Its leaves are 1–2 in (2.5–5 cm) long and are bright green with a purplish V-shaped marking on the upper surface. The pink flowers are borne in small spherical heads. *Persicaria capitata* is a fairly quick-growing species. **ZONES 8–10.**

Persicaria filiformis
syn *Polygonum filiforme*

Up to 4 ft (1.2 m) tall, *Persicaria filiformis* comes from Japan, the Himalayas and northeastern USA. It has 3–6 in (8–15 cm) long elliptical leaves with a covering of short, rough hairs and often marked with rows of chocolate-brown flecks. The flower spikes are slender and the green-white or pale pink flowers, which are borne in summer, are not particularly showy. **ZONES 5–10.**

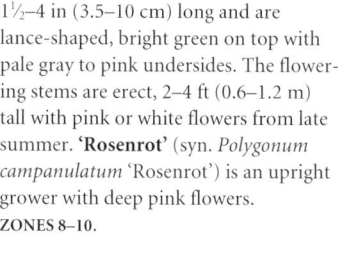

Persicaria campanulata

Persicaria bistorta 'Superba'

Persicaria filiformis

P

Persicaria macrophylla
syn. *Polygonum macrophyllum*

This spreading Himalayan and western Chinese semi-evergreen perennial rarely exceeds 6 in (15 cm) in height, but has leaves up to 4 in (10 cm) long. The foliage forms a basal clump that slowly enlarges and spreads. The pink or red flowers open in summer. **ZONES 5–9.**

Persicaria maculosa
syn. *Polygonum persicaria*
REDSHANK

Widely distributed through Europe and temperate Asia, this species sometimes becomes a weed of arable land. It has a sprawling or creeping habit, rooting at the nodes. The lance-shaped, mid-green leaves have a dark central blotch, and the small pink flowers are borne in summer and fall (autumn). **ZONES 4–10.**

Persicaria macrophylla

Persicaria orientalis

Persoonia pinifolia

Persicaria odorata
syn. *Polygonum odoratum*
VIETNAMESE MINT

This tender perennial species from Southeast Asia grows to around 12 in (30 cm) tall, at which point the stems begin to bend down and take root at the tip. Its leaves have a pungent mint smell with a hint of curry and are used as a culinary herb. In cool regions it is best treated as an annual. **ZONES 10–12.**

Persicaria orientalis
syn. *Polygonum orientale*
PRINCE'S FEATHER, PRINCESS FEATHER

From eastern and Southeast Asia and Australia, this species is an annual that reaches 5 ft (1.5 m) tall. Its leaves are large, up to 8 in (20 cm) long, and are roughly an elongated heart shape. The flowers open from late summer and are bright pink to purple-pink or white and are borne in large, slightly pendulous, branched spikes. **ZONES 8–11.**

Persicaria vacciniifolia
syn. *Polygonum vacciniifolium*

This trailing semi-evergreen perennial from the Himalayan region has woody stems that are reddish when young. It has a spread of around 6 ft (1.8 m). Its deep green leaves are up to 1 in (25 mm) long. From late summer well into fall (autumn), the carpet of foliage is smothered in 1–3 in (2.5–8 cm) long, upright spikes of bright pink flowers. **ZONES 7–10.**

Persicaria vacciniifolia

Petrea volubilis

Petroselinum crispum

Persicaria virginiana
syn. *Polygonum virginianum*

From Japan, the Himalayas and northeastern USA, this perennial grows to 4 ft (1.2 m) high and has sticky, rather hairy leaves. Its flower spikes are greenish white tinted pink and open from summer to early fall (autumn). **'Painter's Palette'** has green and gold variegated foliage with brown markings. **ZONES 5–10.**

PERSOONIA

This unusual Australian genus of the protea family consists of about 60 species of evergreen shrubs, and takes its name from Christian Persoon, the German botanical author who first described ***Persoonia levis***. Some species have a prostrate habit, but most are tall—up to 15 ft (4.5 m)—open-growing shrubs or small trees. Several are gaining attention as garden plants for their attractive foliage. The yellow, 4-petalled flowers are followed by fleshy berries that are edible but rather astringent.
CULTIVATION: The plants grow best in full sun and well-drained, sandy soil. Do not transplant larger specimens. While notoriously difficult to propagate, freshly harvested seeds pre-soaked in warm water for 24 hours occasionally germinate, and soft tip cuttings can be struck using advanced techniques.

Persoonia pinifolia
PINELEAF GEEBUNG

Soft, delicate, bright green, pine-like foliage and long arching stems are the main features of this shrub from eastern Australia, It reaches a height of 12 ft (3.5 m) with a similar spread. Small golden-yellow flowers are borne in large clusters at the branch tips throughout summer and fall (autumn). They are followed by bunches of small, succulent green berries that by winter have attractive red to purple tonings. **ZONES 10–11.**

PETREA

This genus of some 30 species of deciduous or semi-evergreen vines, shrubs and small trees is from Mexico and tropical America. The foliage is variable, but usually broadly elliptical, 6–8 in (15–20 cm) long, deep green with toothed edges and sometimes sticky or covered with fine hairs. They are smothered in 6–24 in (15–60 cm) long inflorescences from late spring. Most species have blue or purple flowers, although mauve and white are also common. The flowers are followed by small drupes.

Petroselinum crispum var. *neapolitanum*

CULTIVATION: Most species are intolerant of frosts, although a few can withstand very occasional light frost. They are best grown in light, well-drained soil in full sun. Propagate from seed or more commonly from cuttings.

Petrea volubilis
PURPLE WREATH, SANDPAPER, QUEEN'S WREATH

Native to Central America and the West Indies, this bushy, evergreen woody stemmed climber is grown for its clusters of delightful, star-like, violet flowers. They appear from late winter to late summer, set among simple, elliptic, rough-textured leaves. It grows to a height of 20 ft (6 m) or more and needs support to maintain its climbing habit. **ZONES 10–12.**

PETROSELINUM
PARSLEY

This is a genus of 3 species of biennial herbs with a long rootstock and a rosette of bright green leaves, each divided into many leaflets with toothed margins. Very small pale greenish yellow flowers borne on flat open umbels are produced in the second year; these are followed by small light brown seeds. Cultivated for thousands of years, parsley is still one of the most popular herbs and makes a decorative foliage plant for edging, either alone or mixed with colorful annuals. It is also an ideal herb for pot culture.
CULTIVATION: Fully frost hardy, these plants do best in full sun or light shade in warm climates. They like moist, well-drained soil and regular feeding. Propagate from seed from spring to late summer; in frost-prone areas, seedlings can be raised indoors. Seed may take up to 6 weeks to germinate and it is helpful to soak in warm water overnight before sowing.

Petroselinum crispum

This clump-forming species, which grows to 30 in (75 cm) in height and 24 in (60 cm) in spread, has triangular leaves and minute, star-shaped flowers. For the best flavor, harvest the leaves before the plant flowers. The most commonly used are the curly-leafed form and the stronger, flat-leafed Italian variety or French parsley ***Petroselinum crispum* var. *neapolitanum***. **ZONES 5–11.**

PETUNIA

PETUNIA

'Petun' means 'tobacco' in a South American Indian dialect, and petunias are indeed relatives of the tobaccos *(Nicotiana)*: their leaves have a similar narcotic effect on humans, and both genera belong to the same family as potatoes (Solanaceae). There are around 35 species in the genus, occurring in warmer parts of South America, including annuals, biennials and shrubby perennials. They have dark green, rather hairy, smooth-edged leaves and trumpet-shaped flowers in white, purple, red, blue, pink or mixed hues. It is doubtful whether any other group of garden annuals has been the subject of such intense selection by plant breeders over such a long period as the petunias have been. Interestingly, from what they have revealed of their work, it seems to have been concentrated almost entirely on the one hybrid combination *(Petunia × hybrida)*.

CULTIVATION: The garden petunias are frost-tender plants always grown as annuals and are popular worldwide as bedding plants and for window boxes, hanging baskets and planters. Fairly fast growing, they like well-drained, fertile soil and a sunny location and thrive where summers are hot, although they do need shelter from wind. Flowers of some of the larger Grandiflora hybrids are damaged by rain but others, mainly the Multiflora hybrids, are more resistant. Sow seed under glass in early spring, or plant purchased seedlings at beginning of summer. Fertilize every month until flowering is well advanced. Pinch back hard to encourage branching and deadhead regularly. Watch for cucumber mosaic and tomato spotted wilt.

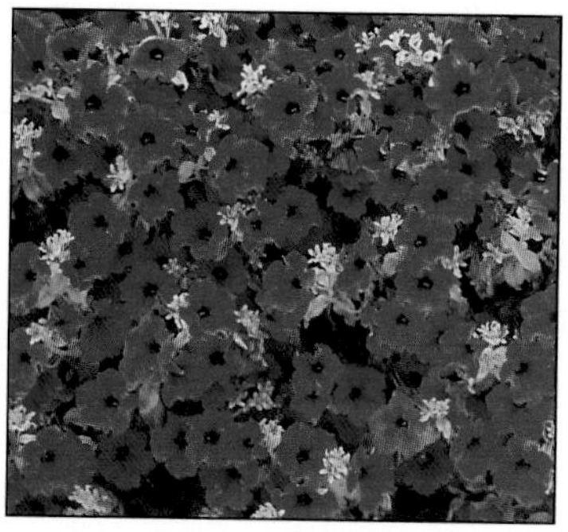

Petunia × hybrida 'Shihi Purple'

Petunia × hybrida

Believed to have originated as a cross between the white-flowered *Petunia axillaris* and the pink to purple-flowered *P. integrifolia*, the garden petunia was a well-known summer bedding plant in Europe by the middle of the nineteenth century. From an early stage, the garden petunias were divided into 4 groups of cultivars and seedling strains, designated by Latin names, and this classification still survives. The 2 most important groups are the **Grandiflora** and **Multiflora** petunias, both with plants around 12 in (30 cm) tall at maturity. Flowers of the former are very wide and shallow, scattered over the somewhat sprawling plants, while Multifloras are more compact in growth with densely massed and somewhat narrower blooms. The **Nana Compacta** petunias are generally less than 6 in (15 cm) high, of compact habit, and with profuse small flowers. The **Pendula** petunias have prostrate, trailing stems and are grown mainly in hanging baskets. It is the Grandiflora petunias that are now the most popular, with a dazzling range of newer F1 hybrids, although they are more easily rain damaged and susceptible to disfiguring botrytis rot; they include the **Cascade** and **Supercascade Series** (or Magic Series), available in a wide range of colors, with single flowers and somewhat trailing stems suitable for hanging baskets. **'Giants of California'** is not so profusely blooming, but individual blossoms are very large with ruffled edges and are white, pink or mauve. The **Multifloras** have smaller blooms but are more prolific flowerers; they include the **Plum Series** with delightfully veined flowers and **Bonanza Series** with frilly, trumpet-shaped double flowers in a multitude of colors. The **Celebrity Series**, including cultivars such as **'Pink Morn'**, also covers a wide color range; they are mainly in pastel shades and are distinguished by their light-throated flowers. The **Madness Series** have small single-color flowers. **'Purple Wave'** is a seedling strain with prolific flowers of a single, magenta-purple color; it has a cascading growth habit and is similar to the vegetatively propagated **'Colorwave'** petunias. ZONES 9–11.

Petunia × hybrida 'Frenzy Rose'

Petunia × hybrida 'Pink Vein'

Petunia × hybrida 'Pink Flamingo'

Petunia × hybrida 'Flamingo'

Petunia Celebrity Series 'Pink Morn'

Petunia integrifolia

Petunia × hybrida cultivar

Petunia integrifolia

syn. *Petunia violacea*

Sometimes sold as **'Burgundy Pet'**, this Argentinian species is a short-lived shrubby perennial that produces masses of small, dark-throated, rose-purple flowers on sprawling plants. It is a weather- and disease-tolerant species that is being increasingly used in hybridizing. Some very free-flowering cultivars recently released under the trade name **Million Bells** may belong to this species. ZONES 9–11.

PHACELIA

SCORPION WEED

This is a genus of around 150 species of annuals, biennials and perennials native to the Americas. They are generally shrubby, but vary considerably in size, ranging from as little as 6 in (15 cm) to over 5 ft (1.5 m) tall. The young shoots and leaves are sometimes downy and the leaves are often toothed or lobed, sometimes to the point of being pinnate. They all have clusters of small 5-petalled flowers at the stem tips. The flowers are usually in blue or purple shades, often

Phacelia bolanderi

Phalaenopsis amabilis

Phaius tankervilleae

with white centers, and can be quite striking. ***Phacelia bolanderi*** is a delicate shade of lilac.

CULTIVATION: Most species are very easily grown in any light but moist, well-drained soil in full sun. They are fully frost hardy. Propagate the annuals and biennials from seed, the perennials from seed or cuttings.

Phacelia campanularia

CALIFORNIAN BLUEBELL, CALIFORNIAN DESERT BLUEBELL

True to its common name, the flowers on this fast-growing annual are blue and shaped like bells. Appearing in spring and early summer, the flowers are small, only 1 in (25 mm) across. This bushy, branching plant is delightful in a rockery or border; it grows 8–18 in (20–45 cm) high, and has dark green, serrated leaves. **ZONES 9–11.**

Phacelia grandiflora

This species from southern California is a 3 ft (1 m) tall annual with serrated-edged, elliptical leaves up to 8 in (20 cm) long. Its flowers are 1½ in (35 mm) wide and are mauve to white. **ZONES 8–11.**

Phacelia grandiflora

Phalaenopsis amabilis

Phacelia tanacetifolia

FIDDLENECK

Found from California to Mexico, this species is widely planted by organic gardeners as a way to attract hoverflies for aphid control. An annual that grows from 6–48 in (15–120 cm) tall, it has deep green, lobed, oblong leaves up to 8 in (20 cm) long. The flowers are deep blue, ½ in (12 mm) in diameter and open through summer. **ZONES 8–11.**

PHAEDRANASSA

QUEEN LILY

This genus of about 6 species of bulbs is from the northern Andean region of South America. They have rather strap-like leaves up to 18 in (45 cm) long. In spring and summer, the bulbs produce flower stems from 12–36 in (30–90 cm) tall, depending on the species. At the top of the stem is a head of 6 to 17, pendulous, 1–2½ in (2.5–6 cm) long tubular flowers with spreading lobes, rather like the flowers of some fuchsia species. The flower color is usually a combination of red tubes with green lobes, or the reverse pattern.

CULTIVATION: Plant these large bulbs near the soil surface or with their necks slightly emergent; in damp areas they can be grown on the surface. Although they tolerate light frosts, they do best in mild climates with a position in sun or part-shade. Propagate from ripe seed or from offsets removed during dormancy.

Phaedranassa carnioli

Found throughout the warmer parts of South America, this species has 24 in (60 cm) stems bearing 6 to 10, 2 in (5 cm) long red flowers tipped with green and yellow. It flowers in spring and summer. **ZONES 8–10.**

PHAENOCOMA

The sole species in this genus is a spreading, daisy-like shrub with semi-succulent

Phaenocoma prolifera

leaves from South Africa. These are little more than small knobs protruding from the stems, and are light green to silvery gray, as are the stems. The main feature of the plant is the massed display of 1½ in (35 mm) wide pink, papery petalled daisies. The flower display peaks in late winter to late spring with odd flowers throughout the year.

CULTIVATION: Grow in light, well-drained, lime-free soil in full sun. Provided the plant is well hardened off in fall (autumn) and is not waterlogged over winter, it will tolerate light frosts. Propagate from seed or small cuttings.

Phaenocoma prolifera

This charming small shrub grows to around 24 in (60 cm) tall with a spread of up to 4 ft (1.2 m). In a warm, sunny position, it flowers freely and is covered for long periods with pink, everlasting, daisy-like flowers. **ZONES 9–11.**

PHAIUS

From Australia, Indonesia, Asia, Africa, Madagascar and islands in the Pacific, the 30 species that make up this genus are evergreen or deciduous, terrestrial and epiphytic orchids. They are grown for their beautiful and colorful flowers, which are borne in multi-flowering racemes. The mid-green, alternate leaves are either elliptical or lance-shaped.

CULTIVATION: These frost-tender orchids require bright light (or full light in winter), rich, leafy soil and constant moisture. Give them plenty of room to grow as their roots are quite extensive. Propagate by division.

Phaius tankervilleae

SWAMP ORCHID, NUN'S ORCHID

This large terrestrial species occurs from India through Southeast Asia to New Guinea and Australia, usually in damp or swampy conditions in full sun or heavy shade. The plants, which can be up to 3 ft (1 m) tall, have a squat pseudobulb about 2½ in (6 cm) long and several thin-textured, pleated leaves up to 3 ft (1 m) long and 8 in (20 cm) wide. The inflorescence is erect, 3–6 ft (1–1.8 m) tall with up to 20 flowers, brownish red inside, each 3 in (8 cm) long; yellow forms occur occasionally. The flowers are produced in spring. **ZONES 10–12.**

PHALAENOPSIS

MOTH ORCHID

The pastel flowers, broad leaves and intricate petals of the nearly 50 species in this genus from tropical Asia to New Guinea and Australia look enough like fluttering butterflies to earn the common name of moth orchid. They do not make pseudobulbs; the leaves, plain green or spotted, spring directly from the rootstock and the arching flower stems rise clear above them. The stem can be 24 in (60 cm) tall, bearing as many as 20 shapely 4 in (10 cm) flowers. They are most commonly shining white, but are sometimes pale pink, and appear at almost any time of year.

CULTIVATION: *Phalaenopsis* require tropical and subtropical climates—or elsewhere a warmed but well-ventilated greenhouse—and filtered light, constant moisture and a rich but open and perfectly drained compost. They are apt to send roots out over the top of the pot: these should be left undisturbed if possible. Their lives as house plants are limited unless they can be retired to a greenhouse when the flowers fade. Propagate by division in spring.

Phalaenopsis amabilis

This is an attractive, small-growing epiphyte (occasionally on rocks) from the humid tropical lowlands of Indonesia, Borneo, New Guinea, the Philippines and Australia. The short stem bears 2 to 5 pendulous, fleshy leaves to 15 in (38 cm) long and 4 in (10 cm) wide. The inflorescences are branched, arching to pendulous, up to 3 ft (1 m) long with 5 to 25 flowers. The flowers are variable in size, up to 4 in (10 cm) across and appear in spring and summer. This large-flowered species is prominent in most hybrids. **ZONES 11–12.**

Phalaenopsis equestris

syn. ***Phalaenopsis rosea***

This small-growing epiphyte occurs in the Philippines and Taiwan at low altitudes. It has 2 to 5 oblong leaves up to 8 in (20 cm) long by 2 in (5 cm) wide. The inflorescence is simple or branched, to about 12 in (30 cm) long and arching, with 10 to 15 flowers, each about 1 in (25 mm) across. This species regularly produces plantlets on the old inflorescences; these are convenient for propagation. *Phalaenopsis equestris* flowers in fall (autumn) and winter. **ZONES 11–12.**

Phalaenopsis gigantea

This large-growing species from Borneo derives its name from its large leaves, which are up to 18 in (45 cm) long and 8 in (20 cm) wide, fleshy and pendulous. It grows in the understory of hillside rainforests at low elevations. It is very rare in the wild and under threat from illegal collecting. The inflorescence is pendulous, up to 15 in (38 cm) long, with many fleshy flowers, each about 2 in (5 cm) across. A slow-growing species, it is best grown on a slab or in a basket. The flowers are produced throughout the year. **ZONES 11–12.**

Phalaenopsis Hybrids

Thousands of hybrids have been produced from the species of this genus.

Phalaenopsis sanderiana

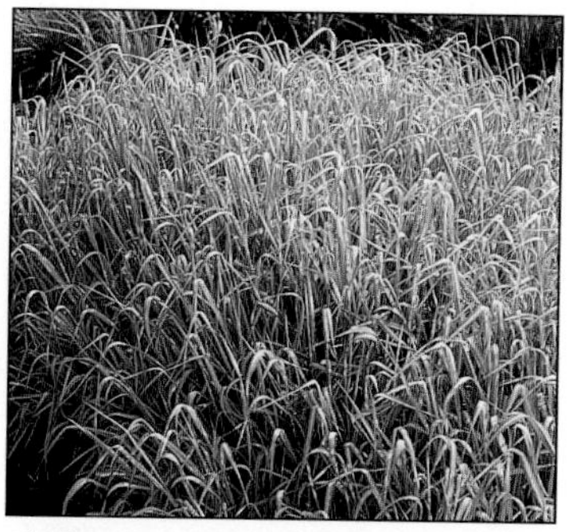

Phalaris arundinacea var. *picta*

Phaseolus coccineus

Phaseolus coccineus 'Achievement'

Breeders have been striving to produce more floriferous plants with larger, more rounded flowers on upright flower spikes and colorful combinations such as striped flowers. Most hybrids are white or pink, and are very popular for the cut flower industry, much-used in floral arrangements and bouquets. Some notable examples are **Alice Gloria 'Cecil Park'**, which is pure white; **Bill Smoothey**, pink with white edgings; **'Carmela's Stripe'**, a striking hybrid with light pink petals with deep red veining and red lips; **Hiramatsua 'Ching Hua'**, with deep pink petals; **Longwood Gardens**, white with brownish yellow lips; and **Plantation Imp 'Moonglow'**, with pinkish orange stripes on its whitish yellow petals, and pinkish orange lips. Some hybrids originating from *P. equestris* as a parent have a multitude of smaller flowers on branched inflorescences. **ZONES 11–12.**

Phalaenopsis sanderiana

syns *Phalaenopsis amabilis* var. *sanderiana*, *P. aphrodite* var. *sanderiana*

This compact plant with large flowers is restricted to the Philippines at low altitudes. There are 2 or 3 leaves marked with purple beneath, up to 10 in (25 cm) long by 3 in (8 cm) wide and pendulous. The inflorescence, sometimes branched, is about 24 in (60 cm) long with several flowers each about 4 in (10 cm) across, in shades of pink or white. This species flowers in late summer. **ZONES 11–12.**

Phalaenopsis schilleriana

This is a robust epiphyte occurring at low altitudes in the Philippines. There are 2 or 3 leaves which are obviously mottled with silver and dark green above and are purple below. They are fleshy, pendulous and about 15 in (38 cm) long by 4 in (10 cm) wide. The inflorescence is branched, arching, becoming pendulous, with up to 250 flowers each about 4 in (10 cm) across. **ZONES 11–12.**

PHALARIS

Found over much of the northern temperate region and in South America, the 15 species of annual and perennial grasses that make up this genus are often rhizomatous and are found growing in damp areas, beside or even in shallow water. They form low clumps of narrow basal leaves up to 15 in (38 cm) long from which emerge upright, wiry flowering stems. These grow 4–5 ft (1.2–1.5 m) tall and are topped with plumes of tiny flowers.

CULTIVATION: Although many species prefer damp environments, they will grow in most garden soils that do not dry out in summer. The green-leafed species will grow in sun or light shade; variegated cultivars are best grown in full sun or they may revert to green. Most species are very frost hardy. Propagate from seed or by division.

Phalaris arundinacea var. *picta*

GARDENERS' GARTERS, REEDY GRASS

This clump-forming perennial grass is easily grown, bearing reed-like leaves with white stripes and, in summer, terminal panicles of purplish or pale green spikelets on stout, upstanding stems. Indigenous to North America and Europe, it can grow to 5 ft (1.5 m) tall, but is generally kept lower in a garden. It can prove invasive. **ZONES 4–10.**

PHASEOLUS

BEAN

This genus, so important as a staple food and commercial crop, is native to warm-temperate to tropical regions of the Americas. There are some 36 annual and perennial species, some familiar as garden crops. They are twining climbing plants with thin, usually bright green, trifoliate leaves. Racemes of white, yellow, red or purple flowers are followed by long, narrow seed pods. In some species the pods are eaten, in others it is the beans they contain.

CULTIVATION: Beans thrive with a long, warm growing season, plenty of sunlight and ample moisture. They prefer a humus-rich yet light and well-drained soil. Some are also suitable for planting in tubs or flower beds. Propagate from seed in fall (autumn) or spring. Watch for attack by slugs.

Phaseolus coccineus

SCARLET RUNNER BEAN

This vigorous climber comes in different varieties and can grow up to 12 ft (3.5 m) high. It needs a sheltered position. Sow seed in late spring in double rows 2 in (5 cm) deep and 12 in (30 cm) apart. Pick pods when they reach 6 in (15 cm) long. These plants are perennial and last for several years, though they bear most heavily in their first year. **'Achievement'** has larger leaves and the flower's keel is orange. **ZONES 9–11.**

Phalaenopsis Hybrid Longwood Gardens

Phalaenopsis Hybrid Bill Smoothey

P. Hybrid Plantation Imp 'Moonglow'

P. Hybrid Alice Gloria 'Cecil Park'

Phalaenopsis Hybrid 'Carmela's Stripe'

Phalaenopsis Hybrid Hiramatsua 'Ching Hua'

P

Phaseolus lunatus
LIMA BEAN

Originally from Central and South America, this twining perennial climber is now widely cultivated in tropical and subtropical countries for its swollen white seeds, which are eaten either fresh or dried. It is normally cultivated as an annual. Because of its tropical origin, the lima bean needs warmer growing conditions than the French bean, but is suited to the same cultural requirements. **ZONES 10–12.**

Phaseolus vulgaris
FRENCH BEAN, KIDNEY BEAN, STRING BEAN, HARICOT BEAN

The major bean species both for green and dried beans, *Phaseolus vulgaris* displays great variation in both pod and seed characters, as well as plant growth habit. It is thought to be a cultivated derivative of a wild species *(P. aborigineus)* of the northern Andes and was already widely planted in the pre-Columbian era. An annual, it was originally a climber but many cultivated strains are 'dwarf beans' that are better adapted to mechanical harvesting. The beans can also be divided into those grown as pulses, including the borlotti, pinto, haricot and navy beans, and those grown as green beans (a few are dual-purpose); these go by many names, including French beans, snap beans, string beans and stringless beans. The pods vary in length, whether they are round or flat, and in color from cream to yellow, green, blue-green, red or purple; seed color may vary almost as much. Popular green bean cultivars include **'Tendercrop'**, a dwarf with straight, plump green stringless pods; **'Blue Lake'**, a climber with very plump, long, tender pods that are slightly bluish green; **'Kentucky Wonder Wax'**, a climber with large golden-yellow pods; and **'Royal Burgundy'**, a dwarf with curved, deep purple pods and purplish foliage. **ZONES 7–11.**

Phaseolus vulgaris

PHELLODENDRON

Elegant, slender and requiring little maintenance, these 10 species of deciduous trees from East Asia grow to 50 ft (15 m) tall with a crown spreading to 12 ft (3.5 m). The shiny, light green pinnate leaves turn a rich shade of yellow in fall (autumn). Small, yellowish green flowers appear in late spring or early summer, followed by blackberry-like fruits.

CULTIVATION: These trees are extremely hardy, tolerating both frost and harsh sun, although they prefer protection from wind. They grow best in full sun with fertile, well-drained soil. Seed may be germinated in spring, or propagate from cuttings or by grafting or layering in summer.

Phellodendron amurense
AMUR CORK TREE

Originally from China and Japan, this is the most common species of the genus in cultivation and earns its common name from its corky older branches. Growing to 40 ft (12 m) tall, it prefers humus-rich soil and summer moisture. Its bright green leaves with 5 to 11 leaflets have an unusual heart-shaped base and a pungent aroma. The 5-petalled flowers, male and female on separate trees, produce berries that are held above the foliage in dense bunches. **ZONES 3–9.**

Phellodendron lavallei
syn. ***Phellodendron amurense* 'Lavallei'**

This species from central Japan is around 30 ft (9 m) tall with thick, corky bark and rusty red young growth. It leaves are 8–15 in (20–38 cm) long with 5 to 13 leaflets, each up to 4 in (10 cm) long. The foliage is yellow-green and slightly hairy underneath. It flowers in summer. **ZONES 6–10.**

Phellodendron sachalinense

Philadelphus 'Natchez'

Philadelphus 'Belle Etoile'

Philadelphus coronarius 'Aureus'

Philadelphus coronarius

Phellodendron sachalinense
syn. ***Phellodendron amurense* var. *sachalinense***
SAKHALIN CORK TREE

This 25 ft (8 m) tall tree from northeast Asia has thin, dark brown bark that, despite its common name, is not corky like many *Phellodendron* species. The young growth is rusty red and the leaves are up to 12 in (30 cm) long with 7 to 11 leaflets. They are deep green above, blue-green below. **ZONES 3–9.**

PHILADELPHUS
MOCK ORANGE, SYRINGA

This genus of 60 species of deciduous shrubs comes from the temperate regions of the northern hemisphere, mainly from East Asia and North America. The cultivated species are all quite similar. They grow to a height and spread of 10 ft (3 m) and have light green, roughly elliptical leaves about 3 in (8 cm) long. They flower in late spring and early summer, bearing 4-petalled white or cream flowers in loose clusters. The flower scent strongly resembles that of orange blossom, hence the common name. *Philadelphus* **'Miniature Snowflake'** is a dwarf cultivar of the popular **'Snowflake'**. **'Natchez'** is another cultivar often grown.

CULTIVATION: Moderately to very frost hardy, they are easily grown, preferring moist, well-drained soil and a position in sun or light shade. They may be pruned after flowering and can be used for informal hedging. Propagate from seed or from cuttings taken in summer.

Phellodendron lavallei

Philadelphus 'Beauclerk'

This is one of a group of hybrids between *Philadelphus* × 'Lemoinei' and *P. coulteri*. It grows to around 6 ft (1.8 m) tall with dark, peeling bark and 1–1$\frac{1}{2}$ in (25–35 mm) long, slightly hairy leaves. Its flowers, borne singly or in groups of 3 to 5, are 1–1$\frac{1}{2}$ in (25–35 mm) wide, white with a small purple center. **ZONES 5–9.**

Philadelphus 'Belle Etoile'

'Belle Etoile' is a relatively narrow, 6 ft (1.8 m) tall species with stems that arch at the top. Starry, 2$\frac{1}{2}$ in (6 cm) wide white flowers with a small central red blotch are borne in late spring and early summer. **ZONES 5–9.**

Philadelphus coronarius

From southern Europe and Asia Minor, this species grows to 6 ft (1.8 m) tall and has very fragrant 2 in (5 cm) wide white flowers. Its oval, bright green leaves are slightly hairy on the undersides. **'Aureus'** has bright yellow new growth and smaller flowers; **'Variegatus'** bears white flowers and has white-edged leaves. **ZONES 2–9.**

Philadelphus 'Lemoinei'
syn. ***Philadelphus* × *lemoinei***

This hybrid between *Philadelphus coronarius* and *P. microphyllus* was bred in the late 1880s by the famous French hybridist Lémoine, who also raised many hydrangeas and lilacs. It grows to 6 ft (1.8 m) and has arching branches. The 1 in (25 mm) flowers are white, very fragrant and are usually carried in clusters of up to 7 blooms. **ZONES 3–9.**

Philadelphus lewisii

Indigenous to the USA and the state flower of Idaho, this species bears clusters of cream flowers up to 2 in (5 cm) across. These appear in mid-spring, occasionally also through the warmer months. The stems reach 10 ft (3 m) and can become woody and untidy if not pruned after flowering. It does best in part-shade and will not tolerate prolonged dry periods. ***Philadelphus lewisii* subsp. *californicus* 'Miniature Schmidt'** is a dwarf cultivar with narrow growth to around 3 ft (1 m) tall and white, fragrant double flowers. **ZONES 4–9.**

Philadelphus 'Manteau d'Hermine'

This is a compact shrub with small leaves and 1 in (25 mm) wide, creamy, double flowers opening from pink to red buds in summer. It grows to a height of 30 in (75 cm) with a 5 ft (1.5 m) spread. **ZONES 5–9.**

Philadelphus mexicanus

MEXICAN MOCK ORANGE, EVERGREEN MOCK ORANGE

Native to Mexico, this evergreen shrub bears very fragrant, cream, single flowers set among oval, green leaves. Moderately frost tender, it grows to a height of 10–20 ft (3–6 m) with a spread of 6 ft (1.8 m). It prefers a part-shaded, protected position. **ZONES 9–10.**

Philadelphus microphyllus

This upright species from southwestern USA grows to 3 ft (1 m) high and wide and has dark peeling bark. The flowers, which appear in summer, are snow white and are highly scented. **ZONES 6–9.**

Philadelphus pendulifolius

Philadelphus 'Lemoinei'

Philadelphus pendulifolius

Possibly a hybrid rather than a true species, this plant grows to about 8 ft (2.4 m) high and wide and bears racemes of cup-shaped white flowers. **ZONES 5–9.**

Philadelphus 'Sybille'

This spreading cultivar, to about 4 ft (1.2 m) tall, has white, 2 in (5 cm) wide, single flowers sometimes with a small pale purple central blotch. **ZONES 3–9.**

Philadelphus 'Virginal'

Very frost hardy, this vigorous, upright shrub grows to a height and spread of a little under 10 ft (3 m). From late spring to early summer, it bears large, fragrant, semi-double flowers set among dark green, oval leaves. **ZONES 3–9.**

PHILESIA

The sole species in this genus is an evergreen shrub from southern Chile. In the wild it is sometimes seen as a semi-climber, but rarely behaves this way in cultivation. It has ½–1½ in (12–35 mm) long lance-shaped leaves. The tubular to bell-shaped flowers, around 2½ in (6 cm) long, open from late summer.
CULTIVATION: A plant for cool, moist but largely frost-free gardens, *Philesia* prefers humus-rich, moist, well-drained soil and part-shade. While the plant will tolerate temperatures down to around 15°F (–10°C), repeated freezing will cause damage and early frosts will cut short the flower display. Propagate from cuttings or by layering.

Philesia magellanica

This erect species from Chile is grown for the delightful, crimson-pink flowers it bears from mid-summer to late fall (autumn). It has dark green, narrow leaves with bluish white undersides. It grows to a height of 3 ft (1 m) with a spread of 6 ft (1.8 m). **ZONES 9–11.**

PHILLYREA

MOCK PRIVET

Closely related and very similar to *Osmanthus*, this genus of 4 evergreen shrubs or small trees is found in the Mediterranean region and the Middle East. They grow 10–30 ft (3–9 m) tall, depending on the species, and have small, leathery leaves, sometimes with toothed edges. Their flowers are very small but fragrant. They are white to greenish cream, clustered in the leaf axils and open in spring, and are followed by small blue-black drupes.

Philadelphus lewisii

Philadelphus 'Virginal'

Philesia magellanica

Phillyrea angustifolia

Phillyrea latifolia 'Spinosa'

CULTIVATION: Reasonably frost hardy, these plants are easily grown in moist, well-drained soil in full sun or part-shade. They will tolerate dry conditions once established and are tough, adaptable plants. Able to withstand frequent trimming, they are suitable for hedging. Propagate from cuttings.

Phillyrea angustifolia

This species from the dry hills around the Mediterranean has an olive-like appearance with narrow, lance-shaped leaves up to 3 in (8 cm) long and clusters of tiny greenish cream flowers in spring. It develops into a dense shrub up to 10 ft (3 m) tall. **ZONES 7–10.**

Phillyrea latifolia 'Spinosa'

This is an unusual cultivar with spiny toothed, oval leaves. It is otherwise similar to the species and if untrimmed will eventually develop into a small tree of great character. Although often found growing in limestone soils in the wild, it is easily cultivated under normal garden conditions. **ZONES 7–10.**

PHILODENDRON

This genus of up to 500 species includes many well-known house plants as well as some shrubs and small trees. Native to tropical America and the West Indies, they are mainly epiphytic, evergreen vines and creepers with aerial roots, some dainty but others quite robust. They are known for their lush foliage, often with a dramatic outline or deep lobes, mostly green but sometimes attractively marked with white, pink or red. The petal-less flowers are inconspicuous. All parts of the plants are poisonous.
CULTIVATION: All species need plenty of moisture and a tropical or subtropical climate to be cultivated outdoors. They need a sheltered, shady spot with well-drained, humus-rich soil. Water and fertilize house plants regularly, reducing

Philodendron bipinnatifidum

watering during the cooler months. Propagate from cuttings taken in spring or from seed.

Philodendron bipennifolium

syn. ***Philodendron panduriforme***

FIDDLE-LEAF PHILODENDRON

This climber attaches itself to suitable supports by means of aerial roots. A decorative plant, it is unusual for the guitar-like shape of its lobed, bright green leaves. It likes medium light, and in a large pot will grow 6–10 ft (1.8–3 m) tall. Cut back if necessary. **ZONES 10–12.**

Philodendron bipinnatifidum

syn. ***Philodendron selloum***

TREE PHILODENDRON

This upright, robust species from Brazil grows to 10 ft (3 m) tall. It is noted for its shiny, oval, deep green leaves, 15–24 in (38–60 cm) long and many-lobed; in some hybrids, the leaves can be up to 3 times as large. The flowers are white or greenish. This species is variable in leaf outline; the common form with irregular lobing is sometimes known under the synonym. Other cultivars and hybrids include some of the most spectacular of all foliage plants. **ZONES 10–12.**

Phlomis chrysophylla

Phlomis tuberosa

Philodendron erubescens

Phlomis fruticosa

Philodendron erubescens

RED-LEAF PHILODENDRON, BLUSHING PHILODENDRON

This climbing species from Colombia has purple-red stems and new growth. Its leaves are more than 15 in (38 cm) long, elongated heart- to arrowhead-shaped, glossy deep green above with purplish undersides. It is usually treated as a house or greenhouse plant, grown in a pot trained up a frame. **'Burgundy'** has 12 in (30 cm) red-flushed leaves with red veins and deep purple-red stems. **ZONES 11–12.**

Philodendron scandens subsp. *oxycardium*

syn. ***Philodendron oxycardium***

SWEETHEART VINE, MONEY PLANT

This widely grown Mexican species is a rapid climber with glossy, heart-shaped, rich green leaves that may grow up a column or trail down. The juvenile foliage is a golden brown. The aerial roots on the trailing stems will attach to anything. **ZONES 11–12.**

PHLEBODIUM

This genus of 10 species of spreading rhizomatous ferns is from tropical America. Their fleshy rhizomes, which are up to 1 in (25 mm) thick and covered in golden scales when young, spread across the ground and also climb short distances up trunks and over rocks. The fronds are leathery and variable in shape. They are often over 3 ft (1 m) long and may be simple, oval and undivided, pinnatifid (deeply lobed to the midrib but without distinct leaflets), or the lobe tips may themselves be lobed. **CULTIVATION:** While these tropical ferns will not tolerate frosts, they do not necessarily require high temperatures and thrive in protected pockets of moist, well-drained soil in the shade and shelter of evergreen trees. Propagate by removing small rooted pieces of rhizome.

Phlebodium aureum

syn. ***Polypodium aureum***

RABBIT'S FOOT FERN, HARE'S FOOT FERN

This evergreen fern has creeping rhizomes with golden scales. The mid-green fronds have orange-yellow sporangia on the undersides. It grows to 5 ft (1.5 m) high 24 in (60 cm) wide and is ideal for hanging baskets. **ZONES 10–12.**

PHLOMIS

This genus consists of around 100 species of often downy-leafed perennials, subshrubs and shrubs found from the Mediterranean region to China. Although variable, in most cases their leaves are large, being over 4 in (10 cm) long, and densely covered with hair-like felting. Typical of members of the nettle family, the leaves occur in whorls on upright stems. The tubular flowers, borne on upright verticillasters, curl downwards and have 2 lips at the tip, the upper lip hooded over the lower. They occur in clusters of 2 to 40 blooms, depending on the species, and are usually in shades of cream, yellow, pink, mauve or purple. **CULTIVATION:** Hardiness varies, though most will tolerate moderate frosts. Species with heavily felted foliage suffer in prolonged wet weather and are best grown in exposed positions where the foliage dries quickly after rain. Plant in moist, well-drained soil in full sun or part-shade. Propagate from seed or from small cuttings of non-flowering shoots, or by division where possible.

Phlomis grandiflora

Phlomis chrysophylla

Native to Lebanon, this 3–4 ft (1–1.2 m) evergreen subshrub has broad, elliptical leaves up to $2\frac{1}{2}$ in (6 cm) long. They are covered with a fine golden down when young that fades to yellow-gray. The flowers are bright golden yellow and open in summer. It is similar to the Jerusalem sage. **ZONES 9–11.**

Phlomis fruticosa

JERUSALEM SAGE

This evergreen shrub, a native of southern Europe, is grown for the strikingly beautiful yellow flowers it bears in whorls from early to mid-summer, among oval, wrinkled, felty green leaves. It tolerates coastal areas quite well and grows to a height and spread of 30 in (75 cm). To keep its habit neat, prune to about half its size in fall (autumn). **ZONES 7–10.**

Phlomis grandiflora

This species is similar to the well-known *Phlomis fruticosa,* but the leaves are greener and less woolly and the yellow flowers are in tighter, more spherical heads. The plant has a rather sprawling habit. **ZONES 8–10.**

Phlomis italica

This 12 in (30 cm) tall evergreen shrub is found on the Balearic Islands, not Italy as its name suggests. It has 2 in (5 cm) long, lance-shaped, sometimes shallow-toothed leaves with a dense covering of white felt. Its 1 in (25 mm) long flowers occur in widely spaced 6-flowered whorls, are pink to lavender and open from late summer. **ZONES 8–10.**

Phlomis russeliana

A native of Syria, this easily grown perennial thrives in any ordinary soil given a reasonable amount of sun. The large, heart-shaped, fresh green leaves make excellent ground cover, forming

Phlomis russeliana

clumps around 12 in (30 cm) high and up to 24 in (60 cm) across. In summer, it bears stout stems 3 ft (1 m) high topped with several whorls of hooded, butter-yellow flowers. **ZONES 7–10.**

Phlomis samia

Found in North Africa, the Balkans and Greece, this perennial species grows to 3 ft (1 m) tall and has long-stemmed, 3–10 in (8–25 cm) leaves with toothed edges. The leaves are felted when young, but this wears to a general hairiness. The flowers, which open from late spring, are pink to pale purple, $1\frac{1}{2}$ in (35 mm) long and in clusters of up to 20 blooms. **ZONES 7–10.**

Phlomis tuberosa

This 5 ft (1.5 m) tall species, which is widespread from southeast Europe to central Asia, develops small tubers on its roots. Its leaves are an elongated heart shape, up to 10 in (25 cm) long with toothed edges. They have a covering of fine hairs, but are not felted. The flowers open in summer, are pink to purple and quite small, although they show up well as there are up to 40 in each whorl. **ZONES 7–10.**

PHLOX

This genus contains more than 60 species of evergreen and semi-evergreen annuals and perennials, mostly native to North America. They are grown for their profuse, fragrant flowers and the symmetry of the flower clusters. The name *phlox* means 'flame', an appropriate epithet for these brightly colored, showy flowers popular in bedding and border displays. ***Phlox purpurea × lutea*** is a colorful hybrid with deep pink flowers with pale yellow centers. **CULTIVATION:** The tall perennial phloxes are easily grown in any temperate climate, though they need a lot of water while they are growing. The annual species will grow in almost any climate from the tropics to the coldest regions. Grow in fertile soil that drains well but remains moist, in a sunny or part-shaded position. Propagate from seed or cuttings or by division. Watch out for red spider mite, eelworm and powdery mildew.

Phlox purpurea × lutea

Phlox bifida 'Petticoat'

Phlox douglasii 'Rosea'

Phlox douglasii 'Waterloo'

Phlox drummondii

Phlox drummondii 'Sternenzauber'

Phlox adsurgens
WOODLAND PHLOX

This is a prostrate to slightly mounding perennial native to Oregon and northern California. Its leaves are rounded, shiny, usually less than 1 in (25 mm) long and slightly hairy. Sprays of bright pink flowers up to 1 in (25 mm) wide open from late spring. It prefers a cool, lightly shaded position. **'Wagon Wheel'** is a popular cultivar with drooping stems of large flowers with strappy petals. **ZONES 6–10.**

Phlox bifida
SAND PHLOX

This low, mounding perennial from central USA has narrow, hairy leaves up to 2½ in (6 cm) long. The flowers, in heads of 6 to 9 blooms, are around ½ in (12 mm) wide, mauve to white and slightly scented. It blooms in spring. **'Petticoat'** is a popular choice with its mass of pale lilac flowers. **ZONES 6–10.**

Phlox caespitosa
CUSHION PHLOX

This small, cushion-forming species is from western USA. The leaves are tiny and overlapping, forming a dense mat that sometimes mounds to 8 in (25 cm) or so. The white to pale blue flowers are around ½ in (12 mm) wide. **ZONES 5–10.**

Phlox carolina
THICK-LEAF PHLOX

Native to central and eastern USA, this perennial grows 3–4 ft (1–1.2 m) tall. It has rather thick, shiny, narrow leaves up to 6 in (15 cm) long. The flowers open early and are about 1 in (25 mm) wide, purple-pink or white with a pale pink to magenta eye. The flowerheads are up to 15 in (38 cm) long and are very showy. **ZONES 5–10.**

Phlox 'Chattahoochee'

This hybrid (possibly ***Phlox divaricata* subsp. *laphamii* × *P. pilosa***) forms a mound of arching stems up to 8 in (20 cm) long. The leaves are narrow and are covered in fine hairs. From late spring, it is smothered in red-centered, bright lavender-blue flowers. **ZONES 5–10.**

Phlox divaricata
WILD SWEET WILLIAM, BLUE PHLOX

A perennial found from Quebec, Canada, to south-central USA, this species has leafy stems to 12 in (30 cm) tall that develop from spreading underground stems. Its leaves are oval and around 2 in (5 cm) long. The flowers are blue, lavender or white, up to 1½ in (35 mm) wide, slightly fragrant and carried in open clusters. It blooms in spring. **ZONES 4–9.**

Phlox douglasii

This evergreen perennial, occurring naturally from Washington to California in the USA, bears white, lavender-blue or pink flowers and grows to 8 in (20 cm) in height. **'Boothman's Variety'** is a dwarf form with blue-centered lavender flowers. **'Crackerjack'** is a compact cultivar with crimson to magenta flowers. **'Red Admiral'** is a strong-growing yet compact form with vivid crimson flowers. **'Rosea'** forms a neat mat with silver-pink flowers. **'Waterloo'** has deep crimson flowers. **ZONES 5–10.**

Phlox caespitosa

Phlox drummondii
ANNUAL PHLOX

This annual grows quickly to a bushy 15 in (38 cm) in height, half that in spread. In summer and fall (autumn), it bears closely clustered, small, flattish flowers with 5 petals in reds, pinks, purples and creams. It has lanceolate, light green leaves and is frost resistant. Cultivars include **'Sternenzauber'** (syn. 'Twinkle') with star-like flowers that have pointed petals, and dwarf strains that grow to 4 in (10 cm). **ZONES 6–10.**

Phlox maculata
MEADOW PHLOX

Phlox maculata is a perennial that grows to 3 ft (1 m) tall and bears scented, white, pink or purple flowers in midsummer. **'Alpha'** is around 30 in (75 cm) tall with deep pink flowers. **'Miss Lingard'** is up to 3 ft (1 m) tall with fragrant white flowers that sometimes have a central pink ring. **'Omega'** is around 30 in (75 cm) in height with fragrant white, lilac-centered flowers. **ZONES 5–10.**

Phlox nana
SANTA FE PHLOX

Native to southwest USA, this perennial grows 4–10 in (10–25 cm) tall with ½–2 in (1.2–5 cm) long, lance-shaped leaves. Its flowers are purple-pink, slightly more than ½ in (12 mm) wide and open in spring. **ZONES 8–10.**

Phlox paniculata

Phlox maculata 'Alpha'

Phlox paniculata
SUMMER PHLOX, PERENNIAL PHLOX

This tall perennial can grow to more than 3 ft (1 m) in height. In summer, it bears long-lasting, terminal flowerheads comprising many small, 5-lobed flowers. Colors range through violet, red, salmon and white according to variety. **'Amethyst'** has violet flowers. **'Brigadier'** has very deep green leaves and pink flowers suffused with orange. **'Bright Eyes'** has pink flowers with red eyes. **'Eventide'** has light mauve or lavender-blue flowers. **'Fujiyama'** has pure white flowers on stems up to 30 in (75 cm) tall. **'Graf Zeppelin'** has white flowers with pinkish red centers. **'Mother of Pearl'** has white to pale pink flowers suffused pink on stems up to 30 in (75 cm) tall. **'Prince of Orange'** has pink flowers strongly flushed orange on stems up to 3 ft (1 m) tall. **'Prospero'** is an award-winning cultivar with white-edged, mauve flowers on plants 3 ft (1 m) tall. **'Sir John Falstaff'** has salmon-pink flowers. **'Snow Hare'** has snow-white flowers. **'White Admiral'** bears pure white flowers on stems up to 3 ft (1 m) tall. **'Windsor'** has deep pink flowers. **ZONES 4–10.**

Phlox paniculata 'Mother of Pearl'

Phlox paniculata 'Graf Zeppelin'

Phlox maculata 'Omega'

Phoenix canariensis

Phlox pilosa subsp. *ozarkana*

Phlox subulata 'Greencourt Purple'

Phlox subulata 'Marjorie'

Phlox pilosa subsp. *ozarkana*
PRAIRIE PHLOX

This form of a perennial widespread in the USA grows to 24 in (60 cm) tall with lance-shaped leaves up to 6 in (15 cm) long. The spring flowers, in large panicles, are up to 1 in (25 mm) wide, white, purple or pink. **ZONES 5–10.**

Phlox × *procumbens* 'Millstream'

'Millstream' has a very compact growth habit, dark green leaves and deep lavender-pink flowers. It grows to a height of only 4 in (10 cm) with a 12 in (30 cm) spread. **ZONES 4–9.**

Phlox subulata

Phlox subulata 'McDaniel's Cushion'

Phlox stolonifera
CREEPING PHLOX

A native of the woodlands of southeast North America, this creeper makes an excellent ground cover in shaded situations. Low mats of deep green, evergreen foliage increase by rhizomes. Spring flowers in pink, blue or white are held above the foliage on 12 in (30 cm) stems. It tolerates sun in cool areas; otherwise it needs shade and a woodsy soil. **'Blue Ridge'** is a neat, compact cultivar with slightly glossy leaves and bright powder-blue flowers. **ZONES 3–10.**

Phlox subulata
MOSS PHLOX

Throughout spring, this prostrate alpine perennial produces terminal masses of 1 in (25 mm) wide, star-shaped flowers in blue, mauve, carmine, pink and white, the petals being notched and open. Its fine-leafed foliage grows carpet-like to 4 in (10 cm) high with a spread twice that. Fully frost hardy and evergreen, it is suitable for sunny rock gardens. **'Greencourt Purple'** is notable for its rich color; it likes a little shade. **'McDaniel's Cushion'** (syn. 'Daniel's Cushion') is best in small groups among shrubs or taller perennials. **'Maischnee'** (syn. 'May Snow') is a beautiful snow-white form. **'Marjorie'** has glowing deep pink flowers, while **'Oakington Blue Eyes'** forms large mats and is smothered with light blue flowers. **ZONES 3–10.**

Phoenix canariensis

PHOENIX

These evergreen feather palms are native to subtropical and tropical parts of Asia, Africa and the Canary Islands. There are 17 very different species; some are an important source of food (dates and palm sugar derived from dates), others are popular as house plants or avenue trees. *Phoenix* includes species with a single trunk as well as some that form clumps of stems. The long fronds have stiff, sharp spines at the base and form a dense crown. The small yellow flowers grow in clusters and are followed by the fruits. *Phoenix* is the ancient Greek name given to the date palm.

CULTIVATION: Male and female plants are needed to ensure pollination. The plants prefer full sun, although they will tolerate part-shade, hot winds and poor soil if given good drainage. Hybrids between species are common. Trim off dead fronds. Propagate from seed in spring.

Phoenix canariensis
CANARY ISLAND DATE PALM

This massive palm from the Canary Islands grows to 50 ft (15 m) tall with a spread of 30 ft (9 m). It has a sturdy trunk up to 3 ft (1 m) across and arching, deep green fronds up to 12 ft (3.5 m) long. Small yellow flowers, borne in drooping clusters in summer, are succeeded by inedible, orange-yellow, acorn-like fruit. This palm needs plenty of room to show off its dramatic symmetrical shape. In areas prone to frosts, plant an advanced specimen when the danger of frost has passed. **ZONES 9–11.**

Phlox stolonifera

Phoenix reclinata

Phoenix dactylifera
DATE PALM

Native to the Middle East and North Africa where they have been cultivated for over 5,000 years, date palms grow to 100 ft (30 m) tall and 20 ft (6 m) wide. The trunk is more slender than that of *Phoenix canariensis*. The fronds have a grayish tinge; those at the top point upwards, the lower ones curve downwards to make a spherical crown. The dates, 1–3 in (2.5–8 cm) long, are cylindrical and yellowish when fresh. **ZONES 10–12.**

Phoenix reclinata
SENEGAL DATE PALM

This African species is smaller than *Phoenix canariensis* and *P. dactylifera*, reaching only 20–30 ft (6–9 m) in height. It is distinctive for its multiple trunks, each gracefully curving out from the center of the clump. The small fruit are yellow to red. **ZONES 10–11.**

Phoenix roebelenii
DWARF DATE PALM

From Laos, this palm is suitable for a hot-climate garden or for use as a potted specimen indoors. Growing to 10 ft (3 m) tall with a similar spread, its dark green, arching fronds give it an elegant, lacy effect. The short, slender stem is rough because the bases of the old leaves persist. The fruit are small, black, egg-shaped drupes. **ZONES 10–12.**

Phlox stolonifera 'Blue Ridge'

Phoenix rupicola

Phoenix roebelenii

Phoenix rupicola

CLIFF DATE, INDIAN DATE PALM

From northern India, this species has a slender 25 ft (8 m) tall trunk topped with a head of gracefully arching, rather glossy fronds up to 8 ft (2.4 m) long. Panicles of yellow flowers are followed by small, dark red fruit. Although the relatively quick growth and size of this species mean it is best grown outdoors, it is suitable for greenhouse cultivation. **ZONES 10–12.**

PHORMIUM

NEW ZEALAND FLAX

Valued for the dramatic effect of their stiff, vertical leaves, these 2 species of large, clumping plants from New Zealand grow well in most conditions. In summer, they produce panicles of flowers that attract nectar-feeding birds. The large, arching, striped leaves appear in clumps and can be anything from dark green to green-yellow; there are many cultivars with variegated or brightly colored foliage. They range in height from 3 ft (1 m) to 6 ft (1.8 m). The fiber of these flaxes has been used commercially, but is now largely confined to traditional Maori crafts. **CULTIVATION:** They make splendid container plants as well as useful garden specimens in almost any climate. They are fairly frost hardy, and respond well to generous watering and permanently moist conditions. Propagate from seed or by division in spring.

Phormium 'Apricot Queen'

This form has dark green, arching leaves to 4 ft (1.2 m) long with apricot striping and bronze edges. The young foliage is creamy yellow. **ZONES 8–11.**

Phormium 'Apricot Queen'

Phormium cookianum 'Maori Maiden'

Phormium cookianum

syn. *Phormium colensoi*

Found throughout New Zealand in a wide range of conditions, this species has leaves 2–5 ft (0.6–1.5 m) long and up to 2½ in (6 cm) wide. Its flowers are yellow to red-brown with yellow interiors, and are carried on stiffly erect stems that extend well above the foliage clump. **'Dark Delight'** has deep wine-red leaves up to 4 ft (1.2 m) long. **'Duet'** is a 12 in (30 cm) tall dwarf cultivar with cream and green foliage. **'Maori Maiden'** (syn. 'Rainbow Maiden) is an upright grower with 3 ft (1 m) long bronze leaves striped red. **'Sundowner'** has extremely long leaves, sometimes almost 6 ft (1.8 m), that are cream with a purple center and cream edges. **'Tricolor'** is an evergreen, upright perennial with bold spiky leaves prettily striped with red, yellow and green, and panicles of tubular, pale yellowish green flowers. **ZONES 8–11.**

Phormium 'Dawn'

The stiff, sword-shaped dark green leaves of this cultivar have red, bronze, salmon-pink and yellow vertical stripes. Panicles of tubular, dull red flowers are borne on short green stems in summer. This plant grows well by the sea. **ZONES 8–11.**

Phormium Hybrids

'Rainbow Warrior' is a recently released cultivar that makes a luxuriant clump of foliage. It has long arching and drooping leaves that are predominantly pinkish red and irregularly striped with bronze green. **ZONES 8–11.**

Phormium cookianum 'Duet'

Phormium Hybrid 'Rainbow Warrior'

Phormium cookianum

Phormium cookianum 'Sundowner'

Phormium cookianum 'Duet'

P

Phormium 'Sea Jade'

This is an upright plant reaching 3–4 ft (1–1.2 m) in height. It has deep green leaves with a strong maroon to bronze midrib stripe. **ZONES 8–11.**

Phormium tenax

The larger of the 2 New Zealand flax species, this has olive-green, strap-like leaves 6–10 ft (1.8–3 m) tall in clumps about 6 ft (1.8 m) across. It grows well by the sea. Hybrids of *Phormium tenax* and *P. cookianum* are often more compact than their parents, and their foliage

Phormium 'Sea Jade'

Phormium tenax

Phormium tenax 'Variegatum'

varies from bronze or purplish chartreuse to pink and salmon; the leaves may be variegated with vertical stripes of 2 or more colors. **'Bronze Baby'** has wide, fibrous, copper-toned leaves with sharply pointed ends. In summer, it bears tubular, bronze-red flowers on a strong stem from the base of the clump. **'Dazzler'** has red leaves edged with plum-purple. **'Purpureum'** has stiff, pointed, plum-purple to dark copper leaves and in summer bears reddish flowers on purplish blue stems. **'Variegatum'** has striped creamy yellow and white foliage. **'Maori Chief'** has green and rose red-striped leaves growing to 5 ft (1.5 m). **'Tom Thumb'** has green leaves with bronze margins growing to 24 in (60 cm). **'Coffee'** is another popular cultivar. **ZONES 8–11.**

PHOTINIA

These 60 species of evergreen or deciduous shrubs and small trees from the Himalayas and East and Southeast Asia are mostly fast growing. They are cultivated for their brilliant young foliage and, if deciduous, for their fall

Phormium tenax

Phormium tenax 'Coffee'

Photinia davidsoniae

Photinia × *fraseri*

(autumn) color. The leaves are alternate and the flowers, mostly white, are followed by either red or dark blue berries. The genus takes its name from a Greek word meaning 'shining'; this is a reference to the gleaming foliage.

CULTIVATION: Plant in sun or part-shade in fertile, well-drained soil with protection from strong winds. They make excellent hedges and should be pruned to promote bushiness and new growth. Propagate from seed or cuttings in summer, or by grafting onto hawthorn or quince stock.

Photinia beauverdiana var. *notabilis*

This variety is a large-leafed form of a deciduous shrub or small tree from western China. It grows to as much as 30 ft (9 m) tall and has leaves up to 6 in (15 cm) long. The leaves are lance-shaped and are edged with small teeth. Cream-flowered inflorescences up to 2 in (5 cm) wide develop in late spring. **ZONES 6–9.**

Photinia davidsoniae

An evergreen shrub or tree to 40 ft (12 m) tall, this central Chinese species has downy young growth with small spines. Its leaves are 3–6 in (8–15 cm) long, elliptical, dark glossy green above with lighter undersides. The inflorescence is also downy and opens in late spring. **ZONES 9–11.**

Photinia × *fraseri*

The young growth of these evergreen shrubs comes in shades of bright red, bronze-red and purple-red that persist in color over a long period. The mature

Photinia beauverdiana var. *notabilis*

Photinia × *fraseri* 'Red Robin'

Photinia × *fraseri* 'Robusta'

leaves are glossy and green. **'Red Robin'** has brilliant red new growth and **'Robusta'** (syn. *Photinia robusta*, *P. glabra* 'Robusta') bears eye-catching, coppery red young leaves. The height of the shrub varies with the cultivar, but most are in the 10–12 ft (3–3.5 m) range. **ZONES 8–10.**

Photinia glabra

Growing to about 10 ft (3 m) tall, this evergreen shrub is often used as a hedge as clipping promotes the reddish bronze new growth. Mature leaves are glossy green. The spring-borne, broad clusters of white flowers give an attractive, smoky effect and are succeeded by blue-black berries. This shrub is frost hardy in short-winter climates, but frost sensitive in prolonged cold conditions. **'Rubens'** bears new growth the color of red sealing wax. **ZONES 7–10.**

Photinia serratifolia

syn. *Photinia serrulata*

CHINESE HAWTHORN, CHINESE PHOTINIA

From China, this evergreen shrub or small tree grows to a height of 20 ft (6 m) with a bushy crown, but can also be kept lower and clipped to form a hedge. The glossy oval leaves are large, serrated and bronze tinted in spring. The small, white spring flowers are followed by small, red berries. **ZONES 7–10.**

Photinia glabra 'Rubens'

Photinia villosa
syn. *Pourthiaea villosa*

This deciduous upright shrub or small tree from Japan, Korea and China grows to 15 ft (4.5 m) tall with a bushy crown. White spring flowers are followed by red berries resembling those of a hawthorn. The oval leaves have serrated edges and a slightly downy surface; bronze tinted when young, they turn scarlet, orange and gold in fall (autumn). ***Photinia villosa* f. *maximowicziana*** is a Korean form that has yellow fall foliage. It is a 15 ft (4.5 m) tall deciduous shrub with 2–3 in (5–8 cm) long, leathery, serrated-edged, dark green leaves and 2 in (5 cm) wide flowerheads. ZONES 3–9.

PHRAGMIPEDIUM
LADY-SLIPPER

This genus consists of 15 to 20 species of epiphytic and terrestrial orchids from Central and South America and Mexico. Similar to *Paphiopedilum*, they share the same pouch-shaped lower flower lobe, but differ in having narrower leaves and more of them. The strappy leaves are 8–12 in (20–30 cm) long. The flowers, borne singly or in small groups on upright stems, usually have narrow arching petals, a hood-like sepal and the pouched lower lip. Colors are variable, but there is usually a base of white or yellow-green overlaid with pink and spotted purple. **CULTIVATION:** Minimum winter temperatures should be 50°–60°F (10°–15°C) for cool-climate species and up to 64°F (18°C) for tropicals. Plant in loose, very free-draining soil in light shade. If flowering ceases, increase the light levels. Never allow to dry out entirely, but keep on the dry side in winter. Propagate by dividing immediately after flowering or from seed.

Phragmipedium caudatum

This species is distributed from Colombia to Bolivia at moderate to high altitudes where it grows on cliff faces, sometimes in full sun. The numerous strap-like leaves are up to 24 in (60 cm) long and are arranged in 2 ranks like a fan, on short rhizomes. The inflorescence is 24 in (60 cm) tall and bears up to 6 large flowers, featuring elongated petals up to 18 in (45 cm) long. This species requires perfect drainage and strong filtered light. ZONES 11–12.

Photinia villosa

Phragmites australis

Phygelius × *rectus*

PHRAGMITES
REED

This genus of the true reeds now includes just 4 widely distributed species of large, perennial, rhizomatous grasses with strong, erect stems 10–12 ft (3–3.5 m) or more tall. Their leaves are narrow, linear and flat, without ribbing, and around 24 in (60 cm) long. In summer and fall (autumn), they produce large plumed panicles of flowers that mature into golden-yellow seed heads. **CULTIVATION:** Although usually found in damp meadows or near standing water in temperate and tropical zones, they will grow in normal garden soil provided it does not dry out in summer. A position in full sun is best. They are very frost hardy. Propagate from seed or by division.

Phragmites australis
syn. *Phragmites communis*
COMMON REED

This species has stems to 12 ft (3.5 m) or more tall and arching, 24 in (60 cm) long, 2 in (5 cm) wide leaves. The floral plumes are 18 in (45 cm) long and usually slightly pendent. They are brown with purple tints when young, ageing to golden yellow. **'Humilis'** is a dwarf form that grows to around 4 ft (1.2 m) tall; **'Rubra'** has red-tinted floral plumes; **'Variegatus'** has yellow-striped leaves that fade to white; and ***Phragmites australis* subsp. *altissimus*** grows to 20 ft (6 m) tall. ZONES 5–11.

Phuopsis stylosa

Phygelius aequalis 'Yellow Trumpet'

Phygelius × *rectus* 'African Queen'

Phygelius × *rectus* 'Pink Elf'

PHUOPSIS

This is a genus of just one species, a small clump- or mat-forming perennial native to the Caucasus and northern Iran. Its whorled foliage is reminiscent of the closely related woodruff *(Galium odoratum)* with tiny, narrow leaves in starry clusters at intervals along the 6–8 in (15–20 cm) stems. Its flowers are bright pink, ½ in (12 mm) long, 5-petalled tubes with a protruding style. They are massed in rounded heads of 30 to 50 blooms and open in summer. **CULTIVATION:** This plant is very frost hardy and is best grown in gritty, humus-rich, moist soil in sun or part-shade. Propagate from seed or cuttings of non-flowering shoots or by division.

Phuopsis stylosa

This charming little plant is most at home in a corner of a rockery that doesn't get too hot and dry in summer. Remove the heads of small pink flowers as they deteriorate and the display should last well into fall (autumn). ZONES 7–9.

PHYGELIUS
CAPE FUCHSIA

Related to *Penstemon* and *Antirrhinum* (the snapdragons) rather than *Fuchsia*, these 2 species of erect, evergreen shrubs or subshrubs—perennials in some winter conditions—are native to the Cape of Good Hope, South Africa. Good rock-garden plants, they grow to 3 ft (1 m) high and 18 in (45 cm) wide. They bear handsome, red flowers in summer, set among dark green, oval leaves. **CULTIVATION:** They do best in sun or part-shade and like a fertile, well-drained soil that is not too dry. Propagate from cuttings in summer.

Phygelius aequalis

This species is a suckering shrub to 3 ft (1 m) tall with dark green leaves and pale pink flowers. **'Yellow Trumpet'** has leaves that are a paler green and creamy yellow flowers. ZONES 8–11.

Phygelius capensis
CAPE FIGWORT, CAPE FUCHSIA

This sprawling, stoloniferous subshrub or shrub can grow up to 4 ft (1.2 m) tall with a spread of 8 ft (2.5 m), although it is usually considerably smaller. It has lance-shaped, 3 in (8 cm) long leaves and is mainly grown for its heads of soft orange-pink, pendulous, tubular flowers, which attract birds into the garden. ZONES 8–11.

Phygelius × *rectus*

These hybrids of *Phygelius aequalis* and *P. capensis* origins tend to be fairly compact plants with large sprays of flowers. They are the best choice for most gardens as they combine the toughness of *P. capensis* with the heavy flowering of *P. aequalis* in compact, non-invasive plants. **'African Queen'** has almost straight-tubed, pendulous, light red flowers with orange-red lobes. **'Pink Elf'** is a dwarf form with red-lobed pale pink flowers; the inflorescences are rather sparse, but the plant flowers over a long season. ZONES 8–11.

PHYLA
FROGFRUIT

This is a genus of some 15 species of spreading or carpeting perennials native

P

Phylica plumosa

Phyla nodiflora

Phyllanthus acidus

to Central and South America. They have loose rosettes or whorls of 1–3 in (2.5–8 cm) long, oval to lance-shaped leaves, often with shallow-toothed edges and a covering of fine hairs. Flat or rounded heads of simple, 4-petalled, white, lilac or purple flowers appear throughout the warmer months.
CULTIVATION: Although most species are rather frost tender, they are otherwise not difficult to grow. Plant in moist, well-drained soil in full sun or part-shade. Propagate from seed or by division in spring or fall (autumn).

Phyla nodiflora
syns *Lippia nodiflora, L. repens*

This widespread tropical to subtropical perennial develops such a dense mat of foliage that it is often used as a lawn substitute. It has 1 in (25 mm) long, gray-green leaves and ½–1 in (12–25 mm) wide heads of lilac flowers. The flowers attract bees, but can be mown off if this is likely to cause problems. ZONES 8–12.

PHYLICA
CAPE MYRTLE

This genus of around 150 species of evergreen shrubs is native to South Africa, the nearby islands and the farther flung Tristan da Cunha. They have bright green, narrow leaves and tiny true flowers that are often largely hidden by the leafy bracts or hairs that surround them. The stems, leaves and bracts are all covered with fine silvery hairs. The flowerheads are used dry or fresh in floral arrangements.
CULTIVATION: They thrive only in warm climates and need full sun and acid soil. Although tolerant of high humidity, they suffer with prolonged rain as it mats the foliage hairs and leads to rotting. They do particularly well in coastal conditions. Little pruning is required if the flowers are used, otherwise trim lightly after flowering. Propagate from seed in spring or cuttings in summer.

Phylica plumosa
syn. *Phylica pubescens*
FLANNEL FLOWER, FLANNEL BUSH

This 3–6 ft (1–1.8 m) tall South African shrub is covered in fine downy hairs; even the flowerheads are hairy. The leaves are 1 in (25 mm) long, narrow, deep green and have rolled-back edges. Although soft, they protrude straight out from the branches, giving a bristly appearance. The flowers, or more accurately the bracts, resemble hairy cream daisies. They appear from early winter and are good cut flowers. ZONES 9–11.

PHYLLANTHUS

This large genus of some 650 species of evergreen or deciduous herbs, shrubs and trees, comes from the tropical and subtropical regions of the world. The stalkless leaves, often red tinted when young, are arranged in two flattened ranks along the branches giving the impression of pinnate foliage. Small, red or yellow-green petal-less flowers appear during spring and summer. Some species have cladophylls rather than true leaves and these become fringed with small flowers, creating an unusual effect as if the leaves are flowering. Although the small pea-sized fruits of most species are inedible, a few produce gooseberry-like fruits that are palatable if cooked.

Phylica plumosa

CULTIVATION: Plant in rich, sandy, well-drained soil with ample water. They are good seaside plants in hot climates. Propagate from seed or cuttings.

Phyllanthus acidus
STAR GOOSEBERRY, OTAHEITE GOOSEBERRY, MALAY GOOSEBERRY

From India and Madagascar, this is the only widely cultivated species. It quickly reaches its mature height of 30 ft (9 m) with a spread of 10 ft (3 m), and has pale green, almost stalkless leaves. In spring, it bears dense clusters of tiny red flowers; these are followed in late summer by tight bunches of ribbed, bright yellow fruit, 1 in (25 mm) long. ZONES 11–12.

× *PHYLLIOPSIS*

This intergeneric hybrid genus results from crossing 2 small North American shrubs of the erica family—*Phyllodoce breweri* and *Kalmiopsis leachiana*—a cross that produces dwarf, evergreen shrubs with dark brown bark and ½–1 in (12–25 mm) long glossy dark green, oblong leaves and bell-shaped flowers.
CULTIVATION: Plant in moist, humus-rich, well-drained soil in dappled shade. They are ideal for moist, shaded rockeries or pots in a cool alpine house, are very frost hardy and are easily propagated from small tip cuttings or by layering.

× *Phylliopsis hillieri*

Growing to a height of 12 in (30 cm), this shrub produces its small racemes of tiny, 5-lobed, red-purple flowers in spring. **'Coppelia'** has relatively large, open lavender-pink flowers. **'Pinocchio'** is a very compact cultivar with small glossy leaves and spikes of bright pink flowers. ZONES 3–9.

PHYLLOCLADUS
CELERY PINE

Five species of evergreen conifers from the southern hemisphere make up this genus. The taller species grow to 70 ft (21 m), but there are some lower growing, shrubby members—reaching a maximum of 6 ft (1.8 m)—that can be made into very attractive bonsai specimens. The stems are erect, with horizontal branches bearing brownish green flattened phylloclades (short stems that act as leaves) that sometimes darken in winter. Male cones are carried in terminal clusters, while the female cones appear on the base of the 'leaves'. The hard, close-grained timber is valued.
CULTIVATION: These conifers are tender to dry conditions. They perform best in well-composted, moist soil in sunny or part-shaded positions away from strong winds. Propagate from seed or cuttings.

Phyllocladus aspleniifolius

From Tasmania in Australia, this slow-growing, 50 ft (15 m) tall conifer has an

× *Phylliopsis hillieri* 'Coppelia'

Phyllocladus aspleniifolius

× *Phylliopsis hillieri* 'Pinocchio'

P

Phyllocladus trichomanoides

idiosyncratic foliage arrangement, producing striking diamond-shaped thick cladodes (modified branchlets) up to 3 in (8 cm) long—these are evergreen, but the true leaves, which appear as tiny scales, are deciduous. Its foliage bears some resemblance to that of celery. **ZONES 8–9.**

Phyllocladus trichomanoides
TANEKAHA, NEW ZEALAND CELERY PINE

In the wild, this symmetrical conifer from New Zealand can reach 50–70 ft (15–21 m) in height, but in cultivation rarely exceeds 20 ft (6 m). Its stems, spreading to 12 ft (3.5 m), radiate in whorls from horizontal branches. The foliage resembles the fronds of maidenhair fern. It prefers cool, moist climates, and its slow growth rate makes it suitable for small gardens. **ZONES 8–10.**

PHYLLODOCE

This genus consists of 8 species of small, evergreen, heath-like shrubs from the Arctic and alpine regions of the northern hemisphere. They have wiry stems and stiff, narrow, leathery leaves less than 1 in (25 mm) long with finely toothed edges and downy undersides. Their pendulous, bell-shaped, 5-lobed flowers develop in small racemes at the stem tips and are produced from spring to early summer.

CULTIVATION: These dainty little shrubs are virtually impervious to cold, but will quickly suffer in hot, dry conditions. Plant them in lime-free, cool, moist, well-drained, humus-rich soil with light shade and do not allow to dry out in summer. Propagate from seed or small tip cuttings of non-flowering stems or by layering.

Phyllodoce caerulea

Found in Asia, Europe and the USA, this species grows to around 12 in (30 cm) tall. It may be erect or spreading, and has ½ in (12 mm) long leaves. Its flowers, borne singly or in groups of 3 to 4, are lilac to purple-pink and open from late spring. **ZONES 2–9.**

Phyllodoce empetriformis
PINK MOUNTAIN HEATHER

This species from the west coast of North America is a mat-forming or mounding shrub 4–12 in (10–30 cm) high. Its leaves are about ½ in (12 mm) long, and in spring and summer is covered in clusters of tiny rose-pink flowers. **ZONES 3–9.**

Phyllodoce empetriformis

Phyllodoce nipponica

Native to northern Japan, this is a wiry stemmed, 8 in (20 cm) shrub with ½ in (12 mm) leaves and 3- to 7-flowered clusters of rose-pink or white flowers in spring and summer. **ZONES 3–9.**

PHYLLOSTACHYS

Made up of 80 species of medium- and large-growing bamboos from Asia, these evergreen plants have spreading rhizomes that may sprout some distance from the parent plant. They are ideally suited to grove planting and are mainly grown for their decorative foliage and graceful habit. They are also useful for preventing soil erosion. The woody stems have nodes at intervals, and the insignificant flowers take several years to appear; as with most bamboos, the plants then die.

CULTIVATION: Temperate-climate plants, they thrive in a sheltered position that is not too dry. Propagate from seed in either spring or fall (autumn), or by division in spring. If they must be confined to a specific area, they can be grown in large tubs.

Phyllostachys aurea
FISHPOLE BAMBOO, GOLDEN BAMBOO

This species has stiffly erect 6–30 ft (1.8–9 m) stems with crowded nodes at the base. It is a spreading species that soon forms large clumps and has dense foliage that makes it a good screen or hedge. **ZONES 6–11.**

Phyllostachys bambusoides
MADAKE, GIANT TIMBER BAMBOO

From China and Japan, this easily grown species reaches 70 ft (21 m) in height. Its large leaves and thick-walled culms (stems) are dark green at first. The young shoots, which are edible, appear in late spring. The flexible wood is widely used in China and Japan. Varieties include **'Allgold'** (syn. 'Holochrysa'), which is smaller growing and has a more open habit with golden-yellow culms, sometimes with green stripes; **'Castillonis'**, with green grooves to the culms; and **'Castillonis Inversa'**, with green culms and yellow grooves. **ZONES 8–11.**

Phyllostachys aurea

Phyllostachys nigra
BLACK BAMBOO

The slender canes of this species, growing to about 20 ft (6 m) tall with prominent joints, are green when young, turning black in their second year. The long, thin leaves are green and pointed. In cool climates, these plants need protection from cold winds, but can become seriously invasive in mild climates. ***Phyllostachys nigra* var. *henonis*** bears a mass of lush dark leaves and yellow-brown canes. **ZONES 5–11.**

Phyllostachys viridiglaucescens

Growing up to 40 ft (12 m) tall but usually much less, this eastern Chinese species has smooth stems that are often slightly curved at the base. They are coated with a white powder and the leaf sheaths are rough. Its leaves are up to 8 in (20 cm) long and densely clothe the stems. **ZONES 7–11.**

PHYMOSIA

The 8 species of evergreen shrubs and small trees that make up this genus are native to Mexico, Guatemala and the Caribbean islands. They have 8–10 in (20–25 cm) wide, hand-shaped leaves with 5 to 7 lobes and serrated or toothed-edged leaves. Abutilon-like flowers develop in the axils of the leaves near the stem tips and are borne in small clusters. They are 1–3 in (2.5–8 cm) wide and usually pink or red, sometimes with white veining.

CULTIVATION: These are largely tropical plants and will not tolerate frost. They prefer moist, well-drained soil but will withstand dry conditions once established. Plant in full or half-day sun. Propagate from seed or cuttings.

Phyllostachys bambusoides

Phymosia umbellata

Up to 20 ft (6 m) tall with 8 in (20 cm) wide leaves, this Mexican species has 1½ in (35 mm) wide, deep pink flowers. It can be trimmed when young to form a multi-trunked shrub or trained as a single-trunked small tree. **ZONES 10–12.**

PHYSALIS
GROUND CHERRY

This is a genus of around 80 species of annuals and perennials with a widespread distribution, especially in the Americas. Most form a clump of upright leafy stems 2–4 ft (0.6–1.2 m) tall. The leaves are variable in shape, usually

Phyllostachys nigra

Phymosia umbellata

P

lance-shaped, oval or deltoid (like a poplar leaf), often with lobes or shallow-toothed edges. The flowers are small, usually white or yellow blotched purple, and are backed by calyces that enlarge to enclose the fruits—yellow, orange or red berries—as they develop. The fruits are often edible and are ripe when the calyces start to dry out.
CULTIVATION: Hardiness varies, but most species tolerate moderate frosts. They prefer moist, well-drained soil and a position in sun or part-shade. Propagate from seed or by division.

Physalis alkekengi
CHINESE LANTERN, WINTER CHERRY

This 24 in (60 cm) tall perennial found from southern Europe to Japan is most notable for the vivid orange calyx that surrounds the ripening fruit, giving rise to one of its common names. The narrow leaves, about 3 in (8 cm) long, are mid-green. The flowers are small and white with yellow centers. The fruiting stems are often used fresh in floral arrangements or dried for winter decoration. ***Physalis alkekengi* var. *franchetii*** has minute, creamy white flowers. **ZONES 6–10.**

Physocarpus opulifolius

Physalis ixocarpa
MEXICAN GROUND CHERRY, TOMATILLO

Raised commercially as an edible berry in Mexico, this perennial grows 3–4 ft (1–1.2 m) tall. It has large greenish yellow fruit borne in papery, purple-veined husks. The pulp is glutinous and is used with chilies in sauces. **ZONES 8–10.**

Physalis peruviana
CAPE GOOSEBERRY, GROUND CHERRY

This perennial South American species grows to around 3 ft (1 m) tall. It is often treated as an annual and is grown for its crop of bright yellow to purple, edible berries. Its leaves are oval to heart-shaped and up to 4 in (10 cm) long. The yellow-blotched purple flowers are ½ in (12 mm) wide and are quickly enveloped by the calyces. **ZONES 8–11.**

Physocarpus monogynus

Physalis alkekengi var. *franchetii*

Physostegia virginiana 'Summer Spire'

Physostegia virginiana

PHYSOCARPUS
NINEBARK

The unusual inflated fruits of this genus of deciduous shrubs from Asia and North America are not edible—the 12 or so species are admired for their flowers and attractive foliage. In the wild, they reach a maximum height of 10 ft (3 m). The leaves are prominently veined, lobed and serrated, and change to a dull yellow in fall (autumn). The 5-petalled white or pink flowers, appearing in spring or early summer, are small but are displayed in decorative clusters along the branches.
CULTIVATION: *Physocarpus* species require fertile, well-drained soil in a sunny position. They are easy to grow in temperate climates, but resent soil with a high lime content and dry roots. Thin out crowded plants by cutting back some of the arching canes after flowering. Propagate from seed or cuttings of semi-ripened wood in summer.

Physocarpus capitatus

This species is an upright shrub native to western North America. Its leaves are up to 3 in (8 cm) wide, sticky when young and covered in fine hairs. They are deeply lobed with serrated edges. Tiny cream flowers open from mid-spring and are densely packed in 3 in (8 cm) wide, flat-topped heads. **ZONES 6–10.**

Physocarpus monogynus
MOUNTAIN NINEBARK

This species from central USA grows to around 3–6 ft (1–1.8 m) tall with arching, spreading stems. The new stems are bright brown, sticky, often with fine hairs; the young leaves are light green. The 2 in (5 cm) wide foliage is 3- to 5-lobed with serrated edges. Flat 2 in (5 cm) wide heads of small white flowers open from late spring. **ZONES 5–10.**

Physocarpus opulifolius

Native to eastern USA, this shrub has a height and spread of 5–10 ft (1.5–3m) and a graceful arching habit. The yellowish green, rounded, heart-shaped leaves complement the dense, pink-tipped white flowers, which are at their best in early summer. Reddish pods with yellow seeds contrast well with the bright fall (autumn) foliage and the dark brown bark that peels off in layers. **'Aureus'** has bright greenish yellow leaves and white flowers. **'Dart's Gold'**, to 4 ft (1.2 m) tall, has bright golden foliage and white flowers flushed pink. **ZONES 2–10.**

PHYSOSTEGIA
OBEDIENT PLANT, FALSE DRAGON HEAD

This is a North American genus of some 12 species of rhizomatous perennials. They are vigorous growers and quickly develop in spring to form clumps of unbranched, upright stems clothed in narrow, lance-shaped, long leaves with toothed edges. Plant size varies from 2–6 ft (0.6–1.8 m) tall and the leaves are 2–6 in (5–15 cm) long. From mid-summer, spikes of flowers develop at the stem tips. The flowers are tubular to bell-shaped with 2 upper lobes and 3 lower lobes. They are usually less than ½ in (12 mm) long and in shades of lavender, pink or purple and white. If a flower is moved, it will not spring back into

Physalis peruviana

position but will stay put, thanks to a stalk with a hinge-like structure.
CULTIVATION: Obedient plants prefer moist, well-drained soil in sun or very light shade. Very easily grown, they can be slightly invasive. Hardiness varies, though all species tolerate at least moderate frosts. Propagate from seed or small basal cuttings or by division.

Physostegia virginiana

The showy flowers of this herbaceous perennial, which bloom in erect terminal spikes late in summer, are tubular, have 2 lips and are available in pale pink, magenta (**'Vivid'**) or white. This native of eastern and central North America grows to 3 ft (1 m) and makes a striking mixed-border display. **'Summer Snow'** is 3 ft (1 m) tall with white flowers. **'Summer Spire'** is around 24 in (60 cm) tall with deep pink flowers. **ZONES 3–10.**

PHYTEUMA
HORNED RAMPION

This Eurasian genus of around 40 species of small perennials is instantly recognizable for the unusually structured flowerheads. The plants vary in size from 4–30 in (10–75 cm) tall. Their basal leaves are usually heart-shaped, while the upper leaves are oval to lance-shaped. The leaves are sometimes sharply toothed. The flowers are borne on rounded heads and are tubular, often swelling at the base, with scarcely open tips from which the stigma protrudes; they are usually in lavender, blue or purple shades tinged with white.
CULTIVATION: The small alpine species should be grown in light, gritty soil with added humus in a rockery or alpine house; the large species will grow in a normal perennial border, but take care that they do not become overgrown by more vigorous plants. Plant in sun or part-shade. Propagate from seed or by division where possible.

Phytolacca dioica

Phytolacca americana

Phytolacca americana

Phyteuma comosum
syn. *Physoplexis comosa*

Native to the European Alps, this tufted perennial rarely exceeds 4 in (10 cm) in height. It has toothed, heart-shaped leaves and heads of violet-blue flowers. A favorite of alpine enthusiasts, it requires a gritty soil with added humus for moisture retention. **ZONES 6–9.**

Phyteuma spicatum
SPIKED RAMPION

Up to 30 in (75 cm) tall, this European species is suitable for general garden use. Its lower leaves are heart-shaped, toothed and around 4 in (10 cm) long. The upper leaves are more oval in shape and are less sharply toothed. The densely packed flowerheads are backed by narrow leafy bracts and the flowers are white, cream or blue. **ZONES 6–10.**

Phyteuma comosum

Phytolacca polyandra

PHYTOLACCA
POKEWEED, POKEBERRY

The 35 species in this genus are native to warm and tropical areas of the Americas, Africa and Asia. The taller plants can grow to 50 ft (15 m). These perennials, evergreen trees and shrubs are valued for their general appearance and decorative, though often poisonous, rounded berries. The leaves can be quite large and have colored stems and attractive hues in fall (autumn); the white flowers are small and are arranged in clusters.
CULTIVATION: They prefer rich soil in a sheltered position in full sun to part-shade and need adequate moisture to thrive. Propagate from seed in spring or fall (autumn).

Phytolacca americana

This soft-wooded shrub from North America is often treated as an herbaceous perennial. The white flowers in summer are followed by purple-blue berries in fall (autumn). All parts of the plant are poisonous. **ZONES 2–11.**

Phytolacca dioica
OMBU, BELLA SOMBRA TREE

From South America, this fast-growing tree reaches 50 ft (15 m) tall with a spread of 10 ft (3 m). Grown chiefly for shade (*bella sombra* means 'beautiful shade'), it has a shallow root system and its sturdy trunk appears swollen. The dense crown consists of elliptical to oval leaves with a pointed tip. The white flowers are followed (on female plants) by yellow, fleshy berries. **ZONES 10–11.**

Phyteuma spicatum

Phytolacca polyandra
syn. *Phytolacca clavigera*

This species from southwest China is a branching, 5 ft (1.5 m) tall, shrubby perennial. It has wavy edged, oval to lance-shaped leaves up to 6 in (15 cm) long and erect 6 in (15 cm) racemes of tiny, petal-less pink flowers. The racemes extend to 12 in (30 cm) long as the $\frac{1}{2}$ in (12 mm) diameter black berries mature. **ZONES 6–10.**

PICEA

SPRUCE

The 30 to 40 members of this genus of evergreen conifers originate in the cool-temperate regions of the northern hemisphere where there are deep pockets of moist, rich, acidic, freely draining soil. Sometimes reaching an impressive 220 ft (66 m) in height, they develop a stiff, narrow, conical, sometimes columnar growth habit with short, horizontal to upward-pointing branches. The leaves are arranged spirally on short pegs and their color varies from bright green to glaucous blue. Able to withstand strong winds, they bear large cones which hang downwards, distinguishing the genus from the superficially similar firs *(Abies)*. The slow growth and contorted habit of some cultivars make them ideal bonsai specimens; others are prostrate and make excellent ground covers. This genus produces valuable timber, plus pitch and turpentine.

CULTIVATION: Plant in full sun in deep, moist but well-drained, neutral to acid soil. Propagate from seed or cuttings in fall (autumn) or by grafting. They will not survive transplantation when large, nor grow well in heavily polluted environments. They may be prone to attack from aphids, red spider mites and, in warm, humid climates, fungal infections.

Picea abies 'Conica'

Picea abies

Picea abies 'Pumila Glauca'

Picea abies

syn. *Picea excelsa*

NORWAY SPRUCE, COMMON SPRUCE

Native to Scandinavia where it can grow to nearly 200 ft (60 m), but less in cultivation, this is the traditional Christmas tree in Europe. Its straight trunk is covered in orange-brown, maturing to reddish, bark which it sheds in scales. The leaves are dark green and rectangular and the reddish cigar-shaped cones, erect at first, become pendulous and grow to 8 in (20 cm) long. Dwarf shrubby cultivars have usually been propagated from witches' brooms, a tight clump of congested foliage that sometimes appears on the plant. Shallow rooted, the Norway spruce can be upended by strong winds. **'Conica'** is a low-growing cultivar (less than 15 ft/4.5 m) with a broad, conical crown. **'Maxwellii'**, the Maxwell spruce, is a low-growing, compact form ideal for rockeries and borders. **'Pumila Glauca'** is a semi-erect dwarf form with bluish green foliage. **'Pygmaea'** is a slow-growing dwarf form. **'Reflexa'** is a weeping cultivar distinguished by growing tips that point upwards when young; it makes a beautiful prostrate shrub. **'Inversa'** is a spreading bush with downward-trailing branches. **'Little Gem'** is a flat-topped dwarf shrub that grows very slowly. **'Nidiformis'**, the bird's nest spruce, is a dwarf form with outward- and upward-curving branches that tend to make a nest-like bowl in the center of the plant. **ZONES 2–9.**

Picea abies 'Maxwellii'

Picea abies 'Pygmaea'

Picea abies 'Reflexa'

Picea abies 'Little Gem'

Picea breweriana

WEEPING SPRUCE, BREWER'S WEEPING SPRUCE

The branchlets of this North American conifer hang its foliage in 3 ft (1 m) long, curtain-like streamers from its horizontally held branches. The needles are blue-green and flattened and the light brown cones grow to 4 in (10 cm) long. The tree forms a strong trunk, reaching a height of 100 ft (30 m) or more, with a broad conical shape that becomes narrow if the tree is grown in crowded conditions. **ZONES 2–9.**

Picea engelmannii

ENGELMANN SPRUCE

Growing slowly to 150 ft (45 m) or more, this is one of the most cold-tolerant evergreen trees; it also grows well in poor soil. The densely textured, pyramid-shaped crown, spreading to 15 ft (4.5 m),

Picea abies

Picea breweriana

Picea engelmannii

Picea glauca var. *albertiana* 'Conica'

Picea glauca var. *albertiana* 'Conica'

Picea omorika × *breweriana*

Picea omorika

is made up of sharply pointed, 4-angled, soft gray to steel-blue needles up to 1 in (25 mm) long. The cones are cylindrical, green and tinged with purple. ZONES 1–9.

Picea glauca
WHITE SPRUCE

From Canada and grown commercially for the paper industry, this slow-growing tree can reach 80 ft (24 m). Bright green shoots appear in spring, and the drooping branchlets carry aromatic, 4-angled needles up to ½ in (12 mm) long. The cones are small and narrow. **'Echiniformis'** is a dwarf, mounding form with a spiky, needle-studded surface. ***Picea glauca* var. *albertiana* 'Conica'**, the dwarf Alberta spruce, is a very densely foliaged, bright green, conical dwarf that is usually seen as a 3 ft (1 m) shrub, though with great age it can reach 10 ft (3 m). ZONES 1–8.

Picea orientalis 'Atrovirens'

Picea koyamai

This species from northeast Asia grows to 60 ft (18 m) tall or more. Its gray-brown bark peels off in small flakes. The foliage forms a dense, conical crown of blue-green to gray-green needles up to ½ in (12 mm) long. The cones are 2–4 in (5–10 cm) long, cylindrical, and turn brown as they mature. ZONES 6–9.

Picea mariana
AMERICAN BLACK SPRUCE

From the USA, this 60 ft (18 m) conifer has a pyramidal crown spreading to 15 ft (4.5 m) composed of whorled branches bearing blunt, bluish green needles. The 1½ in (35 mm) long cones are purplish brown and remain on the tree for up to 30 years. This conifer prefers boggy soil and must have an open, sunny position to thrive. **'Nana'** is a slow-growing dwarf cultivar. ZONES 1–8.

Picea obovata

This fully frost-hardy species can grow to 200 ft (60 m). Its erect, branching crown displays dark green foliage and long brown cones up to 8 in (20 cm) long.

Picea orientalis

Picea obovata

Picea mariana 'Nana'

This spruce produces some of the most attractive 'flowers' (male cones) of the genus, which appear as pinkish red catkins in spring. ZONES 1–8.

Picea omorika
SERBIAN SPRUCE

From Serbia and Bosnia, this spruce reaches 100 ft (30 m) or more with pendulous branches forming a narrow, spire-like crown. The bright green, flattened needles have a square tip and a grayish underside. The purplish cones mature to a deep brown. Happy in a range of soils from acid to limy and more tolerant of urban pollution than most species, it is one of the best *Picea* for large, temperate-climate gardens. ***Picea omorika* × *breweriana*** is a hybrid between the 2 popular, award-winning species. ZONES 4–9.

Picea koyamai

Picea orientalis
CAUCASIAN SPRUCE

Reaching 100 ft (30 m) in its native Turkey and Caucasus, this slow-growing spruce produces abundant, pendent branches from ground level up. The brilliant, glossy green foliage is short and neat; spectacular brick-red male cones appear in spring, and the purple female cones grow 3 in (8 cm) long. This spruce prefers a sheltered site. **'Atrovirens'** displays attractive rich green foliage that flushes to golden-yellow in early summer. **'Aurea'** has golden-yellow juvenile foliage that greens as it ages but retains a hint of gold. ZONES 3–9.

Picea pungens

Picea pungens 'Conica'

Picea pungens 'Glauca'

Picea pungens 'Hoopsii'

Picea pungens 'Iseli Fastigiate'

Picea pungens 'Pendens'

Picea pungens 'Royal Blue'

Picea pungens 'Viridis'

Picea pungens
COLORADO SPRUCE

This frost-hardy species from the west coast of the USA grows to 100 ft (30 m) or more in the wild, although it is usually much smaller in gardens. It has a pyramid of bluish green foliage composed of stiff and sharply pointed needles; the bark is gray. Prune regularly as fresh growth will not bud from dead wood. The many cultivars include **'Aurea'** with golden leaves; **'Caerulea'** with bluish white leaves; **'Conica'** which grows into a cone-shaped cultivar; **'Glauca'**, which is the commonly grown Colorado blue spruce with striking, steel-blue new foliage; **'Globosa'**, which is a rounded, dwarf form with attractive bluish leaves that is very slow-growing taking a decade or more to reach 24 in (60 cm) in height; **'Hoopsii'**, which is prized for its even bluer foliage; **'Iseli Fastigiate'** with upward-pointing branches and very sharp needles; **'Koster'** with foliage maturing from silvery deep blue to green, spiralled branches and tubular, scaled cones about 4 in (10 cm) long; **'Pendens'**, a prostrate, blue cultivar; **'Royal Blue'**, another striking blue cultivar; **'Moerheimii'** from the Netherlands and bred to produce silvery blue foliage that is longer than other forms; and **'Viridis'** with very dark green foliage. ZONES 2–10.

Picea sitchensis
SITKA SPRUCE

Fast growing to 150 ft (45 m), this is one of the few trees in the genus that can survive being transplanted when young. It also enjoys humid sites but needs good summer rainfall. Its trunk has pale bark. The pyramidal crown becomes broader as the tree matures and is composed of whorled branches; the leaves are flattened, stiff and bluish gray. The 4 in (10 cm) long cones are covered with thin papery scales and they release their winged seeds on warm spring days. The timber is not very strong. ZONES 4–9.

Picea smithiana
MORINDA SPRUCE, WEST HIMALAYAN SPRUCE

This spruce, found from Nepal to Afghanistan, develops graceful branches that hang in cascades. The foliage is dark green and composed of fine, 4-angled needles up to $1\frac{1}{2}$ in (35 mm) long. Green cones maturing to shiny brown grow to 8 in (20 cm) long, often at the ends of the branches, accentuating their pendulous effect. ZONES 6–9.

Picea sitchensis

PIERIS

This genus consists of 7 species of evergreen shrubs and, more rarely, small trees from North America, East Asia and the Himalayas. The shrubby species are valued for their neat compact habit, attractive foliage and flowers, their height rarely exceeding 12 ft (3.5 m) and often less. The flower buds are held throughout the winter, and in spring open into clusters of small, bell-shaped, waxy, usually white flowers.

CULTIVATION: These plants require a temperate climate, soil that is moist, peaty and acidic, and a part-shaded site. They appreciate humidity. Propagate from seed in spring or from cuttings in summer, or by layering.

Pieris 'Forest Flame'

This shrub, which grows to 12 ft (3.5 m) in height with a spread of half that, bears its white flowers in terminal panicles in spring. It is named for the way its dark green leaves are brilliant red when young, then turn pink then white and finally green. ZONES 6–9.

Pieris formosa

This dense, bushy shrub from China carries glossy, dark green leathery leaves and bears sprays of small white flowers in mid-spring. Frost resistant, it grows well in cool or mild climates but is not tolerant of dry conditions. It is one of the taller species, growing to 12 ft (3.5 m). The red-leaf pearl flower, ***Pieris formosa* var. *forrestii*** (syn. *P. forrestii*), is usually smaller, growing to a height and spread of 6 ft (1.8 m) with scarlet-bronze young growth against which the flowers gleam in striking contrast. ***P. f.* var. *forrestii* 'Wakehurst'** is a tall shrub that can reach 15 ft (4.5 m) and has large clusters of white flowers and red new growth that fades to pink before greening. ZONES 6–9.

Pieris japonica
LILY-OF-THE-VALLEY SHRUB

This Japanese shrub can grow to 12 ft (3.5 m) high but usually reaches only 6 ft

Picea smithiana

Pieris formosa var. *forrestii*

Pieris formosa var. *forrestii*

Pieris japonica 'Variegata'

Pieris japonica 'Tickled Pink'

Pieris 'Forest Flame'

Pieris japonica

Pieris japonica 'Bert Chandler'

(1.8 m) in cultivation. Its pointed, elliptical, deep green leaves, to 4 in (10 cm) long, are reddish copper when young. Panicles of small, white, bell-shaped flowers appear from early spring. The many cultivars include **'Bert Chandler'** with pink and cream new growth; **'Christmas Cheer'** with early, pale pink flowers; **'Flamingo'** with bright pink flowers; **'Mountain Fire'** with vivid red new growth and white flowers; **'Purity'** with large, pure white flowers; **'Red Mill'**, a vigorous, late-flowering cultivar; **'Tickled Pink'** with pale red new growth and pink-tinted to pale pink flowers; and **'Variegata'** with cream-edged foliage. **ZONES 4–10.**

PILEA

This is a genus of around 600 species of annuals and perennials that are widely distributed in the tropics with the exception of Australia. They may be creeping or erect and are usually small, though the larger species can reach 6 ft (1.8 m) tall. The foliage is variable: many have simple lance-shaped leaves, others have heart-shaped peperomia-like foliage and a few have tiny, clustered, moss-like leaves. The flowers are tiny, cream to pink structures that are easily overlooked. They are sometimes followed by seed pods that forcibly eject their seed when ripe.

CULTIVATION: All very frost tender, pileas are widely grown as house plants; the smaller species generally prefer warm, humid conditions and are ideal candidates for terrariums and heated greenhouses. In subtropical or tropical gardens grow in moist, well-drained, humus-rich soil in part-shade. Propagate from seed or cuttings or by division.

Pilea cadierei
ALUMINIUM PLANT

This Vietnamese species, which is a free-branching, 18 in (45 cm) tall perennial, is very popular as a house plant. It has 3 in (8 cm) long, deep green, lance-shaped leaves striped with bands of metallic silver. Clusters of tiny cream flowers form at the stem tips but are not really a feature. **ZONES 10–12.**

Pilea involucrata
FRIENDSHIP PLANT

From Central and South America, this trailing species which sometimes mounds to 12 in (30 cm) tall has hairy, toothed-edged, 2½ in (6 cm) long oval leaves. The foliage has a puckered surface and is usually reddish purple with bronze and silver markings. There are several cultivated forms with varying leaf colors, shapes and sizes. **ZONES 10–12.**

Pilea involucrata

Pieris japonica 'Red Mill'

Pieris japonica 'Mountain Fire'

Pieris japonica 'Christmas Cheer'

Pilea nummulariifolia

Pilosella laticeps

Pilosocereus palmeri

Pilea microphylla

ARTILLERY PLANT, CREEPING CHARLIE

This annual or short-lived perennial found from Mexico to Brazil gets the common name, artillery plant, from the way its seed pods forcibly eject their contents when touched. It forms mounds of soft green mossy foliage and grows to 12 in (30 cm) tall. A very tender, soft-stemmed plant, it is often best grown in the humid environment of a terrarium. **ZONES 10–12.**

Pilea nummulariifolia

Usually seen spilling from a hanging basket, this trailing perennial from tropical South America and the West Indies has 1 in (25 mm) long, rounded leaves with toothed edges. In summer it produces small cream flowers in the leaf axils and at the stem tips. **ZONES 10–12.**

PILEOSTEGIA

This is a genus of 4 east Asian species of climbing or spreading evergreen shrubs that are closely related to and resemble the climbing *Hydrangea* and

Pileostegia viburnoides

Pimelea spectabilis

Schizophragma species. Unlike those closely related genera, they do not produce separate fertile and sterile flowers. Instead from late summer they have 6 in (15 cm) wide panicles of all-fertile, tiny, creamy white filamentous flowers. They climb up to 30 ft (9 m) using self-clinging aerial roots. The 2–6 in (5–15 cm) long, glossy deep green leaves are leathery with heavy veining underneath.
CULTIVATION: They are easily grown in any moist, humus-rich, well-drained soil in shade or part-shade. They tolerate only light frosts but may reshoot from the rootstock if well insulated. Propagate from seed or cuttings.

Pileostegia viburnoides

This native of India, China and Taiwan has narrow oblong to lance-shaped 4–6 in (10–15 cm) long leaves that are lightly felted when young. Its large panicles of white to cream flowers contrast well with the dark foliage and can brighten a shady corner. **ZONES 9–10.**

PILOSELLA

This is a genus of some 20 species of small, rosette-forming, dandelion-like perennials from Eurasia and North Africa. At least one species, ***Pilosella aurantiaca***, is a serious weed in the western USA and New Zealand. The clump of basal leaves is composed of simple, hairy, oblong, lance- or spatula-shaped leaves, 1–8 in (2.5–20 cm) long depending on the species. Loose, open heads of small yellow or orange daisy-like flowerheads are carried on wiry stems up to 24 in (60 cm) tall. Most species flower continuously through summer.
CULTIVATION: They are not difficult to cultivate in any light, well-drained soil in full sun and are really plants that are more likely to pop up by chance than to be actively cultivated. Most species are very frost hardy. Propagate from seed or by division.

Pilosella laticeps

The species name means 'wide head' and aptly describes the showy golden flowerheads of this uncommon species, larger than those of most other pilosellas. It shows promise as a rock-garden and ground-cover plant; the spatula-shaped leaves are glossy deep green above and whitish beneath. The plant spreads to form a mat of foliage 24 in (60 cm) or more across. **ZONES 8–10.**

PILOSOCEREUS

Native to Central and northern South America and the West Indies, this genus consists of 45 species of large columnar cacti, mostly bluish, that feature felty spines at their crowns. When planted in large containers they make noteworthy additions to the garden. Their nocturnal, funnel-shaped flowers vary in color and bloom only for 24 hours, but release a very strong odor. They are followed by purple or green fruits.
CULTIVATION: These frost-tender plants need full sun and gritty, fertile, very well-drained soil. Water freely from spring to summer, less so at other times. Propagate from seed in spring.

Pilosocereus palmeri

syn. *Pilosocereus leucocephalus*

This upright, pillar-like cactus is native to Mexico and grows to 10–20 ft (3–6 m) tall and up to 3 ft (1 m) in diameter. The silvery blue-green stem readily branches and is prominently ribbed. Areoles sprouting brown spines line the ribs and white, radially spined areoles cover the apex. Glossy, pink flowers develop near the crown on taller trees. **ZONES 9–11.**

PIMELEA

RICE FLOWER

These 80 species of woody evergreen shrubs, belonging to the same family as the daphnes, are native to Australasia and can grow to a height of 6 ft (1.8 m), though most species are smaller. Their great attraction is their terminal flowerheads in white, yellow, pink or purple, often surrounded by prominent colored bracts. Each flower is tubular and star-shaped.
CULTIVATION: They grow best in full sun in light, well-drained soil enriched with organic matter. Windy and seaside sites also suit them, but they dislike heavy frosts and lime. Lightly tip prune after flowering to keep them tidy. Propagate from seed in spring or cuttings in late summer. Attempts to transplant large specimens usually fail.

Pimelea ferruginea

Pimelea ferruginea

This species from Western Australia forms a compact, well-branched, rounded shrub with a height and spread of 3 ft (1 m). Tiny, recurved, oval leaves are crowded opposite each other along the stems. The leaves are smooth and light green on top and grayish green underneath. In spring compact, rounded, rose-pink flowerheads appear, up to 1½ in (35 mm) across. **'Magenta Mist'** has dusky mauve flowers. **ZONES 9–11.**

Pimelea prostrata

This low-spreading, frost-hardy shrub from New Zealand bears profuse white to pink, fragrant flowerheads in summer; the flowers are followed by minute fruit. It grows to a height of 8 in (20 cm) with an 18 in (45 cm) spread, and has gray-green, leathery leaves. **ZONES 8–10.**

Pimelea spectabilis

This Western Australian species is an upright shrub that grows to 4 ft (1.2 m) tall. Its stems are sticky when young and are clothed with 1½ in (35 mm) long narrow leaves with blue-green undersides. The flowers are relatively large, in shades of pink or yellow, and are massed in heads up to 3 in (8 cm) wide. It blooms in early summer. **ZONES 9–11.**

PIMENTA

ALLSPICE, PIMENTO

This is a genus of 5 species of evergreen trees of the myrtle family, native to tropical America and the Caribbean islands. They have leathery, glossy deep green leaves up to 8 in (20 cm) long and all parts of the plants are aromatic. The flowers are small, filamentous and cream and are carried in panicles at the branch tips. Although the trees produce flowers of both sexes only one is functional, so trees are effectively either male or female. The tiny berry-like fruits that follow yield important spices and fragrances.
CULTIVATION: Often found growing in limestone soils in the wild, these tropical trees demand a warm, moist, humid climate that is frost free. They prefer moist, well-drained, humus-rich soil with shade while young. As the plants are propa-

Pimelea ferruginea 'Magenta Mist'

gated from seed and it is not possible to sex the plants until they fruit, several seedlings should be planted to be sure of getting a fruiting tree.

Pimenta dioica

This 40 ft (12 m) evergreen tree is native to Jamaica. It has 6 in (15 cm) long, glossy, deep green oblong to elliptical leaves with prominent veins on the undersides. The foliage has a clove-like scent when crushed. The spring- and summer-borne panicles of tiny white-green filamentous flowers are followed by 1/4 in (6 mm) diameter dark brown fruit. The fruit are strongly scented when crushed and taste of cinnamon, nutmeg and cloves. The most important spice in Caribbean cuisine, it is used in perfume, and is widely exported. **ZONES 10–12.**

Pimenta officinalis
JAMAICA PEPPER

Similar to *Pimenta dioica*, this species does not grow quite as tall and the flavor of its fruit is more peppery. It is used in cooking, as a scent for potpourri and for the production of aromatherapy oils. **ZONES 10–12.**

PIMPINELLA

This is a genus of around 150 species of mostly annuals and perennials with entire or pinnate leaves and dainty, star-shaped flowers borne in umbrella-like heads. These are followed by small, oval-shaped fruits. Species occur naturally in Eurasia, Africa and South America. *Pimpinella anisum* was cultivated by the Egyptians, Greeks and Romans for its aromatic seeds used in medicine and as a condiment.
CULTIVATION: All species are very frost hardy and easy to grow in a sunny, protected position. Provide a moist but well-drained, fertile soil for best results. Propagate from fresh seed in mid- to late spring; seed can be sown directly into the garden. Germination may take up to 3 weeks.

Pimpinella anisum
ANISE, ANISEED

Native to the eastern part of the Mediterranean region, this aromatic annual to 24 in (60 cm) high has brilliant green, fern-like leaves and umbels of tiny white flowers in mid-summer. The light brown seeds are used for flavoring cakes, bread, confectionery and liqueurs. Cut the whole plant back in fall (autumn) and hang the branches in a dark, warm place until the seeds are thoroughly dry. **ZONES 6–10.**

Pimpinella saxifraga
BLACK CARAWAY, WATER PIMPERNEL

This dark green perennial grows to 3 ft (1 m) high. The pinnate leaves have up to 8 pairs of deeply cut oval leaflets. Tiny white flowers with notched petals are borne in flat-topped umbels in summer. Black caraway is not the culinary caraway, *Carum carvi*. The medicinal part of the herb is the long slender root, used as an expectorant and diuretic. **ZONES 4–9.**

PINANGA
PINANG

The great majority of the 120 species of this palm genus come from dense rainforests of Borneo, Java, Sumatra and the Malay Peninsula, but some extend as far as the Himalayan foothills, south China and Papua New Guinea. They are very diverse in growth form, from medium-large single-trunked palms with long feather-like fronds, to tiny undergrowth palms that are usually several-stemmed, with small fronds that may be undivided and often attractively marbled paler green; some species have no above-ground stem. The frond bases usually form a smooth crownshaft terminating the trunk. Small cream flowers appear in panicles from the trunk below the crownshaft, followed by orange, red or black single-seeded fruits of varied shape and size.
CULTIVATION: Outside the tropics they require a conservatory or greenhouse that is heated in winter and maintained at high humidity. The smaller-growing species require shade, and soil with a deep surface layer of humus kept permanently moist. Propagate from freshly collected seed.

Pinanga coronata
syn. *Pinanga kuhlii*
IVORY CANE PALM

A native of Java and Sumatra, this medium-sized, densely clumping species is the most widely cultivated *Pinanga*. Its bamboo-like green stems are less than 2 in (5 cm) thick and usually under 10 ft (3 m) tall in cultivation, with long crownshafts of an attractive ivory to pale orange shade. The elegant fronds are divided into few but broad segments of varying width. Inflorescences branch into several 2-rowed spikes of white flowers, followed by small fruit that ripen from red to black. **ZONES 11–12.**

PINELLIA

This genus of 6 species of perennials is native to China, Japan and Korea. The roots are rhizome-like and are used in oriental medicine, either by themselves primarily for treating digestive complaints, and in combination with other ingredients for a wide range of disorders. The plants are clump forming with narrow-stemmed basal leaves that vary in shape from simple, oval structures to pinnate and from 1½–8 in (3.5–20 cm) long depending on the species. The flowers, which are arum lily–like, typically have purple-veined green spathes and yellow-green spadices. The flowers are held above the foliage on stems with small leaves that sometimes develop bulbils in their axils.
CULTIVATION: Plant in moist, well-drained soil in part-shade. All species are frost hardy and are propagated from seed or offsets or by division in early spring.

Pinguicula moranensis

Pinellia ternata

This species is valued for its interesting flowers and unusual, broad leaves which are split into three. The pale green spathes curl at the tip and are borne on a leafless stem in late summer. It is fully frost hardy and should be grown in acidic, humus-rich soil in shade. Water well, particularly during growth. **ZONES 6–10.**

PINGUICULA
BUTTERWORT

This widely distributed genus consists of about 45 species of carnivorous perennials. Their 1–2½ in (2.5–6 cm), pointed oval leaves in basal rosettes develop from overwintering buds. The leaves are succulent and their sticky surface traps small insects. The leaf coating also contains an anesthetic that immobilizes the insects, and the leaf edges curl in to trap them. After closing, the leaf secretes a substance to digest the prey and extract its nutrients. In summer the long-spurred, 1–2½ in (2.5–6 cm) long flowers, usually purple, are borne singly on 2–12 in (5–30 cm) stems.
CULTIVATION: Growing naturally in wet, mossy bogs, these plants are not easy to cultivate outside their natural environment. Bell jars and terrariums can provide the necessary humidity, but keeping the soil damp but not putrid is difficult. Frost hardiness varies considerably with the species. Propagate from seed or by division.

Pinguicula grandiflora

Found in western Europe including Britain, this species has 1½–2 in (3.5–5 cm) long yellow-green leaves. As its name suggests, the flowers are strikingly large. They are around 1 in (25 mm) wide, purple or pink with a white throat and are on 6 in (15 cm) stems, one per rosette. **ZONES 7–10.**

Pinguicula moranensis

This Mexican species has 2–4 in (5–10 cm) long, rounded leaves. Its flowers are on 4–8 in (10–20 cm) stems and are 1½–2 in (3.5–5 cm) wide, crimson or pink with a red throat. **ZONES 10–11.**

Pinguicula vulgaris

Although the leaves of this European species are small, less than 2 in (5 cm) long, its flower stems are relatively tall, up to 8 in (20 cm). The flowers are around 1 in (25 mm) wide and are violet with a white throat. **ZONES 3–10.**

PINUS
PINE

In everyday speech 'pine' and 'conifer' are almost synonymous but to botanists and foresters the name pine means a tree of the genus *Pinus*, arguably the most important genus of conifers. Consisting of around 120 species of needle-leafed evergreens, *Pinus* is represented in most parts of the northern hemisphere, from northern Scandinavia and Alaska to the equator (in Sumatra), though absent from all but the far north of Africa. The greatest concentrations of species are in the Mexican highlands, southern USA

Pinanga coronata

Pimpinella anisum

P

and China—though the best-known species come from more northern regions, for example, the Scots pine *(P. sylvestris)* of northern Eurasia. Most pines are medium to tall forest trees but a few are small and bushy, though never true shrubs in their typical, wild forms unless stunted by extreme conditions. The characteristic feature of *Pinus* is the way the needles are grouped in bundles, the number per bundle, usually between 2 and 7, is fairly constant for each species. Male (pollen) and female (seed) cones are borne on the same tree. The species of *Pinus* are divided into 2 major groups, namely the **white pines** (soft pines) with typically 5 needles and non-woody cone scales, and the **black pines** (hard pines) with typically 2 to 4 needles and woody cone scales, the cones taking 2 years or longer to mature their seeds. The white pines are typified by the North American *P. strobus* and include some of the tallest conifers; the black pines are typified by *P. sylvestris* or *P. radiata* and account for the majority of species, including nearly all those from the subtropics and tropics. Pines include many of the world's most important forest trees, especially in cool-temperate and subarctic regions, providing lumber for many everyday purposes including house construction, and much of the world's paper pulp. In the past their aromatic resins (pitch) and turpentines had many uses but these have largely been replaced by petroleum products. The seeds of several species (pine nuts) are important foods in some cultures. In recent times the bark of pines, once discarded as saw-mill waste, has become widely used in horticultural growing mediums and as a mulch in landscaping.

For smaller gardens the most suitable pines are some of the dwarf cultivars of species such as *P. sylvestris, P. thunbergii, P. strobus* and *P. mugo,* which can be grown as tub or rock-garden specimens. Many pines can also be used as bonsai subjects, or they can be grown for several years as Christmas trees and discarded when too large.

CULTIVATION: Most pines are easily grown in a wide range of conditions, though their tolerance of both cold and warmth varies and each species has its optimum climate. They are mostly very wind resistant and will thrive on soils of moderate to low fertility, but may need a symbiotic soil fungus to assist nutrient uptake on poorer soils—these fungi are likely to be already present in the pines' native regions, but a handful of decaying needles from a pine forest can be added if planting pines where none have grown before. The majority of pines require well-drained soil, and resent soil disturbance. Seed is normally the only means of propagation, cuttings being almost impossible to strike, but cultivars may be grafted.

Pinus aristata

Pinus aristata
BRISTLE CONE PINE

Slow growing and long lived, this North American pine can reach 30 ft (9 m) or more in height. As a garden plant it forms a dense shrubby tree, making an effective informal windbreak. Its 2 in

Pinus canariensis

Pinus ayacahuite

(5 cm) long, deep green needles flecked with resin press closely to the stem in groups of five. Its cones are glossy and 4 in (10 cm) long. **ZONES 5–9.**

Pinus armandii
ARMAND PINE

This pine from China and Taiwan does not like to dry out. It grows to 60 ft (18 m) or more with spreading branches, and bears green leaves up to 6 in (15 cm) long in groups of five. The thin cones, arranged in pairs or triplets, are as long as the leaves. **ZONES 8–10.**

Pinus ayacahuite
MEXICAN WHITE PINE

Native to Mexico and Guatemala, this pine is proving to be a valuable addition to city parks as it tolerates high levels of pollution. Growing to 100 ft (30 m) or more, it is characterized by the symmetry of its growth, its bluish green, 6 in (15 cm) long needles in groups of 5, and its 12 in (30 cm) cones which contain long-winged seeds. **ZONES 8–11.**

Pinus bungeana
LACEBARK PINE

This tree from China can reach 100 ft (30 m) in the wild but less in cultivation. It branches almost from ground level and can be trained as a large, multi-trunked shrub. The common name comes from the patchwork of colors left by the smooth, flaking bark. It has dark green, 3 in (8 cm) long needles in groups of 3 and small, rounded pale brown cones carried singly or in pairs. It tolerates extremes of cold and heat. **ZONES 5–9.**

Pinus caribaea

Pinus cembra

Pinus bungeana

Pinus bungeana

Pinus canariensis
CANARY ISLANDS PINE

This moderately fast-growing tree from the Canary Islands, though adaptable and tolerant of dry conditions, prefers an open, sunny spot where the soil is rich and moist yet well drained. It matures to a spreading tree, up to 80 ft (24 m) high. The upright trunk has reddish brown, fissured bark. The densely packed, shiny, grass-green needles are 12 in (30 cm) long and are carried in groups of three. The oval, brown cones are 8 in (20 cm) long. **ZONES 8–11.**

Pinus caribaea
CARIBBEAN PINE

From Central America, this species reaches 100 ft (30 m) in height with an open, broad, rounded crown and gray to brown bark exfoliating in large flat plates. Deep green needles 12 in (30 cm) long grow in bundles of 3 to 5; the cones are glossy rust brown. It is used for timber and for making turpentine. ***Pinus caribaea* var. *bahamensis*,** the Bahamas pine, grows to about 70 ft (21 m) tall; and the fast-growing ***P. c.* var. *hondurensis*,** the Honduran pine, grows to 150 ft (45 m). **ZONES 9–12.**

Pinus cembra
AROLLA PINE, SWISS STONE PINE

Growing to 80 ft (24 m) in its native Alps, central Europe and Siberia, this pine is appreciated for its neat, conical shape, dense foliage and long-lived needles. It is tough and disease resistant, but must be kept moist. The 6 in (15 cm) long, dark green, glossy needles occur in groups of five. The 3 in (8 cm) cones mature from purple to deep bluish brown. The seeds are edible. **ZONES 4–9.**

Pinus densiflora 'Oculus Draconis'

Pinus cembroides
MEXICAN PIÑON, MEXICAN NUT PINE

Native to Mexico and southwestern USA, this slow-growing, compact, shrubby tree grows to 25 ft (8 m) or more and tolerates both dry conditions and wind. A short-needled pine, it produces many orange-brown branchlets and bears small, rounded cones that complement its rounded crown. Its bark is silvery gray. The wingless seeds of this species are sold commercially. **ZONES 6–9.**

Pinus contorta
SHORE PINE, BEACH PINE

This species from the west coast of North America grows quickly to 30 ft (9 m) tall then develops horizontal branches and grows slowly to 70 ft (21 m). It has pairs of dark green, 2 in (5 cm) needles and small yellow-brown cones. It is easily trimmed to shape and does well as a garden specimen but does not thrive in hot, dry areas. ***Pinus contorta* var. *latifolia***, the lodgepole pine, is a straight-trunked, tapering tree to 80 ft (24 m) in its native Rocky Mountains but is slow growing, low and bushy in cultivation. It has yellowish green, 2–3 in (5–8 cm) long needles in pairs and small, oval cones that release fine seeds that are carried by wind. **ZONES 7–9.**

Pinus cembroides

Pinus contorta var. *latifolia*

Pinus densiflora 'Umbraculifera'

Pinus densiflora 'Tanyosho Nana'

Pinus coulteri
BIG-CONE PINE, COULTER PINE

This tough pine from California withstands heat, wind and dry conditions and tolerates most soils, including heavy clay. Its spiny brown cones grow to a massive 15 in (38 cm) and weigh 5 lb (2.3 kg). It grows relatively fast to a bushy tree up to 90 ft (30 m) high with attractive, stiff, bluish green needles up to 12 in (30 cm) long held in groups of three. **ZONES 8–10.**

Pinus coulteri

Pinus densiflora

Pinus densiflora 'Pendula'

Pinus densiflora
JAPANESE RED PINE

Used as a timber tree in its native Japan, where it can reach 100 ft (30 m), in cultivation this distinctive pine with red bark and naturally twisted shape is slow growing and often multi-trunked. It can be pruned and makes a popular bonsai specimen. Ovoid, yellow-purplish cones stand out boldly from the bright green, 4 in (10 cm) long foliage. There are many popular cultivars including **'Tanyosho Nana'**. The dwarf cultivar **'Umbraculifera'** has an umbrella-like canopy and orange-red, flaky bark on its multiple trunks; an extremely slow grower, it eventually reaches 15 ft (4.5 m). **'Oculus Draconis'**, the dragon's eye pine, has yellow-banded needles. **'Pendula'** is a strong-growing, semi-prostrate cultivar best grown near ponds or on banks where its weeping form can be most appreciated. **ZONES 4–9.**

Pinus coulteri

Pinus elliottii

Pinus elliottii

Pinus edulis
ROCKY MOUNTAIN PIÑON

Native to southwest USA, this species grows to around 50 ft (15 m) and has a compact domed crown with silver-gray, scaly bark. Its stiff needles are in pairs, 1½ in (35 mm) long and dark green. Its has small, light brown cones. It thrives in hot, dry areas. **ZONES 5–9.**

Pinus elliottii
SLASH PINE

From southeastern USA, this fast-growing species to 80 ft (24 m) copes with most soils. Pyramidal in shape with narrow, deep green leaves up to 4 in (10 cm) long in bundles of 2 or 3, the cones are 6 in (15 cm) long. Each scale is armed with a sharp prickle. It yields turpentine, rosin, timber and wood pulp. **ZONES 9–11.**

Pinus halepensis

Pinus jeffreyi

Pinus montezumae

Pinus engelmannii
APACHE PINE

A 100 ft (30 m) tree from southwest USA and Mexico, this species has deeply fissured dark brown bark and needles in groups of three or four. The needles are very long, more than 12 in (30 cm), bright green or olive green. The cones too are large, 4–8 in (10–20 cm) long, and yellow brown. **ZONES 8–10.**

Pinus halepensis
ALEPPO PINE

From the eastern Mediterranean area, this pine is the most resistant to dry conditions, in fact tolerating most conditions except severe frost when young. Fast growing to 50 ft (15 m), it has a spreading crown and a distinctive rugged character. The young bark is ash gray,

Pinus engelmannii

but ages to reddish brown. The soft, light green needles are 4 in (10 cm) long and are usually carried in pairs; the 3–4 in (8–10 cm) cones are reddish brown. **ZONES 7–10.**

Pinus jeffreyi
JEFFREY PINE

From western North America, this slender, conical pine grows to 180 ft (55 m) but in harsh conditions it is often naturally dwarf. It has 8 in (20 cm) long, thick, aromatic, bluish green needles and curved, often J-shaped cones up to 12 in (30 cm) long. Deep reddish brown fissured bark flakes off to reveal bright new bark. It is susceptible to *Elytroderma deformans,* a disease that causes witches' brooms. **ZONES 6–9.**

Pinus monophylla

Pinus koraiensis

Pinus monticola

Pinus kesiya

Found from northern India through Southeast Asia to the Philippines, this tree grows to 100 ft (30 m) and has thick, deeply fissured bark. Its 6–10 in (15–25 cm) long gray-green needles are held in groups of three. Its cones are 2–4 in (5–10 cm) long and dark brown. *Pinus kesiya* is a rather tender species. **ZONES 9–12.**

Pinus koraiensis
KOREAN PINE

From Korea, Japan and the Amur region of China, this narrow tree grows to 50 ft (15 m) in cultivation with a rounded head. Its unusually rough, deep bluish green needles, up to 4 in (10 cm) long, are carried in bundles of five. Its bark is rough and grayish brown and the cones are 3–6 in (8–15 cm) long. Tough and adaptable, *Pinus koraiensis* prefers well-drained soil. **ZONES 5–9.**

Pinus kesiya

Pinus monophylla
SINGLE-LEAF PIÑON

From western North America, in cultivation this tough pine grows slowly to 25 ft (8 m) and is usually multi-stemmed. It matures from a slender sapling to an interesting, round-headed tree with a crooked trunk. Its single, stiff, prickly leaves are 2 in (5 cm) long. Its spherical, brown, woody cones, 2 in (5 cm) in diameter, produce edible nuts. It is resistant to dry conditions. **ZONES 7–10.**

Pinus montezumae
MONTEZUMA PINE

Found in Mexico and Guatemala, this tree grows quickly to 100 ft (30 m). It has a columnar crown when young and eventually becomes a round-headed tree. Its bark is deep red-brown to near black and is deeply fissured. It has 6–12 in (15–30 cm), slightly blue-green, pendulous needles in groups of 5 and buff-colored cones up to 10 in (25 cm) long. **ZONES 9–11.**

Pinus monticola
WESTERN WHITE PINE

Native to western USA, this grows to 200 ft (60 m). The oldest recorded specimen is 500 years old. Upward-growing branches carry bluish green needles 4 in (10 cm) long in dense clumps of 5, and tapering, purplish cones up to 8 in (20 cm) long occur on the tips. It is prone to white pine blister rust in northwestern USA. **ZONES 5–9.**

Pinus mugo
MOUNTAIN PINE, SWISS MOUNTAIN PINE

In the mountains of Europe this small tree grows slowly to 12 ft (3.5 m). Its

Pinus mugo 'Mops'

Pinus nigra var. *maritima*

Pinus nigra

Pinus nigra

windswept appearance reflects its habitat, making it an interesting bonsai and rock-garden specimen. Its pairs of 2 in (5 cm) long, bright green needles develop from resinous buds. The oval, dark brown cones are 1–2 in (2–5 cm) long. This species does not tolerate extreme heat or dry conditions. **'Aurea'** has golden foliage. **'Gnom'**, a compact bush 6 ft (1.8 m) high with a similar spread, produces whitish new shoots against rich, black-green mature growth. **'Mops'** matures to 5 ft (1.5 m) over 10 years. ***Pinus mugo* var. *pumilo***, the dwarf Swiss mountain pine, develops a compact bun shape, achieving 30 in (75 cm) in 10 years. **ZONES 2–9.**

Pinus muricata
BISHOP PINE

This 70–100 ft (21–30 m) tree from California is dense and compact when young, open and irregularly shaped when mature. It has deeply fissured, dark red-brown bark that splits deeply and pairs of 4–6 in (10–15 cm) long bright green needles. The cones are 2–4 in (5–10 cm) long and slightly glossy. It is usually at its best in coastal conditions. **ZONES 8–10.**

Pinus nigra
AUSTRIAN BLACK PINE, EUROPEAN BLACK PINE

From central and southern Europe, this pine grows to 120 ft (36 m) or more in the wild, though cultivated specimens rarely exceed 50 ft (15 m). It has an open, conical habit with a whitish brown trunk, whorled branches and a dense crown of dark green, 6 in (15 cm) long, paired needles; its cones are 3 in (8 cm) long. It grows in chalk and clay and tolerates coastal conditions. ***Pinus nigra***

Pinus oaxacana

var. *maritima*, the Corsican pine, forms a denser crown and is slower growing; its gray-green twisted needle pairs can exceed 6 in (15 cm) and it has cracking bark and a very straight trunk that is harvested for timber. **ZONES 4–9.**

Pinus oaxacana

Found from southeast Mexico to Honduras, this rather tender tree grows to 100 ft (30 m) tall with a rounded crown and thick, deeply fissured bark. It needles are 8–12 in (20–30 cm) long, gray-green, drooping and in groups of five. The dark brown cones are up to 6 in (15 cm) long. **ZONES 9–11.**

Pinus palustris
LONG-LEAF PINE

From eastern and central USA, this pine grows to 100 ft (30 m) with an open crown. It has blunt, bluish green needles up to 18 in (45 cm) long, arranged in groups of three. Its 6–10 in (15–25 cm) long, reddish brown cones have spines on the tips of their scales and are held on the tree for up to 20 years. This pine will not tolerate strong winds or dry conditions. **ZONES 4–11.**

Pinus parviflora 'Glauca'

Pinus pinaster

Pinus parviflora
JAPANESE WHITE PINE

This pyramid-shaped pine usually grows to 40 ft (12 m) in cultivation but in its native Japan can reach 80 ft (24 m) tall with a similar spread. It produces some of the shortest needles in the genus—1 ½ in (35 mm) long. Its dense, bluish green foliage and slow growth habit make it a popular bonsai or tub subject. **'Brevifolia'** is an upright, sparsely foliaged cultivar. The blue-foliaged **'Glauca'** takes many years to reach 5 ft (1.5 m); its needles have distinctive blue-white bands on their inner sides. **'Adcock's Dwarf'** is a bun-shaped cultivar that grows to only 30 in (75 cm). **ZONES 3–9.**

Pinus patula
MEXICAN WEEPING PINE, SPREADING-LEAFED PINE

The long, slender, drooping needles and spreading canopy make this graceful pine a good shade tree. It is slow growing to 50 ft (15 m) with a 15 ft (4.5 m) spread, branching low to the ground. The 8 in (20 cm) long needles are soft, pale green to grayish green, and grouped in 3s; the oval cones are 4 in (10 cm) long. **ZONES 9–11.**

Pinus parviflora 'Brevifolia'

Pinus pinaster
MARITIME PINE, CLUSTER PINE

From the Mediterranean region and growing quickly to 100 ft (30 m), this pine does not tolerate dry conditions or frost but enjoys coastal locations and is a good windbreak. Its bright reddish brown bark is deeply furrowed. The paired green needles, up to 10 in (25 cm) long, are stiff and shiny. Rich brown, oval cones 6 in (15 cm) or more long persist on the branches for many years without opening. This pine is valued for timber and resin. **ZONES 7–10.**

Pinus pinea
ROMAN PINE, STONE PINE, UMBRELLA PINE

From southern Europe and Turkey, this species can reach 80 ft (24 m) in the wild and has a flattened crown atop a straight, though often leaning trunk with furrowed, reddish gray bark. The rigid, paired needles are 4–8 in (10–20 cm) long and bright green. The globe-shaped cones are shiny and brown; the edible seeds are known as pine nuts. Once established this pine copes with most conditions, including dryness and heat. **ZONES 8–10.**

Pinus pinea

Pinus patula

P

Pinus strobus 'Nana'

Pinus strobus 'Radiata'

Pinus roxburghii

Pinus ponderosa

PONDEROSA PINE, WESTERN YELLOW PINE

Abundant in its native western North America, this pine has a deeply fissured bark with a mosaic of broad, smooth, yellowish brown, reddish brown and pinkish gray plates. An important timber tree, it can reach 200 ft (60 m) but in cultivation is usually smaller. It has dark brown cones on spire-like branches. Its dark green needles, in bundles of 3, are up to 10 in (25 cm) long. **ZONES 5–9.**

Pinus pseudostrobus

SMOOTH-BARK MEXICAN PINE

Found from Mexico to Honduras, this tree is over 100 ft (30 m) tall with a dense, rounded crown. Its branches are in whorls. Its smooth bark is yellow-gray. The bright blue-green needles, in groups of 5, are 6–10 in (15–25 cm) long. Cones are 3–6 in (8–15 cm) long. **ZONES 9–11.**

Pinus radiata

syn. ***Pinus insignis***

MONTEREY PINE, RADIATA PINE, HIMALAYAN PINE

Fast growing to over 100 ft (30 m), this pine from California is an important timber tree in other parts of the world, especially Australia and New Zealand. It grows best in well-drained soil but does not tolerate extreme dry conditions or heat and can be toppled by strong wind. It has a pyramidal shape when young, becoming more columnar with age. The deep green needles are 4–6 in (10–15 cm) long, and the bark is grayish brown. The 4–6 in (10–15 cm) long cones are light brown. **'Aurea'** is a golden-foliaged cultivar that displays its best color in winter; it is smaller than the species but inclined to revert to green and grow normally. **ZONES 8–10.**

Pinus strobus 'Prostrata'

Pinus roxburghii

CHIR PINE, HIMALAYAN LONG-LEAF PINE

From the Himalayan foothills, where it can reach 150 ft (45 m) tall with a 15 ft (4.5 m) spread, this species is smaller in cultivation. It is slender when young, becoming round-headed with age, and cannot withstand severe dry conditions. The bark is mottled with light brown and grayish tones. The drooping 12 in (30 cm) needles are light green and are carried in threes. The cones are oval with reflexed scales and are 8 in (20 cm) long. **ZONES 6–11.**

Pinus radiata

Pinus pseudostrobus

Pinus × *sondereggeri*

This natural hybrid between *Pinus palustris* and ***P. taeda*** is found in southeast USA. It can reach 100 ft (30 m) tall and has bright red-brown bark with buff new growth. Its needles are bright green, around 12 in (30 cm) long, and carried in groups of three. **ZONES 8–10.**

Pinus strobus

EASTERN WHITE PINE, WEYMOUTH PINE

Occurring naturally in eastern North America, where it is valued for its timber, this species grows to 200 ft (60 m) in the wild but to less than 80 ft (24 m) in cultivation. It is characterized by deeply fissured, grayish brown bark and whorled branches. The conical crown becomes flattish with age. Its fine, 4 in (10 cm) long, bluish green needles are soft and are carried in groups of five. The pointed cones, clustered at the branch ends, produce copious amounts of white resin. This species develops rapidly if grown away from a polluted environment and, though cold hardy, it is susceptible to dry conditions and windburn. **'Fastigiata'** has vivid green growth on upward-pointing branches. **'Nana'** is a rounded dwarf cultivar with dense foliage that completely obscures the branches. **'Prostrata'** is a very low-growing, spreading cultivar that eventually mounds to around 18 in (45 cm) high at the center. **'Radiata'** is a dwarf cultivar that develops into a slowly spreading hummock of foliage up to 24 in (60 cm) high. **ZONES 3–9.**

Pinus sylvestris

SCOTS PINE

This fast-growing species, found throughout northern Europe and western Asia and the only pine indigenous to the UK, is the most commonly grown pine in Europe and is often used in forestry. It reaches 100 ft (30 m) with a rounded head of foliage and orange-red bark. Twisted, bluish green needles grow in pairs and are 3 in (8 cm) long. This pine grows well in poor sandy soil but will not tolerate dry conditions. Dwarf cultivars make attractive tub specimens. **'Aurea'** has gold-tinted foliage, especially

Pinus strobus

Pinus strobus 'Fastigiata'

Pinus radiata 'Aurea'

Pinus × *sondereggeri*

Pinus torreyana

the new growth and the winter foliage. **'Beuvronensis'** is a very densely foliaged dwarf cultivar with light blue-green needles that eventually reaches 6 ft (1.8 m) tall but is small for many years. **'Moseri'** is a small pyramidal cultivar with yellow foliage. **'Watereri'** only grows 2–3 in (5–8 cm) a year and can be thought of as a dwarf, blue-foliaged form of the Scots pine. It is ideal for rockeries or collections of dwarf conifers. **ZONES 4–9.**

Pinus thunbergii

syn. ***Pinus thunbergiana***

JAPANESE BLACK PINE

This pine has a rugged trunk, purplish black bark, pairs of thick needles, conspicuous white buds and an intricate framework of irregular, layered, horizontal branches. Widely grown in Japan as an ornamental, it has for centuries inspired artists and bonsai masters. It will stand any amount of pruning and trimming to shape; untrimmed it grows to 120 ft (36 m). It does very well in containers. **'Nishiki'** is a naturally dwarf, gnarled cultivar with corky bark very popular for bonsai. **ZONES 5–9.**

Pinus torreyana

This southern Californian species grows quickly to 50 ft (15 m). It has an irregular, broad, open crown and 8–12 in (20–30 cm) long gray-green needles in groups of five. The dark brown cones are 4–6 in (10–15 cm) long. It grows well in many situations but looks most attractive when shaped by coastal winds. **ZONES 8–10.**

Pinus wallichiana

BHUTAN PINE, BLUE PINE

This ornamental pine is an effective centerpiece for a large lawn, with its conical shape, broad base and graceful long branches bearing drooping, gray-green needles 6–8 in (15–20 cm) long. Its 12 in (30 cm) long cones are eyecatching. If grown in moist, deep soil it can reach 150 ft (45 m). It is cold and disease resistant but suffers in hot, dry conditions. **ZONES 5–9.**

PIPER

PEPPER

This genus of over 1,000 species of shrubs, climbers and trees is found

Pinus wallichiana

throughout the tropics. As might be expected of such a large genus there is little to be said that applies to all of them. The source of pepper and kava, they are often aromatic plants and their leaves are smooth-edged, usually deep green and often heart- or lance-shaped. The flowers are minute, cream or green and are borne on short yellowish spikes that form in the leaf axils. Small green fruits that ripen to red follow.

CULTIVATION: All species are frost tender and need a warm climate with moist, humus-rich soil to grow well. They will grow in sun or shade and in the right conditions can be vigorous. Propagate from seed or cuttings or by division or layering depending on the plant type.

Piper betle

BETEL

Found from India to the Malay peninsula, this 15 ft (4.5 m) tall plant climbs using adventitious roots. Its leaves are heart-shaped, 4–6 in (10–15 cm) long by 3 in (8 cm) wide and are chewed by native peoples along with the nut of the betel palm *(Areca catechu)*. The floral spike is up to 6 in (15 cm) long and becomes a red mass as the fruit develop. **ZONES 10–12.**

Pinus sylvestris

Pinus thunbergii 'Nishiki'

Piper cubeba

CUBEB, CUBEB PEPPER

This Indonesian species climbs to 10 ft (3 m) high. It has heart- to lance-shaped leaves up to 6 in (15 cm) long and a 4 in (10 cm) flower spike. The dried and ground red-brown fruit are used in perfumes, commercial flavorings and as a spice in Indonesian cooking. **ZONES 10–12.**

Piper methysticum

KAVA KAVA

This is a climbing shrub with heart-shaped leaves and short, cylindrical spikes of small flowers followed by small rounded fruit. The people of the South Pacific islands use the upper portion of the root of this plant to make a euphoria-producing, bitter-tasting beverage; it is taken as a ritual sacrament before important ceremonies. **ZONES 11–12.**

Piper nigrum

BLACK PEPPER

Highly regarded as a condiment, this is probably the most widely used spice in the world today. It is a strong, woody climber to 20 ft (6 m) or more high with prominently veined, glossy oval leaves. The inconspicuous flowers, borne in long slender spikes in summer, are followed by red globular fruit. Plants begin bearing in 2 to 5 years and under good conditions may produce for up to 40 years. **ZONES 11–12.**

Pinus sylvestris 'Moseri'

Pinus thunbergii

Piper ornatum

CELEBES PEPPER

Native to the Indonesian island of Sulawesi (Celebes), this sprawling shrub has wiry stems that spread across the ground and climb into low vegetation. It can grow to about 15 ft (4.5 m) tall. The heart-shaped leaves are nearly as wide as they are long (4 in/10 cm). The upper leaf surfaces are a mottled pattern of green, pink and silver while the undersides are flushed purple-red. **ZONES 11–12.**

PIPTANTHUS

This Himalayan and Chinese genus includes just 2 species, evergreen shrubs slightly reminiscent of *Laburnum* when in flower. They form clumps of hollow, gray-green stems up to 15 ft (4.5 m) tall and have trifoliate leaves with leaflets up

Piper ornatum

Piper betle

Pistia stratiotes

Piptanthus tomentosus

Pisonia umbellifera 'Variegata'

to 6 in (15 cm) long. In spring and early summer they produce 6 in (15 cm) racemes of yellow pea-like flowers in the leaf axils and at the stem tips.
CULTIVATION: Both species will tolerate moderate frosts, although in prolonged cold they may lose much of their foliage. Plant in moist, humus-rich, well-drained soil in sun or part-shade. Propagate from seed or small tip cuttings.

Piptanthus nepalensis
syn. *Piptanthus laburnifolius*

The leaves of this species are a bright mid-green and are sparsely hairy with leaflets to 4 in (10 cm) long. The new growth is quite downy. The bright yellow flowers are occasionally blotched purple and usually open in early summer, though it is seldom without a few blooms. **ZONES 8–10.**

Piptanthus tomentosus

This southwest Chinese species flowers from late spring but is primarily grown for its foliage. The leaves are covered in fine silky hairs that are especially dense on the undersides. It grows to a height of

Piptanthus tomentosus

8 ft (2.4 m) with a 6 ft (1.8 m) spread. **ZONES 8–10.**

PISONIA
syn. *Heimerliodendron*

These 35 species of fast-growing, evergreen shrubs, small trees and climbers occur naturally in tropical and subtropical areas, particularly in the Americas, northern Australia and the Malaysian region. They have large, oval leaves somewhat like those of the rubber tree (*Ficus elastica*); variegated foliage cultivars are often grown. The small greenish flowers, though borne in panicles, are not showy but are followed by the extremely sticky fruits for which the genus is best known. These often trap insects and even small birds, although why they do this is unknown.
CULTIVATION: These frost-tender plants require rich, well-drained soil in a sunny or part-shaded site. They will grow in containers and are sometimes used as house plants. The species may be raised from seed or cuttings; the variegated foliage forms are cutting grown.

Pisonia grandis
BIRD LIME TREE

This tree species, growing to 30 ft (9 m) with pale green leaves 12 in (30 cm) or more long, is ideal for avenue planting. The flowers are greenish and appear in late summer. The soft, spongy trunk branches shortly above the ground into a broad, open crown. **ZONES 10–12.**

Pisonia umbellifera
BIRD-CATCHER TREE

Native to the western Pacific region, this erect, branching shrub grows to 15 ft

Pistacia chinensis

(4.5 m) with a spread of 10 ft (3 m). It has large, elliptical, glossy green leaves and insignificant flowers and bears very sticky, purplish fruit all year round. Trees from temperate east Australia and New Zealand are now usually separated as *Pisonia brunoniana* (syn. *Heimerliodendron brunonianum*). **'Variegata'** has oval leaves 12–15 in (30–38 cm) long and beautifully patterned in tones of pale to dark green and creamy white, and small, greenish flowers. **ZONES 10–12.**

PISTACIA
PISTACHIO

This small genus consists of 9 species of deciduous and evergreen trees and shrubs occurring naturally in the warm-temperate regions of the northern hemisphere. It includes the familiar edible pistachio nuts as well as ornamental deciduous species that develop vivid foliage tones in fall (autumn), and species grown for their resins and oils. The tallest species grow to 80 ft (24 m). The leaf arrangements are compound, usually composed of an even number of leaflets. The flowers are generally inconspicuous, male and female flowers occurring on separate plants. Female plants display clusters of small berries or fleshy fruits in fall and early winter.
CULTIVATION: A well-drained soil in full sun is preferred. Propagate from seed sown in fall and winter, or by budding or grafting.

Pistacia chinensis
CHINESE PISTACHIO

Growing to 25 ft (8 m) in gardens, this deciduous species has glossy green leaves consisting of up to 10 pairs of leaflets that in fall (autumn) turn yellow, orange and scarlet. The inconspicuous flowers, borne in panicles, are followed in summer by small red spherical seed pods that turn blue in fall and attract birds. An excellent street tree, it also makes a good canopy for shade-loving shrubs. It often forms a double trunk. **ZONES 5–10.**

Pistacia vera
PISTACHIO NUT

This small deciduous tree reaching a height and spread of 30 ft (9 m) is native to western Asia and the Middle East, but is cultivated worldwide in many temperate areas. The leaves consist of 1 to 5 pairs of oval leaflets and turn red-gold in fall (autumn). Red male and white female flowers are borne on separate trees; at least one of each is needed for a crop of nuts. These are reddish, fleshy and oval with a green or yellow kernel. For a good yield, this tree needs a hot dry summer and a mild to cold winter. **ZONES 8–10.**

PISTIA
WATER LETTUCE, SHELL FLOWER

The sole species in this genus is an aquatic perennial widespread in the tropics and a noxious weed in some areas. The name water lettuce is an apt description: the 6 in (15 cm) wide, floating rosettes of ribbed, wedge-shaped leaves resemble blue-green lettuce heads. The base of the leaves is spongy, which keeps them buoyant, and the fine roots emerging from the base of the rosette extract nutrients directly from the water. Although connected by stolons, the rosettes can survive independently. The arum-like inflorescence is enclosed in a leaf-like spathe that makes it inconspicuous.
CULTIVATION: Apart from needing warm subtropical to tropical conditions, water lettuce is easily grown in any pond or slow-moving water. It multiplies rapidly and can quickly clog streams. It is usually self-propagating.

Pistia stratiotes

Forming large clumps of felted rosettes, this species is an aggressive colonizer that can easily smother a small pond. Although it does not oxygenate the water, fish will feed on its roots. It also helps to shade the surface and keep the water cool. **ZONES 10–12.**

PISUM
PEA

This genus originated in the eastern Mediterranean region and peas have been part of the human diet for at least 5,000 years. Only 2 species are recognized in this genus, the wild pea and the garden pea, *Pisum sativum*, grown for its tender green peas. Garden peas come in two forms: dwarf, or bush and climbing. There are many varieties of each form including the sugar or snow peas which have tender, sweet, edible pods.
CULTIVATION: Peas are a cool-season crop that can be enjoyed both in spring and fall (autumn). They need a sunny, well-drained, previously manured soil that contains some lime and dolomite. A support of stretched wire on short stakes helps keep the dwarf varieties off the ground and increases productivity. Propagate from seed in mild climates from fall until spring. Young plants are not injured by frosts, but the blossoms and pods are. In cold winter areas sowing can be timed to give maturity when frosts have passed. Watch for mildew, mites and blight.

Pisum sativum
GARDEN PEA

This annual species grows to 6 ft (1.8 m) and has branched tendrils. There are from 1 to 4 pairs of leaflets and the flowers, to $1\frac{1}{4}$ in (30 mm) wide, are white, sometimes with pale or dark

Pisum sativum cultivar

purple markings. Plant seedlings 2 in (5 cm) apart in rows 4 in (10 cm) apart. When the seedlings are 3 in (8 cm) high stake them with short twigs. Keep weeds down and water when dry. Pick the pods from the lower stems. Popular cultivars include **'Alderman'**, **'Snow Flake'** and **'Sugar Bon'**. ***Pisum sativum* var. *macrocarpum***, the snowpea or mangetout pea, prefers a temperate climate and a moist sandy soil. Sow 2 in (5 cm) deep when the garden is likely to be frost free and use a trellis for climbing varieties. Pick the pods when they are still immature. **ZONES 3–10.**

PITCAIRNIA

This genus of bromeliads is native to Central and South America, Mexico and the West Indies. Mostly rock dwellers or ground dwellers, they are occasionally epiphytic. They produce clumps of somewhat grass-like foliage and spikes of variously colored tubular flowers with recurved petals. The 260 species vary widely in their styles of growth but all of them require a rest period with minimum water in cold months.
CULTIVATION: Some species like full sun while the evergreen species prefer a part-shaded position. The leaf-dropping species need plenty of water and fertilizer as soon as the first regrowth appears. Generally it is a frost-tender genus. All prefer well-drained soil. Propagate from seed or by division of the rhizomes.

Pitcairnia flammea

Found originally in the granite rocks of the mountains of Rio de Janeiro, this species bears red and white flowers in spring. It is sensitive to cold. **ZONES 10–12.**

Pitcairnia ringens

This is one of the *Pitcairnia* species adapted to drier environments. It has underground growing points which produce sparse tufts of short, narrowly lance-shaped leaves and spreading spikes about 18 in (45 cm) tall of progressively opening scarlet flowers about 2 in (5 cm) long. **ZONES 10–12.**

PITTOSPORUM

This genus consists of some 200 species of evergreen trees and shrubs from the tropical and subtropical regions of

Pitcairnia ringens

Australasia, Africa, Asia and the Pacific Islands. They make good specimen plants, screens and windbreaks or dense hedges in mild-winter climates. The leaves are arranged alternately along the stems or in whorls. Several species have striking foliage prized by flower arrangers. The fragrant flowers are followed by fruits with a hard outer capsule enclosing round seeds with a sticky covering.
CULTIVATION: Grow in fertile, well-drained soil and keep moist over summer to maintain the foliage at its best. They need full sun or part-shade, and a sheltered position in colder areas. Some species are frost tolerant and many are excellent for seaside gardens. Propagate from seed in fall (autumn) or spring, or from tip cuttings in summer.

Pittosporum crassifolium
KARO

Native to New Zealand, this moderately frost hardy species grows to 25 ft (8 m) tall with a spread of 10 ft (3 m). The single trunk bears low-growing branches and a domed canopy. The oblong to oval leaves are dark green and leathery, 3 in (8 cm) long with grayish white, felted undersides. Clusters of fragrant, star-shaped, reddish purple flowers are borne in spring and are followed by fleshy, greenish white, oval fruit up to 1 in (25 mm) long. Tolerant of dry conditions and suitable for seaside locations, it adapts to most soil types but needs an open, sunny aspect. **'Variegatum'** has gray to bright green leaves with an irregular cream edge. **ZONES 8–10.**

Pittosporum eugenioides
TARATA, LEMONWOOD

From New Zealand, this densely foliaged species is pyramidal when young and grows to 40 ft (12 m) tall with smooth, pale gray bark. The shiny, dark green, oval leaves have a wavy edge and a citrus-like aroma when crushed. The terminal clusters of small, star-shaped yellow flowers with a honey-like perfume appear in spring. Large clusters of green oval fruit follow, persisting through winter. Tolerant of both frost and dry conditions, it thrives in most soils if given an open, sunny spot. **'Variegatum'** has beautiful gray-green leaves blotched along the edge with white and grows to 8–15 ft (2.4–4.5 m) tall. The species and its cultivars are suitable for clipped hedges. **ZONES 9–11.**

Pittosporum crassifolium 'Variegatum'

Pittosporum 'Garnettii'

Although often listed under *Pittosporum tenuifolium*, this cultivar appears to be a hybrid. It has rounded leaves up to 2 in (5 cm) long with irregular cream and green variegations, and the foliage develops pink tones in cold weather. It grows 8–10 ft (2.4–3 m) tall. **ZONES 9–11.**

Pittosporum napaulense

Native to India, Bhutan and Nepal, this shrub or small tree can grow to 20 ft (6 m) tall. Its leaves, clustered at the branch tips, are 3–8 in (8–20 cm) long, elliptical and leathery. It carries panicles of sweetly scented yellow flowers from late spring. **ZONES 9–11.**

Pittosporum phillyraeoides
syn. ***Pittosporum phylliraeoides***

BERRIGAN, WEEPING PITTOSPORUM, WILLOW PITTOSPORUM

This species, which ranges across inland Australia, grows to 25 ft (8 m) tall with a graceful weeping habit and open canopy of shiny, dark green, lance-shaped leaves up to 4 in (10 cm) long. It bears creamy yellow flowers singly or in small clusters at the branch tips in spring and summer. Fleshy, oval, 1 in (25 mm) long fruit follow, ripening from yellow to reddish brown. They then split to reveal red seeds against a yellow interior. The seeds were used by Australian Aborigines to treat pain and cramps. **ZONES 9–11.**

Pittosporum eugenioides

Pittosporum napaulense

Pittosporum crassifolium

Pittosporum eugenioides 'Variegatum'

Pittosporum phillyraeoides

Pittosporum rhombifolium
QUEENSLAND LAUREL, AUSTRALIAN LAUREL

This rainforest tree from eastern Australia can reach 80 ft (24 m) tall. Spring-time clusters of star-shaped, creamy white flowers are followed in fall (autumn) and winter by masses of round, bright orange fruit ½ in (12 mm) across that split when ripe to reveal sticky black seeds. Upward-sweeping branches form a dense pyramidal crown; the 4 in (10 cm) long rhomboid leaves are toothed, leathery and shiny green. This tree prefers loamy to heavy soil and a frost-free climate. **ZONES 9–11.**

Pittosporum tenuifolium
KOHUHU, TAWHIWHI

This New Zealand species can reach 30 ft (9 m); young plants are columnar, rounding as they mature. It has pale green oblong leaves, 3 in (8 cm) long, and black twigs and bark. Its small, dark brown flowers, borne in late spring, have an intense honey perfume at night. In late summer its round fruit ripen from green to almost black. It tolerates heavy pruning and prefers an open, sunny site. **'Silver Magic'** has small, silver-gray leaves that develop pink tints, especially in winter. **'Tom Thumb'** is a low-growing form usually under 3 ft (1 m) tall with deep purple-bronze leaves with wavy edges; **'Variegatum'** has olive-green leaves with cream margins. **ZONES 9–11.**

Pittosporum rhombifolium

Pittosporum tobira

Pittosporum tobira
JAPANESE MOCK ORANGE

From Japan and China, this shrubby species eventually reaches 8 ft (2.4 m). Its oval to oblong shiny green leaves, 4 in (10 cm) long, occur in whorls along the stems. Star-shaped, cream flowers with an orange blossom scent appear in late spring and summer. It thrives in mild climates in an open, sunny position. It is a good hedge plant in coastal regions. **'Wheeler's Dwarf'**, a mound-like shrub, grows to 24 in (60 cm); **'Variegatum'** has an irregular silvery white edge to its leaves. **ZONES 9–11.**

Pittosporum undulatum
SWEET PITTOSPORUM, AUSTRALIAN DAPHNE

This popular Australian species reaches 20–40 ft (6–12 m) tall with a wide dome. The dense green leaves are lance-shaped with scalloped edges. Profuse clusters of creamy white, bell-shaped flowers in spring are followed by yellow-brown fruit. Marginally frost hardy, it prefers moderate to warm climates. Watch for white scale and sooty mold. **'Sunburst'** is a popular cultivar. **ZONES 9–11.**

Pittosporum tobira 'Wheeler's Dwarf'

Pittosporum tobira 'Variegatum'

Pittosporum tenuifolium 'Variegatum'

Pittosporum 'Variegatum'
syn. *Pittosporum* 'Silver Queen'

This 12–15 ft (3.5–4.5 m) tall cultivar has leaves with narrrowly feathery margins of cream, or almost white. Often listed as a *Pittosporum tenuifolium* cultivar, its origins are not confirmed and it is best regarded as a possible hybrid. **ZONES 8–11.**

PITYROGRAMMA

This genus consists of about 40 species of evergreen ferns from North and South America and Africa, some of which are invasive and have spread widely in the tropics. They have short, creeping rhizomes that can also climb to 24–36 in (60–90 cm). The fronds have finely cut pinnae (leaflets), and can reach 30 in (75 cm) long on dark, wiry stems. The fronds are usually deep green on the upper surface and silvery white or yellow underneath. When fertile they shed copious quantities of spores.
CULTIVATION: These ferns are easily grown in cool, moist, humus-rich soil in light shade. Frost hardiness varies: many are tropical, but a few of the North American species tolerate moderate frosts. Propagate from the spores or by breaking off rooted pieces of rhizome.

Pityrogramma calomelanos
SILVER FERN

Originally from tropical America, this species is now widespread in the tropics. It has fronds up to 24 in (60 cm) long on deep brown 8–18 in (20–45 cm) stems. The fronds are finely divided and the undersides have a powdery silver coating . **ZONES 11–12.**

Pittosporum undulatum 'Sunburst'

Pittosporum tenuifolium 'Tom Thumb'

Pittosporum tenuifolium 'Silver Magic'

PLAGIANTHUS

This genus consists of *Plagianthus regius*, which is 40 ft (12 m) tall and is one of the few deciduous trees native to New Zealand, and ***P. divaricatus***, a shrub that eventually reaches 6 ft (1.8 m) in height and spread. They have light olive-green leaves with serrated edges and greenish white flowers in summer. They are very tough and adaptable plants.
CULTIVATION: Plant in moist, well-drained soil with light shade when young. Propagate from seed or grow selected male forms from cuttings.

Plagianthus regius
syn. ***Plagianthus betulinus***
RIBBONWOOD

When young this tree is a densely twiggy, spreading shrub and stays in this form

Pityrogramma calomelanos

for several years. The leaves are up to 4 in (10 cm) long. There are separate male and female plants, both producing panicles of yellowish or greenish white flowers; those of the male are slightly larger and more decorative. The name ribbonwood comes from the lacy inner bark. **ZONES 7–9.**

PLANCHONIA

This genus consists of semi-deciduous trees indigenous to the monsoonal regions of Australia and New Guinea. They have an upright habit, reaching 20 ft (6 m), and the trunk is covered with corky bark. The circular leaves are 4 in (10 cm) long. Large, pale green flowers appear on the branch tips in summer. The edible fruits resemble green eggs.
CULTIVATION: They thrive in poor soil if given constant moisture and plenty of sun. Propagate from seed or cuttings.

Planchonia careya
COCKY APPLE

This species forms an open tree with circular leaves held on long stalks. The young foliage is pale green and becomes brilliant orange before dropping during the dry season. The winter and spring flowers appear with long white stamens stained scarlet at the base; they open in the morning but normally fall by the afternoon. This is a useful small tree for gardens in tropical climates. **ZONES 11–12.**

PLANTAGO
PLANTAIN

This is a worldwide genus of around 200 species of annuals, biennials, perennials and shrubs, some of which are considered weeds. Their leaves are primarily basal, form clumps of loose rosettes and are often sparsely hairy. The leaves are

Plagianthus regius

Planchonia careya

Platanus × acerifolia

oval to a broad spatula shape with stout petioles and often develop purple tints in the sun or cold weather. The flowers are usually very small but conspicuous because they are borne on long-stemmed spikes that extend above the foliage.
CULTIVATION: Although a few of the larger-leafed species make attractive border plants, most plantains are rather invasive and need little in the way of cultivation. They prefer well-drained soil with moisture at depth but dry on the surface. Either sun or part-shade is suitable. Propagate from seed or by division in spring.

Plantago lanceolata
NARROW-LEAFED PLANTAIN

This European biennial or perennial species has crowded rosettes of narrow, lance-shaped, 2–15 in (5–38 cm) long leaves. The foliage has finely toothed edges and hairy undersides. The flower spike is up to 24 in (60 cm) tall and is topped with a 1–2 in (2.5–5 cm) cylindrical spike of tiny, very pale green flowers. It is a common weed of waste ground, although the white-variegated **'Marginata'** is occasionally cultivated. **ZONES 6–11.**

Plantago psyllium
FLEAWORT, SPANISH PSYLLIUM

This Mediterranean annual produces clumps of narrow leaves 2–6 in (5–15 cm) long, sometimes with finely toothed edges. The hairy flower stems are up to 24 in (60 cm) tall and are topped by egg-shaped heads of tiny white to pale green flowers. The husks are used as an appetite suppressant—they have no food value. **ZONES 6–10.**

PLATANUS
PLANE, SYCAMORE

This genus consists of 6 species of large, vigorous, wide-crowned, deciduous trees from Eurasia, North America and

Plantago lanceolata

Platanus × acerifolia

Mexico. It contains some of the world's largest shade trees for dry-summer climates, many of which are widely used as street trees. They are called planes or plane trees in some countries, sycamores in others. The most conspicuous feature is the flaking, mottled bark, which is shed in winter. The 5-lobed leaves are large and maple-like, and the brown seed balls hang in clusters on the trees in winter. The flowers are insignificant.
CULTIVATION: They thrive in deep, rich, well-drained soil in a sunny site and can be transplanted. Propagate from seed or cuttings or by layering. Most tolerate severe pruning, air pollution and hard construction (e.g. paving) covering the roots.

Platanus × acerifolia
syns *Platanus × hispanica, P. × hybrida*
LONDON PLANE

Used as a street tree for many years, this fast-growing hybrid can reach 120 ft (36 m) in height. It can withstand poor conditions and is resistant to leaf blight; however, the roots can lift paving and the large, bright green, leathery leaves can block small drains. Its straight, erect trunk is attractively blotched in gray, brown and white. **ZONES 3–10.**

Platanus occidentalis
AMERICAN PLANE, BUTTONWOOD

This large tree with its broad open head can reach a height of 150 ft (45 m). The creamy white bark is dark brown close to

Platanus orientalis

the ground on older trees. Bright green, toothed leaves grow up to 10 in (25 cm) wide. This tree prefers cold winters and hot summers and is prone to leaf blight. In the USA, its timber is used for furniture and firewood. **ZONES 3–9.**

Platanus orientalis
CHINAR, CHENNAR, ORIENTAL PLANE

Ranging from Turkey to the western Himalayas, this large tree grows about 100 ft (30 m) tall with spreading branches. Fully frost hardy, it has a relatively short, stout trunk and flaking gray to greenish white bark. Its deeply incised leaves form 5 to 7 narrow, pointed lobes, and 3 to 5 round, brown seed heads hang like beads on a thread. It is used as a street tree in Australia, southern Africa and southern Europe. The leaves of **'Digitata'** have elongated, narrow lobes that are more deeply cut. **ZONES 3–10.**

Platycladus orientalis 'Aurea Nana'

Platycladus orientalis 'Green Cone'

Platycladus orientalis

Platycladus orientalis 'Filiformis Erecta'

Platycladus orientalis 'Hillieri'

Platycladus orientalis

Platanus racemosa

WESTERN SYCAMORE, CALIFORNIA SYCAMORE, ALISO

From the mountains of California, this tree can fail in areas with long, harsh winters. It grows rapidly to 100 ft (30 m) tall or more, with a canopy about half that, and has a stout, erect trunk that is pale when young. The green leaves have a downy, whitish underside. The greenish flowers hang in clusters, followed by 2 to 7 spiky seed heads hanging on a stalk. **'Wrightii'** is very similar except the seed heads are smooth. **ZONES 7–10.**

PLATYCERIUM

This genus is common to the tropics and subtropics of Africa, Southeast Asia and Australia, although some species can tolerate quite cool temperatures. The 15 species are epiphytic ferns with hanging, spore-bearing divided fronds up to 8 ft (2.4 m) long. They are valued for their dramatic appearance.

CULTIVATION: These ferns can be grown as epiphytes by tying them onto boards that are then attached to a post or tree, or grown in baskets. The sterile nest leaves catch leaf litter and other vegetable matter so that the roots eventually grow into the debris and are protected from wind. The base of the plants should be kept moist. Fertilize the plants with dilute liquid manure. Propagate by division in spring. Check for beetle and moth larvae.

Platycerium bifurcatum

ELKHORN FERN

Native to the northeast coast of Australia, Papua New Guinea and New Caledonia, the elkforn fern is an easily grown plant that does well in sheltered gardens. It grows to a height and spread of about 3 ft (1 m). **ZONES 9–12.**

Platycerium superbum

syn. *Platycerium grande*

STAGHORN FERN

In the wild, clinging to a rainforest tree, this epiphyte can reach up to 6 ft (1.8 m) in height and spread, and its sheer weight can make it fall to the ground. It does well in a fernery or garden, where it grows to about half its natural size. **ZONES 10–12.**

PLATYCLADUS

ORIENTAL ARBOR-VITAE

Platycladus is a genus from China and Korea that contains only a single species, an evergreen conifer featuring flat, fan-like sprays of aromatic foliage. You may also find it listed with the closely related *Thuja*. It is a slender, conical tree but the attraction for gardeners lies in the wide choice of selected small to dwarf cultivars. These offer a diversity of neat, conical or rounded bushes with changing foliage tones through the seasons. As all the branches are retained right down to the ground, they form excellent hedges and screens, rockery features or tub specimens. The leaves are tiny, scale-like needles that clasp the twigs. Female trees have small, erect, rather fleshy cones with overlapping scales which ripen from waxy blue to brown. The species prefers warmer climates than many conifers.

CULTIVATION: Choose a spot sheltered from strong winds, although preferably in full sun. A partly shaded position will also be suitable. Most moist, well-drained soils are appropriate. Prune *Platycladus* lightly in spring, if desired, to shape. Propagate from seed in spring, or from cuttings taken in the cooler months.

Platycladus orientalis

syns *Thuja orientalis, Biota orientalis*

This densely branched large shrub or small tree grows to 40 ft (12 m) tall. Young plants are conical to columnar; older trees have a domed crown of upward-sweeping branches atop the short trunk. Some smaller varieties have very dense, crisp foliage and a symmetrical shape; others are more irregular. They are recognisable by the arrangement of their foliage in narrow, vertical planes. Some dwarf types keep their fuzzy, juvenile foliage. **'Aurea Nana'** is a golden-foliaged cultivar with a low, rounded growth habit seldom more than 3 ft (1 m) tall. **'Blue Cone'** is a dense, upright plant with a conical growth habit and blue-green foliage. **'Elegantissima'** is a neat, 8 ft (2.4 m) tall shrub with a broad columnar growth habit and yellow-tipped foliage sprays that develop golden tones in winter. **'Filiformis Erecta'** has thread-like foliage that droops slightly or lays flat along the stems and grows 5–6 ft (1.5–1.8 m) tall. **'Green Cone'** is similar in shape to 'Blue Cone', but with green foliage. **'Hillieri'** is another rounded dwarf cultivar. **'Raffles'** is a dense, low-growing, rounded cultivar with bright yellow foliage. **'Rosedalis'** looks prickly but feels soft and grows 3–5 ft (1–1.5 m) tall. **ZONES 6–11.**

Platanus racemosa

PLATYCODON

BALLOON FLOWER, CHINESE BELLFLOWER

The sole species in this genus is a semi-tuberous perennial with flower stems up to 30 in (75 cm) tall. Native to China, Japan, Korea and eastern Siberia, in spring it forms a clump of 2–3 in (5–8 cm) long, toothed-edged, elliptical to lance-shaped light blue-green foliage. The leafy flower stems develop quickly from mid-summer and are topped with heads of inflated buds that open into broad, bell-shaped, white, pink, blue or purple flowers up to 2 in (5 cm) wide.

CULTIVATION: Very frost hardy and easily grown in any well-drained soil in full sun, this plant may take a few years to become established. Propagate from seed or by division. Because it resents disturbance, do not divide regularly.

Platycodon grandiflorus

On this species, balloon-like buds open out into 5-petalled flowers like bells, colored blue, purple, pink or white, in summer. The serrated elliptical leaves with a silvery blue cast form in a neat clump up to 24 in (60 cm) high and half that in spread. **'Fuji Blue'** is a very erect cultivar to 30 in (75 cm) tall with very large blue flowers. ***Platycodon grandiflorus* var. *mariesii*** was introduced in the late 1800s. More compact than the species, it grows to 18 in (45 cm) tall and has glossy, lance-shaped leaves. **ZONES 4–10.**

Platycodon grandiflorus 'Fuji Blue'

Platycodon grandiflorus

Plecostachys serpyllifolia

Plectranthus argentatus

Plectranthus ciliatus

PLATYSTEMON

CREAMCUPS

This genus contains one annual species native to California; it grows 12 in (30 cm) tall and may be erect or spreading. Its narrow, nearly stemless, 3 in (8 cm) long, gray-green leaves resemble cornflower foliage in miniature, and they extend right up the wiry stems to within 2–3 in (5–8 cm) of the 1 in (25 mm) diameter, cream, poppy-like flowers. The leaves and young stems have a covering of fine hairs.

CULTIVATION: It is very easily grown as a border or container annual in any light, well-drained soil with occasional watering and full sun. It is moderately frost hardy and may be planted in late winter for an early show. Propagate from seed.

Platystemon californicus

Along with its close relative the California poppy *(Eschscholzia californica)*, this species is ideal for naturalizing in a wildflower garden. Although only an annual, it can usually be relied on to self-sow and soon becomes established. It goes well with larkspurs, cornflowers and nemesia. **ZONES 8–10.**

PLECOSTACHYS

This is a South African genus consisting of just 2 species. They are rangy subshrubs that grow to around 5 ft (1.5 m) tall, although they are often considerably smaller. Their most distinguishing feature is their foliage, which is small and round, usually less than 1 in (25 mm) long, but covered in sticky white hairs on the upper side with dense white felting below. Small, yellow, daisy-like flowers open in spring or after rain following a prolonged dry period.

CULTIVATION: Plant in light, gritty, very well-drained soil in full sun. Although tolerant of light frosts, prolonged cold, wet conditions can lead to rotting. Pinch growing tips to encourage branching. Propagate from seed or small cuttings.

Plecostachys serpyllifolia

Formerly classified as a member of the genus *Helichrysum*, this sprawling, frost-tender subshrub has felt-like stems and tiny leaves of silvery gray. Although the flowers are insignificant, the foliage and form provide an excellent addition to container and window-box gardens in cold regions, or a year-round, low mound of silver for mild gardens. **ZONES 9–10.**

PLECTRANTHUS

This genus contains more than 350 species of annuals, perennials and shrubs native to Africa, Asia and Australia. Most are rather frost tender and several species are grown as house plants, others are garden ornamentals or herbs. They generally have succulent or semi-succulent stems. The leaves, too, are often fleshy and frequently oval to heart-shaped. The flowers are small and tubular, but are borne in sometimes showy spikes that extend above the foliage.

CULTIVATION: Plant in moist, well-drained soil in part-shade. Protect from frost and prolonged dry conditions. Propagate from seed or cuttings or by layering. Many species are spreading and will self-layer.

Plectranthus ecklonii

Plectranthus argentatus

This Australian species is a spreading shrub up to 3 ft (1 m) high. Its branches and leaves are covered with short silver hairs. The leaves are 2–4 in (5–10 cm) long, oval with finely toothed edges. Its flowers are blue and white, in 9- to 11-flowered spikes that are 12 in (30 cm) long. **ZONES 10–11.**

Plectranthus australis

SWEDISH IVY

Commonly grown as an indoor plant, Swedish ivy has quilted leaves and sprays of tubular lilac and white flowers which look very pretty cascading from a hanging basket. *Plectranthus australis* grows to 8 in (20 cm) in height and spreads widely. Its glossy green leaves have attractive scalloped edges. It will thrive if given some direct sunlight and plenty of moisture. Tips should be cut back when the plant becomes untidy. **ZONES 9–11.**

Plectranthus ciliatus

This evergreen perennial with creeping, branched stems with upturned ends reaches a height of about 18 in (45 cm). *Plectranthus ciliatus* is a South African species that will make a rapidly spreading ground cover in the shade of trees. The leaves are bronze-green above and deep purple beneath, with a row of fine, soft bristle-tipped teeth along the margin. In summer and fall (autumn), it bears short sprays of tubular pale mauve flowers. **ZONES 9–11.**

Plectranthus ecklonii

This attractive South African shrub grows to a height of 6 ft (1.8 m) under favorable conditions, preferring a sheltered position and tolerating moderate shade. It has an erect, bushy habit with large deep green leaves that taper into their stalks and are strongly veined on the upper side. The tubular violet flowers are borne in erect terminal panicles in fall (autumn). Cutting the plant back hard in early spring induces a better show of flowers. **ZONES 9–11.**

Plectranthus neochilus

Plectranthus madagascariensis

MINTLEAF

Found in Madagascar and southern Africa, this spreading succulent-stemmed perennial strikes root as it spreads, and mounds to about 24 in (60 cm) tall. Its leaves are 2 in (5 cm) long, rather succulent, toothed edged with slight felting on their undersides. The white or purple flowers are borne on simple 3- to 8-flowered spikes. **ZONES 10–12.**

Plectranthus neochilus

This is one of a group of species allied to *Plectranthus caninus* that range from southeastern Africa to southern Arabia. Its flowers are pale lavender on short dense spikes that terminate in a group of purplish bud bracts, cast off as flowers open. The fleshy eaves have a strong musky smell. They have a mat-forming habit of growth and are fairly drought tolerant. **ZONES 10–12.**

Plectranthus oertendahlii

Often grown as a house plant, this free-branching, spreading, semi-succulent South African perennial has bright green, 2 in (5 cm) long, toothed-edged leaves with silver veins and purple undersides. Its flowers are pink to mauve, around 1/2 in (12 mm) long, and carried on simple 6-flowered spikes. **ZONES 10–12.**

Plectranthus saccatus

From eastern South Africa, this species is a soft-stemmed 4 ft (1.2 m) tall shrub. The stems are tinged purple and its leaves are up to 3 in (8 cm) long, semi-succulent with just a few large teeth. Its flowers are pale blue, in clusters of 1 to 3 on 4 in (10 cm) spikes. **ZONES 10–11.**

Plectranthus saccatus

Plectranthus ciliatus

P

Plectranthus thyrsoideus

syn. *Coleus thyrsoideus*

This fast-growing, bushy perennial is also grown as an annual. This is a larger species, growing to 3 ft (1 m) high with a spread of 24 in (60 cm). Its leaves are oval, mid-green with serrated edges, and panicles of tubular, bright blue flowers are borne in winter. **ZONES 10–11.**

Plectranthus verticillatus

This is a low, spreading, semi-succulent perennial from southern Africa. Its stems are sticky with fine hairs and grow to more than 3 ft (1 m) long. Its 2 in (5 cm) leaves are rounded, finely hairy, with toothed edges and reddish undersides. The relatively large flowers are white with purple spotting. **ZONES 10–12.**

PLEIOBLASTUS

This is a Chinese and Japanese bamboo genus of around 20 species. Most are dwarf to medium sized and seldom exceed 10 ft (3 m) tall. They have rhizomes and some are moderately invasive. They have slender, hollow stems and small narrow leaves that are seldom more than 8 in (20 cm) long, often considerably less and frequently with striped variegations. The leaf sheaths are conspicuous and often bristly.

CULTIVATION: Most species are very frost hardy and not difficult to cultivate. Plant in loose, moist, well-drained soil in sun or part-shade; water well in summer. Running species need to be contained. Propagate by division.

Pleioblastus auricomus

Pleioblastus variegatus

Pleioblastus auricomus

KAMURO-ZASA

A Japanese native, this species has 5 ft (1.5 m) stems and leaves 4–8 in (10–20 cm) long. The leaves are covered with a fine down and are bright yellow with contrasting green stripes. The purple-tinted leaf sheaths are also downy. **ZONES 7–10.**

Pleioblastus pygmaeus

syns *Arundinaria pygmaea, Sasa pygmaea*

DWARF BAMBOO

This spreading, rhizomatous bamboo can be used to help control erosion. Left uncut, the dark green foliage (variegated in most of the commonly available strains) of this evergreen will grow to 18 in (45 cm) and spread indefinitely. Cut back almost to the ground in early spring to ensure a lush crop of fresh new leaves. **ZONES 6–10.**

Pleioblastus variegatus

DWARF WHITE-SHEATHED BAMBOO, CHIGO-ZASA

In common with several other species, this plant is known only from cultivation and has never been found in the wild. It has powdery white, 30 in (75 cm) stems with proportionally large (4–8 in/ 10–20 cm long), deep green leaves with variable cream stripes. The leaf sheaths have purple interiors and downy exteriors. **ZONES 7–10.**

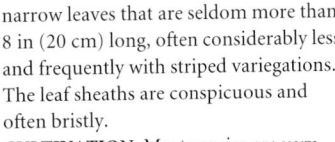

Pleione bulbocodioides

Pleione, Shantung Hybrid

PLEIONE

This is a small genus consisting of about 16 to 20 miniature orchids native to areas in southern and eastern Asia. They are epiphytic or terrestrial, with globose or flask-shaped, crowded pseudobulbs and one or two deciduous leaves. The flowers are large and showy, and arise from the base of the pseudobulb as the new growth is produced.

CULTIVATION: They like a mild, cool-temperate climate and protection from winter wet. They are usually grown in pots in good orchid potting mix and prefer part-shade. Propagate by division.

Pleione bulbocodioides

syns *Pleione formosana, P. pricei*

This species from southern China, Taiwan and Burma grows on trees or rocks at moderate to high altitudes in moist forests. The pseudobulbs are clustered, pear-shaped, about 1 in (25 mm) in diameter with a single leaf to 6 in (15 cm) long and 2 in (5 cm) wide. The shapely, 3 in (8 cm) wide flowers are borne in early spring before the new leaves appear. ***Pleione bulbocodioides* var. *alba*** (syn. *P. formosana* 'Alba') has white flowers. **ZONES 8–10.**

Pleione hookeriana

This small species grows epiphytically or on moss-covered rocks at high elevations in the Himalayas from India, Nepal, Burma, Laos and southern China. The pseudobulbs are spaced apart, oval, about 1½ in (35 mm) long, with a single, deciduous leaf 2–3 in (5–8 cm) long and 1 in (25 mm) broad. The inflorescence stands up to 4 in (10 cm) high, with a single flower about 2 in (5 cm) across.

Pleione bulbocodioides var. *alba*

Pleione Vesuvius

Flowering is in spring and summer. **ZONES 8–10.**

Pleione, Shantung Hybrids

Shantung is one of the most desirable of the fairly new hybrid pleiones. It comes in a number of clones that differ slightly in their blends of cream and pale pink. **'Muriel Fisher'**, named for a New Zealand botanist, is fairly frost hardy but needs a sheltered spot. Enrich its soil liberally with leafmold or compost. **ZONES 8–10.**

Pleione Vesuvius

This hybrid grex is reported to be the result of a cross between *Pleione bulbocodioides* and the natural hybrid *B.* × *confusa*. It has flowering stems that are tall for a pleione, commonly bearing 2 large flowers that are bright purplish pink except for the pale orange labellum, which is strongly frilled at the edge and densely flecked with red. **ZONES 8–10.**

Pleione yunnanensis

This species occurs at altitudes of 4,000–9,330 ft (1,200–2,800 m) in the Yunnan province of China. The crowded pseudobulbs are spherical and about 1 in (25 mm) in diameter with a single leaf that is absent at flowering. The basal inflorescences are up to 6 in (15 cm) tall with a single flower about 4 in (10 cm) across. *Pleione yunnanensis* flowers in spring and summer. **ZONES 8–10.**

PLEIOSPILOS

LIVING GRANITE, LIVING ROCK

These cunning succulents from the deserts of South Africa protect themselves from predators by masquerading as stones. There are 4 species, all of very similar appearance with little clumps of fleshy leaves that look like pebbles or pieces of granite. In early fall (autumn), however, a yellow, salmon-pink or white daisy-like flower emerges from between each pair of leaves. The plants seldom grow higher than 4 in (10 cm), each clump spreading to about 8 in (20 cm).

CULTIVATION: They thrive in warm climates but tolerate light, infrequent frosts. Grow in full sun in very well-drained soil. Propagate from seed or offsets in spring or summer.

Pleiospilos bolusii

LIVING ROCK CACTUS

This evergreen succulent from the African Cape grows 4 in (10 cm) tall. It is clump-forming with green foliage growing 2–3 in (5–8 cm) long. Golden-yellow, daisy-like flowers appear in spring and summer, reaching up to 3 in (8 cm) across. **ZONES 9–11.**

Pleiospilos nelii

SPLIT ROCK PLANT

The stem of this species from Cape Province, South Africa looks like a cluster of small stones until the pale yellow flowers emerge in late summer and early fall (autumn). It grows to 3 in (8 cm) in height with a 6 in (15 cm) spread. **ZONES 9–11.**

Plumbago auriculata

Plumbago auriculata 'Royal Cape'

PLUMBAGO

LEADWORT

This genus of 10 to 15 species of annuals, perennials, evergreen shrubs and scrambling climbers and semi-climbers is found in warm-temperate to tropical regions. The blue, white or red flowers have 5 petals narrowing to a long slender tube and are massed on short stems near the tips of the arching branches. The leaves are arranged alternately.
CULTIVATION: Plumbagos require well-drained soil, perhaps enriched with a little organic matter. They grow best in warm climates; in frost-prone areas they do well in a mildly warmed greenhouse. Established plants are tolerant of dry conditions, but soil should be kept moist during summer for a good flowering display. Prune in late winter to tidy their vigorous stems and remove old wood to encourage new growth and next season's flowers. Propagate from tip cuttings in the warmer months or from semi-hardwood cuttings in fall (autumn).

Plumbago auriculata

syn. ***Plumbago capensis***

BLUE PLUMBAGO, CAPE PLUMBAGO

This fast-growing species from South Africa grows to 6 ft (1.8 m) tall with a similar spread and carries its prolific sky-blue flowers through the warmer months. The pale green, oblong leaves are 2 in (5 cm) long. It suckers readily, and grows higher on supports or by climbing nearby shrubs. It is cultivated as an informal hedge or as a trimmed, formal hedge. **'Alba'** has clear white blooms. **'Royal Cape'** has flowers of a more intense blue and is slightly more tolerant of frost and dry conditions. **ZONES 9–11.**

Plumbago indica

syn. ***Plumbago rosea***

SCARLET LEADWORT

Although smaller and less frost hardy than *Plumbago auriculata*, this species

Pleiospilos bolusii

Plumbago indica

from India is a first-rate pot plant for a lightly shaded spot in subtropical or warm-temperate climates or for mildly warmed greenhouses in cool climates. Its flowers are a beautiful deep glowing pink. **ZONES 10–12.**

PLUMERIA

FRANGIPANI, TEMPLE TREE

Plumeria commemorates Charles Plumier, a seventeenth-century French botanist who described several tropical species. The genus contains 8 species of mainly deciduous shrubs and trees, originally from Central America, known for their strongly fragrant flowers. The trees can reach a height of 30 ft (9 m), though they are generally much smaller. Their fleshy branches contain a poisonous, milky sap. In the tropics, the terminally held flowers (generally white) appear before the leaves and continue to flower for most of the year. In subtropical climates the flowers appear in spring, after the leaves, and continue growing until the next winter. The fruits consist of 2 leathery follicles, although the trees rarely fruit in cultivation. Most plumerias in gardens are hybrids.
CULTIVATION: In colder climates, these trees and shrubs can be grown in a greenhouse. Outdoors, they prefer full sun and moderately fertile, well-drained soil. Propagate in early spring from

Pleiospilos nelii

Plumeria rubra 'Golden Kiss'

Plumeria obtusa 'Singapore White'

cuttings that have been allowed to dry out for a couple of weeks.

Plumeria obtusa

WHITE FRANGIPANI, SINGAPORE PLUMERIA

This small tree grows to 25 ft (8 m) high and is best suited to a tropical climate where, unlike most frangipanis, it is reliably evergreen. It can be grown in frost-free, subtropical climates, but requires a sheltered position and a fairly constant water supply. The broad, blunt-ended leaves are 6 in (15 cm) or more long. The scented, creamy white flowers have a bright yellow center. With its elegant, rounded flowers and soft perfume, **'Singapore White'** is one of the loveliest of all plumerias. **ZONES 10–12.**

Plumeria rubra

This widely cultivated, deciduous large shrub or small tree, with its broadly rounded canopy, can grow to a height of 25 ft (8 m). It is distinguished by its pale pink to crimson flowers, which are used extensively for decoration. ***Plumeria***

Plumeria rubra

Plumeria rubra var. *acutifolia*

rubra* var. *acutifolia is usually seen more commonly than the species and features creamy white flowers, sometimes flushed pink, with a deep yellow center. **'Golden Kiss'** has large heads of golden-yellow flowers with a soft flush of apricot along the lower edge of each petal. **ZONES 10–12.**

POA

This genus of some 500 species of mainly perennial grasses includes several important agricultural species, a few weeds and

Podalyria calyptrata

Poa labillardieri

Podocarpus elatus

some that are widely used for sports fields and as tough lawn grasses. The species are widely distributed in the temperate regions and have narrow but strong stems, seldom more than 3 ft (1 m) tall. Their leaves, which are often thickened and jointed at the base, are narrow and usually bright green or blue-green. Short flower spikes appear throughout the growing season; they are often the same color as the foliage, but may develop red, brown or purple tints.
CULTIVATION: They are easily grown in full sun or part-shade in any well-drained garden soil. Most species are at least moderately frost hardy, some are very frost hardy. Propagate from seed or by division.

Poa labillardieri

This is an Australian species with stems to 3 ft (1 m) tall and narrow, gray-green, 12 in (30 cm) long leaves. Its flower spikelets are purple tinted. **ZONES 8–10.**

Poa pratensis
KENTUCKY BLUE GRASS, MEADOW GRASS

Although producing an appealing blue-green lawn, this perennial native of central Europe will not take the heavy traffic of playgrounds or playing fields and does not survive dry conditions. It does well in cooler climates. It has smooth, erect stems and small, flat, pointed leaves. If left ungroomed it will grow to 6 in (15 cm) in height and spread. In spring and mid-summer, it bears spikelets in spreading panicles. It is vulnerable to attack by rust and other diseases, including fusarium blight brought on by a hot summer. **ZONES 3–9.**

Podalyria calyptrata

PODALYRIA

This is a genus of about 25 species of evergreen shrubs and small trees that occur naturally in the winter rainfall areas of southern Africa. They have oval leaves 1½ in (35 mm) long covered with very fine hairs that create a silvery effect. The flowering season varies, but usually starts in very early spring when fragrant clusters of mauve or white sweet-pea flowers open.
CULTIVATION: Plant in light, well-drained soil in full sun; these plants thrive in coastal conditions. Propagate from seed in spring or cuttings in summer, or by layering. A light trimming after flowering keeps the bushes compact.

Podalyria calyptrata
SWEET PEA BUSH

This species grows to be a rather open, small tree about 12 ft (3.5 m) high and nearly as wide. The silver-gray foliage is as much a feature as the masses of pink spring flowers. This is an undemanding and reliable plant in mild climates. **ZONES 9–10.**

PODOCARPUS
PLUM PINE

Occurring throughout the wet tropics and southern hemisphere continents extending also to Japan and Mexico, the 100 or so species in this coniferous genus are all moderately fast-growing evergreens, ranging from ground covers of 3 ft (1 m) to trees up to 150 ft (45 m) in height. Grown for their dense foliage and attractive habit, they bear a slight resemblance to the yews *(Taxus)*. The flat, generally narrow leaves are spirally arranged. There are separate male and female plants: the males have catkin-like yellow pollen cones; the females have naked seeds held on short stalks that develop into the fleshy blue-black to red berry-like 'fruits' that give them their common name. Some species are harvested for softwood.
CULTIVATION: They are reliable in a range of soils from rich to poor either in full sun or part-shade, depending on the species, although warm-temperate climates, free from heavy frost, suit them best. In cooler areas, plum pines can be successfully grown indoors. Leave unpruned unless a hedge is desired. Propagate from seed or cuttings.

Podocarpus elatus
BROWN PINE

In its native eastern Australia, this species can grow to 120 ft (36 m) with a spreading crown, but is smaller when cultivated as a shade tree or clipped as a hedge. It has flaky, dark brown bark, and its shiny, dark green leaves, 4 in (10 cm) long, are oblong and sharply pointed. The edible fruit are rounded and purplish to black, and 1 in (25 mm) across. This species can tolerate mild frosts, but must be watered in dry periods. **ZONES 9–12.**

Podocarpus hallii

Native to New Zealand and very similar to *Podocarpus totara*, this species is distinguished by its thin papery bark and larger leaves. Hybrids between the 2 species probably occur and it can be very difficult to tell them apart. **ZONES 8–11.**

Podocarpus henkelii
NATAL YELLOWWOOD, HENKEL'S YELLOWWOOD

Native to South Africa, this species has drooping branches and foliage. It has individual leaves 6 in (15 cm) or more long that are often curved. The fruit are rounded and waxy green, up to ½ in (12 mm) across. **ZONES 9–12.**

Podocarpus latifolius

Podocarpus latifolius
REAL YELLOWWOOD

In the forests of southern Africa, this erect species grows to 120 ft (36 m) or more in height; in cultivation it seldom exceeds 50 ft (15 m). Fully grown trees have leaves grouped close to the tips of the branches, and longitudinally grooved bark that shreds in long strips. Male trees produce pinkish, 1½ in (35 mm) long cones. When mature, the fruit from female trees turn blue or purplish. It is slightly frost tender. **ZONES 9–12.**

Podocarpus lawrencii
syn. *Podocarpus alpinus*
MOUNTAIN PLUM PINE

This fairly slow-growing Australian shrub or small tree can withstand frost but requires a sunny position. It ranges in height from 24 in (60 cm) in mountain areas to 25 ft (8 m) in lower woodlands. The trunk is gnarled and twisted and the small, grayish green leaves contrast well with the red, fleshy berries. This species is suitable for container planting. **ZONES 7–9.**

Podocarpus macrophyllus
KUSAMAKI, BUDDHIST PINE, YEW PINE

From the mountains of Japan and China, where it grows to 70 ft (21 m) tall with a spread of 12 ft (3.5 m), this cold-tolerant species prefers moist, rich soil. It has long, thick, dark green leaves up to 6 in (15 cm) long and responds well to pruning, making a good thick hedge. It is often grown in Japanese temple gardens and is also a suitable container plant. The berries are small and black. **'Maki'**, rarely bigger than a shrub, has a distinctly erect habit with almost vertical branches. **ZONES 7–11.**

Podocarpus henkelii

Podocarpus lawrencii

Podocarpus macrophyllus

Podocarpus matudae var. *reichii*

This species, found from northeast Mexico to Costa Rica, grows to 100 ft (30 m) tall and has 4 in (10 cm) long leaves. Often a tree will have several particularly vigorous stems with 6 in (15 cm) leaves. The drupes are red brown. **ZONES 9–12.**

Podocarpus neriifolius

BLACKLEAF PODOCARP

In the warm climate of its native Borneo and New Guinea, this species grows to more than 60 ft (18 m) and is characterized by relatively large leaves and small fruit. The unusually glossy, dark green, thin leaves have prominent midribs and are up to 6 in (15 cm) long. Its flowers appear as catkins: the male brown and the female green. Its fruit are oval, fleshy, green berries. **ZONES 10–12.**

Podocarpus rumphii

Native to mountain forests of the Philippines, eastern Indonesia and New Guinea, this species is a smallish tree growing to 30 ft (9 m) tall or more. It is distinguished by its very large leaves, up to 10 in (25 cm) long and ¾ in (18 mm) wide. These hang almost vertically, are deep green, very leathery, and each leaf persists for many years. The seeds sit on fleshy stalks little different from those of other true *Podocarpus* species. Slow growing when young, this species makes a striking tub specimen. **ZONES 10–12.**

Podocarpus salignus

WILLOWLEAF PODOCARP

This Chilean conifer differs from other members of the genus in its willow-like leaves (hence its common name), which are glossy blue-green and up to 6 in (15 cm) long. The bushy, columnar crown, reaching 60 ft (18 m) or more, is held on a trunk bearing shaggy, orange-brown bark. It does not like to dry out and should be mulched heavily in cultivation. **ZONES 8–9.**

Podocarpus totara

TOTARA, MAHOGANY PINE

Slow growing to a height of 100 ft (30 m), this New Zealand tree is one of the tallest of the genus and can live for much more than 200 years. Its trunk grows to a diameter of 10 ft (3 m) and

Podocarpus macrophyllus 'Maki'

yields a valuable timber. Its dense, sharp-pointed leaves are stiff and bronze green; the bark is reddish brown when fresh, maturing to grayish brown before peeling off in strips. Round crimson fruit, about ½ in (12 mm) in diameter, are carried on red stalks. **'Aureus'** is smaller, growing to 15 ft (5 m) tall, and has a pyramidal form, rich golden yellow foliage and more graceful branches; it can be dwarfed by pruning to suit confined spaces. **ZONES 9–11.**

PODOPHYLLUM

Although the 9 perennials in this genus have a superficial resemblance to trilliums, they are actually in the berberis family. Native to eastern North America, East Asia and the Himalayas, they have stout rhizomes that in early spring sprout large, peltate leaves up to 12 in (30 cm) across. The leaflets are broad with toothed edges and often lobed. Cup-shaped, upward-facing, 6- to 9-petalled flowers soon follow. They are around 2 in (5 cm) wide, white or soft pink and are often followed by red berries up to 2 in (5 cm) across.

CULTIVATION: These essentially woodland plants prefer moist, humus-rich, well-drained soil and dappled shade. Most tolerate hard frosts provided the rootstock is insulated. Propagate from seed or by division.

Podophyllum peltatum

MAY APPLE

This is a popular eastern American wildflower, appearing before the leaves on deciduous forest trees. Deeply lobed, peltate leaves around 12 in (30 cm) long shelter creamy white blossoms resembling single roses, almost hidden under the leaves. Edible yellow fruit follow. It spreads rampantly to form a bold ground cover, so it is not for the small garden. Propagate by dividing the rhizomes in early spring. **ZONES 3–9.**

PODRANEA

PORT ST JOHN CREEPER

This genus contains 2 species of evergreen shrubby climbers, both from South Africa and both very generous throughout summer with their pink or lilac trumpet-shaped flowers. These plants were once classified as bignonias and are related to the Australian pandoreas.

CULTIVATION: Podraneas are subtropical plants and grow strongly in warm, frost-free climates. Grow in part-shade in fertile, moist but well-drained soil. They need stout support and will soon cover a fence or pergola. Water liberally during the growth period. Dense foliage may be pruned in winter and at the beginning of summer. Propagate from cuttings in summer or from seed in spring.

Podranea ricasoliana

syns *Bignonia rosea, Pandorea ricasoliana, Tecoma ricasoliana*

PINK TRUMPET VINE

This climber reaches 12 ft (3.5 m) high on a leathery, twisting stem. Its dark green, fern-like leaves consist of up to 11 finely serrated, lance-shaped to rounded leaflets. From spring until fall (autumn) light pink, funnel-shaped flowers with red markings appear on branched terminal clusters. **ZONES 9–11.**

POGOSTEMON

PATCHOULI

Famed for their aromatic oils, which are used in perfumes and aromatherapy, the patchouli plants are native to tropical East Asia. They are shrubby with upright stems and have large, nettle-like leaves that are roughly heart-shaped with shallowly lobed edges. Their flowers are white, mauve or pink, and are carried on a typical mint-family verticillaster (whorled flower stem).

CULTIVATION: All species have tropical origins and demand warm, frost-free conditions. They prefer moist, humus-rich, well-drained soil in sun or part-shade. Propagate from seed or cuttings.

Podranea ricasoliana

Podocarpus totara

Podophyllum peltatum

Podocarpus matudae var. *reichii*

Podocarpus rumphii

Podocarpus salignus

P

Pogostemon cablin

Native to Indonesia, the Philippines and Malaysia, this is the species most often cultivated. It has narrow leaves and stems. Because it seldom flowers, seeds are rarely available so it is usually grown from cuttings. ***P. heyneanus,*** regarded as a poor substitute for *P. cablin*, has smooth stems and slightly bronze new growth, and flowers reliably. **ZONES 11–12.**

POLEMONIUM

JACOB'S LADDER

This genus of around 25 species of annuals and perennials is distributed over the Arctic and temperate regions of the northern hemisphere. They form clumps of soft, bright green, ferny, pinnate leaves from which emerge upright stems topped with heads of short, tubular, bell- or funnel-shaped flowers usually in white or shades of blue or pink. Completely dormant in winter, they develop quickly in spring and are in flower by early summer.

CULTIVATION: Most species are very frost hardy and easily cultivated in moist, well-drained soil in sun or part-shade. Propagate annuals from seed; perennials from seed or cuttings of young shoots or by division. Some species self-sow freely.

Polemonium boreale

NORTHERN JACOB'S LADDER

Found north of the Arctic tree line, this perennial species has basal leaves made up of 13 to 23, ½ in (12 mm) leaflets. Its flower stems are 3–12 in (8–30 cm) tall, and the blue to purple flowers are about ½ in (12 mm) long. It is a dwarf species for rockeries or alpine troughs. **ZONES 3–9.**

Pogostemon heyneanus

Polemonium 'Brise d'Anjou'

Polemonium 'Brise d'Anjou'

This cultivar of uncertain origin but clearly part of the *Polemonium caeruleum* complex, is distinguished by its neatly variegated foliage—the upper and lower edge of each leaflet has a narrow pale yellow stripe. **ZONES 3–9.**

Polemonium caeruleum

Yellowy orange stamens provide a colorful contrast against the blue of this perennial's bell-shaped flowers when they open in summer. The flowers cluster among lance-shaped leaflets arranged in many pairs like the rungs of a ladder. The plant grows in a clump to a height and spread of up to 24 in (60 cm) or more. The stem is hollow and upstanding. A native of temperate Europe, it suits cooler climates. **ZONES 2–9.**

Polemonium delicatum

SKUNKLEAF JACOB'S LADDER

This native of the Midwest and western USA has leaves less than 4 in (10 cm) long made up of 5 to 11, ½–1 in (12–25 mm) long leaflets. The flowers are also small, blue to violet and open in summer. It is an excellent rockery species. **ZONES 6–9.**

Polemonium pulcherrimum

SKUNKLEAF POLEMONIUM

This perennial species from northwest North America has leaves with up to 37, 1½ in (35 mm) long leaflets. Its flowers open in late spring and summer and are ½ in (12 mm) long, pale blue, violet or white with soft yellow interiors. **ZONES 4–9.**

Polemonium boreale

Polemonium caeruleum

Polemonium delicatum

Polemonium reptans

GREEK VALERIAN, CREEPING POLEMONIUM

This large perennial species from eastern USA forms a 12–24 in (30–60 cm) high foliage clump with leaves composed of 7 to 19 leaflets. The inflorescence is inclined to be lax and the flowers, which are bright blue, are large: ½–1 in (12–25 mm) in diameter. Low-growing and spreading forms have given rise to several cultivars. **ZONES 4–9.**

Polemonium 'Sapphire'

A cultivar probably derived from *Polemonium reptans*, *P.* 'Sapphire' forms a compact clump of foliage with flower stems 12–15 in (30–38 cm) tall. The flowers are light blue and about ½ in (12 mm) wide. **ZONES 4–9.**

POLIANTHES

This is a sun-loving genus of about 13 clump-forming perennials, most of which are native to Mexico and most of which are tender to both frost and dry conditions. The garden-grown species present their leaves from a basal rosette and their flowers on straight, upright stems. The genus includes the well-known tuberose, *Polianthes tuberosa*, which has been grown as a cut flower for centuries and is used extensively in the manufacture of perfumes.

CULTIVATION: These plants do best in open positions in good, well-drained garden loams and with adequate moisture during the summer growing phase. The clumps should be lifted annually and the large bulbs, which once they flower will not flower again, removed. Propagate from seed.

Polianthes tuberosa

TUBEROSE

This species produces a mass of sweetly scented blooms in summer or early fall (autumn). A tall stem up to 3 ft (1 m) in height is topped with a spike bearing clusters of tubular, star-shaped, creamy white flowers. A double variety, **'The Pearl'**, is more widely available than the single. The slender leaves are strap-shaped. **ZONES 9–11.**

POLYALTHIA

This is a genus of tropical trees with large, very glossy, elliptical to lance-shaped leaves. Their narrow-petalled, yellow-green flowers are reminiscent of those of the star magnolia *(Magnolia stellata)* and are followed by clusters of egg-shaped fruits.

CULTIVATION: Plant in moist, well-drained soil and shade when young. Although they will not tolerate frost, they are otherwise tough and adaptable. Propagate from seed or cuttings.

Polemonium 'Sapphire'

Polyalthia longifolia

Polyalthia longifolia

INDIAN MAST TREE

Originating from Sri Lanka, this has become one of the most popular park and avenue trees of tropical Asia, thriving in monsoonal regions such as Thailand and southern India. Growing to about 50 ft (15 m) tall, it has a striking narrowly conical or columnar habit which is sometimes almost pole-like. A curtain of long, glossy green leaves with slightly wavy edges conceals all but the base of the trunk. New foliage flushes are at first yellowish then bronzy green. Small greenish yellow flowers are borne in the wet season (summer) but are hidden under the foliage; the small plum-like fruits are eaten only by animals such as fruit-bats. **ZONES 11–12.**

POLYARRHENA

This South African genus is closely allied to the better known *Felicia* and consists of only 4 species of perennials and subshrubs, all restricted in the wild to southwestern Cape Province. They have smallish, toothed leaves and the daisy-like flowerheads are borne singly at branch ends; these have ray florets that are white or purple-flushed on the upper sides, but a dull reddish color beneath.

CULTIVATION: They require a warm, sunny position and well-drained soil that is not too rich. After flowering has finished, the plants can be cut back to improve shape, but not too hard. Propagate from seed or cuttings.

Polyarrhena reflexa

This species is a rather untidy, straggling subshrub that grows to 3 ft (1 m) tall. Its leaves are lance-shaped and slightly curled. They have toothed edges. In summer it has small white, sometimes flushed pink, daisy flowers with red undersides. **ZONES 9–11.**

POLYGALA

MILKWORT, SENECA, SNAKEROOT

This genus consists of more than 500 species from warm areas all over the world. They include annuals, perennials and some shrubs, only a few of which are cultivated. Some species were used by the ancient Greeks to stimulate the secretion of milk in lactating mothers. The 2 biggest sepals of the pea-like flowers are rose-purple, petal-like and known as wings. The keel terminates in a crown-like tuft that is characteristic of polygalas. The flowers are carried in racemes and are followed by a 2-chambered seed pod.
CULTIVATION: They need light, well-drained soil in a sunny to part-shaded spot. They are suitable for pot culture. To keep the growth dense, prune any straggly stems after the main flowering has finished. Propagate from seed in spring or early summer, or from cuttings in late summer.

Polygala calcarea

This creeping, evergreen perennial from western Europe develops into a small, wiry stemmed shrub about 8 in (20 cm) tall. It has small, narrow leaves and 6- to 20-flowered racemes of blue or white flowers. **'Lillet'** has very bright blue flowers. **ZONES 7–9.**

Polyarrhena reflexa

Polygala chamaebuxus

Polygala chamaebuxus

BASTARD BOX

This evergreen shrub, a native of alpine Europe, grows to 8 in (20 cm) tall with a spread of 15 in (38 cm). Racemes of small yellow and white flowers appear in spring and early summer. It has tiny, oval, dark green leaves and is fully frost hardy. ***Polygala chamaebuxus* var. *grandiflora*** has larger, more obviously pea-like flowers with purple wings and yellow petals. **ZONES 6–9.**

Polygala × dalmaisiana

syn. *Polygala myrtifolia* var. *grandiflora* of gardens

SWEET PEA SHRUB

A hybrid of 2 South American species, *Polygala myrtifolia* and ***P. oppositifolia,*** this shrub bears soft magenta flowers almost non-stop in mild regions. It forms a mound 3–5 ft (1–1.5 m) tall and wide, and has slender, light green leaves. It may become bare at the base. It will tolerate shearing to encourage more dense growth. **ZONES 9–11.**

Polygala myrtifolia

SEPTEMBER BUSH

This evergreen shrub from South Africa grows to 6 ft (1.8 m) tall with an upright habit. Its many twiggy branches are covered with rounded to oval, soft, dull green leaves, 1 in (25 mm) long. The greenish white, 1 in (25 mm) diameter flowers with purple hues occur in large clusters near the branch tips for several months from late winter. This shrub can cope with light frost, but does best in subtropical areas. It may become invasive. **ZONES 9–11.**

Polygala virgata

PURPLE BROOM

This fast-growing 6 ft (1.8 m) tall shrub bears graceful clusters of deep purplish pink, winged flowers. The narrow, lance-like leaves are alternate and simple, up to

Polygala calcarea

Polygala × dalmaisiana

Polygala × dalmaisiana

Polygonatum falcatum

2 in (5 cm) long. It is self-seeding and small plants often appear around the parent plant after the first flowering season; these transplant easily. It has an open habit and is wind resistant. Established plants tolerate dry conditions and some frost. **ZONES 9–11.**

POLYGONATUM

SOLOMON'S SEAL

The 30 or so species in this genus of forest-floor perennials are distributed all over the temperate zones of the northern hemisphere. The most likely explanation of the common name is that the scars left on the creeping rhizomes after the flowering stems die off in fall (autumn) are thought to resemble the 6-pointed star associated with kings Solomon and David. King Solomon is thought to have first discovered the medicinal qualities of the plants, which are credited with healing wounds; the distilled sap of the rhizomes is still used in the cosmetics industry. The plants' fresh greenery and delicate white flowers make them favorites for planting in woodland gardens.
CULTIVATION: They need rich, moist soil and a shady spot. Cut back to the rhizome in fall (autumn) as they are completely dormant in winter. Propagate from seed or by division of the rhizomes in spring or fall.

Polygonatum biflorum

SMALL SOLOMAN'S SEAL

This very frost-hardy, tuberous wood plant is native to southern Canada and eastern USA. It has arching stems that bear many slightly scented, pendulous, green-tipped, tubular, white flowers beneath its glaucous foliage. The foliage clump grows to about 3 ft (1 m) high and may eventually spread to several yards wide. **ZONES 3–9.**

Polygala virgata

Polygonatum multiflorum

Polygonatum × hybridum

Polygonatum falcatum

With stems to 3 ft (1 m) long and long, rather narrow leaves, this Japanese and Korean species is not as attractive as some of the others. Its flowers tend to be small and are carried singly rather than in small clusters. The stems are red tinted. **ZONES 6–9.**

Polygonatum × hybridum

This hybrid species does best in cool to cold areas. In spring, the white, green-tipped, tubular flowers hang down from the drooping 3 ft (1 m) stems at the leaf axils. It is difficult to grow from seed. **ZONES 6–9.**

Polygonatum multiflorum

This Eurasian species has arching 3 ft (1 m) stems with large, broad leaves that point upwards very distinctly. Its flowers are cream with green tips in 2- to 5-flowered clusters. It has vigorous rhizomes and can be invasive. Although often found on limestone soil in the wild, it does not seem fussy about soil type. **ZONES 4–9.**

Polygonatum odoratum

Polystichum proliferum

Polygonatum odoratum

From Europe, Russia, Japan and the Caucasus, this perennial to 3 ft (1 m) tall has long, hairless leaves in 2 rows. The fragrant, tubular, white flowers have green tips and appear in late spring and early summer. They are followed by rounded black fruit. **ZONES 4–9.**

POLYPODIUM

CALIFORNIA POLYPODY, POLYPODY

This widespread, mainly temperate northern hemisphere fern genus includes some 75 species. They may be epiphytic or terrestrial, and a few species grow on rocks. They have scaly, red-brown, creeping rhizomes and long-stemmed, light to mid-green, pinnate or bipinnate fronds usually less than 30 in (75 cm) long. Inclined to produce cristate fronds and other unusual forms, they were very popular with Victorian collectors.
CULTIVATION: Hardiness varies considerably with the species, otherwise they are easily grown in any moist, well-drained soil in dappled shade. Additional humus promotes lush foliage. Propagate by division or by sowing spores.

Polypodium californicum

CALIFORNIA ROCK FERN

This evergreen, epiphytic fern is native to California and grows along rock ledges in humus-rich soil. Emerging from low, creeping rhizomes, the fronds reach heights of 12 in (30 cm) and are deeply incised. Grow this fern in rock crevices filled with humus and water during dry spells. **ZONES 8–11.**

Polypodium scouleri

LEATHER-LEAF FERN, COAST POLYPODY

A native of coastal western North America, this species has leathery fronds

Polystichum munitum

Polystichum retrorsopaleaceum

around 15 in (38 cm) long. The fronds are made up of up to 14 pairs of stiff leaflets and are on wiry 4 in (10 cm) stems. It is a tough, sun-tolerant species that thrives in rockeries. **ZONES 9–10**

Polypodium virginianum

AMERICAN ROCK FERN, ROCK POLYPODY

Native to eastern and central North America, this moderately frost-hardy, evergreen fern forms colonies atop rocks, in rock crevices and along woodland banks. Creeping rhizomes produce glossy green, deeply incised, leathery fronds that grow to 15 in (38 cm) tall. Bright orange spore masses are borne in rows along each side of the mid-veins of the lobes. **ZONES 2–9.**

Polypodium vulgare

COMMON POLYPODY, ADDER'S FERN

This species, widespread in North America, Europe, Africa and Asia, has a rather thick, creeping rhizome that spreads over rocks and tree trunks as well as growing on the ground. Its fronds, evergreen and around 12 in (30 cm) long, are borne on wiry stems of a similar length. The pinnae (leaflets) are sometimes toothed and may become crested. Cultivars with crested fronds, such as **'Bifidum'** and **'Cristatum'**, are popular as both garden and container plants. **ZONES 3–9.**

POLYSCIAS

PANAX, ARALIA

From tropical Asia, Australia and the Pacific, these 100 species of evergreen shrubs and trees are cultivated for their attractive, aromatic foliage. The leaves are usually pinnate with 2 or more pairs of leaflets; the small flowers are borne in branched panicles up to 24 in (60 cm) long. In tropical climates they are appealing outdoor accent plants or they can be grown as hedges. In cooler climates they make useful house plants.
CULTIVATION: They require warm-temperate to tropical climates and plenty of water. They prefer well-drained, humus-rich soil and part-shade. Prune leggy stems in spring. Propagate from seed in spring or cuttings in summer.

Polyscias filicifolia

FERN-LEAF ARALIA

This frost-tender shrub from the Pacific Islands grows to 15 ft (4.5 m) tall with a spread of 6 ft (1.8 m). Its bright green leaves are leathery, deeply dissected with prominent purple veining, and up to 12 in (30 cm) long. The plant is at its best when young as the stems tend to grow straggly. **ZONES 11–12.**

Polyscias fruticosa

MING ARALIA

Probably originating in the western Pacific region, this 25 ft (8 m) tall, large shrub or small tree has very finely cut, bright green often red-tinted, pinnate to tripinnate leaves up to 30 in (75 cm) long. The individual cream flowers are tiny, but are borne on 6–8 in (15–20 cm) panicles at the stem tips. It is a very graceful plant best trained to a canopy with either single or multiple trunks. **ZONES 11–12.**

Polyscias guilfoylei

GERANIUM-LEAF ARALIA, WILD COFFEE

Native to Polynesia, this sparsely branched shrub grows up to 20 ft (6 m) has large, fern-like, dark green leaves composed of serrated leaflets that spread to 18 in (45 cm) and develop white margins. Prune only to remove damaged foliage. **ZONES 11–12.**

Polyscias scutellaria

This many-branched shrub has glossy green, round leaves with prominent midribs and 24 in (60 cm) flower panicles. Growing to 15 ft (4.5 m), it spreads to 6 ft (1.8 m). Decorative in the garden, it is also excellent for growing in a container. **ZONES 11–12.**

POLYSTICHUM

SHIELD FERN

This genus of 200 species of ground- or rock-dwelling ferns is found worldwide in anything from tropical to subantarctic regions. Their fronds are either pinnate or simple and ribbon-shaped. They are known as shield ferns because groups of the spores are covered with a fragile, shield-shaped growth. Ornamental species have become very popular.
CULTIVATION: They prefer part- to full shade and fertile, humus-rich, well-drained soil. The frond tips usually bear an abundance of small buds that become plantlets in their own right when conditions are favorable. Otherwise, propagate by sowing spores in summer or by division of the rhizomes in spring.

Polystichum acrostichoides

CHRISTMAS FERN

From the North American woodlands, this terrestrial fern grows from tufted crowns arising from slowly spreading rhizomes. The leathery, evergreen fronds emerge as silvery white 'fiddleheads' in early spring and mature to lustrous, dark green, pinnate leaves 12–36 in (30–90 cm) tall. It is excellent for naturalizing among low to medium shrubs. **ZONES 3–9.**

Polystichum aculeatum

This European species has short, brown, scaly stems and stiff, slightly arching, glossy deep green, 12–30 in (30–75 cm) long fronds. The young growth is slightly yellow. It forms a clump around 24 in (60 cm) high and is a tough, undemanding plant for woodlands or near water. **ZONES 5–9.**

Polystichum munitum

WESTERN SWORD FERN

Resembling *Polystichum acrostichoides* but much taller, the 3–5 ft (1–1.5 m) fronds of this species are dimorphic: the fertile fronds stand erect at the outer extremity of the sterile fronds. Native to moist, coniferous woods of coastal North America, it is well suited to cool, shady, moist garden sites in humus-rich soil. **ZONES 5–9.**

Polystichum proliferum

MOTHER SHIELD FERN

From southeastern Australia, this shield fern is one of the most reliable and easy to grow. It grows to 3 ft (1 m) tall and is longlasting in tubs or the ground. **ZONES 5–9.**

Polystichum retrorsopaleaceum

This attractive species from Japan has a compact rhizome and rosettes of arching apple-green pinnate fronds, the primary leaflets in turn dissected into neat oblong segments. The central stalk of each frond is clothed in conspicuous brown scales. The plant grows to around 24 in (60 cm) high, with a greater spread. **ZONES 8–10.**

Polystichum richardii

syn. ***Polystichum vestitum* var. *richardii***

COMMON SHIELD FERN, PIKOPIKO, TUTOKE

Originating in New Zealand and Fiji, this robust, variable fern has a squat, upright trunk. The deep green, woody fronds, up to 12 in (30 cm) long, have a paler underside and are composed of bluish to sallow green leaflets. This adaptable species will grow in poor soil and full sun or shade. **ZONES 9–11.**

Polystichum setiferum

SOFT SHIELD FERN

Native to the damp woodlands and valleys of Europe, this large fern has bright green, soft, bipinnate fronds up to 4 ft (1.2 m) long. The central bud head and frond stems have a dense covering of large brown scales. Easily grown it is popular in ferneries and gardens. **'Divisilobum Densum Erectum'** is a form in which each leaflet is itself bipinnate, creating a dense feather duster of a frond. **'Plumosum Bevis'** has elongated, sometimes crested-tipped fronds with widely spaced leaflets creating an airy, open effect. **ZONES 7–9.**

Polystichum setiferum

Pomaderris aspera

Pomaderris prunifolia

POMADERRIS

These woody evergreen shrubs and small trees are natives of Australia and New Zealand. Only a few of the 50 species have become garden subjects. They are most spectacular in late spring when large, feathery masses of small cream, yellow or pale green flowers cover the plants. The foliage consists of alternate hairy green leaves. The twigs and branches are also hairy.
CULTIVATION: They need well-drained, even gravelly soil and shelter from strong winds. Trim to keep a compact shape. They cope with occasional light frosts if grown in a sheltered spot, but may need a greenhouse in colder areas. Propagate from seed or cuttings.

Pomaderris apetala
NEW ZEALAND HAZEL, TAINUI

This erect, evergreen shrub is grown mainly for its foliage—large, wrinkled, prominently veined leaves. Less significant are the long clusters of green flowers it bears in spring. It grows to a height of 15 ft (4.5 m) with a spread of 6 ft (1.8 m). **ZONES 9–10.**

Pomaderris aspera
HAZEL POMADERRIS

Native to shady gullies in eastern Australia, this species grows into an open shrub 15 ft (4.5 m) tall with a spread of about half that. In spring, tiny greenish white flowers mass together into large plumes. The oval leaves have conspicuous veins and are about 4 in (10 cm) long. Keep moist as it does not tolerate dry conditions. **ZONES 8–10.**

Pomaderris kumeraho
KUMARAHOU, GOLDEN TAINUI, GUMDIGGER'S SOAP

This New Zealand shrub was used by the Maoris to treat asthma and other chest problems. It grows to 10 ft (3 m) tall and up to 6 ft (1.8 m) in spread. Its slender branches carry bluish green, wrinkled, oval leaves that are 4 in (10 cm) long and densely hairy underneath. In early spring, it bears masses of tiny yellow flowers in fluffy clusters up to 8 in (20 cm) across. **ZONES 8–10.**

Pomaderris prunifolia

Occurring on rather dry rocky hills of southeastern Australia, this species makes an erect, open shrub up to 10 ft (3 m) tall. It has dense rust-colored hairs on its young shoots. The elliptical leaves are only 1–2 in (2.5–5 cm) long, glossy, deep green above with conspicuously impressed primary veins, and felted beneath with slightly brownish hairs. In spring, it bears profuse small, tight clusters of cream flowers. A prostrate form has recently come into cultivation, making a fine rock-garden plant for mild climates. **ZONES 9–11.**

Poncirus trifoliata

PONCIRUS
TRIFOLIATE ORANGE, BITTER ORANGE

This genus, closely related to *Citrus*, consists of a single species—a small, fast-growing, deciduous tree originally from China and Korea that looks most attractive in winter without its leaves. Although mainly used as a rootstock for oranges and some other *Citrus* species, it is an attractive plant in flower. It also makes an impenetrably thorny hedge.
CULTIVATION: This very frost-hardy plant prefers full sun and fertile, well-drained soil. Shelter it from cold winds. Propagate from seed or cuttings in summer.

Poncirus trifoliata

This species has flattened stems, long, stout spines and trifoliate leaves. It bears white, scented, 5-petalled flowers that open before or with the new growth in spring. These are followed by yellow fruit that become quite fragrant when ripe, but are inedible. Prune in early summer when used in hedging. **ZONES 5–11.**

PONTEDERIA
PICKEREL WEED

The 5 or so aquatic perennials in this genus are all native to river shallows in North and South America. They have distinctive, lance-shaped leaves and bell-shaped, usually blue flowers in terminal spikes. The Latin name has nothing to do with ponds; it honors Guilio Pontedera (1688–1757), who was a professor of botany at the University of Padua.
CULTIVATION: Easily grown, pickerel weed flourishes in almost any climate, from cold to subtropical. Plant it in full sun in up to 10 in (25 cm) of water. Only the spent flower stems need pruning, to encourage successive batches of flowers from spring to fall (autumn). Propagate from seed or by division in spring.

Pontederia cordata

Poncirus trifoliata

Pontederia cordata
PICKEREL RUSH

This species grows from Nova Scotia to Florida, USA. A very frost-hardy, marginal water plant, it grows to 30 in (75 cm) with an 18 in (45 cm) spread. Its tapered, heart-shaped leaves are dark green and shiny. In summer it produces intense blue flowers in dense, terminal spikes. **ZONES 3–10.**

POPULUS
POPLAR, ASPEN, COTTONWOOD

This genus consists of some 35 species of fast-growing, deciduous trees all from temperate regions of the northern hemisphere. Many blaze with yellow or gold in fall (autumn). Poplars are widely cultivated in parks and large gardens and as avenue trees, windbreaks and screens. Their soft white timber is used for making matches and packing cases. Male and female flowers, borne on separate trees, are hanging catkins and appear in late winter and early spring before the leaves, which are set on long, flexible stalks. The

Pomaderris kumeraho

fruits are capsules containing seeds covered with cotton-like hairs. Most species are short lived—60 years or so. **CULTIVATION:** Plant in deep, moist, well-drained, fertile soil in full sun; they dislike arid conditions. Many species have vigorous root systems notorious for blocking drains and lifting paving, and so are not suitable for small gardens; some species sucker freely from the roots. Propagate from cuttings in winter.

Populus alba

WHITE POPLAR, SILVER POPLAR

From Europe and the Middle East, this species reaches 80 ft (24 m). The leaves have 3 to 5 lobes, and their undersides are covered with white, downy hairs that give a silvery effect in the wind. The leaves turn gold in fall (autumn). In spring the tree carries reddish catkins; the bark is grayish white. It can withstand low moisture levels, salt winds and poor alkaline soils. Because of its suckering roots it grows best in open country. **'Pyramidalis'** is conical, and **'Richardii'** bears yellowish leaves. **ZONES 2–10.**

Populus × canescens

A natural hybrid between *Populus alba* and *P. tremula*, this tree from central Europe, Russia and Iran grows to over 100 ft (30 m) tall. It has a rounded head and rough grayish yellow bark. Its leaves resemble those of *P. alba*, being roughly heart-shaped, around 4 in (10 cm) long with gray felting on the undersides. **ZONES 4–10.**

Populus deltoides

EASTERN COTTONWOOD, EASTERN POPLAR

An upright, broad-headed tree from eastern North America growing to 100 ft (30 m), this species is less likely to sucker than other poplars. It is short lived and brittle in high winds. The triangular, glossy green leaves are up to 8 in (20 cm) long and are coarsely toothed; the bark is gray and deeply corrugated. The long catkins are yellow and red. The common name cottonwood refers to the copious quantities of fluff that surround the seeds. This is a tough tree for extreme inland conditions. ***Populus deltoides* var. *monilifera***, the northern cottonwood, bears slightly smaller leaves with the toothed margins more sharply delineated. **ZONES 3–11.**

Populus nigra

Populus deltoides

Populus deltoides

Populus maximowiczii

Populus alba 'Pyramidalis'

Populus fremontii

FREMONT COTTONWOOD, ALAMILLO, WESTERN COTTONWOOD

Growing quite fast to a height of about 100 ft (30 m), this tree from western USA carries a fairly narrow, rounded crown. The $2\frac{1}{2}$ in (6 cm) long leaves are triangular and turn yellow late in the season. The catkins are also yellow. The tree adapts well to most soils and conditions and is tolerant of both frost and dry conditions in cool or mild climates. **ZONES 5–10.**

Populus lasiocarpa

CHINESE NECKLACE POPLAR

Growing more slowly than some members of the genus, this poplar is less inclined to sucker. Usually seen in large gardens and parks, it reaches heights of about 30 ft (10 m) although larger specimens have been known. It carries very large, leathery leaves that are veined in red and are held on red stems with a light green upper side and silvery underside. The leaves can become disfigured when exposed to hot winds. Fat yellow catkins are displayed in spring. **ZONES 7–9.**

Populus lasiocarpa

Populus tremula

Populus maximowiczii

JAPANESE POPLAR

Over 100 ft (30 m) tall when mature, this species from Japan, Korea and northeast China has a broad crown and deeply fissured gray bark. Its young growth is red with fine hairs and the leaves are around 4 in (10 cm) long with toothed edges and pale green undersides. They have a somewhat wrinkled surface with small hairs. **ZONES 4–9.**

Populus nigra

BLACK POPLAR

Its height of 100 ft (30 m) and its suckering habit make this tree unsuitable for small gardens. It has dark, deeply furrowed bark. Its large, diamond-shaped leaves, bronze when young, become bright green and then yellow in fall (autumn); held on thin stalks, they give an impression of constant movement. The male tree produces black catkins in mid-winter. Best known of the many cultivars is **'Italica'** (syn. *Populus pyramidalis*), the Lombardy poplar, a male cultivar that is popular for its narrow, columnar shape and fast growth. **ZONES 6–10.**

Populus tremula

COMMON ASPEN, EUROPEAN ASPEN

A vigorous, spreading tree from Europe suitable for cool climates, this species grows to about 50 ft (15 m). The rounded, toothed leaves are bronze-red when young, gray-green in maturity and turn a clear yellow in fall (autumn). They are held on slim, flat stems and quiver and rustle in the slightest breeze. Long gray catkins are carried in late winter. In large gardens and parks constant mowing will control its suckering habit. **ZONES 1–9.**

Populus tremuloides
QUAKING ASPEN, AMERICAN ASPEN

Fast growing to 50 ft (15 m), this spreading tree from western North America thrives in cool climates and looks best when given plenty of space and planted in groves. The bark is smooth and gray with silvery markings; the glossy, dark green leaves are finely toothed, small and fluttery—hence the common name. The leaves turn golden before dropping in fall (autumn). **ZONES 1–9.**

Populus trichocarpa
BLACK COTTONWOOD, WESTERN BALSAM

A conical, dense tree from western USA, this species can reach 100 ft (30 m) but is usually smaller. This is a balsam poplar with an especially fragrant, young wood. The leaves, which turn yellow in fall (autumn), are oval, glossy and dark green and have white undersides. The tree will endure maritime winds. It is said to be prone to canker in some places and can prove short lived in mild climates. **ZONES 7–10.**

Populus yunnanensis
YUNNAN POPLAR

From Yunnan in southwestern China, this species grows into a broad tree 80 ft (24 m) tall. It bears bright green, triangular leaves 6 in (15 cm) long with reddish stalks and midribs and a whitish underside. The twigs are also reddish. It does not freely sucker and is resistant to poplar rust, a disease that causes premature leaf fall. It adapts to a wide range of soils and copes better with warmer and drier conditions than do other poplars. **ZONES 7–10.**

PORTEA

This bromeliad genus has 7 species of rock or ground dwellers native to Brazil. Generally they are large rosette-forming perennials with stiff-spined green leaves that vary in height from 30 in (75 cm) to over 6 ft (1.8 m) when in flower.

Populus tremuloides

Portulaca oleracea

CULTIVATION: Plants enjoy bright light and warm conditions. Plant in humus-rich, loamy soil. Some species are cold sensitive. Propagate from offsets or seed.

Portea petropolitana
syns *Aechmea petropolitana, Portea gardneri, Streptocalyx podantha*

This is a large species with varying lengths of branches and flower stalks. The plant is stemless, with thick, heavily spined leaves, and reaches over 3 ft (1 m) in height when in bloom. Narrow, blue-violet flowers are $1\frac{1}{2}$ in (35 mm) long and the inflorescences upright in length to 15 in (38 cm) long. **ZONES 9–12.**

PORTULACA

There are about 100 species of semi-succulent annuals or perennials in this genus, indigenous to the warm, dry regions of the world. The fleshy leaves vary in color from white to green or red, but it is for their flowers that they are grown—cup-shaped, white, yellow, apricot, pink, purple or scarlet in color, and resembling roses in form.
CULTIVATION: They are easily grown in all climates. In cooler areas they should not be planted out until the danger of frost has passed. Because they are plants of the deserts they need sun, well-drained soil and only occasional watering. Propagate from seed in spring or cuttings in summer. Check for aphids.

Portulaca grandiflora
ROSE MOSS, SUN PLANT

Native to South America and one of the few annual succulents, this low-growing plant reaches 8 in (20 cm) high and spreads to 6 in (15 cm). It has small, lance-shaped, fleshy, bright green leaves like beads on their reddish stems. Its large, open flowers, usually double and borne in summer, are 3 in (8 cm) wide and come in bright colors including yellow, pink, red or orange. The flowers

Populus trichocarpa

Portulaca grandiflora

Portulacaria afra

Portulacaria afra 'Variegata'

close at night and on cloudy days. It is suitable as a ground cover or in a rockery or border. **ZONES 10–11.**

Portulaca oleracea
PURSLANE

The oldest member of the genus in cultivation, this is a sprawling annual with small, fleshy leaves that are not in the least decorative. An annoying weed in many warm climates, it has a long history of being eaten as a salad vegetable; it reputedly has a high vitamin content. **ZONES 9–11.**

PORTULACARIA
JADE PLANT, ELEPHANT BUSH, ELEPHANT'S FOOD

The single member of this genus is a succulent, evergreen shrub with many branches, often horizontal or twisted. It may reach a height of 12 ft (3.5 m) but looks like a twisted dwarf tree even when very young. In its native hot, dry habitat of southern Africa it bears tiny pink flower clusters, followed by insignificant, pinkish, 3-cornered berries. In dry parts of South Africa the shrub is used to feed livestock and game, hence some of its common names.
CULTIVATION: It adapts well to a wide range of soils and climates. The soil should be well-drained and kept fairly dry, especially during winter. This shrub thrives by the sea. It will grow in sun or shade and tolerates dry conditions but only the lightest frost. Propagate from cuttings in summer and from seed.

Portulacaria afra

The reddish to purplish branches on this species carry opposite pairs of lime green, round to oval, silky smooth leaves, $\frac{1}{2}$ in (12 mm) across, each leaf set directly into the stem or into short spur-like twigs. The tiny pink flowers and berries are rare on cultivated plants. It makes an interesting, low-maintenance rockery and tub plant, and is also a good subject for bonsai. **'Tricolor'** has green, cream and pink tones, and **'Variegata'** has green leaves edged with cream. **ZONES 9–11.**

POTAMOGETON

This genus, with representatives virtually worldwide, is composed of 80 to 100 species of aquatic perennials. Their roots are anchored in the pond bottom and the foliage may be submerged or floating or both, depending on the water's depth. The foliage varies in size and shape depending on the species. The leaves of submerged types are usually larger than those of floating species. The most common species have narrow, elliptical leaves that are light olive green, often tinted red in sunlight. The short flower spikes have tiny white or cream flowers, either submerged or above the surface.
CULTIVATION: They are easily grown in full sun in any pond or slow-moving stream provided the roots have soil to anchor them. Frost hardiness and depth requirements vary. Propagate from cuttings in late spring or early summer.

Potentilla anserina

Potentilla cuneata

Potentilla fruticosa

Potentilla fruticosa 'Tangerine'

Potentilla fruticosa 'Goldstar'

Potentilla fruticosa 'Maanleys'

Potentilla fruticosa 'Red Ace'

Potamogeton crispus
CURLED PONDWEED

Native to Europe and naturalized in the USA, this species has submerged leaves up to 6 in (15 cm) long. They are bronze green and when young are flat with toothed edges. As they mature they curl and twist. **ZONES 6–11.**

Potamogeton natans
BROAD-LEAFED PONDWEED

From Europe and northern USA, this species has long, unbranched stems and both floating and submerged foliage. The submerged leave are small and narrow but the floating leaves are 4–6 in (10–15 cm) long with equally long stems. **ZONES 6–11.**

POTENTILLA
CINQUEFOIL

This genus of 500 or so perennials, some annuals and biennials, and deciduous shrubs is indigenous mainly to the northern hemisphere, from temperate to arctic regions. Many have 5-parted leaves (hence the common name cinquefoil), and range from only 1 in (25 mm) or so tall to about 18 in (45 cm). They bear clusters of 1 in (25 mm), rounded, bright flowers in profusion through spring and summer. Some species are used medicinally—the root bark of one species is said to stop nose bleeds and even internal bleeding.

CULTIVATION: Plant all species in well-drained, fertile soil. Lime does not upset them. Although the species all thrive in full sun in temperate climates, the colors of pink, red and orange cultivars will be brighter if protected from very strong sun. Perennials are generally frost hardy. Propagate by division in spring, or from seed or by division in fall (autumn); propagate shrubs from seed in fall or from cuttings in summer.

Potentilla alba

This low, spreading perennial from Europe rarely exceeds 4 in (10 cm) high. It has hand-shaped basal leaves with 5 leaflets, each up to 2½ in (6 cm) long. The young growth has a dense covering of fine hairs that gives it a silver sheen. The white flowers are 1 in (25 mm) wide, in clusters of up to 5 blooms. **ZONES 5–9.**

Potentilla anserina
GOOSE GRASS, SILVERWEED, WILD TANSY

This trailing herbaceous species occurs widely round the northern hemisphere and grows to 8 in (20 cm) high from a central rosette of long, compound leaves, soft green above with silvery undersides. In spring 5-petalled yellow flowers are borne on slender stems. This is a good ground cover for a sunny bank, but it can become invasive. **ZONES 5–9.**

Potentilla atrosanguinea

One of the larger perennial species, this Himalayan native has flower stems up to 3 ft (1 m) tall. The leaves are trifoliate with 2–3 in (5–8 cm) long leaflets and the foliage has a dense covering of short hairs, particularly the undersides, which are silvery. The flowers are deep blood red, up to 1½ in (35 mm) wide in small clusters. **'Etna'** is a low grower with very silvery leaves. **ZONES 5–9.**

Potentilla aurea

Native to the Alps and Pyrenees of Europe, *Potentilla aurea* is a prostrate perennial spreads to about 12 in (30 cm) wide. It has hand-shaped leaves with 5 small leaflets. It is not a heavy flowering plant but the little golden yellow blooms are very attractive. They appear in loose clusters from early summer. **ZONES 5–9.**

Potentilla cuneata

This Himalayan perennial develops a woody base and can form a rather upright mound or be a low, spreading plant. Its leaves are trifoliate, up to 6 in (15 cm) long, leathery, deep green above and blue-green below. The flowers are bright yellow, 1 in (25 mm) wide and carried singly. **ZONES 5–9.**

Potentilla fruticosa
BUSH CINQUEFOIL

This dense, deciduous shrub, found in many parts of the temperate northern hemisphere, grows to over 3 ft (1 m) tall with a spread of 4 ft (1.2 m) or more. From early summer to fall (autumn) garden varieties bear 1 in (25 mm) wide flowers in shades from white to yellow and orange, the orange ones often fading to salmon pink in the sunshine. The flat, mid-green leaves comprise 5 or 7 narrow elliptical leaflets arranged palmately. **'Tangerine'** has golden orange flowers; **'Goldstar'** is an upright shrub with large, deep yellow flowers; **'Maanleys'** grows up to 4 ft (1.2 m) tall with blue-green foliage and pale yellow flowers; and **'Red Ace'**, a low grower with small leaves and bright orange-red flowers, is inclined to be untidy and short lived. **'Abbotswood'** is a spreading, 24 in (60 cm) tall shrub with white flowers; **'Beesii'** grows to 24 in (60 cm) tall with very silvery leaves and bright yellow flowers; **'Daydawn'** is a 3 ft (1 m) tall shrub with salmon-pink flowers; **'Elizabeth'** is a dense, bushy, 3 ft (1 m) shrub with bright yellow flowers; **'Goldfinger'** is a low grower with narrow, bright green leaflets and very bright yellow flowers; and **'Primrose Beauty'**, up to 3 ft (1 m) tall and 5 ft (1.5 m) wide, has primrose-yellow flowers very reminiscent of a small wild rose. **ZONES 2–9.**

Potentilla 'Gibson's Scarlet'

This red-flowered perennial is one of several attractive summer-flowering hybrids. It grows to18 in (45 cm) tall and wide with somewhat floppy stems. The foliage is a soft green, with each leaf divided into 3 leaflets. **ZONES 5–9.**

Potentilla megalantha

This perennial from Japan forms a mound of foliage about 12 in (30 cm)

Potentilla fruticosa 'Beesii'

Potentilla fruticosa 'Elizabeth'

Potentilla fruticosa 'Goldfinger'

Potentilla fruticosa 'Primrose Beauty'

Potentilla nepalensis

Potentilla nepalensis 'Miss Willmott'

Potentilla neumanniana

Potentilla × *tonguei*

wide. Its leaves are trifoliate with hairy undersides. Its $1\frac{1}{2}$ in (35 mm) wide, bright yellow flowers are carried singly and are produced in summer. **ZONES 5–9.**

Potentilla 'Monsieur Rouillard'

The flowers borne on this cultivar throughout summer are saucer-shaped and double, in deep red hues. Its dark green leaves resemble those of a strawberry plant. This perennial matures into a clump 18 in (45 cm) in height and spread. **ZONES 5–9.**

Potentilla nepalensis

A profusion of flowers in shades of pink or apricot with cherry red centers appears throughout summer on the slim branching stems of this Himalayan perennial. With bright green, strawberry-like leaves, this species grows to 12 in (30 cm) or more high and twice that in width. **'Miss Willmott'** is an 18 in (45 cm) high cultivar with deep cerise-red flowers. **ZONES5–9.**

Potentilla neumanniana
syn. ***Potentilla verna***

This herbaceous, mat-forming perennial grows to 4 in (10 cm) in height. Golden yellow flowers to 1 in (25 mm) are borne from spring onwards. **ZONES 5–9.**

Potentilla recta

This perennial has hairy stems up to 18 in (45 cm) long. Its leaves are hand-shaped with 5 to 7, $1\frac{1}{2}$ in (35 mm) long leaflets. Its flowers are 1 in (25 mm) wide, bright yellow and produced very freely from early summer. **ZONES 4–9.**

Potentilla sterilis
BARREN STRAWBERRY

Now rather rare in the wild, this European perennial is usually found growing in grassy meadows and occurs at quite high altitudes. It closely resembles the common garden strawberry, with deep green trifoliate leaves and small white flowers, though it is smaller and does not produce edible fruit. **ZONES 4–9.**

Potentilla × *tonguei*

This hybrid derives from the Himalayan *Potentilla nepalensis* crossed with ***P. anglica***, a European species. It is a sprawling perennial with attractive leaves and abundant 1 in (25 mm) wide, tangerine-colored flowers in summer. If spent flower stalks are trimmed, the plant usually responds with more flowers. **ZONES 5–9.**

Potentilla 'William Rollison'

This perennial bears its semi-double orange-red flowers in summer. It reaches a height of 18 in (45 cm) and spread of 24 in (60 cm). **ZONES 5–9.**

PRATIA

This genus, closely allied to *Lovelia*, includes 20 species of evergreen perennials native to New Zealand, Australia, Africa, Asia and South America. They have multiple branching stems and little toothed leaves. A profusion of starry flowers is followed by globular berries. Most are carpet forming and make excellent rockery specimens, but tend to overrun the garden.

CULTIVATION: Ranging from very frost hardy to frost hardy, these plants generally enjoy damp but porous soil, total sun or part-shade and protection from the elements. Water liberally during the growth period and sparingly in winter. Some species are susceptible to slugs if over-moist. Propagate by division or from seed in fall (autumn).

Pratia angulata

This very frost-hardy New Zealand creeper has wide, rounded, deep green leaves with roughly serrated edges. In spring white starry flowers with purple veins appear in the leaf axils, followed in fall (autumn) by globular, reddish purple fruit. This species tolerates full sun and enjoys damp soil. **ZONES 7–10.**

Pratia nummularia

This Asian species has small, rounded to heart-shaped leaves with toothed edges. Its flowers are less than $\frac{1}{2}$ in (12 mm) wide, creamy yellow, pink or mauve with a purple lower lip and are followed by red berries. **ZONES 9–11.**

Pratia pedunculata

From eastern Australia, this small-leafed, low-growing species makes a good ground cover, spreading and taking root at its nodes. In spring and early summer it bears profuse star-shaped, 5-petalled flowers, usually mid-blue to white, sometimes purple. These are followed by small berries. It is very frost hardy. **ZONES 7–11.**

Pratia perpusilla

The specific name of this coastal New Zealand species is Latin for 'extremely small'. Its prostrate stems which root at the nodes are very thin and weak, and the narrow, toothed, slightly hairy leaves are little more than $\frac{1}{8}$ in (3 mm) long. The $\frac{1}{4}$ in (6 mm) long white flowers are held just above the foliage on very slender stems. **ZONES 8–10.**

Pratia puberula

Native to Tasmania, Australia, this species is a prostrate, spreading ground cover with tiny pale blue or white flowers that rarely fruits in cultivation. It is a vigorous grower with rooting stems that can become rather invasive. **ZONES 9–10.**

PRIMULA
PRIMROSE

This well-known and much loved genus of perennials consists of around 400 species, found throughout the temperate regions of the northern hemisphere, although most densely concentrated in China and the Himalayas. They also occur on high mountains in the tropics, extending as far south as Papua New Guinea. They are mainly rhizomatous, though some have poorly developed rhizomes and are short lived (*Primula malacoides,* for example). The leaves are usually crowded into a basal tuft or rosette: mostly broadest toward their tips, they generally have toothed or scalloped margins. The flowering stems vary in form, but most often carry successive whorls or a single umbel of flowers or, in a few species, the flowers are tightly crowded into a terminal head or a short spike; in a few others they emerge singly or in small groups from among the leaves on short stalks. Flower shape, size and color vary so much that it is hard to generalize, though basically all have a tubular flower that opens abruptly into a funnel or flat disc, with five or more petals that are often notched at their tips.

CULTIVATION: Primulas like fertile, well-drained soil, part-shade and ample water. Propagate from seed in spring, early summer or fall (autumn), or by division or from root cuttings. Remove dead heads and old foliage after blooming. There is a primula for virtually every position and purpose.

Primula allionii

From the coastal ranges of France and Italy comes this low, evergreen perennial. The leaves, produced in basal rosettes, are sticky, hairy, gray-green and have toothed edges. In winter or early spring stems of up to 5 white, pink or rose flowers, each about 1 in (25 mm) across, rise above the foliage. Plants grow 4–6 in (10–15 cm) tall with a spread of about 8 in (20 cm). **ZONES 7–9.**

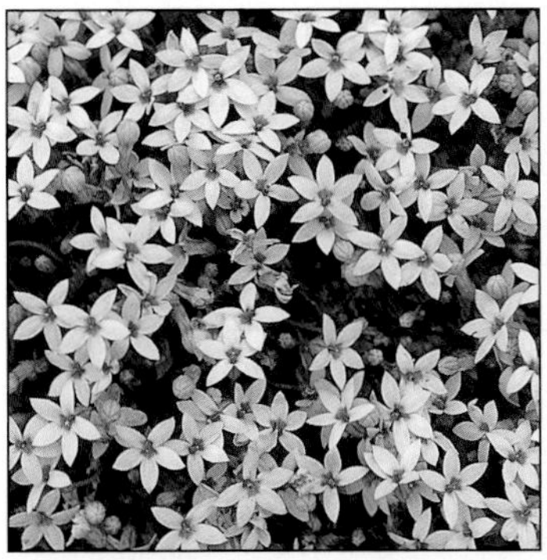
Pratia pedunculata

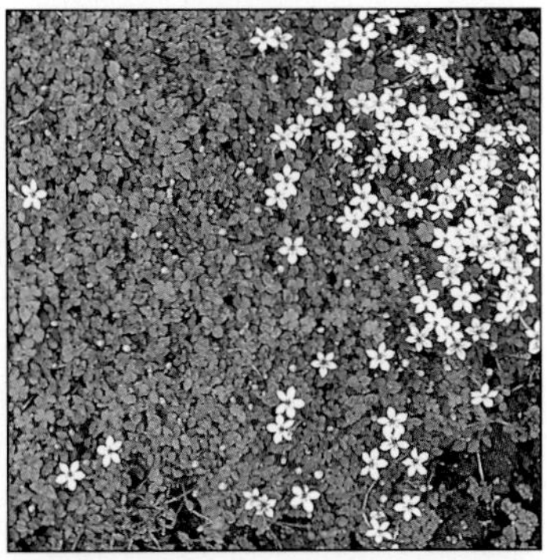
Pratia perpusilla

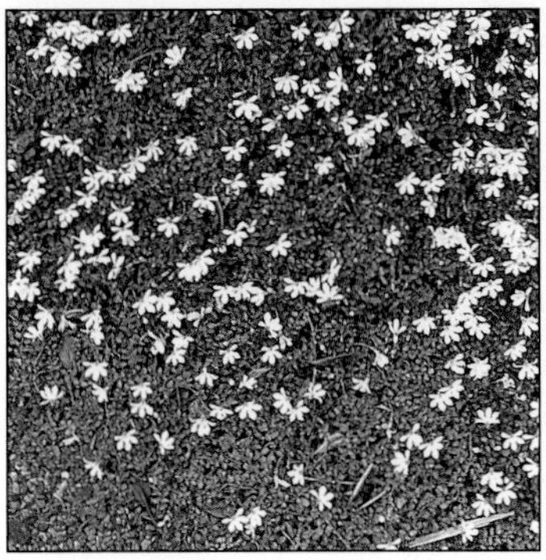
Pratia angulata

Pratia nummularia

P

Primula alpicola

This summer-flowering, herbaceous perennial comes from the mountains of Tibet where it is found in cool, humid, rainy areas. It grows 18–24 in (45–60 cm) tall and just over half as wide, forming rosettes of rounded, toothed leaves each about 4 in (10 cm) long. The flowers are tubular with a flat face and may be white, yellow or purple. They are produced in hanging clusters atop powdery gray stems and are sweetly fragrant. **ZONES 6–9.**

Primula auricula

This small central European perennial has yellow flowers in spring and furry leaves (hence its old common name of bear's ear—*auricula* means a 'little ear'). Garden varieties come in a wide range of colors. In the mid-eighteenth century a mutation resulted in flowers in shades of gray, pale green and almost black with centers covered with a white powder called 'paste'. Such flowers, called show auriculas, were once great favorites, but now have few devotees. **ZONES 3–9.**

Primula beesiana

This candelabra-style primrose from western China has tapering, toothed-edged leaves, which together with their stems are up to 6 in (15 cm) long. The 24 in (60 cm) flower stems hold 5 to 7 whorls of yellow-eyed red-purple flowers. This deep-rooted species is not a bog plant but does require deep watering. **ZONES 5–9.**

Primula auricula

Primula beesiana

Primula bulleyana 'Ceperley Hybrid'

Primula cockburniana

Primula bulleyana

This western Chinese candelabra primrose is very similar to *Primula beesiana* except that its leaves have reddish midribs and its flowers are bright yellow. It dies down completely over winter. **'Ceperley Hybrid'** has yellow, orange and pink flowers. **ZONES 6–9.**

Primula capitata subsp. *mooreana*

This northern Indian subspecies differs from the species in having white powdering on the underside of the foliage and a slightly different leaf shape. Its leaves are up to 6 in (15 cm) long and it has drumstick heads of violet flowers on 12 in (30 cm) stems. **ZONES 5–9.**

Primula cockburniana

Native to China, this candelabra primrose has relatively few 6 in (15 cm) toothed-edged leaves and 12–15 in (30–38 cm) stems with 3 to 5 whorls of orange-red flowers. It is less robust than other candelabra primroses but makes up for that with its vivid color. **ZONES 5–9.**

Primula capitata subsp. *mooreana*

Primula denticulata

Primula florindae

Primula denticulata

DRUMSTICK PRIMROSE

The botanical name of this very frost-hardy Himalayan perennial refers to the toothed profile of the mid-green, broadly lanceolate leaves. A neat and vigorous grower, it reaches a height and spread of 12 in (30 cm). In early to mid-spring its open, yellow-centered flowers of pink, purple or lilac crowd in rounded terminal clusters atop thick hairy stems. ***Primula denticulata* subsp. *alba*** has white flowers usually on slightly shorter stems than the species. **ZONES 6–9.**

Primula elatior

OXLIP

This European species has 2–8 in (5–20 cm) long leaves with finely hairy undersides. Its 4–12 in (10–30 cm) flower stems carry a heavy crop of long-tubed, 1 in (25 mm) wide yellow to orange-yellow flowers. **ZONES 5–9.**

Primula bulleyana 'Ceperley Hybrid'

Primula, Polyanthus Group

Primula flaccida

This is a Chinese species with 4–8 in (10–20 cm) long toothed-edged leaves and flower stems up to 15 in (38 cm) tall. They bear conical heads of downward-facing, funnel-shaped, lavender to violet flowers. **ZONES 6–9.**

Primula florindae

TIBETAN PRIMROSE

In spring this perennial carries up to 60 bright yellow flowers to an umbel, hanging like little bells against a backdrop of broad, mid-green leaves with serrated edges. It grows 24–36 in (60–90 cm) high and likes wet conditions, thriving by the edge of a pond or stream. **ZONES 6–9.**

Primula forrestii

This Chinese species is often found growing in soil pockets among limestone rocks. It has woody rhizomes and 1½–3 in (3.5–8 cm) leaves with toothed edges and powdering on the undersides. The flowers are bright yellow and are carried in polyanthus-like heads on 6–8 in (15–20 cm) stems. **ZONES 6–9.**

Primula forrestii

Primula japonica

Primula poissonii

Primula, Polyanthus Group

Primula frondosa

Native to the Balkans, this species has 4 in (10 cm) long, toothed-edged leaves with powdering on the undersides. Its flower stems are 2–6 in (5–15 cm) tall and carry as few as 1 or as many as 30, ½ in (12 mm) wide yellow-eyed lilac to purple flowers. **ZONES 5–9.**

Primula japonica

JAPANESE PRIMROSE

Forming a clump up to 24 in (60 cm) high and 18 in (45 cm) across, this fully frost-hardy perennial flowers in tiers on tall, sturdy stems like a candelabra in spring and early summer. Its shiny flowers range through pink, crimson and purple to nearly pure white, usually with a distinct eye of another color. The leaves are elliptical, serrated and pale green. This species also does best in a moist situation. **'Postford White'** offers a white, flattish round flower. **ZONES 5–10.**

Primula malacoides

Primula obconica

Primula, Polyanthus Group

Primula juliae

This low-growing, rosette-forming miniature primrose from the Caucasus has 4 in (10 cm) long, dark green leaves. It bears bright purple, yellow-centered flowers and has given rise to a series of garden varieties. **ZONES 5–9.**

Primula × *kewensis*

Usually treated as a greenhouse plant except in cool, frost-free areas, this hybrid has often powdery, coarsely toothed leaves up to 8 in (20 cm) long. Its flowers are golden yellow and are borne in whorls on 12–18 in (30–45 cm) stems. It mainly blooms in winter and spring. **ZONES 9–10.**

Primula malacoides

FAIRY PRIMROSE

This is a native of China. Small, open flowers bloom in spiral masses on this frost-tender perennial, sometimes grown as an annual. The single or double flowers range from white to pink to magenta. Its oval, light green leaves and erect stem have a hairy texture. It reaches a height and spread of 12 in (30 cm) or more. **ZONES 8–11.**

Primula marginata

Occurring naturally in the Cottian Alps between France and Italy, this little clump-forming species has ½–4 in (1.2–10 cm) leaves, powdery and toothed around the edges. Its flower stem is 1–4 in (2.5–10 cm) tall with 2 to 20 white-eyed lilac, light purple or pink flowers that are lightly scented. There are many cultivated forms. **ZONES 7–9.**

Primula polyneura

Primula obconica

POISON PRIMROSE

Dense flower clusters grow in an umbellate arrangement on hairy, erect stems of this perennial. Native to China, it grows to 12 in (30 cm) high and wide and flowers from winter through spring. The yellow-eyed, flattish flowers, 1 in (25 mm) across, range from white to pink to purple. The light green leaves are elliptical and serrated. **ZONES 8–11.**

Primula poissonii

This is a Chinese species with rather open rosettes of 6–8 in (15–20 cm) long, blue-green leaves. Its flower stems are up to 18 in (45 cm) tall with 2 to 6 whorls of yellow-eyed deep pink to crimson flowers. It blooms late, prefers wet soil and can be somewhat sparse. **ZONES 6–9.**

Primula, Polyanthus Group

syn. *Primula* × *polyantha*

These fully frost-hardy perennials, sometimes grown as annuals, reach 12 in (30 cm) in spread and height. Large, flat, scented flowers in every color but green bloom on dense umbels from winter to spring. Polyanthus are cultivars derived from *Primula vulgaris* crossed with *P. veris*, and have been grown since the seventeenth century. **ZONES 6–10.**

Primula polyneura

This Chinese species has light green, rounded, softly hairy leaves 2–10 in (5–25 cm) wide on wiry stems. Its flower stems are 8–18 in (20–45 cm) tall with 1, 2 or several whorls of deep pink to purple-red flowers. It spreads freely. **ZONES 5–9.**

P

Primula pulverulenta

Primula sieboldii

Primula sinopurpurea

Primula veris

Primula vialii

Primula 'Wanda'

Primula vulgaris

Primula vulgaris 'Gigha White'

P

Primula prolifera

Native to the eastern Himalayas and Indonesia, this species has coarsely toothed leaves up to 15 in (38 cm) long. Its flowers stems grow to 3 ft (1 m) tall and carry up to 20 whorls of fragrant golden-yellow flowers. It is a spectacular but rather tender candelabra primrose. **ZONES 8–10.**

Primula pulverulenta

This is a Chinese candelabra primrose with deep green, wrinkled leaves 12 in (30 cm) or more long. Its flower stems are 3 ft (1 m) tall, white powdered with whorls of 1 in (25 mm) wide flowers. The flowers are white, pink or red with a contrasting eye. **ZONES 6–9.**

Primula rosea

This small winter-dormant Himalayan species, suitable for a rockery, flowers before or as the new spring foliage develops. The flowers are bright pink with yellow eyes and are carried in clusters of 4 to 12 blooms on short stems. The leaves, which are smooth edged and bright green, eventually grow 6–8 in (15–20 cm) long. **ZONES 6–9.**

Primula sieboldii

This species from Japan and northeast Asia has large, scalloped-edged leaves 4–15 in (10–38 cm) long. Its flowers, which may be white, pink or purple, are carried in 6- to 20-flowered heads on 6–15 in (10–38 cm) stems. There are several cultivated forms, grown mainly in Japan. **ZONES 5–9.**

Primula sinopurpurea

This late-flowering Chinese species has very distinctive, nearly smooth-edged, narrow, bright green leaves that are 2–12 in (5–30 cm) long. It produces its purple-pink flowers when the stems are around 12 in (30 cm) tall, but the stem continues to grow as the seed matures and eventually reaches 30 in (75 cm). **ZONES 5–9.**

Primula suffrutescens

This species from California has woody rhizomes and small, toothed, spatula-shaped leaves that rarely exceed 1½ in (35 mm) long. Its 2–4 in (5–10 cm) tall flower stems carry 2 to 10 yellow-eyed rose-pink or light purple flowers. **ZONES 8–9.**

Primula veris
COWSLIP

A European wildflower of open woods and meadows, this species blooms a little later than the common primrose does. It is easily distinguished by the clusters of flowers carried on 6 in (15 cm) tall stalks and its sweeter scent. This plant is easy to grow. **ZONES 5–9.**

Primula vialii

This 24 in (60 cm) tall perennial species from Yunnan Province in China is remarkable for carrying its purple flowers in short spikes, quite unlike any other primula. The buds are bright crimson, giving the inflorescence a two-toned effect. The foliage is lush and bright green. It needs a cool, moist climate. **ZONES 7–9.**

Primula vulgaris
ENGLISH PRIMROSE, COMMON PRIMROSE

This common European wildflower likes its cultivated conditions to resemble its cool woodland native environment. Low growing to 8 in (20 cm) and usually frost hardy, it produces a carpet of bright flowers in spring. The flattish flowers are pale yellow with dark eyes (but the garden forms come in every color), and bloom singly on hairy stems above rosettes of crinkled, lance-shaped, serrated leaves. Both the leaves and flowers are edible. **'Gigha White'** has white flowers with yellow centers. **ZONES 6–9.**

Primula 'Wanda'

This little plant disappears entirely over winter and begins to burst into flower as the new foliage develops. The leaves are deep green, heavily crinkled and about 3 in (8 cm) long. The short-stemmed flowers are deep magenta to purple with a yellow eye. It is an easily grown plant that quickly forms a small clump. **ZONES 6–9.**

Prinsepia uniflora

PRINSEPIA

This genus of 3 or 4 deciduous shrubs in the rose family ranges from the Himalayas to northern China and into Taiwan. The arching stems have peeling gray-brown bark and short spines. In spring tiny, 5-petalled, white or yellow flowers with golden anthers develop in the leaf axils along the entire stem length. They are followed by ½ in (12 mm) diameter purple-red, cherry-like fruits.
CULTIVATION: These tough shrubs are easily grown in any well-drained soil in sun or part-shade. Plant them where the thorns will not scratch passersby. Frost hardy, they are propagated from seed or cuttings.

Prinsepia uniflora

A spiny stemmed, spring-flowering shrub from China, this species grows to 6 ft (1.8 m) tall and has narrow, 2½ in (6 cm) long, bright green leaves. The arching yet stiff branches are studded with small 5-petalled white flowers that are followed by purple-red to black, cherry-like fruit. **ZONES 5–9.**

PRITCHARDIA
LOULU PALM

This is a genus of some 37 species of tropical fan palms. Found naturally in Fiji, Hawaii and other Pacific islands, they grow as tall as 70 ft (21 m) and have very large, flat fronds that are divided only about halfway to the midrib. The trunk is straight and smooth for its lower two-thirds; the upper third is often covered with old frond bases and thatch. Branched inflorescences of small cream to orange flowers develop at the base of the crown and are followed by small black fruits.
CULTIVATION: These tropical palms demand a warm, humid climate and suffer in temperatures below 50°F (10°C). They prefer moist, humus-rich, well-drained soil and light shade when young. Propagate from seed.

Pritchardia pacifica
FIJI FAN PALM

There is some doubt that this handsome fan palm is truly native to Fiji, though

Pritchardia pacifica

that is where it first became known to science, and some palm botanists have suggested that it was introduced from Tonga. It is impressive for the crown of luxuriant foliage, consisting of huge, pleated fronds each up to 5 ft (1.5 m) across and only shallowly divided into segments. The flowering branches are shorter than those of many other pritchardias, not extending beyond the fronds and bearing dense clusters of yellow flowers at their ends; the fruit are small, black and round. This palm is easily cultivated and makes rapid growth. **ZONES 10–12.**

PROBOSCIDEA

UNICORN PLANT, DEVIL'S CLAW

This genus of 9 species of annuals and perennials is found from South America north to central USA. They earn their common name of devil's claw from the unusual curved horn shape of the seed pods, which can reach 6 in (15 cm) long. The foliage is rough and hairy, rounded and heart- or kidney-shaped. The flowers are trumpet-shaped, 5-lobed, usually around 2 in (5 cm) long with a prominent yellow flare on the lower lobes. They are followed, of course, by the distinctive seed pods.
CULTIVATION: Many of these plants are subtropical and in colder climates require mildly warmed greenhouses. Outdoors they prefer light, moist, well-drained soil and full sun. Propagation is from seed.

Proboscidea fragrans

SWEET UNICORN PLANT

This Mexican annual has scented violet to magenta flowers borne on long stalks. The flowers are often purple blotched and have a yellow stripe on the lower lobes. **ZONES 10–11.**

Proboscidea louisianica

COMMON UNICORN PLANT

Native to southern USA and Mexico, *Proboscidea louisianica* is an annual species with heart-shaped leaves up to 8 in (20 cm) long. The 2 in (5 cm) long, scented, pale pink, cream or violet flowers have yellow throats and purple blotches. It grows about 15 in (38 cm) tall and makes a handsome pot plant. **ZONES 10–11.**

PROIPHYS

syn. *Eurycles*

There are 3 species of perennial herbs in this genus from Australia and neighboring Southeast Asia. The plants are among the surprisingly few Australian bulbous plants; they are attractive sights with their glossy, almost evergreen leaves and white flowers borne in clusters on 18 in (45 cm) tall stems in early summer. However, they are not cultivated widely even in their native region.
CULTIVATION: They need a tropical or subtropical climate and moist, well-drained soil in a lightly shaded spot. In frosty climates they do very well as a greenhouse pot plants. Propagate from seed or offsets.

Proiphys amboinensis

syns *Eurycles amboinensis, E. sylvestris*

The heart-shaped, almost evergreen leaves of this lily are almost as decorative as the white flowers, and it is surprising that the plant hasn't found more favor in gardens and greenhouses than it has, especially as it is believed to bring good luck to its owner. **ZONES 10–12.**

Proiphys cunninghamii

Native to southeast Queensland and New South Wales, Australia, this species has oval leaves up to 10 in (25 cm) long on 4–10 in (10–25 cm) stems. Its flower stems are up to 30 in (75 cm) tall and are topped with 5- to 12-flowered umbels of white, funnel-shaped blooms. **ZONES 10–12.**

PROSOPIS

MESQUITE

Although typically thought of as trees of the American southwest, this legume genus includes some 44 species of deciduous and evergreen subshrubs, shrubs and trees found not only in the warmer parts of the Americas but also in southwest Asia and Africa. They are often thorny stemmed and have lush, ferny foliage that makes them stand out in the dry, barren areas they often inhabit. The flowers are pea-like, usually creamy green to yellow and are borne on spike-like racemes that form in the leaf axils. Bean-like seed pods follow the flowers.
CULTIVATION: Most species tolerate only very light frosts and prefer a warm, dry climate. The soil should be light and well-drained with moisture at depth. They tolerate dry conditions and alkaline soil. Plant in full sun. Propagate from seed or cuttings.

Prosopis glandulosa

HONEY MESQUITE, TEXAS MESQUITE

This is an important tree in arid regions, where its low, spreading canopy provides needed shade for patios and garden beds. Seldom more than 30 ft (9 m) tall with a similar width, its deciduous leaves are compound with many tiny leaflets giving a fine texture to the foliage mass. Spiny stems discourage close contact. In spring the trees are covered with fluffy spikes of yellow flowers, popular with bees. It has become a problem in some regions where it develops impenetrable thickets. **ZONES 8–11.**

Prosopis pubescens

SCREWBEAN

This 30 ft (9 m) tall shrub is from southwest USA and northwest Mexico. Its branches bear vicious 3 in (8 cm) spines. Its paired leaves are each made up of 5 to 9 pairs of leaflets. The flowers are downy and yellow and are followed by yellowish 2 in (5 cm) seed pods. **ZONES 8–11.**

Prosopis velutina

VELVET MESQUITE, ARIZONA MESQUITE

This tree reaches a height of 15–30 ft (4.5–9 m) with a spread of up to 40 ft (12 m). It is very thorny and has somewhat heavier branches than other mesquites. **ZONES 7–11.**

PROSTANTHERA

MINT BUSH

These 50 species of woody, evergreen shrubs grow naturally in Australia. Glands dotted over the leaves release a minty smell when crushed, hence the common name. The flowers, which appear during spring and summer, are trumpet-like with 2 lips. The upper lip is erect and hooded with 2 lobes; the broader, lower lip has 3 lobes. Flower colors include green, white, blue and purple, and even red and yellow. The fruits are small nuts.
CULTIVATION: A warm climate is essential. They prefer a sunny location sheltered from strong winds and very well-drained soil, which must be kept moist during the growing season. Even with the best of care, some species are notorious for their tendency to die suddenly. Prune after flowering. Propagate new plants from seed or cuttings taken in summer. Some of the more difficult species can be grafted.

Prostanthera caerulea

BLUE MINT BUSH

Native to eastern Australia, this is an upright, densely foliaged shrub 8 ft (2.4 m) tall with a 3 ft (1 m) spread. In spring it bears blue to violet flowers, carried in showy sprays up to 4 in (10 cm) across. The dark green, lance-shaped leaves are up to 2 in (5 cm) long, with toothed edges. It prefers light shade and medium to heavy soil. **ZONES 9–10.**

Prostanthera cuneata

ALPINE MINT BUSH

This compact shrub from southeastern Australia reaches 3 ft (1 m) in height but spreads over 5 ft (1.5 m). In summer it bears small, profuse clusters of white to mauve flowers with purple spots in the throat. The very aromatic, soft, dark green leaves, round and ½ in (12 mm) across, form a dense crown. This plant thrives in medium to heavy soils if kept moist over summer. **ZONES 8–9.**

Prosopis glandulosa

Proiphys amboinensis

Proboscidea louisianica

Prostanthera cuneata

P

Prostanthera lasianthos

Prostanthera nivea var. *induta*

Prostanthera ovalifolia

Prostanthera rotundifolia var. *rosea*

Prostanthera sieberi

Prostanthera lasianthos

VICTORIAN CHRISTMAS BUSH

Native to eastern Australia, this fast-growing, large shrub or small tree grows 15–30 ft (4.5–9 m) tall with an open canopy spreading out from a short trunk. From spring to mid-summer it bears sprays of faintly perfumed, white flowers tinged with either pink or light blue and marked with purple and orange spots in the throat. The lance-shaped leaves are up to 3 in (8 cm) long. It tolerates an occasional light frost. **ZONES 8–10.**

Prostanthera nivea var. *induta*

The species is a bushy shrub to 10 ft (3 m) with white flowers and bright green leaves. *Prostanthera nivea* var. *induta* bears lilac flowers in racemes in spring and summer and has silvery green leaves. **ZONES 9–11.**

Prostanthera ovalifolia

PURPLE MINT BUSH

This spectacular but short-lived mint bush bears large sprays of rich purple flowers in spring. It forms a large shrub or small tree 6 ft (1.8 m) tall, either upright and dense or more spreading. The small, oval leaves are dark green above and grayish green underneath, and are up to ½ in (12 mm) long. Both the foliage and stems are very aromatic. **ZONES 9–11.**

Prostanthera rotundifolia

ROUND-LEAFED MINT BUSH

This shrub features lilac or mauve but sometimes whitish flowers, arranged in large, open or more compact clusters. It has a bushy crown only 6 ft (1.8 m) tall and 5 ft (1.5 m) wide. The dense, dark green leaves are very aromatic, oval to round, and ½ in (12 mm) across with smooth edges. It prefers part-shade. ***Prostanthera rotundifolia* var. *rosea*** has mauve-pink to deep pink flowers and is usually a slightly more compact plant than the species. **ZONES 9–10.**

Prostanthera sieberi

This shrub from southeast Australia is around 6 ft (1.8 m) tall with toothed 1 in (25 mm) leaves. It has mauve to purple flowers in clusters of 4 to 8 blooms. **ZONES 8–10.**

PROTASPARAGUS

syn. *Asparagus*

ASPARAGUS FERN

Primarily native to southern Africa, these tuberous perennials have now been separated from the true rhizomatous asparagus, although some botanists disagree with this reclassification. Widely grown as garden plants in warm-temperate to tropical areas, they are popular house plants everywhere. Grown primarily for their sprays of fern-like foliage, they may be shrubby or semi-climbing. Their stems are often protected by small but vicious thorns. The tiny white, cream or green flowers are inconspicuous but the red or black berries can be a feature.

CULTIVATION: They are undemanding plants that are tolerant of neglect, hence their popularity as house plants. Grow in moist, well-drained, humus-rich soil in sun or part-shade. Propagate from seed or by division, but do not divide into very small pieces as plants so treated seldom recover quickly.

Protasparagus densiflorus

syn. *Asparagus densiflorus*

EMERALD ASPARAGUS FERN

Although frequently used as an indoor plant, this South African species is hardy to about 25°F (–4°C) and can be grown outdoors in many areas. Emerald asparagus fern produces sprays of 24–36 in (60–90 cm) long, wiry, rather spiny stems covered with very fine, almost needle-like bright green leaves. Small but fragrant white flowers are followed by bright red berries. **'Myersii'**, the foxtail fern, has mainly upright stems with dense foliage cover, giving them a tapering, cylindrical shape. **'Sprengeri'** is a sprawling perennial with bright green leaves and bears abundant tiny, white, heavily scented flowers, usually followed by red berries. **ZONES 9–11.**

Protasparagus plumosus

syns *Asparagus plumosus*, *A. setaceus*

This slender, climbing perennial has leaves divided many times into tiny segments, giving an ultra-ferny appearance. It is very easy to grow, provided it is never allowed to dry out entirely and receives good light. Remove old stems and, in early spring, cut over-long stems to the base to encourage new growth. The plant has some hooked and razor-sharp thorns. **ZONES 9–11.**

PROTEA

The 115 species in this outstanding genus of evergreen shrubs and small trees from Africa are prized for their flowerheads, especially by the cut flower industry. Most species grow 3–10 ft (1–3 m) tall. The characteristic cone-shaped flowerheads have a dense central mass of hairy flowers surrounded by brightly colored bracts. These range from yellow to red, crimson, pink, orange, silver or white, and flowering usually extends over several months. The leathery green leaves often have hairy or undulating margins.

CULTIVATION: Often difficult to grow, proteas prefer an open, sunny position with light, usually acidic, well-drained soil. They can cope with occasional light frosts, but young plants need protection during their first two winters. Mulch to suppress weeds. Prune after flowering to maintain shape and to promote new growth. Propagate from seed or cuttings in summer, or by grafting or budding.

Protea aristata

This slow-growing species forms a compact, round shrub 8 ft (2.4 m) tall and 10 ft (3 m) wide. The leaves, 3 in (8 cm) long, are fresh green with a black pointed tip. The blooms, 4–6 in (10–15 cm) long and 4 in (10 cm) across, are cup-shaped with a central cone of dark pink, hairy flowers surrounded by deep pink to red

Protasparagus densiflorus 'Sprengeri'

Protea aristata

Protasparagus densiflorus 'Myersii'

Protea aurea

Protea cynaroides

Protea aurea subsp. *potsbergensis*

bracts. The flowers appear at the branch tips from early to mid-summer. **ZONES 9–10.**

Protea aurea

Restricted in the wild to cool, moist hill slopes in southwest Cape Province, South Africa, this attractive species grows to 15 ft (4.5 m) tall, though often less than half that in gardens, with erect branches from a single trunk at the base. The broad leaves are heart-shaped at the base, and the flowerheads are shuttlecock-shaped, with a funnel of creamy green to crimson bracts and a spreading tuft of long, straight styles extending well beyond the bracts but of the same color. Even more handsome is ***Protea aurea* subsp. *potsbergensis*** with broader, slightly silvery leaves and flowerheads of a pale silvery pink or greenish white. Found naturally on the coast, it is endangered in the wild. **ZONES 9–10.**

Protea 'Clark's Red'

A hybrid between *Protea repens* and *P. aurea*, this New Zealand-raised plant grows to around 8 ft (2.4 m) tall and has narrow, funnel-shaped, red flowerheads throughout the year. It is a reliable performer, a good cut flower and one of the hardiest proteas, capable of surviving in the warmest parts of Zone 8 once established. **ZONES 9–10.**

Protea compacta

BOT RIVER PROTEA

This stiff, upright 10 ft (3 m) shrub has sparse, rangy branches arising from the single main stem. The cup-shaped flowerheads, borne from late fall (autumn) to early spring, are delicate and almost oblong—4–6 in (10–15 cm) long and 3–4 in (8–10 cm) across. Its velvety bracts are rich pinkish tones and are fringed with silver; the flowers are paler. The light green leaves are stemless, varying from oblong to broadly lance-shaped, and grow up to 6 in (15 cm) long. The new leaves are downy, mature leaves smooth. **'Pink Velvet'** is a compact, heavy-flowering cultivar with long-stemmed pure pink flowers. **ZONES 9–10.**

Protea cynaroides

KING PROTEA, GIANT PROTEA

This, South Africa's floral emblem, grows to 5 ft (1.5 m) tall with several sprawling stems. Each flowerhead is a huge, shallow bowl up to 12 in (30 cm) across. Widely spaced, pointed, downy pink bracts enclose a central dome of pink, snowy haired flowers, which are borne from mid-winter to spring. The oval, leathery leaves, 6 in (15 cm) long, are shiny green with a long red stalk. **ZONES 9–10.**

Protea eximia

syn. ***Protea latifolia***

RAY-FLOWERED PROTEA, DUCHESS PROTEA

This dense, upright shrub grows to 15 ft (5 m) tall with few branches. The leaves are broadly oval to heart-shaped and silvery to purplish green. The blooms are 4–6 in (10–15 cm) long and 3–4 in (8–10 cm) across. Their long, spoon-shaped, rose-pink to crimson bracts surround a cone of pink, hairy flowers tipped with purple. These blooms are held well above the foliage. Flowering peaks in the spring months. **'Sylvia'** bears deep pink to red flowers profusely through summer. **ZONES 9–10.**

Protea grandiceps

RED SUGARBUSH, PEACH PROTEA

Slow to mature, this species reaches a height and spread of 5 ft (1.5 m). Deep peach-pink to scarlet bracts surround the flower. These bracts are fringed with reddish purple hairs that protect the showy white stamens within. The flowerheads grow to 6 in (15 cm) across and the dull, grayish green leaves are oval and 4 in (10 cm) long. **ZONES 9–10.**

Protea 'Kurrajong Rose'

This Australian-raised hybrid between *Protea magnifica* and ***P. burchellii*** is moderately frost hardy and grows to at least 6 ft (1.8 m) tall. It has deep red-centered, clear red flowers highlighted with a dusting of silver. **ZONES 9–10.**

Protea grandiceps

Protea compacta 'Pink Velvet'

Protea compacta

Protea eximia

P

Protea longifolia
SIR LOWRY'S PASS PROTEA

Restricted to the winter rainfall areas of southern Africa, this species makes a small spreading shrub up to 5 ft (1.5 m) tall. Blooms 3–6 in (8–15 cm) long and 2–4 in (5–10 cm) across are borne from fall (autumn) until late spring. They consist of pointed cream bracts, tinged with green or yellow, surrounding a mass of fluffy white flowers and a central peak of hairy black flowers. The leaves are long and narrow, pointing upwards, and are 6 in (15 cm) long. **ZONES 9–10.**

Protea magnifica
QUEEN PROTEA

This variable bushy shrub, usually seen as an 8 ft (2.4) tall and nearly as wide, has narrow, 4–6 in (10–15 cm) long gray-green to blue-green leaves. The magnificent spring flowerheads, about 6 in (15 cm) long, are downy, in shades of soft pink and cream with a black-topped central flower mass. **ZONES 9–10.**

Protea neriifolia

Protea neriifolia
BLUE SUGARBUSH, OLEANDER-LEAFED PROTEA

This widely grown species has narrow, gray-green leaves up to 6 in (15 cm) long, covered with fine felting when young. From fall (autumn) to spring upright, 4 in (10 cm) long, goblet-shaped flowerheads open at the tips of the branches. They have a felty central cone surrounded by overlapping, upward-facing, petal-like, deep reddish pink bracts tipped with a fringe of black hairs. There are forms with deeper or paler flowers, as well as a greenish white one. **ZONES 9–10.**

Protea obtusifolia

This species is unusual in that it is lime tolerant. It is a large shrub, over 10 ft (3 m) tall, with leaves up to 6 in (15 cm) long. Flowering through winter and spring, it has greenish cream to pale pink flowers tipped with red. **ZONES 9–10.**

Protea longifolia

Protea sulphurea

Protea 'Pink Ice'

This evergreen shrub, a hybrid of ***Protea susannae*** and *P. neriifolia*, is the cultivar that is most important commercially as a cut flower. Its shiny pink flowerheads, appearing in fall (autumn) and winter, resemble those of *P. neriifolia* minus the soft, black hairs on the bracts. Marginally frost hardy, it grows to 10 ft (3 m) tall with a spread of 6 ft (1.8 m). **ZONES 9–10.**

Protea repens
SUGARBUSH, HONEY PROTEA

One of the easiest of the species to grow, this upright, multi-branched, rounded shrub reaches 10 ft (3 m) tall and wide. It features deep, V-shaped blooms with shiny, sticky bracts, creamish white to crimson or white with candy pink tips surrounding an open cone of downy white flowers. The flowerheads are up to 4 in (10 cm) across, and bloom from early fall (autumn) through winter. The mid-green leaves, 2–6 in (5–15 cm) long, are tipped with a bluish tinge and are narrowly oblong to lance-shaped. **'Guerna'**, one of the first cultivars, bears large, upright, deep red flowers in summer. **ZONES 9–10.**

Protea scolymocephala

From the coastal flats of southern Africa, this small shrub, 3 ft (1 m) high, produces dainty flowers during spring and summer. Cream to greenish flowerheads 2 in (5 cm) across are composed of bracts arranged in the form of a bowl. The shrub is well branched and the narrow leaves, massed along the stems, partly obscure the flowers. Slightly frost tender but wind resistant, it needs sandy soil. **ZONES 9–10.**

Protea sulphurea

Though not very widely cultivated, the combination of blue-green foliage and cream and pale pink flowerheads makes this species very desirable. It is less than 3 ft (1 m) tall but sprawls somewhat wider; it makes a handsome, tall ground cover. **ZONES 9–10.**

Protea 'Pink Ice'

Protea repens

PRUMNOPITYS

This genus of 10 species of evergreen conifers is closely related to *Podocarpus*. They are found in South America, New Zealand, New Caledonia and northeast Australia and are all capable of reaching at least 50 ft (15 m) tall, often more. Their foliage resembles that of the yew, with two rows of ½–1 in (12–25 mm) long, narrow leaflets often slightly twisted. Male cones appear in spring and are ½–1½ in (12–35 mm) long, narrow and cylindrical. The inconspicuous female cones develop into clusters of small red, purple or black drupes.
CULTIVATION: Hardiness varies with the species: some are very frost tender. They prefer deep, moist, humus-rich soil with light shade and shelter when young. Propagate from seed or cuttings.

Prumnopitys elegans
PLUM-FRUITED YEW

The graceful foliage on this elegant Chilean conifer is similar to that of the yew family and is composed of narrow, rich green leaves set opposite each other on thin green branches. It forms a compact, pyramidal shape, reaching 12 ft (3.5 m), and yields valuable timber. Its attractive fruit are round, red and plum-like. **ZONES 8–10.**

Prumnopitys ferruginea
MIRO

This New Zealand tree grows to 80 ft (24 m) tall with a spread of 15 ft (5 m). Its bark is almost black with distinct indentations; the dark green leaves are set in two rows on narrow branchlets. Its bright red, succulent berries—attractive to birds but poisonous to humans—are up to 1 in (25 mm) wide, smell of turpentine and are covered with a waxy bloom when they first appear. This tree prefers well-composted soil. **ZONES 8–10.**

PRUNELLA
SELF-HEAL

This is a genus of 7 species of semi-evergreen perennials from Europe, Asia, North Africa and North America. They form low, spreading clumps and bear opposite pairs of ovate to oblong, sometimes deeply lobed leaves. Erect flowering stems bear whorled spikes of 2-lipped tubular flowers in shades of white, pink or purple.
CULTIVATION: Most species spread from creeping stems that readily take root at the nodes, making them excellent ground covering plants for creating large drifts. They are fully frost hardy and will grow in sun or part-shade in moist, well-drained soil. Propagate from seed or by division in spring or fall (autumn).

Prunella grandiflora
LARGE SELF-HEAL

Purple, 2-lipped flowers grow in erect spikes above leafy stubs in spring and summer on this species. A native of Europe, it is good for ground cover or rock gardens, having a spread and height of 18 in (45 cm). **'Loveliness'** has soft mauve flowers. **ZONES 5–9.**

Prumnopitys ferruginea

Prunella laciniata

This densely pubescent perennial to around 12 in (30 cm) high has a fairly open habit. It has attractive, deeply lobed leaves to 3 in (8 cm) long and dense, upright spikes of yellowish white flowers in summer. Occasionally pink or purple flowering forms are seen. **ZONES 6–9.**

Prunella vulgaris
HEAL-ALL

A creeping, mat-forming plant common in meadows and wastelands throughout most of Europe, this species has hairy, oval to diamond-shaped leaves and bears masses of purplish flowers in short cylindrical terminal heads in mid-summer. The whole of the plant is used in herbal medicine and is especially valued as a gargle for a sore throat or ulcerated mouth. **ZONES 3–10.**

PRUNUS

This large genus, mostly from the northern hemisphere, includes the edible stone fruits—cherries, plums, apricots, peaches, nectarines and almonds—but is also represented in gardens by ornamental species and cultivars with beautiful flowers. While the genus includes several shrubby species, most are trees growing on average to 15 ft (4.5 m), although some can reach as much as 100 ft (30 m). Most of the familiar species are deciduous and bloom in spring (or late winter in mild climates) with scented, 5-petalled, pink or white flowers. The leaves are simple and often serrated and all produce a fleshy fruit containing a single hard stone. Many have attractive foliage colors in fall (autumn), and others have interesting bark. The timber of cherries and plums is sometimes used commercially.

The genus *Prunus* consists of about 430 species, and these are divided among 5 or 6 easily recognized subgenera, treated as distinct genera by botanists in some countries. They are: ***Prunus*** in the narrow sense, which includes all the plums; sometimes included in this subgenus but sometimes kept separate are ***Armeniaca***, the apricots; ***Amygdalus*** includes peaches, nectarines and almonds as well as a few ornamental species with similar stalkless blossoms and pitted stones; ***Cerasus*** includes all the cherries and flowering cherries with few-flowered umbels; while ***Padus*** includes the bird cherries, mainly North American, with small flowers in long racemes; and finally there are the evergreens in subgenus ***Laurocerasus***, also with flowers in racemes and including the well-known cherry laurel and its allies and a large group of tropical rainforest trees from Asia and the Americas.
CULTIVATION: Plant in moist, well-drained soil in full sun but with some protection from strong wind for the spring blossom. Keep the ground around base of trees free of weeds and long grass and feed young trees with a high-nitrogen fertilizer. Many of the fruiting varieties respond well to espaliering. Propagate by grafting or from seed—named cultivars must be grafted or budded onto seedling stocks. Pests and diseases vary with locality.

Prunella grandiflora

Prunella laciniata

Prunella vulgaris

Prunus × *amygdalopersica*
POLLARD ALMOND

This attractive hybrid between a flowering peach and an almond grows to 20 ft (6 m) or so with a broadly spreading crown. It is valued for its large, deep pink flowers, which have protruding purplish red stamens and appear on leafless branches at the end of winter or early spring; inedible green fruit follow. Like the almond it is suited to quite dry climates. Prune while still in bloom and guard against peach curly-leaf fungus. **'Pollardii'**, the original clone of this cross, has large, very bright pink flowers. **ZONES 5–10.**

Prunus armeniaca
APRICOT

Now believed to have originated in northern China and Mongolia, the apricot was introduced to the Middle East more than 1,000 years ago and thence to Europe. It grows to no more than about 25 ft (8 m) tall, the trunk becoming characteristically gnarled with age. White or pinkish blossoms are borne in early spring before the leaves appear. The twigs are reddish, and the smooth, heart-shaped leaves are about 3 in (8 cm) long. The yellow-orange fruit contains a smooth, flattened stone that separates easily from the sweet-tasting flesh. Prune moderately after flowering to encourage a good fruit crop. **ZONES 5–10.**

Prunus avium
GEAN, MAZZARD, SWEET CHERRY, WILD CHERRY

Native to Europe and western Asia, this species is the major parent of the cultivated sweet cherries. It can reach 60 ft (18 m) in height, with a rounded crown and stout, straight trunk with banded reddish brown bark. The pointed, dark green leaves are up to 6 in (15 cm) long and turn red, crimson and yellow before dropping. Profuse white flowers appear in late spring before the leaves and are followed by black-red fruit which in the wild forms may be sweet or somewhat bitter, but not acid. The cultivated cherries are rarely self-fertile, so trees of 2 or more different clones are usually necessary for fruit production. Cherry wood is prone to fungus and so the tree should not be pruned in winter or in wet weather. The ornamental cultivar **'Plena'** carries a mass of drooping, double white flowers. **ZONES 3–9.**

Prunus × *blireana*

Prunus campanulata

Prunus cerasoides

Prunus × *blireana*

DOUBLE FLOWERING PLUM

This popular hybrid originated in the early twentieth century as a cross between the Japanese apricot *Prunus mume* and the purple-leaved plum *Prunus cerasifera* 'Pissardii'. A rounded shrub, it grows to around 12 ft (3.5 m) high and has slender, arching branches and thin, red-purple leaves that change to golden brown in fall (autumn). In early spring it bears fragrant pale rose-pink, double flowers. **ZONES 5–10.**

Prunus campanulata

TAIWAN CHERRY, CARMINE CHERRY

This cherry species from Taiwan, south China and the Ryukyu Islands is less frost tolerant than most other deciduous *Prunus* species and does best in warm-temperate climates. It can reach 30 ft (9 m) in height though is mostly smaller in cultivation, with a vase-shaped habit. It comes into bloom in mid- to late winter in a warm climate, or early spring in cooler climates. The bare branches are festooned with clusters of bell-shaped flowers, bright carmine red in the commonly grown form. The foliage turns bronze-red in fall (autumn). Like most cherries, it responds poorly to pruning. **ZONES 7–11.**

Prunus caroliniana

CAROLINA LAUREL-CHERRY

A native of southeastern USA where it grows in moist, fertile soil in valleys, this is an evergreen species allied to *Prunus laurocerasus* and *P. ilicifolia*, differing in its smaller, thinner leaves with few or no marginal teeth. It makes a bushy-crowned small tree to about 30 ft (9 m) high with glossy dark green foliage; in late winter and early spring it produces short spikes of very small white flowers from the leaf axils, followed by ½ in (12 mm) diameter, juicy black fruit that ripen in late fall (autumn) and persist through winter. Like other laurel cherries its foliage is poisonous to livestock, containing prussic acid. The plants tolerate heavy pruning and shaping and make fine hedges. **'Bright 'n' Tight'** has a compact form and glossy green foliage. **ZONES 7–11.**

Prunus cerasifera

CHERRY PLUM, MYROBALAN, PURPLE-LEAFED PLUM

Native to Turkey and the Caucasus region, this small-fruited thornless plum has long been cultivated in Europe. It grows to about 30 ft (9 m) and is tolerant of dry conditions, with an erect, bushy habit and smallish leaves that are slightly bronze tinted. Profuse, small white flowers appear before the leaves, in spring in cool climates and in late winter in milder ones, followed by edible red plums up to 1¼ in (30 mm) diameter in summer. There are many ornamental cultivars of this species, the most widely grown being those with deep purple foliage. **'Nigra'** is slightly smaller than the normal *Prunus cerasifera* and has vibrant, deep purple leaves turning more blackish purple in late summer; in spring it bears single, pale pink blossoms with red calyx and stamens. The cherry-size red fruit are edible but sour. **'Pissardii'** (syn. 'Atropurpurea') was the original purple-leafed plum, sent to France in 1880 by M. Pissard, gardener to the Shah of Persia. It has new foliage of a deep red color turning dark purple and its pink buds open white. Other purple-leafed cultivars include **'Newport'** and **'Thundercloud'**, of American origin. **'Elvins'** (syn. *P.* 'Elvins'), is an Australian-raised cultivar grown for its white blossom prettily flushed with flesh pink, densely massed on arching branches; it grows only to about 12 ft (3.5 m) and blooms in mid-spring. **ZONES 3–10.**

Prunus cerasoides

A lovely cherry from western China and the eastern Himalayas, this species reaches 25 ft (8 m) in its natural habitat.

Prunus cerasifera 'Nigra'

Prunus cerasifera 'Elvins'

Prunus cerasifera cultivar

Prunus glandulosa 'Sinensis'

It has shiny, grayish brown bark and leathery, sharply toothed leaves; in late spring it bears rose-pink flowers that are deeper pink in bud. It was introduced to cultivation in 1931. **ZONES 7–9.**

Prunus cerasus
SOUR CHERRY, MORELLO CHERRY

The fruiting cherries of Europe and western Asia have been the subject of much confusion concerning their botanical identities. Many of the forms are placed under the name *Prunus cerasus*, characterized by a smaller, more bushy growth form than that of *P. avium*, suckering from the roots, and acid fruit. Its wild origin is unknown and botanists suspect it may have a common ancestry with *P. avium*. The plants are self-fertile, so an isolated tree is capable of setting fruit, but like the sweet cherry, it needs cold winters for successful growth. ***P. c.* var. *austera***, the morello cherry, has pendulous branches and has blackish fruit with purple juice; the red amarelle cherries with clear juice belong to ***P. c.* var. *caproniana***, while the famous maraschino cherries with very small blackish fruit are ***P. c.* var. *marasca*,** which grows in Dalmatia. **ZONES 3–9.**

Prunus 3 *cistena*
PURPLE-LEAF SAND CHERRY

A hybrid between a purple-leafed form of *Prunus cerasifera* and the American sand cherry ***P. pumila***, this rather weak-stemmed 8 ft (2.4 m) tall shrub has red-brown leaves less than $2\frac{1}{2}$ in (6 cm) long. Its white flowers are borne singly or in pairs in spring and are followed in summer by small deep purple fruit. **ZONES 3–10.**

Prunus × *domestica*
PLUM, EUROPEAN PLUM

The common plum of Europe is believed to be an ancient hybrid, its probable ancestors thought to include the blackthorn, *Prunus spinosa*, and the cherry plum, *P. cerasifera*. It has numerous cultivars, most grown for their sweet fruit but some for their display of blossom. It is a vigorous grower to a height of 30 ft (9 m) or even more, with a tangle of strong branches spreading into a broad, dense crown of foliage. Only the vigorous new growths are sometimes spiny. Flowers are white, borne in

Prunus dulcis

profuse small clusters in spring, and the summer fruit are spherical to somewhat elongated with a yellow, red or blue-black skin and green or yellow flesh; they range in length from $1\frac{1}{4}$–3 in (3–8 cm). Not as juicy as the red-fleshed Japanese plums *(**P. salicina**)*, the fruit of most cultivars are best cooked or dried for prunes; one of the best for eating is **'Coe's Golden Drop'** a sweet, juicy, amber-yellow plum with red spots. ***Prunus domestica* subsp. *insititia***, the damson plum or bullace, is a thornier tree that often succeeds in districts too cold for large-fruited varieties; the small purple-black fruit with tart acid flesh are used for jams and jellies. **ZONES 5–9.**

Prunus dulcis
syn. ***Prunus amygdalus***
ALMOND

Closely related to the peach, the almond is believed to have originated in the eastern Mediterranean region and requires a climate with hot dry summers and cool winters to bear well. It grows to well over 20 ft (6 m) high, with a moderately spreading habit. Stalkless pink blossoms are borne in clusters of 5 to 6 on the leafless branches in late winter or early spring. These are followed in summer by the flattened, furry fruit, like a small dried-up peach; this dries and splits to release the weak-shelled stone, which in turn contains the almond kernel. Almonds need a well-drained, salt-free soil and the young trees are frost tender; they are not self-fertile and two varieties that blossom at the same time are needed to produce fruit. They are prone to shot-hole disease, which appears on the fruit as purple spots, spoiling the nut inside. Prune to an open vase shape encouraging 3 or 4 main branches. **ZONES 6–9.**

Prunus glandulosa
DWARF FLOWERING ALMOND, ALMOND-CHERRY

This deciduous shrub from China and Japan belongs to a group of dwarf *Prunus* species that belong in the cherry subgenus *(Cerasus)* but show some of the characteristics of almonds and peaches. It makes a showy late spring-flowering shrub of up to 5 ft (1.5 m) with thin, wiry branches, small leaves, and profuse white to pale pink flowers, borne along the stems. The dark red fruit about half the size of a cherry are edible though rather sour. It is common practice to cut the bushes back almost to ground level as soon as flowering finishes, producing a thicket of strong vertical shoots that bloom very freely the next spring. **'Sinensis'** (syn. 'Rosa Plena') bears double pink flowers. **'Alba Plena'** has double white flowers. **ZONES 6–10.**

Prunus ilicifolia
HOLLY-LEAF CHERRY

This evergreen species of the laurel-cherry group is native to the coastal ranges of California. In cultivation it is normally a dense, mound-like shrub of 8–12 ft (2.4–3.5 m) in height, but in the wild it sometimes reaches 25 ft (8 m) or even more. The thick, glossy green leaves are prickly-toothed like English holly and are only 1–2 in (2.5–5 cm) long. White flowers appear in summer on slender spikes up to 3 in (8 cm) long, followed by small, round, deep red-purple fruit. This shrub makes an excellent screen or hedge, but careful shaping is needed to give it a tree form. It tolerates hot sun and dry conditions once established. **ZONES 8–10.**

Prunus incisa
FUJI CHERRY

It is uncertain whether this cherry species from Japan was named *incisa* for its sharply toothed leaf margins, or for its deeply notched petals. It is a small tree of up to 30 ft (9 m) with oval, sharply toothed leaves that are reddish when unfolding in spring, darkening to green in summer and then orange-red in fall (autumn). The pink buds, opening to white or pale pink blossoms, appear in early spring before the leaves. **'Praecox'** flowers in early winter. **ZONES 7–10.**

Prunus laurocerasus

Prunus laurocerasus
CHERRY LAUREL, LAUREL CHERRY

Both the botanical and common names of this handsome evergreen reflect the resemblance of its foliage to that of the true laurel *(Laurus nobilis)* and the 2 plants are sometimes confused. Native to the Balkans, Turkey and the Caspian region, it has been grown in western Europe since the sixteenth century. It is commonly grown as a hedge, but if unclipped can reach as much as 50 ft (15 m) in height. The shiny, bright green leaves are 6 in (15 cm) or more long; in mid- to late spring it bears upright sprays of small, sweetly scented white flowers, followed by red berries that ripen to black in fall (autumn). One of the toughest of evergreens, cherry laurel tolerates alkaline soils and will grow in shade. **'Otto Luyken'** is a free-flowering dwarf form growing to 3–4 ft (1–1.2 m) in height and spreading 5 ft (1.5 m). **'Zabeliana'** is a horizontally branched cultivar, usually under 3 ft (1 m) in height and 12 ft (3.5 m) or more in width, with narrow, willow-like leaves. **ZONES 6–10.**

Prunus ilicifolia

Prunus cerasus var. *austera*

Prunus lusitanica
PORTUGAL LAUREL

Closely allied to the cherry laurel, this evergreen species from Spain and Portugal makes a large shrub or small tree up to 40 ft (12 m) and can be grown as a tall hedge or screen. The leaves are 4 in (10 cm) or more long, have serrated edges and long-pointed tips; they are yellow-green on the undersides. Profuse drooping spikes of small white flowers appear in early summer, followed by red berries ripening black in fall (autumn). A fine ornamental, it tolerates both cold and dry conditions. ***Prunus lusitanica* subsp. *azorica*** is a smaller plant, rarely exceeding 15 ft (4.5 m), with slightly smaller leaves and shorter spikes of flowers. **ZONES 6–10.**

Prunus lyonii

Prunus maackii

Prunus lyonii
CATALINA CHERRY

This evergreen species from offshore islands of southern California is allied to *Prunus ilicifolia* but without the prickly-toothed leaves of that species. It makes a bushy, small tree 25 ft (8 m) tall and has narrow, 2 in (5 cm) long leaves, sometimes with toothed edges. Short spikes of small white flowers open in spring and are followed by 1 in (25 mm) long red-black fruit. **ZONES 8–11.**

Prunus maackii
MANCHURIAN CHERRY, AMUR CHOKE-CHERRY

This cherry from Korea and nearby parts of China and eastern Siberia grows to around 50 ft (15 m) tall. The 3–4 in (8–10 cm) long leaves are downy when young and often color well in fall (autumn). The small white flowers are carried in short dense spikes at the ends of the previous year's growth and are followed by tiny, dry, black fruit. Its relationships are uncertain, and it seems to show characteristics of both the bird cherries *(P. padus)* and the laurel cherries *(P. laurocerasus)*. **ZONES 2–9.**

Prunus maritima
BEACH PLUM

Native to the eastern USA where it grows close to the seashore in sandy or gravelly soil, this untidy 6 ft (1.8 m) shrub has 2 ½ in (6 cm) long, deep green leaves with downy undersides. Its pale pink flowers are ½ in (12 mm) wide, in clusters of 2 to 3 blooms and are followed by small edible, quite tasty, purple-red fruit. Although not a neat bush, it is useful for shelter and erosion control in coastal areas. **ZONES 3–9.**

Prunus mume 'Pendula'

Prunus lusitanica

Prunus mume
JAPANESE APRICOT

Closely related to the common apricot, this very early flowering species is a native of China but has been cultivated for many centuries in both China and Japan, and has given rise there to hundreds of named cultivars selected for both fruit and flower. It makes a round-headed tree of 15–30 ft (4.5–9 m) high with sharply pointed leaves up to 4 in (10 cm) long. The lightly scented, white to deep pink flowers, 1 in (25 mm) or more across, are carried in small clusters along the branches in late spring and are followed by yellowish, apricot-like fruit. Its blossoms feature in classical Chinese and Japanese paintings and it is also popular for bonsai work. Cultivars include **'Alboplena'** with white double flowers; **'Beni-chidori'**, a later flowerer with fragrant pink double flowers; **'Pendula'** with a weeping habit; and **'Geisha'** with semi-double deep rose flowers. **ZONES 6–9.**

Prunus 'Okame'

This attractive hybrid cherry is a cross between *Prunus campanulata* and *P. incisa*. In spring, before the leaves appear, it bears profuse blossoms of a clear, bright pink opening from more reddish buds. It grows to about 25 ft (8 m) tall and has dark green foliage that turns brilliant orange in fall (autumn). **ZONES 7–10.**

Prunus padus
BIRD CHERRY

This temperate Eurasian tree grows to around 50 ft (15 m) tall, though usually considerably less in gardens. It has 4 in (10 cm) long, serrated-edged leaves with fine hairs, often developing orange tints in fall (autumn). The flowers are white, ½ in (12 mm) wide, on racemes just over 4 in (10 cm) long. Pea-sized black fruit, attractive to birds, follow. **'Watereri'** is a shapely tree with pendulous racemes up to 8 in (20 cm) long. **ZONES 3–9.**

Prunus 'Okame'

Prunus mume 'Geisha'

Prunus sargentii

Prunus persica

PEACH, FLOWERING PEACH, NECTARINE

Believed to have originated in China but introduced to the Mediterranean region over 1,000 years ago, the peach is one of the most important species in the genus for its fruit. Growing to 12 ft (3.5 m) or more, it bears abundant pinkish red flowers in early spring (late winter in mild climates); the narrow, 6 in (15 cm) long, mid-green leaves appear after the blossoms. Its delicious midsummer fruit, varying in color from cream and pale pink to yellow or scarlet, is covered with a velvety down and contains a stone that is deeply pitted and grooved. The numerous cultivars include both fruiting and flowering peaches, the latter mostly with small, hard fruit that are of little use for eating; the fruiting cultivars, though, can be quite showy in flower. Ornamental peach cultivars include the widely grown **'Alba Plena'** with double white flowers ; **'Klara Meyer'** with double peach-pink flowers with frilled petals; **'Magnifica'** noted for its double deep crimson blooms that cover the branches in early spring; and **'Versicolor'** which bears semi-double flowers, some white, others pale pink and variably red-striped, all on the same tree. ***Prunus persica* var. *nectarina***, the nectarine, is almost identical to the peach in habit and flowers but its fruit are smooth skinned, mostly smaller and with a subtly different flavor. There are several named varieties and their seedlings often give rise to normal, downy-skinned peaches. ZONES 5–10.

Prunus persica

Prunus persica 'Versicolor'

Prunus salicifolia

MEXICAN BIRD CHERRY, CAPULIN

One of the American bird cherries allied to *Prunus serotina*, this species from the highlands of Mexico, Central America and northern South America grows to 40 ft (12 m) in height. It has leathery, finely serrated leaves up to 4 in (10 cm) long. The white flowers, ½ in (12 mm) in diameter, are borne in loose racemes. The small, red to blackish fruit are edible. ZONES 6–10.

Prunus sargentii

SARGENT CHERRY

This flowering cherry species is native to Japan, Korea and eastern Siberia, and is one of the tallest of the Japanese flowering cherry group, growing to as much as 80 ft (24 m), with dark chestnut-colored bark. In mid-spring the branches are covered with pink flowers with deeper pink stamens, accompanied by the unfolding leaves which are long-pointed and up to 5 in (12 cm) in length; in fall (autumn) they make a brilliant display of reddish bronze, turning orange and red. This species performs best away from polluted environments. ZONES 4–9.

Prunus, Sato-zakura Group, 'Shirotae'

Prunus, Sato-zakura Group, 'Seykiyama'

P., Sato-zakura Group,'Cheal's Weeping'

Prunus, Sato-zakura Group

These are the main group of Japanese flowering cherries, believed to be derived mainly from the species *Prunus serrulata* (under which name they are commonly to be found), but with probable hybrid influence of several closely related species. Mostly small to medium-sized trees, they can be recognized by their large leaves with fine, even teeth ending in bristle-like points, and their loose umbels of flowers that are mostly over 1½ in (35 mm) in diameter; the bases of the umbels carry conspicuous, toothed bracts, like miniature leaves. They are among the most widely planted trees for spring blossom in cool climates but require good rainfall and a mild summer for the best display of blossom. The numerous cultivars are mostly of Japanese origin and there has been much confusion as to their names. Height and growth form vary with cultivar, as do the color, shape and size of the flowers and the color of the new leaves, which unfold with or just after the opening flowers. **'Amanogawa'** has a narrow habit, growing to 30 ft (9 m) high, and carries fragrant, semi-double white to shell-pink flowers. **'Sekiyama'** (syn. 'Kanzan'), a vigorous grower to 10 ft (3 m), bears double purple-pink flowers in mid-spring. **'Cheal's Weeping'** (syn. 'Kiku-shidare') flowers early, carrying double deep pink flowers on weeping branches. **'Shirotae'** (syn. 'Mount Fuji'), growing to 20 ft (6 m), has slightly drooping,

Prunus persica 'Klara Meyer'

Prunus, Sato-zakura Group, 'Taihaku'

Prunus, Sato-zakura Group, 'Okumiyako'

Prunus, Sato-zakura Group, 'Shirofugen'

Prunus, Sato-zakura Group, 'Takasago'

Prunus, Sato-zakura Group, 'Ukon'

spreading branches; green, lacy-edged leaves appear in early spring and turn orange-red in fall (autumn); in mid-spring it carries a wealth of fragrant, single or semi-double white blossoms. **'Okumiyako'** (syn. 'Shimidsu sakura'), growing to 15 ft (4.5 m), has wide, spreading branches; pink-tinted buds appear in late spring and open to fringed, large, double white flowers, and the leaves turn orange and red in fall. **'Pink Perfection'** is a strong-growing cultivar with clusters of large, deep pink, double flowers that open from red buds. **'Shirofugen'**, strong growing to 20 ft (6 m), blooms late, and the purplish pink buds intermingle attractively with the young, copper leaves; clusters of double flowers open white and turn purplish pink. **'Shogetsu'** makes a 15 ft (4.5 m), spreading tree with arching branches and large clusters of semi-double to fully double, white-centered pale pink flowers; it blooms late. **'Taihaku'**, known as the great white cherry, is a vigorous, spreading tree to 20 ft (6 m) or more; in mid-spring it bears large, pure white flowers and bronze-red, young leaves that mature to dark green. **'Takasago'**, the Naden cherry, with scented pink flowers, is thought by some to be a hybrid with *Prunus* × *yedoensis*. **'Ukon'**, an upright tree to 30 ft (9 m), bears large pink-tinged, greenish cream flowers in mid-spring. ZONES 5–9.

Prunus serotina

Prunus serotina
BLACK CHERRY, RUM CHERRY

This fast-growing species of the bird cherry group reaches heights of over 100 ft (30 m) in its native eastern and central North America, where its timber is highly prized for furniture-making; in cultivation a tree of 50 ft (15 m) would be exceptional. It has dark brown bark and its pointed leaves, up to 6 in (15 cm) long, are green above with paler undersides and often have a downy midrib. They turn yellow and pale scarlet before falling. The small fragrant, white flowers are borne in drooping spikes up to 6 in (15 cm) long in late spring, followed by pea-sized black fruit in summer; these are eaten by birds, which distribute the seeds widely. ZONES 3–9.

Prunus serrula
TIBETAN CHERRY

Native to western China, this deciduous, neatly round-headed tree growing to 50 ft (15 m) is prized in gardens for its gleaming, mahogany red bark. Clusters of small white flowers appear in spring at the same time as the new leaves, which mature to dark green and turn yellow in fall (autumn); the tiny round fruit are red to black. This species requires a cool climate. ZONES 5–9.

Prunus serrulata

Prunus, Sato-zakura Group

Prunus × *subhirtella* 'Pendula'

Prunus serrulata
JAPANESE CHERRY, ORIENTAL CHERRY

This cherry from China is believed to the main ancestor of the Japanese flowering cherries (*Prunus*, Sato-zakura Group). It has similar foliage though the teeth on the leaves are not so noticeably bristle-tipped. It makes a spreading tree of about 30 ft (9 m) in height and bears pink-flushed white flowers before or with the leaves in mid- to late spring. ZONES 5–9.

Prunus spinosa
SLOE, BLACKTHORN

A species of plum, this 12–15 ft (3.5–4.5 m) thorny shrub or small tree is found throughout temperate Eurasia and in North Africa. It has toothed 2 in (5 cm) long leaves and profuse small white flowers borne singly or occasionally in pairs on the leafless branches in early spring. The flowers are followed in summer by ½ in (12 mm) diameter, prune-like fruit that can be used to make a very tart jam or conserve. ZONES 4–9.

Prunus × *subhirtella*
HIGAN CHERRY, ROSEBUD CHERRY

This graceful cherry from Japan is now believed to be of hybrid origin. It grows to 30 ft (9 m) and produces a profusion of pale pink flowers early in spring. The leaves are dark green and pointed, and fade to shades of yellow before dropping. It thrives in cool climates but can be rather short-lived. **'Autumnalis'**, growing to 15 ft (4.5 m), bears pink-budded white flowers intermittently from late fall (autumn) through winter and into early spring; **'Autumnalis Rosea'** is similar but has pale pink flowers. **'Pendula'** has slender, vertically pendulous branches like a weeping willow and is usually grafted onto a standard; it bears a profusion of small pale pink, 5-petalled flowers from late winter into spring, followed by little spherical brown-red fruit. The spring-blooming **'Pendula Rubra'** bears rich pink flowers. **'Accolade'** is a presumed hybrid between *Prunus* × *subhirtella* and *P. sargentii*: it makes a spreading tree to about 25 ft (8 m) with quite large pale pink semi-double flowers opening from deep pink buds in early spring. **'Hally Jolivette'** is the result of a backcross of the hybrid *P.* × *subhirtella* × *yedoensis* onto *P.* × *subhirtella*. It is a large shrub, growing to 8–15 ft (2.4–4.5 m) in height and spread. Of dense growth with many reddish, upright stems, it is covered for 2 to 3 weeks in spring with double white flowers opening from pink buds. ZONES 5–9.

Prunus tenella
DWARF RUSSIAN ALMOND

This vase-shaped shrub from eastern Europe and the Caspian region of Asia is a dwarf relative of the peaches and almonds. Growing to no more than about 5 ft (1.5 m), it bears massed bright pink stalkless flowers on long, slender branches in mid-spring before the glossy, narrow, 3 in (8 cm) long leaves unfold. It makes an excellent tub specimen if repotted and root pruned every second year. It is very frost hardy but dislikes drying out. A common practice is to cut the plants back hard almost to ground level after flowering, to produce a thicket of vigorous summer growths. **'Fire Hill'** has erect stems that are wreathed with brilliant, deep rose flowers. ZONES 4–9.

Prunus × *yedoensis*

Prunus × *yedoensis* 'Shidare Yoshino'

Prunus virginiana
CHOKE-CHERRY, AMERICAN BIRD CHERRY

This species is native to eastern and central North America, where it is often regarded almost as a weed, the seeds being spread abundantly by birds. It is commonly only a shrub of 12–15 ft (3.5–4.5 m) but can make a small tree up to 30 ft (9 m) with finely-toothed 3 in (8 cm) leaves. It bears dense spikes up to 6 in (15 cm) long of small white flowers from early to mid-spring, followed by pea-sized, dark red fruit that are acid and astringent. ZONES 2–9.

Prunus × *yedoensis*
TOKYO CHERRY, YOSHINO CHERRY

Another Japanese cherry that is now regarded as of hybrid origin, the parents probably ***Prunus speciosa*** and *P.* × *subhirtella*. It is a small tree, growing quite rapidly to 30 ft (9 m) high and wide. Massed fragrant white or pale pink flowers usually open before the new foliage develops; the deep green 4 in (10 cm) long leaves color well in fall (autumn). It makes a beautiful lawn specimen or avenue tree and is the main flowering cherry planted in Washington DC. **'Ivensii'** has an arching and weeping growth habit. **'Akebono'** has pure pink flowers. **'Shidare Yoshino'** has a weeping habit and masses of pure white flowers. ZONES 5–9.

PSEUDERANTHEMUM

This genus consists of 60 species of small evergreen perennials, subshrubs and shrubs native to tropical regions worldwide. They are grown for their unusual foliage and spectacular spikes of white flowers which are spotted with red, pink and magenta. Varying in height from 12 in (30 cm) to 5 ft (1.5 m), these

Prunus × *subhirtella*

Prunus × *subhirtella* 'Accolade'

charming plants are cultivated as ground covers or small, ornamental bushes.
CULTIVATION: Well-drained, moist and composted soil in part-shade ensures healthy growth and a good flowering display. They are frost tender. Tip prune to encourage bushiness or, if the plants become too straggly, cut back hard in spring. Propagate year-round from seed or by division.

Pseuderanthemum reticulatum
GOLDEN NETBUSH

This shrub from Vanuatu grows to a height and spread of 3 ft (1 m). The showy foliage varies from green to purplish black with oval leaves growing to 6 in (15 cm); these have an intricate network of golden veins and undulating edges. Large flower spikes at the ends of the branches hold several tubular white blossoms with cerise markings in the centers. It thrives in hot climates, and prefers protection from winds. **ZONES 11–12.**

PSEUDOCYDONIA

The single species in this genus is a small deciduous or semi-evergreen tree from China and, as the Latin name suggests, it resembles its close relative the quince (*Cydonia oblonga*). However, its large, yellow, 4–6 in (10–15 cm) long fruit, while edible, are not as palatable as true quinces but are very fragrant. The glossy green, oval leaves have hairy undersides. The 1 in (25 mm) wide spring-borne flowers are pale pink, carried singly and followed by the fruit. In fall (autumn) the foliage develops red and yellow tones, so that the leaves and fruit make the tree very colorful.
CULTIVATION: It is frost hardy but needs ample summer warmth. It is not fussy about soil type as long as it is well drained. Plant in full sun to ensure that the fruit and foliage color well. Propagate from seed or cuttings or by grafting.

Pseudocydonia sinensis

Pseudocydonia sinensis
syn. *Cydonia sinensis*
CHINESE QUINCE

This species has bark that is gray and cream and peels in patches to reveal greenish new bark. Its stems, downy when young, become shiny with age. **ZONES 6–10.**

PSEUDOLARIX
GOLDEN LARCH

This genus consists of a single species, a deciduous conifer from China. Slow growing to 120 ft (36 m), in cultivation it seldom exceeds 70 ft (21 m). It grows almost as wide as it does high. It differs from the larch (*Larix*) in that the cone scales taper to a point; the male cones are held in clusters, not singly, and the scales on the female cones spread and drop off.
CULTIVATION: Plant in moist, rich, deep, well-drained, acid soil. It requires shelter from strong winds and abundant light. Propagate from seed.

Pseudopanax crassifolius

Pseuderanthemum reticulatum

Pseudolarix amabilis

Pseudolarix amabilis
syn. *Pseudolarix kaempferi*

The horizontal branches on this species form a broad conical crown, held on a trunk with reddish brown bark that is fissured and scaly. Its fine leaves are soft and pale green with bluish undersides and are arranged in rosettes along slender twigs. The foliage turns golden yellow in the cooler months before dropping. Its flowers appear as catkins, followed by green cones that mature to yellow and persist on the tree. It makes an excellent bonsai specimen. **ZONES 3–9.**

Pseudolarix amabilis

PSEUDOPANAX
syns *Neopanax, Nothopanax*

Members of this small genus of evergreen trees and shrubs are grown for their interesting fruits and foliage. Most of the 12 to 20 species are endemic to New Zealand with one each in Tasmania, New Caledonia and Chile. The leaves are simple when young, becoming compound as they mature. The 5-petalled, greenish summer flowers are inconspicuous. They are followed by clusters of berries. These plants make good tub specimens and attractive house plants.
CULTIVATION: Suited to warm-climate gardens, they need well-drained soil enriched with organic matter either in sun or part-shade. Propagate from seed or cuttings taken in summer.

Pseudopanax arboreus
syns *Neopanax arboreus, Nothopanax arboreus*
FIVE FINGERS

This New Zealand species, growing to 20 ft (6 m), has a domed crown and stubby limbs. Large, lustrous, deep green, compound leaves comprise 5 to 7 serrated leaflets, each 6–8 in (15–20 cm) long. Small green flowers with a honey fragrance are followed by bunches of purple-black, spherical fruit. **ZONES 9–11.**

Pseudopanax crassifolius
HOROEKA, LANCEWOOD

This small tree from New Zealand changes dramatically with age. Young plants have a single stem up to 8 ft (2.4 m) tall. The stiff, sword-like, narrow leaves up to 3 ft (1 m) long, dark shiny green above, purplish beneath, with sharply serrated edges and a reddish midrib. Older plants are branched, 30 ft (9 m) or so tall with a rounded canopy 10 ft (3 m) wide. The leaves then become compound, with leathery leaflets 12 in (30 cm) long and edges more deeply toothed. Small, black, ornamental fruit are produced by female plants. **ZONES 9–11.**

Pseudopanax ferox
TOOTHED LANCEWOOD

This species passes through 3 juvenile leaf stages before developing its adult foliage. The first stage is the most impressive: viciously toothed, narrow leaves up to 18 in (45 cm) resemble miniature Asian swords. They hang at a 30° to 60° angle from perfectly straight stems up to 12 ft (3.5 m) tall. As the tree matures to its eventual 25 ft (8 m), the leaves become smaller, broader, rounded and smooth edged. **ZONES 9–10.**

Pseudopanax laetus

Ultimately up to 20 ft (6 m) tall, this species is widely grown as a tub plant when young. It has luxuriant hand-shaped leaves with 5 to 7 leaflets, each of which is up to 10 in (25 cm) long. New leaf buds are enclosed in a jelly and open from purplish young stems. The large heads of tiny green flowers are followed by small purple-red seed capsules. This is a great plant for adding a tropical touch to a temperate garden. **ZONES 9–10.**

Pseudopanax lessonii
HOUPARA

This well-branched, slender shrub or small tree grows to 20 ft (6 m) and has rich green leathery leaves, each consisting of 3 to 5 oval to lance-shaped leaflets up to 4 in (10 cm) long. In warm-temperate areas the leaves may be tinged bronze to purple in winter. The houpara tolerates exposed windy conditions and also makes a good tub specimen. **ZONES 9–10.**

Pseudopanax lessonii Hybrids

In New Zealand these hybrids are widely planted and have largely displaced the typical *Pseudopanax lessonii* in popularity as garden plants. Their other parent species is generally *P. crassifolius.* Some have leaves that are not compound but only lobed, the lobes often very broad and rounded, while others have compound leaves with leaflets of varying width and often purplish. Yellow-variegated cultivars are also offered. **'Cyril Watson'** has leathery, 3-lobed leaves with light-colored veins and multiple stems. **ZONES 9–11.**

PSEUDOSASA

This evergreen, perennial bamboo genus native to China, Korea and Japan consists of 3 to 6 species. In warm, humid climates they have running rhizomes that become invasive; if exposed to cold winters they are clump forming and less vigorous. They have stiffly erect, powdery white, narrow stems with bristly sheaths on each node. Heights range from 6–40 ft (1.8–12 m) depending on the species. The bright green, narrow, lance-shaped leaves are 3–12 in (8–30 cm) long. They are strong growers that make excellent screens or hedges. **CULTIVATION:** They are easily grown in any moist, well-drained soil in sun or part-shade and are very frost hardy. Propagate by division.

Pseudotsuga menziesii

Pseudopanax laetus

Pseudosasa japonica
ARROW BAMBOO, METAKE

Native to Japan, this species has white-powdered stems 10–20 ft (3–6 m) tall but less than 1 in (25 mm) in diameter. The leaves are 8–15 in (20–38 cm) long and blue-green on the undersides for about two-thirds of their length. This is a vigorous grower that can be difficult to contain in areas with mild winters. **ZONES 6–10.**

PSEUDOTSUGA

Among the largest of all conifers, the 6 to 8 *Pseudotsuga* species are seldom seen at their maximum height outside their native North America, China, Taiwan, Japan and Mexico. They can reach 300 ft (90 m) with a cylindrical trunk supporting an attractive, broad pyramidal shape. The leaves are soft, green, flattened and tapered, with two bands of white on their undersides. The brown cones, 2 in (5 cm) long with pointed bracts, hang downwards; they take a year to mature. **CULTIVATION:** These very frost-hardy trees prefer cold climates, cool, deep soil and sunny, open spaces. Propagate from seed or by grafting.

Pseudotsuga menziesii
syns *Pseudotsuga douglasii, P. taxifolia*
DOUGLAS FIR, OREGON PINE

This fast-growing conifer can reach 300 ft (90 m) and live for 400 years. Its timber has long been valued in North America. Its sturdy trunk is covered with dark, reddish brown, thick, corky bark. The branch tips curve upwards and have dense, soft, fragrant, bluish green, needle-like foliage. At each branch tip wine-red buds form in winter, opening as apple-green rosettes of new growth in spring. Pendulous cones appear after the plant is 20 years old. **ZONES 4–9.**

Pseudowintera colorata

Pseudopanax lessonii Hybrid 'Cyril Watson'

Pseudopanax lessonii Hybrids

Pseudosasa japonica

PSEUDOWINTERA

This genus of 3 species of evergreen trees and shrubs is native to New Zealand. They are usually 3–8 ft (1.8–2.4 m) tall, though one species can become a small tree with great age. Their attraction lies in their multicolored, aromatic foliage. The rounded, leathery leaves are 2½ in (6 cm) long by 1½ in (35 mm) wide. They are basically a light greenish cream shade, but they can develop red, purple or orange markings and blotches and lighter silvery undersides. Although the small cream flowers are insignificant, they are followed by large black berries. **CULTIVATION:** Plant in moist, well-drained soil in sun or light shade. They are moderately frost hardy and colorful throughout the year. They may be raised from seed, although particularly good forms should be perpetuated by cuttings.

Pseudowintera colorata
syn. *Drimys colorata*
ALPINE PEPPER TREE, HOROPITO

A spreading, bushy, evergreen shrub, this species grows to a height of 3–6 ft (1–1.8 m) with a spread of 5 ft (1.5 m). The yellow-green leaves, with scarlet markings and a silvery underside, are the main attraction of *Pseudowintera colorata*—these turn purple in the winter months. The greenish spring and summer blooms are insignificant but the black, olive-sized fruit that follow are quite conspicuous. **ZONES 8–10.**

PSIDIUM
GUAVA

Named after the Greek word for pomegranate, this genus of about 100 species of evergreen trees and shrubs, growing to 30 ft (9 m) high, originated in Central and South America. They are grown for their fruits and foliage. Their simple leaves are arranged opposite one another. The clusters of 5-petalled white flowers are usually large and are followed by the decorative fruits. Each fruit is a globular to pear-shaped berry with red or yellow skin. The fruits are mostly used to make jellies, jams and juice but are available fresh in subtropical areas. **CULTIVATION:** Guavas need a warm to hot climate, a protected position and rich, moist, free-draining soil. Tip prune for a compact shape. Propagate from seed or cuttings, or by layering or grafting.

Psychopsis hybrid

Psidium cattleianum

Psidium cattleianum
CHERRY GUAVA

This shrub, growing to 20 ft (6 m), takes its common name from its deep red to purplish fruit about 1 in (25 mm) across. It has an upright trunk with smooth, beautifully mottled bark; the rounded, shiny green leaves, 3 in (8 cm) long, are leathery and form a canopy to 12 ft (3.5 m) across. Its single flowers are 1 in (25 mm) across. ***Psidium cattleianum* var. *littorale*** has yellow fruit; **'Lucidum'** has sweet purplish fruit. ZONES 9–11.

Psidium guajava
YELLOW GUAVA

Grown in all tropical and subtropical regions for its nutritious abundant fruit, this tree reaches 30 ft (9 m) with a dense, bushy canopy. It has scaly, greenish bark. The 6 in (15 cm) long leaves are leathery

Psidium guajava

with prominent veins and downy undersides. Spring flowers bunched in the leaf axils are followed by round, 3 in (8 cm) diameter fruit with pink flesh and yellow skins. ZONES 10–12.

PSILOTUM
FORK FERN, WHISK FERN

Two species make up this genus; they are widespread throughout the tropics and subtropics and are very primitive plants that are not really ferns but more closely allied to the club mosses. Without roots, they are epiphytic or terrestrial and anchor themselves in any available crevice. They have no leaves and instead rely on their branching green stems for photosynthesis. They grow 24–30 in (60–75 cm) tall and resemble small clumps of wiry stemmed broom, except for the flower bud-like spore capsules that form near the stem tips.
CULTIVATION: As they have no roots, they rely on atmospheric moisture; consequently they need a humid environment, or at least periods of high humidity. Frost tender, they are green-

Psidium cattleianum

house plants in temperate areas. Situate in sun or part-shade and peg or wire down to prevent movement. Propagate by division.

Psilotum nudum
SKELETON FORK FERN

The skeleton fork fern grows to around 24 in (60 cm) tall and is usually an erect, wiry stemmed bush but sometimes has a pendulous habit. The stems are bright, slightly yellow- to olive-green with bronze new growth. The spore capsules that develop at the stem tip split open to reveal white spores. ZONES 10–12.

PSORALEA

This genus of perennials and shrubs from the Americas and South Africa includes some 130 species. They have compound, bright green leaves, often trifoliate but sometimes reduced to almost needle-like foliage. Their flowers are pea-like and are usually borne in spikes or racemes clustered near the stem tips. The flowers are usually white or a combination of blue and white.
CULTIVATION: Hardiness varies with the species. Those most widely cultivated are usually fairly frost tender but otherwise are easily grown in any light, well-drained soil in full sun. They are raised from seed, which often self-sows in favorable climates, or from cuttings.

Psoralea pinnata
BLUE PEA

This evergreen South African species grows to about 10 ft (3 m) tall. It has a dense covering of bright green, needle-like foliage that is soft and pliable. Bright blue and white sweet pea-like flowers are carried in terminal clusters in spring. Frost hardy to around 25°F (–4°C), does best in mild coastal areas. ZONES 9–11.

PSYCHOPSIS

There are about 5 evergreen orchid species in this genus, all of which were formerly placed in the genus *Oncidium*. They occur from Costa Rica to Peru at low altitudes in moist forests. The pseudobulbs are compressed with a single, reddish brown leaf with some green blotches. The inflorescences rise from the base of the pseudobulbs with the flowers being produced singly in progression at the apex of the inflorescences.
CULTIVATION: Cultivate in a well-drained medium in a pot, or on a slab, in warm or intermediate conditions. Propagate by division and check for aphids, mealybugs and spider mites.

Psychopsis papilio
syn. *Oncidium papilio*

This species is distributed from the West Indies to Venezuela, Colombia, Ecuador and Peru and is epiphytic in forests at low altitudes. The pseudobulbs are crowded, laterally compressed and about 1–2 in (2.5–5 cm) long with a single leaf up to 8 in (20 cm) long and 2 in (5 cm) wide, olive green, mottled with red or purple. The inflorescences, which are up to 3 ft (1 m) long with only one flower, open one at a time; each flower is about 4 in (10 cm) long. ZONES 10–12.

PSYCHOTRIA
WILD COFFEE

This is a genus of well over 500 species of perennials, shrubs and trees widely distributed through the tropics and subtropics. Their leaves are large (6–12 in/15–30 cm long), usually elliptical to lance-shaped with 2 leafy bracts at their base that are shed as the leaves mature. The foliage is leathery, sometimes with fine hairs. Their flowers, usually white or cream, are tiny but are carried on showy panicles. They are followed by ½ in (12 mm) diameter yellow, red, blue, purple or black berries. Many species yield tryptamine-style drugs that have narcotic and medicinal effects.
CULTIVATION: All species are very frost tender, though the smaller ones make good greenhouse plants in temperate areas. Plant in moist, humus-rich, well-drained soil in sun or part-shade. Propagate from seed or cuttings.

Psilotum nudum

Psoralea pinnata

Pteris tricolor

Pteris umbrosa

Psychotria capensis

This is a South African tree that grows to around 25 ft (8 m) tall. It has lustrous, leathery, elliptical, 6 in (15 cm) long leaves and 6 in (15 cm) panicles of tiny cream to yellow flowers. The fruit are red ageing to black. **ZONES 10–11.**

PSYLLIOSTACHYS

STATICE

This genus of 6 to 8 species of annuals is found in the Middle East and central Asia. Once included with *Statice (Limonium)*, they are now classified separately. Rarely over 15 in (38 cm) tall in flower, they form a clump of basal leaves, sometimes hairy, that are often deeply cut so they are almost pinnate. The papery flowers are white, pink or mauve, tiny and borne on upright spikes that only rarely branch. They are often dried or used fresh in floral arrangements.

CULTIVATION: Plant in moist, well-drained soil in full sun and allow to dry off after flowering. Propagate from seed.

Psylliostachys suworowii

syn. ***Limonium suworowii***

RUSSIAN STATICE, RAT'S TAIL STATICE

Native to Iran, Afghanistan and central Asia, this species has sticky 2–6 in (5–15 cm) leaves and relatively large pink flowers on wavy 6 in (15 cm) spikes. **ZONES 6–10.**

PTELEA

From the cooler parts of North America, this is a genus of 11 species of small, deciduous trees or large shrubs that grow slowly to an eventual height of 25 ft (8 m). The branching stems carry bushy foliage with leaves composed of 3 oblong leaflets. In common with the citrus family, to which they are related, the leaves have oily glands that release a scent when crushed. They turn a beautiful shade of gold in fall (autumn). The small, greenish white flowers are fragrant and appear from late spring to early summer.

CULTIVATION: Plant in a shady site in free-draining soil and keep well watered. Propagate from seed in fall or by layering and grafting in spring.

Ptelea trifoliata

HOP TREE, WATER ASH, STINKING ASH

This tree can grow to 25 ft (8 m), given the shade of taller trees and plenty of mulch in the warmer months to conserve soil moisture. The bark is a rich brown, and the oval, dark green leaflets are up to 4 in (10 cm) long. The fruit resemble bunches of keys. This tree makes an attractive ornamental for cool-temperate gardens. **'Aurea'** has soft yellow leaves when young that mature to lime green. **ZONES 2–9.**

PTERIS

BRAKE FERN

This genus consists of 280 species of deciduous, semi-evergreen and evergreen ferns native to the shady, damp gullies of subtropical and tropical rainforests but also found growing out of rock crevices in full sunlight. They have closely spaced fronds and spores that form at the frond edges, and do well as feature plants.

CULTIVATION: These ferns can adapt to various positions but need a great deal of water during the early growth period and should be kept out of direct sunlight. They are often grown indoors and are generally best propagated from spores or by division. Some species are frost tender, others are frost hardy. Keep an eye out for aphids on the leaf stalks.

Psychotria capensis

Pteris cretica

CRETAN BRAKE FERN

This bushy yet delicate evergreen fern grows to 18 in (45 cm) high. It prefers a moist, sheltered garden or fernery, and makes an attractive indoor plant. There are several cultivated varieties, the best known being **'Albolineata'**, which has almost gray leaves with broad central margins of white. **ZONES 10–12.**

Pteris ensiformis

SLENDER BRAKE FERN

This dainty little evergreen fern grows to 12 in (30 cm) high. Its small fronds are pinnate or bipinnate, with narrow segments rounded at their tip. Cultivars are variegated. It prefers a warm climate, and so in cool areas should be well sheltered. **ZONES 10–12.**

Pteris tricolor

PAINTED BRAKE

This evergreen species reaches a height of 24 in (60 cm) and comes from Malacca. The pinnate fronds grow to 24 in (60 cm) in length, are purple-red when young and mature to mid-green. **ZONES 10–12.**

Pteris umbrosa

JUNGLE BRAKE

This Australian species has 12–24 in (30–60 cm) fronds on 4–12 in (10–30 cm) stems. Its creeping rhizome spreads quickly and enables the plant to colonize large areas. **ZONES 10–12.**

Pteris vittata

Native to tropical and temperate regions throughout the world except America, this evergreen species has broad, brown-scaled fronds up to 3 ft (1 m) long. It develops into a dense clump and can be rather invasive. **ZONES 9–12.**

PTEROCARPUS

Widely distributed in the tropics and also found in South Africa, this genus of legumes includes some 20 species of trees and climbers. They have large, pinnate leaves and are usually deciduous in the dry season, the flowers opening before

Ptelea trifoliata

Psylliostachys suworowii

the foliage develops. The flowers are pea-like, scented, small but brightly colored in shades of yellow and orange and are borne in racemes. Rounded pods follow, their edges extended into a 'wing' in some species and not splitting to release their seeds like pods of most other legumes.
CULTIVATION: Plant in moist, well-drained soil in full sun. These are tropical plants that will not tolerate frosts. Propagate from seed or cuttings.

Pterocarpus rohrii

This species is widespread in tropical America, ranging from Costa Rica to Peru, growing in deciduous lowland rainforest. It makes a broadly spreading tree to 30 ft (9 m) or more in height with drooping outer branches and leaves with broad, deep green leaflets. Attractive sprays of pea-like flowers are followed by pods that are large for this genus, about 4 in (10 cm) across, almost circular and quite woody. **ZONES 11–12.**

PTEROCARYA

WING NUT

Ranging from the Caucasus to China, this genus consists of about 10 species of deciduous trees that are grown for their handsome leaves and pendent flowers. Reaching a height of 100 ft (30 m) or more, they have spreading crowns with abundant, pinnate, bright green leaves, each leaflet 4 in (10 cm) or more long. Members can be readily identified by the spring flowers, which appear as yellowish green catkins and grow to 18 in (45 cm) long. Winged nutlets, forming chains up to 18 in (45 cm) long, hang from the branches in ribbons and are an eye-catching feature.
CULTIVATION: These very frost-hardy trees prefer full sun and fertile, deep, moist but well-drained soil. Propagate from cuttings in summer or from suckers or seed in fall (autumn).

Pterocarpus rohrii

Pterocarpus rohrii

Pterocarya stenoptera var. *brevialata*

Pterocarya carpinifolia

The name of this species means 'with leaves like *Carpinus*' (the hornbeam genus). This presumably refers to the conspicuous, regular veining of the leaflets—though the hornbeams, of course, differ in having simple, not compound leaves. In other respects *Pterocarya carpinifolia* resembles *P. fraxinifolia.* **ZONES 5–9.**

Pterocarya fraxinifolia

CAUCASIAN WING NUT

This large tree quickly reaches 100 ft (30 m) and has a wide crown adorned with numerous leaflets. Its flowers form long, pendulous, greenish golden catkins; these are followed by ribbons of winged fruit. This species needs a sheltered position and is an excellent shade tree for a large garden or park, especially near water. **ZONES 5–9.**

Pterocarya carpinifolia

Pterocarya stenoptera

This Chinese species grows to at least 60 ft (18 m) tall with leaves up to 15 in (38 cm) long made up of up to 23 leaflets. The new foliage and young shoots are covered with fine down. The catkins are as long as or slightly longer than the foliage. ***Pterocarya stenoptera* var. *brevialata*** has short-winged catkins. **ZONES 7–10.**

PTEROCELTIS

Allied to the hackberries (*Celtis* spp.), the single species in this genus is a 30 ft (9 m) tall, round-headed, deciduous tree from northern and central China. It has flaking, grayish bark and 1½–4 in (3.5–10 cm) long, oval to lance-shaped leaves with finely serrated edges, conspicuous veining and a slight down on the undersides. In fall (autumn) the foliage shows little color except hints of yellow and orange.
CULTIVATION: It thrives in any moist, well-drained soil and needs part-shade and shelter from strong winds when young; otherwise it is easily grown, tough and adaptable. It is hardy to at least –5°F (–20°C). Propagate from seed or cuttings or by grafting.

Pteroceltis tatarinowii

There are separate male and female flowers on this species. While inconspicuous, they are followed by sycamore-like winged fruit (samara) up to 1 in (25 mm) wide. This tough tree is particularly well suited to parks and playgrounds. **ZONES 5–9.**

PTEROCEPHALUS

This genus from the Mediterranean area and central to eastern Asia contains 25 species in a range of growth forms: annuals, perennials, subshrubs and shrubs. The most commonly cultivated are tufted, cushion-forming plants bearing hairy, silver-gray, 1½ in (35 mm) leaves with wavy edges. From late spring onwards 1 in (25 mm) wide heads of pink, scabious-like flowers start to open, carried on 2 in (5 cm) stems just above the foliage.
CULTIVATION: Usually treated as rockery plants, they prefer full sun and light, well-drained soil with a little dolomite lime. They also do well on dry-stone walls. Propagate the annuals from seed, the rest from seed or cuttings.

Pterocarya fraxinifolia

Pterocephalus perennis

This Greek species is a small, cushion-forming perennial with 1½ in (35 mm), shallowly toothed, gray-green leaves. It is about 4 in (10 cm) high and spreads to around 12 in (30 cm) wide. From late spring it is studded with 1 in (25 mm) wide, dusky pink flowerheads on short stems. An ideal rockery plant, it appreciates a touch of dolomite lime. **ZONES 6–9.**

PTEROSTYLIS

GREENHOOD ORCHID

This small-growing terrestrial orchid genus of at least 60 species occurs in Australia, New Zealand, New Caledonia and Papua New Guinea. They grow mostly in temperate, seasonal, open forests at sea level to moderate altitudes. The plants consist of underground tubers with a rosette of leaves and an inflorescence, usually arising terminally from the rosette. The flowers have the dorsal sepal and the petals united into a hood, which is often translucent. The lip is hinged and responds to being touched by springing back into the hood. The lateral sepals are also joined. Most species lose their leaves during the dry season.
CULTIVATION: Cultivation requirements are for intermediate to cool conditions in part-shade, with a dry resting period in which water is completely withheld in summer or winter depending on the climate from which they come. The medium should be well drained with composted pine bark, fine

charcoal, leafmold and coarse sand. After the resting period the plants may be repotted and then separated. When well grown, *Pterostylis* species make interesting pot plants with attractive flowers.

Pterostylis baptistii
KING GREENHOOD

This is a small terrestrial species that forms large colonies in moist, open forests and rainforest margins on the eastern coast of Australia. The thin-textured leaves are in a rosette and are up to 3 in (8 cm) long and 1 in (25 mm) broad. The inflorescence is up to 15 in (38 cm) tall with a single flower 1½–2½ in (3.5–6 cm) long. This is the largest species in the genus. Flowering is variable, but occurs mostly in fall (autumn). **ZONES 9–11.**

Pterostylis obtusa
BLUNT TONGUE GREENHOOD

This small terrestrial from southeastern Australia has thin-textured leaves about 1 in (25 mm) long by ½ in (12 mm) wide in a rosette. The inflorescence is up to 8 in (20 cm) tall with a single flower about 1 in (25 mm) long. Flowering is in fall (autumn). **ZONES 9–11.**

Pterostylis taurus
syn. *Pterostylis ophioglossa* var. *fusca*
CHARGING BULL

This small, colony-forming, terrestrial species occurs in the northeastern part of Australia at low to moderate altitudes,

Pterostylis baptistii

Pterostylis obtusa

Pterostyrax hispida

often in strong sunlight and seasonal conditions. The leaves are 1–1½ in (25–35 mm) long by ½–1 in (12–25 mm) wide in a rosette. The inflorescence is 4–10 in (10–25 cm) tall with a single flower ½–1 in (12–25 mm) long. It flowers in fall (autumn). **ZONES 9–11.**

PTEROSTYRAX

This genus from Asia consists of 4 species of deciduous shrubs and trees that reach up to 50 ft (15 m) with a spread of 40 ft (12 m). The slender branches carry serrated leaves that are 6 in (15 cm) or more long, bright green and oval. Creamy white, fluffy flowers are produced in pendulous sprays up to 10 in (25 cm) long. The fruits are bristly seed capsules.
CULTIVATION: Plant in deep, moist, well-drained soil in sun or part-shade. Propagate from seed in the cooler months, from cuttings in summer or by layering. These useful shade trees should be pruned only to control shape and size.

Pterostyrax hispida
EPAULETTE TREE, FRAGRANT EPAULETTE TREE

This species from China and Japan grows to 50 ft (15 m). Rich green, oval leaves with wedge-shaped bases and downy undersides form a dense crown. In summer it displays fragrant white flowers in drooping sprays. Gray, furry, 10-ribbed fruit appear in early fall (autumn) and stay on the bare branches during winter. **ZONES 4–9.**

Pterostylis taurus

Pterostyrax hispida

PTILOTUS

This is a genus of around 100 species of annuals, perennials and subshrubs from Australasia. Their leaves are often rather thick and heavy and are stemless. The foliage tends to be red tinted and frequently has wavy edges. The flowers are tiny, usually a shade of green, pink or purple, and are carried on shaggy spikes up to 6 in (15 cm) long.
CULTIVATION: Apart from being frost tender, they are easily cultivated in any well-drained soil in full sun. Propagate the annuals from seed, the perennials and shrubs from seed or cuttings.

Ptilotus exaltatus
MULLA MULLA, TALL PUSSY TAILS

This perennial, native to the arid inland of Australia, bears lilac-gray to dark pink flowers in feathery, cylindrical clusters on strong, upstanding stems above lance-shaped, gray-green leaves. Flowering occurs from winter through to summer. It grows 24–36 in (60–90 cm) tall with a 24 in (60 cm) spread. **ZONES 9–11.**

Ptilotus manglesii

This is an Australian species that flowers from late winter to early summer when it is covered in rounded, 4 in (10 cm) spikes of pink to purple flowers. Sometimes grown as an annual, it is a short-lived spreading perennial that grows to around 12 in (30 cm) high. The leaves

Ptilotus manglesii

vary in shape: the basal leaves are oval and up to 3 in (8 cm) long, while the upper leaves are narrow. **ZONES 9–11.**

PTYCHOSPERMA

Indigenous to northern Australia, New Guinea and other Pacific islands, this genus consists of 30 species of clump-forming or solitary feather palms that can grow to 30 ft (9 m) on erect, slender trunks. The leaves are dark green and pinnate, forming a canopy up to 12 ft (3.5 m) wide. The cream or yellow flowers occur in large, branching sprays. Red, orange or black berries cluster in bunches along the length of the stems.
CULTIVATION: These tropical plants need humidity, full sun and well-drained soil with plenty of moisture. Propagation from seed is slow, as it takes several months to germinate.

Pulmonaria officinalis 'Sissinghurst White'

Pulmonaria saccharata

Pulmonaria saccharata 'Highdown'

Ptychosperma macarthurii
MACARTHUR PALM

Growing to 30 ft (9 m), this species forms a clump displaying large leaves up to 5 ft (1.5 m) long. Its leaflets have a characteristic 'chewed' appearance at the tip. Yellowish flowers held in long, pendulous sprays are followed by red berries. This species looks good as an understory plant in a mixed palm grove; it also makes a good tub specimen. Prune only to remove badly wind-damaged fronds. **ZONES 11–12.**

PULMONARIA
LUNGWORT

Lungwort is an unappealing name for this Eurasian genus, which consists of 14 species of perennial, rhizomatous, forget-me-not-like plants, but it refers to their former medicinal use not their appearance. The most common species are low, spreading plants 6–10 in (15–25 cm) high with a spread of 24 in (60 cm) or more. The simple oval to lance-shaped leaves are sometimes slightly downy and often spotted silver-white. From very early spring small deep blue, pink or white flowers open from pink or white buds.

CULTIVATION: These woodland plants are easily grown in cool, moist, humus-rich soil in light shade. All are very frost hardy. Propagate from seed or cuttings or by division.

Pulmonaria angustifolia
BLUE COWSLIP, BLUE LUNGWORT

Dark blue flowers, sometimes tinged pink, bloom throughout spring on this frost-resistant European deciduous perennial. The flowerheads have a 5-lobed tubular shape and are held above basal rosettes of mid-green foliage. The plant grows to a height and spread of 10–12 in (25–30 cm). **'Blaues Meer'** produces an extra generous display of big, very bright blue flowers. **ZONES 3–9.**

Pulmonaria 'Blue Ensign'

This species grows to about 12 in (30 cm) in height and has big, deep, bright blue flowers. **ZONES 5–9.**

Pulmonaria longifolia 'Roy Davidson'

Derived from the popular cultivar **'Bertram Anderson'**, this form has broad, strappy, heavily silver white-spotted leaves up to 18 in (45 cm) long and light blue flowers that fade to pink. **ZONES 6–9.**

Pulmonaria 'Mawson's Blue'
syn. *Pulmonaria* 'Mawson's Variety'

'Mawson's Blue' is a deep blue-flowered deciduous perennial with narrow 12 in (30 cm) unspotted leaves and very bristly flower stems. It grows to a height of 15 in (38 cm) with an 18 in (45 cm) spread. **ZONES 5–9.**

Pulmonaria officinalis
JERUSALEM COWSLIP, COMMON LUNGWORT

Often recommended by herbalists as a treatment for coughs, bronchitis and other breathing disorders, this evergreen perennial is widely grown as an ornamental. It has heavily white-spotted 4–6 in (10–15 cm) long leaves and deep blue flowers on stems up to 12 in (30 cm) tall. **'Sissinghurst White'** is an early-blooming, white-flowered cultivar that does not develop pink tints as the flowers age; it grows up to 12 in (30 cm) tall with large leaves. **ZONES 6–9.**

Pulmonaria 'Mawson's Blue'

Pulmonaria rubra
RED LUNGWORT

This evergreen perennial has leaves up to 18 in (45 cm) long, only rarely spotted and relatively hairless. The flower stems are covered with fine bristles and bear purple to blue flowers. Near red-flowered forms occur and there are several cultivars in shades of pink and white. **ZONES 6–9.**

Pulmonaria saccharata
JERUSALEM SAGE, BETHLEHEM SAGE

This evergreen perennial has heavily spotted, hairy, 10 in (25 cm) leaves and has given rise to numerous cultivars with flowers in white and all shades of pink and blue. **'Highdown'** is a 12 in (30 cm) cultivar with silver-frosted leaves and pendulous clusters of deep blue flowers. The **Argentea Group** consists of cultivars with silver leaves and red flowers that turn dark purple with age. **ZONES 3–9.**

Pulmonaria vallarsae

A plant of the highlands and alps of Italy, this herbaceous perennial is found in sun or part-shade in rocky soil near streams. It grows as a clump of spotted, hairy leaves up to 12 in (30 cm) tall but at least twice as wide. The flowers are produced in spring, clustered atop hairy, sticky stems. Blooms open reddish violet but soon change to purple. The award-winning hybrid **'Margery Fish'** has remarkable silver leaves, spotted at the edges, and pink-violet flowers. **ZONES 5–9.**

PULSATILLA
PASQUE FLOWER

These 30 species of spring-flowering, deciduous perennials from Eurasia and North America are closely related to the anemones and were once included in that genus. They form mounding clumps of very finely divided, almost ferny foliaged rosettes. The leaves and flower stems are covered with downy silver-gray hairs. The general effect is that of a hairy anemone with simple large flowers. The flower color range includes white, pink, purple and red.

CULTIVATION: Most often grown in rockeries, these very frost-hardy plants are also suitable for borders and troughs and prefer a moist, gritty, scree soil in sun or part-shade. They do best with cool to cold winters and cool summers and tend to be short lived in mild areas. Propagate from seed or by division.

Pulsatilla albana

Native to the Caucasus and northeast Turkey, this species has deeply divided, very hairy basal leaves and nodding, yellow, bell-shaped flowers on 8 in (20 cm) stems. The outer surface of the flowers is silky. **ZONES 5–9.**

Pulsatilla alpina
ALPINE PASQUE FLOWER

This normally white-flowered species is found in the mountains of central Europe. It forms a dense low clump with rather carrot-like foliage, and the flowering stems, to 18 in (45 cm) tall, bear 2 in (5 cm) wide blooms. **ZONES 5–9.**

Pulsatilla vulgaris 'Rubra'

Pulsatilla alpina

Pulsatilla bungeana

Pulsatilla bungeana

This Siberian species is very small with flower stems scarcely 2 in (5 cm) high. Its flowers are upward facing, bell-shaped and violet-blue when young. They are a little over ½ in (12 mm) wide. **ZONES 4–9.**

Pulsatilla halleri

Found throughout much of southern and eastern Europe and the Caucasus, this species has white, lavender or purple flowers that open from purple-pink to purple buds. Its new growth is a light green and very hairy. The first flowers are usually open before the early leaves are fully unfurled. The whole plant is covered in fine hairs and has a very silky feel. **ZONES 5–9.**

Pulsatilla montana

This species from Switzerland, Romania and Bulgaria has very finely divided leaves, each of the 3 main leaflets having up to 150 lobes. The flowers are 1½ in (35 mm) wide, deep blue to purple, and bell-shaped. They are carried on 6 in (15 cm) stems that continue to grow after flowering and reach 18 in (45 cm) tall when the seed ripens. **ZONES 6–9.**

Pulsatilla patens
EASTERN PASQUE FLOWER

Found in northern Europe and from Russia eastwards through Siberia to western North America, this species has lavender flowers with white or pale yellow exteriors. They are up to 3 in (8 cm) wide and are carried on 3–6 in (8–15 cm) stems. The leaves are less finely divided than those of most species and are quite leathery. **ZONES 4–9.**

Pulsatilla vernalis

After *Pulsatilla vulgaris*, this is probably the most widely cultivated species. Found throughout most of Europe and eastwards to Siberia, it has near prostrate rosettes of very hairy, deeply divided leaves. Its flowers, initially drooping but later erect, are white or white flushed pink. The stems and buds are blue-green. **ZONES 4–9.**

Pulsatilla vulgaris
syns *Anemone pulsatilla, A. vulgaris*

Nodding, 6-petalled flowers bloom in spring on this species from Europe. The yellow centers of the flowers are a stark color contrast to the petals, which can range through white, pink and red to purple. The finely divided leaves are pale green and very hairy. Reaching 10 in

Pulsatilla montana

(25 cm) in height and spread, the species is good in a sunny rock garden. Avoid disturbing the roots. **'Alba'** has pure white flowers and needs protection from sun and frost for the flowers to last. **'Rode Klokke'** (syn. 'Rote Glocke') is a free-flowering form with dark red blooms. **'Rubra'** has purplish red or rusty flowers. **ZONES 5–9.**

PUNICA
POMEGRANATE

This genus, originating from the Mediterranean countries and southern Asia, consists of just 2 species of deciduous shrubs or trees. *Punica granatum*, the only one cultivated, has been valued for centuries for its edible fruit. They have opposite, entire leaves and trumpet-shaped, bright red flowers.
CULTIVATION: Pomegranates can be grown in a wide range of climates, from tropical to warm-temperate, but the red or orange fruit will ripen only where summers are hot and dry. Plant in deep, well-drained soil preferably in a sheltered, sunny position. Propagate from seed in spring or from cuttings in summer or by removing suckers. They can be pruned as a hedge and also make good tub specimens.

Punica granatum

This species, growing to 15 ft (4.5 m) tall and 10 ft (3 m) wide, has 3 in (8 cm) long, blunt-tipped, glossy leaves. Its large, 8-petalled, funnel-shaped, red-orange flowers appear at the branch tips in spring and summer; these are followed by the apple-like fruit. Green before ripening to orange-red, pomegranates have a thick rind surrounding masses of seeds in a reddish, sweet pulp. A range of cultivars is available, the fruit varying from very sweet to acidic and the flowers from red, pink or white. ***Punica granatum* var. *nana***, a dwarf cultivar growing to 3 ft (1 m) high, has single orange-red flowers and small fruit. The commercially grown **'Wonderful'** has double, orange-red flowers and large fruit. **ZONES 9–11.**

Punica granatum

PUSCHKINIA
STRIPED SQUILL, LEBANON SQUILL

This is a genus containing a single species, a strappy-leafed bulb native to the Caucasus, Turkey, northern Iran, northern Iraq and Lebanon. Resembling a small hyacinth or *Scilla*, it has flower stems up to 8 in (20 cm) tall. The flowers are pale blue with darker stripes, tubular, about ½ in (12 mm) long.
CULTIVATION: A tough little bulb well suited to rockeries or pots, it prefers a climate with a distinct winter and a cool summer. Grow in full sun in well-drained soil. It naturalizes well in a suitable climate. Propagate from seed or by dividing well-established clumps.

Puschkinia scilloides
syns *Puschkinia libanotica, P. sicula*

Reaching a height of 4–8 in (10–20 cm), this spring-flowering bulb has 2 semi-erect, mid-green, basal, strap-like leaves and a slim spike of up to 6 pale blue, star-shaped flowers with a darker line down the petals. The small, hyacinth-like flowers have a strong scent. **ZONES 5–9.**

Pulsatilla vulgaris 'Alba'

Pulsatilla vulgaris

Punica granatum var. *nana*

Punica granatum

PUTORIA

Native to the Mediterranean region, this genus is composed of 3 dwarf evergreen shrubs. They are densely branched with small, rather leathery leaves and small clusters of tiny pink flowers at the stem tips. The flowers, which open from mid-spring, are followed by dark red berries that ripen to black. The foliage has an unpleasant odor when crushed.
CULTIVATION: Although not commonly cultivated, they are undemanding. Plant in full sun in well-drained, moist soil. Propagate from seed or cuttings.

Putoria calabrica
STINKING MADDER

This species, ideal for rockeries and alpine troughs, is near prostrate with spreading, mat-forming stems. Its leaves are less than 1 in (25 mm) long, elliptical to landscaped and leathery. Its bright pink flowers are less than ½ in (6 mm) long. **ZONES 8–10.**

PUYA

This large genus of terrestrial bromeliads from South America consists of 170 species. They include the largest of all bromeliads, some species growing to about 20 ft (6 m). They are cultivated in gardens as shrubs. The leaves stand out boldly from a basal rosette and they often have hollow stems. Large blue, purple or yellow flowers are held on unbranched spikes or in dense panicles. The fruit are capsules that enclose winged seeds.
CULTIVATION: These plants can grow in a wide range of soils provided they are well drained, and prefer a sunny position. As with all members of the bromeliad family, keep them away from footpaths because the leaves bear sharp spines along their margins. Prune to remove damaged foliage and propagate by division of offsets or from seed. In cool climates they can be grown in a greenhouse.

Puya alpestris

Puya alpestris

Although plants are often sold under this name, those in cultivation are usually *Puya berteroniana.* The true species is a native of southern and central Chile. It grows 4–5 ft (1.2–1.5 m) tall with spine-edged leaves up to 24 in (60 cm) long. The leaves form dense rosettes from which emerge strong flower stems topped with pyramidal heads of tubular blue green flowers. **ZONES 8–9.**

Puya berteroniana

This species from Chile has blue-green foliage. The stems are prostrate, and the 3 ft (1 m) long narrow leaves are strap-like and arching. During summer, metallic blue flowers with vivid orange stamens form dense panicles up to 6–10 ft (1.8–3 m) tall at the ends of long stems. The rosette of leaves dies after flowering, leaving offsets to carry on. This plant benefits from mulch to prevent water evaporation from its roots. **ZONES 9–10.**

Puya alpestris

Puya berteroniana

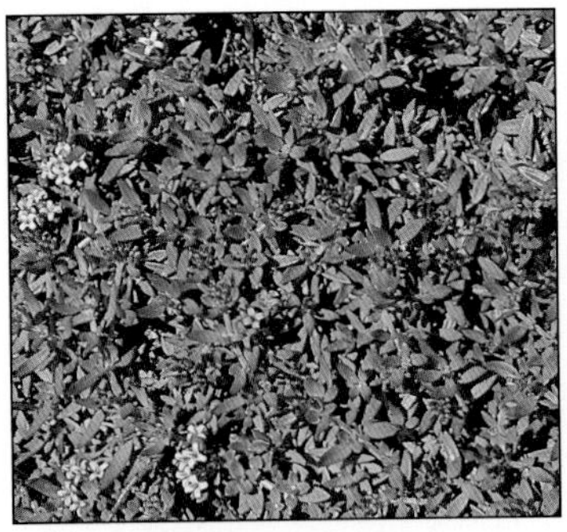

Putoria calabrica

Puya chilensis

This Chilean species has flower stems up to 10 ft (3 m) tall and bright yellow to greenish yellow flowers. Its leaves are spine edged but the spines are not as vicious as those of some species. **ZONES 9–10.**

Puya mirabilis

Native to Argentina and Bolivia, this species has 24–30 in (60–75 cm) long leaves that are silvery brown with fine spines along the edges. Its flower stems are around 5 ft (1.5 m) tall and the flowers are green to white. **ZONES 9–10.**

Puya raimondii

A Peruvian native, this species has very large leaves. They are 3–6 ft (1–1.8 m) long, very stiff, and densely crowded into rosettes. The spines along the edges are ½ in (12 mm) long and viciously hooked. The flower stems are up to 8 ft (2.4 m) tall with yellow green flowers. **ZONES 9–10.**

PYCNANTHEMUM
MOUNTAIN MINT

This genus consists of about 20 species of aromatic perennials closely related to the common mints and sharing their aromas and flavors. They are found in lightly wooded or grassy areas in the higher rainfall parts of North America, where they grow into multi-stemmed herbs up to 5 ft (1.5 m) in height. The leaves are lightly hairy but variable in shape from long and narrow to rounded, with or without toothed edges. The flowers, similar to common mints, are pleasant rather than showy and may be white or pinkish.
CULTIVATION: Grow in moisture-retentive, fairly rich soil that contains plenty of rotted organic matter. Both sun or part-shade are suitable and where winter temperatures fall lower than 20°F (–7°C) it is a good idea to mulch over the

Puya raimondii

Puya mirabilis

roots with a thick layer of straw. Propagate from seed or by division.

Pycnanthemum pilosum

This is an erect-growing perennial 3–5 ft (1–1.5 m) tall with spearhead-shaped leaves that are hairy underneath but mostly smooth above. The pinkish flowers appear on branched inflorescences at the ends of the stems. This very frost-hardy species comes from the eastern half of the USA. **ZONES 4–9.**

PYCNOSORUS

An Australian genus in the daisy family, *Pycnosorus* consists of 6 species of annuals and perennials that until recently were included in the genus *Craspedia.* The plants usually branch from the base into several erect, leafy flowering stems. The leaves are narrow and gray haired and the stems white felted. Each stem terminates in a spherical to egg-shaped flowerhead consisting of tightly packed tiny florets, their color ranging from lemon-yellow to deep gold. The effect is rather striking and they have potential as commercial cut flowers, though as garden plants they are inclined to be rather weak stemmed and untidy.
CULTIVATION: Moderately frost hardy, all species can be treated as annuals and massed in a bed or border in cooler climates. Any normal garden soil suits them, and some species tolerate water-logged soil. Propagate from seed or basal stem cuttings.

Pycnosorus chrysanthus
syn. Craspedia chrysantha
GOLDEN BILLY BUTTONS

Native to eastern Australia, this tufted, short-lived perennial tolerates wet soils. The bright yellow flowerheads measure ½ in (12 mm) across; the foliage is silvery. **ZONES 8–10.**

Pycnosorus globosus
syn. *Craspedia globosa*
DRUMSTICKS

This tufted perennial from southeastern Australia has deep yellow flowerheads 1 in (25 mm) in diameter. Dense hairs on the leaves give them a silvery appearance. The flowers are ideal for cutting. **ZONES 7–10.**

Pycnostachys urticifolia

Pycnosorus globosus

PYCNOSTACHYS

These 40 species of woody stemmed perennials and soft-wooded shrubs come from southern Africa. They can grow to 6 ft (1.8 m) high and have evergreen, narrow, hooked leaves up to 12 in (30 cm) long. In late summer they display cobalt blue flowers on dense spikes 4 in (10 cm) or more long.

CULTIVATION: They need a warm, sheltered position in moist, well-drained soil. In cool climates they can be grown in a greenhouse. Prune back after flowering. Propagate from seed or from cuttings in spring.

Pycnostachys urticifolia
HEDGEHOG SAGE

This much-branched, shrubby plant grows to 5 ft (1.5 m) with 4 in (10 cm) long, oval leaves that are deeply cut and toothed. The bugle-shaped heads of royal blue flowers appear in summer on spikes 4 in (10 cm) high; these can be damaged by frost. It thrives in a warm-temperate to tropical climate. **ZONES 9–12.**

PYRACANTHA
FIRETHORN

Native to temperate Asia and the Mediterranean, these 7 species of large shrubs are grown for their evergreen foliage and abundant, bright red, orange or yellow berries in fall (autumn) and winter. Although tasteless, the berries are edible and much enjoyed by birds. Growing up to 20 ft (6 m), the branches are armed with spines; the foliage is usually glossy green. Clusters of small, white flowers are borne on short spurs along the branches in spring.
CULTIVATION: These temperate-climate plants adapt to a wide range of soils. Firethorns need a sunny position for the brightest berry display, and adequate moisture in dry weather. Propagate from seed or cuttings. Pruning is often necessary to control size, but bear in mind that fruits are produced on second-year wood. They can be espaliered and also make dense, informal hedges and screens. They tend to naturalize and become invasive in favorable conditions. Check for fireblight and scab.

Pyracantha angustifolia
ORANGE FIRETHORN

From western China, this dense shrub with graceful, horizontal branches can reach a height and width of 10 ft (3 m) or more. Its narrow, oblong, dark green leaves, 2 in (5 cm) long have gray downy undersides and are clustered in rosettes on the flowering twigs but arranged spirally on new shoots. It bears clusters of small white flowers from late spring to early summer. Yellow or orange berries persist for most of winter; the flesh has a floury texture. **ZONES 6–11.**

Pyracantha coccinea
SCARLET FIRETHORN

This species, originally from southern Europe, Turkey and the Caucasus, produces a spectacular display of fiery scarlet fruit that resemble tiny apples. Both fruit and foliage become darker if grown in cool climates. It grows to 15 ft (4.5 m) with arching branches spreading to 6 ft (1.8 m). Its narrow leaves are up to $1\frac{1}{2}$ in (35 mm) long, held on slender stalks. Young leaves and twigs are finely downy. **'Kasan'** carries striking orange-red fruit. **'Lalandei'**, developed in France in the 1870s, is a vigorous plant with erect branches that display abundant fruit which ripen to bright orange-red. **'Fructo Luteo'** has bright yellow berries ripening to golden yellow. **ZONES 5–9.**

Pyracantha rogersiana

Pyracantha crenatoserrata
syn. *Pyracantha fortuneana*
YUNNAN FIRETHORN

Native to central and western China, this species has dense, deep green foliage. The rather broad leaves are glossy and hairless on both sides. Its berries are orange, ripening to crimson red. It grows to a height and spread of 12 ft (3.5 m) and looks particularly effective if trained against a brick wall. **'Gold Rush'** bears orange-yellow berries. **ZONES 6–10.**

Pyracantha crenatoserrata 'Gold Rush'

Pyracantha crenatoserrata

Pyracantha coccinea 'Lalandei'

Pyracantha crenulata
syn. *Crataegus crenulata*
NEPAL FIRETHORN

Native to Nepal and China, this sturdy, erect, marginally frost-hardy shrub grows rapidly to a height and spread of 10–12 ft (3–3.5 m). Numerous white, open flowers in early summer are followed by a profusion of small, dark red berries. The glossy leaves are narrow and blunt. **ZONES 7–10.**

Pyracantha koidzumii
FORMOSA FIRETHORN

This species is more irregular in habit than others in the genus and responds less well to pruning and shaping. It is good as a barrier plant or on a bank. **'Santa Cruz'** is a good ground cover, easily kept to under 3 ft (1 m) and producing lots of red berries. **ZONES 7–10.**

Pyracantha 'Mohave'

Pyracantha crenulata

Pyracantha 'Mohave'

This bushy shrub grows to 12 ft (3.5 m) and has dark green leaves, small white flowers and long-lasting orange-red berries. **ZONES 7–10.**

Pyracantha 'Orange Glow'

This upright cultivar, to 10 ft (3 m) in height, is well suited to espaliering. It has vivid orange berries that are very attractive to birds. **ZONES 7–10.**

Pyracantha 'Red Elf'

This is a very compact, mounding bush with deep green leaves and masses of bright red berries. **ZONES 6–9.**

Pyracantha rogersiana

This Chinese species grows to over 8 ft (2.4 m) tall and has 1–1½ in (25–35 mm) long leaves and bright yellow to orange-red berries. The younger shoots are covered with a pale down but mature to red-brown. It flowers heavily and is quite attractive in spring. **ZONES 8–10.**

Pyracantha 'Soleil d'Or'

This spiny shrub grows 10–12 ft (3–3.5 m) tall with a spread of 8 ft (2.4 m). It has shiny, very dark green leaves against which its abundant crops of golden-yellow berries are contrasted beautifully. The berries begin to ripen in late summer and persist on the plant well into fall (autumn). The small white

Pyrostegia venusta

flowers that produce them appear in late spring or early summer. **ZONES 8–10.**

Pyracantha × *watereri*

This ***Pyracantha atalantioides*** × *P. rogersiana* hybrid is densely foliaged and grows to 8 ft (2.4 m) tall. It bears a heavy crop of orange berries. **ZONES 7–10.**

PYROSTEGIA
BRAZILIAN FLAME VINE

This is a genus of 3 or 4 species of climbers and vines native to the warmer parts of Central and South America. They are vigorous twiners with paired, mid-green, 3 in (8 cm) leaves. The flowers are intense orange-red, widely flared trumpets up to 2½ in (6 cm) long. They are carried in clusters of about 15 to 20 blooms. Depending on the climate, flowering starts from early winter to mid-spring and the display lasts for several months.
CULTIVATION: These tropical and subtropical plants require a warm, near frost-free climate and should be grown in moist, well-drained soil in full sun. They may be raised from seed but are usually propagated from cuttings.

Pyrostegia venusta
syns *Pyrostegia ignea, Bignonia venusta*
FLAME VINE, GOLDEN SHOWER

From South America, this magnificent creeper will reach great heights of 30 ft (10 m) or more in warm climates. It is

Pyracantha 'Orange Glow'

Pyrostegia venusta

Pyrrosia lingua

grown chiefly for its brilliant display of orange-gold flowers in fall (autumn), winter or spring, depending on the climate. It will only flower well in full sun. Water well in summer and grow on a strong pergola or arch where the flowers can droop down freely. **ZONES 9–11.**

PYRROSIA
FELT FERN

Found throughout much of the tropics and subtropics, this is a genus of around 100 species of epiphytic or terrestrial ferns with rhizomes that can spread over the ground, across rocks and climb short distances. The rhizomes branch and the ferns eventually form large clumps. The leathery fronds are undivided and leaf-like, 6–18 in (15–45 cm) long depending on the species, with powdery scaling on the upper surface and felting below.
CULTIVATION: These ferns are woodland plants that are often found carpeting large areas in warm-climate forests. Other than an abhorrence of frost, they are easily grown in part-shade in fertile, well-drained soil. Propagate by division.

Pyrrosia lingua
TONGUE FERN

This species is native to China, Taiwan and Japan. It creeping rhizome bears simple 12 in (30 cm) fronds on 2 in (5 cm) stems. There are many cultivated forms with unusually shaped or marked fronds. **ZONES 10–12.**

PYRUS
PEAR

The 30 or so species in this genus from temperate Eurasia and North Africa are related to the apple *(Malus)*. Slow-

P

growing, deciduous and semi-evergreen trees, they occasionally reach 80 ft (24 m) but are often smaller. They have been cultivated since antiquity for their grainy textured, sweet, juicy, yellowish green fruits, not all of which are pear-shaped. They are also valued for their attractive fall (autumn) foliage (for which they need plenty of sun) and their clusters of fragrant, 5-petalled, white flowers (sometimes tinged with pink) which appear with the new leaves, or just before them, in spring. The glossy leaves vary from almost round to quite narrow.
CULTIVATION: With their modest moisture requirements they suit coastal conditions and thrive in heavy, sandy loams with good drainage in a sunny position. They are ideal for cool-temperate climates. They must be cross-pollinated to produce fruit. Prune to remove damaged branches and to improve their shape in late winter or early spring. Propagate from seed or by grafting.

Pyrus calleryana
CALLERY PEAR

Grown as an ornamental, this shapely semi-evergreen tree from China reaches 60 ft (18 m) with a broad canopy. Showy clusters of white flowers appear in early spring and are often followed by small, brown, inedible fruit. The grayish green, 3 in (8 cm) long leaves stay on the tree until late fall (autumn), when they turn shades of rich purplish claret, red, orange or yellow. Tolerating heat, dry conditions, wind and poor soil, it makes an ideal street tree. It is resistant to fire blight but is not very long lived. **'Bradford'** is a common cultivar that flowers profusely and grows well in poor conditions. **'Aristocrat'** is a pyramidal, thornless cultivar with glossy, wavy edged leaves that turn fiery red in fall and yellow to red fruit. **'Chanticleer'** is a narrow-crowned, spiny cultivar with red to magenta fall foliage. **ZONES 5–9.**

Pyrus kawakamii

Pyrus calleryana

Pyrus communis 'Packham's Triumph'

Pyrus communis
COMMON PEAR

The parent of many garden cultivars, the wild pear is grown for its beautiful single, pinkish white flowers with red stamens. Long lived, it reaches 50 ft (15 m) but its short branches can look unappealing when not covered in flowers. The bark is dark gray or brown and cracks into small plates. The dark green, leathery leaves have serrated margins and long stalks. The greenish fruit, up to 2 in (5 cm) long, ripen to yellow and are usually gritty with a dull flavor—the fruit of the cultivars are sweeter and best when picked before fully ripe. **'Beurre Bosc'** is widely cultivated for its heavy crops of large, soft, sweet, brown-skinned pears which are good for baking. **'Bon Chrétien'**, cultivated since medieval times, has medium-sized, succulent, musky-flavored fruit and is the parent of the famous English **Williams** pear; in North America, Australia and New Zealand it is known as the Bartlett pear and is grown for canning—the red-skinned cultivar is known as **'Red Bartlett'**. **'Packham's Triumph'** is an Australian cultivar with large, sweet, green-skinned fruit. **'Conference'** is an early-flowering European pear that produces the best quality fruit if cross-pollinated; fruit start to ripen in mid-fall (mid-autumn) and should be picked before they are fully ripe. **ZONES 2–9.**

Pyrus ussuriensis

Pyrus communis 'Beurre Bosc'

Pyrus communis

Pyrus salicifolia 'Pendula'

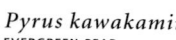

Pyrus kawakamii
EVERGREEN PEAR

From Japan, this graceful, evergreen tree with somewhat pendulous branches grows to 25 ft (8 m) tall and wide. White flowers are produced in quantity in late winter, attractive against the glossy green leaves. The fruit are tiny and hard. It is easily trained as an espalier, but is susceptible to fire blight. **ZONES 8–10.**

Pyrus pyrifolia
JAPANESE PEAR, SAND PEAR

This compact tree, grown for centuries in China and Japan, grows to 50 ft (15 m) and is valued for its beauty and for its fruit. Small flowers appear either just before or at the same time as the oblong, sharply toothed leaves. Glossy green when young, the leaves turn a rich orange-bronze in fall (autumn). The small, round, brown fruit are hard and have a gritty texture. ***Pyrus pyrifolia* var. *culta*** is the name used for all the cultivated forms with larger, edible fruit, including the modern nashi pears. **'Kosui'** is a Japanese cultivar with russet-skinned, globular fruit. **ZONES 4–9.**

Pyrus salicifolia
WILLOW-LEAFED PEAR, SILVER PEAR, WEEPING SILVER PEAR

This popular ornamental pear, growing to about 25 ft (8 m), comes from the Caucasus and Iran. It has graceful, arching branches and the willow-like foliage is long, silver-gray and covered with silky down when young. Small, creamy white flowers are somewhat hidden by the foliage. The small, brown, pear-shaped fruit ripen in fall (autumn). **'Pendula'** has a willowy habit and is more popular than the species itself; its foliage is smaller than that of its parent. Both are very frost hardy. **ZONES 4–9.**

Pyrus salicifolia

Pyrus ussuriensis
MANCHURIAN PEAR, USSURI PEAR

This is the largest growing pear species and can reach 70 ft (21 m) or more. With a broad, pyramidal shape, it makes a neat, attractive street tree. In spring it is covered with a profusion of small, scented white flowers that are followed by small, yellow-brown fruit. Its almost heart-shaped, dark shiny green leaves are up to 4 in (10 cm) wide and turn brilliant red and coral in fall (autumn). **ZONES 3–9.**

Q R

QUERCUS

OAK

Most oaks are from temperate regions but a surprisingly large number of the 600 or so evergreen, semi-evergreen and deciduous species come from tropical and subtropical regions of Mexico, Southeast Asia and even New Guinea. Oaks range from shrubs 3 ft (1 m) high to trees of 120 ft (36 m), and are mostly very long lived; some species have been used for centuries for their hardwood timber. Their leaves, mostly lobed and leathery but in some species thin and lustrous, provide a dense canopy for a multitude of animals, birds and insects and make wonderful compost for acid-loving plants. The leaves of some deciduous oaks develop magnificent hues during the cooler months before they drop. Oaks can be divided into 'white oaks' and 'red oaks', the former with rounded leaf lobes and edible acorns that mature in one year, the latter with pointed leaf lobes and acorns that mature in 2 years and are too bitter to eat. The female flowers are insignificant and greenish, while the male flowers appear as yellow catkins in spring.

CULTIVATION: They thrive in deep, damp, well-drained soil. Some species like full sun; others prefer part-shade when young. They have extensive root systems and do not like to be transplanted. Prune only to remove damaged limbs. Otherwise easy to maintain, oaks are susceptible to oak-leaf miner in humid climates, as well as oak root fungus and aphids. Propagate from fresh seed or by grafting in late winter just before new buds appear.

Quercus acutissima

Quercus acutissima

syn. *Quercus serrata*

JAPANESE OAK, SAWTOOTH OAK

The 6 in (15 cm) long, narrow, glossy green leaves on this deciduous oak from China, Japan and Korea are similar to those of the chestnut and turn yellow in fall (autumn). This slow-growing, lime-hating tree eventually reaches a height of 50 ft (15 m). The narrow foliage remains on the tree until well into winter and attractive long catkins appear in spring. The name sawtooth oak comes from the regular serration of the leaves, as was emphasized by the old name *Quercus serrata*. **ZONES 5–10.**

Quercus alba

Quercus bicolor

Quercus canariensis

Quercus cerris

Quercus agrifolia

CALIFORNIA LIVE OAK

This oak is identified by its stiff, evergreen, spiny toothed leaves and its relatively large acorns maturing to 1 in (25 mm) long. The trunk has black bark and, growing to 60 ft (18 m), supports a rather untidy canopy. This is an important species in California and old specimens are protected by law. It is notably resistant to dry conditions and must be kept dry in summer or its roots will rot; it is difficult to transplant. **ZONES 8–10.**

Quercus alba

AMERICAN WHITE OAK

This deciduous oak grows up to 100 ft (30 m) high with a similar spread. It has scaly, fissured, pale ash-gray bark and oblong, lobed leaves that are up to 8 in (20 cm) long and turn purplish red in fall (autumn). Its acorns are small. Its timber is important commercially, particularly in eastern USA and Canada where it is an important part of mixed hardwood forests. It is one of the stateliest of the American oaks. **ZONES 3–9.**

Quercus bicolor

SWAMP WHITE OAK

This oak is distinguished by its flaking, curling bark, particularly on young trees. Its deciduous foliage forms a round crown and is composed of shallowly lobed, glossy green leaves that are sometimes white and downy beneath. Its small acorns occur in pairs. From eastern USA, it matures to a height of 70 ft (21 m). **ZONES 4–10.**

Quercus castaneifolia

Quercus coccinea

Quercus canariensis

syns *Quercus lusitanica*, *Q. mirbeckii*

CANARY OAK, MIRBECK'S OAK

From North Africa and the Iberian Peninsula, this deciduous or semi-evergreen species keeps its 4 in (10 cm) long, coarsely toothed leaves until well into winter by which time they are a yellowish brown. It grows quickly to 40 ft (12 m) and its long acorns taper to a fine point. To a gardener, this is effectively a larger-leafed version of the English oak that can withstand drier conditions, though it is not suitable for really arid regions. In the wild it grows naturally in river valleys. **ZONES 7–10.**

Quercus castaneifolia

CHESTNUT-LEAFED OAK

This deciduous tree from Iran and the Caucasus is related to the Turkey oak but has leaves remarkably similar to that of a chestnut. These sharply toothed leaves are up to 6 in (15 cm) long and are narrowly tapered with parallel veins. *Quercus castaneifolia* grows to 100 ft (30 m) and forms a broad crown. **'Green Spire'** is a narrow, conical plant that grows to about 30 ft (9 m) tall. **ZONES 6–10.**

Quercus cerris

TURKEY OAK

Originating in central and southern Europe and Turkey, this deciduous oak is one of the grandest in the genus, reaching 120 ft (36 m) with a stout trunk. Its dark, rough bark is deeply fissured and its narrow leaves are gray-green and irregularly toothed, up to 4 in (10 cm) long. It can tolerate alkaline soils and seaside situations, though it rarely reaches its full size there. Its acorns are enclosed within shaggy cups and mature during their second year. **ZONES 7–10.**

Quercus chrysolepis

MAUL OAK, CANYON LIVE OAK, GOLDCUP OAK

From Oregon and California on the west coast of the USA, this evergreen oak grows up to a height of about 70 ft (21 m). *Quercus chrysolepis* is characterized by a short trunk and spreading crown and dark green, glossy leaves up to 4 in (10 cm) long. Its acorn is contained within a cup that is covered in yellow hairs. **ZONES 7–10.**

Quercus coccinea

SCARLET OAK

This deciduous eastern North American oak has deeply lobed, glossy bright green

Q

leaves with bristle tips. The 6 in (15 cm) long leaves turn brilliant scarlet in a cool, dry fall (autumn) and stay on the tree for a long time. It reaches 80 ft (24 m) on a strong central trunk and is distinguished by its drooping branches. The bark is gray and darkens as it matures. *Quercus coccinea* can tolerate pollution and makes a good specimen for urban environments. **'Splendens'** has very deep red fall foliage color. **ZONES 2–9.**

Quercus dentata
DAIMIO OAK

This deciduous oak with stout branches from eastern Asia grows to 50 ft (15 m). Its canopy extends to 40 ft (12 m) and bears dense foliage with very large, coarsely lobed leaves that can be as long as 12 in (30 cm) on young trees. It prefers acid soil. **ZONES 7–9.**

Quercus douglasii
BLUE OAK

This is a very adaptable deciduous tree, native to California. Frost hardy and resistant to dry conditions, it suits most soils and positions and thrives in cold to temperate climates. The blue oak may reach 50 ft (15 m) in height but is often 25–30 ft (8–9 m) in cultivation, erect in form with a crown 10–20 ft (3–6 m) wide. Its leaves are oblong to oblanceolate, up to 4 in (10 cm) long and 2 in (5 cm) wide. The lobes are shallow and undulate, blue-green above and paler below and with a downy midrib. Young shoots are hairy. The acorns on this species are solitary and smallish—to 1 in (25 mm) long—sessile, downy and egg-shaped. **ZONES 8–10.**

Quercus faginea
syn. ***Quercus lusitanica***
PORTUGAL OAK

This deciduous southern European species grows 30–60 ft (9–18 m) tall and can withstand dry conditions. The small, variable leaves are serrated and have a gray, downy underside. The acorns are long and skinny. **ZONES 7–10.**

Quercus falcata
syns ***Quercus digitata, Q. cuneata, Q. trilobata***
SOUTHERN RED OAK

This tall deciduous tree, 80 ft (25 m) or more, is native to southeastern USA. The broad and rounded crown is colored by its young shoots, which are rusty brown and hairy. The leaves are oblong with 1 to 3 pairs of deep lobes, 8 in (20 cm) long with entire to sparsely toothed margins, dark green and glossy above, gray and downy beneath. It prefers dry sites. **ZONES 6–9.**

Quercus gambelii
syn. ***Quercus utahensis***
GAMBEL OAK, UTAH WHITE OAK, ROCKY MOUNTAIN WHITE OAK

This shrubby oak from the foothills of the Rockies is an important tree for the mountain regions of the western USA. Normally 15–30 ft (4.5–9 m) tall and growing in a thicket, it can be pruned into a small tree form. Its deciduous leaves have deeply cut, rounded lobes. Very adaptable to the dry climate of the mountains, it serves many forms of wildlife as a source of food and shelter. **ZONES 4–9.**

Quercus garryana
OREGON OAK, WESTERN OAK, GARRY OAK

This is a large deciduous tree to 100 ft (30 m) with an erect trunk and densely spreading crown although often shrubby in alpine areas. Native to northwestern North America, it is adaptable to most soil types and is resistant to dry conditions. The leaves are glossy green above and paler and downy underneath, oblong to oval, to 6 in (15 cm) long with lobed margins dividing almost to the midrib. The young shoots are orange and downy and the leaf stalks are also hairy as is the cup on the acorn. **ZONES 5–9.**

Quercus × hispanica 'Lucombeana'
LUCOMBE OAK

A hybrid between *Quercus cerris* and *Q. suber*, this semi-evergreen tree with corky bark is fairly tall, to 60 ft (18 m), with a broad, spreading, conical shaped crown often over half its own height. The leaves have 6 to 9 pairs of triangular teeth, are oval to oblong and are glossy green above and downy gray underneath. The acorn is half covered by the cup at its base. **ZONES 6–9.**

Quercus ilex
HOLM OAK, HOLLY OAK

Native to southern Europe and North Africa, near the Mediterranean coast, this round-headed, dense evergreen can grow to 90 ft (27 m). Its oval leaves are toothed (similar to holly) when young, but become entire with age, and are a lustrous dark green above and white and downy underneath. It grows well in an exposed position, particularly on the coast, and makes a good windbreak. **ZONES 7–10.**

Quercus kelloggii
CALIFORNIA BLACK OAK

This deciduous oak is found throughout the mountains of California and Oregon, where it provides some of the best fall (autumn) color of any native tree in the region. The leaves resemble those of the eastern deciduous oaks, with pointed lobes. It grows to 90 ft (27 m) tall in the wild, less in cultivation. It prefers a very well-drained site with plenty of sun. **ZONES 7–10.**

Quercus leucotrichophora
syn. *Quercus incana*

This oak, native to the Himalayas where it is found with *Rhododendron arboreum*, is evergreen, with an erect trunk and peeling, flaky bark which it often sheds in large pieces. It reaches a height of around 60 ft (18 m). Its acorns are small—$\frac{1}{4}$–$1\frac{1}{4}$ in (6–30 mm) long—and half-enclosed by a cup. The leaves are 3–4 in (8–10 cm) long, oblong to lanceolate, with serrated margins. New growth is silvery pink and densely downy; older leaves are deep green above with a grayish downy underside. **ZONES 8–10.**

Quercus lobata
syn. ***Quercus hindsii***
VALLEY OAK, CALIFORNIAN WHITE OAK

This deciduous tree grows to about 100 ft (30 m), sometimes with a spread of 30 ft (9 m) or more of drooping branches from a central trunk. This is an adaptable tree, suiting warm and cooler climates but preferring plenty of water in summer. The leaves are oblong to oval, 3 in (8 cm) long with 5 to 6 pairs of rounded lobes, dark green with stellate hairs above, grayish and downy beneath. The young shoots are also gray and downy. The acorns are set singly or in pairs, from 1 in (25 mm) long. It is a native of California in the USA. **ZONES 9–10.**

Quercus macrocarpa
BUR OAK, MOSSY-CUP OAK

Native to the USA from the Midwest to the Appalachian Mountains, this deciduous species has scaly, deeply furrowed, light brown bark and matures to a height of 70–80 ft (21–24 m). It is identified by its oblong, deeply lobed leaves which are shiny and up to 10 in (25 cm) long. They turn yellowish brown in fall (autumn). The large cup that encloses the acorn has a moss-like fringe. **ZONES 4–9.**

Quercus mongolica
MONGOLIAN OAK

This striking deciduous tree grows to 100 ft (30 m). From Japan and north-eastern Asia, it bears coarsely but regularly toothed leaves grouped at the ends of the branches. These characteristic leaves are 8 in (20 cm) long and have a fine pale down on the undersides. Its acorns are cone-shaped. **ZONES 4–9.**

Quercus muehlenbergii
YELLOW CHESTNUT OAK, CHINKAPIN OAK, CHINQUAPIN OAK

A native of eastern USA and the Great Lakes district of Canada, this deciduous tree to 100 ft (30 m) has grayish, fissured bark. Its leaves are narrow elliptic to oblong, 6 in (15 cm) long and 2 in (5 cm) wide with yellowish petioles, pale and hairy beneath and glossy green and dark yellow above. The leaf margins are coarsely and deeply serrated and incurved. **ZONES 5–9.**

Quercus myrtifolia
MYRTLE OAK

This oak is a small, shrubby evergreen tree with light gray checkered bark. It is native to coastal regions from South Carolina to Florida in the USA. Its leaves are elliptic to oblong, sometimes with a bristly tip; they are dark green and glossy on both sides, sometimes roll backwards and are 1–2 in (2.5–5 cm) long. The sessile acorns appear in pairs and are only $\frac{1}{2}$ in (12 mm) wide. **ZONES 8–10.**

Quercus kelloggii

Quercus ilex

Quercus lobata

Quercus dentata

Quercus falcata

Quercus palustris

Quercus nigra

Quercus robur 'Concordia'

Quercus phellos

Quercus nigra
WATER OAK, POSSUM OAK

The leaves of this mostly deciduous North American oak are bluish green on top, glossy green beneath. Broad toward the tip, they are 3 in (8 cm) long and held on a slender stalk. Growing to 50 ft (15 m) with a broad, rounded crown, it thrives in moist soil. **ZONES 6–10.**

Quercus palustris
PIN OAK

From the eastern and central USA, this species tolerates dry, sandy soil though it is at its best in deep alluvial soils with plenty of water in summer. Moderately fast growing, it matures to 80 ft (24 m) high. Its smooth, gray trunk supports horizontal branches towards the top of the tree, while the lower branches droop gracefully. Its lustrous green leaves are 4 in (10 cm) long with deep, pointed lobes that turn crimson in fall (autumn) and persist on the tree well into winter. It has a shallow root system. **ZONES 3–10.**

Quercus petraea
syn. *Quercus sessiliflora*
DURMAST OAK, SESSILE OAK

A deciduous tree from central and southeastern Europe and western Asia, this species is closely allied to *Quercus robur* and grows to over 100 ft (30 m). Leaves are glossy green and leathery, and it often forms a broad crown. The bark is grayish and fissured and the trunk thick and stout, continuing to the crown of the tree, making it an important timber tree in Europe. This white oak has leaves with 5 to 8 rounded lobes. **ZONES 5–9.**

Quercus phellos
WILLOW OAK

Native to eastern USA south of New York State, this graceful, deciduous tree reaches about 60 ft (18 m) and makes a good shade tree. Its narrow leaves are up to 4 in (10 cm) long and differ from those of most oaks in being willow-like and not lobed. The foliage turns from a shiny, light green to bright orange in fall (autumn). It prefers moist soil. **ZONES 5–9.**

Quercus prinus
SWAMP CHESTNUT OAK, BASKET OAK

From eastern USA, this deciduous oak can grow to 100 ft (30 m) with an open crown. Its shiny, dark green leaves have pale gray, downy undersides and turn rich yellow in fall (autumn). They have shallow, coarse teeth and are up to 6 in (15 cm) in length; the acorns are oval. This species prefers deep, moist soil. The swamp chestnut is a commercial source of tannin and its timber is also valuable. **ZONES 3–9.**

Quercus robur

Quercus robur 'Fastigiata'

Quercus robur
COMMON OAK, ENGLISH OAK, PEDUNCULATE OAK

Arguably the most famous of all the oaks and with a life span of 600 to 700 years, this species has spreading, heavily leafed branches that provide good shade. Its 4 in (10 cm) long leaves are deciduous and remain dark green through fall (autumn). It eventually reaches a height of 120 ft (36 m) and trunks with a circumference of more than 70 ft (21 m) have been recorded. It is one of Europe's most valuable timber trees. **'Fastigiata'** is grown for its narrow, upright habit, while **'Concordia'** is a rounded tree to 30 ft (9 m). **ZONES 3–10.**

Quercus shumardii

Quercus rubra

Quercus rubra
syn. *Quercus borealis*
RED OAK, NORTHERN RED OAK

Originating in eastern USA and eastern Canada, this robust deciduous tree reaches up to 90 ft (27 m) with a broad canopy formed by strong, straight branches. Its shiny gray bark forms flat-topped ridges that become dark brown as it ages. The matt green leaves with pointed lobes are up to 8 in (20 cm) in length and display rich scarlet and red-brown fall (autumn) hues. The large acorn is held in a shallow cup. The red oak grows relatively quickly and does well in sun or part-shade. The young leaves of **'Aurea'** are bright yellow. **ZONES 3–9.**

Quercus salicina

An evergreen species of oak growing to 60 ft (18 m), this native of Japan has slender, grayish brown branches with narrow, smooth-edged, glossy green foliage. White on the undersides, the lance-shaped leaves are 4 in (10 cm) long. The acorns ripen in their second year. This species is occasionally mistaken for ***Quercus bambusifolia*** because the foliage is similar, and for ***Q. myrsinifolia*** because the acorns are similar. **ZONES 8–10.**

Quercus salicina

Quercus rubra 'Aurea'

Quercus tomentella

Quercus virginiana

Quercus shumardii
SHUMARD RED OAK, SHUMARD OAK

The attractive, 6 in (15 cm) long leaves of this oak are deeply lobed and turn red or golden brown in fall (autumn). From southeastern USA, this deciduous species will grow to 80 ft (24 m). It is very similar to the northern red oak *(Quercus rubra)* but prefers a warmer climate and can withstand a moister soil. **ZONES 5–9.**

Quercus suber
CORK OAK

The thick, furrowed, gray bark of *Quercus suber*, principally from Spain and Portugal and growing elsewhere around the Mediterranean, is the source of commercial cork. A short, sturdy, often gnarled and twisted trunk gives the tree character. It reaches 60 ft (18 m) high with a broad, spreading canopy of 50 ft (15 m). The oval, evergreen leaves with a slightly toothed edge are up to 3 in (8 cm) long; they are a dark, shiny green on top and silvery beneath. Single or paired acorns mature to chocolate brown and are held loosely in a cup covering just over a third of the acorn. **ZONES 8–10.**

Quercus tomentella
ISLAND OAK

An evergreen species, this tree is native to California, Baja California and the coastal islands nearby. It grows to 30–60 ft (9–18 m) tall. The leaves are narrow, to 3 in (8 cm) long, smooth above, downy and prominently veined beneath and often roll backwards. The cup, which encloses one-quarter of the acorn, has scales embedded in a dense matting of downy hairs. **ZONES 10–11.**

Quercus velutina
BLACK OAK, YELLOW OAK

This deciduous oak with velvety buds originates in eastern North America but is now cultivated in Europe. Growing to 100 ft (30 m), it has yellow bark that yields tannin. The inner bark is a source of a yellow dye. Its large, glossy dark green leaves, downy beneath, are lobed and grow to 12 in (30 cm). The ovoid acorns are half-enclosed in a deep cup. **ZONES 3–9**

Quercus velutina

Quercus virginiana
syn. *Quercus virens*
LIVE OAK

This evergreen species is native to southeastern USA and Gulf States west to Mexico. It grows to 40–80 ft (12–24 m) tall with a short trunk that supports horizontally spreading branches and a dense, broad-domed crown. The dark green leaves are white and downy underneath, oblong to rounded in shape and up to 4 in (10 cm) long. The acorns are small, arranged singly or in 2s or 3s and ripen to very dark brown within a year, which is unusual for a red oak. **ZONES 7–11.**

Quercus wislizenii
INTERIOR LIVE OAK

An evergreen tree from California, this species matures to 80 ft (24 m) with a rounded crown. It has black to red fissured bark, while the young branches are quite rigid and downy. The glossy green leaves (like holly) can be either entire or toothed and are up to 4 in (10 cm) long. The small acorns are half-enclosed in their cups. **ZONES 8–10.**

QUESNELIA

This bromeliad genus consists of 15 species of stemless, evergreen perennials found originally in rocky outcrops in eastern Brazil. Some species are also epiphytic. They have a medium-sized rosette of lance-shaped, stiff, spiny leaves. The inflorescences, which are either upright or hanging, are composed of tubular or ovoid flowers that appear among showy bracts.
CULTIVATION: These frost-tender plants prefer part-shade and coarse, humus-rich, moist but well-drained soil. They need the protection of a greenhouse where temperatures drop below 55°F (13°C). Water moderately, but reduce watering levels over the winter period. Propagate from seed or offsets.

Quercus wislizenii

Quesnelia liboniana

This species features navy blue flowers and orange-red bracts. It is a stemless plant that grows to 30 in (75 cm) high. The foliage forms a tube-shaped rosette composed of light green leaves with gray scales on the undersides and spines on the leaf edges. **ZONES 11–12.**

QUILLAJA

About 3 species of evergreen shrubs or trees make up this genus from southern South America, but only one, *Quillaja saponaria,* is of economic importance and is sometimes cultivated. They have shiny, thick, leathery foliage and large, white, purple-centered flowers, which appear in spring.
CULTIVATION: Quillajas need moist but well-drained soil in a part-shaded position and protection from strong winds. They can be clipped to form hedges. Propagate from seed or cuttings.

Quillaja saponaria
SOAPBARK TREE, QUILLAI

The distinguishing characteristic of this tree from Chile and Peru is its bark. Thick, rough and dark, it contains a substance called saponin that acts like soap. It is a narrowly, droopily branched tree to a height of 60 ft (18 m) with thick, glossy green, leathery leaves held on short stalks. The unperfumed, greenish white, 5-petalled flowers appear in spring and are followed by capsular fruit that open into a star shape. **ZONES 8–10.**

Quisqualis indica

QUISQUALIS

This is a genus of about 16 species of evergreen shrubs and twining climbers. They bear panicles or racemes of small, tubular, 5-lobed flowers and have simple leaves produced in opposite pairs. The genus name means 'Which? What?'—an expression of amazement at the variable growth pattern of these natives of Africa and tropical Asia.
CULTIVATION: Grow these frost-tender plants in humus-rich, moist but well-drained soil in full sun or part-shade. The stems may need support; pinch out overgrowth in spring. Propagate from seed or cuttings or by layering.

Quisqualis indica
RANGOON CREEPER, RED JASMINE

This strong-growing, evergreen creeper can reach 70 ft (21 m) in tropical areas. The flowers are strongly fragrant, especially at night, opening white and deepening to pink and then red throughout summer. It needs a sturdy support and is useful for covering fences, walls and pergolas. Cut back old stems in spring and remove spent flowers in fall (autumn). **ZONES 10–12.**

Quesnelia liboniana

Quercus suber

RADERMACHERA

This genus contains about 15 species of evergreen trees and shrubs from tropical and subtropical areas of Asia. In sufficiently warm areas they are grown outdoors for their flamboyant blooms and attractive bipinnate foliage. The usually fragrant flowers are tubular- to trumpet-shaped, in tones of yellow, pink, orange and white; a number of species are night blooming. In cooler climates some species are grown in pots as foliage plants.
CULTIVATION: Plant in rich, well-drained soil in full sun or part-shade. Shelter them from wind, and water regularly during the growing season. Prune plants to maintain a neat habit. Propagate from seed or cuttings.

Radermachera sinica
ASIAN BELL-FLOWER

This native of China's southern tropical regions reaches 30 ft (9 m) tall. It has glossy, dark green bipinnate leaves up to 3 ft (1 m) long, with leaflets up to 2 in (5 cm) long. When mature it bears large panicles of trumpet-shaped white or yellow flowers at the branch tips or axils during spring and summer and slender, capsular fruit up to 15 in (38 cm) long. **ZONES 10–12.**

RAFFLESIA

This genus, thought to contain 14 species, is not well understood, as the flowers are impossible to preserve for study and botanists have to be in the right place at the right time to see them. The generic name honors the contributions to science of Sir Thomas Stamford Raffles (1781–1826), perhaps better known as the founder of Singapore.
CULTIVATION: It appears that *Rafflesia* has never been successfully cultivated for any length of time. They are parasites that have particular host plants (usually *Tetrastigma* or *Cissus* vines) and very exacting requirements. In addition, their repugnant smell, should they ever flower, would limit their welcome as garden plants.

Rafflesia arnoldii

This, the largest species in the genus, bears the world's largest flower. The plant shows nothing above the ground except its football-sized bud, which bursts forth from the stem of its host vine and unfolds as a single flower up to 3 ft (1 m) wide. Its 5 fleshy petals surround a central disc with a circular hole revealing the stamens and pistils. It is mottled all over in dull yellow, cream and mahogany red, and smells of rotting meat to attract flies, which pollinate it. It has never been successfully cultivated. **ZONE 12.**

RAMONDA

This genus from Spain, the Pyrenees and the Balkans contains 3 species of evergreen perennials that have rosettes of hairy, usually wrinkled leaves with toothed, wavy edges. Doing well in rock gardens or in cracks in stone walls, they are also grown for their brightly colored, 4- to 5-petalled flowers, which appear in late spring and early summer.
CULTIVATION: Excessive water in the leaf rosettes may cause rotting, so these plants are best grown on an angle in part-shade and very well-drained, humus-rich soil. Propagate from seed or cuttings.

Radermachera sinica

Rafflesia arnoldii

Radermachera sinica

Ramonda nathaliae

Ranunculus asiaticus

R. asiaticus, Bloomingdale Hybrid

Ramonda myconi
syn. *Ramonda pyrenaica*
BALKAN PRIMROSE, PYRENEAN PRIMROSE, ROSETTE MULLEIN

From branched, reddish brown stems this frost-hardy evergreen produces flattish 5-petalled flowers that resemble African violets. The flowers are in hues of white, pink, blue, lavender or purple and have yellow, pointed anthers. From the mountains of southern Europe, it reaches a height and spread of 3–4 in (8–10 cm). **ZONES 6–9.**

Ramonda nathaliae

This species, which reaches a height and spread of 4 in (10 cm), bears panicles of flat, 4-petalled, deep purple flowers with orange-yellow centers. The mid- to dark green leaves, hairier on the undersides than on top, grow to 2 in (5 cm) in length. **ZONES 6–9.**

RANUNCULUS
BUTTERCUP

This is a genus of some 400 species, mostly annuals and perennials, widely distributed throughout temperate regions worldwide. They are grown for their colorful flowers, which are bowl- or cup-shaped, 5-petalled and yellow, white, red, orange or pink. The name derives from the Latin for 'frog', due to the tendency of some species to grow in bogs or shallow water. The genus includes 2 species of buttercups that are popular folk cures for arthritis, sciatica, rheumatism and skin conditions, including the removal of warts.
CULTIVATION: Most species of *Ranunculus* are easy to grow and thrive in well-drained soil, cool, moist conditions and sunny or shady locations. They are mostly fully frost hardy. Propagate from fresh seed or by division in spring or fall (autumn). Water well through the growing season and allow to dry out after flowering. Keep an eye out for powdery mildew and for attacks by slugs, snails and aphids.

Ranunculus acris 'Flore Pleno'

R. asiaticus, Bloomingdale Hybrid

Ranunculus aconitifolius
BACHELOR'S BUTTONS

Cultivated for its pure white single or double flowers, this perennial flowers in terminal clusters on robust, branched stems from spring to summer. Its dark green leaves have 3 or 5 lobes with saw edges. The plant grows to 24 in (60 cm) high and 18 in (45 cm) wide. It is native to southern and central Europe. **'Flore Pleno'** has long-lasting double, white flowers. **ZONES 6–10.**

Ranunculus acris
MEADOW BUTTERCUP

This clump-forming perennial from Europe and western Asia has wiry stems with lobed and cut leaves. Panicles of saucer-shaped, bright yellow flowers appear in mid-summer. It grows from 8–36 in (20–90 cm) in height. **'Flore Pleno'** has double, rosetted, golden-yellow flowers. **ZONES 5–9.**

Ranunculus anemoneus
ANEMONE BUTTERCUP

Known only from the slopes of Mt Kosciuszko, Australia's highest mountain, this evergreen perennial grows to 18 in (45 cm) high and 24 in (60 cm) wide. Its large white, many petalled flowers have a golden yellow eye and appear in spring and summer. The large deep green leaves are oval and dissected. **ZONES 7–9.**

Ranunculus asiaticus
PERSIAN BUTTERCUP

This frost-hardy perennial from the Mediterranean region is parent to many hybrids and cultivars. Masses of single or double flowers are borne on 15 in (38 cm) stems in spring, in many colors including yellow, orange, red, pink and white. The **Bloomingdale Hybrids** are an 8 in (20 cm) strain bred specially for growing in pots. **ZONES 9–10.**

Ranunculus bulbosus
BULBOUS BUTTERCUP

This perennial species from Europe, northern Africa and the Caucasus has a swollen stem base and grows to 15 in (38 cm) in height. It has dark green leaves and bears panicles of saucer-shaped, deep yellow flowers in spring and summer. **ZONES 7–10.**

Ranunculus cortusifolius

Found on the Atlantic islands of the Azores, Canaries and Madeira, this species has thick, rounded, leathery basal leaves with toothed edges and shallow lobes. The flower stems, up to 4 ft (1.2 m) tall, bear reduced leaves and many-flowered corymbs of 2 in (5 cm) wide bright yellow flowers. **ZONES 9–10.**

Ranunculus ficaria
LESSER CELANDINE, PILEWORT

From southwestern Asia, Europe and northwestern Africa, this perennial has single, almost cup-shaped, bright yellow flowers that appear in spring. It reaches only 2 in (5 cm) in height, and has glossy green leaves with silver or gold markings; the leaves die down after the flowers appear. **'Albus'** has single, creamy white flowers with glossy petals. **'Brazen Hussy'** has deep bronze-green leaves and shiny, deep golden-yellow flowers with bronze undersides. **ZONES 5–10.**

Ranunculus gramineus

With hairy, bluish green leaves shaped like grass, this clump-forming perennial from southwestern Europe has a compact spread and grows 18 in (45 cm) tall. In late spring and early summer it produces yellow, cup-shaped flowers. Plant it in rich soil. **ZONES 7–10.**

Ranunculus cortusifolius

Ranunculus ficaria (orange form)

Ranunculus lyallii

Ranunculus lyallii
MT COOK LILY, GIANT MOUNTAIN BUTTERCUP, MOUNTAIN LILY

Native to the subalpine and low-alpine regions of New Zealand's South Island, this thicket-forming perennial grows to 3 ft (1 m) tall. Its broad, leathery leaves, which resemble water lily leaves, can reach 8 in (20 cm) wide and are lustrous deep green. Glossy, white, cup-shaped flowers appear in branched clusters on tall stems in summer. Moderately frost hardy, it can be very difficult to cultivate. **ZONES 7–9.**

Ranunculus montanus 'Molten Gold'

This compact, clump-forming perennial grows to 6 in (15 cm) with a 4 in (10 cm) spread. It is very frost hardy and has rounded, 3-lobed leaves. Its shallowly cup-shaped, shiny golden-yellow flowers are borne in early summer. **ZONES 6–9.**

Ranunculus repens
CREEPING BUTTERCUP

From Europe, Asia and Africa, this perennial has open, glossy yellow flowers that appear in spring and summer. It has 3-lobed leaves and narrow, entire upper leaves, both appearing on prostrate, creeping stems. It grows to 12 in (30 cm) in height. **'Pleniflorus'** is an erect cultivar to 24 in (60 cm) with yellow, double flowers. **ZONES 3–10.**

RAOULIA
VEGETABLE SHEEP

This is a genus of about 20 species of evergreen perennials or subshrubs confined to New Zealand. They mostly form slow-growing, ground-hugging carpets of downy leaves and in summer bear small white or pale yellow, papery textured daisies. They are excellent foliage plants for rock gardens or raised beds. **CULTIVATION:** Most require a cool-temperate climate, moist, acidic, sharply drained soil and protection from heavy winter rain (otherwise they will rot). They prefer an open, sunny position or part-shade in warmer areas. Propagate from fresh seed or by division in spring.

Ranunculus gramineus

Ranunculus repens

Raoulia australis

Raoulia eximia

Raoulia australis
syn. *Raoulia lutescens*
GOLDEN SCABWEED

Suitable for rock gardens, this prostrate, mat-forming perennial native to New Zealand lays down a solid carpet of silvery leaves ½ in (12 mm) deep over a 10 in (25 cm) spread. In summer it produces minuscule flowerheads of fluffy yellow blooms. **ZONES 7–9.**

Raoulia eximia

This perennial makes tight hummocks of growth 3 ft (1 m) across and completely covered with gray hairs. In late spring or summer it bears yellowish white flowerheads. It grows to only 2 in (5 cm) in height. **ZONES 7–9.**

Raoulia haastii

This frost-hardy perennial grows to only ½ in (12 mm) in height with a 12 in (30 cm) spread. The pale green, silky leaves overlap slightly in dense cushions. Yellow flowerheads appear in spring. **ZONES 7–9.**

Raoulia hookeri

This mat-forming New Zealand species, to 24 in (60 cm) wide, has densely packed rosettes of tiny, silver-gray leaves and, in summer, is studded with clusters of small cream bracts that conceal the yellow true flowers. It is suitable for rockeries provided it is not wet in winter, but is best given alpine house conditions. **ZONES 7–9.**

Raoulia haastii

RAPHANUS
RADISH

Eaten by Egyptian slaves and the ancient Chinese, the well-travelled radish has been used for centuries as an important cooked vegetable (the winter variety) and in salads, pickles and garnishes (the summer variety). There are 3 species in the genus; many varieties are grown in different parts of the world and vary in form from globe-shaped, oblong to cylindrical or tapered. The outside of the root varies from white through pink, to red, purple and black; some are 2-toned. **CULTIVATION:** A friable, moisture-retentive, well-drained soil and a little shade for the summer varieties give best results. The summer varieties require a little shade and are sown directly into the soil. Sow in rows 12 in (30 cm) apart through summer at 14-day intervals and thin out seedlings so that the roots are not competing. In hot weather, keep well

Raphanus sativus

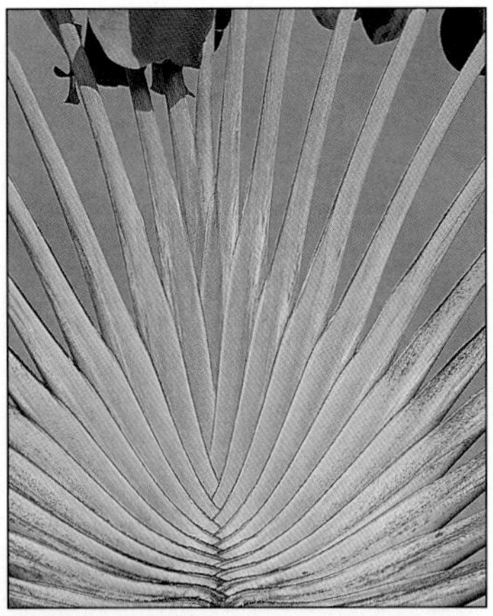

Ravenala madagascariensis

Rauvolfia caffra

watered. Harvest 4 weeks after sowing in warm climates. In cooler climates wait a further 3 weeks. Winter maturing varieties may take up to 60 days to mature and are best sown later in summer or fall (autumn). Do not leave in the ground too long as radishes turn woody. Propagate from seed. Keep birds away from the young leaves.

Raphanus sativus

This Chinese annual grows to 3 ft (1 m) and spreads to 18 in (45 cm). It has an erect, hollow stem and rough, alternate leaves. White or lilac flowers with strongly marked veins and 4 petals appear in branching clusters. **'Rex'** and **'Tarzan F1'** are both very popular cultivars. **ZONES 6–10.**

RATIBIDA

MEXICAN HAT, PRAIRIE CONEFLOWER

This genus from Mexico and North America contains 5 or 6 species of biennials and perennials with erect stems and alternate, pinnate leaves. They are grown mainly for their daisy-like flowerheads, which make good cut flowers, and do very well in wildflower gardens.
CULTIVATION: These very frost-hardy plants prefer full sun and very well-drained, almost dry, moderately fertile soil. They can tolerate dry conditions. Propagate from seed or by division.

Ratibida columnifera

This erect perennial grows to 30 in (75 cm) in height and has a 12 in (30 cm) spread. It bears its flowerheads with reflexed, yellow ray florets and long, green to brown disc florets from summer to fall (autumn). The grayish green, hairy leaves can be up to 6 in (15 cm) long. **ZONES 3–9.**

Ratibida pinnata

DROOPING CONEFLOWER

From central North America, this upright, many branched perennial bears its bright yellow flowerheads from summer to fall (autumn). It has glaucous, toothed leaves and reaches 4 ft (1.2 m) in height. **ZONES 3–9.**

RAUVOLFIA

There are over 50 species in this genus of trees and shrubs, which are found growing in the tropics of both hemispheres. Their large, glossy leaves are held in whorls of three or five. The flowers, held terminally, are either white or greenish and are followed by a berry containing 1 or 2 seeds. Different parts of the plants, including the watery or milky white poisonous sap, have been used as a tranquilizer, poison, purgative or sexual stimulant, or as a treatment for wounds, snakebite and malaria. The genus name commemorates the sixteenth-century German physician Leonhart Rauwolf, who travelled widely to collect medicinal plants.
CULTIVATION: Plant in rich, deep soil in a sunny position and water well. Propagate from seed or cuttings.

Rauvolfia caffra

QUININE TREE

Growing wild in tropical and southern Africa, the quinine tree is the only species of this genus occurring naturally in South Africa. It has a wide, round crown and slightly drooping foliage. Fast growing, it can reach 40 ft (12 m) tall with a single, straight trunk up to 5 ft (1.5 m) in diameter. The bark, cream to gray or dark brown, may be cork-like or smooth and contains reserpine, which is used in tranquilizers. It has glossy, dark

Rebutia arenacea

green leaves up to 8 in (20 cm) long and, in summer, bears fragrant white flowers followed by small, glossy black fruit. The fruit can be eaten by birds and monkeys but is poisonous to humans. **ZONES 9–12.**

RAVENALA

TRAVELLER'S PALM, TRAVELLER'S TREE

A member of a very striking family, this genus is endemic to Madagascar but is now commonly grown throughout the tropics. It has only one species, an evergreen tree with huge, paddle-like leaves on long stalks that are similar to those of the banana *(Musa)*, but spreading fan-like from the base and looking exceptionally graceful when swaying in the breeze although they tend to fray with age.
CULTIVATION: *Ravenala* needs rich, moist but well-drained soil and a sunny spot in a hot climate. Shelter from strong winds. Propagate from seed in spring or by division of suckers at any time.

Ravenala madagascariensis

The bright green leaves of this species grow up to 10 ft (3 m) long, form 2 opposite rows and are held on tightly overlapped long stalks. Its trunk terminates in the sheathing bases of the leaf stalks, which lap together. The whole arrangement grows 30 ft (9 m) tall, spreading out to form a wide, flat fan of foliage. Clusters of white flowers emerge from between the leaf bases in summer. **ZONES 11–12.**

REBUTIA

CROWN CACTUS, HEDGEHOG CACTUS

This genus, native to South America, contains about 40 very small, mostly cluster-forming species, varying from hemispherical to erect and cylindrical. The plants develop tubercles around their bases, from where the flower buds emerge after one or two years. Large, vivid orange, pink, purple, red, yellow or white flowers readily bloom in late spring to early summer.
CULTIVATION: Frost tender, rebutias prefer moderately fertile, very well-drained soil and total sun; they need water only during the budding and blooming period. Propagate from seed or cuttings in spring or summer.

Rebutia albiflora

This small cactus native to Bolivia grows in clusters and has a profusion of white spines. It reaches a height of 4 in (10 cm). Attractive, white, 1 in (25 mm) tubular flowers bloom plentifully from spring to fall (autumn). **ZONES 9–11.**

Rebutia arenacea

This tiny cactus forms cushions of globular plants $1\frac{1}{2}$ in (35 mm) high and 2 in (5 cm) wide. Covered in white spines, it produces large, beautiful, yellow-orange flowers in spring and summer that last about a week. **ZONES 9–11.**

Rebutia aureiflora

Originating in Argentina, this mound-forming cactus averages 2 in (5 cm) tall. Its deep green-purple body is covered with lateral rows of tubercles and rigid, brownish white radial and central spines. At the end of spring yellow, or occasionally purple flowers with white interiors bloom profusely around the base. **ZONES 9–11.**

Rebutia cupperiana

This species grows to 6 in (15 cm) in height and has a purplish green, globose and clustering stem with stiff, dark brown spines 1 in (25 mm) long arranged in groups. The dark red flowers are trumpet-shaped. **ZONES 9–11.**

Rebutia deminuta

This small, dark green, clustering cactus is from Argentina. Each individual plant grows to a height of 4 in (10 cm) and width of $2\frac{1}{2}$ in (6 cm). Attractive orange and red, funnel-shaped flowers grow from around the base of the body, lasting for about a week in summer. **ZONES 9–11.**

Rebutia espinosae

Native to Bolivia, this globular cactus produces a cluster of pale pink flowers in summer. The smooth spines grow in star-like formations. **ZONES 9–11.**

Rebutia famatinensis

From western Argentina, this species has tuberous roots and a squat, cylindrical

Rebutia aureiflora

Rebutia cupperiana

Rebutia espinosae

Rebutia fulviseta

stem that is slightly depressed at the top. The spines, less than ¼ in (6 mm) long, are soft, white and hair-like. The flowers open from felted buds and are around 1 in (25 mm) long with purple outer petals and a yellow-orange interior. **ZONES 9–11.**

Rebutia fiebrigii
syn. ***Rebutia muscula***

Native to Argentina, this globular, deep green cactus has a mound-forming habit, spreading out to 6 in (15 cm). White, silky, short spines and light green tubercles thickly cover the body. Vivid orange flowers blossom at the end of spring to early summer. **ZONES 9–11.**

Rebutia fulviseta

This tiny, dark green cactus, native to Bolivia, reaches just over ½ in (12 mm) in height and diameter. Violet and red, funnel-shaped flowers appear through spring and summer and are followed by small, round fruit. **ZONES 9–11.**

Rebutia hoffmannii

This clustering, gray-green cactus comes from Argentina. Reaching up to 2 in (5 cm) in height and 1½ in (35 mm) in width, it produces a ring of orange, funnel-shaped flowers around its base in summer. **ZONES 9–11.**

Rebutia krainziana

With its brilliant red, trumpet-shaped flowers, this clustering cactus, probably a garden hybrid rather than a true species, is considered the most handsome of all the rebutias. The stems are up to 2 in (5 cm) across and are composed of 20 or more spirally arranged ribs and white areoles with white spines. **ZONES 9–11.**

Rebutia marsoneri

This dark green, cluster-forming cactus is native to Argentina. It grows to about 2 in (5 cm) high and wide, with spiral

Rebutia fiebrigii

Rebutia residua

tubercles and large, funnel-shaped yellow flowers eclipsing the body throughout summer. **ZONES 9–11.**

Rebutia minuscula
syn. ***Rebutia violaciflora***

A species originally from northern Argentina, this cactus features golden yellow spines that grow 1 in (25 mm) long and a yellow-green, globular body. Large, purple and red, funnel-shaped flowers are produced in summer. **ZONES 9–11.**

Rebutia nivea

Bolivia is the native habitat of this cactus, which grows about 2 in (5 cm) high and wide. It grows in clusters and is covered in soft, white spines. Orange-red, funnel-shaped flowers, tinged with yellow, bloom from near the plant base in summer. **ZONES 9–11.**

Rebutia pseudodeminuta
WALLFLOWER CACTUS

This popular miniature cactus from Argentina and Bolivia is just a cluster of stems, 1½ in (35 mm) thick and 4 in (10 cm) tall, with pale prickles, but in early summer it disappears under scarlet flowers with prominent golden stamens. Yellow-flowered forms are also grown. **ZONES 9–11.**

Rebutia senilis

Rebutia residua

Native to Bolivia, this species reaches about 2 in (5 cm) in height and spread. Growing in clumps, it features 1 in (25 mm) wide brilliant orange to scarlet, funnel-shaped flowers, each lasting about a week throughout summer. **ZONES 9–11.**

Rebutia senilis

This clump-forming species has a 2½ in (6 cm) wide stem matted with soft white spines. Trumpet-shaped red, yellow, pink or orange flowers 2 in (5 cm) wide appear in spring. **ZONES 9–11.**

Rebutia tarvitensis

This globular cactus from Bolivia grows from 12 in (25 cm) in height and 1½ in (35 mm) in width. The large, purple-red, funnel-shaped flowers appear in spring and summer. **ZONES 9–11.**

Rebutia verticillacantha var. *aureiflora*
syn. ***Sulcorebutia verticillacantha* var. *aureiflora***

Reaching a height of 2 in (5 cm) and a width of 1½ in (35 mm), this Bolivian cactus is ringed with bright yellow, funnel-shaped flowers in summer. **ZONES 9–11.**

REHMANNIA

The 8 or 9 perennial species of *Rehmannia*, from China, are sometimes classed in the Scrophulariaceae family with the foxgloves and the snapdragons, or assigned to Gesneriaceae as cousins of the gloxinia and the African violet. The uncertainty is due to the fact that the 2-lipped flowers look a bit like foxgloves, somewhat like snapdragons, and somewhat like gloxinias. They all have an attractive shape and delicate color, usually some shade of cool pink with pink and gold at their throats. The leaves are large, oblong, veined and hairy, and form basal rosettes.

CULTIVATION: Plant in a warm-temperate climate (or a mildly warmed greenhouse in cool climates) in a sheltered spot in full sun and in rich, leafy soil. Propagate from seed in winter or cuttings in late fall (autumn). Watch for attack by slugs and snails.

Rehmannia elata
syn. ***Rehmannia angulata* of gardens**
CHINESE FOXGLOVE

This is the best known *Rehmannia* in gardens. From the mountains of China, it bears semi-pendent, tubular, bright pink flowers from summer to fall (autumn) and grows to 3 ft (1 m) high. Though perennial, it is short lived and is usually grown as a biennial. **ZONES 9–10.**

Rehmannia elata

Rebutia nivea

Rebutia tarvitensis

Rebutia krainziana

R

Rehmannia glutinosa

This fully frost-hardy species from northern China bears its pendent, tubular flowers from spring to summer; the flowers have purple-veined, reddish brown petals with yellow lips. It grows to 12 in (30 cm) in height and spread. The mid-green, red-tinted leaves have quite obvious veins. **ZONES 9–10.**

REINECKEA

From Japan and China and allied to *Ophiopogon,* this genus contains a single species, an evergreen, rhizomatous perennial that has arching, glossy green leaves and small, scented flowers.

CULTIVATION: This frost-hardy plant prefers part-shade and moist but well-drained, humus-rich soil. Propagate from seed or by separation of the rhizomes. It may be prone to attack by snails and slugs.

Reineckea carnea

This species, which reaches 8 in (20 cm) in height with a 15 in (38 cm) spread, produces its almost cup-shaped, white or pink flowers to $\frac{1}{2}$ in (12 mm) wide in late spring. If the summer months are warm, round berries will appear in fall (autumn). **ZONES 7–10.**

Reseda odorata

REINWARDTIA

Funnel-shaped, 5-petalled flowers are produced on the single shrub species that makes up this evergreen genus allied to flax *(Linum)* from mountains of southern Asia. The alternate leaves are either toothed or entire.

CULTIVATION: These marginally frost-hardy plants should be grown in a greenhouse or conservatory in cold climates; outdoors, they prefer full sun and fertile, moist but well-drained soil. They can be watered freely when in full growth, less so at other times. Propagate from seed or cuttings.

Reinwardtia indica

syns *Reinwardtia trigyna, Linum trigynum* of gardens

YELLOW FLAX

This winter-flowering shrub grows to about 3 ft (1 m) high and bears sprays of 1 in (25 mm) wide, golden-yellow flowers with 5 overlapping petals, which form a wide-flared funnel. Its leaves are 3 in (8 cm) long, bright green ovals. **ZONES 9–11.**

RENANTHERA

This orchid genus is made up of about 15 species of mostly large, climbing or scrambling plants of low altitudes from northeast India to southern China, mostly from Southeast Asia, the Philippines and Indonesia to New Guinea. The stems have 2 ranks of leaves and the flowers are produced from the apical third of the plants. The flowers are mostly red, but some are orange or yellow; they are borne in large, branched inflorescences. The species have been used extensively in hybridizing with *Vanda, Phalaenopsis, Vandopsis* and *Euanthe.*

CULTIVATION: These plants need room to scramble, a coarse, well-drained mixture, warm conditions and a fairly even climate with year-round watering and strong light. In the tropics they are often grown in raised garden beds in full sun. Propagate by division.

Reineckea carnea

Reinwardtia indica

Renanthera monachica

Renanthera storiei

Reseda luteola

Retama monosperma

Renanthera monachica

This species is more compact than most . The stems are 18–36 in (45–90 cm) long, with dark green, fleshy leaves $2\frac{1}{2}$–6 in (6–15 cm) long. The inflorescences are branched and 8 in (20 cm) long; numerous, long-lasting flowers about 1 in (25 mm) across appear in winter and spring. This is one of the few renantheras suited to pot culture. **ZONES 11–12**

Renanthera storiei

This is a large, scrambling species from the Philippines. It is terrestrial or epiphytic, growing at low altitudes in sunny and shaded conditions. The leafy stems are up to 15 ft (4.5 m) tall, with the fleshy leaves being 4–6 in (10–15 cm) long. The branched inflorescence is held horizontally and is up to 3 ft (1 m) long with numerous, long-lasting flowers 2–3 in (5–8 cm) long. This species has been widely used in hybridizing. **ZONES 11–12**

RESEDA

MIGNONETTE

This genus from Asia, Africa and Europe contains about 60 species of erect or spreading, branching annuals and perennials. They bear star-shaped, greenish white or greenish yellow flowers in spike-like racemes from spring to fall (autumn). These are attractive to bees. Mignonette used to be a favorite with perfumers and the plant is still cultivated in France for its essential oils.

CULTIVATION: Plant in full sun or part-shade in well-drained, fertile, preferably alkaline soil. Deadheading will prolong flowering. Propagate from seed in late winter.

Reseda alba

WILD MIGNONETTE

This upright, 30–36 in (75–90 cm) tall annual or short-lived perennial has deeply cut, 6 in (15 cm) long pointed oval leaves. Upright 8–24 in (20–60 cm) long racemes of $\frac{1}{4}$ in (6 mm) wide, white to cream flowers open in summer. Originally a Mediterranean native, it is now widespread and is considered a weed in some areas. **ZONES 8–10.**

Reseda luteola

WELD, WILD MIGNONETTE, DYER'S ROCKET

This biennial or short-lived perennial from Europe and central Asia yields a yellow dye that has been used as a paint pigment and in textile making. Weld grows to 4 ft (1.2 m) tall with narrow bright green leaves; almost half its height is made up of narrow, sometimes branched flower spikes, composed of whorls of small pale yellow to yellow-green flowers. The flowers appear in the second summer of growth, the first season being spent developing the large tap root. **ZONES 6–10.**

Reseda odorata

COMMON MIGNONETTE

From northern Africa, this moderately fast-growing annual is renowned for the strong fragrance of its flowers. The conical heads of tiny greenish flowers, with touches of red, and dark orange stamens are otherwise unspectacular. They appear from summer to early fall (autumn). The plants will grow to 24 in (60 cm) high and about half that in spread. **ZONES 6–10.**

RETAMA

This small genus of brooms is made up of about 4 species of graceful, deciduous shrubs from the Mediterranean region, the Canary Islands and western Asia. They are a joy in spring when covered with a mass of white or yellow pea-like flowers. These are followed by the fruits: small pea-shaped pods that may be downy. The mid-green leaves are small and last only a couple of days, and the plants reach a height of 5 ft (1.5 m). This genus is related to *Genista.*

CULTIVATION: They are easy to grow providing they have moderately fertile, well-drained soil and plenty of sun. They tolerate a range of climates and dislike humidity. Prune lightly after flowering to keep them bushy. Propagate from seed in spring or cuttings in summer.

R

Rhaphiolepis × delacourii

Rhaphiolepis × delacourii 'Enchantress'

Rhamnus californica 'Curly'

Retama monosperma
syn. *Genista monosperma*
WHITE BROOM

Like all brooms, this shrub is popular for its sweetly scented white flowers borne profusely on bare branchlets, which have a weeping habit from a short trunk and are silvery green. The plant blooms for a long period if protected from strong winds. **ZONES 8–10.**

RHABDOTHAMNUS
MATATA, NEW ZEALAND GLOXINIA, WAIUATUA

This genus of the African violet family contains a single species from New Zealand, a slender, many branched evergreen shrub with rough, hairy leaves. The tubular flowers will bloom throughout the year in favored positions. **CULTIVATION:** This marginally frost-hardy plant prefers a lightly shaded position and open, humus-rich soil. Prune frequently to produce a bushier plant. Propagate from seed or cuttings.

Rhabdothamnus solandri

This species has small, birch-like leaves with coarsely serrated margins and a dark midrib and veins. The small flowers have a narrow corolla tube in shades of orange to orange-red with red veins and a purple throat. It grows to about 6 ft (1.8 m) high and wide. **ZONES 10–11.**

RHAMNUS
syn. *Frangula*
BUCKTHORN

This genus of 125 species of deciduous and evergreen shrubs and small trees occurs in a range of climates, mostly in the northern hemisphere. It tolerates dry conditions and salt-laden atmospheres. They are distinguished by smooth, dark bark and simple green leaves, often with serrated edges. The flowers, borne in clusters, are insignificant. The fruits are fleshy, pea-sized berries popular with birds. Some species are thorny, some produce dyes that are used commercially, and the bark of some species is the source of the purgative cascara sagrada. **CULTIVATION:** These versatile plants require moderately fertile, well-drained soil and full sun or part-shade in hot areas. Propagate the deciduous species from seed and the evergreen species from cuttings in summer.

Rhamnus a. 'Argenteovariegatus'

Rhabdothamnus solandri

Rhamnus alaternus
ITALIAN BUCKTHORN, ALATERNUS

This large, evergreen, multi-stemmed shrub from the Mediterranean is valued in its native lands for its tolerance of dry conditions and polluted environments. It grows quickly to 15 ft (4.5 m) and its thorny branches bear a mass of small, glossy dark green leaves. These hide the tiny greenish yellow flowers, which attract all kinds of insects. Its berries are purple-black. It can become invasive in certain areas. **'Argenteovariegatus'**, which is more decorative than its parent but is less frost hardy, has leaves that are marbled with gray and edged with creamy white. **ZONES 7–10.**

Rhamnus californica
syn. *Frangula californica*
COFFEEBERRY, CALIFORNIA BUCKTHORN

This evergreen or semi-evergreen shrub from western North America bears finely toothed oval leaves up to 2 in (5 cm) long with 12 pairs of veins. It grows to 12 ft (3.5 m) with a 10 ft (3 m) spread. Honey-bees are attracted to the greenish flowers. The fruit change from red to black as they ripen. **'Eve Case'**, **'Sea View'** and **'Curly'** have full-flavored fruit. **ZONES 7–10.**

Rhamnus cathartica
COMMON BUCKTHORN

This thicket-forming, thorny, deciduous species from Europe, Asia and northwestern Africa grows to a height of 20 ft (6 m) with a 15 ft (4.5 m) spread. Its glossy green leaves turn yellow in fall (autumn), and its yellowish green flowers appear in spring and summer. The red fruit ripen to black. **ZONES 3–9.**

Rhaphiolepis indica

Rhamnus californica

Rhamnus frangula
ALDER BUCKTHORN

This deciduous species from Europe, Turkey and northern Africa grows about 10–15 ft (3–4.5 m) tall. It has glossy dark green, oval leaves up to 3 in (8 cm) long. The insignificant green flowers are followed by $\frac{1}{2}$ in (12 mm) diameter fruit that change from red to black as they ripen. **'Tall Hedge'** is an upright form less than 3 ft (1 m) wide. **ZONES 3–9.**

Rhamnus purshiana
syn. *Frangula purshiana*
CASCARA SAGRADA, BEARBERRY

Unlike other *Rhamnus* species, this deciduous tree from western USA prefers an open, sunny position and requires plenty of moisture during dry spells. It grows 25 ft (8 m) tall and at least 10 ft (3 m) wide, and has reddish brown bark. Its 8 in (20 cm), oblong leaves are finely toothed, with prominent veins and downy undersides. They appear after the clusters of greenish flowers. The drug cascara sagrada is produced from its bark. **ZONES 7–10.**

RHAPHIOLEPIS
syn. *Raphiolepis*

The 9 species in this genus are slow-growing, tough, evergreen shrubs native to subtropical Southeast and eastern Asia. Most spread wider than they are tall. Their leathery leaves, up to 3 in (8 cm) long and half as wide, are oblong and dark green, with pale undersides. New shoots are often coppery red. The fragrant, 5-petalled flowers, white or pink, are borne in loose terminal clusters, usually held rigidly away from the foliage. The fruit are blue-black berries. **CULTIVATION:** Moderately frost hardy, these shrubs like plenty of sun, or semi-shade in hot climates. They do best in well-drained, sandy soil enriched with organic matter and thrive in sheltered seaside gardens. Propagate from seed or cuttings or by layering.

Rhaphiolepis × delacourii

This rounded, evergreen shrub to a height and spread of 6 ft (1.8 m) is grown for its rose-pink, early summer flowers and the blue-black berries that follow in winter. Its oval, leathery leaves are toothed at the ends. **'Cootes Crimson'** bears dark pink flowers. **'Enchantress'** is a compact form with rose-pink flowers. **'Springtime'** is a compact cultivar with pink and bronze new growth and large pink flowers. **ZONES 8–11.**

Rhaphiolepis indica
INDIAN HAWTHORN

Despite its common name, this shrub comes from southern China. It grows 8 ft (2.4 m) high and wide, and in late winter and spring bears 3 in (8 cm) clusters of perfumed, star-shaped flowers. These are white with a pink blush and long, pink stamens. Its black berries have a bluish tinge. The shiny dark green, serrated leaves are lanceolate. **ZONES 8–11.**

Rhaphiolepis umbellata

Rhaphithamnus spinosus

Rhapis excelsa

Rhaphiolepis umbellata
YEDDO HAWTHORN

A dense, rounded shrub normally 6 ft (1.8 m) tall, this native of Japan and Korea has paddle-shaped, smooth-edged leaves that are covered with gray, downy hairs when young. Clusters of perfumed white flowers appear in summer; in warm climates they spot bloom for much of the year. The bluish black berries persist into winter. This species has adapted to seashore conditions. **ZONES 8–11.**

RHAPHITHAMNUS

This unusual genus of the verbena family consists of just 2 species, both found in the temperate parts of South America. They are spiny stemmed, evergreen shrubs or small trees with small clusters of flowers along the stems and in the leaf axils, followed by small, berry-like fruits. **CULTIVATION:** They prefer full sun and moist, well-drained soil. Although tolerant of only light frosts, they are easily grown and are adaptable. They can withstand dry conditions once established. Propagate from seed or cuttings.

Rhaphiolepis umbellata

Rhapidophyllum hystrix

Rhaphithamnus spinosus
PRICKLY MYRTLE

This species grows to over 20 ft (6 m) tall and has 1½ in (35 mm) spines. It has simple, elliptical, leathery, glossy green leaves and finely hairy new growth. The flowers occur in the leaf axils and are mauve. Violet-blue fruit around ½ in (12 mm) wide follow the flowers. **ZONES 9–11.**

RHAPIDOPHYLLUM
BLUE PALMETTO, NEEDLE PALM

The single species in this palm genus grows naturally in the American states of South Carolina, Georgia and Florida. It forms a low, dense clump of fan-shaped fronds. The flowers are tiny but densely clustered. The fruit are oval and downy, and are up to 1 in (25 mm) long. **CULTIVATION:** *Rhapidophyllum* prefers part-shade and moist soil with plenty of organic matter. It adapts to a range of climates from cool to warm and can be grown in temperate regions where most palms will not thrive. Propagate from seed, which take up to 6 months to germinate, or from suckers.

Rhapidophyllum hystrix

The common name of needle palm is apt for this species as it conceals many long, black spines among its frond stalks. The stems hug the ground. Each frond, 30 in (75 cm) wide, is bluish green on top and silvery below and is deeply divided into 12 or more segments. The 3-petalled flowers are dark red. **ZONES 8–11.**

RHAPIS
LADY PALM

Rhapis is a small genus of about 12 species of low-growing palms ranging from southern China to Thailand. They form clumps of slender, bamboo-like stems carrying small, deeply divided, fan-shaped fronds. New stem growth is covered with interwoven fibers arising from the base of each frond. The yellow male and female flowers occur on separate plants. The fruits are small berries containing a single seed. **CULTIVATION:** These frost-tender palms are often grown in tubs, as ornamental clumps, or as hedges outdoors in warm, humid climates. Elsewhere they are favorite house plants. They require some shade and rich, moist soil. They are usually propagated by dividing a clump but can be reproduced from seed.

Rhapis excelsa
MINIATURE FAN PALM

The many stems of this palm from southern China form a dense clump up to 15 ft (4.5 m) tall. The fronds, light to rich green, divide into 5 to 8 stiff, finger-like segments. The tiny, bowl-shaped, creamy flowers appear in small panicles among the fronds in summer. It will grow outside in warm climates, but slowly; its leaves may burn in full sun. **ZONES 10–12.**

RHEUM

This genus contains 50 species of rhizomatous perennials, including the edible rhubarb and several ornamental plants. From eastern Europe and central Asia to the Himalayas and China, they are grown for their striking appearance and for their large basal leaves, which are coarsely toothed and have prominent midribs and veins. The minute, star-shaped flowers appear in summer and are followed by winged fruits. **CULTIVATION:** These very frost-hardy plants prefer full sun or part-shade and deep, moist, humus-rich soil. Propagate from seed or by division, and watch out for slugs and crown rot.

Rheum × *cultorum*
syns *Rheum* × *hybridum*, *R. rhabarbarum*
RHUBARB

One of the few plants grown for its edible leaf stalks, rhubarb is a tough, vigorous perennial. Once classified as a species, it is now thought to be a hybrid of *Rheum rhaponticum*. In spring its large leaves quickly expand from the woody, winter-dormant rhizome. The stems, at first green, are ready to eat when they have reddened. Flowering stems are usually removed from cultivated plants, but if left to develop they grow to 5 ft (1.5 m) tall and are topped with heads of small red-flushed cream flowers. It is best grown from root divisions in a fertile, phosphorous-rich soil. Eat the stalks only; the leaves are poisonous. **ZONES 3–9.**

Rheum × *cultorum*

Rheum officinale

Sometimes used in weight control drugs and herbal medicine, this species from western China and Tibetan can grow to 10 ft (3 m) tall. Its leaves are kidney-shaped to round, 5-lobed and up to 30 in (75 cm) wide. In summer it produces large branched heads of white to greenish white flowers. **ZONES 7–10.**

Rheum palmatum
CHINESE RHUBARB

This species bears panicles of small, dark red to creamy green flowers that open early in summer. It has deep green leaves with decoratively cut edges, and reaches up to 8 ft (2.4 m) in height and 6 ft (1.8 m) in spread. **'Atrosanguineum'** has dark pink flowers and crimson leaves that fade to dark green. **ZONES 6–10.**

RHIPSALIS
MISTLETOE, WICKERWORK

This cactus genus consists of 40 to 50 species, mostly native to Central and South America, with the exception of *Rhipsalis baccifera* from Africa and Sri Lanka, the only cactus to occur naturally outside the Americas. They are medium-sized or large epiphytes that mostly bloom in late winter or early spring. Ideal subjects for hanging baskets with their tubular or leaf-like pendent green foliage, they have very small, open-faced, white or pale pink flowers that are followed by white, black or pink berries. **CULTIVATION:** These frost-tender plants prefer humid, warm conditions in full shade. They prefer atmospheric moisture to wet soil but should not be allowed to dry out entirely. Propagate from seed or root cuttings of stem sections.

Rheum officinale

Rheum palmatum 'Atrosanguineum'

Rhodiola rosea

Rhodochiton atrosanguineus

Rhipsalis cereuscula
CORAL CACTUS

This is a 24 in (60 cm) tall, pendulous cactus from Brazil and Argentina. Its green stems are cylindrical in shape, reaching up to 12 in (30 cm) in length. White, star-shaped flowers appear in spring, and are followed by the fruit in late spring and summer. **ZONES 9–11.**

Rhipsalis paradoxa
CHAIN CACTUS, LINK PLANT

Native to South America, this epiphytic cactus grows to 3 ft (1 m), then develops multiple trailing, chain-like stems. From winter to spring small, trumpet-shaped white flowers appear along the margins of the 'chains', followed by resinous, spherical fruit. It requires a dry rest during fall (autumn). **ZONES 9–11.**

RHODANTHE
STRAWFLOWER

The 40 species of erect annuals, perennials and subshrubs in this genus all come from arid areas of Australia and in recent times have mostly been classified in the genus *Helipterum*. Their daisy-like, everlasting, pink, yellow or white summer flowers are keenly sought for cut flowers and in dried arrangements. They have alternate, mid-green to gray-green leaves.
CULTIVATION: These marginally frost-hardy plants prefer full sun and well-drained soil of poor quality. The flowerheads can be cut for drying and hung upside down in a dark, cool place. Propagate from seed.

Rhodanthe anthemoides
syn. *Helipterum anthemoides*

From southeastern Australia,this perennial has wiry stems with small, grayish leaves. Papery, daisy-like, 1 in (25 mm) wide flowers are carried throughout the year in most areas. It has a mounding habit and grows 8 in (20 cm) high and 12 in (30 cm) wide. **ZONES 9–11.**

Rhodiola stephanii

Rhodanthe chlorocephala subsp. *rosea*
syns *Helipterum roseum, Acroclinium roseum*

This annual from southwestern Australia grows to a height of 24 in (60 cm) and a spread of 6 in (15 cm). The flowerheads are composed of white to pale pink bracts surrounding a yellow center, and close in cloudy weather. It is widely grown for cut flowers. **ZONES 9–11.**

Rhodanthe manglesii
syn. *Helipterum manglesii*
SWAN RIVER EVERLASTING

This plant from Western Australia, the best known and most widely cultivated species of *Rhodanthe*, has delicate flowers that carpet the desert after rain. They open deep pink and fade to white as they age, which gives the charming effect of several different colors on the same plant at one time. An upright annual, it grows 12–18 in (30–45 cm) in height and has pointed, gray-green leaves. **ZONES 7–11.**

Rhodanthe 'Paper Star'

This cultivar, possibly a form of *Rhodanthe anthemoides,* has profuse white flowerheads. While not very long lasting as a cut flower, it is an impressive, long-flowering garden specimen of semi-prostrate habit. **ZONES 7–11.**

RHODIOLA

Similar to *Hylotelephium* and the larger *Sedum* species, this genus includes around 50 species of fleshy leafed, rhizomatous perennials widely distributed in the northern hemisphere. The plants are composed of a mass of thickened stems clothed with simple, often toothed, gray-green leaves. The individual, star-shaped flowers, in shades of yellow, orange, red, occasionally green or white, appear in dense, rounded heads.
CULTIVATION: Most are very frost-hardy and undemanding. Plant in an area that remains moist in summer but which is not boggy in winter. A sunny rockery is ideal. Propagate by division in spring or take cuttings of the young growth. They may be attacked by aphids.

Rhodiola heterodonta

Rhodiola heterodonta
syn. *Sedum heterodontum*

This rhizomatous, clump-forming species from Afghanistan, the Himalayas and Tibet grows to a height and spread of 15 in (38 cm). It bears flattish heads of yellow to orange-red or greenish flowers in spring to early summer and has thick, unbranched stems with oval, toothed, blue-green leaves. **ZONES 5–10.**

Rhodiola kirilowii
syn. *Sedum kirilowii*

Found from central Asia to Mongolia, this species has heavy, branched rhizomes from which develop stout, upright stems that grow to 3 ft (1 m) tall. The narrow to lance-shaped leaves are unusually large, sometimes over 10 ft (3 m) long. The flowers are yellow-green to rusty red, and open from early summer. **ZONES 5–10.**

Rhodiola purpureoviridis
syn. *Sedum purpureoviride*

This dense species has rounded, ovate leaves with densely hairy, toothed margins. The flowering stems grow to 18 in (45 cm) and bear pale green-yellow flowers in early summer. It comes from western China and Tibet. **ZONES 6–10.**

Rhodiola rosea
syn. *Sedum rosea*
ROSEROOT

The tightly massed heads of pink buds produced by this perennial in late spring or early summer open to small, star-shaped flowers in pale purple, green or yellow. The saw-edged, elliptical leaves are fleshy. This species grows into a clump 12 in (30 cm) in height and spread. The name comes from the scent of the fleshy roots, used in making perfume. It is a highly sociable species that occurs right around the temperate northern hemisphere. **ZONES 2–9.**

Rhodiola purpureoviridis

Rhodiola kirilowii

Rhodiola stephanii
syn. *Sedum stephanii*

This rhizomatous, branching species from eastern Siberia has bright yellow-green, deeply toothed leaves. The flowering stems, to 10 in (25 cm) in length, bear their creamy white flowers in summer. **ZONES 5–10.**

RHODOCHITON

This genus from Mexico contains 3 species of evergreen, leaf-stalk climbers grown for their unusual flowers. The flowers are pendent and have long-tubed corollas with 5 segments. They perform better when grown as annuals, especially in frost-prone areas.
CULTIVATION: They may be planted against fences or trellises or used as ground cover, and prefer full sun and humus-rich, moist but well-drained soil. Propagate from seed in spring.

Rhodochiton atrosanguineus
syn. *Rhodochiton volubile*
PURPLE BELLS

This twining climber is often grown as an annual and flowers from late spring through to late fall (autumn). The flowers have a long, finger-like, dark purple corolla protruding from a bell-shaped calyx in a redder hue of purple. The leaves are ovate to heart-shaped, with slightly hairy edges and twining stems. It grows to 10 ft (3 m) in height. **ZONES 9–11.**

Rhodanthe chlorocephala subsp. *rosea*

Rhodanthe 'Paper Star'

R

RHODODENDRON

syn. *Azalea*

The rhododendrons are a spectacular genus of around 800 evergreen semi-deciduous and deciduous shrubs and trees. Although largely confined to the northern hemisphere with the majority of species native to southern China and the Himalayan region, many are found in North America, Japan and Southeast Asia, and the tropical branch of the genus extends the range to New Guinea and the far northeast of Australia. Rhododendrons are woody stemmed plants grown mainly for their massed display of flowers, which vary greatly in size from tiny thimbles to 8 in (20 cm) trumpets. They are usually clustered in inflorescences (trusses) at the branch tips and occur in every color except a true bright blue. The flowers may be self- or multi-colored, often with a contrasting throat blotch (flare) or spotting. Some species have scented flowers. Temperate-climate rhododendrons tend to bloom from late winter to early summer, but the tropical rhododendrons are far less seasonal and bloom throughout the year, usually reaching a peak in early fall (autumn). Plant size ranges from near prostrate through to trees over 50 ft (15 m) tall. Yet despite this enormous variety of species, and the thousands of garden hybrids and cultivars, rhododendrons are all remarkably similar in general appearance and unlikely to be mistaken for any other plants. They are mainly broad leafed with roughly elliptical, usually deep green leaves and their 5-petalled (or more) flowers are flat, funnel-, bell- or trumpet-shaped. Rhododendrons also have beautiful foliage. The leaves of the evergreens are usually thick and leathery, often deep green and lustrous. The deciduous and semi-evergreen forms tend to have hairy leaves and their foliage may change color in fall and winter. Leaf size varies enormously. Many of the alpines have tiny leaves under 1 in (25 mm) long, while the foliage of species from mild, high rainfall areas can exceed 24 in (60 cm) long. Rhododendrons are botanically divided by the presence (lepidote species) or absence (elepidote species) of scales on their leaves. While often barely noticeable, these scales sometimes take the form of felting (indumentum) on the foliage. This is usually confined to the leaf undersides and is a feature of many rhododendrons.

As far as gardeners are concerned there are 3 main categories of rhododendrons, namely: azaleas (deciduous and evergreen); tropical or Vireya rhododendrons; and the temperate climate plants we might call 'true' rhododendrons, which includes the small alpine or arctic rhododendrons. All have been extensively developed and hybridized, so in addition to those 800-odd species there now are countless garden forms. With such a huge variety of plants from widely differing backgrounds, it is easy to become confused. Consequently, some of the main hybrid groups are subdivided into smaller blocks of plants with similar characteristics or parentage.

CULTIVATION: As would be expected of such a large group, rhododendrons vary considerably in their climatic preferences. However, they all share the same general cultivation needs. This is because their roots lack the fine feeding hairs at the root tips that are found on most other plants; instead, the entire root ball is a mass of fine roots that serve the same function as root hairs. This lack of heavy, aggressive, spreading roots greatly influences the cultivation and uses of rhododendrons. A compact root ball and no tap roots make rhododendrons ideal for container cultivation and easy to transplant, but there are disadvantages. Fine roots dry out quickly in dry conditions, soon rot if kept waterlogged, suffer in compacted soils and cannot penetrate hard or rocky ground. Rhododendrons need loose, open, well-aerated, acidic soil with plenty of humus to retain moisture. They thrive with regular mulching that enables their predominantly surface roots to spread and develop. In wet areas or gardens with alkaline soil it is best to plant in raised beds filled with specially blended compost. Most rhododendrons are woodland plants that prefer dappled shade or at least protection from the hottest afternoon sun and strong winds. They require little maintenance apart from a light trim after flowering. They are not greatly troubled by pests and diseases but are prone to infestation by thrips, two-spotted mites and spider mites and powdery mildew or rust in humid areas. Evergreen azaleas are sometimes disfigured by azalea leaf gall. Taller varieties make good woodland or shrubbery plants, even hedges, while the dwarf forms are perfect for mass plantings or rock gardens. Azaleas are usually at their best planted *en masse*. Vireya rhododendrons are superb plants for tropical or subtropical gardens or as potted plants in conservatories. Rhodoendrons are propagated from seed or cuttings or by layering, the method and timing varying with the type of plant. Frost hardiness also varies greatly.

Rhododendron argyrophyllum

Rhododendron aurigeranum

Rhododendron arboreum

Rhododendron brookeanum

RHODODENDRON, SPECIES

Although nearly all rhododendron species are worth cultivating, some are rather untidy, rangy growers that have little appeal for gardeners. The following are some of the more attractive, popular or influential species. Many more are available through specialist nurseries and rhododendron societies. The very rare species are often only available as seed. All are evergreen unless otherwise stated.

Rhododendron ciliicalyx

Rhododendron arboreum

From northern India to southern China and over 100 ft (30 m) tall in the wild, this species reaches 40 ft (12 m) in cultivation with a narrow, cylindrical crown. Its leathery, deep bronze-green, 8 in (20 cm) long leaves have whitish or rust-colored undersides. Red, white or deep pink bell-shaped flowers in globular heads of 15 to 20 blooms open in very early spring. This species was an early introduction and is a parent of many cultivars. **ZONES 7–11.**

Rhododendron argyrophyllum

This large shrub or small tree from Sichuan, China, is grown as much for its beautiful, very deep green, glossy foliage as it is for its flowers. The leaves are narrow and up to 3 in (8 cm) long with white scaling on their undersides. White, bell-shaped, 2 in (5 cm) long flowers, occasionally flushed with pink or purple spotted, open from early spring. **ZONES 6–10.**

Rhododendron augustinii

From southern China and Tibet and first described in 1886, this species has bronze-green, 1½–4 in (3.5–10 cm) long leaves that darken in winter. Usually seen as a 5 ft (1.5 m) shrub, it can develop into a 30 ft (9 m) tree. From mid-spring it is smothered in loose, 2- to 6-flowered clusters of 1½ in (35 mm) wide, openly funnel-shaped blue or violet blooms. ***Rhododendron augustinii* subsp. *chasmanthum*** is usually tree-sized, even in cultivation, with mauve flowers. **ZONES 6–9.**

Rhododendron aurigeranum

Native to New Guinea and found in forest clearings, rocky areas or grassy slopes at moderate altitudes, this Vireya rhododendron grows to 8 ft (2.4 m) tall with orange to orange-yellow funnel-shaped flowers. It is popular with hybridizers of modern Vireya cultivars. **ZONES 10–12.**

Rhododendron brookeanum

Native to Malaysia and Indonesia, this Vireya may be epiphytic or terrestrial. At low altitudes it is found as an epiphyte on mangroves and other trees, and terrestrially on sandstone rocks at up to 4,660 ft (1,400 m). It reaches 6–15 ft (1.8–4.5 m) tall with fragrant funnel-shaped flowers that are orange, orange-pink or red, with white to golden yellow centers. **'Titan'** has flowers fading to light pink. **ZONES 10–12.**

Rhododendron calendulaceum
FLAME AZALEA

This deciduous azalea, found from West Virginia to Georgia, USA develops into a spreading bush around 12 ft (3.5 m) tall and wide. Its orange to red (rarely yellow) funnel-shaped flowers open in late spring and are carried in trusses of 5 to 7 blooms. The flower color varies with the season, location and climate. Many orange to flame azaleas derive their color from this species. **ZONES 5–9.**

Rhododendron callimorphum

The species name of this rounded, 2–6 ft (0.6–1.8 m) tall shrub from Yunnan, China and northeast Burma means 'with a lovely shape', which is an apt description as it is a very neat bush with attractive glossy deep green, medium-sized leaves. The bell-shaped flowers, in trusses of 5 to 8 blooms, are white to rose pink, sometimes with purple flecks, and open from mid-spring. **ZONES 7–11.**

Rhododendron campylogynum

This species, found from northern India and Burma to southern China, is a dwarf shrub from 6–48 in (15–120 cm) tall. It has small leaves and from mid-spring produces tiny, wide open bell-shaped flowers that resemble small thimbles. The flowers may be cream, pink, red, claret, purple to black-purple. It is a superb rockery or alpine house plant. **ZONES 7–9.**

Rhododendron calendulaceum

Rhododendron ciliatum

Rhododendron catawbiense
CATAWBA RHODODENDRON, MOUNTAIN ROSEBAY

This shrub from eastern USA is one of the most influential species in the development of frost-hardy hybrids. It grows to around 10 ft (3 m) tall and develops into a dense thicket of shiny, deep green foliage. Its cup-shaped flowers, which open from late spring, are pink, rosy pink, lilac-purple or white and carried in trusses of up to 20 blooms. **'Album'** is a heat-resistant form with white flowers that open from pink buds. **ZONES 4–9.**

Rhododendron ciliatum

Native to the Himalayan region, this species is a compact 4–6 ft (1.2–1.8 m) shrub. It has 2–3 in (5–8 cm) long, shiny deep green leaves with bluish undersides. The bark is red-brown and peeling. From early spring it produces white or white flushed rose, bell-shaped flowers and is an easily grown shrub that tolerates slightly alkaline soil. **ZONES 7–9.**

Rhododendron ciliicalyx

This shrub from western China grows quickly to form a 5–10 ft (1.5–3 m) mound of narrowly elliptical, 3–4 in (8–10 cm) leaves with brown-scaled undersides. Its clusters of 3, open funnel- to bell-shaped flowers open from early spring and are 3 in (8 cm) long, pure white or pink tinged. Occasionally the flowers are lightly scented. **ZONES 7–9.**

Rhododendron cinnabarinum

Native to the Himalayan region and northern Burma, this aromatic species is an upright shrub or small tree 5–20 ft (1.5–6 m) tall. Its peeling red-brown bark and narrowly oval deep green to blue-green leaves are very attractive, as are the 2 in (5 cm) long, pendulous, tubular flowers that open from mid-spring. Usually orange, the 3- to 5-flowered trusses may be red, salmon pink, pink, yellow, apricot or combinations of colors. ***Rhododendron cinnabarinum* subsp. *cinnabarinum* 'Mount Everest'** has apricot flowers that are more widely open than usual. **ZONES 6–9.**

Rhododendron catawbiense

Rhododendron degronianum

Rhododendron campylogynum

Rhododendron davidsonianum

Rhododendron dauricum

Regarded as the earliest flowering frost-hardy species, this semi-deciduous native of Japan, China, Mongolia, and eastern Russia is often in bloom shortly after mid-winter. It grows 2–5 ft (0.6–1.5 m) tall with red-purple, purple, pink, or white ½–1 in (12–25 mm) long funnel-shaped flowers. The scaly, deep green, 1½ in (35 mm) leaves develop bronze tones in winter. **ZONES 5–9.**

Rhododendron davidsonianum

This western Chinese species is an upright, open shrub from 3–20 ft (1–6 m) tall. The leaves are 2½ in (6 cm) long, lance-shaped, deep green on top with scaly undersides. Its trusses of 2 to 6, funnel-shaped, 2 in (5 cm) long flowers are of variable color, usually white or white suffused pink, but often pink or lavender and sometimes green or red flecked. **ZONES 7–9.**

Rhododendron decorum

From western China, northern Burma and Laos, this shrubby species is 4–20 ft (1.2–6 m) tall and has slightly curling, 6 in (15 cm) long, oblong leaves. The flowers, borne in loose trusses of 8 to 14 blooms, are fragrant, funnel-shaped, 3 in (8 cm) long, white to mid-pink, often tinged green and flecked with green, ochre or red. **ZONES 7–10.**

Rhododendron decorum

Rhododendron degronianum

This compact, heavily foliaged shrub has glossy, deep green, oblong leaves with strongly recurved edges. It is 3–10 ft (1–3 m) tall and has 2½ in (6 cm) long, funnel-shaped, pink to pale red flowers with conspicuous flecks and occasional dark stripes, in trusses of 10 to 12 blooms. Native to Japan, it occurs over a wide altitude range in several forms. **ZONES 7–9.**

Rhododendron edgeworthii

This fragrant Himalayan species was popular in the mid-nineteenth century for hybridizing. Unfortunately, it lacks hardiness and is inclined to be rangy. It grows to around 10 ft (3 m) tall and has 2½ in (6 cm) long, deep green, lance-shaped leaves with thick fawn indumentum. The flowers are 4 in (10 cm) long, funnel-shaped, white flushed pink, they open from mid-spring. **ZONES 9–10.**

R

Rhododendron javanicum

Rhododendron elliottii

Rhododendron fastigiatum

Rhododendron fortunei subsp. *fortunei*

Rhododendron elliottii

Native to moderate altitudes in northern India, this species grows to 6–25 ft (1.8–8 m) tall and has deep red flowers with very dark spotting and white-tipped anthers. The flowers open from mid-spring, are funnel- to bell-shaped, around 2 in (5 cm) long and in trusses of around 10 blooms. The leaves are glossy deep green and up to 4 in (10 cm) long. **ZONES 9–10.**

Rhododendron fastigiatum

In the wild this alpine species from Yunnan Province, China, grows at altitudes of up to 15,000 ft (4,500 m). It has ½ in (12 mm) long, blue-gray leaves and is a dense, wiry stemmed, 18–30 in (45–75 cm) tall shrub. It flowers in mid-spring when it is smothered in ½ in (12 mm) purple or lavender blooms, and is a superb plant for a rockery or alpine house. **ZONES 7–9.**

Rhododendron ferrugineum

ALPINE ROSE

Native to the Pyrenees and the Alps and one of the few European rhododendrons, this species was first cultivated in 1739. It is a 2–5 ft (0.6–1.5 m) tall shrub with 1–1½ in (25–35 mm) deep green leaves that have scaly brown undersides. Its flowers open from mid-spring, are tubular to bell-shaped, less than 1 in (25 mm) long and pale crimson or white in trusses of 6 to 8 blooms. **ZONES 4–8.**

Rhododendron forrestii

Found at up to 15,000 ft (4,500 m) in Yunnan, Tibet and Burma, this dwarf, spreading shrub seldom exceeds 6 in (15 cm) high. It has rounded, deep green, 1–3 in (2.5–8 cm) long leaves and bright red, waxy, 1½ in (35 mm) long bell-shaped flowers. The flowers open from early spring and are borne singly or in pairs. It is popular with hybridizers. **ZONES 8–10.**

Rhododendron fortunei

This Chinese species has been extremely influential in the development of garden hybrids. It is a shrub or small tree 4–30 ft (1.2–9 m) tall with matt mid-green oval leaves up to 8 in (20 cm) long. Its 4 in (10 cm) wide flowers open pink, fade to white and are fragrant. They open from mid-spring and are carried in large rounded trusses. ***Rhododendron fortunei* subsp. *discolor*** has flowers with a yellow-green throat blotch; they are not always scented; ***R. f.* subsp. *fortunei*** has scented, pale pink to lavender flowers and leaves with purple-red petioles. **ZONES 6–9.**

Rhododendron griersonianum

This 5–10 ft (1.5–3 m) tall, open shrub from western China and northern Burma has light green lance-shaped leaves up to 8 in (20 cm) long. The leaves, petioles and young stems are bristly. The funnel-shaped flowers are an unusual shade of pinkish orange-red, sometimes with darker flecks. They are 3 in (8 cm) long in trusses of up to 12 blooms. It is a very influential hybridizing species. **ZONES 8–9.**

Rhododendron griffithianum

This extremely influential species from the Himalayan region is a shrub or tree 6–30 ft (1.8–9 m) tall with bright green, oblong, 4–12 in (10–30 cm) long leaves and 4- to 5-flowered trusses of 3 in (8 cm) long, white to rose-pink flowers occasionally spotted green. The flowers are scented and have conspicuous calyces. **ZONES 8–9.**

Rhododendron hanceanum

An 1½–6 ft (0.45–1.8 m) tall shrub from Sichuan, China, this species has upright, open growth and lance-shaped leaves up to 4 in (10 cm) long. Many-flowered trusses of cream to yellow, 1 in (25 mm) long, slightly scented, funnel-shaped flowers open from mid-spring. **'Nanum'** is a compact plant with bright yellow flowers. **ZONES 8–9.**

Rhododendron indicum

Not to be confused with the Indica azaleas, this evergreen azalea from Japan grows to around 6 ft (1.8 m) tall with narrow, lance-shaped, 1½ in (35 mm) long leaves. Its wide open, funnel-shaped flowers bloom from mid-spring and are pink, salmon, cerise, or white. **'Balsaminiflorum'** has orange-pink, rosebud-style double flowers on a dense, wiry stemmed bush. **ZONES 6–10.**

Rhododendron irroratum

Although up to 30 ft (9 m) tall in the wild, this species from China, Vietnam, Indonesia and Laos is a medium-sized shrub in cultivation. It has 4–6 in (10–15 cm) long, light green elliptical leaves and 15-flowered trusses of 2 in (5 cm) long, red-purple spotted, white, cream or pink bell-shaped flowers from early spring. **'Spatter Paint'** has white-flushed flowers bordered with pink and with a dense inner covering of red-purple flecks. **ZONES 7–9.**

Rhododendron jasminiflorum

Native to the Malay Peninsula, this Vireya species can grow to 8 ft (2.4 m) tall. It has 2½ in (6 cm) long, bright green leaves in whorls of three to five. Throughout the year it produces 5- to 8-flowered trusses of 1½–2 in (3.5–5 cm) long, scented, tubular white flowers. **ZONES 10–12.**

Rhododendron javanicum

This 6–12 ft (1.8–3.5 m) tall epiphytic or terrestrial Vireya native to Malaysia and Indonesia has oval leaves up to 8 in (20 cm) long. The often fragrant, large-lobed, funnel-shaped flowers in loose trusses are 1½ in (35 mm) long and wide and are orange to orange-pink or red with cream or yellow centers. **ZONES 10–12.**

Rhododendron johnstoneanum

From northern India, this 8–15 ft (2.4–4.5 m) tall shrub, sometimes epiphytic in the wild, has bristly elliptical leaves up to 3 in (8 cm) long. Its flowers are scented, 3 in (8 cm) long, funnel-shaped, creamy white or pale yellow, sometimes with red or yellow spots, and open from early spring. **'Double Diamond'** has creamy yellow double flowers, often with darker markings. **ZONES 7–9.**

Rhododendron kaempferi

This 4–10 ft (1.2–3 m) tall evergreen azalea from Japan is fully frost hardy, though it loses much of its foliage in very cold conditions. The hairy, elliptical

Rhododendron jasminiflorum

Rhododendron griffithianum

Rhododendron hanceanum 'Nanum'

Rhododendron johnstoneanum

Rhododendron litiense

leaves are 1½ in (35 mm) long. Funnel-shaped flowers open from mid-spring and are red to orange-pink, occasionally white, sometimes with purple or red flecks. It is extensively used in hybridizing for frost hardiness. **ZONES 5–9.**

Rhododendron keiskei

This variable 1–10 ft (0.3–3 m) tall shrub from Japan, has 1–3 in (2.5–8 cm) long, lance-shaped leaves, bronze-green when young. Pale to bright yellow, 1–1½ in (25–35 mm) long, wide open, funnel-shaped flowers bloom from early spring. ***Rhododendron keiskei* var. *cordifolia* 'Yaku Fairy'** is a densely foliaged, near-prostrate form with reddish new growth and bright yellow flowers. **ZONES 5–9.**

Rhododendron kiusianum

Native to Kyushu, Japan, this dense, mounding evergreen azalea is usually less than 3 ft (1 m) tall. It has hairy, ½ in (12 mm) long, purple-green leaves that darken in winter. From mid-spring the foliage is hidden by tiny purple, pink or white flowers. It is an important parent of the Kurume azaleas, and there are many cultivated forms. **'Hinode'** is the brightest red-flowered selection. **'Komokulshan'** has white or pale pink flowers with darker petal tips. **ZONES 6–10.**

Rhododendron laetum

From New Guinea, this Vireya is 5 ft (1.5 m) tall with 3 in (8 cm) long elliptical leaves. Its flowers are wide open, funnel-shaped and 2½ in (6 cm) long, usually deep yellow, sometimes suffused pink, orange or red and occasionally scented. **ZONES 10–12.**

Rhododendron leucaspis

This species from western China grows to around 3 ft (1 m) tall. It has 1–1½ in

Rhododendron kiusianum

(25–35 mm) long, blue-green, bristly leaves and wide open, almost flat, bell-shaped, 1 in (25 mm) wide white flowers with brown anthers. The flowers are often slightly pink tinted. **ZONES 7–9.**

Rhododendron litiense

From western China, this is a 4 ft (1.2 m) tall shrub with oblong, matt, mid-green leaves with waxy blue-green undersides. The 2 in (5 cm) wide, bell-shaped, clear yellow flowers are carried in trusses of 6 to 8 blooms. It is widely considered to be a form of *Rhododendron wardii* var. *wardii*, although the waxy glaucous foliage distinguishes it. **ZONES 6–9.**

Rhododendron lochiae

This Vireya species is found in northeast Queensland, and is the only rhododendron native to Australia. It grows to 6 ft (1.8 m) tall with oval leaves around 3 in (8 cm) long. It has large-lobed, deep red, 1½ in (35 mm) long tubular flowers in trusses of 2 to 7 blooms. **ZONES 10–11.**

Rhododendron luteum

This deciduous azalea is found from eastern Europe to the Caucasus. It grows to 12 ft (3.5 m) and has 2–4 in (5–10 cm) long, bristly, lance-shaped leaves. Its flowers are bright yellow and sweetly scented. They are around 1½ in (35 mm) long, funnel-shaped with a narrow tube in trusses of up to 12 blooms. **ZONES 5–9.**

Rhododendron macabeanum

This species from northern India is a tree up to 50 ft (15 m) tall. It has very dark green, heavily veined, leathery leaves up to 18 in (45 cm) long with white indumentum on the undersides. Pale yellow, bell-shaped, 2–3 in (5–8 cm) long flowers with a basal purple blotch are carried in rounded trusses of up to 20 blooms and open from early spring. **ZONES 8–9.**

Rhododendron lochiae

Rhododendron maddenii

From the Himalayan region eastward to Vietnam, this often epiphytic species is an open, sometimes leggy 4–8 ft (1.2–2.4 m) shrub with 6 in (15 cm) long, scaly, bronze-green leaves. Its flowers are white, sometimes tinted pink, with a yellow basal blotch. They are tubular, up to 4 in (10 cm) long and scented. ***Rhododendron maddenii* subsp. *crassum*** has slightly larger foliage than the species and is rather frost tender; ***R. m.* subsp. *maddenii*** can grow to 15 ft (4.5 m) tall and has flowers that are often pink tinted and occasionally light yellow. **ZONES 9–10.**

Rhododendron maximum

ROSEBAY RHODODENDRON

Native to eastern North America, this 3–15 ft (1–4.5 m) shrub or small tree has slightly hairy, 6 in (15 cm) long, elliptical leaves. It blooms late and has 15- to 20-flowered trusses of white to deep pink, 1 in (25 mm) long, bell-shaped flowers with greenish spotting. **ZONES 3–9.**

Rhododendron molle

This deciduous azalea is found in eastern and central China. It grows 4–6 ft (1.2–1.8 m) tall and bears large, densely packed trusses of 2½ in (6 cm) long, funnel-shaped yellow or orange flowers from mid-spring. The flowers are sometimes fragrant. ***Rhododendron molle* subsp. *japonicum*** (syn. *R. japonicum*), from Japan, is a 3–10 ft (1–3 m) tall shrub with bright red, orange-red, pink or yellow flowers and brightly colored fall (autumn) foliage. This subspecies is the principal parent of the deciduous Mollis Azaleas. **ZONES 7–9.**

Rhododendron mucronulatum

One of the few deciduous rhododendrons not always considered an azalea, this 5–8 ft (1.5–2.4 m) tall shrub from northeast Asia and Japan has scaly, 4 in (10 cm) long, lance-shaped leaves and produces 1½ in (35 mm) long pink to purple, funnel-shaped flowers from late winter. In mild areas it will flower in mid-winter. There are several dwarf forms. **'Cornell Pink'** has very early, soft, pure pink flowers and yellow-orange fall (autumn) foliage. ***Rhododendron mucronulatum* var. *taguetti*** is a very early flowering, near-prostrate variety from Korea. **ZONES 4–9.**

Rhododendron molle subsp. *japonicum*

Rhododendron luteum

Rhododendron macabeanum

Rhododendron laetum

Rhododendron nakaharai

This evergreen Taiwanese azalea is a near-prostrate shrub usually under 12 in (30 cm) tall. The pointed elliptical leaves are hairy and a little under 1 in (25 mm) long. The 1 in (25 mm) long orange-red funnel-shaped flowers open in early summer. It is a good rockery, bonsai or ground-cover plant. **'Mt Seven Star'** is a densely foliaged, prostrate form with large deep orange-red flowers. **ZONES 5–10.**

Rhododendron nuttallii

Native to the Himalayan region, this 8–30 ft (2.4–9 m) shrub or small tree has deep green, leaves up to 12 in (30 cm) long and 3- to 7-flowered trusses of 4–6 in (10–15 cm) long, bell-shaped, creamy white fragrant flowers. The flowers open in mid-spring as the red-tinted new foliage develops. **ZONES 9–10.**

Rhododendron occidentale

WESTERN AZALEA

From western USA, this species is a 6–15 ft (1.8–4.5 m) tall deciduous azalea with slightly hairy, 4 in (10 cm) long elliptical leaves. The fragrant 3 in (8 cm) wide, funnel-shaped flowers are carried in trusses of up to 12 blooms, and are usually white or pale pink with a yellow, occasionally maroon, flare but may be red, yellow or orange-pink. The foliage turns red and copper in fall (autumn). **'Leonard Frisbie'** has large, frilled, fragrant flowers that are white suffused pink with a yellow flare. **ZONES 6–9.**

Rhododendron nakaharai

Rhododendron ponticum

From Europe and the Middle East to Russia, this 6–20 ft (1.8–6 m) shrub has glossy deep green, oblong to lance-shaped leaves up to 8 in (20 cm) long. The 10- to 15-flowered trusses open in late spring and are 2 in (5 cm) long, funnel-shaped, purple, lavender, pink or rarely maroon or white flushed pink, often with yellow, ochre or brown flecks. It is used in hybridizing. **'Variegatum'** has dark green leaves with cream edges and occasional stripes or flecks. **ZONES 6–10.**

Rhododendron prunifolium

PLUMLEAF AZALEA

This 6–15 ft (1.8–4.5 m) tall deciduous azalea from southeast USA flowers very late. It has 4–6 in (10–15 cm) long, narrow oval leaves and 4- to 5-flowered trusses of orange-red to red, occasionally orange or yellow tubular to funnel-shaped flowers. It tolerates more shade than most deciduous azaleas. **ZONES 6–9.**

Rhododendron russatum

An $1\frac{1}{2}$–6 ft (0.45–1.8 m) tall shrub from western China, this alpine species has

Rhododendron saluenense

scaly, $1\frac{1}{2}$ in (35 mm) long, narrowly elliptical leaves. Its funnel-shaped flowers are a little under 1 in (25 mm) wide, indigo, purple, rose pink or sometimes white in trusses of 4 to 10 blooms. The growth habit is variable, with both compact and upright forms. **ZONES 5–9.**

Rhododendron saluenense

This $1\frac{1}{2}$–5 ft (0.45–1.5 m) tall shrub from northern Burma and western China forms a many stemmed mound of spreading branches that are clothed with $\frac{1}{2}$–$1\frac{1}{2}$ in (12–35 mm) long, bristle-edged, rounded leaves. The aromatic, deep green leaves develop purple tones in winter. The flowers open in early spring, are flat, $\frac{1}{2}$–$1\frac{1}{2}$ in (12–35 mm) across in trusses of 2 to 5 and range from pink to deep purple, often with crimson spotting. **ZONES 6–9.**

Rhododendron schlippenbachii

ROYAL AZALEA

This deciduous azalea from Korea, Manchuria and nearby parts of Russia is a

Rhododendron sinogrande

Rhododendron trichostomum

6–15 ft (1.8–4.5 m) tall shrub with 4–6 in (10–15 cm) long leaves in whorls of five. Its 3- to 6-bloom trusses of 3 in (8 cm) wide flowers, which are usually lightly scented and open in mid-spring, vary from white flushed pink to rose pink, often with brown flecks. The foliage colors well in fall (autumn). It prefers light shade. **ZONES 4–9.**

Rhododendron simsii

The main parent of the Indica evergreen azaleas, this shrub found through much of northern Southeast Asia and southern China is 4–8 ft (1.2–2.4 m) tall with 1–3 in (2.5–3 cm) long elliptical leaves. The flowers are funnel-shaped, $2\frac{1}{2}$ in (6 cm) wide, in shades of crimson and red and carried in trusses of 2 to 6 blooms. **ZONES 8–11.**

Rhododendron sinogrande

This species from high rainfall parts of the Himalayan region is famed for its huge leaves, the largest in the genus, which can be up to 3 ft (1 m) long, though usually considerably smaller. The leaves are heavily veined with a buff or fawn indumentum. It grows to 30 ft (9 m) and in early spring bears rounded trusses of 20 or more 3 in (8 cm) long, cream to pale yellow, bell-shaped flowers with a basal crimson blotch. **ZONES 8–10.**

Rhododendron thomsonii

From the Himalayas and western China, this species grows 2–20 ft (0.6–6 m) tall with oval leaves to 4 in (10 cm) long and peeling red-brown bark. Its 10- to 12-flowered trusses, which open from early spring, are usually blood red but also occur in pink with crimson spotting. When mature *Rhododendron thomsonii* is very heavy flowering. **ZONES 6–9.**

Rhododendron trichostomum

This twiggy shrub from western China is $2\frac{1}{2}$–5 ft (0.75–1.5 m) tall with narrow,

Rhododendron nuttallii

Rhododendron occidentale

Rhododendron prunifolium

Rhododendron ponticum

aromatic, scaly, olive-green leaves up to 1 in (25 mm) long. In mid-spring it develops rounded trusses of up to 16 funnel-shaped, white or pink, ½–1 in (12–25 mm) long flowers. **ZONES 7–9.**

Rhododendron wardii

Named after collector and explorer Frank Kingdon Ward, this species from western China is variable and ranges from 3–25 ft (1–8 m) tall. It has deep green, oval, 4 in (10 cm) long leaves and saucer-shaped white to pale yellow, sometimes crimson-blotched flowers in trusses of 7 to 14 blooms from mid-spring. ***Rhododendron wardii* var. *wardii*** has bright yellow flowers, sometimes with a purple blotch, and is used extensively in hybridizing. **ZONES 7–9.**

Rhododendron williamsianum

This densely foliaged shrub from Sichuan, China grows 2–5 ft (0.6–1.5 m) tall and has rounded to heart-shaped, matt mid-green leaves up to 2 in (5 cm) long. The new growth is a contrasting bronze color. The flowers, which appear in mid-spring, are bell-shaped, 2 in (5 cm) long, mid-pink to rose, sometimes with darker flecks and carried in loose clusters of 2 to 3 blooms. **ZONES 7–9.**

Rhododendron wardii var. *wardii*

Rhododendron williamsianum

Rhododendron yunnanense

Rhododendron yakushimanum

Native to Yakushima Island, Japan, this dense, mounding, 3–8 ft (1–2.4 m) tall shrub has 3–4 in (8–10 cm) long, deep green leathery leaves with rolled edges and heavy fawn indumentum. The flowers appear quite early and are white or pale pink opening from deep pink buds and carried in rounded trusses of up to 10 blooms. **'Exbury Form'** makes a perfect dome of deep green, heavily indumented foliage with light pink flowers. **'Koichiro Wada'** is similar to 'Exbury Form' but has white flowers opening from deep pink buds. **ZONES 5–9.**

Rhododendron yedoense var. *poukhanense*

This species from Korea is among the frost hardiest of the evergreen azaleas, though it loses much of its foliage in very cold conditions. It grows to 5 ft (1.5 m) tall with sparsely hairy, 3 in (8 cm) long, lance-shaped leaves and slightly fragrant 2 in (5 cm) wide, funnel-shaped, deep pink to lilac flowers. It has been used in hybridizing to add frost hardiness. **ZONES 5–9.**

Rhododendron yunnanense

From Burma and western China, this upright 5–15 ft (1.5–4.5 m) tall shrub has bristly, narrowly elliptical leaves up to 4 in (10 cm) long. From mid-spring it bears masses of 1½ in (35 mm) long white, pink or lavender, open funnel-shaped flowers in trusses of 3 to 5 blooms. **ZONES 7–9.**

Rhododendron zoelleri

Usually seen as a 4–6 ft (1.2–1.8 m) tall shrub, this Vireya from Indonesia, New Guinea and the Moluccas can reach 20 ft (6 m) tall. Its trumpet-shaped flowers are particularly bright shades of yellow and

Rhododendron 'Annie E. Endtz'

Rhododendron cultivar

orange with orange-red lobes. It is popular with hybridizers for its vivid color. **ZONES 10–12.**

Rhododendron yakushimanum

Rhododendron zoelleri

RHODODENDRON CULTIVARS

Unlike the azaleas, rhododendron cultivars are generally not divided into groups; they are most often simply referred to by their cultivar name. However, there are several recognizable styles. The alpine rhododendrons tend to be dense, twiggy plants with small leaves and masses of tiny flowers; those from high rainfall areas often have large leaves; and many of the fragrant cultivars are similar to one another. Knowledgeable gardeners often use alliance or grex names or refer to a hybrid by its dominant parent. Groups of similar rhododendrons are sometimes grouped as alliances (*maddenii* alliance, *ciliicalyx* alliance, etc.) and their offspring tend to be similar. A grex is a group of sister seedlings from the same cross. Grex names are rare among modern hybrids but are still found among popular old-timers such as Fabia, Naomi and Loderi. You may have heard such terms as *yakushimanum* or 'yak' hybrid, *williamsianum* hybrid or *griersonianum* hybrid. Hybrids of these and other species often closely resemble their parents in terms of foliage and general growth habit, although the flowers can vary markedly. Exact sizes are not given as rhododendrons are notoriously variable. Dwarf is under 18 in (45 cm), small is less than 4 ft (1.2 m), medium is 4–8 ft (1.2–2.4 m) and anything over 8 ft (2.4 m) is large. It is important to realize that rhododendrons are long lived and continue to grow throughout their lives.

Rhododendron 'Alice'

Very old specimens can be extremely large. The flowering season also varies considerably depending on the climate. Generally though, in mild temperate climates early is before the spring equinox, mid-season is from the equinox to 6 weeks later, and late is more than 6 weeks after the equinox.

Rhododendron 'Alice'

This is a *Rhododendron griffithianum* hybrid with 6 in (15 cm) long leaves that becomes large with age. Its large trusses of bright pink blooms with lighter centers appear mid-season. **ZONES 6–9.**

Rhododendron 'Alison Johnstone'

This medium-sized bush has a narrow upright growth habit and blue-green rounded leaves. Funnel-shaped flowers in small clusters are yellow flushed pink and appear early to mid-season. **ZONES 7–9.**

Rhododendron 'Anna-Rose Whitney'

This large shrub has 6–8 in (15–20 cm) long, mid-green oval leaves and late, deep pink, trumpet-shaped flowers up to 4 in (10 cm) wide in trusses of up to 12 blooms. **ZONES 6–9.**

Rhododendron 'Annie E. Endtz'

Developed from 'Pink Pearl' in 1939, this medium-sized hybrid has broad waxy leaves and rounded trusses of frilled pink flowers shortly after mid-season. **ZONES 7–9.**

Rhododendron 'Blue Boy'

Rhododendron 'Arthur J. Ivens'

Rhododendron 'Betty'

Rhododendron 'Billy Budd'

Rhododendron 'Gibraltar'

Rhododendron 'Bibiani'

Rhododendron 'Blue Peter'

Rhododendron 'Brickdust'

Rhododendron 'Britannia'

Rhododendron 'Arthur J. Ivens'

A *Rhododendron williamsianum* hybrid, this small mounding shrub has small oval leaves and early to mid-season, loose trusses of dusky pink bell-shaped flowers. **ZONES 6–9.**

Rhododendron 'Babylon'

This is a medium-sized, dense, mounding bush with 4–6 in (10–15 cm) long, narrow, deep green leaves and conical trusses of 9 to 15 funnel-shaped, white to pale pink flowers with brown throat markings. It flowers early. **ZONES 6–9.**

Rhododendron 'Betty'

This large shrub has lush mid-green foliage and deep pink, funnel-shaped flowers in conical trusses from mid-season. **ZONES 6–9.**

Rhododendron 'Bibiani'

This is a medium-sized *Rhododendron arboreum* hybrid raised in 1934 by the famous English breeder Lionel de Rothschild. It has 4–6 in (10–15 cm) long, dark green, heavy textured leaves and early, deep red, 2 in (5 cm) wide, bell-shaped flowers in trusses of 11 to 15 blooms. **'Gibraltar'** is a hybrid seedling of 'Bibiani' with similar blooms of very deep red. **ZONES 7–10.**

Rhododendron 'Billy Budd'

This small shrub has elliptical leaves with a slight indumentum. It blooms mid-season with flat-topped trusses of 10 to 12 waxy bright red flowers. **ZONES 6–9.**

Rhododendron 'Blue Boy'

This medium-sized shrub has 4–6 in (10–15 cm) long, narrow, deep green leaves and tight rounded trusses of up to 20, violet-blue blotched black, funnel-shaped, 2 in (5 cm) wide flowers. **ZONES 6–9.**

Rhododendron 'Blue Peter'

Probably a *Rhododendron ponticum* hybrid, this medium-sized bush was introduced by the English company Waterer in 1933. It has glossy deep green leaves and frilled trusses of lavender-blue flowers with a prominent purple flare. It flowers mid-season. **ZONES 6–9.**

Rhododendron 'Brickdust'

Typical of a *Rhododendron williamsianum* hybrid, this small plant forms a dense mound of 2 in (5 cm) long, rounded leaves with masses of loose trusses of bell-shaped flowers. The blooms are dusky orange and appear mid-season. **ZONES 6–9.**

Rhododendron 'Britannia'

A medium-sized shrub, 'Britannia' has 4–6 in (10–15 cm) long, narrow, light green, somewhat drooping leaves. From late mid-season it produces large trusses of bright scarlet flowers. **ZONES 6–9.**

Rhododendron 'Bruce Brechtbill'

Rhododendron 'Bruce Brechtbill'

This medium-sized shrub is very similar to its parent 'Unique' except that its flowers are pink flushed yellow. It has heavy, deep green oblong leaves and its conical trusses open early to mid-season. **ZONES 7–9.**

Rhododendron 'Cherry Custard'

This small Canadian hybrid shows its 'Fabia' heritage in its flat 10- to 12-flowered trusses of yellow blooms that open from orange-red buds. It is a low, spreading plant with narrow, pointed elliptical leaves. **ZONES 7–9.**

Rhododendron 'Christmas Cheer'

Always one of the first to bloom, this old, medium-sized *Rhododendron caucasicum* hybrid has 2–4 in (510 cm) long, mid-green elliptical leaves and 5- to 11-flowered trusses of funnel-shaped white and pale pink flowers that open from deep pink buds. Late frosts can destroy the flowers. **ZONES 5–9.**

Rhododendron 'Cinnkeys'

This very unusual plant, a medium-sized hybrid between *Rhododendron cinnabarinum* and *R. keysii*, was introduced in 1926. It has oval, glossy mid-green foliage and distinctive waxy, tubular flowers that are red fading to yellow at the tips. **ZONES 7–9.**

Rhododendron 'Cinnkeys'

Rhododendron 'Cherry Custard'

R

Rhododendron 'Countess of Haddington'

Rhododendron 'Dido'

Rhododendron 'Cornubia'

This large, vigorous *Rhododendron arboreum* hybrid has slightly puckered mid-green leaves up to 6 in (15 cm) long. It blooms early and gives a marvellous display of 7- to 11-flowered trusses of bright red, funnel-shaped flowers; the flowers can be damaged by late frosts. **ZONES 8–10.**

Rhododendron 'Countess of Haddington'

Many fragrant rhododendrons are untidy bushes but this 1862 hybrid of unknown origin is a neat medium-sized bush with 4 in (10 cm) long, slightly glossy, bronze-green foliage. Its large bell-shaped flowers are white flushed pink, pleasantly scented and carried in heads of 3 to 5 blooms. **ZONES 9–10.**

Rhododendron 'Crest'

Raised in England in 1953, this medium-sized shrub was one of the first hybrids to use *Rhododendron wardii* rather than *R. burmanicum* to produce yellow flowers with frost hardiness. It is an open grower with bronze-green foliage and flowers mid-season. **ZONES 6–9.**

Rhododendron 'Dido'

Rhododendron 'Dido', raised in England in 1934, has had more influence as a parent plant than as a garden specimen. Used as one of the parents of 'Lem's Cameo', it has greatly influenced modern American rhododendron development. It grows to 4 ft (1.2 m) and has rounded, light green leaves and lax trusses of yellow-centered, orange-pink, trumpet-shaped flowers. **ZONES 7–9.**

Rhododendron 'Dora Amateis'

One of the few ***Rhododendron minus*** hybrids, this small shrub has 2 in (5 cm) long, pointed elliptical, deep green leaves

Rhododendron 'Crest'

Rhododendron 'Eldorado'

that are aromatic and bronze when young. In early spring the foliage disappears under masses of 3- to 6-flowered clusters of white, funnel-shaped flowers. **ZONES 5–9.**

Rhododendron 'Eldorado'

This medium-sized, open-growing *Rhododendron johnstoneanum* hybrid has small, scaly, deep olive-green leaves and 2 in (5 cm) long, bright yellow, funnel-shaped flowers in clusters of 2 to 3 blooms. The flowers open early. **ZONES 8–10.**

Rhododendron 'Elisabeth Hobbie'

This is a small *Rhododendron forrestii* hybrid with rounded, 2 in (5 cm) long,

Rhododendron 'Elisabeth Hobbie'

Rhododendron Fabia 'Roman Pottery'

deep green leaves. The petioles and new growth are red tinted. Bright to deep red, bell-shaped flowers in clusters of 5 to 7 blooms open mid-season. **ZONES 6–10.**

Rhododendron 'Elizabeth'

This hybrid shows considerable *Rhododendron griersonianum* influence. It is a medium-sized, rather open bush with 3–4 in (8–10 cm) long, narrow pointed leaves and bright red 3 in (8 cm) wide, funnel-shaped flowers in lax 6- to 8-bloom trusses from early mid-season. **ZONES 7–9.**

Rhododendron Fabia

This collection of sister seedlings resulted from a 1934 *Rhododendron dichroanthum* and *R. griersonianum* cross by the Welsh breeder Aberconway. This grex has had enormous influence in the development of modern frost-hardy hybrids in yellow and orange shades. The plants grow to around 3 ft (1 m) tall and slightly wider with 3 in (8 cm) pointed elliptical leaves. The mid-season flowers are in soft orange tones, bell-shaped, and carried in open trusses of 3 to 7 blooms. **'Roman Pottery'** has unusual terracotta-colored flowers. **ZONES 7–9.**

Rhododendron 'Fastuosum Flore Pleno'

Dating from before 1846 and still one of the few double-flowered 'true' rhododendrons, this large shrub has mid-green, 4–6 in (10–15 cm) long

Rhododendron 'Fastuosum Flore Pleno'

Rhododendron 'Elizabeth'

leaves. They open mid-season to late and are semi-double, deep lavender with greenish yellow throat markings in trusses of 7 to 15 blooms. **ZONES 5–8.**

Rhododendron 'Fragrantissimum'

This medium-sized, rather open-growing *Rhododendron edgeworthii* hybrid from before 1868 remains popular because of it large, funnel-shaped, white flushed pink flowers, which are fragrant. They are carried in loose trusses of 3 to 7 blooms and open mid-season. The foliage is bronze green, pointed and 3–4 in (8–10 cm) long. **ZONES 8–10.**

Rhododendron 'Frank Baum'

Named after the author of *The Wizard of Oz*, this 1969 American hybrid is medium-sized and blooms late. It has 10- to 14-flowered trusses of yellow-centered coral flowers that open late. Its heavy leaves are dark green with red-tinted petioles. **ZONES 6–9.**

Rhododendron 'Frank Baum'

Rhododendron 'Fragrantissimum'

Rhododendron 'Furnivall's Daughter'

This is a medium to large shrub with large bright green leaves and tall trusses of bright pink flowers with a darker blotch. It is a vigorous grower that flowers heavily from mid-season. **ZONES 6–9.**

Rhododendron 'George's Delight'

This very distinctively colored small shrub is typical of the modern style of rhododendron hybrid. It has lustrous mid-green leaves and dense growth, and from mid-season it produces spectacular rounded trusses of soft yellow and cream flowers with pink margins. **ZONES 7–9.**

Rhododendron 'Golden Wit'

This small shrub has a spreading habit and 2 in (5 cm) long, rounded, bright green leaves. Its bell-shaped flowers, which open mid-season, are soft golden yellow with red or red-brown markings and carried in loose clusters of up to 9 blooms. **ZONES 7–9.**

Rhododendron 'Good News'

This free-flowering, medium-sized shrub has light green new growth and fawn indumentum. This soon disappears from the upper surfaces but remains on the undersides. Funnel-shaped crimson flowers in 12- to 15-flowered trusses open from bright red buds late in late spring. **ZONES 6–9.**

Rhododendron 'Furnivall's Daughter'

Rhododendron 'Grumpy'

Rhododendron 'George's Delight'

Rhododendron 'Good News'

Rhododendron 'Golden Wit'

Rhododendron 'Hydon Dawn'

Rhododendron 'Grumpy'

This is one of a group of *Rhododendron yakushimanum* hybrids known as The Seven Dwarfs bred by Waterer's in the 1970s. It is a small to medium-sized bush with deep green foliage and cream to pale yellow flowers flushed pink. The rounded trusses open mid-season. **ZONES 6–9.**

Rhododendron 'Halopeanum'
syn. ***Rhododendron* 'White Pearl'**

This is a fast-growing large shrub with deep green foliage and tall conical trusses of pale pink flowers that fade to white. Although largely superseded by better plants, it is still widely grown for its extreme vigor. It flowers mid-season. **ZONES 7–9.**

Rhododendron 'Honeymoon'

Another beautiful hybrid with considerable *Rhododendron wardii* influence, this plant is medium-sized and forms a dense mound of heavy, deep green foliage. The flowers, borne in flat trusses of up to 15 blooms from mid-season, are soft yellow often with a hint of orange. **ZONES 7–9.**

Rhododendron 'Hotei'

A significant hybrid in the development of frost-hardy, yellow-flowered rhododendrons, this small to medium-sized shrub has rounded bright green leaves around 4 in (10 cm) long. Its flowers, borne in rounded trusses of up to 12 blooms from mid-season, are bright yellow and bell-shaped. **ZONES 7–9.**

Rhododendron 'Halopeanum'

Rhododendron 'Honeymoon'

Rhododendron 'Impi'

Rhododendron 'Irene Stead'

Rhododendron 'Hydon Dawn'

This is a *Rhododendron yakushimanum* hybrid of the same cross as the better known **'Hydon Hunter'**. It is a small bush that develops into a mound of glossy, bright green foliage. The flowers, borne in small rounded trusses, open mid-season and are pink, lightening at the edges. **ZONES 7–9.**

Rhododendron 'Impi'

'Impi' combines dark green foliage with very deep purple-red flowers. It is a medium-sized bush that blooms from late mid-season. Its flowers are carried in small rounded trusses. **ZONES 7–9.**

Rhododendron 'Irene Stead'

Of Loderi parentage and very similar to the plants of that grex, this New Zealand-raised hybrid is a large bush with mid-green leaves around 8 in (20 cm) long. Its mid-season, pale pink and white flowers are somewhat waxy and carried in large conical trusses. **ZONES 6–9.**

Rhododendron 'Jingle Bells'

This Fabia hybrid is a neat, small bush with a dense covering of narrow deep green, 3–4 in (8–10 cm) long leaves. Orange bell-shaped flowers in lax trusses of 5 to 9 blooms open from orange-red buds and fade to yellow. They smother the plant in mid-season. **ZONES 7–9.**

Rhododendron 'Max Sye'

Rhododendron 'Kubla Khan'

This medium-sized plant has bright green foliage and striking flowers with calyces so large they create a hose-in-hose effect. The color is a combination of pink, orange and red on a cream background with a large red flare on the upper lobes and calyx. It blooms from late mid-season and needs cool conditions for the flowers to last. **ZONES 6–9.**

Rhododendron 'Lemon Lodge'

Very distinctive foliage and soft pastel yellow flowers distinguish 'Lemon Lodge', a medium to large New Zealand-

Rhododendron 'Jingle Bells'

Rhododendron 'Kubla Khan'

Rhododendron 'Lem's Aurora'

Rhododendron 'Lem's Monarch'

Rhododendron 'Lem's Cameo'

raised *Rhododendron wardii* hybrid. The leaves are a bright light to mid-green, oval, 3–4 in (8–10 cm) with a waxy texture. The flowers are in rather flat trusses that open mid-season. **ZONES 7–10.**

Rhododendron 'Lem's Aurora'

This is a compact small to medium-sized bush with dark green, 4 in (10 cm) leaves and rounded trusses of crimson flowers with light golden-yellow centers and calyces. It blooms mid-season. **ZONES 6–9.**

Rhododendron 'Lem's Cameo'

This beautiful and very influential hybrid is a medium-sized mound of deep green, glossy 3–4 in (8–10 cm) long leaves with rich bronze new growth. The mid-season flowers, borne in trusses of up to 20

Rhododendron 'Lemon Lodge'

Rhododendron 'May Day'

Rhododendron 'Loder's White'

Rhododendron Loderi 'King George'

blooms, are delicate shades of apricot-pink and creamy yellow and funnel-shaped. **ZONES 7–9.**

Rhododendron 'Lem's Monarch'

This impressive large shrub is densely foliaged with rounded, bright mid-green leaves up to 8 in (20 cm) long. The flowers, carried in large conical trusses of 9 to 15 blooms, are funnel-shaped and white to pale pink flushed and edged deep pink to crimson. **ZONES 6–9.**

Rhododendron Loderi

This grex consists of a large group of *Rhododendron griffithianum* × *R. fortunei* seedlings that date from around 1900. They are all very similar to one another and have 6–8 in (15–20 cm) long, mid-green to slightly glaucous leaves and large trusses of white to mid-pink, funnel-shaped, fragrant flowers. They are large, tree-like plants that are very impressive in full bloom. **'King George'** has white flowers opening from pink buds. **'Sir Edmond'** has very large pale pink flowers. **'Sir Joseph Hooker'** has light to mid-pink flowers. **ZONES 6–9.**

Rhododendron 'Loder's White'

Not to be confused with the Loderi grex, which it predates, this medium-sized shrub has attractive bright green, 6 in (15 cm) long leaves and large upright trusses of white flowers opening from pink buds. It blooms from mid-season. **ZONES 6–9.**

Rhododendron 'Mariloo'

This is one of the best known hybrids from *Rhododendron lacteum*. It has heavy

Rhododendron Loderi 'Sir Edmond'

Rhododendron 'Mariloo'

textured, rounded, 6 in (15 cm) long leaves with a blue-green to bronze bloom. New growth is very frost tender. Pale milky yellow, bell-shaped flowers, carried in large trusses, open early mid-season from yellow-green buds. **ZONES 8–10.**

Rhododendron 'Max Sye'

This is an open-growing, medium-sized shrub with narrow dark green leaves up to 6 in (15 cm) long. The flowers are deep red with a very dark blotch and are carried in rounded trusses. It blooms from late mid-season. **ZONES 6–9.**

Rhododendron 'May Day'

This vigorous small bush develops into a spreading mound of 3–4 in (8–10 cm) long, dark green leaves with light brown indumentum on the undersides. Lax trusses of 5 to 9 bright red to orange-red, bell-shaped flowers open from early mid-season. **ZONES 7–9.**

Rhododendron 'Oklahoma'

Rhododendron 'Moonwax'

Rhododendron 'Mrs G. W. Leak'

Rhododendron 'Moonstone'

Rhododendron 'Moonstone'

A small to medium-sized shrub, this *Rhododendron williamsianum* hybrid has 2–3 in (5–8 cm) long, rounded mid-green leaves. From early spring it is smothered in 3- to 5-flowered clusters of greenish white to pale cream, slightly pendulous, bell-shaped flowers. **ZONES 6–9.**

Rhododendron 'Moonwax'

This medium-sized shrub has narrow, oval, 6 in (15 cm) long leaves and waxy cream flowers with mauve tints. The flowers are mildly scented and carried in large trusses of up to 12 blooms that open mid-season. **ZONES 7–9.**

Rhododendron 'Mrs Charles E. Pearson'

An old hybrid still popular because of its frost hardiness, vigor and heavy flowering, this large bush becomes tree-like with age. The leaves are oval, deep green and 4–8 in (10–20 cm) long. The flowers, carried in trusses of 13 to 18 blooms, are funnel-shaped and light pink with darker markings. It is sun and heat tolerant. **ZONES 6–9.**

Rhododendron 'Mrs G. W. Leak'

This medium to large bush is instantly recognizable when in bloom. Its light pink, funnel-shaped flowers have a beautiful red flare and spotting that stands out from a great distance. They are borne in upright trusses of 9 to 12 blooms from early mid-season. The leaves are mid-green, 4–6 in (10–15 cm) long and very sticky, especially when young. **ZONES 6–9.**

Rhododendron 'Nancy Evans'

With 'Hotei' and 'Lem's Cameo' as its parents, this should be something special and so it is. A compact small to medium-sized bush, it is worth growing for its 2–4 in (5–10 cm) long foliage alone. The leaves are deep bronze green with reddish new growth. Deep golden-yellow, bell-shaped flowers open from orange buds in trusses of 15 to 20 blooms. The large calyces create a hose-in-hose effect. **ZONES 7–9.**

Rhododendron Naomi 'Pink Beauty'

Rhododendron 'Mrs Charles E. Pearson'

Rhododendron Naomi

This Rothschild grex, while not greatly influential in hybridizing, nevertheless includes some beautiful plants. The best known form is a large, densely foliaged shrub with mid-green, slightly glaucous, 4–8 in (10–20 cm) long leaves. The flowers are waxy, in light biscuit and pink shades, and carried in large trusses. It blooms mid-season. **'Nautilus'** has excellent foliage and pink flowers flushed orange with a green throat. **'Pink Beauty'** has deep pink flowers. **ZONES 6–9.**

Rhododendron 'Oklahoma'

This late-blooming, medium-sized shrub is not very frost hardy, but in a suitable climate can make an impressive show. Its trusses hold up to 22 large crimson flowers with darker spotting. The anthers and stigma are black. Its narrow, mid-green leaves droop slightly. **ZONES 8–10.**

Rhododendron 'Olin O. Dobbs'

Famed for its heavy, waxy flowers of intense red-purple, this medium-sized American hybrid also has lustrous deep green leaves up to 6 in (15 cm) long. The flowers are funnel-shaped and carried in conical trusses of 11 to 15 blooms that open from mid-season. **ZONES 5–9.**

Rhododendron 'Patty Bee'

This pretty little dwarf hybrid develops into a mound of bright green $\frac{1}{2}$–$1\frac{1}{2}$ in (12–35 mm) long, elliptical deep green leaves. From early mid-season it is smothered in 6-flowered clusters of soft yellow, funnel-shaped flowers up to 2 in (5 cm) wide. It is ideal for rockeries or containers. **ZONES 6–9.**

Rhododendron 'Percy Wiseman'

This beautiful *Rhododendron yakushimanum* × 'Fabia Tangerine' hybrid combines the best characteristics of both its parents. It is a small to medium-sized bush with a dense covering of narrow, deep green, 2–4 in (5–10 cm) long leaves with a hint of indumentum when young. The trusses of 13 to 15 funnel-shaped blooms open mid-season and are pale pink with yellowish throats. **ZONES 6–9.**

Rhododendron 'Percy Wiseman'

Rhododendron 'Olin O. Dobbs'

Rhododendron 'Nancy Evans'

Rhododendron 'Patty Bee'

R

Rhododendron 'Pineapple Delight'

Rhododendron 'Purple Heart'

Rhododendron 'President Roosevelt'

Rhododendron 'Pineapple Delight'

Rhododendron 'Pineapple Delight' forms a small to medium-sized mound of deep green, slightly puckered leaves up to 4 in (10 cm) long. The flowers, in trusses of 12 to 14 blooms, are bright yellow deepening with age, funnel-shaped and up to 4 in (10 cm) wide. **ZONES 7–10.**

Rhododendron 'Pink Gin'

This medium-sized shrub has 2–4 in (5–10 cm) long, deep green leaves with a hint of blue-green bloom. The flowers are funnel-shaped, pale purplish pink fading to orange pink in the center, in 4- to 5-flowered trusses that open mid-season. **ZONES 7–9.**

Rhododendron 'Pink Pearl'

This is a classic, large pink rhododendron, now over 100 years old but still the standard by which others are judged. It has large mid-green leaves and 11- to 15-flowered conical trusses of funnel-shaped, mid-pink blooms opening from deep pink buds and fading to pale pink. It flowers mid-season. **ZONES 6–9.**

Rhododendron 'Pink Gin'

Rhododendron 'Professor Hugo de Vries'

Rhododendron 'Point Defiance'

Of the same parentage as 'Lem's Monarch' (**'Anna'** × **'Marinus Koster'**) and virtually identical in all respects, this is a large bush with 6–8 in (15–20 cm) long rounded leaves and upright trusses of around 17 white, funnel-shaped flowers with deep pink to red edges. **ZONES 6–9.**

Rhododendron 'President Roosevelt'

This old medium-sized Dutch hybrid is still one of the few rhododendrons with boldly variegated foliage. The leaves are deep green with a central yellow splash and 4–6 in (10–15 cm) long. The flowers, which open early and are carried in conical trusses of 5 to 11 blooms, are funnel-shaped and white, edged and flushed red. **ZONES 7–9.**

Rhododendron 'Professor Hugo de Vries'

This is very similar to 'Pink Pearl', one of its parents, except that its flowers are a darker shade of pink. It is a large shrub with leaves up to 8 in (20 cm) long. The flower trusses are large, upright and open late mid-season. **ZONES 6–9.**

Rhododendron 'Rainbow'

Rhododendron 'Point Defiance'

Rhododendron 'Ptarmigan'

This is a dwarf, spreading, alpine-style shrub with scaly 1 in (25 mm) long leaves and pure white, widely funnel-shaped flowers up to 1 in (25 mm) wide. The flowers are in clusters of 2 or 3 blooms and open early mid-season. **ZONES 6–8.**

Rhododendron 'Purple Heart'

This large shrub is similar in shape and foliage to its parent 'Purple Splendour'. Its flowers are violet to purple with yellow-green throats. The upright, conical trusses hold 6 to 11 blooms and open mid-season. **ZONES 6–9.**

Rhododendron 'Purple Splendour'

Raised before 1900, this *Rhododendron ponticum* hybrid is still one of the best purple-flowered rhododendrons. It has narrow, slightly glossy, dark green leaves up to 6 in (15 cm) long. The flowers, which open late mid-season on trusses of 7 to 14 blooms, are deep purple with a near black blotch. **ZONES 6–9.**

Rhododendron 'Queen Elizabeth II'

Rhododendron 'Purple Splendour'

Rhododendron 'Queen Elizabeth II'

This medium to large shrub has striking soft yellow, funnel-shaped flowers over 4 in (10 cm) across. They are carried in trusses of around 12 blooms and open mid-season. The leaves are deep green, up to 6 in (15 cm) long and relatively narrow. **ZONES 7–9.**

Rhododendron 'Queen Nefertiti'

This medium-sized shrub forms a wide, rounded mound of bright green foliage. Its flowers are carried in globular trusses of around 12 blooms and are mid-pink with darker edging and pale spots. They open mid-season. **ZONES 7–9.**

Rhododendron 'Rainbow'

Similar in flower to 'Lem's Monarch' and 'Point Defiance', this large upright shrub has glossy, rather narrow, 6–8 in (15–20 cm) long leaves. The deep pink-edged, white flowers are carried on large trusses that sometimes droop under their own weight. It flowers mid-season. **ZONES 7–9.**

Rhododendron 'Romany Chai'

This is a grex, though only one form appears to be common. It is an upright, medium to large bush with large dark green leaves. The orange-red flowers with brown speckling open from mid-season and are carried in rather lax trusses. This hybrid is reputed to be heat tolerant. The name means 'gypsy children'. The red-flowered form is more properly known as **'Empire Day'**. **ZONES 6–9.**

Rhododendron 'Queen Nefertiti'

Rhododendron 'Rubicon'

Rhododendron 'Seta'

Rhododendron 'Rubicon'

This densely foliaged, medium-sized bush has lush, somewhat puckered, glossy green leaves up to 4 in (10 cm) long. 'Rubicon' has funnel-shaped, attractive deep rich red flowers which are carried in trusses of 9 to 17 blooms. The flowers open early to mid-season. **ZONES 7–9.**

Rhododendron 'Ruby Hart'

In the style of 'Elisabeth Hobbie' and 'Scarlet Wonder' but taller, this small shrub has 2 in (5 cm) long, deep green rounded leaves. The new growth is red-tinted. 'Ruby Hart' has widely funnel-shaped flowers which open early mid-season, and are about 2 in (5 cm) long. They are deep rich red in color and carried in trusses of 5 to 7 blooms. **ZONES 6–9.**

Rhododendron 'Sappho'

Rhododendron 'Sappho' was raised before 1847 but it is still a very distinctive plant today. When not in flower this cultivar looks much like any other large rhododendron but in bloom it cannot be mistaken for any other. Its funnel-shaped flowers, carried in upright conical trusses of 5 to 11 blooms, are pure white in color with a large, sharply contrasting, blackish purple flare. **ZONES 5–8.**

Rhododendron 'Scarlet Wonder'

This spreading *Rhododendron forrestii* hybrid is simply one of the best small rhododendrons available. It has a dense covering of lush deep green, 2 in (5 cm) long round leaves, and from mid-spring is smothered in deep red bell-shaped flowers in loose clusters of 4 to 7 blooms. **ZONES 5–9.**

Rhododendron 'Seta'

Among the earliest rhododendrons to bloom, 'Seta' has 2 in (5 cm) long, slightly blue-green pointed leaves and develops into an open, medium-sized bush. Its flowers, which are tubular to bell-shaped and carried in small clusters, are palest pink with a darker edge. **ZONES 7–8.**

Rhododendron 'Snow Lady'

Rhododendron 'Snow Lady' makes a dwarf to medium-sized bush. It has delightful foliage as well as a brilliant show of white to cream funnel-shaped flowers which appear in early spring. Its leaves are bright green, rounded and about 1½ in (35 mm) in length, and are also covered with fine fuzzy hair. The flowers can be up to 2 in (5 cm) wide. They are carried in loose clusters and are slightly fragrant. The plants are susceptible to damage by late frosts. **ZONES 6–9.**

Rhododendron 'Ruby Hart'

Rhododendron 'Sappho'

Rhododendron 'Sonata'

This spreading, medium-sized bush becomes a dense mass of narrow deep green leaves. *Rhododendron* 'Sonata' flowers late, producing rounded trusses of orange-red flowers edged with lavender to light red-purple, an unusual and distinctive color combination. **ZONES 6–9.**

Rhododendron 'Susan'

Popular ever since its introduction around 1930, *Rhododendron* 'Susan' makes a medium to large shrub. It has superb glossy deep green leaves which are up to 6 in (15 cm) long with a light indumentum. The flowers, which open in the middle of the season, are lavender blue in color with darker spots. They are funnel-shaped and are carried in trusses of between 5 and 11 blooms. **ZONES 6–9.**

Rhododendron 'Susan'

Rhododendron 'Ted's Orchid Sunset'

A stunning hybrid in all respects, 'Ted's Orchid Sunset' makes a medium-sized bush with matt mid-green leaves up to 6 in (15 cm) long. The new growth is bronze-colored. The flowers, over 3 in (8 cm) wide and in trusses of 7 to 11 blooms, open mid-season and are funnel-shaped and a dazzling combination of deep lavender pink shaded orange with orange-bronze throat markings. **ZONES 6–9.**

Rhododendron 'The Honourable Jean-Marie de Montague'

Probably bearing the longest name of any rhododendron, this cultivar is also a very influential and beautiful plant in its own right. It has extremely dark green leaves that are narrow, slightly drooping and up to 6 in (15 cm) long. Its flowers, which open in the middle of the season set the standard for red blooms. They are blood red in color, funnel-shaped and carried in trusses of 10 to 14 blooms. **ZONES 6–9.**

Rhododendron 'Too Bee'

A development of 'Patty Bee', this dwarf shrub has small deep green leaves and masses of thimble-sized, funnel-shaped flowers that are deep pink on the outside with apricot-pink interiors. It blooms from mid-season and is an irresistible plant for rockeries or containers. **ZONES 7–9.**

Rhododendron 'Trude Webster'

This large shrub is superb in all respects. 'Trude Webster' is densely clothed in lush, rounded, mid-green leaves up to 8 in (20 cm) long. From mid-season the plant is smothered in huge trusses of 15 to 20 flowers. These are large, funnel-shaped and clear mid-pink in color. **ZONES 5–9.**

Rhododendron 'Too Bee'

Rhododendron 'Ted's Orchid Sunset'

R

Rhododendron 'Vintage Rose'

Rhododendron 'Virginia Richards'

Rhododendron 'Wonder'

Rhododendron 'Whitney's Orange'

Rhododendron 'Winsome'

Rhododendron 'Unique'

While the color changing flowers of this medium-sized plant are no longer as unusual as when it was introduced around 1930, 'Unique' is still a beautiful and desirable plant. It has slightly glossy, rounded, 4 in (10 cm) long leaves and from early mid-season its bright pink buds begin to open to pale yellow, funnel-shaped flowers that fade to cream. There are 11 to 15 flowers per truss. **ZONES 6–9.**

Rhododendron 'Van Nes Sensation'

This is a large shrub with bright mid-green leaves more than 6 in (15 cm) long. It blooms mid-season with 7- to 11-flowered trusses of large, funnel-shaped, white suffused pink flowers opening from deep pink buds. The flowers are sightly fragrant. **ZONES 6–9.**

Rhododendron 'Vintage Rose'

This medium-sized, spreading, *Rhododendron yakushimanum* hybrid has 4 in (10 cm) long leaves. Its flowers are 2½ in (6 cm) wide, white flushed rose pink with a darker throat and a little red spotting. They open mid-season in compact rounded trusses. **ZONES 6–9.**

Rhododendron 'Virginia Richards'

This neat small to medium-sized bush has mid-green, 3–4 in (8–10 cm) long, pointed elliptical leaves. Its orange buds open in mid-spring to reveal funnel-shaped, red blotched, apricot-orange flowers with soft creamy orange centers. The compact trusses hold 9 to 13 blooms. **ZONES 6–9.**

Rhododendron 'Whitney's Orange'

This medium-sized, rather open-growing bush has 4 in (10 cm) long, narrow, slightly rolled bright green leaves. Its flowers, which open late mid-season, are pinkish orange with yellow centers. They are funnel-shaped in lax trusses. **ZONES 7–9.**

Rhododendron 'Winsome'

This small to medium-sized bush is attractive throughout the year with deep green, 3 in (8 cm) long pointed leaves with a pale buff indumentum. The new growth is bronze. From early mid-season the foliage disappears under 5- to 9-flowered clusters of deep pink bell-shaped flowers. **ZONES 7–9.**

Rhododendron 'Wonder'

One of the hybrids of the 'Tortoiseshell' grex raised by Slocock in the 1940s, this upright hybrid grows to around 4 ft (1.2 m) tall and has narrow, 4–6 in (10–15 cm) long leaves. The flowers, borne in loose clusters, are a delicate combination of pale orange and salmon pink. **ZONES 6–9.**

Rhododendron 'Yaku Prince'

This compact, small, *Rhododendron yakushimanum* hybrid has 4 in (10 cm) long, deep green leaves with a light tan indumentum. The flowers, in rounded trusses of 10 to 14 blooms, are funnel-shaped and light pink with red spotting. They open late mid-season. **ZONES 6–9.**

R. cultivar 'Mrs E. C. Stirling'

Rhododendron 'Yellow Petticoats'

This is a small to medium-sized, densely foliaged bush with deep green, 3–4 in (8–10 cm) long leaves. Its flowers are a bright clear yellow. They are slightly frilled, funnel-shaped, in trusses of 9–13 blooms and open mid-season. This hybrid needs excellent drainage. **ZONES 6–9.**

RHODODENDRON, VIREYAS

Also known as Malesian rhododendrons, the tropical Vireya rhododendrons include around 250 species, many of which are natural epiphytes from high rainfall areas of Southeast Asia through Borneo and New Guinea to northeast Australia. They tend to be rather straggly plants but make up for their untidy growth habit with very brightly colored and often fragrant flowers. Most produce loose heads of 5 to 9 blooms. Vireyas are not strictly seasonal in their blooming, though flowers are most likely in late summer and fall (autumn). Many Vireyas are high-altitude plants and will tolerate prolonged exposure to relatively cool temperatures, but few can withstand any but the lightest frosts. In mild frost-free climates Vireyas can be treated much like any other rhododendron. In colder areas they are generally grown in containers, using a coarse potting mix with added humus. Feed occasionally with dilute liquid fertilizers. In greenhouses it is better to create large beds rather than use pots, as pots tend to dry out quickly and are inclined to tip over as the plants are often very top heavy.

Rhododendron cultivar 'Alarm'

Rhododendron cultivar 'Cynthia'

R. cultivar 'Chelsea Seventy'

Rhododendron cultivar 'Lavender Girl'

Rhododendron 'Gilded Sunrise'

Rhododendron 'George Budgen'

Rhododendron 'Pink Delight'

Rhododendron 'Candy'

Rhododendron 'Candy'

This is very like *Rhododendron jasminiflorum* and is possibly a cultivated form of that species. It has rounded, mid-green leaves, a neat growth habit and fragrant, pale pink, funnel-shaped flowers. ZONES 10–12.

Rhododendron 'Flamenco Dancer'

The widely flared, funnel-shaped flowers of this *Rhododendron aurigeranum* and *R. macgregoriae* hybrid are a soft but bright yellow. It is an upright bush with 3 in (8 cm) elliptical leaves. ZONES 10–12.

Rhododendron 'George Budgen'

This hybrid between *Rhododendron laetum* and *R. zoelleri* has bright golden-yellow, funnel-shaped flowers in 5-flowered trusses. It is an upright, rather open shrub with deep green, 4 in (10 cm) long leaves that tolerates very light irregular frosts. ZONES 10–12.

Rhododendron 'Gilded Sunrise'

This *Rhododendron aurigeranum* × *R. laetum* hybrid has bright golden-yellow, funnel-shaped flowers that darken with age. It is an upright, open shrub. ZONES 10–12.

Rhododendron 'Pink Delight'

This is an old hybrid of unknown parentage. It has vivid pink, funnel-shaped flowers and an upright, rather open growth habit. It is the parent of several modern hybrids. ZONES 10–12.

Rhododendron 'Simbu Sunset'

In common with many other Vireyas with orange and yellow flowers, this cultivar has *Rhododendron laetum* × *R. zoelleri* parentage. The blooms are large with orange tubes, 5 deep orange lobes and yellow centers. It is a compact plant with red-stemmed new growth. ZONES 10–12.

RHODODENDRON, DECIDUOUS AZALEAS

Deciduous azaleas are really quite different from the other rhododendrons. They generally perform best in sunny locations; flower predominantly in yellow and orange shades, not pink, red or mauve; and, of course, they lose all their foliage in winter. Most are very frost hardy and many develop intense fall (autumn) foliage colors. Deciduous azalea hybrids are divided into groups based on their parentage. The main groups are as follows.

Rhododendron, Ghent Azaleas

In the early 1800s Ghent, Belgium, was the main center for azalea breeding. The earliest hybrids were raised from *Rhododendron calendulaceum, R. nudiflorum,*

R., Ghent Azalea, 'Narcissiflora'

R. luteum and *R. viscosum*. Later, *R. molle* was crossed with *R. viscosum* to produce the **Viscosepalum hybrids**, which have now largely disappeared. Further developments include the double Ghent or **Rustica** strain. Introduced from the late 1850s, they were followed in 1890 by a similar group of double-flowered hybrids known as **Rustica Flore Pleno hybrids**. Ghent azaleas tend to be large, late-flowering plants with small flowers in large heads. They are often fragrant. At the height of their popularity over 500 Ghent cultivars were available. Today they have been largely superseded by later styles. **'Coccinea Speciosa'** has bright orange-pink flowers with a striking orange blotch. **'Daviesii'** is a tall, upright Viscosepalum hybrid with fragrant, white to pale yellow flowers late in the season. **'Nancy Waterer'** has large, bright yellow, scented flowers from late spring. **'Narcissiflora'** is a tall, upright hybrid with small, double, fragrant, pale yellow flowers from late spring. **'Norma'** is a Rustica Flore Pleno hybrid with small pink-edged orange-red, double flowers. **'Phebe'** (syn. 'Phoebe') is a Rustica Flore Pleno hybrid with yellow double flowers. **'Vulcan'** is an upright bush with deep red flowers that have an orange-yellow blotch. ZONES 5–9.

Rhododendron, Mollis Azaleas

The mollis azaleas were developed in Belgium and Holland from Ghent azaleas. They show a greater *Rhododendron molle* influence than the Ghents and some may actually be forms of ***R. molle* var. *japonicum*** rather than hybrids. They first appeared in the late 1860s and were further refined over the next 30 years. Mollis azaleas flower from mid-spring and are usually over 6 ft (1.8 m) tall. The flowers are larger than the Ghents, tend to be bright yellow, orange or red and they are all singles. Because mollis azaleas can be difficult to propagate from cuttings, this group includes seedling strains. These reproduce reasonably true to type, but plants are best chosen when in flower because any label description is likely to be an approximation only. **'Anthony Koster'** has bright yellow flowers with a vivid orange blotch. **'Apple Blossom'** has light pink flowers fading to nearly white. **'Christopher Wren'** has large bright yellow flowers with an orange blotch. **'Dr M. Oosthoek'** (syn. 'Mevrouw van Krugten') has large, bright reddish orange flowers with a light orange blotch. **'Floradora'** has bright orange flowers with a red blotch. **'J.C. van Tol'** has apricot-pink flowers with an orange blotch. **'Orange Glow'**, which was developed from 'J. C. van Tol', has apricot flowers with an orange blotch. **'Spek's Orange'** is a relatively small bush with very large orange-blotched red flowers in trusses of up to 9 blooms. **'Winston Churchill'** has orange-red flowers with a red blotch. ZONES 6–9.

Rhododendron, Occidentale Azaleas

Rhododendron occidentale is a fragrant white- to pink-flowered deciduous azalea from the west coast of the USA. It was

Rhododendron, Occidentale Azalea, 'Exquisita'

Rhododendron, Knap Hill Azalea, 'Homebush'

discovered in 1827 and entered cultivation in the 1850s. Occidentale hybrids are among the most fragrant azaleas and usually develop into large plants, although they are quite slow growing. They bloom from mid-spring and the flowers, up to 3 in (8 cm) in diameter, are white or pale pink, often with conspicuous golden throat markings. **'Delicatissima'** has scented creamy white flushed pink flowers with a yellow blotch. **'Exquisita'** has frilled, highly scented white flushed pink flowers with an orange-yellow blotch. **'Magnifica'** has purple-red flowers with a gold blotch. ZONES 6–9.

Rhododendron, Knap Hill, Exbury and Ilam Azaleas

The Knap Hill, Exbury and Ilam hybrids are the most widely grown deciduous azaleas. The original plants were developed from about 1870 at the Knap Hill, England nursery of Anthony Waterer. Starting with Ghent azaleas, he crossbred extensively and selected only the best of the resultant hybrids. Waterer named only one of his plants, 'Nancy Waterer' (officially a Ghent hybrid), and it was not until the seedlings were acquired by Sunningdale Nurseries in 1924 that plants started to be made available to the public. Lionel de Rothschild of Exbury developed the Exbury strain from Knap Hill seedlings. The first of these, 'Hotspur', was introduced in 1934. The collection was almost lost during World War II and relatively few hybrids were introduced until the 1950s. Edgar Stead of Ilam, Christchurch, New Zealand, working with various species and Ghent and Knap Hill hybrids, further refined the strain. Stead's work was continued by Dr. J. S. Yeates. Most are large bushes with vividly colored single flowers. Frost hardiness varies. **'Brazil'**, an Exbury hybrid, has bright orange red flowers. **'Cannon's Double'**, a low-growing Exbury hybrid, has light yellow and cream double flowers. **'Carmen'** (syn. 'Ilam Carmen'), an early-flowering Ilam hybrid, has apricot flowers with a yellow-orange blotch. **'Cecile'**, an Exbury hybrid, has red flowers with an orange-yellow blotch. **'Chaffinch'**, a Knap Hill hybrid, has deep pink flowers and is often sold as a seedling as it is quite variable. **'Gallipoli'**, an Exbury hybrid, has apricot-pink flowers with an orange blotch. **'Gibraltar'**, an Exbury hybrid, has bright orange-red flowers from mid-spring. **'Homebush'**, a Knap Hill hybrid, has semi-double purplish red flowers. **'Hotspur'**, an Exbury hybrid, has bright orange-red flowers. **'Klondyke'**, an Exbury hybrid, has bright orange flowers with an orange-yellow blotch. **'Louie Williams'** (syn. 'Ilam Louis Williams'), an Ilam hybrid, has large, light pink and soft yellow flowers with an orange blotch. **'Maori'**, a low-growing Ilam hybrid, has bright orange-red flowers in large trusses. **'Ming'** (syn. 'Ilam Ming'), an Ilam hybrid, has large orange flowers with a yellow blotch and is among the first to flower. **'Persil'**, a Knap Hill hybrid, has white flowers with a soft yellow blotch. **'Red Rag'**, an Ilam hybrid, has slightly frilled, bright orange-red flowers. **'Strawberry Ice'**, an Exbury hybrid, has yellowish pink flushed mid-pink flowers with an orange blotch. **'Yellow Giant'** (syn. 'Ilam Yellow Giant'), an Ilam hybrid, has very large bright yellow flowers. ZONES 5–9.

Rhododendron, Exbury Azalea, 'Klondyke'

Rhododendron, Other Groups

Many hybridizers have raised deciduous azaleas, but in general they don't vary greatly from the main groups. Most have been developed in the USA and generally have only localized distribution. The Girard and Carlson hybrids are probably the most important of these lesser-known groups.

RHODODENDRON, EVERGREEN AZALEAS

Despite the name, evergreen azaleas are semi-deciduous. They have 2 types of leaf: the lighter textured, often larger spring leaves and the tougher, more leathery fall (autumn) growth. The spring foliage is shed in fall but the summer leaves are largely retained over winter. Although with age many reach 6 ft (1.8 m) tall, they tend to be small to medium-sized shrubs. They occur naturally in Japan, China, Korea and through the cooler parts of Southeast Asia. Evergreen azaleas are divided into groups based on their parentage; the following is a very brief outline of the main groups.

1. *Rhododendron,* Indica Azaleas

The first Indica hybrids were developed in Belgium in the 1850s as house plants. Their main parent is *Rhododendron simsii*, a native of Southeast Asia, which often produces bicolor flowers and is easily forced into bloom in winter. Indicas are the fanciest azaleas with an enormous range of frilly doubles and multicolor flowers. Most Indicas will be badly damaged if regularly exposed to 20°F (–7°C), though if the climate is mild enough they are no more difficult than any other azalea. Most are around 24 in (60 cm) tall by 3 ft (1 m) wide, though some are stronger growing and can reach 5 ft (1.5 m) tall or more. There are several sub-groups, such as Kerrigan and Rutherford Indicas. Many are very similar to one another and simply represent various breeders' efforts along the same lines. ZONES 8–11.

Rhododendron, Ilam Azalea, 'Louie Williams'

1a. *Rhododendron*, Belgian Indica Azaleas

'Albert Elizabeth', which is early flowering, has semi-double white flowers with a broad deep pink edge. **'Anniversary Joy'**, early to mid-season, has semi-double pale pink flowers with darker shading and edges, although the flowers show considerable variation. **'Bertina'**, an early-flowering cultivar often used for forcing, has masses of soft, slightly yellow-tinted pink single flowers. **'Centenary Heritage'**, mid-season, has semi-double bright reddish pink flowers. **'Charly'**, a sport of 'Lucie' that is very striking in full bloom but tender when young, is very early blooming with double, vivid purplish red flowers. **'Comptesse de Kerchove'**, an early-flowering, low-growing, frost-hardy bush with light green foliage, has light apricot-pink double flowers with orange pink shading. **'Deutsche Perle'** has very early pure white double flowers and should be trimmed annually to keep it compact. **'Elsa Kaerger'** has very vibrant, semi-double deep orange-red flowers from early mid-season. **'Gerhardt Nicolai'** has early, very large deep pink semi-double to double flowers; the foliage has a tendency to sunburn and the plant is particularly frost tender when young. **'Goyet'**, early spring, is capable of growing to 4 ft (1.2 m) tall and has very large, frilled, dark red double flowers. **'Hexe'**, mid-season, is a frost-hardy Indica with deep green foliage and small but profuse, vivid purple-red, slightly ruffled hose-in-hose flowers. **'Inga'** is a compact, very early flowering plant with double, bright mid-pink flowers with a white border; it is very heavy flowering and needs shelter when young. **'James Belton'**, mid-season and relatively large and frost hardy, has single, pale pink flowers with a darker center. **'Koli'**, a neat compact plant that is popular for forcing, has semi-double purple-pink flowers from mid-season. **'Leopold Astrid'**, early spring, has double flowers that are white with a red edge, is magnificent in full bloom and also has good foliage but is quite frost tender when young. **'Little Girl'**, mid-season and a heavy flowering compact bush that is a little frost tender when young, has frilled, light pink, hose-in-hose flowers. **'Lucie'**, a popular forcing plant, has very early deep purple-red flowers; it blooms extremely heavily but is frost tender when young. **'Melodie'**, mid-season, is a rather tall yet compact grower with single to semi-double pink flowers with a red blotch. **'Mme Alfred Sander'** is a neat, compact, frost-hardy bush with dark foliage and very well-shaped, formal, double, deep purplish pink flowers that blooms early and very heavily. **'Mrs Gerard Kint'** (syn. 'Mevrouw Gerard Kint'), early to mid-season and frost hardy, is a very showy, compact bush with single to semi-double white to pale flowers with a broad red edge. **'My Fair Lady'** (syn. 'Miss California') has double, mid-pink flowers with a white edge that open early on a nice compact bush. **'Only One Earth'**, frost hardy and named for the 1972 Stockholm Earth Summit, has semi-double, bright purplish pink flowers from mid-season. **'Paul Schaeme'**, an old cultivar that has been very influential in the development of modern forcing azaleas, has masses of double, bright red flowers from early spring. **'Pink Ice'** flowers early and is frost hardy; the flowers, which are at their best just before fully open, are semi-double and pale pink with occasional deep pink flecks and stripes. **'Pink Ruffles'** is a compact bush with frilled, double, light pink flowers with a white edge; it blooms early and forces well. **'Red Poppy'**, an upright, frost-hardy bush with very distinctive single to semi-double, deep red, poppy-shaped flowers, is one of the first azaleas to bloom. **'Red Wings'** is a frost-hardy, spreading bush with deep purple-red, hose-in-hose flowers from early spring; it is a strong grower when young. **'Rosa Belton'** is a

R., Belgian Indica Azalea, cultivar

R., Belgian Indica A., 'Southern Aurora'

R., Belgian Indica Azalea, 'Stella Maris'

R., Belgian Indica Azalea, 'Red Wings'

R., Belgian Indica Azalea, 'Koli'

Rhododendron, Belgian Indica Azalea, 'Bertina'

R., Belgian Indica A., 'Silver Anniversary'

R., Belgian Indica Azalea, cultivar

R., Belgian Indica Azalea, cultivar

heavy flowering bush that blooms early, is frost hardy and has single white flowers with a broad lavender edge and light green, hairy foliage. **'Rosali'**, mid-season and popular as a slightly later-blooming forcing plant, has semi-double purple-red flowers. **'Rosina'** (syn. 'Nelly Kelly') is a vigorous grower with pale pink double flowers from early spring. **'Lavender Rosina'** is a mauve-flowered sport. **'Silver Anniversary'** is a large, upright bush with frilled, light pink hose-in-hose flowers with darker edges that is rather frost tender when young. **'South Seas'** is a neat, compact bush with semi-double purple-pink flowers from early spring that is suitable for use as a forcing plant. **'Southern Aurora'** is a uniquely colored azalea with double white flowers, heavily flushed and edged orange-red. It is spectacular and never fails to attract attention. **'Stella Maris'** is a sport of 'Rosali', has semi-double white flowers with a purple-red blotch, blooms mid-season and is a neat compact grower but is quite frost tender when young. **'The Teacher'** has attractive white, double flowers flushed and edged reddish pink, blooms early but is rather frost tender until established. **'Violacea'** is an upright grower that can become a large, spreading bush with age; it has semi-double, magenta-purple flowers from early spring and benefits from trimming to shape when young. ZONES 9–11.

1b. *Rhododendron,* Southern Indica Azaleas

Not long after the Belgian Indicas became popular in Europe they made their appearance in the USA. Most were too tender to be used as anything but house plants in the north, however, in the milder south they were immediately popular with many acres being planted by the plantation owners. With time the azaleas set seed, some of which germinated. Some of these seedlings were cultivated and sold as new varieties. These new plants were bred with the surviving cultivars to produce the Southern Indicas. The Southern Indicas of today are a mixed bag: old Belgian Indicas, chance seedlings perpetuated, and deliberately bred hybrids. As a group the Southern Indicas are usually hardier to both sun and frost than the Belgians and tend to be larger plants when mature. **'Alphonse Anderson'** (syn. 'George Lindley Taber') has large, single, white flushed with pink flowers with a deep

R., Kerrigan Indica Azalea, 'Gay Paree'

R., Mucronatum Hybrid Azalea, 'Alba Magnifica'

pink throat blotch. It blooms mid-season and grows to 5–6 ft (1.5–1.8 m) tall. **'Fielder's White'** is a large shrub up to 8 ft (2.4 m) tall and widespreading that is used as a background or filler. It has narrow, light green leaves and slightly fragrant, single white flowers with a lemon-yellow throat from mid-spring. Remove any branches with mauve flowers as they may come to predominate. **'Mardi Gras'** is a low, shrubby plant growing to about 24 in (60 cm) tall by 3 ft (1 m) wide with semi-double, orange-pink flowers with a broad white edge. It blooms early to mid-season. **'Modele'**, around 30 in (75 cm) tall by 4 ft (1.2 m) wide, is a heavy flowering shrub with deep purple-red double flowers from mid-season. ZONES 8–11.

1c. *Rhododendron,* Rutherford Indica Azaleas

These hybrids, developed in the USA in the 1920s, were bred for use as greenhouse forcing plants and as such they are very similar to the Belgian Indicas. The name Rutherford comes from the Bobbink and Atkins Nursery of East Rutherford, New Jersey where the hybrids were developed. **'Alaska'** has early, semi-double white flowers with a light green blotch. The flowers can be variable, with single to almost fully double blooms on the one plant. It grows 3 ft (1 m) tall by 4 ft (1.2 m) wide. **'Dorothy Gish'** is a mid-season bloomer with frilled hose-in-hose flowers of an unusual orange-pink shade with a darker blotch. It is an attractive, compact bush around 24 in (60 cm) tall by 3 ft (1 m) wide. **'Purity'** is an early to mid-season bloomer with double white flowers; it

R., Kerrigan Indica A., 'Bride's Bouquet'

R., Mucronatum Hybrid, 'Magnifica Rosea'

R., Rutherford Indica A., 'White Gish'

R., Rutherford Indica A., 'Rose Queen'

grows to 3 ft (1 m) tall and has deep green foliage. **'Rose King'** is a sport of 'Rose Queen' with deep pink flowers. **'Rose Queen'** has semi-double, mid-pink flowers with darker markings from early spring; it is a low, spreading bush growing to around 24 in (60 cm) tall. **'Tickled Pink'** is a sport of 'Purity' with white-edged, light pink hose-in-hose flowers. **'White Gish'** (syn. 'Dorothy White Gish') has white hose-in-hose flowers. ZONES 9–11.

1d. *Rhododendron,* Kerrigan Indica Azaleas

In effect these are just another form of the Belgian Indicas; they were bred in the USA from the 1950s onwards principally as greenhouse plants. Most are fairly frost tender when young but they do have showy flowers. **'Bride's Bouquet'** is a 3 ft (1 m) tall bush with beautiful formal, rosebud, double flowers that are white with greenish throat markings and open mid-season. The blooms need some shade if they are to last. **'Gay Paree'** has spectacular bicolor, semi-double, white flowers with deep pink edges. It blooms mid-season and grows to around 3 ft (1 m) tall. **'Ripples'** is an extremely heavy flowering plant with ruffled, double, deep purple-pink flowers that open from early spring. It is sun tolerant and grows to approximately 24 in (60 cm) tall and 3 ft (1 m) wide. ZONES 8–11.

1e. *Rhododendron,* Indicum and Mucronatum Hybrid Azaleas

When *Rhododendron indicum* is crossed with *R. simsii* the resultant plants are known as Indicum hybrids. Mucronatum hybrids show the influence of ***R. ripense*** as well as possible *R. indicum* parentage. The resulting plants usually have sticky, light green leaves and scented white or mauve flowers. **'Alba Magnifica'** is a Mucronatum hybrid with single white flowers with yellowish markings; the flowers open mid-season and are slightly fragrant. It grows to around 5 ft (1.5 m) tall and wide. **'Magnifica Rosea'** (syn. 'Magnifica') is a Mucronatum hybrid with single, mid-pink to mauve flowers that are slightly fragrant and open mid-season. It is around 5 ft (1.5 m) in height and the same in width. ZONES 8–11.

R., Southern Indica, 'Alphonse Anderson'

R., Southern Indica A., 'Fielder's White'

R

Rhododendron, Kurume Azalea, 'Hinode-giri'

Rhododendron, Kurume A., 'Addy Wery'

Rhododendron, Kurume A., 'Fairy Queen'

Rhododendron, Kurume A., 'Hatsu Giri'

2. *Rhododendron,* Kurume Azaleas

Kurume, on Kyushu, the southernmost main island of Japan, has long been a major azalea growing area. In 1919 the famous plant collector Ernest Wilson visited Kurume and obtained examples of 50 cultivars, which he introduced to Western gardens as Wilson's Fifty. Since then many further hybrids have been raised and introduced. Kurume azaleas clearly show the influence of *Rhododendron kiusianum*, a species that grows wild on Mt. Kirishima. They are dense, compact growers with small leaves and masses of small flowers early in the season. Many Kurume azaleas have hose-in-hose flowers in which the sepals become petal-like and create the effect of a second corolla. Most are best grown in full sun or very light shade; they respond well to trimming to shape after flowering. **'Addy Wery'** has deep orange-red, single flowers and bronze winter foliage color; it grows to around 5 ft (1.5 m) tall. **'Christmas Cheer'** (syn. 'Ima Shojo') is a compact bush with small, rounded, bright green leaves that is smothered in tiny, vivid cerise, hose-in-hose flowers. It grows to about 3 ft (1 m) tall if trimmed, otherwise 6 ft (1.8 m) or more and is No. 36 of Wilson's Fifty. **'Fairy Queen'** (syn. 'Aioi') is a compact shrub with pale apricot-pink, hose-in-hose flowers often with a red blotch. It grows to about 3 ft (1 m) tall by 4 ft (1.2 m) wide and is No. 43 of Wilson's Fifty. **'Hatsu Giri'** is a very twiggy, upright bush with vivid purplish flowers that are occasionally spotted pink. It grows to around 4 ft (1.2 m). **'Hino Crimson'** has bright pinkish red, single flowers that often hide the foliage and is among the last to

Rhododendron, Kurume A., 'Osaraku'

Rhododendron, Kurume A., 'Hinomayo'

Rhododendron, Kurume A., 'Kiritsubo'

bloom. It is a very tough bush that often has brilliant winter foliage color and grows to 5 ft (1.5 m) tall. **'Hinode-giri'** is a dense, heavily foliaged shrub that produces masses of tiny cerise single flowers. It grows to 5 ft (1.5 m) tall and is No. 42 of Wilson's Fifty. **'Hinomayo'** (syn. 'Hinomoyo') is a strong-growing, upright bush that can reach 6 ft (1.8 m) or more. It has vivid purple-pink single flowers. **'Iroha Yama'** (syn. 'Dainty') is a compact bush with small, bright green, rounded leaves and single white flowers that have deep apricot-pink edges. It grows to 4 ft (1.2 m) tall and is No. 8 of Wilson's Fifty. **'Kirin'** (syn. 'Coral Bells) is certainly one of the best of the Kurumes and probably the most popular azalea of all. It is a dense, heavily foliaged bush with rounded bright green leaves that become bronze in winter. From very early spring it becomes a solid mass of soft pastel pink, hose-in-hose flowers and grows to 3 ft (1 m) if trimmed, otherwise 6 ft (1.8 m) or more. It is No. 22 of Wilson's Fifty. **'Kiritsubo'** (syn. 'Twilight') is a strong, upright bush with bright purplish single flowers. It grows to around 4 ft (1.2 m) tall if trimmed, otherwise over 6 ft (1.8 m) and is No. 24 of Wilson's Fifty. **'Mother's Day'** (syn. 'Muttertag') is a Kurume azalea bred to be treated like an Indica. Widely used as a forcing plant, it is a dense, compact bush with vivid cerise hose-in-hose or semi-double flowers that grows to 4 ft (1.2 m) tall unless trimmed. **'Osaraku'** (syn. 'Penelope') has single flowers with very delicate shadings of white suffused light purple. It is very dense and twiggy with tiny leaves, grows to 5 ft (1.5 m) tall and is No. 17 of Wilson's Fifty. **'Red Robin'** (syn 'Waka Kayede') is a relatively low, spreading bush that glows with single, bright orange-red flowers from mid-spring. It grows to 3 ft (1 m) tall by 5 ft (1.5 m) wide and is No. 38 of Wilson's Fifty. **'Sui Yohi'** (syn. 'Sprite') has delicately shaded and textured, single, white flushed pale pink flowers with pink petal tips. It is one of the more frost-tender Kurumes, grows to around 6 ft (1.8 m) tall and is No. 10 of Wilson's Fifty. **'Venus'** is one of an old group known as Sander and Forster azaleas; actually a Kurume/Indica cross, it is usually listed as a Kurume. It has small reddish flowers in abundance and grows to around 6 ft (1.8 m) tall. **'Ward's Ruby'**, usually regarded as the deepest red-flowered evergreen azalea, is an upright, twiggy bush with small single flowers with great intensity of color. It grows to 5 ft (1.5 m) tall and is somewhat frost tender. **ZONES 7–10.**

Rhododendron, Kurume Azalea, 'Venus'

Rhododendron, Kurume Azalea, 'Kirin'

Rhododendron, Kaempferi Azalea, 'John Cairns'

R., Kaempferi Azalea, 'Double Beauty'

R., Gable Hybrid Azalea, 'Lorna'

2a. *Rhododendron,* Amoenum Kurume Azaleas

These plants are very much in the Kurume style. The well-known **'Amoena'** is a form of the plant formerly known as ***Rhododendron obtusum***, which is itself now regarded as a hybrid of *R. sataense, R. kiusianum* and *R. kaempferi.* Always a feature of early spring due to its tremendously prolific flower display, it has tiny, purple, hose-in-hose flowers and is not the most evergreen of azaleas but it becomes a solid block of color. It is extremely tough, makes a good hedge even in exposed positions and grows to 8 ft (2.4 m) tall unless trimmed. **'Princess Maude'** is a tall, twiggy bush with rather open growth and small, vivid deep pink flowers from early spring. It grows to 8 ft (2.4 m) tall and benefits from trimming when young. **ZONES 6–10.**

3. *Rhododendron,* Kaempferi Azaleas

Kaempferis are the frost hardiest of the evergreen azalea hybrids and are derived from *Rhododendron kaempferi* and ***R. yedoense***, both of which will withstand -5°F (20°C). However, when exposed to very low temperatures they drop most of their foliage. Most Kaempferi hybrids originated from the USA and Holland. They have, until recently, been bred primarily for frost hardiness but many of the newer hybrids have quite fancy flowers. Kaempferis often develop red foliage tints in winter and tend to have simple, very brightly colored flowers. **'Double Beauty'** has hose-in-hose, pinkish flowers from early spring. It has light green foliage and a low, spreading habit and grows 30 in (75 cm) tall by 4 ft (1.2 m) wide. **'Johanna'** has deep red, single to semi-double flowers from mid-season. It is a vigorous grower with good bright purple-red fall (autumn) and winter foliage color and grows to 6 ft (1.8 m). **'John Cairns'** has upright, twiggy growth and small bright orange-red single flowers. It grows to around 6 ft (1.8 m) tall. **ZONES 6–10.**

R., Vuyk Hybrid A., 'Vuyk's Scarlet'

3a. *Rhododendron,* Vuyk Hybrid Azaleas

These hybrids, which are very like the original Kaempferis, were developed from 1921 by Vuyk Van Nes Nursery of Boskoop, Holland. **'Palestrina'** has white to pale cream, single flowers with yellow-green spotting. It is a compact, free-flowering bush with bright green foliage that grows to 4 ft (1.2 m). **'Queen Wilhelmina'** is a large, spreading bush with long, narrow, lance-shaped leaves and large single, orange-red flowers with a black-red blotch. It grows to 6 ft (1.8 m) tall by 8 ft (2.4 m) wide and is late blooming. **'Vuyk's Rosy Red'** is very similar to 'Vuyk's Scarlet' except that the growth is not quite as compact and the flowers tend towards cerise rather than red. **'Vuyk's Scarlet'** has masses of large, single, bright red flowers from early spring. It is always impressive and reliably evergreen even under adverse conditions and grows to 3 ft (1 m) tall by 5 ft (1.5 m) wide. **ZONES 6–10.**

3b. *Rhododendron,* Gable Hybrid Azaleas

These hybrids, developed by Joseph Gable of Pennsylvania, were bred with frost hardiness as a prime objective; not only was this achieved but some quite showy double flowers were also raised. **'Lorna'** has very full double, bright mid-pink flowers from mid-season. It is a tough and colorful bush that grows to 5 ft (1.5 m) tall. **'Purple Splendor'** is a low, spreading bush with narrow leaves and frilled, light purple hose-in-hose flowers from mid-season; it grows to 3 ft (1 m) tall by 5 ft (1.5 m) wide. **'Rosebud'** is very like 'Lorna' but with deeper pink flowers and somewhat lower, more compact growth. **ZONES 6–10.**

R., Vuyk Hybrid A., 'Vuyk's Rosy Red'

R., Amoenum Kurume A., 'Amoena'

Rhododendron., Vuyk Hybrid Azalea, 'Palestrina'

Rhododendron, Amoenum Kurume Azalea, 'Princess Maude'

3c. *Rhododendron,* Girard Hybrid Azaleas

Developed from the late 1940s onward by Peter Girard of Ohio, USA, these are good compact hybrids. **'Girard's Border Gem'** is a dwarf, small-leafed bush with deep pink single flowers from mid-season that grows 15 in (38 cm) tall by 24 in (60 cm) wide. **'Girard's Chiara'** has ruffled, deep cerise, hose-in-hose flowers with a reddish blotch. It blooms mid-season and grows 18 in (45 cm) tall and wide. **ZONES 6–10.**

3d. *Rhododendron,* Shammarello Hybrid Azaleas

These bushes are similar to the Gable hybrids, and indeed many have Gable parentage. They are very tough plants. **'Desiree'** has frilled, single white flowers from early spring. It is a strong, spreading bush to around 3 ft (1 m) tall by 5 ft (1.5 m) wide. **'Elsie Lee'** has mid-season, semi-double to double, mauve flowers with darker markings, very attractive flowers in quite an unusual shade. It grows to 3 ft (1 m). **ZONES 5–10.**

4. *Rhododendron,* Satsuki Azaleas

Most gardeners regard the Kurume as the traditional Japanese azalea, however,

Rhododendron, Satsuki, 'Chinzan'

R., Shammarello Hybrid, 'Elsie Lee'

the Satsuki is more revered in Japan. The confusion probably arose because Kurumes have been cultivated in Western gardens for longer than the Satsukis, which have been widely grown only since the 1950s. 'Satsuki' means fifth month, and while not a direct reference to May in the northern hemisphere it does give an indication of the flowering time. Satsukis flower late and their blooms need protection from the summer sun to last. Satsukis have large, highly variable single flowers. One plant can display a wide range of color and pattern in its flowers. They are generally small, spreading plants and are hardy to around 10°F (12°C). **'Benigasa'** (syn 'Red Umbrella') has large, single, deep orange-red flowers from late spring and is intensely colored

R., Satsuki, 'Hitoya No Haru'

Rhododendron, Satsuki, 'Daishuhai'

for a Satsuki. It has rounded deep green leaves and grows to 18 in (45 cm) tall by 3 ft (1 m) wide. **'Chinzan'** (syn. 'Rare Mountain') is a low, spreading bush with small leaves and single, bright pink flowers with a darker blotch from mid-season. It grows 12 in (30 cm) tall by 3 ft (1 m) wide. **'Daishuhai'** (syn. 'Great Vermilion Cup') has single, white flowers with a clearly defined red tip to each petal and more open growth than most Satsukis though it is by no means rangy. It grows to 24 in (60 cm) tall by 3 ft (1 m) wide. **Gumpo** (a group of Phoenixes) is a group of dwarf bushes seldom exceeding 12 in (30 cm) tall by 24 in (60 cm) wide. They have single flowers from late mid-season, are among the most heavy flowering of azaleas and are ideally suited to rockeries or small gardens. Included in the Gumpo group is **Fancy** with mid-pink flowers with a white margin and pink markings; **Light Pink** with pale pink flowers with darker markings; **Salmon** with frilled bright salmon-pink flowers; and **White** with white, heavily frilled, extremely profuse flowers. **'Hitoya No Haru'** (syn. 'Glory of Spring') is among the last of the azaleas to bloom with large, single, bright lavender-pink flowers. It is an outstanding plant with glossy foliage year round and a superb flower display that grows 18 in (45 cm) tall by 3 ft (1 m)

R. Satsuki, 'Issho No Haru'

wide. **'Issho No Haru'** (syn. 'Spring of a Lifetime') has large, single, soft pastel pink flowers with occasional purple splashes; it blooms late spring and grows 15 in (38 cm) tall by 24 in (60 cm) wide. **'Shiko'** (syn. 'Purple Light') has very large, single, lavender-pink flowers from late mid-season. The flowers are highly variable and often have white or purple flakes and sectors. It grows 15 in (38 cm) tall by 3 ft (1 m) wide. **'Shugetsu'** (syn. 'Autumn Moon') has large, single, white flowers edged bright purple, although many patterns can be seen on one bush. It blooms late mid-season and grows to 24 in (60 cm) tall by 3 ft (1 m) wide. **ZONES 7–11.**

5. *Rhododendron,* Inter-Group Azaleas

This catch-all collection of sub-groups includes the hybrids produced by breeding between the other groups and also includes those raised from newly introduced species.

Rhododendron, Girard Hybrid, 'Girard's Chiara'

R., Satsuki, 'Shiko'

R. Satsuki 'Gumpo' 'Shugetsu'

R

Rhododendron, August Kehr Hybrid Azalea, 'Anna Kehr'

5a. *Rhododendron*, Glenn Dale Hybrid Azaleas

In 1935 B.Y. Morrison of the US Department of Agriculture Plant Introduction Section at Glenn Dale, Maryland, USA started breeding azaleas in an attempt to produce frost-hardy plants in a good color range and to fill a then existing mid-season gap in flowering. Thousands of clones were trialled over a ten-year period with the majority of the selected types being released in 1947–49 with the remainder following in 1952. Four hundred and forty clones were released, though many are no longer common. **'Ben Morrison'** has striking single, deep rusty red flowers with darker markings and a broad white border. It blooms mid-season and grows to 5 ft (1.5 m) tall by 6 ft (1.8 m) wide. This hybrid was raised by Morrison but not released by him; it was introduced after his death to commemorate his work. **'Festive'** has single, white flowers flecked and striped with purple. It flowers early and grows to 6 ft (1.8 m). **'Glacier'** has single, white flowers tinted light green. It blooms from early mid-season and has a vigorous upright growth habit to 6 ft (1.8 m) tall. **'Martha Hitchcock'** is a very tough and vigorous bush that has large, single white flowers with a broad purplish pink edge. It flowers from mid-season and grows to 4 ft (1.2 m) tall by 6 ft (1.8 m) wide. **'Vespers'** has single to semi-double white flowers with green markings and occasional pink splashes. It is a very vigorous, early-flowering bush that grows to 5 ft (1.5 m) tall. **ZONES 7–10.**

5b. *Rhododendron*, Back Acres Hybrid Azaleas

Morrison produced these compact hybrids after his retirement from the US Department of Agriculture. **'Debonaire'** has bright pink, single flowers with darker edges and a light center. It blooms mid-season and grows to 3 ft (1 m) tall and wide. **'Fire Magic'** has apricot-red, double flowers with bright red spotting. It flowers mid-season and grows to 4 ft (1.2 m). **'Hearthglow'** has double, mid-pink, camellia-like flowers flushed reddish orange that open from late mid-

R., August Kehr Hybrid, 'White Rosebud'

season. It grows to 4 ft (1.2 m) tall. **'Miss Jane'** has white double flowers with deep pink edges. It is a compact, late-flowering bush that requires shade for the display to last and grows to 24 in (60 cm) tall by 3 ft (1 m) wide. **ZONES 7–10.**

5c. *Rhododendron*, August Kehr Hybrid Azaleas

Developed by another US Department of Agriculture employee, Dr. August Kehr, these hybrids represent a lifetime's work. From the many clones that he bred he released only a handful of the frost hardiest and most beautiful plants. Of all the evergreen azaleas, they probably best combine showy double flowers and frost hardiness. **'Anna Kehr'** has full double, deep pink flowers from mid-season. It often takes time to settle down to serious blooming and requires shaping when young but is well worth the effort, growing to 30 in (75 cm) tall by 24 in (60 cm) wide. **'White Rosebud'** has full double, white flowers with green throats. It blooms mid-season, is sun tolerant for a white and grows 3 ft (1 m) tall and wide. **ZONES 6–10.**

5d. *Rhododendron*, Greenwood Hybrid Azaleas

Developed in Oregon, USA, by using Kurume, Glenn Dale and Gable hybrids, these are very frost-hardy hybrids noted for doing well in cool climates. Most are very compact bushes. **'Greenwood Orange'** has masses of small orange-red, double flowers from mid-season and a rather open growth habit that benefits from trimming to shape when young. It grows to 3 ft (1 m). **'Royal Robe'** is a compact, mound-forming bush with light purple hose-in-hose flowers from mid-season. It is excellent for rockeries and grows to 15 in (38 cm) tall by 24 in (60 cm) wide. **'Tenino'** has hose-in-hose, deep pinkish purple flowers from mid-season. It grows to 15 in (38 cm) tall by 3 ft (1 m) wide. **ZONES 6–10.**

R., Greenwood Hybrid A., 'Royal Robe'

R., Glenn Dale Hybrid A., 'Ben Morrison'

R., Glenn Dale Hybrid A., 'Festive'

R., Glenn Dale Hybrid, 'Martha Hitchcock'

Rhododendron, Back Acres Hybrid Azalea, 'Miss Jane'

Rhododendron, Back Acres Hybrid Azalea, 'Fire Magic'

Rhododendron, Harris Hybrid Azalea, 'Frosted Orange'

Rhododendron, Harris Hybrid Azalea, 'Miss Suzie'

R., Nuccio Hybrid Azalea, 'Happy Days'

R., Harris Hybrid Azalea, 'Gloria Still'

R., Nuccio Hybrid A., 'Purple Glitters'

5e. *Rhododendron*, Harris Hybrid Azaleas

Developed by James Harris from 1970 onwards, these cultivars are very compact and heavy flowering. They are frost hardy once established. **'Fascination'** has large single flowers with a broad deep red border and a white or pale pink center, very much in the Satsuki style. It grows to 3 ft (1 m) tall. **'Frosted Orange'** is a twiggy, spreading bush with white flowers that have striking, broad orange-toned borders. It is spectacular but blooms late and needs shade for the display to last, and grows 30 in (75 cm) tall by 4 ft (1.2 m) wide. **'Gloria Still'** is a compact, slowly spreading plant that grows to 30 in (75 cm) tall by 4 ft (1.2 m) wide. It has variegated pink and white flowers in large clusters. **'Miss Suzie'** is a compact, low-growing bush with bright red hose-in-hose flowers from mid-season. It grows to 24 in (60 cm) tall. ZONES 6–10.

5f. *Rhododendron*, North Tisbury Hybrid Azaleas

When *Rhododendron nakaharai* began to be cultivated a new style of azalea arrived: the ground cover that could be adapted to hanging baskets. Primarily developed by Polly Hill of Massachusetts during the 1960s and 1970s, the resulting plants are low, mounding or trailing bushes grown as much for their form as for their blooms. **'Pink Pancake'** is a near-prostrate cultivar that spreads to about 4 ft (1.2 m) wide. It has small mid-pink flowers with red markings and blooms late and is superb in rockeries or hanging baskets. **'Red Fountain'** has simple single red flowers late in spring. It is excellent spilling over banks or in hanging baskets and grows to around 4 ft (1.2 m) wide. **'Susannah Hill'** has red, hose-in-hose flowers that are sun tolerant, making it one of the best for exposed positions. It grows 12 in (30 cm) high by 4 ft (1.2 m) wide. ZONES 6–10.

5g. *Rhododendron*, Nuccio Hybrid Azaleas

The Nuccios of California, perhaps better known for their camellias, also breed azaleas. They have used a wide range of the material and as a result Nuccio hybrids cover the whole spectrum of flower type, size and frost hardiness. **'Bit of Sunshine'** is a Kurume-style cultivar with masses of vivid pinkish red, hose-in-hose flowers from early spring. It grows 3 ft (1 m) tall by 4 ft (1.2 m) wide. **'Happy Days'** is an Indica-style cultivar with bright mid-purple, rosebud, double flowers from early spring; the flowers last well over a long season. It grows to 30 in (75 cm) and is fairly frost tender when young. **'Purple Glitters'**, a large, upright bush around 5 ft (1.5 m) tall, is a Kurume-style cultivar that is smothered in vivid purplish pink single flowers from early spring. **'Rose Glitters'** is a deep cerise form. ZONES 6–11.

5h. *Rhododendron*, Robin Hill Hybrid Azaleas

These hybrids were bred from 1937 to 1981 by Robert Gartrell of Wyckoff, New Jersey, USA. From 20,000 seedlings trialled he eventually released 69 cultivars. Most are medium-sized, relatively frost-hardy shrubs. **'Betty Ann Voss'** is a vigorous, low, spreading cultivar with late, semi-double to hose-in-hose bright mid-pink flowers. It grows 18 in (45 cm) tall by 3 ft (1 m) wide with glossy foliage. **'Early Beni'** is a mounding, 24–30 in (60–75 cm) tall bush with semi-double, deep orange-red flowers from early spring. It is sun tolerant. **'Lady Louise'** has mid-season, semi-double to double, deep apricot-pink flowers with reddish markings on a spreading, 30 in (75 cm) tall bush; winter foliage is bronze. **'Nancy of Robin Hill'** is a bushy cultivar to 24 in (60 cm) tall with semi-double, light pink flowers with darker markings. It blooms from mid-spring. **'Watchet'** is a dwarf cultivar to about 15 in (38 cm) tall by 24 in (60 cm) wide. It has single, mid-pink flowers with white throats and blooms from just after mid-spring. **'White Moon'** is a Satsuki-like, 15 in (38 cm) tall spreading cultivar. It produces its large, single, white flowers in late spring. The flowers are occasionally splashed with pink and need shade to prevent them burning. ZONES 6–10.

R., Robin Hill Hybrid A., 'Betty Ann Voss'

Rhododendron, Robin Hill Hybrid Azalea, 'Nancy of Robin Hill'

RHODOHYPOXIS
ROSE GRASS

There are 4 to 6 species of these small, colorful, tuberous-rooted, herbaceous perennials from high in the Drakensberg Mountains of South Africa in this genus, but only one, *Rhodohypoxis baurii*, has become common in gardens. Named varieties are available, but sowing seeds from any of them will give quite a range of colors. They have grass- to strap-like hairy leaves and produce white, pink, red or purple flowers on short stalks over long periods in summer.
CULTIVATION: These plants grow well in any temperate climate where soil does not freeze to the depth of the tubers. They prefer full sun and well-drained, fertile, humus-rich soil that retains moisture in summer and is not excessively wet in winter. Propagate from seed in spring or by division in fall (autumn).

Rhodohypoxis baurii

This alpine plant grows 3 in (8 cm) tall, each tuber producing grassy, lightly hairy leaves and, in spring, several starry flowers 3 in (8 cm) wide. Colors range from pure white to various shades of pink and dark red. The central 3 petals close over the heart of the flower to protect it from the weather, and spring open when a pollinating insect alights. It soon forms a dense clump. **ZONES 8–10.**

RHODOLEIA

The leaves of these small evergreen trees native to Southeast Asia are alternate and leathery, waxy underneath. Spring flowers appear in hanging clusters in the leaf axils, each rose-red flower surrounded by colored bracts. The fruits are capsules arranged in clusters. The genus is usually regarded as comprising a single variable species, ranging in the wild from South China to Java, but up to 7 species have been recognized.
CULTIVATION: Frost-tender, they should be grown in full sun or part-shade with shelter from wind. They require a light, slightly acid, well-drained soil enriched with organic matter. Propagate from seed in spring or from cuttings in winter.

Rhodoleia championii
SILK ROSE, HONG KONG ROSE

This tree can grow at least 20 ft (6 m) tall. Thick, obtuse, dark green leaves 6 in (15 cm) long crowd together at the branch tips and have a cream midrib and pink stalks. It bears drooping clusters of 5 to 10 rose-red, bell-shaped flowerheads, each with a whorl of pink to crimson bracts 2 in (5 cm) across. **ZONES 9–11.**

RHODOPHIALA

This genus from South America contains 35 species of bulbous perennials closely related to *Hippeastrum*. They bear umbels of funnel-shaped flowers in summer and fall (autumn) and have mid-green leaves.
CULTIVATION: They are mostly frost tender and prefer full sun and moderately fertile, well-drained soil. They appreciate a deep winter mulch in cold areas. Propagate from seed or by offsets.

Rhodophiala bifida
syn. *Hippeastrum bifidum*

This species from Argentina and Uruguay grows to 12 in (30 cm) tall with a 4 in (10 cm) spread. It bears its bright dark red flowers, 2 in (5 cm) long, before the leaves appear. **ZONES 9–10.**

Rhodophiala bifurcata
CHILEAN LILY

This species bears up to 6 dark red, 2 in (5 cm) long, trumpet-shaped flowers on a 12 in (30 cm) stem. The stem and flowers appear in summer before the blue-green, slender, strap-like foliage. There are also bright red- and yellow-flowered forms. **ZONES 9–10.**

RHODOSPHAERA
YELLOWWOOD, TULIP SATINWOOD

Native to tropical and subtropical areas of northeastern Australia, *Rhodosphaera* contains only one species: a small evergreen tree that produces male and female flowers on separate plants. The genus is closely allied to *Rhus*. Its leathery, pinnate leaves consist of 4 to 12 pairs of leaflets, each leaflet up to 3 in (8 cm) long and covered in minute, soft, erect hairs. The 5-petalled red flowers appear in spring on a dense, branching inflorescence. These are followed by berry-like fruit, each with a single seed.
CULTIVATION: This tree will grow in subtropical areas in full sun or part-shade and needs well-drained soil and moisture during dry periods. Propagate from fresh seed or cuttings in fall (autumn).

Rhodosphaera rhodanthema

This bushy tree reaches 40 ft (12 m) tall in its natural environment and produces a beautiful yellow timber. It sheds its rough, gray-brown bark in thick, scale-like plates. The 15 in (38 cm) leaves have a wavy surface and are glossy dark green above and pale beneath. Glossy brown fruit hang on the tree for a long time. **ZONES 9–12.**

RHODOTYPOS

This genus, closely allied to *Kerria*, contains one species, a 15 ft (4.5 m) deciduous shrub native to China and Japan with soft mid-green leaves and simple, 2 in (5 cm) diameter white flowers. The calyces remain after the flowers fall and enclose $\frac{1}{4}$–$\frac{1}{2}$ in (6–12 mm) glossy black berries. As the sepals dry they fold back to reveal the pea-shaped fruit, which appear to be unattractive to birds and lasts well into winter.
CULTIVATION: This plant grows happily in any well-drained soil in sun or light shade. It is fully frost hardy and may be propagated from cuttings or seed or by layering.

Rhodohypoxis baurii

Rhodotypos scandens

This upright or slightly arching shrub bears its shallowly cupped, single, 4-petalled flowers in late spring and early summer. The sharply toothed leaves are most appealing when young. **ZONES 5–9.**

RHOICISSUS

Native to tropical and southern Africa, the 12 species of vines or scrambling shrubs in this genus climb by tendrils. Their leaves may be simple or compound with up to 5 leaflets, red-tinted when young and up to 8 in (20 cm) wide. In common with other grape family plants, the flowers are inconspicuous but are followed by clusters of deep red berries.
CULTIVATION: These frost-tender plants prefer full sun and moist but well-drained soil. They should be grown in a greenhouse where temperatures fall below 45°F (7°C). Propagate from seed or cuttings or by layering.

Rhoicissus capensis

This vigorous climber reaches 15 ft (4.5 m) in height. It has large, ovate, heart-shaped, glossy green leaves and wiry stems. The flowers are insignificant and are followed by glossy reddish purple, edible berries. **ZONES 9–11.**

Rhodophiala bifida

Rhodoleia championii

Rhoicissus rhomboidea

This southern African species has often been confused with the widely cultivated *Cissus rhombifolia* from tropical America, hardly surprising when both have leaves consisting of 3 diamond-shaped leaflets, rusty hairs on the new shoots, and both have a very compact, bushy habit of growth. The *Rhoicissus* species is said to differ in having tendrils that are not forked. **ZONES 9–11.**

Rhoicissus tomentosa
FOREST GRAPE

Of wide distribution in South Africa, this woody stemmed climber is vigorous and densely foliaged; it grows to a height of at least 15 ft (4.5 m), though it can be kept trimmed to a smaller size. It has simple dark green leaves that are almost semicircular in outline though shallowly toothed around the outer edge. In fall (autumn) and winter it bears small purple-brown berries. **ZONES 9–12.**

RHOPALOSTYLIS

The 3 species in this genus of palms grow naturally in New Zealand, Norfolk Island and the Kermadec Islands. The trunks are topped by a swollen shaft made up of the leaf bases, called the crownshaft. The pinnate leaves, obliquely erect and feather-like, give these palms a distinctive outline. The flowers, carried in a branched cluster below the leaves, are followed by red berry-like fruits.
CULTIVATION: These palms need a sheltered, sunny spot in a frost-free climate. A moist but well-drained, light to medium soil enriched with organic matter is ideal. Propagate from fresh seed in spring.

Rhodotypos scandens

Rhodosphaera rhodanthema

R

Rhopalostylis baueri
NORFOLK PALM, NIAU

The Norfolk Palm has a gray, closely ringed trunk growing up to 40 ft (12 m) high, a wide-spreading crown and leaves 12 ft (3.5 m) long that have a reddish tint when young. Its distinctive crownshaft is stout and very pale green. The fruit are small and slightly conical. This palm is easily shredded by wind. **ZONES 10–11.**

Rhopalostylis sapida
NIKAU PALM, FEATHER DUSTER PALM

This slow-growing New Zealand species is the world's most southerly wild palm. It has a stout 30 ft (9 m) trunk, a shiny green crownshaft bulging at the base, and a mass of short-stalked fronds 10 ft (3 m) long, each divided into many lanceolate leaflets 3 ft (1 m) long. Cream to mauve flower clusters 12 in (30 cm) long appear below the crownshaft. **ZONES 10–11.**

RHUS

Rhus is a large, diverse genus consisting of 200 species of deciduous and evergreen shrubs, trees and scrambling vines found in many parts of the world. One group of species, now separated into a new genus, *Toxicodendron*, contains trees and shrubs notorious for causing allergies. Some deciduous species turn brilliant shades of red, purple, orange, yellow and bronze in fall (autumn); others bear reddish or brownish velvety fruit. Many produce male and female flowers on different trees. Some of the many evergreen species, from regions such as southern Africa and California, are moderately frost tolerant. Many species tolerate pollution.
CULTIVATION: They like a sunny position, moderately fertile, moist but well-drained soil and protection from wind. Propagate from seed or cuttings, or by dividing root suckers.

Rhopalostylis sapida

Rhus aromatica
FRAGRANT SUMAC

This sprawling, deciduous species from eastern USA reaches 3 ft (1 m) tall and 5 ft (1.5 m) wide. Tiny yellow flowers, borne in spikes on bare stems, are followed by downy, deep green, coarsely toothed and aromatic foliage maturing to spectacular shades of orange and purple in fall (autumn). Small berries appear in mid-summer. **'Gro-Low'** is an very low-growing form with fragrant flowers that are a deeper yellow than those of the species. **ZONES 2–9.**

Rhus chinensis
CHINESE SUMAC, NUTGALL TREE

This small, broad-headed, deciduous shrub or small tree, found in Japan as well as China, reaches 20 ft (6 m) or more and is grown for its spectacular fall (autumn) hues. Its compound leaves are coarsely toothed and arranged on winged stalks. Clusters of whitish flowers are borne in late summer and are followed by red, downy berries. **'September Beauty'** is grown for its striking blaze of fall color. **ZONES 8–11.**

Rhus aromatica

Rhopalostylis sapida

Rhus glabra

Rhus copallina
DWARF SUMAC, SHINING SUMAC

This deciduous, upright shrub from northeastern North America grows to 5 ft (1.5 m). Its glossy dark green leaves turn purple-red in fall (autumn). The tiny, greenish yellow flowers appear in dense clusters in mid- to late summer, then develop into egg-shaped, bright red fruit. **ZONES 5–9.**

Rhus aromatica 'Gro-Low'

Rhus copallina

Rhus glabra
SMOOTH SUMAC

This deciduous, bushy shrub from North America and Mexico has reddish purple stems with bluish white blooms and deep blue-green leaves that turn red in fall (autumn). Panicles of greenish red flowerheads appear in summer and are followed by reddish, hairy fruit on female plants. **ZONES 2–9.**

Rhus integrifolia
LEMONADE BERRY, LEMONADE SUMAC, SOURBERRY

This species from southern California is an evergreen shrub or small tree that reaches 30 ft (9 m) in height. The simple leaves are elliptic and 2 in (5 cm) long, and the spring flowers are white or pink. **ZONES 9–11.**

Rhus chinensis 'September Beauty'

Rhus lancea
KARREE, AFRICAN SUMAC

This native of South Africa tolerates dry conditions, growing quickly to 20 ft (6 m). Its rough bark is split and very dark, and its pendent branches grow crookedly. The slender leaves occur in groups of 3, with leaflets 6 in (15 cm) long. It bears yellowish flower clusters in late summer, and yellowish brown fruit. **ZONES 9–11.**

Rhus laurina
syn. *Malosma laurina*
LAUREL SUMAC

Native to southern California and Baja, this frost-tender shrub grows quickly to 10–20 ft (3–6 m) tall. Small, creamy white flowers develop into white fruit which attract birds. **ZONES 9–11.**

Rhus microphylla
LITTLE-LEAF SUMAC, DESERT SUMAC

This twiggy shrub or small tree, native to the dry, southwestern USA, can reach 8–25 ft (2.4–8 m) if enough moisture is available. Normally evergreen, in cold winters its leaves color and drop; they may also drop during extremely dry conditions. It bears white flowers in spring and bright orange-red fruit, popular with wildlife, in summer. **ZONES 9–11.**

Rhus ovata
SUGAR BUSH

A large, evergreen shrub, this native of southern California produces sugar-coated fruit that make a refreshing citrus-like drink. Reaching a height and spread of 10–12 ft (3–3.5 m), it makes a good screening plant. Its oval leaves are very tough and leathery. Clusters of tiny pink and white flowers appear in late winter. It needs little or no water once established. **ZONES 9–11.**

Rhus ovata

Rhus pendulina
syn. *Rhus viminalis*
WHITE KARREE

From South Africa, this 15 ft (4.5 m) evergreen tree is willow-like, with lanceolate leaflets held in 3s, a tawny gray trunk and branches and an abundant crown. Tiny, pale green flowers appear on female trees in summer, followed by fruit resembling miniature mangoes. Resistant to dry conditions and wind, it thrives in mild, coastal regions. It can be propagated simply by planting a branch. **ZONES 9–11.**

Rhus typhina
syn. *Rhus hirta*
STAG'S HORN SUMAC

This deciduous shrub or small tree from temperate eastern North America makes a brilliant fall (autumn) display. It grows a slender erect trunk or thicket of stems up to 15 ft (4.5 m) high and spreads to 12 ft (3.5 m). It bears pinnate leaves with toothed, 6 in (15 cm) leaflets, yellowish green flower clusters and striking 'candles' of velvety red fruit. **'Dissecta'** (syns *Rhus typhina* 'Laciniata', *R. hirta* 'Laciniata') carries its dark fruit well into winter and has deeply dissected, fern-like foliage. **ZONES 3–9.**

RHYNCHOLAELIA

There are only 2 orchid species in this genus, which occurs in Central America in seasonal forests at low to moderate altitudes. The pseudobulbs are cylindrical or club-shaped with a single leathery leaf. The inflorescence arises from a sheath at the apex of the stem with a large single flower. Both species have been used in hybrids with *Laelia*, *Cattleya* and other genera.
CULTIVATION: Plant these epiphytes in orchid compost in full light with shade from hot sun. Water freely in summer, moderately in winter. Propagate by division.

Rhus pendulina

Rhus lancea

Rhus typhina

Ribes alpinum

Rhyncholaelia digbyana
syn. *Brassavola digbyana*

Despite its reputation for being difficult, this Central American orchid is a beautiful plant, important in orchid breeding. It resembles a large, single-leafed *Cattleya* and in summer it bears 6 in (15 cm) wide, lemon-scented flowers, one per pseudobulb. These are pale green or pinkish with a large, deeply fringed lower lip. Crosses with cattleyas are still known as brassocattleyas, the name *Rhyncolaelia* having been adopted only in 1971. They probably now outnumber the pure-bred cattleyas in gardens. **ZONES 11–12.**

RIBES
CURRANT

This genus, from cool-temperate, northern hemisphere regions, contains some 150 species of evergreen and deciduous, ornamental and fruiting shrubs. The white, scarlet, purple, green or black berries are mostly edible. They can grow to 10 ft (3 m) and have long, arching stems. Some have reddish brown branches; some produce prickles on stems or fruit, or on both. The lobed, mid-green leaves, sometimes with downy or felted undersides and toothed edges, may turn red and orange before dropping. Masses of yellow, red or pink blossoms (some fragrant) appear in late winter or early spring.
CULTIVATION: Unisexual species such as this must be planted in groups to ensure vigorous flowering and fruiting. Fully frost hardy, they need moist, rich soil and full sun to semi-shade. In the USA some species host white pine blister rust. Propagate from seed or cuttings.

Ribes alpinum
MOUNTAIN CURRANT, ALPINE CURRANT

This dense, twiggy, deciduous shrub from northern Europe to Russia grows 6 ft (1.8 m) tall and wide. Reddish purple, smooth stems bear 3- to 5-lobed rounded, serrated leaves. The pale, greenish yellow flower clusters carry 7 to 15 blossoms. These are followed by large bunches of scarlet berries, provided both male and female plants are grown. *Ribes alpinum* is a neat and versatile shrub that tolerates heavy shade. **ZONES 5–9.**

Ribes fasciculatum

From Korea and Japan, this deciduous shrub bears smooth stems carrying dark green, deeply serrated leaves. In good soil and a sunny position it grows 5 ft (1.5 m) tall and 6 ft (1.8 m) wide. The fragrant, creamy yellow flower clusters are borne in early summer and, because they are unisexual, the scarlet berries will appear only if plants of both sexes are grown. **ZONES 5–10.**

R

Richea dracophylla

Ribes odoratum

Ribes sanguineum

Ribes nigrum

BLACKCURRANT

Native to Europe and temperate Asia, this shrub reaches 6 ft (1.8 m) and bears greenish white flowers and sweet, black fruit. It thrives if fertilized with potash and nitrogen. Prune old shoots to promote new growth; pick fruit when the upper berries start to fall. Watch for currant borer moth, mites and leaf spot. **'Ben Lomond'** is late-ripening, and high-yielding with large fruit; **'Jet'** has a heavy crop of large, dark fruit. **ZONES 5–9.**

Ribes odoratum

syn. ***Ribes aureum*** **of gardens**

CLOVE CURRANT, BUFFALO CURRANT

A spreading 8 ft (2.4 m) shrub with prickle-free stems, this species is native to the prairies and high plains of midwestern USA. The shiny, 3-lobed leaves color well in fall (autumn). The large, down-turned flowerheads are greenish yellow, deepening with age and followed by black berries. The plant is grown mainly for the spicy, clove-like fragrance of its leaves. **ZONES 6–9.**

Ribes sanguineum

RED FLOWERING CURRANT, WINTER CURRANT, FLOWERING CURRANT

This prickle-free, deciduous shrub from western North America has aromatic, lobed leaves that are held on 12 ft (3.5 m) stems. The deep pink or red flowers, appearing in late spring, are borne on erect to drooping spikes. Bluish black berries follow in summer. There are several named cultivars, including **'King Edward VII'** which bears carmine flowers; **'Brocklebankii'** with golden leaves and pink flowers; **'Tydeman's White'** with white flowers; **'White Icicle'** has pure white clusters of flowers; and **'Pulborough Scarlet'** which carries a mass of deep red flowers. ***Ribes sanguineum*** **var.** ***glutinosum*** has hanging clusters of pink flowers and leaves that are more sparsely pubescent than *R. sanguineum*. **'Barrie Coate'** was found on Fremont Peak in California growing in full sun and has deep rose-colored, pendent clusters of flowers. **'Spring Showers'** is a bushy, vase-shaped shrub with downy bright green leaves and hanging clusters of pink flowers. **ZONES 6–10.**

Ribes uva-crispa

Ribes silvestre

syns ***Ribes rubrum, R. sativum***

REDCURRANT, WHITE CURRANT

Native to western Europe including the UK, this deciduous, prickle-free species is an erect 6 ft (1.8 m) shrub with $2\frac{1}{2}$ in (6 cm) long, lobed leaves that have silvery undersides. Racemes of small flowers open in spring, followed by clusters of small, very juicy, round red or pale amber (white) fruit. They are rather tart and are excellent fresh or cooked. Cultivars of note include **'Viking'**; **'Jonkheer van Tets'**, a vigorous, open redcurrant that flowers and fruits very early; **'Red Lake'**, vigorous, densely branched and disease-resistant with an early crop of dark red, rather small fruit; and **'White Grape'** with large clusters of pale pinkish yellow fruit. **ZONES 6–9.**

Ribes speciosum

FUCHSIA FLOWERING GOOSEBERRY

This deciduous, spiny, bushy shrub from California in the USA reaches 6 ft (1.8 m) in height and spread. Fully frost hardy, it has red juvenile shoots and oval, 3- to 5-lobed glossy green leaves. Its slender, drooping red flowers, which open in late winter, have long red stamens; they are followed by spherical red fruit. **ZONES 7–10.**

Ribes uva-crispa

syn. ***Ribes grossularia***

GOOSEBERRY, EUROPEAN GOOSEBERRY

This stiff, spiny, deciduous shrub is native to central Europe and North America. It grows about 3 ft (1 m) tall, with upright canes and small green leaves held at stiff angles from the stems. Pinkish green flowers are followed by greenish fruit covered with soft bristles. This species rarely fruits well in frost-free climates. There are many cultivars in a variety of sizes and shapes, bearing green, russet green or yellow green fruit. **'Careless'** is a spreading bush with few thorns, the fruit being yellow, elongated and bland; **'Invicta'** (syn. 'Malling Invicta') is an early ripener with a heavy crop of large yellow fruit; **'Leveller'** has well-flavored fruit and is fairly vigorous; and **'Whinham's Industry'** is a slow-growing bush with a good crop of tasty, round, yellow berries with purple red bristles. ***Ribes uva-crispa*** **var.** ***reclinatum*** has bristly, round to slightly elongated fruit that may be yellow or red when ripe. **ZONES 5–9.**

Ribes silvestre

RICHEA

All but 2 of these beautiful but rarely cultivated Australian evergreens of the epacris family are endemic to Tasmania. Most of the 12 species are bushy shrubs, but some can grow as tall as 50 ft (15 m). The strap-like leaves can vary from $\frac{1}{2}$ in (12 mm) to over 3 ft (1 m) long. Dense flower clusters appear in summer and are pink, white, yellow or cream, thrust above the foliage on upright spikes. These plants do well in containers. **CULTIVATION:** They must have humus-rich, moist but well-drained, preferably acid soil and shelter from full sun and wind to produce the best blooms. Plants benefit from an annual mulch of organic matter. Prune spent flowerheads in early fall (autumn). Propagate from seed in fall or from cuttings in summer.

Ribes silvestre 'Viking'

Richea dracophylla

Richea dracophylla is an erect, sparsely branched species from Tasmania. It has narrow leaves to 8 in (20 cm) long in a tapering, zigzag form that crowd at the ends of the stems. Reaching to as much as 15 ft (4.5 m) in height, it bears its terminal spikes of white or pink flowers with purplish bracts in summer.
ZONES 8–9.

Richea pandanifolia
TREE HEATH

In its native Tasmania, this species has grown as high as 50 ft (15 m), though it is generally considerably smaller. It remains unbranched for many years. Its 3 ft (1 m) long, finely tapering leaves have waxy margins. Tiny, cup-shaped flowers of pink or white cluster along the branches in summer.
ZONES 8–9.

RICINUS

This genus from northeastern Africa and southwestern Asia contains a single species, a fast-growing, tree-like shrub grown for its foliage. The spikes of small, cup-shaped flowers appear in summer. All parts of the plant, especially the seeds, are extremely poisonous and can cause death in children; however, the seed oil is used medicinally after heat treatment and purification.

Robinia pseudoacacia 'Tortuosa'

Ricinus communis 'Carmencita'

CULTIVATION: This marginally frost-hardy plant prefers full sun and fertile, humus-rich, well-drained soil. It may need staking. Propagate from seed.

Ricinus communis
CASTOR OIL PLANT

The purgative of universal renown comes from the seeds of this species, which is mostly grown as an annual. Rounded, prickly seed pods follow the summer display of felty clusters of red and greenish flowers. The plant's leaves are large, glossy and divided deeply into elliptical lobes. *Ricinus communis* grows rapidly, reaching 12 ft (3.5 m) in height and in warm climates it often becomes a weed. **'Carmencita'** is a tall form that grows to 10 ft (3 m) with bronze-red foliage and red female flowers. **ZONES 9–11.**

ROBINIA
BLACK LOCUST

These 20 species of leguminous deciduous shrubs and trees from the USA are fast growing and tolerate pollution well. Some *Robinia* species grow 80 ft (24 m) tall although many are shrub-like, reaching only 6 ft (1.8 m). Most of the species spread by suckers and are self-seeding. The pinnate leaves have small oval leaflets, sometimes turning buttery yellow in fall (autumn). There is usually a pair of spines on the branch at each leaf base. They bear pendulous sprays of pink, purple or white, fragrant pea-blossoms in spring. The fruits are flat pods less than 4 in (10 cm) long. Cultivars have been grafted to produce a mop-like head of foliage.
CULTIVATION: Robinias prefer poor but moist soil in a sunny position sheltered from strong winds. Propagate from scarified seed, cuttings or suckers or by division. Cultivars must be grafted.

Robinia pseudoacacia 'Umbraculifera'

Robinia pseudoacacia 'Frisia'

Robinia × *slavinii* 'Hillieri'

Robinia pseudoacacia 'Rozynskiana'

Robinia × *ambigua* 'Idaho'
IDAHO LOCUST

This hybrid of *Robinia pseudoacacia* and *R. viscosa* was selected for its deep reddish purple, fragrant flowers. Other features are similar to *R. pseudoacacia*, although it rarely exceeds 40 ft (12 m) in height. It is equally tolerant of difficult soils, heat and dry conditions, and is a good tough tree for drier mountain regions. **ZONES 3–10.**

Robinia hispida
ROSE ACACIA

Robinia hispida is a deciduous shrub from the dry woods and scrub of southeastern USA. It has pinnate leaves that are fresh green, long and fern-like; the erect stems and branches are clothed in brown bristles. In summer, rose-pink pea-flowers are followed by bristly seed pods up to 3 in (8 cm) long. In favorable conditions the plant quickly reaches 6 ft (1.8 m). This species is sometimes grafted on to stems of *R. pseudoacacia* to produce a small, mop-headed tree. On ***Robinia hispida* var. *kelseyi*** (syn. *R. kelseyi*) only the flower stalks and raceme axes have bristles; it bears glossy rose-pink flowers. **ZONES 5–10.**

Robinia pseudoacacia
FALSE ACACIA, BLACK LOCUST

This fast-growing 80 ft (24 m) tree has dark, deeply grooved bark and prickly branches. The pinnate, fern-like leaves, with about 23 leaflets, turn yellow in fall (autumn). The scented white pea-flowers appear in late spring or summer, followed by reddish brown pods containing black, kidney-shaped seeds. The cultivar **'Frisia'** carries golden foliage deepening in fall, and is thornless. **'Rozynskiana'** is a large shrub or small tree with drooping branches and leaves. **'Tortuosa'** has short, twisted branches. **'Umbraculifera'**, the mop-head acacia, is also thornless and rarely flowers. These cultivars rarely exceed 30 ft (9 m).
ZONES 3–10.

Robinia × *slavinii* 'Hillieri'

Robinia × *slavinii* 'Hillieri' is a small tree with a compact, rounded head of foliage. Its fragrant flowers are lavender pink and open from early summer. It is ideal in large containers or as a feature plant for small gardens.
ZONES 5–10.

Rodgersia aesculifolia

Rodgersia aesculifolia

Rodgersia sambucifolia

Rodgersia pinnata

Robinia viscosa

CLAMMY LOCUST

This 40 ft (12 m) species has sticky, glandular young shoots and smooth, spineless twigs. The trunk and mature stems are dark, and its foliage turns golden yellow in fall (autumn). The 3 in (8 cm) long bunches of flowers, pale rose pink stained with yellow, are very attractive to bees. Though seldom planted, this is one of the most ornamental members of the genus. **ZONES 5–10.**

RODGERSIA

Native to Burma, China, Korea and Japan, this genus consists of 6 species of moisture-loving perennials. They have handsome foliage and flowers, but tend to be grown more for their bold leaves than for their plumes of fluffy flowers, borne in mid- to late summer. The stems unfurl in mid-spring and spread out to form a fan of leaves on top of stout stems.

CULTIVATION: Their liking for moist soil makes them excellent plants for marshy ground at the edge of a pond or in a bog garden in sun or part-shade. They do best in a site sheltered from strong winds, which can damage the foliage. Propagate by division in spring or from seed in fall (autumn).

Rodgersia aesculifolia

This Chinese species has lobed, 10 in (25 cm) wide leaves that are borne on hairy stalks, forming a clump 24 in (60 cm) high and wide. The large, cone-shaped clusters of small, starry flowers are cream or pale pink, and are borne on stout stems up to 4 ft (1.2 m) tall. **ZONES 5–9.**

Rodgersia pinnata

This rhizomatous, clump-forming plant produces bold, dark green leaves arranged in pairs. Star-shaped, yellowish white, pink or red flowers are borne in panicles on reddish green stems in mid- to late summer. It reaches a height of 4 ft (1.2 m) and a spread of 30 in (75 cm). **'Superba'** has bright pink flowers and purplish bronze leaves. **ZONES 6–9.**

Rodgersia podophylla

Suited to pond surrounds, this rhizomatous species has green, copper-tinted leaves comprising 5 to 9 large leaflets. It bears multi-branched panicles of cream, star-shaped flowers. It tolerates full shade but does better in part-shade, and grows 3–4 ft (1–1.2 m) tall by 30 in (75 cm) wide. **ZONES 5–9.**

Rodgersia sambucifolia

This clump-forming, rhizomatous species from western China has emerald-green, occasionally bronze-tinted leaves with large leaflets. It reaches 3 ft (1 m) high and wide and bears sprays of creamy white flowers above the foliage in summer. **ZONES 6–10.**

ROHDEA

Related to lily-of-the-valley *(Convallaria majalis)*, the sole species in this genus is a small woodland perennial from Japan and southwestern China. In spring its rhizomes sprout rosettes of fleshy, sword-shaped, deep green leaves. From the center of each rosette emerges a spike of white, bell-shaped flowers, followed by red or yellow berries. The overall effect is midway between a snowflake *(Galanthus)* and a lily-of-the-valley.

CULTIVATION: This woodland plant prefers cool, moist, humus-rich soil and a position in dappled or full shade. It is reasonably frost hardy and naturalizes freely in a suitable climate. Propagate from seed or by division in late winter.

Rohdea japonica

LILY-OF-CHINA

This charming woodlander is most at home among deciduous trees, where it quickly forms a clump of deep green 8–18 in (20–45 cm) long leaves. Although its flowers are small, less than ½ in (12 mm), they are carried on branching, 3 in (8 cm) spikes and their whiteness contrasts with the dark foliage. In Japan there are numerous cultivars with yellow- or white-striped leaves, prized by collectors. **ZONES 7–10.**

ROLDANA

This genus of 48 species of large annuals, perennials and subshrubs is from Mexico and central America. They have slender stems and alternate leaves and flowers with from 5 to 45 yellow florets.

CULTIVATION: These frost-tender plants prefer moderately fertile, moist but well-drained soil and full sun. Propagate from seed or cuttings, or by division.

Roldana petasitis

syn. *Senecio petasitis*

This weak-stemmed subshrub is found from Mexico to Nicaragua. Growing to around 6 ft (1.8 m) tall, it has large leaves with 7 or more broad, blunt lobes. The daisy-like yellow flowerheads are borne in leafy panicles; each has about 6 ray petals. **ZONES 9–11.**

ROMANZOFFIA

The 4 perennial species in this genus are native to western North America and the Aleutian Islands. Small mat- or mound-forming plants, and their semi-tuberous roots and leathery, deep green leaves may be rounded or kidney-shaped, usually lobed and seldom over 2 in (5 cm) long. Small, white to pale purple and bell-shaped flowers are borne in heads on short stems held above the foliage, opening in late spring or early summer.

CULTIVATION: They prefer moist, humus-rich, well-drained soil and a position in afternoon shade or full shade. Ideal candidates for a deciduous woodland or shady rockery, they prefer cool conditions and suffer in a hot, dry summer. Propagate from seed or by division in early spring.

Romanzoffia sitchensis

Found from Alaska to Montana, this species forms a 4 in (10 cm) mound of foliage with 1–1½ in (25–35 mm) long, deeply lobed, dark green, kidney-shaped leaves. Its flowers are very small, white with yellow petal bases, and are borne on branching, 6 in (15 cm) racemes on stems up to 12 in (30 cm) tall. **ZONES 5–9.**

ROMNEYA

TREE POPPY

The 2 species in this genus from North America and Mexico are summer-flowering, woody based perennials and deciduous subshrubs. They have blue-green foliage composed of alternate leaves and poppy-like, 6-petalled flowers with glossy yellow stamens.

CULTIVATION: They prefer a warm, sunny position and fertile, well-drained

Roldana petasitis

R

Rondeletia amoena

soil. They are difficult to establish (although once established they may become invasive), and they resent transplanting. Protect the roots in very cold areas in winter. Propagate from seed or cuttings.

Romneya coulteri
CALIFORNIA TREE POPPY, MATILIJA POPPY

This shrubby Californian perennial produces large, sweetly scented, poppy-like white flowers highlighted with fluffy gold stamens. The silvery green leaves are deeply divided, their edges sparsely fringed with hairs. Fully frost hardy, it forms a bush up to 8 ft (2.4 m) high with a spread of 3 ft (1 m). ***Romneya coulteri* var. *trichocalyx*** has pointed, rather bristly sepals. **ZONES 7–10.**

ROMULEA

This genus of about 80 species of cormous perennials, which originated in the Mediterranean regions and North and South Africa, takes it name from Romulus, the legendary founder of Rome. The flowers of the common garden species open in spring or summer, are star-like with a curious satin sheen on their petals and only open on sunny days. Although the flowers often include some white, many of the petal colors are somewhat garish. The linear leaves are crocus-like but without the distinctive crocus midrib.
CULTIVATION: Plant in an open, well-drained position in the open garden or in containers. The majority are frost tender and cannot withstand dry conditions during the growing phase, however, when conditions suit their requirements they can become hard to contain. They need water during the growing season but must be kept dry when dormant. In areas with wet summers the corms should be lifted. Propagate from seed or by dividing well-established clumps.

Romulea bulbocodium
SATIN FLOWER

This dainty little plant is native to southern Europe and northern Africa and is excellent in a rock garden. The fine stems grow to 4 in (10 cm), each bearing up to 6 upward-facing, 2 in (5 cm), trumpet-shaped blooms in spring. The flowers are usually violet with white to yellow centers. The flowers close in the evening or on dull days. **ZONES 7–10.**

RONDELETIA

These striking evergreen trees and shrubs are native to tropical America and the West Indies. Only 3 of the 125 to 150 species are commonly cultivated; they grow to 10 ft (3 m) in warm climates. The tough foliage is distinctly veined and remains attractive all year. The red, yellow, pink or white tubular flowers appear in terminal or axillary clusters in spring and summer; being rich in nectar, they attract birds. The fruits are small capsules containing many seeds.
CULTIVATION: Grow in sun or part-shade in well-drained, slightly acid soil enriched with organic matter. If kept in pots, they should be well watered during growth. Cut back the flowered stems each year in early spring. Propagate from seed in spring or from cuttings.

Rondeletia amoena
YELLOW-THROATED RONDELETIA

This erect, branching shrub is native to Central America. Growing to a height of 10 ft (3 m) and spread of 6 ft (1.8 m), it is grown for the dense, rounded clusters of pink scented flowers it bears in spring. It has dark green oval leaves up to 6 in (15 cm) long. **ZONES 10–11.**

Rondeletia odorata

This bushy shrub from Panama and Cuba reaches a height of 10 ft (3 m) on downy stems with wavy margined leaves that are dark green above and pale green beneath. The fragrant, red or orange flowers are tubular and have yellow throats, and are borne in fall (autumn). **ZONES 11–12.**

Rondeletia strigosa

This native of Guatemala is an evergreen shrub of about 4 ft (1.2 m) in height, with arching cane branches springing from the base. The leaves are small, broad at the base and drawn out into a point at the tip, and are mostly arranged in whorls of three. The flowers are rather striking, $\frac{3}{4}$ in (18 mm) across and deep crimson with a golden 'eye' surrounded by a raised circular rim, borne in groups of 3 to 5 at the branch ends. It blooms through summer and fall (autumn), or for much of the year in a sufficiently warm climate. **ZONES 10–12.**

ROSA
ROSE

The 150 species of roses and their countless hybrid derivatives, valued for their beauty and perfume and sometimes for their bright fruits, have been at the forefront of garden design and plant hybridization. In centuries past roses had medicinal uses too, yet even in the Middle Ages when most plants had to have practical uses to justify their cultivation, a few roses were grown for their beauty alone. Found over most of the northern hemisphere, though primarily in the temperate regions, roses are woody stemmed shrubs or scrambling climbers. Almost all are deciduous, and even those regarded as evergreen or semi-evergreen often shed much of their foliage in cold winters. They range from small shrubs under 24 in (60 cm) tall through to the huge spreading climbers such as *Rosa gigantea*, which can have a spread of over 100 ft (30 m). Roses have trifoliate or pinnate leaves with finely toothed leaflets. The foliage may be bright green, very deep lustrous, almost black-green or distinctly blue-tinted. Most species have arching, thorny stems, and both the young stems and new foliage are often tinted red. The thorns of cultivated roses are usually broad based and recurved to a fine point, but many wild species, especially the briars, have a dense covering of prickles rather than thorns. Garden roses often have semi-double to very full double flowers, but that is the result of extensive hybridizing. The species and the less highly developed cultivars most often have single flowers, usually 5-petalled. Flower color among the modern hybrids now covers everything except a true natural blue. The species, too, cover a wide color range but without the flamboyant combinations seen in the hybrids. Clusters of brilliant red or orange fruits known as hips (more rarely heps or haws) sometimes follow the flowers, particularly those of the species or single-flowered hybrids. These add interest in late summer and fall (autumn) and can be almost as much a feature as the flowers.
CULTIVATION: Roses are generally frost-hardy, vigorous plants with a great zest for life. However, they do have some climatic and soil preferences, and though prone to a few pests and diseases these

Rondeletia strigosa

Romneya coulteri

R

problems are lessened or prevented with the right planning and cultivation. Roses prefer a temperate climate and most do best with at least 2 months of winter chilling. They do not actually need exposure to frost, just enough prolonged cold to induce dormancy and proper bud formation. However, light to moderate frosts are useful for killing off any overwintering pests. Roses are adaptable: they can be planted in beds of roses alone or blended into the overall garden design, and a few can even be left to run wild. The miniatures and smaller types mix well with shrubs, perennials and annuals and make marvellous informal hedges along pathways or edging larger beds. Use ground cover roses to carpet sloping ground or for cascading over retaining walls. Climbers can be used on fences, for covering unsightly sheds or old trees and for growing over archways or entrances to provide a fragrant greeting for visitors. Small shrub roses, miniature climbers and trailers grow well in containers provided they are regularly fed and do not dry out.

Siting and planting: Roses require at least half-day sun, good ventilation without being exposed to strong winds; slightly acid, moisture-retentive yet well-drained soil; and limited competition from large shrubs and trees. Shade leads to poor flowering, rank growth and fungal problems. Strong winds damage the foliage and flowers and may break the branches, while poor ventilation is sure to encourage the spread of fungal diseases. Prepare the site well in advance, beginning by planning their layout: large bushes need more width than small, climbers need something to climb and large growers should not overshadow smaller plants. Allow easy access for pruning and spraying. As a rule a bush rose will spread to at least two-thirds its height. Before planting, trim any damaged stems or roots. Examine the main stem near the bud union for a color change that indicates the level at which it was planted in the field, then plant the bush at the same level in the garden. Dig a hole large enough to ensure there is a good depth and spread of loosened soil so the root system can quickly develop. Position the plant, spread its roots, add a light dusting of mild fertilizer and check the depth, then back fill by gently firming the soil into place. Stake standards and tall bushes to prevent damage from wind; position the stake before refilling the hole so that roots are not inadvertently damaged by driving the stake through them. After planting, water and mulch around the new rose.

Pruning: Prune to encourage new growth, rejuvenate plants, improve their shape and to enable light to penetrate to the center of the bush to promote even growth. Hard pruning tends to promote strong stems with fewer but better blooms, while leaving longer stems promotes dense bushy growth with many but smaller blooms. Despite the tradition of pruning to an outward facing bud to create an open vase-shaped bush, recent research suggests that roses will thrive with a far more casual approach to pruning. Just removing the old or damaged wood and trimming to shape should be sufficient. Roses are normally pruned when dormant in winter, although there is no reason why they should not be trimmed and thinned in summer, this in fact being the best option for small roses with masses of fine twiggy stems where careful trimming is impractical.

Pests and diseases: Good ventilation, avoiding overcrowding and providing the right growing conditions will all help to prevent problems with pests and diseases. Should problems occur, the key is early control. Pests such as aphids, thrips and mites can be controlled by systemic insecticides, however it is fungal diseases that are more likely to cause lasting damage. Mildews and black spot lead to premature foliage drop and general debilitation. Rust spreads rapidly, can cause almost total defoliation if allowed to take hold, and may be carried over to the following season. Even with the best of care, mild cases of these diseases will occur and spraying may be unavoidable.

Propagation: Most hybrid roses are budded onto vigorous, disease-resistant, non-suckering rootstocks. Although roses can also be grown from cuttings, some modern varieties do not grow well on their own roots and suckering varieties become nuisances. Propagation from seed is generally restricted to species or raising new hybrids. The seed germinates well but it must be stratified for 8 to 12 weeks before sowing.

Rosa banksiae var. *banksiae*

Rosa banksiae var. *normalis* 'Lutea'

Rosa bracteata

SPECIES AND THEIR CULTIVATED FORMS (WILD ROSES)

Roses have been in existence for at least 35 million years and, although they have only been cultivated for about the last 2,700 of those years, their development from untamed shrubs to the plants we know is a long and complicated story beginning with the wild species. Rose species are divided into 4 main groups: Hulthemia, Hesperhodos, Platyrhodon and Eurosa. The first 3 groups include only 5 species; the rest belong to the Eurosa group, which is itself divided into 10 sections. Plants from almost all those groups and sections have been used for breeding, but relatively few have had a major influence. Most garden roses are hybrids, but some species are cultivated. Species roses are often quite different from modern hybrids, tending to be rather untidy, scrambling bushes, while many smaller growers are covered in thorns, spines or prickles. The flowers are generally rather small, very simple and only appear for a short time in late spring. Yet the species are usually tough and adaptable, able to shrug off pests and diseases, and many produce a marvellous display of rose hips from late summer.

Rosa chinensis 'Viridiflora'

Rosa banksiae

DOUBLE WHITE BANKSIAN ROSE

This climbing species has thornless stems to 40 ft (12 m) in height and half that in spread. The double, rosette-shaped white flowers appear in clusters in spring. ***Rosa banksiae* var. *banksiae*** (syn. *R. b.* 'Alba Plena'), the Lady Banks rose, has long, arching, thornless canes and slender, pointed, dark green, smooth and leathery leaflets, 3 or 5 per stem; the foliage is evergreen and disease free. The sweetly scented, double white flowers appear in spring in clusters of 3 to 7 flowers. The hips, borne rarely, are small and dull red. ***R. b.* var. *normalis* 'Lutea'**, from central and western China, has long, arching, thornless canes and grows to 12 ft (3.5 m) in height and spread. There are 3 to 7 evergreen, slender, dark green, leathery leaflets per leaf. The single yellow spring flowers, with prominent stamens, are sweetly scented and grow in clusters of 3 to 7 flowers. The hips are small and dull red. **ZONES 7–10.**

Rosa bracteata

MACARTNEY ROSE

Introduced from China to England in 1793, this evergreen, climbing species has dark green, glossy foliage made up of leaflets with blunt or rounded apexes, unique among roses. New growth is covered with soft gray-brown hairs and red bristles with double hooked thorns at each node. It flowers from late spring to fall (autumn) with 5-petalled white flowers with very prominent orange-yellow stamens, the flowers either single or in clusters. The hips are globular and orange. It reaches 20 ft (6 m) in height. **ZONES 7–11.**

Rosa chinensis 'Viridiflora'

GREEN ROSE, MONSTOSA

Reported to have been in cultivation in England as early as 1743, this climber has mid-green, smooth foliage and somewhat twiggy, prickly growth. Clusters of 3 to 7 small oval buds of soft blue-green open to flowers with 35 long thin bracts, light green streaked reddish brown bracts, and hairy reddish brown centers. **ZONES 7–10.**

Rosa davidii var. *elongata*

This species is a tall, open shrub of around 10 ft (3 m) with strong, straight, smooth shoots and a few straight prickles. The leaflets are broad, oval, smooth and dark green. The spring flowers are bright pink with prominent golden stamens and long sepals, some $2\frac{1}{2}$ in (6 cm) across, and appear in clusters of three to

Rosa foetida

seven. The hips are orange-red and elongated. **ZONES 6–10.**

Rosa ecae

syn. ***Rosa xanthina*** **var.** ***ecae***

This dense shrub ranges from from Pakistan to northern China. It has twiggy branches and grows to 5 ft (1.5 m) in the wild, larger in cultivation. The brown stems are covered with straight flat thorns and small, fern-like, elliptical leaflets. The small, golden-yellow, 5-petalled flowers are carried singly at each node. The hips are oval and red-brown. **'Golden Chersonese'** grows to 6 ft (1.8 m) tall and has golden-yellow flowers with overlapping petals and prominent golden stamens. **ZONES 7–10.**

Rosa elegantula 'Persetosa'

syn. ***Rosa farrari*** **'Persetosa'**

THREEPENNY BIT ROSE

This shrub grows to 6 ft (1.8 m) tall and double that in spread. Light brown growth with hair-like prickles gives it a mossed effect. The fine, fern-like, mid-green foliage composed of 7 to 9 leaflets also gives the plant a delicate appearance. Lilac-pink flowers no more than $\frac{1}{2}$ in (12 mm) wide appear in spring. Orange-red, flagon-shaped hips appear in profusion. **ZONES 6–10.**

Rosa filipes 'Kiftsgate'

This extremely vigorous rambler can reach 50 ft (15 m) in height, although it is very slow to establish. The reddish tinted new growth has many hooked thorns and can grow to 20 ft (6 m) in a season. The foliage is large, profuse and glossy mid-green, tinted copper on new growth and rich russet in fall (autumn). Fragrant single white flowers appear in spring in huge corymbs that can be 10 in (5 cm) across with upwards of 80 flowers. The hips are orange-red and round. **ZONES 5–10.**

Rosa foetida

syn. ***Rosa lutea***

AUSTRIAN BRIAR, AUSTRIAN YELLOW

This shrub grows to 8 ft (2.4 m) tall with smooth young growth and numerous slender, straight thorns on reddish brown older wood that ages silvery gray. The foliage is dull, with light to grayish green leaves. The rich golden-yellow

Rosa filipes 'Kiftsgate'

flowers, with prominent stamens, appear singly in spring. It has quite an over-powering fragrance, and is prone to black spot. **'Bicolor'** (syn. *Rosa lutea punicea*), the Austrian copper, has single flowers with a golden-yellow reverse, the yellow showing through the thin petal texture of the intense nasturtium red of the flower face. **'Persiana'**, the Persian yellow, has very double, cupped, paler yellow flowers than the species that open flat. **ZONES 4–9.**

Rosa gallica

syn. ***Rosa provincialis***

PROVINS ROSE, FRENCH ROSE

This shrub, thought to have been in cultivation prior to 1500, is the ancestor of garden roses in Europe. It is a sprawling, suckering species around 30 in (75 cm) tall. Stem prickles are usually found on older wood; each stem has from 3 to 7 smooth, bluish green, oval leaflets often with a rounded apex. The sweetly scented spring flowers are 5-petalled, clear pink in color but lighter pink in the center with golden stamens. The hips are oval to round. It is resistant to leaf diseases such as black spot. **ZONES 5–9.**

Rosa gigantea

GIANT ROSE

This vigorous climber grows to 50 ft (15 m) in height. It has strong, hooked prickles and oval, dark green, smooth leaves with reddish stems. The pale apricot buds are tall and slender, and the creamy white flowers are very large and have a subtle fragrance of tea. **ZONES 9–11.**

Rosa glauca

syn. ***Rosa rubrifolia***

This spectacular shrub, native to central Europe, grows to around 15 ft (4.5 m) high with arching canes and purplish red wood. There are 5 to 7 long, slender, gray to purplish leaves. The spring flowers, usually in groups of 4 to 6, are pink with delicate pale pink centers, golden stamens and a subtle fragrance. The brownish red oval hips are around 1 in (25 mm) long. **ZONES 2–9.**

Rosa glauca

Rosa holodonta

This upright shrub grows to 10 ft (3 m) in height and 6 ft (1.8 m) in spread. It has arching, reddish brown canes and a few straight prickles on the old wood. The leaflets are dark green and wrinkled, taking on rufous colors as they age. The spring flowers are a deep rose pink and have prominent stamens. The hips are orange-red and flagon-shaped. **ZONES 6–10.**

Rosa laevigata

syn. ***Rosa sinica*** **'Alba'**

CHEROKEE ROSE

This vigorous climber grows to 20 ft (6 m) with green new wood and many hooked thorns; the old wood is silvery gray. The leaflets are smooth, shiny, light green and oval in shape with a long pointed apex. The large, late winter flowers are single, white with prominent golden stamens and slightly fragrant. **ZONES 7–11.**

Rosa gigantea

Rosa × *macrantha*

This shrub was introduced to cultivation around 1880. It is vigorous and arching with many thorns, growing 5 ft (1.5 m) tall and 6 ft (1.8 m) wide. The mid-green foliage is composed of 5 leaflets, each around $1\frac{1}{2}$ in (35 mm) long. The single flowers are borne in clusters of 3 to 5, and are cream-pink fading to near white with conspicuous stamens and a delicious fragrance. The hips are orange. **ZONES 6–10.**

Rosa macrophylla

LARGE-LEAFED ROSE

Native to the Himalayas, this very large, free-growing shrub bears its delicate, soft pink, sweetly fragrant flowers with golden yellow stamens in late spring. It grows to around 15 ft (4.5 m) tall and has mid-green leaves on deep red to purple stems. It is thornless. The flowers are followed by large, bottle-shaped, scarlet-colored hips, which can be almost 3 in (8 cm) long. **ZONES 7–11.**

Rosa gallica

Rosa laevigata

R

Rosa majalis
syn. ***Rosa cinnamomae***
CINNAMON ROSE

This species, native to Europe and western Asia, was in cultivation prior to 1600. It is an upright shrub to 6 ft (1.8 m) tall with light green canes with a reddish brown hue and slightly hooked prickles and bristles on the old growth. The foliage is long, oval and gray-green in color. The fragrant, single, spring flowers are an attractive pink and are produced singly or in clusters of three. **ZONES 6–9.**

Rosa moschata
MUSK ROSE

This sweetly fragrant shrub or robust climber grows from 10–30 ft (3–9 m) tall. It has smooth branches with very few prickles and mid-green foliage that is smooth and shiny on the face and downy on the reverse composed of oval leaflets in groups of seven. The late summer, single, white flowers, in loose corymbs, open cream and fade white. The hips are oval and hairy. **ZONES 6–10.**

Rosa moyesii

Native to western China, this species is a robust, upright shrub to 10 ft (3 m) high, often with many stems shooting from the base. The mature wood is yellowish tan colored and has a few straight thorns near the base. The leaflets are smooth and oval. The fragrant spring flowers are produced singly or in groups of up to 4, and are red with golden anthers. The flagon-shaped, orange-red hips are produced in profusion. **'Highdownensis'** has more compact, bushy growth and a greater profusion of flowers than the species; the single flowers are displayed in conspicuous clusters of vivid cerise-crimson. **ZONES 5–9.**

Rosa nitida

This eastern North America native is a suckering shrub to around 3 ft (1 m) tall with dark green, upright canes covered with tan-colored bristles and a few straight prickles. The leaflets are narrow, elliptical and shiny dark green, turning deep crimson in fall (autumn). The fragrant flowers are produced singly or in clusters of 3 to 5 in early summer, and are deep rose pink. The red hips are shiny and round. **ZONES 3–10.**

Rosa pimpinellifolia
syn. ***Rosa spinosissima***
SCOTCH BRIAR, BURNET ROSE, SCOTS ROSE

This species forms a low, suckering thicket up to 3 ft (1 m) tall with bristles and prickles the full length of the stems. The smooth leaflets are small and fern-like with good fall (autumn) coloring. The prolific, single, spring to early summer flowers are creamy white often shaded pink, and have golden-yellow stamens. The round hips are purple to shiny black and make almost as good a display as the flowers. **'Altaica'** (syns *Rosa pimpinellifolia* 'Grandiflora', *R. spinosissima* 'Altaica') grows to 6 ft (1.8 m) tall and wide and has large, fragrant, ivory white flowers suffused with primrose yellow and round, shiny dark maroon to black hips. **ZONES 4–9.**

Rosa rugosa

Rosa roxburghii 'Plena'

Rosa nitida

Rosa moschata

Rosa roxburghii 'Plena'
syn. ***Rosa roxburghii***
CHESTNUT ROSE, BURR ROSE

This large, suckering shrub grows to 6 ft (1.8 m) tall and wide, with many upright light silvery brown stems with flaking bark (giving off a pungent aroma) and very sharp, straight thorns in pairs at the nodes. The mid-green foliage is quite striking. The summer flowers are very double, opening flat and reflexing, with upwards of 80 petals, the color of the petals varying from white to deep mauve pink. **ZONES 5–10.**

Rosa rugosa
RUGOSA ROSE, SALTSPRAY ROSE, RAMANUAS ROSE,

This large, suckering shrub grows to 8 ft (2.4 m) tall with stout prickly stems. The foliage is bright glossy green and wrinkled and displays good fall (autumn) colors. The very fragrant, large flowers, which are produced throughout summer either singly or in clusters of 3, vary from purplish rose to violet-carmine. The large tomato-like hips are a feature. ***Rosa rugosa* var. *alba*** has white flowers that open with a pale pink flush to the petals; it is often used for hedging. **ZONES 2–10.**

Rosa sericea subsp. *omeiensis* f. *pteracantha*
syn. ***Rosa omeiensis* f. *pteracantha***
MALTESE CROSS ROSE

This upright shrub grows to 10 ft (3 m) in height with strong arching canes that are adorned with an almost continuous array of large red-winged thorns, popular in flower arrangements. The new wood is gray-green with a reddish hue and is often covered with fine hairs, while the foliage has a fern-like appearance. The 4-petalled white flowers are borne singly at the nodes. The hips are oval and red. **ZONES 6–10.**

R. s. subsp. *omeiensis* f. *pteracantha*

Rosa moyesii

Rosa setigera
PRAIRIE ROSE

This species forms a rambling shrub that can climb to 15–20 ft (4.5–6 m) if supported. The new wood is light green, becoming red as it ages, and the prickles at the nodes are red and hooked. The leaflets grow in 3s, and have a shiny dark green upper surface that is wrinkled and broad with a fine tapered apex. The leaf stems are red. Fragrant early summer flowers, produced in clusters, are crimson paling to white at the center. The hips are small and red. **ZONES 4–9.**

Rosa × *villosa* 'Duplex'
syns ***Rosa* 'Wolley-Dod', *R. pomifera* 'Duplex'**
WOLLEY-DOD'S ROSE

This shrub grows to 10 ft (3 m) high and 15 ft (4.5 m) wide and has arching, prickly canes that are silvery gray-green in color and age reddish brown. The leaflets are grayish green. The flowers are semi-double, clear rosy pink, have soft yellow stamens and are slightly fragrant. The hips are large, red, flagon-shaped and hairy. **ZONES 5–9.**

Rosa wichuraiana
MEMORIAL ROSE

This prostrate, creeping rambler has pliable, smooth green branches to 10 ft (3 m) long with curved prickles that are

R

red on new growth. The foliage is shining green and smooth. The 5-petalled flowers, in loose corymbs of 3 to 15, are white with golden-yellow stamens; they open in succession in early summer, later in cooler climates. The hips are small and orange-red. **ZONES 5–10.**

Rosa willmottiae

This very delicate shrub to 10 ft (3 m) tall has pale mauve to lilac new growth with fine straight prickles; older wood is plum colored. The leaflets are fine, light gray-green and slightly fragrant. Small, fragrant flowers are borne in spring, and are lilac-pink with yellow stamens. The hips are bright red and flagon-shaped, and fall off when ripe. **ZONES 6–10.**

Rosa woodsii var. *fendleri*

Native to North America, this upright shrub was introduced to cultivation in 1888. It has arching canes some 6 ft (1.8 m) tall with wide, flat thorns at the nodes that are red on the new growth. The wood is grayish green to light brown with a reddish hue. The leaflets are long and mid-green. The flowers appear in clusters of 3 and are pale lilac-pink with yellow stamens, while the round hips are orange-red. **ZONES 4–9.**

Rosa xanthina

Found in northern China and Korea, this 4–12 ft (1.2–3.5 m) shrub is thought by some botanists to be a wild form of an old garden plant rather than a true species. Its flowers and foliage are variable and several forms are recognized. The typical plant has 2 in (5 cm) wide, bright yellow semi-double flowers and leaves with 7 to 12 small, toothed leaflets and hairy undersides. It blooms once in early summer. Although described after *Rosa xanthina*, ***R. x.* f. *spontanea***, a vigorous grower with single flowers, is thought to be the true wild species. ***R. x.* f. *hugonis*** (syn. *R. hugonis*) has hairless leaf stems and single flowers. **'Canary Bird'**, a hybrid between *R. x.* var. *hugonis* and *R. x.* f. *spontanea* is regarded as the best garden plant; it is very similar to *R. x.* f. *spontanea* but performs better in cultivation. **ZONES 5–9.**

OLD (HERITAGE) ROSES

The use of wild roses for the production of rose water, scented oils and other fragrances goes back to the Sumerian civilization of Iraq around 2,000 BC. Rose cultivation also goes back to Confucius (551–479 BC), who mentions extensive plantings in the Chinese Imperial gardens, and the Romans and other early European civilizations also grew large quantities for commercial use. The early European garden roses were probably forms of *Rosa gallica*, a plant that grows wild from France to the Caucasus. The period 1200 to 1700 saw several new roses enter cultivation and with them developed the first recognizable hybrid groups. The Damask roses and the 2 color forms of the plant known as the yellow rose of Asia (*R. foetida* and the orange-flowered *R. foetida* 'Bicolor') are generally regarded as the ancestors of most of the European roses. The Damask roses were extremely important because of their fragrance, a tendency to produce double flowers and because their flowering season extended into fall (autumn). Further developments, plants such as the Alba, Centifolia and Moss roses, were really just variations on the earlier themes. This changed with the introduction of the China rose *(**R. chinensis**)*: although first seen in Europe in 1752 and followed in the 1790s by hybrids with *R. gigantea*, it was not until the early 1800s that the full influence of the Chinese introductions became apparent. The first of these new, compact, repeat-flowering plants were the Bourbon roses. The Portland Roses (Perpetual-flowering Damasks) soon followed. These groups, all shrubs, were joined by the climbing Noisettes. The ultimate development of this line was the Hybrid Perpetuals. They resulted from intensive interbreeding between the Bourbon, Portland, Gallica and hybrid China roses and were the roses most popular in the nineteenth century. Tea roses or Tea-scented roses are another development of *R. chinensis*. Although beautiful in their own right, their real significance is that when crossed with the Hybrid Perpetuals they gave rise to the groups that have dominated rose breeding ever since: the Hybrid Teas and the Floribundas.

The progression of rose development is fairly easily traced; nevertheless, there are some groups that have been developed tangentially and do not neatly fit the overall pattern. Neither Old nor Modern roses, in some cases they are rather primitive although they are not species either. These are the Climbing roses, Rambling roses and the Scotch (or Burnet or Pimpinellifolia) roses. They have been included at the end of this section on Old (Heritage) roses.

Rosa, OR, Gallica, 'Officinalis'

Rosa, OR, Gallica, 'Rosa Mundi'

Rosa, OR, Gallica, 'Anaïs Ségales'

Rosa, OR, Gallica, 'Complicata'

Rosa, OR, Gallica, 'Ipsilanté'

Rosa, OR, Gallica, 'Charles de Mills'

Rosa, OR, Gallica, 'Empress Josephine'

Rosa, Old Rose, Gallica, cultivar

1. Gallica Roses

Gallicas are compact, once-flowering, suckering plants with fragrant flowers in a variety of shades from white through pink to red (including bicolors) and in all forms from single to very full doubles. **'Officinalis'** is a deep pink semi-double, introduced into France from the Middle East by thirteenth-century crusaders. Its sport **'Rosa Mundi'** (syn. 'Versicolor') dates from the late sixteenth century and has striped and sectored bicolor white and deep pink flowers. Gallicas are currently enjoying new-found popularity and many of the old cultivars are readily available. **'Anaïs Ségales'** is a small bush with deep pink double flowers. **'Charles de Mills'** (syn. 'Bizarre Triomphant') has very fragrant, rather flattened, fully double, purple-red flowers. The delightful **'Complicata'** has simple but very beautiful white-centered pink, single flowers. **'Ipsilanté'** is a late bloomer with mid-pink double flowers. **'Tuscany Superb'** has small, slightly scented, red, double flowers. **'Empress Josephine'** (syn. 'L'Imperatrice') has large, faintly scented blooms in shades of pink; it is a compact bush. **ZONES 5–10.**

Rosa willmottiae

Rosa woodsii var. *fendleri*

Rosa, Old Rose, Gallica, 'Belle de Crécy'

Rosa, Old Rose, Damask, 'Rose de Rescht'

R., OR, Gallica, 'Duchesse de Montebello'

Rosa, OR, Gallica, 'Hippolyte'

Rosa, Old Rose, Damask, 'Trigintipetala'

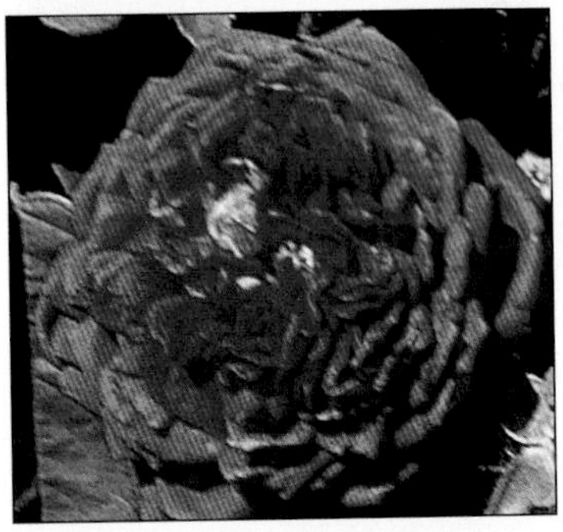

Rosa, OR, Gallica, 'The Bishop'

Rosa, OR, Damask, 'Omar Khayyám'

2. Damask Roses

Derived from *Rosa gallica*, the Damasks were the first true hybrid roses cultivated. There are 2 styles: the once-flowering Summer Damask *(R. gallica × R. phoenicea)* and the repeat-flowering Autumn Damask *(R. gallica × R. moschata)*. Damasks are similar to Gallicas, though they are usually a little taller and not quite as frost hardy. **'Trigintipetala'** (syns 'Kazanlik', 'Kazanluk') is a 6 ft (1.8 m) tall bush with loosely double flowers. The blooms are pink and strongly scented, for which reason they have long been grown for the production of attar of roses. **'Ispahan'** (syn. 'Pompon de Princes') is a fragrant, soft mid-pink double raised before 1832. **'Omar Khayyám'** is a strongly fragrant, mid-pink double dating from 1893. The original pink autumn damask is known as **'Quatre Saisons'** (syn. 'Autumn

R., OR, Damask, 'York and Lancaster'

Damask'). The more modern **'Rose de Rescht'** has deep purple-pink double flowers. **'York and Lancaster'** (syn. 'Versicolor') has loosely double, variable pink and white flowers and has been cultivated since before 1551. ZONES 5–10.

Rosa, Old Rose, Damask, 'Ispahan'

Rosa, OR, Damask, 'Quatre Saisons'

Rosa, OR, Damask, 'Mme Hardy'

Rosa, OR, Damask, 'Botzaris'

R., OR, Centifolia, 'Petite de Hollande'

Rosa, Old Rose, Damask, 'Blush Damask'

Rosa, Old Rose, Centifolia, 'Bullata'

3. Centifolia or Provence Roses

The Centifolia, Provence or Cabbage roses appeared in France near the end of the sixteenth century and were extensively hybridized in seventeenth-century Holland. The name Centifolia means one hundred-petalled and refers to their distinctive, exceptionally full double flowers. Centifolias are usually compact bushes and their flowers are so fully double and heavy with petals that they often droop under their own weight. The cultivar **'Centifolia'** (syn. *Rosa centifolia*), the original Cabbage rose, has richly scented, bright pink flowers. **'Petite de Hollande'** (syn. 'Pompon de Dames') is a small bush with masses of strongly scented pink flowers. **'Bullata'** has fragrant pink flowers and is distinguished by its wrinkled leaves, which are red-tinted when young. **ZONES 5–9.**

Rosa, Old Rose, Centifolia, 'Centifolia'

Rosa, Old Rose, Centifolia, 'Fantin-Latour'

Rosa, Old Rose, Centifolia, 'De Meaux'

R

4. Moss Roses

***Rosa* 'Chapeau de Napoléon'** (syns 'Cristata', 'Crested Moss') and **'Muscosa'** (syn. *R. centifolia* 'Muscosa') are among the most popular Centifolias. They have fragrant, mid-pink, double flowers; their buds are covered in fine tubercles known as moss. Though usually regarded as Centifolias, they could equally be thought of as the first Moss roses because Mosses were developed from these natural mutations of Centifolias and Damasks. They were fashionable in the eighteenth and nineteenth centuries when several hundred forms were raised. Some, such as the deep purple-red flowered **'Capitaine John Ingram'** and the unusually scented pale pink **'Alfred de Dalmas'** (syn. 'Mousseline'), are still grown, though Mosses are not common. **ZONES 5–9.**

5. Alba Roses

Thought to be the white rose of York of the War of the Roses, ***Rosa* × *alba*** is a plant of uncertain origins that may have been introduced to Britain by the Romans. Albas always have light-colored, pleasantly scented flowers and blue-tinted foliage. **'Alba Maxima'** grows to 8 ft (2.4 m) tall with white, double flowers. **'Félicité Parmentier'** dating from 1834, is 5 ft (1.5 m) tall with Damask-like white, double flowers that open from pink buds. known since the fifteenth century, **'Great Maiden's Blush'** is 8 ft (2.4 m) tall with sweetly scented, soft pink flowers. **'Mme Plantier'** is a shrub or 6–12 ft (1.8–3.5 m) climber with cream flowers that age to white. **ZONES 4–9.**

Rosa, OR, Alba, 'Alba Maxima'

Rosa, OR, Alba, 'Félicité Parmentier'

R., OR, Moss, 'Chapeau de Napoléon'

R., OR, Moss, 'Capitaine John Ingram'

Rosa, Old Rose, Alba, 'Königin von Dänemark'

Rosa, OR, Moss, 'Alfred de Dalmas'

Rosa, OR, Moss, 'Henri Martin'

Rosa, Old Rose, Alba, 'Great Maiden's Blush'

Rosa, Old Rose, Moss,'Muscosa'

Rosa, OR, Moss, 'Mme Louis Lévêque'

Rosa, OR, Moss, 'Soupert et Notting'

R., OR, Alba, 'Pompon Blanc Parfait'

6. China Roses

Along with the Tea roses, China roses are intermediate in appearance between the old Cabbage rose style and the modern pointed bud typified by the Large-flowered or Hybrid Tea roses. They result from cross-breeding between several species and early hybrids and consequently are a rather variable lot. Several of the early Chinas were climbers, a trait reflected in the sprawling growth of some of the bushes such as **'Mutabilis'** (syn. 'Tipo Ideale'), which grows to 8 ft (2.4 m) tall and has light yellow-orange flowers that age to crimson. Others like **'Hermosa'** (syn. 'Armosa'), which has scented, pink, double flowers, rarely exceed 4 ft (1.2 m) tall. ZONES 7–11.

7. Tea Roses

These plants, which flower in shades of white, pink and yellow, are *Rosa gigantea* × *R. chinensis* hybrids, a cross known as ***R.* × *odorata***. The name 'Tea' refers to their scent. Although rather tender, they were popular around the 1830s and some, particularly the climbing forms and larger bushes, are once again being grown in numbers. **'Archiduc Joseph'** (syn. 'Monsieur Tillier') is a double in pinkish red with salmon pink. **'Devoniensis'** is a yellow-cream double also available as a climber. **'Lady Hillingdon'** is a climbing form with loosely double, golden yellow flowers. **'Papa Gontier'** is a shrub with semi-double, deep pink to red flowers. **'Souvenir d'un Ami'** is a very fragrant double in rose pink to salmon and buff yellow shades. Among the more popular Climbing Teas are the soft yellow, double-flowered **'Gloire de Dijon'** (syn. 'Old Glory Rose') and **'Jaune Desprez'** (syn. 'Desprez à Fleur Jaune'). ZONES 7–11.

Rosa, Old Rose, Tea, 'Papa Gontier'

Rosa, OR, Tea, 'Lady Hillingdon'

Rosa, Old Rose, Tea, 'Gloire de Dijon'

Rosa, OR, Tea, 'Lady Mary Fitzwilliam'

Rosa, Old Rose, China, 'Mutabilis'

Rosa, Old Rose, Tea, 'Anna Olivier'

Rosa, OR, Tea, 'Lorraine Lee'

Rosa, Old Rose, China, 'Mutabilis'

Rosa, Old Rose, China, 'Echo'

Rosa, OR, Tea, 'Archiduc Joseph'

Rosa, Old Rose, Tea, 'Devoniensis'

Rosa, Old Rose, Tea, 'Souvenir d'un Ami'

R., OR, Portland, 'Comte de Chambord'

Rosa, OR, Bourbon, 'Boule de Neige'

Rosa, OR, Bourbon, 'Bourbon Queen'

R., OR, Bourbon, 'Honorine de Brabant'

Rosa, Old Rose, Bourbon, 'Souvenir de la Malmaison'

Rosa, Old Rose, Bourbon, 'Souvenir de St Anne's'

Rosa, Old Rose, Bourbon, 'Zéphirine Drouhin'

8. Portland Roses

Developed in England in the late eighteenth century, the original plant was a cross between the Autumn Damask and ***Rosa gallica* 'Officinalis'**. The group was named after the 2nd Duchess of Portland and although a few such as the sweetly scented, pink, double-flowered **'Comte de Chambord'** are still grown, their greatest significance is probably as a parent of the Hybrid Perpetual roses. ZONES 5–10.

9. Bourbon Roses

Bourbon roses originated from a chance crossing of ***Rosa chinensis*** and an Autumn Damask that occurred on the once important French outpost of Île de Bourbon (now known as Réunion). Seed of the original plant was sent to France and crossed with Gallica and Damask roses to produce the first Bourbons. These plants, which are long blooming and strongly scented, are still widely grown. **'Boule de Neige'** has white double flowers opening from red buds. **'Bourbon Queen'** grows to 8 ft (2.4 m) tall with a massed display of light pink, double flowers. **'Prince Charles'** has deep purple-red double flowers. **'Souvenir de la Malmaison'** is a small bush with a continuous display of very pale pink double flowers. Its single- to semi-double-flowered sport **'Souvenir de St Anne's'** was introduced in 1950. There are also climbing Bourbons, such as the deep pink, double-flowered **'Zéphirine Drouhin'**. ZONES 6–11.

Rosa, Old Rose, Bourbon, 'Mme Isaac Pereire'

Rosa, OR, Bourbon, 'La Reine Victoria'

R., OR, Bourbon, 'Variegata di Bologna'

Rosa, Old Rose, Bourbon, 'Commandant Beaurepaire'

R., OR, Noisette, 'Alister Stella Gray'

R., OR, Noisette, 'Champney's Pink Cluster'

Rosa, Old Rose, Noisette, 'Autumnalis'

Rosa, OR, Bourbon, 'Prince Charles'

10. Noisette Roses

This hybrid group, the first to originate from the USA, resulted from an 1802 cross between the musk rose (*Rosa moschata*) and the China rose 'Parson's Pink China' (syn. 'Old Blush'). Named after early developer Phillipe Noisette, they are generally strong-growing bushes or climbers with clusters of fairly small flowers in pastel shades of yellow or pink, the climbers recently becoming very popular. **'Alister Stella Gray'** has light golden-yellow, fragrant, double flowers. **'Lamarque'** (syn. 'Thé Maréchal') has fragrant double, pale yellow flowers that age to creamy white. **'Mme Alfred Carrière'** has large pink-blushed white, double flowers. **ZONES 6–10.**

Rosa, Old Rose, Noisette, 'Lamarque'

Rosa, Old Rose, Noisette, 'Mme Alfred Carriére'

R

11. Boursault Roses

Also dating from the early nineteenth century, these now seldom-grown hybrids are usually large shrubs or semi-climbers. They are probably crosses of ***Rosa blanda*** and ***R. chinensis***. **'Amadis'**, a vigorous plant with near-thornless 12–15 ft (3.5–4.5 m) canes, deep green leaves and red, double flowers, is typical of the Boursault style. **ZONES 6–10.**

Rosa, OR, Boursault, 'Amadis'

12. Hybrid Perpetual Roses

This group of repeat-flowering Portland × China hybrids originated around 1835 and enjoyed some 70 years of immense popularity, though very few of the hundreds of nineteenth-century cultivars survive today; however, the recently introduced Canadian **Explorer Series**, based on Hybrid Perpetuals, has raised the interest of modern rose growers. Sturdy bushes, they often have large, strongly scented flowers but are seldom tidy. **'Baron Girod de l'Ain'** has white-edged red, double flowers. **'Baronne Prévost'** is a fully frost-hardy, upright bush with fragrant, deep pink, double flowers. **'Champion of the World'**, with deep pink double flowers, is one of the first roses to bloom. **'Ferdinand Pichard'** has deep pink and white striped bicolor double flowers. **'Mrs John Laing'** is a small bush with fragrant, soft pink, double flowers. **ZONES 5–10.**

Rosa, Old Rose, Hybrid Perpetual, 'Fisher and Holmes'

Rosa, Old Rose, Hybrid Perpetual, 'Mrs John Laing'

Rosa, OR, HP, 'Baronne Prévost'

Rosa, OR, HP, 'Champion of the World'

Rosa, Old Rose, Hybrid Perpetual, 'Baron Girod de l'Ain'

Rosa, Old Rose, Hybrid Perpetual, 'Ferdinand Pichard'

Rosa, Old Rose, Hybrid Perpetual, 'Hugh Dickson'

Rosa, Old Rose, Hybrid Perpetual, 'Le Havre'

Rosa, Old Rose, Climbing Tea, 'Sombreuil'

Rosa, Old Rose, Rambler, 'Rambling Rector'

Rosa, Modern Rose, Climber, 'Alchymist'

Rosa, Old Rose, Rambler, 'Sander's White'

Rosa, OR, Rambler, 'Wedding Day'

13. Climbing and Rambling Roses

Many roses are natural ramblers, scramblers or climbers and the earliest garden examples were often little more than selected forms of wild species. True branching climbers are rare among the Old roses, though there are a few large bushes that can be trained as climbers. **'Sombreuil'**, a Climbing Tea, and the Climbing Boubon **'Zephyrine Drouhin'** are probably the best known. Modern hybridists have bred climbers like **'Alchymist'** that closely resemble old roses.

Rosa, Old Rose, Rambler, 'Düsterhlohe'

Rosa, Old Rose, Rambler, 'Albertine'

Rosa, OR, Rambler, 'Veilchenblau'

Rosa, Old Rose, Rambler, 'Excelsa'

Rosa, Old Rose, Rambler, 'Phyllis Bide'

Rosa, Old Rose, Rambler, 'Albéric Barbier'

Rosa, Old Rose, Rambler, 'Blush Rambler'

Ramblers differ from climbers in that instead of producing long-lived branching stems they send up from ground level strong-growing shoots that flower in the second year and which are then pruned off as they cease to be productive. **'Albéric Barbier'** grows to 20 ft (6 m) tall and bears semi-double, cream flowers. **'Albertine'**, which can also reach 20 ft (6 m) in height, has one magnificent burst of soft apricot pink, double flowers. **'Félicité et Perpétue'** is nearly evergreen, has clusters of small cream double flowers and can grow to over 20 ft (6 m) tall. **'Paul Transon'** has clusters of 3–5 bright pink flowers which are slightly fragrant, and glossy dark green leaves. **'Veilchenblau'** is near thornless and has clusters of small flowers in an unusual shade of bluish-purple.

R., OR, Rambler, 'Félicité et Perpétue'

Rosa, Old Rose, Rambler, 'Paul Transon'

Rosa, OR, Scotch, 'Irish Rich Marbled'

Rosa, OR, Scotch, 'William III'

14. Scotch, Burnet or Pimpinellifolia Roses

The Scotch rose *(Rosa pimpinellifolia)* is a naturally variable shrub that has produced several excellent cultivars. They are low, thorny, suckering bushes that smother themselves in bloom. **'Irish Rich Marbled'** with its striped and flecked, pink and white, double flowers is probably the most striking. Others, such as the pale pink double **'Stanwell Perpetual'**, show the influence of hybridizing, possibly with Damask roses or ***R. pendulina***. Similar work has been done with the sweet briar *(**R. rubignosa**)*. ZONES 4–9.

MODERN ROSES

The Hybrid Perpetual roses were strong, healthy plants that made the Tea roses appear rather weak and spindly, but Tea roses had beautifully shaped buds and flowers in shades of soft yellow that were lacking in the hybrid perpetuals. It was an obvious move to cross the two, and in 1867 the first Hybrid Tea, **'La France'**, a soft pink double, appeared. Although not immediately popular, the development of the Hybrid Tea proved so significant that 1867 is now recognized as the official cut-off date between Old and Modern Garden roses. It wasn't until the bright yellow, double-flowered ***Rosa foetida* var. *persiana*** was introduced into the breeding program by the French breeder Pernet-Ducher that Hybrid Teas started to become the dominant roses. Unfortunately, the early Hybrid Teas were rather tender for European gardens, a situation that was remedied in the mid-1940s by the increased use of *R. wichuraiana*. While Modern roses began with the first Large-flowered roses in 1867, not all roses bred since then are classified as Modern. Roses classed as Hybrid Perpetual or Tea roses bred after that time remain Old Garden roses.

1. Bush Roses

The Bush roses are the most significant of the modern roses, and most likely to be grown in gardens. The Bush roses are divided into Large-flowered (Hybrid Teas), Cluster-flowered (Floribundas) and Polyanthas. Many crosses have been made between Large- and Cluster-flowered roses, and it has become difficult to discriminate between them. There are Large-flowered roses with bigger clusters than some Cluster-flowered roses, and Cluster-flowered roses with bigger flowers than some Large-flowered roses, and in-between varieties that are difficult to classify. In the USA these in-between roses are often classed as **Grandifloras**, a term not commonly used outside America. ZONES 7–10.

Large-flowered (Hybrid Tea) Roses

These constitute probably the most widely grown class, and are considered the more 'classic' rose. The beautiful blooms are borne singly or in groups of three or four. Depending on climate, the flowers can be from 4–8 in (10–20 cm), and grow from 3–5 ft (1–1.5 m) tall. There are hundreds of cultivars. **'Aotearoa'** (syn. 'New Zealand') has large, very fragrant, pale pink, formal double flowers. **'Big Purple'** (syn. 'Nuit d'Orient') has unusual purple, double flowers on a compact bush. **'Deep Secret'** (syn. 'Mildred Scheel') has the deepest of red, double flowers. **'Elina'** (syn. 'Peaudouce') has beautiful cream blooms that age to white. **'First Love'** (syn. 'Premier Amour') has loosely double, soft apricot-pink flowers. **'Fragrant Cloud'** (syns 'Duftwolke', 'Nuage Parfumée') has scented, bright orange-red flowers. **'Ingrid Bergman'** has compact deep red, double flowers on long stems. **'Just Joey'** is famed for the size of its buff to light orange-yellow flowers. **'Loving Memory'** (syns 'Burgund '81', 'Red Cedar') is everyone's idea of the long-stemmed red rose. **'Pascali'** is a tall bush with pure white flowers. **'Peace'** (syns 'Gloria', 'Gloria Dei', 'Mme A. Meilland') has pale yellow blooms suffused with gold and edged pink. **'Royal Dane'** (syn. 'Troika') opens pink and ages to buff with a few pink petals. **'Savoy Hotel'** is a compact bush with light pink, full double flowers. **'Super Star'** (syn. 'Tropicana') has scented, orange-red flowers. **'The World'** (syn. 'Die Welt') has yellow flowers suffused and softly edged with orange. Other cultivars include the dusky pink **'Blue Moon'** (syns 'Blue Monday', 'Mainzer Fastnacht', 'Sissi'); mid-pink **'Esmeralda'** (syn. 'Keepsake'); red **'Granada'** (syn. 'Donatella'); striped red-orange and gold **'Harry Wheatcroft'** (syn. 'Caribia'); rich yellow **'Helmut Schmidt'** (syn. 'Simba'); scarlet and gold fading to purplish pink and cream **'Kronenbourg'** (syn. 'Flaming Peace'); bright yellow **'Landora'** (syn. 'Sunblest'); rich pink **'Maria Callas'** (syn. 'Miss All-American Beauty'); pale apricot-pink **'Paul Shirville'** (syn. 'Heart Throb'); yellow-centered fading to creamy white **'Polar Star'** (syn. 'Polarstern'); vivid red **'Precious Platinum'** (syns 'Opa Potschke', 'Red Star'); white **'Virgo'** (syn. 'Virgo Liberation'); and the pinkish yellow **'Whisky'** (syn. 'Whisky Mac'). ZONES 7–11.

Rosa, Modern Rose, Large-flowered, 'Aotearoa'

Rosa, MR, Large-flowered, 'Aotearoa'

Rosa, MR, Large-flowered, 'Elina'

Rosa, Modern Rose, Large-flowered, 'First Love'

Rosa, MR, Large-flowered, 'Big Purple'

Rosa, MR, Large-flowered, 'Deep Secret'

Rosa, Modern Rose, Large-flowered, 'Just Joey'

Rosa, Modern Rose, Large-flowered, 'Ingrid Bergman'

Rosa, MR, Large-flowered, 'Pascali'

R., MR, Large-flowered, 'Royal Dane'

Rosa, Modern Rose, Large-flowered, 'Fragrant Cloud'

Rosa, Modern Rose, Large-flowered, 'Loving Memory'

Rosa, MR, Large-flowered, 'Peace'

Rosa, MR, Large-flowered, 'Blue Moon'

R

Rosa, MR, Large-flowered, 'Esmeralda'

Rosa, MR, Large-flowered, 'Granada'

Rosa, MR, Large-flowered, 'Maria Callas'

Rosa, MR, Large-flowered, 'Paul Shirville'

Rosa, Modern Rose, Large-flowered,'The World'

Rosa, Modern Rose, Large-flowered, 'Helmut Schmidt'

R., MR, L-f, 'Helmut Schmidt'

R., MR, L-f, 'Harry Wheatcroft'

Rosa, Modern Rose, Large-flowered, 'Precious Platinum'

Rosa, Modern Rose, Large-flowered, 'Kronenbourg'

R

Rosa, MR, Large-flowered, 'Landora'

Rosa, MR, Large-flowered, 'Polar Star'

Rosa, MR, Large-flowered, 'Virgo'

Rosa, MR, Large-flowered, 'Brandy'

Rosa, Modern Rose, Large-flowered, 'Whisky'

Rosa, Modern Rose, Large-flowered, 'Alexander'

Rosa, MR, L-f, 'Charles de Gaulle'

Rosa, MR, L-f, 'Double Delight'

Rosa, Modern Rose, Large-flowered, 'Irish Elegance'

Rosa, Modern Rose, Large-flowered 'Julia's Rose'

Rosa, MR, Large-flowered, 'Ena Harkness'

Rosa, MR, L-f, 'Michèle Meilland'

Rosa, MR, Large-flowered, 'Mister Lincoln'

Rosa, MR, L-f, 'Mrs Herbert Stevens'

Rosa, Modern Rose, Large-flowered, 'Remember Me'

Rosa, Modern Rose, Large-flowered, 'Mme Caroline Testout'

Rosa, Modern Rose, Large-flowered, 'Pristine'

Rosa, Modern Rose, Large-flowered, 'Olympiad'

Rosa, Modern Rose, Large-flowered, 'Pink Panther'

R

Rosa, Modern Rose, Large-flowered, 'Tequila Sunrise'

Rosa, Modern Rose, Large-flowered, 'Silver Jubilee'

Polyantha Roses

The Polyantha rose appeared about the same time as the first Hybrid Teas. It was a low-growing rose with small, double, white flowers borne in clusters, and was introduced as 'Paquerette' in 1875. These compact plants bear their small flowers in large clusters and were produced by crossing dwarf forms of ***Rosa multiflora*** (syn. *R. polyantha*) with either a dwarf China or a small Hybrid Tea. Polyanthas have continued to be grown and new introductions appear occasionally. **'Cécile Brünner'** has small pale pink double flowers. **'Perle d'Or'** is a somewhat rangy grower with buff pink double flowers. **'Strawberry Ice'** is a dense, compact bush with white and cerise double flowers. **'The Fairy'** is a mid-pink double that can be grown as a bush or small climber. **'Marjorie Fair'** (syns 'Red Ballerina', 'Red Yesterday') has sprays of carmine and white flowers. ZONES 6–10.

Rosa, MR, Large-flowered, 'Sheer Bliss'

Rosa, MR, L-f, 'Susan Hampshire'

Rosa, MR, Polyantha, 'Marjorie Fair'

Rosa, MR, Polyantha, 'Perle d'Or'

Rosa, MR, Polyantha, 'The Fairy'

Rosa, MR, Large-flowered, 'Sutter's Gold'

Rosa, Modern Rose, Polyantha, 'Strawberry Ice'

Rosa, Modern Rose, Polyantha, 'Cécile Brünner'

Rosa, MR, C-f, 'Amber Queen'

Rosa, MR, Cluster-flowered, 'Arthur Bell'

Rosa, MR, Cluster-flowered, 'Iceberg'

R., MR, Cluster-flowered, 'Evelyn Fison'

Cluster-flowered (Floribunda) Roses

Although very successful roses, the flowers of the Polyantha roses tended to be very small and poorly formed, so they were crossed with Hybrid Teas by Danish breeder Poulsen to produce the Floribunda roses. Now known as Cluster-flowered roses for their habit of producing several blooms per stem, they are hard to beat for sheer color. **'Amber Queen'** is a compact bush with golden-yellow flowers. **'Arthur Bell'** has bright yellow flowers and has been used in hybridizing. **'Auckland Metro'** (syn. 'Precious Michelle') has pure white blooms that open from pale pink buds. **'Bonfire Night'** (syn. 'Bonfire') is a semi-double in a vivid combination of yellow, orange and red. **'Evelyn Fison'** (syn. 'Irish Wonder') has dense heads of bright red flowers. **'Friesia'** (syns 'Sunsprite', 'Korresia') has highly scented double blooms of the most intense pure yellow. **'Gold Medal'** has bright yellow flowers that open from amber-orange buds. **'Iceberg'** is covered in heads of pure white blooms over a long season. **'Jacqueline du Pré'** has white, semi-double flowers with red anthers. **'Margaret Merril'** has large, semi-double, white flowers. **'Matangi'**, **'Old Master'** and **'Priscilla Burton'** have 'hand-painted' two-tone flowers in shades of deep pink, orange-red and white. **'Playboy'** (syn. 'Cheerio') has single to semi-double orange flowers with a gold center. **'Radox Bouquet'** (syn. 'Rosika') has pleasantly scented, mid-pink double flowers. **'Raspberry Ice'** (syns 'Hannah Gordon', 'Tabris') is compact with long-lasting white and deep pink flowers. **'Sexy Rexy'** is smothered from late spring to late fall (autumn) with light pink double flowers. **'Trumpeter'** has deep green foliage and weather-resistant red flowers. Other Floribundas include the vivid red-flowered **'Color Break'** (syn. 'Brown Velvet'); white **'Edelweiss'** (syn. 'Snow-line'); red-pink **'Elmshorn'** (syn. 'Elmsham'); crimson **'Intrigue'** (syns 'Lavaglow', 'Lavaglut'); apricot-pink **'Sonia'** (syns 'Sonia Meilland', 'Sweet Promise'); and the golden-yellow **'Zonta Rose'** (syn. 'Princess Alice'). ZONES 6–10.

Rosa, MR, Cluster-flowered, 'Friesia'

Rosa, MR, C-f, 'Auckland Metro'

Rosa, Modern Rose, Cluster-flowered, 'Bonfire Night'

Rosa, Modern Rose, Cluster-flowered, 'Gold Medal'

Rosa, Modern Rose, Cluster-flowered, 'Jacqueline du Pré'

R

Rosa, MR, C-f, 'Margaret Merril'

Rosa, MR, Cluster-flowered, 'Matangi'

R., MR, Cluster-flowered, 'Edelweiss'

Rosa, MR, Cluster-flowered, 'Color Break'

Rosa, Modern Rose, Cluster-flowered, 'Playboy'

Rosa, MR, Cluster-flowered, 'Sexy Rexy'

Rosa, MR, Cluster-flowered, 'Trumpeter'

Rosa, MR, C-f, 'Radox Bouquet'

Rosa, MR, Cluster-flowered, 'Zonta Rose'

Rosa, Modern Rose, Cluster-flowered, 'Elmshorn'

Rosa, Modern Rose, Cluster-flowered, 'Old Master'

Rosa, Modern Rose, Cluster-flowered, 'Raspberry Ice'

Rosa, Modern Rose, Cluster-flowered, 'Burma Star'

Rosa, Modern Rose, Cluster-flowered, 'Europeana'

Rosa, MR, C-f, 'Carefree Beauty'

Rosa, MR, Cluster-flowered, 'Escapade'

Rosa, MR, Cluster-flowered, 'French Lace'

Rosa, MR, C-f, 'Madam President'

Rosa, Modern Rose, Cluster-flowered, 'Eyepaint'

Rosa, Modern Rose, Cluster-flowered, 'Old Port'

Rosa, MR, Cluster-flowered, 'Intrigue'

Rosa, MR, Cluster-flowered, 'Sonia'

R., MR, Cluster-flowered, 'Lilli Marlene'

Rosa, MR, Cluster-flowered, 'Pink Parfait'

Rosa, Modern Rose, Cluster-flowered, 'Ripples'

Rosa, Modern Rose, Musk, 'Francis E. Lester'

R., MR, Cluster-flowered, 'Regensberg'

R., MR, Cluster-flowered, 'Rock 'n' Roll'

Rosa, MR, Musk, 'Sally Holmes'

Rosa, Modern Rose, Musk, 'Pax'

Rosa, MR, C-f, 'Queen Elizabeth'

2. Shrub Roses

These roses are perhaps a little bigger, more vigorous or spreading and are hard to classify simply. They range in color and fragrance, but because they are easy to grow are popular with both novices and experienced rosarians. ZONES 7–11.

Hybrid Musk Roses

The first Hybrid Musks were released in 1913 by the Reverend J. H. Pemberton, an English clergyman and rose enthusiast. These vigorous roses bear attractive flowers throughout the season, and can be trained around pillars if desired. **'Autumn Delight'**, with cream flowers that open from amber buds, is at its best in summer despite the name. The flowers of **'Buff Beauty'** open soft yellow, age to cream and are strongly scented. **'Lavender Lassie'** has heads of small, scented, pink double flowers. **'Penelope'** has soft yellow, single to semi-double blooms. **'Sally Holmes'** is a spreading bush with a repeat display of pale apricot-pink, single to semi-double flowers. ZONES 5–10.

Rosa, MR, Musk, 'Autumn Delight'

Rosa, Modern Rose, Musk, 'Penelope'

Rosa, MR, Musk, 'Buff Beauty'

Rosa, Modern Rose, Musk, 'Erfurt'

Rosa, Modern Rose, Musk, 'Felicia'

R., MR, Rugosa, 'Blanc Double de Coubert'

Rosa, MR, Rugosa, 'Delicata'

Rosa, Modern Rose, Rugosa, 'Pink Grootendorst'

Hybrid Rugosa Roses

These shrub, developed from *Rosa rugosa*, usually share that species' lush, dense foliage, vigor and resistance to disease. They are attractive, large bushy shrubs growing to some 6 ft (1.8 m) and responding well to a good pruning. In addition to their flowers, many cultivars also have a prodigious crop of bright orange-red hips. **'Blanc Double de Coubert'** has recurrent, fragrant, semi-double to double, white flowers. **'Delicata'** is a bright pink semi-double. **'Fimbriata'** (syns 'Phoebe's Frilled Pink', 'Dianthiflora') has small white to pale pink, semi-double flowers with unusual serrated edges to the petals. **'Fru Dagmar Hastrup'** (syn. 'Frau Dagmar Hartopp') has large pink, single flowers followed by bright red hips. **'Pink Grootendorst'** resembles 'Fimbriata' except that its flowers are bright pink. **'Roseraie de l'Haÿ'** is a thorny bush with striking deep pink, semi-double blooms. **'Sarah van Fleet'** is a tall, prickly bush with a long-lasting display of scented, double, pink flowers. ZONES 3–10.

Rosa, MR, Rugosa, 'Fimbriata'

R., MR, Rugosa, 'Frau Dagmar Hastrup'

Rosa, Modern Rose, Rugosa, 'Agnes'

Rosa, MR, Rugosa, 'Roseraie de l'Haÿ'

Rosa, MR, Rugosa, 'Sarah van Fleet'

Rosa, MR, Rugosa, 'Parfum de l'Haÿ'

English Roses

The English roses were bred specifically by David Austin to capture the fragrance and charm of Old Garden roses on plants with the vigor, health, color range and repeat flowering of modern roses. **'Abraham Darby'** has large, amber-pink Centifolia-style flowers and may be grown as a bush or small climber. **'Charles Austin'** has large, fragrant blooms in an unusual yellow with soft apricot and pink tones, and has also produced the yellow-flowered sport **'Yellow Charles Austin'**. **'Constance Spry'** is once blooming with large, mid-pink flowers and may be grown as a shrub or climber. **'Gertrude Jekyll'** is an open bush with strongly scented, deep pink flowers. **'Graham Thomas'** has strongly scented yellow flowers over a long season. **'Mary Rose'** is extremely fragrant and has clusters of deep pink flowers that age to pale pink. **'Winchester Cathedral'** is a compact bush with clusters of small white flowers. **'Wise Portia'** is low growing with strongly scented, purple-red flowers. ZONES 6–10.

Rosa, Modern Rose, English, 'Abraham Darby'

Rosa, Modern Rose, English, 'Yellow Charles Austin'

Rosa, Modern Rose, English, 'Constance Spry'

Rosa, MR, English, 'Gertrude Jekyll'

R., MR, English, 'Winchester Cathedral'

Rosa, MR, English, 'Mary Rose'

Rosa, MR, English, 'The Miller'

Rosa, Modern Rose, English, 'Graham Thomas'

Rosa, MR, English, 'Windrush'

Rosa, MR, English, 'Perdita'

Rosa, Modern Rose, English, 'Queen Nefertiti'

Rosa, MR, English, 'Leander'

Rosa, MR, English, 'Othello'

Rosa, Modern Rose, English, 'Wise Portia'

Unclassified Modern Shrub Roses

As the name suggests, these are roses that simply do not fit in any of the other categories. As such they are naturally a rather mixed lot, though they all tend to be reasonably large and vigorous. **'Fritz Nobis'** is a 6 ft (1.8 m) tall shrub with clusters of pale pink to white, semi-double flowers. **'Nevada'** is 10 ft (3 m) tall and wide with masses of single, cream flowers that often develop pink tints. **'Robusta'** is often grown as a climber and has deep glowing red, single flowers. **'Sadler's Wells'** is a long-flowering shrub with single flowers that gradually lighten to pink at the center. **'Sparrieshoop'** is a heavy flowering bush with heads of white-centered, mid-pink, single flowers. **ZONES 4–10.**

Rosa, Modern Rose, Unclassified, 'Sadler's Wells'

Rosa, MR, Unclassified, 'Nevada'

Rosa, MR, Unclassified, 'Fritz Nobis'

Rosa, MR, Unclassified, 'Robusta'

Rosa, MR, Unclassified, 'Sparrieshoop'

Rosa, Modern Rose, Unclassified, 'Bonn'

Rosa, MR, C-f Climber, 'Dortmund'

Rosa, MR, Unclassified, 'Golden Wings'

Rosa, Modern Rose, Unclassified, 'Marguerite Hilling'

Rosa, Modern Rose, Ground Cover, 'White Meidiland'

Rosa, Modern Rose, Large-flowered Climber, 'Compassion'

Rosa, MR, C-f Climber, 'America'

R., MR, L-f Climber, 'Climbing Shot Silk'

Rosa, MR, L-f Climber, 'Casino'

Rosa, MR, C-f Climber, 'Joseph's Coat'

Rosa, Modern Rose, Ground-cover, 'Snow Carpet'

R., MR, L-fC, 'Climbing Etoile de Hollande'

Rosa, MR, L-f Climber, 'Maigold'

Rosa, MR, GC, 'Flower Carpet'

R., MR, L-fC, 'Mme Grégoire Staechelin'

Rosa, MR, Ground-cover, 'Sea Foam'

Rosa, MR, Ground-cover, 'Sea Foam'

3. Ground-cover Roses

The Ground-cover roses form an increasingly important group that has been produced from a wide range of breeding stock. Most are extremely vigorous plants capable of carpeting a wide area and many are similar in flower and foliage to miniature roses. Some, however, are rather sparse and are best used as trailers rather than ground covers. **'Flower Carpet'** is densely foliaged, near evergreen in mild climates and has deep pink, semi-double flowers. **'Sea Foam'** is a trailer with pale pink, double flowers that age to white. **'Snow Carpet'** is often classed as a Miniature rose and has masses of small, white, double flowers. ZONES 4–10.

4. Climbing Roses

Climbing roses are also classified as either Large-flowered and Cluster-flowered. They are often bred from bush roses and, where this happens, they retain their original name prefixed with the word 'Climbing', as in 'Climbing Peace'. Climbing roses, which usually flower in spring, can be trained to grow over walls or verandahs. They usually flower in spring. ZONES 7–10.

Large-flowered Climbing Roses

These have all the bloom characteristics of their shrub cousins, though they need regular deadheading to keep new blooms forming. Light summer pruning is advisable, as their vigorous stems are inclined to be sappy and may be damaged by strong winds if not shortened or tied back. **'Casino'** has bright yellow double flowers; **'Compassion'** (syn. 'Belle de Londres') produces loosely double apricot-pink flowers with a yellow base to the petals; **'Climbing Étoile de Hollande'** has semi-double red flowers; **'Maigold'** bears glowing golden-yellow semi-double flowers in abundance; **'Mme Grégoire Staechelin'** (syn. 'Spanish Beauty') has dusky deep pink flowers; and **'Climbing Peace'** has flowers very like the bush form but on an 8–10 ft (2.4–3 m) tall climber. ZONES 7–11.

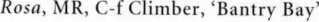

Rosa, MR, C-f Climber, 'Bantry Bay'

Rosa, MR, C-fC, 'Parkdirektor Riggers'

Rosa, Modern Rose, Cluster-flowered Climber, 'Dublin Bay'

Rosa, MR, C-fC,'Golden Showers'

Rosa, MR, C-fC, 'Climbing Iceberg'

Rosa, Modern Rose, Cluster-flowered Climber, 'Gold Bunny'

Cluster-flowered Climbing Roses

These usually flower very heavily and are among the most popular climbing roses. They require little care other than occasional deadheading. Some of the best are **'Bantry Bay'** which has masses of bright pink, semi-double flowers; **'Dublin Bay'** with small, deep red, semi-double to double flowers; **'Golden Showers'**, slightly scented, small, bright yellow semi-double flowers; **'Climbing Iceberg** (syn. 'Fée de Neiges') is floriferous with pure white flowers over a long season; and **'Parkdirektor Riggers'** is tall with vivid red, single flowers. **ZONES 6–10.**

5. Miniature Roses

There are several styles of Miniature rose. While all have small flowers, many bushes can reach 24–36 in (60–90 cm) or more with time. Some of the larger-growing forms are known as Patio roses; others are budded onto tall stems to produce miniature and weeping standards. There are even a few Climbing Miniature roses. **'Anita Charles'** has deep pink, double flowers with an amber reverse to the petals. **'Baby Darling'** has beautifully shaped buds that open to apricot-pink, double flowers. **'Cheers'** has double flowers in an unusual brownish red shade with a light reverse to the petals. **'Gold Coin'** has rounded, golden-yellow flowers. The flowers of **'Green Ice'** open white and age to green with small red markings. **'Jeanne Lajoie'** is a tall bush with bright pink, double flowers that can be used as a climber. **'Lavender Jewel'** bears masses of small, fully double, lavender-pink flowers in dense clusters. **'Magic Carousel'** has white to pale pink, double flowers with a broad pink border. **'Mary Marshall'** has coral-pink, double flowers with a pinkish yellow petal reverse. **'Orange Honey'** has vivid orange, double flowers that are often lighter in the center. **'Rainbow's End'** has golden-yellow flowers tipped and sometimes edged with red. **'Red Cascade'** is a trailer with deep red semi-double to double flowers. **'Rise 'n' Shine'** is probably the most popular Miniature and has golden-yellow, double flowers. **'Si'** has the smallest flowers of all the roses: tiny, perfectly formed pink rosebuds. **ZONES 5–10.**

Rosa, MR, Miniature, 'Anita Charles'

Rosa, MR, Miniature, 'Baby Darling'

Rosa, Modern Rose, Miniature, 'Gold Coin'

Rosa, MR, C-f Climber, 'Altissimo'

Rosa, MR, C-f Climber, 'Clair Matin'

R

Rosa, MR, Miniature, 'Green Ice'

Rosa, MR, Miniature, 'Jeanne Lajoie'

Rosa, MR, Miniature, 'Orange Honey'

Rosa, MR, Miniature, 'Rise 'n' Shine'

Rosa, MR, Miniature, 'Magic Carousel'

Rosa, MR, Miniature, 'Mary Marshall'

Rosa, MR, Miniature, 'Si'

Rosa, MR, Miniature, 'Gold Fever'

Rosa, Modern Rose, Miniature, 'Lavender Jewel'

Rosa, MR, Miniature, 'Jean Kenneally'

Rosa, MR, Miniature, 'Little Girl'

Rosa, MR, Miniature, 'Popcorn'

Rosa, MR, Miniature, 'Tom Thumb'

Rosa, Modern Rose, Miniature, 'Rainbow's End'

Rosa, Modern Rose, Miniature, 'Loving Touch'

ROSCOEA

These 18 species of tuberous perennials from China and the Himalayas are related to ginger *(Zingiber)*, but in appearance are more reminiscent of irises. They are grown for their orchid-like flowers, which have hooded upper petals, wide-lobed lower lips and 2 narrower petals. The leaves are lance-shaped and erect. They are most suitable for open borders and rock and woodland gardens.
CULTIVATION: They prefer part-shade and cool, fertile, humus-rich soil that should be kept moist but well drained in summer. Provide a top-dressing of leafmold or well-rotted compost in winter, when the plants die down. Propagate from seed or by division.

Roscoea cautleoides

Bearing its yellow or orange flowers in summer, this frost-hardy species from China grows to 10 in (25 cm) tall with a 6 in (15 cm) spread. The glossy leaves are lance-shaped and erect and wrap into a hollow stem-like structure at their base. **ZONES 6–9.**

Roscoea humeana

This summer-flowering species from China has rich green leaves that form a stem-like sheath at the base. It bears up to 10 long-tubed, purple flowers and grows to 10 in (25 cm) in height with an 8 in (20 cm) spread. **ZONES 7–10.**

Roscoea purpurea

Growing to a height of 15 in (38 cm) with an 8 in (20 cm) spread, the long-pointed leaves of this species from the Himalayas wrap around each other at the base to form a false stem. The summer flowers are purple, or sometimes white or bicolored. **ZONES 6–10.**

ROSMARINUS
ROSEMARY

Some botanists recognize up to 12 species in this genus, but most suggest there is only one, an evergreen native to the Mediterranean. It has been valued for centuries for its perfume and for medicinal and culinary uses. A small shrub rarely growing more than 4 ft (1.2 m) tall, it has narrow, needle-like leaves that are dark green and aromatic. The blue flowers are held in short clusters.
CULTIVATION: *Rosmarinus* prefers a sunny site and thrives in poor soil if it is well drained; it is salt tolerant. Prune regularly to keep it compact and promote new growth. It can be grown as a specimen shrub or as a low hedge. Propagate from seed or cuttings in summer.

Rosmarinus officinalis

Widely grown as a culinary herb, this species is also ornamental. It is upright with strong woody branches densely clothed with narrow, 1 in (25 mm), deep green leaves. Simple, lavender-blue to deep blue flowers smother the bush in fall (autumn), winter and spring. **'Benenden Blue'** has vivid blue flowers; **'Huntingdon Carpet'** is a low spreader with blue flowers; **'Lockwood de Forest'** has deep blue flowers and a spreading habit; **'Majorca Pink'** is an upright grower with soft pink flowers; **'Miss Jessop's Upright'** grows vigorously to 6 ft (1.8 m); **'Prostratus'** (syn. *Rosmarinus lavendulaceus* of gardens), a ground-cover form, is ideal for spilling over walls or covering banks; and **'Tuscan Blue'** bears dark blue flowers. **ZONES 6–11.**

Roscoea cautleoides

ROSSIOGLOSSUM

This Central American genus is composed of 6 species of epiphytic orchids. They form clusters of flattened, oval, 4 in (10 cm) long pseudobulbs from which develop strap-like, blue-green leaves around 15 in (38 cm) long by 2 in (5 cm) wide. Closely allied to *Odontoglossum*, they have similar but larger flowers that are up to 6 in (15 cm) in diameter, usually ochre to yellow with red to brown barring. They open in fall (autumn) and winter and are carried in clusters of as many as 8 blooms in racemes up to 12 in (30 cm) long.
CULTIVATION: *Rossioglossum* tolerates cool winters and may be grown in shaded places outdoors in frost-free areas. However, winter minimums around 50°F (10°C) are recommended. Plant in coarse, open, very free-draining soil mix and use weak liquid fertilizers in the growing season. Propagate from seed sown on agar or by dividing large plants.

Rossioglossum grande
syn. ***Odontoglossum grande***
CLOWN ORCHID, TIGER ORCHID

This evergreen species from Mexico and Guatemala bears erect racemes of rich yellow flowers heavily marked with chestnut brown and spotted in red, brown or yellow in fall (autumn). The broadly oval, stiff green leaves reach 8 in (20 cm) in length. It grows to 15 in (38 cm) in height. **ZONES 10–12.**

ROSULARIA

This genus of succulents includes some 25 species found from the Iberian Peninsula and North Africa to the Himalayas. Very similar to *Sempervivum,* they have flat rosettes of keeled or spatula-shaped leaves. The leaf size ranges from 1–6 in (2.5–15 cm) long depending on the species. The flowers are funnel-shaped and, though small, are borne in quite showy panicles. White, pink and yellow are the common flower colors.
CULTIVATION: Most species are easily grown in a sunny, open position with gritty, well-drained soil. They need moisture when in growth but are otherwise very tolerant of dry conditions and, in fact, winter wet can cause rotting. Propagation is from seed or cuttings or by breaking off rosettes to use as cuttings.

Rosmarinus officinalis

R. officinalis 'Huntingdon Carpet'

Rosularia sedoides

From the southern Himalayas, this species has rounded leaves that exude a resinous, pine-like scent when crushed. The leaves are up to 1 in (25 mm) long, hairy and not always succulent. The white to green-tinted flowers are around ½ in (6 mm) wide and are borne in short racemes. **ZONES 7–11.**

ROTHMANNIA

There are about 30 species in this genus of evergreen shrubs or small trees native to tropical and southern Africa. They were once classified with *Gardenia,* which they resemble somewhat. Growing to 15 ft (4.5 m) high, they sometimes form several stems. Their lanceolate or oval, opposite leaves, up to 6 in (15 cm) long, are a glossy green. Stalkless, bell-shaped flowers with a strong fragrance appear from spring to summer, and are followed by fleshy, rounded fruits.
CULTIVATION: Grow these frost-tender plants in a sheltered, sunny or semi-shaded spot. A well-drained soil enriched with organic matter is ideal, preferably with a neutral to slightly acid pH. Propagate from seed in spring or from cuttings in summer.

Rothmannia globosa

Rothmannia capensis

Rosmarinus officinalis 'Prostratus'

Rothmannia capensis
CAPE GARDENIA

In cultivation, this fast-growing species from South Africa reaches 15 ft (4.5 m). Its leathery, 4 in (10 cm) leaves have slightly wavy edges, while the gray-brown bark conceals pink underbark. Its cream to yellow 3 in (8 cm) flowers have reddish spots in the throat. The sap of the green fruit was once used to heal wounds. **ZONES 10–11.**

Rothmannia globosa
TREE GARDENIA

This shrub or small tree from South Africa bears masses of creamy white spring flowers, sometimes with yellowish throats, and with a gardenia-like perfume; they occur in the leaf axils or at the branch tips. It reaches 12 ft (3.5 m) in height and has dark-colored bark. Its fruit, 1 in (25 mm) in diameter, are brownish black when ripe. **ZONES 10–11.**

ROYSTONEA
ROYAL PALM

This genus of about 10 species of very tall palms comes from the Caribbean region. Capable of reaching 120 ft (36 m) tall,

R

Roystonea elata

Rubus 'Navajo'

Rubus 'Benenden'

though usually rather less, they have single, erect, pale brown trunks. Their fronds can grow 20 ft (6 m) long and 6 ft (1.8 m) wide. Broom-like panicles of small white flowers are followed by deep purple berries. These palms are often seen planted along avenues or in parks. The genus name honors General Roy Stone, veteran of the US Civil War.

CULTIVATION: They demand a tropical or subtropical climate with full sun and moist, rich, well-drained soil. Propagate from seed in spring. If grown indoors they may be prone to attack from spider mites and scale insects.

Roystonea elata

Very similar to *Roystonea regia*, this native of southern Florida differs visibly only in that the veining of the leaflets is inconspicuous. **ZONES 11–12.**

Roystonea regia
CUBAN ROYAL PALM

When mature, this palm grows 100 ft (30 m) tall and 30 ft (9 m) wide. Its straight trunk often thickens in the middle, and the 20 ft (6 m) fronds are composed of numerous narrow, deep green leaflets. It bears small white flower clusters in pendulous spikes up to 3 ft (1 m) long, and deep purple berries 1 in (25 mm) in diameter. **ZONES 11–12.**

RUBIA
MADDER

This genus of around 60 species of scrambling or weak-stemmed climbing plants is found in Europe, Asia and Africa. The angular stems are often rough or prickly and the leaves are opposite or in whorls of four; the leaf-like stipules give the appearance of additional leaves. The tubular flowers are borne in small terminal or axillary clusters. These are followed by fleshy reddish brown or black berry-like fruits.

CULTIVATION: Frost hardy, *Rubia* are cultivated mainly for use as vegetable dyes or to a lesser extent for herbal medicine. Grow in deep, well-drained soil in full sun or part-shade. Propagate from seed in spring or by division of the creeping rootstock after flowering.

Roystonea regia

Rubia peregrina
WILD MADDER, LEVANT MADDER

This scrambling or creeping shrub grows to 4 ft (1.2 m) in height with rough or prickly upper stems. The leathery leaves are glossy above with prickles on the veins beneath and on the margins. Masses of yellow-green flowers are borne in terminal or axillary clusters in summer. **ZONES 7–11.**

Rubia tinctoria
DYER'S MADDER

This traditional dye plant reaches around 3 ft (1 m) in height. The lanceolate or oblong leaves are 3 in (8 cm) long, and have prickles on the margins and undersurface. The small, star-shaped, yellow flowers are borne in summer. The roots, which are harvested from 2 year old plants, yield shades of red, pink, purple, orange and brown depending on the mordant used. **ZONES 6–11.**

RUBUS

This large genus of 250 or more species of deciduous and evergreen shrubs and scrambling climbers occurs in most parts of the world. The plants range from the tiny cloudberry *(Rubus chamaemorus)* through to viciously armed, 12 ft (3.5 m) high thickets and high forest climbers. Their cane-like stems bear flowers and fruits in their second year. The leaves, usually felted underneath, are mostly compound with 3 to 7 leaflets arranged pinnately or palmately. The summer flowers are white, pink or purple, resembling those of a small single rose, for example, ***Rubus* 'Navajo'**. They are followed by the sweet, juicy fruits, a mass of tiny, usually red or black drupes.

Rubus deliciosus

CULTIVATION: These moderately to fully frost-hardy plants prefer moist, well-drained, moderately fertile soil in a sunny position. Some forms naturalize freely and become a menace. After fruiting, cut the canes back to ground level. Propagate by root division in winter, or from seeds, cuttings or suckers.

Rubus 'Benenden'

This deciduous, arching, thornless shrub has peeling bark and lobed, deep green leaves. Reaching 10 ft (3 m) in height and spread, it bears its large, pure white flowers in late spring and early summer. **ZONES 5–9.**

Rubus chamaemorus
CLOUDBERRY

A native to the arctic and subarctic regions, this creeping perennial grows to about 10 in (25 cm) high and bears white flowers followed by edible yellowish berries in fall (autumn). The berries have a sweet flavor and are eaten as a food or used in preserves, pastries, sweets and vinegar. **ZONES 2–8.**

Rubus cockburnianus

This deciduous shrub from China grows to 8 ft (2.4 m) in height and spread. The black fruit, while edible, are unpalatable; they follow the racemes of purple flowers, which appear in summer. The ovate leaves are deep green above and felty white beneath. **ZONES 6–10.**

Rubus deliciosus
ROCKY MOUNTAIN RASPBERRY

This 10 ft (3 m) deciduous shrub is found in western USA, especially the Rocky Mountains. Its leaves are rounded or kidney-shaped, 3- to 5-lobed and slightly less than 3 in (8 cm) wide. The stems are thornless with peeling bark. Spring-borne, 2 in (5 cm) wide white flowers are followed by purple-red fruit. **ZONES 5–9.**

Rubus fruticosus
BRAMBLE, BLACKBERRY

This widespread, northern European bramble grows wild in woods and hedgerows. It is an aggregate, consisting of over 2,000 micro-species, all differing in small details. The cultivated blackberry's prickly, arching stems grow to 10 ft (3 m) with a similar spread. They bear deep green leaves with 3 to 5 leaflets, white or pink flowers 1 in (25 mm) across, and delicious blackberries with purple juice. **'Himalayan Giant'**

Rubus fruticosus

Rubus idaeus

Rubus idaeus 'Killarney'

(syn. 'Himalaya') is very vigorous with very dark medium-sized berries which are produced over a long season; **'Loch Ness'** has spineless semi-erect canes. **ZONES 5–10.**

Rubus idaeus

RASPBERRY, RED RASPBERRY

The northern hemisphere raspberry is a cool-climate, deciduous, perennial shrub 5 ft (1.5 m) tall and wide. It has smooth, reddish brown stems bearing many or few prickles and serrated leaflets 6 in (15 cm) long. The small, 5-petalled white flowers appear on the side shoots of the branches produced over the previous summer. The succulent, aromatic berries are usually red, but can occasionally be white or yellowish in color. There are many cultivars. **'Autumn Bliss'** is an easily grown, repeat-fruiting cultivar with medium-sized red fruit; **'Taylor'** has large strong canes with late season bright red, medium-sized fruit; and **'Killarney'** and **'Glen May'** produce full-flavored fruit in early summer. **ZONES 4–9.**

Rubus × *loganobaccus*

This evergreen shrub grows to 15 ft (4.5 m) in height with erect stems and has broadly ovate leaves that are white beneath. The white flowers are borne in prickly corymbs. **'Boysen'** (syn. *Rubus* 'Boysen'), the boysenberry, is a rampant grower with long canes that are either thorny or smooth and large, purple-red berries that take 6 weeks to ripen. **'Logan'** (syn. *Rubus* 'Logan'), the loganberry, is a hybrid between a blackberry and a garden raspberry said to have originated in the garden of Judge Logan in California in 1881; its crimson, tart fruit is highly suitable for cooking. **ZONES 5–10.**

Rubus occidentalis

BLACK RASPBERRY

A parent of many cultivars of black raspberries, this erect shrub from North America reaches 8 ft (2.4 m) in height. Its prickly canes arch and root from their tips. The 3-lobed leaves are serrated and whitish underneath. Its small white flowers are held in dense clusters, and the berries are usually black, with some occasionally golden. **'Black Hawk'** and **'Jewel'** are hardy, high-yielding cultivars. **ZONES 3–9.**

Rubus odoratus

ORNAMENTAL RASPBERRY, FLOWERING RASPBERRY, THIMBLEBERRY

This vigorous, thicket-forming, deciduous, prickle-free shrub is from eastern North America. It has peeling stems and can grow to 6 ft (1.8 m) tall. The vine-like leaves are dark green and velvety; the fragrant flower sprays which are produced all through the warmer months, are a warm rose pink, sometimes white. The red fruit are tasteless. **ZONES 2–8.**

Rubus parviflorus

THIMBLEBERRY

Growing to over 15 ft (4.5 m), this deciduous shrub comes from North America and northern Mexico. *Rubus parviflorus* has upright stems which are thornless. The young growth is covered with fine hairs, and when mature the stems have peeling bark. The kidney-shaped leaves are lobed and large: up to 8 in (20 cm) wide. The flowers, which are borne in racemes, are 2 in (5 cm) wide and they are followed by red berries. **ZONES 3–10.**

Rubus pentalobus

syn. *Rubus calycinoides*

This evergreen shrub which comes from Taiwan spreads to 3 ft (1 m) or more, but its height is only 2 in (5 cm). It develops roots easily along its stems where they touch the ground. The shiny, dark, green leaves are deeply veined above and white beneath. *Rubus pentalobus* bears small, white, strawberry-like flowers in mid-summer. **ZONES 9–11.**

Rubus spectabilis

SALMONBERRY

From western North America, this 6 ft (1.8 m) deciduous species has erect, sticky stems covered with fine prickles. Its leaves, up to 6 in (15 cm) wide, are composed of 3-pointed, oval leaflets. *Rubus spectabilis* has pink to pale purple flowers, up to 1½ in (35 mm) wide. These are followed by light orange fruit. **ZONES 5–9.**

Rubus thibetanus

This deciduous, arching shrub from western China has white-bloomed, brownish purple young shoots in winter and fern-like, glossy deep green foliage that is white beneath. Growing to 8 ft (2.4 m) in height and spread, *Rubus thibetanus* bears its small pink flowers from mid- to late summer; the flowers are followed by the black fruit. **ZONES 6–10.**

Rubus xanthocarpus

This 18–24 in (45–60 cm) tall shrub with prickly stems occurs naturally in western China. Its leaves are composed of 3 to 5 oval to lance-shaped leaflets, each of which is around 2½ in (6 cm) long. Flowers appear in small clusters, are white and are less than 1 in (25 mm) in diameter. They are followed by glossy, ½ in (12 mm) golden-yellow fruit. **ZONES 6–10.**

RUDBECKIA

CONEFLOWER

This popular genus from North America has about 15 species of annuals, biennials and perennials. The plants in this genus have bright, daisy-like, composite flowers with prominent central cones (hence the common name). The single, double or semi-double flowers are usually in tones of yellow; cones, however, vary from green through rust, purple and black. Species range in height from 24 in (60 cm) to 10 ft (3 m). A number of species and garden forms make excellent cut flowers.

Rudbeckia cultivar

Rubus pentalobus

Rubus odoratus

Rubus occidentalis

Rudbeckia hirta cultivar

Rudbeckia fulgida var. *speciosa*

Rudbeckia hirta 'Irish Eyes'

R. fulgida var. *sullivantii* 'Goldsturm'

CULTIVATION: Coneflowers prefer loamy, moisture-retentive soil in full sun or part-shade. Propagate from seed or by division in spring or fall (autumn). They are moderately to fully frost hardy. Aphids may be a problem to some species and garden forms.

Rudbeckia fulgida

BLACK-EYED SUSAN, ORANGE CONEFLOWER

This rhizomatous perennial, which reaches 3 ft (1 m) in height, has branched stems, mid-green, slightly hairy leaves with prominent veins, and daisy-like, orange-yellow flowers with dark brown centers. ***Rudbeckia fulgida* var. *deamii*** has very hairy stems and is free flowering; ***R. f.* var. *speciosa*** has elliptic to lance-shaped basal leaves and toothed stem leaves; ***R. f.* var. *sullivantii* 'Goldsturm'** (syn. *R.* 'Goldsturm') grows 24 in (60 cm) tall with crowded stems and narrow, lanceolate, green leaves. ZONES 3–10.

Rudbeckia hirta

BLACK-EYED SUSAN

The flowerheads on this biennial or short-lived perennial are bright yellow, with central cones of purplish brown and its lanceolate leaves are mid-green and hairy. It reaches 12–36 in (30–90 cm) tall, with a spread of 12 in (30 cm). **'Irish Eyes'** is noteworthy for its olive-green center. **'Marmalade'** has large flowerheads with golden-orange ray florets. Many dwarf strains of cultivars such as **'Becky Mixed'** are available in a range of colors from pale lemon to orange and red; they are usually treated as annuals. ZONES 3–10.

Rudbeckia laciniata

CUTLEAF CONEFLOWER

This species is a splendid summer-flowering perennial that can reach 10 ft (3 m) tall, though 6 ft (1.8 m) is more usual. The drooping ray florets give the flowerhead an informal elegance. **'Golden Glow'** is a striking, if somewhat floppy, double cultivar. **'Goldquelle'** grows to around 30 in (75 cm) tall and has large, bright yellow, double flowers. ZONES 3–10.

RUELLIA

syns *Stephanophysum, Arrhostoxylum*

This genus from tropical and subtropical America with a few species in temperate North America contains about 150 species of evergreen perennials, shrubs and subshrubs. The funnel-shaped flowers, usually red, pink or blue, occur in densely packed terminal panicles and axillary clusters. They have smooth-edged, oblong to lance-shaped leaves up to 6 in (15 cm) long and look good in informal borders.
CULTIVATION: The plants are fairly tolerant of dry conditions and like sun or semi-shade, so they do well in dry places at the feet of trees. In cooler climates they are grown indoors or in greenhouses. Plant in humus-rich, fertile, moist soil. Propagate from seed in spring or cuttings in spring or early summer.

Ruellia devosiana

Native to Brazil, this 18 in (45 cm) tall subshrub has a dense covering of fine hairs. Its leaves are deep green, lance-shaped, around 3 in (8 cm) long with pale veins on the upper surfaces and purple-red undersides. The flowers are 1½–2 in (3.5–5 cm) long, funnel-shaped, borne singly in the leaf axils and are lavender blue, suffused white with purple veins. ZONES 10–12.

Ruellia elegans

This bushy Brazilian species reaches 24 in (60 cm) in height and spread and has pointed, oval leaves. It blooms in summer with clusters of large-lobed, tubular, red flowers. Trim in spring to encourage new growth and to keep the plant compact. ZONES 11–12.

Ruellia graecizans

syn. *Ruellia amoena*

This South American subshrub is 24 in (60 cm) tall with a dense, bushy yet spreading habit. Its leaves, up to 8 in (20 cm) long, are narrow and hairless. Its bright red flowers, occurring in small clusters in the leaf axils, are 1 in (25 mm) long and funnel-shaped. ZONES 10–12.

Ruellia macrantha

CHRISTMAS PRIDE

This Brazilian species' common name refers to the fact that its large, deep pink, trumpet flowers are in full bloom during the southern hemisphere Christmas; they are 3 in (8 cm) long with darker veins and appear from fall (autumn) to winter. It reaches 6 ft (1.8 m) in height and 18 in (45 cm) in spread. ZONES 10–12.

RUMEX

DOCK, SORREL

Chiefly found in northern hemisphere temperate regions, this genus comprises around 200 species of annual, biennial and perennial herbs, usually with a deep tap root. Many species have been introduced to other parts of the world and have become invasive weeds. Docks are erect plants, usually with a basal rosette of simple leaves and with or without stem leaves. Flowers are borne in whorls in spikes or panicles, followed by small, oval, pointed fruits. A few species are cultivated for their ornamental foliage or as herbs mainly used as a vegetable.
CULTIVATION: Most docks thrive in full sun in moderately fertile, well-drained soil. They are marginally to fully frost hardy. Propagation is from seed sown in spring or by division in fall (autumn); broken pieces of root will also sprout. Protect young plants from slugs and snails.

Rumex acetosa

syn. *Acetosa sagittata*

GARDEN SORREL

This fast-growing, fully frost-hardy perennial grows to 3 ft (1 m) high and has bright green leaves shaped like arrowheads. Whorls of green flowers, which change to red, are borne during summer. The sour lemon-flavored leaves are eaten as a vegetable and in green salads. ZONES 3–9.

Rudbeckia laciniata

Rudbeckia laciniata 'Goldquelle'

Rumex acetosa

Rumex scutatus

Rumex alpinus
MOUNTAIN RHUBARB, MONK'S RHUBARB

This spreading, rhizomatous perennial from the mountains of Europe has red-tinted flowering stems up to 5 ft (1.5 m) tall. Its foliage is mainly in a basal clump with broad, wavy leaves up to 15 in (38 cm) long. **ZONES 5–9.**

Rumex hymenosephalus
CANAIGRE, WILD RHUBARB

This species is a 3 ft (1 m) tall perennial with thickened, spindle-shaped roots and oblong to lance-shaped leaves up to 12 in (30 cm) long. The leaves are curled or wavy and short stemmed. It is a native of western USA. **ZONES 6–9.**

Rumex scutatus
SORREL, FRENCH SORREL

This low-growing perennial has pale green, oval-shaped leaves and greenish flowers. French sorrel used to be eaten in the same way as spinach, but sorrel's tart flavor is more suitable for sauces, salads or in soups. Sow in spring or plant from divisions, leaving 12 in (30 cm) between plants. Remove flowers to encourage new growth. Sorrel contains oxalic acid, which is toxic in large amounts. **ZONES 6–10.**

RUSCHIA

This is a South African and Namibian genus of some 350 species of succulent perennials and small shrubs. Most have many wiry stems with living leaves only near the tips and the dry remains of older foliage along the rest of their length. The succulent leaves are usually less than 1 in (25 mm) long, gray-green, may be cylindrical or keeled with tubercles or teeth and sometimes develop pink or red tints in the sun. The flowers,

Russelia equisetiformis

usually white, pink, purple or rarely yellow, are daisy-like and from 1–1½ in (25–35 mm) in diameter. In desert conditions they open after rain, otherwise in early summer.
CULTIVATION: Plant in light, gritty, very free-draining soil in full sun or morning shade. Hardiness varies; a few species will tolerate light frosts but all are prone to rotting in cold, wet conditions. Propagate from seed or leaf petiole cuttings or by layering.

Ruschia lineolata

This evergreen succulent from the African Cape has a low-growing habit, reaching a height of only 2 in (5 cm). It has tiny, triangular green leaves and bears large, purple, daisy-shaped flowers in summer. **ZONES 10–11.**

RUSCUS
BUTCHER'S BROOM

This genus from the Mediterranean region, Madeira and the Azores consists of 6 species of evergreen, clump-forming subshrubs grown for their foliage and fruits. The leaves are actually flattened shoots, on which flowers and fruits are borne. The flowers are tiny, star-shaped and green to greenish white and the fruits, for which both male and female plants are required, are red and showy.
CULTIVATION: These plants will tolerate anything from full sun to part-shade and any soil as long as it is not waterlogged. Propagate from seed or by division.

Ruscus aculeatus
BUTCHER'S BROOM, BOX HOLLY

A tough, erect, branching evergreen subshrub, *Ruscus aculeatus* is native to northern Africa. Its spring flowers are followed by bright red berries. The leaves end in spines, and the flowers and fruit are borne in the center. Moderately frost hardy, it grows to a height of 30 in (75 cm) and a spread of 3 ft (1 m). Butcher's broom is so called because in days gone by, butchers used the brush of the spiky stems to brush down their chopping blocks. **ZONES 7–10.**

RUSSELIA

Consisting of around 50 species of evergreen and deciduous subshrubs and shrubs, this genus ranges from Mexico and Cuba to Colombia. They have showy tubular flowers, which are red, pink or white. The scale-like leaves appear on pendent stems.
CULTIVATION: These frost-tender plants prefer full sun and humus-rich, light, well-drained soil. Propagate from cuttings or by dividing rooted layers.

Russelia equisetiformis
syn. *Russelia juncea*
CORAL PLANT, CORAL FOUNTAIN

This erect, slender subshrub with wiry, near-leafless green stems is a native of Mexico. It is grown for the clusters of handsome red flowers it bears all year round, set among tiny, green leaves. Fast growing, it is well suited to spilling over a wall, or as a seaside specimen. It grows to a height and spread of just under 3 ft (1 m). **ZONES 9–12.**

RUTA
RUE

This genus consists of 8 species of subshrubs and shrubs and woody perennials with deeply divided aromatic leaves and small yellow flowers produced in terminal sprays. They are grown for their foliage and flowers and are sometimes used as a medicinal and strewing herb or as an insect repellent. The decorative blue-gray leaves make these plants outstanding in any garden where they can be used for low hedging. They look especially attractive when planted beneath tall-growing roses. Take care when picking or weeding around rue as the foliage can cause an irritating rash in hot weather.

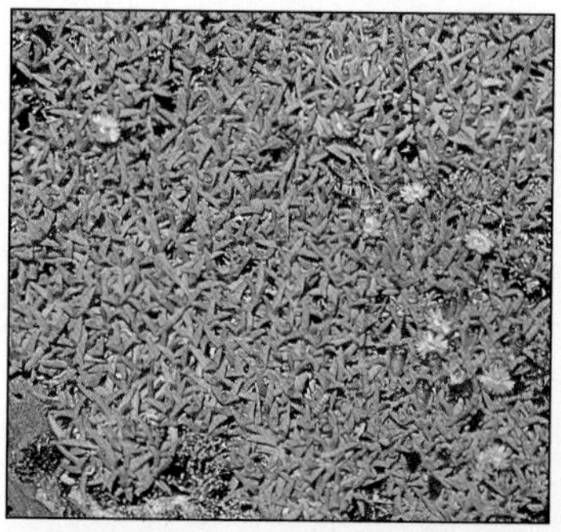

Ruschia lineolata

Ruellia macrantha

CULTIVATION: Marginally to fully frost hardy, they prefer slightly alkaline, well-drained soil in full sun. Protect from strong winds and severe frost in cold climates. Trim after flowering to encourage compact growth. Propagate by division in spring or from stem cuttings in late summer.

Ruta graveolens
COMMON RUE

One of the bitter herbs of classical times believed to ward off disease, this species is also very decorative with very pretty, gray-green, lacy leaves. It is a frost-hardy, evergreen shrub that grows 24 in (60 cm) high, with clusters of small yellow-green flowers in summer. The leaves and flowers make attractive posies. Common rue has been used in the past for medicinal purposes, but can be dangerous if taken in large doses and during pregnancy. **ZONES 5–10.**

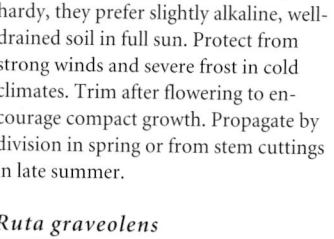

Ruta graveolens

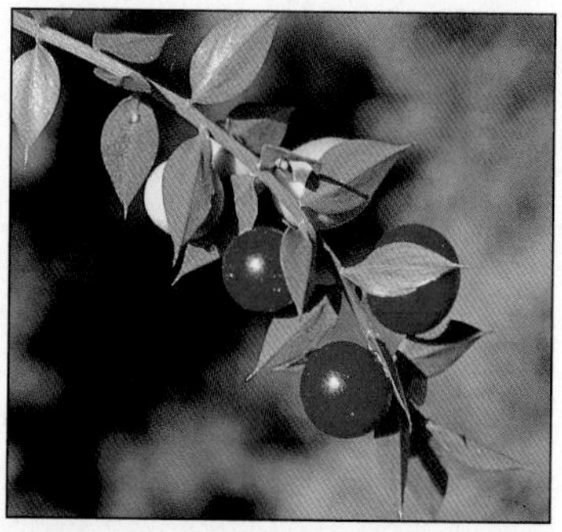

Ruscus aculeatus

S

SABAL

PALMETTO

These 14 species of fan palms are indigenous to southeastern USA and the Caribbean region. Some species have tall erect trunks, while others feature very short stems. The fronds are fan-shaped and deeply cut into segments of regular size, the stalks often persisting for years on the trunk after the fronds have fallen. Long sprays of tiny whitish flowers appear among the fronds, their stalks enclosed by tubular bracts at the base. The fruits are rounded to slightly pear-shaped berries. Palmetto fronds are traditionally used for thatching roofs, while the buds of some species are one source of hearts-of-palm, also known as millionaire's salad.

CULTIVATION: These palms suit warm to hot climates and moist or dry conditions. They prefer a sheltered, sunny spot in well-drained soil rich in organic matter. Propagate from fresh seed.

Sagina subulata

Sagittaria sagittifolia

Sabal minor

Sabal mexicana

TEXAS PALMETTO, OAXACA PALMETTO,

A fan palm from Mexico and the far south of Texas, this species grows slowly to 30–50 ft (9–15 m) tall. The fronds fall completely to reveal a clean, slender trunk. **ZONES 9–12.**

Sabal minor

DWARF PALMETTO, SCRUB PALMETTO

Indigenous to southeastern USA, this shrub-sized palm is usually about 6 ft (1.8 m) tall and half as wide. The stem is mostly underground but can occasionally be upright and short, and leaves appear from the crown at ground level. Each frond is green to bluish green, stiff and almost flat and cut into regular ribbed segments. Flowers are small, white and scented, on slender erect panicles projecting high above the foliage. The small fruit are black and shiny. **ZONES 8–12.**

Sabal palmetto

CABBAGE PALM, CABBAGE PALMETTO

This species is native to southeastern USA, Cuba and the Bahamas and thrives in swampy coastal areas. It can reach a height of 80 ft (24 m) with a sturdy trunk, scarred where the frond bases have been. The fronds are dark green above and grayish underneath, and up to 6 ft (1.8 m) long. Each characteristically twisted frond is divided into regular segments cut two-thirds of the way to the main axis and split at the tips. The small, whitish flowers are held in long, branched clusters while the fruit are small black berries. **ZONES 8–12.**

Saccharum ravennae

Sabal palmetto

SACCHARUM

SUGAR CANE

This genus is made up of about 35 species of perennial grasses with tall stout jointed stems. They occur mainly in tropical and subtropical areas, generally along river flats. The leaves are flat, and the flowerheads form branched plumes at the top of the canes. In the garden, they produce plants of strong vertical form with soft terminal flowers. ***Saccharum arundinaceum*** pulp is used in the making of paper.

CULTIVATION: Species of *Saccharum* are suitable for tropical areas or protected or greenhouse cultivation in temperate areas. They need full sun rich, summer-moist soil and can become invasive under suitable conditions. They are usually propagated from cuttings.

Saccharum officinarum

SUGAR CANE

The tall stout stems on this species grow to 20 ft (6 m). The canes are 2 in (5 cm) thick and very juicy, and bear lance-shaped leaves up to 6 ft (1.8 m) long and 2 ½ in (6 cm) wide with rough edges. The flower plumes are slender and arching, up to 3 ft (1 m) long. Each individual flower spikelet is ⅛ in (3 mm) long and enveloped with long silky hairs. This grass is widely cultivated in tropical areas as the main commercial source of sugar. **ZONES 9–12.**

Saccharum ravennae

syn. ***Erianthus ravennae***

RAVENNA GRASS

This species bears strong smooth stems up to 6 ft (1.8 m) tall that support linear leaves up to 3 ft (1 m) long and covered with a white bloom. This North African plant has plume-like flower panicles on stems 10 ft (3 m) tall. **ZONES 8–11.**

SAGINA

There are about 20 species in this genus of small tufts, both annual and perennial, which are distributed over the northern temperate zones and some tropical mountain areas. The paired linear leaves join where they meet at the stem. The flowers are white and small, with 4 or 5 petals.

CULTIVATION: Plants need a moist but well-drained soil in a sunny position, and will benefit from some shade in the middle of the day in hot climates. Propagate from seed in fall (autumn) or by division in spring.

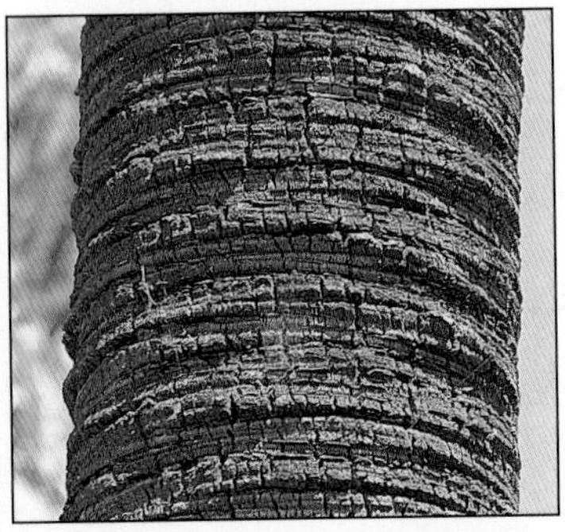

Sabal palmetto

Sagina subulata

IRISH MOSS, SCOTCH MOSS

This plant is grown for its neat dense growth habit. Its short branches are self-rooting and bear bright green ¼ in (6 mm) leaves to form a compact spreading carpet with white flowers in late spring to summer. **'Aurea'** has yellow-green leaves. Both species and cultivar are very suitable for rock gardens, for spaces between paving or towards the front of garden beds. **ZONES 4–10.**

SAGITTARIA

ARROWHEAD, WAPATO, DUCK POTATO

About 20 species of submerged or partially emergent temperate and tropical aquatic perennials, some tuberous, make up this genus. The emersed leaves are often linear to oval, but a few species have sagittate (arrowhead-shaped) leaves, hence the common name. They are usually about 10–12 in (25–30 cm) long. The submerged leaves are ribbon like, up to 4 ft (1.2 m) long including the petioles, and may form dense underwater meadows. In summer showy, purple-spotted white flowers open. They are 3-petalled, borne on branched stems that extend above the foliage and are ½–2 in (1.2–5 cm) wide.

CULTIVATION: Emergent species generally grow in ponds and fully submerged species prefer streams. All are bottom rooting and require a soil base and a position in full sun. Frost hardiness varies considerably according to the species. Propagate from seed or by division of the roots or tubers.

Sagittaria graminea

The corms of this perennial plant grow stems up to 3 ft (1 m) high. The above-water leaves vary from linear to oval, and rarely have lobes at the base. The erect flower spike bears ½ in (12 mm) white flowers with the females more obviously stalked. It occurs down the east coast of USA and Cuba, and has become naturalized in the Panama Canal. **ZONES 6–12.**

Sagittaria lancifolia

With this species from North Carolina down to northern South America and the West Indies, most leaves are above the water, the whole plant growing to 6 ft (1.8 m). The leaves may be linear, oval or elliptical and up to 15 in (38 cm) long, leathery and pale green. The white flowers may be 2 in (5 cm) wide in several whorls. **'Gigantea'** is larger in all aspects, while **'Rubra'** has a reddish tint to its leaves and flowers. **ZONES 9–12.**

Sagittaria sagittifolia

JAPANESE ARROWHEAD, SWAMP POTATO, SWAN PLANT

This plant is widespread in Europe and Asia; it is widely grown in Asia in paddy fields for the edible tuber, while in the West it is often seen in ponds and aquaria. It is similar to *Sagittaria lancifolia*, and although the leaves vary in shape those with a distinct sagittate (arrowhead) form are preferred as ornamentals. The flowers are smaller, about 1 in (25 mm) in diameter, white but with purple spots at the base. **'Flore Pleno'** has double flowers. **ZONES 7–12.**

SAINTPAULIA

AFRICAN VIOLET

Natives of eastern Africa, saintpaulias were originally collected in the late nineteenth century by Baron von Saint-Paul. There are 20 species of these low-growing, evergreen perennials and several thousand varieties, which are some of the most popular flowering indoor plants because of their attractive foliage, compact nature, long flowering periods and wide range of flower colors. Cultivars include **'Chimera Monique'** with purple and white flowers; **'Chimera Myrthe'** with crimson and white flowers; **'Nada'** with white flowers; and **'Ramona'** with flowers a rich crimson. The flowers are 5-petalled and the succulent leaves are usually hairy.

CULTIVATION: Although African violets have a reputation for being difficult to grow, in the right conditions this is generally not so. They do demand certain soil, so plant them in commercial African violet mix. Constant temperature, moderate humidity and bright, indirect light ensure prolonged flowering; in winter they may also need artificial light. Use room temperature water, allowing the surface soil to dry out a little between waterings; avoid splashing the leaves. They bloom best when slightly potbound; repot when very leafy and no longer flowering well. Propagate from leaf cuttings rooted in water or stuck in a layer of pebbles on top of a moist sand and peat mixture. African violets are vulnerable to cyclamen mite, mealybug and powdery mildew.

Saintpaulia 'Chimera Myrthe'

Saintpaulia 'Chimera Monique'

Saintpaulia confusa

This species from the mountains of Tanzania grows to 4 in (10 cm) in height with slender, erect stems. It has rounded, hairy, dark green leaves and bluish violet flowers with yellow anthers; they occur in clusters of four. **ZONES 10–11.**

Saintpaulia ionantha

COMMON AFRICAN VIOLET

This Tanzanian species has clusters of tubular, semi-succulent violet-blue flowers, growing on the stems above the leaves. The mid-green leaves, with reddish green undersides, are scalloped, fleshy and hairy. Thousands of cultivars are available, now far removed from the species; the flowers can be single or double, usually $1\frac{1}{2}$ in (35 mm) across, and come in shades from white through mauve and blue to purple, and pale and deep pink to crimson. **ZONES 11–12.**

Saintpaulia 'Nada'

Saintpaulia 'Ramona'

Saintpaulia magungensis

This plant from Tanzania has purple flowers $\frac{3}{4}$ in (18 mm) across in groups of 2 or 4, held just above the leaves. Branched stems up to 6 in (15 cm) long bear leaves with petioles (leaf stems) up to 2 in (5 cm) long. The leaves are oval or round, about $2\frac{1}{2}$ in (6 cm) across, with a wavy edge and both long and short hairs on the upper surface. **ZONES 10–12.**

Saintpaulia cultivar

Saintpaulia magungensis

Saintpaulia, Miniature and Trailing Types

These African violets are derived from crosses of *Saintpaulia ionantha* and other lesser known *Saintpaulia* species. They can be compact rosettes, no more than 3 in (8 cm) across with leaves and flowers in proportion, or trailing types that may develop stems as much as 4 in (10 cm) long. The leaves and flowers are equally tiny; some flowers are bell-shaped rather than flat. The miniature types have the reputation of being easier to grow than the large ones. **ZONES 11–12.**

Salix babylonica

SALIX

WILLOW, OSIER, SALLOW

This genus includes about 300 species of deciduous trees, shrubs and subshrubs mainly from cold and temperate regions in the northern hemisphere. The fast-growing but relatively short-lived trees are the most widely grown. They are largely grown for their timber, their twigs which are used in basket-making and their strong suckering habit, which aids soil retention. Willow bark was the original source of aspirin. The leaves are usually bright green, lance-shaped and narrow. The flowers, which are borne in fluffy catkins, are conspicuous in some species, appearing before or with the new leaves; male and female catkins are usually borne on separate trees.

CULTIVATION: These frost-hardy plants do best in areas with clearly defined seasons and prefer cool, moist soil with sun or part-shade. Propagation is from seed or cuttings in either winter or summer, or by layering. They are vulnerable to attack by caterpillars, aphids and gall mites as well as canker-causing fungal diseases.

Salix alba

WHITE WILLOW

A very adaptable tree from Europe, northern Africa and central Asia, this species grows to about 80 ft (24 m) high. Its erect branches weep somewhat at the tips and are clothed with 3 in (8 cm) long, narrow leaves that are bright green above with flattened silky hairs on the undersides. The white willow makes a good windbreak tree, albeit with invasive roots. **'Britzensis'** (syn. 'Chermesina') has bright red stems; **'Chrysostela'** has yellow shoots tipped with orange; ***Salix alba* var. *caerulea*** has blue-green leaves and is the willow from which cricket bats are made; ***S. a.* var. *sericea*** has silvery foliage; and **'Vitellina'**, the golden willow, has young growth of a brilliant clear yellow. **ZONES 2–10.**

Salix alba var. *sericea*

Salix alba 'Vitellina'

Salix fragilis

Salix babylonica

S. babylonica var. *pekinensis* 'Tortuosa'

Salix apoda

This prostrate shrub from eastern Europe and the Caucasus grows to about 8 in (20 cm) high and spreads to 24 in (60 cm) wide. The pointed oval leaves are 2½ in (6 cm) long, covered with hair when young, dark green when mature. In early spring reddish brown buds open to reveal striking 1 in (25 mm) silver-gray catkins with a felt-like texture. While larger than the stunted arctic willows, this species has a bonsai-like quality that makes it a marvellous plant for a large rockery. **ZONES 3–9.**

Salix babylonica

WEEPING WILLOW, BABYLON WEEPING WILLOW

Probably the most widely grown and recognized willow, this Chinese species grows to about 50 ft (15 m) high and wide. The narrow, bright green leaves,

Salix apoda

Salix helvetica

3–6 in (8–15 cm) long, densely cover flexible, arching branches that often droop right down to ground level. The catkins are insignificant. **'Crispa'** has twisted leaves and a narrower growth habit. ***Salix babylonica* var. *pekinensis* 'Tortuosa'** has lance-shaped, serrated leaves that turn from bright green to yellow in fall (autumn). **ZONES 4–10.**

Salix 'Blanda'

WISCONSIN WEEPING WILLOW, NIOBE WILLOW

This cultivar has pendulous branches and lance-shaped bluish leaves up to 6 in (15 cm) long. It grows rapidly to a height and width of 40 ft (12 m). **ZONES 4–9.**

Salix × *boydii*

This hybrid between ***Salix lapponum*** and *S. reticulata* originated in the UK. It is slow growing to 12 in (30 cm), but its upright, twisted habit and round grayish leaves on hairy stems create an impression of great age. It is suitable for single or grouped bonsai as well as the garden. **ZONES 5–9.**

Salix × *boydii*

Salix caprea

PUSSY WILLOW, GOAT WILLOW, GREAT WILLOW, FLORIST'S WILLOW

Native to Europe to northeast Asia, this dense shrub or tree grows 10–30 ft (3–9 m) tall. The oval mid-green leaves are 2–4 in (5–10 cm) long with a fleecy gray underside. The male plant has large yellow catkins called 'palm', the female has silvery catkins known as 'pussy willow', both appearing in spring before the foliage. This species grows well in brackish marshlands but its very strong suckering habit can cause great problems in a smaller garden. **'Kilmarnock'** is a stiffly pendulous weeping tree, usually grafted at 6 ft (1.8 m), with a dense head of yellow and brown shoots. **ZONES 5–10.**

Salix chilensis

syn. ***Salix humboldtiana***

SOUTH AMERICAN WILLOW

Almost fully evergreen, this willow occurs naturally in warmer areas of Chile and other parts of Central and South America. It grows to 50 ft (15 m) tall, often with several upright trunks and upward-sweeping branches, giving a columnar shape. The tough, flexible branches are used for making wicker furniture. The bright green, waxy leaves, 4–6 in (10–15 cm) long, are narrow to lance-shaped and similar to those of the familiar weeping willow. New growth can be damaged by frosts. **ZONES 8–11.**

Salix cinerea

GRAY SALLOW, GRAY WILLOW

This willow from Europe and Asia forms a large shrub or small tree up to 15 ft (4.5 m). The leaves have wavy edges with a grayish underside, up to 3 in (8 cm) long. The branches are also grayish and downy. The silky catkins appear in early spring before the leaves. There are variegated forms, some with a yellow and white variegation, some with red. **ZONES 2–9.**

Salix caprea

Salix elaeagnos

syn. ***Salix incana***

HOARY WILLOW, ROSEMARY WILLOW

From the mountains of central Europe and Turkey and southwestern Asia comes this large tree which grows to 10 ft (3 m). Its narrow leaves can be 6 in (15 cm) long, white beneath with margins that curl under. The whole tree has a dense habit with slender reddish brown stems. Catkins appear before or with the leaves in spring. **ZONES 4–9.**

Salix fragilis

CRACK WILLOW, BRITTLE WILLOW

This fast-growing, erect species from Europe and northwestern Asia can reach 50 ft (15 m) tall, its many branches forming a broad crown. The toothed leaves, to 6 in (15 cm) long, turn yellow in fall (autumn). Its wood has been used to produce high-quality charcoal. This tree grows easily and can naturalize and become a problem, spreading along the banks of streams. Several cultivars are known. The common name brittle willow comes from the tree's brittle twigs; old trees rot easily and break apart in storms. **ZONES 5–10.**

Salix gracilistyla

ROSE-GOLD PUSSY WILLOW

This vigorous shrub to 10 ft (3 m) has gray downy leaves and young shoots. The leaves are oblong, up to 4 in (10 cm) long, at first silky but the upper surface becoming smooth. The silky gray male catkins can be up to 2 in (5 cm) long, appearing in spring before the leaves. It is found naturally in eastern Asia. **'Melanostachys'** has black bracts over the catkins, so that the whole catkin appears black. **ZONES 6–10.**

Salix hastata

HALBERD WILLOW

From Eurasia, this is an upright, dense shrub to 4 ft (1.2 m) with twigs often becoming reddish purple. The leaves are about 1–3 in (2.5–8 cm) long and are clearly veined, dull green above but downy beneath; leaf shape varies from elliptical to lance-shaped. Catkins appear before or with the leaves in spring. **'Wehrhahnii'** has a spreading habit with many silver-gray male catkins turning yellow as the anthers mature. **ZONES 6–9.**

Salix helvetica

SWISS WILLOW

This branched, dense shrub to 5 ft (1.5 m) with a soft gray down on the

Salix caprea 'Kilmarnock'

Salix integra 'Hakuro-nishki'

Salix lanata

Salix lindleyana

younger stems, leaves and catkins is from the European Alps. The narrow bright silver foliage turns gray-green on top but remains white underneath. Catkins occur with the leaves in spring. **ZONES 3–9.**

Salix integra

This upright shrub grows to 10 ft (3 m) and is similar to *Salix purpurea*, having purplish branches and 4 in (10 cm) long leaves that are whitish below and mid-green above. **'Hakuro-nishki'** (syn. 'Alba Maculata') has white-mottled leaves, pink at the branch tips. **ZONES 6–10.**

Salix koriyanagi

syn. *Salix* 'Fuji Koriyanagi'

This tall shrub to 15 ft (4.5 m) is from Japan and Korea. Rather similar to *Salix purpurea*, it has gray bark and paired opposite leaves that are ½ in (12 mm) across, rather thick, deep green on top and blue-green beneath. **ZONES 6–10.**

Salix lanata

WOOLLY WILLOW

This small shrub from northern Europe grows to 3 ft (1 m) tall and is of slow spreading habit, becoming gnarled with age. The silvery gray rounded leaves, up to 2 in (5 cm) long, mature to a dull green on top and become slightly wavy. Erect, felty yellow-gray catkins appear in spring after the leaves. **ZONES 2–9.**

Salix lindleyana

syns *Salix hylematica* of gardens, *S. nepalensis*

This dwarf Himalayan species reaches a height of only 1½ in (35 mm) but spreads to 24 in (60 cm). It has glossy green leaves and pinkish male catkins or tiny female catkins, both appearing in spring with the leaves. **ZONES 7–10.**

Salix magnifica

From China, this is a large shrub or small tree to 20 ft (6 m) tall, of rather sparse habit. Its small twigs are purple, gradually becoming reddish. The large, magnolia-like leaves are gray-green above and whitish beneath, and patterned with red veins. They are oval in shape and may reach 10 in (25 cm) by 4 in (10 cm). The catkins may be 8 in (20 cm) long and appear with the leaves in spring. **ZONES 7–10.**

Salix purpurea

PURPLE OSIER, PURPLE WILLOW, BASKET WILLOW

This species from Europe, North Africa to central Asia and Japan grows to about 15 ft (4.5 m) high. In its darkest forms the catkins are an intense reddish purple. The leaves are silver gray, often with a hint of purple on the undersides, and the stems are tinted purple. **'Nana'** is a compact form to 3 ft (1 m) with slender shoots and gray-green leaves. **ZONES 5–10.**

Salix reticulata

This creeping dwarf willow comes from northern Europe, North America and northern Asia where it only grows 3 in (8 cm) high, forming a mat of stems. The dark green rounded leaves are whitish underneath, and ½–1½ in (12–35 mm) across. The catkins—½–1¼ in (12–30 mm) across—appear after the leaves on leafless stems. **ZONES 1–8.**

Salix × *rubens*

syn. *Salix* × *viridis*

This hybrid between *Salix alba* and *S. fragilis* comes from central Europe. It grows to 30 ft (9 m) tall with dark olive branchlets tinged with yellow or red. It bears lance-shaped leaves 3–6 in (8–15 cm) long and has 1–2½ in (2.5–6 cm) catkins. **'Basfordiana'** has more intense coloring. **ZONES 6–10.**

Salix viminalis

COMMON OSIER, HEMP WILLOW, BASKET WILLOW

This vigorous small tree or large shrub to 20 ft (6 m) has long straight flexible stems that are gray when young but soon become olive to yellowish. The long narrow dull green leaves have a silvery bloom on the undersides. The catkins appear before the leaves. This species is found from Europe to northwestern Asia and has long been cultivated for making baskets. **ZONES 4–9.**

Salix purpurea 'Nana'

SALPIGLOSSIS

These natives from the southern Andes are not seen very often in gardens as they can be tricky to grow, but patient gardeners who live in mild climates with fairly cool summers will be rewarded by a short but beautiful display of flowers like petunias (they are related). They come in rich shades of crimson, scarlet, orange, blue, purple and white, all veined and laced with gold. There are 2 species of annuals and perennials providing color in borders or as greenhouse plants in cold climates.

CULTIVATION: Plant in full sun in rich, well-drained soil. Deadhead regularly. *Salpiglossis* species are best sown directly from seed in early spring in the place they are to grow as seedlings do not always survive transplanting. They are prone to attack by aphids.

Salpiglossis sinuata

PAINTED TONGUE

Offering a variety of flower colors including red, orange, yellow, blue and purple, this annual from Peru and Argentina blooms in summer and early fall (autumn). The 2 in (5 cm) wide, heavily veined flowers are like small flaring trumpets, while the lanceolate leaves are light green. A fast grower, it reaches a height of 18–24 in (45–60 cm) and a spread of at least 15 in (38 cm). It is frost tender and dislikes dry conditions. **ZONES 8–11.**

SALVIA

SAGE

The largest genus of the mint family, *Salvia* consists of as many as 900 species of annuals, perennials and soft-wooded shrubs, distributed through most parts of the world except very cold regions and tropical rainforests. Their distinguishing feature is the tubular, 2-lipped flower with the lower lip flat but the upper lip helmet- or boat-shaped; the calyx is also 2-lipped and may be colored. The flowers come in a wide range of colors, including some of the brightest blues and scarlets of any plants, though yellows are rare. Many beautiful sage species are grown as garden plants, including some with aromatic leaves grown primarily as culinary herbs, but even these can be grown for their ornamental value alone. The genus name goes back to Roman times and derives from the Latin *salvus*, 'safe' or 'well', referring to the supposed healing properties of *Salvia officinalis*.

CULTIVATION: Most of the shrubby Mexican and South American species will tolerate only light frosts, but some of the perennials are more frost-hardy. Sages generally do best planted in full sun in well drained, light-textured soil with adequate watering in summer.

Salix reticulata

Salpiglossis sinuata

S

Propagate from seed in spring, cuttings in early summer, or division of rhizomatous species at almost any time. Foliage of many species is attacked by snails, slugs and caterpillars.

Salvia africana-lutea
syn. ***Salvia aurea***
BEACH SALVIA, BROWN SALVIA

Native to coastal areas of South Africa's Cape Province, this is one of the longest-lived and woodiest sages and is also remarkable for its flower color. It makes a spreading tangle of branches about 6 ft (1.8 m) tall, the foliage gray and densely woolly, and through spring and summer produces an abundant succession of 1½ in (35 mm) long flowers shaped like parrots' beaks, opening creamy yellow but soon turning a rich rust brown, with a shrivelled, papery appearance as though they were dead. As well as being tolerant of seashore conditions, it is a bird-attracting plant. **ZONES 9–10.**

Salvia apiana
BEE SAGE, CALIFORNIAN WHITE SAGE

The botanical name of this striking plant means literally 'bee sage' (Latin *apis*, bee) and it is a useful honey producer in its native southern California and Baja California, growing in dry chaparral scrub of coastal ranges. A stiff, coarsely branched, often quite woody shrub of up to about 5 ft (1.5 m) high, it has crowded, long-pointed, very aromatic leaves that are densely coated in silvery white hairs—indeed, it can make one of the finest of all gray-foliaged shrubs, but requires a climate with hot dry summers to perform at its best. Numerous small white or pale violet flowers are borne in summer and fall (autumn) on branched panicles that rise 3–4 ft (1–1.2 m) above the foliage. **ZONES 8–11.**

Salvia argentea

Salvia africana-lutea

Salvia blepharophylla

Salvia argentea
SILVER SAGE

Silver sage is a biennial or short-lived perennial native to southern Europe and North Africa. It has large, silver-felted leaves forming a flat basal rosette that builds up in fall (autumn) and winter to as much as 3 ft (1 m) wide before sending up 3 ft (1 m) panicles of small white flowers in spring and summer. Its main attraction is its foliage, which can be maintained for longer if inflorescence buds are removed. Allow to seed in the second or third year to maintain a supply of replacement seedlings. **ZONES 6–9.**

Salvia austriaca
AUSTRIAN SAGE

From eastern Europe, this is one of a large group of cold-hardy perennial sages with basal rosettes of closely veined, jaggedly toothed or lobed leaves, and long, erect spikes of smallish flowers in regular whorls. In *Salvia austriaca* the stalked leaves may be over 12 in (30 cm) long and the pale yellow flowers with protruding stamens are borne in summer on spikes to 3 ft (1 m) tall. **ZONES 6–10.**

Salvia azurea
BLUE SAGE, PRAIRIE SAGE

A native of southeastern USA, this perennial sage is a variable species that sends up thickets of slender 3–5 ft (1–1.5 m) stems from a rhizomatous rootstock. It has paired narrow, gray-green leaves and in summer and fall (autumn) the stems terminate in long spikes of sky-blue flowers. The form commonly cultivated is ***Salvia azurea* var. *grandiflora*** with flowers up to 1 in (25 mm) long and of a more intense color. White-flowered forms are also available. **ZONES 4–10.**

Salvia austriaca

Salvia chamaedryoides

Salvia chiapensis

Salvia blepharophylla
EYELASH LEAFED SAGE

This Mexican species is a subshrubby perennial of similar style to the better-known *Salvia greggii* and *S. microphylla.* It is almost evergreen and spreads by creeping rhizomes, reaching about 15 in (38 cm) in height and somewhat greater spread, with rich green foliage. Through summer and fall (autumn) it produces a succession of bright red flowers suffused with paler orange or pink. It likes part-shade and moist soil. **ZONES 8–11.**

Salvia buchananii
BUCHANAN'S SAGE

One of the larger-flowered Mexican sages, this plant was discovered in a garden in Mexico City and taken to England, being named in 1963 in honor of its introducer, but has not yet been found in the wild. It is a weak-stemmed perennial 12–24 in (30–60 cm) tall and somewhat wider, many stemmed from the base, with glossy deep green foliage. In summer and fall (autumn) or almost-year-round in mild climates it bears nodding, 2 in (5 cm) long magenta flowers, hairy on the outside, a few at a time per stem. It needs shelter and part-shade. **ZONES 9–11.**

Salvia cacaliifolia
GUATEMALAN BLUE SAGE

From the highlands of Mexico, Guatemala and Honduras, this is one of the most distinctive sages: its name signifies a resemblance between its leaves and those of *Cacalia*, a genus allied to *Senecio*. It is a perennial to about 3 ft (1 m) high with stems springing from a creeping rootstock, bearing pairs of glossy bright green triangular leaves that are about as broad as long, with 3 sharp points. In summer and fall (autumn) it produces a profusion of small deep blue flowers on branched spikes. **ZONES 8–10.**

Salvia chamaedryoides
GERMANDER SAGE

From Texas and Mexico, this tiny leafed perennial is suitable for the rock garden, being multi-branched and very compact. The foliage is gray-blue and masses of small deep violet-blue flowers appear in summer. It grows to 12 in (30 cm) high and 24 in (60 cm) wide. **ZONES 8–11.**

Salvia clevelandii

Salvia chamelaeagnea

This 5 ft (1.5 m) shrub from South Africa has soft gray-green leaves and terminal heads of charming, soft lavender and white flowers. It will flower freely from mid-summer to early winter, when it should be pruned back hard. It prefers full sun and light soil. **ZONES 9–11.**

Salvia chiapensis
CHIAPAS SAGE

This 3 ft (1 m) shrub from Mexico flowers continuously in temperate gardens. The leaves are smooth and dark green on elongating branchlets that bear the pinkish maroon ½ in (12 mm) wide flowers. Some pruning is necessary to induce neatness, even if some flowers have to be sacrificed. It grows best in light shade. **ZONES 8–11.**

Salvia clevelandii
CLEVELAND SAGE

This shrubby sage is a characteristic plant of the dry chaparral and scrublands of California, where its aromatic foliage and flowers add a distinct fragrance to the air. A gray-green mound reaching 3–5 ft (1–1.5 m) tall and wide, its soft lavender-blue flowers are produced on stems rising 12–24 in (30–60 cm) above the foliage. **'Winifred Gilman'** is more compact, with deeper blue flowers. **ZONES 8–10.**

Salvia coccinea
RED TEXAS SAGE

This compact, shrubby, short-lived perennial from South America is treated as an annual in colder climates. It has small mid-green leaves and an abundance of scarlet flowers from early summer to late fall (autumn). It is normally grown in full sun but when placed in light shade and protected from frost it can survive another season or two. Many forms are known, including a pure white and a lovely salmon pink and white bicolor. **'Coral Nymph'** is a compact form with coral-pink flowers; **'Lady in Red'** is also compact, growing just 15 in (38 cm) tall with bright red flowers. **ZONES 8–11.**

S

Salvia confertiflora

Salvia coccinea 'Coral Nymph'

Salvia columbariae

Many species of *Salvia* have rather insignificant flowers, relying on colored bracts to attract pollinating insects. This species is one such, an annual from California that grows about 12 in (30 cm) tall and flowers in summer. Trimming off the faded flower clusters will prolong flowering. **ZONES 7–11.**

Salvia confertiflora
SABRA SPIKE SAGE

From Brazil, this perennial plant can reach a height of 6 ft (1.8 m). It has large, 8 in (20 cm) wide, mid-green oval leaves with downy undersides. The flower spikes are in 12 in (30 cm) unbranched heads with red flowers and deep red calyces during late summer and fall (autumn). **ZONES 9–11.**

Salvia darcyi
DARCY SAGE

This rare perennial from high in the mountains of northeastern Mexico is a recent discovery only named in 1994, although introduced to cultivation in the USA about 5 years earlier. Growing to about 3 ft (1 m) high, it is a little like *Salvia coccinea* but its rich scarlet flowers are larger, about $1\frac{1}{2}$ in (35 mm) long, and borne in greater profusion in erect panicles. It flowers in summer and early fall (autumn) and dies back in winter. Easily grown in fertile soil with ample water in summer, *S. darcyi* is proving an outstanding ornamental. **ZONES 8–10.**

Salvia discolor
ANDEAN SAGE

Salvia discolor is a small Peruvian perennial which grows 18–36 in (45–90 cm) in height. The stems are covered with white hairs, while the leaves are thick and green

Salvia viridis

above but white beneath. The silver calyces hold 1 in (25 mm) long flowers of the deepest indigo. **ZONES 8–11.**

Salvia dolomitica

This native of South Africa is still rare in cultivation. It has gray-green foliage, grows to around 4 ft (1.2 m) tall and spreads slowly by rhizomes to eventually form a dense thicket of stems. Its flowers are dusky lavender-pink and appear in spring. The calyces are purple-red and last well after the flowers have fallen. **ZONES 9–11.**

Salvia dominica

An aromatic shrub to 3 ft (1 m) from Lebanon, Israel and Syria, this plant has hairy, oblong, wavy leaves that are 2 in (5 cm) long. It bears many flowers, white with a yellow tint and some brown markings. The sticky calyx expands as the fruit mature. **ZONES 9–11.**

Salvia dorisiana
FRUIT SCENTED SAGE

Native to Honduras, this is an admirable shade-tolerant plant valued for its late fall (autumn) to winter flowering. It is a multi-branched shrub to 6 ft (1.8 m) tall and 4 ft (1.2 m) wide, with large lime-green heart-shaped leaves, strongly pineapple scented when crushed. The large flowers are deep pinkish magenta, 4 to 8 flowers per truss. **ZONES 10–12.**

Salvia dorri
DORRI SAGE, DESERT SAGE

This southwest American native is a low mound only 24–36 in (60–90 cm) tall with attractive silvery foliage, evergreen except in the coldest of winters. Spring and early summer flowers are produced in dense, fluffy balls of blue and reddish purple. It is a good plant for softening the harshness of a desert garden, tolerating full sun to part-shade and requiring only occasional watering to extend the flowering season. **ZONES 8–10.**

Salvia elegans
PINEAPPLE-SCENTED SAGE

This open-branched perennial or subshrub from Mexico and Guatemala which can reach 6 ft (1.8 m) in milder areas and is grown for its light green foliage, has a distinctive pineapple scent and flavor. Its whorls of small bright red flowers are borne in late summer and fall (autumn). The leaves are used fresh but sparingly in fruit salads, summer drinks and teas. The flowers are delicious, and may be added to desserts and salads for color and flavor. **'Scarlet Pineapple'** (syn. *Salvia rutilans)* is more floriferous with larger scarlet flowers which, in milder areas, will persist to mid-winter and are most attractive to honey-eating birds. **ZONES 8–11.**

Salvia farinacea
MEALY-CUP SAGE

This species is grown as an annual in regions that have cold winters and is at its best when mass planted. It is a short-lived perennial in warmer climates, although if planted in a little shade to protect it from hot afternoon sun and pruned hard in mid-fall (mid-autumn) it can live up to 5 years. Growing to 24–36 in (60–90 cm), it bears lavender-like, deep violet-blue flowers on slender stems. It is a good cut flower and comes from Texas and Mexico. **'Blue Bedder'** is an improved cultivar; **'Strata'** has blue and white flowers; and **'Victoria'** has deep blue flowers. **ZONES 8–11.**

Salvia forsskaolii
syn. *Salvia forskaohlei*

This highly variable perennial from southeastern Europe has slightly hairy basal leaves with small flowers on single 30 in (75 cm) long stems. The flower color will vary from violet to pinkish magenta with white or yellow markings on the lower lip. It is fully frost hardy but prefers drier winters. **ZONES 7–10.**

Salvia fulgens
CARDINAL SAGE

From Mexico, this perennial subshrub up to 30 in (75 cm) tall has oval heart-shaped leaves that are white felted underneath and up to 3 in (8 cm) long. The flowers are scarlet, up to 2 in (5 cm) long, hairy and very showy, appearing in summer. **ZONES 9–11.**

Salvia farinacea 'Strata'

Salvia forsskaolii

Salvia elegans 'Scarlet Pineapple'

Salvia darcyi

Salvia dolomitica

Salvia elegans

S

Salvia gesneriiflora

This erect Colombian and Mexican perennial usually grows to 24 in (60 cm) high, though reportedly can reach 25 ft (8 m). It has oval or heart-shaped leaves about 4 in (10 cm) long that are bright green and finely hairy. It produces its large orange-red flowers from spring to fall (autumn). Each flower is 2 in (5 cm) long but presents no difficulty to nectar-seeking birds. A light pruning is necessary before winter. **ZONES 8–11.**

Salvia greggii

FALL SAGE, CHERRY SAGE, AUTUMN SAGE

This shrub, which can reach 3–4 ft (1–1.2 m) in height, is native from Texas into Mexico and is a long-flowering addition to dryish gardens in California and southwestern USA. The leaves are small and aromatic; above the foliage rise slender stems with broad-lipped sage blossoms in red, orange, salmon, pink, pale yellow, white and blends. The flowers are produced from spring through fall (autumn) in coastal areas, and in fall and winter in the desert. Many hybrids and named selections are available. **ZONES 9–10.**

Salvia gesneriiflora

Salvia guaranitica

Salvia guaranitica

ANISE SCENTED SAGE

Plant this tall-growing perennial from Brazil, Uruguay and Argentina with care as it has a tendency to 'gallop' in its second or third season, choking less valiant plants. Its deep violet-blue flowers are held aloft on strong 6 ft (1.8 m) stems from mid-summer to late fall (autumn). **'Argentine Skies'** was selected for its pale blue flowers, and **'Purple Splendour'** for its intense blackish purple flowers. **ZONES 9–11.**

Salvia indica

This plant from the Middle East forms an erect branched shrub to 5 ft (1.5 m) tall with heart-shaped hairy leaves to 12 in (30 cm). Masses of white and blue or lilac flowers are held by heel-shaped 1/2 in (12 mm) calyces during spring and summer. **ZONES 9–11.**

Salvia indica

Salvia involucrata

ROSELEAF SAGE

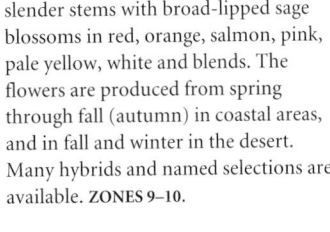

This is a charming tall perennial that remains evergreen in mild climates but even so, is best cut back to the ground every year to promote flowering. From the highlands of central Mexico, it has erect cane-like stems to about 5 ft (1.5 m) high and broad, long-stalked leaves that often develop red veining. The loose flower spikes terminate in groups of large mauve to magenta bracts, which are shed one by one to reveal a trio of developing flowers of the same or deeper color; each flower is up to 2 in (5 cm) long, tubular but swollen in the middle, and the small upper lip is covered in velvety hairs. It blooms over a long summer–fall (autumn) season, and appreciates sun and rich, well drained soil. In the UK it has mainly been known in the form of the cultivar **'Bethellii'**, a superior selection from the wild. **ZONES 9–10.**

Salvia guaranitica 'Purple Splendour'

Salvia involucrata 'Bethellii'

Salvia jurisicii

This charming though atypical sage from Macedonia and Serbia is distinguished by its unusual foliage. The leaves are bright silvery gray, lacy and fern-like, almost prostrate to the ground. The flowers are on lax 8 in (20 cm) stems, and may be either soft lavender or pure white. It is an ideal plant for the rock garden, but needs sharp, well-drained soil. **ZONES 6–10.**

Salvia leucantha

MEXICAN BUSH SAGE

This Mexican and tropical central American native is a woody subshrub grown for its seemingly endless display of downy purple and white flowers on long, arching spikes. The soft, gray-green foliage is attractive all year round. It will reach 3–4 ft (1–1.2 m) in height and spread, making it suitable for the middle of the border; it is often used as a flowering hedge in mild-winter regions. Sun, good drainage and occasional water suit this dependable sage. **ZONES 8–10.**

Salvia greggii

Salvia leucantha

Salvia microphylla var. neurepia

Salvia mellifera

CALIFORNIAN BLACK SAGE

This 3–6 ft (1–1.8 m) tall woody shrub from California has lance-shaped leaves up to 2½ in (6 cm) long, which are hairy underneath. The calyx holds white, blue or lavender flowers about ½ in (12 mm) long. **ZONES 8–11.**

Salvia mexicana

MEXICAN SAGE

This large rounded shrub can reach 12 ft (3.5 m) but is usually smaller in cultivation, around 5 ft (1.5 m) high and wide. It forms a woody base with many multi-branched stems holding pleasant bluish green, heart-shaped leaves and terminal flowerheads, ranging in color from blue to violet purple. An interesting form, **'Limelight'** has lime-green calyces that form in summer and persist well into fall (autumn), its blue-purple flowers emerging in slow succession. Grow in sun or part-shade; a light pruning is all that is necessary. **ZONES 9–11.**

Salvia microphylla

syn. *Salvia grahamii*

LITTLE LEAF SAGE, CHERRY SAGE

This small-leafed, rounded shrub bears rounded leaves and masses of scarlet flowers from late spring to early winter. ***Salvia microphylla* var. *neurepia*** has larger leaves and deeper cherry-red flowers although over a shorter period. Many different color forms are available including some excellent ***S. microphylla* × *greggii*** hybrids. **ZONES 9–11.**

Salvia muelleri
ROYAL PURPLE SAGE

This is a rare subshrub, closely allied to *Salvia greggii*, confined to a small mountain area of northeastern Mexico. It grows to about 30 in (75 cm) tall, with narrow, glossy green leaves forming a dense foliage mass, from which radiate slender spikes of rich purple 2-lipped flowers, less than 1 in (25 mm) long. Drought tolerant, it requires good drainage and full sun. **ZONES 7–10.**

Salvia multicaulis

This low-growing shrubby or mat perennial from southwestern Asia produces erect hairy stems to 18 in (45 cm) tall. The white-felted leaves are mainly basal, oval, $1\frac{1}{2}$ in (35 mm) long and wavy. The hairy calyx can be lime green or purple, the flowers violet or white and up to $\frac{3}{4}$ in (18 mm) long. It is spring and summer flowering and needs full sun in cultivation. **ZONES 8–11.**

Salvia nemorosa
syn. *Salvia virgata* var. *nemorosa*

Many slender, erect spikes of pinkish purple or white flowers bloom in summer on this neat, clump-forming perennial. Growing 3 ft (1 m) high with an 18 in (45 cm) spread, this frost-hardy species has rough leaves of narrow elliptical shape. It is widespread from Europe to central Asia. **ZONES 5–10.**

Salvia officinalis
COMMON SAGE, GARDEN SAGE

From Spain, the Balkans and North Africa, common sage is a decorative, frost-hardy, short-lived perennial that grows to 30 in (75 cm) high and wide, with downy gray-green oval leaves and short racemes of bluish mauve flowers in summer. Its culinary merits are well known, and it has entered folklore over the centuries for its real and supposed medicinal qualities. **'Purpurascens'** has

Salvia officinalis 'Icterina'

Salvia officinalis 'Purpurascens'

gray-green leaves invested with a purplish hue and pale mauve flowers; **'Tricolor'** is a garish combination of green, cream and beetroot red leaves; **'Icterina'** has gold and green leaves; and **'Berggarten'** is a lower-growing form with larger leaves and blue flowers. **ZONES 5–10.**

Salvia patens

This tuberous-rooted, erect, branching perennial from Mexico produces whorls of vivid blue flowers and oval, mid-green leaves. Pale blue and white forms are also available. It grows to 24 in (60 cm) with a spread of 18 in (45 cm). **ZONES 8–11.**

Salvia pratensis
MEADOW CLARY, MEADOW SAGE

This tough, reliable and fully frost-hardy sage from Europe and Morocco bears

Salvia greggii

Salvia multicaulis

Salvia nemorosa

Salvia prunelloides

Salvia puberula

Salvia officinalis

Salvia officinalis 'Tricolor'

oval to oblong basal leaves and shorter leaves along its 3 ft (1 m) flowering stems; the flowers are rather sparsely distributed along these stems. The commonly grown form has violet-purple flowers but in the wild it is immensely variable, from the white and pale blue **'Haematodes'** through to deeper blues and darker purples and even **'Rosea'** with rose-pink flowers, and **'Rubicunda'** with rose-red flowers. **ZONES 3–9.**

Salvia prunelloides

This low, tuberous-rooted perennial to 15 in (38 cm) is from Mexico. The few hairy branches bear oblong leaves to 3 in (8 cm) long. Each silky calyx carries a bright blue flower up to $\frac{3}{4}$ in (18 mm) long. Its flowering time of late summer into fall (autumn) makes it a desirable garden plant. **ZONES 9–11.**

Salvia puberula

This species is closely allied to *Salvia involucrata* and comes from the same highland region of Mexico. It is a perennial of much the same size and growth habit, and the long-pointed leaves are somewhat more downy. The flowers also are very similar but a deeper magenta color and the inflorescence is shorter and has smaller bud bracts. It has been grown in southern USA and makes a fine ornamental, blooming mainly in fall (autumn). **ZONES 8–10.**

Salvia pratensis

Salvia purpurea

This tall shrubby perennial from Mexico and Guatemala grows up to 10 ft (3 m) in height. The stems are smooth, as are the oval leaves which grow to 4 in (10 cm) long. Dense flowerheads carry hairy purplish calyces and 1 in (25 mm) purple or pink flowers. **ZONES 9–12.**

Salvia raemeriana

A small perennial growing to 24 in (60 cm), this species bears wavy, toothed, heart-shaped leaves up to 12 in (30 cm) long. The hairy calyx may vary from green through to purple; the $1\frac{1}{4}$ in (30 mm) flowers are finely hairy and scarlet. It flowers in summer and comes from Texas. **ZONES 8–11.**

Salvia splendens 'Salsa Burgundy'

Salvia × *sylvestris* 'Wesuwe'

Salvia × *sylvestris* 'Mainacht'

Salvia sclarea

Salvia spathacea

Salvia splendens 'Van Houttei'

Salvia regla
MOUNTAIN SAGE

This shrub to 6 ft (1.8 m) high comes from Texas and Mexico. The many smooth branches form a tight bush with smooth kidney-shaped leaves up to 2 in (5 cm) across. The flowers, which appear in fall (autumn), are rather sparse, but the large scarlet $\frac{1}{4}$–$\frac{3}{4}$ in (6–18 mm) calyces and the 2 in (5 cm) downy scarlet petals make a fine show. ZONES 9–11.

Salvia sclarea
BIENNIAL CLARY, CLARY SAGE

This native of southern Europe and Syria is a biennial and grows 3 ft (1 m) tall. Moderately fast growing and erect, it has long, loose, terminal spikes of tubular, greenish white tinged with purple flowers in summer and velvety, heart-shaped leaves. ***Salvia sclarea* var. *turkestanica*** has pink stems and white, pink-flecked flowers. ZONES 5–10.

Salvia sinaloensis
SINALOA SAGE

This perennial from Mexico grows 8–12 in (20–30 cm) tall. Its hairy stems are sometimes purplish. The elliptical leaves may be smooth or hairy, finely toothed and up to $2\frac{1}{2}$ in (6 cm) long. The small hairy calyx holds flowers up to $\frac{3}{4}$ in (18 mm) long, deep blue with white spots on the lower lip. ZONES 9–11.

Salvia × *sylvestris*

Salvia spathacea
PITCHER SAGE, HUMMINGBIRD SAGE, CRIMSON SAGE

This woody perennial with hairy stems up to 3 ft (1 m) tall has leaves which vary from oval to heart- or arrowhead-shaped with a white felt beneath. Many magenta flowers about $1\frac{1}{4}$ in (30 mm) long are held above the bush. It comes from California. ZONES 8–11.

Salvia splendens
SCARLET SAGE

This native of Brazil, which is grown as an annual, produces dense terminal spikes of scarlet flowers in summer through early fall (autumn). The leaves are toothed and elliptical. It grows 3–4 ft (1–1.2 m) tall with a similar spread. In hotter climates, give some shade; it is moderately frost hardy. **'Salsa Burgundy'** has deep burgundy flowers, while **'Van Houttei'** has a deep dull red calyx with large lighter red flowers; both prefer a little shade. ZONES 9–12.

Salvia × *superba*

This hybrid between *Salvia* × *sylvestris* and ***S. villicaulis*** is a clump-forming, erect, branched perennial that bears slender, terminal racemes of purple flowers from mid-summer to early fall (autumn). Reaching a height of 3 ft (1 m), it has lance-shaped, scalloped, mid-green leaves that are 4 in (10 cm) long and slightly hairy underneath. ZONES 5–10.

Salvia × *sylvestris*

This leafy perennial to 12–36 in (30–90 cm) high is a hybrid between *Salvia pratensis* and *S. nemorosa*. It has hairy oblong heart-shaped leaves 2–4 in (5–10 cm) long. The summer flowers are purplish violet in long-branched heads. It comes from western Asia and Europe but is naturalized in North America. There are many cultivars, some of uncertain origin. **'Blauhügel'** ('Blue Mound') is a compact grower with clear blue flowers; **'Ostfriesland'** ('East Friesland') is deep purple; **'Mainacht'** is lower

Salvia × *sylvestris* 'Ostfriesland'

S

growing with blackish purple tones; and **'Wesuwe'** is an early bloomer with dark violet flowers. **ZONES 5–10.**

Salvia taraxacifolia

This perennial from Morocco with upright stems reaching only 18 in (45 cm) has ferny leaves that are white underneath and form rosettes. The flowers, which appear from spring to summer, may be white or pale pink with a yellowish blotch on the lower lip and purple specks on the upper. Each flower attains a length of $1\frac{1}{4}$ in (30 mm). **ZONES 9–11.**

Salvia tiliifolia

This slender perennial has very erect branching stems up to 3 ft (1 m) and rounded leaves that are 1–3 in (2.5–8 cm) long and are rather rough to the touch. The flowers may be white to blue to lilac and rather small, scarcely longer than the calyces. It comes from Mexico and tropical South America. **ZONES 10–12.**

Salvia uliginosa
BOG SAGE

Long racemes of sky-blue flowers appear in summer on this upright branching perennial from South America. The leaves are toothed, elliptical to lance-shaped and up to 3 in (8 cm) long, smooth or only slightly hairy. Growing to 3–6 ft (1–1.8 m), it has slender curving stems. Although widely grown for its blue flowers, in good or moist soil it sends out underground rooting shoots and may become invasive. **ZONES 8–11.**

Salvia viridis

This is an erect annual or biennial plant with oval or oblong leaves up to 2 in (5 cm) long. The green or purple calyx bears $\frac{1}{2}$ in (12 mm) flowers which may be white to lilac to purple. It occurs around the Mediterranean and flowers in summer. There are several named color forms available. **ZONES 7–11.**

Salvia taraxacifolia

Salvia tiliifolia

Salvinia auriculata

SALVINIA

There are about 10 species of these floating annual ferns distributed widely over the tropical northern hemisphere and South America. They have no true roots, but a group of divided leaves under the water take on this function and also produce the fruiting spores. When mature the spores sink and grow just as ferns do.
CULTIVATION: Species of *Salvinia* are easily grown as floating ferns, but winter cool often kills the plant; new plants appear in warm weather from dropped spores. They prefer full sun and still water. Propagate by separating stems in spring or summer.

Salvinia auriculata

This species comes from around the Gulf of Mexico to northern Argentina. The heart-shaped leaves, to $\frac{3}{4}$ in (18 mm) long, are dark green, folded upwards, and have rows of knobs alongside longitudinal veins. They are crowded onto the slender stems. **ZONES 10–12.**

SAMBUCUS
ELDERBERRY, ELDER

This genus includes about 25 species of perennials, deciduous shrubs and softwooded trees, with representatives spread widely over the temperate regions of the world. Although most are rarely cultivated because of their tendency to be somewhat weedy and invasive, some species are useful for their edible flowers and berries and are attractive in foliage and flower. Most have pinnate leaves and in late spring and early summer bear large radiating sprays of tiny white or creamy flowers followed by clusters of usually purple-black, blue or red berries.
CULTIVATION: Usually undemanding, *Sambucus* thrive in any reasonably well-drained, fertile soil in sun or shade. Prune out old shoots and cut young shoots by half. Propagate from seed in fall (autumn) or cuttings in summer or winter.

Salvia uliginosa

Sambucus canadensis

Sambucus australasica

Sambucus australasica
YELLOW ELDERBERRY

A tall shrub up to 10 ft (3 m) in height, yellow elderberry is fern-like in appearance and is found along rivers and in moist gullies in eastern Australia, from Queensland to Victoria. Dense panicles of creamy yellow flowers are produced in spring to early summer, followed by creamy, translucent, berry-like fruit up to $\frac{1}{2}$ in (12 mm) across. **ZONES 9–11.**

Sambucus caerulea
syn. ***Sambucus mexicana***
BLUEBERRY ELDER

This small, deciduous tree from northern and western areas of North America is often seen in California. It grows 10–50 ft (3–15 m) in height; the leaves usually have 7 leaflets and the creamy yellow flowers are borne in early summer in flat-topped sprays. The edible fruit that follow are black but covered with a powdery bloom that makes them look blue. This species is grown commercially for its tasty berries, which should be cooked before they are eaten. **ZONES 4–9.**

Sambucus callicarpa
PACIFIC COAST RED ELDERBERRY

This large shrub from western USA grows 10 ft (3 m) tall and has leaves with 5 to 7 serrated leaflets, each 2–4 in (5–10 cm) long with a hairy midrib and at first felted underneath. The flowers are creamy white in heads up to 4 in (10 cm) across, appearing in summer before the showy scarlet fruit of fall (autumn). **ZONES 6–10.**

Sambucus canadensis 'York'

Sambucus canadensis
AMERICAN ELDER, SWEET ELDER

An upright, deciduous shrub from cold-climate regions in the northeast of North America, this fast-growing species reaches about 10 ft (3 m) tall with a similar spread and has soft pithy stems. The compound leaves have 5 to 11 leaflets and the tiny, white, starry flowers appear in spring, borne in large sprays about 8 in (20 cm) across; they are followed by purple-black berries. **'Aurea'** features golden-yellow foliage and red berries. **'York'** was raised in New York State in 1964 and is considered among the best cultivars; it is a large bush with large fruit and requires cross-pollination by another cultivar to produce its best crops. **ZONES 2–10.**

Sambucus ebulus
DWARF ELDER, DANE'S ELDER, DANEWORT, WALLWORT

From Europe, North Africa, Turkey and Iran, this is an herbaceous perennial growing up to 5 ft (1.5 m) high with strong creeping underground stems. The leaflets, usually 9 to 13, are elliptic, toothed and slightly hairy. It produces flat heads up to 4 in (10 cm) across of white-tinged pink flowers in summer, followed by black fruit. It is considered too invasive for a small garden. **ZONES 5–10.**

Sambucus javanica subsp. *chinensis*

This open shrub from Japan, Taiwan and Southeast Asia has erect branches to 8 ft (2.4 m) and bears 2 to 6 paired, lance-shaped leaflets up to 8 in (20 cm) long. Flat heads of creamy white flowers are followed by black fruit. **ZONES 5–11.**

Sambucus nigra
EUROPEAN ELDER, BLACK ELDER, COMMON ELDER

This species, sometimes regarded as a weed, is cultivated for its large, spring-borne sprays of tiny white flowers and the clusters of purple-black berries that follow. Originally from Europe, northern Africa and western Asia, it is a deciduous shrub or small tree to 20 ft (6 m) high with pinnate leaves made up of 5 to 9 deep green, serrated leaflets. The berries are used in pies, the flowers and fruit to make wine or liqueurs. **'Aurea'** has creamy white, star-shaped, fragrant flowers and yellow leaves; **'Laciniata'** has irregularly, finely cut leaves. **ZONES 4–10.**

Sambucus racemosa
EUROPEAN RED ELDER, RED ELDERBERRY

This shrub or small tree usually grows to 10 ft (3 m) although it may become taller under good conditions. The trunk becomes corky with age. The 5 oval or elliptic leaflets are 2–4 in (5–10 cm) long and sharply toothed. The cream flowers form flat heads up to 8 in (20 cm) in diameter in summer. The scarlet fruit are not often produced in cultivation. **'Plumosa Aurea'** has deeply divided golden leaves and yellowish flowers; and **'Tenuifolia'** slowly forms a low arching mound of fern-like foliage. **ZONES 4–9.**

SANCHEZIA

Native to Central and South America, *Sanchezia* is a genus of some 20 species of large, frost-tender, bushy perennials, shrubs and scrambling climbers. They bear spikes of tubular, showy, yellow, orange, red or purple flowers, each with 5 lobes and often colored bracts, and have opposite pairs of simple leaves.
CULTIVATION: Plant in full sun in fertile, well-drained soil. Tip prune young plants to encourage a branching habit. Propagate from cuttings in spring or summer. Watch for attack by scale insects.

Sanchezia speciosa
syn. *Sanchezia nobilis*

This species has multicolored flowers with yellow petals, bright red bracts and purple stems in summer. An erect, evergreen shrub, it has glossy leaves with white or yellow veins. **ZONES 10–12.**

Sambucus javanica subsp. *chinensis*

Sandersonia aurantiaca

Sanchezia speciosa

Sanguisorba canadensis

SANDERSONIA
CHRISTMAS BELLS, GOLDEN LILY OF THE VALLEY, CHINESE LANTERN LILY

The single species in this South African genus is now rare in the wild but is widely cultivated for the cut flower trade and in gardens. Growing from brittle tubers, the stem carries both the yellow to orange, lantern-shaped flowers and the emerald-green leaves.
CULTIVATION: This frost-tender plant is summer-flowering and winter dormant and should be kept moist and well fed during its growing phase and fairly dry during dormancy. It makes a half-hearted attempt at climbing and needs some form of enclosing support (twigs or a wire circular frame will serve the purpose) if it is to display well. Propagate from seed or by division.

Sandersonia aurantiaca

This beautiful perennial climber which blooms in mid-summer, has climbing stems that grow to around 30 in (75 cm). The ribbed leaves sometimes have tendrils at their tips, which cling to supports. The nodding, $1\frac{1}{2}$ in (35 mm), yellow to orange flowers are borne at the leaf axils, and have a delicate Chinese lantern or chef's hat shape. **ZONES 8–11.**

SANGUINARIA
BLOODROOT, RED PUCCOON

The single species of the genus is a widespread woodland plant from eastern USA, from Nova Scotia through to Florida. It is a low-growing perennial herb grown for its spring display of cup-shaped flowers.
CULTIVATION: It prefers sandy soil but will tolerate clay soil if not too wet. It does well in sun or part-shade, and especially under deciduous trees. Propagation is by division in late summer when the leaves have died back.

Sanguinaria canadensis

Sambucus nigra

Sambucus nigra 'Aurea'

Sanguinaria canadensis

This perennial has a long stout horizontal rootstock. Each bud on the stock sends up a heart-shaped leaf with scalloped edges on stalks 6 in (15 cm) long. Each leaf is up to 12 in (30 cm) across. The solitary white or pink-tinged flowers are up to 3 in (8 cm) across, single, with 8 to 12 petals and many yellow central anthers. They appear in the folds of the leaves in spring before the gray leaves fully expand, and last for about 3 weeks. ***Sanguinaria canadensis* var. *grandiflora*** has larger flowers; the double form **'Flore Pleno'** has more but narrower petals. **ZONES 3–9.**

SANGUISORBA
syn. *Poterium*
BURNET

This is a genus of about 18 species found over the northern temperate zones. They may be rhizomatous perennials or small shrubs, and all have coarsely ferny leaves. The flowerheads resemble small bottlebrushes, and often only the lower half of the bottlebrush has male and female parts to the flowers.
CULTIVATION: They prefer full sun or part-shade and moderately fertile, moist but well-drained soil that should not be allowed to dry out in summer. Propagate from seed or by division.

Sanguisorba canadensis
CANADIAN BURNET

A native of eastern North America, this vigorous perennial loves full sun and moist soil. The handsome, pinnate leaves form a clump around 18 in (45 cm) wide, above which are borne masses of white flowers in late summer. It grows to 6 ft (1.8 m) in height. **ZONES 4–9.**

Sanguisorba minor
syn. *Poterium sanguisorba*
GARDEN BURNET, SALAD BURNET

This perennial to 24 in (60 cm) has 6 to 10 rounded toothed leaflets on each leafstalk. The flowers occur in terminal oblong heads to 1 in (25 mm). They are white, the upper ones female, the lower ones male, with the middle section comprised of both. It occurs across Europe, western Asia and North Africa in dry rocky areas, often on limestone. It is often seen in herb gardens where fresh leaves are picked for soups and salads. It has a taste rather like cucumber and is excellent in cold drinks. **ZONES 5–9.**

Sanguisorba officinalis
GREATER BURNET, BURNET BLOODWORT

The creeping rhizomes of this perennial carry erect stems, sometimes reddish, up to 4 ft (1.2 m) tall. The basal leaves are large with many leaflets up to 2 in (5 cm) long. The ¾ in (18 mm) long, dark reddish purple flowers appear in summer and fall (autumn). It comes from China, Japan, North America and western Europe. **ZONES 4–9.**

SANSEVIERIA
BOWSTRING HEMP, SNAKE PLANT

Native to India, Indonesia and Africa, these 60 species of popular and resilient evergreen perennials are grown for their stiff, fleshy, patterned 12–24 in (30–60 cm) tall leaves. Stems of greenish white, slightly fragrant flowers appear in late spring in warm conditions. In Africa the fibers are used to make hemp.

Santolina c. 'Lemon Queen'

Sansevieria pearsonii

CULTIVATION: Species of *Sensevieria* will tolerate sun or shade and most soil types; over-watering may cause rotting at the leaf bases and at the roots. They are frost tender and need a minimum temperature of 50–60°F (10–15°C). Propagate from leaf cuttings or by division in spring or summer.

Sansevieria pearsonii

The central fan of this species from tropical Africa produces 3 to 5 leaves up to 3 ft (1 m) tall. They are dark mottled green, thinly cylindrical, and taper to a white tip. The flowers have a wattle-like scent. **ZONES 10–12.**

Sansevieria trifasciata
MOTHER-IN-LAW'S TONGUE

From the central rosette of this Nigerian species emerge stiff, lance-shaped leaves 2–4 ft (0.6–1.2 m) long and 2 in (5 cm) or more wide. The dark green leaves are banded with gray-green and yellow. The plant sometimes has racemes of tubular, green flowers but rarely when grown indoors. **'Golden Hahnii'** has broad leaves with golden-yellow vertical stripes; **'Hahnii'** has erect, pointed leaves banded with pale green or white; and **'Laurentii'** has narrow, upright leaves with broad yellow margins. **ZONES 10–12.**

SANTALUM
SANDALWOOD

From low-rainfall areas of Southeast Asia, Australia and the Pacific, these 9 species of evergreen trees and shrubs are semi-parasitic, relying on the roots of other plants to supply their nutrients. Because of this they are considered difficult to cultivate, but research continues as some species bear edible fruits suitable for growing in warm, arid areas. The traditional sandalwood, from which small precious objects are made and fragrant oil is distilled, is *Santalum album*.

Santolina chamaecyparissus

Santalum acuminatum

Sanguisorba minor

Sansevieria trifasciata 'Laurentii'

CULTIVATION: Grow in moist, well-drained soil in sun or part-shade; protect from midday sun in summer and water regularly. Propagate from seed.

Santalum acuminatum
SWEET QUANDONG

This small tree from dry inland regions of Australia grows 10–20 ft (3–6 m) tall with pendulous, leathery, gray-green leaves and small, greenish white, 4-petalled flowers in spring and summer. Bright red succulent fruit resembling small plums are borne after about 4 years and are used for making jam; the kernels within the nut are also edible, being oily and nutritious. **ZONES 9–11.**

Santalum album
INDIAN SANDALWOOD, WHITE SANDALWOOD

The fragrant wood of this small tree to 15 ft (4.5 m) yields sandal oil. The leaves are elliptical, about 1½–2½ in (3.5–6 cm) long, rather dryish in texture and paler underneath. Panicles of reddish flowers are followed by black cherry-sized fruit. Probably from Malaysia, this species is widely cultivated in tropical Asia. The white or yellow wood is widely used for wooden jewellery and boxes. **ZONES 10–12.**

SANTOLINA

Small, aromatic, frost-hardy evergreens from the Mediterranean region, the 18 shrub species in this genus are grown for their scented, usually silvery gray foliage and dainty, button-like yellow flowerheads. They are useful for covering banks and as a ground cover.
CULTIVATION: They require well-drained soil and a sunny situation. Cut back old wood to encourage new growth from the base immediately after flowering, and remove dead flowerheads and stems in fall (autumn). Propagate from cuttings in summer.

Santolina chamaecyparissus
COTTON LAVENDER, LAVENDER COTTON

This low-spreading, aromatic shrub, native to mild, coastal areas of the Mediterranean, grows to a height of 18 in (45 cm) and spread of 3 ft (1 m). It bears bright yellow, rounded flowerheads on long stalks in summer, set among oblong, grayish green leaves divided into tiny segments. **'Lemon Queen'** is a compact form—to 24 in (60 cm)—with lemon-yellow flowerheads. **ZONES 7–10.**

Santolina rosmarinifolia

Santolina pinnata subsp. *neapolitana*

Santolina pinnata

Divided green leaves clothe this 18–30 in (45–75 cm) tall shrub from Italy. Heads of ivory-white flowers occur in summer. ***Santolina pinnata* subsp. *neapolitana*** is not quite as tall, and has gray-green foliage and yellow flowers; ***S. p.* subsp. *neapolitana* 'Sulphurea'** has beautiful pale yellow blooms. **ZONES 7–10.**

Santolina rosmarinifolia

syn. *Santolina virens*

HOLY FLAX

Native to Spain, Portugal and southern France, this species has green, thread-like, 1½ in (35 mm) long leaves and bears heads of bright yellow flowers in mid-summer. It has a dense bushy habit, reaching a height of 24 in (60 cm) with a spread of 3 ft (1 m). **'Morning Mist'** has golden-yellow flowers; **'Primrose Gem'** has paler yellow flowers. **ZONES 7–10.**

SANVITALIA

CREEPING ZINNIA

From southwestern USA and Mexico come these 7 species of annuals or short-lived perennials of the daisy family. The ovate leaves come in pairs and the small white or yellow flowers have a dark purplish black or white center. They make good ground covers, rock-garden plants and hanging basket specimens.
CULTIVATION: Plants do best in full sun in humus-rich, well-drained soil. They are grown as annuals, sown *in situ* or in small pots for replanting with minimal root disturbance. Propagate from seed.

Sanvitalia procumbens

A native of Mexico, this summer-flowering, fully frost-hardy annual

Sapium sebiferum

Santolina rosmarinifolia 'Morning Mist'

produces masses of bright yellow flowerheads like 1 in (25 mm) daisies with blackish centers. It is a prostrate species with mid-green, ovate leaves, growing to 8 in (20 cm) high and spreading at least 15 in (38 cm). **ZONES 7–11.**

SAPINDUS

This genus contains about 13 species of evergreen and deciduous trees, shrubs and climbers, very few of which feature in gardens. Originating in tropical, subtropical and warm-temperate regions worldwide, they are grown as ornamental and shade specimens as well as for their inedible berry-like fruits, which are fleshy and leathery. The fruits contain a substance called saponin, which lathers in water and therefore allows the berries to be used as a soap substitute in their native lands. The leaves are pinnate and the small, 5-petalled summer flowers are in shades of white, yellow or orange with prominent hairy stamens.
CULTIVATION: They prefer full sun and are not fussy about soil as long as it is well-drained. Propagate from seed or cuttings.

Sapindus drummondii

WESTERN SOAPBERRY, WILD CHINA TREE

Indigenous to arid regions of southern USA and Mexico, this deciduous tree reaches a height of 50 ft (15 m). It forms a spreading canopy with pinnate leaves composed of up to 18 leaflets, each 3 in (8 cm) long. The yellowish white summer flowers are held in clusters at the ends of the branches; they are followed by small yellow fruit that ripen to black. This species is tolerant of both cold and drought. **ZONES 8–10.**

Sanvitalia procumbens

SAPIUM

This is a genus of about 100 species of evergreen or semi-deciduous trees and shrubs found naturally in warm-climate areas from eastern Asia to tropical America. Like other members of the euphorbia family, they have a milky sap that is poisonous to humans and animals which congeals on drying; some of the South American species have been tapped for rubber. The leaves are arranged alternately along the stems. The flowers are in spikes but are insignificant, while the fruits are hard-shelled capsules.
CULTIVATION: These plants thrive in full sun in well-drained soil enriched with organic matter. Propagate from freshly collected seed in spring or cuttings in summer. Superior forms of *Sapium sebiferum* are sometimes grafted onto seedling rootstocks.

Sapium sebiferum

CHINESE TALLOW TREE, VEGETABLE TALLOW

From warm-climate areas of China and Japan and the only species commonly seen in cultivation, this fast-growing tree reaches 20–40 ft (6–12 m) with a spreading crown. It is semi-deciduous in hot climates, deciduous where winters are cooler. The bright green leaves, heart-shaped to oval with a pointed tip, color attractively to shades of yellow, orange, red and purple in fall (autumn), even in a frost-free climate. In late spring spikes of tiny greenish yellow flowers are borne at the branch tips. The fall fruit contain 3 seeds that are covered with white wax. **ZONES 8–11.**

SAPONARIA

SOAPWORT

The common name of this genus consisting of 20 species of annuals and perennials comes from the old custom of using the roots for washing clothes. They contain a glucoside called saponin, which is just as good as any detergent for dissolving grease and dirt and which, being edible, has been used as an additive to beer to ensure that it develops a good head when poured. These are good plants for rock gardens, banks and for trailing over walls.
CULTIVATION: Fully frost-hardy, they need sun and well-drained soil. Propagate from seed in spring or fall (autumn) or from cuttings in early summer.

Saponaria ocymoides

Saponaria 'Bressingham'

This perennial forms a loose mat of small oval leaves 3 in (8 cm) high and 4 in (10 cm) wide. The flowers occur in heads above the plant throughout summer, and are a strong deep pink. **ZONES 5–10.**

Saponaria ocymoides

ROCK SOAPWORT

This alpine perennial from Europe forms a thick carpet from which profuse terminal clusters of small, flattish flowers, colored pink to deep red, bloom in late spring and early summer. It has sprawling mats of hairy oval leaves. **ZONES 4–10.**

Saponaria officinalis

BOUNCING BET, SOAPWORT

While this species' pink flowers on their 24 in (60 cm) tall stems are not in the first rank of beauty, they make a pretty show in their summer season and the plant grows almost anywhere; it is a very nice old-fashioned flower for a cottage garden. It has oval, smooth, mid-green leaves. Keep an eye on adjacent plants, as it spreads rapidly. **ZONES 5–10.**

Saponaria × *olivana*

This soapwort forms a tight compact cushion to 3 in (8 cm) and bears profuse pale pink blooms in summer. It needs very good drainage. **ZONES 5–10.**

Saponaria officinalis

Saponaria × *olivana*

Sarcococca ruscifolia

Sarcobatus vermiculatus

SARACA

This leguminous genus consists of 71 species of small evergreen trees from tropical Southeast Asia; they occur naturally as understory trees in forests and are grown for their dense clusters of showy flowers and attractive foliage. The leaves are pinnate with paired leaflets; the new foliage is often soft and bronze red, maturing to mid-green. The flowers have no true petals but a very colorful tubular calyx opening into 4 to 5 flat sepals and long, prominent stamens, and are borne in clusters on older branches, followed by narrow oblong pods.
CULTIVATION: Species of *Saraca* need a hot, humid climate, rich, moist, well-drained soil and some shade. In cooler climates they can be grown in greenhouses. Propagate from seed in fall (autumn) or winter.

Saraca indica
ASOKA, SORROWLESS TREE

The best known species of the genus, this erect evergreen tree occurs naturally from India to the Malay Peninsula. It can grow to 30 ft (9 m) and has long, shiny, compound leaves with 3 to 6 pairs of leaflets that are soft and reddish when young. The flowers, held in dense clusters, appear mainly in summer, though a few can be seen almost all year. They are yellow-orange to scarlet with long, showy, dark red stamens, and the pods that follow are deep reddish purple. **ZONES 11–12.**

SARCOBATUS
GREASEWOOD

The single species in this genus of the rose family from western North America is a rounded, spreading shrub with spines at the ends of the branches and fleshy leaves. The male flowers occur in a dense spike, the female flowers towards the ends of the branches where the enlarging calyx grows into a papery disc about $\frac{1}{3}$ in (8 mm) across.
CULTIVATION: Plants are easily grown in full sun in most soil as long as it is well-drained. Propagation is from seed.

Sarcobatus vermiculatus

This species forms a dense bush to 6 ft (1.8 m) high with a wider spread. Arching branches have whitish new shoots bearing thin gray leaves up to $1\frac{1}{2}$ in (35 mm) long. The enlarging papery discs of the female calyces are in rows about 1 in (25 mm) long on the ends of the branches. **ZONES 5–10.**

SARCOCOCCA
SWEET BOX, CHRISTMAS BOX

This is a genus of 11 species of wiry stemmed, evergreen shrubs from India, China and Southeast Asia with glossy, deep green, elliptical leaves. They produce small white to pink flowers that are not very showy but are sweetly scented. The flowers are followed by conspicuous berries.
CULTIVATION: While often grown in difficult, dry, shady areas, sweet boxes look better with a little care and attention. They prefer a relatively cool, moist climate with well-drained soil. Propagate from seed in fall (autumn), from cuttings in summer or by layers. They are largely trouble free.

Sarcococca confusa

Sarcococca confusa

This dense species with multiple basal green branches slowly grows 6 ft (1.8 m) tall and bears smooth shiny dark green leaves $1\frac{1}{2}$–2 in (3.5–5 cm) long. The small white flowers occur in clusters along the stems during late fall (autumn) and winter. Shiny black berries follow. The origin of this species remains unknown; it could be from China but it has not been found in the wild. It may be a natural hybrid. **ZONES 5–10.**

Sarcococca hookeriana

Indigenous to the Himalayan region, this rhizomatous species develops into a dense clump of upright, somewhat arching stems. Its cream flowers, borne in winter, have reddish pink anthers. The berries are black. ***Sarcococca hookeriana* var. *digyna*** has male flowers with cream anthers and slender leaves. ***S. h.* var. *humilis*** (syn. *S. humilis*) is a low, spreading, evergreen shrub superb for deep shade and with tiny white flowers with a honey-like fragrance. **ZONES 8–10.**

Sarcococca ruscifolia

The most commonly grown, this species is native to central China. It has an upright, arching habit, reaching a height and spread of 3 ft (1 m). The milky white flowers appear in winter, and are followed by brilliant, scarlet berries. The leaves are oval, deep lustrous green above and paler beneath. ***Sarcococca ruscifolia* var. *chinensis*** has lance-shaped to ovate leaves. **ZONES 8–10.**

SARMIENTA

The single species in this genus from southern Chile is a wiry stemmed, evergreen creeper or climber with smooth paired fleshy leaves. The flowers appear from the leaf axils on stalks; they are tubular with a central ballooning before narrowing again at the mouth with 5 small spreading lobes.

Sarcococca hookeriana

Sarcococca hookeriana var. ***humilis***

Saraca indica

CULTIVATION: This plant needs well-drained, peaty soil in a protected shady place and abundant water. Propagate from seed in spring or cuttings in late summer.

Sarmienta scandens
syn. *Sarmienta repens*

Smooth obovate to elliptic leaves 1 in (25 mm) long are toothed at the tip on this wiry clambering perennial. The numerous flowers on long fine stalks are bright scarlet and about $\frac{3}{4}$ in (18 mm) long. **ZONES 5–9.**

SARRACENIA
PITCHER PLANT

The *Sarracenia* genus consists of about 8 insectivorous evergreen or perennial species from the eastern part of North America; although they cover a wide area, they prefer to grow in peat bogs or in the sodden ground at the edges of pools. All the species have curious, many-petalled flowers whose styles develop into a sort of umbrella that shelters the stamens. The flowers are usually purple-red or greenish yellow or a blend of these colors, and the same tints are found in the modified leaves, called pitchers, which are nearly as decorative as the flowers. Insects are attracted to the foliage colors and slide down the slippery sides, drowning in the rainwater that accumulates at the bottom.
CULTIVATION: These moderately to fully frost-hardy plants need sun or part-shade and moist, peaty soil. Keep very wet during the growth period, and cool and moist in winter. Propagate from seed or by division in spring.

Sarracenia leucophylla

Sassafras albidum

Sarracenia alata

Sarracenia alata
YELLOW TRUMPETS

This species from southern USA produces erect, trumpet-like, yellowish green pitchers up to 30 in (75 cm) tall. The upper part of the trumpet and the adjacent part of its lid are often a dull red color. The nodding spring flowers are greenish yellow and up to 2$\frac{1}{2}$ in (6 cm) across. **ZONES 8–11.**

Sarracenia flava
YELLOW PITCHER PLANT, HUNTSMAN'S HORNS, WATCHES

This species has cylindrical, yellowish green pitchers up to 4 ft (1.2 m) long, marked in crimson and with a hooded top. The pitchers secrete nectar that, together with the bright colors of the plant, attract insects which become trapped and are absorbed into the plant. Strongly scented yellow or greenish yellow flowers are borne on long stems in late spring to summer. **ZONES 7–11.**

Sarmienta scandens

Sarracenia leucophylla
syn. *Sarracenia drummondii*

This semi-evergreen perennial bears purple flowers in spring and has erect, slender pitchers up to 4 ft (1.2 m) long with narrow wings and erect lids with wavy margins. These are usually white and have light purple-red netting, gradually merging into green bases. **ZONES 7–11.**

Sarracenia × *mitchelliana*

This hybrid between *Sarracenia leucophylla* and *S. purpurea* produces erect or sprawling pitchers up to 18 in (45 cm) tall. They are open funnels, olive green at the base grading to dark red at the top. The lip is very wavy and stands erect. The spring flowers are large and dark red. **ZONES 7–10.**

Sarracenia purpurea
COMMON PITCHER PLANT, HUNTSMAN'S CUP, INDIAN CUP, SWEET PITCHER PLANT

This species is widespread in eastern North America, from New Jersey to the Arctic. It grows to 6 in (15 cm) in height. The pitchers are slender at the basal rosette, rapidly becoming swollen higher up. They are usually green with purple tints and the lid stands erect. The flowers appear in spring; they are purple or greenish purple and up to 2$\frac{1}{2}$ in (6 cm) wide. It has become naturalized in Europe, particularly Ireland. **ZONES 6–10.**

SASA

This genus of 40 to 50 species of small to medium, rhizomatous, woody bamboos closely is related to *Sasaella*. Native to eastern Asia, they have smooth, cylindrical canes with a waxy white bloom beneath the nodes. A variegated effect is achieved in winter when the large, toothed leaves wither at their edges.
CULTIVATION: Grow these fully frost-hardy plants in fertile, moist, well-drained soil in full sun or shade. They may need to be planted in containers to restrict growth. Propagate from seed in fall (autumn) or by division in spring.

Sasa palmata
syn. *Arundinaria palmata*

This spreading, evergreen bamboo from Japan grows to a height of 6 ft (1.8 m) with an indefinite spread. Its flowers are insignificant but the wide, rich green leaves make it an excellent foliage plant, adding grace and contrast to borders and rock gardens. Its hollow stems are streaked with purple and bear one branch at each node. **ZONES 7–11.**

Sasa veitchii

Sasa veitchii
syns *Arundinaria veitchii, Sasa albomarginata*
KUMA SASA

This species from Japan grows to a height of 6 ft (1.8 m) and spreads indefinitely. Its 10 in (25 cm) long leaves turn white at the edges. Its stems, which branch from each node, are generally purple with a whitish powder beneath the node. **ZONES 8–11.**

SASAELLA

Closely allied to the genus *Sasa, Sasaella* includes 12 species of bamboo, all from Japan. The stems are erect, not arching, and there is a swelling at each node or joint. The plants have very vigorous systems of underground rhizomes and are excellent choices for preventing soil erosion on steep banks.
CULTIVATION: Grow in friable, fertile soil containing rooted organic matter. In humid, frequently rainy climates or where summers are mild they can be planted in full sun but, as the thin leaves easily dry out, dappled shade or part-shade is recommended in warmer areas. They need plenty of water and are generally quite frost hardy. Propagate by division.

Sasaella masumuneana
syn. *Arundinaria purpurea*
SHIYA SASA

The Shiya sasa grows over 6 ft (1.8 m) tall, usually in part-shade at the edge of forests. The leaves are moderately large: 8 in (20 cm) long and 2 in (5 cm) wide. The culms (stems) are slender, erect and an attractive reddish shade. **ZONES 7–10.**

SASSAFRAS

This small genus of the laurel family contains 3 species of tall deciduous trees from China, North America and Taiwan. All parts of the trees have a spicy aroma that repels insects, and the wood has been used to make insect-proof cabinets and furniture. The alternate leaves of the trees can be entire or lobed and it is not unusual to see both on the same plant. The unisexual or bisexual flowers have no petals; usually greenish yellow, they

are borne in clusters and appear with the leaves in spring. The inedible fruits are oval-shaped, blue-black drupes.
CULTIVATION: Plant in deep, fertile, well-drained, acid soil in full sun or light shade. Propagate from seed or suckers in fall (autumn) or from root cuttings in winter.

Sassafras albidum
COMMON SASSAFRAS

This handsome tree occurs naturally in forests on the east coast of North America; it grows to 70 ft (21 m). The leaves are up to 4 in (10 cm) long, sometimes lobed, glossy dark green above and paler beneath; the foliage turns spectacular orange and scarlet shades in fall (autumn). The spring flowers are small, greenish yellow and insignificant, and the fruit are blue-black. The inner bark yields the aromatic oil of sassafras, which was once used medicinally, as a food flavoring and in cosmetics but is now known to be poisonous. **ZONES 5–10.**

SATUREJA
SAVORY

This genus consists of 30 species of annuals, semi-evergreen perennials and subshrubs that make useful additions to rock gardens or dry banks. Native to the northern hemisphere, they were much loved by the Ancient Greeks and Romans for their refreshing flavor. They have aromatic leaves and tubular, stalkless, 2-lipped flowers that appear in summer and which attract insects, especially bees. Savory has many culinary uses.
CULTIVATION: These moderately to fully frost-hardy plants prefer full sun and well-drained soil. Propagate from seed in winter or spring or from cuttings in summer.

Satureja douglasii
syn. *Micromeria chamissonis*
YERBA BUENA

Found from California to British Columbia, this slender-stemmed perennial has stems that root as they spread. It mounds to around 12 in (30 cm) high and 3 ft (1 m) wide and has mint-scented, rounded, 1 in (25 mm) long leaves with finely scalloped edges. Small white or lavender pink-tinged flowers open from spring to fall (autumn). The dried leaves are used to make a herbal tea. The city of San Francisco was originally named Yerba Buena after this plant. **ZONES 6–10.**

Satureja hortensis
SUMMER SAVORY

This bushy annual grows 15 in (38 cm) high and has narrow, dark green leaves and pale lavender flowers in late summer. The leaves have a sweet, spicy taste with a hint of thyme and are traditionally used to flavor bean dishes. They are also used to flavor vinegar, salad dressings and butter. **ZONES 8–11.**

Satureja montana
WINTER SAVORY

A spreading subshrub that grows to 18 in (45 cm), winter savory has dark green, pointed leaves and tiny white flowers with pink markings in summer. It may need winter protection in cold climates and benefits from regular pruning to stimulate fresh growth and prevent legginess. It makes a good edging or border and is often grown to attract bees. The leaves, sharper and more peppery than those of summer savory, are used to flavor meat casseroles and roasts. **ZONES 6–10.**

SAUROMATUM

This genus consists of 2 species of tuberous perennials; they come from the Himalayas and Africa. The solitary leaf arises from a tightly enfolded shiny bud after flowering. Male and female flowers are separated by a long sterile area on the spathe.
CULTIVATION: These frost-tender plants prefer part-shade and humus-rich, fertile, well-drained soil. Propagate by removing offsets in winter when the plants are dormant.

Sauromatum venosum
syn. *Sauromatum guttatum*
VOODOO LILY

This curious bulb from the Himalayas resembles *Dracunculus* in its bold, tropical foliage and strange, yellow, arum-like flower; the purple-spotted, 12 in (30 cm) tall flower releases a foul odor for a short time after opening. The foliage, which consists of a single, rounded leaf 15 in (38 cm) long, appears after the flower. This species reaches 18 in (45 cm) in height and is usually grown in a pot. **ZONES 10–11.**

SAUSSUREA

This genus consists of 300 species of perennials from Europe, Asia and North America. Most are not particularly ornamental, but some species from the high Himalayas have adapted to the harsh conditions by covering themselves with downy hairs. The leaves are simple and alternate, and the flowerheads appear in rosettes but usually die down as the seeds are released.
CULTIVATION: They do best in full sun in humus-rich, moist but very well-drained soil in areas with cool, moist summers. Water well during growth, but protect them from winter wet. Propagate from seed or by division.

Saussurea stella

This plant is from damp grassland and bog tussocks up to 13,000 ft (4,000 m) in the Himalayas. It is a flat rosette of dark green, 8 in (20 cm) long leaves with purple flowers in the center. **ZONES 7–9.**

Satureja montana

SAXEGOTHAEA
PRINCE ALBERT'S YEW

This genus comprises a single species of conifer with yew-like foliage indigenous to cool, moist climates of southern Chile and Argentina. The timber is used in its native countries for general carpentry as it is easy to work. It is of great botanical interest, forming as it does a link between the yews, the podocarps and the pine family. Most botanists place it in the yew family, *Taxaceae.*
CULTIVATION: This fully frost-hardy species prefers full sun or part-shade and moderately fertile, well-drained soil. Propagate from cuttings.

Saxegothaea conspicua

This slow-growing, evergreen conifer can grow to over 70 ft (21 m) tall. In warm-temperate areas it forms a neat conical shape, but it tends to be more columnar and bushy in cooler regions. The needle-like, dark green leaves are about ½ in (12 mm) long and spirally arranged; the young foliage is somewhat pendulous. The cones differ from those of other conifers in being fleshy, spine tipped and powdery blue. **ZONES 8–10.**

SAXIFRAGA
SAXIFRAGE

Both the foliage and blooms on these perennials, biennials and annuals are equally appealing. The genus comprises some 440 species of evergreens and semi-evergreens. Their natural territory includes temperate, alpine and subarctic regions, mostly in the northern hemisphere, but many garden hybrids have been cultivated; they serve well in rock gardens and as ground cover. The flowers are mostly white, sometimes spotted with pink, but other colors are also available. The genus name combines two Latin terms, 'rock' and 'to break', suggestive of either the hardiness of their rooting system or their reputed medicinal effect on bladder stones.
CULTIVATION: Soil and light requirements vary greatly depending on the species; they also vary from being very frost hardy to marginally frost hardy. Propagate from seed in fall (autumn), by division or from rooted offsets in winter.

Saxifraga × *anglica* 'Cranbourne'

This is a mat-forming, frost-hardy perennial with rosettes of dark green leaves and deep violet-purple flowers ¼ in (6 mm) across on short 2 in (5 cm) stems; they appear in spring. This hybrid would seem to have been successful many times, resulting in a large number of named cultivars ranging from the softest pink, to deep carmine through to the deepest of purples. Grow in full sun. **ZONES 6–9.**

Saussurea stella

Saxegothaea conspicua

S

Saxifraga × *apiculata*

This perennial is a hybrid between ***Saxifraga marginata*** and ***S. sancta***. It forms tight rosettes to 4 in (10 cm) high with small lance-shaped leaves and small yellow flowers of 10 to 12 per head. **'Alba'** has white flowers. **'Gregor Mendel'** has soft lemon flowers. Other hybrids are known and all, to various degrees, have a white encrustation to the leaves. They need some protection from heat and are intolerant of drying out. **ZONES 6–9.**

Saxifraga 'Apple Blossom'

The parentage of this plant is unknown. It forms a rounded clump up to 3 in (8 cm) tall and spreads to 24 in (60 cm). The toothed oval green leaves make a dense wall, while the ½ in (12 mm) pale pink flowerbuds, opening to white, are held above the foliage; they appear from spring to early summer. **ZONES 7–9.**

Saxifraga 'Apple Blossom'

Saxifraga bronchialis

This plant forms a tuft to 8 in (20 cm) tall, with stiff linear leaves to ½ in (12 mm) long. The flowers are cream, spotted with red. It comes from North America and Asia. ***Saxifraga bronchialis* subsp. *vespertina*** is found in China, Mongolia and Siberia and bears greenish white flowers spotted with reddish pink. **ZONES 4–9.**

Saxifraga burseriana

BURSER'S SAXIFRAGE

This is a slow-growing evergreen perennial from the eastern Alps that is woody at its base and forms a series of dense conical cushions rather than rosettes with grayish green to silver leaves. The crimson flowers are solitary on 2 in (5 cm) tall stems. Plant in full sun in moderately fertile, well-drained soil. **'Gloria'** is made distinctive by brilliant red flower stems and larger white flowers with deep yellow centers. **ZONES 6–9.**

Saxifraga callosa

LIMESTONE SAXIFRAGE

This species from northeastern Spain and the southwestern Alps has rosettes of long narrow leaves, with the flowering stems appearing from shorter leafed offsets. Each flowering stem grows up to 8 in (20 cm) long, with a cone-shaped panicle of small white flowers occupying half its length. The leaves are lime secreting, forming a downy encrustation. **ZONES 6–9.**

Saxifraga cochlearis 'Minor'

This is a small hummock-forming plant whose leaves are so lime encrusted, even in lime-free soils, as to be totally silvery white. The 4–6 in (10–15 cm) long stem carries 10 to 15 small white flowers. It is a valuable plant for rock crevices. **ZONES 6–9.**

Saxifraga bronchialis subsp. *vespertina*

Saxifraga exarata subsp. *moschata*

Saxifraga longifolia

Saxifraga exarata subsp. *moschata*

syn. *Saxifraga moschata*

This is a delightful downy-leafed cushion-forming plant from central and southern Europe with many round-petalled flowers on 4 in (10 cm) stems. The colors range from white or creamy yellow to pink through to strong carmine pink or red. The tricky combination of full sun and moist soil with perfect drainage in winter will keep it robust and healthy. **ZONES 6–9.**

Saxifraga federici-augusti subsp. *grisebachii*

This species has spoon-shaped, silver-gray leaves and crimson to cherry-red flowers that appear on arching red stems. From the Balkan Peninsula, it reaches 4 in (10 cm) in height. Grow in full sun in well-drained, alkaline soil. **'Wisley Variety'** bears dense racemes of dark red flowers in spring. **ZONES 7–9.**

Saxifraga ferdinandi-coburgi

Small multi-leafed rosettes, rather irregularly formed and haphazard in direction, give rise to quite large yellow flowers on 4 in (10 cm) leafy stems of this species from eastern Macedonia, northern Greece and eastern Bulgaria. **ZONES 6–9.**

Saxifraga fortunei

This deciduous or semi-evergreen, fleshy leafed plant forms rosettes that clump to around 12 in (30 cm) in height. From Japan, it has sprays of dozens of tiny white flowers in fall (autumn). Moist, humus-rich soils in sun or part-shade are needed in hotter areas. **ZONES 7–10.**

Saxifraga × *irvingii*

This hybrid between *Saxifraga burseriana* and ***S. lilacina*** would seem to be of garden origin. It is a dense carpeting plant, consisting of small rosettes, made up of tiny gray-green leaves. The flowers, 1 in (25 mm) across, are stemless and are pink or lilac in color. Many named cultivars are available, including **'Jenkinsiae'** which has a rather looser habit than the type and is a soft pink. **ZONES 6–9.**

Saxifraga × *apiculata* cultivar

Saxifraga longifolia

PYRENEAN SAXIFRAGE

This species forms a tight rosette of long narrow leaves with heavily lime encrusted margins. It bears a single panicle to 18 in (45 cm) long. This is multi-stemmed, each stem holding a ball-shaped head of tiny, round-petalled white flowers in spring. It is unfortunately monocarpic, so must be grown from seed as it dies after flowering. **'Tumbling Waters'** is a particularly fine form. **ZONES 6–9.**

Saxifraga paniculata

syn. *Saxifraga aizoon*

LIVELONG SAXIFRAGE

This summer-flowering evergreen perennial from central Europe bears terminal clusters of 5-petalled white flowers, often with spots of reddish purple, on erect stalks. Other colors include pale pinks and yellows. The bluish green leaves form a rosette below the flower stems. *Saxifraga paniculata* grows to a height and spread of 8–10 in (20–25 cm). Grow in full sun in well-drained, alkaline soil. Many forms have been noted with variations in flower size and color, from white and creams through to yellows and variations in leaf size and the size and shapes of the rosettes. **'Rosea'** has bright pink flowers. **'Minima'** has very small foliage and flowers. ***Saxifraga paniculata* var. *baldensis*** has very small rosettes of leaves and red-tinged flower stems. **ZONES 3–9.**

Saxifraga rotundifolia

ROUND-LEAFED SAXIFRAGE

This species from southwest France to northern Turkey grows from a stout rhizome and forms loose clumps of open rosettes of scalloped roundish leaves. It flowers on a sparsely leafed stem 10 in (25 cm) tall, forming an open truss of small white, often purple-spotted flowers shading to yellow at the center. It is best grown in moist soil in light shade. **ZONES 6–9.**

Saxifraga 'Ruth Draper'

Ruth Draper was a British comedienne of the 1930s, famous for her monologue, 'You should have seen my garden last week'. Her namesake is a pretty example of a mossy saxifrage, a group that likes a moist and lightly shaded position. It bears large, cup-shaped, purple-pink flowers in early spring and grows to 2 in (5 cm) in height. **ZONES 6–9.**

Saxifraga sempervivum

An evergreen perennial with short leaves, this species from the Balkans and northwestern Turkey forms open cushions with minimal lime encrustations. It has tiny reddish purple flowers, 15 to 20 per panicle on a 4 in (10 cm) leafy purple flower stem. Grow in full sun in well-drained soil. **ZONES 7–9.**

Saxifraga stolonifera

syn. *Saxifraga sarmentosa*

MOTHER OF THOUSANDS, STRAWBERRY BEGONIA

Geranium-like leaves are a feature of this perennial, which is a native of eastern

Saxifraga rotundifolia

Asia. The rounded, glossy leaves are olive green with silver veins, purplish pink on the undersides. In spring through early summer oddly petalled white flowers are borne in delicate panicles on thin, erect stalks. One petal on the tiny flowers seems to outgrow its 4 companion petals. Frost tender, it grows to a height of 6–8 in (15–20 cm) and spreads to 12 in (30 cm) by runners. **'Tricolor'** has deeply cut, green leaves patterned with red and white. **ZONES 5–10.**

Saxifraga umbrosa

This species from the Pyrenees forms a spreading leafy rosette of gray-green foliage with small white flowers on multiple 8 in (20 cm) stems. It is best in humus-rich soil and, in full sun or part-shade in hotter areas, it will flower freely from late spring to early summer. Other forms with shell-pink flowers are recorded. **ZONES 7–9.**

Saxifraga paniculata 'Rosea'

Saxifraga stolonifera 'Tricolor'

Saxifraga 'Ruth Draper'

Saxifraga stolonifera

Saxifraga sempervivum

Saxifraga umbrosa

Saxifraga × *urbium*

LONDON PRIDE

This perennial hybrid between ***Saxifraga spathularis*** and *S. umbrosa,* has small mid-pink flowers on 8–12 in (20–30 cm) stems from spring to mid-summer. A splendid border or edging plant, grow in sun or part-shade in hotter areas. **ZONES 7–9.**

SCABIOSA

SCABIOUS, PINCUSHION FLOWER

This genus of 80 species of annuals, biennials and perennials, found widely in temperate climates, bears tall-stemmed, honey-scented flowers ideal for cutting. The blooms, bearing multiple florets with protruding filaments giving a pincushion effect, range from white, yellow, red, blue and mauve to deep purple.

Scabiosa anthemifolia

CULTIVATION: Most species will thrive in full sun in well-drained, alkaline soil. Propagate annuals from seed in spring, and perennials from cuttings in summer, seed in fall (autumn) or by division in early spring.

Scabiosa africana

This mauve-flowering perennial comes from South Africa. It has oblong leaves and flower stems up to 3 ft (1 m) tall. The flowerheads are 1½ in (35 mm) wide. **ZONES 7–11.**

Scabiosa anthemifolia

This is an annual or short-lived perennial with arching stems up to 30 in (75 cm) long bearing 2½ in (6 cm) flowers in shades of mauve, violet or rose. It comes from South Africa. **ZONES 7–11.**

Scabiosa atropurpurea

This bushy biennial or short-lived perennial from southern Europe produces flowers from summer through to early fall (autumn), provided blooms are cut or deadheaded. The dome-shaped flowerheads are about 2 in (5 cm) wide and are fragrant; they are mainly crimson but also come in white, pink, purple and blue. Size varies from 18 in (45 cm) for dwarf forms up to 3 ft (1 m) for taller plants. This fully frost-hardy species has lobed, lance-shaped foliage. **ZONES 7–11.**

Saxifraga paniculata

Saxifraga paniculata var. *baldensis*

Scabiosa caucasica 'Staefa'

Scabiosa caucasica

Scabiosa caucasica 'Mrs Isaac House'

Scabiosa caucasica

Flat, many-petalled flowerheads in pink, red, purple or blue hues with pincushion-like centers often in a contrasting color make this summer-flowering perennial popular for borders and as cut flowers. A bushy plant with lobed mid-green leaves, it reaches a height and spread of 18–24 in (45–60 cm). **'Clive Greaves'** has lilac-blue flowers; **'Miss Wilmott'** has white flowers; **'Staefa'** is a strong grower with blue flowers; and **'Mrs Isaac House'** has creamy white flowers. **ZONES 4–10.**

Scabiosa columbaria

This biennial or perennial grows to 24 in (60 cm) with a spread of 3 ft (1 m). Slender, erect, hairy stems produce globular heads of reddish purple to lilac-blue flowers in 1½ in (35 mm) wide heads during summer and fall (autumn). **'Butterfly Blue'** is a lower growing, dense, fuzzy leafed cultivar with lavender-blue pincushion flowers over a very long period. **ZONES 6–10.**

Scabiosa farinosa

This shrub grows to 3 ft (1 m) in height with smooth, dark green leaves and small mauve flowers held up on 4 in (10 cm) long stalks. **ZONES 6–10.**

Scabiosa ochroleuca

This perennial species bears 30 in (75 cm) long stalks of primrose-yellow flowers 2 in (5 cm) across during summer and fall (autumn). It comes from Europe and western Asia. **ZONES 6–10.**

SCADOXUS

BLOOD LILY

These 9 species of bulbs from Africa and the Arabian Peninsula are closely related to the blood lilies *(Haemanthus)* and at one time were included in that genus. Their bulbs are much alike: that is, big and fat with a preference for growing with their noses just below the ground.

Scadoxus multiflorus

Scabiosa columbaria 'Butterfly Blue'

Both genera flower without their leaves, but *Scadoxus* flower in spring and their leaves are carried in much more conventional bunches (rather than the 2 leaves of *Haemanthus*).

CULTIVATION: These are warm-temperate to subtropical plants needing a greenhouse where winters are frosty. Plant in full sun or dappled shade in humus-rich, well-drained soil. Overwatering while the plants are dormant will prevent them from flowering. Propagate from seed or offsets in spring.

Scadoxus multiflorus

syn. *Haemanthus multiflorus*

This spring- to summer-flowering bulb has lance-shaped, semi-erect leaves forming a basal rosette and a globular umbel with as many as 100 brilliant red starry flowers on an 18 in (45 cm) tall stem. ***Scadoxus multiflorus* subsp. *katherinae*** is a very robust, clump-forming bulb with up to 200 red flowers from spring to summer, while ***S. m.* subsp. *multiflorus*** has a perianth tube to ¾ in (18 mm) in length. **ZONES 10–12.**

Scadoxus puniceus

syns *Haemanthus magnificus, H. natalensis*

PAINTBRUSH LILY, SNAKE LILY

This plant is native to eastern and southern Africa. In spring it bears masses of orange and red flowers wrapped in red bracts and borne on marbled stems. It grows to 18 in (45 cm) in height and makes an attractive potted plant. **ZONES 10–12.**

SCAEVOLA

FAN FLOWER

This genus from Australia and the Pacific region contains 96 species of mainly temperate origin, with a very few occurring in tropical and subtropical regions. They are mainly evergreen perennials, shrubs, subshrubs and small trees, with a number of ground-covering varieties that have proved and adaptable to a wide range of garden conditions, including seaside gardens. Most have leaves that are fleshy, often hairy and occasionally succulent, borne on stout, sometimes brittle stems. Fan-shaped flowers, while generally fairly small at ½–1 in (12–25 mm) across, are profuse and are held on the plant for long periods. The flower color ranges from white to blue, mauve and deep purple.

CULTIVATION: Species of *Scaevola* tolerate a wide range of soils but prefer them light and well drained; they do best in sun or part-shade. Propagate from seed or cuttings in spring or summer.

Scaevola aemula

syn. *Scaevola humilis*

FAIRY FAN FLOWER

The thick, coarsely toothed, dark green leaves on this perennial herb grow along spreading stems to form ground-hugging cover not more than 18 in (45 cm) high with a similar spread. Spikes of large, mauve-blue flowers with yellow throats continue to elongate as new flowers open, blooming from early spring to late summer. Native to the sandy coast and near coastal woodlands of Australia, it resists dry conditions, frost and salt spray. **'Blue Wonder'** bears lilac-blue flowers almost continuously in great profusion. **ZONES 9–11.**

Scadoxus multiflorus subsp. *katherinae*

S

Schefflera actinophylla

Schefflera arboricola

Scaevola 'Blue Fandango'

A dense perennial shrub 24 in (60 cm) tall and wide, this species has upright or ascending stems, seldom trailing. The leaves are serrate or irregularly lobed, soft and with a light covering of hairs. Spikes of violet-blue flowers bloom for most of the year, making this a very desirable garden or container plant. Full sun or filtered light and well-drained soil are preferred. The hybrid **'Diamond Head'** is a parent plant. **ZONES 9–11.**

Scaevola crassifolia

THICK-LEAFED FAN FLOWER

This is a vigorous spreading loose shrub 3 ft (1 m) high and slightly wider of coastal or inland sandy areas of warm-temperate Western Australia. The leaves are thick and serrated, and the light blue to mauve flowers are in terminal heads. **ZONES 10–11.**

Scaevola 'Mauve Clusters'

This frost-hardy, spreading perennial flowers profusely in spring and summer. The small flowers present a mass of mauve against a backdrop of bright green leaves. Growing very close to the ground, it spreads as much as 6 ft (1.8 m). **ZONES 9–11.**

Scaevola taccada

syn. *Scaevola sericea*

SEA LETTUCE

One of the few species occurring beyond Australia, this species grows on tropical beaches and atolls throughout the Pacific and Indian oceans. An attractive evergreen shrub, it grows to 5 ft (1.5 m) high and about as wide. The bright green leaves are 4 in (10 cm) long. The small

Schefflera arboricola 'Samoa Snow'

white flowers, streaked with purple, are borne at the branch ends for most of the year. The fruit are small, succulent, purplish blue berries. **ZONES 10–12.**

SCHEFFLERA

syns *Brassaia, Dizygotheca, Heptapleurum*

This is a vast genus of small trees, shrubs and scrambling climbers, with over 700 species occurring through most wetter tropical and subtropical regions of the world. The leaves consist of similar-sized leaflets arranged like a cartwheel at the ends of long stalks. The small flowers are arranged in branching, usually radiating spikes. The fruits are small, fleshy berries. In their native rainforests many scheffleras grow as epiphytes, high on other trees or on cliffs or rock outcrops. Several species are popular house plants in cool and cold climates; a few species are grown for their luxuriant foliage.
CULTIVATION: In warm to hot climates they can be planted in the garden in a spot sheltered from wind either in the sun or part-shade. Young plants make excellent tub specimens. Grow them in well-drained soil preferably enriched with organic matter, keeping the soil moist over summer. Propagate from fresh seed in late summer, cuttings in summer or by air-layering in spring.

Scaevola taccada

Schefflera actinophylla

syn. *Brassaia actinophylla*

QUEENSLAND UMBRELLA TREE, AUSTRALIAN IVY PALM, OCTOPUS TREE

Each leaf of this species resembles an umbrella and consists of 7 to 15 light green glossy leaflets up to 15 in (38 cm) long. From rainforests of northern Australia and New Guinea, this species reaches to 40 ft (12 m) in cultivation with multiple erect trunks and a dense canopy 20 ft (6 m) wide. Numerous clusters of flowers are arranged in spectacular radiating spikes on red stems; these appear near the top of the plant from late summer to early spring. Each ruby red flower has contrasting cream stamens and is rich in nectar. Reddish fleshy berries follow. **ZONES 10–12.**

Schefflera arboricola

HAWAIIAN ELF SCHEFFLERA

Endemic to Taiwan, this smaller version of *Schefflera actinophylla* makes a shrub 6–15 ft (1.8–4.5 m) tall with a similar spread. It produces many branches near the ground and can be pruned to a rounded shape, making it a popular pot plant for indoors and out. The leaves consist of 5 to 10 leaflets radiating from the leaf stalk; each is shiny green and up to 6 in (15 cm) long. Greenish yellow flowers in sprays appear near the branch tips in spring and summer, followed by orange fruit that ripen to purple. **'Renate'** has variegated leaves, as does **'Samoa Snow'**. **ZONES 10–12.**

Scaevola aemula

Scaevola 'Diamond Head'

Schefflera digitata

This is the only species in the genus native to New Zealand. It has rich green leaves divided into 5 to 10 oval leaflets. In spring there are tiny greenish flowers, followed in fall (autumn) by small, globular, dark violet fruit (this happens rarely indoors). **ZONES 9–11.**

Schefflera elegantissima

syns *Aralia elegantissima, Dizygotheca elegantissima*

FALSE ARALIA

This elegant, erect plant from New Caledonia can grow to 6 ft (1.8 m) indoors, 50 ft (15 m) in the wild. When young, the leaves are bronze green, changing to a lustrous dark green with maturity. On juvenile plants they consist of 7 to 10 narrow, finger-like leaflets with saw-toothed edges while in adult plants the leaflets are much broader and more obscurely toothed. **ZONES 10–12.**

Scaevola 'Mauve Clusters'

Scaevola aemula 'Blue Wonder'

S

SCHIMA

This genus was once regarded as including several species, all of which are now regarded as forms of one very variable species, *Schima wallichii*, from southern and Southeast Asia. An evergreen tree or tall shrub, it is grown for its spirally arranged glossy leaves and for the camellia-like flowers it bears in summer.
CULTIVATION: This tropical or near-tropical plant requires warm, frost-free conditions with moist, humus-rich, well-drained soil and a position in part-shade when young. Propagate from seed or cuttings.

Schima wallichii

This species grows to 30 ft (9 m) tall and has elliptical leaves 3–10 in (8–25 cm) long with shallow-toothed edges. The leaves are reddish purple when young and mature to deep green with blue-green undersides. The flowers develop in the leaf axils and at the branch tips. Bright red buds open to 2½ in (6 cm) wide, white to pale mauve, 5- to 6-petalled flowers with a central boss of golden stamens. **ZONES 9–12.**

SCHINUS

The 30 species of evergreen shrubs and trees that make up this genus are indigenous to Central and South America. They are grown for their graceful habit and great resistance to very dry conditions. The leaves usually consist of many leaflets but are sometimes simple. The flowers are tiny and are arranged in clusters, male and female flowers on the same or separate trees. Female trees feature attractive round berries. They make excellent shade and street trees.
CULTIVATION: Plant these marginally frost-hardy to frost-tender plants in full sun in well-drained, coarse soil; they grow best in warm to hot climates. Propagate from fresh seed in spring or cuttings in summer.

Schinus molle var. *areira*
syn. *Schinus areira*
PEPPER TREE, PEPPERCORN

This fast-growing tree with graceful, drooping leaves and branchlets develops an attractive, gnarled trunk as it ages to a height of 30–50 ft (9–15 m). The dark green, shiny leaves are 6 in (15 cm) long, composed of 10 to 18 pairs of small pointed leaflets; they are resinous and aromatic when crushed. Pendulous clusters of tiny cream flowers appear from late spring to early summer. Decorative sprays of tiny rose-pink berries follow—these have a peppery taste and have been used like pepper, but are somewhat toxic. In hot dry climates it naturalizes readily and may become a weed. **ZONES 9–11.**

Schinus terebinthifolius
BRAZILIAN PEPPER TREE

A round-headed tree up to about 30 ft (9 m) high, this species has bronze-green pinnate leaves usually composed of 7 leaflets. The drooping panicles of tiny cream flowers that appear in summer are followed by small green berries that redden as they ripen in winter. When trimmed it makes an excellent shade tree. In some warm, wet climates, such as in Hawaii, it has become a serious weed. **ZONES 10–12.**

Schinus molle var. *areira*

Schizanthus hookeri

Schinus terebinthifolius

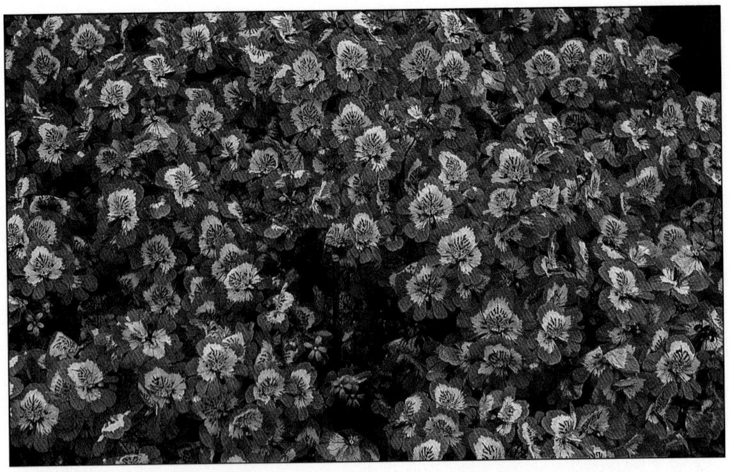

Schizanthus × *wisetonensis*

SCHIZACHYRIUM

This is a genus of about 100 species of deciduous perennial grasses widespread throughout the world. They have solitary, terminal racemes of stalked spikelets, and foliage that turns bronze or chestnut in fall (autumn).
CULTIVATION: These fully frost-hardy plants prefer full sun and moderately fertile, very well-drained soil. Old stems should be cut out in winter; the flowerheads can be dried for indoor decoration. Propagate by division in spring or from seed in fall.

Schizachyrium scoparium
BLUE STEM, BROOM BEARD GRASS, PRAIRIE GRASS

This tough grass is a native of North America. It forms a perennial tuft with upright stems to 3 ft (1 m) and green or blue-green leaves often shaded bronze or purplish. **ZONES 3–10.**

SCHIZANTHUS
POOR MAN'S ORCHID, BUTTERFLY FLOWER

Despite their common name, there is nothing apologetic about the exquisite flowers of these 12 to 15 species of annuals from the Chilean mountains. Although the blooms do look like miniature orchids, *Schizanthus* are in fact related to petunias. They come in shades of pink, mauve, red, purple and white, all with gold-speckled throats. They grow to about 3 ft (1 m) high and 12 in (30 cm) wide. Most of the flowers seen in gardens are hybrids, giving a colorful display over a short spring to summer season.
CULTIVATION: These subtropical mountain plants do not like extremes of heat or cold. They grow best outdoors in a mild, frost-free climate; in colder climates they need the controlled, even temperature of a greenhouse. Grow in full sun in fertile, well-drained soil and pinch out growing tips of young plants to ensure bushy growth. Propagate from seed in summer or fall (autumn).

Schizanthus hookeri

This species grows to 18 in (45 cm) in height with divided leaves and large pink, violet or purple flowers, whose upper lips are yellow blotched. **ZONES 7–11.**

Schizanthus pinnatus

This bush is grown for its exotic blooms and pale green, fern-like foliage. Orchid-like flowers come in a range of colors from white, pink and mauve to scarlet and purple. It grows up to 24 in (60 cm) high and 12 in (30 cm) wide. **ZONES 7–11.**

Schizanthus × *wisetonensis*

This erect species bears tubular to flared, 2-lipped, white, blue, pink or reddish brown flowers often flushed with yellow from spring to summer. It has lance-shaped, light green leaves and grows to 18 in (45 cm) high with a spread of 12 in (30 cm). Most garden strains are derived from this species. **ZONES 7–11.**

SCHIZOLOBIUM

Indigenous to tropical regions of South America, the 2 tall evergreen or deciduous trees of this genus are valued for their huge, feathery, alternate leaves and wonderful display of golden-yellow flowers in spring.
CULTIVATION: They do best in deep, rich, moist soil in full sun but with shelter from strong winds and plenty of water. Propagate from seed in late summer or fall (autumn).

Schizolobium parahybum
TREE-FERN TREE, BACURUBU

This tall, slender-trunked tree, indigenous to tropical Brazil, is fast growing to about 100 ft (30 m) with a sparse, open growth habit. The large, bipinnate, fern-like leaves are up to 4 ft (1.2 m) long, and are borne in crowded whorls at the branch ends. Young trees remain unbranched up to 20 ft (6 m) or more, resembling a slender tree fern. The leaves are shed in late winter, and by late spring the tree is covered with golden-yellow flowers in large clusters. The fruit that follow are brown pods, each holding a single seed. **ZONES 10–12.**

SCHIZOPHRAGMA

Found from the Himalayas across to Japan and Taiwan, there are 2 species of

these woody, deciduous, climbing or creeping plants which attach themselves with strong aerial roots. The paired long-stemmed leaves are oval, sometimes toothed. The small flowers are grouped in flattened heads that are surrounded by a ring of large, white calyx lobes that look like petals.
CULTIVATION: Plant these moderately to fully frost-hardy plants in full sun or part-shade in moderately fertile, humus-rich, moist but well-drained soil. Propagate from cuttings.

Schizophragma hydrangeoides
JAPANESE HYDRANGEA

From Japan and Korea this vigorous climber grows to 30 ft (9 m) or more and makes a spectacular cover for pergolas and large walls. The large, flattened flowerheads, 12 in (30 cm) across, are composed of very small white flowers surrounded by ornamental white sepals and are borne in summer. It has attractive, deep green, toothed leaves 4 in (10 cm) long on green stalks. **'Roseum'** has red leaf stalks and a rose blush on the outer sepals. **ZONES 5–10.**

Schizophragma integrifolium

This climber from China eventually attains 30 ft (9 m). The leaves are 4–8 in (10–20 cm) long, oval or heart-shaped, sometimes with a few small teeth. The white flowerheads reach 8–12 in (20–30 cm) across and appear in summer. **ZONES 7–10.**

SCHIZOSTYLIS

A single species of grassy leafed rhizomatous perennial in the iris family makes up this genus. *Schizostylis* is widely distributed in South Africa where it grows along banks of streams. The long-flowering stems terminate in clusters of bowl-shaped 6-petalled flowers in deep scarlet and pink; it is an excellent cut flower.
CULTIVATION: Frost hardy, it prefers full sun and fertile, moist soil with shelter from the cold in cool-temperate climates. Divide every couple of years when it becomes crowded or propagate from seed in spring.

Schizostylis coccinea 'Mrs Hegarty'

Schizostylis coccinea 'Sunrise'

Schlumbergera 'Santa Cruz'

Schizostylis coccinea
CRIMSON FLAG

This variable species can fail in prolonged dry conditions. The sword-shaped leaves are green and are untidy unless pruned regularly and protected from thrips and slugs. It is valued for its late summer and fall (autumn) display which in some climates, conditions and seasons can extend into winter and beyond. *Coccinea* means scarlet, and that is the usual color of this species. It is a dainty plant reaching a height of 24 in (60 cm) and spread of 12 in (30 cm). Several named varieties are available in shades of pink, including the rose pink **'Mrs Hegarty'**, the salmon pink **'Sunrise'** and the crimson **'Grandiflora'** (syns 'Gigantea', 'Major'). **'Viscountess Byng'** has pale pink flowers with narrow petals. **ZONES 6–10.**

SCHLUMBERGERA
CHRISTMAS CACTUS

Christmas cacti are familiar flowershop pot plants. The genus consists of 6 species of bushy cacti from southeastern Brazil with flattened, spineless and rather weeping branches with indented notches at the margins. While still marketed as *Zygocactus, Schlumbergera* has been the updated name now for some 30 years. Most plants sold are hybrids. The bright flowers appear at the stem tips and are an attractive, asymmetrical shape; they come in shades from palest pink to orange, magenta, scarlet and white. They are often grown in hanging baskets but do not cascade vigorously enough to cover the basket, looking their best in tall pots.
CULTIVATION: Species of *Schlumbergera* prefer mild, frost-free climates; in cooler areas they make excellent indoor plants. Plant in part-shade in rich, well-drained soil. Once they set their flower buds they do not like being moved to another position and could drop their buds. Propagate from stem cuttings in spring or early summer.

Schizostylis coccinea 'Grandiflora'

Schlumbergera hybrids

Schizostylis coccinea 'Viscountess Byng'

Schizostylis coccinea 'Grandiflora'

Schlumbergera × *buckleyi*

Of garden origin, this epiphytic, readily branching cactus produces upright stems that arch in maturity. These stems are composed of flat, rectangular pads or cylindrical links covered with bristly areoles, often with notched edges. Prominent, cylindrical flowers bloom from the tops of the stems in fall (autumn) and winter. **ZONES 9–12.**

Schlumbergera 'Santa Cruz'

'Santa Cruz' is a new cultivar of Christmas cactus with a showy orange-red flower. It was bred in California and introduced there in 1989. **ZONES 9–12.**

Schlumbergera truncata
syn. ***Zygocactus truncatus***
CRAB CACTUS

This species from southeastern Brazil bears deep pink, red, orange or white flowers 3 in (8 cm) long from late fall (autumn) to winter and reaches 12 in (30 cm) in height. The bright green stems have prominent, tooth-like marginal notches. **ZONES 9–12.**

SCHOENOPLECTUS

This genus contains around 80 species of evergreen, rhizomatous, marginal aquatic perennials and annuals with a widespread natural distribution. They usually have very fine, deep green 5–12 ft (1.5–3.5 m) tall, reed-like stems that are leafless or have very reduced leaflets. The stems may be whip-like or stiffly erect, cylindrical or 3-angled, and form clumps to create an effect reminiscent of horsetails *(Equisetum)*. The flower spikes, usually red-brown in color, develop in summer.
CULTIVATION: Although capable of being grown in moist garden soil, these sedges do best in permanently damp soil at the margins of ponds and streams with a position in full sun. Some are invasive and should be planted with caution. Most species are frost hardy to around 5°F (–15°C) and may be propagated from seed or by division.

Schoenoplectus lacustris subsp. *tabernaemontani* 'Zebrinus'
syn. ***Scirpus lacustris* subsp. *tabernaemontani* 'Zebrinus'**
ZEBRA RUSH

This evergreen perennial has white-banded, leafless stems. In summer, it carries brown spikelets. It grows 4 ft (1.2 m) high and 24 in (60 cm) wide. **ZONES 4–10.**

S

Schotia brachypetala

Schotia brachypetala

Sciadopitys verticillata

Schoenoplectus validus

This species from North America has strong rhizomes and stems from $1\frac{1}{2}$–8 ft (0.45–2.4 m) high and $\frac{1}{4}$–1 in (6–25 mm) thick. **ZONES 7–10.**

SCHOTIA

This genus includes 4 or 5 species of evergreen or deciduous shrubs and small trees indigenous to hot, dry areas of central and southern Africa. They are grown for their showy clusters of flowers. The leaves are alternately arranged and are composed of an even number of leaflets. The fruits are protein-rich, oblong leathery pods.

CULTIVATION: They need a warm, frost-free climate and shelter from wind, and grow best in full sun and light to medium, well-drained soil. Propagate from seed or cuttings in fall (autumn).

Sciadopitys verticillata

Schotia brachypetala
WEEPING BOERBOON, TREE FUCHSIA, AFRICAN WALNUT

This large shrub or wide-spreading deciduous tree reaches a height of 30–50 ft (9–15 m). In spring it sheds most of its leaves before producing large clusters of deep red flowers with tiny, bristly petals and projecting red stamens. Copious nectar drips from the flowers, giving rise to the common name weeping boerboon. Birds adore this nectar, which ferments in the sun and makes them drunk. The leaves are shiny green and consist of 4 to 5 pairs of oval to oblong leaflets. The fruit are oblong pods 4 in (10 cm) long. **ZONES 9–12.**

SCIADOPITYS
JAPANESE UMBRELLA PINE

This genus consists of just one species, a very distinctive and handsome conifer from Japan. It is an upright, single-trunked, conical tree that eventually grows to over 100 ft (30 m) tall, though it is very slow growing. It can be kept in a container for long periods and is often used as a bonsai subject.

CULTIVATION: Japanese umbrella pines prefer a cool maritime climate with cool, moist, humus-rich soil and light shade when young. Propagate from seed.

Sciadopitys verticillata

The distinctive foliage of this species is composed of deep green, flattened needles up to 6 in (15 cm) long carried in stiff whorls of 20 to 30 and facing upwards, creating an effect like the ribs of an umbrella. Interestingly, the needles are not true leaves at all but they do photosynthesize; the true 'leaves' are the tiny scales that lie almost flat along the stems. The small oval cones take 2 years to mature. **ZONES 5–10.**

Schoenoplectus validus

SCILLA
SQUILL, BLUEBELL

This is a genus of about 90 species of bulbous perennials from Europe, Asia and Africa dependable for their terminal racemes of usually blue flowers in spring although they also come in pink, purple and white. Varying from 2–20 in (5–50 cm) in height, their tiny, usually star-shaped flowers are clustered above strap-shaped leaves. They look good naturalized under trees and shrubs or in lawns.

CULTIVATION: Most are adaptable to cold-winter climates and naturalize with ease in lawns and gardens. All should be planted in fall (autumn) in average soil in full sun to light shade. Divide in late summer when clumps become crowded, or propagate from seed in fall.

Scilla bifolia

This species bears a one-sided spike with up to 20 star-shaped, 6-petalled, blue, pink or white flowers in early spring. It grows to 6 in (15 cm) high with a spread of 2 in (5 cm) and has long, narrow, dark green leaves that widen toward the tips. **ZONES 6–9.**

Scilla hyacinthoides
HYACINTH

This plant produces 10 to 12 leaves edged with small bristles, each up to 18 in (45 cm) long and $1\frac{1}{2}$ in (35 mm) wide and edged with small bristles. The lilac-blue flowers are numerous, forming an erect spike up to 3 ft (1 m) tall long and 2 in (5 cm) wide in summer. It is found around the Mediterranean. **ZONES 6–10.**

Scilla litardierei

From Croatia and Serbia, this species grows to 10 in (25 cm) in height. The 3 to 6 thin arching leaves can be 12 in (30 cm) long. The flowers are blue, and there are as many as 16 to a head. ***Scilla litardierei* var. *hoogiana*** has up to 36 flowers. **ZONES 6–9.**

Scilla mischtschenkoana
syn. *Scilla tubergeniana*

This winter-flowering species from northwestern Iran, Georgia, Armenia and Azerbaijan has pale blue to white flowers with dark centers occurring on erect, terminal spikes. It reaches 4 in (10 cm) in height. The leaves are long, narrow, mid-green and clump forming. **ZONES 6–9.**

Scilla peruviana
CUBAN LILY, WILD HYACINTH, PERUVIAN SCILLA

This plant, native to southwest Europe and northwest Africa, has a dense cluster

Scilla litardierei var. *hoogiana*

Scilla peruviana 'Alba'

Scilla peruviana

Scrophularia nodosa

Scutellaria costaricana

of up to 50 star-shaped flowers that are borne in summer on a 12 in (30 cm) long stem. The 1 in (25 mm) wide flowers are usually blue, sometimes white or purple. The dark to olive-green foliage is glossy and strap-like. **'Alba'** bears white flowers. **ZONES 6–10.**

Scilla siberica
SIBERIAN SQUILL

In established patches of this Siberian species, rich blue flowers on loose racemes are produced in such quantity as to color the ground blue. The flowers appear in early to mid-spring on 6 in (15 cm) long stems. The foliage dies soon after flowering finishes. It spreads rapidly by division of bulbs and from seed, and does not do well where winters are mild. **ZONES 3–9.**

Scilla verna
SEA ONION, SPRING SCILLA

Blunt, concave leaves up to 8 in (20 cm) long appear before the heads of 6 to 12 bluish flowers on this species from western Europe. The flowerheads are not as tall as the leaves, but the leaves arch away from the flowers so that the blooms are well displayed. **ZONES 6–9.**

SCLERANTHUS
KNAWEL

This genus consists of 10 species of small annuals and perennials of wide distribution in temperate regions of both northern and southern hemispheres, with the exception of North America. They have small, narrow, crowded leaves and tiny white or greenish yellow flowers. The genus name means 'hard flower', a reference to the tough persistent calyx which often remains on the plant for a long time.
CULTIVATION: These plants prefer full sun but midday shade and gritty, free-draining soil. They need protection from prolonged periods of frost and winter wet. Propagate from seed or cuttings, or by division.

Scleranthus biflorus
TWIN-FLOWERED KNAWEL

A tightly mounding plant found in alpine regions of Australia, New Zealand and South America, this species may be covered with snow for 6 months in winter. It forms a spreading, tough, bright green mound 6 in (15 cm) high but spreading slowly up to 24 in (60 cm). Tiny 2-pronged flowers appear during the summer. The bright green 'cushion' appearance makes it a very popular garden and container plant; it will grow quite happily for years given sun, moisture and a cool root system. **ZONES 7–9.**

SCOLOPIA

This genus contains about 37 species of trees and shrubs indigenous to tropical and subtropical areas of southern Africa, Asia and Australia. The species, which can be spiny, have simple alternate leaves and small flowers in unbranched elongated clusters usually borne near the ends of the branches. They produce fleshy, berry-like fruits with 2 to 4 seeds.
CULTIVATION: These plants do best in full sun in well-drained soil with adequate water. Propagate from fresh seed or cuttings.

Scolopia braunii
BROWN BIRCH

From forests of eastern Australia, this erect tree grows to 50 ft (15 m). It has a dense crown of smooth, glossy, sometimes toothed green leaves that are up to 3–4 in (8–10 cm) long; the young foliage is diamond-shaped with toothed edges. The clusters of small, creamy white flowers are followed by $\frac{1}{2}$ in (12 mm) globular, black, red or yellow fruit. It can be pruned hard and is adaptable to pot culture; it makes an attractive house plant. **ZONES 10–12.**

SCROPHULARIA
FIGWORT

This genus consists of about 200 species of perennials and subshrubs that are widespread through the northern temperate zone. Quite variable in appearance, most species have fleshy stems and widely spaced, opposite pairs of elliptical or compound toothed leaves, each of which produces another pair of leaves at the leaf axil. Spikes of small flowers develop at the stem tips and leaf axils. The inconspicuous flowers are usually in dull shades of red, brown or purple.
CULTIVATION: These are tough plants usually treated as foliage fillers for perennial borders or woodlands. Plant in moist, well-drained soil in sun or part-shade. Some species tolerate very wet soil, others need lime. All are fully frost hardy. Propagate from seed or by division.

Scrophularia auriculata
WATER BETONY, WATER FIGWORT

This marginal aquatic perennial grows 24–36 in (60–90 cm) high and has paired leaves and green flowers with a purplish upper lip. It is from western Europe. **'Variegata'** has dark green leaves with cream markings. **ZONES 5–10.**

Scrophularia nodosa

This perennial species from Europe reaches 5 ft (1.5 m) in height. It has similar flowers to *Scrophularia auriculata* in summer. **ZONES 5–10.**

SCUTELLARIA
SKULLCAP, HELMET FLOWER

The name of this genus comes from the Latin *scutella*, meaning a small shield or cup, which is a rough description of the pouch of the upper calyx. There are some 300 known species consisting mainly of summer-flowering perennials, most on a rhizomatous root system, though a few are annuals and rarely subshrubs. They occur mainly in temperate regions throughout the northern hemisphere.
CULTIVATION: They are easily grown in full sun in most reasonable garden soil. None would be happy with parched soil in summer, but they are content with ordinary watering throughout dry weather. Propagation is by division in winter or from seed sown fresh in fall (autumn). Cuttings may be taken in summer.

Scutellaria costaricana

An erect perennial to 3 ft (1 m) tall with dark purple stems, this species has slender oval leaves and $2\frac{1}{2}$ in (6 cm) tubular flowers that are bright orange-scarlet with a golden-yellow lip. It comes from Costa Rica. **ZONES 9–12.**

Scleranthus biflorus

Scolopia braunii

Scilla verna

Scutellaria incana

This is a rounded perennial to 4 ft (1.2 m) in height with lightly serrated oval leaves and large panicles of grayish blue flowers in summer. A light prune will sometimes produce a second flush of flowers in fall (autumn). It is widespread throughout northeastern USA. **ZONES 5–9.**

Scutellaria indica

This is an upright, slowly spreading perennial around 12 in (30 cm) high with light gray-green oval leaves and clumped heads of soft blue-gray, tubular flowers. ***Scutellaria indica* var. *parvifolia*** (syn. *S. i. japonica*) is lower growing to 4 in (10 cm) and clumps more rapidly. It has crowded heads of blue-gray and cream, shortish tubular flowers in late spring; if deadheaded immediately it will reflower in late summer. **ZONES 5–10.**

Scutellaria incana

Scutellaria orientalis

This is a quickly spreading perennial with slightly hairy, oval, light green leaves on gray-green stems. It has upright clusters of golden flowers with brownish lips, 4 to 6 flowers per stem. It is best used as a ground cover and comes from southern Europe to central Asia. **ZONES 7–10.**

SECHIUM

CHOKO, CHAYOTE

The 6 to 8 species in this genus are native to tropical America and from the same family as the melon and cucumber. They are strong-growing perennial bright green vines with 10 in (25 cm) heart-shaped leaves. They are frost tender in temperate climates and require plenty of space to grow, as their tendrils will grip onto and climb almost anything. The large, hairy, green fruits can be boiled, baked or stewed, but not overcooked or they will be tasteless.

CULTIVATION: Grow only in warm regions in well-drained, rather loose soil enriched with plenty of compost. Water well when plant growth is under way. A day length of a little more than 12 hours is required before flowering will commence. Propagate from seed or cuttings or from the whole fruit, which is planted on its side with the narrow end slightly exposed.

Scutellaria indica var. *parvifolia*

Sedum anglicum

Sedum dendroideum

Sechium edule

CHOW CHOW, CHRISTOPHINE, VEGETABLE PEAR

This high-climbing species has thickened, tuberous roots and 3- to 5-lobed leaves with minute teeth. The pale yellow male flowers appear in long racemes; the female flowers have a green tinge. The fruit appear in summer. **ZONES 10–12.**

SEDUM

STONECROP

This large genus contains about 400 species of succulent annuals, biennials, perennials, subshrubs and shrubs native to the northern hemisphere. Quick-growing plants, they vary widely in habit from carpet forming to upright up to 3 ft (1 m) tall. Their leaves may be cylindrical, lanceolate, egg-shaped or elliptical and the 5-petalled flowers appear in terminal sprays. They make excellent hanging basket or pot plants.

CULTIVATION: They range from being frost tender to fully frost hardy. Fertile, porous soil is preferred; however some types are extremely robust and will grow in most soil types. They need full sun. Propagate perennials, shrubs and subshrubs from seed in spring or fall (autumn) or by division or from cuttings in spring through mid-summer. Propagate annuals and biennials from seed sown under glass in early spring or outdoors in mid-spring.

Sedum acre

GOLD MOSS, COMMON STONECROP

This little perennial is one of the hardiest of all succulents. It is native to Europe, Turkey and northern Africa and grows abundantly in Britain, its creeping stems hugging the ground between rocks or growing in the chinks of old walls. The whole plant is only about $1\frac{1}{2}$ in (35 mm) high and, with its bright green leaves, looks like a lush patch of moss—until spring, when it is covered with masses of tiny yellow flowers. **ZONES 5–10.**

Sedum baileyi

Sedum cauticola

Sedum aizoon

Native to Siberia, China and Japan, this is a fully frost-hardy plant differing from the usual run of succulents in not being evergreen—it dies down each winter, to return in spring with 18 in (45 cm) tall stems with fleshy leaves and crowned with clusters of yellow flowers in summer. There are also red-flowered forms. **ZONES 7–10.**

Sedum album

From Europe, North Africa and western Asia, this is a commonly cultivated but variable mat-forming plant with 3–8 in (8–20 cm) oblong, cylindrical or spherical leaves. Dwarf-leafed forms also occur. White flowers are seen in summer, but white, pink or greenish blooms occur in some forms. **ZONES 6–11.**

Sedum allantoides

This perennial succulent is found in Mexico and has medium-sized obovate leaves. In spring it produces small, greenish white, daisy-like flowers. **ZONES 8–11.**

Sedum anglicum

This small mat-forming plant from western Europe has tiny cylindrical leaves. White or pink flowers are held on 1–6 in (2.5–15 cm) long stalks, appearing in early summer. **ZONES 6–10.**

Sedum baileyi

This species is a perennial succulent from China with ovate- to spoon-shaped foliage. It produces star-shaped yellow flowers. **ZONES 7–10.**

Sedum cauticola

syn. *Hylotelephium cauticola*

This trailing, shallow-rooted perennial from northern Japan has a name meaning 'dweller on rocks or cliffs', an ideal position for it to grow. It dies back in winter after the appearance of its $\frac{1}{2}$ in (12 mm), star-shaped, pinkish red flowers. It grows to 3 in (8 cm) in height. **ZONES 4–10.**

S

Sedum hidakanum

Sedum dasyphyllum

This hairy tufted little plant grows to 3 in (8 cm) in height and has summer flowers that open white-backed with pink. It originates in southern Europe and North Africa. **ZONES 8–11.**

Sedum dendroideum

This is a small Mexican shrub to 8 in (20 cm) in height with flat club-shaped leaves. Heads of yellow flowers appear in spring. **ZONES 8–11.**

Sedum ewersii

syn. *Hylotelephium ewersii*

This plant from the northern Himalayas, Mongolia, central Asia and China has branching, spreading low stems up to 12 in (30 cm) high with oval gray-green leaves up to 1 in (25 mm) long. The pink flowers persist from late spring to early fall (autumn). **ZONES 4–9.**

Sedum forsterianum

This is a green mat-forming perennial from western Europe. It has flat leaves on non-flowering stems that form rosettes. Yellow flowers appear in summer. **ZONES 7–10.**

Sedum 'Herbstfreude'

Sedum ewersii

Sedum lucidum

Sedum kamtschaticum

Sedum 'Herbstfreude' ('Autumn Joy')

syn. *Hylotelephium* 'Autumn Joy'

This plant forms a small clump which grows to 24 in (60 cm) tall. It has toothed fleshy leaves. Large heads of pink flowers appear in fall (autumn). These fade to copper tones and then finally turn red. In cold climates it dies back to the ground in winter. **ZONES 5–10.**

Sedum hidakanum

This perennial succulent is a native to Japan. It grows up to $2\frac{1}{2}$ in (6 cm) high and forms mats along the ground. The small, gray-green leaves are roughly oval in shape and the white, star-shaped flowers appear in summer. **ZONES 5–10.**

Sedum 'Herbstfreude'

Sedum forsterianum

Sedum rubrotinctum

S. k. 'Weihenstephaner Gold'

Sedum kamtschaticum

syn. *Hylotelephium pluricaule*

KAMSCHATKA STONECROP

This carpeting semi-evergreen perennial grows 4–8 in (10–20 cm) high with 1 in (25 mm) long green leaves, bluntly toothed towards the tip. Yellow flowers appear in summer. It comes from northern China, eastern Siberia and Japan. **'Variegatum'** has leaves edged with white; **'Weihenstephaner Gold'** has a more trailing habit, with golden-yellow flowers ageing to orange. **ZONES 7–10.**

Sedum lucidum

This shrub grows to 18 in (45 cm) high and has bright green elliptical leaves up to 2 in (5 cm) long and white flowerheads appearing over cooler months. It comes from Mexico. **ZONES 9–12.**

Sedum morganianum

DONKEY'S TAIL, BURRO TAIL

Native to Mexico, this popular, readily branching, evergreen perennial has a compact, upright habit, becoming weeping as the stems lengthen. Growing up to 12 in (30 cm), the attractive stems are composed of bluish green, interlocking leaves that have a plump, lanceolate form. In cultivation clusters of long, pinkish red, starry flowers may bloom at the stem tips in summer. It makes an ideal hanging basket plant but should be handled with care as the leaves readily detach. **ZONES 9–12.**

Sedum morganianum

Sedum pachyphyllum

MANY FINGERS, JELLYBEAN PLANT

This shrub grows to 12 in (30 cm) high with spoon-shaped or triangular leaves up to 3 in (8 cm) long and tipped with red. The yellow flowers are held above the plant in winter and spring. It comes from Mexico. **ZONES 8–11.**

Sedum rubrotinctum

CHRISTMAS CHEER

Small and evergreen, this subshrub grows up to 10 in (25 cm) in height and has yellow winter blooms. Readily branching, its slender, multiple stems are wide spreading and develop vivid green, pulpy, obovate leaves in grape-like bunches that turn red and yellow under arid conditions. A cold, damp climate will maintain the leaf luster. **ZONES 9–12.**

Sedum 'Ruby Glow'

This hybrid between *Sedum cauticolum* and ***S. telephium*** is a strong-growing, deciduous perennial to around 10 in (25 cm). It bears loose sprays of starry ruby-red flowers from mid-summer to early fall (autumn). **ZONES 5–10.**

Sedum rupestre

syn. *Sedum reflexum*

This mat-forming evergreen grows to 4 in (10 cm) with thin cylindrical leaves. The yellow flowers are seen in late spring and early summer. It comes from central and western Europe. **ZONES 7–10.**

Sedum spectabile

Sedum spathulifolium 'Cape Blanco'

Sedum spathulifolium 'Purpureum'

Sedum spurium 'Schorbuser Blut'

Sedum spathulifolium

This evergreen perennial has a carpet-forming habit with tiny rosettes to 4 in (10 cm) high composed of plump, circular, green or frosted gray leaves suffused with a brownish red color. In summer star-shaped yellow flowers appear on short stems. **'Cape Blanco'** has a very compact habit with leaves that are silvery green, often tinged with purple; it will tolerate light shade. **'Purpureum'** has purple leaves. ZONES 7–10.

Sedum spectabile

syn. ***Hylotelephium spectabile***

SHOWY SEDUM, ICE PLANT

Spoon-shaped, fleshy, gray-green leaves grow in clusters on the branching erect stems of this perennial from China and Korea. Butterflies flock to the flattish heads of small, pink, star-like flowers, which bloom in late summer. It grows to a height and spread of 18 in (45 cm) and is resistant to both frost and dry conditions. **'Brilliant'** bears profuse heads of bright rose-pink flowers. **'Stardust'** has rich green leaves. ZONES 5–10.

Sedum spurium

This summer-flowering, evergreen perennial from Turkey and northern Iran bears small blooms in big, rounded flowerheads; colors range from white to purple. Hairy stems carrying saw-edged, elliptical leaves spread widely into a carpet 4 in (10 cm) tall, suitable for covering banks and slopes. **'Schorbuser Blut'** ('Dragon's Blood') is a creeping cultivar with plum-toned leaves and magenta flowers; **'Sunset Cloud'** has deep pinkish orange flowers. ***Sedum stoloniferum*** is similar to *S. spurium* but its stems lie close to the ground and the flowers are pink. ZONES 7–10.

Sedum telephium subsp. *maximum*

syn. ***Hylotelephium telephium***

ORPHINE, LIVE-FOREVER

This perennial from eastern Europe and across Asia to Japan has red 12–24 in (30–60 cm) stems arising from tuberous roots. The oblong leaves are 1–3 in (2.5–8 cm) long, rather upright and stemless. Red-purple flowers appear in late summer. ZONES 6–10.

Sedum spectabile

Sedum spectabile 'Brilliant'

Sedum spectabile

Sedum spectabile 'Stardust'

Sedum spurium

SELAGINELLA

LITTLE CLUB MOSS, SPIKE MOSS

There are about 700 species of evergreen, rhizomatous perennials in this genus, which occur mainly in tropical and warm-temperate zones. They are grown for their attractive branching foliage. Many are suitable for hanging baskets or for growing in pots in greenhouses in cooler areas.

CULTIVATION: These frost-tender plants prefer part-shade and moderately fertile, moist but well-drained soil. Propagate from spores or by division.

Selaginella kraussiana

SPREADING CLUB MOSS, TRAILING SPIKE MOSS, KRAUSS'S SPIKE MOSS

The trailing branched stems of this species from southern Africa and the Azores form a bright green feathery mesh up to 1 in (25 mm) high. Dwarf plants are available, as well as the golden form **'Aurea'** and **'Variegata'** with green and yellow colorings. ZONES 9–11.

Selaginella martensii

Overlapping bright green leaves on 6 in (15 cm) high stems trail and root from the nodes on this species. Some forms have a white variegation. It comes from Central America. ZONES 9–11.

Selaginella uncinata

PEACOCK MOSS, RAINBOW FERN, BLUE SPIKE MOSS

This striking species from China has mid-green leaves that age to a pinkish yellow or plum color with a peacock blue sheen. It is a trailing perennial with

Selaginella kraussiana

Sedum stoloniferum

Sedum telephium subsp. *maximum*

Selaginella martensii

almost leafless stems with densely branched side shoots. It reaches only 2 in (5 cm) in height but has an indefinite spread, and makes a splendid hanging-basket plant. **ZONES 9–11.**

Selaginella willdenovii
WILLDENOW'S SELAGINELLA

This climbing plant from southern China, Indonesia and the Himalayas reaches up to 20 ft (6 m). It branches from the base and bears blue-green or bronze-green oval leaves. **ZONES 10–11.**

SELENICEREUS
MOON CEREUS, MOON CACTUS, NIGHT-BLOOMING CEREUS

From tropical America and the Caribbean comes this group of 20 species of semi-pendent, epiphytic or rock-dwelling cacti. The slender ribbed stems have small spines. The large white or red flowers appear only at night.
CULTIVATION: These frost-tender plants prefer dappled to part-shade and moderately fertile, humus-rich, moist but very well-drained soil. Propagate from seed or cuttings.

Selenicereus grandiflorus
QUEEN OF THE NIGHT

This vine-like, climbing cactus reaches up to 10 ft (3 m) in height and is native to Mexico and the West Indies. It is highly valued for its large, pure white, nocturnal flowers, up to 12 in (30 cm) in diameter, to which the common name refers. They are very sweetly scented. Quick growing and readily branching, its deep bluish green, slender stems bear needle-shaped, short yellow spines. **ZONES 9–12.**

SELLIERA

This small genus is made up of evergreen, fleshy-leafed, creeping perennials found in Australia, New Zealand and Chile. The leaves, which spring from spreading and rooting stems, are about 1 in (25 mm) long. The flowers, usually white, have 5 narrow to rounded petals and are followed by small, many-seeded fruit. Both the foliage and fruit may develop red tints in full sun.
CULTIVATION: They are best grown in a rockery or alpine garden and are undemanding plants. The creeping rootstock can be slightly invasive in loose soil but is easily controlled. Propagate from seed or by division.

Selliera radicans
SWAMP WEED

Found throughout the range of the genus, this is the most common species and is easily recognized by its flattened spatula-shaped leaves and its unusual flowers which have all 5 petals on the lower part of the bloom. The flowers are white, appear throughout the warmer months, and are followed by 1/4 in (6 mm) long, fleshy, red-tinted green fruit. **ZONES 8–10.**

SEMELE
CLIMBING BUTCHER'S BROOM

The single species of the genus is a large evergreen climber from the Canary Islands and the western Mediterranean. Its common name comes from its resemblance to the butcher's broom *(Ruscus aculeatus)*. The base of the plant is a vigorous clump that in just one season can grow 15–25 ft (4.5–8 m) tall. It twines when young, then stiffens and branches with age. The true leaves are reduced to stem scales. Spined 1–3 in (2.5–8 cm) dark green cladophylls perform the function of leaves and tiny cream flowers, singly or in clusters, develop on the edges or faces of these. The flowers are followed by 1/2 in (12 mm) diameter orange berries.
CULTIVATION: This vigorous plant needs a stout climbing support. It prefers moist, humus-rich, well-drained soil and prefers part- or full shade. It tolerates light frosts only and is propagated from seed or by layering.

Semele androgyna

This species may be grown outside in warmer areas, but needs protection in cooler climates. It may climb up to 60 ft (18 m). The leaves are oval, up to 4 in (10 cm) long and rather leathery. Flowering occurs on one-year-old growth. **ZONES 9–11.**

SEMIAQUILEGIA

A genus of 7 species of perennials from eastern Asia, these plants differ from *Aquilegia* in that the flowers are not spurred; most gardeners regard them as just another type of columbine or granny's bonnet. They grow 12–18 in (30–45 cm) tall with 3-part basal leaves from 2–12 in (5–30 cm) long. Each of the 3 purple-tinted leaflets is also divided into 3 parts. Long-stemmed, pendulous, 1 in (25 mm) diameter flowers open in spring and summer.
CULTIVATION: These plants prefer woodland conditions: moist, humus-rich, well-drained soil with shade from the hottest sun. They are frost hardy to at least 5°F (−15°C) and easily grown, though prone to aphid infestation. Propagate from seed or by dividing established clumps.

Semiaquilegia ecalcarata

A perennial with purplish dark green ferny leaves, this species grows to 18 in (45 cm) high. The wine or purple flowers nod in heads of 5 to 8 and look like a small *Aquilegia* without spurs, but are dainty and modest. It comes from western China. **ZONES 6–9.**

SEMIARUNDINARIA

This genus consists of 10 to 20 tall, slow-growing bamboos from China and Japan. The rhizomes tend to run in warmer climates, but remain much more bunched in cooler areas. They form rather open clumps, starting as plum-colored stems but becoming a smooth green flushed with purplish or brownish tints.
CULTIVATION: They will tolerate sun or shade, and prefer a moist, humus-rich soil either in the garden or a tub. Propagate by division.

Semiarundinaria fastuosa
NARIHIRA BAMBOO

The tall hollow stems of this species grow 10–40 ft (3–12 m) high, but only 1/2–2 1/2 in (1.2–6 cm) wide. They have purplish brown markings, with a white powder beneath the nodes. The green leaves are up to 8 in (20 cm) long and appear towards the top of the stems. It comes from southern areas of Japan where it is widely grown as an ornamental plant. **ZONES 7–11.**

SEMPERVIVUM

This is a genus of about 40 evergreen, perennial succulents originating in Europe and western Asia. They almost all have small yellow, pink or white star-shaped flowers in summer, but their chief beauty resides in the symmetry of their rosettes of leaves and the way they spread to form carpets of foliage, making them ideal for rock gardens, walls and banks. Like all succulents they do not mind dry conditions; they take their name from a custom dating from Roman times of growing them on the roofs of houses—it was said that no witch could land her broomstick on a roof on which houseleeks were growing.
CULTIVATION: Plant in full sun in gravelly, well-drained soil. Flowering does not begin for several years; the rosettes die after flowering leaving offsets, from which they can be propagated.

Sempervivum arachnoideum
COBWEB HOUSELEEK

The web of white hairs covering the green, triangular-leafed rosettes of this species no doubt inspired its name. Through summer it produces pink to crimson flowers in loose terminal clusters. A native of the European Alps, it grows to a height of 3 in (8 cm) and spread of 12 in (30 cm). **ZONES 5–10.**

Sempervivum ciliosum

The 1–2 in (2.5–5 cm) rosettes of gray-green hairy leaves on this species from Bulgaria, northwestern Greece and the former Yugoslavia give rise to 4 in (10 cm) stems of greenish yellow flowers, which appear in summer. **ZONES 6–10.**

Sempervivum arachnoideum

Sempervivum ciliosum

Sempervivum × *fauconnetti*

This small, rosette-forming hybrid reaches a maximum spread of 2 in (5 cm) and is characterized by the white cobwebs that envelop it. Small, pink, star-shaped flowers develop in spring. **ZONES 6–10.**

Sempervivum × *funckii*

The 1½ in (35 mm) wide rosettes of this species have leaves with hairy margins. Rose-purple flowers appear in summer on 8 in (20 cm) stalks. **ZONES 5–10.**

Sempervivum tectorum

COMMON HOUSELEEK, ROOF HOUSELEEK, HENS AND CHICKENS

The rosettes of this species are reddish tipped, sometimes red throughout. The flowers are purple to rosy red and appear in one-sided terminal clusters on 12 in (30 cm) high stems in summer. It reaches 4–6 in (10–15 cm) high and 18 in (45 cm) wide. Applying bruised leaves to the skin has a cooling effect and is said to relieve burns, insect bites, skin problems and fever; the juice is used on warts and

Sempervivum × *fauconnetti*

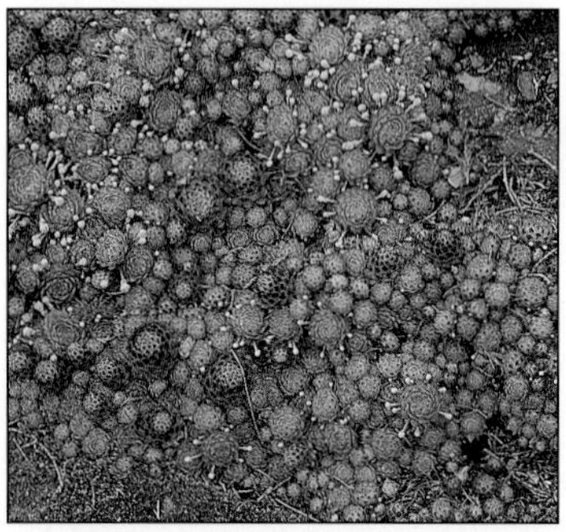

Sempervivum × *funckii*

Senecio articulatus

freckles. **'Commander Hay'** from the UK has large rosettes of red and green; **'Purple Beauty'** has dark violet leaves; and **'Magnificum'** has large rosettes and pink flowers. **ZONES 4–10.**

SENECIO

This large genus of vigorous leafy plants includes some 1,000 species from all over the world. Plants range from annuals, biennials and perennials to evergreen tree-like shrubs and climbers, some of the species being succulent. The daisy-like flowers, usually yellow but sometimes red, orange, blue or purple, are arranged in small to large clusters at the tops of the plants. Some species contain alkaloids and are poisonous to humans and animals.

CULTIVATION: Reasonably fertile, well-drained soil suits these frost-tender to fully frost-hardy plants, as well as a sunny location. Regular tip pruning encourages a bushy habit. Propagate shrubs from cuttings in summer, annuals from seed in fall (autumn) and perennials by division in spring.

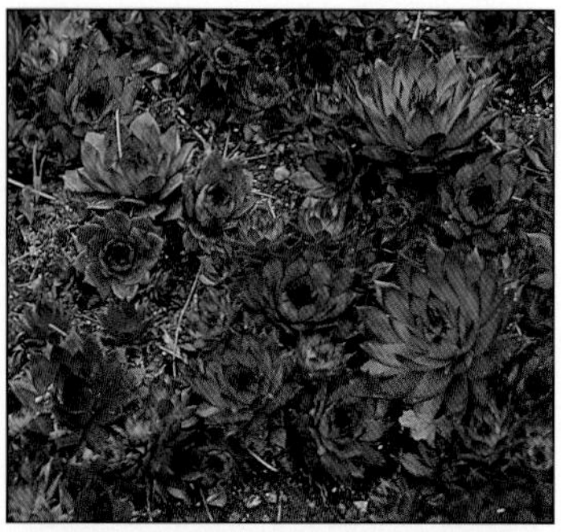

Sempervivum tectorum 'Purple Beauty'

Senecio cineraria

Senecio elegans

Senecio arborescens

This is a tropical species that grows to tree size, found at medium altitudes in the mountains of Costa Rica, in clearings in rainforests. It grows to 20 ft (6 m) or more tall with a thick trunk and large leaves. In summer it bears sprays of numerous small yellow flowerheads that are strongly aromatic. **ZONES 10–12.**

Senecio articulatus

syn. ***Kleinia articulata***

HOT DOG CACTUS, CANDLE PLANT

Native to South Africa, this perennial succulent grows up to 24 in (60 cm) tall. Its multiple grayish blue stems are tubular and weakly jointed. Terminal sprays of yellow-white daisy-like flowers bloom from spring into summer. A marginally frost-hardy species, it is well suited to coastal climates and is an ideal choice for use as a tub or large pot specimen. **ZONES 9–12.**

Senecio cineraria

syns ***Cineraria maritima, Senecio candicans, S. maritimus***

DUSTY MILLER

This evergreen subshrub or shrub, which grows 24 in (60 cm) tall and wide, is a multi-purpose bloomer for grouping or for formal bedding in semi-shaded spots, window boxes, containers on balconies or in protected courtyards. The daisy-like flowers are mustard yellow in color. *Senecio cineraria* is very tolerant of heat, salt air and poor soil, but does poorly in high humidity or excessive rain. **'Silver Dust'** has lacy, almost white leaves. **ZONES 8–11.**

Senecio arborescens

Senecio macroglossus

Senecio confusus

syn. ***Pseudogynoxys chenopodioides***

MEXICAN FLAME VINE

This species dazzles with its clusters of flame-colored flowers throughout summer. It is a bushy, evergreen, twining climber that reaches 20 ft (6 m) or more in height and has thick, toothed, mid-green leaves. It is native to areas from Mexico to Honduras. **ZONES 10–12.**

Senecio elegans

WILD CINERARIA

This marginally frost-hardy, hairy annual is native to South Africa and has an erect habit, growing to 24 in (60 cm) tall. Its branching stems are covered with variable dark green leaves that range from entire to pinnate, up to 3 in (8 cm) long. In spring to summer daisy-like purplish pink flowers appear in dome-shaped terminal clusters. **ZONES 9–11.**

Senecio macroglossus

NATAL IVY, WAX VINE

This is a smooth-leafed evergreen climber with arrowhead-shaped leaves up to 2½ in (6 cm) long. Pale yellow flowers with showy heads appear in summer. It comes from eastern South Africa, Mozambique and Zimbabwe. **'Variegatus'** has variegated leaves of green and yellow. ZONES 10–11.

Senecio rowleyanus
STRING OF BEADS

This perennial succulent forms creeping mats that root at the nodes. The spherical leaves are ¼ in (6 mm) across. The white daisy flowers ½ in (12 mm) across appear on 1½ in (35 mm) stalks in summer. Widely grown in hanging baskets, with pendent stems of gray bead leaves, it is from southwestern Africa. ZONES 9–12.

Senecio serpens
BLUE CHALKSTICKS

The cylindrical blue-green leaves on this 12 in (30 cm) tall, shrubby perennial succulent branch from the base. The white flowers appear in summer. It comes from South Africa. ZONES 9–11.

Senecio tamoides

This South African climber makes a mass of succulent foliage that can mound up on a wall or fence to a height of 10 ft (3 m) or more, though not spreading widely. From late spring to fall (autumn) it bears large clusters of small bright yellow flowerheads. ZONES 8–11.

Senecio viravira
syn. *Senecio leucostachys*
DUSTY MILLER

This species from central Argentina gets its common name from its soft, silver-gray foliage. It is a loosely branched subshrub to 24 in (60 cm) tall with branches from the base all densely covered with white hairs. The 2 in (5 cm) long, slightly furry leaves are dissected into linear segments. White, daisy-like flowerheads with golden centers are held above the foliage in summer. ZONES 8–11.

Senecio rowleyanus

Senecio serpens

Senecio cineraria

Senecio cineraria

Senna alata

SENNA

This large genus consists of 260 species of fast-growing, mostly evergreen shrubs as well as some herbaceous perennials and small trees. It includes several species grown for medicinal use. Formerly classified under *Cassia*, they occur in most warmer parts of the world with most species in the Americas, Africa and Australia. They are grown for their clusters of buttercup-like flowers, mostly golden yellow but sometimes pink. The compound leaves consist of paired leaflets. The fruit are long pods, either flattened or rounded.

CULTIVATION: Most species thrive in light, well-drained soil with full sun and shelter from wind. Prune plants lightly after flowering to maintain dense foliage. Propagate from seed (first soaked in warm water for 24 hours) or from cuttings.

Senna aciphylla

Senna artemisioides

Senna didymobotrya

Senna aciphylla
syn. *Cassia aciphylla*

This shrubby species native to eastern Australia develops into a mound of foliage up to 5 ft (1.5 m) high with a slightly wider spread. Its leaves are less than 2 in (5 cm) long and are made up of 5 to 12 pairs of small leaflets. Its flowers, in clusters of 2 to 4 blooms, appear sporadically, with the heaviest bloom in late spring. ZONES 9–11.

Senna alata
syn. *Cassia alata*
EMPRESS CANDLE PLANT, CANDLE BUSH

This fast-growing, evergreen, tropical shrub grows to about 6–30 ft (1.8–9 m) tall and 15 ft (4.5 m) wide. Its large leaves have up to 14 leaflets and bright yellow, cup-shaped flowers are borne in summer in upright, candle-like spikes; the winged seed pods are 6 in (15 cm) long. The plants are a source of chrysophanic acid, which is used in the treatment of some skin diseases. ZONES 10–12.

Senna artemisioides
syn. *Cassia artemisioides*
SILVER CASSIA, PUNTY, FEATHERY CASSIA

This dense, rounded, evergreen shrub reaches 6 ft (1.8 m) tall and is endemic to dry parts of southern Australia. The foliage is silver gray and silky due to a covering of minute hairs. The leaves are up to 2 in (5 cm) long, with 3 to 8 pairs of narrow leaflets. The flowers are a rich yellow with contrasting brown anthers, arranged in clusters of 10 to 12; flowering extends from winter to early summer. The fruit are flattened pods that mature dark brown. ZONES 9–11.

Senna corymbosa
syn. *Cassia corymbosa*
AUTUMN CASSIA, FLOWERY SENNA

This fast-growing shrub from southern USA, Uruguay and Argentina has light green foliage and large, dense clusters of bright yellow flowers that cover the shrub in fall (autumn). It grows to a height of 8 ft (2.4 m) with a spread of 6 ft (1.8 m). ZONES 9–11.

Senna didymobotrya
syn. *Cassia didymobotrya*

Indigenous to tropical Africa, this evergreen shrub grows to 10 ft (3 m) and has a rounded canopy on a short trunk. Fine downy hairs cover both the leaves and shoots; the foliage has an unpleasant smell when crushed. The leaves may be 12–18 in (30–45 cm) long. From summer to winter yellow flowers are carried near the shoot tips in erect spikes up to 12 in (30 cm) long, bursting from bud scales. The fruit are long, flattened pods. ZONES 10–12.

Senna multiglandulosa
syn. *Cassia tomentosa*

This is a widespread and variable leafy shrub or small tree from Central and South America, southern USA, eastern Australia, India and South Africa. It grows 3–20 ft (1–6 m) high. The new branches of this species are downy but become dark brownish gray with age. The leaves are up to 8 in (20 cm) long and are composed of about 8 paired leaflets with sharp tips. The yellow flowers are up to ¾ in (18 mm) across in heads of up to twenty. The 6 in (15 cm) seed pods are black, softly hairy and hang vertically down. **ZONES 8–12.**

Sequoia sempervirens

Senna multijuga
syn. *Cassia multijuga*

This species from Central and South America is a fast-growing evergreen tree that reaches 25 ft (8 m) in height and forms a rounded crown with attractive, pinnate leaves with 10 to 15 pairs of leaflets. It bears golden-yellow flowers on large, terminal panicles in late summer, followed by long seed pods. **ZONES 10–12.**

Senna occidentalis
COFFEE SENNA, STYPTIC WEED

This dense, rather unpleasant-smelling shrub comes from tropical Africa, southern Asia, northern Australia and the Pacific Islands up to Hawaii. It usually grows to 5 ft (1.5 m) tall with pinnate leaves and a dark pinkish calyx giving rise to yellow flowers. **ZONES 10–12.**

Sequoia sempervirens 'Adpressa'

Sequoia sempervirens

Senna pendula

This shrub or small tree reaches a height of 6–10 ft (1.8–3 m) and forms a broadly spreading mass of evergreen foliage up to 8 ft (2.4 m) across. The bright yellow flowers are borne in large clusters in fall (autumn). The fruit are cylindrical pods. A decorative, fast-growing plant for the subtropics, it is short lived and apt to spread from self-sown seed and become a nuisance. In cool climates it makes a fine plant for a mildly heated greenhouse. **ZONES 9–11.**

Senna phyllodinea
SILVER CASSIA

This is a small shrub of 3–15 ft (1–4.5 m) tall from inland Australia. It is all silvery gray with the true leaves reduced to phyllodes up to 2 in (5 cm) long. The yellow flowers are produced in heads in summer and fall (autumn). **ZONES 9–11.**

Senna siamea
KASSOD TREE

This open-branched tree grows rapidly to around 25 ft (8 m) high with a spread of around 20 ft (6 m). It has felty leaf stalks and up to 12 pairs of oval leaflets. The yellow flowers are in dense heads. It comes from Indonesia and the Malay Peninsula. **ZONES 11–12.**

Senna sophera
syn. *Cassia sophera*

This bushy shrub from tropical Africa, Australia and Central America grows to 6 ft (1.8 m) tall. The leaflets are in 4 to 8 pairs and there are only a few bright yellow flowers to the head. **ZONES 9–12.**

Senna multijuga

Senna pendula

Senna spectabilis
syn. *Cassia spectabilis*

This evergreen species from Central and South America varies greatly in size, ranging from a 6 ft (1.8 m) shrub to a 70 ft (21 m) tree. It is mainly seen as a rangy, small tree with ferny leaves up to 18 in (45 cm) long, covered with fine down when young. In summer it produces clusters of bright yellow flowers, followed by seed pods up to 12 in (30 cm) long. **ZONES 10–12.**

SEQUOIA
CALIFORNIA REDWOOD, COAST REDWOOD

This genus, which contains a single species, boasts the world's tallest tree, at about 360 ft (110 m). The redwood is extremely long lived, with some specimens estimated to be about 3,500 years old. An evergreen conifer indigenous to the west coast of the USA from Monterey, California north to southern Oregon, it is valued for its timber, and it has been necessary to provide statutory protection for the most notable groves in national parks and elsewhere to save it from exploitation.

CULTIVATION: This tree will survive in a wide range of climates; extremely cold weather may affect the foliage but not the plant itself. It grows quickly when young and needs plenty of water, and prefers full sun or part-shade and deep, well-drained soil. Suckers should be removed immediately and general pruning is tolerated. Propagate from seed or heeled cuttings; this is one of the few conifers that will sprout from the cut stump.

Sequoia sempervirens

This single-trunked, conical tree has bright green, flattened, leaf-like needles up to 1 in (25 mm) long. The foliage is held horizontally on small side branches, with the main branches drooping slightly. The whole tree has a resinous

Senna sophera

Senna phyllodinea

aroma like pine wood, especially the red-brown, fibrous bark which is very thick and deeply fissured in parallel lines running straight up the trunk. **'Adpressa'** is very dwarf, remaining for many years about 3 ft (1 m) high and 6 ft (1.8 m) wide, maturing to 20 ft (6 m) high; **'Aptos Blue'** has blue-green foliage and slightly pendulous branch tips; **'Los Altos'** has deep green, heavy-textured foliage on arching branches; and **'Santa Cruz'** has pale green, soft-textured, slightly drooping foliage. **ZONES 8–10.**

SEQUOIADENDRON

GIANT SEQUOIA, BIG TREE

From the Sierra Nevada area of California, the only species in this genus is a true giant of a tree. While not quite as tall as the California redwood *(Sequoia sempervirens)*, it is far more heavily built and contains the largest timber volume of any tree. It is also very long lived, and is an impressive tree for large parks and gardens. Its huge trunk is covered in rough, deeply fissured, reddish brown bark.
CULTIVATION: Trees of this size need a solid base, so plant in deep, well-drained soil in an open, sunny position and water well when young; it is frost resistant but dislikes dry conditions. Propagate from seed or cuttings.

Sequoiadendron giganteum

syns *Sequoia gigantea, Wellingtonia gigantea*

This conifer can grow to 300 ft (90 m) tall, with a trunk up to 40 ft (12 m) in diameter at the base. It is an upright, single-trunked, conical tree with sprays of deep green, slightly prickly, cypress-like foliage. A specimen of this species in the Sequoia National Park in California is said to be 3,800 years old. **'Pendulum'** has pendent side branches. **ZONES 7–10.**

SERENOA

SAW PALMETTO, SCRUB PALMETTO

This genus contains just a single palm species which occurs naturally in southeastern USA. It is an evergreen fan palm with creeping or, rarely, short upright stems. This plant forms immense colonies in its natural habitat.
CULTIVATION: This palm prefers full sun or part-shade and dislikes frost. It grows best in well-drained soil and is very tolerant of exposed coastal locations; it also tolerates boggy conditions. Propagate from seed or suckers.

Serenoa repens

This palm has stems that are mostly prostrate or creeping and grows to 24–36 in (60–90 cm) high and twice as wide, but occasionally grows an upright 10 ft (3 m) stem. The fan-shaped leaves are held stiffly upwards and vary from green to bluish green or even silver; each leaf is 18–30 in (45–75 cm) across and is divided into about 20 strap-like segments. The leaf stalks are toothed along the edges. In summer creamy white, perfumed flowers are hidden among the foliage. The fruit that follow are egg-shaped and blackish when ripe. **ZONES 8–11.**

SERIPHIDIUM

This genus comprises around 130 species of annuals, perennials or subshrubs from dry areas of the northern hemisphere, most of which have formerly been classified under *Artemisia*. The leaves are usually deeply divided, silver or gray and aromatic. It is for these they are grown, as the flowers are not very interesting.
CULTIVATION: These marginally to very frost-hardy plants prefer full sun and poor to moderately fertile, dry, very well-drained soil. Propagate from seed or cuttings.

Seriphidium tridentatum

syn. *Artemisia tridentata*

BIG SAGEBRUSH

This evergreen perennial or spreading subshrub is native to the mountains and basins of western North America. The 3-pointed silvery leaves have a pungent aroma; the feathery, grayish white or yellow flowers are not showy. Height varies from 18 in (45 cm) to over 10 ft (3 m). **ZONES 7–10.**

SERISSA

This genus has only one species, an evergreen shrub to 18 in (45 cm) high with oval, rather thick leaves. It is grown for its neat habit and long flowering time.
CULTIVATION: Suitable for a full sun position in moderately fertile, moist but well-drained soil in areas without frost, it may be grown in greenhouses or indoors with good light and humidity. Propagate from cuttings or by layering.

Serissa foetida

syn. *Serissa japonica*

From Southeast Asia, this species has small, oval, deep green leaves that have an unpleasant smell if they are bruised. From spring to fall (autumn) 4- or 5-lobed, funnel-shaped white flowers appear. Cultivars with double flowers or variegated leaves are also available. **'Pink Snow Rose'** has pale pink flowers and leaves edged off-white. **ZONES 9–12.**

SERRURIA

Members of the protea family, *Serruria* includes about 55 species of evergreen shrubs that are endemic to the southwestern Cape area of South Africa. Each flowerhead consists of a central tuft of flowers surrounded by leafy bracts, often the dominant feature of the bloom. The flowerheads may be solitary at the branch ends or in clusters. Some are given a very feathery appearance by the mass of central stamens. *Serruria* range from prostrate shrubs to plants 5 ft (1.5 m) tall. The leaves are fern-like, with each leaf divided into many fine segments. The fruits are small hard nuts covered with hairs.
CULTIVATION: These plants thrive only in sandy, perfectly drained soil and a warm climate; plant in an open sunny spot. They grow faster than most other proteas and are best propagated from seed or cuttings.

Seriphidium tridentatum

Serruria florida

BLUSHING BRIDE

This species forms a slender shrub to 4 ft (1.2 m) tall. It is rare in the wild, but is popular due to its long-lasting, 2 in (5 cm) wide dainty white to pale pink flowerheads. These consist of showy, broad, papery, creamy white bracts, flushed pink or rarely green, surrounding a central tuft of feathery, silvery white to pinkish flowers and appearing in clusters of 3 to 5 from winter to spring. The leaves are delicate and fern-like and are divided into needle-like segments. **'Sugar 'n' spice'** has white bracts flushed deep rose pink surrounding the central mass of pale pink flowers. **ZONES 9–11.**

SESAMUM

This is a genus of about 15 species of annuals from Africa and tropical Asia, with leaves simple or palmately divided and white, pink, red or purple flowers that are tubular and 2-lipped. The fruits are oblong capsules that open when dry to release numerous small seeds. One species *(Sesamum orientale)* is the crop plant sesame, grown mainly for its seeds which are used to flavor bread, cakes and biscuits and from which sesame oil is extracted. The whole seed is used extensively in cooking in the Middle East and Asia. Tahini is a nut-like cream of ground sesame seeds much used in Lebanese food.
CULTIVATION: These plants require a warm climate for the seeds to mature. Allow a growing season of 90 to 120 days of hot weather. They do best in moderately rich soil in a sunny position. Propagate from seed.

Sesamum orientale

syn. *Sesamum indicum*

SESAME

This erect annual grows to 30 in (75 cm) tall with dark green lance-shaped leaves and axillary pink or white tubular flowers. Harvest the seeds in fall (autumn) before they completely dry out and scatter. **ZONES 9–12.**

Serenoa repens

Serruria florida

Sequoiadendron giganteum

Sequoiadendron giganteum

SESELI

MOON CARROT

These perennials and biennials from Europe, the Caucasus and central Asia are good plants for the meadow or wildflower garden. They are not common but are grown for the light, airy look of their lacy foliage and the rounded umbels of tiny, mostly white flowers. There are over 60 species in all, ranging in size from about 8 in (20 cm) to 5 ft (1.5 m).

CULTIVATION: Demanding only full sun and free-draining soil, moon carrots are not particularly fussy or hard to grow plants. Once established they will tolerate extended dry periods but always look and grow best with adequate water. Fully frost hardy, they are easily raised from seed sown either in fall (autumn) or spring, or established plants can be lifted and divided in late winter.

Seseli dichotomum

This is a summer-flowering perennial from the Caucasus with softly hairy, bipinnate leaves up to 6 in (15 cm) long. White flowers appear at the ends of the branches in rounded umbels. **ZONES 6–10.**

Sesleria albicans

Sesleria autumnalis

Shepherdia argentea

Setaria palmifolia

Seseli gummiferum

From the coasts of the Black and Aegean Seas, this perennial grows 3–4 ft (1–1.2 m) tall producing several strong, stiff stems. The leaves are whitish gray, lobed and hairy, making the plant attractive for its foliage alone. In summer hairy umbels of white or pinkish red flowers dot the plant. The specific name *gummiferum* is a reference to the plant's gum-like sap. **ZONES 6–10.**

SESLERIA

Coming from mountainous regions in Europe, the 33 species in this genus are grown for their brightly colored foliage, which consists of narrow leaves, and for their flowers which appear in dense, spike-like panicles. They are evergreen perennial grasses that, for the best effect, should be planted in mixed borders or rock gardens or in wildflower meadows.

CULTIVATION: Fully frost hardy, they prefer full sun or dappled shade and moderately fertile, well-drained soil that is neutral to slightly alkaline. Propagate from seed or by division.

Sesleria albicans

syn. ***Sesleria caerulea*** **subsp.** ***calcarea***

BLUE MOOR GRASS

This vigorous species forms mounds of densely tufted pale blue-gray leaves that are 12 in (30 cm) long and glossy deep green beneath. Growing to 12 in (30 cm) tall and 10 in (25 cm) wide, it bears its bluish purple flower panicles from mid-spring to early summer. **ZONES 4–10.**

Sesleria autumnalis

AUTUMN MOOR GRASS

This clump-forming grass produces bright green, narrow foliage with a slight yellow cast to 12 in (30 cm) in height. The narrow, 3 in (8 cm) long, silvery white flower panicles are borne among the foliage in late summer to early fall (autumn). **ZONES 5–10.**

SETARIA

BRISTLE GRASS

Consisting of some 100 species of annual and perennial grasses, this genus is widespread throughout the tropical, subtropical and warm-temperate zones. Some have become annual weeds in temperate farmlands. Size ranges from 24 in (60 cm) to 10 ft (3 m) tall with strong, upright stems clothed with very narrow, deep green leaves up to 3 ft (1 m) long. The name bristle grass comes from the stiff, sometimes bottlebrush-like flowerheads that develop in summer. The taller, more ornamental species are useful as screening plants, especially on windy sites.

CULTIVATION: They thrive in any reasonably moist, well-drained soil in full sun. Frost hardiness varies with the species. Propagate the annuals from seed, perennials from seed or by division.

Setaria palmifolia

PALM GRASS

This tall coarse perennial grass from tropical Asia consists of a clump of strong upright stems up to 6 ft (1.8 m) tall. The leaf lobes are folded, up to 18 in (45 cm) long and $2\frac{1}{2}$ in (6 cm) wide, sometimes striped. The flower panicles are held at the top, being up to 15 in (38 cm) long. **ZONES 9–12.**

SHEPHERDIA

BUFFALO BERRY

There are 3 species of these North American evergreen or deciduous shrubs which are grown because they will tolerate dry, rocky conditions. They have minute, tubular flowers borne on spikes or racemes, followed by the simple, opposite leaves. The flowers are also followed by rounded red or yellowish red fruits on female plants.

CULTIVATION: These fully frost-hardy plants prefer full sun and moderately fertile, well-drained soil. The fruit will only be produced if both male and female plants are grown together. Propagate from seed or by division.

Shepherdia argentea

Shepherdia argentea

SILVERBERRY, SILVER BUFFALO BERRY

This dense shrub grows to 12 ft (3.5 m) with thorny branches and intensely silver oblong leaves. The small yellow flowers are followed by single or clustered glossy bright red edible fruit, which can be made into a jelly. There is also a form with yellow fruit (***Shepherdia argentea* f. *xanthocarpa***). This species is sometimes used as a hedge because of its hardiness. **ZONES 2–9.**

SHIBATAEA

The plants of this genus of 8 species of evergreen bamboo from China and Japan appear to form clumps but in fact grow from a running rhizome, though they are not invasive. They range in size from 24 in (60 cm) to 6 ft (1.8 m) tall and have very narrow, leafy stems, somewhat flattened on one side. The sheathless leaves are 2–6 in (5–15 cm) long and up to 1 in (25 mm) wide. The foliage at the top of the stems arches and droops.

CULTIVATION: They are easily grown in any moist, well-drained, lime-free soil in sun or shade. Most species are frost hardy to at least 10°F (–12°C) and make excellent, billowy ground covers for exposed positions provided they do not dry out. Propagate by division at any time.

Shibataea kumasasa

OKAME-ZASA

This small bamboo grows to 6 ft (1.8 m) and is very resistant to low temperatures down to –10°F (–23°C). It is very dense and bushy, with short broad dark green leaves on long stalks. It comes from Japan. **ZONES 6–10.**

SHORTIA

There are 6 species of these evergreen stemless plants with creeping roots. They come from eastern Asia and North America. The long-stalked leaves form a rosette, each leaf being round or heart-shaped and rather glossy. The flowers may be white, blue or pink, either single or in small heads and rather nodding.

CULTIVATION: Species of *Shortia* need a deeply shady spot with humus-rich, moist but well-drained soil. Propagation is by division or from rooted runners.

Shortia galacifolia

OCONEE BELLS

The rather round leaves of this perennial from eastern USA are 2 in (5 cm) in diameter, glossy green, toothed and becoming bronzed in winter. Single white or blue flowers occur on 4 in (10 cm) stalks, each flower reaching 1 in (25 mm) across. **ZONES 5–9.**

Shortia soldanelloides

FRINGED GALAX, FRINGEBELL

This mat-forming perennial from Japan has rounded leaves 2 in (5 cm) in diameter and with coarse teeth. Deep pink, white or bluish flowers occur in groups of 4 to 6 on 3 in (8 cm) stalks; each flower is 1 in (25 mm) across with the petals fringed. It comes from Japan. ***Shortia soldanelloides* var. *ilicifolia*** has leaves which have only a few coarse teeth. **ZONES 7–9.**

SIDALCEA

PRAIRIE MALLOW, CHECKER MALLOW

The 20 to 25 species of upright annuals or perennials with lobed, rounded leaves in this genus are found in western USA, from open grasslands to mountain forests. Pink, purple or white flowers have a silky appearance and feel, and last well as cut flowers.
CULTIVATION: They prefer cool summers and mild winters in good, deep, moisture-retentive soil. They will tolerate a little shade in hot climates. If cut back after flowering they will produce a second flush of blooms. Propagate from seed or by division.

Sidalcea campestris

MEADOW SIDALCEA

This hairy stemmed perennial grows up to 6 ft (1.8 m) tall. The pale pink or white flowers are 3 in (8 cm) across. It comes from northwestern USA. **ZONES 7–10.**

Sidalcea malviflora

CHECKERBLOOM

This erect perennial plant grows to 4 ft (1.2 m) tall with spreading fibrous roots. It has lobed leaves and loose heads of pink or white flowers resembling hollyhocks during spring and summer. It comes from the western states of the USA. Most cultivars included under this name are now believed to be hybrids with other species. **ZONES 6–10.**

Sidalcea 'Rose Queen'

syn. *Sidalcea malviflora* 'Rose Queen'

Large, deep pink, cupped flowers are borne in spikes in summer on this fully frost-hardy perennial. The divided leaves form a basal clump with a spread of 24 in (60 cm). The overall height of this plant is 4 ft (1.2 m) and tall plants may need staking. **'William Smith'** is similar but grows only 3 ft (1 m) tall and produces flowers in 2 tones of deep pink. **ZONES 6–10.**

Sideroxylon inerme

SIDERITIS

This genus consists of over 100 species, including evergreen subshrubs and shrubs, annuals and perennials. They are very tolerant of dry conditions and are grown for their white, often aromatic foliage, which is composed of felted or hairy leaves in opposite pairs. Bell-shaped or tubular 2-lipped flowers appear in spikes in summer.
CULTIVATION: Marginally frost hardy to frost tender, they prefer full sun and very well-drained, fertile soil. Propagate from seed or cuttings or by division.

Sideritis candicans

This 3 ft (1 m) tall shrub has white stems and leaves. The hairy flowers are yellow with white or brown tips, and occur on 12 in (30 cm) stems. It comes from the Canary Islands and Madeira. **ZONES 8–10.**

SIDEROXYLON

COASTAL MILKWOOD

The evergreen trees of this genus from Africa are grown for their timber, which is widely used in ornamental carving. They are elegant, tall trees with trunks flanged at the base and covered with wrinkled, corky, mottled brown bark. The young branchlets are covered with distinctive small, pimple-like swellings. The thick, firm leaves are oval. White bell-shaped flowers appear from spring to fall (autumn); they are mildly fragrant, and clustered in groups of 2 or 6 on hairy stalks. The flesh of the succulent, plum-like berries is edible when made into jam.
CULTIVATION: These trees prefer light to medium, well-drained soil in a protected, sunny or part-shaded position. Propagate from seed or cuttings, or by layering.

Sideroxylon inerme

Sidalcea campestris

Sidalcea malviflora

Sidalcea 'Rose Queen'

Shortia soldanelloides var. *ilicifolia*

Sideroxylon inerme

This smallish, dense, leafy tree to 30 ft (9 m) tall grows along the east coast of South Africa from the Southwestern Cape to Zululand. The glossy green leaves are oval with rounded tips. A milky latex appears whenever the leaves or branches are broken. This superb foliage tree is a good choice for the garden and does well in full sun. It tolerates considerable wind and sea air, but is sensitive to frost. **ZONES 9–12.**

SILENE

CAMPION, CATCHFLY

This genus contains over 500 species of annuals, biennials and deciduous or evergreen perennials featuring 5-petalled summer flowers, baggy calyces and a multitude of small, elliptical, often silky leaves. Some of the species do well potted; others make good ground covers, with numerous stems forming a mound. Many of the weedier species open their flowers only at night, when they can be quite pretty, though all you see during the day is shrivelled petals. Some species exude gum from their stems; passing flies get stuck to this, hence the common name catchfly.
CULTIVATION: Widely distributed throughout temperate and cold climates of the northern hemisphere, these marginally to fully frost-hardy plants like fertile, well-drained soil and full or part-sun. Propagate from seed in spring or early fall (autumn) or from cuttings in spring.

S

Silene armeria

Silene coeli-rosa

Silene fimbriata

Silene acaulis
MOSS CAMPION

This is a mat-forming evergreen perennial with masses of small leaves and shortly stalked pink flowers in summer. It comes from subarctic regions of Europe, Asia and North America, but is often poorly flowering in cultivation. It reaches a height of only 2 in (5 cm) with an 8 in (20 cm) spread. **ZONES 2–9.**

Silene armeria

This European annual or biennial has pink, bell-shaped flowers with 5 notched petals. Growing to a height of 12 in (30 cm) with a spread of 6 in (15 cm), it has slender, erect, branching stems and linear leaves. **ZONES 6–10.**

Silene caroliniana
WILD PINK

This 8 in (20 cm) tall perennial branches from the base and carries heads of pink flowers during summer. It comes from eastern and central USA. **ZONES 5–10.**

Silene laciniata

Silene coeli-rosa
syns *Agrostemma coeli-rosa, Lychnis coeli-rosa, Viscaria elegans*

ROSE OF HEAVEN

This upright annual from the Mediterranean bears pinkish purple flowers in summer. Its lance-shaped, green leaves have a grayish cast. It grows rapidly to 18 in (45 cm) with a spread of 6 in (15 cm). **ZONES 6–11.**

Silene fimbriata

This hairy perennial to 24 in (60 cm) tall with upright leafy stems has loose heads of large white flowers and a persistent light green inflated calyx. It comes from Turkey. **ZONES 6–10.**

Silene keiskei var. *minor*

This evergreen perennial from Japan reaches 4 in (20 cm) tall and 8 in (20 cm) wide, on slender stems with hairy, dark green leaves. Sprays of dark rose-pink flowers appear in late summer. **ZONES 6–10.**

Silene laciniata
INDIAN PINK, MEXICAN CAMPION

This 3 ft (1 m) tall perennial comes from California and northern Mexico.

Silene pendula 'Compacta'

Silene acaulis

The flowers are held in small heads and are bright crimson in color. **ZONES 7–11.**

Silene latifolia
syn. *Silene alba*

WHITE CAMPION, WHITE COCKLE, EVENING CAMPION

This species is a common European wildflower; it wafts a pleasing scent by night. A perennial plant, it grows to a height of 3 ft (1 m). The slender, branching stems produce white, bell-shaped flowers with 5 bilobed petals in spring and summer. The leaves are sticky and hairy. *Silene latifolia* has become naturalized in North America, where it is a weed of cultivated areas. **ZONES 6–11.**

Silene pendula
NODDING CATCHFLY

This moderately fast-growing, bushy annual from the Mediterranean bears clusters of pale pink flowers in summer and early fall (autumn). It has oval, hairy, mid-green leaves and grows to 8 in (20 cm) in height with a similar spread. The cultivar **'Compacta'** is a dense form only growing to 4 in (10 cm). **ZONES 7–11.**

Silene uniflora cultivar

Silene keiskei var. *minor*

Silene vulgaris

Silene schafta

This is a hairy clump-forming, semi-evergreen perennial from western Asia. The deep purplish red flowers appear in late summer and fall (autumn) on stems 10 in (25 cm) high. **ZONES 6–10.**

Silene uniflora
syn. *Silene vulgaris* subsp. *maritima*

SEA CAMPION

This deep-rooted perennial bears a multitude of white flowers like pompons on branched stems in spring or summer. Its calyces are greenish and balloon like; its lanceolate leaves have a grayish cast. Reaching about 8 in (20 cm) in height and spread, it can be grown on top of walls, in beds or containers and grows wild on cliffs along the European seaboard. **'Flore Pleno'** has double white flowers with deeply cut petals. **ZONES 3–10.**

Silene vulgaris
BLADDER CAMPION, MAIDEN'S TEARS

This perennial has stems up to 24 in (60 cm) tall, oval leaves and white flowers with 2-lobed petals; the flowers are either solitary or in heads. It is found through-

Silene uniflora 'Flore Pleno'

Sisyrinchium graminoides

out northern Africa, temperate Asia and Europe. However, most plants sold as *Silene vulgaris* are, in fact, *S. uniflora*. **ZONES 5–10.**

SILYBUM

Two erect annuals or biennials make up this genus from the Mediterranean, southwest Europe, central Asia and Africa. They are grown for their rosettes of intensely spiny, glossy dark green foliage, and the rounded, single, purple-pink flowerheads which are surrounded by thorny bracts.
CULTIVATION: Fully frost hardy, they prefer full sun and poor to moderately fertile, well-drained soil. Propagate from seed and watch out for slugs and snails.

Silybum marianum
BLESSED THISTLE, HOLY THISTLE

Viciously spiny dark green foliage marbled with white forms a rosette of dissected leaves on this biennial. Single stalks produce a head of flowers up to 4 ft (1.2 m) tall in the summer of the second year. It has become naturalized in California and the pampas of Argentina. **ZONES 7–11.**

SIMMONDSIA
JOJOBA, GOAT NUT

There is only one species in this genus, an evergreen shrub that occurs naturally in dry, frost-free areas of southwestern USA and Mexico, despite the specific name *chinensis*. Male and female flowers

Sisyrinchium idahoense

are borne on separate plants; the male flowers are arranged in clusters, while the female flowers are solitary. Jojoba has attracted attention because oil from the capsules is used as a substitute for whale oil and in a range of products including cosmetics.
CULTIVATION: It needs a warm to hot climate and thrives in full sun in any well-drained soil. Propagate from seed or cuttings.

Simmondsia chinensis

This is a stiffly branched, upright shrub to 8 ft (2.4 m) tall. The leathery, dull green leaves have almost no stalks; they are oblong to oval and arranged in opposite pairs. The flowers are carried on short stalks in summer. In spring, leathery nut-like capsules appear. **ZONES 10–12.**

SINNINGIA

This genus of about 40 species of tuberous perennials and deciduous or evergreen shrubs from Central and South America includes the flower-shop gloxinias. The flowers can be as much as 4 in (10 cm) across and come in the richest shades of blue, violet, pink or red, usually with their throats mottled in white or paler shades of the main color and their petals edged in white or a pale color. They make spectacular pot plants, each plant carrying as many as 20 flowers at the center of a rosette of coarsely velvety leaves. Unfortunately they are useless as garden plants because when rain fills the trumpets they collapse.
CULTIVATION: Species of *Sinningia* prefer a humid atmosphere with bright light but not direct sun and moist, peaty soil. The leaves die down after flowering, after which the tubers can be dried out and stored in a frost-free area. Propagate from seed in spring or from stem cuttings in late spring or summer.

Sinningia speciosa
FLORIST'S GLOXINIA, VELVET SLIPPER PLANT

This perennial native of Brazil is highly prized for its large, trumpet-shaped flowers in white, red, blue, purple and pastels; these appear in summer. Nearly stemless with long, velvety leaves, it grows to a height of 12 in (30 cm) with a similar spread. The **Fyfiana Group** has large open flowers in various colors; the **Maxima Group** has nodding flowers. **ZONES 11–12.**

SISYRINCHIUM

These natives of South and North America can self-destruct in seasons of prolific blooming, because the flower stem kills off the leaf stem from which it sprouts. The genus includes 90 marginally to fully frost-hardy species of annuals and rhizomatous perennials. It is easy to mistake the narrow leaves of the seedlings for grass.
CULTIVATION: Establish them in poor to moderately fertile, moist but well-drained soil. Although tolerant of part-shade, they prefer sun. They readily self-seed, otherwise they can be propagated by division in late summer.

Sisyrinchium bellum
CALIFORNIA BLUE-EYED GRASS

Branched stems rise up to 18 in (45 cm) on this perennial species to form a tuft with linear leaves and amethyst-purple (rarely white) flowers. It comes from California. **ZONES 8–11.**

Sisyrinchium californicum
YELLOW-EYED GRASS

This short-lived, semi-evergreen perennial has winged stems to 15 in (38 cm) tall that carry yellow flowers in summer. From western North America, it has sword-shaped, gray-green leaves. **ZONES 5–10.**

Sisyrinchium graminoides
syn. ***Sisyrinchium angustifolium***
BLUE-EYED GRASS

This semi-evergreen perennial from southeastern USA grows 24 in (60 cm) tall. It blooms in spring, producing terminal clusters of small pale to dark purple flowers like irises, with yellow throats, to 5 in (12 cm) across. The stalks are flattened and winged. **ZONES 3–10.**

Sisyrinchium idahoense

Winged unbranched stems grow to 18 in (45 cm) on this semi-evergreen perennial from western USA. The flowers are violet-blue with a yellow center, rarely white. **ZONES 3–9.**

Simmondsia chinensis

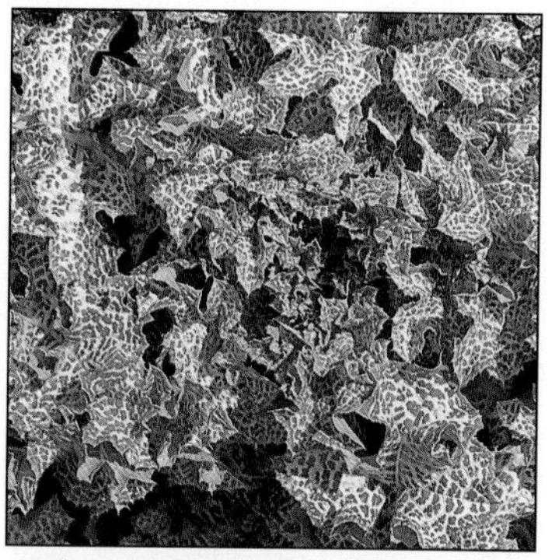

Silybum marianum

Sinningia speciosa

Sinningia speciosa

S

Sisyrinchium striatum
syn. ***Phaiophleps nigricans***
SATIN FLOWER

Long, narrow and sword-shaped, the leaves on this fully frost-hardy, evergreen perennial are gray-green. In summer it bears slender spikes of small cream flowers, striped purple. The species, which originates in Chile and Argentina, grows 18–24 in (45–60 cm) high with a 12 in (30 cm) spread. There is also an attractive variegated form. **ZONES 8–10.**

SKIMMIA

Spread over much of eastern Asia from the Himalayan region to eastern Siberia, Japan, Taiwan and the Philippines, this genus includes 4 species of evergreen shrubs and trees. They have glossy deep green, oval leaves about 4–6 in (10–15 cm) long and about half as wide. The small starry flowers, which open from late winter, are white or cream and densely packed in conical clusters. They are followed by red or black berries depending on the species. Most species require male and female plants to be present for pollination.

CULTIVATION: Skimmias are plants for shade or part-shade and grow very well with rhododendrons, azaleas and camellias. Like them they prefer moist, humus-rich, well-drained soil. They can be raised from seed in fall (autumn) but are most commonly grown from cuttings in late summer.

Skimmia japonica

Skimmia japonica
JAPANESE SKIMMIA

This fully frost-hardy shrub from Japan, China and Southeast Asia grows to about 20 ft (6 m) high and wide. It has 4 in (10 cm) long, glossy, deep green, leathery, oval leaves. In spring terminal clusters of slightly fragrant, creamy white flowers are borne, followed by $\frac{1}{2}$ in (12 mm) long, bright red berries. Both male and female plants are required to obtain berries. **'Rubella'** has red-margined leaves and dark red flower buds. ***Skimmia japonica* subsp. *reevesiana* 'Robert Fortune'** is a hermaphrodite with pale green leaves margined in dark green. **ZONES 7–10.**

SLOANEA

These 120 species of tall, handsome evergreen or deciduous trees come from rainforests in most tropical regions. They are erect and straight with a wide domed crown and buttressed trunk. The dark green leaves, up to 12 in (30 cm) long, have serrated edges, and the flowers, usually cream or white, have broad, fleshy petals. They are held in clusters, followed by capsular berries with a fleshy coating that is eaten by birds; the attractive woody, spiny, seed cases are sometimes used in dried flower arrangements.

CULTIVATION: These trees need a frost-free climate, shelter when young, and plenty of water. Grow them in fertile, humus-rich, moist but well-drained soil. They are propagated from cuttings or seed in spring.

Sloanea woollsii
YELLOW CARABEEN

This tall, subtropical rainforest tree reaches 150 ft (45 m) in the wild, about half that in cultivation; its massive buttressed trunk can be up to 8 ft (2.4 m) in diameter and is covered with wrinkled gray-brown bark. The long, shiny, dark green leaves are ovate with toothed margins and conspicuous veins. The velvety white flowers appear in spring, borne in clusters in the leaf axils; they are followed by prickly, light brown, capsular fruit that hold 2 seeds. **ZONES 10–12.**

Sloanea woollsii

Sisyrinchium striatum

SMILACINA
FALSE SOLOMON'S SEAL

The 25 species in this genus occur in North and Central America and over much of temperate and subtropical Asia. These very attractive perennials with their plumes of white flowers in early summer bear a genus name meaning 'like a *Smilax*', which is a closely related though mainly tropical genus from the roots of which sarsaparilla is made. The common name suggests that their rhizomes might be confused with those of another cousin, *Polygonatum multiflorum* (Solomon's seal). However, while both sarsaparilla and the 'true' Solomon's seal are used medicinally, *Smilacina* species are not. They colonize rapidly, adorning gardens with their luxuriant foliage and pretty flowers.

CULTIVATION: These fully frost-hardy plants prefer dappled or deep shade and humus-rich, moist but well-drained neutral to acid soil. Propagate from seed in fall (autumn) or by division in fall or spring.

Smilacina racemosa
FALSE SOLOMON'S SEAL, FALSE SPIKENARD

Red fleshy fruit appear on this North American and Mexican species after it blooms in spring through mid-summer, producing lemon-scented white flowers in feathery sprays above fresh green, elliptical leaves. It grows to 3 ft (1 m) high with a spread of 24 in (60 cm). **ZONES 4–9.**

Similacina stellata
STAR-FLOWERED LILY OF THE VALLEY, STARFLOWER

This species has stems up to 24 in (60 cm) long that produce lance-shaped 6 in (15 cm) long folded leaves which are finely hairy underneath. Up to 20 white flowers are crowded on a 2 in (5 cm) wide head. The berries are at first green with black stripes, later becoming dark red. It comes from North America and Mexico. **ZONES 3–9.**

SMILAX
SARSAPARILLA, GREENBRIER, CATBRIER

Almost 200 species of deciduous or evergreen vines and herbaceous perennials make up this genus, found in tropical and temperate regions worldwide. They are a variable lot but usually have small, elliptical leaves and tiny white flowers, sometimes fragrant, carried in racemes. The stems usually grow in a zigzag pattern, changing direction at each leaf node, and often have small barbs or spines as climbing aids. The female flowers are followed by $\frac{1}{4}$ in (6 mm) diameter red, blue-black or black berries. The prime attraction of *Smilax* species is the dense light green foliage cover they provide.

CULTIVATION: Grow in moist, well-drained soil in sun or light shade. Frost hardiness varies greatly with the species. Propagate from seed, layers, semi-ripe cuttings or by dividing well-established plants.

Smilax china

This deciduous climber from China, Korea and Japan attains a height of 15 ft (4.5 m). *Smilax china* has oval leaves, which may be up to 3 in (8 cm) across, and the small umbels of yellow-green flowers are borne in spring. They are followed on female plants by red berries. **ZONES 6–10.**

Smilacina racemosa

Similacina stellata

Smilax glyciphylla
SWEET SARSAPARILLA

This vigorous climber is found in moist forests and rainforest margins throughout New South Wales, Australia. The leaves are tough, 3-veined, green above and grayish beneath. Small white, green or pink flowers in clusters appear throughout the year, followed by black berries that are sought after by birds. **ZONES 9–11.**

SMITHIANTHA
TEMPLE BELLS

This genus of 4 small, rosette-forming, fleshy leafed rhizomatous perennials comes from Mexico and Guatemala. They are relatives of the African violets (*Saintpaulia* species) and closely resemble them. The toothed-edged leaves are deep green, sometimes mottled red or purple and round to heart-shaped with a dense covering of fine, velvety hairs. The flowers are tubular to trumpet-shaped with flared lobes. They are ½–1½ in (12–35 mm) long and are bright pink, orange, red or white, usually with red-spotted yellow interiors. They form on flower stems that may reach 24 in (60 cm) tall.
CULTIVATION: Grow in moist, humus-rich, well-drained soil in dappled sunlight. They require winter minimum temperatures of about 60°F (15°C) and outside the tropics are usually grown indoors. Propagate from seed or cuttings or by dividing the rhizomes.

Smithiantha cinnabarina

The deep green leaves of this species are covered with fine red-brown hairs, giving the young growth in particular a very velvety, overall red-brown appearance. The flowers, borne on stems up to 24 in (60 cm) tall, are brick red. **ZONES 11–12.**

SOLANDRA
CHALICE VINE

This genus of 8 species of evergreen, woody stemmed, scrambling climbers was named in honor of the Swedish botanist Daniel Carlsson Solander (1736–82), a pupil of Linnaeus. Natives of tropical America, they are grown for their large, fragrant, trumpet-shaped flowers and shiny, leathery foliage.
CULTIVATION: These plants are susceptible to frost and need a warm climate to thrive; grow in a warmed greenhouse in cold areas. Plant outdoors in full sun in fertile, well-drained soil and water freely during the growing season. Thin out crowded stems after flowering. Propagate from cuttings in summer.

Solanum mauritianum

Solanum jasminoides 'Album'

Solandra maxima
syn. *Solandra nitida*

CUP OF GOLD, HAWAIIAN LILY, GOLDEN CHALICE VINE

A giant climber from Mexico to Colombia and Venezuela valued for its huge flowers and ability to cover very large areas, this is a rampant, woody vine growing to 30 ft (9 m) or more, requiring plenty of space and a sturdy support. The yellow flowers, to 10 in (25 cm) across and with a purplish stripe down the center of each petal, appear in spring and summer. It tolerates wind, dry conditions and salt spray, so it is an excellent plant for seaside gardens. **ZONES 10–12.**

SOLANUM
syn. *Lycianthes*

There are over 1,400 species in this genus including trees, shrubs, annuals, biennials, perennials and climbers from a range of habitats worldwide. Some are evergreen, others semi-evergreen or deciduous. The genus includes important food plants like the potato and eggplant (aubergine), though many species are dangerously poisonous. Ornamental species are grown for their flowers and fruits. The leaves are arranged alternately, while the showy flowers are solitary or in clusters, star-shaped to bell-shaped, ranging in color from white and yellow to blue and purple. The fruits are berries that contain many seeds.
CULTIVATION: These warm-climate plants have a wide range of requirements; most prefer full sun and rich, well-drained soil. They are commonly grown from seed in spring or cuttings in summer. They are prone to attack by spider mite, white fly and aphids.

Solanum aviculare
KANGAROO APPLE, PORO PORO

Indigenous to Australia and New Zealand, this evergreen shrub is fast growing but short lived. Reaching 10–12 ft (3–3.5 m) tall, its single upright stem has spreading branches forming a wide crown. The large, dark green to bluish green leaves are oval to lance-shaped, often with deeply lobed edges. In spring and summer the star-shaped purple flowers, 1½ in (35 mm) across, appear in large clusters at the branch tips. The fruit of *Solanum aviculare,* oval berries about 1 in (25 mm) long, hang from thin stalks and ripen from green to yellow to red. **ZONES 9–11.**

Solanum jasminoides 'Album'

Solandra maxima

Solanum crispum

Solanum aviculare

Solanum crispum
CHILEAN POTATO TREE

This is an evergreen or semi-evergreen scrambling climber to 20 ft (6 m) from Chile, with undulating oval or heart-shaped leaves up to 4 in (10 cm) long that are finely hairy. The heads of lilac-blue flowers are fragrant and are followed by white ¼ in (6 mm) fruit. **'Glasnevin'** is a vigorous form with deep blue flowers. **ZONES 8–11.**

Solanum dulcamara
BITTERSWEET, CLIMBING NIGHTSHADE, POISONOUS NIGHTSHADE

This poisonous woody vine comes from Europe and Asia and has become naturalized in North America. It grows to 15 ft (4.5 m) and its leaves may be simple or quite deeply lobed. The flowers are lilac to blue, the fruit oval or spherical and bright red. **ZONES 4–9.**

Solanum jasminoides
POTATO VINE

From Brazil, this quick-growing, semi-evergreen or evergreen climber reaches 20 ft (6 m) and bears showy clusters of pale blue flowers in summer and fall (autumn), followed by small, purple berries. It is marginally frost hardy; in cool areas it can be potted up in fall to spend the winter under glass. **'Album'** has white flowers. **ZONES 9–11.**

Solanum mammosum
NIPPLE FRUIT, COW'S UDDER PLANT

A tropical plant indigenous to Central America, this perennial herb or soft-wooded subshrub grows to about 4 ft (1.2 m) tall with angular, spiny stems and large hairy leaves. It has smallish white flowers and striking yellow or orange fruit about 2 in (5 cm) long, sometimes waisted, bloated structures resembling a cow's udder with several nipples at the calyx end. Branches bearing the fruit are often cut for indoor use, with the leaves removed; they last for several weeks. **ZONES 11–12.**

Solanum mauritianum

This shrub or small tree originates in Argentina. It grows up to 15 ft (4.5 m) and has gray-green hairy branches and oval leaves up to 12 in (30 cm) long that are softly hairy. The flowers are blue, and the fruit are hairy yellow balls to ½ in (12 mm) long in clusters. **ZONES 10–12.**

S

Solanum rantonnetii

Solanum nigrum

Solanum rantonnetii

Solanum melongena
AUBERGINE, EGGPLANT, MAD APPLE

This tropical vegetable native to Asia has large, purple fruit. It is a relative of the potato and tomato, and needs warm conditions and low level humidity. It is an annual with erect stems that can be spiny, ovate leaves and pale blue or deep purple flowers. Harvest the fruit if it gives slightly when squeezed. **ZONES 9–12.**

Solanum nigrum
BLACK NIGHTSHADE, COMMON NIGHTSHADE

This is a very variable annual with branched stems up to 24 in (60 cm) long bearing oval or lance-shaped leaves, white flowers and yellow or black berries. From Europe and Asia, it has become naturalized in North America and Australia. **ZONES 4–11.**

Solanum pyracanthum

Solanum pseudocapsicum
JERUSALEM CHERRY, WINTER CHERRY, CHRISTMAS CHERRY

This frost-tender, evergreen Mediterranean native produces starry white flowers in summer, followed by small scarlet berries that are poisonous. It grows sedately into a bushy, velvety leafed shrub about 4 ft (1.2 m) high and wide and is perhaps best grown as an annual, even in wild areas, in which case it should grow to 24 in (60 cm) tall. Several varieties with differently colored fruit are available. The species is related to the potato, eggplant and tomato, as well as to some other less edible plants. **ZONES 9–11.**

Solanum pyracanthum

This perennial from tropical Africa grows to 5 ft (1.5 m) tall. The lobed leaves are spiny along the central vein. The flowers are violet. **ZONES 10–12.**

Solanum rantonnetii
syn. *Lycianthes rantonnetii*
PARAGUAY NIGHTSHADE, BLUE POTATO BUSH

This South American relative of the potato is a valuable long-blooming shrub or scrambling vine for warm-climate gardens. Simple green leaves cover the branches and provide a good foil for the summer-long profusion of deep violet-blue flowers. It can be used as a 6–8 ft (1.8–2.4 m) tall background shrub or trained on a trellis or arbor, where it may reach 12 ft (3.5 m) or more. **'Royal Robe'** has deeper purple flowers and nearly year-round bloom in mild-winter areas. **ZONES 9–11.**

Solanum tuberosum

Solanum seaforthianum
ST VINCENT LILAC, GLYDINE, BRAZILIAN NIGHTSHADE

This is a showy, evergreen, slender-stemmed vine growing to 20 ft (6 m) and bearing large nodding clusters of violet-blue flowers with yellow stamens in summer. These are followed by small scarlet berries. From South America, it is frost tender. **ZONES 10–12.**

Solanum tuberosum
POTATO

Native to South America and one of the most widely eaten vegetables, the potato can be scatter grown throughout the garden. A perennial plant, it grows to a height of 30 in (75 cm) with a spread of 18 in (45 cm). It has an erect, hairy, green stem and large—to 15 in (38cm)—pinnate, dark green leaves with 3 or 5 pairs of heart-shaped leaflets. The flowers occur in pendent clusters of white or pale violet flowers. **ZONES 6–11.**

Solanum wendlandii
POTATO VINE, PARADISE FLOWER, GIANT POTATO CREEPER

This robust evergreen or semi-evergreen vine to 20 ft (6 m) has a few hooked spines. The 8 in (20 cm) leaves are very variable, simple or divided. The hanging flowerheads of lilac flowers are up to 6 in (15 cm) across, occurring in summer. It is native to Costa Rica. **ZONES 10–12.**

SOLDANELLA
SNOWBELL

The soldanellas are elegant relatives of the primrose. They come from the mountains of Europe and flower at the end of spring. There are 10 species of evergreen perennials, all rather alike and interbreeding freely both in the wild and in gardens much to the irritation of those who like to be certain of their plants' names. They have nodding to pendent purple to white flowers and leathery leaves and are good plants for rock gardens and tubs.

CULTIVATION: These plants are mostly fully frost hardy, although the flower buds may be destroyed by frost. They need part-shade and humus-rich, well-drained, peaty soil. Propagate from seed in spring or by division in late summer. Watch out for slugs.

Soldanella alpina
ALPINE SNOWBELL

This clump-forming species from the Pyrenees through to the Tyrolean Alps has tufts of green leaves and nodding, fringed, bell-shaped, lilac-colored flowers with attractive red markings on their throats. It grows to 6 in (15 cm) in height. **ZONES 5–9.**

Soldanella carpatica

This alpine species forms a rosette or clump of almost round, 2 in (5 cm) wide, dark green leaves with purple undersides. The violet flowers, appearing at the beginning of spring, are about ½ in (12 mm) wide, fringed and hang from a stem of up to 5 blooms. The plants reach up to 6 in (15 cm) tall with a similar

Solanum pseudocapsicum

Solanum wendlandii

Solidago 'Goldenmosa'

Soleirolia soleirolii 'Aurea'

spread, and produce many flowering stems. **ZONES 5–9.**

Soldanella montana

Growing to about 12 in (30 cm) tall, this mound-forming species comes from the Alps but prefers the alpine woodlands to the bare rocks higher up. It flowers in early spring, often before the snows have quite melted, producing long, pendent, bell-shaped, lavender-blue blossoms with fringed mouths. It has shallow-toothed, rounded leaves. **ZONES 6–9.**

SOLEIROLIA

BABY'S TEARS, MIND-YOUR-OWN-BUSINESS, PEACE-IN-THE-HOME

The single species in this genus from western Mediterranean islands has mat-forming small leaves, and is an intricately branching plant that roots at the nodes. It is an evergreen perennial with soft green foliage that can withstand a broad range of climatic conditions.
CULTIVATION: It prefers well-drained moist soil and some shade in hot climates. Propagation is by division in spring.

Soleirolia soleirolii

syn. *Helxine soleirolii*

This creeping plant has small round leaves and tiny white, pink-tinged flowers, which occur singly in the leaf axils. It grows to a height of 2 in (5 cm) with an indefinite spread. It can be invasive unless contained; hanging baskets are ideal. **'Aurea'** has yellow-green foliage. **ZONES 9–11.**

SOLENOSTEMON

COLEUS, FLAME NETTLE, PAINTED NETTLE

This genus comprises 60 species of low shrubby perennials, often hairy and with variegated leaves, from tropical Africa and Asia. The stems are 4-angled and the opposite leaves are often toothed. The flowers are small with an elongated lower lip.

Solidago 'Golden Wings'

CULTIVATION: These frost-tender plants are easily grown in milder climates with adequate summer moisture and protection from hot sun. They prefer humus-rich, moist but well-drained soil and need to be pinched back to promote bushiness. Propagate from seed or cuttings.

Solenostemon amboinicus

syns *Coleus amboinicus, Plectranthus amboinicus*

ALLSPICE, THREE-IN-ONE SPICE

This short-lived creeping perennial is believed to have originated somewhere in tropical Asia but has been cultivated for so long its true native area is now unknown. It has pairs of pale green, downy, rather fleshy leaves, almost circular but with scalloped edges; they are very aromatic with a pleasantly spicy smell and can be used as a flavoring herb in cooked dishes. The white flowers are rather insignificant and not always produced in cultivation. The plant is seldom more than 12 in (30 cm) high, with weak, fleshy stems that root as it spreads. **ZONES 10–12.**

Solenostemon scutellarioides

syns *Coleus blumei* var. *verschaffeltii, C. scutellarioides*

Native to Southeast Asia, this bushy, fast-growing perennial is grown as an annual in more temperate climates. The leaves are a bright mixture of pink, green, red or yellow and are a pointed, oval shape with serrated edges. It grows 24 in (60 cm) high and 12 in (30 cm) wide. **ZONES 10–12.**

SOLIDAGO

GOLDENROD

The goldenrods are a genus of about 100 species of woody based perennials, almost all indigenous to the meadows and prairies of North America with a few species in South America and Eurasia. They are related to the asters and, like them, flower in fall (autumn). Their effect is quite different, however, as the individual flowers are very much smaller and are bright yellow. Most of the species are too weedy to be allowed into even the wildest garden, but some are worth cultivating for their big flower clusters and there are some very attractive hybrids.
CULTIVATION: These fully frost-hardy plants grow well in sun or shade in any fertile, well-drained soil. Most species self-seed, or they can be propagated by dividing the clumps in fall or spring.

Solidago 'Baby Gold'

syn. *Solidago* 'Golden Baby'

Some garden hybrids are valuable for their bright color in early fall (autumn). This one is an upright plant with feathery spikes of golden flowers. Reaching 3 ft (1 m) in height, it has lance-shaped, green leaves. **ZONES 5–10.**

Solidago canadensis

This strong-growing species reaches 5 ft (1.5 m) in height. The leaves may be up to 4 in (10 cm) long, the largest occurring in the middle of the stem. Pyramidal heads of yellow flowers appear in late summer and fall (autumn). It comes from North America, but has become naturalized in Europe. **ZONES 3–10.**

Solidago 'Goldenmosa'

This hybrid makes a compact, bushy plant to 30 in (75 cm) in height and 18 in (45 cm) in spread. Its bright yellow flowerheads appear in panicles in late summer and fall (autumn). **ZONES 5–10.**

Solidago 'Golden Wings'

This perennial grows to 5 ft (1.5 m) high with a spread of 3 ft (1 m). It has downy, lance-shaped leaves with serrated margins, and produces small, bright yellow flowers in feathery panicles early in fall (autumn). **ZONES 5–10.**

Solidago sphacelata

FALSE GOLDENROD

This species grows 24–36 in (60–90 cm) tall and has serrated, heart-shaped leaves. It eventually forms a large clump but is not invasive. The yellow flowers are borne on narrow arching stems from late summer. **ZONES 4–9.**

Solidago sphacelata

Soldanella montana

Solenostemon amboinicus

Solidago 'Baby Gold'

Solenostemon scutellarioides cultivars

Sollya heterophylla

Solidago virgaurea

Solidago virgaurea

This is a 3 ft (1 m) plant from Europe, flowering in summer and fall (autumn) with dense heads of yellow flowers. ***Solidago virgaurea* subsp. *minuta*** only grows to 4 in (10 cm) and comes from Japan. **ZONES 5–10.**

× *SOLIDASTER*

This is an intergeneric hybrid genus between *Solidago canadensis* and *Aster ptarmicoides*, found as a spontaneous hybrid in a French nursery in 1910. It is grown for its flowerheads of daisy-like blooms, which appear in great numbers from mid-summer to fall (autumn).
CULTIVATION: This fully frost-hardy plant prefers full sun and moderately fertile, well-drained soil. Propagate by division or from basal cuttings.

× *Solidaster luteus*
syns *Aster luteus*, × *Solidaster hybridus*
YELLOW ASTER

When this perennial's flowers first open at their mid-summer blooming, both their discs and rays are gold, although the rays quickly fade to creamy yellow. The flowers cluster in flattish heads 4 in (10 cm) across on downy stems branched near the top. The leaves are narrow and mid-green. It grows to 3 ft (1 m) high and 12 in (30 cm) wide. **ZONES 6–10.**

Sophora japonica with pods

SOLLYA

This Western Australian genus consists of 3 species of small evergreen climbers. They have narrow, thin, smooth-edged leaves and small 5-petalled, bell-shaped flowers borne in small loose clusters at the branch tips.
CULTIVATION: These frost-tender plants grow best in a sunny spot, but like some protection from midday sun and fertile, humus-rich, moist but well-drained soil. Climbing stems need support. Propagate from seed in spring or cuttings in late spring or early summer.

Sollya heterophylla
BLUEBELL CREEPER, AUSTRALIAN BLUEBELL CREEPER

The dainty bells of this species from Western Australia appear from spring to fall (autumn). As well as the usual blue, there are white- and pink-flowered varieties available. The flowers are followed by decorative, navy blue fruit about $\frac{1}{2}$ in (12 mm) long. It reaches a height of 6 ft (1.8 m) and has narrow, lance-shaped or oval leaves. **ZONES 9–11.**

SONERILA

These evergreen perennials and small shrubs come from Southeast Asia and southern China, and over 175 species are known. The leaves are oval, sometimes toothed with 3 to 5 veins, dark green,

Sophora japonica 'Pendula'

spotted, and bristly. The flowers appear in racemes or corymbs and are anything from star- to cup-shaped.
CULTIVATION: They are usually grown as greenhouse plants outside the tropics; outdoors they prefer dappled shade and humus-rich, moist but well-drained soil. Propagate from cuttings.

Sonerila margaritacea

This 10 in (25 cm) high plant comes from Malaysia and Java. The arching or hanging stems are scarlet, and the leaves are dark polished green with white spots in lines in between the veins. Underneath the veins are purple. The rose-colored flowers are in heads of 8 to 10 and up to $\frac{3}{4}$ in (18 mm) across. **ZONES 10–12.**

SOPHORA

This legume genus of some 50 species of deciduous and evergreen trees, shrubs and perennials is scattered widely through warmer parts of the world. All have pinnate leaves and short racemes of clusters of pea-flowers, mostly in shades of yellow, cream, grayish blue or lilac; the seed pods are constricted between the seeds and are often slow to split open, and the very hard, waxy seeds are long lived and resistant to water penetration. Most interesting is a group of closely related species, which some botanists believe should be treated as a separate genus, *Edwardsia*, that are widely scattered around the southern oceans on small islands such as Easter Island, Gough Island and Mauritius as well as larger landmasses such as New Zealand, Hawaii, and the southern tip of South America; typified by the New Zealand *Sophora tetraptera*, they have large yellow flowers and pods with 4 slightly translucent wings. Their seeds are resistant to saltwater, and are believed to have floated around the southern oceans, with limited evolution taking place after establishing in new lands.
CULTIVATION: Sophoras thrive under a wide range of conditions. They can be grown in small groves, or used as shade trees or lawn specimens. Most prefer moist, well-drained soil in sun or part-shade. Propagate from seed or cuttings. In Australia and New Zealand caterpillars of the kowhai moth can defoliate plants in summer.

Sophora microphylla

Sophora japonica
JAPANESE PAGODA TREE, PAGODA TREE

Despite its name, this deciduous tree originates from central China and Korea. It grows to about 100 ft (30 m) high. The light green pinnate leaves are 8 in (20 cm) long, and the cream or occasionally pale pink flowers are borne in long panicles. The pods that follow are like bead necklaces. **'Pendula'** is often grafted onto 8 ft (2.4 m) standards to produce a small weeping tree. **ZONES 4–10.**

Sophora microphylla
WEEPING KOWHAI

This New Zealand evergreen species grows 12–20 ft (3.5–6 m) tall. Its weeping, interlocking, wiry branches form a wide, rounded crown. The leaves are fern-like; many are shed in late winter before the flowers appear. The flowers, lemon to deep orange but usually deep yellow and up to $1\frac{1}{2}$ in (35 mm) long, are borne in dense clusters from late winter to early summer. The fruits are pods about 6 in (15 cm) long. ***Sophora microphylla* var. *longicarinata*** has lemon flowers and smaller, more numerous leaflets. **'Golden Shower'** forms a symmetrical tree with strongly weeping outer branches and golden-yellow flowers. **ZONES 8–10.**

Sophora prostrata

This New Zealand native is much prized for the clusters of pale yellow flowers it bears in summer amid small, oval leaflets. Frost hardy, it is a many-branched, prostrate or bushy semi-evergreen shrub that grows to a maximum height and spread of 6 ft (1.8 m). **'Little Baby'** has very angular twiggy growth, very fine leaves and yellow flowers in early spring. **ZONES 8–10.**

Sophora microphylla

× *Sophrolaeliocattleya* Hybrid Jannine Louise 'Orange Glow'

Sorbaria kirilowii

Sorbaria kirilowii

Sophora secundiflora
MESCAL BEAN, TEXAS MOUNTAIN LAUREL

This large shrub is native to Texas and is valuable throughout southwestern USA for its evergreen foliage and fragrant flowers. Usually with multiple trunks, it grows to 10–30 ft (3–9 m) in height with a spread of at least 10 ft (3 m). Its leaves are pinnately divided into many rounded leaflets. The purple flowers resemble those of wisteria and have a sweet, fruity fragrance. **ZONES 7–10.**

Sophora tetraptera
KOWHAI

This free-flowering, usually evergreen tree from the North Island is New Zealand's national flower. It may grow to 30 ft (9 m) tall but is usually smaller. Mature specimens develop a semi-pendulous habit, with the branches somewhat interlocked. The leaves consist of 20 to 30 pairs of small, gray-green leaflets. The abundant spring pea-flowers are about 1½ in (35 mm) long; pale to golden yellow, they are borne in showy pendulous clusters. The fruit are narrow pods that ripen to dark gray. **ZONES 8–11.**

Sophora tomentosa
SILVERBUSH

This species is a tropical member of a predominantly temperate-zone genus. It is a large, sprawling shrub or small tree to 10 ft (3 m), fairly common on tropical seashores and worth bringing into the garden for its unusual color scheme—the leaves are silver-gray, the flowers lime yellow. **ZONES 10–12.**

× *SOPHROCATTLEYA*

This orchid generic hybrid name covers all crosses between any members of the genera *Sophronitis* and *Cattleya*, including all later generation seedlings and backcrosses. They mostly have slightly smaller flowers than the average *Cattleya* or × *Laeliocattleya* hybrid. Apart from smaller size, *Sophronitis* has contributed brilliant reds, scarlets and oranges to the coloring, a strong tendency to uniform coloring, and a rather flat flower shape with small labellum. × ***Sophrolaeliocattleya*** is the equivalent trigeneric hybrid name for crosses involving *Sophronitis, Laelia* and *Cattleya*—in practice these are much the same as sophrocattleyas, the laelia influence hardly showing. When *Rhyncolaelia* is added to this trigeneric mix to give a quadrigeneric hybrid, the resulting crosses go under the name × ***Potinara***, following the modern convention that names of multigeneric hybrids end in *ara*.

CULTIVATION: All these generic hybrids require much the same conditions as the cooler-growing cattleyas, though perhaps with a little more water supplied during the winter resting period. Propagate by division, though commercial production is usually from flasked seedlings or mericlones.

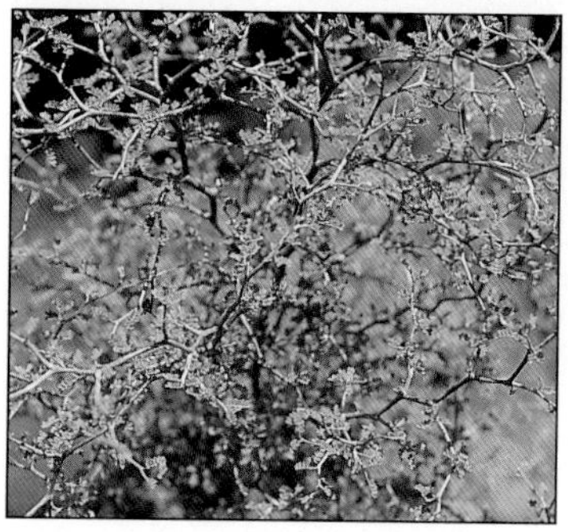

Sophora prostrata 'Little Baby'

× *Sophrocattleya* and × *Sophrolaeliocattleya* Hybrids

It is the infusion of genes from the brilliantly colored *Sophronitis coccinea* that has most influenced these hybrids, the first cross having been made in England as early as 1886; the resulting grex, × ***Sophrocattleya* Batemaniana**, is still in cultivation. Since that time thousands of hybrids have been registered, the sophrolaeliocattleyas now greatly outnumbering the sophrocattleyas. Typical modern hybrids are × ***Sophrolaeliocattleya* Jannine Louise 'Orange Glow'** with orange-yellow flowers tinged reddish on the frilled edges and × ***Sophrolaeliocattleya* Jewel Box 'Scheherazade'**, a compact plant with clusters of rich, shining red flowers. **ZONES 10–12.**

SOPHRONITIS

There are 8 species of these small epiphytic or lithophytic orchids in this genus from eastern Brazil and Paraguay. The small pseudobulbs have one fleshy leaf. The flowers may be red or violet, and are very showy.

CULTIVATION: They need some shade in a protected area without frost. They may be grown in a bark mix or attached to boards. Allow to dry out between waterings in cooler weather. Propagate by division and check regularly for spider mites, aphids and mealybugs.

Sophronitis coccinea
syn. *Sophronitis grandiflora*

This dainty epiphyte from Brazil makes a low-growing clump of dark green leaves, adorned in spring with beautifully shaped, 1½ in (35 mm) wide flowers. They can be pink, orange, red or violet, but it is the scarlet forms that are most admired and which have been crossed with cattleyas to lend them their beautiful color. It grows to 2 in (5 cm) in height. **ZONES 10–12.**

Sophora tetraptera

SORBARIA

The 10 shrub species of this genus originate from the cool to cold mountain regions of Asia. All are deciduous and have pinnate leaves with serrated leaflets. The small, starry white flowers, usually in large terminal panicles, have a cup-shaped calyx, 5 reflexed petals and many prominent stamens. The fruits are berries.

CULTIVATION: Most species sucker freely; they thrive in full sun in rich, moist soil and prefer cool climates. Prune in winter to restrict size; remove some older canes if necessary. Propagate from seed or cuttings in late winter or summer, or by division in fall (autumn).

Sorbaria kirilowii
syns *Sorbaria arborea, Spiraea arborea*
FALSE SPIRAEA

This large, spreading shrub from China and Tibet grows to 20 ft (6 m) tall with cane-like stems and compound leaves consisting of up to 17 long, narrow leaflets. The flowers are held in upright fluffy panicles 12 in (30 cm) long. The young growth is often covered in masses of hair. **ZONES 4–10.**

Sophora tomentosa

× *Sophrolaeliocattleya* Hybrid Jewel Box 'Scheherazade'

S

Sorbaria tomentosa

This tree from the Himalayas has spreading branches and grows up to 20 ft (6 m) tall. There are up to 20 serrated lance-shaped leaflets. The cream flowers occur in heads up to 16 in (40 cm) across. ***Sorbaria tomentosa* var. *angustifolia*** from Afghanistan and Nepal has purplish brown branches. **ZONES 6–10.**

SORBUS

ROWAN, SERVICE TREE, MOUNTAIN ASH

This genus is made up of 100 species of deciduous trees and shrubs from cool-climate regions of the northern hemisphere, grown for their foliage, timber and decorative fruits. Most species have pinnate leaves and terminal clusters of small, creamy white flowers in spring. The flowers, which are often rather unpleasantly scented, are followed by showy berries. A few species have attractive fall (autumn) foliage.

Sorbus aucuparia

Sorbus aria

Sorbaria tomentosa var. *angustifolia*

CULTIVATION: Rowans are easily grown in sun or part-shade in any well-drained, fertile soil and are most at home in areas with distinct winters. The species may be raised from stratified seed; selected forms are usually grafted. They are susceptible to fireblight.

Sorbus americana

AMERICAN MOUNTAIN ASH

This is a vigorous tree to 30 ft (9 m) with ascending reddish branches and red sticky buds. The pinnate leaves are bright green, turning bright golden yellow in fall (autumn). Large dense bunches of small red berries follow. It comes from eastern North America. **ZONES 3–9.**

Sorbus aria

WHITEBEAM

This European species is a 30 ft (9 m) tall tree with coarsely toothed, simple leaves 4 in (10 cm) long with white felting on the undersides. They develop orange and yellow fall (autumn) tones. The ½ in (12 mm) berries are red. This species is very tough, tolerating chalky soil, salt winds and air pollution. **'Aurea'** has light yellowish green leaves; **'Chrysophylla'** has yellow leaves; **'Lutescens'** has young foliage covered with fine silvery hairs; **'Majestica'** has leaves and berries larger than those of the species; and **'Theophrasta'** has orange berries and glossy green foliage. **ZONES 2–9.**

Sorbus aucuparia

ROWAN, MOUNTAIN ASH, EUROPEAN MOUNTAIN ASH

The most commonly grown species, this tree grows to about 50 ft (15 m) high in gardens, much taller in its native European and Asian forests. The pinnate leaves, made up of 11 to 15 small, toothed leaflets, turn rich gold in fall (autumn). The white spring flowers are followed by scarlet berries. **'Asplenifolia'** has very finely cut leaves; **'Edulis'** is a large-berried form used for jams and preserves; **'Fructu Luteo'** has orange-yellow berries; **'Pendula'** has wide-spreading growth and a weeping habit; **'Sheerwater Seedling'** is narrowly upright; and **'Xanthocarpa'** has yellow berries. **ZONES 2–9.**

Sorbus aria 'Theophrasta'

Sorbus commixta

Sorbus cashmiriana

KASHMIR MOUNTAIN ASH

Indigenous to the western Himalayas, this spreading tree can attain a height of 25 ft (8 m), although it is often smaller. Its mid-green leaves are made up of 17 to 19 elliptical leaflets that are gray-green underneath. The pendent clusters of white to pale pink flowers appear in early summer, followed by ½ in (12 mm) wide globular white fruit that endure into winter. **ZONES 5–9.**

Sorbus chamaemespilus

This shrub from central Europe grows to about 10 ft (3 m) tall. Its finely toothed, simple, leathery leaves are 3 in (8 cm) long, deep green above and yellow-green beneath. The young growth tends to be hairy and the clusters of pink flowers are followed by tightly packed bunches of small, bright red fruit. **ZONES 5–9.**

Sorbus cashmiriana

Sorbus commixta

Sorbus commixta

syn. ***Sorbus discolor* of gardens**

JAPANESE ROWAN, KOREAN ROWAN

This erect tree grows to 15–25 ft (4.5–8 m) or more. It is grown for its handsome pinnate leaves, dark green and shiny above, gray-green beneath (in fall/autumn they turn brilliant shades of orange and red) and for the massed clusters of scarlet berries that are borne in summer. Their winter buds are curiously sticky. **'Embley'** has bright red leaves and fruits profusely. **ZONES 4–9.**

Sorbus domestica

SERVICE TREE

This 70 ft (21 m) high, spreading tree, indigenous to southern and eastern Europe and northern Africa, has deeply fissured bark. The leaves are made up of 13 to 21 toothed leaflets. The 1 in (25 mm) long fruit, brownish green with a rosy tint, are somewhat pear-shaped and edible when fully ripe. **ZONES 3–9.**

Sorbus forrestii

This spreading tree grows to 20 ft (6 m) in height and spread. From China, it has very large white berries that appear in fall (autumn) and persist until mid-winter. **ZONES 7–9.**

Sorbus hupehensis

HUBEI ROWAN

Indigenous to Hubei province in central China, this tall, vigorous tree has blue-green pinnate leaves made up of 9 to 17

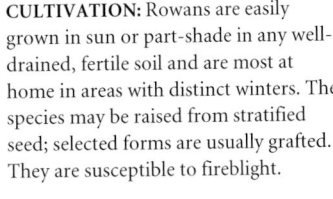

Sorbus megalocarpa

Sorbus hybrida 'Gibbsii'

leaflets. The foliage develops orange, red and purple fall (autumn) tones. The berries are white, tinged pink, and are carried on red stems. ZONES 5–9.

Sorbus hybrida 'Gibbsii'

This small tree grows to 30 ft (9 m) and has a very compact spreading crown. The fruit are deep red. It is a hybrid between *Sorbus aria* and *S. aucuparia.* ZONES 5–9.

Sorbus prattii var. *subarachnoidea*

Sorbus 'Joseph Rock'

This vigorous upright tree of unknown East Asian origin grows to about 30 ft (9 m) high. Its leaves are made up of 15 to 21 sharply toothed leaflets that develop rich red, orange and purple tones in fall (autumn). It produces large clusters of bright yellow berries. ZONES 4–9.

Sorbus megalocarpa

Rare in cultivation but very striking, this tree grows to about 25 ft (8 m) in its natural environment in China and the Himalayas, with large, bright green, obovate, double-toothed leaves and creamy white, downy flowerheads borne at the branch tips in late winter before the leaves appear. The flowers have a rather pungent smell. The brown, egg-shaped fruit are about 1 in (25 mm) long, which is unusually large for the genus. ZONES 4–9.

Sorbus domestica

Sorbus forrestii

Sorbus hupehensis

Sorbus pluripinnata

Sorbus pluripinnata

This large shrub or small tree from China grows to 20 ft (6 m). The young shoots and leaves are gray felted, while fall (autumn) foliage is reddish purple. The white flowers are followed by red fruit. ZONES 6–9.

Sorbus 'Joseph Rock'

Sorbus pohuashanensis 'Pagoda Red'

Sorbus reducta

Sorbus pohuashanensis

Indigenous to mountainous regions of northern China where it reaches 70 ft (21 m) tall, this species is closely related to the European rowan *(Sorbus aucuparia).* The pinnate leaves are up to 8 in (20 cm) long, green above but hairy and blue-green beneath; young shoots and flower buds are also covered in hair. The flat-topped clusters of flowers are held above the foliage, as are the shiny red fruit. The cultivar **'Pagoda Red'** has a fine display of fruit. ZONES 4–9.

Sorbus prattii

From western China comes this tree of 25 ft (8 m), with leaflets that are hairy underneath. ***Sorbus prattii* var. *subarachnoidea*** has rusty colored hairs on the leaves. Both have white fruit. ZONES 6–9.

Sorbus reducta

This small shrub to 5 ft (1.5 m) forms a thicket by suckering. The elliptical leaflets become bronze and purplish in fall (autumn). The flowers are white but sparse, and white or ruby fruit follow. It comes from western China. **'Gnome'** is a smaller, tighter form. ZONES 6–9.

Sparaxis tricolor

Sorbus scopulina

Sorbus vilmorinii

Sorbus sargentiana

This rigidly branched tree from western China grows to 30 ft (9 m). The large sticky crimson buds appear in winter, and the serrated leaflets color red in fall (autumn). Hairy flowerheads up to 6 in (15 cm) across are followed by large round clusters of small scarlet fruit. **ZONES 6–9.**

Sorbus scalaris

This small tree from China grows to 30 ft (9 m) with a wide-spreading habit. The dark green rather glossy leaves are gray and downy underneath, and become red-purple in fall (autumn). Red fruit follow in flattened heads. **ZONES 5–9.**

Sorbus scopulina

This 6 ft (1.8 m) shrub comes from the Rocky Mountains of the USA. It is very upright with smooth serrated leaflets. The large flowerheads are followed by dense bunches of red berries. **ZONES 5–9.**

Sorbus terminalis
WILD SERVICE TREE

This species from the Mediterranean grows to 50 ft (15 m) or more with a rounded crown. The twigs are felted when young, the leaves maple-shaped, dark green and glossy but white and downy beneath, becoming bronzed yellow in fall (autumn). Reddish brown fruit follow the white flowers. **ZONES 6–9.**

Sorbus thibetica

This tree grows to 70 ft (21 m) with stiffly erect branches. The ribbed leaves are sparsely hairy underneath, gray and rather downy when young. The berries are dark yellow spotted with gray. **'Jon Mitchell'** is a fast-growing tree with a narrow crown that becomes rounded with age and large round leaves that are white and downy underneath; the berries are yellow-brown. **ZONES 6–9.**

Sorbus vilmorinii

This shrub or small tree to 20 ft (6 m) tall spreads to 13–16 ft (4–5 m). The buds and shoots are downy and reddish brown. The many leaflets are grayish underneath, becoming red and purple in the fall (autumn). The white flowers are followed by drooping clusters of rosy berries that fade to pinkish white. It is native to China. **ZONES 6–9.**

SPARAXIS
HARLEQUIN FLOWER

This is a genus of 6 species of deciduous perennial herbs from South Africa. They have loose spikes of 5 cup-shaped, brightly colored flowers that are borne in spring and summer and look good in raised beds or borders. The leaves are lance-shaped and ribbed and occur in an erect, basal fan.
CULTIVATION: Grow in moderately fertile, well-drained soil in full sun and provide shelter from cold winds; in colder areas they may need the shelter of a greenhouse. Propagate from seed.

Sparaxis elegans

This species has 2 to 5 unbranched stems that arise from each corm to a height of 12 in (30 cm). The flowers have a yellow tube with vermillion lobes fading to pink. The lobes have a violet band at their base. **ZONES 9–10.**

Sparaxis tricolor
VELVET FLOWER

This marginally frost-hardy native of South Africa is easily grown in warm areas. The 12 in (30 cm) wiry, drooping stems bear a spike of up to 5 funnel-shaped or star-shaped blooms in spring. The 2 in (5 cm) flowers are red to pink or orange, usually with a yellow center outlined in black; they close at night and on dull days. The stiff leaves are lance-shaped. ***Sparaxis tricolor* subsp. *blanda*** is a beautiful white-flowered version. **ZONES 9–10.**

SPARRMANNIA

This small genus of 3 to 7 species of evergreen trees and shrubs is indigenous to tropical and temperate southern Africa and Madagascar. The stems and leaves are covered with soft hairs. The large, soft leaves have a toothed edge and may be lobed. Its attractive flowers, on long stalks, are arranged in clusters near the shoot tips or arise from the leaf axils. The fruits are spiny capsules.
CULTIVATION: These plants need a sunny position with shelter from wind and frost, and well-drained soil enriched with organic matter. Keep the soil moist during the active growth period. These are plants for warm climates, often grown in greenhouses in cooler areas. Propagate from cuttings in late spring.

Sparrmannia africana
AFRICAN HEMP, WILD HOLLYHOCK, AFRICAN LINDEN

This fast-growing shrub or small tree reaches 20 ft (6 m) and bears clusters of striking white flowers with prominent purple and gold stamens. Flowering peaks in winter to early spring but the species flowers sporadically throughout most of the year. The large leaves may be oval to heart-shaped with a pointed tip, or have several finger-like lobes. The stems are erect and woody with many spreading branches. The fruit are rounded. **'Flore Pleno'** has double flowers. **ZONES 9–11.**

SPARTIUM
BROOM, SPANISH BROOM

This genus includes just one species, a deciduous, almost leafless shrub that is indigenous to the Mediterranean region but has naturalized in a few areas with a similar climate. A yellow dye is derived from the flowers.
CULTIVATION: This adaptable plant thrives in well-drained soil enriched with a little organic matter. Full sun is best; it is a shrub for warm to coolish climates. Pruning after flowering will maintain compact, well-shaped bushes. Propagate from seed or cuttings.

Spartium junceum

This shrub bears masses of large, golden-yellow, fragrant pea-flowers carried in loose, 18 in (45 cm) long spikes at the shoot tips. It flowers profusely through spring into early summer. The leaves are bluish green, lance-shaped to linear and up to 1 in (25 mm) long; they are seen only on the new growth, and fall by mid-summer. The broom makes a bushy shrub 6–10 ft (1.8–3 m) tall; on older specimens the stems arch downwards. The fruit are flat, silvery pods maturing to brown. **ZONES 6–11.**

Sparrmannia africana 'Flore Pleno'

Spartium junceum

Sorbus sargentiana

S

Spathiphyllum 'Mauna Loa'

Spathiphyllum wallisii

SPATHIPHYLLUM

Most of the 36 species of this genus of evergreen, rhizomatous perennials come from tropical America, with some native to Malaysia. They are lush, with dark green, oval leaves that stand erect or arch slightly, and beautiful white, cream or green flowers resembling arum lilies that bloom reliably indoors. A NASA study of 'sick building syndrome' found spathiphyllums among the top 10 plants for their ability to 'clean' the air in offices.
CULTIVATION: Grow in loose, fibrous, porous potting soil in filtered light away from the sun. To re-create tropical conditions, increase the humidity by placing the plant on a tray of pebbles and water or mist regularly; sponge any dust from the leaves. Water regularly, keeping the soil moist but not soggy, and allow it to dry out a little in winter. Feed every 4 to 6 weeks with half-strength soluble fertilizer in spring and summer. Propagate by division in spring or summer. They are generally pest free. Too much light may turn the foliage yellow.

Spathiphyllum floribundum

Narrow, oval, white spathes with a green and white spadix are borne intermittently on this tufted, short-stemmed perennial. Reaching 12 in (30 cm) in height, it has clusters of lance-shaped, long, glossy dark green leaves to 6 in (15 cm). **ZONES 11–12.**

Spathiphyllum 'Mauna Loa'
PEACE LILY

The leathery, lance-shaped, glossy, mid-green leaves of this perennial reach

Spathiphyllum 'Sensation'

lengths of 12 in (30 cm). Oval, white, papery spathes surrounding white spadices are borne intermittently, turning green with age. It is the best known of a fairly large number of large-flowered cultivars; others are **'Clevelandii'**, which is shorter, and **'Aztec'**. **ZONES 11–12.**

Spathiphyllum 'Sensation'

This is the largest of the *Spathiphyllum* cultivars. It has dark green foliage with prominent ribbing and large, well-shaped white flowers. It is a very attractive plant even when not in bloom. **ZONES 11–12.**

Spathiphyllum wallisii
WHITE SAILS

This is a dwarf species with clusters of glossy green, lance-shaped leaves on reed-like stems growing to 12 in (30 cm). A white spathe encloses tiny, creamy white spadices of fragrant flowers tightly packed around an upright spike. The color changes to green with age. **ZONES 11–12.**

SPATHODEA
AFRICAN TULIP TREE, FOUNTAIN TREE

This genus contains a single species of evergreen tree that occurs naturally in tropical and subtropical Africa. It is widely planted as a street tree and is ornamental all over the tropics. Its large, bell-shaped, orange or scarlet flowers are produced in dense, terminal clusters. The large pinnate leaves are deep green. The fruit are oblong capsules that split open when ripe to release the seeds. The common name fountain tree refers to the way the buds squirt moisture when they are squeezed.
CULTIVATION: This is a tree for warm, frost-free areas. It prefers rich, well-drained soil, shelter from wind and a sunny position. Propagation is usually from seed, which can be variable.

Spathodea campanulata

This spectacular, fast-growing tree grows to about 80 ft (24 m) tall. The large, flat clusters of velvety, bronze-green buds and big, nectar-rich, orange-red flowers with yellow frilly edges are borne through spring and summer. The leaves are bronze when young, maturing to deep glossy green. The fruit are 8 in (20 cm) long. **ZONES 11–12.**

SPATHOGLOTTIS

The 40-odd species of this genus occur from India through Southeast Asia to the Philippines, New Guinea, Australia and the islands of the Pacific, at low to moderate altitudes. They usually consist of a group of crowded globose pseudobulbs with several long, broad, pleated leaves. The inflorescences arise basally and have several large flowers opening progressively, in shades of purple, yellow and white.
CULTIVATION: They require warm or intermediate conditions depending on the species, and a well-drained mixture such as would be used for *Cymbidium* species. They thrive on copious watering and most species need strong light to flower. In the tropics they are often used in garden beds.

Spathodea campanulata

Spathodea campanulata

Spathoglottis plicata

This medium to large terrestrial species is from India to Tonga and most areas between and north to the Philippines. It grows in lowland areas in seepages and other moist places. The pseudobulbs are ovoid to 2 in (5 cm) in diameter with pleated leaves 18–36 in (45–90 cm) long and 1–2½ in (2.5–6 cm) wide. The inflorescence is about 18–36 in (45–90 cm) tall with 3 to many flowers, variable in size up to 1½ in (35 mm) across. Flowering can be throughout the year, particularly in spring and summer. **ZONES 11–12.**

SPEIRANTHA

This genus consists of only one species, a perennial related to *Convallaria*. From thick spreading rhizomes, stemless leaves form a basal rosette. White flowers are followed by berries.

CULTIVATION: This plant prefers part-shade and moderately fertile, moist, humus-rich soil enriched with leafmold. Propagate from ripe seed or by division.

Speirantha convallarioides

Speirantha convallarioides

This species has stemless leaves 6 in (15 cm) long and 1¼ in (30 mm) wide, tapering to a blunt point. The flower stalk is 4 in (10 cm) tall and carries a loose head of 25 white flowers in spring and summer. This plant for shady places comes from China. **ZONES 8–10.**

SPHAERALCEA

GLOBE MALLOW, FALSE MALLOW

This genus comprises 60 species of annuals, shrubby perennials and deciduous or evergreen subshrubs and shrubs. The round or lance-shaped leaves are sometimes lobed. The clustered flowers are white, pink, lavender, red, yellow or orange. These are plants from very dry areas in the Americas and southern Africa; they have a very long flowering period.

CULTIVATION: They need moderately fertile, very well-drained soil in full sun. Propagation is from seed or cuttings, or by division.

Sphaeralcea ambigua

DESERT MALLOW

This woody perennial grows to 3 ft (1 m) tall with white or yellow felted stems. The leaves are round and thick, and the flowers are orange, up to 3⁄4 in (18 mm) wide. It comes from southwest USA and Mexico. **ZONES 5–10.**

Spiraea cantoniensis

SPINACIA

SPINACH

The Chinese have the first record of the spinach plant in the seventh century; it was later introduced to Spain in the eleventh century and from there spread to the rest of Europe. The genus consists of 3 species of fast-growing annuals with delicate, rich green large leaves that are eaten when young in salads or cooked as a vegetable. Two kinds of spinach are traditionally grown: the smooth seeded or marginally frost-hardy summer spinach and the fully frost-hardy prickly seeded winter type which generally has more lobed leaves. The flowers are insignificant.

CULTIVATION: Spinach develops a long tap root so benefits from a deep, enriched soil with good drainage. It is a cool season, short-day crop and grows best during the cooler temperatures of spring and fall (autumn). Space plants about 10 in (25 cm) apart. Keep the soil free of weeds and well watered so that the plants will not run to seed. Harvest the first leaves in 8 weeks. Propagate from seed. Watch for chewing insects and downy mildew.

Spinacia oleracea

ENGLISH SPINACH

Native to the Middle East and partial to cool climates, this species can be a challenge to grow well. It has stems to 3 ft (1 m) tall and bright green, entire or dentate leaves. The small flowers are unisexual. **ZONES 5–10.**

SPIRAEA

This genus consists of 80 species of deciduous or semi-evergreen shrubs, mostly from Europe, Asia and North America to Mexico, that are valued for their spring and summer flower display and fall (autumn) foliage color. Spiraeas form clumps of wiry stems that shoot up from the base and are densely covered with narrow, toothed leaves. They belong to the rose family, and under a magnifying glass the flowers do resemble tiny roses but they are so small that the individual flower is lost among the mass of blooms carried on each flower cluster.

CULTIVATION: Spiraeas are adaptable plants that thrive under most garden conditions in temperate climates, though they prefer a warm summer. They thrive in moist, well-drained soil and a position sheltered from the hottest sun, especially in warm summer areas where the foliage may burn. Most should be pruned after flowering. Propagate from cuttings in summer.

Spiraea 'Arguta'

GARLAND SPIRAEA, BRIDAL WREATH, FOAM OF MAY

This dense rounded deciduous shrub to 8 ft (2.4 m) high has slender arching branches that carry multitudinous small clusters of pure white flowers all along the stems in spring. **ZONES 4–10.**

Spiraea cantoniensis

REEVES' SPIRAEA

This deciduous or semi-evergreen shrub is very showy when in flower in spring, with rounded 2 in (5 cm) clusters of small, white, 5-petalled flowers densely clothing the reddish, gracefully arching branches. The narrow leaves are dark green above and blue-green below. A 3–6 ft (1–1.8 m) tall species, it originated in China. It can be used for hedging and is the best spiraea for warmer temperate regions. The double-flowered form is the most popular in gardens. **ZONES 5–11.**

Spiraea densiflora

This shrub of up to 7½ ft (2.5 m) from northwestern USA has toothed elliptical leaves and masses of small pink flowers in summer. ***Spiraea densiflora* subsp. *splendens*** has creamy white flowers. **ZONES 6–10.**

Spiraea douglasii

WESTERN SPIRAEA, STEEPLE BUSH

Occurring naturally from northern California to Alaska, this upright deciduous shrub grows to about 6 ft (1.8 m) tall and almost as wide. The oblong leaves are dark green above, velvety white beneath. The rose-pink cylindrical flower clusters, about 8 in (20 cm) long, are borne at the ends of the branches in summer. Prune (if necessary) in early spring, as this species flowers on new season's wood. **ZONES 4–10.**

Spiraea japonica

JAPANESE SPIRAEA

This low, mounding, deciduous shrub bears rose-pink to red flowers from late spring to mid-summer. It grows to a height and spread of about 6 ft (1.8 m). The cream and pink variegated new leaves turn green as they mature. It has the best foliage of any in the genus and many varieties and cultivars, including: **'Little Princess'**, to 3 ft (1 m) tall; **'Anthony Waterer'**, the most commonly cultivated selection; **'Goldflame'**, popular for its bronze new growth which turns golden as it matures; **'Nyewoods'**, with small leaves and dark pink flowers; **'Shirobana'** with both dark pink and white flowers on one plant; and **'Nana'** (syn. 'Alpina'), more compact at only 18 in (45 cm). **ZONES 3–10.**

Spathoglottis plicata

Spinacia oleracea

Spiraea densiflora subsp. *splendens*

Spiraea japonica 'Anthony Waterer'

Spiraea japonica 'Goldflame'

Spiraea myrtilloides
syn. *Spiraea virgata*

This deciduous shrub from western and central China grows to around 6 ft (1.8 m) high. It has very small oval leaves, usually only $\frac{1}{4}$–$\frac{1}{2}$ in (6–12 mm) long and strongly toothed. In early summer the branches are strung with button-like flowerheads less than 1 in (25 mm) wide of crowded, small white flowers. It is rarely grown. ZONES 4–10.

Spiraea prunifolia 'Plena'

Spiraea nervosa

This species has broad oval leaves and masses of white flowers in spring and summer. It comes from China and Japan. ZONES 6–10.

Spiraea nipponica

From Japan, this upright to spreading deciduous shrub reaches 6 ft (1.8 m) high and wide. Its rounded leaves are finely serrated and in early summer it bears pure white flowers in neat, round heads crowded along the branches. **'Snowmound'** is a particularly vigorous cultivar. ZONES 5–10.

Spiraea nipponica

Spiraea nipponica 'Snowmound'

Spiraea myrtilloides

Spiraea japonica 'Shirobana'

Spiraea japonica 'Nana'

Spiraea prunifolia

This deciduous shrub from China, Taiwan and Japan grows to 6 ft (1.8 m) tall. Snowy white, 5-petalled flowers with greenish centers are arranged in small clusters of 3 to 6 all along its pendulous branches in early spring before the leaves appear. These turn red in fall (autumn). The double-flowered **'Plena'** is the only form commonly grown. ZONES 4–10.

Spiraea × *schinabeckii*

This 6 ft (1.8 m) tall hybrid between ***Spiraea schmaedryfolia*** and ***S. trilobata*** has dark yellow shoots and 2 in (5 cm) long rounded serrated leaves. Large white flowers appear in summer. ZONES 6–10.

Spiraea thunbergii

An early flowering species, this dense, arching shrub is indigenous to China but has long been cultivated in Japan. It grows to 5 ft (1.5 m) tall and about 8 ft (1.8 m) wide. The small, white, 5-petalled blossoms on thread-like stalks appear all along its slender, wiry branches in early spring. The lance-like, finely serrated leaves are light green; they may stay on the plant all year in mild climates, while in cooler areas they often turn shades of pink and orange before falling. ZONES 4–10.

Spiraea × *schinabeckii*

Spiraea japonica

Spiraea × *vanhouttei*

This compact, deciduous shrub bears dense clusters of white flowers amid dark green, diamond-shaped leaves in spring. It grows to a height of 6 ft (1.8 m) with a spread of 5 ft (1.5 m). ZONES 4–10.

SPOROBOLUS
DROPSEED, RUSHGRASS

This genus includes 100 species of annual and perennial grasses found worldwide. The panicles may be open or dense, and each spikelet has only one flower. They form attractive clumps. **CULTIVATION:** They will do well in full sun in any soil as long as it is

S

well-drained. Propagate from seed sown *in situ*.

Sporobolus airoides

This delicate grass has a wide distribution in North America. The flowering panicle is very finely branched into a mist of hair-like stalks each terminating in a tiny spikelet, resembling the inflorescence of another grass genus *Aira* (hence the specific name). ZONES 3–9.

Sporobolus heterolepis

PRAIRIE DROPSEED

Native to central North America, this warm-season grass has a restrained growth habit and fine hair-like foliage that moves gracefully in the wind. It develops into a 12 in (30 cm) high rounded mound and is valued for its texture. ZONES 4–9.

SPREKELIA

JACOBEAN LILY, MALTESE CROSS LILY, AZTEC LILY

This genus from Mexico and Guatemala consists of one species of bulbous

Stachys byzantina 'Primrose Heron'

Stachys byzantina

Sporobolus airoides

Stachys coccinea

perennial which forms a clump of strap leaves. It also has a flowering stem that carries only one red flower (rarely white) with 6 segments, giving it the appearance of an orchid.

CULTIVATION: Plant this frost-tender bulb in full sun in moderately fertile, well-drained soil with the neck and shoulders of the bulb above soil level. Propagate by separating offsets during their fall (autumn) dormancy.

Sprekelia formosissima

This beautiful perennial grows to 18 in (45 cm) tall and in summer produces bright red, 6 in (15 cm) long flowers that

Stachys byzantina 'Silver Carpet'

Stachys byzantina 'Cotton Boll'

Sporobolus heterolepis

Stachys byzantina 'Big Ears'

resemble the red cross borne by the Spanish religious order of St Jacob of Cal-atrava, hence one of the common names. The lower 3 petals form an open tube and the upper petals curve upwards and outwards. The green leaves are strap-shaped. ZONES 9–11.

STACHYS

BETONY, WOUNDWORT, HEDGE NETTLE

This genus, in the mint family, contains about 300 species of annuals, perennials and evergreen shrubs. They have long been used in herb gardens, many of them having supposed medicinal value, and come from a range of habitats mostly in northern temperate regions. Many species are aromatic, and most are attractive to bees and butterflies. They bear tubular, 2-lipped, purple, red, pink, yellow or white flowers.

CULTIVATION: They all like well-drained, moderately fertile soil in full sun. Propagate from seed or cuttings or by division.

Stachys affinis

CHINESE ARTICHOKE, KNOTROOT, CHAROGI, CROSNES-DU-JAPAN

This is an erect, hairy perennial to 18 in (45 cm) tall with many slender knotted tubers just under the soil. The oval leaves are round and the flowers are white or light red. It is cultivated in eastern Asia for its edible tubers. ZONES 5–10.

Stachys byzantina

syns *Stachys lanata*, *S. olympica*

LAMBS' EARS, LAMBS' TAILS, LAMBS' TONGUES

The leaves give this perennial its common names: they are lance-shaped and

Sprekelia formosissima

Stachys macrantha

have the same white, downy feel of a lamb. Unfortunately, the leaves turn to mush in very cold, humid or wet weather. It makes a good ground cover or border plant, growing 12–18 in (30–45 cm) high, with a 24 in (60 cm) spread. Mauve-pink flowers appear in summer. **'Silver Carpet'** seldom flowers, remaining more compact than the species; **'Cotton Boll'** (syn. 'Sheila McQueen') has flowers that look like cottonwool balls; **'Primrose Heron'** has yellowish green leaves; and **'Big Ears'** (syn. 'Countess Helen von Stein') is a large-growing cultivar which bears tall spikes of purple flowers. ZONES 5–10.

Stachys coccinea

SCARLET HEDGE NETTLE

This long-flowering perennial native to southwest USA and Mexico bears red flowers, although pink and white forms are now available. The flowers are almost irresistible to hummingbirds. Flowering continues from spring through fall (autumn) on plants that grow 12–36 in (30–90 cm) tall and 18 in (45 cm) wide. ZONES 6–10.

Stachys macrantha

This perennial has erect stems up to 24 in (60 cm) tall bearing heads of hooded, purple-pink flowers from early summer to early fall (autumn). The basal leaves are long and heart-shaped, wrinkled and rough with hairs. ZONES 5–10.

Stachys officinalis

BISHOP'S WORT, WOOD BETONY

This stately erect perennial from Europe grows to 3 ft (1 m) in height. The basal

S

rosette leaves are oblong or heart-shaped. The red-purple flowers are held in dense spikes, although white and pink forms also occur. **ZONES 5–10.**

STACHYTARPHETA

FALSE VERVAIN, SNAKE-WEED

This genus comprises over 60 species of annuals, perennials and shrubs from Central and South America, Southeast Asia and the Pacific. The leaves are usually toothed and wrinkled. White, red, purple or blue flowers occur in terminal spikes.

CULTIVATION: The rather weedy habit of these plants is tolerated because of the flowers. They prefer filtered sun and fertile, well-drained soil. Tip pruning of young plants increases their bushiness. Propagate from seed or cuttings. They are prone to attack from white fly.

Stachytarpheta mutabilis

PINK SNAKE-WEED

This is a rather straggling shrub up to 8 ft (2.4 m) in height. The stems are 5-angled and hairy, and carry small leaves that are rough on top but softly felty underneath. The 24 in (60 cm) long flower stalks carry large showy red flowers that age to tones of pink. It comes from Central and South America. **ZONES 10–12.**

STACHYURUS

This genus includes some 6 species of deciduous or semi-evergreen shrubs and trees from the Himalayas and eastern Asia. Although reminiscent of the witch hazels and *Corylopsis,* they belong in a different family. They are generally not spectacular plants though one species, *Stachyurus praecox,* is fairly widely grown. They bloom in late winter or early spring before or just as the leaves are developing, and produce small cream to pale yellow flowers in drooping racemes at every leaf bud. They also have broadly lance-shaped leaves.

CULTIVATION: These plants prefer humus-rich, well-drained, acidic soil in sun or light shade and are usually propagated from seed or cuttings in summer.

Stachyurus praecox

A 6 ft (1.8 m) high and wide deciduous shrub indigenous to Japan, this species is noted for its early flowering habit.

Stachyurus praecox

Stanhopea tigrina

Its gracefully drooping, 3 in (8 cm) long racemes of buds appear on the bare branches in fall (autumn), opening as small pale yellow flowers in late winter or early spring. The leaves that follow are up to 6 in (15 cm) long and are carried on tiered, reddish brown stems. **ZONES 5–10.**

STANHOPEA

UPSIDE-DOWN ORCHID

Each of the 30 species in this South American genus blooms in a way only an epiphyte could do—the buds burrow upside down through the roots so that the flowers hang below the rest of the plant. Obviously, when cultivated they can only be grown in hanging baskets, not pots. The story is told that when the first *Stanhopea* was grown at Kew Gardens (back in the 1820s) it was planted in an ordinary pot and no one ever saw its flowers until one day a careless gardener broke the pot and discovered the flower buds. The evergreen leaves are broad and glossy, and the curiously shaped waxy flowers are very striking. They appear in summer and are not very long lived but are sweetly fragrant.

CULTIVATION: Stanhopeas grow happily outdoors in warm, frost-free climates in a shaded position, requiring a greenhouse in cooler areas. They should be allowed to dry off in winter. Propagate by division in spring.

Stanhopea tigrina

This perennial epiphyte has clustered pseudobulbs, each with a pendent stem and a solitary, erect, green leaf. It bears pendent racemes of yellow flowers with a white, waxy lip and red sepals spotted with yellow. It is tender to both dry conditions and frost and grows to 18 in (45 cm) high. **ZONES 10–12.**

Stapelia gigantea

Stanhopea wardii

This species bears 4 in (10 cm) wide, unusual golden flowers marked with red dots in summer; the flowers, which look somewhat like a squid, occur in terminal racemes and smell strongly of chocolate and vanilla. The oval, semi-rigid leaves are 8 in (20 cm) long, while the plant itself reaches 18 in (45 cm) in height. **ZONES 10–12.**

STAPELIA

CARRION FLOWER, STARFISH FLOWER

The 45 species in this genus are the carrion flowers *par excellence.* They are perennial succulents from southern Africa, like small cacti in growth habit but without thorns. The flowers are wide open stars, elegant in their symmetry, but they are pollinated by flies that think nothing in the world is more tasty than a piece of rotting meat. Stapelias pander to them both by the odor of the flowers and also by their color, which always includes some variation on the theme of red, brown and purple usually in marbled patterns and sometimes streaked with cream to resemble fatty meat. The flies are sometimes so thoroughly deceived that they lay eggs on them, but the larvae starve to death when they hatch—they can't eat the flower. There are several hybrids and cultivars, some featuring pinkish or yellow tints at the tips of their stems.

CULTIVATION: Plant these frost-tender species in full sun or part-shade and moderately fertile, very well-drained soil. Propagate from seed or stem cuttings in spring or summer.

Stapelia gigantea

The specific name means 'gigantic', but this is a rather modest plant growing 8 in (20 cm) or so tall at most. It earns its name from the size of the flowers, the largest in the genus and often over 12 in (30 cm) across. They are star-shaped, yellow-brown marked with red and have white-haired, recurved edges. **ZONES 9–11.**

Stapelia leendertziae

This species grows to 12 in (30 cm) tall and has lush, slender, upright stems with 4 angles and indented or winged

Stapelia gigantea

margins. Hairy, deep purple, bell-shaped flowers bloom in summer on tubes up to 2½ in (6 cm) long. **ZONES 9–11.**

STAPHYLEA

BLADDERNUT

The 11 species that make up this genus come from northern temperate regions. They are tough deciduous shrubs or small trees from moist woodland habitats with 3 to 7 toothed leaflets and flowers in terminal heads, either white or tinted rose.

CULTIVATION: Fully frost hardy, they prefer full sun or part-shade and moist but well-drained soil. Flowering is best following long hot summers. Propagation is from seed, some needing 12 weeks warmth followed by 12 weeks cold (in the refrigerator), or from cuttings in summer.

Staphylea colchica

BLADDERNUT

This upright shrub is native to the Caucasus in Europe. From spring to early summer it bears delicate, erect, daffodil-like, trumpet-shaped flowers set among serrated, trifoliate leaves. Pale green inflated pods follow the blooms. It grows to a height and spread of 10 ft (3 m). **ZONES 6–9.**

Staphylea trifolia

AMERICAN BLADDERNUT

This tall shrub from eastern USA grows to 15 ft (4.5 m) high with 3 in (8 cm) long, elliptical, finely toothed leaves. It bears ivory flowers in hanging panicles up to 2 in (5 cm) long in spring. **ZONES 5–9.**

Stenocarpus sinuatus

Steirodiscus tagetes

Stauntonia hexaphylla

Steirodiscus tagetes 'Gold Rush'

STAUNTONIA

This genus consists of 16 species of evergreen or semi-evergreen climbers from temperate eastern Asia and Japan. They have 3 to 7 digitate leaves composed of 2–4 in (5–10 cm) long, mid-green leaflets. In spring they bear simple, rose-scented, bell-shaped flowers in loose clusters. By mid-summer the fruits are becoming apparent. They are ovoid, green until they ripen to purplish red and filled with a bland edible pulp.
CULTIVATION: Plant in cool, moist, humus-rich, well-drained soil in light shade or morning sun. The common species are frost hardy to about 15°F (–10°C). They are easily, if slowly, raised from seed but otherwise difficult to propagate—layering is probably the most reliable method for gardeners.

Stauntonia hexaphylla

This vine may grow to 30 ft (9 m) and has leathery leaflets. The fragrant flowers are $^{3}/_{4}$ in (18 mm) long, white, tinged with violet. The edible purple berries are 1–2 in (2.5–5 cm) long. It comes from Korea and Japan. **ZONES 8–10.**

STEIRODISCUS

This genus consists of 5 annuals from South Africa with spirally arranged, toothed, divided leaves. Yellow or orange daisy flowers appear in summer.
CULTIVATION: Frost tender, they prefer full sun and well-drained, humus-rich soil. Propagate from seed or cuttings.

Steirodiscus tagetes

This species grows to 12 in (30 cm) in height with wiry branching stems and 2 in (5 cm) long divided leaves. The bright yellow or orange flowers are $^{3}/_{4}$ in (18 mm) wide. **'Gold Rush'** is a larger yellow form. **ZONES 9–11.**

STELLARIA

CHICKWEED, STARWORT

The 120 or more species of annuals or perennials that make up this genus found in most temperate regions of the world, have a rather brittle branching growth habit. Some are garden weeds but others are modest garden plants. The flowers are usually solitary, 5-petalled and white. They are followed by tiny capsules containing numerous seeds.
CULTIVATION: They prefer full sun and rich, moist, slightly acidic soil. Propagate from seed or cuttings.

Stenotaphrum secundatum

Stellaria holostea

STITCHWORT

Stellaria holostea is a perennial with floppy stems forming a twisted dome up to 24 in (60 cm) tall. The leaves taper to a long point and have rough edges. The flowers are white, large and notched, occuring in spring. It comes from Europe, North Africa and western Asia. **ZONES 5–10.**

STENOCACTUS

This genus consists of some 10 species of cacti and is native to Mexico. Species may be single stemmed or clustering. The stems, which are globose or short and cylindrical, rarely exceed 6 in (15 cm) in height. They are usually blue-green and heavily ribbed with spine-bearing areoles on the ribs. The areoles have 3 to 27 spines depending on the species, and the spines are up to 1 in (25 mm) long. The short funnel-shaped flowers, which cluster around the stem tips in spring and summer, are yellow, pink or purple and are $^{1}/_{2}$–1$^{1}/_{2}$ in (12–35 mm) long and wide.
CULTIVATION: Plant in free-draining, gritty soil in full sun or morning shade. Most species tolerate occasional light frosts but resent cold, wet conditions. Propagate from seed or offsets.

Stenocactus obvallatus

syns *Echinofossulocactus pentacanthus*, *E. violaciflorus*

Native to central Mexico, this is a grayish, blue-green spherical cactus that reaches a height of 4 in (10 cm) and width of 6 in (15 cm). It bears gray-brown spines and in spring produces solitary, yellow or pale pink flowers with purple-red stripes on each petal. **ZONES 9–11.**

STENOCARPUS

This is a genus of 22 species of evergreen shrubs and trees belonging to the protea family and indigenous to Australia, Malaysia and New Caledonia. They bear umbels of tubular, cream to red flowers with knob-shaped stigmas protruding through splits in the tubes. The leaves are alternate and simple.
CULTIVATION: They need full sun and fertile, well-drained soil. Water generously in summer, less in winter. Propagate from seed in spring or from cuttings in summer.

Stenocarpus sinuatus

FIREWHEEL TREE

A handsome but slow-growing tree endemic to rainforests of Australia's warm east coast, this species can reach 30–70 ft (9–21 m); it has an upright, thick trunk with dark brown bark topped by a dense crown of foliage. The leaves are shiny and dark green and up to 12 in (30 cm) long. The interesting skittle-shaped buds, opening to contorted flowers about 3 in (8 cm) across, are orange to red and are arranged in a cluster like spokes on a wheel. The woody, boat-shaped fruit are 2–4 in (5–10 cm) long. **ZONES 9–12.**

STENOCEREUS

These tree-like columnar cacti are native to Mexico, Cuba, the West Indies and Venezuela. The genus consists of 25 species, some featuring very attractive blooms. The flowers are generally white and bell-shaped, growing from the tip of the blue-green stems in spring or summer. The toxic sap of ***Stenocereus gummosus*** has been used in north Mexico to stun fish by throwing the stems in the water.
CULTIVATION: Frost tender, these plants need quite warm conditions and will not do well in very cold regions. Plant in humus-rich, very well-drained soil in full sun. Propagate from seed in spring or cuttings in summer. They are susceptible to aphids and scale when flowering.

Stenocereus beneckei

syn. *Hertrichocereus beneckei*

This interesting cactus from western Mexico only grows 3–6 ft (1–1.8 m) tall, branching from the base and with stems tending to fall over with age. The stems have 7 to 9 broad rounded ribs from which project blunt tubercles with short blackish spines. Younger parts of the stems are striking blue-gray. Nocturnal white or pink-tinged flowers up to 3 in (8 cm) long are borne in summer. **ZONES 9–11.**

STENOTAPHRUM

This genus from tropical and subtropical regions throughout the world is made up of 6 species of annual and perennial grasses with stems that root at the nodes. The leaves are flat, folded and short, lying perpendicular to the stem. Axillary and terminal racemes bear greenish brown spikelets.
CULTIVATION: These frost-tender plants prefer full sun and fertile, moist but well-drained soil. Propagate from cuttings or by division.

Stenotaphrum secundatum

BUFFALO GRASS, ST AUGUSTINE GRASS

Although a coarse-textured grass with wide blades, this spreading perennial makes a good lawn in warmer climates, particularly near the sea where its tolerance to salt spray is an asset. It is light to dark green in color and forms a mat by taking root at the nodes of runners that spread quickly. It grows up to 6 in

Steriphoma paradoxum

(15 cm) high if left uncut. **'Variegatum'** has pale green leaves with ivory stripes. **ZONES 9–12.**

STEPHANANDRA

This genus is made up of 4 species of deciduous shrubs related to *Spiraea.* From the eastern Asian region, they tolerate low temperatures. The toothed and lobed mid-green leaves, which turn orange and gold in fall (autumn), are very ornamental, as are the sepia-tinted bare stems in winter. Tiny, star-shaped, white or greenish flowers appear in summer in soft panicles; each has many stamens.
CULTIVATION: Species of *Stephanandra* grow well in sun or part-shade, preferring rich, moist, loamy soil, and can be pruned to shape in winter if necessary. Propagate from cuttings or by division in fall.

Stephanandra incisa

LACE SHRUB, CUTLEAF STEPHANANDRA

Occurring naturally in Japan, Taiwan and Korea, this shrub grows to about 6 ft (1.8 m) tall with a similar spread. The lace shrub has graceful arching branches with diamond-shaped, deeply toothed leaves. The tiny greenish white flowers appear in summer. This shrub tolerates neglect. **'Crispa'** is a dwarf-growing cultivar with slightly curled leaves. **ZONES 4–10.**

Stephanandra tanakae

Valued for its decorative, arching growth habit and attractive leaves, this shrub from Japan grows to about 10 ft (3 m) tall with a similar spread. The plant's leaves are 2–4 in (5–10 cm) long with shallowly toothed lobes with long points. The new foliage is pinkish brown. The tiny white flowers are borne through summer. **ZONES 4–10.**

STEPHANOTIS

This genus of 5 to 15 species of twining woody stemmed climbers is found in the tropical and subtropical regions of Africa, Madagascar and Asia. Growing 10–20 ft (3–6 m) tall, they have wiry stems clothed with pairs of 4–6 in (10–15 cm) long, waxy, deep green leaves. The foliage is attractive but the primary appeal is the fragrant flowers. Opening from early summer in clusters of around 4 blooms, they are pure white, pendulous, tubular with widely flared lobes, and up to $2\frac{1}{2}$ in (6 cm) long.
CULTIVATION: Plant in moderately fertile, humus-rich, moist but well-drained soil in filtered sunlight as full sun will burn the flowers. Frost tender, they may be grown indoors or in greenhouses where temperatures fall below 59°F (15°C). The stems should be supported and shortened in spring if they become overcrowded. Propagate from seed in spring or cuttings in summer.

Stephanotis floribunda

WAX FLOWER, BRIDAL WREATH, MADAGASCAR JASMINE

This evergreen climber from Madagascar can grow to a height and spread of 10 ft (3 m). It is grown for its pleasant fragrance and attractive foliage of paired, waxy, deep green leaves. The pure white flowers appear in clusters of about 4 blooms from spring to fall (autumn). **ZONES 10–12.**

STERCULIA

This genus consists of 200 species of deciduous or evergreen trees grown for shade and for their ornamental appearance. They have large simple or lobed leaves and flowers with no petals, although the calyx is usually colored. They have a remarkable fruit structure, with the carpels opening soon after pollination so that the seeds develop 'naked', that is, exposed to the air. The follicles themselves are rather leathery and soft.
CULTIVATION: They are marginally frost hardy and prefer full sun and loamy, well-drained soil. Water them regularly and protect from cold winds. They can be pruned if necessary. Propagate from seed in late fall (autumn) or winter.

Stephanotis floribunda

Sterculia coccinea

syn. *Sterculia hamiltonii*

This beautiful species from Southeast Asia has simple, elliptical leaves, though with a jointed leaf-stalk. The follicles are bright scarlet. **ZONES 11–12.**

STERIPHOMA

This tropical American genus consists of 8 species of evergreen shrubs related to Capparis, notable for the very elongated, drooping stamens of each flower. They have simple, leathery leaves and the branches terminate in erect sprays of flowers with the 5 petals much shorter than the stamens. Like other members of the caper family, the ovary of the flower (which becomes the fruit after pollination) is separated from the remainder of the flower by a long stalk. Quite ornamental, *Steriphoma* species are sometimes grown in tropical gardens, or in hothouses of cool-climate botanical gardens.
CULTIVATION: These tropical shrubs require a frost-free climate with humid summers and should be grown in a sheltered position in sun or part-shade, with adequate soil moisture. Propagate from seed or cuttings.

Steriphoma paradoxum

A beautiful shrub when in flower, *Steriphoma paradoxum* is native to Central America and northern South America, from Gautemala to Colombia, and grows at medium altitudes. Reaching a height of about 10 ft (3 m), it has rusty red hairs on the new growths; leaves are elliptical, pointed and glossy deep green. The flower buds are covered in a fuzz of pale red-brown hairs, and the short petals and 3 in (8 cm) long stamens are pinkish cream to more yellowish. **ZONES 10–12.**

STERNBERGIA

AUTUMN CROCUS, AUTUMN DAFFODIL

This genus of 8 species of flowering bulbs ranges from Italy across to Iran and was named in honor of Austrian botanist Count Kaspar von Sternberg (1761–1838), a founder of the National Museum in Prague. They have large, crocus-like flowers that appear in spring or fall (autumn) and are related to daffodils, the bulbs in fact looking like small daffodil bulbs.
CULTIVATION: They need a hot, sunny site in well-drained soil and should be planted against a sunny wall in cool climates. If left undisturbed they will form clumps. Propagate by division in spring or fall.

Sternbergia candida

This spring-flowering species bears a fragrant, trumpet-shaped white flower on a leafless stem. Reaching 8 in (20 cm) in height, it has strap-like, semi-erect, grayish green leaves. **ZONES 7–10.**

Stephanandra incisa

Stephanandra tanakae

Sterculia coccinea

Sternbergia lutea

This delightful species is native to the Mediterranean region. The buttercup-yellow flowers are 2 in (5 cm) long and are borne singly on 6 in (15 cm) stems in fall (autumn). The slender leaves are strap-like. It is only just frost hardy and needs warm, dry conditions when dormant in summer; it is best grown in pots in areas with wet summers and makes an excellent plant in a rock garden. **ZONES 7–10.**

STEWARTIA

syn. *Stuartia*

This eastern Asian and North American genus consists of 15 to 20 species of deciduous or evergreen small trees or shrubs closely allied to the camellias. The flowers are usually white with prominent golden stamens, about 3 in (8 cm) across, and resemble single camellia blooms. The leaves are elliptical, 2–6 in (5–15 cm) long, and often develop bright orange and red fall (autumn) tones. **CULTIVATION:** Species of *Stewartia* grow best in moist, humus-rich, well-drained, slightly acidic soil in sun or part-shade. Propagate from seed in fall or from cuttings in summer.

Stewartia pseudocamellia var. *koreana*

Stewartia pseudocamellia

Stewartia pseudocamellia

Stewartia monadelpha

Stewartia malacodendron

MALLOW TREE, SILKY STEWARTIA

This species is indigenous to southeastern USA and is usually seen as a 20 ft (6 m) high and 10 ft (3 m) wide shrub, though it can reach 30 ft (9 m). It blooms from early summer, its flowers sometimes having purplish stamens. The fall (autumn) foliage is reddish purple. The mallow tree needs warm summers to flower well. **ZONES 7–10.**

Stewartia monadelpha

This tree from Korea and Japan can grow to over 70 ft (21 m), but is usually a large shrub in cultivation. The bark is smooth but peels in thin flakes, while the veins beneath the leaves are silky. The flowers are 2 in (5 cm) wide and white with purple anthers. The leaves turn bright red in fall (autumn). **ZONES 7–10.**

Stewartia ovata

syns *Stuartia ovata, S. pentagyna*

MOUNTAIN CAMELLIA, MOUNTAIN STEWARTIA

A native of North America, this small tree grows slowly to 20 ft (6 m). Its mid-green, oval leaves are downy underneath and turn yellow in early fall (autumn). Bowl-shaped flowers appear in mid-summer and are white with orange-yellow centers. ***Stewartia ovata* var. *grandiflora*** has 4 in (10 cm) wide white flowers with purple stamens resembling big camellias. **ZONES 7–10.**

Stewartia sinensis

Stewartia pseudocamellia

syn. *Stuartia pseudocamellia*

FALSE CAMELLIA, JAPANESE STEWARTIA

Indigenous to Japan (not Hokkaido) and Korea, this species can grow to 70 ft (21 m) high in the wild but is more commonly about 20 ft (6 m) in cultivation. It blooms from late spring to early summer and the white flowers are followed by small, spherical, nut-like seed capsules that are a prominent feature from mid-summer. It has attractive peeling bark and yellow, orange and red fall (autumn) foliage. ***Stewartia pseudocamellia* var. *koreana*** (syn. *Stewartia koreana*) hardly differs from the typical Japanese plants, the main distinction being that the petals spread more widely instead of being cupped and the leaves are broader and less silky when young. **ZONES 6–10.**

Stewartia sinensis

syn. *Stuartia sinensis*

A 30 ft (9 m) tall tree indigenous to China, this species blooms in late spring and summer with small, fragrant, rose-like, white flowers about 2 in (5 cm) across. The color of the flaking bark is a warm reddish brown to purple and the fall (autumn) foliage is crimson. **ZONES 6–10.**

STICHERUS

FAN FERN

This genus contains about 100 species from the tropics and from temperate regions of the southern hemisphere. They are vigorous colonizing ferns, found along waterways and gullies; narrow linear leaf segments are dense and crowded, and give the plants an umbrella-like appearance. **CULTIVATION:** These frost-tender ferns need a protected, shaded position and moist, cool soil. Propagate by division.

Sticherus tener

SILKY FAN FERN

This is a dense multi-layered fern with rough brown scaled creeping rhizomes. The fronds are umbrella-like and erect on straggling stems up to 6 ft (1.8 m) long. The leaflets are up to 1½ in (35 mm) long, narrow and arranged densely along dull green stalks. In the landscape it is a dramatic species when associated with the margins of broad water areas or as understory plants in moist shaded areas such as fern gullies. It is found naturally in cooler areas of southeastern Australia, including Tasmania. **ZONES 8–10.**

Sticherus tener

Stigmaphyllon ciliatum

STIGMAPHYLLON

This genus consists of about 110 species of woody climbers that are grown for their handsome leaves and yellow flowers. They come from tropical North and South America, the Caribbean and the West Indies and remain frost tender in cultivation away from the tropics. **CULTIVATION:** They are generally too strong growing for greenhouse culture, but very heavy pruning can mitigate this. Outdoors they prefer full sun and fertile, moist soil. Climbing stems will need support. Propagate from cuttings or by layering.

Stigmaphyllon ciliatum

GOLDEN VINE, ORCHID VINE, AMAZON VINE

This slender twining vine has oval leaves up to 3 in (8 cm) long, heart-shaped with toothed edges and a long stalk. The rich yellow flowers, which are borne in groups of 3 to 6, are saucer-shaped. It comes from coastal areas of Central and South America. **ZONES 10–12.**

STIPA

syn. *Achnatherum*

FEATHER GRASS, NEEDLE GRASS, SPEAR GRASS

This widely distributed genus consists of 300 species of perennial tufted and frost-hardy grasses. They are noted for their tall flowering spikes with large feathery panicles. The flowers are borne in large,

Stipa calamagrostis

loose panicles with one floret per spikelet, and as the seeds mature they develop long bristles or awns—in some cases as much as 4 in (10 cm) long—which give this genus its particular character. The leaves are narrow and straight-edged. The larger growing species, with flower spikes that can reach over 6 ft (1.8 m), are often grown as specimen plants, sited where they can be seen to best advantage but without overwhelming other plantings.

CULTIVATION: Plant in full sun in well-drained soil. To propagate, sow seed in spring or fall (autumn) or divide the plants in late spring.

Stipa tenacissima

Stipa arundinacea

WIND GRASS, PHEASANT'S TAIL GRASS

This clump-forming evergreen grass from New Zealand is grown for its attractive foliage and flowers. The leaves are long, narrow and dark green tinged orange. In winter the clump turns a rich rusty orange. In summer arching stems of fluffy, pinkish purple flowers are generously produced, creating a halo over the plant. It grows 3 ft (1 m) tall with a slightly wider spread. **ZONES 8–10.**

Stipa barbata

This European grass forms a clump to 24 in (60 cm) wide. The arching leaves are smooth on top but hairy underneath. The flowerheads are narrow. The long awns are hairy at the base and grow 6 in (15 cm) long. **ZONES 8–10.**

Stipa calamagrostis

Strong-growing clumps reach 4 ft (1.2 m) on this grass from southern and central Europe. The leaves are 12 in (30 cm) long. Loose flowerheads grow to 30 in (75 cm) long with purplish spikelets and ½ in (12 mm) curved awns. **ZONES 7–10.**

Stipa gigantea

GOLDEN OATS, GIANT FEATHER GRASS

Native to Spain and Portugal, this evergreen or semi-evergreen, clump-forming grass is best grown as a specimen plant. It is a long-lived species with narrow

Stipa splendens

Stipa barbata

Stipa gigantea

green leaves that can reach 30 in (75 cm). In summer the upright stems bear bristle-like, silver-purple flowers in large, open panicles up to 8 in (20 cm) long. These persist into winter, turning a deep golden color. Cut the flower stems in mid-summer for drying. **ZONES 8–10.**

Stipa pennata

WILD OATS

Golden anthers hang from the long-awned, silver spikelets that form delicate, panicles on this grass from summer to winter. The narrow leaves are about 18 in (45 cm) long. Fully frost-hardy, it grows 8 ft (2.4 m) tall and comes from southern Europe to Asia. **ZONES 7–10.**

Stipa pulchra

PURPLE NEEDLE GRASS

The 3 ft (1 m) long stems on this species have long narrow leaves. The loose open panicle of slender spreading branches has purplish seed heads. It comes from western USA. **ZONES 7–10.**

Stipa ramosissima

BAMBOO GRASS, PILLAR OF SMOKE

This evergreen, clumping grass from eastern Australia grows to a height and

Stipa ramosissima

spread of 6–8 ft (1.8–2.4 m). It has slender bamboo-like stems, soft, deep green leaves and small panicles of feathery, pale green flower spikelets, borne from spring to summer. **ZONES 8–11.**

Stipa splendens

CHEE GRASS

This tall grass to 8 ft (2.4 m) from central Asia, Russia and Chile forms clumps of stout stems with rough leaves. The loose panicles of flowers with white or purple tonings appear in summer. **ZONES 7–10.**

Stipa tenacissima

ESPARTO GRASS

Found in Spain and North Africa, this grass yields a strong fiber that was used in paper manufacture in the nineteenth century. It was also used to make rope and matting. The plant forms a dense tuft of fine, smooth leaves with inrolled edges, and sends up flowering stems to about 6 ft (1.8 m) tall. **ZONES 8–10.**

S

Strelitzia juncea

Stipa tenuissima

Stipa tirsa

Stipa tenuissima
MEXICAN FEATHER GRASS

This grass forms a large tuft of slender stems up to 24 in (60 cm) long. The thin, wiry leaves may reach 12 in (30 cm) or more in length, curled upwards along the leaf blades. The panicles are narrow, soft and nodding, and the awns are about 2 in (5 cm) long. It comes from Texas, Mexico and Argentina. **ZONES 8–10.**

Stipa tirsa

This is a stoutly stemmed grass from southern and central Europe with leaves up to 3 ft (1 m) long. The compact flowerheads have 2 in (5 cm) hairy awns. **ZONES 7–10.**

STOKESIA
STOKES' ASTER

This genus of a single perennial species native to the southeastern states of the USA was named after Englishman Dr Jonathan Stokes (1755–1831). One of the most attractive late-flowering perennials, it grows about 18 in (45 cm) high and flowers from late summer to fall (autumn) if the spent flower stems are promptly removed. It is very good for cutting. **CULTIVATION:** Plant in full sun or part-shade and fertile, well-drained soil. Water well in summer. Propagate from seed in fall or by division in spring.

Stokesia laevis
syn. *Stokesia cyanea*

This fully frost-hardy perennial has evergreen rosettes, its narrow leaves green, basal and divided. The blue-mauve or white blooms have a shaggy appearance reminiscent of cornflowers and are borne freely on erect stems. **ZONES 7–10.**

STRELITZIA
BIRD OF PARADISE

The 5 species of clump-forming perennials that make up this genus have exotic flowers which resemble the head of a bird. Each bloom consists of several spiky flowers arising from a boat-like bract. The leaves are large and dramatic. Strelitzias form large clumps of evergreen banana-like foliage. They occur naturally in South Africa but are grown in warm climates around the world; in cool areas they are enjoyed as greenhouse specimens. The fruits are capsules. **CULTIVATION:** They need full sun or part-shade and prefer well-drained soil enriched with organic matter and dryish conditions in cooler months. New plants can be produced by dividing a clump, but this is hard work as the clump and roots are very dense. They can also be propagated from seed or suckers in spring.

Strelitzia juncea
syn. *Strelitzia reginae* var. *juncea*

Botanists have long disputed whether this should be treated as a species distinct from *Strelitzia reginae* or as a variety of that species. Its appearance is dramatically different with tall, rush-like, straight leaf stalks to 6 ft (1.8 m) high, lacking any leaf blade. The flowerheads are identical with those of *S. reginae*, but their stems are much shorter than the leaf stalks. **ZONES 9–12.**

Strelitzia reginae 'Mandela's Gold'

Strelitzia nicolai
WILD BANANA, GIANT BIRD OF PARADISE

The erect, woody, palm-like stems on this tree-sized species reach a height of 20 ft (6 m) and the clump spreads over 12 ft (3.5 m). It has large dull green leaves over 5 ft (1.5 m) long on long stalks. The flowers appear in summer near the top of the plant from the leaf axils. These striking flowers are greenish blue and white, and open a few at a time from a reddish brown bract. **ZONES 10–12.**

Strelitzia reginae
CRANE FLOWER, BIRD OF PARADISE

This shrub-sized species has blooms of bright orange and blue sitting in a pointed green bract edged with red; the main flowering season is spring to summer. It grows to 6 ft (1.8 m) high and spreads over 3 ft (1 m), forming an erect clump of leaves and smooth flower stalks arising from underground stems. The leaves are grayish green and spoon-like. **'Mandela's Gold'** has yellow-orange and purplish blue blooms. **ZONES 10–12.**

STREPTOCARPUS

This genus consists of 130 species of annuals, perennials and rarely subshrubs from tropical Africa, Madagascar, Thailand, China and Indonesia. There are 3 main groups: shrubby bushy species with vigorous growth; rosetted plants; and single-leafed species producing one very large leaf up to 3 ft (1 m) long. They all bear tubular flowers with 5 lobes and hairy, veined, crinkly leaves. **CULTIVATION:** Frost tender, they prefer part-shade and leafy, humus-rich, moist but well-drained soil. Seeding will be prevented if flowers are deadheaded and stalks are removed. Propagate from seed or cuttings or by division.

Streptocarpus rexii

This is a rosetted perennial from South Africa with leaves that are up to 12 in (30 cm) long and 2½ in (6 cm) wide, scalloped, wavy and hairy. One to six stalks 8 in (20 cm) long bear large white, mauve or bluish 3 in (8 cm) flowers. **ZONES 10–11.**

Strelitzia nicolai

Strelitzia reginae

Streptocarpus Hybrid 'Ruby'

Streptocarpus Hybrid 'Blue Heaven'

Streptocarpus Hybrids

Most *Streptocarpus* hybrids have *S. rexii* as a major parent. They are generally plants with a rosette growth habit and large, showy, trumpet-shaped flowers in bright colors with a white throat. **'Bethan'** bears multitudes of lilac-purple flowers; **'Blue Heaven'** has flowers that are a strong mid-blue to pale purple; **'Falling Stars'** has many small sky-blue to lilac flowers; **'Gloria'** has pinkish flowers; **'Ruby'** has crimson-red flowers; and **'Susan'** has deep red flowers with yellow centers. **ZONES 10–11.**

STREPTOSOLEN

MARMALADE BUSH

This genus consists of only one species, a loosely scrambling shrub with alternate, simple leaves occurring in parts of the northern Andes. It is cultivated mainly for its clusters of brightly colored, long-tubed, funnel-shaped flowers.
CULTIVATION: In the garden it does best in full sun with shelter from strong winds. A light, well-drained soil is ideal, preferably enriched with organic matter, and it needs adequate moisture during warmer months. Light pruning after flowering will keep it compact. Propagate from cuttings in summer.

Streptosolen jamesonii

syn. *Browallia jamesonii*

This fast-growing, evergreen shrub reaches 6 ft (1.8 m) high, with long flexible stems that arch slightly under the weight of the flowerheads. Flowering peaks in spring to summer but continues for much of the year. Individual, bright orange flowers are on a thin stalk, and strangely twisted; they form large dense clusters at the branch tips. The leaves are neat, oval and shiny dark green above, paler underneath. Both foliage and flowers bear fine hairs. The fruit are small capsules. **ZONES 9–11.**

Streptocarpus Hybrid 'Bethan'

Streptocarpus Hybrid 'Gloria'

STROBILANTHES

This genus contains over 250 species of evergreen or deciduous perennials and soft-stemmed shrubs from Asia and Madagascar. The leaves are opposite, while the flowers occur in compact heads, spikes or panicles. They are tubular with 5 terminal unequal lobes.
CULTIVATION: These species are mostly frost tender and prefer full sun to part-shade and fertile, well-drained soil. Propagate from seed or cuttings.

Strobilanthes dyerianus

This evergreen soft-stemmed shrub grows to 4 ft (1.2 m) high with lance-shaped, toothed leaves up to 6 in (15 cm) long, purple underneath and green-purple above. The flowers are funnel-shaped and pale blue to 1¼ in (30 mm) long. It comes from Burma. **ZONES 10–12.**

STROMANTHE

This genus of some 13 species of evergreen, rhizomatous perennials in the arrowroot family is found from Central America to southern Brazil. They often develop short trunks or sturdy, trunk-like stems. The leaves, enclosed in a petiole sheath before expanding, are oblong, heavily veined and 4–18 in (10–45 cm) long depending on the species. They are usually dark green above with purplish

Streptocarpus Hybrid 'Susan'

undersides. Inflorescences of small white, pink or mauve flowers appear in summer. Leafy bracts enclose the flowers and are occasionally brightly colored. Small, ridged fruits follow the flowers.
CULTIVATION: Plant in moist, humus-rich, well-drained soil in light to moderate shade. Principally tropical plants, they will not tolerate frosts and prefer a mild, humid climate. Propagate from seed or by division where possible, or by removing rooted basal offsets.

Stromanthe sanguinea

This is an erect species from Brazil to 5 ft (1.5 m). The oblong 18 in (45 cm) leaves are dark green above, purple underneath. The stem-leaf sheaths are papery and broad and pink or red. White flowers occur in panicles and have red bracts and orange-red calyces. **ZONES 10–12.**

STROMBOCACTUS

The sole species in this genus is a cactus from eastern Mexico. The summer flowers are followed by dry fruit containing minuscule seeds. It does very well in desert gardens.
CULTIVATION: Plant in light, gritty, very free-draining soil and keep dry in winter. It tolerates light frosts but tends to rot in cold, wet conditions. Propagate from seed or offsets, though these rarely form.

Strombocactus disciformis

This cactus has a curious appearance, resembling a knobbly pine cone 1–4 in (2.5–10 cm) high by 1½–6 in (3.5–15 cm) wide with small spines.

Stromanthe sanguinea

The globose or slightly flattened stem is gray-green to pale brown and the weak spines are about ½ in (12 mm) long. Clusters of 3 or so stocky, white or pale yellow flowers develop at the apex of the stem. The widely funnel-shaped flowers are about 1½ in (35 mm) long and wide. **ZONES 9–11.**

STRONGYLODON

This genus from tropical areas in Southeast Asia and the Pacific Islands consists of 20 species of vigorous evergreen shrubs or woody stemmed vines that bear long racemes of pea-flowers. The flowers can be blue-green, blue, red or orange. The tripalmate leaves have lance-shaped or rounded leaflets.
CULTIVATION: These frost-tender plants prefer full sun or part-shade and fertile, humus-rich soil. Propagate from seed, by rooting stem sections or by air layering.

Strongylodon macrobotrys

JADE VINE, EMERALD CREEPER

A large, twining climber up to 70 ft (21 m) tall, this species is valued for its spectacular, 18 in (45 cm) long, pendulous sprays of blue-green flowers borne in summer. It is native to the Philippines. Grow over a pergola or large arch where the long racemes of flowers can hang down. **ZONES 11–12.**

Streptosolen jamesonii

Streptocarpus Hybrid 'Falling Stars'

Stylophorum diphyllum

Styrax japonicus

Strophanthus gratus

Stylidium graminifolium

Styrax obassia

Styrax obassia

Sutera cordata

STROPHANTHUS

This tropical genus from South Africa and Asia consists of 38 species of shrubs that are often climbing and have opposite or whorled leaves with prominent veins. The showy flowers are white, yellow, orange, red or purple, mostly bi-colored, and with the lobes often twisted into a long tail.
CULTIVATION: These frost-tender plants prefer a protected, part-shaded position and fertile, humus-rich, moist but well-drained soil. Propagate from seed or cuttings.

Strophanthus gratus
CLIMBING OLEANDER

This climber from West Africa grows to 25 ft (8 m). The olive-green leaves have prominent veins and a red leaf stalk. The white flowers have a rosy purple tint, becoming yellow with age; they are 2 in (5 cm) long enlarging into $1\frac{1}{2}$ in (35 mm) lobes, but without tails. **ZONES 10–12.**

STYLIDIUM
TRIGGER PLANT

About 140 species of annuals, perennials and subshrubs make up this genus, most native to Australia, but some ranging as far as Southeast Asia. The leaves may be grass-like and basal, or short and narrow on wiry stems. Some species are clump forming, others shrubby, and at least one is a low-growing climber. All share a similar flowering habit with small, lobelia-like, white, pink or yellow flowers. Each flower has an irritable style that snaps over to deposit and receive pollen from visiting insects, hence the common name trigger plant.
CULTIVATION: These are tropical plants and few will tolerate anything other than very light frosts. Plant in well-drained, humus-rich soil with a sunny aspect or cultivate in a greenhouse. Propagate from seed or cuttings or by division.

Stylidium graminifolium
GRASS TRIGGER PLANT

This is a variable species from eastern Australia growing in habitats ranging from coastal to alpine. It forms a clump of grassy leaves, from which arise several stems 12–36 in (30–90 cm) tall; each stem bears a long, gradually opening spike of flowers ranging in color from palest pink to magenta, the latter color most often associated with the alpine forms. **ZONES 9–11.**

STYLOPHORUM
WOOD POPPY

This genus consists of 3 poppy-like perennials from eastern Asia and eastern North America. They form low rosettes of deeply lobed foliage: the basal leaves, which have long petioles, are about 18 in (45 cm) long, while the leaves higher in the rosette have shorter petioles and are correspondingly smaller. Simple 4-petalled, bright yellow flowers up to 2 in (5 cm) in diameter are carried in clusters at the top of leafy stems barely higher than the foliage rosette. They appear in spring and summer.
CULTIVATION: Woodland conditions with cool, moist, humus-rich soil in dappled shade are ideal. However, with occasional watering they can be grown in perennial borders with a sunny exposure. Propagate from seed or by dividing established clumps in late winter.

Stylophorum diphyllum
CELANDINE POPPY

This hairy plant grows to 12 in (30 cm) in height and has deeply toothed leaves. The simple flower stalks give rise to a cluster of bracts holding yellow flowerheads up to 2 in (5 cm) across. It comes from eastern USA. **ZONES 7–10.**

STYRAX
SNOWBELL

This genus consists of about 100 species of deciduous and evergreen shrubs and small trees occurring naturally over a wide area of the Americas and eastern Asia, with one species native to Europe. Several cool-temperate, deciduous species are cultivated for their neat growth habit and attractive spring display of slightly drooping sprays of small, bell-shaped, white flowers, which appear on the previous year's wood.
CULTIVATION: They prefer cool, moist, well-drained soil and cool, moist, summer climates. Usually raised from stratified seed in fall (autumn), they can also be grown from cuttings in summer.

Styrax japonicus
JAPANESE SNOWBELL, JAPANESE SNOWDROP TREE

This species is a native of Japan, Korea and China. It grows to about 25 ft (8 m) high and flowers from mid-spring. Its branches, which are clothed with rather narrow, 3 in (8 cm) long, deep green shiny leaves, tend to be held horizontally which creates a somewhat tiered effect. This species does best shaded from the hottest sun. **ZONES 6–9.**

Styrax obassia
FRAGRANT SNOWBELL

Indigenous to Japan, Korea and northern China, this species grows to 30 ft (9 m) high. Its flowers are not as pendulous as those of other species, but they are slightly fragrant. The large deep green, paddle-shaped leaves are up to 8 in (20 cm) long and are covered in whitish down on the undersides. It is worth growing for the foliage alone. **ZONES 6–9.**

Styrax officinalis
STORAX

This deciduous shrub or small tree to 20 ft (6 m) comes from southeastern Europe and southwestern Asia. The slender branches are felted at first, but become smooth in maturity. The heart-shaped leaves are up to $2\frac{1}{2}$ in (6 cm) long and wide, white felted when young. Groups of 3 to 8 white flowers hang at the ends of the branches in summer. ***Styrax officinalis* var. *californicum*** has smoother leaves. **ZONES 9–10.**

SUTERA
syn. *Bacopa*

There are 130 species in this genus, comprising annuals, perennials and small shrubs from South Africa. The leaves are opposite or clustered and simple or lobed. The flowers come from the leaf axils or are terminal or both, being white, pink, lilac or purple. These compact plants are suitable for the garden in mild climates, and some make excellent hanging basket subjects.
CULTIVATION: Frost tender, they prefer full sun and well-drained, fertile soil. Propagation is from cuttings in summer, from seed or by division.

Sutera cordata

This 24 in (60 cm) woody shrub has opposite elongated heart-shaped leaves and terminal white flowers over a long period in summer and fall (autumn). It is usually sold as *Bacopa* 'Snow Flake'. **ZONES 9–11.**

Sutera grandiflora
PURPLE GLORY PLANT

This woody based perennial grows to 3 ft (1 m) with hairy branches and opposite hairy toothed leaves. Many lavender to deep purple flowers appear over a long period in summer and fall (autumn). The palest lavender form is sold as **'Pink Domino'**. **ZONES 9–11.**

SUTHERLANDIA

This small southern African genus is made up of 5 species of small, evergreen shrubs. The pinnate leaves are soft gray-green and slightly to very hairy. The pea-flowers are borne in small clusters.
CULTIVATION: With regular water the plants grow quickly and flower in the same year. Frost tender but wind

Swainsona formosa

resistant, they prefer full sun and are not fussy about soil—a rockery suits them well. They tend to get straggly with age and should be cut back each year after flowering. Propagate from seed sown in spring or from cuttings in summer.

Sutherlandia frutescens
CANCER BUSH, BALLOON PEA, DUCK PLANT

This soft-wooded shrub from drier parts of southern Africa grows to 5 ft (1.5 m) tall and wide. The compound leaves are divided into small oval leaflets, which give the plant a graceful appearance. Showy, drooping, coral-red pea-flowers are borne from late winter to summer; these are followed by inflated pale green seed pods that often appear simultaneously with the flowers, thus creating a very decorative effect. **ZONES 9–11.**

SWAINSONA
PEA, DESERT PEA

This genus of around 50 species of perennials, annuals and subshrubs or trailing plants is endemic to Australia with one species from New Zealand. Most species are found in dry to arid areas, with some occupying moister sites in cooler regions. The leaflets are mostly gray to gray-green, with the pea-shaped flowers in extended racemes ranging in color from white to blue, mauve and dramatic scarlet.

CULTIVATION: Frost tender, they prefer full sun and moderately fertile, very well-drained soil. Propagate from seed or cuttings.

Swainsona formosa
syns *Clianthus dampieri, C. formosus*
STURT'S DESERT PEA

Native to the dry outback of Australia, this slow-growing, trailing annual has unusually large and showy, brilliant red, black-blotched spring flowers and small, gray leaves. It grows to a height of 6 in (15 cm) and spread of 3 ft (1 m). **ZONES 9–11.**

Swainsona galegifolia
DARLING PEA, SWAN FLOWER

In Australia—where this poisonous, evergreen perennial grows naturally throughout the states of New South Wales and Queensland—the Aborigines are said to make a poultice from its crushed leaves to relieve swelling and bruising. Each of its light to dark green leaves comprises 12 or so narrow, elliptical leaflets. The pea-shaped flowers bloom in spring and summer in dense terminal heads; they can be pink, purple, carmine or white and perhaps red or blue. **ZONES 8–11.**

SWIETENIA
MAHOGANY

This small genus consists of evergreen or semi-deciduous trees from the tropical forests of Central America and the West Indies, prized as the source of one of the world's most precious timbers for fine furniture. The trees grow tall and straight and the timber is dense and finely grained; it is a rich reddish brown when seasoned. The large, pinnate leaves consist of smooth, shiny leaflets, and the small, insignificant flowers are greenish yellow. The fruits that follow are large woody capsules containing winged seeds, which are used for propagation. 'Mahagoni' is their local name in the West Indies; they are widely grown for shade in frost-free areas.

CULTIVATION: They need deep, fertile soil and high rainfall. In subtropical areas with distinct seasons the leaves often turn golden in fall (autumn) and most are shed. Propagate from seed or cuttings in late summer.

Swietenia macrophylla
HONDURAS MAHOGANY

First introduced to the furniture-makers of Europe in the 1600s, this handsome tree supplies one of the world's most coveted timbers. In its native forests it grows straight trunked to over 150 ft (45 m) high, but in cultivation as a shade or street tree it is usually smaller. The compound leaves are 15 in (38 cm) long, and the brown woody fruit are about 6 in (15 cm) long. **ZONES 10–12.**

Swietenia mahagoni
WEST INDIES MAHOGANY

While still majestic, this tree is overall smaller than *Swietenia macrophylla;* it grows to 70 ft (21 m), the pinnate leaves are 4–8 in (10–20 cm) long and the fruit are 4 in (10 cm) in diameter. It is widely grown as a shade and street tree in the tropics. **ZONES 11–12.**

SYAGRUS
syn. *Arecastrum*

The 32 or so palms in this genus are indigenous to drier parts of tropical and subtropical South America. They have single, smooth, horizontally ridged trunks crowned with a mass of feathery, pinnate leaves arising from a fibrous sheath. The leaf stalks are mostly smooth but are sometimes edged with teeth. Separate male and female flowers are borne in a large panicle that bursts from a huge, spindle-shaped enclosing bract, emerging from among the leaves. The fruit are fleshy fibrous drupes. Several species are a commercial source of palm oil.

CULTIVATION: Grow these frost-tender plants in fertile, moist, well-drained soil in full sun or part-shade. Water only as necessary in winter. Propagate from seed in spring.

Syagrus comosa
GUARIROBA DO CAMPO, PALMITO AMARGOSO, BABAO, CATOLE, JERIVA, POTI

This palm has a single or cluster of thin trunks 4 in (10 cm) in diameter, growing to 20 ft (6 m) tall. The leaves may be up to 4 ft (1.2 m) long with up to 80 leaflets per side, clustered in pairs or fours. The branched flowerhead can be 10 in (25 cm) long. **ZONES 10–12.**

Syagrus romanzoffiana
syns *Arecastrum romanzoffiana, Cocos plumosa*
COCOS PALM, QUEEN PALM

Fast growing, this species has a slender, upright, smooth gray trunk to 70 ft (21 m) tall, with a crown of arching, plume-like leaves. Each leaf is green, up to 15 ft (4.5 m) long, with long leaflets radiating from the central stalk on several planes. The flowers are small and inconspicuous. The fruit, which are fat, orange-red, fleshy berries up to 1 in (25 mm) long, are edible and may attract bats and insects. **ZONES 10–12.**

SYMPHORICARPOS
SNOWBERRY

This genus is made up of about 17 species of deciduous shrubs allied to *Lonicera* and from North America, with one rare and obscure species from China. They have elliptical to nearly round leaves and very small, bell-shaped, pink or white flowers in spring. They are mostly grown for their large crops of distinctive berries, which stand out clearly in winter when the branches are bare.

CULTIVATION: They are easily grown in any moist, well-drained soil in sun or shade and are usually propagated from open-ground winter hardwood cuttings. Being resistant to shade, poor soil and pollution, they are very suitable for city gardens.

Symphoricarpos albus
COMMON SNOWBERRY

Found east of the Rocky Mountains from Colorado to Quebec, this wiry stemmed, suckering shrub grows to 6 ft (1.8 m) high and wide. Its small spring flowers are followed by clusters of ½ in (12 mm) white berries that persist well after the leaves have fallen. The striking white berries are the distinguishing feature of this shrub. ***Symphoricarpos albus* var. *laevigatus*** bears pink or white flowers and large white fruit. **ZONES 3–9.**

Swietenia macrophylla

Syagrus comosa

Sutherlandia frutescens

Swietenia mahagoni

Symphoricarpos × *chenaultii*
CHENAULT CORALBERRY

This hybrid is an arching, many-branched shrub with pinkish flowers in spring followed by white fruit tinged pink. It reaches a height and spread of 3–6 ft (1–1.8 m). **'Hancock'** is a dwarf selection only 12 in (30 cm) tall; it is good for ground covering in a shaded area. **ZONES 5–9.**

Symphoricarpos × *doorenbosii*

This strong-growing, multi-stemmed shrub grows to around 6 ft (1.8 m) tall with an indefinite spread. The leaves are rounded to oval in shape, about 2 in (5 cm) long and dark green with a paler underside. In summer spikes of small, white or pinkish white flowers appear; they are bell-shaped and are followed in fall (autumn) by clusters of pink-tinged, white berries each about $\frac{1}{2}$ in (12 mm) across. **'Magic Berry'** has masses of reddish purple fruit; **'White Hedge'** is a smaller and more compact-growing form with upright stems and generous crops of white berries. **ZONES 4–9.**

Symphoricarpos microphyllus

This upright 6 ft (1.8 m) tall shrub has felted shoots. The oval leaves are $1\frac{1}{4}$ in (30 mm) long. The white flowers appear in summer and are followed by small pink-tinged white fruit. It comes from Mexico. **ZONES 9–10.**

Symphoricarpos orbiculatus
INDIAN CURRANT, CORAL BERRY

This tough, adaptable shrub from the USA and Mexico grows to about 6 ft (1.8 m) high and wide. It is very dense and twiggy, with oval leaves around $1\frac{1}{2}$ in (35 mm) long. The fruit are small, under $\frac{1}{4}$ in (6 mm) in diameter, but abundant and a conspicuous bright pink. The berries last long after the leaves have fallen. A hot summer will yield a heavier crop of berries. **ZONES 3–9.**

Symphytum officinale

Symphoricarpos orbiculatus

SYMPHYANDRA

This genus from Asia and Korea to the eastern Mediterranean and the Caucasus consists of around 12 species of short-lived perennials usually grown as biennials. They have long-stalked, hairy leaves and tubular- to bell-shaped flowers and are suitable for large rock gardens or the bases of banks.

CULTIVATION: Fully frost hardy, symphyandras prefer full sun or dappled shade and fertile, well-drained soil. They may die down after flowering. Propagate from seed.

Symphyandra hofmannii

This charming, free-flowering plant from Bosnia and Herzegovina grows to 24 in (60 cm) tall and about half as wide. It produces a rosette of rounded to spearhead-shaped, toothed leaves, each about 6 in (15 cm) long. From the ends of the tall leafy stems pendulous creamy yellow flowers appear in summer. **ZONES 4–9.**

Symphyandra wanneri
syn. *Campanula wanneri*

From the mountains of the Balkans, this is a hairy perennial that feels rough to the touch. The toothed, lanceolate leaves are produced in basal rosettes, each leaf being 4–5 in (10–12 cm) long. In summer tall flower spikes rise bearing many-flowered panicles of pendulous, blue-violet flowers. The total height of the plant is about 12 in (30 cm) with a similar spread. **ZONES 7–9.**

Symphytum 'Goldsmith'

Symphytum × *uplandicum* 'Variegatum'

Symphytum caucasicum

SYMPHYTUM
COMFREY

This genus comprises 25 to 35 species of hairy perennials from damp and shaded places in Europe, North Africa and western Asia. They grow rapidly and may become invasive in the garden. The leaves are alternate and rather crowded at the base of the plant. The flowers are held in shortly branched heads of pink, blue, white or cream. Each flower consists of a tube terminating in 5 triangular lobes.

CULTIVATION: They are easily grown in sun or part-shade in moist, well-dug soil with added manure. Propagate from seed or cuttings, or by division.

Symphytum asperum
PRICKLY COMFREY

This thick-rooted perennial from Europe, Turkey and Iran has oval, heart-shaped or oblong leaves covered with stiff prickly hairs. The flower stems grow up to 5 ft (1.5 m) tall and are openly branched with few hairs. There are many flowers in the head; they open a rose color, soon changing to lilac or blue, and are $\frac{1}{2}$ in (12 mm) long. It has become naturalized in North America where it has been grown as a fodder plant. **ZONES 5–10.**

Symphytum caucasicum

This is a smaller, softly hairy branched perennial growing to 24 in (60 cm). The leaves are hairy on both sides and oval to oblong up to 8 in (20 cm) long; they run back a short way down the stem. The flowers are at first red-purple, changing to blue, and $\frac{3}{4}$ in (18 mm) long in terminal paired heads. It occurs naturally in the Caucasus and Iran. **ZONES 5–10.**

Symphoricarpos × *chenaultii*

Symphytum asperum

Symphytum 'Goldsmith'
syn. *Symphytum* 'Jubilee'

'Goldsmith' grows to 12 in (30 cm) and has leaves edged and blotched with cream and gold; the flowers are blue, pink or white. **ZONES 5–10.**

Symphytum 'Hidcote Blue'

This hybrid cultivar only grows to 18 in (45 cm) tall but is a vigorous and spreading plant. The flowers are soft blue and white. **ZONES 5–10.**

Symphytum ibericum
syn. *Symphytum grandiflorum* of gardens

Creeping rhizomes produce lax hairy stems up to 15 in (38 cm) long on this species from eastern Europe and Turkey; they hold stalked hairy oval or elliptical leaves. There are many pale yellow flowers in each head. **ZONES 5–10.**

Symphytum officinale
COMMON COMFREY, HEALING HERB, BONESET

This robust, clump-forming species from Europe and western Asia grows to 5 ft (1.5 m) with large, lance-shaped leaves and clusters of pretty white, pink or mauve pendent flowers in late spring and summer. It is used as a companion plant because it keeps the surrounding soil rich and moist. However, it often becomes invasive and smothers smaller plants. Wilted leaves are used as a mulch and help activate decomposition in compost heaps; they are rich in nitrogen and other minerals. In the Middle Ages, comfrey was used as an aid in setting broken bones; it is moderately poisonous if too much is eaten. **ZONES 5–10.**

Symphytum tuberosum
TUBEROUS COMFREY

Dense strong creeping rhizomes give rise to 24 in (60 cm) long hairy stems with long-stalked oblong leaves on this species from Europe and Turkey. There are 8 to 16 pale yellow flowers in each head. **ZONES 5–10.**

Symphytum × *uplandicum*
RUSSIAN COMFREY

This coarse hairy perennial hybrid between *Symphytum asperum* and

S. officinale grows to 6 ft (1.8 m) tall. The leaves are oblong, hairy on both surfaces and run a short distance down the stem. The flowers are $^{3}/_{4}$ in (18 mm) long, rosy at first then becoming purple or blue. **'Variegatum'** has an attractive cream leaf variegation, but flower color is poor and the flowers are often removed. **ZONES 5–10.**

SYMPLOCARPUS

SKUNK CABBAGE, POLECAT WEED, FOETID POTHOS

There is only one species in this genus, a deciduous perennial of wet woodlands in northeastern Asia and northeastern America. Large oval leaves grow from a tap-rooted rhizome in clumps after flowering; each is 18 in (45 cm) long, dark green, smooth and soft but gives off a disagreeable smell when damaged.
CULTIVATION: It may be grown in sun or shade in rich, moist or wet soil. Propagate from seed.

Symplocarpus foetidus

The 6 in (15 cm) flowers on this perennial are produced at ground level before the leaves appear. They are purple-brown, blotched with greenish yellow, egg-shaped and with a pointed inward-curving tip. They appear in late winter and spring. The flower spadix can raise its temperature up to 55°F (30°C) above the surrounding conditions, and so prevent frost damage. **ZONES 4–9.**

SYNADENIUM

This is a genus of about 20 species of evergreen shrubs or small trees from tropical and subtropical Africa to the Mascarene Islands. Closely related to *Euphorbia,* they differ only in flower details. They produce heads of greenish yellow flowers and bracts that are quite attractive, but their real appeal lies in the foliage, which is glossy, often leathery and frequently in brilliant shades of red and deep green. The leaves are 4–8 in (10–20 cm) long and roughly oval. All parts of the plant contain a caustic and very poisonous milky latex.
CULTIVATION: Most species tolerate only the lightest frosts and prefer a warm, dry climate. Plant in light, well-drained soil in full sun. Propagate from seed or cuttings.

Synadenium compactum

syn. *Synadenium grantii* of gardens

This shrub or small tree from East Africa may grow to 20 ft (6 m) or more. The oval leaves, a dark glossy green, sometimes splashed purple, grow to 8 in (20 cm) long and have a pronounced central rib that may be keeled underneath. The flowers are greenish yellow, sometimes tinged red. **ZONES 9–12.**

SYNCARPIA

TURPENTINE

This genus consists of 2 species of tall, evergreen trees indigenous to coastal forests of eastern Australia. Not dissimilar to the (related) eucalypts, they grow tall and straight with a domed crown atop a trunk of thick, fibrous bark. The trees are

Syringa laciniata

exploited in Australia for their timber—the dense, straight hardwood has a high silica content that makes it exceptionally resistant to marine borers. ***Syncarpia hillii***, endemic to Queensland's Fraser Island, was used last century for sidings in the construction of the Suez Canal and for wharves worldwide.
CULTIVATION: Turpentines need a frost-free climate, full sun or part-shade, moist, well-drained soil and reliable rainfall. Propagate from seed in fall (autumn).

Syncarpia glomulifera

RED TURPENTINE

Valued as a shade tree as well as for its durable reddish timber, this species is cultivated in subtropical USA and Africa as well as Australia. In the wild it grows to 200 ft (60 m) tall, its straight trunk clothed in red-brown, deeply fissured bark; the leaves, mid-green with paler, hairy undersides, are aromatic when crushed. Small cream flowers with long stamens are fused into fluffy globular flowerheads borne through spring and summer, and the woody fruit are also fused into a spiky ball. **ZONES 9–12.**

SYNGONIUM

There are about 33 species of these robust evergreen epiphytic or terrestrial climbing vines from tropical America. The long-stemmed and lobed leaves carry a milky sap. They are usually produced as potted climbing plants or in hanging baskets, when the juvenile simple or basal-lobed leaves are all that is seen. The flowers are seldom seen in cultivation; they may be red, orange, green or white.
CULTIVATION: They need rich soil, protection from direct sun. Allow the medium to dry out between waterings. Tip pruning encourages compact growth. Propagate from cuttings.

Syngonium podophyllum

syn. ***Nephthytis triphylla*** **of gardens**

ARROWHEAD VINE, GOOSEFOOT

This plant closely resembles its relative the climbing *Philodendron,* with its handsome climbing or trailing foliage. It has an unusual feature of changing leaf shape with maturity. The young, arrow-head-shaped leaves on the ends of erect

Syncarpia glomulifera

Syncarpia glomulifera

stalks become, with age, lobed with 7 to 9 glossy leaflets growing to 12 in (30 cm) long. There are several varieties with variegated leaves in cream or pink. **ZONES 10–12.**

SYRINGA

LILAC

Lilacs are prized for their upright to arching panicles of small, highly fragrant flowers, which are massed in loose heads. They appear from mid-spring and range in color from white and pale yellow to all shades of pink, mauve and purple. Most of the common garden varieties of *Syringa vulgaris* were raised in France in the late 1800s to early 1900s, though new forms appear from time to time; not all cultivars are fragrant. The genus contains about 20 species, all deciduous shrubs and trees from Europe and northeastern Asia. Most reach about 8 ft (2.4 m) high and 6 ft (1.8 m) wide, with opposite leaves. The foliage sometimes colors well in fall (autumn).
CULTIVATION: Lilacs prefer moist, humus-rich, well-drained soil in sun or light shade. They do best where winters are cold because they require at least a few frosts in order to flower well. Any pruning is best done immediately after flowering. Species may be raised from seed or cuttings. Named cultivars are usually grafted but can sometimes be struck from hardwood or semi-ripe cuttings. Established plants produce suckers that can be used for propagation.

Syringa × hyacinthiflora

These cultivars result from the crossing of *Syringa oblata* and *S. vulgaris*. They were originally raised in France; later W. B. Clarke in California produced many of the crosses grown today. They

Syngonium podophyllum cultivar

Syringa josikaea

tend to flower earlier than the *S. vulgaris* varieties, and although similar in appearance are not quite as fragrant. The young leaves are bronzed as in *S. oblata*, and turn purple in fall (autumn). **'Alice Eastwood'** has double claret-pink buds opening to mauve-pink. **'Asessippi'** is early flowering with many single fragrant pale lavender flowers. **'Blue Hyacinth'** has rounded single lavender blue heads. **'Clarke's Giant'** has long panicles of single, large-flowered purple buds opening to lavender-blue. **'Esther Stanley'** is single with red-mauve buds blooming pink. **'Missimo'** has very large single rich purple flowers in a big open flowerhead. **'Pocahontas'** is upright, vigorous and profusely flowering in red-purple shades. **ZONES 4–9.**

Syringa × josiflexa

This is a hybrid between *Syringa josikaea* and ***S. komarowii*** **subsp. *reflexa*.** There is a range of colors of pendulous flowerheads. **'Bellicent'** has large flowerheads of strong pink. **ZONES 5–9.**

Syringa josikaea

HUNGARIAN LILAC

This is an erect shrub to 12 ft (3.5 m) with rigid warty branches. The leaves are glossy on top and gray underneath with felted veins. The richly colored flowers are held upright in loose heads in summer. **ZONES 5–9.**

Syringa laciniata

CUT-LEAF LILAC

This species, a graceful form with prettily dissected 3- to 9-lobed leaves, produces small heads of lilac flowers 4 in (10 cm) long in mid-spring and is a spreading shrub that grows to 6 ft (1.8 m) with a spread of 10 ft (3 m). **ZONES 5–9.**

S

S. pubescens subsp. *patula* 'Miss Kim'

Syringa vulgaris

Syringa × *persica* 'Alba'

Syringa yunnanensis

Syringa meyeri 'Superba'

S. vulgaris 'Andenken an Ludwig Späth'

Syringa vulgaris 'Mme F. Morel'

Syringa vulgaris 'Vestale'

Syringa meyeri 'Palibin'

Syringa vulgaris 'Charles Joly'

Syringa vulgaris 'Katherine Havemeyer'

Syringa vulgaris 'Mme Lemoine'

Syringa oblata

Syringa villosa

Syringa reticulata

Syringa meyeri

From China, this small spreading shrub grows to about 6 ft (1.8 m) tall and wide. The leaves are elliptical and the deep purplish mauve flowers appear in spring in dense heads. **'Palibin'** is a slow-growing dwarf cultivar with violet to rose-pink flowers in small dense clusters. **'Superba'** has dark pink flowers that fade as they mature; it is a long-flowering form with some flowers produced from mid-spring to mid-summer. All forms of *Syringa meyeri* may have a lesser flowering in fall (autumn). **ZONES 4–9.**

Syringa oblata

From China comes this 12 ft (3.5 m) tall shrub with kidney- or heart-shaped leaves up to 4 in (10 cm) long. The lilac flowers are held on dense heads up to 6 in (15 cm) long. This is the earliest flowering lilac and the only species with leaves that color well in fall (autumn). ***Syringa oblata* var. *alba*** has white flowers and smaller leaves. **ZONES 5–9.**

Syringa patula

KOREAN LILAC, MANCHURIAN LILAC

This neat shrub grows to 10 ft (3 m) tall. It has a rounded spreading crown and its branches are tinged purple. The leaves are velvety green and slightly hairy with paler undersides. The flowers, mauve outside and white inside, appear in small terminal heads in late spring. **ZONES 4–9.**

Syringa × *persica*

PERSIAN LILAC

This is thought to be a hybrid of *Syringa laciniata* and ***S. afghanica*** or else a stable juvenile form of *S. laciniata*. Probably native to Afghanistan, it is a deciduous, bushy, compact shrub. In spring it bears profuse heads of small, delightfully fragrant flowers set amid narrow, pointed, dark green leaves. It grows to a height and spread of just under 6 ft (1.8 m) and will grow in warmer winter climates than most lilacs. **'Alba'** has dainty, sweetly scented white flowers. **ZONES 5–9.**

Syringa pubescens subsp. *patula* 'Miss Kim'

syn. *Syringa patula* 'Miss Kim'

MISS KIM LILAC

Syringa pubescens subsp. *patula* 'Miss Kim' is a compact selection of an excellent lilac notable for its late-season flowering. It has relatively large leaves and fragrant flowers that are pale lilac pink. This plant will reach a height of 6–8 ft (1.8–2.4 m) with a similar spread, but is slow growing and will remain only 3–4 ft (1–1.2 m) tall for many years. **ZONES 4–9.**

S

Syringa reflexa

A native of the Hubei province in central China, this species grows to 12 ft (3.5 m) high, and its 8 in (20 cm) pendulous heads of deep pink flowers are borne in abundance from late spring. The pointed, elliptical leaves are up to 8 in (20 cm) long. This beautiful species is just different enough from the common garden lilacs to attract attention. It is the parent of a number of hybrids raised in Canada collectively known as ***Syringa* × *prestoniae***. ZONES 3–9.

Syringa reticulata
JAPANESE TREE LILAC

This Japanese lilac has comparatively small flowers, but they produce a wonderful spring display of creamy white flowerheads at the ends of the branches. Sweetly fragrant, they stand out against the dark green foliage and make excellent cut flowers. Although the Japanese tree lilac can grow to 30 ft (9 m), forming a squat, wide-crowned tree it is usually seen as a large shrub. **ZONES 3–9.**

Syringa villosa
LATE LILAC

This compact shrub from northern China bears large terminal heads of pinkish flowers and has large, deep green, oval leaves. It grows to 12 ft (3.5 m) tall with a similar spread. **ZONES 4–9.**

Syringa vulgaris
COMMON LILAC

This is the species from which most garden cultivars derive. It is native to southeastern Europe and grows to about 20 ft (6 m) high with pointed, oval or heart-shaped leaves up to 4 in (10 cm) long. The flowers are borne in dense pyramidal heads and are strongly fragrant, white or pale mauve. **'Andenken an Ludwig Späth'** (syn. 'Souvenir de Louis Spaeth') has single deep purple large heads in mid-season; **'Aurea'** has yellowish green leaves and darker lilac flowers; **'Charles Joly'** is a double deep reddish purple lilac with very fragrant flowers and strongly upright growth; **'Congo'** has single rich dark purple flowers; **'Edith Cavell'** is white; **'Firmament'** is light blue; **'Katherine Havemeyer'** has fully double large-flowered heads of lavender-purple buds opening to a soft mauve-pink; **'Lavender Lady'** is mid-mauve; **'Marechal Foch'** is purplish pink; **'Miss Ellen Willmott'** has double white flowers with buds tinged green; **'Mme Antoine Buchner'** is pale mauve-pink; **'Mme F. Morel'** is purplish pink; **'Mme Lemoine'** is a double white with medium-sized tight flowerheads on a free-flowering and compact shrub; **'Mrs Edward Harding'** has double reddish purple flowers in large heads; **'President Lincoln'** is light blue; **'Président Poincaré'**, introduced by Lemoine in 1913, has double flowers of a rich claret-mauve in large heads; **'Primrose'** has early soft single lemon flowers on a compact shrub; **'Souvenir d'Alice Harding'** has small heads of white flowers in summer; **'Vestale'** is pure white; **'Volcan'** bears single ruby purple flowers; and **'William Robinson'** bears single royal purple flowers. **ZONES 5–9.**

Syringa yunnanensis

This erect 10 ft (3 m) tall shrub has reddish green felted new growth that holds elliptical 3 in (8 cm) leaves. The shell-pink flowers occur in terminal panicles up to 6 in (15 cm) long in early summer. It comes from the Yunnan Province in China. **ZONES 6–9.**

SYZYGIUM
LILLYPILLY, BRUSH CHERRY

These 400 to 500 species of evergreen trees and shrubs, at one time included in the genus *Eugenia*, are found in tropical and subtropical rainforests of Southeast Asia, Australia and Africa. They are grown for their attractive foliage, flowers and berries. The edible berries—white, pink, magenta or purple—ripen in late summer to fall (autumn). The plants have a dense canopy of shiny green leaves; new growth in spring is often a contrasting red, pink or copper. The spring and summer flowers are mostly small with protruding white to mauve or crimson stamens giving a fluffy appearance.

CULTIVATION: The plants prefer full sun to part-shade and deep, moist, well-drained, humus-rich soil; they do best in warm climates with only occasional light frosts. Prune to shape if necessary. Propagate from fresh seed in spring or cuttings in summer.

Syzygium aromaticum
CLOVE, ZANZIBAR RED HEAD

The cloves used in cooking are the dried flower buds of this tree, which originated in the Moluccas and is now widely cultivated. It grows into a small tree to 50 ft (15 m) of conical shape. The leaves are elliptical, dark green above, paler beneath, dotted with glands and up to 4 in (10 cm) long. The fragrant flowers are in groups of 3, pinkish yellow, becoming darker pink with age. The fruit are elliptical purple berries. **ZONES 11–12.**

Syzygium jambos
syn. *Eugenia jambos*
ROSE APPLE

Indigenous to Southeast Asia, this tree reaches a height of 30–40 ft (9–12 m) with a rounded crown. The leaves are dark green and glossy and the fluffy, greenish white flowers are borne in large rounded clusters. The edible, creamy pink to yellow, fragrant fruit have a decided taste of rose water. **ZONES 10–12.**

Syzygium wilsonii

Syzygium luehmannii
syn. *Eugenia luehmannii*
SMALL-LEAFED LILLYPILLY, RIBERRY

This is a large tree with a buttressed trunk in the wild in eastern Australian rainforests, but when cultivated it usually reaches only 20 ft (6 m) or so with spreading branches low to the ground and a domed crown. An attractive shade and specimen tree for warm to hot climates, it can also be grown as a formal hedge. The leaves are very shiny and oval to lance-shaped with a prominent midrib. New growth is pink to red. The creamy white summer flowers in small clusters are followed by coral-red, pear-shaped fruit. **ZONES 10–12.**

Syzygium malaccense
MALAY APPLE

This 80 ft (24 m) tree from the Malay Peninsula has a buttressed trunk and fibrous brown-red flaky bark. The leaves are elliptical and up to 6 in (15 cm) long. The flowers are cream or reddish purple and held in clusters. The rounded fruit are up to 1 in (25 mm) wide and red or pink, but becoming dark purple when ripe. **ZONES 10–12.**

Syzygium paniculatum
syn. *Eugenia paniculata*
MAGENTA BRUSH CHERRY, AUSTRALIAN BRUSH CHERRY

This small to medium tree from Australia can grow up to 50–60 ft (15–18 m) tall with an irregular rounded and densely foliaged crown. The leaves are shiny green, variable in shape from oval to rounded, coppery brown when young and held on reddish stalks. The fragrant creamy white flowers are ½ in (12 mm) wide and held in dense clusters mainly in late spring. The large, decorative fruit are rose purple, oval to rounded and up to 1 in (25 mm) long. This species is used as a hedge in southeastern and southwestern USA. **ZONES 9–12.**

Syzygium wilsonii
POWDERPUFF LILLYPILLY

This spreading shrub from Australia grows to about 6 ft (1.8 m) tall and wide; in moist, shady spots it scrambles to a greater height and width. The leaves vary from lance-shaped to more rounded; each is 4–6 in (10–15 cm) long, often on a twisted stalk, smooth and dark green. The new foliage is orange-red to red. The flowers have insignificant white petals and showy magenta stamens; they appear in spring and summer and are arranged in dense clusters on the tips of arching stems. The fruit are whitish, round to oval berries. **ZONES 10–12.**

Syzygium malaccense

Syzygium paniculatum

Syzygium jambos

Syzygium luehmannii

S

T

TABEBUIA

TRUMPET TREE

The 100 or so shrubs and trees of this genus occur naturally in tropical America and the West Indies, where some are valued for their highly durable timber. They feature spectacular flowers and attractive foliage, and make excellent shade trees. Many are briefly deciduous during the tropical dry season, but some are almost evergreen. The flowers are trumpet- to bell-shaped and shades of white, yellow, pink, red or purple. They are clustered at the branch tips, usually when the leaves have fallen in late winter to spring. Fruits are bean-like capsules. Leaves vary in shape, and may be simple or palmately compound, with 3 to 7 leaflets, their edges are often toothed.
CULTIVATION: Trumpet trees need a hot to warm frost-free climate and deep, humus-rich soil with good drainage. A sunny position is best, with some shelter from wind to protect the flowers. Propagate from seed or by layering in spring or from cuttings in summer; selected types are grafted.

Tabebuia chrysantha

Tabebuia impetiginosa

Tabebuia chrysotricha

Tabebuia chrysantha

This small deciduous tree from Venezuela grows to a height of 20 ft (6 m) and forms an open crown of slender branches. Its leaves are composed of 5 hairy, finger-like leaflets. It bears a profusion of rich mustard-yellow, trumpet-shaped flowers about 3 in (8 cm) long. These are grouped in large heads at the ends of leafless branches from late winter to spring. The fruit are slightly hairy. **ZONES 11–12.**

Tabebuia chrysotricha

GOLDEN TRUMPET TREE

Native to Central America, this deciduous tree reaches 30–50 ft (9–15 m) in height with a spread of 25 ft (8 m). It develops an open canopy and brownish hairs cover the branches, flower stalks, leaf stalks, lower leaf surfaces and fruit. The dark green leaves, mostly with 3 to 5 oval to oblong leaflets, are held on long stalks. Clusters of flowers almost smother the crown in late winter or early spring; each is trumpet-shaped, about 2 in (5 cm) across, with bright yellow ruffled petals. Brownish lines and golden-brown hairs highlight the throat. The fruit is golden brown. **ZONES 9–11.**

Tabebuia heterophylla

IPE ROXO

This Brazilian species is one of the most magnificent, producing a mass of flowers on leafless branches. The blossoms hang in large, loose clusters and come in various shades of pink, from the palest eggshell to the deepest rose. Valued for its timber, this species is thought by some to be an effective treatment for syphilis. **ZONES 11–12.**

Tabebuia impetiginosa 'Pink Cloud'

Tabebuia pallida

Tagetes 'Disco Orange'

Tabebuia impetiginosa

syns *Tabebuia ipe, T. avellanedae, T. heptaphylla*

PINK TRUMPET TREE, ARGENTINE FLAME TREE, PAU D'ARCO

More upright than *Tabebuia chrysotricha*, this handsome deciduous tree reaches 50 ft (15 m) or more in height. Its rounded crown is formed by a network of branching stems sparsely clad with slender palmate leaves with oval leaflets; the leaves are shed briefly in spring. Spectacular clusters of rose-pink or purple-pink trumpet-shaped flowers are borne on the bare branches in spring. **'Pink Cloud'** is one of a number of attractive cultivars. **ZONES 9–11.**

Tabebuia pallida

CUBAN PINK TRUMPET TREE

This small evergreen or briefly deciduous tree occurs naturally in the West Indies, Mexico and Central America. It reaches 25 ft (8 m) or so in height. This species has a straight trunk and an open, rounded crown, although it may be quite variable in its habit. The leaves consist of 1, 3 or 5 leaflets, each with a prominent yellow midrib. The flowers, borne in terminal clusters, are lilac pink paling to white at the edges; they are usually produced from mid- to late summer, with occasional flowers at other times. *Tabebuia pallida* suits warm coastal areas. **ZONES 11–12.**

TABERNAEMONTANA

Widespread throughout tropical and subtropical regions, this genus consists of around 100 species of evergreen shrubs and small trees. Some resemble gardenias in both leaf and flower but differ in having milky sap. The leaves are deep green and roughly oval; the funnel-shaped flowers are usually white. They are often used as informal hedging in warmer climates.
CULTIVATION: Species of *Tabernaemontana* are nearly all frost tender. They grow best in humus-rich, moist, well-drained soil, in a sheltered position in sun or dappled shade. Water well all year round. Propagate the species from seed and the cultivars from cuttings.

Tabernaemontana divaricata

syns *Ervatamia divaricata, E. coronaria*

CREPE JASMINE, CREPE GARDENIA

Occurring naturally from northern India to China's Yunnan province and north-

Tagetes lemmonii

Tacca integrifolia

ern Thailand, this twiggy, heavily foliaged shrub grows to about 6 ft (1.8 m) high. It has leathery leaves up to 4 in (10 cm) long. White tubular flowers in terminal clusters open throughout the warmer months; their scent is strongest in the evening. **'Flore Pleno'** is a double-flowered cultivar and is much more widely grown than the species. These beautiful shrubs are excellent container plants and can be lightly trimmed to shape. **ZONES 11–12.**

TACCA

This genus of 10 species of rhizomatous perennials is widespread throughout tropical Southeast Asia and Africa. They have basal leaves close to the ground, from which rise a scape with greenish yellow flowers surrounded by bracts. The strange, almost bizarre flowers have earned members of this genus names such as bat flowers, cats' whiskers and devil's tongue.
CULTIVATION: These frost-tender plants can be grown outdoors in the tropics and subtropics, but elsewhere require the protection of a greenhouse. They need a humid atmosphere, some shade and a peaty soil. Water amply in summer, but allow to dry out almost totally in winter. Propagate by division of the rhizomes or from seed, if available, in spring.

Tacca integrifolia

BAT PLANT, BAT FLOWER

Found naturally in Southeast Asia and from eastern India to southern China, this upright species has lance-shaped leaves up to 24 in (60 cm) long. The flowers, which open in summer and are carried in racemes of up to 30 blooms, are purple-red to brown and are backed by 4 green to purple-tinted bracts. Filaments up to 8 in (20 cm) long hang from the flowers. **ZONES 10–12.**

TAGETES

MARIGOLD

These annuals were rare at the time of their discovery in the seventeenth century; today, they are among the most familiar of summer plants and are useful as bedding plants or for edging. The single or double flowers come in cheerful shades of orange, yellow, mahogany, brown and red and contrast brightly with the deep green leaves. Some of the 50 or so species have aromatic foliage, hence ***Tagetes minuta***'s common name of stinking Roger. It is also said that the roots exude substances fatal to soil-borne pests, leading to their extensive use as companion plants.

CULTIVATION: These fast-growing plants thrive in warm, frost-free climates, but the young plants may need to be raised in a greenhouse in cooler climates. Grow in full sun in fertile, well-drained soil. Deadhead regularly to prolong flowering. Propagate from seed in spring after the danger of frost has passed. They may be prone to attack by slugs, snails and botrytis.

Tagetes 'Disco Orange'

Judging by the cultivar name, it's a safe bet that 'Disco Orange' first appeared sometime in the 1970s. It is a cheerful dwarf marigold suitable for the front of a summer border, and produces single, weather-resistant flowerheads from late spring to early fall (autumn). **ZONES 9–11.**

Tagetes erecta

AFRICAN MARIGOLD, AMERICAN MARIGOLD, AZTEC MARIGOLD

The aromatic, glossy dark green leaves of this bushy annual from Mexico have deeply incised margins. With its upstanding, branching stems, it grows to 18 in (45 cm) in height and spread. Orange or yellow daisy-like flowers bloom in summer and early fall (autumn). The flowers can be as large as 4 in (10 cm) across. **'Crackerjack'** has double flowers and grows to a height of 24 in (60 cm). This species is used as a culinary and medicinal herb. **ZONES 9–11.**

Tagetes lemmonii

MOUNTAIN MARIGOLD

Native to Arizona and adjacent regions of Mexico, this species is unusual in being a shrub of 3–5 ft (1–1.5 m) in height, of somewhat sprawling habit. The leaves are light green and pinnately divided into narrow segments; they are very aromatic, giving off a smell like ripe passionfruit when brushed against. In fall (autumn) and winter it bears small golden-yellow flowerheads, sometimes continuing through most of the year (encouraged by cutting back in early summer). A popular shrub in southwestern USA, it likes full sun and a sheltered position. **ZONES 9–11.**

Tagetes patula

Tagetes lucida

MEXICAN MARIGOLD, SWEET MACE, MEXICAN TARAGON

This species grows to a height of about 24 in (60 cm) and has erect stems and linear leaves. The leaves, which have an anise scent, are mostly shed in winter and may be cut back by frost. The 2- to 3-petalled golden-yellow flowerheads are carried in clusters at the top of the plant in summer and will continue until fall (autumn) if regularly deadheaded. Grown as a culinary and medicinal herb, this species was used to flavor the Aztec cocoa-based drink *chocólatl*. **ZONES 9–11.**

Tagetes patula

FRENCH MARIGOLD

This fast-growing, bushy annual reaches 12 in (30 cm) in height and spread. It was introduced to European gardens from its native Mexico via the south of France—hence its common name. The double flowerheads, produced in summer and early fall (autumn), resemble carnations. They bloom in red, yellow and orange. The leaves are deep green and aromatic. **'Dainty Marietta'** is an all-yellow cultivar with single flowerheads; **'Naughty Marietta'** bears single golden-yellow flowerheads with dark red-brown markings on the petal bases; and **'Honeycomb'** has large mahogany-red flowers edged with gold. **ZONES 9–11.**

Tagetes tenuifolia

SIGNET MARIGOLD

More delicate in its lacy foliage than other *Tagetes* species, the signet marigold grows to a height and spread of only 8 in (20 cm), making it suitable for edgings and bedding. The summer and early fall (autumn) flowers are also smaller and are soft yellow or orange. **'Tangerine Gem'** bears small, single, rich orange flowerheads. **ZONES 9–11.**

TAIWANIA

This genus of evergreen conifers occurs naturally in Burma, China and Taiwan. It consists of 2 or possibly 3 species, none of them widely grown, and is closely related to *Cryptomeria*. The juvenile leaves are narrow, grayish green and almost needle-like, while mature leaves are similar but shorter. The seed-bearing cones are cylindrical and woody. In China the wood from these trees has been used for centuries to make coffins; they are now almost extinct in the wild.

CULTIVATION: Very frost hardy, they prefer well-drained soil and a sheltered position with plenty of moisture and sun. Propagate from seed or cuttings.

Talauma hodgsonii

Tagetes tenuifolia

Taiwania cryptomerioides

FORMOSA REDWOOD

This conifer forms an impressive conical tree, reaching 200 ft (60 m) in the wild, with a massive trunk up to 20 ft (6 m) in diameter. Young trees are vigorous and columnar, with gracefully drooping branches and blue-green leaves. The juvenile leaves are rigid, sharply pointed and narrow, about $\frac{1}{2}$ in (12 mm) long and in flattened rows angled away from the stem. The adult leaves are less than half this length, softer, triangular and pressed against the stem. Small, cylindrical brown cones hang from the drooping ends of the branches. **ZONES 8–10.**

TALAUMA

This genus of about 40 evergreen trees is widespread over Central America and subtropical Asia. It is closely related to *Magnolia*, differing only in the way in which the fruits discharge their seeds. Some species were used by the Aztec Indians for medicinal purposes.

CULTIVATION: Members of this genus are not common in cultivation. They require moist, humus-rich soil and a position in sun or part-shade. All species are frost tender.

Talauma hodgsonii

A native of Nepal, *Talauma hodgsonii* has large, leathery, deeply veined leaves and red-tinted new growth. **ZONES 10–11.**

TALINUM

FAMEFLOWER

Widely distributed throughout the tropics and subtropics, the 50 or so species of annuals and perennials in this genus are generally less than 24 in (60 cm) tall. They have somewhat succulent, broad basal leaves that vary in shape from lance-shaped to nearly round. Leaves further up the stems are narrower, sometimes quite needle-like. Many species have deep, fleshy roots. The tiny yellow, red, pink or purple flowers are borne in terminal clusters in summer. They are followed by small green fruits that often have a brightly colored (usually pink or purple), papery covering. Often found in rock gardens, they can be grown in containers and alpine houses. Some species are edible; they are used as vegetables for human consumption or as stock food.

CULTIVATION: These plants are easily grown in any light, well-drained soil in full sun. Most species are very frost tender, although some are frost hardy. Propagate annuals from seed in fall (autumn); perennials from seed or small tip cuttings.

Taiwania cryptomerioides

Taiwania cryptomerioides

Talinum paniculatum

JEWELS OF OPAR

This frost-tender, upright perennial has a height and spread of 24 in (60 cm) or more. The leaves are elliptical to oval; large clusters of yellowish to red flowers are borne in summer. **ZONES 10–12.**

TAMARINDUS

TAMARIND, INDIAN DATE

This legume genus consists of only one species: a tall, slow-growing evergreen tree that originated in eastern Africa, but is now naturalized in many areas of tropical Southeast Asia. Valued as an ornamental shade and street tree, it is also grown for its bean-like pods, which contain large seeds encased in an edible,

Tamarindus indica

Tamarindus indica

Tamarix parviflora

sweet, fibrous pulp. This pulp, with high tartaric acid content, is cooked and strained to produce a tart-sweet syrup that is used to make a refreshing drink in Middle Eastern countries, and is an important ingredient in Asian cuisine and Worcestershire sauce.
CULTIVATION: These frost-tender trees need a tropical climate and a sunny position if they are to thrive, but are not fussy about soil. Once established, they will tolerate drought and exposed positions. The roots can be invasive. Propagate from seed, cuttings or by air layering in spring.

Tamarindus indica

This handsome tree grows to 70 ft (21 m), with a broad spreading crown and dense foliage. The short trunk is covered with shaggy brown bark. The fern-like, compound, vivid green leaves are held on slender, pale brown branchlets. The small flowers, pale orange-yellow or cream with red veins, are borne in small clusters among the leaves in summer. These are followed by the 8 in (20 cm) long pods, which ripen from green to dark brown and have brittle shells. **ZONES 11–12.**

Tamarix tetrandra

Tamarix aphylla

TAMARIX

TAMARISK

The 50 or so species of tough shrubs and small trees in this genus occur naturally in southern Europe, North Africa and temperate Asia in dry riverbeds, often in saline soils. Most *Tamarix* species are deciduous, but a few are evergreen. They develop a short trunk and a graceful dense canopy of drooping branchlets. The leaves are minute and scale-like, and have salt-secreting glands. The flowers are small and white or pink, occurring in abundant, slender spikes; the fruits are capsules.
CULTIVATION: Grown for ornament and as windbreaks, these trees adapt to a wide range of soils and climates and can cope with salt spray and very dry conditions. Very to moderately frost hardy, they do best in deep, sandy soil with good drainage and can be pruned after flowering. Propagate from ripe seed or from hardwood cuttings in winter and semi-ripe cuttings in late spring or fall (autumn). They are prone to attack by stem borers in poorly drained soil.

Tamarix aphylla

syn. *Tamarix articulata*
ATHEL TREE

This vigorous, evergreen tree grows to 30 ft (10 m) in height with a spread of 24 ft (8 m). It is frost hardy and has dense, weeping branches. A spreading crown tops the short, single, grayish trunk. It has slender, grayish twigs and gray-green linear leaves. In summer and fall (autumn), tiny white to pale pink flowers appear, arranged in spikes. This species helps stabilize sandy soil, but its rapid spread along watercourses is causing much concern in warm, arid regions of the USA and Australia. **ZONES 8–11.**

Tamarix chinensis

syns *Tamarix japonica, T. plumosa*
CHINESE TAMARISK, SALT CEDAR

This deciduous shrub does best in mild climates. Although it tolerates hot, dry conditions, it must have a supply of moisture to the roots. It makes an elegant shrub, growing to about 12 ft (3.5 m) with an upright stem and slightly weeping branchlets. The leaves are small, linear and slightly drooping. A haze of massed, tiny bright pink flowers appear in late summer and can last for several months. **ZONES 7–10.**

Tamarix gallica

FRENCH TAMARISK

Native to the Canary Islands and Sicily, this deciduous, irregularly branched, spreading shrub grows to a height of 12 ft (3.5 m) with a spread of 20 ft (6 m). In spring and summer, terminal clusters of pink, star-shaped flowers are borne amid tiny, blue-gray leaves. This species is moderately frost hardy. **ZONES 5–10.**

Tamarix parviflora

syn. *Tamarix tetrandra* var. *purpurea*
EARLY TAMARISK

This species grows well in mild climates; it is frost hardy but drought sensitive. A small, deciduous, spreading tree about 15 ft (4.5 m) in height, it is a pretty sight when smothered in spring with a haze of tiny, pale pink flowers which are carried in small spikes along the previous year's growth. The toothed, mid-green leaves are small and narrow, and turn orange-red in fall (autumn). This tree is often confused with the similar *Tamarix gallica*. **ZONES 5–10.**

Tamarix ramosissima

syn. *Tamarix pentandra*
LATE TAMARISK

Perhaps the most widely grown *Tamarix* species, this elegant, deciduous shrub grows to about 15 ft (4.5 m) with a spread of about 10 ft (3 m). Occurring from eastern Europe to central Asia and very frost hardy, it has tiny blue-green leaves. The branches and twigs are a dark red-brown. Clusters up to 6 in (15 cm) long of profuse, small, pink flowers are borne in plumes during late summer and early fall (autumn). **'Pink Cascade'** is a vigorous cultivar which bears rich rose-pink flowers. **ZONES 2–10.**

Tamarix tetrandra

This species grows to 10 ft (3 m) with arching purplish brown shoots and needle-like leaves. In spring, it bears lateral racemes of 4-petalled, pink flowers on the previous year's growth. **ZONES 6–10.**

Tamarix ramosissima

TANACETUM

syn. *Pyrethrum*

In classical Greek mythology, immortality came to Ganymede as a result of drinking tansy, a species of this genus of rhizomatous perennial daisies. Even in recent times, it has been used (despite being potentially quite poisonous even when applied externally) for promoting menstruation and treating hysteria, skin conditions, sprains, bruises and rheumatism. Confined mainly to temperate regions of the northern hemisphere, the 70 or so species of this genus, relatives of the chrysanthemum, are today more appreciated for their daisy-like flowers and their foliage that is often white-hairy and in many cases finely dissected. The foliage of many of the perennials is strongly aromatic.
CULTIVATION: Moderately to very frost hardy, they prefer full sun in well-drained, dryish soil; in fact, any soil that is not wet and heavy. Do not overwater. A second flowering may be encouraged if faded flowers are cut back. These plants spread readily and need to be kept under control. Propagate by division in spring or from seed in late winter or early spring.

Tanacetum argenteum

syn. *Achillea argentea*

This usually evergreen perennial has a mat-forming habit. It reaches 10 in (25 cm) in height with a spread of 8 in (20 cm). Very frost hardy, it is prized for its fine, silvery green foliage. Masses of small, white, daisy-like flowers are produced in summer. **ZONES 5–10.**

Tanacetum balsamita

syns *Balsamita major, Chrysanthemum balsamita*
ALECOST, COSTMARY

This tough, frost-hardy perennial with strong rhizomatous roots can become somewhat invasive. It grows to 5 ft (1.5 m) tall and produces heads of white flowers with bright yellow disc florets from late summer. The leaves can be used sparingly in salads and as a

Tamarix ramosissima

T

Tanacetum argenteum

Tanacetum coccineum

Tanacetum haradjanii

flavoring in meat and vegetable dishes. The name 'alecost' comes from its former use as a spicy additive to beer. It also has antiseptic properties. ***Tanacetum balsamita* var. *tomentosum*** has leaves densely covered with fine hairs on their undersides. It is commonly known as the camphor plant because of its strongly camphor-scented foliage, which the parent species lacks. **ZONES 6–10.**

Tanacetum cinerariifolium

syns *Chrysanthemum cinerariifolium*, *Pyrethrum cinerariifolium*

PYRETHRUM, DALMATIAN PELLITORY

This frost-hardy species grows to about 30 in (75 cm) with a spread of 12 in (30 cm). It has slender, gray, hairy stems and finely divided gray-green leaves. The solitary flowers are white to pink, with yellow disc florets. They are produced from early summer to early fall (autumn). The dried flowerheads are powdered and used to produce widely available commercial insecticides. **ZONES 6–10.**

Tanacetum coccineum

syns *Chrysanthemum coccineum*, *Pyrethrum roseum*

PAINTED DAISY, PYRETHRUM

This frost-hardy, erect perennial has dark green, feathery, scented leaves that are finely dissected. Its single, or sometimes double, long-stalked flowerheads may be pink, red, purple or white, appearing from late spring to early summer. The species grows 2–3 ft (60–90 cm) tall with a spread of 18 in (45 cm) or more. **'Brenda'** has striking magenta single flowers. **'Eileen May Robinson'** is one of the best single pinks. **'James Kelway'** has deep crimson-pink flowers. It is a native of western Asia. **ZONES 5–9.**

Tanacetum balsamita var. *tomentosum*

Tanacetum corymbosum

Tanacetum corymbosum

This dense, clump-forming species from southern and central Europe and central Russia grows to a height of 3 ft (1 m) with a spread of 12 in (30 cm). The leaves are finely cut and the flowers white. **ZONES 2–10.**

Tanacetum haradjanii

syn. *Chrysanthemum haradjanii*

This woody, evergreen perennial from Syria and Turkey grows to 10–15 in (25–38 cm) in height and spread. Moderately frost hardy, it has a mat-forming habit and a tap root. The broad, lance-shaped leaves are silver-gray and much divided. Terminal clusters of bright yellow flowerheads are borne in summer. *Tanacetum haradjanii* is a suitable plant for a rock garden. **ZONES 8–10.**

Tanacetum niveum

Tanacetum niveum

SILVER TANSY

Growing to about 24 in (60 cm) with a spread of up to 3 ft (1 m), this attractive species has deeply divided gray-green leaves. In mid-summer it produces an abundant display of small white flower-heads with yellow centers. A fine ornamental species, it will often self-seed when grown in a border. **ZONES 7–10.**

Tanacetum parthenium

syn. *Chrysanthemum parthenium*

FEVERFEW

Feverfew is one of those aromatic plants with a long history of medicinal use—it was used to dispel fevers and agues, and as an antidote for over-indulgence in opium. These days it is admired for its pretty clusters of single or double, ½ in (12 mm) wide, white-petalled, daisy-like flowers. These are borne over a long period in summer. Frost hardy, it has yellow-green leaves up to 3 in (8 cm) long. This species reaches 24 in (60 cm) in height with a spread of 18 in (45 cm). Although perennial, it is short lived; many gardeners prefer to sow it afresh each spring. **'Aureum'** has bright golden foliage. **'Golden Moss'** is a dwarf cultivar with a height and spread of 6 in (15 cm); it has golden, moss-like foliage and is often grown as an edging or bedding plant. **'Snowball'** has pompon flowers and grows to 12 in (30 cm) tall. **ZONES 6–10.**

Tanacetum ptarmiciflorum

syn. *Chrysanthemum ptarmiciflorum*

DUSTY MILLER, SILVER LACE

This bushy perennial from the Canary Islands spreads from a woody tap root. Its silvery, lanceolate leaves are strongly divided. Marginally frost-hardy and with a maximum height and spread of 15 in (38 cm), it is good for the rock garden. White flowerheads in terminal clusters are borne in summer. It is very useful in floral arrangements. **ZONES 9–11.**

Tanacetum parthenium 'Golden Moss'

Tanacetum parthenium

Tanacetum vulgare

TANSY

Native to Europe, this is a coarse, strongly aromatic and rather invasive plant. It has a creeping rootstock and grows to a height of 5 ft (1.5 m) with an indefinite spread. Tall stems grow from this rootstock in early spring, together with dark green, fern-like leaves. The stems are topped with clusters of bright golden-yellow, button-like flowers in late summer and fall (autumn). Tansy is used as an insect repellent, particularly against flies and ants. **ZONES 4–10.**

TAPEINOCHILOS

INDONESIAN GINGER

Ranging in the wild from Southeast Asia to northern Australia, members of this genus are plants of the forest floor. There are some 15 tropical species in this genus and, like *Costus* and *Heliconia* species, they make their dramatic statement not so much from the insignificant flowers but from the brilliantly colored bracts that surround them. Unfortunately their splendor is often hidden beneath the handsome foliage. These evergreen perennials make excellent cut flowers, but their short stems and cultivation requirements have cost them popularity.

CULTIVATION: These frost-tender plants need heat and humidity to thrive. In cooler climates they are happy in a

Tanacetum ptarmiciflorum

Tanacetum parthenium 'Snowball'

Tanacetum parthenium 'Aureum'

T

well-warmed greenhouse. Plant in part-shade in humus-rich soil. Propagate from seed or bulbils, or by division in spring.

Tapeinochilos ananassae
syn. *Tapeinochilos queenslandiae*

As the botanical name suggests, this species resembles a hard, scarlet pineapple *(Ananas)*, but without the deep green fronds at the top. The flower spike rises about 15 in (38 cm) directly from the ground and is overtopped by the considerably taller stems, which carry the foliage. The scarlet bracts almost hide the small, tubular, yellow flowers. This species is native to eastern Indonesia, New Guinea and northeastern Australia. **ZONES 11–12.**

TARAXACUM
DANDELION

This genus of humble weeds and wildflowers has been the subject of much disagreement among botanists concerning the number of species it contains. Some place it as low as 60, others as high as several hundred, but the higher number includes many minor variations, especially in Europe, that are *apomicts*, that is, presumed stabilized hybrids that reproduce by seed without genetic recombination. Most taraxacums are perennials with thick tap roots, though some are biennials. They have basal rosettes of crisp green leaves that usually have sharply toothed or lobed edges. Hollow, unbranched flowering stems each bear a solitary flowerhead consisting of numerous narrow ray florets and lacking a central disc. All parts of the plants exude fine droplets of white latex when broken or cut. Some dandelion species, notably *Taraxacum officinale*, have long been used medicinally and their blanched leaves and sliced roots are added to salads; the roots are also roasted and ground as a coffee substitute, in the same way as the related chicory. In Russia it was discovered that the native ***Taraxacum koksaghyz*** yielded sufficient latex to manufacture rubber, and it was cultivated as an emergency source of rubber in World War II.

CULTIVATION: Seldom cultivated for ornament, taraxacums are easy to grow in a sunny position in moist, well-drained soil. If growing as a salad vegetable treat the young plants like lettuce, feeding and watering well and harvesting the leaves before flowering, when they are less bitter. Propagate from seed or from pieces of tap root.

Tapeinochilos ananassae

Tasmannia lanceolata

Taraxacum officinale
COMMON DANDELION

Native to Europe but found naturalized through most of the world except the tropics, this familiar plant has leaves of very variable outline, from almost smooth edged to deeply and closely lobed. The flowering stems, up to about 12 in (30 cm) high, bear bright golden flowerheads up to 1½ in (35 mm) across for much of the year in milder climates, though in cold climates it dies back in winter. The flowers are used to make tonics, beer and wine. The plant has diuretic properties, hence the French common name of *pissenlit* or wet-the-bed. **ZONES 3–10.**

Taxodium ascendens

Taxodium ascendens 'Nutans'

Taxodium mucronatum

TASMANNIA
PEPPER BUSH

This is a genus of a dozen or more species of evergreen, medium-sized shrubs to small trees, ranging in the wild from the Malay Peninsula to eastern Australia and Tasmania. Botanical opinion is divided on whether they should be included in the genus *Drimys*. The flowers are usually creamy white and the fruits are black to dark purple with a hot flavor. The foliage is dark green and shiny; the twigs are reddish.

CULTIVATION: These plants are easy to grow in a mild, moist climate, but do best in humus-rich soil in half to full sun. Propagate from cuttings.

Tasmannia lanceolata
syn. *Drimys lanceolata*
MOUNTAIN PEPPER BUSH

This rounded evergreen shrub from southeastern Australia will grow to a height and spread of 6 ft (1.8 m). The leaves are elliptical and about 2½ in (6 cm) long. Cream summer flowers are followed by black fruit that are sometimes used as a condiment. **ZONES 8–10.**

TAXODIUM

This small genus of deciduous or semi-evergreen conifers consists of 3 species, which occur naturally on the edges of rivers and lakes in eastern North America and parts of Mexico. The genus name comes from the supposed similarity of their foliage to that of the yews *(Taxus)*. *Taxodium* species develop large, spreading branches and shed their leaves in fall (autumn), still attached to the small branchlets. These are feather-like and turn coppery brown. The male (pollen) cones are tiny; the female ones are globular, up to 1 in (25 mm) in diameter. The wood of *Taxodium* species is strong, tough and termite resistant.

CULTIVATION: These trees thrive in boggy soils in full sun and will even grow in shallow water. However, they will grow equally well in a normal well-drained soil that is sufficiently deep and moist. Propagate from seed or cuttings.

Taxodium ascendens
POND CYPRESS

Occurring mainly in the coastal sandy 'pine barrens' of eastern USA, this species grows in shallow pools in the wild. A narrowly conical tree, it reaches a height of 60 ft (18 m) in cultivation and has spirally arranged leaves on erect branchlets. The new spring growth is erect and fresh green, becoming rich brown in fall (autumn). The small cones hang from the branch tips. As its common name suggests, this tree makes an excellent feature beside rivers, ponds and lakes. **'Nutans'** has shoots that are erect at first, becoming nodding as they mature. **ZONES 7–10.**

Taxodium distichum

Taxodium distichum

Taxodium distichum
BALD CYPRESS, SWAMP CYPRESS

Found in the swamp regions of southeastern USA, this fast-growing tree reaches a height of 120 ft (36 m) in the wild, but only about 80 ft (24 m) in cultivation. It is distinguished by its deeply fissured, fibrous, reddish brown bark and knobbly 'knees'. These special structures are vertical woody growths sent up from the roots when the plant is standing in water and are thought to allow the tree to breathe with its root system submerged. It has tiny, light green, slender, pointed leaves which, as they mature, turn rusty red in fall (autumn) then golden brown before falling. It has resinous, round, purple cones, 1 in (25 mm) across. **ZONES 6–10.**

Taxodium mucronatum
MEXICAN BALD CYPRESS, MONTEZUMA CYPRESS

Native to Mexico and southwest Texas, USA, this conifer is only deciduous in cooler climates. It reaches a height of 100 ft (30 m) or more, with a massive trunk and widely spreading branches. The leaves are identical to those of *Taxodium distichum*, while the cones are

Taxus cuspidata

inconspicuous. There are some huge specimens in the Mexican highlands, most notably the great tree of Tulé, which has a trunk more than 30 ft (9 m) in diameter. Although its age has been estimated at thousands of years, observations of the growth rate of this species under good conditions suggest that it is no more than 1,000 years old. **ZONES 9–10.**

TAXUS

YEW

The evergreen conifers of this small genus, from cool-climate regions of the northern hemisphere, are slow growing but very long lived. Young trees are conical in shape, but as they age—over the centuries—they develop a domed crown and a massive, thick trunk clothed in reddish brown or grayish brown bark which peels off in thin scales. The flat green leaves are shortish, needle-like and sharply pointed; male and female flowers appear on separate trees in spring. The single, small brown seed of the female plant is enclosed in a vivid red fleshy cup; this cup is the only part of the plant that is not poisonous to humans and animals. Yews make excellent dense hedges and are often used for topiary.

CULTIVATION: These frost-hardy trees tolerate a wide range of conditions, including heavy shade and chalky soil. However, they do not enjoy warm winters or hot, dry summers. Propagate from seed or cuttings or by grafting.

Taxus baccata

ENGLISH YEW, COMMON YEW

Indigenous to western Asia, North Africa and Europe, this dense, dark tree has had legendary and religious associations for centuries. The wood of this tree was once used for making longbows. It grows best in a moist alkaline soil in an open position. The dark-colored trunk is erect and very thick in maturity; the leaves are dark green. The male tree bears scaly cones, while the female tree bears cup-shaped, scarlet berries which encase a poisonous seed. Old trees may reach 50 ft (15 m), but cultivars rarely achieve this height. **'Aurea'** has golden-yellow foliage when young, turning green in the second year. **'Dovastoniana'**, known as the Westfelton yew because the original tree was planted in 1777 at Westfelton in Shropshire, England, is a distinct form with tiers of wide-spreading, horizontal branches; it normally is found only in the female form. **'Dovastoniana Aurea'**

Taxus cuspidata 'Densiformis'

is similar in habit but the leaves are edged bright yellow. **'Fastigiata'**, the Irish yew, is columnar, while **'Repandens'** has a spreading habit. **'Semperaurea'** is a slow-growing male bush with ascending branches and gold leaves that fade with age to a russet yellow. **ZONES 5–10.**

Taxus brevifolia

PACIFIC YEW, WESTERN YEW

This species is distributed from southeastern Alaska down to central California and inland to the Rocky Mountains. Growing to 50 ft (15 m) high and 30 ft (10 m) wide, it has a conical open crown with slender drooping branches. The bark is scaly and red-purple. The linear-lanceolate leaves are parted on either side of the shoot. It is rare in cultivation and all parts of this tree are extremely poisonous. The bark of this toxic tree is used to produce the drug taxol, which is useful in the treatment of cancers, particularly ovarian cancer. **ZONES 6–10.**

Taxus cuspidata

JAPANESE YEW

Faster growing than *Taxus baccata*, this conifer is popular in cold climates and is tolerant of very dry and shady conditions. It forms a large shrub or small tree to 15 ft (4.5 m) or more in height and spread, with an erect trunk which is covered in grayish brown bark. The dense foliage is composed of small, narrow leaves arranged in V-shaped rows on the stem. The leaves are dull green above and lighter below. Tolerant of pollution, it is one of the few conifers that performs well in difficult urban environments. **'Aurescens'** is a low-growing compact form with deep yellow young leaves that turn green in the second year. Equally compact is the dwarf cultivar **'Densiformis'**, which forms a dense mound about 3 ft (1 m) high. **ZONES 4–9.**

Taxus × media 'Everlow'

Taxus × media

These hybrids between the English and Japanese yews offer a range of sizes and shapes for the garden. **'Brownii'**, a male form, and **'Everlow'** are low and rounded, eventually reaching 8 ft (2.4 m) tall and wide; they are easily kept smaller by pruning. **'Hatfield'** is the broad, upright male form, while **'Hicksii'** is narrow, upright and female; both are good for hedging. **ZONES 5–9.**

TECOMA

syn. *Stenolobium*

This genus of mainly evergreen shrubs and small trees consists of around 12 species native to Central and South America, and closely related to *Tecomaria* and *Tabebuia*—in fact a recent botanical revision includes the African tecomarias in an expanded *Tecoma*. They bear clusters of showy yellow to orange, tubular to trumpet-shaped flowers from spring to fall (autumn). Their leaves can be simple or compound with an odd number of leaflets. The fruits are smooth, bean-like capsules.

CULTIVATION: *Tecoma* species are suitable for warm to hot climates—they can withstand only minimal frosts. They thrive in full sun with shelter from strong winds, and need adequate soil moisture in summer. Propagate from seed in spring or cuttings in summer. Look out for spider mite.

Tecoma stans

syns *Bignonia stans, Stenolobium stans*

YELLOW BELLS, YELLOW TRUMPET FLOWER, YELLOW ELDER

This evergreen shrub or small tree reaches a height of 15–20 ft (4.5–6 m), but can be pruned heavily after flowering

Taxus baccata 'Dovastoniana'

Taxus baccata

to keep it compact. The leaves are composed of 5 or 7 leaflets, each $2\frac{1}{2}$–3 in (6–8 cm) long with deeply serrated edges. This species features bright yellow, trumpet-shaped flowers, 2 in (5 cm) long, arranged in sprays at the branch tips. It has a long flowering season, from early summer to late fall (autumn). The fruit is a capsule about 8 in (20 cm) long, ripening to chocolate brown. **ZONES 10–12.**

TECOMANTHE

This is a genus of 5 species of evergreen twining climbers from Australia, New Zealand, Papua New Guinea and Malaysia. They are grown for their spectacular flowers which bloom profusely in large trusses.

CULTIVATION: These frost-tender plants can be grown outdoors only in warm-temperate to tropical climates; elsewhere they need the protection of a conservatory or greenhouse. They need a humus-rich and well-drained soil, and part-shade in summer. Water liberally during the growth period; less at other times. The climbing stems will need

Tecoma stans

Taxus baccata 'Repandens'

Taxus baccata 'Fastigiata'

some form of support, and should be thinned out as necessary in spring. Propagate from seed in spring or cuttings in summer.

Tecomanthe speciosa

This vigorous twining climber grows to 30 ft (9 m) or more in height. Its compound leaves consist of up to 5 leaflets. In fall (autumn), it bears lush cream, green-tinged flowers rather like foxgloves. This species requires temperatures above 50°F (10°C) and protection from the summer sun. Prune closely packed stems in spring. All plants in cultivation owe their existence to the sole wild specimen found on the Three Kings Islands off the north of New Zealand. **ZONES 9–11.**

TECOMARIA

A single, variable species of semi-climbing evergreen shrub constitutes this genus, native to southern and eastern Africa. Some botanists now merge it with the American *Tecoma*. It has showy trumpet-shaped flowers in shades of yellow, orange or scarlet, which appear in clusters at the ends of shoots. The pinnate leaves are arranged opposite each other or in whorls of 3, and have an odd number of leaflets. The fruits are oblong, narrow capsules.
CULTIVATION: These frost-tender plants grow best in full sun in a position where they are protected from wind; they should be provided with some form of support. Thin out crowded stems in

Tecomaria capensis

Telanthophora grandifolia

spring as necessary. The soil should be well-drained with added organic matter. Water regularly during the warmer months; less so at other times. Propagate from seed in spring or cuttings in summer.

Tecomaria capensis
syn. *Tecoma capensis*
CAPE HONEYSUCKLE

The Cape honeysuckle is a moderately frost hardy, scrambling shrub able to climb to a height of 15–25 ft (4.5–8 m). The branches are slender and sprawling, forming roots where they touch the ground. The glossy green leaves are 6 in (15 cm) long, divided into 5 to 9 rounded to oval leaflets with serrated edges. Orange-red to scarlet, curved flowers, each 2 in (5 cm) long are borne in short spikes from late spring to late summer. **'Aurea'** has yellow flowers. **ZONES 10–12.**

TECOPHILAEA

This genus consists of only 2 species, both native to mountain ranges in Chile, one of them very rare in cultivation. They grow from corms that are covered in a fibrous coating. Both species have beautiful blue flowers, though the color may be variable. The flowers are flattish with short perianth tubes. No more than 3 leaves are usually produced, and these are rather spreading, sheathing the flower stem at the base.
CULTIVATION: Plant in fertile sandy soil in full sun. Tecophilaeas are protected in their native habitats from heavy winter frosts by a blanket of snow, so in frost-prone areas it is best to overwinter them in an alpine house or cool greenhouse. Keep fairly dry in winter. Propagate from seed or corms in spring.

Tecophilaea cyanocrocus
CHILEAN BLUE CROCUS

This spring-flowering species, now thought to be extinct in the wild, grows to a height of 4–6 in (10–15 cm) and produces 1 to 2 flowers on each stem. These are fragrant, funnel-shaped and 2 in (5 cm) in diameter with broad perianth segments; they open out flat and are an intense deep blue with a white throat. The leaves are narrow at the base, sheathing the lower part of the stem. ***Tecophilaea cyanocrocus* var. *leichtlinii*** bears lighter blue, widely funnel-shaped flowers with a more distinct, large, white center. Pure white forms are produced occasionally. **ZONES 8–9.**

Tecophilaea cyanocrocus

Telopea 'Starburst'

TECTONA
TEAK

These fast-growing deciduous trees from tropical India and the monsoonal forests of Southeast Asia form tall, majestic trees, usually with very straight trunks. There are 3 species in the genus. *Tectona grandis* is the only one of note and is renowned for its timber. In tropical Asia, these trees have naturalized widely. They are often planted in parks and gardens, where they are valued for their dense shade and handsome foliage. The fruits are round and a dark purplish red.
CULTIVATION: These trees require high rainfall, heat, humidity and deep, rich soil to make good growth. They need a tropical climate to develop fully. Propagate from seed or cuttings.

Tectona grandis

Harvested since the early nineteenth century by the British, particularly for shipbuilding and fine furniture, this species is still regarded in Europe as a timber for quality furniture. As a result of its early use, many of the largest teak trees have disappeared from the wild. It makes a fine specimen tree and will grow up to about 80 ft (24 m); its large, rounded leaves are up to 24 in (60 cm) long and have wavy edges and prominent veins. In summer, the bluish white flowers are borne in large, upright, clusters up to 15 in (38 cm) across. The fruit are fleshy, plum-like berries. **ZONES 11–12.**

TELANTHOPHORA

This genus consists of 14 species of shrubs and small trees native to Central America formerly included in the huge genus *Senecio*. They have erect stems with few branches and their leaves and stems are covered in fine hairs. The leaves, usually large, have lobed or toothed margins. Broad sprays of yellow daisy-like flowerheads develop at the stem tips and open late in the growing season.

Tellima grandiflora

Telopea 'Sunflower'

CULTIVATION: Apart from being frost tender, they are easily grown in any well-drained soil in sun or part-shade. Propagate from seed.

Telanthophora grandifolia
syn. *Senecio grandifolius*
BIG-LEAF GROUNDSEL

This shrub reaches 15–20 ft (4.5–6 m) in height and spread. The purplish, velvety buds are as attractive as the yellow daisy-like flowers. The leaves have grand proportions and earn the plant its rather dull common name. **ZONES 10–11.**

TELLIMA
FRINGECUPS

Native to North America, this genus consists of only one species. An evergreen perennial, it makes an ideal ground cover in cool part-shaded woodland gardens or under shrubs in sunnier positions.
CULTIVATION: Very frost hardy, it does best in reasonably well-drained soil. Propagate by division in spring or from seed in fall (autumn).

Tellima grandiflora

This clump-forming perennial has heart-shaped, purple-tinted green leaves. Semi-evergreen, they form a neat clump around 24 in (60 cm) high. Racemes of small, bell-shaped, creamy flowers are borne in spring on 24 in (60 cm) stems, well above the foliage. **'Rubra'** (syn. 'Purpurea') has reddish purple leaves underlaid with dark green and pink-tinged cream flowers. It can be grown as a ground cover and in woodland gardens. **ZONES 6–9.**

TELOPEA
WARATAH

These sturdy evergreen shrubs and small trees are indigenous to the open forests of southeastern Australia, including Tasmania; only 4 species exist, but there are also some attractive hybrids such as **'Starburst'** and **'Sunflower'**. They bear spectacular flowerheads in spring, each distinctive bloom a dense head of tubular flowers surrounded by showy red bracts. Flowers develop at the shoot tips. The leathery green leaves are alternate along the woody stems and have long stalks. The fruits are leathery pods.

CULTIVATION: Waratahs can be difficult to grow successfully, needing well-drained, sandy soil with low fertility and an acid pH; they are prone to fungal root and stem rot. Moderately frost hardy, they prefer full sun to part-shade, and need shelter from the wind. Regular pruning after flowering will keep them bushy. Waratahs are best propagated from seed or cuttings in spring, and can also be grafted.

Telopea oreades
GIPPSLAND WARATAH, VICTORIAN WARATAH

Occurring naturally in cool hill forests, this waratah has a slender, upright, well-branched habit and forms an open crown. Mature trees have one to several dominant shoots and masses of shorter stems. They reach a height of 20–25 ft (6–8 m) and bear crimson flowers from spring to early summer. These are arranged in broad, loose, spidery heads, up to 3 in (8 cm) across, and have pale reddish to green oval to oblong bracts at the base. There is also a rare white-flowered form. The fruits are boat-shaped pods. **ZONES 9–10.**

Telopea 'Shady Lady'

This evergreen shrub quickly reaches a height and spread of 10 ft (3 m). In spring, it bears red flowerheads up to 6 in (15 cm) across at the ends of the upright branches. These are set amid dark green, oval leaves. An outstanding cut flower, this hybrid is a cross between *Telopea speciosissima* and *T. oreades* as is the rather more loosely open-flowered **'Starflower'**. **ZONES 9–11.**

Telopea speciosissima
WARATAH

The waratah is the floral emblem of New South Wales, Australia. The leaves vary from oblong to wedge-shaped, often having a serrated edge and are sometimes slightly lobed. Magnificent scarlet to crimson flowers are borne in large, domed heads 4–6 in (10–15 cm) across in spring and early summer. These are surrounded by bright red bracts of variable size and prominence. This sturdy, vigorous shrub grows to 10 ft (3 m) tall with a spread of 6 ft (1.8 m). The fruit are brown. **'Sunflare'** has particularly

Terminalia brassii

Telopea 'Shady Lady'

large, showy bracts and flat-topped flowers. **'Wirrimbirra White'** features creamy white flowers and cream to greenish bracts. **ZONES 9–11.**

Telopea truncata
TASMANIAN WARATAH

This large evergreen shrub grows up to 15 ft (4.5 m) tall with a similar spread. In its native habitat in Tasmania, Australia, it grows in cool, moist hill country. The red flowerheads, produced in late spring, are 2 in (5 cm) in diameter and flatter than in other species. The deep green leaves are narrow, up to 4 in (10 cm) in length and pointed at the tips. **ZONES 9–10.**

TEMPLETONIA
CORAL BUSH

Native to the western deserts of Australia, this genus contains 11 species of evergreen shrubs and subshrubs, some of which have spiny stems. The commonly grown species reach around 6 ft (1.8 m) high and wide, and have simple blue-green oblong leaves $\frac{1}{2}$–$1\frac{1}{2}$ in (12–35 mm) long. Their usually bright to dusky red pea-flowers, 1 in (25 mm) long, open from winter to spring. The flowers are borne either singly in the leaf axils or in small clusters at the branch tips.
CULTIVATION: These plants vary in hardiness from moderately frost hardy to frost tender. Plant in light, free-draining soil in full sun to part-shade. Most species occur in limestone areas and benefit from occasional light liming. Trim after flowering to maintain a neat shape. Propagate from seed in spring or cuttings in summer.

Templetonia retusa
COCKIES' TONGUES

This rounded, spreading shrub grows to 6 ft (1.8 m) high with a spread of 10 ft

Tephrosia grandiflora

Telopea speciosissima

Telopea oreades

(3 m). The oval to oblong leaves are gray to bright green, leathery and indented at the apex. It produces large red flowers with a reflexed standard in winter and early spring; occasionally the flowers may be white, yellow or partly yellow. **ZONES 10–11.**

TEPHROSIA

This large genus of some 300 mainly evergreen, shrubby plants is widespread throughout the tropics and subtropics. All have alternate leaves and paired or clustered flowers, usually in terminal racemes. Most flower in spring and summer.
CULTIVATION: They tolerate arid conditions and grow well in any soil that does not become waterlogged in winter. Hardiness varies considerably with the species.

Tephrosia grandiflora

This erect shrub, native to South Africa, reaches up to 6 ft (1.8 m) in height. The leaves are 2–4 in (5–10 cm) in length and have 11 to 15 leaflets which are hairy on the undersides. The purple to dark pink flowers are formed in clusters, the buds being enclosed in broad bracts. **ZONES 9–11.**

TERMINALIA
TROPICAL ALMOND

This large genus consists of around 200 species of evergreen and deciduous trees occurring in tropical and subtropical regions of Asia, Australia and southern Africa. The bark is often fissured and the branches are arranged in tiers. The leaves

Telopea speciosissima 'Sunflare'

Telopea speciosissima 'Wirrimbirra White'

are generally large and leathery. The 5-petalled, greenish white flowers are small and not showy; they appear on spikes or in clusters. The fruits are yellow, dark red or black drupes, usually angled or winged and sometimes edible, though it is said that eating too many will make one drunk.
CULTIVATION: Frost tender, they need well-drained soil and plenty of sun; some species tolerate salty winds and dry conditions. Propagate from seed in spring.

Terminalia brassii

This tall handsome tree has glossy mid-green ovate leaves. It makes a good shade tree in the tropics and subtropics and is also used as a quick-growing plantation tree in the Solomon Islands, and has been trialled as a source of paper pulp. **ZONES 11–12.**

Terminalia catappa
INDIAN ALMOND, SEA ALMOND, TROPICAL ALMOND

This attractive tree has horizontal, tiered branches and a broad, flattened canopy

T

Terminalia catappa

Tetradium daniellii

Tetradium daniellii

which is often twice as wide as its height of 60 ft (18 m). The leaves are glossy green and broadly oval with prominent veins; as they age they turn bright orange, then red, and fall at any time of year, though the tree is never completely bare. The inconspicuous but lightly fragrant white flowers are held on spikes near the ends of branches from summer to fall (autumn). They are followed by yellow fruit, which are tinged with red when ripe; they consist of fibrous flesh surrounding an almond-like seed of which the kernel is edible, either raw or roasted. **ZONES 11–12.**

TERNSTROEMIA

Most of the 85 species of shrubs and small trees in this genus are native to tropical America, but one occurs in eastern Asia and two in tropical Africa. Their evergreen foliage resembles that of camellias, to which they are closely related. The small flowers are usually solitary, though sometimes appear in small clusters; they are followed by fleshy fruits.

Ternstroemia gymnanthera

Ternstroemia gymnanthera

CULTIVATION: Well-drained, slightly acidic soil suits these plants best, with plenty of moisture during dry spells. They benefit from an annual dressing of organic mulch spread thickly over the roots. Young plants can be transplanted in winter and trained to form a dense hedge. Propagate from ripe seed or from cuttings in fall (autumn).

Ternstroemia gymnanthera

syn. *Ternstroemia japonica*
JAPANESE TERNSTROEMIA

This attractive shrub or small tree is one of the few species in cultivation. Occurring naturally from Japan to southwestern China, it reaches a height of 15 ft (4.5 m) with a rounded crown about 8 ft (2.4 m) wide. The oval, glossy green, pointed leaves are thick and are arranged in spirals; young foliage is coppery red. Borne in late spring and early summer, the small white flowers hang in clusters of 3 and are delicately perfumed. These are followed by berries that ripen to scarlet. **ZONES 7–10.**

TETRADENIA

syns *Iboza, Moschosma*

Belonging to the mint family, this genus contains 9 species of soft-stemmed, deciduous and semi-deciduous shrubs native to southern Africa and Madagascar. They are grown for their masses of small, sweetly scented flowers and aromatic foliage.
CULTIVATION: Marginally frost hardy, they prefer light, well-drained loam, but not prolonged dry conditions. Plant in full sun and provide plenty of water in summer, with protection from strong

Tetradenia riparia

winds. They can be pruned hard each year after the flowers are spent. Propagate from cuttings in spring.

Tetradenia riparia

syns *Iboza riparia, Moschosma riparia*
NUTMEG BUSH, MOSCHOSMA, GINGER BUSH

This semi-deciduous South African shrub grows to 8 ft (2.4 m) tall with a spread of 5 ft (1.5 m). It has an erect, stout habit and is marginally frost hardy. The toothed, velvet-textured, soft green leaves are spicily aromatic when crushed. Long, fragrant clusters of tiny, pale pink to mauve flowers with red stamens are borne at the ends of branches in winter and early spring. **ZONES 10–11.**

TETRADIUM

This genus consists of 9 species of deciduous small trees from East Asia. Grown for their foliage, they are often planted as part of a shrub border. The leaves are pinnate and the leaflets have translucent oil dots and a slightly aromatic smell when crushed. Flowers appear in flat sprays at the ends of new growth. Both the flower and fruit parts of the trees usually occur in 4s; the fruits are poisonous in some species. One species, ***Tetradium ruticarpum,*** has been used in traditional Chinese medicine since the Hang Dynasty.
CULTIVATION: They do best in full sun to part-shade, and prefer deep, fertile, moist but well-drained soil. Although very frost hardy, young growth needs protection from late frosts. Propagate from seed in fall (autumn) or cuttings in late winter.

Tetradium daniellii

syn. *Euodia daniellii*

This tree from the mountain woodlands of northern China and Korea grows to 50 ft (15 m) tall and forms a canopy of broad, spreading, upwardly pointing branches. Its 12 in (30 cm) long leaves are composed of 5 to 11 ovate leaflets, each narrowing to a sharp point. They are smooth and glossy, dark green above and blue-green and hairy below. Sprays of small, white, perfumed flowers appear in late summer. Small, beaked, reddish black capsular fruit are produced in generous clusters in fall (autumn). **ZONES 8–10.**

TETRAGONIA

This genus allied to the ice plants *(Mesembryanthemum)* contains about 50 species, all from the southern hemisphere. They are sprawling or scrambling annuals or perennials or small shrubs. They have flat, rather succulent leaves; green or yellow flowers are held in axillary clusters of between one and five. Many species have edible leaves like miniature spinach leaves.
CULTIVATION: Many are invasive plants that are only too easily grown. They thrive in humus-rich soil in sun or morning shade and prefer ample summer moisture.

Tetragonia tetragonioides

syn. *Tetragonia expansa*
NEW ZEALAND SPINACH

Sir Joseph Banks brought this perennial plant back to England from New Zealand in the eighteenth century, but it became more popular in the USA and Europe. It occurs widely in Australia as well, including exposed seashores. It is a weak, almost prostrate plant up to about 12 in (30 cm) tall but spreading to 3 ft (1 m) or more. Soak the seeds overnight and sow them in spring. Water regularly and harvest the leaves as needed. **ZONES 8–10.**

TETRAPANAX

RICE-PAPER PLANT

This genus consists of one species, an evergreen, suckering shrub or small tree native to Taiwan and possibly another in Japan's Ryukyu Islands. A type of fine 'rice paper' is made from the white pith of the stems of this plant, hence both the common and species names. It is grown in temperate gardens for its very large, fan-like leaves; it works well where an exotic, tropical effect is required and space is available for its often rampant growth.
CULTIVATION: Plants do best in mild climates, in sheltered, preferably lightly shaded spots and well-drained soil. Tolerant of salt winds and sandy soil, they adapt well to seaside conditions. Water container plants freely during warmer months. Prune to remove damaged

Tetragonia tetragonioides

Tetrapanax papyrifer

Teucrium marum

foliage and spent flowerheads, and in winter remove canes at ground level to control the size of the plants. Propagate from seed or cuttings in early spring.

Tetrapanax papyrifer
syns *Aralia papyrifera, Fatsia papyrifera*

This freely suckering shrub grows vigorously to 20 ft (6 m) tall and has a similar spread. The huge, umbrella-like, many lobed leaves are a shiny mid-green above, felty underneath. New growth has a distinctive pale brownish bloom. The flowerheads are creamy white, fluffy balls held in large, loose panicles; they appear during fall (autumn) and are followed by black berries. **'Variegata'** has cream to white leaves tinged with bright to dark green. **ZONES 8–11.**

TETRASTIGMA
JAVAN GRAPE

This genus consists of around 90 species of tendril-bearing climbers occurring naturally from tropical Asia to northern Australia. They are related to the true grapes *(Vitis)* and carry similar bunches of cherry-sized fruit. These develop from inconspicuous green flowers that are often slightly scented. The leaves are usually compound, with 3 to 7 toothed leaflets.
CULTIVATION: Most are frost tender and grow best in subtropical to tropical areas. They prefer moist, humus-rich soil and require strong support as they can cover a large area. Propagate from seed or cuttings, or by layering.

Tetrastigma voinierianum
syns *Cissus voinierana, Vitis voinierana*
CHESTNUT VINE

This evergreen climbing plant occurs naturally in Indo-China and has thick stems with jointed segments. The leaves are divided into 5 glossy green leaflets up to 8 in (20 cm) long; these are densely hairy underneath and have serrate margins and spirally shaped tendrils. The inconspicuous yellow-green flowers appear in summer. This species prefers a part-shaded position. **ZONES 10–12.**

TETRATHECA
BLACK-EYED SUSAN

Native to Australia, this genus consists of 39 species of heath-like evergreen shrubs with nodding, 4-petalled flowers, whose black centers give rise to the common name. Masses of showy pink, mauve or purple flowers are borne on slender red stems; there are some rare white forms.

Teucrium polium 'Aureum'

CULTIVATION: Marginally frost hardy, they prefer light, well-drained, lime-free soil in part-shade, with protection from summer sun. Mulch occasionally with compost or leafmold. Propagate from seed in spring or cuttings in late summer or fall (autumn).

Tetratheca ciliata
PINK EYE, PINK BELLS

A compact, evergreen shrub, this species is native to southern and southeastern Australia. It reaches a height and spread of 3 ft (1 m). The small, rounded leaves are arranged in whorls of 3 on slender branches. In winter and spring, lovely pinkish purple flowers with black centers are borne on fine red stems; occasionally white forms occur. **ZONES 9–11.**

TEUCRIUM
GERMANDER

Mainly native to the Mediterranean, this genus of around 100 species in the mint family was named for King Teucer of Troy, who reputedly used the plants medicinally. Evergreen or deciduous shrubs, subshrubs and perennials, they have 2-lipped flowers and slightly aromatic foliage. These plants are able to withstand hot, dry conditions and poor soils. They can be used as hedges and will grow in sheltered maritime conditions.
CULTIVATION: Mostly fairly frost hardy, they prefer light, well-drained soil and sun. Low-growing species do best in poor soils. Propagate shrubs and subshrubs from cuttings in summer; perennials are propagated by division in fall (autumn) or from seed in spring.

Teucrium chamaedrys
WALL GERMANDER

This hardy, evergreen alpine species of subshrub is native to Europe and southwestern Asia. It grows 1–2 ft (30–60 cm) tall with a spread of 2–3 ft (60–90 cm). The toothed, ovate leaves are glossy deep green above and gray beneath. It is suitable for walls, steep banks and edging, and has long been used as a medicinal herb. Spikes of pale to deep rosy purple flowers are produced in summer and fall (autumn). **'Prostratum'** is, as its name suggests, a prostrate form. **ZONES 5–10.**

Teucrium cossonii

This species is a low spreader with rounded heads of deep pink flowers. Its narrow, gray-green leaves are reminiscent of some *Lavandula* species. **ZONES 8–11.**

Teucrium fruticans
BUSH GERMANDER

This marginally frost-hardy, evergreen from the Mediterranean grows to a height and spread of 4–8 ft (1.2–2.4 m). The attractive blue tubular, double-lipped flowers, set among aromatic, oval, silvery gray leaves, are borne in spring. *Teucrium fruticans* makes a good low, neat hedge, and does well in seaside gardens. Trim old flowerheads to promote new growth. **'Azureum'** has darker blue flowers and is slightly frost tender. **ZONES 8–10.**

Teucrium marum
CAT THYME

This marginally frost-hardy, perennial shrub reaches 12 in (30 cm) in height with a spread of 24 in (60 cm). It has silver-gray leaves and bears red to purple flowers in sprays above the foliage in early summer. This species is attractive to cats—hence its common name. **ZONES 9–11.**

Teucrium polium

This deciduous subshrub with procumbent stems forms low hummocks 1–2 in (2.5–5 cm) in height. Its narrow, gray, felted leaves have scalloped margins and white to yellow or pinkish purple flowers in terminal heads are produced in summer. It is moderately frost hardy. **'Aureum'** has leaves edged with creamy yellow. **ZONES 7–10.**

Teucrium scorodonia
SAGE-LEAVED GERMANDER, WOOD SAGE

This perennial subshrub has square stems with opposite grayish green leaves, similar to those of sage except that the tips are rounded. It grows to a height of 24 in (60 cm); small greenish yellow flowers are borne in spike-like clusters. This plant has a faint smell of garlic and has been used as a substitute for hops in brewing. **ZONES 6–10.**

THALIA
WATER CANNA

The 7 species of this American genus honor a German botanist, Johann Thal, who lived from 1542 to 1583. Deciduous or perennial marginal water plants, they are grown for their spikes of tubular flowers and their oval, long-stalked, blue-green leaves.
CULTIVATION: Grow these frost-tender plants in baskets of fertile, loamy soil or in deep, humus-rich mud in up to 20 in (50 cm) of water and in full sun; some species tolerate cool water. Pick off spent foliage. Propagate from seed or by division in spring.

Thalia dealbata

This aquatic, deciduous perennial from the southeast of North America grows to 6 ft (1.8 m) in height with a spread of 24 in (60 cm) or more. It carries leaves that are broadly elliptical to lanceolate, and have a mealy whitish coating. Its stems are erect and unbranching. The flowers, which occur in tall spikes, are violet and waxy, their 6 petals forming a narrow tube; they are borne in summer and are followed by decorative seed heads. **ZONES 9–10.**

Thalia dealbata

Teucrium chamaedrys

Teucrium cossonii

Tetrastigma voinierianum

Tetratheca ciliata

THALICTRUM
MEADOW RUE

Over 300 species make up this genus of perennials known for their fluffy, showy flowers. The branches of their slender, upstanding stems often intertwine. The leaves are finely divided. Blooming in spring and summer, the flowers have no petals, but instead have 4 or 5 sepals and conspicuous stamen tufts. They serve well in borders, particularly as a contrast to perennials with bolder blooms and foliage, and in the margins of bush gardens. The genus occurs in most temperate regions of the northern hemisphere, extending south into South America, South Africa and New Guinea.
CULTIVATION: Grow these frost-hardy plants in sun or part-shade in any well-drained soil; some species need cool conditions. Propagate from fresh seed in fall (autumn) or by division in spring.

Thalictrum aquilegiifolium
GREATER MEADOW RUE

This clump-forming Eurasian perennial grows to 3 ft (1 m) tall and has a spread of 18 in (45 cm). Pink, lilac or greenish white flowers in fluffy clusters on strong stems are produced in summer. Each gray-green leaf comprises 3 to 7 small, elliptical, toothed leaflets in a feather-like arrangement, resembling the leaves of some *Aquilegia* species. **ZONES 6–10.**

Thalictrum aquilegiifolium

Thalictrum delavayi
syn. ***Thalictrum dipterocarpum*** **of gardens**
LAVENDER SHOWER

Rather than fluffy heads, this graceful, clump-forming perennial from western China bears a multitude of nodding, lilac flowers in loose panicles, with prominent yellow stamens. The flowers are borne from the middle to the end of summer. The finely divided leaves give the mid-green foliage a dainty appearance. Reaching 4 ft (1.2 m) high, this species has a spread of 24 in (60 cm). **'Hewitt's Double'** has rounded, pompon-like, mauve flowers. **ZONES 7–10.**

Thalictrum kiusianum

This mat-forming perennial species from Japan grows to 6 in (15 cm) tall with a spread of 12 in (30 cm). It produces clusters of tiny purple flowers from spring to summer and has small, fern-like, 3-lobed leaves. There is also a white-flowered form. This species prefers shade and moist sandy, peaty soil. It is particularly suitable for peat beds and rock gardens. **ZONES 8–10.**

Thalictrum rochebrunianum
LAVENDER MIST

This very tall species from Japan can reach a height of 6–8 ft (1.8–2.4 m) or more if given full sun and a moist soil. Tiny flowers, produced in late summer and early fall (autumn), are arranged in large, open inflorescences and are pale lavender in color. **ZONES 8–10.**

THELOCACTUS

Native to Texas and Mexico, this cactus genus contains 13 species. They may be flat, globular or conical in shape and feature long, curved or straight spines that grow sparsely or densely from the stem. These plants reach about 8 in (20 cm) in height and can spread to 15 in (38 cm). The flat-faced flowers are variously white, yellow or pink, and the stems are

Thalictrum delavayi

Thalictrum kiusianum

Thelocactus bicolor

Theobroma cacao

Thevetia peruviana

Thevetia thevetioides

green or metallic gray. Small seed pods follow the flowers.
CULTIVATION: These frost-tender cacti enjoy full sun. Do not overwater as they are prone to rot. Propagate from offsets or seed in spring or summer.

Thelocactus bicolor
syn. ***Ferocactus bicolor***
GLORY OF TEXAS

This perennial cactus grows to around 8 in (20 cm) in height and spread. It has a spiny, pillar-like singular stem, which is globe-shaped to erect. The stem has more than 10 prominent ribs, lined with pronounced tubercles sprouting 2-toned yellow and red radial spines, and 4 longer, yellow, central spines. It flowers easily; its pinkish purple trumpet-shaped flowers are $2\frac{1}{2}$ in (6 cm) long and bloom from the crown. **ZONES 9–11.**

Thelocactus setispinus

This species has globose to cylindrical stems and with age develops into a small clump of stems. The ribs are well defined and bear areoles with up to 12 spines, each 2–4 in (5–10 cm) long. The hooked central spines are yellow and the radial spines are red. Red-throated yellow flowers open from summer to fall (autumn). **ZONES 9–11.**

THEOBROMA

This genus consists of about 20 species of evergreen trees from tropical America. The genus name comes from the Greek *theos*, meaning god, and *broma* meaning food, referring to the seeds of *Theobroma cacao*, which is the source of chocolate. They have unlobed, alternate leaves and bisexual, 5-petalled flowers arising directly from the trunk and branches. The fruits are large and fleshy and contain many seeds. The trees grow naturally as understory plants in forests.
CULTIVATION: Frost tender, they do best in well-drained soil containing a large percentage of organic matter, with regular water and shelter from sun and wind. Propagate from seed in fall (autumn) or by grafting.

Theobroma cacao
COCOA, CACAO

In its native tropical forests of Central America, this erect tree grows to 30 ft (9 m) or more; in commercial cultivation, it is generally kept smaller to facilitate harvesting. The pointed, oval, glossy green leaves are up to 10 in (25 cm) long, and leathery. Small, creamy yellow flowers are borne in late spring on the trunk and larger woody branches. These are followed by the fruit: large, ribbed pods, about 12 in (30 cm) long and 8 in (20 cm) wide, which ripen to a rich, glossy reddish brown. The seeds of the fruit are used to make cocoa and chocolate. **ZONES 11–12.**

THERMOPSIS

This genus of about 20 rhizomatous perennials is distributed over North America and northeastern Asia. All have trifoliate leaves and resemble lupins in appearance. Some species are cultivated for their large showy racemes of yellow or sometimes purple, pea-like flowers.
CULTIVATION: Very frost hardy, they prefer sun and rich, light soil. Propagate by division during dormancy or from seed in fall (autumn) or spring.

Thermopsis macrophylla
GOLDEN PEA, FALSE LUPINE

Growing to 1–6 ft (0.3–1.8 m) tall, this species from western USA has elliptical leaflets with downy undersides. The yellow flowers are borne in racemes of 6 or so blooms at the branch tips. **ZONES 7–10.**

Thermopsis villosa
CAROLINA LUPINE

This species from southeastern USA grows to as much as 5 ft (1.5 m) tall and has elliptical blue-green leaves with slightly downy undersides. Yellow flowers in loose spikes open from spring to summer. **ZONES 7–10.**

THESPESIA
PORTIA TREE

Widespread in the tropics, the 17 species of this genus closely related to *Hibiscus* are evergreen shrubs or small trees. The leaf shape is variable, from heart-shaped to oval or sometimes palmate with up to 9 lobes. Some species exude a sticky nectar from glands near the midribs of the leaves; others have dense scales on the leaf underside. The long-stemmed, 5-petalled flowers are usually bell-shaped, yellow or orange with red or purple centers. They arise from the leaf axils and may be borne singly or in small clusters. The dark red wood is used for making small utensils and ornamental articles.
CULTIVATION: These tropical trees demand a warm, frost-free climate and prefer moist, well-drained soil with full sun or morning shade. Water freely during warmer months. Propagate from seed in spring or cuttings in summer.

Thespesia populnea
PORTIA OIL NUT, INDIAN TULIP TREE

This evergreen tree from tropical seashores around the world grows to 40 ft (12 m) or more with a spread of 10–20 ft (3–6 m). It has heart-shaped leaves and cup-shaped yellow flowers that are produced intermittently throughout the year. Each flower has a maroon eye that ages to purple. **ZONES 11–12.**

THEVETIA

All 8 species of this genus of evergreen trees and shrubs have a poisonous milky sap; in fact, all parts of the plants are very poisonous. Relatives of the oleander *(Nerium)*, they are indigenous to tropical America. They feature clusters of showy, mostly yellow, funnel-shaped flowers at the shoot tips; flowering peaks in summer. The fruits are berry-like. The leaves are arranged spirally on the branchlets. **CULTIVATION:** These frost-tender plants grow best in a sandy, well-drained soil enriched with organic matter. They need plenty of water while in flower. The ideal location provides shelter from wind, plus full sun to part-shade. Prune the plants after flowering to maintain their dense growth. Propagate from seed in spring or from cuttings in summer.

Thevetia peruviana
syn. *Thevetia neriifolia*
YELLOW OLEANDER, LUCKY NUT

This domed tree grows to 25 ft (8 m) tall. The long, shiny, rich green leaves are hard and strap-like to narrowly lance-shaped, with barely any stalk. The yellow to soft orange, slightly perfumed flowers, each 2 in (5 cm) across, are held on long stalks. They bloom on and off for most of the year in their native habitat; in cooler climates, they bloom in summer. The fruit are oddly shaped, fleshy drupes, rounded and with prominent ridges. They ripen from green through red to black and are regarded by some as a lucky charm, even though dangerously poisonous. **ZONES 10–12.**

Thladiantha dubia

Thryptomene calycina

Thevetia thevetioides
LARGE-FLOWERED YELLOW OLEANDER, BE-STILL TREE, GIANT THEVETIA

This species grows to 15 ft (4.5 m) tall. Its erect but rather weak stems form an untidy crown. The leaves are narrowly lance-shaped, 4 in (10 cm) long and ½ in (12 mm) wide, with a pointed tip and prominent veins. The flowers, about 3 in (8 cm) across, are orange or pale to strong yellow, and more open than those of *Thevetia peruviana*. The fruit are green drupes. **ZONES 10–12.**

THLADIANTHA

Related to the cucumbers, the 23 species in this East Asian and African genus are annual or perennial trailers or climbers. They have simple oval or trifoliate leaves and bell-shaped yellow flowers borne singly or in small clusters; these are followed by small, sometimes ribbed fruits. **CULTIVATION:** Except for a few species, they are only moderately frost hardy. They prefer moist, humus-rich soil and a position in full sun. Propagate from seed or cuttings, or by layering.

Thladiantha dubia

Among the hardier species, this summer-flowering native of Korea and northeastern China climbs by means of tendrils and has 2–4 in (5–10 cm) heart-shaped leaves. **ZONES 7–11.**

THRYPTOMENE

This Australian genus is made up of about 40 species of wiry-stemmed, woody evergreen shrubs, only a few of which are in cultivation. They grow up to 5 ft (1.5 m) high with a similar spread, and have tiny, heath-like, green leaves that are aromatic when crushed. An abundance of small, starry flowers appear all along the branches. **CULTIVATION:** Thryptomenes make good cut flowers and, as they need regular trimming to keep them compact, cutting for flowers is a good way to prune. They prefer light, lime-free, well-drained soil in full sun or part-shade, and a mild climate, frost free or almost so. They are usually propagated from cuttings.

Thryptomene calycina
GRAMPIANS THRYPTOMENE

This species from a limited area of western Victoria, Australia—in particular, the rugged sandstone Grampians mountains—has slightly pointed leaves and white flowers with dark centers carried in great profusion through winter and spring. The species is widely cultivated for cut flowers. A distinctive characteristic of *Thryptomene calycina* is that the 5 sepals are identical in shape, size and color to the 5 petals. There are several cultivars. **ZONES 9–11.**

Thryptomene saxicola

Thuja occidentalis 'Micky'

Thuja occidentalis 'Rheingold'

Thryptomene saxicola
syn. *Thryptomene* 'Paynei'

This open, slightly pendulous species has somewhat rounded leaves and light pink or white flowers which occur mainly in winter and spring. It is a neat, compact plant that seldom exceeds 4 ft (1.2 m) high with a spread of 5 ft (1.5 m), and only requires light trimming after flowering. **ZONES 9–11.**

THUJA
ARBOR-VITAE

This small genus contains 5 evergreen conifers that come from high-rainfall, cool-temperate regions of northeastern Asia and North America. All are valuable timber trees, and several are widely cultivated on a commercial basis. They feature erect, straight trunks covered in deeply fissured, fibrous bark and are columnar to pyramidal. The aromatic foliage consists of sprays of scale-like leaves, often flattened. The egg-shaped cones are covered with overlapping scales and are green, maturing to brown; they are notably small for such large trees, mostly under ½ in (12 mm) long. Dwarf cultivars, some no more than 15 in (38 cm) high, make excellent rockery or container specimens; most are juvenile forms. **CULTIVATION:** These plants tolerate cold and are not fussy about soil as long as it is well drained; most species prefer full sun and dislike dry conditions. Propagation is from seed or cuttings in winter.

Thuja occidentalis 'Lutea Nana'

Thuja occidentalis 'Smaragd'

Thuja occidentalis

Thuja occidentalis
AMERICAN ARBOR-VITAE, WHITE CEDAR

Growing to 50 ft (15 m) in height with a pyramidal crown, this species has attractive, reddish brown, peeling bark. Its dense foliage is composed of yellow-green glandular leaves with bluish undersides held on flat, spreading branchlets. The leaves turn bronze in fall (autumn); it has tiny, yellow-green cones which ripen to brown. This species has given rise to more than 140 cultivars, ranging from dwarf shrubs to large trees. **'Ericoides'** is a small dense bush to 18 in (45 cm) tall and has soft, loose, bronze juvenile foliage which becomes brownish green as it matures. **'Lutea'** grows to 8 ft (2.4 m) in 10 years; its leaves become rich golden bronze in winter. **'Lutea Nana'** is a small conical bush, very dense, with golden-yellow foliage in winter. **'Micky'** is a bun-shaped, green-foliaged cultivar. Slow-growing **'Rheingold'** forms a spreading, semi-prostrate dome 30 in (75 cm) high and 5 ft (1.5 m) wide, and has leaves that turn rich golden brown in winter. **'Smaragd'**, with a compact pyramidal habit, has bright green foliage all year round and forms a dense hedge 6 ft (1.8 m) high. **ZONES 4–10.**

T

Thuja plicata 'Zebrina'

Thuja plicata

Thuja plicata
WESTERN RED CEDAR

This fast-growing conifer reaches about 80 ft (24 m) in cultivation, but is much taller in its natural habitat. It has long been harvested for its durable and versatile softwood timber. Of conical habit, it becomes columnar in maturity, with branches sweeping the ground. When the rich, coppery green foliage is crushed, it exudes a sweet, tangy aroma. The dwarf cultivar **'Rogersii'** forms a round bun shape 18 in (45 cm) across. Compact **'Zebrina'**, growing to 20 ft (6 m) high and 5 ft (1.5 m) wide, has glossy bright green foliage striped with yellow. **'Aurea'** has rich, old gold foliage. **'Stoneham Gold'** is slow growing, but eventually makes a large bush with dense foliage and a narrowly conical form; the foliage is bright gold topped with copper bronze. Similar to 'Stoneham Gold', and also slow growing, **'Collyer's Gold'** has brighter yellow foliage. **'Atrovirens'** is a compact shrub ideal for hedging. **ZONES 5–10.**

THUJOPSIS
MOCK THUJA, HIBA, FALSE ARBORVITAE

This genus from Japan contains only a single species, *Thujopsis dolabrata*. It resembles *Thuja*, but is distinguished by several important features, namely round, woody cones, winged seeds and larger leaves. It is the parent of several cultivars, which vary in habit and foliage color.

CULTIVATION: Tolerant of cold, this plant thrives in moist, well-drained, acidic or alkaline soil and an open, sunny position. Propagation is from seed, or cuttings for selected forms.

Thujopsis dolabrata

This evergreen conifer is variable in growth habit, from upright and pyramidal to spreading and bushy. It reaches a height of 20–50 ft (6–15 m) with a spread of 25–30 ft (8–9 m). Its foliage is composed of flattened, scale-like leaves which are dark green above with frosted white undersides. Its small cones are bluish gray, round and scaly. The dwarf cultivar **'Nana'** forms a spreading, bun

Thuja plicata 'Collyer's Gold'

shape 24 in (60 cm) high by 5 ft (1.5 m) wide, with fresh green foliage, sometimes tinged bronze. The slow-growing **'Variegata'** matures to a broad pyramid 10 ft (3 m) high and 5 ft (1.5 m) wide; its vivid green, shiny foliage is splashed with white. **ZONES 5–10.**

THUNBERGIA

This genus of 90 to 100 species of mainly twining climbers and evergreen, clump-forming shrubs, was named after the eighteenth-century Swedish botanist Dr Carl Peter Thunberg, who collected in Africa and Japan. Native to Africa, Asia and Madagascar, their leaves are entire or lobed, and the mostly trumpet-shaped blooms are borne individually from the leaf axils or in trusses.

CULTIVATION: The species range from marginally frost hardy to frost tender, and prefer temperatures above 50°F (10°C). They will grow in any reasonably rich soil with adequate drainage. Full sun is preferred, except during the summer months, when part-shade and liberal water should be provided. Support the stems and prune densely packed foliage during early spring. Propagate from seed in spring and cuttings in summer.

Thunbergia alata
BLACK-EYED SUSAN

Native to tropical Africa, this vigorous annual or perennial (in frost-free areas) climber grows quickly to 10 ft (3 m). It is

Thujopsis dolabrata 'Variegata'

marginally frost hardy. Its deep green, cordate leaves are up to 3 in (8 cm) long. It bears masses of 2 in (5 cm) wide orange flowers with black throats from early summer to fall (autumn). **ZONES 9–12.**

Thunbergia battiscombei

This species from tropical Africa is a scrambler with 4 in (10 cm) elliptical leaves and racemes of yellow-throated purple trumpet flowers. **ZONES 11–12.**

Thunbergia grandiflora
BLUE TRUMPET VINE, SKY FLOWER

Originally from India, this fast-growing, vigorous, evergreen climber grows to around 15 ft (4.5 m) high. It is

Thujopsis dolabrata

Thujopsis dolabrata 'Nana'

Thunbergia alata

Thunbergia grandiflora

grown for its drooping clusters of large, sky blue to deep violet trumpet-shaped flowers, borne in summer and fall (autumn). It has large-toothed, heart-shaped leaves up to 8 in (20 cm) long and looks best when grown on a trellis, fence or pergola. It is frost tender and requires protection from dry summer winds. **ZONES 10–12.**

Thunbergia gregorii

syn. ***Thunbergia gibsonii***

ORANGE CLOCKVINE

Performing as a perennial in mild climates and as an annual in harsher ones, this evergreen, twining vine climbs to 6 ft (1.8 m) or sprawls as a ground cover to 6 ft (1.8 m) in diameter. The leaves are triangular to oval, with winged stalks. The very showy, brilliant orange tubular flowers are borne nearly all year round where climates permit; but only in summer when treated as an annual. **ZONES 9–11.**

Thunbergia mysorensis

This evergreen, woody stemmed climber comes from tropical mountains in the south of India and thrives in frost-free conditions similar to that of its homeland. It reaches 20 ft (6 m) and has narrow green leaves. The pendent flower spikes are a cheerful combination of brownish red and yellow, and appear from spring to fall (autumn). **ZONES 10–11.**

Thunbergia natalensis

This very attractive species from South Africa is not a climber but a soft-wooded shrub that reaches 3 ft (1 m) in height. It bears its soft blue flowers throughout summer and dies down completely in

Thunbergia battiscombei

winter. Subtropical and warm-temperate climates suit it best. **ZONES 10–11.**

Thunbergia togoensis

This semi-climbing African shrub produces hairy buds, opening into dark blue flowers with yellow centers. **ZONES 10–12.**

THUNIA

This group of about 4 or 5 medium to large, deciduous terrestrial orchids is distributed in China, India and Southeast Asia. The stems are close together, up to 4 ft (1.2 m) tall, bearing many leaves in 2 rows. The leaves are thin, deciduous and up to 8 in (20 cm) long and 2 in (5 cm) wide. The drooping inflorescences are borne terminally on the young shoots, with a few large, short-lived flowers.

CULTIVATION: Grow in a moisture-retaining mixture such as is used for *Cymbidium*. The plants need copious watering during the growing and flowering seasons in spring and summer, with a dry resting period in winter when the plants are dormant.

Thunia alba

syn. ***Thunia marshalliana***

BAMBOO ORCHID, ORCHID OF BURMA

This tall terrestrial orchid is the most commonly grown species. It reaches more than 3 ft (1 m) in height and is native to Burma, Thailand and southern China, where it grows at moderate altitudes. As it has no pseudobulbs, it is effectively a regular, frost-tender herbaceous plant. The pale green leaves are about 6–8 in (15–20 cm) long. The pendent clusters of 5 in (12 cm) wide, white flowers with pink and gold veins on the labellum are borne on the ends of the reed-like stems. The stems die down after the summer flowering, when the plants can be divided if desired. It likes intermediate conditions, summer shade and regular watering; it should not be allowed to dry out, even in winter. Give the plants fairly large pots of ordinary orchid compost, and allow them to build up into generous, many-flowered clumps. **ZONES 11–12.**

Thunbergia gregorii

Thymus caespititius

THYMUS

THYME

This genus consists of over 300 evergreen species of herbaceous perennials and subshrubs, ranging from prostrate to 8 in (20 cm) high. Chosen for their aromatic leaves, these natives of southern Europe and Asia are frequently featured in rockeries, between stepping stones or for a display on banks. Some species are also used in cooking. The flowers are often tubular and vary from white through pink to mauve. Historically, thyme has been associated with courage, strength, happiness and wellbeing.

CULTIVATION: These plants are mostly frost hardy. For thick, dense plants, the flowerheads should be removed after flowering. Plant out from early fall (autumn) through to early spring in a sunny site with moist, well-drained soil. Propagate from cuttings in summer or by division.

Thymus caespititius

syn. ***Thymus micans***

This species is found naturally on dry, stony slopes in the Azores, northwestern Spain and Portugal. An evergreen, mat-forming subshrub, this moderately frost-hardy plant has slender woody stems and minute hairy, aromatic mid-green leaves. Small lilac or lilac-pink flowers are produced in late spring and summer. It grows to little more than 2 in (5 cm) high. **ZONES 7–10.**

Thunbergia mysorensis

Thunbergia natalensis

Thunia alba

Thunbergia togoensis

Thymus camphoratus

This Portuguese species has camphor-scented foliage, as its name suggests. It is a small, wiry stemmed shrub around 18 in (45 cm) high with slightly hairy leaves and purple flowers. **ZONES 7–10.**

Thymus × citriodorus

syn. *Thymus serpyllum* var. *citriodorus*

LEMON-SCENTED THYME

This delightful rounded, frost-hardy shrub grows 12 in (30 cm) high and has tiny oval lemon-scented leaves and pale lilac flowers. The leaves are used fresh or dry in poultry stuffings or to add lemon flavor to fish, meat and vegetables. **'Anderson's Gold'** is a yellow-foliaged spreader that is inclined to revert to green; **'Argenteus'** has silver edges to the leaves; **'Aureus'** has golden variegated leaves; **'Doone Valley'** is prostrate with gold variegated leaves that develop red tints in winter; and **'Silver Queen'** has silvery white foliage. **ZONES 7–10.**

Thymus doerfleri

This low spreader is ideal for carpeting a rockery or filling the cracks between

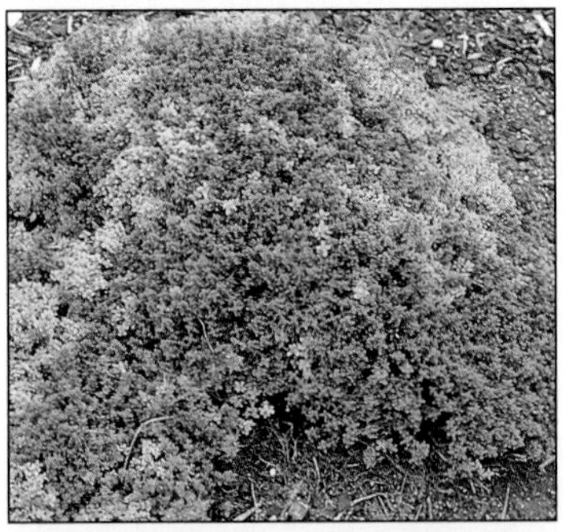

Thymus × citriodorus 'Anderson's Gold'

Thymus camphoratus

paving stones. It is native to Albania and has hairy, ½ in (12 mm) long leaves and pink to purple flowers. **ZONES 5–10.**

Thymus herba-barona

CARAWAY THYME

With a species name meaning 'prince of herbs', this caraway-scented Corsican native grows to 6 in (15 cm) tall with a spread of 10 in (25 cm). A subshrub, it has prostrate, woody, branching stems and lanceolate, deep green leaves. Tubular, rose-pink flowers with 2 lips are borne in terminal clusters in spring. It is marginally frost hardy. **ZONES 9–11.**

Thymus longicaulis

This species from southern Europe is a dwarf spreading shrub. The flowering stems are up to 4 in (10 cm) tall and carry pink to purple flowers. **ZONES 7–10.**

Thymus mastichina

From Spain and Portugal, this is an 18 in (45 cm) high, wiry stemmed shrub. The flowers are usually white but pink- and purple-flowered forms are also common. **ZONES 7–10.**

Thymus × citriodorus 'Argenteus'

Thymus × citriodorus 'Doone Valley'

Thymus longicaulis

Thymus pannonicus

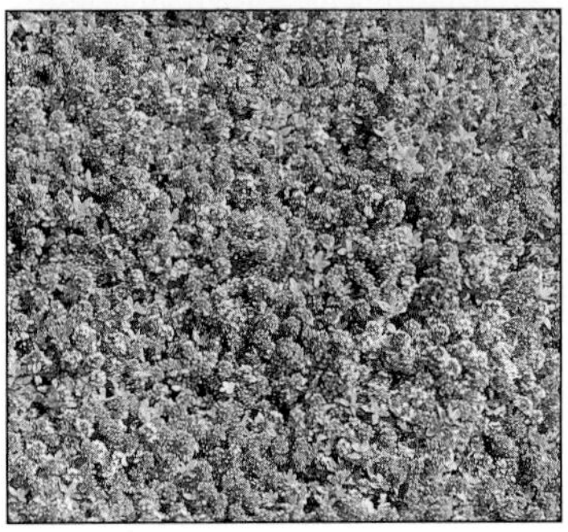

Thymus polytrichus

Thymus polytrichus 'Porlock'

Thymus pannonicus

This species usually behaves as an herbaceous perennial, although in mild climates it may be evergreen. It is a low spreader or trailer with pink flowers and is native to southwestern and central Europe. **ZONES 5–10.**

Thymus polytrichus

syn. *Thymus praecox*

CREEPING THYME, WILD THYME

This evergreen creeping perennial grows to ½ in (12 mm) high, with prostrate woody stems covered in minute oval to oblong aromatic green leaves. The flowers are produced in clusters in summer; they are small, 2-lipped, and may be purple, mauve or white. This species is fully frost hardy. **'Porlock'** has rounded dark green leaves and fragrant pink flowers. **ZONES 5–10.**

Thymus pseudolanuginosus

syn. *Thymus lanuginosus*

WOOLLY THYME

This very low-growing, frost-hardy thyme, which reaches only 1 in (25 mm) in height, accentuates the contour of the

Thymus herba-barona

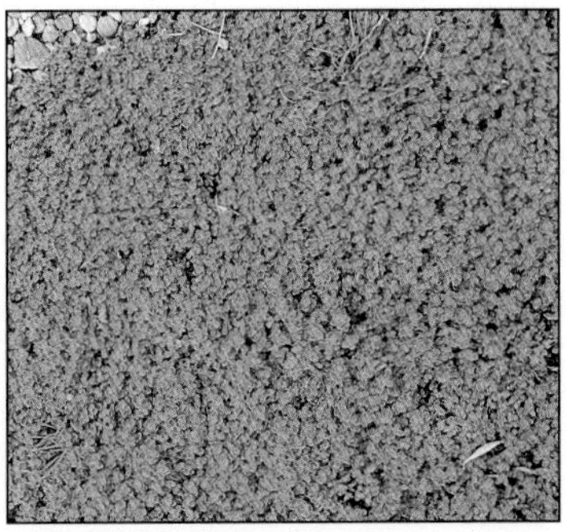

Thymus pseudolanuginosus

Thymus doerfleri

Thymus mastichina

ground below as it spreads to form broad, oval mats of densely hairy, gray-green foliage. It bears terminal spikes of tubular, 2-lipped, pale pink flowers in mid-summer and has tiny leaves. **ZONES 3–9.**

Thymus serpyllum

WILD THYME, CREEPING THYME, MOTHER OF THYME

This native of Europe grows to a height of 10 in (25 cm) and spread of 18 in (45 cm), forming a useful ground cover. Its creeping stem is woody and branching, and the scented, bright green leaves are elliptical to lanceolate. The bluish purple flowers are small and tubular with 2 lips, and are borne in spring and summer in dense terminal whorls. It is very frost hardy and will take moderate foot traffic, but needs replanting every few years to maintain a dense cover. Cultivars include: **'Annie Hall'**, which has rounded leaves and pink flowers; **'Coccineus Minor'**, with crimson-pink flowers; and **'Pink Ripple'**, with bronze-pink flowers. **ZONES 3–9.**

Thymus vulgaris

COMMON THYME

This is the most popular culinary thyme, producing the strongest aromatic leaves. It is a frost hardy subshrub that grows to 12 in (30 cm) high. White to pale purple flowers are produced in summer. The tiny, mid-green leaves are used in vinegars, butters and to flavor a variety of meat or vegetable dishes. Thyme tea is used to aid digestion, sore throats and coughs. **ZONES 7–10.**

Thymus serpyllum

Thymus vulgaris

THYSANOLAENA

TIGER GRASS

The sole species in this genus is a perennial grass from tropical Asia. It forms a large clump of arching stems with narrow, lance-shaped leaves. Its large flower spikes are produced in summer to fall (autumn).

CULTIVATION: Plant *Thysanolaena* species in moist, humus-rich soil and keep moist during the growing season. If allowed to dry out, the foliage may fall—leaving the plant rather sparse. It is only marginally frost hardy. Propagate from seed or by division.

Thysanolaena maxima

At up to 12 ft (3.5 m) tall, this bamboo-like grass is nearly impenetrable in the wild. Its flower panicles are 12–24 in (30–60 cm) long and make a bold display. **ZONES 9–11.**

TIARELLA

FOAMFLOWER

The foamflowers are a genus of 5 species of forest-floor perennials, all of which are native to North America. They resemble their relatives, the heucheras, and can be hybridized with them. They all grow from thick rootstocks, with their decorative leaves growing close to the ground. The airy sprays of small white flowers are borne on bare stems about 12 in (30 cm) tall; pale pink forms occur rarely.

CULTIVATION: Very frost hardy, they are easy to grow in cool-temperate climates, and make good ground covers for a woodland-style garden. Plant in part- to deep shade in moist, well-drained soil. Propagate from seed or by division in early spring.

Thymus serpyllum 'Coccineus Minor'

Thymus serpyllum 'Pink Ripple'

Tiarella polyphylla

Tiarella cordifolia

FOAMFLOWER, COOLWORT

This vigorous spreading evergreen blooms profusely in early to late spring, producing terminal spikes of tiny, creamy white flowers with 5 petals. Its leaves are mostly pale green, lobed and toothed, with dark red marbling and spots; the basal leaves take on an orange-red hue in winter. When in flower, it has a height and spread of 12 in (30 cm) or more. **ZONES 3–9.**

Tiarella polyphylla

This perennial species is native to China and the Himalayas. It grows to a height of 18 in (45 cm) with a similar spread. It has a stout, erect stem and heart-shaped leaves about 2 in (5 cm) in length. In late spring and summer, 5-petalled pink or white flowers are borne in terminal clusters. **ZONES 7–10.**

Tiarella wherryi

An almost evergreen perennial, this slow-growing, clump-forming species reaches 8 in (20 cm) high and wide. The late spring flowers make a decorative mass of soft pink or white star shapes and last quite well when cut. The hairy, green leaves turn crimson in fall (autumn). **ZONES 6–10.**

Thymus serpyllum 'Annie Hall'

Thysanolaena maxima

Tiarella wherryi

Tiarella cordifolia

TIBOUCHINA

LASIANDRA, GLORY BUSH

There are more than 300 species in this genus of evergreen perennials, shrubs, small trees and scrambling climbers from South America. The flowers are large and vivid, commonly purple, pink or white, with 5 satiny petals. They are borne either singly or in clusters at the shoot tips, and sometimes the whole plant is smothered with blooms over several months, usually from late summer to early winter. The flower buds are rounded and fat, while the leaves are simple and hairy, deeply marked with 3 to 7 veins. New growth is often a contrasting reddish bronze, and stems are square; the fruits are capsules.

CULTIVATION: They prefer full sun and do best in light soil with added organic matter and a slightly acidic to neutral pH. Keep plants moist during the growing season. Prune after flowering. They

T

Tibouchina urvilleana

Tibouchina clavata

Tibouchina granulosa

have brittle stems and need shelter from wind; they do not like frost. Propagate from cuttings in late spring or summer.

Tibouchina clavata

This rather straggling species, native to Brazil, grows to 8 ft (2.4 m) tall. Attractive lilac or white flowers are produced in early fall (autumn). The blooms are not very large, but are gathered in elegant open clusters. **ZONES 10–12.**

Tibouchina granulosa

Indigenous to Brazil, this fast-growing species is usually a large shrub 12–15 ft (3.5–4.5 m) in height and spread. It sometimes becomes tree-like, reaching a height of 30–40 ft (9–12 m). The flower clusters are 12 in (30 cm) long and may completely hide the foliage in fall (autumn); each bloom is rose purple to violet or pink and 2 in (5 cm) across. The branching stems are thick and woody. The leaves are lance-shaped to oblong and 6–8 in (15–20 cm) long. They are dark green and shiny on top, bright green and hairy underneath, and hairy along the edges. **ZONES 10–12.**

Tibouchina heteromalla

This evergreen spreading shrub grows to a height of 3 ft (1 m) with a spread of 4 ft (1.2 m). The erect stems rise directly from the base; the 4–6 in (10–15 cm) long leaves are velvety and whitish green on the underside. Five-petalled, violet-petalled flowers are produced in terminal panicles which may be up to 8 in (20 cm) long and 2–3 in (5–8 cm) in diameter. Blooms usually appear mid-summer, but they can extend until late fall (autumn) in warm areas. **ZONES 10–12.**

Tibouchina 'Jules'

This is like a miniature version of *Tibouchina urvilleana.* Its rich purple flowers and velvety green leaves are half the size of *T. urvilleana* and the bush grows to only about 3 ft (1 m) tall. It flowers in late summer. **ZONES 10–11.**

Tibouchina lepidota

Native to Ecuador and Colombia, this leafy shrub usually has a short trunk to 12 ft (3.5 m) high. However, it can become tree-like, growing to 40 ft (12 m) tall with a neat round canopy. The leaves

Tibouchina heteromalla

Tibouchina 'Jules'

are dark green and shiny, oblong to lance-shaped, with 5 main veins and 2 outer minor ones; they are paler and hairy underneath. Its violet to purple flowers are borne in clusters; the flower buds are enclosed by pink silky bracts and the stems have reddish hairs. **'Alstonville'** has particularly vibrant flowers. **ZONES 10–12.**

Tibouchina urvilleana

syns *Lasiandra semidecandra, Tibouchina semidecandra*

PRINCESS FLOWER, GLORY BUSH

This slender-branched species develops a short trunk topped by a bushy rounded crown and reaches 15 ft (4.5 m) in height. The young stems are reddish and slightly hairy, turning brown later. The oval to slightly oblong leaves are 2–4 in (5–10 cm) long, shiny dark green above and slightly hairy below. The rich purple to violet, satiny flowers, 3 in (8 cm) wide with purple stamens, are borne singly or in small groups. The flower buds are large, reddish and hairy. **ZONES 9–12.**

TIGRIDIA

TIGER FLOWER

This genus of the iris family contains about 35 species of cormous plants native to Central and South America. The distinctive flowers inspire admiration for their strikingly spotted centers and 3 bold outer petals in red, orange, pink, yellow, purple or white. They are short lived, usually each lasting only a day, but they make up for this by blooming in succession for weeks during summer.

CULTIVATION: Tigridias are subtropical plants but will tolerate light frosts. In cooler areas, the corms should be lifted and stored during winter or the plants grown in a greenhouse. They need a position in full sun in well-drained soil; water amply in summer. Propagate from seed in spring.

Tigridia pavonia

JOCKEY'S CAP LILY, PEACOCK FLOWER, TIGER FLOWER

This Mexican native blooms in summer. The 6 in (15 cm) triangular flowers are usually red with a yellow center spotted with purple, borne on 24 in (60 cm) stems. The foliage is iris-like, sword-shaped and pleated. **ZONES 8–10.**

TILIA

LIME TREE, LINDEN

From temperate regions of Asia, Europe and North America, this genus consists of 45 species of tall, handsome, deciduous trees, often planted in avenues and streets because they are fast growing and withstand regular heavy pruning and atmospheric pollution. They are generally upright, with thick, buttressed trunks, and have a tendency to sucker. Rounded to heart-shaped leaves, held on thin stalks, briefly turn yellow in fall (autumn). The small, fragrant, cup-shaped cream flowers are borne in clusters in summer; each cluster has a whitish bract which persists and helps to disperse the fruits on the wind. Both flowers and bracts are dried to make linden tea. The fruits are small, round, hard, green berries. Several species are valued for their pale, strong but lightweight wood.

CULTIVATION: Very frost hardy, they do best in cool climates and prefer full sun, neutral, well-drained soil and plenty of water in dry periods. Even quite large trees

Tigridia pavonia

Tibouchina lepidota

T

Tilia 'Petiolaris'

Tilia × *europaea* 'Wratislaviensis'

can be readily transplanted during their winter dormancy. Propagate from seed in fall, from cuttings or by layering; selected forms and hybrids can be grafted in late summer.

Tilia americana
BASSWOOD, AMERICAN LINDEN

This attractive, sturdy tree from eastern-central USA and Canada grows to 120 ft (36 m) tall. It has an erect trunk with smooth gray bark which becomes fissured with age. Its young branches are green and form a compact, narrow crown. The heart-shaped, dull green leaves are up to 6 in (15 cm) long and have toothed edges. Yellowish white, fragrant flowers in pendent clusters appear in summer, followed by small, hairy fruit. **'Redmond'**, a selected form raised in Nebraska in about 1926, has a dense conical habit. **ZONES 3–9.**

Tilia cordata
syn. *Tilia parvifolia*
SMALL-LEAFED LINDEN, LITTLE-LEAF LINDEN

An inhabitant of European woodlands, this species grows to 100 ft (30 m) tall with a dome-shaped crown. Its leathery, round leaves, 2 in (5 cm) across, are bright green on top with pale undersides. Its small flowers are pale yellow and sweetly scented; the fruit are gray. This long-lived species can make a handsome specimen for parks and formal gardens where it has plenty of space. The soft whitish timber is often used for wood carving and musical instruments. **'Greenspire'** is a fast-growing American selection with an upright habit and oval-shaped crown. **'June Bride'** is heavy-flowering with conical growth and glossy leaves. **ZONES 2–9.**

Tilia cordata

Tilia cordata

Tilia × *euchlora*
syn. *Tilia* 'Euchlora'
CRIMEAM LINDEN

This elegant hybrid between *Tilia cordata* and *T. dasystyla* reaches 70 ft (21 m) in height. The leaves are dark green on the upper surface and paler, almost glaucous underneath. It has arching branches, with the lower branches becoming pendulous in maturity. The flowers are said to have a narcotic effect on bees. **ZONES 4–9.**

Tilia × *europaea*
syn. *Tilia* × *vulgaris*
EUROPEAN LINDEN, COMMON LIME TREE

Widely grown in Europe, this handsome, vigorous hybrid between *Tilia cordata* and *T. platyphyllos* grows to 100 ft (30 m) tall. It is characterized by a dense, shapely crown held on a stout trunk that has a strong tendency to sucker. Shoots should be removed from the bur at the base from time to time. The smooth green shoots grow in a distinct zigzag pattern and the bright green, rounded to heart-shaped leaves have toothed edges. Its pale yellow flowers appear among the leaves in early summer; they are sometimes infused and drunk as a tea. The rounded fruit are faintly ribbed. The foliage of **'Wratislaviensis'** is golden yellow when young, maturing to a dark green. **ZONES 3–9.**

Tilia heterophylla
WHITE BASSWOOD

Rarely seen outside its native eastern USA, this species reaches 100 ft (30 m) in height, with a rounded crown supported by a network of smooth branches. The dark green leaves are large, broad and oval, with coarsely toothed edges and pale, hairy undersides. **ZONES 4–9.**

Tilia japonica
JAPANESE LIME

Indigenous to Japan and east China, this species is a distinctive and attractive medium-sized tree with small leaves. It is similar to *Tilia cordata* but the leaves are slightly larger, narrowing to a sharp point. It has a columnar growth habit and the underside of its foliage is blue-green. **ZONES 6–10.**

Tilia americana

Tilia heterophylla

Tilia mongolica
MONGOLIAN LIME

Native to Mongolia and northern China, this 60 ft (18 m) tall tree has a rounded, compact habit and dense twiggy growth with reddish shoots and stalks. The dark green leaves, up to $2\frac{1}{2}$ in (6 cm) long, are similar to ivy and coarsely toothed with 3 to 5 lobes. **ZONES 3–9.**

Tilia 'Petiolaris'
syn. *Tilia petiolaris*
WEEPING SILVER LINDEN, PENDENT SILVER LIME, WEEPING LIME

Possibly no more than a form of *Tilia tomentosa*, this weeping tree reaches 60–80 ft (18–24 m) in height. It has a spreading, conical form which expands with age. The pointed, cordate leaves are 2–4 in (5–10 cm) long, deep green on

Tilia heterophylla

Tilia japonica

top and silver-felted underneath. Creamy yellow flowers bloom in terminal clusters and are followed by bumpy, nut-like seed pods. **ZONES 5–9.**

Tilia platyphyllos
BROAD-LEAFED LINDEN, BIG-LEAF LINDEN

Reaching a height of 80 ft (24 m), this vigorous European species has a straight, rough, gray trunk and a rounded crown spreading to a broad shape. The young shoots are reddish brown and downy; the large, dark green leaves are heart-shaped and bluish underneath. Pale yellow flowers in groups of 3 are followed by hard, pear-shaped, ribbed fruit. In **'Rubra'**, the bark of the young twigs is a vivid red. **ZONES 5–9.**

Tilia tomentosa
SILVER LINDEN, SILVER LIME

This graceful tree native to eastern Europe and Turkey is distinguished by its young shoots, which are pale gray and felted. Growing to 90 ft (27 m) tall, its ascending branches are often pendulous at the tips. Large round leaves, with serrated edges and whitish undersides, seem to shimmer in the wind. The highly fragrant, lime-green flowers, which are borne in summer and are toxic to bees, are followed by rough, oval fruit. This species is tolerant of dry conditions and smog-laden atmospheres. **ZONES 5–9.**

TILLANDSIA
AIR PLANT

This genus contains more than 350 species of evergreen, mainly epiphytic plants, often rosette-forming and some with branching stems and spirally arranged leaves. They are found from southeastern USA to the southernmost tip of South America. These bromeliads are grown for foliage and their unusual flowers, which are usually carried on spikes, heads or panicles and range in color from white to purple and green to red. Plants vary from 2½ in (6 cm) to more than 12 ft (3.5 m) high. Foliage may be gray, green or red-brown and leaves are covered with silver scales. The fruits are small capsules.

CULTIVATION: All species are frost tender. Generally, the stiff, silver-leafed varieties are grown in hardier conditions in full sun, while the softer, green-leafed varieties prefer part-shade. Plant in well-drained sphagnum moss or on slabs of bark or driftwood; equal parts of bark and coarse sand can be used. They are often placed high up in hanging baskets to catch the rising heat. Mist regularly and water moderately in summer; sparingly at other times. Propagate from offsets or by division in spring to summer.

Tillandsia ionantha

Tillandsia bergeri

Tillandsia cyanea

Tillandsia flabellata

Tillandsia lindenii

Tillandsia aeranthos

From the Latin meaning 'air blooming', this epiphyte is often confused with its close relative *Tillandsia bergeri*. It is a bromeliad with dark purple to red flowers. The plant is rosette-shaped with a spread of 4–6 in (10–15 cm). The leaves are narrow and taper to a point. **ZONES 9–11.**

Tillandsia argentea

This small bromeliad grows 4–6 in (10–15 cm) wide, with a bulbous base and heavily scaled, silver, thread-like leaves. The leaves are arranged spirally around the short stem so that they resemble an onion. The red to violet flowers, held almost perpendicularly, are offset by red stems and red and green bracts. It grows best when mounted on trees or driftwood in filtered sunlight. Ensure good air circulation and a moderately humid atmosphere. **ZONES 10–12.**

Tillandsia bergeri

Native to Argentina, this epiphyte grows in thick clumps with an average height of 4 in (10 cm) and a spread of 6 in (15 cm) and requires frequent watering. Its leaf blades are slightly channelled and thickly scaled. The flowers grow to 1½ in (35 mm) long with blue petals that turn to pink as they fade. Both leaves and flowers are arranged spirally. **ZONES 9–11.**

Tillandsia caulescens

This species from Bolivia and Peru grows to 18 in (45 cm) high. It has compact, spiralled, gray-green foliage, red bracts and white to purple flowers; these are 1 in (25 mm) long with recurved tips to the petals. In its native habitat, it is epiphytic on trees or cliffs at high altitudes. It is easy to grow. **ZONES 10–12.**

Tillandsia cyanea
PINK QUILL

The dense rosettes of grass-like, arching leaves on this species are usually deep green, but often reddish brown when young. In summer to fall (autumn) the spectacular, paddle-shaped flowerheads rise on tall stems from among the foliage. They consist of overlapping pink or red bracts with deep violet-blue flowers emerging. It needs maximum humidity and is best grown in a compost of tree fern fiber, peat and sand. **ZONES 9–11.**

Tillandsia flabellata

Native to the cloud forests of Mexico and Guatemala, this is a very decorative plant when in flower. The foliage is rosette-shaped and either red or green; the bracts are pointed and bright red. Its long, narrow bloom spikes grow upright in a fan-like arrangement to a height of 15 in (38 cm). The flowers are blue with petals up to 2 in (5 cm) long, fused into a tube. It needs a moderately humid atmosphere. **ZONES 10–12.**

Tillandsia ionantha

This small stemless bromeliad from Mexico usually grows in thick clumps. It has a tight, bulb-like rosette with narrow, densely scaly, triangular leaves. When in flower, the inner rosette complements the white-tipped, violet blooms by turning brilliant red. It likes moderately damp conditions and its size makes it suitable for terrariums; it can be grown outdoors in summer. **ZONES 9–11.**

Tillandsia lindenii

This species grows in a typical rosette. The arching leaves are thin, smooth, pointed, and marked with red-brown lines. In fall (autumn), a large flower spike of crimson or pink-tinted bracts overlaps dense clusters of pansy-shaped, deep blue or purple-blue flowers rising just above the leaves. **ZONES 10–12.**

Tillandsia aeranthos

Tillandsia argentea

Tilia platyphyllos 'Rubra'

Tilia platyphyllos

Tillandsia caulescens

Tillandsia pruinosa

This small, stemless epiphytic bromeliad grows 3–8 in (8–20 cm) high. The green leaves have furry white scales and are strongly channeled. The short bracts are held upright and are pink when the plant is in flower; petals are blue, tubular and 1½ in (35 mm) long. This decorative plant is easily grown in cultivation and needs infrequent watering. **ZONES 9–11.**

Tillandsia stricta

syns *Tillandsia krameri, T. meridionalis, T. stricta* var. *krameri*

This epiphytic species may have a short stem or be stemless, and usually grows in thick clumps. The foliage is green and covered in silver-gray scales on both sides. The flowers form a rigid, upright, sometimes one-sided rosette; the bracts are bright carmine and the petals blue with flared tips. It prefers a moderately damp and shady position, but is easy to grow. When in flower, it is one of the most beautiful species of the entire genus. **ZONES 9–11.**

Tillandsia usneoides

SPANISH MOSS, GRAY BEARD

This remarkable epiphytic and rootless plant hangs in pendulous festoons from the branches. Inconspicuous, greenish yellow or pale blue flowers appear in summer and are almost hidden among the foliage. Repeatedly branched stems bear fine, curled leaves, which are densely covered in silvery white scales. Spanish moss is widely distributed from the Deep South of the USA (including the Louisiana bayous) to northern South America. **ZONES 8–11.**

TIPUANA

This legume genus is made up of just a single species of tree from subtropical South America. It is evergreen in warm, wet climates, deciduous in cooler or drier climates. Clusters of cassia-like flowers are borne at the branch tips. The pinnate leaves consist of many small leaflets. They make good shade trees and are grown for their attractive appearance and blooms.

CULTIVATION: It needs full sun and a mild to warm climate. Prune young specimens to shape in winter. Fast growing, it thrives in deep, well-drained soil. Propagate from fresh scarified seed in spring.

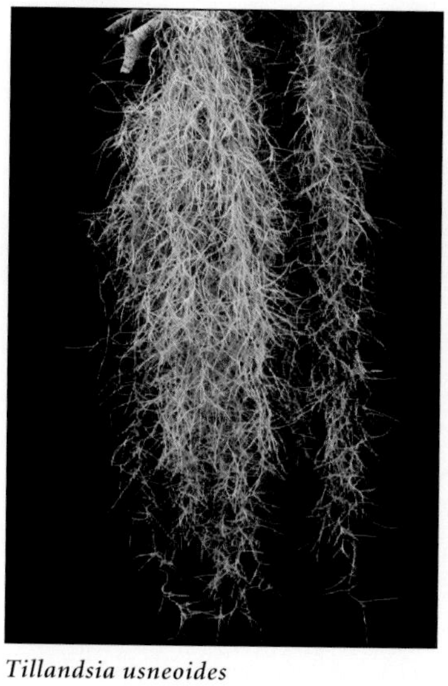

Tillandsia usneoides

Titanopsis calcarea

Tipuana tipu

syn. *Tipuana speciosa*

TIPU TREE, PRIDE OF BOLIVIA

This attractive shade tree with spreading branches and an irregular crown reaches a height of 50–70 ft (15–21 m) with a similar spread. The dark green leaves are up to 10 in (25 cm) long, composed of 15 to 19 oblong leaflets. The yellow to orange flowers, arranged in terminal clusters, bloom for several weeks in spring, followed in fall (autumn) and winter by brown, winged pods 2–4 in (5–10 cm) long. **ZONES 9–12.**

TITANOPSIS

Included among the southern African succulents known as 'living stones', this genus consists of 6 species with highly succulent foliage. They are small rosette plants, each shoot composed of 6 to 8 leaves and developing into small clumps. The thick, gray leaves are spatula-shaped to triangular, and often have a dense covering of ochre to light brown, warty tubercles. Bright yellow to orange daisy-like flowers up to 1 in (25 mm) in diameter open after rain in the wild or in fall (autumn) in cultivation.

CULTIVATION: Plant in very free-draining, gritty soil in full sun; keep dry in winter, water sparingly as the new leaves appear. While most species tolerate light frosts, they quickly rot in cold, wet conditions. Propagate from seed in summer or fall.

Tillandsia pruinosa

Tithonia diversifolia

Tipuana tipu

Titanopsis calcarea

JEWEL PLANT

Found in the western Cape region, this species has 1 in (25 mm) long gray-green leaves. Small tubercles cover the foliage tips and may be white, gray, bluish or light red. **ZONES 9–11.**

TITHONIA

MEXICAN SUNFLOWER

This genus of 10 species consists mainly of annuals, biennials and perennials, *Tithonia diversifolia* being the only one that becomes a true shrub. Originating in Central America and the West Indies, they are related to sunflowers and bear large, vivid yellow, orange or scarlet daisy-like flowerheads in summer and fall (autumn). The leaves are often hairy on the undersides and sharply lobed.

CULTIVATION: Marginally frost hardy, these plants thrive in hot, dry conditions, but require a plentiful supply of water. They grow best in well-drained soil and need full sun; they may need staking. Deadhead regularly to promote a longer flowering season and prune hard after flowering to encourage new growth. Propagate from seed sown under glass in late winter or early spring.

Tithonia diversifolia

TREE MARIGOLD

A very large, robust perennial or shrub growing to 15 ft (4.5 m) tall, this species has large, oval to oblong, hairy leaves with lobed margins. It is best suited to the rear of a shrub border where it can supply visual impact during the late summer months with its large, orange-yellow flowerheads. Dead flowers may be difficult to remove because of its height; the seed heads themselves are of interest. **ZONES 9–11.**

Tithonia rotundifolia

This bulky annual needs plenty of room in the garden as it can easily grow to 5 ft (1.5 m) tall with a spread of 3 ft (1 m). Its leaves are heart-shaped. It is a great plant for hot color schemes, both in the garden and as a cut flower, with its 4 in (10 cm) wide, zinnia-like flowers of orange or scarlet. **'Torch'** bears bright orange or red flowerheads and grows to 3 ft (1 m). **ZONES 8–11.**

Tithonia rotundifolia

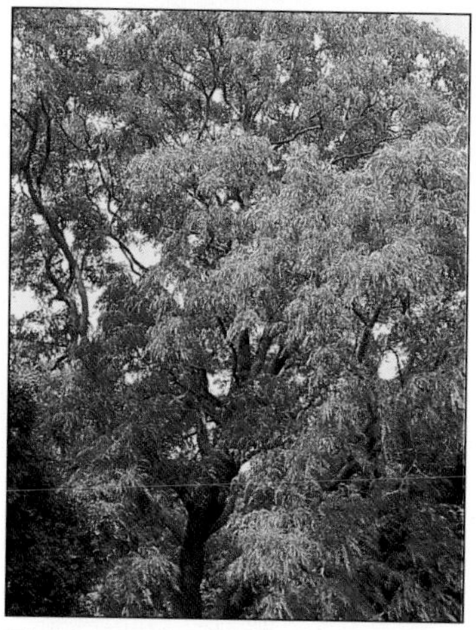

Tipuana tipu

TOLMIEA

PIGGYBACK PLANT, YOUTH-ON-AGE, MOTHER-OF-THOUSANDS

A relative of *Heuchera* and *Saxifraga*, this genus consists of a single species of evergreen perennial from west-coastal North America, from northern California to Alaska. Its dark green leaves are very like those of some heucheras, heart-shaped and coarsely toothed—but the plant's most distinctive feature is the production of a plantlet at the point where the leaf joins its stalk, on many of the leaves at least; as the leaves age and droop, these plantlets take root and grow, allowing the plant to spread quite extensively over the shaded forest floor which is its normal habitat. The slender, erect flowering stems bear inconspicuous flowers, again very like those of some heucheras.

CULTIVATION: For many years it has been popular as an indoor plant, as well as being useful as a ground cover for shade in regions of mild, moist climate. It adapts particularly well to being planted in hanging baskets, making a ball of luxuriant foliage. Keep soil moist but not soggy and water sparingly in winter. Feed every 2 months in the warmer season with half-strength soluble fertilizer. Attacks by spider mites cause browning of the leaves, requiring immediate treatment. It is easily propagated by detaching well-developed plantlets.

Tolmiea menziesii

Toona sinensis

Toona sinensis 'Flamingo'

Tolmiea menziesii

The pale green leaves of this perennial are dull and somewhat hairy, 2–4 in (5–10 cm) long, and arise in dense clumps from short surface rhizomes. In late spring and early summer the plant produces sparse flowering stems 12–24 in (30–60 cm) tall bearing dull red-brown flowers with tiny narrow petals. **ZONES 7–10.**

TOONA

Previously included in the closely related genus *Cedrela*, the 4 or 5 species of deciduous and evergreen trees in this genus are found naturally from China and the Himalayas to eastern Australia. They are valued for their fine, often aromatic timber. Attractive pinnate leaves have many oval to lance-shaped leaflets.
CULTIVATION: *Toona* species grow best in moist climates with full sun and a deep, rich soil; water regularly. Their cold tolerance depends on their country of origin; *Toona ciliata* and *T. sinensis* thrive in subtropical climates, with shelter from wind. Propagate from fresh seed or suckers in late summer. Tip moth larvae and mites attack some species.

Toona ciliata

Toona ciliata

Toona ciliata

syns *Cedrela toona, Toona australis*

TOON, AUSTRALIAN RED CEDAR

This variable species extends over most of the range of the genus, but its beautiful reddish, aromatic timber reaches its finest quality in subtropical eastern Australian rainforests, where most larger trees of the species were felled in the nineteenth century; it was used as a substitute for imported mahogany *(Swietenia)* for furniture and interior fittings. It grows to over 100 ft (30 m) tall and the straight trunk is up to 6 ft (1.8 m) in diameter, the bark is dark gray and broken into small squarish scales. The crown is spreading and the foliage turns yellowish in fall (autumn), while the new foliage in late spring is bronzy red. Growth is fast in the young stages but the tree's growth is usually checked by the larvae of the cedar tip moth, or heavy infestations of spider mite on the leaflets. **ZONES 9–12.**

Toona sinensis

syn. *Cedrela sinensis*

CHINESE TOON

Occurring in eastern and southern China and Southeast Asia, this species is also very variable, and only some forms have found their way into cultivation. It may become a large, single-trunked tree, but is also seen as a clump of stems to about 30 ft (9 m) high. The leaves are up to 24 in (60 cm) long, with dark green leaflets and a reddish central stalk. The young shoots are used as a vegetable in China, smelling strongly of onions when broken. In recent years there has appeared in Western gardens the striking cultivar **'Flamingo'**, which has brilliant pink spring foliage turning cream and finally green; first noticed in Australia and New Zealand, it spreads widely by root suckers, sending up slender stems to no more than 20 ft (6 m) high. **ZONES 6–11.**

TORENIA

WISHBONE FLOWER

This genus of 40 to 50 species of erect to spreading, bushy annuals and perennials comes from tropical African and Asian woodlands. They have oval to lance-shaped, entire or toothed, opposite leaves. In summer, they bear racemes of trumpet-shaped, 2-lipped flowers with 2-lobed upper lips and 3-lobed lower lips.
CULTIVATION: Torenias prefer a warm, frost-free climate. In cooler climates, they should not be planted out until the last frost. They make attractive pot plants and in cool climates are grown in greenhouses. Grow in fertile, well-drained soil in part-shade in a sheltered position. Pinch out the growing shoots of young plants to encourage a bushy habit. Propagate from seed in spring.

Torenia fournieri

BLUEWINGS

This branching annual has light to dark green ovate or elliptical leaves with toothed edges. Frost tender, it grows fairly rapidly to a height of 12 in (30 cm) and a spread of 8 in (20 cm). Its flowers, borne in summer and early fall (autumn), are pansy-like and a deep purplish blue, turning abruptly paler nearer the center, and with a touch of yellow. Red, pink and white varieties are also available. **ZONES 9–12.**

TORREYA

The yew-like evergreen coniferous trees and shrubs of this small genus of 6 or so species occur naturally in eastern Asia and North America. The spiny pointed leaves are spirally arranged on twisted shoots and are often paler on the undersides. The fruits are oval drupes which contain a single seed.
CULTIVATION: They adapt to a wide variety of soils, from chalk to heavy clay and poor sand, and are reasonably cold tolerant provided they are planted in a sheltered position. All demand adequate water during dry spells. Propagate from seed or by grafting.

Torreya californica

CALIFORNIA NUTMEG

This neat, erect tree grows to a height of 70 ft (21 m); conical in habit, its horizontal branches sweep the ground in maturity. The dark green, needle-like leaves, about $2\frac{1}{2}$ in (6 cm) long, are yellowish green beneath. Male and female organs are borne on separate trees; woody, olive-like fruit, similar to the nutmeg of commerce, follow on female trees. It is moderately frost hardy. **ZONES 7–10.**

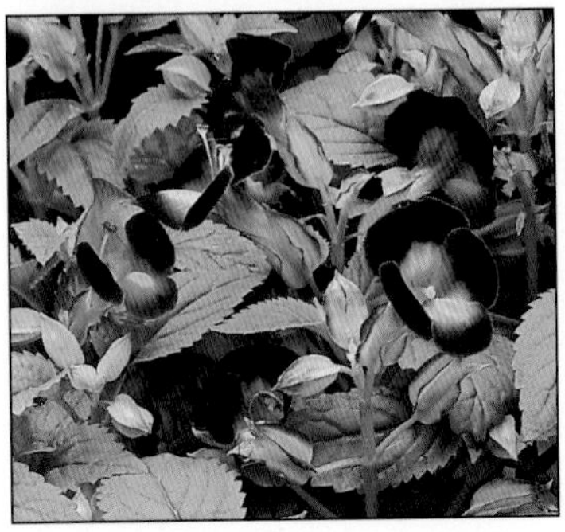

Torenia fournieri

Torreya nucifera

NAYA

Native to Japan, this attractive, symmetrical conifer reaches about 70 ft (21 m) in height. Its stiff, spiky, yew-like foliage is dark gray-green and pleasantly pungent when crushed. The bark is a smooth reddish brown. The fruit are edible green drupes which ripen to purple with a white bloom; they contain a rich oil. **ZONES 7–10.**

TOWNSENDIA

This North American genus comprises around 20 species of annual, biennial and perennial daisies. They form mats of narrow or spatula-shaped leaves, often silvery to gray-green in color. Most species are less than 6 in (15 cm) high and less than 18 in (45 cm) wide. The $\frac{1}{2}$–$1\frac{1}{2}$ in (12–35 mm) diameter flowers, which open in spring and summer, resemble a single-flowered Michaelmas daisy. They are white, pink, mauve or purple, with a yellow central disc.
CULTIVATION: Most species are extremely hardy alpines that prefer to grow in well-drained soil that stays moist in summer. Plant in sun or morning shade. Despite their hardiness, they tend to be short lived and often do better in alpine houses, where they are protected from cold, wet conditions that may cause rotting. Propagate from seed.

Townsendia exscapa

Probably the most widely cultivated species and a favorite of rockery enthusiasts, this little white-flowered, silver-leafed

Townsendia exscapa

Torreya californica

T

daisy occurs naturally from central Canada to Mexico. It demands perfectly drained soil and shelter from winter rain, protection it receives in the wild from a covering of snow. **ZONES 3–9.**

Townsendia hookeri
EASTER DAISY

From central USA and nearby parts of Canada, this species forms a small, tufted clump of silky foliage. Its flowers, slightly over $\frac{1}{2}$ in (12 mm) wide, have white petals with pink undersides. **ZONES 4–9.**

Townsendia leptotes

The leaves of this western USA species are among the larger in the genus, up to $2\frac{1}{2}$ in (6 cm) long. The flowers, just under 1 in (25 mm) wide, are white with a hint of blue or pink. **ZONES 7–10.**

TOXICODENDRON

The exact status of this genus and the closely related *Rhus* is somewhat confused. *Toxicodendron* is made up of trees, shrubs and root-climbers. The milky or resinous sap of all species is highly caustic and an irritant to the skin; mere contact with the leaves can cause a severe allergic reaction, sometimes life threatening. For this reason, cultivation is prohibited in some places. The genus includes the noxious *T. radicans* (the poison ivy of North America). Toxicodendrons occur naturally in temperate and subtropical regions of North America and East Asia; several are grown for their brilliant fall (autumn) foliage. The leaves are ash-like, with a few to many paired leaflets. The small flowers are arranged in clusters, with separate male and female flowers. The fruits are small, rounded, gray, slightly flattened drupes with dry flesh.
CULTIVATION: These plants prefer full sun, and adapt to most well-drained soils. Propagate from seed in summer or cuttings.

Toxicodendron radicans
syn. *Rhus radicans*
POISON IVY, MARKWEED

This shrub or vine has variably sized compound leaves usually with 3 toothed, elliptical leaflets, but they can have up to 7 leaflets and they may be smooth-edged. This variability makes identification difficult, which is very unfortunate because the plant causes severe skin irritations if handled. The flower panicle is up to 4 in (10 cm) long. Subspecies with differing leaf shapes and degrees of hardiness can be found throughout North America, south to Guatemala. **ZONES 5–10.**

Toxicodendron succedaneum
syn. *Rhus succedanea*
RHUS TREE, WAX TREE, POISON SUMAC

This East Asian deciduous shrub or small tree grows 20–25 ft (6–8 m) tall, and has a single trunk and a spreading crown. The large, compound leaves have 9 to 15 oblong, slightly drooping leaflets; they are shiny green and turn vibrant scarlet and orange in fall (autumn), even in warm-temperate climates. In summer, clusters of inconspicuous yellowish green flowers are followed by large clusters of black to brown drupes that persist for a long time. A wax is derived from the berries and a lacquer from the substance that exudes from the stem. **ZONES 5–10.**

TRACHELIUM

This is a genus of small perennials that are useful for rock gardens and mixed borders; some are suitable for alpine houses. Several species are normally grown as annuals and make excellent cut flowers.
CULTIVATION: These plants are fully to moderately frost hardy, but some may need protection in winter. All species resent damp conditions and must be grown in a very well drained soil. Propagate from seed in early to mid-spring or cuttings, also in spring.

Trachelium caeruleum
THROATWORT

This moderately fast-growing, erect species from the Mediterranean makes a tuft of serrated, oval leaves with slender leafy stems. These bear dense clusters of rounded flowerheads with tiny tubular pink, blue or white flowers in summer, rather like valerian but with more prominent styles. It was once used medicinally for throat infections. **ZONES 9–11.**

TRACHELOSPERMUM

This genus of about 20 evergreen species from east to Southeast Asia, with one from the USA, consists of twining or root-clinging shrubs suitable for all but the coldest climates. They bear sweet-scented jasmine-like flowers in late summer. Both the stems and leaves exude a milky sap when cut.
CULTIVATION: Moderately frost hardy, they will grow in any fertile, well-drained soil in sun or part-shade. Prune congested or straggly branches in fall (autumn). Propagate from seed in spring, by layering in summer or from cuttings in late summer or fall.

Trachelospermum asiaticum

This species from Japan and Korea grows to a height of 20 ft (6 m) or more with a similar spread. The oval leaves are 1–2 in (2.5–5 cm) long, dark green and glossy. The fragrant flowers, borne in summer, are creamy white with a buff yellow center that fades to yellow. More compact in its habit than *Trachelospermum jasminoides* and with smaller leaves and flowers, it will grow prostrate on the ground or cling to a wall, making a dense foliage cover in either case. **ZONES 7–11.**

Trachelospermum jasminoides

Trachelospermum jasminoides
syn. *Rhynchospermum jasminoides*
CONFEDERATE JASMINE, STAR JASMINE

Valued for its perfumed, star-shaped flowers, this attractive evergreen, twining climber from China grows up to 20 ft (6 m) tall. It has lance-shaped leaves, and hanging clusters of white flowers are produced in summer. This plant does best in a sunny position. Although slow growing during the early stages, it will flourish once established and can be trained on pillars, pergolas and arches. It can also be used as a ground cover. **ZONES 8–11.**

TRACHYCARPUS
WINDMILL PALM, FAN PALM

This genus is made up of 6 species of highly ornamental palms bearing large, fan-shaped leaves. They are valued for their ability to tolerate cooler climates than most palms. Indigenous to southern China and the Himalayas, they often occur at high altitudes. They are small to medium trees, and their trunks are usually covered with coarse, shaggy fiber. The dark green fronds are divided into narrow, pointed segments and can be up to 5 ft (1.5 m) across. Small yellowish flowers, borne in summer, are followed by dark-colored berries.
CULTIVATION: Provided adequate moisture is available, these palms will adapt to any free-draining soil in part-shade or full sun. Protect plants from cold winds, especially when young. These palms are shallow-rooted and can be transplanted quite easily. Windmill palms make excellent tub specimens for patios and larger greenhouses. Propagate from seed.

Trachycarpus fortunei
CHINESE FAN PALM, CHUSAN PALM, WINDMILL PALM

Moderately frost hardy, this remarkable palm has been cultivated in Europe for 160 years, where it is prized for its exotic appearance and tolerance of cold. It reaches 30 ft (9 m) tall and the trunk is swathed in brownish fiber. The leaves are held on long stalks and are dark green above, blue-green below; dead leaves tend to persist as a 'skirt' on the tree. Dense, showy clusters of small yellow flowers precede the marble-sized, dark blue berries, which have a coating of whitish wax. **ZONES 8–11.**

Trachelospermum asiaticum

Trachycarpus taki

Very similar to *Trachycarpus fortunei*, this species comes from the western Himalayas where it grows in damp oak forests. It is compact and slow growing with a shorter trunk than *T. fortunei*, seldom exceeding 20 ft (6 m), and covered in brown fibres. It bears 30 to 40 dark green fronds with narrow segments. The inflorescence is branched with white flowers; the fruit are kidney-shaped and purplish. **ZONES 9–11.**

TRACHYMENE
BLUE LACE FLOWER

From Australia and the western Pacific come the 12 species of annuals and perennials that make up this genus. They develop into a mat of branching decumbent stems (ascending then bending to spread along the ground). In summer they bear 2 in (5 cm) wide umbels of white or dusky blue flowers reminiscent of the European *Scabiosa*. The light green to gray-green leaves may be finely divided, narrow and linear or lobed, and up to 4 in (10 cm) long.
CULTIVATION: Plant in a sunny position with moist, well-drained soil. The flowering stems often need supporting with canes. Hardiness varies with the species, but few will stand anything but light frosts. Propagate annuals from seed in spring; perennials from seed, cuttings, or by layering.

Toxicodendron succedaneum

Trachycarpus fortunei

Trachymene coerulea
syn. *Didiscus coeruleus*
BLUE LACE FLOWER

This branching annual is moderately fast growing and marginally frost hardy. It reaches a height of 18 in (45 cm) with a spread of 8 in (20 cm). The pale green leaves are deeply divided. In summer, spherical heads of tiny blue to mauve flowers are produced. They make very good cut flowers. **ZONES 9–12.**

TRACHYSTEMON

Two species of coarse, hairy perennials related to borage make up this genus from open woodlands in eastern Europe and the mountains of the Caucasus. They make good, weed-suppressing ground cover in moist, less manicured parts of the garden but because they can spread aggressively they are usually only seen in larger gardens.

CULTIVATION: Although these very frost-hardy plants will grow satisfactorily in almost any soil, they look best in leaf-rich, moisture-retentive yet free-draining soil in part- or dappled shade. Propagate from seed sown in fall (autumn), in a cold frame where winters are cold, or by division in early spring.

Trachystemon orientalis

This species makes big patches of wavy edged, heart-shaped leaves at ground level with smaller, rounded or oval leaves along the flowering stems. The leaves are hairy and dark green. In spring, blue-purple flowers each ½ in (12 mm) wide appear on hairy, few-branched stems. The stamens are black and are joined to form a small, protruding cone. Plants grow up to 24 in (60 cm) tall and spread rapidly. **ZONES 7–10.**

TRADESCANTIA
syns *Rhoeo, Setcreasea, Zebrina*
SPIDERWORT

This genus consists of 50 or more species of perennials, some of them evergreen, from North and South America. Some are rather weedy, but the creeping species (wandering jew) make useful ground covers and are grown for their attractive foliage. Some of the upright species are cherished for their pure blue flowers, a color not easy to find for the late-summer garden. Most of the trailing types are rather frost tender and are usually grown as greenhouse pot plants, except in mild-winter climates where they make good ground cover—admired for their richly toned foliage.

CULTIVATION: Grow in full sun or part-shade in fertile, moist to dry soil. Cut back ruthlessly when they become straggly. Propagate by division or from tip cuttings in spring, summer or fall (autumn).

Tradescantia cerinthoides

Tradescantia fluminensis 'Variegata'

T., Andersoniana Group 'J. C. Weguelin'

T., Andersoniana Group 'Red Cloud'

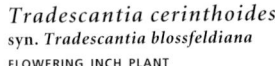

Tradescantia, Andersoniana Group 'Jazz'

Tradescantia, Andersoniana Group 'Alba'

Tradescantia sillamontana

Tradescantia pallida 'Purple Heart'

Tradescantia, Andersoniana Group

This group of hybrids covers a range of plants formerly listed under ***Tradescantia × andersoniana*** or ***T. virginiana***. They are mainly low-growing perennials with fleshy, strap-like leaves and heads of 3-petalled flowers. Although the foliage clump seldom exceeds 18 in (45 cm) high, the flower stems can reach 24 in (60 cm). There are many hybrids in a range of white, mauve, pink and purple flower shades. Those of **'Alba'** are white; **'J. C. Weguelin'** has lavender-blue flowers; **'Jazz'** has magenta flowers; and **'Red Cloud'** is cerise-red. **ZONES 7–10.**

Tradescantia cerinthoides
syn. *Tradescantia blossfeldiana*
FLOWERING INCH PLANT

Native to southeastern Brazil, this species has glossy deep green, oval leaves up to 6 in (15 cm) long that are purple and hairy on the undersides. From spring to fall (autumn) it bears heads of purple-pink flowers. It is a sprawling plant of up to about 24 in (60 cm) in height. **ZONES 7–11.**

Tradescantia fluminensis
syn. *Tradescantia albiflora*
WANDERING JEW

This is a frost-tender, evergreen perennial with trailing rooting stems and oval

Tradescantia, Andersoniana Group hybrid

Tradescantia zebrina

Tradescantia spathacea 'Vittata'

fleshy leaves about 1.5 in (35 mm) long that clasp the stem. The leaves are a glossy green with purple undersides. Tiny white flowers are produced intermittently, enclosed in leaf-like bracts. It is invasive. **'Variegata'** has glossy green leaves irregularly striped with white, cream and yellow; they are tinged with purple on the undersides. **ZONES 9–12.**

Tradescantia pallida
syn. *Setcreasea purpurea*

This species from eastern Mexico forms a dense clump of foliage and has small pink flowers in summer. The slightly succulent, lance-shaped, 3–6 in (8–15 cm) long, leaves often develop red tints if grown in full sun. **'Purple Heart'** (syn. 'Purpurea') has purple foliage. **ZONES 8–11.**

Tradescantia sillamontana
syns *Tradescantia pexata, T. velutina*

This evergreen erect perennial has oval, stem-clasping leaves that are densely covered in fine white hairs. It produces clusters of small purplish pink flowers in spring and summer. It has a height and spread of 12 in (30 cm) and is frost tender. **ZONES 9–11.**

Tradescantia spathacea
syns *Rhoeo discolor, R. spathacea*
BOAT LILY, MOSES-IN-THE-CRADLE

This evergreen, clump-forming, frost-tender species reaches 18 in (45 cm) high and 10 in (25 cm) wide. It has a short stem bearing a rosette of fleshy, lance-shaped leaves up to 12 in (30 cm) long. The leaves are glossy green with purple undersides. Tiny white flowers, held in leaf-like bracts, are produced throughout the year. **'Vittata'** has yellow-striped, glossy green leaves. **ZONES 9–11.**

Tradescantia zebrina
syn. *Zebrina pendula*
SILVER INCH PLANT

This evergreen mat-forming perennial has bluish green leaves with 2 broad silver bands and tinged with purple on the undersides. The flowers are pink to violet-blue and are borne in spring and summer. It will grow to a height of 6 in (15 cm) and is frost tender. **'Purpusii'** is a trailer with purple foliage and pink flowers. **'Quadricolor'** has leaves striped with green, pink, red and white. Its tiny pink flowers are also produced mainly in spring and summer. **ZONES 9–12.**

TRAGOPOGON

Widely distributed over Europe and temperate Asia, this genus consists of over 100 species of annuals, biennials and perennials belonging to the daisy family. They have solitary or sparsely branched stems, grass-like leaves and terminal, star-shaped flowerheads that are followed by large heads of thistle down.
CULTIVATION: Most species are frost hardy and adaptable to most soils. All prefer a sunny position. Propagate from seed sown in spring.

Tragopogon dubius
GOATSBEARD

This European species is an erect biennial herb that grows to 3 ft (1 m) tall. It has basal grass-like leaves that half sheathe the base of the stem. The lemon-yellow, star-shaped flowerheads open in the morning and close during the day. **ZONES 5–10.**

Tragopogon porrifolius
SALSIFY, OYSTER PLANT

This plant is valued for its edible white tap roots. It prefers a light soil, free from stones, and grows best in temperate climates. Sow the large seeds in lots of 3 in spring. Keep 8 in (20 cm) between the groups and 12 in (30 cm) between the rows. Mulch with compost to keep weeds down and water to maintain moisture. Harvest the root from fall (autumn) onwards. It can be baked, roasted, boiled or made into soup. The flowerheads are pinkish mauve in color and borne on hollow stems. This species is fairly pest and disease free, and is often grown as a companion plant. **ZONES 5–10.**

TRAPA
WATER CHESTNUT

This genus of aquatic perennials includes some 15 species found from central Europe to East Asia and Africa. The lower or submerged leaves are attached directly to the stem and are cleft at the tips. The diamond-shaped floating leaves have toothed edges and are around $1\frac{1}{2}$ in (35 mm) wide, with fibrous roots below. The small flowers have 4 white petals with 4 green sepals. They are followed by 4-spined, nut-like fruits.
CULTIVATION: These plants are easy to cultivate in still water at the edge of rivers or streams and in any pond that does not freeze solid. A position in full sun is best. Most species are very frost hardy

Tragopogon dubius

and easily propagated from seed or by division in spring. They are considered a noxious weed in some areas.

Trapa natans
JESUIT'S NUT, WATER CALTROP

This widespread annual aquatic plant occurs naturally in tropical Africa and from central Europe to eastern Asia. It has submerged, root-like feathery leaves and rosettes of almost triangular floating leaves with inflated leaf stalks. The white flowers, borne in summer, are followed by 4-angled, spiny black fruit up to 2 in (5 cm) across. **ZONES 5–10.**

TREVESIA

Members of the aralia family, the 12 species of shrubs and trees in this genus are found in the Himalayas, southern China and Southeast Asia. They form clumps of erect, often prickly stems clothed with large palmate leaves that are palmately lobed or dissected. Large inflorescences of small cream flowers form at the stem tips in summer.
CULTIVATION: Apart form being frost tender, they only require a moist, humus-rich soil and reliable moisture to thrive. They are propagated from cuttings or seed and small plants can sometimes be divided.

Trevesia palmata

This small evergreen tree from tropical Asia grows to a height of 20 ft (6 m) with a spread of about 6 ft (1.8 m). It has an erect, slender trunk. The large, glossy leaves are up to 24 in (60 cm) wide and may be either entire or lobed; new leaves are quite prickly. The greenish white flowers have 8 to 12 petals and are produced in clusters in spring. This species is frost tender and is often grown as an indoor pot plant in cool areas. **'Micholitzii'** is the form commonly grown, known as the snowflake plant on account of the snowflake pattern of dissection of its large leaves. **ZONES 10–12.**

TRICHILIA

This genus includes about 300 species of tropical and subtropical trees and shrubs, mostly from the Americas, but with a few species found in southern and eastern Africa. The large, compound leaves are alternate; the leaflets untoothed. Male and female flowers are borne in sprays in the leaf axils. The fruits are about $1\frac{1}{2}$ in (35 mm) across and contain several black seeds almost covered by a scarlet, fleshy aril. Oil

Trevesia palmata

Trevesia palmata 'Micholitzii'

Trichilia emetica

Trichodiadema bulbosum

Trichodiadema intonsum

Trichostema lanatum

derived from the fruits have a number of uses in traditional medicine in the trees' native countries.
CULTIVATION: Suitable only for subtropical or tropical areas, *Trichilia* species prefer moist, humus-rich soil and will not tolerate drought. Propagate from seed or summer cuttings.

Trichilia emetica
RED ASH, NATAL MAHOGANY

This handsome evergreen shade tree is indigenous to southern Africa and is widely seen in warm, humid areas. It grows to 30 ft (9 m) tall with a rounded, spreading crown and brownish gray bark. The leaves have 7 to 11 leaflets and are dark green, with shiny upper surfaces and paler undersides. In summer, small creamy white, fragrant, bell-shaped flowers are borne in long sprays. The fruit are small, creamy brown and shaped like figs. **ZONES 10–12.**

TRICHODIADEMA

This genus of bushy succulents is native to South Africa and is made up of 36 species. They are mostly miniature shrubs with long branches and woody or fleshy roots. Bristles radiate from the tips of the small cylindrical leaves. Species of *Trichodiadema* flower readily, with red and white, medium-sized flowers in evidence for most of the year. The smaller species will grow well on window sills.
CULTIVATION: These frost-tender plants prefer a sunny position with good air circulation and well-drained soil. Water generously in summer, sparingly or not at all in winter. Propagate from cuttings or seed in spring and summer.

Trichodiadema bulbosum

This succulent species has very small, fleshy gray leaves and magenta flowers. It is a low-growing perennial, reaching about 6 in (15 cm) in height with a similar spread. The stem is low and branching, and carries the glossy, daisy-like flowers in spring and summer. These open only in full sun. **ZONES 9–11.**

Trichodiadema intonsum

From the Eastern Cape, this prostrate to mounding species has $\frac{1}{2}$ in (12 mm) leaves with a few brown bristles. The flowers—red or white—are slightly less than 1 in (25 mm) in diameter. **ZONES 9–11.**

TRICHOSTEMA
BLUE CURLS

Resembling some of their close relatives the sages *(Salvia)*, the 16 species in this genus are natives of North America. They are annuals, perennials or small shrubs and are 1–5 ft (0.3–1.5 m) tall

Tricyrtis hirta

Tricyrtis suzukii

Trifolium pratense

Trifolium repens

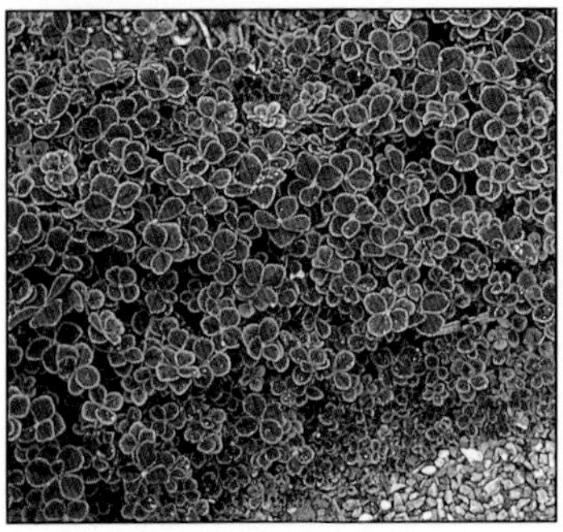

T. repens **'Purpurascens Quadrifolium'**

Trillium albidum

depending on the species. Their simple lance-shaped leaves are often slightly sticky and blue-tinted. Their flowers, borne on upright spikes, are tubular and slightly upcurved, hence the common name, blue curls. Flower colors are in the pink, mauve-blue to purple range.
CULTIVATION: Suited to a perennial border, blue curls prefer moist, humus-rich soil. Some species are very lime tolerant. Propagate from seed or cuttings.

Trichostema lanatum
WOOLLY BLUE CURLS

This Californian species is a shrub growing up to 5 ft (1.5 m) tall. Its 3 in (8 cm) long leaves have sticky upper surfaces and felted undersides. The flower spike, also felted, is around 18 in (45 cm) long and carries blue flowers. **ZONES 6–10.**

TRICYRTIS
TOAD LILIES

The common name of this genus of about 20 species seems to have biased gardeners against the toad lilies—no one thinks of toads as attractive—but these clumping rhizomatous summer-flowering perennials from the woodlands of Asia are really quite attractive in their quiet colorings and markings. The flowers, which are star-, bell- or funnel-shaped, with opened-out tips, are held in the axils of the leaves. The leaves are pointed and pale to dark green, appearing on erect or arching, hairy stems.
CULTIVATION: Grow these very frost-hardy plants in part-shade in humus-rich, moist soil; in areas with cool summers, they need a warm spot. Propagate from seed in fall (autumn) or by division in spring.

Tricyrtis formosana

This upright plant will grow 24–36 in (60–90 cm) high. The flowers are spurred, heavily spotted with purplish pink and have a yellow tinged throat; they are produced in terminal cymes in early fall (autumn). The glossy dark green leaves clasp the stems. **ZONES 7–9.**

Tricyrtis hirta

This upright species bears 2 in (5 cm) wide, star-shaped white flowers spotted with purple from late summer to fall (autumn). The branching stems are about 3 ft (1 m) long. **ZONES 5–9.**

Tricyrtis macranthropsis
syn. ***Tricyrtis macrantha*** **subsp.** ***macranthopsis***

This native of Japan is one of the best garden species. It has nodding, pale yellow flowers with brownish purple dots. The stems are long and unbranched, and the leaves are narrowly lanceolate with a long tapering apex. **ZONES 6–9.**

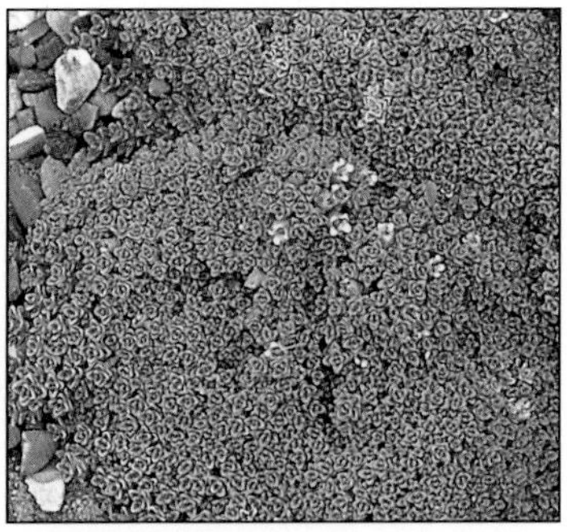

Trifolium uniflorum

Tricyrtis suzukii

The flowers in this species from Taiwan are white with purple spots, but otherwise it is similar to *Tricyrtis formosana.* It is seldom found in cultivation. **ZONES 7–10.**

TRIFOLIUM
CLOVER

This large genus of annuals, biennials or perennials consists of about 230 species, some of which are semi-evergreen. Widespread throughout temperate and subtropical regions, they are absent from Australia. Species have rounded, usually 3-parted leaves and heads of pea-like flowers. The individual blooms are often very small, making the head resemble a single bloom. Many species become invasive, but have agricultural uses; others are suitable for banks or in rock gardens.
CULTIVATION: All species are very frost hardy. Clovers will grow in sun or part-shade. Propagate from seed in fall (autumn) or by division in spring. Most species self-seed readily.

Trifolium pratense
RED CLOVER

This coarse, erect or decumbent perennial is up to 24 in (60 cm) tall. From late spring to early fall (autumn) it bears large, globose heads of pink to purple flowers. Native to Europe, it is a popular pasture clover. It is occasionally sold in cultivated forms and its flowers are popular with apiarists. **ZONES 6–10.**

Trifolium repens
WHITE CLOVER

This European species has low creeping stems which root at the nodes. The trifoliate leaves have leaflets with serrated margins and a whitish mark at the base. The white or green flowers are produced in globular terminal clusters from spring to fall (autumn) and into winter in warmer climates. **'Purpurascens Quadrifolium'** is grown for its bronze-green 4-parted foliage that is variably edged with bright green. Although unwelcome in fine turf, white clover is an important pasture plant and honey source. **ZONES 4–10.**

Trifolium uniflorum

This is a low-growing creeping and clump-forming species from the eastern Mediterranean. It has trifoliate leaves and the lilac flowers are borne in terminal clusters in summer. **ZONES 7–10.**

TRIGONELLA
FENUGREEK

This is a genus of about 80 species of slender annual legumes with light green trifoliate leaves and small pea-like white or pink flowers. These are followed by narrow sickle-shaped pods which contain up to 20 brownish yellow seeds. The dried seeds of *Trigonella foenum-graecum* have a strong spicy odor and have long been used as a food-flavoring and medicine. Fenugreek often appears as a spice in curry powders and chutneys, and is a herb much used in North African and Egyptian cooking. One kind of fenugreek is used to flavor special cheeses.
CULTIVATION: Although often sprouted year round for domestic use, fenugreeks are strictly summer annuals outdoors. Grow in moderately rich, well-drained soil in a sunny position. Propagate from seed sown directly into the soil in spring. Thin to 4 in (10 cm) apart.

Trigonella foenum-graecum
FENUGREEK

This aromatic annual grows to 24 in (60 cm) high and has clover-like trifoliate leaves. Small white pea-flowers are borne in summer and are followed by a long narrow pod. This species is used as a fodder plant in central and southern Europe. It is also extensively cultivated as a spice in many countries, particularly in the Middle East and Asia. Pick the seeds when ripe and dry them in a warm, dry spot indoors. They can be used as a sprouting vegetable and will sprout in 3 to 4 days. They add spice to almost any kind of salad. **ZONES 7–10.**

TRILLIUM
WAKE ROBIN, WOOD LILY

Among North America's most beautiful wildflowers, this genus in the lily family contains 30 species of rhizomatous, deciduous perennials; they also occur naturally in northeastern Asia. Upright or nodding, solitary, funnel-shaped flowers with 3 simple petals are held just above a whorl of 3 leaves. The numerous species are found in woodland habitats, flowering in spring before the deciduous leaves which remain green until fall (autumn). They make good ornamentals in wild gardens and shady borders.
CULTIVATION: Very frost hardy, they prefer a cool, moist soil with ample water and shade from the hot afternoon sun. Slow to propagate from seed in fall or by division in summer, they are long lived once established.

Trillium albidum

Native to western USA, this species has 8 in (20 cm) leaves, grows to over 18 in (45 cm) tall and is similar to *Trillium chloropetalum*. Its flowers are white flushed pink and are up to 4 in (10 cm) long. **ZONES 6–9.**

Trillium cernuum
NODDING WOOD LILY, NODDING TRILLIUM

This species from eastern USA and Canada grows to no more than 2 in (5 cm) high and frequently less. It has

Trillium cuneatum

Trillium cernuum

Trillium chloropetalum

almost stalkless foliage, 2–6 in (5–15 cm) long and narrower at the tips, and produces 2 or 3 stems in spring. These stems carry small, drooping white flowers, rarely pink, up to 1 in (25 mm) long and with the same diameter. **ZONES 6–9.**

Trillium chloropetalum
GIANT TRILLIUM

The giant trillium is found from California to Washington in western USA, in wooded or streamside situations. Growing up to 24 in (60 cm) tall, its flowers may be green, white, pink or maroon, with the 3 petals held upright. This species is more tolerant of dry shade than others. **ZONES 6–9.**

Trillium cuneatum
WHIPPORWILL FLOWER

Native to southern USA, this species bears reddish brown to maroon flowers in early spring. It grows to a height of 12–24 in (30–60 cm). It prefers a soil that is slightly alkaline. **ZONES 6–9.**

Trillium erectum
BETHROOT, BIRTHROOT, WAKE-ROBIN

This species comes from northern USA and Canada where it grows in large groups 12 in (30 cm) in diameter. They often produce more than one stem with stalkless leaves which narrow to a point. The flowers can be variable with white, yellow and green forms, sometimes with reddish hues. Each flower, 1 in (25 mm) long and slightly wider, is normally held at an angle to the stem. This species was used as a medicinal plant by Native Americans for gynaecological and obstetric problems, ranging from sore nipples to inducing labor. **ZONES 4–9.**

Trillium grandiflorum
SNOW TRILLIUM, WAKE-ROBIN

This showy, clump-forming trillium is the easiest to grow, reaching 12–18 in (30–45 cm) in height. The pure white flowers, borne in spring, fade to pink as they age. The double-flowered white form, **'Flore Pleno'**, is beautiful but rare, and has arching stems and oval, dark green leaves. **ZONES 3–9.**

Trillium luteum
syns *Trillium sessile* var. *luteum*, *Trillium viride*
WOOD TRILLIUM

From Appalachian woodlands of eastern USA, this species is distinguished by its rather pointed leaves that are spotted and splashed with paler green, and small, stalkless yellow-green flowers that do not open very widely. **ZONES 6–9.**

Trillium rivale
BROOK WAKE ROBIN

In this species, both the oval leaves and the cup-shaped flowers have long stems, often 2 in (5 cm) or more. Borne in spring, the white or pinkish flowers have heart-shaped, dark-spotted petals. Although they are 1½ in (35 mm) in diameter, the whole plant is quite short, usually no more than 4 in (10 cm) tall. **ZONES 5–9.**

Trillium rugelii
SOUTHERN NODDING TRILLIUM

Endemic to Tennessee, USA, this trillium is now regarded as rather rare and endangered in the wild. However, it is becoming more common in cultivation. **ZONES 5–9.**

Trillium sessile
TOAD-SHADE, WAKE-ROBIN

This upright, clump-forming perennial reaches 12–15 in (30–38 cm) in height with a spread of 12–18 in (30–45 cm). It has deep green leaves marbled with pale green, gray and maroon. They bear stalkless, maroon flowers with lance-shaped petals in late spring. ***Trillium sessile* var. *californicum*** bears white flowers. **ZONES 4–9.**

Trillium grandiflorum **'Flore Pleno'**

TRIPLEUROSPERMUM
SCENTLESS FALSE CHAMOMILE, TURF DAISY

Consisting of some 30 species of annuals and perennials allied to *Matricaria*, this genus is widespread in the northern temperate regions. They have finely divided leaves, often with narrow, needle-like leaf segments. Daisy-like flowerheads with white ray florets around a wide boss of bright yellow disc-florets usually open through spring and summer. Once grouped with the chamomiles, the transferred species have few herbal uses. **CULTIVATION:** These tough plants are easily grown in any sunny position with well-drained soil. Seed germinates freely and often self-sows; perennial species can also be propagated from small cuttings or by division if large enough.

Tripleurospermum maritimum
syn. *Matricaria maritima*

This native of coastal areas of western and northern Europe may be prostrate or upright to about 3 ft (1 m). Although a short-lived perennial, it is often treated as an annual to obtain compact growth. Its leaves have short, fleshy segments. It flowers from mid-spring to mid-fall (mid-autumn). **ZONES 5–10.**

TRIPTERYGIUM

This genus consists of just 2 species of deciduous scrambling climbers from China, Taiwan, Japan and Korea. They have simple pointed, elliptical leaves and their flowers, borne in loose panicles in summer, are greenish white with darker tints. Green fruit follow the flowers. **CULTIVATION:** These undemanding plants will grow in any well-drained soil in sun or part-shade. The 2 species differ considerably in hardiness. Propagate from seed, cuttings or by layering.

Tripterygium regelii

This species has long reddish brown warty branches grows to 20 ft (6 m) high. Its leaves are 6 in (15 cm) long, dark green on the upper surface and paler underneath. Small flowers are borne in late summer, followed by pale green, 3-winged fruit. **ZONES 5–9.**

TRISTAGMA

This genus closely allied to *Ipheion* and *Triteleia* species consists of 5 bulbs native to southern Chile and Argentina. They bear only a few grassy leaves and small yellow and green to pale blue flowers with curled tips to the petals. Rarely cultivated, they are charming plants for rock gardens and alpine house pans. **CULTIVATION:** Plant the small bulbs in fall (autumn) in full sun or part-shade in well-drained soil. They are only moderately frost hardy and like plenty of water through winter and spring.

Tripterygium regelii

Trillium rugelii

Trillium sessile var. *californicum*

Trillium sessile

Trillium grandiflorum

Trillium luteum

Tristagma nivale

This small bulb occurs wild near the far southern tip of South America. In summer it produces umbels of 2 to 5 small, greenish yellow flowers on stems mostly less than 6 in (15 cm) high. **ZONES 8–9.**

TRISTANIA

WATER GUM

Most species previously included in *Tristania* are now in the genera *Lophostemon* and *Tristaniopsis,* leaving the revised genus with just one species, a shrub native to southeastern Australia. The narrow leaves are in opposite pairs, making 4 ranks. The yellow, 5-petalled flowers make a showy display.
CULTIVATION: It does not do well in waterlogged soils, at least not in cultivation. It prefers moist but well-drained, humus-rich soil and full sun.

Tristania neriifolia

This shrub to 12 ft (3.5 m) high has smooth but slightly flaky bark. The narrow, lance-shaped leaves are $1\frac{1}{2}$–$2\frac{1}{2}$ in (35–60 mm) long. The flowers are borne in loose clusters in the upper axils in mid-summer. **ZONES 9–11.**

Triteleia laxa 'Queen Fabiola'

Tristaniopsis laurina

Tristaniopsis laurina

TRISTANIOPSIS

This genus of 30 species of evergreen trees or shrubs is closely related to *Tristania* and used to be included in that once larger genus. Species have obscurely veined leaves and 5-petalled yellow to white flowers. The seeds are usually winged. The genus contains several species indigenous to the high-rainfall coastal forests of eastern Australia and others from Southeast Asia, Papua New Guinea and New Caledonia. These plants make excellent screen or hedge plants.
CULTIVATION: Marginally frost hardy, they adapt to a range of situations, but grow best in deep, well-drained, moist soil in shade or part-shade. Water freely during the warmer months and prune to size as necessary. Propagate from seed in late summer.

Tristaniopsis laurina

syn. *Tristania laurina*

WATER GUM, KANUKA

A conical tree to 30–50 ft (9–15 m) high, the water gum has a smooth, creamy brown trunk attractively streaked with gray. The branches start low to the ground and form a dense canopy. The leaves are oblong to lance-shaped and 4 in (10 cm) long. Their upper surfaces are dark green and the undersides paler; in colder areas, they turn red. New leaves are pinkish. Clusters of small, deep yellow flowers appear in summer, each blossom rich with nectar. The fruit are round capsules. **ZONES 10–12.**

TRITELEIA

The name of this bulb genus of 15 species comes from the Latin *tri* meaning 'three parts', and refers to the fact that the flowers are arranged in threes. The genus is closely related to *Brodiaea*, under which name species are often listed. Most are native to the west coast of North America. They usually produce grass-like foliage, with the onion-like leaves often dying before the flowerheads appear. The well-held umbels of starry flowers, usually borne in late spring, are blue and resemble the *Allium* species.
CULTIVATION: These bulbs like moist, well-drained soil, with drier conditions from late summer to early fall (autumn); they should never be waterlogged. Plant where there is full sun for at least part of the day during the growing period. In cold areas, they may need some winter protection. The corms, which should be planted in a sunny but sheltered position in fall, can be dry-stored during the mid- to late summer dormancy.

Triticum durum

Trithrinax acanthocoma

Triteleia grandiflora

syn. *Brodiaea grandiflora*

HOWELL'S TRITELEIA

In this species, 10 in (25 cm) stems carry dark to medium blue flowers held in a compact flowerhead 1 in (25 mm) long and the same diameter. It is a useful rock-garden plant, but must have very good drainage and is best left undisturbed for several years. **ZONES 5–9.**

Triteleia hyacinthina

syn. *Brodiaea hyacinthina*

Occurring from British Columbia south to California, this species grows to 18 in (45 cm) high. It produces 3 in (8 cm) umbels with individual flowers, milk white in color and occasionally purple tinged, up to 1 in (25 mm) across. These flowers, borne from late spring to early summer, are useful for drying. Spring moisture is preferred and in general this species is easily grown. **ZONES 4–9.**

Triteleia ixioides

syn. *Brodiaea ixioides*

PRETTY FACE, GOLDEN BRODIAEA

This species reaches 18 in (45 cm) in height with a spread of 3–4 in (8–10 cm). It has semi-erect basal leaves. In early summer, loose flowerheads are produced at the ends of the stems and are up to 5 in (12 cm) across. They bear yellow flowers with a purple stripe on each petal. **ZONES 7–10.**

Triteleia laxa

syn. *Brodiaea laxa*

GRASS NUT, TRIPLET LILY, ITHURIEL'S SPUR

The showy *Triteleia laxa*, whose flowers vary between milky blue and purple blue, is a popular and easily grown garden plant. It has the largest flower umbels—up to 6 in (15 cm) in diameter—of any species in the genus. The umbels, however, are not as tight as in other species, with flower stalks over 2 in (5 cm) long. The flowers are borne from late spring to early summer; the stems are strong and wiry. **'Queen Fabiola'** is a little taller and has even stronger stems. **ZONES 7–10.**

Trithrinax campestris

TRITHRINAX

The 5 species of single-trunked or clump-forming palms in this genus come from Bolivia to southern Brazil and Argentina, where they grow in sandy marshes and along riverbeds in dry areas. They are usually grown for their distinctive spiny, fiber-covered trunks and because of their tolerance to cold. Plant with care, avoiding paths, entrances and areas of high foot traffic, as the spines are quite sharp and can be dangerous.
CULTIVATION: These palms prefer a moderately alkaline soil, full sun and ample moisture. They are suitable for warm-temperate to tropical areas, but are not widely grown in cultivation.

Trithrinax acanthocoma

SPRING FIBER PALM

This species has a thick single trunk up to 12 ft (3.5 m) high which is covered in brown spiky webbing and old leaf bases. The fan leaves are green above and paler on the undersides, with narrow segments. The inflorescence is heavy with cream flowers; the round creamy white fruit are 1 in (25 mm) in diameter. **ZONES 10–11.**

Trithrinax campestris

This species forms a compact clump of trunks with blue-green fan leaves which are fuzzy white on the upper surface. The fruit are about 1 in (25 mm) in diameter and the seeds often take 3 months or more to germinate. It needs to be protected from wind. **ZONES 10–11.**

TRITICUM

WHEAT

One of the oldest and most important of the cereal crops, this annual grows in most temperate climates. Winter and spring wheat are the 2 major classes, with the severity of the winter determining which type is cultivated. Hard wheats, best suited for breadmaking, are generally grown in dry climates. The wheats of wetter areas are softer and are primarily used for pastry products.
CULTIVATION: A well-cultivated, weed-free soil produces the best grain. Hoe or rake just before planting to eliminate newly emerged weeds. Propagate from certified seed, which is sown by broadcasting, and cover the ground as evenly as possible. Spring wheat is grown in the colder areas. It requires at least a 90-day growing season and is usually planted as soon as the ground can be worked. Winter wheat is always sown in the fall (autumn) and grows best where fall rainfall is good and the winter temperatures not too severe.

Triticum aestivum
WHEAT

This is the most important bread wheat. It is an annual grass to about 4 ft (1.2 m) with long slender leaves, hollow stems and spikelets composed of varying numbers of flowers and with bristles (awns) of greatly varying length. Wheat is usually harvested when the stalks are entirely golden and the grains hard. Stems should be cut close to the ground on a dry sunny day after the dew has dried. **ZONES 5–11.**

Triticum durum
DURUM WHEAT

When ripe, this wheat is amber in color with pointed kernels. It is higher in protein than bread wheat and is used almost entirely for making pasta. Although the texture will be heavier, home-grown durum wheat can be made into a highly nutritious bread. **ZONES 5–11.**

TRITONIA

The name of this genus of corms comes from the Greek *triton*, which the author thought to mean a weathercock, and refers to the stamens in some species which change direction. There are 28 species in the genus, all native to South Africa and most of them to Cape Province. There they are found growing in meadows where there is plenty of moisture during the growing season, followed by a dry period. They are closely related and similar to *Crocosmia*. The corms have a thin, dry covering and are usually no more than ½ in (12 mm) in diameter. The sword-shaped leaves are rigid and vary in width. The flower spike emerges from the center of the leaves and is sometimes branched, usually with at least 6 flowers per stem, arranged alternately.
CULTIVATION: Marginally frost hardy, they need well-drained soil in a sunny, sheltered position. In cold areas, corms should be lifted and stored over winter or protected with a thick mulch. With the exception of ***Tritonia rubrolucens***, which is planted in winter, corms should be planted in fall (autumn). Water well during the growing season, but allow to dry out after flowering. Propagate from new corms, which are produced on top of the old ones and can be separated when they become overcrowded, or from seed in fall.

Tritonia crocata
syn. ***Tritonia hyalina***
BLAZING STAR, ROOIKALKOENTJIE

This freesia-like plant has wiry stems which grow to 20 in (50 cm) and bear a spike of pretty, cup-shaped blooms. The 2 in (5 cm) wide flowers appear in late spring to summer and are bright orange to red with yellow throats and purple anthers. The erect green leaves grow from the base. *Tritonia crocata* makes a good cut flower. It is marginally frost hardy so it needs some protection. **ZONES 9–10.**

TROCHODENDRON
WHEEL TREE

This genus contains just one species, an evergreen shrub or small tree found in

Trochodendron aralioides

the forests of Japan, Korea and Taiwan. Known to reach 70 ft (21 m) in height, it usually remains shrubby for many years before developing its final form. It has simple, long-stemmed, 2–6 in (5–15 cm) long, lance-shaped leaves in whorled clusters at the branch tips. The many-stamened bright green flowers, borne in raceme-like clusters of up to 20 blooms, are around ½ in (12 mm) wide.
CULTIVATION: This tree is moderately frost hardy and easily grown in any well-drained soil. It prefers dappled shade and shelter when young. Propagate from seed or cuttings.

Trochodendron aralioides

This species is slow growing with a spreading habit. The bark is aromatic and in some regions it is used to make birdlime. The leathery leaves are a bright apple green to yellowish green and scalloped on the margins. The bright green flowers are an unusual and attractive choice as cut blooms. **ZONES 8–10.**

TROLLIUS
GLOBE FLOWER

The perennial globe flowers resemble their cousins the buttercups in their bright yellow flowers and their liking for wet ground, but they are much more sedate in their habits—no chance of the garden being taken over here. The flowers are also often bigger—to about 3 in (8 cm)—and their larger number of petals give them the appearance of being double. From Europe and temperate Asia, any of the 30 species is worth growing. Spring is the main flowering season, but do not be surprised to see some fall (autumn) flowers, too.
CULTIVATION: Very frost hardy, they can be grown in regular flowerbeds in moist soil provided they are watered generously, but the boggy edge of a pond or stream suits them better. They are among the few water's edge plants that actually prefer a little shade. Propagate from seed in spring or fall or by division in early fall or early spring.

Trollius chinensis
syn. ***Trollius ledebourii***
CHINESE GLOBE FLOWER

This is one of the lesser known but still very desirable species. It grows 2–3 ft (60–90 cm) tall and bears its shining flowers in spring above handsomely slashed foliage. The flower color varies from light to deep yellow. It is a fast grower, but is not invasive. **ZONES 5–9.**

Trollius chinensis

Tropaeolum majus

Trollius × cultorum

This is a clump-forming hybrid between *Trollius europaeus* and *T. chinensis* and has given rise to a popular race of garden globe flowers with good foliage and beautiful incurved global-shaped flowers like big double buttercups. There are many named forms, with either yellow or orange flowers. **'Byrne's Giant'** is a butter yellow; **'Canary Bird'** is lemon yellow; **'Goldquelle'** (syn. 'Golden Fountain') provides a good late show of deep yellow flowers; and **'Orange Princess'** is bright orange. **ZONES 5–9.**

Trollius europaeus
COMMON GLOBE FLOWER

The stem on this clump-forming perennial from northern and central Europe is smooth, hollow and upstanding, branching at the apex. Its spring flowers are yellow and terminal; the 5 to 15 petal-like sepals forming a rounded shape 2 in (5 cm) across. Each mid-green leaf has 3 to 5 lobes arranged palmately, with each lobe deeply incised. This species grows to a height of 24 in (60 cm) with an 18 in (45 cm) spread. **ZONES 5–9.**

TROPAEOLUM
NASTURTIUM

The 87 species of annuals, perennials and twining climbers in this genus from Chile to Mexico, are admired for their brightly colored flowers. In warm areas, nasturtiums can survive for several years, self-sowing freely and flowering all year. The flowers can be single or double, about 2 in (5 cm) across, and come in red, orange, russet, yellow, cream and even blue. In the nineteenth century a white cultivar was bred, only to be lost.
CULTIVATION: Frost hardy to frost tender, most species prefer moist, well-drained soil in full sun or part-shade. Propagate from seed, basal stem cuttings or tubers in spring. Watch out for aphids and cabbage moth caterpillars.

Trollius europaeus

Tropaeolum majus Alaska Hybrids

Tropaeolum pentaphyllum

Tropaeolum azureum

This rare perennial climber grows to around 3 ft (1 m) and has pale or mid-green lance-shaped leaflets. In late spring, short-spurred, pale blue flowers with creamy or yellow centers are borne. **ZONES 9–10.**

Tropaeolum majus
GARDEN NASTURTIUM, INDIAN CRESS

The stem is trailing and climbing on this fast-growing, bushy annual. Its leaves are rounded and marked with radial veins. It blooms in summer and fall (autumn); its 5-petalled flowers spurred, open and trumpet-shaped, come in many shades from deep red to pale yellow. It grows to a spread of 3 ft (1 m) and a height of up to 18 in (45 cm). The hot-tasting leaves and flowers of this species are sometimes added to salads. There are several varieties with single or double flowers, and a compact or trailing habit. The **Alaska Hybrids** have single flowers in a range of colors and prettily variegated leaves. **ZONES 8–11.**

Tropaeolum pentaphyllum

Native to Bolivia, this is an unusual, tuberous-rooted trailer (or rather weak climber). It blooms in summer, when the red and yellow flowers look very striking against the 5-lobed, blue-green leaves. **ZONES 8–11.**

Tropaeolum peregrinum

Tsuga canadensis 'Pendula'

Tsuga canadensis

Tropaeolum peregrinum
syn. *Tropaeolum canariense*
CANARY CREEPER, CANARY BIRD FLOWER

This frost-tender vine climbs to more than 6 ft (1.8 m) in height. Its gray-green leaves have 5 broad lobes and radial veins. In summer to early winter, it bears small, trumpet-shaped yellow flowers; the upper pair of its 5 petals are bigger and are fringed. In cold climates, it is best grown as an annual. **ZONES 10–11.**

Tropaeolum speciosum
FLAME CREEPER, FLAME NASTURTIUM

A herbaceous perennial climber with slender stems reaching up to 10 ft (3 m), this species has a tuberous rhizome and attractive, bright green foliage composed of 6 oval leaflets. Scarlet flowers, borne in summer, are followed by blue fruit. This species is frost hardy. **ZONES 8–10.**

Tropaeolum tricolorum
syn. *Tropaeolum tricolor*

This perennial climber has unusually shaped, 1½ in (35 mm) flowers that blaze in scarlet, purple and bright yellow. It grows to 6 ft (1.8 m) high and has green leaves with 5 to 7 lobes. **ZONES 8–10.**

Tropaeolum tricolorum

Tsuga canadensis

Tsuga chinensis

Tropaeolum tuberosum

This perennial climber has large, purple-marbled yellow tubers and grayish green leaves. Cup-shaped flowers with orange-red sepals and deep yellow petals with brown veins are produced from mid-summer to fall (autumn). It grows to 12 ft (3.5 m) in height. **'Ken Aslet'** has bright orange flowers. **ZONES 8–10.**

TSUGA
HEMLOCK

The 10 or so species of elegant evergreen conifers from cool-temperate areas of North America and East Asia that make up this genus are widely grown as ornamentals in cool climates. They range from tall trees to (in the case of dwarf cultivars) small shrubs good for hedging and rockeries. Conical to pyramidal in habit, the spreading branches droop gracefully. Both male and female cones are small, the latter with thin scales and containing winged seeds. The common name hemlock has no link to the poisonous herb—the trees are not poisonous.
CULTIVATION: These frost-hardy trees are tolerant of shade and thrive in slightly acid, deep, well-drained soil containing plenty of organic matter. They do not enjoy urban environments or very exposed positions, and dislike being transplanted. Propagate from seed in spring or cuttings in fall (autumn).

Tsuga caroliniana

Tsuga canadensis
EASTERN HEMLOCK, CANADIAN HEMLOCK

From the cool northeast of North America, this slow-growing tree reaches a height of 80 ft (24 m), with a trunk that is often forked at the base. It forms a broad pyramidal crown, the thin branches with pendulous tips. The short, oblong needles are arranged in 2 rows and are grayish brown and hairy when young, maturing to dark green with 2 grayish bands on the undersides. Oval cones 1 in (25 mm) long are borne at the ends of the branchlets and disperse their seeds in fall (autumn). **'Pendula'** forms a semi-prostrate mound to 6 ft (1.8 m) tall and wide; its lime-green juvenile foliage becomes grayish green with age. **ZONES 2–9.**

Tsuga caroliniana
CAROLINA HEMLOCK

From southeastern USA, this species grows to 70 ft (21 m) tall in the wild but much less in cultivation. It has attractive bark: dark purple-brown and fissured. The shiny young shoots are gray, red or yellowish brown, and the needles are a soft mid-green. It is a better garden tree than *Tsuga canadensis*. **ZONES 4–9.**

Tsuga chinensis
CHINESE HEMLOCK

This conifer reaches a height of 70 ft (21 m) in the wild, less in cultivation. It has been in cultivation for thousands of years and is often a feature of formal Japanese gardens. It forms a narrow crown with a spread of around 12 ft (3.5 m) and is one of the neatest members of the genus. Its yellowish young shoots precede glossy green needles that are distinctly notched at the tip. **ZONES 6–10.**

Tsuga heterophylla

Tsuga heterophylla
WESTERN HEMLOCK

From northwestern North America, this large, fast-growing tree can reach nearly 200 ft (60 m) in the wild (generally less in cultivation) and is harvested commercially for its pale yellow timber and tannin-rich bark. As with *Sequoia*, the harvest comes almost entirely from natural forests, to the great concern of environmentalists. As a specimen in parks and large gardens it is particularly elegant, with a spire-like habit, weeping branchlets and a rusty brown, fissured trunk. New young shoots are grayish, and the flat needles are deep green. **ZONES 6–10.**

Tsuga mertensiana
MOUNTAIN HEMLOCK

One of the smallest species in the genus, *Tsuga mertensiana* seldom exceeds 50 ft (15 m) in height and performs best in areas similar to the mild coastal regions of its native western Canada and Alaska. Narrow and columnar, with a straight single trunk and pendent branches, it bears blue-green, distinctly rounded needles that are banded top and bottom. These are arranged spirally on the branches and habitually point forward. Its comparatively large, cylindrical, purplish black cones mature to 3 in (8 cm) long. A slow grower, it is susceptible to pollution and dry conditions. **ZONES 4–9.**

TSUSIOPHYLLUM

The sole species in this genus is a charming semi-evergreen dwarf shrub native to Japan, which was once included in the genus *Rhododendron* because of its similarity to azaleas. It is usually a dense, rounded bush but under extremely harsh conditions it is almost prostrate. This shrub is a mass of fine twigs clothed with ½ in (12 mm) long, deep green oval leaves. In late spring and summer it bears flowers that are at first enclosed in an orange-red bud cap which springs off as the flowers open.
CULTIVATION: Very frost hardy, *Tsusiophyllum* is best treated in the same way as a miniature rhododendron. Plant it in moist, well-drained, humus-rich soil in part-shade. Propagate from seed sown on sphagnum moss or from cuttings.

Tsuga mertensiana

Tsusiophyllum tanakae
syn. *Rhododendron tsusiophyllum*

This small shrub grows 12–18 in (30–45 cm) tall. It has a dense twiggy habit and masses of tiny leaves that are glaucous on the undersides. The small tubular, bell-shaped white flowers, less than ½ in (12 mm) long, are borne in clusters of two to six. **ZONES 7–9.**

TULBAGHIA

Linnaeus named this African genus of 20 rhizomatous, tuberous or cormous perennials for Ryk Tulbagh, the Dutch Governor of Cape Province from 1751to 1771, with whom he corresponded (in Latin). The plants are generally evergreen with clump-forming, narrow leaves. The dainty flowers, which are carried in long-stalked umbels, appear spasmodically over a long period during the warmer months. Some species are onion scented; others smell pleasantly of hyacinths.

CULTIVATION: When consideration is given to their native habitat, these plants withstand moderate frost, provided the drainage is good and there is protection from cold, wet winds. They need full sun and moisture while the foliage is developing; water should be withheld once the flowers appear. Propagate from offsets, which can be removed while the plant is dormant.

Tulbaghia simmleri
syn. *Tulbaghia fragrans*

This species has scented, deep mauve to bright blue, occasionally white, flowers. It grows to a height of 18 in (45 cm) with broad strap-shaped gray-green leaves and strong wiry stems. It flowers from spring through summer. **ZONES 8–10.**

Tulbaghia violacea
SOCIETY GARLIC

Robust and clump-forming, this plant grows to 30 in (75 cm) in height. It thrives in dry or wet summer climates, in a garden bed or container, and exudes a garlic-like odor. The flowers range from deep lilac to white and appear sporadically between mid-spring and late fall (autumn). The narrow, gray-green leaves are more or less evergreen. It is good as a border plant or in a rock garden. The bulbs are edible. **'Silver Lace'** is a variegated form whose leaves are edged in white. It is slightly less robust than the species and is said to be a good mole deterrent. **ZONES 7–10.**

TULIPA
TULIP

Tulips are one of the world's major commercial flower crops, both for cut flowers and horticulture. Wild species of these bulbs come from central and western Asia. They were introduced into Europe in about 1554 and rapidly became so popular that 90 years later speculators were risking vast sums of money on bulbs they had never seen. This 'Tulipomania' ended in a disastrous crash but the popularity of tulips survived, with new cultivars continuously being developed. There are more than 100 species of *Tulipa*, but most of those we know are cultivars of only a few species, chiefly *Tulipa gesneriana*. Tulips sport freely and the origin of many very old tulips is unknown. Cultivars run into thousands, with new ones being developed every year. Their names sometimes vary between different countries. Cultivars have been classified into groups for hundreds of years, but modern revisions have led to our present set of 15 groups or divisions. Characteristics are those which are produced in the Royal General Bulbgrowers' Association (KAVB) trial garden in Holland; they are classified according to characteristics such as stem length, flower features and time of flowering. By choosing bulbs from across the groups, you can have a sequence of flowering throughout spring. They range in height from 4 in (10 cm) up to 27 in (70 cm). The blooms come in any number of colors, including bronze, brown, black, yellow, white, red, pink, purple, lilac, violet, green and blue; these colors may vary with soil type or environmental conditions.

CULTIVATION: Climate crucially affects tulip flowering; they require dry, warm summers but cold winters and should not be grown in warm climates unless the bulbs have been suitably chilled. Plant in late fall (autumn), preferably in a sunny position, about 6 in (15 cm) deep in rich, preferably alkaline, well-drained soil. Water well during their growth period. Remove spent flowers, but allow leaves to die off naturally in order to replenish the bulb. In areas with wet summers, lift bulbs and store under cool, dry, well-ventilated conditions. Tulips are prone to aphid attack and the fungal disease tulip fire, caused by *Botrytis tulipae*, which thrives under moist conditions. Propagate from offsets or seed in fall.

Tulipa acuminata
HORNED TULIP

A most unusual tulip, *Tulipa acuminata* is thought not to be a true species, but an ancient cultivar of Turkish origin. It grows to about 20 in (50 cm) tall and is distinguished by its curious, long, narrow, tapering tepals of scarlet and yellow, which are sometimes twisted. **ZONES 5–9.**

Tulipa aucheriana
syn. *Tulipa humilis*

A hardy, dwarf species from Iran, *Tulipa aucheriana* produces star-shaped, scented, flowers in late spring. They are lilac with yellow-brown blotches and may grow to a height of 4 in (10 cm), though in practice they rarely reach more than 3 in (8 cm). The leaves may, on occasions, appear after the flowers. **ZONES 5–9.**

Tulipa batalinii

With its distinctive, wedge-like tepals, this charming tulip exactly fits the ancient Turkish ideal of pointed tepals in red or yellow. At only 6 in (15 cm) tall its stout, sturdy stems support dainty, pale lemon-yellow flowers with brown bases, which fade to apricot as they age. They are ideal for rock gardens. It is possible that this species is actually a yellow form of *Tulipa linifolia*. *T. batalinii* has produced several cultivars, including **'Yellow Jewel'**, which has yellow flowers, tinged rose, with a greenish yellow base, and **'Bright Gem'**, an early flowering, 15 in (38 cm) tall form with orange-tinged, rich bright yellow flowers, each tepal having a darker orange base. **ZONES 5–9.**

Tulipa clusiana
syns *Tulipa aitchisonii, T. stellata*
LADY TULIP, PEPPERMINT STICK TULIP

One of the most graceful of all tulips, this lovely species produces elegant, star-like flowers, white inside with a violet base and outer tepals which are carmine on the outside. They grow to about 10 in (25 cm) tall and require minimal chilling, making them a delightful permanent garden plant, even in milder climates. Occasionally more than one flower per stem is produced. ***Tulipa clusiana* var. *chrysantha*** (syn. *T. chrysantha*) is also very popular. It is smaller than *T. clusiana*, reaching only 8 in (20 cm) in height, but its small flowers, deep yellow inside, are long and slimly elegant in bud. The outer tepals may have a yellow edge. **ZONES 5–9.**

Tulipa fosteriana

This dramatic representative type of the Fosteriana Group is a variable species, first described in 1906. Its large, vivid scarlet flowers are not as elegant as those of most species, but it is very easy to grow and its combination of fresh, green foliage and glowing color make it a striking addition to beds and borders. It reaches a height of 15 in (38 cm). According to some authorities, it is synonymous with *Tulipa lanata*. **ZONES 5–9.**

Tulipa gesneriana

This is not actually a species, but the collective name originally given to a large number of ancient cultivars in 1753 by the father of taxonomy, Carl Linnaeus. Cultivars and varieties of this 'species' are placed in different groups and are named as *Tulipa* cultivars. **ZONES 5–9.**

Tulipa greigii

The attractive, heavily streaked or mottled leaves of this, the type species of the Greigii Group, make it easy to identify. Its large flowers are brilliant scarlet with bases marked with a black blotch and edged with yellow. It reaches a height of 24 in (60 cm). Although vigorous, *Tulipa greigii* should be lifted after the foliage discolors. It has been used to produce a range of hybrids, all of which are attractive and good increasers. **ZONES 5–9.**

Tulbaghia violacea 'Silver Lace'

Tsusiophyllum tanakae

Tulbaghia violacea

Tulipa acuminata

Tulipa batalinii 'Yellow Jewel'

Tulipa clusiana

Tulipa kaufmanniana
WATERLILY TULIP

This beautiful species has been used as the parent of many hybrids. Its flowers, with their bright carmine outer tepals, open right out, exposing their creamy white insides and bases of deep, golden-yellow. *Tulipa kaufmannia* may not be tall, reaching a height of only 8 in (20 cm), but it is one of the earliest tulips to flower and its lack of fussiness and ease of cultivation make it ideally suitable for home gardens. **ZONES 5–9.**

Tulipa linifolia

First described in 1884, this is a dwarf species from Asia Minor that only grows to 4 in (10 cm) high. Its narrow, undulating leaves lie flat and the flowers, with their tepals in shades of bright red, have greenish outer bases, large jet black inner bases with paler edges and grayish purple anthers. Some botanists believe that *T. maximowiczii* and *T. batalinii* are synonyms of this species and properly treated as cultivars. **ZONES 5–9.**

Tulipa maximowiczii

Tulipa maximowiczii resembles *T. linifolia* and is believed by some to be a cultivar of that species. However, it differs in having a tiny, deep blue base, upright leaves and a slightly earlier time of flowering. **ZONES 5–9.**

Tulipa praestans

This fine species comes from Bokhara. It is one of the multi-flowering varieties, producing 2 to 4 brick-red cups per stem. A very pretty feature is its large, apple green leaves which have dark red edges. It grows to 15 in (38 cm) tall and is lovely in a rock garden. Of its several cultivars and sports, **'Fusilier'** is the most popular. Exceptionally beautiful with its orange-scarlet cups, 4 to 6 per stem, and dark green leaves, it is superb planted in clusters of 12 or more. **ZONES 5–9.**

Tulipa saxatilis
syn. *Tulipa bakeri*

This very showy species was first described in 1825 in Crete. It reaches a height of 8 in (20 cm) and usually produces 2 cups per stem. They are rosy lilac with yellow bases. Minimal chilling requirements make it very easy to grow and suitable for naturalizing, although deep planting is advisable. It spreads by underground stolons, rarely sets seed and has very glossy, fresh green leaves which often appear in late fall (autumn) and make it through the winter unmarked. Its slightly smaller cultivar, **'Lilac Wonder'**, has an exterior of pinkish purple, the inner ring of tepals being somewhat lighter, and a pale yellow base. The interior is pastel mauve with a large, circular, lemon-yellow base and yellow anthers. It grows to only 6 in (15 cm). **ZONES 5–9.**

Tulipa sprengeri
syn. *Tulipa brachyanthera*

Tulipa sprengeri comes from the Black Sea coast of Turkey and tolerates wetter summers than most species. The last of the tulips to flower, it appears at the end of spring and grows to 15 in (38 cm) tall. The flowers are bright scarlet with olive bases on tall, elegant stems and the narrow, lanceolate leaves are bright green with shiny surfaces. It grows well in shade and moist conditions. Although slow to multiply, it flowers quickly from seed. **ZONES 5–9.**

Tulipa sylvestris
syns *Tulipa florentina*, *T. repens*, *T. tchitounyi*, *T. thirkeana*

This sweetly scented, reliable old favorite dates from 1753. One of the most widely distributed of all species, it is easy to grow and is suitable for rock gardens, borders or naturalizing in woodlands or grasslands. Its elegant, star-like flowers are yellow, somewhat greenish on the outside, but clear and bright within. Each bulb produces 1 to 2 flowers and the globular, pendent buds turn upwards as they mature, opening out into reflexed tepals. It is variable in size, reaching a height of up to 12 in (30 cm) and is usually free flowering, although it may not be so when it is left to spread undisturbed. Its environmental requirements are also variable, although it generally requires minimal chilling and tolerates wetter summers. ***Tulipa sylvestris* var. *major*** is a large-flowered form, with 8 yellow tepals. **ZONES 5–9.**

Tulipa tarda
syn. *Tulipa dasystemon*

This is a most attractive, multi-flowered species from Turkestan. It produces 1 to 8 star-like flowers per stem in late spring. They are white with brownish purple exteriors and have a bright yellow base. A true miniature, this tulip reaches only 4 in (10 cm) tall and its long leaves are almost prostrate. It is easy to grow, especially in sunny places, and tolerates wetter conditions in summer. **ZONES 5–9.**

Tulipa turkestanica

Although its flowers are somewhat dull, being white with grayish violet exteriors to the outer tepals and an orange-yellow base, this hardy species is in fact quite useful. Its robust flowers appear very early, are very long-lasting and often number 5 to 9 per stem. It grows to a height of 8 in (20 cm) and can be left to multiply undisturbed. **ZONES 5–9.**

Tulipa urumiensis

Another useful, very hardy species, *Tulipa urumiensis* often produces 3 or 4 star-like flowers per stem. The anthers are yellow and their clear yellow outer tepals are much pigmented on the inside with olive and red, giving them a dull, slightly flushed appearance. Although this dwarf species reaches only 4 in (10 cm) in height, it nonetheless makes a pleasing sight against foliage and is ideal for rock gardens. **ZONES 5–9.**

Tulipa, Single Early Group

These single-flowered cultivars, mainly short stemmed and early flowering, are mostly derived from *Tulipa gesneriana*. They may be difficult to obtain in some countries. **'Apricot Beauty'** is a fragrant cultivar dating from 1953; salmon rose tinged red, it reaches a height of 18 in (45 cm) and is suitable as a bedding plant and for clumps of color. A mutation of **'Imperator'**, it has itself produced several sports, including **'Beauty Queen'** which has an exterior of feathered rose on a salmon ground with a red midrib. Its outer base is whitish; the star-shaped inner base is yellowish green edged with yellow, sitting within a cup of scarlet, edged in red and supporting gray anthers. **'Keizerskroon'** (syn. 'Grand Duc') was developed in 1750 and has never lost its popularity; its bright red cups have broad yellow borders and it grows to 15 in (38 cm) tall. It also shows a propensity to sport. **ZONES 5–9.**

Tulipa, Double Early Group

This group of early flowering, mainly short-stemmed cultivars produces double flowers which resemble gardenias in appearance. **'Monte Carlo'** has sulfur-yellow double flowers, slightly feathered red, which make this a very showy tulip; it is fragrant and reaches 12 in (30 cm) high. The delicate and fragrant **'Murillo'** is white, flushed pink and grows to a height of 10 in (25 cm). It has produced numerous sports, including **'Peach Blossom'** introduced in 1890. With its large, deep rose cups, it is the most popular of all the double pink tulips. **'Yellow Baby'** makes a sumptuous golden contribution to the garden in early spring. Its gardenia-like flowers are rich yellow and the anthers are pale yellow. **ZONES 5–9.**

Tulipa, Triumph Group

The single-flowered cultivars of this group, with medium stem lengths and mid-season flowering, originate from hybridization between cultivars of the Single Early Group and the Single Late Group. They are ideal for exposed positions in beds and borders, and make graceful cut flowers. **'Attila'** is a sturdy, strong cultivar well deserving of its name. Its large, single cups of heavily textured, violet flowers are supported on

Tulipa maximowiczii

Tulipa saxatilis

Tulipa sprengeri

Tulipa saxatilis 'Lilac Wonder'

Tulipa turkestanica

T., Single Early Group, 'Beauty Queen'

T., Double Early Group, 'Yellow Baby'

Tulipa, Triumph Group, 'Cantor'

Tulipa, Triumph Group, 'Ile de France'

Tulipa, Triumph Group, 'Orleans'

Tulipa, Triumph Group, 'Rosario'

Tulipa, Triumph Group, 'Walter Scheel'

stiff stems. Dating from 1945, it has produced many sports since then. It reaches a height of 20 in (50 cm) and is weather resistant. **'Cantor'** is coral pink with a white base and black anthers; combined with long stems, it is a tulip of serene elegance. **'Don Quichotte'** is Tyrian rose in color and reaches a height of 20 in (50 cm); it works well in exposed positions. **'Ile de France'** has a cardinal-red exterior and blood-red interior and the variable base is sometimes dark bronze green with a narrow yellowish edge. It grows to about 18 in (45 cm) tall and makes a good cut flower. **'Kees Nelis'** has large, blood-red flowers edged orange-yellow; its strong stems grow to 18 in (45 cm) high. It has sported several times. **'Orléans'** is an interesting member of this group, with its shades of yellow and white. The exterior is a small mimosa yellow flame, somewhat green, on an ivory-white ground, whilst the interior is barium yellow fading to white, and the base is buff yellow with lemon-yellow blotches. Even the anthers are yellow. It grows to a height of 24 in (60 cm) and makes an ideal cut flower. **'Prinses Irene'**, a sport of **'Couleur Cardinal'**, has unique coloring—orange and purple. The sturdy stems grow to 15 in (38 cm) tall; it has a tendency to sport. **'Rosario'** has a carmine-rose exterior with a large, white base. The interior is also carmine, with a base of ivory white; it grows to 20 in (50 cm) tall. **'Shirley'** is a late-flowerer which reaches 24 in (60 cm) in height. It features creamy flowers, each tepal faintly edged in plum. **'Walter Scheel'** is a fantasy in yellow. Its exterior is flamed barium yellow with a canary yellow edge, the interior is bright canary yellow with lemon-yellow anthers. It grows to 20 in (50 cm) tall. ZONES 5–9.

Tulipa, Darwin Hybrid Group

This group consists of the single-flowered, long-stemmed cultivars that flower mid-season. These are the most frequently grown varieties for the cut-flower market. They are the result of hybridization either between cultivars of the former Darwin Group with *Tulipa fosteriana* or between other cultivars and botanical tulips which have the same habit and in which the wild plant is not evident. The popular **'Apeldoorn'** is very tall with large flowers and is best used as a background to a mixed border or alone as a feature. With black anthers, an outside of cherry red edged in signal red, with a yellow base and its inside signal red with a black base edged with yellow, it is very striking. It grows to a height of 22 in (55 cm) and has produced many sports. **'Apeldoorn's Elite'** has an exterior of cherry red and light mandarin-red feathered on buttercup yellow with a yellowish green base. Its narrow, black anthers rise from a black-brown base edged in yellow within a cup of Orient-red feathered on buttercup yellow. **'Golden Apeldoorn'** is golden yellow with a base consisting of a black star on bronzy green ground, and black anthers. **'Gudoshnik'** is a large, yellow tulip, spotted red and flamed rose. Its base is bluish black, and it grows to a height of 24 in (60 cm). **'Oxford'**, a fragrant tulip, has a scarlet exterior flushed purple-red and is pepper red inside with a base of sulfur yellow. It grows to 22 in (55 cm) tall and has produced several sports. These include: **'Golden Oxford'**, which is pure yellow with a narrow red margin, a yellow base and black anthers; and **'Oxford's Elite'**, which has a cherry-red exterior edged with orange-yellow, and an interior feathered and spotted poppy red on an orange-yellow ground. Both inner and outer bases are lemon yellow, the anthers are bluish black. ZONES 5–9.

Tulipa, Darwin Hybrid

Tulipa, Single Late Group

This late-flowering group, which includes the former Darwin and Cottage Groups, comprises single-flowered, mainly long-stemmed cultivars. They are generally excellent garden plants and as cut flowers. **'Clara Butt'** has good-sized, salmon-pink cups supported by strong, erect stems. It reaches a height of 22 in (55 cm). **'Dreamland'** is a striking cultivar with its exterior of deep pink with creamy flaming and a rose-pink inside containing a white base and yellow anthers. It grows 24 in (60 cm) tall. **'Grand Style'** has a strong red exterior and pale yellow anthers inside a purple interior on a yellow base edged with blue; it grows about 26 in (65 cm) tall. **'Halcro'** has large, carmine flowers with yellow bases edged in green. It grows to more than 27 in (70 cm) tall and is excellent for naturalizing. **'Kingsblood'** is cherry red with scarlet edging and makes a bold splash of color in late spring. Its stems grow to 24 in (60 cm) tall. **'Queen of Night'** is one of the best of the 'black' tulips. Its beautiful, stately cups are actually a deep velvety maroon and it grows 24 in (60 cm) tall. ZONES 5–9.

Tulipa, Single Late, 'Queen of Night'

Tulipa, Single Late, 'Grand Style'

Tulipa, Single Late, 'Halcro'

Tulipa, Darwin Hybrid, 'Oxford'

Tulipa, Single Late, 'Dreamland'

Tulipa, Darwin Hybrid, 'Apeldoorn'

Tulipa, Darwin Hybrid, 'Gudoshnik'

Tulipa, Lily-flowered Group

The single-flowered cultivars of this group of mid-season or late-flowering tulips date from the twentieth century. They produce elegant flowers with pointed, reflexed tepals which form a star on opening and have stems of variable length. **'Ballade'** is an exquisite cultivar with reddish magenta tepals, edged white, and a yellow base, also edged white. It reaches a height of 22 in (55 cm). **'Lilac Time'** produces flowers of intense violet-purple with white bases and yellow anthers. It grows to a height of 18 in (45 cm). **'Red Shine'** is a deep red with a striking blue base. It grows to a height of 22 in (55 cm). **ZONES 5–9.**

Tulipa, Fringed Group

This is a distinctive group of single-flowered cultivars; tepals are edged with crystal-shaped fringes. They flower mid-season or late, and stems are of variable length. **'Aleppo'** has pink and apricot-pink tones over a yellow base; **'Redwing'** is red with a lighter fringe. **ZONES 5–9.**

Tulipa, Viridiflora Group

This late-flowering group consists of single-flowered cultivars with partly greenish tepals. Their stems are of variable length. The muted colors of **'Spring Green'**, a 1969 cultivar, make a lovely massed display. Its tepals are ivory white with green feathering and the anthers are light green. Its stems reach a height of 20 in (50 cm). **ZONES 5–9.**

Tulipa, Rembrandt Group

This long-stemmed group is not commercially available and is known only in historical collections or through paintings. These are the famous cultivars with 'broken' flowers—striped or marked brown, bronze, black, red, pink or purple on red, white or yellow ground—which resulted from a viral infection. **'Absalon'** has brown markings on a yellow base; **'May Blossom'** has striking maroon markings on a cream base. **ZONES 5–9.**

Tulipa, Parrot Group

This is a group of rather strange, often bizarrely colored, single-flowered cultivars with laciniate, curled and twisted tepals. Mainly late flowering and with stems of variable length, they may have very big flowers with deeply cut, fringed tepals on long but weak stems. They may be difficult to obtain in some countries. **'Apricot Parrot'** illustrates the propensity of the *Tulipa* genus to sport. It is a sport of a sport: **'Alberio'** sported, among several, **'Karel Doorman'** which sported to produce 'Apricot Parrot' in 1961. A popular, showy tulip of pale apricot-yellow, tinged creamy white and rose with purple anthers, it grows to 20 in (50 cm) tall. **'Flaming Parrot'**, like so many tulips, is the product of several sports: **'Gloria Swanson'** sported **'Red Parrot'**, which in turn sported 'Flaming Parrot', first described in 1968. With an exterior of barium yellow, lighter to the edge and flamed crimson, primrose yellow inside flamed glowing red, a base of primrose yellow and black-purple anthers, it is a showy cultivar. It grows to 27 in (70 cm) and is better used in clumps rather than in borders. **ZONES 5–9.**

Tulipa, Lily-flowered, 'Lilac Time'

Tulipa, Lily-flowered, 'Red Shine'

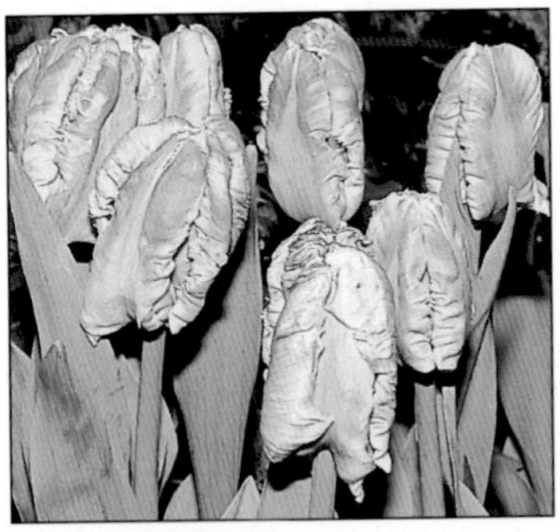

Tulipa, Parrot, 'Apricot Parrot'

Tulipa, Parrot, 'Flaming Parrot'

Tulipa, Double Late, 'Angelique'

Tulipa, Gregii, 'Oriental Splendour'

Tulipa, Greigii, 'Red Riding Hood'

Tulipa, Greigii, 'Sweet Lady'

Tulipa, Greigii, 'Toronto'

Tulipa, Double Late Group

This group contains late-flowering, mainly long-stemmed cultivars, similar to those of the Parrot Group. Their beautiful double flowers resemble peonies and for this reason they are sometimes known as peony-flowering tulips. They generally show excellent weather resistance. **'Granda'** has gorgeous carmine-rose flowers with white bases; it reaches a height of 18 in (45 cm) and can tolerate light shade. Its only sport, **'Angelique'**, comes in shades of pale and darker pink with lighter edges; it has itself sported. **ZONES 5–9.**

Tulipa, Kaufmanniana Group

This group of very early-flowering tulips contains *Tulipa kaufmanniana* with its cultivars, subspecies, varieties and hybrids; all resemble *T. kaufmanniana*. Their foliage is sometimes mottled. The flower, with its multi-colored base and an exterior which normally has a clear carmine blush, opens fully and reaches a height of up to 8 in (20 cm). They require minimal chilling only. The flowers of **'Ancilla'** have exteriors of soft pink with rose-red, and pure white insides and a distinctive red ring in the center. Their short stems grow to about 8 in (20 cm). **'Giuseppe Verdi'** has golden-yellow flowers with outer tepals vertically striped in red. The leaves also bear longitudinal, reddish purple stripes. It grows to 8 in (20 cm) tall. **'Heart's Delight'** has a dramatic combination of 2-toned pink tepals splashed red and yellow at their bases. The leaves are also striped reddish purple. It grows 8–10 in (20–25 cm) tall. **'Shakespeare'** has tepals that are hot red, edged pink on the outside, yellow on the base and bright red and pink on the inside. It grows to 10 in (25 cm) tall. **ZONES 5–9.**

Tulipa, Fosteriana Group

The most brilliant of all tulips, this early flowering group comprises *Tulipa fosteriana* with its cultivars, subspecies, varieties and hybrids; all resemble *T. fosteriana*. Their leaves are very broad, green or gray-green, and sometimes mottled or striped. Stems are medium to long and they have large, long flowers with variable bases. **'Golden Eagle'** is a vivid combination of yellow and orange with a dark orange exterior; **'Robassa'** is red with a yellow base and cream edges. **ZONES 5–9.**

Tulipa, Greigii Group

This group includes *Tulipa greigii* with its cultivars, subspecies, varieties and hybrids; all resemble the type species. The foliage is usually mottled or striped, with leaves normally spreading on the ground, and mostly strongly undulated. Flowering occurs later than in *T. kaufmanniana* and their flower shape is variable. Heights are variable, but generally in the middle ranges. The cups of **'Oriental Splendour'** have carmine exteriors edged lemon yellow and lemon-yellow interiors with green basal blotches within a blood-red ring. The large leaves are mottled and striped with purple. It grows to 20 in (50 cm) tall. **'Plaisir'** comes in shades of bright red with sulfur-yellow edging inside and a base of black and yellow. It reaches a height of 10 in (25 cm). **'Red Riding Hood'** describes this charming tulip's character: carmine cups whose insides are scarlet with black bases, and striking foliage mottled purplish brown. It grows to a height of 12 in (30 cm). **'Sweet Lady'** is one of the more charmingly colored of this group, being pinkish orange with a base of bronzy green, tinged yellow. Its mottled leaves add to its interest; it reaches 12 in (30 cm) in height. **'Toronto'** has tepals in several shades of red, a base of bronzy green on buttercup yellow and bronze anthers. It has striking, mottled leaves and reaches a height of about 15 in (38 cm). **ZONES 5–9.**

Tulipa, Miscellaneous, 'Anodrona'

Tulipa, Miscellaneous, 'Bokassa'

Tulipa, Single Late, 'Clara Butt'

Tussilago farfara

Tulipa, Single Late, 'Golden Beryl'

Tulipa, Single Early, 'Mellow Yellow'

Tulipa, Miscellaneous, 'Monet White'

Tweedia caerulea

T., Miscellaneous, 'Monet Orange'

Tulipa, Miscellaneous, 'Princess'

Tulipa, Double Early, 'Schoonoord'

Typha latifolia

Tulipa, Miscellaneous

Not, in fact, a cultivar group, this is rather the collection of all species, varieties and their cultivars in which the wild species is evident and which do not belong to any of the above-mentioned cultivar groups. **ZONES 5–9.**

TUSSILAGO

This genus of about 15 species of perennials from cooler parts of the northern hemisphere is a rather humble relative of the more stately ligularias. Only one species is known in cultivation, and that is grown more for its medicinal uses than for any ornamental qualities—it has been renowned for centuries as a cough remedy, hence the genus name, from the Latin *tussis*, cough, and *-ago*, act upon. They are plants with long-running rhizomes that send up widely spaced tufts of often almost circular leaves. The flowerheads are borne on stems separate from the leafy shoots and often appearing before the leaves; they are daisy-like with numerous narrow ray-florets and a small central disc.
CULTIVATION: These plants are easily grown in a temperate climate, preferring heavy soils and damp ground, and where conditions suit them they may become invasive. They will thrive in full sun or part-shade. Propagate from seed or by division of rhizomes.

Tussilago farfara
COLTSFOOT

Of wide occurrence in Europe, temperate Asia and North Africa, coltsfoot grows on moist banks, screes or river gravels. Its distinctively shaped leaves (hence the common name) are glossy green above and white-felted beneath, mostly 4–8 in (10–20 cm) across. From early spring onward tight groups of scaly flowering stems about 6 in (15 cm) high emerge from the ground, each stem bearing a gold flowerhead up to $1\frac{1}{2}$ in (35 mm) across; the leaves emerge while later flowerheads are opening; they are commonly dried and then smoked like tobacco as a remedy for coughs and chest complaints. **ZONES 3–9.**

TWEEDIA

This is now a genus of one species, a straggling or semi-climbing subshrub from southern Brazil and Uruguay. It is grown primarily for its clear pale blue, star-shaped flowers, which are long lasting and popular as cut blooms. White- and pink-flowered forms, usually sold as **'Alba'** and **'Rosea'** are occasionally offered. In common with other asclepiads, the seed pods are filled with seeds that have downy 'parachute' tufts.
CULTIVATION: Plant in full sun in a well-drained soil that is a little on the dry side. *Tweedia* is marginally frost hardy but otherwise undemanding. Propagate from seed.

Tweedia caerulea
syn. *Oxypetalum caeruleum*

This subshrub to 3 ft (1 m) has heart-shaped, gray-green, downy leaves. The pale blue flowers, ageing to purple, are borne in summer and early fall (autumn) and are followed by 6 in (15 cm) long, boat-shaped, green seed pods. **ZONES 9–11.**

TYPHA
BULRUSH, REEDMACE, CAT TAIL

This cosmopolitan genus includes some 10 very similar species. They have tough, fibrous, spear-shaped leaves that can form a dense thicket of foliage around the margins of ponds or slow-moving streams. Their most distinguishing feature is their cylindrical seed heads that develop on stems up to 10 ft (3 m) high.
CULTIVATION: These very frost-hardy plants demand permanently moist soil and will grow in shallow water. They tend to fill and drain a pond (they are an important source of peat) so plant only where they can be controlled. Propagate from seed or by division in spring.

Typha angustifolia
LESSER BULRUSH

Native to the northern hemisphere, this species grows to a height of 5 ft (1.5 m). It has erect stems with leaves up to 3 ft (1 m) long but no more than $\frac{1}{4}$ in (6 mm) wide. The flowers are held in terminal spikes and are produced in summer; the dark brown male flowers are below the female flowers. In its natural habitat, it grows in salty marshes in sunny positions. **ZONES 3–9.**

Typha domingensis

This species occurs in most warmer regions of the world. It reaches a height of 6 ft (1.8 m) or more. The stout, erect stems are sheathed with dark green, narrow, reed-like leaves $\frac{1}{2}$–$\frac{3}{4}$ in (12–18 mm) wide. The light brown or rust-colored flowers are borne on dense cylindrical spikes in summer. It will grow in wet soils and shallow pools, but is a troublesome weed in some areas. **ZONES 5–11.**

Typha latifolia
REEDMACE, BULRUSH

This species from most temperate regions of the northern hemisphere is one of the tallest in the genus, reaching a height of 10 ft (3 m). It has large clumps of mid-green foliage and the erect stems carry leaves up to $\frac{3}{4}$ in (18 mm) wide. The flowers are cigar-like spikes 12 in (30 cm) in length, the male on the upper part and the female below. It can be extremely invasive. **ZONES 3–10.**

T

U V

UGNI

This small genus of evergreen shrubs to 10 ft (3 m) tall is closely related to *Myrtus* and was formerly included in that genus. Indigenous to areas of South and Central America and Mexico, the species most commonly found in cultivation is *Ugni molinae*, which is grown for its attractive, edible fruit and glossy, deep green leaves.
CULTIVATION: Species need well-drained, moist, lime-free soil and prefer partial to full sun. Prune in winter to keep the plants compact and bushy. Propagate from seed or cuttings in summer.

Ugni molinae
syn. ***Myrtus ugni***
CHILEAN GUAVA, CHILEAN CRANBERRY

Indigenous to Chile and Bolivia, this species bears fragrant, purplish red, berry-like fruit. These are edible, though tart, and are often made into jam or conserves. The abundant small, bell-shaped flowers are pink or white with prominent stamens, and are borne in the leaf axils. Its dense growth and height of 6 ft (1.8 m) or more makes *Ugni molinae* suitable for hedges; it needs partial shade in hot climates. **ZONES 8–10.**

Ugni montana
syn. ***Myrtus montana***

This species is native to the mountains of southern Mexico, at altitudes of around 7,000 ft (2,100 m). It makes a densely branched shrub of perhaps 6 ft (1.8 m) in height, the twigs clothed in very short white hairs and the thick, oblong leaves less than ½ in (12 mm) long, with recurved margins. The small white flowers and dark red fruit are similar to those of *Ugni molinae*. **ZONES 8–10.**

ULEX

GORSE

This genus consists of about 20 species of leafless or almost leafless, densely spiny shrubs from western Europe and North Africa. It belongs to the broom tribe of legumes along with *Cytisus, Genista* and *Spartium*. Young plants have small, compound leaves with 3 leaflets, but on mature plants the leaves are reduced to sharp spines, as are the branch tips. The flowers are profuse, mostly golden yellow and fragrant, borne singly or in small clusters. Small, hairy pods release their seeds explosively in mid-summer. Gorses are valued for their ability to thrive on sites too exposed or infertile for most other shrubs. Common gorse (*Ulex europaeus*) is apt to become a nuisance, however, especially in regions other than its native Europe.
CULTIVATION: Fully frost hardy, gorses thrive under most conditions (though not in the tropics or subtropics) as long as they receive full sun. They are tolerant of very poor sandy soils and exposure to salt-laden winds. In more sheltered positions, they may need pruning to keep a compact form. Propagate from seed in fall (autumn) or spring, or from cuttings in summer.

Ulex europaeus
COMMON GORSE, FURZE

This species is a broad, mound-like shrub which reaches about 6 ft (1.8 m) in height. When it blooms in spring, it is completely covered in pea-flowers in groups of 2s or 3s; their fragrance resembles that of coconut. The double-flowered form, **'Flore Pleno'**, has rather distorted blooms, but is more compact; it is also preferred for cultivation because it cannot form seeds and is thus not invasive. **ZONES 6–9.**

Ugni molinae

Ulex europaeus

Ulmus × hollandica

Ulmus americana

Ulmus minor

ULMUS

ELM

The 30 or so species in this genus of trees occur naturally in temperate regions of the northern hemisphere. During the 1920s and 1930s, and again in the 1960s and 1970s, elm trees in Europe and North America were devastated by Dutch elm disease, caused by the fungus *Ophiostoma ulmi*, which is transmitted by the elm bark beetle. Except for a few East Asian species, they are deciduous, turning yellow in fall (autumn). The leaves are usually one-sided at the base, with prominent, parallel lateral veins and regularly toothed margins; the small, disc-like fruits have a membranous wing and are carried in clusters. Most elms are large limbed with furrowed gray bark and high, domed crowns.
CULTIVATION: Mostly very frost hardy, they require cool to cold winters and prefer full sun and deep, moist, fertile soil. Propagate from semi-ripe cuttings in summer, from suckers or by grafting or budding in fall. They can be propagated from seed in fall, but the germination rate is often low.

Ulmus americana
AMERICAN ELM, WHITE ELM

The largest North American elm, this species occurs naturally over eastern and central USA, and southern Canada. It can reach a height of 120 ft (36 m) in the wild—about half that in cultivation—and has high-arching limbs. Mature trees develop a broad crown and may become strongly buttressed at the base; the ash-gray bark is deeply fissured. The leaves, 4–6 in (10–15 cm) long, have smooth upper sides with slightly downy undersides, and unforked lateral veins. **'Delaware'** is broadly vase-shaped, fast growing and claimed to be resistant to Dutch elm disease. **'Princeton'** is also vase-shaped, and vigorous with some resistance to elm leaf beetle. **'Washington'** is thought to be a hybrid of *Ulmus americana* and an unknown species. **ZONES 3–9.**

Ulmus americana

Ulmus glabra 'Camperdownii'

Ulmus glabra
syns ***Ulmus montana, U. scabra***
SCOTCH ELM, WYCH ELM

One of the major European elms, this species can grow to more than 100 ft (30 m) high with a wide, spreading crown, and does not sucker from the roots. Its dull, dark green leaves, up to 6 in (15 cm) long and broadest near the apex, have a rough raspy upper surface. **'Camperdownii'** forms a dome-like mound of weeping branches when grafted onto a standard; **'Lutescens'**, the common golden elm, has spring and summer foliage colored lime green and tipped with pale yellow. **ZONES 3–9.**

Ulmus × hollandica
DUTCH ELM, HYBRID ELM

This hybrid name covers several clones believed to originate from crosses between *Ulmus glabra* and *U. minor*. Their glossy dark green leaves, yellowing in fall (autumn), are mostly smaller and less raspy than *U. glabra* leaves, and broader and shorter stalked than those of *U. minor*. The original, now referred to as **'Hollandica'**, has broad, rounded leaves. **'Jacqueline Hillier'** is a small bushy shrub growing 8 ft (2.4 m) in height. **'Purpurascens'**, a vigorous, open tree, has purplish green new growth. **'Vegeta'**, the Huntingdon elm (an old clone), bears pale yellowish green leaves in flattened sprays. **ZONES 4–9.**

Ulmus laevis
RUSSIAN ELM, EUROPEAN WHITE ELM

From central and eastern Europe and east to the Caucasus region, the Russian elm is a large, 100 ft (30 m) tall, vigorous tree. Its coarse, dark green leaves resemble those of *Ulmus americana*, a close relative, but are shorter and relatively broader with gray down underneath. The crown is broad, even on young trees, and the dark gray bark is strongly furrowed. **ZONES 3–9.**

Ulmus minor
syn. ***Ulmus carpinifolia***
FIELD ELM, SMOOTH-LEAFED ELM

Widespread throughout Europe, western Asia and North Africa, this deciduous species is usually smaller than the other

European elms and the crown is pointed. It reaches a height of 100 ft (30 m) with a spread of up to 70 ft (21 m) in the wild. The leaves are also smaller, tapering at both ends, with smooth upper sides and a slender stalk. Due to its suckering habit, a single tree may form a small, dense grove. **'Variegata'**, with white-streaked leaves, is just as vigorous, but is less inclined to sucker. ***Ulmus minor* 'Cornubiensis'** (syn. *U. angustifolia* var. *cornubiensis*) is a tall, slender tree growing 60–70 ft (18–21 m) tall and 20 ft (6 m) wide. Commonly known as Cornish elm, it forms a dense conical head of ascending branches, later becoming more open and loose. The leaves are smooth and glossy above and conspicuously tufted beneath. It thrives in coastal situations. **ZONES 4–9.**

Ulmus parvifolia
CHINESE ELM, LACEBARK ELM

Native to China and Japan, this elm grows to 60 ft (18 m) tall and has a spreading, sinuous habit and bark mottled with dark gray, reddish brown and cream. It is semi-evergreen in mild climates. The small, leathery, dark green leaves, smooth and shiny on top, have small, blunt teeth. The fruit mature in fall (autumn), much later than those of most other elms. It is relatively resistant to Dutch elm disease. **'Frosty'** is a shrubby, slow-growing form with small, neatly arranged leaves bearing white teeth. **ZONES 5–10.**

Ulmus procera
ENGLISH ELM

This elm, which can reach 150 ft (45 m) in height, has a high-branched, billowing crown and straight or slightly sinuous trunk. In the UK, few have survived

Ulmus minor

Ulmus parvifolia

Ulmus laevis

Dutch elm disease. Cultivated in the southern hemisphere, it produces a compact, rounded crown up to 80 ft (24 m) high. Its smallish, rounded leaves have a rough surface. Seldom setting fertile seed, it is usually propagated from suckers. The rare cultivar **'Louis van Houtte'** has golden-green leaves. **ZONES 4–9.**

Ulmus pumila
SIBERIAN ELM, DWARF ELM

Occurring naturally from eastern Siberia right across northern China and central Asia, this small, fast-growing elm is valued for its hardiness in drought and severe cold. It is easily distinguished by its slender-stalked, small leaves, almost completely symmetrical at the base; they are dark green and toothed. Its branches tend to brittleness, but as it appears resistant to Dutch elm disease it has been used to breed hybrid cultivars such as **'Sapporo Autumn Gold'**, which has dense foliage turning deep golden yellow in fall (autumn). **ZONES 3–9.**

Ulmus rubra
SLIPPERY ELM, RED ELM

This tree is native to southern and central North America. It develops a broad, open crown and spreading branches, reaching a height of 60 ft (18 m). The oval leaves are large, 6–8 in (15–20 cm), tinged red when opening, dark green and rough above with a paler, downy underside giving a velvety appearance. The flowers are greenish and insignificant, and carried in clusters near the branch tips in spring. This species prefers an open, sunny position but does not tolerate dry conditions. The leaves turn dull yellow in fall (autumn). **ZONES 3–10.**

UMBELLULARIA
CALIFORNIA BAY TREE, CALIFORNIA LAUREL, PEPPERWOOD, OREGON MYRTLE, HEADACHE TREE

This genus consists of a single species, an evergreen tree indigenous to California

Ulmus parvifolia 'Frosty'

Ulmus procera

Ulmus pumila

Ulmus procera 'Louis van Houtte'

and Oregon. It is sometimes called 'headache tree' because when its leaves are crushed under the nose, their pungent smell can cause an instant (though temporary) headache. It has nonetheless been used as a traditional headache cure; Native Americans also used the leaves as an insect repellent.

CULTIVATION: Frost hardy once established, it prefers full sun and deep, moist, but well-drained soil. Propagate from seed in fall (autumn).

Umbellularia californica

The California laurel reaches 80 ft (24 m) in height and forms a dense, spreading crown. The trunk has scaly bark, and its leathery leaves are oval to lance-shaped, 4 in (10 cm) long, dark green and shiny on top. Inconspicuous yellowish green flowers are carried in clusters near the branch tips in spring. The fruit are purple and olive-like. The timber is valued for delicate woodworking. **ZONES 7–10.**

UNCINIA
HOOK SEDGE

This sedge genus consists of 35 to 45 species of tussocky, grass-like, evergreen perennials. They occur naturally in moist or swampy, open or lightly wooded areas in New Zealand, Australia, South America and islands of the southern oceans. The leaves are long and narrow, sometimes with a central groove and very often colored a deep brownish red. The flowers are not showy, but the small nutlike fruits have a hooked apex, allowing them to cling to fur or feathers.These plants are sometimes grown in collections of ornamental grasses or in permanently damp parts of the garden.

CULTIVATION: Although not aquatic, they do need consistent moisture around their roots and do best in rich, peaty soil that allows excess water to drain away, or they can be grown in containers standing in a saucer of water. Grow in full sun or dappled or part-shade. Propagate by division in spring to retain good color forms, as seedlings can be somewhat variable.

Uncinia uncinata
RED SEDGE, RED HOOK SEDGE

Growing to a height of around 18 in (45 cm), the New Zealand red sedge forms a clump of narrow, channeled, evergreen leaves that are a pleasant mahogany color. The insignificant flowers are brown and appear towards the end of summer. It is moderately frost hardy. **ZONES 8–10.**

URGINEA

This genus, allied to *Scilla*, consists of about 100 species of bulbs, mostly occurring naturally in Africa with a few species from the Mediterranean region. They have 12–24 in (30–60 cm) long, sword-like, gray- to blue-green leaves that do not appear until fall (autumn), after the flower spike has developed. The cultivated species produce 18 in–5 ft (45 cm–1.5 m) flower stems with 12 in (30 cm) or longer lupin-like heads of 6-petalled, starry, white flowers in late summer.

Urginea maritima

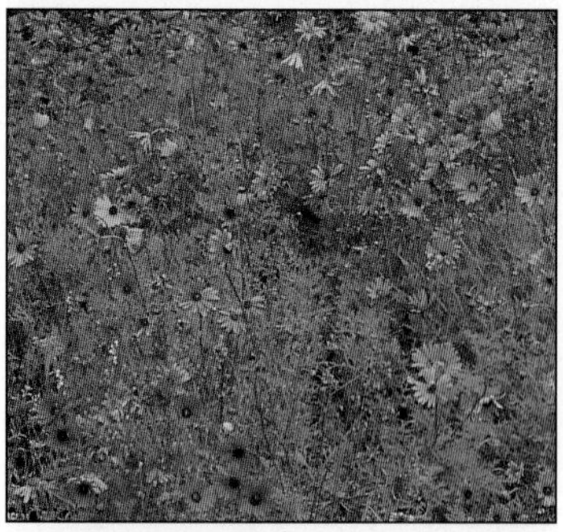

Ursinia cakilefolia

Ursinia sericea

CULTIVATION: Plant the large bulbs with their upper half protruding from the soil. Marginally frost hardy, they prefer light, sandy, well-drained soil in full sun; do not water in summer until the flower spikes begin to develop. If left undisturbed, large clumps develop, which can then be broken up. Otherwise, propagate from ripe seed, bulbils or bulb scaling.

Urginea maritima

syns *Scilla maritima, Drimia maritima*
SEA SQUILL, SEA ONION

Native to Mediterranean coastal regions, where it grows in sand and gravel often under very harsh conditions, this species has been known since ancient times for the medicinal value of the sliced and dried bulbs (squills), still used in some cough mixtures though dangerously poisonous in large doses. *Urginea maritima* has half-buried bulbs 3–5 in (8–12 cm) in diameter, building into clumps with age and each producing several broad, wavy edged gray-green leaves up to 24 in (60 cm) long. In spring each bulb sends up a stout spike 12–36 in (30–90 cm) tall bearing a large number of starry white flowers, each of which is less than $\frac{1}{2}$ in (12 mm) wide and slender stalked. The sea squill is easily grown in a dry, sunny position in sandy soil. **ZONES 8–10.**

Ursinia anthemoides

Ursinia calenduliflora

URSINIA

Native to southern Africa and Ethiopia, this genus contains up to 40 species of annuals, perennials, subshrubs and shrubs. The plants have pinnate, fern-like foliage. They bear open, terminal clusters of yellow, white, orange or occasionally red flowers with purple or yellow centers.

CULTIVATION: Ranging from marginally frost hardy to frost tender, they require warm, dry climates, full sun and well-drained, moderately fertile soil. Propagate from cuttings or seed in spring. Protect from aphids.

Ursinia anthemoides

STAR OF THE VELD

This bushy, frost-tender annual, with its pale green, feathery foliage, blooms in summer and early fall (autumn). Its flowerheads are like orange-yellow daisies with dark purple or coppery centers. It grows 15 in (38 cm) tall and 8 in (20 cm) wide. **ZONES 9–11.**

Ursinia cakilefolia

Indigenous to the Cape Province area, this sun-loving annual grows to a height of 18 in (45 cm) and bears deep yellow or orange flowerheads, about 2 in (5 cm) across, with a darker central disc. The collar at the base of the flower is rigid and purple-tipped. The leaves are somewhat fleshy and coarsely divided and the stems are straw colored. **ZONES 9–11.**

Ursinia calenduliflora

SPRINGBOK ROCK URSINIA

This South African annual grows to 15 in (38 cm) tall. *Ursinia calenduliflora* has pinnate, $2\frac{1}{2}$ in (6 cm) long leaves which consist of narrow to rounded leaflets. The daisy-like flowers, $2\frac{1}{2}$ in (6 cm) in diameter, are yellow and are frequently marked with dark purple near the base. **ZONES 9–11.**

Ursinia sericea

This subshrub grows to about 30 in (75 cm) in height and bears large yellow flowers in summer. The leaves are tapered, hairy and about 3 in (8 cm) long. **ZONES 9–11.**

URTICA

NETTLE

Many of the 100 or so species in this genus have stinging hairs on their leaves and stems, which is referred to in their generic name, derived from the Latin *uro*, meaning 'I burn'. From temperate regions of both northern and southern hemispheres, nettles are erect annuals or perennials with opposite, toothed leaves. Minute green and white unisexual flowers in axillary, tassel-like clusters are borne in summer. Nettles, especially ***Urtica dioica, U. pilulifera*** and *U. urens*, are valued in herbal medicines and as a dye. Their young, fresh green leaves, rich in vitamins and minerals, can be eaten as a cooked vegetable or in salads or soups. The stinging hairs are destroyed during cooking. At one time nettles were cultivated in Scotland and Norway and used in cloth manufacture—a craft with a 2,000 year history.

CULTIVATION: Mostly very frost hardy, nettles are easy to grow in sun or shade in most soils. Propagate from seed or by division of roots in spring.

Urtica urens

SMALL NETTLE

Native to Europe, but now extensively naturalized elsewhere, this branching annual grows to a height of 24 in (60 cm). It has hairy, oval to heart-shaped serrated gray-green leaves. Short branched clusters of greenish unisexual flowers are produced throughout most of the year. **ZONES 5–10.**

UTRICULARIA

BLADDERWORT

This large genus with worldwide distribution consists of more than 200 species of annual or perennial carnivorous plants including terrestrial, epiphytic and aquatic forms. A peculiarity of all species is that they do not possess any kind of root, but instead form long, occasionally branching stems or stolons. Most are found growing in water or wet places, some with submersed stems and leaves; some tropical species are epiphytic. The most remarkable feature of each plant are the stalked and bladder-like traps scattered on the stems or leaves of the plant, ingeniously adapted to catch tiny aquatic creatures. The 2-lipped, spurred flowers vary in size, form and color.

Urtica urens

CULTIVATION: The diversity of these variably frost-hardy to frost-tender species necessitates different treatments. The aquatic species are best grown in aquaria or shallow pans of water with sphagnum moss; terrestrial species can be grown in pots of peat moss. They require full sun if grown outdoors. Propagate by division in spring and summer.

Utricularia gibba

syn. Utricularia exoleta

This aquatic and sometimes partly terrestrial species thrives in a humid tropical climate. Occurring naturally in the USA, Israel, South Africa, China, Australia and New Zealand, its habitat is lakes, ponds and sphagnum hollows. It forms a thick mat of tangled leaves and bladders. The hair-like leaves are held on thread-like stems; the small flowers, produced in mid-summer, are sulfur yellow with a red tinge in the center. **ZONES 10–12.**

Utricularia sandersonii

RABBIT EARS

This small perennial species grows naturally among moss-covered rocks in the Cape Province to Natal area of South Africa. The leaves are light green to pale yellow and fan-shaped. The flowers, which appear throughout the year, are white with mauve veins and a yellow center. This terrestrial bladderwort is one of the prettiest and easiest to grow, and multiplies freely. **ZONES 9–11.**

UVULARIA

BELLWORT, MERRY-BELLS

The 5 species of rhizomatous perennials in this genus are native to eastern North America. These herbaceous woodland plants are usually found growing in

Uvularia perfoliata

Utricularia sandersonii

U

Vaccinium corymbosum 'Blue Ray'

Vaccinium cylindraceum

moist but well-drained leafy soil in the shade of deciduous trees. The stems are either simple or branched, erect to arching and the leaves are perfoliate in some species. The pendulous, bell-shaped flowers are borne either solitary and terminal, or in axillary clusters. They usually come in shades of yellow and appear in spring.
CULTIVATION: Very frost hardy, they can be grown in rock gardens and beside water features provided they are in at least part-shade and the acidic soil contains plenty of organic matter. Propagate by division in late winter or early spring or from ripe seed.

Uvularia grandiflora
BELLWORT, MERRYBELLS

This easily grown herbaceous, clump-forming perennial has fresh green leaves on arching stems reaching about 30 in (75 cm) in height. The straw-yellow flowers, produced in spring, are 1–2 in (2.5–5 cm) long and hang delicately from the stems, rather like Solomon's seal *(Polygonatum)* to which it is related. It needs protection from slugs when young. **ZONES 3–9.**

Uvularia perfoliata

This species has markedly stem-clasping leaves, glabrous and paler underneath, and reaches a height of about 24 in (60 cm). The flowers are up to 2 in (5 cm) long, pale yellow with rather twisted, upturned segments and are carried conspicuously above the leaves in spring. It forms a clump that can be easily divided for propagation. **ZONES 4–9.**

VACCINIUM

This is a large and varied genus of about 450 species of deciduous and evergreen shrubs and occasionally small trees and vines. The species seen in gardens are shrubs valued for either their edible berries or their notable fall (autumn)

Vaccinium corymbosum 'Earliblue'

color. The berries, known according to the species as bilberry, blueberry, cranberry, huckleberry or whortleberry, are red or blue-black and are often covered with a bloom when ripe. They are grown commercially for fresh fruit, as well as for juicing and canning. Vacciniums are indigenous mainly to the northern hemisphere in a wide range of habitats, stretching from the Arctic to the tropics. The leaves are bright green, often leathery and sometimes coppery red when young; their edges can be toothed or smooth. Small bell-shaped flowers, pale pink, white, purple or red, appear in late spring or early summer.
CULTIVATION: *Vaccinium* species are generally frost hardy and shade loving; many form dense, thicket-like shrubs. The plants need acidic, well-drained soil with plenty of humus and regular water; some, indeed, prefer boggy ground. Propagate by division or from cuttings in fall.

Vaccinium arboreum
TREE SPARKLEBERRY, FARKLEBERRY

Native to southeastern USA, this medium to large deciduous or semi-evergreen shrub can achieve tree-like proportions in the wild. Its glossy, dark green leaves are 2 in (5 cm) long and leathery, with downy undersides. The foliage colors well in fall (autumn), but the berries appeal as a food only to birds. **ZONES 7–10.**

Vaccinium corymbosum
HIGHBUSH BLUEBERRY

This deciduous species from New England, USA, has a preference for boggy soils. It is grown mainly for its edible, blue-black berries. It also displays fine scarlet fall (autumn) foliage. Forming a dense thicket of upright stems with a height and spread of 6 ft (1.8 m), its new leaves are bright green. The clusters of pendulous flowers are pale pink. **'Blue Ray'** has delicious, sweet, juicy fruit. **'Earliblue'** is tall and vigorous with very large berries. For heavier cropping, grow 2 cultivars together. **ZONES 2–9.**

Vaccinium cylindraceum

Native to the Azores, this deciduous or semi-evergreen, medium-sized shrub has dark green, glossy, finely toothed leaves and produces flowers in short dense racemes on the previous year's shoots. The flowers are cylindrical and about $\frac{1}{2}$ in (12 mm) long. Red when in bud, they open to pale yellow-green and are produced in summer and fall (autumn). They are followed by cylindrical, blue-black berries covered with a bloom. **ZONES 10–11.**

Vaccinium glaucoalbum

This evergreen shrub has a suckering habit and occurs naturally in the Himalayas. It reaches 2–4 ft (0.6–1.2 m) in height. The large, oval, leathery leaves are mid-green above and vividly blue-white beneath. The tiny cylindrical flowers, white flushed pink with silvery white bracts, are produced in racemes in early summer. The berries are black with a glaucous bloom and often last well into winter. It prefers a moist, shaded position. **ZONES 9–11.**

Vaccinium macrocarpon
syn. *Oxycoccus macrocarpon*
AMERICAN CRANBERRY

Native to eastern North America, this evergreen is commercially grown there and several cultivars are known. Prostrate in habit, it forms mats of interlacing wiry stems with alternate leaves spreading to around 3 ft (1 m) when fully mature. Pink, nodding flowers are produced in summer, followed by relatively large, tart red fruit. **ZONES 2–9.**

Vaccinium myrtillus
BILBERRY, WHORTLEBERRY

This European and north Asian species is a compact, semi-deciduous shrub around 18 in (45 cm) tall. It has small oval leaves with finely toothed edges, and in spring bears $\frac{1}{4}$–$\frac{1}{2}$ in (6–12 mm) wide dusky red, bell-shaped flowers. Edible blue-black berries follow. This tough little shrub is ideal for rock gardens. **ZONES 3–9.**

Vaccinium ovatum
EVERGREEN HUCKLEBERRY

Occurring naturally from Oregon through to southern California, this is a dense, compact shrub. Its dark green, glossy foliage is much in demand by florists as it lasts well in water; in fact, this demand has driven the wild plants very nearly to extinction. The plant forms a spreading clump 3 ft (1 m) high and 5 ft (1.5 m) wide and can reach 8–10 ft (2.4 –3 m) in shady spots. The white or pink flowers appear in early summer. Its tangy, edible berries are red when young, maturing to blue-black. **ZONES 7–10.**

Vaccinium vitis-idaea
COWBERRY, FOXBERRY

Native to North America, Europe and Asia, this vigorous, evergreen, prostrate shrub forms hummocks 6–12 in (15–30 cm) high. The small, dark green, leathery leaves become bronzed in winter. Its flowers are bell-shaped, white, tinged pink and borne in short terminal racemes during summer. The globular red berries, produced in late fall (autumn), are edible but acid to the taste. **'Koralle'** is an especially abundant cropper that has won the Award of Garden Merit from the Royal Horticultural Society in the UK. **ZONES 2–9.**

VALERIANA
VALERIAN

This genus consists of more than 150 species of herbaceous perennials, herbs and subshrubs mostly distributed throughout the woodlands of Europe, with some species indigenous to North America and tropical South America. Few of the plants are of any ornamental value in the garden. Those that are, are

Vaccinium ovatum

Vaccinium macrocarpon

Vaccinium glaucoalbum

suitable for borders and rock gardens. The name derives from the Latin *valere*, meaning 'keep well', in recognition of the medicinal properties of some species. Before modern tranquilizers were introduced, the root from *Valeriana officinalis* was used to treat nervous conditions.
CULTIVATION: Very frost hardy, they will thrive in almost any soil, in sun or part-shade. Propagate from seed or by division of established plants in fall (autumn).

Valeriana arizonica

A low-growing plant with a creeping rhizome, this species is a native of Arizona and can grow up to 12 in (30 cm) in height. It has fleshy leaves and clusters of rounded flowerheads of tiny pink flowers appearing in late spring. **ZONES 7–10.**

Valeriana officinalis

CAT'S VALERIAN, COMMON VALERIAN, GARDEN HELIOTROPHE

This clump-forming, fleshy perennial, which is attractive to cats, grows to 4 ft (1.2 m) tall with a spread of 3 ft (1 m). It occurs naturally throughout Europe and eastwards to Russia and western Asia. It bears rounded flowerheads of white to dark pink flowers in summer on erect, hollow, hairy stems. The leaves are opposite with serrated margins. **ZONES 3–9.**

Valeriana phu

This native of the Caucasus is an easily grown plant, reaching about 24 in (60 cm) in height. It is often planted in gardens for its attractive oval to oblong, fleshy green leaves. The small flowers are white and produced in clusters of rounded flowerheads in late summer. **'Aurea'** has bright yellow young leaves and white flowers in summer. **ZONES 3–9.**

VALERIANELLA

LAMB'S LETTUCE

This genus consists of 50 to 60 species of annual and biennial herbs which occur naturally in North America, Europe, North Africa and Asia. The 2–5 in (5–12 cm), linear to lanceolate leaves are rather succulent and usually in a rosette; the flowers may be white, rose or blue, and are borne in terminal cymes. Some species occur as weeds of arable land, but improved selections are widely cultivated in western Europe where they form a useful winter salad crop.
CULTIVATION: Most species are frost resistant, but will not tolerate continual dryness. They can be grown in any sunny position in well-drained soil. Propagate from seed in fall (autumn) and spring.

Valerianella locusta

CORN SALAD

Rampant in corn fields in cool to cold climates and a hardy grower, this is a good substitute for lettuce in winter. Sow the seeds in late summer and early fall (autumn) in a sunny spot in the garden. Place seeds 10 in (25 cm) apart. Make sure the soil is lightly raked and forked. Ideally, it should be situated where another crop was previously grown. Keep the soil moist and harvest the leaves as they are needed. Watch for slugs. **ZONES 4–9.**

VALLISNERIA

EEL GRASS, TAPE GRASS

This genus consists of 2 species of submerged, bottom-rooting aquatic perennials with a wide distribution in the temperate zones and tropics. They spread by runners and often cover large areas. The grassy leaves grow in clusters from the roots and are about 1 in (25 mm) wide and up to 6 ft (1.8 m) long. The tiny flowers float on the water's surface. The male flowers are inconspicuous; the white, 3-petalled, female flowers are more visible, though scarcely a feature. The flowers are followed by small, curved seed capsules. These plants can be grown in pools and aquariums.

Valeriana arizonica

Valeriana officinalis

Vancouveria hexandra

Vancouveria planipetala

CULTIVATION: These frost-tender plants grow in still or flowing water with a depth of 3 ft (1 m) or more. They do best with constantly warm water, but are hardy enough to survive anywhere the water temperature stays above 40°F (5°C) in winter. Plant in sun or morning shade. Propagate by division in spring or summer.

Vallisneria spiralis

RIBBON WEED

A native of Africa, Europe and Asia, this plant adapts to both cold water or tropical ponds provided it is in a sunny position. It grows to about 6 ft (1.8 m) tall with a similar spread. The short stem is submerged and the translucent green leaves are long, linear and ribbon-like. The male flowers are small and insignificant; the white female flowers are carried on spiral, terminal spikes which, after pollination, twist and carry the young fruit to the bottom to ripen. **ZONES 8–12.**

VANCOUVERIA

There are 3 species in this genus of graceful, creeping, woodland plants with slender rhizomes. These perennial herbs and shrubs are native to western North America and are related to *Epimedium.* The leaves are rounded and often 3 lobed; the flowering stem, 8–16 in (20–40 cm) long, is normally leafless. The small pendulous flowers are white or yellow, and borne in spring or summer.
CULTIVATION: Useful as a ground cover in cool shaded areas, these frost-hardy plants usually prefer a cool position in peaty soil. Propagate by division, or from fresh ripe seed in spring.

Vancouveria chrysantha

SISKIYOU INSIDE-OUT FLOWER

Found growing naturally on rocky hillsides in Oregon and California, this small evergreen shrub spreads to about 3 ft (1 m) and reaches 12 in (30 cm) in height. The leaves are dark green and stiff in texture, somewhat leathery and hairy underneath. The 5-petalled flowers are golden yellow and are produced in pendent clusters on glandular stalks in spring. This species is suitable for a warm, sheltered position in sandy soil. Propagate by division. **ZONES 7–9.**

Vancouveria hexandra

This deciduous shrub reaches a height of 18 in (45 cm) and a spread of up to 3 ft (1 m). It is distributed from Washington to California, and is found in shady woods. The white flowers are tinged with pink and borne in pendent clusters in mid-summer. The leaves are divided into almost hexagonal leaflets and are thin but not leathery. **ZONES 5–9.**

Vancouveria planipetala

REDWOOD IVY, INSIDE-OUT FLOWER

This plant is found growing in the redwood forests of North America in sunny or part-shaded positions which are sheltered in winter. It grows to 18 in (45 cm) in height with a 3 ft (1 m) spread. The stems are creeping, prostrate and branching. The evergreen leaves are thick and leathery with a wavy margin. The flower stem is leafless, up to 18 in (45 cm) tall, and the flowers are white, tinged with lavender and borne in spring. **ZONES 7–9.**

VANDA

The most celebrated species of this epiphytic orchid genus from Southeast Asia to northern Australia is *Vanda caerulea* from the mountains of Thailand and Burma, where was once quite common. Sadly, the greed of Western gardeners has brought it to an endangered state—and it is not often seen in gardens either, its place having been taken by more easily grown hybrids. Some of the 35 or so species of this genus are spring or summer flowering, and the color range is from white through cream and pink to orange—blue is rare. Many have interesting markings and mottlings of other colors. These orchids range from miniatures to large robust plants.
CULTIVATION: They are all warm-growing epiphytes, liking a very coarse compost and strong light, though preferably not full sunshine; they are outdoor plants only in the tropics. Keep them warm and watered all year, as they rarely take a winter rest. Most will need staking; if this is a piece of tree fern trunk they will cling to it by aerial roots. Feed regularly during the growing season. Propagate by removing rooted offsets.

Vanda Hybrids

The *Vanda* species have been used to develop a large number of hybrids over the past 100 years. Many of these have been used in the cut flower industry as the flowers are large and long lasting, and are readily grown in tropical countries. Major trends have been with the terete-leafed species (now usually regarded as a separate genus—*Papilonanthe*) and with the larger-flowered species such as ***V. sanderiana*** (syn. *Euanthe sanderiana*) and *V. caerulea*. There are also numerous intergeneric crosses with *Ascocentrum* and other smaller genera which have given rise to more compact hybrids. **ZONE 12.**

Vanda caerulea

This perennial species grows to 5 ft (1.5 m) tall with an erect stem and pale green, strap-shaped leaves. Terminal racemes bear up to 15 blooms—blue flowers tinged with white and with twisted petals; the flowers are 4 in (10 cm) across and appear in early fall (autumn). **ZONE 12.**

Vanda Josephine van Brero

One of the many popular Vanda hybrids, Josephine van Brero has large sprays of pink flowers, usually twice a year. **ZONE 12.**

Vanda Nellie Morley

Derived from *Vanda sanderiana*, this has become perhaps the most popular of the *Vanda* hybrids, with many named clones available. It usually has 4 in (10 cm) wide flowers in shades of rich pink or coral. Unusually, it flowers twice a year, in spring and again in fall (autumn). It likes warm conditions, but plenty of fresh air. **ZONE 12.**

Vanda Rothschildiana
BLUE ORCHID

This hybrid between *Vanda caerulea* and *Euanthe sanderiana* is easier to grow than its parents and hence more often encountered in gardens than other hybrids. It bears sprays of 6 in (15 cm) or larger, long-lasting flowers in winter. They range in the different clones from light to deep violet blue, the flowers being distinctly veined with a deeper shade; a well-grown plant can carry several sprays of flowers. It has itself given rise to further hybrids. **ZONE 12.**

Vanda tricolor

This species is restricted to the island of Java, Indonesia, where it grows as an epiphyte at low elevations. It is a large plant with stems up to 18 in (45 cm) long, often branched to form a dense tangle of stems and roots. The leaves are strap-like, about 15 in (38 cm) by 2 in (5 cm) and curved. The inflorescence is up to 10 in (25 cm) long with 6 to 9 long-lasting, variously colored fragrant flowers about 3 in (8 cm) across. This species does best in a well-lit position in a mixture of coarse rubble; it requires regular watering. Flowering occurs throughout the year. **ZONE 12.**

VANILLA

The members of this genus are vine-like climbing orchids with stems known to reach lengths of up to 120 ft (36 m). There are about 100 species distributed throughout tropical and subtropical regions of the world. They have fleshy leaves scattered along their stems and roots develop opposite the leaves to attach to host trees. Inflorescences are short, each with several fragrant, large and showy flowers opening progressively, however, they are not long lasting. The flowers are followed by capsules with large seeds.
CULTIVATION: The plants grow well if potted in a mixture such as would be used for *Cymbidium* and need something on which to climb. They require bright filtered light and regular watering and fertilizing. The plants do not flower until they have reached a large size. Propagate from stem cuttings.

Vanilla planifolia

This large climber occurs naturally in the West Indies and Central America, but is now cultivated around the world for the vanilla essence which is extracted from the seed pods. The fleshy leaves are up to 8 in (20 cm) long and 2 in (5 cm) broad. The pale yellow inflorescence is about 2 in (5 cm) long and has several fragrant, short-lived flowers which open successively, each about $2\frac{1}{2}$ in (6 cm) long. The seed pod, the source of vanilla flavoring, is fleshy, turning black as it ages and exuding a strong odor. *Vanilla*

Veitchia merrillii

planifolia flowers throughout the year. **ZONE 12.**

VEITCHIA

The elegant, feather-leafed palms of this genus occur naturally in tropical forests of Fiji, Vanuatu and the Philippines. The 15 or so species range in height from 20–100 ft (6–30 m) and most have a slender, pale gray, smooth or lightly ringed trunk. The bright green, gently arching fronds form an umbrella-like crown. Bunches of insignificant flowers are followed by dense clusters of bright red or orange berries.
CULTIVATION: They need a tropical or warm subtropical climate, protection from wind and moist, well-drained soil; they do best in full sun or part-shade. Mature trees make attractive lawn and landscape specimens, while young plants grow well in tubs, even indoors in well lit conditions. Propagation from seed is slow.

Veitchia merrillii
MANILA PALM

Native to the Philippines, this is an attractive, small palm widely grown in tropical gardens. Maturing to 20 ft (6 m) tall, it has a slender trunk marked with rings. The feathery, bright green leaves, springing from a short crownshaft, form a compact crown. The bright red fruit, about $1\frac{1}{2}$ in (35 mm) long, hang in clusters below the crown in fall (autumn) and winter. This species is often seen planted in the shelter of buildings where its delicate fronds are protected from wind damage. **ZONES 11–12.**

VELLA

The name of this genus from the western Mediterranean region is derived from the Celtic *veller*, meaning cress, and the genus is related to the cabbage family. It consists of 4 species of deciduous or evergreen low shrubs which are much branched. The yellow flowers, occasionally veined with violet, have 4 petals and are borne in racemes.
CULTIVATION: These are plants suitable for a rock garden in a sunny, rather dry position, but they are liable to be damaged or killed by severe winters. Prune only to remove dead wood after flowering. Propagate from cuttings taken in fall (autumn) and plant out in spring.

Vanda Nellie Morley

Vanda Josephine van Brero

Vella spinosa

Native to the limestone mountains in Spain, this small, rounded, deciduous shrub grows 12 in (30 cm) tall with the upper branches of the stems tipped with spines. The leaves are gray-green, fleshy and dull; the creamy summer flowers are veined with violet. **ZONES 8–10.**

VELTHEIMIA
VELDT LILY

The 2 species of bulbous perennials that make up this South African genus produce rosettes of basal leaves and dense spikes of pendent, tubular flowers in winter or spring. The flowers are similar in form to those of *Kniphofia*.
CULTIVATION: Plant bulbs in fall (autumn) in moist, rich, well-drained soil in good light to keep foliage compact and properly develop flower colors. Reduce watering after flowering. Frost tender, they should be grown in pots in cold areas. Propagate from seed or offsets in fall.

Veltheimia bracteata
syn. *Veltheimia viridifolia*
FOREST LILY

Found wild in the Eastern Cape of South Africa, this species has wavy, glossy green leaves growing in a rosette. Rocket-like inflorescences on strong, erect stalks are produced in spring and early summer. The drooping, tubular flowers are pink, red or pale yellow. Growing 18 in (45 cm) tall and 12 in (30 cm) wide, it thrives in part-shade under trees or shrubs. It is a good potted specimen. **ZONES 9–11.**

Veltheimia capensis
syn. *Veltheimia glauca*

This species produces a strong stem growing up to 18 in (45 cm), which bears a dense spike of pendent, tubular, 1 in (25 mm) blooms in spring. The rosy pink to red flowers are sometimes tipped with green. The glossy, dark green leaves have wavy edges. **ZONES 9–11.**

Veltheimia bracteata

Vanda Rothschildiana

Vella spinosa

VERATRUM

This genus consists of about 45 species of perennial herbs found in Europe, Siberia and North America. They grow from a thick rhizome, which is poisonous, and from this arises erect, leafy stems which make arching mounds of foliage. The leaves are large, pleated and very decorative. The flowers, often on tall, leafless stalks, are broadly bell-shaped in terminal panicles. The powdered rhizome of *Veratrum album,* called hellebore powder, was once used to destroy caterpillars.
CULTIVATION: Very frost hardy, these are easy plants to grow given a rich, moist soil. When the plants need to be divided, this should be done in fall (autumn) as they start into growth very early in spring. They can also be propagated from seed in fall. Protect from snails. All species are poisonous.

Veratrum album

Veratrum nigrum

Verbascum bombyciferum

Verbascum chaixii

Verbascum chaixii 'Album'

Veratrum album

WHITE FALSE HELLEBORE, EUROPEAN WHITE HELLEBORE

This clump-forming perennial grows to 6 ft (1.8 m) tall with a spread of 24 in (60 cm). The large, striking leaves are clear green and appear to be folded like a fan. The leafless flower stalk bears dense terminal panicles of pale green to almost white bell-shaped flowers in late summer. This species does best when grown in a shaded, protected position. **ZONES 5–9.**

Veratrum nigrum

BLACK FALSE HELLEBORE

This species is a rare perennial from southern Europe and Asia. It carries long, narrow, terminal spikes of small, purplish brown flowers with 6 petals that bloom from late summer. The large, pleated, elliptical leaves are arranged spirally into a sheath around the stout, erect stems. It grows to a height of 6 ft (1.8 m) and half as wide. **ZONES 6–9.**

V

VERBASCUM

MULLEIN

This genus consists of semi-evergreen to evergreen perennials, biennials and shrubs from Europe and the more temperate zones of Asia. Including some very large and some very coarse species, the genus offers much variety in the foliage with leaves ranging from glossy to velvety. They develop large, often complex, basal rosettes. Many of the 250 or so species are scarcely better than weeds. However, several are desirable in the garden for their stately habit, gray foliage and long summer-flowering season—the flowers do not open from the bottom up as, for example, delphiniums or foxgloves do, but a few at a time along the spike.

CULTIVATION: These plants are fully to moderately frost hardy but will not tolerate winter-wet conditions. Establish all species in well-drained soil and an open, sunny location, although they do tolerate shade. Propagate from seed in spring or late summer or by division in winter. Some species self-seed readily.

Verbascum bombyciferum

This biennial from Asia Minor has silvery gray, furry, large leaves and grows 6 ft (1.8 m) tall. It bears golden-yellow, cup-shaped flowers in summer, sometimes in terminal spikes. **ZONES 6–10.**

Verbascum chaixii

This species from southern Europe can be relied on to live long enough to form clumps. The flowers, borne on 3 ft (1 m) tall stems in summer, are normally yellow. The white form **'Album'** is usually finer. **ZONES 5–10.**

Verbascum dumulosum

This evergreen, low-spreading perennial from southwest Turkey grows 6–12 in (15–30 cm) tall with a spread of about 18 in (45 cm). The gray-green leaves are felty in texture. In late spring is produces a succession of bright yellow flowers, each with 5 lobes, on short clusters. It will not tolerate wet soil. **ZONES 8–10.**

Verbascum 'Gainsborough'

This plant is probably a hybrid of *Verbascum phoeniceum* and is a short-lived perennial often treated as an annual. It grows to 3–4 ft (1–1.2 m) tall, has gray leaves and produces spikes of sulfur-yellow flowers, marked with purple. **ZONES 6–10.**

Verbascum 'Letitia'

This small-growing hybrid between *Verbascum dumulosum* and *V. spinosum* has slender, felted, silver-gray foliage. From mid-spring onwards, it produces masses of delicate lemon-yellow flowers on short, branched stems. It is ideal for a rock garden or as a container plant in a sunny position. The flowers are sterile, so propagation is by division. **ZONES 8–10.**

Verbascum nigrum

BLACK MULLEIN, HAG TAPER

Native to Morocco, this semi-evergreen, clump-forming perennial is very frost hardy and grows to a height and spread of about 3 ft (1 m). Long spikes of yellow flowers with purple centers appear from summer through to fall (autumn). Its mid-green leaves taper to a point and carry a dense layer of hairs. Black mullein is used as a herbal remedy for colic, coughs and spitting blood. So-called witches of the Middle Ages were thought to use the plant in their love potions and brews, hence the common name hag taper. **ZONES 5–10.**

Verbascum olympicum

Not a long-lasting species, this semi-evergreen perennial grows sedately up to 5 ft (1.5 m) tall with a spread of 24 in (60 cm). Its stems and leaves are hairy. The leaves are large, elliptical and silver gray, and spikes of 5-lobed, yellow flowers appear in summer. **ZONES 6–10.**

Verbascum phoeniceum

PURPLE MULLEIN

A native of Europe, this species forms basal rosettes of dark green, broad leaves from which rise branching stems bearing clusters of violet, pink or purple flowers. It is reliably perennial and self-sows quite prolifically when in a warm, well-drained situation. It is one of the parents of the many beautiful garden hybrids. It grows to a height of 2–4 ft (0.6–1.2 m) and can make a strong focal point in a border. **ZONES 6–10.**

Verbascum 'Pink Domino'

This hybrid mullein, a cross between *Verbascum phoeniceum* and *V. olympicum*, produces flowers of a gentle rose color with a coral red eye. It grows to 3–4 ft (1–1.2 m) tall and flowers in mid-summer. When the flower spikes are cut back, secondary spikes can be induced. Not truly perennial, it should be propagated from root cuttings. **ZONES 6–10.**

Verbascum thapsus

This species has soft, velvety, pale green leaves and yellow, stalkless flowers produced in dense, terminal spikes in summer. It grows on freely draining hillsides, often in very poor soil. The flowers, once dried, form an ingredient in herbal teas and cough mixtures. **ZONES 3–9.**

VERBENA

Originating in Europe, South America and North America, this genus of 250 or more species of biennials and perennials is characterized by small, dark, irregularly shaped and toothed leaves. They bloom in late spring, summer and fall (autumn). An agreeably spicy aroma is associated with most verbenas.

CULTIVATION: Marginally frost hardy to frost tender, they do best where winters are not severe. Establish in medium, well-drained soil in full sun or at most part-shade. Propagate from seed in fall or spring, stem cuttings in summer or fall, or by division in late

Verbascum 'Letitia'

Verbascum nigrum

Verbena bonariensis

Verbena canadensis

Verbena × *hybrida*

Verbena × *hybrida* 'Silver Ann'

Verbena × *hybrida* 'Sissinghurst'

winter. They can also be propagated in spring by division of young shoots.

Verbena bonariensis

This tall South American perennial is often grown as an annual, primarily for its deep purple flowers which top the sparsely foliaged 4–5 ft (1.2–1.5 m) stems from summer to fall (autumn). The deeply toothed leaves cluster in a mounded rosette, which easily fits in the front or middle of a border; the floral stems give a vertical line without much mass. Frost hardy, it self-seeds readily and survives with only minimal water, even in dry areas. **ZONES 7–10.**

Verbena canadensis
ROSE VERBENA, CREEPING VERVAIN

This native of eastern North America is a trailing or sprawling, short-lived perennial easily grown as an annual. It grows to 18 in (45 cm) in height with a spread of 24 in (60 cm). The dark purplish pink flowers appear from summer through fall (autumn). **ZONES 5–10.**

Verbena hastata
BLUE VERVAIN

Native to Canada and the USA, this stiffly erect plant with pointed leaves grows to a height of 4–5 ft (1.2–1.5 m) and is very frost hardy. The stems become branched at the top and produce

Verbena × *hybrida* 'Homestead Purple'

Verbena × *hybrida* 'Sissinghurst'

tiny purple flowers from purple bracts. The flowers appear in summer and last for many weeks. It is easily grown in any fertile soil and can be propagated by division or from seed. **ZONES 3–9.**

Verbena × *hybrida*
GARDEN VERBENA

This trailing perennial bears slightly hairy leaves and blooms in summer to fall (autumn). Its fragrant flowers appear in dense clusters 1 in (25 mm) across, many showing off white centers among the hues of red, mauve, violet, white and pink. It is suitable for use in summer beds and containers. Avoid being heavy handed with fertilizers or the plants will yield more leaves than flowers. **'Homestead Purple'** is a sturdy cultivar with rich red-purple flowers. **'La France'** has bright pink flowerheads. **'Silver Ann'** has heads of light pink flowers with darker blooms at the center. **'Sissinghurst'** has mid-green leaves and bears stems of brilliant pink flowerheads in summer; it reaches a height of 6–8 in (15–20 cm). **ZONES 9–10.**

Verbena laciniata
syn. *Verbena erinoides*

This marginally frost-hardy, prostrate South American perennial grows to only 12–18 in (30–45 cm) tall, but spreads widely. It bears finely divided, gray-green

Verbena laciniata

Verbena × *hybrida* 'La France'

leaves and abundant heads of blue, magenta or violet flowers. Trim back after flowering and avoid mildew by not over-watering. **ZONES 8–10.**

Verbena officinalis
VERRAIN, COMMON VERBENA

Indigenous to many parts of Europe, this is an annual or sometimes biennial species with 4-angled, branched stems up to 3 ft (1 m) high. The tiny flowers on slender spikes are purplish or lavender. **ZONES 4–10.**

Verbena peruviana
syn. *Verbena chamaedrifolia*

This low, creeping perennial from Brazil and Peru has stems rooting at the nodes and oval, toothed, mid-green leaves forming a carpet. The heads of small, tubular, intense scarlet flowers with spreading petals are produced in summer and fall (autumn). It reaches a height of 3 in (8 cm) with a spread of about 3 ft (1 m). Propagate from cuttings. **'Red Cascade'** has particularly bright flowers. **ZONES 9–11.**

Verbena rigida
syn. *Verbena venosa*

A South American native, this tuberous-rooted perennial is an excellent species for seaside cultivation. It reaches a height of 18–24 in (45–60 cm) with a spread of

Verbena rigida 'Silver Jubilee'

Verbena peruviana

12 in (30 cm). The dense spikes of pale violet to magenta flowers are borne from mid-summer. **'Silver Jubilee'** bears a mass of red flowers right through the growing season. **ZONES 8–10.**

Verbena tenera var. *maonettii*
syn. *Verbena alpina* of gardens

This low-spreading perennial, native to South America, has oval, deeply cut and toothed green leaves on spreading stems. It is often confused with other species. The terminal clusters of small tubular flowers are rose violet with a white margin on the petals and appear in summer. Marginally frost hardy, it grows 6 in (15 cm) tall. **ZONES 9–11.**

Verbena tenuisecta
MOSS VERBENA

Native to Chile and Argentina, this evergreen perennial gets its common name from its dense, prostrate habit and minute, finely divided, vivid green foliage which forms a flat, moss-like covering over the ground. Through late spring and summer, it bears masses of lilac flowers in small, rounded inflorescences. It requires a hot, fairly dry position and is frost tender. **ZONES 9–11.**

VERNICIA

Formerly included in *Aleurites*, this small genus consists of mainly deciduous trees

Verbena tenuisecta

Verbena rigida

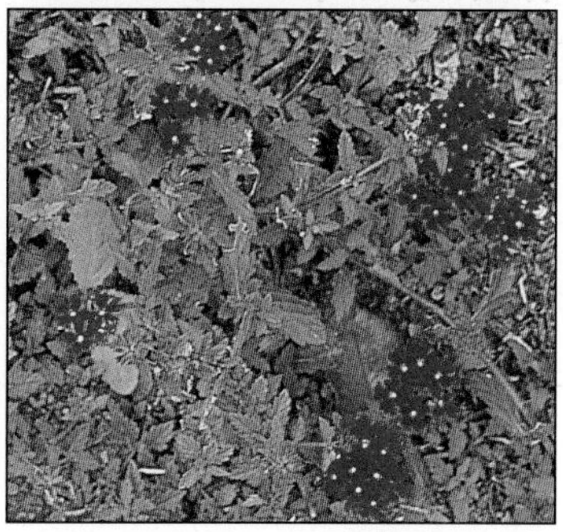
Verbena peruviana 'Red Cascade'

from China and Indo-China. They are grown commercially for their seeds which contain chinawood oils—drying oils used extensively in paints and varnishes—and are also valued as shade trees. The large seeds are poisonous; they are enclosed in large rounded fruits that look a bit like walnuts. The leaves are oval to heart-shaped, sometimes lobed, and the flowers appear in clusters at the branch tips. Profuse hairs cover the attractive flowers, as well as the young stems and leaves.
CULTIVATION: These trees grow best in full sun in an open position and in light, well-drained soil. They thrive in warm climates. Propagate from seed sown *in situ,* or from cuttings.

Vernicia fordii
syn. *Aleurites fordii*
TUNG-OIL TREE

From southern China, the tung-oil tree grows to 20–30 ft (6–9 m) tall. The branches extend horizontally from the trunk, forming a round to flat-topped canopy. The leaves are oval, about 6 in (15 cm) long, with 3 lobes; each has 2 red glands at the base where it joins the long stalk. Mature leaves are held horizontally and are light yellowish green. The spring flowers are trumpet-shaped and cream, streaked with orange or red, each 1 in (25 mm) long on a long thin stalk. The fruit are 2–3 in (5–8 cm) across, ripening from green to brown. **ZONES 10–11.**

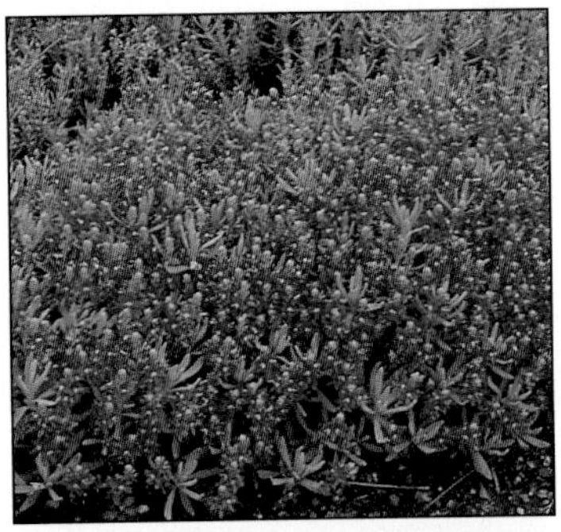

Veronica cinerea

Veronica chamaedrys

Vernicia fordii

VERNONIA
IRONWEED

Named after William Vernon, a seventeenth-century North American botanist, this genus of the daisy family consists of around 1,000 species of annuals, perennials, shrubs or small trees, occurring in most warmer parts of the world. The flowers are usually red, purple, blue or rarely white, and usually terminal. While very few of the species have any horticultural value, the perennial species tend to flower in fall (autumn) and are useful to combine with other daisy-type flowers. They are suitable for the wild garden or in the vicinity of a pond or stream.
CULTIVATION: These plants will grow in practically any type of soil. Propagate from seed in spring, cuttings or by division in spring or fall, depending on the nature of the plant.

Vernonia lindheimeri
WOOLLY IRONWEED

This perennial species from Texas grows to about 30 in (75 cm) tall and has long, narrow leaves which are whitish in color, entire and hairy. The purple flowers are produced in summer. **ZONES 8–10.**

Vernonia noveboracensis
NEW YORK IRONWEED

Native to eastern USA, this perennial grows to 5 ft (1.5 m) tall. It has stiff, upright stems surmounted by flat heads of daisy-like flowers in a crimson-purple shade in summer. The leaves are long and undistinguished. **ZONES 5–10.**

Veronica austriaca **'Royal Blue'**

Veronica austriaca

Veronica gentianoides

VERONICA
SPEEDWELL

Saint Veronica was the woman who, pious legend relates, wiped the face of Christ with her veil and was rewarded with having his image imprinted on it. Her connection with this flower is that the savants of the Middle Ages thought they could see a face in it; they must have peered rather closely, because veronica flowers are not exactly large—½ in (12 mm) wide is big for the genus. The shrubby species are now given a genus of their own, *Hebe*, and all the remaining 200 or so are herbaceous perennials. They range from prostrate, creeping plants suitable for the rock garden to 6 ft (1.8 m) high giants. Small as the flowers are, they make quite an impact, being gathered in clusters of various sizes and coming in great abundance in summer. Blue is the predominant color, although white and pink are also common.
CULTIVATION: Fully to moderately frost hardy, these plants are easy to grow in any temperate climate, warm or cool, and are not fussy about soil or position. Propagate from seed in fall (autumn) or spring, from cuttings in summer or by division in early spring or early fall.

Veronica austriaca
syn. *Veronica teucrium*

Distributed from southern Europe to northern Asia, this species grows in grassland and open woods. This clump-forming perennial grows to 10–18 in (25–45 cm) tall with long, slender stems bearing bright blue, saucer-shaped flowers in late spring. The leaves vary in shape from broadly oval to narrow and are either entire or deeply cut. Propagate by division in fall (autumn) or from softwood cuttings in summer. **'Crater Lake Blue'** is 12 in (30 cm) tall and has deep blue flowers; **'Royal Blue'** is taller with royal blue flowers. In late summer, ***Veronica austriaca* subsp. *teucrium*** bears 12 in (30 cm) high flower stems, comprising many tiny blooms in deep true blue; it prefers full sun and well-drained soil. **ZONES 6–10.**

Veronica austriaca **'Crater Lake Blue'**

Veronica longifolia **'Rosea'**

Veronica beccabunga
BROOKLIME

This Eurasian species is a spreading perennial. It is usually evergreen and is often found as a marginal aquatic plant in the wild. It has small, fleshy, rounded, toothed leaves and produces 4–6 in (10–15 cm) spikes of lavender-blue flowers in late summer. **ZONES 5–9.**

Veronica chamaedrys
BIRDS' EYES, ANGELS' EYES

Native to Europe and Asia, this herbaceous perennial reaches up to 18 in (45 cm) in height and has a creeping rootstock and roundish, toothed leaves. It is common in the wild and has become naturalized in eastern North America. In late spring, bright blue flowers are borne in compact, terminal spikes up to 6 in (15 cm) long in the leaf axils. It prefers sun or part-shade. **ZONES 3–9.**

Veronica cinerea

This mat-forming, many-branched perennial from Turkey has small, narrow or occasionally oval leaves with the margins inrolled and silver gray in color. The flowers are borne on trailing stems in summer and are purplish blue with white eyes. Growing to 6 in (15 cm) tall, it makes a good plant for a sunny rock garden. **ZONES 5–9.**

Veronica gentianoides
GENTIAN SPEEDWELL

This mat-forming perennial has wide, dark green leaves from which rise spikes of pale blue or white flowers in late spring. It reaches 18 in (45 cm) in height and spread. **ZONES 4–9.**

Veronica longifolia
BEACH SPEEDWELL

From northern and central Europe and Asia, this perennial plant grows up to 3 ft (1 m) tall. Its narrow, tapering leaves are arranged in whorls and toothed on the edges. The flowers are lilac blue and closely packed on a long, erect infloresence. **'Rosea'** has pink flowers and branched stems. **ZONES 4–9.**

Veronica officinalis
COMMON SPEEDWELL, GYPSYWEED

Native to Europe, Asia and North America, this mat-forming perennial has stems either prostrate or ascending to 18 in (45 cm) long. The leaves are oval to oblong in shape, 2 in (5 cm) long and serrated. The pale blue flowers are produced in dense racemes in late spring to summer. **ZONES 3–9.**

Veronica peduncularis

Ranging from the Ukraine and the Caucasus to western Asia, this spreading and mounding perennial has tiny oval leaves and 2–4 in (5–10 cm) sprays of pink-veined blue, white or pink flowers from late spring to early summer. **'Georgia Blue'** (syn. 'Oxford Blue') is a vigorous grower with bright blue flowers. **ZONES 6–9.**

Veronica prostrata
syn. *Veronica rupestris*

This perennial from Europe and parts of Asia has woody, branching stems and variable foliage, although all are tooth edged. The flowers are small and blue with widely flared petals, occurring in upright spikes in spring and early summer. This species spreads widely into a mat of indefinite coverage; however, it only reaches 12 in (30 cm) in height. **ZONES 5–9.**

Veronica repens

Native to Corsica and Spain, this is an attractive prostrate species with small, vivid green leaves. It is excellent as a ground cover for bulbs, for the rock garden or in paving. It grows rapidly in a sunny or part-shaded position, and bears intensely blue, minute flowers in late spring and early summer. **ZONES 5–9.**

Veronica spicata 'Blaufuchs'

Veronicastrum virginicum

Veronica spicata
DIGGER'S SPEEDWELL, SPIKE SPEEDWELL

A European species, this very frost-hardy perennial reaches a height of 24 in (60 cm) and a spread of up to 3 ft (1 m). Its stems are erect, hairy and branching. Spikes of small, star-shaped, blue flowers with purple stamens bloom in summer. The leaves of this species are mid-green, linear to lanceolate in shape. ***Veronica spicata*** **subsp.** ***incana*** is notable for its spreading clumps of silvery, felty leaves and deep violet-blue flowers. **'Blaufuchs'** is bright lavender blue; **'Blue Peter'** has dark blue flowers in very compact spikes; **'Heidekind'**, a compact form to 12–15 in (30–38 cm) tall, has hot-pink flowers and silver-gray foliage; **'Red Fox'** has crimson flowers; and **'Rosea'** is a pink-flowered form. **ZONES 3–9.**

Veronica spuria

This erect species from southeast Europe grows 12–36 in (30–90 cm) tall and has dense and downy foliage. The leaves are arranged in whorls and are slightly toothed. The flowers, produced in summer, are blue and in large terminal panicles. **ZONES 3–9.**

VERONICASTRUM
CULVER'S PHYSIC

This genus consists of 2 species of tall, slender, perennial herbs closely related to *Veronica*, found in eastern North America and East Asia. Formerly used medicinally, they are now grown as ornamentals only. Pale blue or white flower spikes open in summer.
CULTIVATION: Plant in a humus-rich, moist soil and do not allow to dry out in summer. Any exposure from full sun to part-shade will do. Propagate from seed or by division.

Veronica spicata 'Blue Peter'

Veronicastrum virginicum

Veronica spuria

Veronicastrum virginicum
BLACK ROOT, CULVER'S ROOT, BOWMAN'S ROOT

Native to the USA, this perennial prefers moist, swampy soils in a protected, shaded position. Although frost hardy, it does not tolerate dry conditions. This plant grows to about 5 ft (1.5 m), and has slender, erect stems and lance-shaped, finely serrated leaves. The tubular, purplish blue or white flowers are produced in summer. **ZONES 3–9.**

VESTIA

Like its relative the potato, the evergreen shrub that is the only member of this genus comes from temperate areas of South America. The leaves have an unpleasant smell when crushed. The flowers are pendent and borne singly or in clusters.
CULTIVATION: This shrub appreciates shelter from strong winds and does best in rich, well-drained soil with plenty of water in warmer months. Full sun or light shade suit it best. In warm-temperate or even subtropical climates, it can be cut back hard in winter and will shoot from the base in spring. Propagate from seed in fall (autumn) or spring or cuttings in summer.

Vestia foetida
syn. *Vestia lycioides*

Indigenous to Chile, this fast-growing shrub reaches 6 ft (1.8 m) in height with many erect stems. Its shiny green leaves are thin and narrow, crowding down the stems. Dainty, lemon yellow, tubular flowers with prominent stamens are produced through spring and summer, followed by small, inedible, blue berries. The sap has a most unpleasant smell, hence the specific name 'foetida' meaning stinking. **ZONES 9–11.**

Vestia foetida

Veronica spicata

VIBURNUM

This important genus is made up of some 150 species of evergreen, semi-evergreen and deciduous cool-climate shrubs or small trees, primarily of Asian origin with fewer species from North America, Europe and northern Africa. Many of the cultivated species and forms are noted for their fragrant, showy flowers and may also produce colorful berries or bright fall (autumn) foliage. In several species, flowers are arranged in a similar way to those of the lacecap hydrangeas, with small fertile flowers and large sterile ones on the same plant; these have all given rise to cultivars with all-sterile flowerheads known as 'snowball viburnums'. The evergreen species are often used for hedging.
CULTIVATION: Fully to moderately frost hardy, most species are remarkably trouble-free plants, growing in any well-drained soil in sun or light shade. They can be trimmed heavily after flowering, although this will prevent fruit forming. They are usually propagated from cuttings in summer or from seed in fall.

Viburnum acerifolium
MAPLE-LEAF VIBURNUM

One of the lesser known viburnums but one of the most appealing for a woodland garden, this deciduous species has slender stems that grow 4–6 ft (1.2–1.8 m) tall from a clump that spreads underground. The maple-shaped leaves are a soft green through the growing season, turning subtle shades of pink to purple in fall (autumn). The yellowish flowers appear in small clusters in early summer, followed by black fruit in fall. It is very tolerant of shade, forming natural colonies in the eastern American forests to which it is native. **ZONES 3–8.**

Viburnum davidii

Viburnum × *burkwoodii*

Viburnum × *burkwoodii* 'Park Farm'

Viburnum davidii 'Femina'

Viburnum carlesii 'Aurora'

Viburnum carlesii

Viburnum × *bodnantense*

A hybrid between *Viburnum farreri* and ***V. grandiflorum***, this deciduous shrub reaches 10 ft (3 m) in height. It has slightly glossy, deep green, oval leaves that are pale green on the undersides. Before they drop in fall (autumn), they develop intense orange, red and purple tones. The heavily scented flowers, which bloom from fall to early spring depending on the climate, are bright pink in the bud, open pale pink and fade to white. **'Dawn'** has slightly darker flowers, especially those that open in spring; and **'Deben'** has light pink to white, somewhat tubular flowers. **ZONES 7–10.**

Viburnum × *burkwoodii*

BURKWOOD VIBURNUM

A hybrid between *Viburnum carlesii* and ***V. utile***, this 8–10 ft (2.4–3 m) high semi-evergreen shrub has glossy, deep green, pointed oval leaves to about 3 in (8 cm) long. They are pale sage green on the undersides and those that drop in fall (autumn) develop bright yellow and red tones. From early to late spring ball-shaped clusters of small, starry, fragrant flowers open; they are pink in the bud, opening white. **'Anne Russell'**, the result of a backcross with *V. carlesii*, has clusters of fragrant flowers. **'Park Farm'** has a more spreading habit and larger flowers. **'Mohawk'** has dark glossy leaves that turn to orange in fall and fragrant red-blotched white flowers that open from red buds. **ZONES 5–10.**

Viburnum × *carlcephalum*

FRAGRANT VIBURNUM

This is a deciduous, spring-flowering hybrid with large, rounded heads of fragrant, creamy white flowers that are pink when in bud. The dark green foliage often turns red in fall (autumn). It has a rounded, bushy habit and grows to a height and spread of about 8 ft (2.4 m). **ZONES 3–9.**

Viburnum carlesii

KOREAN VIBURNUM, KOREAN SPICE VIBURNUM

Indigenous to Korea and Tsushima Island, this densely foliaged deciduous shrub grows to about 5 ft (1.5 m) tall with a similar spread. It has pointed oval leaves 2–3 in (5–8 cm) long with finely serrated edges. The starry flowers open from mid- to late spring; they are pale pink ageing to white, around ½ in (12 mm) across and sweetly scented. The flowers are carried in rounded clusters up to 3 in (8 cm) in diameter. The fruit ripen to black. Several cultivars are available, including **'Aurora'**, with deep pink buds; **'Cayuga'**, with very fragrant white flowers and a heavy crop of black berries; **'Charis'**, with white flowers; and **'Diana'**, with deep pink buds. **ZONES 9–10.**

Viburnum 'Chesapeake'

syn. *Viburnum carlesii* 'Chesapeake'

This viburnum bears pinkish white, fragrant flowers that open from pink buds in mid- to late spring. It is a dense, mound-forming shrub that reaches a height of 6 ft (1.8 m) and spread of 10 ft (3 m). The leaves are leathery, glossy and dark green. **ZONES 8–10.**

Viburnum cinnamomifolium

A native of China, this is a large, handsome, evergreen shrub which can grow up to 20 ft (6 m) tall and almost as wide. It has dark green, leathery leaves that are paler underneath. The clusters of summer flowers, 4–6 in (10–15 cm) across, are dull white. They are followed in fall (autumn) by small, shiny, oval, blue black fruit. It prefers a sheltered position in sun or part-shade. **ZONES 7–9.**

Viburnum dilatatum 'Iroquois'

Viburnum × *carlcephalum*

Viburnum davidii

DAVID VIBURNUM

This evergreen species from Sichuan, China, grows 3–5 ft (1–1.5 m) tall and spreads slowly to form a densely foliaged shrub up to 6 ft (1.8 m) across. If massed, it makes an excellent, large-scale ground cover. The pointed oval leaves are bright glossy green and up to 6 in (15 cm) long; leaf petioles and new wood are reddish brown. The spring-borne clusters of white flowers are not spectacular, but are followed by turquoise blue berries. **'Femina'** is a reliable, heavy-fruiting cultivar. **ZONES 7–10.**

Viburnum dentatum

SOUTHERN ARROW-WOOD

The Native Americans used the stems of this shrub from eastern USA for the shafts of arrows. Today, its uses are purely decorative, as it makes an attractive deciduous shrub which reaches

Viburnum dentatum

Viburnum × *bodnantense*

Viburnum 'Chesapeake'

Viburnum odoratissimum

Viburnum × globosum 'Jermyn's Globe'

8–15 ft (2.4–4.5 m) in height and has a spread of about 6 ft (1.8 m). Its rounded, prominently veined, toothed leaves are occasionally tufted beneath. Glossy green when young, they turn rich red in fall (autumn). Flowering in early summer, its white blooms are borne in clusters on the ends of long stalks. The egg-shaped fruit are bluish black. **ZONES 2–9.**

Viburnum dilatatum
LINDEN VIBURNUM

From Japan and China, this 10 ft (3 m) tall deciduous shrub has coarsely toothed, hairy oval leaves. Its flowers are white and abundant and carried in heads 4–6 in (10–15 cm) wide; bright red fruit follow. **'Iroquois'** is slightly smaller and bushier than the species with flowers more of a creamy white. **ZONES 5–10.**

Viburnum farreri
syn. ***Viburnum fragrans***

Discovered in mountain regions of western China at the beginning of the twentieth century by Reginald Farrer, this deciduous shrub grows to about 8–10 ft (2.4–3 m) tall. Its lightly arching branches are clad in oval, deeply toothed leaves with prominent veins; bronze when young, they mature to rich green and turn red before falling. The pink buds open to white, sweetly smelling flowers clustered at the branch tips in early spring before the leaves appear. Glossy red fruit are produced only occasionally. **'Candidissimum'** has pure white flowers and buds bright green leaves. **ZONES 6–10.**

Viburnum × globosum 'Jermyn's Globe'

A hybrid raised in England in 1964 from a cross between *Viburnum davidii* and ***V. calvum***, this is a small, evergreen shrub with a dense, rounded habit. The toothed, dark green leaves are narrow

Viburnum japonicum

and leathery on slender, reddish petioles. The white flowers are followed by bluish black fruit. **ZONES 7–10.**

Viburnum japonicum
JAPANESE VIBURNUM

Growing to 6–15 ft (1.8–4.5 m) tall, this handsome evergreen shrub from Japan has large oval, leathery leaves, dark green above, paler beneath. The fragrant white flowers are borne in large, flattened trusses, followed by red berries in fall (autumn). It often takes some years before flowers appear. **ZONES 7–10.**

Viburnum × juddii

This hybrid between 2 fragrant species, ***Viburnum bitchiuense*** and *V. carlesii*, is a deciduous medium-sized shrub up to 8 ft (2.4 m) tall with a bushy, spreading habit. It was raised in 1920 by the propagator William Judd. It freely produces sweetly scented, pink-tinted flowers in terminal clusters during spring and these are useful for cut flowers. **ZONES 5–9.**

Viburnum lantana
WAYFARING TREE

Often used as hedging, this deciduous species from Europe and northwestern Asia is tolerant of cold climates. It forms a tall, branching shrub 15 ft (4.5 m) high and is distinguished by its new shoots, which are unusually furry for a viburnum. The oval leaves have hairy undersides and turn burgundy red in fall (autumn). In early summer, small, creamy white flowers are profusely borne in flat clusters. The oblong red fruit ripen to black. **'Rugosum'** has larger and more wrinkled leaves and larger flower clusters. **ZONES 3–9.**

Viburnum lantana

Viburnum lantana 'Rugosum'

Viburnum macrocephalum
CHINESE SNOWBALL TREE

The distinctive characteristic of this species native to China is the presence of small, fertile flowers and large sterile ones, but the cultivar **'Sterile'** has all-sterile flowers. Huge, rounded trusses of white flowers, up to 6 in (15 cm) across, give a spectacular display in early summer on this upright shrub. The dark green, leathery leaves are oval, 4 in (10 cm) long and tinted red and yellow in fall (autumn); normally deciduous, this species may be semi-evergreen in milder climates. It grows to 6–10 ft (1.8–3 m) tall. **ZONES 6–10.**

Viburnum odoratissimum
SWEET VIBURNUM

This fast-growing species forms a dense, rounded shrub or small tree 15–20 ft (4.5–6 m) tall, developing a remarkably thick, low-branching trunk with age. Its very fragrant flowers are white and star-shaped, in dense clusters 4 in (10 cm) across. The red berries mature to black. This species occurs naturally from the Himalayas to the Philippines and Japan. Evergreen, its shiny green leaves are thick, leathery and rounded and 6 in (15 cm) long. Frost tender, it is one of the few viburnums to thrive in warm to hot climates. **ZONES 9–11.**

Viburnum × juddii

Viburnum macrocephalum

Viburnum odoratissimum

Viburnum opulus

GUELDER ROSE, EUROPEAN CRANBERRY BUSH

This lovely deciduous shrub from Europe and North Africa produces splendid clusters of snowy white, lacy flowers in summer. It has attractive fruit and fall (autumn) color, and can be grown in wet or boggy situations. A large shrub growing to 12 ft (3.5 m) tall, it has gray bark and a spreading habit with long, pale green shoots. Its leaves turn deep crimson in fall. Generous bunches of shiny, translucent, orange-red fruit remain on the bush until well into winter. **'Aureum'** has bronze-colored shoots turning yellow then green, and yellowish leaves which may burn in the sun; **'Compactum'** is a dense, compact shrub bearing large quantities of flowers and fruit; **'Nanum'** has small leaves and seldom flowers or fruits; **'Roseum'** (syn. *Viburnum opulus* 'Sterile'), the snowball bush, has snowball-like heads of pale green to white, sterile flowers so large they weigh the branches down; **'Pink Sensation'** is similar to 'Roseum' except the flowers have a pinkish hue; and **'Xanthocarpum'** has clear yellow fruit which are quite translucent when ripe. **ZONES 2–10.**

Viburnum plicatum 'Pink Beauty'

Viburnum plicatum

Viburnum plicatum

syn. *Viburnum tomentosum*

This deciduous shrub from Japan and China grows to about 15 ft (4.5 m) tall with a similar spread. It has hazel-like, 3 in (8 cm) long, mid-green, pointed oval leaves with serrated edges and a somewhat tiered growth habit, a feature emphasized in the cultivar **'Mariesii'**. The large, creamy white flower clusters with a mass of tiny fertile flowers in the center, surrounded by large sterile flowers, open in spring; they are followed by small berries that are red at first, ripening to black. **'Lanarth'** is a fine cultivar, with branches less arching than the species; **'Pink Beauty'** has a pale pink tinge to the flowers; and **'Sterile'** (syn. *Viburnum plicatum* var. *plicatum*) is a sterile form. **'Rosace'** has overlapping horizontal branches and foliage that colors well in fall (autumn); it has sterile heads of mixed white and pink flowers and bronze spring foliage. **ZONES 4–9.**

Viburnum plicatum 'Mariesii'

Viburnum plicatum 'Lanarth'

Viburnum prunifolium

BLACK-HAW

This shrub species from eastern USA features deciduous leaves that turn orange and red in fall (autumn); broadly oval to round with a finely toothed edge, each is 3 in (8 cm) long on a reddish stalk. *Viburnum prunifolium* grows to about 15 ft (4.5 m) tall. In spring the small white flowers are borne in flat-topped clusters 4 in (10 cm) across. The berries are bluish black in flattened clusters, each one measuring just over ½ in (12 mm) long. The root of this plant is used for medicinal purposes. **ZONES 3–9.**

Viburnum opulus

Viburnum opulus 'Aureum'

Viburnum opulus 'Pink Sensation'

Viburnum opulus 'Xanthocarpum'

Viburnum opulus 'Compactum'

Viburnum opulus 'Nanum'

Viburnum opulus 'Roseum'

Viburnum plicatum 'Rosace'

Viburnum rafinesquianum
RAFINESQUE VIBURNUM

This deciduous shrub from eastern North America grows to 8 ft (2.4 m) high and has coarsely toothed leaves with felted undersides. White flowers are followed by blue-black berries. ***Viburnum rafinesquianum* var. *affine*** has large, slightly sticky leaves. **ZONES 2–9.**

Viburnum rhytidophyllum
LEATHERLEAF VIBURNUM

This fast-growing, evergreen shrub from China has distinctive, handsome foliage. Its long leaves are corrugated, deeply veined and dark glossy green, with gray felted undersides. Growing to 10–15 ft (3–4.5 m) tall and almost as wide, it tolerates alkaline soil. Small, creamy white spring flowers appear in large, flat clusters at the ends of branches; the fruit are oval berries, red at first, later turning black. Plant in groups to ensure fruiting. **ZONES 6–10.**

Viburnum rhytidophyllum

Viburnum sargentii
SARGENT VIBURNUM

From northeastern Asia, this 10–15 ft (3–4.5 m) deciduous shrub has 4 in (10 cm) wide, 3-lobed leaves, yellow-green when young, ageing to dark brown. The large, individual flowers are carried on heads up to 4 in (10 cm) wide. The berries are red. **'Onondaga'** has maroon young growth that becomes purple-red in fall (autumn). **ZONES 4–9.**

Viburnum rafinesquianum var. *affine*

Viburnum prunifolium

Viburnum setigerum

This deciduous species from China grows to about 12 ft (3.5 m) tall and can be trimmed to keep it compact. The rich orange-yellow fall (autumn) foliage is matched in beauty by the oval, yellow fruit which mature to a brilliant red. The unspectacular flowers appear as white clusters in early summer. The leaves were said to be made into tea by Chinese monks. **ZONES 5–9.**

Viburnum sargentii 'Onondaga'

Viburnum setigerum

Viburnum tinus

Viburnum trilobum

Viburnum tinus
LAURUSTINUS

This densely foliaged evergreen shrub from the Mediterranean region may eventually grow to 15 ft (4.5 m) tall and 20 ft (6 m) wide, although it is usually kept smaller through trimming. The dark green, pointed elliptical leaves are up to 4 in (10 cm) long and develop purplish tones in cold weather. Cream and yellow variegated foliage forms are available. Clusters of white flowers open from pink buds from late winter, followed by blue-black berries. **'Compactum'** (syn. 'Spring Bouquet') is a smaller form with dense compact growth; **'Eve Price'** has smaller leaves, carmine buds and pink-tinged flowers; **'Gwenllian'** has pink buds that open into pinkish white flowers followed by clusters of blackish seeds; and **'Pink Prelude'** has white flowers becoming deep pink. **ZONES 7–10.**

Viburnum trilobum
syns *Viburnum americanum*, *V. opulus* var. *americanum*

HIGHBUSH CRANBERRY, AMERICAN CRANBERRY BUSH

The North American equivalent of *Viburnum opulus*, this species has showy flowers, fruit and fall (autumn) foliage. A tall shrub growing 8–12 ft (2.4–3.5 m) tall and wide, it is useful as a hedge or screening plant. The white flowers appear in spring in flat-topped clusters. The bright red fruit appear in fall and last through winter. **'Wentworth'** has a very heavy crop of fruit. **ZONES 3–9.**

Viburnum wrightii

Viburnum wrightii
WRIGHT VIBURNUM

Indigenous to Japan, Korea and China, this medium-sized, 8 ft (2.4 m) tall, deciduous shrub is valued for its foliage and fruits. The clusters of white flowers produced in spring are followed by glistening red fruit. The metallic green, oval leaves color to a rich crimson in fall (autumn). **ZONES 5–9.**

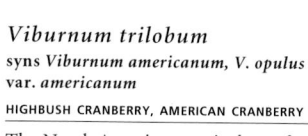

Victoria amazonica × *cruziana* 'Longwood Hybrid'

Vicia faba

Vigna caracalla

VICIA

VETCH, TARE

This legume genus of around 140 species of annuals and perennials occurs wild mostly in temperate regions of the northern hemisphere, with a few species in the Andes of South America and mountains of East Africa. It is closely related to the sweet-pea genus *Lathyrus* and most species have the same tendrils at the ends of their pinnate leaves, by which they scramble through long grass or over shrubs and dead twigs; an exception is *Vicia faba*, the broad bean, which has an erect habit and lacks tendrils. The small flowers, usually borne in short spikes or clusters from the leaf axils, are typical pea-flowers in form though not opening very wide, and are mostly white, pink, purple or pale yellow. The pods that follow mature rapidly, are often hairy or downy and contain a row of small to large seeds. Many vetches are pasture plants or weeds of waste ground, but a few would make attractive additions to meadow or rock gardens. **CULTIVATION:** Most vetches are easily grown in ordinary garden soil. They self-seed freely and can quickly become a nuisance, although the plants are easily pulled up. Propagate from seed; perennial species may also be divided in fall (autumn). For cultivation of broad beans see under *Vicia faba*.

Vicia cracca

TUFTED VETCH, COW VETCH

Occurring wild through cooler-temperate regions of the northern hemisphere, this perennial is one of the more vigorous species and also has showier flowers than most. The scrambling stems are up to 6 ft (1.8 m) long and the deep green pinnate leaves are about 3 in (8 cm) long, bearing tendrils at the tips.Violet to purple flowers are crowded onto spikes up to 4 in (10 cm) long, appearing all through summer. It is an attractive plant, but should be kept away from vegetable crops. **ZONES 3–10.**

Vicia faba

BROAD BEAN, FAVA BEAN

The broad bean is believed to be one of the earliest domesticated crop plants, its seeds found in Middle Eastern archaeological excavations going back thousands of years. It is not known in the wild but may have been derived in cultivation from the Mediterranean species ***Vicia narbonense***. It is an annual growing to about 30 in (75 cm) in height with thick, erect stems and coarse, gray-green foliage. The white flowers (red in some cultivars) with a blackish central blotch are clustered in the upper leaf axils and are followed by large, downy green pods, up to 24 in (60 cm) long in some cultivars but usually much less; the large seeds, tender when immature, are white, green, or rarely crimson. As well as the vegetable strains there are races of this species cultivated for fodder, known as horse beans and tic beans. Broad beans are a winter to spring crop and successful cultivation requires a temperate climate. They are mostly sown in fall (autumn) in well-drained, limed and manured soil (mounded into ridges if necessary), preferably following a non-leguminous crop in the same plot; where frosts are very severe delay sowing until early spring. Young plants may need staking and should not be over-watered. Beans are harvested while still green and tender, usually 2 to 3 months after planting. Watch for aphids. Popular broad bean cultivars are **'Early Long Pod'**, **'Green Windsor'**, **'Red Epicure'** and **'Aquadulce Claudia'**, an especially frost-hardy cultivar. **ZONES 7–10.**

Vicia sativa

COMMON VETCH, SPRING VETCH

This temperate Eurasian species is naturalized in many other parts of the world. It is variable, and several subspecies are recognized, some preferred as fodder plants, while others are common weeds. They are scrambling annuals, the stems up to about 4 ft (1.2 m) long, the leaves with several pairs of narrow leaflets and terminating in tendrils. Purplish flowers are borne in 1s or 2s in the leaf axils and are up to 1½ in (35 mm) long in ***Vicia sativa* subsp. *sativa***. **ZONES 6–10.**

VICTORIA

GIANT LILY, ROYAL WATERLILY

This genus of just 2 species of rhizomatous, deep-water aquatic annuals or perennials comes from tropical South America. Their strong rhizomes support huge floating leaves and bear nocturnal, waterlily-like flowers. Joseph Paxton (1801–65), gardener to the Duke of Devonshire, was the first to make them flower in Britain, and based his design for the Crystal Palace on the structure of its leaves—so strong they could bear the weight of his 7-year-old daughter. **CULTIVATION:** These frost-tender plants need at least 3 ft (1 m) of water in which to grow and a position in full sun. Plant them in containers of rich loamy soil with added organic matter. Propagate from seed in early spring.

Victoria amazonica

syn. ***Victoria regia***

AMAZON WATERLILY

This is the largest known waterlily, with leaves reaching to 6 ft (1.8 m) across. It grows quickly, achieving its huge size just 7 months after planting from seed. The flat, prickly leaves have upturned margins of 2–4 in (5–10 cm). Leaf size is determined by the depth of the water in which the plant is growing—the deeper the water, the bigger the leaves. The flowers, white outside and pink inside, have as many as 60 petals each; they are more than 12 in (30 cm) wide. Only one flower blooms at a time. **'Longwood Hybrid'**, a hybrid between *Victoria amazonica* and *V. cruziana*, has white flowers that age pink. **ZONES 11–12.**

Victoria cruziana

SANTA CRUZ WATERLILY

This perennial species grows to 4 in (10 cm) above the water surface and has leaves with hairy undersurfaces up to 6 ft (1.8 m) across. The white fragrant flowers, which open through the growing season, are nocturnal. **ZONES 11–12.**

VIGNA

This genus of beans consists of about 150 species of leguminous plants found mostly in the tropical parts of the world. The leaves are divided into 3 leaflets and the pea-flowers are produced in terminal clusters on long stems. Seed pods can vary in size from 3–36 in (8–90 cm) long and contain small kidney-shaped or round seeds in various colors. Several species are grown for cattle food and for green manure, but the seeds of all are edible. Some species are grown for bean sprouts, especially in Asian countries. **CULTIVATION:** All can be readily raised from seed in a warm climate. Plant in fertile, moist but well-drained soil in full sun. Water these plants well during the growing season, but less during winter. Frost tender, vignas can be grown in a greenhouse in cooler climates.

Vigna caracalla

syn. ***Phaseolus caracalla***

SNAIL CREEPER, SNAIL VINE

This is a decorative, evergreen, twining climber with soft green foliage. The perfumed flowers in shades of purple and white are produced from mid-summer to early fall (autumn). Frost tender, it is best suited to warm-temperate and tropical areas where it will grow rapidly to 10–20 ft (3–6 m) tall. Grow in full sun in humus-rich, well-drained soil and protect from drying winds. Prune tangled growth in spring. **ZONES 10–11.**

Vigna radiata

MUNG BEAN, BEAN SPROUT

Native to Burma and India, mung beans are popular as sprouting vegetables and have been an important part of the diet of the people in Asia for thousands of years. It is the green type of mung bean which is commonly used to sprout. They can be grown on a small scale at home and only take a few days to sprout. Mung beans are eaten raw in salads and lightly steamed in Oriental dishes. **ZONES 10–11.**

Vigna unguiculata

COWPEA

Originally from tropical Africa, this species is now widely cultivated for its immature pods and seeds which are cooked as a green vegetable or dried and cooked like dried beans. *Vigna unguiculata* subsp. *susquipedalis* is the asparagus bean or yard-long bean with succulent pods sometimes reaching 3 ft (1 m) in length. It is popular as a green vegetable in some countries. With sufficient warm weather, cowpeas do best in a nitrogen- and lime-rich, well-drained soil. Water thoroughly in dry weather. **ZONES 10–11.**

VINCA

PERIWINKLE

This genus contains 7 species of slender-stemmed, evergreen subshrubs and herbaceous perennials from Russia, Europe and North Africa. With their opposite, simple, lance-shaped leaves, they make useful ground covers, although they may be invasive. The flowers are widely flared

Vinca major

Vinca minor

with 5 lobes. Ingestion of any part of the plant may cause a mild stomach upset. **CULTIVATION:** Hardiness ranges from frost and drought resistant to fully frost hardy. Any soil is suitable provided it is not too dry. If ground cover is desired, provide these evergreens with shade to part-shade. If flowers are desired, let them have more sun. Propagate by division in fall (autumn) through spring, or from cuttings in summer.

Vinca difformis

This low-growing, shrubby perennial comes from the western Mediterranean countries of Europe and North Africa. The leaves are spearhead-shaped, dark green and glossy, usually under 3 in (8 cm) long. The flowers, white or pale blue, are produced in spring but only on the erect growing shoots. Stems that spread sideways never bloom. It grows to about 12 in (30 cm) in height with a virtually indefinite spread. It tolerates light frosts only. **ZONES 8–10.**

Vinca major
GREATER PERIWINKLE

This tenacious evergreen creeper from the Mediterranean has mid-green, glossy leaves that are heart-shaped to pointed ovate. Widely spreading with an erect woody stem, it climbs as high as 10 ft (3 m). The brilliant violet flowers, 2 in (5 cm) across, are borne in late spring through early fall (autumn). Drought and moderately frost resistant, it can also be aggressive and invasive. **'Variegata'** has leaves blotched and margined creamy white and large lavender-blue flowers. **ZONES 7–10.**

Vinca minor
LESSER PERIWINKLE, DWARF PERIWINKLE

The slender, woody stems on this European evergreen creeper will cover ground over a distance of 10 ft (3 m) to lay down a mat of glossy, dark green

Vinca major 'Variegata'

leaves of pointed elliptical shape. The small flowers, produced in mid-spring through early summer, are bluish lilac, purple or white. This species, like *Vinca major,* is often aggressive and invasive if not trimmed back. **'Alba'** has white flowers and a more vigorous growth; **'Gertrude Jekyll'** has small white flowers and narrower foliage; **'Grape Cooler'** has deep pink flowers that become pale with age; and **'La Grave'** has large flowers and broad foliage. A variegated form is also available. **ZONES 4–9.**

VIOLA
VIOLET, HEARTSEASE, PANSY

This well-known and much-loved genus of annuals, perennials and subshrubs consists of as many as 500 species, found in most temperate regions of the world including high mountains of the tropics, though with the greatest concentrations of species in North America, the Andes and Japan. Most are creeping plants, either deciduous or evergreen, with slender to thick rhizomes and leaves most often kidney-shaped or heart-shaped, though in some species they are divided into narrow lobes. Flowers of the wild species are seldom more than 1 in (25 mm) across and characteristically have 3 spreading lower petals and 2 erect upper petals, with a short nectar spur projecting to the rear of the flower. Many species also produce *cleistogamous* flowers, with smaller petals that do not open properly, and able to set seed without cross-pollination. A few Eurasian species have been hybridized extensively to produce the garden pansies, violas and violettas, with showy flowers in very bright or deep colors; these are nearly always grown as annuals, though potentially some are short-lived perennials. **CULTIVATION:** Most of the cultivated *Viola* species will tolerate light frosts at least, and many are fully frost hardy. The more compact perennial species suit

Vinca minor 'Alba'

rock gardens where they do best in cooler, moister spots, while the more spreading species make effective ground covers beneath trees and taller shrubs, requiring little or no attention. Pansies and violas *(Viola × wittrockiana)* are grown as annuals or pot plants in full sun, but appreciate shelter from drying winds; sow seed in late winter or early spring, under glass if necessary, planting out in late spring in soil that is well-drained but not too rich. Water well and feed sparingly as flowers develop. Propagate perennial species by division or from cuttings.

Viola adunca
WESTERN DOG VIOLET, HOOKED SPUR VIOLET

This species is widespread through North America and grows as a compact little plant 2–4 in (5–10 cm) high. The flowers are deep to light violet or lavender with a white eye; the lower petals are veined with dark violet and a short, hooked spur is present. This species prefers part-sun or shade. The leaves are shaded purple. **ZONES 4–9.**

Viola canadensis
CANADIAN VIOLET

Widespread in the mountain woodlands of North America under deciduous trees, this relatively tall-growing species, 12–24 in (30–60 cm), has a rather lanky growth habit. It has shiny, oval, rich green leaves and the flowers are white, tinged with violet and yellowish at the base. It flowers in summer and prefers a cool, moist position. **ZONES 4–9.**

Viola canina

Native to Europe, this species has many characteristics of the well-known *Viola odorata*, but is of larger and completely without perfume. It has dark green, pointed and toothed leaves and large violet-blue flowers. An unusual feature of the plant is that the leaves grow to double their normal size after flowering has finished in summer. Propagate by division. **ZONES 6–10.**

Viola cornuta
HORNED VIOLET

Native to the Pyrenees, this is a broad-faced violet with a short spur at the back, in shades of pale blue to deeper violet and borne in spring and summer. The plants spread by rhizomes, sending up flowering stems to 6 in (15 cm) long. The horned violet is one of the major parent species of pansies and violas. **'Minor'** has smaller leaves and flowers. **ZONES 6–9.**

Viola cornuta 'Minor'

Viola cornuta

Vinca minor 'Gertrude Jekyll'

Viola elatior

This species is found in the damp meadows and marshy areas of central and eastern Europe and northwest China. It has long, tapered leaves and grows up to 18 in (45 cm) tall. The stems are erect and tufted; the large flowers are lilac blue and appear in early summer. The plants grow well in leafy, peaty soil in sun or part-shade. **ZONES 5–9.**

Viola hederacea

syns *Erpetion reniforme, Viola reniformis*
AUSTRALIAN NATIVE VIOLET

The small, scentless flowers borne on short stems on this creeping evergreen perennial from southeastern Australia are mostly white with a lilac blotch in the throat; they appear from spring to fall (autumn). Its stems are prostrate, suckering and mat forming, spreading widely and growing 2–4 in (5–10 cm) in height. Its leaves are kidney-shaped with irregular edges. **ZONES 8–10.**

Viola elatior

Viola labradorica

LABRADOR VIOLET

Native to North America through to Greenland, this low-growing, spreading species has light purple flowers in spring. It does well in shady places, but can become invasive. **ZONES 2–9.**

Viola nuttalii

YELLOW PRAIRIE VIOLET

This species is indigenous to western North America and has small yellow flowers rather hidden beneath the leaves. It grows to 6 in (15 cm) tall. **ZONES 4–10.**

Viola odorata

SWEET VIOLET

A sweet perfume wafts from the flowers of this much-loved species: they are the well-known florists' violets, sold in small bunches for their perfume. It is a spreading, rhizomatous perennial from Europe, which grows 3 in (8 cm) tall and may spread indefinitely on cool, moist ground. Its dark green leaves are a pointed kidney shape with shallowly toothed edges. Spurred, flat-faced flowers in violet, white or rose appear from late winter through early spring. It boasts many cultivars. **ZONES 6–10.**

Viola hederacea

Viola labradorica

Viola odorata

Viola, Perennial Cultivar, 'Magic'

Viola pedata

BIRD'S-FOOT VIOLA

A beautiful and variable species found in eastern North America, it has a tufted habit with the basal leaves divided into segments like a bird's foot. The flowers have 2 upper petals of dark violet and the 3 lower ones are pale lilac with darker veins. Unlike most violets, it thrives in a sunny, dry position in acidic sandy soil, although it needs some shade in hot conditions. It flowers in early spring and again in late summer, and can be propagated from seed. **ZONES 4–9.**

Viola, PC, 'Huntercombe Purple'

Viola, Perennial Cultivars

Primarily of *Viola lutea, V. amoena* and *V. cornuta* parentage, these hardy perennial plants are long flowering, year round in mild climates. **'Huntercombe Purple'** has creamy centered purple flowers; **'Jackanapes'** has brown upper petals and yellow lower petals; **'Maggie Mott'** has bright purple-blue flowers; **'Nellie Britten'** (syn. 'Haslemere') has lavender-pink flowers; and **'Magic'** is rich purple with a small eye of dark purple and yellow. **ZONES 6–10.**

Viola reichenbachiana

WOOD VIOLET

This perennial bears small, pink, mauve or pale blue flowers in spring and summer. Its kidney-shaped leaves are green. Although invasive—spreading widely but growing to only 2 in (5 cm) tall—it can be planted over a bank or in a woodland setting. **ZONES 8–11.**

Viola riviniana

DOG VIOLET

Found in Europe, Iceland, North Africa and Madeira, this tufted little violet produces colonies from sucker shoots. The flowers are blue-violet, scentless and are borne from spring through summer.

Viola, Perennial Cultivar, 'Jackanapes'

V

Viola riviniana 'Purpurea'

The leaves are long-stemmed and rounded. **'Purpurea'** has purple-green leaves and purple flowers; it reaches 2–4 in (5–10 cm) in height, with a spread of 10 in (25 cm). **ZONES 5–10.**

Viola septentrionalis
NORTHERN BLUE VIOLET

This spring-flowering perennial from North America bears large flowers with a spur, in hues usually of bluish purple but sometimes white. The hairy green leaves are pointed and oval to heart-shaped and have toothed edges. The plant has creeping and suckering stems and grows 6–8 in (15–20 cm) high and wide. **ZONES 7–10.**

Viola tricolor 'Bowles' Black'

Viola sororia
syn. *Viola papilionacea*
WOOLLY BLUE VIOLET

This stemless, herbaceous perennial has scalloped, thickly hairy leaves 4 in (10 cm) long. It bears short-spurred white flowers speckled with violet blue from spring to summer; the flowers are sometimes deep violet blue. **'Freckles'** has white flowers speckled with violet-purple. Both the species and the cultivar reach 4–6 in (10–15 cm) in height. ***Viola sororia* var. *priceana*** has grayish white flowers with violet-blue stems. **ZONES 4–10.**

Viola tricolor
WILD PANSY, JOHNNY JUMP UP, LOVE-IN-IDLENESS

Of wide occurrence in Europe and temperate Asia, this annual, biennial or short-lived perennial produces neat flowers with appealing faces, in shades of yellow, blue, violet and white, in fall (autumn) and winter in mild climates if cut back in late summer. It has soft, angular, branching stems and lobed oval to lance-shaped leaves. It grows to a height and spread of 6 in (15 cm) and self-seeds readily. *Viola tricolor* **'Bowles' Black'** is a striking cultivar with black velvety petals and a yellow center. **ZONES 4–10.**

Viola tricolor

Viola sororia

Viola sororia 'Freckles'

Viola septentrionalis

Viola × *wittrockiana* cultivar

Viola × *wittrockiana* cultivar

Viola × *wittrockiana* cultivar

Viola × *wittrockiana* 'Padparadja'

Viola × *wittrockiana* 'Sky Clear Purple'

Viola × *wittrockiana* 'Princess Deep Purple'

Viola × *wittrockiana* 'Penny Azure Wing'

Viola × *wittrockiana*

PANSY, VIOLA

This hybrid group of compactly branched perennials are almost always grown as biennials or annuals. Offering flowers of a great many hues, the numerous cultivars bloom in late winter through spring and possibly into summer in cooler climates. The flowers are up to 4 in (10 cm) across and have 5 petals in a somewhat flat-faced arrangement. The mid-green leaves are elliptical, with bluntly toothed margins. The plants grow slowly, reaching about 8 in (20 cm) in height and spread. This is a complex hybrid group, including both pansies and violas, the latter traditionally distinguished by the flowers lacking dark blotches, but there are now intermediate types with pale-colored markings. Hybrids in the **Imperial Series** are large-flowered pansies. **'Gold Princess'** is a good example, producing bicolored flowers in golden yellow and red. The **Joker Series** are of an intermediate type, with a range of very bright contrasting colors such as orange and purple. The **Accord Series** of pansies covers most colors and has a very dark central blotch. **'Padparadja'** has vibrant orange flowers. **'Magic'** has purple flowers with a bright face. Other seedling strains include the **Universal** and **Sky Series**. ZONES 5–10.

Viola × *wittrockiana* 'Accord Red Blotch'

Viola × *wittrockiana* 'Jolly Joker'

Virgilia oroboides

Virgilia divaricata

VIRGILIA

Only 2 species belong to this genus, both evergreen trees and both indigenous to South Africa. They are notable for their fast growth and have a tendency to fall over as they age. Over the warmer months, they make a great display of showy pea-flowers. The fruits are flat pods, while the leaves are fern-like with an odd number of leaflets.
CULTIVATION: Very adaptable, they grow best in an open, sunny position and well-drained soil. They cope well with wind and suit warm climates, as they are frost tender, particularly when young. Propagate in spring from seed pre-soaked in warm water for 24 hours.

Virgilia divaricata
SPRING-FLOWERED VIRGILIA

This small evergreen tree grows rapidly to a mature height of about 20 ft (6 m) with relatively horizontal branches. It bears clusters of pea-shaped pink flowers in spring followed by flat pods. The fern-like leaves are divided into many leaflets. It comes true to type when grown from seed. **ZONES 9–11.**

Viola × *wittrockiana* 'Universal Orange'

Virgilia oroboides
syn. ***Virgilia capensis***
CAPE LILAC, TREE-IN-A-HURRY

This species features masses of small, mauve-pink, fragrant flowers in clusters scattered through the crown from early summer to fall (autumn). It is called tree-in-a-hurry because of its speedy growth habit—up to 15 ft (4.5 m) in only 2 years. However, it is often short lived and older trees become quite straggly, so it is mainly useful for new gardens or as a nursery plant. It makes a rounded shrub to small tree 20–30 ft (6–9 m) tall. The leaves are dark green, up to 8 in (20 cm) long, with 13 to 21 oblong, leathery leaflets. The pod is 2–3 in (5–8 cm) long. **ZONES 9–11.**

Viola × *wittrockiana* 'Universal True Blue'

Vitex lucens

VITEX

This genus is made up of about 250 mainly tropical and subtropical trees and shrubs—some evergreen, some deciduous. The leaves are compound with 3 to 7 leaflets radiating from the stalk—less commonly, the leaves are simple. Highlights are the sprays of tubular flowers in shades of white, yellow, red, blue or purple; the fleshy drupes are usually not a feature. In some species, both the leaves and the flowers are aromatic.
CULTIVATION: Moderately to marginally frost hardy, *Vitex* adapt to most soils, but do best in fertile soil with good drainage and with plenty of summer moisture. A sheltered spot in full sun is ideal. Propagate from seed in fall (autumn) or spring or cuttings in summer.

Vitex agnus-castus
CHASTE TREE

This moderately frost-hardy shrub, indigenous to southern Europe and western Asia, has aromatic leaves; these are 6–8 in (15–20 cm) long with 5 to 7 lance-shaped to rounded leaflets, deep green on top and felty gray underneath. The chaste tree is a deciduous, rounded shrub or small tree, 10–20 ft (3–6 m) tall with an upright, branching, woody stem. From early summer to fall (autumn) it bears dense, erect sprays of faintly

Vitex agnus-castus

perfumed, lavender flowers up to 12 in (30 cm) long. Small purple fruit follow. White-flowered and variegated-leaf forms are also available. ***Vitex agnus-castus* var. *latifolia*** has shorter, broader leaves. **ZONES 7–10.**

Vitex lucens
PURIRI, NEW ZEALAND CHASTE TREE

This fine evergreen tree from New Zealand reaches a height of 30–60 ft (9–18 m) and features a rounded crown and a smooth pale trunk. Sprays of bright red or pink flowers are a winter bonus, each flower 1 in (25 mm) long. The large, bright red drupes mature in spring. The leaves consist of 3 to 5 large, oval to round leaflets, smooth and shiny rich green with a wavy edge. It is moderately frost hardy. **ZONES 9–11.**

Vitex negundo

This useful shrub or small tree, native to warm-climate areas from southern and eastern Asia, is grown for its pleasantly aromatic foliage and fragrant flowers. It grows to 25 ft (8 m) tall and produces long leaves composed of deeply cut leaflets which are dark green above with pale, furry undersides. The fragrant flowers are mauve and appear in loose sprays in spring. **ZONES 8–11.**

Vitex trifolia

An evergreen, rounded shrub or bushy small tree to 10 ft (3 m) high, this species occurs naturally in coastal areas from eastern Australia to Southeast Asia. The leaves usually have 3 leaflets and are oblong to lance-shaped, mid-green above, white and downy on the undersides. The blue to purple flowers, in sprays to 8 in (20 cm) long, are borne from late spring to fall (autumn). The flower stalks are white and hairy; the fruit are black drupes. **'Purpurea'** has leaves with deep purple undersides, while **'Variegata'** has bright green leaves edged with creamy yellow. **ZONES 10–12.**

Vitex negundo

VITIS

GRAPE VINE, VINE

This genus of around 65 deciduous, tendril-climbing shrubs and vines has huge commercial significance as the source of grapes. Only a few species yield fruits suitable for wine or the table, and almost all wine grapes are derived from *Vitis vinifera*. The foliage is standard through much of the genus—roughly heart-shaped with 3 to 7 lobes—and often colors well in fall (autumn). Spring-borne sprays of small 5-petalled flowers develop into the familiar fruits.

CULTIVATION: Grow in humus-rich, moisture-retentive but well-drained soil in full sun or part-shade. Fully to marginally frost hardy, they need cool winters and low summer humidity or mildew will be a major problem. Train on a sturdy pergola or fence where it is sunny, and in deep soil so that the vine can dig its roots down. Pruning depends on grape type and upon the way the vine is being grown. For pergola vines, train on a single trunk until it reaches the horizontal beams, then allow it to spread out. Birds are a nuisance, so cover the vines with bird netting or put paper bags around the grape clusters. Cut the grapes with sharp scissors when fully ripe. Vines need annual pruning in mid-winter to control their growth and encourage heavy fruiting. They are traditionally propagated from cuttings in late winter.

Vitis vinifera 'Purpurea'

Vitis vinifera 'Cabernet Sauvignon'

Vitis 'Brandt'

Especially popular in the UK, this vigorous plant reaches 20 ft (6 m) or more. Its bright green leaves turn coppery in fall (autumn); the abundant fruit are edible. **ZONES 6–10.**

Vitis californica

Vitis labrusca

Vitis californica

This species from western USA climbs to as much as 30 ft (9 m) high or wide. The young growth has a covering of fine gray down; the mature leaves are 3-lobed, about 4 in (10 cm) across, turning crimson in fall (autumn). The fruit are very small and purple with a whitish bloom. **'Roger's Red'** is grown for its rich red fall foliage. The small leaves are dull green above and gray beneath, distinctly toothed and of variable size. A vigorous cultivar, it will attain heights of 15–20 ft (4.5–6 m) in full sun. **ZONES 6–10.**

Vitis coignetiae

CRIMSON GLORY VINE

This rapid-growing climber from Japan and Korea reaches 50 ft (15 m) in height, with green, slightly lobed leaves which turn deep crimson, orange and scarlet in fall (autumn). Clusters of small black berries with a glaucous bloom are borne in late summer. Its tendrils coil around supports and need plenty of room to spread. Fully frost hardy, the leaf color is best in cool climates. **ZONES 5–10.**

Vitis labrusca

FOX GRAPE

The parent of most of the non-*Vitis vinifera* grapes cultivated in the USA, this native of the eastern seaboard produces long, felty young shoots that require trellising for support. The large, shallowly 3-lobed leaves are deep green above and felty white beneath. Full sun and well-drained, fertile soil are ideal for the production of the large, purple-black fruit, which have a musky or 'foxy' flavor. **'Concord'**, **'Catawba'** and **'Niagara'** are commonly grown cultivars in areas where winters are cold and summers are cool and short. **ZONES 4–9.**

Vitis vinifera

GRAPE

This species is native to Europe and the Mediterranean and has been cultivated since antiquity. A vigorous, fully frost-hardy vine, it has given rise to a

V

multitude of varieties with either black or white (pale green or yellow) fruit, some being better for wine, others for eating fresh or dried. It is best grown where summers are dry. **'Albany Surprise'** is a sweet white table grape; **'Cabernet Sauvignon'**, a black wine grape, produces many of the best quality red wines; **'Chardonnay'** is a white wine grape that has become very popular in recent years; **'Ganzin Glory'** is widely grown for its brilliant crimson fall (autumn) foliage which colors reliably, even in mild-winter areas; **'Merlot'** is a black wine grape often blended with 'Cabernet Sauvignon'; **'Muller Thurgau'** is a white grape often used for bulk production wines; **'Pinot Noir'** is a black grape used in red wine manufacture and in the production of champagne, in which it is fermented without its skin to prevent the wine reddening—some skin contact is allowed for pink champagne; **'Purpurea'** has spectacular bright crimson foliage in fall; **'Riesling'**, and its derivatives, is a white grape responsible for a range of wines depending on its degree of ripeness and is one of the main grapes of German vineyards; **'Schiava Grossa'** (syn. 'Black Hamburgh') is a black table grape often grown in greenhouses in cool areas; **'Semillon'** is a white wine grape; and **'Shiraz'** (syn. 'Syrah') is a black wine grape widely grown in Australia. Other cultivars include **'Festivee'** and **'Perlette'**. Wine grape cultivars are often grafted onto *Vitus labrusca* rootstock, resistant to the *Phylloxera* root aphid. ZONES 6–10.

Vitis vinifera 'Perlette'

Vitis vinifera 'Festivee'

VRIESEA

Native to Central and South America, this genus consists of around 250 species of epiphytes, among the most popular bromeliads and closely related to *Tillandsia*. The smooth-margined leaves are often coated in mealy scales and have colored cross-bandings. The spectacular flower spikes vary in shape, with petals free or fused into a tube. They can be red, orange or yellow. Different species flower at different times of the year. Many hybrid cultivars have been developed, for example **'Christine'**. **CULTIVATION:** These plants are frost tender. Plant in part-shade in well-drained orchid medium. Water moderately during growth periods, always ensuring the rosette centers are filled with water. Propagate from offsets or seed from spring to summer.

Vriesea carinata
LOBSTER CLAWS

The striking flattened spike of crimson and gold bracts gives this Brazilian bromeliad its common name. It grows to 10 in (25 cm) and has soft, arching, light green leaves. An excellent pot plant, be aware that this species needs a big pot as it has a larger root system than most bromeliads. ZONES 11–12.

Vriesea fosteriana
RED CHESTNUT

This large attractive bromeliad is native to Mexico, Brazil and Argentina. Its broad, mid-green leaves have a band of reddish brown on both sides, grow up to 3 ft (1 m) long and form a dense rosette. This species has a prominent flower spike up to 5 ft (1.5 m) tall with yellow flowers. Ensure a position with adequate air circulation. ZONES 11–12.

Vriesea psittacina

This small to medium-sized species has soft, light-green leaves and spreads to 24 in (60 cm). Its delicate, feather-like inflorescence and yellow flowers, when offset by yellow, red or green bracts, provide a vivid array of colors. ZONES 11–12.

Vriesea 'Christine'

Vriesea carinata

Vriesea splendens

×*Vuylstekeara* 'Susan Bigelow'

Vriesea splendens
syns *Tillandsia splendens, Vriesea speciosa*
FLAMING SWORD

This very striking bromeliad earned its common name from its sword-shaped flower spike of bright red or orange. It has medium-sized, soft green leaves with purple-black bands and an 18 in (45 cm) high inflorescence. ZONES 11–12.

× VUYLSTEKEARA

The almost unpronounceable name of this genus honors Charles Vuylsteke (1844–1927), the Belgian orchid grower who first realized the possibilities of combining in one hybrid the broad petals and summer-flowering habit of the pansy orchids *(Miltonia),* the extravagant ruffles and marbled patterns of *Odontoglossum crispum,* and the brilliant reds and oranges of the various species of *Cochlioda*, all epiphytic orchids from the upland forests of Brazil and Colombia. The results are considered by many orchid fanciers to be the most successful of all the many multigeneric orchid hybrids. The plants will flower when they are quite small, though they are seen at their best when allowed to develop into 18 in (45 cm) wide, many-flowered clumps. The flowers, which can appear at almost any time of year, can only be described as baroque in their splendid ruffles and beautiful colors, usually red, strong pink or burgundy, all with marblings and mottlings of white. There are many fine cultivars. **CULTIVATION:** They are not difficult to grow, needing only moderate warmth but liking bright light and regular watering and feeding. Plant in coarse compost and propagate by division in spring.

× *Vuylstekeara* Cambria 'Plush'

There are many other members of this hybrid genus, but Cambria 'Plush' is by far the most famous—and, thanks to mericlonal propagation, one of the most widely available. It is a compact plant, with round pseudobulbs each carrying a few long leaves; the flowers can appear at any time from spring to fall (autumn). They are about 3 in (8 cm) wide, carried in sprays of 12 or so, and an attractive shade of dull red with very pretty white markings on the labellum. ZONES 11–12.

× *Vuylstekeara* 'Susan Bigelow'

The broad and handsome labellum of this plant comes from its *Miltonia* ancestors, the extraordinary pattern of white spots and stripes from the *Odontoglossum* side of the family, and the rich crimson on which they are displayed from *Cochlioda*. As it matures, the blossoms in the cluster increase to about 12 in number. The flowers are long lived, usually about 3 weeks. ZONES 11–12.

W X Y Z

Washingtonia filifera

Wachendorfia thyrsiflora

Wahlenbergia stricta 'Tasmanian Sky'

Wahlenbergia albomarginata

Wahlenbergia gloriosa

Wahlenbergia communis

WACHENDORFIA

RED ROOT

Only one or two of the 25 or so species of this genus of cormous perennials from South Africa are known in cultivation outside their own country. Wachendorfias have basal tufts of long, narrow, pleated leaves and bear erect spikes of starry, golden flowers in spring and summer. Their common name comes from the red sap of the corms, used as a dye, and the bright red-orange color of the roots themselves.

CULTIVATION: Only moderately frost hardy, they thrive best when grown outdoors in warm, near frost-free climates. They require a moist but well-drained soil in a sunny position and are ideal for bog gardens. They spread readily throughout the garden by seed. Propagate from seed or by division in spring.

Wachendorfia thyrsiflora

RED ROOT

This is the best known species. It grows to 7 ft (2 m) and bears thick, straight spikes of bright yellow flower clusters in spring and early summer. The narrow, lance-shaped leaves are pleated, strong and strap-like—up to 3 ft (1 m) long. It tolerates light frost. **ZONES 8–11.**

WAHLENBERGIA

BLUEBELLS

A genus of about 200 species of annual or perennial herbs with a wide distribution, mostly in the southern hemisphere. They have variable foliage and the flowers range from wide open stars to tubular bells, all with 5 prominent lobes, in shades of blue, purple or white. They are usually small in stature and are suitable for the rock garden or border.

CULTIVATION: Unless otherwise stated, all the species described are fully frost hardy. Grow in a well-drained, humus-rich soil in full sun or light shade. Propagate from seed or by division in spring.

Wahlenbergia albomarginata

NEW ZEALAND BLUEBELL

This tufted perennial to 8 in (20 cm) high forms basal rosettes of lance-shaped oval or spoon-shaped hairy leaves. Underground rhizomes spread to form new rosettes and these may develop into mat-like colonies. The nodding, usually solitary bell-shaped pale blue to white flowers with spreading lobes are borne on fine stems in summer. This marginally frost-hardy, short-lived plant grows best in part-shade. **ZONES 7–10.**

Wahlenbergia communis

syn. ***Wahlenbergia bicolor***

TUFTED BLUEBELL, GRASS-LEAF BLUEBELL

This perennial tufted herb is native to Australia where it occurs in all mainland states, sometimes in fairly arid areas. It grows up to 30 in (75 cm) high and has linear leaves to 3 in (8 cm) long, sometimes with small teeth. Masses of star-shaped light blue flowers are borne on slender stems in spring and summer. **ZONES 8–11.**

Wahlenbergia gloriosa

ROYAL BLUEBELL, AUSTRALIAN BLUEBELL

This perennial herb with spreading rhizomes and erect stems to about 8 in (20 cm) high is a native of Australian alpine regions and is the floral emblem of the Australian Capital Territory. It has dark green lance-shaped leaves to 1½ in (35 mm) long with wavy, toothed margins and bears a profusion of royal-blue or purple bell-shaped flowers on separate fine stems in summer. **ZONES 8–10.**

Wahlenbergia hederacea

IVY-LEAVED BELLFLOWER

This wahlenbergia is native to western Europe, but is rare in the UK. It grows in acidic soils on moors and peat bogs, and produces its pale blue flowers in summer. As its common name suggests, its leaves are ivy-shaped, ½ in (12 mm) across, growing on slender trailing stems and giving the plant a creeping or sprawling form. **ZONES 7–10.**

Wahlenbergia stricta

syn. ***Wahlenbergia consimilis***

TALL BLUEBELL

This tufted perennial herb to 3 ft (1 m) tall has a wide distribution throughout southern Australia and is quite common in open forests and grasslands. The basal obovate leaves with wavy margins become linear up the stem. Lower stems and leaves have spreading, long white hairs. Small, blue star-shaped flowers are borne in spring and summer. **'Tasmanian Sky'** has light purple flowers. **ZONES 9–10.**

WALDSTEINIA

Found over much of the northern temperate zone, the 6 species in this genus are clump-forming, rhizomatous perennials. They are semi-evergreen, creeping ground covers with 3-parted leaves resembling those of their close allies, the strawberries. The hairy leaves are usually bright green with bronze tints if grown in the sun. In spring and summer, bright yellow 5-petalled flowers are borne singly or in clusters of up to 8 blooms.

CULTIVATION: Most species are quite frost hardy and easily grown in any well-drained soil in sun or part-shade. Propagate by division or by self-rooted offsets from the runners.

Waldsteinia ternata

syn. ***Waldsteinia trifoliata***

Native to central Europe through Russia to China and Japan, this herbaceous or semi-evergreen creeping perennial grows to a height of about 6 in (15 cm). Golden-yellow, buttercup-like flowers appear from late spring, mostly on the new growth. Each bloom is about ½ in (12 mm) across. It spreads quite fast and makes a thick ground cover in moist soil in part-shade beneath trees. In ideal conditions, *Waldsteinia ternata* can become invasive. **ZONES 3–9.**

WASHINGTONIA

WASHINGTONIA PALM

This genus is made up of 2 species of fan-leafed palms from arid parts of western Mexico, southern California and Arizona. Their stately appearance makes them ideal specimen or avenue trees. They have an upright, single trunk, and are sometimes called petticoat palms because the dead fronds hang down in a mass around the trunk, almost to the ground. The large fronds have many long, tapering segments and spiny stalks. The small white flowers cluster at intervals on long flowering branches that arch out well beyond the fronds. The fruits are small dark drupes.

CULTIVATION: These palms enjoy warm to hot climates, full sun, well-drained soil and an open position. Propagate from seed in spring.

Washingtonia filifera

syn. ***Washingtonia filamentosa***

CALIFORNIA FAN PALM, COTTON PALM

From southern California and Arizona, this palm develops a fat trunk and grows 20–60 ft (6–18 m) tall. The grayish green fronds form a broad, spherical crown

Watsonia borbonica

Watsonia galpinii

Watsonia pillansii 'Watermelon Shades'

Washingtonia robusta

about 15 ft (4.5 m) across. The common name cotton palm comes from the white, cotton-like threads on and between the frond segments. Its small hard black berries ripen in winter. **ZONES 9–11.**

Washingtonia robusta

MEXICAN WASHINGTONIA PALM, MEXICAN FAN PALM

This species, taller and more slender than *Washingtonia filifera* and with a more tapering trunk, occurs naturally in northwestern Mexico. It grows to 80 ft (24 m) and its crown is 10 ft (3 m) across. The shiny, bright green fronds, almost circular, are less deeply segmented than those of *W. filifera*. The fruit are tiny dark brown berries. **ZONES 10–11.**

WATSONIA

This is a genus of about 60 species of cormous perennials, allied to *Gladiolus* and native to South Africa and Madagascar. They produce spikes of fragrant, tubular, orange, pink, red or white flowers resembling gladioli, although somewhat more tubular in form. Flowers usually appear from spring to summer. The leaves are also similar to those of gladioli, being sword-shaped and erect. There are evergreen and deciduous species available.

CULTIVATION: The corms should be planted in fall (autumn) in light, well-drained soil in a sunny spot. They like plenty of water during the growing season, and will tolerate only light frost.

Watsonia pillansii

Clumps are best left undisturbed and allowed to spread freely. Propagate from seed in the fall (autumn) or by division when clumps become overcrowded.

Watsonia aletroides

From South Africa, this species forms clumps of erect, sword-shaped shiny leaves to 16 in (40 cm) high. It produces unbranched spikes to 24 in (60 cm) high of up to 12 tubular scarlet flowers, each 2 in (5 cm) long, from late winter to spring. **ZONES 9–10.**

Watsonia borbonica

syn. ***Watsonia pyramidata***

PINK WATSONIA

This species grows to 5 ft (1.5 m). It bears a spike of lilac to rose pink, 2 in (5 cm), funnel-shaped flowers in summer. The slender green leaves are sword-shaped. This plant is almost evergreen, especially if grown in boggy soil. The white-flowering ***W. borbonica* subsp. *ardernei*** (syn. *W. ardernei*) is sometimes classed as a species in its own right. **ZONES 9–10.**

Watsonia galpinii

The stems on this watsonia reach 3 ft (1 m) in height. There are usually 4 to 8 basal leaves, 12–15 in (30–38 cm) in length and ½ in (15 mm) wide. They are stiff and erect, the margins of the leaves being thickened. The 8 to 10 orange-red flowers are borne on flower spikes in late summer. The curved tube is about ⅔ of the length of the flower with the ends turned out; the anthers and pollen are white. **ZONES 9–10.**

Watsonia humilis

This clump-forming, spring-flowering species has lance-shaped leaves to 12 in (30 cm) in length. It bears unbranched spikes to 18 in (45 cm) high of 12 tubular, pink flowers with spreading lobes. This deciduous species is dormant in the summer months. **ZONES 9–10.**

Watsonia meriana

This watsonia also has a clumping form, and grows to a height of 3 ft (1 m). Its leaves are erect and sword-shaped, growing both from the base and up the stems. Flowers are pink to red, tubular, with 6 spreading lobes and blackish anthers. Its attractive flowers and vigorous growth have made this species, like other watsonias, a popular garden plant, but its ability to spread rapidly and densely from corms and small bulbils (produced on stems after flowering) make it a weed in some areas. The larger-flowered **'Bulbillifera'** produces bulbils among the flower spikes. **ZONES 9–10.**

Watsonia pillansii

syn. ***Watsonia beatricis***

BEATRICE WATSONIA

This evergreen species grows to 4 ft (1.2 m) in height. The flower spike bears salmon pink, tubular, star-shaped flowers 3 in (8 cm) long in late summer to fall (autumn). The green foliage is sword-shaped. Hardier than other species, it can withstand some frost. A number of hybrids have been developed from this species, including **'Watermelon Shades'**, and there is some doubt about whether this plant, common in nurseries under this name, is the true wild species. **ZONES 7–10.**

Watsonia spectabilis

syn. ***Watsonia coccinea***

This species makes an upright clump to about 15 in (38 cm) tall and has narrow, linear or lance-shaped leaves. In winter and spring it bears spikes of 3 to 6 tubular flowers with spreading lobes in shades of red, purple or pink. **ZONES 9–10.**

Watsonia tabularis

A very large and colorful clumping plant, this species has stout, rigid stems of 6 ft (1.8 m) with 4 to 5 leaves arising from the base. These are 3 ft (1 m) long and up to 2 in (5 cm) wide with transparent margins. Several flowers are borne on each flower spike, the main stem of which is purple, in early summer. They are deep coral red outside the tube and a pale salmon pink on the inside. The tube, with turned-out ends, is 3 in (8 cm) long and the anthers are a striking dark purple-blue with white pollen. **ZONES 9–10.**

WEDELIA

There are around 70 species of this genus of the daisy family distributed throughout the tropics and subtropics. They range from annuals or perennials through to small shrubs. The former often have prostrate stems which root at the nodes giving the plant a creeping form; some are scrambling climbers. The leaves are in opposite pairs with the uppermost sometimes alternate. The flowers are typical of the daisy family, with small bell-shaped bisexual flowers in the center and female ray flowers radiating out, both of which are yellow. They are either solitary or occur in small clusters on long stalks. They set single-seeded fruits.

CULTIVATION: Frost-tender, wedelias prefer well-drained soil in either sun or shade. Propagate from seed or cuttings, or by division.

Wedelia trilobata

CREEPING DAISY

This daisy is native to the West Indies and northern South America. It is a trailing herb with many slender, flexible stems sometimes up to 6 ft (1.8 m) long rooting at the nodes. The leaves are elliptic to oblong, green, notched and a little fleshy. They can be up to 4 in (10 cm) long and slightly lobed. With its golden flowers, 1 in (25 mm) across, and sprawling habit, this species makes a popular ground cover or hanging basket plant. It also grows well under trees, provided the ground is dry. **ZONES 10–12.**

WEIGELA

This genus includes about 12 species of arching deciduous shrubs from Japan, Korea and northeastern China. Most grow 6–10 ft (1.8–3 m) high and wide, and have pointed, elliptical, deep green leaves about 4 in (10 cm) long. The foliage often develops orange, red and purple tones in fall (autumn). In spring,

Watsonia borbonica subsp. *ardernei*

Watsonia tabularis

Watsonia spectabilis

masses of white, pink or crimson, sometimes yellowish, bell- or trumpet-shaped flowers appear, 1½ in (35 mm) long.

CULTIVATION: Fully frost hardy, most species prefer full sun or light shade in moist, fertile, well-drained soil. Prune out older branches after flowering to maintain vigor. Propagate from summer cuttings.

Weigela 'Bristol Ruby'

This erect hybrid, bred from *Weigela florida* and *W. coraeensis*, is grown for the profusion of crimson flowers which adorn the shrub from late spring to early summer. It grows to 6 ft (1.8 m) tall, with slender, arching branches and dark green oval leaves. **ZONES 4–10.**

Weigela coraeensis

syns *Weigela amabilis, W. grandiflora*

On maturity, this large deciduous shrub from Japan may reach 15 ft (4.5 m). It

Weigela florida 'Foliis Purpureis'

Weigela floribunda

Weigela japonica

Weigela coraeensis

Weigela praecox

Weigela florida

Weigela florida 'Eva Rathke'

Weigela florida 'Aureovariegata'

has long, broad, pointed leaves, 3–5 in (8–12 cm) long, with hairy veins. It is distinguished from other species by being mostly non-hairy along the stems and leaf surface. The sessile flowers are tubular, the 5 petals opening out at the apex, whitish pink to rose. **ZONES 6–10.**

Weigela floribunda

syn. *Diervilla floribunda*

From Japan, this deciduous shrub reaches about 10 ft (3 m) in height and has slender, pointed leaves which are hairy on both sides. Young shoots are also hairy, as are the outsides of the flowers. These are deep crimson, crowded on short lateral branchlets, tubular in form with the style projecting out from the opened petals. **ZONES 6–10.**

Weigela florida

This arching, deciduous shrub from Japan, Korea and northeastern China, which grows up to 10 ft (3 m) or so, is grown for its lavish spring display of rose pink, trumpet-shaped flowers. **'Appleblossom'**, with variegated leaves, has flowers that open white and age to pink. **'Aureovariegata'** has bright green, cream-edged leaves and wide, bright pink, trumpet-shaped flowers to 1½ in (35 mm) wide. **'Eva Rathke'** bears crimson flowers from purplish red buds. Fully frost hardy, it grows 5 ft (1.5 m) tall and wide with a dense, erect habit. **'Foliis Purpureis'** has purplish green leaves. The flowers are deep pink, paler inside the tube and appear from late spring to early summer and sometimes again in fall (autumn). **ZONES 4–10.**

Weigela japonica

As the name suggests, this deciduous shrub is from Japan. It reaches 10 ft (3 m) in height with a spread of about half that. The leaves, elliptic to oblong, are coarsely serrated, up to 4 in (10 cm) long and very hairy beneath—especially the veins. The young branchlets are, however, non-hairy. The flowers are white with a reddish base, trumpet-shaped and occur in 3s on loose terminal clusters in late spring. **ZONES 6–10.**

Weigela middendorffiana

This species grows to a height and width of about 6 ft (1.8 m). Its distinctive, plump, bell-shaped, spring flowers range in color from pale creamy yellow to deep amber, with reddish markings in the throat. It can tolerate heat, but prefers part-shade and needs shelter from strong winds to perform at its best. **ZONES 4–10.**

Weigela praecox

This weigela is from Korea, China and Japan. It is deciduous and grows to about 6 ft (1.8 m) and is characterized by having arching branches. The leaves are slender, ovate, pointed and hairy on both sides. The rose-pink trumpet flowers are yellow on the inside of the tube, which opens out at the end with pointed petals giving it a star-like appearance. The outside of the tube is hairy. The flowers occur in loose terminal clusters in spring—it is the earliest flowering weigela. **'Variegata'** has leaves green in the center and cream around the margin, which is entire. It has pink trumpet flowers with a star-shaped appearance. **ZONES 5–10.**

Weinmannia pinnata

WEINMANNIA

This genus of about 190 species of evergreen trees and shrubs is found in Central and South America, Madagascar, the Malay Archipelago and islands of the west Pacific. They have opposite, usually pinnate leaves that may be different in juvenile and adult stages. The small white or yellow flowers in erect often showy racemes are followed by a shiny, reddish brown 2-celled capsule. They are grown for their attractive foliage, flowers and fruit and value as shade cover.

CULTIVATION: Frost tender, they grow best in slightly acid peaty soil with good drainage. Light requirements range from part-shade to full sun. A plentiful water supply is needed during the flowering season. They will tolerate pruning. Propagate from seed or cuttings.

Weinmannia pinnata

This shrub or small tree from Mexico to Brazil and the West Indies grows to about 30 ft (10 m) tall with downy young branches and pinnate leaves to 3 in (8 cm) long. The elliptical leaflets have serrated margins. It bears small white flowers. **ZONES 10–12.**

Weinmannia racemosa
KAMAHI

This New Zealand evergreen tree grows 40–60 ft (12–18 m) tall. The glossy leaves are heart-shaped with a sharp point and slightly serrated edges, which in juvenile leaves may be divided into 3 leaflets. During spring and summer white or pink, bottlebrush-like flower-spikes appear; they are about 4 in (10 cm) long. The flowers are followed by red fruit. **ZONES 9–11.**

WELWITSCHIA

This bizarre genus consists of a single species, native to the desert regions of southern Angola and Namibia. It is a gymnosperm, occasionally cultivated for its curiosity value. Its short, hollow, woody stems terminate in a 2-lobed disc-like apex. From opposite sides of the disc sprout 2 long strap-like leaves. These 2 leaves persist for the full lifetime of the plant, splitting lengthwise with age. Male or female cones are borne on separate plants on branched stalks that arise from the center of the disc.
CULTIVATION: This is a very slow-growing frost-tender plant requiring dry, hot conditions and adequate soil depth for a long tap root. It needs full sun and perfect drainage. Water moderately during the growing season and keep completely dry during winter. Propagation is from seed.

Welwitschia mirabilis
syn. *Welwitschia bainesii*

This species' leaves are leathery and long, up to 8 ft (2.4 m), and 3 ft (1 m) wide, splitting with age into multiple strips. Scarlet cones are set in groups of up to 20 on stalks up to 12 in (30 cm) long, each female cone bearing many winged seeds under its scales. Male cones are smaller and insignificant. It is adapted to desert conditions. **ZONES 9–10.**

WESTRINGIA

These 25 or so species of evergreen shrubs are indigenous to Australia. The square, woody stems are clothed in small stiff leaves arranged in whorls of 3 or 4. The tubular flowers are 2 lipped, the upper lip with 2 lobes, the lower with 3; they appear for many months in the leaf axils, peaking in spring. The fruits are tiny and nut like.
CULTIVATION: Westringias grow best in mild-winter climates. Many grow naturally near the sea and thrive on coastal conditions. They prefer an open, sunny site and adapt to most well-drained soils; some species benefit from the addition of organic matter. All species thrive if adequately watered over summer. Clip the bushes annually to keep them compact. Propagate from seed in spring or from cuttings in late summer.

Welwitschia mirabilis

Westringia eremicola

This species from the eastern States of Australia is as easy to grow as the better known *Westringia fruticosa*, though it is not so bushy. It can be pruned, however, to a more compact form if desired. The white or mauve flowers appear in summer. *W. eremicola* tolerates poor soil. **ZONES 9–11.**

Westringia fruticosa
syn. *Westringia rosmariniformis*
COAST ROSEMARY, AUSTRALIAN ROSEMARY

This eastern Australian species has somewhat rosemary-like foliage, and makes a compact, rounded shrub to 6 ft (1.8 m) high and about as wide with rather stiffly spreading branches. The narrow leaves, arranged in 4s, are gray-green on top, white-felted underneath. The small flowers, white with purple blotches in the throat, appear most of the year. Coast rosemary will tolerate salt-laden winds and can be grown as a hedge in seaside gardens. **'Morning Light'** is a smaller variegated form to 3 ft (1 m) high. The green leaves are surrounded by a cream band. **ZONES 9–11.**

Westringia glabra
VIOLET WESTRINGIA

This species is native to southeastern Australia. It is a fast-growing, bushy shrub which grows to about 4 ft (1.2 m). The dark bluish green, oval-shaped

Westringia fruticosa

Westringia eremicola

Westringia fruticosa 'Morning Light'

Wigandia caracasana

Westringia raleighii

leaves to ½ in (12 mm) long are set in whorls of four. Bluish mauve flowers are produced from late winter to early summer. **ZONES 9–11.**

Westringia raleighii
syn. *Westringia brevifolia*

This native of Tasmania is a rounded shrub to about 5 ft (1.5 m) high and has small elliptical leaves to ½ in (12 mm) long arranged in whorls of 4 around the stem. Pale bluish mauve flowers are produced in winter and spring. **ZONES 9–11.**

WIGANDIA

These 5 species of striking, evergreen shrubs from Central and South America have huge, oval to heart-shaped, scalloped, deep green leaves with white, often stinging hairs beneath. The leaves are 18 in (45 cm) long and the bushes grow to 10 ft (3 m) or more tall, although they can be pruned. Violet-blue flowers appear in large terminal panicles of one-sided spikes from spring to fall (autumn). *Wigandia caracasana* from Venezuela is the best known of the 5 species.
CULTIVATION: Plant in moist but well-drained soil in full light. Frost tender, they are grown under glass in cool climates. They can be grown in pots and need abundant water during the growth

Welwitschia mirabilis

period, moderate amounts at other times. Propagate from seed or cuttings in spring. Sometimes white fly can be a problem.

Wigandia caracasana
syn. *Wigandia urens* var. *caracasana*

Native to Mexico and South America, *Wigandia caracasana* is a variable species of erect evergreen shrub that grows to 10 ft (3 m) or even more. It has leaves which are very large, up to 18 in (45 cm) long, oval and wavy edged and deep green above with a hairy white underside. The hairs can be sticky and sometimes mixed with longer stinging hairs. The flowers are violet to purple, in large terminal clusters. This species is often grown for its 'jungle effect' on a garden. It can grow in full light in a protected situation, but is frost- and drought-tender. **ZONES 10–12.**

× WILSONARA

Under this name are found a group of tri-generic orchid hybrids that include genes of *Oncidium*, *Odontoglossum* and *Cochlioda*. The first of them, × *Wilsonara* Insignis, was flowered in 1916, the result of a cross between

Odontoglossum illustrissimum and × *Oncidioda* Charlesworthii but its blooms were of inferior quality. In the 1980s interest in wilsonaras revived and many more crosses have now been named. They are rather varied but often combine the long flower sprays of oncidiums with the larger star-shaped flowers, heavily barred with purple or chocolate, of odontoglossums.
CULTIVATION: A cool greenhouse with a minimum night temperature in winter of 50°F (10°C) is suitable for these orchids. Grow in a standard epiphytic orchid potting mix. During the summer growing season provide a high level of humidity, plenty of water and some form of shade. Water sparingly during winter and increase the light. Propagate by division.

× *Wilsonara* Hybrids

Like all 3 parent genera these plants feature strongly flattened pseudobulbs closely spaced on short rhizomes, each bearing 1 or 2 smooth, strap-like leaves from the apex. Inflorescences are often many flowered and the flowers are mostly 2–3 in (5–8 cm) across. Purple or chocolate coloring usually predominates on the pointed petals and the lip may be of contrasting color. **Maduida** has purple-tinged red petals and a white lip patterned orange and yellow. **ZONES 10–11.**

Wisteria brachybotrys

Wisteria floribunda 'Alba'

Wisteria floribunda 'Honbeni'

× *Wilsonara* Hybrid Maduida

Wisteria sinensis

WISTERIA

WISTERIA

These deciduous, woody stemmed, twining climbers are among the most popular plants for pergolas, prized for their large, drooping sprays of perfumed flowers and the summer shade of their soft, light green, luxuriant foliage. This genus of legumes consists of about 10 species from China, Korea, Japan and the USA. Their leaves are pinnate and they bear pendent, bean-like, seed pods.
CULTIVATION: Wisterias like a sunny position and humus-rich, well-drained soil. Although they take some time to establish, they become large, vigorous plants and need strong support. Prune after flowering; prune again in winter only if really necessary to control size. With regular pruning and some support in the early years, a wisteria can be grown as a large, free-standing shrub or standard. All wisterias are frost hardy. Seedlings are easily raised but take many years to flower. Propagate from cuttings or seed, or by layering or grafting in late summer.

Wisteria brachybotrys

syn. *Wisteria venusta*

SILKY WISTERIA

This deciduous climber can reach 30 ft (9 m). Its deep green leaves, 15 in (38 cm) long, have 9 to 13 leaflets. The white, scented flowers hang in 6 in (15 cm) long racemes, and have yellow markings on the petals. They appear in early summer, but can spot flower again during fall (autumn). There are 2 cultivars of this wisteria: **'Murasaki Kapitan'** (syn. *Wisteria venusta* 'Violacea'), which has lavender-blue flowers with white markings, and **'Shiro Kapitan'** (syn. 'Alba'), which bears white flowers but may differ little from the true species. Occasionally double flowers are produced. **ZONES 5–10.**

Wisteria frutescens

Wisteria floribunda cultivar

Wittrockia superba

Wisteria floribunda

JAPANESE WISTERIA

From Japan, this vigorous climber grows up to 30 ft (9 m). It bears pendulous racemes of fragrant, purple-blue flowers 18 in (45 cm) or more long. These are often produced after the leaves expand, in spring. Large velvety oblong pods are produced in fall (autumn). **'Alba'** (syn. 'Shiro Noda'), a beautiful, white-flowering form, has drooping sprays up to 24 in (60 cm) long. **'Domino'** (syn. 'Issai') is a more dwarfed form with violet flowers and is suited to a more restricted environment. **'Honbeni'** (syn. 'Rosea') has pale pink flowers with purple tips. **'Macrobotrys'** (syn. Multijuga') bears spectacular racemes of lilac flowers up to 3 ft (1 m) long. **'Violacea Plena'** (syn. 'Double Black Dragon') produces its double dark violet-blue flowers in early summer. **ZONES 5–10.**

Wisteria frutescens

Native to the eastern USA, *Wisteria frutescens* has lilac to purple flowers, each about ½ in (12 mm) long in dense racemes of 2–5 in (5–12 cm) in length. The leaves consist of 9 to 15 ovate leaflets. It sets fruit in pods up to 4 in (10 cm) long. **ZONES 5–10.**

Wisteria sinensis

syn. *Wisteria chinensis*

CHINESE WISTERIA

Native to China and the most widely grown of the wisterias, this vigorous deciduous climber is known to reach 100 ft (30 m). The sprays of slightly fragrant, lavender blue flowers, up to 12 in (30 cm) long, appear in spring on bare branches before the leaves, making a magnificent sight. The leaves are composed of 7 to 13 leaflets. **'Alba'** has strongly scented pea-like white flowers, set in drooping racemes up to 24 in (60 cm) long in early summer. **'Caroline'** bears highly fragrant, dark purplish blue flowers. **ZONES 5–10.**

WITTROCKIA

This small genus of 7 species of bromeliads is found only in southern coastal mountains of Brazil. They are epiphytic, terrestrial or rock-dwelling plants that form stemless rosettes. Most species have colorful thinly textured linear leaves with a few marginal spines. Spikes of flowers nestled in the heart of the plant have colorful bracts and blue or white petals.
CULTIVATION: In warm, frost-free areas they may be grown outdoors in an open, well-drained soil in filtered shade. When grown as pot plants in a greenhouse, use an open, porous bromeliad potting mix. Indoors they need warm humid conditions and bright, filtered light. Propagation is from seed or offsets.

Wittrockia superba

syns *Nidularium karatas, N. superbum, Canistrum cruentum*

In its natural habitat this rosette-forming bromeliad, to 3 ft (1 m) high and across, grows on trees, on rocks or in leaf litter on the ground. The long stiff leaves are a glossy green with red tips and sharp terminal spines. The flowers, arranged in a cone-shaped spike, are nestled in the heart of the plant. These are blue and white, surrounded by red bracts and are produced in summer. **ZONES 11–12.**

WODYETIA

FOXTAIL PALM

This palm genus contains only one species, endemic to Australia's Cape York Peninsula where it grows among huge granite boulders. Identified only in the early 1980s, it is already widely grown in the tropics and subtropics in many countries. At one stage fears were held for the future of wild populations due to seed poaching, but fortunately planted specimens are now bearing abundantly. The genus is named after

Wodyeti, the last male Aborigine of his clan, who died in the 1970s.
CULTIVATION: *Wodyetia*, easily grown in warm, frost-free areas, needs very well-drained soil but will tolerate dry conditions and hot sun. Strong winds damage the fronds. Propagate from seed.

Wodyetia bifurcata

This palm has bright green, 8 ft (2.4 m) long, plumose fronds—their form suggestive of a fox's tail—and grows to 30 ft (9 m) tall. The trunk, slightly bottle-shaped, smooth and banded, has a prominent, pale green crownshaft. Large branched flower clusters occur at the crownshaft base. The oval fruit are $2\frac{1}{2}$ in (6 cm) long and ripen orange-red. **ZONES 10–12.**

WOLFFIA

WATER MEAL, DUCKWEED

Allied to *Lemna*, this is a genus of 8 species of floating aquatics distributed over most of the tropical to warm-temperate regions of the world. They are among the smallest known flowering plants, having minuscule, bright green plant bodies or 'fronds', from which emerge very fine, hair-like roots. The fronds mass together to cover large areas of still water, each one producing a minute green flower in a central cavity.
CULTIVATION: Often introduced to ponds as food for water fowl or used as cold-water aquarium plants, they vary in hardiness depending on the species, but are generally easily grown in any still water with sun or part-shade.

Wolffia arrhiza

This species is found in Eurasia, Africa and Australia. It is semi-evergreen, sometimes dying off in less favorable months but often producing its tiny green flowers all year round if conditions are good. The small leaves are rounded and $\frac{1}{16}$ in (1 mm) long and each plant can spread out to cover about 3 ft (1 m) in diameter. **ZONES 7–11.**

WOLLEMIA

WOLLEMI PINE

This conifer genus, endemic to a very restricted area in the Blue Mountains of southeastern Australia, was discovered in late 1994. The only known species is *Wollemia nobilis*. Closely related to *Agathis* and *Araucaria*, *Wollemia* belongs to an ancient family of conifers. One of the world's rarest plants, with only 20 or so adult trees surviving in a deep, moist sandstone canyon, it is considered a 'living fossil'. Slender and columnar, it grows 120 ft (36 m) tall. The bark of mature trees features many spongy nodules; on young stems it peels in thin, reddish brown scales. Its unique branching habit produces a double crown effect. Branches near the crown apex terminate in a male or female cone, then each whole branch is shed from the trunk. Buds lower down on the trunk grow out to produce a 'second crown'.
CULTIVATION: To date there are few cultivation details. In the wild it grows in moist soil derived from sandstone and high in organic matter. Propagation has been effected from both seed and cuttings.

Wollemia nobilis

On the lower lateral branches of this tree the leaves are long, narrow and flexible, in 2 comb-like rows; at the top of the crown they are short, broad and rigid, in 4 rows, all directed upwards. The globular female (seed) cones, 4 in (10 cm) long, have bristle-pointed scales; the cylindrical male (pollen) cones, 6 in (15 cm) long, occur further down the tree. **ZONES 9–11.**

WOODSIA

This genus of deciduous ferns numbers 20 to 30 species, occurring in temperate and subarctic regions mainly of the northern hemisphere but extending through the Andes in South America. They are plants of moist woodland areas, often growing in rock crevices, and have short rhizomes and tufts of narrow fronds that are divided pinnately, the primary divisions deeply toothed or further divided. The spore bodies (sori) on the frond undersides are half-enclosed in cup-like structures.
CULTIVATION: Most are very frost hardy and can be grown outdoors in cool climates, preferring a moist, shaded position in a rock garden. They should be planted in a crevice or among pebbles, and require constant moisture and good soil drainage.

Woodsia andersonii

Native to western China and the Himalayas, *Woodsia andersonii* is an alpine fern growing at altitudes of 9,000–11,000 ft (2,700–3,300 m). **ZONES 6–9.**

WOODWARDIA

CHAIN FERN

Indigenous to warm-temperate areas of Europe, Asia and North America, this is a genus of about 12 species of vigorous evergreen or deciduous ferns. They have large, bipinnate arching or spreading fronds which emerge red then turn deep green. The spore bodies are set in chain-like rows parallel to the midrib. Some species can be grown in a bog garden, such as the magnificent ***Woodwardia gigantea***, or near the edge of a pond.
CULTIVATION: Species vary from moderately frost hardy to frost hardy. They prefer a humid atmosphere, part-shade and a very moist peaty, neutral to slightly acidic soil. In cool climates woodwardias can be grown in a conservatory or greenhouse. Propagate from spores or plantlets.

Woodwardia fimbriata

GIANT CHAIN FERN

Native to western North America, *Woodwardia fimbriata* produces large oval to lanceolate fronds from a stout, creeping rhizome. The dark green fronds, growing to 6–8 ft (1.8–2.4 m) long, have deeply incised, ragged-edged leaflets with pointed lobes. The spore bodies are borne in chain-like formations on the undersides of fertile fronds. **ZONES 7–9.**

Wollemia nobilis

Worsleya rayneri

Woodwardia radicans

Woodsia andersonii

Woodwardia gigantea

Woodwardia radicans

EUROPEAN CHAIN FERN

This evergreen species, which can reach 6 ft (1.8 m) in height and almost twice the spread, is native to southwestern Europe. Its long fronds are lance shaped and coarsely divided, with curved pinnules to 3 in (8 cm) long. This species has been popular in cultivation for over 200 years, being easy to propagate from plantlets produced at the end of the frond stems. *Woodwardia radicans* is frost hardy. **ZONES 8–10.**

Woodwardia virginica

VIRGINIA CHAIN FERN

A smaller version of *Woodwardia fimbriata*, this eastern North American native produces deep green, 3–4 ft (1–1.2 m) long fronds with striking shiny black stripes. Found growing naturally in bogs, they require acidic, humus-rich soil in full sun to shade. **ZONES 4–10.**

WORSLEYA

BLUE AMARYLLIS, EMPRESS OF BRAZIL

This genus, closely allied to *Hippeastrum*, consists of only one species. The fat bulb has a long neck protruding above the ground, topped by a few strap-shaped leaves; in winter a short-stemmed cluster of large trumpet-shaped flowers emerges from the leafless bulb.
CULTIVATION: This bulb needs a subtropical climate (or warm greenhouse), full sun and perfect drainage. Most gardeners grow it in tall pots, the favored potting mix being a combination of granite chips with a little compost. Never allow the soil to dry out. Propagate from seed in spring.

Worsleya rayneri

syns *Hippeastrum procerum*, *Worsleya procera*

This species was discovered on a mountainside near Rio de Janeiro in 1860, but it was not until 1899 that it was introduced to gardens by the Englishman whose name it bears, Arthington Worsley (1861–1943); it remains an expensive rarity. In the wild it grows in crevices of granite cliffs, the long bulb necks lifting the flowers into the air and sunshine. The color of the 4 in (12 cm) wide trumpets varies, from almost white to deep lilac-blue, sometimes with spotted petals. **ZONES 10–12.**

WULFENIA

This is a genus of about 6 species of small evergreen tufted perennials, native to southeastern Europe, western Asia and the Himalayas. Leaves are usually rough-textured with scalloped margins, set from a basal point on long stalks. Flowers are borne on spike-like racemes from the base of the plant—these are blue to purple, tubular in shape with 4 lobes. The fruits are capsules.

Wulfenia carinthiaca

Xanthorrhoea malacophylla

Xeranthemum annuum Mixed Hybrids

CULTIVATION: Fully frost hardy and suited to cold climates, plants resent high humidity and excessive moisture in winter. They prefer full sun and moist, but well-drained soil. Propagate from seed or by division in spring.

Wulfenia carinthiaca

Native to the Alps and the Balkan Peninsula, this species has a height and spread of about 8 in (20 cm). Leaves are in a basal rosette and are lance-shaped to oval, about 7 in (18 cm) long, toothed, dark green and hairy underneath. The top quarter of the flower stem is a one-sided spike of tubular flowers; violet blue with rounded lobes, which are borne in summer. **ZONES 5–9.**

XANTHOCERAS

YELLOW HORN

Native to China, this genus consists of only one species. Although related to *Koelreuteria*, it is very different in general appearance. Except for its vulnerability to occasional injury by late spring frosts, this deciduous shrub or small tree is easily grown. The fragrant, erect flower spikes recall those of the horse chestnut.

Xanthoceras sorbifolium

Xanthorrhoea preissii

CULTIVATION: While it tolerates low winter temperatures, the yellow horn should be protected from late frosts and needs long hot summers to flower well. It prefers well-drained, good loamy soil and will tolerate mild alkalinity. It requires plenty of sunshine but does well in cooler areas if sited in a warm sheltered position. Propagate from stratified seed in spring or root cuttings or suckers in late winter; prune lightly to maintain shape. It is susceptible to coral spot fungus.

Xanthoceras sorbifolium

This deciduous upright shrub or small tree to about 15 ft (4.5 m) is native to China. The bright green leaves are composed of many sharply toothed leaflets. The white flowers are borne in erect sprays from the leaf axils in late spring and summer; each flower has a carmine red blotch at the base of the petals. The common name refers to the horn-like growths between the petals. The large fruiting capsules are pear-shaped and contain small seeds like chestnuts. It has thick, fleshy yellow roots. **ZONES 6–10.**

XANTHORRHOEA

GRASS TREE

This is a small genus of evergreen plants with grass-like foliage, all indigenous to Australia; they are very slow growing but long lived. Mature plants are stemless or develop a thick, sometimes branching trunk topped by a dense crown of long, arching, rather rigid leaves. Young plants are stemless, and may take 20 years or more to form a trunk. Long, spear-like flower spikes are produced spasmodically, usually in spring or in response to burning. The spikes, up to 5 ft (1.5 m)

Xanthostemon chrysanthus

long, consist of many densely packed, small white flowers, held on woody stalks up to 6 ft (1.8 m) long. The fruits are leathery capsules, packed along the spikes and surrounded by the blackened floral bracts. The glassy resin which exudes from the trunks was formerly used in varnishes and other products. The grass trees have, in the past, been variously classified with the rushes and the lilies, but are now recognized as constituting their own unique family.
CULTIVATION: Marginally frost hardy, grass trees need an open, sunny spot and well-drained soil as they are susceptible to root rot. They can also be grown in containers. Propagate from seed in fall (autumn) or spring.

Xanthorrhoea australis

This species is confined to the rocky hills of southeastern Australia. A dense tuft of narrow, arching, grassy leaves 3 ft (1 m) long sprout from a trunk made up of a mass of old leaf bases held together by natural resin. It takes 30 years or more for the leaf tuft to rise above the trunk. Spears of small white or cream flowers, smelling of honey, appear after 10 to 15 years, but only erratically; often it will bloom after a bushfire. **ZONES 9–11.**

Xanthorrhoea malacophylla

This grass tree, one of the tallest species, has a trunk as much as 20 ft (6 m) high and often branched when older, each branch terminating in a luxuriant rosette of long, bright green leaves that are rather soft and drooping. Each rosette may send up a flower spike to 5 ft (1.5 m) long on top of a stout stalk to 6 ft (1.8 m) long. The numerous small white flowers open from late fall (autumn) to mid-spring. The species is confined to wet coastal ranges of northeastern New South Wales, Australia. **ZONES 10–11.**

Xanthorrhoea preissii

From mild-climate areas of Western Australia, this species has an upright or slightly twisted trunk, often black and scorched, which can reach 20 ft (6 m) with maturity, with a crown of long, arching, grass-like leaves. The small, creamy yellow flowers are densely packed at the top of a long spike which stands high above the crown. Brownish capsular fruit follow. **ZONES 10–11.**

XANTHOSOMA

TANNIA, MALANGA

Occurring naturally in tropical America, this genus of the arum family consists of 45 or so species of tuberous perennials, somewhat similar to taro *(Colocasia)*. A few are cultivated, either for their ornamental foliage or for their tuberous roots, which in some species are edible. Above ground they have short, trunk-like stems and long-stalked, heart- to arrowhead-shaped, leaves that are up to 5 ft (1.5 m) long depending on the species. Simple green or cream spathes around 4 in (10 cm) long largely hide the yellow or white flower spikes (spadix) within.
CULTIVATION: These tropical aroids require rich moist soil, humid conditions and a warm climate. The winter minimum temperature should be above 50°F (10°C) or the foliage will start to die off. Propagation is from seed, stem cuttings or by division of tubers in spring or summer.

Xanthosoma sagittifolium

TANNIA

This species with its yam-like tuber is also grown for its edible arrowhead-shaped leaves. It thrives in lowlands throughout the tropics and is particularly popular as a vegetable in the West Indies and West Africa. Only the lateral tubers are eaten; the main tubers are left in the ground. The flowers are greenish white and appear throughout the year. **ZONES 11–12.**

Xanthosoma violaceum

BLUE TARO

This species has attractively veined arrowhead-shaped leaves on dark purple stalks to 3 ft (1 m) long. Pale yellow arum-like flowers are produced throughout the year. This is an attractive foliage plant for warm tropical gardens. The edible tubers have pink flesh. **ZONES 11–12.**

XANTHOSTEMON

The 40 or so species of evergreen trees of this genus in the myrtle family range from northeastern Australia through the Malay Archipelago and New Caledonia. The leathery oval leaves are glossy dark green, the new growth often bronze-pink. The 5-petalled flowers are white, gold or yellow with long stamens and are held in clusters at the ends of branches.
CULTIVATION: These trees need a warm, frost-free climate. They prefer full sun or light shade, humus-rich soil and plenty of moisture. Shelter from strong winds is beneficial. Propagate from seed or cuttings in fall (autumn).

Xanthostemon chrysanthus

BLACK PENDA

Popular in tropical and subtropical gardens in Australia, this tree reaches 25 ft (8 m) or so in cultivation, although it is taller in its native habitat. The showy heads of bright acid-yellow flowers with masses of long stamens are borne mainly in winter, but rain may stimulate flowering at other times. The large leaves have a pale green mid-vein. **ZONES 10–12.**

XERANTHEMUM

IMMORTELLE

The 5 or 6 annuals in this genus are natives of the Mediterranean region, extending to Iran. They are known as immortelles or everlasting flowers because their dried flowerheads retain their color and form for many years. The erect, branching stems have narrow, hoary leaves. The flowerheads are solitary on long stems and the small fertile flowers are surrounded by papery bracts which may be white, purple or pink.
CULTIVATION: Moderately frost hardy, they grow best in a sunny position in fertile, well-drained soil. Propagate from seed which should be sown in spring where the plants are to grow.

Xeranthemum annuum

IMMORTELLE

A good source of dried flowers, this annual blooms in summer, producing heads of purple daisy-like flowers; whites, pinks and mauves, some with a 'double' appearance are also available. The leaves are silvery and lance-shaped and the plants grow to around 24 in (60 cm) high and 18 in (45 cm) wide. **Mixed Hybrids** include singles and doubles in shades of pink, purple, mauve, red or white. **ZONES 7–10.**

XERONEMA

There are only two species in this genus and neither has ever been common in the wild or in gardens. Found naturally in New Caledonia and on the rocky volcanic terrain of the Poor Knights Islands off the northeast of New Zealand, they are striking plants that appeal to all who see them. There is nothing quite like their brilliant red flowers borne on one-sided racemes among iris-like, leathery, sword-shaped leaves.
CULTIVATION: Although able to be grown from seed or by careful division, tissue culture propagation has been the key to success and plants are now readily available to gardeners. It needs a frost-free climate and, even in a rich soil, can take a few years to settle down to flowering. Plant in a humus-rich soil with added pumice or scoria to ensure good drainage.

Xeronema callistemon

POOR KNIGHTS LILY

The unique and beautiful flowers of this perennial are a rare sight. A vivid red in color, their long stamens are massed to create a 6 in (15 cm) brush. They are held horizontally to provide a perch for the honey-eating birds that pollinate them. They are strictly greenhouse plants in cool-temperate climates. **ZONES 10–11.**

XEROPHYLLUM

ELK GRASS

This North American lily genus consists of 3 species of clump-forming rhizomatous perennials. The foliage is seldom more than a rather untidy clump of long, tough grassy leaves. The flowerheads are far more impressive; they are composed of massed, starry white blooms. The heads are carried on stiff stems up to 6 ft (1.8 m) high and open in summer.
CULTIVATION: Plant in moist, humus-rich soil in full sun. Although frost hardy, elk grass can be difficult to establish. However, once growing well, it requires little attention and should be left undisturbed. Propagate from seed in fall (autumn).

Xerophyllum tenax

BEAR GRASS

An elegant, clump-forming, rhizomatous perennial, this species is native to western North America. It has grassy basal leaves, 3 ft (1 m) long, from which arise flowering stems up to 5 ft (1.5 m) tall, carrying a dense spike of white, starry flowers during summer. It needs a sunny position in damp, peaty soil. **ZONES 5–9.**

XYLOMELUM

WOODY PEAR

This small Australian genus consists of 5 species of evergreen small trees with leathery leaves and short spikes of flowers resembling those of grevilleas and hakeas, which are members of the same family. Occurring in warmer temperate and tropical regions, these unusual plants have unique woody, pear-shaped large seed capsules, hence their common name.
CULTIVATION: Marginally frost hardy, they need fertile, well-drained, sandy soil and full sun. Young plants need to be given ample water and protection from frosts. Prune when young to encourage a compact shape. Propagate from seed in winter.

Xylomelum occidentale

WESTERN WOODY PEAR

This Western Australian tree reaches 25 ft (8 m) tall, with a spreading crown and dark brown, flaky bark. The large, deep green leaves resemble those of some oaks and have prickly edges. Sprays of creamy flowers appear in summer; these are followed by the showy, pear-shaped fruit, up to 4 in (10 cm) long. They ripen to reddish brown and persist on the plant after they have split open to release their seeds. They can be used in arrangements of dried flowers. **ZONES 9–11.**

YUCCA

The 40 or so species of unusual evergreen perennials, shrubs and trees in this genus are found in drier regions of North America. Often slow growing, they form rosettes of stiff, sword-like leaves usually tipped with a sharp spine; as the plants mature, some species develop an upright woody trunk, often branched. Yuccas bear showy, tall panicles of drooping, white or cream, bell- to cup-shaped flowers. The fruits are either fleshy or dry capsules, but in most species are rarely seen away from the plants' native lands as the flowers must be pollinated by the yucca moth.
CULTIVATION: Yuccas do best in areas of low humidity; they prefer full sun and sandy soil with good drainage. Depending on the species, they are frost hardy to frost tender. Propagate from seed (if available), cuttings or suckers in spring.

Yucca aloifolia

SPANISH BAYONET, SPANISH DAGGER

This species gets its common name from its very sharp, sword-like, grayish green leaves, each 24 in (60 cm) long and 1–2 in (2.5–5 cm) wide with smooth edges. It develops a branched trunk up to 25 ft (8 m) high, but in cultivation is often much smaller. The flowers are carried in an upright spike up to 24 in (60 cm) long, mainly in summer but sometimes continuing into fall (autumn). Each bell-shaped flower is white flushed with purple and about 2 in (5 cm) across. The fruit are fleshy. There are several cultivars with variegated leaves: **'Marginata'** has yellow-edged leaves; **'Tricolor'** has white or yellow in the center of the leaf; and **'Variegata'** has leaves edged with creamy white. **ZONES 8–11.**

Yucca australis

TREE YUCCA, ST PETER'S PALM

The epithet *australis* means simply 'of the south' and is found in the names of many plant species. In this case it refers to the south of Mexico, where this yucca species is native. *Yucca australis* is one of the larger species and in cultivation has achieved impressive size—there is an old specimen in Valencia, Spain, that has a trunk 30 ft (9 m) in girth, and about 25 ft (7.5 m) tall overall; it branches into numerous heads of foliage with narrow, sword-shaped leaves and erect panicles of white flowers. This yucca has been used medicinally in Mexico, as a purgative or laxative. **ZONES 9–12.**

Yucca baccata

BLUE YUCCA, BANANA YUCCA, DATIL YUCCA

Yucca baccata comes from southwestern USA and northern Mexico and grows to 5 ft (1.5 m) in height. Its twisted leaves are flexible near the base and are dark green tinged with yellow or blue. The pendent flowers are bell-shaped, white or cream and often tinged with purple. **ZONES 9–11.**

Yucca australis

Yucca aloifolia 'Marginata'

Yucca aloifolia

Yucca baccata

Xeronema callistemon

Xylomelum occidentale

X Y

Yucca baileyi
ALPINE YUCCA

Occurring naturally on compacted sandy soils and thinly scattered in grasslands and woodlands in highlands of northern Mexico, this species makes a small, dense clump with leaves pale or yellow green with a white margin. Its inflorescence is a simple raceme of greenish white flowers deeply tinged with purple, appearing in early summer. **ZONES 9–11.**

Yucca brevifolia
JOSHUA TREE

Of striking if somewhat misshapen appearance, this well-known tree reaches 40 ft (12 m) tall in its natural habitat. The short leaves are narrow and sharply pointed, with minute teeth along the edges. Its greenish white flowers about 2 ½ in (6 cm) long, arranged on a long erect spike, are followed by dry capsules. Extremely slow growing, it can be difficult to cultivate, even in its native regions of southern USA and northern Mexico. Flowering is irregular and dependent on rain in the wild; in cultivation, late spring is the usual flowering season. **ZONES 7–10.**

Yucca elephantipes

Yucca carnerosana
SPANISH DAGGER

This tree-like species from Texas and northern Mexico grows to 15 ft (4.5 m) or more high. The rigid leaves are 3 ft (1 m) long and about 3 in (8 cm) wide with smooth margins. The bark is pale gray, tinted red-brown. The flower infloresence reaches 6 ft (1.8 m) high and consists of white bracts and white flowers. Its fruit are fleshy. **ZONES 9–11.**

Yucca desmetiana

This species, named from cultivated plants of uncertain origin, is now thought to be from Mexico. It grows to 6 ft (1.8 m) tall with multiple stems and the short leaves are crowded and recurved. They are green, tinged purple, though in full sun turn purple-bronze. Flowers are rarely seen. **ZONES 9–11.**

Yucca elephantipes
syn. ***Yucca gigantea***
SPINELESS YUCCA, GIANT YUCCA

This yucca occurs naturally in southern Mexico and Central America. It develops a rough, thick trunk that often branches and reaches a height of 30 ft (9 m); in cultivation it is usually smaller. The leaves are 4 ft (1.2 m) long and 3 in (8 cm) wide, shiny dark green with finely serrated edges. White, often somewhat drooping, bell-shaped flowers are clustered in large panicles from summer to fall (autumn). **ZONES 10–12.**

Yucca brevifolia

Yucca glauca

Yucca recurvifolia

Yucca filamentosa
ADAM'S NEEDLE-AND-THREAD

The leaves on this plant form basal rosettes and are edged with white threads. Up to 3 ft (1 m) long, they are thin-textured and a slightly bluish gray-green. The nodding, white flowers are 2 in (5 cm) long, borne on erect panicles to 6 ft (1.8 m) tall in summer. It is native to eastern USA and is the most frost hardy of the yuccas. **ZONES 4–10.**

Yucca filifera

Normally seen as a low clump of foliage, this Mexican species may eventually become tree-like, reaching up to 30 ft (9 m) in height and eventually much branched. When young it resembles *Yucca filamentosa*, but the leaves are shorter and thinner, with the margins sparsely threaded. The flowers on the tall summer panicles are creamy white and pendulous. **'Golden Sword'** has yellow leaf margins; **'Ivory'** has creamy white flowers tinged green. **ZONES 7–10.**

Yucca filifera 'Golden Sword'

Yucca gloriosa

Yucca rostrata

Yucca glauca
syn. ***Yucca angustifolia***
DWARF YUCCA, SOAPWEED

Native to central USA, this small, stemless, clump-forming species has glaucous, blue-green, narrow spear-like leaves with white margins and a few gray threads. In summer, the flower spike, up to 3 ft (1 m) tall, bears fragrant greenish white flowers which are often tinged reddish brown. **ZONES 4–9.**

Yucca gloriosa
SPANISH DAGGER, MOUND LILY

The stiff, sword-like leaves of this species start out with a grayish cast, turning a deeper green as they mature. White, bell-shaped flowers, tinged flesh-pink on the outside, appear in erect panicles to 8 ft (2.4 m) tall from summer to fall (autumn). Native to southeastern USA, it is usually seen as a stemless clump of leaves, but with age can develop trunks to 6 ft (1.8 m) or more tall. **ZONES 7–10.**

Yucca recurvifolia
syn. ***Yucca pendula***
WEEPING YUCCA

This striking plant from southeastern USA reaches 6–10 ft (1.8–3 m) in height, with several short trunks and long, dark blue-green leaves that often bend and droop at the tips. The 3 ft (1 m) tall flower spike bears creamy white blooms in summer. **ZONES 8–11.**

Yucca carnerosana

Yucca filamentosa

Yucca filifera

Yucca treculeana

Yucca rostrata
BEAKED YUCCA

Native to southern USA and northern Mexico, this tree-like species grows to 15 ft (4.5 m) tall with its very narrow, rigid leaves in a symmetrical rosette. They have a grayish bloom and yellow, minutely toothed margins. The spiked inflorescence of small white flowers is borne in fall (autumn). **ZONES 8–11.**

Yucca treculeana
SPANISH DAGGER, PALMA PITA

This summer-flowering species from Texas and western Mexico reaches 15 ft (4.5 m) in height, the trunk crowned by a symmetrical rosette of stiff, bluish green, sword-shaped leaves up to 4 ft (1.2 m) long. The flower spike is pyramidal in shape and its white flowers are often tinged purple. Its fruit are up to 4 in (10 cm) long. **ZONES 9–11.**

Yucca whipplei
OUR LORD'S CANDLE, CANDLE YUCCA

This is distinguished from most other yuccas by its very narrow, gray-green leaves which form a nearly perfect sphere. Native to the coastal lower ranges of California, in late summer and fall (autumn) it sends up a straight, flowering spike to 12 ft (3.5 m) high that is densely covered in creamy white flowers, sometimes tinged with purple. It is very tolerant of dry conditions. **ZONES 8–11.**

ZAMIA

This is the largest and most diverse of the American genera of cycads. They are distributed from Florida through the wide Caribbean region and northern South America, growing in a variety of habitats. There are thought to be 60 or more species, and they include some of the most diminutive cycads. They usually have a short subterranean or above-ground stem, and arching fronds divided into few or many leaflets. The leaflets are mostly smooth, often with toothed or serrated margins. Male and female cones are borne on different plants and vary in shape. The stems in some species have been used as a source of edible starch.
CULTIVATION: These cycads are suited to a range of climates, but most grow best in the tropics and subtropics. A few are marginally frost hardy. Grow in part-shade in well-drained soil; water liberally during growth and sparingly at other times. They make excellent container plants. Propagate in spring

Yucca whipplei

from fresh seed after removing the fleshy outer covering.

Zamia pumila
COONTIE, FLORIDA ARROWROOT

A native of the grasslands and open forests of the whole Caribbean region, this small cycad grows from freely branching, underground stems. The dark green, leathery, fern-like leaves are erect to spreading and are less than 3 ft (1 m) long. The male cones are cylindrical, while the female cones are ovoid; both are rusty red. Best grown in full sun, this species makes an attractive addition to a border or as a container specimen. **ZONES 10–12.**

ZANTEDESCHIA
ARUM LILY, CALLA LILY, PIG LILY

Indigenous to southern and eastern Africa, this well-known genus of the arum family consists of 6 species of tuberous perennials. The inflorescence consists of a showy white, yellow or pink spathe shaped like a funnel, with a central finger-like, yellow spadix. The leaves are glossy green and usually arrowhead-shaped.
CULTIVATION: Consisting of both evergreen and deciduous species, this genus includes frost-tender to moderately frost-hardy plants; most are intolerant of dry conditions. Most prefer well-drained soil in full sun or part-shade, although *Zantedeschia authiopica* will grow as a semi-aquatic plant in boggy ground that is often inundated. Propagate from offsets in winter.

Zantedeschia aethiopica
WHITE ARUM LILY, LILY OF THE NILE

Although normally deciduous, in summer and early fall (autumn) this species can stay evergreen if given enough moisture. It can also be grown in water up to 6–12 in (15–30 cm) deep. This species reaches 24–36 in (60–90 cm) in height and spread, with large clumps of broad, dark green leaves. The large flowers, produced in spring, summer and fall (autumn), are pure white with a yellow spadix. **'Crowborough'** is more cold tolerant and better suited to cool climates such as the UK and the northwest USA. It grows to about 3 ft (1 m) tall. **'Green Goddess'** has interesting green markings on the spathes. **ZONES 8–11.**

Zantedeschia aethiopica

Zantedeschia elliottiana
GOLDEN ARUM LILY

This summer-flowering species has a yellow spathe surrounding a yellow spadix, sometimes followed by a spike of bright yellow berries that are attractive to birds. It grows 24–36 in (60–90 cm) tall with a spread of 24 in (60 cm). The heart-shaped, semi-erect leaves have numerous white spots or streaks. **ZONES 8–11.**

Zantedeschia, New Zealand Mixed Hybrids

These hybrids of *Zantedeschia rehmannii* and *Z. elliottiana* have flowers in a range of colors from red, pink and bronze to orange. Some have spotted leaves. Although there are miniatures, most reach a height of 24 in (60 cm) or more with a spread of 8 in (20 cm). Not as easy to grow as their parents, they need warmth and very rich soil. The flowers of **'Brigadier'** are washed a reddish orange; and the orange-red tones of **'Mango'** varies with cultivation, a slightly alkaline soil giving richer color than an acid one. The 'flower' is about 6 in (15 cm) wide and the leaves are spotted. **ZONES 8–11.**

Zantedeschia, NZMH, 'Brigadier'

Zantedeschia aethiopica 'Green Goddess'

Zantedeschia rehmannii
PINK ARUM LILY, PINK CALLA

The spathe on this summer-flowering plant is mauve to rose-purple with paler margins, enclosing a yellow spadix. Its green, unmarked leaves are semi-erect and not arrowhead-shaped as in other species. It grows 15 in (38 cm) tall and 12 in (30 cm) wide. Marginally frost hardy, it likes well-composted soil, a protected location and part-shade. **ZONES 8–11.**

ZAUSCHNERIA

From southwestern USA and Mexico, this genus consists of about 4 species of shrubby perennials. Although very similar, for horticultural purposes they can be considered variations on *Zauschneria californica.* They are grown for their masses of orange to scarlet, tubular flowers. Some botanists now believe these species belong in the *Epilobium* genus.
CULTIVATION: These plants are marginally frost hardy. Grow in full sun in well-drained soil in a warm, sheltered position. Propagate from seed or by division in spring, or from side-shoot cuttings in summer.

Zantedeschia, NZMH, 'Mango'

Zantedeschia rehmannii

Zantedeschia elliottiana

Zauschneria californica

Zauschneria californica subsp. *cana*

Zauschneria septentrionalis

Zea mays

Zelkova serrata

Zauschneria californica

syn. *Epilobium canum* subsp. *canum*

CALIFORNIAN FUCHSIA

The common name refers both to the species' Californian origin and to its flowers, which are indeed like the related fuchsias. These are bright red, appearing in terminal spikes on erect, slender stems in late summer and early fall (autumn). This evergreen shrub has lance-like, 1 in (25 mm) long leaves, is highly variable and grows 12–24 in (30–60 cm) tall and 3–6 ft (1–1.8 m) wide. It needs only occasional water and is hardy to around 15°F (–9°C). ***Zauschneria californica* subsp. *cana*** (syn. *Zauschneria cana*), a small suckering shrub, reaches 24 in (60 cm) high. It has felty gray foliage and its larger flowers are a brilliant vermilion red. ***Z. c.* subsp. *canum* 'Dublin'** (syn. 'Glasnevin'), more compact to 12 in (30 cm) tall with bright orange-red flowers, was selected at Glasnevin Gardens in Ireland . **ZONES 8–10.**

Zauschneria septentrionalis

syn. *Epilobium septentrionale*

HUMBOLDT COUNTY FUCHSIA

Native to western North America, this species is more or less mat-forming and grows to 8 in (20 cm) tall. The leaves are gray-white and felted; the flowers are bright orange-red. **ZONES 8–10.**

ZEA

The maize or sweet corn genus is now thought to include 4 species of annual and perennial grasses from Central America; the crop species may be an ancient hybrid, its grains found in archeological excavations up to 5,600 years old. They bear terminal male panicles with solitary 'ears'; the female inflorescences have numerous spikelets in rows on a thick axis enclosed within a 'husk', from which only the long silky styles emerge; these are followed by a 'cob' of fleshy kernels. Ornamental cultivars are grown for their variegated leaves and multi-colored cobs.
CULTIVATION: Grow in full sun in fertile, moist, well-drained soil. Propagate from seed in late winter or early spring. They may be prone to aphids.

Zea mays

SWEET CORN, MAIZE, MEALY

This robust annual grass grows to 12 ft (3.5 m) tall with arching, lance-shaped, waxy leaves. It produces terminal panicles of male flowers to 8 in (20 cm) in length, and female inflorescences of the same length. The flowers are followed in late summer or early fall (autumn) by cobs with usually yellow, sweet, edible grains. **'Golden Beauty'** is a much-admired cultivar. **ZONES 7–11.**

ZELKOVA

Occurring naturally from Asia Minor across cool-climate areas of western Asia to China and Japan, these deciduous trees are cultivated for their attractive habit and handsome foliage. They are important timber trees in China and Japan. The leaves resemble those of the English or American elms, but are smaller, giving an effect of airy elegance. Although related to the elms, they are not plagued by the same diseases and are becoming popular as elm substitutes. The small, greenish flowers, borne in spring, are sometimes perfumed; both these and the fruits are insignificant.
CULTIVATION: Although frost hardy, they prefer some shelter. They need full sun and deep, fertile, well-drained soil and plenty of water during summer. Propagate from seed or root cuttings in fall (autumn), or by grafting.

Zelkova carpinifolia

ELM ZELKOVA

From the Caucasus and Asia Minor, this slow-growing tree can live to a great age, reaching 100 ft (30 m) high and 50 ft (15 m) wide. It has a dense, rounded head, slender upright branches and weeping branchlets. The mid-green, pointed leaves have serrated edges; their upper sides are rough to the touch. Fragrant but insignificant flowers appear in spring. **ZONES 4–10.**

Zelkova serrata

JAPANESE ZELKOVA

This ornamental tree from Japan, Korea and Taiwan grows to a height of 80 ft (24 m) or more with a wide, spreading crown. It has smooth bark dappled gray and brown and new shoots are tinged purple. The pointed, oblong, sharply serrated leaves are light green and slightly hairy above, with shiny undersides. The foliage turns golden yellow to rusty brown in fall (autumn). Cultivars include **'Village Green'**, and **'Green Vase'** growing to 40 ft (12 m) tall in a graceful vase shape. **ZONES 3–10.**

ZENOBIA

This genus consists of only one species, a semi-evergreen or deciduous shrub from southeastern USA, where it grows in heathland and around the edges of pine forests. It has slightly arching branches and is grown for its attractive flowers.
CULTIVATION: This shrub is very frost hardy. Plant in moist, acid, well-drained soil in part-shade. Water well in summer and feed with an acidic fertilizer. Trim to shape after flowering if necessary. Propagate from seed, layers, suckers or cuttings in summer.

Zenobia pulverulenta

This species can grow 6 ft (1.8 m) tall but is often considerably smaller. A characteristic of this shrub is the blue-gray bloom on the stems and the underside of the oval, bluntly toothed leaves when young. During summer, clusters of 20 or more fragrant, white, bell-shaped flowers are borne along 8 in (20 cm) flower stalks. **ZONES 5–10.**

ZEPHYRANTHES

WINDFLOWER, ZEPHYR LILY, RAIN LILY

There are about 70 species in this genus of charming bulbs, all indigenous to the Americas. They would be much better known if they were just a little more frost hardy. Most species have open flowers like small Asiatic lilies and are deciduous. They vary in height from about 6–15 in (15–38 cm) and can be white, yellow or various shades of warm pink. All bear one flower to a stem; most close up their petals at night.
CULTIVATION: Moderately to marginally frost hardy, they do well in sun or part-shade. They like fertile, well-drained but moist soil, but usually flower best when they have had a chance to thicken into clumps. In colder climates, they do well in pots in a mildly warmed greenhouse. Propagate from seed in fall (autumn) or spring.

Zephyranthes atamasco

ATAMASCO LILY

Among the most frost hardy of the zephyr lilies, this native of southeastern USA has pure white to purple-tinged, fragrant flowers. Its stems, up to 12 in (30 cm) tall, emerge from grassy, dark green leaves. The flowers appear in late spring and early summer. **ZONES 8–11.**

Zephyranthes candida

syn. *Argyropsis candida*

FLOWER OF THE WEST WIND, STORM LILY

Indigenous to Uruguay and Argentina, this vigorous species grows to a height of 6 in (15 cm). The starry, cup-shaped, white flowers, 2 in (5 cm) wide, are borne singly on the slender stems in summer and early fall (autumn). It is said to flower mainly in cloudy weather. The grass-like foliage is evergreen. **ZONES 9–10.**

Zephyranthes candida

Zephyranthes grandiflora

Zephyranthes pulchella

Zeugites americana

Zieria buxijugum

Zieria granulata

Zephyranthes grandiflora
syns *Zephyranthes carinata, Z. rosea*
PINK STORM LILY

A native of Mexico, this popular species grows to 10 in (25 cm) tall. The 4 in (10 cm) flowers, produced in summer, are funnel shaped, white throated and dusky pink, while the slender leaves are strap shaped. There are many forms, some with smaller flowers. **ZONES 9–10.**

Zephyranthes pulchella

This species from Texas has a small bulb to only 1 in (25 mm) in diameter, globose and dark brown. Flowering stems reach 8 in (30 cm) in height and bear erect, bright yellow flowers in late summer and fall (autumn). **ZONES 9–10.**

ZEUGITES

This genus of grasses consists of 12 species, all native to tropical America. They are all perennials with creeping or erect, leafy stems, sometimes scrambling over shrubs or rocks to 8 ft (2.4 m) or more high. The leaf blades are quite short and broad, each narrowed at the base into a short stalk. The inflorescence is an open panicle with individual flower spikelets held on fine stalks. Shade-loving grasses, they grow mostly in moist, sheltered ravines and wooded hillsides. **CULTIVATION:** Cultivation in suitably mild climates should present few difficulties in any sheltered situation, provided soil moisture is adequate. Propagate from seed or rooted divisions or runners.

Zeugites americana

This is the most widespread member of the genus, distributed through North and Central America and Andean South America from southern USA to Bolivia, also the West Indies. **ZONES 8–12.**

ZIERIA

This genus consists of about 20 species of evergreen shrubs, all native to eastern Australia. From 2–8 ft (0.6–2.4 m) tall, they are erect and often spreading, and can be kept compact by light pruning after flowering. The leaves are small and compound with 3 leaflets; they contain aromatic oils in small translucent dots. Small, starry flowers are white or shades of pale to deep pink, with bright yellow stamens.
CULTIVATION: Zierias need humus-rich, sandy soil with good drainage; like the related boronias, they tolerate light frosts and prefer shade, though some tolerate full sun. Propagate from cuttings.

Zieria buxijugum

This is one of a number of rare and localized species discovered recently on rocky hilltops in southeastern Australia. Its ornamental qualities and ease of cultivation have attracted native plant enthusiasts. Growing to 6 ft (1.8 m) tall, its fine lacy foliage consists of leaves with very narrow leaflets with finely warted surfaces that are velvety to the touch. In spring, it bears numerous small sprays of starry, white flowers on fine stalks. **ZONES 9–10.**

Zieria granulata

This erect shrub, growing to about 5 ft (1.5 m) high, has a strong odor. The leaflets are long and thin with the margins strongly recurved and the plant is covered with prominent yellowish worts. It produces small white flowers in loose panicles in spring, and is found in coastal areas and adjoining plateaux of New South Wales, Australia. **ZONES 9–11.**

Zieria pilosa

This straggling shrub, to about 3 ft (1 m) high, has hairy, cylindrical branches. It has small, narrow, downy leaflets and small white flowers are borne in spring. It is widespread on heathlands in New South Wales, Australia. **ZONES 9–10.**

ZIGADENUS

This genus of bulbous or rhizomatous lilies is native to North America and northeastern Asia. Of the 18 or so known species, some are poisonous to stock. The long leaves are clustered at the base of erect stems and the flowers, borne in a terminal, branched raceme, are usually white, yellowish white or greenish white.
CULTIVATION: Hardiness varies, although most are frost hardy. They prefer moist, peaty soils and can be propagated by division or from seed.

Zigadenus fremontii
STAR LILY, STAR ZYGADENE

This bulbous plant is found from southern Oregon to California. A 3 ft (1 m) flowering stem arises from strap-like basal leaves 24 in (60 cm) long and 1 in (2.5 cm) wide with a rough margin. The flowers are yellowish white borne in racemes or panicles. It is among the more tender species. **ZONES 8–10.**

ZINGIBER
GINGER

This genus consists of about 100 species of evergreen perennials with thick, branching, aromatic rhizomes and leafy, reed-like stems. They bear flowers in axils of colorful, waxy bracts in short spikes or globular heads on stalks arising from the rhizomes. One species produces the culinary root and stem ginger.
CULTIVATION: These frost-tender plants need a hot position with high humidity and plentiful water in summer, less in winter. Give them plenty of space to spread. Propagate from rhizome divisions in spring.

Zingiber officinale
COMMON GINGER, HALIA

Originating in southern Asia, this species can reach up to 6 ft (1.8 m) high in hot areas and has narrow, lance-shaped leaves. Spikes of white flowers with purple streaks are produced in summer. The fresh root, peeled and finely chopped or grated, is used to flavor many Asian dishes, curries and chutneys. Dried and powdered ginger is used in sweet dishes and cakes. Also used medicinally, it was once thought to safeguard against marauding tigers. **ZONES 10–12.**

Zingiber zerumbet
WILD GINGER

This clump-forming, upright species is native to India and Southeast Asia. It has narrow, 12 in (30 cm) long leaves. On separate, tall stems are overlapping green bracts ageing to red, surrounding white or gold flowers. The rhizomes are bitter to eat, but can be used in potpourri. **ZONES 10–12.**

ZINNIA
ZINNIA

This genus of 20 species of erect to spreading annuals, perennials and subshrubs has daisy-like, terminal flowerheads in many colors including white, yellow, orange, red, purple and lilac. Found throughout Mexico and Central and South America, some are grown for cut flowers and in mixed borders.
CULTIVATION: These plants are marginally frost hardy and should be grown in a sunny position in fertile soil that drains well. They need frequent deadheading. Propagate from seed sown under glass early in spring.

Zinnia elegans
YOUTH-AND-OLD-AGE

This sturdy Mexican annual is the best known of the zinnias. The wild form has purple flowerheads, and blooms from summer to fall (autumn). It grows fairly rapidly to 24–30 in (60–75 cm), with a smaller spread. Garden varieties offer hues of white, red, pink, yellow, violet, orange or crimson in flowers up to 6 in (15 cm) across. **'Envy'** has pale green semi-double flowers. The **Dreamland** series is compact and heavy flowering—typical of F1 Hybrid bedding zinnias. **'F1 Dreamland Ivy'** has pale greenish yellow flowers. The **Thumbelina** series has 2 in (5 cm) wide flowerheads on plants only 6 in (15 cm) high. **ZONES 8–11.**

Zigadenus fremontii

Zingiber officinale

Zinnia elegans

Zingiber zerumbet

Ziziphus jujuba

Zinnia elegans 'F1 Dreamland Ivy'

Zygopetalum crinitum

Zygopetalum mackaii

Zygopetalum intermedium

Zinnia grandiflora

Flowering through the warmer months, this shrubby species grows in dense little clumps up to 10 in (25 cm) in height. The disc flowers are red or green, and the ray florets are yellow. It occurs naturally from Colorado and Kansas south to Mexico. **ZONES 4–11.**

Zinnia haageana

syn. *Zinnia mexicana, Z angustifolia*

This Mexican annual reaches 24 in (60 cm) in height with a spread of 8 in (20 cm). The small but profuse yellow, orange and bronze flowerheads, more than 1½ in (35 mm) wide, appear in summer and early fall (autumn). **'Old Mexico'** is an old but valuable cultivar that is drought resistant. **ZONES 8–11.**

Zinnia peruviana

This species ranges in the wild from Arizona to Argentina. An erect-growing, summer-flowering annual, it reaches a height of 3 ft (1 m). The hairy stems are green, changing to yellow or purple. Its flowerheads are yellow to scarlet. **ZONES 8–11.**

ZIZANIA

WILD RICE

This genus from North America and eastern Asia is made up of 3 species of annual and perennial aquatic grasses. Growing at the edges of marshes, lakes and rivers, they have semi-erect, narrow, 5 ft (1.5 m) long leaves with rough edges. The flower stems, up to 10 ft (3 m) tall, are thick and spongy. A 24 in (60 cm) long inflorescence develops at the top of each stem and opens into a multi-branched panicle. The yellow to reddish grains that follow are edible.

CULTIVATION: Wild rice can be grown in any damp or boggy area in full sun. Hardiness varies with the species, though all will tolerate some frost. Propagate from seed sown in early spring; the perennial species may also be divided.

Zizania aquatica

WILD RICE, INDIAN RICE

Native to North America, most common in the Great Lakes region, this coarse annual grass grows to 10 ft (3 m) tall. The nutritious, rather long, dark brown grains, now considered a delicacy, have long been an important food of Native Americans. Wild rice grows naturally in still shallow water in marshes and along streams, and this is the ideal growing situation for cultivation; harvest in late summer. **ZONES 5–10.**

Zoysia tenuifolia

ZIZIPHUS

This genus of about 80 or so species of deciduous or evergreen trees and shrubs occurs naturally in warm- to hot-climate areas of both the northern and southern hemispheres. Some have spiny branches. Their leaves are usually marked with 3 veins and there are spines at the base of each leaf stalk. The insignificant flowers are small, greenish, whitish or yellow, arranged in clusters in the leaf axils. The small, fleshy fruits of some species are edible. *Ziziphus macronata* is widespread in riverine areas.

CULTIVATION: Frost tender, grow ziziphus species in open, loamy, well-drained soil in full sun, and provide plenty of water. Tip prune to maintain compact growth. Propagate from seed or root cuttings in late winter, or by grafting.

Ziziphus jujuba

JUJUBE, CHINESE DATE

This deciduous tree, distributed from western Asia to China, grows to 40 ft (12 m) tall. The oval to lance-shaped leaves are 1–2 in (2.5–5 cm) long and green in color, with 2 spines at the base of the leaf stalk, one of which is usually bent backwards. Small greenish flowers are borne in spring. The reddish, oblong to rounded fruit are up to 1 in (25 mm) long; they ripen from fall (autumn) to winter on the bare branches. Apple-like in taste, the fruit may be stewed, dried or used in confections. **ZONES 7–10.**

ZOYSIA

This genus consists of around 5 species of creeping, perennial grasses native to East and Southeast Asia, Polynesia, Australia and New Zealand. Some form a dense turf that is useful for lawns in warm climates. Most species become brown and dry in winter.

CULTIVATION: Established either by sowing seed or planting 'plugs' of stolons, Zoysia grass is undemanding provided frosts are rare. Do not mow the grass too close or the surface rhizomes may be damaged.

Zoysia japonica 'Meyeri'

syn. *Meyer zoysia*

MEYER ZOYSIA

This very drought-tolerant, perennial, Japanese grass is extensively used for lawns in the arid zones of southern and southwestern USA where frosts are of short duration. Resembling bluegrass, the wide blades are dark green and up to 6 in (15 cm) long. It is the first species of its genus to turn brown in winter and the last to green up in spring. **ZONES 8–11.**

Zoysia tenuifolia

MASCARENE GRASS, KOREAN GRASS

Of uncertain origin, this grass is known from the Mascarene and Solomon Islands, Japan and Taiwan among other lands. It has thread-like, bristly leaves up to 4 in (10 cm) long. The stolons are very slender and produce a dense turf. It is sometimes cultivated as a lawn grass in the USA. **ZONES 10–12.**

ZYGOPETALUM

This orchid genus consists of 12 or so rather similar species of evergreen epiphytes from Central and South America. The scented flowers are admired for their unusual color—the petals and sepals are usually green, spotted with red, and the labellum finely striped in purple and white. These tones may be distributed in different patterns in some species. Zygopetalums are low-growing, clumpy plants with glossy, mid-green leaves. Their flower stems grow up to 24 in (60 cm) long and can carry up to a dozen flowers. The plants usually flower in fall (autumn) or early winter.

CULTIVATION: Zygopetalums prefer subtropical and frost-free, warm-temperate climates when grown outdoors; under these conditions, they are very easy orchids to grow in a shaded position. In cooler climates, they will need to be protected in a greenhouse. Grow in orchid compost in a position with filtered light and water freely. Propagate by division.

Zygopetalum crinitum

This colorful medium-sized species is native to eastern Brazil. The pseudobulbs are crowded, compressed and about 2½ in (6 cm) by 1½ in (35 mm). They have 3 to 5 leaves at the apex. The leaves are strap-like, 10–15 in (25–38 cm) long and 1–2 in (2.5–5 cm) broad. The inflorescence is erect, 18 in (45 cm) tall with up to 10 very fragrant flowers about 3 in (8 cm) in diameter. It flowers in summer and fall (autumn). **ZONES 10–12.**

Zygopetalum intermedium

This South American species has lustrous, bright green leaves and grows to 18 in (48 cm). It bears waxy green to yellow-green flowers blotched with red-brown or crimson in fall (autumn) and winter; they smell strongly of hyacinths. It is separated from the closely related *Zygopetalum mackaii* by its petals which are the same length as the sepals, not shorter as in *Z. mackaii*. **ZONES 10–12.**

Zygopetalum mackaii

This is an epiphytic species from Brazil and bears long sprays of perfumed, brown-spotted, green flowers with purple-veined, white lips to 3 in (8 cm). It grows to 30 in (75 cm) tall and has oval, ribbed leaves. **ZONES 10–12.**

An Explanation of Plant Names

The plants featured in this book are arranged alphabetically by their scientific names. Because these names are in Latin they may not be familiar to every gardener, but there are many difficulties associated with using plants' common names.

One of the greatest problems would be that many plants share the same common name—for example, 'cedar' refers to quite unrelated trees in Asia, North America, South Africa and Australia. Another problem is that many plants have more than one common name even in the one language, not to mention common names that the same plant may have in different languages of the world. And to these difficulties should be added the fact that a large proportion of the world's plants have never received a common name, on account of being too rare, hard to distinguish, or found only in wilderness areas.

The reason that scientific names are in Latin is that, when the systematic description of plants began to receive attention in the Renaissance period, the common language of European scholarship was Latin. But for the next two or three centuries the names of plants were clumsy Latin phrases, which might be translated as, for example, 'Oak with lobed leaves and long-stalked nuts, its bark used for tanning'.

It was the famous Swedish naturalist Carolus Linnaeus (1707–78) who first hit on the idea of identifying each plant by two names. At first, in his book *Species Plantarum* of 1753, he showed the differentiating names merely as marginal annotations beside the longer phrase-names of the text, but it was not long before the convenience of this system was appreciated and these names were coupled with the genus names to give the Latin two-word names (binomials) we now use. These follow a similar principle to people's names, though with the surname and given name reversed, and so *Quercus alba* and *Quercus rubra* are both members of the 'family' *Quercus*, in the same way that Elizabeth Mann and Manfred Mann are both members of the family Mann. The parallel can be extended, in that the second part of the name, for example, *rubra*, can be the 'given' name in unrelated 'families'—thus there is an *Ulmus rubra* and a *Morus rubra* as well as a *Quercus rubra*.

The first part of the botanical name is the *genus* name, which is unique and can stand on its own: thus *Quercus* is the genus of oaks and no other plant genus can share the name. Each genus (plural: genera) may consist of several or many (or sometimes only one) *species*, each designated by a two-part name as just described—thus the name of the white oak species is *Quercus alba*, not just *alba*, the latter word being referred to by botanists as the 'specific epithet'.

There are standard ways of using botanical names: when appearing in other text they are distinguished by a different typeface, usually italic; and the genus name is usually abbreviated to its initial letter when additional species are itemized.

But in a way the use of binomials was not Linnaeus' most important contribution to the study of plants. He also put forward a comprehensive system of classification of plants and animals, with a full hierarchy of names from kingdom at the top to species at the bottom. Every plant known at the time could be allotted a place in his system, including the wealth of new species recently discovered in the Americas and tropical Asia. His classification of plants was based on the flower and in particular its organs of fertilization, the stamens and pistils. This revolutionary 'sexual system' used the respective numbers of stamens and pistils to place plants in a series of classes and subclasses—for example, a plant whose flowers have 5 stamens and 3 pistils would be placed in Linnaeus's *Pentandria Trigyna*. The advantage of this system was that all plants could be reliably pigeon-holed, but the disadvantage was that many plants that were obviously closely allied were placed in different classes simply on the basis of an extra stamen!

Linnaeus' successors soon realized this shortcoming and began to place species and genera in 'natural orders', now known as plant *families*, defined on the basis of a wider range of characters of flowers, fruits and foliage. By the late nineteenth century family names had stabilized into the form we now use, that is, using the name of the genus that typifies the family but with the ending *-aceae*. Thus *Rosa* gives its name to the family Rosaceae, of which it is a typical member.

Just as it is possible for a genus to consist of only one species or many species (over 1,000 in some cases), so a family may consist of only one genus or many genera. Family, genus and species are only the best known levels in the whole hierarchy of botanical names, which runs in descending order from kingdom, subkingdom, phylum or division, class, order, family, subfamily, tribe, genus, section, species, subspecies and cultivar.

There are other levels that can be squeezed in between some of these levels, for example, subsection between section and species. We should also emphasize that there are many different classifications of plants possible, depending on judgments of different botanists about the closeness of relationship between different genera, families and so on.

Often disagreement hinges on whether a botanist favors more broadly or more narrowly defined families, genera, etc. For example, the genus *Casuarina* has generally been regarded as the only genus in family Casuarinaceae, but recent study has shown that there is an argument for splitting this into 4 genera, of which 3, *Allocasuarina*, *Gymnostoma* and *Ceuthostoma* are newly named, while *Casuarina* itself is narrowed in scope to only 17 species out of the original 90. However, some botanists have rejected the arguments for this reclassification and choose to still treat *Casuarina* in the broad sense. Under the *International Code for Botanical Nomenclature* they are quite free to choose either classification—what this code governs is the correct use of names once a classification has been chosen, determined on rather legalistic grounds according to rules based on priority of publication. Thus the correct botanical name of the common larch is *Larix decidua*, not *L. europaea*, because the former name was published earlier and there is no dispute that both names refer to the same species.

Another subject that may need explanation is levels of classification below the rank of species. Linnaeus listed varieties (*varietas*) after some of the species in his *Species Plantarum*, indicating them with the Greek letters α, β, etc. Botanists in the nineteenth century continued to recognize mainly varieties, treating them as variants of the 'typical' species, thus *Acer saccharum* var. *leucoderme* was treated as distinct from *A. saccharum.* In the mid-twentieth century there was a move towards classifications that reflected evolving biological entities and many botanists moved to using *subspecies* in the same way as zoologists used it. In such a classification a species is divided into two or more subspecies, often regarded as species still in the process of evolving, with each subspecies usually having its own geographical range. The species *includes* all subspecies rather than being distinct from them, and one of them always repeats the species name. For example, the European *Pinus nigra* is now treated as consisting of three (sometimes more) subspecies: subsp. *nigra* is the Austrian pine, ranging from the Austrian Alps to Greece; subsp. *laricio* is the Corsican pine, restricted to Corsica, Sicily and Calabria; and subsp. *pallasiana* is the Crimean pine, occurring in the Balkans, Crimea and the Caucasus.

Variant forms of species that have been created or perpetuated by gardeners are now named as *cultivars* rather than varieties and must now be given names in modern languages, not Latin. We are all familiar with cultivar names such as those of roses ('Papa Meilland') and camellias ('Great Western'), names in this style having been in use for over 150 years. Note that a cultivar name is always in a different typeface from the botanical name, and has an initial capital letter; they are also usually in single quotes, though an alternative is to prefix them with the abbreviation cv.

You may notice that some cultivar names are attached to a species name while for others only the genus is mentioned. The latter is the practice for many plants of hybrid origin, particularly where more than two species are involved in the parentage, or for those cases where the species cannot readily be identified. Again, roses would be a major group where species name is seldom mentioned.

Cultivars, at least of trees and shrubs, are normally assumed to be single clones: that is, all individual plants of, for example, *Rosa* 'Peace' are derived from the original hybrid seedling by vegetative propagation, in this case by grafting or budding. A particular hybrid crossing may produce many seedlings with differing combinations of the parental characters; breeders select the best seedlings and perpetuate them as clones, naming the commercially promising ones as cultivars. An example of a hybrid is the cross between *Camellia japonica* and *C. saluenensis*, which has been repeated several times producing numerous seedlings. All seedling plants must take the hybrid name *C.* × *williamsii*, but some have been named as cultivars including the favorites 'Donation' and 'Caerhays'.

Because botanists the world over use the same system of plant nomenclature and follow its conventions, plants from all parts of the world can be identified and described without confusion. There are about 300,000 species of flowering plants, conifers, cycads, and ferns and allies in the world, and the development of a simple system by which they can all be named and enumerated has been a triumph of human ability and cooperation. And having named and classified them, we have taken the first step towards understanding their part in the complex web of life. For the gardener, knowing the names of plants and how they relate to each other can help in understanding the conditions in which they flourish.

Glossary

Acid (of soils) Containing relatively little lime, to give a pH reaction of less than 7, the sort of soil needed to grow such plants as azaleas, camellias, rhododendrons and the like, and in which hydrangeas flower blue. A very acid soil is described as 'sour'.
Adpressed (or appressed) (of leaf or stem hairs, or of leaves) Bent forward and pressing closely against the surface from which they arise.
Aerial root A root that springs from the stem of a plant above ground. The aerial roots of ivy are short and used by the plant to cling to its support. In such plants as monsteras, philodendrons or some of the tropical figs they eventually reach the ground; before they do they draw moisture from the air.
Air-layering A method of propagation applicable to a wide range of trees and shrubs which involves wounding the stem and then packing the wound with damp sphagnum moss, held in place and kept from drying by wrapping in plastic. When roots show, the branch can be severed and planted.
Alkaline (of soils) Containing a great deal of calcium (lime) to give a pH reaction of more than 7. It is the sort of soil preferred by such plants as bearded irises and the cabbage tribe. Some gardeners refer to alkaline soils as 'sweet'.
Alpine A plant from high mountain regions, usually from above the treeline and hence herbaceous or a very compact shrub, and adapted to overwintering beneath deep snow where they remain moist and are protected from extremely low temperatures.
Alpine house A type of greenhouse designed to meet the specialized requirements of alpines, usually kept cool in summer by shading the glass, and unheated in winter but providing protection from severe frosts.
Alternate (of leaves) Arising, one by one, first from one side of the stem and then the other. Whether the leaves are alternate or opposite is an important aid in plant identification. Most leaf arrangements called 'alternate' are in fact spiral.
Amphibious (of plants) Able to grow both in the water (aquatic) and on exposed soil, usually moist or boggy, when the water recedes.
Annual A plant that lives for only a year—often less—or which is customarily treated as such in gardens. Annuals are normally propagated from seed.
Anther The part of the stamen that actually contains the pollen, released when the anther opens (dehisces) through a slit or pore.
Apex The growing tip of a shoot; the uppermost part of any plant organ, or the part furthest from its stalk or base. The plural of apex is apices.
Aphid Member of the order Aphididae of small sap-sucking insects with delicate translucent bodies, often infesting foliage in large numbers and weakening the plant. Aphids secrete a sugary 'honeydew' eaten by ants, which in return protect the aphids from other predators.
Apomictic Reproducing by seed but without fertilization by the pollen nucleus (though sometimes stimulated by pollination), so that the resulting seedlings are genetically identical to the mother plant. Plant varieties that habitually reproduce thus are called apomicts.
Appendage A small lobe or projection from any plant organ, for example, from a petal or stamen, sometimes with no evident function.
Aquatic A plant able to grow with at least its base immersed in water. Aquatics come in many different forms, including submerged, emergent and floating. Gardeners use aquatics mostly in ponds and streams, but they are also grown in tanks by aquarium fanciers.
Arbor A structure, usually freestanding, designed to be covered with climbing plants to provide shade. The term is more or less interchangeable with pergola.
Areole A specialized structure characteristic of the cactus family, consisting of a small pad of tissue from which arise spines, hairs, and flowers. Areoles are always positioned along the ribs of a cactus stem or at apices of stem tubercles; they are interpreted as highly modified and condensed lateral shoots.
Aromatic Having a strong, usually pleasant but not just sweet smell. Aromatic plants often have resin glands on their stems and leaves, releasing the strongest aroma when the sun is hottest; many others contain essential oils in tiny leaf cavities, releasing their aroma when foliage is crushed or bruised.
Awn A projecting bristle found in a particular position on a plant organ. The best known awns are on spikelets of some grasses, for example, barley and wild oats.
Axil The 'armpit' of a leaf; that is, the angle between the leaf base and the stem, where there is usually a bud which may elongate to produce a lateral branch, a flower, or a group of flowers—these are then termed axillary.
Bamboo A member of the tribe Bambuseae of the grass family (Poaceae), though used primarily for those species which produce substantial aerial stems, often rather woody and with lateral branches from the nodes. Bamboos grow from underground rhizomes that are long-running or short and crowded. The stems (culms) are hollow in most bamboos.
Bark The protective surface layer of the trunk or branches of a tree or shrub, generated from a layer of dividing cells at the bark-wood interface (cambium) and often from additional layers of dividing cells (cork cambium). Bark may build up in thickness as the tree grows, often becoming fissured or checkered as it is stretched; or outer layers of bark may be shed annually leaving a smooth new surface; or layers may peel in irregular flakes.
Basal (of branches, leaves, etc.) Springing directly from the base of the plant rather than from an aerial stem; or may simply mean the opposite of apical, as in the basal lobes of a leaf.
Bedding (of plants) A plant, usually low growing, suitable for a mass planting display of flowers or foliage. Most are annuals or short-lived perennials.
Berry In normal use, a small juicy fruit which is eaten entire and unpeeled, or a small ornamental fruit that appears similar; but in botany often with the restrictive meaning of a fruit with seeds embedded in the flesh, lacking a hard stone (see *drupe*), and which does not open when ripe—for example, a tomato.
Biennial A plant which dies in its second year after germination; it may flower in both the first and second years, or in the second year only.
Bifoliate (of cattleya orchids and their hybrids) Plants which have two leaves per pseudobulb.
Bipinnate (of leaves) Twice pinnate: that is, compound with leaflets arranged in feather-like form, but each leaflet is again compound with leaflets similarly arranged.
Blade The flat part of a leaf.
Bloom A general term for a flower, or any inflorescence or portion of an inflorescence that has the appearance of a flower; a coating of whitish or bluish wax on a leaf, stem or fruit, as on some grapes.
Blossom Much the same as *bloom*, except that it is used for the massed flowering of deciduous orchard trees, and to signify the position of the withered floral remains of a fruit, as in 'blossom end'.
Bog garden An area of garden in which soil moisture is maintained at a saturated level, by restricting drainage; most easily achieved at the margin of a pond or permanent stream. Used to grow plants from bog and marsh habitats.
Bole The lowest part of the trunk of a tree; the part of the trunk below the first branch.
Bottom heat Arrangement for propagating plants, generally striking of cuttings or germinating seeds, consisting nowadays of electric heating cables running through base of propagating medium.
Bract A modified leaf associated with a flower or group of flowers, usually differing in size, shape or color from a normal foliage leaf. In many plants the bracts are the showiest part of the 'flower', for example, in poinsettias.
Branch Any plant stem arising from the primary stem in a lateral position, including flowering stems, though most commonly used for the lateral shoots of a tree which become thick and woody.
Bristle An outgrowth from any plant organ (leaf, stem, fruit etc.) that is thicker and stiffer than a hair but thinner and weaker than a spine or prickle.
Bud An immature flower before its petals have unfolded; the embryonic stage of a leafy shoot before it expands, especially on deciduous trees when it is usually protected by tough scales.
Budding A form of grafting in which a (vegetative) bud of the desired clone (scion) is inserted in a slit in the bark of the stock plant.
Bulb A (usually) underground storage organ consisting of swollen leaf bases, each encircling the next inner one, as in an onion, or consisting of overlapping scales, as in liliums. The flowering stem of bulbous plants grows up through the middle of the bulb.
Bulbil or bulblet A small bulb, produced either from the base of the parent bulb, or budding from the aerial stem or inflorescence. The term 'offset' is sometimes used.
Buttress A wedge-shaped outgrowth of a tree trunk at the base, expanding the tree's area of contact with the soil. Buttresses allow a stronger and more stable connection between the tree's trunk and the large mat

of shallow roots characteristic of tree species that grow in shallow or poorly drained soil.
Cacti Plural of cactus.
Cactus A member of the large plant family Cactaceae, almost wholly native to the Americas and the most significant family of succulent plants, most species with very sharp spines. Used loosely by some gardeners to refer to any succulent or spiky plant.
Calyx The outermost whorl of enclosing organs in a flower, often green and leafy in contrast to the colored petals, but in some plants quite showy and substituting for the petals (for example, in *Daphne*, *Clematis*). The individual segments of the calyx are the sepals.
Cane A branch or stem that is slender, straight and not very woody, usually produced by a single season's growth.
Capsule A fruit developing from 2 or more fused carpels which when ripe dries and splits open to release the seeds. If formed from a single carpel, such a fruit is usually termed a pod or follicle.
Carpel The basic female organ of the flower, containing the developing seed; a single flower may have from one to many carpels, and they may be separate (as in buttercups) or fused together (as in poppies). Each carpel or group of fused carpels consists of an ovary, in which the seeds develop, a stigma, which receives pollen, and frequently a style, an elongated section between ovary and stigma. The carpels of a flower are collectively called the pistil.
Catkin The type of flower cluster, usually pendulous, found on such plants as willows or alders. The individual flowers, usually of one sex only on each catkin, are tiny and generally have no petals, pollination being effected by the wind.
Caudex Literally just the trunk of a tree in Latin, but used in botany to denote a stem that is long-lived, thick and not quite woody enough to be termed a trunk, for example, as in cycads. Succulent enthusiasts use it for the swollen stems of some desert shrubs, which they rather pretentiously refer to as 'caudiciforms', for example, *Cyphostemma juttae*.
Cephalium A head of flowers, that is a type of inflorescence in which the flowers are crowded onto the apex of a stem with their individual stalks reduced to zero length; or used in cacti for a specialized area of the stem, usually with a dense mass of wool, hairs or bristles, from which the flowers emerge year after year, for example, *Cephalocereus*.
Chalk A kind of soft, porous limestone that on weathering produces very fine, powdery, alkaline soil in which many garden plants are difficult to grow. Chalk soils are common in parts of the UK.
Circumpolar Literally, occurring right around the Arctic (or Antarctic) Zone. Applied mainly to northern hemisphere plant species that occur in the far north of both Eurasia and North America, often extending south to high mountain ranges such as the Rocky Mountains and the Alps.
Cladode A stem or branch with green tissues that performs the photosynthetic functions normally performed by leaves, as in many of the brooms. In many plants with cladodes true leaves are either absent or very small and short-lived. The term is often used in a narrower sense, for stems that are flattened and imitate leaves, but these are correctly phylloclades.
Clay A major component of soils, consisting of very fine particles of mineral origin that swell and become sticky when they take up water. A high proportion of clay in a soil makes it difficult to dig and impedes both root penetration and drainage.
Climber A plant with stems too long and flexible to be self-supporting and which raises itself to the light by climbing into and over other plants. It may attach itself to its support by twining around it, as jasmine or honeysuckle do; by means of tendrils (grapes, peas); by short aerial roots (ivy); or by suckers (Virginia creeper); or by a grappling onto tree branches with thorns (bougainvillea), prickles (roses) or reflexed branchlets.
Cloche A miniature, portable greenhouse placed over crops in the open ground to protect them from cold or encourage early development. Traditionally made from two or four pieces of glass in a wire frame, but can be simply a wire frame clad in transparent polythene.
Clone A group of plants propagated asexually (that is, by cuttings, grafting, division, etc.) from a single individual and thus genetically all identical. Named cultivars of woody plants such as roses, camellias and fruit trees are always clonal—that is, each cultivar consists of a single clone—but a clone need not be named as a cultivar.
Clubroot A disease of cabbages and related vegetables and ornamental plants in the brassica family, such as stocks, caused by the slime mold fungus *Plasmodiophora brassica*.
Colony A group of apparently separate plants in the one small area of ground, spreading from a single initial plant by vegetative means such as rhizomes, stolons, bulbils on flowering stems, or even fallen leaves in the case of some succulents of the 'mother-of-millions' type.
Columnar Shaped like column or narrow cylinder, used to describe the crown shape of certain trees.
Common name The name by which a plant is commonly known by non-botanists, though many plants that are not well known or have only a short history of cultivation lack a common name. Common names may be genuine folk names such as 'lad's love', or book names, coined by writers as an alternative to the scientific name, though these are often merely a translation of the Latin or Greek—thus 'regal lily' for *Lilium regale*. Common names vary from country to country or even from person to person, whereas botanical (scientific) names are used internationally.
Composite Botanist's term for any member of the large daisy family (Asteraceae or Compositae), characterized by their composite flowerheads often resembling a single flower, with a disc consisting of small, tightly packed disc florets, commonly surrounded by rays or ray florets, which have much longer petals fused into a strap-like form.
Compost Material resulting from the breakdown by fungi and bacteria of waste organic matter such as leaves, grass clippings, vegetable peelings, animal manure and many other items—used in gardens as fertilizer and for improvement of soil texture. The term is also used for soilless growing mixes used for potting of orchids and other indoor plants.
Compound (of any plant organ) Consisting of smaller, simple units—thus a compound leaf consists of 2 to many leaflets arranged in regular fashion (see *pinnate, bipinnate, palmate*); a compound umbel consists of many small umbels on stalks which are themselves arranged in an umbel (as in carrots); and a compound fruit consists of many fruits pressed or fused together on a single stalk (as in pineapple).
Cone The structure that encloses the seeds of most conifers and cycads, consisting of scales arranged around a central axis, each scale having one or more seeds attached to its surface or embedded in its tissues; also used for the pollen-bearing organs (pollen cones) of these plants which consist of smaller scales bearing many tiny pollen sacs which shed their pollen into the wind.
Conifer A member of the major subgroup of the gymnosperms the Pinopsida, flowerless seed-bearing woody plants mostly with needle-like or scale-like leaves, representing a lower and earlier evolutionary level than the flowering plants. Some conifers, using the term in the broad sense, do not bear their seed in recognisable cones but in more fleshy structures (for example, yews, podocarps, junipers) but belong with the conifers nonetheless.
Conservatory A glassed-in area for growing frost-tender plants, usually attached to or forming part of a house.
Container Any item that can contain soil or other growing medium, in which a plant can be grown, sold, and moved around to any desired position—including pots, tubs and hanging baskets.
Cool-temperate (of climates) Those in the cooler half of the temperate zones, essentially those regions between about 40 and 60 degrees latitude though extending closer to the equator in highlands and large continental landmasses of the northern hemisphere. Regions between 60 degrees north and the Arctic Circle are usually termed subarctic.
Cordate (of leaves) Heart-shaped, with stalk attached to notch at broader end.
Corm A bulb-like organ, usually growing underground but without the scales (fleshy modified leaves) of a bulb; a corm is in fact a kind of tuber, a condensed stem that stores food material, differing from other tubers in that it forms new corms at the apex and dies off behind at the base. Most cormous plants form a new corm annually. Gardeners often group cormous plants under the general heading of bulbs.
Cormlet A small corm that grows from around the base of a corm, often numerous and able to be used for propagation.
Cormous (of plant species) Characterized by the possession of corms.
Corolla The whole collection of petals that forms the eye-catching part of most flowers. The petals can be separate, as in roses, or fused together in a bell or trumpet form, as in rhododendrons or campanulas, when the free tips of the petals are termed the corolla lobes.
Corona A crown-like structure in the center of a flower, formed from fused stamens (as in *Hoya*) or their filament bases (as in *Hymenocallis*) or from fused appendages of the petals (as in *Narcissus*).
Creeper A plant that makes long shoots that grow along the ground or up a wall, in the latter case clinging by aerial roots (for example, ivy).
Creeping (of perennials and shrubs) With stems running along the ground, in many cases putting out roots (for example, *Juniperus conferta*).
Crest An apex that is stretched laterally to form a line, often wavy or wrinkled, used in various ways for plant parts—for example, crested cacti are plants with aberrant growing points that form bizarre shapes, while crested irises are a group of *Iris* species with erect crests on their style branches.
Crop A mass planting, usually of annual plants and usually running into acres at a time, grown for food or some other economic purpose. Crop plants are species commonly grown in this way, for example, wheat, potatoes, sunflowers.
Cross Another name for a hybrid, though somewhat vaguer in meaning.
Crown The more or less permanent base of a perennial plant from which the leaves and flower stems grow upwards and the roots downwards; the upper part of a tree, consisting of the foliage and its supporting branches; the collective fronds of a palm, tree fern or cycad.
Crownshaft (of palms) An apparent upward extension of the trunk in certain palms, being a pseudostem (as in banana plants) made up of tightly furled sheathing bases of the fronds. Only one large group of feather palms, mainly from the wet tropics, includes species with well developed crownshafts.
Culinary herb A plant grown for its strong flavor, used to flavor cooked dishes or salads—usually it is

the leaves, flowers or bulbs that are used, as plants of which the seeds, fruits or rhizomes are used tend to be termed spices.

Cultivar A variety of plant which has arisen or been selected in the course of cultivation, commonly as the result of hybridization. It may be propagated by any means that preserves its distinctive character, and the Code of Nomenclature states that it must not be named in Latin but should be given in Roman type with single quotes, for example, 'Iceberg', 'Jeanne d'Arc'. Cultivars that arose before this ruling and were given Latin names are treated similarly, giving rise to such names as *Acer palmatum* 'Dissectum Atropurpureum'. Most cultivars of woody or long-lived plants represent single clones and are propagated from cuttings, divisions or grafts, but cultivars of annuals may be true-breeding lines, F1 hybrids, or mixed-color strains and are grown from seed. A cultivar name may follow a species name if derived from that species alone, or follow directly after the genus name if of unknown or hybrid origin.

Cultivar group Used in many commercially important plant species and hybrids to distinguish major groups of cultivars sharing common characteristics. An example is the brassica vegetables, most of which are cultivars of the variable species *Brassica oleracea*. The cabbages, the cauliflowers, Brussels sprouts, broccolis and kales each constitute a cultivar group of this species. Cabbages, for example, were once designated *Brassica oleracea* var. *capitata* but modern principles of nomenclature demand that they now be named *Brassica oleracea* Capitata Group—this name covers numerous cultivars, some of which form subgroups, such as the Savoy cabbages. The thousands of cultivars in such complex hybrid groups as the roses, tulips and dahlias are generally classified into cultivar groups, sometimes in quite artificial ways.

Cultivated (of plants) Domesticated for use in gardens, agriculture or forestry, with the implication that cultivation techniques appropriate to the plant have been worked out.

Cutting A piece of stem or root cut from a plant and used for propagation, producing roots and new growth if kept in a suitable environment. According to the state of maturity of the stem from which it is taken, a cutting may be classed as a softwood cutting, a half-hardened (or -ripened) cutting, or a hardwood cutting.

Cycad The other major group of gymnosperms apart from the conifers, consisting of long-lived flowerless plants with palm-like or fern-like, leathery fronds springing from a short trunk or caudex. Male (pollen) and female (seed) cones are borne on separate plants and may be quite large. Cycads are an ancient group, most abundant in the 'age of dinosaurs' (Jurassic and Cretaceous) just before the flowering plants began to diversify. Less than 200 species survive today, confined to warmer regions of the world. Examples are *Cycas, Encephalartos, Zamia.*

Daisy A type of bloom characteristic of the large composite family of plants, though by no means all composites have a typical daisy 'flower'. It is in fact a whole inflorescence (or unit of a larger inflorescence), consisting of a disc of tiny disc florets surrounded by a ring of more showy rays or ray florets. The common or English daisy is *Bellis perennis.*

Deadhead (dead head) To remove dead flowers, with the twofold aim of tidying up the plant and preventing it wasting energy in unwanted seed. In some plants it may also help prevent diseases, such as petal blight of azaleas.

Deciduous (of trees and shrubs) Losing all the leaves each year, growing a fresh set later. Typically the leaves drop in fall (autumn), sometimes assuming brilliant colors before they do so, and new leaves grow in spring. Many tropical trees drop their leaves at any time of the year in anticipation of a prolonged dry season. A tree that does not drop all its leaves is called semi-deciduous. (of perennials) Dying back to the ground in winter—such plants are alternatively called herbaceous perennials, though this is not the correct botanical meaning of 'herbaceous'.

Deltoid (of leaves) Triangular in shape, though commonly with rounded corners, usually with the stalk joining the blade at the center of the base.

Dicotyledons One of the two major subdivisions of the flowering plants (the other, lesser one is the monocotyledons). Characterized by a pair of seed leaves, the leaves mostly with a reticulate pattern of veining, and flower parts mostly in fours or fives (or multiples thereof). Most broad-leafed trees and shrubs are dicotyledons, as are major plant families such as the daisy, rose, legume, carrot and mint families.

Die-back The death of the tips of shoots or branches, often progressing downward with time until the whole plant dies—mostly caused by diseases or pests attacking the root system, preventing uptake of sufficient water to support the foliage.

Diffuse Forming many branches, usually used of shrubs to suggest an open, rangy habit of growth rather than a compact one.

Digitate (of leaves) Compound with the leaflets attached to the main leaf-stalk like the spokes of an umbrella, or (in the literal sense of the term) like the fingers of a hand. Also used of leaves that are not truly compound but only deeply lobed, described as digitately lobed. Palmate has much the same meaning.

Dioecious (of plant species) Bearing male and female flowers on different plants, so that for fruit and seed production to take place there needs to be a male plant present as well as the female. This is not the same as self-incompatibility, as in apples and pears, in which flowers are bisexual but unable to be fertilized by pollen from the same plant or clone, and hence require the presence of a different clone or cultivar for pollination.

Disease An ailment of a plant caused by an infectious micro-organism, either fungal, bacterial or viral, or by a defect of environment such as a mineral deficiency in the soil, or an air pollutant. Infestations of most insects and other fauna are not regarded as diseases, except maybe for nematodes (eelworms) and some gall-producing insects.

Disjunct distribution (of plant species, genera or families) Having a natural distribution consisting of two or more occurrences separated by large geographical gaps, for example, the occurrence of *Magnolia* in eastern Asia and eastern North America.

Disc floret (of plants of the composite family) One of the tiny flowers that make up the disc, or center of the flowerhead, as opposed to the ring of more showy ray florets.

Dissected (of leaves, or sometimes of petals) Deeply divided or lobed into many small segments, though not truly compound (as in many *Artemisia* species).

Division The simplest method of propagation, whereby a clump-forming plant is dug up and broken or cut apart into several pieces which are then replanted.

Dormant (of plants) In a state of non-growth, usually leafless or with leaves and stems having died back to the ground and the plant surviving as underground storage organs, thus evading winter cold or a dry season. (of seeds) In a state adapted to long-term survival and in which germination is not readily initiated. Seed dormancy can be broken in a variety of ways, including stratifying and scarifying of the seeds.

Dorsal Situated on the back of an organ—(of leaves or flowers) this means the side furthest away from the stem when in bud, thus the underside of a leaf. But orchid specialists always talk about the *dorsal sepal,* meaning the one at the *top* of the typical orchid flower. The apparent contradiction is due to the fact that most orchid flowers have a stalk that twists through 180 degrees, turning the flowers upside-down.

Double (of flowers) Having more than the 'natural' number of petals. The extra petals are in most cases mutated stamens, and where all of these are completely transformed the flower is apt to be sterile. A flower with stamens still showing in the center is said to be semi-double'.

Downy (of leaves, fruits) Having a coating of fine, short hairs, as on the skin of a peach.

Drupe A type of fruit, for example, plums or cherries, in which the fruit wall is differentiated into a fleshy, usually juicy outer layer and a bony, woody or fibrous inner layer (the 'stone') enclosing one or more seeds.

Ellipsoid (mainly of fruits) Elliptic in outline but three-dimensional.

Elliptic(al) (of leaves) More or less oval in shape though tending to a point at each end—one of the most common leaf shapes, the term used more loosely in botany than its strict geometrical meaning.

Embryo The earliest detectable stage of a seedling enclosed in the developing seed, shortly after fertilization; or the plantlet that can be observed when a mature seed is dissected.

Emergent (of aquatic plants) With part of the plant's foliage projecting above the water surface.

Endemic (of a species, subspecies, genus or family) Confined in the wild to one clearly delimited geographical region or state—thus the genus *Carpenteria* is endemic to California (or is a Californian endemic).

Entire (of leaves) Having margins that are smooth, not toothed, scalloped, lobed or dissected in any way (though they may be recurved or revolute and still entire).

Epiphyte A plant that grows on the trunk, branches, twigs, or in some cases even on the leaves of another plant, but does not steal nourishment from its host as does a parasite; many orchids and bromeliads are examples familiar to gardeners, though epiphytes also include numerous ferns, mosses and lichens, common in humid forest environments.

Erect Standing up almost vertically, applied to stems, branches, leaves or inflorescences.

Ergot A fungal disease of cereal grains and other grasses, most notoriously of rye, in which the ripe grains are replaced by masses of blackish fungal tissue. Caused by the fungus *Claviceps purpurea,* ergot is very poisonous and in Europe whole towns were once poisoned by eating infected bread.

Escape A plant that is on the away to becoming naturalized, having 'escaped' from cultivation.

Espalier The technique of training a tree or shrub, most typically a fruit tree such as a peach or a fig, to grow flat against a wall or trellis. It was originally designed to encourage earlier ripening by holding the fruit close to the reflected warmth of the wall, but can also be used for decorative effect.

Essential oil An aromatic oil found in minute cavities in the leaves or flowers of plants, or exuded as droplets mixed with resin. Plants are harvested and distilled to obtain commercial quantities of certain oils, used for perfumery and food flavoring. So-called because each type of oil was said to be the 'essence' of a particular fragrance—as in lavender oil, lemon oil, eucalyptus oil—but most such plants contain mixtures of oils of differing chemical composition.

Evergreen Any plant that retains foliage all year. Evergreen trees and shrubs do drop old leaves, though not until after the new ones have been

formed and usually only a few at a time.
Exotic A plant that is not native to the country or region in which it is grown, though the term is often used to signify any kind of plant seen as strange, alluring or glamorous.
F1 hybrid A hybrid strain created by crossing two very carefully selected parents, created afresh for every batch of seed. The resulting seedlings usually show great vigor and uniformity and many strains of annuals and vegetables are F1 hybrids. It is useless to save seeds from these.
Fall The American term for autumn; each of the lower three petals of an iris.
Family The next major unit of classification above the level of genus. A plant family may consist of few to many genera, or in rare cases of a single genus only. The cacti (family Cactaceae) constitute an easily recognized family, as do the orchids (family Orchidaceae). Family names end in -aceae.
Fan palm A palm with roughly circular (palmate) fronds or leaves, the ribs radiating from the end of the supporting stalk, like those of an old-fashioned hand fan. Most palms fall into one of two groups, fan palms and feather palms.
Feather palm A palm with elongated, pinnately divided fronds or leaves, the leaflets arising along the whole length of a central rib or stalk (the rachis), giving the appearance of a feather.
Female (of plants) Those bearing only female reproductive organs, hence able to bear fruit and seeds. Most flowering plants are in fact bisexual, commonly bearing hermaphrodite flowers.
Fern Any member of the major subgroup of the *pteridophytes*, plants with well developed stems containing conducting tissues, but lacking the seeds which characterize the gymnosperms and flowering plants. The visible fern plant is asexual, producing minute spores from small patches *(sori)* on its fronds: the spores germinate in cool, moist places to produce tiny plantlets (the gametophytes) that bear male and female organs, fertilization requiring water droplets.
Fertile (of soils) Containing an abundance of the mineral nutrients (chiefly nitrogen, phosphorus and potassium) necessary for good plant growth, as well as decomposed organic materials producing a good tilth and moisture retention. (of plants and flowers) Possessing fully functioning sexual organs, ensuring successful production of fruit or seed.
Fertilizer Anything added to the soil to maintain or increase its fertility. Fertilizer may be organic, that is, derived from once-living matter, as are manure, compost, and bone meal; or inorganic (artificial), such as sulphate of ammonia or superphosphate, which are prepared in chemical factories.
Fibrous root A fine, young root, usually one of very many. These are the roots that take up moisture and nourishment from the soil.
Filament The stalk of a stamen, which carries the anther.
Fireblight A bacterial disease of the pome-fruit trees and shrubs of family Rosaceae, most feared by apple and pear growers but affecting also genera such as *Sorbus*, *Cotoneaster* and *Crataegus*. Its symptoms include shrivelled and blackened leaves and oozing patches on the branches and the plant may eventually die.
Fissured (of bark) With many fissures or furrows, occurring on trees with persistent bark and caused by the growth in diameter of the underlying wood, resulting in stretching of the bark layer. Each tree species has its characteristic pattern of bark behaviour.
Floret A single flower, used of flowers that are mostly small and aggregated into a large, dense inflorescence or partial inflorescence—for example, hydrangeas.
Flower The organ of reproduction of the flowering plants, basic in determining to what genus and species the plant belongs. They are normally composed of three parts: the calyx, the corolla, and the sexual organs proper, the male stamens and the female carpels. Not all may be present in any given flower (*Clematis*, for instance has no petals), and they may be, as in orchids or cannas, modified into the most fantastic forms.
Flowerhead A cluster of flowers, which may be so compact as to look like a single flower, as in a daisy.
Fodder Plants grown for animal feed, usually in the form of foliage or grains.
Forage Plants on which grazing animals browse while still growing, often in the wild and including trees and shrubs as well as grasses and other herbs.
Frame A miniature greenhouse, designed mainly for propagation. The traditional style is an enclosed bed with wood to a height of about 16 in (40 cm) with an old window across the top. A hot frame is heated, a cold one not.
Frond A large compound or much-divided leaf, as that of a fern, a palm or a cycad. Used for convenience to circumvent the botanical distinction between leaves and their component leaflets or segments, which non-botanists often find difficult to comprehend.
Frost hardy (of plants) Able to survive winter frosts without damage to leaves (in the case of evergreens) or of dormant stems, buds or roots (in the case of deciduous plants). Frost hardiness is a relative concept, in that many plants able to survive a frost of 20 F (–7 C) in, say, southern England would be killed outright by the –30 F (–34 C) frosts experienced in northern USA. See Hardiness Zone Map on page 16.
Frost tender (of plants) Damaged or killed by even the lightest winter frosts. Many frost tender plants (mostly of tropical origin) may in fact suffer tissue damage when exposed to temperatures well above freezing-point, as high as 50 F (10 C) in the case of some species.
Fruit The part of the plant which contains the seed or seeds: in the strict sense of the term, fruits are found only on flowering plants, developing from the fertilized ovary of the flower. A fruit may or may not be edible; some of the edible 'fruits' are in fact false fruits, for example, apples, strawberries, consisting largely of tissues derived from the floral receptacle, not the ovary. The plural of fruit is fruits when considered as different kinds, fruit when considered in a mass.
Fruit fly A small insect pest that lays its eggs beneath the surface of developing fruits, in particular soft fruits such as peaches and tomatoes. The small, soft larvae develop rapidly and exit the fully ripe fruit via small holes, but not before causing pockets of fermentation and rot in the fruit, thus spoiling it.
Fungal disease Any of a great number of diseases of plants caused by a fungal organism.
Fungi (plural of fungus) A very large group of organisms, now considered to belong to a kingdom separate from both plants and animals, with vegetative bodies consisting of fine, almost invisible threads, or single cells, or even aggregations of naked protoplasm (the slime molds). Many fungi produce more conspicuous spore-bearing organs, as in the mushrooms, toadstools and puffballs. Fungi, unlike green plants, cannot synthesize their food from soil minerals but must utilize organic foods that have been synthesized by other organisms: they may feed either on dead matter (saprophytes) or living plants or animals (parasites). Many plant diseases are caused by parasitic fungi, but saprophytic fungi play a vital role in breaking down dead plant material, channeling it back into the nutrient cycle.
Gametophyte See *fern*.
Genera Plural of genus.
Genus The next major unit of plant classification above species—thus a group of species with many features in common may be grouped together and named as a genus. The name given to a genus is of Latin form (or Latinised Greek). A genus name can stand on its own, referring then to all its members, but a species name must always consist of 2 words, the first being the genus name. All roses belong to the genus *Rosa*, which consists of about 150 species including *Rosa canina* and *Rosa rugosa*.
Glabrous (of leaves, stems, fruits etc.) Smooth, lacking any covering of hairs, scales or bristles.
Gland In botany used for a variety of plant organs, mainly very small, associated with the secretion of any fluid such as nectar, resin, oil or even water. Most flowers have one or more nectar glands (or nectaries) secreting nectar as the 'bait' for pollinating birds or insects, but nectar glands can also be found on leaves or stems of some plants. Glands are often vestigial and no longer secrete anything.
Glasshouse A structure, traditionally roofed and clad with glass but now often with polythene sheeting, designed to trap the sun's heat and thus allow warmth-loving plants to be grown in cool climates. Supplementary heating may be provided.
Glaucous (of leaves and stems) Bluish gray or whitish, usually due to a thin coating or 'bloom' of wax which reflects light strongly. The Latin epithet *glauca* is applied indiscriminately by nurseries to any conifer plants with a bluish or grayish cast to the foliage.
Globose Botanist's term for globular or spherical.
Globular Approximately spherical in shape.
Grafting A method of propagation which involves the uniting of a piece of stem of a desirable plant, the scion, to that of a less desirable but hardier one, the stock or understock, to give a stronger root system than the scion would have naturally. Many different techniques for grafting have been employed.
Grass Any member of the very large grass family (Poaceae or Gramineae), though usually excluding larger members of the bamboo tribe of this family. Grasses are mostly tufted or creeping plants with narrow leaves and much-reduced flowers born in large inflorescences, consisting of spikelets each containing one to several florets. The cereals are grasses which produce edible grains (seeds) in large quantities. Lawns are almost invariably composed of grasses. Enthusiasts for ornamental grasses often include superficially similar plants such as the sedges (Cyperaceae) in their concept of 'grass'.
Green manure A crop of annual plants grown to be dug into the soil at maturity to improve or restore its fertility; most useful are some annual legumes, such as lupins and cowpeas, as these absorb nitrogen from the air and convert it to plant food; green manures also improve soil texture.
Greenhouse Originally a lavishly windowed structure where evergreen plants were placed to keep them from winter cold; but now synonymous with 'glasshouse'.
Grex A group of hybrid plants of the same parentage, whether the parent plants be species or previous hybrid grexes; the term is used mainly in the context of orchid breeding, though used also for rhododendrons. A grex usually consists of many clones, representing the individual seedlings from the cross, the most desirable of which may be named as cultivars. Grex names are given without quotes in Roman type, and may be followed by a cultivar name, distinguished by being in quotes—thus the orchid name × *Brassolaeliocattleya* Yellow Ribbons 'Starfire'.
Ground cover An extensive planting of a single species of low-growing plants.
Growing season The time of year in which a

particular plant makes its maximum growth of stems and foliage; usually late spring and summer, though for some plants from mild climates with dry summers it may be fall (autumn) or winter.

Gymnosperm Plants bearing naked seeds, that is, not enclosed in a fruit, and without true flowers. The gymnosperms are now seen as representing an evolutionary level rather than a group that evolved from a single ancestor; they first appeared in the Palaeozoic era, at least 100 million years before the first flowering plants. The largest living group of gymnosperms is the conifers, followed by the cycads. Other small relic groups are the ginkgo, the ephedras, the gnetums, and the amazing *Welwitschia.*

Habit (or growth habit) The complete picture of the way a plant grows; a species may be described as being of 'compact', 'weeping' or 'upright' habit, for instance.

Habitat The environment in which a plant is usually found growing—the concept of habitat encompasses many factors, the most important being climate and soils, but microclimate is also significant, as are a plant's interactions with all the other plants, animals and micro-organisms present.

Hair A fine hair-like protuberance from the surface of a leaf, stem, bract, flower or fruit. Plant hairs come in many shapes, sizes, textures and orientations. Together they make up the *indumentum* of a plant surface, which may be described by a variety of terms, for example, pubescent, tomentose, pilose, hispid, sericeous, lanuginose—sometimes even in plain English words, for example, woolly, silky, velvety.

Hanging basket A container designed to be suspended in order to show trailing plants such as ivy, Christmas cactus or fuchsias to their best advantage.

Hardiness In a wide sense, the ability to withstand adverse conditions, but in gardening the use of this term has narrowed to mean frost hardiness, at least in those parts of the world where frost is a major factor in determining what plants can be grown. The opposite of hardy is tender, and tenderness likewise is commonly taken to mean frost tenderness.

Haws Small pome fruits, especially those of *Crataegus*, the hawthorn genus.

Head Any dense aggregation of flowers, their individual stalks absent or very short. The composite or daisy family (Asteraceae) is characterized by its flowerheads, but they are found in may other plants as well, for example, *Monarda, Scabiosa, Platanus.*

Heath Any plant of the genus *Erica*, or sometimes used in a wider sense for other small-leafed shrubs of the family Ericaceae or its Australasian equivalent Epacridaceae; or a type of vegetation (also called heathland) in which shrubs like heaths and heathers *(Calluna)* dominate, usually occurring on shallow, poorly drained, acid soils on exposed hills or moors—as in the 'blasted heath' in Macbeth.

Hedge A close planting of trees or shrubs, their branches intertwining and acting as a barrier or fence. Hedges can be almost any height or width, depending on the species used, but the typical garden hedge is 5–10 ft (1.5–3 m) high and composed of a single species of shrub or small tree such as box, holly, yew or privet, plants that respond to regular clipping by producing very dense, compact foliage and that are very long-lived.

Heel A sliver of old wood retained at the base of a cutting. It is traditional in taking cuttings of carnations and roses.

Hemisphere Any half of the earth's surface, but most commonly taken to mean the northern or southern hemisphere, divided by the equator—though in earlier times an equally significant distinction was seen to be that between the eastern (Europe, Asia, Africa) and western (Americas) hemispheres. Climatically, there is a considerable difference between the northern and southern temperate zones, the latter having milder winters for equivalent latitudes due to the greater extent of oceans and the unimpeded circulation of their currents.

Herb In botany, any plant that does not have permanent woody stems, such as petunias and zinnias. In gardening, a plant whose leaves or shoots are added to food to enhance its flavor or used in the preparation of medicines.

Herbaceous In botany, the adjective describing herbs. But among gardeners it is used for perennial plants which die down to the ground each year, for example, delphiniums; a herbaceous border is a planting composed entirely of such plants.

Horticulture The art and science of gardening. Commercial horticulture is traditionally distinguished from agriculture in covering fruit, flower and small-scale vegetable growing, as well as the nursery industry, whereas agriculture covers broadacre farming activities.

House plant Any kind of plant that can be grown for ornamental purposes inside a house. The house plants of temperate regions mostly originate from warmer parts of the world, many being known as outdoor garden plants in subtropical climates (for example, abutilons, poinsettias). The most widely grown house plants are those that will tolerate the most adverse conditions, in particular very low light levels, low humidity, dust, and air polluted by gas combustion. Aspidistras and sansevierias are renowned for their hardiness in these respects.

Humus The organic content of soil, in nature derived mostly from fallen leaves, twigs, bark, and dead roots. These are broken down by insects and other ground fauna at the same time as they are being decomposed by fungi and bacteria. Earthworms are important in distributing humus throughout the topsoil. The humus content of soil can be enriched with many organic materials, including manure, compost, dead leaves, peat, and composted sawdust or pine bark. Humus returns nutrients to the soil and improves its texture and water retentiveness.

Hybrid A plant originating from the cross-pollination, either in the wild or as the result of matchmaking by the gardener, of two different species. If hybrids are crossed, the resulting plants may carry the genes of several species. Hybrids between plants of different genera are rare, though quite common among orchids. In plant breeding the term hybrid is extended to include crosses between cultivated different strains of the one species, for example, of maize or wheat.

Hybrid group See *cultivar group.*

In situ Applied to the sowing of seeds or rooting of cuttings directly in the ground where they are to grow.

Incurved (of leaves, petals, leaf margins, etc.) Curving upward and inward, toward the center or base of the organ in question. The opposite is recurved, which means curving downward and outward.

Indigenous Of plant species in relation to any country or geographical region: native to that region—that is, growing there in the wild and believed always to have occurred there in the wild (at least for the span of human history).

Indoor (of plant cultivation) Within any enclosed structure, such as a house, conservatory or greenhouse, that a person can enter (thus excluding frames and cloches). Indoor cultivation both avoids winter frosts and raises temperatures in the growing season.

Inflorescence The structure that carries the flowers. It may take any one of a number of forms: a spike (gladiolus), a raceme (as in delphiniums), a panicle (as in lilacs), an umbel (as in onions); gardeners often refer simply to a 'cluster' or 'spray'. Inflorescences are described as 'terminal' when they grow at the ends of shoots, or axillary, when they arise in the axils of the leaves.

Insectivorous plant An alternative term for carnivorous plants; they trap and digest insects to supply them with extra nitrogen, which is difficult to obtain from the swampy soils where they usually grow. 'Carnivorous' is preferred by pedantic botanists because these plants may trap other small fauna (spiders for example) in addition to insects.

Intergeneric hybrid A hybrid involving species of two or more different genera, whether first generation or any subsequent generations or backcrosses. They are uncommon in the plant world generally, due to the greater genetic distance between genera than between species of the same genus, but are quite numerous among orchid hybrids—for example, the various hybrid combinations of the genera *Cattleya, Laelia, Sophronitis* and *Rhyncholaelia.* Bigeneric hybrid names are formed from parts of the names of the parent genera, with a multiplication sign placed before the name, thus × *Sophrocattleya* for hybrids between *Sophronitis* and *Cattleya.* Where 3 or more genera are involved the convention is now to attach the ending *-ara* to a personal name, thus × *Wilsonara* for hybrids involving *Odontoglossum, Oncidium* and *Cochlioda.*

Invasive (of plant species) Apt to spread rapidly, either by self-sown seedlings or by rhizomes or stolons, crowding out or smothering other garden plants or native vegetation.

Irregular (of flowers) Having the petals arranged in some way other than radial symmetry, though almost always bilaterally symmetrical, such as on orchids and violets. The scientific term is 'zygomorphic'. A few flowers lack even bilateral symmetry, for example, cannas.

Kernel The edible inner part of a nut, which is usually the seed, as in almonds.

Labellum The lowest of the three petals of an orchid, usually larger and more elaborately shaped and colored than the others. Also called a 'lip'.

Lanceolate (of leaves) Lance-shaped, applied in botany to leaves that taper to both ends, their length 4 to 9 times their width, and broadest at or below the middle. Broader leaves are mostly termed ovate or elliptic, narrower leaves linear.

Lateral A side shoot, growing from the axil of a leaf of the main stem. In many fruit trees it is these shoots that bear the flowers and ultimately the fruit.

Lax Weak-stemmed and consequently of rather floppy habit, for instance *Clianthus puniceus*, the opposite of erect or stiff.

Layering A method of propagation by which a branch of a plant is bent down to the ground where it takes root; the rooted section can then be severed from its parent and transplanted. It is most useful for plants that can be slow or reluctant to root from cuttings; some plants will layer themselves naturally.

Leader The main central growing shoot of a sapling, which eventually thickens to form the trunk of the adult tree. A double leader results when the leader forks at a narrow angle, regarded as undesirable because it weakens the tree.

Leaf The primary photosynthetic organ of green plants above the level of mosses (though even mosses have leaves of a sort).

Leaflet One of the several leaves into which a compound leaf such as a rose leaf is divided. A leaf has a bud in its axil; a leaflet does not.

Legume A member of the large pea family (Fabaceae or Leguminosae), which includes peas, beans, clover, lupins, wisteria, acacias, the various brooms, and some trees such as the cassias and locusts. They all share the ability to draw nitrogen straight from the air, by courtesy of bacteria that live in nodules on their roots.

Lime Compounds of calcium (principally calcium carbonate and calcium hydroxide) added to soil to make it more alkaline, and also to improve the structure of clay soil; a tropical fruit of the genus *Citrus*; deciduous trees of the genus *Tilia*, also known as lindens.
Linear (of leaves) Very long and narrow, such as the leaves of most grasses; in botany, used for any leaf with length more than about 9 times the width.
Lip In orchids, the same as labellum. In many tubular flowers, the upper and lower lobes at the mouth of the flower, where these are evident.
Lithophytic (of plants such as orchids) Growing on the naked surfaces of rocks and deriving nourishment from any litter they can accumulate around their roots—contrasted with epiphytic, which means growing perched on other plants. Many lithophytes are also epiphytes, growing on either rocks or trees but not in the ground.
Loam Soil of light texture, with a low clay content and roughly equal proportions of silt and sand (defined as the medium and large particle sizes of mineral soil), usually with a good humus content as well. Loams are valued as garden soils, being easily worked and allowing good root penetration, though varying in fertility.
Lobe Any division of a leaf or any other flat part of a plant, formed by the deep indentation of its margin. A typical maple leaf is a lobed leaf, though the lobes of maples are commonly toothed as well. Lobes can take many forms and shapes. A lobed leaf is not the same as a compound leaf, though the leaflets of some compound leaves may be lobed (for example, those of *Koelreuteria paniculata*)
Male Any plant that lacks functioning female organs and hence cannot produce seeds. Male plants produce pollen, required to fertilize the female organs if seed is to result. The majority of flowering plants are bisexual, bearing male and female organs on the one plant, though often in different flowers, which are then called male and female flowers (as in oaks and chestnuts).
Mallow A member of the moderately large plant family Malvaceae, though more narrowly of some of its herbaceous genera allied to *Malva*. A feature of the family (to which hibiscuses also belong) is the presence of a slimy mucilage layer under the very tough bark, often with mucilage also in leaves and roots. Marsh mallow is *Althaea officinalis*, its mucilage used in the original marshmallow.
Manure The dung of animals, used as fertilizer. Like all materials of organic origin it adds humus to the soil but may also be a rich source of nitrogen and sometimes phosphorus, depending on which animal it comes from and their diet at the time.
Margin The edge of any flat organ such as a leaf or petal. Features of the leaf margin such as teeth are important in plant identification.
Marginal plant One which in the wild grows in the swampy margins of ponds or lakes, and which can be cultivated in similar positions around a garden pond, such as *Iris ensata*. Most do not mind having their roots submerged for at least part of the year.
Mealybug Small sap-sucking insects of the family Coccidae, to which scale insects also belong. Mealybugs are tiny but easily seen, flattened and slow-moving, with a whitish water-repellent coating like flour dusted over cobwebby hairs. They hide on the undersides of leaves, among sheathing leaf bases, and among plant roots, thriving best on plants grown indoors in very open potting mix. They are persistent and difficult to eradicate.
Mediterranean (of plant distributions) Countries bordering the Mediterranean Sea, or at least those parts of them that are climatically influenced by the Mediterranean—for example, the southeastern thirds respectively of France and Spain, most of Italy, all the southern Balkans and much of Turkey. Only a narrow fringe of the coast and mountains of North Africa is truly Mediterranean. The Mediterranean climate is characteristically mild and wet in winter but hot and dry in summer. Similar climates in other parts of the world, notably California, western South Africa and coastal southern Australia are often termed 'Mediterranean'.
Mericlones Plants of the one clone raised by growing tiny pieces of tissue dissected from a plant's shoot tip (a meristem) in a sterile nutrient medium using laboratory techniques. Manipulation of growth with plant hormones is needed to make the tissue differentiate into stem, leaves and roots. Mericloning is mainly used for orchid hybrids and can produce a large number of plants of a desirable clone in a quite short period. Painstaking research is required to find successful techniques for mericloning each different group of plants.
Midrib The main central vein of a leaf; the central stalk to which the leaflets of a pinnate leaf are attached.
Mildew Certain kinds of fungi that form fine webs on the surfaces of organic materials, or on the leaves of live plants. Mildews thrive in warm, humid conditions and mainly affect plants that are not adapted to such conditions. Downy mildews are virulent plant diseases, the most notorious being downy mildew of grape.
Monocarpic A plant which flowers only once in its life and then dies, for example, *Agave victoriae-reginae* and the talipot palm *(Corypha umbraculifera)*.
Monocotyledon One of the two major subdivisions of the flowering plants (the other, larger one is the dicotyledons). Characterized by a single seed leaf, leaves mostly with parallel veining, and flower parts in threes or sixes. Major groups of monocotyledons are the grasses, sedges, lilies, orchids and palms.
Monoecious Having organs of both sexes on the one plant, though necessarily in the one flower.
Monopodial A plant has a monopodial growth habit if it continues apical growth of the same shoot indefinitely. In the orchids there is an obvious distinction between the monopodial habit and its main alternative, the sympodial habit, in which each shoot grows to a predetermined length (often terminating in an inflorescence) and new shoots branch from the base in succession. Vandas are monopodial, cattleyas sympodial.
Monsoonal A term applied to regions of the tropics and subtropics that experience a long dry season followed by a wet season with frequent heavy rain and thunderstorms, derived ultimately from an Arabic word 'mausim', for the rainy season. Plants adapted to monsoonal climates sometimes grow poorly in different climates.
Moss A large group of primitive non-flowering plants which normally grow on moist soil or rocks. Most are of very diminutive stature; some are occasionally cultivated as ground cover, for example, in Japanese gardens.
Mulch A blanket spread over the bare surface of soil to block the loss of moisture and to discourage the growth of weeds. Most mulches are of such organic matter as manure, compost, straw, bark chips, etc. which eventually rot and add humus to the soil, thus enhancing its fertility. Inorganic materials such as pebbles may also be also used.
Native Much the same as *indigenous*: a term denoting the relationship of a plant species to a particular geographical region.
Naturalized (of a plant species) Behaving like a native plant of a particular geographical region, though originally introduced from a distant region, either as a cultivated plant or accidentally as a weed.
Nectar The sugary liquid secreted by glands in the center of many flowers. Nectar is the most common reward for the insects, birds, bats or other fauna that effectively transfer pollen between flowers, thereby allowing the plant to reproduce. Honey is derived from nectar, concentrated by bees who store it in their hives.
Needle A leaf that is needle-like in form—most commonly used for the leaves of pines *(Pinus)*.
Neutral (of soils) Neither acid nor alkaline, that is having a pH of 7.
Node The point on a stem, often with a slight swelling, where a leaf is attached and its axillary bud grows. It is the place to cut when pruning, and also where the base of a cutting should be cut.
Noxious Used of particular weeds, also animal pests, that are universally disliked for the economic damage they cause, and generally implying the existence of a legal prohibition, or a requirement to take steps to control them.
Nut In botany, any fruit that is non-fleshy and does not release its seed or seeds when ripe; in normal use a nut is a dry fruit or seed that contains one or few edible kernels, or one of those kernels.
Nutrient In respect to plant growth, nutrients are the water-soluble substances taken up by the roots. The major nutrients, required in high concentration, are the elements nitrogen, phosphorus and potassium, while the minor nutrients include the elements iron, magnesium, calcium, manganese, zinc, boron, sulfur and molybdenum. These do not actually form the plant 'food', which consists of carbohydrates manufactured by photosynthesis from water and carbon dioxide, using the sun's energy, but they all have key positions in the protein and enzyme molecules essential to plant growth.
Oblong In botany, the shape of a leaf or any other flat plant organ that does not taper to each end, and of which the length is no more than about 8 times the width. An oblong leaf, unlike the oblong (or rectangle) of geometry, may have ends that are rounded to some degree.
Obovate (of leaves) More or less egg-shaped in outline but with the broadest part closer to the apex than to the stalk end.
Offset A shoot arising from the base of a plant which can be detached and used for propagation.
Opposite (of leaves) Arising in pairs, one opposite the other on either side of the stem. See *alternate*.
Orchid Any member of the family Orchidaceae, the second largest plant family after the composites, consisting of around 18,500 species occurring in nearly all parts of the world but most abundant in tropical rainforests, where they mostly grow as epiphytes. Orchids have flowers of complex structure, with bilateral symmetry and elaborate pollination mechanisms. Their seeds are the smallest of any flowering plant seeds, sometimes a million or more present in the one capsule, and contain no stored plant food. The growth of orchids depends on a symbiotic fungus in their fleshy roots.
Organic matter Material derived from things that were once alive, such as manure and compost, and which breaks down to form humus. The addition of organic matter improves the structure and fertility of any soil.
Ornamental A plant grown purely for its aesthetic attractions, rather than for food or any other economic use.
Ovary The lowest part of a carpel, containing the embryonic seeds (ovules). Ovaries positioned above the calyx are called 'superior', while those below the calyx are called 'inferior'.
Ovate (of leaves, bracts or petals) Egg-shaped in outline, with the widest point closer to the base than the apex (see *obovate*).

Palm Any member of the family Arecaceae (or Palmae), though in a loose sense used for certain other large monocotyledons such as bananas and *Ravenala*. The true palms, all but a small number of them from the tropics, are divided between feather palms, with pinnately divided leaves or fronds, and fan palms with palmately divided leaves. They are very diverse in growth habit but are nearly always long-lived.

Palmate (of leaves) Divided into lobes or leaflets that spread out from the end of the leaf stalk like the fingers of a hand, as in a maple leaf. *Digitate* has much the same meaning.

Panicle A type of inflorescence, strictly a compound raceme, as typified by that of the lilac.

Pantropical (of plant distributions) Occurring right around the world in the tropical zone, though many plants described as pantropical do spill over into some warmer parts of the temperate zones.

Parasite A plant which grows upon or within another, stealing moisture and nourishment from its host. Mistletoe is an example; more common and less welcome are the parasitic fungi that cause plant diseases.

Peat The preserved and compressed remains of dead bog plants, usually either sphagnum moss or sedges. The natural acidity of some bogs prevents the dead plant material from decaying, so that it accumulates and over time forms thick deposits. Peat is extracted from these deposits and used for many purposes, including horticultural uses. It is termed *moss peat* (or peat moss) when derived mainly from sphagnum, or *sedge peat* when formed from sedges.

Pendent or pendulous Hanging, the way the flower sprays of the wisteria do.

Perennial In botany, any plant that lives for three or more years; trees and shrubs are woody perennials, in contrast to herbaceous perennials which have no woody above-ground parts. In this book 'perennial' is used in the sense of herbaceous perennial.

Pergola A structure built in the garden, usually with walls or posts and a roof of open beams, on which climbing plants can be grown. A pergola may be circular or square, or elongated and open at the ends, forming a passageway.

Persistent A structure that stays on the plant after it serves its purpose, instead of falling off. The sepals of the rose which stay on the ripening rose hip are an example.

Pest Any of various kinds of fauna that infest garden plants, or disturb a garden. Insect pests are of most concern in gardens, causing much damage to prized plants, also slugs and snails. *Diseases* differ from pests in being caused by micro-organisms such as fungi and bacteria, or minute internal fauna such as eelworms.

Petals The whorl of enclosing organs of a flower that comes between sepals and stamens; the most colorful and conspicuous part of most flowers. The petals collectively form the *corolla*.

Petiole The stalk of a leaf. The stalk of a leaflet of a compound leaf is termed the *petiolule*.

pH The scale on which the acidity or alkalinity of soil is measured. It ranges from 1, an acid of fearsome strength, to 14, an alkali of equal ferocity, with 7 being the neutral point. Most garden soils fall somewhere between about pH 5.5 and 8.6.

Phyllode A kind of leaf in which the blade has dwindled, in the evolutionary sense, to the point of being absent or almost absent, and the leaf stalk (petiole) has expanded to take over the leaf's photosynthetic function. Many of the Australian species of *Acacia* are characterized by having phyllodes in the adult state, though their early seedling leaves are bipinnate.

Picotee A pattern of coloration in flowers, achieved mainly in carnation *(Dianthus)* cultivars, in which the petals each have a narrow border of strongly contrasting color giving the flower a lacy effect.

Pinch out The operation of removing the tip of a growing shoot, usually with the fingers, to encourage lateral shoots to grow and make the plant bushier.

Pinna, pinnule Botanist's terms for the leaflet of a pinnate and bipinnate leaf respectively.

Pinnate (of leaves) Compound and consisting of leaflets arranged on either side of a central stalk or rachis, as in a rose leaf or those of many palms and ferns. From the Latin pinna, a feather.

+ (plus sign) Though grafts do not usually hybridize, it does happen on very rare occasions, and the resulting plant is designated with the + sign, as with + *Laburnocytisus adamii*, a freak that occurred in a Paris nursery last century when a purple broom was grafted to laburnum stock to create a standard broom.

Pod Any fruit that is more or less elongated, thin-walled and with a hollow cavity containing the seeds. Most often used of the fruits of legumes.

Pollen The tiny grains of plant substance containing genetic material, which unite with the embryonic seeds contained in the ovary to create the fruit and hence a new generation of flowering plants—a process termed pollination. The transfer is usually carried out by insects, but can also be carried out by nectar-eating birds and sometimes by the wind.

Pollination The act of transference of pollen between flowers.

Pome A type of fruit, for example, apples or quinces, in which the true fruit, with several carpels each containing one or more seeds, is fused to and almost enclosed in a 'false fruit' derived from the receptacle (calyx-tube) of the flower, which enlarges greatly as the fruit develops. The *pome fruits* are this whole class of edible and ornamental fruits in the rose family, principally apples and pears but also including genera such as *Sorbus, Amelanchier, Crataegus, Chaenomeles* and *Mespilus.*

Pot A container for growing plants, roughly cylindrical in shape with a drainage hole or holes in the bottom. Traditionally made from terracotta, pots are now mostly plastic. Pots larger than about 15 in (50 cm) diameter are generally referred to as *tubs*.

Potpourri A mix of sweet-smelling dried herbs and petals, usually placed in a bowl or a small muslin bag to perfume a room. Rose petals and lavender flowers are common ingredients.

Prickle A sharp-pointed projection from a plant stem, leaf or fruit, as found in roses or blackberries. In botany prickles are distinguished from *thorns*, which are modified branchlets (as in hawthorn), and *spines*, which are modified leaves or stipules (as in cacti).

Propagate To intentionally multiply a particular plant, whether by sowing seed, taking cuttings, grafting, budding, division, or using tissue culture techniques in a laboratory.

Prostrate A plant of low-growing, ground-hugging habit, such as the prostrate junipers.

Pruning The art of cutting off parts of a plant to encourage more of the sort of growth the gardener desires, or to maintain a compact habit of growth.

Pseudobulb The fleshy, bulb-like stem found on many orchids.

Pseudostem The structure apparently supporting the leaves of some plants such as bananas and cannas that is in fact formed from the sheathing bases of the leaves, tightly furled around one another.

Pseudowhorls Apparent whorls of leaves, which on close examination are seen to be spirally arranged, the result of seasonal growth patterns in which the leaves are crowded at the end of a branch's growth spurt. Rhododendrons are an example.

Pteridophyte A large class of plants, some fossil members of which were among the earliest land plants, characterized by a lack of seeds and flowers, their means of dispersal being primarily minute spores that are carried by the wind. The ferns are the largest class of existing pteridophytes but they also include the clubmosses *(Lycopodium* and *Selaginella)* and the horsetails *(Equisetum)*.

Pubescent (of surfaces of leaves, stems, fruits) Having a covering of short, fine hairs, sometimes hardly visible to the eye except when lit from behind.

Pulses The dried, edible seeds of certain legumes, for example, chickpeas, lentils and peanuts.

Raceme A type of inflorescence, where the flowers are arranged around an elongated stem, each flower having a separate stalk, as in delphiniums.

Radial spine In cacti, those spines arising from each areole that radiate in much the same plane as the stem surface, as opposed to the central spine or spines that project outward. The relative number, size, thickness, coloration and curvature of the radial and central spines are important in cactus identification.

Rainforest Dense forest growing in regions of high rainfall, mainly in the tropics. True rainforest is characterized by an unbroken foliage canopy and the presence of many large climbing plants and epiphytes, though in cooler areas the epiphytes are mostly smaller mosses, liverworts and lichens.

Ray floret One of the apparent 'petals' of a daisy (or composite) flower, actually a small flower.

Reed A tall grass that grows in shallow water or boggy ground. The common reed is *Phragmites australis*, a species of worldwide occurrence.

Reflexed (Of leaves, leaf-tips, sepals etc.) Bent sharply downwards or backwards.

Revert To return to normal, as when a variegated plant starts producing plain green leaves.

Rhizomatous (of plant species) Characterized by having rhizomes.

Rhizome A stem that creeps on or below the surface, rooting as it goes, usually thickened and containing stored food, commonly the overwintering organ of perennials. The rhizomes are the edible part of the ginger plant.

Rock garden A garden or area of a larger garden constructed mainly of large rocks, carefully arranged as they might occur in nature. Not to be confused with the more humble rockery, which is usually smaller and less ambitious in scope.

Root The underground parts of a plant, which anchor tit in position and take up water and nutrients from the soil.

Rootstock The understock of a grafted plant; the base of a perennial where the roots grow.

Rosette A group of leaves radiating from the same point on a short stem, to give an effect like a green flower, as in sempervivums.

Runner A horizontally growing stem that roots at each node where it touches the ground, as in strawberries and violets.

Rush Any of a large group of monocotyledonous plants, commonly found in boggy and marshy areas, with erect tufts of thin, straight, green stems and heads of tiny drab-colored flowers. The true rushes belong to the large genus *Juncus* but the term is also used for certain of the sedges (family Cyperaceae). The flowering rush is *Butomus umbellatus.*

Rust fungus Any of a large group of plant-parasitic fungi characterized by the production of tiny but profuse spore-bodies that erupt from the host plant's leaves or stems, usually yellow, orange or rusty brown in color. Wheat rust is the most economically significant, but poplar rust is one of the most commonly and easily seen.

Sand The coarsest of the mineral components of soils, easily detected as grit by rubbing a pinch of soil between the fingers. Most sand is almost pure silica (quartz), one of the hardest and most insoluble minerals and containing no plant nutrients. Washed sand has many horticultural uses.

Savannah A kind of very open woodland, characteristic of many regions of the dry tropics and subtropics.

Scale insect Small sap-sucking insects of the family Coccidae (coccids), which in their adult phase are stationary on leaf and stem surfaces, coating themselves with an adhesive waxy shell which repels water and makes them difficult to eradicate. They can cause considerable damage to longer-lived plants such as trees and shrubs and are unsightly as well.

Scape A leafless flower stem that arises directly from the base of the plant, especially common in bulbs. The stems of narcissi and agapanthus are examples.

Scarify To break or soften the hard coat on the seeds of certain plants, especially legumes such as sweet peas and wattles, to allow water to penetrate and thus speed up germination. It can be done by rubbing carefully with fine sandpaper or soaking the seed for a little while in hot water.

Scientific name The internationally recognized Latin name of a plant which may be descriptive of a feature of the plant, or commemorate some person connected with it. The name of a species consists of two parts, the genus name and the species name. The system was first devised by the Swedish botanist Linnaeus in 1753.

Scion In grafting, the piece of plant stem of the desired variety that is grafted onto the rooted stock (or rootstock) and subsequently grows, comprising all the branches, flowers and fruit of the grafted plant.

Sedge Any member of the large plant family Cyperaceae, though sometimes used in a narrower sense for plants of its largest genus *Carex.*

Seed The organ of dispersal of flowering plants and gymnosperms. Seeds are not immortal, and it is not worth saving leftover seeds of vegetables and flowers for the following year; the percentage that will germinate decreases markedly.

Seed leaf (cotyledon) The leaves contained in the seed which are the first to appear when a seedling germinates; they are different from those that follow. The flowering plants are subdivided into 2 major classes, the *monocotyledons* and *dicotyledons*, according to whether they have one or two seed leaves.

Seedhead A general term for a dry, inedible fruit that contains seeds, or an inflorescence with developing seeds, as in grasses.

Self-sow, self-seed A plant's habit of shedding seeds around itself which germinate without the gardener's assistance.

Sepal One of the parts of the calyx, usually green, leaflike and sometimes colored and showy, as in hellebores and clematis. In many monocotyledonous plants the sepals are almost indistinguishable from the petals, as in lilies and tulips.

Series (also strain) A group of plants developed by a plant breeder and raised from seed and thus not genetically identical but sufficiently alike to be treated as a garden variety. A series may include several named cultivars, usually with the series name incorporated in their names. Most modern annual and vegetable seed is sold under a series name, though a true-breeding line of seedlings can be treated as a single cultivar.

Serrated (of leaf margins) Toothed, but with the teeth all forward-pointing, as the teeth of a saw.

Sessile (of leaves or flowers) Having no stalk, as the flowers of most camellias for example.

Sheath The expanded base of a leaf that wraps around the stem or shoot tip; a large bract that encloses a group of flowers in bud, as in the onion inflorescence.

Shoot Any aerial part of a plant that bears leaves, though in normal usage a shoot is an actively elongating stem or branch.

Shrub A woody perennial plant of low stature, generally less than about 15 ft (4.5 m) tall, and generally branching at or just above the ground into many stems. The distinction between a shrub and a tree is rather vague, some claiming that any plant with a single trunk is a tree, regardless of size, but this definition goes against general usage.

Silky Used of plant hairs that are colorless and lie flat and parallel, reflecting light and appearing somewhat like silk.

Simple (of leaves) Not compound, in the strict botanical meaning, though a heavily dissected leaf would not normally be called simple.

Single (of garden flowers) Having only a single row of petals: the opposite of double.

Smut A fungal disease characterized by spore-bodies appearing like small masses of black soot, usually infecting the seedheads of grasses.

Soft-wooded (of plants) Having stems and branches lacking very strong woody tissue, usually with a core of pith.

Solitary (of flowers) Not grouped into an inflorescence but appearing singly in leaf axils, ends of branches, or on a flowering stem.

Sorus (plural sori) Each group or patch of minute spore sacs (sporangia) on the fertile frond of a fern. They can take a variety of forms and are often shielded by a flap or hood of leafy tissue, the indusium.

Spadix A fleshy flower stalk which bears many tiny flowers—a speciality of the arum family.

Spathe Any bract that encloses the whole inflorescence (or partial inflorescence) in bud. Most commonly used of the arum family, where the spathe may be a large and specialized structure, but also applicable to, for example, the sheath of an onion flowerhead or the bracts enclosing the buds in irises.

Spatulate (or spathulate) Shaped like a traditional spatula, that is, rather narrowly wedge-shaped but rounded at the broad end.

Species A population of wild plants which are sufficiently alike to carry the same name, and which will freely breed with one another to give rise to offspring like themselves. The honor of naming a species goes to the scientist who discovers or describes it.

Sphagnum Moss of the genus *Sphagnum*, which grows in vast masses in bogs in cooler areas of the world, creating acid conditions in the water which inhibits decay when the lower parts of the moss eventually die, resulting in deep deposits of the dead moss (see *peat*). The dead moss is very spongy and can absorb large quantities of water; it is much used when dried as an ingredient in potting mixes, especially for orchids. Sphagnum often appears to come back to life when kept wet, but this may be due to the growth of green algae among its leaves.

Spike A type of inflorescence where the flowers are borne on an elongated, usually upright stem. Unlike a raceme, a spike has flowers lacking individual stalks. An example is gladiolus. In gardening the term spike is used more loosely for any elongated, unbranched inflorescence.

Spikelet The basic unit of the inflorescences of grasses, consisting of one or more tiny petal-less flowers hidden between bracts, which may be arranged in overlapping rows.

Spine In botanical usage a stiff, sharply pointed organ usually considered to be a modification of a leaf, stipule, bract or sepal. See *thorn* and *prickle.*

Spore The equivalent of a seed in non-flowering plants such as ferns and fungi. Much tinier than seeds, they are produced in great numbers and blow about on the wind.

Spreading A plant which grows much wider than it does tall, perhaps with mainly horizontal branches, perhaps by rooting in the ground and making an ever-expanding clump.

Spur A hollow projection from a petal, often containing nectar; the short flowering shoots on such plants as apples, pears or hoyas, which normally continue to flower and fruit for several years.

Stalk, stem The two terms are almost interchangeable, but in horticulture a stem usually has leaves growing from its sides while a stalk does not.

Stamen The basic male organ in a flower. The stamens usually form the next whorl in from the whorl of petals and are often partly fused to the petals. A stamen typically consists of a *filament* or stalk bearing at its tip the *anther*, the hollow organ containing the pollen. The pollen is released in most cases when the anther opens by slits or pores.

Standard The big petal that stands up at the back of a pea flower; a tree or shrub with a single, rather tall stem before the branches begin. Many trees grow thus naturally; shrubs like roses or fuchsias have to be trained to the form artificially. A half-standard has a shorter stem than usual.

Stem The main body of a plant, that connects the roots to the leaves and flowers, or any part of it. Trunks, branches and twigs are all stems.

Sterile Incapable of bearing seeds or pollen or both (flowers) or spores (the fronds of ferns). A plant may produce perfectly normal flowers but not mature fertile seed due to some aberration in its genetic make up, something which often occurs in hybrids; or the reproductive parts of the flower may have been transformed into the extra petals of a double flower.

Stigma The upper part of a carpel with specialized receptive cells on its surface, often slightly sticky and hence able to capture pollen grains from visiting insects or birds, or wind-borne pollen. The chemical environment of the stigma allows the pollen grain to germinate, sending a fine tube down through the style of the carpel, this tube containing the pollen parent's genetic material which then impregnates the ovules, resulting in seeds. Stigmas may be knob-like in form or have various other shapes, including star-shaped.

Stipule Leafy outgrowths at the base of a leaf stalk, as in roses or sweet peas. Stipules may be modified into spines, as in *Robinia* or may assume the same size and form as normal leaves, as in *Galium.*

Stock In grafting, the rooted plant (rootstock) onto which the scion is grafted. Any subsequent regrowth from the stock must be trimmed off as soon as it appears, otherwise it will rob food and water from the more desirable scion.

Stolon A slender, rapidly elongating rhizome, generally rooting only at long intervals. The stolons of strawberries are produced above ground, but stolons may also be buried, such as those produced by some bulbs as a means of extending their colonies.

Stoloniferous (of a plant species) Having stolons.

Stone The inner fruit wall of a drupe, when of a hard, bony or woody nature. The stone incloses the seed. Plums and cherries have stones.

Stratify A technique used to break the dormancy of seeds of such plants as roses and apples, which need a period of cold before they can germinate. In its simplest form, it involves bundling them up in damp sphagnum moss or peat and putting them in a refrigerator for a few weeks.

Strewing herb Term used for certain herbaceous plants of which the fragrant foliage was once strewn over the floors of such rooms as the dining halls of manor houses, to mask the bad smells from drains and putrefying food scraps. In England woodruff *(Galium)* and sweet vernal grass *(Anthoxanthum)* were typical strewing herbs.

Striate (or striated) (of leaves or stems) Ridged or

fluted along the length, as in *Sisyrinchium striatum.*
Strike The emergence of roots of a cutting.
Subarctic (of regions) The coolest parts of the northern temperate zone, close to the Arctic Circle.
Subshrub A perennial with more or less permanent aboveground but hardly woody stems, such as many pelargoniums ('geraniums'), or thyme.
Subspecies The next rank in plant classification below species, applied mainly to wild populations: thus a species may be subdivided into 2 or more subspecies, each usually with its own geographical distribution though these may sometimes overlap. As soon as the first subspecies name is published under any plant species, there is automatically created the concept of the typical subspecies, which normally repeats the name of the species. Thus *Veronica spicata* is now subdivided into the gray-leafed *V. spicata* subsp. *incana* and the 'normal' green-leafed *V. spicata* subsp. *spicata*. In this and other horticulturally oriented books the typical subspecies name is omitted but implied, in particular when one of the other subspecies is listed. The abbreviation 'subsp.' is preferred as the alternative 'ssp.' is easily confused with 'spp.' (plural of 'sp.').
Subtropical Applied to regions of the world usually no more than 5 to 10 degrees higher in latitude than the Tropics of Cancer or Capricorn and enjoying a climate that is virtually tropical.
Succulent A plant which has evolved swollen organs, either stems or leaves, which store water and help it to survive in arid climates. The cacti include many extreme examples, as do the African euphorbias and the large mesembryanthemum tribe, but other plants show succulence to a lesser degree, as many orchids do in their pseudobulbs.
Sucker A shoot or stem that arises from the roots or trunk base of a tree or shrub or, undesirably, from the understock of a grafted specimen.
Synonym (usually abbreviated to 'syn.') A scientific name which, though no longer accepted, still lingers in use, *Cyrtostachys renda* syn. *C. lakka.*
Taproot The main root of a plant, which plunges straight down to anchor it; the swollen taproots of carrots are some of the most familiar. Most trees have them too, and resent them being damaged.
Temperate Strictly speaking, those regions lying between the tropic of Capricorn and the Arctic Circle and between the Tropic of Cancer and the Antarctic Circle, known as the north and south temperate zones respectively. Used in a more general way to refer to climates without extremes of heat or cold. Often subdivided approximately into cool-temperate, warm-temperate, and subtropical, the latter applying to regions no more than 5 to 10 degrees of latitude beyond the tropic.
Tendril A cord-like structure which some climbing plants wrap around a branch or wire to support themselves. They are modifications of other plant organs, usually leaf-tips (gloriosa), leaflets of compound leaves (sweet peas), stipules (clematis) or inflorescences (grapes).
Terete (of plant organs such as stems and leaves) Approximately circular in cross-section, and elongated.
Terminal (of inflorescences and flowers) Appearing at the end of a shoot, as with roses, marigolds and poinsettias.
Terrestrial (of plant species) Growing in the ground, the way most plants do, rather than in water (aquatic) or perched on trees (epiphytic).
Thorn A short lateral branch with a sharp point, as in hawthorns *(Crataegus)* and firethorns *(Pyracantha)*. See *prickle* and *spine.*
Throat The inside part of a trumpet- or tube-shaped flower, often displaying, as in foxgloves and gloxinias, a different pattern or color to guide insects.
Toothed (of leaves) with teeth or serrations on the margin, as in rose leaves. In botanical usage toothing is distinguished as dentate, with teeth pointing straight out, or serrate, with teeth pointing forward as in a saw.
Topiary The art of clipping suitable trees or shrubs such as yew, privet or box into artificial shapes, such as pyramids, globes, peacocks, etc.
Tree A woody plant, usually reaching a height of more than about 15 ft (4.5 m) and tending to have a single main trunk at least in the sapling stage. There is some overlap in definition between a small tree and a tall shrub, but this is virtually confined to plants in the 10–20 ft (3–6 m) height range, and it is only in these cases that habit of growth may be the deciding issue.
Tree fern A fern with a straight, erect stem usually reaching a height of more than 6 ft (1.8 m) or sometimes as much as 50 ft (15 m) tall, bearing at its apex a crown of large fronds. Most of the world's tree ferns belong to the genera *Cyathea, Cibotium* or *Dicksonia* and come from high-rainfall regions of the tropics and subtropics.
Trellis A structure or arrangement of wires or rods held up by posts or frames, specifically for the support of climbing plants. It may be freestanding in a garden, or attached to the wall of a house. The most highly developed forms of trellis are those on which grapes are grown commercially for wine or fruit; they are also used for peas, beans, hops and cucumbers.
Tri- In compound words, indicating three, as trifoliate, tripinnate, etc.
Trifoliate (of compound leaves) Consisting of 3 leaflets. The more pedantic botanists insist that the correct word is *trifoliolate* from the Latin *foliolum* for leaflet.
Tripinnate (of compound leaves) Like bipinnate but carried to one further stage of division, so that the leaflets (of a basically pinnate leaf) are themselves pinnate and the resulting leaflets are again pinnate. Many tree ferns have tripinnate (sometimes even quadripinnate) leaves.
Tropical (of regions) Lying anywhere between the Tropic of Capricorn and the Tropic of Cancer, in what was once known as the 'torrid zone'—defined as the part of the globe in which the sun is directly overhead at least once each year. Plants do not observe these strict divisions and many tropical plant groups spill over into the subtropics. Also many plants coming from mountain areas of the tropics are moderately frost-tolerant, whereas lowland tropical plants are nearly always frost tender.
Trunk The central stem of a tree: at least that part of it below the first branches, and often continuing upward as the dominant supporting element of the tree's canopy, as in firs, spruces and most pines. The stems of larger palms are also referred to as trunks, though of different structure and behaviour from the trunks of true (dicotyledonous) trees.
Truss Used for certain inflorescences with a tight grouping of large flowers held above the foliage, as in many rhododendron hybrids.
Tuber A swollen, starchy underground organ designed to store food for a plant during its dormancy. Many tubers, such as those of the potato, provide food for humans too.
Tubercle An outgrowth from a stem, leaf or fruit, usually hemispherical to rather more cylindrical. The stems of many kinds of cacti are covered in a regular arrangement of tubercles, most notably *Mammillaria.*
Tuberous root A root that is swollen to resemble a tuber, as in dahlias. Most root tubers will not sprout again when cut away, unless a small piece of the stem or rootstock is taken as well.
Twig Any of the smallest branches of a tree or shrub, though only used for those that are thin and weak.
Twining (of climbing plants) Gaining height by growing in a spiral manner around a support that is more or less vertically oriented, such as a stake or a tree sapling. A species of twiner is nearly always constant in its direction of twining, whether clockwise or anticlockwise (hence 'the right-handed honeysuckle and the left-handed bindweed'). The shoot apex of a twiner can sweep in a broad circle up to several times in a day in order to detect a possible support, which it then 'senses' and begins to twine around.
Umbel A type of inflorescence in which several to many flower stalks arise from one point, as in onions, agapanthus or parsley.
Upright A growth habit in which at least the main branches grow more or less vertically.
Variegated Variegated plants have patterns of other colors as well as green on their leaves, and usually grow less strongly than their plain-leafed counterparts, as they have less chlorophyll. They are usually the result of cultivation and are sometimes caused by viruses though some species, notably *Coleus blumei,* are variegated naturally.
Variety Strictly speaking, a group of plants arising in the wild which though not sufficiently different from the norm of their species to be of great interest to botanists (they may only differ in flower color, for instance) are different enough to be of interest to gardeners. A variety is designated as, for instance, *Acacia longifolia* var. *sophorae*, the var. being short for *varietas*. Varieties created by gardeners are supposed to be called cultivars and not given Latin names.
Vein Any one of the strands of conducting tissue visible through the surface of a leaf or flower petal, though also used for the linear patterns on some petals designed to guide pollinating insects to the nectar. The pattern of venation of a leaf is characteristic for each plant species and is an important aid to identification. The primary vein is often called the midvein or midrib and secondary veins are alternatively called lateral veins; tertiary veins commonly form a reticulate pattern in dicotyledons, but in most monocotyledons (for example, grasses, lilies) nearly all the leaf veins lie parallel.
Viability The capacity for germination or renewed growth in a stored seed or bulb. Seeds vary greatly in the time they remain viable, from a few days in some tropical trees such as cocoa, to a few weeks in camellias, to more than 20 years in the case of many hard-seeded legumes. Viability is also greatly affected by storage conditions, being improved by low temperature and humidity.
Vine Historically, a grape plant *(Vitis vinifera)*, but used more loosely for climbing plants generally, or even for some sprawling plants such as pumpkins.
Virus The infective agents of a wide range of plant diseases, which as in human viral diseases, cannot be eliminated by any chemical agent and are thus incurable. They may be fatal or very debilitating to the plants and some viral diseases are much feared by commercial growers. However, some viruses are relatively benign, such as the one that makes tulips 'break' into stripes.
Warm-temperate Usually applied to the upper-middle parts of the temperate zones, between about 30 and 40 degrees of latitude, where at least in coastal areas frost is absent or very light. See *cool-temperate* and *subtropical.*
Water plant The same as aquatic.
Weed Any plant that is unwanted and a nuisance in the context of a particular environment, whether it be a garden, a cultivated field, a pasture or in natural woodland or forest. In natural vegetation weeds are almost by definition exotic to the region, but in gardens they may include some native plants. Weeds cause much economic loss and there is a large

industry devoted to their control. They compete with cultivated plants for water, nutrients and sunlight as well as contaminating harvested crops, or spoiling the aesthetics of ornamental plantings.

Weeping Used mostly for trees and shrubs with pendulous branches or branchlets, as in weeping willows.

White fly Very small, winged, sap-sucking insects of the family Aleyrodidae, which belongs to the same order of insects as the aphids. They settle on some cultivated plants, for example, cabbages, in large numbers and affect their health. White flies are a particularly bad pest of greenhouse and indoor plants, but are fairly easily controlled by spraying.

Whorl Usually of leaves, an arrangement where three or more arise at the same node, as in oleanders. Flowers can arise in whorls around the stalks also, as in *Primula malacoides*.

Wing A thin, flat projection running lengthwise down a stem or leaf stalk; a flat projection from a seed of dry fruit, aiding its dispersal by wind.

Wood A feature of dicotyledonous trees and shrubs, being the tissue laid down inside the bark cylinder by the dividing cells of the cambium layer. It consists largely of a cellulose framework with the denser carbohydrate lignin deposited in the cell walls. The living outer part (sapwood) is the main tissue by which water and dissolved nutrients are conducted upward through the tree, and its cells contain starch (which provides food for borers). 'Woods' is an alternative term for forest, especially in the USA, while in gardening 'wood' is used with various qualifying adjectives to indicate the stage of maturity of a plant's branches or twigs, as in 'new wood', 'old wood', 'previous year's wood', and so on.

Woodland garden A garden established beneath trees (usually deciduous) in partial shade or even quite deep shade. It suits plants that require shelter and humidity and whose roots need to remain undisturbed.

Woody (of plant species) Developing stems which, although they may not be big enough to use as timber, contain permanent woody tissue. Trees and shrubs are characteristically woody, but many climbers, such as the grape, are also woody.

× **(multiplication sign)** A sign placed in front of the Latin name of a plant to indicate that the plant is of hybrid origin, whether natural or artificial; as in *Camellia* × *williamsii* or × *Brassolaeliocattleya* Sylvia Fry.

Plant Families and Their Relationships

In the following pages every genus of plants in this book is listed under the plant family to which it belongs. The families in turn are arranged under headings which reflect successively higher levels of relationship. (For an explanation of plant names, see page 946.)

For the last two centuries, botanists have been refining systems of classification of the whole plant kingdom. Modern classifications, based on improved knowledge of plant structures, show radical differences from some of the traditional classifications—the fungi, for example, are not now regarded as even belonging to the plant kingdom, but rather form a kingdom of their own. But the vast amount of scientific data available can be interpreted in many different ways, with different botanists placing emphasis on different characteristics, and so even at the present time there are a number of rival systems of plant classification. This is particularly the case for the higher levels of classification, where the plant kingdom is divided into major groups such as algae, mosses, ferns and their allies, conifers and flowering plants; there is a plethora of scientific names for these groups and their subdivisions and no two published classifications use the same names.

The division of the plant kingdom most familiar to gardeners is the **Flowering Plants**. Although the most recent group to appear in the geological record, they now form the great bulk of the world's land vegetation and show an extraordinary degree of diversity. Well over 90 per cent of the entries in this book are flowering plants, the remainder being divided between gymnosperms (mainly conifers) and pteridophytes (mainly ferns); no algae or mosses are included in this book. A glance at the list below will show the predominance of flowering plant families and genera.

The scheme of classification of the flowering plants used here is based rather loosely on that of Dahlgren, a recent Danish botanist. Dahlgren's system recognizes a larger number of plant families than another well known recent system, that of the American Cronquist. This is particularly the case in the 'lily' group of monocotyledon families, where Cronquist's single large family Liliaceae is divided by Dahlgren into more than thirty families (about twenty of them listed here). In these and other cases of alternative classifications, we have shown both possible family names, separated by an oblique stroke, **Hyacinthaceae/Liliaceae** is an example. In a few cases three alternative names are shown.

As well as differences in classification which reflect differing scientific judgements, there are differences in nomenclature of some family names that persist among botanists, to the irritation and confusion of gardeners and others. The general convention for forming a family name is to take a genus name (or its etymological stem) and add the ending -aceae (pronounced ay-see-ee)—thus we have Pinaceae, based on the genus name *Pinus*. But botanists traditionally allowed a number of exceptions to this rule, best known being the family names Leguminosae, Compositae and Gramineae. The present-day practice is to disallow these traditional names and insist that all family names be properly formed: thus Leguminosae becomes Fabaceae, Compositae becomes Asteraceae, Gramineae becomes Poaceae. This practice is followed below, but the traditional names are given in brackets, for example, **Asteraceae (Compositae)**.

Most confusing are the many styles of referring to the legume family, here called **Fabaceae:** these involve both disagreement as to whether this is a single family consisting of three subfamilies or should be split into three separate families, and the names to be used for both the one and the three families. The confusion is compounded by the existence of a third name, Papilionaceae, which has been used in place of either Fabaceae or Leguminosae. Here we place the legumes in a single family divided into three subfamilies, and indicate only some of the alternative names.

The families are grouped into larger units of classification known variously as divisions, subdivisions, classes, subclasses and superorders by botanists. Their exact status is of little concern to gardeners, but they are shown here to allow some sort of overview of the way plant families relate to one another, and how they fit into the larger scheme of things. In the case of the flowering plants, the units under which families are grouped are Dahlgren's superorders, all of which end in -florae.

The classification outlined below gives a number to each plant family. It is followed by an alphabetical listing of all genera found in the book, with each genus given the number of the family to which it belongs.

Pteridophytes

Psilotopsida
1 Psilotaceae
Psilotum

Lycopsida (clubmosses)
2 Lycopodiaceae
Lycopodium
3 Selaginellaceae
Selaginella

Equisetopsida (horsetails)
4 Equisetaceae
Equisetum

Filicopsida (true ferns)
5 Osmundaceae
Osmunda
6 Schizaeaceae
Anemia, Lygodium
7 Gleicheniaceae
Sticherus
8 Cyatheaceae
Cyathea
9 Dicksoniaceae
Dicksonia
10 Pteridaceae/Adiantaceae
Pteris
11 Taenitidaceae/Adiantaceae
Pityrogramma
12 Hemionitidaceae/Adiantaceae
Hemionitis
13 Sinopteridaceae/Adiantaceae
Pellaea
14 Adiantaceae
Adiantum, Doryopteris, Onychium
15 Davalliaceae
Davallia, Nephrolepis
16 Polypodiaceae
Hymenolepis, Microsorum, Phlebodium, Platycerium, Polypodium, Pyrrosia
17 Dryopteridaceae/Aspleniaceae
Cyrtomium, Dryopteris, Polystichum
18 Athyriaceae/Aspleniaceae
Athyrium
19 Onocleaceae/Aspleniaceae
Onoclea
20 Aspleniaceae
Asplenium, Elaphoglossum, Gymnocarpium, Matteuccia, Woodsia,
21 Blechnaceae
Blechnum, Doodia, Woodwardia
22 Marsileaceae
Marsilea
23 Azollaceae
Azolla
24 Salviniaceae
Salvinia

Gymnosperms

Ginkgoopsida (ginkgo)
25 Ginkgoaceae
Ginkgo

Cycadopsida (cycads)
26 Cycadaceae
Cycas
27 Zamiaceae/Cycadaceae
Dioon, Encephalartos, Lepidozamia, Macrozamia, Zamia

Pinopsida (conifers)
28 Podocarpaceae
Afrocarpus, Dacrycarpus, Dacrydium, Lagarostrobos, Phyllocladus, Podocarpus, Prumnopitys, Saxegothaea
29 Taxaceae
Taxus, Torreya
30 Cephalotaxaceae/Taxaceae
Cephalotaxus
31 Araucariaceae
Agathis, Araucaria, Wollemia
32 Pinaceae
Abies, Cedrus, Larix, Picea, Pinus, Pseudolarix, Pseudotsuga, Tsuga
33 Taxodiaceae/Cupressaceae
Athrotaxis, Cryptomeria, Cunninghamia, Glyptostrobus, Metasequoia, Sciadopitys, Sequoia, Sequoiadendron, Taiwania, Taxodium
34 Cupressaceae
Austrocedrus, Callitris, Calocedrus, Chamaecyparis, ×Cupressocyparis, Cupressus, Fitzroya, Fokienia, Juniperus, Libocedrus, Microbiota, Platycladus, Thuja, Thujopsis, Widdringtonia

Gnetopsida
35 Welwitschiaceae
Welwitschia
36 Ephedraceae
Ephedra

Flowering Plants (Magnoliopsida) A – Dicotyledons

Magnoliiflorae
37 Winteraceae
Drimys, Pseudowintera, Tasmannia
38 Magnoliaceae
Liriodendron, Magnolia, Manglietia, Michelia, Talauma
39 Myristicaceae
Myristica
40 Annonaceae
Annona, Artabotrys, Asimina, Cananga, Polyalthia
41 Nelumbonaceae
Nelumbo
42 Atherospermataceae/Monimiaceae
Atherosperma
43 Calycanthaceae
Calycanthus, Chimonanthus, Idiospermum
44 Lauraceae
Beilschmiedia, Cinnamomum, Laurus, Lindera, Persea, Sassafras, Umbellularia
45 Hernandiaceae
Hernandia
46 Illiciaceae
Illicium
47 Schisandraceae
Kadsura
48 Aristolochiaceae
Aristolochia, Asarum
49 Rafflesiaceae
Rafflesia

Nymphaeiflorae
50 Saururaceae
Anemopsis, Houttuynia
51 Piperaceae
Macropiper, Piper
52 Peperomiaceae/Piperaceae
Peperomia
53 Nymphaeaceae
Euryale, Nuphar, Nymphaea, Victoria
54 Cabombaceae
Cabomba
55 Ceratophyllaceae
Ceratophyllum

Ranunculiflorae
56 Ranunculaceae
Aconitum, Actaea, Adonis, Anemone, Anemonella, Anemonopsis, Aquilegia, Caltha, Cimicifuga, Clematis, Consolida, Delphinium, Eranthis, Helleborus, Hepatica, Nigella, Pulsatilla, Ranunculus, Semiaquilegia, Thalictrum, Trollius,
57 Berberidaceae
Berberis, Caulophyllum, Epimedium, Mahonia, Vancouveria
58 Nandinaceae/Berberidaceae
Nandina
59 Podophyllaceae/Berberidaceae
Diphylleia, Jeffersonia, Podophyllum
60 Lardizabalaceae
Akebia, Decaisnea, Holboellia, Stauntonia
61 Menispermaceae
Menispermum
62 Coriariaceae
Coriaria
63 Papaveraceae
Argemone, Bocconia, Chelidonium, Dendromecon, Eomecon, Eschscholzia, Glaucium, Hunnemannia, Macleaya, Meconopsis, Papaver, Platystemon, Romneya, Sanguinaria, Stylophorum
64 Fumariaceae/Papaveraceae
Adlumia, Corydalis, Dicentra

Caryophylliflorae
65 Phytolaccaceae
Ercilla, Phytolacca
66 Nyctaginaceae
Abronia, Bougainvillea, Mirabilis, Pisonia
67 Aizoaceae
Aptenia, Argyroderma, Carpobrotus, Cheiridopsis, Conophytum, Cylindrophyllum, Delosperma, Dorotheanthus, Drosanthemum, Faucaria, Fenestraria, Gibbaeum, Glottiphyllum, Lampranthus, Lithops, Malephora, Mesembryanthemum, Ophthalmophyllum, Oscularia, Pleiospilos, Ruschia, Tetragonia, Titanopsis, Trichodiadema
68 Cactaceae
Aporocactus, Ariocarpus, Astrophytum, Browningia, Carnegiea, Cephalocereus, Cereus, Chamaecereus, Cleistocactus, Denmoza, Echinocactus, Echinocereus, Echinopsis, ×Epicactus, Epiphyllum, Epithelantha, Escobaria, Espostoa, Eulychnia, Ferocactus, Frailea, Gymnocalycium, Haageocereus, Hatiora, Hylocereus, Leuchtenbergia, Lophocereus, Lophophora, Mammillaria, Matucana, Melocactus, Myrtillocactus, Neoporteria, Nopalxochia, Opuntia, Oreocereus, Pachycereus, Parodia, Pelecyphora, Pereskia, Pilosocereus, Rebutia, Rhipsalis, Schlumbergera, Selenicereus, Stenocactus, Stenocereus, Strombocactus, Thelocactus
69 Chenopodiaceae
Atriplex, Bassia, Beta, Spinacia
70 Amaranthaceae
Achyranthes, Alternanthera, Amaranthus, Celosia, Gomphrena, Iresine, Ptilotus
71 Portulacaceae
Calandrinia, Ceraria, Claytonia, Lewisia, Neopaxia, Portulaca, Portulacaria, Talinum
72 Basellaceae
Anredera, Basella
73 Caryophyllaceae
Agrostemma, Arenaria, Cerastium, Dianthus, Gypsophila, Lychnis, Minuartia, Paronychia, Sagina, Saponaria, Scleranthus, Silene, Stellaria

Polygoniflorae
74 Polygonaceae
Antigonon, Coccoloba, Eriogonum, Fagopyrum, Fallopia, Homalocladium, Muehlenbeckia, Persicaria, Rheum, Rumex

Theiflorae
75 Dilleniaceae
Dillenia, Hibbertia
76 Paeoniaceae
Glaucidium, Paeonia
77 Ochnaceae
Ochna
78 Theaceae
Camellia, Cleyera, Eurya, Franklinia, Gordonia, Schima, Stewartia, Ternstroemia
79 Actinidiaceae
Actinidia
80 Clusiaceae (Guttiferae)
Calophyllum, Clusia, Garcinia, Hypericum
81 Lecythidaceae
Barringtonia, Couroupita, Planchonia

Malviflorae
82 Elaeocarpaceae
Aristotelia, Crinodendron, Elaeocarpus, Sloanea
83 Tiliaceae
Grewia, Sparrmannia, Tilia
84 Sterculiaceae
Brachychiton, Chiranthodendron, Dombeya, Firmiana, Fremontodendron, Heritiera, Hermannia, Sterculia, Theobroma
85 Bombacaceae
Adansonia, Bombax, Ceiba, Chorisia, Durio, Pachira
86 Malvaceae
Abelmoschus, Abutilon, Alcea, Althaea, Alyogyne, Anisodontea, Gossypium, Hibiscus, Hoheria, Lagunaria, Lavatera, Malva, Malvastrum, Malvaviscus, Pavonia, Phymosia, Plagianthus, Sidalcea, Sphaeralcea, Thespesia
87 Plumbaginaceae
Acantholimon, Armeria, Ceratostigma, Limonium, Plumbago, Psylliostachys
88 Elaeagnaceae
Elaeagnus, Hippophae, Shepherdia

89 Thymelaeaceae
Dais, Daphne, Edgeworthia, Pimelea
90 Ulmaceae
Celtis, Hemiptelea, Pteroceltis, Ulmus, Zelkova
91 Cannabidaceae
Cannabis, Humulus
92 Moraceae
Artocarpus, Broussonetia, Dorstenia, Ficus, Maclura, Morus
93 Cecropiaceae/Moraceae
Cecropia
94 Urticaceae
Elatostema, Pilea, Soleirolia, Urtica
95 Euphorbiaceae
Acalypha, Aleurites, Breynia, Codiaeum, Euphorbia, Hevea, Jatropha, Manihot, Omalanthus, Pedilanthus, Phyllanthus, Ricinus, Sapium, Synadenium, Vernicia
96 Rhamnaceae
Ceanothus, Colletia, Discaria, Hovenia, Paliurus, Phylica, Pomaderris, Rhamnus, Ziziphus

Violiflorae

97 Flacourtiaceae
Azara, Berberidopsis, Dovyalis, Idesia, Oncoba, Scolopia
98 Bixaceae
Bixa
99 Cochlospermaceae/Bixaceae
Cochlospermum
100 Cistaceae
Cistus, ×Halimiocistus, Halimium, Helianthemum
101 Stachyuraceae
Stachyurus
102 Violaceae
Hymenanthera, Viola
103 Tamaricaceae
Tamarix
104 Frankeniaceae
Frankenia
105 Passifloraceae
Passiflora
106 Caricaceae
Carica
107 Cucurbitaceae
Benincasa, Citrullus, Cucumis, Cucurbita, Ecballium, Kedrostis, Lagenaria, Luffa, Sechium, Thladiantha
108 Begoniaceae
Begonia
109 Loasaceae
Mentzelia
110 Salicaceae
Populus, Salix
111 Capparidaceae
Capparis, Cleome, Crateva, Steriphoma
112 Brassicaceae (Cruciferae)
Aethionema, Alliaria, Alyssum, Arabis, Armoracia, Aubrieta, Aurinia, Barbarea, Brassica, Cardamine, Cochlearia, Crambe, Draba, Eruca, Erysimum, Hesperis, Iberis, Isatis, Lobularia, Lunaria, Malcolmia, Matthiola, Nasturtium, Peltaria, Raphanus, Vella
113 Moringaceae
Moringa
114 Resedaceae
Reseda

Corniflorae

115 Cyrillaceae
Cyrilla
116 Clethraceae
Clethra
117 Epacridaceae
Epacris, Richea
118 Ericaceae
Agapetes, Agarista, Andromeda, Arbutus, Arctostaphylos, Bruckenthalia, Calluna, Cassiope, Cavendishia, Comarostaphylis, Daboecia, Enkianthus, Erica, Gaultheria, Kalmia, Kalmiopsis, Ledum, Leiophyllum, Leucothoë, Lyonia, Macleania, Menziesia, Oxydendrum, ×Phylliopsis, Phyllodoce, Pieris, Rhododendron, Tsusiophyllum, Vaccinium, Zenobia
119 Diapensiaceae
Galax, Shortia
120 Eucommiaceae
Eucommia
121 Sarraceniaceae
Darlingtonia, Heliamphora, Sarracenia
122 Nepenthaceae
Nepenthes
123 Droseraceae
Dionaea, Drosera
124 Fouquieriaceae
Fouquieria
125 Alangiaceae
Alangium
126 Cornaceae
Aucuba, Cornus, Davidia, Griselinia
127 Nyssaceae/Cornaceae
Camptotheca, Nyssa
128 Corokiaceae/Cornaceae
Corokia
129 Garryaceae
Garrya
130 Caprifoliaceae
Abelia, Diervilla, Dipelta, Kolkwitzia, Leycesteria, Linnaea, Lonicera, Sambucus, Symphoricarpos, Viburnum, Weigela
131 Valerianaceae
Centranthus, Valeriana, Valerianella
132 Dipsacaceae
Cephalaria, Dipsacus, Knautia, Pterocephalus, Scabiosa
133 Morinaceae
Morina

Araliiflorae

134 Araliaceae
Aralia, Brassaia, Cussonia, Eleutherococcus, Fatshedera, Fatsia, Hedera, Kalopanax, Meryta, Panax, Polyscias, Pseudopanax, Schefflera, Tetrapanax, Trevesia
135 Apiaceae (Umbelliferae)
Aciphylla, Actinotus, Aegopodium, Ammi, Anethum, Angelica, Anthriscus, Apium, Astrantia, Azorella, Bolax, Bupleurum, Carum, Centella, Coriandrum, Cuminum, Daucus, Eryngium, Ferula, Foeniculum, Hacquetia, Heracleum, Hydrocotyle, Levisticum, Meum, Myrrhis, Oenanthe, Pastinaca, Petroselinum, Pimpinella, Seseli, Trachymene
136 Rubiaceae
Alberta, Asperula, Bouvardia, Burchellia, Carrierea, Coffea, Coprosma, Emmenopterys, Galium, Gardenia, Hamelia, Hedyotis, Ixora, Luculia, Manettia, Mitchella, Mussaenda, Nauclea, Nertera, Pentas, Phuopsis, Psychotria, Putoria, Rondeletia, Rothmannia, Rubia, Serissa
137 Pittosporaceae
Billardiera, Bursaria, Hymenosporum, Pittosporum, Sollya

Primuliflorae

138 Sapotaceae
Sideroxylon
139 Ebenaceae
Diospyros
140 Styracaceae
Halesia, Pterostyrax, Styrax
141 Myrsinaceae
Ardisia, Myrsine
142 Primulaceae
Anagallis, Androsace, Cyclamen, Dionysia, Dodecatheon, Hottonia, Lysimachia, Primula, Soldanella

Rosiflorae

143 Trochodendraceae
Trochodendron
144 Cercidiphyllaceae
Cercidiphyllum
145 Platanaceae
Platanus
146 Hamamelidaceae
Corylopsis, Disanthus, Exbucklandia, Fothergilla, Hamamelis, Liquidambar, Loropetalum, Parrotia, Rhodoleia
147 Buxaceae
Buxus, Pachysandra, Sarcococca, Simmondsia
148 Juglandaceae
Carya, Juglans, Pterocarya
149 Myricaceae
Myrica
150 Fagaceae
Castanea, Chrysolepis, Fagus, Lithocarpus, Nothofagus, Quercus
151 Betulaceae
Alnus, Betula
152 Carpinaceae/Betulaceae
Carpinus, Ostrya
153 Corylaceae/Betulaceae
Corylus
154 Casuarinaceae
Allocasuarina, Casuarina, Gymnostoma
155 Eucryphiaceae
Eucryphia
156 Cunoniaceae
Callicoma, Ceratopetalum, Cunonia, Weinmannia
157 Baueraceae/Cunoniaceae
Bauera
158 Hydrangeaceae/Saxifragaceae
Carpenteria, Decumaria, Deinanthe, Deutzia, Hydrangea, Kirengeshoma, Philadelphus, Pileostegia, Schizophragma
159 Grossulariaceae/ Saxifragaceae
Ribes
160 Escalloniaceae
Anopterus, Carpodetus, Escallonia, Itea
161 Greyiaceae
Greyia
162 Bruniaceae
Berzelia
163 Crassulaceae
Adromischus, Aeonium, Aichryson, Bryophyllum, Chiastophyllum, Cotyledon, Crassula, Dudleya, Echeveria, Graptopetalum, Greenovia, Jovibarba, Kalanchoe, Pachyphytum, ×Pachyveria, Rhodiola, Rosularia, Sedum, Sempervivum
164 Saxifragaceae
Astilbe, Bergenia, Boykinia, Chrysosplenium, Darmera, Francoa, Heuchera, ×Heucherella, Mitella, Parnassia, Rodgersia, Saxifraga, Tellima, Tiarella, Tolmiea
165 Gunneraceae/Haloragaceae
Gunnera
166 Rosaceae
Acaena, Adenostoma, Agrimonia, Alchemilla, Amelanchier, Aronia, Aruncus, Cercocarpus, Chaenomeles, Chamaebatiaria, Cotoneaster, Cowania, +Crataegomespilus, Crataegus, ×Crataemespilus, Cydonia, Dryas, Duchesnea, Eriobotrya, Exochorda, Fallugia, Filipendula, Fragaria, Geum, Gillenia, Heteromeles, Holodiscus, Kerria, Lyonothamnus, Malus, Margyricarpus, Mespilus, Neviusia, Osteomeles, Photinia, Physocarpus, Potentilla, Prinsepia, Prunus, Pseudocydonia, Pyracantha, Pyrus, Quillaja, Rhaphiolepis, Rhodotypos, Rosa, Rubus, Sanguisorba, Sarcobatus, Sorbaria, Sorbus, Spiraea, Stephanandra, Waldsteinia
167 Chrysobalanaceae
Chrysobalanus

Fabiflorae (legumes)

168.1 Fabaceae subfam. Caesalpinioideae /Caesalpiniaceae
Acrocarpus, Amherstia, Barklya, Bauhinia, Brownea, Caesalpinia, Cassia, Ceratonia, Cercidium, Cercis, Colvillea, Delonix, Gleditsia, Gymnocladus, Parkinsonia, Peltophorum, Saraca, Schizolobium, Schotia, Senna, Tamarindus
168.2 Fabaceae subfam. Mimosoideae / Mimosaceae
Acacia, Albizia, Calliandra, Mimosa, Neptunia, Paraserianthes, Prosopis
168.3 Fabaceae subfam. Faboideae / Leguminosae/Papilionaceae
Abrus, Adenocarpus, Amorpha, Arachis, Argyrocytisus, Astragalus, Baptisia, Bolusanthus, Brya, Butea, Cajanus, Calpurnia, Canavalia, Caragana, Carmichaelia, Castanospermum, Chamaecytisus, Chordospartium, Chorizema, Cicer, Cladrastis, Clianthus, Clitoria, Colutea, Coronilla, Crotalaria, Cytisus, Desmodium, Dipogon, Erinacea, Erythrina, Galega, Genista, Glycine, Glycyrrhiza, Halimodendron, Hardenbergia, Hedysarum, Indigofera, Jacksonia, Kennedia, Lablab, +Laburnocytisus, Laburnum, Lathyrus, Lens, Lespedeza, Lotus, Lupinus, Maackia, Medicago, Millettia, Mucuna, Mundulea, Myroxylon, Notospartium, Olneya, Oxytropis, Pachyrhizus, Parochetus, Phaseolus, Piptanthus, Pisum, Podalyria, Psoralea, Pterocarpus, Retama, Robinia, Sophora, Spartium, Strongylodon, Sutherlandia, Swainsona, Templetonia, Tephrosia, Thermopsis, Tipuana, Trifolium, Trigonella, Ulex, Vicia, Vigna, Virgilia, Wisteria

Proteiflorae

169 Proteaceae
Alloxylon, Banksia, Brabejum, Buckinghamia, Darlingia, Dryandra,

Embothrium, Gevuina, Grevillea, Hakea, Isopogon, Leucadendron, Leucospermum, Lomatia, Macadamia, Mimetes, Persoonia, Protea, Serruria, Stenocarpus, Telopea, Xylomelum

Myrtiflorae

170 Haloragaceae
Myriophyllum
171 Lythraceae
Cuphea, Lagerstroemia, Lawsonia, Lythrum
172 Trapaceae
Trapa
173 Myrtaceae
Acmena, Agonis, Angophora, Astartea, Austromyrtus, Backhousia, Baeckea, Beaufortia, Callistemon, Calothamnus, Calytrix, Chamelaucium, Corymbia, Darwinia, Eucalyptus, Eugenia, Feijoa, Homoranthus, Kunzea, Leptospermum, Lophomyrtus, Lophostemon, Luma, Melaleuca, Metrosideros, Myrtus, Pimenta, Psidium, Syncarpia, Syzygium, Thryptomene, Tristania, Tristaniopsis, Ugni, Xanthostemon
174 Punicaceae
Punica
175 Onagraceae
Clarkia, Epilobium, Fuchsia, Gaura, Oenothera, Zauschneria
176 Melastomataceae
Bertolonia, Centradenia, Heterocentron, Medinilla, Melastoma, Osbeckia, Sonerila, Tibouchina
177 Combretaceae
Combretum, Quisqualis, Terminalia

Santaliflorae

178 Santalaceae
Santalum
179 Loranthaceae
Amylotheca, Nuytsia
180 Celastraceae
Celastrus, Euonymus, Maytenus, Paxistima, Tripterygium
181 Aquifoliaceae
Ilex
182 Corynocarpaceae
Corynocarpus
183 Vitaceae
Ampelopsis, Cissus, Cyphostemma, Parthenocissus, Rhoicissus, Tetrastigma, Vitis

Rutiflorae

184 Tremandraceae
Tetratheca
185 Polygalaceae
Polygala
186 Staphyleaceae
Euscaphis, Staphylea
187 Melianthaceae
Melianthus
188 Sapindaceae
Alectryon, Cardiospermum, Castanospora, Cupaniopsis, Dodonaea, Koelreuteria, Litchi, Nephelium, Sapindus, Xanthoceras
189 Hippocastanaceae
Aesculus
190 Aceraceae
Acer
191 Cneoraceae
Cneorum
192 Meliaceae
Azadirachta, Cedrela, Chukrasia, Ekebergia, Melia, Swietenia, Toona, Trichilia
193 Rutaceae
Acradenia, Adenandra, Agathosma, Boronia, Calodendrum, Choisya, ×Citrofortunella, Citrus, Clausena, Coleonema, Correa, Crowea, Dictamnus, Eriostemon, Flindersia, Fortunella, Melicope, Murraya, Phellodendron, Poncirus, Ptelea, Ruta, Skimmia, Tetradium, Zieria
194 Simaroubaceae
Ailanthus
195 Anacardiaceae
Anacardium, Cotinus, Harpephyllum, Malosma, Mangifera, Pistacia, Rhodosphaera, Rhus, Schinus, Toxicodendron
196 Linaceae
Linum, Reinwardtia
197 Malpighiaceae
Malpighia, Stigmaphyllon
198 Oxalidaceae
Averrhoa, Oxalis
199 Geraniaceae
Erodium, Geranium, Pelargonium
200 Tropaeolaceae
Tropaeolum
201 Balsaminaceae
Impatiens
202 Limnanthaceae
Limnanthes

Gentianiflorae

203 Loganiaceae
Buddleja, Desfontainea, Fagraea, Gelsemium, Nuxia
204 Gentianaceae
Eustoma, Exacum, Gentiana, Orphium
205 Apocynaceae
Acokanthera, Adenium, Allamanda, Alstonia, Amsonia, Apocynum, Beaumontia, Carissa, Catharanthus, Cerbera, Mandevilla, Nerium, Pachypodium, Plumeria, Rauvolfia, Strophanthus, Tabernaemontana, Thevetia, Trachelospermum, Vinca
206 Asclepiadaceae
Araujia, Asclepias, Ceropegia, Hoodia, Hoya, Huernia, Orbea, Stapelia, Stephanotis, Tweedia
207 Periplocaceae/Asclepiadaceae
Periploca
208 Oleaceae
Chionanthus, Fontanesia, Forestiera, Forsythia, Fraxinus, Jasminum, Ligustrum, Olea, Osmanthus, Phillyrea, Syringa
209 Goodeniaceae
Dampiera, Goodenia, Lechenaultia, Scaevola, Selliera

Solaniflorae

210 Nolanaceae
Nolana
211 Solanaceae
Atropa, Browallia, Brugmansia, Brunfelsia, Capsicum, Cestrum, Cyphomandra, Datura, Fabiana, Iochroma, Jaborosa, Lycium, Lycopersicon, Mandragora, Nicotiana, Nierembergia, Petunia, Physalis, Salpiglossis, Schizanthus, Solandra, Solanum, Streptosolen, Vestia
212 Convolvulaceae
Argyreia, Calystegia, Convolvulus, Dichondra, Ipomoea, Merremia
213 Menyanthaceae
Menyanthes, Nymphoides
214 Polemoniaceae
Cantua, Cobaea, Gilia, Ipomopsis, Phlox, Polemonium
215 Hydrophyllaceae
Hydrophyllum, Nemophila, Phacelia, Romanzoffia, Wigandia
216 Boraginaceae
Alkanna, Anchusa, Arnebia, Borago, Brunnera, Caccinia, Cerinthe, Cynoglossum, Echium, Eritrichium, Heliotropium, Lindelofia, Lithodora, Mertensia, Moltkia, Myosotidium, Myosotis, Omphalodes, Onosma, Pulmonaria, Symphytum, Trachystemon
217 Ehretiaceae/Boraginaceae
Cordia

Lamiiflorae

218 Verbenaceae
Aloysia, Callicarpa, Caryopteris, Citharexylum, Clerodendrum, Duranta, Holmskioldia, Lantana, Petrea, Phyla, Rhaphithamnus, Stachytarpheta, Tectona, Verbena, Vitex
219 Avicenniaceae/Verbenaceae
Avicennia
220 Lamiaceae (Labiatae)
Acinos, Agastache, Ajuga, Ballota, Calamintha, Cedronella, Colquhounia, Dracocephalum, Glechoma, Hemiandra, Horminum, Hyssopus, Lamium, Lavandula, Leonotis, Marrubium, Melissa, Mentha, Moluccella, Monarda, Monardella, Nepeta, Ocimum, Origanum, Perilla, Perovskia, Phlomis, Physostegia, Plectranthus, Pogostemon, Prostanthera, Prunella, Pycnanthemum, Pycnostachys, Rosmarinus, Salvia, Satureja, Scutellaria, Sideritis, Solenostemon, Stachys, Tetradenia, Teucrium, Thymus, Trichostema, Westringia
221 Callitrichaceae
Callitriche
222 Plantaginaceae
Plantago
223 Scrophulariaceae
Alonsoa, Angelonia, Antirrhinum, Asarina, Bacopa, Bowkeria, Calceolaria, Chelone, Collinsia, Derwentia, Diascia, Digitalis, Erinus, Halleria, Hebe, Isoplexis, Jovellana, Keckiella, Lathraea, Leucophyllum, Linaria, Lindernia, Lophospermum, Maurandya, Mazus, Mimulus, Nemesia, Otacanthus, Parahebe, Penstemon, Phygelius, Rhodochiton, Russelia, Scrophularia, Sutera, Torenia, Verbascum, Veronica, Veronicastrum, Wulfenia
224 Globulariaceae
Globularia
225 Myoporaceae
Eremophila, Myoporum
226 Gesneriaceae
Achimenes, Aeschynanthus, Columnea, Episcia, Haberlea, Kohleria, Mitraria, Nautilocalyx, Nematanthus, Ramonda, Rehmannia, Rhabdothamnus, Saintpaulia, Sarmienta, Sinningia, Smithiantha, Streptocarpus
227 Acanthaceae
Acanthus, Aphelandra, Barleria, Crossandra, Dicliptera, Duvernoia, Eranthemum, Fittonia, Graptophyllum, Hemigraphis, Hypoestes, Justicia, Mackaya, Megaskepasma, Pachystachys, Pseuderanthemum, Ruellia, Sanchezia, Strobilanthes, Thunbergia
228 Pedaliaceae
Sesamum
229 Martyniaceae
Martynia, Proboscidea
230 Bignoniaceae
Amphitecna, Bignonia, Campsis, Catalpa, Chilopsis, Clytostoma, Distictis, Dolichandrone, Eccremocarpus, Incarvillea, Jacaranda, Kigelia, Macfadyena, Markhamia, Pandorea, Paulownia, Podranea, Pyrostegia, Radermachera, Spathodea, Tabebuia, Tecoma, Tecomanthe, Tecomaria
231 Lentibulariaceae
Pinguicula, Utricularia

Asteriflorae

232 Asteraceae (Compositae)
Achillea, Ageratina, Ageratum, Ajania, Amberboa, Ammobium, Anaphalis, Antennaria, Anthemis, Arctotheca, Arctotis, Argyranthemum, Arnica, Artemisia, Aster, Asteriscus, Baccharis, Baileya, Bellis, Bellium, Berkheya, Berlandiera, Bidens, Boltonia, Brachycome, Brachyglottis, Brachylaena, Bracteantha, Calendula, Callistephus, Calomeria, Carlina, Carthamus, Cassinia, Catananche, Celmisia, Cenia, Centaurea, Chamaemelum, Chrysanthemoides, Chrysanthemum, Chrysocephalum, Chrysogonum, Cicerbita, Cichorium, Cineraria, Cirsium, Cladanthus, Coreopsis, Cosmos, Cotula, Craspedia, Cynara, Dahlia, Dendranthema, Dimorphotheca, Doronicum, Dymondia, Echinacea, Echinops, Edmondia, Encelia, Erigeron, Eriocephalus, Eriophyllum, Espeletia, Eumorphia, Eupatorium, Euryops, Farfugium, Felicia, Gaillardia, Gazania, Gerbera, Grindelia, Gynura, Haplopappus, Helenium, Helianthus, Helichrysum, Heliopsis, Heterotheca, Hieracium, Inula, Kalimeris, Kleinia, Lactuca, Layia, Leontopodium, Leptinella, Leucanthemum, Leucogenes, Leucophyta, Liatris, Ligularia, Lindheimera, Matricaria, Melampodium, Montanoa, Mutisia, Oldenburgia, Olearia, Onopordum, Osteospermum, Otanthus, Othonna, Ozothamnus, Pachystegia, Pericallis, Phaenocoma, Pilosella, Plectostachys, Polyarrhena, Pycnosorus, Raoulia, Ratibida, Rhodanthe, Roldana, Rudbeckia, Santolina, Sanvitalia, Saussurea, Senecio, Seriphidium, Silybum, Solidago, ×Solidaster, Steirodiscus, Stokesia, Tagetes, Tanacetum, Taraxacum, Telanthophora, Tithonia, Townsendia, Tragopogon, Tripleurospermum, Tussilago, Ursinia, Vernonia, Wedelia, Xeranthemum, Zinnia

233 Campanulaceae
Adenophora, Campanula, Canarina, Codonopsis, Edraianthus, Jasione, Michauxia, Ostrowskia, Phyteuma, Platycodon, Trachelium, Wahlenbergia
234 Lobeliaceae/Campanulaceae
Lobelia, Monopsis, Pratia
235 Pentaphragmataceae
Pentaphragma
236 Stylidiaceae
Stylidium

Flowering Plants (Magnoliopsida) B – Monocotyledons

Liliiflorae
237 Dioscoreaceae
Dioscorea
238 Taccaceae
Tacca
239 Trilliaceae/Liliaceae
Paris, Trillium
240 Smilacaceae/Liliaceae
Smilax
241 Philesiaceae/Liliaceae
Lapageria, Philesia
242 Convallariaceae/Liliaceae
Aspidistra, Convallaria, Liriope, Ophiopogon, Polygonatum, Reineckea, Rohdea, Smilacina, Speirantha
243 Asparagaceae/Liliaceae
Asparagus, Myrsiphyllum
244 Ruscaceae/Liliaceae
Danae, Ruscus, Semele
245 Dracaenaceae/Liliaceae/Agavaceae
Dracaena, Sansevieria
246 Nolinaceae/Liliaceae/Agavaceae
Beaucarnea, Dasylirion, Nolina
247 Asteliaceae/Liliaceae
Astelia, Cordyline
248 Dasypogonaceae/ Xanthorrhoeaceae
Kingia
249 Lomandraceae/Xanthorrhoeaceae
Lomandra
250 Blandfordiaceae/Liliaceae
Blandfordia
251 Xanthorrhoeaceae/Liliaceae
Xanthorrhoea
252 Agavaceae/Amaryllidaceae
Agave, Beschorneria, Furcraea, Hesperaloe, Polianthes, Yucca
253 Hypoxidaceae/Amaryllidaceae
Hypoxis, Molineria, Rhodohypoxis
254 Tecophilaeaceae
Tecophilaea
255 Phormiaceae/Liliaceae
Dianella, Phormium, Xeronema
256 Doryanthaceae/Agavaceae
Doryanthes
257 Hemerocallidaceae/Liliaceae
Hemerocallis
258 Asphodelaceae/Liliaceae
Aloe, Asphodeline, Asphodelus, Bulbine, Bulbinella, Eremurus, Gasteria, Haworthia, Kniphofia, Paradisea
259 Anthericaceae/Liliaceae
Anthericum, Arthropodium, Chlorophytum
260 Aphyllanthaceae/Liliaceae
Aphyllanthes
261 Funkiaceae/Liliaceae
Hesperocallis, Hosta
262 Hyacinthaceae/Liliaceae
Albuca, Bowiea, Brimeura, Camassia, Chionodoxa, ×Chionoscilla, Eucomis, Galtonia, Hyacinthoides, Hyacinthus, Lachenalia, Ledebouria, Muscari, Ornithogalum, Puschkinia, Scilla, Urginea, Veltheimia
263 Alliaceae/Liliaceae/Amaryllidaceae
Agapanthus, Allium, Bessera, Bloomeria, Brodiaea, Dichelostemma, Ipheion, Leucocoryne, Milla, Nectaroscordum, Tristagma, Triteleia, Tulbaghia
264 Amaryllidaceae/Liliaceae
Amaryllis, Argyropsis, Boophone, Brunsvigia, Calostemma, Chlidanthus, Clivia, Crinum, Cyrtanthus, Eucharis, Galanthus, Habranthus, Haemanthus, Hippeastrum, Hymenocallis, Leucojum, Lycoris, Narcissus, Nerine, Pancratium, Phaedranassa, Proiphys, Rhodophiala, Scadoxus, Sprekelia, Sternbergia, Worsleya, Zephyranthes
265 Melanthiaceae/Liliaceae
Helonias, Heloniopsis, Veratrum, Xerophyllum, Zigadenus
266 Alstroemeriaceae/Amaryllidaceae
Alstroemeria, Bomarea
267 Colchicaceae/Liliaceae
Colchicum, Gloriosa, Littonia, Onixotis, Sandersonia
268 Uvulariaceae/Liliaceae
Clintonia, Disporum, Maianthemum, Tricyrtis, Uvularia
269 Calochortaceae/Liliaceae
Calochortus
270 Liliaceae sensu stricto
Cardiocrinum, Erythronium, Fritillaria, Lilium, Nomocharis, Tulipa
271 Iridaceae
Anomatheca, Aristea, Babiana, Belamcanda, Chasmanthe, Crocosmia, Crocus, Cypella, Dierama, Dietes, Diplarrena, Ferraria, Freesia, Geissorhiza, Gladiolus, Gynandriris, Herbertia, Hermodactylus, Homeria, Iris, Ixia, Libertia, Moraea, Neomarica, Orthrosanthus, Romulea, Schizostylis, Sisyrinchium, Sparaxis, Tigridia, Tritonia, Watsonia
272 Cypripediaceae/Orchidaceae
Cypripedium, Paphiopedilum, Phragmipedium
273 Orchidaceae
Ada, Aerangis, Aerides, Angraecum, Anguloa, ×Angulocaste, Anoectochilus, ×Ascocenda, Ascocentrum, Bifrenaria, Bletilla, Brassavola, Brassia, ×Brassocattleya, ×Brassolaeliocattleya, Bulbophyllum, Calanthe, Cattleya, Coelogyne, Cymbidium, Dactylorhiza, Dendrobium, Dendrochilum, Disa, Dracula, Epidendrum, Epipactis, Euanthe, Goodyera, Laelia, ×Laeliocattleya, Lycaste, Masdevallia, Maxillaria, Miltoniopsis, ×Odontioda, ×Odontocidium, Odontoglossum, Oncidium, Ophrys, Orchis, Phaius, Phalaenopsis, Pleione, Psychopsis, Pterostylis, Renanthera, Rhyncholaelia, Rossioglossum, ×Sophrocattleya, ×Sophrolaeliocattleya, Sophronitis, Spathoglottis, Stanhopea, Thunia, Vanda, Vanilla, ×Vuylstekeara, ×Wilsonara, Zygopetalum

Ariflorae
274 Araceae
Acorus, Aglaonema, Alocasia, Amorphophallus, Anthurium, Arisaema, Arisarum, Arum, Biarum, Caladium, Calla, Colocasia, Cryptocoryne, Dieffenbachia, Dracunculus, Epipremnum, Lysichiton, Monstera, Orontium, Philodendron, Pinellia, Pistia, Sauromatum, Spathiphyllum, Symplocarpus, Syngonium, Xanthosoma, Zantedeschia
275 Lemnaceae
Lemna, Wolffia

Alismatiflorae
276 Aponogetonaceae
Aponogeton
277 Butomaceae
Butomus
278 Limnocharitaceae
Hydrocleys
279 Alismataceae
Alisma, Baldellia, Damasonium, Sagittaria
280 Hydrocharitaceae
Elodea, Vallisneria
281 Potamogetonaceae
Potamogeton

Bromeliiflorae
282 Bromeliaceae
Abromeitiella, Acanthostachys, Aechmea, Ananas, Billbergia, Bromelia, Canistrum, Catopsis, Cryptanthus, Dyckia, Fascicularia, Guzmania, Neoregelia, Nidularium, Orthophytum, Pitcairnia, Portea, Puya, Quesnelia, Tillandsia, Vriesea, Wittrockia
283 Haemodoraceae/Amaryllidaceae
Anigozanthos, Wachendorfia
284 Pontederiaceae
Eichhornia, Pontederia
285 Sparganiaceae
Sparganium
286 Typhaceae
Typha

Zingiberiflorae
287 Musaceae
Ensete, Musa
288 Heliconiaceae/Musaceae
Heliconia
289 Strelitziaceae/Musaceae
Ravenala, Strelitzia
290 Zingiberaceae
Achasma, Alpinia, Curcuma, Etlingera, Globba, Hedychium, Hornstedtia, Kaempferia, Roscoea, Zingiber
291 Costaceae/Zingiberaceae
Costus, Tapeinocheilos
292 Cannaceae
Canna
293 Marantaceae
Calathea, Ctenanthe, Maranta, Stromanthe, Thalia

Commeliniflorae
294 Commelinaceae
Callisia, Commelina, Cyanotis, Dichorisandra, Tradescantia
295 Juncaceae
Juncus, Luzula
296 Cyperaceae
Carex, Cyperus, Eleocharis, Eriophorum, Isolepis, Schoenoplectus, Uncinia
297 Poaceae (Gramineae)
Agropyron, Agrostis, Alopecurus, Andropogon, Arrhenatherum, Arundo, Avena, Bambusa, Briza, Bromus, Buchloe, Calamagrostis, Chasmanthium, Chimonobambusa, Chionochloa, Chusquea, Coix, Cortaderia, Cymbopogon, Cynodon, Dactylis, Deschampsia, Elymus, Fargesia, Festuca, Glyceria, Hakonechloa, Helictotrichon, Holcus, Hordeum, Imperata, Indocalamus, Lagurus, Lamarckia, Leymus, Lolium, Melica, Melinis, Milium, Miscanthus, Molinia, Muehlenbergia, Nassella, Oplismenus, Oryza, Panicum, Pennisetum, Phalaris, Phragmites, Phyllostachys, Pleioblastus, Poa, Pseudosasa, Saccharum, Sasa, Sasaella, Schizachyrium, Semiarundinaria, Sesleria, Setaria, Shibataea, Sporobolus, Stenotaphrum, Stipa, Thysanolaena, Triticum, Zea, Zeugites, Zizania, Zoysia
298 Restionaceae
Chrondopetalum, Elegia

Areciflorae
299 Arecaceae (Palmae)
Acanthophoenix, Acoelorrhaphe, Aiphanes, Archontophoenix, Areca, Arenga, Borassodendron, Brahea, Butia, Calamus, Caryota, Chamaedorea, Chamaerops, Chrysalidocarpus, Coccothrinax, Cocos, Copernicia, Corypha, Cyrtostachys, Elaeis, Hedyscepe, Howea, Hyophorbe, Jubaea, Licuala, Livistona, Lodoicea, Neodypsis, Orbignya, Phoenix, Pinanga, Pritchardia, Ptychosperma, Rhapidophyllum, Rhapis, Rhopalostylis, Roystonea, Sabal, Serenoa, Syagrus, Trachycarpus, Trithrinax, Veitchia, Washingtonia, Wodyetia

Pandaniflorae
300 Pandanaceae
Pandanus

Alphabetical list of Genera

The number following each genus is the number of its family in the preceding table of families, **not** a page number

Index of Common Names and Synonyms

B

C

D

M

N

O

P

S

T

U

V

Index of Plant Groups

This index lists plants according to their plant group, such as Annuals and perennials, Trees, Bromeliads, Vegetables, Herbs, etc.

Annuals and perennials

Annuals and perennials *continued*

Bromeliads

Bulbs, corms and tubers

Cacti and succulents

Climbers and creepers

Climbers and creepers *continued*

Ferns

Fruit trees, nut trees and other fruits

Groundcovers

Herbs

Lawngrasses

Orchids

Ornamental grasses and bamboos

Palms and cycads

Shrubs

Trees

Trees *continued*

Vegetables